W9-BLE-021

Lake Superior

SOTA

WISCONSIN

MICHIGAN

Lake Michigan

Lake Huron

Lake Ontario

St. Lawrence R.

MAINE

VT.

N.H.

MASS.

CONN.

R.I.

NEW YORK

IOWA

ILLINOIS

INDIANA

OHIO

PENNSYLVANIA

Lake Erie

THE ORIGINAL THIRTEEN COLONIES

NEW JERSEY

MASON-DIXON LINE

MARYLAND

DELAWARE

WEST VIRGINIA

Ohio R.

KENTUCKY

VIRGINIA

MISSOURI

**THE ORIGINAL
UNITED STATES**
(By Treaty with Britain, 1783)

NORTH CAROLINA

36°30' N

TENNESSEE

ARKANSAS

Mississippi R.

SOUTH CAROLINA

MISSISSIPPI

ALABAMA

GEORGIA

LOUISIANA

(Seized from Spain, 1810, 1813)

ATLANTIC OCEAN

**Territorial Growth
of the
United States**

**FLORIDA**
(By Treaty with
Spain, 1819)

FLORIDA

GULF OF MEXICO

BAHAMAS

**PUERTO RICO**
(Acquired from
Spain, 1898)

**VIRGIN IS.**
(Acquired from
Denmark, 1916-1917)

PUERTO RICO

VIRGIN ISLANDS

0    50    100 Miles

0    50    100 Kilometers

0    200    400 Miles

0    200    400 Kilometers

Albers Equal-Area Projection

CUBA

DOMINICAN
REPUBLIC

HAITI

# The Enduring Vision

# THE *Enduring* VISION
*Fourth Edition*

## A History of the American People

Paul S. Boyer
*University of Wisconsin*

Clifford E. Clark, Jr.
*Carleton College*

Joseph F. Kett
*University of Virginia*

Neal Salisbury
*Smith College*

Harvard Sitkoff
*University of New Hampshire*

Nancy Woloch
*Barnard College*

Houghton Mifflin Company
Boston   New York

Editor-in-chief: Jean Woy
Sponsoring editor: Jeffrey Greene
Senior project editor: Rosemary Winfield
Production/design coordinator: Jennifer Meyer
Senior cover design coordinator: Deborah Azerrad Savona
Senior manufacturing coordinator: Marie Barnes
Senior marketing manager: Sandra McGuire


Cover design: Deborah Azerrad Savona; cover art: *Landscape with Covered Wagon,*
Thomas Birch. Wadsworth Atheneum, Hartford. Bequest of Mrs. Clara Hinton Gould.

Printed in the U.S.A.

Library of Congress Catalog Number: 99-72038

ISBN: 0-395-96077-0

123456789-VH-03  02  01  00  99

# Brief Contents

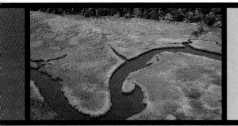

# Contents

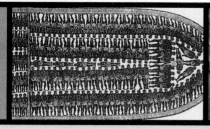

## 4

### The Bonds of Empire, 1660–1750

#### 80

## 5

### Roads to Revolution, 1744–1776

#### 112

# 12

## The Old South and Slavery, 1800–1860

### 320

# 11

## Life, Leisure, and Culture, 1840–1860

### 294

## 16

## The Crises of Reconstruction, 1865–1877
### 440

## 17

## The Trans-Mississippi West
### 472

# 21
## Politics and Expansion in an Industrializing Age
### 584

# 22
## The Progressive Era
### 616

# 24
## The 1920s
678

# 25
## Crash, Depression, and New Deal
706

# 26

## American Life in a Decade of Crisis at Home and Abroad

### 734

# 27

## Waging Global War, 1939–1945

### 758

# 28

## Cold War America, 1945–1952

### 788

# 29

## America at Midcentury
### 812

# 30

## The Turbulent Sixties
### 840

# 31

## A Troubled Journey: From Port Huron to Watergate
866

# 32

## Turning Inward: Society and Politics from Ford to Bush
892

# Maps

# *Charts, Graphs, and Tables*

# Preface

Each new edition of a textbook presents a different challenge. While the first edition is the most exciting—because of the chance to see our vision in print and the years of hard work it takes to write—subsequent editions assume their own identity as well. The second edition affords an opportunity to attend to those details that schedule or other circumstances made difficult to get just right in the first edition. However, the gratification of being successful enough to warrant a second edition is soon superseded by the unexpected amount of work a revision requires. But all that work to get everything just right meant in the third edition we could reexamine decisions we made in the first edition regarding issues of organization and content. So the major thrust of the third edition was to provide more attention to the borderland communities in the South and West and to continue weaving in the story of Americans' encounters with the natural environment.

In making these decisions about what to change and what new areas to emphasize, we, of course, rely on the criticism and suggestions we get from those who have used our book as well as from colleagues and on our own teaching experience and scholarly pursuits. The success of *The Enduring Vision* is a wonderful confirmation of our original ideas for what a textbook for the U.S. history survey should be. And while we continue to make substantive changes in each new edition, these changes all conform to the framework we established in the first edition. In that first edition, our desire was to write a book that established a sturdy political and chronological framework into which we could integrate the best scholarship in social, cultural, and environmental history. *The Enduring Vision* was to be a book that synthesized much of the best scholarship in these areas and presented it to students in an engaging and challenging narrative. To that end, we labored long and hard to get the writing just right, to communicate to students through vigorous prose that American history is a dynamic story of many parts. Names, dates, and places are important but only as they help inform the nature of the actions and decisions that shaped our history.

## New to This Edition

In its three editions, *The Enduring Vision* has established the identity we desired. In the fourth edition, the challenge was how to build on that solid foundation and make improvements. In considering this challenge, we decided to look again at the writing style as well as the usual issues raised by new scholarship and the comments of our users. We cover a lot of ground in *The Enduring Vision* and this attempt to be as comprehensive as possible means there is a lot for students to absorb. And in their efforts to absorb all this material, they also have to be able to discern what is most important in each chapter and be able to recognize the themes we are emphasizing and the arguments we are making. This can be challenging for even the best students. So in this edition we decided to offer some help. We've gone through each chapter thoroughly to ensure that the level of detail of the writing provides just the right amount of information and emphasis to the reader. Where we found that the amount of information threatened to overwhelm the student, we either eliminated some of it or rewrote passages to make them more clear. Essentially, we wanted to make the same points, while in some cases actually saying less. The result is a shorter book that should be more accessible to students.

In addition to tightening the prose, we have added a new feature to each chapter—focus questions. These questions follow the chapter-opening vignettes and serve to introduce students to the main points that will be discussed in the chapter. They will help provide a framework into which students can fit what follows. The conclusions have also been reconceived to revisit the issues raised in the focus questions and to wrap up the chapter.

Of course a key aspect of the revision process is to examine each chapter to see where new scholarship might fit and to respond to the concerns of our users. Adding our own judgment to this process, we have made the following substantive changes in the fourth edition as well as many more minor changes to each chapter.

In Chapter 2, new material has been added on the history of Africa and Europe that illustrates that they had some shared history prior to and aside from the trans-Atlantic slave trade. Chapter 3 incorporates new scholarship on the household economy and gender in New England. With an additional discussion comparing the Spanish and French colonies with the English, there are now allusions to the colonial histories of many more states than the original thirteen in Chapter 4. Some sections of Chapters 5 to 7 have been reorganized and rewritten, and those chapters provide more attention to women, African Americans, native Americans, frontier conflicts, and the economy.

In Chapter 9, there is increased emphasis on the role of industrial outwork, and especially on the role of women in this type of manufacturing. New scholarship in Chapter 10 focuses on the election of 1836 and a new explanation of Jackson's early popularity as an outgrowth of popular ire against corruption. Chapter 12 features a revised discussion of proslavery arguments and of slave rebellions, as well as new material on southern evangelicals and white values. There is a new discussion in Chapter 13 on the non-inevitability of the Monroe Doctrine and more attention to the opinions of Mexicans regarding the Mexican War.

Chapter 15, on the Civil War, includes an expanded discussion of the Thirteenth Amendment and of self-emancipation during the war. There is greater attention to the Chinese in the West and the connection between the Homestead Act and the political ideology of the Republican Party in Chapter 17. In Chapter 18 new material has been added on the character of industrial change, including the ambiguous impact of industrialization on the independence of single women. The notion of regional centers has been expanded to include Chicago and San Francisco, as have the industrialization of the West and the impact of standardization on everyday life. There is new emphasis on the impact of immigrant life on nineteenth-century cities by the rich mix of ethnic groups that created a diverse, competitive civic culture in Chapter 19. Chapter 20 continues the emphasis on immigration and class by demonstrating how racial discrimination reinforced class distinctions and served as a barrier to advancement for African Americans, Italians, Chinese, and others.

Discussion of the Grange movement has been moved into Chapter 21 for better chronological coherence. Additional material has been added on the impact of *Plessy* v. *Ferguson,* why Cleveland beat Harrison in 1892, the role of African Americans in the Spanish American War, and the economic sources of expansionism. In Chapter 22, new material has been added on the antiprostitution crusade, immigration procedures, and water resources in the West. There is expanded treatment of the Wilson administration's response to the Bolshevik Revolution in Russia in Chapter 23 and more material has been added on the Mellon tax cuts, farmers' defection from the GOP in the 1928 election, falling immigration in the 1920s, anti-Japanese laws in California, and the spread of the KKK in the Northeast in Chapter 24.

In Chapter 25, discussion of the Supreme Court's turnaround in 1937 has been broadened, new material on unions has been added, and the discussion of the New Deal's impact on the evolution of the American state has been expanded. In addition, there is new material on FDR's use of wartime imagery in his efforts to build a spirit of national unity, the New Deal arts program, and the New Deal and the West. In Chapter 26, coverage of Japanese and Filipino agricultural workers has been added as well as further discussion of the later importance of the Munich analogy, more on Walter Reuther and the tensions between radicals and moderates in the 1930s labor movement, the New Deal policy toward Indians, and the strategic calculations underlying FDR's Good Neighbor Policy.

The discussion of the war economy in the West and the Sunbelt has been expanded as well as coverage of women in the military and the homefront, and of gays and Hispanics in Chapter 27. In Chapter 28, the beginnings of the modern conservative movement in American politics are introduced and new scholarship on Alger Hiss, the Rosenbergs, and Senate action against gays has been added. In Chapter 29, the effects of defense and government spending on the economic development of the West receives more attention and a new discussion of the beginnings of Silicon Valley has been added. The discussion of the development of modern conservatism continues in Chapter 30, and a new discussion of Indian agency has been introduced.

In Chapter 31, there is a new treatment of the New Left and youth culture, and continued development of the rise of conservatism. Chapter 32 features more on *Roe* v. *Wade,* the relationship of the ERA defeat to the antifeminist backlash, affirmative action, President Reagan's effect on the federal judiciary, and campus protests of the Gulf War. And finally, Chapter 33 has been updated through the Senate trial of President Clinton and material has been added on the federal tobacco bill, campaign-finance reform, the Lewinsky scandal,

North Korea's nuclear program, and the nuclear tests by India and Pakistan, the bombings of American embassies in Africa, and the impact of the Russian and East Asian economic crises on the U.S.

In addition to these changes, we have replaced 25 percent of the "A Place in Time" features. Throughout, we have also updated the bibliographies and suggestions for further reading. Those familiar with the third edition will note that we have placed the works that were listed at the end of chapters under "Additional Bibliography" in a separate appendix at the end of the book.

## Special Features

A range of useful study aids has been built into *The Enduring Vision.* Each chapter begins with a vignette of a person or an event that both swiftly draws the reader into the atmosphere and issues of the times and establishes the chapter's main themes, and is followed by focus questions. The chronology of events and developments has been moved to near the beginning of the chapter. In every chapter a two-page, illustrated essay called "A Place in Time" delves into a single community's experiences. Tables and chronological charts on special topics occur regularly throughout the text, and each chapter closes with a conclusion and annotated For Further Reading recommendations for the student. The Appendix provides statistical tables; handy reference lists; the bibliography; and the text of the Declaration of Independence, the Articles of Confederation, and the Constitution (with its amendments). The full-color design of *The Enduring Vision* features hundreds of photographs, paintings, and cartoons and almost 200 maps and graphs. Informative captions enrich the art program.

## Supplementary Resources

The most exciting addition to our extensive list of supplementary resources is *@history,* a combination CD-ROM and web site that presents approximately 1,000 primary sources—text, audio, video, and animations—that cover the span of American history and include sources on political, social, economic, diplomatic, environmental, and cultural history. Half of these sources include suggested activities to be used for discussion or assignments. A gateway on the *@history* web site provides access to hundreds more sites, all of which have

been categorized for easy searching. In addition to the gateway, the web site offers instructor's resources, primary sources, and ACE, a self-testing program that allows students to assess their knowledge. The contents of the CD-ROM and web site have been selected and the activities prepared by Paula Petrik of the University of Maine and Kelly Woestman of Pittsburgh State University.

There is both a student version of the CD-ROM and an instructor's version. The instructor's version contains everything that is on the student version plus additional notes suggesting ways to use a particular source with students. The activities have also been classified by level of skill required to complete them. This is also available exclusively on the instructor's version. For instructors who want to create multimedia lectures and use these sources as presentation material, there are sample e-lectures that offer examples of how to create a multimedia lecture. Instructors can use the sample e-lectures as is or edit them by importing sources on the CD-ROM or by importing their own material. Flexibility and customization are built into this package.

In addition to *@history,* we offer:

- *Student Guide with Map Exercises,* Fourth Edition, by Barbara Blumberg

  Keyed chapter-by-chapter to the textbook, the *Student Guide with Map Exercises,* available in two volumes, provides an outline-summary of major topics and themes and includes several features guiding the student in chapter review and self-testing. Map exercises sharpen students' knowledge of and skills in understanding U.S. historical geography.

- *Enduring Voices Document Sets,* Fourth Edition, by James J. Lorence

  This one-of-a-kind, two-volume reader, organized to follow the chapter sequence of *The Enduring Vision,* presents discrete sets of primary sources, with each set built around a problem closely related to a major theme in the corresponding textbook chapter.

- *Instructor's Guide,* Fourth Edition, by Robert Grant and James J. Lorence

  This indispensable instructor's resource provides introductory how-to essays and student handouts, followed by teaching suggestions and strategies tied to each chapter of *The Enduring Vision,* Fourth

Edition. Also included are detailed guidelines for using the *Enduring Voices Document Sets* in the classroom.

- *Test Item File,* Fourth Edition, by Kenneth Blume

  This rich bank of identification, multiple-choice, essay, and map questions covers all the main topics and themes of *The Enduring Vision.* Questions suitable for midterm and final exams are included.

- *Computerized Testing* for IBM and Macintosh computers

  Available for Macintosh and IBM-compatible computers, this electronic test generator provides the same questions as the printed test bank, but in convenient electronic format.

- The Houghton Mifflin *U.S. History Transparency Set*

  Approximately 130 full-color maps and graphs are offered in this valuable two-volume collection of overhead-transparency acetates.

## *Acknowledgments*

In the supplements program as well as in the textbook, our goal has been to make teaching and learning American history enjoyable and stimulating. We would value any comments you and your students have as you navigate through your course using *The Enduring Vision* and its supplements; don't hesitate to write to us.

We have had the help of many people in preparing this edition of *The Enduring Vision.* In particular, Neal Salisbury would like to thank his research assistants, Amy Tanzer and Stephanie Ziegler, who provided invaluable assistance. In addition we have benefited from the sage advice of many of our colleagues who provided comments for this edition. Our thanks to:

L. Anthony Wise, Jr., *Pellissippi State Technical Community College*
Robert Phelps, *California State University, Hayward*
Robert Olwell, *University of Texas, Austin*
Lester J. Rodney, *Morehouse University*
Mark Kleinman, *University of Wisconsin, Oshkosh*
Diane F. Britton, *University of Toledo*
Ronald C. McArthur, *Atlantic Community College*
Joseph A. McCartin, *SUNY Geneseo*
Stephen W. Haley, *Shelby State Community College*
Myles L. Clowers, *San Diego City College*
Richard Frucht, *Northwest Missouri State University*
Nancy G. Isenberg, *University of Northern Iowa*
Mark Grimsley, *The Ohio State University*
David B. Castle, *Ohio University Eastern*
Sherry L. Smith, *University of Texas, El Paso*
John L. Rector, *Western Oregon University*
Hal K. Rothman, *University of Nevada, Las Vegas*

And finally, we would like to thank all the instructors and students who have taken the time to send us their thoughtful and constructive suggestions. *The Enduring Vision* is a much better book as a result.

|       |       |
|-------|-------|
| P. B. | N. S. |
| C. C. | H. S. |
| J. K. | N. W. |

# About the Authors

**Paul S. Boyer,** Merle Curti Professor of History at the University of Wisconsin, Madison, earned his Ph.D. from Harvard University. An editor of *Notable American Women, 1607–1950* (1971), he also coauthored *Salem Possessed: The Social Origins of Witchcraft* (1974), for which, with Stephen Nissenbaum, he received the John H. Dunning Prize of the American Historical Association. His other published works include *Urban Masses* and *Moral Order in America, 1820–1920* (1978), *By the Bomb's Early Light: American Thought and Culture at the Dawn of the Atomic Age* (1985), *When Time Shall Be No More: Prophecy Belief in Modern American Culture* (1992), and *Promises to Keep: The United States Since World War II,* 2nd ed. (1999). He is also editor-in-chief of the *Oxford Companion to United States History* (forthcoming). His articles and essays have appeared in the *American Quarterly, New Republic,* and other journals. He is an elected member of the American Antiquarian Society, the Society of American Historians, and the American Academy of Arts and Sciences.

**Clifford E. Clark, Jr.,** M. A. & A. D. Hulings Professor of American Studies and professor of history at Carleton College, earned his Ph.D. from Harvard University. He has served as both the chair of the History Department and director of the American Studies program at Carleton. Clark is the author of *Henry Ward Beecher: Spokesman for a Middle-Class America* (1978), *The American Family Home, 1800–1960* (1986), *The Intellectual and Cultural History of Anglo-America Since 1789* in the General History of the Americas, and with Carol Zellie, *Northfield: The History and Architecture of a Community* (1997). He also has edited and contributed to *Minnesota in a Century of Change: The State and Its People Since 1900* (1989). A past member of the Council of the American Studies Association, Clark is active in the fields of material culture studies and historic preservation, and he serves on the Northfield, Minnesota, Historical Preservation Commission.

**Joseph F. Kett,** Commonwealth Professor of History at the University of Virginia, received his Ph.D. from Harvard University. His works include *The Formation of the American Medical Profession: The Role of Institutions, 1780–1860* (1968), *Rites of Passage: Adolescence in America, 1790–Present* (1977), *The Pursuit of Knowledge Under Difficulties: From Self-Improvement to Adult Educa-* tion in America, 1750–1990* (1994), and *The Dictionary of Cultural Literacy* (1988), of which he is coauthor. A former History Department chair at Virginia, he also has participated on the Panel on Youth of the President's Science Advisory Committee, has served on the Board of Editors of the *History of Education Quarterly,* and is a past member of the Council of the American Studies Association.

**Neal Salisbury,** professor of history at Smith College, received his Ph.D. from the University of California, Los Angeles. The author of *Manitou and Providence: Indians, Europeans, and the Making of New England, 1500–1643* (1982) and editor of *The Sovereignty and Goodness of God,* by Mary Rowlandson. He also has contributed numerous articles to journals and edited collections. He has been awarded fellowships by the Smithsonian Institution, the National Endowment for the Humanities, the Charles Warren Center for Studies in American History at Harvard University, the National Humanities Center, and the American Antiquarian Society. Formerly chair of the History Department at Smith, he is active in the fields of colonial and Native American history, has served as president of the American Society for Ethnohistory, and coedits a book series, Cambridge Studies in North American Indian History.

**Harvard Sitkoff,** professor of history at the University of New Hampshire, earned his Ph.D. from Columbia University. He is the author of *A New Deal for Blacks* (1978) and *The Struggle for Black Equality, 1954–1992* (1981, 1992), coeditor of *A History of Our Time* (1982, 1987, 1991), and editor of *Fifty Years Later: The New Deal Evaluated* (1985). A contributor to numerous edited collections, he also has published articles in many journals, among them the *American Quarterly, Journal of American History, Journal of Southern History,* and *Wilson Quarterly.*

**Nancy Woloch** received her Ph.D. from Indiana University. She is the author of *Women and the American Experience* (1984, 1994, 1996, 2000), editor of *Early American Women: A Documentary History, 1600–1900* (1992, 1997), and coauthor, with Walter LaFeber and Richard Polenberg, of *The American Century: A History of the United States Since the 1890s* (1986, 1992, 1998). She is also the author of *Muller v. Oregon: A Brief History with Documents* (1996). She teaches American history and American Studies at Barnard College, Columbia University.

# The Enduring Vision

# *Prologue*

# Enduring Vision,
# Enduring Land

**Eroded Lava Badlands,** by Alexandre Hogue, 1982

This is the story of America and of the visions that Americans have shared. The first vision was of the land itself. For the Native Americans who spread over the land thousands of years ago, for the Europeans who began to arrive in the sixteenth century, and for the later immigrants who poured in by the tens of millions from all parts of the world, North America offered a haven for new beginnings. If life was hard elsewhere, it would be better here. And once here, the lure of the land continued. If times were tough in the East, they would be better in the West. New Englanders migrated to Ohio; Ohioans migrated to Kansas; Kansans migrated to California. For Africans the migration to America was forced and brutal. But after the Civil War, newly freed southern blacks embraced the vision and dreamed of new opportunities elsewhere:

> I got my ticket,
> Leaving the thicket,
> And I'm a-heading for the Golden Shore!

For most of American history, the vision of the land celebrated its beauty, its diversity, and its ability to provide sustenance and even wealth to those who exploited its fertility and its resources. But within this shared vision were deep-seated tensions. Whereas Native Americans regarded the land and other natural phenomena as spiritual forces to be feared and respected, many Europeans and their descendants considered nature a force to be conquered. The very abundance of America's natural resources led them to think of these resources as infinitely available and exploitable. In moving from one locale to another, some sought only to escape starvation or oppression, while others pursued wealth and power despite the environmental consequences. Regardless of their motives

and conditions, migrants often left behind a land bereft of wild animals, its fertility depleted by intensive farming, its waters dammed and polluted or dried up altogether. If the land today remains part of the vision, it is only because we realize its vulnerability, rather than its immunity, to pollution and exploitation.

But the vision involves more than simply a love of the land. It also entails a commitment to an ongoing process: the process of creating a just social order. In pursuing this goal, Americans have sought to blend the best from their intellectual and cultural traditions with new, experimental social forms, a pattern often leading to bitter debates. Over thousands of years, Native Americans worked in this way to construct ideal social orders as they refined their relationships with one another and with the land around them. For the past five hundred years, immigrants from all over the world have pursued comparable ideals, both within their communities and in the nation at large.

Central to the American vision of the good society is the notion of individual freedom. To be sure, our commitment to freedom has frequently faltered in practice. The Puritans who sought freedom of worship for themselves denied it to others. Southern whites who cheered the Declaration of Independence lived by the labor of black slaves. Many a wealthy employer conveniently forgot that economic exploitation can extinguish freedom as effectively as political tyranny or military force. And through much of our history, women—half the population—were relegated to second-class status. Yet the battered vision endured, prodding a sometimes reluctant nation to confront and explore its full meaning.

But freedom can be an empty and cheerless thing unless one is also part of a social group. The novelist

O. E. Rölvaag, describing the emotions of a nineteenth-century Norwegian immigrant farm woman on the Great Plains, captured this feeling of social isolation:

> A sense of desolation so profound settled upon her that she seemed unable to think at all. . . . She threw herself back in the grass and looked up into the heavens. But darkness and infinitude lay there, also—the sense of utter desolation still remained. . . . Suddenly, for the first time, she realized the full extent of her loneliness. . . .

Thus the vision must also be one of community. Puritan leader John Winthrop, addressing a group of fellow immigrants aboard the *Arbella* on their way to America in 1630, eloquently summed up this dimension of the vision: "We must delight in each other, make others' conditions our own, rejoice together, mourn together, labor and suffer together: always having before our eyes our commission and community . . . as members of the same body."

The family, the town, the neighborhood, the church, the ethnic group, and the nation itself have been ways by which Americans have woven into their lives a web of social meaning. And *community* is not just a high-sounding abstraction; it has political implications. If we are not just a fragmented collection of self-absorbed individuals but also a *people,* what obligations do we owe one another? What limitations on our freedom are we willing to accept in order to be part of a social group? In struggling with tough questions like these, we have further defined our vision of America.

Finally, this vision is one of renewal and new beginnings. The story of America is part of the human story, and thus it has its dark and shameful passages as well as its bright moments of achievement. Arrogance, injustice, callous blindness to suffering, and national self-delusion have all figured in our history. But balancing the times when we lost our way are the moments when we found our bearings and returned to the hard task of defining what America at its best might truly be.

This, then, is the essence of the vision: a vision not of a foreordained national destiny unfolding effortlessly but of a laborious, often frustrating struggle to define what our common life as a people shall be. For all the failures and the wrong turns, it remains a vision rooted in hope, not despair. In 1980 Jesse de la Cruz, a Mexican-American woman who had fought for years to improve conditions for California's migrant workers, summed up the philosophy that kept her going: "Is America progressing toward the better? . . . We're the ones that are gonna do it. We have to keep on struggling. . . . With us, there's a saying: *La esperanza muere al último.* Hope dies last. You can't lose hope. If you lose hope, that's losing everything."

No sentiment could better sum up the enduring vision of American history.

## An Ancient Heritage

"The land was ours before we were the land's." So begins "The Gift Outright," which poet Robert Frost read at President John F. Kennedy's inauguration in 1961. Frost's poem meditates on the interrelatedness of history, geography, and human consciousness. At first, wrote Frost, North American settlers merely possessed the land; but then, in a subtle spiritual process, they became possessed by it. Only by entering into this deep relationship with the land itself—"such as she was, such as she would become"—did their identity as a people fully take shape.

Frost's poem speaks of the encounter of English colonists with a strange new continent of mystery and promise; but of course, what the Europeans called the "New World" was in fact the homeland of Native American peoples whose ancestors had been "possessed by" the land for at least fifteen thousand years. Native Americans had undergone an immensely long process of settling the continent, developing divergent cultures, discovering agriculture, and creating a rich spiritual life tightly interwoven with the physical environment that sustained them. We cannot fully comprehend the past five hundred years of American history without first understanding how, for thousands of years before then, Indians created the human habitats that non-Indians and their descendants would occupy and transform.

To comprehend the American past, we first must know the American land itself. The patterns of weather; the undulations of valley, plain, and mountain; the shifting mosaic of sand, soil, and rock; the intricate network of rivers, streams, and lakes—these have profoundly influenced U.S. history. North America's fundamental physical characteristics have shaped human events from the earliest migrations from Asia to the later cycles of agricultural and industrial development, the rise of cities, the course of politics, and even the basic themes of American literature, art, and music. Geology, geogra-

## CHRONOLOGY

**c. 3,000,000,000 B.C.**   Formation of oldest known rocks in present-day North America.

**c. 500,000,000 B.C.**   Precambrian era ends; Paleozoic era begins. Earliest forms of animal life appear.

**c. 250,000,000 B.C.**   Supercontinent of Pangaea forms.

**c. 225,000,000 B.C.**   Paleozoic era ends; Mesozoic era begins. First dinosaurs appear.

**c. 210,000,000 B.C.**   Appalachian Mountains emerge.

**c. 180,000,000 B.C.**   Pangaea begins to break up.

**c. 65,000,000 B.C.**   Mesozoic era ends; Cenozoic era begins. Dinosaurs become extinct. Rocky Mountains form.

**c. 50,000,000 B.C.**   Hawaiian Islands emerge.

**c. 20,000,000 B.C.**   Grand Canyon begins to form.

**c. 5,000,000 B.C.**   Earliest human ancestors appear in Africa.

**c. 2,000,000 B.C.**   Ice Age begins.

**c. 300,000–100,000 B.C.**   Humans spread throughout Eastern Hemisphere.

**c. 120,000 B.C.**   Wisconsin glaciation begins.

**c. 40,000–15,000 B.C.**   Ancestors of Native Americans cross Alaska-Siberian land bridge.

**c. 10,000 B.C.**   Ice Age ends. Wisconsin glaciation retreats from North America. Native Americans begin to spread throughout Western Hemisphere.

**A.D. 1492**   Christopher Columbus makes his first voyage to Western Hemisphere.

---

phy, and environment are among the fundamental building blocks of human history.

This prologue tells the story of the land itself: its geological origins; its reshaping by eons of lifting, sinking, erosion, and glaciation; the opportunities and limitations that it presents to human endeavor. It reminds us of the ultimate dependence of human beings on their environment.

It is sobering to begin the study of American history by contrasting the recent rise of a rich, complex human society on this continent with the awesomely slow pace by which the North American environment took form. Geologists trace the oldest known rocks on the continent back some 3 billion years when a single landmass, which they call Pangaea, encompassed all the earth's dry surfaces. The rocky "floor" known as the Canadian Shield first became visible on the surface of what is now Canada during the earliest geologic era, the Precambrian, which ended 500 million years ago. Halfway between that remote age and the present, during the Paleozoic ("ancient life") era, forests covered much of what would eventually be the United States. From this organic matter, America's enormous coal reserves would be created, the largest yet discovered in the entire world. About 180 million years ago, during the Mesozoic ("middle life") era—the age of the dinosaurs—Pangaea began to break apart. By a process

known as continental drift—which continues today at the rate of a few centimeters a year—today's continents were eventually formed. As a result, most plant and animal life in each of the earth's major landmasses—the Americas, Eurasia-Africa, Australia, and Antarctica—evolved thereafter in isolation from life in the others. As environmental historian Alfred W. Crosby puts it, "The ancestors of American buffalos, Eurasian cattle, and Australian kangaroos shambled and hopped down diverging paths of evolution." The overseas expansion of Europeans in the past five centuries has brought an abrupt end to that isolation, with some far-reaching consequences in North America that are noted in the chapters that follow.

So enormous a gulf of time separates the origins of North America from the beginning of its human history that, if those 180 million years were compressed into the space of a single twenty-four-hour day, everything that has happened since the Indians' ancestors arrived would flash by in the last half-second before midnight, and America's history since Columbus would occupy about five-thousandths of a second. In considering the sweep of geologic time, one inevitably wonders how ephemeral human history itself may yet prove to be.

Many millions of years after North America's initial separation, violent movements of the earth's crust thrust up the Pacific Coastal, Sierra Nevada, and Cas-

## Formation of the Continents

*After the breakup of the supercontinent of Pangaea, drifting landmasses gradually formed today's continents.*

**180 million years ago**

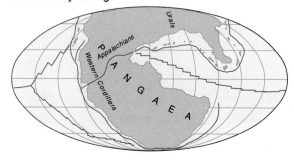

**125 million years ago**

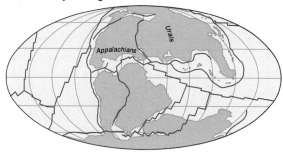

**55 million years ago**

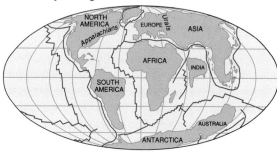

**Today**

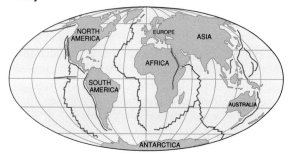

cade ranges on the continent's western edge. As the dinosaurs were dying out, toward the end of the Mesozoic some 65–70 million years ago, the vast, shallow sea that washed over much of west-central North America disappeared, having been replaced by the Rocky Mountains. By then, the decay and fossilization of plant and animal life were creating North America's once great petroleum deposits, which until a generation ago seemed almost limitless. Within the last 50 million years, volcanic eruptions raised the cones that now form the Hawaiian Islands, twenty-five hundred miles southwest of California. Active Pacific-rim volcanoes and powerful earthquakes all over the continent dramatically demonstrate that the molding of the American landscape still continues.

Between 2 million and ten thousand years ago, four great glaciations left a tremendous imprint on the land. The Ice Age staggers the imagination. During periods of maximum glacial expansion, a carpet of ice as thick as thirteen thousand feet extended over most of Canada and crept southward into what is now New England, New York State, and much of the Midwest.

Like the slow but relentless shaping of the planet itself, the origins of the human species extend back to the mists of prehistoric time. More than 5 million years ago, direct human ancestors evolved in the temperate grasslands of Africa. Between three hundred thousand and one hundred thousand years ago, humans began migrating throughout the Eastern Hemisphere. During the last glaciation, which geologists term Wisconsin, hunting bands pursuing large game animals moved

**Volcanic Eruption, Hawaii**

from Central Asia into Siberia. Between forty thousand and fifteen thousand years ago, most scientists believe, some of these bands crossed the broad land bridge then connecting Siberia to Alaska. In so doing, they became the first Americans.

While the earth has been relatively stable during the last few thousand years, earthquakes in California and elsewhere remind us that the continents continue to drift and that the world as we know it is not static but in a state of steady change.

## The Continent and Its Regions

As the glacial ice melted, raising the world's oceans to their present levels, North America slowly warmed. The ensuing differences in climate, physical features, and organic life were the basis of America's extraordinary geographic diversity. Geographic diversity contributed, in turn, to the remarkable diversity of regional cultures that later emerged, first among American Indians and then among the nonnative peoples who settled in America after Columbus's voyages. Geographic variety also contributed to the United States' rise to political and economic preeminence in the modern world.

### *The West*

With its severe climate and profuse wildlife, Alaska still evokes the land that ancient North America's earliest migrants discovered. Indeed, Alaska's far north resembles a world from which ice caps have just retreated—a treeless tundra of grasses, lichens, and stunted shrubs. This region, the Arctic, is a stark wilderness in winter, reborn in fleeting summers of colorful flowers and returning birds. In contrast, the subarctic of central Alaska and Canada is a heavily forested country known as taiga. Here rises North America's highest peak, 20,320-foot Mt. McKinley, or Denali. Average temperatures in the subarctic range from the fifties above zero in summer to well below zero in the long, dark winters, and the soil is permanently frozen except during summer surface thaws.

The expanse from Alaska's glacier-gouged and ruggedly mountainous Pacific shore southward to northern California forms the Pacific Northwest. Only a few natural harbors break the shoreline, but they include the magnificent anchorages of Puget Sound and San Francisco Bay. Offshore, cool currents and warm winds make possible rich coastal fisheries.

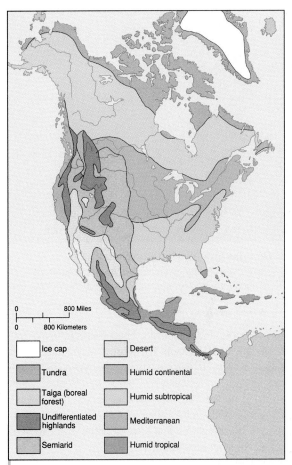

**North American Climatic Regions**

The Pacific coastal region is in some ways a world apart. Vegetation and animal life, isolated from the rest of the continent by mountains and deserts, include many species unfamiliar farther east. Warm, wet westerly winds blowing off the Pacific create a climate more uniformly temperate than anywhere else in North America. From Anchorage and the Alaska panhandle to a little south of San Francisco Bay, winters are cool, humid, and foggy, and the coast's dense forest cover includes the largest living organisms on earth, the giant redwood trees. Along the southern California coast, winds and currents generate a warmer, "Mediterranean" climate, and vegetation includes a heavy growth of shrubs and short trees, scattered stands of oak, and grasses able to endure prolonged seasonal drought.

The rugged Sierra Nevada, Cascade, and coastal ranges stretch the length of British Columbia, Washing-

**Douglas Firs, Washington State**
*The impact of clear-cutting timber to meet worldwide demand for wood is made vividly clear in this photograph.*

Well east of the Pacific coastal band lies the Great Basin, encompassing Nevada, western Utah, southern Idaho, and eastern Oregon. The few streams here have no outlet to the sea. Much of the Great Basin was once covered by an inland sea holding glacial meltwater, a remnant of which survives in Utah's Great Salt Lake. Today, however, the Great Basin is dry and severely eroded, a cold desert rich in minerals, imposing in its austere grandeur and lonely emptiness. North of the basin, the Columbia and Snake rivers, which drain the plateau country of Idaho and eastern Washington and Oregon, provide plentiful water for farming.

Western North America's "backbone" is the Rocky Mountains. In turn, the Rockies form part of the immense mountain system that reaches from Alaska to the Andes of South America. Elevations in the Rockies rise from a mile above sea level in Denver at the foot of the mountains to permanently snowcapped peaks more than fourteen thousand feet above sea level. Beyond the front range of the Rockies lies the Continental Divide, the watershed separating the rivers flowing eastward into the Atlantic from those draining westward into the Pacific. The climate and vegetation of the Rocky Mountain high country resemble Arctic and subarctic types.

ton, Oregon, and California. Their majestic peaks trap abundant Pacific Ocean moisture that gigantic clockwise air currents carry eastward. Between the ranges nestle flat, fertile valleys—California's Central Valley (formed by the San Joaquin and Sacramento rivers), Oregon's Willamette Valley, and the Puget Sound region in Washington—that have become major agricultural centers in recent times.

Arizona, southern Utah, western New Mexico, and southeastern California form America's southwestern desert. The climate is arid, searingly hot on summer

**Coastal Farming Belt, Northern California**

days and cold on winter nights. Adapted to stringent environmental conditions, many plants and animals that thrive here could not survive elsewhere. Dust storms, cloudbursts, and flash floods have everywhere carved, abraded, and twisted the rocky landscape. Nature's fantastic sculpture appears on the most monumental scale in the Grand Canyon, where for 20 million years the Colorado River has been cutting down to Precambrian bedrock.

In the face of such tremendous natural forces, human activity might well seem paltry and transitory. Yet here the first crop cultivation began in what is now the continental United States.

## The Heartland

North America's heartland comprises the area extending eastward from the Rockies to the Appalachians. This vast region forms one of the world's largest drainage systems. From it the Great Lakes empty into the North Atlantic through the St. Lawrence River, and the Mississippi-Missouri-Ohio river network flows southward into the Gulf of Mexico. Where the drainage system originates, at the northern and western reaches of the Great Lakes region, lie some of the world's richest deposits of iron and copper ore. In our own time, the heartland's waterways have offered a splendid means of carrying this mineral wealth to nearby coal-producing areas for processing but in so doing have spawned widespread environmental pollution.

The Mississippi—the "Father of Waters" to nearby Algonquian-speaking Indians, and one of the world's longest rivers—carries a prodigious volume of water

**Night View of Aspen, Colorado**
*By the late twentieth century, even outdoor recreation has an enormous effect on the environment.*

**Lakes and Marshes in the Great Basin During the Last Ice Age**
*The Great Basin's extensive lakes and marshes during the last Ice Age contrast starkly with the diminished amount of surface water in the region today.*

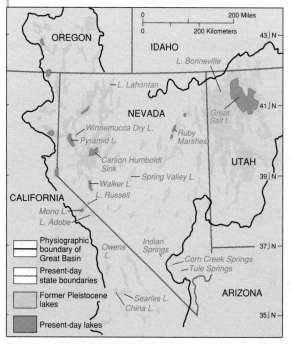

*Source:* W. F. Ruddiman and H. E. Wright, Jr., eds. "North America and Adjacent Oceans During the Last Deglaciation." *The Geology of North America* K–3 (1987): 241.

**Bonneville, Salt Flats, Utah**

## Present-Day U.S. Agriculture, Industry, and Resources

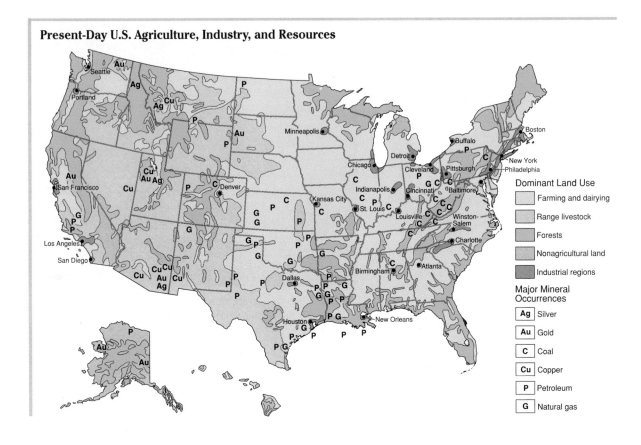

**Dominant Land Use**
- Farming and dairying
- Range livestock
- Forests
- Nonagricultural land
- Industrial regions

**Major Mineral Occurrences**

| | |
|---|---|
| **Ag** | Silver |
| **Au** | Gold |
| **C** | Coal |
| **Cu** | Copper |
| **P** | Petroleum |
| **G** | Natural gas |

**Mississippi River Flood, 1993, at Davenport, Iowa**
*The river's most severe floods disrupt human routines in cities as well as in the countryside.*

and silt. It has changed course many times in geological history. The lower Mississippi (below the junction with the Ohio River) meanders constantly. In the process, the river deposits rich sediments throughout its broad, ancient floodplain. Indeed, the Mississippi has carried so much silt over the millennia that in its lower stretches, the river flows *above* the surrounding valley, which it catastrophically floods when its high banks (levees) are breached. Over millions of years, such riverborne sediment covered what was once the westward extension of the Appalachians in northern Mississippi and eastern Arkansas. Only the Ozark Plateau and Ouachita Mountains remain exposed, forming the hill country of southern Missouri, north-central Arkansas, and eastern Oklahoma. These uplands have evolved into an economically and culturally distinctive region—beautiful but isolated and impoverished.

Below New Orleans the Mississippi empties into the Gulf of Mexico through an enormous delta with an intricate network of grassy swamps known as bayous. The Mississippi Delta offers rich farm soil, capable of supporting a large population. Swarming with water-

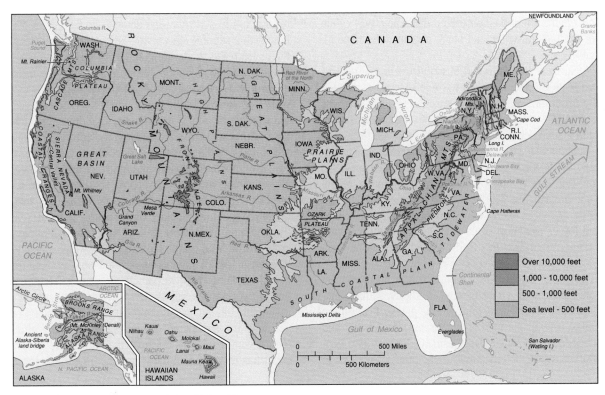

*Above,* **Physiographic Map of the United States**
*Below,* **Natural Vegetation of the United States**

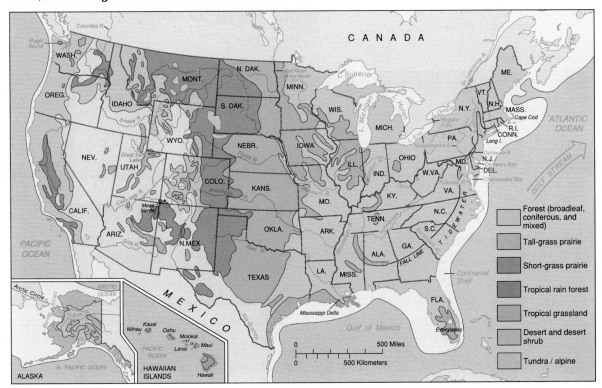

fowl, insects, alligators, and marine plants and animals, this environment has nurtured a distinctive way of life for the Indian, white, and black peoples who have inhabited it.

North of the Ohio and Missouri rivers, themselves products of glacial runoff, Ice Age glaciation molded the American heartland. Because the local terrain was generally flat prior to glaciation, the ice sheets distributed glacial debris quite evenly. Spread even farther by wind and rivers, this fine-ground glacial dust slowly created the fertile farm soil of the Midwest. Glaciers also dug out the five Great Lakes (Superior, Huron, Michigan, Ontario, and Erie), collectively the world's largest body of fresh water. Water flowing from Lake Erie to the lower elevation of Lake Ontario created Niagara Falls, comparable only to the Grand Canyon as testimony to nature's power.

Most of the heartland's eastern and northern sectors were once heavily forested. To the west thick, tall-grass prairie covered Illinois and parts of adjoining states, as well as much of the Missouri River basin and the middle Arkansas River basin (Oklahoma and central Texas). Beyond the Missouri the prairie gave way to short-grass steppe—the Great Plains, cold in winter, blazing hot in summer, and always dry. The great distances that separate the heartland's prairies and Great Plains from the moderating effects of the oceans have made this region's annual temperature range the most extreme in North America. As the traveler moves westward, elevations rise gradually, winds howl ceaselessly, trees grow only along streambeds, long droughts alternate with violent thunderstorms and tornadoes, and water and wood are ever scarcer.

Now much of this forested, grassy world is forever altered. The heartland has become open farming country. Gone are the flocks of migratory birds that once darkened the daytime skies of the plains; gone are the free-roaming bison. Forests now only fringe the heartland: in the lake country of northern Minnesota and Wisconsin, on Michigan's upper peninsula, and across the hilly uplands of the Appalachians, southern Indiana, and the Ozarks. The settlers who displaced the region's Indian inhabitants have done most of the plowing up of prairie grass and felling of trees since the early nineteenth century. Destruction of the forest and grassy cover has made the Midwest both a "breadbasket" for

**America's Heartland**
*Grain harvesting (right).*
*Bison on South Dakota prairie (below).*

the world market and, during intervals of drought, a bleak "dust bowl."

## The Atlantic Seaboard

The eastern edge of the heartland is marked by the ancient Appalachian Mountain chain, which over the course of 200 million years has been ground down to gentle ridges paralleling one another southwest to northeast. Between the ridges lie fertile valleys such as Virginia's Shenandoah. The Appalachian hill country's wealth is in thick timber and mineral beds—particularly the Paleozoic coal deposits—whose heavy exploitation since the nineteenth century has accelerated destructive soil erosion in this softly beautiful, mountainous land.

Descending gently from the Appalachians' eastern slope is the piedmont ("foot of the mountain"). In this broad, rolling upland extending from Alabama to Maryland, the rich red soil has been ravaged in modern times by excessive cotton and tobacco cultivation. The piedmont's modern piney-woods cover constitutes "secondary growth" replacing the sturdy hardwood trees that Native Americans and pioneering whites and blacks once knew. The northward extension of the piedmont from Pennsylvania to New England has more broadleaf vegetation, a harsher winter climate, and

(through the Hudson and Connecticut river valleys) somewhat better access to the piedmont itself. But unlike the piedmont, upstate New York and New England were shaped by glaciation: the terrain here comprises hills contoured by advancing and retreating ice, and numerous lakes scoured out by glaciers. Belts of debris remain, and in many places granite boulders shoulder their way up through the soil. Though picturesque, the land is the despair of anyone who has tried to plow it.

From southeastern Massachusetts and Rhode Island to south-central Alabama runs the fall line, the boundary between the relatively hard rock of the interior and the softer sediment of the coastal plain. Rivers crossing the fall line drop quickly to near sea level, thus making a series of rapids that block navigation upstream from the coast.

The character of the Atlantic coastal plain varies strikingly from south to north. In the extreme south, at the tip of the Florida peninsula, the climate and vegetation are subtropical. The southern coastal lands running north from Florida to Chesapeake Bay and the mouth of the Delaware River compose the tidewater region. This is a wide, rather flat lowland, heavily wooded with a mixture of broadleaf and coniferous forests, ribboned with numerous small rivers, occasionally swampy, and often miserably hot and humid in summer. North of Delaware Bay, the coastal lowlands nar-

**Cades Cove, Great Smoky Mountains** (right)
**Tennessee Strip Mining** (below)
*The impact of human hands is dramatically apparent in these two starkly contrasting Appalachian hill country scenes.*

**Saltwater Marsh, Outer Banks, North Carolina**

**The Tip of Cape Cod, Massachusetts** *(below)*

**Oyster Men, Chesapeake Bay, Maryland**

ward through eastern Canada; the Connecticut in New England; the Hudson, Delaware, Susquehanna, and Potomac in what are now the Middle Atlantic states; the Savannah in the South. Most of these originally carried glacial meltwater. The Susquehanna and the Potomac filled in the broad, shallow Chesapeake Bay, teeming with marine life and offering numerous anchorages for oceangoing ships.

North America's true eastern edge is not the coastline but the offshore continental shelf, whose relatively shallow waters extend as far as 250 miles into the Atlantic before plunging deeply. Along the rocky Canadian and Maine coasts, where at the end of the Ice Age the rising ocean half-covered glaciated mountains and valleys, oceangoing craft may find numerous small anchorages. South of Massachusetts Bay, the Atlantic shore and the Gulf of Mexico coastline form a shoreline of sandy beaches and long barrier islands paralleling the mainland. Tropical storms boiling up from the open seas regularly lash North America's Atlantic shores, and at all times brisk winds make coastal navigation treacherous.

row and flatten to form the New Jersey pine barrens, Long Island, and Cape Cod—all of these created by the deposit of glacial debris. Here the climate is noticeably milder than in the interior. North of Massachusetts Bay, the land back of the immediate shoreline becomes increasingly mountainous.

Many large rivers drain into the Atlantic: the St. Lawrence, flowing out of the Great Lakes northeast-

Crossing the Atlantic east to west can daunt even skilled mariners, particularly those battling against powerful winds by sail. Here, on one of the world's stormiest seas, the mighty Gulf Stream current sweeps from southwest to northeast. Winds off the North American mainland also trend steadily eastward, and dangerous icebergs floating south from Greenland's waters threaten every ship. Little wonder that in 1620 the *Mayflower* Pilgrims' first impulse on landing was to sink to their knees in thanks to God for having transported them safely across "the vast and furious ocean." Many a vessel went to the bottom.

**Pemigewasset Wilderness, White Mountains, New Hampshire**

But for millions, the Atlantic coastal region of North America offered a welcoming haven to settlers. For example, ten thousand years ago, ancient Indian hunters followed a warming climate eastward across the Appalachians to the coast. During the first millennium A.D., eastern peoples adopted the Woodland culture and agriculture of the heartland. Offshore, well within their reach, lay such productive fishing grounds as the Grand Banks and Cape Cod's coastal bays, where cool-water upwellings on the continental shelf had lured swarms of fish and crustaceans. "The abundance of sea-fish are almost beyond believing," wrote a breathless English settler in 1630, "and sure I should scarce have believed it, except I had seen it with my own eyes."

## A Legacy and a Challenge

At least three thousand miles of open sea separates North America from Europe and Africa; and Asia, except for the subarctic region where Alaska and Siberia once joined, lies even more distant.

A lingering sense of isolation stimulated European-descended Americans' hopes of keeping "Old World" problems away from the pristine "New World," just as North America's fertile soil, extensive forests, and rich mineral resources long conjured up visions of limitless wealth. But population growth, intensive agriculture, industrialization, urbanization, and a hunger for consumer goods have stretched to the limits the American land's ability to maintain a modern society without irreversible ecological damage. And only in the twentieth century did Americans learn that global transportation networks and instantaneous communication make isolation impossible. At last, as ecologist Aldo Leopold put it, they began discovering that the earth's people "are only fellow voyagers in the odyssey of evolution." And that lesson has been hard learned. "It required 19 centuries to define decent man-to-man conduct and the process is only half-done," Leopold admonished; "it may take as long to evolve a code of decency for man-to-land conduct."

It is in evolving such a code, however, that the Native American legacy may yet prove most enduring. Interacting constantly with their physical environments, Indians considered themselves spiritually related to the land and all living beings that shared it. In recapturing a sense that the land—its life-sustaining bounty and its soul-sustaining beauty—is itself of inestimable value and not merely a means to the end of material growth, future American generations may reestablish a sense of historical and cultural continuity with their Native American precursors. Thereby they can truly be possessed by their land instead of simply being its possessors.

# 1

# America
# Begins

**Woman Grinding Maize,** Stone Effigy Pipe, Spiro Mound,
Oklahoma *c. A.D. 1250–1500*

Hiawatha had known the depths of despair. For years his people, the group of Indian nations known as the Iroquois, had been beset by a destructive, seemingly endless cycle of violence and revenge. Families, villages, and nations fought one another, and neighboring Indians attacked relentlessly. When Hiawatha tried to restore peace among his own Onondaga people, an evil sorcerer who opposed peace caused the deaths of his seven beloved daughters. Grief-stricken and angry, Hiawatha wandered alone into the forest. After several days he reached the shore of a lake, where he experienced a series of visions. First he saw a flock of wild ducks suddenly fly up from the lake, taking the water with them. Hiawatha walked onto the dry lake bed, gathering and stringing the beautiful purple and white shells that lay there. He saw the shells, called wampum, as symbolic "words" of condolence that, when properly presented, would soothe grief, no matter how intense. Then he met a holy man named Deganawidah ("the Peacemaker"), who presented him with the beads and spoke the appropriate words, one to dry his weeping eyes, another to open his ears to the words of peace and reason, a third to clear his throat so that he himself could once again speak peacefully and reasonably. Deganawidah and Hiawatha then took the wampum to the five Iroquois nations. To each they introduced the ritual of condolence as a new message of peace. The Iroquois subsequently submerged their differences and created a council of chiefs and a confederacy, based on the condolence ritual. Thus was born the powerful League of the Iroquois.

Although it is an oral tradition couched in spiritual language, the story of Hiawatha and Deganawidah depicts a concrete event in American history. Archaeological evidence at Iroquois sites corroborates the sequence of bloody warfare followed by peace and dates the league's origins at some time between the late-fourteenth and the mid-fifteenth century. As with all of American history before the arrival of Europeans and their system of writing, archaeological evidence and oral traditions, examined critically, are our principal sources of knowledge about the past. In this case the story refers to an event of importance not only for pre-Columbian history but for the period of European contact with Native Americans as well. For the Iroquois Confederacy was a significant diplomatic and military force throughout the colonial period and has inspired and intrigued many non-Indians down to the present, despite the fact that it was established prior to, and entirely independently of, the Europeans' arrival.

The founding of the League of the Iroquois marked just one moment in a long history that began more than ten thousand years before Christopher Columbus's first voyage. Over that time an indigenous American history unfolded, one characterized by cultural diversity and by extensive interactions among communities. Some native peoples eked out their existences in precarious environments, whereas others enjoyed affluence and prosperity; some lived in small bands, whereas others lived in large cities; some believed that the first humans came from the sky, whereas others maintained that they originated underground. Wherever and however they lived and whatever they believed, native peoples together made North America a human habitat and gave it a history.

This chapter will focus on three major questions:

- What was the relationship between environmental changes in North America and cultural changes among its Indian inhabitants?

- What were the nature and consequences of Native American communities' interactions and exchanges with one another?

**Iroquois canoe model**

♦ What basic values did Native Americans have in common despite the vast cultural differences that often separated them? How would these shared values compare with those of the Europeans who arrived after 1500?

## The First Americans

Precisely when and how the vast Western Hemisphere was first peopled remains uncertain. The most widely accepted theory is that sometime during the last Ice Age, bands of Siberian hunters crossed the expanse of land still linking North America and Asia in the far northern Pacific (see Prologue). Drifting southward from the glacier-covered north, they discovered a hunter's paradise. Giant mammoths, mastodons, horses, camels, bison, caribou, and moose, as well as smaller species, roamed the continent innocent of the ways of human predators. By 9000 B.C. the Paleo-Indians, as archaeologists call these hunters, had dispersed throughout the Western Hemisphere.

Most Native Americans are descended from these earliest migrants. A few, however, trace their lineage to later arrivals. About nine thousand years ago, Athapaskan-speaking peoples likewise crossed from northeastern Asia and spread over much of northern and western Canada and southern and central Alaska. Some of them later migrated southward to form the Apaches and Navajos in the Southwest, as well as smaller groups elsewhere. Eskimos and Aleuts began crossing the Bering Sea—which had submerged the land bridge—from Siberia between five thousand and four thousand years ago, and the Hawaiian Islands remained uninhabited until after A.D. 300.

### The Peopling of North America

Paleo-Indians established some of the foundations upon which their Native American descendants would build families and communities over the next twelve thousand years. Archaeologists surmise that Paleo-Indians dwelled in bands of about fifteen to fifty people. The men hunted; the women prepared the food and cared for the children. Members of a band lived together during the spring and summer and split into smaller groups of one or two families for the fall and winter. Although they moved constantly, they generally remained within informally defined boundaries. An exception occurred when they traveled to favored quarries to obtain jasper or flint for making tools and spear points. At such sites they encountered other bands, with whom they exchanged ideas and goods, intermarried, and participated in religious ceremonies. By such means, Paleo-Indians developed a cultural life that transcended their small bands.

Around 9000 B.C. many of the prized big-game species such as the mammoths and mastodons became extinct. The effectiveness of the Paleo-Indian hunters may have contributed to this demise, but the animals were also doomed by the warming climate, which brought ecological changes that undermined the food chain on which they depended. In other words, the replacement of the big-game mammals by humans marked part of a larger process of ecological change associated with the end of the Ice Age.

### Archaic Societies

The warming of the earth's atmosphere continued until about 4000 B.C., with far-reaching effects on the North American continent. Sea levels rose, flooding shallow offshore areas, and glacial runoff in the interior filled the Great Lakes, the Mississippi River basin, and other waterways. As the glaciers receded northward, so did the arctic and subarctic environments that had previously extended far into what are now the "lower 48" states of the United States. Treeless plains and evergreen forests gave way to deciduous forests in the East, grassland prairies on the Plains, and desert in much of

## CHRONOLOGY

**c. 10,000–9000 B.C.**   Paleo-Indians spread throughout Western Hemisphere.

**c. 9000 B.C.**   Extinction of big-game mammals.

**c. 8000 B.C.**   Archaic era begins.

**c. 7000 B.C.**   Athapaskan-speaking peoples arrive in North America.

**c. 5000 B.C.**   First domesticated plants grown in Western Hemisphere.

**c. 3500 B.C.**   First domesticated plants grown in North America.

**c. 3000–2000 B.C.**   Inuit and Aleut peoples arrive in North America.

**c. 1500 B.C.**   Archaic era ends.
Bow and arrow and ceramic pottery introduced in North America.

**c. 1200 B.C.**   Poverty Point flourishes in Louisiana.

**c. 400–100 B.C.**   Adena culture flourishes in Ohio Valley.

**c. 250 B.C.**   Hohokam culture begins in Southwest.

**c. 100 B.C.**   Anasazi culture begins in Southwest.

**c. 100 B.C.–A.D. 600**   Hopewell culture thrives in Midwest.

**c. A.D. 300**   First people arrive at Hawaiian Islands.

**c. A.D. 700**   Mississippian culture begins.

**c. A.D. 900**   Stockade and first mounds built at Cahokia.
Anasazi expansion begins.

**c. A.D. 1000–1100**   Norse settlement of Vinland flourishes on Newfoundland.

**c. A.D. 1150**   Anasazi peoples disperse to form pueblos.

**c. A.D. 1200–1300**   Cahokia declines.

**c. A.D. 1400**   League of the Iroquois formed.

**A.D. 1492**   Christopher Columbus begins permanent European colonization of Western Hemisphere.

---

the West. An immense range of flora and fauna, both on land and in the waters, came to characterize the American landscape. We are familiar with many of these same plants and animals today.

Whereas Paleo-Indians had focused most of their food gathering energy on big game, Archaic peoples, as archaeologists term native North Americans from c. 8000 B.C. to 1500 B.C., lived off wide varieties of smaller mammals, fish, and wild plants. As they used the resources of their environments more efficiently, their communities required less land area and could support larger populations. Although hunting-gathering bands in the Great Basin and Southwest changed little from Paleo-Indian times, many people in the East and Midwest now resided in villages with larger populations for all or most of the year. For example, a year-round village that flourished near Kampsville, Illinois, from 3900 to 2800 B.C., supported 100 to 150 people. It could do so because the residents knew how and when to procure fish and mussels from local lakes, in addition to the deer and other mammals, birds, nuts, and seeds available in the surrounding area.

Archaic peoples diversified other aspects of their lives as well. Besides using many more varieties of stone, they utilized bone, shell, copper, horn, ivory, as-

phalt, clay, and leather to make such objects as tools, weapons, utensils, and ornaments. Although many of these materials were available locally, Native Americans obtained others through exchanges, both with neighbors and through long-distance trade networks. Archaeological evidence gives some indication of the extent and importance of long-distance trade. Obsidian (a glassy black volcanic rock) from the Yellowstone region, copper from the Great Lakes, and marine shells from the coasts appear at sites hundreds and even thousands of miles from their points of origin. A few large

**Archaic Hunting Aid**
*This duck decoy was made two to three thousand years ago by a hunter living at Lovelock Cave in west-central Nevada.*

sites, among them Indian Knoll in western Kentucky, which dates to 2500–2000 B.C., served as major centers of interregional trade.

Trade networks were routes not only for materials but also for ideas about their uses. By means of these pathways, the techniques developed in one locale for making material objects, procuring food, or utilizing the medicinal properties of plants were carried to other areas, overriding the narrow boundaries of community, language, and ethnicity. Out of such diffusions of ideas arose regional cultural patterns (see below). Trade also served to spread religious beliefs, as exemplified in ideas and practices relating to death. Human burials became more elaborate during the Archaic era as Native Americans in many regions buried the dead with their personal possessions as well as with objects fashioned from obsidian, copper, shell, and other highly valued substances. They often sprinkled the flexed corpses with bright red hematite, a source of iron, so that they resembled a baby at birth. Ideas of death as a kind of rebirth remained widespread in North America at the time Europeans began arriving many centuries later.

Over time, Archaic Americans sharpened many of the distinctions between women's and men's roles. Men took responsibility for fishing as well as hunting, whereas women harvested and prepared the products of wild plants, including the grinding and milling of seeds. Men and women each made the tools needed for their tasks. In general, men's activities entailed travel, and women's activities kept them close to the village, where they bore and raised children. These role distinctions are apparent in the burials at Indian Knoll, where tools relating to hunting, fishing, woodworking, and leatherworking were usually buried with men and those relating to nut cracking and seed grinding with women. Yet gender-specific distinctions by no means applied to all activities, for objects used by shamans, or religious healers, were distributed equally between male and female graves.

## The Indians' Continent

By 1500 B.C. Indians in parts of North America were shaping new ways of life and new institutions, transcending the Archaic cultures developed over the preceding millennia. Most post-Archaic Americans remained in small bands consisting of a few families and continued to rely on combinations of hunting, fishing, and gathering. But others developed more specialized methods of food production and more actively shaped their environments to their own needs. In the Southwest, the Southeast, and the Northeast the advent of agriculture and of large centers of trade and population marked a radical departure from Archaic patterns and from the foraging way of life still followed by Indians in other regions.

Despite the discrepancies emerging among native societies, the ties between them grew strong. Trade networks carrying goods and ideas over geographic distances and across linguistic, ethnic, and cultural divides continued to proliferate. In this way the bow and arrow and ceramic pottery spread throughout the Americas, from the smallest bands to the largest cities. And Indians virtually everywhere retained their preferences for seasonal food procurement and for living in communities based on kinship, often abandoning or resisting more centralized systems that proved unworkable or oppressive.

## The Northern and Western Perimeters

In western Alaska, where the first Americans had arrived thousands of years earlier, the post-Archaic period marked the beginning of a new way of life. The Eskimos and Aleuts had brought highly sophisticated tools and weapons from their Siberian homeland. Combining ivory, bone, and other materials, they fashioned harpoons and spears for the pursuit of sea mammals and—in the case of the Eskimos—caribou. Through their continued contacts with Siberia, the Eskimos made and used the first bows and arrows, the first ceramic pottery, and the first pit houses (structures set partially below ground level) in the Americas. As they perfected their ways of living in the cold tundra environment, many Eskimos spread across upper Canada to the shores of Labrador, western Newfoundland, and Greenland.

Long before the arrival of Columbus, the Eskimos made contact with Europeans and used some of their material goods. From about A.D. 1, a few iron tools were reaching western Alaska by way of Russia and Siberia. However, they were too few in number to affect Eskimo culture in any substantial way. Contacts with Europeans were more direct and sustained in areas of Greenland, Newfoundland, and Labrador, where Norse people from Scandinavia attempted to colonize,

**Major Language Groups of North American Indians and Locations of Selected Peoples, A.D. 1500**
*Most of the several hundred languages spoken by North American native peoples on the eve of European coloniza-
tion were derived from just a dozen basic language groups.* (Source: Dean Snow, *The Archaeology of North America:
American Indians and Their Origins* (London: Thames and Hudson, Ltd., 1976)).

beginning in the late tenth century A.D. The Norse exchanged metal goods for ivory with the Eskimos and
with the Beothuk Indians near their settlement in Newfoundland. But peaceful trade gave way to hostile encounters. By the eleventh century the native peoples'
resistance to the newcomers' colonizing ambitions led
the Norse to withdraw from Vinland, as they called

Newfoundland. As a Norse leader, dying after losing a
battle with some natives, put it, "There is fat around
my belly! We have won a fine and fruitful country, but
will hardly be allowed to enjoy it." Several more centuries would pass before Europeans would enjoy, at
the expense of native peoples, the fruits of a "New
World."

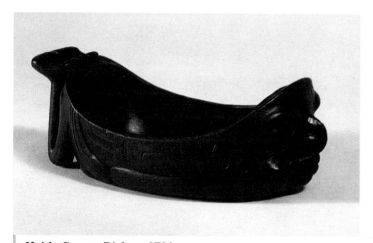

**Haida Grease Dish, c. 1700**
*Northwest Coast artists crafted even the most seemingly mundane objects with an eye for beauty and form.*

Along the Pacific coast, from Alaska to southern California, improvements in the production and storage of certain key foods enabled Indians to develop more settled ways of life. On the Northwest coast, from the Alaskan panhandle to northern California, and in the Columbia Plateau, natives devoted brief periods of each year to catching salmon and other spawning fish. After drying the fish, the Northwest Coast Indians stored it in quantities sufficient to last the year round. As a result, their seasonal movements gave way to a settled lifestyle in permanent villages consisting of cedar-plank houses. Plateau Indians constructed villages of pit houses where they subsisted on salmon through the summer. They left the villages in spring and fall for hunting and gathering.

By A.D. 1 many villages on the Northwest coast numbered several hundred people. Trade and warfare with interior groups strengthened the power of chiefs and other leading figures, whose families were distinguished from those of commoners by their wealth and prestige. These leading families proclaimed their status most conspicuously in elaborate totem poles depicting supernatural beings supposedly linked to their ancestors and in potlatches, ceremonies in which they gave away or destroyed much of their material wealth. From the time of the earliest contacts, Europeans were awestruck by the artistic and architectural achievements of the Northwest Coast Indians. "What must astonish most," wrote a French explorer in 1791, "is to see paint-

ing everywhere, everywhere sculpture, among a nation of hunters."

At about the same time as native peoples in the Northwest, Indians on the coast and in the interior valleys of what is now California also became more settled. Residing in villages of about one hundred people, they devoted extensive time and effort to processing acorns. After the fall harvest, the Indians ground the acorns into meal, leached them of their bitter tannic acid, and then roasted, boiled, or baked the nuts prior to eating or storing them. In the face of intense competition for acorns, native Californians defined territorial boundaries more rigidly than elsewhere in pre-Columbian North America and combined several villages under the leadership of a single chief. The chiefs conducted trade, diplomacy, and religious ceremonies with neighboring groups and, when necessary, led their people in battle. Along with the resources of game, fish, and plants available to them, acorns enabled the Indians of California to prosper. As a Spanish friar arriving in California from Mexico in 1770 wrote, "This land exceeds all the preceding territory in fertility and abundance of things necessary for sustenance."

**Chumash Baskets**
*California Indians, including the Chumash, gathered, prepared, and stored acorns and other foods in baskets crafted by specialized weavers.*

The end of the Archaic period is less noticeable in the Great Basin than almost anywhere else in North America. This region's warm, dry climate was almost as forbidding to humans as that of the frigid Arctic. Foraging bands continued to move over the area, depending primarily on hunting small mammals and harvesting seeds and piñon (pine) nuts. Little change occurred until about the fourteenth or fifteenth century A.D., when Paiute, Ute, and Shoshone Indians fanned over the Great Basin from their homeland in southeastern California, absorbing or displacing the earlier inhabitants. Although the newcomers' way of life was essentially the same as that of the older groups, their more efficient seed processing enabled them to support larger populations, which in turn occupied ever-larger territories.

## The Southwest

Although the peoples of the Northwest coast and California cultivated tobacco, they never farmed food-bearing plants. With their abundant food sources, they had little incentive to hazard the additional risks that agriculture would have entailed, especially in California, with its dry summers. However, elsewhere in North America agriculture became central to Indian life. In the arid Southwest, natives concentrated much of their communities' energy on irrigation in order to feed themselves by farming. In the humid Eastern Woodlands, on the other hand, plant cultivation came more easily. But in both regions, the advent of agriculture was a long, slow process that never entirely displaced other food-procuring activities.

Farming began in the Western Hemisphere about 5000 B.C.—just as agriculture was being introduced to Europe from southwestern Asia—when Indians living in the Tehuacán Valley of central Mexico experimentally planted the seeds of certain wild plants they customarily harvested. Among these were squash, maize (corn), and eventually beans. Slowly, the techniques of plant domestication spread in all directions, reaching the Southwest by about 3500 B.C. But substantial changes in southwestern life began only after 400 B.C., when the introduction (probably from Mexico) of a more drought-resistant strain of maize enabled the inhabitants to move from the highlands to the drier lowlands. In the centuries that followed, populations rose, and native culture was transformed. The two most influential new cultural traditions were the Hohokam and the Anasazi.

**Mimbres Bowl, C. A.D. 1100**
*The women of Mimbres, in southwestern New Mexico, produced some of the finest pottery north of Mexico. This bowl depicts the guardians of the four cardinal directions, considered sacred in many Native American cultures.*

The Hohokam emerged during the third century B.C. when ancestors of the Pima and Tohono O'odham Indians began farming in the Gila River and Salt River valleys of southern Arizona. Hohokam peoples built elaborate canal systems for irrigation that enabled them to harvest two crops per year, an astonishing achievement in such an arid environment. To construct and maintain their canals, the Hohokam people needed large, coordinated work forces. They built permanent villages, usually consisting of several hundred people. Although many such villages remained independent, others joined confederations in which several towns were linked by canals. The central village in each confederation coordinated labor, trade, and religious and political life for all the communities connected to it.

Essentially a local creation, Hohokam culture nevertheless drew extensively on materials and ideas from outside the Southwest. From about the sixth century A.D., the large villages had ball courts and platform mounds like those found throughout Mexico at the time. As in Mexico, ball games were major public events in Hohokam villages. Although no evidence of their rules survives, they probably resembled the Mexican game, in which play was rough, players could not use their hands, and the losers relinquished some of

**Pueblo Bonito, Chaco Canyon, New Mexico**
*Pueblo Bonito illustrates the richness and grand scale of Anasazi architecture.*

their material possessions. Mexican influence was also apparent in the creations of Hohokam artists, who worked in clay, stone, turquoise, and shell. Archaeologists have unearthed such artifacts as rubber balls, macaw feathers, and copper bells among the Mexican items found at Hohokam sites. Artists used seashells from California in pottery, as backing for turquoise mosaics, and as material for intricate etchings.

Among the last southwesterners to take up farming were a people known as the Anasazi, a Navajo term meaning "ancient ones." Their culture originated in the Four Corners area where Arizona, New Mexico, Colorado, and Utah meet. By the sixth century A.D., the Anasazi people were only beginning to harvest beans, live in permanent villages with pit houses, and make pottery. Yet over the next six centuries, these ancestors of the modern Pueblo Indians expanded over a wide area and became the most powerful people in the Southwest.

One of the distinguishing characteristics of Anasazi culture was its architecture. Early Anasazi people lived in pit houses that featured underground storage cists, ventilator shafts, and small holes in the floor known as *sipapus.* The Anasazis and modern Pueblos maintain

that the first humans reached the earth from underground, following a long and tortuous journey through several underworlds. Symbolizing this journey, the sipapu was a sacred place in each family's house. As village populations increased after the sixth century, often reaching one hundred or more houses, the Anasazis shifted to above-ground, rectangular apartments. However, they retained the form of the pit house in their *kivas,* round, partly underground structures in which the men held religious ceremonies. To this day Anasazi-style apartments and kivas are central features of Pueblo Indian architecture in the Southwest.

From the beginning of the tenth century to the middle of the twelfth, during an unusually wet period in the Southwest, the Anasazis expanded over much of what is today northern New Mexico and Arizona. The population of some villages grew to more than a thousand. In Chaco Canyon in present-day northwestern New Mexico, a cluster of twelve large towns forged a powerful confederation numbering about fifteen thousand people. A system of roads radiated out of the canyon to satellite towns located as far as sixty-five miles away. These roads were perfectly straight; their builders even carved out stairs or footholds in the sides of steep cliffs rather than go around them. The largest of the towns, Pueblo Bonito, had about twelve hundred inhabitants and was the home of two Great Kivas, each about fifty feet in diameter. People traveled from the outlying towns to Chaco Canyon for religious rituals. In addition, the canyon was the center of a turquoise industry that manufactured beads for trade with Mexico. By controlling rainwater runoff through small dams, terraces, and other devices, the towns fed themselves as well as their satellites.

The classic Anasazi culture, as manifested at Chaco Canyon, Mesa Verde in southwestern Colorado, Canyon de Chelly in northeastern Arizona, and other sites, came to an end in the twelfth and thirteenth centuries. Although Chaco Canyon's somewhat earlier collapse may have been triggered by a cutoff of its turquoise trade with Mexico, the overriding cause of the Anasazi demise was drought. Suddenly, the amount of available farmland was drastically reduced for a population that had grown rapidly during the preceding centuries. The great Anasazi centers were abandoned as the inhabitants dispersed. Most formed new pueblos on or near the upper Rio Grande, whereas others moved south to establish the Zuni and Hopi pueblos. Descendants of the Anasazis still inhabit many of these pueblos. Other large agricultural communities, such as those of the Hohokam, also dispersed when drought came. With farming peoples now clustered in the few areas with enough water, the drier lands of the Southwest attracted the foraging Apaches and Navajos, whose arrival at the end of the fourteenth century ended their long migration from northwestern Canada.

### The Eastern Woodlands

Whereas the Hohokam and Anasazi peoples built large villages and created centralized or confederated political systems as a consequence of deciding to farm for most of their food, natives on the Northwest coast and in California enlarged and consolidated their societies in the absence of agriculture. Nonfarming Indians in much of the Eastern Woodlands—that vast stretch of land from the Mississippi Valley to the Atlantic Ocean—likewise experimented with village life and political centralization without farming. But after doing so, they developed an extraordinarily productive agriculture.

In 1200 B. C. about five thousand people had concentrated in a single village at Poverty Point on the Mississippi River in Louisiana. The village was flanked by two large constructed mounds and surrounded by six concentric embankments, the outermost of which spanned more than half a mile in diameter. During the spring and autumn equinoxes, a person standing on the larger mound could watch the sun rise directly over the village center. As with similar communities of the period in Mexico, solar observations were the basis for religious beliefs as well as for a calendar. Poverty Point also lay at the center of a much larger political and economic unit. The settlement imported large quantities of quartz, copper, obsidian, crystal, and other materials considered sacred from throughout eastern North America and then redistributed them to nearby communities. These communities almost certainly supplied some of the labor for the earthworks. Although Poverty Point was built by local inhabitants, its general design and organization suggest the influence of the Olmec peoples of Mexico. For reasons that are unclear, Poverty Point flourished for only about three centuries and then declined. Nevertheless, it foreshadowed later developments in the Mississippi Valley.

A different kind of mound-building culture, called Adena, emerged in the Ohio Valley in the fifth century B.C. Adena villages were smaller than Poverty Point, rarely exceeding four hundred inhabitants. But Adena people spread over a wide area and built hundreds of mounds, most of them containing graves. The largest, Grave Creek Mound in West Virginia, was 240 feet in diameter, 70 feet high, and contained 72,000 tons of soil. The treatment of Adena dead varied widely, indicating differences in social or political status. Some corpses were cremated, others were placed in round clay basins, and still others were given elaborate tombs. Some burials contained just a few utilitarian grave goods, whereas others had many more and varied goods including pipes and other finely crafted objects.

During the first century B.C., Adena culture evolved into a more complex and widespread culture known as Hopewell. Hopewell ceremonial centers were even larger and more elaborate than their Adena predecessors. They proliferated not only in the Ohio Valley but also in the Illinois River Valley. Some centers contained two or three dozen mounds within enclosures of several square miles. The variety and quantity of goods buried with members of the elite were also greater. Some Hopewell corpses were surrounded with thousands of freshwater pearls or copper ornaments or with sheets of mica, quartz, or other sacred substances. Hopewell artisans fashioned a wide variety of effigies,

**Great Serpent Mound, Ohio**

*This well-known mound, built for religious ceremonies rather than for burials, depicts a 1,254-foot-long snake devouring an egg or a frog.*

**Poverty Point, Louisiana**

*This perspective sketch shows the large mound located just outside the concentric rings, as well as a smaller mound in the upper right. The earthworks symbolized Poverty Point's importance as a regional center for trade and religious ceremonies.*

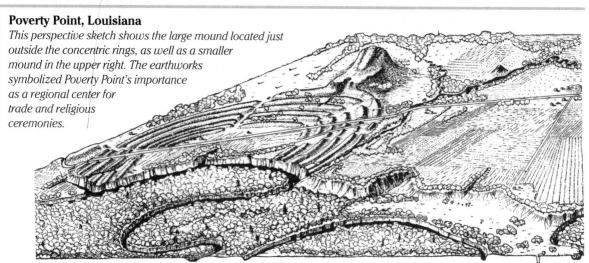

ornaments, and jewelry, which their owners wore to their graves. The raw materials for these objects originated in locales throughout America east of the Rockies. Through far-flung trade networks Hopewell influence spread over much of the Eastern Woodlands—to communities as far away as Wisconsin, Missouri, Florida, and New York. Some of these, such as Marksville in Louisiana, emulated the Ohio centers in almost every detail, but others were more selective, imitating Hopewell mounds, copper work, or pottery. Although the great Hopewell centers of the Ohio and Illinois valleys were abandoned in the fifth century A.D. for reasons that are unclear, they had an enormous influence on subsequent developments in eastern North America.

Remarkably, the people who created the sophisticated Hopewell culture were hunter-gatherers but not farmers. Archaic Indians in Kentucky and Missouri had cultivated small amounts of squash as early as 2500 B.C., and maize first appeared in eastern North

America by 300 B.C. But agriculture became a dietary mainstay for Woodlands people only between the seventh and twelfth centuries A.D., as women moved beyond gathering and minor cultivating activities to become the major producers of food.

The first full-time farmers in the East were Indians living on the floodplains of the Mississippi River and its major tributaries. They developed a new culture, called Mississippian, that incorporated elements of Hopewell culture and ideas from Mexico into their indigenous traditions. The volume of Mississippian craft production and long-distance trade dwarfed those of Adena and Hopewell cultures. At the same time, Mississippian towns, numbering hundreds or even thousands of people, were built around open plazas like those of central Mexico. Large platform mounds stood next to the plazas, topped by sumptuous religious temples and the residences of chiefs and other elites. Religious ceremonies focused on the worship of the sun as the source of agricultural fertility. The people considered chiefs to be related to the sun. When a chief died, his wives and servants were killed so that they could accompany him to the afterlife. Largely in connection with their religious and funeral rituals, Mississippian artists produced highly sophisticated work in clay, stone, shell, copper, wood, and other materials.

Many Mississippian centers were built not by local natives but by outsiders seeking to combine farming and riverborne trade (see map). Local natives often were coerced into bringing corn and goods to a new center and paying homage to its chief. By the tenth century most Mississippian centers were part of even larger systems, based on trade and on shared religious beliefs and dominated by a single "super-center." The most powerful such system centered around Cahokia (see A Place in Time), located near modern St. Louis.

For two and a half centuries, Cahokia reigned supreme in the American heartland. Beginning in the thirteenth century, however, Cahokia and its allied centers began to experience shortages of food and other resources. Soon they were challenged militarily by neighboring peoples and, as a result, the inhabitants, fled to the countryside. By the fifteenth century, Indians in the central Mississippi Valley were living (like their Archaic forebears) in small villages linked by reciprocity rather than coercion. Similar developments led to the decline of some temple-mound centers in the Southeast, but in this region new centers arose to take their place.

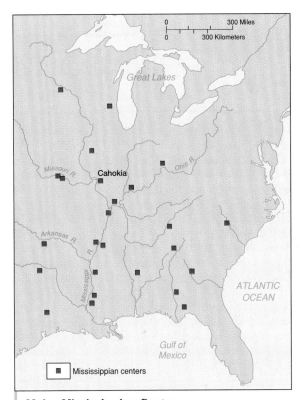

**Major Mississippian Centers**
(Source: Jay A. Levenson, ed., *Art in the Age of Exploration: Circa 1492* (New Haven, Conn.: Yale University Press, 1991)).

In spite of Cahokia's decline, however, Mississippian culture profoundly affected Native Americans in the East. Mississippians spread new strains of maize and beans, along with many of the techniques and tools to cultivate these crops, enabling women to weave agriculture into the fabric of village life among the Iroquois and other Indians throughout the region. Only in portions of northern New England and the upper Great Lakes was the growing season generally too short for maize (which required 100 frost-free days) to be a reliable crop. Some eastern Indians, searching for new farmlands, moved to the river valleys of the plains, where they interacted peacefully with the region's hunting peoples.

Indian hands tended eastern North America's lands with skill and care. Over much of the region, great expanses of hardwood trees formed open, parklike tracts, free of underbrush (which Indians systematically burned) but rich with grass and berry bushes that at-

## Cahokia in 1200

Between the tenth and thirteenth centuries, a city of about twenty thousand people flourished near the confluence of the Mississippi and Missouri rivers. Called Cahokia, it filled more than six square miles and contained more than 120 earthworks. At its center a four-terraced structure called Monk's Mound covered fifteen acres (more than the Great Pyramids of Egypt) and rose 100 feet at its highest point. Surrounding the city, a 125-square-mile metropolitan area encompassed ten large towns and more than fifty farming villages. In addition, Cahokia dominated a vast network of commercial and political alliances extending over much of the American heartland.

Cahokia's beginnings lay in the seventh century A.D., as Native Americans in the East were shifting to farming as their primary means of procuring food. In search of better soil, several small villages moved to the low floodplain extending eastward from the Mississippi around what is now the Illinois side of greater St. Louis. Around A.D. 900 these villages began their transformation into a city with the construction of several mounds. Within another two centuries, a stockade enclosed Monk's Mound and numerous other public structures, and most of the city's residents lived outside the walled precincts.

Cahokia was ideally situated for a position of preeminence in mid-America. Its fertile land yielded surplus agricultural crops, which the women harvested, and the river provided rich supplies of fish and mussels. Game and wild plants abounded in nearby uplands. The city had ready access not only to the Mississippi and Missouri rivers but to the Ohio and Illinois, where Adena and Hopewell peoples had previously developed extensive trade networks based on shared religious beliefs. Cahokia and other Mississippian societies drew on Hopewell be-

### Cahokia Mounds
*This contemporary painting conveys Cahokia's grand scale. Not until the late eighteenth century did another North American city (Philadelphia) surpass the population of Cahokia, c. 1200.*

liefs and new ideas from Mexico as they erected even more complex political, economic, and religious institutions. By the twelfth century, some scholars believe, Cahokia was the capital of a potential nation-state.

Archaeology provides evidence of what Cahokians made and left in the ground as well as clues to their social structure, trade networks, and beliefs. Work gangs dug the soil for the mounds with shovels made of wood and stone and then carried the dirt in baskets to construction sites, often more than half a mile away. Much of the workforce for this backbreaking labor undoubtedly was drawn from neighboring towns, which also contributed agricultural surpluses to feed specialized artisans and elites in the city. The artisans produced pottery, shell beads, copper ornaments, clothing, stone tools, and a range of other goods. The raw materials for these objects were brought to Cahokia from locations all over eastern and central North America as tribute—payment by Indian societies dependent on Cahokia—or in return for the finished products. The coordination of labor, trade, and other activities also required a sizable class of managers or overseers. Atop all these were the political and religious leaders, whose overpowering roles are confirmed by French accounts, recorded in the eighteenth century, of a similar society among the Natchez Indians of the lower Mississippi River.

Archaeologists also find evidence of social ranking at Cahokia in the treatment of the dead. Most people were buried in mass graves outside the city, but more prestigious commoners were placed in ridgetop mounds, and those of highest status in conical mounds. In the single most remarkable mound, an adult male was laid out on a platform of twenty thousand beads, made from shells originating in the Gulf of Mexico. He was surrounded by bushels of mica from the Appalachians, a sheet of rolled copper from Lake Superior, and quivers of arrows from communities throughout the Mississippi Valley. This extraordinary man did not go to his grave alone. An adjacent pit contained the bodies of fifty young females in their late teens and early twenties; another held the remains of four men whose heads and hands were cut off; and a third included three men and three women. French witnesses describe how, when a Natchez ruler died, his wife, servants, guards, and others personally attached to him were killed so that they could accompany him in the afterlife. The people called this ruler the Great Sun to denote his position as earthly representative of the sun, the central focus of Mississippian religion. This and burials like it at Cahokia appear to be based on similar beliefs.

By 1200 Cahokia had reached its peak. During the century that followed, it declined in size and power, while other centers in the Southeast and Midwest surpassed it. Although the causes of this decline are not certain, the archaeological evidence provides clues. First, neighboring communities were straining to produce enough crops to feed themselves and the many Ca-

**Stone Spud**
*A spud was used in ceremonies as a symbol of authority.*

hokians who did not grow their own food. Second, the city's demands for fuel and construction materials were seriously reducing the supply of wood in and around Cahokia. This depletion of the forests also deprived residents of the animals and wild plants on which they depended for food. Third, the strengthening of the stockade surrounding central Cahokia suggests that the elites were facing a military challenge from inside or outside the city, or both. Finally, the trade networks that formerly brought tribute to Cahokia and carried away the city's finished products had collapsed. Taken together, these trends indicate that a combination of environmental factors and resistance to centralized authority probably led to Cahokia's downfall. By the time the French explorer La Salle passed through in 1682, Cahokia was a small village of Illinois Indians who, like other native peoples of the region, had abandoned Mississippian religious and political systems for the autonomous villages of their ancestors.

**Sandstone Tablet Depicting Birdman**

**Guale Indians Planting Crops, 1564**
*A French explorer sketched this scene on the Carolina coast in which men are breaking up the soil while women sow corn, bean, and squash seeds.*

tracted a profusion of game. The Woodland peoples' "slash-and-burn" method of land management was environmentally sound and economically productive. Men cleared the land by burning underbrush and destroying the larger trees' bark. Then, amid the leafless deadwood, women planted corn, beans, and pumpkins in soil enriched by ash. After several years of abundant harvests, yields declined, and the Indians moved on to a new site to repeat the process. Soon groundcover reclaimed the abandoned clearing, restoring fertility naturally, and the Indians could return. Meanwhile, Native Americans engaged in diverse food-producing activities (fishing, hunting, and gathering wild plants, as well as farming) to avoid dependence on a single food source.

By A.D. 1500 the North American continent presented a remarkable variety of human cultures, societies, and historical experiences. As they had for thousands of years, small, mobile hunting bands peopled the Arctic, Subarctic, Great Basin, and much of the Plains. More sedentary societies, based on fishing or gathering, predominated along the Pacific coast, whereas village-based agriculture was typical in the Eastern Woodlands and the river valleys of the Southwest and Plains. Finally, Mississippian urban centers still prevailed in portions of the Southeast.

Despite the vast differences among Native Americans, much bound them together. Trade facilitated the exchange not only of goods but of ideas, techniques, and beliefs. Thus the bow and arrow, ceramic pottery, and certain beliefs and rituals surrounding the burial of the dead came to characterize Indians everywhere. Indians also shared a preference for the independent, kin-based communities that generally had characterized indigenous North America, a preference that probably was reinforced by the failure of such highly centralized systems as Cahokia and the Anasazi centers during the thirteenth century.

## American Peoples on the Eve of European Contact

In 1492 the entire Western Hemisphere had a population of about 75 million. Native Americans clustered most thickly in Mexico and Central America, the Caribbean islands, and Peru. But North America was not an empty wasteland. Between 7 million and 10 million Indians lived north of present-day Mexico, unevenly distributed. Sparse populations of nomads inhabited the Great Basin, the high plains, and the northern forests. Fairly dense concentrations, however, thrived along the Pacific coast, in the Southwest and Southeast, in the Mississippi Valley, and along the Atlantic coast. All these peoples grouped themselves in several hundred nations and tribes, speaking many diverse languages and dialects. But the most important Indian social groups were the family, the village, and—in many societies—the clan. Within these spheres Native Americans fed themselves, reared their children, and interacted with one another and with the spiritual forces surrounding them.

## Family and Community

Kinship cemented all Indian societies together. Ties to cousins, aunts, and uncles created complex patterns of social obligation. So did membership in clans—the large networks of kin groups that reckoned their descent from a common ancestor who embodied the admired qualities of a particular animal. Depending on the culture, clan membership could descend from either the mother or the father. Clans linked widely scattered groups within a tribe. Members of different clans usually dwelled together in a single village.

Kinship bonds counted for much more in Indian societies than did the nuclear families that married couples and their children formed. Indians did not necessarily expect spouses to be bound together forever, but kinship lasted for life. Thus Native Americans could accept the divorce of a married couple without feeling a threat to the social order. Customs regulating marriages varied considerably, but strict rules always prevailed. In most cultures young people married in their teens, after winning social acceptance as adults and (generally) after a period of sexual experimentation. Sometimes male leaders took more than one wife, but nuclear families never stood alone. Instead, strong ties of residence and deference bound each couple to one or both sets of parents, producing what social scientists call extended families.

Kinship was also the basis for armed conflict. Indian societies typically considered homicide a matter to be resolved by the extended families of the victim and the perpetrator. If the perpetrator's family offered a gift that the victim's family considered appropriate, the question was settled. If not, the victim's kin might seek to avenge the killing by armed retaliation. If necessary, chiefs and other leaders intervened to resolve disputes between families within the same band, village, or

tribe. But disputes between members of different groups could escalate into war. Densely populated societies that competed for scarce resources, as on the Northwest and California coasts, and centralized societies that attempted to dominate trade networks through coercion, such as Hopewell and Mississippian, experienced frequent and intense intergroup warfare. Still, warfare remained a low-level affair in most of North America. An exasperated New England officer, writing of his effort to obtain Indian allies in the early seventeenth century, described a battle between two Indian groups as "more for pastime than to conquer and subdue enemies." He concluded that "they might fight seven years and not kill seven men."

Women did the cultivating among most agricultural Indians outside the Southwest. For Indian women, field work easily meshed with child care, as did such other tasks as preparing animal hides and gathering wild vegetation. Men did jobs that took them away from the women and children: hunting, fishing, trading, negotiating, and fighting. With women producing the greater share of the food supply, these communities accorded women more power than did European societies. Among the Iroquois of upstate New York, for example, the women collectively owned the fields and distributed food, and leading women played a weighty role in deliberations regarding war. In New England, women sometimes served as *sachems*, or chiefs.

In the Southwest, wresting a living from the severe environment demanded concentrated effort, but the native peoples succeeded remarkably well. The population was comparatively dense: a hundred thousand people may have lived in the pueblos in the early sixteenth century, and intensive cultivation also supported large river-valley settlements. As in the rest of North America, extended families formed the foundation of southwestern village life in both the pueblos and the river valleys.

Southwestern patterns of property ownership and gender roles differed from those of Native Americans elsewhere. Unlike Indians in other regions, here men and women shared agricultural labor. Some peoples owned land privately and passed it through the male line, and men dominated decision making. In pueblo society (which in this respect resembled societies in the Northeast and Southeast), land was communally owned, and women played an influential role in community affairs. A pueblo woman could end a marriage simply by tossing her husband's belongings out the door and sending him back to his kinfolk. Moreover, clan membership passed through the mother's line. Yet pueblo communities depended on secret male societies to perform the rituals that would secure the gods' blessing and ensure life-giving rain. More than other Indians, pueblo society strictly subordinated the individual to the group and demanded rigorous cooperation.

### Indian Spiritual and Social Values

Most Indians explained the origin and destiny of the human race in myths told by storytellers during religious ceremonies. In the beginning, said the Iroquois, was the sky world of unchanging perfection. From it fell a beautiful pregnant woman, whom the birds saved from plunging into the limitless ocean. On the back of a tortoise that rose from the sea, birds created the earth's soil, in which the woman planted seeds carried during her fall. From these seeds sprang all nature; from her womb, the human race.

Native American religions revolved around the conviction that all nature was alive, pulsating with a spiritual power—*manitou,* in the Algonquian languages, *orenda* in the Iroquoian, *wakan* in the Siouan. A mysterious, awe-inspiring force that could affect human life for both good and evil, such power united all nature in an unbroken web. Manitou encompassed "every thing which they cannot comprehend," reported the Puritan leader Roger Williams, one of the few Europeans who genuinely tried to understand the northeastern Indians' spiritual world. Their belief in supernatural power led most Native Americans to seek constantly to conciliate all the spiritual forces in nature: living things, rocks and water, sun and moon, even ghosts and witches. For example, Indians were careful to pray to the spirits of the animals they hunted, thanking them for the gift of food.

Indians had many ways of gaining access to spiritual power. One was through dreaming: most Native Americans took very seriously the visions that came to them in sleep. Some also sought access to the supernatural through difficult physical ordeals. Young men in many societies gained recognition as adults through a "vision quest"—a solitary venture into a forest or up a mountain, involving fasting and awaiting the appearance of an animal spirit that would reveal itself as a protective guide and offer a glimpse of the future. Girls went through comparable rituals at the onset of menstruation to initiate them into the spiritual world from which female reproductive power flowed. Moreover, entire communities often practiced collective power-seeking rituals such as the Sun Dance, performed by Indians of the Plains and Great Basin (see Chapter 17).

Although on occasion all Indians tried to communicate directly with the spiritual world, they normally relied on shamans for help in understanding the unseen. The shamans were healers who used both medicinal plants and magical chants. They also interpreted dreams, guided vision quests, invoked war or peace spirits, and figured prominently in community councils. Chiefs had to maintain respectful relations with shamans, who by the sixteenth century were organized into priesthoods in some societies.

Even as they grew larger and more complex, Indian societies maintained the strong sense of interdependence forged over thousands of years by Paleo-Indians and their successors. As a result, they demanded a strong degree of cooperation. From early childhood Indians learned to be accommodating and reserved—slow to reveal their own feelings before they could sense others'. Although few Native American peoples favored physical punishment in child rearing, Indian parents punished psychologically, by shaming. Communities made decisions by consensus, and leaders articulated slowly emerging agreements in memorable, persuasive, often passionate oratory. Shamans and chiefs therefore had to be dramatic orators. Noted John Smith, they spoke in public "with vehemency and so great passions that they sweat till they drop and are so out of breath they scarce can speak."

Because Indians highly valued consensus building in everyday life, their leaders' authority depended primarily on the respect that they invoked rather than what they could demand by compulsion. Distributing gifts was central to establishing and maintaining leadership within a Native American community, as a French observer in early-seventeenth-century Canada clearly understood: "For the savages have that noble quality, that they give liberally, casting at the feet of him whom they will honor the present that they give him. But it is with hope to receive some reciprocal kindness, which is a kind of contract, which we call . . . 'I give thee, to the end thou shouldst give me.' "

Thus for Indians, trade was not merely an economic activity by which they acquired useful goods. It was also a means of ensuring goodwill with other peoples and of building their own prestige. European visitors almost always found Native Americans eager to barter. For many centuries, trade among the Indians

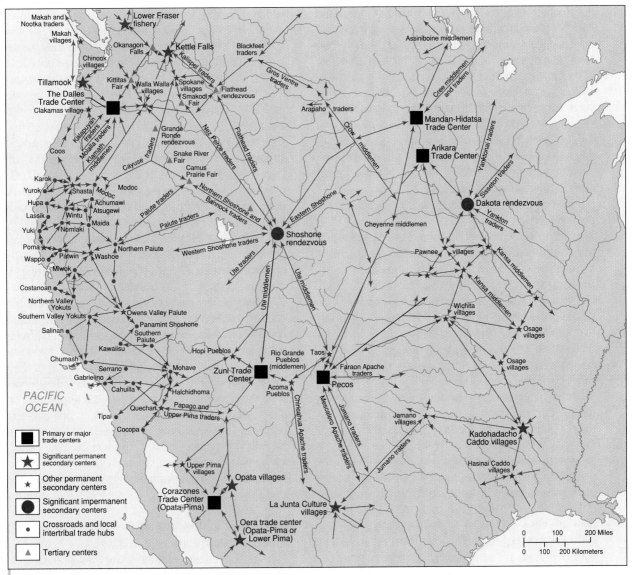

**Native American Trade Networks**

*Well before the arrival of Europeans, North American Indians participated in extensive trade relations not only locally but over vast distances.*

had spanned the continent. The Hurons of southern Ontario and the Pueblo Indians of the Southwest produced large agricultural surpluses for trade, and southwestern turquoise found its way to Mexico and the Great Plains. Flint and other tool-making materials, salt, dyes, furs, exotic minerals and shells, and (in hard times) food and seeds were major objects of trade. So was tobacco, which Indians regarded primarily as a

ceremonial drug, its fragrant smoke symbolizing the union of heaven and earth.

Scholars have used the word *reciprocity* to characterize Native American religious and social values. Reciprocity involved mutual give-and-take, but its aim was not to confer equality. Instead, societies based on reciprocity tried to maintain equilibrium and interdependence between individuals of unequal power and prestige. In their religious thinking, too, Indians applied the concept of reciprocity, in viewing nature as a web of interdependent spiritual powers into which humans had to fit. And in social organization, the Indians' principle of reciprocity required that communities be places of face-to-face, lifelong interaction. Trade and gift giving solidified such reciprocal bonds. The Indians' faith in social reciprocity also underlay their idea of property rights. They believed that the people of one area might agree to share with others the right to use the land for different but complementary purposes: hunting, gathering, farming, trapping, or traveling.

But Native American society was hardly a noncompetitive world.

Even in the Southwest, where stress on cooperation minimized competition, Indian life had an intensely competitive side. Individuals and communities eagerly strove to show physical prowess in ritualized games like lacrosse, and some bet enthusiastically on the outcome. "They are so bewitched with these . . . games, that they will lose sometimes all they have," said an Englishman of the Massachusett Indians about 1630. Such games served not only as recreation but also as a means of acquiring prestige.

All Indian cultures possessed a strong sense of order. Custom, the demands of social conformity, and the rigors of nature strictly regulated life, and the people's everyday affairs mingled with the spiritual world at every turn. Nature and the supernatural world could sometimes be frightening. For example, Indians feared ghosts and believed that nonconformists could invoke evil spirits by witchcraft—the most dreaded crime in Indian cultures.

It follows that the breakdown of order in Indian communities could bring fearful consequences: accusations of witchcraft, demands for revenge against wrongdoers, war against enemies. Going to war or exacting personal revenge was a ritualized way of restoring order that had broken down. A captured male could expect death after prolonged torture. Indian men learned from early childhood to inflict (and to bear) physical pain out of loyalty to kin and neighbors; they knew that they must withstand torture without flinching and death without fear. Endurance was central to Indian life.

## CONCLUSION

When Europeans "discovered" America in 1492, they did not, as they thought, enter a static world of simple savages. Instead, for thousands of years, native cultures and societies had transformed the North American continent into a human habitat. Indians had tapped the secrets of the land and the environment so as to be able to sustain themselves and flourish in almost every ecological zone. Over the millennia they learned the properties, uses, and values of plants, animals, soils, rocks, and other minerals, as well as the cycles of months, seasons, and years. And Native Americans transformed the landscape, as evidenced by their hunting camps, villages, and cornfields and by the web of roads and trails connecting them to one another. But for Indians, these discoveries and accomplishments were not the basis for pride in their ability to conquer nature. Rather, they saw themselves as participants in a natural and spiritual order that pervaded the universe, and their attitudes, as expressed in their religious practices, were ones of gratitude and constant concern lest they violate that order.

These beliefs did not necessarily make all Indians careful conservationists. Plains hunters, stampeding herds of bison (an essential food source) over cliffs, often killed more animals than they could eat. And eastern Indians may sometimes have lost control of their fires and burned more land than intended. But the depletion of species in such cases was only temporary; Indians did not act consistently enough to prevent their renewal. However, other Indian actions were more consistent and hence more consequential. One reason for the decline of the great Anasazi centers in the Southwest and of the Mississippian center of Cahokia was the excessive demands placed on their environments by large concentrations of people. In these instances, Indians seemed to have learned the obvious lessons and abandoned destructive ways of life.

After 1500 a new attitude toward the land made itself felt in North America. "A people come from under the world, to take their world from them"—thus an early-seventeenth-century Virginia Indian characterized the English invaders of his homeland. Certain that God had given humanity dominion over nature, Europeans claimed vast expanses of territory for their crowned heads. They then divided much of the land into plots, each to be owned by an individual or family and to be valued according to the wealth it produced. All the while they ignored and even belittled strategies that would have allowed natural resources to renew themselves. The modern society that since the seventeenth century has arisen on the Indians' ancient continent bears little resemblance to the world that the Native Americans once knew.

## FOR FURTHER READING

John Bierhorst, *The Mythology of North America* (1985). An excellent introduction to Native American mythology, organized regionally.

Brian Fagan, *Ancient North America: The Archaeology of a Continent* (1991). An informative, comprehensive introduction to the continent's history before the Europeans' arrival.

Gwyn Jones, *The Norse Atlantic Saga*, rev. ed. (1986). A single volume combining recent scholarship on Norse, Eskimos, and Indians with translations of their most important sagas.

Alvin M. Josephy, Jr., *America in 1492: The World of the Indian Peoples Before the Arrival of Columbus* (1992). Regional and thematic essays on life in the Western Hemisphere on the eve of European contact.

William C. Sturtevant, gen. ed., *Handbook of North American Indians* (20 vols. projected, 1978–   ). A partially completed reference work providing basic information on the history and culture of virtually every known native society, as well as surveys of regional archaeology and essays on topics of special interest.

Bruce G. Trigger and Wilcomb E. Washburn, eds., *The Cambridge History of the Native Peoples of the Americas*, vol. I (in two parts): North America (1996). A collection of authoritative essays by archaeologists and historians, covering the entire expanse of Native American history.

# Transatlantic Encounters and Colonial Beginnings 1492–1630

**Bartholomew Gosnold Trading with Wampanoag Indians at Martha's Vineyard, Massachusetts,** by Theodore De Bry, 1634

At ten o'clock on a moonlit night, the tense crew spotted a glimmering light. Then at two the next morning came the shout "Land! Land!" At daybreak they entered a shallow lagoon. The captain, Christopher Columbus, rowed ashore, the royal flag fluttering in the breeze. "And, all having rendered thanks to the Lord, kneeling on the ground, embracing it with tears of joy for the immeasurable mercy of having reached it, [he] rose and gave this island the name San Salvador." The date was October 12, 1492. The place was a tiny tropical island less than four hundred miles southeast of present-day Florida.

Besides his crew, the only witnesses to Columbus's landing were a band of Taíno Indians peering from the jungle as he claimed for the Spanish queen the island that they called Guanahaní. Soon curiosity overcame their fears. Gesturing and smiling, the Taínos walked down to the beach, where the newcomers quickly noticed the cigars they offered and the gold pendants in their noses.

The voyagers learned to savor the islanders' tobacco and to trade for golden ornaments as they sailed on among the West Indies, searching for the emperor of China's capital city. Although Columbus had found no potentates, he sensed that fabulous wealth lay within his grasp. He was sure that he had reached Asia—the Indies. Two months later, bringing with him some "Indians" and various souvenirs, he sailed home to tell of "a land to be desired and, once seen, never to be left."

Perhaps some Taínos would have agreed with the astonished Canadian Indian who saw his first shaggily bearded white man in 1632: "O, what an ugly man! Is it possible that any woman would look with favor on such a man?" Later Indians' accounts of their first sightings of Europeans also speak of wonder at seeing white-sailed "canoes" descending as from the sky and of fascination with the strangers' "magic"—their guns, gunpowder, durable metal pots and tools, and glass beads. Because the strangers were seldom prepared to survive unaided, the hospitable native people had ample opportunity to make themselves useful.

But the potential for deep misunderstanding was already present. From his first day in the New World, Columbus thought like a benevolent colonial master. "They should be good servants and of quick intelligence, . . . and I believe that they would easily be made Christians, for it appeared to me that they had no creed." The Europeans would soon realize that Native Americans were neither gullible fools nor humble servants. Disillusioned, the newcomers would begin to see the Indians as lazy and deceitful "savages." Meanwhile, the Native Americans found much of the Europeans' "magic"—which included their diseases as well as their material goods—very destructive. In much of what is now Latin America, the coming of the Europeans quickly turned into conquest. In the future United States and Canada, European mastery would come more slowly. More than one hundred years would pass before truly self-sustaining colonies were established. Nevertheless, from the moment of Columbus's landing on October 12, 1492, the American continents became the stage for the encounter of Native American, European, and African peoples.

This chapter will focus on four major questions:

- How did trade and warfare affect West African and western European societies in the sixteenth century?

- Which developments *within* Europe were most critical in facilitating expansion to the Americas?

- Why were other European powers unable to match Spain's imperial successes in the early sixteenth century, and why were some of Spain's rivals able to compete effectively by the early seventeenth century?

♦ Why did Native Americans sometimes welcome, and other times resist, European traders and colonizers?

# African and European Peoples

Although separated by the vast Sahara Desert, West Africa and Europe were linked indirectly by trade long before coming into direct contact in the fifteenth century. Thereafter the two continents spawned the largest movement of peoples until then in world history, from the Eastern Hemisphere to the Western. But whereas most Europeans migrated with some degree of freedom, most Africans crossed the Atlantic in chains.

## *Mediterranean Crossroads*

One of the most vibrant and tumultuous areas in the Eastern Hemisphere was the Mediterranean Sea, around which African, Asian, and European peoples had interacted in both peace and war since ancient times. By 1400 hundreds of small ships criss-crossed the sea annually between port cities, unloading luxury goods from one part of the world and loading others for the next leg of their journeys. Thus it was that West African gold enriched Turkish sultans, European guns strengthened North African armies, and Indian spices stimulated Italian palates. In Africa and Asia, many of these goods moved to and from the Mediterranean by caravans that traveled thousands of miles across forbidding deserts like the Sahara and rugged mountains such as the Himalayas. Seagoing merchant vessels linked east and south Asia with the Arabian peninsula and East Africa, and others connected northern and southern Europe. But before the fifteenth century, intercontinental travel and trade were unknown on the Atlantic.

Mediterranean commerce was closely intertwined with religion and politics. From the seventh to the fourteenth centuries, Muslim conquerors spread Islam from Southeast Asia to West Africa and much of southern Europe. During the same period, Roman Catholic rulers introduced Christianity to new areas of central and northern Europe. Political leaders sought to capture some of the wealth being generated by commerce while merchants valued the security afforded by close

ties with strong rulers. Above all the two religions provided a common faith and identity to peoples spread over vast distances, reinforcing the political and economic links being forged between them.

Religion did not always divide people along political or economic lines. Christian and Muslim rulers on the Mediterranean frequently signed treaties with one another in order to secure commercial ties and protect against piracy. Christians, Jews, and Muslims, especially merchants, frequently traveled and lived in lands where they were in the minority. In the fourteenth century, Morocco in particular was a stable, pluralistic society that welcomed and tolerated Jews, many of them fleeing persecution in Christian portions of Spain, as well as Christians.

**Christopher Columbus**
*Although he thought he was in Asia, Columbus's landfall inaugurated European expansion to the Americas.*

But over time, religious strife between Christians and Muslims became more common. Beginning in the eleventh century, European Christians undertook a long series of crusades to recapture formerly Christian territories in Europe and the Middle East from Muslim "infidels," and some Muslim leaders waged *jihad* (holy war) against Christians. In southwestern Europe, the kingdoms of Castile and Aragon led a gradual "reconquest" of the Iberian peninsula to rid it of non-Christians. That effort culminated in 1492 when the last Muslim rulers were driven from Spain and all remaining Jews were forced by decree to convert to Catholicism. Meanwhile, Spain's small neighbor, Portugal, had launched a series of increasingly bold voyages southward in the Atlantic, seizing Moroccan ports and taking over the trade in gold and other commodities between Europe and West Africa.

## *West Africa and Its Peoples*

Before the advent of long-distance travel on the Atlantic, the only link between sub-Saharan Africa and the Mediterranean was the broad belt of grassland known as the Sudan (from which the modern African nation gets its name) that separates the desert from the

## CHRONOLOGY

**c. 1000**   Muslim conquest of Ghana.
Norse establish a small settlement at Vinland (Newfoundland).

**c. 1300**   Rise of Mali.

**c. 1400–1600**   Renaissance era—first in Italy, then elsewhere in Europe.

**c. 1400**   Rise of Songhai.
Rise of Guinea.

**1440**   Portuguese slave trade in West Africa begins.

**1488**   Bartolomeu Días reaches the Cape of Good Hope.

**1492**   Christian "reconquest" of Spain.
Christopher Columbus lands at San Salvador.

**1497**   John Cabot reaches Nova Scotia and Newfoundland.

**1512–1521**   Juan Ponce de León explores Florida.

**1513**   Vasco Núñez de Balboa views the Pacific Ocean.

**1517**   Protestant Reformation begins in Germany.

**1519**   Ferdinand Magellan embarks on round-the-world voyage.
Hernán Cortés begins conquest of Aztec empire.

**1524**   Giovanni da Verrazano explores the Atlantic coast of North America.

**1534**   Church of England breaks from Roman Catholic Church.

**1534–1542**   Jacques Cartier explores eastern Canada for France.

**1539–1543**   Hernando de Soto explores the southeastern United States.

**1540–1542**   Francisco Vásquez de Coronado explores the southwestern United States.

**1558**   Elizabeth I becomes queen of England.

**1565**   St. Augustine founded by Spanish.

**1565–1580s**   English attempt to subdue Ireland.

**1577**   Francis Drake circumnavigates the globe.

**1584–1587**   Roanoke colony explored and founded.

**1588**   English defeat the Spanish Armada.

**1598**   New Mexico colony founded.

**1603**   James I becomes king of England.

**1607**   English found colonies at Jamestown and Sagadahoc.

**1608**   Samuel de Champlain founds Quebec.

**1609**   Henry Hudson explores the Hudson River for the Dutch Republic.

**1610–1614**   First Anglo-Powhatan War.

**1614**   New Netherland colony founded.

**1619**   Large exports of tobacco from Virginia begin.
First Africans arrive in Virginia.

**1620**   Mayflower Compact signed; Plymouth Plantation founded.

**1622–1632**   Second Anglo-Powhatan War.

**1624**   James I revokes Virginia Company's charter.

forests to the south. Here the growth of the trans-Saharan caravan trade stimulated the rise of kingdoms and empires whose size and wealth rivaled any in Europe at the time. The richest portion of the savanna was in West Africa, with its ample stores of gold (see map on page 22). In the eleventh century, Muslim conquerors toppled the empire of Ghana in order to supply a growing European demand for gold. Although Ghana soon overthrew the invaders, its rulers retained Islam and the lucrative contacts with wealthy rulers and merchants in North Africa and the Middle East that the Muslim network provided.

In the fourteenth century, Ghana collapsed and a new empire, Mali, arose in its place. Mali expanded westward into the Senegal and Gambia river valleys,

leading to the Atlantic, and southward to the mighty Niger River. Every market town in Mali was staffed with royal agents who facilitated trade, collected duties, and protected merchants against robbery. Traders objecting to high duties imposed by agents could appeal directly to the emperor. Mali's attentiveness to commercial conditions, along with its geographic expanse, brought it great wealth as well as fame in the outside world. Although its principal import was salt from the Sahara, it also imported brass, copper, cloth, spices, manufactured goods, and Arabian horses. Its best known city, Timbuktu, was widely recognized for its intellectual and academic vitality and for its beautiful mosque, designed and built by a Spanish Muslim architect.

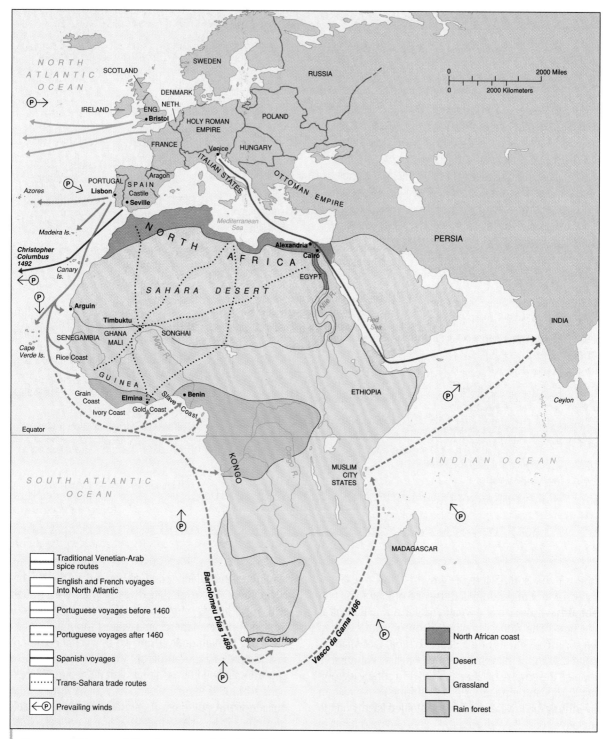

**Europe, Africa, and Southwestern Asia in 1492**

*In 1492 Europeans had little knowledge of the outside world apart from the Mediterranean basin and Africa's west coast. Since the Azores, the Canary Islands, and the Cape Verde Islands had been explored recently in the eastern Atlantic, many Europeans were not surprised when Columbus encountered new islands farther west in 1492.*

Early in the fifteenth century, divisions within Mali's royal family severely weakened the empire, leading many territories to secede. A successor empire, Songhai, arose briefly and forcibly united most of the seceded territory. But by the sixteenth century, most of Mali and Songhai had both been absorbed by Morocco to the north.

Compared with the Sudan and its mighty empires, coastal West Africa remained relatively undeveloped for many centuries. In Senegambia at Africa's westernmost bulge, several small Islamic states took root. Infestation by the tsetse fly, the carrier of sleeping sickness, kept livestock-herding peoples out of Guinea's coastal forests, but many small states arose here, too. Among these was Benin, where artisans had been fashioning magnificent metalwork for centuries.

In the fifteenth century, Guinea's population rose. With gold having recently been made the standard for nearly all Europe's currencies, demand for the precious metal was greater than ever. During the fifteenth century, this demand brought thousands of newcomers from the Sudan and Central Africa to the region later known as Africa's "Gold Coast." New states emerged to take advantage of the opportunities afforded by exporting gold, though none was as extensive or powerful as Mali at its height. Similarly eager to capitalize on its neighbor's resources were the Portuguese, who in the mid-fifteenth century used new maritime techniques to sail up and down West Africa's coast in search of gold and slaves (see below).

West African political leaders differed sharply in the amounts and kinds of political power they wielded. Some emperors enjoyed semigodlike status, which they only thinly disguised if they adopted Islam. Rulers of smaller kingdoms depended largely on their ability to persuade, to conform to custom, and sometimes to redistribute wealth justly among their people.

In sub-Saharan Africa, the cohesiveness of kinship groups knitted society together. From childhood, Africans found themselves in a network of interlocking mutual obligations to kinfolk. Not just parents but also aunts, uncles, distant cousins, and persons sharing clan ties formed an African's kin group and claimed his or her first loyalty. Africans held their grandparents in highest esteem and accorded village or clan elders great deference. In centuries to come, the tradition of strong extended families would help enslaved Africans in the New World to endure the breakup of nuclear families by sale.

**Mali Horseman, c. 13th–14th century**
*This terra-cotta figure originated in Mali, one of several powerful empires in West Africa before the arrival of Europeans.*

West Africans viewed marriage as a means by which extended families forged alliances for their mutual benefit. A prospective husband made a payment to his bride's kin before marriage. In so doing, he did not "buy" a wife; in effect, he posted bond for good behavior and acknowledged the relative prestige of his own and his bride's kin groups. A man of wealth and elite status could further strengthen his family's standing by marrying more than one woman. West African wives generally kept lifelong links with their own kin groups, and in many societies children traced descent through the mother's, not the father's, bloodline. All this buttressed women's standing.

Kinship also informed attitudes toward land and property. To West Africans, kin groups not only enjoyed inalienable rights to the soil that their ancestors had always cultivated but also had a duty to honor ancestors and earth spirits by properly cultivating the land. Like Native Americans, Africans did not treat land as a commodity to be bought and sold.

Cultivation was difficult in Africa and required the labor of both men and women. As in all tropical regions, scorching sunlight and frequent downpours prevented humus (slowly decaying vegetative matter) from accumulating in the African soil. Like Indians in eastern North America, Africans maintained soil fertility by practicing slash-and-burn tillage. In the coastal rain forests, Africans grew root crops, primarily yams. On the grasslands the staff of life was grain—millet, sorghum, and rice—though farming was supplemented by cattle-raising and fishing.

By the fifteenth century, the market economy fostered by long-distance trade extended to many small families. Farmers traded surplus crops at local marketplaces for other food or cloth. Artisans wove cloth, made clothing, and crafted tools and other objects of iron and wood. While gold was the preferred currency among wealthy rulers and merchants, cowrie shells served as a medium of exchange for most people.

Religion permeated African life. West African, like Native American, religions recognized spiritual presences pervading nature. The power of earth spirits and of agricultural ancestors reinforced the esteem that Africans accorded to cultivators. In the eighteenth century, Europeans got an authentic glimpse of African religion from Olaudah Equiano, a West African who had managed to buy his freedom from slavery:

> The natives believe that there is one Creator of all things, and that he lives in the sun, [and] . . . that he governs events. . . . Some . . . believe in the transmigration of souls [reincarnation] to some degree. Those spirits, who are not transmigrated, such as their dear friends or relations, they believe always attend them, and guard them from the bad spirits of their foes. For this reason, they always, before eating . . . put some small portion of the meat and pour some of their drink, on the ground for them; and they often make oblations [offerings] of the blood of beasts or fowls at their graves.

Magic and the placating of spiritual powers were important in West African life, and, as with Native Americans, the responsibility for maintaining contact with the spirit world fell to shamans. Africans explained misfortunes in terms of witchcraft, much as did Native Americans and Europeans. But African religion differed from other traditions in its focus on ancestor worship, in which departed forebears were venerated as spiritual guardians.

Africa's magnificent artistic traditions were also steeped in religion. The ivory, cast iron, and wood sculpture of West Africa, whose bold designs would help mold the twentieth-century Western world's modern art, was used in ceremonies reenacting creation myths and honoring spirits. A strong moralistic streak ran through African folk tales. Oral reciters transmitted these stories in dramatic public presentations with ritual masks, dance, and music of a highly complex rhythmic structure now appreciated as one of the foundations of jazz.

Much in traditional African culture seemed to clash with the great monotheistic religions, Islam and Christianity. Among Africans, Islam appealed primarily to merchants trading with Muslim North Africa and the Middle East and to kings and emperors eager to consolidate their power. Some Muslim rulers, however, tempered Islam as a concession to popular opinion. By the sixteenth century, Islam had only begun to affect the daily lives of some cultivators and artisans in the Sudan. Christianity, arriving in West Africa with the Portuguese in the fifteenth and sixteenth centuries, demanded that Africans break even more radically with their traditional culture but, until the nineteenth century, had limited impact.

## European Culture and Society

When Columbus landed on San Salvador in 1492, Europe was approaching the height of a mighty cultural revival, the Renaissance. Contemporary intellectuals and poets believed that their age was witnessing a return to the standards of ancient Greek and Roman civilization. After a century-long economic recession, money had accumulated to pay for magnificent architecture, and wealthy patrons commissioned master painters and sculptors to create works glowing with idealized human beauty. Renaissance scholars strove to reconcile ancient philosophy with Christian faith, to explore the mysteries of nature, to map the world, and to explain the motions of the heavens.

But European society was quivering with tension. The era's artistic and intellectual creativity was partly inspired by intense social and spiritual stress, as Renaissance Europeans groped for stability by glorifying order, hierarchy, and beauty. A concern for power and rank ("degree") dominated European life between the fifteenth and seventeenth centuries. William Shakespeare (1564–1616), who expressed Renaissance values with incomparable eloquence, wrote,

The heavens themselves, the planets and this
    center [earth]
Observe degree, priority, and place . . .
Take but degree away, untune that string,
And hark, what discord follows!

Gender, wealth, inherited position, and political power affected every European's status, and few lived outside the reach of some political authority's burden of taxes and laws. But this order was shaky. Conflicts between states, between religions, and between social classes constantly threatened the balance.

At the heart of these conflicts lay deep-seated forces of economic, political, and religious change. Several western European political rulers, traditionally dependent on the nobility (or aristocracy) of their countries for financial support, sought to balance that dependence by turning to bankers and overseas merchants, whose ambitions for expansion matched the rulers' own. In this way, monarchs hoped to distance themselves from the inward-looking nobles, who preferred to pour their inherited fortunes into lavish living rather than embrace the forces of change sweeping the continent. Moreover, the rise of merchants and a market economy in western Europe was elevating the importance of the town, where business was conducted, instead of the countryside, which was dominated by the nobility and was home to most of Europe's population.

Most Europeans, in fact 70 to 80 percent of the population, were peasants. Peasants ranged from a few prosperous families with large holdings, such as the English yeomen, to landless laborers who barely scraped by on odd jobs. Taxes, rents, and other dues to landlords and Catholic Church officials were heavy, and poor harvests or war drove even well-to-do peasants to starvation. Not surprisingly, peasant revolts were common, but the authorities mercilessly suppressed such uprisings.

Conditions among the peasants were made even worse by a sharp rise in population, from about 55 million in 1450 to almost 100 million by 1600, and by agricultural methods whose yields were pitifully low. Families had to cooperate in plowing, sowing, and harvesting, as well as in grazing their livestock on the fallow field and the jointly owned "commons," or pastureland and forest. With new land at a premium, the commons were a tempting prize for landlords, especially the English gentry, to "enclose"—that is, to convert to private property. Peasants who had no *written* title to their land were especially vulnerable, but yeomen with strong titles often kept their land, and a few even profited by enclosing.

**The Woman Spinning** *by Geertruyd Roghman (c. 1650) (detail)*
*In early modern Europe, mothers introduced their daughters to spinning at an early age. Roghmann, one of the few women engravers of her time, specialized in depicting the daily lives of women.*

European towns were numerous but small, typically with several thousand inhabitants each. A great metropolis like London, whose population ballooned from 55,000 in 1550 to 200,000 in 1600, was quite exceptional. But all towns were dirty and disease-ridden, and townspeople lived close-packed with their neighbors.

Unappealing as sixteenth-century towns might seem today, many men and women of the time viewed them as preferable to the villages and tiny farms they left behind. Immigration from the countryside—rather than an excess of urban births over deaths—accounted for towns' expansion. Most people who flocked into towns remained at the bottom of the social order as servants or laborers who often failed to accumulate enough money to marry and live independently. Manufacturing took place in household workshops, where subordinate workers were dependent on an artisan master. Successful artisans and merchants formed guilds to control employment, prices, and the sale of goods. Dominated by the richest citizens, urban governments enforced social conformity by "sumptuary laws" that forbade dressing inappropriately to one's social rank.

The consequences of rapid population growth were particularly acute in England, where the number of people doubled from about 2.5 million in 1500 to 5 million in 1620. In parts of the countryside, landowners united to divide the commons among themselves, raise sheep, and grow rich selling wool. But with textile-manufacturing technology largely unchanged, per capita output and real household income among textile workers fell. In effect, more workers competed for fewer jobs in the face of diminishing European markets for English cloth and rapidly rising prices for food. Enclosures aggravated unemployment, forcing large numbers of people to wander the countryside in search of work and so making England's population highly mobile. To the upper and middle classes, these poor vagabonds seemed to threaten law and order. To control them, Parliament passed "Poor Laws" that ordered vagrants whipped and sent home, where hard-pressed taxpayers maintained them on relief.

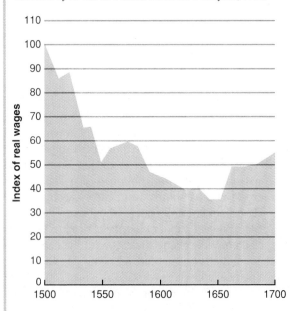

### Decline in Real Wages in England, 1500–1700

*This index measures the drop in purchasing power due to inflation and declining wages. It indicates that by around 1630, living standards for English workers had declined by about two-thirds since the base year, 1500.*

Source: E. H. Phelps Brown and S. V. Hopkins, "Builders' Wage-Rates, Prices and Population: Some Further Evidence," *Economica*, XXVI (1959): 18–38; adapted from D. C. North and R. P. Thomas, *The Rise of the Western World: A New Economic History* (Cambridge: Cambridge University Press, 1973), 111.

As in America and Africa, traditional society in Europe rested on maintaining long-term, reciprocal relationships. But because its aim was the smooth functioning of social relationships between individuals of unequal status, European reciprocity required the upper classes to act with self-restraint and dignity, and the lower classes to show deference to their "betters." It also demanded strict economic regulation to ensure that sellers charged a "just price"—one that covered costs and allowed the seller a "reasonable" living standard but that barred him from taking advantage of buyers' and borrowers' misfortunes or of shortages to make "excessive" profits.

Yet for several centuries Europeans had been compromising the ideals of traditional economic behavior. "In the Name of God and of Profit," thirteenth-century Italian merchants had written on their ledgers. By the sixteenth century, nothing could stop the charging of interest on borrowed money or sellers' price increases in response to demand. New forms of business organization slowly spread in the commercial world—especially the impersonal joint-stock company with many investors, the ancestor of the modern corporation. Demand rose for capital investment, and so did the supply of accumulated wealth. Slowly a new economic outlook took form that justified both the unimpeded acquisition of wealth and unregulated economic competition, and insisted that individuals owed one another nothing but the money necessary to settle each market transaction. This new outlook, the central value system of capitalism or the "market economy," was the opposite of traditional demands for the strict regulation of economic activity to ensure social reciprocity and maintain "just prices."

Sixteenth- and seventeenth-century Europeans therefore held conflicting attitudes toward economic enterprise and social change, and their ambivalence remained unresolved. In Europe itself and in transplanted Europeans' colonial communities, a restless desire for fresh opportunity kept life simmering with competitive tension. But those who prospered still sought the security and prestige provided by traditional social distinctions, whereas the poor longed for the age-old values that they hoped would restrain irresponsible greed.

Perhaps the most sensitive barometer of social change was the family. Throughout Europe the typical household consisted of a small nuclear family—two parents and two or three children—in which the husband and father functioned as a head whose authority was not to be questioned. The role of the wife and mother was to bear and rear children as well as assist her husband in the unending labor of providing for the family's subsistence. Children were regarded as potential laborers who would assist in these tasks until they left home to start their own families. The household, then, was not only a family of intimately related people but the principal economic unit in European society. Peasants on their tiny farms, artisans and merchants in their shops, and even nobles in their castles all lived and worked in households. People who did not live with their own families resided as dependents in the households of others as servants, apprentices, or simply as relatives. Europeans regarded those who lived outside households with extreme suspicion, often accusing them of crime or even witchcraft.

In a common cliché of the age, the nuclear family was a "little commonwealth." The father's government within the family was supposed to mirror God's rule over Creation and the king's lordship over his subjects. Even grown sons and daughters regularly knelt for their father's blessing. The ideal, according to a German writer, was that "wives should obey their husbands and not seek to dominate them; they must manage the home efficiently. Husbands . . . should treat their wives with consideration and occasionally close an eye to their faults." In practice, the father's sovereignty often had to make room for the wife's responsibility in managing family affairs and helping to run the farm or the workshop. And repeated male complaints (such as that of an English author in 1622) about wives "who think themselves every way as good as their husbands, and no way inferior to them," suggested that male domination had its limits.

### Religious Upheavals

"In the beginning God created the heaven and the earth. . . . And God said, Let us make man in our image . . . and let them have dominion . . . over all the earth. . . . So God created man in his own image, . . . male and female he created them." Most sixteenth-century Europeans firmly believed in this biblical explanation of the origins of the world and its peoples. Christianity, to which the vast majority adhered, taught that Jesus Christ, God's Son, had redeemed sinners by suffering crucifixion and rising from the dead. Equally vivid was their belief in the devil, Satan, whom God had hurled from heaven soon after the Creation and who ceaselessly lured people to damnation by tempting

**The Banker and His Wife, by Quentin Metsys, 1514**
*Despite religious admonitions against excessive material gain, some sixteenth-century Europeans sought to reconcile profit with piety. In this portrait, a banker weighs gold coins to ensure their accurate value as his wife, watching him, holds a prayer book.*

them to do evil. The non-Christian European minority encompassed small Jewish communities and Muslims in the Balkans and in Spain. But all Europe's population—Christians, Jews, and Muslims—worshiped a single supreme being, based on the God of the Old Testament.

Although Christianity had sunk deep roots into Europeans' consciousness by the sixteenth century, many also retained beliefs that originated outside the Christian tradition. Many Europeans feared witches, and many thought that individuals could manipulate nature by invoking unseen spiritual powers—that is, by magic. Others looked to astrology, which insisted that a person's fate depended on the conjunction of various planets and stars. Such supernaturalism had more in common with Native Americans and African mind sets than any of these traditional belief systems have with more modern world views.

The Catholic Church, based in Rome, taught that Christ's sacrifice was repeated every time a priest said Mass, and that divine grace flowed to sinners through

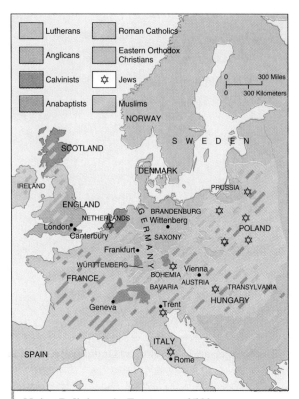

**Major Religions in Europe, c. 1560**
*Sixteenth-century Europe teemed with religious change and conflict.*

the sacraments that consecrated priests alone could administer—above all, baptism, confession, and the Eucharist (communion). The Church was a huge network of clergymen, set apart from laypeople by the fact that they did not marry. At the top was the pope, the "vicar (representative) of Christ," whose authority reached most of central and western Europe.

The papacy wielded awesome spiritual power. Fifteenth- and early-sixteenth-century popes dispensed extra blessings, or "indulgences," to repentant sinners in return for such "good works" as donating money to the Church. Indulgences promised time off from future punishment in purgatory, where souls atoned for sins they had already confessed and been forgiven. (Hell, from which there was no escape, awaited those who died unforgiven.) Given people's anxieties over "sinful" behavior, indulgences were enormously popular. The jingle of one successful indulgence seller in early-sixteenth-century Germany promised that

As soon as the coin in the cash box rings,
The soul from purgatory's fire springs.

The sale of indulgences provoked charges that the materialism and corruption infecting economic life had spread to the Church. In 1517 the German friar Martin Luther (1483–1546) attacked the practice. When the papacy tried to silence him, Luther broadened his criticism to encompass the Mass, purgatory, priests, and the pope. Luther's revolt initiated the Protestant* Reformation, which changed Christianity forever.

To Luther, indulgence selling and similar examples of clerical corruption were evil not just because they bilked people. The Church, he charged, also gave people false confidence that they could "earn" salvation by doing good works. His own agonizing search for salvation had convinced Luther that God alone chose whom to save from damnation and that believers could trust only God's love. "I did not love a just and angry God, but rather hated and murmured against him," recalled Luther, "until I saw the connection between the justice of God and the [New Testament] statement that 'the just shall live [be saved] by faith.' . . . Thereupon I felt myself to be reborn and to have gone through open doors into paradise." Luther's spiritual struggle and experience of being "reborn" constituted a classic conversion experience—the heart of Protestant religion as it soon would be preached and practiced in northern Europe and North America.

Other reformers arose to challenge Luther's interpretation of God's Word. Whereas Luther stressed faith in Christ as the key to salvation, the great French reformer John Calvin (1509–1564) insisted on the stark doctrine of predestination, in which an omnipotent God "predestined" most sinful humans to hell, saving only a few to exemplify his grace. And Calvinists and Lutherans, as the followers of the two Reformation leaders came to be called, were equally horrified by more radical Protestants such as the Anabaptists, who appealed strongly to women and common people with their criticisms of the rich and powerful and sought to restrict baptism to "converted" adults. Judging the Anabaptists a threat to the social order, governments and mainstream churches persecuted them.

But Protestants also shared much common ground. For one thing, they placed a high value on reading. Luther's own conversion had sprung from his long study of the Bible, and Protestants demanded that

---

* The word *Protestant* comes from the *protest* of Luther's princely supporters against Holy Roman Emperor Charles V's anti-Lutheran policies.

God's Word be translated from Latin into spoken languages and read carefully by believers, not solely by priests. The new faith was spread best by the newly invented printing press; wherever Protestantism became established, basic education and religious indoctrination followed. Protestantism also denied that God had endowed priests with special powers. Instead, Luther claimed, the church was a "priesthood of all believers." Protestant reformers insisted that laypeople take responsibility for their own spiritual and moral conditions. Finally, Protestantism represented a yearning in many people for the simplicity and purity of the ancient Christian church. More than Catholicism, it condemned the replacement of traditional reciprocity by marketplace values. In a world of troubling change, it could forge individuals of strong moral determination and equip them with the fortitude to survive and prosper amid the temptations of worldly wealth. Protestantism's greatest appeal was to all those—ordinary individuals, merchants, and aristocrats alike—who brooded over their chances for salvation and valued the steady performance of duty.

In the face of the Protestant challenge, Rome was far from idle. Catholic reform had begun in Spain even before Luther's revolt, and soon the papacy vigorously attacked corruption and combated Protestant viewpoints on major religious issues. The popes also sponsored a new religious order fervently committed to the papacy: the Jesuits, whose members would distinguish themselves for centuries as missionaries and royal advisers. This Catholic revival, the Counter-Reformation, brought into existence the modern Roman Catholic Church.

Together the Reformation and Counter-Reformation reinforced a new crusading spirit in Europe, recently bolstered by Spain's fifteenth-century expulsions of Muslims and of Jews who refused to become Christians. Coinciding with the emergence of nation-states and overseas expansion, this spirit frequently gave Europeans a justification for assuming themselves superior to the non-Christian peoples of the Americas and Africa and for seizing their land, resources, and labor.

The Reformation also changed the map of western Europe. While the tiny states comprising the modern nations of Germany and Switzerland were divided among Catholics, Lutherans, and Calvinists, Lutheranism became the state religion in the Scandinavian countries and Calvinism made significant inroads in France, the Netherlands (ruled by Spain), and England, where it competed with Catholicism and with the moderately reformed Church of England.

## The Rise of Puritanism in England

England's Reformation began not with the writings of a theologian or with cries of the people, but with the actions of a king and Parliament. King Henry VIII (ruled 1509–1547) wanted a male heir but his queen, Catherine of Aragon, failed to bear a son. Frustrated and determined, Henry asked the pope to annul his marriage; equally determined, the pope refused. Henry then persuaded Parliament, in a series of acts in 1533–1534, to dissolve his marriage and proclaim him "supreme head" of the Church of England (or Anglican Church).

Religion remained a source of trouble in England for well over a century after Henry's break with Rome. Under Edward VI (ruled 1547–1553), the church veered sharply toward Protestantism; then Mary I (ruled 1553–1558) tried to restore Catholicism, in part by burning several hundred Protestants at the stake.

The reign of Elizabeth I (ruled 1558–1603) marked a crucial watershed. After "Bloody Mary," most English people were ready to become Protestant; *how* Protestant was the divisive question. A militant Calvinist movement called Puritanism had arisen. Puritans demanded a wholesale "purification" of the Church of England from "popish [Catholic] abuses." As Calvinists, they affirmed salvation by predestination, denied Christ's presence in the Eucharist, and believed that a learned sermon was the heart of true worship. They wished to free each congregation and its minister from outside interference by bishops and encouraged lay members (nonclergy) to participate in parish affairs. Above all, Puritans argued that membership in a true Christian church must be reserved exclusively for those who had had a *conversion experience*. At this moment, a soul confronted the horrifying truth of its own unworthiness and felt the transcending power of God's saving grace. Through a process known as sanctification, the new convert was cemented to God as a "saint," or member of the "elect," chosen by God for salvation. Whereas membership in the Church of England was automatic for anyone born in England, only saints could join Puritan congregations.

The severe self-discipline and moral uprightness demanded of Puritans appealed to only a few from the titled nobility, with their inherited wealth and privileges, and from the desperate poor, whose lives were consumed by the quest for physical survival. Puritanism's primary appeal lay instead among the small but growing number of people between the extremes of English society—landowning gentry, university-educated clergymen and intellectuals, merchants, shopkeepers, artisans, and yeoman farmers. Self-discipline had become central to both the secular and spiritual dimensions of these people's lives. From their ranks, and particularly from the farmers, artisans, and clergymen, would later come the settlers of New England (see Chapter 3).

Elizabeth distrusted Puritan militancy but, after 1570, when the pope declared her a heretic and urged Catholics to overthrow her, she regarded English Catholics as even more dangerous. Thereafter, she courted influential Puritans and embraced militant anti-Catholicism.

Under Elizabeth, most Puritans had come to expect that they would eventually transform the Church of England into independent congregations of "saints." But her successor, James I (ruled 1603–1625), the founder of England's Stuart dynasty, bitterly opposed Puritan efforts to eliminate the office of bishop, making clear that he saw Puritan attacks on bishops as a direct threat to the throne when he snapped, "No bishop, no king." After Charles I became king in 1625, Anglican authorities undertook a systematic campaign to eliminate Puritan influence within the church. With the king's backing, bishops insisted that services be conducted according to the Book of Common Prayer, which prescribed rituals similar to Catholic practices, and they dismissed Puritan ministers who refused to perform these "High Church" rites. Church courts, which judged cases involving religious law, harassed the Puritan laity with fines or excommunication.

Religious oppression, along with dwindling economic opportunities, made leading a godly life difficult for many Puritans. One minister wrote that everyone in England was tempted "to pluck his means, as it were, out of his neighbor's throat." Such conditions led many Puritans to consider migrating to New England after 1620 (see below and Chapter 3).

# European Expansion

Whereas European wealth at the beginning of the fifteenth century centered on Mediterranean city-states such as Florence and Venice, the ensuing hundred years witnessed the rise of Atlantic nation-states whose monarchs had consolidated their power over vast territories. Among these, the most prominent were Portu-

gal, Spain (recently formed through the marriage of Queen Isabella of Castile and King Ferdinand of Aragon), France, and England. During the sixteenth century, these nations would lead Europe's expansion over the oceans of the world and set the stage for the colonization of North America.

## *Seaborne Expansion*

The earliest efforts at European expansion were primarily commercial rather than territorial. While European merchants had long traded with Asia and Africa by way of the Mediterranean (see above), some recognized that such trade would yield only limited profits unless Europeans could establish more direct contacts with the sources of prized imports and with overseas markets for exports. During the fifteenth century, tiny Portugal led the way in overcoming impediments to long-distance travel on the Atlantic Ocean. The most significant outcome of Portuguese pioneering was to begin Europe's massive trade in black African slaves. By the following century, the most powerful nations of western Europe had transformed the Atlantic from a barrier to a busy passageway for both people and goods.

Important changes in maritime technology occurred in the early fifteenth century. Shipbuilders and mariners along Europe's stormy Atlantic coast added the triangular Arab sail to the heavy cargo ships they used for voyaging between England and the Mediterranean. They created a more maneuverable vessel, the caravel, that could sail against the wind. Sailors also mastered the compass and astrolabe, by which they got their bearings on the open sea. Without this "maritime revolution," European exploration would have been impossible.

Renaissance scholars' search for more accurate readings of ancient texts forced fifteenth-century Europeans to look at their world with new eyes. The great ancient Greek authority on geography was Ptolemy, but cartographers had to correct his data when they tried to draw accurate maps. Thus Renaissance "new learning" combined with older Arabic and European advances in mathematics to sharpen Europeans' geographic sense.

Led by Prince Henry "the Navigator" (1394–1460), Portugal was the first nation to capitalize on these developments. Henry gained the support of merchants seeking to circumvent Moroccan control of the African-European gold trade and of religious zealots eager to confront Muslim power. At the same time he hoped eventually to find a sea route to Asia that would enable Portugal to bypass Mediterranean traders in tapping the markets of that continent as well. Henry encouraged Portuguese seamen to pilot the new caravels farther down the African coast, searching for weak spots in Muslim defenses and for opportunities to trade profitably. At the time of his death, the Portuguese operated a successful gold-making factory at Arguin and had established trade ties south of the Sahara. In 1488 Bartolomeu Días reached the Cape of Good Hope at Africa's southern tip. A decade later Vasco da Gama led a Portuguese fleet around the Cape of Good Hope and on to India.

Ultimately the Portuguese failed to destroy older Euro-Asian commercial links, although for a century they remained an imperial presence in the Indian Ocean and present-day Indonesia. Meanwhile, they had brought Europeans face-to-face with black Africans and an already flourishing slave trade.

### The "New Slavery" and Racism

Slavery was well established in fifteenth-century West Africa. Kings and emperors, as well as many families, depended on slaves. But most slaves or their children were absorbed into African families over time. The eighteenth-century West African Olaudah Equiano, who had suffered enslavement by the British, explained the fate of war captives in his native society:

> How different was their condition from that of the slaves in the West Indies! With us they do no more work than other members of the community, even their master. Their food, clothing, and lodging, were nearly the same as [free people's], except that they were not permitted to eat with those who were born free. . . . Some of these slaves even have slaves under them, as their own property, and for their own use.

Outsiders—first Middle Eastern and North African Muslims then European Christians—turned African slavery into an intercontinental business and tore slaves from their native societies. One fifteenth-century Italian who witnessed Portuguese and Muslim slave trading noted that the Arabs "also have many Berber horses, which they trade, and take to the Land of the Blacks, exchanging them with the rulers for slaves. Ten or fifteen slaves are given for one of these horses, according to their quality. . . . These slaves are brought to the market town of Hoden; there they are divided. . . . [Some] are taken . . . and sold to the Portuguese leaseholders [of

**An Astrolabe**

*A device for calculating the position and elevation of the sun, stars, and planets, the astrolabe is one of the world's oldest scientific instruments. It was known to the ancient Greeks and perfected by the medieval Arabs. Ocean navigators found it indispensable. This brass English astrolabe, dating to 1326, may be the oldest such European instrument extant.*

Arguin]. As a result every year the Portuguese carry away from [Arguin] a thousand slaves."

Equiano's eighteenth-century testimony starkly captures slaves' experience in earlier centuries too. Brought on a European slave ship, he wrote,

> I was now persuaded that I had got into a world of bad spirits, and that they were going to kill me. Their complections differing so much from ours, their long hair, and the languages they spoke . . . united to confirm me in this belief. . . . Quite overpowered with shock and horror, I . . . fainted. When I recovered a little, I found some black people around me, who I believed were some of those who brought me on board, and had been receiving their pay. . . . I asked them if we were not to be eaten by those white men. . . . They told me I was not. [But] soon after this the blacks who had brought me on board went off, and left me abandoned to despair. . . . I found some of my own nation [and] inquired . . . what was to be done with us? They gave me to understand that we were to be carried to these white people's country to work for them. I then was a little revived . . . but still I feared I should be put to death, the white people looked, as I thought, so savage. . . .

**African View of Portuguese, c. 1650–1700**

*A carver in the kingdom of Benin, on Africa's west coast, created this saltholder depicting Portuguese officials and their ship.*

The Portuguese found slave trading lucrative and kept out competitors until after 1600. Although in 1482 they built an outpost, Elmina, on West Africa's Gold Coast, they exploited existing African commercial and social patterns. Often Portuguese merchants traded slaves and local products to other Africans for gold. The local African kingdoms were too strong for the Portuguese to attack, and black rulers traded—or chose not to trade—according to their own self-interest.

West African societies changed with the coming of Portuguese slavers. In Guinea and Senegambia, which supplied the bulk of sixteenth-century slaves, small kingdoms expanded to "service" the trade. Some of their rulers became comparatively rich. Farther south, in present-day Angola, the kings of Kongo used the slave trade to consolidate their power and voluntarily adopted Christianity, just as earlier rulers had converted to Islam. Kongo flourished until the late sixteenth century, when rival powers from the interior destroyed it.

African political leaders and their communities used the trade as a way of disposing of "undesirables," including slaves whom they already owned, lawbreakers, and persons accused of witchcraft. But most slaves were simply victims of raids or wars. Muslim and European slave trading greatly exacerbated conflicts among African communities.

Although European societies had used slaves since the time of ancient Greece and Rome, there were ominous differences in the European slavery that arose once the Portuguese began voyaging to West Africa. First, the unprecedented scale of the trade resulted in a demographic catastrophe for West Africa and its peoples. Before the Atlantic slave trade finally ended in the nineteenth century, nearly 12 million Africans would be shipped in terrible conditions across the sea. Slavery on this scale had been unknown to Europeans since the collapse of the Roman Empire. Second, African slaves were subjected to new extremes of dehumanization. In medieval Europe and in West Africa itself slaves had lived in their masters' households and primarily performed domestic service. But by 1450 the Portuguese and Spanish created large slave-labor plantations on their Atlantic and Mediterranean islands. These plantations produced sugar for European markets, using capital supplied by Italian investors to buy African slaves who toiled until death. In short, the African slaves owned by Europeans were regarded as property rather than merely as persons of low status; as such, they were consigned to labor that was unending, exhausting, and mindless. By 1600 the "new slavery" had become a brutal link in a commerce that ultimately would encompass all major Western nations.

Finally, race became the explicit basis of the "new slavery." Africans' blackness and their alien religion dehumanized them in European eyes. As their racial prejudice hardened, Europeans justified enslaving blacks with increasing ease. From the fifteenth century onward, European Christianity made few attempts to soften slavery's rigors, and race defined a slave. Because the victims of the "new slavery" were physically distinctive as well as culturally alien, slavery became a lifelong, hereditary, and despised status.

## Europeans Reach America

Europeans' varying motivations for expanding their horizons converged in the fascinating, contradictory figure of Christopher Columbus (1451–1506), the son of a weaver from the Italian port of Genoa. Columbus's maritime experience, self-taught geographical learning, and keen imagination led him to conclude that Asia could be reached by sailing westward across the Atlantic. By the early 1480s this idea obsessed him. Religious fervor led Columbus to dream of carrying Christianity around the globe and liberating Jerusalem from Muslim rule, but he also burned with ambition to win wealth and glory.

Columbus would not be the first European to venture far out into the Atlantic. Besides the early Norse, fifteenth-century English fishermen may already have sailed as far west as the Grand Banks and even the North American coast. But Columbus was unique in the persistence with which he hawked his "enterprise

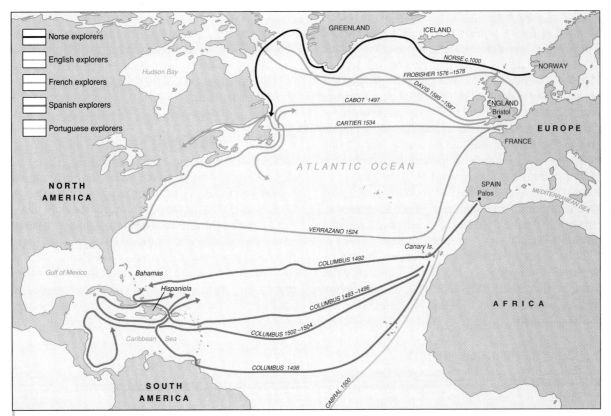

### Major Transatlantic Explorations, 1000–1587

*Following Columbus's 1492 voyage, Spain's rivals soon began laying claim to parts of the New World based on the voyages of Cabot for England, Cabral for Portugal, and Verrazano for France. Later English and French exploration focused on finding a passage to Asia around or through Canada.*

of the Indies" around the royal courts of western Europe. John II of Portugal showed interest until Días's discovery of the Cape of Good Hope promised a surer way to India. Finally, in 1492, hoping to break a threatened Portuguese monopoly on direct trade with Asia, the rulers of newly united Spain—Queen Isabella of Castile and King Ferdinand of Aragon—accepted Columbus's offer. Picking up the westward-blowing trade winds at the Canary Islands, Columbus's three small ships reached San Salvador within a month.

Word of Columbus's discovery caught Europeans' imaginations. To forestall potential rivals, Isabella and Portugal's King John II in 1494 signed the Treaty of Tordesillas, which divided all future American discoveries between Castile and Portugal. Meanwhile, Isabella had sent Columbus back to explore further, and he established a colony on Hispaniola, the Caribbean island today occupied by Haiti and the Dominican Republic. Columbus proved a poor administrator, and after his

last voyages (1498–1502), he was shunted aside. He died an embittered man, convinced that he had reached the threshold of Asia, only to be cheated of his rightful rewards.

England's Henry VII (ruled 1485–1509) ignored the Treaty of Tordesillas and in 1497 sent an Italian navigator, John Cabot, westward into the Atlantic. Cabot claimed for England Nova Scotia, Newfoundland, and the rich Grand Banks fisheries. Like Columbus, Cabot thought that he had reached Asia.

The more Europeans explored, the more apparent it became that a vast landmass blocked the route to Asia. In 1500 the Portuguese claimed Brazil, and other voyages soon revealed a continuous coastline from the Caribbean to Brazil. In 1507 this landmass got its name when a publisher brought out a collection of voyagers' tales. One of the chroniclers was an Italian named Amerigo Vespucci. With a shrewd marketing touch, the publisher devised a catchy name for the new continent: America.

Getting past America and reaching Asia remained the early explorers' primary aim. In 1513 the Spaniard Vasco Núñez de Balboa chanced upon the Pacific Ocean when he crossed the narrow isthmus of Panama. Then in 1519 the Portuguese Ferdinand Magellan, sailing under the Castilian flag, began a voyage around the world by way of the stormy (later named for him) straits at South America's southern tip. In an incredible feat of endurance, he crossed the Pacific to the Philippines, only to die fighting with local natives. One of his five ships and fifteen emaciated sailors finally returned to Spain in 1522, the first people to have sailed around the world. But Europeans hoped for easier access to East Asia's fabled wealth. The French king Francis I led the search for a "northwest passage" to Asia. In 1524 he dispatched the Italian navigator Giovanni da Verrazano, who explored the North American coast from the Carolinas to Newfoundland. In three subsequent voyages between 1534 and 1542 the French explorer Jacques Cartier carefully probed the coasts of Newfoundland, Quebec, and Nova Scotia and ascended the St. Lawrence as far as present-day Montreal. Although encountering large numbers of Native Americans, Verrazano and Cartier found no gold and no northwest passage.

## *Spain's* Conquistadores

Columbus was America's first slave trader and the first Spanish conqueror, or *conquistador.* At his struggling colony on Hispaniola, he began exporting Indian slaves and created *encomiendas*—grants for the right to extract labor and other tribute from the Indians of a designated district. Other *conquistadores* would soon transplant this practice to the American mainland.

From the beginning *encomiendas* harshly exploited the native people, who died in droves from overwork, malnutrition, and disease. Then Portuguese slavers

**Spanish Map of the Antilles, 1519**
*This map offers a rare glimpse of Spain's initial stronghold in the Caribbean islands, centering on what is now Haiti. The decorative figures are Africans, imported to replace Indian labor lost to disease and harsh treatment.*

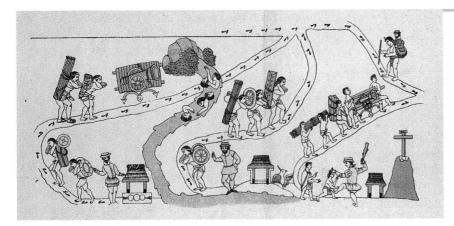

**Cortés's Entrance into Veracruz, c. 1550**

*The ancient Mexicans called Veracruz the "Place of Precious Stones." Mexican Lienzo de Tlaxcala's pictorial description shows Cortés transporting cannons on his march through Mexico.*

stepped in, supplying shiploads of Africans to replace the perishing Indians. Spanish friars who came to Hispaniola to convert the Indians quickly sent back grim reports of Indian exploitation; and King Ferdinand (who had made money by selling *encomiendas*) felt sufficiently shocked to attempt to forbid the practice. No one, however, worried about the African slaves' fate.

Soon Spanish settlers were fanning out through the Caribbean in search of Indian slaves and gold. In 1519 the restless nobleman Hernán Cortés (1485–1547) led a small band of followers to the Mexican coast. Destroying his boats and gathering Indian allies, he marched inland over towering mountain passes to conquer Mexico.

Spaniards had dreamed of a prize such as Mexico ever since they reached America. Mexico was rich: an impressive civilization had been evolving there for three thousand years, culminating in the mighty Aztec Empire. It was exotic: the priests and soldiers who dominated the empire raided neighboring peoples to seize victims for ceremonial human sacrifices. And Mexico was highly organized. The 300,000 inhabitants of the capital, Tenochtitlán, enjoyed fresh water supplied by means of elaborate engineering works; their urban society was highly stratified; and artisans produced a profusion of finely crafted pottery as well as stone, copper, silver, and gold implements. "We were amazed and said that it was like the enchantments they tell of [in stories], and some of our soldiers even asked whether the things that we saw were not a dream," recalled one of Cortés's soldiers of his first glimpse of Tenochtitlán's pyramids, lakes, and causeways. Certainly the golden gifts that the Aztecs offered in the vain hope of buying off the invaders were no dream. "They picked up the gold and fingered it like monkeys," recalled an Indian. "Their bodies swelled with greed, and their hunger was ravenous. They hungered like pigs for that gold."

Cortés attacked and swiftly prevailed. He owed his astonishing victories partly to firearms and horses, which terrified the Aztecs, and partly to initial Aztec suppositions that the Spanish were the white, bearded gods whose return ancient legends had foretold. His success also resulted from his boldness and cunning, the Aztec emperor Moctezuma's fears, epidemics among the Indians, and the revolt of the Aztecs' subject peoples. By 1521 Cortés had overthrown the Aztecs and begun to build Mexico City on the ruins of Tenochtitlán. Soon the last Aztec emperor suffered defeat and execution, and within twenty years Central America lay at the Spaniards' feet. New Spain was born.

During the rest of the sixteenth century, other *conquistadores* and officials consolidated a great Hispanic empire stretching from New Spain (Mexico) to Chile. The human cost of the conquest was enormous. Mourned a vanquished Aztec,

> Broken spears lie in the roads;
> We have torn our hair in our grief.
> The houses are roofless now . . .
> And the walls are splattered with gore . . .
> We have pounded our hands in despair
> Against the adobe walls.

When Cortés landed in 1519, central Mexico's population had been about 25 million. By 1600 it had shrunk to between 1 million and 2 million. Peru and other regions experienced similar devastation. America had witnessed the greatest demographic disaster in world history.

### The Columbian Exchange

Warfare, forced labor, starvation, and mass slaughter accounted for some of the catastrophe of European conquest, but the greatest killers were microbes. Native Americans lacked antibodies to European and African infections—above all, the deadly, highly communicable smallpox. From the first years of contact, frightful epidemics decimated Indian communities. In the West Indian islands, the entire native population perished within fifty years, and devastation from disease facilitated the colonization of mainland North America. "The people began to die very fast, and many in a short space," an Englishman later remarked, adding that the deaths invariably occurred after Europeans had visited an Indian village. From early in the sixteenth century, raging epidemics of smallpox and other alien maladies scourged the defenseless Indians. Whole villages perished at once, with no one left to bury the dead. Up to 90 percent of the native population in some areas was lost.

Yet the "Columbian exchange"—the biological encounter of the Eastern and Western Hemispheres—was not limited to deadly germs. In addition to diseases, sixteenth-century Europeans brought horses, cattle, sheep, swine, chickens, wheat and other grains, coffee, sugar cane, numerous fruits and garden vegetables, and an astonishing variety of weeds, insects, and rodents to America. In the next century, African slaves carried rice and yams with them across the Atlantic. The list of American gifts to the Eastern Hemisphere was equally impressive: corn, many varieties of beans, white and sweet potatoes, the tropical root crop manioc, tomatoes, squash, pumpkins, peanuts, vanilla, cacao, avocados, pineapples, chilis, tobacco, and turkeys. Often several centuries passed before new plants became widely accepted across the ocean; for example, many Europeans suspected that potatoes and tomatoes were either poisons or aphrodisiacs until the nineteenth century, and few Indians were eager to grow wheat. European weeds and domestic animals drastically altered many environments in the Western Hemisphere, especially in North America, overwhelming indigenous plantlife and thereby driving away wild animals who fed on those plants. In this way, colonists' ways of life impinged directly on the lives of native peoples. Settlers' crops, intensively cultivated on lands never replenished by lying fallow, often exhausted American soil. But the worldwide exchange of food products also enriched human diets and later made possible enormous population growth.

Another dimension of the transatlantic encounters was the mixing of peoples. During the sixteenth century, about 300,000 Spaniards immigrated, 90 percent of them male. Particularly in towns, a racially blended people emerged as these men married Indian women, giving rise to the large *mestizo* (mixed Spanish-Indian) population of Mexico and other Latin American countries. *Métis*, as the French termed people of both Indian and European descent, would appear in lesser proportions in the French and English colonies of North America. Throughout the Americas, particularly in plantation colonies, European men fathered *mulatto* children with African women, most of them slaves, and African-Indian unions occurred in nearly all regions. But the context for these population transfers and mixtures was the massive migrations of Europeans and enslaved Africans and the wholesale extermination of Native Americans through disease and violence.

The Americas supplied seemingly limitless wealth for Spain. Not only did some Spaniards grow rich from West Indian sugar plantations and Mexican sheep and cattle ranches, but immense quantities of silver crossed the Atlantic after rich mines in Mexico and Peru began producing in the 1540s. A robust trade between America and Spain grew up, which Castilian officials tried to regulate. Spain took in far more American silver than its economy could absorb, setting off inflation that eventually engulfed all Europe. Bent on dominating Europe, the Spanish kings needed ever more American silver to finance their wars. Several times they went bankrupt, and their efforts to squeeze more taxes from their subjects provoked in the 1560s the revolt of Spain's rich Netherlands provinces. In the end, gaining access to American wealth cost Spain dearly.

## Footholds in North America

As early as 1510, the flow of wealth from the Americas to Spain attracted swarms of Europeans. While most flocked to Mexico, the Caribbean, and points farther south, some Europeans grew familiar with the North American coast through exploratory voyages, fishing expeditions, a small-scale fur trade, and piracy and smuggling. But except for a Spanish base at St. Augustine, Florida, their attempts to plant colonies failed. These failures did not stem from lack of effort. Would-be conquerors and colonizers tried many times to establish the presence of Spain, France, or England on North American soil. But they predicated their efforts on unrealistic expectations of fabulous wealth and pliant natives.

As the seventeenth century dawned, the ravaging of Indian populations owing to disease, and the rise of English, French, and Dutch power finally made colonization possible. By 1614 Spain, England, France, and the Netherlands had established secure North American bases. Within another decade, each colony developed a distinct economic orientation, as well as patterns of Indian relations and geographic expansion. Thus the first quarter of the seventeenth century marked the formative period of North America's modern history.

## New Spain's Northern Frontier

The Spanish had built their American empire by subduing the Aztec and other Indian states, whose riches had attracted the invaders like a magnet. The dream of more such finds drew would-be *conquistadores* to the borderlands north of Mexico. "As it was his object to find another treasure like that . . . of Peru," a witness wrote of one such man, Hernando de Soto, he "would not be content with good lands nor pearls."

The earliest of these invaders was Juan Ponce de León, the conqueror of Puerto Rico, who in 1512–1513 and again in 1521 trudged through Florida in search of gold and slaves. His quest ended in death in an Indian skirmish. The most astonishing early expedition began in Florida in 1527. After provoking several attacks by Apalachee Indians, the three hundred explorers were separated into several parties. All were thought to have perished until eight years later, when four survivors, led by Alvar Nuñez Cabeza de Vaca and including an African slave, Estevanico, arrived in northern Mexico. Cabeza de Vaca's account of their journey from Florida through Texas and New Mexico is the most compelling European literary work on North America before permanent colonization.

Cabeza de Vaca provided direct inspiration for the two most formidable attempts at Spanish conquest. De Soto and his party in 1539–1543 blundered from Tampa Bay to the Appalachians to southern Texas. Scouring the land for gold, de Soto harried the Indians mercilessly. "Think, then," an Indian chief appealed to him vainly,

> what must be the effect on me and mine, of the sight of you and your people, whom we have at no time seen, astride the fierce brutes, your horses, entering with such speed and fury into my country, that we had no tidings of your coming—things so absolutely new, as to strike awe and terror into our hearts.

Although de Soto died without finding any gold or conquering any Indians, his and other expeditions caused epidemics that destroyed most of the remaining Mississippian societies (see Chapter 1). By the time Europeans returned to the southeastern interior late in the seventeenth century, only the Natchez on the lower Mississippi River still inhabited their sumptuous temple-mound center and remained under the rule of a Great Sun monarch. Depopulated groups like the Cherokees and Creeks had adopted the less centralized village life of other eastern Indians.

As de Soto roamed the Southeast, some Spanish officials in Mexico were drawn by rumors that the fabled Seven Golden Cities of Cíbola lay to the north. In 1540–1542, Francisco Vásquez de Coronado led a massive expedition bent on locating, and subjugating, these cities of gold. Coronado plundered several pueblos and wandered from the Grand Canyon to Kansas before returning to Mexico, finding no gold but embittering many Native Americans. Other expeditions, along the

**The Spanish and Portuguese Empires, 1610**
*By 1610 Spain dominated Latin America, including Portugal's possessions. Having devoted its energies to exploiting Mexico and the Caribbean, Spain had not yet expanded into what is now the United States, aside from establishing outposts in Florida and New Mexico.*

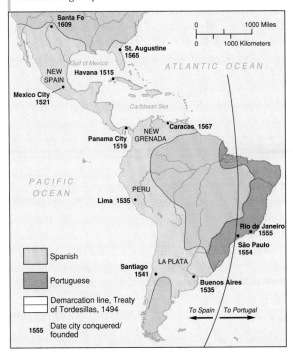

**Navajo View of Spanish Colonizers**
*This pictograph—a painting or drawing on rock—was sketched in the early colonial period in Cañón del Muerto, Arizona.*

California coast and up the Colorado River, likewise proved fruitless.

For several decades after these failed ventures, Spain's principal interest north of Mexico and the Caribbean lay in establishing strategic bases to keep out French and English intruders. In 1565 Spain established the first successful European settlement in North America, a powerful fortress at St. Augustine, Florida. Despite efforts to strengthen Florida and to build forts linking it to Mexico, St. Augustine remained only a military stronghold and a base for a chain of religious missions extending north to Chesapeake Bay. Rejecting missionary efforts to reorder their lives, the Indians rebelled and forced the closing of all the missions before 1600.

Franciscan missionaries renewed their efforts in Florida in the early seventeenth century and secured the nominal allegiance of about sixteen thousand Guale and Timucuan Indians. But epidemics in the 1610s killed about half the converts.

Meanwhile, in the 1580s, Spanish friars had returned to the Southwest, preaching Christianity and scouting the area's potential wealth. Encouraged by their reports, in 1598 Juan de Oñate led five hundred Spaniards, mestizos, Mexican Indians, and African slaves into the upper Rio Grande Valley, where he proclaimed the royal colony of New Mexico, distributed *encomiendas,* and demanded tribute from the pueblo-dwelling Indians.

The new colony barely survived. The Spanish government replaced Oñate in 1606 because of misman-agement and excessive brutality toward the Indians. His successor founded Santa Fe in 1610, but many colonists established ranches nearer the pueblos in order to exploit Indian labor. New Mexico survived primarily through the efforts of Franciscan missionaries. By 1630 they had converted about twenty thousand Indians and established more than fifty missions in the Rio Grande Valley and westward 250 miles to the Hopi villages in Arizona.

## France: Initial Failures and Canadian Success

The voyages of Verrazano and Cartier (see above) began France's interest in North America. France made the first attempt at colonizing in North America in 1541, when Jacques Cartier led ten ships carrying four hundred soldiers, three hundred sailors, and a few women to the St. Lawrence Valley. Cartier had already alienated many Indians along the St. Lawrence during two previous expeditions, and his construction of a fortified settlement on Indian land cut off all possibility of native support. Over the next two years, the French suffered heavy casualties from Indian attacks and from scurvy (for which the Indians could have shown them a cure) before abandoning the colony.

The failed French expedition seemed to verify the Spanish opinion, voiced by the cardinal of Seville, that "this whole coast as far [south] as Florida is utterly unproductive." The next French effort at colonization came in 1562, when French Huguenots (Calvinists)

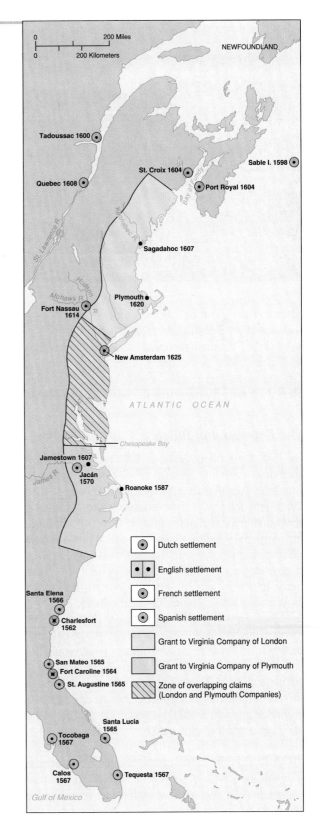

### European Settlements in Eastern North America, 1565–1625

*Except for St. Augustine, Florida, and Santa Fe, New Mexico, all European settlements founded before 1607 were abandoned by 1625. Despite the migration of ten thousand Europeans to North America's Atlantic coast by 1625, the total number of Spanish, English, French, and Dutch on the continent was then about eighteen hundred, of whom two-thirds lived in Virginia.*

briefly established a base in what is now South Carolina. In 1564 the Huguenots founded a settlement near modern-day Jacksonville, Florida, which the Spanish destroyed a year later, massacring all 132 male defenders. These failures, along with a civil war between French Catholics and Huguenots, temporarily hindered the French from further attempts at colonization.

Meanwhile, French and other European fishers were working the plenteous Grand Banks fisheries of the North Atlantic. Going ashore to dry their fish, some French sailors bartered with coastal Indians for skins of the beaver, a species almost extinct in Europe. By the late sixteenth century, as European demand for beaver hats skyrocketed, a French-dominated fur trade blossomed. Before the end of the century, French traders were returning annually to sites from Newfoundland to Maine and along the lower St. Lawrence.

Unlike explorers such as de Soto and colonizers such as those at Roanoke (see below), the traders recognized the importance of reciprocity in dealing with the Indians. Consequently, they were generally more successful. In exchange for pelts, they traded metal tools such as axes and knives, cloth, and glass beads. Seen by the Europeans as "trinkets," glass beads to the Indians had the same supernatural power as quartz, mica, and other sacred substances obtained via trade networks for thousands of years. By the next century specialized factories in Europe would be producing both cloth and glass for the "Indian trade."

Between 1598 and 1604, a series of government-sponsored French fur-trading outposts appeared in Acadia (modern-day Nova Scotia). And in 1608 the first enduring French settlement on Canadian soil was founded by Samuel de Champlain at Quebec, far up the St. Lawrence River. Champlain wintered there with twenty-eight men, of whom twenty died.

In order to strengthen the fragile colony, Champlain the next year allied with nearby Indians and aided them in defeating their Mohawk Iroquois enemies (see A

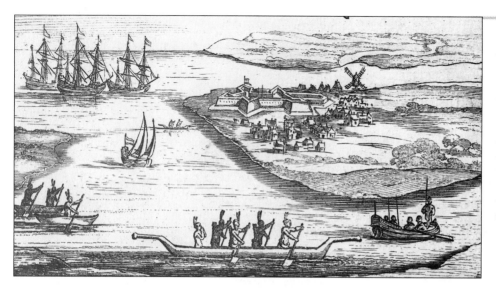

**New Amsterdam**

*After the Dutch "purchase" of Manhattan Island, the fortified settlement of New Amsterdam grew only slowly, as this view from 1651 (the earliest known depiction) clearly shows. Except for the tip, the island remained farmland or forest. Corn brought by canoe-paddling Indians also helped feed the settlement. Note the windmill, where grain was ground.*

Place in Time). Through their alliance with the powerful Hurons, the French gained access to the thick beaver pelts of the Canadian interior in exchange for providing protection from the Iroquois. These economic and diplomatic arrangements defined the course of New France's history for the rest of the seventeenth century.

### The Enterprising Dutch

By 1588 the independence of the Protestant, Dutch-speaking part of Spain's rebellious Netherlands provinces was secure, although the southern Netherlands—modern Belgium and Luxembourg—would remain under Spanish rule until 1713. The Dutch Republic, one of the seventeenth century's great powers, built an empire stretching from Brazil to West Africa to what is now Indonesia. North America was for them a relatively minor sphere of activity. Even so, the Dutch played a key role in colonizing the continent.

Having established lucrative ties with Indians on the lower Hudson River (see A Place in Time), Dutch traders in 1614 built Fort Nassau near what would become Albany, and established the colony of New Netherland. In 1626 the Dutch bought an island at the mouth of the Hudson from local Indians and began a second settlement there. The Dutch named the island Manhattan and the settlement New Amsterdam.

New Netherlanders lived by the fur trade. Through the Mohawks, they relied on the Iroquois Confederacy, much as the French depended on the Hurons. To stimulate a flow of furs to New Netherland, in the 1620s Dutch traders obtained from Indians near Long Island

Sound large quantities of wampum (tiny seashells denoting spiritual power, which Native Americans had long traded throughout the continent's interior) and used it to buy beaver pelts inland. Backed respectively by the French and the Dutch, Hurons and Iroquois became embroiled in an ever-deepening contest to control the movement of goods between Europeans and Indians.

### Elizabethan England and the Wider World

In 1558, when Elizabeth I became queen, England was a minor power and stood on the sidelines as Spain and France grappled for supremacy in Europe. At that time, England and Spain were enjoying friendly relations. But the English worried about Spain's intervention in France's religious wars and its determined effort to crush the Dutch revolt, as well as about the pope's call for Elizabeth's overthrow. Furthermore, in 1568 the Spanish authorities in Mexico had chased pesky English privateers, including John Hawkins and Francis Drake, from the Caribbean. Secretly, Elizabeth stepped up her aid to Calvinist rebels in France and the Netherlands, and to "sea dogs" like Hawkins and Drake—from whose voyages she took a share of the plunder. In the 1570s she encouraged merchants to invest in Atlantic-oriented ventures.

Meanwhile, England's position in Ireland was deteriorating. As early as 1565, English troops fought to impose colonial rule throughout the island. The conflict intensified when the pope and the Spanish began directly aiding Irish Catholics' resistance to the English. In the ensuing war that ground on through the 1580s, the English drove the Irish clans out of their strongholds, especially in northern Ireland, or Ulster, and established their own settlements ("plantations") of En-glish and Scottish Protestants. The English practiced total war to break the rebellious population's spirit, inflicting starvation and mass slaughter by destroying villages in the winter.

Elizabeth's generals justified these atrocities by claiming that the Irish were "savages." Ireland thus furnished precedents for strategies that the English later employed against North American Indians, whose customs, religion, and method of fighting likewise seemed to absolve the English from guilt in waging exceptionally cruel warfare.

England had two objectives in the Western Hemisphere in the 1570s. The first was to find the northwest passage to Asia and if possible to discover gold on the way; the second, in Drake's words, was to "singe the king of Spain's beard" by raiding Spanish fleets and ports from Spain to the West Indies. The search for the northwest passage only led to such embarrassments as explorer Martin Frobisher's return from the Canadian Arctic with a shipload of "fool's gold." However, privateering raids on the Spanish were both spectacularly successful and profitable for Drake's and Hawkins's financial backers, including merchants, gentry, government leaders, and Elizabeth herself. The most breathtaking enterprise was Drake's voyage around the world (1577–1580) in quest of sites for colonies. During this voyage he sailed up the California coast and entered Drake's Bay, north of San Francisco, where he traded with Miwok Indians.

Now deadly rivals, Spain and England sought to outmaneuver one another in America. In 1572 the Spanish tried to fortify a Jesuit mission on the Chesapeake Bay. They failed, largely because Powhatan Indians resisted. After an attempt to colonize Newfoundland failed, Raleigh obtained a royal patent (charter) to start an English colony farther south, closer to the Spanish—the region that the English had already named Virginia in honor of their virgin queen. Raleigh dispatched Arthur Barlowe to explore the region, and Barlowe returned singing the praises of Roanoke Island and its peaceable natives. Raleigh then persuaded Elizabeth to dispatch ships and a company of soldiers to launch a colony at Roanoke.

At first all went well. The Roanoke Indians eagerly traded and shared their corn—which they grew with amazing ease. Given such abundance and native hospi-tality, the colonists wondered why they should work at all. Refusing to grow their own food, they expected the Indians to feed them. By the first winter, they had outlived their welcome. Fearing that the Roanokes were about to attack, English soldiers killed Winginia, the Roanoke leader, in June 1586. When Raleigh's friend Drake stopped in soon after on his way back to England, most of the English joined him.

**Elizabeth I:
The Armada Portrait**

Thereafter the growing Anglo-Spanish conflict repeatedly prevented English ships from sailing back to Roanoke. When a rescue party finally arrived in 1590, it found only rusty armor, moldy books, and the word *CROATOAN* cut into a post. What had happened to the "lost colony"? Historians will never know with certainty.

Roanoke's brief history illustrates several stubborn realities about early European experiences in North America. First, even a large-scale, well-financed colonizing effort could fail, given the settlers' unpreparedness for the American environment. Second, colonists did not bring enough provisions for the first winter and consistently disdained growing their own food. Although some early English settlers were curious and open-minded about the Indians' way of life, all assumed that the natives would submit to their authority and feed them while they looked for gold—a sure recipe for trouble. Third, colonizing attempts would have to be self-financing: financially strapped monarchs like Elizabeth I would not throw good money after bad into America. Fourth, conflict with the Spanish hung menacingly over every European attempt to gain a foothold in North America.

While Roanoke struggled, England in 1588 won a spectacular naval victory over the Armada, a huge invasion fleet sent into the English Channel by Spain's Philip II. This famous victory preserved England's independence and confirmed its status as a major power in the Atlantic.

**1609**

## Lake Champlain

For thousands of years before the seventeenth century, Lake Champlain had been central to the lives of Native Americans. The lake and its many tributaries abounded with fish and waterfowl as well as beaver, otter, and other mammals. The surrounding Champlain Valley's forests were rich in edible plants and home to deer, bear, and wild turkey. And its fertile soil supported Indian cultivation of corn, beans, and squash while its stone outcrops served as quarries for making tools. Arriving in 1609, the French colonizer, Samuel de Champlain (who named the lake for himself) described the valley as "a fine, fertile region," its waters as "very full of fish," and its land as having "many butternut trees and vines, and beautiful meadows with much game." Besides being a habitat, Lake Champlain was a high-way over which Indian traders, diplomats, and warriors passed between the Northeast's two major river systems— the St. Lawrence and the Hudson. It was as a warrior that Champlain sailed on to the lake that summer day in 1609.

Champlain had arrived in Canada the year before and established France's first successful North American colony at Quebec on the St. Lawrence. The French government planted the colony in order to control the lucrative Canadian fur trade and to keep out English, Dutch, and independent French competitors. Having previously explored much of the Northeast and headed a short-lived French settlement at Acadia, Champlain was familiar with Indian politics and diplomacy in the region. Building on this understanding, he shrewdly allied with the Montagnais and Algonquians of the St. Lawrence and the Hurons of the lower Great Lakes and agreed to help them defeat their enemies, the Mohawks of the Iroquois Confederacy, who had long sought direct access to European traders visiting the St. Lawrence. Champlain's new allies were equally shrewd in recognizing the advantage that French guns would give them against the usually dreaded Mohawks.

In mid-July Champlain and two other Frenchmen accompanied sixty Montagnais and Huron warriors to the Mohawk-controlled lake. In the days that followed, the Indians and French learned much about each other's methods of waging war. Champlain particularly admired the Indian leaders' sophisticated discussions of strategy, their thorough drilling of their men, and their smooth coordination of fighting, scouting, and provisioning operations. On the other hand, he scoffed at the Indians' belief that dreams would foretell the outcome of the battle and at an elaborate ceremony in which a religious leader (whom Champlain considered a fraud) attempted to determine whether the Indians "would come upon their enemies and kill many of them."

On the evening of July 29, the party encountered two hundred Mohawks at Point Ticonderoga near the lake's southern tip. Instead of taking up weapons (for the Indians rarely fought at night), the warriors on each side exchanged boasts and taunts, each side predicting that it would humiliate the other on the following day. All the while the French remained hidden. In the morning, Champlain's party went ashore, the main body moving directly toward the Mohawks and the rest taking cover behind nearby trees. As the main column neared its opponents, Champlain stepped ahead and confronted the Mohawks' three spectacularly attired war leaders.

**French and Dutch Expeditions in the Northeast, 1608–1609**

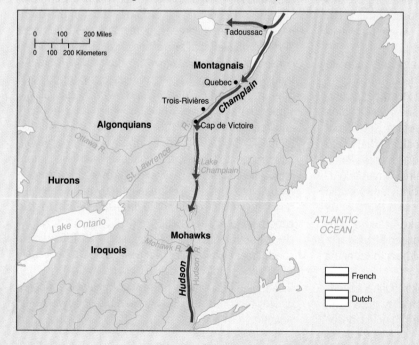

I was thirty paces from the enemy, who as soon as they caught site of me halted and gazed at me and I at them. When I saw them make a move to draw their bows upon us, I took aim with my arquebus [*a kind of gun*] and shot straight at one of the three chiefs, and with this same shot two fell to the ground, and one of their companions was wounded and died a little later. . . . The Iroquois were much astonished that two men should have been killed so quickly, . . . As I was reloading my arquebus, one of my [French] companions fired a shot from within the woods, which astonished them again so much that, seeing their chiefs dead, they lost courage and took to flight, abandoning the field and their fort, and fleeing into the depths of the forest, whither I pursued them and laid low still more of them.

Thereafter the French and their allies pursued the fleeing Mohawks, killing about fifty and capturing about a dozen prisoners. A few of the pro-French Indians suffered minor arrow wounds.

What took place that day on the shore of Lake Champlain was nothing less than revolutionary. Although the Spanish had used firearms extensively in their conquests to the south, such weapons remained unknown to northeastern Indians except in a few coastal communities. The fact that Europeans—whose goods of glass and metal were already becoming highly prized by the region's Indians—also possessed such a powerful weapon made alliance with them all the more imperative for Native Americans. Just as the French were routing the Mohawks, Henry Hudson sailed up the river later named for him and traded with various Indians while claiming the land for the Dutch Republic. When Dutch traders returned the following year, some of their most eager customers were—not surprisingly—Mohawk Iroquois. There began an economic and diplomatic tie that would serve the Iroquois and Dutch as a counterweight to the power of the French and their native allies. Dutch traders later sold guns to the Iroquois, making them the most feared and the most heavily armed Indian force in North America. The French-Iroquois rivalry did not abate until a series of wars at the end of the century finally exhausted both sides. The battle of Lake Champlain marked the end of casual Indian-European encounters in the Northeast and the beginning of a deadly era of trade, diplomacy, and warfare.

**Montagnais Indians**

**(Above) Samuel de Champlain**
*The explorer is considered the "father of New France"*; **(right)** *Battle of Lake Champlain*

### The Beginnings of English Colonization: Virginia

Anglo-Spanish relations took a new turn after 1603, when Elizabeth died and her cousin, the king of Scotland, ascended the English throne as James I. The cautious and peace-loving king signed a truce with Spain in 1604. Seriously alarmed by Dutch naval victories, the Spanish considered England the lesser danger. The new Spanish king, Philip III, therefore conceded what his predecessors had always refused: a free hand to another power in part of the Americas. Spain renounced its claims to Virginia; England could now colonize unmolested.

The question now was: How would England's colonies be financed? Neither the English crown nor Parliament would agree to spend money on colonies, and Roanoke's failure had proved that private fortunes were inadequate to finance successful settlements. Only joint-stock companies—business corporations that would amass capital through sales of stock to the public—could raise funds for American settlement. Such stock offerings produced large sums, but with limited risk for each investor.

On April 10, 1606, James I granted a charter authorizing overlapping grants of land in Virginia to two separate joint-stock companies, one based in London and the other in Plymouth. The Virginia Company of Plymouth received a grant extending south from modern Maine to the Potomac River, and the Virginia Company of London's lands ran north from Cape Fear to the Hudson River. Both companies dispatched colonists in 1607.

The Virginia Company of Plymouth sent 120 men to Sagadahoc, at the mouth of the Kennebec River. Half left in 1608 after alienating the Abenaki Indians and enduring a hard Maine winter, and the rest went back to England a year later. Soon thereafter the company disbanded.

The Virginia Company of London barely avoided a similar failure. Its first expedition included many gentlemen who disdained work and expected riches to fall into their laps. They chose a site on the James River in May 1607 and named it Jamestown. Discipline quickly fell apart and, as at Roanoke, the colonists neglected to plant crops. When relief ships arrived in January 1608 with reinforcements, only 38 survivors remained out of 105 immigrants.

Short of workers who could farm, fish, hunt, and do carpentry, Virginia also lacked effective leadership. The council's first president hoarded supplies, and its second was lazy and indecisive. In September 1608 the desperate councilors turned to a brash soldier of fortune, Captain John Smith.

Only twenty-eight years old and of yeoman origin, Smith had experience fighting Spaniards and Turks that prepared him well to assume control in Virginia. Organizing all but the sick in work gangs, he ensured sufficient food and housing for winter. Applying lessons learned in his soldiering days, he laid down rules for maintaining sanitation and hygiene to limit disease. Above all, he brought order through military discipline. During the winter of 1608–1609, Virginia lost just a dozen men out of two hundred.

Smith also became the colony's best diplomat. After local Native Americans captured him in late 1607, Smith displayed such courage that Powhatan, the leader of the nearby Powhatan Confederacy, arranged an elaborate reconciliation ceremony in which his daughter, Pocahontas, "saved" Smith's life during a mock execution. Smith maintained satisfactory relations with the Powhatan Confederacy in part through his personality, but he also employed calculated demonstrations of English military strength to mask the settlers' actual weakness.

John Smith prevented Virginia from disintegrating as Sagadahoc had. But when he returned to England in 1609 after being wounded in a gunpowder explosion, discipline again crumbled. Expecting the Indians to provide them with corn, the colonists had not laid away sufficient food for the winter. Consequently, relations with the Powhatans deteriorated. A survivor of the winter wrote,

> So lamentable was our scarcity, that we were constrained to eat dogs, cats, rats, snakes, toadstools, horsehides, and what not; one man out of the misery endured, killing his wife powdered her up [with flour] to eat her, for which he was burned. Many besides fed on the corpses of dead men.

Of the five hundred residents at Jamestown in September 1609, about four hundred died by May 1610. But an influx of new recruits, coupled with the imposition of military rule, enabled Virginia to win the First Anglo-Powhatan War (1610–1614). The English population remained small, however, just 380 in 1616, and it had yet to produce anything of value for the stockholders.

Tobacco emerged as Virginia's economic salvation. John Rolfe, an Englishman who married Pocahontas after the war, spent several years perfecting a salable variety of tobacco and began planting it in Virginia. By 1619 the product commanded high prices, and that year Virginia exported large amounts of the crop. Thereafter the Virginia Company poured supplies and settlers into the colony.

To attract labor and capital, the company awarded fifty-acre grants ("headrights") to anyone paying his or her own passage or the transit of a laborer. By paying the passage of their indentured servants, some enterprising planters accumulated sizable tracts of land. Thousands of single young men and a few hundred women calculated that uncertainty in Virginia was preferable to continued unemployment and poverty in England. In return for their passage, the servants worked for a fixed term, usually four to seven years. The Virginia Company also abandoned military rule and provided for an assembly to be elected by the "inhabitants" (apparently meaning only the planters). Although the assembly's actions were subject to the company's veto, its establishment in 1619 did mark the beginnings of representative government in North America.

By 1622 Virginia faced three serious problems. First, local officials systematically defrauded the shareholders by embezzling treasury funds, overcharging for supplies, and using company laborers to work their own tobacco fields. They profited, but the company sank deep into debt. Second, the colony's population suffered from an exceptionally high death rate. The majority of fatalities stemmed from malnutrition owing to the poor diets of the servants, or from salt poisoning, typhus, or dysentery, contracted when the settlers drank the salty, polluted water from the lower James River. Most of the 3,500 immigrants entering Virginia from 1618 to 1622 died within three years. Finally, relations with the Powhatans steadily worsened after Pocahontas died in England in 1617, and Powhatan a year later. Leadership passed to Opechancanough, who at first sought to accommodate the English. But relentless expansion led to Indian discontent and to the rise of a powerful shaman, Nemattenew, who urged the Powhatans to resist the English to the death. After some settlers killed Nemattenew, the Indians launched a surprise attack in 1622 that killed 347 of the 1,240 colonists. With much of their livestock destroyed, spring planting prevented, and disease spreading through cramped fortresses, hundreds more colonists died in the ensuing months.

After the Virginia Company sent more men, Governor Francis Wyatt reorganized the settlers and took the offensive during the Second Anglo-Powhatan War

**Carolina Indians Fishing, by John White, 1585**
*Using canoes, weirs, nets, and spears, coastal Indians depended on fishing as an important source of their food.*

(1622–1632). Using tactics developed during the Irish war, Wyatt inflicted widespread starvation by destroying food supplies, conducted winter campaigns to drive Indians from their homes when they would suffer most, and fought (according to John Smith) as if he had "just cause to destroy them by all means possible." By 1625 the English had effectively won the war, and the Indians had lost their best chance of driving out the intruders.

The clash left the Virginia Company bankrupt and James I concerned over complaints against its officers. After receiving a report critical of the company's management, James revoked its charter in 1624 and Virginia became a royal colony. Only about five hundred colonists now lived in Virginia, including a handful of Africans who had been brought in since 1619.* So the roots from which Virginia's Anglo-American and African-American peoples later grew were fragile indeed.

---

* The emergence of Virginia's African-American population will be traced in Chapter 3.

## The Origins of New England: Plymouth Plantation

Still another colonial venture was begun in the early seventeenth century by the English who settled New England. In 1614 the ever-enterprising John Smith, exploring its coast, gave New England its name. "Who," he asked, "can but approve this most excellent place, both for health and fertility?" An admirer of Cortés, Smith planned to conquer its "goodly, strong, and well-proportioned [Indian] people" and establish an English colony there. But his hopes came to naught. As for the region's native peoples, a terrible epidemic devastated the coastal tribes by about 90 percent in 1616–1618. Later visitors found the ground littered with the "bones and skulls" of the unburied dead, and acres of overgrown cornfields.

Against this tragic backdrop, in 1620 the Virginia Company of London gave a patent to some London merchants headed by Thomas Weston for a settlement. Weston sent over twenty-four families (a total of 102 people) in a small, leaky ship called the *Mayflower*. The colonists promised to send lumber, furs, and fish back to Weston in England for seven years, after which they would own the tract.

The expedition's leaders—but only half its members—belonged to a small religious community from the town of Scrooby in northern England. The group was made up of Separatist Puritans who had with-drawn from the Church of England and fled to the Netherlands to practice their religion freely. But fearing that their children were assimilating into Dutch culture, they decided to immigrate to America.

In November 1620 the *Mayflower* landed at Plymouth Bay, outside the bounds of Virginia. Knowing that they had no legal right to be there, the expedition's leaders insisted that all the adult males in the group (including Non-Separatists) sign the Mayflower Compact before they landed. By this document they constituted themselves a "civil body politic"—that is, a civil government—under James I's sovereignty and established the colony of Plymouth Plantation.

Weakened by their journey and unprepared for winter, half the Pilgrims, as they came to be known, died within four months of landing. Those still alive in the spring of 1621 owed much to the aid of two English-speaking Indians. One was Squanto, a local Patuxet Indian who had been taken to Spain as a slave some years earlier, escaped to England, and made himself useful to potential colonizers. Returning, he learned that most of the two thousand Patuxets had perished in the recent epidemic. The other friendly Indian, an Abenaki from Maine named Samoset, had experience trading with the English. To prevent the Pilgrims from stealing their food, the Indians taught the newcomers how to grow corn. The Pilgrims' first harvest of 1621 was marked by a ceremony cementing the relationship, "at which time . . . we exercised our arms, many of the Indians coming amongst us, . . . some 90 men, whom for three days we entertained and feasted." This ceremony was the basis for Thanksgiving, a holiday established in the nineteenth century.

Plymouth's relations with the Native Americans worsened, however. The alliance that Squanto and Samoset had arranged between Plymouth and local Wampanoag Indians headed by Chief Massasoit united two weak parties. But with their firearms the colonists became the dominant partner, forcing the Indians to acknowledge English sovereignty. News of the Virginia massacre of 1622 hastened the colony's militarization under the leadership of a professional soldier, Miles Standish, who threatened Plymouth's Indian "allies" with its monopoly of firepower. For although Massasoit remained loyal, many other Indians were offended by the colonists' conduct.

Relations with Native Americans also enabled Plymouth to become economically self-sufficient. After the colony turned from communal farming to individually owned plots, its more prosperous farmers pro-

**Early Plymouth Colony**

*After barely surviving their first winter, the settlers ensured their future by building simple houses and using Indian techniques to grow corn.*

duced corn surpluses, which they traded to nonfarming Abenakis in Maine for furs. In 1627 Plymouth agreed with the Dutch to divide the fur and wampum trade in New England. Within a decade, the Plymouth colony had grown to several hundred people in the southeastern corner of present-day Massachusetts.

At first an almost insignificant group, the Pilgrims were only one of several small English bands that immigrated to New England in the 1620s. Their lasting importance was twofold. First, they would help inspire the later American vision of sturdy, self-reliant, God-fearing folk crossing the Atlantic to govern themselves freely. Second, they foreshadowed the methods that later generations of European Americans would use to gain mastery over Indians. In both respects, the Pilgrims were the vanguard of a massive, voluntary migration of Puritans to New England in the 1630s.

## CONCLUSION

The sixteenth century marked the emergence of a new "Atlantic world," linking Europe, Africa, and the Americas. Europe haltingly entered a new, "modern" era characterized by commercial capitalism, nation-states, and postmedieval Christianity. These new forces did not entirely displace economies based on subsistence and reciprocity, local communities rooted in centuries-old customs, and widespread beliefs in supernatural forces independent of the Christian God. Expansion and colonization strengthened the "modern" forces by providing new fields for investment and profit, and new foundations for national power. The overseas ventures also enabled European leaders and ideologues to portray Native Americans and Africans as "savages" whose cultures and customs "civilized" Europeans should avoid at all cost.

The Atlantic world brought few benefits to West Africans and Native Americans. Initial Portuguese incursions on West Africa's coast promised to expand the region's trade ties with Europe. But by century's end, Europe's overwhelming demand for slave labor was shaping trade, politics, and warfare throughout West Africa. Africa's notorious underdevelopment, which persists in our own time, had begun.

During the sixteenth century, indigenous peoples in Mexico, Peru, and elsewhere felt the terrible violence of Spanish conquest, suffering untold losses of population as well as the shattering of political, social, and religious institutions and practices. All the while, Indians in North America held would-be conquerors and coloniz-

ers at bay. But new colonizing efforts by British, French, Dutch, as well as Spanish at the dawn of the seventeenth century made clear that native North Americans now faced challenges as serious as those confronted earlier by peoples to the south.

Nevertheless, Europe's presence north of the Caribbean and Mexico remained limited in 1625. In New Mexico and Florida, Spain advanced as far north as seemed worthwhile to protect Mexican and Caribbean conquests. Virginia's victory over the Indians there strengthened the English position in the Chesapeake, where tobacco had become the principal commercial crop. Here and in the fragile Plymouth colony, English settlers relied primarily on farming. New France and New Netherland existed mainly to trade in furs. To one degree or another, all these enterprises depended for their success or security on maintaining stable relations with at least some Native Americans. The transplantation of Europeans into North America was hardly a story of inevitable triumph.

## FOR FURTHER READING

Robert J. Berkhofer, Jr., *The White Man's Indian: Images of the American Indian from Columbus to the Present* (1978). A penetrating analysis of the shaping of European and American attitudes, ideologies, and policies toward Native Americans.

Alfred W. Crosby, Jr., *Ecological Imperialism: The Biological Expansion of Europe, 900–1900* (1986). A far-reaching discussion of the environmental and medical history of European overseas colonization.

Olwen Hufton, *The Prospect Before Her: A History of Women in Western Europe*, vol. I: 1500–1800 (1995). An outstanding interpretive synthesis.

D. W. Meinig, *The Shaping of America*, vol. I: Atlantic America, 1492–1800 (1986). A geographer's engrossing study of Europeans' encounter with North America and the rise of colonial societies.

David B. Quinn, *North America from Earliest Discoveries to First Settlements: The Norse Voyages to 1612* (1977). A thorough, learned account of European exploration, based on a wide range of scholarship.

Kirkpatrick Sale, *The Conquest of Paradise: Christopher Columbus and the Columbian Legacy* (1990). A polemical but informed critique of Columbus and his role in opening the Americas to European exploitation.

John Thornton, *Africa and Africans in the Making of the Atlantic World, 1400–1680*, 2d ed. (1998). An insightful perspective on the place of West Africa and its peoples in the colonization of the Americas.

Eric Wolf, *Europe and the People Without History* (1982). An anthropologist's sweeping view of the causes and consequences of Europe's worldwide expansion.

# 3

## Expansion and Diversity:
## The Rise of Colonial America

**Ninigret, Eastern Niantic Sachem**
*Artist Unknown, c. 1684*

On the West Indian island of Barbados in 1692, a widowed Englishwoman named Sarah Horbin counted up her relatives to see who might deserve bequests of property in case her only son—a sailor being held for ransom in a North African prison—died. Through her kinsman John Seabury of Barbados, she had kept in contact with a dozen Seabury cousins in New England. She had also remained in touch with several Virginia relatives in the Empereur family and with a kinsman of her husband's, Andrew Rouse, who lived in Carolina.

Sarah Horbin and her far-flung clan were part of a great migration of English, Dutch, French, Spanish, and other European women and men who built new communities in North America and the Caribbean during the seventeenth century. By 1700 there were more than 250,000 people of European birth or parentage, most of them English, within the modern-day United States. The vast exodus provided North America with its first large wave of immigrant settlers.

In 1665 another newly widowed immigrant, Mary Johnson of Somerset County, Maryland, conducted a similar survey of her kin. Her two sons, living nearby, each had a wife and two children. Johnson's other relatives were undoubtedly as widely scattered as Horbin's, but unlike Horbin, she had no idea where they were. For Mary Johnson had arrived in Virginia thirty years earlier not as a free person but as a slave. Although Mary's origins are unknown, her husband Anthony had previously been called Antonio, indicating that he had been enslaved first by the Portuguese. Soon after their marriage in 1625, the Johnsons somehow gained their freedom (all pertinent records have been lost), as did a few dozen other slaves in Virginia's early decades. Thereafter they managed not only to survive as free persons but to own some land and even a few slaves. Nevertheless they faced not only the uncertainties confronting all small tobacco planters in the seventeenth-century Chesapeake region, but the even more daunting legal restrictions based on race.

Most of the Johnsons' fellow Africans were less fortunate. Whereas Europeans might at least hope to realize economic opportunity or religious freedom, most Africans and their progeny would be the property of others for as long as they lived. Even the Johnsons' grandchildren disappear from the records after the turn of the eighteenth century, most likely the victims of legislation forcing most free blacks into slavery.

The vast majority of the 300,000 Africans taken to the Caribbean and North America during the seventeenth century went to the sugar plantations of Sarah Horbin's neighbors in Barbados and elsewhere in the West Indies; a small but distinct minority, to the mainland plantation colonies of the Southeast; and a scattered few to other regions.

Patterns of European and African immigration contributed significantly to the emergence of distinct regions in colonial North America. The preponderance of immigrants from England ensured that nation's domination of North America's eastern coast as well as the Caribbean, forcing the Dutch out of North America altogether and leaving France and Spain with lands less attractive to colonists. Within England's mainland colonies, four distinct regions emerged: New England, the Chesapeake, Carolina, and the middle colonies. Several factors distinguished these regions from one another, including their physical environments, the motives of white immigrants, and the concentrations of enslaved Africans.

The vast migrations of Europeans and Africans were possible only because of yet another demographic upheaval, the depopulation and uprooting of Native Americans. Having begun in the sixteenth century, the process continued in the seventeenth, primarily as a result of epidemic diseases but also because of warfare and other factors arising from the European invasion of Indian lands. Although many native populations partly recovered, it is likely that about 1 million Indians died as a result of contact with Europeans by 1700. Sarah Horbin, Mary Johnson, and their various kin settled not in wildernesses but in lands long inhabited and worked by Native Americans.

Although dominated by European immigrants, the wealth and vitality of the North American colonies at the end of the seventeenth century resulted from the unequal encounter of peoples from three continents.

This chapter will focus on four major questions:

♦ How and why did the four regions of English North America develop in such different ways during the seventeenth century?

♦ Why did indentured servitude give way to racial slavery in England's plantation colonies? Why were both these institutions more limited in the nonplantation colonies?

♦ How would you characterize and compare Indian–European relations in the various colonial regions of North America during the seventeenth century? How do you explain the similarities and differences you find?

♦ What factors contributed most significantly to England's supremacy among European powers colonizing North America during the seventeenth century?

## The New England Way

In the late 1620s, as England's religious and political environment grew threatening and the economy worsened, many Puritans became interested in colonizing New England. Separatist Puritans (the "Pilgrims") had established Plymouth in 1620, and a few hundred others had drifted into the region over the next decade. But not until 1630 did large-scale migration begin (see map on page 50). Building communities based on religious ideals, this larger, more formidable group of Puritans endeavored to build America's first utopian, or ideal, society.

### *A City upon a Hill*

In 1628 several Puritan merchants obtained a charter to settle north of Plymouth colony between the Charles and Merrimack Rivers. Organizing as the Massachusetts Bay Company, they took advantage of a gap in their charter and in 1629 moved the seat of their colony's government to New England. Like Plymouth, Massachusetts Bay would be self-governed rather than controlled from England by stockholders, proprietors, or the crown.

After four hundred Puritans arrived at Salem, Massachusetts, in 1629, the company in 1630 sent out its "great fleet" of eleven ships and seven hundred passengers under Governor John Winthrop. In midvoyage Winthrop delivered a lay sermon titled "A Model of Christian Charity," describing the colony as a utopian alternative to old England.

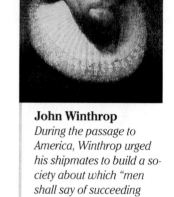

**John Winthrop**
*During the passage to America, Winthrop urged his shipmates to build a society about which "men shall say of succeeding plantations: 'The Lord make it like that of New England.'"*

Winthrop boldly announced that "we shall be as a city upon a hill, the eyes of all people are upon us." The settlers would build a godly community whose example would shame England into repenting. The English government would then truly reform the church, and a revival of piety would create a nation of saints.

Winthrop denounced the economic jealousy that bred class hatred. God intended that "in all times some must be rich and some poor," he explained. The rich had an obligation to show charity and mercy; those less wealthy should live out their faith in God's will by demonstrating patience and fortitude. God expected the state to keep the greedy among the rich from exploiting the needy and to prevent the lazy among the poor from burdening their fellow citizens. In outlining a divine plan in which all people, rich and poor, depended on one another, Winthrop expressed a conservative European's understanding of social reciprocity (see Chapter 2) and voiced the Puritans' deep dismay with the economic forces battering—and changing— English society.

Winthrop's address exemplified the main difference between New England's settlement and English colonization elsewhere. Other colonists would display the acquisitive impulses transforming England, but in New England, as one minister put it, "Religion and

## CHRONOLOGY

| | |
|---|---|
| **1627** | English establish Barbados. |
| **1629** | Massachusetts Bay colony founded. |
| **1630** | John Winthrop, "A Model of Christian Charity." |
| **1633** | First English settlements in Connecticut. |
| **1634** | Cecilius Calvert (Lord Baltimore) founds proprietary colony of Maryland. |
| **1636** | Roger Williams founds Providence, Rhode Island. |
| | Harvard College established. |
| **1637** | Anne Hutchinson banished from Massachusetts Bay. |
| | Pequot War in Connecticut. |
| **1638** | New Sweden established. |
| **1639** | Connecticut formally established. |
| **1640s** | Large-scale slave-labor system takes hold in the West Indies. |
| **1642–1648** | English Civil War. |
| **1644–1646** | Third Anglo-Powhatan War in Virginia. |

| | |
|---|---|
| **1649** | Maryland's Act for Religious Toleration. |
| | King Charles I beheaded. |
| | Five Iroquois Nations disperse Hurons. |
| **1655** | New Netherland annexes New Sweden. |
| **1660** | Charles II becomes king of England. |
| **1661** | Maryland defines slavery as a lifelong, inheritable racial status. |
| **1662** | Half-Way Covenant drafted. |
| **1663** | Carolina founded as English colony. |
| | New France made a royal colony. |
| **1664** | English conquer New Netherland; rename it New York. |
| | New Jersey established. |
| **1670** | Settlement of southern Carolina begins. |
| | Virginia defines slavery as a lifelong, inheritable racial status. |
| **1672** | Louis Jolliet and Jacques Marquette explore the Mississippi River. |
| **1675–1676** | King Philip's War in New England. |

| | |
|---|---|
| **1676** | Bacon's Rebellion in Virginia. |
| **1680–1692** | Pueblo revolt in New Mexico. |
| **1681** | William Penn founds Pennsylvania. |
| **1682** | La Salle descends the Mississippi River to the Gulf of Mexico and claims the Mississippi basin for France. |
| **1690s** | Collapse of the Royal African Company's monopoly on selling slaves to the English colonies; large shipments of Africans begin reaching the Chesapeake. |
| **1691** | Spain establishes province of Texas. |
| **1692–1693** | Salem witchcraft trials. |
| **1698** | French begin settlements near the mouth of the Mississippi River. |
| **1702** | New Jersey made a royal colony. |
| **1704** | Delaware established. |
| **1711–1713** | Tuscarora War in Carolina. |
| **1715–1716** | Yamasee War in Carolina. |

profit [would] jump together." While hoping for prosperity, Puritans believed there were limits to legitimate commercial behavior. They thought that moral self-restraint—or if need be, the government—should prevent merchants from taking advantage of shortages to squeeze out "excessive" profits. Above all, they hoped to turn religious idealism into a renewed sense of community. "It is a great thing," wrote an early New Englander, "to be a foundation stone in such a spiritual

building." Massachusetts Bay would not be an extension of England but an alternative to it.

Winthrop and the great fleet arrived in June 1630 at Boston harbor, and by fall six towns had sprung up nearby. During the unusually severe first winter, 30 percent of Winthrop's party died, and another 10 percent went home in the spring. By mid-1631, however, thirteen hundred new settlers had landed, and more were on the way. The worst was over. The colony would

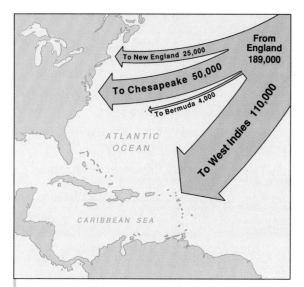

**English Migration, 1610–1660**
*During the first phase of English transatlantic migration, the West Indies attracted more than twice as many colonists as went to the Chesapeake, and over four times as many as settled in New England.*

never suffer another starving time. In contrast to early Virginia, Massachusetts Bay attracted pious, disciplined men and women of modest means who established the colony on a firm basis within a year.

## The Pequot War

Also in contrast to the settlement of Virginia, the colonization of New England began with little sustained resistance from Native Americans, whose numbers were drastically reduced by the ravages of disease. After one epidemic killed about 90 percent of New England's coastal Indians between 1616 and 1618 (see Chapter 2), a second inflicted comparable casualties on Indians throughout the Northeast in 1633–1634. Having dwindled from twenty thousand in 1600 to a few dozen survivors by the mid-1630s, the Massachusett Indians were pressed to sell most of their land to the English. During the 1640s Massachusetts Bay passed laws prohibiting them from practicing their own religion and encouraging missionaries to convert them to Christianity. Thereafter they moved into "praying towns" like Natick, a reservation established by the colony. In the praying towns Puritan missionary John Eliot hoped to teach the Native Americans Christianity and English ways.

The expansion of English settlement farther inland, however, aroused Indian resistance. As settlers moved into the Connecticut River Valley, beginning in 1633, friction developed with the Pequots, who controlled the trade in furs and wampum with New Netherland. After tensions escalated into violence, the English in 1637 took decisive action. Having gained the support of the Mohegan and Narragansett Indians, they waged a ruthless campaign, using tactics similar to those devised by the English to break Irish resistance during the 1570s (see Chapter 2). In a predawn attack English troops surrounded and set fire to a Pequot village at Mystic, Connecticut, and then cut down all who tried to escape. Several hundred Pequots, mostly women and children, were killed. Although their Narragansett allies protested that "it is too furious, and slays too many men," the Puritans found in the grisly massacre a cause for celebration. Wrote Plymouth's Governor William Bradford,

> It was a fearful sight to see them [the Pequots] thus frying in the fire and the streams of blood quenching the same, and horrible was the stink and scent thereof; but the victory seemed a sweet sacrifice, and they [the English] gave the praise to God, who had wrought so wonderfully for them, thus to enclose their enemies in their hands and give them so speedy a victory over so proud and insulting an enemy.

By late 1637 Pequot resistance was crushed, with surviving Pequots being taken by pro-English Indians as captives or by the English as slaves. English establishment of the new colonies of Connecticut (1639) and New Haven (1643) could now proceed unimpeded. (New Haven was absorbed by Connecticut in 1662.)

## The Development of a Puritan Orthodoxy

Although most New England Puritans considered themselves spiritual members of the Church of England, they created a system of self-governing congregations (congregationalism) that completely ignored the authority of Anglican bishops. (The Separatist Puritans of Plymouth and Rhode Island explicitly disavowed Anglican authority over their congregations.) Control of each congregation lay squarely in the hands of the male saints (church members). By majority vote these men chose their minister, elected a board of "elders" to handle finances, decided who else deserved recognition as saints, and otherwise ran the church. In contrast, in a typical English parish, a powerful gentry family would

**Attack on Mystic Fort, Pequot War**
*This print, published in an English participant's account of the war, shows English troops, backed by allied Indians, surrounding the Pequot village while soldiers prepare to burn it.*

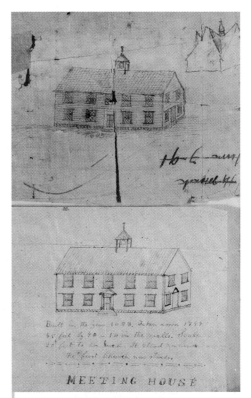

**Sketches of an Early Plymouth Meetinghouse**
*One early New Englander boasted that his community's meetinghouse had been erected "by our own vote, framed by our own hammers and saws, and by our own hands set in the convenientest place for us all."*

select a new pastor (subject to a bishop's formal approval), and all other important decisions would be made by the parish council, or vestry, which was virtually always composed of wealthy landlords. New England congregationalism thus allowed for broader-based control of the church than did Anglicanism.

While saints controlled a congregation's internal affairs, the colonies obliged all adults to attend services and pay set rates (or tithes) to support their local churches. New England thus had a state-sponsored, or "established," church, whose relationship to civil government was symbolized by the fact that a single building—called a meetinghouse rather than a church—was used for both religious services and town business.

This "New England Way" also diverged from English practices by setting higher standards for identifying the elect. English Puritans usually accepted as saints those who could correctly profess the faith, had repented their sins, and lived free of scandal. Massachusetts Puritans, however, insisted that candidates for membership provide a soul-baring "relation," or account, of their conversion before the congregation.

English Puritans strongly criticized the conversion relation as an unnecessary barrier to membership that would intimidate humble saints who were hesitant to reveal their spiritual travails in public. Many early Puri-

tans shared the reluctance of Jonathan Fairbanks, who refused to give a public profession of grace before the church in Dedham, Massachusetts, for several years, until the faithful persuaded him with many "loving conferences." The conversion relation would emerge as the New England Way's most vulnerable point and a major cause of its eventual demise.

New Englanders, like most European Protestants, could scarcely imagine conversion without literacy. Young people read the Bible to feel the quickening of God's grace, and saints often recorded their lapses and spiritual insights in diaries. In 1647 Massachusetts Bay ordered every town of fifty or more households to appoint one teacher to whom all children could come for instruction, and every town of at least one hundred households to maintain a grammar school. This and similar laws in other Puritan colonies represented New

England's first step toward public education. But none of these laws required school attendance, and boys were more likely to be taught reading and especially writing than were girls.

However diligent laypeople might be in reading the Bible and indoctrinating their children, clergymen had responsibility for leading saints to repentance and stimulating piety. The minister's role was to stir his parishioners' faith with direct, logical, and moving sermons that spoke to all saints, not just to a well-educated elite. The Puritans' preference for this "plain style" of preaching did not contradict their desire for a highly educated clergy, for ministers also had to uphold orthodoxy and be alert for signs of heresy.

To produce learned ministers, Massachusetts founded Harvard College in 1636. From 1642 to 1671, the college produced 201 graduates, including 111 ministers. Harvard's alumni made New England the only part of England's overseas empire to possess a college-educated elite during the seventeenth century, and they ensured that the New England Way would not falter for lack of properly trained clergy.

### Dissenting Puritans

The values articulated by Winthrop and other New England leaders reinforced social order and religious conformity. Without order and conformity, the leaders feared, divisiveness among Puritans over questions such as church-state relations, church membership, economic individualism, and the role of women would lead to a splintering of the colonists and their failure in the eyes of God. Despite the leaders' efforts, some Puritans entertained quite radical ideas and insisted on expressing them.

Puritans agreed that the church must be free of state control, and they opposed theocracy (government run by clergy). But most believed that a holy commonwealth required cooperation between church and state. Roger Williams, who arrived in 1631, took a different stance. He argued that civil government should remain absolutely uninvolved with religious matters, whether blasphemy (cursing God), failure to pay tithes, refusal to attend worship, or swearing oaths on the Bible in court. Williams also opposed any kind of compulsory church service or government interference with private religious beliefs, not because all religions deserved equal respect but because the state (a creation of sinful human beings) would corrupt the church.

Believing that the very purpose of founding Massachusetts Bay was to protect true religion and prevent heresy, the political authorities declared Williams's opinions subversive and banished him in 1635. Williams moved south to a place that he called Providence, which he purchased from the Narragansett Indians. At Williams's invitation, a steady stream of dissenters drifted to the group of settlements near Providence on Narragansett Bay, which in 1647 joined to form Rhode Island colony. (Orthodox Puritans scorned the place as "Rogues Island.") True to Williams's ideals, Rhode Island was the only New England colony to practice religious toleration. Growing slowly, the colony's four towns had eight hundred settlers by 1650.

A second major challenge to the New England Way came from Anne Hutchinson, whom Winthrop described as "a woman of haughty and fierce carriage, of a nimble wit and active spirit." The controversy surrounding Hutchinson was especially ironic because it centered on her repudiation of the Catholic idea that one's "good works" in this life were the key to salvation thereafter (see Chapter 2). Supposedly, all Puritans agreed that "good works" were a false road to heaven, instead following John Calvin in maintaining that God had predetermined who would and would not be saved. But Hutchinson argued that most Puritan ministers were hypocritical on the question of salvation. By insisting that they could scrutinize a person's outward behavior for "signs" of salvation, especially when that person was relating his or her conversion experience, the clergymen discarded God's judgment in favor of their own. Such ministers, she went on to say, impeded rather than aided their parishioners' conversions. Only by looking inward and by ignoring such false prophets could individuals hope to find salvation. Hutchinson eventually alleged that all the colony's ministers except two had not been saved and so lacked authority over saints like herself.

By casting doubt on the clergy's spiritual state, Hutchinson undermined its authority over laypersons. Critics charged that her beliefs would delude individuals into imagining that they were accountable to no one but themselves. Winthrop branded her followers Antinomians, meaning those opposed to the rule of law. Hutchinson bore the additional liability of being a woman who stepped outside her prescribed role. As one of her accusers put it, "You have stepped out of your place; you [would] have rather been a husband than a wife, a preacher than a hearer; and a magistrate than a subject."

By 1636 Massachusetts Bay split into two camps. Hutchinson's supporters included Boston merchants (like her husband) who disliked the government's economic restrictions on their business; young men chafing against the rigid control of church elders; and women, protesting their second-class status in church affairs. In 1636 the Antinomians were strong enough to have their candidate elected governor, but they suffered defeat with Winthrop's return to office in 1637.

The victorious Winthrop brought Hutchinson to trial for heresy before the Massachusetts Bay legislature (the General Court), whose members peppered her with questions. Hutchinson's knowledge of Scripture was so superior to that of her interrogators, however, that she would have been acquitted had she not claimed to have been converted through a direct revelation from God. Like virtually all Christians, orthodox Puritans believed that God had ceased to make known matters of faith by personal revelation since New Testament times. Thus Hutchinson's own words were sufficient to condemn her.

The General Court banished the leading Antinomians from the colony, and some of the others voluntarily followed them to Rhode Island, New Hampshire, or back to England. The largest group, led by Hutchinson, settled in Rhode Island.

Antinomianism's defeat was followed by new restrictions on women's independence and on equality within those Puritan congregations that had previously acted more evenhandedly on matters of gender. Increasingly, women were prohibited from assuming the kind of public religious roles claimed by Hutchinson, and were even required to relate their conversion experiences in private to their ministers rather than publicly before their congregations.

The most fundamental threat to Winthrop's city upon a hill was that the people would abandon the ideal of a close-knit community to pursue self-interest. Although most Puritans welcomed the chance to found villages dedicated to stability, self-discipline, and a sense of mutual obligation, a large minority had come to America to find prosperity and social mobility. The most visibly ambitious colonists were merchants, whose activities fueled New England's economy but whose way of life challenged its ideals.

Merchants fit uneasily into a religious utopia that idealized social reciprocity and equated financial shrewdness with greed. They protested when government leaders tried to regulate prices so that consumers would not suffer from the chronic shortage of manufactured goods that afflicted New England.

In 1635, when the Massachusetts General Court forbade the sale of any item above 5 percent of its cost, Robert Keayne of Boston and other merchants objected. These men argued that they had to sell some goods at higher rates in order to offset their losses from other sales, shipwrecked cargoes, and inflation. In 1639, after selling nails at 25 percent to 33 percent above cost, Keayne was fined heavily in court and was forced to make a humiliating apology before his congregation.

Controversies like the one involving Keayne were part of a struggle for New England's soul. At stake was the Puritans' ability and desire to insulate their city upon a hill from a market economy that, they feared, would strangle the spirit of community within a harsh new world of frantic competition.

### Power to the Saints

To preserve the New England Way, the Puritans evolved political and religious institutions with far more popular participation than those in England. Unlike the Virginia Company of London, the Massachusetts Bay Company established its headquarters in America (see above). Massachusetts did not require voters or officeholders to own property but bestowed full citizenship on every adult male accepted as a saint. By 1641 about 55 percent of the colony's 2,300 men could vote. By contrast, English property requirements allowed fewer than 30 percent of adult males to vote.

In 1634, after public protest that the governor and council held too much power, each town gained the option of sending two delegates to the General Court. In 1644 the General Court became a bicameral (two-chamber) lawmaking body when the towns' deputies separated from the Governor's Council to form the House of Representatives.

England's basic unit of local government was the county court. Its justices of the peace not only decided legal cases but also performed administrative tasks and assessed taxes. Gaining office by royal appointment, English justices were always members of the gentry selected because of their wealth and political connections. By contrast, New England's county courts functioned primarily as courts of law, and the vital unit of

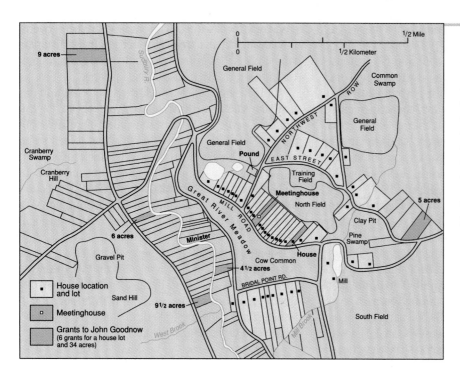

**Land Divisions in Sudbury, Massachusetts, 1639–1656**
*Like other first-generation settlers, John Goodnow lived on a small house lot near the meetinghouse. He grazed his livestock on "common" fields owned by the town and grew crops in five fields at varying distances from his house.* (Source: Sumner Chilton Powell, *Puritan Village: The Formation of a New England Town* (Middletown, Conn.: Wesleyan University Press, 1963). Reprinted by permission.)

local administration was the town meeting. Town meetings decentralized authority over political and economic decisions to a degree unknown in either England or its other colonies.

New England legislatures established a town by awarding a grant of land to several dozen heads of families. These men then laid out the settlement, organized its church, distributed land among themselves, set local tax rates, and made local laws. Each town determined its own qualifications for voting and holding office in the town meeting, although custom dictated that all male taxpayers (including nonsaints) be allowed to participate. The meeting could exclude anyone from settling in town, and it could grant the right of sharing in any future land distributions to newcomers, whose children would inherit this privilege.

## Community Life

The local economy and environment left their stamp on New England towns. Of these communities the seaports often seemed least tight-knit because of their transient population, whereas most other towns resembled traditional English villages.

A town's founders usually granted each family a one-acre house lot (just enough for a vegetable garden) within a half-mile of the meetinghouse. They also gave each household strips of land or small fields farther out for its crops and livestock. Often an individual owned several parcels of land in different locations and had the right to graze a few extra animals on the town "commons."

Few aspects of early New England life are more revealing than the first generation's attempt in many, but not all, towns to keep settlement tightly clustered by granting families no more land than they needed to support themselves. Dedham's forty-six founders, for example, received 128,000 acres from Massachusetts Bay in 1636 yet gave themselves just 3,000 acres by 1656, or about 65 acres per family. The rest remained in trust for future generations.

With families clustered within a mile of one another, New England towns' physical settings were conducive to traditional reciprocity. They also fostered an atmosphere of mutual watchfulness that Puritans hoped would promote godly order. For the enforcement of such order, they relied on the women of each town as well as male magistrates.

Although women's public roles had been sharply curtailed following the Antinomian crisis, women—especially those who were church members—continued to be a social force in their communities. With their husbands and older sons usually attending the family's scattered fields, women remained at home in the tightly clustered neighborhoods at the center of each town. Neighboring women exchanged not only goods—say, a pound of butter for a section of spun wool—but advice and news of other neighbors as well. They also gathered at the bedside when one of them gave birth, a setting that was entirely closed to men. In these settings, women confided in one another, creating a "community of women" within each town that contributed to the enforcement of morals and the protection of the poor and vulnerable. In 1663 Mary Rolfe of Newbury, Massachusetts, was being sexually harassed by a high-ranking gentleman while her fisherman husband was at sea. Rolfe confided to her mother who in turn consulted with a neighboring woman of influence before filing formal charges. A jury found the gentleman guilty of attempted adultery. When a gentlewoman, Patience Dennison, charged her maidservant with stealing food and clothing for more than a year and giving them to a poor young wife, a fourth woman testified that the provisions had kept the young wife's family from perishing. And the servant herself testified that her mistress was stingy, giving Dennison a reputation she never lived down.

## Puritan Families

To Puritans, society's foundation rested not on the individual but on the "little commonwealth"—the nuclear family at the heart of every household. "*Well ordered families,*" declared minister Cotton Mather in 1699, "naturally produce a *Good Order* in other *Societies.*" In a proper Puritan family, the wife, children, and servants dutifully obeyed the household's male head. According to John Winthrop, a "true wife" thought of herself "in subjection to her husband's authority."

New Englanders defined matrimony as a contract subject to state regulation rather than a religious sacrament and so were married by justices of the peace instead of ministers. As a civil institution, a marriage could be dissolved by the courts in cases of desertion, bigamy, adultery, or physical cruelty. By permitting divorce, Puritans diverged radically from practices in England, where Anglican authorities rarely annulled marriages and civil divorces required a special act of Parliament. Still, New Englanders saw divorce as a remedy fit only for extremely wronged spouses, such as the Plymouth woman who discovered that her husband was also married to women in Boston, Barbados, and England. Massachusetts courts allowed just twenty-seven divorces from 1639 to 1692.

Because Puritans believed that healthy families were crucial to the community's welfare, they intervened whenever they discovered truly serious problems in a household. The courts disciplined unruly youngsters, disobedient servants, disrespectful wives, and violent or irresponsible husbands whose behavior seemed dangerous or unusually disruptive to a family. Churches also censured, and sometimes expelled, spouses who did not maintain domestic tranquillity. Negligent parents, one minister declared, "not only wrong each other, but they provoke God by breaking his law."

New England wives enjoyed significant legal protections against spousal violence and nonsupport and also had more freedom than their English counterparts to escape a failed marriage. But they also suffered the same legal disabilities as all Englishwomen. An English wife had no property rights independently of her husband unless he consented to a special prenuptial agreement giving her control over any property that she already owned. Only if a husband had no other heirs or wrote a will awarding his widow full control over their possessions could she claim rights over household property, although the law reserved lifetime use of a third of the estate for her support.

In contrast to England, New England benefited from a remarkably benign disease environment. Al-

**Mary Hollingsworth Embroidered Sampler**
*Many women found in embroidery a creative outlet that was compatible with their domestic duties.*

though settlements were compact, minimal travel occurred between towns, especially in the winter, when people were most susceptible to infection. Furthermore, easy access to land allowed most families an adequate diet, which improved resistance to disease and lowered death rates associated with childbirth.

Consequently, New Englanders lived longer and raised larger families than almost any society in the world in the seventeenth century. Life expectancy for men reached 65, and women lived nearly that long. More than 80 percent of all infants survived long enough to get married. The 58 men and women who founded Andover, Massachusetts, for example, had 247 children; by the fourth generation, the families of their descendants numbered 2,000 (including spouses who married in from other families). Despite the relatively small size and short duration of the Puritan exodus to New England (just 20,000 immigrants landed from 1630 to 1642, after which few newcomers arrived), the fact that most settlers came as members of family groups soon resulted in a population evenly divided between males and females. This balance permitted rapid population growth without heavy immigration.

Most immigrants had little or no cash; instead they relied on the labor of their large, healthy families to sustain them and secure their futures. Male heads of households managed the family's scattered crops and livestock, conducted most of its business transactions, and represented it in town government. Their wives bore, nursed, and reared their children. The women also had charge of most labor in the house, barn, and garden, including the making of most food and clothing from raw materials. In addition, they contributed to their communities by assisting at childbirths and aiding the poor and vulnerable, especially women living alone.

More than in England and the other colonies, the sons of New England's founding generation depended on their parents to provide them with acreage for a farm. With eventual land ownership guaranteed and few other opportunities available, sons delayed marriage and worked in their fathers' fields until finally receiving their own land. Because the average family raised three or four boys to adulthood, parents could depend on thirty to forty years of work if their sons delayed marriage beyond age twenty-five.

While daughters performed equally vital labor, their future lay with another family—the one into which they would marry. Being young, with many childbearing years ahead of them, enhanced their value

to that family. Thus first-generation women, on average, were only twenty-one when they married.

Families with more sons and daughters enjoyed a labor surplus that allowed them to send their children to work as apprentices or hired hands for others. However, this system of family labor was inefficient for two reasons. First, the available supply of labor could not expand in times of great demand. Second, parents were reluctant to force their own children to work as hard as strangers. Nevertheless, family labor was the only system that most New Englanders could afford.

Saddled with the burdens of a short growing season, rocky soil salted with gravel, and a system of land distribution in which farmers cultivated widely scattered strips, the colonists managed to feed large families and keep ahead of their debts, but few became wealthy from farming. Seeking greater fortunes than agriculture offered, some seventeenth-century New Englanders turned lumbering, fishing, fur trading, shipbuilding, and rum distilling into major industries. As its economy became more diversified, New England prospered. But in the process, its inhabitants grew more worldly, only to discover that fewer and fewer of their children were emerging as saints.

### The Demise of the Puritan Errand

As New Englanders struggled to make a living and create a utopia, England fell into chaos. Charles I's efforts to impose taxes without Parliament's consent sparked a civil war in 1642. Alienated by years of religious harassment, Puritans gained control of the revolt, beheaded Charles in 1649, and eventually replaced the king with "Lord High Protector" Oliver Cromwell. After Cromwell's death, however, a provisional English government "restored" the Stuarts and in 1660 crowned Charles II king.

The Restoration left American Puritans without a mission. A generation of New England ministers had inspired their congregations to hope that their example would shame England into establishing a truly reformed church. However, having conquered a wilderness and built their city upon a hill, New Englanders discovered after 1660 that the eyes of the world were no longer fixed on them.

Simultaneously with the Restoration, an internal crisis gripped the New England Way. The turmoil stemmed from the failure of the founding generation's children to declare themselves saints. The first generation believed that they had accepted a holy contract, or covenant, with God, which obliged them to establish a scripturally ordained church and charge their descendants with its preservation. In return for upholding this New England Way, God would make the city upon a hill prosper and shield it from corruption.

Relatively few second-generation Puritans, on the other hand, were willing to join the elect. By 1650, for example, fewer than half the adults in John Winthrop's congregation were saints. The principal reason was the second generation's reluctance to subject themselves to a grilling before relatives and friends. All children who matured in Puritan towns must have witnessed at least one person suffer an ordeal like that of Sarah Fiske. For more than a year, Fiske answered petty charges of speaking uncharitably about her relatives—especially her husband—and then was admitted to the Wenham, Massachusetts, church only after publicly denouncing herself as worse "than any toad."

Because Puritan churches baptized only babies born to saints, the unwillingness of the second generation to submit to the conversion relation confronted their parents with the prospect that their own grandchildren would remain unbaptized unless standards for church membership were loosened. In 1662 a convention of clergy devised a compromise known as the Half-Way Covenant, which permitted the children of all baptized adults, including nonsaints, to receive baptism. This covenant allowed the founders' descendants to transmit potential church membership to their grandchildren, but it left their adult children "halfway" members who could not take communion or vote in church affairs. When forced to choose between a church system founded on a pure membership of the elect and one that embraced the entire community, New Englanders, after bitter struggles in many congregations, sacrificed purity for community.

The Half-Way Covenant signaled the eventual end of the New England Way. The elect had been unable to bring up a new generation of saints whose religious fervor equaled their own. Most adults chose to remain in "halfway" status for life, and the saints became a shrinking minority as the third and fourth generations matured. Sainthood tended to flow in certain families, and by the 1700s there were more women among the elect than men. But because women could not vote in church affairs, religious authority stayed in male hands. Nevertheless, ministers publicly recognized women's role in upholding piety and the church itself.

## Expansion and Native Americans

As settlements grew and colonists prospered, Native Americans declined. Although Indians began to recover from the initial epidemics by midcentury, the settlers brought new diseases such as diphtheria, measles, and tuberculosis, as well as new outbreaks of smallpox, that took heavy tolls. New England's Indian population was reduced from 125,000 in 1600 to 10,000 in 1675.

Native Americans felt the English presence in other ways. The fur trade, which initially benefited interior natives, became a liability after midcentury. Once Indians began hunting for trade instead of just for their own subsistence needs, they quickly depleted the beavers and other fur-bearing animals of the region. And because English traders customarily advanced trade goods on credit to Indian hunters before the hunting season, the lack of pelts pushed many natives into debt. In this situation traders such as John Pynchon of Springfield, Massachusetts, began taking Indian land as collateral and selling it to settlers.

Elsewhere, English townsmen, eager to expand their agricultural output and provide land for their sons, voted themselves larger amounts of land after 1660 and insisted that their scattered parcels be consolidated. For example, Dedham, Massachusetts, which distributed only three thousand acres from 1636 to 1656, allocated five times as much in the next dozen years. Rather than continue living closely together, many farmers built homes on their outlying tracts, thereby coming into closer proximity to native settlements and the Indians' hunting, gathering, and fishing areas.

As English settlements expanded, they put new pressures on the natives and the land alike. As early as 1642, Miantonomi, a Narragansett sachem (chief), warned other New England Indians,

> These English having gotten our land, they with scythes cut down the grass, and with axes fell the trees; their cows and horses eat the grass, and their hogs spoil our clam banks, and we shall all be starved.

Within a generation, Miantonomi's fears were being borne out. By clearing away extensive stands of trees for fields and for use as fuel and building material, colonial farmers altered an entire ecosystem. Deer were no longer attracted, and the wild plants upon which the Indians depended for food and medicine

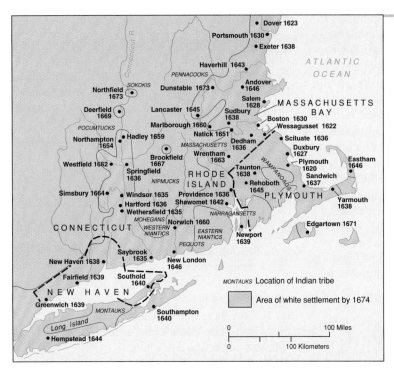

**Colonizing New England, 1620–1674**

*White expansion reached its maximum extent in the seventeenth century just before King Philip's War, which erupted as a result of the pressure on Indian communities. Frontier expansion did not resume in New England until after 1715.*

(Source: Frederick Merk, *History of the Westward Movement.* Copyright © 1979 by Lois Bannister Merk. Reprinted by permission of Alfred A. Knopf, Inc.)

could not grow. The soil became drier and flooding more frequent in the face of this deforestation. The settlers also introduced domestic livestock, which, according to English custom, ran wild. Pigs damaged Indian cornfields (until the natives adopted the alien practice of fencing their fields) and shellfish gathering sites. English cattle and horses quickly devoured native grasses, which the settlers then replaced with English varieties.

With native religious leaders powerless to halt the alarming decline of Indian population, land, and food sources, many Indians became demoralized. In their despair some turned to alcohol, increasingly available during the 1660s despite colonial efforts to suppress its sale to Native Americans. Interpreting the crisis as one of belief, other Indians joined those who had already converted to Christianity. By 1675 Puritan missionaries had established about thirty praying towns in eastern Massachusetts and Plymouth and on the islands of Martha's Vineyard and Nantucket. Supervised by missionaries, each praying town had its own Native American magistrate, usually a sachem, and many congregations had Indian preachers. Although the missionaries struggled to convert the Indians to "civilization," by which they meant English culture and lifestyles as well as to Christianity, most praying Indians integrated the

new faith with their native cultural identities. This practice reinforced the hostility of most settlers, who believed that all Indians were irrevocably "savage" and heathen.

Anglo-Indian conflict became acute during the 1670s because of pressure imposed on unwilling Indians to sell their land and to accept missionaries and the legal authority of colonial courts. Tension ran especially high in the Plymouth colony, where the English had engulfed the Wampanoags and forced a number of humiliating concessions on their leader Metacom, or "King Philip," the son of Massasoit, the Pilgrims' one-time ally.

In 1675 Plymouth hanged three Wampanoags for killing a Christian Indian and threatened to arrest Metacom. A minor incident in which several Wampanoags were shot while burglarizing a farmhouse led to a steady escalation of violence. About two-thirds of the Native Americans, including some Christian Indians, rallied around Metacom, igniting the conflict known as King Philip's War.

Metacom's forces—unlike the Indian combatants in the Pequot War, few of whom had fought with guns—were as well armed as the colonists. The Indians attacked 52 of New England's 90 towns (of which 12 were entirely destroyed), burned 1,200 houses, slaughtered 8,000 head of cattle, and killed 600 colonists.

The tide turned against Metacom in 1676 after the Mohawk Indians of New York and many Christian Indians joined the English against him. English militiamen destroyed their enemies' food supplies and sold hundreds of captives into slavery, including Metacom's wife and child. "It must have been as bitter as death to him," wrote Puritan clergyman Cotton Mather, "to lose his wife and only son, for the Indians are marvellously fond and affectionate toward their children." Perhaps three thousand Indians starved or fell in battle, including Metacom himself, and many more fled to New York and Canada.

King Philip's War reduced southern New En-gland's Indian population by almost 40 percent and eliminated overt resistance to white expansion. It also deepened English hostility toward Native Americans, even the Christian Indians who fought Metacom. In Massachusetts ten praying towns were disbanded and all Indians restricted to the remaining four; all Indian courts were dismantled; and "guardians" were appointed to supervise the reservations. "There is a cloud, a dark cloud upon the work of the Gospel among the poor Indians," mourned John Eliot. In the face of poverty and discrimination, remaining Indians managed to maintain their communities and cultural identities. To make up for the loss of traditional sources of sustenance, many worked as seamen or indentured servants, served in England's wars against the French in Canada, or made and sold baskets and other wares.

### Economics, Gender, and Satan in Salem

After the Half-Way Covenant's adoption in 1662, social and economic changes continued to undermine the New England Way. The dispersal of settlers away from town centers, besides putting pressure on Native Americans, generated friction between townspeople settled near the meetinghouse, who usually dominated politics, and "outlivers," whose distance from the town center generally limited their influence over town affairs. Moreover, the region's economy had become more complex, especially in its several port cities, and its distribution of wealth more uneven. These developments undermined the Puritan ideal of community by fostering anxiety that a small minority might be profiting at the majority's expense. They also led many individuals—in both cities and the countryside—to act more competitively, aggressively, and im-

personally toward one another. John Winthrop's vision of a religiously oriented community sustained by a sense of reciprocity and charity was giving way to a world increasingly like the materialistic, acquisitive society that the original immigrants had fled in England.

Nowhere in New England did these trends have more disturbing effects than in Salem, Massachusetts, which grew rapidly after 1660 to become the region's second largest port. Trade made Salem prosperous but also destroyed the relatively equal society of humble fishermen and farmers that had once existed. A sharp distinction emerged between the port's residents—especially its rich merchants—and outlying farmers.

Salem's divisions were especially sharp in the precinct of Salem Village (now Danvers), an economically stagnant district located north of Salem Town. Those who lived in the village's eastern section farmed richer soils and benefited from Salem Town's prosperity. In contrast, residents of Salem Village's less fertile western half did not share in Salem Town's commercial expansion and had lost the political influence that they once held in town.

In late 1691 several Salem Village girls encouraged an African slave woman, Tituba, to tell fortunes and talk about sorcery. When the girls later began behaving strangely, villagers assumed that they were victims of witchcraft. Pressed to identify their tormenters, the girls named two local white women and Tituba.

So far the incident was not unusual. Until the late seventeenth century, belief in witchcraft was very strong at all levels of European and American society. Witches were people (nearly always women) whose pride, envy, discontent, or greed supposedly led them to sign a pact with the devil. Thereafter they allegedly used *maleficium* (the devil's supernatural power of evil) to torment neighbors and others by causing illness, destroying property, or—as with the girls in Salem Village—inhabiting or "possessing" their victims' bodies and minds. Apart from *maleficium,* witnesses usually claimed that witches displayed aggressive, unfeminine behavior. A disproportionate number of the 342 accused witches in New England were women who had inherited, or stood to inherit in the future, property beyond the one-third of a husband's estate normally bequeathed to widows. In other words, most witches were assertive women who had or soon might have more economic power and independence than many men. For New Englanders, who felt the need to limit both female independence and economic individualism, witches symbolized the dangers awaiting those who disregarded such limits. In most earlier witchcraft accusations in New England, there was only one defendant and the case never went to trial. The few exceptions to this rule were tried with little fanfare. Events in Salem Village, on the other hand, led to a colonywide panic.

By April 1692 the girls had denounced two locally prominent farm wives and had identified the village's former minister as a wizard (male witch). Fears of witchcraft soon overrode doubts about the girls' credibility and led local judges to sweep aside normal procedural safeguards. Specifically the judges ignored the law's ban on "spectral evidence"—testimony that a spirit resembling the accused had been seen tormenting a victim. Thereafter accusations multiplied until the jails overflowed with accused witches.

The pattern of hysteria in Salem Village reflected that community's internal divisions. Most charges came from the village's troubled western division, and most of those accused came from wealthier families in the eastern village or in Salem Town.

Patterns of gender and age were also apparent in the accusations. Two-thirds of all accusers were "possessed" girls or young women aged eleven to twenty, and more than half had lost one or more parents in conflicts between Indians and settlers in Maine. They and other survivors had fled to Massachusetts, where most were now servants in other families' households. They most frequently named as witches middle-aged wives and widows—women who had avoided the poverty and uncertainty they themselves faced. At the same time, the "possessed" accusers gained momentary power and prominence by voicing the anxieties and

---

**Petition of Mary Easty, 1690**

(Detail) *In her petition Easty swore that "I know not the least thing of witchcraft."*

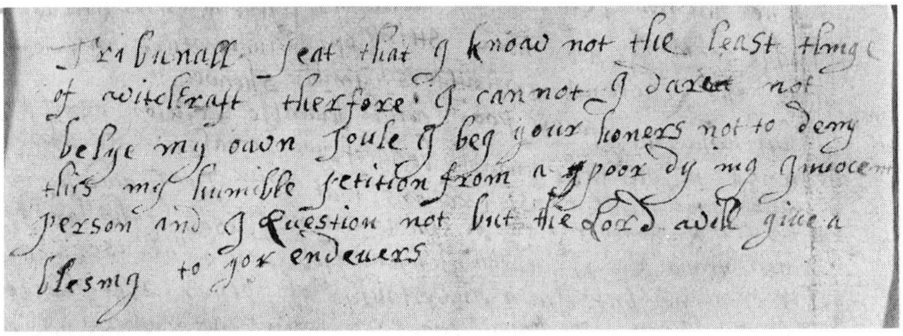

---

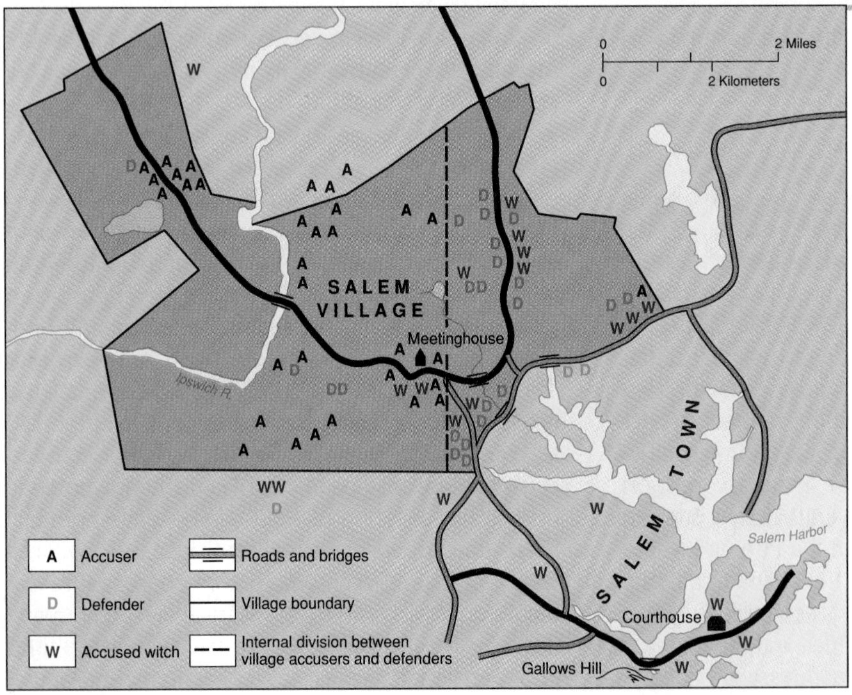

**The Geography of Witchcraft: Salem Village, 1692**

*Geographic patterns of witchcraft testimony mirrored tensions within Salem Village. Accused witches and their defenders lived mostly in the village's eastern division or in Salem Town, whereas their accusers overwhelmingly resided in the village's western sector.*

(Source: Adapted from Paul Boyer and Stephen Nissenbaum, *Salem Possessed: The Social Origins of Witchcraft* (Cambridge, Mass.: Harvard University Press, 1974).)

| | |
|---|---|
| A | Accuser |
| D | Defender |
| W | Accused witch |

hostilities of many others in their community and by virtually dictating the course of events in and around Salem for several months.

The number of persons facing trial multiplied quickly. Those found guilty desperately tried to stave off death by implicating others. As the pandemonium spread beyond Salem, fear dissolved ties of friendship and family. A minister heard himself condemned by his own granddaughter. A seven-year-old girl helped send her mother to the gallows. Fifty persons saved themselves by confessing. Twenty others who would neither disgrace their own name nor betray the guiltless went to their graves. Shortly before she was hanged, a victim of the witch hunters named Mary Easty begged the court to come to its senses: "I petition your honors not for my own life, for I know I must die . . . [but] if it be possible, that no more innocent blood be shed."

By late 1692 most Massachusetts ministers had come to doubt that justice was being done. They objected that spectral evidence, which was crucial in most convictions, lacked legal credibility because the devil could manipulate it. New Englanders, concluded Increase Mather, a leading clergyman, had fallen victim to a deadly game of "blind man's buffet" set up by Satan and were "hotly and madly, mauling one another in the dark." Backed by the clergy (and alarmed by an accusation against his wife), Governor William Phips forbade any further imprisonments for witchcraft in October—by which time over a hundred individuals were in jail and twice that many stood accused—and shortly thereafter he suspended all trials. Phips ended the terror in early 1693 by pardoning all those convicted or suspected of witchcraft.

The witchcraft hysteria reflected profound anxieties over social change in New England. The underlying causes for this tension were evident in the antagonism of Salem Village's communally oriented farmers toward the competitive, individualistic, and impersonal way of life represented by Salem Town. In this clash of values, the rural villagers assumed the symbolic role of purging their city upon a hill of its commercial witches, only to leave the landscape desecrated by their gallows.

By the last years of the seventeenth century, the New England Way had lost its relevance for the generation reaching maturity. Eighteenth-century New Englanders would be far less willing to accept society's right to restrict their personal behavior and economic freedom. True to their Puritan roots, they would retain their strong religious convictions and their self-discipline, which many began applying to the pursuit of material gain.

Throughout the seventeenth century, as New England moved away from its roots, the Chesapeake region to the south also underwent a radical transformation that gave it a new prominence. But the differences between the two regions remained as great as ever.

# Chesapeake Society

Virginia's survival was no longer at stake when James I took control of the colony in 1624 from the bankrupt Virginia Company. The company had built a successful colony but destroyed itself in the process. Thereafter Virginia and its neighbor, Maryland, devoted themselves single-mindedly to the production of tobacco for export. In this pursuit, the Chasapeake was quite unlike New England, where farm families sought primarily to feed themselves. Also unlike New England, Chesapeake society was sharply divided between a few wealthy planters who dominated a majority consisting of indentured servants and small but growing numbers of black slaves and poor white farmers.

## *State and Church in Virginia*

King James I disliked representative government and planned to rule Virginia through a governor of his own choosing, who would appoint and dismiss advisers to a newly created council. But Virginians petitioned repeatedly that their elected assembly be revived. In 1628 the new king, Charles I, grudgingly relented, but only to induce the assembly to lay a tax on tobacco exports that would transfer the cost of the colony's government from the crown to Virginia's taxpayers.

After 1630 the need for additional taxes led royal governors to call regular assemblies. The small number of elected representatives, or burgesses, initially met as a single body with the council to pass laws. During the 1650s the legislature split into two chambers—the House of Burgesses and the Governor's Council, whose members held lifetime appointments. Later other royal colonies all established bicameral legislatures like Virginia's.

Local government varied widely during Virginia's first quarter-century. After experimenting with various institutions of local administration, in 1634 Virginia's settlers adopted England's county-court system. The courts' members, or justices of the peace, acted as judges; they also set local tax rates, paid county officials, and saw to the construction and maintenance of roads, bridges, and public buildings. As in England, the justices and the sheriffs, who administered the counties during the courts' recesses, gained office by the royal governor's appointment instead of by citizens' votes. Everywhere south of New England, unelected county courts would become the basic unit of local government by 1710.

In contrast to Puritan New England, Virginia had as its established church the Church of England. First instituted in 1618, Anglican vestries governed each parish. The six vestrymen handled all church finances, determined who was deserving of poor relief, and investigated complaints against the minister. The taxpayers, who were legally obliged to pay fixed rates to the Anglican Church, elected vestries until 1662, when the assembly made them self-perpetuating and independent of the voters.

Because few counties supported more than one parish, many residents could not conveniently attend services. A chronic shortage of clergymen left many communities without functioning congregations. In 1662 just ten ministers served Virginia's forty-five parishes. Compared to New Englanders, Chesapeake dwellers felt religion's influence lightly.

### Virginia's First Families

Virginia encountered great difficulty in developing a social elite able and willing to provide disinterested public service. By 1630 all but a few of the gentlemen sent by the Virginia Company had either died or returned to England.

The next cycle of leaders were primarily middle class in origins, but over time they acquired great wealth. Some built large estates by defrauding Virginia Company stockholders. Others were rough-hewn gamblers who risked all on tobacco and won big. From 1630 to 1660, these individuals dominated Virginia's council and became even richer through land grants, tax exemptions, and public salaries. Because they had few or no children to assume their place in society, however, their influence died with them.

From 1660 to 1675, a third cycle of immigrants, who generally arrived after 1645, assumed political power. Principally members of English merchant families engaged in trade with Virginia, they had become planters. They usually emigrated with wealth, education, and burning ambition. By 1670 they controlled the council. Most of them profited from "public" service by obtaining huge land grants.

Unlike their predecessors, this group bequeathed their wealth and power to future generations, later known as the First Families of Virginia. Among them were the Burwell, Byrd, Carter, Harrison, Lee, Ludwell, Randolph, and Taylor families. The First Families would dominate Virginia politics for two centuries, and four of the first five American presidents would be descended from them.

### Maryland

Until 1632 successful English colonization had resulted from the ventures of joint-stock companies, but afterward the crown repeatedly made presents of the Virginia Company's forfeited territory to reward English politicians. Overseas settlement thereafter resulted from grants of crown land to proprietors, who assumed the responsibility for peopling, governing, and defending their colonies.

In 1632 the first such grant went to Lord Baltimore (Cecilius Calvert) for a large tract of land north of the Potomac River and east of Chesapeake Bay, which he named Maryland in honor of England's Queen Henrietta Maria. Lord Baltimore also secured freedom from royal taxation, the power to appoint all sheriffs and judges, and the privilege of creating a local nobility. The only checks on the proprietor's power were the crown's control of war and trade and the requirement that an elected assembly approve all laws.

With Charles I's consent, Lord Baltimore intended to create an overseas refuge for English Catholics, who constituted about 2 percent of England's population. Although English Catholics were rarely molested and many (like the Calverts) were very wealthy, they could not worship in public, had to pay tithes to the Anglican Church, and were barred from holding political office.

In making Maryland a Catholic haven, Baltimore had to avoid antagonizing English Protestants. He sought to accomplish this by transplanting to the Chesapeake the old English institution of the manor— an estate on which a lord could maintain private law courts and employ as his chaplain a Catholic priest. Local Catholics could then come to the manor to hear Mass and receive the sacraments privately. Baltimore adapted Virginia's headright system (see Chapter 2) by offering wealthy English Catholic aristocrats large land grants on condition that they bring settlers at their own cost. Anyone transporting five adults (a requirement raised to twenty by 1640) received a two-thousand-acre manor. Baltimore hoped that this arrangement would

### Artifacts from Early Virginia

*This double-edged sword (shown with fragments of its guard and pommel) and elaborate pipe tamper (featuring a man wearing armor and smoking a pipe) were unearthed at Flowerdew Hundred, an early English settlement near present-day Hopewell, Virginia, and date from the first half of the seventeenth century.*

allow Catholics to survive and prosper in Maryland while making it unnecessary to pass any special laws alarming to Protestants.

Maryland's initial colonization proceeded quite smoothly. In 1634 the first two hundred settlers landed. Maryland was the first colony spared a starving time, thanks to the Calvert family's careful study of Virginia's early history. The new colony's success showed that English overseas expansion had come of age. Baltimore, however, stayed in England, governing as an absentee proprietor, and few Catholic settlers went to Maryland. From the outset, Protestants formed the majority of the population. Maryland became a society of independent landowners because land prices were low and few settlers consequently were willing to become tenants on the manors. These conditions doomed the Calvert family's dream of creating a manorial system of mostly Catholic lords collecting rents. By 1675 all of Maryland's sixty nonproprietary manors had evolved into plantations.

There was little religious tension in Maryland in the colony's first years, but the situation worsened over time. The Protestant majority dominated the elected assembly, but many Catholics (including several Calvert relatives) became large landowners, held high public office, and dominated the appointive upper house. Serious religious problems first emerged in 1642, when Catholics and Protestants in the capital at St. Mary's argued over use of the city's chapel, which the two groups had shared until then. As antagonisms intensified, Baltimore drafted the Act for Religious Toleration, which the assembly passed in 1649. The toleration act was America's first law affirming liberty of worship. However, it did not protect non-Christians, nor did it separate church and state, since it empowered the government to punish religious offenses such as blasphemy.

The toleration act also failed to secure religious peace. In 1654 the Protestant majority barred Catholics from voting, ousted Governor William Stone (a pro-tolerance Protestant), and repealed the toleration act. In 1655 Stone raised an army of both faiths to regain the government but was defeated at the Battle of the Severn River. The victors imprisoned Stone and hanged three Catholic leaders. Catholics in Maryland actually experienced more trouble than had their counterparts during the English Civil War, in which Catholics were seldom molested by the victorious Puritans.

Maryland remained in Protestant hands until 1658. Ironically, Lord Baltimore resumed control by order of the Puritan authorities then ruling England. Even so, the Calverts encountered enormous obstacles in governing Maryland during the next four decades because of Protestant resistance to any political influence by Catholics.

## Tobacco Shapes a Way of Life

Compared to colonists in New England's compact towns (where five hundred people often lived within a mile of the meetinghouse), Chesapeake residents had few neighbors. A typical community comprised about two dozen families in an area of twenty-five square miles, or about six persons per square mile. Friendship networks seldom extended beyond a three-mile walk from one's farm and rarely included more than twenty adults. Many, if not most, Chesapeake inhabitants lived in a constricted world much like that of Robert Boone, a Maryland farmer described by an Annapolis paper as having died at age seventy-nine "on the same Plantation where he was born in 1680, from which he never went 30 Miles in his Life."

### Pattern of Settlement in Surry County, Virginia, 1620–1660

*Unlike the New England colonists, whose settlements were usually nucleated around a town center (see the map of Sudbury, Massachusetts, on p. 54), the Chesapeake population distributed itself thinly along the banks of rivers and creeks.*

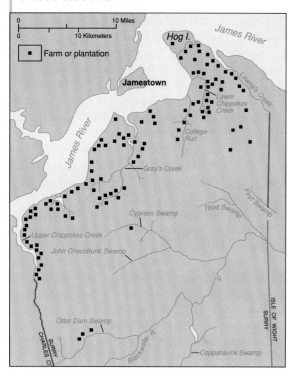

(Source: Thad W. Tate and David Ammerman, eds., *The Chesapeake in the Seventeenth Century* (Chapel Hill: University of North Carolina Press, 1979). Published for the Institute of Early American History and Culture. Reprinted by permission.)

The isolated folk in Virginia and Maryland and in the unorganized settlements of what would become North Carolina shared a way of life shaped by one overriding fact: their future depended on the price of tobacco. Tobacco had dominated Chesapeake agriculture since 1618, when demand for the crop exploded and prices spiraled to dizzying levels. The boom ended in 1629 after prices sank a stunning 97 percent. After stabilizing, tobacco rarely again fetched more than 10 percent of its former price.

Despite the plunge, tobacco stayed profitable as long as it sold for over two pence per pound *and* was cultivated on fertile soil near navigable water. The plant grew best on level ground with good internal drainage, so-called light soil, which was usually found beside rivers. Locating a farm along Chesapeake Bay or the region's web of rivers also minimized transportation costs by permitting tobacco to be loaded on ships at wharves near one's home. Perhaps 80 percent of all Chesapeake homes lay within a half-mile of a riverbank, and most within just six hundred feet of the shoreline.

From such waterfront bases, wealthy planters built wharves that served not only as depots for tobacco exports but also as distribution centers for imported goods. The planters' control of both export and import commerce stunted the growth of towns and the emergence of a powerful merchant class. Urbanization therefore proceeded slowly in the Chesapeake, even in a capital like Maryland's St. Mary's, which as late as 1678 was still a mere hamlet of thirty scattered houses.

Although the tobacco crash left small producers struggling to support themselves, cultivating the "weed" could generate a large income for anyone with a sizable work force. Tobacco thus sustained a sharp demand for labor that lured about 110,000 English to the Chesapeake from 1630 to 1700. Ninety percent of these immigrants were indentured servants. Men were more valued as field hands than women, so 80 percent of servants were males, usually in their twenties.

## Mortality, Gender, and Kinship

So few women immigrated to the Chesapeake in the early years of colonization that barely a third of all male servants could find brides before 1650. Furthermore, marriage occurred relatively late because most inhabitants immigrated as servants whose indentures forbade them to wed before completing their term of labor. Their own scarcity gave women a great advantage in negotiating favorable marriages. Female indentured servants often found prosperous planters to be their suitors and to buy their remaining time of service.

Death ravaged seventeenth-century Chesapeake society mercilessly and left domestic life exceptionally fragile. Before 1650 the greatest killers were diseases contracted from contaminated water: typhoid, dysentery, and salt poisoning. After 1650 malaria became endemic as sailors, arriving from Africa, along with a few Africans, carried it into the marshy lowlands, where the disease was spread rapidly by mosquito bites. Life expectancy in the 1600s was about forty-eight for men and forty-four for women—slightly less than in England but nearly twenty years less than in New England. Servants died at horrifying rates, with perhaps 40 percent going to their graves within six years of arrival, and 70 percent by age forty-nine. Such high death rates severely crippled family life. Half of all people married in Charles County, Maryland, during the late 1600s became widows or widowers within seven years. The typical Maryland family saw half of its four children die in childhood.

Chesapeake women who lost their husbands tended to enjoy greater property rights than widows elsewhere. To ensure that their own children would inherit the family estate in the event that their widows remarried, Chesapeake men often wrote wills giving their wives perpetual and complete control of their estates. A widow in such circumstances gained economic independence yet still faced enormous pressure to marry a man who could produce income by farming her fields.

The prevalence of early death produced complex households in which stepparents might raise children with two or three different surnames. Mary Keeble of Middlesex County, Virginia, bore seven children before being widowed at age twenty-nine, whereupon she married Robert Beverley, a prominent planter. Mary died in 1678 at age forty-one after having five children by Beverley, who then married Katherine Hone, a widow with one child. Upon Beverley's death in 1687, Katherine quickly wed Christopher Robinson, who had just lost his wife and needed a mother for his four children. Christopher and Katherine's household included children named Keeble, Beverley, Hone, and Robinson. This tangled chain of six marriages among seven people eventually produced twenty-five children who lived at least part of their lives with one or more stepparents.

The combination of predominantly male immigration and devastating death rates notably retarded population growth. Although the Chesapeake had received perhaps 89,000 English immigrants between 1630 and 1700, its white population stood at just 85,000 in 1700. By contrast, a benign disease environment and a more balanced gender ratio among the 28,000 immigrants to New England during the 1600s allowed that region's white population to more than triple to 91,000 by 1700.

The Chesapeake's dismal demographic history began improving in the late seventeenth century. By then resistance acquired from childhood immunities allowed native-born residents to survive into their fifties, or ten years longer than immigrants. As the number of families slowly rose, the ratio of men to women became more equal, since half of all children were girls. By 1690 an almost even division existed between males and females. Thereafter, the white population grew primarily through an excess of births over deaths rather than through immigration, so that by 1720 the Chesapeake was primarily a native-born society.

## Tobacco's Troubles

The massive importation of servants into the seventeenth-century Chesapeake widened the gap between rich and poor. Taking advantage of the headright system, a few planters built up large landholdings and then earned substantial incomes from their servants' labor. The servants' lot was harsh. Most were poorly fed, clothed, and housed. The exploitation of labor in the Chesapeake was unequaled anywhere in the English-speaking world outside the West Indies.

Servants faced a bleak future when their indentures ended. Having received no pay, they entered into freedom almost penniless. Virginia obliged masters to provide a new suit of clothes and a year's supply of corn to a freed servant. Maryland required these items plus a hoe and an ax and gave the right to claim fifty acres whenever an individual could pay to have the land surveyed and deeded.

Maryland's policy of reserving fifty acres for former servants permitted many of its freedmen to become landowners. Two-thirds of all Chesapeake servants went to Virginia, however, where no such entitlement existed. After 1650 Virginia speculators monopolized most of the light soil along riverbanks so essential for a profitable farm, and freedmen found land ever more unaffordable. Upward mobility was possible, but few achieved it.

After 1660 upward mobility almost vanished from the Chesapeake as the price of tobacco fell far below

### Tobacco Prices, 1618–1710

*Even after its great plunge in the 1620s, tobacco remained profitable until about 1660, when its price fell below the break-even point—the income needed to support a family or pay off a farm mortgage.*

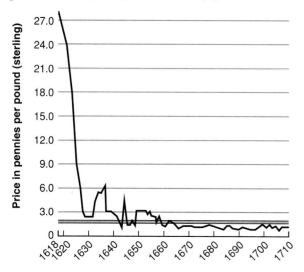

*Source:* Russell R. Menard, "The Chesapeake Economy, 1618–1720: An Interpretation" (unpublished paper presented at the Johns Hopkins University Seminar on the Atlantic Community, November 20, 1973) and "Farm Prices of Maryland Tobacco, 1659–1710," *Maryland Historical Magazine,* LVIII (Spring 1973): 85.

profitable levels, to a penny a pound. So began a depression lasting over fifty years. Despite their own tobacco losses, large planters earned other income from rents, interest on loans, some shopkeeping, and government fees.

Most landowners held on by offsetting tobacco losses with small sales of corn and cattle to the West Indies. A typical family nevertheless inhabited a shack barely twenty feet by sixteen feet and owned no more property than Adam Head of Maryland possessed when he died in 1698: three mattresses without bedsteads, a chest and barrel that served as table and chair, two pots, a kettle, "a parcel of old pewter," a gun, and some books. Most tobacco farmers lacked furniture, lived on mush or stew because they had just one pot, and slept on the ground—often on a pile of rags. Having fled poverty in England or the Caribbean for the promise of a better life, they found utter destitution in the Chesapeake.

Servants who completed their indentures after 1660 fared even worse, for the depression slashed wages well below the level needed to build savings and in this way placed landownership beyond their means. Lacking capital, those living as tenants could not afford to breed cattle for the West Indies, and they had little corn to sell after meeting their own needs. Ex-servants formed a frustrated and embittered underclass that seemed destined to remain landless and poor.

### Bacon's Rebellion

By the 1670s these bleak conditions trapped most Virginia landowners in a losing battle against poverty and left the colony's laborers and freedmen verging on despair. Both groups were capable of striking out in blind rage if an opportunity presented itself to stave off economic disaster. In 1676 this human powder keg exploded in violence that left hundreds of Indians dead, dozens of plantations looted, and Virginia's capital, Jamestown, burned. The person who lit the match was Nathaniel Bacon, a wealthy, well-educated young Englishman who had immigrated to Virginia in 1674 and established a plantation. He was a bold man and an inspiring speaker, and Governor William Berkeley, a distant relative, had immediately appointed him to the council.

Virginia had been free of serious conflict with Native Americans since the Third Anglo-Powhatan War (1644–1646). During that struggle, forces under Opechancanough, then nearly a century old but able to direct battles from a litter, killed five hundred of the colony's eight thousand whites before meeting defeat. By 1653 tribes encircled by English settlement began agreeing to remain within boundaries set by the government—in effect, on reservations. White settlement then expanded north to the Potomac River, and by 1675 Virginia's four thousand Indians were greatly outnumbered by forty thousand whites.

As in New England, tensions flared between natives struggling against depopulation and nearby settlers bent on altering the landscape. In Virginia tensions ran particularly high because Governor Berkeley and a few friends held a fur-trade monopoly that profited from friendly relations with some of the frontier Indians. As a result, settler resentments against the governor became fused with those against Indians. In June 1675 a dispute between some Doeg Indians and a Virginia farmer escalated until a force of Virginia and Maryland militia pursuing the Doegs murdered fourteen friendly Susquehannocks and then executed five of their leaders during a peace conference. The violence was now unstoppable.

Governor Berkeley proposed defending the panic-stricken frontier with an expensive chain of forts linked by patrols. Stung by low tobacco prices and taxes that took almost a quarter of their yearly incomes, small farmers preferred the less costly solution of waging a war of extermination. Despite orders from Berkeley not to retaliate, three hundred settlers elected Bacon to lead them against nearby Indians in April 1676. Bacon's expedition found only peaceful Indians but massacred them anyway.

When he returned in June 1676, Bacon sought authority to wage war "against all Indians in generall." Bacon's newfound popularity forced the governor to grant his demand. The legislature voted a program designed to appeal to both hard-pressed taxpayers and ex-servants desperate for land. The assembly defined as enemies any Indians who left their villages without English permission (even if they did so out of fear of attack by Bacon), and declared their lands forfeited. Bacon's troops were free to plunder all "enemies" of their furs, guns, wampum, and corn harvests and also to keep Indian prisoners as slaves. The assembly's incentives for enlisting were directed at land-bound buccaneers eager to get rich quickly by seizing land and enslaving any Indians who fell into their clutches.

But Berkeley soon had second thoughts about letting Bacon's thirteen hundred men continue their frontier slaughter and called them back. The governor's order spared more Indians from attack, leading Bacon's men to rebel and march on Jamestown. Forcing Berkeley to flee across Chesapeake Bay, the rebels burned Jamestown, offered freedom to any Berkeley supporters' servants or slaves who joined the uprising, and then looted their enemies' plantations. At the very moment of triumph, however, Bacon died of dysentery in late 1676, and his followers dispersed.

The tortured course of Bacon's Rebellion revealed a society under deep internal stress. The revolt began as an effort to displace escalating tensions within white society onto local Indians. Because social success in Virginia depended on accumulating land and labor, farmers and landless ex-servants alike responded enthusiastically to the prospect of taking Indian lands, stealing their furs, wampum, and harvests, and enslaving prisoners. So easily did the insurrection disintegrate into an excuse for settlers of all classes to plunder other whites, however, that it appears that the rebels were driven by economic opportunism as well as by racism. Bacon's Rebellion was an outburst of long pent-up frustrations by marginal taxpayers and ex-servants, dri-

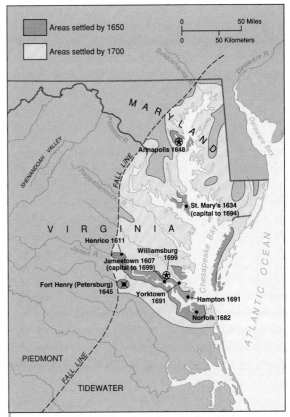

**Colonizing the Chesapeake, 1607–1660**
*The native-settler frontier moved slowly westward until after Indian defeat in the Third Anglo-Powhatan War (1644–1646). By 1700, when the European and African population had reached 110,000, newcomers had spread virtually throughout the tidewater.*

ven to desperation by the tobacco depression, as well as by wealthier planters excluded from Berkeley's circle of favorites.

## Slavery

Bacon's Rebellion exposed the crackling tensions underlying class relations among Chesapeake whites. This social instability derived in large part from the massive importation of indentured servants, who later became free agents in an economy that offered them little but poverty while their former masters seemingly prospered. But even before Bacon's Rebellion, the acute potential for class conflict was diminishing as Chesapeake planters gradually substituted black slaves for white servants.

Racial slavery developed in three stages in the Chesapeake. Africans first began appearing from 1619 to 1640. Although Anglo-Virginians carefully distinguished blacks from whites in official documents—in a manner that seems to show a tendency to discriminate according to race—they did not assume that every African sold was a slave for life. The same was true for Indians captured in the colony's wars. Some Africans gained their freedom, and a few, such as Anthony and Mary Johnson, owned their own tobacco farms. During the second phase, spanning the years 1640–1660, unmistakable evidence survives that growing numbers of blacks and some Indians were treated as slaves and that their children inherited that status, in contrast to white indentured servants, who had fixed terms of service. At the same time there is ample evidence from this period of white and black laborers running away or rebelling against a master together, and occasionally marrying one another. Perhaps in reaction to such incidents, the colonies, after 1660, officially recognized slavery and regulated it by law. Maryland first defined slavery as a lifelong, inheritable, racial status in 1661. Virginia followed suit in 1670. This hardening of status lines did

not prevent some black and white laborers from joining Bacon's Rebellion. Indeed the last contingent of rebels to lay down their arms consisted entirely of slaves and servants. By 1705 strict legal codes defined the place of slaves in society and set standards of racial etiquette. By then free blacks like Mary Johnson's grandchildren had all but disappeared from the Chesapeake. Although this period saw racial slavery become fully legalized, many of the specific practices enacted into law had evolved into custom before 1660.

The English never considered slavery a status appropriate for any European or any Christian. Although they could have enslaved enemies such as the Irish and Spanish, they always reserved this complete denial of human rights for nonwhites.

Emerging gradually in the Chesapeake, slavery was formally codified by planter elites attempting to stabilize Chesapeake society and defuse the resentment of whites. In deeming nonwhite "pagans" unfit for freedom, the elites created a common, exclusive identity for whites as free or potentially free persons.

Chesapeake planters began formulating this racial caste system before slavery itself became economically significant. As late as 1660, fewer than a thousand slaves lived in Virginia and Maryland. The number in bondage first became truly significant in the 1680s, when the Chesapeake's slave population (by now almost entirely black, owing to Indian decline) almost tripled, rising from forty-five hundred to about twelve thousand. By 1700 slaves made up 22 percent of the inhabitants and over 80 percent of all unfree laborers.

Having been made possible by racism, slavery replaced indentured servitude for economic reasons. First, it became more difficult to import indentured servants as the seventeenth century advanced because a gradual decline in England's population between 1650 and 1700 reduced the number of people willing to emigrate overseas. As England's population decreased, labor became more valuable at home, and wages rose by about 50 percent. Second, before 1690 the Royal African Company, which held a monopoly on selling slaves to the English colonies, shipped nearly all its cargoes to the West Indies. During the 1690s this monopoly was broken, and rival companies began shipping large numbers of Africans directly to the Chesapeake.

The emergence of slavery relaxed the economic strains within white society that had helped precipitate Bacon's Rebellion. Gradually after 1690, non–slave-owning whites came to see themselves as sharing a common interest with upper-class planters in maintaining social control over a black race regarded as alien and

### Tobacco Label
*The slave's central role in growing tobacco and serving his white master (here enjoying a smoke) is depicted.*

*Kositzky's* Beſt Virginia *LONDON.*

threatening. Slavery's establishment as the principal form of labor in the Chesapeake was part of a larger trend among England's plantation colonies, one that began in the Caribbean and spread to the new mainland colony of Carolina.

# The Spread of Slavery: The Caribbean and Carolina

Simultaneously with the expansion of European colonization in mainland North America, a second wave of settlement swept the West Indies. Between 1630 and 1642 almost 60 percent of the seventy thousand English who emigrated went to the Caribbean. In the 1640s the English West Indians began adapting their economy to large-scale slave labor and devising a code of social conduct for nonwhites. In this way, the West

Indies pioneered techniques of racial control that would later appear in the mainland colonies' plantation societies.

After 1660 a large outmigration of English islanders added significantly to English North America's population. Most of the migrants went to the Chesapeake and to Carolina, thereby introducing the habits and prejudices of plantation slaveholding, as well as some slaves, to the mainland colonies. By 1710, the population of Carolina, like that of the Caribbean colonies, was predominantly black and enslaved.

### *Sugar and Slaves*

As in the Chesapeake, a strong demand for tobacco led the first English settlers in the Caribbean to cultivate that plant almost exclusively. Although low prices inhibited upward mobility, through the 1630s the English

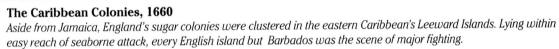

**The Caribbean Colonies, 1660**
*Aside from Jamaica, England's sugar colonies were clustered in the eastern Caribbean's Leeward Islands. Lying within easy reach of seaborne attack, every English island but Barbados was the scene of major fighting.*

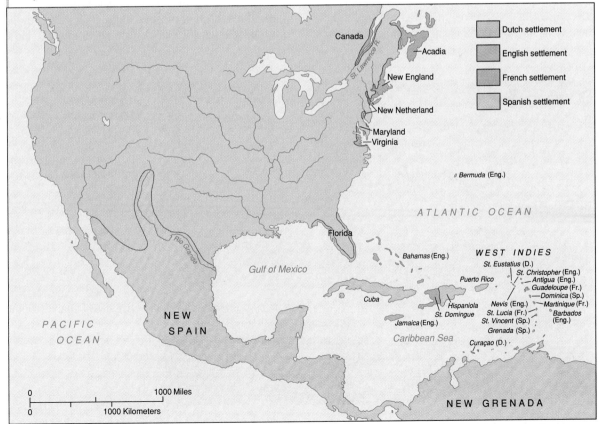

West Indies remained a society with a large percentage of independent landowners, an overwhelmingly white population, and no extreme inequality of wealth.

During the early 1640s an alternative to tobacco appeared that rapidly revolutionized the islands' economy and society. Dutch merchants familiar with Portuguese methods of sugar production in Brazil began encouraging English planters to raise and process sugar cane, which the Dutch would then market.

Because planters needed three times as many workers per acre to raise cane as tobacco, rising sugar production greatly multiplied the demand for labor. Before 1640 West Indians had imported white servants who signed an indenture, or contract, to work without pay for four to six years in return for free passage to America. After 1640, however, sugar planters increasingly purchased enslaved Africans from the Dutch to do common field work and used the indentured servants as overseers or skilled artisans.

Although slavery had died out in England after the eleventh century, English immigrants to the Caribbean quickly copied the example set there by Spanish slaveowners. On Barbados, for example, English newcomers imposed slavery on both blacks and Indians immediately after settling on that island in 1627. The Barbadian government in 1636 condemned every black brought there to lifelong bondage. Planters on other English islands likewise plunged into slaveowning with gusto.

Sugar planters like Sarah Horbin's husband preferred black slaves to white servants because slaves could be driven harder and maintained less expensively. Moreover, most servants ended their indentures after four years, but slaves toiled on until death. Although slaves initially cost two to four times more than servants, they proved a more economical long-term investment. In this way the profit motive and the racism that emerged with the "new slavery" (see Chapter 2) reinforced one another.

By 1670 the sugar revolution had transformed the British West Indies into a predominantly slave society. In 1713 blacks outnumbered whites by a margin of four to one. Although the number of blacks shot up from approximately 40,000 in 1670 to 130,000 in 1713, the white population remained stable at about 33,000 because the planters' preference for slave labor greatly reduced the importation of indentured servants after 1670.

Declining demand for white labor in the West Indies diverted the flow of English immigration from the islands to mainland North America and so contributed to population growth there. Furthermore, because the expansion of West Indian sugar plantations priced land beyond the reach of most whites, perhaps thirty thousand people left the islands from 1655 to 1700. Most

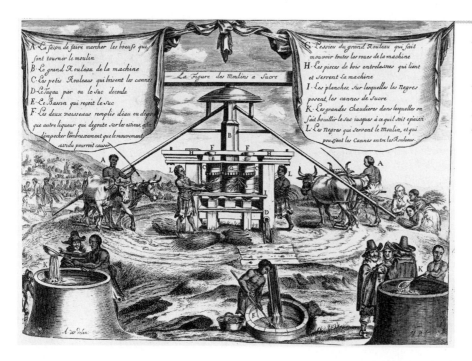

**African Slaves Making Sugar**

*This drawing, published in 1665, shows slaves feeding sugar cane into a cattle-driven mill, which turns it into juice. Other slaves then boil the liquid.*

**Tuscarora Resistance, 1711**
*Defending their homeland against an influx of settlers, the Tuscaroras captured Baron Christopher von Graffenried, leader of the Swiss community at New Bern. Graffenried drew this sketch, which depicts him being held along with an English trader, John Lawson, and an African slave. Lawson was later executed.*

whites who quit the West Indies also migrated to the mainland colonies—especially Carolina.

## Carolina: The First Restoration Colony

During the 1650s settlers from New England and the English West Indies established several unauthorized outposts along the swampy coast between Virginia and Spanish Florida. In 1663 King Charles II (who had assumed the throne when the Stuart monarchy was restored in 1660) bestowed this unpromising coast on several English supporters, making it the first of several Restoration colonies. The grateful proprietors named their colony Carolina in honor of Charles (*Carolus* in Latin).

Carolina grew haltingly until 1669, when one of the proprietors, Anthony Ashley Cooper, speeded up settlement by offering immigrants fifty-acre land grants for every family member, indentured servant, or slave they brought in. Cooper's action marked a turning point. In 1670 settlement of southern Carolina began when two hundred Barbadian and English settlers landed near modern-day Charleston, "in the very chops of the Spanish." Here, in the settlement they called Charles Town, they formed the colony's nucleus, with their own bicameral legislature distinct from that of the northern district.

Cooper and his secretary—John Locke, later acclaimed as one of the great philosophers of the age—devised an intricate plan for Carolina's settlement and government. Their Fundamental Constitutions of Carolina attempted to ensure the colony's stability by decreeing that political power and social rank should accurately reflect settlers' landed wealth. Thus they invented a three-tiered nobility that would hold two-fifths of all land, make laws through a Council of Nobles, and dispense justice through manorial law courts. Ordinary Carolinians with smaller landholdings were expected to defer to this nobility, although they would enjoy religious toleration and the benefits of English common law. Until the 1680s most settlers were small landowners from Barbados or the mainland colonies, along with some French Huguenots. Obtaining all the land they needed, they saw little reason to obey pseudofeudal lords and all but ignored most of the plans drawn up for them across the Atlantic. Southern Carolinians raised livestock and exported deerskins and Indian slaves (see below), and colonists in northern Carolina exported tobacco, lumber, and pitch, giving local people the name tarheels. These activities did not at first produce enough profit to warrant maintaining many slaves, and so self-sufficient white families predominated in the area.

But many southern Carolinians were not content merely to eke out a marginal existence. Like the first Virginians, they sought a staple crop that could make them rich. By the early eighteenth century, they found it—rice. The grain was familiar to slaves from Senegambia, where it constituted the basic foodstuff. Because rice, like sugar, enormously enriched a few men with capital to invest in costly dams, dikes, and slaves, it remade southern Carolina into a society resembling that of the West Indies. By earning annual profits of 25 percent, rice planters within a generation became the only colonial elite whose wealth rivaled that of the Caribbean sugar planters.

The Carolina rice planters' huge profits had to be reaped at someone's expense, however. No matter how inhumanly they might be driven, indentured English servants simply did not survive in humid rice paddies swarming with malaria-bearing mosquitoes. The planters' solution was to import an ever-growing force of African slaves, who possessed two major advantages for masters. First, perhaps 15 percent of the Africans taken to Carolina had cultivated rice in their homeland, and their expertise was vital in teaching whites how to raise the unfamiliar crop. Second, many Africans had developed partial immunity to malaria, the infectious and deadly disease transmitted by mosquito bites, which was endemic to coastal regions of West Africa and which African-born slaves (and infected slave ships' crews) carried to the New World. (Tragically, the antibody that helps ward off malaria also tends to produce the sickle-cell trait, a genetic condition often fatal to those children who inherit it.) These two advantages made possible commercial rice production in Carolina. A great demand for black slave labor resulted, for a typical rice planter farming 130 acres needed sixty-five slaves. The proportion of slaves in southern Carolina's population spurted from 17 percent in 1680 to 67 percent in 1720. Carolina was Britain's sole mainland colony with a black majority.

Rice thrived only within a forty-mile-wide coastal strip extending from Cape Fear to present-day Georgia. The hot, humid, marshy lowlands quickly became infested with malaria. Carolinians grimly joked that the rice belt was a paradise in spring, an inferno in summer, and a hospital in the wet, chilly fall. In the worst months, planters' families usually escaped to the relatively cool and more healthful climate of Charles Town and let overseers supervise their harvests.

As long as Europeans outnumbered Africans, race relations could be somewhat relaxed. But as a black majority emerged and swelled, whites increasingly relied on force and fear to control their slaves, adopting many of the galling restrictions and gruesome punishments imposed on slaves in Barbados. Bondage in the mainland colony was becoming as cruel and harsh as in the West Indies.

White Carolinians' attitudes toward Native Americans likewise hardened into exploitation and violence. In the 1670s traders in southern Carolina armed nearby Indians and encouraged them to raid Spanish missions in Florida. These allies captured unarmed Guale, Apalachee, and Timucua Indians at the missions and traded them, along with deerskins, to the Carolinians for guns and other European goods. The English then sold the enslaved Indians, mostly to planters in the West Indies. By the mid-1680s the Carolinians had extended the trade inland through alliances with the Yamasees (Guale Indians who had fled the inadequate protection of the Spanish in Florida) and the Creeks, a powerful confederacy centered in what is now western Georgia and northern Alabama. For three decades these Indians terrorized the Spanish and other Indians in the region with their slave raids. No statistical records of Carolina's Indian slave trade survive, but a recent study estimates that the number of Native Americans enslaved was in the tens of thousands. Once shipped to the West Indies, most died quickly because they lacked immunities to both European and tropical diseases.

Conflict came to northern Carolina in 1711 when the Tuscarora Indians, provoked by white encroachments on their land and by several instances of whites kidnapping Indians as slaves, destroyed New Bern, a frontier settlement of seven hundred Swiss immigrants. Northern Carolina enlisted the aid of southern Carolina and its well-armed Indian allies. By 1713, with a thousand of their people killed or enslaved (about one-fifth of the total population), the Tuscaroras surrendered. Nearly half the survivors eventually migrated to New York, where they became the sixth nation of the Iroquois Confederacy.

Having helped defeat the Tuscaroras, Carolina's Indian allies resented a growing number of incidents of cheating, violence, and enslavement perpetrated by English traders, and encroachments on their land by settlers. In 1715 the Yamasees, who were most seriously affected by these incidents, led a coordinated series of attacks on English trading houses and settlements. Only by enlisting the aid of the Cherokee Indians, and allowing four hundred slaves to bear arms, could the colony crush the uprising. Yamasees not killed or captured were driven back to Florida or to Creek towns.

The first two generations of white settlers and black slaves had cleared the unhealthy coastal regions and developed Carolina's profitable exports. With help from Indian allies, they had extinguished resistance from hostile Native Americans. In realizing these formidable accomplishments, they had received little aid from the absentee proprietors, whose main activities had been grabbing land for themselves, vetoing laws passed by the assemblies, and appointing unpopular governors. Carolinians came to regard the proprietors as indifferent even to their defense. After southern Carolinians overthrew proprietary rule in 1719 (Carolina's fourth major rebellion), the British monarchy intervened and by 1729 created two royal colonies, North Carolina and South Carolina.

## The Middle Colonies

Between the Chesapeake and New England, a fourth mainland colonial region, the middle colonies, took shape, slowly at first. New Netherland and New Sweden were small commercial outposts, although the Dutch colony began to grow and flourish at midcentury. But in 1664, England seized New Netherland from the Dutch, and in 1681 King Charles II authorized a new colony where New Sweden had stood. These actions resulted in three additional Restoration colonies—New York, New Jersey, and Pennsylvania. By the end of the seventeenth century, the middle colonies composed North America's fastest-growing region.

### *Precursors: New Netherland and New Sweden*

New Netherland became North America's first multiethnic society. Barely half its colonists were Dutch; most of the rest were Germans, French, Scandinavians, and Africans, free as well as enslaved. In 1643 the population included Protestants, Catholics, Jews, and Muslims, and eighteen European and African languages were spoken. But religion counted for little (in 1642 the colony had seventeen taverns but not one place of worship), and the settlers' get-rich-quick attitude had long sapped company profits as private individuals persisted in trading illegally in furs. In 1639 the company bowed to mounting pressure and legalized private fur trading.

Privatization led to a rapid influx of guns into the hands of New Netherland's Iroquois allies, giving them a distinct advantage over other natives. As overhunting depleted local supplies of beaver skins and as smallpox epidemics took their toll, the Iroquois encroached on pro-French rival Indians in a quest for pelts and for captives, who could be adopted into Iroquois families to replace the dead. After 1648 the Iroquois, in a series of bloody "beaver wars," dispersed the Hurons and other French allies, incorporating many members of these nations into their own ranks. Then they attacked the French settlements along the St. Lawrence. "They come like foxes, they attack like lions, they disappear like birds," wrote a French Jesuit of the Iroquois.

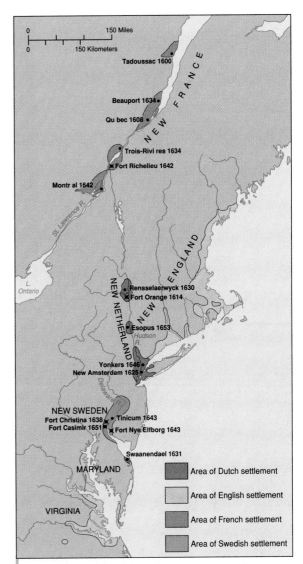

**The Riverine Colonies of New France, New Netherland, and New Sweden, c. 1650**
*So that they could easily buy furs trapped by Indians farther inland, England's imperial rivals located their colonies along major river routes to the interior. The French settled along the St. Lawrence, the Dutch along the Hudson, and the Swedes along the Delaware.*

Although the Dutch allied successfully with the Iroquois, their relations with their nearer Indian neighbors were the worst of any Europeans. With its greedy settlers and military weakness, New Netherland had largely itself to blame. In 1643 all-out war erupted when Dutch forces massacred previously friendly Algonquian-speaking Indians and by 1645 the Dutch could temporarily prevail only with English help and by in-

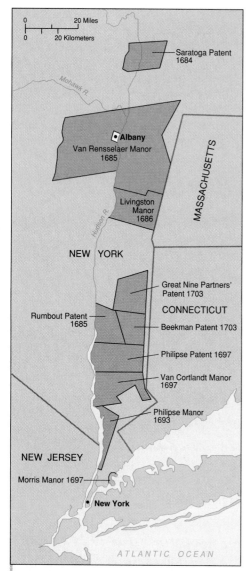

## The New York Manors and Land Grants

*Between 1684 and 1703, English governors awarded most of the best land east of the Hudson River as manors to prominent politicians—the majority of them Dutch—whose heirs became the wealthiest elite in the rural northern colonies.*

**Peter Stuyvesant c. 1660**

*The last governor of New Netherland was handicapped by lack of support from Holland and an overbearing personality that alienated most people with whom he worked.*

furs from New Netherland. Annoyed, in 1655 the Dutch colony's governor, Peter Stuyvesant, marched his militia against New Sweden. The four hundred residents of the rival colony peacefully accepted Dutch annexation.

Tiny though they were, the Dutch and Swedish colonies were historically significant. New Netherland had attained a population of nine thousand and featured a wealthy, thriving port city by the time it came under English rule in 1664. Even short-lived New Sweden left a mark—the log cabin, that durable symbol of the American frontier, which Finnish settlers in the Swedish colony first introduced to the continent. Above all, the two colonies bequeathed an environment characterized by ethnic and religious diversity that would continue in England's "middle colonies."

## English Conquests: New York and the Jerseys

Like Carolina, the English colonies of New York and New Jersey had their origins in the speculative enterprise of Restoration courtiers close to King Charles II. Here too upper-class proprietors hoped to create a hierarchical society in which they could profit from settlers' rents. These plans for the most part failed in New Jersey, as in Carolina. Only in New York did they come close to success.

In 1664, waging war against the Dutch Republic, Charles II dispatched a naval force to conquer New Netherland. Weakened by clashes with local Indians, Dutch governor Peter Stuyvesant and four hundred poorly armed civilians surrendered peacefully. Nearly all the Dutch (including Stuyvesant himself) remained in the colony on generous terms.

Charles II made his brother James, Duke of York, proprietor of the new province and renamed it New York. When the duke became King James II in 1685, he proclaimed New York a royal colony. Immigration from New England, Britain, and France boosted the popula-

flicting terrible atrocities. But the fighting had cut New Netherland's Indian population from 1,600 to 700.

Another European challenger dangerously distracted the Dutch in their war with the Algonquians. In 1638 Sweden had planted a small fur-trading colony in the lower Delaware Valley. Trading with the Delaware (or Lenni Lenape) Indians, New Sweden diverted many

tion from 9,000 in 1664 to 20,000 in 1700; just 44 percent were descended from the original New Netherlanders.

New York's governors rewarded their most influential political supporters, both Dutch and English, with large land grants. By 1703 five families held approximately 1.75 million acres (about half the area east of the Hudson River and south of Albany), which they withheld from sale in hope of creating manors with numerous rent-paying tenants. Earning an enormous income from their rents over the next half-century, the New York *patroons* (the Dutch name for manor lords) by 1750 formed a landed elite second in wealth only to the Carolina rice planters.

Ambitious plans likewise collided with American realities in New Jersey, which also was carved out of New Netherland. Immediately after the Dutch province's conquest in 1664, the Duke of York awarded New Jersey to a group of proprietors headed by William Penn, John Lord Berkeley, and Sir Philip Carteret. The area at the time was inhabited by about four thousand Delaware Indians and a few hundred Dutch and Swedes. From the beginning the New Jersey proprietors had difficulty controlling their province. By 1672 several thousand New Englanders had settled along the Atlantic shore. After the quarrelsome Puritans renounced allegiance to them, Berkeley and Carteret sold the region to a group of even more contentious religious dissenters, called Quakers, who split the territory into the two colonies of West Jersey (1676) and East Jersey (1682).

The Jerseys' Quakers, Anglicans, Puritans, Scottish Presbyterians, Dutch Calvinists, and Swedish Lutherans got along poorly with one another and even worse with the proprietors. The governments collapsed between 1698 and 1701 as mobs disrupted the courts. In 1702 the disillusioned proprietors finally surrendered their political powers to the crown, which proclaimed New Jersey a royal province.

### Quaker Pennsylvania

The noblest attempt to carry out European concepts of justice and stability in founding a colony began in 1681. That year Charles II paid off a huge debt by making a supporter's son, William Penn, the proprietor of the last unallocated tract of American territory at the king's disposal. Penn (1644–1718) had two aims in developing his colony. First, he was a Quaker and wanted to launch a "holy experiment" based on the teachings of the radical English preacher George Fox. Second, "though I desire to extend religious freedom," he explained, "yet I want some recompense for my trouble."

Quakers in late-seventeenth-century England stood well beyond the fringe of respectability. Quakerism appealed strongly to men and women at the bottom of the economic ladder, and its adherents challenged the conventional foundation of the social order. George Fox, the movement's originator, had received his inspiration while wandering civil war–torn England's byways and searching for spiritual meaning among distressed common people. Tried on one occasion for blasphemy, he warned the judge to "tremble at the word of the Lord" and was ridiculed as a "quaker." Fox's followers called themselves the Society of Friends, but the name Quaker stuck. They were among the most radical of the many religious sects born in England during the 1640s and 1650s.

The core of Fox's theology was his belief that the Holy Spirit or "Inner Light" could inspire every soul. Mainstream Christians, by contrast, found any such claim of special communication with God highly suspicious, as Anne Hutchinson's banishment from Massachusetts Bay colony in 1637 had revealed. Although trusting direct inspiration, Quakers also took great pains to ensure that individual opinions would not be mistaken for God's will. They felt confident that they understood Inner Light only after having reached near-unanimous agreement through intensive and searching discussion led by "Public Friends"—ordinary laypeople. In their simple religious services ("meetings"), Quakers sat silently until the Inner Light prompted one of them to speak.

Some of their beliefs led English Quakers to behave in ways that seemed disrespectful to government and the social elite and so aroused fierce hostility. For example, insisting that individuals deserved recognition for their spiritual state rather than their wealth or family status, Quakers refused to tip their hats to their social betters. For the same reason, they would not use the pronoun *you* (customarily employed when commoners spoke to members of the gentry), instead addressing everyone *thee* and *thou* as a token of equality. By wearing their hats in court, moreover, Quakers appeared to mock the state's authority; and by taking literally Scripture's ban on swearing oaths, they seemed to place themselves above the law. The Friends' refusal to bear arms appeared unpatriotic and cowardly to many. Finally, Quakers accorded women unprecedented equality. The Inner Light, Fox insisted, could "speak in the female as well as the male." Acting on these beliefs, Quakers suffered persecution, and occasionally death, in England, Massachusetts, and Virginia.

Not all Quakers came from the bottom of society. The movement's emphasis on quiet introspection and its refusal to adopt a formal creed also attracted some well-educated and well-to-do individuals disillusioned by the quarreling of rival faiths. The possessor of a great fortune, William Penn was hardly a typical Friend, but there were significant numbers of merchants among the estimated sixty thousand Quakers in the British Isles in the early 1680s. Moreover, the industriousness that the Society of Friends encouraged in its members ensured that many humble Quakers were already accumulating money and property.

Much care lay behind the Quaker migration to Pennsylvania that began in 1681, and it resulted in the most successful initial transplantation of Europeans in any North American colony. Penn sent an advance party to the Delaware Valley, where about five thousand Delaware Indians and one thousand Swedes and Dutch already lived. After an agonizing voyage in which one-third of the passengers died, Penn arrived in 1682. Choosing a site for the capital, he named it Philadelphia—the "City of Brotherly Love." By 1687 some eight thousand settlers had joined Penn across the Atlantic. Most were Quakers from the British Isles, but they also included Presbyterians, Baptists, Anglicans, and Catholics, as well as Lutherans and radical sectarians from Germany—all attracted by Pennsylvania's religious toleration. Because most Quakers immigrated in family groups rather than as single males, a high birthrate resulted, and the population grew rapidly. In 1698 one Quaker reported that in Pennsylvania one seldom met "any young Married Woman but hath a Child in her belly, or one upon her lap."

After wavering between authoritarian and more democratic plans, Penn finally gave Pennsylvania a government with a strong executive branch (a governor and governor's council) and granted the lower legislative chamber (the assembly) only limited powers. Friends, forming the majority of the colony's population, dominated this elected assembly. Penn named Quakers and their supporters as governor, judges, and sheriffs. Hardly a democrat, he feared "the ambitions of the populace which shakes the Constitution," and he intended to check "the rabble" as much as possible. Because he also insisted on the orderly disposition of property and hoped to avoid unseemly wrangling, he carefully oversaw land sales in the colony. To prevent haphazard growth and social turmoil in Philadelphia, Penn designed the city with a grid plan, laying out the streets at right angles and reserving small areas for parks.

Good planning ensured that Pennsylvania suffered no initial starving time. The colony was also fortunate in experiencing no large-scale wars for seventy years. Partly this resulted from the reduced Native American population in the Delaware Valley. To the Indians, Penn

**William Penn's Map of Philadelphia,** *c. 1681*
*Central to William Penn's master plan for Philadelphia was the idea that each residence should stand in the middle of its plot, encircled by gardens and orchards. This pastel portrait is thought to be the most accurate likeness of Penn extant.*

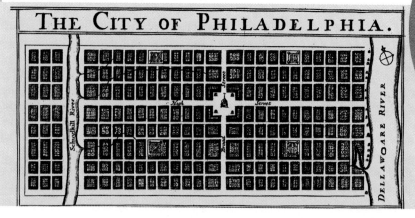

THE CITY OF PHILADELPHIA.

**Portrait of Penn,**
*by Francis Place*

expressed a wish "to live together as Neighbours and Friends," and he tried to buy land fairly from them.

Pennsylvania seemed an ideal colony—intelligently organized, well financed, tolerant, open to all industrious settlers, and largely at peace with the Indians. Rich, level lands and a lengthy growing season produced bumper crops. Sharp West Indian demand for its grain quickly generated widespread prosperity and by 1700 made Philadelphia a major port.

But like other attempts to base new American societies on preconceived plans or lofty ideals, Penn's "peaceable kingdom" soon bogged down in human bickering. In 1684 the founder returned to England and in his absence (until 1699) the settlers quarreled incessantly. An opposition party attacked Penn's efforts to monopolize foreign trade and to make each landowner pay him a small annual fee. Bitter struggles between Penn's supporters in the governor's council and opponents in the assembly deadlocked the government. From 1686 to 1688, the legislature passed no laws and the council once ordered the lower house's speaker arrested. Penn's brief return to Pennsylvania from 1699 to 1701 helped little, but just before he sailed home, he made the legislature a unicameral (one-chamber) assembly and allowed it to initiate measures.

In addition, religious conflict shook Pennsylvania during the 1690s, when George Keith, a college-educated Public Friend, urged Quakers to adopt a formal creed. This would have changed the democratically functioning Quaker sect—in which the humblest member had equal authority in interpreting the Inner Light—into a more traditional church dominated by an educated clergy. The majority of Quakers rejected Keith's views in 1692, whereupon he joined the Church of England, taking some Quakers with him. Keith's departure began a major decline in the Quaker share of Pennsylvania's population. The proportion fell further once Quakers ceased immigrating in large numbers after 1710.

William Penn met his strongest opposition in the counties on the lower Delaware River, where the best lands had been taken up by Swedes and Dutch. In 1704 these counties became the separate colony of Delaware, but Penn continued to name their governors.

The middle colonies soon demonstrated that British America could benefit by encouraging pluralism. New York and New Jersey successfully integrated New Netherland's Swedish and Dutch population; and Pennsylvania, New Jersey, and Delaware refused to require residents to pay support for any official church. Meanwhile, England's European rivals, France and Spain, were also extending their claims in North America.

# Rivals for North America

In marked contrast to England's compact settlements, France and Spain established far-flung inland networks of fortified trading posts and missions. To offset the English colonists' superiority in numbers, France and Spain enlisted Native Americans as trading partners and military allies, and the two Catholic nations had far more success than English Protestants in converting Indians to Christianity. By 1720 missionaries, fur traders, soldiers, and merchants—and relatively few farmers and ranchers—had spread French and Spanish influence through two-thirds of the present-day United States.

England's rivals exercised varying degrees of control in developing their American colonies. Louis XIV's France, the supreme power in late-seventeenth-century Europe, poured in state resources, whereas Spain, then in deep decay, made little attempt to influence North American affairs from afar. In both cases, local officials and settlers assumed the primary burden for extending imperial control.

## *France Claims a Continent*

France's King Louis XIV (reigned 1661–1715) sought to subordinate his American colony to French interests. His principal adviser, Jean-Baptiste Colbert, was a forceful proponent of the doctrine of *mercantilism* (see Chapter 4), according to which colonies should provide their home country with raw materials it lacked and with markets for its manufactured goods. In this way, the nation would not have to depend on rival countries for trade. Accordingly, Colbert and Louis hoped that New France could increase its output of furs, ship agricultural surpluses to France's new sugar-producing colonies in the West Indies, and export timber for those colonies and for the French navy. To begin realizing these goals, they revoked the charter of the private New France Company in 1663 and placed the colony under royal direction. They then sought to stifle the Iroquois threat to New France's economy and to encourage French immigration to Canada.

For more than half a century, and especially since the "beaver wars," the Iroquois had limited New France's productivity by intercepting convoys of beaver

## Taos Pueblo, New Mexico

Since 1675 Native American leaders from many New Mexico pueblos had gathered regularly at Taos to plan the overthrow of Spanish rule. Hostile to the Spanish from the time of their arrival, Taos had become the center of a wider movement after Popé, a religious leader of San Juan Pueblo, fled there to avoid persecution by the Spanish.

In August 1680 Popé and his cohorts were ready to act. On the morning of August 10, some Taos Indians and

### Diego de Vargas

*Leader of the Spanish reconquest of New Mexico.*

their Apache allies attacked the homes of the seventy Spanish colonists residing near Taos and killed all but two. Then, with Indians from neighboring pueblos, they proceeded south and joined a massive siege of New Mexico's capital, Santa Fe. Thus began the Pueblo Revolt of 1680, the most significant event in the history of the colonial Southwest.

Taos's leading role in the revolt is not surprising, for it had long been a meetingplace for Native Americans from near and far and a center of anti-Spanish resistance. Before the Spanish arrived, Taos was a major center of trade between the farming Pueblo Indians and the buffalo-hunting Apaches to the north and east. An early Spanish expedition reported some Apaches returning from Taos, "where they sell meat, hides, tallow, suet, and salt in exchange for cotton, blankets, pottery, maize, and some small green stones [turquoise]."

After establishing New Mexico in 1598, the Spanish collected corn as tribute from the pueblos. As a result, Pueblo Indians could no longer send their surplus crops to Taos and other trade centers for exchange with the Apaches. Having come to depend on corn, Apaches now raided pueblos for the grain. When Taos resisted colonial rule in 1602, Spanish troops waged a punitive raid on the pueblo. Four years later, Taos, two other trade centers, and several Apache bands urged the other pueblos to join them in overthrowing the Spanish. But most of the pueblos, fearing the Apaches, responded by strengthening their ties to the Spanish.

For the next seven decades, the Taos Indians struggled to retain their independence from the Spanish. On two occasions they destroyed Franciscan missions in their pueblo, only to watch as the churches were rebuilt under the protection of Spanish soldiers. The Taos also maintained their ties with the Apaches. In 1640 some Taos fled to live near friendly Apaches in Kansas, where they remained until Spanish troops forcibly returned them home in 1662. Meanwhile, the Spanish raided Taos and another pueblo where some Apaches lived, slaying all Apache men and enslaving Apache women and children.

For more than half a century, most of the other pueblos tried to accommodate Spanish rule and Catholicism. But during the 1660s they grew disillusioned. For several consecutive years their crops withered under the effects of sustained drought. Drought-induced starvation plus deadly epidemic diseases sent their population plummeting from about 80,000 in 1598 to just 17,000 in the 1670s. Riding horses stolen from the Spanish, Apaches inflicted more damage than ever in their raids. Reeling under the effects of these catastrophes, Christian Indians returned to traditional Pueblo beliefs and ceremonies in hopes of restoring the spiritual balance that had brought ample rainfall, good health, and peace before the Spanish arrived. Seeking to suppress Pueblo religion as "witchcraft" and "idolatry," missionaries entered sacred, underground kivas, destroyed religious objects, and publicly whipped native religious leaders and their followers.

Matters came to a head in 1675 when Governor Juan Francisco Treviño ordered soldiers to sack the kivas and to arrest the religious leaders. Three leaders were sent to the gallows, a

fourth hanged himself, and forty-three others—including Popé—were jailed, whipped, and sentenced to be sold as slaves. In response, armed warriors from several pueblos converged on Santa Fe and demanded the prisoners' release. With most of his soldiers off fighting the Apaches, Governor Treviño complied.

Despite this concession, there was now no cooling of Pueblo resentment against the Spanish. Besides Popé and his Taos host, El Saca, the leaders gathered at Taos included Luis Tupatú, Antonio Malacate, and others whose Christian names signified that earlier they had been baptized. Some were of mixed Pueblo-Spanish ancestry, and

one leader, Domingo Naranjo, combined Pueblo, Mexican Indian, and African ancestors. They and many of their followers had attempted to reconcile conversion to Christianity and subjection to Spanish rule with their identities as Indians. But the natives' deteriorating conditions and the cruel intolerance of the Spanish turned them against Catholicism. At each pueblo, rebels destroyed the churches and religious paraphernalia and killed those missionaries who did not escape. Then they "plunge[d] into the rivers and wash[ed] themselves with amole," a native root, in order to undo their baptisms. As a follower later testified, Popé also called on the Indians "to break and enlarge their cultivated fields, saying now they were as they had been in ancient times, free from the labor they had performed for the religious and the Spaniards." In rejecting Christianity and the Spanish, Pueblo Indians from throughout New Mexico did what many Taos had urged them to do for decades.

The siege of Santa Fe led to the expulsion of the Spanish from New Mexico for twelve years. By the time Diego de Vargas, leading the Spanish reconquest, reached Taos in September 1692, most pueblos had already resubmitted to Spanish rule. Suspicious as always of Spanish intentions, the Taos retreated to the mountains until Vargas consented to pardon them. Once returned to their community, ninety-six of them agreed to be baptized, and two leaders told Vargas of a new plot against him. Nevertheless, many Taos people continued to resent the Spanish, and in 1696 they joined Indians from several other villages in an abortive uprising. Thereafter suspicions of the Spanish lingered, but Taos did not again attempt to overthrow them. Like recently defeated Indians in New England and the Chesapeake, they sought thereafter to survive and to sustain their cultural identities within, rather than outside, the bounds of colonial rule.

**Taos Pueblo, North House Block, 1880**

**View of Quebec, 1699**
*New France's security was built on its rising commercial economy and its close ties to Canada's Indians.*

pelts from the interior. After assuming control of the colony, the royal government sent fifteen hundred soldiers to stop Iroquois interference with the French fur trade. In 1666 these troops sacked and burned four Mohawk villages well stocked with winter food. After the Iroquois Confederacy made a peace that lasted until 1680, New France enormously expanded its North American fur exports.

Meanwhile, the French crown energetically built up New France's population. Within a decade of the royal takeover, the number of colonists rose from 2,500 to 8,500. The vast majority were indentured servants who were paid wages and given land after three years' work. Others were former soldiers and their officers, who were encouraged to remain in New France and farm while strengthening the colony's defenses. The officers were encouraged to marry among the "king's girls," female orphans shipped over with dowries.

The upsurge in French immigration petered out after 1673. Tales of disease and other hazards of the transatlantic voyage, of Canada's hard winters, and of

wars with the "savage" Iroquois were spread by the two-thirds of French immigrants who returned to their native land over the next century. New France would grow slowly, relying on the natural increase of its small population rather than on newcomers from Europe.

Colbert had encouraged immigration in order to enhance New France's agricultural productivity. But many men who remained spurned farming in the St. Lawrence Valley, instead swarming westward in search of furs. By 1670 one-fifth of them were *coureurs de bois*—independent traders unconstrained by government authority or dubious pasts. Living and intermarrying with Indians, the *coureurs* built for France an empire based on alliances with Canadian and Great Lakes Indians from whom the French obtained furs in exchange for European goods, including guns to use against the Iroquois and other rivals.

Alarmed by the rapid expansion of England's colonies and by Spanish plans to link Florida with New Mexico, France boldly sought to dominate the North American heartland. As early as 1672, fur trader Louis Jolliet and Jesuit missionary Jacques Marquette became the first Europeans known to have reached the upper Mississippi River (near modern Prairie du Chien, Wisconsin); they later paddled twelve hundred miles downstream, to the Mississippi's junction with the Arkansas River. Ten years later, the Sieur de La Salle, an ambitious upper-class adventurer, descended the entire Mississippi to the Gulf of Mexico. When he reached the delta, La Salle formally claimed all the Mississippi basin—half the territory of the present-day continental United States—for Louis XIV, in whose honor he named the territory Louisiana.

Having asserted title to this vast empire, the French began settling the southern gateway into it. In 1698 the first colonizers arrived near the mouth of the Mississippi. A year later, the French erected a fort near present-day Biloxi, Mississippi. In 1702 they occupied what is now Mobile, Alabama, as a fur-trading station.

### The Spanish Borderlands

English and French expansion did not go unnoticed by the Spanish. They grew alarmed when La Salle temporarily occupied an outpost near modern-day Houston from 1685 to 1687. To defend their border holdings, Spanish authorities in Mexico proclaimed the province of Texas (Tejas) in 1691. But no permanent Spanish settlements appeared there until 1716 (see Chapter 4).

Spanish preoccupation with New Mexico was a primary reason for this neglect of Texas. By 1680 about 2,300 Europeans—many of them scattered on isolated *ranchos* (ranches)—and 17,000 Pueblo Indians lived in New Mexico's Rio Grande Valley, compared with 80,000 natives in 1598 when the Spanish arrived. That year a Pueblo religious leader named Popé led a revolt, culminating nearly a century of grievances and sparked by Spanish efforts to outlaw the rituals central to the Pueblo peoples' way of life (see A Place in Time). The Indians killed 400 colonists (including most priests), captured Santa Fe, and drove the survivors south to El Paso. The Pueblo peoples held New Mexico until 1692, and their resistance continued to threaten Spanish rule until the end of the century.

In Florida, an even older colony than New Mexico, the Spanish fared no better. Before 1680 the colony faced periodic rebellions from Guale, Timucua, and Apalachee Indians protesting forced labor and the religious discipline imposed by Franciscan missionaries. Beginning in the 1680s, Creek and other slave raiders allied to Carolina added to the effects of recurrent diseases in reducing the number of Indians in Florida. When a new round of warfare erupted in Europe at the end of the decade, Spain was ill prepared to defend its beleaguered North American colonies.

## CONCLUSION

In less than a century, from 1630 to 1700, the far-flung dispersals of European, African, and Native American peoples transformed the map of North America. The kin of Sarah Horbin, Mary Johnson, and others had spread far and wide among colonial regions in the Americas. Native Americans in communities like Taos either reconciled themselves to one or another form of coexistence with European colonizers or left their homelands in order to avoid contact with the intruders. Among the colonizing powers, England was by far the most successful. By 1700 the population of its North American colonies was about 250,000, compared with 15,000 for the French holdings and 4,500 for the Spanish.

Within the English colonies, what had begun as four distinct regions was becoming only two. After beginning with a labor force consisting primarily of white indentured servants, the tobacco planters of the Chesapeake followed their counterparts in the West Indies

and Carolina by turning to enslaved Africans. In the process, the Chesapeake and Carolina came to constitute a single, southern region dominated by planter-slaveowners and containing the vast majority of North America's slaves. To the north, New England's Puritanism had grown less utopian and more worldly as the inhabitants gradually reconciled their religious views with the realities of a commercial economy. In between New England and the South, the middle colonies, with their ethnic and religious pluralism, embraced the market economy with less hesitation. Despite continued differences between them, New England and the middle colonies were merging into a single, northern region oriented toward commerce and dominated by merchants. Yet while planters and merchants rose to prominence, most whites in both south and north continued to live on family farms. During the first half of the eighteenth century, these rapidly expanding colonial regions would be effectively integrated into the first empire in history rooted in commercial capitalism.

## FOR FURTHER READING

Paul Boyer and Stephen Nissenbaum, *Salem Possessed: The Social Origins of Witchcraft* (1974). A study of the witchcraft episode as the expression of social conflict in one New England community.

William Cronon, *Changes in the Land: Indians, Colonists, and the Ecology of New England* (1983). A pioneering study of the interactions of Native Americans and European settlers with the New England environment.

W. J. Eccles, *France in America*, rev. ed. (1991). An interpretive overview of French colonization in North America and the Caribbean by a distinguished scholar.

Jack P. Greene, *Pursuits of Happiness: The Social Development of Early Modern British Colonies and the Formation of American Culture* (1988). A brilliant synthesis of the colonial history of British America.

Edmund S. Morgan, *American Slavery, American Freedom: The Ordeal of Colonial Virginia* (1975). A penetrating analysis of the origins of southern slavery and race relations.

Mary Beth Norton, *Founding Mothers and Fathers: Gendered Power and the Forming of American Society* (1996). A major study of female and male power in the seventeenth-century colonies.

David J. Weber, *The Spanish Frontier in North America* (1992). A masterful synthesis of Spanish colonial history north of the Caribbean and Mexico.

Betty Wood, *The Origins of American Slavery: Freedom and Bondage in the English Colonies* (1997). A concise discussion of the rise of slavery and racism, and the varying forms they took in the seventeenth-century colonies.

# The Bonds of Empire

## 1660–1750

**Mrs. Harme Gansevoort (Magdalena Bouw)** by Pieter Vanderlyn, c. 1740

Alexander Garden was furious with the young Anglican minister George Whitefield (page 82). Just over from England, Whitefield was asserting publicly that Garden's ministers were unsaved and endangering their parishioners' souls. Garden, as the bishop of London's commissary (representative) in Charles Town, South Carolina, was responsible for the Church of England's well-being in the southern British colonies. Resenting this challenge to his authority, Garden summoned Whitefield and demanded a retraction. But he got more than he bargained for. Whitefield claimed that Garden "was as ignorant as the rest" of the local clergy because he failed to teach the central Calvinist doctrine of salvation by predestination (see Chapter 2). And Whitefield threatened to widen his attacks if Garden refused to condemn dancing and other "sinful" entertainments. Garden shot back that Whitefield would be suspended if he preached in any church in the province—to which Whitefield retorted that he would treat such an action as he would an order from the pope. The meeting ended with Garden shouting, "Get out of my house!"

Garden got Whitefield out of his house but not out of his hair. The two men carried their dispute to the public. Garden accused Whitefield of jeopardizing the stability of colonial society. Whitefield charged the Anglican clergy with abandoning piety in favor of the cold heresy of reason. An extraordinary orator, Whitefield stirred his listeners' passions, calling forth an "enthusiasm" for religion that undermined traditional order and deference. He inspired members of congregations to think themselves as good as, if not superior to, their ministers; wives, to question their husbands' piety; children, to claim divine grace that their parents did not feel; and common people, including slaves and subjugated Indians, to insist that they were the equal of anyone else.

That was Whitefield's greatest crime—to be heard throughout America. He became the first intercolonial celebrity in North America, traveling thousands of miles to spread his critique of the established religious order. Everywhere he went, the people poured out by the thousands to listen and feel, to sense individually the overwhelming power of a direct connection with God.

Whitefield represented one of two European cultural currents that crossed the Atlantic during the middle decades of the eighteenth century. Indeed the preacher was the greatest English-speaking prophet of a powerful revival of religious piety sweeping the Protestant world. The second current was the Enlightenment—the dissemination among the educated public of faith in reason rooted in an appreciation of natural science—which found its foremost American exponent in Benjamin Franklin. Franklin's emphasis on reason might seem at odds with Whitefield's conscious efforts to tap his audience's deepest emotions. But both men repudiated the relatively self-contained hierarchical communities of the past in favor of a more dynamic society that was intercolonial and transatlantic in its orientation.

Sweeping through British North America in the 1740s, Whitefield encountered a vibrant society, a rapidly growing economy, and the beginnings of a richly diverse culture. By 1750 the colonies could claim the world's largest concentration of overseas Europeans; besides those with English backgrounds, significant numbers descended from Welsh, German, Irish, Scottish, Dutch, and French settlers. North America was also the enforced home of a burgeoning African population, by now slowly becoming both English-speaking and Christian. And everywhere the pace of colonial expansion was blurring once-distinct boundaries separating Native Americans from colonists.

**George Whitefield**
*By the mid-eighteenth century, the Protestant revivalist from England was the most prominent figure in the British colonies.*

The peace and prosperity that characterized mid-eighteenth-century British North America would have astonished seventeenth-century colonists, clinging to their uncertain footholds on the edge of the wilderness. But even though by 1740 life was becoming reasonably stable and secure, especially for upper-class Anglo-Americans, the Great Awakening let loose spiritual and social tremors that jolted colonial self-confidence. Alexander Garden's nervousness was hardly unreasonable.

This chapter will focus on four major questions:

♦ Why were France and Spain unable to match Britain's imperial success in mainland North America during the first half of the eighteenth century?

♦ What were the advantages and disadvantages of British mercantilism for the mainland colonies?

♦ In what ways was the racial and ethnic composition of North America transformed during the first half of the eighteenth century? What were the principal causes of these changes?

♦ What were the most fundamental differences between the Enlightenment and the Great Awakening? What, if anything, did the two movements have in common?

# Rebellion and War

Although the English had established colonies as early as 1607, with the founding of Jamestown, Virginia, England made no serious effort to weld its colonies into a coherent empire until King Charles II (ruled 1660–1685) assumed the throne. Charles's ascension, marking the "restoration" of the Stuart monarchy in England, ended two decades of civil war and experimentation with republican rule. Almost immediately, English authorities undertook a concerted policy that sought to expand the nation's overseas trade at the ex-

pense of its rivals and to subordinate its colonies to English commercial interests and political authority. Efforts to tighten royal control over the colonies ended in 1689 after the "Glorious Revolution" in England forced King James II into exile.

## *Royal Centralization*

As the sons of a king (Charles I) executed by Parliament, the last two Stuart monarchs disliked representative government. Charles II called Parliament into session rarely after 1674, and not at all from 1681 until his death in 1685. James II (ruled 1685–1688) hoped to reign as an "absolute" monarch like France's Louis XIV, who never had to face a national parliament. Not surprisingly, neither English king had much sympathy for the American colonial assemblies.

**The Restoration Colonies**
*England's Restoration colonies were carved out of the claims or earlier colonial territories of rival European powers. Spain claimed the territory chartered as Carolina in 1663. Out of England's takeover of Dutch New Netherland in 1664 came the colonies of New York, New Jersey, West Jersey, Pennsylvania, and Delaware.*

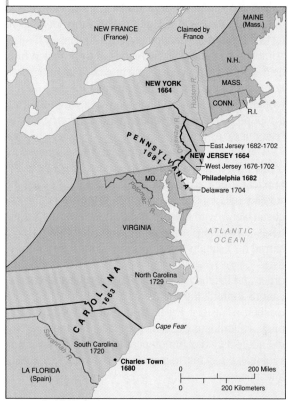

## CHRONOLOGY

**1651–1733** Parliament enacts the Navigation Acts to regulate British imperial commerce.

**1660** Restoration of the Stuart dynasty to English throne.

**1685** Duke of York becomes King James II of England.

**1686–1689** Dominion of New England.

**1688** Glorious Revolution in England; James II deposed.

**1689** William and Mary ascend to English throne.

Protestant Association seizes power in Maryland.

Leisler's Rebellion in New York.

**1689–1697** King William's War (in Europe, War of the League of Augsburg).

**1690** John Locke, *Essay Concerning Human Understanding.*

**1698** French begin settlements near the mouth of the Mississippi River.

**1701** Iroquois adopt neutrality policy toward European powers.

**1702–1713** Queen Anne's War (in Europe, War of the Spanish Succession).

**1716** San Antonio de Béxar founded.

**1718** New Orleans founded.

**1729–1730** French war on Natchez Indians in Louisiana.

**1732** Georgia colony chartered.

Benjamin Franklin begins publishing *Poor Richard's Almanack.*

**1735** Jonathan Edwards leads revival in Northampton, Massachusetts.

**1737** Walking Purchase of Delaware Indians in Pennsylvania.

**1739** Great Awakening begins with George Whitefield's arrival in British colonies.

Stono Rebellion in South Carolina.

**1739–1744** Anglo-Spanish War.

**1743** Benjamin Franklin founds American Philosophical Society.

**1750** Slavery legalized in Georgia.

---

Royal intentions of extending direct political control to North America first became evident in New York. The proprietor, Charles II's brother James, the Duke of York, considered elected assemblies "of dangerous consequence" and until 1682 forbade them to meet. He relented from 1682 to 1686 but thereafter called none. Meanwhile, Charles appointed former army officers to about 90 percent of all gubernatorial positions, thereby compromising the time-honored English tradition of holding the military strictly accountable to civilian authority. By 1680 such "governors general" ruled 60 percent of all American colonists. James II later continued this policy.

Ever resentful of outside meddling, New Englanders proved most stubborn in defending self-government and resisting Stuart policies. As early as 1661, the Massachusetts assembly politely but firmly declared its citizens exempt from all laws and royal decrees from England except for a declaration of war. The colony ignored the Navigation Acts and continued welcoming Dutch traders. Charles II responded by targeting Massachusetts for special punishment. In 1679 he carved out of its territory a new royal colony, New Hampshire. Then in 1684 he declared Massachusetts itself a royal colony and revoked its charter, the very foundation of the Puritan city upon a hill. Puritan minister Increase Mather repudiated the King's actions, calling on colonists to resist even to the point of martyrdom.

Royal centralization in America culminated after James II ascended to the throne. In 1686 the new king consolidated Massachusetts, New Hampshire, Connecticut, Rhode Island, and Plymouth into a single administrative unit, the Dominion of New England. He added New York and the Jerseys in 1688. With this bold stroke, all legislatures in these colonies ceased to exist, and still another former army officer, Sir Edmund Andros, became the governor of the Dominion of New England, at Boston.

Massachusetts burned with hatred for the new governor. By "Exercise of an arbitrary Government," preached Salem's minister, "ye wicked walked on Every Side & ye Vilest of men ware [sic] exalted." Andros was indeed arbitrary. He suppressed the legislature, limited towns to a single annual meeting, and strictly enforced toleration of Anglicans and the Navigation Acts. "You have no more privileges left you," Andros reportedly told a group of outraged colonists, "than not to be sold for slaves." Other than his soldiers and a handful of recently arrived Anglican immigrants, however, Andros had no base of support in Massachusetts.

Tensions also ran high in New York, where Catholics held high political and military posts under the Duke of York's rule. By 1688 citizens feared that these Catholic officials would betray the colony to France. When Andros's local deputy, Captain Francis Nicholson, allowed the harbor's forts to deteriorate and reacted skeptically to rumors of Indian hostility, New Yorkers suspected the worst.

## The Glorious Revolution in England and America

New England Puritans' fury at Andros's forcing them to tolerate Anglicanism was matched by English Protestants' growing worries about the Stuarts' predilection for Catholicism. The Duke of York became a Catholic in 1676, and Charles II converted on his deathbed. Both rulers violated Parliament's laws by issuing decrees that allowed Catholics to hold high office and worship openly. English Protestants' fears that they would have to accept Catholicism intensified after both kings expressed their preference for allying with France just as Louis XIV was launching new persecutions of that country's Protestant Huguenots in 1685.

The English tolerated James II's Catholicism only because his heirs, his daughters Mary and Anne, had re-

**King William and Queen Mary**
*This plate, made in England in about 1700, depicts the monarchs who assumed the throne after the Glorious Revolution.*

mained Anglican. Then in 1688 James's wife bore a son, who would be raised—and might someday reign—as a Catholic. Aghast at the thought of a Catholic successor to the monarchy, some English politicians asked Mary and her husband, William of Orange (head of the Dutch Republic) to intervene. When William and Mary led a small army to England in November 1688, most royal troops defected to them, and James II fled to France.

This bloodless revolution of 1688, also called the Glorious Revolution, created a "limited monarchy" as defined by England's Bill of Rights of 1689. The crown promised to summon Parliament annually, sign all its bills, and respect traditional civil liberties. The Glorious Revolution's vindication of limited representative government burned deeply into the English political consciousness, and Anglo-Americans never forgot it. Colonists struck their own blows for liberty when Massachusetts, New York, and Maryland all rose up against local representatives of the Stuart regime.

News that England's Protestant leaders had rebelled against James II electrified New Englanders. On April 18, 1689, well before confirmation of the English revolt's success, Boston's militia arrested Andros and his councilors. (The governor tried to flee in women's clothing but was caught after an alert guard spotted a "lady" in army boots.) Massachusetts' political leaders acted in the name of William and Mary, risking their necks should James return to power in England.

William and Mary gave official consent to dismantling the Dominion of New England and restored to the citizens of Connecticut and Rhode Island the right of electing their own governors. However, they acted to reduce Massachusetts' power and influence. While allowing the province to absorb Plymouth and Maine, they refused to let it regain New Hampshire. More seriously, the new royal charter of 1691 reserved to the crown the right of appointing the governor. In addition, property ownership, not church membership, became the criterion for voting. Finally, the Puritan colony had to tolerate Anglicans, who were proliferating in the port towns. In a society trembling at divine displeasure over its ungodliness (see Chapter 3), this was indeed bitter medicine to swallow.

New York's counterpart of the anti-Stuart uprising was Leisler's Rebellion. Emboldened by news of Boston's coup, the city's militia—consisting mainly of Dutch and other non-English artisans and shopkeepers—seized the harbor's main fort on May 31, 1689. Captain Jacob Leisler of the militia took over command of the colony, repaired its rundown defenses, and called elections for an assembly. When English troops arrived at New York in 1691, Leisler denied them entry to key forts for fear that their commander was loyal to James II. A skirmish resulted, and Leisler was arrested.

"Hott brain'd" Leisler unwittingly had set his own downfall in motion. He had jailed many elite New Yorkers for questioning his authority, only to find that his former enemies had gained the new governor's ear and persuaded him to charge Leisler with treason for firing on royal troops. In the face of popular outrage, a packed jury found Leisler and his son-in-law, Jacob Milborne, guilty. Both men went to the gallows insisting that they were dying "for the king and queen and the Protestant religion."

News of England's Glorious Revolution heartened Maryland's Protestant majority, which had long chafed under Catholic rule. Hoping to prevent a repetition of religion-tinged uprisings that had flared in 1676 and 1681, Lord Baltimore sent a messenger from England in early 1689 to command Maryland's obedience to William and Mary. But the courier died en route, leaving the colony's unknowing Protestants in fear that their Catholic proprietor was a traitor who supported James II.

Soon John Coode and three others organized the Protestant Association to secure Maryland for William and Mary. These conspirators seem to have been motivated far more by their exclusion from high public office than by religious zeal, for three of the four had Catholic wives. Coode's group seized the capital in July 1689, removed all Catholics from office, and requested that the crown take over the colony. They got their wish. Maryland became a royal province in 1691, and in 1692 it made the Church of England the established religion. Catholics, who composed less than one-fourth of the population, lost the right to vote and thereafter could worship only in private. Maryland stayed in royal hands until 1715, when the fourth Lord Baltimore joined the Church of England and regained his proprietorship.

The revolutionary events of 1688–1689 decisively changed the colonies' political climate by reestablishing legislative government and ensuring religious freedom for Protestants. Dismantling the Dominion of New England and directing governors to call annual assemblies, William and Mary allowed colonial elites to reassert control over local affairs and encouraged American political leaders to identify their interests with England. A foundation was thus laid for an empire based on voluntary allegiance rather than submission to raw power imposed from faraway London. The crowning of William and Mary opened a new era in which Americans drew rising confidence from their relationship to the English throne. "As long as they reign," wrote a Bostonian who helped topple Andros, "New England is secure."

## A Generation of War

The bloodless Revolution of 1688 ironically ushered in a quarter-century of warfare that convulsed both Europe and the colonies. In 1689 England joined a general European coalition against France's Louis XIV, who supported James II's claim to the English crown. The resulting War of the League of Augsburg (which Anglo-Americans called King William's War) was the first struggle to embroil the colonies in European rivalries.

With the outbreak of King William's War, New Yorkers and Yankees launched a two-pronged invasion of New France in 1690, with one prong aimed at Montreal and the second at Quebec. After both invasions failed, the war took the form of cruel but inconclusive border raids against civilians, carried out by both English and French troops and their Indian allies.

Already weary from a new wave of wars with pro-French Indians in the Ohio Valley, the Five Nations of the Iroquois bore the bloodiest fighting in King William's War. Standing almost alone against their foes, the Five Nations faced overwhelming odds. Not only did their English allies meet with little success intercepting enemy war parties, but the French had enlisted virtually all other Indians from Maine to the Great Lakes as combatants. In 1691 every Mohawk and Oneida war chief died in battle; by 1696 French armies had destroyed the villages of every Iroquois nation but the Cayugas and Oneidas.

Although the Anglo-French war ended in 1697, the Iroquois staggered under Algonquian invasions until 1700. By then one-quarter of the Five Nations' 2,000 warriors had been killed or taken prisoner, or had fled to Canada. The total Iroquois population declined 20 percent over twelve years, from 8,600 to 7,000. (By comparison, about 1,300 English, Dutch, and French died during the same period.)

By 1700 Iroquois society was divided into three factions—pro-English, pro-French, and neutralists. Under the impact of war, the neutralists succeeded in defining a new direction for Iroquois diplomacy. In the "Grand

Settlement" of 1701, the Five Nations of the Iroquois made peace with France and its Indian allies in exchange for access to western furs while redefining their British alliance to exclude military cooperation. Skillful negotiations brought the exhausted Iroquois far more success than had war by allowing them to keep control of their lands, rebuild their decimated population, and gain recognition as keys to the balance of power in the Northeast.

In 1702 European war again erupted when England fought France and Spain in the War of the Spanish Succession, called Queen Anne's War by England's American colonists. This conflict reinforced Anglo-Americans' awareness of their military weakness. French and Indian raiders from Canada destroyed several towns in Massachusetts and Maine. The Spanish invaded southern Carolina and nearly took Charles Town in 1706. Enemy warships captured many colonial vessels and landed looting parties along the Atlantic coast. Meanwhile, colonial sieges of Quebec and St. Augustine ended as expensive failures.

English forces had more success than those of the colonies, seizing the Hudson Bay region, as well as Newfoundland and Acadia (henceforth called Nova Scotia). Although Great Britain kept these gains in the peace of 1713, the French and Indian hold on the continent's interior remained unbroken.

The most important consequence of the colonial wars for Anglo-Americans was political, not military. The wars instilled in them a profound sense of dependence on the newly formed United Kingdom of Great Britain (created by the formal union of England and Scotland in 1707). The clashes with France vividly reminded the colonists of the loyalty they owed William and Mary for ousting James II, who many believed would have persecuted Protestants and ruled despotically. Anglo-Americans also came to recognize their own military weakness and the extent to which their shipping needed the Royal Navy's protection. Even as a new generation of English colonists matured, war was thus reinforcing their sense of British identity by buttressing their loyalty to the crown.

# Colonial Economies and Societies

The achievement of peace in 1713 enabled the European powers to concentrate on competing economically rather than militarily. For the next three decades the two principal powers, Britain and France, sought to enhance their advantages over each other by integrating their American colonies into single imperial economies. Spain pursued a similar course but was hampered by small wars with both its rivals and by a structurally weakened economy.

## *Mercantilist Empires in America*

The policies followed by Britain, France, and Spain were all rooted in a set of political-economic assumptions known as *mercantilism.* Mercantilism was not a carefully elaborated economic theory. Rather, the word refers to a set of policies aimed at guaranteeing prosperity by making a nation as self-sufficient as possible—by eliminating dependence on foreign suppliers, damaging foreign competitors' commercial interests, and increasing its nation's net stock of gold and silver by selling more abroad than buying. Mercantilist policies generally had the additional effect of favoring special interests such as chartered companies and merchants' guilds. Mercantilism would not be effectively challenged until Adam Smith's *The Wealth of Nations,* published in 1776, argued for a competitive free-market system.

Britain's mercantilist policies were articulated above all in a series of "Navigation Acts" governing commerce between Britain and its overseas colonies. Parliament enacted the first Navigation Act in 1651 to undercut the Dutch Republic's economic preponderance. After the Stuart restoration, Parliament enacted the Navigation Acts of 1660 and 1663, barring colonial merchants from exporting such commodities as sugar and tobacco anywhere except to England, and from importing goods in non-English ships. An act of 1672 provided administrative machinery to enforce these rules. Finally, the Molasses Act of 1733 taxed all foreign molasses (a liquid drained from sugar plants and used to distill rum) from entering the mainland colonies at sixpence per gallon. This act was intended less to raise revenue than to serve as a protective tariff that would benefit British West Indian sugar producers at the expense of their French rivals. By 1750 a long series of Navigation Acts were in force, affecting the colonial economy in four major ways.

First, the laws limited all imperial trade to *British* ships, defined as those with British ownership and whose crews were three-quarters British. For purposes of this legislation, Parliament classified all colonists, including slaves, as British. This restriction not only contributed to Great Britain's rise as Europe's foremost shipping nation but also laid the foundations for an American shipbuilding industry and merchant marine. By the 1750s one-third of all imperial vessels were American-owned, mostly by merchants in New England and the middle colonies. The swift growth of this merchant marine diversified the northern colonial economy and made it more self-sufficient. The expansion of colonial shipping in turn hastened urbanization by creating a need for centralized docks, warehouses, and repair shops in the colonies. By 1770 Philadelphia and New York City had emerged as two of the British Empire's busiest ports.

The second major way in which the Navigation Acts affected the colonies lay in their barring the export of certain "enumerated goods" to foreign nations unless these items first passed through England or Scotland. The mainland's chief "controlled" items were tobacco, rice, furs, indigo (a Carolina plant that produced a blue dye), and naval stores (masts, hemp, tar, and turpentine). Parliament never restricted grain, livestock, fish, lumber, or rum, which altogether made up 60 percent of colonial exports. Furthermore, Anglo-American exporters of tobacco and rice—the chief commodities affected by enumeration—had their burdens reduced by two significant concessions. First, Parliament gave tobacco growers a monopoly over the British market by excluding foreign tobacco, even though this hurt British consumers. (Rice planters enjoyed a natural monopoly because they had no competitors.) Second, Parliament tried to minimize the added cost of landing tobacco and rice in Britain (where customs officials collected duties on both) by refunding these duties on all tobacco and rice that the colonists later shipped to other countries. About 85 percent of all American tobacco and rice was eventually reexported and sold outside the British Empire.

The navigation system's third impact on the colonies was to encourage economic diversification. Parliament used British tax money to pay modest bounties to Americans producing such items as silk, iron, dyes, hemp, and lumber, which Britain would otherwise have had to import from other countries, and it raised the price of commercial rivals' imports by imposing protective tariffs on them. The trade laws did prohibit Anglo-Americans from competing with *large-scale* British manufacturing of certain products, most notably clothing. However, colonial tailors, hatters, and housewives could continue to make any item of dress in their households or small shops. Manufactured by low-paid labor, British clothing imports generally undersold whatever the colonists could have produced given their higher labor costs. The colonists were also free to produce iron, and by 1770 they had built 250 ironworks employing thirty thousand men, a work force larger than the entire population of Georgia or of any provincial city.

Finally, the Navigation Acts made the colonies a protected market for low-priced consumer goods and other exports from Britain. Steady overseas demand for colonial products spawned a prosperity that enabled white colonists to consume ever larger amounts not only of clothing but of dishware, home furnishings, tea, and a range of other items both produced in Britain and imported by British and colonial merchants from elsewhere. Consequently, the share of British exports sold to the colonies spurted from just 5 percent in 1700 to almost 40 percent by 1760. Cheap imported goods enabled many colonists to adopt a lifestyle similar to that of middle-class Britons. "You may depend upon it," remarked Pennsylvanian William Allen, "this is one of the best poor man's countries in the world."

**Philadelphia**
*Founded just four decades earlier, Philadelphia was already one of British America's largest and wealthiest cities.*

Although some colonists complained about the navigation system in the late seventeenth century, few did so between 1700 and 1760. The trade regulation primarily burdened tobacco and rice exporters, whose income nevertheless was reduced by less than 3 percent. The commercial laws did increase the cost of non-British merchandise imported into the colonies, but seldom by enough to encourage smuggling (except in the case of tea from India and molasses from the French Caribbean).

Although Parliament intended the laws to benefit only Britain, the colonies also benefited. British North America's economy grew at a per capita rate of 0.6 percent annually from 1650 to 1770, a pace twice that of Great Britain.

The economic development of the French and Spanish colonies paled beside that of British North America. Although France's Jean-Baptiste Colbert (see Chapter 3) was the most forceful proponent of mercantilism, he and his successors had great difficulty implementing mercantilist policies. New France gradually developed agricultural self-sufficiency and, in good years, exported some of its wheat to France's West Indian colonies. It also exported small amounts of fish and timber to the Caribbean and to France. The colony's chief imports were wine and brandy, its chief export, furs. Although furs were no longer very profitable by the eighteenth century, the French government maintained and even expanded the fur trade because it would need Native American military support in another war with England. The government actually lost money by sending large amounts of cloth, firearms, and other manufactured commodities to Indian allies in exchange for furs. Moreover, France maintained a sizable army in its Canadian colony that, like the trade with Indians, was a drain on the royal treasury. Meanwhile, Canada attracted little private investment either from France or from within the colony. French Canadians enjoyed a standard of living comparable with that of English colonists but lacked the private investment, the extensive commercial infrastructure, the vast consumer market, and the manufacturing capacity of the British colonies.

France's greatest economic success in the Americas was in the West Indies where French planters emulated the English by importing large numbers of slaves to produce sugar under appalling conditions. Ironically this success was partly a result of French planters' defying mercantilist policies. In St. Domingue, Martinique, and Guadeloupe, many planters built their own sugar refineries and made molasses instead of shipping their raw sugar to refineries in France, as mercantilism prescribed. They then sold much of their molasses to merchants from Britain's mainland colonies, especially Massachusetts. France attempted to duplicate its Caribbean success in Louisiana but quickly found that, as in Canada, dependence on Native Americans and other factors rendered the colony economically unprofitable.

Spain was even weaker economically than France. The monarchy's early success in extracting bullion (gold and silver) from the Americas set off a general surge in prices that undermined Spain's already weak manufacturing sector. Spaniards at home and in the Americas sought to obtain cheaper goods from other countries but were hampered by mercantilist quotas, duties, and other regulations that rendered imports scarce or expensive. In response many Spanish colonists turned to smuggling goods to and from Spain's supposed enemies. On the frontier between Texas and Louisiana, Spanish traders offered Louisianans horses in exchange for French goods. Spaniards in Florida interacted with English, French, and the Indian allies of both—even for commodities as basic as food. Without the flourishing of contraband trade, Spain's colonies in North America might not have survived.

At bottom, the difference between England's colonies and those of France and Spain reflected a fundamental difference in their respective economies and societies. While all three nations were governed according to mercantilist principles, France and Spain remained societies in which most wealth was controlled by the monarchy, the nobility, and the Catholic Church. Most private wealth was inherited and took the form of land rather than liquid assets. England, on the other hand, had made the transition to a mercantile-commercial economy in which much of the nation's wealth was in the form of capital held by merchants who reinvested it in commercial and shipping enterprises. For its part the British government used much of its considerable income from duties, tariffs, and other taxes to enhance commerce. For example, the government strengthened Britain's powerful navy to protect the empire's trade and created the Bank of England in 1694 to ensure a stable money supply and lay the foundation for a network of lending institutions. By the mid-eighteenth century, investments in British enterprises were moving the country from a strictly commercial economy to the world's first industrial one.

## A Burgeoning, Diversifying Population

Britain's economic advantage over its rivals was reinforced by the demographic disparities between its colonies and those of France and Spain. In 1700 approximately 250,000 non-Indians resided in English America whereas French colonists numbered only 15,000 and the Spanish just 4,500. During the first half of the eighteenth century, all three colonial populations at least quadrupled in size—the British to 1,170,000, the French to 60,000, and the Spanish to 19,000. With the passage of time, Britain's advantage only magnified.

Immigrants from Spain could choose among that nation's many Latin American colonies, most of which offered more opportunities than poorly developed Florida, Texas, and New Mexico. Most potential French immigrants were trapped at home by poverty. Those who could seek opportunities elsewhere were deterred by reports of the harsh Canadian winter and of Louisiana's poor economy. With few exceptions, neither France nor Spain attempted to attract colonists from outside their own empires, and both limited non-slave immigration to Roman Catholics, a restriction that diverted many French Huguenot emigrants to the English colonies instead. The English colonies, on the other hand, boasted good farmlands, a healthy economy, and a willingness to absorb members of all European nationalities and of most Protestant denominations. (Although anti-Catholicism remained strong, small Jewish communities formed in several colonial cities.)

Spain regarded its colonies north of Mexico and the Caribbean less as centers of population than as buffers against French and English penetration of their more valued colonies to the south. While hoping to lure civilian settlers, the Spanish relied heavily on soldiers stationed in *presidios* (forts) for defense plus missionaries who would, they hoped, settle loyal Native Americans at strategically placed missions. Most immigrants to the colonies came not from Spain itself but from Mexico and other Spanish colonies in Latin America and, in the case of Texas, the Canary Islands (a Spanish colony off the West African coast).

Although boasting a larger population than the Spanish colonies, New France and Louisiana experienced similar limitations. Here too the military played a strong role while missionaries and traders worked to enhance the colony's relations with Native Americans. Canada's population growth in the eighteenth century was largely a result of natural increase rather than of immigration. Some members of Canada's burgeoning rural population established new settlements along the Mississippi River in upper Louisiana, now part of Illinois and Missouri. But on the lower Mississippi, Louisiana acquired a foul reputation, and too few French immigrated there willingly. To boost its population, the government sent paupers and criminals, recruited some German refugees, and encouraged large-scale slave imports. By 1732 two-thirds of lower Louisiana's 5,800 people were slaves.

The British colonies outpaced the population growth of not only their French and Spanish rivals but Britain itself. White women in the colonies had an average of eight children and forty-two grandchildren; British women at the same time typically bore five children and had fifteen grandchildren. The ratio of England's population to that of the mainland colonies plummeted from 20 to 1 (1700) to 3 to 1 (1775).

In the eighteenth century, immigration continued to contribute significantly to colonial population growth, although it became less important than natural increase. In the forty years after Queen Anne's War, the colonies absorbed 350,000 newcomers, 40 percent of them (140,000) African-born slaves who had survived a sea crossing of sickening brutality. All but a few enslaved immigrants originated along the west coast of Africa between Senegambia and Angola. Whereas most planters made few distinctions as to Africans' backgrounds, many in South Carolina expressly sought slaves from Gambia and nearby regions for their rice-growing experience.

Conditions aboard slave ships were appalling by any standard. Olaudah Equiano was an enslaved Ibo from the area that today is Nigeria. Equiano, who eventually became free, Christian, and an abolitionist, recalled being put aboard a Barbados-bound ship in 1756:

> I was soon put down under the decks, and there I received such salutation in my nostrils as I had never experienced in my life; so that, with the loathsomeness of the stench, and crying together, I became so sick and low that I was not able to eat, nor had I the least desire to taste any thing. . . . On my refusing to eat, one of them [white men] held me fast by the hands, and laid me across I think the windlass while the other flogged me severely. . . . Could I have got over the nettings, I would have jumped over the side, but I could not.

From 1713 to 1754, five times as many slaves poured onto mainland North America as in all the preceding years. The proportion of blacks in the colonies dou-

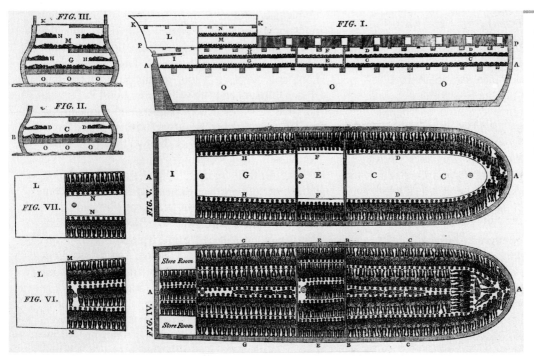

**Architect's Plan of a Slave Ship**

*This plan graphically depicts the crowded, unsanitary conditions under which enslaved Africans were packed like cargo and transported across the Atlantic.*

bled, rising from 11 percent at the beginning of the century to 20 percent by midcentury. Slavery was primarily a southern institution, but 15 percent of its victims lived north of Maryland, mostly in New York and New Jersey. By 1750 every seventh New Yorker was a slave.

Because West Indian and Brazilian slave buyers outbid the mainland colonists, a mere 5 percent of transported Africans were ever sold within the present-day United States. Unable to buy as many male field hands as they needed, mainland masters had no choice but to accept numerous female workers, and they protected their investments by maintaining the slaves' health. These factors promoted family formation and increased life expectancy far beyond the levels in the Caribbean, where family life was unstable and high death rates resulted from overwork and disease (see Chapter 3). On the mainland by 1750, the rate of natural increase for blacks almost equaled that for whites, and in some areas American-born slaves outnumbered those born in Africa.

The approximately 210,000 whites who immigrated during these years included a sharply reduced share from England compared to the seventeenth century. Whereas between 1630 and 1700 an average of 2,000 English settlers landed annually (constituting 90

percent of all European immigrants), after 1713 the English contribution dropped to about 500 a year. Rising employment and higher wages in eighteenth-century England simply made voluntary immigration to America far less attractive than before. But economic hardship elsewhere in the British Isles and northern Europe supplied a steady stream of immigrants, and their coming ensured that white North Americans were growing more ethnically diverse.

The largest European contingent comprised 100,000 newcomers from Ireland, two-thirds of them "Scots-Irish" descendants of sixteenth-century Scottish Presbyterians who had settled in northern Ireland. After 1718 Scots-Irish fled to America to escape rack renting (frequent increases in farm rents), and they commonly came as complete families. In contrast, 90 percent of all Catholic Irish immigrants arrived as unmarried male indentured servants. Rarely able to find Catholic wives, they generally abandoned their faith to marry Protestant women.

Meanwhile, from Germany came a wave of 65,000 settlers, most of them refugees from terrible economic conditions in the Rhine Valley. Wartime devastation had compounded the misery of Rhenish peasants, many of whom were squeezed onto plots of land too small to feed a family. One-third of these people financed their voyage as "redemptioners"—that is, they had sold themselves or their children as indentured servants. Most Germans were either Lutherans or Calvinists. But a significant minority belonged to small, pacifist religious sects that desired above all to be left alone.

Overwhelmingly, the eighteenth-century immigrants were poor. Those who became indentured servants had to give one to four years of work to an urban or rural master, who might well exploit them cruelly. Servants could be sold or rented out, beaten, granted minimal legal protection, kept from marrying, and sexually harassed; and attempted escape usually meant an extension of their service. But at the end of their term, most managed to collect "freedom dues," which could help them to marry and acquire land.

Few immigrants settled permanently in those parts of North America where land was relatively scarce and expensive—New England, New Jersey, lower New York, and the southern tidewater. New Englanders in particular did not welcome people who might become public charges: "these confounded Irish will eat us all up," snorted one Bostonian. Philadelphia became the immigrants' primary port of entry. So many foreigners went to Pennsylvania that by 1755 the English accounted for only one-third of that colony's population; the rest were mostly Germans and Scots-Irish.

Rising numbers of immigrants also traveled to the piedmont region, stretching along the eastern slope of the Appalachians. A significant German community developed in upper New York, and thousands of other Germans as well as Scots-Irish fanned southward from Pennsylvania into western Maryland. Many more from Germany and Ireland arrived in the second-most popular gateway to eighteenth-century America, Charles Town, whence they moved on to settle the Carolina piedmont. There they raised grain, livestock, and tobacco, generally without slaves. After 1750 both streams of immigration merged with an outpouring of Anglo-Americans from the Chesapeake in the rolling, fertile hills of western North Carolina. In 1713 few Anglo-Americans had lived more than fifty miles from the sea, but by 1750 one-third of all colonists resided in the piedmont.

English-descended colonists did not relish the influx of so many foreigners. Franklin spoke for many when he asked in his 1751 essay on population,

> why should the Palatine boors [Germans] be suffered to swarm into our settlements, and, by herding together, establish their language and manners, to the exclusion of ours? Why should Pennsylvania,

### Distribution of Non-Indian Nationalities Within the British Mainland Colonies, 1700–1755

*The impact of heavy immigration from 1720 to 1755 can be seen in the reduction of the English and Welsh from four-fifths of the colonial population to a slight majority; in the doubling of the African population; and in the sudden influx of Germans and Irish, who together comprised a fifth of all Anglo-Americans by 1755. For a more detailed breakdown of African origins, see the map on page 92.*

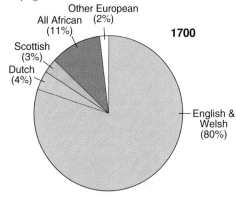

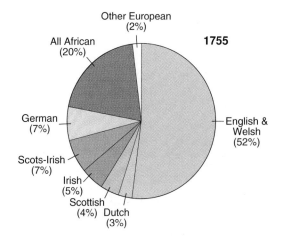

*Source:* Thomas L. Purvis, "The European Ancestry of the United States Population," *William & Mary Quarterly,* LXI (1984): 85–101.

founded by the English, become a colony of aliens, who will shortly be so numerous as to Germanize us instead of us Anglicizing them, and will never adopt our language or customs any more than they can acquire our complexion?

In the same ungenerous spirit, Franklin objected to the slave trade largely because it would increase America's black population at the expense of industrious whites.

On another occasion, Franklin suggested that the colonists send rattlesnakes to Britain in return for the

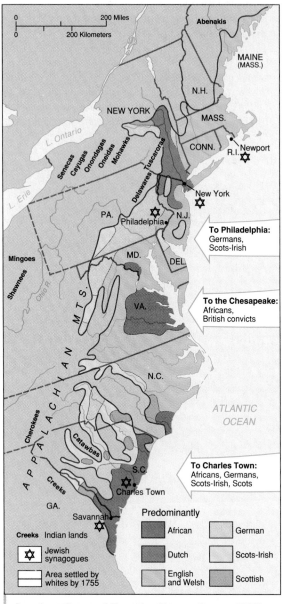

**Immigration and Frontier Expansion, to 1755**

*A sharp rise in the importance of African slaves made much of the southern tidewater a predominantly black region. Immigrants from Germany, Ireland, and Scotland tended to settle in the piedmont. A significant Jewish population emerged in the seaports.*

convict laborers dumped on American shores. Deportation of lawbreakers to America had been common enough in the seventeenth century, and between 1718 and 1783, some thirty thousand convicts arrived. A few were murderers; most were thieves; some were guilty of the most trivial offenses, like a young Londoner who "got intoxicated with liquor, and in that condition attempted to snatch a handkerchief from the body of a person in the street to him unknown. . . ." Convicts were sold as servants on arrival. Relatively few committed crimes in America, and some managed eventually to establish themselves as backcountry farmers. But like many contemporary Americans, colonists seldom wished to absorb the victims of other nations' social problems.

## Rural Men and Women

Although the benefits of rising living standards in the British colonies were widespread, the colonial population enjoyed these advantages unevenly. With few exceptions—Benjamin Franklin is the best known—true affluence was reserved for those born wealthy. For the rest, personal success was limited and came only through hard work, if at all.

Because the vast majority of farm families owned just enough acreage for a working farm, they could not provide their children with land of their own when they married. Moreover, since couples typically started having children in their midtwenties, had their last babies sometime after forty, and lived past sixty, all but their youngest children would be approaching middle age before receiving any inheritance. Young adults rarely got more than a sixth or seventh of their parents' estate, because most families wrote wills that divided property evenly—or almost so—among all daughters and sons. A young male had to build savings to buy farm equipment by working (from about age sixteen to twenty-three) as a field hand for his father or neighbors. Because mortgages usually required down payments of 33 percent, a young husband normally supported his growing family by renting a farm from a more prosperous landowner until his early or midthirties. In some areas, most notably the oldest colonized areas of New England, the continued high birthrates of rural families combined with a shortage of productive land to limit farming opportunities altogether. As a result, many young men turned elsewhere to make their livings— the frontier, the port cities, or the high seas.

Even after acquiring their own land, many farmers supplemented their incomes through seasonal or part-time work. Some learned a craft like carpentry that earned money year-round. Many more trapped furs, gathered honey and beeswax, or made cider, shingles, turpentine, or wampum. Whenever possible, farmers found wintertime jobs draining meadows, clearing fields, or fencing land for wealthier neighbors.

Families worked off mortgages slowly because the long-term cash income from a farm (6 percent) about equaled the interest on borrowed money (5–8 percent). After making a down payment of one-third, a husband and wife generally satisfied the next third upon inheriting shares of their deceased parents' estates. They paid off the final third when their children reached their teens and the family could thus expand farm output with two or three full-time workers. Only by their late fifties, just as their youngest offspring got ready to leave home, could most colonial parents hope to free themselves of debt.

In general, the more isolated a community or the less productive its farmland, the more self-sufficiency and bartering its people practiced, although only the remotest settlements were completely self-sufficient. Rural families depended heavily on wives' and daughters' production. Women contributed to their household's financial success by manufacturing items that the family would otherwise have had to purchase. Besides cooking, cleaning, and washing, wives preserved food, boiled soap, made clothing, and tended the garden, dairy, orchard, poultry house, and pigsty. Women often sold dairy products to neighbors or export merchants, spun yarn into cloth for tailors, knitted various garments for sale, and even vended their own hair for wigs. A farm family's ability to feed itself and its animals was worth about half of its cash income (a luxury that few European peasants enjoyed), and women did no less than men in meeting this end.

Legally, however, women in the British colonies found themselves constrained (see Chapter 3). A woman's single most autonomous decision was her choice of a husband. Once married, she lost control of her dowry, unless she was a New Yorker subject to Dutch custom, which allowed her somewhat more authority. Women in the French and Spanish colonies retained ownership of, and often augmented, the property they brought to a marriage. Widows did control between 8 and 10 percent of all property in eighteenth-century Anglo-America, and a few—among them Eliza Pinckney of South Carolina, a prominent political leader and the mother of two Revolutionary-era leaders—owned and managed large estates.

## Colonial Farmers and the Environment

The rapid expansion of European settlement hastened the transformation of the environment east of the Appalachians. Whereas the earliest colonists farmed land already cleared and cultivated by Native Americans,

**Women's Work**
*Rural women were responsible for most household and garden tasks. This print, dating to 1780, shows young women tending onions in Wethersfield, Connecticut.*

eighteenth-century settlers usually first had to remove trees from their plots. Despite the labor involved, farmers and planters, especially those using slave labor, preferred the most heavily forested areas, where the soil was most fertile. New England farmers also had to clear innumerable heavy rocks—debris from the last Ice Age—with which they then built walls around their fields. And colonists everywhere used timber to construct their houses, barns, and fences and to provide fuel for heating and cooking. Farmers and planters also sold firewood to the inhabitants of colonial cities and towns. Only six years after Georgia's founding, a colonist noted that there was "no more firewood in Savannah; . . . it must be bought from the plantations for which reason firewood is already right expensive."

In removing the trees (deforestation), farmers drove away bears, panthers, wild turkeys, and other forest animals while attracting grass- and seed-eating rabbits, mice, and possums. By removing protection from winds and, in summer, from the sun, deforestation also produced warmer summers and colder winters, so that it actually reinforced the demand for wood as fuel. By hastening the runoff of spring waters, it led both to heavier flooding and drier streambeds in most areas and, where water could not escape, to more extensive swamps. In turn, less stable temperatures and water levels, along with impediments created by mills and by the floating of timbers downstream, rapidly reduced the number of fish in colonial waters. Writing in 1766, naturalist John Bartram noted that fish "abounded formerly when the Indians lived much on them & was very numerous," but that "now there is not the 100[th] or perhaps the 1000th [portion of] fish to be found."

Deforestation dried and hardened the soil, but colonists' crops had even more drastic effects. Native Americans, recognizing the soil-depleting effects of intensive cultivation, rotated their crops regularly so that fields could lie fallow (unplanted) and thereby be replenished with vital nutrients. But many colonial farmers either did not have enough land to leave some unplanted or were unwilling to sacrifice short-term profits for possible long-term benefits. As early as 1637, one New England farmer discovered that his soil "after five or six years [of planting corn] grows barren beyond belief and puts on the face of winter in the time of summer." Chesapeake planters' tobacco yields declined after only three or four years in the same plot. Like farmers elsewhere, they used animal manure to fertilize their food crops but not their tobacco, fearing that manure would spoil the taste for consumers. As Chesapeake tobacco growers moved inland to hillier areas, away from rivers and streams, they also contributed to increased soil erosion. By 1750, to remain productive, many Chesapeake farmers were shifting their crop from tobacco to wheat.

Because they confronted a more serious shortage of land and resources, well-to-do farmers in Europe were already turning their attention to conservation and "scientific" farming. But most colonists ignored such techniques, either because they could not afford to implement them or because they believed that American land, including that still held by Indians, would sustain them and future generations indefinitely.

### The Urban Paradox

The cities were British North America's economic paradox. As the ports of entry and exit, they were keys to colonial prosperity; yet most of their inhabitants were caught in a downward spiral of declining opportunity.

After 1740 economic success proved ever more elusive for the 4 percent of colonists who lived in the three major seaports of Philadelphia, New York, and Boston. Debilitating ocean voyages left many immigrants too weak to work, and every incoming ship from Europe carried numerous widows and orphans. Moreover, the cities' poor rolls always bulged with the survivors of mariners lost at sea, as well as with unskilled, landless men, women (often widowed), and children from the countryside. High population density and poor sanitation in urban locales allowed contagious diseases to run rampant, so that half of all city children died before age twenty-one and urban adults lived ten years less on average than country folk.

Even the able-bodied found cities economically treacherous. Early-eighteenth-century urban artisans typically trained apprentices and employed them as journeymen for many years until the latter opened their own shops. After 1750, however, more and more employers kept their labor force only as long as business was brisk, and released workers when sales slowed; in 1751 a shrewd Benjamin Franklin recommended this practice as an intelligent way to use expensive labor. Recessions hit more frequently after 1720 and created longer spells of unemployment. As urban populations ballooned, wages correspondingly tended to shrink, and the cost of rents, food, and firewood shot up.

Urban poverty grew from insignificance before 1700 into a major problem in the mid-eighteenth century. By 1730 Boston could no longer shelter its destitute in the almshouse built in 1685, and by 1741 the town had declared every sixth citizen too poor to pay taxes. Not until 1736 did New York need a poorhouse (for just forty people), but by 1772, 4 percent of its residents (over eight hundred people) required public assistance to survive. The number of Philadelphia families listed as poor on tax rolls jumped from 3 percent in 1720 to 11 percent by 1760.

Wealth, on the other hand, remained highly concentrated in eighteenth-century colonial cities. For example, New York's wealthiest 10 percent (mostly merchants) owned about 45 percent of the property throughout the eighteenth century. Similar patterns existed in Boston and Philadelphia. Set alongside the growth of a poor underclass in these cities, such statistics underscored the polarization of status and wealth in urban America on the eve of the Revolution.

Most southern cities were little more than large towns. Charles Town, however, became North America's fourth-largest city. South Carolina's capital offered gracious living to the wealthy planters who flocked to their townhouses during the months of worst heat and insect infestation on their plantations. But shanties on the city's outskirts sheltered a growing crowd of destitute whites. The colony encouraged whites to immigrate in hopes of reducing blacks' numerical preponderance, but some European newcomers could not reach frontier farms or find any work except as ill-paid roustabouts. Like their counterparts in northern port cities, Charles Town's poor whites competed for work with urban slaves whose masters rented out their labor, and racial tensions simmered.

Although middle-class women in cities and large towns performed somewhat less manual drudgery than their country cousins, they nonetheless managed complex households that often included servants, slaves, apprentices, and other nonfamily members. While raising poultry and vegetables as well as sewing and knitting, urban wives purchased their cloth and most of their food in daily trips to public markets. Many had one or more household servants, usually young single women or widows, to help with cooking, cleaning, and laundering—tasks that required more attention than in the country because of higher urban standards of cleanliness and appearance. Wives also worked in family businesses or their own shops, located (unlike in modern times) in owners' homes.

Less affluent wives and widows housed boarders rather than servants, and many spun and wove cloth in their homes for local merchants. But especially in Boston, where conditions were the grimmest, many widows with children had to look to the community for relief. Whereas their Puritan forebears had deemed it one's Christian duty to care for poor dependents, affluent Bostonians turned an increasingly wary eye toward the needy. Preaching in 1752, the city's leading minister, Charles Chauncy, lamented "the Swarms of Children, of both Sexes, that are continually strolling and playing about the Streets of our Metropolis, cloathed in Rags, and brought up in Idleness and Ignorance," and another clergyman warned that charity for widows and their children was money "worse than Lost."

### Slavery's Wages

For slaves, the economic progress achieved in colonial America meant only that most masters could afford to keep them healthy. Rarely, however, did masters choose to make their human chattels comfortable. A visitor to a Virginia plantation from Poland (where

**Newspaper Ads**
*Women shopkeepers were common in the cities, especially in trades that required only a small investment. These three Boston women advertised imported garden seeds..*

most peasants lived in dire poverty) recorded this impression of slaves' quality of life:

> We entered some Negroes huts—for their habitations cannot be called houses. They are far more miserable than the poorest of the cottages of our peasants. The husband and wife sleep on a miserable bed, the children on the floor . . . a little kitchen furniture amid this misery . . . a teakettle and cups . . . five or six hens, each with ten or fifteen chickens, walked there. That is the only pleasure allowed to the negroes.

To maintain slaves, masters normally spent just 40 percent of the amount paid for the upkeep of indentured servants. Whereas white servants ate two hundred pounds of beef or pork yearly, most slaves consumed only fifty pounds of meat. The value of the beer and hard cider given to a typical servant alone equaled the expense of feeding and clothing the average slave. Masters usually provided adult slaves with eight quarts of corn and a pound of pork each week but expected them to grow their own vegetables, forage for wild fruits, and perhaps raise poultry.

Slaves worked for a far longer portion of their lives than whites. Slave children went to the fields as part-time helpers soon after reaching seven years and began working full-time between eleven and fourteen. Whereas most white women worked in their homes, barns, and gardens, female slaves routinely tended tobacco or rice crops, even when pregnant, and often worked outdoors in winter. Most slaves toiled until they died, although those who survived to their sixties rarely performed hard labor.

Despite the rigors of bondage, slaves proved resourceful at maximizing opportunities within this harsh, confining system. For example, some slaves gained exclusive rights to their own gardens and poultry, and a few sold food to their masters. In 1769, for example, Thomas Jefferson made several purchases like the following:

| | |
|---|---|
| gave negro for watermelon | 7 pence |
| paid Fanny for 6 chickens | 2 shillings |
| paid Cato for 1 doz eggs | 3 pence |

House slaves widely insisted on being tipped by guests for shining shoes and stabling horses. They sometimes sought presents aggressively on holidays, as a startled New Jersey tutor on a Virginia plantation discovered in 1774 when slaves demanding gifts of cash roused him from bed early Christmas morning.

**Asante Drum**
*Enslaved Africans carried their cultures with them to the Americas. This drum, made from African wood, was found in Virginia.*

In the South Carolina and Georgia rice country, slaves working under the task system had control of about half their waking hours. Under tasking, each slave spent some hours caring for a quarter-acre—usually a half-day—after which his or her duties ended. By 1750 this system permitted certain slaves to keep hogs and sell surplus vegetables in Charles Town. A remarkable but atypical slave named Sampson earned enough money in his off-hours to hire another to work his own task, and became free in 1728.

But the independence of South Carolina's slaves and the fact that they constituted a majority of the colony's population aroused planters' fears that they were losing control of "their" blacks. For example, a 1735 law, noting that many Africans wore "clothes much above the condition of slaves," imposed a dress code limiting slaves' apparel to fabrics worth less than ten shillings per yard and even prohibited their wearing the cast-off clothes of their owners. Of even greater concern were gatherings of large numbers of blacks uncontrolled by whites. In 1721 Charles Town enacted a 9:00 P.M. curfew for blacks, while South Carolina's assembly placed all local slave patrols under the colonial militia. Slaves responded to the colony's vigilance and harsher punishments with increased instances of arson, theft, flight, and violence.

Tensions erupted in 1739 when South Carolina was rocked by a powerful slave uprising, the Stono Rebellion. It began when twenty slaves robbed guns and ammunition from a store twenty miles from Charles Town, at the Stono River Bridge. Marching under a makeshift flag and crying "Liberty!" they collected eighty men and headed for Spanish Florida, a well-known refuge for runaways (see A Place in Time). Along the way they burned seven plantations and killed twenty whites, but they spared a Scottish innkeeper who "was a good Man and kind to his slaves." Within a day mounted militia surrounded the slaves by a riverbank, cut them down mercilessly, and spiked a rebel head on every milepost between that spot and Charles Town. Disturbances elsewhere in the colony required more than a month to suppress, with insurgents generally "put to the most cruel Death." Thereafter white apprehension ran high, expressed in a new slave code that would remain essentially in force until the Civil War. The code kept South Carolina slaves under constant surveillance. Furthermore, it threatened masters with fines for not disciplining slaves and required legislative approval for manumission (freeing of individual slaves). The Stono

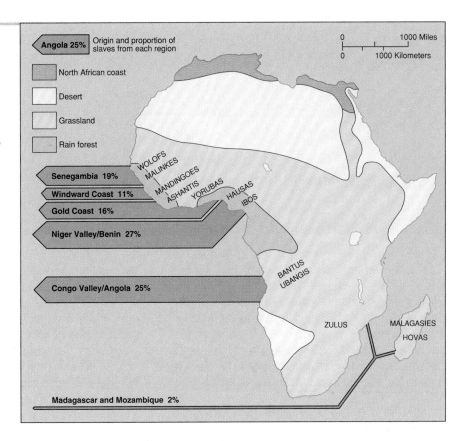

**African Origins of North American Slaves, 1690–1807**

*Virtually all slaves brought to English North America came from West Africa, between Senegambia and Angola. Most were captured or bought inland and marched to the coast, where they were sold to African merchants who in turn sold them to European slave traders.*

Rebellion thus speeded South Carolina's emergence as a rigid, racist, and fear-ridden society.

Slavery and racial tensions were by no means confined to plantations. By midcentury slaves made up 20 percent of New York City's population and formed a majority in Charles Town and Savannah. City life offered slaves advantages, most notably the chance for those with skills to hire themselves out and keep part of their wages. By 1770 one-tenth of Savannah's slaves lived in rented rooms away from their owners. Though still in bondage, these blacks forced urban whites to allow them a substantial measure of personal freedom. But although city life afforded slaves greater freedom of association than the plantation did, it did not extend to them the opportunities being realized by their owners. In 1712 rebellious slaves in New York City killed nine whites in a calculated attack. As a result thirteen slaves were hanged, one was starved to death, three were burned at the stake, and one was broken on the wheel. Six others committed suicide to avoid similar tortures. In 1741 a wave of thefts and fires attributed to New York slaves led to the torture and hanging of thirteen slaves

and four white accomplices, the burning of an additional thirteen slaves, and the sale of seventy more to the West Indies.

## The Rise of the Colonial Elites

"A man who has money here, no matter how he came by it, he is everything, and wanting [lacking] that he's a mere nothing, let his conduct be ever so irreproachable." Thus a Rhode Islander in 1748 described how colonial Americans defined high status. But once having achieved wealth, a man was expected by his contemporaries to behave with an appropriate degree of responsibility, to display dignity and generosity, and to be a community leader. His wife must be a skillful household manager and, in the presence of men, a refined yet deferring hostess. In short, they were to act like a "gentleman" and a "lady."*

---

* In the eighteenth century, the words *gentleman* and *lady* referred to individuals who not only conformed to socially accepted standards of behavior but also belonged to the upper class, or *gentry*.

**John Potter and His Family**
*The Potters of Matunuck, Rhode Island, relax at tea. In commissioning a portrait depicting themselves at leisure and attended by a black slave, the Potters proclaimed their elite status.*

Before 1700 the colonies' class structure was less readily apparent, because the elite's more limited resources were spent buying land, servants, or slaves instead of luxuries. As late as 1715 a traveler visiting one of Virginia's richest planters, Robert Beverley, noticed that his host owned "nothing in or about his house but just what is necessary, . . . [such as] good beds but no curtains and instead of cane chairs he hath stools made of wood."

After 1720 British mercantilist trade flourished. Higher incomes enabled well-to-do colonists to display their wealth more openly, particularly in their housing. The greater gentry—the richest 2 percent, who held about 15 percent of all property—constructed residences such as the Low House, New Jersey's most splendid home in 1741, and the Shirley mansion in Virginia. The lesser gentry, or second-wealthiest 2 to 10 percent, who held about 25 percent of all property, typically lived in a more modest fieldstone dwelling such as Pennsylvania's Lincoln homestead or a wood-frame house such as Whitehall in Rhode Island. In contrast, middle-class farmers commonly inhabited one-story wooden buildings with four small rooms and a loft.

Colonial gentlemen and ladies also exhibited their wealth after 1720 by living in imitation of the European "grand style." They wore costly English fashions, drove carriages instead of wagons, and bought expensive chinaware, books, furniture, and musical instruments. They pursued a gracious life by studying foreign languages, learning formal dances, and cultivating polite manners. In sports men's preference shifted to horse racing (on which they bet avidly) and away from cockfighting, a less elegant diversion. A few young colonial males even got an English education. By midcentury the elite's taste for consumer goods was spreading to the middle class and helping to fuel a "consumer revolution" in the British Empire.

For Chesapeake gentlemen, debt was a problem even if they lived thriftily. Tobacco planters were perpetually short of cash and in debt to British merchants who bought their crops and sold them imported goods on credit at high prices. Planters could respond only in two ways. First, they could strive for as much self-sufficiency as possible on their estates—for example, by training their slaves to manufacture glass, bricks, tools, nails, and carriages. Second, they could diversify away from the region's tobacco monoculture (dependence on a single staple crop) by growing wheat or cutting timber. Self-sufficiency and diversification became more widely accepted objectives as the eighteenth century wore on, and after 1750 respected landowners like George Washington and Thomas Jefferson strongly advocated them.

### Elites and Colonial Politics

Colonial gentlemen not only monopolized wealth but also dominated politics. Governors invariably appointed members of the greater gentry to sit on their councils and as judges on the highest courts. Most representatives elected to the legislatures' lower houses (assemblies) also ranked among the wealthiest 2 percent, as did majors and colonels in the militia. In contrast, members of the lesser gentry sat less often in the legislature, but they commonly served as justices of the peace on the county courts and as militia officers up to captain.

Colonial America's only high-ranking elected officeholders were the members of the legislature's lower house. But outside New England (where any voter could hold office), legal requirements barred 80 percent of white men from running for the assembly, most often by specifying that a candidate must own a minimum of a thousand acres. (Farms then averaged 180 acres in the South and 120 acres in the middle colonies.) Even had there been no such property qualifications, however, few ordinary citizens could have afforded the high costs of elective office. Assemblymen received only living expenses, which might not fully cover the cost of staying at their province's capital, much less compensate a farmer or an artisan for his absence from farm or shop for six to ten weeks a year. Even members of the gentry grumbled about legislative duty, many of them viewing high office as "a sort of tax on them to serve the public at their own Expense besides the neglect of their business," according to Governor Lewis Morris of New Jersey.

For these reasons, political leadership fell to certain wealthy families with a tradition of public service. Nine families, for example, provided one-third of Virginia's royal councilors during the century after 1680. John Adams, a rising young Massachusetts politician, estimated that most towns in his colony chose their legislators from among just three or four families.

The colonies set liberal qualifications for male voters, but all provinces excluded women, blacks (free as well as enslaved), and Indians from elections. In seven colonies voters had to own land (usually forty to fifty acres), and the rest demanded that an elector have enough property to furnish a house and work a farm with his own tools. About 40 percent of free men could not meet these requirements, mostly indentured servants, single sons still living with parents, or young men just beginning family life. Most white males in British North America would vote by age forty, whereas two-thirds of all men in England and nine-tenths in Ireland could not and would never vote.

In rural areas voter participation was low unless a vital issue was at stake. The difficulties of voting limited the average rural turnout to about 45 percent. (This rate of participation was, however, better than in typical U.S. elections today, apart from those for president.) Most governors called elections according to no set pattern, so that elections might lapse for years and suddenly be held on very short notice. Voters in isolated areas thus often had no knowledge of an upcoming contest. The fact that all polling took place at the county seat discouraged many electors from traveling long distances over poor roads to vote. In several colonies voters had to state their choice publicly, often

face-to-face with the candidates. This procedure naturally inhibited participation on the part of those who might dissent. Finally, the absence of political parties also played a role in the turnout: no institutional means existed to stimulate popular interest in politics and to mobilize voters in support of candidates. Office seekers nominated themselves and usually ran on their reputation rather than issues that might spur public interest.

In view of these factors, indifference toward politics was not uncommon by the mid-eighteenth century. For

### Charles County, Maryland, Courthouse and Ordinary

*In the Chesapeake colonies, community life usually centered on the county courthouse and a few other buildings on a cleared parcel. On election days, voters were treated to drinks in the nearby ordinary (tavern) by candidates before proceeding to the courthouse and voting orally and publicly.*

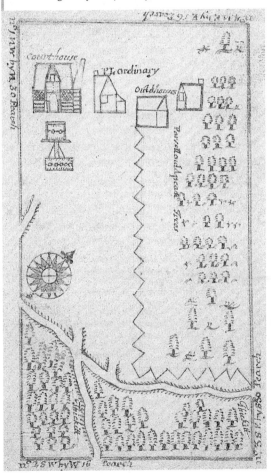

example, to avoid paying legislators' expenses at the capital, numerous Massachusetts towns refused to choose assemblymen; in 1763, 64 of 168 towns held no elections. Thirty percent of men elected to South Carolina's assembly neglected to take their seats from 1731 to 1760, including a majority of those chosen in 1747 and 1749. Apathy would have been even greater had candidates not freely plied voters with alcohol. This "swilling the planters with bumbo" was most popular among Virginians: George Washington dispensed almost two quarts of liquor for each voter at the courthouse when first elected to the assembly in 1758. Such practices helped the elite in most eighteenth-century colonies build up a tradition of community leadership that would serve them well in the years of revolutionary crisis after 1763.

Only in the major seaports did a truly competitive political life flourish. Voter turnout was relatively high in the cities because of greater population density, better communications, and the use of secret ballots (except in New York). Furthermore, the cities' acute economic difficulties stimulated political participation among urban voters, ever hopeful that the government might ease their problems. In politics as in economics, cities were an exception to the general pattern for Anglo-America.

The most significant political development after 1700 was the rise of the assembly as the preponderant force in American government. Except in Connecticut and Rhode Island (where voters elected their governor), the crown or the proprietors in England chose each colony's governor, who except in Massachusetts in turn named a council, or upper house of the legislature. Thus the assembly became the vehicle through which members of the gentry asserted their own interests. Until 1689 governors and councils took the initiative in drafting laws, and the assemblies rather passively followed their lead; but thereafter, the assemblies assumed a more central role in politics.

Colonial leaders argued that their legislatures should exercise the same rights as those won by Parliament in its seventeenth-century struggle with royal authority. Indeed, Anglo-Americans saw their assemblies as miniature Houses of Commons, and they assumed that governors possessed only those powers exercised by the British crown. Since Parliament had won supremacy over the monarchy through the Bill of Rights in 1689, colonials felt that their governors had strictly limited powers and should defer to the assemblies in cases of disagreement.

The lower houses steadily asserted their prestige and authority by refusing to permit outside meddling in their proceedings, taking firm control over taxes and budgets, and especially by keeping a tight rein on executive salaries. Although governors had considerable powers (including the right to veto acts, call or dismiss assembly sessions at will, and schedule elections anytime), they were vulnerable to legislatures' financial pressure because they received no salary from British sources and relied on the assemblies for income. Only through this "power of the purse" could assemblies force governors to sign laws opposed by the crown.

Moreover, because the British government had little interest in eighteenth-century colonial politics, the assemblies could seize considerable power at the governors' expense. The Board of Trade, which Parliament established in 1696, was charged with monitoring American developments and advising the crown on colonial affairs. The board could have easily frustrated the assemblies' rise to power by persuading the crown to disallow objectionable colonial laws signed by the governors; but of 8,563 acts sent from the mainland between 1696 and 1776, the board had just 469 disapproved. The Board of Trade's ineffectiveness left a vacuum in royal policy that allowed the colonies to become self-governing in most respects except for trade regulation, restrictions on printing money, and declaring war. This autonomy, reinforced by self-assertive assemblies, would haunt British authorities when they attempted to exercise more direct rule after 1763 (see Chapter 5).

Thus during the first half of the eighteenth century, many colonists flourished and some grew wealthy. At the same time, however, class distinctions became more sharply etched. Far less than in the French and Spanish colonies, power and authority in British North America were disconnected from hereditary titles, royal appointment, the imperial army, and the state church. Instead, a homegrown provincial elite dominated public life.

## Competing for a Continent

The first half of the eighteenth century witnessed the rapid transformation of North America as Europeans competed among themselves in expanding their territorial claims, engaging in more intensive trade and warfare alike with Native Americans, and opening up new areas for settlement by colonists. Native Americans

**Intercultural Trade in Colonial Louisiana**

*Alexandre de Batz, a French visitor in 1735, depicted an important dimension of Louisiana's economy in this drawing of Indians from several nations gathering to trade near New Orleans. Trade goods, including cured skins, kegs of fat, and bear oil, are lined up in the foreground.*

welcomed some of these new developments and resisted others, depending on how they thought their livelihoods would be affected.

## *France and Native Americans*

With the conclusion of the War of Spanish Succession in 1713, France aggressively resumed expanding and strengthening its North American empire, particularly the colony of Louisiana. Founded in 1718, New Orleans soon became the colony's capital and port. Louisiana's staunchest Indian allies were the Choctaws, through whom the French hoped to counter both the rapidly expanding influence of Carolina's traders and the weakening presence of the Spanish in the Southeast. But inroads by the persistent Carolinians led the Choctaws by the 1730s to become bitterly divided into pro-English and pro-French factions.

Life was dismal in Louisiana, for whites as well as blacks. A thoroughly corrupt government ran the colony. With Louisiana's sluggish export economy failing to sustain them, settlers and slaves found other means of survival. Like the Indians, they hunted, fished, gathered wild plants, and cultivated gardens. In 1727 a priest described how some free settlers eventually prospered: "A man with his wife or partner clears a little ground, builds himself a house on four piles, covers it with sheets of bark, and plants corn and rice for his provisions; the next year he raises a little more for food, and has also a field of tobacco; if at last he succeeds in having three or four Negroes, then he is out of difficulties."

But many red, white, and black Louisianans depended on exchanges with one another in order to be "out of difficulties." Indians provided corn, bear oil, tallow (for candles), and above all deerskins to European merchants in return for blankets, kettles, axes, chickens, hogs, guns, and alcohol. Indians from west of the Mississippi brought horses and cattle, usually stolen from Spanish ranches in Texas. Familiar with cattle from their homelands, West African slaves managed many of Louisiana's herds, and some became rustlers and illicit traders of beef.

With Canada and Louisiana secure, the French sought to counter growing British influence in and around the Ohio Valley. After the valley was largely emptied of natives during wars with the Iroquois in the seventeenth century, the Iroquois' adoption of neutrality in 1701 (see Chapter 3) encouraged Indian refugees to settle there. Nations such as the Kickapoos and Mascoutens returned from the upper Great Lakes, while others, among them Shawnees and Delawares, arrived from the east to escape English encroachments. Hoping to secure commercial and diplomatic ties with these natives, the French expanded their trade activities. Detroit and several other French posts ballooned into sizable villages housing Indians, French, and mixed-ancestry *métis*. But with English traders increas-

**Huron (Wyandotte) Woman**
*Her cloth dress, glass beads, and iron hoe reflect the influence of French trade on this woman and other Indians of the Great Lakes–Ohio region in the eighteenth century.*

ingly active in the region, most Indians preferred a more independent course.

Although the French generally were more successful among Indians than the English, by no means did they enjoy universal success. The Carolina-supported Chickasaws frequently attacked the French and their native allies on the Mississippi River. Although ultimately unsuccessful, the Mesquakie, or Fox, Indians led a long effort to prevent French traders from making direct contact with Sioux Indians to the west. And the French in 1729–1730 brutally suppressed the Natchez Indians, the last of the Mississippian peoples, in order to open up land in Louisiana for tobacco and sugar production.

By 1744 French fur traders had explored as far west as North Dakota and Colorado and were buying beaver pelts and Indian slaves on the Great Plains. At the instigation of these traders and their British competitors, trade goods, including guns, spread to Native Americans throughout central Canada and then to the Plains. Meanwhile, Indians in the Great Basin and southern Plains were acquiring horses, thousands of which had been left behind by the Spanish when they fled New Mexico during the Pueblo Revolt of 1680. Adopting the horse and gun, Indians such as the Lakota Sioux and Comanches moved to the Plains and built a new, highly mobile way of life based on the pursuit of buffalo. By 1750 France had an immense domain, but one that depended on often precarious relations with Native Americans.

### Native Americans and British Expansion

As in the seventeenth century, British colonial expansion was made possible by the depopulation and dislocation of Native Americans. Epidemic diseases, envi-

ronmental changes, war, and political pressures on Indians to cede land and to emigrate all combined to open up new lands for white immigrants. Pennsylvania, where William Penn's idealism was rapidly waning, coerced the Delaware Indians into selling more than fifty thousand acres between 1729 and 1734. In the latter year, the colony's leaders (William Penn's sons and his former secretary) produced a patently fraudulent treaty in which the Delawares allegedly had agreed in 1686 to sell their land as far west as a man could walk in a day and a half. In 1737, Pennsylvania blazed a trail and hired three men to walk west as fast as they could. The men covered nearly sixty miles, meaning that the Delawares, in what became known as the Walking Purchase, had to hand over an additional twelve hundred square miles of land. Despite the protests of Delaware elders who had been alive in 1686 and remembered no such treaty, the Delawares were forced to move under Iroquois supervision. The proprietors then sold these lands to settlers and speculators at a large profit. Within a generation the Delawares' former lands were among the most productive in the British Empire.

In helping to remove the Delawares from Pennsylvania, the Iroquois sought to accommodate the English while consolidating their own power. Late in the seventeenth century, the Iroquois had agreed with several colonies, from Maryland to Massachusetts, to relocate Indians whose lands were sought by colonists. Under these agreements, known collectively as the Covenant Chain, Indians were moved to areas of what are now New York and Pennsylvania on the periphery of the Iroquois' own homeland, where they could serve as buffers against English expansion. The removal of the Delawares marked Pennsylvania's entry into the Covenant Chain. In so grouping other Native Americans around them and in incorporating the Tuscaroras as the sixth nation of their confederacy (see Chapter 3), the Iroquois established a center of Native American power distinct from, but cooperative with, the British.

Indians elsewhere along the frontier of settlement likewise confronted pressures from settlers on one side and from the Iroquois on the other. Typical of these were the Catawbas of the Carolina piedmont. After the defeat of the Yamasees (whose cause the Catawbas supported) in 1716, Carolina settlers moved uncomfortably close to some Catawba villages, provoking the kind of environmental upheavals experienced earlier by Indians in New England and other settled regions (see Chapter 3). Most Catawbas abandoned these villages to join more remote Catawbas who engaged in the deerskin trade. Having escaped the settlers, the Catawbas, however, faced rising conflict with the Iroquois, who, after making peace with the Indian allies of New France in 1701, looked south when launching raids for captives to adopt into their ranks. To counter the Iroquois, whose alliances with most of the northern colonies left them well armed, the Catawbas turned to South Carolina. By ceding land and helping defend that colony against outside Indians, the Catawbas received guns, food, and clothing. Their relationship with the English allowed the Catawbas the security they needed to strengthen their traditional institutions. However, the growing gap in numbers between them and the settlers, and their competition with the settlers for resources, made the Indians vulnerable and dependent.

### British Expansion in the South: Georgia

Parliament's chartering of the colony of Georgia in 1732 represented a new expansionist thrust. Parliament intended Georgia as a refuge where bankrupt debtors would be settled on land that England had agreed, in a 1670 treaty, belonged to Spain. Meanwhile, the new colony's sponsors hoped that Georgia would flourish by exporting expensive commodities like wine and silk. Parliament even spent money to ensure the success of the colony, which became the only North American province besides Nova Scotia in which the British government actually invested funds.

Under tough-minded James Oglethorpe (1696–1785), who dominated the provincial board of trustees, Georgia took shape slowly during its first decade. Oglethorpe founded the port of entry, Savannah, in 1733, and by 1740 a small contingent of 2,800 colonists had settled in the colony. Almost half the immigrants came from Germany, Switzerland, and Scotland, and most had their overseas passage paid by the government. A small number of Jews were among the early settlers. Georgia thus began as the least English of all the colonies. In 1740 Oglethorpe led a massive assault on Florida. Although failing to seize St. Augustine, he led 650 men in repelling 3,000 Spanish troops and refugee South Carolina slaves who counterattacked Georgia in 1742. When peace returned in 1744, Georgia's survival was assured.

Oglethorpe hated slavery and tried to ban it from Georgia. "They live like cattle," he wrote to the trustees after viewing Charles Town's slave market. "If we allow slaves, we act against the very principles by which we associated together, which was to relieve the distressed." Slavery, he thought, degraded blacks, made whites lazy, and presented a terrible risk. Oglethorpe

**Creek Delegation to London**
*In 1734 James Oglethorpe visited London with Creek Indians who had sold him land. Here the Creeks meet with Englishmen who have invested in the Georgia colony.*

**Yuchi Ceremony, 1736**
*A German visitor to Georgia painted this watercolor, which he titled A Festival. The guns hanging inside the shelter were probably acquired from English traders in South Carolina.*

worried that wherever whites relied on a slave labor force, they courted slave revolts, which the Spanish could then exploit. But most of all, he recognized that slavery undermined the economic position of poor whites like those he sought to settle in Georgia.

At Oglethorpe's insistence, Parliament made Georgia the only colony where slavery was forbidden. He also pushed through a requirement that landholdings be no larger than five hundred acres. These measures were aimed at keeping rural Georgia populated by white, independent farmer-soldiers, ready to leap to the colony's defense and uncorrupted by the urge to speculate in real estate or build up slave-labor plantations.

But Oglethorpe's well-intentioned plans failed completely. Few debtors arrived because Parliament set impossibly stringent conditions for their release from prison. Limitations on settlers' rights to sell or enlarge their holdings, as well as the ban on slavery, also kept settlement low. Raising exotic export crops proved impractical; as in South Carolina, only rice yielded a profit. Oglethorpe struggled against economic reality for a decade and then gave up. In 1750 the trustees finally legalized slavery, and restrictions on the market for land also fell by the wayside. As a result, Georgia boomed. The population rose from four thousand residents in 1750 (including up to a thousand slaves) to twenty-three thousand inhabitants in 1770, 45 percent of them blacks.

Having held Georgia against Spain and pushed the frontier west 150 miles, British expansion virtually halted after 1750. Anglo-Americans would not settle beyond the Appalachians until the 1760s.

## Spain's Struggles

While endeavoring to maintain its empire in the face of Native American, French, and British adversaries, Spain spread its language and culture over much of North America, especially in the Southwest.

Seeking to repopulate New Mexico with settlers after the Pueblo Revolt (see Chapter 3), Spain gave land grants of approximately twenty-six square miles wherever ten or more families founded a town. Strong fortifications arose to protect against Indian attacks, now coming primarily from the Apaches. As in the early New England towns, the settlers built homes on small lots around the church plaza, farmed separate fields nearby, grazed livestock at a distance, and shared a community woodlot and pasture.

The livestock-raising *ranchos,* radiating out for many miles from little clusters of houses, monopolized vast tracts along the Rio Grande and blocked further town settlement. On the *ranchos* mounted cattle and sheep herders (*vaqueros*) created the way of life later associated with the American cowboy—featuring lariat and roping skills, cattle drives, roundups, and livestock brandings.

By 1750 the population of New Mexico numbered just 3,800 Spanish, half of them in four towns, and 8,400 Pueblo Indians (an astonishing 50 percent reduction

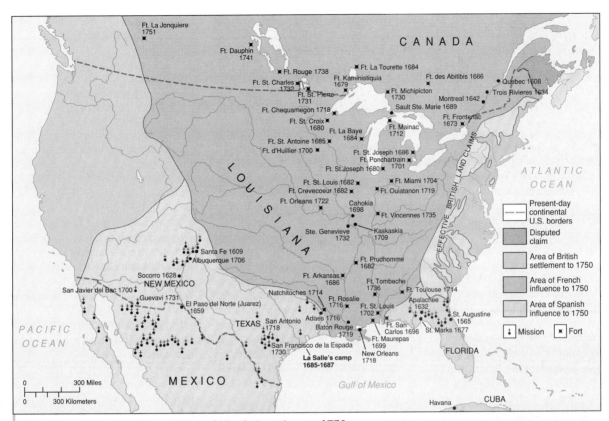

**French and Spanish Occupation of North America, to 1750**
*French fur traders became entrenched along the Great Lakes and Upper Mississippi River between 1666 and 1700, after which they built many settlements in territory claimed by Spain along the Gulf of Mexico. Spanish colonization was concentrated in Florida, central Texas, and the Rio Grande Valley.*

since 1680). Most Pueblos now cooperated with New Mexico's government, and although many had converted to Catholicism, they also practiced their traditional religion. On the colony's borders, the Navajos and Apaches, whose raids once menaced Spanish and Pueblos alike, had made peace with New Mexico in order to gain its support against even more fearsome raids by armed and mounted Utes from the north and Comanches from the east.

Spain established Texas in order to counter growing French influence among the Comanches and other Native Americans on the southern Plains. Colonization began after 1716, when Spaniards established several outposts on the San Antonio and Guadalupe rivers. The most flourishing center was at San Antonio de Béxar, where two towns, a *presidio,* and a mission (later known as the Alamo) were clustered. But most Indians

**The Alamo**
*As the center of Franciscan missionary efforts in Texas, this San Antonio church was a critical bulwark for Spain on its fragile northern frontier. It later became the symbol of Texan independence from Mexico (see Chapter 13).*

## Mose, Florida

The Spanish presence in Florida was always tenuous and, after English colonists established Charles Town in Carolina in 1670, vulnerable to outside attack. During the eighteenth century Spain retained its hold in Florida by enlisting the support of Native Americans and Africans alienated by the English. In particular, by promising freedom to slaves who fled from Carolina to Florida and converted to Catholicism, the Spanish bolstered their population and defenses. The black community of Mose, established near St. Augustine in 1738, vividly demonstrated the importance of these immigrants.

Blacks had lived in Florida since the founding of St. Augustine in 1565. In 1683, after Indians armed by Carolina began attacking and capturing Florida mission Indians for sale into slavery, the Spanish colony formed a black militia unit. In 1686 fifty-three blacks and Indians conducted a counterraid into Carolina and returned with, among other prizes, thirteen of the governor's slaves. In subsequent diplomatic negotiations between the two colonies, Florida's governor, Diego de Quiroga, refused English demands that he return the blacks, instead giving them wage-paying jobs. Soon other Carolina slaves were making their way to Florida. Spain's King Charles II ruled in 1693 that all arriving slaves should be given their freedom, "so that by their example and my liberality others will do the same."

With Spain deliberately encouraging Carolina slaves to escape to Florida, the numbers rose further, especially during the Yamasee War (1715–1716), when the English were nearly crushed by a massive uprising of Indians. In 1726 a former South Carolina slave, Francisco Menéndez, was appointed to command a militia unit consisting of his fellow Carolinians to defend against an expected English invasion. The Spanish built a fortified village for Menéndez's men and their families in 1738 and called it Gracia Real de Santa Teresa de Mose, usually shortened to Mose, an Indian name for the location.

Mose was strategically placed just two miles north of St. Augustine, so that its residents served as both sentries and a buffer for the capital. Spanish and English documents, along with recent archaeological excavations, reveal that it had sturdy earthen walls "lined round with prickly royal" (a thorny plant) and was surrounded by a moat. A stone fort was the most prominent structure inside the walls. Outside the fort the one hundred residents planted fields and gathered shellfish from the banks of a nearby saltwater stream. In a letter to the Spanish king, Florida's governor, Manuel de Montiano, praised Menéndez for having "distinguished himself in the establishment and cultivation of Mose, . . . [and] doing all he could so that the rest of his subjects, following his example, would apply themselves and learn good customs."

For its residents Mose symbolized their new status as

**English Map of St. Augustine and Mose, 1762**
*Mose is indicated as "Negroe Fort"; "Indian Town" is a settlement of pro-Spanish Indians.*

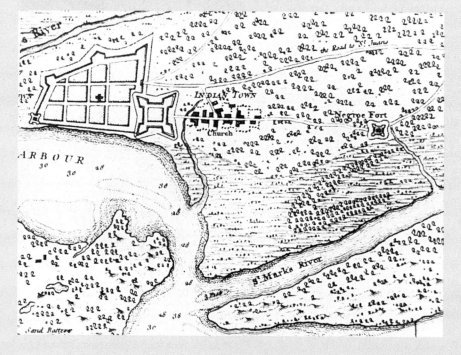

freed men and women. Most had been born in West Africa and then enslaved and carried to Carolina. After escaping they had lived among friendly Indians who helped them make their way to the Spanish colony. Mose was their own community, their first since being taken from Africa. In agreeing to live there, they understood the price they might have to pay. Writing to the king in 1738, they declared themselves "the most cruel enemies of the English," who were ready to shed their "last drop of blood in defense of the Great Crown of Spain and the Holy Faith."

The importance of Florida's free blacks and their town was demonstrated in 1740 when Georgia's governor, James Oglethorpe, led a massive force of Georgia and South Carolina troops, Indian allies, and seven warships in an invasion of Florida. The English captured Mose in May after all its residents were evacuated, but Menéndez's militia and other troops recaptured the town a month later in a fierce battle that helped Oglethorpe decide to withdraw. (The British called the battle Bloody Mose.) But English destruction of the town and the Spanish crown's refusal to fund its rebuilding led Mose's residents to move into St. Augustine. For twelve years they lived among the Spanish as laborers, seamen, and hunters and in other capacities. In 1752 a new governor had Mose rebuilt and ordered the blacks to return to their former town despite their express "desire to live in complete liberty." To go back to the town, which they once had cherished as a symbol of their freedom, now, after twelve years of assimilation in the capital city, seemed relegation to second-class citizenship.

In 1763 Spain ceded Florida to Britain in the Treaty of Paris (see Chapter 5). Spanish authorities evacuated the people of Mose and allotted them homesteads in Matanzas, Cuba. But the meager provisions given the blacks proved inadequate, and many, including Francisco Menéndez, soon moved to Havana. In 1783 another Treaty of Paris returned Florida to Spain (see Chapter 6), and the following year, a new Florida governor resumed the policy of granting freedom to escaped slaves. Hearing the news and recalling Florida's earlier reputation, hundreds of slaves responded. But now Spain proceeded more cautiously with the slaveholders' government to Florida's north; in 1790 U.S. Secretary of State Thomas Jefferson persuaded the Spanish to rescind the policy of granting freedom to escaped slaves. In 1819 the United States annexed Florida, and in 1845 it joined the Union as a slave state.

**Puerto Rican Sergeant**
*This seventeenth-century free black sergeant belonged to a Spanish militia unit in Puerto Rico, similar to the one based at Mose.*

**Ft. Mose Watercolor**
*Artist's reconstruction of Mose, based on archaeological and documentary evidence.*

in Texas preferred trading with the French to farming, Christianity, and the ineffective protection of the Spanish. Lack of security also deterred Hispanic settlement, so that by 1760 only 1,200 Spaniards faced periodic raids by French, Comanches, and other Indians.

Spain's position in Florida was equally precarious. After 1715 the neutrality of the Creeks enabled the Spanish to compete with the English and French in the southeastern deerskin trade, though with limited effectiveness, and to sponsor Indian counterraids into Carolina. In addition, the Spanish offered freedom to any English-owned slaves who escaped and made their way to Florida (see A Place in Time).

The Spanish saw Georgia's founding in 1733 as a bold new threat to Florida, and planned, but then cancelled, an invasion in 1737. When war broke out between England and Spain in 1739, the two sides attempted invasions of each other without success. Spain had resisted the English, but its reputation as "the sick man of Europe" clearly applied equally in North America.

By the mid-eighteenth century, Spain controlled much of the Southeast and Southwest, while France exercised influence in the Mississippi, Ohio, and Missouri River valleys, as well as around the Great Lakes and in Canada. Both empires, spread thin, depended heavily on Indian goodwill or acquiescence. In contrast, British North America was compact, wealthy, densely populated by non-Indians, and aggressively expansionist.

# Enlightenment and Awakening

Anglo-America was probably the world's most literate society in the eighteenth century. Perhaps 90 percent of New England's adult white male population and 40 percent of the women could write well enough to sign documents, thanks to the region's traditional support for primary education. Among white males elsewhere in the colonies, the literacy rate varied from about 35 percent to more than 50 percent. (In England, by contrast, no more than one-third of all males could read and write.) But how readily most of these people could (or would) read a book or write a letter was another matter. Ordinary Americans' reading fare at best encompassed only a few well-thumbed books: an almanac, a psalter, and the Bible. They inhabited a world of oral culture, in which ideas and information passed through the spoken word—a conversation with neighbors, an exchange of pleasantries with the local gentle-

man, a hot debate at the town meeting, a sermon by the minister. When uttered with feeling and sincerity, spoken words could move them with tremendous force.

However, members of the gentry, well-to-do merchants, educated ministers, and some self-improving artisans and farmers also lived in the world of print culture. Though costly, books, newspapers, and writing paper could open up eighteenth-century European civilization to reading men and women. And a rich, exciting world it was. Great advances in natural science seemed to explain the laws of nature; human intelligence appeared poised to triumph over ignorance and prejudice; life itself looked as if it would at last become pleasant. For those who had the time to read and think, an age of optimism and progress had dawned: the Enlightenment. Upper-class Americans could not resist its charms and could be powerfully moved by the promise of its written words.

## *The Enlightenment in America*

Anglo-American intellectuals like the self-taught scientist Benjamin Franklin drew their inspiration from Enlightenment ideals, which combined confidence in human reason with skepticism toward beliefs not founded on science or strict logic. One source of Enlightenment thought lay in the writings of English physicist Sir Isaac Newton (1642–1727), who in 1687 explained how gravitation ruled the universe. Newton's work captured Europe's imagination by demonstrating the harmony of natural laws and stimulated others to search for rational principles in medicine, law, psychology, and government.

In the second quarter of the eighteenth century, no American more fully embodied the Enlightenment spirit than Franklin. Born in Boston in 1706, Franklin migrated to Philadelphia at age seventeen. He brought along skill as a printer, considerable ambition, and insatiable intellectual curiosity. In moving to Philadelphia, Franklin put himself in the right place at the right time, for the city was growing much more rapidly than Boston and was attracting English and Scottish merchants who shared Franklin's zest for learning. These men nudged Franklin's career along by lending him books and securing him printing contracts. In 1732 Franklin began to publish *Poor Richard's Almanack,* a collection of maxims and proverbs that made him famous. By age forty-two Franklin had earned enough money to retire and devote himself to science and community service.

These dual goals—science and community benefit—were intimately related in Franklin's mind, for he believed that all true science would be useful in the sense of making everyone's life more comfortable. For example, experimenting with a kite, Franklin demonstrated in 1752 that lightning was electricity, a discovery that led to the useful lightning rod. Franklin organized the American Philosophical Society in 1743 to encourage "all philosophical experiments that let light into the nature of things, tend to increase the power of man over matter, and multiply the conveniences and pleasures of life." By 1769 this society had blossomed into an intercolonial network of amateur scientists.

Although several southern plantation owners, including Thomas Jefferson, ardently championed progress through science, the Enlightenment's primary centers in America were the seaboard cities, where the latest books and ideas from Europe circulated and gentlemen and self-improving artisans met in small societies to investigate nature. In the eyes of many of these individuals, the ideal was the Royal Society in London, the foremost learned society in the English-speaking world. In this respect, the Enlightenment, at least initially, strengthened the ties between colonial and British elites. Although confident that science would benefit everyone, the Enlightenment's followers envisioned progress as gradual and proceeding from the top down. They trusted reason far more than they trusted the common people, whose judgment, especially on religious matters, seemed too easily deranged.

Just as Newton inspired the scientific bent of Enlightenment intellectuals, English philosopher John Locke's *Essay Concerning Human Understanding* (1690) led many to embrace "reasonable" or "rational" religion. Locke contended that ideas, including religion, are not inborn but are acquired by toilsome investigation of and reflection upon experience. To most Enlightenment intellectuals, the best argument for the existence of God seemingly could be derived through study of the harmony and order of nature, which pointed to a rational Creator. Some individuals, including Franklin and Jefferson, carried this argument a step further by insisting that where the Bible conflicted with reason, one should follow the dictates of reason rather than the Bible. Called Deists, they concluded that God, having created a perfect universe, did not miraculously intervene in its workings but rather left it alone to operate according to natural laws.

Most colonists influenced by the Enlightenment described themselves as Christians and attended church.

**Meeting of the Tuesday Club**
*Like Franklin's Junto and similar groups in other colonial cities, the Tuesday Club of Annapolis, Maryland, appealed to the elite white men who cultivated the literary and cultural tastes of "gentlemen."*

But they feared Christianity's excesses, particularly as indulged in by those who persecuted others in religion's name, and by "enthusiasts" who emphasized emotion rather than reason in the practice of piety. Mindful of Locke's caution that a human can never be *absolutely* certain of anything but his or her own existence, they distrusted zealots. Typically, Franklin contributed money to most of the churches in Philadelphia but thought that religion's value lay in its encouragement of virtue and morality rather than in theological hair splitting.

Prior to 1740 colonial intellectuals usually associated fanaticism and bigotry with Catholics and the early

Puritans, and they looked on their own time as an era of progressive reasonableness. But a series of religious revivals known as the Great Awakening would soon shatter their complacency.

### The Great Awakening

Viewing the world as orderly and predictable, rationalists were inclined to a sense of smug self-satisfaction. Writing his will in 1750, Franklin thanked God for giving him "such a mind, with moderate passions" and "such a competency of this world's goods as might make a reasonable mind easy." But many Americans lacked a comfortable competency of worldly goods and lived neither orderly nor predictable lives. For example, in 1737 and 1738 an epidemic of diphtheria, a contagious throat disease, killed every tenth child under sixteen from New Hampshire to Pennsylvania. Such an event starkly reminded the colonists of the fragility of earthly life and turned their thoughts to religion.

Throughout the colonial period, religious fervor had occasionally quickened within a denomination or region and then died down. But in 1739, an outpouring of European Protestant revivalism spread to British North America. This "Great Awakening" cut across lines of class, status, and education. Above all, the revivals represented an unleashing of anxiety and longing among ordinary people living in a world of oral culture—anxiety about sin, and longing for salvation. And the answers that they received were conveyed through the spoken word. Some revivalists were themselves intellectuals, comfortable amid the books and ideas of the print culture. But for all, religion was primarily a matter of emotional commitment.

In contrast to rationalists, who stressed the human potential for betterment, the ministers who roused their congregations into outbursts of religious fervor during the revivals depicted the emptiness of material comfort, the utter corruption of human nature, the fury of divine wrath, and the need for immediate repentance. Although he was a brilliant thinker, well aware of contemporary philosophy and science, the Congregationalist Jonathan Edwards, who led a revival at Northampton, Massachusetts, in 1735, drove home this message with breathtaking clarity. "The God that holds you over the pit of Hell, much as one holds a spider or other loathsome insect over the fire, abhors you," Edwards intoned in one of his famous sermons, "Sinners in the Hands of an Angry God." "His wrath toward you burns like fire; He looks upon you as worthy of nothing else but to be cast into the fire."

Even before Edwards's Northampton revival, two New Jersey ministers, Presbyterian William Tennent and Theodore Frelinghuysen of the Dutch Reformed Church, had stimulated conversions in prayer meetings called Refreshings. But the event that brought these various threads of revival together was the arrival in 1739 of the charismatic George Whitefield, an English clergyman who had been stoking the fires of revival in the Anglican Church. So overpowering was Whitefield's presence that some joked that he could make crowds swoon simply by uttering "Mesopotamia." Crowds exceeding twenty thousand could hear his booming voice clearly, and many wept at his eloquence.

Whitefield's American tour inspired thousands to seek salvation. Most converts were young adults in their late twenties. In Connecticut alone, the number joining churches jumped from 630 in 1740 to 3,217 in 1741, and within four years of Whitefield's arrival, every fifth man and woman under forty-five had reportedly been saved by God's grace. Whitefield's allure was so mighty that he even awed potential critics. Hearing him preach in Philadelphia, Benjamin Franklin first vowed to contribute nothing to the collection. But so admirably did Whitefield conclude his sermon, Franklin recalled, "that I empty'd my Pocket wholly into the Collector's Dish, Gold and all."

Divisions over the revivals quickly developed in Whitefield's wake and were often exacerbated by social and economic tensions. For example, after leaving Boston in October 1740, Whitefield invited Gilbert Tennent (William's son) to follow "in order to blow up the divine flame lately kindled there." Denouncing Boston's established clergymen as "dead Drones" and lashing out at aristocratic fashion, Tennent built a following among the city's poor and downtrodden. So did the Congregationalist James Davenport, who was expelled for having said that Boston's clergy were leading the people blindfolded to hell.

Exposing colonial society's social divisions, Tennent and Davenport corroded support for the revivals among established ministers and officials. As Whitefield's exchange with Alexander Garden showed, the lines hardened between the revivalists, known as New Lights, and the rationalist clergy, or Old Lights, who dominated the Anglican, Presbyterian, and Congregational Churches. In 1740 Gilbert Tennent published *The Danger of an Unconverted Ministry*, which hinted that

**Baptist Meetinghouse and Anglican Church Interiors, Eighteenth-Century Virginia**
*The New Light Baptist structure (above) reflects the members' poverty as well as their preference for equality, simplicity, and intimacy in their services. The Old Light Anglican Church (right) expresses an emphasis on hierarchy, formality, and distance among members. In particular, compare the relationship of minister to congregation in each church.*

most Presbyterian ministers lacked saving grace and hence were bound for hell, and urged their parishioners to abandon them for the New Lights. By thus sowing the seeds of doubt about individual ministers, Tennent was undermining one of the foundations of social order, for if the people could not trust their own ministers, whom could they trust?

Old Light rationalists fired back. In 1742 Charles Chauncy, a well-known Boston Congregationalist, condemned the revival as an epidemic of the "enthusiasm" that Enlightened intellectuals so loathed. Chauncy particularly blasted those who mistook the ravings of their overheated imaginations for the experience of divine grace. He even provided a kind of checklist for spotting enthusiasts: look for "a certain wildness" in their eyes, the "quakings and tremblings" of their limbs, and foaming at the mouth, Chauncy suggested. Put simply, the revival had unleashed "a sort of madness."

The Great Awakening opened unprecedented splits in American Protestantism. In 1741 New and Old Light Presbyterians formed rival branches that did not reunite until 1758, when the revivalists emerged victorious. The Anglicans lost many members to New Light preachers,

especially to Presbyterians and Baptists. Congregationalists splintered so badly that within twenty years of 1740, New Lights had seceded from one-third of all New England churches and formed separate parishes.

In Massachusetts and Connecticut, where the Congregational Church was established by law, the secession of New Light parishes provoked bitter conflict. To force New Lights into paying tithes to their former church, Old Lights repeatedly denied new parishes legal status. Connecticut passed repressive laws forbidding revivalists to preach or perform marriages, and the colony expelled many New Lights from the legislature. In Connecticut's Windham County, an extra story had to be added to the jail to hold all the New Lights arrested for not paying tithes. Elisha Paine, a revivalist imprisoned at Windham for illegal preaching, continued giving sermons from his cell and drew such crowds that his followers built bleachers nearby to hear him. Paine and his fellow victims generated widespread sympathy for the New Lights, who finally won control of Connecticut's assembly in 1759.

Although New Lights made steady gains until the 1770s, the Great Awakening peaked in 1742. The revival then crested everywhere but in Virginia, where its high point came after 1755 with an upsurge of conversions by Baptists, who also suffered legal harassment.

For all the commotion it raised at the time, the Great Awakening's long-term effects exceeded its immediate impact. First, the revival started the decline in the influence of Quakers (who were not significantly affected by the Great Awakening), Anglicans, and Congregationalists. As these churches' importance waned, the number of Presbyterians and Baptists increased after 1740, and that of Methodists (revivalist offshoots of Anglicanism) rose after 1770. Ever since the late 1700s, these three churches have dominated American Protestantism. Second, the Great Awakening stimulated the founding of new colleges, for existing colleges were scarred in their opponents' eyes by their affiliations with either Old or New Lights. In 1746 New Light Presbyterians established the College of New Jersey (Princeton). Then followed King's College (Columbia) for Anglicans in 1754, the College of Rhode Island (Brown) for Baptists in 1764, Queen's College (Rutgers) for Dutch Reformed in 1766, and Dartmouth College for Congregationalists in 1769. Third, the revival went beyond the ranks of white society to draw many African-Americans and Native Americans to Protestantism for the first time. The revivals' oral and communal dimensions, along with their emphasis on piety over intellectual learning as the key to God's grace, enabled some Africans and Native Americans to combine aspects of their traditional cultures with Protestant Christianity. The Great Awakening marked the real emergence of black Protestantism, which was almost nonexistent before 1740. New Lights reached out to slaves, some of whom joined white churches and even preached at revival meetings. Conversions came slowly, but by 1790 many blacks were Christians. Meanwhile, a few New Light preachers became missionaries to Indians still residing in the colonies. Among their converts were some Indians who had previously rejected Protestant missionaries. A few Christian Indians, such as Samson Occom, a Mohegan born in Connecticut, became widely known as preachers themselves. Despite these breakthroughs, blacks and Indians still faced considerable discrimination in colonial churches, even among New Lights.

The Great Awakening also gave added prominence to women in colonial religion. For several decades ministers had singled out women—who constituted the majority of church members—as embodying the Christian ideal of piety. Now some of the New Light churches, mostly Baptist and Congregationalist, began to grant women the right to speak and vote in church meetings. And like Anne Hutchinson a century earlier, some women moved from leading women's prayer and discussion groups to presiding over meetings that included men. One such woman, Sarah Osborn of Newport, Rhode Island, conducted "private praying Societies Male and female" that included black slaves in her home. In 1770 Osborn and her followers won a bitter fight over their congregation's choice of a new minister. While most assertive women were prevented by detractors from exercising as much power as Osborn, none was persecuted as Hutchinson had been in Puritan New England.

**Reverend Samson Occom, Mohegan Indian Preacher**
*Born in a wigwam in Connecticut, Occom converted to Christianity under the influence of the Great Awakening and preached to other Native Americans. But he grew disillusioned with the treatment of his people by whites and, after the American Revolution, joined an exodus of Indians from New England to upstate New York.*

Finally the revivals had the unintended effect of fostering religious toleration by blurring theological differences among New Lights. Although an Anglican who helped found Methodism, George Whitefield preached with Presbyterians such as Gilbert Tennent and Congregationalists like Jonathan Edwards. By emphasizing inner experience over doctrinal and institutional fine points, revivalism helped to prepare Americans to accept denominational pluralism, which emerged after the Revolution as the best means of accommodating religious diversity.

Historians have disagreed over whether the Great Awakening had political as well as religious effects. Although Tennent and Davenport called the poor "God's people" and flayed the wealthy, they never advocated a social revolution, and the Awakening did not produce any distinct political ideology. Yet by empowering ordinary people to criticize those in authority, the revivals laid some of the groundwork for political revolutionaries a generation later, who would contend that royal government in America had grown corrupt and unworthy of obedience.

## CONCLUSION

By the 1750s the British mainland colonies had taken on the look of mature societies. For fifty years their population and wealth had been rising impressively, and they now participated fully in the British-dominated Atlantic economy. White British colonists' standard of living far exceeded those of lower Louisiana and the Spanish colonies, and equaled that of England. The influence of Europe's Enlightenment had spread widely in the colonies, and by 1766 Anglo-America had more institutions of higher learning than England, Scotland, and Ireland together. A self-confident Anglo-American upper class had garnered expertise in law, trade, finance, and politics. The Great Awakening, with its European origins and its intercolonial appeal, further signaled the colonies' emergence from provincial isolation. Above all, the burgeoning of newspaper and book publishing, along with the proliferation of far-reaching commercial, intellectual, and religious networks, enabled eighteenth-century white colonists to identify more closely than had their predecessors with developments in Britain and in other colonies.

French and Spanish achievements on the North American mainland contrasted starkly with those of Britain. The two nations' territories were only thinly colonized, mostly on lands that were remote from the more dynamic centers of Atlantic commerce. Despite their mercantilist orientations, neither France nor Spain developed North American colonies that substantially enriched their respective home countries.

For all of its evident wealth and progress, Anglo-America was rife with tensions. In some areas, vast discrepancies in the distribution of wealth and opportunities fostered a rebellious spirit among whites who were less well off. The Enlightenment and the Great Awakening revealed deep-seated religious and ideological divisions. Slave resistance and Anglo-Indian warfare demonstrated the depths of racial antagonisms. After France was vanquished and Spain further weakened in the Seven Years' War (1756–1763), these tensions fused with newly emergent differences between Britain and its colonies. The result was a revolutionary explosion.

## FOR FURTHER READING

Bernard Bailyn and Philip D. Morgan, eds., *Strangers Within the Realm: Cultural Margins of the First British Empire* (1991). Leading historians examine the interplay of ethnicity and empire in North America, the Caribbean, Scotland, and Ireland.

Ira Berlin, *Many Thousands Gone: The First Two Centuries of Slavery in North America* (1998). A major study illuminating slave existence and culture in mainland North America, from the earliest African arrivals through the age of the American Revolution.

Ronald Hoffman et al., eds. *Through a Glass Darkly: Reflections on Personal Identity in Early America* (1997). Essays that explore issues of personal identity for individual Americans during the seventeenth and eighteenth centuries.

Rhys Isaac, *The Transformation of Virginia, 1740–1790* (1982). Pulitzer Prize–winning study of class, race relations, and culture during the Great Awakening and American Revolution.

Susan Juster, *Disorderly Women: Sexual Politics and Evangelicalism in Revolutionary New England* (1994). A major study of the gendered dimensions of the religious revivals.

John J. McCusker and Russell R. Menard, *The Economy of British America, 1607–1789*, rev. ed. (1991). A comprehensive discussion of the economy in light of current scholarship.

James H. Merrell, *The Indians' New World: Catawbas and Their Neighbors from European Contact Through the Era of Removal* (1989). A pathbreaking examination, with broad implications for understanding the Native American past.

Gary B. Nash, *The Urban Crucible: Social Change, Political Consciousness, and the Origins of the American Revolution* (1979). A masterful study of social, economic, and political change in Boston, New York, and Philadelphia.

# Roads to Revolution

## 1744–1776

**The Boston Massacre, 1770,** Engraving by Paul Revere
*Shortly after this incident, one Bostonian observed that "unless there is some great alteration in the state of things, the era of the independence of the colonies is much nearer than I once thought it, or now wish it."*

On the evening of March 5, 1770, an angry crowd of poor and working-class Bostonians gathered in front of the guard post outside the Boston customs house. The crowd was protesting a British soldier's abusive treatment a few hours earlier of a Boston apprentice who was trying to collect a debt from a British officer. Suddenly shots rang out, and when the smoke and dust had cleared, five Bostonians lay dead and six more were wounded. Among those in the crowd was an impoverished, twenty-eight-year-old shoemaker named George Robert Twelves Hewes. Hewes had joined earlier Boston crowds in their protests against British authorities, but it was the "Boston Massacre" (facing page), as the shooting became known, that led Hewes to see his and the other protesters' actions in political terms. Four of the five dead men were personal friends; he himself had received a serious blow to the shoulder from a soldier's rifle butt; and he had had an earlier run-in with the guards' arrogant commanding officer. Over the next several days, Hewes attended meetings and signed public petitions denouncing British conduct in the shooting, and he later testified against the soldiers. Thereafter he participated far more prominently in such anti-British actions as the Boston Tea Party.

How did it come to be that British troops were stationed on the streets of Boston in 1770? What had brought those troops and the city's citizens to the verge of war? And what led obscure, humble people like George Robert Twelves Hewes to become angry political activists in an age when the lowborn were expected to defer to their social superiors? The Boston Massacre was but one of a long chain of events that resulted finally in the complete rupture of Britain's relationship with its American colonies.

The conflict between Britain and the colonies arose suddenly after 1763, when Parliament attempted to reorganize its suddenly enlarged empire by tightening control over economic and political affairs in the colonies. Long accustomed to benefiting economically from the empire while legislating for themselves, colonists were shocked by this unexpected effort to centralize decision making in London. Many colonial leaders, such as Benjamin Franklin, interpreted Britain's clampdown as calculated antagonism, intended to deprive the colonists of their prosperity and their relative independence. Others, such as Massachusetts lieutenant governor and chief justice, Thomas Hutchinson, stressed the importance of maintaining order and authority.

For many ordinary colonists like Hewes, however, the conflict was more than a constitutional crisis. In the port cities, crowds of poor and working people engaged in direct, often violent demonstrations against British authority. Sometimes they acted in concert with elite radicals; at other times, in defiance. Settlers in the remote backcountry of several colonies invoked the language and ideas of urban radicals when resisting the monopolies of large landowners and the policies of colonial governments dominated by seaboard elites. These movements reflected social-economic tensions within the colonies and the emergence of distinctly nonelite views on the crisis. By the same token, the growing participation of white women in colonial resistance brought to the fore yet another perspective on the crisis. Moreover, colonial protests did not arise in a vacuum but rather drew from ideas and opposition movements in Britain and elsewhere in Europe.

Taken as a whole, colonial resistance involved many kinds of people with many outlooks. It arose most immediately from a constitutional crisis within the British Empire, but it also reflected deep democratic stirrings in America and in the Atlantic world generally. These stirrings would erupt in the American Revolution, beginning in 1776, then in the French Revolution, which began in 1789, and spread subse-

**The Female Combatants, 1776**
*Britain, the fashionable mother, tries to subdue her rebellious daughter, America, an Indian princess.*

quently over much of Europe and the Americas.

Despite their apprehension over parliamentary taxes, colonial politicians usually expressed their opposition peacefully from 1763 to 1775, through such tactics as legislative resolutions and commercial boycotts. Few lost their lives during the twelve years prior to the battles at Lexington and Concord, the first military clashes of the Revolution, and all of those killed were American civilians rather than royal officials or soldiers. Even after fighting broke out, some colonists agonized for more than a year over whether to sever their political relationship with England—which even native-born Americans sometimes referred to affectionately as "home." Of all the world's colonial peoples, none became rebels more reluctantly than did Anglo-Americans in 1776.

This chapter focuses on four major questions:

♦ How and why did the Seven Years' War lead to a rupture between Britain and its North American colonies?

♦ What were the fundamental differences between British officials and their colonial opponents with respect to the status and role of the colonies within the British Empire?

♦ In what ways did protests against British policies affect political life *within* the colonies?

♦ How did colonial protesters overcome the distinct histories and identities of the various colonies to mount a united front against British policies?

## Imperial Warfare

After 1713, when Queen Anne's War ended, the American colonies enjoyed a generation of peace as well as prosperity. The peace was shattered in 1739 by an Anglo-Spanish war in the Southeast that quickly merged with a second one in central Europe, the War of the

Austrian Succession, known as King George's War in British America (1740–1748). After a "diplomatic revolution" in which Austria dropped its alliance with Britain for one with France, leading Britain to align with Prussia, the conflict resumed as the Seven Years' War (1756–1763). In both wars the Anglo-French conflict was fought not in Europe but on the high seas; in India (where the two powers competed for influence among local rulers); and in North America. Although these conflicts originated in rivalries among the great powers of Europe, few colonists doubted that King George's War was also *their war,* or that their prosperity depended on a British victory in the Seven Years' War.

### King George's War

King George's War largely followed the pattern of earlier conflicts under William and Mary and Queen Anne (see Chapter 4). Few battles involved more than six hundred men, and most of the skirmishes consisted of raids and counterattacks in the Northeast, in which many civilians were killed and others captured, especially by French and Indians attacking New England frontier towns. Although prisoners were exchanged at the end of each conflict, some captives, particularly women and children, elected to remain with the French or Indians.

King George's War produced just one major engagement. In 1745 almost four thousand New Englanders under William Pepperell of Maine besieged and, after seven weeks of intense, heroic fighting, captured the French bastion of Louisbourg, which guarded the entrance to the St. Lawrence River. But after three more years of inconclusive warfare, Britain and France signed the Treaty of Aix-la-Chapelle in 1748, exchanging Louisbourg for a British outpost in India that the French had taken during the war. The memory of how their stunning achievement at Louisbourg went for naught would rankle the colonists for a decade.

### A Fragile Peace

King George's War failed to establish either Britain or France as the dominant power in North America, and each side soon began preparations for another war. Although there were many points of contention between the two powers, it was the Ohio Valley that became the tinderbox for conflict.

For more than half a century, the region had attracted refugee Indians—Delawares from Pennsylvania, Shawnees returning to their homeland from Penn-

## CHRONOLOGY

**1744–1748** King George's War (in Europe, the War of Austrian Succession, 1740–1748).

**1755–1760** Seven Years' War (in Europe, 1756–1763).

**1760** George III becomes king of Great Britain.

Massachusetts controversy over writs of assistance.

**1763–1766** Indian uprising in Ohio Valley and Great Lakes.

**1763** Proclamation of 1763.

**1764** Sugar Act.

**1765** Stamp Act.

First Quartering Act.

Loyal Nine formed in Boston to oppose the Stamp Act.

Sons of Liberty band together throughout the colonies.

Stamp Act Congress.

Colonists begin boycott of British goods.

**1766** Stamp Act repealed.

Declaratory Act.

**1767** New York Suspending Act.

Revenue Act (Townshend duties).

John Dickinson, *Letters from a Farmer in Pennsylvania*.

American Board of Customs Commissioners created.

**1768** Massachusetts "circular letter."

Boston merchants adopt the colonies' first nonimportation agreement.

John Hancock's ship *Liberty* seized by Boston customs commissioner.

British troops arrive in Boston.

First Treaty of Fort Stanwix.

John Wilkes elected to Parliament; arrested.

St. George's Fields Massacre in London.

**1770** Townshend duties, except tea tax, repealed.

Boston Massacre.

**1771** Battle of Alamance Creek in North Carolina.

**1772** Committees of correspondence begin in Massachusetts and rapidly spread.

**1773** Tea Act.

Boston Tea Party.

Lord Dunmore's War.

**1774** Coercive Acts.

Quebec Act.

First Continental Congress meets in Philadelphia and adopts Suffolk Resolves.

Continental Association.

**1775** Battles of Lexington and Concord.

Second Continental Congress meets.

Olive Branch Petition.

Battles at Breed's Hill and Bunker Hill.

**1776** Thomas Paine, *Common Sense*.

Declaration of Independence.

---

sylvania and South Carolina, and others driven there by colonial expansion and fur-trade rivalries (see Chapter 4). Even some Iroquois, eager for new trading opportunities, had moved to the area, where they became known as Mingos. Initially welcomed as trade partners and bulwarks against English expansion, these Indians increasingly irritated the French by their independence, in particular the willingness of some to deal with Pennsylvania traders and even to fight against the French in King George's War. The French derided these Indians as "republicans" for their defiance of all outside authority—French, English, and Iroquois.

For the next decade and a half, the "republican" Indians sought to balance the English and French against each other while the two powers grew ever less patient with the Indians' neutrality. After the war Virginia pressured some Iroquois leaders into ceding land occupied by Delawares so that the colony's agents could build a fortified trading post at the junction of the Allegheny and Monongahela rivers—the site of modern Pittsburgh. As a result the Delawares and other "republican" Indians began to fear that the English were the greater threat to their independence.

By 1752 the Ohio Valley was the subject of competing claims by Virginia, Pennsylvania, France, and the Iroquois, as well as by the Indians who actually lived there. The next year the French began building a chain of forts in order to recapture control of trade with the Indians from Virginians and Pennsylvanians. Virginia retaliated by sending a twenty-one-year-old surveyor and speculator, George Washington, to force the French out through either persuasion or force. But in 1754, French troops drove Washington and his militiamen back to their homes.

**"Join, or Die," 1754**
*Benjamin Franklin published this well-known cartoon just before the Albany Congress convened. The snake symbolized the colonies' considerable divisions—a disunity that political leaders would have to struggle against in years to come.*

Sensing the need to resolve differences among themselves and to restore the confidence of the Indians, delegates from seven colonies north of Virginia gathered in mid-1754 at Albany, New York, to lay plans for their mutual defense. By showering the wavering Iroquois with thirty wagonloads of presents, the colonists kept them neutral for the moment. (But virtually all Indians in Ohio itself now supported the French.) The delegates then endorsed a proposal for a colonial confederation, the so-called Albany Plan of Union, largely based on the ideas of Pennsylvania's Franklin and Massachusetts's Thomas Hutchinson. The plan called for a "Grand Council" representing all the colonial assemblies, with a crown-appointed "president general" as its executive officer. The Grand Council would devise policies regarding military defense and Indian affairs, and, if necessary, it could demand funds from the colonies according to an agreed-upon formula. Although it provided a precedent for later American unity, the Albany Plan came to nothing, primarily because no colonial legislature would surrender the least control over its powers of taxation, even to fellow Americans and in the face of grave mutual danger.

### The Seven Years' War in America

Although France and Britain remained at peace in Europe until 1756, Washington's 1754 clash with French troops created a virtual state of war in North America. In response, the British dispatched General Edward Braddock and a thousand regular troops to North America to take Fort Duquesne at the headwaters of the Ohio.

Stiff-necked and scornful of colonial soldiers as well as Native Americans, Braddock expected his disciplined British regulars to make short work of the enemy and only dimly perceived the strength and resourcefulness of the forces gathering against him. On July 9, 1755, about 850 French, Canadians, and Indians ambushed Braddock's force of 2,200 Britons and Virginians nine miles east of Fort Duquesne. Riddled by three hours of steady fire from an unseen foe, Braddock's troops retreated. Nine hundred regular and provincial soldiers died in Braddock's defeat, including the general himself, compared to just twenty-three on the French and Indian side.

Following this engagement, Indian raids convulsed Pennsylvania, Maryland, Virginia, and even parts of New Jersey—all colonies that had escaped attack in previous wars.

Confronted by the numerically superior but disorganized Anglo-Americans, the French seized Fort Oswego on Lake Ontario in 1756 and took Fort William Henry on Lake George in 1757. The French now threatened central New York and western New England. In Europe, too, the war was going badly for Britain, which by 1757 seemed to be facing defeat on all fronts.

In this dark hour, two developments turned the tide for the British. First, the Iroquois and most Ohio Indians, sensing that the French were gaining too decisive an advantage, agreed at a treaty conference at Easton, Pennsylvania, in 1758 to abandon their support of the French. Their subsequent withdrawal from Fort Duquesne enabled the British to capture it and other French forts. Although some Indians stayed out of the fighting, others actively joined the British cause.

The second decisive development occurred when William Pitt took control of military affairs in the British cabinet and reversed the downward course. Imaginative and single-minded in his conception of Britain's imperial destiny, Pitt saw himself as the man of the hour. "I know," he declared, "that I can save this country and that no one else can." True to his word, Pitt reinvigorated British patriotism throughout the empire. By the war's end, he was the colonists' most popular hero, the symbol of what Americans and the English could accomplish when united.

Hard pressed in Europe by France and its allies (which included Spain after 1761), Pitt chose not to send large numbers of additional troops to America.

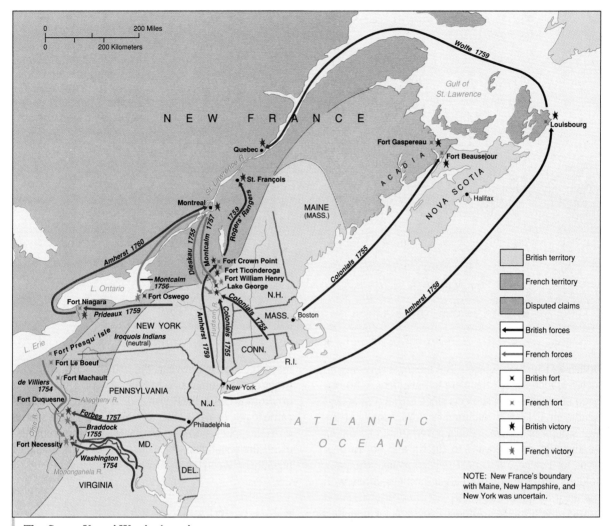

### The Seven Years' War in America

*After experiencing major defeats early in the war, Anglo-American forces turned the tide against the French by taking Fort Duquesne in late 1757 and Louisbourg in 1758. After Canada fell in 1760, the fighting shifted to Spain's Caribbean colonies.*

Rather, he believed that the key to crushing New France lay in the mobilization of colonial soldiers. To encourage the colonies to assume the military burden, he promised that if they raised the necessary men, Parliament would bear most of the cost of fighting the war.

Pitt's offer to free Anglo-Americans from the war's financial burdens generated unprecedented support. The colonies organized more than forty thousand troops in 1758–1759, far more soldiers than the crown sent to the mainland during the entire war. The impact of Pitt's decision was immediate. Anglo-American troops under General Jeffery Amherst captured Fort Duquesne and Louisbourg by late 1758 and drove the French from northern New York the next year. In September 1759 Quebec fell after General James Wolfe defeated the French commander-in-chief, Louis Joseph Montcalm, on the Plains of Abraham outside that city, where both commanders died in battle. French resistance ended in 1760, when Montreal surrendered.

France ceded all its territories on the North American mainland by the Treaty of Paris of 1763, which officially ended the Seven Years' War in both America and Europe. As a result, several thousand French colonists, stretching from Quebec to Illinois to Louisiana, became

**New British Fort, 1759**
*After the French abandoned Crown Point on Lake Champlain, British troops occupied it and built a greatly expanded fortress. This watercolor was painted by a British officer.*

British and Spanish subjects. But the most adversely affected Franco-Americans were the Acadians, who had been nominal British subjects since England took over Acadia in 1713 and renamed it Nova Scotia. At the war's outbreak, Nova Scotia's government ordered all Acadians to swear loyalty to Britain and not to bear arms for France. After most refused to take the oath, soldiers drove them from their homes—often with nothing more than they could carry in their arms—and burned their villages. Almost 5 percent of Canada's population was eventually deported in this way to the British colonies, especially Maryland and Pennsylvania. But facing poverty and intense anti-French, anti-Catholic prejudice, most Acadians moved on to Louisiana. There they became known as Cajuns.

Under terms of the Treaty of Paris, France gave Britain all of its lands east of the Mississippi and transferred title to its claims west of that river to Spain, which also gained New Orleans. In return for Cuba, which a British expedition had taken over in 1762, Spain ceded Florida to Britain. Spain's vast American empire thus remained intact, but France's formerly extensive holdings were reduced to a few tiny fishing islands off Newfoundland and several thriving sugar islands in the West Indies. Britain reigned supreme in eastern North America.

King George's War and the Seven Years' War produced an ironically mixed effect. On one hand, they fused the bonds between the British and the Anglo-Americans. Fighting side by side, shedding their blood in common cause, the British and the American colonists came to rely on each other as rarely before. At the same time, the conclusion of each war planted the seeds first of misunderstanding, then of suspicion, and finally of hostility between the two former compatriots.

## Imperial Reorganization

Following the Seven Years' War, Britain sought to finance its greatly expanded empire through a series of revenue measures imposed on Britons and colonists alike, and to exercise more direct control over its colonies. Opposition movements arose in Britain and in its mainland colonies, from Massachusetts to Georgia, to protest not only the new measures' economic costs but what many people regarded as a dangerous extension of tyrannical power. In America this confrontation quickly escalated into a principled conflict over the colonies' relationship with Parliament in Britain.

The new revenue measures coincided with the beginning of the reign of George III (ruled 1760–1820), who ascended to the throne at age twenty-two. In contrast to his immediate predecessors, George I and George II, who had been largely content to let veteran politicians run the country, the new king distrusted the British political establishment. He was determined to have a strong influence on government policy, but he wished to reign as a constitutional monarch who cooperated with Parliament and worked through prime ministers. However, neither his experience, his temperament, nor his philosophy suited George III to the formidable task of selecting satisfactory prime ministers to oversee the passage of imperial laws. Clashes of personality and policy prompted the king to make frequent abrupt changes in government leadership at the very time Britain was trying to implement a massive reorganization of its empire.

### Friction Among Allies

An extraordinary coalition of Britons, colonists, and Native Americans had achieved the victory over France in North America. But the return of peace brought deep-seated tensions among these allies back to the surface.

During the war, British officers regularly complained about the quality of colonial troops, not only their inability to fight but also their tendency to return home—even in the midst of campaigns—when their terms were up or when they were not paid on time. For their part, colonial soldiers complained of British officers who, as one put it, contemptuously treated their troops "but little better than slaves."

Tensions between British officers and colonial civilians also flared, with officers complaining about colonists' unwillingness to provide food and shelter and colonists resenting the officers' arrogant manners. One general groused that South Carolina planters were "extremely pleased to have Soldiers to protect their Plantations but will feel no inconveniences for them." Quakers in the Pennsylvania assembly, acting from their pacifist convictions, refused to vote funds to support the war effort, while assemblies in New York and Massachusetts opposed the quartering of British troops on their soil as an encroachment on their English liberties. English authorities regarded such actions as affronts to the king's prerogative and as stifling Britain's efforts to defend its territories.

Pitt's promise to reimburse the colonial assemblies for their military expenses also angered many Britons, who concluded that the colonists were escaping scot-free from the war's financial burden. The colonies had already profited enormously from the war, as military contracts and spending by British troops brought an influx of British currency into the hands of farmers, arti-

**George III,** Studio of A. Ramsay, c. 1767
*Although unsure of himself and emotionally little more than a boy upon his accession to the English throne, George III possessed a deep moral sense and a fierce determination to rule as well as to reign.*

sans, and merchants. Some colonial merchants, moreover, had continued their illicit trade with the French West Indies during the conflict, so that they were not only violating the Navigation Acts but trading with the enemy. Meanwhile, Britain's national debt had nearly doubled during the war, from £72 million to over £132 million. At a time when the total debt of all the colonies collectively amounted to £2 million, the interest charges alone on the British debt came to more than £4 million a year. This debt was assumed by British landowners through a land tax and, increasingly, by ordinary consumers through excise duties on a wide variety of items, including beer, tea, salt, and bread.

But many colonists felt equally burdened. Those who profited during the war spent their additional incomes on goods imported from Britain, the annual

**Queen Anne Dining Room**
*Virtually everything in this recreated dining room was imported from England. Whereas early colonial houses were devoted entirely to feeding and sheltering family members, eighteenth-century elite houses featured specialized rooms including lavishly furnished dining rooms for entertainment.*

value of which doubled during the war's brief duration. Along with a parallel movement in Britain, the consumption of tea, wine, mass-produced textiles, ceramics, and metalware by members of the middle class was fueling Britain's economy, particularly its manufacturing sector. And it was transforming the habits and tastes of thousands of people who previously had made or purchased locally nearly everything they consumed. But the wartime boom in the colonies ended as abruptly as it had begun when peace returned in 1760. To maintain their new middle-class lifestyles, colonists went into debt. British creditors obliged their American merchant customers by extending the usual period for remitting payments from six months to a year. Nevertheless, many recently prosperous colonists suddenly found themselves overloaded with debts and in many cases bankrupt. As colonial indebtedness to Britain grew, some Americans began to suspect the British of deliberately plotting to "enslave" the colonies.

Victory over the French did not end the British need for revenue, for the settlement of the war spurred new Anglo-Indian conflicts that drove the British debt even higher. With the French vanquished, Ohio and Great Lakes Indians recognized that they could no longer play the two imperial rivals off against each other. Their

fears that the British would treat them as subjects rather than allies were confirmed when General Jeffrey Amherst, Britain's commander in North America, decided to cut expenses by refusing to distribute food, ammunition, and other gifts. Moreover, squatters from the colonies were moving onto Indian lands in some areas and harassing the occupants, and many Indians feared that the British occupation was intended to support these incursions.

As tensions mounted, a Delaware religious prophet named Neolin attracted a large following by calling for a complete repudiation by Indians of European culture, material goods, and alliances. Meanwhile, other Native Americans hoped that the French would return so they could once again manipulate an imperial balance of power. Political leaders such as Pontiac, an Ottawa Indian, drew on these sentiments to forge an explicitly anti-British movement. During the spring and summer of 1763, they and their followers sacked eight British forts near the Great Lakes and besieged two others at Pittsburgh and Detroit. But over the next three years, shortages of food and ammunition, a smallpox epidemic (triggered when British officers at Fort Pitt deliberately distributed infected blankets at a peace parley), and a recognition that the French would not return led the Indians to make peace with Britain.

Although word of the uprising spread to Indians in the Southeast and Mississippi Valley, the effective diplomacy of British agent John Stuart prevented violence from erupting in these areas.

Despite the uprising's failure, the Native Americans had not been decisively defeated. Hoping to conciliate the Indians and end the frontier fighting, the British government issued the Proclamation of 1763, by which it asserted direct control of land transactions, settlement, trade, and other activities of non-Indians west of the Appalachian crest. The government's goal was to restore order to the process of colonial expansion by replacing the authority of the various (and often competing) colonies with that of the crown. The proclamation recognized existing Indian land titles everywhere west of the "proclamation line" until such time as tribal governments agreed to cede their land through treaties. Although calming Indian fears, the proclamation angered the colonies by subordinating their western claims to imperial authority and by slowing expansion.

The uprising was also a factor in the British government's decision that ten thousand soldiers should remain in North America to occupy its new territories and to intimidate the Indian, French, and Spanish inhabitants. But the burden of maintaining control over the western territories would reach almost half a million pounds a year, fully 6 percent of Britain's peacetime budget. Britons considered it perfectly reasonable for the colonists to help offset this expense, which the colonists, however, saw as none of their responsibility. Although the troops would help to offset the colonies' unfavorable balance of payments with Britain, they appeared to many Americans as a "standing army" that in peacetime could only threaten their liberty. With the French menace to their security removed, increasing numbers of colonists saw westward expansion onto Indian lands as a way to prosperity, and they viewed British troops, enforcing the Proclamation of 1763, as hindering rather than enhancing that expansion.

### *The Writs of Assistance*

Even before the Seven Years' War was over, British authorities began attempts to halt American merchants from trading with the enemy in the French West Indies. In 1760 the royal governor of Massachusetts authorized revenue officers to employ a document called a writ of assistance to seize illegally imported goods. The writ was a general search warrant that permitted customs

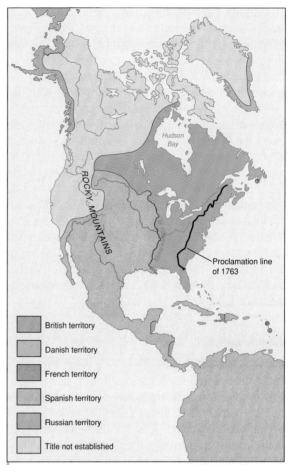

**European Powers in North America 1763**
*The Treaty of Paris (1763) divided France's North American empire between Britain and Spain. Hoping to prevent unnecessary violence between whites and Indians, Britain forbade any new white settlements west of the Appalachians' crest in the Proclamation of 1763.*

officials to enter any ships or buildings where smuggled goods might be hidden. Because the document required no evidence of probable cause for suspicion, most English legal authorities considered it unconstitutional. The writ of assistance also threatened the traditional respect accorded the privacy of a family's place of residence, since most merchants conducted business from their homes.

Writs of assistance proved a powerful weapon against smuggling. In quick reaction to the writs, merchants in Boston, virtually the smuggling capital of the colonies, hired lawyer James Otis to challenge the constitutionality of these warrants. Arguing his case before the Massachusetts supreme court in 1761, Otis proclaimed that "an act against the Constitution is void"—even one passed by Parliament. But the court, influenced by the opinion of Chief Justice Thomas Hutchinson, who noted the use of identical writs in England, ruled against the Boston merchants.

Despite losing the case, Otis expressed with absolute clarity the fundamental conception of many, both in Britain and in the colonies, of Parliament's role under the British constitution. The British constitution was not a written document but a collection of customs and accepted principles that guaranteed certain rights to all citizens. Most British politicians assumed that Parliament's laws were themselves part of the constitution and hence that Parliament could alter the constitution at will. Like other colonists, Otis contended that Parliament possessed no authority to violate any of the traditional "rights of Englishmen," and he asserted that there were limits "beyond which if Parliaments go, their Acts bind not."

### The Sugar Act

In 1764, just three years after Otis's court challenge, Parliament passed the Sugar Act. The measure's goal was to raise revenues that would help offset Britain's military expenses in North America, and thus end Britain's long-standing policy of exempting colonial trade from revenue-raising measures. The Navigation Acts had not been designed to bring money into the British treasury but rather to benefit the imperial economy indirectly, by stimulating trade and protecting English manufacturers from foreign competition. The taxes that Parliament levied on colonial products entering Britain were paid by English importers who passed them on to consumers; they were not taxes paid by American producers. So little revenue did the Navigation Acts bring in (just £1,800 in 1763) that they did not even pay for the cost of their own enforcement.

The Sugar Act amended the old Molasses Act of 1733 (see Chapter 4), which amounted to a tariff on French West Indian molasses entering British North America. But colonists simply continued to import the cheaper French molasses, bribing customs officials into taking 1½ pence per gallon to look the other way when it was unloaded. Aware of the widespread bribery, Parliament assumed, erroneously, that rum drinkers could stomach a threepence duty per gallon.

New taxes were not the only feature of the Sugar Act objectionable to American merchants. The act also stipulated that colonists could export lumber, iron, skins, and many other commodities to foreign countries only if the shipments landed first in Britain. Previously, American ships had taken these products directly to the Netherlands or the German states, where captains purchased local goods and then returned directly to the colonies. By channeling this trade through Britain, Parliament hoped that colonial shippers would purchase more *imperial* wares for the American market and buy fewer goods from foreign competitors.

The Sugar Act also vastly complicated the requirements for shipping colonial goods. A captain now had to fill out a confusing series of documents to certify his trade as legal, and the absence of any of them left his entire cargo liable to seizure. The law's petty regulations made it virtually impossible for many colonial shippers to avoid committing technical violations of the Sugar Act, even if they traded in the only manner possible under local circumstances.

Finally, the Sugar Act disregarded many traditional English protections for a fair trial. First, the law allowed customs officials to transfer smuggling cases from the colonial courts, in which juries decided the outcome, to vice-admiralty courts, where a judge alone gave the verdict. Because the Sugar Act (until 1768) awarded vice-admiralty judges 5 percent of any confiscated cargo, judges had a financial incentive to find defendants guilty. Second, until 1767 the law did not permit defendants to be tried where their offense allegedly had taken place (usually their home province) but required all cases to be heard in the vice-admiralty court at Halifax, Nova Scotia. Third, the law reversed normal courtroom procedures, which presumed innocence until guilt was proved, by requiring the defendant to disprove the prosecution's charge.

The Sugar Act was no idle threat. British prime minister George Grenville ordered the navy to enforce the measure, and it did so vigorously. A Boston resident complained in 1764 that "no vessel hardly comes in or goes out but they find some pretense to seize and detain her." That same year, Pennsylvania's chief justice reported that customs officers were extorting fees from small boats carrying lumber across the Delaware River to Philadelphia from New Jersey and seemed likely "to destroy this little River-trade."

Rather than pay the threepence tax, Americans continued smuggling molasses until 1766. Then, to discourage smuggling, Britain lowered the duty to a penny—less than the customary bribe American shippers paid to get their cargoes past inspectors. The law thereafter raised about £30,000 annually in revenue.

Opposition to the Sugar Act remained fragmented and ineffective. The law's burden fell overwhelmingly on Massachusetts, New York, and Pennsylvania; other provinces had little interest in resisting a measure that did not affect them directly. In the end, the Sugar Act's immediate impact was minor. Soon a far more controversial issue would overshadow it—the Stamp Act.

## The Stamp Act

The revenue raised by the Sugar Act did little to ease Britain's financial crisis. The national debt continued to rise, and the British public groaned under the weight of the second-highest tax rates in Europe. Particularly irritating to Britons was the fact that by 1765 their rates averaged 26 shillings per person, whereas the colonial tax burden varied from ½ to 1½ shillings per inhabitant, or barely 2–6 percent of the British rate. Well aware of how lightly the colonists were taxed, Grenville thought that fairness demanded a larger contribution to the empire's expenses in North America.

To raise such revenues, Parliament passed the Stamp Act in March 1765. The law obliged colonists to purchase and use special stamped (watermarked) paper for newspapers, customs documents, various licenses, college diplomas, as well as legal forms used for recovering debts, buying land, and making wills. As with the Sugar Act, any violators would face prosecution in vice-admiralty courts, without juries. The prime minister projected yearly revenues of £60,000 to £100,000, which would offset 12–20 percent of North American military expenses. Unlike the Sugar Act, which was an *external* tax—one levied on imports as they entered the colonies—the Stamp Act was an *internal* tax, or a duty levied directly on property, goods, and government services in the colonies. Whereas external taxes were intended to regulate trade and fell mainly on merchants and ship captains, internal taxes were designed to raise revenue for the crown and had far wider effects. In the case of the Stamp Act, anyone who made a will, transferred property, borrowed money, or bought playing cards or newspapers would pay the tax.

To Grenville and his supporters, the new tax seemed a small price for the benefits of the empire, especially since Britons had been paying a similar tax since 1695. Nevertheless, some in England, most notably William Pitt, objected in principle to Britain's levying an internal tax on the colonies. They emphasized that the colonists had never been subject to

British revenue bills and noted that they taxed themselves through their own elected assemblies.

Grenville and his followers agreed that Parliament could not tax any British subjects unless they enjoyed representation in that body. But they contended that Americans shared the same status as the majority of British adult males who either lacked sufficient property to vote or lived in large cities which had no seats in Parliament. Such people were considered to be "virtually" represented in Parliament.

**Tax Stamps**
*Under the Stamp Act, all legal and commercial documents had to bear tax stamps such as the one shown here in close-up.*

The theory of virtual representation held that every member of Parliament stood above the narrow interests of his constituents and considered the welfare of *all* subjects when deciding issues. By definition, then, no Briton was represented by any particular individual in the House of Commons, but rather all imperial subjects, including Americans, could depend on each member of Parliament to protect their well-being.

Grenville and his supporters also denied that the colonists were entitled to any exemption from British taxation because they elected their own assemblies. These legislative bodies were allegedly no different from English or Scottish town councils, whose local powers to pass laws and taxes did not nullify Parliament's authority over them. Accordingly, colonial assemblies were an adaptation to unique American circumstances and possessed no more power than Parliament allowed them to exercise. But Grenville's position clashed directly with the stance of many colonists who had been arguing for several decades that their assemblies exercised legislative powers equivalent to those of the House of Commons in Great Britain (see Chapter 4).

To many colonists the Stamp Act seemed to force them either to confront the issue of parliamentary taxation head-on or to surrender any claim to meaningful rights of self-government. However much they might admire and respect Parliament, few colonists imagined that it represented them. They accepted the theory of virtual representation as valid for England and Scotland but denied that it could be extended to the colonies. Instead they argued that they enjoyed a substantial measure of self-governance similar to that of Ireland, whose Parliament alone could tax its people but could not interfere with laws, like the Navigation Acts, passed by the British Parliament. In a speech before the Boston town meeting opposing the Sugar Act, James Otis expressed Americans' basic argument: "that by [the British] Constitution, every man in the dominions is a free man: that no parts of His Majesty's dominions can be taxed without consent: that every part has a right to be represented in the supreme or some subordinate legislature." In essence, the colonists assumed that the empire was a loose federation in which their legislatures possessed considerable autonomy, rather than an extended nation governed directly from London.

### Resisting the Stamp Act

Unlike the Sugar Act, the Stamp Act generated a political storm that rumbled through all the colonies in 1765. To many colonists Parliament's passage of the Stamp Act demonstrated both its indifference to their interests and the shallowness of the theory of virtual representation. Colonial agents in London had lobbied against passage of the law, and provincial legislatures had sent petitions—carefully worded statements of principle—warning against passage, but all to no avail. Parliament had dismissed the petitions without a hearing. Parliament "must have thought us Americans all a parcel of Apes and very tame Apes too," concluded Christopher Gadsden of South Carolina, "or they would have never ventured on such a hateful, baneful experiment."

In late May 1765, Patrick Henry, a twenty-nine-year-old Virginia lawyer with a talent for fiery oratory, dramatically conveyed the rising spirit of resistance. Henry persuaded the Virginia House of Burgesses to adopt several strongly worded resolutions denying Parliament's power to tax the colonies, and in the debate over the resolutions, the Speaker of the House cut him off just short of his uttering a treasonous wish that "some good American would stand up for his country"—presumably by assassinating the British tyrant responsible. Rather garbled accounts of Henry's resolutions electrified other Americans, and by the year's end, eight other colonial legislatures took a firm stand against British taxation.

Meanwhile, grass-roots resistance to the law was taking shape. In Boston by late summer, a group of mostly middle-class artisans, shopkeepers, and businessmen joined together as the Loyal Nine to fight the Stamp Act. They recognized that the stamp distributors, who alone could accept money for watermarked paper, were the law's weak link. If the public could pressure them into resigning before taxes became due on November 1, the Stamp Act would become inoperable. The Loyal Nine would propel Boston to the forefront of resistance.

It was no accident that Boston set the pace in opposing Parliament. Bostonians lived primarily by trade and distilling, and in 1765 they were not living well. No other port suffered so much from the Sugar Act's trade restrictions. The law burdened rum producers with a heavy tax on molasses, dried up a flourishing business of importing Portuguese wines, and prohibited the direct export of many New England products to profitable overseas markets. The city, moreover, was still struggling to recover from a great fire in 1760 that had burned 176 warehouses and left every tenth family homeless.

Widespread economic distress produced an explosive situation in Boston. A large segment of its population blamed British policies for the town's hard times. The situation was unusually dangerous because Bostonians were accustomed to forming large crowds to engage in pointed but symbolic political expression. The high point of each year was November 5, Guy Fawkes Day, when thousands gathered to commemorate the failure of a Catholic plot in England in 1605 to blow up Parliament and kill King James I. On that day each year, crowds from the North End and the South End customarily burned gigantic effigies of the pope as well as of local political leaders and other elite figures, and generally satirized the behavior of the "better sort." High spirits sometimes overflowed into violent confrontations in which the two crowds battled each other with fists, stones, and barrel staves. In August 1765 the Loyal Nine oversaw a truce between the two groups that united them under a South End shoemaker named Ebenezer MacIntosh.

The morning of August 14 found a likeness of Boston's stamp distributor, Andrew Oliver, swinging from a tree guarded by a menacing crowd. Oliver apparently did not realize that the Loyal Nine were warning him to resign immediately, so at dusk MacIntosh and several hundred followers demolished a new building of Oliver's at the dock. Thereafter, the Loyal Nine withdrew and the crowd continued on its own. The men surged toward Oliver's house, where they ceremoniously beheaded his effigy and "stamped" it to pieces. The crowd then shattered the windows of his home, smashed his furniture, and even tore out the paneling. When Lieutenant Governor Thomas Hutchinson and the sheriff tried to disperse the crowd, they were driven off under a barrage of rocks. Surveying his devastated home the next morning, Oliver announced his resignation.

Bitterness against the Stamp Act unleashed spontaneous, contagious violence. Twelve days after the first Boston riot, Bostonians demolished the elegant home of Thomas Hutchinson. This attack occurred in part because smugglers held grudges against Hutchinson for certain decisions he had given as chief justice and also because many financially pinched citizens saw him as a symbol of the royal policies crippling Boston's already troubled economy and their own livelihoods. In their view, wealthy officials "rioted in luxury," with homes and fancy furnishings that cost hundreds of times the annual incomes of most Boston working men. They were also reacting to Hutchinson's efforts to stop the destruction of his brother-in-law Andrew Oliver's house. Ironically, Hutchinson privately opposed the Stamp Act.

Meanwhile, groups similar to the Loyal Nine but calling themselves Sons of Liberty began forming throughout the colonies. After the assault on Hutchinson's mansion and an even more violent incident in Newport, Rhode Island, the leaders of the Sons of Liberty sought to prevent more such rampages, lest they alienate elite opponents of the tax. Thereafter they directed their violence against property and invariably left avenues of escape for their victims. Especially fearful that a royal soldier or revenue officer might be shot or killed, the Sons of Liberty forbade their followers to carry weapons, even when facing armed adversaries. Realizing the value of martyrs, they resolved that the only lives lost over the issue of British taxation would come from their own ranks.

In October 1765 representatives of nine colonial assemblies met in New York City in the so-called Stamp Act Congress. The session was remarkable for the colonies' agreement on and bold articulation of the general principle that Parliament lacked authority to levy taxes outside Great Britain and to deny any person a jury trial. Only once before had a truly intercolonial meeting taken place—the Albany Congress, in 1754—and its plea for unity had fallen on deaf ears. In 1765 the

**Stamp Act Protest**
*A Boston crowd burns bundles of the special water-marked paper intended for use as stamps.*

colonial response was entirely different. "The Ministry never imagined we could or would so generally unite in opposition to their measures," wrote a Connecticut delegate to the congress, "nor I confess till I saw the Experiment made did I."

By late 1765 most stamp distributors had resigned or fled, and without the watermarked paper required by law, most royal customs officials and court officers were refusing to perform their duties. In response, legislators compelled the reluctant officials to resume operation by threatening to withhold their pay. At the same time, merchants obtained sailing clearances by insisting that they would sue if cargoes spoiled while delayed in port. By late December the courts and harbors of almost every colony were again functioning.

Thus the colonial upper class assumed control of the public outcry against the Stamp Act. Respectable gentlemen moved to keep an explosive situation from getting out of hand by taking over leadership of local

Sons of Liberty groups, by coordinating protest through the Stamp Act Congress, and by having colonial legislatures restore normal business. Colonial leaders feared that chaos was about to break out, particularly if British troops landed to enforce the Stamp Act. An influential Pennsylvanian, John Dickinson, summed up how colonial elites envisioned the dire consequences of revolutionary turmoil: "a multitude of Commonwealths, Crimes, and Calamities, Centuries of mutual jealousies, Hatreds, Wars of Devastation, till at last the exhausted provinces shall sink into savagery under the yoke of some fortunate Conqueror."

Such extreme consequences did not come to pass, though the Stamp Act remained in effect. To force its repeal, New York's merchants agreed on October 31, 1765, to boycott all British goods, and businessmen in other cities soon followed their example. Because American colonists purchased about 40 percent of England's manufactures, this nonimportation strategy put the English economy in danger of recession. The colonial boycotts consequently triggered panic within England's business community, whose members descended on Parliament to warn that the Stamp Act's continuation would stimulate a wave of bankruptcies, massive unemployment, and political unrest.

For reasons unconnected with the Stamp Act, George Grenville had fallen from George III's favor in mid-1765 and had been succeeded by the Marquis of Rockingham. The new prime minister hesitated to advocate repeal because the overwhelming majority within the House of Commons was outraged at colonial defiance of the law. Then in January 1766 William Pitt, a steadfast opponent of the Stamp Act, boldly denounced all efforts to tax the colonies, declaring, "I rejoice that America has resisted." Parliamentary support for repeal thereafter grew, though only as a matter of practicality, not as a surrender of principle. In March 1766 Parliament revoked the Stamp Act, but only in conjunction with passage of the Declaratory Act, which affirmed parliamentary power to legislate for the colonies "in all cases whatsoever."

Because the Declaratory Act was written in general language, Americans interpreted its meaning to their advantage. Most colonial political leaders recognized that the law was modeled after an earlier statute of 1719 regarding Ireland, which was considered exempt from British taxation. The measure therefore seemed no more than a parliamentary exercise in saving face to compensate for the Stamp Act's repeal, and Americans ignored it. The House of Commons, however, intended that the colonists take the Declaratory Act literally to mean that they could not claim exemption from *any* parliamentary statute, including a tax law. The Stamp Act crisis thus ended in a fundamental disagreement between Britain and America over the colonists' political rights.

Although the Stamp Act crisis had not resolved the underlying philosophical differences between Britain and America, most colonists eagerly put the events of 1765 behind them, and they showered both king and Parliament with loyal statements of gratitude for the Stamp Act's repeal. The Sons of Liberty disbanded. Anglo-Americans manifestly still possessed a deep emotional loyalty to "Old England" and concluded with relief that their active resistance to the law had slapped Britain's leaders back to their senses. Nevertheless, the crisis led many to ponder British policies and actions more deeply than ever before.

## Ideology, Religion, and Resistance

The Stamp Act and the conflicts that arose around it revealed a chasm between England and its colonies that startled Anglo-Americans. For the first time, some sensed a sinister quality to the imperial relationship that they previously had taken for granted and valued. In their efforts to grasp the significance of their new perceptions, a number of educated colonists turned to the works of philosophers, historians, and political writers. Many more, both educated and uneducated, looked to religion.

By the 1760s the colonists already were widely familiar with the political writings of European Enlightenment thinkers, particularly John Locke (see Chapter 4). Locke argued that humanity originated in a state of nature in which people enjoyed the "natural rights" of life, liberty, and property. Thereafter, people entered into a "social contract" in order to form governments that would protect those rights. A government that encroached on natural rights, then, broke its contract with the people. In such cases, people could resist their government, although Locke cautioned against outright rebellion except in the most extreme cases. To many colonial readers, Locke's concept of natural rights appeared to justify opposition to arbitrary legislation by Parliament.

Among the most widely read authors in the colonies were a group of English political writers known as oppositionists. According to John Trenchard, Thomas Gordon, and others belonging to this group, Parliament—consisting of the freely elected representatives of the people—formed the foundation of England's unique political liberties and protected those liberties against the inherent corruption and tyranny of executive power. But since 1720, the oppositionists argued, prime ministers had exploited the treasury's vast resources to provide pensions, contracts, and profitable offices to politicians or had bought elections by bribing voters in small boroughs. Most members of Parliament, in their view, no longer represented the true interests of their constituents; rather, they had sold their souls for financial gain and joined in a "conspiracy against liberty." Often referring to themselves as the "country party," these oppositionists feared that a power-hungry "court party" of nonelected officials close to the king was using a corrupted Parliament to gain absolute power for themselves.

During the 1760s and 1770s, a group of English radicals, most notably Joseph Priestley and James Burgh, drew on both Enlightenment and oppositionist authors to fashion a wide-ranging critique of English government and a new way of thinking about politics. At the heart of all political relationships, they argued, a struggle raged between the aggressive extension of artificial *power,* as represented by corrupt governments, and the natural *liberty* of the people. To protect their liberty, a free people had to avoid moral corruption in their own lives and resist the encroachments of power, or tyranny. Above all, they had to remain alert for "designs" or "conspiracies" against liberty wherever they might appear.

Influenced by such ideas, a number of colonists detected a diabolical conspiracy behind British policy during the Stamp Act crisis. James Otis characterized a group of pro-British Rhode Islanders as a "little, dirty, drinking, drabbing, contaminated knot of thieves, beggars, and transports . . . made up of Turks, Jews, and other infidels, with a few renegade Christians and Catholics." Joseph Warren of Massachusetts noted that the act "induced some to imagine that the minister designed by this to force the colonies into a rebellion, and from thence to take occasion to treat them with severity, and, by military power, to reduce them to servitude." Over the next decade, a proliferation of pamphlets denounced British efforts to "enslave" the colonies through excessive taxation and the imposition of officials, judges, and a standing army directed from

**A Patriot View of British Officials, 1766**
*This Boston editorial cartoon depicts two British officials as enslaved to the devil.*

London. In such assaults on liberty and natural rights, some Americans found principled reasons for opposing British policies and actions.

Many colonists also followed the lead of Massachusetts assemblyman Samuel Adams, who expressed hope that America would become a "Christian Sparta." By linking Christian piety and classical antiquity, Adams was combining two of colonial leaders' most potent rhetorical appeals in rallying public protest. Almost every eighteenth-century American had been steeped in Protestantism since childhood; and all whose education had gone beyond the basics had imbibed Greek and Latin learning, as well as seventeenth-century English literature. All these hallowed traditions, Americans believed, confirmed the legitimacy of their cause.

Recalling in later years the inspiring debate over the Stamp Act that he had witnessed in Virginia's House of Burgesses in 1765, Thomas Jefferson said of Patrick Henry that "he appeared to me to speak as Homer wrote." Jefferson was a typical educated man of his day in revering the ancient republics of Greece and Rome for their supposedly stern, virtuous devotion to liberty. The pamphlets, speeches, and public declarations that gentlemen like Jefferson and John Dickinson wrote resounded with quotations from the ancient classics. These allusions served as constant reminders to upper-class Americans of the righteous dignity of their cause. But appeals to ordinary Americans had to draw upon deeper wellsprings of belief. Significantly, the power of Henry's oratory also reflected his ability (unique among Virginia political leaders) to evoke the religious fervor of the Great Awakening.

Beginning with the Stamp Act protest, New England's clergymen mounted their pulpits and summoned their flocks to stand up for God and liberty. "A just regard to our liberties . . . is so far from being displeasing to God that it would be ingratitude to him who has given them to us to . . . tamely give them up," exhorted one minister. With equally heartfelt intensity, Baptist and other dissenting preachers took up the cause. Only Anglican ministers, whose church was headed by the king, tried to stay neutral or opposed the protest; and many pacifist Quakers kept out of the fray. But to most American Protestant clergymen, memories of battling for the Lord in the old Calvinist tradition proved too powerful to resist.

Voicing such a message, clergymen exerted an enormous influence on public opinion. Far more Americans heard sermons than had access to newspapers or pamphlets, and ministers always got a respectful hearing at town meetings. Community leaders' proclamations of days of "fasting and public humiliation"—in colonial America, a familiar means of focusing public attention on an issue and invoking divine aid—inspired sermons on the theme of God's sending the people woes only to strengthen and sustain them until victory. Even Virginia gentlemen not notable for their piety felt moved by such proclamations. Moreover, protest leaders' calls for boycotting British luxuries meshed neatly with traditional pulpit warnings against frivolity and wastefulness. Few ordinary Americans escaped the unceasing public reminders that community solidarity against British tyranny and "corruption" meant rejecting sin and obeying God.

The ebbing of the Stamp Act crisis momentarily took the urgency out of such extreme views. But the alarm that Britain's actions raised in the minds of many colonists was not easily put to rest. After a hiatus of two years, it was clear that British and American views of the colonies' place in the empire remained as far apart as ever.

# The Deepening Crisis

From 1767 to 1773, Parliament pursued a confrontational policy that gradually corroded Americans' trust of Britain. The British government's actions in these years created a climate of fear and alienation that left most colonists convinced that the Stamp Act had not been an isolated mistake but part of a deliberate design to undermine colonial self-governance. In this they were joined by many in Britain who questioned policies that were economically costly and actions that seemed to threaten Britons and colonists alike.

## *The Quartering Act*

In August 1766, in a move arising out of British politics, George III dismissed the Rockingham government and summoned William Pitt to form a cabinet. Opposed to taxing the colonies, Pitt might have repaired the Stamp Act's damage, for no man was more respected in America. But Pitt's health collapsed in March 1767, and effective leadership passed to his chancellor of the exchequer (treasurer) Charles Townshend.

Just as Townshend took office, a conflict arose with the New York legislature over the Quartering Act of 1765. This law ordered colonial legislatures to pay for certain goods needed by soldiers stationed within their respective borders. The necessary items were relatively inexpensive barracks supplies such as candles, windowpanes, mattress straw, polish, and a small liquor ration.

Despite its seemingly petty stipulations, the law aroused resentment, for it constituted an *indirect* tax; that is, although it did not (like the Stamp Act) empower royal officials to collect money directly from the colonists, it obligated assemblies to raise a stated amount of revenue by whatever means they considered appropriate. The act fell lightly or not at all on most colonies; but New York, where more soldiers were stationed than in any other province, found compliance very burdensome and refused to grant any supplies.

New York's resistance to indirect taxation produced a torrent of anti-American feeling in the House of Commons, whose members remained bitter at having had to withdraw the Stamp Act. Townshend responded by drafting the New York Suspending Act, which threatened to nullify all laws passed by the colony if the assembly refused to vote the supplies. By the time that George III signed the measure, however, New York had appropriated the necessary funds.

Although New York's retreat averted further confrontation, the conflict over the Quartering Act demonstrated that British leaders would not hesitate to defend Parliament's sovereignty through the most drastic of all steps: by interfering with American claims to self-governance.

## The Townshend Duties

The new wave of parliamentary resentment toward the colonies coincided with an outpouring of British frustration over the government's failure to cut taxes from wartime levels. Dominating the House of Commons, members of the landed gentry slashed their own taxes by 25 percent in 1767. This move cost the government £500,000 and prompted Townshend to propose laws that would tax imports entering America and increase colonial customs revenue.

Townshend sought to tax the colonists by exploiting an oversight in their arguments against the Stamp Act. In confronting the Stamp Act, Americans had emphasized their opposition to *internal* taxes, but had said little about Parliament's right to tax imports as they entered the colonies. Townshend and other British leaders chose to interpret this silence as evidence that the colonists accepted Britain's right to tax their trade—to impose *external* taxes. Yet not all British politicians were so mistaken. "They will laugh at you," predicted a now wiser George Grenville, "for your distinctions about regulations of trade." Brushing aside Grenville's warnings, Parliament passed Townshend's Revenue Act of 1767 (popularly called the Townshend duties) in June and July 1767. The new law taxed glass, paint, lead, paper, and tea imported into the colonies.

On the surface, Townshend's contention that the Americans would submit to this external tax on imports was convincing, for the colonists had long accepted Parliament's right to regulate their overseas trade and had in principle acknowledged taxation as a legitimate form of regulation. But Townshend's Revenue Act differed significantly from what Americans had long seen as a legitimate way of regulating trade through taxation. To the colonists, charging a duty was a lawful way for British authorities to control trade only if that duty excluded foreign goods by making them prohibitively expensive to consumers. The Revenue Act of 1767, however, set moderate rates that did not price goods out of the colonial market; clearly, its purpose was to collect money for the treasury. Thus from the

colonial standpoint, Townshend's duties were taxes just like the Stamp Act duties.

Although Townshend had introduced the Revenue Act in response to the government's budgetary problems, he had an ulterior motive for establishing an American source of revenue. Traditionally, royal governors had depended on colonial legislatures to vote their salaries; for their part, the legislatures had often refused to allocate these salaries until governors signed certain bills they themselves opposed. Through the Revenue Act, Townshend hoped to establish a fund that would pay the salaries of governors and other royal officials in America, thus freeing them from the assemblies' control. In effect, by stripping the assemblies of their most potent weapon, the power of the purse, the Revenue Act threatened to tip the balance of constitutional power away from elected colonial representatives and toward unelected royal officials.

In reality the Revenue Act would never yield anything like the income that Townshend anticipated. Of the various items taxed, only tea produced any significant revenue—£20,000 of the £37,000 that the law was expected to yield. And because the measure would serve its purpose only if British tea were affordable to colonial consumers, Townshend eliminated £60,000 worth of import fees paid on Dutch East Indian tea entering Britain before transshipment to America. On balance, the Revenue Act *worsened* the British treasury's deficit by £23,000. By 1767 Britain's financial difficulties were more an excuse for, than the driving force behind, political demands to tax the colonies. From Parliament's standpoint, the conflict with America was becoming a test of national will over the *principle* of taxation.

## The Colonists' Reaction

Parliament gave the colonists little time to plan resistance against the Townshend duties. Americans only learned of the Revenue Act shortly before it went into operation, and they hesitated over the appropriate response. The strong-arm tactics that sent stamp tax collectors into panicky flight would not work against the Townshend duties, which the navy could easily collect offshore, safe from any Sons of Liberty.

Resistance to the Revenue Act remained weak until December 1767, when John Dickinson published twelve essays entitled *Letters from a Farmer in Pennsylvania*. The essays, which appeared in nearly every colonial newspaper, emphasized that although

Parliament could regulate trade by voting duties capable of providing small amounts of "incidental revenue," it had no right to tax commerce for the single purpose of raising revenue. In other words, the legality of any external tax depended on its intent. No tax designed to produce revenue could be considered constitutional unless a people's elected representatives voted for it. Dickinson said nothing that others had not stated or implied during the Stamp Act crisis. Rather, his contribution lay in persuading many Americans that the arguments that they had marshaled against the Stamp Act also applied to the Revenue Act.

Soon after publication of Dickinson's *Letters,* James Otis, the Boston lawyer famed for his arguments in the writs-of-assistance case, chaired a Boston town meeting that asked the Massachusetts legislature to oppose the Townshend duties. In response, the assembly in early 1768 called on Samuel Adams to draft a "circular letter" to every other legislature. Adams's letter forthrightly condemned both taxation without representation and the threat to self-governance posed by Parliament's making governors and other royal officials financially independent of the legislatures. But it ac-

knowledged Parliament as the "supreme legislative Power over the whole Empire," and it advocated no illegal activities. Virginia's assembly warmly approved Adams's message and sent out a more strongly worded circular letter of its own, urging all colonies to oppose imperial policies that would "have an immediate tendency to enslave them." But most colonial legislatures reacted indifferently to these letters. In fact, resistance to the Revenue Act might have disintegrated had the British government not overreacted to the circular letters.

Parliamentary leaders regarded even the mild Massachusetts letter as "little better than an incentive to Rebellion." Disorganized by Townshend's sudden death in 1767, the king's Privy Council directed Lord Hillsborough, first appointee to the new post of secretary of state for the colonies, to express the government's displeasure. Hillsborough flatly told the Massachusetts assembly to disown its letter, forbade all assemblies to endorse it, and commanded royal governors to dissolve any colonial legislature that violated his instructions. George III later commented that he never met "a man of less judgment than Lord Hillsborough." A wiser man might have tried to divide the colonists by appealing to their sense of British patriotism, but Hillsborough had chosen a course guaranteed to unite them in anger.

To protest Hillsborough's crude bullying, many legislatures previously indifferent to the Massachusetts circular letter now adopted it enthusiastically. The Massachusetts House of Representatives voted 92–17 not to recall its letter. The number 92 immediately acquired symbolic significance for Americans; colonial politicians on more than one occasion drank 92 toasts in tipsy salutes to Massachusetts's action. In obedience to Hillsborough, royal governors responded by dismissing legislatures in Massachusetts and elsewhere. These moves played directly into the hands of Samuel Adams, James Otis, and John Dickinson, who wanted nothing more than to ignite widespread opposition to the Townshend duties.

Although increasingly outraged over the Revenue Act, the colonists still needed some effective means of pressuring Parliament for its repeal. One approach, nonimportation, seemed especially promising because it offered an alternative to violence and would distress Britain's economy. In August 1768 Boston's merchants therefore adopted a nonimportation agreement, and the tactic slowly spread southward. "Save your money,

**Samuel Adams**

*A central player in the drive for American liberty, Adams wrote in 1774, "I wish for a permanent union with the mother country, but only in terms of liberty and truth. No advantage that can accrue to America from such a union, can compensate for the loss of liberty."*

and you save your country!" became the watchword of the Sons of Liberty, who began reorganizing after two years of inactivity. Not all colonists supported nonimportation, however. Its effectiveness ultimately depended on the compliance of merchants, whose livelihood relied, in turn, on buying and selling imports. In several major communities, including Philadelphia, Baltimore, and Charles Town (Charleston), South Carolina, merchants continued buying British goods until 1769. Far from complete, the boycott probably kept out about 40 percent of all imports from Britain.

### *"Wilkes and Liberty"*

The exclusion of 40 percent of imports seriously affected many people in Britain and thus heightened pressure there, too, for repeal of the Townshend duties. Hardest hit were merchants and artisans dealing in consumer goods. Their protests formed part of a larger movement that arose during the 1760s to oppose the domestic and foreign policies of George III and a Parliament dominated by wealthy landowners. The leader of this movement was John Wilkes, a fiery London editor and member of Parliament who had first gained notoriety in 1763, when his newspaper regularly and irreverently denounced George III's policies. The government had finally arrested Wilkes for seditious libel, but to great popular acclaim, he had won his case in court. The government, however, had succeeded in shutting down his newspaper and in persuading members of the House of Commons to deny Wilkes his seat. After again offending the government with a publication, Wilkes had fled to Paris.

Wilkes returned to England in 1768, defying a warrant for his arrest, and ran again for Parliament. By this time the Townshend acts and other government policies were stirring up widespread protests. Merchants and artisans in London, Bristol, and other cities demanded the dismissal of the "obnoxious" ministers who were "ruining our manufactories by invidiously imposing and establishing the most impolitic and unconstitutional taxations and regulations on your Majesty's colonies." They were joined by (nonvoting) weavers, coal heavers, seamen, and other workers who protested low wages and high prices that stemmed in part from government policies. All these people rallied around the cry, "Wilkes and liberty!"

After he again was elected to Parliament, Wilkes was arrested. The next day, twenty to forty thousand an-

**The Alternative of Williamsburg,** by Philip Dawe, 1775
*In this cartoon, armed patriots in Williamsburg, Virginia, obtain a merchant's written agreement not to import British goods. The "alternative" is the containers of tar and feathers hanging in the background.*

gry "Wilkesites" massed on St. George's Fields, outside the prison where he was being held. When members of the crowd began throwing stones, soldiers and police responded with gunfire, killing eleven protesters. The "massacre of St. George's Fields" had given the movement some martyrs. Wilkes and an associate were elected to the seat twice more and were both times denied their seats by other legislators. Meanwhile, the imprisoned Wilkes was besieged by outpourings of popular support, from the colonies as well as from Britain. Some Virginians sent him tobacco, and the South Carolina assembly voted to contribute £1,500 to help defray his debts. He maintained a regular correspondence with the Boston Sons of Liberty and, upon his release in April 1770, was hailed in a massive Boston celebration as "the illustrious martyr to Liberty."

Wilkes's cause sharpened the political thinking of government opponents in Britain and the colonies alike. Thousands of voters in English cities and towns signed petitions to Parliament protesting its refusal to seat Wilkes as an affront to the electorate's will. Like the colonists, they regarded the theory of "virtual representation" in Parliament as a sham. Fearing arbitrary government actions, some of them formed a Society of the Supporters of the Bill of Rights "to defend and maintain the legal, constitutional liberty of the subject." And while more "respectable" opponents of the government such as William Pitt and Edmund Burke disdained Wilkes for courting the "mob," his movement emboldened them to speak more forcefully against the government, especially on its policies toward the colonies. For the colonists themselves, Wilkes and his following made clear that Parliament

and the government represented a small if powerful minority whose authority could be legitimately questioned.

## Women and Colonial Resistance

The tactical value of nonimportation was not restricted to damaging Britain's economy. It also hinged on colonists convincing the British—and one another—that they were determined to sustain resistance, and on demonstrating that their cause rested on the foundations of morality and moderation. In this respect, the nonimportation movement provided a unique opportunity for white women to join the protest against unconstitutional laws.

White women's participation in public affairs had been widening slowly and unevenly among the colonies for several decades. Women far outnumbered men among white church members, especially in New England where ministers frequently hailed them as superior to most men in piety and morality. By the 1760s, when colonial protests against British policies began, colonial women such as Sarah Osborn (see Chapter 4) had become well known as religious activists. Calling themselves the Daughters of Liberty, a contingent of upper-class female patriots had played a minor part in defeating the Stamp Act. Some had attended political rallies during the Stamp Act crisis, and many more had expressed their opposition in discussions and correspondence with family and friends.

In contrast, women assumed a highly visible role during the Townshend crisis. To protest the Revenue Act's tax on tea, more than three hundred "mistresses of families" in Boston denounced the consumption of the beverage in early 1770. In some ways, such nonconsumption was a more effective tactic than nonimportation, for although a minority of merchants might ignore nonimportation on the basis of principle or financial interest, a refusal by colonists to consume imports would chill merchants' incentive to continue importing English products.

Nonconsumption agreements soon became popular and were extended to include English manufactures (mostly clothing) as well as tea. Again women played a vital role, because the boycott would fail unless the colonists replaced British imports with apparel of their own making. Responding to leaders' pleas that they expand domestic cloth production, women of all social ranks, even those who customarily did not weave their own fabric or sew their own clothing, organized spin-

**Mr. and Mrs. Thomas Mifflin,** by John Singleton Copley, 1773. *The Mifflins were prominent Philadelphians. Thomas, a merchant in his early years, sat in the Pennsylvania assembly and the First Continental Congress and was later an officer in the Continental Army. An ardent supporter of the American cause, Sarah Morris Mifflin here demonstrates her patriotism by spinning her own thread.*

ning bees. These events attracted intense publicity as evidence of American determination to fight parliamentary taxation. One historian calculates that more than 1,600 women participated in spinning bees in New England alone from 1768 to 1770. The colonial cause, noted a New York woman, had enlisted "a fighting army of amazons . . . armed with spinning wheels."

Spinning bees not only helped undermine the notion that women had no place in public life but also endowed spinning and weaving, previously considered routine household tasks, with special political virtue. "Women might recover to this country the full and free enjoyment of all our rights, properties and privileges," exclaimed the Reverend John Cleaveland of Ipswich, Massachusetts, in 1769, adding that this "is more than the men have been able to do." For many colonists, such logic enlarged the arena of supposed feminine virtues from strictly religious matters to include political issues.

Spinning bees, combined with female support for boycotting tea, dramatically demonstrated that American determination ran far deeper than the protests of a few male merchants and the largely male crowds in American seaports. Women's participation showed that colonial protests extended into the heart of many American households and congregations, and were leading to broadened popular participation in politics.

### Customs Racketeering

Besides taxing colonial imports, Townshend sought to increase revenues through stricter enforcement of the Navigation Acts. While submitting the Revenue Act of 1767, he also introduced legislation creating the American Board of Customs Commissioners. This law raised the number of port officials, funded the construction of a colonial coast guard, and provided money for secret informers. It also awarded an informer one-third of the value of all goods and ships appropriated through a conviction of smuggling. The fact that fines could be tripled under certain circumstances provided an even greater incentive to seize illegal cargoes. Smuggling cases were heard in vice-admiralty courts, moreover, where the probability of conviction was extremely high.

In the face of lax enforcement, including widespread bribery of customs officials by colonial shippers and merchants, Towshend wanted the board to bring honesty, efficiency, and more revenue to overseas customs operations. But the law quickly drew protests because of the ways it was enforced and because it assumed those accused to be guilty until or unless they could prove otherwise.

Under the new provisions, revenue agents commonly filed charges for technical violations of the Sugar Act, even when no evidence existed of intent to conduct illegal trade. They most often exploited the provision that declared any cargo illegal unless it had been loaded or unloaded with a customs officer's written authorization. Customs commissioners also fanned angry passions by invading the traditional rights of sailors. Long-standing maritime custom allowed a ship's crew to supplement their incomes by making small sales between ports. Anything stored in a sailor's chest was considered private property that did not have to be listed as cargo on the captain's manifest. After 1767, however, revenue agents began treating such belongings as cargo, thus establishing an excuse to seize the entire ship. Under this new policy, crewmen saw their trunks ruthlessly broken open by arrogant inspectors and then lost trading stock worth several months' wages because it was not listed on the captain's loading papers.

To merchants and seamen alike, the commissioners had embarked on a program of "customs racketeering" that constituted little more than a system of legalized piracy. The board's program fed an upsurge in popular violence. Above all, customs commissioners' use of informers provoked retaliation. The *Pennsylvania Journal* in 1769 scorned these agents as "dogs of prey, thirsting after the fortunes of worthy and wealthy men." By betraying the trust of employers, and sometimes of friends, informers aroused wild hatred in their victims and were roughly handled whenever found.

Nowhere were customs agents and informers more detested than in Boston, where in June 1768 citizens finally retaliated against their tormentors. The occasion was the seizure, on a technicality, of the colonial merchant John Hancock's sloop *Liberty*. Hancock, reportedly North America's richest merchant and a leading opponent of British taxation, had become a chief target of the customs commissioners. Now they fined him £9,000, an amount almost thirteen times greater than the taxes he supposedly evaded on a shipment of Madeira wine. A crowd tried to prevent the towing of Hancock's ship and then began assaulting customs agents. Growing to several hundred as it surged through the streets, the mob drove all revenue inspectors from Boston.

Hancock's case forced colonists to reevaluate their former acceptance of the principle that Parliament had limited authority to pass laws for them. Prior to 1768 colonial leaders had single-mindedly denied Britain's power to tax them, without considering that freedoms of equal importance might also be jeopardized by other kinds of legislation. But by 1770 many argued that measures like the Sugar Act and the act creating the American Board of Customs Commissioners seriously endangered property rights and civil liberties. They expanded their opposition from a rejection of taxation without representation to a more broadly based rejection of legislation without representation. By 1774 there would emerge a new consensus that Parliament possessed no lawmaking authority over the colonies except the right to regulate imperial commerce through statutes like the old Navigation Acts.

### The Boston Massacre

Responding to the violence stirred up by the customs commissioners, the British government dispatched seventeen hundred British troops to Boston during the six weeks after October 1, 1768. Regarding the troops as a "standing army" that threatened their liberty, as well as a financial burden, Bostonians resented the soldiers' presence.

Boston rapidly took on the atmosphere of an occupied city and crackled with tension as armed sentries and resentful civilians traded insults. The mainly Protestant townspeople found it especially galling that many soldiers were Irish Catholics. The poorly paid enlisted men, moreover, were free to seek employment following the morning muster. Often agreeing to work for less than local laborers, they generated fierce hostility in a community that was plagued by persistently high unemployment.

Although Bostonians endured their first winter as a garrison town without undue trouble, relations between the remaining soldiers and the city's poorer civilians only worsened. The deep-seated resentment against all who upheld British authority suddenly boiled over on February 22, 1770, when a customs informer shot into a crowd picketing the home of a customs-paying merchant, killing an eleven-year-old boy. While elite Bostonians had disdained the unruly exchanges between soldiers and crowds, the horror at a child's death momentarily united the community. "My Eyes never beheld such a funeral," wrote John Adams. "A vast Number of Boys walked before the Coffin, a vast Number of Women and Men after it. . . . This Shews

there are many more Lives to spend if wanted in the Service of their country."

Although the army had played no part in the shooting, it became a natural target for popular frustration and rage. A week after the boy's funeral, tensions between troops and a crowd led by Crispus Attucks, a seaman of African and Native American descent, and including George Robert Twelves Hewes, erupted at the guard post protecting the customs office. When an officer tried to disperse the civilians, his men endured a steady barrage of flying objects and dares to shoot. A private finally did fire, after having been knocked down by a block of ice, and then shouted, "Fire! Fire!" to his fellow soldiers. The soldiers' volley hit eleven persons, five of whom, including Attucks, died.

The shock that followed the March 5 bloodshed marked the emotional high point of the Townshend crisis. Royal authorities in Massachusetts tried to defuse the situation in Boston by isolating all British soldiers on a fortified island in the harbor, and Governor Thomas Hutchinson promised that the soldiers who had fired would be tried. Patriot leader John Adams, an opponent of crowd actions, served as their attorney. Adams appealed to the Boston jury by claiming that the soldiers had been provoked by a "motley rabble of saucy boys, negroes and mulattoes, Irish teagues, and outlandish jack tarres," in other words, people not considered "respectable" by the city's elites and middle class. All but two of the soldiers were acquitted, and the ones found guilty suffered only a branding on their thumbs.

Burning hatreds produced by an intolerable situation underlay the Boston Massacre, as it came to be called in conscious recollection of the St. George's Fields Massacre of Wilkesites in London two years earlier. The shooting of unarmed American civilians by British soldiers, and the light punishment given the soldiers, forced the colonists to confront the stark possibility that the British government was bent on coercing and suppressing them through naked force. In a play written by Mercy Otis Warren, a character predicted that soon, "Murders, blood and carnage/Shall crimson all these streets," as patriots rose to defend their republican liberty against tyrannical authority.

### Lord North's Partial Retreat

As the Boston Massacre raged, a new British prime minister, Lord North, quietly worked to stabilize relations between Britain and its colonies. North was a

**Mercy Otis Warren** by John Singleton Copley, 1763
*Essayist and playwright Mercy Otis Warren was the most
prominent woman intellectual of the Revolutionary era.*

shrewd politician who would remain in office until 1782. North favored eliminating most of the Townshend duties to prevent the American commercial boycott from widening, but to underscore British authority, he insisted on retaining the tax on tea. Parliament agreed, and in April 1770, giving in for the second time in three years to colonial pressure, it repealed most of the Townshend duties.

Parliament's partial repeal produced a dilemma for American politicians. They considered it intolerable that taxes remained on tea, the most profitable item for the royal treasury. Colonial leaders were unsure whether they should press on with the nonimportation agreement until they achieved total victory, or whether it would suffice to maintain a selective boycott of tea. When the nonimportation movement collapsed in July 1770, colonists resisted external taxation by voluntary agreements not to drink British tea. Through nonconsumption they succeeded in limiting revenue from tea to about one-sixth the level originally expected. This amount was far too little to pay the salaries of royal governors as Townshend had intended.

Yet colonial resistance leaders took little satisfaction in having forced Parliament to compromise. The tea duty remained as a galling reminder that Parliament refused to retreat from the broadest possible interpretation of the Declaratory Act.

Meanwhile, the British government, aware of officers' excesses, took steps to rein in the powers of the American Board of Customs Commissioners. The smuggling charges against Hancock were finally dropped because the prosecution feared that Hancock would appeal a conviction to England, where honest officials would take action against the persons responsible for violating his rights.

## The Committees of Correspondence

In the fall of 1772, Lord North's ministry was preparing to implement Townshend's goal of paying the royal governors' salaries out of customs revenue. The colonists had always viewed this intention to free the governors from legislative domination as a fundamental threat to representative government. In response, Samuel Adams persuaded Boston's town meeting to request that every Massachusetts community appoint persons responsible for exchanging information and coordinating measures to defend colonial rights. Of approximately 260 towns, about half immediately established "committees of correspondence," and most others did so within a year. From Massachusetts the idea spread throughout New England.

The committees of correspondence were the colonists' first attempt to maintain close and continuing political cooperation over a wide area. By linking almost every interior community to Boston through a network of dedicated activists, the system allowed Adams to conduct a campaign of political education for all of New England. Adams sent out messages for each town's local committee to read at its own town meeting, which would then debate the issues and adopt a formal resolution. Forcing tens of thousands of citizens to consider evidence that their rights were in danger, the system committed them to take a personal stand by voting.

Adams's most successful venture in whipping up public alarm came in June 1773, when he publicized certain letters of Massachusetts governor Thomas Hutchinson that Benjamin Franklin had obtained. Massachusetts town meetings discovered through the letters that their own chief executive had advocated "an abridgement of what are called English liberties" and "a great restraint of natural liberty." The publication of the Hutchinson correspondence confirmed American suspicions of a plot to destroy basic freedoms.

In March 1773, Patrick Henry, Thomas Jefferson, and Richard Henry Lee proposed that Virginia establish colony-level committees of correspondence. Within a year every province but Pennsylvania had followed its example. By early 1774 colonial leaders were linked by a communications web for the first time since 1766.

In contrast to the brief, intense Stamp Act crisis, the dissatisfaction spawned by the Townshend duties and the American Board of Customs Commissioners persisted and gradually poisoned relations between Britain and America. In 1765 feelings of loyalty and affection toward Britain had remained strong in America and thus had helped disguise the depth of the division over the constitutional issue of taxation. By 1773, however, colonial allegiance was becoming conditional and could no longer be assumed.

## Frontier Tensions

Although most of the conflicts between colonists and British officials took place in the eastern seaports, tensions along the frontier contributed to a continuing sense of crisis among natives, settlers, and colonial authorities. These stresses were rooted in the rapid growth that had spurred the migration of people and capital to the Appalachian frontier, where colonists and their governments sought access to Indian land.

Land pressures and the lack of adequate revenue from the colonies left the British government utterly helpless in enforcing the Proclamation of 1763. Speculators such as George Washington sought western land because "any person who . . . neglects the present opportunity of hunting out good Lands will never regain it." Settlers, traders, hunters, and thieves also trespassed on Indian land, and a growing number of instances of violence by colonists toward Indians were going unpunished. In the meantime, the British government was unable to maintain garrisons at many of its forts, to enforce violations of laws and treaties, or to provide gifts to its native allies. Under such pressure, Britain and its Iroquois allies agreed in the Treaty of Fort Stanwix (1768) to grant land along the Ohio River that was occupied by the Shawnees, Delawares, and Cherokees to the government of Pennsylvania and Virginia. The Shawnees now assumed leadership of the "republican" Indians who, along with the Cherokees, sensed

that no policy of appeasement could stop colonial expansion.

The treaty served only to heighten rather than ease frontier tensions, especially in the Ohio country where settlers agitated to establish a new colony, Kentucky. Growing violence there culminated in 1774 in the unprovoked slaughter by colonists of thirteen Shawnees and Mingos, including eight members of the family of Logan, until then a moderate Mingo leader. The outraged Logan led a force of Shawnees and Mingos who retaliated by killing an equal number of white Virginians. The colony in turn opened a campaign against the Indians known as Lord Dunmore's War (1774), for Virginia's governor. The two forces met at Point Pleasant on the Virginia side of the Ohio River, where the colonists soundly defeated the Indians. During the peace conference that followed, the Virginians gained uncontested rights to lands south of the Ohio in exchange for all claims on the northern side. But resentments remained strong on both sides and fighting would resume once Britain and its colonies went to war.

The Treaty of Fort Stanwix resolved the conflicting claims of Pennsylvania and Virginia in Ohio at the Indians' expense. But other frontier disputes led to conflict among the colonists themselves. Settlers moving west in Massachusetts in the early 1760s found their titles challenged by some of New York's powerful landlords. When two landlords threatened to evict tenants in 1766, the New Englanders joined the tenants in an armed uprising, calling themselves Sons of Liberty after the Stamp Act protesters. In 1769, in what is now Vermont, settlers from New Hamshire also came into conflict with New York. After four years of guerrilla warfare, the New Hampshire settlers, calling themselves the Green Mountain Boys, established an independent government. Unrecognized at the time, it eventually became the government of Vermont. A third group of New England settlers, from Connecticut, settled in the Wyoming Valley of Pennsylvania, where they clashed in 1774 with Pennsylvanians claiming title to the same land.

Expansion also provoked conflicts between frontier settlers and their colonial governments. In North Carolina a group known as the Regulators aimed to redress the grievances of settlers living in the colony's western regions. The westerners, underrepresented in the colonial assembly, had found themselves exploited by dishonest officeholders appointed by eastern politicians. The Regulator movement climaxed on May 16, 1771, at the battle of Alamance Creek. Leading an army of perhaps thirteen hundred eastern militiamen, North Carolina's royal governor defeated about twenty-five hundred Regulators in a clash that produced almost three hundred casualties. Although the Regulator uprising then disintegrated, it crippled the colony's subsequent ability to resist British authority.

An armed Regulator movement also arose in South Carolina, in this case to counter the government's unwillingness to prosecute bandits who were terrorizing settlers. But the South Carolina government did not dispatch its militia to the frontier for fear that the colony's restive slave population might use the occasion to revolt. Instead it conceded to the principal demands of the Regulators by establishing four new judicial circuits and allowing jury trials in the newly settled areas.

Although not directly related to one another, these frontier episodes all reflect the tensions generated by a rising land-hungry population and its willingness to defy established authorities and resort to violence. As tensions mounted between colonists and British authorities in older settled areas, the frontier dwellers' anxious mood spread.

## Toward Independence

Although the British Empire remained superficially tranquil in early 1773, it had resolved none of its underlying constitutional problems. To a large degree, Americans ignored the continued taxation of tea because of a widespread expectation that Lord North would eventually have the duty repealed. Parliament suddenly blasted this unrealistic hope when it passed the Tea Act in 1773. This measure set off a chain reaction that started with the Boston Tea Party in late 1773 and was followed by Parliament's Coercive Acts in 1774, the First Continental Congress in September 1774, the outbreak of fighting in April 1775, and the colonists' declaration of their independence in July 1776.

### *The Tea Act*

Colonial smuggling and nonconsumption had taken a heavy toll on the East India Company, which enjoyed a legal monopoly on importing tea into the British Empire. By 1773, with tons of tea rotting in its warehouses, the company was teetering on the brink of bankruptcy. But Lord North could not let the company fail. Not only

did it pay substantial duties on the tea it imported into Britain, but it also provided huge indirect savings for the government by maintaining British authority in India at its own expense.

If the company could only control the colonial market, North reasoned, its chances for returning to profitability would greatly increase. Americans supposedly consumed more than a million pounds of tea each year, but by 1773 they were purchasing just one-quarter of it from the company. In May 1773, to save the beleaguered East India Company from financial ruin, Parliament passed the Tea Act, which eliminated all remaining import duties on tea entering England and thus lowered the selling price to consumers. (Ironically, the same saving could have been accomplished by repealing the Townshend tax, which would have ended colonial objections to the company's tea and produced enormous goodwill toward the British government.) To lower the price further, the Tea Act also permitted the company to sell its tea directly to consumers rather than through wholesalers. These two concessions reduced the cost of East India Company tea in the colonies well below the price of all smuggled competition. Parliament expected simple economic self-interest to overcome American scruples about buying taxed tea.

But the Tea Act alarmed many Americans, above all because they saw in it a menace to colonial representative government. By making taxed tea competitive in price with smuggled tea, the law would raise revenue, which the British government would use to pay royal governors. The law thus threatened to corrupt Americans into accepting the principle of parliamentary taxation by taking advantage of their weakness for a frivolous luxury. Quickly, therefore, the committees of correspondence decided to resist the importation of tea, though without violence and without the destruction of private property. Either by pressuring the company's agents to refuse acceptance or by intercepting the ships at sea and ordering them home, the committees would keep East India Company cargoes from being landed. In Philadelphia an anonymous "Committee for Tarring and Feathering" warned harbor pilots not to guide any ships carrying tea into port.

In Boston, however, this strategy failed. On November 28, 1773, the first ship came under the jurisdiction of the customhouse, where duties would have to be paid on its cargo within twenty days. Otherwise, the cargo would be seized from the captain and the tea claimed by the company's agents and placed on sale.

When Samuel Adams, John Hancock, and other lead-ing citizens repeatedly asked the customs officers to is-sue a special clearance for the ship's departure, they were blocked by Thomas Hutchinson's refusal to com-promise.

On the evening of December 16, Samuel Adams convened a meeting in Old South Church. He informed the five thousand citizens of Hutchinson's insistence upon landing the tea, told them that the grace period would expire in a few hours, and announced that "this meeting can do no more to save the country." Dis-guised as Indians, about fifty young men, including George Robert Twelves Hewes, then yelled a few war whoops and headed for the wharf, followed by most of the crowd.

The disciplined band assaulted no one and dam-aged nothing but the hated cargo. Thousands lined the waterfront to see them heave forty-five tons of tea over-board. For almost an hour, the onlookers stood silently transfixed, as if at a religious service, while they peered through the crisp, cold air of a moonlit night. The only sounds were the steady chop of hatchets breaking open wooden chests and the soft splash of tea on the water. When their work was finished, the participants left qui-etly, and the town lapsed into a profound hush—"never more still and calm," according to one observer.

### The Coercive Acts

Boston's "Tea Party" inflamed the British. Lord North fumed that only "New England fanatics" could imagine themselves oppressed by inexpensive tea. A Welsh member of Parliament drew wild applause by declar-ing that "the town of Boston ought to be knocked about by the ears, and destroy'd." In vain did the great parlia-mentary orator Edmund Burke plead for the one action that could end the crisis. "Leave America . . . to tax her-self. . . . Leave the Americans as they anciently stood. . . ." The British government, however, swiftly asserted its authority by enacting four Coercive Acts that, together with the unrelated Quebec Act, became known to many colonists as the "Intolerable Acts."

The first of the Coercive Acts, the Boston Port Bill, became law on April 1, 1774. It ordered the navy to close Boston harbor unless the Privy Council certified by June 1 that the town had arranged to pay for the ru-ined tea. Lord North's cabinet deliberately imposed this impossibly short deadline in order to ensure the har-bor's closing, which would lead to serious economic distress.

The second Coercive Act, the Massachusetts Gov-ernment Act, revoked the Massachusetts charter and re-structured the government to make it less democratic. The colony's upper house would no longer be elected annually by the assembly but appointed for life by the crown. The governor gained absolute control over the naming of all judges and sheriffs. Jurymen, previously elected, were now appointed by sheriffs. Finally, the new charter forbade communities to hold more than one town meeting a year without the governor's per-mission. These changes brought Massachusetts into line with other royal colonies, but the colonists inter-preted them as evidence of hostility toward representa-tive government.

The final two Coercive Acts—the Administration of Justice Act and a new Quartering Act—rubbed salt into the wounds. The first of these permitted any person charged with murder while enforcing royal authority in Massachusetts (such as the British soldiers indicted for the Boston Massacre) to be tried in England or in other colonies. The second went beyond the Quartering Act of 1766 by allowing the governor to requisition *empty* private buildings for housing troops. These measures, along with the appointment of General Thomas Gage, Britain's military commander in North America, as the new governor of Massachusetts, struck New Englan-ders as proof of a plan to place them under a military tyranny.

Americans learned of the Quebec Act along with the previous four statutes and associated it with them. Intended to cement loyalty to Britain among conquered French-Canadian Catholics, the law established Roman Catholicism as Quebec's official religion. This provi-sion alarmed Protestant Anglo-Americans, who widely believed that Catholicism went hand in hand with despotism. Furthermore, the Quebec Act gave Canada's governors sweeping powers but established no legisla-ture. It also permitted property disputes (but not crimi-nal cases) to be decided by French law, which did not use juries. Additionally, the law extended Quebec's ter-ritorial claims south to the Ohio River and west to the Mississippi, a vast area populated by Native Americans and some French. Although designated off-limits by the Proclamation of 1763, portions of the region were claimed by several colonies.

The "Intolerable Acts" convinced New Englanders that the crown was plotting to corrode traditional En-glish liberties throughout North America. Many believed that after starving Boston into submission, the governor of Massachusetts would appoint corrupt sheriffs and

**"Boston Cannonaded"**

*In this pro-resistance cartoon, Britain's ministers harass and force tea down the throat of America, depicted as an innocent woman. Note that one minister carries a copy of the (Boston) Port Bill (1774) that forced the closing of the city's harbor.*

judges to crush political dissent through rigged trials. The Quartering Act would repress any resistance by forcing troops on an unwilling population. The Administration of Justice Act, which the colonists cynically called the Murder Act, would encourage massacres by preventing local juries from convicting soldiers who killed civilians. Once resistance in Massachusetts had been smashed, the Quebec Act would serve as a blueprint for extinguishing representative government throughout the colonies. Parliament would revoke every colony's charter and introduce a government like Quebec's. Elected assemblies, freedom of religion for Protestants, and jury trials would all disappear.

Intended by Parliament simply to punish Massachusetts—and particularly that rotten apple in the barrel, Boston—the acts instead pushed most colonies to the brink of rebellion. Repeal of these laws became, in effect, the colonists' nonnegotiable demand. Of the twenty-seven reasons justifying the break with Britain that the Americans later cited in the Declaration of Independence, six concerned these statutes.

### The First Continental Congress

In response to the "Intolerable Acts," the extralegal committees of correspondence of every colony but Georgia sent delegates to a Continental Congress in Philadelphia. Among those in attendance when the Congress assembled on September 5, 1774, were many of the colonies' most prominent politicians: Samuel and John Adams of Massachusetts; John Jay of New York; Joseph Galloway and John Dickinson of Pennsylvania; and Patrick Henry, Richard Henry Lee, and George Washington of Virginia. The fifty-six delegates had come together to find a way of defending the colonies' rights in common, and in interminable dinner parties and cloakroom chatter, they took one another's measure.

The First Continental Congress opened by endorsing a set of statements of principle called the Suffolk Resolves that recently had placed Massachusetts in a state of passive rebellion. Adopted by delegates at a convention of Massachusetts towns just as the Continental Congress was getting under way, the resolves declared that the colonies owed no obedience to any of the Coercive Acts, that a provisional government should collect all taxes until the former Massachusetts charter was restored, and that defensive measures should be taken in the event of an attack by royal troops. The Continental Congress also voted to boycott all British goods after December 1 and to cease exporting almost all goods to Britain and its West Indian possessions after September 1775 unless a reconciliation had been accomplished. This agreement, the Continental Association, would be enforced by locally elected committees of "observation" or "safety," whose members in effect were usurping control of American trade from the royal customs service.

Such bold defiances were not to the liking of all delegates. Jay, Dickinson, Galloway, and other moderates who dominated the middle-colony contingent most feared the internal turmoil that would surely accompany a head-on confrontation with Britain. These "trimmers" (John Adams's scornful phrase) vainly opposed nonimportation and tried unsuccessfully to win endorsement of Galloway's plan for a "Grand Council," an American legislature that would share with Parliament the authority to tax and govern the colonies.

Finally, however, the delegates summarized their principles and demands in a petition to the king. This document conceded to Parliament the power to regulate colonial commerce, but it argued that all previous parliamentary efforts to impose taxes, enforce laws through admiralty courts, suspend assemblies, and unilaterally revoke charters were unconstitutional. By addressing the king rather than Parliament, Congress was imploring George III to end the crisis by dismissing those ministers responsible for passing the Coercive Acts.

## The Fighting Begins

Most Americans hoped that their resistance would jolt Parliament into renouncing all authority over the colonies except trade regulation. But tensions between moderates and radicals ran high, so that bonds between men formerly united in outlook sometimes snapped. John Adams's onetime friend Jonathan Sewall, for example, charged that the Congress had made the "breach with the parent state a thousand times more irreparable than it was before." Fearing that Congress was enthroning "their *High Mightinesses,* the MOB," he and like-minded Americans fell back on their loyalty to the king. In England meanwhile, George III sniffed rebellion in the Congress's actions. His instincts, and those of American loyalists, were correct. A revolution was indeed brewing.

To solidify their defiance, the American resistance leaders coerced waverers and loyalists (or "Tories," as they were often called). Thus the elected committees that Congress had created to enforce the Continental Association often turned themselves into vigilantes, compelling merchants who still traded with Britain to burn their imports and make public apologies, browbeating clergymen who preached pro-British sermons, and pressuring Americans to adopt simpler diets and dress in order to relieve their dependence on British imports. Additionally, in colony after colony, the commit-

tees took on government functions by organizing volunteer military companies and extralegal legislatures. By the spring of 1775, colonial patriots had established provincial "congresses" that paralleled and rivaled the existing colonial assemblies headed by royal governors.

The uneasy calm was broken in April 1775, in Massachusetts. There as elsewhere, citizens had prepared for the worst by collecting arms and organizing extralegal militia units (locally known as minutemen) whose members could respond instantly to an emergency. The British government ordered Massachusetts governor Gage to quell the "rude rabble" by arresting the principal patriot leaders. Aware that most of these had already fled Boston, Gage instead sent seven hundred British soldiers on April 19, 1775, to seize military supplies that the colonists had stored at Concord. Two couriers, William Dawes and Paul Revere, quickly alerted nearby towns of the British troops' movements and target. At Lexington about seventy minutemen confronted the soldiers. After a confused skirmish in which eight minutemen died and a single redcoat was wounded, the British pushed on to Concord. There they found few munitions but encountered a growing swarm of armed Yankees (see A Place in Time). When some minutemen mistakenly became convinced that the town was being burned, they exchanged fire with the British regulars and touched off a running battle that continued most of the sixteen miles back to Boston. By day's end the redcoats had lost 273 men, and they had gained some respect for Yankee courage.

These engagements awakened the countryside, and by the evening of April 20, some twenty thousand New Englanders were besieging the British garrison in Boston. On May 10 the Green Mountain Boys, led by Ethan Allen, overran Fort Ticonderoga on Lake Champlain, partly with the intent of using its captured cannon in the siege of Boston. That same day, the Second Continental Congress convened in Philadelphia. Most delegates still opposed independence and at Dickinson's urging agreed to send a "loyal message" to George III. Dickinson composed what became known as the Olive Branch Petition; excessively polite, it nonetheless presented three demands: a cease-fire at Boston, repeal of the Coercive Acts, and negotiations to establish guarantees of American rights. Events quickly overtook this effort at reconciliation. The Olive Branch Petition reached London at the same time as news of a battle fought just outside Boston on June 17. In this engagement British troops attacked colonists entrenched on Breed's Hill and Bunker Hill. Although successfully dislodging the Americans, the British suffered 1,154 casualties out of 2,200 men, compared to a loss of 311 patriots. After Bunker Hill many Britons wanted retaliation, not reconciliation, and on August 23 the king proclaimed New England in a state of rebellion. In December Parliament declared all the colonists rebellious and made their ships subject to seizure.

### The Failure of Reconciliation

Despite the turn of events, most colonists clung to hopes of reconciliation. Even John Adams, who believed in the inevitability of separation, described himself as "fond of reconciliation, if we could reasonably entertain Hopes of it on a constitutional basis." Yet while pleading for peace, delegates to the Continental Congress passed measures that Britain could only construe as rebellious. In particular, they voted in May 1775 to establish an "American continental army" and appointed George Washington its commander.

Still, most colonists resisted independence, partly because they clung to the notion that evil ministers rather than the king were forcing unconstitutional measures on them and partly because they expected that saner heads would rise to power in Britain. On both counts they were wrong. The Americans exaggerated the influence of Pitt, Burke, Wilkes (who finally took his seat in Parliament in 1774), and their other friends in Britain. For example, when Burke proposed in March 1775 that Parliament acknowledge the colonists' right to raise and dispose of taxes, he was voted down by a thumping majority in Parliament. In August George III declared the colonies to be in "open and avowed rebellion," and four months later Parliament outlawed all trade with them.

The colonists' sentimental attachment to the king, the last emotional barrier to their accepting independence, finally crumbled in January 1776 with the publication of Thomas Paine's *Common Sense*. A failed corsetmaker and schoolmaster, Paine immigrated to the colonies from England late in 1774 with a letter of introduction from Benjamin Franklin, a penchant for radical politics, and a gift for writing plain and pungent prose that anyone could understand.

Paine told Americans what they had been unable to bring themselves to say: monarchy was an institution rooted in superstition, dangerous to liberty, and inappropriate to Americans. The king was "the royal brute" and a "hardened, sullen-tempered Pharaoh." Whereas previous writers had maintained that an English conspiracy against American liberty was being directed by certain corrupt politicians, Paine argued that such a conspiracy was rooted in the very institutions of monarchy and empire. Moreover, he argued, America had no economic need for the British connection. As he put it, "The commerce by which she [America] hath enriched herself are the necessaries of life, and will always have a market while eating is the custom in Europe." In addition, he pointed out, the events of the preceding six months had made independence a reality. Finally, Paine linked America's awakening nationalism with the sense of religious mission felt by many in New England and elsewhere when he proclaimed, "We have it in our power to begin the world over again. A situation, similar to the present, hath not happened since the days of Noah until now." America, in Paine's view, would be not only a new nation but a new *kind* of nation, a model society founded on new principles and unburdened by the oppressive beliefs and institutions of the European past.

**Thomas Paine**
*Having arrived in the colonies less than two years earlier, Paine became a best-selling author with the publication of* Common Sense *(1776).*

Printed in both English and German, *Common Sense* sold more than 100,000 copies within three months, equal to one for every fourth or fifth adult male. The Connecticut Gazette described it as "a landflood that sweeps all before it." By the spring of 1776, Paine's pamphlet was stimulating local gatherings of colonists—in artisan guilds, town meetings, militia musters, and numerous other settings—to pass resolutions favoring American independence. *Common Sense* had dissolved lingering allegiance to George III and removed the last psychological barrier to independence.

### Declaring Independence

John Adams described the movement toward independence as a coach drawn by thirteen horses, which could not reach its destination any faster than the slowest ones were willing to run. New England was already in rebellion, and Rhode Island declared itself indepen-

## Concord, Massachusetts

About 2 A.M. on April 19, 1775, the alarm bell in Concord, Massachusetts, started to ring furiously. Normally, it summoned men to turn out with fire buckets, but on this night drowsy citizens (including the town's minister, Reverend William Emerson) ambled toward the town square clutching muskets. Concord's minutemen were gathering to oppose 750 British troops marching to seize arms and ammunition stored in their town. Concord's mobilization on that chilly spring night was sure evidence that the colonies were teetering on the brink of revolution.

Until recently, the citizens had been loyal British subjects. Like other rural New Englanders, they had been indifferent to the British Empire's political crisis until they had debated Boston's circular letter of November 20, 1772. Thereafter, Concord's town meeting endorsed a steady flow of correspondence from Boston denouncing unconstitutional parliamentary laws. In June 1774, 80 percent of Concord's men signed a strongly worded pledge to boycott British goods until the Coercive Acts were repealed. By March 6, 1775, all but three men in town had sworn to uphold the Continental Congress against Massachusetts's royal governor, General Thomas Gage. Within the brief span of thirty months, Concord had shed its apathy and become united in resisting the Coercive Acts.

As dawn approached, the townspeople hid bullets and gunflints throughout their houses, concealed gunpowder in the woods, and buried cannon and muskets. Fifteen-year-old Milicent Barrett, the granddaughter of the minutemen's colonel, supervised teenage girls in the manufacture of cartridges. Reinforcements for Concord's 150 minutemen arrived from nearby towns. Word came that the British had opened fire on Lexington's minutemen, but no one knew if blood had been shed.

At daybreak Captain David Brown marched his company toward Lexington and promptly ran into the British. Sizing up the situation, Brown swung back to Concord with drums beating and fifes squealing. "We had grand music," Corporal Amos Barrett later recalled. Badly outnumbered, Colonel James Barrett evacuated the town center and took up position on high ground overlooking the Concord River bridge to await reinforcements.

After posting a guard at the bridge, just out of the minutemen's range, the British scoured the town for military equipment. Much of what little remained behind was saved by the town's women, who outwitted redcoats sent to search their homes. Mrs. Amos Wood tricked an officer who correctly suspected the presence of hidden ammunition into believing that a locked room sheltered panic-stricken women. "I forbid anyone entering this room," commanded the chivalrous Englishman. Hannah Barnes bluffed a search party out of entering a room that contained a chest filled with money needed to buy additional military supplies.

The British regulars dumped five hundred pounds of bullets into a pond, destroyed sixty barrels of flour, and found two cannon. They also accidentally set fire to the courthouse and a blacksmith shop, which they saved before serious damage resulted. But the minutemen on the ridge became enraged by the rising smoke.

"Will you let them burn the town down?" screamed Lieutenant Joseph Hosmer at Colonel Barrett. Now commanding four hundred men, Barrett decided to reenter the town and led his men toward the hundred redcoats guarding the bridge. The British withdrew across the river and fired several warning shots. One round wounded Luther Blanchard, a fifer who had been merrily playing a marching tune. Suddenly, smoke billowed from the British ranks and musketballs whistled across the water. Captain Isaac Davis and Private Abner Hosmer, volunteers from nearby Acton, fell dead. "For God's sake, fire," shouted Captain Jonathan Buttrick to his Concord company, which shot a volley at the British that killed three soldiers and wounded nine others.

The skirmish lasted only two or three minutes. The British withdrew to the town center. The minutemen

**"The White Cockade"**
*Fifer Luther Blanchard and drummer Francis Barker played this martial tune shortly before the skirmish near the bridge.*

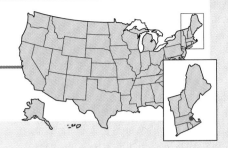

crossed the river but then broke ranks and milled about in confusion. Both sides kept their distance until noon, when the British started to march back to Boston.

The British delay in leaving Concord allowed hundreds of minutemen to arrive from neighboring towns. At Meriam's Corner, these reinforcements began harassing the redcoats in a running battle that continued for sixteen miles. "Every man," recalled Private Thaddeus Blood, "was his own commander." By day's end almost three hundred royal troops were killed, wounded, or missing, and eighty colonists lay dead or injured.

Concord citizens escaped the day with slight losses: four men wounded, none dead. The war, however, had barely begun, and during the coming months, Concord sent off every able-bodied man between the ages of eighteen and forty to serve in the army. After the war the fight at the bridge assumed mythic dimensions for Americans, who celebrated the patriots who dared death at "the rude bridge that arched the flood" and "fired the shot heard 'round the world." But Concord citizens were too familiar with the events to romanticize them. In 1792 they unsentimentally tore up the historic bridge and built a more convenient crossing several hundred yards downriver.

**British Looters**
*A colonial cartoonist caught the red-coats in a looting spree during their retreat from Concord.*

**A View of the Town of Concord, 1775**, by Ralph Earl

dent in May 1776. The middle colonies hesitated to support revolution because they feared, correctly, that the war would largely be fought over control of Philadelphia and New York. Following the news in April that North Carolina's congressional delegates were authorized to vote for independence, the South began pressing for separation. Virginia's extralegal legislature instructed its delegates at the Second Continental Congress to propose independence, which Richard Henry Lee did on June 7. Formally adopting Lee's resolution on July 2, Congress created the United States of America.

The task of drafting a statement to justify the colonies' separation from England fell to a committee of five, including John Adams, Benjamin Franklin, and Thomas Jefferson, with Jefferson as the principal author. Among Congress's revisions to Jefferson's first draft were its insertion of the phrase "pursuit of happiness" in place of "property" in the Declaration's most famous sentence, and its deletion of a statement blaming George III for foisting the slave trade on unwilling colonists. The Declaration of Independence never mentioned Parliament by name—even though the central point of dispute since 1765 had been Parliament's legislative powers—because Congress was unwilling to imply, even indirectly, that it held any authority over America. Jefferson instead followed England's own Bill of Rights, which had sharply reduced monarchical power after the Glorious Revolution (see Chapter 4), as well as Paine, and focused on the king. He listed twenty-seven "injuries and usurpations" committed by George III against the colonies. And he drew on a familiar line of radical thinking when he added that the king's actions had as their "direct object the establishment of an absolute tyranny over these states."

Also like Paine, Jefferson elevated the colonists' grievances from a dispute over English freedoms to a struggle of universal dimensions. In the tradition of Locke and other Enlightenment figures, Jefferson argued that the English government had violated its contract with the colonists, thereby giving them the right to replace it with a government of their own design. His eloquent emphasis on the equality of all individuals and their natural entitlement to justice, liberty, and self-fulfillment expressed the Enlightenment's deepest longing for a government that would rest on neither legal privilege nor exploitation of the majority by the few.

Jefferson addressed the Declaration of Independence as much to Americans uncertain about the wis-

dom of independence as to world opinion, for even at this late date a significant minority opposed independence or hesitated to endorse it. Above all he wanted to convince his fellow citizens that social and political progress could no longer be accomplished within the British Empire. But he left unanswered just who among Americans was and was not included among those considered equal to one another and entitled to liberty. All the colonies endorsing the declaration countenanced, on grounds of racial inequality, the enslavement of blacks and severe restrictions on the freedoms of blacks who were not enslaved. Moreover, all had property qualifications that prevented many white men as well as African Americans from voting. The declaration's proclamation that "all men" were created equal accorded with the Anglo-American assumption that women could not and should not function politically or legally as autonomous individuals. And Jefferson's accusation that George III had unleashed "the merciless Indian savages" on innocent colonists seemed to place Native Americans outside the bounds of humanity.

Was the Declaration of Independence, then, a statement that expressed the sentiments of but a minority of colonists? In a very narrow sense it was, but it was at the same time something much greater. For the ideas motivating Jefferson and his fellow delegates had also moved thousands of ordinary colonists to political action over the preceding eleven years, both on their own personal behalf and on that of the colonies in their quarrel with Britain. For better or worse, the struggle for national independence had hastened, and become intertwined with, a quest for equality and personal independence that, for many Americans, transcended boundaries of class, race, or gender. In their reading, the declaration never claimed that perfect justice and equal opportunity existed in the United States; rather, it challenged the Revolutionary generation and all who later inherited the nation to bring this ideal closer to reality.

## CONCLUSION

In 1763 Britain emerged from its conflict with France as the world's most powerful nation. Yet just over a decade later, its mighty empire was shattered by the North American colonies' Declaration of Independence. In attempting to centralize imperial authority and, particularly, to force the colonies to contribute more revenue to the British treasury, English officials confronted the ambitions and attitudes of Americans who felt themselves to be in every way equal to Britons.

Throughout the long imperial crisis, Americans had repeatedly pursued the goal of reestablishing the empire as it had functioned before 1763, when colonial trade had been protected and encouraged by the Navigation Acts, and when colonial assemblies had exercised exclusive power over taxation and internal legislation. But political and social dynamics in both Britain and the colonies had brought about an entirely different outcome.

The conflict between empire and colonies quickly passed from differences over the merits of various revenue-raising measures to more fundamental issues. First, people asked, who had the authority, as the people's representatives, to levy taxes on the colonists? Failing to resolve that question to everyone's satisfaction, colonists began to debate whether Parliament had any authority at all in the colonies. Finally, Americans were led—with help from the recent English immigrant Thomas Paine—to challenge the legitimacy of Britain's monarchy itself.

Americans by no means followed a single path to the point of advocating independence. Ambitious elites resented British efforts to curtail colonial autonomy as exercised almost exclusively by members of their own class in the assemblies. They and many more in the middle classes were angered by British policies that made commerce less profitable as an occupation and more costly to consumers. But others, including both frontier dwellers and poor and working urban people, like George Robert Twelves Hewes, defied conventions demanding that humble people defer to the authority of their social superiors. Sometimes resorting to violence,

they directed their wrath toward British officials and colonial elites alike. In so doing they contributed to antiauthoritarian, republican sentiments that were beginning to sweep throughout the Atlantic world.

America's reluctant revolutionaries now had to face the might of Europe's greatest imperial power and win their independence on the battlefield. They also had to struggle over interpreting and implementing the idealistic vision evoked in Jefferson's declaration. Neither task would prove simple or easy.

## FOR FURTHER READING

Bernard Bailyn, *The Ideological Origins of the American Revolution* (1967). A probing discussion of the ideologies that shaped colonial resistance to British authority.

Linda Colley, *Britons: Forging the Nation, 1707–1837* (1992). A major study of the formation of political identity in Great Britain, providing an important perspective on relations between the empire and its North American colonies.

Edward Countryman, *The American Revolution* (1985). An outstanding introduction to the Revolution, its background, and its consequences.

Robert A. Gross, *The Minutemen and Their World* (1976). An eloquent and evocative examination of Concord, Massachusetts, in the Revolutionary era.

Pauline Maier, *From Resistance to Revolution: Colonial Radicals and the Development of American Opposition to Britain, 1765–1776* (1972). An insightful, definitive account of how colonial elite leaders mobilized colonists to resist British policies, eventually arriving at the point of open rebellion.

Mary Beth Norton, *Liberty's Daughters: The Revolutionary Experience of American Women, 1750–1800* (1980). A wide-ranging discussion of the experiences and roles of women in eighteenth-century colonial society and the American Revolution.

Richard White, *The Middle Ground: Indians, Empires, and Republics in the Great Lakes Region, 1650–1815* (1991). An innovative study of the contest for control of the Ohio Valley.

# 6 Securing Independence, Defining Nationhood 1776–1788

**George Washington [1777]** by Charles Peale Polk, c. 1792–1793

In November 1775 General George Washington ordered Colonel Henry Knox (page 151) to bring the British artillery recently captured at Fort Ticonderoga to reinforce the siege of Boston. Washington knew firsthand of the difficulties of wilderness travel, especially in the winter, and he must have wondered if this city-bred officer was up to the task. Only twenty-five years old and a Boston bookseller with little experience in the woods, Knox was nevertheless the army's senior artillerist, largely because he had read several books on the subject while business in his store was dull.

Knox and his men built crude sleds to haul their fifty-nine cannons through dense forest covered by two feet of snow. On good days they moved these sixty tons of artillery about seven miles. On two very bad ones, they shivered for hours in freezing water while retrieving guns that had fallen through the ice at river crossings. As their oxen grew weak from overexertion and poor feed, the men had to throw their own backs into pulling the cannons across New York's frozen landscape. On reaching the Berkshire Mountains in western Massachusetts, their pace slowed to a crawl as they trudged uphill through snow-clogged passes. Forty days and three hundred miles after leaving Ticonderoga, Knox and his exhausted New Yorkers reported to Washington in late January 1776. The Boston bookseller had more than proved himself: he had accomplished one of the Revolution's great feats of endurance.

The guns from Ticonderoga placed the outnumbered British in a hopeless position and forced them to evacuate Boston on March 17, 1776. A lifelong friendship formed between Washington and Knox. Knox served on the Virginian's staff throughout the war and accepted his request to be the nation's first secretary of war in 1789.

Friendships like the one between Washington and Knox were almost as revolutionary as the war that produced them. Because inhabitants of different colonial regions had little opportunity to become acquainted before 1775, their outlooks were largely confined within those regions. This regionalism was well entrenched at the start of the war. George Washington at first described New Englanders as "an exceeding dirty and nasty people." Yankee soldiers irritated troops from the southern colonies with smug assumptions of superiority expressed in their popular marching song "Chester," whose rousing lyrics rang out:

Let tyrants shake their iron rod,
and slavery clank her galling chains.
We fear them not, we trust in God.
New England's God forever reigns.

The Revolution gave northerners and southerners their first real chance to learn what they had in common, and they soon developed mutual admiration. George Washington, who in the war's early days dismissed New England officers as "the most indifferent kind of people I ever saw," changed his mind after meeting men like Henry Knox.

In July 1776 the thirteen colonies had out of desperation declared independence and joined together in a loosely knit confederation of states. But only as a result of the collective hardships experienced during eight years of terrible fighting did the inhabitants of the thirteen states cease to see themselves simply as military allies and begin to accept one another as fellow citizens.

Even while the war was still under way, a nation was formalized with the adoption of the Articles of Confederation. But Americans remained divided over a number of basic political questions relating to the distribution of power and authority. These divisions were apparent in some states' struggles to adopt constitutions and, even more forcefully, in the contests over writing and ratifying a new national Constitution. The ratification of the Constitution marked the passing of America's short-lived Confederation and a triumph for those favoring more centralization of power at the national level.

This chapter focuses on three major questions:

♦ What were the most critical factors enabling the Americans to win the War of Independence with Britain?

♦ In what ways did the Revolution advance the ideals of liberty and equality in American society, and in what ways did it stifle them?

♦ Why did it take the new nation twelve years, from the Declaration of Independence until the ratification of the Constitution, to design a lasting form of national government?

# America's First Civil War

The Revolution was both a collective struggle that marched a sizable portion of the American people against Britain and a civil war between inhabitants of North America. Eventually, it would degenerate into a brothers' war of the worst kind, conducted without restraint, mutual respect, or compassion. From a military standpoint, the Revolution's outcome depended not only on the ability of the supporters of independence, called the patriots, or Whigs, to wear down the British army but also on the rebels' success in suppressing fellow Americans' opposition to independence.

## *Loyalists and Other British Sympathizers*

As late as January 1776, most colonists still hoped that declaring independence from Britain would not be necessary. Not surprisingly, when separation came six months later, many Americans remained unconvinced that it was justified. About 20 percent of all whites either opposed the rebellion actively or refused to support the Continental Congress unless threatened with fines or imprisonment. Although these internal enemies of the Revolution called themselves loyalists, they were "Tories" to their Whig foes. Whigs remarked, but only half in jest, that "a tory was a thing with a head in England, a body in America, and a neck that needed stretching."

Loyalists avowed many of the same political values as did the patriots. Like the rebels, they usually opposed Parliament's claim to tax the colonies. Many loyalists thus found themselves fighting for a cause with which they did not entirely agree, and as a result many of them would change sides during the war. Most doubtless shared the apprehension expressed in 1775 by the Reverend Jonathan Boucher, a well-known Maryland loyalist, who preached with two loaded pistols lying on his pulpit cushion: "For my part I equally dread a Victory by either side."

**A British View of the Loyalists**
*This British cartoon depicts Americans as "savage" Indian warriors massacring helpless loyalists. It is also critical of Prime Minister Lord Shelburne for failing to protect the loyalists.*

## CHRONOLOGY

**1770** Yearly meeting of New England Quakers prohibits slaveowning—first American ban on slaveholding.

**1772** *Somerset* decision in England.

**1775** Virginia governor Lord Dunmore promises freedom to any slave assisting in the restoration of royal authority.

**1776** British troops evacuate Boston.

British drive American forces from New York City.

American victory in Battle of Trenton.

Cherokees attack North Carolina frontier.

**1777** American victory in Battle of Princeton.

British general John Burgoyne surrenders at Saratoga.

Battle of Brandywine Creek; British occupy Philadelphia.

British victory in Battle of Germantown.

Congress approves Articles of Confederation.

**1778** France formally recognizes the United States.

France declares war on Britain.

British troops evacuate Philadelphia; American victory in Battle of Monmouth Court House (New Jersey).

Joseph Brant leads Iroquois attacks in western Pennsylvania and New York.

**1779** Spain declares war on Britain.

George Rogers Clark recaptures Vincennes.

John Sullivan leads U.S. raids in Iroquois country.

Judith Sargent Murray writes "On the Equality of the Sexes" (published 1790).

**1780** British seize Charles Town.

Dutch Republic declares war on Britain.

**1781** Articles of Confederation become law.

Battle of Yorktown; British general Cornwallis surrenders.

**1782** Paris peace negotiations begin.

Rhode Island rejects national import duty.

**1783** Peace of Paris.

Newburgh Conspiracy.

Treaty of Augusta.

**1784** Spain closes New Orleans to American trade.

Economic depression begins.

Second Treaty of Fort Stanwix.

**1785** Ordinance of 1785.

Treaty of Fort McIntosh.

**1786** Congress rejects Jay-Gardoqui Treaty.

Treaty of Fort Finney.

Joseph Brant organizes Indian resistance to U.S. expansion.

Virginia adopts Thomas Jefferson's Statute for Religious Freedom.

**1786–1787** Shays's Rebellion in Massachusetts.

**1787** Northwest Ordinance.

Philadelphia Convention; federal Constitution signed.

**1788** Alexander Hamilton, James Madison, and John Jay, *The Federalist.*

Federal Constitution ratified.

---

Loyalists disagreed, however, with the patriots' insistence that only independence could preserve the colonists' constitutional rights. The loyalists denounced separation as an illegal act certain to ignite an unnecessary war. Above all, they retained a profound reverence for the crown and deeply believed that if they failed to defend their king, they would sacrifice their personal honor.

Toward loyalists collectively, patriot Whigs reserved an intense hatred, far greater than their antipathy toward the British army, and loyalists responded with equal venom. Each side saw its cause as so sacred that opposition by a fellow American was an unforgivable act of betrayal. The worst atrocities committed during the war were inflicted by Americans upon each other.

The most important factor in determining loyalist strength in any area was the degree to which local Whigs successfully convinced the public that representative government was endangered by the king and Parliament. Town leaders in New England, the Virginia gentry, and the rice planters of South Carolina's seacoast had vigorously pursued a program of political education and popular mobilization from 1772 to 1776. Repeatedly explaining the issues at public meetings, these elites persuaded the overwhelming majority in favor of resistance. As a result, probably no more than 5 percent of whites in these areas were committed loyalists in 1776. Where leading families acted indecisively, however, their communities remained divided when the fighting began. Because the gentry of New York and New Jersey were especially reluctant to declare their allegiance to either side, the proportion of loyalists was highest there. Those two states eventually furnished about half of the 21,000 Americans who fought in loyalist military units.

The next most significant factor influencing loyalist military strength was the geographic distribution of recent British immigrants, who remained closely identified with their homeland. Among these newcomers were thousands of British soldiers who had served in the Seven Years' War and then stayed on in the colonies, usually in New York, where they could obtain land grants of two hundred acres. Furthermore, more than 125,000 English, Scots, and Irish landed from 1763 to 1775—the greatest number of Britons to arrive during any dozen years of the colonial era. In New York, Georgia, and the backcountry of North and South Carolina, where native-born Britons were heavily concentrated, the proportion of loyalists among whites probably ranged from 25 percent to 40 percent in 1776. In wartime the British army organized many Tory units comprising immigrants from the British Isles, including the Loyal Highland Emigrants, the North Carolina Highlanders, and the Volunteers of Ireland. After the war foreign-born loyalists composed a majority of those compensated by the British for property losses during the Revolution—including three-quarters of all such claimants from the Carolinas and Georgia.

Other North Americans supported the British cause, not out of loyalty to the crown but from a perception that an independent American republic would pose the greater threat to their own liberty and independence. A few German, Dutch, and French religious congregations doubted that their rights would be as safe in an independent nation dominated by Anglo-Americans. Yet on balance, these groups provided few loyalists. The great majority of German colonists in Pennsylvania, Maryland, and Virginia, for example, had embraced emergent American republicanism by 1776 and would overwhelmingly support the Revolutionary cause.

Canada's French Catholics comprised the most significant white minority to hold pro-British sympathies. Although the British had conquered them in the Seven Years' War, the Quebec Act of 1774 reversed Britain's failed policy in Acadia (see Chapter 5) by guaranteeing Canadians' religious freedom and their continued, partial use of French civil law. Remembering that the American colonists had denounced this measure and demanded its repeal, French Catholics worried that their privileges would disappear if they were absorbed into an independent Protestant America. Canadian anxieties intensified in 1775, when Continental forces marched into Canada and attacked Quebec but suffered defeat. French Catholics emerged from the shock of invasion more loyal to the crown than ever before.

The rebels never even attempted to win over three other mainland colonies—Nova Scotia and East and West Florida—whose small populations of mainly recent immigrants were firmly dominated by British military authorities. Nor was independence seriously considered in Britain's thirteen West Indian colonies, which were dominated by absentee plantation owners who lived in England and depended on the protected British market for selling their sugar exports.

The British cause would also draw significant wartime support from nonwhites. As a deeply alienated group within society, slaves quickly responded to calls for "liberty" and "equality." In 1766, when a group of African-American slaves, inspired by the protests against the Stamp Act, had marched through Charles Town, South Carolina, shouting "Liberty!" they had faced arrest for inciting a rebellion. Thereafter unrest among slaves—usually in the form of violence or escape—kept pace with that among free colonists. Then in 1772 a court decision in England electrified much of the African-American population. A Massachusetts slave, James Somerset, whose master had taken him to England, sued for his freedom. Writing for the King's Court, Lord Chief Justice William Mansfield ruled that because Parliament had never explicitly established slavery, no court could compel a slave to obey an order depriving him of his liberty.

Although the *Somerset* decision applied only within England, African Americans seized upon it in a number of ways. In January 1773 some of Somerset's fellow Massachusetts slaves filed the first of three petitions to the legislature, arguing that the decision should be applied in the colony as well. In Virginia and Maryland, dozens of slaves ran away from their masters and sought passage aboard ships bound for England. As Anglo-American tensions mounted in 1774, many slaves looked for war and the arrival of British troops as a means to their liberation. The young James Madison feared that "if America and Britain come to a hostile rupture, I am afraid an insurrection among the slaves may and will be promoted" by England.

Madison's fears were borne out in 1775 when Lord Dunmore, governor of Virginia, promised freedom to any slave who enlisted in the cause of restoring royal authority. About eight hundred blacks joined him before he fled the colony. Meanwhile, hundreds of South Carolina slaves had escaped and taken refuge on British ships in Charles Town's harbor. During the war at least twenty thousand enslaved African Americans ran away to sign on as laborers or soldiers in the Royal Army. Among the slaveholders who saw many of his slaves escape to British protection was Thomas Jefferson.

Although the Native American population was divided, most supported the British. Indians along the frontier recognized the danger to their homelands posed by expansion-minded Anglo-Americans. As had been the case since midcentury, tensions ran especially high in the Ohio Country. There, Shawnees, Delawares, Mingos, and other Indians continued to bristle at white incursions, as did the Cherokees to the south. Native Americans in the Upper Great Lakes, after the uprising of 1763 (see Chapter 5), had developed good rapport with British agents in the former French forts and were solidly in the British camp. The Iroquois and Creek confederacies, whose neutrality had been a source of strength until the French defeat in 1760, were now divided. The Creeks' allegiance reflected each village's earlier trade ties with either Britain or Spain (the latter leaned toward the colonists' cause). Most Iroquois followed the lead of the English-educated Mohawk chief Joseph Brant in supporting Britain. Only the Oneidas and Tuscaroras, influenced by Congregationalist missionary Samuel Kirkland, sided with the rebels. Native Americans in upper New England and the Canadian maritime provinces and in the Illinois and Wabash Valleys initially took an anti-British stand because of earlier ties with the French, though many of them became alienated from the colonists during the war. Most of the relatively small number of Indians living in the established colonies supported the rebellion.

### *The Opposing Sides*

Britain entered the war with two major advantages. First, in 1776 the 11 million inhabitants of the British Isles greatly outnumbered the 2.5 million colonists, one-third of whom were either slaves or loyalists. Second, Britain possessed the world's largest navy and one of its best professional armies. Nevertheless, the royal military establishment grew during the war years to a degree that strained Britain's resources. The army more than doubled from 48,000 to 111,000 men, not only in North America but also in the British Isles and the West Indies. To meet its manpower needs, the British government hired 30,000 German mercenaries known as Hessians and later enlisted 21,000 loyalists.

Despite its smaller population, the new nation mobilized about 220,000 troops—compared to the 162,000 who served in the British army. But most Americans served short terms, and the new nation would have been hard-pressed had it not been for the contributions of its French allies in the war's later stages.

**Woodcut from "A New Touch on the Times . . . By a Daughter of Liberty, Living in Marblehead," 1779**
*Americans on the home front as well as in the front lines experienced crippling wartime hardships. This illustration of a female partisan holding a musket accompanied a poem by Molly Gutridge, whose theme was women's sacrifice and suffering in a seaport economy upset by war.*

Britain's ability to crush the rebellion was further weakened by the decline in its seapower that had resulted from peacetime budget cuts after 1763. Midway through the war, half of the Royal Navy's ships sat in dry dock awaiting major repairs. Although the navy expanded rapidly from 18,000 to 111,000 sailors, it lost 42,000 men to desertion and 20,000 to disease or wounds. In addition, Britain's merchant marine suffered mightily from raids by American privateers. During the war rebel privateers and the fledgling U.S. Navy would capture over 2,000 British merchant vessels and 16,000 crewmen.

Britain could ill afford these losses, for it faced a colossal task in trying to supply its troops in America. In fact, almost all the food consumed by the army, a third of a ton per soldier per year, had to be imported from Britain. Seriously overextended, the navy barely kept the army supplied and never effectively blockaded American ports.

Mindful of the enormous strain that the war imposed, British leaders faced serious problems maintaining their people's support for the conflict. The war more than doubled the national debt, thereby adding further to the burdens of a people already paying record taxes. The politically influential landed gentry could not be expected to vote against their pocketbooks forever.

The new nation faced different but no less severe wartime problems. One-fifth of its free population, a large but uncertain proportion of enslaved southerners, and most Native Americans favored the British. Although the state militias sometimes performed well in hit-and-run guerrilla skirmishes and were also effective in intimidating loyalists and in requisitioning war supplies, they lacked the training to fight pitched battles against professional armies like Britain's. Congress recognized that independence would never be secured if the new nation relied on guerrilla tactics, avoided major battles, and allowed the British to occupy all major population centers. Moreover, because European powers would interpret dependence on guerrilla warfare as evidence that Americans could not drive out the British army, that strategy would doom efforts by the Continental Congress to gain foreign loans, diplomatic recognition, and military allies.

The Continental Army thus had to fight in the standard European fashion of the times. Professional eighteenth-century armies relied on expert movements of mass formations. Victory often depended on rapid maneuvers to crush an enemy's undefended flank or rear. Attackers needed exceptional skill in close-order drill in order to fall on an enemy before the enemy could re-form and return fire. Because muskets had a range of under one hundred yards, armies in battle were never far apart. Battles usually occurred in open country with space for maneuver. The troops advanced within musket range of each other, stood upright without cover, and fired volleys at one another until one line weakened from its casualties. Discipline, training, and nerve were essential if soldiers were to stay in ranks while comrades fell beside them. The stronger side then attacked at a quick walk with bayonets drawn and drove off its opponents.

In 1775 Britain possessed a well-trained army with a strong tradition of discipline and bravery under fire. In contrast, the Continental Army had neither an inspirational heritage nor many experienced officers or sergeants who might turn raw recruits into crack units. Consequently, the Americans experienced a succession of heartbreaking defeats in the war's early years. Yet to win the war, the Continentals did not have to destroy the British army but only prolong the rebellion until Britain's taxpayers lost patience with the struggle. Until then, American victory would hinge heavily on the ability of one man to keep his army fighting despite defeat. He was George Washington.

### George Washington

Few generals ever looked and acted the role as much as Washington. He spoke with authority and comported himself with dignity. At six feet two inches, he stood a half-foot taller than the average man of his day. Powerfully built, athletic, and hardened by a rugged outdoor life, he was one of the war's few generals whose presence on the battlefield could inspire troops to heroism.

Washington's military experience began at age twenty-two, when he had taken command of a Virginia regiment raised to resist French claims. Washington's early military experience—his mistakes and lost battles in the Ohio Valley (see Chapter 5)—taught him lessons that he might not have learned from easy, glorious victories. He discovered the dangers of overconfidence and the need for determination in the face of defeat. He also learned much about American soldiers, especially that they performed best when led by example and treated with respect.

With Virginia's borders safe from attack in 1758, Washington had resigned his commission and become a tobacco planter. He had sat in the Virginia House of Burgesses, where his influence had grown, not because he thrust himself into every issue but because others respected him and sought his opinion. Having emerged as an early, though not outspoken, opponent of parliamentary taxation, he had also sat in the Continental Congress. In the eyes of the many who valued his advice and remembered his military experience, Washington was the logical choice to head the Continental Army.

### War in Earnest

Henry Knox's successful transport of artillery from Ticonderoga to Boston prompted the British to evacuate Boston in March 1776 and to move on to New York, which they wished to seize and use as a base for conquering New England. Under two brothers—General William Howe and Admiral Richard, Lord Howe—130 warships carrying 32,000 royal troops landed near New York harbor in the summer of 1776. Defending New

York, America's second-largest city, were 18,000 poorly trained soldiers under George Washington.

By the end of the year, William Howe's men had killed or taken prisoner one-quarter of Washington's troops and had driven the survivors into headlong retreat from New York across New Jersey and the Delaware River into Pennsylvania. Thomas Paine accurately described these demoralizing days as "the times that try men's souls."

With the British in striking distance of Philadelphia, Washington decided to seize the offensive before the morale of his army and country collapsed completely. On Christmas night, 1776, he led his troops back into New Jersey and attacked a Hessian garrison at Trenton, where he captured 918 Germans and lost only 4 Continentals. Washington then attacked 1,200 British at Princeton on January 3, 1777, and killed or took captive one-third of them while sustaining only 40 casualties.

These American victories at Trenton and Princeton had several important consequences. At a moment when defeat seemed inevitable, they boosted civilian and military morale. In addition, they drove a wedge between New Jersey's five thousand loyalists and the British army. Washington's victories forced the British early in 1777 to remove virtually all their New Jersey garrisons to New York, while Washington established winter quarters at Morristown, New Jersey, only twenty-five miles from New York City.

New Jersey loyalism never recovered from the blow it received when the British evacuated the state. The state militia disarmed known loyalists, jailed their leaders, and kept a constant watch on suspected Tories. Ironically, the British themselves contributed to the undermining of New Jersey loyalism, for prior to the Battle of Trenton, British commanders had failed to prevent an orgy of looting by their troops that victimized loyalists and Whigs equally. Surrounded by armed enemies and facing constant danger of arrest, most loyalists who remained in the state bowed to the inevitable and swore allegiance to the Continental Congress; more than a few ex-loyalists themselves joined the rebel militia.

**Henry Knox**
*One of Washington's most trusted officers, Knox went on to serve as the first president's Secretary of War.*

**The Battle of Princeton (1777)** by James Peale, c. 1790
*In the battle's first phase, fought south of the town, the American advance guard clashed with redcoats who were en route to Trenton, where they planned to link up with Lord Cornwallis. The British had the upper hand until George Washington and the main Continental force arrived, attacked, and drove them off.*

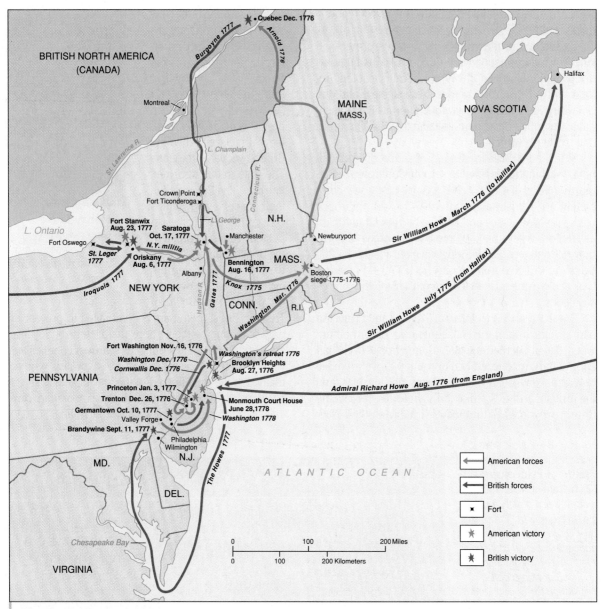

**The War in the North, 1776–1779**
*Following the British evacuation of Boston, the war shifted to New York City, which the British held from 1776 to
1783. In 1777 Britain's success in taking Philadelphia was offset by defeat in upstate New York. The hard-fought battle of Monmouth Court House, New Jersey, ended the northern campaigns in 1778.*

### The Turning Point

Shortly after the battles of Trenton and Princeton, the
Marquis de Lafayette, a young French aristocrat, joined
Washington's staff. Lafayette was twenty years old,
highly idealistic, very brave, and infectiously optimistic.
Given Lafayette's close connections with the French
court, his presence in America indicated that the

French king, Louis XVI, might recognize American independence and perhaps declare war on Britain. Before recognizing the new nation, however, Louis
wanted proof that the Americans could win a major
battle, a feat they had not yet accomplished.

Louis did not have to wait long. In the summer of
1777, the British planned a two-pronged assault in-

tended to crush American resistance in New York State and thereby isolate New England. Pushing off from Montreal, a force of regulars and their Iroquois allies, marching under Lieutenant Colonel Barry St. Leger, would proceed south along Lake Ontario and invade central New York from Fort Oswego in the west. At the same time General John Burgoyne would lead the main British force south from Quebec through eastern New York and link up with St. Leger near Albany.

Nothing went according to British plans in New York. St. Leger's force of 1,900 British and Iroquois advanced 100 miles and halted to besiege 750 New York Continentals at Fort Stanwix. Unable to take the post after three weeks, St. Leger retreated in late August 1777.

Burgoyne's campaign appeared more promising after his force of 8,300 British and Hessians took Fort Ticonderoga, about a hundred miles north of Albany. But Burgoyne's supply lines were overstretched, and he lost at Bennington, Vermont. Meanwhile General Horatio Gates gathered nearly 17,000 American troops for an attack. Gates fought two indecisive battles near Saratoga in the fall, inflicting another 1,200 casualties on Burgoyne. Surrounded and hopelessly outnumbered, Burgoyne's 5,800 troops honorably laid down their arms on October 17, 1777. The diplomatic impact of the Battle of Saratoga rivaled its military significance and made it the war's turning point.

The victory at Saratoga convinced France that the Americans could win the war and thus deserved diplomatic recognition. In February 1778 France formally recognized the United States. Four months later, it went to war with Britain. Spain declared war on Britain in 1779, but as an ally of France, not the United States, and the Dutch Republic joined them in the last days of 1780. Now facing a coalition of enemies, Britain had no allies.

The American allies soon made their presence felt. Between 1779 and 1781, Spanish troops based in Louisiana drove the British from West Florida, effectively preventing Britain from taking the Mississippi Valley. Beginning in 1781, French troops also contributed to rebel victories. Moreover, Britain sent thousands of soldiers to Ireland and the West Indies to guard against French invasion, thus reducing the manpower available to fight in North America. The French and Spanish navies, which together approximately equaled the British fleet, won several large battles, denied Britain control of the sea, and punctured the Royal Navy's blockade.

### The Continentals Mature

While Gates and Burgoyne maneuvered in upstate New York, General Howe landed 18,000 troops near Philadelphia in late August. With Washington at their head and Lafayette at his side, 16,000 Continentals occupied the imperiled city.

The two armies collided on September 11, 1777, at Brandywine Creek, Pennsylvania. In the face of superior British discipline, not only did most Continental units crumble but Congress soon fled Philadelphia in panic, enabling Howe to occupy the city. Howe again defeated Washington at Germantown on October 4. In one month's bloody fighting, 20 percent of the Continentals were killed, wounded, or captured.

While the British army wintered comfortably eighteen miles away in Philadelphia, the Continentals huddled in the bleak hills of Valley Forge. Despite severe shortages of food, clothing, and shelter, the troops somehow preserved a sense of humor, which they occasionally demonstrated by joining together in a thousand voices to squawk like crows watching a cornfield. Underlying these squawks was real hunger: James Varnum reported on December 20 that his Connecticut and Rhode Island troops had gone the two previous days without meat and three days without bread.

The army slowly regained its strength but still lacked training. The Continentals had forced Burgoyne to surrender more by their overwhelming numbers than by their skill. Indeed, when Washington's men had met Howe's forces on equal terms, they lost badly. The Americans mainly lacked the ability to march as compact units and maneuver quickly. Regiments often straggled single-file into battle and then wasted precious time forming to attack, and few troops were expert in bayonet drill.

The Continental Army's ill-trained recruits received a desperately needed boost in February 1778, when the

**Thaddeus Kosciuszko,** engraving by Gabriel Fiesinger, 1798
*A Polish military engineer, Kosciuszko contributed significantly to several American victories during the Revolution. After the war, he led an unsuccessful effort to overthrow Poland's king.*

German soldier of fortune Friedrich von Steuben arrived at Valley Forge. The short, squat Steuben did not look like a soldier, but this earthy German instinctively liked Americans and became immensely popular. He had a talent for motivating men (sometimes by staging humorous tantrums featuring a barrage of German, English, and French swearing); but more important, he possessed administrative genius. In a mere four months, General Steuben almost single-handedly turned the army into a formidable fighting force.

General Henry Clinton, now British commander-in-chief, evacuated Philadelphia in mid-1778 and marched to New York. The Continental Army got its first opportunity to demonstrate Steuben's training when it caught up with Clinton's rear guard at Monmouth Court House, New Jersey, on June 28, 1778. The battle raged for six hours in one-hundred-degree heat until Clinton broke off contact. Expecting to renew the fight at daybreak, the Americans slept on their arms, but Clinton's army slipped away before then. The British would never again win easily, except when they faced more militiamen than Continentals.

The Battle of Monmouth ended the contest for the North. Clinton occupied New York, which the Royal Navy made safe from attack. Washington kept his army nearby to watch Clinton. Meanwhile, the Whig militia hunted down the last few Tory guerrillas and extinguished loyalism.

### Frontier Campaigns

A different kind of war developed west of the Appalachians and along the western borders of New York and Pennsylvania. The numbers engaged in these frontier skirmishes were relatively small, but the fighting was fierce and the stakes—for the new nation, for the British, and for Indians in the region—were high. In 1776 few Americans had a clear notion of their nation's western boundaries; by 1783, when the Peace of Paris concluded the war, the Confederation could assert its claim to the Mississippi River as its western border. So although the frontier campaigns did not determine the outcome of the war, they had a significant impact on the future shape of the United States.

Frontier fighting erupted first in the South, where Cherokees began attacking settlers from Virginia to Georgia in 1776. After suffering heavy losses, the southern colonies recovered and organized retaliatory expeditions. Within a year these expeditions had burned most Cherokee towns, forcing the Cherokees

to sign treaties that ceded most of their land in South Carolina and substantial tracts in North Carolina and Tennessee.

Elsewhere the intense fighting lasted longer. Largely independent of American and British coordination, natives and settlers fought for two years in Kentucky with neither side gaining a clear advantage (see A Place in Time). But after British troops occupied French settlements in what are now Illinois and Indiana, Colonel George Rogers Clark led 175 Kentucky militiamen north of the Ohio River. After capturing and losing the French community of Vincennes on the Wabash River, Clark retook the settlement for good in February 1779. With the British unable to offer assistance, the Indians were vulnerable. In May, John Bowman led a second Kentucky unit in a campaign that destroyed most Shawnee villages, and in August a move northward from Pittsburgh by Daniel Brodhead inflicted similar damage on the Delawares and the Seneca Iroquois. Although these raids depleted their populations and food supplies, most Ohio Indians resisted the Americans until the war's end.

In the East pro-British Iroquois, led by the gifted Mohawk leader Joseph Brant, devastated the Pennsylvania and New York frontiers in 1778. They killed 340 Pennsylvania militia at Wyoming, Pennsylvania, and probably slew an equal number in their other raids. In 1779 the American general John Sullivan retaliated by invading Iroquois country with 3,700 Continentals and several hundred Tuscaroras and Oneidas. Sullivan fought just one battle, near present-day Elmira, New York, in which his artillery routed Brant's warriors. After he burned two dozen Indian villages and destroyed a million bushels of corn, most Iroquois fled without food into Canada. Untold hundreds starved during the next winter, when more than 60 inches of snow fell.

In 1780 Brant's thousand warriors fell upon the Tuscaroras and Oneidas and then laid waste to Pennsylvania and New York for two years. But this final whirlwind of Iroquois fury masked reality: Sullivan's campaign had destroyed the Iroquois peoples' heartland, and their population declined by about one-third during the eight-year war.

### Victory in the South

After 1778 the war's focus shifted to the South. With the entry of France and Spain into the war, the conflict had acquired international dimensions; Britain was suddenly locked in a struggle that raged from India to

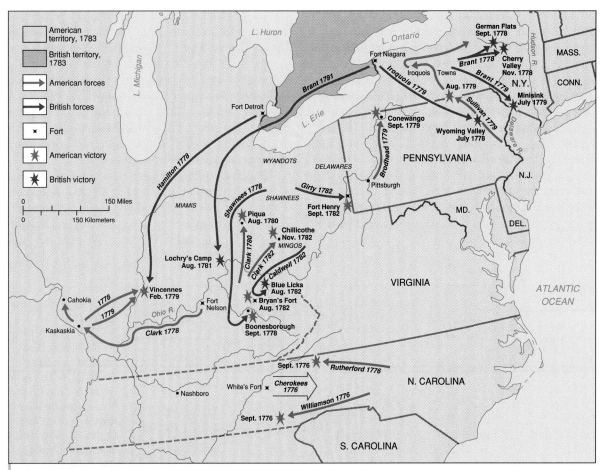

**The War in the West, 1776–1779**
*George Rogers Clark's victory at Vincennes in 1779 gave the United States effective control of the Ohio Valley. Carolina militiamen drove attacking Cherokees far back into the Appalachians in 1776. In retaliation for their raids on New York and Pennsylvania, John Sullivan inflicted widespread starvation on the Iroquois by burning their villages and winter food supplies in 1779.*

Gibraltar to the West Indies and the American mainland. By securing ports in the South, the British would acquire the flexibility to move their forces back and forth between the West Indies and the United States as necessity dictated. In addition, the South looked like a relatively easy target. General Henry Clinton expected that a renewed invasion of the South would tap a huge reservoir of loyalist support. In sum, the British plan was to seize key southern ports and, with the aid of loyalist militiamen, move back toward the North, pacifying one region after another.

The plan unfolded smoothly at first. Sailing from New York with 9,000 troops, Clinton forced the surrender of Charles Town, South Carolina, and its 3,400-man garrison on May 12, 1780. Clinton then left mopping-up operations in the South to Lord Charles Cornwallis. However, the British quickly found that there were fewer loyalists than they had expected. Southern loyalism had suffered several serious blows since the war began. When the Cherokees had attacked the Carolina frontier in 1776, they killed whites indiscriminately. Numerous Tories had switched sides, joining the rebel militia to defend their homes. Then, as in Virginia earlier, the arrival of British troops sparked a mass exodus of enslaved Africans from their plantations. About one-third of Georgia's blacks and one-fourth of South Carolina's—25,000 in all—fled to British lines or to British-held Florida in quest of freedom. However, the

British had no interest in emancipating slaves, and British officials made every effort to return the runaways to loyalist owners or otherwise to keep them in bondage. But plantation owners were angry about the loss of many slaves and fearful that the wholesale rupturing of their authority would lead to a black uprising. Despite British efforts to placate them, many former loyalists abandoned their support of the British and welcomed the return to power of the rebels in 1782. Those who remained loyalists, embittered by countless instances of harsh treatment under patriot rule, lost little time in taking revenge. Patriots struck back whenever possible. So began an escalating cycle of revenge, retribution, and retaliation that engulfed the Lower South through 1782.

But the southern conflict was not all personal feuds and guerrilla warfare. After the capture of Charles Town, General Horatio Gates took command in the South. With only a small force of Continentals at his disposal, however, Gates had to rely on poorly trained militiamen. In August 1780 Cornwallis inflicted a crushing defeat on Gates at Camden, South Carolina. Fleeing after firing a single volley, Gates's militia left his badly outnumbered Continentals to be overrun. Camden was the worst rebel defeat of the war.

Washington and Congress responded by relieving Gates of command and sending General Nathanael Greene to confront Cornwallis. Greene subsequently fought three major battles between March and September 1781, and he lost all of them. "We fight, get beat,

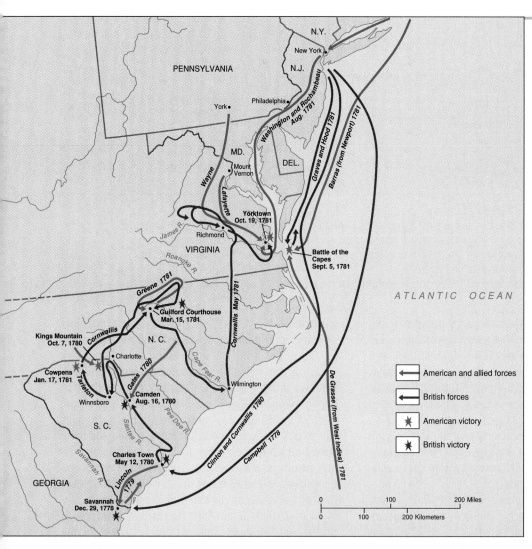

### The War in the South, 1778–1781

*By 1780 Britain held the South's major cities, Charles Town and Savannah, but could not establish control over the backcountry because of resistance from Nathanael Greene's Continentals. By invading Virginia, Lord Cornwallis placed himself within striking distance of American and French forces, a decision that rapidly led to the British surrender at Yorktown in October 1781.*

**Surrender of the British**

*French naval power combined with American military savvy to produce the decisive defeat of the British at Yorktown.*

rise, and fight again," he wrote back to Washington. Still, Greene won the campaign, for he gave the Whig militia the protection they needed to hunt down loyalists, stretched British supply lines until they began to snap, and sapped Cornwallis's strength by inflicting much heavier casualties than the British general could afford. Greene's dogged resistance forced Cornwallis to leave the Carolina backcountry in American hands and to lead his battered troops into Virginia.

Secure in New York City, Clinton wanted Cornwallis to return to Charles Town and renew his Carolina campaign; but Cornwallis had a mind of his own and established a new base at Yorktown, Virginia, near the coast. From Yorktown Cornwallis hoped to fan out into Virginia and Pennsylvania, but he never got the chance. Cornwallis's undoing began on August 30, 1781, when a French fleet dropped anchor off the Virginia coast and landed troops near Yorktown. Soon Lafayette joined them, leading a small force of Continentals. Meanwhile, Washington made enough feints at New York City to prevent Clinton from coming to Cornwallis's aid and then moved his army south to tighten the noose around the British. Trapped in Yorktown, Cornwallis's 6,000 British stood off 8,800 Americans and 7,800 French for three weeks. They finally surrendered with military honors on October 19, 1781.

## The Peace of Paris

"Oh God!" Lord North exclaimed upon hearing of Yorktown, "It's all over." Indeed, Cornwallis's surrender drained the will of England's overtaxed people to fight and forced the government to commence peace negotiations. John Adams, Benjamin Franklin, and John Jay were America's principal diplomats at the peace talks in Paris, which began in June 1782.

Military realities largely influenced the terms of the peace. Britain recognized American independence and agreed to the evacuation of all royal troops from the new nation's soil. Although the vast majority of Americans lived in the thirteen states clustered near the eastern seaboard, the British had little choice but to award the Confederation all lands east of the Mississippi, for by 1783 twenty thousand Anglo-Americans lived west of the Appalachians, and Clark's victories had given Americans control of the Northwest. The treaty also gave the new nation important fishing rights off the Grand Banks of Canada.

On the whole, the settlement was highly favorable to the Confederation, but it did not resolve all disputes. In a separate treaty, Britain transferred East and West Florida back to Spain, but the boundaries designated by this treaty were ambiguous. Spain interpreted the treaty to mean that it regained the same Florida territory that it had ceded to Britain in 1763. But Britain's treaty with the Confederation named the thirty-first parallel as the Floridas' northern border, well south of the area claimed by Spain. Spain and the new nation would dispute the northern boundary of Florida until 1795.

The Peace of Paris also planted the seeds of several future disputes between Britain and the Americans. Although the new nation promised to urge the state legislatures to compensate loyalists for their property losses and agreed that no legal bars would prevent British creditors from collecting prewar debts, several state governments later refused to pay back loyalists and erected barriers against British creditors. In response, the British failed to honor their treaty pledge to return slaves confiscated by their troops.

Notably missing in the Peace of Paris was any reference to Native Americans, most of whom had supported the British in order to avert the alternative—an independent American republic that would be no friend to Indian interests. In effect the treaty left the native peoples to deal with this new republic on their own, without any provision for their status or treatment. Not surprisingly, many Native Americans did not acknowledge the new nation's claims to sovereignty over their territory.

The Peace of Paris ratified American independence, but winning independence had exacted a heavy price. At least 5 percent of all free white males aged sixteen to forty-five died in the war. If the present-day U.S. population fought a war with comparable casualties, 12.5 million people would be killed. Only the Civil War produced a higher ratio of casualties to the nation's popu-

lation. Furthermore, the war drove perhaps one of every six loyalists and several thousand slaves into exile in Canada, Britain, or the West Indies. Fleeing loyalists accounted for perhaps as much as 20 percent of New York's white population. When the British evacuated Savannah in 1782, 15 percent of Georgia's whites accompanied them. Most whites who departed were recent British immigrants. Finally, although the war secured American independence, it did not settle two important issues: what kind of society America was to become and what sort of government the new nation would possess. Yet the war had a profound impact on both questions.

# Revolutionary Society

Two forces shaped the social effects of the Revolution: first, the principles articulated in the Declaration of Independence; and second, the dislocations caused by the war itself. These factors combined to change relationships between members of different classes, races, and genders momentously.

### Egalitarianism

Between 1700 and 1760, social relations between elites and the common people had grown more formal, distant, and restrained. Members of the colonial gentry had emphasized their social position by living far beyond the means of ordinary families. By the late 1760s, however, many in the upper classes began wearing homespun rather than imported English clothes in support of the boycott of British goods and subsequently watched their popularity soar. When Virginia planters organized minutemen companies in 1775, they threw away their expensive militia uniforms and dressed in homespun hunting shirts; then even the poorest farmer would not be too embarrassed to enlist because of his humble appearance. By 1776 the anti-British movement had persuaded many elites to maintain the appearance, if not the substance, of equality with common people.

Then came war, which accelerated the erosion of class differences by forcing the gentry, who held officers' rank, to show respect to the ordinary folk serving as privates. Indeed, the soldiers demanded to be treated with consideration, especially in light of the ringing words of the Declaration of Independence, "All men are created equal." The soldiers would follow

**American Foot Soldiers, Yorktown Campaign**
by Jean-Baptiste-Antoine DeVerger, 1781

commands, but not if they were addressed as inferiors.

The best officers realized this fact immediately. Some, among them General Israel Putnam of Connecticut, went out of their way to show that they felt no superiority to their troops. While inspecting a regiment digging fortifications around Boston in 1776, Putnam saw a large stone nearby and told a noncommissioned officer to throw it onto the outer wall. The individual protested, "Sir, I am a corporal." "Oh," replied Putnam, "I ask your pardon, sir." The general then dismounted his horse and hurled the rock himself, to the immense delight of the troops working there.

A majority of men of military age were exposed to treatment of this sort in the course of the war. Soldiers came to expect that their worth as individuals would be recognized by their officers, at least within the limits of the army. After these common soldiers returned to civilian life, they retained a sense of self-esteem and insisted on respectful treatment. As these feelings of personal pride gradually translated into political behavior and beliefs, many candidates took care not to scorn the common people. The war thus subtly but fundamentally democratized Americans' political assumptions.

The gentry's sense of social rank also diminished as they met men who rose through ability rather than through advantages of wealth or family. The war produced numerous examples like James Purvis, the illiterate son of a nonslaveowning Virginia farmer, who joined the First Virginia Regiment as a private in 1775, soon rose to sergeant, and then taught himself to read and write so that he could perform an officer's duties. Captain Purvis fought through the entire war and impressed his well-born officers as "an uneducated man, but of sterling worth." As elites saw more and more men like Purvis performing responsibilities previously thought to be above their station in life, many developed a new appreciation that a person's merit was not always related to his wealth.

Not all those who considered themselves republicans welcomed the apparent trend toward democracy. Especially among elites, many continued to insist that each social class had its own particular virtues and that a chief virtue of the lower classes was deference to those possessing the wealth and education necessary to govern. Writing to John Adams in 1778, Mercy Otis Warren observed that while "a state of war has ever been deemed unfavorable to virtue, . . . such a total change of manners in so short a period . . . was never

known in the history of man. Rapacity and profusion, pride and servility, and almost every vice is contrasted in the same heart."

Nevertheless, most Revolutionary-generation Americans came to insist that virtue and sacrifice defined a citizen's worth independently of his wealth. Voters widely began to view members of the "natural aristocracy"—those who had demonstrated fitness for government service by personal accomplishments—as the ideal candidates for political office. This natural aristocracy had room for a few self-made men such as Benjamin Franklin, as well as for those, like Jefferson and John Hancock, born into wealth. Voters still elected the wealthy to office, but not if they flaunted their money. The new emphasis on equality did not extend to propertyless males, women, and nonwhites, but it undermined the tendency to believe that wealth or distinguished family background conferred a special claim to public office.

## A Revolution for Black Americans

The wartime situation of African Americans contradicted the ideals of equality and justice for which Americans were fighting. About 500,000 black persons—20 percent of the total population—inhabited the United States in 1776, of whom all but about 25,000 lived in bondage. Even those who were free could not vote, lived under curfews and other galling restrictions, and lacked the guarantees of equal justice held by the poorest white criminal. Free blacks could expect no more than grudging toleration, and few slaves ever gained their freedom.

Although the United States was a "white man's country" in 1776, the war opened some opportunities to African Americans. Amid the confusion of war, some slaves, among them Jehu Grant of Rhode Island, ran off and posed as free persons. Grant later recalled his excitement "when I saw liberty poles and the people all engaged for the support of freedom, and I could not but like and be pleased with such a thing."

In contrast to the twenty thousand who joined British forces, approximately five thousand African Americans served in the Continental forces, most from the North. Even though the army late in 1775 forbade the enlistment of any African Americans, black soldiers were already fighting in units during the siege of Boston, and the ban on black enlistments started to collapse in 1777. The majority were slaves serving with their masters' consent, usually in integrated units.

## Boonesborough, Kentucky

In the half-century of war that consumed North America, nowhere was the fighting more intense and bitter than in the Ohio River valley, or "Ohio country." For imperial visionaries in France, Britain, and the newly independent United States, the Ohio country—linking the eastern seaboard to the vast Mississippi Valley—was the key to continental and even global power. For Native Americans and white settlers, it was a means of securing liberty and a livelihood. Among the region's original inhabitants were the Shawnees, driven from the upper Ohio in the 1680s by Iroquois warriors and dispersed to other parts of eastern North America. A half-century later, Shawnees began returning to find a homeland where English and French traders visited Indian towns regularly and sometimes married native women and Native Americans used scissors and needles to fashion European cloth into

garments and iron tools to build log cabins and guns, powder, and shot to hunt. Alcohol was a staple at Indian social gatherings. Delawares, Mingos, Miamis, and other Native Americans were, like the Shawnees, moving to the Ohio country to be near traders and far from English or Iroquois neighbors. Despite the changes, the Ohio country was at peace and remained Indian country where Shawnees and other Native Americans maintained the customs and beliefs of their grandparents.

Midcentury saw a sudden influx of European settlers from Pennsylvania into what colonists called the "back-country" (the Appalachian Mountains and lands west). They too came to extract a living without being bound by scarce resources or outside authorities and adopted many Indian practices. Many immigrant men spent fall and winter hunting deer and trapping beaver, learned from Native Americans

the lay of the land, the ways of its animals, and the advantage of Indian moccasins and buckskin.

A young North Carolinian named Daniel Boone pursued game in the upper Ohio country, where in 1769 he was seized by Shawnees and held for two years. Undaunted, Boone attempted to lead kinfolk and neighbors into the land known as Kentucky in 1773 but was turned back by attacking Indians. Two years later, Boone was hired by land speculators to guide a roadbuilding crew through the Cumberland Gap and founded the town of Boonesborough on the upper Kentucky River in April 1775.

Although Boonesborough celebrated news of the Declaration of Independence in July 1776, veterans of the North Carolina Regulator movement sided against their eastern enemies who favored independence. Others wanted no contact with outside authorities and tried to remain neutral. Many were animated by anti-British sentiments and tried to preserve personal independence by siding with the patriots. Finally, many simply followed other family members in joining either Tories or Whigs.

Some Shawnees too sought to remain neutral. Others sided with Blackfish, a renowned war leader from Chillicothe who felt the war would allow Shawnees to regain lands south of the Ohio, which the Iroquois had ceded to Britain and the colonies in 1768. Finally, some Shawnees saw no hope for peace and moved west.

In 1777 Blackfish led two war parties against Boonesborough and in February 1778 captured Boone and 26 other Boonesborough men. The men were publicly paraded before Chillicothe villagers seeking to adopt individuals to replace dead family members. Half the captives were taken to British authorities in Detroit for bounties. The

**Daniel Boone Escorting Settlers Through the Cumberland Gap, 1851–52** by George Coleb Bingham
*Bingham's is the best known of the many prints and paintings depicting this singular moment in colonial westward expansion.*

rest, including Boone, were adopted, Boone by Blackfish himself to replace a son killed in an earlier raid on Boonesborough. Boone was bathed in the river, plucked of all hair except for a scalplock that hung from the top of his head to one side, and dressed for his naming ceremony. Blackfish then welcomed his adopted son Sheltowee ("Big Turtle") into his family.

Several captives feared that Boone's adoption meant he might betray them to the Shawnees or British, but in June he escaped and returned to Boonesborough. Townspeople suspected Boone's intentions but agreed to prepare for an anticipated attack by securing the stockade and expanding the food supply. On the morning of September 7, 1778, 60 fighting men and other residents of Boonesborough watched as 400 Shawnees plus a British militia unit from Detroit emerged from the woods to within rifle range of the stockade. A young African man, Pompey, captured as a boy from a Virginia plantation and Chillicothe's English translator, stepped forward to summon Boone to come out and speak with his father Blackfish. After the two men embraced and exchanged gifts, Blackfish lamented his son's escape and hoped they could now reunite, with the townspeople surrendering and accompanying the Shawnees to Detroit. Boone agreed to consult with his men and report back the next day. Although Boone would have been willing to take his chances and surrender, the rest of the men vowed to fight to the death. Boone then said, "Well, well, I'll die with the rest."

The next day Boonesborough's leading men emerged from the stockade to welcome their Shawnee counterparts to join them in an elaborate feast. They were repaying Blackfish and his people for their earlier hospitality but also wanted to imply they had enough provisions to withstand a prolonged siege. When Blackfish asked his son for Boonesborough's decision, Boone replied that the men had vowed to fight to the death. Blackfish expressed great sorrow and made another offer: the adversaries would recognize the Ohio as the boundary dividing them but allow one another to cross the river freely to hunt or visit. The Americans asked for time to consider the offer. What happened next occurred so suddenly that participants could not later recall the details. Declaring that peace was now at hand, Blackfish called on his leading men to embrace their Boonesborough counterparts, but the white men sensed a trap and fought their way past the approaching Shawnees and into the stockade, while riflemen on both sides unleashed torrents of gunfire.

For 17 days, both sides fired rifles while the Shawnees tried to burn the fort and tunnel toward it. Inside, men, women, children, free and slave, fired guns and prepared and distributed food. Boone's daughter, Gamma Calloway, was wounded while tending to the wounds of others. After a downpour collapsed their nearly completed tunnel, the exhausted and demoralized Shawnees withdrew.

The siege of Boonesborough had virtually no military significance in the colonies' war with Britain but was later remembered as a symbolic moment in the history of Kentucky (admitted to the union in 1792) and the American frontier, when outnumbered settlers defended their tiny world against a "savage" onslaught and made possible America's future growth and pros-

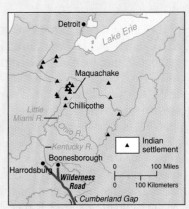

**Boonesborough During the Revolutionary Era**

perity. Such remembering overlooked what settlers and Shawnees had shared and forgot that the siege's hero was far from certain of his own loyalties.

**Early drawing of Fort Boonesborough**
*The townspeople of Boonesborough completed their stockade just in time to face the Shawnee-British siege of September 1778.*

For the most part, these wartime opportunities for African-American men grew out of the army's need for personnel rather than a white commitment to equal justice. In fact, until the mid-eighteenth century, few in the Western world had criticized slavery at all. Like disease and sin, slavery was considered part of the natural order. But in the decade before the Revolution, American opposition to slavery had swelled, especially as resistance leaders increasingly compared the colonies' relationship with Britain to that between slaves and a master. The first American prohibition against slave-owning came from the yearly meeting of the New England Quakers in 1770. The yearly meetings of New York and Philadelphia Quakers followed suit in 1776, and by 1779 Quaker slaveowners had freed 80 percent of their slaves.

Although the Quakers aimed mainly to abolish slaveholding within their own ranks, the Declaration of Independence's broad assertion of natural rights and human equality spurred a more general attack on the institution of slavery. Between 1777 and 1784, Vermont, Pennsylvania, Massachusetts, Rhode Island, and Connecticut ended slavery. New York did so in 1799, and New Jersey in 1804. New Hampshire, unmoved by petitions like that written in 1779 by Portsmouth slaves demanding liberty "to dispose of our lives, freedom, and property," never freed its slaves; but by 1810 there were none in the state.

The movement against slavery reflected the Enlightenment's emphasis on realizing equality through gradual change, initiated by leaders who carefully primed public opinion. The Revolutionary generation, rather than advocating slavery's immediate abolition, favored steps that would weaken the institution and in this way bring about its eventual demise. Most state abolition laws provided for gradual emancipation, typically declaring all children born of a slave woman after a certain date—often July 4—free. (Such individuals still had to work, without pay, for their mother's master for up to twenty-eight years.) Furthermore, the Revolution's leaders did not press for decisive action against slavery in the South, out of fear that widespread southern emancipation would either bankrupt or end the Union. They argued that the Confederation, already deeply in debt as a result of the war, could not finance immediate abolition in the South, and any attempt to do so without compensation would drive that region into secession. "Great as the evil is," observed Virginia's James Madison in 1787, "a dismemberment of the union would be worse."

Yet even in the South, slavery worried the consciences of some Whigs. When one of his slaves ran off to join the British and later was recaptured, Madison concluded that it would be hypocritical to punish the runaway "merely for coveting that liberty for which we have paid the price of so much blood." Still, Madison did not free the slave, and no state south of Pennsylvania abolished slavery. Nevertheless, every state but North Carolina passed laws making it possible for masters to manumit (set free) slaves without posting large sums of money as bond for their good behavior. By 1790 the number of free blacks in Virginia and Maryland had risen from about 4,000 in 1775 to nearly 21,000, or about 5 percent of all African Americans there.

These "free persons of color" faced the future as destitute, second-class citizens. Most had purchased their freedom by spending their small cash savings earned in off-hours and were past their physical prime. Once free, they found whites reluctant to hire them or to pay equal wages. Black ship carpenters in Charleston (formerly Charles Town), South Carolina, for example, earned one-third less than their white coworkers in 1783. Under such circumstances, most free blacks remained poor laborers, domestic servants, and tenant farmers. Even under such extreme disadvantages, some free blacks became landowners or skilled artisans, and a few gained recognition from whites. One of the best known was Benjamin Banneker of Maryland, a self-taught mathematician and astronomer. In 1789 Banneker was one of three surveyors who laid out the new national capital in Washington, D.C., and after 1791 he published a series of widely read almanacs. Sending a copy of one to Thomas Jefferson, Banneker chided the future president for holding views of black inferiority that contradicted his own words in the Declaration of Independence. Another prominent African American was the Boston poet and slave, Phillis Wheatley. Several of Wheatley's poems explicitly linked the liberty sought by colonists with a plea for the liberty of slaves, including one that was autobiographical:

> I, young in life, by seeming cruel fate
> Was snatch'd from Afric's fancy'ed happy seat:
>
> . . . . . .
>
> Such, such my case. And can I then but pray
> Others may never feel tyrannic sway?

Free blacks relied on one another for help. Self-help among African Americans flowed largely through

**Phillis Wheatley,
African-American Poet**

*Though a slave, Wheatley was
America's best-known poet at
the time of the Revolution.
Despite her fame, Wheatley
died in poverty in 1784.*

religious channels. Because many white congregations spurned them and because racially separate churches provided mutual support, self-pride, and a sense of accomplishment, free blacks began founding their own Baptist and Methodist congregations after the Revolution. In 1787 black Methodists in Philadelphia started the congregation that by 1816 would become the African Methodist Episcopal church. Black churches, a great source of inner strength and community cohesion for African Americans ever since, had their origins in the Revolutionary period.

Most states granted important civil rights to free blacks during and after the Revolution. Free blacks had not participated in colonial elections, but those who were male and met the property qualification gained this privilege everywhere by the 1780s. Most northern states repealed or stopped enforcing curfews and other colonial laws restricting African Americans' freedom of movement. These same states generally changed their laws to guarantee free blacks equal treatment in court hearings.

The Revolution neither ended slavery nor brought equality to free blacks, but it did begin a process by which slavery eventually could be extinguished. In half the nation, human bondage had been outlawed and white southerners increasingly viewed slavery as a necessary evil—an attitude that implicitly recognized its immorality. Slavery had begun to crack, and free blacks had made some gains. But this shift would prove short-lived when events in the 1790s squelched the move toward egalitarianism.

### White Women in the New Republic

"To be adept in the art of Government is a prerogative to which your sex lay almost exclusive claim," wrote Abigail Adams to her husband John in 1776. She was one of the era's shrewdest political commentators and her husband's political confidante and best friend, but she had no public role. Indeed, for most white women as well as men in the 1780s, a woman's duty was to maintain her household and raise her children.

Apart from the fact that some states eased women's difficulties in obtaining divorces, the Revolution did not significantly affect the legal position of white women. Women did not gain any new political rights, although New Jersey's 1776 constitution did not exclude white female property holders from voting, which they did in significant numbers until barred (along with free blacks) in 1807. The assumption that women were naturally dependent—either as children subordinate to their parents or as wives to their husbands—continued to dominate discussions of the female role. Nevertheless, the Revolutionary War and contemporary ideological currents emphasizing liberty and equality were significant for white American women.

White women's support of colonial resistance before Independence (see Chapter 5) broadened into an even wider range of support activities during the war. Female "camp followers," many of them soldiers' wives, served military units on both sides by cooking and laundering and by nursing the wounded. A few women, by disguising themselves as men, even joined in the fighting. Many more women remained at home, where they managed families, households, farms, and businesses on their own. After her civilian husband was seized by loyalists and turned over to the British on Long Island, Mary Silliman of Fairfield, Connecticut, tended to her four children (and bore a fifth), oversaw several servants and slaves, ran a commercial farm that had to be evacuated when the British attacked Fairfield, and launched appeals for her husband's release. Despite often enormous struggles, such experiences boosted white women's confidence in their abilities to think and act on matters traditionally reserved for men. "I have the vanity," wrote another Connecticut woman, Mary Fish, to a female friend, "to think I have in some measure acted the *heroine* as well as my dear Husband the Hero."

As with African Americans, the Revolutionary era witnessed the beginnings of a challenge to whites' traditional attitudes toward women. American republicans increasingly recognized the right of a woman to choose her husband—a striking departure from the practice, still prevalent among some elites, whereby marriages were approved or even arranged by fathers.

Thus in 1790, on the occasion of his daughter's marriage, Jefferson wrote to a friend that, following "the usage of my country, I scrupulously suppressed my wishes, [so] that my daughter might indulge her sentiments freely." Outside elite circles, such independence was even more apparent. Especially in the Northeast, daughters increasingly got pregnant by prospective husbands, thus forcing their fathers to consent to their marrying in order to avoid a public scandal. For example, Mary Brown's father objected to her wedding John Chamberlain in Hallowell, Maine, in May 1792. In December he finally consented and the couple wed, just two days before their daughter's birth. By becoming pregnant, northeastern women secured for themselves economic support in a region where an exodus of young, unmarried men left a growing number of women single.

**Judith Sargent Stevens (Murray)** by John Singleton Copley, c. 1770
*Drawing on discussions then going on in Europe, Judith Sargent Murray became the foremost advocate of women's rights at the end of the eighteenth century.*

White women also had fewer children overall than their mothers and grandmothers. In Sturbridge, Massachusetts, women in the mid-eighteenth century averaged nearly nine children per marriage, compared with just six in the first decade of the nineteenth century. Whereas 40 percent of Quaker women had nine or more children before 1770, only 14 percent bore that many thereafter. Such statistics testify to declining farm sizes and urbanization, both of which were incentives for having fewer children. But they also indicate that women were finding some relief from the near-constant state of pregnancy and nursing that consumed their forebears.

As white women's roles expanded, so too did republican notions of male-female relations. "I object to the word 'obey' in the marriage-service," wrote a female author calling herself Matrimonial Republican, "because it is a general word, without limitations or definition." "The obedience between man and wife," she continued, "is, or ought to be mutual." Lack of mutuality was one reason for a rising number of divorce petitions from women, from fewer than 14 per year in Connecticut before the Revolution, to 45 in 1795. A few women also challenged the sexual double standard that allowed men to indulge in extramarital affairs while their female partners, single or married, were condemned. Writing in 1784, an author calling herself Daphne pointed out how a woman whose illicit affair was exposed was "forever deprive[d] . . . of all that renders life valuable," while "the base [male] betrayer is suffered to triumph in the success of his unmanly arts, and to pass unpunished even by a frown." Daphne called on her "sister Americans" to "stand by and support the dignity of our own sex" by publicly condemning seducers rather than their victims.

Gradually, the subordination of women, which once was taken for granted among most whites, became the subject of debate. In the essay "On the Equality of the Sexes," written in 1779 and published in 1790, essayist and poet Judith Sargent Murray contended that the genders had equal intellectual ability and deserved equal education. "We can only reason from what we know," she wrote, "and if an opportunity of acquiring knowledge hath been denied us, the inferiority of our sex cannot fairly be deduced from there." Murray hoped that "sensible and informed" women would improve their minds rather than rush into marriage (as she had at eighteen), and would instill republican ideals in their children.

Like many of her contemporaries, Murray supported "republican motherhood." Republicans emphasized the importance of educating white women in the values of liberty and independence in order to strengthen virtue in the new nation. It was the duty of women to inculcate these values in their sons as well as their daughters. Even so conservative a man as John Adams reminded his daughter that she was part of "a young generation, coming up in America . . . [and] will be responsible for a great share of the duty and opportunity of educating a rising family, from whom much will be expected." After 1780 the urban upper class founded numerous private schools, or academies, for girls, and these provided to American women their first widespread opportunity for advanced education. Massachusetts also established an important precedent in 1789, when it forbade any town to exclude girls from its elementary schools.

By itself, however, the expansion of educational opportunities for white women would have little effect. "I acknowledge we have an equal share of curiosity with the other sex," wrote Mercy Otis Warren to Abigail Adams, but men "have the opportunities of gratifying their inquisitive humour to the utmost, in the great school of the world, while we are confined to the narrow circle of domesticity." Although the great struggle for female political equality would not begin until the next century, Revolutionary-era assertions that women were intellectually and morally men's peers provoked scattered calls for political equality. In 1793 Priscilla Mason, a young woman graduating from one of the female academies, blamed "*Man,* despotic man" for shutting women out of the church, the courts, and government. In her salutatory oration, she urged that a women's senate be established by Congress to evoke "all that is human—all that is *divine* in the soul of woman."

Warren and Mason had pointed out a fundamental limitation to republican egalitarianism: besides being a virtuous wife and mother, there was little a woman could *do* with her education.

### Native Americans and the Revolution

For Native Americans, the consequences of the United States' triumph over Britain were less certain. Whereas Revolutionary ideology held out at least an abstract hope for blacks, white women, and others seeking equal rights and status in American society, it made no provision for the many Indians who sought to maintain their political and cultural independence. Moreover, in an overwhelmingly agrarian society like the United States, the Revolution's implicit promise of equal economic opportunity for all male citizens set the stage for territorial expansion beyond the areas already settled, thereby threatening Native American landholdings. Even where Indians retained land, the influx of settlers posed dangers to them in the form of deadly diseases, farming practices inimical to Indian subsistence (see Chapter 3), and alcohol. Indians were all the more vulnerable because, during the three decades encompassed by the Seven Years' War and the Revolution (1754–1783), the native population east of the Mississippi had declined by about half, and many Indian communities had been uprooted.

In the face of these uncertainties, Native Americans continued their efforts to incorporate the most useful aspects of European culture into their own. From the beginning of the colonial period, Indians had selectively adopted European-made goods of cloth, metal, glass, and other materials into their lives. But Native Americans did not give up their older ways altogether; rather, their clothing, tools, weapons, utensils, and other material goods combined elements of the old and the new. Indians, especially those no longer resisting American expansion, also selectively participated in the American economy by working occasionally for wages or by selling food, crafts, or other products. This interweaving of the new with the traditional characterized Indian communities up and down the newly independent states. Even Indians west of the settled areas, who hoped to avert the takeover of their lands by the new republic, looked to the British in Canada or the Spanish in Florida for trade as well as for diplomatic and military support.

Native Americans, then, did not remain stubbornly rooted in traditional ways, nor did most of them resist participation in a larger world dominated by Europeans or Euro-Americans. But they did insist on retaining control of their communities and their ways of life. Ten years after the Treaty of Paris, an intertribal delegation bluntly told some American commissioners seeking their lands,

> You have talked to us about concessions. It appears strange that you should expect any from us, who have only been defending our just rights against your invasion. We want peace; restore to us our country and we shall be enemies no longer.

In the Revolution's aftermath, it appeared doubtful that the new nation would accommodate Native Americans on such terms.

### The Revolution and Social Change

The American Revolution left the overall distribution of wealth in the nation unchanged. Because the 3 percent of Americans who fled abroad as loyalists represented a cross-section of society, their departure left the new nation's class structure unaltered. Loyalists' confiscated estates tended to be bought up by equally well-to-do Whig gentlemen. Overall, the American upper class seems to have owned about as much of the national wealth in 1783 as it did in 1776.

In short, the Revolution did not obliterate social distinctions or even challenge most of them. Class distinctions, racial injustice, and the subordination of women persisted into the nineteenth century. In particular, the institution of slavery survived intact in the South, where the vast majority of African Americans lived. Yet the Revolutionary era set in motion significant social changes. Increasingly, the members of the gentry had to earn respect by demonstrating their competence and by treating the common people with dignity. The Revolution dealt slavery a decisive blow in the North, greatly enlarged the free-black population, and awarded free people of color important political rights. Although the momentous era did not bring white women political equality, it placed new issues pertaining to the relations between the genders on the agenda of national debate. And inevitably, the social changes wrought by the Revolution shaped the new nation's momentous political debates.

## Forging New Governments

Americans had drawn many political conclusions from the imperial crisis of the 1760s, including the conviction that without vigilance by the people, governments would become despotic. But before the Declaration of Independence was written, few colonists had given much thought to forming governments of their own. Although guiding and inspiring the Americans, the Continental Congress lacked the sovereign powers usually associated with governments, including the authority to impose taxes.

During the war years, rebels quickly recognized the need to establish government institutions to sustain the war effort and to buttress the United States' claim to independent nationhood. But the task of forging a government would prove arduous, in part because of the inevitable upheavals of war. In addition, the state governments that Americans formed after the Declaration of Independence reflected two different and often conflicting impulses: on one hand, the traditional ideas and practices that had guided Anglo-Americans for much of the eighteenth century; on the other, the republican ideals that found a receptive audience in America in the 1760s and early 1770s.

"Can America be happy under a government of her own?" asked Thomas Paine in 1776. He answered his own question: "as happy as she pleases: she hath a blank sheet to write upon."

### Tradition and Change

In establishing the Revolutionary state governments, patriots relied heavily on ideas about government inherited from the colonial experience. For example, most Whigs took for granted the value of bicameral legislatures. As we have seen, the colonial legislatures had consisted of two houses: an elected lower chamber (or assembly) and an upper chamber (or council) appointed by the governor or chosen by the assembly. These two-part legislatures resembled Parliament's division into the House of Commons and House of Lords and symbolized the assumption that a government should give separate representation to aristocrats and common people.

Despite the Revolution's democratic tendencies, few questioned the long-standing practice of setting property requirements for voters and elected officials. In the prevailing view, only the ownership of property, especially land, made it possible for voters to think and act independently. Whereas tenant farmers and hired laborers might sell their votes, mindlessly follow a demagogue, or vote to avoid displeasing their landlords or employers, property holders had the financial means and the education to express their opinions at the ballot box freely and responsibly. The association between property and citizenship was so deeply ingrained that even radicals such as Samuel Adams opposed allowing all males—much less women—to vote and hold office.

The notion that elected representatives should exercise independent judgment in leading the people rather than simply carry out the popular will also survived from the colonial period and restricted the democratization of politics. Although Americans today take political parties for granted, the idea of parties as necessary instruments for identifying and mobilizing public opinion was alien to the eighteenth-century political temper, which equated parties with "factions"—selfish groups that advanced their own interests at the expense of the public good. In general, candidates for office did not present voters with a clear choice between policies calculated to benefit rival interest groups; instead, they campaigned on the basis of their personal reputations and fitness for office. As a result, voters did not know where office seekers stood on specific issues and hence found it hard to influence government actions.

Another colonial practice that persisted into the 1770s and 1780s was the equal (or nearly equal) division of legislative seats among all counties or towns, regardless of differences in population. Inasmuch as representation had never before been apportioned according to population, a minority of voters normally elected a majority of assemblymen. Additionally, many offices that later would become elective—such as sheriffs and justices of county courts—were appointive in the eighteenth century.

In sum, the colonial experience provided no precedent for a democratization of the United States during the Revolutionary era. Yet without intending to extend political participation, political elites found themselves pulled in a democratic direction by the logic of the imperial crisis of the 1760s and 1770s. The colonial assemblies, the most democratic parts of colonial government, had led the fight against British policy during Americans' ideological clash with England, whereas the executive branch of colonial governments, filled by royal governors and their appointees, had repeatedly locked horns with the assemblies. Colonists entered the Revolution dreading executive officeholders and convinced that even elected governors could no more be trusted with power than could monarchs. Recent history seemed to confirm the message hammered home by British "country party" ideology (see Chapter 5) that those in power tended to become either corrupt or dictatorial. Consequently, Revolutionary statesmen proclaimed the need to strengthen legislatures at the governors' expense.

Despite their preference for vesting power in popularly elected legislatures, Revolutionary leaders described themselves as republicans rather than democrats. Although used interchangeably today, these words had different connotations in the eighteenth century. At worst, democracy suggested mob rule; at best,

it implied the concentration of power in the hands of an uneducated multitude. In contrast, republicanism presumed that government would be entrusted to capable leaders, elected for their superior talents and wisdom. For most republicans, the ideal government would delicately balance the interests of different classes to prevent any one group from gaining absolute power. Some, including John Adams, thought that a republic could include a hereditary aristocracy or even a monarchy as part of this balance, but most thought otherwise. Having blasted one king in the Declaration of Independence, most political leaders had no desire to enthrone another. Still, their rejection of hereditary aristocracy and monarchy posed a problem for republicans as they set about drafting state constitutions: how to maintain balance in government amid pervasive distrust of executive power.

### *From Colonies to States*

The state governments that Americans constructed during the Revolution reflected a struggle between more radical, democratic elements and elites who would minimize popular participation. In keeping with colonial practice, eleven of the thirteen states maintained bicameral legislatures. In all but a few states, the great majority of officeholders, at both the state and the county level, were still appointed rather than elected. The most radical constitution, Pennsylvania's, attempted to ensure that election districts would be roughly equal in population, so that a minority of voters could not elect a majority of legislators. Nine of the thirteen states reduced property requirements for voting, but none abolished such qualifications entirely, and most of the reductions were modest.

Yet the persistence of these conservative features should not obscure the pathbreaking components of the state constitutions. Above all, they were *written* documents whose adoption usually required popular ratification and which could be changed only if voters chose to amend them. In short, Americans jettisoned the British conception of a constitution as a body of customary arrangements and practices, insisting instead that constitutions were written compacts that defined and limited the powers of rulers. Moreover, as a final check on government power, the Revolutionary constitutions spelled out citizens' fundamental rights. By 1784 all state constitutions included explicit bills of rights that outlined certain freedoms beyond government control. In sum, governments were no longer to serve as the final judge of the constitutionality of their activities.

The earliest of those new state constitutions severely limited executive power in particular. In most states the governor became an elected official, and elections themselves occurred far more frequently. (Pennsylvania actually eliminated the office of governor altogether.) Prior to 1776 most colonial elections were called at the governor's pleasure, usually about every three or four years. In contrast, after 1776 each state scheduled annual elections except South Carolina, which held them every two years. In most states the power of appointments was transferred from the governor to the legislature. Legislatures usually appointed judges and could reduce their salaries or impeach them (try them for wrongdoing). By relieving governors of most appointive powers, denying them the right to veto laws, and making them subject to impeachment, the constitutions turned governors into figureheads who simply chaired an executive council that made militia appointments and supervised financial business.

As the new state constitutions weakened the executive branch and vested more power in the legislatures, they also made the legislatures more responsive to the will of the people. Nowhere could the governor appoint the upper chamber. Eight constitutions written before 1780 allowed voters to select both houses of the legislature, one (Maryland) used a popularly chosen "electoral college" for its upper house, and the remaining "senates" were filled by vote of their assemblies. Pennsylvania and Georgia abolished the upper house and substituted a unicameral (single-chamber) legislature. Americans' assault on the executive branch and their enhancement of legislative authority reflected their bitter memories of royal governors who had acted arbitrarily to dismiss assemblies and control government through their power of appointment, and it underscored the influence of "country-party" ideologues, who had warned that republics' undoing began with executive usurpation of authority.

In the first flush of revolutionary enthusiasm, elites had to content themselves with state governments dominated by popularly elected legislatures. Gradually, however, wealthier landowners, bankers, merchants, and lawyers reasserted their desires for centralized authority and the political prerogatives of wealth. In Massachusetts an elite-dominated convention in 1780 pushed through a constitution stipulating stiff property qualifications for voting and holding office, state senate

districts that were apportioned according to property values, and a governor with considerable powers in making appointments and vetoing legislative measures. The Massachusetts constitution signaled a general trend. Georgia and Pennsylvania substituted bicameral for unicameral legislatures by 1790. Other states raised property qualifications for members of the upper chamber in a bid to encourage the "senatorial element" and to make room for men of "Wisdom, remarkable integrity, or that Weight which arises from property."

The later state constitutions revealed a central feature of elites' thought. Gradations among social classes and restrictions on the expression of popular will troubled them far less than the prospect of tyranny by those in power. But some republican elites believed that social divisions, if deep-seated and permanent, could jeopardize liberty, and attempted to implement major social changes through legislation. In Virginia, for example, Thomas Jefferson in 1776 persuaded the Virginia legislature to abolish entails, legal requirements that prevented an heir and all his descendants from selling or dividing an estate. Although entails were easy to break through special laws—Jefferson himself had escaped the constraints of one—he hoped that their elimination would strip wealthy families of the opportunity to amass land continuously and become an overbearing aristocracy. Through Jefferson's efforts, Virginia also ended primogeniture, the legal requirement that the eldest son inherit all a family's property in the absence of a will. Jefferson hoped that these laws would ensure a continuous division of wealth. By 1791 no state provided for primogeniture, and just two still allowed entails.

These years also witnessed the end of state-established churches in most of the country. New England resisted this reform, and the Congregational church continued to collect tithes (church taxes) until 1817 in New Hampshire, 1818 in Connecticut, and 1833 in Massachusetts. But in states where colonial taxpayers had supported the Anglican Church, such support was abolished by 1786. Thomas Jefferson best expressed the ideal behind disestablishment in his Statute for Religious Freedom (1786), whose preamble resounded with a defense of religious freedom at all times and places. "Truth is great," proclaimed Jefferson, "and will prevail if left to itself."

The American Revolution, wrote Thomas Paine in 1782, was intended to ring in "a new era and give a new turn to human affairs." This was an ambitious declara-

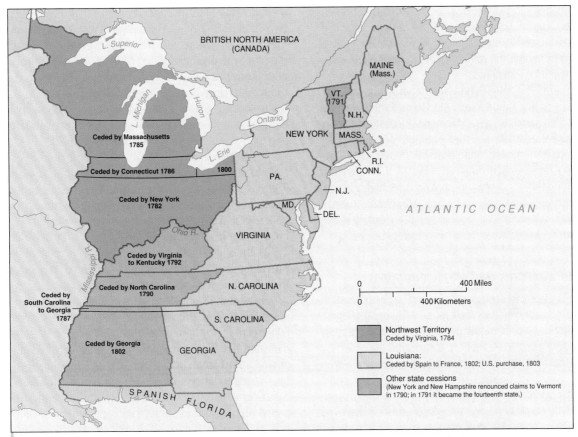

**State Claims to Western Lands, and State Cessions to the Federal Government, 1782–1802**

*Eastern states' surrender of land claims paved the way for new state governments in the West. Georgia was the last state to cede its western lands, in 1802.*

tion and seemed to conflict with the states' retention of institutions such as state senates and property requirements for voting. But Paine's point was that *all* political institutions, new and old alike, now were being judged by the standard of whether they served the public good rather than the interests of the powerful few. More than any single innovation of the era, it was this new way of thinking that made American politics revolutionary.

## The Articles of Confederation

As with their revolt against Britain and their early state constitutions, Americans' first national government reflected widespread fears of centralized authority and its potential for corruption. In 1776 John Dickinson, who had stayed in Congress despite having refused to sign the Declaration of Independence, drafted a proposal for a national government, which he called the Articles of Confederation. Congress adopted a weakened version of the Articles and sent it to the states for ratification in 1777.

The Articles explicitly reserved to each state "its sovereignty, freedom and independence" and established a form of government in which Americans were citizens of their own states first and of the United States second. As John Adams later explained, the Whigs of 1776 never thought of "consolidating this vast Continent under one national Government" but instead erected "a Confederacy of States, each of which must have a separate government."

Under the Articles, the national government consisted of a single-chamber Congress, elected by the state legislatures, in which each state had one vote. Congress could request funds from the states but could enact no tax of its own without every state's approval, nor could it regulate interstate or overseas commerce.

The Articles did not provide for an executive branch. Rather, congressional committees oversaw financial, diplomatic, and military affairs. Nor was there a judicial system by which the national government could compel allegiance to its laws.

By 1781 the Articles had been approved by all thirteen states' legislatures and the Confederation was in place. The new nation had taken a critical step in defining the role of national sovereignty in relation to the sovereignty of the individual states. Whereas the Continental Congress had directed most of the war effort without defined powers, the nation now had a formal government. Nevertheless, many Americans' misgivings about centralized power left the Confederation government severely limited in important respects.

### Finance, Trade, and the Economy

Perhaps the greatest challenge facing the Confederation was putting the nation on a sound financial footing. Winning the war had cost the nation's 600,000 taxpayers a staggering $160 million, a sum that exceeded by 2,400 percent the taxes raised to pay for the Seven Years' War. To finance the War for Independence, which cost far more than could be immediately collected through taxation, the government borrowed funds from abroad and printed its own paper money, called Continentals. Lack of public faith in the government destroyed 98 percent of the value of the Continentals from 1776 to 1781, an inflationary disaster that gave rise to the expression "not worth a Continental."

Faced with a desperate financial situation, Congress turned to a wealthy, self-made Philadelphia merchant, Robert Morris, who in 1781 became the nation's superintendent of finance. Morris proposed that the states authorize the collection of a national import duty of 5 percent to finance the congressional budget and to guarantee interest payments on the war debt. Because the Articles stipulated that every state had to approve the levying of national taxes, the import duty failed to pass in 1782 when Rhode Island alone rejected it.

Hoping to panic the country into creating a regular source of national revenue, Morris and New York congressman Alexander Hamilton then engineered a dangerous gamble known later as the Newburgh Conspiracy. In 1783 the two men secretly persuaded some army officers, then encamped at Newburgh, New York, to threaten a coup d'état unless the treasury obtained the taxation authority needed to raise their pay, which was months in arrears. But George Washington, learning of the conspiracy before it was carried out, ended the plot by delivering a speech that appealed to his officers' honor and left them unwilling to proceed. Although Morris may never have intended that a coup actually occur, his willingness to take such a risk demonstrated the new nation's perilous financial straits and the vulnerability of its political institutions.

When peace came in 1783, Morris found it impossible to secure adequate funding for the United States. That year, Congress sent another tax measure to the states, but once again a single legislature, this time New York's, blocked it. From then on, the states steadily decreased their contributions to Congress. By the late 1780s, the states had fallen behind nearly 80 percent in providing the funds that Congress requested to operate the government and honor the national debt.

Nor did the Confederation succeed in prying trade concessions from Britain. Before independence, almost 60 percent of northern exports had gone to the West Indies, and New England's maritime community had employed approximately 15 percent of all adult males. After independence, however, Britain prohibited American trade with its Caribbean colonies and imposed high customs fees for landing products in Great Britain. Because half of all American exports went to Great Britain and its colonies, these restrictions allowed British shippers to increase their share of Atlantic trade at American expense.

The decline in trade with Britain contributed substantially to an economic depression that gripped parts of the nation beginning in 1784. New Englanders were the least fortunate. A short growing season and poor soil kept yields so low, even in the best of times, that farmers barely produced enough grain for local consumption. New Englanders also faced both high taxes to repay the money borrowed to finance the Revolution and a tightening of credit that spawned countless lawsuits against debtors. Economic depression only aggravated the region's chronic overpopulation. Young New England men continued migrating to the frontier or to the cities, and their discontent and restless mobility loosened the bonds of parental authority and left many women without marriage prospects.

British restrictions against trading with the West Indies fell especially hard on New England. Resourceful captains took cargoes to the French West Indies, Scandinavia, and even China. Some even smuggled food-

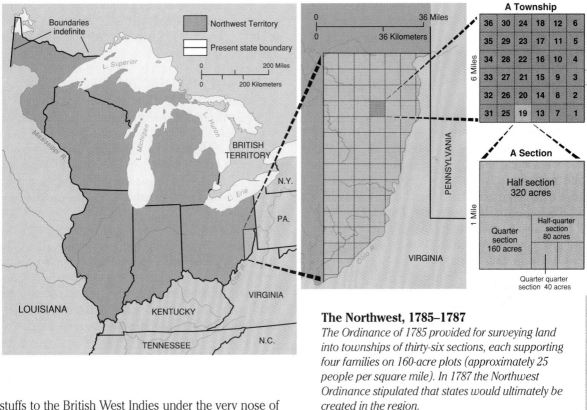

**The Northwest, 1785–1787**
*The Ordinance of 1785 provided for surveying land into townships of thirty-six sections, each supporting four families on 160-acre plots (approximately 25 people per square mile). In 1787 the Northwest Ordinance stipulated that states would ultimately be created in the region.*

stuffs to the British West Indies under the very nose of the Royal Navy. Nevertheless, by 1791 discriminatory British treatment had reduced the number of seamen in the Massachusetts cod and whale fisheries by 42 percent compared to the 1770s.

The mid-Atlantic states, on the other hand, were less dependent on British-controlled markets for their exports. As famine stalked Europe, farmers in Pennsylvania and New York prospered from climbing export prices—much as Thomas Paine had predicted (see Chapter 5). By 1788 the region had largely recovered from the Revolution's ravages.

Southern planters faced frustration at the failure of their principal crops, tobacco and rice, to return to prewar export levels. Whereas nearly two-thirds of the mainland colonies' exports originated in the South in 1770, less than half the new nation's exports were produced by southern states in 1790. In an effort to stay afloat, many Chesapeake tobacco growers shifted to wheat, and others expanded their production of hemp. But these changes had little effect on the region as a whole. The South's failure to recover its export base, along with barriers to westward expansion, contributed to nagging uncertainties about its future.

## The Confederation and the West

Another formidable challenge confronting the Confederation was the postwar settlement and administration of western lands. Settlers and speculators were determined to possess these lands, and Native Americans were just as determined to keep them out. At the same time, Britain and Spain sought to contain the new nation's territorial expansion.

After the states surrendered claims to more than 160 million acres north of the Ohio River, Congress established uniform procedures for surveying this land in the Ordinance of 1785. The law established as the basic unit of settlement a township six miles square. Every township would be subdivided into thirty-six sections of 640 acres each, one of which would be reserved as a source of income for schools. Subsequently, in the Northwest Ordinance of 1787, Congress defined the steps for the creation and admission of new states. This law designated the area north of the Ohio River as the Northwest Territory and provided for its later division into states. It forbade slavery while the region remained a territory, although the citizens could legalize the institution after statehood (as Illinois almost did in 1824).

The Northwest Ordinance outlined three stages for admitting states into the Union. First, during the initial years of settlement, Congress would appoint a territorial governor and judges. Second, as soon as five thousand adult males lived in a territory, voters would approve a temporary constitution and elect a legislature that would pass the territory's laws. Third, when the total population reached sixty thousand, voters would ratify a state constitution, which Congress would have to approve before granting statehood.

The Ordinance of 1785 and the Northwest Ordinance became the Confederation's major contributions to American life. These laws set the basic principles for surveying the frontier, allowed territorial government at an early stage of settlement, and provided reasonable standards for obtaining statehood. Both measures served as models for organizing territories later acquired west of the Mississippi River. The Northwest Ordinance also established a significant precedent for banning slavery from certain territories. But because Indians, determined to keep out Confederation immigrants, controlled virtually the entire region north of the Ohio River, the Confederation's ordinances respecting the Northwest had no immediate effect.

The Northwest Territory seemed to offer enough rich land to guarantee future citizens landownership for centuries. This fact satisfied American republicans who feared that the rapidly growing white population would quickly exhaust available land east of the Appalachians and so create a large class of tenants and poor laborers who would lack the property needed to vote. By poisoning politics through class conflict, such a development would undermine the equality that republicans thought essential for a healthy nation.

The realization of these republican dreams was by no means inevitable. Most "available" territory from the Appalachians to the Mississippi River belonged to those peoples whom the Declaration of Independence had condemned as "merciless Indian savages." Divided into more than eighty tribes and numbering perhaps 150,000 people in 1789, these Native Americans were struggling to preserve their way of life. At post-

war treaty negotiations, they repeatedly heard federal commissioners scornfully declare, "You are a subdued people . . . we claim the country by conquest." Under threats of continued warfare, some Indian leaders initially gave in. The Iroquois, who had suffered heavily during the war, lost about half their land in New York and Pennsylvania in the second Treaty of Fort Stanwix (1784). In the treaties of Fort McIntosh (1785) and Fort Finney (1786), the Delawares and Shawnees, respectively, were obliged to recognize American sovereignty over their lands. But most Indians reacted with outrage and repudiated these treaties on the grounds that their negotiators lacked the authority to give up their nations' lands.

The Indians' resistance to Confederation encroachments also stemmed from their confidence that the British—still a presence in the West—would provide the arms and ammunition they needed to defy the Confederation. Britain had refused to abandon seven forts on the new nation's northwestern frontier, citing certain states' failure to compensate loyalists for confiscated property and to honor prewar debts owed by citizens. But well before Britain knew about the violation of these provisions of the peace treaty, its colonial office had secretly ordered the governor of Canada to hold those forts. With Indian support, Britain hoped eventually to reestablish its claim to the Northwest Territory. Meanwhile, the lingering British presence in the Northwest allowed Canadian fur traders to maintain a brisk business there.

The Mohawk Joseph Brant emerged as the initial inspiration behind Indian resistance in the Northwest. Courageous in battle, skillful in diplomacy, and highly educated (he had translated an Anglican prayer book and the Gospel of Mark into Mohawk), Brant became a minor celebrity when he visited King George at London in 1785. At British-held Fort Detroit in 1786, he helped organize the northwestern Indians into a military alliance to exclude Confederation citizens north of the Ohio River. But Brant and his Mohawks, who had relocated beyond American reach in Canada, could not win support from Senecas and other Iroquois who had chosen to remain in New York, where they now lived in peace with their white neighbors.

Seizing on disunity within Indian ranks, Kentuckians and others organized militia raids into the Northwest Territory. These raids gradually forced the Miamis, Shawnees, and Delawares to evacuate southern Indiana and Ohio. The Indians' withdrawal northward, toward the Great Lakes, tempted whites to make their first settlements in what is now Ohio. In the spring of 1788, about fifty New Englanders sailed down the Ohio River in a bullet-proof barge named the *Mayflower* and founded the town of Marietta. That same year, some Pennsylvanians and New Jerseyites established a second community north of the Ohio, on the site of modern-day Cincinnati. By then the contest for the Ohio Valley was nearing a decisive stage.

The Confederation confronted similar problems in the Southeast, where Spain and its Indian allies took steps to prevent American settlers from advancing on their lands. The Spanish found a brilliant ally in the Creek leader Alexander McGillivray. In a series of fraudulent treaties, two Creeks had surrendered extensive territory to Georgia that McGillivray intended to re-

**Joseph Brant,** by Wilhelm von Moll Berczy, c. 1800
*In the 1780s several Indian leaders—among them Brant (a Mohawk), Blue Jacket (a Shawnee), and Little Turtle (a Miami)—worked to create a northwestern Indian confederation that would strengthen Native American resolve not to bargain with land-hungry whites.*

gain. Patiently holding back his followers for three years, McGillivray negotiated a secret treaty with Spain that promised the Creeks weapons so that they could protect themselves "from the Bears and other fierce Animals." When the Creeks finally attacked in 1786, they assaulted only occupants on the disputed lands and shrewdly offered Georgia a cease-fire after winning their objective. Eager to avoid voting taxes for a costly war, Georgia politicians let the Creeks keep the land.

Spain also sought to prevent American infiltration by denying western settlers permission to ship their crops down the Mississippi River to New Orleans. Having negotiated a separate treaty with Britain (see above), Spain had not signed the Peace of Paris, by which Britain promised the United States export rights down the Mississippi, and in 1784 the Spanish closed New Orleans to Anglo-American commerce. To negotiate trading privileges at New Orleans, the United States sent John Jay to Spain. Jay returned in 1786 with a treaty that opened up valuable Spanish markets to eastern merchants and renounced Spanish claims to disputed southwestern lands—at the cost, however, of relinquishing American export rights through New Orleans for twenty years. Westerners and southerners charged that this Jay-Gardoqui Treaty sacrificed their interests to benefit northern commerce, and Congress rejected it.

### Shays's Rebellion

Without an outbreak of violence in Massachusetts late in 1786, the Confederation might have tottered on indefinitely. The depression that had begun in 1784 struck especially hard in Massachusetts after the state lost its best market, the British West Indies. To worsen matters, the state legislature voted early in 1786 to pay off its Revolutionary debt in three years. This ill-considered policy necessitated a huge tax hike. Meanwhile, the state's unfavorable balance of payments with Britain had produced a shortage of specie (gold and silver coin) because British creditors refused any other currency. Fearing a flood of worthless paper notes, Massachusetts bankers and merchants insisted that they, too, be paid in specie, while the state mandated the same for payment of taxes. At the bottom of this cycle of debt were thousands of small family farmers who rarely handled hard currency. As with small farmers throughout America, those in Massachusetts were accustomed to paying each other and local creditors in goods such as grain and wool and sometimes with a service such as shoeing a horse or helping to build a barn. Creditors allowed debts from local customers to run for months and years at a time. The notion of immediately paying all debts and taxes owed in hard currency was not only alien to but impossible for many.

The plight of Massachusetts farmers was especially severe in the western counties, where agriculture was least profitable. Farmers held public meetings, as they had more than a decade earlier, to discuss "the Suppressing of tyrannical government." This time, however, they meant the Massachusetts government rather than the British. Late in 1786 farmer and former Revolutionary War officer Daniel Shays led some two thousand angry men in an attempt to shut down the courts in three of these western counties, and thereby stop sheriffs' auctions for unpaid taxes and prevent foreclosures on farm mortgages. Although routed by state troops after several skirmishes, sympathizers of Shays won control of the Massachusetts legislature in 1787, cut taxes, and secured a pardon for their leader.

Shays's supporters had limited objectives, were dispersed with relatively little bloodshed, and never seriously posed the danger of anarchy. But his uprising, and similar but less militant movements in other states, symbolized for many the republic's fragility under the Confederation. By threatening to seize weapons from a federal arsenal at Springfield, Massachusetts, the Shaysites unintentionally enabled nationalists to argue that the United States had become vulnerable to "mobocracy." At the same time, rumors were flying that the Spanish had offered export rights at New Orleans to westerners if they would secede from the Union. Nationalists sowed fears that the United States was on the verge of coming apart.

Not everyone shared these apprehensions. In contrast to New England, the mid-Atlantic and southern states were emerging from the depression, thanks to rising tobacco and food exports to Europe. Taxpayers in these sections, moreover, were paying off war debts easily. Furthermore, the regions' numerous small farming families, living in relatively isolated communities and trading largely with neighbors, were in quiet times widely indifferent to national politics. But the minority of people intensely dissatisfied with the Confederation was growing. Urban artisans, for example, hoped for a stronger national government that would impose a uniformly high tariff and thereby protect them from foreign competition. Merchants and shippers wanted a government powerful enough to secure trading privileges for them, and land speculators and western settlers preferred a government capable of pursuing a more activist policy against the Indians. To these groups were now added economic and political elites who saw in Shays's Rebellion a sign of worse things to come.

Shortly before the outbreak of the rebellion, delegates from five states had assembled at Annapolis, Maryland. They had intended to discuss means of promoting interstate commerce but instead called for a general convention to propose amendments to the Articles of Confederation. Accepting their suggestion, Congress asked the states to appoint delegations to meet in Philadelphia.

### The Philadelphia Convention

In May 1787 fifty-five delegates from every state but Rhode Island began gathering at the Pennsylvania State House in Philadelphia, later known as Independence Hall. Among them were established figures like George Washington and Benjamin Franklin, as well as talented newcomers such as Alexander Hamilton and James Madison. Most were wealthy and in their thirties or forties, and nineteen owned slaves. More than half had legal training.

The convention immediately closed its sessions to the press and the public, kept no *official* journal, and even appointed chaperones to accompany the aged and talkative Franklin to dinner parties lest he disclose details of what was happening. Although these measures opened the members of the convention to the charge of acting undemocratically and conspiratorially, the delegates thought secrecy essential to ensure themselves freedom of debate without fear of criticism from home.

The delegates shared a "continental" or "nationalist" perspective, instilled through their extended involvement with the national government. Thirty-nine had sat in Congress, where they had seen the Articles' defects firsthand. In the postwar years, they had become convinced that unless the national government were freed from the state legislatures' control, the country would fall victim to foreign aggression or simply disintegrate.

The convention faced two basic issues. The first was whether to tinker with the Articles, as the state leg-

**The Assembly Room in Independence Hall**

*Much history was made in this room. The Declaration of Independence was signed here in 1776, and the constitutional convention delegates met in this chamber in 1787.*

islatures had formally instructed the delegates to do, or to scrap the Articles and draw up an entirely new frame of government. The second fundamental question was how to balance the conflicting interests of large and small states. James Madison of Virginia, who had entered Congress in 1780 at twenty-nine, proposed an answer to each issue. Despite his youth and almost frail build, Madison commanded enormous respect for his profound knowledge of history and the passionate intensity that he brought to debates.

Madison's Virginia Plan, introduced in late May, boldly called for the establishment of a national government rather than a federation of states. Madison's blueprint gave Congress virtually unrestricted rights of legislation and taxation, the power to veto any state law, and authority to use military force against the states. As one delegate immediately saw, the Virginia Plan was designed "to abolish the State Govern[men]ts altogether." The Virginia Plan specified a bicameral legislature and fixed representation in both houses of Congress proportionally to each state's population. The voters would elect the lower house, which would then choose delegates to the upper chamber from nominations submitted by the legislatures. Both houses would jointly name the country's president and judges.

Madison's scheme aroused immediate opposition, however, especially his call for state representation according to population—a provision highly favorable to his own Virginia. On June 15 William Paterson of New Jersey offered a counterproposal, the so-called New Jersey Plan, which recommended a single-chamber congress in which each state had an equal vote, just as under the Articles.

Despite their differences over representation, Paterson's and Madison's proposals alike would have strengthened the national government at the states' expense. No less than Madison, Paterson wished to empower Congress to raise taxes, regulate interstate commerce, and use military force against the states. The New Jersey Plan, in fact, was the first to define congressional laws and treaties as the "supreme law of the land"; it would also have established courts to force reluctant states to accept these measures.

The two plans exposed the convention's great stumbling block: the question of representation. The Virginia Plan would have given the four largest states a majority in both houses. The New Jersey Plan would have allowed the seven smallest states, which included just 25 percent of all Americans, to control Congress. By July 2 the convention had arrived "at a full stop," as one delegate put it. To end the impasse, the delegates as-

collect taxes, to regulate interstate commerce, and to conduct diplomacy. States could no longer coin money, interfere with contracts and debts, or tax interstate commerce. All acts and treaties of the United States became "the supreme law of the land." All state officials had to swear to uphold the Constitution, even against acts of their own states. The national government could use military force against any state.

These provisions added up to a complete abandonment of the principle on which the Articles of Confederation had rested: that the United States was a federation of independent republics known as states, with all authority concentrated in their legislatures. Yet still concerned about too centralized a federal system, the Constitution's framers devised two ways to restrain the power of the new central government. First, they established three distinct branches—executive, legislative, and judicial—within the national government; and second, they designed a system of checks and balances to prevent any one branch from dominating the other two. The framers systematically applied to the national government the principle of a *functional* separation of powers, an idea that had been evolving in the states since about 1780. In the bicameral Congress, states' equal representation in the Senate was offset by the proportional representation, by population, in the House; and each chamber could block hasty measures demanded by the other. Furthermore, where the state constitutions had deliberately weakened the executive, the Constitution gave the president the power to veto acts of Congress; but to prevent capricious use of the veto, Congress could override the president by a two-thirds majority in each house. The president could conduct diplomacy, but only the Senate could ratify treaties. The president named his cabinet, but only with Senate approval. The president and all his appointees could be removed from office by a joint vote of Congress, but only for "high crimes," not for political disagreements.

To further ensure the independence of each branch, the Constitution provided that the members of one branch would not choose those of another, except for judges, whose independence was protected by lifetime appointment. For example, the president was to be selected by an electoral college, whose members the states would select as their legislatures saw fit. The state legislatures also elected the members of the Senate, whereas the election of delegates to the House of Representatives was achieved by direct popular vote.

**James Madison**
*Although one of the Philadelphia Convention's youngest delegates, Madison of Virginia was among its most politically astute. He played a central role in the Constitution's adoption.*

signed a member from each state to a "grand committee" dedicated to compromise. The panel adopted a proposal offered earlier by the Connecticut delegation: an equal vote for each state in the upper house and proportional voting in the lower house. Madison and the Virginians doggedly fought this so-called Connecticut Compromise, but they were voted down on July 17. The convention overcame the remaining hurdles rather easily in the next two months.

As finally approved on September 17, 1787, the Constitution of the United States was an extraordinary document, and not merely because it reconciled the conflicting interests of the large and small states. Out of hard bargaining among different states' representatives emerged the Constitution's delicate balance between the desire of nearly all delegates for a stronger national government and their fear that governments tended to grow despotic. The Constitution augmented national authority in several ways. Although it did not incorporate Madison's proposal to give Congress a veto over state laws, it vested in Congress the authority to lay and

In addition to checks and balances, the founders improvised a novel form of federalism—that being a system of shared power and dual lawmaking by the national and state governments—in order to place limits on central authority. Not only did the state legislatures have a key role in electing the president and senators, but the Constitution could be amended by the votes of three-fourths of the state legislatures. Thus, the convention devised a form of government that differed significantly from Madison's plan to establish a "consolidated" national government entirely independent of, and superior to, the states.

A key assumption behind federalism was that the national government would limit its activities to foreign affairs, national defense, regulating interstate commerce, and coining money. Most other political matters were left to the states. Regarding slavery in particular, each state retained full authority.

The dilemma confronting the Philadelphia Convention centered not on whether slavery should be allowed in the new republic but rather on the much narrower question of whether slaves could be counted as persons when it came to determining a state's representation at the national level. For most legal purposes, slaves were regarded not as persons but rather as the *chattel* property of their owners, meaning that they were on a par with other living property such as horses and cattle. But southern states saw their large numbers of slaves as a means of augmenting their numbers in the House of Representatives and in the electoral colleges that would elect the nation's presidents every four years. So strengthened, they could prevent northerners from ever abolishing slavery. Representing states that were abolishing slavery, northern delegates hesitated to give southern states a political advantage by allowing them to count people who had no civil or political rights. But as property owners themselves, northern delegates were also hesitant to question southern planters' notions of property rights, no matter what form the property took. Southerners also played on northern fears of disunion. After Georgia and South Carolina threatened to secede if their demands were not met, northerners agreed to allow three-fifths of all slaves to be counted for congressional representation. The Constitution also forbade any state's people to prevent the return of runaway slaves to another state. The Constitution limited slavery only to the extent of permitting Congress to ban the importation of slaves after 1808, and by not repudiating Congress's earlier ban on slavery in the Northwest Territory.

Although leaving much authority to the states, the Constitution established a national government clearly superior to the states in several spheres, and it utterly abandoned the notion of a federation of virtually independent states. Having thus strengthened national authority, the convention had to face the issue of ratification. For two reasons, it seemed unwise to submit the Constitution to state legislatures for ratification. First, the framers realized that the state legislatures would reject the Constitution, which shrank their power relative to the national government. Second, most of the framers repudiated the idea—implicit in ratification by existing state legislatures—that the states were the foundation of the new government. The opening words of the Constitution—"We the People of the United States"—underlined the delegates' growing conviction that the government had to be based on the consent of the American people themselves, "the fountain of all power" in Madison's words.

In the end, the Philadelphia Convention provided for the Constitution's ratification by special state conventions composed of delegates elected by the people. Approval by only nine such conventions would put the new government in operation. Because any state refusing to ratify the Constitution would remain under the Articles, the possibility existed that the country might divide into two nations.

Under the Constitution the framers expected the nation's "natural aristocracy" to continue exercising political leadership; but did they also intend to rein in the democratic currents set in motion by the Revolution? In one respect they did, by curtailing what most nationalists considered the excessive power of popularly elected legislatures. But the Constitution made no attempt to control faction and disorder by suppressing liberty—a "remedy," wrote Madison, that would be "worse than the disease." The framers did provide for one crucial democratic element in the new government, the House of Representatives. Equally important, the Constitution recognized the American people as the ultimate source of political legitimacy. Moreover, by making the Constitution flexible and amendable (though not easily amendable) and by dividing political power among competing branches of government, the framers made it possible for the national government to be slowly democratized in ways unforeseen in 1787, without turning into a tyranny of ideologues or tempo-

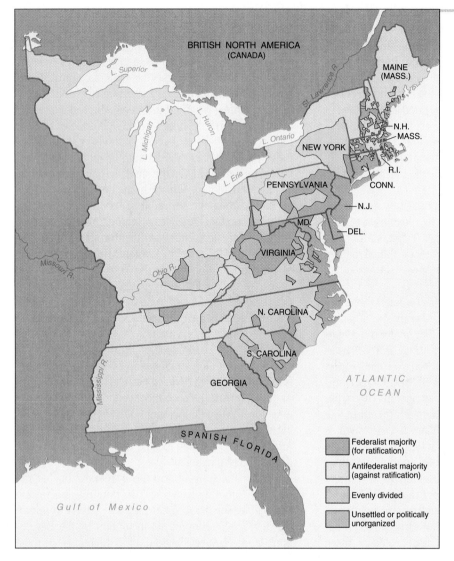

**Federalist and Antifederalist Strongholds, 1787–1790**
*Federalists drew their primary backing from densely populated areas along major transportation routes, where trade, mobility, and frequent contact with people in other states encouraged a nationalistic identity. Antifederalist support came from interior regions where geographic isolation bred a localistic perspective. However, some frontier regions, among them Georgia and western Virginia, voted for a strong central government that would push back the Indians or the Spanish.*

rary majorities. Madison eloquently expressed the founders' intention of controlling the dangers inherent in any society:

> If men were angels, no government would be necessary. If angels were to govern men, neither external nor internal controls on government would be necessary. In framing a government which is to be administered by men over men, the great difficulty lies in this: You must first enable the government to control the governed; and in the next place, oblige it to control itself. A dependence on the people is no doubt the primary control on the government; but experience has taught mankind the necessity of external precautions.

## The Struggle Over Ratification

The Constitution's supporters began the campaign for ratification without significant national support. Most Americans had expected that the Philadelphia Convention would offer only limited amendments to the Articles. A majority therefore hesitated to adopt the radical restructuring of government that had been proposed. Undaunted, the Constitution's friends moved decisively to marshal political support. In a clever stroke, they called themselves Federalists, a term that implied that the Constitution balanced the relationship between the national and state governments and thereby lessened the opposition of those hostile to a centralization of national authority.

The Constitution's opponents commonly became known as Antifederalists. This negative-sounding title probably hurt them, for it did not convey the crux of their argument against the Constitution—that it was not "federalist" at all since it failed to balance the power of the national and state governments. By augmenting national authority, Antifederalists maintained, the Constitution would ultimately doom the states.

The Antifederalist arguments reflected a deep-seated Anglo-American suspicion of concentrated power, expressed from the time of the Stamp Act crisis (see Chapter 5) through the War of Independence and during the framing of the first state constitutions and the Articles of Confederation. Unquestionably, the Constitution gave the national government unprecedented authority in an age when almost all writers on politics taught that the sole means of preventing despotism was to restrain the power of government officials. Compared to a distant national government, state governments struck Antifederalists as far more responsive to the popular will. True, the framers had devised a system of checks and balances to guard against tyranny, but no one could be certain that the untried scheme would work. To Mercy Otis Warren, the proposed government was "of such motley mixture that its enemies cannot trace a feature of Democratick or Republican extract," and one that would "have passed through the short period of its existence without a name, had not Mr. [James] Wilson . . . suggested the happy epithet of a *Federal Republic*." For all its checks and balances, in addition, the Constitution nowhere contained ironclad guarantees that the new government would protect the liberties of individuals or the states. The absence of a bill of rights made an Antifederalist of Madison's nationalist ally and fellow Virginian, George Mason, the author of the first such state bill in 1776.

Although the Antifederalists advanced some formidable arguments, they confronted a number of disadvantages in publicizing their cause. While Antifederalist ranks included prominent figures, among them Patrick Henry, Richard Henry Lee, and Mercy Otis Warren, the Federalists claimed most of the country's wealthiest and most honored men. And no Antifederalist had the stature of George Washington or Benjamin Franklin. Moreover, most American newspapers were pro-Constitution and did not hesitate to bias their reporting in favor of the Federalist cause. Finally, as state and local leaders, the Antifederalists lacked their opponents' contacts and experience at the national level, acquired through service in the officer corps of the Continental Army or in Congress.

The Federalists' advantages in funds and political organizing proved decisive. The Antifederalists failed to create a sense of urgency among their supporters, assuming incorrectly that a large majority would rally to them. Only one-quarter of the voters turned out to elect delegates to the state ratifying conventions, however, and most had been mobilized by Federalists.

Federalist delegates prevailed in eight conventions between December 1787 and May 1788, in all cases except one by margins of at least two-thirds. Such lopsided votes reflected the Federalists' organizational skills and aggressiveness rather than the degree of popular support for the Constitution. Advocates of the new plan of government did indeed ram through approval in some states "before it can be digested or deliberately considered," in the words of a Pennsylvania Antifederalist. Only Rhode Island and North Carolina rejected the Constitution and thus refused to join the new United States.

But unless Virginia and New York ratified, the new government would not be workable. In both states (and elsewhere) Antifederalist sentiment ran high among small farmers, who saw the Constitution as a scheme favoring city dwellers and monied interests. Prominent political leaders in these two states called for refusing ratification, including New York governor George Clinton and Virginia's Richard Henry Lee, George Mason, Patrick Henry, and future president James Monroe.

The Constitution became the law of the land on June 21, 1788, when the ninth state, New Hampshire, ratified by the close vote of 57–47. At that moment debate was still under way in the Virginia convention. The Federalists won crucial support from the representatives of the Allegheny counties—modern West Virginia—who wanted a strong national government capable of ending Indian raids across the Ohio River. Western Virginians' votes, combined with James Madison's logic and the growing support for the Constitution among tidewater planters, proved too much for Henry's spellbinding oratory. On June 25 the Virginia delegates ratified by a narrow 53 percent majority.

The struggle was even closer and more hotly contested in New York. Antifederalists had solid control of the state convention and would probably have voted down the Constitution, but then news arrived of New Hampshire's and Virginia's ratification. The Federalist forces, led by Alexander Hamilton and John Jay, began hinting strongly that if the convention voted to reject, pro-Federalist New York City would secede from the state and join the Union alone, leaving upstate New York a landlocked enclave. When a number of Antifederalist delegates took alarm at this threat and switched sides, New York ratified on July 26, by a 30–27 vote.

So the Antifederalists went down in defeat, and they did not survive as a political movement. Yet they left an important legacy. At their insistence, the Virginia, New York, and Massachusetts conventions ratified the Constitution with the accompanying request that the new charter be amended to include a bill of rights protecting Americans' basic freedoms. So widespread was the public demand for a bill of rights that it became an inevitable item on the new government's agenda, even as the states were choosing members of Congress and as presidential electors were unanimously designating George Washington president of the United States.

Antifederalists' objections in New York also stimulated a response in the form of one of the great classics of political thought: *The Federalist,* a series of eighty-five newspaper essays penned by Alexander Hamilton, James Madison, and John Jay. *The Federalist* papers probably had little or no influence on the voting in the New York State convention. Rather, their importance lay in providing a glimpse of the framers' intentions in designing the Constitution, and thus powerfully shaping the American philosophy of government. The Constitution, insisted *The Federalist's* authors, had a twofold purpose: first, to defend the minority's rights against majority tyranny; and second, to prevent a stubborn minority from blocking well-considered measures that the majority believed necessary for the national interest. Critics, argued *The Federalist,* had no reason to fear that the Constitution would allow a single economic or regional interest to dominate. In the most profound essay in the series, *Federalist* No. 10, Madison rejected the Antifederalist argument that establishing a republic for a nation as large as the United States would unleash a chaotic contest for power and ultimately leave the majority exploited by a minority. "Extend the sphere," Madison insisted, "and . . . you make it less probable that a majority of the whole will have a common motive to invade the rights of other citizens, . . . [or will be able to] act in unison with each other." The country's very size and diversity would neutralize the attempts of factions to push unwise laws through Congress.

Madison's analysis was far too optimistic, however. As the Antifederalists predicted, the Constitution afforded enormous scope for special interests to influence the government. The great challenge for Madison's generation would be how to maintain a government that would provide equal benefits to all but at the same time accord special privileges to none.

## CONCLUSION

The entry of North Carolina into the Union in late 1789 and of Rhode Island in May 1790 marked the final triumph of the uncertain nationalism born of the War for Independence. The devastating eight-year conflict swept up half of all men of military age and made casualties of one-fifth of these. Among whites, blacks, and Native Americans alike, the conflict was a civil war as well as a war for American independence from Great Britain. The fighting also affected large numbers of civilians because it took place in America's cities, towns, and countryside, and because troops needed provisions and other forms of local support. Never before had so many Americans participated together in an event of such magnitude.

Fueled by ideals of liberty and equality and by their suffering and sacrificing on behalf of American independence, most Americans recognized the democratic aspirations that the conflict had unleashed. For many these aspirations were intrinsic to the new nation's identity, to what made it distinct from the other nations of the world. For such people, democracy would be achieved by maximizing the power of the white male electorate in choosing officeholders and making and enforcing laws, and by decentralizing power and authority. But for others, America's democratic tendencies needed to be held firmly in check by vesting most power in the hands of men of property and virtue. The conflict between these competing visions was played out in the protracted debates over several state constitutions and, most decisively, in the efforts to frame and ratify the new federal Constitution. By itself the Constitution did not make America a democracy; rather it created the legal and institutional framework within which Americans could struggle to attain democracy. In that way its conception was a fundamental moment in the history of America's enduring vision.

## FOR FURTHER READING

Colin G. Calloway, *The American Revolution in Indian Country: Crisis and Diversity in Native American Communities* (1995). A powerful study of eight distinct societies, from Canada to Florida, that demonstrates the variety of Indian experiences during and immediately after the Revolution.

Edward Countryman, *The American Revolution* (1985). An excellent introduction to developments from the 1760s through ratification of the Constitution.

Sylvia R. Frey, *Water from the Rock: Black Resistance in a Revolutionary Age* (1991). A major study of southern African Americans during and after the Revolution.

Linda K. Kerber, *Women of the Republic: Intellect and Ideology in Revolutionary America* (1980). A major study of women and of ideologies of gender during the Revolutionary and early republican eras.

Robert Middlekauff, *The Glorious Cause: The American Revolution, 1763–1789* (1982). A narrative of military and political developments through the ratification of the Constitution.

Jack N. Rakove, *Original Meanings: Politics and Ideas in the Making of the Constitution* (1996). A thorough study of the Constitution's framing, rooted in historical context.

Charles Royster, *A Revolutionary People at War: The Continental Army and American Character* (1980). An illuminating analysis of how Revolutionary Americans created and fought in an army.

Gordon S. Wood, *The Radicalism of the American Revolution* (1991). A sweeping interpretation of the Revolution's long-range impact on American society.

# Launching The New Republic
## 1789–1800

**Wife and Children of Major Marsh and Servants c. 1790**

Early in 1789 a mysterious stranger from New Orleans named André Fagot appeared in Nashville, Tennessee. Fagot was officially there to talk business with local merchants, but in reality he was a Spanish agent sent to exploit discontent. For years, westerners had agonized over the American government's failure to win Spanish permission for them to export crops through New Orleans (page 182), without which their settlements would never flourish. Fagot made westerners a tempting offer—unrestricted export privileges at New Orleans, which promised to ensure them prosperity. But in return, they would have to request that Spain annex Tennessee to its Louisiana colony.

Fagot found many local residents willing to discuss becoming Spanish subjects. One of his more enthusiastic contacts was a young lawyer recently arrived from the Carolinas. Aware that poor communities could support only poor lawyers, the Carolinian was drawn irresistibly to the plot. Learning that Spain would give valuable land grants in the lower Mississippi Valley to anyone who renounced U.S. citizenship, the lawyer began visiting Spanish Louisiana regularly to investigate settling there. Fagot probably placed little reliance on this brash conspirator, who had a wild temper and a reputation for gambling and drinking, and who seemed just another frontier opportunist. The obscure lawyer's name was Andrew Jackson.

The fact that a future patriot and president such as Jackson was talking secession with a Spanish agent underscores the fragility of the United States in 1789, the year of George Washington's first inauguration. North Carolina (which controlled Tennessee territory) and Rhode Island had not yet joined the Union. Thousands of recently arrived western settlers appeared to be abandoning the new government. The United States' claims to western territories were being effectively challenged by Native Americans and their Spanish and British allies. The development of American economic power was severely limited by foreign restrictions on U.S. exports and by the government's inability to obtain credit abroad.

During the 1790s Americans fought bitterly over the social and economic course their new nation should take, and these conflicts merged with the dissension between Americans loyal to revolutionary France and those favoring its British opponents. By 1798 voters had divided into two parties, each of which accused the other of threatening republican liberty. Only when the election of 1800 had been settled—by the narrowest of margins—could it be said that the United States had managed to avoid dissolution and preserve civil liberties for those defined as citizens.

This chapter focuses on four major questions:

◆ How and why did the political consensus prevailing at the time of Washington's first inauguration fracture into a two-party system by 1796?

◆ Why was the United States at various times at odds with Spain, Britain, and France at the end of the eighteenth century?

◆ What principal issues divided Federalists and Republicans in the presidential election of 1800?

◆ What were the primary factors contributing to the declining status and welfare of nonwhites in the new republic?

**New Orleans**

*The French and Spanish developed this port city during the eighteenth century. By century's end many in the United States saw New Orleans as a key to the new nation's future expansion and prosperity.*

# Constitutional Government Takes Shape

Traveling slowly over the nation's miserable roads, the men entrusted with launching the federal experiment began assembling in New York, the new national capital, in March 1789. Because so few members were on hand, Congress opened its session a month late. George Washington did not arrive until April 23 and only took his oath of office a week later.

The slowness of these first halting steps disguised the seriousness of the tasks at hand. The country's elected leaders had to make far-reaching decisions on several critical questions left unresolved by the Constitution's framers. For example, the Constitution gave the president no formal responsibility for preparing a legislative agenda, although it allowed him wide discretion by directing him to make periodic reports on the state of the Union and by permitting him to recommend matters for Congress's consideration. The Philadelphia Convention likewise had not specified whether cabinet officers would be accountable to Congress or to the president. Nor did the Constitution say how the federal court system should be structured. Finally, widespread distrust of any government unrestrained by a bill of rights required that Congress pre-

pare amendments for the states' consideration, but the exact scope and character of these amendments remained to be determined. "We are in a wilderness," wrote James Madison, "without a footstep to guide us."

## Defining the Presidency

No office in the new government aroused more suspicion than the presidency. Many feared that the president's powers could make him a virtual king. Public apprehension remained in check only because of George Washington's reputation for honesty. Washington tried to calm fears of unlimited executive power.

The Constitution mentioned the executive departments only in passing, required the president to obtain the Senate's approval for his nominees to head these bureaus, and made all executive personnel liable to impeachment. Otherwise, Congress was free to determine the organization and accountability of what became known as the cabinet. The first cabinet, established by Congress, consisted of four departments, headed by the secretaries of state, treasury, and war and by the attorney general. Vice President John Adams's tie-breaking vote defeated a proposal that would have forbidden the president from dismissing cabinet officers without Senate approval. This outcome reinforced the president's authority to make and carry out policy; it also separated the powers of the executive and legislative branches beyond what the Constitution required, and so made the president a more equal partner with Congress.

President Washington suggested few laws to Congress. Rarely did he speak out against opponents of government policy, and generally he limited his public statements to matters of foreign relations and military affairs. He generally deferred to congressional decisions concerning domestic policy and cast only two vetoes during his eight-year tenure (1789–1797).

Washington tried to reassure the public that he was above favoritism and conflicts of interest. Accordingly, he strove to understand the aspirations of the two groups that dominated American society—northeastern merchants and entrepreneurs, and southern planters—and he balanced his cabinet between them. When Secretary of State Thomas Jefferson opposed certain policies of Secretary of the Treasury Alexander Hamilton, Washington implored Jefferson not to leave his post, even though the president supported Hamilton. Like most republican leaders, Washington believed

**1789** First Congress convenes in New York.

George Washington sworn in as first president.

Judiciary Act of 1789.

French Revolution begins.

**1790** Alexander Hamilton submits his Report on the Public Credit and Report on a National Bank to Congress.

Treaty of New York.

**1791** Bank of the United States is granted a twenty-year charter.

Vermont admitted to the Union.

Bill of Rights ratified.

Slave uprising begins in French colony of Saint Domingue.

Society for the Encouragement of Useful Manufactures founded.

Hamilton submits his Report on Manufactures to Congress.

**1792** Washington reelected president.

Kentucky admitted to the Union.

**1793** Fugitive Slave Law.

*Chisholm* v. *Georgia.*

Large-scale exodus of French planters from Saint Domingue to the United States.

France declares war on Britain and Spain.

Washington's Neutrality Proclamation.

Citizen Genet arrives in United States.

First Democratic societies established.

**1794** Whiskey Rebellion in western Pennsylvania.

General Anthony Wayne's forces rout Indians in the Battle of Fallen Timbers.

**1795** Treaty of Greenville.

Jay's Treaty with Britain ratified.

**1796** *Hylton* v. *United States.*

*Ware* v. *Hylton.*

Tennessee admitted to the Union.

Treaty of San Lorenzo (Pinckney's Treaty) ratified.

Washington's Farewell Address.

John Adams elected president.

**1798** XYZ Affair.

Alien and Sedition Acts.

Eleventh Amendment to the Constitution ratified.

**1798–1799** Virginia and Kentucky Resolutions.

**1798–1800** United States fights Quasi-War with France.

**1799** Fries Rebellion in Pennsylvania.

**1800** Gabriel's Rebellion in Virginia.

Thomas Jefferson elected president.

that the proper role for ordinary citizens was not to set policy through elections but rather to choose well-educated, politically sophisticated men who would make laws in the people's best interest, though independently of direct popular influence.

The president endured rather than enjoyed the pomp of office. Suffering from a variety of ailments that grew as the years passed, Washington longed to escape the presidency and Philadelphia (the nation's capital from 1790 to 1800). Only with difficulty was he persuaded to accept reelection in 1792. He dreaded dying while in office and thus setting the precedent for a lifetime presidency. With great anxiety he realized that "the preservation of the sacred fire of liberty and the destiny of the republican model of government are . . . *deeply,* perhaps *finally,* staked on the experiment entrusted to the hands of the American people." Should he contribute to that experiment's failure, he feared, his name would live only as an "awful monument."

## National Justice and the Bill of Rights

The Constitution merely authorized Congress to establish federal courts below the level of the Supreme Court; it offered no guidance as to how the judicial system should be structured. And although the Constitution specifically barred the federal government from committing such abuses as passing ex post facto laws* and bills of attainder,[†] the absence of a comprehensive bill of rights had led several delegates at Philadelphia to refuse to sign the Constitution and had been a major point of attack by Antifederalists. The task of filling in these gaps fell to the First Congress.

---

\* Ex post facto law: a law criminalizing previously legal actions and punishing those who have been engaging in such actions.

[†] Bill of attainder: a legislative act proclaiming a person's guilt and stipulating punishment without a judicial trial.

In 1789 many citizens feared that the new federal courts would ride roughshod over local customs. Every state had gradually devised a unique, time-honored blend of judicial procedures appropriate to local circumstances. Any attempt to force states to abandon their legal heritages would have produced strong counterdemands that federal justice be narrowly restricted.

In passing the Judiciary Act of 1789, Congress managed to quiet popular apprehensions by establishing in each state a federal district court that operated according to local procedures. As the Constitution stipulated, the Supreme Court exercised final jurisdiction. Congress had struck a reasonable compromise that respected state traditions while offering wide access to federal justice.

Behind the movement for a bill of rights lay Americans' long-standing fear that a strong central government would lead to tyranny. Many Antifederalists believed that the best defense against tyranny would be to strengthen the powers of state governments at the expense of the federal government, but many more Americans wanted simply to guarantee basic personal liberties. James Madison, who had been elected to the House of Representatives, played the leading role in drafting the ten amendments that became known as the Bill of Rights when ratified by the states in December 1791.

Madison insisted that the first eight amendments guarantee personal liberties, not strip the national government of any necessary authority. The First Amendment guaranteed the most fundamental freedoms of expression—religion, speech, press, and political activity—against federal interference. The Second Amendment ensured that each state could form its own citizen militia. Like the Third Amendment, it sought to protect citizens from what eighteenth-century Britons and Americans alike considered the most sinister embodiment of tyrannical power: standing armies. The Fourth through Eighth amendments limited the police powers of the state by guaranteeing individuals' fair treatment in legal and judicial proceedings. The Ninth and Tenth amendments reserved to the people or to the states powers not allocated to the federal government under the Constitution, but Madison headed off proposals to limit federal power more explicitly. In general, the Bill of Rights imposed no serious check on the framers' nationalist objectives.

Once the Bill of Rights was in place, the federal judiciary moved decisively to establish its authority. In 1793, in *Chisholm* v. *Georgia,* the Supreme Court ruled that a state could be sued in federal courts by nonresidents. In 1796 the Court declared its right to determine the constitutionality of congressional statutes in *Hylton* v. *United States* and to strike down state laws in *Ware* v. *Hylton.* But Congress decided that the Court had encroached too far on states' authority in *Chisholm,* and in 1794 it voted to overturn this decision through a constitutional amendment. Ratified in 1798, the Eleventh Amendment revised Article III, Section 2, so that private citizens could no longer use federal courts to sue another state's government in civil cases. The defeat of *Chisholm* stands as one of the handful of instances in American history whereby the Supreme Court was subsequently overruled by a constitutional amendment.

By endorsing the Eleventh Amendment, Congress expressed its recognition that federal power could threaten vital local interests. Such awareness had been growing since the early 1790s, rupturing the nationalist coalition that had written the Constitution, secured its ratification, and dominated the First Congress. The catalyst of this split was Alexander Hamilton, whose bold program raised fears that federal policies could be shaped to reward special interests.

# National Economic Policy and Its Consequences

Washington's reluctance to become involved with pending legislation and with domestic affairs enabled his energetic secretary of the treasury, Alexander Hamilton, to set many of the administration's priorities. Hamilton quickly emerged as the country's most imaginative and dynamic statesman by formulating a sweeping program for strengthening the federal government and promoting economic development.

## *Hamilton and His Objectives*

Born in the British Caribbean island of Nevis in 1755, Hamilton had sailed to New York in 1772 and entered the Continental Army in 1775. Serving four years on Washington's staff, the brilliant Hamilton gained extraordinary influence over Washington, who despite misgivings frequently supported the younger man's policies.

Hamilton formulated his financial proposals to strengthen the nation against foreign enemies and also to lessen the threat of disunion. In his mind, the most immediate danger concerned national security: the possibility of war with Great Britain, Spain, or both. The Republic could finance a full-scale war only by borrowing heavily, but because Congress under the Articles of Confederation had failed to redeem or pay interest on the Revolutionary debt, the nation's credit had been seriously weakened abroad and at home. The country's economy also seemed unequal to fighting a major European power. Unless the United States achieved self-sufficiency in the manufacture of vital industrial products and maintained a strong merchant marine ready for combat, Hamilton reasoned, its chances of surviving a second war with Britain would be slim.

Hamilton also feared that the Union might disintegrate because of Americans' tendency to think first of their local loyalties and interests. Born outside the thirteen colonies, he felt little personal identification with his adopted state, New York, or any other American locale. Instead, his six years in the Continental Army produced a burning nationalistic faith. For him, the Constitution's adoption had been a close victory of national over state authority. Now he worried that the states might reassert power over the new government. If this happened, he doubted whether the nation could prevent ruinous trade discrimination between states, deter foreign aggression, and avoid civil war.

Both his wartime experiences and his view of human nature forged Hamilton's political beliefs. An enthusiastic young patriot who had fought bravely during the Revolution's darkest hours, Hamilton had, like many nationalists, come to believe that the Republic's population was incapable of displaying limitless self-sacrifice and virtue. Hamilton concluded that the federal government's survival depended on building support among politically influential citizens through a straightforward appeal to their financial interests. Private ambitions would then serve the national welfare.

Charming and brilliant, vain and handsome, a notorious womanizer, and thirsting for fame and power, Hamilton himself exemplified the worldly citizen whose fortunes he hoped to link to the Republic's future. But to his opponents, Hamilton embodied the dark forces luring the Republic to its doom—a man who, Jefferson wrote, believed in "the necessity of either force or corruption to govern men."

### Report on the Public Credit

Seeking guidance on how to restore the nation's creditworthiness, in 1789 Congress directed the Treasury Department to evaluate the status of the Revolutionary debt. Hamilton seized the opportunity to devise policies that would at once strengthen the country's credit, enable it to defer paying its debt, and entice a key sector of the upper class to place their prestige and capital at its service. Congress received his Report on the Pub-

**New York, 1792, (Detail)**
*Merchants conduct business at the Tontine Coffee House, at the intersection of Wall and Water streets, while laborers, shopkeepers, and women fill the streets below.*

lic Credit in January 1790. The report listed $54 million in U.S. debt: $42 million owed to Americans, and the rest to foreigners. Hamilton estimated that on top of the national debt, the states had debts of $25 million, an amount that included several million dollars that the United States had promised to reimburse, such as Virginia's expenses in defending settlements in the Ohio Valley.

Hamilton's first major recommendation was that the federal government support the national debt by "funding" it—that is, raising the $54 million needed to honor the debt by selling an equal sum in new securities. Purchasers of these securities would choose from several combinations of federal "stock" and western lands. Those who wished could retain their original bonds and earn 4 percent interest. All of the options would reduce interest payments on the debt from the full 6 percent set by the Confederation Congress. Hamilton knew that creditors would not object to this reduction because their investments would now be more valuable and more secure.

Second, the report proposed that the federal government pay off the state debts remaining from the Revolution. Such obligations would be funded along with the national debt in the manner described above.

Hamilton exhorted the government to use the money earned by selling federal lands in the West to pay off the $12 million owed to Europeans as quickly as possible. The Treasury could easily accumulate the interest owed on the remaining $42 million by collecting customs duties on imports and excise taxes on whiskey distillers. In addition, Hamilton proposed that money owed to American citizens should be made a permanent debt. That is, he urged that the government *not* attempt to repay the $42 million principal but instead keep paying interest to people wishing to hold bonds as an investment. If Hamilton's recommendation were adopted, the only burden on the taxpayers would be the small annual cost of interest. It would then be possible to uphold the national credit at minimal expense, without ever having to pay off the debt itself.

Hamilton advocated a perpetual debt above all as a lasting means of uniting the economic fortunes of the nation's creditors to the United States. In an age when financial investments were notoriously risky, the federal government would protect the savings of wealthy bond holders through conservative policies but still offer an interest rate competitive with the Bank of England's. The guarantee of future interest payments would act as the explicit link uniting the interests of the moneyed class with those of the government. Few other investments would entail so little risk.

Hamilton's Report on the Public Credit provoked immediate controversy. Although no one in Congress doubted that its provisions would fully restore the country's fiscal reputation, many objected that those least deserving of reward would gain the most. The original owners of more than three-fifths of the debt certificates issued by the Continental Congress (ranging from George Washington to Revolutionary patriots of modest means) had long before sold theirs at a loss, many out of dire financial necessity. Foreseeing Hamilton's intentions, wealthy speculators had thereby accumulated large holdings at the expense of unsuspecting original owners. Now these speculators stood to reap huge gains, even collecting interest that had fallen due before they had purchased the certificates. "That the case of those who parted with their securities from necessity is a hard one, cannot be denied," Hamilton admitted. But making exceptions would be even worse.

To Hamilton's surprise, Madison—his longtime colleague and initially a supporter of the plan—emerged as one of the chief opponents of reimbursing current holders at face value. Sensing opposition to the plan in his home state of Virginia, Madison now tried but failed to obtain compensation for original owners who had sold their certificates. Congress rejected his suggestions primarily because some members feared that they would weaken the nation's credit. Hamilton's policy generated widespread resentment because it rewarded

**Continental Currency**

rich profiteers while ignoring the wartime sacrifices of ordinary citizens.

Opposition to assuming the state debts also ran high. Only Massachusetts, Connecticut, and South Carolina had failed to make effective provisions for paying their creditors. Understandably, the issue stirred the fiercest indignation in the South, which except for South Carolina had extinguished 83 percent of its debt. Madison and other southerners maintained that to allow residents of the laggard states to escape heavy taxes while others had liquidated theirs at great expense was to reward irresponsibility. South Carolina became the sole southern state that supported Hamilton's policies.

Southern hostility almost defeated assumption. In the end, however, Hamilton managed to save his proposal by exploiting the strong desire among Virginians to relocate the national capital in their region. Virginians expected that moving the capital would make their state the crossroads of the country and thus help preserve its position as the nation's largest, most influential state. In return for the northern votes necessary to transfer the capital to the Potomac River, Hamilton secured enough Virginians' support to win the battle for assumption. Yet the debate over state debts alienated most southerners by confirming their suspicions that other regions monopolized the benefits of a stronger union.

Congressional enactment of the Report on the Public Credit dramatically reversed the nation's fiscal standing. Thereafter, Europeans grew so enthusiastic for U.S. bonds that by 1792 some securities were selling at 10 percent above face value.

## Reports on the Bank and Manufactures

Having significantly expanded the stock of capital available for investment, Hamilton intended to direct that money toward projects that would diversify the national economy through a federally chartered bank. Accordingly, in December 1790 he presented Congress with a second message, the Report on a National Bank.

The proposed bank would raise $10 million through a public stock offering. Private investors could purchase shares by paying for three-quarters of their value in government bonds. In this way, the bank would capture a significant portion of the recently funded debt and make it available for loans; it would also receive a substantial and steady flow of interest payments from the Treasury. Anyone buying shares under these circumstances had little chance of losing money and was positioned to profit handsomely.

Hamilton argued that the Bank of the United States would cost the taxpayers nothing and greatly benefit the nation. It would provide a safe place for the federal government to deposit tax revenues, make inexpensive loans to the government when taxes fell short, and help relieve the scarcity of hard cash by issuing paper notes that would circulate as money. Furthermore, it would possess authority to regulate the business practices of state banks. Above all, the bank would provide much needed credit to expand the economy.

Finally, Hamilton called for American economic self-sufficiency. He admired the "prodigious effect" on Great Britain's national wealth that the recent expansion of factories had stimulated in that nation, and he wanted to encourage similar industrialization in the United States. His December 1791 Report on Manufactures advocated protective tariffs on foreign imports to foster domestic manufacturing, which in turn would both attract immigrants and create national wealth. Elsewhere the secretary called for assisting the merchant marine against British trade restrictions by reducing duties on goods imported into the United States on American ships and by offering subsidies (called bounties) for fishermen and whalers. These measures would also indirectly protect the national bank's loans to industrialists and shippers.

Hamilton's critics denounced his proposal for a national bank, interpreting it as a dangerous scheme that would give a small, elite group special power to influence the government. These critics believed that the Bank of England had undermined the integrity of government in Britain. Shareholders of the new Bank of the United States could just as easily become the tools of unscrupulous politicians. If significant numbers in Congress owned bank stock, they would likely support the bank even at the cost of the national good. To Thomas Jefferson, the bank was "a machine for the corruption of the legislature [Congress]." Representative John Taylor of Virginia predicted that its vast wealth would enable the bank to take over the country, which would thereafter, he quipped, be known as the United States of the Bank.

Opponents also argued that the bank was unconstitutional. The Constitution gave Congress no specific authorization to issue charters of incorporation; indeed the Philadelphia Convention had rejected a proposal giving Congress just such power. Unless Congress ad-

**Alexander Hamilton,** by John Trumbull, 1792
*Hamilton's self-confident pride clearly shines through in this portrait, painted at the height of his influence in the Washington administration.*

hered to a "strict interpretation" of the Constitution, critics argued, the central government might oppress the states and trample individual liberties, just as Parliament had done to the colonies. Strictly limiting the powers of the government seemed the surest way of preventing the United States from degenerating into a corrupt despotism.

Congress approved the bank by only a thin margin. Doubtful of the bank's constitutionality, Washington turned for advice to both Jefferson and Hamilton. Like many southern planters, whose investments in slaves left them short of capital and often in debt, Jefferson distrusted banking. Moreover, his fear of excessively concentrated economic and political power led him to oppose extending government authority beyond the letter of the Constitution. "To take a single step beyond the boundaries thus specifically drawn around the powers

of Congress is to take possession of a boundless field of power no longer susceptible of any definition," warned Jefferson. Hamilton fought back, urging Washington to sign the bill. Because Congress could enact all measures "necessary and proper" (Article I, Section 8), Hamilton contended that the only unconstitutional activities were those actually *forbidden* to the national government. In the end, the president accepted Hamilton's cogent argument for a "loose interpretation" of the Constitution. In February 1791 the Bank of the United States obtained a charter guaranteeing its existence for twenty years. Washington's acceptance of the principle of loose interpretation was an important victory for those advocating an active, assertive national government.

Madison and Jefferson also strongly opposed Hamilton's proposal to encourage industry through protective tariffs on foreign manufactures. Representing a region that depended on planters' ability to market their exports as cheaply as possible, they viewed tariffs as a threat to southern prosperity. They also viewed such protectionism as an unfair subsidy promoting uncompetitive industries that would founder without government support. Moreover, tariffs imposed heavy import taxes that were passed on to consumers. Together these results unjustifiably raised prices. The only beneficiaries would be those shielded from overseas competition and institutions, like the bank, that lent them money. Fearing that American cities might develop a dangerous class of dependent and politically volatile poor people, Jefferson and Madison saw industrialization as a potential menace to the Republic's stability.

Congress ultimately refused to approve a high protective tariff. Nevertheless, Hamilton succeeded in setting higher duties on goods imported into the United States by British vessels than on items carried by American ships. As a result, the tonnage of such goods carried by the American merchant marine more than tripled from 1789 to 1793. Congress also approved subsidies for New England's beleaguered whale and cod fisheries in 1792.

### Hamilton's Legacy

Hamilton's attempt to erect a base of political support by appealing to economic self-interest proved highly successful but also divisive. His arrangements for rescuing the nation's credit provided enormous gains for the speculators, merchants, and other "monied men" of the port cities who by 1790 held most of the Revolutionary debt. As holders of bank stock, these same groups had yet another reason to use their prestige on behalf of national authority. Assumption of the state debts liberated taxpayers from a crushing burden in New England, New Jersey, and South Carolina. Hamilton's efforts to promote industry, commerce, and shipping struck a responsive chord among the Northeast's budding entrepreneurs and hard-pressed artisans.

Those attracted to Hamilton's policies called themselves Federalists, in order to associate themselves with the Constitution and to imply (incorrectly) that their opponents had formerly been Antifederalists. In actuality, Federalists favored a "consolidated" (centralized) national government instead of a truly "federal" system with substantial powers left to the states. Federalists dominated public opinion in New England, New Jersey, and South Carolina and enjoyed considerable support in Pennsylvania and New York.

Hamilton's program sowed dissension in sections of the country where Federalist economic policies provided few benefits. Resentment ran high among those who felt that the government appeared to be rewarding special interests. Southern reaction to Hamilton's program, for example, was overwhelmingly negative. Outside a few urban centers, most notably Charleston, South Carolina, few southerners retained Revolutionary certificates in 1790. The Bank of the United States attracted few southern stockholders, and it allocated very little capital for loans there.

Hamilton's plans offered little to the West, where agriculture promised to be exceptionally profitable if only the right to export through New Orleans would be guaranteed. In Pennsylvania and New York, too, the uneven impact of Hamiltonian policies generated dissatisfaction. Resentment against a national economic program whose main beneficiaries seemed to be eastern "monied men" and Yankees who refused to pay their debts gradually united westerners, southerners, and many individuals in the mid-Atlantic region into a political coalition that challenged the Federalists for control of the government and called for a return to the "true principles" of republicanism.

### The Whiskey Rebellion

Hamilton's financial program not only sparked an angry political debate in Congress but also helped ignite a civil insurrection called the Whiskey Rebellion. Severely testing the federal government's authority, this insurrection was the young republic's first serious crisis.

To augment the national government's revenue from import duties, Hamilton had recommended an excise tax on domestically produced whiskey. He insisted that his proposal would distribute the expense of financing the national debt evenly across the United States. He even alleged that the country's morals would improve if higher prices induced Americans to drink less liquor, a contention enthusiastically endorsed by Philadelphia's College of Physicians. Though Congress complied with Hamilton's request in March 1791, many members doubted that Americans (who on average annually imbibed six gallons of hard liquor per adult) would submit tamely to sobriety. James Jackson of Georgia, for example, warned the administration that his constituents "have long been in the habit of getting drunk and that they will get drunk in defiance of a dozen colleges or all the excise duties which Congress might be weak or wicked enough to pass."

The accuracy of Jackson's prophecy became apparent in September 1791, when a crowd tarred and feathered an excise agent near Pittsburgh. Western Pennsylvanians found the new tax especially burdensome. Unable to ship their crops to world markets through Spanish New Orleans, most farmers had grown accustomed to distilling their rye or corn into alcohol, which could be carried across the Appalachians at a fraction of the price charged for bulky grain. Hamilton's excise equaled 25 percent of whiskey's retail value, enough to wipe out a frontier farmer's profit.

The law furthermore specified that all trials concerning tax evasion be conducted in federal courts. Any western Pennsylvanian indicted for noncompliance thus had to travel three hundred miles to Philadelphia. Not only would the accused then face a jury of unsympathetic easterners, but he would have to bear the cost of a long journey and lost earnings while at court, in addition to fines and other court penalties if found guilty. Moreover, Treasury officials rarely enforced the law rigorously outside western Pennsylvania. Consequently, western Pennsylvanians complained, local circumstances made the whiskey tax excessively burdensome.

In a scene reminiscent of colonial protests against Britain, large-scale resistance erupted in July 1794. One hundred men attacked a U.S. marshal serving sixty delinquent taxpayers with summonses to appear in court at Philadelphia. A crowd of five hundred burned the chief revenue officer's house after a shootout with federal soldiers assigned to protect him. Roving bands torched buildings, assaulted tax collectors, chased government supporters from the region, and flew a flag symbolizing an independent country that they hoped to create from six western counties.

Echoing British denunciation of colonial protests, Hamilton blasted the rebellion as simple lawlessness, in particular because Congress had reduced the tax rate per gallon in 1792 and just recently had voted to allow state judges in western Pennsylvania to hear trials. Washington concluded that failure to respond strongly to the uprising would encourage similar outbreaks in other frontier areas where lax enforcement had allowed distillers to escape paying taxes.

Washington accordingly mustered 12,900 militiamen from Pennsylvania, Maryland, Virginia, and New Jersey to march west under his command. Opposition evaporated once the troops reached the Appalachians, and the president left Hamilton in charge of making arrests. Of about 150 suspects seized, Hamilton sent twenty in irons to Philadelphia. Two men received death sentences, but Washington eventually pardoned them both, noting that one was a "simpleton" and the other "insane."

The Whiskey Rebellion was a milestone in determining limits on public opposition to federal policies. In the early 1790s, many Americans still assumed that it was legitimate to protest unpopular laws using the same tactics with which they had blocked parliamentary measures like the Stamp Act. Indeed, western Pennsylvanians had justified their resistance with exactly such reasoning. Before 1794 the question of how far the people might go in resisting federal laws remained unresolved because, as Washington declared, "We had given no testimony to the world of being able or willing to support our government and laws." But by firmly suppressing the first major challenge to national authority, Washington served notice that if citizens wished to change the law, they could do so only through constitutional procedures—by making their dissatisfaction known to their elected representatives and if necessary by electing new representatives.

# The United States on the World Stage

By 1793 disagreements over foreign affairs had emerged as the primary source of friction in American public life. The political divisions created by Hamilton's financial program hardened into ideologically oriented factions that argued vehemently over whether the country's foreign policy should favor industrial and overseas mercantile interests or those of farmers, planters, small businesses, and artisans. Moreover, having ratified its Constitution in the year that the French Revolution began (1789), the new United States government entered the international arena as European tensions were once again exploding. The rapid spread of pro-French revolutionary ideas and organizations alarmed Europe's monarchs and aristocrats. Perceiving a threat to their social orders as well as their territorial interests, most European nations declared war on France by early 1793. For most of the next twenty-two years—until Napoleon's final defeat in 1815—Europe and the Atlantic world remained in a state of war.

While most Americans hoped that their nation could avoid this latest European conflict, the fact was that the interests and ambitions of many of their compatriots collided at critical points with those of Britain, France, Spain, or some combination of these powers. Thus it was that differences over foreign policy fused with those over domestic affairs, further intensifying the partisanship of American politics.

## *Spanish Power in the Far West*

The late eighteenth century marked a brief, limited revival of Spanish fortunes in North America. Influenced by the Indian policies of France and Britain, Spanish officials shifted from futilely attempting to conquer their Indian enemies in the Southwest and southern Plains to a policy of peaceful trade. Under the new plan, they would, as Louisiana's Governor Bernardo de Gálvez put it, provide Native Americans with the "sundry conveniences of life of whose existence they previously knew nothing, and which they now look upon as indispensable." Among the "conveniences" Gálvez had in mind were poorly made guns, which the Indians would be obliged to have regularly repaired by Spanish gunsmiths, and alcohol. By the end of the century, the new policy had enabled Spain to make peace with the Comanches, Utes, Navajos, and most of the Apache nations that had previously threatened their settlements in New Mexico and Texas.

These reforms were part of a larger effort by Spain to counter potential rivals for North American territory and influence. The first challenge came in the north Pacific Ocean, where Spain enjoyed an unchallenged monopoly. Lacking any maritime rivals, Spain every year dispatched its "Manila galleons," which sailed

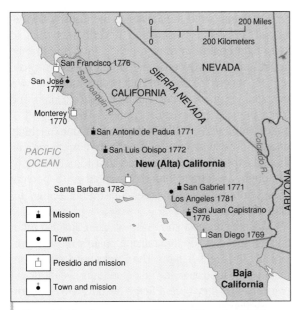

**Spanish Settlements in New California, 1784**
*While the United States was struggling to establish its independence, Spain was extending its empire northward along the Pacific coast.*

north from Mexico's Pacific coast to Monterey Bay in California and then turned eastward for the long voyage to Asia's shores. But meanwhile, in the 1740s, Russian traders in Siberia had crossed the Bering Sea and had begun trading with Alaskan natives for sea-otter pelts, frequently using brutal force and spreading deadly diseases in the process. Soon the Russians moved farther south to trade with the wealthy Indians of the Northwest Coast. By the 1770s the exploring voyages of Britain's Captain James Cook and others revealed the wealth such pelts were bringing to Russian merchants. The Russians carried the otterskins overland through Siberia to China where they exchanged them for silk cloth, porcelain ware, and other fine objects. Sensing the profits such trade could generate, British and American maritime traders began plying Northwest coastal waters in the 1780s. Trading cloth, metal tools, and other goods to the Indians, they carried furs to Hawaii—also made known to Europeans and Americans by Cook—and traded them to China-bound merchants for Chinese goods. These luxuries were then carried back to Europe and America and sold to affluent consumers who prized them for their exotic designs and fine craftsmanship. Thus began the "China trade," which brought tidy profits to many a

Boston merchant and fueled American dreams of expanding to the Pacific.

Responding to these inroads, Spain boldly expanded its empire northward from Mexico. In 1769 it established "New California," a long stretch of coast from San Diego to Sonoma (north of San Francisco). Efforts to encourage large-scale Hispanic immigration to New California failed, so that the colony was sustained primarily by its religious missions to coastal Native Americans, several *presidios* (forts), and a few large *ranchos* (ranches). Seeking refuge from inland adversaries, the Indians welcomed the Spanish at first. But the Franciscan missionaries sought to convert them to Catholicism and "civilize" them by imposing rigid disciplinary measures and putting them to work in vineyards and in other enterprises. Meanwhile, Spanish colonists' spreading of epidemic and venereal diseases among natives precipitated a decline in the Indians' numbers from about 72,000 in 1770 to about 18,000 by 1830.

Having strengthened its positions in Texas, New Mexico, and California, Spain attempted to befriend Indians in the area later known as Arizona. In this way, Spain hoped to dominate North America from the Pacific to Louisiana on the Gulf of Mexico. But these hopes were thwarted by resistance from the Hopi, Quechan (Yuma), and other Native Americans. Fortunately for Spain, this region had not yet attracted the interest of other outside powers. Spain's tenuous hold on the Southwest would later be inherited by the independent republic of Mexico (see Chapter 13).

### The Trans-Appalachian Frontier

East of the Mississippi River, Spain, Britain, the United States, and the various local Indian nations jockeyed for advantage in a region that all considered central to their interests and which Native Americans regarded as homelands.

Unable to prevent American settlers from occupying territory it claimed in the Southeast, Spain sought to win the newcomers' allegiance by offering them citizenship. Noting that Congress under the Articles of Confederation seemed ready to accept the permanent closing of New Orleans in return for Spanish concessions elsewhere (see Chapter 6), many westerners began talking openly of secession. "I am decidedly of the opinion," wrote Kentucky's attorney general in 1787, "that this western country will in a few years Revolt from the Union and endeavor to erect an Independent

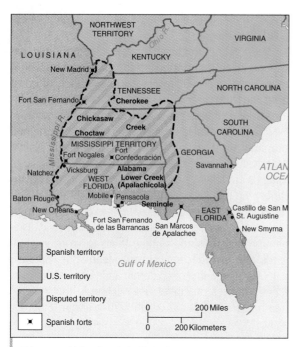

### Disputed Territorial Claims, Spain and the United States, 1783–1796

*The two nations' claims to lands east of the Mississippi and north of the thirty-first parallel were a principal point of contention until the Treaty of San Lorenzo was ratified in 1796.*

Government." In 1788 Tennessee conspirators boldly advertised their flirtation with Spain by naming a large district along the Cumberland River after Spain's governor in New Orleans. Most westerners who accepted Spanish favors and gold meant only to pocket badly needed cash in return for vague promises of goodwill. The episode showed, however, that leading citizens were susceptible to foreign manipulation and subversion. As young Andrew Jackson concluded in 1789, making some arrangements with the Spanish seemed "the only immediate way to obtain peace with the Savage [Indians]."

In the early years of Washington's administration, Spanish officials continued to bribe well-known political figures in Tennessee and Kentucky, among them a former general on Washington's staff, James Wilkinson. Thomas Scott, a congressman from western Pennsylvania, meanwhile schemed with the British. Between 1791 and 1796, the federal government anxiously admitted Vermont, Kentucky, and Tennessee to the Union, partly in the hope of strengthening their sometimes flickering loyalty to the United States.

Consulting with the Senate as the Constitution required, President Washington nevertheless tried to keep tight control of foreign policy. Realizing that he could not quickly resolve the complex western problem, he pursued a course of patient diplomacy that was intended "to preserve the country in peace if I can, and to be prepared for war if I cannot." The prospect of peace improved in 1789 when Spain unexpectedly opened New Orleans to American commerce, although exports remained subject to a 15 percent duty. Although westerners bitterly resented a 15 percent Spanish duty on exports, secessionist sentiment gradually subsided.

Washington now moved to weaken Spanish influence in the West by neutralizing Spain's most important ally, the Creek Indians. The Creeks numbered more than twenty thousand, including perhaps five thousand warriors, and they bore a fierce hostility toward Georgian settlers, whom they called *Ecunnaunuxulgee,* or "the greedy people who want our lands." In 1790 the Creek leader Alexander McGillivray signed the Treaty of New York with the United States. The treaty permitted American settlers to occupy lands in the Georgia piedmont fought over since 1786, but in other respects preserved Creek territory against U.S. expansion. Washington insisted that Georgia restore to the Creeks' allies, the Chickasaws and Choctaws, the vast area along the Mississippi River known as the Yazoo Tract, which Georgia claimed and had begun selling off to white land speculators (see Chapter 8).

Washington adopted a harsher policy toward Great Britain's Indian allies in the Great Lakes region. In 1790 his first effort to force peace through military action failed when General Josiah Harmar was defeated by an alliance of Indians, losing nearly two hundred of his soldiers. A second campaign ended in disaster on November 4, 1791, when Ohio Indians killed nine hundred men out of a force of fourteen hundred led by General Arthur St. Clair.

While employing military force, the Washington administration, led by Secretary of War Henry Knox, also sought to pacify the Indians through a benevolent policy similar to that proclaimed by the British in 1763 (see Chapter 5). Alarmed by the chaos on the frontier, where trespassers invaded Indian lands and the native peoples rejected U.S. claims to sovereignty, the government formally recognized Indian title as secure and inalienable except by the "free consent" of the Indians themselves. To reinforce this policy, Congress enacted laws prohibiting trespassing on Indian lands, punishing crimes committed there by non-Indians, outlawing alcohol, and, in the Indian Non-Intercourse Act (1790), regulating trade. In addition, the administration sought to encourage Indians to leave off their "savage" ways and become "civilized," by which it meant above all abandoning communal landownership and seasonal migrations for hunting, gathering, and fishing. By adopting private property and a strictly agricultural way of life, Knox and others thought, Indians would find a niche for themselves in American society while making much additional land available for non-Indians.

Knox recognized that his "civilization" policy would have limited appeal. Although most Indians were receptive to European material goods, they were unwilling to give up their traditional ways entirely and assimilate into an alien culture. And most whites were equally averse to integrating Native Americans into their society. Accordingly, the United States continued to pressure most Native Americans to sell their lands and move farther west.

With many Indians opposed to abandoning both their lands and their cultures, and with St. Clair's defeat in 1791, Washington's frontier policy lay in a shambles. Not only had two military expeditions suffered defeat in the Northwest Territory, but in 1792 the Spanish had persuaded the Creeks to renounce their two-year-old treaty with the federal government and to resume hostilities. Ultimately, the damage done to U.S. prestige by these setbacks convinced many Americans that the combined strength of Britain, Spain, and the Native Americans could be counterbalanced only by an alliance with France.

## France and Factional Politics

One of the most momentous events in history, the French Revolution began in 1789 with the meeting (for the first time in almost two centuries) of France's legislative assembly, the Estates General. Americans remained fundamentally sympathetic to the revolutionary cause as the French abolished nobles' privileges, wrote a constitution, and bravely repelled invading armies from Austria and Prussia. France became a republic early in 1793; it then proclaimed a war of all peoples against all kings, in which it assumed that the United States would eagerly enlist.

Enthusiasm for a pro-French foreign policy raged in the South and on the frontier, in particular after France went to war against Spain and Great Britain in 1793. Increasingly, western settlers and southern speculators in

**Stimafachki of the Koasati Creeks,**
by John Trumbull, 1790
*This portrait was sketched during the U.S.–Creek conference that resulted in the Treaty of New York.*

frontier lands hoped for a decisive French victory in Europe that, they reasoned, would leave Britain and Spain militarily too exhausted to continue meddling in the West. The United States could then insist on free navigation of the Mississippi, force the evacuation of British garrisons, and end both nations' support of Indian resistance.

Moreover, a slave uprising in France's Caribbean colony of Saint Domingue (later renamed Haiti) soon generated passionate anti-British sentiment in the South. White southerners grew alarmed for the future of slavery and their own lives as thousands of terrified French planters fled to the United States from Saint Domingue with accounts of how British invaders in 1793 had supported the rebellious slaves. The blacks had fought with determination and inflicted heavy casualties on the French. Assuming that Africans were incapable of rebelling on their own, southern whites concluded that the British had intentionally sparked the bloodbath and would do the same in the South. Anti-British hysteria even began to undermine South Carolina's loyalty to Federalist policies.

Northern and southern reactions to the French Revolution also diverged for economic reasons. In the North merchants' growing antagonism toward France reflected not only their conservatism but also their awareness that good relations with Britain were essential for their region's prosperity. Virtually all the nation's merchant marine operated from northern ports, and by far the largest share of U.S. foreign trade was with Great Britain. Merchants, shippers, and ordinary sailors in New England, Philadelphia, and New York feared that an alliance with France would provoke British retaliation against this valuable commerce, and they argued that the United States could win valuable concessions by demonstrating friendly intentions toward Great Britain. Indeed, important members of Parliament, including Prime Minister William Pitt the Younger, seemed to favor liberalizing trade with the United States.

Southerners had no such reasons to favor Britain. Southern spokesmen viewed Americans' reliance on British commerce as a menace to national self-determination and wished to divert most U.S. trade to France. Jefferson and Madison repeatedly demanded that British imports be reduced through the imposition of steep discriminatory duties on cargoes shipped from England and Scotland in British vessels. In the heat of the debate, Federalist opponents of a discriminatory tariff warned that Britain, which sold more manufactured goods to the United States than to any other country, would not stand by while a weak French ally pushed it into depression. If Congress adopted this program of trade retaliation, Hamilton predicted in 1792, "there would be, in less than six months, an open war between the United States and Great Britain."

Many southern citizens also had personal stakes in trans-Appalachian affairs because Virginia and North Carolina had rewarded Revolutionary soldiers with western land. Whether these veterans intended to move west themselves or to profit by selling their rights to others, all wanted to see the western territories prosper. Hoping to make a quick fortune in land speculation, southern planters (including George Washington) had borrowed heavily to buy frontier real estate; but uncertainty about the West's future made them worry that land prices would crash. By 1789 a potent combination of small farmers and landed gentry in the South had become enraged at foreign barriers to frontier expansion and eagerly supported politicians such as Jefferson and Madison who advocated strong measures against the British and Spanish.

After declaring war on Britain and Spain in 1793, France actively tried to embroil the United States in the conflict. The French dispatched Edmond Genet as minister to the United States with orders to mobilize republican sentiment in support of France, enlist American mercenaries to conquer Spanish territories and attack British shipping, and strengthen the treaty of alliance between the two nations. Much to the French government's disgust, however, President Washington issued a proclamation of American neutrality on April 22.

Meanwhile, Citizen Genet (as he was known in French Revolutionary style) had arrived on April 8. He found no shortage of southern volunteers for his American Foreign Legion despite America's official neutrality. Making generals of George Rogers Clark of Kentucky and Elisha Clarke of Georgia, Genet directed them to seize the Spanish garrisons at New Orleans and St. Augustine. Clark openly defied Washington's Neutrality Proclamation by advertising for recruits for his mission in Kentucky newspapers; Clarke began drilling three hundred troops on the Florida border. But the French failed to provide adequate funds for either campaign. Although the American recruits were willing to fight for France, few were willing to fight for free, and so both expeditions eventually disintegrated.

However, Genet did not need funds to outfit privateers, whose crews were paid from captured plunder. By the summer of 1793, almost a thousand Americans were at sea in a dozen ships flying the French flag. These privateers seized more than eighty British vessels and towed them to U.S. ports, where French consuls sold the ships and cargoes at auction.

### The British Crisis

Even though the Washington administration swiftly closed the nation's harbors to Genet's buccaneers and requested the French ambassador's recall, his exploits provoked an Anglo-American crisis. George III's ministers decided that only a massive show of force would deter further American aggression. Accordingly, on November 6, 1793, the Privy Council issued secret orders confiscating any foreign ships trading with French islands in the Caribbean. The council purposely delayed publishing these instructions until after most American ships carrying winter provisions to the Caribbean left port, so that their captains would not know that they were sailing into a war zone. The Royal Navy then seized more than 250 American vessels.

Meanwhile, the U.S. merchant marine was suffering a second galling indignity—the drafting of its crewmen into the Royal Navy. Thousands of British sailors, including numerous naval deserters, had previously

**Negotiating the Treaty of Greenville**

*In this detail of a contemporary painting believed to have been done by a member of General Wayne's staff, Chief Little Turtle of the Miamis speaks to Wayne, who stands with one hand behind his back.*

fled to U.S. ships, where they hoped to find an easier life than under the tough, poorly paying British system. In late 1793 British naval officers began routinely inspecting American crews for British subjects, whom they then impressed (forcibly enlisted) as the king's sailors. Overzealous commanders sometimes broke royal orders by taking U.S. citizens, and in any case the British did not recognize former subjects' right to adopt American citizenship. Impressment scratched a raw nerve in most Americans, who recognized that their government's willingness to defend its citizens from such contemptuous abuse was a critical test of national character.

Next the British boldly challenged the United States for control of the West. In February 1794 Canada's royal governor delivered an inflammatory speech at an Indian council, denying U.S. claims north of the Ohio River and urging his listeners to destroy every white settlement in the Northwest. Soon British troops were building an eighth garrison on U.S. soil, Fort Miami, near present-day Toledo, Ohio. Meanwhile, the Spanish encroached further upon territory owned by the United States by building Fort San Fernando in 1794 at what is now Memphis, Tennessee.

Hoping to halt the drift toward war, Washington launched a desperate diplomatic initiative in 1794. He sent Chief Justice John Jay to Great Britain, dispatched Thomas Pinckney to Spain, and authorized General Anthony Wayne to negotiate a treaty with the Indians of the Ohio Valley.

Having twice defeated federal armies, the Indians scoffed at Washington's peace offer. But the tide turned as "Mad Anthony" Wayne led three thousand U.S. troops deep into Indian homelands and ruthlessly razed every village within his reach. On August 20, 1794, his troops routed a thousand Indians at the Battle of Fallen Timbers just two miles from British Fort Miami. Wayne's army then built an imposing stronghold to challenge British authority in the Northwest, appropriately named Fort Defiance. Indian morale plummeted. In August 1795 Wayne compelled twelve northeastern tribes to sign the Treaty of Greenville, which opened most of modern-day Ohio to white settlement and ended U.S.–Indian hostilities in the region for sixteen years.

Wayne's success allowed John Jay to win a major diplomatic victory in London: a British promise to withdraw troops from American soil. He also managed to gain access to West Indian markets for small American ships, but only by bargaining away U.S. rights to load cargoes of sugar, molasses, and coffee from the Caribbean. On other points, Jay found the British unyielding. Aside from fellow Federalists, few Americans could interpret Jay's Treaty as preserving peace with honor.

Jay's Treaty left Britain free not only to violate American neutrality but also to ruin a profitable commerce by restricting U.S. trade with French ports during wartime. Many opponents, moreover, passionately decried Jay's failure to end impressment and predicted that Great Britain would thereafter force even more Americans into the Royal Navy. And southerners resented that Jay had not achieved their long-sought goal of compensation for slaves taken away by the British army during the Revolution. As the Federalist-dominated Senate ratified the treaty by a one-vote margin in 1795, Jay nervously joked that he could find his way across the country by the fires of rallies burning him in effigy.

Despite its unpopularity, Jay's Treaty defused an explosive crisis with Great Britain before war became inevitable and ended a twelve-year British occupation of U.S. territory. Although the Senate rejected the provision granting limited trading rights with the West Indies in return for a British monopoly over certain commodities, Jay's Treaty played a critical role in stimulating an enormous expansion of American trade. British governors in the West Indies used the treaty's ratification as an excuse to proclaim their harbors open to U.S. ships. Other British officials permitted Americans to develop a thriving commerce with India, even though this trade infringed on the East India Company's monopoly. Within a few years after 1795, American exports to the British Empire shot up 300 percent.

On the heels of Jay's Treaty came an unqualified diplomatic triumph engineered by Thomas Pinckney. Ratified in 1796, the Treaty of San Lorenzo with Spain (also called Pinckney's Treaty) won westerners the right of unrestricted, duty-free access to world markets via the Mississippi River. Spain also promised to recognize the thirty-first parallel as the United States' southern boundary, to dismantle all fortifications on American soil, and to discourage Indian attacks against western settlers.

By 1796 the Washington administration thus had successfully defended the country's territorial integrity, restored peace to the frontier, opened the Mississippi for western exports, made it possible for northeastern shippers to regain British markets, and kept the nation out of a dangerous European war. As the popular outcry over Jay's Treaty demonstrated, however, the nation's foreign policy had left Americans much more deeply divided in 1796 than they had been in 1789.

# Battling for the Nation's Soul

Besides distrusting centralized executive authority, colonial and Revolutionary Americans feared organized political parties. Labeling parties "factions," Americans (and many Britons) assumed that such groups were formed by corrupt conspirators operating against the liberties of the people. Neither the Constitution nor *The Federalist* had envisioned political parties, and none existed in 1789 when Washington became president. By the end of his second term, however, politically conscious Americans had split into two hostile parties, Federalists and Republicans, as instruments for advancing their interests, ambitions, and ideals.

The unfolding struggle transcended the economic and sectional differences so evident in earlier disputes about Hamiltonian finance and the possibility of war with Britain. After 1796 a battle raged over the very future of representative government, culminating in the election of 1800, whose outcome would determine whether the nation's political elite could accommodate demands from ordinary citizens for a more active and influential role in determining government policy. No issue was more important or hotly argued than the matter of officeholders' accountability to their constituents.

## *Ideological Confrontation*

By the mid-1790s the French Revolution had led many Americans to reassess their political values. American attitudes toward events in France divided sharply after that nation's revolutionary regime turned radical in 1793–1794, sending thousands of "counterrevolutionaries" to the guillotine. The polarization of American opinion assumed a strongly, though not completely, regional dimension.

For northern Federalists, revolutionary France became an abomination—"an open hell," thundered Massachusetts Federalist Fisher Ames, "still ringing with agonies and blasphemies, still smoking with sufferings and crimes." New England was the United States' most militantly Protestant region, and most of its middle-class and elite citizens came to detest the French government's disregard for civil rights and its attempt to substitute the adoration of Reason for the worship of God. Middle Atlantic elites, who were perhaps less religious than New Englanders but even more conservative, condemned French leaders as evil radicals who incited the poor against the rich.

Federalists trembled at the thought of guillotines and "mob rule" looming in the United States' future. Memories of Shays's Rebellion and the Whiskey Rebellion reinforced their fears. So did the tendency of artisans in Philadelphia and New York to bandy the French revolutionary slogan "Liberty, Equality, Fraternity" and to admire pro-French politicians such as Jefferson. Moreover, Citizen Genet had openly encouraged opposition to the Washington administration and, even more troubling, he had found hundreds of Americans willing to fight for France. Federalists worried that all of this was just the tip of an iceberg.

By the mid-1790s Federalist leaders had concluded that it was dangerous to involve the public too deeply in politics. The people, they believed, were not evil-minded but simply undependable and could easily fall prey to a rabble rouser such as Genet. As Senator George Cabot of Massachusetts put it, "The many do not think at all." For Federalists, democracy meant "government by the passions of the multitude." They consequently argued that ordinary white male property owners should not be presented with choices over policy during elections; instead, voters ought to choose among elite candidates according to their personal merits. Thus Federalists favored a government in which elected officials would rule in the people's name but would be independent of direct popular influence.

A very different understanding of republican ideology surfaced in urban areas of New England and the Middle Atlantic states, and ran particularly high in the South. Republican opponents of Federalist measures stressed the corruption inherent in a powerful government dominated by a highly visible few, and insisted that liberty would be safe only if power were diffused among virtuous, independent citizens. Whereas Federalists denounced self-interest as inimical to the public good, their opponents argued that self-interest could be pursued virtuously in a society in which property and other means to economic independence were widely available rather than being monopolized by the wealthy few. Jefferson, Madison, and other republicans interpreted the American and French revolutions as opening the way to a new kind of human community in which self-interested individuals recognized their common interest in maintaining a stable society responsive to the needs of all.

A radical ideology like republicanism, with its emphasis on liberty and equality, might seem anomalous among southern slaveowners. In fact, however, such men were among its most forceful proponents. Although a few southern republicans advocated abolishing slavery gradually, most declined to trouble themselves unduly over their ownership of human beings. The liberty and equality they advocated were intended for white men only, even though articulated in universal terms. With their own labor force consisting of enslaved blacks rather than of free white wage workers, southern elites feared popular participation in politics

**The Republican Court,**
by Daniel Huntington
*Federalists emphasized the dignity of the national government by staging sumptuous balls and formal receptions. Administration critics saw these affairs as an effort to emulate European court life. Washington, although mindful of upholding presidential dignity, found public functions tedious, and his stiff formality often masked his personal discomfort.*

far less than did their northern counterparts. Overlooking the possibility that their slaves understood their ideas and their debates, they maintained a confidence built on the loyalty toward them of nonelite whites.

Self-interest, too, drove men like Jefferson and Madison to rouse ordinary citizens' concerns about civic affairs. The widespread awe in which Washington was held inhibited open criticism of him, his policies, and his fellow Federalists. If, however, the Federalists could be held accountable to the public, they would think twice before enacting measures opposed by the majority; or if they persisted in advocating misguided policies, they would ultimately be removed from office. Such reasoning led Jefferson, a wealthy landowner and large slaveholder, to say, "I am not among those who fear the people; they and not the rich, are our dependence for continued freedom."

Organized efforts to turn public opinion against the Federalists had begun in October 1791 with the publication of the nation's first opposition newspaper, the *National Gazette.* Then in 1793–1794, popular dissatisfaction with the government's policies led to the formation of dozens of Democratic (or Republican) societies, primarily in seaboard cities but also in the rural South and in frontier towns. Their memberships ranged from planters and merchants to artisans and sailors. Conspicuously absent were clergymen, the poor, and nonwhites.

Sharply critical of the Federalists, the societies spread dissatisfaction with the Washington administration's policies. Federalists interpreted their emotional appeals to ordinary people as demagoguery and denounced the societies' followers as "democrats, mobocrats, & all other kinds of rats." They feared that the societies would grow into revolutionary organizations. During the Whiskey Rebellion, Washington publicly denounced "certain self-created societies." So great was his prestige that the societies temporarily broke up. But by attacking them, Washington had at last ended his nonpartisan stance and identified himself unmistakably with the Federalists. The censure would cost him dearly.

### The Republican Party

Neither Jefferson nor Madison belonged to a Democratic society. However, these private clubs helped publicize administration critics' views, and they initiated into political activity numerous voters who would later support Jefferson's and Madison's Republican party.

Prior to the mid-1790s, politically aware Americans believed that deliberately organizing a political faction or party was a corrupt, subversive action. The Constitution's framers had neither wanted nor planned for political parties. In *The Federalist* No. 10, Madison (the future partisan) had claimed that the Constitution would prevent the rise of national political factions. Republican ideology commonly assumed that factions or parties would fill Congress with politicians of little ability and less integrity, pursuing selfish goals at the expense of national welfare. Good citizens, it was assumed, would shun partisan scheming. These ideals, however, began to waver as controversy mounted over Hamilton's program and foreign policy. Jefferson finally resigned from the cabinet in 1793, and thereafter even the president could not halt the widening political split. Each side saw itself as the guardian of republican virtue and attacked the other as an illegitimate "cabal" or "faction."

In 1794 party development reached a decisive stage. Shortly after Washington had openly identified himself with Federalist policies, followers of Jefferson who called themselves Republicans (rather than the more radical-sounding "Democrats") successfully attacked the Federalists' pro-British leanings in many local elections and won a slight majority in the House of Representatives. The election signaled the Republicans' transformation from a coalition of officeholders to a broad-based party capable of coordinating local political campaigns throughout the nation.

Federalists and Republicans alike used the press to mold public opinion. In the 1790s American journalism came of age as the number of newspapers multiplied from 92 to 242, mostly in New England and the Middle Atlantic states. By 1800 newspapers had perhaps 140,000 paid subscribers (about one-fifth of the eligible voters), and their secondhand readership probably exceeded 300,000. Newspapers of both camps were libelous and irresponsible. They cheapened the quality of public discussion through incessant fear mongering and character assassination. Republicans stood accused of plotting a reign of terror and of wishing to turn the nation over to France. Federalists faced charges of favoring a hereditary aristocracy and even of planning to establish an American dynasty by marrying off John Adams's daughter to George III. Such tactics whipped up mutual distrust and made political debate emotional and subjective. Nevertheless, the newspaper warfare stimulated many citizens to become politically active.

**George Washington's Inaugural Journey Through Trenton, 1789**
*Washington received a warm welcome in Trenton, site of his first victory during the Revolutionary War.*

Behind the inflammatory rhetoric, the Republicans' central charge was that the Federalists had evolved into a faction bent on enriching wealthy citizens at the taxpayers' expense. In 1794 a Republican writer claimed that Federalist policies would create "a privileged order of men . . . who shall enjoy the honors, the emoluments, and the patronage of government, without contributing a farthing to its support." The Republicans wildly exaggerated when claiming that their opponents were scheming to introduce legal privilege, aristocracy, and monarchy. But they correctly identified the Federalists' fundamental assumption: that citizens' worth could be measured in terms of their money.

Republican charges that the president secretly supported alleged Federalist plots to establish a monarchy enraged Washington. "By God," Jefferson reported him swearing, "he [the president] would rather be in his grave than in his present situation . . . he had rather be on his farm than to be made *emperor of the world.*" Furthermore, the president took alarm at the stormy debate over Jay's Treaty, and he dreaded the nation's polarization into hostile factions. Republicans' abuse sharply stung him. Lonely and surrounded by mediocre advisers after Hamilton's return to private life, Washington decided in the spring of 1796 to retire after two terms. Four years earlier, Madison had drafted the president's parting message to the nation; but now Wash-

ington called on Hamilton to give a sharp political twist to his Farewell Address.

The heart of Washington's message was a vigorous condemnation of political parties. Partisan alignments, he insisted, endangered the republic's survival, especially if they became entangled in disputes over foreign policy. Washington warned that the country's safety depended on citizens' avoiding "excessive partiality for one nation and excessive dislike of another." Otherwise, independent-minded "real patriots" would be overwhelmed by demagogues championing foreign causes and paid by foreign governments. Aside from scrupulously fulfilling its existing treaty obligations and maintaining its foreign commerce, the United States must avoid "political connection" with Europe and its wars. If the United States gathered its strength under "an efficient government," it could defy any foreign challenge; but if it became sucked into Europe's quarrels, violence, and corruption, then the republican experiment was doomed. Washington and Hamilton had skillfully turned the central argument of republicanism against their Republican critics. They had also evoked a vision of America virtuously isolated from foreign intrigue and power politics, which would remain a potent inspiration until the twentieth century.

Washington left the presidency in 1797 and died in 1799. Like many later presidents, he went out amid a barrage of criticism. During his brief retirement, the nation's political division into Republicans and Federalists hardened into a two-party system.

### The Election of 1796

As the election of 1796 approached, the Republicans cultivated a large, loyal body of voters. Their efforts to marshal support marked the first time since the Revolution that the political elite had effectively mobilized ordinary Americans to take an interest in public affairs. The Republicans' constituency included the Democratic societies, workingmen's clubs, and immigrant-aid associations.

Immigrants became a prime target for Republican recruiters. During the 1790s the United States absorbed perhaps twenty thousand French refugees from Saint Domingue and more than sixty thousand Irish, including some who had been exiled for their opposition to British rule. Although potential immigrant voters were few—comprising less than 2 percent of the electorate—the Irish in particular could exert crucial influence in Pennsylvania and New York, where public opinion was closely divided and a few hundred immi-

**John Adams,** by Gilbert Stuart, 1826 (Detail)
*The Adamses hailed from Quincy, Massachusetts. Soon after the elder Adams's death, John Quincy Adams, now president, commissioned a final portrait of his father. This gentle and distinguished canvas was the result.*

grant voters could tip the balance away from the Federalists.

In 1796 the presidential candidates were Vice President John Adams, supported by the Federalists, and the Republicans' Jefferson. Republicans expected to win as many southern electoral votes and congressional seats as the Federalists counted on in New England, New Jersey, and South Carolina. The crucial "swing" states were Pennsylvania and New York, where the Republicans fought hard to win the large immigrant (particularly Irish) vote with their pro-French and anti-British rhetoric. In the end, however, the Republicans took Pennsylvania but not New York, and so Jefferson lost the presidency by just three electoral votes. The Federalists narrowly regained control of the House and maintained their firm grip on the Senate. But by a political fluke possible under the Constitution at the time, Jefferson became vice president.*

Adams's brilliance, insight, and idealism have rarely been equaled among American presidents. Like many intellectuals, however, Adams was more comfortable with ideas than with people, more theoretical than practical, and rather inflexible. He inspired trust and often admiration but could not command personal loyalty. His wisdom and historical vision were drowned out in highly emotional political debate. Adams's rational, reserved personality was likewise ill suited to inspiring the electorate, and he ultimately proved unable to unify the country.

### The French Crisis

Adams was initially fortunate, however, that French provocations produced a sharp backlash against the Republicans. The French interpreted Jay's Treaty as an American attempt to assist the British in their war against France. On learning of Jefferson's defeat, the French ordered the seizure of American ships carrying goods to British ports; and within a year the French had plundered more than three hundred vessels. The French government rubbed in its contempt for the United States by directing that every American captured on a British naval ship (even those involuntarily impressed) should be hanged.

---

\* The Constitution then stipulated that the presidential candidate with the second-highest electoral vote would become vice president. This was one example of the Constitution's failure to provide for political partisanship.

Hoping to avoid war, Adams sent a peace commission to Paris. But the French foreign minister, Charles de Talleyrand, refused to meet the delegation, instead promising through three unnamed agents ("X, Y, and Z") that talks could begin after he received $250,000 and France obtained a loan of $12 million. This barefaced demand for a bribe became known as the XYZ Affair. Americans reacted to it with outrage. "Millions for defense, not one cent for tribute" became the nation's battle cry as the 1798 congressional elections began.

The XYZ Affair discredited the Republicans' foreign policy views, but the party's leaders compounded the damage by refusing to condemn French aggression and opposing Adams's call for defensive measures. The Republicans tried to excuse French behavior, whereas the Federalists rode a wave of militant patriotism. In the 1798 elections, Jefferson's supporters were routed almost everywhere, even in the South.

Congress responded to the XYZ Affair by arming fifty-four ships to protect American commerce. During the Quasi-War—an undeclared Franco-American naval conflict in the Caribbean from 1798 to 1800—U.S. forces seized ninety-three French privateers at the loss of just one vessel. The British navy meanwhile extended the protection of its convoys to America's merchant marine. By early 1799 the French were a nuisance but no longer a serious threat at sea.

Meanwhile, the Federalists in Congress tripled the regular army to ten thousand men in 1798, with an automatic expansion of land forces to fifty thousand in case of war. But the risk of a land war with the French was minimal. In reality, the Federalists primarily wanted a military force ready in the event of a civil war, for the crisis had produced near-hysteria about conspiracies that were being hatched by French and Irish malcontents flooding into the United States.

Federalists were well aware that the French legation was not only engaged in espionage but also making treasonous suggestions to prominent persons. The government knew, for example, that in 1796 General Victor Collot had traveled from Pittsburgh to New Orleans under orders to investigate the prospects for establishing a pro-French, independent nation west of the mountains, and also that he had examined strategic locations to which rebellious frontier dwellers might rally. The State Department heard in 1798 that France had created in the West "a party of mad Americans ready to join with them at a given Signal."

## The Alien and Sedition Acts

The Federalists also insisted that the likelihood of open war with France required stringent legislation to protect national security. In 1798 the Federalist-dominated Congress accordingly passed four measures known collectively as the Alien and Sedition Acts. Adams neither requested nor particularly wanted these laws, but he deferred to Federalist congressional leaders and signed them.

The least controversial of the four laws, the Alien Enemies Act, outlined procedures for determining whether the citizens of a hostile country posed a threat to the United States as spies or saboteurs; if so, they were to be deported or jailed. The law established fundamental principles for protecting national security and respecting the rights of enemy citizens. It was to operate only if Congress declared war and so was not used until the War of 1812 (see Chapter 8).

Second, the Alien Friends Act, a temporary peacetime statute, authorized the president to expel any foreign residents whose activities he considered dangerous. The law did not require proof of guilt, on the assumption that spies would hide or destroy evidence of their crime. Republicans maintained that the law's real purpose was to deport prominent immigrants critical of Federalist policies.

Republicans also denounced the third law, the Naturalization Act. This measure increased the residency requirement for U.S. citizenship from five to fourteen years (the last five continuously in one state), with the purpose of reducing Irish voting.

Finally came the Sedition Act, the only one of these measures enforceable against U.S. citizens. Its alleged purpose was to distinguish between free speech and attempts at encouraging others to violate federal laws or to overthrow the government. But the act nevertheless defined criminal activity so broadly that it blurred any real distinction between sedition and legitimate political discussion. Thus it forbade an individual or group "to oppose any measure or measures of the United States"—wording that could be interpreted to ban any criticism of the party in power. Another clause made it illegal to speak, write, or print any statement about the president that would bring him "into contempt or disrepute." Under such restrictions, for example, a newspaper editor might face imprisonment for disapproving of an action by Adams or his cabinet members. The Federalist *Gazette of the United States* expressed the

**Congressional Pugilists,** 1798
*A cartoonist satirizes the fiercely partisan debates in Congress surrounding the Alien and Sedition acts.*

twisted logic of the Sedition Act perfectly: "It is patriotism to write in favor of our government—it is sedition to write against it."

Sedition cases were heard by juries, which could decide if the defendant had really intended to stir up rebellion or was merely expressing political dissent. But however one looked at it, the Sedition Act interfered with free speech. Ingeniously, the Federalists wrote the law to expire in 1801 (so that it could not be turned against them if they lost the next election) and to leave them free meanwhile to heap abuse on the *vice* president, Jefferson.

The principal target of Federalist repression was the U.S. opposition press. Four of the five largest Republican newspapers were charged with sedition just as the election of 1800 was getting under way. The attorney general used the Alien Friends Act to threaten Irish journalist John Daly Burk with expulsion (Burk went underground instead). Scottish editor Thomas Callender was being deported when he suddenly qualified for citizenship. Now unable to expel Callender, the government tried him for sedition before an all-Federalist jury, which sent him to prison for criticizing the president.

Federalist leaders never intended to fill the jails with Republican martyrs. Rather, they wanted to use a small number of highly visible prosecutions to intimidate most journalists and candidates into keeping quiet during the election of 1800. The attorney general charged seventeen persons with sedition and won ten convictions. Among the victims was the Republican congressman Matthew Lyon of Vermont ("Ragged Matt, the democrat," to the Federalists), who spent four months in prison for publishing a blast against Adams.

Vocal criticism of Federalist repression erupted during the summer of 1798 in Virginia and Kentucky. Militia commanders in these states mustered their regiments, not to drill but to hear speeches demanding that the federal government respect the Bill of Rights. Entire units then signed petitions denouncing the Alien and Sedition Acts. The symbolic implications of these protests were sobering. Young men stepped forward to sign petitions on drumheads with a pen in one hand and a gun in the other, as older officers who had fought in the Continental Army looked on approvingly. It was not hard to imagine Kentucky rifles being substituted for quill pens as the men who had led one revolution took up arms again.

Ten years earlier, opponents of the Constitution had warned that giving the national government extensive powers would eventually endanger freedom. By 1798 their prediction seemed to have come true. Shocked Republicans realized that because the Federalists controlled all three branches of the government, neither the Bill of Rights nor the system of checks and balances protected individual liberties. In this context, the doctrine of states' rights was advanced as a means of preventing the national government from violating basic freedoms.

Madison and Jefferson anonymously wrote two manifestos on states' rights that the assemblies of Virginia and Kentucky officially endorsed in 1798. Madison's Virginia Resolutions and Jefferson's Kentucky Resolutions declared that the state legislatures had never surrendered their right to judge the constitutionality of federal actions and that they retained an authority called interposition, which enabled them to protect the liberties of their citizens. A set of Kentucky Resolutions adopted in November 1799 added that objectionable federal laws might be "nullified" by the states. The terms *interposition* and *nullification* were not defined, but the intention was to invalidate the enforcement of any federal law in a state that had deemed the law unconstitutional. Interposition challenged the jurisdiction of federal courts and could have led state militias to march into a federal courtroom to halt proceedings at bayonet point.

Although no other states endorsed these resolutions (most in fact expressed disapproval), their passage demonstrated the great potential for violence in the late 1790s. So did a minor insurrection called the Fries Rebellion, which broke out in 1799 when crowds of Pennsylvania German farmers released prisoners jailed for refusing to pay taxes needed to fund the national army's expansion. But the disturbance collapsed just as federal cavalry arrived.

The nation's leaders increasingly acted as if a crisis were imminent. Vice President Jefferson hinted that events might push the southern states into secession from the Union, while President Adams hid guns in his home. After passing through Richmond and learning that state officials were purchasing thousands of muskets for the militia, an alarmed Supreme Court justice wrote in January 1799 that "the General Assembly of Virginia are pursuing steps which will lead directly to civil war." A tense atmosphere hung over the Republic as the election of 1800 neared.

### The Election of 1800

In the election the Republicans rallied around Jefferson for president and the wily New York politician Aaron Burr for vice president. The Federalists meanwhile became mired in wrangling between Adams and the more extreme "High Federalists" who looked to Alexander Hamilton for guidance. That the nation survived the election of 1800 without a civil war or the disregard of voters' wishes owed much to the good sense of the more moderate leaders of both parties. Thus Jefferson and Madison discouraged radical activity that might provoke intervention by the national army, while Adams rejected High Federalist demands that he ensure victory by deliberately sparking an insurrection or asking Congress to declare war on France.

"Nothing but an open war can save us," argued one High Federalist cabinet officer. But when Adams suddenly discovered the French willing to seek peace in 1799, he proposed a special diplomatic mission. "Surprise, indignation, grief & disgust followed each other in quick succession," said a Federalist senator on hearing the news. Adams obtained Senate approval for his envoys only by threatening to resign and so make Jefferson president. Outraged High Federalists tried unsuccessfully to dump Adams, but this ill-considered maneuver rallied most New Englanders around their stubborn, upright president.

Adams's negotiations with France did not achieve a settlement until 1801, but the expectation that normal—and perhaps friendly—relations with the French would resume prevented the Federalists from exploiting charges of Republican sympathy for the enemy. Without the immediate threat of war, moreover, voters grew resentful that in merely two years, taxes had soared 33 percent to support an army that had done nothing except chase terrified Pennsylvania farmers. As the danger of war receded, voters gave the Federalists less credit for standing up to France and more blame for ballooning the national debt by $10 million.

Two years after their triumph in the 1798 elections, support for the Federalists had eroded sharply. High Federalists who had hoped for war spitefully withheld the backing that Adams needed to win. The Republicans meanwhile redoubled their efforts to elect Jefferson. They were especially successful in mobilizing voters in Philadelphia and New York, where artisans, farmers, and some entrepreneurs were ready to forsake the Federalists, whom they saw as defenders of entrenched privilege and upstart wealth. As a result, popular interest in politics rose sharply. Voter turnouts in 1800 leaped to more than double those of 1788, rising from about 15 percent to almost 40 percent, and in hotly contested Pennsylvania and New York more than half the eligible voters participated.

Playing on their opponent's reputation as a religious free thinker, the Federalists forged a case against Jefferson that came down to urging citizens to vote for "GOD—AND A RELIGIOUS PRESIDENT; or impiously declare for JEFFERSON—AND NO GOD!!!" The ploy did not prevent thousands of deeply religious Baptists, Methodists, and other dissenters from voting Republican. (The Federalists overlooked the fact that Adams was scarcely more conventional in his religious views than Jefferson.)

Adams lost the presidency by just 8 electoral votes out of 138. He would have won if his party had not lost control of New York's state senate, which chose the electors, after a narrow defeat in New York City. Unexpectedly, Jefferson and his running mate Burr also carried South Carolina because their backers made lavish promises of political favors to that state's legislators.

Although Adams lost, Jefferson's election was not assured. Because all 73 Republican electors voted for both their party's nominees, the electoral college deadlocked in a Jefferson-Burr tie.* The choice of president devolved upon the House of Representatives, where thirty-five ballots over six days produced no result. Finally, Delaware's only representative, a Federalist, abandoned Burr and gave Jefferson the presidency by history's narrowest margin.

# Economic and Social Change

The growing partisanship of American politics mirrored the growing complexity of American society after independence. Three principal components contributed to this complexity: first, the shift away from small-scale, largely subsistence farming by substantial numbers of northeasterners; second, the migration westward of thousands of white Americans and black slaves, and the consequent pressures on Native Americans' lands; and third, the renewal of slavery as a viable economic system. Together these trends triggered a sharpening of conflicts between economic interests, social classes, and regions that was frequently manifested in party politics. But the changes also led to a hardening of the lines separating Americans by race. And because racial divisions worked primarily to the disadvantage of people excluded from the electorate, they were ignored in partisan discourse.

### *The Household Economy*

For centuries the backbone of European societies and their colonial offshoots had been an economy in which most production took place in household settings. At the core of each household was a patriarchal family—the male head, his wife, and their unmarried children. Beyond these family members, most households included other people. Some outsiders were relatives but most were either boarders or workers—apprentices and journeymen in artisan shops, servants and slaves in well-off households, and slaves, "hired hands," and tenant farmers in rural settings. (Even slaves who dwelled

in separate "quarters" on large plantations labored in an enterprise centered on their owners' household.) Unlike in our modern world, nearly everyone before the nineteenth century worked at what was temporarily or permanently "home." The notion of "going to work" would have struck them as odd.

Although households varied in size and economic orientation, the vast majority until the late eighteenth century were those of small farms with few or no members beyond the owner and his family. Such farm families typically included four or five children who contributed to production while requiring no outlays of cash. While husbands and older sons worked in fields at some distance from the house, women, daughters, and small children maintained the barns and gardens near the house and provided food and clothing for all family members. Women, of course, bore and reared all the children as well. As in the colonial period (see Chapter 4), most farm families produced foods and other products largely for their own consumption, adding small surpluses for bartering with neighbors or local merchants. Such families handled relatively little cash.

In the aftermath of the American Revolution, households in the more heavily settled regions of the Northeast, especially New England, began to change. Small plots of land on New England's thin, rocky soil no longer sufficed to support large families, leading young people to look beyond their immediate locales for means of support. While many young men and young couples moved west, unmarried daughters more frequently remained at home where they could help satisfy a growing demand for manufactured cloth. Before the Revolution, affluent colonists had imported cloth as well as finished clothing, but the boycott of British goods led many women to either spin their own or purchase it from other women. After the Revolution, enterprising merchants began catering to urban consumers as well as southern slaveowners seeking to clothe their slaves as cheaply as possible. Making regular circuits through rural areas, the merchants supplied cloth to mothers and daughters in farm households. A few weeks later they would return and pay the women in cash for their handiwork. A comparable transition began in some households of artisans. The shoemakers of Lynn, Massachusetts, had expanded their production during the Revolution when filling orders from the Continental Army. After the war, some more successful artisans began supplying

---

* The Twelfth Amendment (ratified in 1804) eliminated the possibility of such problems. It stipulated that electors vote for presidential and vice-presidential candidates as a pair; no longer would the runner-up in the presidential contest become vice president.

leather to other shoemakers and then paying them for the finished product. By 1800 these merchants were taking leather to farm families beyond Lynn in order to fill an annual demand that had risen from 189,000 pairs in 1789 to 400,000. Numerous other enterprises likewise emerged, employing men as well as women to satisfy demands that self-contained households could never have met on their own. For example, a traveler passing through Middleborough, Massachusetts, observed,

> In the winter season, the inhabitants . . . are principally employed in making nails, of which they send large quantities to market. This business is a profitable addition to their husbandry; and fills up a part of the year, in which, otherwise, many of them would find little employment.

In these enterprises lay the seeds of America's later industrialization.

Behind the new industries was an ambitious, aggressive class of businessmen. Most of these individuals had begun as merchants, and they now used their profits to invest in factories, ships, government bonds, and banks (see A Place in Time). Supporters of Hamilton's economic policies, they believed that the United States would gain strength if Americans balanced agriculture with banking, manufacturing, and commerce, and they wanted to limit American dependence on imported British manufactures. They also insisted that the nation needed a healthy merchant marine standing ready to augment U.S. naval forces in wartime.

Such entrepreneurs stimulated a flurry of innovative business ventures that pointed toward the future. The country's first private banks were founded in the 1780s in Philadelphia, Boston, and New York. Philadelphia merchants created the Pennsylvania Society for the Encouragement of Manufactures and the Useful Arts in 1787. This organization promoted the immigration of English artisans familiar with the latest industrial technology, including Samuel Slater (see Chapter 9), a pioneer of American industrialization who helped establish a cotton-spinning mill at Pawtucket, Rhode Island, in 1793. In 1791 investors from New York and Philadelphia started the Society for the Encouragement of Useful Manufactures, which attempted to demonstrate the potential of large-scale industrial enterprises by building a factory town at Paterson, New Jersey. That same year, New York merchants and insurance underwriters organized America's first formal association

for trading government bonds, out of which the New York Stock Exchange evolved.

## Indians in the New Republic

By 1795 Native Americans who had come under the authority of the United States had suffered severe reductions in population and territory. Innumerable deaths had resulted from battle, famine, exposure to the elements during flight from enemies, and disease. From 1775 to 1795, the Cherokees declined from 16,000 to 10,000 and the Iroquois fell from about 9,000 to 4,000. Meanwhile, in the quarter-century before 1800, Indians forfeited more land than the area inhabited by whites in 1775. Ignoring the Indian Non-Intercourse Act, the states seized Indian lands without congressional approval, crowding Native Americans onto tiny, widely separated reservations. Settlers, liquor dealers, and criminals trespassed on Indian lands, and government agents and missionaries pressured Native Americans to give up their communal lands and traditional cultures. Indians who sold land or worked for whites were often paid in the unfamiliar medium of cash and then found little to spend it on in their isolated communities except liquor.

In the face of such losses and pressures, many Indians became demoralized. Unable to strike back at

**Sauk Chief,** c. 1805
*This portrait probably depicts Wa Pawni Ha, a seventeen-year-old leader of the Sauk nation.*

## Philadelphia in the 1790s

From 1790 to 1800, Philadelphia was the United States' capital, largest city, main financial market, and intellectual and scientific center. Home to 44,000 people in 1790, by 1800 Philadelphia almost doubled its population. This growth occurred despite a series of frightful yellow-fever epidemics, which cost thousands of lives and sent wealthier residents (including President Washington and the entire federal government) fleeing each summer while the disease raged. A constant stream of country people and foreign immigrants poured in, and large numbers of African Americans, Germans, French, Irish, and Scots kept Philadelphia's population diverse.

The dynamism and diversity of Philadelphia's economy made for a society consisting of several distinct layers. The richest 10 percent of Philadelphians owned about half the city's wealth. This upper crust included old Quaker merchant families, recent wartime profiteers, and hustling new entrepreneurs. Philadelphia was still a preindustrial city entirely dependent on foreign trade for its existence, and most of its wealthiest men made their fortunes in commerce.

Philadelphia's economic environment was treacherous, however. Given rapidly changing market conditions, merchants had to be ever ready to act decisively. They repeatedly gambled everything in hopes of developing new overseas markets for Delaware Valley foodstuffs or of expanding the sphere within which they could retail European-made imports. But overseas trade was the most nerve-wracking of all Philadelphia businesses. From 1785 to 1791, bankruptcies reduced the number of trading firms from 514 to 440. Of the sixty-five wealthiest traders operating in 1779, only nine were still in business seventeen years later. The survivors were calculating, daring, and grasping.

In 1776 into this competitive commercial world came the half-blind French immigrant Stephen Girard. Relying on a quick mind and a scrappy, abrasive personality, Girard struggled for years just to avoid bankruptcy. But he exemplified the traits necessary for commercial success in Philadelphia—a determination to conduct his business personally (even when laid up with a painful head wound) and a willingness to take chances. "Since I have not as much as I desire, it seems necessary for me to take some risks or remain always poor." By 1795 he ranked high among the city's wealthiest individuals.

Girard's phenomenal success stemmed from his refusal to imitate conservative businessmen, who demonstrated a "prudence that will risk nothing." He and his fellow entrepre-

**The City or Port of Philadelphia on the River Delaware from Kensington** by William Birch, 1800
*This engraving illustrates Philadelphia's remarkable growth in little more than a century. From the large elm under which William Penn was said to have first negotiated with the Delaware Indians (see Chapter 4), it looks across the Delaware River to the busiest port in North America.*

neurs helped propel Philadelphia into the industrial age. They provided two essential elements that would transform the city's economy—capital amassed from foreign trade and a readiness to take chances by investing in manufacturing.

Amid the shifting sands of precarious commerce and embryonic industrial capitalism, the wealthier families in the 1790s helped a flourishing, cultured city continue to prosper. The well-to-do could even afford to send their daughters to the Young Ladies' Academy, founded in 1787 by Dr. Benjamin Rush. "The patriot—the hero—the legislator," Dr. Rush grandly proclaimed, "would find the sweetest reward for their toils, in the approbation of their wives"—and how better could young women bestow this approval than by being educated themselves? Among the subjects that they studied was bookkeeping.

Most Philadelphians belonged to artisan families practicing such trades as carpentry, bricklaying, tailoring, and leatherworking. These crafts supplied the city's elite with elegant imitations of the latest European styles in dress, furniture, and housing. The better endowed artisans, along with small merchants and professional men, lived fairly comfortably, if not opulently.

Such was not the case for the thousands of Philadelphians known to those in the upper and middle ranks as the "lower sort." Employed as porters, woodcutters, washer-women, dock workers, seamen, and in dozens of other occupations, the lower sort provided vital services but led lives of uncertainty. When they had work at all, it was temporary and low paying. They had higher rates of illness and death than other Philadelphians because of their poor diets and living conditions and their inability to afford smallpox immunizations. Many received relief and charity or spent time in the almshouse, workhouse, or jail. Among these unfortunates in 1790 were 1,840 African Americans, all but 301 of whom were free. (Pennsylvania had enacted gradual emancipation in 1780.) Whereas some slaves had been trained in a skilled trade such as blacksmithing, young free men of color found themselves excluded from crafts and relegated to menial work. Still, free blacks strove to improve their lot: this largest free-black community in North America maintained seven schools and three churches, all of which were segregated.

Philadelphia's bustling commerce and unequal distribution of wealth produced social strain. Journeymen printers and leatherworkers, for example, organized and struck in a vain attempt to avoid becoming permanent wage earners. Yet the so-called lower sort largely avoided politics, and the city's most notable political pressure group of the 1790s did not promote class conflict. In this organization, Philadelphia's Democratic Society, artisan masters rubbed shoulders with members of the professional elite like Dr. Rush and famed scientist David Rittenhouse—and with entrepreneur Stephen Girard. What united these republican enthusiasts were a conviction that individuals of talent and ambition ought not be held back by special interests, an admiration for revolutionary France, and a determination to preserve the liberty so hard won in the American Revolution.

**Absalom Jones,**
by Raphael Peale, 1810
*Born a slave, Jones was allowed to study and work for pay; eventually he bought his freedom. He became a businessman, a cofounder of the African Methodist Episcopal Church, and a stalwart in Philadelphia's free black community.*

**Philadelphia City Directory, 1796**
*Like other city directories of its time, Philadelphia's listed all heads of households from the most prominent to the most humble.*

> **DIRECTORY.** 593
>
> Warren Mary, school-miftrefs, Shipherds court.
> Warrington Cefar, labourer, 73, So. Fifth ft.
> Wartman Sarah, widow, boarding-houfe, 15, Branch ft.
> Warts John, fea-captain, near 19, Vernon ft.
> WASHINGTON GEORGE, PRESIDENT of the UNITED STATES, 190, High Street.
> Waftlie John, fkin-drefler, 53, So. Fifth St.
> Waterman Jeffe, fchool-mafter, 28, North alley.
> Waters Mary, widow, doctorefs, Willings alley.
> Waters Nathaniel, fcrivener, 52, Walnut ft.

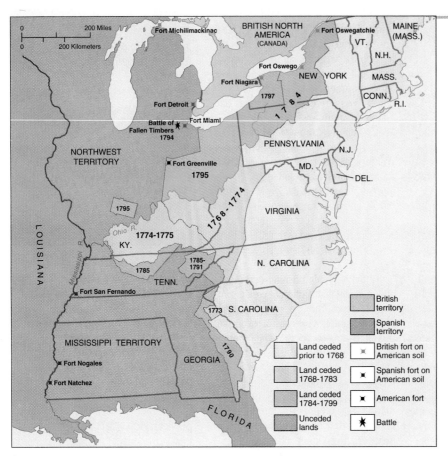

**Indian Land Cessions, 1768–1799**

*Between 1768 and 1775, western Indians sold off vast territories, mostly hunting grounds in mountainous regions. The upheavals of the Revolutionary War, followed by conflicts with U.S. military forces from 1784 to 1799, led to large cessions of inhabited Indian lands.*

whites, Indians often consumed enormous quantities of whiskey and inflicted violence on one another. All too typical were the tragedies that beset Mary Jemison, born a half-century earlier to white settlers but a Seneca since her wartime capture at age ten. Jemison saw two of her sons murdered by a third in alcohol-related instances before the third met a similar fate.

The Indians' predicament spawned a profound social and moral crisis within tribes threatened by the settlers' expansion. Among those most afflicted were the Seneca Iroquois. But beginning in 1799, a Seneca prophet, Handsome Lake, led his people in one of the most resourceful efforts to resolve this crisis. Overcoming his own problems with liquor, he sought to end alcoholism among Indians by appealing to their religious traditions. At the same time, he welcomed Quaker missionaries and federal aid earmarked for teaching Euro-American agricultural methods to Iroquois men, who had to look for new livelihoods after the loss of most of their lands and the demise of the fur trade. More traditional Indians rejected the notion that Indian men should work like white farmers; said one, only "squaws and hedgehogs are made to scratch the ground." But many Iroquois men welcomed the change. It was the women who resisted most, because they stood to lose their collective ownership of farmland, their control of the food supply, and their considerable political influence. Women who did not accept Handsome Lake's and the Quakers' urging to exchange farming for housewifery found themselves accused of witchcraft, and some were killed. As a result of such conflicts between traditional and new ways, cultural change among the Senecas and other Native Americans within the United States proceeded fitfully.

### Redefining the Color Line

The Republic's first years marked the high tide of African Americans' Revolutionary era success in bettering their lot. Although racism had not disappeared, Jefferson's eloquent words "all men are created equal" had stirred blacks' aspirations and awakened many

## Number and Percentage of Free Blacks, by State, 1800

*Within a generation of the Declaration of Independence, a large free-black population emerged that included every ninth African American. In the North, only in New Jersey and New York did most blacks remain slaves. Almost half of all free blacks lived in the South. Every sixth black in Maryland was free by 1800.*

Source: U.S. Bureau of the Census.

| State | Total Number of Free Blacks | Free Blacks as a Percentage of Total Black Population |
|---|---|---|
| Massachusetts | 7,378 | 100% |
| Vermont | 557 | 100% |
| New Hampshire | 855 | 99% |
| Rhode Island | 3,304 | 90% |
| Pennsylvania | 14,564 | 89% |
| Connecticut | 5,300 | 85% |
| Delaware | 8,268 | 57% |
| New York | 10,374 | 33% |
| New Jersey | 4,402 | 26% |
| Maryland | 19,587 | 16% |
| Virginia | 20,124 | 6% |
| North Carolina | 7,043 | 5% |
| South Carolina | 3,185 | 2% |
| Georgia | 1,019 | 2% |
| Kentucky | 741 | 2% |
| Tennessee | 309 | 2% |
| UNITED STATES | 108,395* | 11% |

* Total includes figures from the District of Columbia, Mississippi Territory, and Northwest Territory. These areas are not shown on the chart.

whites' consciences. By 1790, 8 percent of all African Americans enjoyed freedom—many having purchased liberty or earned it through wartime service. Ten years later, 11 percent controlled their own fate. Various state reforms meanwhile attempted to improve slaves' conditions. In 1791, for example, the North Carolina legislature declared that the former "distinction of criminality between the murder of a white person and one who is equally an human creature, but merely of a different complexion, is disgraceful to humanity" and authorized the execution of whites who murdered slaves. By 1794 most states had outlawed the Atlantic slave trade.

Hesitant measures to ensure free blacks' legal equality also appeared in the 1780s and early 1790s. Most states dropped restrictions on African Americans' freedom of movement and protected their property. Of the sixteen states in the Union by 1796, all but three either permitted free blacks to vote or made no specific attempt to exclude them. But by then a countertrend was reversing many of the Revolutionary era advances for free blacks. Before the 1790s ended, abolitionist

sentiment ebbed, slavery became more entrenched, and whites resisted accepting even free blacks as fellow citizens.

Federal law led the way in restricting blacks' rights. When Congress established procedures for naturalizing aliens in 1790, it limited eligibility to foreign whites. The federal militia law of 1792 required whites to enroll in local units but allowed states to exclude free blacks, an option that state governments increasingly chose. The navy and the marine corps forbade nonwhite enlistments in 1798. Delaware stripped free blacks of the vote in 1792, and by 1807 Maryland, Kentucky, and New Jersey had followed suit. Free blacks continued to vote and serve in integrated militia organizations in many localities after 1800 (including the slave states of North Carolina and Tennessee), but the number of places that treated them as the political equals of whites dropped sharply in the early 1800s.

An especially revealing indication of changing racial attitudes occurred in 1793, when Congress enacted the Fugitive Slave Law. This law required judges to award possession of a runaway slave upon any formal request by a master or his representative. Accused runaways not only were denied a jury trial but also were sometimes refused permission to present evidence of their freedom. Slaves' legal status as property disqualified them from claiming these constitutional privileges, of course, but the Fugitive Slave Law denied *free* blacks the legal protections that the Bill of Rights guaranteed them as citizens. Congress nevertheless passed this measure without serious opposition. The law marked a striking departure from the atmosphere of the 1780s, when state governments had invariably given whites and free blacks the same legal privileges. By 1793 white Americans clearly found it easy to forget that the Constitution had not limited citizenship to their race, and fewer of them felt honor-bound to protect black rights.

The bloody slave revolt on Saint Domingue notably undermined the trend toward abolition and reinforced the kind of fears that spawned racism. Reports of the slaughter of French slaveowners made white Americans more reluctant to criticize slavery in the United States and helped transform the image of blacks from that of victims of injustice to one of a potential menace. In August 1800 smoldering southern white fears were kindled when a slave insurrection broke out near Virginia's capital, Richmond. Amid the election campaign that year, in which Federalists and Republicans accused one another of endangering liberty and hinted at violence, a slave named Gabriel thought that the split among whites afforded blacks an opportunity to gain their freedom. Having secretly assembled weapons, more than a thousand slaves planned to march on Richmond. But the plot was leaked on the eve of the march. Obtaining confessions from some participants, the authorities rounded up the rest and executed some thirty-five slaves, including Gabriel. "I have nothing more to offer than what General Washington would have had to offer, had he been taken by the British officers and put to trial by them," said one rebel before his execution. "I have ventured my life in endeavoring to obtain the liberty of my countrymen, and I am a willing sacrifice to their cause."

Gabriel's Rebellion confirmed whites' anxieties that Saint Domingue's terrifying experience could be replayed on American soil. For years thereafter, isolated uprisings occurred, and rumors persisted that a massive revolt was brewing. Antislavery sentiment diminished quickly. By 1810 abolitionists ceased to exert political influence, and not until the 1830s would the antislavery movement recover from the damage inflicted by the Saint Domingue revolt.

A different kind of development also strengthened slavery. During the 1790s demand in the British textile industry stimulated the cultivation of cotton in coastal South Carolina and Georgia. The soil and climate were ideal for growing long-staple cotton, a variety whose fibers could be separated easily from its seed by squeezing it through rollers. In the South's upland and interior regions, however, the only cotton that would thrive was the short-staple variety, whose seed stuck so tenaciously to the fibers that rollers crushed the seeds and ruined the fibers. It was as if southerners had discovered gold only to find that they could not mine it. But in 1793 a Connecticut Yankee, Eli Whitney, rescued the South by inventing a cotton gin that successfully separated the fibers of short-staple cotton from the seed. Quickly copied and improved upon by others, Whitney's invention removed a major obstacle to the spread of cotton cultivation. It gave a new lease on life to plantation slavery and undermined the doubts of those who considered slavery economically outmoded.

By the time Thomas Jefferson assumed the presidency in 1801, free blacks had suffered a noticeable erosion of the political gains made since 1776, and slaves were no closer to freedom. Two vignettes poignantly communicate the plight of African Ameri-

**Doing His Duty** by Benjamin Henry Latrobe
*Despite the beginning of its abolition in the North and efforts to extend abolition to the South, slavery persisted at century's end as the foundation of society and the economy in the southern states.*

cans. By arrangement with her late husband, Martha Washington freed the family's slaves in 1800, a year after George died. But many of the freed blacks remained impoverished and dependent on the Washington estate because Virginia law prohibited the education of blacks and otherwise denied them opportunities to realize their freedom. Meanwhile, across the Potomac, work was proceeding on the new national capital that would bear the first president's name. Enslaved blacks performed most of the labor. African Americans were manifestly losing ground.

## CONCLUSION

The United States had survived the perils of birth. First George Washington had steered the country through the initial uncertain years under the new Constitution. But even before his retirement, an outbreak of bitter political strife led to the formation of distinct political parties and threatened the unity of the still fragile new nation. Then a peaceful transfer of power, unprecedented in history, occurred when the Federalists allowed Thomas Jefferson to become president.

The election of 1800 restored political stability to the American political mainstream and marked the triumph of a new understanding of republican virtue. This new understanding recognized both the potential for virtue in all independent (or potentially independent) white men and the political reality that citizens would form coalitions across regional, social, and occupational lines. But the price of this new understanding was a retreat from the limited idealism of the Revolution on matters of race and the exclusion of nonwhites from the ranks of the virtuous.

## FOR FURTHER READING

Joyce Appleby, *Capitalism and a New Social Order: The Republican Vision of the 1790s* (1984). A brief, penetrating analysis of Jeffersonian ideology.

Douglas R. Egerton, *Gabriel's Rebellion: The Virginia Slave Conspiracies of 1800 and 1802* (1993). A thorough, well-written narrative that presents slave resistance against the backdrop of post-Revolutionary society and politics.

Stanley Elkins and Eric McKitrick, *The Age of Federalism: The Early American Republic, 1788–1800* (1993). A magisterial account of politics and diplomacy through the election of 1800.

Richard Hofstadter, *The Idea of a Party System: The Rise of Legitimate Opposition in the United States, 1780–1840* (1969). A classic discussion of how and why America's founders, originally fearing political parties, came to embrace them.

Alan Taylor, *William Cooper's Town: Power and Persuasion on the Frontier of the Early American Republic* (1995). A compelling account of the fall of one elite Federalist in the face of the Republicans' rise to power.

Laurel Thatcher Ulrich, *A Midwife's Tale: The Life of Martha Ballard, Based on Her Diary, 1785–1812* (1990). A Pulitzer Prize–winning study of a woman's life in rural America.

Anthony F. C. Wallace, *The Death and Rebirth of the Seneca* (1969). A masterful narrative of the Senecas' devastation during the Revolution and their remarkable cultural recovery afterward.

# Jeffersonianism and the
# Era of Good Feelings

**Portrait of Samuel Chester Reid** by John Wesley Jarvis, 1815

On March 4, 1801, Vice President Thomas Jefferson walked from his boarding house to the Capitol to be inaugurated the nation's third president. His decision to walk rather than ride in a coach reflected his distaste for pomp and circumstance, which he thought had grown out of hand in the Washington and Adams administrations. The stroll was also practical, for the new capital, Washington, had scarcely any streets. Pennsylvania "Avenue" was no more than a path cut through swamp and woods (so dense that congressmen got lost in them) to connect the unfinished Capitol with the city's only other building of note, the president's mansion. By later standards, the government that Jefferson would head was a dwarf. There were more congressmen (138) than employees of all executive departments in the city (132, counting the president)! Officials called the place "hateful," "this abode of splendid misery," a "desert city," and the "abomination of desolation."

After arriving at the Capitol, Jefferson was sworn in by the new chief justice, John Marshall, a John Adams appointee whom Jefferson already had begun to distrust. The notable absence of the outgoing president reminded everyone of the bitterness of the 1800 election, which Federalists had interpreted as a victory for the "worthless, the dishonest, the rapacious, the vile and the ungodly" over the men of "talents, virtues, probity, peace and public services." The presence of Vice President Aaron Burr scarcely reassured Jefferson, who suspected Burr of having intrigued with Federalists in the House of Representatives to secure his own election as president.

Nevertheless, in his inaugural address, Jefferson struck a conciliatory note. The will of the majority must prevail, but the minority had "their equal rights," he assured the beaten Federalists. He then traced the political convulsions of the 1790s to differing responses to the French Revolution, an external event whose fury had passed, and he thereby suggested that the source of American discord was foreign and distant. What Americans needed to recognize was that they agreed on essentials, that "every difference of opinion is not a difference of principle," that "we are all republicans, we are all federalists."

Newspapers added capitals and printed the last clause as "we are all Republicans, we are all Federalists," but in Jefferson's manuscript the words appear generic: *republicans* and *federalists.* The distinction is critical, for Jefferson's point was not that the Federalist and Republican parties would merge or dissolve. Compared to President Adams, Jefferson would play a much more active role as leader of his party. Rather, he hoped that, since the vast majority of Americans accepted the federal union (federalism) and representative government (republicanism), they would develop a more harmonious spirit in politics.

Jefferson's expectations met with disappointment. The Federalist party began to disintegrate during his two terms and collapsed under his successors, James Madison and James Monroe, but like a wounded beast, it could still lash out. In addition, the Federalist decline opened the way to intensified factionalism within the Republican party, first during Jefferson's second term (1805–1809) and next during the misleadingly named Era of Good Feelings (1817–1824). Contrary to Jefferson's hopes, events in Europe would continue to agitate American politics, which experienced a dizzying sequence of events between 1800 and 1820. In swift succession the United States would double its land area; survive a bizarre scheme by Aaron Burr to dismember the Union; end all trade with Europe in an effort to avoid war, then go to war anyway and nearly lose; conclude a peace more favorable than it had a right to expect; and almost disintegrate in a battle over statehood for Missouri, while simultaneously extracting from European powers concessions that would extend its territorial claims from the Atlantic to the Pacific.

This chapter focuses on five major questions:

♦ How did Jefferson's philosophy of government shape his policies toward the public expenditures, the judiciary, and the Louisiana Purchase?

♦ What divisions emerged within Jefferson's Republican party during his second term?

♦ What led James Madison to abandon Jefferson's policy of "peaceable coercion" and go to war with Britain in 1812?

♦ How did the War of 1812 influence American domestic politics?

♦ How did conflict in Europe work to the advantage of the United States between 1800 and 1820?

## The Age of Jefferson

Unemotional himself, Jefferson aroused deep emotions in others. His admirers saw him as a vigilant defender of equal rights for all. His detractors, pointing to his doubts about certain Christian doctrines and his early defense of the French Revolution, portrayed him as an infidel and frenzied radical. Jefferson had so many sides that it was hard *not* to misunderstand him. Trained in law, he had spent much of his life in public service—as governor of Virginia, Washington's secretary of state, and Adams's vice president. He designed his own mansion, Monticello (see A Place in Time); studied the violin and numerous languages (including several Native American tongues); and served twenty years as president of America's oldest and most important scientific organization, the American Philosophical Society. He viewed himself as a stronger friend of equality than either Washington or Adams, but he owned scores of slaves.

History convinced Jefferson that the real threat to republics arose less from hostile neighbors than from taxes, standing armies, and public corruption, which turned governments into the masters rather than the servants of the people. France offered a case in point. He had greeted the French Revolution with hope and then watched in dismay as Napoleon Bonaparte assumed despotic power in 1799.

To prevent the United States from sinking into tyranny, Jefferson advocated that state governments retain considerable authority. He reasoned that in a vast republic marked by strong local attachments, state governments were more immediately responsive to the popular will than was the government in Washington. He also believed that popular liberty required popular

**Man of the People**
*Foreign diplomats in the United States were often shocked when Thomas Jefferson greeted them dressed in every-day working clothes and carpet slippers. But Jefferson thought of himself as a working politician and man of the people, not as an aristocratic figurehead.*

## CHRONOLOGY

**1800–1801** John Adams's "midnight" judiciary appointments.

**1801** Thomas Jefferson's inauguration.

**1802** Repeal of the Judiciary Act of 1801.
Yazoo land compromise.
American right of deposit at New Orleans revoked.

**1803** *Marbury* v. *Madison*.
Conclusion of the Louisiana Purchase.

**1804** Judge John Pickering convicted by the Senate.
Impeachment of Justice Samuel Chase.
Aaron Burr kills Alexander Hamilton in a duel.
Jefferson elected to a second term.

**1804–1806** Lewis and Clark expedition.

**1805** Start of the Burr conspiracy.
Chase acquitted by the Senate.
*Essex* case.

**1806** British government issues the first Order in Council.

**1807** Burr acquitted of treason.
*Chesapeake* Affair.
Embargo Act passed.

**1808** James Madison elected president.

**1809** Non-Intercourse Act passed; Embargo Act repealed.

**1810** Macon's Bill No. 2.

**1811** Battle of Tippecanoe.

**1812** Orders in Council revoked.
United States declares war on Britain.
Madison reelected to a second term.
General William Hull surrenders at Detroit.
USS *Constitution* defeats HMS *Guerrière*.
Battle of Queenston.

**1813** Battle of Lake Erie (Put-in-Bay).
Battle of the Thames.

**1814** Battles of Chippewa and Lundy's Lane.
Battle of Bladensburg.

**1814** British burn Washington, D.C.
Captain Thomas Macdonough's naval victory at the Battle of Plattsburgh.
Hartford Convention.
Treaty of Ghent signed.

**1815** Battle of New Orleans.

**1816** James Monroe elected president.
Second Bank of the United States chartered.

**1817** Rush-Bagot Treaty.

**1818** British-American Convention of 1818.
Andrew Jackson invades East Florida.

**1819** Adams-Onís (Transcontinental) Treaty.
*Dartmouth College* v. *Woodward*.
*McCulloch* v. *Maryland*.

**1820** Monroe reelected to a second term.

**1820–1821** Missouri Compromise.

**1823** Monroe Doctrine.

virtue. For republican theorists like Jefferson, virtue consisted of a disposition to place the public good ahead of one's private interests and to exercise vigilance to keep governments from growing out of control. To Jefferson, the most vigilant and virtuous people were educated farmers, who were accustomed to act and think with sturdy independence. The least vigilant were the inhabitants of cities. Jefferson regarded cities as breeding grounds for mobs and as menaces to liberty. When the people "get piled upon one another in large cities, as in Europe," he wrote, "they will become corrupt as in Europe."

Despite his deep philosophical beliefs, Jefferson was not impractical. Of all the charges leveled at him by contemporaries, the most inaccurate was that he was a dreamy philosopher incapable of governing. "What is practicable," he wrote, "must often control pure theory." He studied science not because he liked to ponder abstract puzzles but because he believed that every scientific advance would increase human happiness. All true knowledge was useful knowledge. This practical cast of mind revealed itself both in his inventions—he designed an improved plow and a gadget for duplicating letters—and in his presidential agenda.

## Monticello, Virginia

"Architecture is my delight," Thomas Jefferson wrote, "and putting up, and pulling down, one of my favorite amusements." In this as in other respects, he was an unsual American. Most wealthy Anglo-Americans of the eighteenth century had copied the Georgian style of English country houses, with their irregular roof lines and obtrusive chimneys. Monticello ("Little Mountain"), the house in central Virginia that Jefferson designed for his family and whose construction he oversaw between 1769 and 1809, drew its inspiration from ancient Rome and the classic revival of the eighteenth century. Although Rome had turned itself into a lavish, indulgent empire, Jefferson associated the classical style with spare simplicity and elegant balance of parts, qualities he thought appropriate to a republic.

Visitors to the mansion instantly recognized that Monticello was an extension of Jefferson, for it looked like no other house in America and gave off a shower of sparks of Jefferson's distinctive creativity. Most great houses of Virginia had been designed to appear imposing, for example by greeting the visitor with a grand staircase in the entrance hall. In contrast, Jefferson designed Monticello to look smaller than it was; it actually contains three stories but appears from the outside to contain just one. Jefferson designed a mezzanine level whose windows were cleverly placed just above the windows of the main floor, so that they appear to be merely upper sashes of the first-floor windows. In place of the grand staircase he designed an entrance hall filled with instructive objects that traced the history of civilization through maps and through displays of mammoth bones

and tusks that had been unearthed in Kentucky.

The museum-like foyer also reminded visitors of Jefferson's keen interest in the history of North America. It displayed Indian artifacts brought back by Meriwether Lewis and William Clark from their exploration of the Louisiana Purchase, including a Mandan chief's headdress, a buffalo robe, mocassins, and a bone whistle. Jefferson intended that even the mammoth bones have a patriotic purpose, for their massive size disproved the theory, advanced by French philosophers, that all species shriveled in the New World.

From the entrance hall the visitor proceeded into the other public rooms, which included a dining room and parlor, both filled with finely upholstered furniture that Jefferson had purchased while ambassador to France in the 1780s. Jefferson described his purchases

**The World of Thomas Jefferson at Monticello**

*Jefferson spent much of his adult life building and remodeling Monticello, his "simple and elegant" Virginia mansion, and he died there on July 4, 1826, fifty years to the day after the signing of the Declaration of independence.*

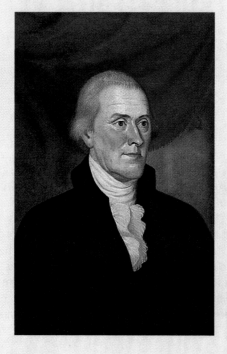

in Paris as "moderate," but eighty-seven crates of furniture, damask, paintings, and books followed him back to the United States.

Few visitors ever saw the inside of Jefferson's private apartment. Had they, they would have found more evidence of Jefferson's far-ranging interests and of his conviction that nothing was worth knowing unless it could be put to use. His study, for example, contained several gadgets, including a device for duplicating his letters. This certainly was useful, since Jefferson wrote approximately twenty thousand letters in the course of his life and kept copies of every letter he wrote after 1785. In addition, a revolving book stand, whose design he improved, enabled him to consult up to five books at once. By 1814, when he sold his library to the government (it became the nucleus of the Library of Congress), he owned seven thousand books touching on virtually every field of knowledge and written in

so many languages that one Federalist advised the government against the purchase because, aside from spreading Jefferson's "infidel" philosophy, many were in "languages which many can not read, and most ought not."

Just beyond Jefferson's private apartment lay the greenhouse, where he kept a workbench for designing and repairing everything from parlor chairs to plows, and flat boxes for experimenting with seeds. Monticello was both a mansion and a working plantation, which produced the beef, vegetables, and fruits that fed Jefferson's distinguished visitors. Recognizing that Virginia's tobacco boom was over, Jefferson was ever experimenting with new crops and farm implements. His interest in improvements should not disguise his plantation's fundamental dependence on slave labor. Jefferson believed that slavery was unwise, but he also thought that he would have to live with the institution until, somehow, it was extinguished. He occasionally freed slaves, especially skilled craftsmen whom he thought could survive on their own, but he kept most of those he acquired.

Jefferson died at Monticello on July 4, 1826, fifty years to the day after the signing of the Declaration of Indepen-

dence. By a remarkable coincidence, John Adams died in Massachusetts the same day. The eulogies to both men that resounded across the nation tactfully omitted the fact that Jefferson had died broke. A slave once said that Jefferson was rich only in his learning. Jefferson's economic ideal had been to secure the "independence" that he expected agriculture to provide to most white Americans—peace of mind and freedom from debt. In reality, his not always "moderate" expenditures, fluctuations in agricultural prices, and the ruinations of bad weather sank him ever deeper into debt. Even many of his slaves were mortgaged to his creditors. Soon after his death Jefferson's family was forced to sell the house, its possessions, and his slaves. For the rest of the century Monticello passed through the hands of a succession of private owners, none of whom could halt its gradual deterioration. A local militia company used the grounds for target practice. Finally, in 1923 a foundation purchased Monticello and commenced its restoration. Today it is a major national landmark.

### Monticello, a "Simple and Elegant" Mansion
*Preferring the useful to the showy, Jefferson omitted the grand staircase evident in other mansions, designed the house to appear smaller than it actually was, and filled it with labor-saving gadgets.*

### Thomas Jefferson's Polygraph, 1806
*Jefferson judged this "polygraph" to be the finest invention of his age. He used it to make copies of his letters from 1806 till his death.*

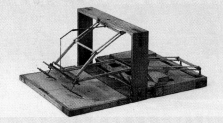

## Jefferson's "Revolution"

Jefferson described his election as a revolution, but the revolution he sought was to restore the liberty and tranquillity that (he thought) the United States had enjoyed in its early years and to reverse the drift toward despotism that he had seen in Alexander Hamilton's economic program and John Adams's Alien and Sedition Acts. One alarming sign of this drift was the growth of the national debt by $10 million under the Federalists. Jefferson and his secretary of the treasury Albert Gallatin rejected Hamilton's idea that a national debt would strengthen the government by giving creditors a stake in its health. Paying the interest alone would require taxes, which would suck money from industrious farmers, the backbone of the Republic, and put it into the hands of wealthy creditors, parasites who lived off others' misfortune. Increased tax revenues might also tempt the government to create a standing army, always a threat to liberty.

Jefferson and Gallatin induced Congress to repeal most internal taxes, and they slashed expenditures by closing some embassies overseas and reducing the army. The navy was a different matter. In 1801 Jefferson ordered a naval squadron into action in the Mediterranean against the so-called Tripolitan (or Barbary) pirates of North Africa. For centuries, the Muslim rulers of Tripoli, Morocco, Tunis, and Algiers had solved their own budgetary problems by engaging in piracy and extorting tribute in exchange for protection; seamen whom they captured were held for ransom or sold into slavery. Most European powers handed over the fees demanded, but Jefferson calculated that going to war would be cheaper than paying high tribute to maintain peace. Although suffering its share of reverses during the ensuing fighting, the United States did not come away empty-handed. In 1805 it was able to conclude a peace treaty with Tripoli for roughly half the price that it had been paying annually for protection.

Jefferson was not a pacifist and would continue to use the navy to gain respect for the American flag, but he and Gallatin placed economy ahead of military preparedness. Gallatin calculated that the nation could be freed of debt in sixteen years if administrations held the line on expenditures. In Europe, the Peace of Amiens (1802) brought a temporary halt to the hostilities between Britain and France that had threatened American shipping in the 1790s, and buoyed Jefferson's confidence that minimal military preparedness was a sound policy. The Peace of Amiens, he wrote, "removes the only danger we have to fear. We can now proceed without risks in demolishing useless structures of expense, lightening the burdens of our constituents, and fortifying the principles of free government." This may have been wishful thinking, but it rested on a sound economic calculation, for the vast territory of the United

**Explosion of the *Intrepid***
*In September 1804 the American fireship* Intrepid, *loaded with powder and intending to penetrate Tripoli harbor and explode enemy ships, blew up before reaching its target, killing Captain Richard Somers and his crew. Seven months earlier, commanded by Lieutenant Stephen Decatur, the* Intrepid *had destroyed the American frigate* Philadelphia, *which had fallen into Tripolitan hands. Britain's Lord Nelson reportedly described Decatur's exploit as "the most bold and daring act of the age."*

States could never be secured from attack without astronomical expense.

## Jefferson and the Judiciary

Jefferson had hoped to conciliate the moderate Federalists, but conflicts over the judiciary derailed this objective. When Jefferson came to office, not a single Republican sat on the federal judiciary. Still bitter about the zeal of federal courts in enforcing the Alien and Sedition Acts, Jefferson saw the Federalist-sponsored Judiciary Act of 1801 as the last straw. By reducing the number of Supreme Court justices from six to five, the act threatened to strip Jefferson of his first opportunity to appoint a justice. At the same time, the act created sixteen new federal judgeships, which outgoing president John Adams filled by last-minute "midnight" appointments of Federalists. To Jefferson, this was proof that the Federalists intended to use the judiciary as a stronghold from which "all the works of Republicanism are to be beaten down and erased." Accordingly, in 1802 he won congressional repeal of the Judiciary Act of 1801.

Jefferson's troubles with the judiciary were not over. On his last day in office, Adams appointed an obscure Federalist, William Marbury, as justice of the peace in the District of Columbia but failed to deliver Marbury's commission before midnight. When Jefferson's secretary of state, James Madison, refused to release the commission, Marbury petitioned the Supreme Court to issue a writ compelling delivery. In *Marbury* v. *Madison* (1803), Chief Justice John Marshall, an ardent Federalist and the reputed author of the Judiciary Act of 1801, ruled that, although Madison should have delivered Marbury's commission, he was under no legal obligation to do so because Congress had exceeded its constitutional authority when, in the Judiciary Act of 1789, it had granted the Court the authority to issue such a writ.

For the first time the Supreme Court had declared an act of Congress unconstitutional. Jefferson had no quarrel with the principle of judicial review (that courts had the power to declare legislative acts unconstitutional), but he was enraged that Marshall had used part of his decision to lecture Madison on his moral duty (as opposed to his legal obligation) to have delivered Marbury's commission. This gratuitous lecture—really directed at Jefferson as Madison's superior—struck Jefferson as another example of Federalist partisanship.

While the *Marbury* decision was brewing, the Republicans had already taken the offensive against the judiciary by moving to impeach (charge with wrongdoing) two Federalist judges. One, John Pickering, was an insane alcoholic; the other, Supreme Court justice Samuel Chase, was a partisan Federalist notorious for his jailing of several Republican editors under the Sedition Act of 1798. These cases raised the same issue: was impeachment, which the Constitution restricted to cases of treason, bribery, and "high Crimes and Misdemeanors," an appropriate remedy for judges who were insane or excessively partisan?

**John Marshall,**
by Chester Harding
*In his three decades as chief justice of the Supreme Court, Marshall greatly strengthened the power of both the Court and the national government, each of which he thought vital to preserving the intrinsic rights of life, liberty, and property.*

Pickering was removed from office, but the Senate narrowly failed to convict Chase, in part because moderate Republicans were coming to doubt whether impeachment was a solution to judicial partisanship.

Chase's acquittal ended Jefferson's skirmishes with the judiciary. Although his radical followers continued to attack the principles of judicial review and an appointed judiciary as undemocratic, Jefferson objected to neither. He merely challenged Federalist use of judicial power for political goals. Yet there was always a gray area between law and politics. Federalists did not necessarily see a conflict between protecting the Constitution and advancing their party's cause. Nor did they use their control of the federal judiciary to undo Jefferson's "revolution" of 1800. The Marshall court, for example, upheld the constitutionality of the repeal of the Judiciary Act of 1801. For his part, Jefferson never proposed to impeach Marshall. In supporting the impeachments of Pickering and Chase, Jefferson was trying to make the judiciary more responsive to the popular will by challenging a pair of judges whose behavior had been outrageous. No other federal judge would be impeached for more than fifty years.

## The Louisiana Purchase

Jefferson's goal of avoiding foreign entanglements would remain beyond reach as long as European powers had large landholdings in North America. In 1800 Spain, a weak and declining power, controlled East and West Florida as well as the vast Louisiana Territory. The latter alone was equal in size to the United States at that time. In the Treaty of San Ildefonso (October 1, 1800), Spain ceded the Louisiana Territory to France, which was fast emerging under Napoleon Bonaparte as the world's foremost military power. It took six months for news of the treaty to reach Jefferson and Madison but only a few minutes for them to grasp its significance.

Jefferson had long dreamed of an "empire of liberty" extending across North America and even into South America, an empire to be gained not by military conquest but by the inevitable expansion of the free and virtuous American people. An enfeebled Spain constituted no real obstacle to this expansion. As long as Louisiana had belonged to Spain, time was on the side of the United States. But Bonaparte's capacity for mischief was boundless. What if Bonaparte and the British reached an agreement that gave England a free hand in the Mediterranean and France a license to expand into North America? Then the United States would be sandwiched between the British in Canada and the French in Louisiana. What if Britain refused to cooperate with France? In that case, Britain might use its naval power to seize Louisiana before the French took control, thereby trapping the United States between British forces in the South and West as well as in the North and West.

Although Americans feared these two possibilities, Bonaparte actually had a different goal. During the 1790s he had dreamed of a French empire in the Middle East, but his defeat by the British fleet at the Battle of the Nile in 1798 had blasted this dream. Now Bonaparte devised a plan for a new French empire, this one bordering the Caribbean and the Gulf of Mexico. The fulcrum of the empire was to be the Caribbean island of Santo Domingo (modern Haiti and the Dominican Republic). He wanted to use Louisiana not as a base from which to threaten the United States but as a breadbasket for an essentially Caribbean empire. His immediate task was to subdue Santo Domingo, where a bloody slave revolution in the 1790s had resulted by 1800 in the takeover of the government by the black statesman Toussaint L'Ouverture (see Chapter 7). Bonaparte dispatched an army to reassert French control and

to reestablish slavery, but yellow fever and fierce resistance on the part of former slaves combined to destroy the army.

As a slaveholder himself, Jefferson tacitly approved Bonaparte's attempted reconquest of Santo Domingo; as a nationalist, he continued to fear a French presence in Louisiana. This fear intensified in October 1802, when the Spanish colonial administrator in New Orleans issued an order prohibiting the deposit of American produce in New Orleans for transshipment to foreign lands. Because American farmers west of the Appalachians depended on New Orleans as a port for the cash crops that they shipped down the Mississippi River, the order was a major provocation to Americans. The order had in fact originated in Spain, but most Americans assumed that it had come from Bonaparte, who, although he now owned Louisiana, had not yet taken possession of it. An alarmed Jefferson wrote to a friend that "the day that France takes possession of N. Orleans . . . we must marry ourselves to the British fleet and nation."

The combination of France's failure to subdue Santo Domingo and the termination of American rights to deposit produce in New Orleans stimulated two crucial decisions, one by Jefferson and the other by Bonaparte, that ultimately resulted in the United States' purchase of Louisiana. First, Jefferson nominated James Monroe and Robert R. Livingston to negotiate with France for the purchase of New Orleans and as much of the Floridas as possible. (Because West Florida had repeatedly changed hands between France, Britain, and Spain, no one was sure who owned it.) Meanwhile, Bonaparte, mindful of his military failure in Santo Domingo and of American opposition to French control of Louisiana, had concluded that his projected Caribbean empire was not worth the cost. In addition, he planned to recommence the war in Europe and needed cash. So he decided to sell *all* of Louisiana. After some haggling between the American commissioners and Bonaparte's minister, Talleyrand, a price of $15 million was settled upon. (One-fourth of the total represented an agreement by the United States to pay French debts owed to American citizens.) For this sum the United States gained an immense, uncharted territory west of the Mississippi River. No one knew its exact size; Talleyrand merely observed that the bargain was noble. But the purchase virtually doubled the area of the United States at a cost, omitting interest, of 13½¢ an acre.

Because Jefferson's commissioners had exceeded their instructions, however, the president had doubts

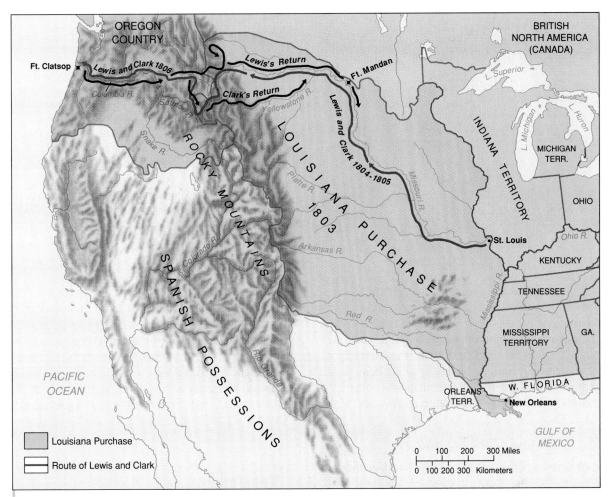

**The Louisiana Purchase and the Exploration of the West**
*The explorations of Lewis and Clark demonstrated the vast extent of the area purchased from France.*

about the constitutionality of the purchase. No provision of the Constitution explicitly gave the government authority to acquire new territory or to incorporate it into the Union. Jefferson therefore drafted a constitutional amendment that authorized the acquisition of territory and prohibited the American settlement of Louisiana for an indefinite period. Fearing that an immediate and headlong rush to settle the area would lead to the destruction of the Native Americans and to an orgy of land speculation, Jefferson wanted to control development so that Americans could advance "compactly as we multiply." Few Republicans, however, shared Jefferson's constitutional reservations, and the president himself soon began to worry that ratification of an amendment would take too long and that Bona-

parte might in the meantime change his mind about selling Louisiana. Consequently, he quietly dropped the amendment and submitted the treaty to the Senate, where it was quickly ratified.

It is easy to make too much of Jefferson's dilemma over Louisiana. He was wedded to strict construction of the Constitution, believing that the Constitution should be interpreted according to its letter. But he was also committed to the principle of establishing an "empire of liberty." Doubling the size of the Republic would guarantee land for American farmers, the backbone of the nation and the true guardians of liberty. Like the principle of states' rights to which Jefferson also subscribed, strict construction was not an end in itself but a means to promote republican liberty. If that end could

**William Clark and Meriwether Lewis,** by Charles Willson Peale
*Clark, the brother of the famed Indian fighter George Rogers Clark, fought at the Battle of Fallen Timbers. He later became the governor of Missouri and an outspoken advocate of the interests of the Native Americans, whom he had opposed in his youth. Lewis grew up near Jefferson's Virginia home and later served as his personal secretary.*

be achieved by some way other than strict construction, so be it. In addition, Jefferson was alert to practical considerations. Most Federalists opposed the Louisiana Purchase on the grounds that it would decrease the relative importance of their strongholds on the eastern seaboard. As the leader of the Republican party, Jefferson saw no reason to hand the Federalists an issue by dallying over ratification of the treaty.

### The Lewis and Clark Expedition

Louisiana dazzled Jefferson's imagination. Here was an immense territory about which Americans knew virtually nothing. No one was sure of its western boundary. A case could be made for the Pacific Ocean, but Jefferson was content to claim that Louisiana extended at least to the mountains west of the Mississippi. No one, however, was certain of the exact location of these mountains because few Americans had ever seen them. Jefferson himself had never been more than fifty miles west of his home in Virginia. Thus the Louisiana Purchase was both a bargain and a surprise package.

Even before the acquisition of Louisiana, Jefferson had planned an exploratory expedition; picked its leader, his personal secretary and fellow Virginian Lieutenant Meriwether Lewis; and sent him to Philadelphia for a crash course in sciences such as zoology, astronomy, and botany that were relevant to exploration. Jefferson instructed Lewis to trace the Missouri River to its source, cross the western highlands, and follow the best water route to the Pacific. In requesting congressional funding for the expedition, Jefferson stressed its commercial possibilities; along the line of the Missouri

and beyond, the Indians' trade in pelts might be diverted from Canada to the south. But the advance of scientific knowledge probably had a higher priority for Jefferson. His specific instructions to Lewis focused on the need to obtain accurate measurements of latitude and longitude; to gather information about Native American languages and customs; and to learn about climate, plants, birds, reptiles, insects, and volcanoes.

**Plains Pipe Bowl**
*Instructed by Jefferson to acquaint themselves with the Indians' "ordinary occupations in the arts," Lewis and Clark collected this Lakota sacred pipe, whose red stone symbolized the flesh and blood of all people and whose smoke represented the breath that carries prayers to the Creator. Considering pipes sacred objects, Indians used them to seal contracts and treaties and to perform ceremonial healing.*

Setting forth from St. Louis in May 1804, Lewis, his second-in-command William Clark, and about fifty others followed the Missouri River and then the Snake and Columbia Rivers. In the Dakota country, Lewis and Clark hired a French-Canadian fur trader, Toussaint Charbonneau, as a guide and interpreter. Slow-witted and inclined to panic in crises, Charbonneau proved a mixed blessing, but his wife, Sacajawea, who accompanied him on the trip, made up for his failings. A Shoshone and probably no more than sixteen years old in 1804, Sacajawea had been stolen by a rival tribe and then claimed by Charbonneau, perhaps in settlement for a gambling debt. When first encountered by Lewis and Clark, she had just given birth to a son; indeed, her infant's presence helped to reassure Native American tribes of the expedition's peaceful intent. Additionally, Sacajawea showed Lewis and Clark how to forage for wild artichokes and other plants, often their only food, by digging into the dens where rodents stored them. Clutching her baby, she rescued most of the expedition's scientific instruments after a storm capsized one of its boats on the Missouri River.

The group finally reached the Pacific Ocean in November 1805 and then returned to St. Louis, but not before collecting a mass of scientific information, including the disturbing fact that more than three hundred miles of mountains separated the Missouri from the Columbia. It also produced a sprinkling of tall tales, many of which Jefferson believed, about gigantic Indians, soil too rich to grow trees, and a mountain composed of salt. Jefferson's political opponents railed that he would soon be reporting the discovery of a molasses-filled lake. For all the ridicule, the expedition stimulated rather than dampened interest in the West.

### The Election of 1804

Jefferson's acquisition of Louisiana left the Federalists dispirited and without a popular national issue. As the election of 1804 approached, the main threat to Jefferson was not the Federalist party but his own vice president, Aaron Burr. In 1800 Burr had tried to take advantage of a tie in the electoral college to gain the presidency, a betrayal in the eyes of most Republicans, who assumed that he had been nominated for the vice presidency. Although the adoption in 1804 of the Twelfth Amendment, which required separate and distinct ballots in the electoral college for the presidency and vice presidency, put an end to the possibility of an electoral tie for the chief executive, it did not put an end to Burr.

### The Election of 1804

| Candidates | Parties | Electoral Vote |
|---|---|---|
| THOMAS JEFFERSON | Democratic-Republican | 162 |
| Charles C. Pinckney | Federalist | 14 |

Between 1801 and 1804, Burr entered into enough intrigues with the Federalists to convince the Republicans that it would be unsafe to renominate him for the vice presidency. The Republicans in Congress rudely dumped Burr in favor of George Clinton. Without a hope of success, the Federalists nominated Charles C. Pinckney and Rufus King and then watched their candidates go down in complete and crushing defeat in the election. The Federalists carried only two states, failing to hold even Massachusetts. Jefferson's overwhelming victory brought his first term to a fitting close; between 1801 and 1804, the United States had doubled its territory, taken steps to pay off its debt, and remained at peace. In short, Jefferson basked in the sun of success.

## The Gathering Storm

The sky was not cloudless for long. In gaining control of Louisiana, the United States had benefited from the preoccupation of European powers with their own struggles. But between 1803 and 1814, the renewal of the Napoleonic Wars in Europe turned the United States into a pawn in a chess game played by others and helped to make Jefferson's second term far less successful than his first. In fact, the very success of his first administration contained the germs of problems that would plague his second term. As long as the two parties could compete on a more or less even basis, as in the election of 1800, leaders within each party could demand unity as a prerequisite for victory. But as the Federalist opposition weakened, unity among Republicans became less important, and they increasingly fell victim to internal squabbles.

### Jefferson's Coalition Fragments

For the moment, the election of 1804 eliminated the Federalists as a force in national politics. More troubling to Republicans than Federalist opposition was factionalism within their own party, much of it the product of the inventive and perverse mind of Aaron Burr. Burr suffered a string of reverses in 1804. After being denied renomination as vice president, he entered into a series of intrigues with a faction of despairing and extreme (or "High") Federalists in New England. Led by Senator Timothy Pickering of Massachusetts, these High Federalists plotted to sever the Union by forming a pro-British "Northern Confederacy," composed of Nova Scotia (part of British-owned Canada), New England, New York, and even Pennsylvania. Although most Federalists disdained the plot, Pickering and others settled on Burr as their leader and helped him gain the Federalist nomination for the governorship of New York. Alexander Hamilton, who had thwarted Burr's plans for the presidency in 1800 by throwing his weight behind Jefferson, now foiled Burr a second time by allowing the publication of his "despicable opinion" of Burr. Defeated by a Republican in the election for New York's governor, Burr challenged Hamilton to a duel and mortally wounded him at Weehawken, New Jersey, on July 11, 1804.

Under indictment in two states for his murder of Hamilton, Burr, still vice president, now hatched a scheme so bold that it gained momentum initially because his political opponents seriously doubted that even Burr was capable of such treachery. He allied himself with the unsavory general James Wilkinson, the military governor of the Louisiana Territory. Wilkinson had been on Spain's payroll intermittently as a secret agent since the 1780s. Together, Burr and Wilkinson conspired to separate the western states into an independent confederacy south of the Ohio River. In addition, Wilkinson had long entertained the idea of an American conquest of Mexico, and Burr now added West Florida as a possible target. They presented these ideas to westerners as having the covert support of the administration, to the British as a way to attack Spanish-owned Mexico and West Florida, and to the Spanish (removing Mexico and West Florida as targets) as a way to divide up the United States.

Jefferson, who described Burr as a crooked gun that never shot straight, let the plot germinate for more than a year before taking action. By the fall of 1806, Burr and about sixty followers had left their staging ground, an island in the upper Ohio River, and were making their way down the Ohio and Mississippi Rivers to join Wilkinson at Natchez. But Wilkinson was not there to greet Burr and his several boatloads of conspirators. Recognizing that Jefferson was now moving

against Burr and that the British were uninterested in supporting the plot, Wilkinson wrote to Jefferson to report the conspiracy and then took refuge in New Orleans, where he proclaimed himself the most loyal of the president's followers.

A few weeks later, in October 1806, Jefferson officially denounced the conspiracy. Now Burr panicked. He tried to escape to West Florida but was intercepted; brought back to Richmond, he was put on trial for treason. Chief Justice Marshall presided at the trial and charged the jury that the prosecution had to prove not merely that Burr had treasonable intentions but also that he had committed treasonable acts, a virtually impossible task inasmuch as the conspiracy had fallen apart before Burr accomplished what he had planned. Jefferson was furious, but Marshall was merely following the clear wording of the Constitution, which deliberately made treason difficult to prove. The jury returned a verdict of "not proved," which Marshall entered as "not guilty." Still under indictment for his murder of Hamilton, Burr fled to Europe, where he tried to interest Napoleon in making peace with Britain as a prelude to a proposed Anglo-French invasion of the United States and Mexico. He returned to the United States in 1812 and, in keeping with his reputation as a womanizer, fathered two illegitimate children in his seventies and was divorced for adultery at eighty. Perhaps the most puzzling man in American history, he died in 1836.

### Jefferson and the Quids

Besides the Burr conspiracy, Jefferson faced a challenge from a group of Republicans known as the Quids,* who were led by the president's fellow Virginian John Randolph, a man of abounding eccentricities and acerbic wit. Randolph still subscribed to the "country" ideology of the 1770s, which celebrated the wisdom of farmers against rulers and warned of government's tendency to encroach on liberty. Originally, Jefferson had shared these beliefs, but he recognized them as an ideology of opposition, not power; once in office, he compromised. In contrast, Randolph remained frozen in the 1770s, denouncing every change as decline and proclaiming that he would throw all politicians to the dogs if he had less respect for dogs.

---

* Quid: a name taken from the Latin *tertium quid,* or "third thing"; roughly, a dissenter.

Not surprisingly, Randolph turned on Jefferson, most notably for backing a compromise in the Yazoo land scandal. In 1795 the Georgia legislature had sold the huge "Yazoo" tract (35 million acres comprising most of present-day Alabama and Mississippi) for a fraction of its value to land companies that had bribed virtually the entire legislature. The next legislature canceled the sale, but many investors, knowing nothing of the bribery, had already bought land in good faith. The scandal posed a moral challenge to Jefferson because of these good-faith purchases and a political dilemma as well, for some purchasers were northerners whom Jefferson hoped to woo to the Republican party. In 1803 a federal commission compromised with an award of 5 million acres to Yazoo investors. For Randolph, the compromise was itself a scandal—further evidence of the decay of republican virtue.

## The Suppression of American Trade

Burr's acquittal and Randolph's taunts shattered the aura of invincibility that had surrounded Jefferson in the wake of the Louisiana Purchase and the election of 1804. In 1803 the Peace of Amiens collapsed. As Britain and France resumed their war, the United States prospered at Britain's expense by carrying sugar and coffee from the French and Spanish Caribbean colonies to Europe. This trade not only provided Napoleon with supplies but also drove down the price of sugar and coffee from the British colonies by adding to the glut of these commodities on the world market. Understandably, the British concluded that American prosperity was the cause of Britain's economic difficulties.

America's boom was being fueled by the reexport trade. According to the British Rule of 1756, any trade closed in peacetime could not be reopened during war. For example, France usually restricted the sugar trade to French ships during peacetime and thus could not open it to American ships during war. The American response to the Rule of 1756 was the "broken voyage" by which American vessels would carry sugar from the French West Indies to American ports, unload it, pass it through customs, and then reexport it as *American* produce. Britain tolerated this dodge for nearly a decade but in 1805 initiated a policy of total war toward France, including the strangulation of French trade. In the *Essex* case (1805), a British court declared the broken voyage illegal.

The British followed the *Essex* decision in May 1806 with the first of several trade regulations known as Orders in Council, which established a blockade of French-controlled ports on the continent of Europe. Napoleon responded with his so-called Continental System, a series of counterproclamations that ships obeying British regulations would be subject to seizure by France. In effect, this Anglo-French war of decrees outlawed virtually all U.S. trade: if an American ship complied with British regulations, it became a French target, and vice versa.

Both Britain and France seized American ships, but British seizures were far more humiliating to Americans. France was a weaker naval power than Britain; much of the French fleet had been destroyed by the British at the Battle of Trafalgar in October 1805. Accordingly, most of France's seizures of American ships occurred in European ports where American ships had been lured by Napoleon's often inconsistent enforcement of his Continental System. In contrast, British warships hovered just beyond the American coast. Off New York, for example, the Royal Navy stopped and searched virtually every American vessel. At times, U.S. ships had to line up a few miles from the American coast to be searched by the Royal Navy.

## Impressment

To these provocations the British added impressment. At issue was Britain's seizing purported Royal Navy deserters from American merchant ships and forcing them back into service. British sailors had good reason to be discontented with their navy. Discipline on the Royal Navy's "floating hells" was often brutal and the pay low; sailors on American ships made up to five times more than those on British ships. Consequently, at a time when war intensified Britain's need for sailors, the Royal Navy suffered a high rate of desertion to American ships. In 1807, for example, 149 of the 419 sailors on the American frigate *Constitution* were British subjects.

Impressed sailors led harrowing lives that included frequent escapes and recaptures. One seaman suffered impressment eleven times. Another, facing his third recapture, drowned himself rather than spend another day in the Royal Navy. Impressment was, moreover, galling to American pride. Many deserters who had become American citizens were impressed anyway on the principle that once a Briton, always a Briton. The

British also impressed U.S.–born seamen, including those who could prove their American birth. Between 1803 and 1812 six thousand Americans were impressed. Although impressment did less damage to the American economy than the seizure of ships, it was more offensive.

Any doubts Americans had about British arrogance evaporated in June 1807 when a British warship, HMS *Leopard,* patrolling off Hampton Roads, Virginia, attacked an unsuspecting American frigate, USS *Chesapeake,* and forced it to surrender. The British then boarded the vessel and seized four supposed deserters. One, a genuine deserter, was later hanged; the other three were former Britons, now American citizens, who had "deserted" only from impressment. Even the British had never before asserted their right to seize deserters off government ships. The so-called *Chesapeake* Affair enraged the country. Jefferson remarked that he had not seen so belligerent a spirit in America since 1775. Yet while making some preparations for war, the president sought peace—first by conducting fruitless negotiations with Britain to gain redress for the *Chesapeake* outrage, and second by steering the Embargo Act through Congress in December 1807.

### The Embargo Act

By far the most controversial legislation of either of Jefferson's administrations, the Embargo Act prohibited vessels from leaving American ports for foreign ports. Technically, it prohibited only exports, but its practical effect was to stop imports as well, for few foreign ships would venture into American ports if they had to leave without cargo. Amazed by the boldness of the act, a British newspaper described the embargo as "little short of an absolute secession from the rest of the civilized world."

Jefferson advocated the embargo as a means of "peaceable coercion." By restricting French and British (especially British) trade with the United States, he hoped to pressure both nations into respecting American neutrality. But the embargo did not have the effect that Jefferson intended. Although British sales to the United States dropped 50 percent between 1807 and 1808, the British quickly found new markets in South America, where rebellions against Spanish rule had flared up, and in Spain itself, where a revolt against Napoleon had opened trade to British shipping. Furthermore, the Embargo Act itself contained some loopholes. For example, it allowed American ships blown off course to put in at European ports if necessary; suddenly, many captains were reporting that adverse winds had forced them across the Atlantic. Treating the embargo as a joke, Napoleon seized whatever American ships he could lay hands on and then informed the United States that he was only helping to enforce the embargo. The British were less amused, but the embargo confirmed their view that Jefferson was an ineffectual philosopher, an impotent challenger compared with Napoleon.

The harshest effects of the embargo were felt not in Europe but in the United States. Some thirty thousand American seamen found themselves out of work. Merchants stumbled into bankruptcy by the hundreds, and jails swelled with debtors. A New York City newspaper ruefully noted that the only activity still flourishing in the city was prosecution for debt. Farmers, too, were devastated. Unable to export their produce or sell it at a decent price to hard-pressed urban dwellers, many farmers could not earn enough cash to pay their debts. In desperation, one farmer in Schoharie County, New York, sold his cattle, horses, and farm implements,

#### The Brig *Reaper,* 1809
*Although damaged by the Embargo, shipbuilding was among the principal industries of New England. Here the hull of the brig* Reaper *is readied for launch in Medford, Massachusetts. Shipwrights spead tallow on the launching way so that the ship could slide into the water. The small box on the left was used to steam oak panels to make them pliable for installation.*

worth eight hundred dollars before the embargo, for fifty-five dollars. Speculators who had purchased land expecting to sell it later at a higher price also took a beating because cash-starved farmers stopped buying land. "I live and that is all," wrote one New York speculator. "I am doing no business, cannot sell anybody property, nor collect any money."

The embargo fell hardest on New England and particularly on Massachusetts, which in 1807 had twice the ship tonnage per capita of any other state and more than a third of the entire nation's ship tonnage in foreign trade. For a state so dependent on foreign trade, the embargo was a calamity. Wits reversed the letters of *embargo* to form the phrase "O grab me."

The picture was not entirely bleak. The embargo forced a diversion of merchants' capital into manufacturing. In short, unable to export produce, Americans began to make products. Before 1808 the United States had only fifteen mills for fashioning cotton into textiles; by the end of 1809, an additional eighty-seven mills had been constructed. But none of this comforted merchants already ruined or mariners driven to soup kitchens. Nor could New Englanders forget that the source of their misery was a policy initiated by one of the "Virginia lordlings," "Mad Tom" Jefferson, who knew little about New England and who had a dogmatic loathing of cities, the very foundations of New England's prosperity. A Massachusetts poet wrote,

> Our ships all in motion once whitened the ocean,
> They sailed and returned with a cargo;
> Now doomed to decay they have fallen a prey
> To Jefferson, worms, and embargo.

## The Election of 1808

Even before the Embargo Act, Jefferson had announced that he would not be a candidate for reelection. With his blessing, the Republican congressional caucus nominated James Madison and George Clinton for the presidency and vice presidency, whereas the Federalists countered with Charles C. Pinckney and Rufus King, the same ticket that had made a negligible showing in 1804. In 1808 the Federalists staged a modest comeback, gaining twenty-four congressional seats. Still, Madison won 122 of 175 electoral votes for president, and the Republicans retained comfortable majorities in both houses of Congress.

The Federalist revival, modest as it was, rested on two factors. First, the Embargo Act gave the party the national issue it long had lacked. Second, younger Fed-

### The Election of 1808

| Candidates | Parties | Electoral Vote |
|---|---|---|
| JAMES MADISON | Democratic-Republican | 122 |
| Charles C. Pinckney | Federalist | 47 |
| George Clinton | Democratic-Republican | 6 |

eralists had abandoned their elders' "gentlemanly" disdain for campaigning and deliberately imitated vote-winning techniques such as barbecues and mass meetings that had worked for the Republicans.

## *The Failure of Peaceable Coercion*

To some contemporaries, the diminutive "Little Jemmy" Madison (he was only five feet, four inches tall) seemed a weak and shadowy figure alongside the commanding presence of Jefferson. But in fact, Madison brought to the presidency an intelligence and a capacity for systematic thought that matched Jefferson's. Like Jefferson, Madison believed that American liberty had to rest on the virtue of the people and that that virtue was critically tied to the growth and prosperity of agriculture. More clearly than Jefferson, Madison also recognized that agricultural prosperity depended on the vitality of American trade, for Americans would continue to enter farming only if they could get their crops to market. In particular, the British West Indies, dependent on the United States for much of their lumber and grain, struck Madison as a natural trading partner for the United States. Britain alone could not fully supply the West Indies. Therefore, if the United States embargoed its own trade with the West Indies, Madison reasoned, the British would be forced to their knees before Americans could suffer severe losses from the embargo. Britain, he wrote, was "more vulnerable in her commerce than in her armies."

The American embargo, however, was coercing no one. Increased trade between Canada and the West Indies made a shambles of Madison's plan to pressure Britain. On March 1, 1809, Congress replaced the Embargo Act with the weaker, face-saving Non-Intercourse Act, which opened trade to all nations except Britain and France and then authorized Congress to restore trade with those nations if they stopped violating neutral rights. But neither complied. In May 1810 Congress substituted a new measure, Macon's Bill No. 2, for the Non-Intercourse Act. This legislation opened trade with Britain and France, and then offered each a clumsy bribe: if either nation repealed its restrictions on neutral shipping, the United States would halt trade with the other.

None of these steps had the desired effect. While Jefferson and Madison lashed out at France and Britain as moral demons ("The one is a den of robbers and the other of pirates," snapped Jefferson), the belligerents saw the world as composed of a few great powers and many weak ones. When great powers went to war, there were no neutrals. Weak nations like the United States should logically seek the protection of a great power and stop babbling about moral ideals and neutral rights. Despite occasional hints to the contrary, neither Napoleon nor the British intended to accommodate the Americans.

As peaceable coercion became a fiasco, Madison came under fire from militant Republicans demanding more aggressive policies. Coming mainly from the South and West, regions where honor was a sacred word, the militants were infuriated by insults to the American flag. In addition, economic recession between 1808 and 1810 had convinced the firebrands that British policies were wrecking their regions' economies. The election of 1810 brought several young malcontents, christened "war hawks," to Congress. Led by thirty-four-year-old Henry Clay of Kentucky, who preferred war to the "putrescent pool of ignominious peace," the war hawks included John C. Calhoun of South Carolina, Richard M. Johnson of Kentucky, and William King of North Carolina, all future vice presidents. Clay was elected Speaker of the House.

### Tecumseh and the Prophet

Voicing a more emotional and pugnacious nationalism than Jefferson and Madison, the war hawks called for the expulsion of the British from Canada and the Spanish from the Floridas. Their demands merged with western settlers' fears that the British in Canada were actively recruiting the Indians to halt the march of American settlement. These fears, groundless but plausible, became intense when the Shawnee chief

**Tenskwatawa, the Prophet**
*In periods of crisis, the Native American cultures often gave rise to prophets—religious revivalists of sorts—such as Tecumseh's brother Tenskwatawa. Known to non-Indians as the Prophet, Tenskwatawa tried to revive traditional Indian values and customs such as the common ownership of land and the wearing of animal skins and furs. His religious program blended with Tecumseh's political program to unite the western tribes.*

Tecumseh and his half-brother the Prophet sought to unite several tribes in Ohio and the Indiana territory against American settlers. Demoralized by the continuing loss of Native American lands to the whites and by the ravages of Native American society by alcoholism, Tecumseh and the Prophet (himself a reformed alcoholic) tried to unify their people and revive traditional Native American virtues. Both men believed that the Indians had to purge themselves of liquor and other corrupting messengers of white civilization as part of this revival. For example, to express his rejection of the whites' ways, Tecumseh long refused to learn English.

The aspirations of these Shawnee leaders set them on a collision course with Governor William Henry Harrison of the Indiana Territory. A wily bargainer, Harrison had purchased much of central and western Indiana from the Miami and Delaware tribes in the Treaty of Fort Wayne (1809) for a paltry ten thousand dollars. After Tecumseh's Shawnees refused to sign the treaty, Harrison saw the charismatic leader as an enemy and even as a British cat's paw. Accordingly, in September 1811 Harrison led an army against a Shawnee encampment at the junction of the Wabash and Tippecanoe rivers. Two months later, when the Prophet prematurely attacked Harrison (Tecumseh was away, recruiting Creek Indians), Harrison won a decisive victory. Ironically, the Battle of Tippecanoe, which made Harrison a national hero, accomplished what it had been designed to prevent. Never before a British agent, Tecumseh now joined with the British.

### Congress Votes for War

By the spring of 1812, President Madison had reached the decision that war with Britain was inevitable. On June 1 he sent his war message to Congress. Meanwhile, an economic depression struck Britain, partly because the American policy of restricting trade with that country had finally started to work. Under pressure from its merchants, Britain repealed the Orders in Council on June 23, but by then Congress, unaware that the British were contemplating repeal of the orders, had passed the declaration of war. It was still possible, of course, for Madison to revoke the declaration now that the maritime issue had been partly settled. The British cabinet believed that he would do so. What the British failed to comprehend, however, was how much more belligerent American political leaders, particularly Republicans, had become between 1810 and 1812.

Although both war hawks and westerners had contributed to this hostile mood, neither held the key to the vote in favor of war. The war hawks comprised a minority within the Republican party; the West was still too sparsely settled to have many representatives in Congress. Rather, the votes of Republicans in populous states like Pennsylvania, Maryland, and Virginia were the main force propelling the war declaration through Congress. Most opposition to war came from Federalist strongholds in Massachusetts, Connecticut, and New York. Because Federalists were so much stronger in the Northeast than elsewhere, congressional opposition to war revealed a sectional as well as a party split. In general, however, southern Federalists opposed the war declaration, whereas northern Republicans supported it. In other words, the vote for war followed party lines more closely than sectional lines. Much like James Madison himself, the typical Republican advocate of war had not wanted war in 1810 nor even in 1811 but had been led by the accumulation of grievances to demand it in 1812.

### The Causes of the War

In his war message, Madison listed impressment, the continued presence of British ships in American waters, and British violations of neutral rights as grievances that justified war. But none of these complaints was new. Taken together, they do not fully explain why Americans went to war in 1812 rather than earlier—for example, in 1807 after the *Chesapeake* Affair. Madison also listed British incitement of the Indians as a stimulus for war. This grievance of recent origin contributed to war feeling in the West. "The War on the Wabash," a Kentucky newspaper proclaimed, "is purely British. The British scalping knife has filled many habitations both in this state as well as in the Indiana Territory with widows and orphans." But the West had too few American inhabitants to drive the nation into war. A more important underlying cause was the economic recession that affected the South and West after 1808—and the conviction, held by John C. Calhoun and others, that British policy was damaging America's economy. Finally, the fact that Madison rather than Jefferson was president in 1812 was of major importance. Jefferson had believed that the only motive behind British seizures of American ships was Britain's desire to block American trade with Napoleon. Hence Jefferson had concluded that time was on America's side; the seizures would stop as soon as the war in Europe ceased. In contrast, Madison had become persuaded that Britain's real motive was to strangle American trade once and for all and thereby eliminate the United States as a trading rival. War or no war in Europe, Madison saw Britain as a menace to America. In his war message, he stated flatly that Britain was meddling with American trade not because that trade interfered with Britain's "belligerent rights" but because it "frustrated the monopoly which she covets for her own commerce and navigation."

## The War of 1812

Maritime issues had dominated Madison's war message, but the United States lacked a navy strong enough to challenge Britain at sea. American frigates, notably the *Constitution,* would win a few sensational duels with British warships, but the Americans would prove unable to prevent the British from clamping a naval blockade on the American coast. Canada, which Madison viewed as a key prop of the British Empire, became the principal target. With their vastly larger population and resources, few Americans expected a long or difficult struggle. To Jefferson, the conquest of Canada seemed "a mere matter of marching."

**The *Constitution* Ranging Alongside the *Guerrière*** by Michael Felice Corne, 1812 *The* Constitution *won more battles than any other early American frigate. Its most famous victory was over H.M.S.* Guerrière *in August 1812. Known affectionately as Old Ironsides, it was saved from demolition in 1830 by the poet Oliver Wendell Holmes, became a schoolship for the U.S. Naval Academy, was nearly confiscated by the fledgling Confederate navy in 1861, and today survives as a naval relic in Boston harbor.*

Little justified this optimism. Although many of the best British troops were in Europe fighting Napoleon, the British in Canada had an invaluable ally in the Native Americans, who struck fear in beholders by dangling scalps from their belts. The British played on this fear, in some cases forcing Americans to surrender by hinting that the Indians might be uncontrollable in battle. Too, the American state militias were filled with Sunday soldiers who "hollered for water half the time, and whiskey the other." Few militiamen really understood the goals of the war. In fact, outside Congress there simply was not much blood lust in 1812. Opposition to the war ran strong in New England, and even in Kentucky, the home of war hawk Henry Clay, only four hundred answered the first call to arms. For many Americans, local attachments were still stronger than national ones.

### On to Canada

From the summer of 1812 to the spring of 1814, the Americans launched a series of unsuccessful attacks on Canada. In July 1812 General William Hull led an American army from Detroit into Canada, then quickly returned when Tecumseh cut his supply line, and surrendered two thousand men to thirteen hundred British and Indian troops. In the fall of 1812 a force of American regulars was crushed by the British at the Battle of Queenston, near Niagara Falls, while New York militia, contending that they had volunteered only to protect

their homes and not to invade Canada, looked on from the New York side of the border. A third American offensive of 1812, a projected attack on Montreal from Plattsburgh, New York, via Lake Champlain, fell apart when the militia again refused to advance into Canada.

The Americans renewed their offensive in 1813 when General William Henry Harrison tried to retake Detroit. A succession of reverses convinced Harrison that offensive operations were futile as long as the British controlled Lake Erie. During the winter of 1812–1813, Captain Oliver H. Perry constructed a little fleet of vessels and then destroyed a British squadron at Put-in-Bay on the western end of the lake on September 10, 1813. "We have met the enemy, and they are ours," Perry triumphantly reported. Losing control of Lake Erie, the British pulled back from Detroit, but Harrison overtook and defeated a combined British and Indian force at the Battle of the Thames on October 5. Tecumseh died in the battle; Colonel Richard Johnson's claim, never proved, to have killed Tecumseh later contributed to Johnson's election as vice president of the United States. These victories by Perry and Harrison cheered Americans, but efforts to invade Canada continued to falter.

### The British Offensive

With fresh reinforcements from Europe, where Napoleon had abdicated as emperor after his disastrous invasion of Russian, the British took the offensive

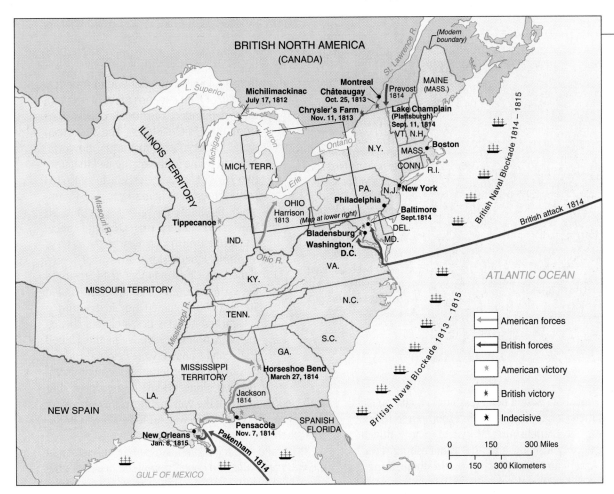

in the spring of 1814. Stiffening resistance by Americans, who now were defending their homes rather than invading Canada, dealt reverses to the attacking redcoats at the battles of Chippewa (July 5) and Lundy's Lane (July 25). Next, General Sir George Prevost led a force of ten thousand British veterans, the largest and best-equipped British force ever sent to North America, in an offensive meant to split the New England states, where opposition to the war was strong, from the rest of the country. They advanced down Lake Champlain until meeting the well-entrenched American forces at Plattsburgh. Resolving that he had to control the lake before attacking Plattsburgh, Prevost called up his fleet, but an American naval squadron under Captain Thomas Macdonough defeated their British counterparts on September 11. Dispirited, Prevost abandoned the campaign.

Ironically, the British achieved a far more spectacular success in an operation originally designed merely as a diversion from their main thrust down Lake Champlain. In 1814 a British army sailed from Bermuda for

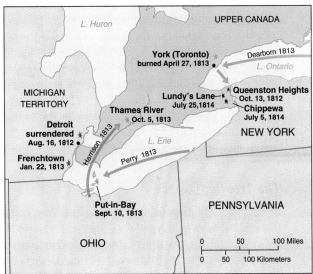

**Major Battles of the War of 1812**
*Most of the war's major engagements occurred on or near the United States' northern frontier; but the Royal Navy blockaded the entire Atlantic coast, and the British army penetrated as far south as Washington and New Orleans.*

**Dolley Madison** by Gilbert Stuart, 1804
*As the attractive young wife of Secretary of State James Madison, Dolley Madison acted virtually as the nation's First Lady during the administration of Jefferson, a widower. Friendly, tactful, and blessed with an unfailing memory for names and events, she added to her reputation as an elegant hostess after her husband became president.*

Chesapeake Bay, landed near Washington, and on August 24 met a larger American force, composed mainly of militia, at Bladensburg, Maryland. The Battle of Bladensburg quickly became the "Bladensburg races" as the American militia fled, almost without firing a shot. The British then descended on Washington. Madison, who had witnessed the Bladensburg fiasco, escaped into the Virginia hills. His wife, Dolley, pausing only long enough to load her silver, a bed, and a portrait of George Washington onto her carriage, hastened to join her husband, while British troops ate the supper prepared for the Madisons at the presidential mansion. Then they burned the mansion along with other public buildings in Washington. A few weeks later, the British attacked Baltimore, but after failing to crack its defenses, they broke off the operation.

### The Treaty of Ghent

In August 1814 negotiations to end the war commenced between British and American commissioners at Ghent, Belgium. The British appeared to command a strong position. Having frustrated American designs on Canada, they stood poised for their Lake Champlain initiative. In reality, however, their position was not as strong as it appeared and would grow weaker as negotiations progressed.

With Napoleon's abdication as emperor, Britain's primary goal had become a favorable and lasting peace in Europe; the British had little to gain from prolonging a minor war in America. Mindful of their superior military position, they demanded territorial concessions from the United States. The American naval victory at Plattsburgh, however, brought home to Britain the fact that after two years of fighting, the British controlled neither the Great Lakes nor Lake Champlain. Similarly, the spectacular raid on Washington had no strategic significance, and so the British gave way on the issue of territorial concessions. The final treaty, signed on Christmas Eve 1814, restored the status quo ante bellum*: the United States neither gained nor lost territory. Several additional issues, including the fixing of a boundary between the United States and Canada, were referred to joint commissions for future settlement. Nothing was done about impressment, but with Napoleon out of the way, neutral rights became a dead issue. Because there was no longer a war in Europe, there were no longer neutrals.

Ironically, the most dramatic American victory of the war came after the conclusion of the peace negotiations. In December 1814 a British army, composed of veterans of the Napoleonic Wars and commanded by General Sir Edward Pakenham, descended on New Orleans. On January 8, 1815, two weeks after the signing of the Treaty of Ghent but before word of the treaty had reached America, Pakenham's force attacked an American army under General Andrew ("Old Hickory") Jackson. Already a legend for his ferocity as an Indian fighter, Jackson inspired little fear among the British, who advanced into battle far too confidently, but he did strike enough terror in his own men to prevent another American rout. In an hour of gruesome carnage, Jackson's troops shredded the line of advancing redcoats, killing Pakenham and inflicting more than two thousand casualties while losing only thirteen Americans.

### The Hartford Convention

Because the Treaty of Ghent had already concluded the war, the Battle of New Orleans had little significance for

---

* Status quo ante bellum: Latin for the state of affairs before the war.

**Two Ottawa Chiefs**
*These two Ottawa chiefs proudly wear the medals bestowed on them by the British. Expecting British support for their land claims at the war's end, they instead were abandoned by the British.*

diplomats. Indirectly, however, it had an impact on domestic politics by eroding Federalist strength.

The comeback that the Federalists had made in the election of 1808 had continued into the 1812 campaign. Buoyed by hostility to the war in the Northeast, the Federalists had thrown their support behind DeWitt Clinton, an antiwar Republican. Although Madison won the electoral vote 128 to 89, Clinton carried all of New England except Vermont, as well as New York and New Jersey. American military setbacks in the war intensified Federalist disdain for the new Madison administration. Federalists saw a nation misruled for over a decade by Republican bunglers. Jefferson's attack on the judiciary had seemed to threaten the rule of law. His purchase of Louisiana, a measure of doubtful constitutionality, had enhanced Republican strength and reduced the relative importance of Federalist New England in the Union. The Embargo Act had severely damaged New England's commerce. Now "Mr. Madison's War" was bringing fresh misery to New England in the form of the British blockade. A few Federalists began to talk of New England's secession from the Union. Most, however, rejected the idea, believing that they would soon benefit from popular disfavor with the war and spring back into power.

In late 1814 a Federalist convention met in Hartford, Connecticut. Although some advocates of secession were present, moderates took control and passed a series of resolutions summarizing New England's griev-

**The Election of 1812**

| Candidates | Parties | Electoral Vote |
|---|---|---|
| JAMES MADISON | Democratic-Republican | 128 |
| DeWitt Clinton | Federalist | 89 |

**The Election of 1816**

| Candidates | Parties | Electoral Vote |
|---|---|---|
| JAMES MONROE | Democratic-Republican | 183 |
| Rufus King | Federalist | 34 |

**The Election of 1820**

| Candidates | Parties | Electoral Vote |
|---|---|---|
| JAMES MONROE | Democratic-Republican | 231 |
| John Quincy Adams | Independent Republican | 1 |

ances. At the root of these grievances lay the belief that New England was becoming a permanent minority in a nation dominated by southern Republicans who failed to understand New England's commercial interests. Accordingly, the convention proposed to amend the Constitution to abolish the three-fifths clause (which gave the South a disproportionate share of votes in Congress by allowing it to count slaves as a basis of representation), to require a two-thirds vote of Congress to declare war and to admit new states into the Union, to limit the president to a single term, to prohibit the election of two successive presidents from the same state, and to bar embargoes lasting more than sixty days. As bold as these proposals were, their timing was disastrous for the Federalists. News of the Treaty of Ghent and of Jackson's victory at New Orleans dashed the Federalists' hopes of gaining broad popular support. The goal of the Hartford Convention had been to assert states' rights rather than disunion, but to many the proceedings smelled of a traitorous plot. The restoration of peace, moreover, stripped the Federalists of the primary grievance that had fueled the convention. In the election of 1816, Republican James Monroe, Madison's hand-picked successor, swept the nation over negligible Federalist opposition. He would win reelection in 1820 with only a single dissenting electoral vote. As a force in national politics, the Federalists were finished.

# The Awakening of American Nationalism

The United States emerged from the War of 1812 bruised but intact. In its first major war since the Revolution, the American Republic had demonstrated not only that it could fight on even terms against a major power but also that republics could fight wars without turning themselves into despotisms. The war produced more than its share of symbols of American nationalism. Whitewash cleared the smoke damage to the presidential mansion; thereafter, it became known as the White House. The British attack on Fort McHenry, guarding Baltimore, prompted a young observer, Francis Scott Key, to compose "The Star-Spangled Banner." The Battle of New Orleans boosted Andrew Jackson onto the stage of national politics and became a source of legends about American military prowess. It appears to most scholars today that the British lost because Pakenham's men, advancing within range of Jackson's ri-

flemen and cannon, unaccountably paused and became sitting ducks. But in the wake of the battle, Americans spun a different tale. The legend arose that Jackson owed his victory not to Pakenham's blundering tactics but to hawk-eyed Kentucky frontiersmen whose rifles picked off the British with unerring accuracy. In fact, many frontiersmen in Jackson's army had not carried rifles; even if they had, gunpowder smoke would have obscured the enemy. But none of this mattered at the time. Just as Americans preferred militia to professional soldiers, they chose to believe that their greatest victory of the war was the handiwork of mere amateurs.

## Madison's Nationalism and the Era of Good Feelings

The War of 1812 had three major political consequences. First, it eliminated the Federalists as a national political force. Second, it went a long way toward convincing the Republicans that the nation was strong and resilient, capable of fighting a war while maintaining the liberty of its people. The third consequence was an outgrowth of the first two. With the Federalists tainted by disloyalty and with fears about the fragility of republics fading, Republicans increasingly embraced some doctrines long associated with the Federalists. In a message to Congress in December 1815, Madison called for federal support for internal improvements, tariff protection for the new industries that had sprung up during the embargo, and the creation of a new national bank. (The charter of the first Bank of the United States had expired in 1811.) In Congress another Republican, Henry Clay of Kentucky, proposed similar measures, which he called the American System, with the aim of making the young nation economically self-sufficient and free from dependency on Europe. In 1816 Congress chartered the Second Bank of the United States and enacted a moderate tariff. Federal support for internal improvements proved to be a thornier problem. Madison favored federal aid in principle but believed that a constitutional amendment was necessary to authorize it. Accordingly, he vetoed an internal-improvements bill passed in 1817.

As Republicans adopted positions that they had once disdained, an "Era of Good Feelings" dawned on American politics. A Boston newspaper, impressed by the warm reception accorded President Monroe while touring New England, coined the phrase in 1817. It has

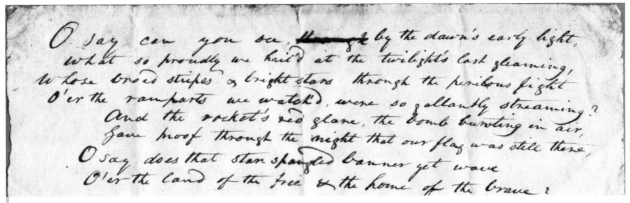

**Manuscript for "The Star-Spangled Banner"**

stuck as a description of Monroe's two administrations, from 1816 to 1824. Compared with Jefferson and Madison, Monroe was neither brilliant, polished, nor wealthy, but he keenly desired to heal the political divisions that a stronger intellect and personality might have inflamed. The phrase "Era of Good Feelings" reflects not only the war's elimination of some divisive issues but also Monroe's conscious effort to avoid political controversies. But the good feelings were paper-thin. Madison's 1817 veto of the internal-improvements bill revealed the persistence of disagreements about the role of the federal government under the Constitution. Furthermore, the embargo, the War of 1812, and the continuation of slavery had aroused sectional animosities that a journalist's phrase about good feelings could not dispel. Not surprisingly, the postwar consensus began to unravel almost as soon as Americans recognized its existence.

### John Marshall and the Supreme Court

In 1819 Jefferson's old antagonist John Marshall, still chief justice, issued two opinions that stunned Republicans. The first case, *Dartmouth College* v. *Woodward,* centered on the question of whether New Hampshire could transform a private corporation, Dartmouth College, into a state university. Marshall concluded that the college's original charter, granted to its trustees by George III in 1769, was a contract. Since the Constitution specifically forbade states to interfere with contracts, New Hampshire's effort to turn Dartmouth into a state university was unconstitutional. The implications of Marshall's ruling were far-reaching. Charters or acts

of incorporation provided their beneficiaries with various legal privileges and were sought by businesses as well as by colleges. In effect, Marshall said that once a state had chartered a college or business, it surrendered both its power to alter the charter and, in large measure, its authority to regulate the beneficiary.

A few weeks later, the chief justice handed down an even more momentous decision in the case of *McCulloch* v. *Maryland.* The issue here was whether the state of Maryland had the power to tax a national corporation, specifically the Baltimore branch of the Second Bank of the United States. The bank was a national corporation, chartered by Congress, but most of the stockholders were private citizens who reaped whatever profits the bank made. Speaking for a unanimous Court, Marshall ignored these private features of the bank and concentrated instead on two issues. First, did Congress have the power to charter a national bank? Nothing in the Constitution, Marshall conceded, explicitly granted this power. But the Constitution did authorize Congress to lay and collect taxes, to regulate interstate commerce, and to declare war. Surely these enumerated powers, he reasoned, implied a power to charter a bank. Marshall was clearly engaging in a broad, or "loose," rather than strict, construction (interpretation) of the Constitution. The second issue was whether a state could tax an agency of the federal government that lay within its borders. Marshall argued that any power of the national government, express or implied, was supreme within its sphere. States could not interfere with the exercise of federal powers. A tax by Maryland on the Baltimore branch was such an interference and hence was plainly unconstitutional.

Marshall's decision in the *McCulloch* case dismayed many Republicans. Although Madison and Monroe had supported the establishment of the Second Bank of the United States, the bank had made itself unpopular by tightening its loan policies during the summer of 1818. This contraction of credit triggered a severe depression, the Panic of 1819, that gave rise to considerable distress throughout the country, especially among western farmers. At a time when the bank was widely blamed for the panic, Marshall's ruling stirred controversy by placing the bank beyond the regulatory power of any state government. His decision, indeed, was as much an attack on state sovereignty as it was a defense of the bank. The Constitution, Marshall argued, was the creation not of state governments but of the people of *all* the states and thus was more fundamental than state laws. His reasoning assailed the Republican theory, best expressed in the Virginia and Kentucky resolutions of 1798–1799, that the Union was essentially a compact among states. Republicans had continued to view state governments as more immediately responsive to the people's will than was the federal government and to regard the compact theory of the Union as a guarantor of popular liberty. As Republicans saw it, Marshall's *McCulloch* decision, along with his decision in the *Dartmouth College* case, stripped state governments of the power to impose the will of their people upon corporations.

## The Missouri Compromise

The fragility of the Era of Good Feelings became even more apparent in the two-year-long controversy over the territory of Missouri. Early in 1819, as the House of Representatives was considering a bill to admit Missouri as a slave state, a New York Republican offered an amendment that prohibited the further introduction of slaves and provided for the emancipation, at age twenty-five, of all slave offspring born after Missouri's admission as a state. Following rancorous debate, the House accepted the amendment and the Senate rejected it. Both chambers voted along sectional lines.

Sectional divisions had long troubled American politics, but prior to 1819 slavery had never been the primary source of division. In the 1790s Republicans had worried that Alexander Hamilton's economic program favored northern commercial interests over southern agricultural ones. After 1800 Federalist opposition to the Louisiana Purchase and the War of 1812 had sprung from the fear that the now dominant Republicans were sacrificing New England's political and commercial interests to those of the South and West.

For various reasons, the Missouri question thrust slavery into the center of this long-standing sectional conflict. In 1819 the Union had eleven free and eleven slave states. The admission of Missouri as a slave state would upset this balance to the advantage of the South. Noting that every president since John Adams had been a Virginian, Federalists portrayed the admission of Missouri as part of a conspiracy to perpetuate the rule of Virginia slaveholders. Republicans countered by pointing to the relatively sudden emergence in the House of Representatives of a vocal antislavery block, which included many northern Federalists, and to the growing number of Federalist-dominated societies in the North that promoted the manumission (freeing) of slaves. In response to these developments, some Republicans began to view all efforts to restrict slavery as part of a plot by the Federalists to divide northern and southern Republicans and thus regain political power. In sum, by 1819 the slavery issue had become intertwined with the prevailing distrust between the parties and between the sections.

Virtually every issue that was to wrack the Union during the next forty years was present in the controversy over Missouri: southern charges that the North was conspiring to destroy the Union and to end slavery; accusations by northerners that southerners were conspiring to extend the institution. For a while, leaders doubted that the Union would survive the crisis. House Speaker Henry Clay wrote that the words *civil war* and *disunion* were commonly uttered, almost without emotion. But a series of congressional agreements in 1820 and 1821, known collectively as the Missouri Compromise, resolved the crisis.

The first of these agreements involved the balance between slave states and free states. At the same time that Congress was considering statehood for Missouri, Maine was seeking admission as a free state. In 1820 Congress agreed to admit Maine as a free state, to pave the way for Missouri's admission as a slave state, and to prohibit slavery in the remainder of the Louisiana Purchase territory north of 36° 30′ (the southern boundary of Missouri). But compromise did not come easily. The components of the eventual compromise passed by close and ominously sectional votes. Additionally, no sooner had the compromise been forged than it nearly

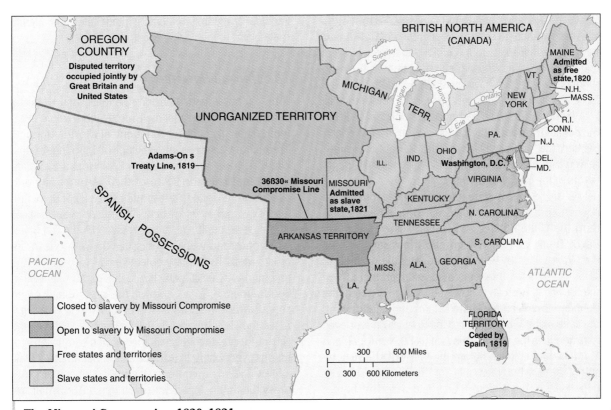

## The Missouri Compromise, 1820–1821

*The Missouri Compromise temporarily quelled controversy over slavery by admitting Maine as a free state and Missouri as a slave state, and by prohibiting slavery in the remainder of the Louisiana Purchase north of 36° 30′.*

fell apart. As a prelude to statehood, Missourians drafted a constitution that prohibited free blacks from entering their territory. This provision raised a thorny question, for some eastern states recognized free people of color as citizens, who, as such, were protected from discrimination by the federal Constitution, which clearly stated that "Citizens of each State shall be entitled to all Privileges and Immunities of Citizens in the several States." Balking at Missourians' exclusion of free blacks, antislavery northerners barred Missouri's admission into the Union until 1821, when Henry Clay engineered a new agreement. This second Missouri Compromise prohibited Missouri from discriminating against citizens of other states but left open the issue of whether free blacks were citizens.

The Missouri Compromise was widely viewed as a southern victory. The South had gained admission of Missouri, whose acceptance of slavery was controversial, while conceding to the North the admission of Maine, whose rejection of slavery inspired no controversy at all. Yet the South had conceded to freedom a vast block of territory north of 36° 30′. Although much of this territory was unorganized Indian country that some viewed as unfit for white habitation, it would not remain a wilderness for long. Also, the Missouri Compromise reinforced the principle, originally set down by the Northwest Ordinance of 1787, that Congress had the right to prohibit slavery in some territories. Southerners had implicitly accepted the argument that slaves were not like other forms of property that could be moved from place to place at will.

### Foreign Policy Under Monroe

American foreign policy between 1816 and 1824 reflected more consensus than conflict. The end of the Napoleonic Wars and the signing of the Treaty of Ghent had removed most of the foreign-policy disagreements between Federalists and Republicans. Moreover, Monroe was fortunate to have as his secretary of state an extraordinary diplomat, John Quincy Adams. An austere and scholarly man whose library equaled his house in monetary value, Adams was a tough negotiator and a fervent nationalist. Although he was the son of the last Federalist president, he had been the only Federalist in the Senate to support the Louisiana Purchase. He later backed the embargo, joined the Republican party, served as minister to Russia, and was one of the negotiators of the Treaty of Ghent.

As secretary of state, Adams moved quickly to strengthen the peace with Great Britain. During his term the United States and Britain signed the Rush-Bagot Treaty of 1817, which effectively demilitarized the Great Lakes by severely restricting the number of ships that the two powers could maintain there. Next the British-American Convention of 1818 fixed the boundary between the United States and Canada from the Lake of the Woods west to the Rockies and restored to Americans the same fishing rights off Newfoundland that they had enjoyed before the War of 1812. As a result of these two agreements, for the first time since independence, the United States had a secure border with British-controlled Canada and could turn its attention southward and westward.

Adams's dealings with the Spanish, who still owned East Florida and claimed West Florida, were also successful. It had never been clear whether the Louisiana Purchase included West Florida. Acting as if it did, the United States in 1812 had simply added a slice of West Florida to the state of Louisiana and another slice to the Mississippi Territory. In 1818 Andrew Jackson, the American military commander in the South, seizing upon the pretext that Florida was both a base for Seminole Indian raids into American soil and a refuge for fugitive slaves, invaded East Florida, hanged two British subjects, and captured Spanish forts. Jackson had acted without explicit orders, but Adams supported the raid, guessing correctly that it would panic the Spanish into further concessions. In 1819 Spain agreed to the Adams-Onís (or Transcontinental) Treaty. By its terms, Spain ceded East Florida to the United States, renounced its claims to all of West Florida, and agreed to a southern border of the United States west of the Mississippi that ran north along the Sabine River (separating Texas from Louisiana) and then westward along the Red and Arkansas Rivers to the Rocky Mountains, finally following the forty-second parallel to the

Pacific. For the first time, the United States had a legitimate claim to the Pacific coast.

## *The Monroe Doctrine*

John Quincy Adams had long believed that God and nature had ordained that the United States would eventually span the entire continent of North America. Throughout his negotiations leading up to the Adams-Onís Treaty, he made it clear to Spain that if the Spanish did not concede some of their territory in North America, the United States might seize all of it, including Texas and even Mexico. Americans were fast acquiring a reputation as an aggressive people. Yet Spain was concerned with larger issues than American encroachment. Its primary objective was to suppress the revolutions against Spanish rule that had broken out in South America. To accomplish this goal, Spain sought support from the European monarchs who had organized the Holy Alliance in 1815. The brainchild of the tsar of Russia, the Holy Alliance aimed to quash revolutions everywhere in the name of Christian principles, and by 1822 its members talked of helping Spain suppress the South American revolutions. But Britain refused to join the Holy Alliance; British foreign minister George Canning proposed that the United States and Britain issue a joint statement opposing any European interference in South America while pledging that neither would annex any part of Spain's old empire in the New World.

While sharing Canning's opposition to European intervention in the New World, Adams preferred that the United States make a declaration of policy on its own rather than "come in as a cock-boat in the wake of the British man-of-war." Specifically, Adams rejected Canning's insistence on a joint Anglo-American pledge never to annex any part of Spain's former territories, for Adams wanted to keep the United States' freedom to annex Texas or Cuba, should their inhabitants one day "solicit a union with us."

This was the background of the Monroe Doctrine, as President Monroe's message to Congress on December 2, 1823, later came to be called. The message, written largely by Adams, announced three key principles: that unless American interests were involved, the United States' policy was to abstain from European wars; that the "American continents" were not "subjects for future colonization by any European power"; and that the United States would construe any attempt at European colonization in the New World as an "unfriendly act."

Europeans widely derided the Monroe Doctrine as a mere unilateral pronouncement by the United States. Fear of the British navy, not the Monroe Doctrine, prevented the Holy Alliance from intervening in South America. With hindsight, however, the Europeans would have taken the doctrine more seriously, for it had important implications. First, by pledging itself not to interfere in European wars, the United States was excluding the possibility that it would support revolutionary movements in Europe. For example, Adams opposed the United States' recognition of Greek patriots, who were then fighting against Turkish domination. Second, by keeping open its options to annex territory in the Americas, the United States was using the Monroe Doctrine to claim a preeminent position in the New World.

### CONCLUSION

The election of 1800 brought the Republicans from opposition to power. Seeking to make the federal government more responsive to the people's will, Jefferson moved quickly to slash public expenditures and to contest Federalist control of the judiciary. His purchase of the Louisiana territory in 1803 would bring new states, dominated by Republicans, into the Union. As the Federalist party waned, Jefferson had to face down challenges from within his own party, notably from the mischief of Aaron Burr and from die-hard old Republicans like John Randolph, who charged that Jefferson was abandoning pure Republican doctrines.

The outbreak of war between Napoleon's France and Britain and the threat each posed to American neutrality preoccupied Jefferson's second term and both

terms of his successor James Madison. The failure of the embargo and "peaceable coercion" to force Europeans to respect American neutrality led the United States into war with Britain in 1812. The war destroyed the Federalists, who committed political suicide at the Hartford Convention, and spurred nationalism, evident in Madison's call for a new national bank, federal support for internal improvements, and protective tariffs, and also in the Monroe Doctrine's bold pronouncement that European powers must not meddle in the affairs of the Western Hemisphere.

Conflict was never far below the surface of the apparent consensus and assertive nationalism of the Era of Good Feelings. In the absence of Federalist opposition, Republicans began to fragment into sectional factions, most ominously in the conflict over Missouri's admission to the Union as a slave state.

### FOR FURTHER READING

Henry Adams, *History of the United States During the Administrations of Jefferson and Madison*, 9 vols. (1889–1891). A classic study by the great-grandson of John Adams.

Stephen Ambrose, *Undaunted Courage* (1997). Fine new study of the Lewis and Clark Expedition.

Drew R. McCoy, *The Last of the Fathers: James Madison and the Republican Legacy* (1989). The best recent book on Madison.

Dumas Malone, *Jefferson and His Time*, vols. 4 and 5 (1970, 1974). An extremely comprehensive biography.

Merrill Peterson, *Thomas Jefferson and the New Nation: A Biography* (1970). The best one-volume biography of Jefferson.

Marshall Smelser, *The Democratic Republic, 1801–1815* (1968). A thorough general work.

J. C. A. Stagg, *Mr. Madison's War: Politics, Diplomacy and Warfare in the Early Republic* (1983). An important reinterpretation of the causes of the War of 1812.

G. Edward White, *The Marshall Court and Cultural Change, 1815–1835* (1991). A seminal reinterpretation of the Supreme Court under John Marshall.

# 9 The Transformation of American Society 1815–1840

**View of the Detriot Waterfront,** by William James Bennett, 1836.

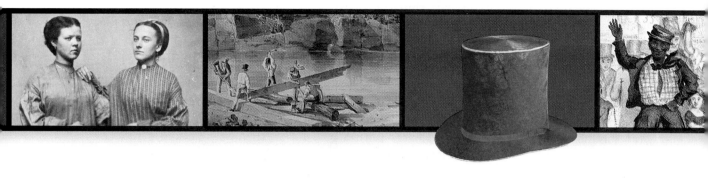

In 1835 William Kirkland and his wife, Caroline, left the private school that they had run in Geneva, New York, and moved to Detroit, in the Michigan Territory. William's plan was simple. He and Caroline would teach in Detroit long enough to earn money to invest in land. Detroit was being flooded by immigrants from the East who, as Caroline wrote, "came to buy land,—not to clear and plough, but as men buy a lottery ticket or dig for gold—in the hope of unreasonable and unearned profits." Although William intended to found a settlement in the wilderness rather than merely to buy and sell land, he, too, hoped to get rich in the West.

Reared in cultivated refinement in New York City and educated at excellent Quaker schools, Caroline had her own notions about the West. The novels and travelers' accounts that she had read projected conflicting but invariably rosy images of the frontier: the West was a land of boundless treasure, a vast garden eager to yield the fruits of its soil, and a romantic wilderness through which one could easily drive a carriage on a moonlit night.

After serving for a year as the principal of a school for young women in Detroit, William acquired thirteen hundred acres of land in Livingston County, sixty miles northwest of Detroit, and laid out his settlement around the village of Pinckney. But life in Pinckney failed to live up to the Kirklands' expectations. Instead of a quaintly romantic cottage, Caroline found herself forced to live in a tiny log cabin, far too small for her fancy eastern furniture. Equally disconcerting to the Kirklands was westerners' attitude toward others' possessions. Frontier neighbors thought that they had a right to borrow anything that Caroline owned, with no more than a blunt declaration that "you've got plenty." "For my own part," Caroline related, "I have lent my broom, my thread, my tape, my spoons, my cat, my thimble, my scissors, my shawl, my shoes; and have been asked for my combs and brushes: and my husband, for his shaving apparatus and his pantaloons."

Other surprises were in store for the Kirklands. Accustomed to servants, Caroline found that even poor western girls refused to hire themselves out permanently as household help. As William noted, occasionally a poor girl would enter service long enough to earn money for a new dress, "but never as a regular calling, or with an acknowledgement of inferior station." Yet the Kirklands gradually realized that the peculiarities of westerners sprang not from selfishness or laziness but from an underlying belief in equality. For example, westerners' penchant for borrowing arose from their attitude that frontier men and women had to share and share alike, or all go under.

Caroline turned her experiences in Michigan to good advantage by writing a fictionalized account of them, *A New Home—Who'll Follow?* (1839). Justly hailed as the first realistic account of western life, *A New Home* established Caroline's literary reputation, which she continued to build after she and William returned to New York in 1843.

Between 1815 and 1840, many Americans like the Kirklands ventured into the West and had their visions of easy living punctured by the harsh realities of the frontier. Even those who remained in the East had to adjust—to the successive waves of economic and social change that swept the nation after the conclusion of the War of 1812. For westerners and easterners alike, improvements in transportation (the so-called transportation revolution) were spearheaded by the completion in 1825 of the Erie Canal. This "revolution" both stimulated interregional trade and migration and encouraged an unprecedented development of towns and cities. The new urban dwellers, in turn, formed a market not only for agricultural produce but also for the products of the industries springing up in New England and the major northeastern cities.

Viewed superficially, these changes did not greatly affect the way most Americans lived. Whether in 1815 or 1840, the majority of Americans dwelled outside of cities, practiced agriculture for a living, and traveled on foot or by horse. Yet this surface impression of continuity is misleading, because by 1840 many farmers had moved to the West. The nature of farming had also changed, as farmers increasingly raised crops for sale in distant markets rather than merely for their families' consumption. Although most Americans still depended on agriculture, by 1840 alternatives to farming abounded. The rise of such alternatives, in turn, affected some of the most basic social relationships: between parents and children, and between wives and husbands.

This chapter focuses on five major questions:

♦ What caused the upsurge of westward migration after the War of 1812?

♦ How did the rise in the prices of farm commodities after 1815 relate to the growth of banks, and how did the spread of banks relate to the Panic of 1819?

♦ How do you account for the vast public investment in canals during this era, and how did the rise of canals and railroads affect where Americans lived and how they made their living?

♦ How did the combined effects of the transportation revolution and the rise of industry influence relationships within families and communities?

♦ Who were the winners and the losers in this period of swift change?

# Westward Expansion and the Growth of the Market Economy

The spark that ignited these changes was the spread of Americans across the Appalachian Mountains. In 1790 the vast majority of the people resided east of the mountains and within a few hundred miles of the Atlantic Ocean. But by 1840 one-third lived between the Appalachians and the Mississippi River. In this area, known at the time as the West, settlers were buffeted by a succession of unexpected social and economic forces.

**American Log House**
*Settlers thinned the western forests, whose lumber they used to build, heat, and fence their houses.*

## The Sweep West

This outward thrust of the population occurred in a series of bursts. The first began even before the 1790s and was reflected in the admission of four new states into the Union between 1791 and 1803: Vermont, Kentucky, Tennessee, and Ohio. Then, after an interlude of over ten years that saw the admission of only one new state, Louisiana, six states entered the Union between 1816 and 1821: Indiana, Mississippi, Illinois, Alabama, Maine, and Missouri. Even as Indiana and Illinois were gaining statehood, settlers were pouring farther west into Michigan. Ohio's population jumped from 45,000 in 1800 to 581,000 by 1820 and 1,519,000 by 1840; Michigan's, from 5,000 in 1810 to 212,000 by 1840.

An adventuring spirit carried Americans far beyond the Mississippi. On an exploring expedition in the Southwest in 1806, Zebulon Pike sighted the Colorado peak that was later named after him. The Lewis and Clark expedition whetted interest in the Far West. In 1811 a New York merchant, John Jacob Astor, founded the fur-trading post of Astoria at the mouth of the Columbia River in the Oregon Country. In the 1820s and 1830s, fur traders also operated along the Missouri River from St. Louis to the Rocky Mountains and beyond. At first, whites relied on the Native Americans to bring them furs, but during the 1820s white trappers or "mountain men"—among them, Kit Carson, Jedediah Smith, and the mulatto Jim Beckwourth—gathered furs on their own while performing astounding feats of survival in harsh surroundings.

Jedediah Smith was representative of these men. Born in the Susquehanna Valley of New York in 1799, Smith moved west with his family to Pennsylvania and

C H R O N O L O G Y

| | | |
|---|---|---|
| **1790** Samuel Slater opens his first Rhode Island mill for the production of cotton yarn. | **1817** Erie Canal started. | **1831** *Cherokee Nation* v. *Georgia.* Alexis de Tocqueville begins visit to the United States to study American penitentiaries. |
| **1793** Eli Whitney invents the cotton gin. | **1819** Economic panic, ushering in four-year depression. | |
| **1807** Robert R. Livingston and Robert Fulton introduce the steamboat *Clermont* on the Hudson River. | **1820–1850** Growth of female moral-reform societies. | **1832** *Worcester* v. *Georgia.* |
| | **1820s** Expansion of New England textile mills. | **1834** First strike at the Lowell mills. |
| **1811** Construction of the National Road begins at Cumberland, Maryland. | **1824** *Gibbons* v. *Ogden.* | **1835** Treaty of New Echota. |
| **1813** Incorporation of the Boston Manufacturing Company. | **1825** Completion of the Erie Canal. | **1837** Economic panic begins a depression that lasts until 1843. |
| **1816** Second Bank of the United States chartered. | **1828** Baltimore and Ohio Railroad chartered. | **1838** The Trail of Tears. |
| | **1830** Indian Removal Act passed by Congress. | **1840** System of production by interchangeable parts perfected. |

Illinois and in 1822 signed on with an expedition bound for the upper Missouri River. In the course of this and subsequent explorations, he was almost killed by a grizzly bear in the Black Hills of South Dakota, learned from the Native Americans to trap beaver and shoot buffalo, crossed the Mojave Desert into California, explored California's San Joaquin Valley, and hiked back across the Sierras and the primeval Great Basin to the Great Salt Lake, a trip so forbidding that even the Native Americans avoided it.

Their exploits popularized in biographies, the mountain men became legends in their own day. They were, however, atypical migrants. For most pioneer settlers, the West meant the area between the Appalachians and the Mississippi River, the region today known as the Midwest, and before 1840 very few ventured into the Far West. In contrast to Jedediah Smith, whose unquenchable thirst for adventure led to his death at the hands of Comanches in 1831, most pioneers sought stability and security. The newspaper reports, pamphlets, and letters home that told easterners what to expect in the West usually stressed that western living was bountiful rather than harsh or even risky. A legislator in the Missouri Territory wrote in 1816 that in the states west of the Appalachians, "there neither is, nor, in the nature of things, can there ever be, any thing like poverty there. All is ease, tranquility and comfort."

## Western Society and Customs

In their desire for stability, pioneers usually migrated as families rather than as individuals. Because they needed to get their crops to market, most settlers between 1790 and 1820 clustered near the navigable rivers of the West, especially the magnificent water system created by the Ohio and Mississippi Rivers. Only with the spread of canals in the 1820s and 1830s, and later of railroads, did westerners feel free to venture far from rivers. In addition, westerners often clustered with people who hailed from the same region back east. For instance, in 1836 a group of farmers from nearby towns met at Castleton, Vermont, listened to a minister intone from the Bible, "And Moses sent them to spy out the land of Canaan," and soon established the town of Vermontville in Michigan. Other migrants to the West were less organized than these latter-day descendants of the Puritans, but most hoped to settle among familiar faces in the West. Finding southerners already well entrenched in Indiana, for example, New Englanders tended to prefer Michigan.

Far from seeking isolation, most westerners craved sociability. Even before there were towns and cities in the West, farm families joined with their neighbors in group sports and festivities. Men met for games that, with a few exceptions like marbles (popular among all

### The Mountain Men

*Rocky Mountain trappers or "mountain men" were among the most colorful and individualistic of nineteenth-century Americans. Entrepreneurs who trapped beavers for their pelts (which were used until the 1830s to make hats), the mountain men were also hunters, explorers, and adventurers who lived "a wild Robin Hood kind of life" with "little fear of God and none at all of the Devil."*

ages), were tests of strength or agility. These included wrestling, lifting weights, pole jumping (for distance rather than height), and a variant of the modern hammer toss. Some of these games were brutal. In gander pulling, horseback riders competed to pull the head off a gander whose neck had been stripped of feathers and greased. Women usually combined work and play in quilting and sewing parties, carpet tackings, and even chicken and goose pluckings. Social activities brought the genders together. Group corn huskings usually ended with dances; and in a variety of "hoedowns" and "frolics," even westerners who in theory might disapprove of dancing promenaded to singing and a fiddler's tune.

Within western families, there was usually a clear division of labor between men and women. Men performed most of the heaviest labor such as cutting down trees and plowing fields, but women had many chores. Women usually rose first in the morning because their work included milking the cows as well as preparing breakfast. Women also fashioned the coverlets that warmed beds in unheated rooms, and prior to the spread of factory-made clothing in the 1830s, they spun yarn and thread on spinning wheels and fashioned shirts, coats, pants, and dresses for family use. They often helped butcher hogs. They knew that the best way

to bleed a hog was to slit its throat while it was still alive, and after the bleeding, they were adept at scooping out the innards, washing the heart and liver, and hanging them to dry. There was nothing dainty about the work of pioneer women.

Most western sports and customs had been transplanted from the East. Gander pulling, for example, had been a popular pastime in Virginia before it made its way to the frontier. Yet the West had a character of its own. Before 1830 few westerners could afford elegant living. Cowpaths did double duty as sidewalks in country towns. The West contained no more than a sprinkling of elegant mansions. Even in the wealthy cotton-growing regions of Alabama and Mississippi, most planters lived in rough conditions prior to 1830. Their relative lack of refinement made westerners easy targets for easterners' contemptuous jibes. Criticisms of the West as a land of half-savage yokels tended, in turn, to give rise to counterassertions by westerners that they lived in a land of honest democracy and that the East was soft and decadent. The exchange of insults fostered a regional identity among westerners that further shaped their behavior. Priding themselves on their simple manners, westerners were often not only hostile to the East but also intolerant of those westerners who had pretensions to gentility. On one occasion, a traveler

**"Barroom Dancing"** by John Lewis Krimmel, 1820
*We can only guess what George Washington, looking soberly down from the wall, would have thought of these tipsy celebrants at a country tavern.*

who hung up a blanket in a tavern to cover his bed from public gaze had it promptly ripped down. On another, a woman who improvised a screen behind which to retire in a crowded room was dismissed as "stuck up." And a politician who rode to a public meeting in a buggy instead of on horseback lost votes.

### The Federal Government and the West

Of the various causes of expansion to the Mississippi from 1790 to 1840, the one that operated most generally and uniformly throughout the period was the growing strength of the federal government. Even before the Constitution's ratification, several states had ceded their western land claims to the national government, thereby creating the bountiful public domain. The Land Ordinance of 1785 had set forth plans for surveying and selling parcels of this public treasure to settlers. The Northwest Ordinance of 1787 provided for the orderly transformation of western territories into states. The Louisiana Purchase of 1803 brought the entire Mississippi River under American control, and the Transcontinental Treaty of 1819 wiped out the last vestiges of Spanish power east of the Mississippi. The federal government directly stimulated settlement of its expanding landholdings by inducing soldiers to enlist during the

War of 1812 in return for promises of land after the war. With 6 million acres allotted to these so-called military bounties, many former soldiers pulled up roots and tried farming in the West. To facilitate westward migration, Congress authorized funds in 1816 for continued construction of the National Road, a highway begun in 1811 that reached Wheeling, Virginia, on the Ohio River, in 1818 and Vandalia, Illinois, by 1838. Soon the road was thronged with settlers. "Old America seems to be breaking up," a traveler on the National Road wrote in 1817. "We are seldom out of sight, as we travel on this grand track towards the Ohio, of family groups before and behind us."

Although whites gained innumerable advantages from having a more powerful national government behind them, the rising strength of that government brought misery to the Indians. Virtually all the foreign-policy successes during the Jefferson, Madison, and Monroe administrations worked to the Native Americans' disadvantage. Both the Louisiana Purchase and the Transcontinental Treaty stripped them of Spanish protection. In the wake of the Louisiana Purchase, Lewis and Clark bluntly told the Indians that they must "shut their ears to the counsels of bad birds" and listen henceforth only to the Great Father in Washington. The outcome of the War of 1812 also worked against the Native Americans; indeed, the Indians were the only real losers of the war. Early in the negotiations leading to the Treaty of Ghent, the British had insisted on the creation of an Indian buffer state in the Old Northwest, between the United States and Canada. But after the American victory at the Battle of Plattsburgh, the British dropped the demand and essentially abandoned the Indians to the Americans.

### The Removal of the Indians

Westward-moving white settlers found sizable numbers of Native Americans in their path, particularly in the South, home to the so-called Five Civilized Tribes: the Cherokees, Choctaws, Creeks, Chickasaws, and Seminoles. Years of commercial dealings and intermarriage with whites had created in these tribes, especially the Cherokees, an influential minority of mixed-bloods who embraced Christianity, practiced agriculture, built gristmills, and even owned slaves. One of their chiefs, Sequoyah, devised a written form of their language; others published a bilingual newspaper, the *Cherokee Phoenix.*

The "civilization" of the southern Indians impressed New England missionaries more than southern whites, who viewed the Civilized Tribes with contempt and their land with envy. Presidents Monroe and John Quincy Adams had concluded several treaties with Indian tribes providing for their voluntary removal to public lands west of the Mississippi River. Although some assimilated mixed-bloods sold their tribal lands to the government, other mixed-bloods, mindful that their prosperity depended on commercial dealings with whites, resisted removal. In addition, full-bloods, the

### Political Cartoon of Jackson and Native Americans

*This cartoon, which depicts Native Americans as children or dolls subject to father Andrew Jackson, was intended as a satire on Jackson's policy of forcibly removing the Indians to reservations. The painting in the upper right corner pointedly depicts the goddess Liberty trampling a tyrant.*

majority even in the "civilized" tribes, clung to their land and customs, which included living near the burial grounds of their ancestors, and condemned those mixed-bloods who bartererd away tribal lands to whites. When the Creek mixed-blood chief William McIntosh sold to the government all Creek lands in Georgia and two-thirds of Creek lands in Alabama in the Treaty of Indian Springs (1825), other Creeks executed him.

During the 1820s whites in Alabama, Georgia, and Mississippi intensified pressure on the Indians by surveying tribal lands and squatting on them. Southern legislatures, loath to restrain white settlers, passed laws that threatened to expropriate Indian lands unless the Indians moved west, extended state jurisdiction over the tribes (which effectively outlawed tribal government), and declared that no Indian could be a witness in a court case involving whites (which made it difficult for Indians to collect debts owed them by whites).

These measures delighted President Andrew Jackson. Reared on the frontier and sharing its contempt for Indians, Jackson believed that it was ridiculous to treat the Indians as independent nations; rather, they should be subject to the laws of their states of residence. This position spelled doom for the Indians, who could not vote or hold state office. In 1834 Cherokee Chief John Ross got a taste of what state jurisdiction meant; Georgia, without consulting him, put his house up as a prize in the state lottery.

In 1830 Jackson secured passage of the Indian Removal Act, which authorized him to exchange public lands in the West for Indian territories in the East and appropriated $500,000 to cover the expenses of removal. But the real costs of removal, human and monetary, were vastly greater. During Jackson's eight years in office, the federal government exchanged 100 million acres of Indian lands for 32 million acres of public lands at a cost of roughly $68 million. In the late 1820s and early 1830s the Creeks, Choctaws, and Chickasaws started their "voluntary" removal to the West. French visitor Alexis de Tocqueville witnessed the arrival of the Choctaws along the Mississippi. "I saw them embark to cross the great river, and the sight will never fade from my memory. Neither sob nor complaint rose from that silent assembly. Their afflictions were of long standing, and they felt them to be irremediable." In 1836 Creeks who clung to their homes were forcibly removed, many in chains. Most Seminoles were removed from Florida, but only after a bitter war between 1835 and 1842 that cost the federal government $20 million.

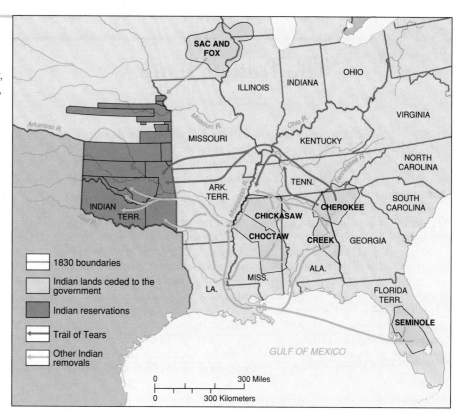

### The Removal of the Native Americans to the West, 1820–1840

*The so-called Trail of Tears, followed by the Cherokees, was one of several routes along which various tribes migrated on their forced removal to reservations west of the Mississippi.*

Ironically, the Cherokees, whose leaders were the most accommodating to American political institutions, suffered the worst fate of all. In 1827 the Cherokees proclaimed themselves an independent republic within Georgia. When the Georgia legislature subsequently extended the state's jurisdiction over this "nation," the Cherokees petitioned the U.S. Supreme Court for an injunction to halt Georgia's legislation. In the case of *Cherokee Nation* v. *Georgia* (1831), Chief Justice John Marshall denied the Cherokees' claim to status as a republic within Georgia; rather, they were a "domestic dependent nation," a kind of ward of the United States. But he added that prolonged occupancy had given the Cherokees a claim to their lands within Georgia. A year later he clarified the Cherokees' legal position in *Worcester* v. *Georgia* by holding that they were a "distinct" political community entitled to federal protection from tampering by Georgia.

But Marshall's decision had little impact. Jackson ignored it, reportedly sneering, "John Marshall has made his decision; now let him enforce it." Next, federal agents persuaded some minor Cherokee chiefs to sign the Treaty of New Echota (1835), which ceded all Cherokee lands in the United States for $5.6 million and free passage west. Congress ratified this treaty (by one vote), but the vast majority of Cherokees denounced it, and in 1839 a Cherokee party took revenge by murdering its three principal signers, including a former editor of the *Cherokee Phoenix.*

The end of this story is simple and tragic. In 1838 the Cherokees were forcibly removed to the west along what became known as "The Trail of Tears" (see A Place in Time).

Indians living in the Northwest Territory fared no better. A series of treaties extinguished their land titles, and most moved west of the Mississippi. The removal of the northwestern Indians was notable for two uprisings. The first, led by Red Bird, a Winnebago chief, began in 1827 but was quickly crushed. The second was led by a Sac and Fox chief, Black Hawk, who resisted removal until 1831 and then moved his people west of the Mississippi, only to return the following year. In June 1832 federal troops and Illinois militia furiously attacked his band and virtually annihilated Black Hawk's followers as they tried to recross the Mississippi into Iowa. Black Hawk's downfall induced the other Old

## The Trail of Tears

"I fought through the civil war and have seen men shot to pieces and slaughtered by the thousands, but the Cherokee removal was the cruelest work I ever knew." So recollected a former colonel in the Confederate Army who, as a youth, had participated in the forced removal in 1838 of some sixteen thousand Cherokees from their lands east of the Mississippi River—in the area where North Carolina, Georgia, Alabama, and Tennessee more or less converge—to the new Indian Territory in what is now Oklahoma. The Cherokees named the journey "the trail of tears."

The event that precipitated this tragic episode was the refusal of the vast majority of Cherokees, whom the governor of Georgia dismissed as "too ignorant and depraved to entitle their opinion to any weight or consideration in these matters," to accept the Treaty of New Echota and voluntarily exchange their ancestral lands in the east for new territory west of the Mississippi River. Far from ignorant, the Cherokees were sufficiently sophisticated to distrust the federal government's promise that they could occupy their new western lands "forever." Too, they knew about the disasters that had afflicted the "voluntary" removal of the Choctaws and Creeks.

No one is certain just how many Cherokees died as a result of the removal. In 1835 a census counted 16,542 eastern Cherokees, but some of these escaped to the hills to avoid forced removal. Approximately 5,000 Cherokees already lived west of the Mississippi in 1835, for a total tribal population of roughly 21,500. The usual estimate is that 4,000, nearly a fifth of the nation, died as a result of the removal, but that figure is based solely on a contemporary's guess. Recent scholarship, which projects from earlier and later censuses the likely size of the Cherokee population had events followed a normal course, points to 8,000 deaths,

**Trail of Tears,** by Robert Lindneux

more than one-third of the nation, as a consequence of removal.

Many of the Cherokees died soon after arriving in Oklahoma, hardly surprising in view of the conditions of removal. In the spring of 1838, federal troops entered Cherokee territory and evicted entire families at bayonet point, often during the dinner hour (when everyone would be home), with the result that cooking utensils and even clothes often were left behind. Next came the confinement of Cherokees in stockades, virtual concentration camps, preparatory to removal. They were then moved to collecting points near the Tennessee River and set out in thirteen detachments of roughly 750–1500 men, women, and children. The "trail" itself consisted of several different improvised routes across Tennessee, through Nashville, and into southwestern Kentucky. Some then proceeded through Arkansas, others through southern Illinois and Missouri, to Indian territory. Responsible for provisioning the emigrants, the federal government supplied one wagon for every twenty Cherokees and let contracts for food, but many wagons were lost crossing rivers and innumerable Cherokees had to walk three hundred and fifty miles. Provisioners, who had obtained contracts by bidding low, often supplied rotten meat. The summer of 1838 was so hot that the Cherokees were able to persuade federal officials to allow an interruption of the journey until the fall, a decision that probably worsened matters. Movement even in autumn was slow, partly because hunger and disease had weakened the hardiest and partly because of pauses to bury the dead. Soon winter set in; those too weak or sick to move lay in wagons or just on the ground, with no more than a blanket or sheet

for protection. The final detachments did not reach their new home until March 1839.

On December 3, 1838, President Martin Van Buren blandly assured Congress that the removal had gone smoothly and "without any apparent reluctance" on the part of the Cherokees. Now, it would seem, the Native Americans were not just out of sight, but also out of mind.

**Trail of Tears** by Brummet Echohawk
*This depiction of the Trail of Tears was painted by the modern-day Native American artist Brummet Echohawk.*

Northwest tribes to cede their lands. Between 1832 and 1837, the United States acquired nearly 190 million acres of Indian land in the Northwest for $70 million in gifts and annuities.

## The Agricultural Boom

In pushing Indians from the path of white settlers, the federal government was responding to whites' demands for land and more land. Depleted soil and overcrowding had long driven eastern farmers west, but after the War of 1812, a new incentive—the bounding prices of agricultural commodities such as wheat, corn, and cotton—drew settlers westward in search of better farmland. Several factors accounted for the skyrocketing farm prices. First, Britain and France, exhausted by the Napoleonic Wars, were importing wheat and corn from America, and the United States had swiftly captured former British markets in the West Indies and former Spanish markets in South America. In addition, the beginnings of industrialization in New England even before the war combined with the westward migration of New England farmers to create a demand in the eastern United States for western foodstuffs. So as domestic and foreign demand intensified, commodity prices rose between 1815 and 1819. The West's splendid river systems made it possible for farmers in Ohio to ship wheat and corn down the Ohio River to the Mississippi and then down the Mississippi to New Orleans. There wheat and corn were either sold or transshipped to the East, the West Indies, South America, or Europe. Just as government policies made farming in the West possible, high prices for foodstuffs made it attractive.

As the prospect of raising wheat and corn pulled farmers toward the Old Northwest, Eli Whitney's invention of the cotton gin in 1793 (see Chapter 7) cleared the path for settlement of the Old Southwest, particularly the states of Alabama and Mississippi on the Gulf of Mexico. After the War of 1812, the explosive thrust of small farmers and planters from the seaboard South into the Old Southwest resembled a gold rush. By 1817 "Alabama fever" gripped the South; settlers bid the price of good land up to thirty to fifty dollars an acre. By 1820 Alabama and Mississippi produced half of the nation's cotton. Stimulated by the seemingly bottomless demand of the British textile industry for raw cotton, cotton production tripled between 1816 and 1826, and the story was only beginning. Between 1831 and 1836, the value of cotton exports rose 300 percent. Accounting for less than a quarter of all American ex-

ports between 1802 and 1807, cotton comprised just over half by 1830, and nearly two-thirds by 1836.

## The Rise of the Market Economy

To farmers, the high prices of agricultural commodities between 1815 and 1819 appeared an unmixed blessing. Most planned to grow enough food to feed their families (called subsistence agriculture) *and* a cash crop like wheat or cotton to sell in local or distant markets (called commercial agriculture, or the "market economy"). Farming for markets was not new; many farmers had done so during the colonial era. What was new after the War of 1812 was the extent to which farmers entered the market economy. High crop prices tempted many former subsistence farmers into the commercial economy. Often these individuals had little experience with commercial dealings and little idea of what they were getting into. Commercial agriculture exposed farmers to innumerable new risks. First, cash crops like wheat and cotton were sold to people whom the farmers themselves frequently never met, in places that they never saw. Second, farmers had no control over the fluctuations of distant markets. Furthermore, there was inevitably an interval, often a long one, between harvesting a cash crop and selling it. To sustain themselves during the interval, farmers had to borrow money. Thus commercial agriculture forced farmers into short-term debt in the hope of long-term profit.

The debt was frequently worse than most had expected. In the first place, many western farmers had to borrow money to buy their land. The roots of this indebtedness for land lay, in turn, in the federal government's inability to devise an effective policy for transferring the public domain directly into the hands of small farmers.

## Federal Land Policy

Partisan and sectional pressures buffeted federal land policy like a kite in a March wind. The result was a succession of land laws passed between 1796 and 1820, each of which sought to undo the damage caused by its predecessors.

At the root of early federal land policy lay a preference for the orderly settlement of the public domain. To this end, the Ordinance of 1785 divided public lands into townships of six miles square each and then subdivided each township into one-mile-square lots (usually called sections) of 640 acres. The architects of the ordinance did not expect that ordinary farmers could afford to purchase 640-acre sections; rather, they assumed that farmers who shared ties based on religion or region of origin would band together to purchase sections. This outcome would ensure that compatible settlers would live on adjoining lots in what amounted to rural neighborhoods, and it would make the task of government much easier than if settlers were to live in isolation on widely scattered homesteads.

Political developments in the 1790s undermined the expectations of the ordinance's framers. Because their political bases lay in the East, the Federalists were reluctant to encourage headlong settlement of the West, but at the same time they were eager to raise revenue for the federal government from land sales. They reconciled these goals—retarding actual settlement while gaining revenue—by encouraging the sale of huge tracts of land to wealthy speculators who did not intend to farm the land but instead planned to hold it until its value rose, and then sell off parcels to farmers. In the 1790s land speculators swarmed through the area east of the Appalachians. The Holland Land Company, for example, composed mainly of Dutch investors, bought up much of western New York and western Pennsylvania. A federal land law passed in 1796 reflected Federalist aims by maintaining the minimum purchase at 640 acres at a minimum price of two dollars an acre, and by allowing only a year for complete payment.

Believing that the small farmer was the backbone of the Republic, and fully aware of Republican political strength in the West, Thomas Jefferson and the Republicans took a different tack. Starting in 1800, federal land laws increasingly reflected the Republicans' desire to ease the transfer of the public domain to farmers. Accordingly, the land law of 1800 dropped the minimum purchase to 320 acres and allowed up to four years for full payment but kept the minimum purchase price at $2.00 an acre. In 1804 the minimum purchase came down to 160 acres, in 1820 to 80 acres, and in 1832 to 40 acres. The minimum price also declined from $2.00 an acre in 1800 to $1.64 in 1804 and to $1.25 in 1820.

Although the government steadily liberalized its land policy, speculators always remained one step ahead of Congress. Long before 1832, speculators were selling 40-acre lots to farmers. Farmers actually preferred these small lots (and rarely bought more than 160 acres), because the "farm" they purchased typically was a forest. A new landowner could clear no more than ten to twelve acres of trees a year. But small lots carried a price. All land in the public domain was sold at auction, usually for much more than the two-dollar minimum. With agricultural prices soaring, speculators assumed that land would continue to rise in value and accordingly were willing to bid high on new land, which they resold to farmers at hefty prices.

The growing availability of credit after the War of 1812 fed speculation. The chartering of the Second Bank of the United States in 1816 had the dual effect of increasing the amount of money in circulation and stimulating the chartering of private banks within states (state banks). The circulation of all banks grew from $45 million in bank notes in 1812 to $100 million in 1817. The stockholders and directors of these banks viewed them less as a sound investment for their capital (many directors actually had very little capital when they started state banks) than as agencies that could lend them money for land speculation. Secretary of the Treasury William H. Crawford observed in 1820 that banks had been incorporated "not because there was capital seeking investment, not because the places where they were established had commerce and manufacturers which required their fostering aid; but because men without active capital wanted the means of obtaining loans, which their standing in the community would not command from banks or individuals having real capital and established credit." In short, banks were founded so that they could lend their directors money for personal investment in land speculation. The result was an orgy of land speculation between 1815 and 1819. In 1819 sales of public land were over 1,000 percent greater than the average in 1800–1814.

### The Speculator and the Squatter

Nevertheless, most of the public domain eventually found its way into the hands of small farmers. Because speculators gained nothing by holding land for prolonged periods, they were only too happy to sell it when the price was right. In addition, a familiar frontier type, the squatter, exerted a restraining influence on the speculator.

Even before the creation of the public domain, squatters had helped themselves to western land; George Washington himself had been unable to drive squatters off lands that he owned in the West. Squatters were an independent and proud lot, scornful of their fellow citizens, who were "softened by Ease, enervated by Affluence and Luxurious Plenty, & unaccustomed to Fatigues, Hardships, Difficulties or dangers." Disdaining land speculators above all, squatters formed claims associations to police land auctions and prevented speculators from bidding up the price of land. Squatters also pressured Congress to allow them "preemption" rights—that is, the right to purchase at the minimum price land that they had already settled on and improved. Seeking to undo the pernicious effects of its own laws, Congress responded by passing special preemption laws for squatters in specific areas and finally, in 1841, acknowledged a general right of preemption.

But preemption laws were of no use to farmers who arrived after speculators had already bought up land. Having spent their small savings on livestock, seed, and tools, these settlers then had to buy land from speculators on credit at vicious interest rates that ranged as high as 40 percent. Saddled by steep indebtedness, many western farmers had no choice but to skimp on subsistence crops while expanding cash crops in the hope of paying off their creditors. Farmers in these years were not merely entering the market economy; they were lunging into it.

Countless farmers who had carried basically conservative expectations to the West and who had hoped to establish self-sufficient farms in a land of abundance quickly became economic adventurers. Wanting land that they could call their own, but forced to raise cash crops in a hurry, many farmers worked their acreage to exhaustion and thus had to keep moving in search of new land. The phrase "the moving frontier" refers not only to the obvious fact that with each passing decade the line of settlement shifted farther west but also to the fact that the same people kept moving. The experience of Abraham Lincoln's parents, who migrated from the East through several farms in Kentucky and then to Indiana, was representative of the westward trek.

### The Panic of 1819

In 1819 the land boom collapsed like a house of cards, the victim of a financial panic. The state banks' loose practices contributed mightily to the panic. Like the Bank of the United States, these banks issued their own bank notes. In the absence of any national system of paper money, these notes served as a circulating medium. A bank note was just a piece of paper with a printed promise from the bank's directors to pay the bearer ("redeem") on demand a certain amount of specie (gold or silver coinage). State banks had long emitted far more bank notes than they could redeem, and these notes had fueled the economic boom after 1815. With credit so readily available, farmers borrowed money to buy more land and to plant more

crops, confident that they could repay their loans when they sold their crops. After 1817, however, the combination of bumper crops in Europe and a business recession in Britain trimmed the foreign demand for U.S. wheat, flour, and cotton—at the very time when American farmers were becoming more dependent on agricultural exports to pay their debts.

In reaction to the overemission of state bank notes, the Bank of the United States, in the summer of 1818, began to insist that state banks redeem in specie their notes that were held by the Bank of the United States. Because the Bank of the United States had more branches than any state bank, notes of state banks were often presented by their holders to branches of the Bank of the United States for redemption. Whenever the Bank of the United States redeemed a state bank note in specie, it became a creditor of the state bank. In turn, to pay their debts to the Bank of the United States, the state banks had no choice but to force farmers and land speculators to repay loans. The result was a general curtailment of credit throughout the nation, but particularly in the West.

The biggest losers were the land speculators, who had bought huge tracts with the expectation that prices would rise but now found prices tumbling. Land that had once sold for as much as $69 an acre dropped to $2 an acre. Land prices fell, in turn, because the credit squeeze drove down the market prices of staples like wheat, corn, cotton, and tobacco. Cotton, which sold for 32¢ a pound in 1818, sank as low as 17¢ a pound in 1820. Since farmers could not get much cash for their crops, they could not pay the debts that they had incurred to buy land. Since speculators could not collect money owed them by farmers, the value of land that they still held for sale collapsed.

The significance of the panic lay not only in the economic damage it did but also in the conclusions that many Americans drew from it. First, the panic left a bitter taste about banks, particularly the Bank of the United States, which was widely blamed for the hard times. In addition, the panic dramatized the vulnerability of American factories to cheap foreign competition (a vulnerability evident even before the economic downturn) and thereby stimulated demands for the protection of domestic industries. These demands would lead to the passage of higher tariffs in 1824 and 1828. Finally, plummeting prices for cash crops demonstrated how much farmers were coming to depend on distant markets. In effect, it took a severe business reversal to show farmers the extent to which they had become entrepreneurs. The fall in the prices of cash crops accelerated the search for better forms of transportation to reach those faraway markets. If the cost of transporting crops could be cut, farmers could keep a larger share of the value of their crops and thereby adjust to falling prices.

## The Transportation Revolution: Steamboats, Canals, and Railroads

The transportation system linking Americans in 1820 had severe weaknesses. The great rivers west of the Appalachians ran north to south and hence could not by themselves connect western farmers to eastern markets. Roads were expensive to maintain, and horse-drawn wagons could carry only limited produce. Consequently, after 1820 attention and investment shifted to the development of waterways.

In 1807 Robert R. Livingston and Robert Fulton introduced the steamboat *Clermont* on the Hudson River. They soon gained a monopoly from the New York legislature to run a New York–New Jersey ferry service. Spectacular profits lured competitors, who secured a license from Congress and then filed suit to break the Livingston-Fulton monopoly. After a long court battle, the Supreme Court in 1824 decided against the monopoly in the famous case of *Gibbons* v. *Ogden*. Speaking for a unanimous court, Chief Justice John Marshall ruled that Congress's constitutional power to regulate interstate commerce applied to navigation as well as to the exchange of goods among states, and thus had to prevail over New York's power to license the Livingston-Fulton monopoly. In the aftermath of this decision, other state-granted monopolies collapsed and steamboat traffic increased rapidly. The number of steamboats operating on western rivers jumped from 17 in 1817 to 727 by 1855.

Steamboats assumed a vital role along the Mississippi-Ohio River system. They were vastly superior to flatboats, often just rafts that could carry produce only downstream, and to keelboats (flatboats with rudders), which could navigate upstream at a snail's pace. It took a keelboat three or four months to complete the 1,350-mile voyage from New Orleans to Louisville; in 1817 a steamboat made the trip in twenty-five days. The development of long, shallow hulls permitted the navigation of the Mississippi-Ohio system even when hot, dry summers lowered the river level. Steamboats became more ornate as well as practical. To compete for passengers, they began to offer luxurious cabins

**Interior of a Flatboat,** by Charles-Alexandre Lesueur, 1826
*Not all flatboats that carried produce and pioneers on American rivers were floating rafts. Many had roomy interiors that accommodated whole families, provisions, and even barn animals.*

and lounges, called saloons. The saloon of the *Eclipse*, a Mississippi steamboat, was the length of a football field and featured skylights, chandeliers, a ceiling criss-crossed with Gothic arches, and velvet-upholstered mahogany furniture.

Once steamboats had demonstrated the feasibility of upriver navigation, popular enthusiasm for internal improvements shifted away from turnpikes and toward canals. Although the cost of canal construction was mind-boggling—Jefferson dismissed the idea as little short of madness—canals offered the prospect of connecting the superb Mississippi-Ohio River system with the Great Lakes, and the Great Lakes with eastern markets.

Completion of the Erie Canal started a canal boom during the late 1820s and 1830s. Ohio constructed a network of canals that made it possible for its farmers to send their wheat by water to Lake Erie. After transport across Lake Erie, the wheat would be milled into flour in Rochester, New York, and then shipped on the Erie Canal to Albany and then down the Hudson River to New York City. Throughout the nation, canals reduced shipping costs from 20–30¢ a ton per mile in 1815 to 2–3¢ a ton per mile by 1830.

When another economic depression hit in the late 1830s, various states found themselves overcommitted to costly canal projects and ultimately scrapped many.

**Erie Canal,** by John William Hill, 1831
*Construction of the Erie Canal was a remarkable feat—all the more so because the United States did not possess a single school of engineering at the time. The project's heros were lawyers and merchants who taught themselves engineering, and brawny workmen, often Irish immigrants, who hacked a waterway through the forests and valleys of New York.*

Yet even as the canal boom was ending, railroads were spreading. In 1825 the world's first railroad devoted to general transportation began operation in England, and by 1840 some three thousand miles of track had been laid in America, about the same as the total canal mileage in 1840. During the 1830s, investment in American railroads actually exceeded that in canals. Cities like Baltimore and Boston, which lacked major inland waterway connections, turned to railroads to enlarge their share of the western market. The Baltimore and Ohio Railroad, chartered in 1828, took business away from the Chesapeake and Ohio Canal farther south. Blocked by its Berkshire Mountains from building a canal to the Erie, Massachusetts chartered the Boston and Worcester Railroad in 1831 and the Western Railroad (from Worcester to Albany) in 1833.

Cheaper to build, faster, and able to reach more places, railroads had obvious advantages over canals and also contributed to the growth of communities that were remote from waterways. But railroads' potential was only slowly realized. Most early railroads ran between cities in the East rather than from east to west and carried more passengers than freight. Not until 1849 did freight revenues exceed passenger revenues, and not until 1850 was the East Coast connected by rail to the Great Lakes.

Several factors explain the relatively slow spread of interregional railroads. Unlike canals, which were built directly by state governments, most railroads were con-

structed by private corporations seeking quick profits. To minimize their original investment, railroad companies commonly resorted to cost-cutting measures such as covering wooden rails with iron bars. As a result, although relatively cheap to build, American railroads needed constant repairs and were even more vulnerable than canals to economic fluctuations. In contrast, although expensive to construct, canals needed relatively little maintenance and were kept in operation for decades after railroads appeared. Moreover, it remained cheaper to ship bulky commodities such as iron ore, coal, and nonperishable agricultural produce by canal.

### The Growth of the Cities

By vastly increasing the opportunities for trades that could conveniently be conducted in urban places—bankers to lend money, insurers to cover risks of transport, warehousers and brokers to store and sell goods—the transportation revolution speeded the growth of towns and cities. In relative terms, the most rapid urbanization in American history occurred between 1820 and 1860. New York City's population rose from 124,000 in 1820 to 800,000 by 1860. An even more revealing change saw the transformation of sleepy villages of a few hundred people into thriving towns of several thousand. For example, the Erie Canal turned Rochester, New York, from home to a few hundred vil-

**Major Rivers, Roads, and Canals, 1825–1860**
*Railroads and canals increasingly tied the economy of the Midwest to that of the Northeast.*

lagers in 1817 into the Flour City, a boom town with nine thousand residents by 1830.

City and town growth occurred with dramatic suddenness, especially in the West. Pittsburgh, Cincinnati, and St. Louis were little more than hamlets in 1800. The War of 1812 stimulated the growth of Pittsburgh, whose iron forges provided shot and weapons for American soldiers, and Cincinnati, which became a staging ground for attacks on the British in the Old Northwest. Meanwhile, St. Louis acquired some importance as a fur-trading center. Then between 1815 and 1819, the agricultural boom and the introduction of the

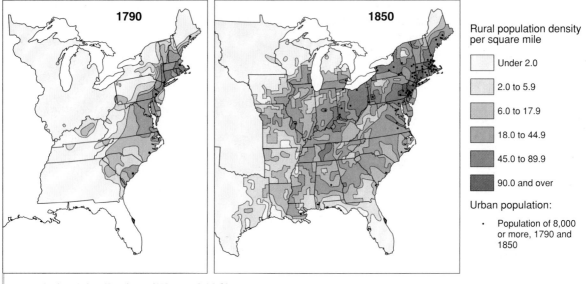

**Population Distribution, 1790 and 1850**

*By 1850 high population density characterized parts of the Midwest as well as the Northeast.*

Source: *1900 Census of Population, Statistical Atlas,* plates 2 and 8.

steamboat transformed all three places from outposts with transient populations of hunters, traders, and soldiers into bustling cities. Cincinnati's population, for example, nearly quadrupled between 1810 and 1820 and doubled in the 1820s.

With the exception of Lexington, Kentucky, whose lack of access to water forced it into relative stagnation after 1820, all the prominent western cities were river ports: Pittsburgh, Cincinnati, and Louisville on the Ohio; St. Louis and New Orleans on the Mississippi. Except for Pittsburgh, all were essentially commercial hubs rather than manufacturing centers and were flooded by individuals extremely eager to make money. In 1819 land speculators in St. Louis were bidding as much as a thousand dollars an acre for lots that had sold for thirty dollars an acre in 1815. Waterfronts endowed with natural beauty were swiftly overrun by stores and docks. "Louis Ville, by nature is beautiful," a visitor wrote, "but the handy Work of *Man* has instead of improving destroy'd the works of Nature and made it a detestable place."

The transportation revolution acted like a fickle god, selecting some cities for growth while sentencing others to relative decline. Just as the steamboat had elevated the river cities over land-locked Lexington, the completion of the Erie Canal shifted the center of western economic activity toward the Great Lakes. The re-

sult was a gradual decline in the importance of river cities and a rise between 1830 and 1860 in the importance of lake cities such as Buffalo, Cleveland, Detroit, Chicago, and Milwaukee. In 1830 nearly 75 percent of all western city dwellers lived in the river ports of New Orleans, Louisville, Cincinnati, and Pittsburgh, but by 1840 the proportion had dropped to 20 percent.

The growth of cities and towns was spurred initially by the transportation revolution and the development of interregional trade. Urban expansion received an added boost from the rise of manufacturing between 1815 and 1840.

## The Rise of Manufacturing

Today we customarily equate manufacturing with industrialization—that is, with large factories, complex machinery, and mass production. But manufacturing literally means "making by hand." During the colonial era, most products were made by hand, either in the households or in the shops of skilled artisans. The period between 1815 and 1860 saw the emergence of modern manufacturing, especially in the production of cotton textiles and shoes. By 1860, 20 percent of the work force engaged in manufacturing, and it produced about 30 percent of the national output.

Industrialization, however, was not a tidal wave that washed away traditional forms of manufacturing. Rather, it was a gradual process with manufacturing, the subdivision of tasks, and the emergence of large factories preceding the introduction of power-driven machinery. Because industrialization grew gradually and unevenly, people did not always recognize that traditional manufacturing by skilled artisans was becoming obsolete and that artisans themselves would soon be replaced by machines.

## Causes of Industrialization

A host of factors stimulated industrialization. The Embargo Act of 1807 persuaded merchants barred from foreign trade to redirect their capital into factories. The Era of Good Feelings saw general agreement that the United States needed tariffs; once protected from foreign competition, American cloth production rose by an average of 15 percent *every* year from 1815 to 1833. Improvements in transportation spurred eastern manufacturers to increase production for markets in the South and West. Too, wherever the transportation revolution reached, farmers concentrated on their farming and bought manufactured shoes and cloth.

Immigration was also vital. Five million people migrated from Europe to the United States between 1790 and 1860, most of them to pursue economic opportunity. The majority were German or Irish, but the smaller number of British immigrants played the key role in launching industrialization. In Britain industrialization was a generation ahead of the United States, and by 1790 Britain had a class of artisans who understood the workings of machines. For example, Samuel Slater, who immigrated to the United States in 1789, had learned the "mystery" of textile production in England. Although British laws forbade emigration by skilled "mechanics," Slater disguised himself and brought his knowledge of machines to eager Americans.

Although Britain had a head start in developing the technology relevant to industrialization, Americans made contributions of their own. Unlike Britain, America had no craft organizations (called guilds) that tied artisans to a single trade. As a result, American artisans freely experimented with machines outside their craft. In the 1790s wagon maker Oliver Evans of Delaware, for example, built an automated flour mill that required only a single supervisor to look on as the grain poured in from one side and was discharged from the other as flour. In addition, the relatively high wages paid to

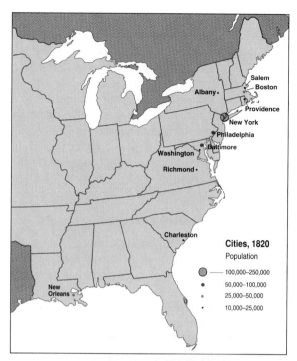

**American Cities, 1820 and 1860**

*In 1820 most cities were seaports. By 1860, however, cities dotted the nation's interior and included San Francisco on the West Coast. This change occurred in large measure because of the transportation revolution.*

Source: *Statistical Abstract of the United States.*

American workers gave manufacturers an incentive to find substitutes for expensive hand labor in order to make products as quickly and cheaply as possible. After inventing the cotton gin, Eli Whitney in 1798 filled a government contract for ten thousand muskets by using unskilled workers to make identical parts that could be interchanged from musket to musket. The idea of interchangeable parts actually originated in Europe, but the United States led all nations in applying the idea in factories—so much so that it came to be called the American system of manufacturing.

### The Faces of Industrialization

New England became America's first industrial region. The trade wars leading up to the War of 1812 had devastated its commercial economy and persuaded its wealthy merchants to invest in manufacturing. Its many swift rivers were ideal sources of waterpower for mills. The westward migration of New England's young men, unable to wrest a living from its rocky soil, left a surplus of young women, who supplied cheap industrial labor.

Cotton textiles led the way. Samuel Slater arrived in Pawtucket, Rhode Island, in 1790 and helped to design and build a mill for spinning cotton into yarn by using the spinning frame invented by the Englishman Richard

**Mill Girls**
*New England's humming textile mills were a magnet for untold numbers of independence-seeking young women in antebellum America.*

Arkwright. Slater's work force quickly grew from nine to one hundred, and his mills multiplied. Slater's mills performed only two of the operations needed to turn raw cotton into clothing: carding (separating broad laps of cotton into fine strands) and spinning these strands into yarn. In what was essentially "cottage" manufacturing, he contracted the weaving to women working in their homes.

The incorporation in 1813 of the Boston Manufacturing Company opened a new chapter in American industrialization. Financed by merchants known as the Boston Associates, this company had ten times the capital of the typical Rhode Island mill and in quick succession built textile mills in the Massachusetts towns of Waltham and Lowell. By 1836 the Boston Associates controlled eight companies employing more than six thousand workers.

Unlike Slater's mills, the Waltham and Lowell mills turned out finished products, and they upset the traditional order of New England society to a degree that Slater had never contemplated. Slater had sought to preserve tradition, not only by contracting weaving to farm families but also by hiring entire families for carding and spinning in his mill complexes. Men raised crops on nearby company lands, while women and children tended the machines inside. In contrast, 80 percent of the workers in Waltham and Lowell, places that had not even existed in the eighteenth century, were young unmarried women who had been lured from farms by the promise of wages. Mary Paul, a Vermont teenager, settled her doubts about leaving home for Lowell by concluding that "I . . . must work where I can get more pay."

In place of traditional family discipline, the workers ("operatives") experienced new restraints. They had to live either in company boardinghouses or in licensed private dwellings, attend church on the Sabbath, observe a 10:00 P.M. curfew, and accept the company's "moral police." Regulations were designed to give the mills a good reputation so that New England farm daughters would continue to be attracted to factory work. Yet mill conditions were far from attractive. To provide the humidity necessary to keep the threads from snapping, overseers nailed factory windows shut and sprayed the air with water. Operatives also had to contend with flying dust and the deafening roar of the machines. Then, keener competition and a worsening economy in the late 1830s led the mill owners to reduce wages and speed up work schedules. The system's impersonality intensified the harshness of the work environment. Each of the major groups that contributed to the system lived in a self-contained world. The Boston Associates raised capital but rarely visited the factories. Their agents, all men, gave orders to the operatives, mainly women. Some 800 Lowell mill women quit work in 1834 to protest a wage reduction. Two years later, there was another "turnout," this time involving 1,500 to 2,000 women. These were the largest strikes in American history to that date, noteworthy as strikes not only of employees against employers but of women against men.

The Waltham and Lowell mills were the most conspicuous examples of industrialization before 1840, but they were not typical of industrial development. As late as 1860, the average manufacturing establishment contained only eight workers. Outside of textiles, many industries continued to depend on industrial outwork. For example, supplied with raw materials by local merchants, more than fifty thousand New England farm women, mainly daughters and widows, earned wages in their homes during the 1830s by making hats out of straw and palm leaves. Similarly, before the 1850s, when the introduction of the sewing machine led to the concentration of all aspects of shoe manufacture in large factories, women often sewed parts of shoes at home and then sent the piecework to factories for finishing.

Manufacturing in cities like New York and Philadelphia also depended on outwork. These cities lacked the fast-flowing rivers that churned machines in New England, and their high population densities made it unnecessary to gather workers into large factories. Nonetheless, they became industrial centers. Lured by the prospect of distant markets, some urban artisans and merchants started to scour the country for orders, which they filled by hiring unskilled workers, often women, to work in small shops or homes fashioning parts of shoes or saddles or dresses anywhere that light would enter. A New York reporter wrote,

> We have been in some fifty cellars in different parts of the city, each inhabited by a shoemaker and his family. The floor is made of rough plank laid loosely down, and the ceiling is not quite so high as a tall man. The walls are dark and damp and . . . the miserable room is lighted only by . . . the little light that struggles from the steep and rotting stairs. In this apartment often lives the man and his work-bench, the wife, and five or six children of all ages; and per-

haps a palsied grandfather or grandmother and often both. . . . Here they work, here they cook, they eat, they sleep, they pray.

New York and Philadelphia were home to artisans with proud craft traditions and independence. Those with highly marketable skills like cutting leather or clothing patterns continued to earn good wages. Others grew rich by turning themselves into businessmen who spent less time making products than making trips to obtain orders. But many artisans found themselves on the downslope in the face of competition from cheap, unskilled labor.

In the late 1820s, skilled artisans in New York, Philadelphia, and other cities began to form trade unions and "workingmen's" political parties to protect their interests. Disdaining association with unskilled workers, most of these groups initially sought to restore privileges and working conditions that artisans had once enjoyed rather than to act as leaders of unskilled workers. But the steady deterioration of working conditions in the early 1830s tended to throw skilled and unskilled workers into the same boat. When coal heavers in Philadelphia struck for a ten-hour day in 1835, they were quickly joined by carpenters, cigar makers, shoemakers, leather workers, and other artisans in the United States' first general strike.

The emergence of organized worker protest underscored the mixed blessings of economic development. Although some benefited from the new commercial and industrial economy, others found their economic position worsening. By the 1830s many Americans wondered whether their nation was truly a land of equality.

## Equality and Inequality

Observers of antebellum (pre–Civil War) America sensed changes sweeping the country but had trouble describing them or agreeing on their direction. Some insisted that wealth was "universally diffused." Others, like the New York merchant Philip Hone, portrayed an unhappy society marked by extremes of "costly luxury" and "squalid misery."

One of the most astute of these observers was the French nobleman Alexis de Tocqueville, who spent nine months in America in 1831–1832. Although Tocqueville filled his private journals with references to inequality, in his two-volume *Democracy in America*

(1835, 1840) he cited the "general equality of condition among the people" as the fundamental shaping force of American society. Inclined to view everything in comparative terms, Tocqueville, while certainly recognizing inequality, thought that wealth was more evenly distributed in the United States than in France and that, regardless of an individual's wealth, Americans believed that one person was as good as another. American servants insisted on being called the "help" and viewed as neighbors invited to assist in running a household rather than as permanent menials. Similarly, whereas in France merchants were disdained by the titled nobility, in America merchants thought themselves equal to anyone.

Historians continue to argue about the meaning and extent of equality in antebellum America, but by using refined techniques of measurement they have drawn a more detailed portrait of antebellum society than the profile sketched by contemporaries. The following discussion applies mainly to northern society. We examine the South, whose "peculiar institution" of slavery created a distinctive social structure and set of social relationships, in Chapter 12.

## Growing Inequality: The Rich and the Poor

The gap between the rich and the poor, which had increased during the late eighteenth century, widened further during the first half of the nineteenth century. Although Americans portrayed them as oases of equality, farm areas contained a good deal of inequality. In 1850 the poorest 40 percent of native-born farmers owned less than one hundred dollars worth of property, whereas the richest 30–40 percent of farmers owned three-fourths or more of the total farm property. But the truly striking inequalities developed in the cities, where a small fraction of the people owned a huge share of urban wealth. In Boston, for example, the richest 10 percent of the population owned a little over half of the city's real estate and personal property in 1771. By 1833 the richest 4 percent owned 59 percent of the wealth, and by 1848 nearly two-thirds of the wealth. By 1848, 81 percent of Boston's population owned only 4 percent of its wealth. In New York City, the richest 4 percent owned nearly half the wealth in 1828 and more than two-thirds by 1845. These statis-

### Cincinnati in 1843

*The population of Cincinnati, the Queen City of the West, rose from 2,540 in 1800 to 161,044, 45 percent of them foreign born, in 1860. Downriver traffic on the Ohio and Mississippi Rivers tied its commerce to the South.*

tics are representative of trends that affected all major cities.

Although commentators celebrated the self-made American who rose "from rags to riches," few individuals actually accumulated their wealth in this way. The vast majority of those who became extremely rich started out with considerable wealth. Fewer than five of every hundred wealthy individuals started poor, and close to ninety of every hundred started rich. The old-fashioned way to make money was to inherit it, marry into more, and then invest wisely. There were just enough instances of fabulously successful poor boys like John Jacob Astor, who built a fur-trading empire, to sustain popular belief in the rags-to-riches myth, but not enough to turn that myth into a reality.

Splendid residences and social clubs also set the rich apart. In 1828 over half of the five hundred wealthiest families in New York City lived on only 8 of the city's more than 250 streets. By the late 1820s New York City had a club so exclusive that it was called simply The Club. Tocqueville noted that in America "the wealthiest and most enlightened live among themselves." Yet Tocqueville was also struck by how the rich feigned respect for equality when they moved about in public. They rode in ordinary rather than sumptuous carriages, brushed elbows easily with the less privileged, and avoided the conspicuous display of wealth that marked their private lives.

At the opposite end of the social ladder were the poor. By today's standards, most antebellum Americans were poor: they lived "close to the margin" of poverty, depended heavily on their children's labor to meet expenses, had little money to spend on medical care or recreation, and were subject to unemployment, not just during general economic downturns but from month to month, even in times of prosperity. Freezing weather, for instance, could temporarily throw day laborers, factory workers, and boatmen out of work. In 1850 an estimated three out of eight males over the age of twenty owned little more than their clothing and the cash in their pockets.

In evaluating economic status, it is important to recognize that statistics on the distribution of wealth to some extent mask the fact that the accumulation of property takes place over an entire lifetime and increases with age. With its extraordinarily high birthrate, antebellum America was overwhelmingly a nation of young people with little property; not all of them would remain propertyless as they grew older.

Also keep in mind that when antebellum Americans themselves spoke of poverty, they were not thinking of the condition of hardship that affected most people. Instead, they were referring to a state of dependency, a total inability to fend for oneself, that affected *some* people. They often called this dependency *pauperism.* The absence of health insurance and old-age pensions condemned many infirm and aged people to pauperism. Widows whose children had left home might also have a hard time avoiding pauperism. Contemporaries usually classified all such people as the "deserving" poor and contrasted them with the "undeserving" poor—such as indolent loafers and drunkards whose poverty was self-willed. Most moralists claimed that America was happily free of a permanent class of paupers. They assumed that since pauperism resulted either from circumstances beyond anyone's control, such as old age and disease, or from voluntary decisions to squander money on liquor, it could not afflict entire groups generation after generation.

This assumption was comforting but also misleading, because a class of people who could not escape poverty was emerging in the major cities during the first half of the nineteenth century. One source of this class was immigration. As early as 1801, a New York newspaper called attention to boatloads of immigrants with large families, without money or health, and "*expiring from the want of sustenance.*" The arrival of huge numbers of Irish immigrants during the 1840s and 1850s made a bad situation worse. The Irish were among the poorest immigrants ever to arrive in America. Fleeing famine in Ireland, they found even worse conditions in noxious slums like New York's infamous Five Points district. Starting with the conversion of a brewery into housing for hundreds of people in 1837, the Five Points became probably the worst slum in America.

The Irish not only were poor but, as Catholics, also belonged to a church despised by the Protestant majority. In short, they were different and had little claim on the kindly impulses of most Protestants. But even the Protestant poor came in for rough treatment in the years between 1815 and 1840. The more Americans convinced themselves that success was within everyone's grasp, the less they accepted the traditional doctrine that poverty was ordained by God, and the more they were inclined to hold the poor responsible for their own misery. Ironically, even as many Americans

DANCING FOR EELS

**"Dancing for Eels"** by James Brown, 1848
*Expressive dancing was part of African-American street festivals in the eighteenth-century cities. Fearing that such street dancing perpetuated white stereotypes of blacks, antislavery whites and black leaders tried to suppress it after 1800, but black dancing survived in dance cellars in New York City's Five Points slum. As this sketch indicates, blacks sometimes danced in public for applause, "a bunch of eels" or other fish, and perhaps money. The black at the left is "patting juba," which meant keeping time by hand clapping or by beating hands against legs. "Juba" also became the nickname of William Henry Lane. After seeing Lane perform in 1842 in a Five Points cellar, the novelist Charles Dickens labeled him "the greatest dancer known."*

blamed the poor for being poor, they practiced discrimination that kept some groups mired in enduring poverty. Nowhere was this more true than in the case of northern free blacks.

### Free Blacks in the North

Prejudice against blacks was deeply ingrained in white society throughout the nation. Although slavery had largely disappeared in the North by 1820, laws penalized blacks in many ways. One form of discrimination was to restrict the blacks' right to vote. In New York State, for example, a constitutional revision of 1821 eliminated property requirements for white voters but kept them for blacks. Rhode Island banned blacks from voting in 1822; Pennsylvania did so in 1837. Throughout the half-century after 1800, blacks could vote on equal terms with whites in only one of the nation's major cities, Boston. Efforts were made to bar free blacks from migrating to other states and cities. Missouri's original constitution authorized the state legislature to prevent blacks from entering the state "under any pretext whatsoever." Free blacks were often barred from public conveyances and facilities and were either excluded from public schools in major cities or forced into segregated schools. Segregation was the rule in northern jails, almshouses, and hospitals. But of all restrictions on free blacks, the most damaging was the social pressure that forced them into the least skilled and lowest-paying occupations throughout the north-

ern cities. Recollecting his youthful days in Providence, Rhode Island, in the early 1830s, the free black William J. Brown wrote: "To drive carriages, carry a market basket after the boss, and brush his boots, or saw wood and run errands was as high as a colored man could rise." Although a few free blacks became successful entrepreneurs and grew moderately wealthy, urban free blacks were only half as likely as city dwellers in general to own real estate.

### The "Middling Classes"

The majority of antebellum Americans lived neither in splendid wealth nor in grinding poverty. Most belonged to what men and women of the time called the middling classes. Even though the wealthy owned an increasing proportion of all wealth, most people's standard of living rose between 1800 and 1860, particularly between 1840 and 1860, when per capita income grew at an annual rate of around 1.5 percent.

Americans applied the term *middling classes* to farmers and artisans, whose ideal was self-employment. Commentators viewed them as steady and dependable, the nation's sturdy "producers." Yet life in the middle was unpredictable, filled with jagged ups and downs. Words like *farmer* and *artisan* were often misleading, for they gave a greater impression of steadiness and stability than was really the case. For example, Asa G. Sheldon, born in Massachusetts in 1788, described himself in his autobiography as a farmer, offered advice on growing corn and cranberries, and gave speeches about the glories of farming. Although Sheldon undoubtedly knew a great deal about farming, he actually spent very little time tilling the soil. In 1812 he began to transport hops from New England to brewers in New York City, and he soon extended this business to Philadelphia and Baltimore. He invested his profits in land, but rather than farm the land, he made money selling its timber. When a business setback forced him to sell his property, he was soon back in operation "through the disinterested kindness of friends," who lent him money with which he purchased carts and oxen. These he used to get contracts for filling in swamps in Boston and for clearing and grading land for railroads. From all this and from the backbreaking labor of the Irish immigrants he hired to do the shoveling, Sheldon the "farmer" grew prosperous. But his prosperity in fact owed little to farming.

The increasingly commercial and industrial economy of antebellum America created opportunities for success and forced individuals like Sheldon to adapt. Not everyone, though, had an opportunity for success. Had it not been for the intervention of wealthy friends, Sheldon would have ended up in a poorhouse. Many lacked kindly friends with money to lend. Some, like Sheldon, rose. Others, like Allan Melville, father of novelist Herman Melville, slipped down the slope. An enterprising import merchant, Allan Melville had an abounding faith in his nation, in "our national Eagle, 'with an eye that never winks and a wing that never tires,' " and in the inevitable triumph of honesty and prudence. The Melvilles lived comfortably in Albany and New York City, but in the late 1820s, Melville's business, never robust, sagged. By 1830 he was begging his father for a loan of $500, proclaiming that "I am destitute of resources and without a shilling—without immediate assistance I know not what will become of me." He got the $500 plus an additional $3,000, but the downward spiral continued. In 1832 he died, broken in spirit and nearly insane.

The case of artisans also illustrates the perils of life in the middling classes. During the colonial period, artisans had formed a proud and cohesive group whose members often attained the goal of self-employment. They owned their own tools, made their own products on order from customers, boarded their apprentices and journeymen in their homes, and passed their skills on to their children. By 1850, in contrast, artisans had entered a new world of economic relationships. This was true even of a craft like carpentry that did not experience any industrial or technological change. Town and city growth in the wake of the transportation revolution created a demand for housing. Some carpenters, usually those with access to capital, became contractors who took orders for more houses than they could build themselves and who then hired large numbers of journeymen to do the construction work. Likewise, as we have seen, in the early industrialization of shoe manufacturing during the 1820s, some shoemakers spent less time crafting shoes than making trips to obtain orders for their products, then hired workers to fashion parts of shoes. In effect, the old class of artisans was splitting into two new groupings. On one side were artisans who had become entrepreneurs; on the other, journeymen with little prospect of self-employment.

An additional characteristic of the middling classes (one that they shared with the poor) was a high degree of transiency, or "spatial mobility." Farmers who cultivated land intensively in order to raise a cash crop and so get out of debt exhausted their land quickly and had to move on. Artisans displaced from skilled jobs by machines found that much unskilled work was seasonal and that they had to move from job to job to survive. Canal workers and boatmen had to secure new work when waterways froze. Even for city dwellers, to shift jobs often meant changing residences, for the cities were spreading out at a much faster rate than was public transportation. Some idea of the degree of transiency can be gained from a survey made by the Boston police on Saturday, September 6, 1851. At a time when Boston's population was 145,000, the survey showed that from 6:30 A.M. to 7:30 P.M., 41,729 people entered the city and 42,313 left.

The multiplying risks and opportunities that confronted Americans both widened the gap between social classes and increased the psychological burdens on individuals. Commercial and industrial growth also placed pressure on such basic social relationships as those between lawyers and their clients, ministers and their parishioners, and children and their parents.

## The Revolution in Social Relationships

Following the War of 1812, the growth of interregional trade, commercial agriculture, and manufacturing disrupted many traditional social relationships and forged new ones. Two broad generalizations encompass these changes. First, Americans questioned authority to an unprecedented degree. In 1775 they had rebelled against their king. Now, it seemed, they were rebelling as well against their lawyers, physicians, ministers, and even their parents. An attitude of individualism sprouted and took firm root in antebellum America. Once *individualism* had meant nothing more than selfishness, but now Americans used the word to signify positive qualities: self-reliance and the conviction that each person was the best judge of his or her own true interests. Ordinary Americans might still agree with the opinions of their leaders, but only after they had thought matters through on their own. Those with superior wealth, education, or social position could no longer expect the automatic deference of the common people.

Second, even as Americans widely proclaimed themselves a nation of self-reliant individualists and questioned the traditional basis of authority, they sought to construct new foundations for authority. For example, among middle-class women, the idea developed that they possessed a "separate sphere" of authority in the home. In addition, individuals increasingly joined with others in these years to form voluntary associations through which they might influence the direction that their society would take.

### The Attack on the Professions

The first phase in this alteration of social relationships witnessed the erosion of traditional forms of authority. In the swiftly changing antebellum society, claims to social superiority were questioned as never before. The statesman Harrison Gray Otis put it in a nutshell in 1836: "Everywhere the disposition is found among those who live in the valleys to ask those who live on the hills, 'How came we here and you there?' "

Intense criticism of lawyers, physicians, and ministers exemplified this assault on authority. As far back as the 1780s, Benjamin Austin, a radical Boston artisan, had complained that lawyers needlessly prolonged and confused court cases so that they could charge high fees. Between 1800 and 1840, a wave of religious revivals known as the Second Great Awakening (see Chapter 10) sparked new attacks on the professions. Some revivalists blasted the clergy for creating complicated theologies that ordinary men and women could not comprehend, for drinking expensive wines, and for fleecing the people. One religious revivalist, Elias

Smith, extended the criticism to physicians, whom he accused of inventing Latin and Greek names for diseases in order to disguise their own ignorance of how to cure them.

Attacks on the learned professions peaked between 1820 and 1850. In medicine a movement arose under the leadership of Samuel Thomson, a farmer's son with little formal education, to eliminate all barriers to entry into the medical profession. Thomson believed that anyone could understand the principles of medicine and become a physician. His crusade was remarkably successful. By 1845 every state had repealed laws that required licenses and education to practice medicine. Meanwhile, attacks on lawyers sharpened, and relations between ministers and their parishioners grew tense and acrimonious. In colonial New England, ministers had usually served a single parish for life, but by the 1830s a rapid turnover of ministers was becoming the norm as finicky parishioners commonly dismissed clergymen whose theology displeased them. Ministers themselves were becoming more ambitious—more inclined to leave small, poor congregations for large, wealthy ones.

The increasing commercialization of the economy contributed both to the growing number of professionals and to the attacks on them. The rise of the market economy intensified the demand for lawyers and physicians; the number of medical schools, for example, grew from one in 1765 to twenty in 1830 and sixty-five in 1860. Like so many other antebellum Americans, these freshly minted lawyers and doctors often were transients without deep roots in the towns that they served and without convincing claims to social superiority. Describing lawyers and physicians, a contemporary observer wrote: "Men dropped down into their places as from clouds. Nobody knew who or what they were, except as they claimed, or as a surface view of their character indicated." A horse doctor one day would the next day hang up his sign as "Physician and Surgeon" and "fire at random a box of his pills into your bowels, with a vague chance of hitting some disease unknown to him, but with a better prospect of killing the patient, whom or whose administrator he charged some ten dollars a trial for his marksmanship."

The questioning of authority was particularly sharp on the frontier. Here, to eastern and foreign visitors, it seemed that every man they met was a "judge," "general," "colonel," or "squire." In a society in which everyone was new, such titles were easily adopted but just as easily challenged. Where neither law nor custom sanctioned claims of superiority, would-be gentlemen substituted an exaggerated sense of personal honor. Obsessed with their fragile status, many of these "gentlemen" reacted testily to the slightest insult. Dueling became a widespread frontier practice. At a Kentucky militia parade in 1819, an officer's dog jogged onto the field and sat at his master's knee. Enraged by this breach of military decorum, another officer ran the dog through with his sword. A week later, both officers met with pistols at ten paces. One was killed; the other maimed for life.

### The Challenge to Family Authority

In contrast to the public, philosophical attacks on the learned professions, children engaged in a quiet questioning of parental authority. Economic change created new opportunities that forced young people to choose between staying at home to help their parents and venturing out on their own. Writing to her parents in Vermont shortly before taking a job in a Lowell textile mill, eighteen-year-old Sally Rice quickly got to the point: "I must of course have something of my own before many more years have passed over my head and where is that something coming from if I go home and earn nothing. You may think me unkind but how can you blame me if I want to stay here. I have but one life to live and I want to enjoy myself as I can while I live."

A similar desire for independence tempted young men to leave home at earlier ages than in the past and to strike out on their own. Although the great migration to the West was primarily a movement of entire families, movement from farms to towns and cities within regions was frequently spearheaded by restless and single young people. Two young men in Virginia put it succinctly: "All the promise of life seemed to us to be at the other end of the rainbow—somewhere else—anywhere else but on the farm. . . . And so all our youthful plans had as their chief object the getting away from the farm."

Antebellum Americans also widely wished to be free of close parental supervision, and their changing attitudes influenced courtship and marriage. Many young people who no longer depended on their parents for land insisted on privacy in courting and wanted to decide for themselves when and whom to marry. Increasingly, too, romantic love between the partners rather than parental preferences determined decisions to marry. Whereas seventeenth-century Puritans had advised young people to choose marriage partners whom they *could* love, by the early 1800s, young men and women viewed romantic love as the indispensable basis for a successful marriage. "In affairs of love," a young lawyer in Maine wrote, "young peoples hearts are generally much wiser than old peoples heads."

One sign of young people's growing control over courtship and marriage was the declining likelihood that the young women of a family would marry in their exact birth order. Traditionally, fathers had wanted their daughters to marry in the order of their birth, to avoid planting the suspicion that there was something wrong with one or more of them. Toward the end of the eighteenth century, however, the practice ceased to be customary, as daughters were making their own marital decisions. Another mark of the times was the growing number of long engagements. Having made the decision to marry, some young women were reluctant to tie the knot, fearing that marriage would snuff out their independence. For example, Caroline and William Kirkland were engaged for seven years before their marriage in 1828. Equally striking was the increasing number of young women who chose not to marry. Catharine Beecher, the daughter of the prominent minister Lyman Beecher, broke off her engagement to a young man during the 1820s, despite her father's pressure to marry him. She later renewed the engagement, but after her fiancé's death in a shipwreck, she remained single for the rest of her life.

Thus young people lived more and more in a world of their own. Not surprisingly, moralists reacted with alarm and flooded the country with books of advice to youth such as William Alcott's *The Young Man's Guide*, which went through thirty-one editions between 1833 and 1858. The number of such advice books sold in antebellum America was truly vast, but to an amazing extent, they all said the same thing. They did not advise young men and women to return to farms, and they assumed that parents had little control over them. Rather, their authors exhorted youths to develop habitual rectitude, self-control, and "character." It was an age not just of the self-made adult but also of the self-made youth.

### Wives, Husbands

Another class of advice books pouring from the antebellum presses counseled wives and husbands on their rights and duties. These were a sign that relations between spouses, too, were changing. Young men and

**Ingersell Family in 1818**

*This watercolor of a Maine family captures the large size of antebellum families and the importance they attached to children. The parents point toward the infant Peggy. But childhood was short. Five-year-old Solomon on the bottom left is dressed as a child, but his older brothers to his left, respectively twelve and nine, are clothed as adults, and Eli grips a paper scroll rather than Solomon's butterfly.*

were changing during the 1820s and 1830s toward a form of equality.

One source of the change was the rise of a potent ideology known as the doctrine of separate spheres. Traditionally, women had been viewed as subordinate to men in all spheres of life. Now middle-class men and women developed a kind of separate-but-equal doctrine that portrayed men as superior in making money and governing the world and women as superior for their moral influence on family members. One of the most important duties assigned to the sphere of women was the raising of children. During the eighteenth century, ministers had addressed sermons to fathers to remind them of their duty to govern the family, but by the 1830s child-rearing manuals increasingly appealed to mothers rather than fathers. "How entire and perfect is this dominion over the unformed character of your infant," the popular writer Lydia Sigourney proclaimed in her *Letters to Mothers* (1838). Advice books instructed mothers to discipline their children by loving them and withdrawing affection when they misbehaved rather than by using corporal punishment. A whipped child might become more obedient but would remain sullen and bitter. In contrast, the gentler methods advised in manuals promised to penetrate to the child's heart, to make the child want to do the right thing.

The idea of a separate women's sphere blended with a related image of the family and the home as secluded refuges from a society marked by commotion and disorder. The popular culture of the 1830s and 1840s painted an alluring portrait of the pleasures of home life through songs like "Home, Sweet Home" and poems such as Henry Wadsworth Longfellow's "The Children's Hour" and Clement Moore's "A Visit from St. Nicholas." The publication of Moore's poem coincided with the growing popularity of Christmas as a holiday season in which family members gathered to exchange warm affection. Even the physical appearance of houses changed as architects offered new designs for the ideal home. The prominent architect Andrew Jackson Downing published plans for peaceful single-family homes that he hoped would offset the "spirit of unrest" and the feverish pace of American life. He wrote of the ideal home: "There should be something to love. There must be nooks about it, where one would love to linger; windows, where one can enjoy the quiet landscape at his leisure; cozy rooms, where all fireside joys are invited to dwell."

women who, as teenagers, had grown accustomed to making decisions on their own were more likely than their ancestors to approach wedlock as a compact between equals. Of course, wives remained unequal to their husbands in many tangible ways, the most obvious being the continuation into the 1830s of the traditional legal rule that married women could not own property. But relations between wives and husbands

As a prophet, Downing deserves high marks because one of the motives that has impelled many Americans to flee cities for suburbs in the twentieth century has been the desire to achieve ownership of a single-family residence. However, in the 1820s and 1830s, this ideal was beyond the reach of most people—not just blacks, immigrants, and sweatshop workers, but much of the middle class as well. In the countryside, although middle-class farmers still managed productive households, these were anything but tranquil: wives milked cows and bled hogs, and children fetched wood, drove cows to pasture, and chased blackbirds from cornfields. In the cities, middle-class families often had to sacrifice their privacy by taking in boarders to supplement family income.

Despite their distortions, the doctrine of separate spheres and the image of the home as a refuge from a harsh world intersected with reality at *some* points. The rising number of urban families headed by lawyers and merchants (who worked away from home) gave mothers more time to spend on child rearing. Above all, even if they could not afford to live in a Downing-designed house, married women found that they could capitalize on these notions to gain new power within their families. A subtle implication of the doctrine of separate spheres was that women should have control not only over the discipline of children but also over the more fundamental issue of the number of children that they would bear.

In 1800 the United States had one of the highest birthrates ever recorded. The average American woman bore 7.04 children. It is safe to say that married women had become pregnant as often as possible. In the prevailing farm economy, children were valuable for carrying out essential tasks and, as time passed, for relieving aging parents of the burden of heavy farm labor. Most parents had assumed that the more children, the better. However, the spread of a commercial economy raised troublesome questions about children's economic value. Unlike a farmer, a merchant or lawyer could not send his children to work at the age of seven or eight. The average woman, who had borne 7.04 children in 1800, was bearing only 5.02 by 1850, and 3.98 by 1900. The birthrate remained high among blacks and among many immigrant groups, but it slumped drastically among native-born whites, particularly in towns and cities. The birthrate also declined in rural areas, but more sharply in rural villages than on farms, and more sharply in the East, where land was scarce, than in the West, where abundant land created continued incentives for parents to have many children.

For the most part, the decline in the birthrate was accomplished by abstinence from sexual intercourse, by *coitus interruptus* (withdrawal of the penis before ejaculation), or by abortion. By the 1840s such abortionists as New York City's notorious Madame Restell advertised remedies for "female irregularities," a common euphemism for unwanted pregnancies. There were no foolproof birth-control devices, and as much misinformation as information circulated about the techniques of birth control. Nonetheless, interest in birth-control devices was intensifying. In 1832 Charles Knowlton, a Massachusetts physician, described the procedure for vaginal douching in his book *Fruits of Philosophy*. Although Knowlton was frequently prosecuted and once jailed for obscenity, efforts to suppress his ideas only resulted in their being publicized even more. By 1865 popular tracts had familiarized Americans with a wide range of birth-control methods, including the rubber condom and the vaginal diaphragm. Whatever the method, the decision to limit family size was usually reached jointly by wives and husbands. Economic and ideological considerations blended together. Husbands could note that the economic value of children was declining; wives, that having fewer children would give them more time to nurture each one and thereby carry out domestic duties.

Supporters of the ideal of separate spheres did not advocate full legal equality for women. Indeed, the idea of separate spheres was an explicit *alternative* to legal equality. But the concept did enhance women's power within marriage by justifying their demands for influence over such vital issues as child rearing and the frequency of pregnancies. In addition, it allowed some women a measure of independence from the home. For example, it sanctioned Catharine Beecher's travels to lecture women on better ways to raise children and manage their households.

## Horizontal Allegiances and the Rise of Voluntary Associations

As some forms of authority, such as that of parents over their children and of husbands over their wives, were weakening, Americans devised new ways through which individuals could extend their influence over others. The pre–Civil War period witnessed the widespread substitution of *horizontal* allegiances for *vertical* allegiances. An example of vertical allegiance is found in the traditional patriarchal family, wherein a wife and children looked up to the father for leadership. Another example occurs in the small eighteenth-century workshop, where apprentices and journeymen took direction from the master craftsman and even lived in the craftsman's house, subject to his authority. Common to these examples is the idea of authority flowing from the top down. In a vertical allegiance, people in a subordinate position identify their best interests with the interests of their superiors rather than with those of other individuals in the same subordinate position.

When social relationships began to assume a horizontal form, several new patterns emerged. Although the older kind of vertical relationships did not disappear, they became less important in people's lives. Relationships now arose that linked those in a similar position. For example, in large textile mills during the 1830s, many operatives discovered that they had more in common with one another than with their managers and overseers. Similarly, wives were increasingly inclined to form associations that bound them with other married women. Young men formed associations with other young men. None of these associations was intended to overthrow traditional authority. Many of them in fact professed to strengthen the family or community. But all represented the substitution of new allegiances for old ones.

A sign of the change can be seen in the large number of voluntary associations formed in the 1820s and 1830s. These were associations that arose apart from government and sought to accomplish some goal of value to their members. Tocqueville observed that in France the government stood at the head of every enterprise but that in America "you will be sure to find an association."

At the most basic level, the voluntary associations encouraged sociability. As transients and newcomers flocked into towns and cities, they tended to join with others who shared similar characteristics, experiences, or interests. Gender was the basis of many voluntary societies. Of twenty-six religious and charitable associations in Utica, New York, in 1832, for instance, one-third were exclusively for women. Race was still another basis for voluntary associations. Although their names did not indicate it, Boston's Thompson Literary and Debating Society, its Philomathean Adelphic Union for the

Promotion of Literature and Science, and New York City's Phoenix Society were all organizations for free blacks.

The pleasures of sociability were not the only benefit of voluntary associations. These associations also allowed their members to assert their influence at a time when traditional forms of authority were weakening. For example, voluntary associations proved compatible with the idea that women had a separate sphere. As long as a woman could argue that her activities were in the best interests of the home, she could escape the kitchen long enough to join maternal associations (where mothers exchanged ideas about child rearing), temperance associations (where they promoted abstinence from alcoholic beverages), and moral-reform societies. These latter societies, which multiplied in the 1830s and 1840s, combated prostitution.

Temperance and moral-reform societies had a dual purpose. They sought to suppress well-known vices *and* to enhance women's power over men. Temperance advocates assumed that intemperance was a male vice. Moral reformers attributed the prevalence of prostitution to the lustfulness of men who, unable to control their passions, exploited poor and vulnerable girls. While exhorting prostitutes to give up their line of work, moral reformers also tried to shame brothel patrons into chastity by publishing their names in newspapers. Just as strikes in Lowell in the 1830s were a form of collective action by working women, temperance and moral-reform societies represented collective action by middle-class women to increase their influence in society. Here, as elsewhere, the tendency of the times was to forge new forms of horizontal allegiance between like-minded Americans.

## CONCLUSION

The expansion of the white population to the Mississippi River burgeoned after 1815. European demand for American agricultural products, especially cotton, federal policies that eased the sale of public lands and encouraged the removal of Indians from the path of white settlement, and the availability of loose-lending banks and paper money all contributed to the postwar boom. The collapse of the boom in 1819 reminded farmers of how dependent they had become on distant markets and prompted improvements in transportation during the 1820s and 1830s. The introduction of steamboats, the building of canals, and the gradual spread of railroads—the transportation revolution—encouraged a turn to commercial occupations and the growth of towns and cities. Now able to reach distant consumers, merchants plunged capital into manufacturing enterprises.

These changes carved new avenues to prosperity for some, and to penury for others. They challenged traditional hierarchies and created new forms of social alignment based on voluntary associations. By joining voluntary associations based on shared interests or opinions, footloose Americans forged new identities that paralleled and often supplanted older allegiances to their parents or places of birth.

## FOR FURTHER READING

Rowland Berthoff, *An Unsettled People: Social Order and Disorder in American History* (1971). A stimulating interpretation of American social history.

Ray A. Billington, *Westward Expansion: A History of the American Frontier* (1949). The standard study of westward movement and settlement.

Carl Degler, *At Odds: Women and the Family in America from the Revolution to the Present* (1980). A fine overview of the economic and social experiences of American women.

Harry N. Scheiber, *The Ohio Canal Era: A Case Study of Government and the Economy, 1820–1861* (1969). An analysis that speaks volumes about economic growth in the early republic.

Charles Sellers, *The Market Revolution: Jacksonian America, 1815–1846* (1991). A major, and controversial, reinterpretation of the period.

Alan Taylor, *William Cooper's Town* (1995). A compelling portrait of the New York frontier in the late eighteenth and early nineteenth centuries.

Sean Wilentz, *Chants Democratic: New York City and the Rise of the American Working Class, 1788–1850* (1983). A stimulating synthesis of economic, social, and political history.

# 10 Politics, Religion, and Reform in the Age of Jackson

**Reading the News,** by Christian Friederck Mayr, 1844

In 1824 the Marquis de Lafayette, former major general in the Continental Army and a Revolutionary War hero, accepted the invitation of President James Monroe and Congress and revisited the United States. For thirteen months as "the Nation's Guest," Lafayette traveled to every state and received a welcome that fluctuated between warm and tumultuous. There seemed no limits to what Americans would do to show their admiration for this "greatest man in the world." "There were," one contemporary wrote, "*La Fayette* boots—*La Fayette* hats—*La Fayette* wine—and *La Fayette* everything." In New York City, some fervid patriots tried to unhitch the horses from Lafayette's carriage and pull it up Broadway themselves.

Lafayette had contributed mightily to the Revolution's success. Americans venerated him as a living embodiment of the entire Revolutionary generation fast passing from the scene. The majority of Americans alive in 1824 had been born since George Washington's death in 1799. John Adams and Thomas Jefferson survived, but they were along in years. Both would die on July 4, 1826, fifty years to the day after the signing of the Declaration of Independence. Seizing on Washington's remark that he loved Lafayette "as my own son," Americans toasted the Frenchman as a cherished member of the family of Revolutionary heroes. In Charleston the toast ran: "WASHINGTON, our Common Father—*you* his favorite *son*"; in New Jersey, "LA FAYETTE, a living monument of greatness, virtue, and faithfulness still exists—a second Washington is now among us."

The festive rituals surrounding Lafayette's visit symbolized Americans' conviction that they had remained true to their heritage of republican liberty. The embers of conflict between Federalists and Republicans that once had seemed to threaten the Republic's stability had cooled; the Era of Good Feelings still reigned over American politics in 1824. Yet even as Americans were turning Lafayette's visit into an affirmation of their ties to the Founders, those ties were fraying in the face of new challenges. Westward migration, growing economic individualism, and increasing sectional conflict over slavery shaped politics mightily between 1824 and 1840. The impact of economic and social change shattered old assumptions and contributed to a vigorous new brand of politics.

This transformation led to the birth of a second American party system, in which two new parties, the Democrats and the Whigs, replaced the Republicans and the Federalists. More was at work here than a change of names. The new parties took advantage of the transportation revolution to spread their messages to the farthest corners of the nation and to arouse voters in all sections. The new parties' leaders were more effective than their predecessors at organizing grass-roots support, more eager to make government responsive to the popular will, and more likely to enjoy politics and welcome conflict as a way to sustain interest in political issues.

Not all Americans looked to politics as the pathway to their goals. Some, in fact, viewed politics as suited only to scoundrels and could identify with the sentiments of the Detroit workingman who wrote in 1832 that he "did not vote. I'll [have] none of sin." Despairing of politics, many men and women became active in reform movements pursuing various goals, among them the abolition of slavery, the suppression of the liquor trade, improved public education, and equality for women. Strongly held religious beliefs impelled reformers into these causes, while simultaneously increasing their distrust of politics. Yet even reformers hostile to politics gradually found that the success of their reforms depended on their ability to influence the political process.

**Lafayette Pitcher**

*The craze for Lafayette artifacts included tableware.*

During the 1820s and 1830s, the political and reform agendas of Americans diverged increasingly from those of the Founders. The Founders had feared popular participation in politics, enjoyed their wine and rum, left an ambiguous legacy on slavery, and displayed only occasional interest in women's rights. Yet even as Americans shifted their political and social priorities, they continued to venerate the Founders, who were revered in death even more than in life. Histories of the United States, biographies of Revolutionary patriots, and torchlight parades that bore portraits of Washington and Jefferson alongside those of Andrew Jackson all helped to reassure the men and women of the young nation that they were remaining loyal to their republican heritage.

This chapter focuses on four major questions:

♦ In what ways had American politics become more democratic by 1840 than at the time of Jefferson's election in 1800?

♦ What factors explain Andrew Jackson's popularity? How did Jackson's policies contribute to the rise of the rival Whig party?

♦ How did the Panic of 1837 and its aftermath solidify the two parties, Democrats and Whigs?

♦ What new assumptions about human nature lay behind the religious and reform movements of the period?

# The Transformation of American Politics, 1824–1832

In 1824 Andrew Jackson and Martin Van Buren, who would guide the Democratic party in the 1830s, and Henry Clay and John Quincy Adams, who would become that decade's leading Whigs, all belonged to the same political party, the Republican party of Thomas Jefferson. Yet by 1824 the Republican party was coming

apart at the seams under pressures generated by industrialization in New England, the spread of cotton cultivation in the South, and westward expansion. These forces sparked issues that would become the basis for the new political division between Democrats and Whigs. In general, those Republicans (augmented by a few former Federalists) who retained Jefferson's suspicion of a strong federal government and preference for states' rights became Democrats; those Republicans (along with many former Federalists) who believed that the national government should actively encourage economic development became Whigs.

Regardless of which path a politician chose, all leaders in the 1820s and 1830s had to adapt to the rising democratic idea of politics as a forum for the expression of the will of the common people rather than as an activity that gentlemen conducted for the people. Gentlemen could still be elected to office, but their success now depended less on their education or wealth than on their ability to identify and follow the will of the majority. Americans still looked up to their political leaders, but the leaders could no longer look down on the people.

## *Democratic Ferment*

Political democratization took several forms. One of the most common was the substitution of poll taxes for the traditional requirement that voters own property. None of the new western states required property ownership for voting, and eastern states gradually liberalized their laws. Moreover, written ballots replaced the custom of voting aloud (called *viva voce* or "stand-up" voting), which had enabled superiors to influence, or intimidate, their inferiors at the polls. Too, appointive office increasingly became elective. The electoral college survived, but the choice of presidential electors by state legislatures gave way to their direct election by the voters. In 1800, rather than voting for Thomas Jefferson or John Adams, most Americans could do no more than vote for the men who would vote for the men who would vote for Jefferson or Adams. By 1824, however, legislatures chose electors in only six states, and by 1832 only in South Carolina.

The fierce tug of war between the Republicans and the Federalists in the 1790s and early 1800s chipped away at the old barriers to the people's expression of their will. First the Republicans and then the Federalists learned to woo voters by staging grand barbecues at which men from Massachusetts to Maryland washed down free clams and oysters with free beer and whiskey. Wherever one party was in a minority, it sought to become the majority party by increasing the electorate. Jefferson's followers showed more interest in registering new voters in New England, where they were weak, than in their southern strongholds. Federalists played the same game; the initiator of suffrage reform in Maryland was an aristocratic Federalist.

Political democratization developed at an uneven pace. In 1820 both the Federalists and Republicans were still organized from the top down. To nominate candidates, for example, both parties relied on the caucus (a conference of party members in the legislature) rather than on popularly elected nominating conventions. Further, even as they recruited new voters in practice, few party leaders embraced the *principle* of universal white manhood suffrage. Nor did the democratization of politics necessarily draw more voters to the polls. The collapse of the Federalists after 1816 stripped national politics of clear issues and turned off voters.

Yet no one could mistake the tendency of the times: to oppose the people or democracy had become a formula for political suicide. The people, a Federalist moaned, "have become too saucy and are really beginning to fancy themselves equal to their betters." Whatever their convictions, politicians learned to adjust.

## The Election of 1824

Sectional tensions brought the Era of Good Feelings to an end in 1824, when five candidates, all Republicans, vied for the presidency. John Quincy Adams emerged as New England's favorite. South Carolina's brilliant

**The Election of 1824**

| Candidates | Parties | Electoral Vote | Popular Vote | Percentage of Popular Vote |
|---|---|---|---|---|
| JOHN QUINCY ADAMS | Democratic-Republican | 84 | 108,740 | 30.5 |
| Andrew Jackson | Democratic-Republican | 99 | 153,544 | 43.1 |
| William H. Crawford | Democratic-Republican | 41 | 46,618 | 13.1 |
| Henry Clay | Democratic-Republican | 37 | 47,136 | 13.2 |

John C. Calhoun contended with Georgia's William Crawford, an old-school Jeffersonian, for southern support. Out of the West marched Henry Clay of Kentucky, ambitious, crafty, and confident that his American System of protective tariffs and federally supported internal improvements would endear him to manufacturing interests in the East as well as to the West.

Clay's belief that he was holding a solid block of western states was punctured by the rise of a fifth candidate, Andrew Jackson of Tennessee. At first, none of the other candidates took Jackson seriously. But he was popular on the frontier and in the South and stunned his rivals by gaining the support of opponents of the American System from Pennsylvania and other northern states.

Although the Republican congressional caucus chose Crawford as the party's official candidate early in 1824, the caucus could no longer unify the party. Three-fourths of the Republicans in Congress had refused to attend the caucus. Crawford's already diminished prospects evaporated when he suffered a paralyzing stroke. Impressed by Jackson's support, Calhoun withdrew from the race and ran unopposed for the vice presidency. In the election, Jackson won more popular and electoral votes than any other candidate (Adams, Crawford, and Clay) but failed to gain a majority, as required by the Constitution. Thus the election was thrown into the House of Representatives, whose members had to choose from the three top candidates—Jackson, Adams, and Crawford. Hoping to forge an alliance between the West and Northeast in a future bid for the presidency, Clay gave his support to Adams. Clay's action secured the presidency for Adams, but when Adams promptly appointed Clay his secretary of state, Jackson's supporters raged that a "corrupt bargain" had cheated Jackson of the presidency. Although there is no evidence that Adams had traded Clay's support for an explicit agreement to appoint Clay his secretary of state (an office from which Jefferson, Madison, Monroe, and Adams himself had risen to the presidency), the allegation of a corrupt bargain was widely believed. It formed a cloud that hung over Adams's presidency.

### John Quincy Adams as President

Failing to understand the changing political climate, Adams made several other miscalculations that would cloak his presidency in controversy. For example, in 1825 he proposed a program of federal aid for internal improvements. Strict Jeffersonians had always opposed such aid as unconstitutional, but now they were joined by pragmatists like New York's senator Martin Van Buren. Aware that New York had just completed construction of the Erie Canal with its own funds, Van Buren opposed federal aid to improvements on the grounds that it would enable other states to build rival canals. Adams next proposed sending American delegates to a conference of newly independent Latin American nations, a proposal that infuriated southerners because it would imply U.S. recognition of Haiti, the black republic created by slave revolutionaries. Instead of seeking new bases of support, Adams clung to the increasingly obsolete notion of the president as custodian of the public good, aloof from partisan politics. He alienated his supporters by appointing his opponents to high office, and wrote loftily, "I have no wish to fortify myself by the support of any party whatever." Idealistic though his view was, it guaranteed him a single-term presidency.

### The Rise of Andrew Jackson

As Adams's popularity declined, Andrew Jackson's rose. Although Jackson's victory over the British in the Battle of New Orleans had made him a hero, veteran politicians distrusted his notoriously hot temper and his penchant for duels. (Jackson had once challenged an opposing lawyer to a duel for ridiculing his legal arguments in a court case.) But as the only presidential candidate in the election of 1824 with no connection to the Monroe administration, Jackson benefited from what Calhoun recognized as "a vague but widespread discontent" in the wake of the Panic of 1819 that left people with "a general mass of disaffection to the Government" and "looking out anywhere for a leader." To many Americans, Jackson, who as a boy had fought in the Revolution, seemed like a living link to a more virtuous past.

**"Cinque"** by Nathaniel Joselyn *In 1839, fifty-three Africans who had been illegally transported to Cuba as slaves rose up and seized control of the Cuban schooner Amistad. After an American revenue schooner intercepted the Amistad off Long Island, the slaves were imprisoned in New Haven, Connecticut, while the courts considered the claims of their Cuban owners to restitution. After an impassioned plea for their freedom by former president John Quincy Adams, the U.S. Supreme Court ruled in favor of their leader, Joseph Cinque, and his men and ordered them returned to Africa as free people.*

Jackson's supporters swiftly established committees throughout the country. Two years before the election of 1828, towns and villages across the United States buzzed with furious but unfocused political activity. With the exception of the few remaining Federalists, almost everyone called himself a Republican. Some Republicans were "Adams men," others were "Jackson men," and still others styled themselves "friends of Clay." Amid all the confusion, few realized that a new political system was being born. The man most alert to the signs of the times was Martin Van Buren, who was to become vice president during Jackson's second term and president upon Jackson's retirement.

Van Buren exemplified a new breed of politician. A tavernkeeper's son, he had started his political career in county politics and worked his way up to New York's governorship. In Albany he built a powerful political machine, the Albany Regency, composed mainly of men like himself from the lower and middling ranks. His archrival in New York politics, DeWitt Clinton, was all that Van Buren was not—tall, handsome, aristocratic, and brilliant. But Van Buren had a geniality that made ordinary people feel comfortable and an uncanny ability to sense in which direction the political winds were about to blow. Van Buren loved politics, which he viewed as a wonderful game; he was one of the first prominent American politicians to make personal friends from among his political enemies.

The election of 1824 convinced Van Buren of the need for renewed two-party competition. Without the discipline imposed by a strong opposition party, the Republicans in 1824 had splintered into sectional pieces. No candidate had secured an electoral majority, and the House of Representatives had decided the outcome amid charges of intrigue and corruption. It would be better, Van Buren concluded, to let all the shades of opinion in the nation be reduced to two. Then the parties would clash, and a clear popular winner would emerge. Jackson's strong showing in the election persuaded Van Buren that "Old Hickory" could lead a new political party. In the election of 1828, this party, which gradually became known as the Democratic party, put up Jackson for president and Calhoun for vice president. Its opponents, calling themselves the National Republicans, rallied behind Adams and his running mate, treasury secretary Richard Rush. Slowly but surely, the second American party system was taking shape.

### The Election of 1828

The 1828 campaign was a vicious, mudslinging affair. The National Republicans attacked Jackson as a drunken gambler, an adulterer, and a murderer. In fact, between duels and military executions he was directly responsible for several men's deaths; and in 1791 he had married Rachel Robards, erroneously believing that her divorce from her first husband had become final. "Ought a convicted adulteress and her paramour husband," the Adams men taunted, "be placed in the highest office of this free and Christian land?" Jackson's supporters replied in kind. They accused Adams of wearing silk underwear, being rich, being in debt, and having gained favor with the tsar of Russia by trying to provide him with a beautiful American prostitute.

Although both sides engaged in tossing barbs, Jackson's men had better aim. Charges by Adams's supporters that Jackson was an illiterate backwoodsman only added to Jackson's popular appeal by making him seem like just an ordinary citizen. Jackson's supporters portrayed the clash as one between "the *democracy* of the *country*, on the one hand, and a *lordly purse-proud aristocracy* on the other." Jackson, they said, was the common man incarnate—his mind unclouded by learning, his morals simple and true, his will fierce and resolute. In contrast, Jackson's men represented Adams as an aristocrat, a dry scholar whose learning obscured the truth, a man who could write but not fight. Much of this, of course, was wild exaggeration. Jackson was a wealthy planter, not a simple frontiersman. But it was what people wanted to hear. Uncorrupt, natural, plain, Jackson was presented as the common man's image of his better self.

The election swept Jackson into office with more than twice the electoral vote of Adams. Yet the popular vote, much closer, made it clear that the people were not simply responding to the personalities or images of the candidates (though these factors dominated the campaign). The vote also reflected the strongly sec-

tional bases of the new parties. The popular vote was close only in the middle states and the Northwest. Adams gained double Jackson's vote in New England; Jackson received double Adams's vote in the South, and nearly triple Adams's vote in the Southwest.

### Jackson in Office

Jackson rode to the presidency on a wave of opposition to corruption and privilege. As president, his first policy was to support "rotation in office"—the removal of officeholders of the rival party, which critics called the "spoils system." Jackson did not invent this policy, but his conviction that the federal civil service was riddled with corruption led him to apply it more harshly than his predecessors by firing nearly half of the higher civil servants. So many Washington homes were suddenly put up for sale by ousted officeholders that the real estate market slumped.

Jackson defended rotation on new, democratically flavored grounds: the duties of most officeholders were so simple that as many plain people as possible should be given a chance to work for the government. Jackson never quite grasped the extent to which this elevated principle opened the gates to partisan appointments. Jackson himself was inclined to appoint his loyal friends to office, but the future belonged to Martin Van Buren's view that federal jobs should become rewards for loyalty to the victorious party.

Jackson's application of rotation ruffled feathers, but the issues of internal improvements and tariffs ignited real controversy. Like most southerners, Jackson believed that federal support for internal improvements was a lavish giveaway. Further, it was an unconstitutional violation of the principle that Congress could appropriate money only for objectives shared by all Americans, such as national defense, not for the objectives of particular sections or interests. Accordingly, in 1830 he vetoed a bill providing federal support for a road in Kentucky between Maysville and Lexington.

The Maysville Road veto, along with the almost simultaneous passage of the Indian Removal Act (see Chapter 9) enhanced Jackson's popularity in the South. The tariff issue, however, would test the South's loyalty to Jackson. In 1828, while Adams was still president, some of Jackson's supporters in Congress had contributed to the passage of a high protective tariff that was as favorable to western agriculture and New England manufacturing as it was unfavorable to southerners, who had few industries to protect and who now

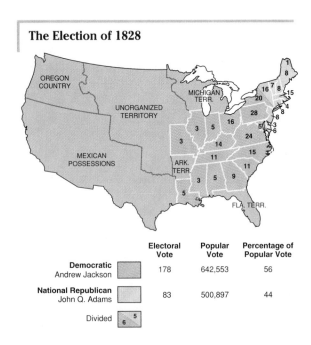

**The Election of 1828**

| | Electoral Vote | Popular Vote | Percentage of Popular Vote |
|---|---|---|---|
| **Democratic** Andrew Jackson | 178 | 642,553 | 56 |
| **National Republican** John Q. Adams | 83 | 500,897 | 44 |
| Divided | 5 / 6 | | |

would have to pay more for manufactured goods. Taking for granted the South's support for Jackson in the coming election, Jackson's supporters had calculated that southerners would blame the Adams administration for this "Tariff of Abominations." In reality, Jackson, not Adams, bore the South's fury over the tariff.

## Nullification

The tariff of 1828 laid the basis for a rift between Jackson and his vice president, John C. Calhoun, that was to shake the foundations of the Republic. Early in his career, Calhoun had been an ardent nationalist. He had entered Congress in 1811 as a "war hawk," supported the protectionist tariff of 1816, and dismissed strict construction of the Constitution as refined philosophical nonsense. During the late 1820s, however, Calhoun the nationalist gradually became Calhoun the states' rights sectionalist. The reasons for his shift were complex. He had supported the tariff of 1816 essentially as a measure conducive to national defense in the wake of the War of 1812. By encouraging fledgling industries, he had reasoned, the tariff would free the United States from dependence upon Britain and provide revenue for military preparedness. By 1826, however, few Americans perceived national defense as a priority. Furthermore, the infant industries of 1816 had grown into troublesome adolescents that demanded higher and higher tariffs.

Calhoun also burned with ambition to be president. Jackson had stated that he would only serve one term, and as vice president Calhoun assumed that he would succeed Jackson. To do so, however, he had to maintain the support of the South, which was increasingly taking an antitariff stance. As the center of cotton production had shifted to the Southwest—Alabama and Mississippi—Calhoun's home state, South Carolina, had suffered an economic decline throughout the 1820s that its voters blamed on high tariffs. Tariffs not only drove up the price of manufactured goods but also threatened to reduce the sale of British textile products in the United States. Such a reduction might eventually lower the British demand for southern cotton and cut cotton prices. The more New England industrialized, the clearer it became that tariff laws were pieces of sectional legislation. New Englanders like Massachusetts's eloquent Daniel Webster swung toward protectionism; southerners responded with militant hostility.

Calhoun followed the Virginia and Kentucky resolutions of 1798–1799 in viewing the Union as a compact by which the states had conferred limited and specified powers on the federal government. Although the Constitution did empower Congress to levy tariffs, Calhoun insisted that only tariffs that raised revenue for such common purposes as defense were constitutional. Set so high that it deterred foreign exporters from shipping their products to the United States, the tariff of 1828 could raise little revenue, and hence it failed to meet Calhoun's criterion of constitutionality: that federal laws benefit everyone *equally*. In 1828 Calhoun anonymously wrote the widely circulated *South Carolina Exposition and Protest,* in which he spelled out his argument that the tariff of 1828 was unconstitutional and that aggrieved states therefore had the right to nullify, or override, the law within their borders.

Vehement opposition to tariffs in the South, and especially in South Carolina, rested on more than economic considerations, however. Southerners feared that a federal government that passed tariff laws favoring one section over another might also pass laws meddling with slavery. Because Jackson himself was a slaveholder, the fear of federal interference with slavery was perhaps far-fetched. But South Carolinians, long apprehensive of assaults on their crucial institution of slavery, had many reasons for concern. South Carolina was one of only two states in which blacks comprised a majority of the population in 1830. Moreover, in 1831 a bloody slave revolt led by Nat Turner boiled up in Virginia. That same year in Massachusetts, William Lloyd Garrison established *The Liberator,* an abolitionist newspaper. These developments were enough to convince many troubled South Carolinians that a line had to be drawn against tariffs and possible future interference with slavery.

## Jackson Versus Calhoun

Like Calhoun, Jackson was strong-willed and proud. Unlike Calhoun, he was already president and the leader of a national party that included supporters in pro-tariff states like Pennsylvania (which had gone for Jackson in the election of 1828). Thus to retain key northern support while soothing the South, Jackson devised two policies.

The first was to distribute surplus federal revenue to the states. Tariff schedules kept some goods out of the United States but let many others in for a price. The price, in the form of duties on imports, became federal revenue. In these years before federal income taxes, tariffs were a major source of federal revenue. Jackson hoped that this revenue, fairly distributed among the states, would remove the taint of sectional injustice from the tariff and force the federal government to restrict its own expenditures. All of this was good Jeffersonianism. Second, Jackson hoped to ease tariffs down from the sky-high level of 1828.

Calhoun disliked the idea of distributing federal revenue to the states because he believed that such a policy could become an excuse to maintain tariffs forever. But he was loath to break openly with Jackson. Between 1828 and 1831, Calhoun muffled his protest, hoping that Jackson would lower the tariff and that he, Calhoun, would retain both Jackson's favor and his chances for the presidency. Congress did pass new, slightly reduced tariff rates in 1832, but these did not come close to satisfying South Carolinians.

Before passage of the tariff of 1832, however, two personal issues had ruptured relations between Calhoun and Jackson. In 1829 Jackson's secretary of war, John H. Eaton, married the widowed daughter of a Washington tavernkeeper. By her own account, Peggy O'Neale Timberlake was "frivolous, wayward, [and] passionate." While still married to a naval officer away on duty, Peggy had acquired the reputation of flirting with Eaton, who boarded at her father's tavern. After her husband's death and her marriage to Eaton, she and Eaton were snubbed socially by Calhoun's wife and by his friends in the cabinet. Jackson, who never forgot how his own wife had been wounded by slander during the campaign of 1828, not only befriended the Eatons but concluded that Calhoun had initiated the snubbing to discredit him and to advance Calhoun's own presidential aspirations.

To make matters worse, in 1830 Jackson received convincing documentation of his suspicion that in 1818, Calhoun, as secretary of war under President Monroe, had urged that Jackson be punished for his unauthorized raid into Spanish Florida. The revelation that Calhoun had tried to stab him in the back in 1818, combined with the spurning of the Eatons, convinced Jackson that he had to "destroy [Calhoun] regardless of what injury it might do me or my administration." A symbolic confrontation occurred between Jackson and Calhoun at a Jefferson Day dinner in April 1830. Jackson proposed the toast, "Our Union: It must be preserved." Calhoun responded: "The Union next to Liberty the most dear. May we always remember that it can only be preserved by distributing equally the benefits and burdens of the Union."

The stage was now set for a direct clash between the president and his vice president over nullification. In 1831 Calhoun acknowledged his authorship of the *South Carolina Exposition and Protest.* In November 1832 a South Carolina convention nullified the tariffs of 1828 and 1832 and forbade the collection of customs duties within the state. Jackson reacted quickly. He despised nullification, calling it an "abominable doctrine" that would reduce the government to anarchy, and he berated the South Carolina nullifiers as "unprincipled men who would rather rule in hell, than be subordinate in heaven." Jackson even began to send arms to loyal Unionists in South Carolina, and in December 1832 he issued a proclamation that while promising South Carolinians further tariff reductions, lambasted nullification as itself unconstitutional. The

**John C. Calhoun,** by Charles Bird King, c. 1825 *Jackson, defeated in the presidential election of 1824, won handily four years later. The magnetic Calhoun, Jackson's vice president, broke with Jackson over nullification and the Peggy Eaton affair and resigned the vice presidency in 1832.*

**Andrew Jackson**
*After the election of 1836, Jackson retired to his home near Nashville, the Hermitage. This photo was taken shortly before his death in 1845, at the age of 78.*

Constitution, he emphasized, had established "a single nation," not a league of states.

The crisis eased in March 1833, when Jackson signed into law two measures—"the olive branch and the sword," in one historian's words. The olive branch was the tariff of 1833 (also called the Compromise Tariff), which provided for a gradual but significant lowering of duties between 1833 and 1842. The sword was the Force Bill, authorizing the president to use arms to collect customs duties in South Carolina. Although South Carolina did not abandon nullification in principle—in fact, it nullified the Force Bill—it construed the Compromise Tariff as a concession and rescinded its nullification of the tariffs of 1828 and 1832.

Like most of the accommodations by which the Union lurched from one sectional crisis to the next before the Civil War, the Compromise of 1833 grew out of a mixture of partisanship and statesmanship. The moving spirit behind the Compromise Tariff was Kentucky's senator Henry Clay, who had long favored high tariffs. A combination of motives brought Clay and the nullifiers together in favor of tariff reduction. Clay feared that without concessions to South Carolina on tariffs, the Force Bill would produce civil war. Furthermore, he was apprehensive that without compromise, the principle of protective tariffs would disappear under the wave of Jackson's immense popularity. In short, Clay would rather take responsibility for lowering tariffs than allow the initiative on tariff questions to pass to the Jacksonians. For their part, the nullifiers hated Jackson and defiantly toasted "Andrew Jackson: On the soil of South Carolina he received an humble birthplace. May he not find in it a traitor's grave!" Although recognizing that South Carolina had failed to gain support for nullification from other southern states and that they would have to bow to pressure, the nullifiers preferred that Clay, not Jackson, be the hero of the hour. So they supported Clay's Compromise Tariff. Everywhere Americans now hailed Clay as the Great Compromiser. Even Martin Van Buren frankly stated that Clay had "saved the country."

## The Bank Veto

In contrast to Jackson's open-mindedness on the subject of tariffs, his disastrous financial speculations early in his career led him to suspect all banks, paper money, and monopolies. On each count, the Bank of the United States was guilty.

The Bank of the United States had received a twenty-year charter from Congress in 1816. As a credi-

tor of state banks, the Bank of the United States restrained their printing and lending of money by its ability to demand the redemption of state bank notes in specie (gold or silver coinage). The bank's power enabled it to check the excesses of state banks, but also provoked hostility. In fact, it was widely blamed for precipitating the Panic of 1819. Further, at a time of mounting attacks on privilege, the bank was undeniably privileged. As the official depository for federal revenue, its capacity to lend money vastly exceeded that of any state bank. Its capital of $35 million amounted to more than double the annual expenditures of the federal government. Yet this institution, more powerful than any bank today, was only remotely under the government's control. Its stockholders were private citizens—a "few monied capitalists" in Jackson's words. Although chartered by Congress, the bank was located in Philadelphia, not Washington, and its directors enjoyed considerable independence. Its president, the aristocratic Nicholas Biddle, viewed himself as a public servant duty-bound to keep the bank above politics.

Urged on by Henry Clay, who hoped to ride a probank bandwagon into the White House in 1832, Biddle secured congressional passage of a bill to recharter the bank. In vetoing the recharter bill, Jackson denounced the bank as a private and privileged monopoly that drained the West of specie, was immune to taxation by the states, and made "the rich richer and the potent more powerful." Failing to persuade Congress to override Jackson's veto, Clay now pinned his hopes on gaining the presidency himself.

## The Election of 1832

By 1832 Jackson had made his views on major issues clear. He was simultaneously a staunch defender of states' rights *and* a staunch Unionist. Although he cherished the Union, he believed that the states were far too diverse to accept strong direction from Washington. The safest course was to allow the states considerable freedom so that they would remain contentedly within the Union and reject dangerous doctrines like nullification.

Throwing aside earlier promises to retire, Jackson ran again for the presidency in 1832, with Martin Van Buren as his running mate. Henry Clay ran on the National Republican ticket, touting his American System of protective tariffs, national banking, and federal support for internal improvements. Jackson's overwhelming personal popularity swamped Clay. Secure in office for another four years, Jackson was ready to finish dismantling the Bank of the United States.

## The Election of 1832

| Candidates | Parties | Electoral Vote | Popular Vote | Percentage of Popular Vote |
|---|---|---|---|---|
| ANDREW JACKSON | Democrat | 242 | 688,242 | 54.5 |
| Henry Clay | National Republican | 49 | 473,462 | 37.5 |
| William Wirt | Anti-Masonic | 7 | 101,051 | 8.0 |
| John Floyd | Independent Democrat | 11 | * | * |

*Electors chosen by South Carolina legislature

# The Bank Controversy and the Second Party System

Jackson's veto of the recharter of the Bank of the United States ignited a searing controversy that threatened to engulf all banks between 1833 and 1840. In part, tempers flared over banking because the U.S. government did not issue paper currency of its own; there were no "official" dollar bills as we know them today. Paper currency consisted of notes (promises to redeem in specie) emitted by private banks. These IOUs fueled economic development by making it easier for businessmen and farmers to acquire loans to build factories or buy land. But if a note depreciated after its issuance (because of public doubts about a bank's solvency), wage earners who had been paid in paper rather than specie would suffer. Further, paper money encouraged a speculative economy, one that raised profits *and* risks. For example, paper money spurred farmers to buy land on credit in the expectation that its price would rise, but a sudden drop in agricultural prices would leave them mired in debt. Would the United States embrace swift economic development, even at the price of allowing some to get rich quickly off investments while others languished? Or would it opt for more modest growth within traditional molds that were based on "honest" manual work and frugality?

Before the answer to any of these questions was clear, the banking issue dramatically transformed American politics. It contributed mightily to the emergence of opposition to the Democrats and to the steady expansion of popular interest in politics.

## *The War on the Bank*

Once reelected, Jackson could have allowed the bank to die a natural death when its charter ran out in 1836.

But Jackson and several of his rabid followers viewed the bank as a kind of dragon that would grow new limbs as soon as old ones were cut off. As one radical Jacksonian put it, were the bank allowed to escape with a breath of life, "it will soon recover its wonted strength, its whole power to injure us, and all hope of its destruction must forever be renounced." When Biddle, anticipating further moves against the bank by Jackson, began to call in the bank's loans and contract credit during the winter of 1832–1833, Jacksonians saw their darkest fears confirmed. The bank, Jackson assured Van Buren, "is trying to kill me, but I will kill it." Accordingly, Jackson embarked on a controversial policy of removing federal deposits from the Bank of the United States and placing them in state banks.

Once in place, the policy of removing deposits only raised a new and even thornier issue. Those state banks that became the depositories for federal revenue could use that revenue as the basis for issuing more paper money and for extending more loans. In short, the removal policy enabled state banks to increase their lending capacity. But Jackson hated both paper money and a speculative economy in which capitalists routinely took out large loans. The policy of removal seemed a formula for producing exactly the kind of economy that Jackson wanted to abolish. Jackson recognized the danger and hoped to sharply limit the number of state banks that would become depositories for federal revenue. But as state banks increasingly clamored for the revenue, the number of state-bank depositories soon multiplied beyond Jackson's expectations. There were twenty-three by the end of 1833. Critics dubbed them "pet banks" because they were usually selected for their loyalty to the Democratic party. During the next few years, fueled by paper money from the pet banks and by an influx of foreign specie to purchase cotton and for investment in canal projects, the economy entered a heady expansion. Jackson could not stem the tide. In 1836, pressured by Congress, he reluctantly signed into law the Deposit Act, which both increased the number of deposit banks and loosened federal control over them.

Jackson's policy of removing deposits deepened a split within his own Democratic party between advocates of soft money (paper) and those of hard money (specie). Both sides agreed that the Bank of the United States was evil, but for different reasons. Soft-money Democrats resented the bank's role in periodically contracting credit and restricting the lending activities of state banks; their hard-money counterparts disliked the bank because it sanctioned an economy based on paper money. Prior to the Panic of 1837, the soft-money position was more popular among Democrats outside Jackson's inner circle of advisers than within that circle. For example, western Democrats had long viewed the Bank of the United States' branch in Cincinnati as inadequate to supply their need for credit and favored an expansion of banking activity.

Aside from Jackson and a few other figures within the administration, the most articulate support for hard money came from a faction of the Democratic party in New York called the Locofocos. The Locofocos grew out of various "workingmen's" parties that had sprouted during the late 1820s in northern cities and that called for free public education, the abolition of imprisonment for debt, and a ten-hour workday. Most of these parties had collapsed within a few years, but in New York the "workies" had gradually been absorbed by the Democratic party. Once in the party, the workingmen were hard to keep in line. Composed of a mixture of intellectuals and small artisans and journeymen threatened by economic change, they worried about inflation, preferred to be paid in specie, and distrusted banks and paper money. In 1835 a faction of workingmen had broken away from Tammany Hall, the main Democratic party organization in New York City, and held a dissident meeting in a hall whose candles were illuminated by a newfangled invention, the "loco foco," or match. Thereafter, these radical workingmen were known as Locofocos.

**Jackson Versus the Bank**

*Andrew Jackson, aided by Martin Van Buren (center), attacks the Bank of the United States, which, like the many-headed serpent Hydra of Greek mythology, keeps sprouting new heads. The largest head belongs to Nicholas Biddle, the bank's president.*

## The Rise of Whig Opposition

During Jackson's second term, the opposition National Republican party changed its name to the Whig party. More important, the opposition began to broaden its base in both the South and the North. Jackson's magnetic personality had swept him to victory in 1828 and 1832. But as the profile of Jackson's administration became more sharply delineated—as Jackson's vague Jeffersonianism of 1829 gave way to hard-and-fast positions against the Bank of the United States, federal aid for internal improvements, protective tariffs, and nullification—the opposition drew into its fold increasing numbers alienated by Jackson's policies.

Jackson's crushing of nullification, for example, led some of its southern supporters into the Whig party, not because the Whigs favored nullification but because they opposed Jackson. Jackson's war on the Bank of the United States produced the same result. His policy of removing deposits from the bank pleased some southerners but dismayed others who had been satisfied with the bank and who did not share westerners' mania for even cheaper and easier credit. Jackson's opposition to federal aid for internal improvements also alienated some southerners who feared that the South would languish behind the North unless it began to push ahead with improvements. Because so much southern capital was tied up in slavery, pro-improvement southerners looked to the federal government for aid, and when they were met with a cold shoulder, they drifted into the Whig party. None of this added up to an overturning of the Democratic party in the South; the South was still the Democrats' firmest base. But the Whigs were making significant inroads, particularly in southern market towns and among planters who had close ties to southern bankers and merchants.

Meanwhile, in the North, social reformers were infusing new vitality into the opposition to Jackson. These reformers wanted to improve American society by attacking the sale of liquor, opposing slavery, bettering public education, and elevating public morality. Most opponents of liquor (temperance reformers) and most public-school reformers gravitated to the Whigs. Whig philosophy was more compatible with the reformers' goals than with Democratic ideals. Where Democrats maintained that the government should not impose a uniform standard of conduct on a diverse society, the Whigs' commitment to Clay's American System implied an acceptance of active intervention by the government to change society. Reformers wanted the government to play a positive role specifically by suppressing the liquor trade and by establishing centralized systems of public education. Thus a shared sympathy for active government programs tended to unite Whigs and reformers.

Reformers also indirectly stimulated new support for the Whigs from native-born Protestant workers. The reformers, themselves almost all Protestants, widely distrusted immigrants, especially the Irish, who viewed drinking as a normal recreation and who, as Catholics, suspected (correctly) that the public schools favored by reformers would teach Protestant doctrines. The rise of reform agitation and its frequent association with the Whigs drove the Irish into the arms of the Democrats but, by the same token, gained support for the Whigs from many native-born Protestant workers who were contemptuous of the Irish.

No source of Whig strength, however, was more remarkable than Anti-Masonry, a protest movement against the secrecy and exclusiveness of the Masonic lodges, which had long provided prominent men with fraternal fellowship and exotic rituals. The spark that set off the Anti-Masonic crusade was the abduction and disappearance in 1826 of William Morgan, a stonema-

son in Genesee County, New York, who had threatened to expose Masonic secrets. Every effort to solve the mystery of Morgan's disappearance ran into a stone wall because local officials were themselves Masons seemingly bent on obstructing the investigation. Throughout the Northeast the public became increasingly aroused against the Masonic order, and rumors spread that Masonry was a powerful conspiracy of the rich to suppress popular liberty, a secret order of men who loathed Christianity, and an exclusive retreat for drunkards.

By 1836 the Whigs had become a national party with widespread appeal. In both the North and South, they attracted those with close ties to the market economy—commercial farmers, planters, merchants, and bankers. In the North they also gained support from reformers, evangelical clergymen (especially Presbyterians and Congregationalists), Anti-Masons, and manufacturers. In the South they appealed to some former nullificationists; Calhoun himself briefly became a Whig. Everywhere the Whigs assailed Jackson as an imperious dictator, "King Andrew I"; indeed, they had taken the name "Whigs" to associate their cause with that of the American patriots who had opposed King George III in 1776.

## The Election of 1836

When it came to popularity, Jackson was a hard act to follow. In 1836 the Democrats ran Martin Van Buren, whose star had risen as Calhoun's had fallen, for the presidency. Party rhetoric reminded everyone that Van Buren was Jackson's favorite, and then contended that the Democratic party itself, with Van Buren as its mere agent, was the real heir to Jackson, the perfect embodiment of the popular will. Less cohesive than the Democrats, the Whigs could not unite on a single candidate. Rather, four anti–Van Buren candidates emerged in different parts of the country. These included three Whigs—William Henry Harrison of Ohio, Daniel Webster of Massachusetts, and W. P. Mangum of North Carolina—and one Democrat, Hugh Lawson White of Tennessee, who distrusted Van Buren and who would defect to the Whigs after the election.

Democrats accused the Whigs of a plot to so divide the vote that no candidate would receive the required majority of votes in the electoral college. That would throw the election into the House of Representatives, where, as in 1824, deals and bargains would be struck. In reality, the Whigs had no overall strategy, and Van

### The Election of 1836

| Candidates | Parties | Electoral Vote | Popular Vote | Percentage of Popular Vote |
|---|---|---|---|---|
| MARTIN VAN BUREN | Democratic | 170 | 765,483 | 50.9 |
| William H. Harrison | Whig | 73 | | |
| Hugh L. White | Democrat/Whig | 26 | 739,795 | 49.1 |
| Daniel Webster | Whig | 14 | | |
| W. P. Mangum | Whig | 11 | | |

Buren won a clear majority of the electoral votes. But there were signs of trouble ahead for the Democrats. The popular vote was close, notably in the South, where the Democrats had won two-thirds of the votes in 1832 but barely half in 1836.

## The Panic of 1837

Jackson left office in a burst of glory and returned to his Nashville home in a triumphal procession. But the public's mood quickly became less festive, for no sooner was Van Buren in office than a severe depression struck.

In the speculative boom of 1835 and 1836, born of Jackson's policy of removing federal deposits from the Bank of the United States and placing them in state ("pet") banks, the total number of banks doubled, the value of bank notes in circulation nearly tripled, and both commodity and land prices soared skyward. Encouraged by easy money and high commodity prices, states made new commitments to build canals. Then in May 1837, prices began to tumble, and bank after bank suspended specie payments. After a short rally, the economy crashed again in 1839. The Bank of the United States, which had continued to operate as a state bank with a Pennsylvania charter, failed. Nicholas Biddle himself was charged with fraud and theft. Banks throughout the nation once again suspended specie payments.

The ensuing depression was far more severe and prolonged than the economic downturn of 1819. Those lucky enough to find work saw their wage rates drop by roughly one-third between 1836 and 1842. In despair, many workers turned to the teachings of William Miller, a New England religious enthusiast whose reading of the Bible convinced him that the end of the world was imminent. Dressed in black coats and stovepipe hats, Miller's followers roamed urban sidewalks and rural villages in search of converts. Many Millerites sold their possessions and purchased white robes to ascend into heaven on October 22, 1843, the date on which Millerite leaders calculated the world would end. Ironically, by then the worst of the depression was over; but at its depths in the late 1830s and early 1840s, the economic slump fed the gloom that made poor people receptive to Miller's predictions.

The origins of the depression were both national and international. In July 1836 Jackson had issued a proclamation called the Specie Circular, which provided that after August 15 only specie was to be accepted in payment for public lands. The Specie Circular was one of Jackson's final affirmations of his belief that paper money encouraged people to embark on speculative, get-rich-quick schemes, sapped "public virtue," and robbed "honest labour of its earnings to make knaves rich, powerful and dangerous." He hoped that the Specie Circular would reverse the damaging effects of the Deposit Act of 1836, which he had signed reluctantly. The Specie Circular took the wind out of the speculative boom by making banks hesitant to issue more of the paper money that was fueling the boom, because western farmers eager to buy public lands would now demand that banks immediately redeem their paper in specie. Although the Specie Circular chilled bankers' confidence, it was not the sole or even the major reason for the depression. There were international causes as well, most notably the fact that in 1836, Britain, in an effort to restrain the outflow of British investment, checked the flow of specie from its shores to the United States.

## The Search for Solutions

Called the "sly fox" and the "little magician" for his political craftiness, Van Buren would need these skills to confront the depression, which was causing misery not only for ordinary citizens but for the Democratic party. Railing against "Martin Van Ruin," the Whigs in 1838 swept the governorship and most of the legislative seats in Van Buren's own New York.

To seize the initiative, Van Buren called for the creation of an Independent Treasury. The idea was simple: instead of depositing its money in banks, which would then use federal funds as the basis for speculative loans, the government would hold its revenues and keep them from the grasp of corporations. When Van Buren finally signed the Independent Treasury Bill into law on July 4, 1840, his supporters hailed it as America's second Declaration of Independence.

The Independent Treasury reflected the deep Jacksonian suspicion of an alliance between government and banking. But the Independent Treasury Act failed to address the banking issue on the state level, where newly chartered state banks—more than nine hundred in number by 1840—lent money to farmers and businessmen. Blaming the depression on Jackson's Specie Circular rather than on banks themselves, Whigs continued to encourage the chartering of banks as a way to spur economic development. In contrast, a growing number of Democrats blamed the depression on banks and paper money and swung toward the hard-money stance long favored by Jackson and his inner circle. In Louisiana and Arkansas, Democrats successfully pro-

hibited banks altogether, and elsewhere they imposed severe restrictions on banks—for example, by banning the emission of paper money in small denominations. In sum, after 1837 the Democrats became an antibank, hard-money party.

### The Election of 1840

Despite the depression, Van Buren gained his party's renomination. Avoiding their mistake of 1836, the Whigs settled on a single candidate, Ohio's William Henry Harrison, and ran former Virginia senator John Tyler as vice president. Harrison, sixty-seven years old and barely eking out a living on a farm, was picked because he had few enemies. Early in the campaign, the Democrats made a fatal mistake by ridiculing Harrison as "Old Granny," a man who desired only to spend his declining years in a log cabin sipping cider. Without knowing it, the Democrats had handed the Whigs the most famous campaign symbol in American history. The Whigs immediately reminded the public that Harrison had been a rugged frontiersman, the hero of the Battle of Tippecanoe, and a defender of all frontier people who lived in log cabins.

Refusing to publish a platform, the Whigs ran a "hurrah" campaign. They used log cabins for headquarters, sang log-cabin songs, gave out log-cabin cider, and called their newspaper the *Log Cabin*. For a slogan, they trumpeted "Tippecanoe and Tyler too." When not celebrating log cabins, they attacked Van Buren as a soft aristocrat who lived in "regal splendor." Whereas Harrison was content to drink hard cider from a plain mug, the Whigs observed, Van Buren had turned the White House into a palace fit for an oriental despot and drank fine wines from silver goblets while he watched people go hungry in the streets.

The election results gave Harrison a clear victory. Van Buren carried only seven states and failed even to hold his own New York. The depression would have made it difficult, if not impossible, for any Democrat to have triumphed in 1840, but Van Buren had other disabilities besides the economic collapse. Unlike Harrison and Jackson, he had no halo of military glory. Moreover, Van Buren ran a surprisingly sluggish campaign. Prior to 1840 the Whigs had been slower than the Democrats to mobilize voters by new techniques. But in 1840 it was Van Buren who directed his campaign the old-fashioned way by writing encouraging letters to key supporters, whereas Harrison broke with

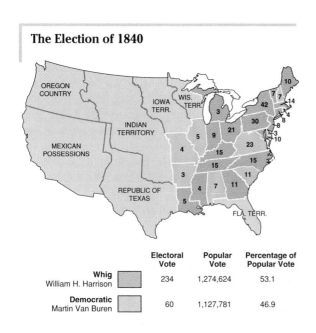

**The Election of 1840**

| | Electoral Vote | Popular Vote | Percentage of Popular Vote |
|---|---|---|---|
| **Whig** William H. Harrison | 234 | 1,274,624 | 53.1 |
| **Democratic** Martin Van Buren | 60 | 1,127,781 | 46.9 |

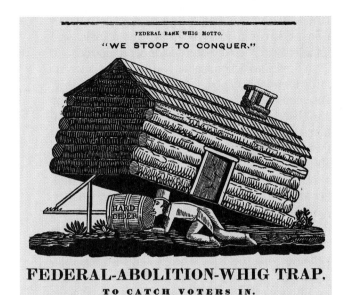

FEDERAL BANK WHIG MOTTO.

**"WE STOOP TO CONQUER."**

**FEDERAL-ABOLITION-WHIG TRAP,**

TO CATCH VOTERS IN.

**The Federal-Abolition–Whig Trap**

*This Democratic cartoon from the 1840 campaign linked the Whigs to the discredited Federalists and to the unpopular abolitionists. An unwary voter, seeking a harmless sip of hard cider, is about to be entrapped by the log cabin, the campaign symbol of the Whig William Henry Harrison.*

tradition and went about the country (often on railroads) campaigning. Ironically, Van Buren, the master politician, was beaten at his own game.

### *The Second Party System Matures*

In losing the presidency in 1840, Van Buren actually received 400,000 more popular votes than any previous presidential candidate. The total number of votes cast in presidential elections had risen from 1.2 million in 1828 to 1.5 million in 1836 to 2.4 million in 1840. The leap in the size of the popular vote between 1836 and 1840, 60 percent, is the greatest proportional jump between consecutive elections in American history. Neither lower suffrage requirements nor population growth was the main cause of this increase. Rather, the spurt in the popular vote resulted from a jump in the percentage of eligible voters who *chose* to vote. In the three elections before 1840, the proportion of white males who voted had fluctuated between 55 percent and 58 percent; in 1840 it rose to 80 percent.

Both the depression and the frenzy of the log-cabin campaign had jolted previously indifferent voters into going to the polls. Yet voter turnouts stayed up even after prosperity returned in the 1840s. The second party system, which had been developing slowly since 1828, reached a high plateau in 1840 and remained there for more than a decade. What gave politicians their appeal in the eyes of ordinary people were not only their rousing campaign techniques but also the strong contrasts and simple choices that they could present. The gradual hardening of the line between the two parties stimulated enduring popular interest in politics.

No less than the tariff and banking issues, reform also aroused partisan passions by 1840. Yet the seeds of many of the reform movements that burst upon the national scene in the 1830s were initially sown in the field of religion rather than politics.

## The Rise of Popular Religion

In *Democracy in America,* Alexis de Tocqueville pointed out an important difference between France and the United States. "In France I had almost always seen the spirit of religion and the spirit of freedom pursuing courses diametrically opposed to each other; but in America I found that they were intimately united, and that they reigned in common over the same country." From this assertion Tocqueville drew a startling conclusion: religion was "the foremost of the political institutions" of the United States.

In calling religion a political institution, Tocqueville did not mean that Americans gave special political privileges to any particular denomination. Rather, he was referring to the way in which religious impulses reinforced American democracy and liberty. Just as Americans demanded that politics be made accessible to the average person, they insisted that ministers preach doctrines that appealed to ordinary people. The most successful ministers were those who used plain words to move the heart, not those who tried to dazzle their listeners with theological complexities. Increasingly, too, Americans demanded theological doctrines that put individuals in charge of their own religious destiny. They thrust aside the Calvinist creed that God had arbitrarily selected some people for salvation and others for damnation and substituted the belief that anyone could attain heaven.

Thus heaven as well as politics became democratized in these years. This harmony between religious and democratic impulses owed much to a series of religious revivals known as the Second Great Awakening.

## The Second Great Awakening

The Second Great Awakening had begun in Connecticut during the 1790s and set ablaze one section of the nation after another during the following half-century. At first, educated Congregationalists and Presbyterians such as Yale University's president Timothy Dwight had dominated the revivals. But as they moved from Connecticut to frontier states like Tennessee and Kentucky, the revivals had undergone striking changes that were typified by the rise of camp meetings. Camp meetings were gigantic revivals in which members of several denominations gathered together in sprawling open-air camps for up to a week to hear revivalists proclaim that the Second Coming of Jesus was near and that the time for repentance was now. The most famous camp meeting had occurred at Cane Ridge, Kentucky, in August 1801, when a huge crowd had come together on a hillside to listen to thunderous sermons and to sing hymns and experience the influx of divine grace. One eyewitness vividly described the meeting:

> At night, the whole scene was awfully sublime. The ranges of tents, the fires, reflecting light amidst the branches of the towering trees; the candles and lamps illuminating the encampment; hundreds moving to and fro, with lights or torches, like Gideon's army; the preaching, praying, singing, and shouting, all heard at once, rushing from different parts of the ground, like the sound of many waters, was enough to swallow up all the powers of contemplation.

The Cane Ridge revival had been an episode of the larger Great Kentucky Revival of 1800–1801. Among the distinguishing features of these frontier revivals was the appearance of "exercises" in which men and women rolled around like logs, jerked their heads furiously (a phenomenon known simply as "the jerks"), and grunted like animals (the "barking exercise"). Observing the apparent pandemonium that had broken loose, critics had blasted the frontier frenzy for encouraging fleshly lust more than spirituality and complained that in revivals, "more souls were begot than saved." In fact, the early frontier revivals had challenged traditional religious customs. The most successful frontier revivalist preachers were not college graduates but ordinary farmers and artisans who had experienced powerful religious conversions and who had contempt for learned ministers with their dry expositions of orthodoxy.

No religious denomination had been more successful on the frontier than Methodists. With fewer than seventy thousand members in 1800, the Methodists had by 1844 become America's largest Protestant denomination, claiming a little over a million members. in contrast to New England Congregationalists and Presbyterians, Methodists emphasized that religion was primarily a matter of the heart rather than the head. Too, the frontier Methodists disdained a "settled" ministry—that is, ministers tied to fixed parishes. Instead, they preferred itinerant circuit riders—young, unmarried men—who moved on horseback from place to place and preached in houses, open fields, or wherever else listeners gathered.

Although the frontier revivals disrupted religious custom, they also worked to promote law, order, and a sense of morality on the frontier. Drunken rowdies who tried to invade camp meetings met their match in brawny itinerants like the Methodist Peter Cartwright. It was not only in camp meetings that Cartwright and his peers sought to raise the moral standard of the frontier. The basic unit of Methodist discipline on the frontier was the "class." When revivals broke up, the converted formed these small groups of twelve or so members who met weekly to provide mutual encouragement of both religion and morality. During these class meetings, Methodists chastised one another for drunkenness, fighting, fornication, gossiping, and even slippery business practices.

## Eastern Revivals

By the 1820s the Second Great Awakening had begun to shift back to the East. The hottest revival fires blazed in an area of western New York known as the Burned-Over District. No longer a frontier, western New York teemed with descendants of Puritans who hungered for religious experience and with people drawn by the hope of wealth after the completion of the Erie Canal. At this time it was a fertile field of high expectations and bitter discontent.

The man who harnessed these anxieties to religion was Charles G. Finney. Finney began his career as a lawyer, but after a religious conversion in 1821, which he described as a "retainer from the Lord Jesus Christ to plead his cause," he became a Presbyterian minister and conducted revivals in towns along the canal like

**Methodist Camp Meeting**

*Frontier revivals occurred outdoors, lasted for days, and attracted an abundance of women and children as well as men. Note the separate seating of women.*

Rome and Utica. Although he also found time for trips to New York and Boston, his greatest "harvest" came in the thriving canal city of Rochester in 1830–1831.

The Rochester revival had several features that justify Finney's reputation as the "father of modern revivalism." First, it was a citywide revival in which all denominations participated. Finney was a pioneer of cooperation among Protestant denominations. In addition, in Rochester and elsewhere, Finney introduced devices for speeding conversions. Among these were the "anxious seat," a bench to which those ready for conversion were led so that they could be made objects of special prayer, and the "protracted meeting," which went on nightly for up to a week. Finney's emphasis on special revival techniques sharply distinguished him from eighteenth-century revivalists, including Jonathan Edwards. Whereas Edwards had portrayed revivals as the miraculous work of God, Finney made them out to be human creations. The divine spirit flowed in revivals, but humans made them happen. Finally, although a Presbyterian, Finney flatly rejected the Calvinist belief that humans had a natural and nearly irresistible inclination to sin (the doctrine of "human depravity"). Rather, he affirmed, sin was purely a voluntary act; no one *had* to sin. Men and women could will themselves out of sin just as readily as they had willed themselves into it. Indeed, he declared, it was theoretically possible for men and women to will themselves free of all sin—to live perfectly. Those who heard Finney and similar revivalists came away convinced that they had experienced the washing away of all past guilt and the beginning of a new life. "I have been born again," a young convert wrote. "I am three days old when I write this letter."

The assertions that people could live without sin ("perfectionism") and that revivals were human contrivances made Finney a controversial figure. Yet his ideas came to dominate "evangelical" Protestantism, forms of Protestantism that focused on the need for an emotional religious conversion. He was successful because he told people what they wanted to hear: that their destinies were in their own hands. A society that celebrated the "self-made" individual found plausible Finney's assertion that even in religion, people could make of themselves what they chose. Moreover, compared to most frontier revivalists, Finney had an unusually dignified style. Taken together, these factors gave him a potent appeal to merchants, lawyers, and small manufacturers in the towns and cities of the North. Finally, more than most revivalists, Finney recognized that without the mass participation of women, few revivals would have gotten off the ground. During the Second Great Awakening, female converts outnumbered male converts by about two to one. Finney encouraged women to give public testimonies of their religious experiences in church, and he often converted husbands by first converting their wives and daughters. After a visit by Finney, Melania Smith, the wife of a Rochester physician who had little time for religion, greeted her husband with a reminder of "the woe which is denounced against the families which call not on the Name of the Lord." Soon Dr. Smith heeded his wife's pleading and joined one of Rochester's Presbyterian churches.

### Critics of Revivals: The Unitarians

Whereas some praised revivals for saving souls, others doubted that they produced permanent changes in behavior and condemned them for encouraging "such extravagant and incoherent expressions, and such enthusiastic fervor, as puts common sense and modesty to the blush."

One small but influential group of revival critics was the Unitarians. The basic doctrine of Unitarianism—that Jesus Christ was less than fully divine—had gained quiet acceptance among religious liberals during the eighteenth century. However, it was not until the early nineteenth century that Unitarianism emerged as a formal denomination with its own churches, ministry, and national organization. In New England in these years, hundreds of Congregational churches were torn apart by the withdrawal of socially prominent families who had embraced Unitarianism and by legal battles over which group—Congregationalists or Unitarians—could occupy church property. Although Unitarians won relatively few converts outside New England, their tendency to attract the wealthy and educated gave them influence beyond their numbers.

Unitarians criticized revivals as uncouth emotional exhibitions and argued that moral goodness should be cultivated by a gradual process of "character building," in which the individual learned to model his or her behavior on that of Jesus rather than by a sudden emotional conversion as in a revival. Yet Unitarians and revivalists shared the belief that human behavior could be changed for the better. Both rejected the Calvinist emphasis on innate human wickedness. William Ellery Channing, a Unitarian leader, claimed that Christianity had but one purpose: "the perfection of human nature, the elevation of men into nobler beings."

### The Rise of Mormonism

The Unitarians' assertion that Jesus Christ was human rather than divine challenged a basic doctrine of ortho-dox Christianity. Yet Unitarianism proved far less controversial than another of the new denominations of the 1820s and 1830s, the Church of Jesus Christ of Latter-day Saints, or Mormons. Its founder, Joseph Smith, grew to manhood in one of those families that seemed in constant motion to and fro but never up. After moving his family nearly twenty times in ten years, Smith's ne'er-do-well father settled in Palmyra, New York, in the heart of the Burned-Over District. As a boy, Smith's imagination teemed with plans to find buried treasure, while his religious views were convulsed by the conflicting claims of the denominations that thrived in the region. "Some were contending for the Methodist faith, some for the Presbyterian, and some for the Baptists," Smith later wrote. He wondered who was right and who wrong, or whether they were "all wrong together."

The sort of perplexity that Smith experienced was widespread in the Burned-Over District, but his resolution of the confusion was unique. Smith claimed that an angel led him to a buried book of revelation and to special stones for use in translating it. He completed his translation of this Book of Mormon in 1827. The Book of Mormon tells the story of an ancient Hebrew prophet, Lehi, whose descendants came to America and created a prosperous civilization that looked forward to the appearance of Jesus as its savior. Jesus had actually appeared and performed miracles in the New World, the book claimed, but the American descendants of Lehi had departed from the Lord's ways and quarreled among themselves. God had cursed some with dark skin; these were the American Indians, who, when later discovered by Columbus, had forgotten their history.

Despite his astonishing claims, Smith quickly gathered followers. The appeal of Mormonism lay partly in its positioning of America at the center of Christian history and partly in Smith's assertion that he had discovered a new revelation. The idea of an additional revelation beyond the Bible appeared to some to resolve the turmoil created by the Protestant denominations' inability to agree on what the Bible said or meant.

Smith and his followers steadily moved west from New York to Ohio and Missouri. Then they migrated to Illinois, where they built a model city, Nauvoo, and a magnificent temple supported by thirty huge pillars. By moving to these areas, the Mormons hoped to draw closer to the Indians, whose conversion was one of their goals, and to escape persecution. Smith's claim to have received a new revelation virtually guaranteed a hostile reception for the Mormons wherever they went,

**Mormon Migrants**

*Persecution of the Mormons raged in Missouri in the 1830s, and in 1838 the state's governor ordered the militia to kill the Mormons or drive them from the state. By 1839 most Mormons had left. Many resettled in Nauvoo, Illinois, only to migrate again to Deseret in the late 1840s.*

because Smith had seemingly undermined the authority of the Bible, one of the two documents (the other being the Constitution) upon which the ideals of the American Republic rested.

Smith added fuel to the fire when he reported in 1843 that he had received still another revelation, this one sanctioning the Mormon practice of having multiple wives, or polygyny. Although Smith did not publicly proclaim polygyny as a doctrine, its practice among Mormons was a poorly kept secret. Smith's self-image also intensified the controversy that boiled around Mormonism. He refused to view himself merely as the founder of another denomination; instead, he saw himself as a prophet of the kingdom of God and was called a "Second Mohammed." Mormonism would be to Christianity what Christianity had been to Judaism: an all-encompassing, higher form of religion. In 1844 he announced his candidacy for the presidency of the United States. But the state of Illinois was already moving against him. Charged with treason, he was jailed in Carthage, Illinois, and along with his brother, murdered there by a mob in June 1844.

Despite persecution, the Mormons won converts, not only in the United States but in the teeming slums of English factory cities from which Mormon agents brought thousands to America. In the thirty years after 1840, the number of Mormons grew from 6,000 to 200,000. After Smith's death a new leader, Brigham Young, led the main body of Mormons from Nauvoo to the Great Salt Lake Valley in Utah, which then was still under the control of Mexico. There Mormons established an independent republic, the state of Deseret. A thousand miles from Illinois, they prospered. Their isolation, combined with the firm control of Young, the "Old Boss," kept the rank and file in line. Polygyny, which Young officially proclaimed as a church doctrine, did not produce the hoped-for increase in Mormon numbers, but it did guarantee that Mormons would remain a people apart from the mainstream of American society. Above all, the Mormons were industrious and deeply committed to the welfare of other Mormons. Cooperation among Mormons took several forms, not the least of which was the practice of devoting each Mormon's "surplus" production to public projects like irrigation. Mormons transformed the valley into a rich oasis. When Utah came under American control after the Mexican War, Mormons dominated its government.

Although Mormonism is one of the few religions to have originated in the United States, the antebellum Mormons pushed against the currents of standard American religion and society. They rejected the Bible as the sole source of revelation, substituted polygyny for monogamy, and elevated economic cooperation above competitiveness. Mormonism appealed to the downtrodden and insecure rather than to the prosperous and secure. It offered the downcast an explicit alternative to dominant religious and social practices. In this respect, Mormonism mirrored the efforts of several religious communal societies whose members resolutely set themselves apart from society. In general, these religious communitarians were less numerous, controversial, and long-lasting than the Mormons, but one group among them, the Shakers, has continued to fascinate Americans.

### The Shakers

The leader of the Shakers (who derived their name from a convulsive religious dance that was part of their ceremony) was Mother Ann Lee, the illiterate daughter of an English blacksmith. Lee had set sail for America in 1774, and her followers soon organized a tightly knit community in New Lebanon, New York. In this and in other communities, the Shakers proved themselves able artisans. Shaker furniture became renowned for its beauty and strength. But for all their achievements as artisans, the Shakers were fundamentally other-worldly and hostile to materialism. Lee insisted that her followers abstain from sexual intercourse, believed that the end of the world was imminent, and derived many of her doctrines from trances and heavenly visions that she claimed to have experienced. Among these doctrines was her conviction that at the Second Coming, Jesus would take the form of a woman, herself.

Her teachings about the evils of sexual relations would quickly have doomed the Shakers to extinction had it not been for the spread of religious revivalism in 1790. Turning up at Cane Ridge and other revival sites, Shaker missionaries made off with converts whom the revivals had loosened from their traditional religious moorings. At their peak during the second quarter of the nineteenth century, the Shakers numbered about six thousand in eight states.

Shakers and Mormons chose to live apart from society. But the message of most evangelical Protestants, including Charles G. Finney, was that religion and economic individualism—a person's pursuit of wealth—were compatible. Most revivalists told people that getting ahead in the world was acceptable as long as they were honest, temperate, and bound by the dictates of their consciences. By encouraging assimilation into

rather than retreat from society, evangelicalism provided a powerful stimulus to the manifold reform movements of the 1820s and 1830s.

## The Age of Reform

Despite rising popular interest in politics between 1824 and 1840, large numbers of people were excluded from politics. Women were not allowed to vote, and blacks generally suffered rather than benefited from the gradual liberalization of voting requirements. By 1860 most northern states denied free people of color the right to vote. Moreover, the political parties did not welcome the intrusion of controversial issues like slavery, nor did they show much interest in women's rights.

During the 1820s and 1830s, unprecedented numbers of men and women overcame these limits of political parties by joining organizations that aimed to improve society. Slavery's abolition, women's rights, temperance, better treatment of criminals and the insane, public education, and even the establishment of utopian communities were high on various reformers' agenda. Although they occasionally cooperated with political parties, especially the Whigs, reformers gave their loyalty to their causes, not to parties. Indeed, politics struck most reformers as a sorry spectacle that allowed a man like Andrew Jackson, a duelist who married a divorcee, to become president and that routinely rewarded persons who would sacrifice any principle for victory at the polls.

Reformers believed that they were on God's side on any given issue. Religious revivalism contributed to their intense moralism. Virtually all prominent temperance reformers of the 1820s and 1830s, for example, had been inspired initially by revivals. But revivalism and reform were not always so intimately linked. Influential school reformers and women's rights advocates were frequently religious liberals either hostile or indifferent to revivals. And although some abolitionists owed their first flush of idealism to revivals, others did not, and almost all came to criticize the churches for condoning slavery. Yet even those reformers opposed to revivalism borrowed the evangelical preachers' language and psychology by portraying drunkenness, ignorance, and inequality as sins that called for immediate repentance.

Reform had a dark side. Reformers did not hesitate to coerce people into change by calling for the legal prohibition of liquor and for compulsory education. For criminals, they designed penitentiaries on highly repressive principles. While assailing intemperance with fury, they frequently ignored the pathetic living and working conditions that stimulated drinking among slum dwellers.

Although the reform movements appealed to those excluded from or repelled by politics, most lacked the political parties' national organizations. New England and those parts of the Midwest settled by New Englanders were hotbeds of reform. In contrast, southerners actively suppressed abolition, displayed only mild interest in temperance and education reform, ignored women's rights, and saw utopian communities as proof of the mental instability of northern reformers.

### The War on Liquor

Agitation for temperance (either total abstinence from alcoholic beverages, or moderation in their use) intensified during the second quarter of the nineteenth century. Temperance reformers addressed a growing problem. The spread of the population across the Appalachians stimulated the production and consumption of alcohol. Before the transportation revolution, western farmers, unable to get their grain to markets, commonly distilled it into spirits. Annual per capita consumption of rum, whiskey, gin, and brandy rose until it exceeded seven gallons by 1830, nearly triple today's rate. By the late 1820s, the average adult male drank a half-pint of liquor a day. With some justification, reformers saw alcoholic excess as a male indulgence whose bitter consequences (spending wages on liquor instead of food) fell on women and children. Not surprisingly, millions of women would march behind the temperance banner during the nineteenth century.

There had been agitation against intemperance before 1825, but that year the Connecticut revivalist Lyman Beecher ushered in a new phase when, in six widely acclaimed lectures, he thundered against all use of alcohol. A year later, evangelical Protestants created the American Temperance Society, the first national temperance organization. By 1834 some five thousand state and local temperance societies were loosely affiliated with the American Temperance Society. Whereas previous temperance supporters had advised moderation in the use of spirits, the American Temperance Society followed Beecher in demanding total abstinence. The society flooded the country with tracts denouncing the "amazing evil" of strong drink and urged churches to expel any members who condoned alcohol.

Among the main targets of the evangelical temperance reformers were moderate drinkers among the laboring classes. In the small shops where a handful of journeymen and apprentices worked informally, passing the jug every few hours was a time-honored way to relieve fatigue and monotony. But with the rise of large factories, new demands arose for a disciplined work force. Factory owners with precise production schedules to meet needed orderly and steady workers. Thus evangelical temperance reformers quickly gained manufacturers' support. In East Dudley, Massachusetts, for example, three factory owners refused to sell liquor in factory stores, calculating that any profits from the sale would be more than offset by lost working time and "the scenes of riot and wickedness thus produced."

Workers showed little interest in temperance before the late 1830s. But after the Panic of 1837, a new stage of temperance agitation sprang up in the form of the Washington Temperance Societies. Starting in Baltimore in 1840, the Washingtonians were more likely to be mechanics (workingmen) and laborers than ministers and manufacturers. Many were reformed drunkards, and most had concluded that their survival in the harsh climate of depression depended on their commitment to sobriety and frugality. For example, Charles T. Woodman, a baker, had been forced by the collapse

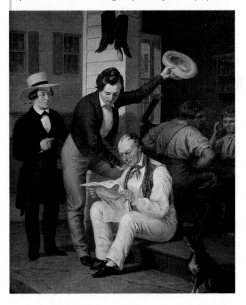

**Reading the News,** by Christian Friederck Mayr, 1844
*Visitors were often struck by the Americans' penchant for reading, especially newspapers.*

of his business to flee Boston for Philadelphia to escape his creditors. Like most Washingtonians, Woodman blamed his ruin on a relapse into his "old habit" of drink. The forces dislocating workers in the late 1830s were often far beyond their control. Part of the appeal of temperance was that it lay *within* their control. Take care of temperance, a Washingtonian assured a Baltimore audience, and the Lord would take care of the economy.

For all their differences from earlier temperance associations, the Washingtonians reflected the impact of revivals even more than did the American Temperance Society. Viewing drinking as sinful, they held "experience meetings," in which members described their "salvation" from liquor and their "regeneration" through abstinence (or "teetotalism"*). Their wives joined "Martha Washington" societies, in which they pledged to smell their husbands' breath each night and paraded with banners that read "Teetotal or No Husband." The Washingtonians spread farther and faster than any other antebellum temperance organization.

As temperance won new supporters, anti-alcohol crusaders gradually shifted their tactics from calls that individuals abstain to demands that cities and towns, and even states, ban all traffic in liquor. This shift from moral suasion to legal prohibition was controversial even within the movement. But by the late 1830s, prohibition was scoring victories. In 1838 Massachusetts prohibited the sale of distilled spirits in amounts less than fifteen gallons, thereby restricting small purchases by individual drinkers; in 1851 Maine banned the manufacture and sale of all intoxicating beverages. Controversial though these laws were, the temperance movement earned a measure of success. After rising steadily between 1800 and 1830, per capita consumption of distilled spirits began to fall during the 1830s. The rate of consumption during the 1840s was less than half that in the 1820s.

### Public-School Reform

No less than temperance reformers, school reformers worked to encourage orderliness and thrift in the common people. Rural America's so-called district schools provided reformers with one of their main targets. One-room log or clapboard cabins containing pupils aged anywhere from three to twenty or more, the district schools taught farmers' children to read and count but

little more. Those who attended the district schools never forgot their primitive conditions or harsh discipline: "the wood-pile in the yard, the open fireplace, the backless benches," and the floggings until "the youngster vomited or wet his breeches."

For all their drawbacks, the district schools enjoyed popular and financial support from rural parents. But reformers saw these schools in a different light, insisting that schools had to equip children for the emerging competitive and industrial economy. The most articulate and influential of the reformers, Horace Mann of Massachusetts, in 1837 became the first secretary of his state's newly created board of education, and for the next decade, he promoted a sweeping transformation of public education. Mann's goals included shifting the burden of financial support for schools from parents to the state, grading the schools (that is, classifying pupils by age and attainment), extending the school term from two or three months to as many as ten months, introducing standardized textbooks, and compelling attendance. In place of loosely structured schools that were mere appendages of the family, Mann and other reformers advocated highly structured institutions that would occupy most of the child's time and energy.

School reformers hoped not only to combat ignorance but to spread uniform cultural values by exposing all children to identical experiences. Children would arrive at school at the same time and thereby learn punctuality. Graded schools that matched children against their age peers would stimulate the competitiveness needed in a rapidly industrializing society. Children would all read the same books and absorb such common sayings as "Idleness is the nest in which mischief lays its eggs." The McGuffey readers, which sold 50 million copies between 1836 and 1870, created a common curriculum and preached industry, honesty, sobriety, and patriotism.

Although school reform made few gains in the South (see Chapter 12), much of the North remodeled its schools along the lines advocated by Mann, and in 1852 Massachusetts passed the nation's first compulsory school law. Success did not come easily, however. Educational reformers faced challenges from farmers, who were satisfied with the informality of the district schools, and from urban Catholics led by New York City's Bishop John Hughes, who pointed out that the textbooks used in public schools dispensed anti-Catholic and anti-Irish epithets. And in both rural and urban areas, the laboring poor opposed compulsory education as a menace to parents dependent on their children's wages.

---

* Teetotal: coined by an English laborer at a temperance meeting in 1834, *teetotal* was merely an emphatic form of *total*.

Yet school reformers prevailed, in part because their opponents, rural Protestants and urban Catholics, were incapable of cooperating with each other. In part, too, reformers succeeded by gaining influential allies. For example, their stress on free, tax-supported schools won the backing of the urban workingmen's parties that arose in the late 1820s; and their emphasis on punctuality appealed to manufacturers, who needed a disciplined work force. The new ideas also attracted reform-minded women, who recognized that the grading of schools would ease women's entry into teaching. People of the times widely believed that a woman could never control the assortment of three- to twenty-year-olds found in a one-room schoolhouse, but managing a class of eight- or nine-year-olds was a different matter. Catharine Beecher accurately predicted that school reform would render teaching a suitable profession for women. Women gradually did take the place of men in the classroom wherever school reform left its mark. By 1900 about 70 percent of the nation's schoolteachers were women.

School reform also appealed to native-born Americans alarmed by the swelling tide of immigration. The public school emerged as the favorite device by which reformers forged a common American culture out of an increasingly diverse society. "We must decompose and cleanse the impurities which rush into our midst" through the "one infallible filter—the SCHOOL."

School reformers were assimilationists in the sense that they hoped to use public education to give children common values through shared experiences. In one respect, however, these reformers wore blinders on the issue of assimilation, for few stressed the integration of black and white children. When black children were fortunate enough to get any schooling, it was usually in segregated schools. Black children who entered integrated public schools met with such virulent prejudice that black leaders in northern cities frequently preferred segregated schools.

## Abolition

Antislavery sentiment among whites flourished in the Revolutionary era but declined in the early nineteenth century. The main antislavery organization founded between 1800 and 1830 was the American Colonization Society (1817), which displayed little moral outrage against slavery. The society proposed a plan for gradual emancipation, with compensation to the slaveowner, and the shipment of freed blacks to Africa. This proposal attracted support from some slaveholders in the Upper South who would never have dreamed of a general emancipation.

At its core, colonization was hard-hearted and soft-headed. Colonizationists assumed that blacks were a degraded race that did not belong in American society, and they underestimated the growing dependence of the South's economy on slavery. Confronted by a soaring demand for cotton and other commodities, few southerners were willing to free their slaves, even if compensated. In any event, the American Colonization Society never had enough funds to buy freedom for more than a fraction of slaves. Between 1820 and 1830, only 1,400 blacks migrated to Liberia, and most were already free. In striking contrast, the American slave population, fed by natural increase (the excess of births over deaths), rose from 1,191,000 in 1810 to more than 2,000,000 in 1830.

During the 1820s the main source of radical opposition to slavery was blacks themselves. Blacks had little enthusiasm for colonization. Most American blacks were native- rather than African-born. How, they asked, could they be sent back to a continent that they had never left? "We are *natives* of this country," a black pastor in New York proclaimed. "We only ask that we be treated as well as *foreigners*." In opposition to colonization, blacks formed scores of abolition societies. In 1829 the Boston free black David Walker published an *Appeal* for a black rebellion to crush slavery.

Not all whites acquiesced to the continuance of slavery. In 1821 the Quaker Benjamin Lundy began a newspaper, the *Genius of Universal Emancipation*, and put forth proposals that no new slave states be admitted, that the internal slave trade be outlawed, that the three-fifths clause of the Constitution be repealed, and that Congress abolish slavery wherever it had the authority to do so. In 1828 Lundy hired a young New Englander, William Lloyd Garrison, as an assistant editor. Prematurely bald and with steel-rimmed glasses, and typically donning a black suit and black cravat, Garrison looked more like a schoolmaster than a rebel. But in 1831, when he launched his own newspaper, *The Liberator*, he quickly established himself as the most famous and controversial white abolitionist. "I am in earnest," Garrison wrote. "I will not equivocate—I will not excuse—I will not retreat a single inch—AND I WILL BE HEARD."

Garrison's battle cry was "immediate emancipation." In place of exiling blacks to Africa, he substituted the truly radical notion that blacks should enjoy civil (or legal) equality with whites. He greeted slaves as "a Man and a Brother," "a Woman and a Sister." Even Garrison,

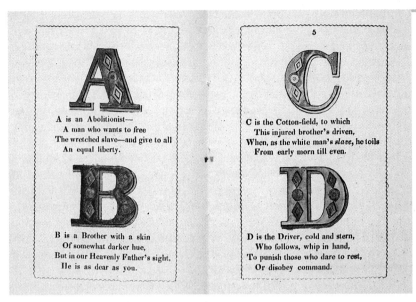

A is an Abolitionist—
A man who wants to free
The wretched slave—and give to all
An equal liberty.

B is a Brother with a skin
Of somewhat darker hue,
But in our Heavenly Father's sight,
He is as dear as you.

C is the Cotton-field, to which
This injured brother's driven,
When, as the white man's *slave*, he toils
From early morn till even.

D is the Driver, cold and stern,
Who follows, whip in hand,
To punish those who dare to rest,
Or disobey command.

**The Antislavery Alphabet**
*Viewing children as morally pure and hence as natural opponents of slavery, abolitionists produced antislavery toys, games, and, as we see here, alphabet books.*

however, did not think that all slaves could be freed overnight. "Immediate emancipation" meant that all people had to realize that slavery was sinful and its continued existence intolerable.

Garrison quickly gained support from the growing number of black abolitionists. A black barber in Pittsburgh sent Garrison sixty dollars to help with *The Liberator*. Black agents sold subscriptions and three-fourths of *The Liberator*'s subscribers in the early years were black. The escaped slave Frederick Douglass and a remarkable freed slave who named herself Sojourner Truth proved eloquent lecturers against slavery. Douglass could rivet an audience with an opening line. "I appear before the immense assembly this evening as a thief and a robber," he gibed. "I stole this head, these limbs, this body from my master, and ran off with them."

Relations between black and white abolitionists were not always harmonious. White abolitionists called for legal equality for blacks but not necessarily for social equality. Not without racial prejudice, they preferred light- to dark-skinned Negroes and, Garrison excepted, were hesitant to admit blacks to antislavery societies. Yet the prejudices of white abolitionists were mild compared to those of most whites. A white man or woman could do few things less popular in the 1830s than become an abolitionist. Mobs, often including colonizationists, repeatedly attacked abolitionists. For example, a Boston mob, searching for a British abolitionist in 1835, found Garrison instead and dragged him

through town on the end of a rope. An abolitionist editor, Elijah Lovejoy, was murdered by a mob in Alton, Illinois, in 1837.

Abolitionists drew on the language of revivals and described slavery as sin, but the Protestant churches did not rally behind abolition as strongly as behind temperance. Lyman Beecher roared against the evils of strong drink but whimpered about those of slavery and in 1834 tried to suppress abolitionists at Cincinnati's Lane Theological Seminary. In response, Theodore Dwight Weld, an idealistic follower of Charles G. Finney, led a mass withdrawal of students. These "Lane rebels" formed the nucleus of abolitionist activity at the antislavery Oberlin College.

As if external hostility were not enough, abolitionists argued continually with each other. The American Anti-Slavery Society, founded in 1833, was the scene of several battles between Garrison and prominent New York and midwestern abolitionists such as the brothers Lewis and Arthur Tappan, Theodore Dwight Weld, and James G. Birney. One of the issues between the two sides was whether abolitionists should enter politics as a distinct party. In 1840 Garrison's opponents ran Birney for president on the ticket of the newly formed Liberty party. As for Garrison himself, he was increasingly rejecting *all* laws and governments, as well as political parties, as part of his doctrine of "nonresistance." In 1838 he and his followers had founded the New England Non-Resistance Society. The starting point of the doctrine was the fact that slavery depended on force.

Garrison then added that all governments ultimately rested on force; even laws passed by elected legislatures needed police enforcement. Because Garrison viewed force as the opposite of Christian love, he concluded that Christians should refuse to vote, hold office, or have anything to do with government. It is a small wonder that many abolitionists thought of Garrison as extreme, or "ultra."

The second issue that divided the American Anti-Slavery Society concerned the role of women in the abolitionist movement. In 1837 Angelina and Sarah Grimké, daughters of a South Carolina slaveholder, embarked on an antislavery lecture tour of New England. Women had become deeply involved in antislavery societies during the 1830s, but always in female auxiliaries affiliated with those run by men. What made the Grimké sisters so controversial was that they drew mixed audiences of men and women to their lectures at a time when it was thought indelicate for women to speak before male audiences. Clergymen chastised the Grimké sisters for lecturing men rather than obeying them.

Such criticism backfired, however, because the Grimkés increasingly took up the cause of women's rights. In 1838 each wrote a classic of American feminism. Sarah produced her *Letters on the Condition of Women and the Equality of the Sexes,* and Angelina contributed her *Letters to Catharine E. Beecher* (Lyman Beecher's daughter and a militant opponent of female equality). Some abolitionists tried to dampen the feminist flames. The abolitionist poet John Greenleaf Whittier dismissed women's grievances as "paltry" compared to the "great and dreadful wrongs of the slave." Even Theodore Dwight Weld, who had married Angelina Grimké, wanted to subordinate women's rights to antislavery. But the fiery passions would not be extinguished. Garrison, welcoming the controversy, promptly espoused women's rights and urged that women be given positions equal to men in the American Anti-Slavery Society. In 1840 the election of a woman, Abby Kelley, to a previously all-male committee split the American Anti-Slavery Society wide open. A substantial minority of pro-feminist delegates left— some to join the Liberty party, others to follow Lewis Tappan into the new American and Foreign Anti-Slavery Society.

The disruption of the American Anti-Slavery Society did not greatly damage abolitionism. The national society had never had much control over the local societies that had grown swiftly during the mid-1830s. By 1840 there were more than fifteen hundred local societies, principally in Massachusetts, New York, and Ohio. By circulating abolitionist tracts, newspapers, and even chocolates with antislavery messages on their wrappers, these local societies kept the country ablaze with agitation.

One of the most disruptive abolitionist techniques was to flood Congress with petitions calling for an end to slavery in the District of Columbia. Congress had no time to consider all the petitions, but to refuse to address them meant depriving citizens of their right to have petitions heard. In 1836 southerners secured congressional adoption of the "gag rule," which automatically tabled abolitionist petitions and thus prevented discussion of them in Congress. Ex-president John Quincy Adams, then a representative from Massachusetts, led the struggle against the gag rule and finally secured its repeal in 1845. The debate over the gag rule subtly shifted the issue from the abolition of slavery to the constitutional rights of free expression and petitioning Congress. Members of Congress with little sympathy for abolitionists found themselves attacking the South for suppressing the right of petition. In a way, the gag-rule episode vindicated Garrison's tactic of stirring up emotions on the slavery issue. By holding passions over slavery at the boiling point, Garrison kept the South on the defensive. The less secure southerners felt, the more they were tempted into clumsy overreactions like the gag rule.

## Women's Rights

The position of American women in the 1830s contained many contradictions. Women could not vote. If married, they had no right to own property (even inherited property) or to retain their own earnings. Yet the spread of reform movements provided women with unprecedented opportunities for public activity without challenging the prevailing belief that their proper sphere was the home. By suppressing liquor, for example, women could claim that they were transforming wretched homes into nurseries of happiness.

The argument that women were natural guardians of the family was double-edged. It justified reform activities on behalf of the family, but it undercut women's demands for legal equality. Let women attend to their sphere, the counterargument ran, and leave politics and finance to men. So deeply ingrained was sexual inequality, indeed, that most feminists did not start out intending to attack it. Instead, their experiences in other

### Lucretia Mott

*Most newspapers ridiculed the Seneca Falls convention that Stanton and Mott organized to advance women's rights. More than three hundred people attended.*

**Elizabeth Cady Stanton**

**Lucretia Mott**

reform movements, notably abolition, led them to the issue of women's rights.

Among the early women's rights advocates who started their reform careers as abolitionists were the Grimké sisters, the Philadelphia Quaker Lucretia Mott, Lucy Stone, and Abby Kelley. Like abolition, the cause of women's rights revolved around the conviction that differences of race and gender were unimportant and incidental. "Men and women," Sarah Grimké wrote, "are CREATED EQUAL! They are both moral and accountable beings, and whatever is *right* for man to do, is *right* for woman." The most articulate and aggressive advocates of women's rights, moreover, tended to gravitate to William Lloyd Garrison rather than to more moderate abolitionists. Garrison, himself a vigorous feminist, repeatedly stressed the peculiar degradation of women under slavery. The early issues of *The Liberator* contained a "Ladies' Department" headed by a picture of a kneeling slave woman imploring, "Am I Not a Woman and a Sister?" It was common knowledge that slave women were vulnerable to the sexual demands of white masters. Garrison denounced the South as a vast brothel and described slave women as "treated with more indelicacy and cruelty than cattle."

Although their involvement in abolition aroused advocates of women's rights, the discrimination they encountered within the abolition movement infuriated them and impelled them to make women's rights a separate cause. In the 1840s Lucy Stone became the first abolitionist to lecture solely on women's rights. When Lucretia Mott and other American women tried to be seated at the World's Anti-Slavery Convention in London in 1840, they were relegated to a screened-off section. The incident made a sharp impression not only on Mott but on Elizabeth Cady Stanton, who had elected to accompany her abolitionist husband to the meeting as a honeymoon trip. In 1848 Mott and Stanton organized a women's rights convention at Seneca Falls, New York, that proclaimed a Declaration of Sentiments. Modeled on the Declaration of Independence, the Seneca Falls Declaration began with the assertion that "all men and women are created equal." The convention passed twelve resolutions, and only one, a call for the right of women to vote, failed to pass unanimously; but it did pass. Ironically, after the Civil War, the call for woman suffrage became the main demand of women's rights advocates for the rest of the century.

Although its crusaders were resourceful and energetic, women's rights had less impact than most other reforms. Temperance and school reform were far more popular, and abolitionism created more commotion. Women would not secure the right to vote throughout the nation until 1920, fifty-five years after the Thirteenth Amendment would abolish slavery. One reason for the relatively slow advance of women's rights was that piecemeal gains—such as married women securing the right to own property in several states by the Civil War—satisfied many women. The cause of women's rights also suffered from a close association with abolitionism, which was unpopular. In addition, the advance of feminism was slowed by the competition that it faced from the alternative ideal of domesticity. By sanctioning activities in reforms such as temperance and education, the cult of domesticity provided many women with worthwhile pursuits beyond the family. In this way, it blunted the edge of female demands for full equality.

## Penitentiaries and Asylums

Other reform efforts took shape during the 1820s to combat poverty, crime, and insanity by establishing highly regimented institutions, themselves products of striking new assumptions about the causes of deviancy. As poverty and crime had increased and grown more visible in the cities of the early nineteenth century, alarmed investigators concluded that indigence and deviant behavior resulted not from defects in human nature, as colonial Americans had thought, but from drunken fathers and broken homes. The failure of parental discipline, not the will of God or the wickedness of human nature, lay at the root of evil. Both religious revivalists and secular reformers increasingly concluded that human nature could be altered by the right combination of moral influences. Most grasped the optimistic logic voiced by William Ellery Channing: "The study of the *causes* of crime may lead us to its *cure.*"

To cure crime, reformers created substitutes for parental discipline, most notably the penitentiary. Penitentiaries were prisons marked by an unprecedented degree of order and discipline. Of course, colonial Americans had incarcerated criminal offenders, but jails had been used mainly to hold prisoners awaiting trial or to lock up debtors. For much of the eighteenth century, the threat of the gallows rather than of imprisonment had deterred wrongdoers. In contrast, nineteenth-century reformers believed that rightly managed, penitentiaries would bring about the sincere reformation of offenders.

To purge offenders' violent habits, reformers usually insisted on solitary confinement. Between 1819 and 1825, New York built penitentiaries at Auburn and Ossining ("Sing Sing"), in which prisoners were confined by night in small, windowless cells. By day they could work together but never speak and rarely even look at each other. Some reformers criticized this "Auburn system" for allowing too much contact and preferred the rival "Pennsylvania system," in which each prisoner spent all of his or her time in a single cell (each with a walled courtyard for exercise) and received no news or visits from the outside.

Antebellum America also witnessed a remarkable transformation in the treatment of poor people. The prevailing colonial practice of offering relief to the poor by supporting them in a household ("outdoor relief") gradually gave way to the construction of almshouses for the infirm poor and workhouses for the able-bodied poor ("indoor relief"). The argument for indoor relief was much the same as the rationale for penitentiaries: plucking the poor from their demoralizing surroundings and exposing them to a highly regimented institution could change them into virtuous, productive citizens. However lofty the motives behind workhouses and almshouses, the results were often abysmal. In 1833 a legislative committee found that the inmates of the Boston House of Industry were packed seven to a room and included unwed mothers, the sick, and the insane as well as the poor.

As for insane people, those living in a workhouse such as the Boston House of Industry were relatively well off, for many experienced even worse treatment

**Pennsylvania's Eastern State Penitentiary**
*Begun in 1822 in Philadelphia, this penitentiary was the showcase of the so-called Pennsylvania or "Separate" system of prison discipline. Each inmate occupied a single cell and at all times was kept from contact with other inmates. This sketch was done by inmate 2954 in 1855.*

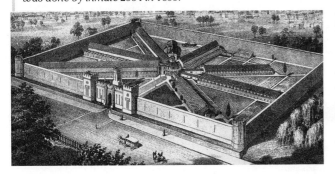

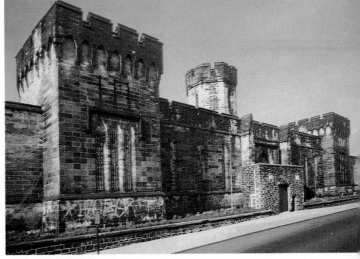

## The Oneida Community, New York

The most controversial of the antebellum experiments in communitarian utopianism, the Oneida community in New York State challenged conventional notions of religion, property, gender roles, marriage, sex, dress, and motherhood. Contemporaries dismissed its founder, John Humphrey Noyes, as a licentious crackpot, and Oneida as the "utopia of obscenity." Yet by the standards of utopian experiments, Oneida passed the test of time, achieved considerable economic prosperity, and continued to attract new members long after the collapse of less radical utopian experiments.

Little in Noyes's background—he had been born in 1811 into a well-connected Vermont family—marked him as an iconoclast. But Noyes came of age at a time when America was boiling over with radical religious doctrines that contained the seeds of still more unsettling social principles, and he possessed a penchant for carrying ideas to their logical conclusions, however extreme, and for leading his willing followers into uncharted regions of experience.

Converted in a Vermont revival in 1831, Noyes studied theology at Yale, where he came under the influence of Nathaniel W. Taylor, a theologian who pried Congregationalism from its Calvinist heritage by emphasizing that sin resulted from the individual's choice rather than from any divine plan. This interpretation left open the possibility that some people could achieve freedom from all sin—the doctrine of perfectionism. In 1834 Noyes startled his peers by asserting that he had achieved this perfect state. When, in response, the orthodox clergy revoked his license to preach, he announced that he would go on preaching just as they were free to go on sinning.

In the late 1830s Noyes began to gather disciples at Putney, Vermont, and to attack monogamous marriage. Because monogamy involved an exclusive attachment to one person, Noyes viewed it as selfish and suited only to sinners. Soon he put his theory into practice by acknowledging his love for Mary Cragin, the wife of one of the Putney perfectionists, while Noyes's wife Harriet disclosed her own affection for Mary's husband. Noyes did not intend to divorce Harriet; rather, he proclaimed that among the perfect, all men would be married to all women and all women to all men—the doctrine of "complex marriage." When the Putney perfectionists recruited two young sis-

**Bag Bee**

*Communal work, shown here in the form of a "bee" (gathering) for making traveling bags, complemented Noyes's belief in the communal ownership of property.*

ters from the village—one only fifteen years old—to their circle, the villagers exploded in outrage. Indicted for adultery with Mary Cragin, Noyes moved his little colony of the sinless to Oneida County in western New York in 1848.

To ordinary minds, Noyes was an advocate of free love. In reality, Noyes tied complex marriage to "male continence"; that is, men could engage in sexual intercourse with women, but they had to discipline themselves to withhold ejaculation (*coitus reservatus*). In this way, they not only practiced birth control but also demonstrated their perfect self-mastery. Like the Shakers, the Oneida community grew at first by attracting converts rather than by natural increase.

Consistent with Noyes's loathing of any form of proprietorship, whether of people or things, Oneidans renounced private property and practiced communism. But they accepted the profit motive in dealing with outsiders, the "worldlings." When an Oneidan invented an improved animal trap, the community marketed it through a Chicago dealer. In contrast to most other utopian communities, which cherished agriculture as a soothing alternative to the frenzied pace of industry, Oneidans fabricated and sold a wide array of products, including embroidered gentlemen's slippers, silk goods, mop handles, wheel spokes, and silverware. As the community prospered, its membership rose from under one hundred in 1849 to nearly three hundred by 1875.

Yet Noyes's unconventional ideas left their stamp even on work routines in Oneida's homes and factories. Although Noyes believed that women were less perfect than men, he mechanized domestic work wherever possible, insisted that males perform kitchen duties alongside women, and allowed

women to work in the community's stores and factories. Indeed, Noyes bitterly criticized the idea of a separate sphere for women, with its exclusive assignment of females to household duties. Oneida women not only worked outside the home but *looked* as if they did. They preferred pantaloons to unwieldy hoop skirts and cut their hair short in an age when middle-class women enhanced their coiffures by purchasing false hair.

Obsessed by the dream of elevating all humanity to perfection, Noyes in 1867 launched Oneida on its boldest experiment: the breeding of a perfect race by means of "stirpiculture." Stirpiculture* necessitated modifying male continence to allow consummation, but Noyes continued to abhor free love. Although individuals could voice preferences for sexual mates and veto proposed candidates, the final decision was left to a committee of elders, headed by "Father" Noyes. Like most educated people of his day, Noyes believed that moral and spiritual as well as physical qualities would be transmitted to children (the doctrine of "acquired characteristics"), and accordingly, he saw to it that the "more perfect," usually the older members of the community, mated with "less perfect" younger members—old men with young women, and young men with older women.

Noyes's influence over matings provoked dissent from Oneida's younger women, who faced criticism and even expulsion whenever they fell in love with men their own age and who suspected that stirpiculture too conveniently rationalized the lust of old men (including the ever prolific "Father" Noyes) for young women. Mounting outside criticism in the 1870s found the community weak and divided. In 1879 Noyes exiled himself to Canada to avoid prosecution (although local and state officials could not identify any law that he had broken); that same year, Oneidans renounced the doctrine of

**Harriet Holton**
*Having heard of Noyes's doctrine of perfection, Harriet Holton had rushed to hear him preach, judged his face to "shine like an angel's," and fallen in love.*

complex marriage. In 1881 they formally abandoned communism.

Oneida is more remarkable for its persistence than for its ultimate collapse. Despite the hostility of the clergy, Noyes usually maintained good relations with nearby worldlings, who found jobs in Oneida's factories. At the same time, the radical doctrines on which the experiment rested gave Oneida a degree of cohesion lacking at Brook Farm. By embracing a seemingly outlandish sexual doctrine, Oneidans, like Mormons, effectively burned their bridges to the world, and when they abandoned complex marriage, their unity dissolved.

### John Humphrey Noyes
*Noyes possessed a magnetic attraction for women and commanded the unswerving loyalty of his female followers.*

---

* Stirpiculture: from the Latin *stirps*—a root or strain.

by confinement in prisons. In 1841 an idealistic Unitarian schoolteacher, Dorothea Dix, was teaching a Sunday School class in a jail in East Cambridge, Massachusetts, and discovered there insane people kept in an unheated room. Dix pursued her investigation and visited jails and almshouses throughout the state. In 1843 she presented a memorial to the state legislature, which described the insane confined "in *cages, closets, cellars, stalls, pens! Chained, naked, beaten with rods, and lashed into obedience.*" With the support of Horace Mann and the Boston reformer Samuel G. Howe, she encouraged legislatures to build insane asylums, and by the time of the Civil War, twenty-eight states, four cities, and the federal government had constructed public mental institutions.

Penitentiaries, workhouses, and insane asylums all reflected the same optimistic belief that deviancy could be erased by resettling deviants in the right environment. But what was the "right" environment? In some aspects, the answer was clear-cut. Heated rooms were better than frigid ones, and sober parents preferable to drunkards. But reformers demanded much more than warm rooms and responsible parents. Reformers were convinced that the unfettered freedom and individualism of American society were themselves defects in the environment and that the poor, criminal, and insane needed extraordinary regimentation if they were to change. Prison inmates were to march around in lock step; in workhouses the poor, treated much like prisoners, were often forbidden to leave or receive visitors without permission. The idealism behind such institutions was genuine, but later generations would question reformers' underlying assumptions.

## Utopian Communities

The belief that individuals could live perfectly, which tinged most antebellum reform movements, took its most extreme form in the experimental societies or "utopian" communities that flourished in these years. Although varying widely in their philosophies and arrangements, utopian communities had some common features. Their founders were intellectuals who designed their communities as alternatives to the prevailing competitive economy and as models whose success would inspire imitation. Unlike the Shakers and the Mormons, the utopians did not claim to have visions of God or visits from angels. Nor did they burn their bridges to society.

American interest in utopian communities first surfaced during the 1820s. In 1825 British industrialist and philanthropist Robert Owen founded the New Harmony community in Indiana. Owen had already acquired a formidable reputation (and a fortune) from his management of cotton mills at New Lanark, Scotland. His innovations at New Lanark had substantially improved his workers' educational opportunities and living conditions and left him convinced that similar changes could transform the lives of working people everywhere. He saw the problem of the early industrial age as social rather than political. If social arrangements could be perfected, all vice and misery would disappear; human character was formed, "without exception," by people's surroundings or environment. The key to perfecting social arrangements lay, in turn, in the creation of small, planned communities—"Villages of Unity and Mutual Cooperation," each to contain a perfect balance of occupational, religious, and political groups.

Lured to the United States by cheap land and by Americans' receptivity to experiments, Owen confidently predicted that by 1827 the northern states would embrace the principles embodied in New Harmony. Unfortunately, by 1827 there was little left to embrace, for the community had quickly fallen apart. New Harmony had attracted more than its share of idlers and fanatics, and Owen had spent too much time on the road publicizing the community and not enough time managing it. He had clashed with clergymen, who still believed that Original Sin, not environment, shaped human character. Yet Owenism survived the wreckage of New Harmony. The notions that human character was formed by environment and that cooperation was superior to competition had a potent impact on urban workers for the next half-century. Owen's ideas, for example, impelled workingmen's leaders to support educational reform during the late 1820s.

In the early 1830s, the utopian impulse weakened, only to revive amid the economic chaos of the late 1830s and 1840s. Appalled by the misery that came with economic depression, small bands of idealists gathered anew in experimental communities whose names—Hopedale, Fruitlands, Brook Farm—suggested idyllic retreats. Their founders' visions were fired by intense but unconventional forms of Christianity. Adin Ballou, a Universalist minister who founded Hopedale, near Milford, Massachusetts, described it as a "miniature Christian republic." Brook Farm, near Boston, was mainly the creation of a group of religious philosophers called transcendentalists. Most transcendentalists, including Ralph Waldo Emerson and George Ripley, had started as Unitarians but sought to revitalize Unitarianism—and indeed all denominations—by proclaiming the infinite spiritual capacities of ordinary men and women.

Like other utopias, Brook Farm was both a retreat and a model. Convinced that the competitive commercial life of the cities was unnatural, philosophers welcomed the opportunity to engage in elevated discussions after a day perspiring in the cabbage patch. Although Brook Farm never had more than a hundred residents, it attracted several renowned writers. Emerson visited it, and novelist Nathaniel Hawthorne lived there for a period; Brook Farm's literary magazine, *The Dial,* became a forum for transcendentalist ideas about philosophy, art, and literature (also see Chapter 11).

Few utopias enjoyed success to match their ambitions. Brook Farm disbanded in 1849; Hopedale, in 1853. In general, utopian communities were less durable and attracted fewer people than religious communities such as those of the Shakers and Mormons. In contrast to the religious communitarians, the utopians kept open their avenues to society and moved back and forth between their communities and antislavery or women's rights conventions. With the notable exception of the Oneida community (see A Place in Time), utopians neither sought nor attained the kind of grip on the allegiance of their members held by a Mother Ann Lee or a Joseph Smith.

Widely derided as fit only for eccentrics, the antebellum utopias nevertheless exemplified in extreme form the idealism and hopefulness that permeated nearly all reform in the Age of Jackson.

## CONCLUSION

The voice of the common people resounded through politics and religion during the 1820s and 1830s. The gentlemanly leadership and surface harmony of the Era of Good Feelings gave way to the raucous huzzahs of mass political parties. Calvinist clergymen found their doctrine of human depravity hammered by the popular revivalists' stress on Americans' capacity to remake themselves.

The louder the people spoke, the less unified they became. The cries of "foul" that had enveloped the election of 1824 catapulted Andrew Jackson as the em-

bodiment of the popular will. But Jackson's seemingly dictatorial manner and his stands on internal improvements, tariffs, nullification, and banking divided the electorate and contributed to the emergence of the Whig party. The Panic of 1837 deepened party divisions by shoving wavering Democrats toward a hard-money, antibank position. Similarly, revivals, which aimed to unite Americans in a religion of the heart, spawned critics of religious excess (Unitarians) and indirectly gave rise to hotly controversial religious groups (Mormons).

In an unsettling age many Americans sought to forge order out of seeming chaos. Reformers thought that they could rehabilitate the entire society by constructing regimented institutions that would cultivate the basic goodness of human nature. Both reformers and politicians sought to slay the demons that threatened the Republic. Often disdaining politics as corrupt, reformers blasted liquor, ignorance, and slavery with the same fervor that Jacksonians directed at banks and monopolies. Yet reformers who called for the legal prohibition of liquor and the reform of public education or who organized an abolitionist political party were reluctantly acknowledging that in a mass democracy everything sooner or later became political.

## FOR FURTHER READING

Lee Benson, *The Concept of Jacksonian Democracy: New York as a Test Case* (1961). A major revisionist interpretation of the period.

Donald B. Cole, *The Presidency of Andrew Jackson* (1993). Fine account, incorporating the latest scholarship.

William W. Freehling, *Prelude to Civil War* (1966). A major study of the nullification crisis.

Richard P. McCormick, *The Second American Party System: Party Formation in the Jacksonian Era* (1966). An influential work stressing the role of political leaders in shaping the second party system.

Robert V. Remini, *Henry Clay: Statesman for the Union* (1991). An important new biography of the leading Whig statesman of the period.

Arthur M. Schlesinger, Jr., *The Age of Jackson* (1945). A classic study, now dated in some of its interpretations but still highly readable.

Fred Somkin, *Unquiet Eagle: Memory and Desire in the Idea of American Freedom, 1815–1860* (1967). A penetrating study of American political values.

Ronald G. Walters, *American Reformers, 1815–1860* (1978). A balanced study that addresses the negative as well as positive aspects of nineteenth-century reform.

Chilton Williamson, *American Suffrage: From Property to Democracy, 1760–1860* (1960). The standard study of changing requirements for voting.

# 11 Life, Leisure, and Culture
## 1840–1860

**Chess Game,** *mid-1860s*

In 1867 a syndicate headed by Cyrus West Field secured the world's largest ship to lay a submarine telegraph cable from Ireland to Newfoundland. It worked. Completion of the cable set off jubilation from Kansas City to Siberia. Land cables were being laid nearly everywhere by 1867, but the greatest obstacle of all, the Atlantic Ocean, had now been bridged by the marvel of electromagnetism.

Field's accomplishment was all the more astounding in light of the problems he had faced since 1853, when, as a wealthy retired businessman living in New York City, he had first conceived the idea for a transatlantic cable. Samuel F. B. Morse had transmitted the first telegraphic message in 1844, from Baltimore to Washington, D.C. But an underwater cable across the Atlantic? Over 1,600 miles separated the closest North American and European points. The ocean was known to be two or three miles deep in places, so a lot more than 1,600 miles of cable would have to be manufactured (2,500 miles as it turned out). Unlike air, water conducts electricity, so unless some way could be found to insulate the cable, its electric energy would dissipate on the ocean floor. No one knew for sure what that floor was like. Perhaps currents would tear the cable to shreds. In Britain, the royal astronomer pronounced the idea mathematically impossible.

Field's first effort, in 1857, failed when the cable snapped 300 miles west of Ireland. Despite threats posed to the venture by storms and frolicking whales, his second attempt, a year later, appeared to succeed. Messages were transmitted for a few weeks, and Americans hailed Field as the new Columbus and danced to the "Atlantic Telegraph Cable Polka." Queen Victoria cabled a message of congratulation, and the London *Times* praised Field for undoing the damage to Anglo-American relations wrought by the American Revolu-

tion. Shares in the company he had formed to finance the expedition (he had also secured financial aid from Congress and the British government) quadrupled. Then the messages stopped; somewhere under the Atlantic the current was leaking. Now Field faced more than failure; he was wrongly accused of having engaged in a fraud to drive up the price of his stock. Like a spent rocket, his reputation fizzled. What proof was there that any messages had been transmitted by the cable, angry investors asked. Actually, many messages had been transmitted, but most, technical communications between electricians, had been discarded, and few believed Field's evidence of a message from Queen Victoria. Poor Field wanted to try again, but now the outbreak of the Civil War forced him to wait until 1865, when once more a remorseless ocean managed to snap the cable.

What kept Field going until he ultimately succeeded was his belief that God had ordained a better future for man in this world. By declaring God the prime mover behind material betterment, Field secularized the teaching of his father, a New England Calvinist clergyman who believed that God's will governs all. No matter how many obstacles one encountered, God expected humans to persist in the improvement of society, would be angry if they did not, and had so arranged the natural world that industry and energy would invariably reap material rewards. One of Field's supporters, the naval officer and oceanographer Matthew Fontaine Maury, assured him that God had shaped a "telegraphic plateau" at the bottom of the Atlantic, just waiting to embrace the cable.

Americans of Field's generation believed that technology, a word popularized after 1829 to describe the application of science to improving the conveniences of life, was God's chosen means of progress. Like Field and Morse, who saw the telegraph as an instrument of world peace, they equated material and moral progress. But progress had its darker side. Periodic cholera epidemics reminded Americans that technology, in the shape of steamboats and railroads, could spread disease as well as food. Philosophers and artists began to worry about the despoliation of the landscape, and conservationists launched conscious efforts to preserve enclaves of nature as parks and retreats safe from progress.

This chapter focuses on three major questions:

♦ In what ways did technology transform the daily lives of ordinary Americans between 1840 and 1860?

♦ Technological change contributed to new kinds of national unity and also to new forms of social division. What were the main unifying features of technology? the principal dividing or segmenting features?

♦ How did technological advances and the expansion of the marketplace affect American intellectual and artistic life? Which features of technological progress did writers and artists welcome, and which ones dismayed or alarmed them?

## Technology and Economic Growth

Widely hailed as democratic, the benefits of *technology*, a word popularized after 1829 to describe how an understanding of scientific principles could be used to transform the practical conveniences of life, drew praise from all sides. Conservatives like Daniel Webster praised machines for doing the work of ten people without consuming food or clothing, while Sarah Bagley, a Lowell mill operative and labor organizer, traced the improvement of society to the development of technology.

The technology that transformed life in antebellum America included the steam engine, the cotton gin, the reaper, the use of interchangeable parts in manufacturing, the sewing machine, and the telegraph. Some of these originated in Europe but Americans had a flair for investing in others' inventions and perfecting their own. Improvements in Eli Whitney's cotton gin between 1793 and 1860, for example, led to an eightfold increase in the amount of cotton that could be ginned in a day. Of course, technology did not benefit everyone. Improvements in the cotton gin served to rivet slavery more firmly in place by making the South more dependent on cotton. Technology also rendered many traditional skills obsolete and thereby undercut the position

**"Lagonda Agricultural Workers"** by Edwin Forbes, 1859
*The manufacture of agricultural implements was becoming a major industry by 1860. Now the farmers shown on the fringe could put down their scythes and let the mechanical reaper do the work.*

**McCormick Ad**
*Cyrus McCormick patented his invention of the reaper in 1834. After failing to renew his patent in 1848, he outdistanced his rivals by investing in advertising and by offering money-back guarantees and deferred payments.*

CHRONOLOGY

**1820**  Washington Irving, *The Sketch Book.*

**1823**  Philadelphia completes the first urban water-supply system.

James Fenimore Cooper, *The Pioneers.*

**1826**  Cooper, *The Last of the Mohicans.*

**1831**  Mount Auburn Cemetery opens.

**1832**  A cholera epidemic strikes the United States.

**1833**  The *New York Sun,* the first penny newspaper, is established.

**1834**  Cyrus McCormick patents the mechanical reaper.

**1835**  James Gordon Bennett establishes the *New York Herald.*

**1837**  Ralph Waldo Emerson, "The American Scholar."

**1841**  P. T. Barnum opens the American Museum.

**1842**  Edgar Allan Poe, "The Murders in the Rue Morgue."

**1844**  Samuel F. B. Morse patents the telegraph.

The American Art Union is established.

Poe, "The Raven."

**1846**  W. T. G. Morton successfully uses anesthesia.

**1849**  Second major cholera epidemic.

Astor Place theater riot leaves twenty dead.

**1850**  Nathaniel Hawthorne, *The Scarlet Letter.*

**1851**  Hawthorne, *The House of the Seven Gables.*

Herman Melville, *Moby-Dick.*

Erie Railroad completes its line to the West.

**1852**  Pennsylvania Railroad completes its line between Philadelphia and Pittsburgh.

**1853**  Ten small railroads are consolidated into the New York Central Railroad.

**1854**  Henry David Thoreau, *Walden.*

**1855**  Walt Whitman, *Leaves of Grass.*

**1856**  Pennsylvania Railroad completes Chicago link.

Illinois Central completed between Chicago and Cairo, Illinois.

**1857**  Baltimore–St. Louis rail service completed.

**1858**  Frederick Law Olmsted is appointed architect in chief for Central Park.

of artisans. But technology contributed to improvements in transportation and increases in productivity, which in turn lowered commodity prices and raised the living standards of a sizable body of free Americans between 1840 and 1860.

### Agricultural Advancement

Although few settlers ventured onto the treeless, semiarid Great Plains before the Civil War, settlements edged westward after 1830 from the woodlands of Ohio and Kentucky into parts of Indiana, Michigan, and Illinois, where flat grasslands (prairies) alternated with forests. The prairie's matted soil was difficult to break for planting, but in 1837 John Deere invented a steel-tipped plow that halved the labor to clear acres to till. Timber for housing and fencing was available in nearby woods, and settlements spread rapidly.

Wheat became to midwestern farmers what cotton was to their southern counterparts. "The wheat crop is the great crop of the North-west, for exchange pur-

poses," an agricultural journal noted in 1850. "It pays debts, buys groceries, clothing and lands, and answers more emphatically the purposes of trade among farmers than any other crop." Technological advances speeded the harvesting as well as the planting of wheat on the midwestern prairies. Using the traditional hand sickle consumed huge amounts of time and labor, all the more so because cut wheat had to be picked up and bound. Inventors in Europe had experimented since the eighteenth century with horse-drawn machines to replace sickles. But until Cyrus McCormick came on the scene, the absence of the right combination of technical skill and business enterprise had relegated mechanical reapers to the realm of tinkerers' dreams. In 1834 McCormick, a Virginian, patented a mechanical reaper that drew on but improved previous designs. Opening a factory in Chicago in 1847, McCormick manufactured reapers by mass production and introduced aggressive marketing techniques such as deferred payments and money-back guarantees. By harvesting grain seven times more rapidly than traditional methods, and with half the labor force, the reaper guaranteed the preeminence of wheat on the midwestern prairies of Illinois, Indiana, Iowa, and Missouri. McCormick sold 80,000 reapers by 1860, and this was only the beginning. During the Civil War, he made immense profits by selling more than 250,000 reapers.

Ironically, just as a Connecticut Yankee, Eli Whitney, had stimulated the foundation of the Old South's economy by his invention of the cotton gin, Cyrus McCormick, a proslavery southern Democrat, would help the North win the Civil War. Indeed, the North provided the main market for McCormick's reaper and for the models of his many competitors; the South, with its reliance on slave labor, had far less incentive to mechanize agriculture. The reaper would keep northern agricultural production high at a time when labor shortages caused by troop mobilization might otherwise have slashed production.

Although Americans proved resourceful at inventing and marketing machines to speed planting and harvesting, they farmed wastefully. With land abundant, farmers were more inclined to look for virgin soil than to improve "worn out" soil. But a movement for agricultural improvement in the form of more efficient use of the soil did develop before 1860, mainly in the East. Confronted by the superior fertility of western soil, easterners who did not move west or take jobs in factories increasingly experimented with new agricultural techniques. In Orange County, New York, for example, farmers fed their cows the best clover and bluegrass and emphasized cleanliness in the processing of dairy products. Through these practices, they produced a superior butter that commanded more than double the price of ordinary butter. Still other eastern farmers turned to the use of fertilizers to keep their wheat production competitive with that of the bountiful midwestern prairies. By fertilizing their fields with plaster left over from the construction of the James River Canal, Virginia wheat growers raised their average yield per acre to fifteen bushels by the 1850s, up from only six bushels in 1800. Similarly, during the 1840s American cotton planters began to import guano, left by the droppings of sea birds on islands off Peru, for use as a fertilizer. Fertilizers helped eastern cotton farmers close the gap created by the superior fertility of southwestern soil for cotton.

### Technology and Industrial Progress

The early growth of American manufacturing had relied primarily on imported technology. That depen-

**Woman at Singer Sewing Machine**
*Asked to repair a sewing machine that did not do continuous stitching, Isaac M. Singer invented one that did. Patented in 1851, the Singer machine quickly dominated the market. Although most early sewing machines were used in factories, some had made their way into households by 1860.*

dence lessened after 1830 as American industries became more innovative. For example, in 1853 a small-arms factory in England reequipped itself with machine tools (tools that shaped metal products) manufactured by two firms in the backwoods of Vermont. After touring American factories in 1854, a British engineer concluded that Americans "universally and willingly" resorted to machines as a substitute for manual labor.

Eli Whitney had pioneered the application of interchangeable parts in the United States in 1798, but the manufacture of guns and other products using interchangeable parts still required a great deal of hand-filing before the parts could be fitted together. By the 1840s, however, improved machine tools had greatly reduced the need for handwork. In 1853 the superintendent of the Springfield, Massachusetts, armory staged a spectacular demonstration of interchangeable parts for a British commission investigating American technology. Rifles that had been produced in ten consecutive years were stripped and their parts reassembled at random.

The American system of manufacturing contained several distinctive advantages. Traditionally, damage to any part of a mechanical contrivance had rendered the whole useless, for no new part would fit. With the perfection of manufacturing by interchangeable parts, however, replacements could be ordered for damaged parts. In addition, the improved machine tools upon which the American system depended enabled entrepreneurs to push inventions swiftly into mass production. The likelihood that inventions would quickly enter production in turn attracted investors. By the 1850s Connecticut firms like Smith and Wesson were mass-producing the revolving pistol, which Samuel Colt had invented in 1836. Sophisticated machine tools made it possible, a manufacturer wrote, to increase production "by confining a worker to one particular limb of a pistol until he had made two thousand." The sewing machine, invented in 1846 by Elias Howe, entered mass production only two years later.

Americans also seized enthusiastically on the telegraph's promise to eliminate the constraints of time and space. The speed with which Americans formed telegraph companies and strung lines stunned a British engineer, who noted in 1854 that "no private interests can oppose the passage of a line through any property." Although telegraph lines usually transmitted political and commercial messages, some cities adapted them for reporting fires. By the early 1850s, Boston had an elaborate system of telegraph stations which could alert fire companies throughout the city to a blaze in any neighborhood. Whatever their use, telegraph lines spread rapidly. By 1852 more than fifteen thousand miles of lines connected cities as distant as Quebec, New Orleans, and St. Louis.

### The Railroad Boom

Even more than the telegraph, the railroad dramatized technology's democratic promise. In 1790 even European royalty could travel no faster than fourteen miles an hour and that only with frequent changes of horses. By 1850 an ordinary American could travel three times as fast on a train, and with considerable comfort. American railroads offered only one class of travel, in contrast to the several classes on European railroads. With the introduction of adjustable upholstered seats that could serve as couches at night, Americans in effect traveled first class—except for African Americans, who often were forced to sit separately.

Americans loved railroads "as a lover loves his mistress," one Frenchman wrote, but there was little to love about the earliest railroads. Sparks from locomotives showered passengers riding in open cars, which were common. In the absence of brakes, passengers often had to get out and pull trains to stops. Lacking

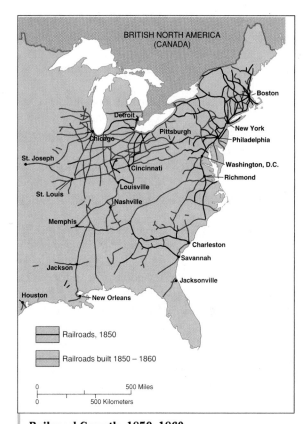

**Railroad Growth, 1850–1860**
*Rail ties between the East and the Midwest greatly increased during the railroad "boom" of the 1850s.*

lights, trains rarely ran at night. Before the introduction of standard time zones in 1883 (see Chapter 18), scheduling was a nightmare; at noon in Boston it was twelve minutes before noon in New York City. Delays were frequent, for trains on single-track lines had to wait on sidings for oncoming trains to pass. Because a train's location was a mystery once it had left the station, these waits could seem endless.

Between 1840 and 1860 the size of the rail network and the power and convenience of trains underwent stunning transformation. Railroad track went from three thousand to thirty thousand miles, flat-roofed coaches replaced open cars, kerosene lamps made night travel possible, and increasingly powerful engines let trains climb even the steepest hills. Fifty thousand miles of telegraph wire enabled dispatchers to communicate with trains en route and thus to reduce delays.

Problems nonetheless lingered. Sleeping accommodations remained crude, and schedules erratic. Because individual railroads used different gauge track, frequent changes of train were necessary; eight changes interrupted a journey from Charleston to Philadelphia in the 1850s. Yet nothing slowed the advance of railroads or cured Americans' mania for them. By 1860 the United States had more track than all the rest of the world.

Railroads spearheaded the second phase of the transportation revolution. Canals remained in use; the Erie Canal, for example, did not reach its peak volume until 1880. But railroads, faster and less vulnerable to winter freezes, gradually overtook them, first in passengers and then in freight. By 1860 the value of goods transported by railroads greatly surpassed that carried by canals.

As late as 1860, few rail lines extended west of the Mississippi, but railroads had spread like spiderwebs east of the great river. The railroads turned southern cities like Atlanta and Chattanooga into thriving commercial hubs. Most important, the railroads linked the East and the Midwest. The New York Central and the Erie railroads joined New York City to Buffalo; the Pennsylvania Railroad connected Philadelphia to Pittsburgh; and the Baltimore and Ohio linked Baltimore to Wheeling, Virginia (now West Virginia). Simultaneously, intense construction in Ohio, Indiana, and Illinois created trunk lines that tied these routes to cities farther west. By 1860 rail lines ran from Buffalo to Cleveland, Toledo, and Chicago; from Pittsburgh to Fort Wayne; and from Wheeling to Cincinnati and St. Louis.

Chicago's growth illustrates the impact of these rail links. In 1849 it was a village of a few hundred people with virtually no rail service. By 1860 it had become a city of 100,000, served by eleven railroads. Farmers in the Upper Midwest no longer had to ship their grain, livestock, and dairy products down the Mississippi to New Orleans; they could now ship their products directly east. Chicago supplanted New Orleans as the interior's main commercial hub.

The east-west rail lines stimulated the development of the settlement and agricultural development of the Midwest. By 1860 Illinois, Indiana, and Wisconsin had replaced Ohio, Pennsylvania, and New York as the leading wheat-growing states. Enabling farmers to speed their products to the East, railroads increased the value of farmland and promoted additional settlement. In turn, population growth triggered industrial development in cities such as Chicago, Davenport, Iowa, and Minneapolis, for the new settlers needed lumber for fences and houses and mills to grind wheat into flour.

Railroads also propelled the growth of small towns along their routes. The Illinois Central Railroad, which had more track than any other railroad in 1855, made money not only from its traffic but also from real estate speculation. Purchasing land for stations along its path, the Illinois Central then laid out towns around the stations. The selection of Manteno, Illinois, as a stop of the Illinois Central, for example, transformed the site from a crossroads without a single house in 1854 into a bustling town of nearly a thousand in 1860, replete with hotels, lumberyards, grain elevators, and gristmills. (The Illinois Central even dictated the naming of streets. Those running east and west were always named after trees, and those running north and south were numbered. Soon one rail town looked much like the next.) By the Civil War, few thought of the railroad-linked Midwest as a frontier region or viewed its inhabitants as pioneers.

As the nation's first big business, the railroads transformed the conduct of business. During the early 1830s, railroads, like canals, depended on financial aid from state governments. With the onset of depression in the late 1830s, however, state governments scrapped overly ambitious railroad projects. Convinced that railroads burdened them with high taxes and blasted hopes, voters turned against state aid, and in the early 1840s, several states amended their constitutions to bar state funding for railroads and canals. The federal government took up some of the slack, but federal aid did not provide a major stimulus to railroads before 1860. Rather, part of the burden of finance passed to city and county governments in agricultural areas that wanted to attract railroads. Municipal governments, for example, often gave railroads rights-of-way, grants of land for stations, and public funds.

### The Express Train

*Antebellum depictions of trains usually showed their smoke as harmless, cloudlike puffs, but this picture renders the real color more accurately and menacingly.*

The dramatic expansion of the railroad network in the 1850s, however, strained the financing capacity of local governments and required a turn toward private investment, which had never been absent from the picture. Well aware of the economic benefits of railroads, individuals living near them had long purchased railroad securities issued by governments and had directly bought stock in railroads, often paying by contributing their labor to building the railroads. But the large railroads of the 1850s needed more capital than such small investors could generate. Gradually, the center of railroad financing shifted to New York City, and in fact, it was the railroad boom of the 1850s that helped make Wall Street the nation's greatest capital market. The securities of all the leading railroads were traded on the floor of the New York Stock Exchange during the 1850s. In addition, the growth of railroads turned New York City into the center of modern investment firms. The investment firms evaluated the securities of railroads in Toledo or Davenport or Chattanooga and then found purchasers for these securities in New York, Philadelphia, Paris, London, Amsterdam, and Hamburg. Controlling the flow of funds to railroads, the investment bankers began to exert influence over the railroads' internal affairs by supervising administrative reorganizations in times of trouble. A Wall Street analyst noted in 1851 that railroad men seeking financing "must remember that money is power, and that the [financier] can dictate to a great extent his own terms."

## Rising Prosperity

Technological advances also improved the lives of consumers by bringing down the prices of many commodities. For example, clocks that cost $50 to fabricate by hand in 1800 could be produced by machine for 50¢ by 1850. In addition, the widening use of steam power contributed to a 25 percent rise in the average worker's real income (actual purchasing power) between 1840 and 1860. Early-nineteenth-century factories, which had depended on water wheels to propel their machines, of necessity had to shut down when the rivers or streams that powered the wheels froze. With the spread of steam engines, however, factories could stay open longer and workers could increase their annual wages by working more hours. Cotton textile workers were among those who benefited: although their hourly wages showed little gain, their average annual wages rose from $163 in 1830 to $176 in 1849 to $201 by 1859.

The growth of towns and cities also contributed to an increase in average annual wages. Farmers experienced the same seasonal fluctuations as laborers in the early factories. In sparsely settled rural areas, the onset of winter traditionally brought hard times; as demand for agricultural labor slumped, few alternatives existed to take up the slack. "A year in some farming states such as Pennsylvania," a traveler commented in 1823, "is only of eight months duration, four months being lost to the laborer, who is turned away as a useless animal." In contrast, densely populated towns and cities offered more opportunities for year-round work. The urban dockworker thrown out of his job as a result of frozen waterways might find work as a hotel porter or an unskilled indoor laborer.

Towns and cities also provided women and children with new opportunities for paid work. (Women and children had long performed many vital tasks on farms, but rarely for pay.) The wages of children between the ages of ten and eighteen came to play an integral role in the nineteenth-century family economy. Family heads who earned more than $600 a year might have been able to afford the luxury of keeping their children in school, but most breadwinners were fortunate if they made $300 a year. Although the cost of many basic commodities fell between 1815 and 1860 (another consequence of the transportation revolution), most families lived close to the margin. Budgets of working-class families in New York City and Philadelphia during the early 1850s reveal annual expenditures of $500–$600, with more than 40 percent spent on food, 25–30 percent on rent, and most of the remainder on clothing and fuel. Such a family obviously could not survive on the annual wages of the average male head of the household. It needed the wages of the children and, at times, those of the wife as well.

Life in urban wage-earning families was not necessarily superior to life in farming communities. A farmer who owned land, livestock, and a house did not have to worry about paying rent or buying fuel for cooking and heating, and rarely ran short of food. Many Americans continued to aspire to farming as the best of all occupations. But to purchase, clear, and stock a farm involved a considerable capital outlay that could easily amount to five hundred dollars, and the effort promised no rewards for a few years. The majority of workers in agricultural areas did not own farms and were exposed to the seasonal fluctuations in demand for agricultural labor. In many respects, they were worse off than urban wage earners.

The economic advantages that attended living in cities help explain why so many Americans moved to urban areas during the first half of the nineteenth century. As a further attraction, during the 1840s and 1850s, cities also provided their residents with an unprecedented range of comforts and conveniences.

## The Quality of Life

"Think of the numberless contrivances and inventions for our comfort and luxury," the poet Walt Whitman exclaimed, "and you will bless your star that Fate has cast your lot in the year of Our Lord 1857." Changes in what we now call the standard of living affected housing and such daily activities as eating, drinking, and washing in the 1840s and 1850s. The patent office in Washington was flooded with sketches of reclining seats, beds convertible into chairs, street-sweeping machines, and fly traps. Machine-made furniture began to transform the interiors of houses. Stoves revolutionized heating and cooking. Railroads brought fresh vegetables to city dwellers.

Despite all the talk of comfort and progress, however, many Americans experienced little improvement in the quality of their lives. Technological advances made it possible for the middle class to enjoy luxuries formerly reserved for the rich but often widened the distance between the middle class and the poor. At a time when the interiors of urban, middle-class homes were becoming increasingly lavish, the urban poor congregated in cramped and unsightly tenements. In addition, some aspects of life remained relatively unaffected by scientific and technical advances. Medical science, for example, made a few advances before 1860, but none that rivaled the astonishing changes wrought by the railroad and the telegraph.

The benefits rather than the limitations of progress, however, gripped the popular imagination. Few Americans accepted the possibility that progress could neglect such an important aspect of everyday life as health. Confronted by the failure of the medical profession to rival the achievements of Cyrus McCormick and Samuel F. B. Morse, Americans embraced popular health movements that sprang up outside the medical profession and that promised to conquer disease by the precepts of diet and regimen.

### Dwellings

Whereas most city dwellers in the eighteenth century had lived in unattached frame houses, all of which looked different and faced in different directions, their nineteenth-century counterparts were more likely to inhabit brick row houses. Typically narrow and long, row houses were practical responses to rising urban land values (as much as 750 percent in Manhattan between 1785 and 1815).

Some praised row houses as democratic; others condemned "their extreme uniformity—when you have seen one, you have seen all." But they were not all alike. In the mid-nineteenth century, middle-class row houses were larger (3 to 3½ stories) than working-class row houses (2 to 2½ stories). In addition, soaring land values led to the subdividing of many row houses for occupancy by several families. The worst of these subdivided row houses were called tenements and became the usual habitats of Irish immigrants and free blacks.

The most fashionable urban residences usually surrounded small parks ringed by iron fences and their addresses contained *Place* or *Square* rather than *Street.* The wealthy also had a taste for elegant doors, curved staircases, carved columns for walls, and rooms with fanciful, asymmetrical shapes. All of this was beyond the resources of the urban middle class, but the rise of mass production in such furniture centers as Grand Rapids, Michigan, and Cincinnati between 1840 and 1860 brought the so-called French antique, or rococo, furniture style within the financial reach of the middle class.

Rococo furniture was by definition ornate. Upholstered chairs, for example, displayed intricate scrolls depicting vines, leaves, or flowers, and rested on curved legs with ornamental feet (called cabriole legs). The heavily upholstered backs of sofas were often trimmed with floral designs topped by carved medallions. Mirrors with gilded moldings that depicted birds, flowers, and even young women frequently weighed so much that they threatened to tumble from the wall. Technological advances in the fabrication of furniture tended to level taste between the middle and upper classes while simultaneously setting off those classes from everyone else.

In rural areas the quality of housing depended as much on the date of settlement as on social class. In recently settled areas the standard dwelling was a rude one-room log cabin, with planked floors, crude clay chimneys, and windows covered by oiled paper or cloth. As rural communities matured, log cabins gave way to frame houses of two or more rooms and better insulation. Most of these houses were built on a principle known as the *balloon frame.* In place of foot-thick

**Family Group**
*This daguerreotype, taken about 1852, reveals the little things so important to etching a middle-class family's social status: curtains; a wall hanging; a piano with scrolled legs; a small desk with elegantly curved legs; a pet; ladies posed in nonproductive but "improving" activities (music, reading); and a young man seemingly staring into space—and perhaps pondering how to pay for it all.*

posts and beams laboriously fitted together, the balloon-frame house had a skeleton of thin-sawn timbers nailed together in such a way that every strain ran against the grain of the wood. The simplicity and cheapness of such houses endeared them to western builders who had neither the time nor the skill to cut and fit heavy beams.

## Conveniences and Inconveniences

By today's standards, everyday life in the 1840s and 1850s was primitive, but contemporaries were struck by how much better it was becoming. The transportation and industrial revolutions were affecting heating, cooking, and diet. In urban areas, where wood was expensive, coal-burning stoves were rapidly displacing open hearths for heating and cooking. Stoves made it possible to cook several dishes at once and thus contributed to the growing variety of the American diet, while railroads brought in fresh vegetables, which in the eighteenth century had been absent from even lavish banquet tables.

Too, contemporaries were struck by the construction of urban waterworks—systems of pipes and aqueducts that brought fresh water from rivers or reservoirs to street hydrants. New York City completed the Croton aqueduct, which carried water into the city from reservoirs to the north, in the 1840s, and by 1860 sixty-eight public water systems operated in the United States.

Despite these improvements, newly acquired elegance still bumped shoulders with squalor. Coal burned longer and hotter than wood, but it left a dirty residue that polluted the air and blackened the snow, and a faulty coal stove could fill the air with poisonous carbon monoxide. Seasonal fluctuations continued to affect diets. Only the rich could afford fruit out of season, since they alone could afford to use sugar to preserve it. Indeed, preserving almost any kind of food presented problems. Home iceboxes were rare before 1860, so salt remained the most widely used preservative. One reason antebellum Americans ate more pork than beef was that salt affected pork's taste less negatively. Although public waterworks were among the most impressive engineering feats of the age, their impact is easily exaggerated. Since the incoming water usually ended its trip at a street hydrant, and only a fraction of the urban population lived near hydrants, houses rarely had running water. Taking a bath was a major operation, for the water had to be heated first, pot by pot, on a stove. A New England physician claimed that not one in five of his patients took one bath a year.

Infrequent baths meant pungent body odors, which mingled with a multitude of strong scents. In the absence of municipal sanitation departments, street cleaning was let to private contractors, who gained a reputation for slack performance of their duties, and so urbanites relied on hogs, which they allowed to roam freely and scavenge. (Hogs that turned down the wrong street often made tasty dinners for the poor.) Stables backed by mounds of manure and outdoor privies added to the stench. Flush tiolets were rare outside cities, and within cities sewer systems lagged behind water systems. Boston had only five thousand flush toilets in 1860 for a population of 178,000, a far higher ratio of toilets to people than most cities.

Expensive conveniences like running water and flush toilets became another of the ways in which progress set the upper and middle classes apart from the poor. Conveniences also sharpened gender differences. In her widely popular *Treatise on Domestic Economy* (1841), Catharine Beecher told women that technological advances made it their duty to make every house a "glorious temple" by utilizing space more efficiently. Women who no longer made articles for home consumption now were expected to achieve fulfillment by obsessively sweeping floors and polishing furniture. Home, a writer proclaimed, had become woman's "royal court," where she "sways her queenly

authority." Skeptical of this trend toward fastidiousness, another writer cautioned women in 1857 against "ultra-housewifery."

## Disease and Health

Despite the slowly rising standard of living, Americans remained vulnerable to disease. Epidemics swept through antebellum cities and felled thousands. Yellow fever and cholera killed one-fifth of New Orleans's population in 1832–1833, and cholera alone carried off 10 percent of St. Louis's population in 1849.

With grim irony, the transportation revolution increased the peril from epidemics. The cholera epidemic of 1832, the first truly national epidemic, followed shipping routes: one branch of the epidemic ran from New York City up the Hudson River, across the Erie Canal to Ohio, and then down the Ohio River to the Mississippi and south to New Orleans; the other branch followed shipping up and down the East Coast from New York City.

Each major antebellum epidemic of cholera or yellow fever intensified public calls for the establishment of municipal health boards, and by the 1850s most major cities had formed such agencies. However, so few powers did city governments give them that the boards could not even enforce the reporting of diseases. The inability of physicians to find a satisfactory explanation for epidemic diseases led to a general distrust of the medical profession and contributed to making public health a low-priority issue.

Prior to 1860 no one understood that tiny organisms called bacteria caused both cholera and yellow fever. Rather, rival camps of physicians battled furiously and publicly over the merits of the "contagion" theory versus those of the "miasm" theory. Insisting that cholera and yellow fever were transmitted by touch, contagionists called for vigorous measures to quarantine affected areas. In contrast, supporters of the miasm theory argued that poisonous gases (miasms) emitted by rotting vegetation or dead animals carried disease through the air. The miasm theory led logically to the conclusion that swamps should be drained and streets cleaned. Neither theory, however, was consistent with the evidence. Quarantines failed to check cholera and yellow fever (an argument against the contagionist theory), and many residents of filthy slums and stinking, low-lying areas contracted neither of the two diseases (a refutation of the miasm theory). Confronted by this inconclusive debate between medical experts, municipal

**"Philadelphia Association for the Relief of Disabled Firemen"** by John Rubens, 1830–1840
*Volunteer fire companies competed with each other to put out fires in antebellum cities. Sometimes they were accused of setting fires and then claiming credit for extinguishing them.*

**Auction at Chatham Square**
*Most antebellum auctions were held outdoors in crowded neighborhoods. Auctioneers did a thriving business.*

leaders refused to delegate more than advisory powers to health boards dominated by physicians. After the worst epidemic in the city's history, a New Orleans editor stated in 1853 that it was "much safer to follow the common sense and unbiased opinion of the intelligent mass of the people than the opinions of medical men . . . based upon hypothetical theories."

Although most epidemic diseases baffled antebellum physicians, a basis for forward strides in surgery was laid during the 1840s by the discovery of anesthetics. Prior to 1840 young people often entertained themselves at parties by inhaling nitrous oxide, or "laughing gas," which produced sensations of giddiness and painlessness; and semicomical demonstrations of laughing gas became a form of popular entertainment. (Samuel Colt, the inventor of the revolver, had begun his career as a traveling exhibitor of laughing gas.) But nitrous oxide had to be carried around in bladders, which were difficult to handle, and in any case, few recognized its surgical possibilities. Then in 1842 Crawford Long, a Georgia physician who had attended laughing-gas frolics in his youth, employed sulfuric ether (an easily transportable liquid with the same properties as nitrous oxide) during a surgical operation. Long failed to follow up on his discovery, but four years later William T. G. Morton, a dentist, successfully employed sulfuric ether during an operation at Massachusetts General Hospital in Boston. Within a few years, ether came into wide use in American surgery.

The discovery of anesthesia improved the public image of surgeons, long viewed as brutes who hacked away at agonized patients. Furthermore, by making longer operations possible, anesthesia encouraged surgeons to take greater care than previously during surgery. Nevertheless, the failure of most surgeons to recognize the importance of clean hands and sterilized instruments partially offset the benefits of anesthesia before 1860. In 1843 Boston physician and poet Oliver Wendell Holmes, Sr., published an influential paper on how the failure of obstetricians to disinfect their hands often spread a disease called puerperal fever among mothers giving birth in hospitals. Still, the medical profession only gradually accepted the importance of disinfection. Operations remained as dangerous as the diseases or wounds that they tried to heal. The mortality rate for amputations hovered around 40 percent, and during the Civil War, 87 percent of soldiers who suffered abdominal wounds died from them.

### Popular Health Movements

Doubtful of medicine and cynical toward public health, antebellum Americans turned to a variety of therapies and regimens that promised to give them healthier and longer lives. One popular response to disease was hydropathy, or the "water cure," which filtered into the United States from Europe during the 1840s. By the mid-1850s the United States had twenty-seven hydropathic sanatoriums, which claimed to offer by cold baths and wet packs "an abundance of water of dewy softness and crystal transparency, to cleanse, renovate, and rejuvenate the disease-worn and dilapidated system." The water cure held a special attraction for well-off women, partly because hydropathics professed to relieve the pain associated with childbirth and menstruation and partly because hydropathic sanatoriums were congenial gathering places in which middle-class women could relax and exercise in private.

In contrast to the water cure, which necessitated the time and expense of a trip to a sanatorium, a health system that anyone could adopt was propounded by Sylvester Graham, a temperance reformer turned popular health advocate. Alarmed by the 1832 cholera epidemic, Graham counseled changes in diet and regimen as well as total abstinence from alcohol. Contending that Americans ate too much, he urged them to substitute vegetables, fruits, and coarse, whole-grain bread (called Graham bread) for meat and to abstain from spices, coffee, and tea as well as from alcohol. Soon Graham added sexual "excess" (by which he meant most sex) to his list of forbidden indulgences. Vegetables were preferable to meat, according to Graham, because they provoked less hunger. The food cravings of the "flesh-eater" were "greater and more imperious" than those of the vegetarian.

Many of Graham's most enthusiastic disciples were reformers. Grahamites had a special table at the Brook Farm community. Until forced out by indignant parents and hungry students, one of Graham's followers ran the student dining room at reformist Oberlin College. Much like Graham, reformers traced the evils of American society to the unnatural cravings of its people. Abolitionists, for example, contended that slavery intensified white men's lust and contributed to the violent behavior of white southerners. Similarly, Graham believed that eating meat stimulated lust and other aggressive impulses.

Yet Graham's doctrines attracted a broad audience that extended beyond the perimeters of the reform movements. Many towns and cities had boarding houses whose tables were set according to his principles. His books sold well, and his public lectures were thronged. Like hydropathy, Grahamism addressed the popular desire for better health

at a time when orthodox medicine seemed to do more damage than good. Graham used religious phrases that were familiar to churchgoers and then channeled those concepts toward nonreligious goals. Luxury was "sinful," disease resembled hell, and health was a kind of heaven on earth. In this way, he provided simple and familiar assurances to an audience as ignorant as he was of the true causes of disease.

## Phrenology

The belief that each person was master of his or her own destiny underlay not only evangelical religion and popular health movements but also the most popular of the antebellum scientific fads: phrenology. Imported from Europe, phrenology rested on the idea that the human mind comprised thirty-seven distinct faculties, or "organs," each located in a different part of the brain. Phrenologists thought that the degree of each organ's development determined skull shape, so that they could analyze a person's character by examining the bumps and depressions of the skull.

In the United States two brothers, Orson and Lorenzo Fowler, became the chief promoters of phrenology in the 1840s. Originally intending to become a Protestant missionary, Orson Fowler became instead a missionary for phrenology and opened a pub-

**"The Illustrated Phrenological Almanac, 1859"**
*By dividing the brain into a large number of "faculties," phrenologists like Lorenzo Fowler, editor of the Phrenological Almanac for 1859, made the point that each person, regardless of whether born high or low, had an abundance of improvable talents.*

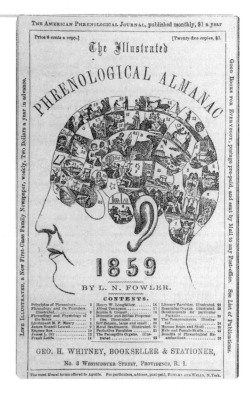

lishing house in New York City (Fowler and Wells) that mass-marketed books on phrenology. The Fowlers' critics were legion, but so were their responses to criticism. Accused of propounding a godless philosophy, they pointed to a huge organ called "Veneration" to prove that people were naturally religious, and they answered charges that phrenology was pessimistic by claiming that exercise could improve every desirable mental organ. Lorenzo Fowler reported that several of his skull bumps had actually grown. Orson Fowler wrapped it all into a tidy slogan: "Self-Made, or Never-Made."

Phrenology appealed to Americans as a "practical" science. In a mobile, individualistic society, it promised a quick assessment of others. Some merchants used phrenological charts to pick suitable clerks, and some women even induced their fiancés to undergo phrenological analysis before tying the knot.

Phrenologists had close ties to popular health movements. Fowler and Wells published the *Water-Cure Journal* and Sylvester Graham's *Lectures on the Science of Human Life.* Orson Fowler filled his phrenological book with tips on the evils of coffee, tea, meat, spices, and sex that could have been plucked from Graham's writings.

Easily understood and practiced, and filled with the promise of universal betterment, phrenology was ideal for antebellum America. Just as Americans had invented machines to better their lives, they could invent "sciences" that promised human betterment.

# Democratic Pastimes

Between 1830 and 1860 technology increasingly transformed leisure by making Americans more dependent on recreation that could be manufactured and sold. People purchased this commodity in the form of cheap newspapers and novels as well as affordable tickets to plays, museums, and lectures.

Just as the Boston Associates had daringly capitalized on new technology to produce textiles at Lowell and Waltham, imaginative entrepreneurs utilized technology to make and sell entertainment. Men like James Gordon Bennett, one of the founders of the penny press in America, and P. T. Barnum, the greatest showman of the nineteenth century, amassed fortunes by sensing what people wanted and then employing available technology to satisfy their desires. To a degree, indeed, these men induced the public to want what they had to

sell. Barnum, for example, had a genius for using newspaper publicity to pique popular interest in curiosities that he was about to exhibit.

Bennett and Barnum thought of themselves as purveyors of democratic entertainment. They would sell their wares cheaply to anyone. Barnum's famous American museum in New York City catered to a wide variety of social classes that paid to view paintings, dwarfs, mammoth bones, and other attractions. By marketing the American Museum as family entertainment, Barnum helped break down barriers that had long divided the pastimes of husbands from those of their wives. Similarly, the racy news stories in Bennett's *New York Herald* provided its vast audience with a common stock of information and topics for conversation. In these ways, the impact of technology on amusement was democratic.

Technology also ignited the process by which individuals became spectators rather than the creators of their own amusements. Americans had long found ways to enjoy themselves. Even the gloomiest Puritans had indulged in games and sports. After 1830, however, the burden of providing entertainment began to shift from individuals to entrepreneurs who supplied ways to entertain the public.

## Newspapers

In 1830 the typical American newspaper was a mere four pages long, with the front and back pages devoted almost wholly to advertisements. The second and third pages contained editorials, details of ship arrivals and cargoes, reprints of political speeches, and notices of political events. Few papers depended on their circulation for profit; even the most prominent papers had a daily circulation of only one thousand to two thousand. Rather, papers often relied on subsidies from political parties or factions. When a party gained power, it inserted paid political notices only in papers loyal to it. "Journalists," a contemporary wrote, "were usually little more than secretaries dependent upon cliques of politicians, merchants, brokers, and office seekers for their prosperity and bread."

As a result, newspapers could be profitable without being particularly popular. Because of their potential for profit, new papers were constantly being established. But most had limited appeal. The typical paper sold for six cents an issue at a time when the average daily wage was less than a dollar. Papers often seemed little more than published bulletin boards. Merely records of events, they typically lacked the exciting news stories and eye-catching illustrations that later generations would take for granted.

The 1830s witnessed the beginnings of a stunning transformation. Technological changes, most of which originated in Europe, vastly increased both the supply of paper (still made from rags) and the speed of printing presses. The substitution of steam-driven cylindrical presses for flatbed hand presses led to a tenfold increase in the number of printed pages that could be produced in an hour. Enterprising journalists, among them the Scottish-born James Gordon Bennett, grasped the implications of the new technology. Newspapers could now rely on vast circulation rather than on political subsidies to turn a profit. To gain circulation, journalists like Bennett slashed the price of newspapers. In 1833 the *New York Sun* became America's first penny newspaper, and Bennett's *New York Herald* followed in 1835. By June 1835 the combined daily circulation of New York's three penny papers reached 44,000; in contrast, before the dawn of the penny press in 1833, the city's eleven dailies had a combined daily circulation of only 26,500. Spearheaded by the penny papers, the combined daily circulation of newspapers throughout the nation rose from roughly 78,000 in 1830 to 300,000 by 1840. The number of weekly newspapers spurted from 65 in 1830 to 138 in 1840.

Affordability was not the only feature of the penny papers. Dependent on circulation and advertising rather than on subsidies, the penny press revolutionized the marketing and format of papers. Where single copies of the six-cent papers were usually available only at the printer's office, newsboys hawked the penny papers on busy street corners. Moreover, the penny papers subordinated the recording of political and commercial events to human-interest stories of robberies, murders, rapes, and abandoned children. They dispatched reporters to police courts and printed transcripts of trials. As sociologist Michael Schudson observes, "The penny press invented the modern concept of 'news.'" Rather than merely recording events, the penny papers wove events into gripping stories. They invented not only news but also news reporting. Relying on party stalwarts to dispatch copies of speeches and platforms, and reprinting news items from other papers, the older six-cent papers did little, if any, reporting. In contrast, the penny papers employed their own correspondents and were the first papers to use the telegraph to speed news into print.

Some penny papers were little more than scandal sheets, but the best, like Bennett's *New York Herald* and Horace Greeley's *New York Tribune* (1841), pioneered modern financial and political reporting. From its inception, the *Herald* contained a daily "money article" that substituted the analysis and interpretation of financial events for the dull recording of commercial facts. "The spirit, pith, and philosophy of commercial affairs is what men of business want," Bennett wrote. The relentless snooping of the *Tribune's* Washington reporters outraged politicians. In 1848 *Tribune* correspondents were temporarily barred from the House floor for reporting that Representative Sawyer of Ohio ate his lunch (sausage and bread) each day in the House chamber, picked his teeth with a jackknife, and wiped his greasy hands on his pants and coat.

### The Theater

Like newspapers, theaters increasingly appealed to a mass audience. Antebellum theaters were large (twenty-five hundred to four thousand seats in some cities) and crowded by all classes. With seats as cheap as twelve cents and rarely more than fifty cents, the typical theater audience included lawyers and merchants and their wives, artisans and clerks, sailors and noisy boys, and a sizable body of prostitutes. Prostitutes usually sat in the top gallery, called the third tier, "that dark, horrible, guilty" place. The presence of prostitutes in theaters was taken for granted; the only annoyance came when they left the third tier to solicit customers in the more expensive seats.

The prostitutes in attendance were not the only factor that made the antebellum theater vaguely disreputable. Theatrical audiences were notoriously rowdy. They showed their feelings by stamping their feet, whistling, hooting at villains, and throwing potatoes or garbage at the stage when they did not like the characters or the acting. Individual actors developed huge followings, and the public displayed at least as much interest in the actors as in the plays. In 1849 a long-running feud between the leading American actor, Edwin Forrest, and the popular British actor William Macready ended with a riot at New York City's Astor Place that left twenty people dead.

The Astor Place riot demonstrated the broad popularity of the theater. Forrest's supporters included a following of Irish workers who loathed the British and appealed to the "working men" to rally against the "aristocrat" Macready. Macready, who projected a more polished and intellectual image than Forrest, attracted the better-educated classes. Had not all classes patronized the theater, the deadly riot probably would never have occurred.

The plays themselves were as diverse as the audiences. Most often performed were melodramas in which virtue was rewarded, vice punished, and the heroine married the hero. Yet the single most popular dramatist was William Shakespeare. In 1835 audiences in Philadelphia witnessed sixty-five performances of Shakespeare's plays. Americans who may never have read a line of Shakespeare grew familiar with Othello, King Lear, Desdemona, and Shylock. Theatrical managers adapted Shakespeare to a popular audience. They highlighted the swordfights and assassinations, cut some speeches, omitted minor characters, and pruned words or references that might have offended the audience's sense of propriety. For example, they substituted *pottels* for *urinals* and quietly advanced Juliet's age at the time that she falls in love with Romeo from fourteen to eighteen. They occasionally changed sad endings to happy ones. The producers even arranged for short performances or demonstrations between acts of Shakespeare—and indeed, of every play. During such an interlude, the audience might have observed a brief impersonation of Tecumseh or Aaron Burr, jugglers and acrobats, a drummer beating twelve drums at once, or a three-year-old who weighed a hundred pounds.

### Minstrel Shows

The Yankee or "Brother Jonathan" figure who served as a stock character in many antebellum plays helped audiences to form an image of the ideal American as rustic, clever, patriotic, and more than a match for city slickers and decadent European blue bloods. In a different way, the minstrel shows that Americans thronged to see in the 1840s and 1850s forged enduring stereotypes that buttressed white Americans' sense of superiority by diminishing black people.

Minstrel shows arose in northern cities in the 1840s, as blackfaced white men took to the stage to present an evening of songs, dances, and humorous sketches. Minstrelsy borrowed some authentic elements of African-American culture, especially dances characterized by the sliding, shuffling step of southern blacks, but most of the songs had origins in white culture. Such familiar

**Dan Bryant, the Minstrel**
*Bryant was one of many antebellum popularizers of black minstrelsy. One of the earliest known minstrelsy performances occurred in Boston in 1799, when the white man Gottlieb Graupner, reportedly made up as a black, sang and accompanied himself on the banjo.*

American songs as Stephen Foster's "Camptown Races" and "Massa's in the Cold Ground," which first aired in minstrel shows, reflected white Americans' notions of how blacks sang more than it represented authentic black music. In addition, the images of blacks projected by minstrelsy both catered to and reinforced the prejudices of the working-class whites who dominated the audience of minstrel shows. Minstrel troupes usually depicted blacks as stupid, clumsy, and obsessively musical and emphasized the Africanness of blacks by giving their characters names like the Ethiopian Serenaders and their acts titles like the Nubian Jungle Dance and the African Fling. At a time of intensifying political conflict over race, minstrel shows planted images and expectations about blacks' behavior through stock characters. These included Uncle Ned, the tattered, humble, and docile slave, and Zip Coon, the arrogant urban free black who paraded around in a high hat, long-tailed coat, and green vest and who lived off his girlfriends' money. Minstrels lampooned blacks who assumed public roles by portraying them as incompetent stump speakers who called Patrick Henry "Henry Patrick," referred to John Hancock as "Boobcock," and confused the word *statute* with *statue*.

By the 1850s major cities from New York to San Francisco had several minstrel theaters. Touring professional troupes and local amateur talent even brought minstrelsy to small towns and villages. Mark Twain later recalled how minstrelsy had burst upon Hannibal, Missouri, in the early 1840s as "a glad and

## Cincinnati, Ohio

Words like *pioneer* and *frontier* still evoke images of a West of majestic forests and wide, rushing rivers, of buckskin-clad settlers and Indians in loincloths. But in fact, throughout the early-nineteenth-century westward migrations, cities were a colorful and vital part of the western fabric.

Located on the Ohio River in a vast agricultural basin that spread from Ohio to parts of Kentucky and Indiana, Cincinnati was positioned astride the major east-west and north-south trade routes, and its growth was nothing short of remarkable. A mere village of 750 inhabitants in 1788, it had become the West's leading city and the nation's ninth-largest city by 1820. By 1850 its industrial and commercial output was exceeded only by that of New York and Philadelphia.

Early Cincinnatians developed an edginess about criticism, to which they responded by crowning their city with one grand title after another: Queen of the West; Athens of the West; Wonder of the West; the Second Boston; and the Infant Hercules. Cincinnati's very success in attracting settlers aroused envy in the East, especially among journalists, who routinely disparaged it as a pestilence-ridden haven of roughnecks, devoid of culture and refinement.

Already sensitive to these insults, Cincinnati dwellers, especially its fledgling high society of merchants, professionals, and their spouses, found more cause to complain with the publication in 1832 of Frances Trollope's *The Domestic Manners of the Americans*. This account of the British-born Trollope's four-year residence in America, including two in Cincinnati, made Cincinnati famous as a symbol of American crassness and materialism. Wealthy men there, she related, spent their time spitting, talking about the price of produce and hogs (a leading hog-packing center, Cincinnati acquired "Porkopolis" as another of its many nicknames), and spitting again. Excluded from all conversation about business or politics, the city's society ladies were ignored even by their husbands and passed their hours evaluating each other's dresses down to the last pin.

*The Domestic Manners of the Americans* would earn a small fortune for Frances Trollope, and not a moment too soon. When she composed the book, she was in her early fifties, with four children and a husband in England who was on the verge of financial and nervous collapse. Accompanied by her son Henry and Henry's tutor, a French artist and political refugee named Auguste Hervieu, Trollope had arrived in Cincinnati in 1828 after a brief sojourn at Nashoba, an interracial utopian community in Tennessee. Nothing about her seemed quite right to Cincinnatians, who did not relish an intellectual woman, particularly one with utopian and abolitionist leanings and most especially a married woman who traveled without her husband but accompanied by a handsome Frenchman. But like the country boy P. T. Barnum in New York City, she was an outsider who recognized something that the locals missed: that urban resources could be marshaled to create new forms of popular entertainment.

Reasoning that Cincinnatians probably found the place as dull as she did and that they would pay to experience the weird and exotic, she soon grasped the commercial possibilities of one of the city's few cultural institutions, the Western Museum. Founded in 1819 to house western scientific collections, the museum had been sliding into financial ruin: Cincinnatians would not pay to look at stuffed birds and animal bones, even if western. Trollope and the museum's director, the French-born Joseph Dorfeuille, boldly conceived the idea of replacing the scientific exhibits with displays evoking mystery, dread, and romance.

**Frances Trollope,**
by Auguste Hervieu, c. 1832
*With the publication of* Domestic Manners of the Americans *at the age of fifty-three, Frances Trollope began a new life as a writer of novels and travel books. She made enough money to overcome the financial catastrophes that overtook her husband and to keep her family together, and she communicated her self-discipline to her son Anthony, who became a famous novelist. Not surprisingly, her fictional heroines were as strong and aggressive as she herself.*

With Hervieu's aid, she helped Dorfeuille to construct two such exhibits. The first, "The Invisible Girl," was housed in a room exotically decorated with wax figures drawn from characters in ancient Greek and Egyptian mythology. A mysterious voice rose from behind a machine-made cloud to answer questions (three to a customer) from the audience in a variety of known and unknown languages. The voice of this "Invisible Girl" was actually that of Trollope's son, Henry, who had studied Latin and Greek in England and who could fake or invent other languages. Most of the time the "girl" spoke gibberish, but customers considered her a multilingual wonder. So successful was this show that the team of Trollope, Hervieu, and Dorfeuille quickly mounted another, "The Infernal Regions," a fancifully fearsome exhibit of hell with mechanical and wax figures depicting imps, snakes, demons, goblins, and the Evil One, and with the tension heightened by blackouts punctuated by "horrid groans" and "terrible shrieks." The view, one observer recorded, "is calculated to awaken serious but not unprofitable reflections." Such was the crush of visitors to the exhibit that an electrified fence had to be installed to deter them from touching the figures.

Trollope's next scheme was a "bazaar," a kind of nineteenth-century shopping mall rolled into a single building. Designed in the exotic Egyptian or "arabesque" style, the emporium boasted a coffeehouse, a bar, an art gallery, and sundry rooms devoted to selling jewelry, sculpture, and clothing. Unlike her other ventures, the bazaar failed dismally, partly because she ran out of (borrowed) money to construct it and partly because, in contrast to her silent partnership in the museum exhibits, her sponsorship of the bazaar was public knowledge. With additional backing someone else probably would have succeeded, for Trollope had grasped what Barnum would later discover: that there was a hungry market for popular culture as long as exhibits, whether mysterious or outlandish, were lifelike, made at least a pretense at edification, and did not remind Americans too much of America.

Trollope left the city after the collapse of her bazaar, sorry that she had ever entered it. But she had left her mark. Successful purveyors of popular culture not only in Cincinnati but also in the East would follow her formula. Painters, for example, found that, although Cincinnatians lacked interest in western landscapes, they would pay to see "panoramas." Popular artists accordingly painted football-field–long canvases that depicted such subjects as events in the life of Napoleon and that were gradually unrolled before their viewers. These "moving pictures" foreshadowed the newsreels of the twentieth century.

Compared to the paintings of the Hudson River school (see page 318), popular art was notable for its lack of symbolism or abstraction. Popular cultural exhibits catered to their viewers' pretensions toward refinement by routinely drawing on classical, mythological, or European themes, but they also featured an obsession with the "authentic" and the lifelike that gave customers the feeling that they were part of the scene itself.

**Republicans at Theatre**

*Snoring or chatting their way through a performance of Shakespeare's* Hamlet, *these Americans display the boorish manners that so annoyed Frances Trollope.*

**The Bazaar**

*Detractors called it Trollope's Folly, but with its arabesque windows, Egyptian columns, and Moorish dome, Frances Trollope's Bazaar was splendid relief from Cincinnati's monotony. Its plans called for a basement housing a barroom and coffee house, a main floor for the bazaar itself, and a top floor with a ballroom and arched mosaics in the style of the Alhambra in Spain.*

stunning surprise." So popular was the craze that minstrels even visited the White House and entertained Presidents John Tyler, James K. Polk, Millard Fillmore, and Franklin Pierce.

## P. T. Barnum

Like Frances Trollope (see A Place in Time) but on a grander scale, P. T. Barnum understood how to turn the antebellum public's craving for entertainment into a profitable business. As a young man in his native Bethel, Connecticut, Barnum savored popular journalism by starting a newspaper, the *Herald of Freedom,* that assailed wrongdoing in high places. Throughout his life, he thought of himself as a public benefactor and pointed to his profits as proof that he gave people what they wanted. Yet honesty was never his strong suit. As a small-town grocer in Connecticut, he regularly cheated his customers on the principle that they were trying to cheat him. Barnum, in short, was a hustler raised in the land of the Puritans, a cynic and an idealist rolled into one.

After moving to New York City in 1834, Barnum started a new career as an entrepreneur of popular entertainment. His first venture exhibited a black woman, Joice Heth, whom Barnum billed as the 169-year-old

former slave nurse of George Washington. Barnum neither knew nor cared how old Joice was (in fact, she was probably around 80); it was enough that people would pay to see her. Strictly speaking, he cheated the public, but he knew that many of his customers shared his doubts about Joice's age. Determined to expose Barnum's gimmick, some poked her to see whether she was really a machine rather than a person. He was playing a game with the public, and the public with him.

In 1841 Barnum purchased a run-down museum in New York City, rechristened it the American Museum, and opened a new chapter in the history of popular entertainment. The founders of most earlier museums had intended an educational purpose. They exhibited stuffed birds and animals, specimens of rock, and portraits. Most of these museums, however, had languished for want of public interest. Barnum, in contrast, made piquing public curiosity the main goal. To attract people, he added collections of curiosities and faked exhibits. Visitors to the American Museum could see ventriloquists, magicians, albinos, a five-year-old midget whom Barnum named General Tom Thumb and later took on a tour of Europe, and the "Feejee Mermaid," a shrunken oddity that Barnum billed as "positively asserted by its owner to have been taken alive in the Feejee Islands." By 1850 the American Museum had become the best-known museum in the nation and a model for popular museums in other cities.

Blessed with a genius for publicity, Barnum recognized that newspapers could invent as well as report news. One of his favorite tactics was to puff his exhibits by writing letters (under various names) to newspapers in which he would hint that the scientific world was agog over some astonishing curiosity of nature that the public could soon see for itself at the American Museum. But Barnum's success rested on more than publicity. A staunch temperance advocate, he provided regular lectures at the American Museum on the evils of alcohol and soon gave the place a reputation as a center for safe family amusement. Finally, Barnum tapped the public's insatiable curiosity about natural wonders. In 1835 the editor of the *New York Sun* had boosted his circulation by claiming that a famous astronomer had discovered pelicans and

**Tom Thumb**
*Barnum helped to arrange the 1863 wedding of "General" Tom Thumb and another midget in his employ, Lavinia Warren. On their wedding tour, Tom and Lavinia visited President Abraham Lincoln in the White House.*

winged men on the moon. At a time when each passing year brought new technological wonders, the public was ready to believe in anything, even the Feejee Mermaid.

# The Quest for Nationality in Literature and Art

Europeans took little notice of American poetry or fiction before the 1820s. "Who ever reads an American book?" a British literary critic taunted in 1820. Americans responded by pointing to Washington Irving, whose *Sketch Book* (1820) contained two famous stories, "Rip Van Winkle" and "The Legend of Sleepy Hollow." Naming hotels and steamboats after Irving, Americans soaked him in applause, but they had to concede that Irving had done much of his best writing while living in England between 1815 and 1832. Americans also responded to British dismissals by claiming that their great political orations and essays were themselves works of art. This assertion cut little ice in Europe, but in the early nineteenth century *literature* was defined very broadly and included orations, essays, works of history, drama, poetry, and (least important) fiction. In the prevailing view inherited from the eighteenth-century movement known as classicism, a work of literature was distinguished by its elegance and refinement, its conformity to supposedly universal standards of taste and excellence that could best be acquired by study of the ancient Latin and Greek classics. Those wedded to classicism viewed literature as a pastime of educated gentlemen, who wrote only for one another (and never for profit), and who used literature as a vehicle for displaying their learning.

In the 1820s and 1830s two developments challenged these assumptions about the nature of literature and the relationship between the writer and the reader. First, the transportation revolution created a national market for books, especially fiction. Initially, this worked to the advantage of British authors, especially the Scot Sir Walter Scott. With the publication of *Waverley* (1814), a historical novel set in Britain of the 1740s, Scott's star began its spectacular ascent on the American horizon. Americans named more than a dozen towns Waverley; advertisements for Scott's subsequent novels bore the simple caption, "By the author of *Waverley*." Scott's success demonstrated that the public wanted to read fiction. Although American publishers continued to pirate British novels (reprinting them without paying copyright fees), Scott's success prompted Americans like James Fenimore Cooper to write fiction for sale. In 1800 American authors accounted for a negligible proportion of the output of American publishers. By 1830, 40 percent of the books published in the United States—and by 1850, 75 percent—were written by Americans.

Second, Americans adapted the literary and philosophical movement known as romanticism to their own purposes. Originating in Europe in the second half of the eighteenth century as a challenge to classicism's insistence that standards of beauty were universal, romanticism stressed that literature should reveal both the distinctive features of the author's nation and the longings of the author's soul. Romantics expected a literary work to be emotionally charged, a unique reflection of its creator's inner feelings.

The emergence of a national market for books and the influence of romanticism tended to elevate fiction, a comparatively democratic form of literature, over other writings. Whereas college-educated men filled orations and essays with classical allusions, writing (and reading) fiction did not require a knowledge of Latin and Greek or a familiarity with ancient history and mythology. Significantly, many of the best-selling novels of the antebellum period—for example, Harriet Beecher Stowe's *Uncle Tom's Cabin*—were written by women, who were still barred from higher education. In addition, the novel had a certain subversive quality that contributed to its popularity. Authors could create unconventional characters, situations, and outcomes. The oration or the essay usually had an unmistakable conclusion. In contrast, the novel left more room for interpretation by the reader. A novel might well have a lesson to teach, but the reader's interest was likely to be aroused less by the moral than by the development of characters and plot.

Although he wrote no novels, Ralph Waldo Emerson emerged in the late 1830s as the most influential spokesman for American literary nationalism. As the leading light of the transcendentalist movement, an American offshoot of romanticism, Emerson broke with the traditional view that our ideas arose from the toil of human reason, which gathered evidence from the senses. Rather, he contended, our ideas of God and freedom were inborn; knowledge resembled sight—an instantaneous and direct perception of truth. That being so, Emerson concluded that learned people enjoyed no special advantage in pursuing truth. All persons could glimpse the truth if only they would trust the promptings of their hearts. Transcendentalist doctrine pointed to the exhilarating conclusion that the United States, a young and democratic society, could produce as noble a literature and art as the more traditional societies of Europe. "Our day of dependence, our long apprenticeship to the learning of other lands draws to a close," Emerson announced in his address, "The American Scholar" (1837). The time had come for Americans to trust themselves. Let "the single man plant himself indomitably on his instincts and there abide," he proclaimed, and "the huge world will come around to him."

### The American Renaissance

"The American Scholar" coincided with the so-called American Renaissance, a flowering of literature and art that had been gaining momentum since the 1820s.

James Fenimore Cooper stands as the first important figure in this literary upsurge. His most important innovation was to introduce a distinctively American fictional character, the frontiersman Natty Bumppo ("Leatherstocking"). In *The Pioneers* (1823), Natty appears as an old man settled on the shores of Lake Otsego in upstate New York. A hunter, Natty blames the farmers for the wanton destruction of game and for turning the majestic forests into deserts of tree stumps. As a spokesman for nature against the march of civilization, Natty immediately became a popular figure, and in subsequent novels such as *The Last of the Mohicans* (1826), *The Pathfinder* (1840), and *The Deerslayer* (1841), Cooper unfolded Natty's earlier life for an appreciative reading public.

Emerson admired Cooper's fiction but his own version of American literary nationalism was expressed mainly in his essays, which mixed broad themes—"Beauty," "Wealth," and "Representative Men"—with pungent and vivid language. For example, he wrote in praise of independent thinking that the scholar should not "quit his belief that a popgun is a popgun, though the ancient and honorable of the earth affirm it to be the crack of doom." Equally remarkable was Emerson's way of developing his subjects. A contemporary compared listening to Emerson to trying to see the sun in a fog; one could see light but never the sun itself. Believing that knowledge reflected God's voice within each person and that truth was intuitive and individual, he never amassed persuasive evidence or presented systematic arguments to prove his point. Rather, he relied on a sequence of vivid if unconnected assertions whose

**Louisa May Alcott, c. 1858**
*Raised in bleak if genteel poverty, Louisa May Alcott first gained recognition for sketches of her experiences as a nurse in a military hospital during the Civil War. The publication of* Little Women, *her largely autobiographical novel of New England family life, brought her fame and enough money to support herself and her sisters.*

truth the reader would instantly see. (They did not always see it—one complained that she might have understood Emerson better if she had stood on her head.)

Emerson had a magnetic attraction for intellectually inclined young men and women who did not fit neatly into American society. In the 1830s several of these gathered in Concord, Massachusetts, to share Emerson's intellectual pursuits. Henry David Thoreau was representative of the younger Emersonians. Yet a crucial difference separated the two men. Adventurous in thought, Emerson was unadventurous in action. Thoreau was more of a doer. At one point he went to jail rather than pay his poll tax. This revenue, he knew, would support the war with Mexico, which he viewed as part of a southern conspiracy to extend slavery. The experience led Thoreau to write *Civil Disobedience* (1849), in which he defended a citizen's right to disobey unjust laws.

In the spring of 1845, Thoreau moved a few miles from Concord to the woods near Walden Pond. There he constructed a cabin on land owned by Emerson and spent the next two years providing for his wants away from civilization. His stated purpose in retreating to Walden was to write a description (later published) of a canoe trip that he and his brother had taken in 1839. During his stay in the woods, however, he conceived and wrote a much more important book, *Walden* (1854). A contemporary described *Walden* as "the logbook of his woodland cruise," and indeed, Thoreau filled its pages with descriptions of hawks and wild pigeons, his invention of raisin bread, his trapping of the woodchucks that ate his vegetable garden, and his construction of a cabin for exactly $28.50. But true to transcendentalism, Thoreau had a larger message. His rustic retreat taught him that he (and by implication, others) could satisfy material wants with only a few weeks' work each year and thereby leave more time for reexamining life's purpose. The problem with Americans, he said, was that they turned themselves into "mere machines" to acquire wealth without asking why. Thoreau bore the uncomfortable truth that material and moral progress were not as intimately related as Americans liked to think.

Among the most remarkable figures in Emerson's circle, Margaret Fuller's peculiar status as an intellectual woman distanced her from conventional society. Disappointed that his first child was not a boy, her Harvard-educated father, a prominent Massachusetts politician, determined to give Margaret the sort of education a male child would have acquired at Harvard. Drilled by her father in Latin and Greek, her reading branched into modern German romantics and the English literary classics. Her exposure to Emerson's ideas during a sojourn to Concord in 1836 pushed her toward transcendentalism, with its vindication of the free life of the spirit over formal doctrines and of the need for each person to *discover* truth on his or her own. Ingeniously, she turned transcendentalism into an occupation of sorts; between 1839 and 1844 she supported herself by presiding over "Conversations" for fee-paying participants drawn from Boston's elite men and women. Transcendentalism also influenced her classic of American feminism, *Woman in the Nineteenth Century* (1845). Breaking with the prevailing notion of separate spheres for men and women, Fuller contended that no woman could achieve the kind of personal fulfillment lauded by Emerson unless she developed her intellectual abilities and overcame her fear of being called masculine.

One of Emerson's qualities was a curious ability to sympathize with such dissimilar people as the reclusive and critical Thoreau, the scholarly and ethereal Fuller,

and the outgoing and earthy Walt Whitman. Self-taught and in love with virtually everything about America except slavery, Whitman left school at eleven and became a printer's apprentice and later a journalist and editor for various newspapers in Brooklyn, Manhattan, and New Orleans. A familiar figure at Democratic party functions, he marched in party parades and put his pen to the service of its antislavery wing.

Journalism and politics gave Whitman an intimate knowledge of ordinary Americans; the more he knew them, the more he liked them. His reading of Emerson nurtured his belief that America was to be the cradle of a new citizen in whom natural virtue would flourish unimpeded by European corruption, a man like Andrew Jackson, that "massive, yet most sweet and plain character." The threads of Whitman's early career came together in his major work *Leaves of Grass,* a book of poems first published in 1855 and reissued with additions in subsequent years.

*Leaves of Grass* shattered most existing poetic conventions. Not only did Whitman write in free verse (that is, most of his poems had neither rhyme nor meter), but the poems were also lusty and blunt at a time when delicacy reigned in the literary world. Whitman wrote of "the scent of these armpits finer than prayer" and "winds whose soft-tickling genitals rub against me." No less remarkably, Whitman intruded himself into his poems, one of which he titled "Song of Walt Whitman" (and later retitled "Song of Myself"). Although Whitman thought well of himself, it was not egotism that moved him to sing of himself. Rather, he viewed himself—crude, plain, self-taught, and passionately democratic—as the personification of the American people. He was

> Comrade of raftsmen and coalmen, comrade
>   of all who shake hands and welcome to
>   drink and meat,
> A learner with the simplest, a teacher of the
>   thoughtfullest.

By 1860 Whitman had acquired a considerable reputation as a poet. Nevertheless, the original edition of *Leaves* (a run of only about eight hundred copies) was ignored or derided as a "heterogeneous mass of bombast, egotism, vulgarity, and nonsense." One reviewer suggested that it was the work of an escaped lunatic. Only Emerson and a few others reacted enthusiastically. Within two weeks of publication, Emerson, never having met Whitman, wrote: "I find it the most extraordinary piece of wit and wisdom that America has yet contributed." Emerson had long called for the appearance of "the poet of America" and knew in a flash that in Whitman that poet had arrived.

### Hawthorne, Melville, and Poe

Emerson, Fuller, Thoreau, and Whitman expressed themselves in essays and poetry. In contrast, two major writers of the 1840s and 1850s—Nathaniel Hawthorne and Herman Melville—primarily wrote fiction, and another, Edgar Allan Poe, both fiction and poetry. Although major contributors to the American Renaissance, Hawthorne, Melville, and Poe paid little heed to Emerson's call for a literature that would comprehend the everyday experiences of ordinary Americans. Hawthorne, for example, set *The Scarlet Letter* (1850) in New England's Puritan past, *The House of the Seven Gables* (1851) in a mansion haunted not by ghosts but by memories of the past, and *The Marble Faun* (1859) in Rome. Poe set several of his short stories such as "The Murders in the Rue Morgue" (1841), "The Masque of the Red Death" (1842), and "The Cask of Amontillado" (1846) in Europe; as one critic has noted, "His art could have been produced as easily had he been born in Europe." Melville did draw materials and themes from his own experiences as a sailor

**Edgar Allen Poe**
*Hounded by poverty, Poe scratched out a living as an ill-paid "magazinist." Today, his reputation easily outdistances that of many of his better-paid contemporaries.*

and from the lore of the New England whaling industry, but for his novels *Typee* (1846), *Omoo* (1847), and *Mardi* (1849), he picked the exotic setting of islands in the South Seas; and for his masterpiece *Moby-Dick* (1851), the ill-fated whaler *Pequod.* If the only surviving documents from the 1840s and 1850s were its major novels, historians would face an impossible task in describing the appearance of antebellum American society.

The unusual settings favored by these three writers partly reflected their view that American life lacked the materials for great fiction. Hawthorne, for example, bemoaned the difficulty of writing about a country "where there is no shadow, no antiquity, no mystery, no picturesque and gloomy wrong, nor anything but a commonplace prosperity in broad and simple daylight, as is happily the case with my dear native land." In addition, psychology rather than society fascinated these three writers; each probed the depths of the human mind rather than the intricacies of social relationships. Their preoccupation with analyzing the mental states of their characters grew out of their underlying pessimism about the human condition. Emerson, Whitman, and (to a degree) Thoreau optimistically believed that human conflicts could be resolved if only individuals followed the promptings of their better selves. In contrast, Hawthorne, Melville, and Poe saw individuals as bundles of conflicting forces that, despite the best intentions, might never be reconciled.

Their pessimism led them to create characters obsessed by pride, guilt, a desire for revenge, or a quest for perfection and then to set their stories along the byways of society, where they would be free to explore the complexities of human motivation without the jarring intrusion of everyday life. For example, in *The Scarlet Letter* Hawthorne turned to the Puritan past in order to examine the psychological and moral consequences of the adultery committed by Hester Prynne and the minister Arthur Dimmesdale. So completely did Hawthorne focus on the moral dilemmas of his central characters that he conveyed little sense of the social life of the Puritan village in which the novel is set. Melville, who dedicated *Moby-Dick* to Hawthorne, shared the latter's pessimism. In the novel's Captain Ahab, Melville created a frightening character whose relentless and futile pursuit of the white whale fails to fill the chasm in his soul and brings death to all of his mates save the narrator, Ishmael. Poe also channeled his pessimism into creative achievements of the first rank. In perhaps his finest short story, "The Fall of the House of

Usher" (1839), he demonstrated an uncanny ability to weave the symbol of a crumbling mansion with the mental agony of a crumbling family.

Hawthorne, Melville, and Poe ignored Emerson's call to write about the everyday experiences of their fellow Americans. Nor did they follow Cooper's lead by creating distinctively American heroes. Yet each contributed to an indisputably American literature. Ironically, their conviction that the lives of ordinary Americans provided inadequate materials for fiction led them to create a uniquely American fiction, one marked less by the description of the complex social relationships of ordinary life than by the analysis of moral dilemmas and psychological states. In this way, they unintentionally fulfilled a prediction made by Alexis de Tocqueville that writers in democratic nations, while rejecting many of the traditional sources of fiction, would explore the abstract and universal questions of human nature.

## *Literature in the Marketplace*

No eighteenth-century gentleman-author imagined that he was writing for the public or that he would make money from his literary productions. Such notions were unthinkable. That suspicion that commercialism corrupted art did not disappear during the American Renaissance. The shy and reclusive poet Emily Dickinson, who lived all of her fifty-six years on the same street in Amherst, Massachusetts ("I do not go from home," she wrote with characteristic pithiness) and who wrote exquisite poems that examined, in her words, every splinter in the groove of the brain, refused to publish her work. But in an age lacking university professorships or foundation fellowships for creative writers, authors were both tempted and often compelled to write for profit. For example, Poe, a heavy drinker and always pressed for cash, scratched out a meager living writing short stories for popular magazines. Despite his reputation for aloof self-reliance, Thoreau craved recognition by the public and in 1843 tried, unsuccessfully, to market his poems in New York City. Only after meeting disappointment as a poet did he turn to detailed narratives of nature, and these did prove popular.

Emerson, too, wanted to reach a broader public, and after abandoning his first vocation as a Unitarian minister he virtually invented a new one, that of "lyceum" lecturer. Lyceums, local organizations for sponsoring lectures, spread throughout the northern tier of states between the late 1820s and 1860; by 1840 3,500 towns had lyceums. Most of Emerson's published essays originated as lectures before lyceums in the Northeast and Midwest. He delivered some sixty speeches in Ohio alone between 1850 and 1867, and lecture fees provided him with his main form of income. Thanks to newly built railroads and cheap newspapers that announced their comings and goings, others followed in his path. Thoreau presented a digest of *Walden* as a lyceum lecture before the book itself was published. One stalwart of the lyceum circuit said that he did it for "F-A-M-E—Fifty and My Expenses," and Herman Melville pledged, "If they will pay my expenses and give a reasonable fee, I am ready to lecture in Labrador or on the Isle of Desolation off Patagonia."

In an age that offered women few opportunities for public speaking, most lyceum lecturers were men. But women discovered ways to tap into the growing market for literature. Writing fiction was the most lucrative occupation open to women before the Civil War. For example, the popular novelist Susan Warner had been brought up in luxury and then tossed into poverty by the financial ruin of her father in the Panic of 1837. Writing fiction supplied her cash as well as pleasure. Warner and others benefited from advances in the technology of printing that brought down the price of books. Before 1830 the novels of Sir Walter Scott had been issued in three-volume sets that retailed for as much as thirty dollars. As canals and railroads opened crossroads stores to the latest fiction, publishers in New York and Philadelphia vied to deliver inexpensive novels to the shelves. By the 1840s cheap paperbacks that sold for as little as seven cents began to flood the market. Those who chose not to purchase books could read fiction in so-called story newspapers such as the *New York Ledger,* which was devoted mainly to serializing novels and which had an astonishing weekly circulation of 400,000 by 1860. In addition, the spread of (usually) coeducational public schools and academies contributed to higher literacy and a widening audience, especially among women, for fiction.

The most popular form of fiction in the 1840s and 1850s was the sentimental novel, a kind of women's fiction—written by women about women and mainly for women. The tribulations of orphans and the deaths of children filled these tearjerkers. In Susan Warner's *The Wide, Wide World* (1850), the heroine wept on an average of every other page for two volumes. But women's fiction dealt with more than the flow of tears. It challenged the image of males as trusty providers and of females as delicate dependents by portraying men as dissolute drunkards or vicious misers and women as resourceful and strong-willed. In the typical plot, a female orphan or spoiled rich girl thrown on hard times by a drunken father learned grittily to master every situation. The moral was clear. Women could overcome trials and improve their worlds. Few of the novelists were active feminists but their writings provide a glimpse into the private feelings of their female readers.

Such authors as Emerson, Hawthorne, Poe, and Melville, who now are recognized as major figures, had to swim in the sea of popular culture represented by the story newspapers and sentimental novels. Emerson, the intellectual, competed on the lecture circuit with P. T. Barnum, the showman. Hawthorne complained about the popularity of the "female scribblers." Poe thought that the public's judgment of a writer's merits was nearly always wrong. Indeed, the public did fail to see Melville's genius; the qualities of *Moby-Dick* were not widely recognized until the twentieth century. By and large, however, the major writers were not ignored by their society. Emerson's lectures made him famous. Hawthorne's *The Scarlet Letter* enjoyed respectable sales. Poe's poem "*The Raven*" (1844) was so popular that some suggested substituting the raven for the eagle as the national bird. What these writers discovered, sometimes the hard way, was that to make a living as authors they had to meet certain popular expectations. For example, *The Scarlet Letter* had greater popular appeal than *Moby-Dick* in part because the former told a love story while the latter, with its all-male cast and high-seas exploits, was simply not what the public looked for in a novel.

### American Landscape Painting

American painters also sought to develop nationality in art between 1820 and 1860. Lacking the mythic past that European artists drew on—the legendary gods and goddesses of ancient Greece and Rome—Americans subordinated history and figure painting to landscape painting. Yet just as Hawthorne had complained about the flat, dull character of American society, the painters of the Hudson River school recognized that the American landscape lacked the European landscape's "poetry of decay" in the form of ruined castles and crumbling temples. Like everything else in the United States, the landscape was fresh, relatively untouched by the human imprint. This fact posed a challenge to the Hudson River school painters.

The Hudson River school flourished from the 1820s to the 1870s. Numbering more than fifty painters, it was best represented by Thomas Cole, Asher Durand, and Frederick Church. All three men painted scenes of the region around the Hudson River, a waterway that Americans compared in majesty to the Rhine. But none was exclusively a landscapist. Some of Cole's most popular paintings were allegories, including *The Course of Empire*, a sequence of five canvases depicting the rise and fall of an ancient city and clearly implying that luxury doomed republican virtue. Nor did these artists paint only the Hudson. Church, a student of Cole and internationally the best known of the three, painted the Andes Mountains during an extended trip to South America in 1853. After the Civil War, the German-born Albert Bierstedt applied many Hudson River school techniques in his monumental canvases of the Rocky Mountains.

The works of Washington Irving and the opening of the Erie Canal had sparked artistic interest in the Hudson during the 1820s. After 1830 the writings of Emerson and Thoreau popularized a new view of nature. Intent on cultivating land, the pioneers of Kentucky and Ohio had deforested a vast area. One traveler complained that Americans would rather view a wheat field or a cabbage patch than a virgin forest. But Emerson, Thoreau, and landscape architects like Frederick Law Olmsted glorified nature; "in wildness is the preservation of the world," Thoreau wrote. Their outlook blended with growing popular fears that, as one contemporary expressed it in 1847, "The axe of civilization is busy with our old forests." As the "wild and picturesque haunts of the Red Man" became "the abodes of commerce and the seats of civilization," he concluded, "it behooves our artists to rescue from its grasp the little that is left before it is too late."

The Hudson River painters wanted to do more than preserve a passing wilderness. Their special contribution to American art was to emphasize emotional effect over accuracy. Cole's use of rich coloring, billowing clouds, massive gnarled trees, towering peaks, and deep chasms so heightened the dramatic impact of his paintings that the poet and editor William Cullen Bryant compared them to "acts of religion." Similar motifs marked Church's paintings of the Andes Mountains, which used erupting volcanoes and thunderstorms to evoke dread and a sense of majesty. Lacking the poignant antiquities that dotted European landscapes, the Americans strove to capture the natural grandeur of their own landscape.

**The Author Painting a Chief at
the Base of the Rocky Mountains, 1850**

*George Catlin's paintings preserved the faces, customs, and
habitats of the Indian tribes whose civilization was collapsing
in the face of white advance.*

**Tchow-ee-put-o-kaw, 1834**

**Rainmaking Among the Mandan, 1837–1839**

Like Cole, the painter George Catlin also tried to preserve a vanishing America. Observing a delegation of Indians passing through Philadelphia in 1824, Catlin resolved on his life's work: to paint as many Native Americans as possible in their pure and "savage" state. Journeying up the Missouri River in 1832, he sketched at a feverish pace, and in 1837 he first exhibited his "Indian gallery" of 437 oil paintings and thousands of sketches of faces and customs from nearly fifty tribes.

Catlin's Indian paintings made him famous, but his romantic view of Indians as noble savages ("the Indian mind is a beautiful blank") was a double-edged sword. Catlin's admirers delighted in his portrayals of dignified Indians but shared his view that such noble creatures were "doomed" to oblivion by the march of progress.

While painters sought to preserve a passing America on canvas, landscape architects aimed at creating little enclaves of nature that might serve as sources of spiritual refreshment to harried city dwellers. Starting with the opening of Mount Auburn Cemetery near Boston in 1831, "rural" cemeteries with pastoral names such as "Harmony Grove" and "Greenwood" sprang up

near major cities and quickly became tourist attractions, so much so that one orator described them as designed for the living rather than the dead. In 1858 New York City chose a plan drawn by Frederick Law Olmsted and Calvert Vaux for its proposed Central Park. Olmsted (who became the park's chief architect) and Vaux wanted the park to look as much like the countryside as possible, showing nothing of the surrounding city. A bordering line of trees screened out buildings, drainage pipes were dug to create lakes, and four sunken thoroughfares were cut across the park to carry traffic. The effect was to make Central Park an idealized version of nature, "picturesque" in that it would remind visitors of the landscapes that they had seen in pictures. Thus nature was made to mirror art.

## CONCLUSION

Typified by the invention of the telegraph, technological advances began to transform the lives of millions of Americans between 1840 and 1860. The mechanical

**"The Course of Empire: Destruction"** by Thomas Cole, 1836
*This painting, part of Thomas Cole's sequence of five canvasses,* The Course of Empire, *depicts the ruination that inevitably follows luxury and opulence. Although his subject was an ancient city, Americans had little difficulty identifying the painting's relevance for them.*

reaper increased wheat production and enabled agriculture to keep pace with the growing population. Steam power reduced the vulnerability of factories to the vagaries of the weather, stretched out the employment season, and increased productivity and income. Railroads gave rise to communities wherever tracks were laid and brought greater variety to the American diet. Technology also left an enduring mark on leisure pursuits by stimulating the rise of the penny press and the inexpensive novel and by contributing to the widening of the reading public. Advocates of progress hailed these developments as instruments of ever rising popular happiness. Even disease came to be seen less as a divine punishment for human depravity than as God's warning to those who ate or drank too much. To Ralph Waldo Emerson it seemed only natural that a progressive, bustling, and democratic society would soon create a literature and art to match its material accomplishments.

Progress carried a price. By bringing commodities once available only to the rich within the financial reach of the middle class, technology narrowed the social distance between these classes. At the same time, though, it set them off more sharply from the poor and intensified the division between the lifestyles of middle-class men and women. Progress also posed moral and spiritual challenges. It threatened unspoiled nature, a truth grasped by Henry David Thoreau and by the painters of the Hudson River school. For their part,

Nathaniel Hawthorne and Herman Melville challenged the easy confidence that technology and democracy could liberate Americans from the dilemmas of the human condition.

## FOR FURTHER READING

Carl Bode, *The Anatomy of American Popular Culture, 1840–1861* (1959). A useful general survey.

Lawrence Buell, *New England Literary Culture* (1986). An excellent study of the relationship between writers and their culture.

Mary Kupiec Cayton, *Emerson's Emergence: Self and Society in the Transformation of New England, 1800–1845* (1989). A sensitive interpretation of the major figure in the American Renaissance.

Ann Douglas, *The Feminization of American Culture* (1977). An analysis of the role of the middle-class women and liberal ministers in the cultural sphere during the nineteenth century.

Siegfried Giedion, *Mechanization Takes Command* (1948). An interpretive overview of the impact of technology on Europe and America.

Richard R. John, *Spreading the News: The American Postal System from Franklin to Morse* (1996). A revealing look at the age.

Barbara Novak, *Nature and Culture: American Landscape Painting, 1825–1875* (1982). An insightful study of the relationships between landscape painting and contemporary religious and philosophical currents.

Gwendolyn Wright, *Building the Dream: A Social History of Housing in America* (1981). An exploration of the ideologies and policies that have shaped American housing since Puritan times.

# 12

# The Old South and Slavery
## 1800–1860

**Slave Auction, Virginia,** by Leferre James Cranstone, 1862

In the early morning hours of August 22, 1831, Nat Turner and six other slaves slipped into the house of Joseph Travis in Southampton County in Virginia's Southside region and began their work of destruction. Nat had been preparing for this moment since February, when he had interpreted a solar eclipse as a long-awaited sign from God that the time had come for him to lead his people against slavery by murdering slaveholders. Employing hatchets and axes, Nat and his band quickly slaughtered Travis, his wife Sally (the widow of a former owner of Nat), and two other whites in the house. Later, two of them returned to murder the Travis infant in its cradle. And so it went as the Turner band moved through the countryside, picking up muskets, horses, and recruits; shooting, clubbing, and hacking whites to death. Soon "General" Nat had over forty followers. His hopes ran high. He knew that blacks outnumbered whites in Southampton, and his deeply religious strain, which had led the slaves to acknowledge him as a preacher and prophet, convinced him that God was his greatest ally.

By noon Turner's army, now grown to sixty to seventy followers, had murdered about sixty whites. But as word of trouble spread, militia and vigilantes, thousands strong, poured into Southampton from across the border in North Carolina and from other counties in Virginia. Following the path of destruction was easy. One farmstead after another revealed its horrors: dismembered bodies and fresh blood. Now it was the whites' turn for vengeance. Scores of blacks who had no part in the rebellion were killed. Turner's band was overpowered and those not shot on sight were jailed, to be tried and hanged in due course. Turner himself slipped away and hid in the woods until his capture on October 30. After a trial, he too was hanged.

Revenge was one thing, understanding another. Before Turner, white Virginians had worried little about a slave rebellion. There had been a brief scare in 1800 when a plot led by a slave named Gabriel Prosser was discovered and nipped in the bud. Overall, slavery in Virginia seemed mild to whites, a far cry from the harsh regimen of the new cotton-growing areas like Alabama and Mississippi. On hearing of trouble in Southside, many whites jumped to the conclusion that the British were invading and only gradually absorbed the more menacing thought that the slaves were rebelling. Turner's subsequently published "Confessions" (recorded by his court-appointed lawyer) did not evidence his mistreatment by owners. What they did reveal was an intelligent and deeply religious man, who had somehow learned to read and write as a boy and who claimed to have seen heavenly visions of white and black spirits fighting each other. Turner's mystical streak, well known in the neighborhood, had never before seemed dangerous. White Baptist and Methodist preachers had converted innumerable slaves to Christianity at the turn of the century. Christianity was supposed to make slaves more docile, but Nat Turner's ability to read had enabled him to find passages in the Bible that threatened death to him who "stealeth" a man, a fair description of slavery. Asked by his lawyer if he now found himself mistaken, Turner replied: "Was not Christ crucified?" Small wonder that a niece of George Washington concluded that she and all other white Virginians were now living on a "smothered volcano."

"What is to be done?" an editorial writer in the *Richmond Enquirer* moaned. "Oh my God, I don't know, but something must be done." In the wake of Turner's insurrection many Virginians, especially nonslaveholding whites in the western part of the state, urged that Virginia follow the lead of northern states and emancipate its slaves.

During the winter of 1831–1832, the Virginia legislature wrangled over emancipation proposals. The narrow defeat of these proposals marked a turning point; thereafter, opposition to slavery steadily weakened, not only in Virginia but throughout the region known to history as the Old South. As late as the Revolution, *south* referred more to a direction than to a place. In 1775 slavery had known no sectional boundaries in America. But as one northern state after another embraced emancipation, slavery became the distinguishing feature, the "peculiar institution," to whose defense the Old South dedicated itself.

A rift of sorts split the Old South into the Upper South (Virginia, North Carolina, Tennessee, and Arkansas) and the Lower, or Deep, South (South Carolina, Georgia, Florida, Alabama, Mississippi, Louisiana, and Texas). With its variegated economy based on the raising of wheat, tobacco, hemp, vegetables, and livestock, the Upper South relied far less than the Lower South on slavery and cotton, and in 1861 it approached secession more reluctantly than its sister states. Yet in the final analysis slavery forged the Upper and Lower Souths into a single Old South where it scarred all social relationships: between blacks and whites, among whites, and even among blacks. Without slavery there never would have been an Old South.

This chapter focuses on three major questions:

♦ What major social divisions segmented the white South?

♦ Why did nonslaveholding whites come to see their futures as bound up with the survival of slavery?

♦ What conditions in the Old South made it possible for a distinctive culture to develop among the slaves, and what were the predominant features of that culture?

# King Cotton

In 1790 the South was essentially stagnant. Tobacco, its primary cash crop, had lost its economic vitality even as it had depleted the once-rich southern soils. The growing of alternative cash crops, rice and cotton, was confined to coastal areas. Three out of four southerners still lived along the Atlantic seaboard, specifically in the Chesapeake and the Carolinas. One of three resided in Virginia alone.

The contrast between that South and the dynamic South of 1850 was stunning. By 1850 southerners had moved south and west. Now only one of every seven southerners lived in Virginia, and cotton reigned as king, shaping this new South. The growth of the British textile industry had created a huge demand for cotton, while Indian removal (see Chapter 9) had made way for southern expansion into the "Cotton Kingdom," a broad swath of land that stretched from South Carolina, Georgia, and northern Florida in the east through Alabama, Mississippi, central and western Tennessee, and Louisiana, and from there on to Arkansas and Texas.

### *The Lure of Cotton*

To British traveler Basil Hall, it seemed that all southerners could talk about was cotton. "Every flow of wind from the shore wafted off the smell of that useful plant; at every dock or wharf we encountered it in huge piles or pyramids of bales, and our decks were soon choked with it. All day, and almost all night long, the captain, pilot, crew, and passengers were talking of nothing else." With its warm climate, wet springs and summers, and relatively dry autumns, the Lower South was especially suited to the cultivation of cotton. In contrast to the

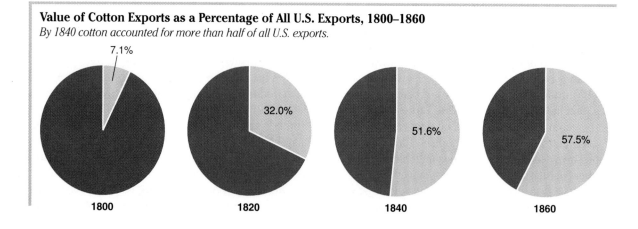

**Value of Cotton Exports as a Percentage of All U.S. Exports, 1800–1860**
*By 1840 cotton accounted for more than half of all U.S. exports.*

7.1%     32.0%     51.6%     57.5%

1800          1820          1840          1860

CHRONOLOGY

**1790s** Methodists and Baptists start to make major strides in converting slaves to Christianity.

**1793** Eli Whitney invents the cotton gin.

**1800** Gabriel leads a slave rebellion in Virginia.

**1808** Congress prohibits external slave trade.

**1812** Louisiana, the first state formed out of the Louisiana Purchase, is admitted to the Union.

**1816–1819** Boom in cotton prices stimulates settlement of the Southwest.

**1817** Mississippi enters the Union.

**1819** Alabama enters the Union.

**1819–1820** Missouri Compromise.

**1822** Denmark Vesey's conspiracy is uncovered in South Carolina.

**1831** William Lloyd Garrison starts *The Liberator.*

Nat Turner leads a slave rebellion in Virginia.

**1832** Virginia legislature narrowly defeats a proposal for gradual emancipation.

Virginia's Thomas R. Dew writes an influential defense of slavery.

**1835** Arkansas admitted to the Union.

**1837** Economic panic begins, lowering cotton prices.

**1844–1845** Methodist Episcopal and Baptist Churches split into northern and southern wings over slavery.

**1845** Florida and Texas admitted to the Union.

**1849** Sugar production in Louisiana reaches its peak.

**1849–1860** Period of high cotton prices.

**1857** Hinton R. Helper, *The Impending Crisis of the South.*

**1859** John Brown's raid on Harpers Ferry.

**1860** South Carolina secedes from the Union.

sugar industry, which thrived in southeastern Louisiana, cotton required neither expensive irrigation canals nor costly machinery. Sugar was a rich man's crop that demanded a considerable capital investment to grow and process. But cotton could be grown profitably on any scale. A cotton farmer did not even need to own a gin; commercial gins were available. Nor did a cotton farmer have to own slaves; in 1860, 35 percent to 50 percent of all farmers in the cotton belt owned no slaves. Cotton was profitable for anyone, even nonslaveholders, to grow; it promised to make poor men prosperous and rich men kings.

Although modest cotton cultivation did not require slaves, large-scale cotton growing and slavery grew together. As the southern slave population nearly doubled between 1810 and 1830, cotton employed three-fourths of all southern slaves. Owning slaves made it possible to harvest vast tracts of cotton speedily, a crucial advantage because a sudden rainstorm at harvest time could pelt cotton to the ground and soil it. Slaveholding also enabled planters to increase their cotton acreage and hence their profits.

An added advantage of cotton lay in its compatibility with the production of corn. Corn could be planted earlier or later than cotton and harvested before or af-

ter. Since the cost of owning a slave was the same whether or not he or she was working, corn production enabled slaveholders to utilize slave labor when slaves were not employed on cotton. Nonslaveholding cotton growers also found it convenient to raise corn, and by 1860 the acreage devoted to corn in the Old South actually *exceeded* that devoted to cotton. Corn fed both families and the livestock that flourished in the South (in 1860 the region had two-thirds of the nation's hogs). From an economic standpoint, corn and cotton gave the South the best of both worlds. Fed by intense demands in Britain and New England, the price of cotton remained high, with the result that money flowed into the South. Because of southern self-sufficiency in growing corn and in raising hogs that thrived on the corn, money was not drained out of the region to pay for food produced in the North. In 1860 the twelve wealthiest counties in the United States were all in the South.

### Ties Between the Lower and Upper South

Two giant cash crops, sugar and cotton, dominated agriculture in the Lower South. The Upper South, a region of tobacco, vegetable, hemp, and wheat growers, depended far less on the great cash crops. Yet the Upper

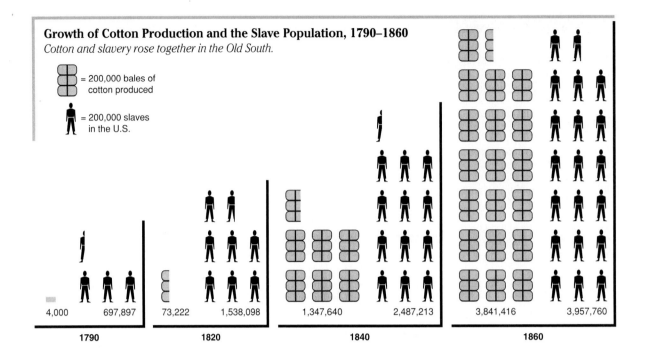

**Growth of Cotton Production and the Slave Population, 1790–1860**
*Cotton and slavery rose together in the Old South.*

= 200,000 bales of
   cotton produced

= 200,000 slaves
   in the U.S.

| 4,000 | 697,897 | 73,222 | 1,538,098 | 1,347,640 | 2,487,213 | 3,841,416 | 3,957,760 |

**1790**                    **1820**                       **1840**                          **1860**

South identified with the Lower South rather than with the agricultural regions of the free states.

A range of social, political, and economic factors promoted this unity. First, many settlers in the Lower South had come from the Upper South. Second, all white southerners benefited from the three-fifths clause of the Constitution, which enabled them to count slaves as a basis for congressional representation. Third, all southerners were stung by abolitionist criticisms of slavery, which drew no distinction between the Upper and Lower South. Economic ties also linked the Souths. The profitability of cotton and sugar increased the value of slaves throughout the entire region. The sale of slaves from the declining plantation states of the Upper South to the booming Lower South became a huge business. "Virginia," an observer stated in 1832, "is, in fact, a *negro* raising State for other States; she produces enough for her own supply, and six thousand a year for sale." Without the sale of its slaves, he concluded, "Virginia will be a desert."

### The North and South Diverge

The changes responsible for the dynamic growth of the South widened the distance between it and the North. At a time when the North was rapidly urbanizing, the South remained predominantly rural. In 1860 the pro-

portion of the South's population living in urban areas was only one-third that of New England and the mid-Atlantic states, down from one-half in 1820.

One reason for the rural character of the South was its lack of industries. Although one-third of the American population lived there in 1850, the South accounted for only 10 percent of the nation's manufacturing. The industrial output of the entire South in 1850 was less than that of New Hampshire and only one-third that of Massachusetts.

Some southerners, including J. D. B. De Bow of New Orleans, advocated factories as a way to revive the economies of older states like Virginia and South Carolina, to reduce the South's dependency on northern manufactured products, and to show that the South was not a backwater. After touring northern textile mills, South Carolina's William Gregg established a company town for textiles at Graniteville in 1845. By 1860 Richmond boasted the nation's fourth-largest producer of iron products, the Tredegar Iron Works, which contributed greatly to the Confederate cause during the Civil War. But these were exceptions. Compared to factories in the North, most southern factories were small, produced for nearby markets, and were closely tied to agriculture. The leading northern factories turned hides into tanned leather and leather into shoes, or cotton into threads and threads into suits. In

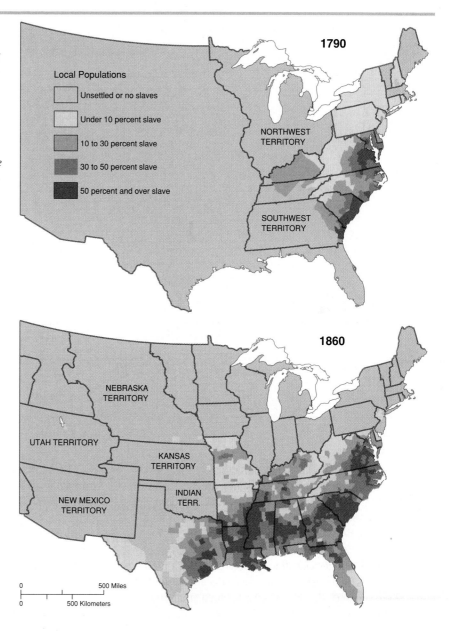

**Distribution of Slaves, 1790 and 1860**

*In 1790 the majority of slaves resided along the southeastern seaboard. By 1860, however, slavery had spread throughout the South, and slaves were most heavily concentrated in the Deep South states.*

*Source:* Reprinted with permission of McGraw-Hill, Inc. from *Ordeal by Fire: The Civil War and Reconstruction* by James M. McPherson. Copyright 1982 by Alfred A. Knopf, Inc.

Local Populations

Unsettled or no slaves

Under 10 percent slave

10 to 30 percent slave

30 to 50 percent slave

50 percent and over slave

contrast, southern factories, only a step removed from agriculture, turned grain into flour, corn into meal, and logs into lumber.

Slavery posed a major obstacle to southern industrialization, but not because slaves were unfit for factories. The Tredegar Iron Works employed slaves in skilled positions. But industrial slavery troubled southerners. Slaves who were hired out to factory masters sometimes passed themselves off as free and acted as if they were free by negotiating better working condi-

tions. A Virginia planter who rented slaves to an iron manufacturer complained that they "got the habit of roaming about and *taking care of themselves.*"

But the chief brake on southern industrialization was money, not labor. To raise the capital needed to build factories, southerners would have to sell slaves. They had little incentive to do so. Cash crops like cotton and sugar were proven winners, whereas the benefits of industrialization were remote and doubtful. Successful industrialization, further, threatened to disrupt

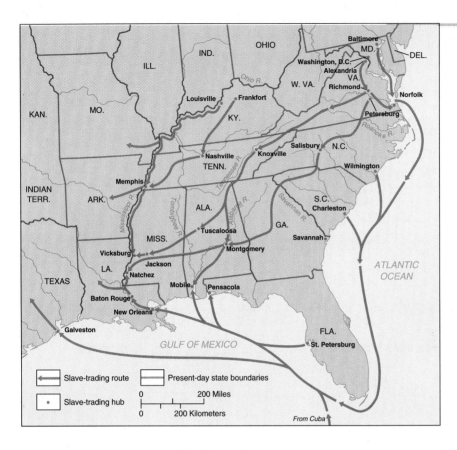

**The Internal Slave Trade, 1810–1860**

*An internal slave trade developed after the slave trade with Africa ended in 1808. With the growth of cotton production, farmers in the Upper South found it profitable to sell their slaves to planters in the Lower South.*

southern social relations by attracting antislavery white immigrants from the North. As long as southerners believed that an economy founded on cash crops would remain profitable, they had little reason to leap into the uncertainties of industrialization.

The South also lagged behind the North in provisions for public education. As was true of southern arguments for industrialization, pro-education arguments were bountiful, but these issued from a small segment of the South's leadership and usually fell on deaf ears. Southerners rejected compulsory education and they were reluctant to tax property to support schools. They abhorred the thought of educating slaves, so much so that southern lawmakers made it a crime to teach slaves to read. Some public aid flowed to state universities, but for most whites the only available schools were private. As a result, white illiteracy, which had been declining in the North, remained high in the South. For example, nearly 60 percent of the North Carolinians who enlisted in the United States Army before the Civil War were illiterate. The comparable proportion for northern enlistees was less than 30 percent.

Agricultural, self-sufficient, and independent, the middling and poor whites of the South remained unconvinced of the need for public education. They had little dependency on the printed word, few complex economic transactions, and infrequent dealings with urban people. Even the large planters, some of whom did support public education, had less commitment to it than did northern manufacturers. Whereas many northern businessmen accepted Horace Mann's argument that public schools would create a more orderly and alert work force, planters had no need for an educated white work force. They already had a black one that they were determined to keep illiterate lest it acquire through books ideas of freedom.

## Cotton and Southern Progress

Because the South diverged so sharply from the North, it is tempting to view the South as backward and lethargic, doomed to be bypassed by the more energetic northern states. Increasingly, northerners associated the spread of cities and factories with progress. Finding few cities and factories in the South, they concluded that the region was a stranger to progress as well. A northern journalist wrote of white southerners in the 1850s: "They work little, and that little, badly; they earn little, they sell little; they buy little, and they have little—very little—of the common comforts and consolations of civilized life."

Yet the white South did not lack progressive features. In 1840 per capita income in the white South was only slightly below the national average, and by 1860 it exceeded the national average. Although it is true that southerners made few contributions to technology to rival those of northerners, many southerners had a progressive zeal for agricultural improvement. The Virginian Edmund Ruffin, who allegedly touched off the Civil War by firing the first cannon on Fort Sumter in 1861 and committed suicide in despair at the South's defeat in 1865, was an enthusiastic supporter of crop rotation and of the use of fertilizer and an important figure in the history of scientific agriculture.

Rather than viewing the Old South as economically backward, it is more accurate to see it merely as different. Cotton was a wonderful crop, and southerners could hardly be blamed for making it their ruler. "No! You dare not make war upon cotton; no power on earth dares to make war upon it," a senator from South Carolina proclaimed in 1858. "Cotton is king."

**Giant Steamboats on the Levee at New Orleans, 1853**

## Social Relations in the White South

Antislavery northerners often charged that slavery twisted the entire social structure of the South out of shape. By creating a permanent black underclass of bond servants, they alleged, slavery robbed lower-class whites of the incentive to work, reduced them to shiftless misery, and rendered the South a premodern throwback in an otherwise progressive age. Stung by northern allegations that slavery turned the white South into a region of rich planters and poor common folk, southerners retorted that the real center of white inequality was the North, where merchants and financiers paraded in fine silks and never soiled their hands with manual labor.

In reality, the white South was a curious mix of aristocratic and democratic, premodern and modern features. Although it contained considerable class inequality, property ownership was widespread. Rich planters occupied seats in state legislatures out of proportion to their numbers in the population, but they did not necessarily get their way, nor did their political agenda always differ from that of other whites. Practices like slaveholding and dueling not only survived but intensified in the Old South at a time when they were dying out elsewhere in the civilized world. Visitors to the South sometimes thought that they were traveling backward in time. "It seems as if everything had stopped growing, and was growing backwards," novelist Harriet Beecher Stowe wrote of the South. Yet like northerners, white southerners were restless, acquisitive, eager to make money, skillful at managing complex commercial enterprises, and when they chose, capable of becoming successful industrialists.

### The Social Groups of the White South

Although all agricultural regions of the South contained slaveholders and nonslaveholders, there was considerable diversity within each group. Some slaveholders in every southern state owned vast estates, magnificent homes, and hundreds of slaves, but most lived more modestly. In 1860 one-quarter of all white families in

**Charlotte Helen and Nurse Lydia, 1857**
*Slavery did not prevent white children and
their slave nurses from forming attachments
to each other.*

the South owned slaves. Of these, nearly half owned fewer than five slaves, and nearly three-quarters had fewer than ten slaves. Only 12 percent owned twenty or more slaves, and only 1 percent had a hundred or more. Large slaveholders clearly were a minority within a minority. Nonslaveholders also formed a diverse group. Most were landowners whose farms drew on the labor of family members, but the South also contained nonslaveholding whites who squatted on land in the so-called pine barrens or piney woods and who scratched out a livelihood by raising livestock, hunting and fishing, and planting a few acres of corn, oats, or sweet potatoes.

Despite all the diversity, one might reasonably divide the South's social structure into four main groups—the planters, the small slaveholders, the yeomen (or family farmers), and the people of the pine barrens—although even this classification is a little arbitrary. Historians usually classify as planters those who owned twenty or more slaves, the minimum number considered necessary for specialized plantation agriculture. Yet in any group of twenty slaves, some were likely to be too old and others too young to work. Arguably, a planter needed more than twenty slaves to run a plantation. Similarly, those with fewer than twenty slaves are usually described as small slaveholders, but an obvious difference separated an individual who owned ten to nineteen slaves and one who owned fewer than

five. The former was close to becoming a planter; the latter was only a step removed from a yeoman. A great deal depended on where one lived. In the low country and delta regions of the South, the planters dominated; most small slaveholders in these areas had dealings with the planters and looked to them for leadership. In the hilly upland regions, the yeomen were dominant, and small slaveholders tended to acquire their outlook.

Of course, many lawyers, physicians, merchants, and artisans, who did not fall into any of these four main groups, also made the Old South their home. But because the South was fundamentally rural and agricultural, those outside of agriculture usually identified their interests with one or another of the four agricultural groups. Rural artisans and merchants had innumerable dealings with the yeomen. Urban merchants and lawyers depended on the planters and adopted their viewpoint on most issues. Similarly, slave traders relied on the plantation economy for their livelihood. Nathan Bedford Forrest, the uneducated son of a humble Tennessee blacksmith, made a fortune as a slave trader in Natchez, Mississippi. When the Civil War broke out, Forrest enlisted in the Confederate army as a private and rose swiftly to become the South's greatest cavalry general. "That devil Forrest," the Yankees called him. Plantation slavery directed Forrest's allegiances as surely as it did those of planters like Jefferson Davis, the Confederacy's president.

### Planters and Plantation Mistresses

With porticoed mansion and fields teeming with slaves, the plantation still stands at the center of the popular image of the Old South. This romanticized view, reinforced by novels and motion pictures like *Gone with the Wind,* is not entirely misleading, for the South contained plantations that travelers found "superb beyond description." Whether devoted to cotton, tobacco, rice, or sugar, the plantations were characterized by a high degree of division of labor. In the 1850s Bellmead, a tobacco plantation on Virginia's James River, was virtually an agricultural equivalent of a factory village. Its more than one hundred slaves were classified into the domestic staff (butlers, waiters, seamstresses, laundresses, maids, and gardeners), the pasture staff (shepherds, cowherds, and hog drivers), outdoor artisans (stonemasons and carpenters), indoor artisans (blacksmiths, carpenters, shoemakers, spinners, and weavers), and field hands. Such a division of labor was inconceivable without abundant slaves and land. Wade Hampton's cotton plantation near Columbia, South Carolina, encompassed 2,400 acres. With such resources, it is not surprising that large plantations could generate incomes that contemporaries viewed as immense ($20,000–$30,000 a year).

During the first flush of settlement in the piedmont and trans-Appalachian South, in the eighteenth century, most well-off planters had been content to live in simple log cabins. In contrast, between 1810 and 1860, elite planters often vied with one another to build stately mansions. Some, like Lyman Hardy of Mississippi, hired architects. Hardy's Auburn, built in 1812 near Natchez, featured Ionic columns and a portico thirty-one feet long and twelve feet deep. Others copied designs from books like Andrew Jackson Downing's *The Architecture of Country Houses* (1850), which sold sixteen thousand copies between 1850 and 1865.

However impressive, these were not typical planters. The wealth of most planters, especially in states like Alabama and Mississippi, consisted primarily in the value of their slaves rather than in such finery as expensive furniture or silver plate. In monetary terms, slaves were worth a great deal, as much as seventeen hundred dollars for a field hand in the 1850s. Planters could convert their wealth into cash for purchasing luxuries only by selling slaves. A planter who sold his slaves ceased to be a planter and relinquished the South's most prestigious social status. Not surprisingly, most planters clung to large-scale slaveholding, even if it meant scrimping on their lifestyles. A northern journalist observed that in the Southwest, men worth millions lived as if they were not worth hundreds.

Planters had to worry constantly about profitability, for the fixed costs of operating plantations—including hiring overseers, housing and feeding slaves, and maintaining cotton gins and other equipment—were considerable. Their drive for profits led planters to search constantly for more and better land, to organize their slaves into specialized work gangs for maximum efficiency, and to make their plantations self-sufficient in food. Their quest for profits also impelled planters to cultivate far-flung commercial connections. Like any commodity, cotton went up and down in price. Sometimes the fluctuations were long term; more often, the price fluctuated seasonally. In response to these rises and falls, planters assigned their cotton to commercial agents in cities. These agents held the cotton until the price was right and extended credit to enable the planters to pay their bills before the cotton was sold.

**Colonel and Mrs. James A. Whiteside, Son Charles and Servants,** by James A. Cameron, c. 1858–1859 *This portrait captures the patriarchy as well as the graciousness that whites associated with the ideal plantation. Not only the slave waiter and nurse but the planter's wife appear overshadowed by the master's presence.*

Thus indebtedness became part of the plantation economy. Persistent debt intensified the planters' quest for more profits to escape from the burden of debt. Planters enjoyed neither repose nor security.

Plantation agriculture placed psychological strains as well as economic burdens on planters and their wives. Frequent moves disrupted circles of friends and relatives, all the more so because migration to the Southwest carried families into progressively less settled, more desolate areas. In 1850 those regions of the South with thriving plantation economies—notably Alabama, Mississippi, and southeastern Louisiana—had only recently emerged from the frontier stage.

For plantation women, migration to the Southwest often amounted to a fall from grace, for many of them had grown up in seaboard elegance, only to find themselves in isolated regions, surrounded by slaves, and bereft of the companionship of white social peers. "I am sad tonight, sickness preys on my frame," wrote a bride who moved to Mississippi in 1833. "I am alone and more than 150 miles from any near relative in the wild woods of an Indian nation." At times wives lacked even their husbands' companionship. Plantation agriculture kept men on the road, scouting new land for purchase, supervising outlying holdings, and transacting business in New Orleans or Memphis.

Planters and their wives found various ways to cope with their isolation from civilized society. Many spent long periods of time in cities and left the management of plantations to overseers. In 1850 fully one-half the planters in the Mississippi Delta were absentees living in or near Natchez or New Orleans rather than on their plantations. Yet in 1850 only 30 percent of planters with a hundred or more slaves employed white overseers; the majority managed their own estates. In response, many made plantation life more sociable by engaging in lavish hospitality. But hospitality imposed enormous burdens on plantation wives, who might have to entertain as many as fifteen people for breakfast and attend to the needs of visitors who stayed for days. Indeed, in the plantation economy, wives had even less leisure than their husbands. Aside from raising their own children and caring for guests, plantation mistresses supervised house slaves, made carpets and clothes, looked after outbuildings such as smokehouses and dairies, and planted garden fruits and vegetables. Plantation women were anything but the delicate idlers of legend. In the absence of their husbands or fathers, they frequently kept the plantation accounts.

Among the greatest sorrows of some plantation mistresses was the presence of the mulatto children, who stood as daily reminders of their husbands' infidelity. Mary Boykin Chesnut, an astute Charleston woman and famous diarist, commented, "Any lady is ready to tell you who is the father of all the mulatto children in everybody's household but her own. These, she seems to think, drop from clouds." Insisting on sexual purity for white women, southern men followed a looser standard for themselves. After the death of his wife, the brother of the famous abolitionist sisters Sarah and Angelina Grimké fathered three mulatto children. The gentlemanly code usually tolerated such transgressions as long as they were not paraded in public—but at times, even if they were. Richard M. Johnson of Kentucky, the man who allegedly killed Tecumseh during the War of 1812, was elected vice president of the United States in 1836 despite having lived openly for years with his black mistress.

The isolation, drudgery, and humiliation that planters' wives experienced turned very few against the system. When the Civil War came, they supported the Confederacy as enthusiastically as any group. However much they might hate living as white islands in a sea of slaves, they recognized no less than their husbands that their wealth and position depended on slavery.

## The Small Slaveholders

In 1860, 88 percent of all slaveholders owned fewer than twenty slaves, and most of these possessed fewer than ten slaves. Some slaveowners were not even farmers: one out of every five was employed outside of agriculture, usually as a lawyer, physician, merchant, or artisan.

As a large and extremely diverse group, small slaveholders experienced conflicting loyalties and ambitions. In the upland regions, they absorbed the outlook of yeomen (nonslaveowning family farmers), the numerically dominant group. Typically, small upland slaveholders owned only a few slaves and rarely aspired to become large planters. In contrast, in the low country and delta regions, where planters formed the dominant group, small slaveholders often aspired to planter status. In these planter-dominated areas, someone with ten slaves could realistically look forward to the day when he would own thirty. The deltas were thus filled with ambitious and acquisitive individuals who linked success to owning more slaves. Whether

# Social Relations in the White South

one owned ten slaves or fifty, the logic of slaveholding was much the same. The investment in slaves could be justified only by setting them to work on profitable crops. Profitable crops demanded, in turn, more and better land. Much like the planters, the small slaveholders of the low country and delta areas were restless and footloose.

The social structure of the deltas was fluid but not infinitely so. Small slaveholders were usually younger than large slaveholders, and many hoped to become planters in their own right. But as the antebellum period wore on, a clear tendency developed toward the geographical segregation of the small slaveholders from the planters in the cotton belt. Small slaveholders led the initial push into the cotton belt in the 1810s and 1820s, whereas the large planters, reluctant to risk transporting their hundreds of slaves into the still turbulent new territory, remained in the seaboard South. Gradually, however, the large planters ventured into Alabama and Mississippi. Colonel Thomas Dabney, a planter originally from tidewater Virginia, made several scouting tours of the Southwest before moving his family and slaves to the region of Vicksburg, Mississippi, where he started a four-thousand-acre plantation. The small slaveholders already on the scene at first resented Dabney's genteel manners and misguided efforts to win friends. He showed up at house raisings to lend a hand, but the hands he lent were not his own, which remained gloved, but those of his slaves. The small slaveholders muttered about transplanted Virginia snobs. Dabney responded to complaints simply by buying up much of the best land in the region. In itself, this was no loss to the small slaveholders. They had been first on the scene, and it was their land that the Dabneys of the South purchased. Dabney and men like him quickly turned the whole region from Vicksburg to Natchez into one of large plantations. The small farmers took the proceeds from the sale of their land, bought more slaves, and moved elsewhere to grow cotton. Small slaveholders gradually transformed the region from Vicksburg to Tuscaloosa, Alabama, into a belt of medium-size farms with a dozen or so slaves on each.

## The Yeomen

Nonslaveholding family farmers, or yeomen, comprised the largest single group of southern whites. Most were landowners. Landholding yeomen, because they owned no slaves of their own, frequently hired slaves at

**Ye Southern Planter, 1838**
*Although they aspired to be leisured gentlemen and live in mansions, most planters resided in modest dwellings and actively managed their estates.*

harvest time to help in the fields. In an area where the land was poor, like eastern Tennessee, the landowning yeomen were typically subsistence farmers, but most grew some crops for the market. Whether they engaged in subsistence or commercial agriculture, they controlled landholdings far more modest than those of the planters—more likely in the range of fifty to two hundred acres than five hundred or more acres. Yeomen could be found anywhere in the South, but they tended to congregate in the upland regions. In the seaboard South, they populated the piedmont region of Georgia, South Carolina, North Carolina, and Virginia; in the Southwest they usually lived in the hilly upcountry, far from the rich alluvial soil of the deltas. A minority of yeomen did not own land. Typically young, these men resided with and worked for landowners to whom they were related.

The leading characteristic of the yeomen was the value that they attached to self-sufficiency. As nonslaveholders, they were not carried along by the same logic that impelled slaveholders to acquire more land and plant more cash crops. Although most yeomen raised cash crops, relative to planters, they devoted a higher proportion of their acreage to subsistence crops like corn, sweet potatoes, and oats than to cash crops. The ideal of the planters was profit with modest self-sufficiency; that of the yeomen, self-sufficiency with modest profit.

Yeomen dwelling in the low country and delta regions dominated by planters were often dismissed as "poor white trash." But in the upland areas, where they constituted the dominant group, the yeomen were highly respectable. There they coexisted peacefully with the slaveholders, who typically owned only a few slaves (large planters were rare in the upland areas). Both the small slaveholders and the yeomen were essentially family farmers. With or without the aid of a few slaves, fathers and sons cleared the land and plowed, planted, and hoed the fields. Wives and daughters planted and tended vegetable gardens, helped at harvest, occasionally cared for livestock, cooked, and made clothes for the family.

In contrast to the far-flung commercial transactions of the planters, who depended on distant commercial agents to market their crops, the economic transactions of yeomen usually occurred within the neighborhood of their farms. Yeomen often exchanged their cotton, wheat, or tobacco for goods and services from local artisans and merchants. In some areas they sold their surplus corn to the herdsmen and drovers who made a living in the South's upland regions by specializing in the raising of hogs. Along the French Broad River in eastern Tennessee, some twenty to thirty thousand hogs were fattened for market each year; at peak season, a traveler would see a thousand hogs a mile. When driven to market, the hogs were quartered at night in huge stock stands, veritable hog "hotels," and fed with corn supplied by the local yeomen.

### The People of the Pine Barrens

One of the most controversial groups in the Old South comprised independent whites of the wooded pine barrens. Making up about 10 percent of southern whites, they usually squatted on the land; put up crude cabins; cleared some acreage on which they planted corn between tree stumps; and grazed hogs and cattle in the woods. They neither raised cash crops nor engaged in the daily routine of orderly work that characterized family farmers. With their ramshackle houses and handful of stump-strewn acres, they appeared lazy and shiftless.

Antislavery northerners cited the pine barrens people as proof that slavery degraded poor whites, but southerners shot back that while the pine barrens people were poor, they could at least feed themselves, unlike the paupers of northern cities. In general, the people of the pine barrens were self-reliant and fiercely independent. Pine barrens men were reluctant to hire themselves out as laborers to do "slave" tasks, and the women refused to become servants.

Neither victimized nor oppressed, these people generally lived in the pine barrens by choice. The grandson of a farmer who had migrated from Emanuel County, Georgia, to the Mississippi pine barrens explained his grandfather's decision: "The turpentine smell, the moan of the winds through the pine trees, and nobody within fifty miles of him, [were] too captivating . . . to be resisted, and he rested there."

### Conflict and Consensus in the White South

Planters tangled with yeomen on several issues in the Old South. With their extensive economic dealings and need for credit, planters and their urban commercial allies inclined toward the Whig party, which was generally more sympathetic to banking and economic development. Cherishing their self-sufficiency, and economically independent, the yeomen tended to be Democrats.

The occasions for conflict between these groups were minimal, however, and an underlying political unity reigned in the South. Especially in the Lower South, each of the four main social groups—planters, small slaveholders, yeomen, and pine barrens people—tended to cluster in different regions. The delta areas that planters dominated contained relatively small numbers of yeomen. In other regions small slaveowners, families with ten to fifteen slaves, predominated. In the upland areas far from the deltas, the yeomen congregated. And the people of the pine barrens lived in a world of their own. There was more geographical intermingling of groups in the Upper South than in the Lower, but throughout the South each group attained a degree of independence from the others. With widespread landownership and relatively few factories, the Old South basically was not a place where whites worked for other whites, and this tended to minimize friction among whites.

In addition, the white South's political structure was sufficiently democratic to prevent any one social group from gaining exclusive control over politics. It is true that in both the Upper and the Lower South, the majority of state legislators were planters. Large planters, those with fifty or more slaves, were represented in legislatures far out of proportion to their numbers in the population. Yet these same planters owed their election to the popular vote. The white South was affected by the same democratic currents that swept northern politics between 1815 and 1860, and the newer states of the South had usually entered the Union with democratic constitutions that included universal white manhood suffrage—the right of all adult white males to vote.

Although yeomen often voted for planters, the non-slaveowners did not issue their elected representatives a blank check to govern as they pleased. During the 1830s and 1840s, Whig planters who favored banks faced intense and often successful opposition from Democratic yeomen. These yeomen blamed banks for the Panic of 1837 and pressured southern legislatures to restrict bank operations. On banking issues, nonslaveholders got their way often enough to nurture their belief that they ultimately controlled politics and that slaveholders could not block their goals.

### Conflict over Slavery

Nevertheless, there was considerable potential for conflict between the slaveholders and nonslaveholders. The white carpenter who complained in 1849 that "unjust, oppressive, and degrading" competition from slave labor depressed his wages surely had a point. Between 1830 and 1860, slaveholders gained an increasing proportion of the South's wealth while declining as a proportion of its white population. The size of the slaveholding class shrank from 36 percent of the white population in 1831 to 31 percent in 1850 to 25 percent in 1860. A Louisiana editor warned in 1858 that "the present tendency of supply and demand is to concentrate all the slaves in the hands of the few, and thus excite the envy rather than cultivate the sympathy of the people." That same year, the governor of Florida proposed a law guaranteeing to each white person the ownership of at least one slave. Some southerners began to support the idea of Congress's reopening the African slave trade to increase the supply of slaves, bring down their price, and give more whites a stake in the institution.

As the debate over slavery in Virginia during 1831–1832 (see this chapter's introduction) attests, slaveholders had good reasons for uncertainty over the allegiance of nonslaveholders to the "peculiar institu-

tion" of slavery. The publication in 1857 of Hinton R. Helper's *The Impending Crisis of the South,* which called upon nonslaveholders to abolish slavery in their own interest, revealed the persistence of a degree of white opposition to slavery. On balance, however, slavery did not create profound and lasting divisions between the South's slaveholders and nonslaveholders. Although antagonism to slavery flourished in parts of Virginia up to 1860, proposals for emancipation dropped from the state's political agenda after 1832. In Kentucky, a state with a history of antislavery activity that dated back to the 1790s, calls for emancipation were revived in 1849 in a popular referendum. But the pro-emancipation forces went down to crushing defeat. Thereafter, the continuation of slavery ceased to

*Proslavery propagandists contrasted what they believed to be the black's African savagery with the blessings of civilization on an American plantation.*

THE NEGRO IN HIS OWN COUNTRY.

THE NEGRO IN AMERICA.

be a political issue in Kentucky and elsewhere in the South.

The rise and fall of pro-emancipation sentiment in the South raises a key question. Since the majority of white southerners were nonslaveholders, why did they not attack the institution more consistently? To look ahead, why were so many of them to fight ferociously and die bravely during the Civil War in defense of an institution in which they appeared not to have had any real stake? There are various answers to these questions. First, some nonslaveholders hoped to become slaveholders. Second, most simply accepted the racist assumptions upon which slavery rested. Whether slaveholders or nonslaveholders, white southerners dreaded the likelihood that emancipation might encourage "impudent" blacks to entertain ideas of social equality with whites. Blacks might demand the right to sit next to whites in railroad cars and even make advances to white women. "Now suppose they [the slaves] was free," a white southerner told a northern journalist in the 1850s; "you see they'd all think themselves just as good as we; of course they would if they was free. Now just suppose you had a family of children, how would you like to hev a niggar steppin' up to your darter?" Slavery, in short, appealed to whites as a legal, time-honored, and foolproof way to enforce the social subordination of blacks. Finally, no one knew where the slaves, if freed, would go or what they would do. After 1830 a dwindling minority of northerners and southerners still dallied with the idea of colonizing freed blacks in Africa, but that alternative increasingly seemed unrealistic in a society where slaves numbered in the millions. Without colonization, southerners concluded, emancipation would produce a race war. In 1860 Georgia's governor sent a blunt message to his constituents, many of them nonslaveholders: "So soon as the slaves were at liberty thousands of them would leave the cotton and rice fields . . . and make their way to the healthier climate of the mountain region [where] we should have them plundering and stealing, robbing and killing." There was no mistaking the conclusion. Emancipation would not merely deprive slaveholders of their property, it would jeopardize the lives of nonslaveholders.

### The Proslavery Argument

Between 1830 and 1860 southern writers constructed a defense of slavery as a positive good rather than a nec-

essary evil. Southerners answered northern attacks on slavery as a backward institution by pointing out that the slave society of ancient Athens had produced Plato and Aristotle and that Roman slaveholders had laid the basis of western civilization. A Virginian, George Fitzhugh, launched another line of attack by contrasting the plight of northern factory workers, "wage slaves" who were callously discarded by their bosses when they were too old or too sick to work, with the southern slaves, who were fed and clothed even when old and ill because they were the property of conscientious masters.

Many proslavery treatises were aimed less at northerners than at skeptics among the South's nonslaveholding yeomanry. Southern clergymen, who wrote roughly half of all the proslavery tracts, invoked the Bible, especially St. Paul's order that slaves obey their masters. Too, proslavery writers warned southerners that the real intention of abolitionists, many of whom advocated equal rights for women, was to destroy the family as much as slavery by undermining the "natural" submission of children to parents, wives to husbands, and slaves to masters.

As southerners closed ranks behind slavery, they increasingly suppressed open discussion of the institution within the South. In the 1830s southerners seized and burned abolitionist literature mailed to the South. In Kentucky the abolitionist editor Cassius Marcellus Clay positioned two cannons and a powder keg to protect his press, but in 1845 a mob dismantled it anyway. By 1860 any southerner found with a copy of Helper's *The Impending Crisis* had every reason to fear for his life.

The rise of the proslavery argument coincided with a shift in the position of the southern churches on slavery. During the 1790s and early 1800s, some Protestant ministers had assailed slavery as immoral. By the 1830s, however, most members of the clergy had convinced themselves that slavery was not only compatible with Christianity but also necessary for the proper exercise of the Christian religion. Like the proslavery intellectuals, clergymen contended that slavery provided the opportunity to display Christian responsibility toward one's inferiors, and it helped blacks develop Christian virtues like humility and self-control. With this conclusion solidified, southerners increasingly attacked antislavery evangelicals in the North for disrupting the allegedly superior social arrangement of the South. In 1844 the Methodist Episcopal Church split into northern and southern wings. In 1845 Baptists formed a separate Southern Convention. Even earlier, southerners and conservative northerners had combined in 1837 to drive the antislavery New School Presbyterians out of that denomination's main body. All this added up to a profound irony. In 1800 southern evangelicals had been more critical of slavery than southerners as a whole. Yet the evangelicals effectively seceded from national church denominations, long before the South seceded from the Union.

# Honor and Violence in the Old South

Almost everything about the Old South struck northern visitors as extreme. Although inequality certainly flourished in the North, no group in northern society was as deprived as the slaves. The Irish immigrants who arrived in the North in great waves in the 1840s often owned no property, but unlike the slaves, they were not in themselves a form of property. Not only did northerners find the gap between the races in the South extreme, but individual southerners seemed to run to extremes. One minute they were hospitable and gracious; the next, savagely violent. Abolitionists were not the only ones to view the Old South as a land of extremes. "The Americans of the South," Alexis de Tocqueville asserted, "are brave, comparatively ignorant, hospitable, generous, easy to irritate, violent in their resentments, without industry or the spirit of enterprise."

## *Violence in the White South*

No one who lived in a southern community, a northern journalist noted in the 1850s, could fail to be impressed with "the frequency of fighting with deadly weapons." Throughout the colonial and antebellum periods, violence deeply colored the daily lives of white southerners. In the 1760s a minister described backcountry Virginians "biting one anothers Lips and Noses off, and gowging one another—that is, thrusting out anothers Eyes, and kicking one another on the Cods [genitals], to the Great damage of many a Poor Woman." In the 1840s a New York newspaper described a fight between two raftsmen on the Mississippi that started when one accidentally bumped the other into shallow water. When it was over, one raftsman was dead; the other gloated, "I can lick a steamboat. My fingernails is related to a sawmill on my mother's side, . . . and the

brass buttons on my coat have all been boiled in poison." Gouging out eyes became a specialty of sorts among poor whites. On one occasion, a South Carolina judge entered his court to find a plaintiff, a juror, and two witnesses all missing one eye. Stories of eye gougings and ear bitings lost nothing in the telling and became part of the folklore of the Old South. Mike Fink, a legendary southern fighter and hunter, boasted that he was so mean that in infancy, he refused his mother's milk and cried out for a bottle of whiskey. Yet beneath the folklore lay the reality of violence that gave the Old South a murder rate as much as ten times higher than that of the North.

## *The Code of Honor and Dueling*

At the root of most violence in the white South lay intensified feelings of personal pride that themselves reflected the inescapable presence of slaves. Every day of their lives, white southerners saw slaves who were degraded, insulted, and powerless to resist. This experience had a searing impact on whites, for it encouraged them to react violently to even trivial insults in order to demonstrate that they had nothing in common with slaves. Among gentlemen this exaggerated pride took the form of a code of honor. In this context, honor can best be defined as an extraordinary sensitivity to one's reputation, a belief that one's self-esteem depends on the judgment of others. In the antebellum North, moralists celebrated a rival ideal, character—the quality that enabled an individual to behave in a steady fashion regardless of how others acted toward him or her. A person possessed of character acted out of the promptings of conscience. In contrast, in the honor culture of the Old South, the slightest insult, as long as it was perceived as intentional, could become the basis for a duel (see A Place in Time).

Formalized by British and French officers during the Revolutionary War, dueling gained a secure niche in the Old South as a means by which gentlemen dealt with affronts to their honor. To outsiders, the incidents that sparked duels seemed so trivial as to be scarcely credible: a casual remark accidentally overheard, a harmless brushing against the side of someone at a public event, even a hostile glance. Yet dueling did not necessarily terminate in violence. Dueling constituted part of a complex code of etiquette that governed relations among gentlemen in the Old South and, like all forms of etiquette, called for a curious sort of self-

## Edgefield District, South Carolina

Located on the western edge of South Carolina near the Georgia border, Edgefield District combined features of the aristocratic low country, to which it was linked by the Savannah River, and the yeoman-dominated upland regions of the Old South. Most Edgefield whites were small farmers or agricultural workers. In 1860 a majority did not own any slaves, and a sizable minority had no land. Yet the invention of the cotton gin had attracted wealthy low-country planters to Edgefield, and by 1860 the district had become the state's leading cotton producer. These planters formed the nucleus of the district's elite. By 1860 the wealthiest 10 percent of white heads of household in Edgefield controlled 57 percent of the district's real and personal property. Intermarriage strengthened ties within the elite. By the Civil War, the leading families, among them the Butlers, Bonhams, Brookses, Simkinses, and Pickenses, had intermarried.

Black slaves were the basis of upper-crust Edgefield's wealth. By 1860 slaves outnumbered whites by 50 percent in the district. The vast majority of Edgefield's black bond servants were field slaves. Almost all of those dwelling on the great plantations worked under the "gang" system, by which they were divided into a number of groups, each performing a specified amount of work. (The gang system stood in contrast to the "task" system, in which individual slaves carried out designated chores.) The plantations' "plow gangs" comprised strong young men and occasionally some women, whereas "hoe gangs" generally included elderly slaves and women. A small number of Edgefield's slaves were skilled artisans who did blacksmithing and carpentry on the district's omnipresent farms. Whether field hands or skilled artisans, most slaves lived with their families in simple, rude one-room cabins in close proximity to the dwellings of other slaves. An Edgefield black born into slavery in 1852 recalled that the slaves "had houses of weatherboards, big enough for [a] chicken coop—man, wife, and chillun [live] dere."

Only one-quarter of Edgefield's whites owned twenty or more of such slaves in 1860. This elite minority accounted for possession of nearly two-thirds of the district's slaves. Using their slaves not only as agrarian workers but as collateral for loans, the great planters agreed with John C. Calhoun's northern-bred son-in-law Thomas Green Clemson—the owner of the Edgefield plantation called Canebreak—that "slaves are the most valuable property in the South, being the basis of the whole southern fabric." Yet despite the yawning gap between the wealth of the planters and the income

### Pierce Mason Butler

*A leading Edgefield politician, Butler was befriended early in his career by John Calhoun, who secured an army commission for him. Joining Calhoun in the early 1830s in support of nullification, Butler was elected governor of South Carolina in 1836. He led the Palmetto regiment in the Mexican War and was killed in action in 1847.*

### Francis Wilkinson Pickens

*Pickens came to Edgefield to study and practice law. A relative of Calhoun, he favored nullification. Elected governor of South Carolina just before its secession from the Union in 1860, Pickens once said that "before a free people can be dragged into a war, it must be in defense of great national right as well as national honor."*

of most other whites, class conflict did not convulse antebellum Edgefield's white society, which as a whole was tightly unified. Verbal assaults on "aristocrats" did sweep through the district from time to time, but lawyers (whom the people treated with suspicion because they did not work with their hands) rather than planters bore the brunt of these attacks.

Religion contributed mightily to this harmony reigning within Edgefield's white society. Indeed, religion was at the core of both family life and community life in the district and significantly molded the world view of the people. Although many churches dotted the countryside, so dispersed was Edgefield's population—the district contained only two incorporated towns—that ministers were limited. Thus devout Episcopalian planters and

zealous Baptist yeomen farmers often found themselves sitting side by side listening to whatever traveling preacher had happened through their neighborhood. As a further boon to white solidarity, Edgefield's small farmers depended on the plantation lords to gin and market their cotton, and during the harvest they often rented slaves from the great planters. Nonslaveholding yeomen were likelier than small slaveowners to be dissatisfied with their lot in life, and many moved west into the states of Georgia, Alabama, Mississippi, and Louisiana rather than stay and complain about the rich. Nearly 60 percent of Edgefield's white heads of household in 1850 no longer resided in the district in 1860.

The code of honor further unified the whites. Like southern gentlemen elsewhere, Edgefield's male elite saw affronts to honor behind every bush. Two military officers once fought a duel be─____

numerable challenges to duels. Yet however much the code of honor set individual against individual, it could unify a region. For example, in 1856 Preston Brooks, a U.S. congressman from Edgefield, brutally caned Massachusetts senator Charles Sumner on the Senate floor after Sumner had delivered an antislavery oration that dealt roughly with one of Brooks's relatives. As Representative Brooks later wrote to his constituents, it was not just the honor of a relative that he sought to defend. Rather, he had set himself up as a "sentinel" guarding the honor of every white South Carolinian against the slanderous tongues of northerners. By the mid-1850s growing attitudes like this were demonstrating that the battle lines clearly had been drawn between southerners and northerners. The time seemed to be fast approaching when, as Edgefield newspaper editor Arthur Simkins observed, southern planters' ___ . . . inherited from a vir─____ " would lead them to ___ to strongly oppose ___ ndencies in American ___ ning in the Northeast's ___ more populous manu─ ___ "

**Presentation Sword and Ceramic Jar**

*Decorative arts in Edgefield ranged from this ___ P. M. Butler, which symbolized the valor and ___ role of the southern planter class, to slave-m___ in one of the district's ten or so clayworks. W___ alkaline glazes, the jar gets its distinctive app___ from the kiln while red-hot and then thrust in___*

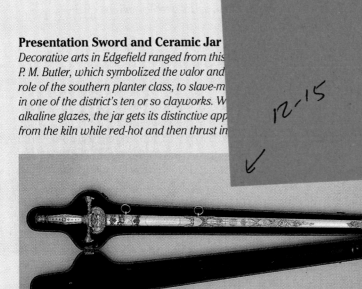

12-15

12-16

restraint. Gentlemen viewed dueling as a refined alternative to the random violence of lower-class life. The code of dueling did not dictate that the insulted party leap at his antagonist's throat or draw his pistol at the perceived moment of insult. Rather, he was to remain cool, bide his time, settle on a choice of weapons, and agree to a meeting place. In the interval, negotiations between friends of the parties sought to clear up the "misunderstanding" that had evoked the challenge. In this way, most confrontations ended peaceably rather than on the field of honor at dawn.

Although dueling was as much a way of settling disputes peaceably as of ending them violently, the ritual could easily terminate in a death or maiming. Dueling did not allow the resolution of grievances by the courts, a form of redress that would have guaranteed a peaceful outcome. As a way of settling personal disputes that involved honor, recourse to the law struck many southerners as cowardly and shameless. Andrew Jackson's mother told the future president, "The law affords no remedy that can satisfy the feelings of a true man."

In addition, dueling rested on the assumption that a gentleman could recognize another gentleman and hence would know when to respond to a challenge. Nothing in the code of dueling compelled a gentleman to duel someone beneath his status because such a person's opinion of a gentleman hardly mattered. An insolent porter who insulted a gentleman might get a whipping but did not merit a challenge to a duel. Yet it was often difficult to determine who was a gentleman. The Old South teemed with pretentious would-be gentlemen. A clerk in a country store in Arkansas in the 1850s found it remarkable that ordinary farmers who hung around the store talked of their honor and that the store's proprietor, a German Jew, kept a dueling pistol.

### The Southern Evangelicals and White Values

With its emphasis on the personal redress of grievances and its inclination toward violence, the ideal of honor had a potential for conflict with the values preached by the southern evangelical churches, notably the Baptists, Methodists, and Presbyterians. These evangelical denominations were on the rise even before the Great Kentucky Revival of 1800–1801 and continued to grow in the wake of the revival. With just 48,000 southern members in 1801, for example, the Methodists reported 80,000 by 1807. All of the evangeli-

cal denominations stressed humility and self-restraint, virtues that stood in contrast to the entire culture of show and display that buttressed the extravagance and violence of the Old South.

Evangelicals continued to rail against dueling, but by the 1830s their values had changed in subtle ways. In the late eighteenth century evangelical preachers had reached out to the South's subordinate groups: women, slaves, and the poor. They had frequently allowed women and slaves to exhort in biracial churches. In contrast, by the 1830s evangelical women were expected to remain silent in church. Pushed to the periphery of white churches, slaves increasingly conducted their own worship services in black churches. In addition Methodists and Baptists increasingly attracted well-to-do converts, and they began to open colleges such as Randolph-Macon (Methodist, 1830) and Wake Forest (Baptist, 1838).

With these developments, the once-antagonistic relationship between evangelicals and the gentry became a two-way street. Evangelical clergymen absorbed some gentry values, including a regard for their honor and reputation that prompted them to throw taunts and threats back at their detractors. In turn, the gentry embraced evangelical virtues. By the 1860s the South contained many Christian gentlemen like the Bible-quoting Presbyterian general Thomas J. "Stonewall" Jackson, fierce in a righteous war but a sworn opponent of strong drink, the gaming table, and the duel.

## Life Under Slavery

Slavery, the institution that lay at the root of the code of honor and other distinctive features of the Old South, has long inspired controversy among historians. Some have portrayed slavery as a benevolent institution in which blacks lived contentedly under kind masters; others, as a cruel and inhuman system that drove slaves into constant rebellion. Neither view is accurate, but both contain a germ of truth. There were kind masters who accepted the view expressed by a Baptist minister in 1854: "Give your servants that which is just and equal, knowing that you also have a Master in heaven." Moreover, some slaves developed genuine affection for their masters. Yet slavery was an inherently oppressive institution that forcefully appropriated the life and labor of one race for the material benefit of another. Despite professions to the contrary by apologists for slavery, the vast majority of slaveholders exploited the labor of blacks to earn a profit. Kind masters might complain about cruel overseers, but the masters hired and paid the overseers to get as much work as possible out of blacks. When the master of one plantation chastised his overseer for "barbarity," the latter replied, "Do you not remember what you told me the time you employed me that [if] I failed to make you good crops I would have to leave?" Indeed, kindness was a double-edged sword, for the benevolent master came to expect grateful affection from his slaves and then interpreted that affection as loyalty to the institution of slavery. In fact, blacks felt little, if any, loyalty to slavery. When northern troops descended upon plantations during the Civil War, masters were dismayed to find many of their most trusted slaves deserting to Union lines.

Although the kindness or cruelty of masters made some difference to slaves, the most important determinants of their experiences under slavery depended on such impersonal factors as the kind of agriculture in which they were engaged, whether they resided in rural or urban areas, and whether they lived in the eighteenth or nineteenth century. The experiences of slaves working on cotton plantations in the 1830s differed drastically from those of slaves in 1700, for reasons unrelated to the kindness or brutality of masters.

## The Maturing of the Plantation System

Slavery changed significantly between 1700 and 1830. In 1700 the typical slave was a young man in his twenties who had recently arrived aboard a slave ship from Africa or the Caribbean and worked in company with other recent arrivals on isolated small farms. Drawn from different African regions and cultures, few such slaves spoke the same language. Because commercial slave ships contained twice as many men as women, and because slaves were widely scattered, blacks had difficulty finding sexual partners and creating a semblance of family life. Furthermore, as a result of severe malnutrition, black women who had been brought to North America on slave ships bore relatively few children. Thus the slave trade had a devastating effect on natural increase among blacks. Without importations,

**Black Women and Men on a Trek Home, South Carolina**
*Much like northern factories, large plantations made it possible to impose discipline and order on their work force. Here black women loaded down with cotton join their men on the march home after a day in the fields.*

the number of slaves in North America would have declined between 1710 and 1730.

In contrast, by 1830 the typical North American slave was as likely to be female as male, had been born in America, spoke a form of English that made possible communication with other slaves, and worked in the company of numerous other slaves on a plantation. The key to the change lay in the rise of plantation agriculture in the Chesapeake and South Carolina during the eighteenth century. Plantation slaves had an easier time finding mates than those on the remote farms of the early 1700s. As the ratio between slave men and women fell into balance, marriages occurred with increasing frequency between slaves on the same or nearby plantations. The native-born slave population rose after 1730 and soared after 1750. Importations of African slaves gradually declined after 1760, and Congress banned them in 1808.

## Work and Discipline of Plantation Slaves

In 1850 the typical slave experience was to work on a large farm or plantation with at least ten fellow bond servants. Almost three-quarters of all slaves that year were owned by masters with ten or more slaves, and just over one-half lived in units of twenty or more slaves. To understand the daily existence of the typical antebellum slave, then, requires an examination of the work and discipline routines common on large-scale farming operations.

The day of antebellum plantation slaves usually began an hour before sunrise with the sounding of a horn or bell. After a sparse breakfast, slaves marched to the fields. A traveler in Mississippi described a procession of slaves on their way to work. "First came, led by an old driver carrying a whip, forty of the largest and strongest women I ever saw together; they were all in a simple uniform dress of bluish check stuff, the skirts reaching little below the knee; their legs and feet were bare; they carried themselves loftily, each having a hoe over the shoulder, and walking with a free, powerful swing." Then came the plow hands, "thirty strong, mostly men, but few of them women. . . . A lean and vigilant white overseer, on a brisk pony, brought up the rear."

As this account indicates, slave men and women worked side by side in the fields. Female slaves who did not labor in the fields scarcely idled their hours away. A former slave, John Curry, described how his mother milked cows, cared for the children whose mothers

worked in the fields, cooked for field hands, did the ironing and washing for her master's household, and took care of her own seven children. Plantations never lacked tasks for slaves of either gender. As former slave Solomon Northup noted, "ploughing, planting, picking cotton, gathering the corn, and pulling and burning stalks, occupies the whole of the four seasons of the year. Drawing and cutting wood, pressing cotton, fattening and killing hogs, are but incidental labors." Regardless of the season, the slave's day stretched from dawn to dusk. Touring the South in the 1850s, Frederick Law Olmsted prided himself on rising early and riding late but added, "I always found the negroes in the field when I first looked out, and generally had to wait for the negroes to come from the field to have my horse fed when I stopped for the night." When darkness made field work impossible, slaves toted cotton bales to the ginhouse, gathered up wood for supper fires, and fed the mules. Weary from their labors, they slept in log cabins on wooden planks. "The softest couches in the world," a former bondsman wryly observed, "are not to be found in the log mansions of a slave."

Although virtually all antebellum Americans worked long hours, no laboring group experienced the same combination of long hours and harsh discipline as did slave field hands. Northern factory workers did not have to put up with drivers who, like one described by Olmsted, walked among the slaves with a whip, "which he often cracked at them, sometimes allowing the lash to fall lightly upon their shoulders." The lash did not always fall lightly. The annals of American slavery contain stories of repulsive brutality. Pregnant slave women were sometimes forced to lie in depressions in the ground and endure whipping on their backs, a practice that supposedly protected the fetus while abusing the mother. The disciplining and punishment of slaves was often left to white overseers and black drivers rather than to masters. "Dat was de meanest devil dat ever lived on the Lord's green earth," a former Mississippi slave said of his driver. The barbaric discipline meted out by others twinged the conscience of many a master. But even masters who professed Christianity viewed the disciplining of slaves as a priority—indeed, as a Christian duty to ensure the slaves' proper "submissiveness." The black abolitionist Frederick Douglass, once a slave, recalled that his worst master had been converted at a Methodist camp meeting. "If religion had any effect on his character at all," Douglass related, "it made him more cruel and hateful in all his ways."

Despite the relentless, often vicious discipline, plantation agriculture gave a minority of slaves opportunities for advancement, not from slavery to freedom but from unskilled and exhausting field work to semiskilled or skilled indoor work. Some slaves developed skills like blacksmithing and carpentry and learned to operate cotton gins. Others were trained as cooks, butlers, and dining-room attendants. These house slaves became legendary for their arrogant disdain of field hands and poor whites. The legend often distorted the reality, for house slaves were as subject to discipline as field slaves. "I liked the field work better than I did the house work," a female slave recalled. "We could talk and do anything we wanted to, just so we picked the cotton." Such sentiments were typical, but skilled slave artisans and house servants were greatly valued and treated accordingly; they occupied higher rungs than field hands on the social ladder of slavery.

**The Land of the Free and the Home of the Brave,**
by Henry Byam Martin, 1833
*White southerners could not escape the fact that much of the Western world loathed their "peculiar institution." In 1833, when a Canadian sketched this Charleston slave auction, Britain abolished slavery in the West Indies.*

## The Slave Family

Masters thought of slaves as naturally promiscuous and flattered themselves into thinking that they alone held slave marriages together. Masters did have an incentive to encourage slave marriages in order to bring new slaves into the world and to discourage slaves from running away. Some masters baked wedding cakes for slaves and later arbitrated marital disputes. James Henry Hammond, the governor of South Carolina and a large slaveholder, noted in his diary how he "flogged Joe Goodwyn and ordered him to go back to his wife. Ditto Gabriel and Molly and ordered them to come together. Separated Moses and Anny finally."

Yet this picture of benevolent masters holding together naturally promiscuous slaves is misleading. The keenest challenge to the slave family came not from the slaves themselves but from slavery. The law provided neither recognition of nor protection for the slave family. Although some slaveholders were reluctant to break slave marriages by sale, such masters could neither bequeath this reluctance to their heirs nor avoid economic hardships that might force them to sell off slaves. The reality, one historian has calculated, was

that on average, a slave would witness in a lifetime the sale of eleven family members.

Naturally, the commonplace buying and selling of slaves severely disrupted the slaves' attempts to create a stable family life. Poignant testimony to the effects of sale on slave families, and to the desire of slaves to remain near their families, was provided by an advertisement for a runaway slave in North Carolina in 1851. The advertisement described the fugitive as presumed to be "lurking in the neighborhood of E. D. Walker's, at Moore's Creek, who owns most of his relatives, or Nathan Bonham's who owns his mother; or, perhaps, near Fletcher Bell's, at Long Creek, who owns his father." Small wonder that a slave preacher pronounced a slave couple married "until death or *distance* do you part."

Aside from their disruption by sale, slave families experienced separations and degradations from other sources. The marriage of a slave woman gave her no protection against the sexual demands of a master nor, indeed, of any white. The slave children of white masters at times became targets of the wrath of white mistresses. Sarah Wilson, the daughter of a slave and her white master, remembered that as a child, she was "picked on" by her mistress until the master ordered his wife to let Sarah alone because she "got big, big blood in her." Slave women who worked in the fields usually were separated from their children by day; young sons and daughters often were cared for by the aged or by the mothers of other children. When slave women took husbands from nearby (rather than their own) plantations, the children usually stayed with the mother. Hannah Chapman remembered that her father tried to visit his family under cover of darkness "because he missed us and us longed for him." But if his master found him, "us would track him the nex' day by de blood stains."

Despite enormous obstacles, the relationships within slave families were often intimate and, where possible, long-lasting. In the absence of legal protection, slaves developed their own standards of family morality. A southern white woman observed that slaves "did not consider it wrong for a girl to have a child before she married, but afterwards were extremely severe upon anything like infidelity on her part." When given the opportunity, slaves sought to solemnize their marriages before clergymen. White clergymen who accompanied the Union army into Mississippi and Louisiana in the closing years of the Civil War conducted thousands of marriage rites for slaves who had long viewed themselves as married and who now desired a formal ceremony and registration.

On balance, slave families differed profoundly from white families. Even on large plantations, where roughly equal numbers of black men and women made marriage a theoretical possibility, planters, including George Washington, often divided their holdings into several dispersed farms and distributed their slaves among them without regard to marriage ties. Conditions on small farms and new plantations discouraged the formation of families, and everywhere spouses were vulnerable to being sold as payment for the master's debts. Slave adults were more likely than whites never to marry, or to marry late, and slave children were more likely to live with a single parent (usually the mother) or with neither parent. In white families, the parent-child bond overrode all others; slaves, in contrast, emphasized ties between children and their grandparents, uncles, and aunts as well as their parents. Such broad kinship ties marked the West African cultures from which many slaves had originally been brought to America, and they were reinforced by the separations between children and one or both parents that routinely occurred under slavery. Frederick Douglass never knew his father and saw his mother infrequently, but he vividly remembered his grandmother, "a good nurse, and a capital hand at making nets for catching shad and herring." In addition, slaves often created "fictive" kin networks; in the absence of uncles

and aunts, they simply named friends their uncles, aunts, brothers, or sisters. In effect, slaves invested non-kin relations with symbolic kin functions. In this way, they helped protect themselves against the involuntary disruption of family ties by forced sale and established a broader community of obligation. When plantation slaves greeted each other as "brudder," they were not making a statement about actual kinship but about kindred obligations they felt for each other. Apologists for slavery liked to argue that a "community of interests" bound masters and slaves together. In truth, the real community of interests was the one that slaves developed among themselves in order to survive.

### The Longevity, Diet, and Health of Slaves

In general, slaves in the United States reproduced faster and lived longer than slaves elsewhere in the Western Hemisphere. The evidence comes from a compelling statistic. In 1825, 36 percent of all slaves in the Western Hemisphere lived in the United States, whereas Brazil accounted for 31 percent. Yet of the 10–12 million African slaves who had been imported to the New World between the fifteenth and nineteenth centuries, only some 550,000 (about 5 percent) had come to North America, whereas 3.5 million (nearly 33 percent) had been taken to Brazil. Mortality had depleted the slave populations of Brazil and the Caribbean to a far greater extent than in North America.

Several factors account for the different rates between the United States on the one hand and Brazil and the Caribbean on the other. First, the gender ratio among slaves equalized more rapidly in North America, encouraging earlier and longer marriages and more children. Second, because growing corn and raising livestock were compatible with cotton cultivation, the Old South produced plenty of food. The normal ration for a slave was a peck of cornmeal and three to four pounds of fatty pork a week. Slaves often supplemented this nutritionally unbalanced diet with vegetables grown in small plots that masters allowed them to farm and with catfish and game. In the barren winter months, slaves ate less than in the summer; in this respect, however, they did not differ much from most whites.

As for disease, slaves had greater immunities to both malaria and yellow fever than did whites, but they suffered more from cholera, dysentery, and diarrhea. In the absence of privies, slaves usually relieved themselves behind bushes; urine and feces washed into the sources of drinking water and caused many diseases. Yet slaves developed some remedies that, though commonly ridiculed by whites, were effective against stomach ailments. For example, the slaves' belief that eating white clay would cure dysentery and diarrhea rested on a firm basis, for we know now that kaolin, an ingredient of white clay, is a remedy for these ailments.

Although slave remedies were often more effective than those of white physicians, slaves experienced higher mortality rates than whites. At any age, a slave faced a shorter life than a white, but most strikingly in infancy. Rates of infant mortality for slaves were at least twice those of whites. Between 1850 and 1860, fewer than two out of three black children survived to the age of ten. Whereas the worst mortality occurred on plantations in disease-ridden, low-lying areas, pregnant, overworked field hands often miscarried or gave birth to weakened infants even in healthier regions. Masters allowed pregnant women to rest, but rarely enough. "Labor is conducive to health," a Mississippi planter told a northern journalist; "a healthy woman will rear most children."

### Slaves Off Plantations

Although plantation agriculture gave some slaves, especially males, opportunities to acquire specialized skills, it imposed a good deal of supervision on them. The greatest opportunities for slaves were reserved for those who worked off plantations and farms, either as laborers in extractive industries like mining and lumbering or as artisans in towns and cities. Because lucrative cotton growing attracted so many whites onto small farms, a perennial shortage of white labor plagued almost all the nonagricultural sectors of the southern economy. As a consequence, there was a steady demand for slaves to drive wagons, to work as stevedores (ship-cargo handlers) in port cities, to man river barges, and to perform various tasks in mining and lumbering. In 1860 lumbering employed sixteen thousand workers, most of them slaves who cut trees, hauled them to sawmills, and fashioned them into useful lumber. In sawmills black engineers fired and fixed the steam engines that provided power. In iron-ore ranges and ironworks, slaves not only served as laborers but occasionally supervised less skilled white workers. In addition, just as mill girls comprised the labor force of the booming textile industry in New England, slave women and children worked in the South's fledgling textile mills.

Slave or free, blacks found it easier to pursue skilled occupations in southern cities than in northern ones, partly because southern cities attracted few immigrants to compete with blacks for work, and partly because the profitability of southern cash crops long had pulled white laborers out of towns and cities, and left behind opportunities for blacks, slave or free, to acquire craft skills. Too, slaves who worked in factories, mining, or lumbering usually were hired rather than owned by their employers. If working conditions deteriorated to the point where slaves fell ill or died, masters would refuse to provide employers with more slaves. Consequently, working conditions for slaves off plantations usually stayed at a tolerable level. Watching workers load cotton onto a steamboat, Frederick Law Olmsted was amazed to see slaves sent to the top of the bank to roll the bales down to Irishmen who stowed them on the ship. Asking the reason for this arrangement, Olmsted was told, "The niggers are worth too much to be risked here; if the Paddies [Irish] are knocked overboard, or get their backs broke, nobody loses anything."

### Life on the Margin: Free Blacks in the Old South

Free blacks were more likely than southern blacks in general to live in cities. In 1860 one-third of the free blacks in the Upper South and more than half in the Lower South were urban.

**Woman in Tignon, 1844**

**Black Society in the Old South, c. 1860**

*Slaves greatly outnumbered free blacks in the Old South. Most slaves were owned by masters with ten or more slaves.*

Slaves in groups of 10 – 99 (60.5%)

Slaves in groups of 1 – 9 (24.1%)

Slaves in groups of 100 or more (9.4%)

Free (6%)

Free (6%)

Slaves (94%)

(For all states in which slavery was legal in 1860)

*Sources:* Eighth Census of the United States, 1860: Population by Age, Sex, Race; and Lewis C. Gray, History of Agriculture in the Southern United States (New York: Kelley, 1933).

The relatively specialized economies of the cities provided free people of color with opportunities to become carpenters, coopers (barrel makers), barbers, and even small traders. A visitor to an antebellum southern market would find that most of the meat, fish, vegetables, and fruit had been prepared for sale by free blacks. Urban free blacks formed their own fraternal orders and churches; a church run by free blacks was often the largest house of worship in a southern city. In New Orleans free blacks had their own literary journals and opera. In Natchez a free black barber, William Tiler Johnson, invested the profits of his shop in real estate, acquired stores that he rented out, purchased slaves and a plantation, and even hired a white overseer.

As Johnson's career suggests, some free blacks were highly successful. But free blacks were always vulnerable in southern society and became more so as the antebellum period wore on. Although free blacks continued to increase in absolute numbers (a little more than a quarter-million free people of color dwelled in the South in 1860), the rate of growth of the free-black population slowed after 1810. Between 1790 and 1810,

this population had more than tripled, to 108,265. The reason for the slowdown after 1810 was that fewer southern whites were setting slaves free. Until 1820 masters with doubts about the rightness of slavery frequently manumitted (freed) their black mistresses and mulatto children, and some set free their entire work forces. In the wake of the Nat Turner rebellion in 1831, laws restricting the liberties of free blacks were tightened. During the mid-1830s, for example, most southern states made it a felony to teach blacks to read and write. Every southern state forbade free blacks to enter that state, and in 1859 Arkansas ordered all free blacks to leave.

So although a free-black culture flowered in cities like New Orleans and Natchez, that culture did not reflect the conditions under which most free blacks lived. Free blacks were tolerated in New Orleans, in part because there were not too many of them. A much higher percentage of blacks were free in the Upper South than in the Lower South. Furthermore, although a disproportionate number of free blacks lived in cities, the majority lived in rural areas, where whites lumped them together with slaves. Even a successful free black like William Tiler Johnson could never dine or drink with whites. When Johnson attended the theater, he sat in the colored gallery.

The position of free blacks in the Old South contained many contradictions. So did their minds. As the offspring, or the descendants of offspring, of mixed liaisons, a disproportionate number of free blacks had light brown skin. Some of them were as color-conscious as whites and looked down on "darky" field hands and coal-black laborers. Yet as whites' discrimination against free people of color intensified during the late antebellum period, many free blacks realized that whatever future they had was as blacks, not as whites. Feelings of racial solidarity grew stronger among free blacks in the 1850s, and after the Civil War, the leaders of the freed slaves were usually blacks who had been free before the war.

## Slave Resistance

The Old South was a seedbed of organized slave insurrections. In the delta areas of the Lower South, where blacks outnumbered whites, slaves experienced continuous forced labor on plantations and communicated their bitterness to each other in the slave quarters. Free blacks in the cities could have provided leadership for

**St. Catherine's Island, Georgia, Slave Quarters**
*Judged by their whitewashed exteriors, these slave cabins attached to a large cotton plantation belonged to the better class of slave housing, which did not differ much from the accommodations available to the white working class. Southern agricultural periodicals advised the regular white-washing of slave cabins as a health measure. But the quality of slave cabins varied and most fell below this standard.*

rebellions. Rumors of slave conspiracies flew around the southern white community, and all whites shuddered over the massive black insurrection that had destroyed French rule in Santo Domingo.

Yet Nat Turner's 1831 insurrection in Virginia (see chapter opening) was the only slave rebellion that resulted in the deaths of whites. A larger but more obscure uprising occurred in Louisiana in 1811, when some two hundred slaves sought to march on New Orleans. Other, better known, slave insurrections were merely conspiracies that never materialized. In 1800 Virginia slave Gabriel Prosser's planned slave uprising was betrayed by other slaves, and Gabriel and his followers were executed. That same year, a South Carolina slave, Denmark Vesey, won fifteen hundred dollars in a lottery and bought his freedom. Purchasing a carpentry shop in Charleston and becoming a preacher at that city's African Methodist Episcopal Church, Vesey built a cadre of black followers, including a slave of the governor of South Carolina and a black conjurer named Gullah Jack. In 1822 they devised a plan to attack Charleston and seize all the city's arms and ammunition, but other slaves informed authorities and the conspirators were executed.

For several reasons, the Old South experienced far fewer rebellions than the Caribbean region or South America. First, although slaves formed a majority in South Carolina and a few other states, they did not constitute a *large* majority in any state. Second, in contrast to the Caribbean, an area of absentee landlords and sparse white population, the white presence in the Old South was formidable, and the whites had all the guns and soldiers. The rumors of slave conspiracies that periodically swept the white South demonstrated to blacks the promptness with which whites could muster forces and mount slave patrols. Third, the development of family ties among slaves made them reluctant to risk death and leave their children parentless. Finally, blacks who ran away or plotted rebellions had no allies. Southern Indians routinely captured runaway slaves and exchanged them for rewards; some Indians even owned slaves.

Short of rebellion, slaves could try to escape to freedom in the North. Perhaps the most ingenious, Henry Brown, induced a friend to ship him from Richmond to Philadelphia in a box and won immediate fame as "Box" Brown. Some light mulattoes passed as whites. More often, fugitive slaves borrowed, stole, or forged passes from plantations or obtained papers describing themselves as free. Frederick Douglass borrowed a sailor's papers in making his escape from Baltimore to New York City in 1838. Some former slaves, among them Harriet Tubman and Josiah Henson, made repeated trips back to the South to help other slaves escape. These sundry methods of escape fed the legend of the "Underground Railroad," supposedly an organized network of safe houses owned by white abolitionists who spirited blacks to freedom. In reality, fugitive slaves owed very little to abolitionists. Some white sympathizers in border states did provide safe houses for blacks, but these houses were better known to watchful slave catchers than to most blacks.

Escape to freedom was a dream rather than an alternative for most blacks; out of millions of slaves, probably fewer than a thousand escaped to the North. Yet slaves often ran away from masters, not to escape to freedom but to visit spouses or avoid punishment. Most runaways remained in the South; indeed, some returned to former, kinder masters. During the eighteenth century, African slaves had often run away in groups to the interior and sought to create self-sufficient colonies or villages of the sort that they had known in Africa. But once the United States had acquired Florida, long a haven for runaways, few uninhabited places remained in the South to which slaves could flee.

Despite poor prospects for permanent escape, slaves could disappear for prolonged periods into the free-black communities of southern cities. Because whites in the Old South depended so heavily on black labor, slaves enjoyed a fair degree of practical freedom to drive wagons to market and to come and go when they were off plantations. Slaves hired out or sent to a city might overstay their leave and even pass themselves off as free. The experience of slavery has sometimes been compared to the experience of prisoners in penitentiaries or on chain gangs, but the analogy is misleading. The supervision that slaves experienced was sometimes intense (for example, when working at harvest time under a driver), but often lax; it was irregular rather than consistent.

The fact that antebellum slaves frequently enjoyed some degree of practical freedom did not change the underlying oppressiveness of slavery. But it did give slaves a sense that they had certain rights on a day-to-day basis, and it helped to deflect slave resistance into forms that were essentially furtive rather than open and violent. Theft was so common that planters learned to keep their tools, smokehouses, closets, and trunks under lock and key. Overworked field hands might leave valuable tools out to rust, or feign illness, or simply refuse to work. As an institution, slavery was vulnerable to such tactics; unlike free laborers, slaves could not be fired for negligence or malingering. Frederick Law

Olmsted found slaveholders in the 1850s afraid to inflict punishment on slaves "lest the slave should abscond, or take a sulky fit and not work, or poison some of the family, or set fire to the dwelling, or have recourse to any other mode of avenging himself."

Olmsted's reference to arson and poisoning reminds us that not all furtive resistance was peaceful. Arson and poisoning, both common in African culture as forms of vengeance, were widespread in the Old South, and the fear of each was even more so. Masters afflicted by dysentery and similar ailments never knew for sure that they had not been poisoned.

Arson, poisoning, work stoppages, and negligence were alternatives to violent rebellion. Yet these furtive forms of resistance differed from rebellion. The goal of rebellion was freedom from slavery. The goal of furtive resistance was to make slavery bearable. The kind of resistance that slaves usually practiced sought to establish customs and rules that would govern the conduct of masters as well as that of slaves without challenging the institution of slavery as such. Most slaves would have preferred freedom but settled for less. "White folks do as they please," an ex-slave said, "and the darkies do as they can."

# The Emergence of African-American Culture

A distinctive culture emerged among blacks in the slave quarters of antebellum plantations. This culture drew on both African and American sources, but it was more than a mixture of the two. Enslaved blacks gave a distinctive twist to the American as well as African components of their culture.

## *The Language of Slaves*

Before slaves could develop a common culture, they had to be able to communicate with one another. During the colonial period, verbal communication among slaves had often been difficult, for most slaves had been born in Africa, which contained an abundance of cultures and languages. The captain of a slave ship noted in 1744,

> As for the languages of *Gambia* [in West Africa], they are so many and so different that the Natives on either Side of the River cannot understand each other; which, if rightly consider'd, is no small happiness to the *Europeans* who go thither to trade for slaves.

In the pens into which they were herded before shipment and on the slave ships themselves, however, Africans developed a "pidgin"—that is, a language that has no native speakers but in which people with different native languages can communicate. Pidgin is not unique to black people. When Tarzan announced, "Me Tarzan, you Jane," he was speaking English pidgin. Nor is English pidgin the only form of pidgin; slaves that were sent to South America developed Spanish and Portuguese pidgins.

Many of the early African-born slaves learned English pidgin poorly or not at all, but as American-born slaves came to comprise an increasingly large proportion of all slaves, English pidgin took root. Indeed, it became the only language most slaves knew. Like all pidgins, this was a simplified language. Slaves usually dropped the verb *to be* (which had no equivalent in African tongues) and either ignored or confused genders. Instead of saying "Mary is in the cabin," they said, "Mary, he in cabin." To negate, they substituted *no* for *not,* saying, "He no wicked." English pidgin contained several African words. Some, like *banjo,* became part of standard English; others, like *goober* (peanut), became part of southern white slang. Although they picked up pidgin terms, whites ridiculed field hands' speech. Some slaves, particularly house servants and skilled artisans, learned to speak standard English but had no trouble understanding the pidgin of field hands. However strange pidgin sounded to some, it was indispensable for communication among slaves.

### African-American Religion

The development of a common language marked the first step in the forging of African-American culture. No less important was the religion of the slaves.

Africa was home to rich and diverse religious customs and beliefs. Some of the early slaves were Muslims; a few had acquired Christian beliefs either in Africa or in the New World. But the majority of the slaves transported from Africa were neither Muslims nor Christians but rather worshipers in one of many native African religions. Most of these religions, which whites lumped together as heathen, drew little distinction between the spiritual and the material worlds. Any event or development, from a storm to an earthquake or an illness, was assumed to stem from supernatural forces. These forces were represented by God, by spirits that inhabited the woods and waters, and by the spirits of ancestors. In addition, the religions of West Africa,

the region from which most American slaves originally came, attached special significance to water, which symbolized life and hope.

The majority of the slaves brought to America in the seventeenth and eighteenth centuries were young men who may not have absorbed much of this religious heritage before their enslavement. In any case, Africans differed from each other in their specific beliefs and practices. For these reasons, African religions could never have unified blacks in America. Yet some Africans probably clung to their beliefs during the seventeenth and eighteenth centuries, a tendency made easier by the fact that whites undertook few efforts before the 1790s to convert slaves to Christianity. Furthermore, dimly remembered African beliefs such as the reverence for water may have predisposed slaves to accept Christianity when they were finally urged to do so, because water had a symbolic significance for Christians, too, in the sacrament of baptism. The Christianity preached to slaves by Methodist and Baptist revivalists during the late eighteenth and nineteenth centuries, moreover, resembled African religions in that Christianity also drew few distinctions between the sacred and the secular. Just as Africans believed that a crop-destroying drought or a plague resulted from supernatural forces, the early revivalists knew in their hearts that every drunkard who fell off his horse and every Sabbath-breaker struck by lightning had experienced a deliberate and direct punishment from God.

**Reed Basket, 1860**
*A Florida slave artisan used traditional African skills in making this basket.*

By the 1790s blacks formed about a quarter of the membership of the Methodist and Baptist denominations. Yet masters continued to fear that a Christianized slave would be a rebellious slave. Converted slaves in fact played a significant role in each of the three major slave rebellions in the Old South. The leaders of Gabriel's rebellion in 1800 used the Bible to prove that slaves, like the ancient Israelites, could prevail against overwhelming numbers. Denmark Vesey read the Bible, and most of the slaves executed for joining his conspiracy belonged to Charleston's African Methodist Church. Nat Turner was both a preacher and a prophet.

Despite the "subversive" impact of Christianity on some slaves, however, these uprisings, particularly the Nat Turner rebellion, actually stimulated Protestant missionaries to intensify their efforts to convert slaves. Missionaries pointed to the self-taught Turner to prove that slaves would hear about Christianity in any event and that organized efforts to convert blacks were the only way to ensure that slaves learned correct versions of Christianity, which emphasized obedience rather than insurgence. Georgia missionary and slaveholder Charles Colcock Jones reassuringly told white planters of the venerable black preacher who, upon receiving some abolitionist tracts in the mail, promptly turned them over to the white authorities for destruction. A Christian slave, the argument ran, would be a better slave rather than a bitter slave. For whites, the clincher was the split of the Methodists, Baptists, and Presbyterians into northern and southern wings by the mid-1840s. Now, they argued, it had finally become safe to convert slaves, for the churches had rid themselves of their antislavery wings. Between 1845 and 1860, the number of black Baptists doubled.

The experiences of Christianized blacks in the Old South illustrate many of the contradictions of life under slavery. Urban blacks often had their own churches, but in the rural South, where the great majority of blacks lived, slaves worshiped in the same churches as whites. Although the slaves sat in segregated sections, they heard the same sermons and sang the same hymns as whites. Some black preachers actually developed followings among whites, and Christian masters were sometimes rebuked by biracial churches for abusing Christian slaves in the same congregation. The churches were, in fact, the most interracial institutions in the Old South. Yet none of this meant that Christianity was an acceptable route to black liberation. Ministers went out of their way to remind slaves that spiritual equality was not the same as civil equality. The effort to convert slaves gained momentum only to the extent that it was becoming certain that Christianity would not change the basic inequality of southern society.

Although they listened to the same sermons as whites, slaves did not necessarily draw the same conclusions. It was impossible to Christianize the slaves without telling them about the Chosen People, the ancient Jews whom Moses led from captivity in Pharaoh's Egypt into the Promised Land of Israel. Inevitably, slaves drew parallels between their own condition and the Jews' captivity. Like the Jews, blacks concluded, they themselves were "de people of de Lord." If they kept the faith, then, like the Jews, they too would reach the Promised Land. The themes of the Chosen People and the Promised Land ran through the sacred songs, or "spirituals," that blacks sang, to the point where Moses and Jesus almost merged:

> Gwine to write to Massa Jesus,
> To send some Valiant Soldier
> To turn back Pharaoh's army, Hallelu!

A listener could interpret a phrase like "the Promised Land" in several ways; it could refer to Israel, to heaven, or to freedom. From the perspective of whites, the only permissible interpretations were Israel and heaven, but some blacks, like Denmark Vesey, thought of freedom as well. The ease with which slaves constructed alternative interpretations of the Bible also reflected the fact that many plantations contained black preachers, slaves trained by white ministers to spread Christianity among blacks. When in the presence of masters or white ministers, these black preachers usually just repeated the familiar biblical command, "Obey your master." Often, however, slaves met for services apart from whites, usually on Sunday evenings but during the week as well. Then the message changed. A black preacher in Texas related how his master would say "tell them niggers iffen they obeys the master they goes to Heaven." The minister quickly added, "I knowed there's something better for them, but I daren't tell them 'cept on the sly. That I done lots. I tells 'em iffen they keep praying, the Lord will set 'em free."

Some slaves privately interpreted Christianity as a religion of liberation from the oppression of slavery, but most recognized that their prospects for freedom were slight. On the whole, Christianity did not turn them into revolutionaries. Neither did it necessarily turn them into model slaves. It did, however, provide slaves with a

**Mary Edmonia Lewis and "Forever Free"**
*Named Wildfire by her Chippewa mother and black father, Mary Edmonia Lewis adopted a Christian name upon entering Oberlin College. Later she studied sculpture in Boston and Rome. Her "Forever Free" (1867) commemorated the abolition of slavery.*

view of slavery different from their masters' outlook. Where the masters argued that slavery was a benign and divinely ordained institution in blacks' best interests, Christianity told them that slavery was really an affliction, a terrible and unjust institution that God had allowed in order to test their faith. For having endured slavery, he would reward blacks. For having created it, he would punish masters.

### Black Music and Dance

Compared to the prevailing cultural patterns among elite whites, the culture of blacks in the Old South was extremely expressive. In religious services, blacks shouted "Amen" and let their bodily movements reflect their feelings long after white religious observances, some of which had once been similarly expressive, had grown sober and sedate. Frederick Law Olmsted recorded how, during a slave service in New Orleans during the 1850s, parishioners "in indescribable expression of ecstasy" exclaimed every few moments: "Glory! oh yes! yes!—sweet Lord! sweet Lord!"

Slaves also expressed their feelings in music and dance. Drawing on their African musical heritage, which used hand clapping to mark rhythm, American slaves made rhythmical hand clapping—called patting

juba—an indispensable accompaniment to dancing, because southern law forbade them to own "drums, horns, or other loud instruments, which may call together or give sign or notice to one another of their wicked designs and intentions." Slaves also played an African instrument, the banjo, and beat tin buckets as a substitute for drums. Whatever instrument they played, their music was tied to bodily movement. Sometimes slaves imitated white dances like the minuet, but in a way that ridiculed the high manners of their masters. More often, they expressed themselves in a dance African in origin, emphasizing shuffling steps and bodily contortions rather than the erect precision of whites' dances.

Whether at work or at prayer, slaves liked to sing. Work songs describing slave experiences usually consisted of a leader's chant and a choral response:

> I love old Virginny
> So ho! boys! so ho!
> I love to shuck corn
> So ho! boys! so ho!
> Now's picking cotton time
> So ho! boys! so ho!

Masters encouraged such songs, believing that singing induced the slaves to work harder and that the innocent content of most work songs proved that the slaves were happy. Recalling his own past, Frederick Douglass came closer to the truth when he observed that "slaves sing most when they are most unhappy. The songs of the slave represent the sorrows of his heart; and he is relieved by them, only as an aching heart is relieved by its tears."

Blacks also sang religious songs, later known as spirituals. The origin of spirituals is shrouded in obscurity, but it is clear that by 1820 blacks at camp meetings had improvised what one white described as "short scraps of disjointed affirmations, pledges, or prayers lengthened out with long repetition choruses." As this description suggests, whites usually took a dim view of spirituals and tried to make slaves sing "good psalms and hymns" instead of "the extravagant and nonsensical chants, and catches, and hallelujah songs of their own composing." Indeed, when around whites, blacks often sang hymns like those of Isaac Watts and other great white evangelicals, but nothing could dampen slaves' enthusiasm for songs of their own making.

Spirituals reflected the potent emphasis that the slaves' religion put on deliverance from earthly travails. To a degree, the same was true of white hymns, but spirituals were more direct and concrete. Slaves sang, for example,

> In that morning, true believers,
>    In that morning,
> We will sit aside of Jesus
>    In that morning,
> If you should go fore I go,
>    In that morning,
> You will sit aside of Jesus
>    In that morning,
> True believers, where your tickets
>    In that morning,
> Master Jesus got your tickets
>    In that morning.

Another spiritual proclaimed, "We will soon be free, when the Lord will call us home."

## CONCLUSION

Slavery gave a distinctive unity to the Old South. Although most whites did not own any slaves, all concluded that their region's prosperity, their ascendancy over blacks, perhaps even their safety, depended on

perpetuating slavery. Slavery also shaped the North's perception of the South. Whether or not northerners believed that the federal government should tamper with slavery, they grew convinced that slavery had cut the South off from progress and had turned it into a region of "sterile lands and bankrupt estates."

Conversely, to most white southerners, the North, and especially the industrial Northeast, appeared as the region that deviated from the march of progress. In their eyes, most Americans—indeed, most people throughout the world—practiced agriculture and agriculture rendered the South a more comfortable place than factories rendered the North. In reaction to northern assaults on slavery, southerners portrayed the institution as a time-honored and benevolent response to the natural inequality of the black and white races. Southerners pointed to the slaves' adequate nutrition, their embrace of Christianity, the affection of some slaves for their masters, and even their work songs as evidence of the slaves' contentment.

These white perceptions of the culture that developed in the slave quarters were misguided. In reality, few if any slaves accepted slavery. Although slaves rebelled infrequently and had little chance for permanent escape, they often engaged in covert resistance to their bondage. The slaves embraced Christianity, but they understood it differently from whites. Whereas whites heard in the Christian gospel the need to make slaves submissive, slaves learned of the gross injustice of human bondage, and the promise of eventual deliverance.

## FOR FURTHER READING

Orville Vernon Burton, *In My Father's House Are Many Mansions: Family and Community in Edgefield, South Carolina* (1985). An extremely valuable study of the South Carolina upcountry.

Wilbur J. Cash, *The Mind of the South* (1941). A brilliant interpretation of southern history.

Bruce Collins, *White Society in the Antebellum South* (1985). A very good, brief synthesis of southern white society and culture.

William J. Cooper, *Liberty and Slavery: Southern Politics to 1860* (1983). A valuable synthesis and interpretation of recent scholarship on the antebellum South in national politics.

Clement Eaton, *The Growth of Southern Civilization, 1790–1860* (1961). A fine survey of social, economic, and political change.

Robert W. Fogel, *Without Consent or Contract: The Rise and Fall of American Slavery* (1989). A comprehensive reexamination of the slaves' productivity and welfare.

Robert W. Fogel and Stanley L. Engerman, *Time on the Cross: The Economics of American Negro Slavery* (1974). A controversial book that uses mathematical models to analyze the profitability of slavery.

Eugene D. Genovese, *Roll, Jordan, Roll: The World the Slaves Made* (1974). The most influential work on slavery in the Old South written during the last thirty years; a penetrating analysis of the paternalistic relationship between masters and their slaves.

Christine Leigh Heyrman, *Southern Cross: The Beginnings of the Bible Belt* (1997). An intriguing new account of southern religious culture.

Peter Kolchin, American Slavery, 1619–1877 (1993). A valuable summary of recent scholarship.

James Oakes, *The Ruling Race: A History of American Slaveholders* (1982). An important attack on the ideas of Eugene D. Genovese.

U. B. Phillips, *American Negro Slavery* (1918) and *Life and Labor in the Old South* (1929). Works marred by racial prejudice but containing a wealth of information about slavery and the plantation system.

Kenneth M. Stampp, *The Peculiar Institution: Slavery in the Ante-Bellum South* (1956). A standard account of the black experience under slavery.

# 13

# Immigration, Expansion, and Sectional Conflict 1840–1848

**Miners in the Sierras,** by Carles Christian Nahl, 1851–1852

In the year 1846 Americans seemed everywhere to be on the move, tiny restless dots representing the spirit that a journalist labeled their "Manifest Destiny" to spread over the whole continent. In Springfield, Illinois, hard times prompted three families, those of the brothers George and Jacob Donner and that of James Reed, a wealthy cabinetmaker, to embark for California in April 1846. Thus was born the ill-fated Donner party, which, with the addition of several new families, soon swelled to eighty-seven men, women, and children, along with wagons, mules, cattle, and oxen.

The Donner party knew that California was still part of Mexico and that the Sierra Nevada mountains, which run in a forbidding wall most of the length of California's eastern border, had induced most westward emigrants to head farther north, toward Oregon. But reports of California's mild climate made an impact on the aging Donner brothers, both in their sixties, and on Margaret, James Reed's ailing wife. All knew that war with Mexico was impending and each expected an American victory, which would add California to the eagle's growing nest.

When the emigrants pushed off for California, they thought that their main problem would be the Indians. In reality, their nemesis turned out to be one Lansford Hastings, the author of a recent guide book for emigrants. Hastings was a plausible fellow who reported, accurately, that a pass through the Sierra Nevada had been discovered. What he did not report was that crossing the pass required unloading each wagon and lugging every item, and then each wagon, through it. Nor did he reveal his own motive in encouraging California's settlement: he wanted to populate California with Americans, then engineer a revolt against Mexico and establish himself as California's leader.

The Donner party's troubles began in August, when it followed a Hastings-advised route through the Wasatch range of the Rockies that took a month instead of the promised week. Now, exhausted and behind schedule, the party struggled across the Great Salt Desert (whose size Hastings had underestimated), losing cattle and oxen to thirst-inspired stampedes. In October, blistering heat gave way to blizzards that forced the party into winter camp in the snowbound Sierras. Starvation was now added to exhaustion. The remaining cattle were slaughtered, their meat for food and their hides for shelter. Soon even the hides had to be eaten, and when the hides ran out, survivors took the most gruesome of all measures: eating their own dead.

The Donner brothers died, but forty-two members of the party survived, including James Reed and his twelve-year-old stepdaughter Virginia, who, along with her mother, almost succeeded in crossing the Sierra summit in the dead of winter to bring back food for the rest of the party. Virginia eventually made it through and lived to write magazine articles about the ordeal. In fact, she lived to age ninety-eight. By the time of her death in 1931, highways were making the western mountains a tourist attraction and the Donner tragedy was remembered mainly by haunting place names: Donner Lake, Donner Pass, Donner Summit.

Inasmuch as Hastings had never actually taken the route he told the Donner party to follow, no one will ever know whether he was a fraud or just an optimist inclined to wishful thinking. If the latter, he had plenty of company. "Americans regard this continent as their birthright," thundered Sam Houston, the first president of the Republic of Texas, in 1847. Indians and Mexicans had to make way for "our mighty march." This was not idle talk. In less than a thousand fevered days during President James K. Polk's administration (1845–1849), the United States increased its land area by 50 percent. It annexed Texas, negotiated Britain out of half of the vast Oregon territory, and fought a war with Mexico that led to the annexation of California and New Mexico. Meanwhile, immigrants poured into the United States, mainly from Europe. The number of immigrants during the 1840s and 1850s exceeded the nation's entire population in 1790.

Immigration and territorial expansion were linked. Most immigrants gravitated to the expansionist Democratic party, and the immigrant vote helped to tip the election of 1844 to Polk, an ardent expansionist. Further, waves of immigrants caused tensions, reflected in ugly outbursts of anti-immigrant feeling, between immigrants and the native-born. Influential Democrats concluded that the best solution to the intensifying class and ethnic conflicts lay in expanding the national boundaries, bringing more land under cultivation, and recapturing the ideal of America as a nation of self-sufficient farmers.

Democrats also saw expansion as a way to reduce strife between the sections: Oregon would gratify the North; Texas, the South; and California, everyone. In reality, expansion brought sectional antagonisms to the boiling point, split the Democratic party in the late 1840s, and set the nation on the path to Civil War.

This chapter focuses on three major questions:

♦ Why did the Whig party, which had won a thumping victory in 1840, suffer a reversal of fortunes in the next four years?

♦ Why was the annexation of Texas so critical an issue? How did the Democrats "sell" Texas annexation to the North in the election of 1844? Why were the results of that election so important?

♦ How did the outcome of the Mexican War intensify intersectional conflict? Why, specifically, did it split the Democratic party?

## Newcomers and Natives

Between 1815 and 1860, 5 million European immigrants landed in the United States. Of these, 4.2 million arrived between 1840 and 1860; 3 million of them came in the single decade from 1845 to 1854. This ten-year period witnessed the largest immigration propor-

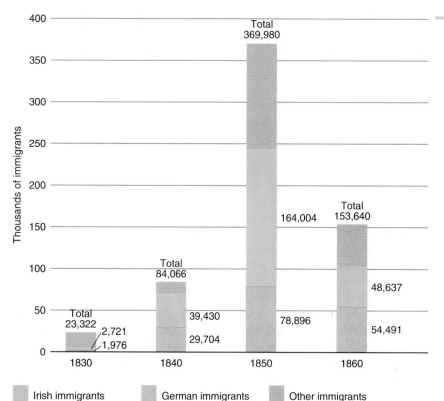

**German, Irish, and Total Immigration, 1830–1860**
*Irish and German immigrants led the more than tenfold growth of immigration between 1830 and 1860.*

(Source: U.S. Bureau of the Census, *Historical Statistics of the United States, Colonial Times to 1970,* Bicentennial Edition (Washington, D.C., 1975).)

## CHRONOLOGY

**1818** The United States and Britain agree on joint occupation of Oregon for a ten-year period.

**1819** Transcontinental (Adams-Onís) Treaty.

**1821** Mexico gains independence from Spain.

**1822** Stephen F. Austin founds the first American community in Texas.

**1824–1825** Russia abandons its claims to Oregon south of 54°40′.

**1826** Haden Edwards leads an abortive rebellion against Mexican rule in Texas.

**1827** The United States and Britain renew their agreement on joint occupation of Oregon for an indefinite period.

**1830** Mexico closes Texas to further American immigration.

**1834** Antonio López de Santa Anna comes to power in Mexico.

Austin secures repeal of the ban on American immigration into Texas.

**1835** Santa Anna invades Texas.

**1836** Texas declares its independence from Mexico.

Fall of the Alamo.

Goliad massacre.

Battle of San Jacinto.

**1840** William Henry Harrison elected president.

**1841** Harrison dies; John Tyler becomes president.

Tyler vetoes Whig National Banking Bill.

**1842** Whigs abandon distribution.

Webster-Ashburton Treaty.

**1843** Tyler launches campaign for Texas annexation.

**1844** Philadelphia Bible Riots.

Senate rejects treaty annexing Texas.

James K. Polk elected president.

**1845** Congress votes joint resolution to annex Texas.

Texas accepts annexation by the United States.

Mexico rejects Slidell mission.

**1846** Congress ends the joint occupation of Oregon.

Zachary Taylor defeats the Mexicans in two battles north of the Rio Grande.

The United States declares war on Mexico.

John C. Frémont proclaims the Bear Flag Republic in California.

Congress votes to accept a settlement of the Oregon boundary issue with Britain.

Tariff of 1846.

Colonel Stephen Kearny occupies Santa Fe.

Wilmot Proviso introduced.

Taylor takes Monterrey.

**1847** Taylor defeats Santa Anna at the Battle of Buena Vista.

Vera Cruz falls to Winfield Scott.

Mexico City falls to Scott.

Lewis Cass's principle of "squatter sovereignty."

**1848** Gold discovered in California.

Treaty of Guadalupe Hidalgo signed.

Taylor elected president.

---

tionate to the total population (then around 20 million) in American history. The Irish led the way as a source of immigration between 1840 and 1860, with the Germans running a close second. Smaller contingents continued to immigrate to the United States from England, Scotland, and Wales, and a growing number came from Norway, Sweden, Switzerland, and Holland. But by 1860 three-fourths of the 4.1 million foreign-born Americans were either Irish or German.

### Expectations and Realities

A desire for religious freedom drew some immigrants to the United States. For example, when Mormon missionaries actively recruited converts in the slums of English factory towns, a number of English migrated to America. Many emigrants from Norway were Quakers fleeing persecution by the official Lutheran clergy. But a far larger number of Europeans sailed for America to better their economic condition. Their hope was fed by a continuous stream of travelers' accounts and letters from relatives describing America as a utopia for poor people. German peasants learned that they could purchase a large farm in America for the price of renting a small one in Germany. English men and women were told that enough good peaches and apples were left rotting in the orchards of Ohio to sink the British fleet.

Hoping for the best, emigrants often encountered the worst. Their problems began at ports of embarkation, where hucksters frequently sold them worthless tickets and where ships scheduled to leave in June might not sail until August. Countless emigrants spent precious savings in waterfront slums while awaiting departure. The ocean voyage itself proved terrifying;

many emigrants had never set foot on a ship. Most sailed on cargo ships as steerage passengers, where, for six weeks or more, they endured quarters almost as crowded as on slave ships.

For many emigrants, the greatest shock came when they landed. "The folks aboard ship formed great plans for their future, all of which vanished quickly after landing," wrote a young German from Frankfurt in 1840. Immigrants quickly discovered that farming in America was a perilous prospect at best. Aside from lacking the capital to start a farm, most immigrants had to confront the fact that farming in the United States bore little resemblance to farming in Europe. European farmers valued the associations of their communities. Their social and cultural lives revolved around villages that were fringed by the fields that they worked. In contrast, as many immigrants quickly learned, American farmers lived in relative isolation. They might belong to rural neighborhoods in which farmers on widely scattered plots of land met occasionally at revivals or militia musters. But they lacked the compact village life of European farmers, and they possessed an individualistic psychology that led them to speculate in land and to move frequently.

Despite the shocks and dislocations caused by migration, certain patterns emerged in the distribution of immigrants within the United States. Initially shaped by trade routes, these patterns were then perpetuated by custom. Most of the Irish settlers before 1840 departed from Liverpool on sailing ships that carried English manufactures to eastern Canada and New England in return for timber. On arrival in America, few of these Irish had the capital to become farmers, and hence they crowded into the urban areas of New England, New York, Pennsylvania, and New Jersey, where they could more easily find jobs. In contrast, German emigrants usually left from continental ports on ships engaged in the cotton trade with New Orleans. However, deterred from settling in the South by the presence of slavery, the oppressive climate, and the lack of economic opportunity, the Germans congregated in the upper Mississippi and Ohio valleys, especially in Illinois, Ohio, Wisconsin, and Missouri. Geographical concentration also characterized most of the smaller groups of immigrants. More than half of the Norwegian immigrants, for example, settled in Wisconsin, where they typically became farmers.

Immigrants were usually less likely to pursue agriculture in the New World than in Europe. Both the Germans and, to an even greater degree, the Irish tended to concentrate in cities. By 1860 these two groups formed more than 60 percent of the population of St. Louis; nearly half the population of New York City, Chicago, Cincinnati, Milwaukee, Detroit, and San Francisco; and well over a third that of New Orleans, Baltimore, and Boston. These fast-growing cities created an intense demand for the labor of people with strong backs and a willingness to work for low wages. Irish construction gangs built the houses, new streets, and aqueducts that were changing the face of urban America and dug the canals and railroads that threaded together the rapidly developing cities. A popular song recounted the fate of the thousands of Irishmen who died of cholera contracted during the building of a canal in New Orleans:

> Ten thousand Micks, they swung their picks,
>   To build the New Canal
> But the choleray was stronger 'n they.
>   An' twice it killed them awl.

The cities provided the sort of community life that seemed lacking in farming settlements. Immigrant societies like the Friendly Sons of St. Patrick took root in cities and combined with associations like the Hibernian Society for the Relief of Emigrants from Ireland to welcome the newcomers.

### The Germans

In the mid-nineteenth century, the Germans were an extremely diverse group. In 1860 Germany was not a nation-state like France or Britain, but a collection of principalities and small kingdoms. German immigrants thought of themselves as Bavarians, Westphalians, or Saxons rather than as Germans. Moreover, the German immigrants included Catholics, Protestants (usually Lutherans), and Jews as well as a sprinkling of freethinkers who denounced the ritual, clergy, and doctrines of all religions. Although few in number, these critics were vehement in their attacks on the established churches. A pious Milwaukee Lutheran complained in 1860 that he could not drink a glass of beer in a saloon "without being angered by anti-Christian remarks or raillery against preachers."

German immigrants came from a wide range of social classes and occupations. The majority had engaged in farming, but a sizable minority were professionals, artisans, and tradespeople. Heinrich Steinweg, an obscure piano maker from Lower Saxony, arrived in New York City in 1851, anglicized his name to Henry Steinway, and in 1853 opened the firm of Steinway and Sons,

**German Winter Gardens**
*A well-known beer hall on lower Manhattan's Bowery, the German Winter Gardens were famous for music and sociability.*

which quickly achieved international acclaim for the quality of its pianos. Levi Strauss, a Jewish tailor from Bavaria, migrated to the United States in 1847. Upon hearing of the discovery of gold in California in 1848, Strauss gathered rolls of cloth and sailed for San Francisco. When a miner told him of the need for durable work trousers, Strauss fashioned a pair of overalls from canvas. To meet a quickly skyrocketing demand, he opened a factory in San Francisco; his cheap overalls, later known as blue jeans or Levi's, made him rich and famous.

For all their differences, the Germans were bound together by their common language, which strongly induced recent immigrants to the United States to congregate in German neighborhoods. Even prosperous Germans bent on climbing the social ladder usually did so within their ethnic communities. Germans formed their own militia and fire companies, sponsored parochial schools in which German was the language of instruction, started German-language newspapers, and organized their own balls and singing groups. The range of voluntary associations among Germans was almost as broad as among native-born Americans.

Other factors beyond their common language brought unity to the German immigrants. Ironically, the Germans' diversity also promoted their solidarity. For example, because they were able to supply their own doctors, lawyers, teachers, journalists, merchants, artisans, and clergy, the Germans had little need to go outside their own neighborhoods. Moreover, economic self-sufficiency conspired with the strong bonds of their language to encourage a clannish psychology among the German immigrants. Although they admired the Germans' industriousness, native-born Americans resented their economic success and disdained their clannishness. German refugee Moritz Busch complained that "the great mass of Anglo-Americans" held the Germans in contempt. The Germans responded by becoming even more clannish. In turn, their psychological separateness made it difficult for the Germans to be as politically influential as the Irish immigrants.

### The Irish

Between 1815 and 1860, Irish immigration to the United States passed through several stages. Irish soldiers who fought against the United States in the War of 1812 had returned to their homeland with reports that America was a paradise filled with fertile land and abundant game, a place where "all a man wanted was a gun and sufficient ammunition to be able to live like a prince." Among the Irish who subsequently emigrated between 1815 and the mid-1820s, Protestant small landowners and tradespeople in search of better economic opportunity predominated.

From the mid-1820s to the mid-1840s, the character of Irish immigration to the United States gradually changed. Increasingly, the immigrants were Catholics drawn from the poorer classes, many of them tenant farmers whom Protestant landowners had evicted as "superfluous." Protestant or Catholic, rich or poor, 800,000 to a million Irish immigrants entered the United States between 1815 and 1844. Then, between 1845 and the early 1850s, a blight destroyed every harvest of Ireland's potatoes, virtually the only food of the peasantry, and spawned one of the most gruesome famines in history. The Great Famine inflicted indescribable suffering on the Irish peasantry and killed perhaps a million people. One landlord characterized the surviving tenants on his estate as no more than "famished and ghastly skeletons." To escape the ravages of famine, 1.8 million Irish migrated to the United States in the decade after 1845.

Overwhelmingly poor and Catholic, the Irish usually entered the work force at or near the bottom. The popular image of Paddy with his pickax and Bridget the maid contained a good deal of truth. Irish men in the cities dug cellars and often lived in them; outside the cities, they dug canals and railroad beds. Irish women often became domestic servants. Compared to other immigrant women, a high proportion of Irish women entered the work force, if not as maids then often as textile workers. By the 1840s Irish women were displacing native-born women in the textile mills of Lowell and Waltham. Poverty drove Irish women to work at early ages, and the outdoor, all-season work performed by their husbands turned many of them into working widows. Winifred Rooney became a nursemaid at the age of seven and an errand girl at eleven. She then learned needlework, a skill that helped her support her family after her husband's early death. The high proportion of employed Irish women reflected more than their poverty. Compared to the predominantly male German immigrants, more than half of the Irish immigrants were women, most of whom were single adults. In both Ireland and America, the Irish usually married late, and many never married. For Irish women to become self-supporting was only natural.

The lot of most Irish people was harsh. One immigrant described the life of the average Irish laborer in America as "despicable, humiliating, [and] slavish"; there was "no love for him—no protection of life—[he] can be shot down, run through, kicked, cuffed, spat upon—and no redress, but a response of 'served the damn son of an Irish b____ right, damn him.'" Yet some Irish struggled up the social ladder. In Philadelphia, which had a more varied industrial base than Boston, Irish men made their way into iron foundries, where some became foremen and supervisors. Other Irish rose into the middle class by opening grocery and liquor stores.

The varied occupations pursued by Irish immigrants brought them into conflict with two quite differ-

**The Bay and Harbor of New York,** by Samuel Waugh, c. 1855
*Smaller than Philadelphia in the eighteenth century, New York City became the leading import depot first for goods, and then for people. Between 1820 and 1860 two-thirds of all immigrants to the United States landed here.*

ent groups. The poorer Irish who dug canals and cellars, hauled cargo on the docks, washed laundry for others, and served white families competed directly with equally poor free blacks. This competition stirred up Irish animosity toward blacks and a hatred of abolitionists. At the same time, enough Irish men eventually secured skilled or semiskilled jobs that clashes with native-born white workers became unavoidable.

## Anti-Catholicism, Nativism, and Labor Protest

The hostility of native-born whites toward the Irish often took the form of anti-Catholicism. Anti-Catholicism had been a strong, if latent, impulse among American Protestants since the early Puritan days. The surge of Irish immigration during the second quarter of the nineteenth century revived anti-Catholic fever. For example, in 1834 rumors circulated among Boston Protestants that a Catholic convent in nearby Charlestown contained dungeons and torture chambers. The mother superior turned away a delegation of officials demanding to inspect the convent. Soon the building lay in ashes, the victim of a Protestant mob. In 1835 Samuel F. B. Morse, the future inventor of the telegraph, warned that the despotic governments of Europe were systematically flooding the United States with Catholic immigrants as part of a conspiracy to destroy republican institutions. "We must first stop this leak in the ship," he wrote, "through which the muddy waters from without threaten to sink us." That same year, the combative evangelical Protestant Lyman Beecher issued *A Plea for the West*, a tract in which he warned faithful Protestants of an alleged Catholic conspiracy to send immigrants to the West in sufficient numbers to dominate the region. A year later, the publication of Maria Monk's best-selling *Awful Disclosures of the Hotel Dieu Nunnery in Montreal* rekindled anti-Catholic hysteria. Although Maria Monk was actually a prostitute who had never lived in a convent, she professed to be a former nun. In her book, she described how the mother superior forced nuns to submit to the lustful advances of priests who entered the convent by a subterranean passage.

As Catholic immigration swelled in the 1840s, Protestants mounted a political counterattack. It took the form of nativist (anti-immigrant) societies with names like the American Republicans and the United Order of Americans. Although usually started as secret or semisecret fraternal orders, most of these societies

developed political offshoots. One, the Order of the Star-Spangled Banner, would evolve by 1854 into the "Know-Nothing," or American, party and would become a major political force in the 1850s. During the 1840s, however, nativist parties enjoyed only brief moments in the sun. These occurred mainly during flare-ups over local issues, such as whether students in predominantly Catholic neighborhoods should be allowed to use the Catholic Douay rather than Protestant King James version of the Bible for the scriptural readings that began each school day. In 1844, for example, after the American Republican party (which opposed any concessions to Catholics) won some offices in Philadelphia elections, fiery Protestant orators mounted soapboxes to denounce "popery," and Protestant mobs descended on Catholic neighborhoods. Before the militia quelled these "Bible Riots," thirty buildings lay in charred ruins and at least sixteen people had been killed.

Nativism fed on an explosive mixture of fears and discontents. Protestants thought that their doctrine that each individual could interpret the Bible was more democratic than Catholicism, which made doctrine the province of the pope and bishops. In addition, at a time when the wages of native-born artisans and journeymen were being depressed by the subdivision of tasks and by the aftermath of the Panic of 1837 (see Chapter 10), many Protestant workers concluded that Catholic immigrants, often desperately poor and willing to work for anything, were threats to their jobs. In reaction, Protestant artisans joined nativist societies.

Nativist outbursts were not labor's only response to the wage cuts that accompanied the depression. Some agitators began to advocate land reform as a solution to workers' economic woes. Americans had long cherished the notion that a nation so blessed by abundant land as the United States need never give rise to a permanent class of factory "wage slaves." In 1844 the English-born radical George Henry Evans organized the National Reform Association and rallied supporters with the slogan "Vote Yourself a Farm." Evans advanced neo-Jeffersonian plans for the establishment of "rural republican townships," composed of 160-acre plots for workers. He quickly gained the backing of artisans who preferred such "agrarian" notions to a further advance of the industrial order that was undermining their position.

Land reformers argued that workers' true interests could never be reconciled with an industrial order in which factory operatives sold their labor for wages. By engaging in wage labor, they said, workers abandoned any hope of achieving economic independence. These reformers most appealed to articulate and self-consciously radical workers, particularly artisans and small masters whose independence was being threatened by factories and who feared that American labor was "fast verging on the servile dependence" common in Europe. But land reform offered little to factory operatives and wage-earning journeymen who completely lacked economic independence. In an age when a horse cost the average worker three months' pay and most factory workers dreaded "the horrors of wilderness life," the idea of solving industrial problems by resettling workers on farms seemed a pipe dream.

Labor unions appealed to workers left cold by the promises of land reformers. For example, desperately poor Irish immigrants, refugees from an agricultural society, believed that they could gain more by unions and strikes than by plowing and planting. Even women workers organized unions in these years; the leader of a seamstresses' union proclaimed, "Too long have we been bound down by tyrant employers."

Probably the most important development for workers in the 1840s was a state court decision. In *Commonwealth* v. *Hunt* (1842), the Massachusetts Supreme Court ruled that labor unions were not illegal monopolies that restrained trade. But because less than 1 percent of the work force belong to labor unions in the 1840s, this decision initially had little impact. Massachusetts employers brushed aside the *Commonwealth* decision, firing union agitators and replacing them with cheap immigrant labor. "Hundreds of honest laborers," a labor paper reported in 1848, "have been dismissed from employment in the manufactories of New England because they have been suspected of knowing their rights and daring to assert them." This repression effectively blunted demands for a ten-hour workday in an era when the twelve- or fourteen-hour day was typical.

Ethnic and religious tensions also split the antebellum working class during the 1830s and 1840s. Friction between native-born and immigrant workers inevitably became intertwined with the political divisions of the second party system.

### Labor Protest and Immigrant Politics

Very few immigrants had ever cast a vote in an election prior to their arrival in America, and only a small fraction were refugees from political persecution. Political upheavals had erupted in Austria and several of the German states in the turbulent year of 1848 (the so-called Revolutions of 1848), but among the million German immigrants to the United States, only about ten thousand were political refugees, or "Forty-Eighters."

Once they had settled in the United States, however, many immigrants became politically active. They quickly found that urban political organizations, some of them dominated by earlier immigrants, would help them to find lodging and employment—in return for votes. Both the Irish and the Germans identified overwhelmingly with the Democratic party. An obituary of 1837 that described a New Yorker as a "warm-hearted Irishman and an unflinching Democrat" could have been written of millions of other Irish. Similarly, the Germans became stalwart supporters of the Democrats in cities like Milwaukee and St. Louis.

Immigrants' fears about jobs partly explain their widespread Democratic support. Former president Andrew Jackson had given the Democratic party an anti-aristocratic coloration, making the Democrats seem more sympathetic than the Whigs to the common people. In addition, antislavery was linked to the Whig party, and the Irish loathed abolitionism because they feared that freed slaves would become their economic competitors. Moreover, the Whigs' moral and religious values seemed to threaten those of the Irish and Germans. Hearty-drinking Irish and German immigrants shunned temperance-crusading Whigs, many of whom were also rabid anti-Catholics. Even public-school reform, championed by the Whigs, was seen as a menace to the Catholicism of Irish children and as a threat to German language and culture.

Although liquor regulations and school laws were city or state concerns rather than federal responsibilities, the Democratic party schooled immigrants in broad, national principles. It taught them to venerate George Washington, to revere Thomas Jefferson and Andrew Jackson, and to view "monied capitalists" as parasites who would tremble when the people spoke. It introduced immigrants to Democratic newspapers, Democratic picnics, and Democratic parades. The Democrats, by identifying their party with all that they thought best about the United States, helped give immigrants a sense of themselves as Americans. By the same token, the Democratic party introduced immigrants to national issues. It redirected political loyalties that often had been forged on local issues into the arena of national politics. During the 1830s the party had persuaded immigrants that national measures like the Bank of the United States and the tariff, seemingly remote from their daily lives, were vital to them. Now during the 1840s, the Democrats would try to convince immigrants that national expansion likewise advanced their interests.

## The West and Beyond

As late as 1840, Americans who referred to the West still meant the area between the Appalachian Mountains and the Mississippi River or just beyond, a region that included much of the present-day Midwest. Beyond the states bordering the Mississippi lay an inhospitable region unlike any that the earlier settlers had ever known. Those who ventured west of Missouri encountered the Great Plains, a semiarid plateau with few trees. Winds sucked the moisture from the soil. Bands of nomadic Indians—including the Pawnees, Kiowas, and Sioux—roamed this territory and gained sustenance mainly from the buffalo. They ate its meat, wore its fur, and covered their dwellings with its hide. Aside from some well-watered sections of northern Missouri and eastern Kansas and Nebraska, the Great Plains presented would-be farmers with massive obstacles.

The formidable barrier of the Great Plains did not stop settlement of the West in the long run. Temporarily, however, it shifted public interest toward the verdant region lying beyond the Rockies, the Far West.

### *The Far West*

With the Transcontinental (or Adams-Onís) Treaty of 1819, the United States had given up to Spain its claims

### Trails to the West, 1840

*By 1840 several trails carried pioneers from Missouri and Illinois to the West.*

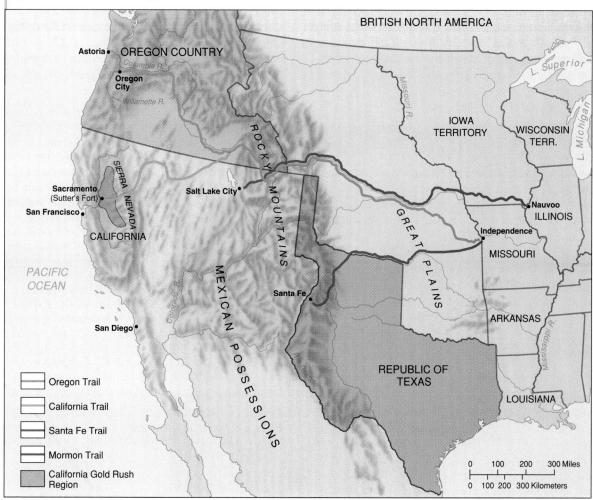

to Texas west of the Sabine River. This had left Spain in undisputed possession not only of Texas but also of California and the vast territory of New Mexico. Combined, California and New Mexico included all of present-day California and New Mexico as well as modern Nevada, Utah, and Arizona, and parts of Wyoming and Colorado. Two years later, a series of revolts against Spanish rule had culminated in the independence of Mexico and in Mexico's takeover of all North American territory previously claimed by Spain. The Transcontinental Treaty also had provided for Spain's ceding to the United States its claims to the country of Oregon north of the forty-second parallel (the northern boundary of California). Then in 1824 and 1825, Russia abandoned its claims to Oregon south of 54°40′ (the southern boundary of Alaska). In 1827 the United States and Britain, each of which had claims to Oregon based on discovery and exploration, revived an agreement (originally signed in 1818) for joint occupation of the territory between 42° and 54°40′, a colossal area that contemporaries could describe no more precisely than the "North West Coast of America, Westward of the Stony [Rocky] Mountains" and that included all of modern Oregon, Washington, and Idaho as well as parts of present-day Wyoming, Montana, and Canada.

Collectively, Texas, New Mexico, California, and Oregon comprised an area larger than Britain, France, and Germany combined. Such a vast region should have tempted any nation, but during the 1820s Mexico, Britain, and the United States viewed the Far West as a remote and shadowy frontier. By 1820 the American line of settlement had only reached Missouri, well over 2,000 miles (counting detours for mountains) from the West Coast. El Paso on the Rio Grande and Taos in New Mexico lay, respectively, 1,200 and 1,500 miles north of Mexico City. Britain, of course, was many thousands of miles from Oregon.

### Far Western Trade

The earliest American and British outposts on the West Coast were trading centers established by merchants who had reached California and Oregon by sailing around South America and up the Pacific. Between the late 1790s and the 1820s, for example, Boston merchants had built a thriving exchange of coffee, tea, spices, cutlery, clothes, and hardware—indeed, anything that could be bought or manufactured in the eastern United States—for furs (especially those of sea otters), cattle, hides, and tallow (rendered from cattle fat

**Mission San Gabriel,** by Ferdinand Deppe, 1832 *The San Gabriel Mission was founded in 1771 in southern California, partly with the intent of converting the local Indians, who are shown here settled in a thatched hut, to Catholicism. In 1781 the Spanish governor set out from this mission to found El Pueblo de Nuestra Señora la Reina de Los Angelos Porciúncula, now usually known simply as Los Angeles.*

and used for making soap and candles). Between 1826 and 1828 alone, Boston traders took more than 6 million cattle hides out of California; in the otherwise undeveloped California economy, these hides, called "California banknotes," served as the main medium of exchange. During the 1820s the British Hudson's Bay Company developed a similar trade in Oregon and northern California.

The California trade occasioned little friction with Mexico. Producing virtually no manufactured goods, Hispanic people born in California (called *californios*) were as eager to buy as the traders were to sell—so eager that they sometimes rowed out to the vessels laden with goods, thus sparing the traders the trip ashore. Those traders who did settle in California, like the American Thomas O. Larkin and the Swiss-born John Sutter, quickly learned to speak Spanish and became assimilated into Mexican culture.

Farther south, trading links developed during the 1820s between St. Louis and Santa Fe along the famed Santa Fe Trail. The Panic of 1819 left the American Midwest short of cash and its merchants burdened by unsold goods. Pulling themselves up from adversity, however, plucky midwesterners loaded wagon trains with tools, utensils, clothing, windowpanes, and household sundries each spring and rumbled westward to Santa Fe, where they traded their merchandise for mules and New Mexican silver. To a far greater extent than had Spain, Mexico welcomed this trade. Indeed, by the 1830s more than half the goods entering New Mexico by the Santa Fe Trail trickled into the mineral-rich interior provinces of Mexico such as Chihuahua and Sonora, with the result that the Mexican silver peso, which midwestern traders brought back with them, quickly became the principal medium of exchange in Missouri.

Some Americans ventured north from Santa Fe to trap beaver in what is today western Colorado and eastern Utah. The profitability of the beaver trade also encouraged merchants and trappers like the "mountain man" Jeddiah Smith (see Chapter 9) to venture directly from St. Louis into the Rockies in competition with both the Santa Fe traders and agents of the Hudson's Bay Company. On the Green River in Mexican territory, the St. Louis–based trader William Ashley in 1825 inaugurated an annual rendezvous or encampment where traders exchanged beaver pelts for supplies, thereby saving themselves the trip to St. Louis. With the aid of Ashley's encampments, the St. Louis traders gradually wrested the beaver trade from their competitors in Santa Fe.

For the most part, American traders and trappers operating on the northern Mexican frontier in the 1820s and 1830s posed more of a threat to the beaver than to Mexico's provinces. (If silk hats had not become fashionable in Europe in the mid-1830s, the beaver might have been hunted to extinction.) Not only did the Mexican people of California and New Mexico depend on the American trade for manufactured goods, but Mexican officials in both provinces relied on customs duties to support their governments. In New Mexico the government often had to await the arrival of the annual caravan of traders from St. Louis before it could pay its officials and soldiers.

Although the relations between Mexicans and Americans were mutually beneficial during the 1820s, the potential for conflict was never absent. Spanish-speaking, Roman Catholic, and accustomed to a more hierarchical society, the Mexicans formed a striking contrast to the largely Protestant, individualistic Americans. And although few American traders themselves became permanent residents of Mexico, many returned with glowing reports of the climate and fertility of Mexico's northern provinces. By the 1820s American settlers were already moving into eastern Texas. At the same time, the ties that bound the central government of Mexico to its northern frontier provinces were starting to fray.

## The American Settlement of Texas

During the 1820s Americans began to settle the eastern part of the Mexican state known as Coahuila-Texas, which lacked the deserts and mountains that formed a natural barrier along the boundaries of New Mexico and California. Initially, Mexico encouraged this migration, partly to gain protection against Indian attacks that had intensified with the erosion of the Spanish/Mexican system of missions.

Spain, and later Mexico, recognized that the key to controlling the frontier provinces lay in promoting their settlement by civilized Hispanic people—that is, by Spaniards and Mexicans, and by Indians who had embraced Catholicism and agriculture. The key instrument of Spanish expansion on the frontier had long been the mission. Staffed by Franciscan priests, the missions endeavored to convert Native Americans and settle them as farmers on mission lands. To protect the missions, the Spanish often had constructed forts, or *presidios,* near them. San Francisco was the site of a mission and a presidio founded in 1776, and did not develop as a town until the 1830s.

Dealt a blow by the successful struggle for Mexican independence, Spain's system of missions declined in the late 1820s and 1830s. The Mexican government gradually "secularized" the missions by distributing their lands to ambitious government officials and private ranchers who turned the mission Indians into forced laborers. As many Native Americans fled the missions, returned to their nomadic ways, and joined with Indians who had always resisted the missions, lawlessness surged on the Mexican frontier and few Mexicans ventured into the undeveloped territory.

In 1824 the Mexican government began to encourage American colonization of Texas by bestowing generous land grants on agents known as *empresarios* to recruit peaceful American settlers for Texas. Initially, most Americans, like the empresario Stephen F. Austin, were content to live in Texas as naturalized Mexican citizens. But trouble brewed quickly. Most of the American settlers were southern farmers, often slaveholders. Having emancipated its own slaves in 1829, Mexico in 1830 closed Texas to further American immigration and forbade the introduction of more slaves. But the Americans, white and black, kept coming, and in 1834 Austin secured repeal of the 1830 prohibition on American immigration. Two years later, Mexican general Manual Mier y Téran ran a sword through his heart in despair over Mexico's inability to stem and control the American advance. By 1836 Texas contained some 30,000 white Americans, 5,000 black slaves, and 4,000 Mexicans.

As American immigration swelled, Mexican politics (which Austin compared to the country's volcanic geology) grew increasingly unstable. In 1834 Mexican president Antonio López de Santa Anna instituted a policy of restricting the powers of the regimes in Coahuila-Texas and other Mexican states. His actions ignited a series of rebellions in those regions, the most important of which became known as the Texas Revolution.

### The Texas Revolution

Santa Anna's brutality in crushing most of the rebellions alarmed Austin and others. Austin initially had taken a moderate position. He hoped to cooperate with Mexican liberals to restore the Mexican Constitution of 1824 and to secure greater autonomy for Texas within Mexico. At the outset, he did not favor Texas's independence from Mexico. When Santa Anna invaded Texas in the fall of 1835, however, Austin cast his lot with the more radical Americans who wanted independence.

At first, Santa Anna's army met with success. In late February 1836, his force of 4,000 men laid siege to San Antonio, whose 200 Texan defenders retreated into an abandoned mission, the Alamo. After repelling repeated attacks and inflicting more than 1,500 casualties on Santa Anna's army, the remaining 187 Texans, including such famed frontiersmen as Davy Crockett and Jim Bowie, were wiped out to the last man on March 6. A few weeks later, Mexican troops massacred some 350 Texas prisoners at Goliad.

Even before these events, Texas delegates had met in a windswept shed in the village of Washington, Texas, and declared Texas independent of Mexico. The rebels by then had settled on a military leader, Sam Houston, for their president. A giant man who wore leopard-skin vests, Houston retreated east to pick up recruits (mostly Americans who crossed

**"Entirro de un Angel" (Funeral of an Angel),** by Theodore Gentilz
*Protestant Americans who ventured into Texas came upon a Hispanic culture unlike anything they had seen. Here a San Antonio procession follows the coffin of a baptized infant who, in Catholic belief, will become an angel in heaven.*

the border to fight Santa Anna). Once reinforced, Houston turned and surprised Santa Anna on a prairie near the San Jacinto River in April. Shouting "Remember the Alamo," Houston's army of eight hundred tore through the Mexican lines, killing nearly half of Santa Anna's men in fifteen minutes and taking Santa Anna himself prisoner. Houston then forced Santa Anna to sign a treaty (which the Mexican government never ratified) recognizing the independence of Texas.

## American Settlements in California, New Mexico, and Oregon

California and New Mexico, both less accessible than Texas, exerted no more than a mild attraction for American settlers during the 1820s and 1830s. Only a few hundred Americans resided in New Mexico in 1840; that same year, California contained perhaps four hundred Americans. A contemporary observed that the Americans living in California and New Mexico during these years "are scattered throughout the whole Mexican population, and most of them have Spanish wives. . . . They live in every respect like the Spanish."

Yet the beginnings of change were already evident. California's Hispanic population generally welcomed American immigration as a way to encourage economic development. In addition, some Americans who settled in California before 1840 sent back highly favorable reports of the region to induce immigration. One story, tongue-in-cheek, told of a 250-year-old man who had to leave the idyllic region in order, finally, to die. Such reports produced their intended effect. During the 1840s an ever-widening stream of Americans migrated to the interior Sacramento Valley, where they lived geographically and culturally apart from the Mexicans. For these land-hungry settlers, no sacrifice seemed too great if it led to California.

Oregon, with its abundant farmland, beckoned settlers from the Mississippi Valley. During the 1830s missionaries like the Methodist Jason Lee moved into Oregon's Willamette Valley, and by 1840 the area contained some five hundred Americans. Enthusiastic reports sent back by Lee piqued interest in Oregon. An orator in Missouri described Oregon as a "pioneer's paradise" where "the pigs are running around under the great acorn trees, round and fat and already cooked, with knives and forks sticking in them so that you can cut off a slice whenever you are hungry." Indeed, to some, Oregon seemed even more attractive than California. Oregon was already jointly occupied by Britain

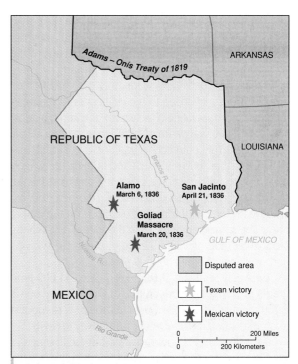

**Major Battles in the Texas Revolution, 1835–1836**
*Sam Houston's victory at San Jacinto was the decisive action of the war and avenged the massacres at the Alamo and Goliad.*

and the United States, and its prospects for eventual U.S. annexation appeared better than California's.

## The Overland Trail

Whether bound for California or Oregon, the pioneers faced a four-month journey across terrain that was all the more terrifying because little was known about it. The eastern press teemed with horror stories, mostly fictitious, of Indian massacres. Assuming that they would have to fight their way across the plains, settlers prepared for the trip by buying enough guns for an army from merchants in the rival jump-off towns of Independence and St. Joseph, Missouri. In reality, the pioneers were more likely to shoot themselves or each other by accident than to be shot by the usually cooperative Indians, and much more likely to be scalped by the inflated prices charged by merchants in Independence or "St. Joe" than by the Native Americans.

Once embarked, the emigrants faced new hardships and hazards: kicks from mules, oxen that collapsed from thirst, overloaded wagons that broke down. Trails were difficult to follow—at least until they became littered by the debris of broken wagons and by the bleached bones of oxen. As the Donner party's experience revealed, guidebooks were more like guessbooks.

Emigrants responded to the challenges of the overland trail by cooperating closely with one another. Most set out in huge wagon trains rather than as individuals. Reflecting firmly entrenched traditions, husbands depended on their wives to pack and unpack the wagon each day, to milk the cows brought along to stock the new farms in the West, and to cook. Women, too, assisted with the childbirths that occurred on the trail at about the same frequency as in the nation as a whole. Men yoked and unyoked the oxen, drove the wagons and stock, and formed hunting parties.

Between 1840 and 1848, an estimated 11,500 emigrants followed an overland trail to Oregon, and some 2,700 reached California. These numbers were modest and concentrated in the years from 1844 to 1848. Yet even small numbers could make a huge difference in the Far West, for the British could not effectively settle Oregon at all, and the Mexican population in California was small and scattered. By 1845 California clung to Mexico by the thinnest of threads. The territory's Hispanic population, the *californios*, felt little allegiance to Mexico, which they contemptuously referred to as the "other shore." Nor did they feel any allegiance to the United States. Some *californios* wanted independence from Mexico; others looked to the day when California might become a protectorate of Britain or perhaps even France. But these californios, with their shaky allegiances, now faced a growing number of American settlers whose political sympathies were not at all divided.

## The Politics of Expansion

The major issue that arose as a by-product of westward expansion was whether the United States should annex the independent Texas republic. In the mid-1840s the Texas-annexation issue generated the kind of political passions that banking questions had ignited in the 1830s, and became entangled with equally unsettling issues relating to California, New Mexico, and Oregon. Between 1846 and 1848, a war with Mexico and a dramatic confrontation with Britain settled all these questions on terms favorable to the United States.

Yet at the start of the 1840s, western issues occupied no more than a tenuous position on the national political agenda. From 1840 to 1842, questions relating to economic recovery—notably, banking, the tariff, and internal improvements—dominated the attention of political leaders. Only after politicians failed to address the economic issues coherently did opportunistic leaders thrust issues relating to expansion to the top of the political agenda.

### *The Whig Ascendancy*

The election of 1840 brought the Whig candidate William Henry Harrison to the presidency and installed Whig majorities in both houses of Congress. The Whigs had raced to power with a program, based on Henry Clay's American System, to stimulate economic recovery, and they had excellent prospects of success. They quickly repealed Van Buren's darling, the Independent Treasury. They then planned to substitute some kind of national "fiscal agent," which, like the defunct Bank of the United States, would be a private corporation chartered by Congress and charged with regulating the currency. The Whigs also favored a tariff, but with a twist. In the past, Whigs had supported a "protective" tariff, one set so high as to discourage the importation of goods that would compete with the products of American industries. Now the Whigs proposed a modification in the form of a "revenue" tariff, one high enough to provide "incidental" protection for

**Conestoga Wagon**
*Originating in southeastern Pennsylvania around 1750, drawn by four or six horses or mules, and distinguished by its slanting gates and its cloth cover supported by bows of bent wood, the Conestoga wagon served for a century as the ship of American inland commerce.*

American industries but low enough to allow most foreign products to enter the United States. The duties collected on these imports would accrue to the federal government as revenue. The Whigs then planned to distribute this revenue to the states for internal improvements, a measure as popular among southern and western Whigs as the tariff was among northeastern Whigs.

The Whig agenda might have breezed into law had it not been for the untimely death of Harrison after only one month in office. With Harrison's demise, Vice President John Tyler, an upper-crust Virginian who had been put on the ticket in 1840 to strengthen the Whigs' appeal in the South, assumed the presidency. From virtually every angle, the new president proved a disaster for the Whigs.

A former Democrat, Tyler had broken with Jackson over nullification, but he continued to favor the Democratic philosophy of states' rights. As president, he repeatedly used the veto to shred his new party's program. In August 1841 a Whig bill to create a new national bank became the first casualty of Tyler's veto. Stunned, the Whig majority in Congress quickly passed a modified banking bill, only to see Tyler veto it as well.

Congressional Whigs fared little better on the issues of the tariff and the distribution of tariff revenues to the states. The Compromise Tariff of 1833 had provided for a gradual scaling down of tariff duties, until none was to exceed 20 percent by 1842. Amid the depression of the early 1840s, however, the provision for a 20 percent maximum tariff appeared too low to generate revenue. Without revenue, the Whigs would have no money to distribute among the states for internal improvements and no program with national appeal. In response, the Whig congressional majority passed two bills in the summer of 1842 that simultaneously postponed the final reduction of tariffs to 20 percent and ordered distribution to the states to proceed. Tyler promptly vetoed both bills. Tyler's mounting vetoes infuriated the Whig leadership. "Again has the imbecile, into whose hands accident has placed the power, vetoed a bill passed by a majority of those legally authorized to pass it," screamed the *Daily Richmond Whig*. Some Whigs talked of impeaching Tyler. Finally, in August, Tyler, needing revenue to run the government, signed a new bill that maintained some tariffs above 20 percent but abandoned distribution to the states.

Tyler's erratic course confounded and disrupted his party. By maintaining some tariffs above 20 percent, the tariff of 1842 satisfied northern manufacturers, but by abandoning distribution, it infuriated many southerners

and westerners. Northern Whigs succeeded in passing the bill with the aid of many northern Democrats, particularly pro-tariff Pennsylvanians, whereas large numbers of Whigs in the Upper South and West opposed the tariff of 1842.

In the congressional elections of 1842, the Whigs paid a heavy price for failing to enact their program. Although retaining a slim majority in the Senate, they lost control of the House to the Democrats. Now the nation witnessed one party in control of the Senate, its rival in control of the House, and a president who appeared to belong to neither party.

### Tyler and the Annexation of Texas

Although a political maverick disowned by his party, Tyler ardently desired a second term as president. Domestic issues offered him little hope of building a popular following, but foreign policy was another matter. In 1842 Tyler's secretary of state, Daniel Webster, concluded a treaty with Great Britain, represented by Lord Ashburton, that settled a long-festering dispute over the boundary between Maine and the Canadian province of New Brunswick. Awarding more than half of the disputed territory to the United States, the Webster-Ashburton Treaty was popular in the North. Tyler reasoned that if he could now arrange for the annexation of Texas, he would build a national following.

The issue of slavery, however, had long clouded every discussion of Texas. By the late 1830s antislavery northerners viewed proposals to annex Texas as part of an elaborate southern conspiracy to extend American territory south into Mexico, Cuba, and Central America, thus allowing for an unlimited number of new slave states while the British presence in Canada would limit the number of free states. In fact, some southerners talked openly of creating as many as four or five slave states out of the vast territory encompassed by Texas.

Nevertheless, in the summer of 1843, Tyler launched a propaganda campaign for Texas annexation. He justified his crusade by reporting that he had learned of certain British designs on Texas, which Americans, he argued, would be prudent to forestall. Tyler's campaign was fed by reports from his unofficial agent in London, Duff Green, a protégé of John C. Calhoun and a man whom John Quincy Adams contemptuously dismissed as an "ambassador of slavery." Green assured Tyler that as a prelude to undermining slavery in the United States, the British would pressure Mexico to recognize the independence of Texas in return for the abolition of slavery there. Calhoun, who became Tyler's secretary of state early in 1844, embroidered these reports with fanciful theories of British plans to use abolition as a way to destroy rice, sugar, and cotton production in the United States and gain for itself a monopoly on all three staples.

In the spring of 1844, Calhoun and Tyler submitted to the Senate for ratification a treaty, secretly drawn up, annexing Texas to the United States. Among the supporting documents accompanying the treaty was a letter from Calhoun to Richard Pakenham, the British foreign minister in Washington, that defended slavery as beneficial to blacks, the only way to protect them from "vice and pauperism." Antislavery northerners no longer had to look under the carpet for evidence that the impulse behind annexation lay in a desire to protect and extend slavery; now they needed only to read Calhoun's words. Both Martin Van Buren, the leading northern Democrat, and Henry Clay, the most powerful Whig, came out against immediate annexation, on grounds that annexation would provoke the kind of sectional conflict that each had sought to bury. By a vote of 35 to 16, the treaty went down to crushing defeat in the Senate. Decisive as it appeared, however, this vote only postponed the final decision on annexation to the upcoming election of 1844.

## The Election of 1844

Tyler's ineptitude turned the presidential campaign into a free-for-all. The president hoped to succeed himself in the White House, but he lacked a base in either party. Testing the waters as an independent, he could not garner adequate support and was forced to drop out of the race.

Henry Clay had a secure grip on the Whig nomination. Martin Van Buren appeared to have an equally firm grasp on the Democratic nomination, but the issue of Texas annexation split his party. Trying to appease all shades of opinion within his party, Van Buren stated that he would abide by whatever Congress might decide on the annexation issue. Van Buren's attempt to evade the issue succeeded only in alienating the modest number of northern annexationists, led by Michigan's former governor Lewis Cass, and the much larger group of southern annexationists. At the Democratic convention, Van Buren and Cass effectively blocked each other's nomination. The resulting deadlock was broken by the nomination of James K. Polk of Tennessee, the first "dark-horse" presidential nominee in American history.

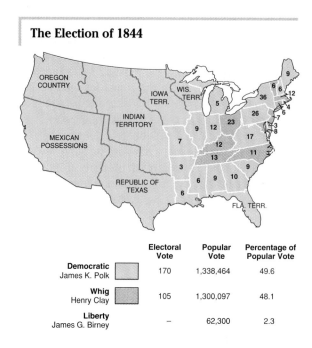

**The Election of 1844**

| | Electoral Vote | Popular Vote | Percentage of Popular Vote |
|---|---|---|---|
| **Democratic** James K. Polk | 170 | 1,338,464 | 49.6 |
| **Whig** Henry Clay | 105 | 1,300,097 | 48.1 |
| **Liberty** James G. Birney | – | 62,300 | 2.3 |

Although little known outside the South, the slaveholding Polk was the favorite of southern Democrats, who accurately described him as the "bosom friend of [Andrew] Jackson, and a pure whole-hogged Democrat, the known enemy of banks and distribution." On the Texas issue, Polk supported immediate "reannexation," a curious turn of phrase that reflected Andrew Jackson's belief that Texas had been part of the Louisiana Purchase until unwisely ceded to Spain by the Transcontinental Treaty of 1819. Indeed, Polk followed Old Hickory's lead so often that he became known as Young Hickory.

Jeering "Who is James K. Polk?" the Whigs derided the nomination. Polk himself marveled at his turn of fortune, for he had lost successive elections for the governorship of Tennessee. Yet Polk, a wily campaigner, persuaded many northerners that annexation of Texas would benefit them. Conjuring an imaginative scenario, Polk and his supporters argued that if Britain succeeded in abolitionizing Texas, slavery would not be able to move westward, racial tensions in existing slave states would intensify, and the chances of a race war, which might spill over into the North, would increase. However far-fetched, this argument played effectively on northern racial fears and helped Polk to detach annexation from Calhoun's narrow, prosouthern defense of it.

In contrast to the Democrats, who established a clear direction in their arguments, Clay kept muddying the waters. In the spring of 1844, he had opposed the annexation treaty. Then he sent conflicting messages to his followers throughout the summer of 1844, saying that he had nothing against annexation as long as it would not disrupt sectional harmony. Finally, in September 1844 he again came out against annexation. Clay's shifts on annexation alienated his southern supporters and prompted a small but influential body of northern antislavery Whigs to desert to the Liberty party, which had been organized in 1840. Devoted to the abolition of slavery by political action, the Liberty party nominated Ohio's James G. Birney for the presidency.

Annexation was not the sole issue of the campaign. The Whigs infuriated Catholic immigrant voters by nominating Theodore Frelinghuysen as Clay's running mate. A leading Presbyterian layman, Frelinghuysen gave "his head, his hand, and his heart" to temperance and an assortment of other Protestant causes. His presence on their ticket fixed the image of the Whigs as the orthodox Protestant party and roused the largely Catholic foreign-born voters to turn out in large numbers for the Democrats.

On the eve of the election in New York City, so many Irish marched to the courthouse to be qualified for voting that the windows had to be left open for people to get in and out. "Ireland has reconquered the country which England lost," an embittered Whig moaned. Polk won the electoral vote 170–105, but his margin in the popular vote was only 38,000 out of 2.6 million votes cast, and he lost his own state of Tennessee by 113 votes. In most states the two main parties contended with each other on close terms, a sign of the maturity of the second party system. A shift of 6,000 votes in New York, where the immigrant vote and Whig defections to the Liberty party hurt Clay, would have given Clay both the state and the presidency.

### Manifest Destiny

The election of 1844 demonstrated one incontestable fact: the annexation of Texas had more national support than Clay had realized. The surging popular sentiment for expansion that made the underdog Polk rather than Clay the man of the hour reflected a growing conviction among the people that America's natural destiny was to expand into Texas and all the way to the Pacific Ocean.

Expansionists emphasized extending the "area of freedom" and talked of "repelling the contaminating

proximity of monarchies upon the soil that we have consecrated to the rights of man." For contemporary young Americans like Walt Whitman, such restless expansionism knew few limits. "The more we reflect upon annexation as involving a part of Mexico, the more do doubts and obstacles resolve themselves away," Whitman wrote. "Then there is California, on the way to which lovely tract lies Santa Fe; how long a time will elapse before they shine as two new stars in our mighty firmament?"

Americans awaited only a phrase to capture this ebullient spirit of continentalism. In 1845 John L. O'Sullivan, a New York Democratic journalist, wrote of "our manifest destiny to overspread and to possess the whole of the continent which Providence has given us for the development of the great experiment of liberty and federated self-government entrusted to us."

Advocates of Manifest Destiny used lofty language and routinely invoked God and Nature to sanction expansion. Inasmuch as most proponents of Manifest Destiny were Democrats, many of whom supported the annexation of Texas, northern Whigs frequently dismissed Manifest Destiny as a smoke screen aimed at concealing the evil intent of expanding slavery. In reality, many advocates of Manifest Destiny were neither supporters of slavery nor zealous annexationists. Oregon and California loomed more prominently in their minds than Texas. For despite their flowery phrases, these expansionists rested their case on hard material calculations. Most blamed the post-1837 depression on the failure of the United States to acquire markets for its agricultural surplus and saw the acquisition of Oregon and California as solutions. A Missouri Democrat observed that "the ports of Asia are as convenient to Oregon as the ports of Europe are to the eastern slope of our confederacy, with an infinitely better ocean for navigation." An Alabama Democrat praised California's "safe and capacious harbors," which, he assured, "invite to their bosoms the rich commerce of the East."

Expansionists desired more than profitable trade routes, however. At the heart of their thinking lay an impulse to preserve the predominantly agricultural character of the American people and thereby to safeguard democracy. Most expansionists associated the industrialization that was transforming America with social stratification and class strife, and many saw the concentration of impoverished Irish immigrants in cities and factory towns as evidence of the common people's shrinking opportunities for economic advancement. After a tour of New England mill towns in 1842, John L.

O'Sullivan warned Americans that should they fail to encourage alternatives to factories, the United States would sink to the level of Britain, a nation that the ardent Democratic expansionist James Gordon Bennett described as a land of "bloated wealth" and "terrible misery."

Most Democratic expansionists came to see the acquisition of new territory as a logical complement to their party's policies of low tariffs and decentralized banking. Where tariffs and banks tended to "favor and foster the factory system," expansion would provide farmers with land and with access to foreign markets for their produce. As a consequence, Americans would continue to become farmers, and the foundations of the Republic would remain secure. The acquisition of California and Oregon would provide enough land and harbors to sustain not only the 20 million Americans of 1845 but the 100 million that some expansionists projected for 1900 and the 250 million that O'Sullivan predicted for 1945.

The expansionists' message, especially as delivered by the penny press in such newspapers as Bennett's *New York Herald,* made sense to the laboring poor of America's antebellum cities. The *Herald,* the nation's largest-selling newspaper in the 1840s, played upon the anxieties of its working-class readers by arguing relentlessly for the expulsion of the British from Oregon and for thwarting alleged British plans to abolitionize the United States. These readers, many of them fiercely antiblack, anti-British Irish immigrants, welcomed any efforts to open up economic opportunities for the common people. Most also favored the perpetuation of slavery, for the freeing of slaves would throw masses of blacks into the already intense competition for jobs.

The expansionists with whom these laboring-class readers sided drew ideas from Thomas Jefferson, John Quincy Adams, and other leaders of the early Republic who had proclaimed the American people's right to displace uncivilized or European people from the path of their westward movement. Early expansionists, however, had feared that overexpansion might create an ungovernable empire. Jefferson, for example, had proposed an indefinite restriction on the settlement of Louisiana. In contrast, the expansionists of the 1840s, citing the virtues of the telegraph and the railroad, believed that the problem of distance had been "literally annihilated." James Gordon Bennett claimed that the telegraph would render the whole nation as compact and homogeneous as New York City. Ironically, although many expansionists pointed with alarm to the negative effects of industrialization on society, their confidence in technology convinced them that the nation could expand with minimal risk to the people.

## Polk and Oregon

The most immediate impact of the growing spirit of Manifest Destiny was to escalate the issue of Oregon. To soften northern criticism of the still-pending annexation of Texas, the Democrats had included in their platform for the election of 1844 the assertion that American title "to the whole of the Territory of Oregon is clear and unquestionable." Taken literally, the platform committed the party to acquire the entire area between California and 54°40′, the southern boundary of Alaska. Since Polk had not yet been elected, the British could safely ignore this extraordinary claim for the moment, and in fact, the Oregon issue had aroused far less interest during the campaign than had the annexation of Texas. But in his inaugural address, Polk reasserted the "clear and unquestionable" claim to the "country of Oregon." If by this Polk meant all of Oregon, then the United States, which had never before claimed any part of Oregon north of the forty-ninth parallel, had executed an astounding and belligerent reversal of policy.

Polk's objectives in Oregon, however, were more subtle than his language. He knew that the United States could never obtain all of Oregon without a war with Britain, and he wanted to avoid that. He proposed to use the threat of hostilities to persuade the British to accept what they had repeatedly rejected in the past: a division of Oregon at the forty-ninth parallel. Such a division would give the United States both the excellent deep-water harbors of Puget Sound and the southern tip of British-controlled Vancouver Island. For their part, the British had long held out for a division along the Columbia River, which entered the Pacific Ocean far south of the forty-ninth parallel.

Polk's comments in his inaugural speech roused among westerners a furious interest in acquiring the whole territory. Mass meetings adopted such resolutions as "We are all for Oregon, and *all* Oregon in the West" and "The Whole or None!" Furthermore, each passing year brought new American settlers into Oregon. Even John Quincy Adams, who advocated neither the annexation of Texas nor the 54°40′ boundary for Oregon, believed that the American settlements in Oregon gave the United States a far more reasonable claim to the territory than mere exploration and discovery gave the British. The United States, not Britain, Adams

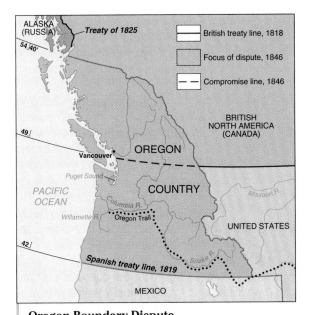

**Oregon Boundary Dispute**
*Although demanding that Britain cede the entire Oregon Territory south of 54°40', the United States settled for a compromise at the forty-ninth parallel.*

preached, was the nation bound "to make the wilderness blossom as the rose, to establish laws, to increase, multiply, and subdue the earth," all "at the first behest of God Almighty."

In April 1846 Polk secured from Congress the termination of joint British-American occupation of Oregon and promptly gave Britain the required one-year's notice. With joint occupation abrogated, the British could either go to war over American claims to 54°40' or negotiate. They chose to negotiate. Although the British raged against "that ill-regulated, overbearing, and aggressive spirit of American democracy," they had too many domestic and foreign problems to welcome a war over what Lord Aberdeen, the British foreign secretary, dismissed as "a few miles of pine swamp." The ensuing treaty provided for a division at the forty-ninth parallel, with some modifications. Britain retained all of Vancouver Island as well as navigation rights on the Columbia River. The Senate ratified the treaty (with the proviso that Britain's navigation rights on the Columbia were merely temporary) on June 15, 1846.

## The Origins of the Mexican War

Even as Polk was challenging Britain over Oregon, the United States and Mexico moved steadily toward war.

The impending conflict had both remote and immediate causes. One long-standing grievance lay in the failure of the Mexican government to pay some $2 million in debts owed to American citizens. In addition, bitter memories of the Alamo and of the Goliad massacre continued to arouse in Americans a loathing of Mexicans. Above all, the issue of Texas embroiled relations between the two nations. Mexico still hoped to regain Texas or at least to keep it independent of the United States.

Behind Mexican anxieties about Texas lay a deeper fear. Mexicans viewed the United States with a mixture of awe and aversion. Americans struck them as marked by industriousness and political stability, qualities Mexicans found lacking in themselves (the Mexican presidency changed hands twenty times between 1829 and 1844). But Mexicans also saw this "Colossus of the North" as extremely aggressive, prone to trample on anyone in its path and then disguise its intentions with high-sounding phrases like Manifest Destiny. Once in control of Texas, the Mexicans feared, the United States might seize other provinces, perhaps even Mexico itself, and treat the citizens of Mexico much as it treated its slaves.

Unfortunately for Mexico, Polk's election increased the strength of the pro-annexationists, as his campaign had persuaded many northerners that enfolding Texas would bring national benefits. In February 1845 both houses of Congress responded to popular sentiment by passing a resolution annexing Texas. However, Texans balked, in part because some Texans feared that union with the United States would provoke a Mexican invasion and war on Texas soil.

Confronted by Texan timidity and Mexican belligerence, Polk moved on two fronts. To sweeten the pot for the Texans, he supported their claim to the Rio Grande as the southern boundary of Texas. This claim ran counter to Mexico's view that the Nueces River, a hundred miles northeast of the Rio Grande, bounded Texas. The area between the Nueces and the Rio Grande was largely uninhabited, but the stakes were high. Although only a hundred miles southwest of the Nueces at its mouth on the Gulf of Mexico, the Rio Grande meandered west and then north for nearly two thousand miles and encircled a huge slice of territory, including part of New Mexico. The Texas that Polk proposed to annex thus encompassed far more land than the Texas that had gained independence from Mexico in 1836. Reassured by Polk's largesse, a Texas convention voted overwhelmingly on July 4, 1845, to accept annexation.

**James K. Polk, 1846**

*Lacking charm, Polk bored even his friends, but few presidents could match his record of aquiring land for the United States.*

In response to Mexican war preparations, Polk then made a second move, ordering American troops under General Zachary Taylor to the edge of the disputed territory. Taylor took up a position at Corpus Christi, a tiny Texas outpost situated just south of the Nueces and hence in territory still claimed by Mexico.

Never far from Polk's thoughts in his insistence on the Rio Grande boundary lay his desire for California and for its fine harbors of San Diego and San Francisco. In fact, Polk had entered the White House with the firm intention of extending American control over California. By the summer of 1845, his followers were openly proclaiming that if Mexico went to war with the United States over Texas, "the road to California will be open to us." Then in October 1845, Polk received a dispatch from Thomas O. Larkin, the American consul at Monterey, California, that warned darkly of British designs on California but ended with the optimistic assurance that the Mexicans in California would prefer American to British rule. Larkin's message gave Polk the idea that California might be acquired by the same methods as Texas: revolution followed by annexation.

With Texans' acceptance of annexation and Taylor's troops at Corpus Christi, the next move belonged to Mexico. In early 1845 a new Mexican government agreed to negotiate with the United States, and Polk, locked into a war of words with Britain over Oregon, decided to give negotiations a chance. In November 1845 he dispatched John Slidell to Mexico City with instructions to gain Mexican recognition of the annexation of Texas with the Rio Grande border. In exchange, the United States government would assume the debt owed by Mexico to American citizens. Polk also authorized Slidell to offer up to $25 million for California and New Mexico. But by the time Slidell reached Mexico City, the government there had become too weak to

make concessions to the United States, and its head, General José Herrera, refused to receive Slidell. Polk then ordered Taylor to move southward to the Rio Grande, hoping to provoke a Mexican attack and unite the American people behind war.

The Mexican government, however, dawdled over taking the bait. Polk was about to send a war message to Congress when word finally arrived that Mexican forces had crossed the Rio Grande and ambushed two companies of Taylor's troops. Now the prowar press had its martyrs. *"American blood has been shed on American soil!"* one of Polk's followers proclaimed. On May 11 Polk informed Congress that war "exists by the act of Mexico herself" and called for a $10 million appropriation to fight the war.

Polk's disarming assertion that the United States was already at war provoked furious opposition in Congress, where John C. Calhoun briefly united with antislavery Whigs to protest the president's high-handedness. Polk's opponents pointed out that the Mexican attack on Taylor's troops had occurred in territory that no previous administration had claimed as part of the United States. By announcing that war already existed, moreover, Polk seemed to be undercutting Congress's power to declare war and using a mere border incident as a pretext for plunging the nation into a general war to acquire more slave territory. The pro-Whig *New York Tribune* warned its readers that Polk was "precipitating you into a fathomless abyss of crime and calamity." Antislavery poet James Russell Lowell of Massachusetts wrote of the Polk Democrats,

> They just want this Californy
>     So's to lug new slave-states in
> To abuse ye, an' to scorn ye,
>     An' to plunder ye like sin.

But Polk had maneuvered the Whigs into a corner. Few Whigs could forget that the opposition of the Federalists to the War of 1812 had wrecked the Federalist party, and few wanted to appear unpatriotic by refusing to support Taylor's beleaguered troops. Swallowing their outrage, most Whigs backed appropriations for war against Mexico.

Throughout the negotiations with Britain over Oregon and with Mexico over Texas, Polk had demonstrated his ability to pursue his goals unflinchingly. A humorless, austere man who banned dancing and liquor at White House receptions, Polk inspired little personal warmth, even among his supporters. But he possessed clear objectives and a single-mindedness in their pursuit. At every point, he had encountered opposition on the home front: from Whigs who saw him as a reckless adventurer; from northerners of both parties opposed to any expansion of slavery; and from John C. Calhoun, who despised Polk for his high-handedness and fretted that a war with Britain would strip the South of its market for cotton. Yet Polk triumphed over all opposition, in part because of his opponents' fragmentation, in part because of expansion's popular appeal, and in part because of the weakness of his foreign antagonists. Reluctant to fight over Oregon, Britain chose to negotiate. Too weak to negotiate, Mexico chose to fight over territory that it had already lost (Texas) and for territories over which its hold was feeble (California and New Mexico).

## The Mexican War

Most European observers expected Mexico to win the war. With a regular army four times the size of the American forces, Mexico had the added advantage of fighting on home ground. The United States, which had botched its one previous attempt to invade a foreign nation, Canada in 1812, now had to sustain offensive operations in an area remote from American settlements.

In contrast to the Europeans, expansionists in the United States hardly expected the Mexicans to fight at all. A leading Democrat confidently predicted that Mexico would offer only "a slight resistance to the North American race" because its mixed Spanish and Indian population had been degraded by "amalgamation." Newspaper publisher James Gordon Bennett proclaimed that the "imbecile" Mexicans were "as sure to melt away at the approach of [American] energy and enterprise as snow before a southern sun."

In fact, the Mexicans fought bravely and stubbornly, although unsuccessfully. In May 1846 Taylor, "Old Rough and Ready," routed the Mexican army in Texas and pursued it across the Rio Grande, eventually capturing the major city of Monterrey in September. War enthusiasm surged in the United States. Recruiting posters blared, "Here's to old Zach! Glorious Times! Roast Beef, Ice Cream, and Three Months' Advance." Taylor's conspicuously ordinary manner—he went into battle wearing a straw hat and a plain brown coat—endeared him to the public, which kicked up its heels in celebration to the "Rough and Ready Polka" and the "General Taylor Quick Step."

After taking Monterrey, Taylor, starved for supplies, halted and granted Mexico an eight-week armistice. Eager to undercut Taylor's popularity—the Whigs were already touting him as a presidential candidate—Polk stripped him of half his forces and reassigned them to General Winfield Scott. Scott was to mount an amphibious attack on Vera Cruz, far to the south, and proceed to Mexico City, following the path of Cortés and his *conquistadores.* Events outstripped Polk's scheme, however, when Taylor defeated a far larger Mexican army at the Battle of Buena Vista, on February 22–23, 1847.

While Taylor was winning fame in northern Mexico, and before Scott had launched his attack on Vera Cruz, American forces farther north were dealing decisive blows to the remnants of Mexican rule in New Mexico and California. In the spring of 1846, Colonel Stephen Kearny marched an army from Fort Leavenworth, Kansas, toward Santa Fe. Like the pioneers on the Oregon Trail, Kearny's men faced immense natural obstacles as they marched over barren ground. Finally reaching New Mexico, Kearny took the territory by a combination of bluff, bluster, and perhaps bribery, without firing a shot. The Mexican governor, following his own advice that "it is better to be thought brave than to be so," fled at Kearny's approach. After suppressing a brief rebellion by Mexicans and Indians, Kearny sent a detachment of his army south into Mexico. There, having marched fifteen hundred miles from Fort Leavenworth, these troops joined Taylor in time for the Battle of Buena Vista.

Like New Mexico, California fell easily into American hands. In 1845 Polk had ordered Commodore John D. Sloat and his Pacific Squadron to occupy California's ports in the event of war with Mexico. To ensure victory, Polk also dispatched a courier overland with secret orders for one of the most colorful and important actors in the conquest of California, John C. Frémont. A Georgia-born adventurer, Frémont had married Jessie Benton, the daughter of the powerful senator Thomas Hart Benton of Missouri. Benton used his influence to have accounts of Frémont's explorations in the Northwest (mainly written by Jessie Benton Frémont) published as government documents. All of this earned glory for Frémont as "the Great Pathfinder." Finally overtaken by Polk's courier in Oregon, Frémont was dispatched to California to "watch over the interests of the United States." Interpreting his orders liberally, Frémont rounded up some American insurgents, seized the town of Sonoma, and proclaimed the independent

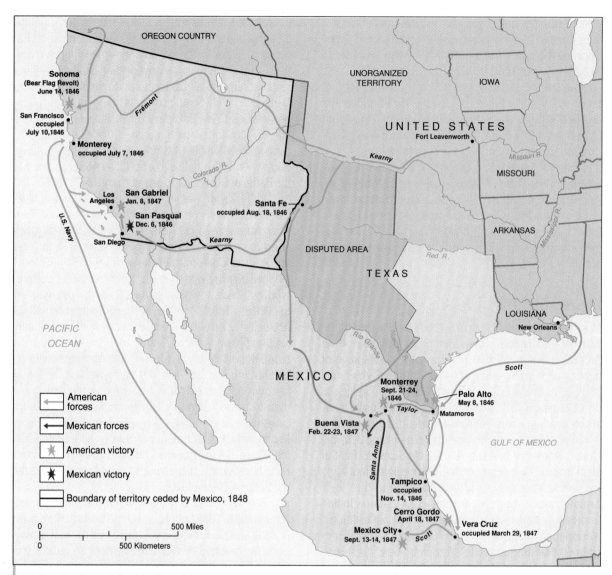

**Major Battles of the Mexican War**
*The Mexican War's decisive campaign began with General Winfield Scott's capture of Vera Cruz and ended with his conquest of Mexico City.*

"Bear Flag Republic" in June 1846. The combined efforts of Frémont, Sloat, his successor David Stockton, and Stephen Kearny (who arrived in California after capturing New Mexico) quickly established American control over California.

The final and most important campaign of the war saw the conquest of Mexico City itself. In March 1847 Winfield Scott landed near Vera Cruz at the head of twelve thousand men and quickly pounded the city into submission. Moving inland, Scott encountered Santa Anna at the seemingly impregnable pass of Cerro Gordo, but a young captain in Scott's command, Robert E. Lee, helped to find a trail that led around the Mexican flank to a small peak overlooking the pass. There Scott planted howitzers and, on April 18, stormed the pass and routed the Mexicans. Scott now moved directly on Mexico City. Taking the key fortresses of Churubusco and Chapultepec (where another young captain, Ulysses S. Grant, was cited for bravery), Scott took the city on September 13, 1847.

**Patriotism and the Mexican War**
*U.S. soldiers commonly wore tall hats known as shako caps during the Mexican War. The caps were adorned with decorative plates showing the eagle spreading its wings, the symbol of Manifest Destiny. Inexpensive and mass-produced lithographs such as the one above, depicting the Battle of Sacramento, aroused patriotic support for the war.*

In virtually all these encounters on Mexican soil, the Mexicans were numerically superior. In the final assault on Mexico City, Scott commanded 11,000 troops against Santa Anna's 25,000. But doom stalked the Mexican army. Hampered by Santa Anna's nearly unbroken string of military miscalculations, the Mexicans fell victim to the vastly superior American artillery and to the ability of the Americans to organize massive military movements. The "barbarians of the North" (as the Mexicans called the American soldiers) died like flies from yellow fever, and they carried into battle the agonies of venereal disease, which they picked up (and left) in every Mexican town they took. But the Americans benefited from the unprecedented quality of their weapons, supplies, and organization.

By the Treaty of Guadalupe Hidalgo (February 2, 1848), Mexico ceded Texas with the Rio Grande boundary, New Mexico, and California to the United States. In return, the United States assumed the claims of American citizens against the Mexican government and paid Mexico $15 million. Although the United States gained the present states of California, Nevada, New Mexico, Utah, most of Arizona, and parts of Colorado and Wyoming, some rabid expansionists in the Senate denounced the treaty because it failed to include all of Mexico. But the acquisition of California, with its excellent Pacific ports of San Diego and San Francisco, satisfied Polk. Few senators, moreover, wanted to annex the mixed Spanish and Indian population of Mexico. A writer in the *Democratic Review* expressed the prevailing view that "the annexation of the country [Mexico] to the United States would be a calamity," for it would incorporate into the United States "ignorant and indolent half-civilized Indians," not to mention "free negroes and mulattoes" left over from the British slave trade. In this way, the virulent racism of American leaders allowed the Mexicans to retain part of their nation. On March 10, 1848, the Senate ratified the treaty by a vote of 38 to 10.

### Intensifying Sectional Divisions

Wartime patriotic enthusiasm did not stop sectional conflict from sharpening between 1846 and 1848. Questions relating to territorial expansion intensified this conflict, but so too did President Polk's uncompromising and literal-minded Jacksonianism.

Polk had restored the Independent Treasury, to the Whigs' dismay, and had eroded Democratic unity by pursuing Jacksonian policies on tariffs and internal improvements. Despite his campaign promise, applauded by many northern Democrats, to combine a revenue tariff with a measure of protection, his administration's Tariff of 1846 had slashed duties to the minimum necessary for revenue. Polk then disappointed western Democrats, thirsting for federal aid to internal improvements, by vetoing the Rivers and Harbors Bill of 1846.

Important as these issues were, territorial expansion sparked the Polk administration's major battles. To Polk, it mattered little whether new territories were slave or free. Expansion would serve the nation's interests by dispersing population and retaining its agricultural and democratic character. Focusing attention on slavery in the territories struck him as "not only unwise but wicked." The Missouri Compromise, prohibiting slavery north of 36°30′, impressed him as a simple and permanent solution to the problem of territorial slavery.

But many northerners were coming to see slavery in the territories as a profoundly disruptive issue that neither could nor should be solved simply by extending the 36°30′ line westward. Antislavery Whigs who opposed any extension of slavery on moral grounds, still a minority within their party, posed a lesser threat to Polk than northern Democrats who feared that expansion of slavery into California and New Mexico (parts of each lay south of 36°30′) would deter free laborers from settling those territories. These Democrats argued that competition with slaves degraded free labor, that the westward extension of slavery would check the westward migration of free labor, and that such a barrier would aggravate the social problems already beginning to plague the East: class strife, social stratification, and labor protest.

### The Wilmot Proviso

A young Democratic congressman from Pennsylvania, David Wilmot, became the spokesman for these disaffected northern Democrats. On a sizzling night in August 1846, he introduced an amendment to an appropriations bill for the upcoming negotiations with Mexico over Texas, New Mexico, and California. This amendment, known as the Wilmot Proviso, stipulated that slavery be prohibited in any territory acquired by the negotiations. Neither an abolitionist nor a critic of

Polk on tariff policy, Wilmot spoke for those loyal Democrats who had supported the annexation of Texas on the assumption that Texas would be the last slave state. Wilmot's intention was not to split his party along sectional lines but to hold Polk to what Wilmot and other northern Democrats took as an implicit understanding: Texas for the slaveholders, California and New Mexico for free labor. With strong northern support, the proviso passed in the House but stalled in the Senate. Polk refused to endorse it, and most southern Democrats opposed any barrier to the expansion of slavery south of the Missouri Compromise line. Accepting the view that the westward extension of slavery would reduce the concentration of slaves in the older regions of the South and thus lessen the chances of a slave revolt, southern Democrats tried to put as much distance as possible between themselves and Wilmot.

The proviso raised unsettling constitutional issues. Calhoun and fellow southerners contended that since slaves were property, slaveholders enjoyed the Constitution's protection of property and could carry their slaves wherever they chose. This position led to the conclusion (drawn explicitly by Calhoun) that the Missouri Compromise of 1820, prohibiting slavery in the territories north of 36°30′, was unconstitutional. On the other side were many northerners who cited the Northwest Ordinance of 1787, the Missouri Compromise, and the Constitution itself, which gave Congress the power to "make all needful rules and regulations respecting the territory or other property belonging to the United States," as justification for congressional legislation over slavery in the territories. With the election of 1848 approaching, politicians of both sides, eager to hold their parties together and avert civil war, searched frantically for a middle ground.

### The Election of 1848

Having asserted that their policies of national banking and high tariffs alone could pull the nation out of the depression, the Whigs had watched in dismay as prosperity returned under the Democrat Polk's program of an independent treasury and low tariffs. Never before had Clay's American System seemed so irrelevant. But the Wilmot Proviso gave the Whigs a political windfall; originating in the Democratic party, it enabled the Whigs to portray themselves as the South's only dependable friends.

These considerations inclined the majority of Whigs toward Zachary Taylor. As a Louisiana slaveholder, he had obvious appeal to the South. As a political newcomer, he had no loyalty to the discredited American System. And as a war hero, he had broad national appeal. Nominating Taylor as their presidential candidate in 1848, the Whigs presented him as an ideal man "without regard to creeds or principles" and ran him without any platform.

The Democrats faced a greater challenge because David Wilmot was one of their own. They could not ignore the issue of slavery in the territories, but if they embraced the position of either Wilmot or Calhoun, the party would split along sectional lines. When Polk declined to run for reelection, the Democrats nominated Lewis Cass of Michigan, who solved their dilemma by announcing the doctrine of "squatter sovereignty," or popular sovereignty as it was later called. Cass argued that Congress should let the question of slavery in the territories be decided by the people who settled there. Squatter sovereignty appealed to many because of its arresting simplicity and vagueness. It neatly dodged the divisive issue of whether Congress had the power to prohibit territorial slavery. In fact, few Democrats wanted a definitive answer to this question. As long as the doctrine remained ambiguous, northern and southern Democrats alike could interpret it to their respective benefits.

In the campaign both parties tried to ignore the issue of territorial slavery but neither succeeded. A pro–Wilmot Proviso faction of the Democratic party in New York, called the Barnburners, broke away from the party, linked up with former Liberty party abolitionists, and courted antislavery "Conscience" Whigs to create the Free-Soil party. Declaring their dedication to "Free Trade, Free Labor, Free Speech, and Free Men," the Free-Soilers nominated Martin Van Buren on a platform opposing any extension of slavery.

Zachary Taylor benefited from the Democrats' alienation of key northern states over the tariff issue, from Democratic disunity over the Wilmot Proviso, and

**"Union" Woodcut** by Thomas W. Strong, 1848
*This 1848 campaign poster for Zachary Taylor reminded Americans of his military victories, unmilitary bearing (note the civilian dress and straw hat), and deliberately vague platform. As president, Taylor finally took a stand on the issue of slavery in the Mexican Cession, but his position angered the South.*

from his war-hero stature. He captured a majority of electoral votes in both North and South. Although failing to carry any state, the Free-Soil party ran well enough in the North to demonstrate the grass-roots popularity of opposition to slavery extension. Defections to the Free-Soilers, for example, probably cost the Whigs Ohio. By showing that opposition to the spread

## The Election of 1848

| Candidates | Parties | Electoral Vote | Popular Vote | Percentage of Popular Vote |
|---|---|---|---|---|
| ZACHARY TAYLOR | Whig | 163 | 1,360,967 | 47.4 |
| Lewis Cass | Democratic | 127 | 1,222,342 | 42.5 |
| Martin Van Buren | Free-Soil | | 291,263 | 10.1 |

## San Francisco, California

San Francisco became a favorite destination for newcomers in the gold rush. Its population spurted from 1,000 in 1849 to 50,000 in 1856. Few American towns had presented less likely prospects for growth. The Spanish had constructed a *presidio* and a mission on the site in 1776, and a small town, Yerba Buena, had sprung up around the mission. But when the United States took possession of Yerba Buena in July 1846, the town stretched for only a few streets in each direction and contained a mere 150 people who huddled amid its low mountains and fog-enshrouded sand hills. Arriving in the summer of 1846, a boatload of 200 Mormons more than doubled the population of Yerba Buena, which became San Francisco in 1847.

The gold rush transformed the town into "a pandemonium of a city" in the words of John Woodhouse Audubon, who became stranded there by Christmas 1849, on his way to the gold fields. San Francisco quickly emerged as the main supply depot for miners and prospectors in the interior. At first, virtually all commodities that passed through the city originated outside of California. Lumber came from Maine and Oregon, flour from Chile and Virginia, sugar from Hawaii, and manufactured goods from the eastern states and Britain. This reliance on imports shaped the town's occupational structure between 1849 and 1853. San Francisco's economy was so top-heavy with merchants and storekeepers that those willing to drive carts (draymen) or un-

load ships or build houses could command wages that elsewhere would have seemed unbelievable. A New England–born lawyer seriously considered giving up his practice to become a drayman, for "they pay a man to drive a cart fifteen to twenty dollars a day," a generous wage at the time. By the mid-1850s the establishment of iron foundries and flour mills relieved the growing city's dependence on imports, but the supply of commodities remained uncertain, and commodity prices continued to gyrate crazily. Flour that cost $10 a barrel one month might jump to $19 the next. Real-estate prices also soared during the early rush, particularly near the waterfront. The city's economy was vulnerable to crashes as precipitous as its booms. A commercial

**Montgomery Street, San Francisco, 1850,** daguerreotype by Frederick Coombs *In the view of historian William H. Goetzmann and art historian William N. Goetzmann, San Francisco was "the final living embodiment of Manifest Destiny, a golden dream city of great instant wealth."*

panic in 1855 produced nearly two hundred bankruptcies and left close to $7 million in uncollectable debts.

The variety of San Francisco's population rivaled the volatility of its economy. Emigrants came from all around the world. By the 1850s the Irish outnumbered every other group of foreign-born immigrants. Many Irish were convicts who arrived by way of Australia, to which they had been exiled as punishment for their crimes. China, France, and Italy, nations that did not contribute many immigrants to other parts of the United States before 1860, all sent sizable contingents to San Francisco. Part of the city's tiny black population was also foreign-born. Richard Dalton, for example, came from the West Indies as a steward on a steamer and then labored on the ships that plied the Sacramento and San Joaquin Rivers to Sacramento and Stockton. Indeed, no other U.S. city contained people from more parts of the world, and only two, St. Louis and Milwaukee, had a higher proportion of foreign-born residents in 1860. In addition, by the early 1850s, San Francisco contained six to ten times as many men as women.

In a city bursting with rival ethnic and racial groups and lacking the constraints imposed by family responsibilities, violence became a principal noncommercial activity. Audubon reported how the place teemed with men "more blasphemous, and with less regard for God and his commands than all I have ever seen on the Mississippi." A young clergyman wrote in 1851 that "most of our citizens if not all go armed" and confessed that he carried a harmless-looking cane, which "will be found to contain a sword two-and-a-half feet long." The city's small fledgling police force posed little challenge to criminals. For protection, some entrepreneurs organized disbanded soldiers into an ex-tralegal force called the Hounds. Unfortunately, the Hounds soon terrorized the people whom they were supposed to protect. In response, in 1851 San Francisco's merchants organized the first of several Committees of Vigilance, which patrolled the streets, deported undesirables, and tried and hanged thieves and murderers.

The vigilantes turned out during subsequent outbursts of lawlessness. In 1855 a gambler named Charles Cora insulted the wife of William Richardson, a U.S. marshal. Richardson then insulted Cora's mistress, a prostitute. A crusading editor, William King, joined the fight on Richardson's side, and a political hack and longtime antagonist of King, James Casey, added his barbs to the fray. The outcome revealed much about law and order in early San Francisco. Richardson armed himself and sought out Cora in a saloon, only to be shot to death by Cora; Casey shot and killed King on a street. Vigilantes then seized Cora and Casey, tried them in secret, and hanged them.

These incidents underscore the city's religious and ethnic tensions as well as its atmosphere of easy violence. Richardson was a southerner and a Protestant, and his supporter King crusaded against the Catholic Church. Although less than models of virtue, their opponents Cora and Casey had been raised Catholic and resented attacks on the religion of their parents. Americans thought of the Far West as a land of opportunity where past antagonisms and traditions would be eradicated, but all the divisions of the larger society were reproduced in San Francisco. The major racial, regional, religious, and ethnic groups kept their distance from one another. Blacks were forced to sit in segregated parts of theaters and to attend segregated schools. Southern and New England Protestants worshiped at different churches. Emigrants from Europe also divided on the basis of language and nationality. German, Polish, Russian, and Anglo-American Jews each maintained separate religious congregations.

Regional and ethnic antagonisms even threatened at times to disrupt the harmony within the city's political parties. Transplanted southerners and Irish immigrants, for example, vied with each other for control of the Democratic party. But at election time, these groups laid aside their discord and united against the rival parties. The Germans usually joined the Irish to ally with the Democrats, whereas the Whigs (and later the Republicans) drew support from former New Englanders, from temperance advocates, and from some immigrants who resented the brash and brawling Irish. In this way, party politics gave coherence to the city's divisions and provided a generally peaceful outlet for the populace's overheated tempers.

**San Francisco Saloon,** by Frank Marryat
*Mexicans, Chinese, Yankees, and southerners drink together in an ornate San Francisco saloon in the booming gold-rush days.*

of slavery had far greater appeal than the staunch abolitionism of the old Liberty party, the Free-Soilers sent the Whigs and Democrats a message that they would be unable to ignore in future elections.

## The California Gold Rush

When Wilmot had first made public his proviso, the issue of slavery in the Far West was more abstract than practical because Mexico had not yet ceded any territory and relatively few Americans resided in either California or New Mexico. Nine days before the signing of the Treaty of Guadalupe Hidalgo, however, an American carpenter discovered gold while constructing a sawmill in the foothills of California's Sierra Nevada range. A frantic gold rush was on within a few months. A San Francisco paper complained that "the whole country from San Francisco to Los Angeles, and from the shore to the base of the Sierra Nevada, resounds

**California Forty-Niner, c. 1850**
*The Forty-Niners, one of them wrote, included "professors, mechanics, sailors, salesmen, and traders," all united in one purpose: "to find gold."*

with the sordid cry to gold, GOLD, GOLD! while the field is left half-planted, the house half-built, and everything neglected but the manufacture of shovels and pickaxes." (Deprived of its staff, advertisers, and subscribers, the newspaper then suspended publication.) By December 1848 pamphlets with titles like *The Emigrant's Guide to the Gold Mines* had hit the streets of New York City. To speed the gold-rushers to their destination, builders constructed sleek clipper ships like Donald McKay's *Flying Cloud,* which made the 18,000-mile trip from New York to San Francisco around Cape Horn in a record eighty-nine days on its maiden voyage in 1851. But most gold-rushers traveled overland. Overland immigrants to California rose from 400 in 1848 to 25,000 in 1849 and to 44,000 in 1850 (see A Place in Time).

With the gold rush, the issue of slavery in the Far West became practical as well as abstract, and immediate rather than remote. In 1849 gold attracted a hundred thousand newcomers to California, including Mexicans, free blacks, and slaves brought by planters from the South. White prospectors loathed the thought of competing with any of these groups and wanted to drive all of them out of the gold fields. Spawned by disputed claims and prejudice, violence mounted, and demands grew for a strong civilian government in California to replace the ineffective military government in place since the war. Polk began to fear that without a satisfactory congressional solution to the slavery issue, Californians might organize a government independent of the United States. The gold rush thus guaranteed that the question of slavery in the Mexican cession would be the first item on the agenda for Polk's successor and, indeed, for the nation.

## CONCLUSION

Nothing went according to plan in the 1840s. Buoyed by their triumph in 1840, the Whigs fully expected that the prosperity stimulated by their program of national banking and tariffs would ensure their political ascendancy. But the Whigs were victimized by a mixture of bad luck and miscalculation. William H. Harrison's untimely death brought John Tyler, a Democrat in Whig clothing, to the presidency, and Tyler's vetoes of the Whig economic program cost the Whigs credibility with voters. Whigs suffered additional reverses as recent immigrants gravitated to the Democrats. For their part, the Democrats devised ingenious arguments to persuade northern voters that the annexation of Texas would prevent southern racial tensions from spilling over into the North. In the election of 1844, critical because the rival candidates held such contrasting views about expansion, the triumph of Polk over Clay committed the nation to policies that nearly led to war with Britain over Oregon and that did lead to war with Mexico over Texas.

Now it was the Democrats' turn to unravel. The Wilmot Proviso exposed their deep sectional divisions that had only been papered over by the ideal of Manifest Destiny and that would explode in the secession of Free-Soil Democrats in 1848. Victorious over Mexico and enriched by the discovery of gold in California, Americans counted the blessings of expansion but began to fear its costs.

## FOR FURTHER READING

Ray A. Billington, *The Far Western Frontier, 1830–1860* (1956). A comprehensive narrative of the settlement of the Far West.

William R. Brock, *Parties and Political Conscience: American Dilemmas, 1840–1850* (1979). An excellent interpretive study of the politics of the 1840s.

William H. Goetzmann, *When the Eagle Screamed: The Romantic Horizon in American Diplomacy, 1800–1860* (1966). A lively overview of antebellum expansionism.

Maldwyn A. Jones, *American Immigration* (1960). An excellent brief introduction to immigration.

Patricia Nelson Limerick, *Legacy of Conquest* (1987). A provocative interpretation of western history.

Charles G. Sellers, *James K. Polk: Continentalist, 1843–1846* (1966). An outstanding political biography.

Henry Nash Smith, *Virgin Land: The American West as Symbol and Myth* (1950). A classic study of westward expansion in the American mind.

# 14

# From Compromise to Secession 1850–1861

**The Last Moments of John Brown** (detail)
*by Thomas Hovdenden, 1884*

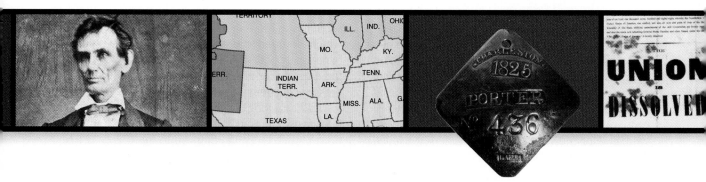

In early July 1859 a man calling himself Isaac Smith and claiming to be a cattle dealer rented a dilapidated farmhouse some seven miles from Harpers Ferry, located in northern Virginia's Blue Ridge mountains. Neighbors soon noticed that others had joined "Smith," including two young women, and perhaps they observed a wagon loaded with fifteen boxes pull up to the farm one day. But nothing seemed out of the ordinary. True, the men stayed out of sight, but the women chatted amiably with neighbors, and "Smith" referred to the contents of the boxes merely as "hardware." In reality, everything *was* out of the ordinary. "Smith" was John Brown, a brooding abolitionist with a price on his head for the massacre of white southerners in Kansas in 1856 and with a conviction that God had ordained him "to purge this land with blood" of the evil of slavery. One of the women was his daughter, the other his daughter-in-law. The boxes contained rifles and revolvers, with which Brown and his recruits—a mixture of white idealists (including three of Brown's sons), free blacks, and fugitive slaves—planned to raid Harpers Ferry, the site of a federal arsenal and armory, as a prelude to igniting a slave insurrection throughout the South.

In some respects, Brown was a marginal figure in the abolitionist movement. Unlike better-known abolitionists, he had written no stirring tracts against slavery. But in Kansas, where civil war between free-staters and slave-staters had broken out in the mid-1850s, Brown had acquired a reputation as someone who could handle the rough stuff. Eastern abolitionists—most of whom were philosophical pacifists but who were starting to suspect that only violence would end slavery—were fast developing a fascination with Brown. Little suspecting his plans for Harpers Ferry, they accepted his disavowal of a role in the Kansas massacre and endorsed, with contributions, his plans to carry on the

fight against those who would forcibly turn Kansas into a slave state.

On the moonless evening of October 16, 1859, Brown and eighteen recruits (three were left behind to guard the farmhouse) entered Harpers Ferry and quickly seized the arsenal and armory. Expecting slaves—half of Harpers Ferry's population was enslaved—to rally at once to his cause, Brown then did nothing, while local whites, jumpy about the possibility of a slave insurrection ever since Nat Turner's 1831 rebellion (see Chapter 12), spread the alarm. Soon armed locals, their courage steeled by liquor, militia from surrounding areas, and U.S. Marines dispatched by President James Buchanan and under the command of Col. Robert E. Lee, clogged the streets of Harpers Ferry. On October 18 the marines stormed the armory, where Brown and most of his men had taken refuge, severely wounded and captured Brown, and killed or mortally wounded ten others, including two of Brown's sons. Five men, including one of Brown's sons, escaped; the remaining recruits were eventually captured and executed. Brown himself was speedily tried, convicted, and hanged.

In the immediate wake of Brown's capture, prominent northerners distanced themselves from him. His lawyers contended that he was insane and hence not culpable for his deeds. But Brown himself derided the insanity defense. His conduct during his brief imprisonment was serene, his words eloquent. He told his captors that he had rendered to God the "greatest service man can." For their part, white southerners came to reject the notion that Brown's plot was the work of an isolated lunatic. A search of the farmhouse after Brown's capture quickly turned up incriminating correspondence between Brown and leading northern abolitionists. As proslavery southerners saw it, Brown had botched the raid, but his plan—to arm nonslaveholding

**379**

southern whites with guns and disaffected slaves with pikes (Brown had contracted for the manufacture of a thousand pikes)—was plausible: in all the southern states slaveholding whites were outnumbered by people who did not own slaves (slaves, free blacks, and nonslaveholding whites) by more than three to one. Finally, northern opinion increasingly shifted toward sympathy for Brown. Ralph Waldo Emerson exulted that Brown's execution would "make the gallows as glorious as the cross."

This chapter focuses on five major questions:

♦ To what extent did the Compromise of 1850 represent a genuine meeting of the minds between northerners and southerners? How, specifically, did the controversy over enforcement of the Fugitive Slave Act and the presidential election of 1852 contribute to the undoing of the Compromise?

♦ Why did the Whig party collapse in the wake of the Kansas-Nebraska Act? Why did the Democratic party not also collapse?

♦ How did the outbreak of conflict in Kansas influence the rise of the Republican party? Why was the Republican doctrine of free soil able to unify northerners against the South?

♦ What led southerners to conclude that the North was bent not merely on restricting territorial slavery but on extinguishing slavery in southern states?

♦ Was the Civil War inevitable? If so, when did it become inevitable?

# The Compromise of 1850

Ralph Waldo Emerson's grim prediction that an American victory in the Mexican War would be like swallowing arsenic proved disturbingly accurate. When the war ended in 1848, the United States contained an equal number (fifteen each) of free and slave states, but the vast territory acquired by the war threatened to upset this balance. Any solution to the question of slavery in the Mexican cession ensured controversy, if not hostility. The doctrine of free soil, which insisted that Congress prohibit slavery in the territories, horrified southerners. The idea of extending the Missouri Compromise line of 36° 30′ to the Pacific angered free-soilers because it would allow slavery in New Mexico and southern California, and southern proslavery extremists because it conceded that Congress could bar slavery in

some territories. A third solution, popular sovereignty, which promised to ease the slavery extension issue out of national politics by allowing each territory to decide the question for itself, pleased neither free-soilers nor proslavery extremists.

As the rhetoric escalated, events plunged the nation into crisis. Utah and then California, both acquired from Mexico, sought admission to the Union as free states. Texas, admitted as a slave state in 1845, aggravated matters by claiming the eastern half of New Mexico, where the Mexican government had long since abolished slavery.

By 1850 these territorial issues had become intertwined with two other concerns. Northerners increasingly attacked slavery in the District of Columbia, within the shadow of the Capitol; southerners complained about lax enforcement of the Fugitive Slave Act of 1793. Any broad compromise would have to take both troublesome matters into account.

## Zachary Taylor at the Helm

Although elected president in 1848 without a platform, Zachary Taylor came to office with a clear position on the issue of slavery in the Mexican cession. A slaveholder himself, he took for granted the South's need to defend slavery. Taylor insisted that southerners would best protect slavery if they refrained from rekindling the issue of slavery in the territories. He rejected Calhoun's idea that the protection of slavery in the southern states ultimately depended on the expansion of slavery into the western territories. In Taylor's eyes, neither California nor New Mexico was suited to slavery; in 1849 he told a Pennsylvania audience that "the people of the North need have no apprehension of the further extension of slavery."

Although Taylor looked to the exclusion of slavery from California and New Mexico, his position differed from that embodied in the Wilmot Proviso, the free-soil measure proposed in 1846 by a northern Democrat. The proviso had insisted that *Congress* bar slavery in the territories ceded by Mexico. Taylor's plan, in contrast, left the decision to the states. Recognizing that most Californians opposed slavery in their state, Taylor had prompted California to bypass the territorial stage that normally preceded statehood, to draw up its constitution in 1849, and to apply directly for admission as a free state. The president strongly hinted that he expected New Mexico to do the same.

Taylor's strategy appeared to guarantee a quick, practical solution to the problem of slavery extension. It

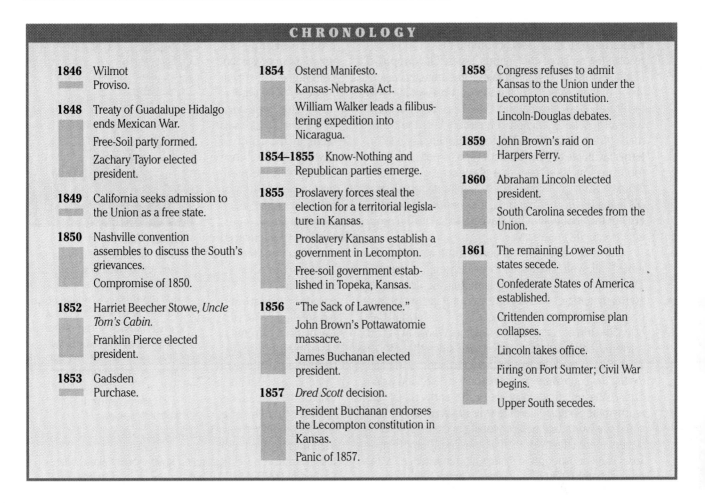

## CHRONOLOGY

**1846** Wilmot Proviso.

**1848** Treaty of Guadalupe Hidalgo ends Mexican War.

Free-Soil party formed.

Zachary Taylor elected president.

**1849** California seeks admission to the Union as a free state.

**1850** Nashville convention assembles to discuss the South's grievances.

Compromise of 1850.

**1852** Harriet Beecher Stowe, *Uncle Tom's Cabin.*

Franklin Pierce elected president.

**1853** Gadsden Purchase.

**1854** Ostend Manifesto.

Kansas-Nebraska Act.

William Walker leads a filibustering expedition into Nicaragua.

**1854–1855** Know-Nothing and Republican parties emerge.

**1855** Proslavery forces steal the election for a territorial legislature in Kansas.

Proslavery Kansans establish a government in Lecompton.

Free-soil government established in Topeka, Kansas.

**1856** "The Sack of Lawrence."

John Brown's Pottawatomie massacre.

James Buchanan elected president.

**1857** *Dred Scott* decision.

President Buchanan endorses the Lecompton constitution in Kansas.

Panic of 1857.

**1858** Congress refuses to admit Kansas to the Union under the Lecompton constitution.

Lincoln-Douglas debates.

**1859** John Brown's raid on Harpers Ferry.

**1860** Abraham Lincoln elected president.

South Carolina secedes from the Union.

**1861** The remaining Lower South states secede.

Confederate States of America established.

Crittenden compromise plan collapses.

Lincoln takes office.

Firing on Fort Sumter; Civil War begins.

Upper South secedes.

would give the North two new free states. At the same time, it would acknowledge a position upon which all southerners agreed: a *state* could bar or permit slavery as it chose. This conviction in fact served as the very foundation of the South's defense of slavery, its armor against all the onslaughts of the abolitionists. Nothing in the Constitution forbade a state to act one way or the other on slavery.

Despite its practical features, Taylor's plan dismayed southerners of both parties. Having gored the Democrats in 1848 as the party of the Wilmot Proviso, southern Whigs expected more from the president than a proposal that in effect yielded the proviso's goal—the banning of slavery in the Mexican cession. Many southerners, in addition, questioned Taylor's assumption that slavery could never take root in California or New Mexico. To one observer, who declared that the whole controversy over slavery in the Mexican cession "related to an imaginary negro in an impossible place," southerners pointed out that both areas already con-

tained slaves and that slaves could be employed profitably in the mining of gold and silver. "California is by nature," a southerner proclaimed, "peculiarly a slaveholding State." Calhoun trembled at the thought of adding more free states. "If this scheme excluding slavery from California and New Mexico should be carried out—if we are to be reduced to a mere handful . . . wo, wo, I say to this Union." Disillusioned with Taylor, nine southern states agreed to send delegations to a southern convention that was scheduled to meet in Nashville in June 1850.

### Henry Clay Proposes a Compromise

Taylor might have been able to contain mounting southern opposition if he had held a secure position in the Whig party. But the leading Whigs, among them Daniel Webster of Massachusetts and Kentucky's Henry Clay, each of whom had presidential aspirations, never reconciled themselves to Taylor, a political novice. Early in 1850 Clay boldly challenged Taylor's leadership by forging a set of compromise proposals to resolve the range of contentious issues. Clay proposed (1) the admission of California as a free state; (2) the division of the remainder of the Mexican cession into two territories, New Mexico and Utah (formerly Deseret), without federal restrictions on slavery; (3) the settlement of the Texas–New Mexico boundary dispute on terms favorable to New Mexico; (4) as a pot-sweetener for Texas, an agreement that the federal government would assume the considerable public debt of Texas; (5) in the District of Columbia, the continuance of slavery but the abolition of the slave trade; and (6) a more effective fugitive slave law.

Clay rolled all of these proposals into a single "omnibus" bill, which he hoped to steer through Congress. The debates over the omnibus during the late winter and early spring of 1850 witnessed the last major appearances on the public stage of Clay, Webster, and Calhoun, the trio of distinguished senators whose lives had mirrored every public event of note since the War of 1812. Clay played the role of the conciliator, as he had during the controversy over Missouri in 1820 and again during the nullification crisis in the early 1830s. He warned the South against the evils of secession and assured the North that nature would check the spread of slavery more effectively than a thousand Wilmot Provisos. Gaunt and gloomy, a dying Calhoun listened as another senator read his address, in which Calhoun summarized what he had been saying for years: the North's growing power, enhanced by protective tariffs and by the Missouri Compromise's exclusion of slaveholders from the northern part of the Louisiana Purchase, had created an imbalance between the sections. Only a decision by the North to treat the South as an equal could now save the Union. Three days later, Daniel Webster, who believed that slavery, "like the cotton-plant, is confined to certain parallels of climate," delivered his memorable "Seventh of March" speech. Speaking not "as a Massachusetts man, nor as a Northern man, but as an American," Webster chided the North for trying to "reenact the will of God" by legally excluding slavery from the Mexican cession and declared himself a forthright proponent of compromise.

However eloquent, the conciliatory voices of Clay and Webster made few converts. With every call for compromise, some northern or southern speaker would rise and inflame passions. The antislavery New York Whig William Seward, for example, enraged southerners by talking of a "higher law than the Constitution"—namely, the will of God against the extension of slavery. Clay's compromise became tied up in a congressional committee. To worsen matters, Clay, who at first had pretended that his proposals were in the spirit of Taylor's plan, broke openly with the president in May, and Taylor attacked Clay as a glory-hunter.

As the Union faced its worst crisis since 1789, a series of events in the summer of 1850 eased the way toward a resolution. When the Nashville convention assembled in June, extreme advocates of "southern rights," called the fire-eaters because of their recklessness, boldly made their presence felt. But talk of southern rights smelled suspiciously like a plot to disrupt the Union. "I would rather sit in council with the six thousand dead who have died of cholera in St. Louis," Senator Thomas Hart Benton of Missouri declared, "than go into convention with such a gang of scamps." Only nine of the fifteen slave states, most in the Lower South, sent delegates to the convention, where moderates took control and isolated the extremists. Then Zachary Taylor, after eating and drinking too much at an Independence Day celebration, fell ill with gastroenteritis and died on July 9. His successor, Vice President Millard Fillmore, quickly proved himself more favorable than Taylor to the Senate's compromise measure by appointing Daniel Webster as his secretary of state. Next, after the compromise suffered a devastating series of amendments in late July, Illinois Democrat Stephen A. Douglas took over the floor leadership from the exhausted Clay. Recognizing that Clay's "omnibus" lacked majority support in Congress, Douglas chopped it into a series of separate measures and sought to secure passage of each bill individually. To secure support from Democrats, he included the principle of popular sovereignty in the bills organizing New Mexico and Utah. By summer's end, Congress had passed each

**Henry Clay**
*Eloquent but at the same time earthy, Clay was first elected to the Senate during Jefferson's administration. Subsequently, Clay himself made five unsuccessful bids for the presidency. A European visitor was struck by his penchant for chewing tobacco, drinking whiskey, putting his legs on the table, and spitting "like a regular Kentucky hog-driver."*

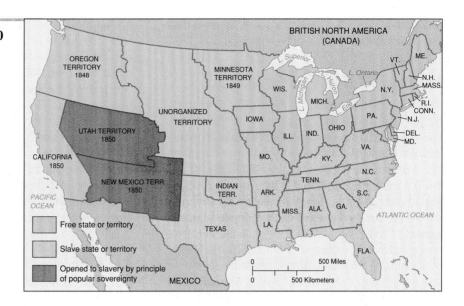

**The Compromise of 1850**

*The Compromise of 1850 admitted California as a free state. Utah and New Mexico were left open to slavery or freedom on the principle of popular sovereignty.*

component of the Compromise of 1850: statehood for California; territorial status for Utah and New Mexico, allowing popular sovereignty; resolution of the Texas–New Mexico boundary disagreement; federal assumption of the Texas debt; abolition of the slave trade in the District of Columbia; and a new fugitive slave law.

## Assessing the Compromise

President Fillmore hailed the compromise as a "final settlement" of sectional divisions, and Clay's reputation for conciliation reached new heights. Yet the compromise did not bridge the underlying differences between the two sections. Far from leaping forward to save the Union, Congress had backed into the Compromise of 1850; the majority of congressmen in one or another section opposed virtually all of the specific bills that made up the compromise. Most southerners, for example, voted against the admission of California and the abolition of the slave trade in the District of Columbia; the majority of northerners opposed the Fugitive Slave Act and the organization of New Mexico and Utah without a forthright congressional prohibition of slavery. These measures passed only because the minority of congressmen who genuinely desired compromise combined with the majority in either the North or the South who favored each specific bill.

Each section both gained and lost from the Compromise of 1850. The North won California as a free state, New Mexico and Utah as likely future free states, a favorable settlement of the Texas–New Mexico

boundary (most of the disputed area was awarded to New Mexico, a probable free state), and the abolition of the slave trade in the District of Columbia. The South's benefits were cloudier. By stipulating popular sovereignty for New Mexico and Utah, the compromise, to most southerners' relief, had buried the Wilmot Proviso's insistence that Congress formally prohibit slavery in these territories. But to southerners' dismay, the position of the free-soilers remained viable, for the compromise left open the question of whether Congress could prohibit slavery in territories outside of the Mexican cession.

Not surprisingly, southerners reacted ambivalently to the Compromise of 1850. In southern state elections during the fall of 1850 and in 1851, procompromise, or Unionist, candidates thrashed anticompromise candidates who talked of southern rights and secession. But even southern Unionists did not dismiss the possibility of secession. Unionists in Georgia, for example, forged the celebrated Georgia platform, which threatened secession if Congress either prohibited slavery in New Mexico or Utah or repealed the fugitive slave law.

The one clear advantage gained by the South, a more stringent fugitive slave law, quickly proved a mixed blessing. Because few slaves had been taken into the Mexican cession, the question of slavery there had a hypothetical quality. However, the issues raised by the new fugitive slave law were far from hypothetical; the law authorized real southerners to pursue real fugitives on northern soil. Here was a concrete issue to which the average northerner, who may never have seen a slave and who cared little about slavery a thousand miles away, would respond with fury.

### *Enforcement of the Fugitive Slave Act*

Northern moderates accepted the Fugitive Slave Act as the price the North had to pay to save the Union. But the law contained a string of features distasteful to moderates and outrageous to staunchly antislavery northerners. It denied alleged fugitives the right of trial by jury, did not allow them to testify in their own behalf, permitted their return to slavery merely on the testimony of the claimant, and enabled court-appointed commissioners to collect ten dollars if they ruled for the slaveholder but only five dollars if they ruled for the fugitive. In authorizing federal marshals to raise posses to pursue fugitives on northern soil, the law threatened to turn the North into "one vast hunting ground." In addition, the law targeted not only recent runaways but also those who had fled the South *decades* earlier. For example, it allowed slave-catchers in 1851 to wrench a former slave from his family in Indiana and return him to the master from whom he had fled in 1832. Above all, the law brought home to northerners the uncomfortable truth that the continuation of slavery depended on their complicity. By legalizing the activities of slave-catchers on northern soil, the law reminded northerners that slavery was a national problem, not merely a peculiar southern institution.

Antislavery northerners assailed the law as the "vilest monument of infamy of the nineteenth century." "Let the President . . . drench our land of freedom in blood," proclaimed Ohio's Whig congressman Joshua Giddings, "but he will never make us obey that law." His support for the law turned Senator Daniel Webster of Massachusetts into a villain in the eyes of the very people who for years had revered him as the "godlike Daniel." The abolitionist poet John Greenleaf Whittier wrote of his fallen idol,

> All else is gone; from those giant eyes
>   The soul has fled:
> When faith is lost, when honor dies,
>   The man is dead.

Efforts to catch and return fugitive slaves inflamed feelings in both the North and the South. In 1854 a Boston mob, aroused by antislavery speeches, broke into a courthouse and killed a guard in an abortive effort to rescue the fugitive slave Anthony Burns. Determined to prove that the law could be enforced "even in Boston," President Franklin Pierce sent a detachment of federal troops to escort Burns to the harbor, where a ship carried him back to slavery. No witness would ever forget the scene. As five platoons of troops marched with Burns to the ship, some fifty thousand people lined the streets. As the procession passed, one Bostonian hung from his window a black coffin bearing the words "THE FUNERAL OF LIBERTY." Another draped an American flag upside down as a symbol that "my country is eternally disgraced by this day's proceedings." The Burns incident shattered the complacency of conservative supporters of the Compromise of 1850. "We went to bed one night old fashioned conservative Compromise Union Whigs," the textile manufacturer Amos A. Lawrence wrote, "and waked up stark mad Abolitionists." A Boston committee later successfully purchased Burns's freedom, but the fate of many fugitives was far less happy. One such unfortunate was Margaret Garner, who, about to be captured and sent back to Kentucky as a slave, slit her daughter's throat and tried to kill her other children rather than witness their return to slavery.

In response to the Fugitive Slave Act, vigilance committees sprang up in many northern communities to spirit endangered blacks to safety in Canada. As another ploy, lawyers used obstructive tactics to drag out legal proceedings and thus raise the slave-catchers' expenses. Then during the 1850s, nine northern states passed "personal-liberty laws." By such techniques as forbidding the use of state jails to incarcerate alleged fugitives, these laws aimed to preclude state officials from enforcing the law.

The frequent cold stares, obstructive legal tactics, and occasional violence encountered by slaveholders who ventured north to capture runaway slaves helped demonstrate to southerners that opposition to slavery boiled just beneath the surface of northern opinion. In the eyes of most southerners, the South had gained little more from the Compromise of 1850 than the Fugitive Slave Act, and now even that northern concession seemed to be a phantom. After witnessing riots against the Fugitive Slave Act in Boston in 1854, a young Georgian studying law at Harvard wrote to his mother, "Do not be surprised if when I return home you find me a *confirmed disunionist*."

### *Uncle Tom's Cabin*

The publication in 1852 of Harriet Beecher Stowe's novel *Uncle Tom's Cabin* aroused wide northern sympathy for fugitive slaves. Stowe, the daughter of the famed evangelical Lyman Beecher and the younger sister of Catharine Beecher, the stalwart advocate of domesticity for women, greeted the Fugitive Slave Act with horror and outrage. In a memorable scene from the novel, she depicted the slave Eliza escaping to freedom, clutching her infant son while bounding across ice floes on the Ohio River. Yet Stowe targeted slavery itself more than merely the slave-catchers who served the institution. Much of her novel's power derives from its intimation that even good intentions cannot prevail against so evil an institution. Torn from his wife and children by sale and shipped on a steamer for the Lower South, the black slave Uncle Tom rescues little Eva, the daughter of kindly Augustine St. Clare, from drowning. In gratitude, St. Clare purchases Tom from a slave trader and takes him into his home in New Orleans. But after St. Clare dies, his cruel widow sells Tom to the vicious (and northern-born) Simon Legree, who whips Tom to death. Stowe played effectively on the emotions of her audience by demonstrating to an age that revered family life how slavery tore the family apart.

Three hundred thousand copies of *Uncle Tom's Cabin* were sold in 1852, and 1.2 million by the summer of 1853. Dramatized versions, which added dogs to chase Eliza across the ice, eventually reached perhaps fifty times the number of people as the novel itself. As a play, *Uncle Tom's Cabin* enthralled working-class audiences normally indifferent, if not hostile, to abolitionism. During one stage performance, a reviewer for a New York newspaper observed that the gallery was filled with men "in red woollen shirts, with countenances as hardy and rugged as the implements of industry employed by them in the pursuit of their vocations." Astonished by the silence that fell over these men at the point when Eliza escapes across the river, the reviewer turned to discover that many of them were in tears.

The impact of *Uncle Tom's Cabin* cannot be precisely measured. Although the novel stirred deep feelings, it reflected the prevailing stereotypes of blacks far more than it overturned commonly held views. Stowe portrayed only light-skinned blacks as aggressive and intelligent; she depicted dark-skinned blacks such as Uncle Tom as docile and submissive. In addition, some of the stage dramatizations softened the novel's antislavery message. In one version, which P. T. Barnum produced, Tom was rescued from Legree and returned happily as a slave to his original plantation.

**Frederick Douglass**

*Born into slavery, Frederick Douglass became a commanding orator and writer in the 1840s and 1850s. He bitterly attacked the Fugitive Slave Act. The only way to make the law a "dead letter," he vowed, was to make "half a dozen or more dead kidnappers." In an Independence Day speech in 1852, he reminded white Americans that "This Fourth of July is yours, not mine."*

Surgery on the plot, however, could not fully excise the antislavery message of *Uncle Tom's Cabin*. Though the novel hardly lived up to the prediction of a proslavery lawyer that it would convert 2 million people to abolitionism, it did push many waverers toward a more aggressively antisouthern and antislavery stance. Indeed, fear of its impact inspired a host of southerners to pen anti–Uncle Tom novels. As historian David Potter has concluded, the northern attitude toward slavery "was never quite the same after *Uncle Tom's Cabin*."

### The Election of 1852

The Fugitive Slave Act fragmented the Whig party. By masterminding defiance of the law, northern Whigs put the southern Whigs, who long had come before the southern electorate as the party best able to defend slavery within the Union, on the spot.

In 1852 the Whigs' nomination of Mexican War hero Winfield Scott as their presidential candidate widened the sectional split within the party. Although a Virginian, Scott owed his nomination to the northern free-soil Whigs. His single feeble statement endorsing the Compromise of 1850 undercut southern Whigs trying to portray the Democrats as the party of disunion and themselves as the party of both slavery and the Union.

The Democrats bridged their own sectional division by nominating Franklin Pierce of New Hampshire, a dark-horse candidate whose chief attraction was that

**The Election of 1852**

| Candidates | Parties | Electoral Vote | Popular Vote | Percentage of Popular Vote |
|---|---|---|---|---|
| FRANKLIN PIERCE | Democratic | 254 | 1,601,117 | 50.9 |
| Winfield Scott | Whig | 42 | 1,385,453 | 44.1 |
| John P. Hale | Free-Soil | | 155,825 | 5.0 |

no faction of the party strongly opposed him. The "ultra men of the South," a friend of Pierce noted, "say they can cheerfully go for him, and none, none, say they cannot." North and South, the Democrats rallied behind both the Compromise and the idea of applying popular sovereignty to *all* the territories. In the most one-sided election since 1820, Pierce swept to victory. Defeat was especially galling for southern Whigs. Compared to the 49.8% of the South's popular vote won by Zachary Taylor in 1848, Scott limped home with only 35%. In state elections during 1852 and 1853, moreover, the Whigs were devastated in the South; one Whig stalwart lamented "the decisive breaking-up of our party."

# The Collapse of the Second Party System

Franklin Pierce had the dubious distinction of being the last presidential candidate for eighty years to win the popular and electoral vote in both the North and the South. Not until 1932 did another president, Franklin D. Roosevelt, repeat this accomplishment. Pierce was also the last president to hold office under the second party system—Whigs against Democrats. For two decades the Whigs and the Democrats had battled, often on even terms. Then, within the four years of Pierce's administration, the Whig party disintegrated. In its place two new parties, first the American (Know-Nothing) party, and then the Republican party, arose.

Unlike the Whig party, the Republican party was a purely sectional, northern party. Its support came from former northern Whigs and from discontented northern Democrats. The Democrats survived as a national party, but with a base so shrunken in the North that in 1856, the Republican party, although scarcely a year old, swept two-thirds of the free states.

For decades the second party system had kept the conflict over slavery in check by giving Americans other issues—banking, internal improvements, tariffs, and temperance—to argue about. By the 1850s the debate over slavery extension was pushing such issues into the background and exposing raw divisions in each party. Of the two parties, Whig and Democratic, the Whigs had the larger, more aggressive free-soil wing, and hence they were more vulnerable than the Democrats to disruption. When Stephen A. Douglas in 1854 put forth a proposal to organize the vast Nebraska territory without restrictions on slavery, he ignited a firestorm that consumed the Whig party.

## The Kansas-Nebraska Act

Signed by President Pierce at the end of May 1854, the Kansas-Nebraska Act dealt a shattering blow to the already weakened second party system. Moreover, the law triggered a renewal of the sectional strife that many Americans believed the Compromise of 1850 had satisfactorily silenced. The origins of the act lay in the seemingly uncontroversial advance of midwestern settlement. Farm families in Iowa and Missouri had long dreamed of establishing homesteads in the vast prairies to their west, and their congressional representatives had repeatedly introduced bills to organize the territory west of these states, so that Native American land titles could be extinguished and a basis for government provided. Too, since the mid-1840s, advocates of national expansion had looked to the day when a railroad would link the Midwest to the Pacific; and St. Louis, Milwaukee, and Chicago had vied to become the eastern end of the projected Pacific railroad.

In January 1854 Senator Stephen A. Douglas of Illinois proposed a bill to organize Nebraska as a territory. An ardent expansionist, Douglas had formed his political ideology in the heady atmosphere of Manifest Destiny during the 1840s. As early as the mid-1840s, he had embraced the ideas of a Pacific railroad and the organization of Nebraska as ways to promote a continuous line of settlement between the Midwest and the Pacific.

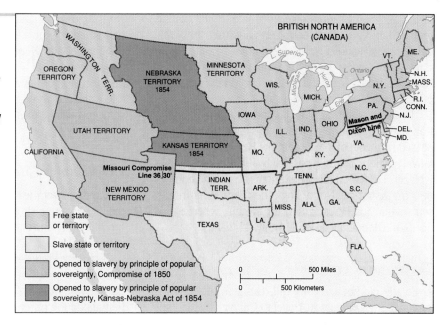

**The Kansas-Nebraska Act, 1854**

*Kansas and Nebraska lay within the Louisiana Purchase, north of 36°30', and hence were closed to slavery until Stephen A. Douglas introduced his bills in 1854.*

Although he preferred a railroad from his hometown of Chicago to San Francisco, Douglas dwelled on the national benefits that would attend construction of a railroad from *anywhere* in the Midwest to the Pacific. Such a railroad would enhance the importance of the Midwest, which could then hold the balance of power between the older sections of the North and South and guide the nation toward unity rather than disruption. In addition, westward expansion through Nebraska with the aid of a railroad struck Douglas as an issue, comparable to Manifest Destiny, around which the contending factions of the Democratic party would unite.

Douglas recognized two sources of potential conflict over his Nebraska bill. First, some southerners advocated a rival route for the Pacific railroad that would start at either New Orleans or Memphis. Second, Nebraska lay within the Louisiana Purchase and north of the Missouri Compromise line of 36°30', a region closed to slavery. Unless Douglas made some concessions, southerners would have little incentive to vote for his bill; after all, the organization of Nebraska would simultaneously create a potential free state and increase the chances for a northern, rather than a southern, railroad to the Pacific. As the floor manager of the Compromise of 1850 in the Senate, Douglas thought that he had an ideal concession to offer to the South. The Compromise of 1850 had applied the principle of popular sovereignty to New Mexico and Utah, territories outside of the Louisiana Purchase and hence unaffected by the Missouri Compromise. Why

not assume, Douglas reasoned, that the Compromise of 1850 had taken the place of the Missouri Compromise *everywhere*? Believing that expansion rather than slavery was uppermost in the public's mind, Douglas hoped to avoid controversy over slavery by ignoring the Missouri Compromise. But he quickly came under pressure from southern congressmen, who wanted an explicit repudiation of the Missouri Compromise. Soon southerners forced Douglas to state publicly that the Nebraska bill "superseded" the Missouri Compromise and rendered it "void." Still under pressure, Douglas next agreed to a division of Nebraska into two territories: Nebraska to the west of Iowa, and Kansas to the west of Missouri. Because Missouri was a slave state, most congressmen assumed that the division aimed to secure Kansas for slavery and Nebraska for free soil.

The modifications of Douglas's original bill set off a storm of protest. Congress quickly tabled the Pacific railroad (which, in the turn of events, would not be built until after the Civil War) and focused on the issue of slavery extension. A group of "Independent Democratic" northern congressmen, composed of antislavery Whigs and free-soil Democrats, assailed the bill as "part and parcel of an atrocious plot" to violate the "sacred pledge" of the Missouri Compromise and to turn Kansas into a "dreary region of despotism, inhabited by masters and slaves." Their rage electrified southerners, many of whom initially had reacted indifferently to the Nebraska bill. Some southerners had opposed an explicit repeal of the Missouri Compromise from fear of stimulating sectional discord; others doubted that Kansas would attract many slaveholders. But the furious assault of antislavery northerners united the South behind the Kansas-Nebraska bill by turning the issue into one of sectional pride as much as slavery extension.

Despite the uproar, Douglas successfully guided the Kansas-Nebraska bill through the Senate, where it passed by a vote of 37 to 14. In the House of Representatives, where the bill passed by little more than a whisker, 113 to 100, the true dimensions of the conflict became apparent. Not a single northern Whig representative in the House voted for the bill, whereas the northern Democrats divided evenly, 44 to 44.

### The Surge of Free Soil

Amid the clamor over his bill, Douglas ruefully observed that he could now travel to Chicago by the light of his own burning effigies. Neither a fool nor a political novice, he was the victim of a political bombshell that exploded under his feet.

Support for free soil united northerners who agreed on little else. Some free-soilers opposed slavery on moral grounds and rejected racist legislation, but others were racists who opposed allowing any African-Americans, slave or free, into the West. An abolitionist traced the free-soil convictions of many westerners to a "perfect, if not supreme" hatred of blacks. Racist free-soilers in Iowa and Illinois secured laws prohibiting settlement by black people.

One opinion shared by free-soilers of all persuasions was that slavery impeded whites' progress. Because a slave worked for nothing, the argument ran, no free laborer could compete with a slave. A territory might contain only a handful of slaves or none at all, but as long as Congress refused to prohibit slavery in the territories, the institution would gain a foothold and free laborers would flee. Wherever slavery appeared, a free-soiler proclaimed, "labor loses its dignity; industry sickens; education finds no schools; religion finds no churches; and the whole land of slavery is impoverished." Free-soilers also blasted the idea that slavery had natural limits. One warned that "slavery is as certain to invade New Mexico and Utah as the sun is to rise"; others predicted that if slavery gained a toehold in Kansas, it would soon invade Minnesota.

To free-soilers, the Kansas-Nebraska Act, with its erasure of the Missouri Compromise, was the last straw, for it revealed, one wrote, "a continuous movement by slaveholders to spread slavery over the entire North." For a Massachusetts Whig congressman, who had voted for the Compromise of 1850 and opposed abolitionists, the Kansas-Nebraska Act, "that most wanton and wicked act, so obviously designed to promote the extension of slavery," was too much to bear. "I now advocate the freedom of Kansas under all circumstances, and the prohibition of slavery in all territories now free."

### The Ebbing of Manifest Destiny

The uproar over the Kansas-Nebraska Act embarrassed the Pierce administration. It also doomed Manifest Destiny, the one issue that had held the Democrats together in the 1840s.

Franklin Pierce had come to office championing Manifest Destiny, but increasing sectional rivalries sidetracked his efforts. In 1853 his emissary James Gadsden negotiated the purchase from Mexico of a strip of land south of the Gila River (now southern Arizona and part of southern New Mexico), an acquisition favored by advocates of a southern railroad route to the Pacific. Fierce opposition to the Gadsden Purchase revealed mounting free-soilers' suspicion of expansion, and the Senate approved the treaty only after slashing nine thousand square miles from the parcel. The sectional rivalries beginning to engulf the Nebraska bill clearly threatened any proposal to gain new territory.

Cuba provided even more vivid proof of the change in public attitudes toward expansion. In 1854 a former Mississippi governor, John A. Quitman, planned a filibuster (an unofficial military expedition) to seize Cuba from Spain. Eager to acquire Cuba, Pierce may have encouraged Quitman, but Pierce forced Quitman to scuttle the expedition when faced with intense opposition from northerners, who saw filibusters as just another manifestation of the Slave Power conspiracy to grab more territory for slavery.

Pierce still hoped to purchase Cuba, but events quickly slipped out of his control. In October 1854 the American ambassadors to Great Britain, France, and Spain, two of them southerners, met in Belgium and issued the unofficial Ostend Manifesto, calling on the United States to acquire Cuba by any means, including force. Beset by the storm over the Kansas-Nebraska Act and the furor over Quitman's proposed filibuster, Pierce rejected the mandate.

Despite Pierce's disavowal of the Ostend Manifesto, the idea of expansion into the Caribbean continued to attract southerners, including the Tennessee-born adventurer William Walker. Slightly built and so unassuming that he usually spoke with his hands in his pockets, Walker seemed an unlikely soldier of fortune. Yet between 1853 and 1860, the year a firing squad in Honduras executed him, Walker led a succession of filibustering expeditions into Central America. Taking advantage of civil chaos in Nicaragua, he made himself the chief political force there, reinstituted slavery, and talked of making Nicaragua a U.S. colony.

For all the proclamations and intrigues that surrounded the movement for southern expansion, its strength and goals remained open to question. With few exceptions, the adventurers were shady characters whom southern politicians might admire but on whom they could never depend. Some southerners, among them Louisiana sugar planters who opposed acquiring Cuba because Cuban sugar would compete with their product, were against expansion. But expansionists stirred enough commotion to worry antislavery northerners that the South conspired to establish a Caribbean slave empire. Like a card in a poker game, the threat of expansion southward was all the more menacing for not being played. As long as the debate on the extension of slavery focused on the continental United States, slavery's prospects for expansion were limited. However, adding Caribbean territory to the pot changed all calculations.

### The Whigs Disintegrate

While straining Democratic unity, the Kansas-Nebraska Act wrecked the Whig party. In the law's immediate aftermath, most northern Whigs hoped to blame the Democrats for the act and to entice free-soil Democrats to their side. In the state and congressional elections of 1854, the Democrats were decisively defeated. But the Whig party failed to benefit from the backlash against the Democrats. However furious they felt at Douglas for initiating the act, free-soil Democrats could not forget that the southern Whigs had supported Douglas. In addition, the northern Whigs themselves were deeply divided between antislavery "Conscience" Whigs, led by Senator William Seward of New York, and conservatives, led by former president Millard Fillmore, who were convinced that the Whig party had to adhere at all costs to the Compromise of 1850 to maintain itself as a national party.

Divisions within the Whig party not only repelled antislavery Democrats from affiliating with it but also prompted many antislavery Whigs to look for an alternative party. By 1856 the new Republican party would become the home for most of these northern refugees

from the traditional parties; but in 1854 and 1855, when the Republican party was only starting to organize, the American, or Know-Nothing, party emerged as the principal alternative to the established parties.

### The Rise and Fall of the Know-Nothings

The Know-Nothings evolved out of a secret nativist organization, the Order of the Star-Spangled Banner, founded in 1850. (The party's popular name, Know-Nothing, derived from the standard response of its members to inquiries about its activities: "I know nothing.") One of many such societies that mushroomed in response to the unprecedented immigration of the 1840s, the Order of the Star-Spangled Banner had sought to rid the United States of immigrant and Catholic political influence by pressuring the existing parties to nominate and appoint only native-born Protestants to office, and by advocating an extension of the naturalization period before immigrants could vote.

Throughout the 1840s nativists usually voted Whig, but their allegiance to the Whigs started to buckle during Winfield Scott's campaign for the presidency in 1852. In an attempt to revitalize his party, which was badly split over slavery, Scott had courted the traditionally Democratic Catholic vote. But Scott's tactic backfired, for most Catholics voted for Franklin Pierce. Nativists, meanwhile, felt betrayed by their party, and after Scott's defeat, many gravitated toward the Know-Nothings. The Kansas-Nebraska Act cemented their allegiance to the Know-Nothings, who in the North opposed both the extension of slavery and Catholicism. Indeed, an obsessive fear of conspiracies unified the Know-Nothings. Just as they denounced the pope for allegedly conspiring to subvert the American republic, they saw the evil influence of Slave Power everywhere.

The Know-Nothings' surge was truly stunning. In 1854 they captured the governorship, all the congressional seats, and almost all the seats in the state legislature in Massachusetts. Know-Nothings were sufficiently strong in the West to retard the emergence of the Republican party, and so strong in the East that they exploded any hopes that the Whigs had of capitalizing on hostility to the Kansas-Nebraska Act.

After rising spectacularly between 1853 and 1855, the star of Know-Nothingism nevertheless plummeted and gradually disappeared below the horizon after 1856. The Know-Nothings proved as vulnerable as the Whigs to sectional conflicts over slavery. Although primarily a force in the North, the Know-Nothings had a southern wing, composed mainly of former Whigs who loathed both the antislavery northerners who were abandoning the Whig party and the southern Democrats, whom they viewed as disunionist firebrands. In 1855 these southern Know-Nothings combined with northern conservatives to make acceptance of the Kansas-Nebraska Act part of the Know-Nothing platform, and thus they blurred the attraction of Know-Nothingism to those northern voters who were more antislavery than anti-Catholic. One such Whig refugee, Illinois congressman Abraham Lincoln, asked pointedly: "How can anyone who abhors the oppression of negroes be in favor of degrading classes of white people?" "We began by declaring," Lincoln continued, "that 'all men are created equal.' We now practically read it 'all men are created equal except negroes.' When the Know-Nothings get control, it will read 'all men are created equal, except Negroes and foreigners and Catholics.' " Finally, even most Know-Nothings eventually came to conclude that, as one observer put it, "neither the Pope nor the foreigners ever can govern the country or endanger its liberties, but the slavebreeders and slavetraders *do* govern it, and threaten to put an end to all government but theirs." Consequently, the Know-Nothings proved vulnerable to the challenge posed by the emerging Republican party, which did not officially embrace nativism and which had no southern wing to blunt its antislavery message.

### The Origins of the Republican Party

Born in the chaotic aftermath of the Kansas-Nebraska Act, the Republican party sprang up in several northern states in 1854 and 1855. With the Know-Nothings' demise after 1856, the Republicans would become the main opposition to the Democratic party, and they would win each presidential election from 1860 through 1880; but in 1855 it was unclear whether the Republicans had any future. While united by opposition to the Kansas-Nebraska Act, the party held various shades of opinion in uneasy balance. At one extreme were conservatives who merely wanted to restore the Missouri Compromise; at the other was a small faction of former Liberty party abolitionists; and the middle held a sizable body of free-soilers.

In addition to bridging these divisions, the Republicans confronted the task of building organizations on the state level, where the Know-Nothings were already well established. Politicians of the day knew that the voters' allegiances were often shaped by state issues,

including temperance. Maine's passage of the nation's first statewide prohibition law in 1851 spurred calls elsewhere for liquor regulation. Linking support for temperance with anti-Catholicism and antislavery, the Know-Nothings were well positioned to answer these calls.

Frequently, the same voters who were antislavery were also pro-temperance and anti-Catholic. The common thread here was the belief that addiction to alcohol and submission to the pope were forms of enslavement that had to be eradicated. Intensely moralistic, such voters viewed the traditional parties as controlled by unprincipled hacks, and they began to search for a new party. In competing with the Know-Nothings on the state level, the Republicans faced a dilemma, stemming from the fact that both parties were targeting many of the same voters. The Republican leadership had clearer antislavery credentials than did the Know-Nothing leadership, but this fact alone did not guarantee that voters would respond more to antislavery than to anti-Catholicism or temperance. Thus, if the Republicans attacked the Know-Nothings for stressing anti-Catholicism over antislavery, they ran the risk of alienating the very voters whom they had to attract. If they conciliated the Know-Nothings, they might lose their own identity as a party.

Sometimes attacking, sometimes conciliating, the Republicans won some successes in state elections in 1855; but as popular ire against the Kansas-Nebraska Act cooled, they also suffered setbacks. Even at the start of 1856, they were organized in only half the northern states and lacked any national organization. The Republicans desperately needed a development that would make voters worry more about the Slave Power than about rum or Catholicism. No single occurrence did more to unite the party around its free-soil center, to galvanize voters' antislavery feelings, and, consequently, to boost the Republicans' fortunes than the outbreak of violence in Kansas, which quickly gained for the territory the name Bleeding Kansas.

### Bleeding Kansas

In the wake of the Kansas-Nebraska Act, Boston-based abolitionists had organized the New England Emigrant Aid Company to send antislavery settlers into Kansas. The abolitionists' aim was to stifle escalating efforts to turn Kansas into a slave state. But antislavery New Englanders arrived slowly in Kansas; the bulk of the territory's early settlers came from Missouri or elsewhere in the Midwest. Very few of these early settlers opposed slavery on moral grounds. Some, in fact, favored slavery; others wanted to keep all blacks, whether slave or free, out of Kansas. "I kem to Kansas to live in a free state," exclaimed a clergyman, "and I don't want niggers a-trampin' over my grave."

Despite most settlers' racist leanings and utter hatred of abolitionists, Kansas became a battleground between proslavery and antislavery forces. In March 1855 thousands of proslavery Missourian "border ruffians," led by Senator David R. Atchison, crossed into Kansas to vote illegally in the first election for a territorial legislature. Drawing and cocking their revolvers, they quickly silenced any judges who questioned their right to vote in Kansas. These proslavery advocates probably would have won an honest election because they would have been supported by the votes both of slaveholders and of nonslaveholders horrified at rumors that abolitionists planned to use Kansas as a colony for fugitive slaves. But by stealing the election, the proslavery forces committed a grave tactical blunder. A cloud of fraudulence thereafter hung over the proslavery legislature subsequently established at Lecompton, Kansas. "There is not a proslavery man of my acquaintance in Kansas," wrote the wife of an antislavery farmer, "who does not acknowledge that the Bogus Legislature was the result of a gigantic and well planned fraud, that the elections were carried by an invading mob from Missouri." This legislature then further darkened its image by expelling several antislavery legislators and passing a succession of outrageous acts. These laws limited officeholding to individuals who would swear allegiance to slavery, punished the

harboring of fugitive slaves by ten years' imprisonment, and made the circulation of abolitionist literature a capital offense.

The territorial legislature's actions set off a chain reaction. Free-staters, including a small number of abolitionists and a much larger number of settlers enraged by the proceedings at Lecompton, organized a rival government at Topeka, Kansas, in the summer and fall of 1855. In response, the Lecompton government in May 1856 dispatched a posse to Lawrence, where free-staters, heeding the advice of antislavery minister Henry Ward Beecher that rifles would do more than Bibles to enforce morality in Kansas, had taken up arms and dubbed their guns "Beecher's Bibles." Riding under flags emblazoned "SOUTHERN RIGHTS" and "LET YANKEES TREMBLE AND ABOLITIONISTS FALL," the proslavery posse tore through the town like a hell-bent mob. Although the intruders did not kill anyone, they burned several buildings and destroyed two free-state printing presses—enough for the Republican press to label their actions "THE SACK OF LAWRENCE."

The next move belonged to John Brown. The sack of Lawrence convinced Brown that God now beckoned him, in the words of a neighbor, "to break the jaws of the wicked." In late May, Brown led seven men, including his four sons and his son-in-law, toward the Pottawatomie Creek near Lawrence. Setting upon five men associated with the Lecompton government, they shot one to death and hacked the others to pieces with broadswords. Brown's "Pottawatomie massacre" struck terror into the hearts of southerners and completed the transformation of Bleeding Kansas into a battleground between the South and the North. A month

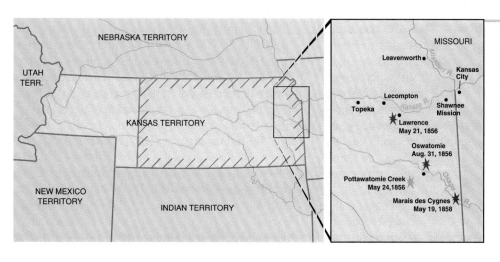

**Bleeding Kansas**
*Kansas became a battleground between free-state and slave-state factions in the 1850s.*

after the massacre, a South Carolinian living in Kansas wrote to his sister:

> I never lie down without taking the precaution to fasten my door and fix it in such a way that if it is forced open, it can be opened only wide enough for one person to come in at a time. I have my rifle, revolver, and old home-stocked pistol where I can lay my hand on them in an instant, besides a hatchet and an axe. I take this precaution to guard against the midnight attacks of the Abolitionists, who never make an attack in open daylight, and no Proslavery man knows when he is safe in this Ter[ritory.]

In Kansas popular sovereignty flunked its major test. Instead of quickly resolving the issue of slavery extension, popular sovereignty merely institutionalized the division over slavery by creating two rival governments, in Lecompton and Topeka. The Pierce administration then shot itself in the foot by denouncing the Topeka government and recognizing only its Lecompton rival. Pierce had forced northern Democrats into the awkward position of appearing to ally with the South in support of the fraudulently elected legislature at Lecompton. Nor did popular sovereignty keep the slavery issue out of national politics. On the day before the sack of Lawrence, Republican senator Charles Sumner of Massachusetts delivered a bombastic and wrathful speech, "The Crime Against Kansas," in which he verbally whipped most of the United States Senate for complicity in slavery and singled out Senator Andrew Butler of South Carolina for his choice of "the harlot, slavery" as his mistress and for the "loose expectoration" of his speech (a nasty reference to the aging Butler's tendency to drool). Sumner's oration stunned most senators. Douglas wondered aloud whether Sumner's real aim was "to provoke some of us to kick him as we would a dog in the street." Two days later a relative of Butler, Democratic representative Preston Brooks of South Carolina, strode into the Senate chamber, found Sumner at his desk, and struck him repeatedly with a cane. The hollow cane broke after five or six blows, but Sumner required stitches, experienced shock, and did not return to the Senate for three years. Brooks became an instant hero in the South, and the fragments of his weapon were "begged as sacred relics." A new cane, presented to Brooks by the city of Charleston, bore the inscription "Hit him again."

Now Bleeding Kansas and Bleeding Sumner united the North. The sack of Lawrence, Pierce's recognition of the proslavery Lecompton government, and Brooks's actions seemed to clinch the Republican argument that an aggressive slaveocracy held white northerners in contempt. Abolitionists remained unpopular in northern opinion, but southerners were becoming even less popular than abolitionists. Northern migrants to Kansas coined a name reflecting their feelings toward southerners: "the pukes." Other northerners attacked the slaveholding migrants to Kansas as the "Missouri savages." By denouncing the Slave Power more than slavery itself, Republican propagandists sidestepped the issue of slavery's morality, which divided their followers, and focused on portraying southern planters as arrogant aristocrats and the natural enemies of the laboring people of the North.

## The Election of 1856

The election of 1856 revealed the scope of the political realignments of the preceding few years. In this, its first presidential contest, the Republican party nominated John C. Frémont, the famed "pathfinder" who had played a key role in the conquest of California during the Mexican War. The Republicans then maneuvered the northern Know-Nothings into endorsing Frémont. The southern Know-Nothings picked the last Whig president, Millard Fillmore, as their candidate, and the Democrats dumped Pierce for the seasoned James Buchanan of Pennsylvania. A four-term congressman and long an aspirant to the presidency, Buchanan finally secured his party's nomination because he had the good luck to be out of the country (as minister to Great Britain) during the furor over the Kansas-Nebraska Act. As a signer of the Ostend Manifesto, he was popular in the South: virtually all of his close friends in Washington were southerners.

The campaign quickly turned into two separate races—Frémont versus Buchanan in the free states and Fillmore versus Buchanan in the slave states. In the North the candidates divided clearly over slavery extension; Frémont's platform called for a congressional prohibition of slavery in the territories, whereas Buchanan pledged congressional "non-interference." In the South Fillmore appealed to traditionally Whig voters and called for moderation in the face of secessionist threats. But by nominating a well-known moderate in Buchanan, the Democrats undercut some of Fillmore's appeal. Although Fillmore garnered more than 40 percent of the popular vote in ten of the slave states, he carried only Maryland. In the North Frémont outpolled Buchanan in the popular vote and won eleven of the sixteen free states; if Frémont had carried Pennsylvania and either Illinois or Indiana, he would have won the

**The Election of 1856**

| Candidates | Parties | Electoral Vote | Popular Vote | Percentage of Popular Vote |
|---|---|---|---|---|
| JAMES BUCHANAN | Democratic | 174 | 1,832,955 | 45.3 |
| John C. Frémont | Republican | 114 | 1,339,932 | 33.1 |
| Millard Fillmore | American | 8 | 871,731 | 21.6 |

election. As it turned out, Buchanan, the only truly national candidate in the race, secured the presidency.

The election yielded three clear conclusions. First, the American party was finished as a major national force. Having worked for the Republican Frémont, most northern Know-Nothings now joined that party, and in the wake of Fillmore's dismal showing in the South, southern Know-Nothings gave up on their party and sought new political affiliations. Second, although in existence scarcely more than a year, lacking any base in the South, and running a political novice, the Republican party did very well. A purely sectional party had come within reach of capturing the presidency. Finally, as long as the Democrats could unite behind a single national candidate, they would be hard to defeat. To achieve such unity, however, the Democrats would have to find more James Buchanans—"doughface" moderates who would be acceptable to southerners and who would not drive even more northerners into Republican arms.

# The Crisis of the Union

No one ever accused James Buchanan of impulsiveness or fanaticism. Although he disapproved of slavery, he believed that his administration could neither restrict nor end the institution. In 1860 he would pronounce secession a grave wrong, but he would again affirm that his administration could not stop it. Understandably, contemporaries hailed his election as a victory for moderation. Yet his administration encountered a succession of controversies, first over the famed *Dred Scott* decision of the Supreme Court, then over the proslavery Lecompton constitution in Kansas, next following the raid by John Brown on Harpers Ferry, and finally concerning secession itself. Ironically, a man who sought to avoid controversy presided over one of the most controversy-ridden administrations in American history. Buchanan's problems arose less from his own actions than from the fact that the forces driving the na-

tion apart were already spinning out of control by 1856. By the time of Buchanan's inauguration, southerners who looked north saw creeping abolitionism in the guise of free soil, whereas northerners who looked south saw an insatiable Slave Power. Once these images had taken hold in the minds of the American people, politicians like James Buchanan had little room to maneuver.

## The Dred Scott Case

Pledged to congressional "non-interference" with slavery in the territories, Buchanan had long looked to the courts for a nonpartisan resolution of the vexatious issue of slavery extension. A case that appeared to promise such a solution had been winding its way through the courts for years; on March 6, 1857, two days after Buchanan's inauguration, the Supreme Court handed down its decision in *Dred Scott* v. *Sandford.*

Dred Scott, a slave, had been taken by his master during the 1830s from the slave state Missouri into Illinois and the Wisconsin Territory, areas respectively closed to slavery by the Northwest Ordinance of 1787 and by the Missouri Compromise. After his master's death, Scott sued for his freedom on the grounds of his residence in free territory. In 1856 the case finally reached the Supreme Court.

The Court faced two key issues. Did Scott's residence in free territory during the 1830s make him free? Next, regardless of the answer to this question, did Scott, again enslaved in Missouri, have a right to sue in the federal courts? The Court could have resolved the case on narrow grounds by answering the second question in the negative, but Buchanan wanted a far-reaching decision that would deal with the broad issue of slavery in the territories.

In the end, Buchanan got the broad ruling that he sought, but one so controversial that it settled little. In the most important of six separate majority opinions, Chief Justice Roger B. Taney, a seventy-nine-year-old Marylander whom Andrew Jackson had appointed to succeed John Marshall in 1835, began with the narrow conclusion that Scott, a slave, could not sue for his freedom. Then the thunder started. No black, whether a slave or a free person descended from a slave, could become a citizen of the United States, Taney continued. Next Taney whipped the thunderheads into a tornado. Even if Scott had been a legal plaintiff, Taney ruled, his residence in free territory years earlier did not make him free, because the Missouri Compromise, whose provisions prohibited slavery in the Wisconsin Territory, was *itself* unconstitutional. The compromise, declared Taney, violated the Fifth Amendment's protection of property (including slaves).

Contrary to Buchanan's hopes, the decision touched off a new blast of controversy over slavery in the territories. The antislavery press flayed it as a "willful perversion" filled with "gross historical falsehoods." Taney's ruling gave Republicans more evidence that a fiendish Slave Power conspiracy gripped the nation. Although the Kansas-Nebraska Act had effectively repealed the Missouri Compromise, the Court's majority now rejected even the *principle* behind the compromise, the idea that *Congress* could prohibit slavery in the territories. Five of the six justices who rejected this principle were from slave states. The Slave Power, a northern paper bellowed, "has marched over and annihilated the boundaries of the states. We are now one great homogenous slaveholding community."

Like Stephen Douglas after the Kansas-Nebraska Act, President Buchanan now appeared as another northern dupe of the slaveocracy. Republicans restrained themselves from open defiance of the decision only by insisting that it did not bind the nation; Taney's comments on the constitutionality of the Missouri Compromise, they contended, amounted merely to *obiter dicta*, opinions superfluous to settling the case.

Reactions to the decision underscored the fact that by 1857 no "judicious" or nonpartisan solution to slavery extension was possible. Anyone who still doubted this needed only to read the fast-breaking news from Kansas.

### The Lecompton Constitution

While the Supreme Court wrestled with the abstract issues raised by the expansion of slavery, Buchanan sought a concrete solution to the gnawing problem of Kansas, where the free-state government at Topeka and the officially recognized proslavery government at Lecompton viewed each other with profound distrust.

Buchanan's plan for Kansas looked simple: an elected territorial convention would draw up a constitution that would either permit or prohibit slavery; Buchanan would submit the constitution to Congress; Congress would then admit Kansas as a state.

Unfortunately, no sooner had Buchanan devised his plan than it began to explode in his face. Popular sovereignty, the essence of Buchanan's plan, demanded fair play, a scarce quality in Kansas. The territory's history of fraudulent elections left both sides reluctant to commit their fortunes to the polls. An election for a constitutional convention took place in June 1857, but free-staters, by now a majority in Kansas, boycotted the election on grounds that the proslavery side would rig it. Dominated by proslavery delegates, a constitutional convention then met and drew up a frame of government, the Lecompton constitution, that protected the rights of those slaveholders already living in Kansas to their slave property and provided for a referendum in which voters could decide whether to allow in more slaves.

The Lecompton constitution created a dilemma for Buchanan. A supporter of popular sovereignty, he had gone on record in favor of letting the voters in Kansas decide the slavery issue. Now he was confronted by a constitution drawn up by a convention that had been elected by less than 10 percent of the eligible voters, by plans for a referendum that would not allow voters to remove slaves already in Kansas, and by the prospect that the proslavery side would conduct the referendum no more honestly than it had other ballots. Yet Buchanan had compelling reasons to accept the Lecompton constitution as the basis for Kansas's admission as a state. The South, which had provided him with 112 of his 174 electoral votes in 1856, supported the constitution. Buchanan knew, moreover, that only about two hundred slaves resided in Kansas, and he believed that the prospects for slavery in the remaining territories were slight. The contention over slavery in Kansas struck him as another example of how extremists could turn minor issues into major ones. To accept the constitution and speed the admission of Kansas as either a free state or a slave state seemed the best way to pull the rug from beneath the extremists and quiet the ruckus in Kansas. Accordingly, in December 1857 Buchanan formally endorsed the Lecompton constitution.

Buchanan's decision provoked a bitter attack from Senator Stephen A. Douglas. What rankled Douglas and many others was that the Lecompton convention, having drawn up a constitution, then allowed voters to decide only whether more slaves could be brought into the territory. "I care not whether [slavery] is voted down or voted up," Douglas declared. But to refuse to allow a vote on the constitution itself, with its protection of existing slave property, smacked of a "system of trickery and jugglery to defeat the fair expression of the will of the people."

Even as Douglas broke with Buchanan, events in Kansas took a new turn. A few months after electing delegates to the convention that drew up the Lecompton constitution, Kansans had gone to the polls to elect a territorial legislature. So flagrant was the fraud in this election—one village with thirty eligible voters returned more than sixteen hundred proslavery votes—that the governor disallowed enough proslavery returns to give free-staters a majority in the legislature. After the drafting of the Lecompton constitution, this territorial legislature called for a referendum on the entire document. Whereas the Kansas constitutional convention's goal had been to restrict the choice of voters to the narrow issue of the future introduction of slaves, the territorial legislature sought a referendum that would allow Kansans to vote against the protection of existing slave property as well as the introduction of more slaves.

In December 1857 the referendum called earlier by the constitutional convention was held. Boycotted by free-staters, the constitution with slavery passed overwhelmingly. Two weeks later, in the election called by the territorial legislature, the proslavery side abstained, and the constitution went down to crushing defeat. Having already cast his lot with the Lecompton convention's election, Buchanan simply ignored this second election. But he could not ignore the obstacles that the division in Kansas created for his plan to bring Kansas into the Union under the Lecompton constitution. When he submitted the plan to Congress, a deadlock in the House forced him to accept a proposal for still another referendum. This time, Kansans were given the choice between accepting or rejecting the entire constitution, with the proviso that rejection would delay statehood. Despite the proviso, Kansans overwhelmingly voted down the constitution.

Not only had Buchanan failed to tranquilize Kansas, but he had alienated northerners in his own party. His support for the Lecompton constitution confirmed the suspicion of northern Democrats that the southern Slave Power pulled all the important strings in their party. Douglas became the hero of the hour for northern Democrats and even for some Republicans.

"The bone and sinew of the Northern Democracy are with you," a New Yorker wrote to Douglas. Yet Douglas himself could take little comfort from the Lecompton fiasco, as his cherished formula of popular sovereignty increasingly looked like a prescription for civil strife rather than harmony.

## The Lincoln-Douglas Debates

Despite the acclaim he gained in the North for his stand against the Lecompton constitution, Douglas faced a stiff challenge in Illinois for reelection to the United States Senate. Of his Republican opponent, Abraham Lincoln, Douglas said: "I shall have my hands full. He is the strong man of his party—full of wit, facts, dates—and the best stump speaker with his droll ways and dry jokes, in the West."

Physically as well as ideologically, the two men formed a striking contrast. Tall (6′4″) and gangling, Lincoln once described himself as "a piece of floating drift-

**The Little Giant in the Character of Gladiator,** *1858. Douglas and his supporters are shown as gladiators menacing President Buchanan and his administration's newspaper, the* Washington Union, *for approving the Lecompton constitution.*

wood." Energy, ambition, and a passion for self-education had carried him from the Kentucky log cabin where he was born in 1809 through a youth filled with odd occupations (farm laborer, surveyor, rail-splitter, flatboatman, and storekeeper) into law and politics in his adopted Illinois. There he had capitalized on westerners' support for internal improvements to gain election to Congress in 1846 as a Whig. Having opposed the Mexican War and the Kansas-Nebraska Act, he joined the Republican party in 1856.

Douglas was fully a foot shorter than the towering Lincoln. But his compact frame contained astonishing energy. Born in New England, Douglas appealed primarily to the small farmers of southern origin who populated the Illinois flatlands. To these and others, he was

the "little giant," the personification of the Democratic party in the West. The campaign quickly became more than just another Senate race, for it pitted the Republican party's rising star against the Senate's leading Democrat and, thanks to the railroad and the telegraph, received unprecedented national attention.

Although some Republicans extolled Douglas's stand against the Lecompton constitution, to Lincoln nothing had changed. Douglas was still Douglas, the author of the infamous Kansas-Nebraska Act and a man who cared not whether slavery was voted up or down as long as the vote was honest. Opening his campaign with the "House Divided" speech ("this nation cannot exist permanently half slave and half free"), Lincoln reminded his Republican followers of the gulf that still

**Stephen A. Douglas**
*Douglas's politics were founded on his unflinching conviction that most Americans favored national expansion and would support popular sovereignty as the fastest and least controversial way to achieve it. Douglas's self-assurance blinded him to rising northern sentiment for free soil.*

**Abraham Lincoln**
*Clean-shaven at the time of his famous debates with Douglas, Lincoln would soon grow a beard to give himelf a more distinguished appearance.*

separated his doctrine of free soil from Douglas's popular sovereignty. Douglas dismissed the house-divided doctrine as an invitation to secession. What mattered to him was not slavery, which he viewed as merely an extreme way to subordinate an allegedly inferior race, but the continued expansion of white settlement. Like Lincoln, he wanted to keep slavery out of the path of white settlement. But unlike his rival, Douglas believed that popular sovereignty was the surest way to attain this goal without disrupting the Union.

The high point of the campaign came in a series of seven debates held from August to October 1858. The Lincoln-Douglas debates mixed political drama with the atmosphere of a festival. For the debate at Galesburg, for example, dozens of horse-drawn floats descended on the town from nearby farming communities. One bore thirty-two girls dressed in white, one for each state, and a thirty-third, who dressed in black with the label "Kansas" and carried a banner proclaiming "THEY WON'T LET ME IN."

Douglas used the debates to portray Lincoln as a virtual abolitionist and advocate of racial equality. Both charges were calculated to doom Lincoln in the eyes of the intensely racist Illinois voters. In response, Lincoln affirmed that Congress had no constitutional authority to abolish slavery in the South, and in one debate he asserted bluntly that "I am not, nor ever have been in favor of bringing about the social and political equality of the white, and black man." However, fending off charges of extremism was getting Lincoln nowhere; so in order to seize the initiative, he tried to maneuver Douglas into a corner.

In view of the *Dred Scott* decision, Lincoln asked in the debate at Freeport, could the people of a territory lawfully exclude slavery? In essence, Lincoln was asking Douglas to reconcile popular sovereignty with the *Dred Scott* decision. Lincoln had long contended that the Court's decision rendered popular sovereignty as thin as soup boiled from the shadow of a pigeon that had starved to death. If, as the Supreme Court's ruling affirmed, Congress had no authority to exclude slavery from a territory, then it seemingly followed that a territorial legislature created by Congress also lacked power to do so. To no one's surprise, Douglas replied that notwithstanding the *Dred Scott* decision, the voters of a territory *could* effectively exclude slavery simply by refusing to enact laws that gave legal protection to slave property.

Douglas's "Freeport doctrine" salvaged popular sovereignty but did nothing for his reputation among southerners, who preferred the guarantees of the *Dred Scott* ruling to the uncertainties of popular sovereignty. Whereas Douglas's stand against the Lecompton constitution had already tattered his reputation in the South ("he is already dead there," Lincoln affirmed), his Freeport doctrine stiffened southern opposition to his presidential ambitions.

Lincoln faced the problem throughout the debates that free soil and popular sovereignty, although distinguishable in theory, had much the same practical impact. Neither Lincoln nor Douglas doubted that popular sovereignty, if fairly applied, would keep slavery out of the territories. In order to keep the initiative and sharpen their differences, Lincoln shifted in the closing debates toward attacks on slavery as "a moral, social, and political evil." He argued that Douglas's view of slavery as merely an eccentric and rather unsavory southern custom would dull the nation's conscience and facilitate the legalization of slavery everywhere. But Lincoln compromised his own position by rejecting both abolition and equality for blacks.

Neither man scored a clear victory in argument, and the senatorial election itself settled no major issues. Douglas's supporters captured a majority of the seats in the state legislature, which at the time was responsible for electing U.S. senators. But despite the racist leanings of most Illinois voters, Republican candidates for the state legislature won a slightly larger share of the popular vote than did their Democratic rivals. Moreover, in its larger significance, the contest solidified the sectional split in the national Democratic party and made Lincoln famous in the North and infamous in the South.

### The Legacy of Harpers Ferry

Although Lincoln rejected abolitionism, he called free soil a step toward the "ultimate extinction" of slavery. Similarly, New York's Republican senator William H. Seward spoke of an "irrepressible conflict" between slavery and freedom. Predictably, many southerners ignored the distinction between free soil and abolition and concluded that Republicans and abolitionists were joined in an unholy alliance against slavery. To many in the South, the North seemed in the lock of demented leaders bent on civil war. One southern defender of slavery equated the doctrines of the abolitionists with those of "Socialists, of Free Love and Free Lands, Free Churches, Free Women and Free Negroes—of No-Marriage, No-Religion, No-Private Property, No-Law and No-Government."

Nothing did more to freeze this southern image of the North than the evidence of northern complicity in

John Brown's raid on Harpers Ferry and northern sermons that turned Brown into a martyr. In Philadelphia, some 250 outraged southern students seceded from the city's medical schools to enroll in southern schools. True, Lincoln and Seward condemned the raid, but southerners suspected that they regretted the conspiracy's failure more than the attempt itself.

Brown's abortive raid also rekindled southern fears of a slave insurrection. Rumors flew around the South, and vigilantes turned out to battle conspiracies that existed only in their minds. Volunteers, for example, mobilized to defend northeastern Texas against thousands of abolitionists supposedly on their way to pillage Dallas and its environs. In other incidents, vigilantes rounded up thousands of slaves, tortured some into confessing to nonexistent plots, and then lynched them. The hysteria fed by such rumors played into the hands of the extremists known as fire-eaters, who encouraged the witch hunt by spreading tales of slave conspiracies in the press so that southern voters would turn to them as alone able to "stem the current of Abolition."

More and more southerners concluded that the Republican party itself directed abolitionism and deserved blame for Brown's raid. After all, had not influential Republicans assailed slavery, unconstitutionally

tried to ban it, and spoken of an "irrepressible conflict" between slavery and freedom? The Tennessee legislature reflected southern views when it passed resolutions declaring that the Harpers Ferry raid was "the natural fruit of this treasonable 'irrepressible conflict' doctrine put forth by the great head of the Black Republican party and echoed by his subordinates."

## The South Contemplates Secession

A pamphlet published in 1860 embodied in its title the growing conviction of southerners that *The South Alone Should Govern the South.* Southerners reached this conclusion gradually, and often reluctantly. In 1850 few southerners could have conceived of transferring their allegiance from the United States to some new nation. Relatively insulated from the main tide of immigration, southerners thought of themselves as the most American of Americans. But the events of the 1850s persuaded many southerners that the North had deserted the true principles of the Union. Southerners interpreted northern resistance to the Fugitive Slave Act and to slavery in Kansas as either illegal or unconstitutional, and they viewed headline-grabbing phrases such as "irrepressible conflict" and "a higher law" as virtual declarations of war on the South. To southerners, it was the North, not the South, that had grown peculiar.

This sense of the North's deviance tinged reports sent home by southern visitors to the North in the 1850s. A Mississippi planter, for example, could scarcely believe his eyes when he witnessed a group of northern free blacks refusing to surrender their seats to white women. When assured by northern friends of their support for the South, southerners could only wonder why northerners kept electing Republicans to office. Southerners increasingly described their visits to the North as forays into "enemy territory." More and more they agreed with a South Carolinian's insistence that the South had to sever itself "from the rotten Northern element."

Viewed as a practical tactic to secure concrete goals, secession did not make a great deal of sense. Some southerners contended that secession would make it easier for the South to acquire more territory for slavery in the Caribbean; yet the South was scarcely united in desiring additional slave territory in Mexico, Cuba, or Central America. States like Alabama, Mississippi, and Texas contained vast tracts of unsettled land that could be converted to cotton cultivation far more easily than the Caribbean. Other southerners continued to complain that the North blocked the access of slaveholders to territories in the continental United States.

**John Brown,** c. 1850

*Brown ran to extremes of kindness and brutality, sympathy and egotistic self-righteousness, all threaded together by his Calvinist religious beliefs. Convinced of humans' utter dependency on God, he was sure that God had destined him to start a slave insurrection. Brown contracted for the production of one thousand pikes like the one shown here, with which he planned to arm the slaves.*

But it is unclear how secession would solve this problem. If the South were to secede, the remaining continental territories would belong exclusively to the North, which could then legislate for them as it chose. Nor would secession stop future John Browns from infiltrating the South to provoke slave insurrections.

Yet to dwell on the impracticality of secession as a choice for the South is to miss the point. Talk of secession was less a tactic with clear goals than an expression of the South's outrage at the irresponsible and unconstitutional course that southerners viewed the Republicans as taking in the North. It was not merely that Republican attacks on slavery sowed the seeds of slave uprisings. More fundamentally, southerners believed that the North was treating the South as its inferior—indeed, as no more than a slave. "Talk of Negro slavery," exclaimed southern proslavery philosopher George Fitzhugh, "is not half so humiliating and disgraceful as the slavery of the South to the North." Having persuaded themselves that slavery made it possible for them to enjoy unprecedented freedom and equality, white southerners took great pride in their homeland. They bitterly dismissed Republican portrayals of the South as a region of arrogant planters and degraded white common folk. Submission to the Republicans, declared the Democratic senator Jefferson Davis of Mississippi, "would be intolerable to a proud people."

Nevertheless, as long as the pliant James Buchanan occupied the White House, southerners did no more than *talk* about secession. Once aware that Buchanan had declined to seek reelection, however, they approached the election of 1860 with anxiety.

### The Election of 1860

As a single-issue, free-soil party, the Republicans had done well in the election of 1856. To win in 1860, however, they would have to broaden their appeal in the North, particularly in states like Pennsylvania and Illinois, which they had lost in 1856. To do so, Republican leaders had concluded, they needed to forge an economic program to complement their advocacy of free soil.

A severe economic slump following the so-called Panic of 1857 furnished the Republicans a fitting opening. The depression shattered more than a decade of American prosperity and thrust economic concerns to the fore. In response, in the late 1850s, the Republicans developed an economic program based on support for a protective tariff (popular in Pennsylvania) and on two issues favored in the Midwest, federal aid for internal improvements and the granting of free 160-acre homesteads to settlers out of publicly owned land. By proposing to make these homesteads available to immigrants who were not yet citizens, the Republicans went far in shedding their nativist image that lingered from their early association with the Know-Nothings. Carl Schurz, an 1848 German political refugee who had campaigned for Lincoln against Douglas in 1858, now labored mightily to bring his antislavery countrymen over to the Republican party.

The Republicans' desire to broaden their appeal also influenced their choice of a candidate. At their convention in Chicago, they nominated Abraham Lincoln over the early front-runner, William H. Seward of New York. Although better known than Lincoln, Seward failed to convince his party that he could carry the key states of Pennsylvania, Illinois, Indiana, and New Jersey. (Rueful Republicans remembered that their presidential candidate John C. Frémont would have won in 1856 if he had carried Pennsylvania and one of the other three states.) Lincoln held the advantage not only of hailing from Illinois but also of projecting a more moderate image than Seward on the slavery issue. Seward's penchant for controversial phrases like "irrepressible conflict" and "higher law" had given him a radical image. Lincoln, in contrast, had repeatedly affirmed that Congress had no constitutional right to interfere with slavery in the South and had explicitly rejected the "higher law" doctrine. The Republicans now needed only to widen their northern appeal.

The Democrats, still claiming to be a national party, had to bridge their own sectional differences. The *Dred Scott* decision and the conflict over the Lecompton constitution had weakened the northern Democrats and strengthened southern Democrats. While Douglas still desperately defended popular sovereignty, southern Democrats stretched *Dred Scott* to conclude that Congress now had to protect slavery in the territories.

The Democratic party's internal turmoil boiled over at its Charleston convention in the spring of 1860. Failing to force acceptance of a platform guaranteeing federal protection of slavery in the territories, the delegates from the Lower South stalked out. The convention adjourned to Baltimore, where a new fight broke out over the question of seating hastily elected, pro-Douglas slates of delegates from the Lower South states that had seceded from the Charleston convention. The decision to seat these pro-Douglas slates led to a walkout by delegates from Virginia and other states in the Upper South. The remaining delegates nominated Douglas; the seceders marched off to another hall in Baltimore and nominated Buchanan's vice president, John C.

## The Election of 1860

| | Electoral Vote | Popular Vote | Percentage of Popular Vote |
|---|---|---|---|
| **Republican** Abraham Lincoln | 180 | 1,865,593 | 39.8 |
| **Democratic, Southern** John C. Breckinridge | 72 | 848,356 | 18.1 |
| **Democratic, Northern** Stephen A. Douglas | 12 | 1,382,713 | 29.5 |
| **Constitutional Union** John Bell | 39 | 592,906 | 12.6 |
| Divided | 3  4 | | |

Breckinridge of Kentucky, on a platform calling for the congressional protection of slavery in the territories. Unable to rally behind a single nominee, the divided Democrats thus ran two candidates, Douglas and Breckinridge. The disruption of the Democratic party was now complete.

The South still contained an appreciable number of moderates, often former Whigs who had joined with the Know-Nothings behind Fillmore in 1856. In 1860 these moderates, aided by former northern Whigs who opposed both Lincoln and Douglas, forged the new Constitutional Union party and nominated John Bell, a Tennessee slaveholder who had opposed both the Kansas-Nebraska Act and the Lecompton constitution. Calling for the preservation of the Union, the new party took no stand on the divisive issue of slavery extension.

With four candidates in the field, voters faced a relatively clear choice. Lincoln conceded that the South had a constitutional right to preserve slavery but demanded that Congress prohibit its extension. At the other extreme, Breckinridge insisted that Congress had to protect slavery in any territory that contained slaves. This left the middle ground to Bell and Douglas, the latter still committed to popular sovereignty but in search of a verbal formula that might reconcile it with the *Dred Scott* decision. Despite this four-way race, Lincoln won

a clear majority of the electoral vote, 180 to 123 for his three opponents combined. Although Lincoln gained only 39 percent of the popular vote, his popular votes were concentrated in the North, the majority section, and were sufficient to carry every free state. Douglas ran a respectable second to Lincoln in the popular vote but a dismal last in the electoral vote. As the only candidate to campaign in both sections, Douglas suffered from the scattered nature of his votes and carried only Missouri. Bell won Virginia, Kentucky, and Tennessee, and Breckinridge captured Maryland and the Lower South.

### *The Movement for Secession*

As the dust from the election settled, southerners faced a disconcerting fact: a man so unpopular among southerners that his name had not even appeared on the ballot in much of their section was now president. Lincoln's election struck most of the white South as a calculated northern insult. The North, a South Carolina planter told a visitor from England, "has got so far toward being abolitionized as to elect a man avowedly hostile to our institutions." Few southerners believed that Lincoln would fulfill his promise to protect slavery in the South, and most feared that he would act as a mere front man for more John Browns. "Now that the black radical Republicans have the power I suppose they will Brown us all," a South Carolinian lamented. An uneducated Mississippian residing in Illinois expressed his reaction to the election more bluntly:

> It seems the north wants the south to raise cotton and sugar rice tobacco for the northern states, also to pay taxes and fight her battles and get territory for the purpose of the north to send her greasy Dutch and free niggers into the territory to get rid of them. At any rate that was what elected old Abe President. Some professed conservative Republicans Think and say that Lincoln will be conservative also but sir my opinion is that Lincoln will deceive them. [He] will undoubtedly please the abolitionists for at his election they nearly all went into fits with Joy.

Some southerners had threatened secession at the prospect of Lincoln's election; now the moment of choice had arrived. On December 20, 1860, a South Carolina convention voted unanimously for secession; and by February 1, 1861, Alabama, Mississippi, Florida, Georgia, Louisiana, and Texas had followed South Carolina's lead (see A Place in Time). On February 4 delegates from these seven states met in Montgomery, Al-

**Jefferson Davis**
*Davis brought an abundance of public experience to the Confederate presidency. Wounded in the Mexican War, he had served in the U.S. Senate, become secretary of war under President Franklin Pierce, and negotiated the Gadsden Purchase.*

abama, and established the Confederate States of America.

Despite the abruptness of southern withdrawal from the Union, the movement for secession had been, and continued to be, laced with uncertainty. Many southerners had resisted calls for immediate secession. Even after Lincoln's election, fire-eating secessionists had met fierce opposition in the Lower South from so-called cooperationists, who called upon the South to act in unison or not at all. Many cooperationists had hoped to delay secession in order to wring concessions from the North that might remove the need for secession. Jefferson Davis, who was inaugurated in February 1861 as the first president of the Confederacy, was a most reluctant secessionist, and he remained in the United States Senate for two weeks after his own state of Mississippi had seceded. Even zealous advocates of secession had a hard time reconciling themselves to secession and believing that they were no longer citizens of the United States. "How do you feel now, dear Mother," a Georgian wrote, "that *we* are in a foreign land?"

In the month after the establishment of the Confederate States of America, moreover, secessionists suffered stinging disappointments in the Upper South. Virginia, North Carolina, Tennessee, Arkansas, and the border slave states of Maryland, Kentucky, Delaware, and Missouri all rejected calls for secession. Various factors account for the Upper South's unwillingness to embrace the movement. In contrast to the Lower South, which had a guaranteed export market for its cotton, the Upper South depended heavily on economic ties to the North, bonds that would be severed by secession. Furthermore, with proportionately far fewer slaves than the Lower South, the states of the Upper South and the border states doubted the loyalty of their sizable non-slaveholding populations to the idea of secession. Virginia, for example, had every reason to question the allegiance to secession of its nonslaveholding western counties, which would soon break away to form Unionist West Virginia. Few in the Upper South could forget the raw nerve touched by the publication in 1857 of Hinton R. Helper's *The Impending Crisis of the South.* A nonslaveholding North Carolinian, Helper had described slavery as a curse upon poor white southerners and thereby questioned one of the most sacred southern doctrines, the idea that slavery rendered all whites equal. If secession were to spark a war between the states, moreover, the Upper South appeared to be the likeliest battleground. Whatever the exact weight assignable to each of these factors, one point is clear: the secession movement that South Carolina so boldly started in December 1860 seemed to be falling apart by March 1861.

### The Search for Compromise

The lack of southern unity confirmed the view of most Republicans that the secessionists were more bluster than substance. Seward described secession as the work of "a relatively few hotheads," and Lincoln believed that the loyal majority of southerners would soon wrest control from the fire-eating minority.

This perception stiffened Republican resolve to resist compromise. Moderate John J. Crittenden of Kentucky proposed compensation for owners of runaway slaves, repeal of northern personal-liberty laws, a constitutional amendment to prohibit the federal government from interfering with slavery in the southern states, and another amendment to restore the Missouri Compromise line for the remaining territories and protect slavery below it. But in the face of steadfast Republican opposition, the Crittenden plan collapsed.

Lincoln's faith in a "loyal majority" of southerners exaggerated both their numbers and their devotion to the Union. Many southern opponents of the fire-eating secessionists were sitting on the fence and hoping for major concessions from the North; their allegiance to the Union thus was conditional. Lincoln can be faulted for misreading southern opinion, but even if his assessment had been accurate, it is unlikely that he would have accepted the Crittenden plan. The sticking point was the proposed extension of the Missouri Compromise line. To Republicans this was a surrender, not a compromise, because it hinged on the abandonment of free soil, the founding principle of their party. In addition, Lincoln well knew that some southerners still talked of seizing more territory for slavery in the Caribbean. In proposing to extend the 36°30′ line, the Crittenden plan specifically referred to territories "here-

## Charleston, South Carolina

After securing the nomination of Pennsylvania's James Buchanan for the presidency in 1856, northern Democrats made a conciliatory gesture to the South. They agreed to hold their party's 1860 convention in Charleston, South Carolina. Time would give northerners many opportunities to regret that gesture. Long in decline, with only a few overpriced hotels, Charleston offered little as a convention city. The supporters of Stephen A. Douglas had to convert the second floor of a meeting hall into a giant dormitory, where they slept in rows of beds and baked in one-hundred-degree heat. Far more troubling to the delegates who descended on the city in April 1860 was the hysteria that consumed Charleston in reaction to John Brown's raid on Harpers Ferry in Virginia six months earlier. Mounted police, armed with swords and muskets, patrolled the streets, and vigilantes combed the byways in search of abolitionists. Panicked Charlestonians viewed every northerner in the city—whether a politician, a traveling salesman, or a schoolteacher—as "necessarily imbued with doctrines hostile to our institutions."

Suspicion and harassment greeted northern sojourners, but Charleston's blacks endured a virtual reign of terror after "the late outrage at Harpers Ferry." A little under half the city's population in 1860 was black, and 81 percent of the blacks were slaves. White southerners distrusted urban slaves, most of whom lived apart from their rural masters and were hired out to city employers. Indeed, some slaves took advantage of their distance from their masters to hire themselves out for wages, a practice that whites feared would infect slaves with the notion that they were free. In addition, white workingmen resented competition from urban slaves in the skilled trades, and they used the furor over John Brown's raid to pressure the city's mayor into enforcing an old and long-neglected ordinance that slaves working away from their masters wear badges. Those without badges were rounded up and jailed, and their masters fined.

Charleston's enslaved blacks were not the sole targets of the city's increasingly repressive mood. Few southern cities had more visible or well-organized communities of free blacks than Charleston. Composed mainly of mulattos who took pride in their light skin and assembled in the Brown Fellowship Society, Charleston's free people of color formed a brown aristocracy of skilled tailors, carpenters, and small tradesmen. Free blacks like John Marsh Johnson worshiped in the same Episcopal church as such elite whites as Christopher G. Memminger, a prominent lawyer and politician who would soon become the Confederacy's secretary of the treasury. The financial prosperity of these free blacks depended on the white aristocrats who frequented their stores, admired their thrift and sobriety, and took comfort in their apparent loyalty. When a bill calling for the enslavement or expulsion of South Carolina's free blacks came before the state legislature in 1859, Memminger reminded the legislators that a free black had helped to expose Denmark Vesey's planned uprising of slaves back in 1822. Heartened by the support of Memminger and others, John Marsh Johnson congratulated himself for predicting "from the onset that nothing would be done affecting our position."

Johnson little realized the extent to which the world of Charleston's free blacks was in danger of falling apart. The city had been a center of southern-rights radicalism since the days of the nullification crisis. Charleston was the home of the fire-eater, Robert Barnwell Rhett; and it always rolled out the welcome carpet for Edmund Ruffin, a Virginia drumbeater for slavery. Furthermore, after John Brown's raid, even moderate citizens, including former Unionists, were embracing secession. The cause of secession demanded, in turn, that elite whites unite with working-class whites in a common front

**Slave Badges**

*The badges that they were forced to wear constantly reminded Charleston's slaves of their bondage.*

against the North. During the 1850s Charleston's working-class whites had grown increasingly powerful and aggressive; the increase in their numbers gave the city a white majority in 1860, for the first time in its history. Working-class whites feared competition from any blacks but had a special loathing for free blacks, who on Sundays dared "to draw up in fine clothes" and "wear a silk hat and gloves" and who celebrated weddings by drinking champagne and riding to the church in elegant carrages.

Soon free blacks became the victims of the growing cooperation between elite and working-class whites. Indeed, by August 1860 Charleston was in the grip of an "enslavement crisis." The same police dragnets that had snared urban slaves without badges now trapped innumerable free blacks as well. Unenslaved blacks suddenly had to prove that they were free, a tall order inasmuch as South Carolina had long prohibited the freeing of slaves. For decades white masters who wanted to free favored slaves had resorted to complicated legal ruses, with the result that many blacks who had lived for years as free people could not prove that they were free and were forced back into slavery. Abandoning his initial optimism, John Marsh Johnson wrote nervously to his brother-in-law to report "cases of persons who for 30 yrs. have been paying capitation Tax [as free persons of color] & one of 35 yrs. that have to go back to bondage & take out their Badges." Many other free African Americans fled to the North.

A religious man, Johnson believed that God helped those who helped themselves. Rather than "supinely wait for the working of a miracle by having a Chariot let down to convey us away," he resolved in late August 1860 to stay and endure the "present calamity." By then, however, the Democratic party had snapped apart under the pressure of southern demands for the congressional recognition of slavery in all the territories. "The last party pretending to be a national party, is broken up," the secessionist Charleston *Mercury* exulted, "and the antagonism of the sections of the Union has nothing to arrest its fierce collision." In December 1860 another convention meeting in Charleston would proclaim South Carolina's secession from the United States. In April 1861, only a year after the Democratic delegates had assembled in Charleston for their party's convention, shore batteries along Charleston's harbor would open fire on Fort Sumter. This action set in motion a train of events leading to the extinction of slavery itself. Ironically, after the Civil War, the free blacks who had weathered the enslavement crisis of 1860 would emerge as the leaders of the city's black people, all of them now free.

**Saluda Sentinels, Always Ready**
*Secessionist sentiment also flared in interior areas of South Carolina such as Saluda. This militia flag of the Saluda Sentinels, featuring an officer in Revolutionary War garb, shows how secessionists invoked memories of the American struggle for independence.*

**First Shots of the Civil War**
*Stunned Charleston residents crowded the city's rooftops to view the firing on Fort Sumter—a siege that lasted thirty-four hours.*

after acquired." Lincoln feared that it would be only a matter of time "till we shall have to take Cuba as a condition upon which they [the seceding states] will stay in the Union."

Beyond these considerations, the precipitous secession of the Lower South subtly changed the question that Lincoln faced. The issue was no longer slavery extension but secession. The Lower South had left the Union in the face of losing a fair election. For Lincoln to have caved in to such pressure would have violated majority rule, the principle upon which the nation, not just his party, had been founded.

### The Coming of War

By the time Lincoln took office in March 1861, little more than a spark was needed to ignite a war. Lincoln pledged in his inaugural address to "hold, occupy, and possess" federal property in the seven states that had seceded, an assertion that committed him to the de-

fense of Fort Pickens in Florida and Fort Sumter in the harbor of Charleston, South Carolina. William Seward, whom Lincoln had appointed secretary of state, now became obsessed with the idea of conciliating the Lower South in order to hold the Upper South in the Union. In addition to advising the evacuation of federal forces from Fort Sumter, Seward proposed a scheme to reunify the nation by provoking a war with France and Spain. But Lincoln brushed aside Seward's advice. Instead, the president informed the governor of South Carolina of his intention to supply Fort Sumter with much-needed provisions, but not with men and ammunition. To gain the dubious military advantage of attacking Fort Sumter before the arrival of relief ships, Confederate batteries began to bombard the fort shortly before dawn on April 12. The next day, the fort's garrison surrendered.

Proclaiming an insurrection in the Lower South, Lincoln now appealed for 75,000 militiamen from the loyal states to suppress the rebellion. His proclamation

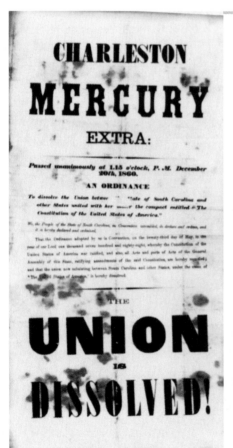

### Secession

*Four key states—Virginia, Arkansas, Tennessee, and North Carolina—did not secede until after the fall of Fort Sumter. The border slave states of Maryland, Delaware, Kentucky, and Missouri stayed in the Union.*

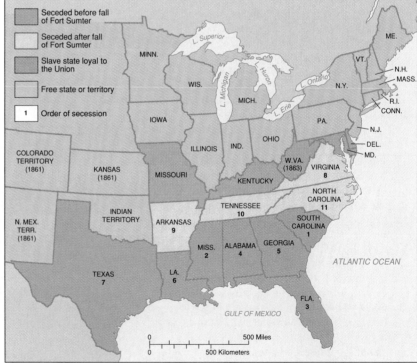

pushed citizens of the Upper South off the fence upon which they had perched for three months. "I am a Union man," one southerner wrote, "but when they [the Lincoln administration] send men south it will change my notions. I can do nothing against my own people." In quick succession, Virginia, North Carolina, Arkansas, and Tennessee leagued with the Confederacy. After acknowledging that "I am one of those dull creatures that cannot see the good of secession," Robert E. Lee resigned from the United States Army rather than lead federal troops against his native Virginia.

The North, too, was ready for a fight, less to abolish slavery than to punish secession. Worn out from his efforts to find a peaceable solution to the issue of slavery extension, and with only a short time to live, Stephen Douglas assaulted "the new system of resistance by the sword and bayonet to the results of the ballot-box" and affirmed: "I deprecate war, but if it must come I am with my country, under all circumstances, and in every contingency."

## CONCLUSION

The expectation of most American political leaders that the Compromise of 1850 would finally resolve the vexing issue of slavery extension had a surface plausibility. In neither 1850 nor 1860 did the great majority of Americans favor the abolition of slavery in the southern states. Rather, they divided over slavery in the territories, an issue seemingly settled by the Compromise. Stephen A. Douglas, its leading architect and a man who assumed he always had his finger on the popular pulse, was sure that slavery had reached its natural limits, that popular sovereignty would keep it out of the territories, and that the furor over slavery extension would die down.

Douglas believed that only a few hotheads had kept the slavery extension issue alive. He was wrong. The differences between northerners and southerners over slavery extension were grounded on different understandings of liberty, which to northerners meant their freedom to pursue self-interest without competition from slaves, and to southerners their freedom to dispose of their legally acquired property, slaves, as they chose. The Compromise, which had barely scraped through Congress, soon unraveled. Enforcement of the Fugitive Slave Act brought to the surface widespread northern resentment of slaveholders, people who seemingly lived off the work of others, and a determi-

nation to exclude the possibility of slavery in the territories. Southern support for Douglas's Kansas-Nebraska bill, with its repeal of the Missouri Compromise and its apparent invitation to southerners to bring slaves into Kansas, persuaded many northerners that the South harbored the design of extending slavery. For their part, southerners, already angered by northern defiance of the Fugitive Slave Act, interpreted northern outrage against Douglas's bill as further evidence of the North's disrespect for the rule of law.

By the mid-1850s the sectional division was spinning out of the control of politicians. The Whigs collapsed and the ties between northern and southern Democrats nearly snapped. The outbreak of civil strife in Kansas pushed former northern Whigs and many northern Democrats toward the new, purely sectional, Republicans, a party whose very existence southerners interpreted as a mark of northern contempt for them. The South was not yet ready for secession. Before it took that drastic step, it had to convince itself that the North's real design was not merely to restrict slavery extension but to destroy slavery and, with it, the South itself. Northern hostility to the *Dred Scott* decision and sympathy for John Brown struck southerners as proof of just such an intent.

As an expression of principled outrage, secession capped a decade in which each side had clothed itself in principles that were deeply embedded in the nation's political heritage. Both sides subscribed to the rule of law, which each accused the other of deserting. In the end, war broke out between siblings who, although they claimed the same heritage and inheritance, had become virtual strangers to each other.

## FOR FURTHER READING

William W. Freehling, *The Road to Disunion: Secessionists at Bay, 1776–1854* (1990). A major study that traces the roots of secession.

Eric Foner, *Free Soil, Free Labor, Free Men: The Ideology of the Republican Party Before the Civil War* (1970). An outstanding analysis of the thought, values, and components of the Republican party.

William E. Gienapp, *The Origins of the Republican Party, 1852–1856* (1987). A comprehensive account of the birth of a major party.

Michael F. Holt, *The Political Crisis of the 1850s* (1978). A lively reinterpretation of the politics of the 1850s.

Allan Nevins, *The Ordeal of the Union* (vols. 1–2, 1947). A detailed, highly regarded account of the coming of the Civil War.

David Potter, *The Impending Crisis, 1848–1861* (1976). The best one-volume overview of the events leading to the Civil War.

# Freedom Reborn: Civil War
## 1861–1865

*The Death of General Sedgwick,
Spotsylvania, May 9, 1864*
by Julian Scott

"We have very exciting times here now . . . the war is all the talk," wrote a young Illinois farmer, James P. Welsh, on May 12, 1861, to his brother John in Virginia. Since Fort Sumter's fall a month before, war fever had swept through Woodford County, Illinois, followed by rallies, recruitment, and heavy enrollment. "Every one wants a place," James Welsh reported. "This county has got three companies, two more than her share, and some are snorting mad because they cannot get to go." James Welsh avidly endorsed the Unionist stance. He thought little of the secessionists—"Jeff Davis and his crew of pirates and rebels"—and less of their actions. "It is treason and nothing more nor less, and will as surely meet the fate of treason," he declared.

James P. Welsh and his brother John Welsh had grown up in Rockbridge County, Virginia, four miles north of Lexington, in the fertile Shenandoah Valley. Sons of a Scots-Irish pioneer, the brothers were Whigs and nonslaveowners; each had farmed 275 acres. In 1853 James had migrated to Illinois, where he became a Republican and voted for Lincoln in 1860. Back in Virginia, at the family home, Turtle Hill, John Welsh disparaged his brother's political views. On May 23, 1861, just as Virginians voted to ratify the state's ordinance of secession, John Welsh sent an angry reply to James in Illinois.

"[T]he North expects to crush the South at once, but they are mistaken," John Welsh declared. "We are prepared for a protracted war; we look upon it as a just cause and are united . . . all contribute without stint." Rockbridge County had raised five companies; men were drilling everywhere. John Welsh especially resented his brother's betrayal of their native state. "[To] think that I have a brother who would advocate sending men here to butcher his own friends and relations," John exclaimed. James, he believed, had been "im-posed upon by false statements." Nor did John Welsh cling to his former Whig opinions. "I have always opposed secession but I shall vote for it today," he explained, because he was unable to accept Republican rule. "We don't intend to trouble the North," John Welsh concluded, "but they must let us alone."

James P. Welsh, however, had the final word. "How can you be expected to be let alone when you are taking the course you now are?" he asked John Welsh in a letter of May 26 that crossed his brother's response. "I once more entreat you not to place yourself in opposition to your country." A week later, when he continued his argument, James P. Welsh hurled back the accusation of disloyalty. He voiced disbelief "that I have a brother that would raise a hand to tear down the glorious Stars and Stripes." He mocked his brother's rebel grievances. "What is it that you complain of? Only that there is a Republican president and you are afraid that he will do something to injure your dear institution of slavery." The administration had done nothing, James insisted, "to interfere with slavery where it exists. But because South Carolina wants to secede you are fool enough to follow." Secession, moreover, would bring its own perils, James warned. Even if Virginia severed itself from the United States, he posited, "What next? Political questions will arise in your Southern Confederacy and you have set the precedent of secession and cannot object to any part of your union going." Finally, James P. Welsh upheld the cause of patriotism. "My country has been assailed and my country's flag has been insulted," he declared. "I would strike down my own brother if he dares to raise a hand to destroy that flag."

After exchanging charges and countercharges, both brothers enlisted. In Virginia, John Welsh joined the 27th Virginia Infantry Regiment, where he became captain of his company and served until fatally wounded at Gettysburg in 1863. James P. Welsh enrolled in the 78th

Illinois Infantry, and in 1864–1865, he marched with the triumphant Union army into Georgia and the Carolinas. Though unusual in their split allegiances, the Welsh brothers were neither unique nor different in sentiment from their respective comrades-in-arms. Like each of the Welsh brothers, Union and Confederate volunteers responded to the rush to arms that engulfed both regions after Fort Sumter fell. Like the brothers, as well, soldiers on both sides claimed the ideals of liberty, loyalty, and patriotism as their own. Like the brothers, finally, most Americans of 1861 harbored their own combinations of prophetic insights and false expectations.

Unlike John Welsh, few volunteers or even politicians anticipated a protracted war. Most northern estimates ranged from one month to a year; rebels, too, counted on a speedy victory. Neither northerners nor southerners anticipated the carnage that the war would bring. One out of every five soldiers who fought in the Civil War died in it; the 620,000 soldiers who lost their lives between 1861 and 1865 nearly equaled the number of American soldiers killed in all the nation's earlier and later wars combined. Once it became clear that the war would not end with a few battles, leaders on both sides contemplated strategies once unpalatable or even unthinkable. The South, where the hand of government had always fallen lightly on the citizenry, found that it had to impose a draft and virtually extort supplies from its civilian population. By the war's end, the Confederacy was even ready to arm its slaves in an ironically desperate effort to save a society founded on slavery. The North, which began the war with the limited objective of overcoming secession and explicitly disclaimed any intention of interfering with slavery, found that in order to win it had to shred the fabric of southern society by destroying slavery. For politicians as well as soldiers, the war defied expectations and turned into a series of surprises.

This chapter focuses on five major questions:

♦ What changes in administration did the war impose on the North and South?

♦ How successfully did the Union and the Confederacy respond to the pressures of war?

♦ How did the issues of slavery and emancipation transform the war?

♦ What factors determined the military outcome of the war?

♦ In what lasting ways did the Civil War change the United States as a nation?

# Mobilizing for War

North and South alike were unprepared for war. In April 1861 the Union had only a small army of sixteen thousand men, scattered all over the country, mostly in the West. One-third of the officers of the Union army had resigned to join the Confederacy. The nation had not had a strong president since James K. Polk in the 1840s. Its new president, Abraham Lincoln, struck many observers as a yokel. That such a government could marshal its people for war seemed a doubtful proposition. The federal government had levied no direct taxes for decades, and it had never imposed a draft. The Confederacy was even less prepared, for it had no tax structure, no navy, only two tiny gunpowder factories, and poorly equipped, unconnected railroad lines.

During the first two years of the war, both sides would have to overcome these deficiencies, raise and supply large armies, and finance the heavy costs of war. In each region mobilization for war expanded the powers of the central government to an extent that few had anticipated.

## *Recruitment and Conscription*

The Civil War armies were the largest organizations ever created in America; by the end of the war, over 2 million men would have served in the Union army and 800,000 in the Confederate army. In the first flush of enthusiasm for war, volunteers rushed to the colors. "I go for wiping them out," a Virginian wrote to his governor. "War! and volunteers are the only topics of conversation or thought," an Oberlin College student told his brother in April 1861. "I cannot study. I cannot sleep. I cannot work, and I don't know as I can write."

At first, the raising of armies depended on local efforts rather than on national or even state direction. Citizens opened recruiting offices in their hometowns, held rallies, and signed up volunteers; regiments were usually composed of soldiers from the same locale. In the South cavalrymen were expected to provide their own horses, and uniforms everywhere were left mainly to local option. In both armies officers up to the rank of colonel were elected by other officers and enlisted men.

This informal and democratic way of raising and organizing soldiers could not long withstand the stress of war. As early as July 1861, the Union instituted examinations for officers. Also, as casualties mounted, military demand soon exceeded the supply of volunteers. The Confederacy felt the pinch first and in April

1862 enacted the first conscription law in American history. All able-bodied white males aged eighteen to thirty-five would be required to serve in the military for three years. Subsequent amendments raised the age limit to forty-five and then to fifty, and lowered it to seventeen.

The Confederacy's Conscription Act antagonized southerners. Opponents charged that the draft was an assault on state sovereignty by a despotic regime and that the law would "do away with all the patriotism we have." Exemptions that applied to many occupations, from religious ministry to shoemaking, angered the nonexempt. So did a loophole, closed in 1863, that allowed the well-off to hire substitutes. Hostility also mounted over an amendment, the so-called 20-Negro law, that exempted an owner or overseer of twenty or more slaves from service. Although southerners widely feared that the slave population could not be controlled if all able-bodied white males were away in the army, the 20-Negro law evoked complaints about "a rich man's war but a poor man's fight."

Despite opposition, the Confederate draft became increasingly hard to evade, and this fact stimulated volunteering. Only one soldier in five was a draftee, but four out of every five eligible white southerners served in the Confederate army. A new conscription law of 1864, which required all soldiers then in the army to stay in for the duration of the war, ensured that a high proportion of Confederate soldiers would be battle-hardened veterans.

Once the army was raised, the Confederacy had to supply it. At first, the South relied on arms and ammunition imported from Europe, weapons confiscated from federal arsenals, and guns captured on the battlefield. These stopgap measures bought time until an industrial base was established. By 1862 the Confederacy had a competent head of ordnance (weaponry), Josiah Gorgas. Working through Gorgas and other officials, the Confederacy assigned ordnance contracts to privately owned factories like the Tredegar Iron Works in Richmond, provided loans to establish new factories, and created government-owned industries like the gi-

## Brothers in Combat: The Opposing Armies of the Civil War

*"They sing and whoop, they laugh: they holler to de people on de ground and sing out 'Good-bye,' " remarked a slave watching rebel troops depart. "All going down to die." Longing for the excitement of battle, the first volunteers signed up with hopes of adventure and zest for combat. "[O]ur men are Almost Crazy to Meet the Enemy," a North Carolinian declared. A New Yorker who sent two teenaged sons to enlist marveled how the war provided "so much manhood suddenly achieved," and in early letters home, soldiers exulted over their transformation in battle. "With your first shot you become a new man," an Alabama volunteer told his father. Actual battlefield experiences scarcely conformed to the early volunteers' visions. For most soldiers, war meant surviving in fetid army camps and inuring themselves to the stench of death. As these graphs show, the Civil War had profound human costs. North and South, there was hardly a family that did not grieve for a lost relative or friend. Injured veterans became a common sight in cities, towns, and rural districts well into the twentieth century.*

**Union Forces**     **Confederate Forces**

| Category | Union Forces | Confederate Forces |
|---|---|---|
| Total size | 2,100,000 | 800,000 |
| Draftees | 46,000 | 120,000 |
| Substitutes | 118,000 | 70,000 |
| Desertions | 200,000 | 104,000 |
| Desertees caught and returned | 80,000 | 21,000 |
| Deaths from battle wounds | 110,070 | 94,000 |
| Deaths from disease | 249,930 | 166,000 |

**Total Civil War Deaths Compared to U.S. Deaths in Other Wars**

|  |  |
|---|---|
| Civil War | 620,000 |
| World War II | 318,000 |
| World War I | 115,000 |
| Vietnam War | 56,227 |
| Korean War | 33,000 |
| Mexican War | 13,270 |
| Spanish-American War and Philippine Insurrection | 9,700 |
| Revolutionary War | 4,044 |
| War of 1812 | 2,200 |

ant Augusta Powder Works in Georgia. The South lost few, if any, battles for want of munitions.

Supplying troops with clothing and food proved more difficult. Southern soldiers frequently went without shoes; during the South's invasion of Maryland in 1862, thousands of Confederate soldiers had to be left behind because they could not march barefoot on Maryland's gravel-surfaced roads. Late in the war, Robert E. Lee's Army of Northern Virginia ran out of food but never out of ammunition. Southern supply problems had several sources: railroads that fell into disrepair or were captured, an economy that relied more heavily on producing tobacco and cotton than growing food, and Union invasions early in the war that overran the livestock and grain-raising districts of central Tennessee and Virginia. Close to desperation, the Confederate Congress in 1863 passed the Impressment Act, which authorized army officers to take food from reluctant farmers at prescribed rates. This unpopular law also empowered agents to impress slaves into labor for the army, a provision that provoked yet more resentment.

The industrial North could more easily supply its troops with arms, clothes, and food than could the South. However, keeping a full army was another matter. When the initial tide of enthusiasm for enlistment ebbed, Congress followed the Confederacy's example and turned to conscription. The Enrollment Act of March 1863 made every able-bodied white male citizen aged twenty to forty-five eligible for draft into the Union army.

Like the Confederate conscription law of 1862, the Enrollment Act granted exemptions, although only to high government officials, ministers, and men who were the sole support of widows, orphans, or indigent parents. It also offered two means of escaping the draft: substitution, or paying another man who would serve instead; and commutation, paying a $300 fee to the government. The law divided each state into enrollment districts and gave them quotas to meet, first through volunteers and then through the draft. The new system was difficult to administer and chaotic in practice. Enrollment districts often competed for volunteers by offering cash payments (bounties); dishonest "bounty jumpers" repeatedly registered and deserted after collecting their payment. Democrats denounced conscription as a violation of individual liberties and states' rights. Ordinary citizens of little means resented the commutation and substitution provision and leveled their own "poor man's fight" charges. Still, as the Confederates had learned, the law stimulated volunteering. Only 8 percent of Union soldiers were draftees or substitutes.

## Financing the War

The recruitment and supply of huge armies lay far beyond the capacity of American public finance at the start of the war. In the 1840s and 1850s, annual federal spending had averaged only 2 percent of the gross national product.* With such meager expenditures, the

---

* Gross national product (GNP): the sum, measured in dollars, of all goods and services produced in a given year. By contrast, in the 1980s the federal budgets averaged about 25 percent of the GNP.

federal government met its revenue needs from tariff duties and income from the sale of public lands. In fact, the government had not imposed any direct taxes on its citizens for thirty years. During the war, however, annual federal expenditures gradually rose to 15 percent of the gross national product, and the need for new sources of revenue became urgent. Yet neither the Union nor the Confederacy initially showed much enthusiasm for imposing taxes. Americans were unaccustomed to paying taxes to their national government, both sides expected the war to be short, and neither wanted the knock of the tax collector to dampen patriotic spirit. In August 1861 the Confederacy enacted a small property tax and the Union an income tax, but neither raised much revenue.

Both sides therefore turned to war bonds; that is, to loans from citizens, to be repaid by future generations. Patriotic southerners quickly bought up the Confederacy's first bond issue ($15 million) in 1861. That same year, a financial wizard, Philadelphia banker Jay Cooke, induced the northern public to subscribe to a much larger bond issue ($150 million). But bonds had to be paid for in gold or silver coin (specie), which was in short supply. Soaking up most of its available specie, the South's first bond issue threatened to be its last. In the North many hoarded their gold rather than spend it on bonds.

Recognizing the limitations of taxation and of bond issues, the Union and the Confederacy began to print paper money. Early in 1862 Lincoln signed into law the Legal Tender Act, which authorized the issue of $150 million of the so-called greenbacks. Christopher Memminger, the Confederacy's treasury secretary, and Salmon P. Chase, his Union counterpart, shared a distrust of paper money, but each came around to the idea because, as Chase bluntly put it, *The Treasury is nearly empty.* The availability of paper money would make it easier to pay soldiers, to levy and raise taxes, and to sell war bonds.

Yet doubts about paper money lingered. Unlike gold and silver, which had established market values, the value of paper money depended mainly on the public's confidence in the government that issued it. To bolster that confidence, Union officials made the greenbacks legal tender (that is, acceptable in payment of most public and private debts) and overcame their early reservations about taxes by imposing increasingly stiff taxes on everything from income to liquor and billiard tables. The steady flow of tax revenue into the federal treasury strengthened public confidence in the government's ability to meet its obligations and helped check the inflationary tendency inherent in paper money.

In contrast, the Confederacy never made its paper money legal tender, and suspicions arose that the southern government lacked confidence in its own paper issues. To compound the problem, the Confederacy raised less than 5 percent of its wartime revenue from taxes. (The comparable figure for the North was 21 percent.) The Confederacy did enact a comprehensive tax measure in 1863, but Union invasions and the South's relatively undeveloped system of internal transportation made tax collection a hit-or-miss proposition. For example, the Confederacy's tax measures of 1863 included a tax-in-kind, a sort of tithe. After feeding their families, farmers had to pledge one-tenth of their crops to the government. But the tax-in-kind fell disproportionately on farmers who lived near the railroads traveled by tax collectors, and some of the food collected rotted in government warehouses. To many farmers, the Confederacy's tax policies seemed unfair and incompetently administered.

In the face of the Confederacy's sorry performance in collecting taxes, confidence in the South's paper money quickly evaporated, and the value of Confederate paper in relation to gold plunged. The Confederacy responded by printing more paper money, a billion dollars by 1865, but this action merely accelerated southern inflation. Whereas prices in the North rose about 80 percent during the war, the Confederacy suffered an inflation rate of over 9,000 percent. What cost a southerner one dollar in 1861 cost forty-six dollars by 1864.

By raising taxes, floating bonds, and printing paper money, both the Union and the Confederacy broke with the hard-money, minimal-government traditions of American public finance. For the most part, these changes occurred as unanticipated and often reluctant adaptations to wartime conditions. But in the North the Republicans took advantage of the departure of the southern Democrats from Congress to push through one measure that they and their Whig predecessors had long advocated, a system of national banking. Passed in February 1863 over the concerted opposition of the northern Democrats, the National Bank Act established criteria by which a bank could obtain a federal charter and issue national bank notes (notes backed by the federal government). It also gave private bankers an incentive to purchase war bonds. The North's ability to revolutionize its system of public finance reflected not only its longer experience with complex financial transactions but its greater political cohesion during the war.

## Political Leadership in Wartime

The Civil War pitted rival political systems as well as armies and economies against each other. The South entered the war with several apparent political advantages. Lincoln's call for militiamen to suppress the rebellion had transformed hesitators in the South into tenacious secessionists. "Never was a people more united or more determined," a New Orleans resident wrote in the spring of 1861. "There is but one mind, one heart, one action." Southerners also claimed a strong leader. A former war secretary and U.S. senator, President Jefferson Davis of the Confederacy possessed experience, honesty, courage, and what one officer described as "a jaw sawed in *steel*."

In contrast, the Union's list of political liabilities appeared lengthy. Loyal but contentious, northern Democrats wanted to prosecute the war without conscription, without the National Bank Act, and without the abolition of slavery. Within the rival Republican party, Lincoln had trouble commanding respect. Unlike Davis, he had served in neither the cabinet nor the Senate, and his informal western manners dismayed eastern Republicans. Northern setbacks early in the war convinced most Republicans in Congress that Lincoln was an ineffectual leader. Criticism of Lincoln sprang from a group of Republicans who became known as the Radicals and who included Secretary of the Treasury Salmon P. Chase, Senator Charles Sumner of Massachusetts, and Representative Thaddeus Stevens of Pennsylvania. The Radicals never formed a tightly knit cadre; on some issues they cooperated with Lincoln. But they did berate him early in the war for failing to make emancipation a war goal and later for being too eager to readmit the conquered rebel states into the Union.

Lincoln's distinctive style of leadership encouraged and simultaneously disarmed opposition within the Republican party. Keeping his counsel to himself until ready to act, he met complaints with homespun anecdotes that caught his opponents off guard. The Radicals frequently concluded that Lincoln was a prisoner of the conservative wing of the party, whereas conservatives complained that Lincoln was too close to the Radicals. But Lincoln's cautious reserve had the dual benefit of leaving open his lines of communication with both wings of the party and fragmenting his opposition. He also co-opted some of his critics, including Chase, by bringing them into his cabinet.

In contrast, Jefferson Davis had a knack for making enemies. A West Pointer, he would rather have led the

**Abraham Lincoln**
*When Lincoln became president in March 1861, he faced more severe problems than any predecessor. Washington photographer Mathew Brady captured this image of the solemn president-elect on February 23, 1861, a few weeks after the formation of the Confederacy and shortly before Lincoln's inauguration.*

army than the government. His cabinet suffered from frequent resignations; the Confederacy had five secretaries of war in four years, for example. Davis's relations with his vice president, Alexander Stephens of Georgia, bordered on disastrous. A wisp of a man, Stephens weighed less than a hundred pounds and looked like a boy with a withered face. But he compensated for his slight physique with a tongue as acidic as Davis's. Leaving Richmond, the Confederate capital, in 1862, Stephens spent most of the war in Georgia, where he sniped at Davis as "weak and vacillating, timid, petulant, peevish, obstinate."

The clash between Davis and Stephens involved not just personalities but also an ideological division, a rift, in fact, like that at the heart of the Confederacy. The Confederate Constitution, drafted in February 1861, explicitly guaranteed the sovereignty of the Confederate states and prohibited the Confederate Congress from enacting protective tariffs and from supporting internal

improvements (measures long opposed by southern voters). For Stephens and other influential Confederate leaders—among them, governors Joseph Brown of Georgia and Zebulon Vance of North Carolina—the Confederacy existed not only to protect slavery but, equally important, to enshrine the doctrine of states' rights. In contrast, Davis's main objective was to secure the independence of the entire South from the North, a goal that frequently led him to override the wishes of state governors for the good of the Confederacy as a whole.

This difference between Davis and Stephens bore some resemblance to the discord between Lincoln and the northern Democrats. Like Davis, Lincoln believed that winning the war demanded an enhancement of the central government's power; like Stephens, northern Democrats resisted governmental centralization. But Lincoln could control his opponents more effectively than Davis because, by temperament, he was more suited to conciliation and also because the nature of party politics in the two sections differed.

In the South the Democrats and the remaining Whigs agreed to suspend party rivalries for the duration of the war. Although intended to promote southern unity, this decision actually encouraged disunity. Without the institutionalization of conflict that party rivalry provided, southern politics disintegrated along personal and factional lines. Lacking a party organization to back him, Davis could not mobilize votes to pass measures that he favored, nor could he depend on the support of party loyalists. In contrast, in the Union, northern Democrats' organized opposition to Lincoln tended to unify the Republicans. In the 1862 elections, which occurred at a low ebb of Union military fortunes, the Democrats won control of five large states, including Lincoln's own Illinois. Republican leaders learned a lesson: no matter how much they disdained Lincoln, they had to rally behind him or risk being driven from office. Ultimately, the Union would develop more political cohesion than the Confederacy, not because it had fewer divisions but because it managed its divisions more effectively.

### Securing the Union's Borders

Even before large-scale fighting began, Lincoln moved to safeguard Washington, which was bordered by two slave states (Virginia and Maryland) and filled with Confederate sympathizers. A week after Fort Sumter, a Baltimore mob attacked a Massachusetts regiment bound for Washington, but enough troops slipped through to protect the capital. Lincoln then dispatched federal troops to Maryland, where he suspended the writ of habeas corpus*; federal troops could now arrest prosecession Marylanders without formally charging them with specific offenses. Cowed by Lincoln's bold moves, the Maryland legislature rejected secession. Delaware, another border slave state, followed suit.

Next Lincoln authorized the arming of Union sympathizers in Kentucky, a slave state with a Unionist legislature, a secessionist governor, and a thin chance of staying neutral. Lincoln also stationed troops under General Ulysses S. Grant just across the Ohio River from Kentucky, in Illinois. When a Confederate army invaded Kentucky early in 1862, the state's legislature turned to Grant to drive it out. Officially, at least, Kentucky became the third slave state to declare for the Union. The fourth, Missouri, was ravaged by four years of fighting between Union and Confederate troops and between sundry bands of guerrillas and bushwackers, including William Quantrill, a Confederate desperado, and his murderous apprentices, Frank and Jesse James. Despite savage fighting and the divided loyalties of its people, Missouri never left the Union.†

By holding these four border slave states—Maryland, Delaware, Kentucky, and Missouri—in the Union, Lincoln kept open his lines to the free states and gained access to the river systems in Kentucky and Missouri that led into the heart of the Confederacy. Lincoln's firmness, particularly in Maryland, scotched charges that he was weak-willed. The crisis also forced the president to exercise long-dormant powers. In the case *Ex parte* Merryman (1861), Chief Justice Roger B. Taney ruled that Lincoln had exceeded his authority in suspending the writ of habeas corpus in Maryland, but the president, citing the Constitution's authorization of the writ's suspension in "Cases of Rebellion" (Article I, Section 9), insisted that he, rather than Congress, would determine whether a rebellion existed; and he ignored Taney's ruling.

---

\* Habeas corpus: a court order requiring that the detainer of a prisoner bring the person in custody to court and show cause for his or her detention.

---

† Admitted to the Union in 1863, West Virginia became the fifth border state. This state originated in the refusal of thirty-five counties in the predominantly nonslaveholding region of Virginia west of the Shenandoah Valley to follow the state's leaders into secession in 1861.

# In Battle, 1861–1862

The Civil War was the first war to rely extensively on railroads, the telegraph, mass-produced weapons, joint army-navy tactics, iron-plated warships, rifled guns and artillery, and trench warfare. All of this lends some justification to its description as the first modern war. But to the participants, slogging through muddy swamps and weighed down with equipment, the war hardly seemed modern. In many ways, the soldiers had the more accurate perspective, for the new weapons did not always work, and both sides employed tactics that were more traditional than modern.

## *Armies, Weapons, and Strategies*

Compared to the Confederacy's 9 million people, one-third of them slaves, the Union had 22 million people in 1861. The North also had 3.5 times as many white men of military age, 90 percent of all U.S. industrial capacity, and two-thirds of its railroad track. Yet the Union faced a daunting challenge. Its goal was to force the South back into the Union, whereas the South was fighting merely for its independence. To subdue the Confederacy, the North would have to sustain offensive operations over an area comparable in size to the part of Russia that the French emperor Napoleon had invaded in 1812 with disastrous results.

Measured against this challenge, the Union's advantages in population and technology shrank. The North had more men, but needing to defend long supply lines and occupy captured areas, it could commit a smaller proportion of them to frontline duty. The South, which relied on slaves for labor, could assign a higher proportion of its white male population to combat. As for technology, the North required, and possessed, superior railroads. Fighting defensively on so-called interior lines, the South could shift its troops relatively short distances within its defensive arc without using railroads, whereas the North had to move its troops and supplies huge distances around the exterior of the arc. Not only could guerrillas easily sabotage northern railroads, but once Union troops moved away from their railroad bases, their supply wagons often bogged down on wretched southern roads that became watery ditches in bad weather. Even on good roads, horses and mules, which themselves consumed supplies, were needed to pull wagons; an invading army of 100,000 men required 35,000 horses or mules. Finally, southerners had an edge in soldiers' morale,

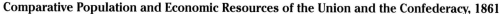

## Comparative Population and Economic Resources of the Union and the Confederacy, 1861

*At the start of the war, the Union enjoyed huge advantages in population, industry, railroad mileage, and wealth produced.*

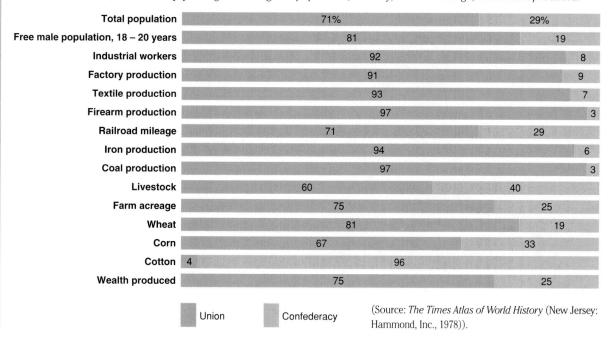

| | Union | Confederacy |
|---|---|---|
| Total population | 71% | 29% |
| Free male population, 18 – 20 years | 81 | 19 |
| Industrial workers | 92 | 8 |
| Factory production | 91 | 9 |
| Textile production | 93 | 7 |
| Firearm production | 97 | 3 |
| Railroad mileage | 71 | 29 |
| Iron production | 94 | 6 |
| Coal production | 97 | 3 |
| Livestock | 60 | 40 |
| Farm acreage | 75 | 25 |
| Wheat | 81 | 19 |
| Corn | 67 | 33 |
| Cotton | 4 | 96 |
| Wealth produced | 75 | 25 |

(Source: *The Times Atlas of World History* (New Jersey: Hammond, Inc., 1978)).

for Confederate troops battled on home ground. "No people ever warred for independence," a southern general acknowledged, "with more relative advantages than the Confederates."

The Civil War witnessed experiments with a variety of newly developed weapons, including the submarine, the repeating rifle, and the multibarreled Gatling gun, the forerunner of the machine gun. Yet these futuristic innovations had less impact on the war than did the perfection in the 1850s of a bullet whose powder would not clog a rifle's spiraled internal grooves after a few shots. Like the smoothbore muskets that both armies had employed at the start of the war, most improved rifles had to be reloaded after each shot. But where the smoothbore musket had an effective range of only eighty yards, the Springfield or Enfield rifles widely employed by 1863 could hit targets accurately at four hundred yards.

The development of the rifle posed a challenge to long-accepted military tactics. Manuals used at West Point in the 1840s and 1850s had identified the mass infantry charge against an opponent's weakest point as the key to victory. These manuals assumed that defenders armed with muskets would be able to fire only a round or two before being overwhelmed. The same assumption led tacticians to disdain trenches; against assaulting infantry, trenches would become mere traps for defenders. Armed with rifles, however, a defending force could fire several rounds before closing with the enemy. Attackers would now have far greater difficulty getting close enough to thrust bayonets; fewer than 1 percent of the casualties in the Civil War resulted from bayonet wounds.

Thus the rifle produced some changes in tactics during the war. Both sides gradually came to understand the value of trenches, which provided defenders protection against withering rifle fire. By 1865 trenches pockmarked the landscape in Virginia and Georgia. In addition, growing use of the rifle forced generals to rely less on cavalry. Traditionally, the cavalry had ranked among the most prestigious components of an army, in part because cavalry charges were often devastatingly effective and in part because the cavalry helped maintain class distinctions within the army. But rifles reduced the effectiveness of cavalry by increasing the firepower of foot soldiers. Bullets that might miss the rider would at least hit the horse. Thus as cavalry charges against infantry became more difficult, both sides relegated cavalry to reconnaissance missions and to raids on supply trains.

**Scott's Great Snake, 1861**
*General Winfield Scott's scheme to surround the South and await a seizure of power by southern Unionists drew scorn from critics who called it the Anaconda plan. In this lithograph, the "great snake" prepares to thrust down the Mississippi, seal off the Confederacy, and crush it.*

Although the rifle exposed traditional tactics to new hazards, it by no means invalidated those tactics. On the contrary, some historians contend, high casualties reflected the long duration of battles rather than the new efficacy of rifles. In any case, the attacking army still stood an excellent chance of success if it achieved surprise. The South's lush forests provided abundant opportunities for an army to sneak up on its opponent. For example, at the Battle of Shiloh in 1862, Confederate attackers surprised and almost defeated a larger Union army despite the rumpus created by green rebel troops en route to the battle, many of whom fired their rifles into the air to see if they would work.

Achieving such complete surprise normally lay beyond the skill or luck of generals. In the absence of any element of surprise, an attacking army might invite disaster. At the Battle of Fredericksburg in December 1862, Confederate troops inflicted appalling casualties on Union forces attacking uphill over open terrain, and at Gettysburg in July 1863, Union riflemen and artillery shredded charging southerners. But generals might still achieve partial surprise by hitting an enemy before it had concentrated its troops; in fact, this is what the North tried to do at Fredericksburg. Because surprise

often proved effective, most generals continued to believe that their best chance of success lay in striking an unwary or weakened enemy with all the troops they could muster rather than in relying on guerrilla or trench warfare.

Much like previous wars, the Civil War was fought basically in a succession of battles during which exposed infantry traded volleys, charged, and countercharged. Whichever side withdrew from the field usually was thought to have lost the battle, but the losing side frequently sustained lighter casualties than the supposed victor. Both sides had trouble exploiting their victories. As a rule, the beaten army moved back a few miles from the field to lick its wounds; the winners stayed in place to lick theirs. Politicians on both sides raged at generals for not pursuing a beaten foe, but it was difficult for a mangled victor to gather horses, mules, supply trains, and exhausted soldiers for a new attack. Not surprisingly, for much of the war, generals on both sides concluded that the best defense was a good offense.

To the extent that the North had a long-range strategy in 1861, it lay in the so-called Anaconda plan. Devised by the Mexican War hero General Winfield Scott, the plan called for the Union to blockade the southern coastline and to thrust, like a huge snake, down the Mississippi River. Scott expected that sealing off and severing the Confederacy would make the South recognize the futility of secession and restore southern Unionists to power. The Anaconda plan promised a relatively bloodless end to the war, but Scott, a southern Unionist, overestimated the strength of Unionist spirit in the South. Furthermore, although Lincoln quickly ordered a blockade of the southern coast, the North hardly had the troops and naval flotillas to seize the Mississippi in 1861. So while the Mississippi remained an objective, northern strategy did not unfold according to any blueprint like the Anaconda plan.

Early in the war, the pressing need to secure the border slave states, particularly Kentucky and Missouri, dictated Union strategy west of the Appalachian Mountains. Once in control of Kentucky, northern troops plunged southward into Tennessee. The Appalachians tended to seal this western theater off from the eastern theater, where the Confederacy's decision to move its capital from Montgomery, Alabama, to Richmond, Virginia, shaped the Union strategy. "Forward to Richmond" became the Union's first war cry in 1861.

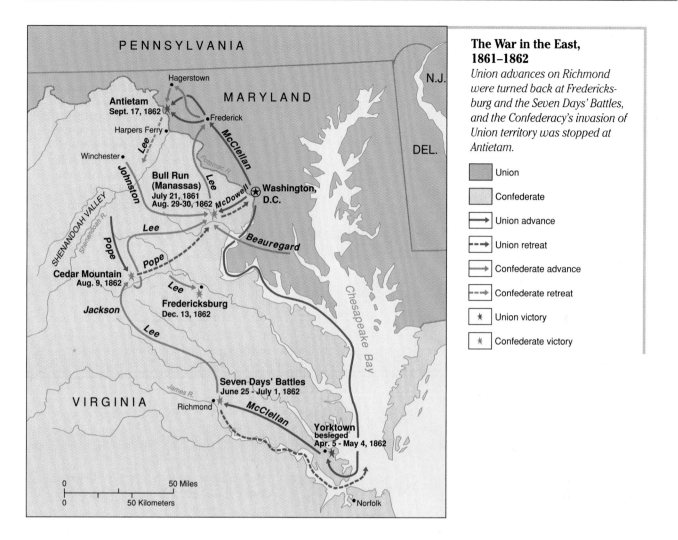

**The War in the East, 1861–1862**

*Union advances on Richmond were turned back at Fredericksburg and the Seven Days' Battles, and the Confederacy's invasion of Union territory was stopped at Antietam.*

| | |
|---|---|
| ▨ | Union |
| ▨ | Confederate |
| → | Union advance |
| ⇢ | Union retreat |
| → | Confederate advance |
| ⇢ | Confederate retreat |
| ★ | Union victory |
| ★ | Confederate victory |

## Stalemate in the East

Before they could reach Richmond, one hundred miles southwest of Washington, Union troops would have to dislodge a Confederate army brazenly encamped at Manassas Junction, only twenty-five miles from the Union capital. Lincoln ordered General Irvin McDowell to attack his former West Point classmate, Confederate general P. G. T. Beauregard. "You are green, it is true," Lincoln told McDowell, "but they are green also; you are all green alike." In the resulting First Battle of Bull Run (or First Manassas),* amateur armies clashed in bloody chaos under a blistering July sun. Well-dressed,

---

\* Because the North sometimes named battles after local landmarks, often bodies of water, and the South after the nearest town, several Civil War battles are known by two names.

picnicking Washington dignitaries gathered to view the action. Aided by last-minute reinforcements and by the disorganization of the attacking federals, Beauregard routed the larger Union army.

After Bull Run, Lincoln replaced McDowell with General George B. McClellan as commander of the Union's Army of the Potomac. Another West Pointer, McClellan had served with distinction in the Mexican War and mastered the art of administration by managing midwestern railroads in the 1850s. Few generals could match his ability to turn a ragtag mob into a disciplined fighting force. His soldiers adored him, but Lincoln quickly became disenchanted. Lincoln believed that the key to a Union victory lay in simultaneous, coordinated attacks on several fronts so that the North could exploit its advantage in manpower and resources. McClellan, a proslavery Democrat, hoped to

*A painting of the Antietam battlefield by James Pope, a Union soldier of the Second Vermont Infantry, shows three brigades of Union troops advancing under Confederate fire. In the photograph of Antietam, dead rebel gunners lie next to the wreckage of their battery at Antietam. The building in both painting and photograph, a Dunker church, was the scene of furious fighting.*

maneuver the South into a relatively bloodless defeat and then negotiate a peace that would readmit the Confederate states with slavery intact.

McClellan soon got a chance to demonstrate his strategy. After Bull Run, the Confederates had pulled back behind the Rappahannock River and awaited the Union onslaught against Richmond. Rather than directly attack the Confederate army, McClellan formulated a plan in the spring of 1862 to move the Army of the Potomac by water to the tip of the peninsula formed by the York and James Rivers and then move northwestward up the peninsula to Richmond. McClellan's plan had several advantages. Depending on water transport rather than on railroads (which Confederate cavalry could cut), the McClellan strategy reduced the vulnerability of northern supply lines. By dictating an approach to Rich-

mond from the southeast, it threatened the South's supply lines. By aiming for the capital of the Confederacy rather than for the Confederate army stationed northeast of Richmond, finally, McClellan hoped to maneuver the southern troops into a futile attack on his army in order to avert a destructive siege of Richmond.

By far the most massive military campaign in American history to that date, the Peninsula Campaign at first unfolded smoothly. Three hundred ships transported 70,000 men and huge stores of supplies to the tip of the peninsula. Reinforcements swelled McClellan's army to 100,000. Although Confederate troops also poured into the peninsula, by late May McClellan was within five miles of Richmond. But after luring the Confederacy to the brink of defeat, McClellan hesitated. Overestimating the Confederates' strength, he refused to launch a final attack on Richmond without further reinforcements, which were turned back by Confederate general Thomas "Stonewall" Jackson in the Shenandoah Valley. While McClellan delayed, General Robert E. Lee took command of the Confederacy's Army of Northern Virginia. A foe of secession and so courteous that at times he seemed too gentle, Lee possessed the qualities that McClellan most lacked, boldness and a willingness to accept casualties. Seizing the initiative, Lee attacked McClellan in late June 1862. The ensuing Seven Days' Battles, fought in the forests east of Richmond, cost the South nearly twice as many men as the North and ended in a virtual slaughter of Confederates at Malvern Hill. Unnerved by his own casualties, McClellan sent increasingly panicky reports to Washington. Lincoln, who cared little for McClellan's peninsula strategy, ordered McClellan to call off the campaign and return to Washington.

With McClellan out of the picture, Lee and his lieutenant, Stonewall Jackson, now boldly struck north and, at the Second Battle of Bull Run (Second Manassas), routed a Union army under General John Pope that had been held back from the peninsula to guard Washington. Lee's next stroke was even bolder. Crossing the Potomac River in early September 1862, he invaded western Maryland, where the forthcoming fall harvest could provide him with desperately needed supplies. By seizing western Maryland, moreover, Lee could threaten Washington, indirectly relieve pressure on Richmond, improve the prospects of peace candidates in the North's upcoming fall elections, and possibly induce Britain and France to recognize the Confederacy as an independent nation. But McClellan met Lee at the Battle of Antietam (or Sharpsburg) on September 17. Although a tactical draw, Antietam proved a strategic victory for the North, for Lee subsequently called off his invasion and retreated south of the Potomac. Heartened by the apparent success of northern arms, Lincoln then issued the Emancipation Proclamation, a war measure that freed all slaves under rebel control (see below). The carnage of the 24,000 casualties at Antietam, however, made it the bloodiest day of the entire war. A Union veteran recollected that one part of the battlefield contained so many bodies that a man could have walked through it without stepping on the ground.

Complaining that McClellan had "the slows," Lincoln faulted his commander for not pursuing Lee after the battle. McClellan's replacement, General Ambrose Burnside, thought himself and soon proved himself un-

fit for high command. In December 1862 Burnside led 122,000 federal troops against 78,500 Confederates at the Battle of Fredericksburg. Burnside captured the town of Fredericksburg, northeast of Richmond, but then sacrificed his army in futile charges up the heights west of the town. Even Lee was shaken by the northern casualties. "It is well that war is so terrible—we should grow fond of it," he told an aide during the battle. Richmond remained, in the words of a southern song, "a hard road to travel." The war in the East had become a stalemate.

## The War in the West

The Union fared better in the West. There, the war shifted over a vast and crucial terrain that provided access to rivers leading directly into the South. The West also spawned new leadership. During the first year of war, an obscure Union general, Ulysses S. Grant, proved his competence. A West Point graduate, Grant had fought in the Mexican War and retired from the army in 1854 with a reputation for heavy drinking. He then failed at ventures in farming and in business. When the Civil War began, he gained an army commission through political pressure.

In 1861–1862 Grant retained control of two border states, Missouri and Kentucky. Moving into Tennessee, he captured two strategic forts, Fort Henry on the Tennessee River and Fort Donelson on the Cumberland. Grant then headed south to attack Corinth, Mississippi, a major railroad junction.

In early April 1862, Confederate forces under generals Albert Sidney Johnston and P. G. T. Beauregard tried to relieve the Union pressure on Corinth by a surprise attack on Grant's army, encamped twenty miles north of the town, in southern Tennessee near a church named Shiloh. Hoping to whip Grant before the imminent arrival of 25,000 Union reinforcements under General Don Carlos Buell, the Confederates exploded from the woods near Shiloh before breakfast and almost drove the federals into the Tennessee River. Beauregard cabled Richmond with news of a splendid Confederate victory. But Grant and his lieutenant, William T. Sherman, steadied the Union line. Buell's reinforcements arrived in the night, and a Union counterattack drove the Confederates from the field the next day. Although Antietam would soon erase the distinction, the Battle of Shiloh was the bloodiest in American history to that date. Of the 77,000 men engaged, 23,000 were killed or wounded, including Confederate general Albert Sidney

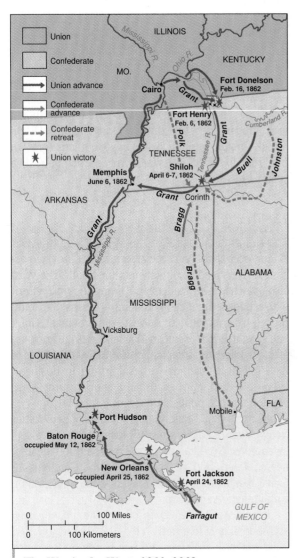

**The War in the West, 1861–1862**
*By the end of 1862, the North held New Orleans and the entire Mississippi River except for the stretch between Vicksburg and Port Hudson.*

his list of conquests. Meanwhile, another Union flotilla moved down the Mississippi and captured Memphis in June. Now the North controlled the entire river, except for a two-hundred-mile stretch between Port Hudson, Louisiana, and Vicksburg, Mississippi.

Union and Confederate forces also clashed in 1862 in the trans-Mississippi West, the vast region of states and territories stretching from the Midwest to the Pacific coast. On the banks of the Rio Grande, Union volunteers, joined by Mexican-American companies, drove a Confederate army from Texas out of New Mexico. A thousand miles to the east, in northern Arkansas and western Missouri, armies vied to secure the Missouri River, a crucial waterway that flowed into the Mississippi. In Pea Ridge, Arkansas, in March 1862, forewarned northern troops scattered a Confederate force of sixteen thousand that included three Cherokee regiments. (Indian units fought on *both* sides in Missouri, where guerrilla combat raged until the war's end.)

These Union victories changed the nature of the trans-Mississippi war. As the rebel threat faded, regiments of western volunteers that had mobilized to crush Confederates turned to fighting Indians. Conflict between the Dakota Sioux and Minnesota volunteers in the fall of 1862 spread to the north and west. Indian wars erupted in Arizona, Nevada, Colorado, and New Mexico, where California volunteers and the New Mexico cavalry, led by Colonel Kit Carson, overwhelmed the Apaches and Navajos. After 1865 federal troops moved west to complete the rout of the Indians that had begun in the Civil War (see Chapter 17).

## Ironclads and Cruisers: The Naval War

By plunging its navy into the Confederacy like a dagger, the Union exploited one of its clearest advantages. The North began the war with over forty active warships against none for the South, and by 1865 the United States had the largest navy in the world. Steam-driven ships could penetrate the South's excellent river system from any direction and thereby turn a peacetime advantage into a wartime liability. For example, the Confederacy had stripped New Orleans's defenses in the belief that the real threat to the city would come from the north, only to find Farragut slipping in from the south.

Despite its size, the Union navy faced an extraordinary challenge in its efforts to blockade the South's 3,500 miles of coast. Early in the war, small, sleek Confederate blockade-runners darted in and out of southern harbors and inlets with little chance of capture. The

Johnston, who bled to death from a leg wound. Defeated at Shiloh, the Confederates soon evacuated Corinth.

To attack Grant at Shiloh, the Confederacy had stripped the defenses of New Orleans, leaving only three thousand militia to guard its largest city. A combined Union land-sea force under General Benjamin Butler, a Massachusetts politician, and Admiral David G. Farragut, a Tennessean loyal to the Union, quickly capitalized on the opportunity. Farragut took the city in late April and soon added Baton Rouge and Natchez to

North gradually tightened the blockade by outfitting tugs, whalers, excursion steamers, and ferries as well as frigates to patrol southern coasts. The proportion of Confederate blockade-runners that made it through dropped from 90 percent early in the war to 50 percent by 1865. Northern seizure of rebel ports and coastal areas shrank the South's foreign trade even more. In daring amphibious assaults during 1861 and 1862, the Union captured the excellent harbor of Port Royal, South Carolina, the coastal islands off South Carolina (see A Place in Time), and most of North Carolina's river outlets. Naval patrols and amphibious operations shrank the South's ocean trade to one-third its prewar level.

Despite meager resources, the South made impressive efforts to offset the North's naval advantage. Early in the war, the Confederacy raised the scuttled Union frigate *Merrimac,* sheathed its sides with an armor of iron plate, rechristened it *Virginia,* and dispatched it to attack wooden Union ships in Hampton Roads, Virginia. The *Merrimac* quickly destroyed two northern warships but met its match in the hastily built Union ironclad the *Monitor.* In the first engagement of ironclads in history, the two ships fought an indecisive battle on March 9, 1862. The South constructed other ironclads and even the first submarine, which dragged a mine through the water to sink a Union ship off Charleston in 1864. Unfortunately, the "fish" failed to resurface and went down with its victim. But short of mechanics and iron-fabricating shops, the South could never build enough ironclads to overcome the North's supremacy in home waters. The Confederacy had more success on the high seas, where wooden, steam-driven commerce raiders like the *Alabama* and the *Florida* (both built in England) wreaked havoc on the Union's merchant marine. Commerce raiding, however, would not tip the balance of the war in the South's favor because the North, unlike its opponent, did not depend on imports for war materials. The South would lose the naval war.

## *The Diplomatic War*

While armies and navies clashed in 1861–1862, conflict developed on a third front, diplomacy. At the outbreak of the war, the Confederacy began a campaign to gain European recognition of its status as an independent nation. Southern confidence in a swift diplomatic victory ran high. Planning to establish a colonial empire in Mexico, Napoleon III of France had grounds to welcome the permanent division of the United

**Deck of the *Monitor***
*Although much smaller than its famous rival the* Merrimac *(C.S.S.* Virginia*), the Union ironclad* Monitor *benefited from its shallow draft, speed, and maneuverability. Its flat, raftlike shape made it hard to hit.*

States. Moreover, the upper classes in France and Britain seemed sympathetic to the aristocratic South and eager for the downfall of the brash Yankee republic. Furthermore, influential southerners had long contended that an embargo of cotton exports would bring Britain to its knees. These southerners reasoned that Britain, dependent on the South for four-fifths of its cotton, would break the Union blockade and provoke a war with the North rather than watch its textile workers sink into revolutionary discontent under the weight of an embargo.

Leaving nothing to chance, the Confederacy in 1861 dispatched emissaries James Mason to Britain and John Slidell to France to lobby for recognition of the South as an independent nation. When a Union ship captain, acting without orders, boarded the British vessel the *Trent,* which was carrying Mason and Slidell, and brought the two men to Boston as prisoners, British tempers exploded. Considering one war at a time enough, President Lincoln released Mason and Slidell. But settling the *Trent* affair did not eliminate friction between the United States and Britain. The construction in British shipyards of two Confederate commerce raiders, the *Florida* and the *Alabama,* evoked protests from Union diplomats. In 1863 the U.S. minister to London, Charles Francis Adams (the son of for-

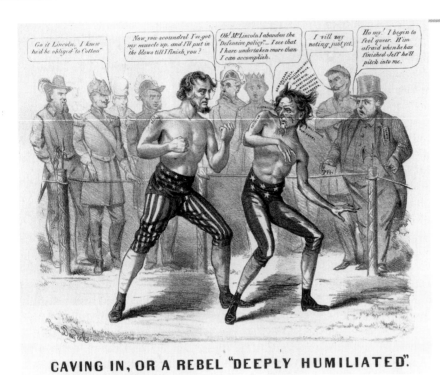

CAVING IN, OR A REBEL "DEEPLY HUMILIATED".

### Lincoln Battles Davis in an 1863 Cartoon

*In the first years of war, European nations played a waiting game without making commitments to Union or Confederacy. By 1863, the North seemed to gain the advantage in the diplomatic war, as this cartoon suggests. Still, the European leaders watching the contest from behind a rope consider self-interest and avoid involvement.*

mer president John Quincy Adams), threatened war if two British-built ironclads commissioned by the Confederacy, the so-called Laird rams, were turned over to the South. Britain capitulated to Adams's protests and purchased the rams for its own navy.

On balance, the South fell far short of its diplomatic objectives. Although recognizing the Confederacy as a belligerent, neither Britain nor France ever recognized it as a nation. Basically, the Confederacy overestimated the power of its vaunted "cotton diplomacy." The Confederate government talked of embargoing cotton exports in order to bring the British to their knees, but in reality, the government never controlled more than 15 percent of the South's cotton. Planters conducted business as usual by raising cotton and trying to slip it through the blockade. Still, the South's share of the British cotton market slumped from 77 percent in 1860 to only 10 percent in 1865. This loss resulted from forces beyond southern control. Bumper cotton crops in the late 1850s had glutted the British market by the start of the war and weakened British demand for cotton. In addition, Britain had found new suppliers in Egypt and India, thereby buffering itself from southern pressure. Gradually, too, the North's tightened blockade restricted southern exports.

The South also exaggerated Britain's stake in helping the Confederacy. As a naval power that had fre-

quently blockaded its own enemies, Britain's diplomatic interest lay in supporting the Union blockade in principle; from Britain's standpoint, to help the South break the blockade would set a precedent that could easily boomerang. Finally, although France and Britain often talked of recognizing the Confederacy, the timing never seemed quite right. The Union's success at Antietam in 1862 and Lincoln's subsequent issuance of the Emancipation Proclamation dampened Europe's enthusiasm for recognition at a crucial juncture. By transforming the war into a struggle to end slavery, the Emancipation Proclamation produced an upsurge of pro-Union feeling in antislavery Britain, particularly among liberals and the working class. Workingmen in Manchester, England, wrote Lincoln to praise his resolve to free the slaves. The proclamation, declared Henry Adams (diplomat Charles Francis Adams's son) from London, "has done more for us here than all of our former victories and all our diplomacy."

## Emancipation Transforms the War

"I hear old John Brown knocking on the lid of his coffin and shouting 'Let me out! Let me out!'" abolitionist Henry Stanton wrote to his wife after the fall of Fort Sumter. "The Doom of Slavery is at hand." In 1861 this prediction seemed wildly premature. In his inaugural that year, Lincoln had stated bluntly, "I have no purpose, directly or indirectly, to interfere with the institution of slavery in the states where it exists." Yet in two years, the North's priorities underwent a decisive transformation. A mix of practical necessity and ideological conviction thrust the emancipation of the slaves to the forefront of northern war goals.

The rise of emancipation as a Union war goal reflected the changing character of the war itself. As late as July 1862, General George McClellan had restated to Lincoln his conviction that "neither confiscation of property . . . or forcible abolition of slavery should be contemplated for a moment." As the struggle dragged on, however, demands for the prosecution of "total war" intensified in the North. Even northerners who saw no moral value in abolishing slavery started to recognize the military value of emancipation as a tactic to cripple the South's resources.

## From Confiscation to Emancipation

Union policy on emancipation developed in stages. As soon as northern troops began to invade the South, questions arose about the disposition of captured rebel property, including slaves. Slaves who fled behind the Union lines were sometimes considered "contraband"—enemy property liable to seizure—and were put to work for the Union army. Some northern commanders viewed this practice as a useful tool of war, others did not, and the Lincoln administration was evasive. To establish an official policy, Congress in August 1861 passed the first Confiscation Act, which authorized the seizure of all property used in military aid of the rebellion, including slaves. Under this act, slaves who had been employed directly by the Confederate armed services and who later fled to freedom became "captives of war." But nothing in the act actually freed these contrabands, nor did the law apply to contrabands who had not worked for the Confederate military.

Several factors underlay the Union's cautious approach to the confiscation of rebel property. Officially maintaining that the South's rebellion lacked any legal basis, Lincoln argued that southerners were thus still entitled to the Constitution's protection of property. The president also had practical reasons to walk softly. The Union not only contained four slave states but also held a sizable body of proslavery Democrats who flatly opposed turning the war into a crusade against slavery. If the North in any way tampered with slavery, these Democrats feared, "two or three million semi-savages" might come north and compete with white workers. Aware of strong northern opposition to turning a limited policy of confiscation into a general program of emancipation, Lincoln assured Congress in December 1861 that the war would not become a "remorseless revolutionary struggle."

From the start of the war, however, Lincoln faced pressure from the loosely knit but determined Radical Republicans to adopt a policy of emancipation. Pennsylvanian Thaddeus Stevens urged that the Union "free every slave—slay every traitor—burn every Rebel mansion, if these things be necessary to preserve this temple of freedom." Radicals agreed with black abolitionist Frederick Douglass that "to fight against slaveholders without fighting against slavery, is but a half-hearted business." With every new northern setback, support for the Radicals' stance grew. Each Union defeat reminded northerners that the confederacy, with a slave labor force in place, could commit a higher proportion of its white men to battle. As a military measure, the idea of emancipation thus gained increasing favor in the North, and in July 1862 Congress passed the second Confiscation Act. This law authorized the seizure of the property of all persons in rebellion and stipulated that slaves who came within Union lines "shall be forever free." Finally, the law opened the door to blacks' military service by authorizing the president to employ blacks as soldiers.

Nevertheless, Lincoln continued to stall, even in the face of rising pressure for emancipation. "My paramount object in this struggle *is* to save the Union, and is *not* either to save or destroy slavery," Lincoln told antislavery journalist Horace Greeley. "If I could save the Union without freeing *any* slave, I would do it, and if I could save it by freeing *all* the slaves, I would do it; and if I could save it by freeing some and leaving others alone, I would also do that." Yet Lincoln had always loathed slavery, and by the spring of 1862, he had come around to the Radical position that the war must lead to its abolition. He hesitated principally because he did not want to be stampeded by Congress into a measure that might disrupt northern unity and because he feared that a public commitment to emancipation in the summer of 1862, on the heels of the northern defeat at Second Manassas and the collapse of the Peninsula Campaign, might be interpreted as an act of frantic desperation. After failing to persuade the Union slave states to emancipate slaves in return for federal compensation, he drafted a proclamation of emancipation, circulated it within his cabinet, and waited for a right moment to issue it. Finally, after the Union victory in September 1862 at Antietam, Lincoln issued the Preliminary Emancipation Proclamation, which declared all slaves under rebel control free as of January 1, 1863. Announcing the plan in advance softened the surprise, tested public opinion, and gave the states still in rebellion an opportunity to preserve slavery by returning to the Union—an opportunity that none, however, took. The final Emancipation Proclamation, issued on January 1, 1863, declared "forever free" all slaves in areas in rebellion.

The proclamation had limited practical impact. Applying only to rebellious areas, where the Union had no authority, it exempted the Union slave states and those parts of the Confederacy then under Union control (Tennessee, West Virginia, southern Louisiana, and sections of Virginia). Moreover, it mainly restated what the second Confiscation Act had already stipulated: if rebels' slaves fell into Union hands, those slaves would be free. Yet the proclamation was a brilliant political stroke. By issuing it as a military measure, in his role as commander-in-chief, Lincoln pacified northern conservatives. Its aim, he stressed, was to injure the Confederacy, threaten its property, heighten its dread, sap its morale, and thus hasten its demise. By issuing the proclamation himself, Lincoln stole the initiative from the Radicals in Congress and mobilized support for the Union among European liberals far more dramatically than could any act of Congress. Furthermore, the declaration pushed the border states toward emancipation: by the end of the war, Maryland and Missouri would abolish slavery. Finally, it increased slaves' incentives to escape as northern troops approached. Fulfilling the worst of Confederate fears, it enabled blacks to join the Union army.

The Emancipation Proclamation did not end slavery everywhere or free "*all* the slaves." But it changed the war. From 1863 on, the war for the Union would also be a war against slavery.

### Crossing Union Lines

The attacks and counterattacks of the opposing armies turned many slaves into pawns of war. Some slaves became free when Union troops overran their areas. Others fled their plantations at the approach of federal troops to take refuge behind Union lines. A few

**Emancipation Triumphant**
*An anonymous painting to celebrate the Emancipation Proclamation shows President Lincoln and the Union army liberating grateful slaves.*

were freed by northern assaults, only to be reenslaved by Confederate counterthrusts. One North Carolina slave celebrated liberation on twelve occasions, as many times as Union soldiers marched through his area. By 1865 about half a million slaves were in Union hands.

In the first year of the war, when the Union had not yet established a policy toward contrabands (fugitive slaves), masters were able to retrieve them from the Union army. After 1862, however, the thousands of slaves who crossed Union lines were considered free. Many freedmen served in army camps as cooks, teamsters, and laborers. Some worked for pay on abandoned plantations or were leased out to planters who swore allegiance to the Union. In camps or outside them, freedmen had reason to question the value of their liberation. Deductions for clothing, rations, and medicine ate up most, if not all, of their earnings. Labor contracts frequently tied them to their employers for prolonged periods. Moreover, freedmen encountered fierce prejudice among Yankee soldiers, many of whom feared that emancipation would propel blacks north after the war. The best solution to the "question of what to do with the darkies," wrote one northern soldier, "would be to shoot them."

But this was not the whole story. Contrabands who aided the Union army as spies and scouts helped to break down ingrained bigotry. "The sooner we get rid of our foolish prejudice the better for us," a Massachusetts soldier wrote home. Before the end of the war, northern missionary groups and freedmen's aid societies sent agents into the South to work among the freed slaves, distribute relief, and organize schools. In March 1865, just before the hostilities ceased, Congress created the Freedmen's Bureau, which had responsibility for the relief, education, and employment of former slaves. The Freedmen's Bureau law also stipulated that forty acres of abandoned or confiscated land could be leased to each freedman or southern Unionist, with an option to buy after three years. This was the first and only time that Congress provided for the redistribution of confiscated Confederate property.

### Black Soldiers in the Union Army

During the first year of war, the Union had rejected black soldiers. Northern recruiting offices sent black applicants home, and black companies that had been formed in the occupied South were disbanded. After the second Confiscation Act, Union generals formed black regiments in occupied New Orleans and on the Sea Islands off the coasts of South Carolina and Georgia (see A Place in Time). Only after the Emancipation Proclamation did large-scale enlistment begin. Leading blacks such as Frederick Douglass and Harvard-educated physician Martin Delany worked as recruiting agents in northern cities. Douglass linked black military service to black claims as citizens. "Once let the black man get upon his person the brass letters, U.S.; let him get an eagle on his button, and a musket on his shoulder and bullets in his pocket, and there is no power on earth which can deny that he has earned the right to citizenship." Union drafts now included blacks, recruiting offices arose in the loyal border states, and freedmen in refugee camps throughout the occupied South were enlisted. By the end of the war, 186,000 blacks had served in the Union army, one-tenth of all Union soldiers. Fully half came from the Confederate states.

White Union soldiers commonly objected to the new recruits on racial grounds. But some, including Colonel

Thomas Wentworth Higginson, a liberal minister and former John Brown supporter who led a black regiment, welcomed the black soldiers. "Nobody knows anything about these men who has not seen them in battle," Higginson exulted after a successful raid in Florida in 1863. "There is a fierce energy about them beyond anything of which I have ever read, except it be the French Zouaves [French troops in North Africa]." Even Union soldiers who held blacks in contempt pragmatically came to approve of "anything that will kill a rebel." Furthermore, black recruitment offered new opportunities for whites to secure commissions, for blacks served in separate regiments under white officers. Colonel Robert Gould Shaw of the 54th Massachusetts Infantry, an elite black regiment, died in combat—as did half his troops—in an attack on Fort Wagner in Charleston harbor in July 1863.

Black soldiers suffered a far higher mortality rate than white troops. Typically assigned to labor detachments or garrison duty, blacks were less likely than whites to be killed in action but more likely to die of disease in the bacteria-ridden garrisons. In addition, the Confederacy refused to treat captured black soldiers as

**Come and Join**
*A recruitment poster urges black men to enlist in the Union Army. African American volunteers served in black regiments led by white officers.*

## The Sea Island Experiments

In November 1861 a Union fleet sailed into Port Royal Sound, an inlet among the South Carolina Sea Islands, and bombarded the port's defenses. Before Union troops could occupy the islands, the white residents, many of them slaveowning planters, fled to the mainland. Left behind were elegant mansions, sprawling cotton plantations, and ten thousand slaves, who would remember the invasion as the "gun shoot at Bay Point."

Lying just off the southern coast between Charleston and Savannah, the conquered islands—including Port

### The Sea Islands
*The island chain, famous for the production of what was called sea-island cotton, was the site of unique wartime experiments in new social policies.*

Royal, Hilton Head, and St. Helena—provided an operating base for the Union blockade fleet. They were of potential value to the Treasury Department, too. The Sea Islands were known for their high-grade cotton, which could be used to supply northern textile mills and to bolster the Union economy. But the takeover of the islands presented the Union with a challenge as well as a triumph.

Before the invasion, slaves had composed 83 percent of the Sea Island population. Long isolated from the mainland, they retained a distinctive culture and perpetuated many African customs. Their syntax and vocabulary were West Indian, and their Gullah dialect was almost incomprehensible to outsiders. Since the late eighteenth century, they had endured a harsh slave system similar to that of the West Indies. To the northerners who now arrived on the Sea Islands—army personnel, treasury agents, plantation managers, teachers, and missionaries—the very numbers of the black inhabitants seemed overwhelming. "Negroes, negroes, negroes," wrote Elizabeth Botume, a Boston teacher. "They hovered around like bees in a swarm. . . . Every doorstep, box, or barrel was covered with them." With the war barely under way and victory still a vision on the distant horizon, the Union suddenly had to forge a policy toward these thousands of "contrabands." While warfare occupied the rest of the nation, Sea Island administrators embarked on a series of experiments in emancipation.

These experiments revealed deep divisions in northerners' thinking about the future of blacks. Some northerners on the scene focused on blacks' potential as soldiers. In May 1862 General David Hunter, who commanded the Union forces occupying the Sea Islands, formed a black army regiment; by Au-

gust Sea Island men were being impressed into the 1st South Carolina "Volunteers," commanded by Massachusetts minister Thomas Wentworth Higginson. The drafting of blacks infuriated idealistic teachers and missionaries, who saw education as the blacks' primary need. "The negroes . . . will do anything for us, if we will only teach them," another teacher from Boston claimed. "The majority learn with wonderful rapidity," reported the free black Charlotte Forten of Philadelphia, "and they are said to be among the most degraded negroes of the South."

Equally sharp disagreements swirled around the question of economic opportunity for blacks. Edward Philbrick of Boston, an engineer who worked as a plantation superintendent on the islands, embodied one approach to the issue. Philbrick hoped to make the islands a showcase for free labor by turning the freed slaves into wage earners on the large cotton plantations there. For blacks to produce more cotton as wage earners than they had as slaves, Philbrick reasoned, would squelch northern "gabble about the danger of immediate emancipation" and buttress the position of those northerners who wanted emancipation to become the Union's main war goal. But the freedmen themselves had little enthusiasm for working in gangs on plantations, even if for wages. The practice smacked too much of their conditions under slavery. Instead, most Sea Island blacks would have preferred to plant food for themselves rather than cotton for northern factories, and many dreamed of owning their own land. "I should like to buy the very spot on which I live," an elderly freedman wrote to President Abraham Lincoln in a dictated letter. "I had rather work for myself . . . than work for a gentleman for wages."

Union administrators made some concessions to blacks' wishes. When, in the fall of 1863, Sea Island officials sold sixty thousand acres of confiscated rebel estates, only sixteen thousand acres were reserved for freedmen. The rest of the land was open to purchase by northern investors and speculators. Protesting the injustice of reserving a mere quarter of the acreage for those who composed the vast majority of the Sea Island residents, General Rufus Saxton, the islands' military governor and a "thoroughgoing Abolitionist, of the radical sort," secured approval in Washington for a plan to allow blacks to claim unsold land merely by squatting on it (a practice called preemption). Pressured by Saxton's rivals, however, the federal government reversed itself early in 1864 and forbade squatter claims.

The policy shifts continued. In December 1864 General William T. Sherman, fresh from his sweep across Georgia, arrived on the Sea Islands in the

**Sea Island Wage Labor**
*Free blacks sort cotton on an Edisto Island plantation. Northern managers who ran plantations on the Sea Islands during the war hoped to prove the virtues of free labor by turning freedmen into wage earners.*

company of thousands of black camp followers who had gathered around his army during its march to the sea. To provide for these people, Sherman took steps to establish a class of black freeholders. General Sherman's Order No. 15 granted blacks the right to preempt unsold land not only on the Sea Islands but for thirty miles inland, on the main-

land. By 1865 the islands had become a haven for black refugees from all over the South.

The new land policy would yet again be reversed: in August 1865 President Andrew Johnson would order all Sea Island lands returned to their original owners, thus dispossessing most of the blacks anew and leaving them no better or worse off than emancipated slaves elsewhere in the South. But during the Civil War, the islands had fulfilled a unique function. They had provided an arena wherein the Union first supervised emancipation and abolitionists first confronted large numbers of slaves. The scene of pioneer ventures in freedmen's education, black wage labor, and land redistribution, the Sea Islands had served as a testing ground for new social policies.

## Sea Island Teachers

*The teachers and missionaries who arrived in the Sea Islands to work among the freed slaves were known as Gideon's Band. Below, a Gideonite group gathers in front of a stately home in Port Royal.*

prisoners of war, a policy that denied captured blacks the opportunity to be exchanged for Confederate prisoners. Instead, Jefferson Davis ordered all blacks taken in battle to be sent back to the states from which they came, where they were reenslaved or executed. In an especially gruesome incident, when Confederate troops captured Fort Pillow, Tennessee, in 1864, they massacred 262 blacks—an action that provoked outcries but no retaliation from the North.

Well into the war, black soldiers faced inequities in their pay. In contrast to white soldiers, who earned $13.00 a month plus a $3.50 clothing allowance, black privates received only $10.00 a month, with clothing deducted. "We have come out Like men and we Expected to be Treated as men but we have bin Treated more Like Dogs then men," a black soldier complained to Secretary of War Edwin Stanton. In June 1864 Congress belatedly equalized the pay of black and white soldiers.

Although fraught with hardships and inequities, military service became a symbol of citizenship for blacks. It proved that "black men can give blows as well as take them," Frederick Douglass declared. "Liberty won by white men would lose half its lustre." Above all, the use of black soldiers, especially former slaves, was seen by northern generals as a major strike at the Confederacy. "They will make good soldiers," General Grant wrote to Lincoln in 1863, "and taking them from the enemy weakens him in the same proportion they strengthen us."

### Slavery in Wartime

Anxious white southerners on the home front felt as if they were perched on a volcano. "We should be practi-cally helpless should the negroes rise," declared a Louisiana planter's daughter, "since there are so few men left at home." When Mary Boykin Chesnut of South Carolina learned that her cousin had been murdered in bed by two trusted house slaves, she became almost frantic. "The murder," Chesnut wrote, "has clearly driven us all wild." To maintain control over their 3 million black slaves, white southerners resorted to a variety of measures. They tightened slave patrols, at times moved entire plantations to relative safety in Texas or in the upland regions of the coastal South, and spread scare stories among the slaves. "The whites would tell the colored people not to go to the Yankees, for they would harness them to carts . . . in place of horses," reported Susie King Taylor, a black fugitive from Savannah.

Wartime developments had a significant effect on the slaves. Some remained faithful to their owners and helped hide family treasures from marauding Union soldiers. Others were torn between loyalty and lust for freedom: one slave, for example, accompanied his master to war, rescued him when he was wounded, and then escaped on his master's horse. Given a viable choice between freedom and bondage, slaves usually chose freedom. Few slaves helped the North as dramatically as Robert Smalls, a hired-out slave boatman who turned over a Confederate steamer to the Union navy, but most who had a chance to flee to Union lines did so. The idea of freedom held irresistible appeal. Upon learning from a Union soldier that he was free, a Virginia coachman dressed in his master's clothes, "put on his best watch and chain, took his stick, and . . . told him that he might for the future drive his own coach."

**Fording the Rappahannock River**
*When federal troops came within reach, those slaves who could do so liberated themselves by fleeing behind Union lines. These Virginia fugitives, lugging all their possessions, move toward freedom in the summer of 1862, after the Second Battle of Bull Run.*

The majority of slaves, however, had no escape and remained on their plantations under the nominal control of their owners. Despite the fears of southern whites, no general uprising of slaves occurred; and the Confederacy continued to impress thousands of slaves to toil in war plants, army camps, and field hospitals. But even slaves with no chance of flight were alert to the opportunity that war provided and swiftly tested the limits of enforced labor. As a Savannah mistress noted as early as 1861, the slaves "show a very different face from what they have had heretofore." Moreover, wartime conditions reduced the slaves' productivity. With most of the white men off at war, the master-slave relationship weakened. The women and boys who remained on plantations complained of their difficulty in controlling slaves, who commonly refused to work, performed their labors inefficiently, or even destroyed property. A Texas wife contended that her slaves were "trying all they can, it seems to me, to aggravate me" by neglecting the stock, breaking plows, and tearing down fences. "You may give your Negroes away," she finally wrote despairingly to her husband in 1864.

Whether southern slaves fled to freedom or merely stopped working, they effectively acted to defy slavery, to liberate themselves from its regulations, and to undermine the plantation system. Thus southern slavery disintegrated even as the Confederacy fought to preserve it. Hard pressed by Union armies, short of manpower, and unsettled by the erosion of plantation slavery, the Confederate Congress in 1864 considered the drastic step of impressing slaves into its army as soldiers in exchange for their freedom at the war's end. Robert E. Lee favored the use of slaves as soldiers on the grounds that if the Confederacy did not arm its slaves, the Union would. Others, however, were adamantly opposed. "If slaves will make good soldiers," a Georgia general argued, "our whole theory of slavery is wrong." Originally against arming slaves, Jefferson Davis changed his mind in 1865. In March 1865 the Confederate Congress narrowly passed a bill to arm 300,000 slave soldiers, although it omitted any mention of emancipation. As the war ended a few weeks later, however, the plan was never put into effect.

Although the Confederacy's decision to arm the slaves came too late to affect the war, the debate over arming them damaged southern morale. By then, the South's military position had started to deteriorate.

## The Turning Point of 1863

In the summer and fall of 1863, Union fortunes dramatically improved in every theater of the war. Yet the year began badly for the North. The slide, which had started with Burnside's defeat at Fredericksburg, Virginia, in December 1862, continued into the spring of 1863. Burnside's successor, General Joseph "Fighting Joe" Hooker, a windbag fond of issuing pompous proclamations to his troops, devised a plan to dislodge the Confederates from Fredericksburg by crossing the Rappahannock River north of the town and descending on the rebel rear. But Lee and Stonewall Jackson routed Hooker at Chancellorsville, Virginia, early in May 1863. The battle proved costly for the South because Jackson was accidentally shot by Confederate pickets and died a few days later. Still, Hooker had twice as many men as Lee, so the Union defeat at Chancellorsville was humiliating for the North. "What will the country say?" Lincoln moaned. Reports from the West brought no better news. Although repulsed at Shiloh in western Tennessee, the Confederates still had a powerful army in central Tennessee under General Braxton Bragg.

**The War in the East, 1863**

*Victorious at Chancellorsville in May 1863, Lee again invaded Union territory but was decisively stopped at Gettysburg.*

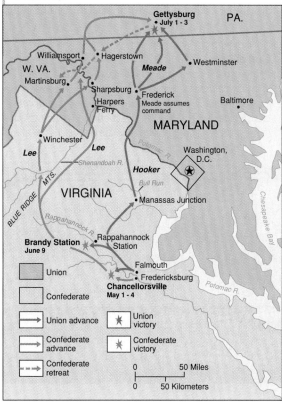

Furthermore, despite repeated efforts, Grant was unable to take Vicksburg; the two-hundred-mile stretch of the Mississippi between Vicksburg and Port Hudson remained in rebel hands.

The upswing in Union fortunes began with Lee's decision after Chancellorsville to invade the North. The decision provoked dissent within the Confederate government, but Lee needed supplies that war-wracked Virginia could no longer provide. He also hoped to panic Lincoln into moving troops from besieged Vicksburg to the eastern theater. Lee envisioned a major Confederate victory on northern soil that would tip the balance in northern politics to the pro-peace Democrats and gain European recognition of the Confederacy. Moving his 75,000 men down the Shenandoah Valley, Lee crossed the Potomac into Maryland and pressed forward into southern Pennsylvania. At this point, with Lee's army far to the west of Richmond,

Hooker recommended a Union stab at the Confederate capital. But Lincoln brushed aside the advice. "Lee's *army,* and not *Richmond,* is your true objective," Lincoln shot back, and then he replaced Hooker with the more reliable George G. Meade.

Early in July 1863, Lee's offensive ground to a halt at a Pennsylvania road junction, Gettysburg. Confederates foraging for shoes in the town encountered some Union cavalry. Soon both sides called for reinforcements, and the war's greatest battle commenced. On July 1 Meade's troops installed themselves in hills south of town along a line that resembled a fishhook: the shank ran along Cemetery Ridge and a northern hook encircled Culp's Hill. By the end of the first day of fighting, most of the troops on both sides had arrived: Meade's army outnumbered the Confederates 90,000 to 75,000. On July 2 Lee rejected advice to plant the Confederate army in a defensive position between Meade's forces and Washington and instead attacked the Union flanks, with some success. But because the Confederate assaults were uncoordinated, and some southern generals disregarded orders and struck where they chose, the Union was able to move in reinforcements and regain its earlier losses.

By the afternoon of July 3, believing that the Union flanks had been weakened, Lee attacked Cemetery Ridge in the center of the North's defensive line. After

### Gettysburg, 1863

*The failure of Pickett's charge against the Union center on July 3 was the decisive action in the war's greatest battle.*

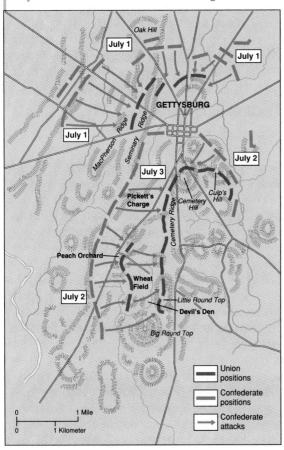

### Gettysburg, 1863

*At the end of the three-day Battle of Gettysburg, Lee's army had suffered over 25,000 casualties. These uninjured Confederate captives, who refuse to face the camera and stare off in different directions, may have spent the rest of the war in northern prison camps.*

southern cannon shelled the line, a massive infantry force of fifteen thousand Confederates, Pickett's charge, moved in. But as the Confederate cannon sank into the ground and fired a shade too high, and as Union fire wiped out the rebel charge, rifled weapons proved their deadly effectiveness. At the end of the day, Confederate bodies littered the field. "The dead and the dying were lying by the thousands between the two lines," a dazed Louisiana soldier wrote. "The enemy seemed to be launching his cavalry to sweep the remaining handful of men from the face of the earth." A little more than half of Pickett's troops were dead, wounded, or captured in the horrible encounter. When Lee withdrew to Virginia on July 4, he had lost seventeen generals and over one-third of his army. Total Union and Confederate casualties numbered almost fifty thousand. Despite the Confederate defeat, Meade failed to pursue and destroy the retreating rebels. Still, because he had halted Lee's foray into the North, the Union rejoiced.

Almost simultaneously, the North won a less bloody but more strategic victory in the West, where Grant finally solved the puzzle posed by Vicksburg's defenses. Situated on a bluff on the east bank of the Mississippi, Vicksburg was protected on the west by the river and on the north by hills, forests, and swamps. Vicksburg could be attacked only over a thin strip of dry land to its east and south. Positioned to the north of Vicksburg, Grant had to find a way to get his army south of the city and onto the Mississippi's east bank. His solution lay in moving his troops far to the west of the city and down to a point on the river south of Vicksburg. Meanwhile, Union gunboats and supply ships ran past the Confederate batteries overlooking the river at Vicksburg (not without sustaining considerable damage) to rendezvous with Grant's army and transport it across to the east bank. Grant then swung in a large semicircle, first northeastward to capture Jackson, the capital of Mississippi, and then westward back to Vicksburg. After a six-week siege, during which famished soldiers and civilians in Vicksburg were reduced to eating mules and even rats, General John C. Pemberton surrendered his thirty-thousand-man garrison to Grant on July 4, the day after Pickett's charge at Gettysburg. Port Hudson, the last Confederate holdout on the Mississippi, soon surrendered to another Union army. "The Father of Waters flows unvexed to the sea," Lincoln declared.

Before the year was out, the Union won another crucial victory in the West. General William S. Rose-

**The War in the West, 1863: Vicksburg**
*Grant first moved his army west of Vicksburg to a point on the Mississippi south of the town. Then he marched northeast, taking Jackson, and finally west to Vicksburg.*

crans fought and maneuvered Braxton Bragg's Confederate army out of central Tennessee and into Chattanooga, in the southeastern tip of the state, and then forced Bragg to evacuate Chattanooga. Bragg defeated the pursuing Rosecrans at the Battle of Chickamauga (September 19–20, 1863), one of the bloodiest of the war, and drove him back into Chattanooga. But the arrival of Grant and of reinforcements from the Army of the Potomac enabled the North to break Bragg's siege of Chattanooga in November. With Chattanooga secure, the way lay open for a Union strike into Georgia.

Coming on the heels of reverses that had driven northern morale to its lowest point of the war, Union successes in the second half of 1863 stiffened the North's will to keep fighting and plunged some rebel leaders into despair. Hearing of the fall of Vicksburg, Confederate ordnance chief Josiah Gorgas wrote, "Yesterday we rode the pinnacle of success—today absolute ruin seems our portion. The Confederacy totters to its destruction."

Totter it might, but the South was far from beaten. Although the outcome at Gettysburg quashed southerners' hopes for victory on northern soil, it did not significantly impair Lee's ability to defend Virginia. The loss of Vicksburg and the Mississippi cut off the Confederate states west of the river—Arkansas, Louisiana, and Texas—from those to the east; but these western states could still provide soldiers. Even with the loss of Chattanooga, the Confederacy continued to hold most of the Carolinas, Georgia, Florida, and Mississippi. Few contemporaries thought that the fate of the Confederacy had been sealed.

# War and Society, North and South

Extending beyond the battlefields, the Civil War engulfed two economies and societies. By 1863 stark contrasts emerged: with its superior resources, the Union could meet wartime demands as the imperiled Confederacy could not. But both regions experienced labor shortages and inflation. As the conflict dragged on, both societies confronted problems of disunity and dissent, for war issues opened fissures between social classes. In both regions war encroached on everyday life. Families were disrupted and dislocated, especially in the South. Women on both sides took on new roles at home, in the workplace, and in relief efforts.

### The War's Economic Impact: The North

The war affected the Union's economy unevenly. Some industries fared poorly. For instance, the loss of southern markets damaged the shoe industry in Massachusetts, and a shortage of raw cotton sent the cotton-textile industry into a tailspin. On the other hand, industries directly related to the war effort, such as the manufacture of arms and clothing, benefited from huge government contracts. By 1865, for example, the ready-made clothing industry received orders for more than a million uniforms a year. Military demand also meant abundant business for the railroads. Some privately owned lines, which had overbuilt before the war, doubled their volume of traffic. In 1862 the federal government itself went into the railroad business by establishing the United States Military Railroads (USMRR) to carry troops and supplies to the front. "The quicker you build the railroad," Union general William T. Sherman told his troops, "the quicker you'll get something to eat." By 1865 the USMRR was the largest railroad in the world.

The Republicans in Congress actively promoted business development during the war. Holding 102 of 146 House seats and 29 of 36 Senate seats in 1861, they overrode Democratic foes and hiked the tariff in 1862 and again in 1864 to protect domestic industries. The Republican-sponsored Pacific Railroad Act of 1862 provided for the development of a transcontinental railroad, an idea that had foundered before the war on disagreements over which route such a railroad should follow. With the South out of the picture and no longer able to demand a southern route from New Orleans across the Southwest, Congress chose a northern route from Omaha to San Francisco. Chartering the Union Pacific and Central Railroad corporations, Congress then gave to each large land grants and generous loans. These two corporations combined received more than 60 million acres in land grants and $20 million in loans from the government. The issuance of greenbacks and the creation of a national banking system, meanwhile, brought a measure of uniformity to the nation's financial system.

The Republicans designed these measures to benefit a variety of social classes, and to a degree, they succeeded. Republican laws such as the Homestead Act, passed in 1862, embodied the party's ideal of "free soil, free labor, free men" by granting 160 acres of public land to settlers after five years of residence on the land. By 1865 twenty thousand homesteaders occupied new land in the West under the Homestead Act. The Republicans also secured passage in 1862 of the Morrill Land Grant Act, which gave to the states proceeds of public lands—to fund the establishment of universities emphasizing "such branches of learning as are related to agriculture and mechanic arts." The Morrill Act spurred the growth of large state universities, mainly in the Midwest and West. Michigan State, Iowa State, and Purdue universities, among many others, profited from the law.

Despite the idealistic goals behind some Republican laws, the war benefited the wealthy more than the average citizen. Corrupt contractors grew fat by selling the government substandard merchandise such as the notorious "shoddy" clothing made from compressed rags, which quickly fell apart. Speculators who locked their patriotism in the closet made millions in the gold market. Because the price of gold in relation to greenbacks rose whenever public confidence in the government fell, those who bought gold in the hope that its price would rise actually gained from Union defeats, and even more from Union disasters. Businessmen with access to scarce commodities also reaped astounding profits. For example, manpower shortages stimulated wartime demand for the mechanical reaper that Cyrus McCormick had patented in 1834. When paid for reapers in greenbacks, which he distrusted, McCormick immediately reinvested them in pig iron and then watched in glee as wartime demand drove the price of pig iron from twenty-three dollars to forty dollars a ton.

The war had a far less happy impact on ordinary workers. Protected from foreign competition by higher tariffs, northern manufacturers hoisted the prices of finished goods. Wartime excise taxes and inflation combined to push prices still higher. At the same time, wages lagged 20 percent or more behind cost increases for most of the war. Common in most periods of rapid inflation, lagging wages became especially severe during the war because boys and women poured into government offices and factories to replace adult male workers who had joined the army. Employers' mere threats of hiring more low-paid youths and females undercut the bargaining power of the men who remained in the work force.

Some workers organized to decry their low wages. "We are unable to sustain life for the price offered by contractors who fatten on their contracts," Cincinnati seamstresses declared in a petition to President Lincoln. Cigar makers and locomotive engineers formed national unions, a process that would accelerate after the war. But protests had little impact on wages; employers often denounced worker protests as unpatriotic hindrances to the war effort. In 1864 army troops were diverted from combat to put down protests in war industries from New York to the Midwest.

## The War's Economic Impact: The South

The war shattered the South's economy. Indeed, if both regions are considered together, the overall impact of the war was to retard *American* economic growth. For example, the commodity output of the American economy, which had registered huge increases of 51 percent and 62 percent in the 1840s and 1850s, respectively, rose only 22 percent during the 1860s. Even this modest gain depended wholly on the North, for in the 1860s commodity output in the South actually *declined* 39 percent.

Substantial wartime industrial growth by the South was more than offset by other factors. For example, the war wrecked the South's railroads; in 1864 Union troops, marching through Georgia under General William T. Sherman, tore up railroad tracks, heated them in giant fires, and twisted them into "Sherman neckties." Cotton production, once the foundation of

**Destroying Railroad Track**

*As the Union general William T. Sherman invaded Georgia, his troops demolished Confederate property of military value, such as arsenals and railroads. These Union soldiers in Atlanta break up a railroad track before setting forth on their march to the sea. The damaged rails that they left behind, often bent out of shape to form "Sherman neckties," may still be found in parts of the South.*

the South's prosperity, sank from more than 4 million bales in 1861 to 300,000 bales in 1865 as Union invasions took their toll on production, particularly in Tennessee and Louisiana.

Invading Union troops also occupied the South's food-growing as well as cotton-producing regions. Moreover, in agricultural areas under Confederate control, the drain of manpower into the army decreased the yields per acre of crops like wheat and corn. Even the loss of a few carpenters and blacksmiths could disrupt the economy of rural districts. Food shortages abounded late in the war. "The people are subsisting on the ungathered crops and nine families out of ten are left without meat," a Mississippi citizen lamented in 1864. Agricultural shortages worsened the South's already severe inflation. By 1863 salt selling for $1.25 a sack in New York City cost $60.00 in the Confederacy. Food riots erupted in 1863 in Mobile, Atlanta, and Richmond; in Richmond the wives of ironworkers paraded to demand lower food prices.

Part of the blame for the South's food shortages rested with the planter class. Although some planters heeded government pleas to shift from cotton to food production, and cotton crops declined sharply overall, many planters still raised more cotton than they could market abroad. The consequences were far-reaching. Slave labor, which could have been diverted to army camps, remained essential on the cotton plantations. This increased the Confederacy's reliance on its unpopular conscription laws. Moreover, cotton continued to sprout from land that could have been used for food production. To feed its hungry armies, the Confederacy had to impress food from civilians. This policy not only elicited resentment of planters but contributed to the South's mounting military desertions. Food-impressment agents usually concentrated on the easiest targets—farms run by the wives of active soldiers, who found it hard to resist desperate pleas to return home. The wife of an Alabama soldier wrote to him: "We haven't got nothing in the house to eat but a little bit o meal. I don't want you to stop fighting them Yankees . . . but try and get off and come home and fix us all up some and then you can go back." By the end of 1864, half of the Confederacy's soldiers were absent from their units.

In one respect, the persistence of cotton growing did aid the South because cotton became the basis for the Confederacy's flourishing trade with the enemy. The U.S. Congress virtually legalized this trade in July 1861 by allowing northern commerce with southerners

loyal to the Union. In practice, of course, it proved impossible to tell loyalists from disloyalists, and for most traders it hardly mattered. As long as Union textile mills stood idle for lack of cotton, northern traders happily swapped bacon, salt, blankets, and other necessaries for southern cotton. The Union's penetration of the Confederate heartland eased business dealings between the two sides. By 1864 traffic through the lines was providing the South with enough food daily to feed Lee's Army of Northern Virginia. To a northern congressman, it seemed that the Union's policy was "to feed an army and fight it at the same time."

Trading with the enemy alleviated the South's food shortages but intensified its morale problems. The prospect of traffic with the Yankees gave planters an incentive to keep growing cotton, and it fattened merchants and middlemen. "Oh! the extortioners," complained a Confederate war-office clerk in Richmond. "Our patriotism is mainly in the army and among the ladies of the South. The avarice and cupidity of men at home could only be exceeded by ravenous wolves."

### Dealing with Dissent

Both wartime governments faced mounting dissent and disloyalty. Within the Confederacy, dissent took two basic forms. First, a vocal group of states' rights activists, notably Vice President Alexander Stephens and governors Zebulon Vance of North Carolina and Joseph Brown of Georgia, spent much of the war attacking Jefferson Davis's government as a despotism. Second, loyalty to the Union flourished among a segment of the Confederacy's common people, particularly those living in the Appalachian Mountain region that ran from western North Carolina through eastern Tennessee and into northern Georgia and Alabama. The nonslaveholding small farmers who predominated here saw the Confederate rebellion as a slaveowners' conspiracy. Resentful of such measures as the 20-Negro exemption from conscription, they were reluctant to fight for what a North Carolinian defined as "an adored trinity, cotton, niggers, and chivalry." "All they want," an Alabama farmer complained of the planters, "is to get you pupt up and to fight for their infurnal negroes and after you do there fighting you may kiss there hine parts for o they care." On the whole, the Confederate government responded mildly to popular disaffection. In 1862 the Confederate Congress gave Jefferson Davis the power to suspend the writ of habeas corpus, but Davis used his power only sparingly, by occasionally and briefly putting areas under martial law, mainly to aid tax collectors.

Lincoln faced similar challenges in the North, where the Democratic minority opposed both emancipation and the wartime growth of centralized power. Although "War Democrats" conceded that war was necessary to preserve the Union, "Peace Democrats" (called Copperheads by their opponents, to suggest a resemblance to a species of easily concealed poisonous snakes) demanded a truce and a peace conference. They charged that administration war policy was intended to "exterminate the South," make reconciliation impossible, and spark "terrible social change and revolution" nationwide.

Strongest in the border states, the Midwest, and the northeastern cities, the Democrats mobilized the support of farmers of southern background in the Ohio Valley and of members of the urban working class, especially recent immigrants, who feared losing their jobs to an influx of free blacks. In 1863 this volatile brew of political, ethnic, racial, and class antagonisms in northern society exploded into antidraft protests in several cities. By far the most violent eruption occurred in July in New York City. Catalyzed by the first drawing of names under the Enrollment Act, and by a longshoremen's strike in which blacks had been used as strikebreakers, mobs of Irish working-class men and women roamed the streets for four days until suppressed by federal troops. The city's laboring Irish loathed the idea of being drafted to fight a war on behalf of the slaves, who, once emancipated, might migrate north to compete with them for low-paying jobs. They also bitterly resented the provision of the draft law that allowed the rich to purchase substitutes. The rioters lynched at least a dozen blacks, injured hundreds more, and burned draft offices, the homes of wealthy Republicans, and the Colored Orphan Asylum.

President Lincoln's speedy dispatch of federal troops to quash these riots typified his forceful response to dissent. Lincoln imposed martial law with far less hesitancy than Davis. After suspending the writ of habeas corpus in Maryland in 1861, he barred it nationwide in 1863 and authorized the arrest of rebels, draft resisters, and those engaged in "any disloyal practice." The contrasting responses of Davis and Lincoln to dissent underscored the differences between the two regions' wartime political systems. As we have seen, Davis lacked the institutionalization of dissent provided by party conflict and thus had to tread warily, lest his opponents brand him a despot. In contrast, Lincoln and

other Republicans used dissent to rally patriotic fervor against the Democrats. After the New York City draft riots, for example, the Republicans blamed the violence on New York's antidraft Democratic governor, Horatio Seymour.

Forceful as he was, Lincoln did not unleash a reign of terror against dissent. In general, the North preserved freedom of the press, speech, and assembly. In 1864 the Union became the first warring nation in history to hold a contested national election. Moreover, although some fifteen thousand civilians were arrested during the war, most were quickly released. A few cases, however, aroused widespread concern. In 1864 a military commission sentenced an Indiana man to be hanged for an alleged plot to free Confederate prisoners. The Supreme Court reversed his conviction two years later when it ruled that civilians could not be tried by military courts when the civil courts were open (*Ex parte* Milligan, 1866). Of more concern were the arrests of politicians, notably Clement L. Vallandigham, an Ohio Peace Democrat. Courting arrest, Vallandigham challenged the administration, denounced the suspension of habeas corpus, proposed an armistice, and in 1863 was sentenced to jail for the rest of the war by a military commission. When Ohio Democrats then nominated him for governor, Lincoln changed the sentence to banishment. Escorted to enemy lines in Tennessee, Vallandigham was left in the hands of bewildered Confederates and eventually escaped to Canada. The Supreme Court refused to review his case.

## The Medical War

Despite the discontent and disloyalty of some citizens, both the Union and the Confederacy witnessed a remarkable wartime patriotism that impelled civilians, especially women, to work tirelessly to alleviate soldiers' suffering. The United States Sanitary Commission, organized early in the war by civilians to assist the Union's medical bureau, depended on women volunteers. Described as a "great artery that bears the people's love to the army," the commission raised funds at "sanitary fairs," bought and distributed supplies, ran special kitchens to supplement army rations, tracked down the missing, and inspected army camps. The volunteers' exploits became legendary. One poor widow, Mary Ann "Mother" Bickerdyke, served sick and wounded Union soldiers as both nurse and surrogate mother. When asked by a doctor by what authority she

**Women's Central Relief Association**

*A civilian agency formed early in the war, the United States Sanitary Commission helped the Army Medical Bureau solve health problems. Seven thousand local auxiliaries, staffed by women volunteers, collected supplies, raised funds, and offered nursing services. These New York women, under commission auspices, gather at Cooper Union.*

demanded supplies for the wounded, she shot back, "From the Lord God Almighty. Do you have anything that ranks higher than that?"

Women also reached out to aid the battlefront through the nursing corps. Before the war ended, some 3,200 women served the Union and the Confederacy as nurses. Already famed for her tireless campaigns on behalf of the insane, Dorothea Dix became the head of the Union's nursing corps. Clara Barton began the war as a clerk in the U.S. Patent Office, but she, too, greatly aided the medical effort, finding ingenious ways of channeling medicine to the sick and wounded. Catching wind of Union movements before Antietam, Barton showed up at the battlefield on the eve of the clash with a wagonload of supplies. When army surgeons ran out of bandages and started to dress wounds with corn husks, she raced forward with lint and bandages. "With what joy," she wrote, "I laid my precious burden down among them." After the war, in 1881, she would found the American Red Cross. The Confederacy, too,

had extraordinary nurses. One, Sally Tompkins, was commissioned a captain for her hospital work; another, Belle Boyd, served the Confederacy as both a nurse and a spy and once dashed through a field, waving her bonnet, to give Stonewall Jackson information. Danger stalked nurses even in hospitals far from the front. Author Louisa May Alcott, a nurse at the Union Hotel Hospital in Washington, D.C., contracted typhoid. Wherever they worked, nurses witnessed haunting, unforgettable sights. "About the amputating table," one reported, "lay large piles of human flesh—legs, arms, feet, and hands . . . the stiffened membrances seemed to be clutching oftentimes at our clothing."

Pioneered by British reformer Florence Nightingale in the 1850s, nursing was a new vocation for women and, in the eyes of many, a brazen departure from women's proper sphere. Male doctors were unsure about how to react to women in the wards. Some saw the potential for mischief, but others viewed nursing and sanitary work as potentially useful. The miasm theory of disease (see Chapter 11) won wide respect among physicians and stimulated some valuable sanitary measures, particularly in hospitals behind the lines. In partial consequence, the ratio of disease to battle deaths was much lower in the Civil War than in the Mexican War. Still, for every soldier killed during the Civil War, two died of disease. "These Big Battles is not as Bad as the fever," a North Carolina soldier wrote. The scientific investigations that would lead to the germ theory of disease were only commencing during the 1860s. Arm and leg wounds frequently led to gangrene or tetanus, and typhoid, malaria, diarrhea, and dysentery raged through army camps.

Prison camps posed a special problem. Prisoner exchanges between the North and the South, common early in the war, collapsed by midwar, partly because the South refused to exchange the black prisoners it held and partly because the North gradually concluded that exchanges benefited the manpower-short Confederacy more than the Union. As a result, the two sides had far more prisoners than either could handle. Prisoners on both sides suffered gravely from camp environments, but the worst conditions plagued southern camps. Squalor and insufficient rations turned the Confederate prison camp at Andersonville, Georgia, into a virtual death camp; 3,000 prisoners a month (out of a total of 32,000) were dying there by August 1864. After the war an outraged northern public secured the execution of Andersonville's commandant. Although the commandant was partly to blame, the deterioration of

**Andersonville Prison**
*Started in early 1864, the overcrowded Andersonville prison in southwest Georgia provided no shelter for its inmates, who built tent-like structures out of blankets, sticks, or whatever they could find. Exposure, disease, and poor sanitation contributed to a mortality rate almost double that in other Confederate prison camps and made Andersonville a scandal that outlived the war.*

the southern economy had contributed massively to the wretched state of southern prison camps. The Union camps were not much better, but the fatality rate among northerners held by the South exceeded that of southerners imprisoned by the North.

### The War and Women's Rights

Female nurses and Sanitary Commission workers were not the only women to serve society in wartime. In both northern and southern government offices and mills, thousands of women took over jobs vacated by men. Moreover, home industry revived at all levels of society. In rural areas, where manpower shortages were most acute, women often did the plowing, planting, and harvesting.

Few women worked more effectively for their region's cause than Philadelphia-born Anna E. Dickinson. After losing her job in the federal mint (for denouncing General George McClellan as a traitor), Dickinson threw herself into hospital volunteer work and public lecturing. Her lecture "Hospital Life," recounting the soldiers' sufferings, won the attention of Republican politicians. In 1863, hard pressed by the Democrats, these politicians invited Dickinson, then scarcely twenty-one, to campaign on behalf of the Republican tickets in New Hampshire and Connecticut. This decision paid handsome dividends for the party. Articulate and poised, Dickinson captivated her listeners. Soon Republican candidates who had dismissed the offer of aid from a woman begged her to campaign for them.

Northern women's rights advocates hoped that the war would yield equality for women as well as for slaves. Not only should a grateful North reward women for their wartime services, these women reasoned, but it should recognize the link between black rights and women's rights. In 1863 Elizabeth Cady Stanton and Susan B. Anthony organized the National Woman's Loyal League. Although the league's main activity was to gather 400,000 signatures on a petition calling for a constitutional amendment to abolish slavery, Stanton and Anthony used the organization to promote woman suffrage as well.

Despite high expectations, the war did not bring women significantly closer to economic or political equality. Women in government offices and factories continued to be paid less than men. Sanitary Commission workers and most wartime nurses, as volunteers, earned nothing. Nor did the war alter the prevailing definition of woman's sphere. In 1860 that sphere already included charitable and benevolent activities; during the war the scope of benevolence grew to embrace organized care for the wounded. Yet men continued to dominate the medical profession, and for the rest of the nineteenth century, nurses would be classified in the census as domestic help.

The keenest disappointment of women's rights advocates lay in their failure to capitalize on rising sentiment for the abolition of slavery to secure the vote for women. Although the North had compelling reasons to abolish slavery in the rebellious areas of the South, northern politicians could see little practical value in woman suffrage. The *New York Herald,* which supported the Loyal League's attack on slavery, dismissed its call for woman suffrage as "nonsense and tomfoolery." Stanton wrote bitterly, "So long as woman labors to second man's endeavors and exalt his sex above her own, her virtues pass unquestioned; but when she dares to demand rights and privileges for herself, her motives, manners, dress, personal appearance, and character are subjects for ridicule and detraction."

# The Union Victorious, 1864–1865

Despite successes at Gettysburg and Vicksburg in 1863, the Union stood no closer to taking Richmond at the start of 1864 than in 1861, and most of the Lower South still remained under Confederate control. The press of Union invasion had taken its toll on the South's home front, but the North's inability to destroy the main Confederate armies had eroded the Union's will to keep attacking. Northern war weariness strengthened the Democrats and jeopardized Lincoln's prospects for reelection in 1864.

The year 1864 proved crucial for the North. While Grant occupied Lee in the East, a Union army under William T. Sherman attacked from Tennessee into northwestern Georgia and took Atlanta in early September. Atlanta's fall boosted northern morale and helped to reelect Lincoln. Now the curtain rose on the last act of the war. After taking Atlanta, Sherman marched across Georgia to Savannah, devastated the state's resources, and cracked its morale. Pivoting north from Savannah, Sherman then moved into South Carolina. Meanwhile, having backed Lee into trenches around Petersburg and Richmond, Grant forced the evacuation of both cities and brought on the Confederacy's collapse.

## *The Eastern Theater in 1864*

Early in 1864 Lincoln made Grant commander of all Union armies and promoted him to lieutenant general. At first glance, the stony-faced Grant seemed an unlikely candidate for so exalted a rank, held previously only by George Washington. Grant's only distinguishing characteristics were his ever-present cigars and a penchant for whittling sticks into chips. "There is no glitter, no parade about him," a contemporary noted. But Grant's success in the West had made him the Union's most popular general. With his promotion, Grant moved his headquarters to the Army of the Potomac in the East and mapped a strategy for final victory.

Like Lincoln, Grant believed that the Union had to coordinate its attacks on all fronts in order to exploit its numerical advantage and prevent the South from shifting troops back and forth between the eastern and western theaters. (The South's victory at Chickamauga in September 1863, for example, had rested in part on reinforcements sent by Lee to Braxton Bragg in the West.) Accordingly, Grant planned a sustained offensive against Lee in the East while ordering William T. Sherman to attack the rebel army in Georgia commanded by Bragg's replacement, General Joseph Johnston. Sherman's mission was "to break it [the Confederate army] up, and to get into the interior of the enemy's country . . . inflicting all the damage you can."

In early May 1864, Grant led 118,000 men against Lee's 64,000 in a forested area near Fredericksburg, Virginia, called the Wilderness. Checked by Lee in a series of bloody engagements (the Battle of the Wilderness, May 5–7), Grant then tried to swing around Lee's right flank, only to suffer new reverses at Spotsylvania on May 12 and Cold Harbor on June 3. These engagements were among the war's fiercest; at Cold Harbor, Grant lost 7,000 men in one hour. Oliver Wendell Holmes, Jr., a Union lieutenant and later a Supreme Court justice, wrote home how "immense the butcher's bill has been." But Grant refused to interpret repulses as defeats. Rather, he viewed the engagements at the Wilderness, Spotsylvania, and Cold Harbor merely as less-than-complete victories. Pressing on, he forced Lee to pull back to the trenches guarding Petersburg and Richmond.

Grant had accomplished a major objective, because once entrenched, Lee could no longer swing around to the Union rear, cut Yankee supply lines, or as at Chancellorsville, surprise the Union's main force. Lee did dispatch General Jubal A. Early on raids down the Shenandoah Valley, which the Confederacy had long used both as a granary and as an indirect way to menace Washington. But Grant countered by ordering General Philip Sheridan to march up the valley from the north and so devastate it that a crow flying over would have to carry its own provisions. The time had come, a Union chaplain wrote, "to peel this land." After defeating Early at Winchester, Virginia, in September 1864, Sheridan controlled the valley.

### Sherman in Georgia

While Grant and Lee grappled in the Wilderness, Sherman advanced into Georgia at the head of 98,000 men. Opposing him with 53,000 Confederate troops (soon reinforced to 65,000), General Joseph Johnston retreated toward Atlanta. Johnston's plan was to conserve strength for a final defense of Atlanta while forcing Sherman to extend his supply lines. But Jefferson Davis, dismayed by Johnston's defensive strategy, replaced him with the adventurous John B. Hood. Hood, who lost the use of an arm at Gettysburg and a leg at Chickamauga, had to be strapped to his saddle; but for all his disabilities, he liked to take risks. In a prewar poker game, he had bet $2,500 with "nary a pair in his hand." Hood gave Davis what he wanted, a series of attacks on Sherman's army. The forays, however, failed to dislodge Sherman and severely depleted Hood's army. No longer able to defend Atlanta's supply lines, Hood evacuated the city, which Sherman took on September 2, 1864.

### The Election of 1864

Atlanta's fall came at a timely moment for Lincoln, who was in the thick of a tough reelection campaign. Indeed, Lincoln had secured the Republican renomination with difficulty. The Radicals, who had earlier flayed Lincoln for delay in adopting emancipation as a war goal, now dismissed his plans to restore the occupied parts of Tennessee, Louisiana, and Arkansas to the Union. The Radicals insisted that Congress, not the president, could alone set the requirements for readmission of conquered states and criticized Lincoln's reconstruction standards as too lenient. The Radicals rallied around Secretary of the Treasury Salmon P. Chase for the nomination. The Democrats, meanwhile, had never forgiven Lincoln for making emancipation a war goal, and now the Copperheads, or Peace Democrats, demanded an immediate armistice, followed by negotiations between the North and the South to settle outstanding issues.

Facing formidable challenges, Lincoln benefited from both his own resourcefulness and his foes' problems. Chase's challenge failed, and by the time of the Republican convention in July, Lincoln's managers were firmly in control. Moreover, to isolate the Peace Democrats and attract prowar Democrats, the Republicans formed a temporary organization, the National Union party, and replaced Lincoln's vice president, Hannibal Hamlin, with a prowar southern Unionist, Democratic senator Andrew Johnson of Tennessee. This tactic helped exploit the widening division among the Democrats, who nominated George B. McClellan, the former commander of the Army of the Potomac and an advocate of continuing the war until the Confederacy's collapse. But McClellan, saddled with a platform written by the Peace Democrats, spent much of his campaign distancing himself from his party's peace-without-victory plank.

**The Election of 1864**

| Candidates | Parties | Electoral Vote | Popular Vote | Percentage of Popular Vote |
|---|---|---|---|---|
| ABRAHAM LINCOLN | Republican | 212 | 2,206,938 | 55.0 |
| George B. McClellan | Democratic | 21 | 1,803,787 | 45.0 |

Despite the Democrats' disarray, as late as August 1864, Lincoln seriously doubted that he would be reelected. Leaving little to chance, he arranged for furloughs so that Union soldiers, most of whom supported him, could vote in states lacking absentee ballots. But the timely fall of Atlanta aided him even more. The Confederate defeat had punctured the northern antiwar movement and saved Lincoln's presidency. With 55 percent of the popular vote and 212 out of 233 electoral votes, Lincoln swept to victory.

The convention that nominated Lincoln endorsed a constitutional amendment to abolish slavery, which Congress passed early in 1865. The Thirteenth Amendment would be ratified by the end of the year.

### Sherman's March Through Georgia

Meanwhile, Sherman gave the South a new lesson in total war. After evacuating Atlanta, Hood led his Confederate army north toward Tennessee in the hope of luring Sherman out of Georgia. But Sherman refused to chase Hood around Tennessee and stretch his own supply lines to the breaking point. Rather, Sherman proposed to abandon his supply lines altogether, march his army across Georgia to Savannah, and live off the countryside as he moved along. He would break the South's will to fight, terrify its people, and "make war so terrible . . . that generations would pass before they could appeal again to it."

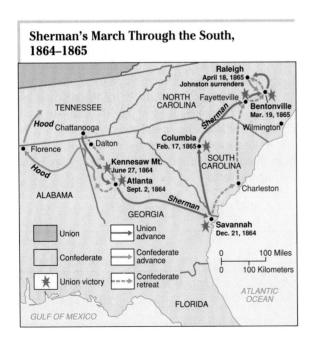

**Sherman's March Through the South, 1864–1865**

Sherman began by burning much of Atlanta and forcing the evacuation of most of its civilian population. This harsh measure relieved him of the need to feed and garrison the city. Then, sending enough troops north to ensure the futility of Hood's campaign in Tennessee, he led the bulk of his army, 62,000 men, out of Atlanta to start the 285-mile trek to Savannah. Soon thousands of slaves were following the army. "Dar's de man dat rules the world," a slave cried on seeing Sherman. Sherman's four columns of infantry, augmented by cavalry screens, moved on a front sixty miles wide and at a pace of ten miles a day. They destroyed everything that could aid southern resistance—arsenals, railroads, munitions plants, cotton gins, cotton stores, crops, and livestock. Although Sherman's troops were told not to destroy civilian property, foragers carried out their own version of total war, ransacking and sometimes demolishing homes. Indeed, the havoc seemed a vital part of Sherman's strategy. By the time he occupied Savannah, he estimated that his army had destroyed about a hundred million dollars worth of property.

After taking Savannah in December 1864, Sherman's army wheeled north toward South Carolina, the first state to secede and, in the general's view, one "that deserves all that seems in store for her." Sherman's columns advanced unimpeded to Columbia, South Carolina's capital. After fires set by looters, slaves, soldiers of both sides, and liberated Union prisoners gutted much of the city, Sherman headed for North Carolina. By the spring of 1865, his army had left in its wake over four hundred miles of ruin. Other Union armies moved into Alabama and Georgia and took thousands of prisoners. Northern forces had penetrated the entire Confederacy, except for Texas and Florida, and crushed its wealth. "War is cruelty and you cannot refine it," Sherman wrote. "Those who brought war into our country deserve all the curses and maledictions a people can pour out."

### Toward Appomattox

While Sherman headed north, Grant renewed his assault on the entrenched Army of Northern Virginia. His objective was Petersburg, a railroad hub south of Richmond. Although Grant had failed on several occasions to overwhelm the Confederate defenses in front of Petersburg, the devastation wrought by Sherman's army had taken its toll on Confederate morale. Accustomed to shortages of food and clothing, rebel soldiers now felt hopeless, and rebel desertions reached epidemic

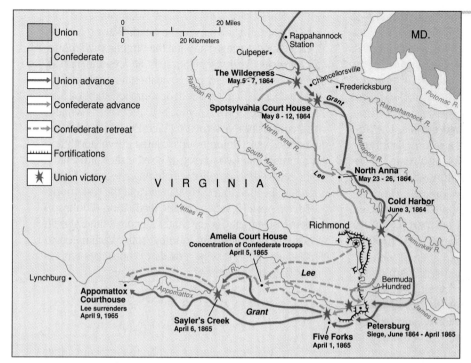

### Union
### Confederate
### Union advance
### Confederate advance
### Confederate retreat
### Fortifications
### Union victory

**VIRGINIA**

Rappahannock Station
Culpeper
The Wilderness
May 5 - 7, 1864
Chancellorsville
Fredericksburg
Spotsylvania Court House
May 8 - 12, 1864
Grant
North Anna
May 23 - 26, 1864
Lee
Cold Harbor
June 3, 1864
Richmond
Amelia Court House
Concentration of Confederate troops
April 5, 1865
Lee
Bermuda Hundred
Lynchburg
Appomattox
Courthouse
Lee surrenders
April 9, 1965
Sayler's Creek
April 6, 1865
Grant
Five Forks
April 1, 1865
Petersburg
Siege, June 1864 - April 1865
MD.

**The Final Virginia Campaign, 1864–1865**

*Refusing to abandon his campaign in the face of enormous casualties, Grant finally pushed Lee (below) into defensive fortifications around Petersburg, whose fall doomed Richmond. When Lee tried to escape to the west, Grant cut him off and forced his surrender.*

proportions. Reinforced by Sheridan's army, triumphant from its campaign in the Shenandoah Valley, Grant late in March 1865 swung his forces around the western flank of Petersburg's defenders. Lee could not stop him. On April 2 Sheridan smashed the rebel flank at the Battle of Five Forks. A courier bore the grim news to Jefferson Davis, attending church in Richmond: "General Lee telegraphs that he can hold his position no longer."

Davis left his pew, gathered his government, and fled the city. In the morning of April 3, Union troops entered Richmond, pulled down the Confederate flag, and ran up the Stars and Stripes over the capitol. As white and black regiments entered in triumph, explosions set by retreating Confederates left the city "a sea of flames." "Over all," wrote a Union officer, "hung a canopy of dense smoke lighted up now and then by the bursting shells from the numerous arsenals throughout the city." Fires damaged the Tredegar Iron Works. Union troops liberated the town jail, which housed slaves awaiting sale, and its rejoicing inmates poured into the streets. On April 4 Lincoln toured the city and, for a few minutes, sat at Jefferson Davis's desk with a dreamy expression on his face.

Lee made a last-ditch effort to escape from Grant and reach Lynchburg, sixty miles west of Petersburg.

**Grant in 1864**

*Exuding determination and competence, General Ulysses S. Grant posed in front of his tent in 1864. Within a year, Grant's final assault on Petersburg and the Union Army's triumphant march into Richmond would bring the war to an end.*

He planned to use the rail connections at Lynchburg to join General Joseph Johnston's army, which Sherman had pushed into North Carolina. But Grant and Sheridan swiftly choked off Lee's escape route, and on April 9 Lee bowed to the inevitable. He asked for terms of surrender and met Grant in a private home in the village of Appomattox Courthouse, Virginia, east of Lynchburg. While stunned troops gathered outside, Lee appeared in full dress uniform, with a sword. Grant entered in his customary disarray, smoking a cigar. When Union troops began to fire celebratory salutes, Grant put a stop to it. The final surrender of Lee's army occurred four days later. Lee's troops laid down their arms between federal ranks. "On our part," wrote a Union officer, "not a sound of trumpet . . . nor roll of drum; not a cheer . . . but an awed stillness rather." Grant paroled Lee's 26,000 men and sent them home with their horses and mules "to work their little farms." The remnants of Confederate resistance collapsed within a month of Appomattox. Johnston surrendered to Sherman on April 18, and Davis was captured in Georgia on May 10.

Grant returned to a jubilant Washington, and on April 14 he turned down a theater date with the Lincolns. That night at Ford's Theater, an unemployed pro-Confederate actor, John Wilkes Booth, entered Lincoln's box and shot him in the head. Waving a knife, Booth leaped onstage shouting the Virginia state motto, *"Sic semper tyrannis"* ("Such is always the fate of tyrants") and then escaped, despite having broken his leg. That same night, a Booth accomplice stabbed Secretary of State Seward, who later recovered, while a third conspirator, assigned to Vice President Johnson, failed to attack. Union troops hunted down Booth and shot him within two weeks, or else he shot himself. Of eight accused accomplices, including a woman boardinghouse keeper, four were hanged and the rest imprisoned. On April 15, when Lincoln died, Andrew Johnson became president. Six days later Lincoln's funeral train departed on a mournful journey from Washington to Springfield, Illinois, with crowds of thousands gathering at stations to weep as it passed.

## CONCLUSION

The Civil War took a larger human toll than any other war in American history. The death count stood at 360,000 Union soldiers and 260,000 Confederates. Most families in the nation suffered losses. Vivid reminders of

**Lincoln's Funeral Procession**

*After Lincoln's funeral in Washington D.C., a nine-car train brought the martyred president's body to Springfield, Illinois. Thousands of mourners filled New York streets on April 25, 1865, as the procession passed.*

the price of Union remained beyond the end of the century. For many years armless and legless veterans gathered at regimental reunions. Citizens erected monuments to the dead in front of town halls and on village greens. Soldiers' widows collected pensions well into the twentieth century.

The economic costs were staggering, but the war did not ruin the national economy, only the southern part of it. The vast Confederate losses, about 60 percent of southern wealth, were offset by northern advances. At the war's end, the North had almost all of the nation's wealth and capacity for production. Spurring economic modernization, the war provided a hospitable climate for industrial development and capital investment. No longer the largest slaveowning power in the world, the United States would now become a major industrial nation.

The war had political as well as economic ramifications. It created a "more perfect Union" in place of the prewar federation of states. The doctrine of states' rights did not disappear, but it was shorn of its extreme features. There would be no further talk of secession, nor would states ever again exercise their antebellum range of powers. The national banking system, created in 1863, gradually supplanted state banks. The greenbacks provided a national currency. The federal government had exercised powers that many in 1860 doubted it possessed. By abolishing slavery and imposing an income tax, it asserted power over kinds of private property once thought untouchable. The war also promoted large-scale organization in both the business world and public life. The giant railroad corporation, with its thousands of employees, and the huge Sanitary Commission, with its thousands of auxiliaries and volunteers, pointed out the road that the nation would take.

Finally, the Civil War fulfilled abolitionist prophecies as well as Unionist goals. The war produced the very sort of radical upheaval within southern society that Lincoln originally said that it would not induce. Beaten Confederates had no idea of what to expect. Some wondered whether blacks and Yankees would permanently take over the South. The same thought occurred to the freedmen. "Hello, massa," a black Union soldier called out when he spotted his former owner among a group of Confederate prisoners whom he was guarding. "Bottom rail top dis time." The nation now turned its attention to the reconstruction of the conquered South and to the fate of 3.5 million newly freed slaves.

## FOR FURTHER READING

Iver Bernstein, *The New York Draft Riots: The Significance for American Society and Politics in the Age of the Civil War* (1990). An exploration of the social, economic, and political facets of the riots, and their ramifications.

David Herbert Donald, *Lincoln* (1995). A compelling biography that reveals connections between Lincoln's private and public lives.

Drew Gilpin Faust, *Mothers of Invention: Women of the Slaveholding South in the American Civil War* (1996). Examines elite women's relation to slavery, southern culture, and the deprivations of war.

Leon Litwack, *Been in the Storm So Long: The Aftermath of Slavery* (1979). A prizewinning examination of slaves' responses to the process of emancipation, continuing into the Reconstruction era.

James M. McPherson, *Battle Cry of Freedom: The Civil War Era* (1988). An award-winning study of the war years, skillfully integrating political, military, and social history.

George C. Rable, *The Confederate Republic: A Revolt Against Politics* (1994). Discusses the tension between nationalism and individualism in Confederate political life.

Charles Royster, *The Destructive War: William Tecumseh Sherman, Stonewall Jackson, and the Americans* (1991). An exploration of the meaning of violence and nationality in the Civil War era.

# The Crises of Reconstruction
## 1865–1877

Former slaves in Jacksonville, Florida
*443*

"The war weren't so great as folks suppose," declared former slave Felix Heywood. "It was the endin' of it that made the difference. That's when we all wakes up that somethin' had happened." To Heywood, who was twenty years old at the Civil War's end, emancipation was breathtaking. "We was all walkin' on golden clouds," he recalled. "Everybody went wild . . . we all felt like heroes and nobody made us that way but ourselves. We was free! Just like that, we was free!"

Heywood's parents had been purchased in Mississippi by his owner, William Gudlow, and brought west to Bexar County in southern Texas, where the Gudlows ran a ranch. There, Heywood and his five brothers and sisters were born. As a teenager, Felix Heywood had been a sheepherder and cowpuncher, and the war, he claimed, left his routine intact. "The ranch went on just like it always had. . . . Church went on," he observed. But after the war, Heywood noticed an important change in the African-American community: the impulse among newly freed people to move from wherever they had lived as slaves to somewhere else. "Nobody took our homes away," Heywood recalled. "But right off colored folks started on the move. They seemed to want to get closer to freedom so they'd know what it was—like it was a place or a city."

Felix Heywood himself did not change place at once. Instead, he "stuck close as a lean tick to a sick chicken." At the outset, his former owners, the Gudlows, provided Heywood and his father with ranchland, where they rounded up cattle that had wandered astray to find water. Then local ranchers gave the two Heywoods a herd of seventy cattle and they ran their own ranch. Eventually, however, like many other former slaves, Felix Heywood migrated to the nearest city. He moved to San Antonio, the county seat, a booming cattle town, where he found a job with the waterworks.

In old age, after raising a family, Felix Heywood still lived in San Antonio, now with his youngest sister. Looking back on his long life, he dwelled on the era right after the war and on the instant that emancipation arrived. "We know'd freedom was on us, but we didn't know what was to come with it," he recalled. "We thought we was goin' to be richer and better off than the white folks; cose we was stronger and knowed how to work, and the whites didn't and they didn't have us to work for them anymore. Hallelujah! But it didn't turn out like that. We soon found out that freedom could make folks proud but it didn't make 'em rich."

For the nation, as for Felix Heywood, the Civil War's end was a crucial turning point and a moment of uncharted possibilities. It was also a time of unresolved conflicts. While former slaves exulted over freedom, the postwar mood of ex-Confederates was often as grim as the wasted southern landscape. Unable to face "southern Yankeedom," some planters considered emigrating to the American West or to Europe, Mexico, or Brazil, and a few thousand did. The morale of the vanquished rarely concerns the victors, but the Civil War was a special case, for the Union had sought not merely military triumph but the return of national unity. The questions that the federal government faced in 1865 were therefore unprecedented.

First, how could the Union be restored and the defeated South reintegrated into the nation? Would the Confederate states be treated as conquered territories, or would they quickly rejoin the union with the same rights as other states? Who would set the standards for readmission—Congress or the president? Would Confederate leaders be punished for treason? Would their property be confiscated and their political rights curtailed? Most important, what would happen to the more than 3.5 million former slaves? The future of the freedmen constituted the crucial issue of the postwar

**The Devastated South**
*After the Civil War, parts of the defeated Confederacy resembled a wasteland. Homes, crops, and railroads had been destroyed; farming and business had come to a standstill; and uprooted southerners wandered about. Above, the remains of a plantation at Fredericksburg, Virginia.*

era, for emancipation had set in motion the most profound upheaval in the nation's history. Before the war slavery had determined the South's social, economic, and political structure. What would replace it in the postwar South? The end of the Civil War, in short, posed two problems that had to be solved simultaneously: how to readmit the South to the Union and how to define the status of free blacks in American society.

Between 1865 and 1877, the nation met these challenges but not without discord and turmoil. Indeed, the crises of Reconstruction—the restoration of the former Confederate states to the Union—reshaped the legacy of the Civil War.

This chapter focuses on five major quesitons:

♦ How did Radical Republicans gain control of Reconstruction politics?

♦ What impact did federal Reconstruction policy have on the former Confederacy, and on ex-Confederates?

♦ In what ways did newly freed southern slaves reshape their lives after emancipation?

♦ What factors contributed to the end of Reconstruction in the 1870s, and which was most significant?

♦ To what extent should Reconstruction be considered a failure?

# Reconstruction Politics

At the end of the Civil War, President Johnson might have exiled, imprisoned, or executed Confederate leaders and imposed martial law indefinitely. Demobilized Confederate soldiers might have continued armed resistance to federal occupation forces. Freed slaves might have taken revenge on former owners and the rest of the white community. But none of these drastic possibilities occurred. Instead, intense *political* conflict dominated the immediate postwar years. In national politics unparalleled disputes produced new constitutional amendments, a presidential impeachment crisis, and some of the most ambitious domestic legislation ever enacted by Congress, the Reconstruction Acts of 1867–1868. The major outcome of Reconstruction politics was the enfranchisement of black men, a development that few—black or white—had expected when Lee surrendered.

In 1865 only a small group of politicians supported black suffrage. All were Radical Republicans, a minority faction that had emerged during the war. Led by Senator Charles Sumner of Massachusetts and Congressman Thaddeus Stevens of Pennsylvania, the Radicals had clamored for the abolition of slavery and a demanding reconstruction policy, in wartime and after. Any valid plan to restore the Union, Stevens contended, must "revolutionize Southern institutions, habits, and manners . . . or all our blood and treasure have been spent in vain." But the Radicals, outnumbered in Congress by other Republicans and opposed by the Democratic minority, faced long odds. Still, they managed to win broad Republican support for parts of their Reconstruction program, including black male enfranchisement. Just as civil war had led to emancipation, a goal once supported by only a minority of Americans, so Reconstruction policy became bound to black suffrage, a momentous change that originally had only narrow political backing.

## *Lincoln's Plan*

Conflict over Reconstruction began even before the war ended. In December 1863 President Lincoln issued the Proclamation of Amnesty and Reconstruction,

CHRONOLOGY

**1863** President Abraham Lincoln issues Proclamation of Amnesty and Reconstruction.

**1864** Wade-Davis bill passed by Congress and pocket-vetoed by Lincoln.

**1865** Freedmen's Bureau established.

Civil War ends.

Lincoln assassinated.

Andrew Johnson becomes president.

Johnson issues Proclamation of Amnesty and Reconstruction.

Ex-Confederate states hold constitutional conventions (May–December).

Black conventions begin in the ex-Confederate states.

Thirteenth Amendment added to the Constitution.

Presidential Reconstruction completed.

**1866** Congress enacts the Civil Rights Act of 1866 and the Supplementary Freedmen's Bureau Act over Johnson's vetoes.

Ku Klux Klan founded in Tennessee.

Congress proposes the Fourteenth Amendment.

**1866** *(continued)*
Tennessee readmitted to the Union.

Race riots in southern cities.

Republicans win congressional elections.

Thirty-ninth Congress begins debates over Reconstruction policy.

**1867** Reconstruction Act of 1867.

William Seward negotiates the purchase of Alaska.

Constitutional conventions meet in the ex-Confederate states.

Howard University founded.

**1868** President Johnson is impeached, tried, and acquitted.

Omnibus Act.

Fourteenth Amendment added to the Constitution.

Ulysses S. Grant elected president.

**1869** Transcontinental railroad completed.

**1870** Congress readmits the four remaining southern states to the Union.

Fifteenth Amendment added to the Constitution.

Enforcement Act of 1870.

**1871** Second Enforcement Act.

Ku Klux Klan Act.

**1872** Liberal Republican party formed.

Amnesty Act.

*Alabama* claims settled.

Grant reelected president.

**1873** Panic of 1873 begins (September–October), setting off a five-year depression.

**1874** Democrats gain control of the House of Representatives.

**1875** Civil Rights Act of 1875.

Specie Resumption Act.

**1876** Disputed presidential election: Rutherford B. Hayes versus Samuel J. Tilden.

**1877** Electoral commission decides election in favor of Hayes.

The last Republican-controlled governments overthrown in Florida, Louisiana, and South Carolina.

**1879** "Exodus" movement spreads through several southern states.

---

which outlined a path by which each southern state could rejoin the Union. Under Lincoln's plan a minority of voters (equal to at least 10 percent of those who had cast ballots in the election of 1860) would have to take an oath of allegiance to the Union and accept emancipation. This minority could then create a loyal state government. But Lincoln's plan excluded some southerners from taking the oath: Confederate government officials, army and naval officers, as well as those military or civil officers who had resigned from Congress or from U.S. commissions in 1861. All such persons would have to apply for presidential pardons. Also excluded, of course, were blacks, who had not been voters in

1860. Lincoln hoped through his "10 percent plan" to undermine the Confederacy by establishing pro-Union governments within it. Characteristically, Lincoln had partisan goals, too. He wanted to win the allegiance of southern Unionists (those who had opposed secession), especially former Whigs, and to build a southern Republican party.

Radical Republicans in Congress, however, envisioned a slower readmission process that would bar even more ex-Confederates from political life. Most Republicans agreed that Lincoln's program was too weak. Thus in July 1864 Congress passed the Wade-Davis bill, which provided that each former Confederate state would be ruled by a military governor. Under the Wade-Davis plan, after at least half the eligible voters took an oath of allegiance to the Union, delegates could be elected to a state convention that would repeal secession and abolish slavery. But to qualify as a voter or delegate, a southerner would have to take a second, "ironclad" oath, swearing that he had never voluntarily supported the Confederacy. Like the 10 percent plan, the congressional plan did not provide for black suffrage, a measure then supported by only some Radicals. Unlike Lincoln's plan, however, the Wade-Davis scheme would have delayed the readmission process almost indefinitely.

Claiming that he did not want to bind himself to any single restoration policy, Lincoln pocket-vetoed* the Wade-Davis bill. The bill's sponsors, Senator Benjamin Wade of Ohio and Congressman Henry Winter Davis of Maryland, blasted Lincoln's act as an outrage. By the end of the war, the president and Congress had reached an impasse. Arkansas, Louisiana, Tennessee, and parts of Virginia under Union army control moved toward readmission under variants of Lincoln's plan. But Congress refused to seat their delegates, as it had a right to do. Lincoln, meanwhile, hinted that a more rigorous Reconstruction policy might be in store. What Lincoln's ultimate policy would have been remains unknown. But at the time of his death, Radical Republicans turned with hope toward his successor, Andrew Johnson of Tennessee, in whom they felt they had an ally.

### Presidential Reconstruction Under Johnson

The only southern senator to remain in Congress when his state seceded, Andrew Johnson had served as military governor of Tennessee from 1862 to 1864. He had taken a strong anti-Confederate stand, declaring that "treason is a crime and must be made odious." Above all, Johnson had long sought the destruction of the planter aristocracy, a goal that dominated his political career. A self-educated man of humble North Carolina origins, Johnson had moved to Greenville, Tennessee, in 1826 and become a tailor. His wife, Eliza McCardle, had taught him how to write. An ardent Jacksonian, he had entered politics in the 1830s as a spokesman for nonslaveowning whites and risen rapidly from local of-

---

* Pocket veto: failure to sign a bill within ten days of the adjournment of Congress.

ficial to congressman to governor to senator. Once the owner of eight slaves, Johnson reversed his position on slavery during the war. When emancipation became Union policy, he supported it. But Johnson neither adopted abolitionist ideals nor challenged racist sentiments. He hoped mainly that the fall of slavery would injure southern aristocrats. Andrew Johnson, in short, had his own political agenda, which, as Republicans would soon learn, did not coincide with theirs. Moreover, he was a lifelong Democrat who had been added to the Republican, or National Union, ticket in 1864 to broaden its appeal and who had become president by accident.

Many Republicans voiced shock when Johnson announced a new plan for the restoration of the South in May 1865—with Congress out of session and not due to convene until December. In two proclamations, the president explained how the seven southern states still without reconstruction governments—Alabama, Florida, Georgia, Mississippi, North Carolina, South Carolina, and Texas—could return to the Union. Almost all southerners who took an oath of allegiance would receive a pardon and amnesty, and all their property except slaves would be restored. Oath takers could elect delegates to state conventions, which would provide for regular elections. Each state convention, Johnson later added, would have to proclaim the illegality of secession, repudiate state debts incurred when the state belonged to the Confederacy, and ratify the Thirteenth Amendment, which abolished slavery. (Proposed by an enthusiastic wartime Congress early in 1865, the amendment would be ratified in December of that year.) As under Lincoln's plan, Confederate civil and military officers would be excluded from the oath needed for voting. But Johnson also disqualified all well-off ex-Confederates, those with taxable property worth $20,000 or more. This purge of the plantation aristocracy, said Johnson, would benefit "humble men, the peasantry and yeomen of the South, who have been decoyed . . . into rebellion." Poorer whites would now be in control.

Presidential Reconstruction took effect in the summer of 1865, but with unforeseen consequences. Those southerners disqualified on the basis of wealth or high Confederate position applied for pardons in droves, and Johnson handed out pardons liberally— some thirteen thousand of them. He also dropped plans for the punishment of treason. By the end of 1865, all seven states had created new civil governments that in effect restored the status quo ante bel-

**Andrew Johnson**

*When Vice President Johnson became president at Lincoln's death in April 1865, many Republicans expected him to impose "harsh terms" upon the defeated South.*

lum. Confederate army officers and large planters assumed state offices. Former Confederate congressmen, state officials, and generals were elected to Congress. Georgia sent Alexander Stephens, the former Confederate vice president, back to Washington as a senator. Some states refused to ratify the Thirteenth Amendment or to repudiate their Confederate debts.

Most infuriating to Radicals, all states took steps to ensure a landless, dependent black labor force: they passed "black codes" to replace the slave codes, state laws that had regulated slavery. Because the ratification of the Thirteenth Amendment was assured by the terms of Johnson's Reconstruction plan, all states guaranteed the freedmen some basic rights. They could marry, own property, make contracts, and testify in court against other blacks. But the codes harshly restricted freedmen's behavior. Some codes established racial segregation in public places; most prohibited racial intermarriage, jury service by blacks, and court testimony by blacks against whites. All codes included economic restrictions that would bar former slaves from leaving the plantations. South Carolina required special licenses for blacks who wished to enter nonagricultural employment. Mississippi prohibited blacks from buying and selling farmland. Most states required annual contracts between landowners and black agricultural workers and provided that blacks without lawful employment would be arrested as vagrants and auctioned off to employers who would pay their fines.

The black codes left freedmen no longer slaves but not really liberated either. Although "free" to sign labor contracts, for instance, those who failed to sign them would be considered in violation of the law and swept back into involuntary servitude. In practice, many clauses in the codes never took effect: the Union army and the Freedmen's Bureau swiftly suspended the enforcement of racially discriminatory provisions of the new laws. But the black codes revealed white southern

intentions. They showed what "home rule" would have been like without federal interference.

When former abolitionists and Radical Republicans decried the black codes, Johnson defended them and his restoration program. Ex-Confederates, he contended, should not be forced back into the Union as "a degraded and debased people." Many northerners, however, perceived signs of southern defiance: voters had elected ex-rebels to public office; southern conventions had been reluctant to repudiate secession or slow to pronounce slavery dead; and new laws had robbed freedmen of basic rights. "What can be hatched from such an egg but another rebellion?" asked a Boston newspaper. Republicans in Congress agreed. When the Thirty-ninth Congress convened in December 1865, it refused to seat the delegates of the ex-Confederate states. Establishing the Joint (House-Senate) Committee on Reconstruction, Republicans prepared to dismantle the black codes and lock ex-Confederates out of power.

### Congress Versus Johnson

The status of the southern blacks now became the major issue in Congress. "This is not a 'white man's government,' " exclaimed Republican congressman Thaddeus Stevens. "To say so is political blasphemy." But Radical Republicans like Stevens—who hoped to impose black suffrage on the former Confederacy and delay the readmission of the southern states into the Union—still constituted a congressional minority. Conservative Republicans, who tended to favor the Johnson plan, formed a minority too, as did the Democrats, who also supported the president. Moderate Republicans, the largest congressional bloc, agreed with the Radicals that Johnson's plan was too feeble. But they thought that northern voters would oppose black suffrage, and they wanted to avoid a dispute with the president. Since none of the four congressional blocs could claim the two-thirds majority required to overturn a presidential veto, Johnson's program would prevail unless the moderates and the Radicals joined forces. Ineptly, Johnson alienated a majority of moderates and pushed them into the Radicals' arms.

The moderate Republicans supported two proposals drafted by one of their own, Senator Lyman Trumbull of Illinois, to invalidate the black codes. These measures won wide Republican support. In the first, Congress voted to continue the Freedmen's Bureau, established in 1865, whose term was ending. This federal agency, headed by former Union general O. O. Howard and staffed mainly by army officers, provided relief, rations, and medical care. It also built schools for the freed blacks, put them to work on abandoned or confiscated lands, and tried to protect their rights as laborers. Congress extended the bureau's life for three years and gave it new power: it could run special military courts to settle labor disputes and could invalidate labor contracts forced on freedmen by the black codes. In February 1866 Johnson vetoed the Freedmen's Bureau bill. The Constitution, he declared, did not sanction military trials of civilians in peacetime, nor did it support a system to care for "indigent persons."

### King Andrew

*This Thomas Nast cartoon, published in* Harper's Weekly *just before the 1866 congressional elections, conveyed Republican antipathy to Andrew Johnson. The president is depicted as an autocratic tyrant. Radical Republican Thaddeus Stevens, upper right, has his head on the block and is about to lose it. The Republic sits in chains.*

In March 1866 Congress passed a second measure proposed by Trumbull, a bill that made blacks U.S. citizens with the same civil rights as other citizens and gave the federal government the right to intervene in the states to ensure black rights in court. Johnson vetoed the civil rights bill also. He argued that it would "operate in favor of the colored and against the white race." But in April Congress overrode his veto; the Civil Rights Act of 1866 was the first major law ever passed over a presidential veto. Then in July Congress enacted the Supplementary Freedmen's Bureau Act over Johnson's veto as well. Johnson's vetoes bewildered many Republicans because the new laws did not undercut presidential Reconstruction. The president insisted, however, that both bills were illegitimate because southerners had been shut out of the Congress that passed them. His stance won support not only from the South but from northern Democrats. But the president had alienated the moderate Republicans, who began to work with the Radicals against him. Johnson had lost "every friend he has," one moderate legislator declared.

Some historians view Andrew Johnson as a political incompetent who, at this crucial turning point, bungled both his readmission scheme and his political future. Others contend that he was merely trying to forge a coalition of the center, made up of Democrats and non-Radical Republicans. In either case, Johnson underestimated the possibility of Republican unity. Once united, the Republicans moved on to a third step: the passage of a constitutional amendment that would prevent the Supreme Court from invalidating the new Civil Rights Act and would block Democrats in Congress from repealing it.

### The Fourteenth Amendment

In April 1866 Congress adopted the Fourteenth Amendment, which had been proposed by the Joint Committee on Reconstruction. To protect blacks' rights, the amendment declared in its first clause that all persons born or naturalized in the United States were citizens of the nation and citizens of their states and that no state could abridge their rights without due process of law or deny them equal protection of the law. This section nullified the *Dred Scott* decision of 1857 (see Chapter 14), which had declared that blacks were not citizens. Second, the amendment guaranteed that if a state denied suffrage to any of its male citizens, its representation in Congress would be proportionally reduced. This clause did not guarantee black suffrage, but it threatened to deprive southern states of some legislators if black men were denied the vote. Third, the amendment disqualified from state and national office *all* prewar officeholders—civil and military, state and federal—who had supported the Confederacy, unless Congress removed their disqualifications by a two-thirds vote. In so providing, Congress intended to invalidate Johnson's wholesale distribution of amnesties and pardons. Finally, the amendment repudiated the Confederate debt and maintained the validity of the federal debt.

The most ambitious step that Congress had yet taken, the Fourteenth Amendment revealed growing receptivity among Republican legislators to the Radicals' demands, including black male enfranchisement. It reflected the Republican consensus that southern states would not deal fairly with blacks unless forced to do so. Most important, it was the first national effort to limit state control of civil and political rights. Its passage created a firestorm. Abolitionists decried the second clause as a "swindle" because it did not explicitly ensure black suffrage. Southerners and northern Democrats condemned the third clause as vengeful. Southern legislatures, except for Tennessee's, refused to ratify the amendment, and President Johnson denounced it. His intransigence solidified the new alliance between moderate and Radical Republicans, and turned the congressional elections of 1866 into a referendum on the Fourteenth Amendment.

Over the summer Johnson set off on a whistle-stop train tour from Washington to St. Louis and Chicago and back. But this innovative campaign tactic—the "swing around the circle," as Johnson called it—failed. Humorless and defensive, the president made fresh enemies, and doomed his hope of creating a new National Union party that would sink the Fourteenth Amendment. Moderate and Radical Republicans, meanwhile, defended the amendment, condemned the president, and branded the Democratic party "a common sewer . . . into which is emptied every element of treason, North and South."

Republicans carried the congressional elections of 1866 in a landslide, winning almost two-thirds of the House and almost four-fifths of the Senate. They had secured a mandate to overcome southern resistance to the Fourteenth Amendment and to enact their own Re-

**The Reconstruction Congress**
*A triumph at the polls in the fall of 1866 gave Republicans in Congress the power to enact their own Reconstruction plan, passed over Andrew Johnson's persistant vetoes in1867–1868. Moderate Republicans and Radical Republicans then joined forces to impeach the president for trying to obstruct the congressional plan.*

construction program, even if the president vetoed every part of it.

### Congressional Reconstruction

The congressional debate over reconstructing the South began in December 1866 and lasted three months. To stifle a resurgence of Confederate power, Radical Republican leaders called for black suffrage, federal support for public schools, confiscation of Confederate estates, and an extended period of military occupation in the South. Moderate Republicans, who once would have found such a plan too extreme, now accepted parts of it. Legislators debated every ramification, and in February 1867, after complex legislative maneuvers and many late-night sessions, Congress passed the Reconstruction Act of 1867. Johnson vetoed the law, and on March 2, Congress passed it over his veto. Later that year and in 1868, Congress passed three further Reconstruction acts, all enacted over presidential vetoes, to refine and enforce the first.

The Reconstruction Act of 1867 invalidated the state governments formed under the Lincoln and Johnson plans. Only Tennessee, which had ratified the Fourteenth Amendment and had been readmitted to the Union, escaped further reconstruction. The new law di-

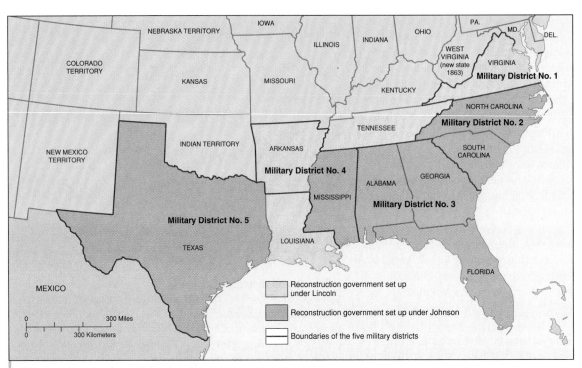

### The Reconstruction of the South

*The Reconstruction Act of 1867 divided the former Confederate states, except Tennessee, into five military districts and set forth the steps by which new state governments could be created.*

vided the other ten former Confederate states into five temporary military districts, each run by a Union general. Voters—all black men, plus those white men who had not been disqualified by the Fourteenth Amendment—could elect delegates to a state convention that would write a new state constitution granting black suffrage. When eligible voters ratified the new constitution, elections could be held for state officers. Once Congress approved the state constitution, once the state legislature ratified the Fourteenth Amendment, and once the amendment became part of the federal Constitution, Congress would readmit the state into the Union—and Reconstruction, in a constitutional sense, would be complete.

The Reconstruction Act of 1867 was far more radical than the Johnson program because it enfranchised blacks and disfranchised many ex-Confederates. It fulfilled a central goal of the Radical Republicans: to delay the readmission of former Confederate states until Republican governments could be established and thereby prevent an immediate rebel resurgence. But the new law was not as harsh toward ex-Confederates as it might have been. It provided for only temporary military rule. It did not prosecute Confeder-

ate leaders for treason or permanently exclude them from politics. Finally, it made no provision for the confiscation or redistribution of property.

During the congressional debates, Radical Republican congressman Thaddeus Stevens had argued for the confiscation of large Confederate estates to "humble the proud traitors" and to provide for the former slaves. He had proposed subdividing such confiscated property into forty-acre tracts to be distributed among the freedmen and selling the rest, some 90 percent of it, to pay off war debts. Stevens wanted to crush the planter aristocracy and create a new class of self-sufficient black yeoman farmers. His land-reform bill won the support of other Radicals, but it never made progress, for most Republicans held property rights sacred. Tampering with such rights in the South, they feared, would jeopardize those rights in the North. Moreover, Stevens's proposal would alienate southern ex-Whigs from the Republican cause, antagonize other white southerners, and thereby endanger the rest of Reconstruction. Thus land reform never came about. The "radical" Reconstruction acts were a compromise.

Congressional Reconstruction took effect in the spring of 1867, but it could not be enforced without

## Major Reconstruction Legislation

| Law and Date of Congressional Passage | Provisions | Purpose |
|---|---|---|
| Civil Rights Act of 1866 (April 1866)* | Declared blacks citizens and guaranteed them equal protection of the laws. | To invalidate the black codes. |
| Supplementary Freedmen's Bureau Act (July 1866)* | Extended the life of the Freedmen's Aid Bureau and expanded its powers. | To invalidate the black codes. |
| Reconstruction Act of 1867 (March 1867)* | Invalidated state governments formed under Lincoln and Johnson. | To replace presidential Reconstruction with a more stringent plan. |
| | Divided the former Confederacy into five military districts. | |
| | Set forth requirements for readmission of ex-Confederate states to the Union. | |
| Supplementary Reconstruction Acts | | To enforce the First Reconstruction Act. |
| Second Reconstruction Act (March 1867)* | Required military commanders to initiate voter enrollment. | |
| Third Reconstruction Act (July 1867)* | Expanded military commanders' powers. | |
| Fourth Reconstruction Act (March 1868)* | Provided that a majority of voters, however few, could put a new state constitution into force. | |
| Army Appropriations Act (March 1867)* | Declared in a rider that only the general of the army could issue military orders. | To prevent President Johnson from obstructing Reconstruction. |
| Tenure of Office Act (March 1867)* | Prohibited the president from removing any federal official without the Senate's consent. | To prevent President Johnson from obstructing Reconstruction. |
| Omnibus Act (June 1868)[†] | Readmitted seven ex-Confederate states to the Union. | To restore the Union, under the terms of the First Reconstruction Act. |
| Enforcement Act of 1870 (May 1870)[‡] | Provided for the protection of black voters. | To enforce the Fifteenth Amendment. |
| Second Enforcement Act (February 1871) | Provided for federal supervision of southern elections. | To enforce the Fifteenth Amendment. |
| Third Enforcement Act (Ku Klux Klan Act) (April 1871) | Strengthened sanctions against those who impeded black suffrage. | To combat the Ku Klux Klan and enforce the Fourteenth Amendment. |
| Amnesty Act (May 1872) | Restored the franchise to almost all ex-Confederates. | Effort by Grant Republicans to deprive Liberal Republicans of a campaign issue. |
| Civil Rights Act of 1875 (March 1875)[§] | Outlawed racial segregation in transportation and public accommodations and prevented exclusion of blacks from jury service. | To honor the late senator Charles Sumner. |

*Passed over Johnson's veto.

[†]Georgia was soon returned to military rule. The last four states were readmitted in 1870.

[‡]Sections of the law declared unconstitutional in 1876.

[§]Invalidated by the Supreme Court in 1883.

military power. When Johnson, as commander-in-chief, impeded the congressional plan by replacing military officers sympathetic to the Radical cause with conservative ones, Republicans seethed. More suspicious than ever of the president, congressional moderates and Radicals once again joined forces to block Johnson from obstructing Reconstruction.

## The Impeachment Crisis

In March 1867 Republicans in Congress passed two laws to limit presidential power. The Tenure of Office Act prohibited the president from removing civil officers without Senate consent. Cabinet members, the law stated, were to hold office "during the term of the president by whom they may have been appointed" and could be fired only with the Senate's approval. The goal was to bar Johnson from dismissing Secretary of War Stanton, the Radicals' ally, whose support Congress needed to enforce the Reconstruction acts. The other law, a rider to an army appropriations bill, barred the president from issuing military orders except through the commanding general, Ulysses S. Grant, who could not be removed without the Senate's consent.

The Radicals' enmity toward Johnson, however, would not die until he was out of office. They began to seek grounds on which to impeach and convict him and thereby remove all potential obstacles to congressional Reconstruction. The House Judiciary Committee, aided by private detectives, could at first uncover no valid charges against Johnson. But just as impeachment efforts seemed a lost cause, Johnson again rescued his foes by providing the charges they needed.

In August 1867, with Congress out of session, Johnson suspended Secretary of War Stanton and replaced him with General Grant. In early 1868 the reconvened Senate refused to approve Stanton's suspension, and Grant, sensing the Republican mood, vacated the office. Johnson then removed Stanton and replaced him with an aged general, Lorenzo Thomas. Johnson's defiance forced Republican moderates, who had at first resisted impeachment, into yet another alliance with the Radicals: the president had "thrown down the gauntlet," a moderate charged. The House approved eleven charges of impeachment, nine of them based on violation of the Tenure of Office Act. The other charges accused Johnson of being "unmindful of the high duties of office," of seeking to disgrace Congress, and of not enforcing the Reconstruction acts.

Johnson's trial, which began in the Senate in March 1868, riveted public attention for eleven weeks. Seven congressmen, including leading Radical Republicans, served as prosecutors or "managers." Johnson's lawyers maintained that he was merely seeking a court test by violating the Tenure of Office Act, which he thought was unconstitutional. They also contended,

## The Reconstruction Amendments

| Amendment and Date of Congressional Passage | Provisions | Ratification |
| --- | --- | --- |
| Thirteenth (January 1865) | Prohibited slavery in the United States. | December 1865. |
| Fourteenth (June 1866) | Defined citizenship to include all persons born or naturalized in the United States. | July 1868, after Congress made ratification a prerequisite for readmission of ex-Confederate states to the Union. |
| | Provided proportional loss of congressional representation for any state that denied suffrage to any of its male citizens. | |
| | Disqualified prewar officeholders who supported the Confederacy from state or national office. | |
| | Repudiated the Confederate debt. | |
| Fifteenth (February 1869) | Prohibited the denial of suffrage because of race, color, or previous condition of servitude. | March 1870; ratification required of Virginia, Texas, Mississippi, and Georgia for readmission to the Union. |

somewhat inconsistently, that the law did not protect Secretary Stanton, an appointee of Lincoln, not Johnson. Finally, they asserted, Johnson was guilty of no crime indictable in a regular court.

The congressional "managers" countered that impeachment was a political process, not a criminal trial, and that Johnson's "abuse of discretionary power" constituted an impeachable offense. Although Senate opinion split along party lines and Republicans held a majority, some of them wavered, fearing that the removal of a president would destroy the balance of power among the three branches of the federal government. They also distrusted Radical Republican Benjamin Wade, the president pro tempore of the Senate, who, because there was no vice president, would become president if Johnson were thrown out.

Intense pressure weighed on the wavering Republicans, whose votes would prove crucial. Late in May 1868, the Senate voted against Johnson 35 to 19, one vote short of the two-thirds majority needed for conviction. Seven Republicans had risked political suicide and sided with the twelve Senate Democrats in voting against removal. In so doing, they set a precedent. Future presidents would not be impeached solely on political grounds or because two-thirds of Congress disagreed with them. But the anti-Johnson forces had also achieved their goal: Andrew Johnson had no future as president. After serving out the rest of his term, he returned to Tennessee, where he was reelected to the Senate five years later. Republicans in Congress, meanwhile, pursued their last major Reconstruction objective: to guarantee black male suffrage.

### *The Fifteenth Amendment*

Black suffrage was the linchpin of congressional Reconstruction. Only with the support of black voters could Republicans secure control of the ex-Confederate states. The Fourteenth Amendment had promoted black suffrage indirectly, by threatening a penalty where it was denied. The Reconstruction Act of 1867, however, forced every southern state legislature to enfranchise black men as a prerequisite for readmission to the Union. But though black voting had begun in the South, much of the North rejected it. Congressional Republicans therefore had two aims. They sought to protect black suffrage in the South against future repeal by Congress or the states and to enfranchise northern and border-state blacks, who would presumably vote Republican. To achieve these goals, Congress in 1869 proposed the Fifteenth Amendment, which prohibited the denial of suffrage by the states to any citizen on account of race, color, or previous condition of servitude.

Democrats argued that the proposed amendment violated states' rights by denying each state the power to determine who would vote. But Democrats did not control enough states to defeat the amendment, and it was ratified in 1870. Four votes came from those ex-Confederate states—Mississippi, Virginia, Georgia, and Texas—that had delayed the Reconstruction process and were therefore forced to approve the Fifteenth Amendment, as well as the Fourteenth, in order to rejoin the Union. Some southerners contended that the new amendment's omissions made it acceptable, for it had, as a Richmond newspaper pointed out, "loopholes through which a coach and four horses can be driven." What were these loopholes? The Fifteenth Amendment did not guarantee black officeholding, nor did it prohibit voting restrictions such as property requirements and literacy tests. Such restrictions might be used to deny blacks the vote, and indeed, ultimately they were so used.

The debate over black suffrage drew new participants into the political fray. Since the end of the war, a small group of abolitionists, men and women, had sought to revive the cause of women's rights. In 1866, when Congress adopted the Fourteenth Amendment, women's rights advocates tried to join forces with their old abolitionist allies to promote both black suffrage and woman suffrage. Most Radical Republicans, however, did not want to be saddled with the woman-suffrage plank; they feared it would impede their primary goal, black enfranchisement.

This defection provoked disputes among women's rights advocates. Some, who continued to support black suffrage, argued that it would pave the way for the women's vote and that black men deserved priority. "If the elective franchise is not extended to the Negro, he is dead," explained Frederick Douglass, a longtime women's rights supporter. "Woman has a thousand ways by which she can attach herself to the ruling power of the land that we have not." But the women's rights leaders Elizabeth Cady Stanton and Susan B. Anthony disagreed. The amendment, insisted Stanton, would establish an "aristocracy of sex" and thereby increase women's disabilities. The battle over black suffrage and the Fifteenth Amendment divided women's rights advocates into two rival suffrage associations, both formed in 1869. It also severed reformers such as Stanton and Anthony from former abolitionist allies and

**Stanton and Anthony, c. 1870**

*Women's rights advocates Susan B. Anthony and Elizabeth Cady Stanton began to promote woman suffrage in 1866 when the issue of black suffrage arose, and subsequently assailed the proposed Fifteenth Amendment for excluding women. By the end of the 1860s, activists had formed two competing suffragist organizations.*

inspired the development of an independent women's rights movement.

By the time the Fifteenth Amendment was ratified in 1870, Congress could look back on five years of momentous achievement. Since the start of 1865, federal legislators had broadened the scope of American democracy by passing three constitutional amendments. The Thirteenth Amendment abolished slavery, the Fourteenth affirmed the rights of federal citizens, and the Fifteenth prohibited the denial of suffrage on the basis of race. Congress had also readmitted the former Confederate states into the Union. But after 1868 congressional momentum slowed. And in 1869, when Ulysses S. Grant became president, the fierce battle between Congress and the chief executive ceased. The theater of action now shifted to the South, where an era of tumultuous change was under way.

# Reconstruction Governments

During the unstable years of presidential Reconstruction, 1865–1867, the southern states had to create new governments, revive the war-torn economy, and face the impact of emancipation. Social and economic problems abounded. War costs had cut into southern wealth, cities and factories lay in rubble, plantation-

labor systems disintegrated, and racial tensions flared. Beginning in 1865, freedmen organized black conventions, political meetings at which they protested ill treatment and demanded equal rights. These meetings took place in a climate of violence. Race riots erupted in major southern cities. In Memphis in May 1866, white crowds attacked black veterans, charged through black neighborhoods, and killed forty-six people; in New Orleans two months later, a white mob and police assaulted black delegates on their way to a political convention and left forty people dead. Even when Congress imposed military rule, ex-Confederates did not feel defeated. "Having reached bottom, there is hope now that we may rise again," a South Carolina planter wrote in his diary.

Congressional Reconstruction, supervised by federal troops, took effect in the spring of 1867. The Johnson regimes were dismantled, state constitutional conventions met, and voters elected new state governments, which Republicans dominated. In 1868 a majority of the former Confederate states rejoined the Union, and two years later, the last four states—Virginia, Mississippi, Georgia, and Texas—followed.

Readmission to the Union did not end the *process* of Reconstruction, for Republicans still held power in the South. But Republican rule was very brief, lasting less than a decade in all southern states, far less in most of them, and on average under five years. Opposition from southern Democrats, the landowning elite, thousands of vigilantes, and indeed, most white voters proved insurmountable. Still, the governments formed under congressional Reconstruction were unique, because black men, including ex-slaves, participated in them. In no other society where slaves had been liberated—neither Haiti, where slaves had revolted in the 1790s, nor the British Caribbean islands, where Parliament had ended slavery in 1833—had freedmen gained democratic political rights.

## A New Electorate

The Reconstruction laws of 1867–1868 transformed the southern electorate by temporarily disfranchising 10–15 percent of potential white voters and by enfranchising more than 700,000 freedmen. Outnumbering white voters by 100,000, blacks held voting majorities in five states.

The new electorate provided a base for the Republican party, which had never existed in the South. To their Democratic foes, southern Republicans comprised three types of scoundrels: northern "carpetbaggers," who had allegedly come south seeking wealth and power (with so few possessions that they could be stuffed into traveling bags made of carpet material); southern "scalawags," predominantly poor and ignorant, who sought to profit from Republican rule; and hordes of uneducated freedmen, who were ready prey for Republican manipulators. Although the "carpetbag" and "scalawag" labels were derogatory and the stereotypes that they conveyed inaccurate, they remain in use as a form of shorthand. Crossing class and racial lines, the hastily established Republican party was in fact a loose coalition of diverse factions with often contradictory goals.

To northerners who moved south after the Civil War, the former Confederacy was an undeveloped region, ripe with possibility. The carpetbaggers' ranks included many former Union soldiers who hoped to buy land, open factories, build railroads, or simply enjoy the warmer climate. Albion Tourgee, a young lawyer who had served with the New York and Ohio volunteers, for example, relocated in North Carolina after the war to improve his health. There he worked as a journalist, politician, and Republican judge, until Republican rule collapsed. Perhaps no more than twenty thousand northern migrants like Tourgee—including veterans, missionaries, teachers, and Freedmen's Bureau agents—headed south immediately after the war, and many returned north by 1867. But those who remained played a disproportionate part in Reconstruction politics, for they held almost one out of three state offices.

Scalawags, white southerners who supported the Republicans, included some entrepreneurs who applauded party policies such as the national banking system and high protective tariffs as well as some prosperous planters, former Whigs who had opposed secession. They also comprised a few prominent politicians, among them James Orr of South Carolina and Mississippi's governor James Alcorn, who became Republicans in order to retain influence and limit Republican radicalism. Most scalawags, however, were small farmers from the mountain regions of North Carolina, Georgia, Alabama, and Arkansas. Former Unionists who had owned no slaves and had no allegiance to the landowning elite, they sought to improve their economic position. Unlike carpetbaggers, they lacked commitment to black rights and black suffrage; most came from regions with small black populations and cared little whether blacks voted or not. Scalawags held the most political offices during Reconstruction, but they proved the least stable element of the southern Republican coalition: eventually, many drifted back to the Democratic fold.

Freedmen, the backbone of southern Republicanism, provided eight out of ten Republican votes. Republican rule lasted longest in states with the largest black populations, such as South Carolina, Mississippi, Alabama, and Louisiana. Introduced to politics in the black conventions of 1865–1867, the freedmen sought land, education, civil rights, and political equality and remained loyal Republicans. As an elderly freedman announced at a Georgia political convention in 1867, "We know our friends." Although Reconstruction governments would have collapsed without black votes, freedmen held at most one in five political offices.

**The Carpetbaggers**

*Southern Democrats disparaged carpetbaggers as interlopers who hoped to "fatten on our misfortunes." In reality, most were Union army officers, businessmen, and professionals with capital and energy to invest in the South. This 1869 sheet-music cover caricatures the carpetbaggers by depicting a predatory northern migrant casting a greedy eye upon the defeated Confederacy.*

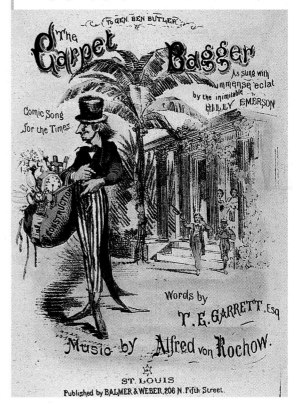

Blacks served in all southern legislatures and filled many high posts in Louisiana, Mississippi, and South Carolina. They constituted a majority, however, only in the legislature of South Carolina, whose population was more than 60 percent black. No blacks won the office of governor, and only two served in the U.S. Senate, Hiram Revels and Blanche K. Bruce, both of Mississippi. In the House of Representatives, a mere 6 percent of southern members were black, and almost half of these came from South Carolina.

Black officeholders on the state level formed a political elite. They often differed from black voters in background, education, wealth, and complexion. A disproportionate number were literate blacks who had been free before the Civil War. (Many more former slaves held office on the local level than on the state level.) South Carolina's roster of elected officials illustrates some distinctions between high-level black officeholders and the freedmen who voted for them.

Among those sent to Congress, almost all claimed some secondary education, and some held advanced degrees. In the state legislature, most black members, unlike their constituents, came from large towns and cities; many had spent time in the North; and some were well-off property owners or even former slaveowners. Color differences were evident, too: 43 percent of South Carolina's black state legislators were mulattos, as were only 7 percent of the state's black population.

High-level black officials and black voters often had different priorities. Most freedmen cared mainly about their economic future, especially about acquiring land, whereas black officeholders cared most about attaining equal rights. Still, both groups shared high expectations and prized enfranchisement. "We'd walk fifteen miles in wartime to find out about the battle," a Georgia freedman declared. "We can walk fifteen miles and more to find how to vote."

## Republican Rule

Large numbers of blacks participated in American government for the first time in the state constitutional conventions of 1867–1868. The South Carolina convention had a black majority, and in Louisiana half the delegates were freedmen. The conventions forged democratic changes in their state constitutions. Delegates abolished property qualifications for officeholding, made many appointive offices elective, and redistricted state legislatures more equitably. All states established universal manhood suffrage, and Louisiana and South Carolina opened public schools to both races. These provisions integrated the New Orleans public schools as well as the University of South Carolina, from which whites withdrew. But no state instituted land reform. When proposals for land confiscation and redistribution arose at the state conventions, they fell to defeat, as they had in Congress. Hoping to attract northern investment to the reconstructed South, southern Republicans hesitated to threaten property rights or to adopt land-reform measures that northern Republicans had rejected. South Carolina did set up a commission to buy land and make it available to freedmen, and several states changed their tax structures to force uncultivated land onto the market, but in no case was ex-Confederate land confiscated.

Once civil power shifted from the federal army to the new state governments, Republican administrations began ambitious programs of public works. They

### Republicans in the South Carolina Legislature, c. 1868

*Only in South Carolina did blacks comprise a majority in the legislature and dominate the legislative process during Reconstruction. This photographic collage of "Radical" legislators, black and white, suggests the extent of black representation. In 1874, blacks won the majority of seats in South Carolina's state senate as well.*

RADICAL MEMBERS OF THE So. CA LEGISLATURE.

built roads, bridges, and public buildings; endorsed railroad bonds; and funded institutions to care for orphans, the insane, and the disabled. Republican regimes also expanded state bureaucracies, raised salaries for government employees, and formed state militia, in which blacks were often heavily represented. Finally, they created public-school systems, almost nonexistent in the South until then.

Because rebuilding the devastated South and expanding state government cost millions, state debts and taxes skyrocketed. State legislatures increased poll taxes or "head" taxes (levies on individuals); enacted luxury, sales, and occupation taxes; and imposed new property taxes. Before the war southern states had taxed property in slaves but had barely taxed landed property at all. Now for the first time, state governments assessed even small farmers' holdings, and big planters paid what they considered an excessive burden. Although northern tax rates still exceeded southern rates, southern landowners resented the new levies. In their view, Reconstruction punished the propertied, already beset by labor problems and falling land values, in order to finance the vast expenditures of Republican legislators, or what one Alabamian called the "no property herd."

To Reconstruction's foes, moreover, Republican rule was wasteful and corrupt, if not the "most stupendous system of organized robbery in history." A state like Mississippi, which had an honest government, provided little basis for such charges. But critics could justifiably point to Louisiana, where the governor pocketed thousands of dollars of state funds and corruption permeated all government transactions (as indeed it had before the war). Or they could cite South Carolina, where bribery ran rampant. The main postwar profiteers, besides government officials who took bribes, were the railroad promoters who doled them out, not necessarily Republicans. Nor did the Republican regimes in the South hold a monopoly on corruption. After the war bribery pervaded government transactions North and South, and far more money changed hands in the North. But critics assailed Republican rule for additional reasons.

## Counterattacks

Ex-Confederates especially chafed at black enfranchisement and spoke with dread about the "horror of Negro domination." As soon as congressional Reconstruction took effect, a clamorous campaign began to under-

mine it. Democratic newspapers assailed delegates to North Carolina's constitutional convention as an "Ethiopian minstrelsy . . . baboons, monkeys, mules . . . and other jackasses," and demeaned Louisiana's constitution as "the work of ignorant Negroes cooperating with a gang of white adventurers."

The Democrats delayed political mobilization until the southern states were readmitted to the Union. Then they swung into action, calling themselves Conservatives in order to attract former Whigs. At first they sought to win the votes of blacks; but when that effort failed, they tried other tactics. In 1868–1869 Georgia Democrats challenged the eligibility of black legislators and expelled them from office. In response, the federal government reestablished military rule in Georgia, but determined Democrats still undercut Republican power. In every southern state, they contested elections, backed dissident Republican factions, elected some Democratic legislators, and also made inroads among scalawags, siphoning some of their votes from the Republicans.

Vigilante efforts to reduce black votes bolstered the Democrats' campaigns to win white ones. Antagonism toward free blacks, long a motif in southern life, resurged after the war. During presidential Reconstruction, antiblack violence erupted. Freedmen's Bureau agents in 1865 itemized a variety of outrages against blacks, including shooting, murder, rape, arson, roasting, and "severe and inhuman beating." Vigilante groups sprang up spontaneously in all parts of the former Confederacy under names like moderators, regulators, and in Louisiana, Knights of the White Camelia. A new group soon rose to dominance. In the spring of 1866, when the Johnson governments were still in power, six young Confederate war veterans in Tennessee formed a social club, the Ku Klux Klan, distinguished by elaborate rituals, hooded costumes, and secret passwords. New Klan dens spread through the state, and within a year Democratic politicians and former Confederate officers took control of them. By the election of 1868, when black suffrage took effect, Klan dens existed in all the southern states, and Klansmen embarked on night raids to intimidate black voters. No longer a social club, the Ku Klux Klan was now a widespread terrorist movement and a violent arm of the Democratic party.

The Klan sought to suppress black voting, reestablish white supremacy, and topple the Reconstruction governments. Its members attacked Union League officers, Freedmen's Bureau officials, white Republicans,

### The Ku Klux Klan

*The menacing symbol and hooded disguise characterized the Ku Klux Klan's campaign of intimidation during Reconstruction. A Klan flag of 1866 features a fierce emblem and a threatening Latin motto: "Because it always is, because it is everywhere, because it is abominable." Hooded Klansmen like this Tennessee nightrider wore robes with astrological symbols, such as the moon and stars. The Klan strove to end Republican rule, restore white supremacy, and obliterate, in a southern editor's words, "the proposterous and wicked dogma of negro equality."*

black militia units, economically successful blacks, and black voters. Concentrated in areas where the black and white populations were most evenly balanced and racial tensions greatest, Klan dens adapted their tactics and timing to local conditions. In Mississippi the Klan targeted black schools; in Alabama it concentrated on Republican officeholders. In Arkansas terror reigned in 1868; in Georgia and Florida Klan strength surged in 1870. Some Democrats denounced Klan members as "cut-throats and riff-raff." But prominent ex-Confederates were also known to be active Klansmen, among them General Nathan Bedford Forrest, the leader of the 1864 Fort Pillow massacre (see Chapter 15). Vigilantism united southern whites of different social classes and drew on the energy of many Confederate veterans. In areas where the Klan was inactive, other vigilante groups took its place.

Republican legislatures outlawed vigilantism through laws providing for fines and imprisonment of offenders. But the state militia could not enforce the laws, and state officials turned to the federal government for help. In May 1870 Congress passed the Enforcement Act to protect black voters, but witnesses to violations were afraid to testify against vigilantes, and local juries refused to convict them. The Second En-

forcement Act, which provided for federal supervision of southern elections, followed in February 1871. Two months later Congress passed the Third Enforcement Act, or Ku Klux Klan Act, which strengthened sanctions against those who prevented blacks from voting. It also empowered the president to use federal troops to enforce the law and to suspend the writ of habeas corpus in areas that he declared in insurrection. President Grant suspended the writ in nine South Carolina counties that had been devastated by Klan attacks. The Ku Klux Klan Act generated thousands of arrests; most terrorists, however, escaped conviction.

By 1872 the federal government had effectively suppressed the Klan, but vigilantism had served its purpose. Only a large military presence in the South could have protected black rights, and the government in Washington never provided it. Instead, federal power in the former Confederacy diminished. President Grant steadily reduced troop levels in the South; Congress allowed the Freedmen's Bureau to die in 1869; and the Enforcement acts became dead letters. White southerners, a Georgia politician told congressional investigators in 1871, could not discard "a feeling of bitterness, a feeling that the Negro is a sort of instinctual enemy of ours." The battle over Reconstruction was in essence a battle over the implications of emancipation, and it had begun as soon as the war ended.

# The Impact of Emancipation

"The master he says we are all free," a South Carolina slave declared in 1865. "But it don't mean we is white. And it don't mean we is equal." Emancipated slaves faced extreme handicaps. They had no property, tools, or capital and usually possessed meager skills. Only a minority had been trained as artisans, and more than 95 percent were illiterate. Still, the exhilaration of freedom was overwhelming, as slaves realized, "Now I am for myself" and "All that I make is my own." At emancipation they gained the right to their own labor and a new sense of autonomy. Under Reconstruction the freed blacks asserted their independence by seeking to cast off white control and shed the vestiges of slavery.

## *Confronting Freedom*

For the former slaves, mobility was often the first perquisite of liberty. Some moved out of the slave quarters and set up dwellings elsewhere on their plantations; others left their plantations entirely. Landowners found that one freed slave after another vanished, with house servants and artisans leading the way. "I have never in my life met with such ingratitude," one South Carolina mistress exclaimed when a former slave ran off. Field workers, who had less contact with whites, were more likely to stay behind or more reluctant to leave. Still, flight remained tempting. "The moment they see an opportunity to improve themselves, they will move on," diarist Mary Chesnut observed.

Emancipation stirred waves of migration within the former Confederacy. Some freed slaves left the Upper South for the Deep South and the Southwest—Florida, Mississippi, Arkansas, and Texas—where planters desperately needed labor and paid higher wages. Even more left the countryside for towns and cities, traditional havens of independence for blacks. Urban black populations sometimes doubled or tripled after emancipation (see A Place in Time). Overall during the 1860s, the urban black population rose by 75 percent, and the number of blacks in small rural towns grew as well. Many migrants eventually returned to their old locales, but they tended to settle on neighboring plantations rather than with their former owners. Freedom

was the major goal. "I's wants to be a free man, cum when I please, and nobody say nuffin to me, nor order me roun'," an Alabama freedman told a northern journalist.

Freed blacks' yearnings to find lost family members prompted much movement. "They had a passion, not so much for wandering as for getting together," a Freedmen's Bureau official commented. Parents sought children who had been sold; husbands and wives who had been separated by sale, or who lived on different plantations, reunited; and families reclaimed youngsters from masters' homes. The Freedmen's Bureau helped former slaves get information about missing relatives and travel to find them. Bureau agents also tried to resolve entanglements over the multiple alliances of spouses who had been separated under slavery.

Reunification efforts often failed. Some fugitive slaves had died during the war or were untraceable. Other ex-slaves had formed new partnerships and could not revive old ones. "I am married," one husband wrote to a former wife (probably in a dictated letter), "and my wife [and I] have two children, and if you and I meet it would make a very dissatisfied family." But there were success stories, too. "I's hunted an' hunted till I track you up here," one freedman told his wife, whom he found in a refugee camp twenty years after their separation by sale.

Once reunited, freed blacks quickly legalized unions formed under slavery, sometimes in mass ceremonies of up to seventy couples. Legal marriage affected family life. Men asserted themselves as household heads; wives and children of able-bodied men often withdrew from the labor force. "When I married my wife, I married her to wait on me and she has got all she can do right here for me and the children," a Tennessee freedman explained. Black women's desire to "play the lady," as southern whites described it, caused planters severe labor shortages. Before the war at least half of field workers had been women; in 1866, a southern journal claimed, men performed almost all the field labor. Still, by the end of Reconstruction, many black women had returned to agricultural work as part of sharecropper families. Others took paid work in cities, as laundresses, cooks, and domestic servants. (Many white women sought employment as well, for the war had incapacitated white breadwinners, reduced the supply of future husbands, and left families destitute or in diminished circumstances.) However, former slaves continued to view stable, independent domestic life, especially the right to bring up their own children, as a

**1860–1890**

## Atlanta Reconstructed

At the Civil War's end, Atlanta presented "a scene of charred and desolate ruins." Before abandoning the city in September 1864, General John Bell Hood and his Confederate army had destroyed its railroads, locomotives, depots, ammunition, and any other property that could help the enemy. Arriving amid smoke and flames, after a six-week siege, General William T. Sherman and the Union Army finished the fiery job that Hood had begun. By mid-November, Union troops had destroyed up to five thousand buildings; renegade soldiers pillaged private homes. When Sherman moved on, about four hundred buildings remained, amid burned-out ruins and twisted rails. One 1865 visitor found "a wilderness of mud, with a confused jumble of railroad sheds" and the bones and skulls of animals lying in the street.

Perched at the southern edge of the Appalachian mountains in the wooded hills of upland Georgia, Atlanta had long been known for enterprise. A railroad center since the 1840s, with rail lines that extended to the west and to the sea,

*Atlanta's depot in ruin after Sherman's siege of the city, 1864.*

Atlanta was a portal for freight en route between the South and other regions. Always bustling, this southern town exuded Yankee energy; prewar city builders included many northerners. During the war, the city had grown rapidly especially as a center for the manufacture and distribution of war supplies. Even after war turned the city to rubble, Atlanta swiftly leapt back to life.

"From all this ruin and devastation, a new city is springing up with marvelous rapidity," wrote the young northern journalist Sidney Andrews during his visit in the fall of 1865. Its narrow streets, he reported, were "alive from morning till night with drays and carts and hand-barrows and wagons . . . with a never-ending throng of pushing and crowding and scrambling and eager and enterprising men, all bent on building and trading and swift-fortune-making." Other observers confirmed this view. "Busy life is resuming its sway," wrote merchant Samuel Richards in July 1865. All kinds of stores had appeared, he noted, "as if by magic." As a new Atlanta arose from the ruins, commerce flourished. "The one sole idea first in everyone's mind is to make money," Andrews declared. To Whitelaw Reid, another northern visitor, "These people were taking lessons from Chicago."

Atlanta's phenomenal postwar growth, like that of Chicago, depended on railroads. Even in 1865, as Andrews

observed, "The four railroads entering here groan with the freight and passenger traffic." Converging at the very center of the city, in a thriving commercial district near the most prosperous residential area, these rail lines made Atlanta the trading hub of the postwar South. The volume of cotton shipped out of the city leapt from 17,000 bales in 1867 to 76,000 in 1876. The Georgia convention of 1868, moreover, voted to move the state capitol from the small town of Milledgeville to Atlanta. Legislators and lobbyists arrived, and real estate values rose. "Our friends in Atlanta are a fast people," a Milledgeville newspaper sniffed in 1867. "They make money fast and they spend it fast. . . . To a stranger the whole city seems to be running on wheels."

Atlanta's vibrant economy boasted diversity. Local manufacturers produced food products, such as flour, cornmeal, meat, candy, coffee, beer, and whiskey, and consumer goods, such as tobacco, dry goods, clothing, boots, shoes, furniture, books, and hardware. Armies of "drummers," or traveling sales agents, who dealt directly with store owners in small towns, canvassed the South. Banks and financial institutions arose, city boosters planned extravagant expositions, and newspapers touted the city's success. Henry W. Grady, editor of the *Atlanta Constitution*, celebrated the "sturdy genius of Atlanta's self-made men," such as cotton magnate S. M. Inman and

**Atlanta's Population**

|        | 1860  | 1870   | 1880   | 1890   |
|--------|-------|--------|--------|--------|
| White  | 7,615 | 11,860 | 21,079 | 39,416 |
| Black  | 1,939 | 9,929  | 16,330 | 28,098 |
| % Black | 20   | 46     | 44     | 43     |

*Source:* Howard N. Rabinowitz, *Race Relations in the Urban South, 1865–1890* (1978), p. 19.

*Domestic workers with tools of their trades—bridle, pot, broom, duster, wheelbarrow, and wagon—pose in front of their employer's home.*

druggist Asa Griggs Candler, who had bought some formulas for patent medicines. One of these, a headache remedy, earned him a fortune. Selling Coca-Cola out of his drugstore, Candler reached an expanding market.

As the economy boomed, Atlanta's population surged, leaping from 9,500 in 1860 to 22,000 in 1870 to 37,000 in 1880 and 65,000 in 1890. A high proportion of newcomers were African-American. One-fifth of the city's residents in 1860, blacks accounted for 46 percent in 1870 and 44 percent in 1880. Like freed people elsewhere, many in Georgia moved to cities. Settling first in tents and shanties, postwar black migrants faced adversities, such as food shortages, unpaved streets, and poor sanitation. Employment was limited. Men found jobs as servants, porters, and laborers, and some worked in industry. Black women, the majority of African-American migrants to Atlanta, labored as cooks, laundresses, nurses,

*Bustling Whitehall Street, a center of commerce, 1882.*

and maids. Still, urban life represented liberty, opportunity, and even a measure of refuge from harassment. "The military is here and nobody interferes with us," declared a black Republican legislator in 1866. "We cannot stop anywhere else so safely."

By 1870 groups of blacks lived in every ward. But trends toward residential segregation were under way. African Americans moved away from the central city, with its business district and elite residential area, to lower elevations on the perimeter. By the 1880s over a third of Atlanta's blacks lived in a handful of areas, such as Sumner Hill, a tract of land in the southeast—including an area once used as the city dump—that had been plundered by Sherman's troops. They also lived in Shermantown to its north, in Diamond Hill on the west side of town, or in smaller clusters in Mechanicsville and Pittsburg in the southeast. In all these areas, schools and churches emerged. In Sumner Hill, in 1867, the African Methodist Episcopal denomination started a

chapel and the American Missionary Association built a school. Northern Methodists founded Clarke University (1869). Diamond Hill welcomed the Atlanta Baptist Seminary, which later became Morehouse College (1879), the Atlanta Baptist Female Seminary (1881), which later became Spelman College, and Atlanta University, which acquired land in 1879. Within black communities, too, enterprises arose to serve a black clientele—grocery stores, barber shops, funeral parlors, and other small businesses. Atlanta's black enclaves created an economic base for the growth of an African-American business class.

Atlanta's new black voters boosted the fortunes of the Republican party, but the Republicans never won control of city government. Reconstruction in fact was brief. By 1871 Democratic power was secure and the spirit of reconciliation firmly in place. City business leaders welcomed northern capital and championed reunion. They embraced the conquering federal troops in the late 1860s, and in 1879 hosted the triumphant Union war hero, General Sherman. By the 1880s dynamic Atlanta symbolized the enterprise and energy of the "New South." Meanwhile, in Shermantown and Sumner Hill, Atlanta's large black population lived a life apart. "[B]y far the largest proportion of Negroes are never really known to us," a reporter observed in 1881. "They . . . drift off to themselves and are almost as far from the white people . . . as if the two races never met."

major blessing of freedom. In 1870 eight out of ten black families in the cotton-producing South were two-parent families, about the same proportion as among whites.

## Black Institutions

The freed blacks' desire for independence also led to the postwar growth of black churches. In the late 1860s, some freedmen congregated at churches operated by northern missionaries; others withdrew from white-run churches and formed their own. The African Methodist Episcopal church, founded by Philadelphia blacks in the 1790s, gained thousands of new southern members. Negro Baptist churches sprouted everywhere, often growing out of plantation "praise meetings," religious gatherings organized by slaves.

The black churches offered a fervent, participatory experience. They also provided relief, raised funds for schools, and supported Republican policies. From the outset black ministers assumed leading political roles, first in the black conventions of 1865–1866 and later in the Reconstruction governments. After southern Democrats excluded most freedmen from political life at Reconstruction's end, ministers remained the main pillars of authority within black communities.

Black schools played a crucial role for freedmen as well. The ex-slaves eagerly sought literacy for themselves and even more for their children. At emancipa-tion blacks organized their own schools, which the Freedmen's Bureau soon supervised. Northern philanthropic societies paid the wages of instructors, about half of them women. In 1869 the bureau reported more than four thousand black schools in the former Confederacy. Within three years each southern state had a public-school system, at least in principle, generally with separate schools for blacks and whites. Advanced schools for blacks opened as well, to train tradespeople, teachers, and ministers. The Freedmen's Bureau and northern organizations like the American Missionary Association helped to found Howard, Atlanta, and Fisk universities (all started in 1866–1867) and Hampton Institute (1868).

Despite these advances, black education remained limited. Few rural blacks could reach the freedmen's schools, located in towns. Underfunded black public schools, similarly inaccessible to most rural black children, held classes only for very short seasons and were sometimes the targets of vigilante attacks. At the end of Reconstruction, more than 80 percent of the black population were illiterate. Still, the proportion of youngsters who could not read and write had declined and would continue to fall (see table, p. 459).

School segregation and other forms of racial separation were taken for granted. Some black codes of 1865–1866 had segregated public-transit conveyances and public accommodations. Even after the invalidation of the codes, the custom of segregation continued

### The Freedmen's School
*Supported by the Freedmen's Bureau, northern freedmen's aid societies, and black denominations, freedmen's schools reached about 12 percent of school-age black children in the South by 1870. Here, a northern teacher poses with her students at a school in rural North Carolina.*

on streetcars, steamboats, and trains as well as in churches, theaters, inns, and restaurants. On railroads, for example, whites could ride in the "ladies' car" or first-class car, whereas blacks had to stay in smoking cars or boxcars with benches. In 1870 Senator Charles Sumner began promoting a bill that would desegregate schools, transportation facilities, juries, and public accommodations. After Sumner's death in 1874, Congress honored him by enacting a new law, the Civil Rights Act of 1875, which encompassed many of his proposals, except for the controversial school-integration provision. But the law was rarely enforced, and in 1883, in the *Civil Rights Cases,* the Supreme Court invalidated it. The Fourteenth Amendment did not prohibit discrimination by individuals, the Court ruled, only that perpetrated by the state.

White southerners rejected the prospect of racial integration, which they insisted would lead to racial amalgamation. "If we have social equality, we shall have intermarriage," one white southerner contended, "and if we have intermarriage, we shall degenerate." Urban blacks sometimes challenged segregation practices, and black legislators promoted bills to desegregate public transit. Some black officeholders decried all forms of racial separatism. "The sooner we as a people forget our sable complexion," said a Mobile official, "the better it will be for us as a race." But most freed blacks were less interested in "social equality," in the sense of interracial mingling, than in black liberty and community. The newly formed postwar elite—teachers, ministers, and politicians—served black constituencies and therefore had a vested interest in separate black institutions. Rural blacks, too, widely preferred all-black institutions. They had little desire to mix with whites. On the contrary, they sought freedom from white control. Above all else, they wanted to secure personal independence by acquiring land.

### Land, Labor, and Sharecropping

"The sole ambition of the freedman," a New Englander wrote from South Carolina in 1865, "appears to be to become the owner of a little piece of land, there to erect a humble home, and to dwell in peace and security, at his own free will and pleasure." Indeed, to freed blacks everywhere, "forty acres and a mule" promised emancipation from plantation labor, from white domination, and from cotton, the "slave crop." Just as garden plots provided a measure of autonomy under slavery, so did landownership signify economic independence afterward. "We want to be placed on

**Percentage of Persons Unable to Write, by Age Group, 1870–1890, in South Carolina, Georgia, Alabama, Mississippi, and Louisiana**

| Age Group | 1870 | 1880 | 1890 |
|---|---|---|---|
| 10–14 | | | |
| Black | 78.9 | 74.1 | 49.2 |
| White | 33.2 | 34.5 | 18.7 |
| 15–20 | | | |
| Black | 85.3 | 73.0 | 54.1 |
| White | 24.2 | 21.0 | 14.3 |
| Over 20 | | | |
| Black | 90.4 | 82.3 | 75.5 |
| White | 19.8 | 17.9 | 17.1 |

*Source:* Roger Ransom and Richard Sutch, *One Kind of Freedom* (Cambridge: Cambridge University Press, 1978), 30.

land until we are able to buy it and make it our own," a black minister had told General Sherman in Georgia during the war. Some freedmen defended their right to the land they lived on by pointing out that they and their forebears had worked on it for decades without pay.

But freedmen's visions of landownership failed to materialize, for, as we have seen, large-scale land reform never occurred. Some freedmen did obtain land with the help of the Union army or the Freedmen's Bureau, and black soldiers sometimes pooled resources to buy land, as on the Sea Islands (see Chapter 15). The federal government also attempted to provide ex-slaves with land. In 1866 Congress passed the Southern Homestead Act, which set aside 44 million acres of land in five southern states for freedmen and loyal whites. This acreage contained poor soil, and few former slaves had the resources to survive even until their first harvest. About four thousand blacks resettled on homesteads under the law, but most were unable to establish farms. (White southern homesteaders fared little better.) By the end of Reconstruction, only a small minority of former slaves in each state owned working farms. In Georgia in 1876, for instance, blacks controlled a mere 1.3 percent of total acreage. Without large-scale land reform, the obstacles to black landownership remained overwhelming.

What were these obstacles? First, most freedmen lacked the capital to buy land and the equipment needed to work it. Furthermore, white southerners on the whole opposed selling land to blacks. Most important, planters sought to preserve a black labor force.

They insisted that freedmen would work only under coercion, and not at all if the possibility of landownership arose. As soon as the war ended, the white South took steps to make sure that black labor would remain available where it was needed, on the plantations.

During presidential Reconstruction, southern state legislatures tried to limit black mobility and to preserve a captive labor force through the black codes. Under labor contracts in effect in 1865–1866, freedmen received wages, housing, food, and clothing in exchange for fieldwork. With cash so scarce, wages usually took the form of a very small share of the crop, often one-eighth or less, divided among the entire plantation work force. Freedmen's Bureau agents promoted the new labor system; they urged freedmen to sign labor contracts and tried to ensure adequate wages. Imbued with the northern free-labor ideology, which held that wage workers could rise to the status of self-supporting tradesmen and property owners, bureau officials endorsed black wage labor as an interim arrangement that would lead to economic independence. "You must begin at the bottom of the ladder and climb up," Freedmen's Bureau head O. O. Howard exhorted a group of Louisiana freedmen in 1865.

But the freedmen disliked the new wage system, especially the use of gang labor, which resembled the

### Reading the Contract

*When Union forces invaded the South Carolina Sea Islands during the Civil War, emancipated slaves there began to work for wages. These free laborers on a plantation near Beaufort, South Carolina, in 1863 listen to the terms of their labor contract.*

work pattern under slavery. Planters had complaints, too. In some regions the black labor force had shrunk to half its prewar size or less, due to the migration of freedmen and to black women's withdrawal from fieldwork. Once united in defense of slavery, planters now competed for black workers. Moreover, their labor problems mounted, for the freedmen, whom planters often scorned as lazy and incorrigible, did not intend to work as long or as hard as they had labored under slavery. One planter estimated that workers accomplished only "two-fifths of what they did under the old system"; and as productivity fell, so did land values. Some planters considered importing white immigrant labor, but they doubted that whites would perform black fieldwork for long. To top off the planters' woes, cotton prices plummeted, for during the war northern and foreign buyers had found new sources of cotton in Egypt and India, and the world supply had vastly increased. Finally, the harvests of 1866 and 1867 were extremely poor. By then an agricultural impasse had been reached: landowners lacked labor and freedmen lacked land. But free blacks, unlike slaves, had the right to enter into contracts—or to refuse to do so—and thereby gained some leverage.

Planters and freedmen began experimenting with new labor schemes, including the division of plantations into small tenancies. Sharecropping, the most widespread arrangement, evolved as a compromise. Under the sharecropping system, landowners subdivided large plantations into farms of thirty to fifty acres, which they rented to freedmen under annual leases for a share of the crop, usually half. Freedmen preferred this system to wage labor because it represented a step toward independence. Heads of households could use the labor of family members. Moreover, a half-share of the crop far exceeded the fraction that freedmen had received as wages under the black codes. Planters often spoke of sharecropping as a capitulation, but they gained as well. Landowners retained power over tenants, because annual leases did not have to be renewed; they could expel undesirable tenants at the end of the year. Planters also shared the risk of planting with tenants: if a crop failed, both suffered the loss. Most important, planters retained control of their land and in some cases extended their holdings. The most productive land, therefore, remained in the hands of a small group of owners, as before the war. Sharecropping forced planters to relinquish daily control over the labor of freedmen but helped to preserve the planter elite.

Sharecropping arrangements varied widely and were not universal. On sugar and rice plantations, the

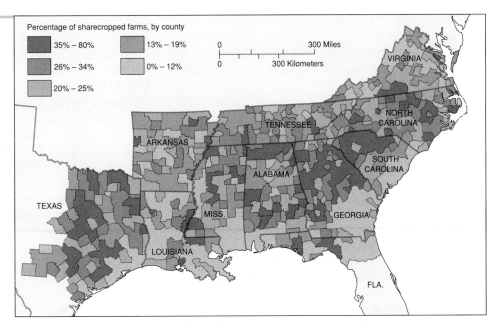

**Southern Sharecropping, 1880**

*The depressed economy of the late 1870s caused poverty and debt, increased tenancy among white farmers, and forced many renters, black and white, into sharecropping. By 1880 the sharecropping system pervaded most southern counties, with the highest concentrations in the cotton belt from South Carolina to eastern Texas.*

(Source: U.S. Census Office, Tenth Census, 1880, *Report of the Production of Agriculture* (Washington, D.C.: Government Printing Office, 1883), Table 5.)

wage system continued. Some freedmen remained independent renters. Some landowners leased areas to white tenants who then subcontracted with black labor. But by the end of the 1860s, sharecropping prevailed in the cotton South, and the new system continued to expand. A severe depression in 1873 drove many black renters into sharecropping. By then thousands of independent white farmers had become sharecroppers as well. Stung by wartime losses and by the dismal postwar economy, they sank into debt and lost their land to creditors. Many backcountry residents, no longer able to get by on subsistence farming, shifted to cash crops like cotton and suffered the same fate. At the end of Reconstruction, one-third of the white farmers in Mississippi, for instance, worked as sharecroppers.

By 1880, 80 percent of the land in the cotton-producing states had been subdivided into tenancies, most of it farmed by sharecroppers, white and black. Indeed, white sharecroppers now outnumbered black ones, although a higher proportion of southern blacks, about 75 percent, were involved in the system. Changes in marketing and finance, meanwhile, made the sharecroppers' lot increasingly precarious.

## Toward a Crop-Lien Economy

Before the Civil War, planters had depended on factors, or middlemen, who sold them supplies, extended credit, and marketed their crops through urban merchants. These long-distance credit arrangements were backed by the high value and liquidity of slave property.

When slavery ended, the factorage system collapsed. The postwar South, with hundreds of thousands of tenants and sharecroppers, needed a far more localized network of credit.

Into the gap stepped the rural merchants (often themselves planters), who advanced supplies to tenants and sharecroppers on credit and sold their crops to wholesalers or textile manufacturers. Because renters had no property to use as collateral, the merchants secured their loans with a lien, or claim, on each farmer's next crop. They charged exorbitant interest of 50 percent or more and quickly drew many tenants and sharecroppers into a cycle of indebtedness. Owing part of the crop to a landowner for rent, a sharecropper also owed a rural merchant a large sum (perhaps amounting to the rest of his crop, or more) for supplies. Often, an illiterate tenant could not keep track of his financial arrangements, and a merchant could easily take advantage of him. "A man that didn't know how to count would always lose," an Arkansas freedman later explained. Once a tenant's debts or alleged debts exceeded the value of his crop, he was tied to the land, to cotton, and to sharecropping.

By the end of Reconstruction, sharecropping and crop liens had transformed southern agriculture. They bound the region to staple production and prevented crop diversification, for despite plunging cotton prices, creditors—landowners and merchants—insisted that tenants raise only easily marketable cash crops. Short of capital, planters could no longer invest in new equipment or improve their land by such techniques as crop rotation and contour plowing. Soil depletion, land erosion, and agricultural backwardness soon locked much of the South into a cycle of poverty. Overall, postwar changes in agriculture left the South with bleak economic prospects.

But the chief victims of the new agricultural order were indebted tenant farmers, who had been trapped in a system of what has been called debt peonage. Raising cotton for distant markets, for prices over which they had no control, remained the only survival route open to poor farmers, regardless of race. But the low income thus derived often forced them into sharecropping and crop liens, from which escape was difficult. Black tenants, who attained neither landownership nor economic independence, suffered further handicaps. Not only were their rights as workers limited, but when Reconstruction ended, their political rights dwindled too. As one southern regime after another returned to Democratic control, freedmen could no longer look to the state governments for protection. Nor could they turn to the federal government, for northern politicians were preoccupied with their own problems.

## New Concerns in the North

The nomination of Ulysses S. Grant for president in 1868 launched a chaotic era in national politics. Grant's two terms in office featured political scandals, a party revolt, a massive depression, and a steady retreat from Reconstruction policies. By the mid-1870s, northern voters cared more about the economic climate, unemployment, labor unrest, and currency problems than about the "southern question." Responsive to the shift in popular mood, Republicans became eager to end sectional conflict and consequently turned their backs on the freedmen of the South.

### *Grantism*

Republicans had good reason to pass over long-time party leaders and nominate the popular Grant. A war

hero, Grant was endorsed by Union veterans, widely admired in the North, and unscathed by the bitter feuds of Reconstruction politics. To oppose Grant in the 1868 election, the Democrats nominated New York governor Horatio Seymour, arch-critic of the Lincoln administration during the war. Seymour opposed Reconstruction and advocated "sound money," or the withdrawal of greenbacks from circulation. Grant, who defended Reconstruction, ran on his personal popularity more than on issues. Although he carried all but eight states in the election, the popular vote was very close; in the South, newly enfranchised freedmen provided the margin of victory. When he was inaugurated, Grant vowed to execute all the laws whether he agreed with them or not, to support sound money, and to follow a humane policy toward the Indians.

A strong leader in war, Grant proved a passive president. Although he lacked Johnson's instinct for disaster, he had little skill at politics. Many of his cabinet appointees—business executives, army men, and family friends—were mediocre if not unscrupulous; scandals plagued his administration. In 1869 financier Jay Gould and his partner Jim Fisk attempted to corner the gold market with the help of Grant's brother-in-law, a New York speculator. When gold prices tumbled, Gould salvaged his own fortune, but investors were ruined and Grant's reputation was tarnished. Then before the president's first term ended, his vice president, Schuyler Colfax, was found to be linked to the Crédit Mobilier, a fraudulent construction company created to skim off the profits of the Union Pacific Railroad. Using government funds granted to the railroad, the Union Pacific directors awarded padded construction contracts to the Crédit Mobilier, of which they were also the directors. Discredited, Colfax was dropped from the Grant ticket in 1872. More trouble lay ahead. Grant's private secretary, Orville Babcock, was unmasked in 1875 after taking money from the "whiskey ring," a group of distillers who bribed federal agents to avoid paying millions in whiskey taxes. And in 1876 voters learned that Grant's secretary of war, William E. Belknap, had taken bribes to sell lucrative Indian trad-

**The Election of 1868**

| Candidates | Parties | Electoral Vote | Popular Vote | Percentage of Popular Vote |
|---|---|---|---|---|
| ULYSSES S. GRANT | Republican | 214 | 3,013,421 | 52.7 |
| Horatio Seymour | Democratic | 80 | 2,706,829 | 47.3 |

**Boss Tweed**

*Thomas Nast's cartoons in* Harper's Weekly *helped topple New York Democratic boss William M. Tweed, who, with his associates, embodied corruption on a large scale. The Tweed Ring had granted lucrative franchises to companies they controlled, padded construction bills, practiced graft and extortion, and exploited every opportunity to plunder the city's funds.*

ing posts in Oklahoma. Impeached and disgraced, Belknap resigned.

Although uninvolved in the scandals, Grant loyally defended his subordinates. To his critics, "Grantism" came to stand for fraud, bribery, and political corruption, evils that spread far beyond Washington. In Pennsylvania, for example, the Standard Oil Company and the Pennsylvania Railroad controlled the legislature. Urban politics also provided rich opportunities for graft and swindles. The New York City press revealed in 1872 that Democratic boss William M. Tweed, the "Grand Sachem" of Tammany Hall, led a ring that looted the city treasury and collected an estimated $200 million in kickbacks and payoffs. When Mark Twain and coauthor Charles Dudley Warner published their satiric novel *The Gilded Age\** (1873), readers recognized the book's speculators, self-promoters, and maniacal opportunists as familiar types in public life.

Grant had some success in foreign policy. In 1872 his competent secretary of state, Hamilton Fish, engineered the settlement of the *Alabama* claims with England. To compensate for damage done by British-built raiders sold to the Confederacy during the war, an international tribunal awarded the United States $15.5 million. But the Grant administration faltered when it

\* The term "Gilded Age" was subsequently used to refer to the decades from the 1870s to the 1890s.

tried to add nonadjacent territory to the United States, as the Johnson administration had done. In 1867 Johnson's secretary of state, William H. Seward, had negotiated a treaty in which the United States bought Alaska from Russia at the bargain price of $7.2 million. Although the press mocked "Seward's Ice Box," the purchase kindled expansionists' hopes. In 1870 Grant decided to annex the Caribbean island nation of Santo Domingo. Formerly known as Hispaniola and today called the Dominican Republic, Santo Domingo had been passed back and forth since the late eighteenth century among France, Spain, and Haiti. Annexation, Grant believed, would promote Caribbean trade and provide a haven for persecuted southern blacks. American speculators anticipated windfalls from land sales, commerce, and mining in Santo Domingo. But Congress disliked Grant's plan. Senator Charles Sumner denounced the scheme as an imperialist "dance of blood." The Senate rejected the annexation treaty and further diminished Grant's reputation.

As the election of 1872 approached, dissident Republicans expressed fears that "Grantism" at home and abroad would ruin the party. Even Grant's new running mate, Henry Wilson, referred to the president privately as a burden on his fellow Republicans. The dissidents took action. Led by a combination of former Radicals and other Republicans left out of Grant's "Great Barbecue," the president's critics formed their own party, the Liberal Republicans.

### The Liberals' Revolt

The Liberal Republican revolt marked a turning point in Reconstruction history. By splitting the Republican party, it undermined support for Republican southern policy. The Liberals attacked the "regular" Republicans on several key issues. Denouncing "Grantism" and

## The Election of 1872

| Candidates | Parties | Electoral Vote | Popular Vote | Percentage of Popular Vote |
|---|---|---|---|---|
| ULYSSES S. GRANT | Republican | 286 | 3,596,745 | 55.6 |
| Horace Greeley* | Democratic | | 2,843,446 | 43.9 |

*Upon Greeley's death shortly after the popular election, the electors supporting him divided their votes among minor candidates.

"spoilsmen" (political hacks who gained party office), they demanded civil-service reform to bring the "best men" into government. Rejecting the usual Republican high-tariff policy, they espoused free trade. Most important, the Liberals condemned "bayonet rule" in the South. Even some Republicans once known for radicalism now claimed that Reconstruction had achieved its goal: blacks had been enfranchised and could henceforth manage for themselves. Corruption in government, North and South, they asserted, posed a greater danger than Confederate resurgence. In the South, indeed, corrupt Republican regimes were *kept* in power, the Liberals said, because the "best men"— the most capable politicians—were ex-Confederates who had been barred from officeholding.

For president the new party bypassed Charles Sumner and nominated *New York Tribune* editor Horace Greeley, who had inconsistently supported both a stringent reconstruction policy and leniency toward former rebels. The Democrats endorsed Greeley as well, despite his long-time condemnation of them. Their campaign slogan explained their support: "Anything to Beat Grant." Horace Greeley proved so diligent a campaigner that he worked himself to death making speeches from the back of a campaign train. He died a few weeks after the election. Grant, who won 56 percent of the popular vote, carried all the northern states and most of the sixteen southern and border states. But the division among Republicans affected Reconstruction. To deprive the Liberals of a campaign issue, Grant Republicans in Congress, the "regulars," passed an amnesty act that allowed all but a few hundred ex-Confederate officials to hold office. The flood of private amnesty acts that followed convinced white southerners that any ex-Confederate save Jefferson Davis could rise to power. During Grant's second term, Republican desires to discard the "southern question" mounted as a depression of unprecedented scope gripped the whole nation.

## The Panic of 1873

The postwar years brought accelerated industrialization, rapid economic expansion, and frantic speculation. Investors rushed to profit from rising prices, new markets, high tariffs, and seemingly boundless opportunities. Railroads provided the biggest lure. In May 1869 railroad executives drove a golden spike into the ground at Promontory Point, Utah, joining the Union Pacific and Central Pacific lines (see Chapter 17). The first transcontinental railroad heralded a new era. By 1873 almost four hundred railroad corporations crisscrossed the Northeast, consuming tons of coal and miles of steel rail from the mines and mills of Pennsylvania and neighboring states. Transforming the economy, the railroad boom led entrepreneurs to overspeculate, with drastic results.

Philadelphia banker Jay Cooke, who had helped finance the Union effort with his wartime bond campaign, had taken over a new transcontinental line, the Northern Pacific, in 1869. Northern Pacific securities sold briskly for several years, but in 1873 the line's construction costs outran new investments. In September of that year, his vaults full of bonds he could no longer sell, Cooke failed to meet his obligations, and his bank, the largest in the nation, shut down. Smaller firms collapsed, as did the stock market. This Panic of 1873 triggered a five-year depression that wrought widespread devastation. Banks closed, farm prices plummeted, steel furnaces stood idle, and one out of four railroads failed. Within two years, eighteen thousand businesses went bankrupt, and by 1878 3 million employees were out of jobs. Those still at work suffered repeated wage cuts, labor protests mounted, and industrial violence spread (see Chapter 18). The depression of the 1870s revealed that conflicts born of industrialization had replaced sectional divisions.

The depression also fed a dispute over currency that had begun in 1865. The Civil War had created fiscal chaos. During the war, Americans had used both national bank notes, yellow in color, which would eventually be converted into gold, and greenbacks, a paper currency not "backed" by a particular weight in gold. To stabilize the postwar currency, greenbacks would have to be withdrawn from circulation. This "sound-money" policy, favored by investors, was implemented by Treasury Secretary Hugh McCulloch with the backing of Congress. But those who depended on easy credit, both indebted farmers and manufacturers, wanted an expanding currency; that is, more greenbacks. Once the depression began, demands for such "easy money" rose. The issue divided both major parties and was compounded by another one: how to repay the federal debt.

During the war the Union government had borrowed what were then astronomical sums, on whatever terms it could get, mainly through the sale of war bonds—in effect, short-term federal IOUs—to private citizens. By 1869 the issue of war-debt repayment afflicted the Republican party, whose support came from voters with diverse financial interests. To pacify bondholders, Senator John Sherman of Ohio and other Republican leaders obtained passage of the Public Credit Act of 1869, which promised to pay the war debt in "coin." Holders of war bonds expected no less, although many had bought their bonds with greenbacks!

With investors reassured by the Public Credit Act, Sherman guided legislation through Congress that swapped the old short-term bonds for new ones payable over the next generation. In 1872 another bill in effect defined "coin" as "gold coin" by dropping the traditional silver dollar from the official coinage. Through a feat of ingenious compromise, which placated investors and debtors, Sherman preserved the public credit, the currency, and Republican unity. In 1875 he engineered the Specie Resumption Act, which promised to put the nation effectively on the gold standard in 1879, while tossing a few more immediate but less important bones to Republican voters who wanted "easy money."

Republican leaders acted not a moment too soon because when the Democrats gained control of the House in 1875, with the depression in full force, a verbal storm broke out. Many Democrats and some Republicans demanded that the silver dollar be restored in order to expand the currency and relieve the depression. These "free-silver" advocates secured passage of the Bland-Allison Act of 1878, which partially restored silver coinage. The law required the treasury to buy

$2–4 million worth of silver each month and turn it into coin but did not revive the silver standard. In 1876 other expansionists formed the Greenback party, which adopted the debtors' cause and fought to keep greenbacks in circulation. But despite the election of fourteen Greenback congressmen, they did not get even as far as the free-silver people had. As the nation emerged from depression in 1879, the clamor for "easy money" subsided, only to resurge in the 1890s (see Chapter 21). The controversial "money question" of the 1870s, never resolved, gave politicians and voters another reason to forget about the South.

### *Reconstruction and the Constitution*

The Supreme Court of the 1870s also played a role in weakening northern support for Reconstruction. In the wartime crisis, few cases of note had come before the Court. After the war, however, constitutional questions surged into prominence.

First, would the Court support congressional laws to protect freedmen's rights? The decision in *Ex parte* Milligan (1866) suggested not. In this case, the Court declared that a military commission established by the president or Congress could not try civilians in areas remote from war where the civil courts were functioning. Thus special military courts to enforce the Supplementary Freedmen's Bureau Act were doomed. Second, would the Court sabotage the congressional Reconstruction plan, as Republicans feared? Their qualms were valid, for if the Union was indissoluble, as the North had claimed during the war, then the concept of *restoring* states to the Union would be meaningless. In *Texas* v. *White* (1869), the Court ruled that although the Union was indissoluble and secession was legally impossible, the process of Reconstruction was still constitutional. It was grounded in Congress's power to ensure each state a republican form of government and to recognize the legitimate government in any state.

The 1869 decision protected the Republicans' Reconstruction plan. But in the 1870s, when cases arose involving the Fourteenth and Fifteenth amendments, the Court backed away from Reconstruction policy. In the *Slaughterhouse* cases of 1873, the Supreme Court began to chip away at the Fourteenth Amendment. The cases involved a business monopoly rather than freedmen's rights, but they provided an opportunity to interpret the amendment narrowly. In 1869 the Louisiana legislature had granted a monopoly over the New Orleans slaughterhouse business to one firm and had closed down all other slaughterhouses in the interest of public health. The excluded butchers brought suit. The state had deprived them of their lawful occupation without due process of law, they claimed, and such action violated the Fourteenth Amendment, which guaranteed that no state could "abridge the privileges or immunities" of U.S. citizens. The Supreme Court upheld the Louisiana legislature by issuing a doctrine of "dual citizenship." The Fourteenth Amendment, declared the Court, protected only the rights of *national* citizenship, such as the right of interstate travel or the right to federal protection when on the high seas. It did not protect those basic civil rights that fell to citizens by virtue of their *state* citizenship. Therefore, the federal government was not obliged to protect such rights against violation by the states. The *Slaughterhouse* decision came close to nullifying the intent of the Fourteenth Amendment—to secure freedmen's rights against state encroachment.

The Supreme Court again backed away from Reconstruction in two cases involving the Enforcement Act of 1870. The case of *U.S.* v. *Reese* (1876) centered on Kentucky officials who, after barring blacks from voting, had been indicted in 1873 by a Kentucky federal court under the First Enforcement Act. Deciding for the officials, the Supreme Court stated that the Fifteenth Amendment did not "confer the right of suffrage upon anyone." It merely prohibited the hindrance of voting on the basis of race, color, or previous condition of servitude. Since the Enforcement Act barred the hindrance of *anyone* from voting for *any* reason (that is, since it did not repeat the exact wording of the amendment), the Court declared its crucial sections, and the Kentucky indictment, invalid. Another 1876 case, *U.S.* v. *Cruikshank*, concerned the indictment under the 1870 Enforcement Act of white Louisianians after the Colfax massacre, a battle between armed whites and black state militiamen in which seventy blacks had surrendered, half of whom were then murdered. The Fourteenth Amendment, contended the Court, prohibited only the encroachment on individual rights by a *state,* not by other individuals; "ordinary crime" was not the target of federal law. The decision threw out the indictments and, with them, the effectiveness of the Enforcement Act.

Continuing its retreat from Reconstruction, the Supreme Court in 1883 invalidated both the Civil Rights Act of 1875 and the Ku Klux Klan Act of 1871 and later upheld segregation laws (see Chapter 21). These decisions cumulatively dismantled the Reconstruction policies that Republicans had sponsored after the war and confirmed rising northern sentiment that Reconstruction's egalitarian goals could not be enforced.

## Republicans in Retreat

The Republicans did not reject Reconstruction suddenly but rather disengaged from it gradually. The withdrawal process began with Grant's election to the presidency in 1868. Although not one of the architects of Reconstruction policy, Grant defended it. But he shared with most Americans a belief in decentralized government and a reluctance to assert federal authority in local and state affairs.

In the 1870s, as the northern military presence shrank in the South, Republican idealism waned in the North. The Liberal Republican revolt of 1872 eroded what remained of radicalism. Although the "regular" Republicans, who backed Grant, continued to defend Reconstruction in the 1872 election, many held ambivalent views. Commercial and industrial interests now dominated both wings of the party, and Grant supporters had greater zeal for doing business in and with the South than for rekindling sectional strife. After the Democrats won control of the House in the 1874 elections, Reconstruction became a political liability.

By 1875 the Radical Republicans, so prominent in the 1860s, had vanished from the political scene. Chase, Stevens, and Sumner were dead. Other Radicals had lost office or had abandoned their former convictions. "Waving the Bloody Shirt," or defaming Democratic opponents by reviving wartime animosity, now struck many Republicans, including former Radicals, as counterproductive. Party leaders reported that voters were "sick of carpet-bag government" and tiring of both the "southern question" and the "Negro question." It now seemed pointless to continue the unpopular and expensive policy of military intervention in the South to prop up Republican regimes that even President Grant found corrupt. Finally, few Republicans shared the egalitarian spirit that had animated Stevens and Sumner. Politics aside, Republican leaders and voters generally agreed with southern Democrats that blacks, although worthy of freedom, were inferior to whites. To insist on black equality would be a thankless, divisive, and politically suicidal undertaking. Moreover, it would quash any hope of reunion between the regions. The Republicans' retreat from Reconstruction set the stage for its demise in 1877.

# Reconstruction Abandoned

"We are in a very hot political contest just now," a Mississippi planter wrote to his daughter in 1875, "with a good prospect of turning out the carpetbag thieves by whom we have been robbed for the past six to ten years." Similar contests raged through the South in the 1870s, as the resentment of white majorities grew and Democratic influence surged. By the end of 1872, the Democrats had regained power in Tennessee, Virginia, Georgia, and North Carolina. Within three years they won control in Texas, Alabama, Arkansas, and Mississippi. As the 1876 elections approached, Republican rule survived in only three states—South Carolina, Florida, and Louisiana. Democratic victories in the state elections of 1876 and political bargaining in Washington in 1877 abruptly ended what little remained of Reconstruction.

## *Redeeming the South*

After 1872 the Republicans' collapse in the South accelerated. Congressional amnesty enabled almost all ex-Confederate officials to regain office, divisions among the Republicans loosened their party's weak grip on the southern electorate, and attrition diminished Republican ranks. Some carpetbaggers gave up and returned

**The White League**
*Alabama's White League, formed in 1874, strove to oust Republicans from office by intimidating black voters. To political cartoonist Thomas Nast, such vigilante tactics suggested and alliance between the White League and the outlawed Ku Klux Klan.*

North; others shifted to the Democratic party. Scalawags deserted in even larger numbers. Southerners who had joined the Republicans to moderate rampant radicalism tired of northern interference;

## The Duration of Republican Rule in the Ex-Confederate States

| Former Confederate States | Readmission to the Union Under Congressional Reconstruction | Democrats (Conservatives) Gain Control | Duration of Republican Rule |
|---|---|---|---|
| Alabama | June 25, 1868 | November 14, 1874 | 6½ years |
| Arkansas | June 22, 1868 | November 10, 1874 | 6½ years |
| Florida | June 25, 1868 | January 2, 1877 | 8½ years |
| Georgia | July 15, 1870 | November 1, 1871 | 1 year |
| Louisiana | June 25, 1868 | January 2, 1877 | 8½ years |
| Mississippi | February 23, 1870 | November 3, 1875 | 5½ years |
| North Carolina | June 25, 1868 | November 3, 1870 | 2 years |
| South Carolina | June 25, 1868 | November 12, 1876 | 8 years |
| Tennessee | July 24, 1866* | October 4, 1869 | 3 years |
| Texas | March 30, 1870 | January 14, 1873 | 3 years |
| Virginia | January 26, 1870 | October 5, 1869[†] | 0 years |

*Admitted before start of congressional Reconstruction.    [†]Democrats gained control before readmission.

*Source:* John Hope Franklin, *Reconstruction After the Civil War* (Chicago: University of Chicago Press, 1962), 231.

once "home rule" by Democrats became a possibility, staying Republican meant going down with a sinking ship. Scalawag defections ruined Republican prospects. Unable to win new white votes or retain the old ones, the always precarious Republican coalition crumbled.

Meanwhile, the Democrats mobilized formerly apathetic white voters. The resurrected southern Democratic party was divided: businessmen who envisioned an industrialized "New South" opposed an agrarian faction called the Bourbons, or the old planter elite. But all Democrats shared a major goal: to oust Republicans from office. Their tactics varied from state to state. Alabama Democrats won by promising to cut taxes and by getting out the white vote. In Louisiana the "White League," a vigilante organization formed in 1874, undermined the Republicans' hold. Intimidation also proved effective in Mississippi, where violent incidents—like the 1874 slaughter in Vicksburg of about 300 blacks by rampaging whites—terrorized black voters. In 1875 the "Mississippi plan" took effect:

local Democratic clubs armed members, dispersed Republican meetings, patrolled voter-registration places, and marched through black areas. "The Republicans are paralyzed through fear and will not act," the anguished carpetbag governor of Mississippi wrote to his wife. "Why should I fight a hopeless battle?" In 1876, South Carolina's "Rifle Clubs" and "Red Shirts," armed groups that threatened Republicans, continued the scare tactics that had worked so well in Mississippi.

New outbursts of intimidation did not completely squelch black voting, but the Democrats deprived the Republicans of enough black votes to win state elections. In some counties they encouraged freedmen to vote Democratic at supervised polls where voters publicly placed a card with a party label in a box. In other instances employers and landowners impeded black suffrage. Labor contracts included clauses barring attendance at political meetings; planters used the threat of eviction to keep sharecroppers in line. Since the Enforcement acts could not be enforced, intimidation and economic pressure succeeded.

### The Exodus to Kansas

*Benjamin "Pap" Singleton, once a fugitive slave from Kentucky, returned there to promote the "exodus" movement of the late 1870s. Forming a real-estate company, Singleton traveled the South recruiting parties of freedmen who were disillusioned with the outcome of Reconstruction. These emigrants, boarding a riverboat at Vicksburg, Mississippi, looked forward to political equality, freedom from violence, and homesteads in Kansas.*

*Redemption*, the word Democrats used to describe their return to power, meant more than a mere rotation in personnel. When the Democrats took office, they made sweeping changes. Some states called constitutional conventions to reverse Republican policies. All cut back expenses, wiped out social programs, lowered taxes, and revised their tax systems to relieve landowners of large burdens. State courts limited the rights of tenants and sharecroppers. Most important, the Democrats used the law to ensure a stable black labor force. Legislatures restored vagrancy laws, revised crop-lien statutes to make landowners' claims superior to those of merchants, and rewrote criminal law. Local ordinances in heavily black counties might restrict hunting, fishing, gun carrying, and ownership of dogs and thereby curtail the everyday activities of freedmen who lived off the land. States passed severe laws against trespassing and theft; stealing livestock or wrongly taking part of a crop became grand larceny with a penalty of up to five years at hard labor. By the end of Reconstruction, a large black convict work force had been leased out to private contractors, who profited from their labor.

For the freedmen, whose aspirations had been raised by Republican rule, redemption was demoralizing. The new laws, Tennessee blacks contended at an 1875 convention, would impose "a condition of servitude scarcely less degrading than that endured before the late civil war." In the late 1870s, as the political climate grew more oppressive, an "exodus" movement spread through Mississippi, Tennessee, Texas, and Louisiana. Seeking a way out of the South, some freed blacks decided to become homesteaders in Kansas. After a major outbreak of "Kansas fever" in 1879, four thousand "exodusters" from Mississippi and Louisiana joined about ten thousand who had reached Kansas in smaller groups earlier in the decade. But the vast majority of freedmen, devoid of resources, had no migration options or escape route. Mass movement of southern blacks to the North and Midwest would not gain momentum until the twentieth century.

## The Election of 1876

By the autumn of 1876, with redemption almost complete, both parties moved to discard the heritage of animosity left by the war and Reconstruction. The Republicans nominated Rutherford B. Hayes, three times Ohio's governor, for president. Untainted by the scandals of the Grant years and popular with all factions in

his party, Hayes presented himself as a "moderate" on southern policy. He favored "home rule" in the South and a guarantee of civil and political rights for all—two planks that were clearly contradictory. The Democrats nominated Governor Samuel J. Tilden of New York, a millionaire corporate lawyer and political reformer. Known for his assaults on the rapacious Tweed Ring that had plundered New York City's treasury, Tilden campaigned against fraud and waste. Both candidates were fiscal conservatives, favored sound money, endorsed civil-service reform, and decried corruption, an irony since the 1876 election would be extremely corrupt.

Tilden won the popular vote by a small margin and seemed destined to capture the 185 electoral votes needed for victory. But the Republicans challenged the pro-Tilden returns from South Carolina, Florida, and Louisiana. If they could deprive the Democrats of these nineteen electoral votes, Hayes would triumph. The Democrats, who needed only one of the disputed electoral votes for victory, challenged the validity of Oregon's single electoral vote, which the Republicans had won, on a technicality. Twenty electoral votes, therefore, were in contention. But Republicans still controlled the electoral machinery in the three unredeemed southern states, where they threw out enough Democratic ballots to declare Hayes the winner.

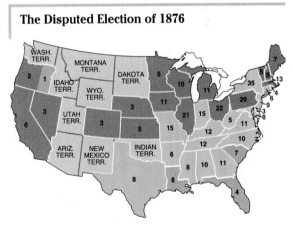

**The Disputed Election of 1876**

| | Uncontested Electoral Vote | Electoral Vote | Popular Vote | Percentage of Popular Vote |
|---|---|---|---|---|
| **Republican** Rutherford B. Hayes | 165 | 185 | 4,034,311 | 48.0 |
| **Democratic** Samuel J. Tilden | 184 | 184 | 4,288,546 | 51.0 |
| **Greenback** Peter Cooper | – | – | 75,973 | 1.0 |

Disputed

The nation now faced an unprecedented dilemma: each party claimed victory in the contested states, and each accused the other of fraud. In fact, both sets of southern results involved fraud: the Republicans had discarded legitimate Democratic ballots, and the Democrats had illegally prevented freedmen from voting. To resolve the conflict, Congress in January 1877 created a special electoral commission to determine which party would get the contested electoral votes. Made up of senators, representatives, and Supreme Court justices, the commission included seven Democrats, seven Republicans, and one independent, Justice David Davis of Illinois. When Davis resigned to run for the Senate, Congress replaced him with a Republican, and the commission gave Hayes the election by an 8 to 7 vote.

Congress now had to certify the new electoral vote. But since the Democrats controlled the House, a new problem loomed. Some Democrats threatened to obstruct debate and delay approval of the electoral vote. Had they carried out their scheme, the nation would have been without a president on inauguration day. But there remained room for compromise, for many southern Democrats accepted Hayes's election. Among them were former scalawags with commercial interests to protect, who still favored Republican financial policies, and railroad investors, who hoped that a Republican administration would help them build a southern transcontinental line. Other southerners cared mainly about Democratic state victories and did not mind conceding the presidency as long as the new Republican administration would leave the South alone. Republican leaders, although sure of eventual triumph, were willing to bargain as well, for candidate Hayes desired not merely victory but southern approval.

A series of informal negotiations ensued, at which politicians exchanged promises. Ohio Republicans and southern Democrats who met at the Wormley House, a Washington hotel, reached an agreement that if Hayes won the election, he would remove federal troops from South Carolina and Louisiana, and Democrats could gain control of those states. In other bargaining sessions, southern politicians asked for federal patronage, federal aid to railroads, and federal support for internal improvements. In return, they promised to drop the filibuster, to accept Hayes as president, and to treat freedmen fairly.

With the threatened filibuster broken, Congress ratified Hayes's election. Once in office, Hayes fulfilled some of the promises his Republican colleagues had made. He appointed a former Confederate as postmaster general and ordered federal troops who guarded the South Carolina and Louisiana statehouses back to their barracks. Although federal soldiers remained in the South after 1877, they no longer served a political function. The Democrats, meanwhile, took control of state governments in Louisiana, South Carolina, and Florida. When Republican rule toppled in these states, the era of Reconstruction finally ended, though more with a whimper than with a resounding crash.

But some of the bargains struck in the Compromise of 1877, such as Democratic promises to treat southern blacks fairly, were forgotten, as were Hayes's pledges to ensure freedmen's rights. "When you turned us loose, you turned us loose to the sky, to the storm, to the whirlwind, and worst of all . . . to the wrath of our infuriated masters," Frederick Douglass had charged at the Republican convention in 1876. "The question now is, do you mean to make good to us the promises in your Constitution?" The answer provided by the 1876 election and the 1877 compromises was "No."

## CONCLUSION

Between 1865 and 1877, the nation experienced a turbulent era of revolution and reaction. In Washington conflict between President Johnson and Congress led to a stringent Republican plan for restoring the South, a plan that included the radical provision of black enfranchisement. In the ex-Confederate states, governments were reorganized, Republicans took over, and far-reaching changes occurred. Emancipation reshaped black communities, where former slaves sought new identities as free people, and transformed the southern economy as a new labor system replaced slavery. The North, meanwhile, hurtled headlong into an era of industrial growth, labor unrest, and financial crises. By the mid-1870s, northern politicians were ready to discard the Reconstruction policies that Congress had imposed a decade before. Simultaneously, the southern states returned to Democratic control, as Republican regimes toppled one by one. Reconstruction's final collapse in 1877 reflected not only a waning of northern resolve but a successful ex-Confederate campaign of violence, intimidation, and protest that had started in the 1860s.

The end of Reconstruction gratified both political parties. Although unable to retain a southern constituency, the Republican party was no longer burdened by the unpopular "southern question." The Democrats, who had regained power in the former Confederacy, would remain entrenched there for over a century. To be sure, the South was tied to sharecropping and economic backwardness as securely as it had once been tied to slavery. But "home rule" was firmly in place. Reconstruction's end also signified a triumph for nationalism and the spirit of reunion. In the fall of 1877, President Hayes toured the South to champion reconciliation, and similar celebrations continued through the 1880s and 1890s. When former President Grant died in 1885, veterans of both Civil War armies served as pallbearers. Jefferson Davis, imprisoned for two years after the war but never brought to trial, urged young men to "lay aside all rancor, all bitter sectional feeling." The federal government turned battlefields into national parks where veterans of both armies could gather for reunions.

As the nation applauded reunion, Reconstruction's reputation sank. Looking back on the 1860s and 1870s, most late-nineteenth-century Americans dismissed the congressional effort to reconstruct the South as a fiasco—a tragic interlude of "radical rule" or "black reconstruction," fashioned by carpetbaggers, scalawags, and Radical Republicans. With the hindsight of a century, historians continued to regard Reconstruction as a failure, though of a different kind.

No longer viewed as a misguided scheme that collapsed because of radical excess, Reconstruction is now widely seen as a democratic experiment that did not go far enough. Historians cite two main causes. First, Congress did not promote freedmen's independence through land reform; without property of their own, southern blacks lacked the economic power to defend their interests as free citizens. Property ownership, however, does not necessarily ensure political rights, nor does it invariably provide economic security. Considering the depressed state of southern agriculture in the postwar decades, the freedmen's fate as independent farmers would likely have been perilous. Thus the land-reform question, like much else about Reconstruction, remains a subject of debate. A second cause of Reconstruction's collapse is less open to dispute: the federal government neglected to back congressional Reconstruction with military force. Given the choice between protecting blacks' rights at whatever cost and promoting reunion, the government opted for reunion. Reconstruction's failure, therefore, was the federal government's failure to fulfill its own goals and create a biracial democracy in the South. As a result, the na-

tion's adjustment to the consequences of emancipation would continue into the twentieth century.

The Reconstruction era left some significant legacies, including the Fourteenth and Fifteenth amendments. Although neither amendment would be used to protect minority rights for almost a century, they remain monuments to the democratic zeal that swept Congress in the 1860s. The Reconstruction years also hold a significant place in African-American history. During this brief respite between slavery and repression, southern blacks reconstituted their families, created new institutions, took part in the transformation of southern agriculture, and participated in government, for the first time in American history. The aspirations and achievements of the Reconstruction era left an indelible mark on black citizens. But other Americans of the 1880s consigned Reconstruction to history and turned their energies to their economic futures—to railroads, factories, and mills, and to the exploitation of the country's bountiful natural resources.

## FOR FURTHER READING

Eric Foner, *Reconstruction: America's Unfinished Revolution, 1863–1877* (1988). A thorough exploration of Reconstruction that draws on recent scholarship and stresses the centrality of the black experience.

John Hope Franklin, *Reconstruction After the Civil War* (1961). An overview that dismantles the traditional view of Reconstruction as a disastrous experiment in radical rule.

William Gillette, *Retreat from Reconstruction, 1869–1879* (1979). A survey of the era's national politics, indicting Republican policy makers for vacillation and lack of commitment to racial equality.

Tera W. Hunter, *To 'Joy My Freedom: Southern Black Women's Lives and Labors After the Civil War* (1997). Explores the experience of women workers in Atlanta from Reconstruction into the twentieth century.

Leon Litwack, *Been in the Storm So Long: The Aftermath of Slavery* (1979). A comprehensive study of the black response to emancipation in 1865–1866.

Roger L. Ransom and Richard Sutch, *One Kind of Freedom: The Economic Consequences of Emancipation* (1977). Two economists' assessment of the impact of free black labor on the South and explanation of the development of sharecropping and the crop-lien system.

Kenneth M. Stampp, *The Era of Reconstruction, 1865–1877* (1965). A classic revisionist interpretation of Reconstruction, focusing on the establishment and fall of Republican governments.

Joel Williamson, *The Negro in South Carolina During Reconstruction, 1861–1877* (1965). A pioneer study of black life and institutions after emancipation.

# 17 The Trans-Mississippi West

Red Cloud's Delegations, 1868

In January 1855, braving freezing winds and deep snows, forty-year-old John W. North, a New England abolitionist, lawyer, and land speculator, searched for a town site along the Cannon River in the southern Minnesota Territory. He found the perfect spot fourteen miles downstream from Faribault. Six months later the new community, bearing the name Northfield in honor of its founder, consisted of a small store, two mills, several houses, and a ramshackle hotel with a cloth roof.

The following year, town resident E. J. Doolittle, writing to a friend back east, glowingly described the community:

> Northfield commenced new a year ago last April. we have one flowering mill that cost thirteen thousand dollars   1 water saw mill . . . three hotels, one of them cost Eleven thousand dollars   4 stores well filled with goods & our other Building a school house that cost nine hundred   a meeting house building about 40 good nice dwelling houses . . . it is a very healthy place, & is going to be a great Farming country . . . I have just been up West of here about 75 miles   I found it to be a fine country   I set out to drive my team through a prairie to get to a piece of timbered land   was obliged to stop   the grass was so thick & high that I could not get through, it was on an average 9 feet high for some way, you may think it a great story   If you don't believe it come out here & I will show to you wild geese, Ducks, Pigeons & fish in abundance.

Doolittle's enthusiastic letter, which portrayed the West as a land of boundless opportunity, obscured the difficulties of starting afresh. North himself went bankrupt in the depression of 1857, left Northfield, and was appointed surveyor-general of Nevada in 1861. Eventually he ended up in California where he founded the city of Riverside in 1870.

Despite the setbacks that North and others experienced, their journey westward was part of one of the great migrations in modern history, exploring and developing the vast interior midsection of the North American continent. Lured by the image of the West as a land of inexhaustible natural resources, other mid-century migrants—including farmers, land speculators, and railroad developers—had first flooded onto the fertile prairies of Iowa, Minnesota, and eastern Kansas, carving the land into farms and communities. Then, coveting the million square miles of territory within this region that had been wrenched from the Native Americans by force, settlers swarmed into the Great Plains and the semiarid regions beyond them.

The same impulse that inspired settlers such as North and Doolittle to view the West as a symbol of economic opportunity drove some individuals to plunder the land's natural resources ruthlessly. The pell-mell quest for property and profit proved destructive to the Native Americans, to the environment, and often to the settlers themselves. Under the banner of civilization and progress, industrious western entrepreneurs exploited Native American, Chinese, and Mexican laborers alike. They also slaughtered millions of buffalo for their hides, skinned the mountainsides in search of minerals, and tore up the prairie sod to build farms.

Although these same entrepreneurs commonly attributed their economic achievements to American individualism and self-reliance, it is obvious that the West's economic development depended heavily on the federal government for military intervention, land subsidies, and aid to railroad builders. Investments by eastern banks and foreign capitalists were also crucial, as was access to international markets. Yet westerners clung to their ideal of the self-reliant, independent individual who could successfully contend with any obstacle, whether natural, human, or economic. That ideal,

**Indians Hunting Buffalo**
*Even before the arrival of the horse on the plains, Indians used many techniques for hunting buffalo, by far their most important food source. The two hunters shown in this George Catlin illustration are disguised in wolf skins, permitting them to creep close to the unsuspecting herd.*

though often sorely tested, survived to form the bedrock of western Americans' outlook even today.

This chapter will focus on five major questions:

- What were the major forces that drove westward expansion? What were the roles of the army and industrial capitalism in the settlement of the West?

- How was the frontier myth of boundless economic opportunity used to justify westward settlement and the displacement of Native Americans? How did Native Americans respond to the directive to move to reservations?

- What was the political impact of settling the vast interior midsection of the continent? Why were women given more political rights there than in the East?

- How was the Wild West image of cowboys and Indians created? Why has it remained so popular?

- How did the process of westward expansion make some Americans more aware of the need to conserve natural resources by setting them aside in national parks?

## Native Americans and the Trans-Mississippi West

The trans-Mississippi West was far from empty when the newcomers arrived. An estimated 360,000 Indians lived in this region in the mid-nineteenth century. Con-

tact with non-Indians had powerfully shaped these native cultures. Many southwestern pueblo peoples such as the Hopis and Zuñis, who initially had been subjugated by Hispanic conquerors, had gradually achieved accommodation with the relatively small Spanish-speaking population. Maintaining their traditional way of life based on agriculture and sheepherding, the Hopis and Zuñis traded mutton and produce with the Mexican *rancheros* (ranchers) for metal hoes, glass beads, knives, and guns. Pueblo Indians and rancheros alike endured terrifying raids by the Jicarilla Apaches and the Navajos, although by the nineteenth century, even these fierce fighters were trading extensively with non-Indians for manufactured goods, and the Navajos were gradually giving up migratory life in favor of settled agriculture.

Among the Indians dwelling on the Great Plains, the introduction of horses by the Spanish at the end of the sixteenth century, and of firearms by British traders in the eighteenth century, had created the armed and mounted warrior tribes encountered by nineteenth-century westward migrants. Commercial and other contacts with the non-Indian world continued to be important to the Plains Indians as new settlers moved in.

But beyond these generally positive exchanges, contact with advancing non-Indians massively disrupted Indian life everywhere. Disease, which had devastated Native Americans since the earliest European contact, continued its ravages among nineteenth-century western Indians. All tribes suffered severely from measles, diphtheria, and other diseases con-

## CHRONOLOGY

**1849** California gold rush.

**1858** Henry Comstock strikes gold on the Carson River in Nevada.

Gold discovered at Clear Creek, Colorado.

**1862** Homestead Act.

**1864** Nevada admitted to the Union.

Massacre of Cheyennes at Sand Creek, Colorado.

George Perkins Marsh, *Man and Nature.*

**1866** Teton Sioux wipe out Captain William J. Fetterman's troops.

Railroad Enabling Act.

**1867** Joseph McCoy organizes cattle drives to Abilene, Kansas.

New Indian policy of smaller reservations adopted.

Medicine Lodge Treaty.

**1868** Fort Laramie Treaty.

**1869** Board of Indian Commissioners established to reform Indian reservation life.

**1872** Mark Twain, *Roughing It.*

Yellowstone National Park established.

**1873** Panic allows speculators to purchase thousands of acres in the Red River valley of North Dakota cheaply.

Timber Culture Act.

Biggest strike on Nevada's Comstock Lode.

**1874** Invention of barbed wire.

Gold discovered in the Black Hills of South Dakota.

Red River War pits the Kiowas, Comanches, and Cheyennes against the United States Army.

Grasshopper infestations ruin crops in Iowa and Kansas.

**1875** John Wesley Powell, *The Exploration of the Colorado River.*

**1876** Colorado admitted to the Union, gives women the right to vote in school elections.

Massacre of Colonel George Armstrong Custer and his troops at Little Bighorn.

**1877** *Munn* v. *Illinois.*

Desert Land Act.

**1878** Timber and Stone Act.

John Wesley Powell, *Report on the Lands of the Arid Regions of the United States.*

**1879** Massacre of northern Cheyennes at Fort Robinson, Nebraska.

**1881** Helen Hunt Jackson, *A Century of Dishonor.*

**1883** William ("Buffalo Bill") Cody organizes Wild West show.

**1886** Severe drought on the Plains destroys cattle and grain.

*Wabash* v. *Illinois.*

**1887** Dawes Severalty Act.

**1888** *Las Gorras Blancas* (The White Caps) raid ranchers in northern New Mexico.

**1889** Oklahoma Territory opened for settlement.

**1889–1896** Theodore Roosevelt, *The Winning of the West.*

**1890** Ghost Dance movement spreads to the Black Hills.

Massacre of Teton Sioux at Wounded Knee, South Dakota.

Yosemite National Park established.

**1891** Hamlin Garland, *Main-Travelled Roads.*

**1892** John Muir organizes the Sierra Club.

**1893** Frederick Jackson Turner, "The Significance of the Frontier in American History."

**1902** Owen Wister, *The Virginian.*

---

tracted from traders and settlers. By 1840 two major smallpox epidemics had reduced the Pawnees in Nebraska by nearly a third, to about six thousand people. The scattered tribes in California were similarly scourged by smallpox epidemics after the gold rush of 1849. Farther north, in present-day Oregon and Washington, the peaceful Klamath, Chinook, Yurok, and Shasta tribes, who lived in permanent villages and fished extensively, were periodically decimated by disease. So were the native inhabitants of Nevada's starkly beautiful Great Basin.

However, by the mid-nineteenth century, it was the physical disruption of Indian life on the Great Plains, where nearly half the Native Americans of the trans-Mississippi West dwelled, that caught the public eye and weighed on the public conscience. Military defeat and occasional massacres, forced removal to reservations, and devastation by disease, alcohol, and impoverishment demoralized the Plains Indian peoples. Neither the occasional Indian victories over federal troops nor the well-meaning but misguided efforts of reformers to "uplift" the surviving Indians reversed the downward spiral. By the 1890s relocation to distant, often inferior, and generally inadequate lands had become the fate of almost every Indian nation of the Great Plains. But there were also signs that the Native Americans were evolving a strong cultural response to conquest and forced modernization.

### The Plains Indians

The Indians of the Great Plains inhabited two major subregions. The northern Plains, from the Dakotas and Montana southward to Nebraska, were dominated by several large tribes who spoke Siouan languages, as well as by the Flatheads, Blackfeet, Assiniboins, northern Cheyennes, Arapahos, and Crows. Some of these were allies, but others were bitter enemies perpetually at war.

The other major concentration of Plains Indians lived in the central and southern Plains. The so-called Five Civilized Tribes driven there from the Southeast in the 1830s (see Chapter 9) pursued an agricultural life in their new home in the Indian Territory (present-day Oklahoma). In western Kansas the Pawnees maintained the older, more settled tradition characteristic of Plains river valley culture before the introduction of horses,

**Buffalo Skulls at the Michigan Carbon Works, 1895.**
*Once the vast herds of bison had been decimated, resourceful entrepreneurs, such as those pictured here, collected the skulls and sold them for industrial use. In all, nearly two million tons of bones were processed.*

spending at least half the year in villages of earthen lodges along watercourses. Surrounding these were the truly migratory tribes of western Kansas, Colorado, eastern New Mexico, and Texas—the Comanches, Kiowas, southern Arapahos, and Kiowa Apaches.

Considerable diversity flourished among the Plains tribes, and customs varied even within subdivisions of the same tribe. For example, the easternmost branch of the great Sioux Nation, the Dakota Sioux of Minnesota, who inhabited the wooded edge of the prairie, led a semisedentary life based on small-scale agriculture, deer and bison hunting, wild-rice harvesting, and maple-sugar production. In contrast, the Lakota Sioux, who roamed the high Plains to the west, followed the buffalo migrations.

Despite the diversity, however, life for all the Plains Indians revolved around extended family ties and tribal cooperation. Within the various Sioux-speaking tribes, for example, children were raised without physical punishment and were taught to treat each adult clan member with the respect accorded to relatives. Families and clans joined forces to hunt and farm and reached decisions by consensus.

For the various Sioux bands, religious and harvest celebrations provided the cement for village and camp life. Sioux religion was complex and entirely different from the Judeo-Christian tradition. The Lakota Sioux thought of life as a series of circles. Living within the daily cycles of the sun and moon, Lakotas were born into a circle of relatives, which broadened to the band, the tribe, and the Sioux Nation. The Lakotas also believed in a hierarchy of plant and animal spirits that were often more powerful than human beings and whose help could be invoked in the Sun Dance. To gain access to spiritual power and to benefit the weaker members of the community, young men would "sacrifice" themselves by suffering self-torture—for example, by fastening skewers to their chest from which they dragged buffalo skulls; by hanging suspended from poles; or by cutting pieces of their own flesh and placing them at the foot of the Sun Dance pole. Painter George Catlin, who recorded Great Plains Indian life before the Civil War, described such a ceremony: "Several of them, seeing me making sketches, beckoned me to look at their faces, which I watched through all this horrid operation, without being able to detect anything but the pleasantest smiles as they looked me in the eye, while I could hear the knife rip through the flesh, and feel enough of it myself, to start involuntary and uncontrollable tears over my cheeks."

Many Plains tribes—not only the Lakota Sioux but also the Blackfeet, Crows, and Cheyennes—followed the buffalo migration. The huge herds, which at their peak contained an estimated 32 million bison, filled an amazing array of tribal needs. The Indians utilized every part of the animal. They ate its meat and used its hide for tepee covers, shields, and robes. Sinews became bowstrings; bones were fashioned into hoes, knives, and fishhooks. They even used the skull for religious purposes, as in the Sun Dance.

By the 1870s the eastern vogue for wearing buffalo robes on carriages and sleighs, coupled with the use of the animals' hides for industrial belting, encouraged white hunters to slaughter the herds upon which the Plains peoples depended. Ruthless entrepreneurs used the expanding railroad networks to kill the animals and transport their prized pelts swiftly to market. William F. "Buffalo Bill" Cody, a famous scout, Indian fighter, and organizer of Wild West shows, in 1867–1868 killed nearly 4,300 bison in eight months to feed construction crews building the Union Pacific railroad. Army commanders, seeing in the destruction of the buffalo a means of undermining the resistance of buffalo-dependent Indians, encouraged the slaughter. The carnage that resulted was almost inconceivable in its scale.

Between 1872 and 1875, hunters killed 9 million buffalo, taking only the skin and leaving the carcass to rot. By the 1880s the once thundering herds had been reduced to a few thousand animals, a Native American way of life dependent on the buffalo had been ruined, and the path was cleared for American farmers to settle on former Indian hunting grounds.

### The Transformation of Indian Life

In the 1860s the federal government abandoned its previous policy of treating much of the West as a vast Indian reserve and introduced a system of smaller, separate tribal reservations where the Indians were to be concentrated, by force if necessary, and where they were expected to exchange nomadism for a settled agricultural life. Some Native Americans, like the Pueblos of the Southwest, the Crows of Montana, and the Hidatsas of North Dakota, peacefully accepted their fate. Others, among them the Navajos of Arizona and New Mexico, as well as the Dakota Sioux, initially opposed the new policy, but to no avail.

The remaining tribes, however, with a population of more than 100,000, resisted. From the 1860s through the 1890s, these tribes—the western Sioux, Cheyennes, Arapahos, Kiowas, and Comanches on the Great Plains; the Nez Percés and Bannocks in the northern Rockies; and the Apaches in the Southwest—faced the U.S. Army in a series of final battles for the West.

In this protracted and bitter conflict, precipitated by the expansion of western settlement and by Washington's new reservation policy, both sides committed atrocities. Two examples illustrate the tragic pattern. In 1864 the Cheyennes and Arapahos of southern Colorado, weary of fighting the gold miners who had intruded upon their traditional lands in the Pikes Peak region, sued for peace and encamped by Sand Creek. There they were viciously attacked by the Colorado militia. Even after the Native Americans had raised a white surrender flag, the militia clubbed and scalped the terrified Indian women and children. "Kill and scalp all, big and little," shouted Colonel John M. Chivington, the militia leader; "Nits make lice." Two years later the Teton Sioux, defending hunting lands along Wyoming's Powder River that in their view had been fraudulently ceded to the United States by their Crow enemies, fought a ferocious war with the U.S. cavalry. Trying to stop the use of the Bozeman Trail (a trail angling northwestward from Fort Laramie, Wyoming, to the gold fields of Virginia City, Montana), the Teton Sioux killed Captain William J. Fetterman and his seventy-nine soldiers and mutilated their bodies.

These massacres—one, of Indian families; the other, of white soldiers—rekindled public debate over federal Indian policy. Western settlers had long pressed Congress to set up a tighter reservation policy controlled by the army rather than by the civilian "Indian agents" employed by the Bureau of Indian Affairs. Other critics, led by Wisconsin senator James R. Doolittle and supported by an Episcopal bishop from Minnesota, Henry Benjamin Whipple, opposed army control and simply urged a cessation of violence on both sides.

Responding to this debate in 1867, Congress halted work on the Bozeman Trail, sent a peace commission to end the fighting, and set aside two large districts, one north of Nebraska, the other south of Kansas. There, it was hoped, the tribes would settle down and convert to Christianity. Behind the federal government's persuasion lay the threat of force. Any Native Americans who refused to "locate in [the] permanent abodes provided for them," warned Commissioner of Indian Affairs Ely S. Parker (himself a Seneca Indian), "would be subject wholly to the control and supervision of military authorities, [and] ... treated as friendly or hostile as circumstances might justify."

At first the plan appeared to work. Representatives of 68,000 southern Kiowas, Comanches, Cheyennes, and Arapahos signed a treaty at Medicine Lodge Creek, Kansas, and pledged to live on land in present-day Oklahoma recently taken from Choctaw and Chickasaw reservations. The following year, scattered bands of Sioux, representing nearly 54,000 northern Plains Indians, agreed to move to reservations on the so-called Great Sioux Reserve in the western part of what is now South Dakota in return for money and provisions.

But Indian dissatisfaction with the treaties ran deep. As a Sioux chief, Spotted Tail, told the commissioners, "We do not want to live like the white man. ... The Great Spirit gave us hunting grounds, gave us the buffalo, the elk, the deer, and the antelope. Our fathers have taught us to hunt and live on the Plains, and we are contented." Rejecting the new system, many Indians refused to move to the reservations or to remain on them once there.

In August 1868 war parties of defiant Cheyennes, Arapahos, and Sioux raided settlements in Kansas and Colorado, burning homes and killing whites. In retaliation, army troops attacked Indians, even peaceful ones, who refused confinement. That autumn Lieutenant Colonel George Armstrong Custer's raiding party struck a sleeping Cheyenne village, killing more than a hundred warriors, shooting their more than eight hundred horses, and taking fifty-three women and children prisoner. Other hostile Cheyennes and Arapahos were pursued, captured, and returned to the reservations.

Spurred on by Christian reformers, Congress in 1869 established the Board of Indian Commissioners to mold reservation life along lines that the reformers thought desirable. The new board delegated to the major Protestant denominations the responsibility for appointing the agents who would run the reservations. The board's goal was to break, once and for all, the Indians' nomadic tradition and force them to remain on their reservations, where, under the supervision of benevolent agents, they would be Christianized, taught to farm on individual plots of land, and given government assistance.

The new and inexperienced church-appointed Indian agents quickly encountered obstacles in trying to implement the board's policies. The pacifist Quaker agent Lawrie Tatum, a big-boned Iowa farmer, failed to persuade the Comanches and Kiowas to stay on their reservations in Oklahoma rather than raid Texas settlements; two Kiowa chiefs, Satanta and Big Tree, insisted that they could be at peace with the federal government while remaining at war with Texans. Other agents were unable to restrain scheming whites who fraudulently purchased reservation lands from the Indians. By the 1880s the federal government, frustrated with the churches, ignored their nominations for Indian agents and made its own appointments.

Caught in the sticky web of an ambiguous and faltering federal policy, and enraged by continuing non-Indian settlement of the Plains, defiant Native Americans struck back in the 1870s. On the southern Plains, the Kiowas, Comanches, and Cheyennes raided a trading post called Adobe Walls in the Texas panhandle in 1874, setting off the so-called Red River War. In this conflict regular army troops, in a fierce winter campaign, destroyed Indian supplies and slaughtered a hundred Cheyenne fugitives near the Sappa River in Kansas. With the exile of seventy-four "ringleaders" in this uprising to reservations in Florida, Native American independence on the southern Plains came to an end. In the Southwest, in present-day Arizona and New Mexico, the Apaches fought an intermittent guerrilla war until their leader, Geronimo, surrendered in 1886.

## Custer's Last Stand

Of all the acts of Indian resistance against the new reservation policy, none aroused more passion or caused more bloodshed than the conflict between the western Sioux tribes and the U.S. Army in the Dakotas, Montana, and Wyoming. The problems went back to the 1868 Treaty of Fort Laramie, which had ended the Powder River War and had set aside the Great Sioux Reserve "in perpetuity." But not all the Sioux bands had fought in the war or signed the treaty. For example, the highly respected chief Sitting Bull had carefully kept his band of Hunkpapa Sioux away from the fighting. Furthermore, certain western Sioux bands that did sign the treaty, among them the Oglala Sioux and the Brulé Sioux, had no intention of actually moving to the reservation.

Skillfully playing local officials against the federal government, Chief Red Cloud's Oglala band and Chief Spotted Tail's Brulé band in 1873 won the concession of staying on their traditional lands near the Indian agencies along the upper reaches of the White River in Nebraska. To protect their precious hunting grounds, they raided encroaching non-Indian settlements in Nebraska and Wyoming, intimidated federal agents, and harassed

### Indian Chiefs

*Early photographs of the Indian leaders Chief Joseph (left) and Sitting Bull (right) captured both their pride and the frustration they felt after years of alternately negotiating and battling with the U.S. Army. "I don't want a white man over me," Sitting Bull insisted. "I want to have the white man with me, but not to be my chief. I ask this because I want to do right by my people...."*

miners, railroad surveyors, and others who ventured onto their lands.

The Indian agents' inability to prevent the Sioux from entering and leaving the reservations at will, coupled with increasing pressures from would-be settlers and developers, prompted the army to take action. In 1874 General William Tecumseh Sherman sent a force under Colonel George Armstrong Custer into the Black Hills of South Dakota, near the western edge of the Great Sioux Reserve. Lean and mustachioed, with shoulder-length reddish-blond hair, the thirty-four-year-old Custer had been a celebrity since his days as an impetuous young Civil War officer, known for the black velvet uniform, embellished with gold braid, that he wore on the battlefield. Now he had switched to a fringed buckskin uniform set off by a crimson scarf.

Custer's ostensible purpose was to find a location for a new fort and to keep an eye on renegade Indians. But his real objective was to confirm rumors about the existence of gold there. In this he was spurred on by the Northern Pacific Railroad, which wanted to attract settlers to the area. While Custer's troops mapped the lush meadows and chose a site for the fort, two "practical miners" panned the streams for gold. In a report that he telegraphed to the *New York World*, Custer described the region as excellent farm country and casually mentioned finding "gold among the roots of the grass." The gold stampede that predictably followed gave the army a new justification for interceding against the Indians.

Custer had in fact become part of a deliberate army plan to force concessions from the Sioux. In November 1875, when negotiations to buy the Black Hills broke down because the Indians' asking price was deemed too high, President Grant and his generals decided to remove all roadblocks to the entry of miners. Indians still outside the reservations after January 31, 1876, the government announced, would be hunted down by the army and taken in by force.

When the Indians refused to return to the reservations, the army mobilized for an assault. In June 1876, leading 600 troops of the 7th Cavalry, Custer proceeded to the Little Bighorn River area of present-day Montana, a hub of Indian resistance. On the morning of June 25, seriously underestimating the Indian enemy and unwisely dividing his force, Custer, with 209 men, recklessly advanced against a large company of Indians encamped along the Little Bighorn. Soon the outnumbered troops found themselves surrounded and under heavy fire. Custer and his entire force were quickly wiped out. Two days later, another company of cavalry troops came upon the scene of carnage and buried the bodies where they lay. A single creature was found alive: a horse that had belonged to one of Custer's captains.

Americans reeled from this unexpected Indian victory. Metropolitan newspaper columnists groped to assess the meaning of "Custer's last stand." Some went beyond criticism of Custer's leadership to question the

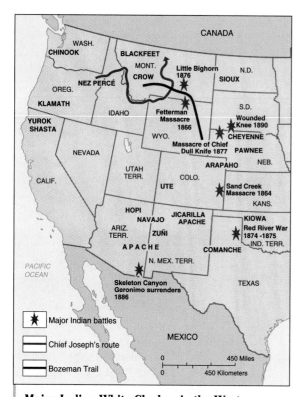

**Major Indian-White Clashes in the West**

*Although they were never recognized as such in the popular press, the battles between Native Americans and the U.S. Army on the Great Plains amounted to a major undeclared war.*

slaughter of the buffalo had wiped out his tribe's major food supply. For a time after his surrender, Sitting Bull suffered the ignominy of appearing as an attraction in Buffalo Bill's Wild West show.

Similar measures were used elsewhere in the West against Chief Joseph and his Nez Percés of Oregon and against the Northern Cheyennes, who had been forcibly transported to Oklahoma after the Battle of Little Bighorn. Some 150 survivors, including men, women, and children, led by Chief Dull Knife, escaped north in September 1878 to join the Sioux. But the army chased them down and imprisoned them in Fort Robinson, Nebraska. When the army denied their request to stay nearer to their traditional northern lands, tribal leaders refused to leave the fort. The post commander then withheld all food, water, and fuel. On a frigid night in January 1879, a desperate Dull Knife and his followers shot the guards and broke for freedom. Members of the startled garrison chased the Indians and gunned down half of them in the snow, including women and children as well as Dull Knife himself. The *Atlanta Constitution* condemned the incident as "a dastardly outrage upon humanity and a lasting disgrace to our boasted civilization." But although sporadic Indian resistance continued until the end of the century, these brutal tactics had sapped the Indians' will to resist.

### *"Saving" the Indians*

A growing number of Americans, most of them well-educated easterners, were outraged not only by bloody atrocities like the Fort Robinson massacre but also by the federal government's flagrant abuse of its Indian treaties. A lecture tour by Chief Standing Bear, whose peaceful Ponca tribe had been driven from land north of the Missouri River guaranteed them by an 1865 treaty, further aroused the reformers' indignation. The Women's National Indian Rights Association, founded in 1883, and other groups took up the cause. Standing Bear's eloquence particularly affected Helen Hunt Jackson, a Massachusetts widow who had recently moved to Colorado. In *A Century of Dishonor* (1881), Jackson sought to rally public opinion against the government's record of broken treaty obligations: "It makes little difference . . . where one opens the record of the history of the Indians; every page and every year has its dark stain."

Genuinely concerned about the Indians' plight, well-intentioned humanitarians concluded that the Indians' interests would best be served by breaking up

wisdom of current federal policy toward the Indians. Others worried that an outraged public would demand retaliation and the outright extermination of the Sioux. Most, however, endorsed the federal government's determination to quash the Native American rebellion. "It is inconsistent with our civilization and with common sense," trumpeted a writer in the *New York Herald*, "to allow the Indian to roam over a country as fine as that around the Black Hills, preventing its development in order that he may shoot game and scalp his neighbors. That can never be. This region must be taken from the Indian."

The Indians' surprising coup at Little Bighorn made the army more cautious. In Montana troops harassed various Sioux bands for more than five years. The army attacked Indian camps in the dead of winter and destroyed all supplies. Even Sitting Bull, a leader at Little Bighorn, who had led his tribe to Canada to escape the army, surrendered in 1881 for lack of provisions: the

the reservations, ending all recognition of the tribes, and propelling individual Native Americans into mainstream society. In short, they proposed to eliminate the "Indian problem" by eliminating the Indians as a culturally distinct entity. Inspired by this vision, they threw their support behind a plan that resulted in the passage in 1887 of the Dawes Severalty Act.

The Dawes Act was designed to reform what well-meaning whites perceived to be the weaknesses of Indian life—the absence of private property and the native peoples' nomadic tradition—by turning Indians into landowners and farmers. The law emphasized severalty, or the treatment of Indians as individuals rather than as members of tribes, and called for the breakup of the reservations. It provided for the distribution of 160 acres of reservation land for farming, or 320 acres for grazing, to each head of an Indian family who accepted the law's provisions. The remaining reservation lands (often the richest) were to be sold to speculators and settlers, and the income thus obtained would go toward purchase of farm tools. To prevent unscrupulous people from gaining control of the lands granted to individual Indians, the government would hold the property of each tribal member in trust for twenty-five years. Under the Dawes Act, those Indians who accepted allotments would in twenty-five years also be declared citizens of the United States with all the rights and responsibilities that attended such status, including the protection of federal laws and the requirement to pay taxes.

Western speculators who coveted reservation lands, as well as military authorities who wanted to break up the reservations for security reasons, had lobbied heavily for the Dawes Act. Nevertheless, the bill's strongest support had come from the "friends of the Indian" like Helen Hunt Jackson. Convinced that citizenship would best protect the Indians, and that full assimilation into society would enable them to get ahead, the reformers systematically tried to "civilize" the Indian peoples and wean them from their traditional culture (see A Place in Time).

The Dawes Act did not specify a timetable for the breakup of the reservations. Because land surveys took time, few allotments were made to the Indians until the 1890s. The act eventually proved to be a boon not to the Indians but to speculators, who commonly evaded the law and obtained the Indians' most arable land. By 1934 the act had slashed the total Indian acreage by 65 percent. Much of what remained in Indian hands was too dry and gravelly for farming.

Although some Native Americans who received land under the Dawes Act prospered enough to expand their holdings and go into large-scale farming or ranching, countless others languished. Hunting restrictions on the former reservation lands prevented many Indians from supplementing their limited farm yields. At the same time, various forms of government support steadily increased Indians' dependence on federal aid. Alcoholism, a continuing problem, and one exacerbated by the prevalence of whiskey as a trade item (and by the boredom that resulted from the disruption of hunting and other traditional pursuits), became more prevalent as Native Americans strove to adapt to the constraints of reservation life.

## The Ghost Dance and the End of Indian Resistance on the Great Plains

The plight of the Sioux became desperate in the late 1880s as the federal government reduced their meat rations and saddled them with more and more restrictions, and as disease killed a third of their cattle. The Sioux, who still numbered almost 25,000, turned to Wovoka, a new prophet popular among the Great Basin Indians in Nevada. Wovoka promised to restore the Sioux to their original dominance on the Plains if they performed the Ghost Dance.

Wearing sacred Ghost Shirts—cotton or leather vestments decorated to ward off evil—the dancers moved in a circle, accelerating until they reached a trancelike state and experienced visions of the future. Many believed that the Ghost Shirts would protect them from harm. Rituals such as the Ghost Dance enabled Indians to reaffirm their own culture.

In the fall of 1890, as the Ghost Dance movement spread among the Sioux in the Dakota Territory, Indian officials and military authorities grew alarmed. The local reservation agent, Major James McLaughlin, decided that Chief Sitting Bull, whose cabin on the reservation had become a rallying point for the Ghost Dance movement, must be arrested. On a freezing, drizzly December morning, McLaughlin dispatched a company of forty-two Indian policemen from the agency to take Sitting Bull into custody. As two policemen pulled the chief from his cabin, his bodyguard Catch-the-Bear shot one of them. As the policeman fell, he in turn shot Sitting Bull at point-blank range. Bloody hand-to-hand fighting immediately broke out. As bullets whizzed by, Sitting Bull's horse began to perform the tricks remembered from its days in the Wild West show. Some

## Carlisle, Pennsylvania

*I*n the fall of 1879, Ota Kte, or Plenty Kill—later named Luther Standing Bear—a young Lakota Sioux boy from the Pine Ridge reservation in South Dakota, set out by steamer on the Missouri River to attend a new boarding school for Indians in Carlisle, Pennsylvania. Standing Bear was one of sixty boys and twenty-five girls who had been recruited on the Sioux reservations for the school. For these children, the trip east proved traumatic. After leaving the steamboat, Standing Bear and the other young Lakotas climbed into what appeared to be little houses lined up on long pieces of iron. They had never seen a train, and when it moved, they were terrified.

Luther Standing Bear and his classmates had been gathered by Captain Richard Henry Pratt, a cavalry officer who shared the notion of other late-nineteenth-century eastern reformers that the only humane way to civilize the Indian was to provide Native American children with formal schooling in English. His optimism for the project had been bolstered during the previous year when he had enrolled seventeen Indians, freed captives from earlier fighting, in the Hampton Normal and Industrial Institute in Hampton, Virginia.

The Hampton Institute had opened a decade earlier to educate freed slaves. Supported financially by the American Missionary Association and led by the charismatic Samuel Chapman Armstrong, the Hampton Institute combined cultural enlightenment with moral and manual training. Students learned blacksmithing, carpentry, and other practical skills thought necessary for living an independent life.

Modeling his school after the Hampton Institute, Pratt opened his new institution at a former military facility in the fall of 1879. Pratt, who would become the most important spokesman for Indian education in the next twenty-five years, liked Indians. He also believed that Native American children, when separated from their tribe and parents, could be uplifted, "civilized," and fully assimilated into American life. What held the Indians back, he believed, was their inferior culture, customs, and languages. Pratt's motto therefore became "Kill the Indian in him and save the man."

Part of a campaign by reformers to bring formal schooling to Native Americans, Carlisle thus became the first government-supported off-reservation Indian boarding school to be established. By 1900 it enrolled 1,218 students from seventy-six tribes. But that same year the federal government also ran eighty-one on-reservation boarding schools with an average yearly attendance of over 8,000.

Although some students were forcibly sent to Carlisle by the Bureau of Indian Affairs, others were urged by their elders to attend. When Apache chief Geronimo was finally captured in 1886, he ordered his nephew, Asa Daklugie, to attend Carlisle, explaining, as Daklugie remembered, that "without this training in the ways of White Eyes, our people could never compete with them. So it was necessary that those destined for leadership prepare themselves to cope with the enemy."

Life at Carlisle was not easy. Designed to destroy every vestige of "savage" Indian life, the schools forced the children to cut their hair, a practice that traditional Native American cultures associated with mourning. "I remember

*Luther Standing Bear and family*

being dragged out," wrote one young Indian girl, "though I resisted by kicking and scratching wildly. In spite of myself, I was carried downstairs and tied fast in a chair. I cried aloud, shaking my head all the while, until I felt the cold blades of the scissors against my neck, and heard them gnaw off one of my thick braids. Then I lost my spirit."

Humiliated by this shearing, the children were then given an English name, taught Victorian manners, and forbidden to speak their native tongue. In a symbolic move that signaled not only the transformation of their outward appearance but also the destruction of their old sense of self, their leggings, moccasins, and other clothes were bundled up and sent back to the reservation. The students were then dressed in prim uniforms and the school proudly displayed before and after pictures to document the transformation.

The ideal, as one Indian agent put it, was to overcome the "barbarism" and "vices" of their parents and turn the children into "refined, cultured, educated beings [who] will assume the title of an American citizen, with all the rights, privileges, and aspirations of that favored individual."

The school day was closely regimented. Bells rang for meals and morning classes, which were devoted to instruction in English and other subjects. Afternoons were spent learning vocations such as carpentry, tailoring, tinsmithing, printing, sewing, and agriculture. Harsh, military-style discipline, often combining humiliation and physical punishment, was used to teach the children obedience, self-control, western conceptions of time, and the Protestant work ethic. Although students worked for a few months each year for selected white families and firms, sup-

posedly to gain experience with white life, the system often simply supplied cheap menial labor for white households.

Although Pratt and the other reformers insisted that their goal was to assimilate the Indians into American life, in practice the vocational training in menial occupations created a level of economic self-sufficiency on the reservations that left the Indians citizens yet simultaneously dependent wards, under the guardianship of the federal government.

In their assessment of the impact of the Indian boarding schools, scholars have noted the destructive impact that the education often had upon the young children. They also point out, however, that many of these same students went on to use their mastery of English to document and preserve their changing traditional native cultures.

Luther Standing Bear's own career shows how he was able to use his education to further the cause of Native Americans. After graduating from Carlisle, he was employed briefly at Wanamaker's department store in Philadelphia. Then, in the 1890s, he returned to the Pine Ridge reservation where he taught school, served as agency clerk, opened a small store, and owned a ranch. Four years later, having

*Richard Henry Pratt*

worked for Buffalo Bill's Wild West show in Europe, Standing Bear returned to be made chief of his tribe. In his published works, *My People the Sioux* (1928), *My Indian Boyhood* (1931), *Land of the Spotted Eagle* (1933), and *Stories of the Sioux* (1934), he had a significant impact on reshaping federal Indian policy in the 1930s. Critical of the Indian school movement, he wrote, "Can a real, true, genuinely superior social order work such havoc [on the native peoples]? Did not the Native American possess human qualities of worth had the Caucasian but been able to discern and accept them; and did not an overweening sense of superiority bring about this blindness?"

*Pratt with students and teachers at the Carlisle School*

**Wounded Knee**
*Piled up like cordwood, the frozen bodies of the Sioux slaughtered at Wounded Knee were a grim reminder that the U.S. Army would brook no opposition to its control of Indian reservation life.*

**General Colby and Child**
*In keeping with his missionary vision, Brigadier General L. W. Colby, commander of the Nebraska National Guard, proudly holds his adopted Indian daughter whose parents had been killed in the bloody massacre.*

observers were terrified, convinced that the spirit of the dead chief had entered his horse.

Sitting Bull's violent death preceded by only two weeks one of the bloodiest episodes of Indian-white strife on the Plains. On December 29, 1890, the 7th Cavalry was rounding up 340 starving and freezing Sioux at Wounded Knee, South Dakota, when an excited Indian fired a gun hidden under a blanket. The soldiers retali-

ated with Hotchkiss cannons. Within minutes 300 Indians, including 7 infants, were slaughtered. Three days later, a baby who had miraculously survived was found wrapped in a blanket under the snow. She wore a buckskin cap on which a beadwork American flag had been embroidered. Brigadier General L. W. Colby, who adopted the baby, named her Marguerite, but the Indians called her Lost Bird.

As the frozen corpses at Wounded Knee were dumped into mass graves, a generation of Indian-white conflict on the Great Plains shuddered to a close. Lost Bird, with her poignantly patriotic beadwork cap, highlights the irony of the Plains Indians' response to the tragic dilemma confronting them. Many did try, with varying success, to adapt to alien non-Indian ways. But few succeeded fully, and many others were understandably devastated at being forced to abandon age-old religious beliefs and a way of life rooted in hunting, cooperative living, and nomadism. Driven onto reservations, the Plains Indians were reduced to a status of almost complete dependency. By 1900 the Plains Indian population had shrunk from nearly a quarter of a million to just over a hundred thousand. Nevertheless, after 1900 the population began slowly to rise. Against overwhelming odds, the pride, group memory, and cultural identity of the Plains Indians survived all efforts to eradicate them.

Unlike the nomadic western Sioux, for whom the encounter with onrushing white civilization was most traumatic, the more settled Navajos of the Southwest

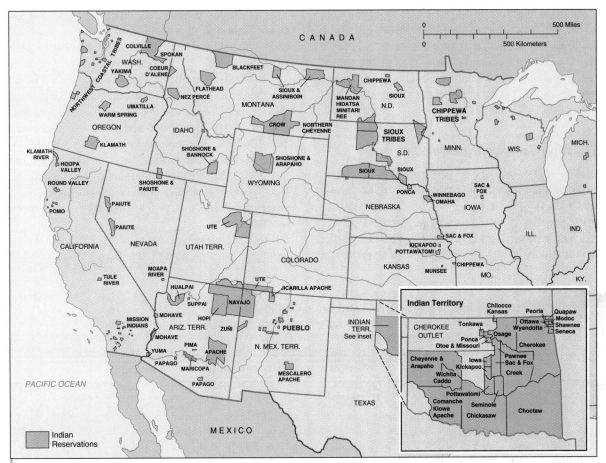

**Western Indian Reservations, 1890**

*Native-American reservations were almost invariably located on poor-quality lands. Consequently, when the Dawes Severalty Act broke up the reservations into 160-acre farming tracts, many of the semiarid divisions would not support cultivation.*

adjusted more successfully to the reservation system, preserving traditional ways while incorporating elements of the new order in a complex process of cultural adaptation. By 1900 the Navajos had tripled their reservation land, dramatically increased their numbers and their herds, and carved out for themselves a distinct place in Arizona and New Mexico.

These extraordinary changes were forced on the Indian population by the advance of non-Indian settlement. In the name of civilization and progress, non-Indians in the generation after the Civil War pursued a course that involved a strong mixture of sincere (if misguided) benevolence, coercion wrapped in an aura of legality, and outbursts of naked violence. Many white Americans felt toward the Indians only contempt, hatred, and greed for their land. Others, however, like General Colby in his gesture of adopting the infant sur-

vivor, viewed themselves as divinely chosen instruments for uplifting and Christianizing the Indians. Both groups, however, were equally blind to any inherent value in Native American life and traditions. The humanitarians, no less than the most brutal advocates of extermination, played their part in shattering a proud people and an ancient culture. The Indians' fate would weigh on the American conscience for generations.

## Settling the West

The successive defeats of the Native Americans opened up for settlement a vast territory that reached from the prairie Plains to the Sierra Nevada and the Cascade Mountains. In the 1840s, when nearly a quarter-million Americans had trudged overland to Oregon and California, they had typically endured a six- to eight-month trip in ox-drawn wagons. After 1870 railroad expansion made the trip to the vast interior of the nation not only faster but considerably easier. In the next three decades, more land was parceled out into farms than in the previous 250 years of American history combined, and agricultural production doubled.

## The First Transcontinental Railroad

On May 10, 1869, Americans celebrated the completion of the first railroad spanning North America. As the two sets of tracks—the Union Pacific's, stretching westward from Omaha, Nebraska, and the Central Pacific's, reaching eastward from Sacramento, California—met at Promontory Point, Utah, beaming officials drove in a

final ceremonial golden spike. With the coming of the transcontinental, Americans could make in a week's time the same coast-to-coast journey that earlier took several *months.*

Building the railroad took backbreaking work. Searching for inexpensive labor, the railroads turned to immigrants. The Central Pacific employed numerous Chinese to chip and blast railbed out of solid rock in the Sierra Nevada. The railroad preferred the Chinese laborers because they worked hard for low wages, did not drink, and furnished their own food and tents. Nearly twelve thousand Chinese graded the roadbed while Irish, Mexican-American, and black workers put down the track.

The Pacific Railroad Act of July 1, 1862, had authorized the construction of the transcontinental (see

### Transcontinental Railroads and Federal Land Grants, 1850–1900

*Despite the laissez-faire ideology that argued against government interference in business, Congress heavily subsidized American railroads and gave them millions of acres of land. As illustrated in the box, belts of land were reserved on either side of a railroad's right of way. Until the railroad claimed the exact one-mile-square sections it chose to possess, all such sections within the belt remained closed to settlement.*

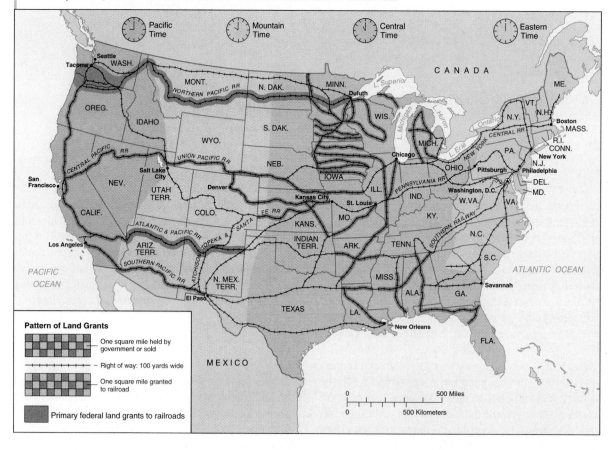

Chapter 15). The grants of land and other subsidies given to the railroads for each mile of track laid made them the single largest landholders in the West. Ultimately nine major routes ran from the South or Midwest to the West.

### Settlers and the Railroad

By 1872, under the Pacific Railroad Act, Congress had awarded the railroads 170 million acres, worth at the time over half a billion dollars. By 1893 the states of Minnesota and Washington had also deeded to railroad companies a quarter of their state lands; Wisconsin, Iowa, Kansas, North Dakota, and Montana had turned over to them a fifth of their acreage. As mighty landowners, the railroads had a unique opportunity to shape settlement in the region—and to reap enormous profits.

The railroads used several different ploys to attract inhabitants. They created land bureaus and sent agents to the East Coast and Europe to recruit settlers. While the agents glorified the West as a new Garden of Eden, the land bureaus offered long-term loans and free transportation to prospective buyers. Acknowledging that life on the Great Plains could be lonely, the promoters advised young men to bring their own wives (because "maidens are scarce") and to emigrate as entire families and with friends.

In addition to the millions of Americans who migrated from nearby states, the railroads between 1870 and 1900 helped bring nearly 2.2 million foreign-born settlers to the trans-Mississippi West. Some agents recruited whole villages of Germans and eastern Europeans to relocate to the North Dakota plains. Irish laborers, hired to lay track, could be found in every town along the rail lines. By 1905 the Santa Fe Railroad alone had transported sixty thousand Russian Mennonites to the fertile Kansas plains.

The railroads influenced agriculture as well. To ensure quick repayment of the money owed to them, the railroads urged new immigrants to specialize in cash crops—wheat on the northern Plains, corn in Iowa and

**Railroads and Horse Trains**
*Railroad advertisements, like the one shown (right), in the Czech language, lured immigrants by promising a lush landscape where entire farming communities could be established in only six years. The reality, as the Montana horse train (below) suggests, was a much slower process.*

Kansas, cotton and tobacco in Texas. Although these crops initially brought in high revenues, many farmers grew dependent on income from a single crop and ultimately became vulnerable to fluctuating market forces.

### Homesteaders on the Great Plains

Liberalized land laws were another powerful magnet pulling settlers westward. The Homestead Act, passed in 1862, reflected the Republican party's belief that free land would enable the poor to achieve economic independence. It offered 160 acres of land to any individual who would pay a $10 registration fee, live on the land for five years, and cultivate and improve it. Because getting to the Great Plains was costly, most settlers migrated from nearby states.

The Homestead Act also proved quite attractive to immigrants from the British Isles as well as from Scandinavia and other regions of Europe where good-quality land was prohibitively expensive. Urged on by land promoters, waves of English, Irish, Germans, Swedes, Danes, Norwegians, and Czechs immigrated to the United States in the 1870s and 1880s and formed their own communities.

**Corn Palace, Sioux City, South Dakota, 1890**
*Urban promoters went to great lengths to publicize the productivity of their region's farm economy.*

Although nearly 400,000 families claimed land under the provisions of the Homestead Act between 1860 and 1900, the law did not function as Congress had envisioned. Advance agents representing unscrupulous speculators filed false claims for the choicest locations, and railroads and state governments acquired huge landholdings. Despite the good intentions of the Homestead Act's authors, only one acre in every nine went to the pioneers for whom it was intended.

A second problem resulted from the 160-acre limit specified by the Homestead Act. On the rich soils of Iowa or in the fertile lands in California, Oregon, and Washington, a 160-acre farm was ample, but in the drier areas west of the hundredth meridian, a farmer needed more land. To rectify this problem, Congress in 1873 passed the Timber Culture Act, which gave homesteaders an additional 160 acres if they planted trees on 40 acres. For states with little rainfall, Congress enacted the Desert Land Act in 1877, which made available 640 acres at $1.25 an acre on condition that the owner irrigate part of it within three years. However, this act, along with the Timber and Stone Act of 1878, which permitted the purchase of up to 160 acres of forest land for $2.50 an acre, was abused by grasping speculators, lumber-company representatives, and cattle ranchers seeking to expand their holdings. But even though families did not receive as much land as Congress had intended, federal laws kept alive the dream of the West as a place for new beginnings.

### New Farms, New Markets

Railroad expansion and the liberalization of the land laws coincided with advances in farm mechanization and the development of improved strains of wheat and corn. Progress on these fronts enabled farmers to boost production dramatically. Efficient steel plows; spring-tooth harrows that broke up the dense prairie soil more effectively than earlier models; specially designed wheat planters; and improved grain binders, threshers, and windmills all allowed the typical Great Plains farmer of the late nineteenth century to grow and harvest ten times more wheat than would have been possible a few decades earlier. Another crucial invention was barbed wire, patented in 1874, which permitted farmers to keep roving livestock off their land—and which touched off violent clashes between farmers and the cattle ranchers, who demanded the right to let their herds roam freely until the roundup. Generally the farmers won.

Fueling the leap in wheat production was a spiraling demand for the commodity, attributable to a 400 percent increase in the eastern urban population between 1870 and 1910. This demand was further stimulated by the development of milling techniques that improved the taste and texture of wheat flour. In 1876 Minnesota millers used steel rollers to crack the kernel, allowing the husk to be blown off and the bran to be separated. This technique produced a silky, all-white flour that won first prize at the Philadelphia World's Fair that year.

Farming seemed to be entering a period of unparalleled prosperity, and enthusiastic promoters nourished the idea that anyone could make an easy living in the West. But few fully understood the costs and perils of pursuing agriculture as a livelihood. Land was expensive, even at the reduced prices offered by the federal government and the railroads. The cost of the horses, machinery, and seed needed to start up a farm could exceed twelve hundred dollars, far more than the annual earnings of the average industrial worker. Faced with substantial mortgage payments, many farmers had to specialize in a crop such as wheat or corn that would fetch high prices. This specialization, in turn, made them dependent on the railroads for shipping and put them at the mercy of the international grain market's shifting prices.

Far from being an independent producer, the western grain grower was a player in a complex world market economy. Railroad and steamship transport allowed the American farmer to compete in the international market. High demand could bring prosperity, but when world overproduction forced grain prices down, the heavily indebted grower faced ruin. Confronted with these realities, many Plains farmers quickly abandoned the illusion of frontier independence and easy wealth.

Exacerbating homesteaders' difficulties on the western Great Plains, normal rainfall was less than twenty inches a year. Farmers compensated through "dry farming"—plowing deeply to stimulate the capillary action of the soils and harrowing lightly to raise a covering of dirt that would retain precious moisture after a rainfall. They also built windmills and diverted creeks for irrigation. But the onset of unusually dry years in the 1870s, together with grasshopper infestations and the major economic depression that struck the United States between 1873 and 1878 (see Chapter 16), made the plight of some midwesterners desperate.

**The Washburn Flouring Mills**
*The mills, pictured here in the 1890s, were known for their efficient operation and prize-winning baking products.*

## Building a Society and Achieving Statehood

Whether they hailed from the East, the nearby Midwest, or foreign lands, homesteaders faced difficult psychological adjustments to frontier life. Working from dawn to dusk in an unfamiliar place and facing fierce storms and natural disasters, many settlers became discouraged and returned east. But those who persisted eventually established ties to the land and built successful communities.

The first years of settlement were the most difficult. Toiling to build a house, plow the fields, plant the first crop, and drill a well, the pioneers put in an average of sixty-eight hours of tedious, backbreaking work a week, in isolated surroundings. Howard Ruede, a Pennsylvania printer who migrated to Kansas to farm, wrote home in 1877 complaining about the mosquitoes and bedbugs infesting his sod house. He and countless others coping with the severe Plains conditions saw their shining vision of Edenic farm life quickly dim. For blacks who emigrated from the South to Kansas and other parts of the Plains after the Civil War, prejudice and racism compounded the psychological burdens of adjusting to a different life.

Many middle-class women settlers, swept up in the romantic conventions of the day, found adaptation to Plains frontier life especially difficult. At least initially, some were enchanted by the haunting landscape, and in letters they described the undulating open plains as arrestingly beautiful. But far more were struck by the "horrible tribes of Mosquitoes"; the violent weather—drenching summer thunderstorms with hailstones as "big as hen's eggs" and blinding winter blizzards; and the crude sod huts that served as their early homes because of the scarcity of timber. One woman burst into tears upon first seeing her new sod house. The young bride angrily informed her husband that her father had built a better house for his hogs.

The high transiency rate on the frontier in these years reflected the frequent failures in adapting to the new environment. Nearly 66 percent of those who settled in Wapello County, Iowa, in 1850 had left within ten years. However, in places like Minnesota or the Pacific Northwest that were populated largely by Germans, Norwegians, and other immigrants with a tradition of family prosperity tied to continuous landownership, the persistence rate (or percentage of people staying for a decade or more) could be considerably higher.

Many who weathered the lean early years eventually came to identify closely with the land. Within a decade, the typical Plains family that had "stuck it out" had moved into a new wood-frame house and had fixed up the front parlor. The women of these surviving households worked hard and learned to accept their lot. "Just done the chores," wrote one such woman to a friend. "I went fence mending and getting out cattle . . . and came in after sundown. I fed my White Leghorns, and then sat on the step to read over your letter. I forgot my wet feet and shoes full of gravel and giggled joyously." Despite their arduous existence, such settlers often spoke positively about life on the Great Plains. But they missed their old friends.

Some remote farm settlements blossomed into thriving communities. Churches and Sunday schools, among the first institutions to appear, became humming centers of social activity as well as of worship. Farmers gathered

## The Settlement of the Trans-Mississippi West, 1860–1890

*The West was not settled by a movement of peoples gradually creeping westward from the East. Rather, settlers first occupied California and the Midwest and then filled up the nation's vast interior.*

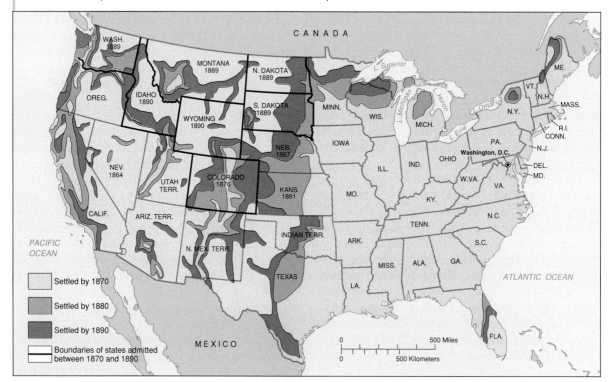

for barn raisings and group threshings, and families pooled their energies in quilting and husking bees. Neighbors readily lent a hand to the farmer whose barn had burned or whose wife or child was sick. Cooperation was a practical necessity and a form of insurance in a rugged environment where everyone was vulnerable to instant misfortune or even disaster.

As settlements grew into small towns, their inhabitants labored to reverse easterners' images of the Midwest as unrefined and backward. They eagerly set up lyceums and libraries to uplift and enlighten local residents. Masonic lodges and social clubs soon followed. Larger communities established fashionable hotels, the symbol of urban sophistication and culture, and brought in entertainers to perform at their new "opera houses."

Like the farmers in the surrounding countryside, townspeople closed ranks when misfortune struck. At the first outbreak of fire or violence, the whole town mobilized. When the notorious ex-Confederate raider and outlaw Jesse James rode into Northfield, Minnesota, and held up the town bank in 1876, local merchants grabbed their shotguns and drove him off, killing two of his gang.

The new settlers on the frontier tended to be conservative. They patterned their churches, schools, courts, and government structures after familiar institutions in the communities from which they had come. Achieving statehood required that the residents of a territory petition Congress to pass an enabling act establishing the territory's boundaries and authorizing an election to select delegates for a state constitutional convention. Once the state constitution had been drawn up and ratified by popular vote, the territory applied to Congress for admission as a state.

Under these procedures Kansas entered the Union in 1861, followed by Nevada in 1864 and Nebraska in 1867. Colorado joined in 1876. Not until 1889 did North Dakota, South Dakota, Montana, and Washington gain statehood. Wyoming and Idaho came into the Union the following year. Utah, long prevented from joining because of the Mormon practice of polygamy, finally declared plural marriages illegal and entered in 1896. With Oklahoma's admission in 1907 and Arizona's and New Mexico's in 1912, the process of creating permanent political institutions in the trans-Mississippi West was complete.

Although generally conservative, the new state governments did support woman suffrage. As territories became states, pioneer women, encouraged by women's rights activists like Susan B. Anthony and Elizabeth Cady Stanton, battled for the vote. Seven western states held referenda on this issue between 1870 and 1910. Success came first in the Wyoming Territory, where the tiny legislature enfranchised women in 1869 in hopes of improving the territory's rowdy reputation. The Utah Territory followed in 1870 and reaffirmed its support for woman suffrage when it became a state. Nebraska in 1867, and Colorado in 1876, permitted women to vote in school elections. Although these successes were significant, by 1910 only four states—Idaho, Wyoming, Utah, and Colorado—had granted women full voting rights. The very newness of their place in the Union may have sensitized legislators in these states to women's important contributions to settlement and made them open to experimentation; but by and large, familiar traditions persisted.

## The Southwestern Frontier

Until 1848, when the Treaty of Guadalupe Hildalgo ended the Mexican War and ceded to the United States an immense territory—part of which became California, Arizona, and New Mexico—Mexicans had controlled wide-open expanses of the Southwest. They had built their own churches, maintained large ranching operations, and as we have seen, traded with the Indians. Although the peace treaty pledged the United States to protect the liberty and property of Mexicans who remained on American soil, in the next three decades, aggressive American ranchers and settlers took over the territorial governments and forced the Spanish-speaking population off much of the land. Mexicans who stayed behind adapted to the new Anglo society with varying degrees of success.

In Texas, where the struggle for independence from Mexico and the Mexican War had left a legacy of bitterness and misunderstanding, Anglos in the 1840s and 1850s frequently harassed local Mexican-Americans and confiscated their lands. Small numbers of Mexican bandits retaliated by raiding American communities, stealing from the rich and giving to the poor. Tensions peaked in 1859, when Juan Cortina, a local Mexican rancher, attacked the Anglo border community of Brownsville, Texas, and freed all the prisoners in jail. Pursued by the U.S. Army, Cortina battled the Americans for years, slipping back and forth across the border until the Mexican government, fearing a U.S. invasion, imprisoned him in 1875.

**Santa Fe Plaza, New Mexico, in the 1880s,** by Francis X. Grosshenney
*After the railroad went through in 1878, Santa Fe became a popular tourist attraction known for its historic adobe buildings. Although the town retained a large Spanish-speaking population with their own newspaper, by the 1880s American and German immigrants monopolized most positions in business, government, the professions, and the skilled trades.*

Similar violence erupted in California in the 1850s and 1860s after a cycle of flood and drought, together with a slumping cattle industry, ruined many of the large southern California ranches owned by the *californios,* the Spanish-speaking descendants of the original Spanish settlers. The collapse of the ranch economy forced many of these Mexican-Americans to retreat into socially segregated urban neighborhoods, called *barrios.* In Santa Barbara, California, Spanish-surnamed citizens made up nearly half the town's 2,640 residents in 1870. Ten years later, however, overwhelmed by an influx of Anglos, they comprised barely a quarter of the population. Maintaining a tenacious hold on their traditions, Spanish-speaking people in Santa Barbara and other towns survived by working as low-paid day laborers.

In California, in particular, the pattern of racial discrimination, manipulation, and exclusion was similar for Mexicans, Native Americans, and Chinese. As the number of Anglo newcomers increased, they quickly labeled minority racial, cultural, and language differences as marks of inferiority. Laws were passed and legal decisions were handed down that made ownership of property difficult for non-Anglos. Relegated to a migratory labor force, they were tagged as shiftless and irresponsible. Yet their labor made possible increased prosperity for the farmers, railroads, and households that hired them.

The cultural adaptation of Spanish-speaking Americans to Anglo society unfolded more smoothly in Arizona and New Mexico, where the initial Spanish settlement was sparse and a small class of wealthy Mexican landowners had long dominated a poor illiterate peasantry. Moreover, beginning in the 1820s, well-to-do Mexicans in Tucson, Arizona, had educated their children in the United States and had formed trading partnerships and business alliances with Americans. Perhaps the most successful was Estevan Ochoa, who began a long-distance freighting business in 1859 with a U.S. partner and then expanded it into a lucrative merchandising, mining, and sheep-raising operation.

The success of hard-working businessmen such as Ochoa, who became mayor of Tucson, helped moderate American settlers' antagonistic attitudes toward the indigenous Mexican-American population. So, too, did the work of popular writers like Bret Harte and Helen Hunt Jackson. By sentimentalizing the old Spanish-Mexican ways in their writings, these authors increased public sympathy for Spanish-speaking Americans. Jackson's 1884 romance *Ramona,* a tale of doomed love set on a California Spanish-Mexican ranch overwhelmed by the onrushing tide of Anglo civilization, was enormously popular.

Not all was harmony, however. In Arizona and New Mexico, Mexican-American and Anglo ranchers became embroiled in fiery land disputes in the 1880s. Organizing themselves as *Las Gorras Blancas* (The White Caps) in 1888, Mexican-American ranchers tore up railroad tracks and intimidated and attacked both Anglo newcomers and those Hispanics who had fenced acreage in northern New Mexico previously considered public grazing land. But this vigilante action gained them little, as Anglo-dominated corporate ranching steadily impinged on their operations. Relations changed in the urban centers as well, as Mexican-American businessmen increasingly restricted their business dealings to their own people, and the Spanish-speaking population as a whole became more impoverished. Even in Tucson, where the Mexican-American elite enjoyed considerable economic and political success, 80 percent of the Mexican-Americans in the work force were laborers in 1880, taking jobs as butchers, barbers, cowboys, and railroad workers.

As increasing numbers of Mexican-American males lost title to their land and were forced to search for seasonal migrant work, Mexican-American women bore the responsibility of holding families and communities together. Households were headed by women when their husbands were away, and women fostered group identification through their emphasis on traditional customs, kinship, and allegiance to the Catholic Church. They served as *madrinas,* or godmothers, for others' children; tended garden plots; and traded food, soap, and produce with other women. This economy, invisible to those outside the village, stabilized the community in times of drought or persecution by Anglos.

Violence and discrimination against Spanish-speaking citizens of the Southwest escalated in the 1890s, a time of rising racism in the United States. Riots against Mexican-Americans broke out in the Texas communities of Beeville and Laredo in 1894 and 1899. Expressions of anti-Catholicism, as well as verbal attacks on the Mexican-Americans as violent and lazy, increased among hostile Anglos. For Spanish-speaking citizens, the battle for fair treatment and cultural respect would continue into the twentieth century.

# Exploiting the West

For a generation of Americans who watched enviously as astounding fortunes were being made in railroading, steel, and other businesses (see Chapter 18), the spectacular gold-mining, cattle-raising, and farming enterprises that lit up the western landscape from the 1850s to the 1880s appeared to offer great opportunities for the individual to strike it rich. Publicized in banner headlines across the land, these "bonanzas" promised unheard of wealth and seemed to confirm the myth of the frontier as a place of boundless opportunity. In reality, however, the bonanzas set in motion a boom-and-bust economy in which a few people became fabulously wealthy but most barely survived or lost their shirts. Of all the groups that surged onto the Great Plains and be-

yond in the late nineteenth century, none had to revise their expectations more radically than the speculators and adventurers thirsting for quick fortunes.

## The Mining Frontier

Beginning with the California gold rush in 1849, a series of mining booms over the next three decades swept from the Southwest northward into Canada. The sensational discoveries in California's Sierra Nevada that produced more than $81 million worth of gold bullion in 1852 were followed by gold strikes on the Fraser River in British Columbia in 1857. The following year, Henry Comstock stumbled upon the rich Comstock Lode along Nevada's Carson River. Months later, feverishly pursuing rumors of new strikes, prospectors swarmed into the Rocky Mountains near present-day Denver and uncovered deep veins of gold and silver along a little stream called Clear Creek. Over the next two decades, gold was discovered in Idaho, Montana, Wyoming, South Dakota, and, in 1896, in the Alaskan Klondike. Although the popular press clearly exaggerated reports of miners scooping up gold by the panful, by 1900 more than a billion dollars worth of gold had been mined just in California.

The early discoveries of "placer" gold, panned from riverbeds and streams, reinforced the myth of the mining country as "a poor man's paradise." By 1860, when census takers asked Californians to report their occupations, more than 82,000 out of a population of 380,000 described themselves as miners. Of these, 35,000 were Chinese, many of whom were forced by prejudice to work claims that others had abandoned.

Although a few prospectors became fabulously wealthy, the experience of Henry Comstock, who sold out one claim for eleven thousand dollars and another for two mules, was more typical. Most of the West's mining wealth fell into the hands of investment bankers and corporations. Because the larger gold and silver deposits lay buried in veins of quartz deep within the earth, extracting them required huge investments in expensive equipment. No sooner had the major discoveries been made, therefore, than large mining companies, backed by eastern or British capital, took them over.

But if the Comstock Lode and the other ore discoveries failed to bring great riches to the average miner, they did dramatically transform normal patterns of behavior. During the heyday of the Comstock Lode in the 1860s and 1870s, Virginia City, Nevada, erupted in an

**Miners of Placerville**
*Despite its get-rich-quick image, mining for gold was hard, tedious work, as shown above in this 1855 painting by A.D.O. Browere. From the start, cheap Chinese labor (right) was often used for the most backbreaking labor.*

orgy of speculation and building. Started as a shanty-town in 1859, it swelled by 1873 into a thriving metropolis of twenty thousand people, complete with elaborate mansions, a six-story hotel, an opera house, 131 saloons, 4 banks, and uncounted brothels. Males outnumbered females by three to one. Money quickly earned was even more rapidly lost.

The boom-and-bust cycle evident in Virginia City was repeated in towns across the west between 1870 and 1900. Mark Twain captured the thrill of the mining "stampedes" in his book *Roughing It* (1872). "Every few days," wrote Twain, "news would come of the discovery of a brand-new mining region: immediately the papers would teem with accounts of its richness, and away the surplus population would scamper to take possession. By the time I was fairly inoculated with the disease, 'Esmeralda' had just had a run and 'Humboldt' was beginning to shriek for attention. 'Humboldt! Humboldt!' was the new cry, and straightway Humboldt, the newest of the new, the richest of the rich, the most marvelous of the marvelous discoveries in silver-land, was occupying two columns of the public prints to 'Esmeralda's' one."

Word of new ore deposits lured to the mining towns transient populations salivating to get rich. Min-

ers typically earned about $2,000 a year at a time when teachers made $450 to $650 and domestic help $250 to $350. Although the mine owners got rich, most miners at best earned only enough to go elsewhere, perhaps buy some land, and try again. Nevertheless, the production of millions of ounces of gold and silver stimulated the economy, lured new foreign investors, and helped usher the United States into the mainstream of the world economy.

### Cowboys and the Cattle Frontier

As Mark Twain had so colorfully related, the popular press's rousing accounts of big gold strikes had helped fuel the feverish expansion of the mining frontier during the 1860s and 1870s. Similar stories, romanticizing the life of the hardy cowboy, driving large herds of longhorns northward from Texas through Oklahoma to markets in Dodge City and Abilene, Kansas, sparked the transformation of the cattle industry in these same decades. In this case, astute businessmen and railroad entrepreneurs, eager to fund their new investments in miles of track, promoted cattle herding as the new route to fame and fortune, and the eastern press took up the theme. The cowboy, once scorned as a ne'er-do-

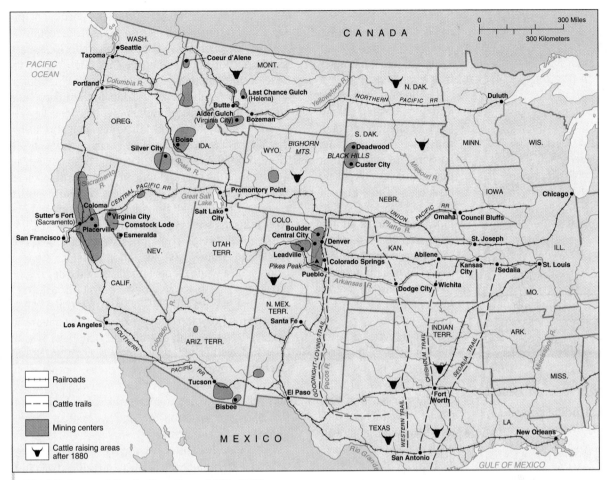

### The Mining and Cattle Frontiers, 1860–1890

*The western mining and ranching bonanzas lured thousands of Americans hoping to get rich quick.*

well and drifter, was now glorified as a man of rough-hewn integrity and self-reliant strength.

In 1868 Joseph G. McCoy, a young cattle dealer from Springfield, Illinois, shrewdly combined organizational and promotional skills to make the cattle industry a new bonanza. With the relocation of the Plains Indians onto reservations and the extension of the railroads into Kansas in the post–Civil War period, McCoy realized that cattle dealers could now amass enormous fortunes.

Forming a partnership with his brothers, McCoy built a new stockyard in Abilene, Kansas. By guaranteeing to transport his steers in railcars to hungry eastern markets, he obtained a five-dollar kickback from the railroads on each cattle car shipped. To make the overland cattle drives from Texas to Abilene easier,

McCoy also helped survey and shorten the Chisholm Trail in Kansas. Finally, in a clever feat of showmanship, he organized the first Wild West show, sending four Texas cowboys to St. Louis and Chicago, where they staged roping and riding exhibitions that attracted exuberant crowds. At the end of his first year in business, 35,000 steers were sold in Abilene; the following year the number more than doubled.

The great cattle drives of the 1860s and 1870s turned into a bonanza for herd owners. Steers purchased in Texas at $9 a head could be sold in Abilene, after deducting $4 in trail expenses, for $28. A herd of two thousand head could thus bring a tidy $30,000 profit. But the cattlemen, like the grain growers farther north on the Great Plains, lived at the mercy of high interest rates and an unstable market. During the

**Ned Huddleston, alias Isom Dart**

*Outlaws and gunfighters, although small in number, created an image of the trans-Mississippi West as lawless and dangerous. Isom Dart, a member of Brown's Park outlaw faction in Colorado and Wyoming, here poses with his six-shooters.*

financial panic of 1873, cattle drovers, unable to get extensions on their loans, fell into bankruptcy by the hundreds.

Continually searching for the quick dollar, thousands of ambitious Americans turned to ranching. Foreign investors sank huge sums into the cattle business. The English alone put $45 million into ranch companies in the 1870s and 1880s—and by 1883 owned or controlled nearly 20 million acres of western grazing land. American businesses followed suit.

As in mining, little of the money made by large-scale ranchers found its way into the pockets of the cowboys themselves. The typical cowpunchers who drove two-thousand-head herds eight hundred miles through the dirt and dust from southern Texas to Abilene during the 1870s earned a mere thirty dollars a month, about the same as common laborers. They also braved the gangs of cattle thieves that operated along the trails.

The most notorious of the cattle rustlers, William H. Bonney, better known as Billy the Kid, may have murdered as many as eleven men before he was killed by a sheriff in 1881 at the age of twenty-one. The long hours, low pay, and hazardous work discouraged older ranch hands from applying. Most cowboys were young men in their teens and twenties who worked for a year or two and then pursued different livelihoods.

Of the estimated 35,000–55,000 men who rode the trails in these years, nearly one-fifth were black or Mexican. Barred by discrimination from many other trades, black cowboys enjoyed the freedom of life on the trail.

Although they were excluded from the position of trail boss, they distinguished themselves as resourceful and shrewd cowpunchers. Nat Love, the son of Tennessee slaves, left for Kansas after the Civil War to work for Texas cattle companies. As chief brander, he moved through Texas and Arizona "dancing, drinking, and shooting up the town." By his own account, he was "wild, reckless, free," and "afraid of nothing." On July 4, 1876, when the Black Hills gold rush was in full swing, Love delivered three thousand head of cattle to a point near the hills and rode into Deadwood to celebrate. Local miners and gamblers had raised prize money for roping and shooting contests, and Nat Love won both, as well as a new title, Deadwood Dick. Close relationships sometimes developed between black and white cowboys. Shortly before Charles Goodnight, a white pioneer trailblazer, died in 1929, he recalled of the black cowboy Bose Ikard, a former slave, that "he was my detective, banker, and everything else in Colorado, New Mexico, and the other wild country I was in. The nearest and only bank was at Denver, and when we carried money I gave it to Bose." Goodnight revealed much about the economic situation of blacks on the Plains, however, when he added that "a thief would never think of robbing him [Ikard]—never think of looking in a Negro's bed for money."

Although the typical real-life cowboy led a lonely, dirty, and often boring existence, a mythic version of the frontier cowboy who might with equal ease become a gunslinging marshal or a dastardly villain was glamorized in the eastern press as early as the 1870s. The image of the West as a wild and lawless land where vigilantes battled with brutish bandits fired easterners' imaginations. Edward L. Wheeler, a writer for the publishing house of Beadle and Adams, in 1877 penned his first dime novel, *Deadwood Dick, The Prince of the Road: or, the Black Rider of the Black Hills.* Over the next eight years, Wheeler turned out thirty-three Deadwood Dick novels relating the adventures of the muscular young hero who wore black clothes and rode a black horse. Cast alternately as outlaw, miner, gang leader, and cowboy, Deadwood Dick turned his blazing six-shooters on ruthless ruffians and dishonest desperadoes. He had much in common with the real-life Deadwood Dick except that Wheeler, to please his white readership, made him a white man.

The reality was a good deal less picturesque. Although Abilene, for example, went through an early period of violence that saw cowboys pulling down the walls of the jail as it was being built, the town had quickly established a local police force to maintain law and order. City ordinances forbade the carrying of firearms and regulated saloons, gambling, and prostitution. James B. ("Wild Bill") Hickok served as town marshal in 1871, but his tenure was less eventful than legend had it. Dime novelists described him as "a veritable terror to bad men on the border," but during his term as Abilene's lawman, Hickok killed just two men, one of them by mistake.* Transient, unruly types certainly gave a distinctive flavor to cattle towns like Abilene, Wichita, and Dodge City, but the overall homicide rates there were not unusually high.

More typical of western conflicts were the "range wars" that pitted "cattle kings" (who thought that the open range existed for them alone to exploit) against farmers. Gaining the upper hand in state legislatures, farming interests sought to cripple the freewheeling cattlemen with quarantine laws and inspection regulations. Ranchers retaliated against the spread of barbed-wire farm fencing, first by cutting the settlers' fences and then by buying up and enclosing thousands of acres of their own. Meanwhile, dozens of small-scale shooting incidents broke out between inhabitants of isolated farms and livestock drovers, as well as between rival cattlemen and sheep ranchers.

Peaking during 1880–1885, the bonanza produced more than 4.5 million head of cattle for eastern markets. Prices began to sag as early as 1882, however, and many ranchers, having expanded too rapidly, plunged heavily into debt. When President Grover Cleveland, trying to improve federal observance of Indian treaties, ordered cattlemen to remove their stock from the Cheyenne-Arapaho reservation in 1885, 200,000 more cattle were crowded onto already overgrazed ranges. That same year and the following, two of the coldest and snowiest winters on record combined with summer droughts and Texas fever to destroy nearly 90 percent of the cattle in some regions, pushing thousands of ranchers into bankruptcy. The cattle industry lived on, but railroad expansion and the increasing numbers of steers raised outside the Great Plains brought the days of the open range and the great cattle drives to an end. As had the mining frontier, the early years of the cattle frontier left behind memories of individual daring, towering fortunes for some, and hard times for many.

## Bonanza Farms on the Plains

The heady enthusiasm that permeated mining and ranching in the 1870s and 1880s also percolated into agriculture. Like the gold rushes and cattle bonanzas, the wheat boom in the Dakota Territory started small but rapidly attracted large capital investments that produced the nation's first "agribusinesses."

The boom began during the Panic of 1873, when the failure of numerous banks caused the price of Northern Pacific Railroad bonds to plummet. The railroad responded by exchanging land for its depreciated bonds. Speculators, including the railroad's own president, George W. Cass, jumped at this wonderful opportunity and purchased more than 300,000 acres in the fertile Red River valley of North Dakota for between fifty cents and a dollar an acre.

Operating singly or in groups, the speculators established enormous, factorylike ten-thousand-acre farms, each run by a hired manager, and invested heavily in labor and equipment. On the Cass-Cheney-Dalrymple farm near Fargo, North Dakota, which covered an area six miles long by four miles wide, fifty or sixty plows rumbled across the flat landscape in unison on a typical spring day. The *New York Tribune* reported that Cass, who had invested fifty thousand dollars for land and equipment, paid all his expenses plus the cost of the ten thousand acres with his first harvest alone.

The publicity generated by the tremendous success of a few large investors like Cass and Oliver Dalrymple, the "king" of the wheat growers, led to an unprecedented wheat boom in the Red River valley in 1880. Eastern banking syndicates and small farmers alike rushed to buy land. North Dakota's population tripled in the 1880s. Wheat production skyrocketed to almost 29 million bushels by the end of the decade. But the profits so loudly celebrated in the eastern press soon evaporated. By 1890 some Red River valley farmers were destitute.

The wheat boom collapsed for a variety of reasons. Overproduction, high investment costs, too little or too much rain, excessive reliance on one crop, and depressed grain prices on the international market all undercut farmers' earnings. Large-scale farmers who had invested in hopes of getting rich felt lucky just to sur-

---

* Hickok eventually moved on to Deadwood, South Dakota, where he was murdered in 1876 by Jack McCall as he played poker, ensuring his place in the pantheon of western heroes.

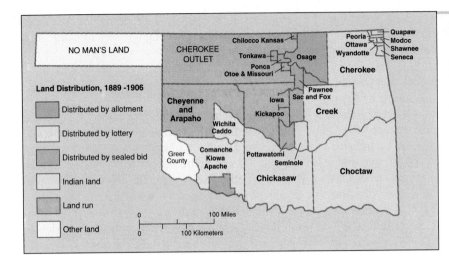

**The Oklahoma Land Rush, 1889–1906**

*Lands in Oklahoma not settled by "Sooners" were sold by lotteries, allotments, and sealed-bid auctions. By 1907 the major reservations had been broken up, and each Native American had been given a small farm.*

vive. Oliver Dalrymple lamented in 1889 that "it seems as if the time has come when there is no money in wheat raising."

### The Oklahoma Land Rush

Even as farmers in the Dakotas and Minnesota were enduring poor harvests and falling prices, hard-pressed would-be homesteaders greedily eyed the enormous Indian Territory, as present-day Oklahoma was then known. The federal government, considering much of the land in this area virtually worthless, had reserved it for the Five Civilized Tribes, who had dwelled there since the 1830s. Because these tribes (except for some Cherokees) had sided with the Confederacy during the Civil War, Washington had punished them by settling thousands of Indians from *other* tribes on lands in the western part of the territory. By the 1880s, recognizing the actual value of the Oklahoma lands, land-hungry non-Indians argued that the Civilized Tribes' betrayal of the Union justified further federal confiscation of their land.

Over the Native Americans' protests, Congress in 1889 transferred to the federally owned public domain nearly 2 million acres in the central part of the Oklahoma Territory that had not been specifically assigned to any Indian tribe. At noon on April 22, 1889, thousands of men, women, and children in buggies and wagons stampeded into the new lands to stake out homesteads. (Other settlers, the so-called Sooners, had earlier infiltrated the lands illegally and were already plowing the fields.) Before nightfall tent communities

had risen at Oklahoma City and Guthrie near stations on the Santa Fe Railroad. Nine weeks later, six thousand homestead claims had been filed. During the next ten years, as the Dawes Severalty Act freed up additional acres by breaking up the Indian reservations into individual allotments and opening the surplus to non-Indian settlement, homesteaders continued to pour into the territory.

The Oklahoma land rush demonstrated the continuing power of the frontier myth, which tied "free" land to the ideal of economic opportunity. Despite early obstacles—the 1889 rush occurred too late in the season for most settlers to plant a full crop, and a drought parched the land the following year—Oklahoma farmers remained optimistic about their chances of "making it" on the last frontier. Most did survive because they were fortunate enough to have obtained fertile land in an area where the normal rainfall was thirty inches, ten inches more than in the semiarid regions farther west. Still, a combination of exploitative farming, poor land management, and sporadic drought would within two generations place Oklahoma at the desolate center of what in the 1930s would be called the dust bowl.

## The West of Life and Legend

In 1893, four years after the last major tract of Western Indian land, the Oklahoma Territory, was opened to non-Indian settlement, a young Wisconsin historian,

Frederick Jackson Turner, delivered a lecture entitled "The Significance of the Frontier in American History." "[T]he frontier has gone," declared Turner, "and with its going has closed the first period of American history." Although Turner's assertion that the frontier was closed was inaccurate (more land would be settled there in the twentieth century than in the nineteenth), his linking of economic opportunity with the development of the trans-Mississippi West caught the popular imagination and launched a new school of historical inquiry into the effects of the frontier on U.S. history.

Scholars now recognize that Turner's inaccurate "frontier thesis," with its ethnocentric omission of Native Americans' claims to the land, was part of an idealized view of the West that became popular in the 1890s. As farmers, miners, ranchers, Indian agents, and prostitutes had pursued their varied activities in the *real* West, a parallel *legendary* West had taken deep root in the American imagination. In the nineteenth century, this mythic West was a product of novels, songs, and paintings. In the twentieth century, it would be perpetuated by movies, radio programs, and television shows. The legend merits attention, for its evolution is fascinating, and its influence far-reaching.

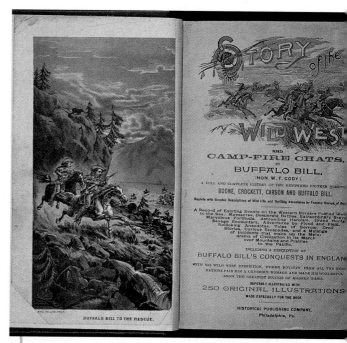

**Legends of the West**
*Buffalo Bill's Wild West and Congress of Rough Riders of the World: Historical Sketches and Programme, Chicago, 1893.*

### The American Adam and the Dime-Novel Hero

In the early biographies of frontiersmen like Daniel Boone and in the wilderness novels of James Fenimore Cooper, the western hero's personal development sometimes parallels, but more often runs counter to, the interests of society. Mid-nineteenth-century writers, extending the theme of the western wilderness as an alternative to society, presented the frontiersman as a kind of mythic American Adam—simple, virtuous, and innocent, untainted by a corrupt social order. For example, an early biographer of Kit Carson, the Kentucky-born guide who in 1830 made one of the first recorded crossings of California's Mojave Desert, depicted him as a perfect antidote to the evils of refined society, an individual of "genuine simplicity, ... truthfulness ... [and] bravery." At the end of Mark Twain's *Huckleberry Finn*, Huck rejects the constraints of settled society as represented by Aunt Sally and heads west with the declaration, "I reckon I got to light out for the territory ahead of the rest, because Aunt Sally she's going to adopt me and sivilize me, and I can't stand it. I been

there before." In this version of the legend, the West is a place of adventure, romance, or contemplation where one can escape from society and its pressures.

But even as this conception of the myth was being popularized, another powerful theme had emerged as well. The authors of the dime novels of the 1860s and 1870s offered the image of the western frontiersman as a figure deeply immersed in society and its concerns. In *Buffalo Bill: King of the Border Men* (1869), a dime novel loosely based on real-life William F. ("Buffalo Bill") Cody, Edward Judson (who published under the name Ned Buntline) created an idealized hero who is a powerful force for morality and social order as he drives off treacherous Indians and rounds up horse thieves and no-good cattle rustlers.

So enthusiastically did the public welcome this new fictional frontiersman that Cody was inspired in 1883 to start his Wild West show. A former army scout and pony express rider, Cody was a natural showman, and his exhibitions proved immensely popular. Cody presented mock "battles" of army scouts and Indians—in effect, morality dramas of good versus evil. Along with entertainment, in short, the Wild West show reinforced the dime-novel image of the West as an arena of moral encounter where virtue always triumphed.

### Revitalizing the Frontier Legend

Both versions of the myth—the West as a place of escape from society and the West as a stage on which the moral conflicts confronting society were played out—figured prominently in the histories and essays of young Theodore Roosevelt, the paintings and sculptures of artist Frederic Remington, and the short stories and novels of writer Owen Wister. These three young members of the eastern establishment spent much time in the West in the 1880s, and each was intensely affected by the adventure. All three had felt thwarted by the constraints and enervating influence of the genteel urban world in which they had grown up, and each went West to experience the physical challenges extolled in the dime novels. When Roosevelt arrived in 1884 at the ranch he had purchased in the Dakota Badlands, he at once bought a leather scout's uniform, complete with fringed sleeves and leggings.

Each man also found in the West precisely what he was looking for. The frontier that Roosevelt glorified in such books as *The Winning of the West* (four volumes, 1889–1896), and that the prolific Remington portrayed in his work, was a stark physical and moral environment that stripped away all social artifice and tested an individual's true ability and character. Drawing on a popular version of English scientist Charles Darwin's evolutionary theory, which characterized life as a struggle in which only the fittest survived, Roosevelt and Remington exalted the disappearing frontier as the last outpost of an honest and true social order.

This version of the frontier myth reached its apogee in Owen Wister's enormously popular novel *The Virginian* (1902), later reincarnated as a 1929 Gary Cooper movie and a 1960s television series. In Wister's tale the elemental physical and social environment of the Great Plains produces individuals like his unnamed cowboy hero, "the Virginian," an honest, strong, and compassionate man, quick to help the weak and fight the wicked. The Virginian is one of nature's aristocrats—ill-educated and unsophisticated but upright, steady, and deeply moral. The Virginian sums up his own moral code in describing his view of God's justice: "He plays a square game with us." For Wister, as for Roosevelt

and Remington, the cowboy was the Christian knight on the Plains, indifferent to material gain as he upheld virtue, pursued justice, and attacked evil.

Needless to say, the western myth in all its forms was far removed from the actual reality of the West. Critics delighted in pointing out that not one scene in *The Virginian* actually showed the hard physical labor of the cattle range. The idealized version of the West also glossed over the darker underside of frontier expansion—the brutalities of Indian warfare, the forced removal of the Indians to reservations, the racist discrimination against Mexican-Americans and blacks, the risks and perils of commercial agriculture and cattle growing, and the boom-and-bust mentality rooted in the selfish exploitation of natural resources.

Further, the myth obscured the complex links between the settlement of the frontier and the emergence of the United States as a major industrialized nation increasingly enmeshed in a global economy. Eastern and foreign capitalists controlled large-scale mining, cattle, and agricultural operations in the West. The technical know-how of industrial America underlay the marvels of western agricultural productivity. And without the railroad, that quintessential symbol of the new industrial order, western expansion would have been quite unthinkable.

### Beginning a Conservation Movement

Despite its one-sided and idealistic vision, Owen Wister's celebration of the western experience reinforced a growing popular recognition that many unique features of the western landscape were being threatened by overeager entrepreneurs. One important byproduct of the western legend, therefore, was a surge of public support for creating national parks and the beginning of an organized conservation movement.

Those who went west in the 1860s and 1870s to map the rugged terrain of the high Plains and the Rocky Mountains were often awed by the natural beauty of the landscape. Major John Wesley Powell, the one-armed veteran of the Civil War who charted the Colorado River in 1869, waxed euphoric about its towering rock formations and powerful cataracts. *In The Exploration of the Colorado River of the West and Its Tributaries* (1875), he wrote that, in coursing through one stretch of rapids: "A beautiful view is presented. The river turns sharply to the east, and seems enclosed by a wall, set with a million brilliant gems. . . . On coming nearer, we

**The Grand Canyon of the Yellowstone,** by Thomas Moran, 1872
*Dazzled by the monumental beauty of the scene, painters strove to portray the western landscape as one of God's wonders. In the process, they stimulated a new popular interest in preserving the spectacular features of the land.*

find fountains bursting from the rock, high overhead, and the spray in the sunshine forms the gems which bedeck the way. . . . We name it Vasey's Paradise. . . ." In his important study, *Report on the Lands of the Arid Regions of the United States* (1878), Powell not only recognized the unique beauty of the Colorado River basin, but he also argued that settlers needed to readjust their expectations about the use of water in the dry western terrain.

As Powell educated the public about the significant differences between the natural landscape of the East Coast and that of the far West, and focused attention on the beauty of the Colorado River and the Grand Canyon in the Southwest, a group of adventurers, led by General Henry D. Washburn, visited the hot springs and geysers near the Yellowstone River in northwestern Wyoming and eastern Montana in 1870. They were stunned by what they saw. "You can stand in the valley of the Yosemite," wrote one of the party, "and look up its mile of vertical granite, and distinctly recall its minutest feature; but amid the canyon and falls, the boil-

ing springs and sulphur mountain, and, above all, the mud volcano and the geysers of the Yellowstone, your memory becomes filled and clogged with objects new in experience, wonderful in extent, and possessing unlimited grandeur and beauty." Overwhelmed by the view, the Washburn explorers changed their plan to claim this area for the Northern Pacific Railroad and instead petitioned Congress to protect it from settlement, occupancy, and sale. Congress responded in 1872 by creating Yellowstone National Park to "provide for the preservation . . . of all time, mineral deposits, natural curiosities, or wonders within said park . . . in their natural condition."

These first steps to conserve the West's finest natural resources and safeguard them against exploitation by unscrupulous entrepreneurs represented the beginning of a changed awareness of the environment. In this same period George Perkins Marsh, an architect and politician from Vermont, in his influential study *Man and Nature* (1864), attacked the older view that nature existed to be tamed and conquered. Cautioning

Americans to curb their destructive use of the landscape, he warned the public to change its ways. "Man," he wrote, "is everywhere a disturbing agent. Wherever he plants his foot, the harmonies of nature are turned to discords."

Marsh's impassioned plea for conservation of natural resources found its most eloquent support in the work of John Muir, a Scottish immigrant who had grown up in Wisconsin. Temporarily blinded by an accident, Muir left for San Francisco in 1869 and quickly fell in love with the redwood forests of the nearby Yosemite Valley. For the next forty years he tramped the rugged mountains of the West and campaigned for their preservation. A romantic at heart, he struggled to experience the wilderness at its most elemental level. Once trekking high in the Rockies during a summer storm, he climbed the tallest pine he could find and swayed back and forth in the raging wind.

Muir became the late nineteenth century's most articulate publicist for wilderness protection. "Climb the mountains and get their good tidings," he advised city dwellers. "Nature's peace will flow into you as the sunshine into the trees. The winds will blow their freshness into you, and the storms their energy, while cares will drop off like autumn leaves." Muir's spirited campaign to protect the wilderness contributed strongly to the establishment in 1890 of Yosemite National Park and the creation two years later of the Sierra Club, an organization committed to encouraging the enjoyment and protection of the wilderness in the mountain region of the Pacific Coast.

Despite the crusades of Muir, Powell, and Marsh to educate the public about the rapacious destruction of the environment, the campaign for wilderness preservation ironically reaffirmed the image of the West as a unique region whose magnificent landscape produced tough individuals of superior ability. Overlooking the senseless violence and ruthless exploitation of the land, contemporary writers, historians, and publicists proclaimed that the settlement of the final frontier marked a new stage in the history of civilization, and they kept alive the legend of the western frontier as a seedbed of American virtues.

## CONCLUSION

It is precisely the divergence between the mythic West and the real West that offers a clue to the disruptive nature of social change in late-nineteenth-century Amer-

ica. In an era when industrialization, urbanization, and immigration were altering the nation in unsettling ways, many Americans embraced the legend of the West as an uncomplicated, untainted Eden of social simplicity and moral clarity. The mythic West represented what the entire society had once been like (or so Americans chose to believe), before the advent of cities, factories, and masses of immigrants.

The myth was the cumulative work of many hands, from dime-novel writers, newspaper correspondents, and railroad publicists to novelists, politicians, and artists. It sank deeply into the American consciousness and soothed the public's qualms over social change.

But the reality of westward expansion was more complex than the mythmakers acknowledged. Under the banner of economic opportunity and individual achievement, nineteenth-century Americans used the army to drive out the Indians and ruthlessly exploited the region's vast natural resources. In less than three decades they had killed off the enormous buffalo herds, depleted the region's extensive deposits of gold and silver, and plowed up the prairie grasslands into farms.

Thus the mythic view of the frontier West as the arena for society building and economic opportunity obscured the dark side of the expansion onto the Great Plains and beyond. In their scramble for wealth, Americans ravaged the environment, conquered the Native Americans, and destroyed the Indians' traditional way of life. Large business enterprises in mining, ranching, and agribusiness, financed by eastern and European bankers, shoved aside the small entrepreneur and took control of much of the natural resources of the area.

Nevertheless, the settlement of the vast internal continental land did reinforce the popular image of the United States as a land of unprecedented economic opportunity and as a seedbed for democracy. Although the exclusion of blacks, Indians, and Spanish-speaking Americans belied the voiced commitment to an open society, the founding of new towns, the creation of new territorial and state governments, and the interaction of peoples of different races and ethnicities tested these ideals and, with time, forced their rethinking. The increasing inclination to give women the vote in many of the new western states would be more broadly accepted within the next two decades.

Although the persistence of the mythic view of the West served to hide the more ruthless and destructive features of western expansionism, the experiences gained from settling the interior territories and the utilization of the region's extensive physical resources led to the beginnings of the conservation movement and a reassessment of traditional American views of the environment. By the turn of the century, the thriving farms, ranches, mines, and cities of that region would help make the United States into one of the world's most prosperous nations.

## FOR FURTHER READING

Peter Iverson, *The Navajos* (1990). A brief, insightful history of the Navajos' culture and everyday life.

Patricia Nelson Limerick, *The Legacy of Conquest: The Unbroken Past of the American West* (1987). A critique of writing on the history of the West that argues for replacing Turner's frontier thesis with a theory of cultural conquest and domination.

Clyde A. Milner II, Carol A. O'Connor, and Martha A. Sandweiss, eds., *The Oxford History of the American West* (1994). A comprehensive reference work with chapters on many facets of the western experience.

Douglas Monroy, *Strangers: The Making of Mexican Culture in Frontier California* (1990). A perceptive study of the interaction between Mexicans, Native Americans, and whites in California.

Ruth B. Moynihan, Susan Armitage, and Christiane Fischer Dichamp, eds., *So Much to Be Done: Women Settlers on the Mining and Ranching Frontier* (1990). Firsthand accounts by women who struggled to adapt to living in the West.

Richard White, *"It's Your Misfortune and None of My Own": A New History of the American West* (1991). An excellent overview of the ways in which different racial and ethnic groups interacted in the trans-Mississippi West and exploited the area's natural resources.

# The Rise of
# Industrial America

"Breaker Boys," 1900

On October 21, 1892, before a crowd of more than 200,000 onlookers, presidential candidate Grover Cleveland stepped proudly into the Grand Court of Honor to open the World's Columbian Exposition in Chicago. Grasping a small electric key connected to a two-thousand-horsepower engine, he proclaimed, "As by a touch the machinery that gives life to this vast Exposition is now set in motion, so in the same instant let our hopes and aspirations awaken forces which in all time to come shall influence the welfare, the dignity, and the freedom of mankind." A moment later, amid enthusiastic cheers, electric fountains shot streams of water high into the air, officially marking the exposition's opening.

The Chicago world's fair represented the triumph of thirty years of industrial development. The country's largest corporations displayed their newest products. In the Electricity Building, the Westinghouse Company's dynamos mysteriously lit a tower of incandescent light bulbs; American Bell Telephone offered the first long-distance telephone calls to the East Coast; and inventor Thomas A. Edison exhibited his latest phonograph.

The fair's splendor dazzled the more than 25 million visitors who entered the gates between October 1892 and October 1893. General Lew Wallace, author of the popular novel *Ben-Hur*, described the exposition as "the fairest city that ever the sun shown [*sic*] on." But Isabelle Garland, mother of writer Hamlin Garland, who visited the fair from a small midwestern farm community, was simply stunned. "[M]y mother sat in her chair, visioning it all yet comprehending little of its meaning," Garland later observed. "Her life had been spent among homely small things, and these gorgeous scenes dazzled her, . . . letting in upon her in one mighty flood a thousand stupefying suggestions of art and history and poetry of the world. . . . At last utterly overcome, she leaned her head against my arm, closed her eyes and said, 'Take me home, I can't stand any more of it.'"

Isabelle Garland's emotional reaction captured the ambivalence of many late-nineteenth-century Americans, who found themselves both unsettled and exhilarated as the nation was transformed by industrialization. In less than thirty years, through innovations in management, technology, production, and distribution, business leaders had built the United States into the world's greatest industrial power. Manufacturing output soared and a host of new products now entered into urban, small-town, and rural homes across the country. All the more remarkably, this growth came amid the disruptions of a boom-and-bust business cycle that produced labor unrest and crippling depressions in 1873–1879 and 1893–1897.

This chapter will focus on five major questions:

- ◆ What innovations in technology and business practices helped launch the vast increases in the size and scale of industrial production in the post–Civil War period?

- ◆ How were Andrew Carnegie, John D. Rockefeller, and other business leaders able to dominate their rivals and consolidate control over their industries?

- ◆ Why did the South's experience with industrialization differ from that of the North and the Midwest?

- ◆ What was the workers' response to the changing nature of work and to the growth of national corporations?

- ◆ In the clash between industry and labor, what tactics enabled corporate executives in the 1890s to undercut labor's bargaining power?

# The Character of Industrial Change

Six features dominated the birth of modern industrial America after the Civil War: first, the exploitation of immense coal deposits as a source of cheap energy; second, the rapid spread of technological innovation and the factory system; third, the need for enormous numbers of new workers who could be carefully controlled; fourth, the constant pressure on firms to compete tooth-and-nail by cutting costs and prices—as well as the impulse to eliminate rivals and create monopolies; fifth, the relentless drop in price levels (a stark contrast to the inflation of other eras); and finally, the failure of the money supply to keep pace with productivity, a development that drove up interest rates and restricted the availability of credit.

All six factors were closely related. The great bituminous coal deposits in Pennsylvania, West Virginia, and Kentucky provided the cheap energy that fueled the

**Bessemer Converter**

*Although Bessemer converters, like this one at the Pennsylvania Steel Company in the 1890s, dramatically improved steel production, their presence made steel-making a dangerous occupation.*

railroads, the factories, and explosive urban growth. Exploiting these inexpensive energy sources, new technologies stimulated productivity and catalyzed breathtaking industrial expansion. Technology also enabled manufacturers to cut costs and hire cheap unskilled or semiskilled labor. This cost cutting in turn drove firms to undersell one another, destroying weaker competitors and prompting stronger, more efficient (and more ruthless) ones to consolidate. At least until the mid-1890s, cost reduction, new technology, and fierce competition forced down overall price levels.

But almost everyone suffered terribly during the depression years, when the government did nothing to relieve distress. "The sufferings of the working classes are daily increasing," wrote a Philadelphia worker in 1874. "Famine has broken into the home of many of us, and is at the door of all." Above all, business leaders' unflagging drive to maximize efficiency both created colossal fortunes at the top of the economic ladder and forced millions of wage earners to live near the subsistence level.

Out of the new industrial system poured dismal clouds of haze and soot—as well as the first tantalizing trickle of what would become an avalanche of consumer goods. In turn, mounting demands for consumer goods stimulated heavy industry's production of "capital goods"—machines to boost even further farm and factory output. Together with the railroads, the corporations that manufactured capital goods, refined petroleum, and made steel became the driving force in the nation's economic growth.

A stunning expansion in the *scale* of industry offered tangible evidence of the magnitude of economic change. By the turn of the century, mammoth corporations, located in urban centers like New York, Chicago, and San Francisco, reached out to the surrounding countryside and dominated production in the railroad, meatpacking, steel, sugar, and oil industries.

Competition among the aggressive and innovative capitalists who headed American heavy industry was intense—and as the post–Civil War era opened, nowhere was it more intense than among the nation's railroads, which to many Americans most symbolized industrial progress.

### *Railroad Innovations*

By 1900, 193,000 miles of railroad track crisscrossed the United States—more than in all of Europe, including Russia. These rail lines connected every state in the

CHRONOLOGY

**1837** Magnetic telegraph invented.

**1859** First oil well drilled in Titusville, Pennsylvania.

**1866** National Labor Union founded.

**1869** First transcontinental railroad completed.

Knights of Labor organized.

**1870** Standard Oil Company established.

**1873** Panic of 1873 triggers a depression lasting until 1879.

**1876** Alexander Graham Bell invents and patents the telephone.

Thomas A. Edison opens research laboratory at Menlo Park, New Jersey.

**1877** Edison invents the phonograph.

Railway workers stage the first nationwide strike.

**1879** Henry George, *Progress and Poverty.*

Edison perfects the incandescent lamp.

**1881** Standard Oil Trust established.

**1882** Edison opens the first electric power station on Pearl Street in New York City.

Chinese Exclusion Act.

**1883** Railroads divide the country into time zones.

William Graham Sumner, *What Social Classes Owe to Each Other.*

Lester Frank Ward, *Dynamic Sociology.*

**1886** American Federation of Labor (AFL) formed.

Police and demonstrators clash at Haymarket Square in Chicago.

**1887** Interstate Commerce Act establishes the Interstate Commerce Commission.

**1888** Edward Bellamy, *Looking Backward.*

**1889** Andrew Carnegie, "The Gospel of Wealth."

**1890** Sherman Anti-Trust Act.

**1892** Standard Oil of New Jersey and General Electric formed.

Steelworkers strike at Homestead, Pennsylvania.

World's Columbian Exposition opens in Chicago.

Miners strike at Coeur d'Alene, Idaho.

**1893** Panic of 1893 triggers a depression lasting until 1897.

**1894** Pullman Palace Car workers strike, supported by the National Railway Union.

**1901** J. Pierpont Morgan organizes United States Steel.

---

Union and opened up an immense new internal market. Most important, railroad companies pioneered crucial aspects of large-scale corporate enterprise, including the issuance of stock to meet their huge capital needs, the separation of ownership from management, the creation of national distribution and marketing systems, and the formation of new organizational and management structures.

Early railroad entrepreneurs such as Thomas A. Scott, who in the 1850s integrated seventy-three smaller companies into the Pennsylvania Railroad, faced enormous financial and organizational problems. The cost of buying land, laying track, building engines, and setting up stations was horrendous. To meet these start-up costs, railroads needed staggering sums. For large lines like the Pennsylvania, the necessary level of capitalization could approach $35 million.

How were sums like this raised? The railroads, of course, received generous land and loan subsidies from federal, state, and local governments. But even so, the larger lines had to borrow heavily by selling bonds to the public. Another way the railroads raised capital was by selling stock. Unlike bond holders, who earned a fixed rate of interest, stockholders received dividends only when the company earned a profit. By 1900 the combined debt of all U.S. railroads stood at an astounding $5.1 billion, nearly five times that of the federal government.

In addition to developing ways to raise large amounts of capital, the railroads created new systems for collecting and using information. To coordinate the complex flow of cars across the country, railroads relied heavily on the magnetic telegraph, invented in 1837. To improve efficiency, the railroads set up clearly defined, hierarchical organizational structures and divided their lines into separate geographic units, each with its own superintendent. Elaborate accounting systems documented the cost of every operation for each division, from coal consumption to the repair of engines and cars. Using these reports, railroad officials could set rates and accurately predict profits as early as the 1860s, a time when most businesses had no idea of their total profit until they closed their books at year's end. Railroad management innovations thus became a model for many other businesses seeking a national market.

## Creativity, Cooperation, and Competition

Collis P. Huntington, Jay Gould, James J. Hill, and the other larger-than-life figures who reorganized and expanded the railroad industry in the 1870s and 1880s were often depicted by their contemporaries as villains and robber barons who manipulated stock markets and company policies to line their own pockets. For example, newspaper publisher Joseph Pulitzer called Jay Gould, the short, secretive president of the Union Pacific, "one of the most sinister figures that have ever flitted batlike across the vision of the American people." Recent historians, however, have pointed out that the great industrialists were a diverse group, and far from all bad. Although some were ironfisted pirates who engaged in fraudulent practices, others were upstanding businessmen who managed their companies with sophistication and innovation. Indeed, some of their ideas were startling in their originality and inventiveness.

The expansion and consolidation of railroading reflected both the ingenuity and the dishonesty flourishing on the corporate management scene. Although by the 1870s railroads had replaced the patchwork of canal and stagecoach operations that dominated domestic transportation before the Civil War, the industry itself was in a state of chaos. Hundreds of small companies used widely different standards for car couplers, rails, track width, and engine size. Financed by large eastern and British banks, Huntington, Gould, and others devoured these smaller lines to create large, integrated track networks. In the Northeast four major trunk lines emerged. West of the Mississippi five great lines—the Union Pacific (1869); the Northern Pacific (1883); the Atchison, Topeka, and Santa Fe (1883); the Southern Pacific (1883); and the Great Northern (1893)—controlled most of the track by 1893.

As they consolidated a hodgepodge of small railroads into a few interlocking systems, the masterminds of the giant trunk lines standardized all basic equipment and facilities, from engines and cars to automatic couplers, air brakes, signal systems, and outhouses (now provided in standard one-, two-, and three-hole sizes). In 1883, independently of the federal government, the railroads unilaterally divided the country into four time zones. Then in May 1886 all railroads shifted simultaneously to the new standard 4′8½″–gauge track. Finally, cooperative billing arrangements enabled the railroads to ship cars from other roads, including dining and sleeping cars owned by the Pullman Palace Car Company, at uniform rates nationwide.

This newly integrated transportation and communications network brought advantages to factory owners and consumers alike. Companies gained access to a national market and across the country people could buy food, hardware, and clothing once available only in the major East Coast cities. Moreover, the standardization of a wide range of products from 2″ x 4″ framing timbers and one pound loaves of bread to milk (now sold in pint or quart bottles) helped reshape everyday life in countless ways.

But the expansion and consolidation of the railroads had its costs. Competition between lines saddled the great trunk lines with massive debts. In 1879 Jay Gould, the guiding force behind the expansion of the

**Jay Gould**

*In a commentary on Gould's vicious manipulation of the railway industry, a disapproving cartoonist depicted him as having amassed his fortune by destroying others' lives with as little concern as a bowler knocking down ninepins.*

Union Pacific, gained control of the Kansas Pacific Railroad. To squeeze out his southwestern competition, he ran tracks parallel to those of his rivals, engineered fluctuations in the price of their stock, and undercut their business by setting his rates below his own cost. One by one his competitors toppled into bankruptcy while he consolidated his holdings. Meanwhile, to increase his own income, he "watered" the company's stock by issuing stock certificates far in excess of the actual value of the assets.

Entangled in heavy indebtedness, overextended systems, and crooked business practices, the railroads fought each other recklessly for traffic. They cut rates for large shippers, offered special arrangements for handling bulk goods, showered free passes on politicians who supported their operations, and granted substantial rebates and kickbacks to favored clients. None of these tactics, however, shored up the railroads' precarious financial position. A pooling agreement between two railroads would soon be undermined by pressure from a third. Rebates given by one system prompted retaliation from another. And the continuous push to expand drove some overbuilt lines into bankruptcy.

Caught in the middle of the railroads' tug-of-war and stung by exorbitant rates and secret kickbacks, farmers and small business owners turned to state governments for help. In the 1870s many midwestern state legislatures, responding to farmer-led protests, outlawed rate discrimination. Initially upheld by the Supreme Court, these and other decisions were negated in the 1880s as the Court broke down local autonomy and supported the capitalist integration of the economy. Then in 1887, persuaded by Illinois senator Shelby M. Cullom's detailed study of devious railroad practices, Congress passed the Interstate Commerce Act, which established the five-member Interstate Commerce Commission (ICC) to oversee the practices of railroads passing through more than one state. The law also banned monopolistic activity like pooling, rebates, and discriminatory short-distance rates. The railroads challenged the commission's rulings in the federal courts, however, and of sixteen cases brought to the Supreme Court before 1905, the justices found in favor of the railroads in all but one, essentially nullifying the ICC's regulatory clout. The Hepburn Act (see Chapter 22), passed in 1906, strengthened the ICC by finally empowering it to set rates.

The railroads' vicious competition did not abate until a national depression that began in 1893 forced a number of roads into the hands of J. Pierpont Morgan and other investment bankers. Morgan, a massively built man with piercing eyes and a commanding presence, took over the weakened systems, reorganized their administration, refinanced their debts, and built intersystem alliances. By 1906, thanks to the bankers' centralized management, seven giant networks controlled two-thirds of the nation's rail mileage.

In short, by the late nineteenth century, competition, corruption, mismanagement, and overextension had created a paradox in the railroad industry. The massive trunk systems had become the largest business enterprises in the world, towering over state and federal governments in the size and scale of their operations. They had pioneered the most advanced methods of accounting and large-scale organization. Yet despite their enormous power and many innovations, the railroads remained unstable. Cutthroat expansion had inflated operating costs, reduced revenues, and made them particularly vulnerable to economic downswings. During the depression of 1893, only intervention by investment bankers saved the industry from collapse.

### Applying the Lessons of the Railroads to Steel

The close connections between railroad expansion and the growth of heavy industry are well illustrated in the career of steelmaker Andrew Carnegie. A diminutive dynamo of a man, only 5′3″ tall, Carnegie was born in Dunfermline, Scotland, and immigrated to America in 1848, at the age of twelve, with his father, a skilled handloom weaver who never found steady employment once the industry mechanized. Ambitious and hard-working, young Carnegie took a job at $1.20 a week as a bobbin boy in a Pittsburgh textile mill. Although he worked a sixty-hour week, the aspiring youngster also enrolled in a night course to learn double-entry bookkeeping.

The following year, Carnegie became a Western Union messenger boy. Taking over when the telegraph operators wanted a break, he soon became the city's fastest telegraph operator. Because he had to decode the messages for every major business in Pittsburgh, Carnegie gained an insider's view of their operations.

Carnegie's big break came in 1852, when Tom Scott, superintendent of the Pennsylvania Railroad's western division, hired him as his secretary and personal telegrapher. When Scott became vice president of the Pennsylvania Railroad seven years later, the

## Iron and Steel Production, 1875–1915

*New technologies, improved plant organization, economies of scale, and the vertical integration of production brought a dramatic spurt in iron and steel production.*

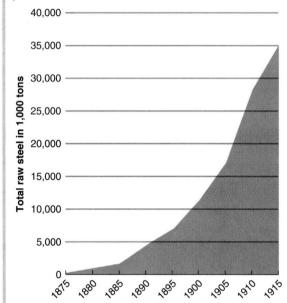

*Note:* short ton = 2,000 pounds.
*Source:* Historical Statistics of the United States.

twenty-four-year-old Carnegie took over as head of the line's western division.

A daring innovator, Carnegie, in his six years as division chief, used the complex cost-analysis techniques developed by Scott to more than double the road's mileage and quadruple its traffic. He slashed commuter fares to keep ridership at capacity and developed various cost-cutting techniques. By 1868 Carnegie was earning more than $56,000 dollars a year from his investments alone, a substantial fortune in that era.

In the early 1870s, Carnegie decided to build his own steel mill. His connections within the railroad industry, the country's largest purchaser of steel, made this a logical choice. Starting with the J. Edgar Thomson Mills, named for the president of the Pennsylvania Railroad, he introduced the new Bessemer production technology, which shot a blast of air through an enormous crucible of molten iron to burn off carbon and impurities. Carnegie combined the new technology with the cost-analysis approach learned from his railroad experience and became the first steelmaker to establish the actual production cost per ton of steel. Using

this data, he not only cut expenses but also developed a solid basis for deciding when to invest in new furnaces and machine tools.

Carnegie's philosophy was deceptively simple: "Watch the costs, and the profits will take care of themselves." From the start he priced his rails below the competition. Then, through rigorous cost accounting and by limiting wage increases to his workers, he lowered his production costs even further. Moreover, he was not above asking for favors from his railroad-president friends or giving "commissions" to railroad purchasing agents.

As output climbed, Carnegie discovered the benefits of vertical integration—that is, controlling all aspects of manufacturing, from extracting raw materials to selling the finished product. In Carnegie's case this control embraced every stage from the mining and smelting of ore to the selling of steel rails. His movement toward vertical integration prompted him in 1881 to establish a partnership with Henry Clay Frick, the owner of a large coke* company, who in 1889 would become the chairman of Carnegie Steel while continuing as head of Frick Coke Company. In 1892 Carnegie also bought into an ore company in the newly opened Mesabi Range in Minnesota. Under Frick's aggressive leadership, Carnegie Steel's annual profits rose each year, reaching $40 million in 1900. Carnegie Steel thus became the classic example of how sophisticated new technology might be combined with innovative management (and brutally low wages) to create a mass-production system that could slash consumer prices.

Frick's management of daily operations left Carnegie free to pursue philanthropic activities. While still in his early thirties, Carnegie resolved to donate his money to charitable projects. (He also knew full well that such actions would buttress his popularity.) Carnegie set up foundations and eventually gave more than $300 million to libraries, universities, and international-peace causes.

By 1900 Carnegie Steel, employing twenty thousand people, had become the world's largest industrial corporation. Yet many of Carnegie's able lieutenants chafed under his domineering management style. In January 1900, when Frick, who had verbally agreed to sell coke to Carnegie Steel at a price considerably below the market rate, tried to raise his price, Carnegie forced him out in an angry confrontation. Said

---

* Coke: the solid residue obtained from coal after the removal of volatile material, used to heat the blast furnaces.

Carnegie of his former partner (who was fourteen years his junior): "He's too old, too infirm in health *and mind*. . . . I have nothing but pity for Frick." (Later, when Carnegie suggested that they renew their old friendship, Frick responded, "Tell Mr. Carnegie I'll meet him in Hell.")

The competitive challenge came from Federal Steel, a large complex put together in 1898 by J. Pierpont Morgan, and from Illinois Steel. The success of these imposing rivals threatened to choke off Carnegie's sales to the wire, nail, and pipe industries. Carnegie responded with typical cunning, by cornering the patents (exclusive rights to manufacturing and sales) on a new process for producing seamless pipes and by announcing plans to build a new pipe plant. His competitors immediately sought a compromise. At Morgan's request Charles Schwab, Carnegie Steel's president, met Carnegie on the golf course early in 1901 to ask what he wanted for his share of Carnegie Steel. The next day Carnegie gave Schwab a penciled note asking for nearly half a billion dollars. Morgan's response was simple: "Tell Carnegie I accept his price." Combining Carnegie's companies with Federal Steel, Morgan set up the United States Steel Corporation, the first business capitalized at more than $1 billion. The corporation, with its two-hundred-member companies employing 168,000 people, marked a new scale in industrial enterprise.

Throughout his chain of corporate-world triumphs, Carnegie consistently portrayed himself as an entrepreneur who had risen through self-discipline and hard work. The full story was more complex. Carnegie did not mention his uncanny ability to see the larger picture, his cleverness in hiring talented associates who would drive themselves (and the company's factory workers) mercilessly, his ingenuity in transferring organizational systems and cost-accounting methods from railroads to steel, and his callousness in keeping wages as low as possible. To a public unaware of corporate

### Andrew Carnegie Sums Up the Cost Savings of Vertical Integration*

The eighth wonder of the world is this:
two pounds of iron-stone purchased on
the shores of lake Superior and
    transported to Pittsburgh;
two pounds of coal mined in Connellsville
and manufactured into coke and
    brought to Pittsburgh;
one half pound of limestone mined
east of the Alleghenies and
    brought to Pittsburgh;
a little manganese ore,
mined in Virginia and
    brought to Pittsburgh.
And these four and one half pounds of
material manufactured into one pound of
solid steel and sold for one cent.
That's all that need be said
    about the steel business.

*Vertical integration: The control of all aspects of production from the mining of raw materials to the selling of the final product. *Source:* Harold C. Livesay, Andrew Carnegie and the Rise of Big Business (Boston: Little, Brown, 1975), 189.

**Andrew Carnegie**
*Although his contemporaries called him "the world's richest man," Andrew Carnegie was careful that his official portraits played down his wealth and pictured him as direct and straightforward.*

management techniques, however, Carnegie's success simply reaffirmed the openness of the American economic system. For the new immigrants flooding the nation's shores, Carnegie's career gave credence to the idea that anyone might rise from rags to riches.

## Consolidating the Industrial Order

Between 1870 and 1900, the same grasping competition that had stimulated consolidation in the railroad and steel industries (see table) also swept the oil, salt, sugar, tobacco, and meatpacking industries. Like steel, these highly competitive businesses required large capital investments. Entrepreneurs in each industry therefore raced to reduce costs and dominate rivals. Chicago meatpackers Philip Armour and Gustavus Swift, for example, raised the process of making bacon, pork chops, and steak from hogs and cattle to a high level of efficiency. Using refrigerated railcars, they reaped a fortune supplying eastern cities with meat.

The evolution of the oil industry typifies the consolidation process. After Edwin L. Drake drilled the first successful petroleum (or "crude-oil") well in 1859 near Titusville in northwestern Pennsylvania, entry into the oil business came relatively easily. Entrepreneurs sank

## Industrial Consolidation:
## Iron and Steel Firms, 1870 and 1900

|  | 1870 | 1900 |
|---|---|---|
| No. of firms | 808 | 669 |
| No. of employees | 78,000 | 272,000 |
| Output (tons) | 3,200,000 | 29,500,000 |
| Capital invested | $121,000,000 | $590,000,000 |

*Source:* Robert L. Heilbroner and Aaron Singer, *The Economic Transformation of America: 1600 to Present,* 2d ed. (San Diego: Harcourt Brace Jovanovich, 1984), 92.

wells, erected small refineries nearby, and distilled the petroleum into oil, which soon replaced animal tallow as the major lubricant, and into kerosene, which became the leading fuel for household and public lighting. By the 1870s the landscape near Pittsburgh and Cleveland, the sites of the first discoveries, was littered with rickety drilling rigs, assorted collection tanks, and ramshackle refineries. The almost festive atmosphere that pervaded this early oil boom—speculators flew homemade flags and banners over their rigs—diverted attention from the environmental pollution created at the drilling sites. "So much oil is produced," reported one Pennsylvania newspaper in 1861, "that it is impossible to care for it, and thousands of barrels are running into the creek; the surface of the river is covered with oil for miles. . . ."

In this rush for riches, John D. Rockefeller, a young Cleveland merchant, gradually achieved dominance. Although he did not share Andrew Carnegie's outgoing personality, the solemn Rockefeller resembled the opportunistic steelmaker in other respects. Like Carnegie, Rockefeller had a passion for cost cutting and efficiency. Having founded the Standard Oil Company in 1870, he daily scrutinized every aspect of the firm's operation. In one case he insisted that a manager find 750 missing barrel stoppers. He realized that in a mass-production enterprise, small changes could save thousands of dollars.

Rockefeller constantly stressed the importance of providing a reliable product in winning consumer loyalty. He built a system of bulk depots and tank wagons for local kerosene distribution and insisted that all equipment be kept neat and clean. Like Carnegie, he adopted the latest refining technologies to improve the quality of his fuels and lubricants. To boost sales volume, he advertised heavily. Packaged in a familiar red five-gallon can, Standard Oil kerosene was instantly recognizable by consumers.

Rockefeller resembled Carnegie, too, in his extraordinary ability to understand the inner workings of an entire industry. He particularly focused on transportation. The firm that controlled the shipment of oil between the well and the refinery, and between the refinery and the retailers, he realized, could dominate the industry. Accordingly in 1872 he purchased his own tanker cars and obtained not only a 10 percent rebate from the railroads for hauling his oil shipments but also a kickback on his competitors' shipments. When new pipeline technology became available, Rockefeller set up his own massive interregional pipeline network.

Like Carnegie, Rockefeller used aggressiveness and deception to force out his competitors. When local refineries rejected his offers to buy them out, he priced his product line below cost and strangled their business. When rival firms teamed up against him, Rockefeller set up a pool—an agreement among several companies—that established production quotas and fixed prices. "The Standard Oil Company brooks no competition," a congressional investigating committee observed; ". . . its settled policy and firm determination is to crush out all who may be rash enough to enter the field against it; . . . it hesitates at nothing in the accomplishment of this purpose." Using such tactics, Rockefeller had seized control of 90 percent of the country's oil-refining capacity by 1879.

Convinced that competition wasted resources, Rockefeller tried to eliminate it in 1882 by establishing the Standard Oil Trust. Where the pool lacked legal status, the trust was a legal device that centralized control over a number of different companies by setting up a board of trustees to run all of them. To implement his trust, Rockefeller and his associates persuaded the stockholders of forty companies to exchange their stock for trust certificates. Within three years the Standard Oil Trust had consolidated crude-oil buying throughout its member firms and slashed the number of refineries by half. In this way Rockefeller integrated the petroleum industry both *vertically,* by controlling every function from production to local retailing, and *horizontally,* by merging the competing oil companies into one giant system.

Taking a leaf from Rockefeller's book, companies in other industries such as copper, sugar, whiskey, and lead established their own trust arrangements. But their rapacious tactics, monopolistic control, and sky-high earnings soon provoked a public outcry. Beginning in

## Mergers in Mining and Manufacturing, 1895–1910

*A wave of business mergers occurred after the Supreme Court's 1897 and 1898 rulings that any firms concluding price-fixing or market-allocating agreements violated the Sherman Anti-Trust Act. But the merger mania died down when business leaders quickly discovered that companies could remain profitable only through vertical integration.*

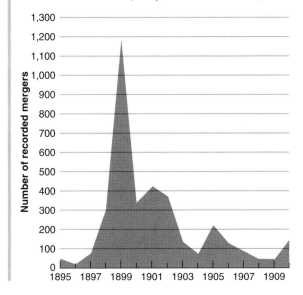

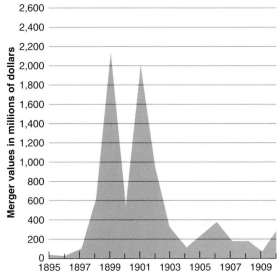

New York State in 1879 and progressing to the federal level, legislative committees exposed the unscrupulous practices of these national trusts, and in the presidential election of 1888, both parties denounced them. When Rockefeller testified that the Standard Oil Trust had greatly reduced prices, his opponents pointed out that monopolies in the copper and sugar industries had pushed prices higher.

Fearful that the trusts would stamp out all competition, Congress, in 1890, under the leadership of Senator John Sherman of Ohio, passed the Sherman Anti-Trust Act, which outlawed trusts and any other contracts or combinations in restraint of trade and slapped violators with fines of up to five thousand dollars and a year in jail. But the loosely worded act failed to define clearly either *trust* or *restraint of trade.* As a result, between 1890 and 1904, the government prosecuted only eighteen antitrust suits. When Standard Oil's structure was challenged in 1892, its lawyers, invoking a New Jersey law that permitted corporations to own property in other states, simply reorganized the trust as an enormous holding company.* The same nine trustees became the new board of directors for Standard Oil (New

Jersey), and the business made more money than ever.

The Supreme Court further hamstrung congressional antitrust efforts by interpreting the Sherman Act in ways sympathetic to big business. In 1895, for example, the federal government brought suit against the sugar trust in *United States* v. *E. C. Knight Company,* arguing that the Knight firm, together with four other corporations, controlled more than 90 percent of all U.S. sugar refining and therefore operated in illegal restraint of trade. The Court threw out the suit, however, drawing a distinction between commerce and manufacturing and defining the latter as a local concern, not a part of interstate commerce. The Court's decision ignored the fact that most trusts dominated the market through their extensive interstate distribution webs. Thus vindicated, corporate mergers and consolidations surged ahead at the turn of the century. By 1900 these mammoth firms accounted for nearly two-fifths of the capital invested in the nation's manufacturing sector.

### The Triumph of Technology

Along with business mergers and consolidations, the invention and patenting of new machines offered another means of driving up profits, lowering costs, and improving efficiency. Furthermore, mechanical inven-

---

* Holding company: a corporation that owns a controlling share of the stock of one or more other firms.

tions had the added advantage of piquing demand for new products. The development of a safe, practical system of generating electricity, for example, made possible an ever-growing range of electrical motors and household appliances. After 1870 business corporations stepped up their research efforts and introduced a remarkable variety of consumer goods.

The major inventions that stimulated industrial output and underlay mass production in these years were largely hidden from public view. Few Americans had heard of the Bessemer process for manufacturing steel or of the improved technologies that facilitated bottle and glassmaking, canning, flour milling, match production, and petroleum refining. Fewer still knew much about the refrigerated railcars that enabled Gustavus Swift's company to slaughter beef in Chicago and ship it east or about the Bonsack cigarette-making machine that could roll 120,000 cigarettes a day, replacing sixty skilled handworkers.

The innovations that people did see were the fruits of this technology—products like the sewing machine,

mass-produced by the Singer Sewing Machine Company beginning in the 1860s; the telephone, developed by Alexander Graham Bell in 1876; and the light bulb, perfected by Thomas A. Edison in 1879. These inventions eased the drudgery of everyday life and in some cases reshaped social interactions. With the advent of the sewing machine, for example, women were relieved of the tedium of sewing the family apparel by hand; inexpensive mass-produced clothing thus led to a considerable expansion in personal wardrobes. The spread of telephones—by 1900 the Bell Telephone Company had installed almost eight hundred thousand in the United States—not only transformed communication but undermined social conventions for polite behavior that had been premised on face-to-face or written exchanges. The light bulb, by further freeing people from dependence on daylight, made possible longer and more regular working hours. These wonders in turn inspired optimism that future technologies might lead to the betterment of society itself. The commissioner of patents proudly declared in 1892, "America has become known the world around as the home of invention."

In the eyes of many, Thomas A. Edison epitomized the inventive impulse. Born in 1847 in Milan, Ohio, Edison, like Andrew Carnegie, was largely self-educated and got his start in the telegraphic industry. Also like the shrewd Scot, Edison was a born salesman and self-promoter. When he modestly averred that "genius is one percent inspiration and ninety-nine percent perspiration," he tacitly accepted the popular identification of himself as an inventing "wizard." Edison moreover shared Carnegie's vision of a large, interconnected industrial system resting on a foundation of technological innovation.

In his early work, Edison concentrated on the telegraph. His experimentation led in 1868 to his first major invention, a stock-quotation printer. The money earned from the patents on this machine enabled Edison to set up his first "invention factory," in Newark, New Jersey, a research facility that he moved to nearby Menlo Park in 1876. Assembling a staff that included university-trained scientists, Edison boastfully predicted "a minor invention every ten days, and a big one every six months."

When the telegraph market was undercut by Bell's invention of the telephone, Edison turned his attention to the electric light. He realized that practical electrical lighting had to be part of a complete system containing generators, voltage regulators, electric meters, and insulated wiring—a system that could be easily installed

**Singer Sewing Machines**

*The Singer Company's success was built not only on its innovative use of interchangeable parts but also on advertising campaigns that stressed how easy its machines were to use.*

### Bell's Liquid Telephone

*Alexander Graham Bell's first telephone consisted of a liquid transmitter(left). Words spoken into a cup, which was filled with acidulted water, made a wire in the liquid vibrate, varying the resistance of the circuit. Bell's subsequent models used a thin metal diaphragm. Sensing the opportunity to better this device, Thomas A. Edison used two carbon buttons to dramatically improve sound quality. Edison later developed a movie projector called the Vitascope (vita from the Latin for "life" and scope from the Greek to "see") in 1896 to make movie-viewing an audience activity.*

and repaired. It also had to be cheaper and more convenient than lighting with kerosene or natural gas, its main competitors.

Buoyed by the success and popularity of his invention in 1877 of a phonograph, or "sound writer" (*phono:* "sound"; *graph:* "writer"), Edison set out to develop a new filament for incandescent light bulbs. Characteristically, he announced his plans for an electricity-generation process before he perfected his inventions and then scrambled feverishly, testing hundreds of materials before he found a carbon filament that would glow dependably in a vacuum. Backed financially by banker J. Pierpont Morgan, the Edison Illuminating Company in 1882 opened a power plant in the heart of New York City's financial district, furnishing lighting for eighty-five buildings.

On the heels of Edison's achievement, other inventors rushed into the electrical field. Edison angrily sued many of his competitors for patent violation. Although he successfully defended his electric light from patent infringement, the lawsuits cost him more than $2 million. Embittered by the legal battles, Edison relinquished control of his enterprises in the late 1880s. In 1892, with financier Morgan's help, Edison's company merged with a major competitor to form the General Electric Company (GE). Four years later, GE and Westinghouse agreed to exchange patents under a joint Board of Patent Control. Such corporate patent-pooling agreements became yet another mechanism of market domination.

Although no longer a corporate leader, Edison continued to pump out invention after invention, including the mimeograph machine, the microphone, the motion-picture camera and film, and the storage battery. By the time of his death in 1931, he had patented 1,093 inventions and had amassed an estate worth more than $6 million. Yet Edison's greatest achievement remained his laboratory at Menlo Park. A model for the industrial research labs established at the turn of the century by Kodak, General Electric, and Du Pont, Edison's laboratory demonstrated that the systematic use of science in support of industrial technology paid large dividends. Invention itself, in short, had become big business.

## *Mass Production, Mass Marketing*

The technological and managerial innovations of such figures as Edison, Carnegie, and Rockefeller proved readily adaptable throughout American industry, spurring marvels of productivity. Indeed, late-nine-teenth-century industrialists often discovered that their factories spewed out more goods than the market could absorb. This was particularly true in two kinds of businesses: those that manufactured devices for individual use such as sewing machines and farm implements, and those that mass-produced consumer goods such as matches, flour, soap, canned foods, and processed meats. Not surprisingly, these industries were trailblazers in developing advertising and marketing techniques. Strategies for whetting consumer demand and for differentiating one product from another represented an important component of the post–Civil War industrial transformation.

The growth of the flour industry illustrates both the spread of mass production and the emergence of new marketing concepts. In the 1870s the nation's flour mills adopted the most advanced European manufac-

turing technologies and installed continuous-process machines that graded, cleaned, hulled, ground, and packaged their product in one rapid operation. These companies, however, soon produced more flour than they could sell. To unload this excess, the mills thought up new product lines such as cake flours and breakfast cereals and sold them using easy-to-remember brand names like Quaker Oats.

Through brand names, trademarks, guarantees, slogans, endorsements, and other gimmicks, manufacturers built demand for their products and won remarkable consumer loyalty. Americans bought Ivory Soap, first made in 1879 by Procter and Gamble of Cincinnati, because of the absurdly overprecise but impressive pledge that it was "99 and $^{44}/_{100}$ths percent pure." James B. ("Buck") Duke's American Tobacco Company used trading cards, circulars, boxtop premiums, prizes, testimonials, and scientific endorsements to convert Americans to cigarette smoking.

In the photographic field, George Eastman in the 1880s developed a paper-based photographic film as an alternative to the bulky, fragile glass plates then in use. Manufacturing a cheap camera for the masses, the Kodak, and devising a catchy slogan ("You press the button, we do the rest"), Eastman introduced a system whereby customers returned the one-hundred-exposure film *and the camera* to his Rochester factory, where the film was developed, the camera reloaded, and everything shipped back to them—for a charge of ten dollars. In marketing a new technology, Eastman had revolutionized an industry and democratized a visual medium previously confined to a few.

**Product Merchandising**
*Eye-catching Jello and Campbell Soup advertisements helped turned the products they touted into household words.*

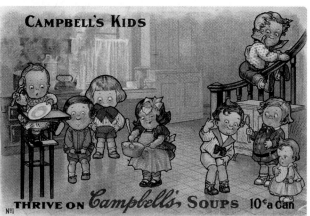

## Industrialization: Costs and Benefits

By 1900 the chaos of early industrial competition, when thousands of small companies had struggled to enter a national market, had given way to an economy dominated by a few enormous firms. An industrial transformation that had originated in railroading and expanded to steel and petroleum had spread to every nook and cranny of American business. For those who fell by the wayside in the era's unforgiving economic environment, the cost could be measured in ruined fortunes, bankrupted companies, and shattered dreams. John D. Rockefeller put things with characteristic bluntness. In the Standard Oil Trust, he said he wanted "only the big ones, only those who have already proved they can do a big business. As for the others, unfortunately they will have to die."

The cost was high, too, for millions of American workers, immigrant and native-born alike. The new industrial order was built on the backs of a vast army of laborers who were paid subsistence wages and who could be fired on a moment's notice when hard times or new technologies made them expendable. Moreover, industrialization often devastated the environment. Polluted rivers fouled by oil or chemical waste, smoky skies filled with clouds of soot, and a landscape littered with reeking garbage and toxic materials bore mute witness to the relentless drive for efficiency and profit.

To be sure, what some called the second industrial revolution brought social benefits as well, in the form of labor-saving products, lower prices, and advances in transportation and communications. The benefits and liabilities sometimes seemed inextricably interconnected. The sewing machine, for example, created thousands of new factory jobs, made available a wider variety of clothing, and eased the lives of millions of housewives. At the same time, it encouraged avaricious entrepreneurs to operate sweatshops in which the immigrant poor—often vulnerable young women—toiled long hours for pitifully low wages.

Whatever the final balance sheet of social gains and costs, one thing was clear: the United States had muscled its way onto the world stage as an industrial titan. The ambition and drive of countless inventors, financiers, managerial innovators, and marketing wizards had combined to lay the groundwork for a new social and economic order in the twentieth century.

# The New South

The South entered the industrial era far more slowly than the North. As late as 1900, total southern cotton-mill output, for example, remained little more than half that of the mills within a thirty-mile radius of Providence, Rhode Island. Moreover, the South's $509 average per capita income was less than half the $1,165 yearly income of northerners.

The reasons for the South's late economic blossoming are not hard to discern. The Civil War's physical devastation, the scarcity of southern towns and cities, lack of capital, illiteracy, northern control of financial markets and patents, and a low rate of technological innovation crippled efforts by southern business leaders to promote industrialization and urban expansion.

Economic progress was also impeded by the myth of the Lost Cause, which, through its nostalgic portrayal

**Industrial Boston**
*For many Americans, the price of progress was often pollution. Lacking the technology to filter carbon and gases from smoke, factory owners had no choice but to fill the skies with soot.*

of pre–Civil War society, perpetuated an image of the South as traditional and unchanging. So although sharing many features of northern industrial growth, including the use of new technology, southern industrialization inched forward haltingly and was shaped in distinctive ways.

## Obstacles to Southern Economic Development

Much of the South's difficulty in industrializing arose from its lack of capital. Although the South had relatively few banks before the Civil War, the average loanable assets of southern banks had been high. Furthermore, a long-standing barter economy had functioned well for whites living in hilly upcountry areas where, as small farmers, they had raised their own food and paid their bills through trade of farm produce.

But the Civil War shattered the South's credit system. Four years of fierce fighting saw cities burned, fields trampled, livestock slaughtered, and farms and plantations ruined. Moreover, the war caused banks to fail in large numbers. By 1865 the South, with more than a quarter of the nation's population, possessed just 2 percent of its banks.

Federal government policies adopted during the war further restricted the expansion of the southern banking system. The Republican-dominated wartime Congress, which had created a national currency and banking structure, required anyone wishing to start a bank to have fifty thousand dollars in capital. Few southerners could meet this test after the war. With limited assets and restricted loan options, southern banks in effect were confined to urban centers and could lend only considerably smaller amounts than their northern counterparts.

With banks in short supply, country merchants and storekeepers became bankers by default, lending supplies rather than cash to local farmers in return for a lien, or mortgage, on their crops (see Chapter 16). Short of cash to pay their own debts, many southern storekeepers insisted that farmers increase their cotton and tobacco acreage because those crops initially brought the highest returns. Yet even though they marked up the goods sold on credit to farmers by 40–70 percent, storekeepers rarely became rich. Few merchants in Georgia during the last quarter of the century had a net worth over five thousand dollars.

The shift from planting corn to raising cotton and tobacco made small southern farmers particularly vulnerable to the fluctuations of commercial agriculture. By the 1880s many southerners who had been largely self-sufficient now depended on outside producers for food, shoes, and agricultural implements. Selling cotton in a national and international market, postbellum farmers fell prey to forces beyond their control. When the price of cotton tumbled from eleven cents per pound in 1875 to less than five cents in 1894, well under the cost of production, many southern farmers grew desperate.

The South not only suffered from an overspecialization in cash crops, particularly cotton, and a shortage of cash and banking facilities, but it also remained the victim of federal policies designed to aid northern industry. High protective tariffs raised the price of machine technology imported from abroad; the demonetization of silver (see Chapter 16) further limited capital availability; and discriminatory railroad freight rates hiked the expense of shipping finished goods and raw materials to outside markets.

The South's chronic shortage of funds affected the economy in indirect ways as well, by limiting the resources available for education. During Reconstruction northern philanthropists such as Georgia-born George Peabody, together with the Freedmen's Bureau, the American Missionary Association, and other relief agencies, had begun a modest expansion of public schooling for both blacks and whites. But Georgia and many other southern states operated segregated schools and refused to tax property for school support until 1889. As a result, school attendance remained low, severely limiting the number of educated people able to staff technical and managerial positions in business and industry.

Southern states, like those in the North, often contributed what modest funds they had to war veterans' pensions. In this way, southern state governments built a white patronage system for Confederate veterans and helped reinforce southerners' lingering idealization of the old Confederacy—the South's Lost Cause. As late as 1911, veterans' pensions in Georgia ate up 22 percent of the state's entire budget, leaving little for economic or educational development.

### The New South Creed and Southern Industrialization

Despite the limited availability of state and federal funds for industrialization, energetic southern newspaper editors such as Henry W. Grady of the *Atlanta Constitution* and Henry Watterson of the *Louisville Courier Journal* championed what became known as the New South creed. The South's unprecedented natural resources and cheap labor, they argued, made it a natural site for industrial development. As one editor declared, "The El Dorado* of the next half century is the South. The wise recognize it; the dull and the timid will ere long regret their sloth or their hesitancy."

The movement to industrialize the South gained momentum in the 1880s. To attract northern capital, southern states offered tax exemptions for new businesses, set up industrial and agricultural expositions, and leased convicts from the state prisons to serve as cheap labor. Florida, Texas, and other states gave huge tracts of lands to railroads, which expanded dramatically throughout the South and in turn stimulated the birth of new towns and villages. Other states sold forest and mineral rights on nearly 6 million acres of federal lands to speculators, mostly from the North, who significantly expanded output. The production of iron, sulfur, and coal catapulted. Denuding the forests of Alabama and Louisiana, northern lumber syndicates between 1869 and 1899 increased lumber production by 500 percent.

---

* El Dorado: a legendary place in Spanish America fabled for its precious metals and jewels.

Following the lead of their northern counterparts, the southern iron and steel industries expanded as well. Birmingham, Alabama, founded in 1871 in the heart of a region blessed with rich deposits of coal, limestone, and iron ore, grew in less than three decades to a bustling iron-producing city with noisy railroad yards and roaring blast furnaces. By 1900 it was the nation's largest pig-iron shipper. In these same years, Chattanooga, Tennessee, housed nine furnaces, seventeen foundries, and numerous machine shops.

As large-scale recruiters of black workers, the southern iron and steel mills contributed to the migration of blacks cityward. By 1900, 20 percent of the southern black population was urban. Many of these urban blacks toiled as domestics or in similar menial capacities, but others entered the industrial work force in places like Birmingham and Chattanooga. Southern industry reflected the patterns of racism permeating other aspects of southern life. Tobacco companies used black workers, particularly women, to clean the tobacco leaves while white women, at a different location, ran the machines that made cigarettes. The burgeoning textile mills of the piedmont were lily-white, whereas in the iron and steel industry, blacks, who comprised 60 percent of the work force by 1900, had practically no chance of advancement. Nevertheless, in a rare reversal of the usual pattern, southern blacks in the iron and steel industry on average earned more than did southern white textile workers.

### The Southern Mill Economy

Unlike the urban-based southern iron and steel industry, the textile mills that mushroomed in the South in the 1880s took southern industrialization down a path different from that of the North and Midwest. Above the Mason-Dixon line, factories and mills were concentrated in cities. But the southern textile industry sprang up in the countryside and often became a catalyst for the formation of new towns and villages. (This same pattern had occurred in rural New England in the 1820s.) In those southern districts that underwent the gradual transition from an agricultural to a mill economy, country ways and values suffused the new industrial workplace.

The cotton-mill economy grew largely in the piedmont, a beautiful country of rolling hills and rushing rivers stretching from central Virginia to northern Georgia and Alabama. The piedmont had long been the South's backcountry, a land of subsistence farming and limited roads. After the Civil War, falling cotton and tobacco prices, laws that required the fencing of livestock, and higher taxes to support railway and road construction trapped farmers in the new commercial economy and undercut their semi-independent existence.

But postwar railroad construction also opened the region to outside markets and sparked a period of intense town building and textile-mill expansion. Between 1880 and 1900, track mileage in North Carolina grew dramatically; the number of towns and villages jumped, quickening the pulse of commerce; and the construction of textile mills accelerated. During this same period, some 120 new mills were built in North Carolina alone; Augusta, Georgia, with 2,800 mill workers, became known as the Lowell of the South. The

**Pig Iron Scene, Birmingham, Alabama,** by Charles Graham, 1886
*Although Birmingham, Alabama's, extensive foundries turned out inexpensive iron ingots, the northern owners forced factory operators to price their products at the same rate as ingots produced in Pittsburgh.*

expansion of the textile industry nurtured promoters' visions of a new, more prosperous, industrialized South.

Even sharecroppers and tenant farmers at first hailed the new cotton mills as beacons of progress. Realizing that a deepening agricultural depression was driving them into destitution and despair, sharecropper Eula Durham recalled a day spent picking cotton. "I got through picking that evening, . . . and [the owner of the cotton field] said 'Well, I don't know, I reckon you're worth a dime.' And he give me a dime for picking cotton all day. I went home and I cried, I was so mad. Papa said, 'If you don't sit down and hush I'm going to tear you all to pieces. That's all that old man had.' I said, 'Well, he ought to have told me that before I picked that cotton.' " For Eula Durham and countless others like her, the mills seemed to offer a way out of rural poverty.

But appearances were deceptive. The chief cotton-mill promoters were drawn from the same ranks of merchants, lawyers, doctors, and bankers who had profited from the commercialization of southern agriculture (and from the misfortunes of poor black and white tenant farmers and sharecroppers enmeshed in the new system). R. R. Haynes, a planter and merchant

from North Carolina's Rutherford County, was typical of the new entrepreneurs. Starting out as a storekeeper, he purchased land and water rights on Second Broad Creek in 1884 and formed a company to finance construction of the Henrietta Mills. By 1913 Haynes owned not only one of the South's largest gingham-producing operations but also banks, railroads, lumber businesses, and a line of general stores.

To run the mills that Haynes and other prosperous southern textile industrialists had built, mill superintendents commonly hired whole families (almost exclusively poor whites) from impoverished nearby farms. In their public pronouncements, they promised that textile work would free these families from poverty and instill in them the virtues of punctuality and industrial discipline. While chanting these benefits, however, the cotton-mill entrepreneurs shamelessly exploited the South's deep pool of cheap labor. By the 1880s, when the mills were earning their investors substantial profits, the superintendents were paying mill workers from seven to eleven cents an hour, a rate 30 percent to 50 percent less than comparable mill wages in New England.

The mill dominated most piedmont textile communities. The mill operator not only built and owned the workers' housing and the company store but also supported the village church, financed the local elementary school, and pried into the morals and behavior of the mill hands. To curb the workers' tendency to move from one mill to another seeking better opportunities, the mill owner usually paid them just once a month, often in scrip—a certificate redeemable only in goods from the company store. Since few families had enough money and supplies to get through a month without buying on credit, they usually overspent and fell behind in their payments. In these cases, the charges were deducted from the workers' wages the following month. In this way, the mill drew workers and their families into a cycle of indebtedness very much like that faced by sharecroppers and tenant farmers.

Southern mill superintendents accommodated themselves to local customs. Unlike northern mill workers, predominantly female and single, southern mill employees comprised men, married and single women, and children. Mothers commonly brought babies into the mills and kept them in baskets nearby while tending their machines. Little children visiting older siblings in the mills sometimes learned to operate the machines themselves. Laboring a twelve-hour day,

**Textile Workers**

*Young children like this one were often used in the textile mills because their small fingers could tie together broken threads more easily than those of adults.*

the mill hands relieved their tedium by deliberately stationing themselves near friends so that they might talk as they worked. Ties among the workers were strong. One employee put it simply: "The mill community was a close bunch of people . . . like one big family. We just loved one another."

To help make ends meet, mill workers kept their own garden patches and raised chickens and an occasional cow and pig. Southern mill hands thus brought communal farm values, nurtured through cooperative planting and harvesting, into the mills and mill villages. Although they had to adapt to machine-paced work and received barely enough pay to live on, the working poor in the mill districts, like their prewar counterparts in the North, eased the shift from rural to village-industrial life by clinging to a cooperative country ethic.

Like northern cotton mills before the Civil War, southern textile companies exploited the cheap rural labor around them, settling transplanted farm people in paternalistic company-run villages. Using these tactics, the industry underwent a period of steady growth. Between 1860 and 1900, cotton-mill capacity shot up 1,400 percent, and by 1920 the South was the nation's leading textile-mill center.

### The Southern Industrial Lag

Still, industrialization in the South occurred on a smaller scale and at a slower rate than industrialization in the North and also depended far more on outside financing, technology, and expertise. Despite leaps in southern lumber, iron, and cotton production, the late-nineteenth-century southern economy remained essentially in a colonial status, subject to control by northern industries and financial syndicates. U.S. Steel, for example, controlled the foundries in Birmingham, and in 1900 its executives began to price Birmingham steel according to the "Pittsburgh plus" formula based on the price of Pittsburgh steel, plus the freight costs of shipping from Pittsburgh. As a result, southerners paid higher prices for steel than did northerners, despite the fact that southern steel production was less costly than northern production.

An array of factors thus combined to retard industrialization in the South. Restrictive banking regulations, scarce capital, absentee ownership, unfavorable railroad rates, cautious state governments, wartime debts, lack of industrial experience, and control by profit-hungry northern enterprises all hampered the region's economic development. Dragged down by a poorly educated white population unskilled in modern technology and by an equally poorly trained, indigent black population excluded from skilled jobs, southern industry languished. Not until after the turn of the century did southern industry as a whole undergo the restructuring and consolidation that had occurred in northern business enterprise two decades earlier. As in the North, industrialization brought significant environmental damage, including polluted rivers and streams, decimated forests, grimy coal-mining towns, and soot-infested steel-making cities. Although Henry Grady's vision of a New South may have inspired many southerners to work toward industrialization, economic growth in the South, limited as it was by outside forces, progressed in its own distinctly regional way.

## Industrial Work and the Work Force

As we have seen in the contrasting experiences of the North and South, industrialization proceeded unevenly nationwide. In fact, during the late nineteenth century, *most* Americans still worked in small factories and locally run businesses. In cities like Philadelphia and Cincinnati, a variety of small-scale work settings coexisted. But in more and more locales as the century unfolded, large factories sprang onto the industrial scene with armies of workers who turned out leather soles for shoes and castings for plows. Thus for all the variety, the pattern of change was evident. Between 1860 and 1900, the number of industrial workers jumped from 885,000 to 3.2 million, and the trend toward large-scale production became unmistakable.

### From Workshop to Factory

The transition to a factory economy came not as an earthquake but rather as a series of jolts varying in strength and duration. But whether they occurred quickly or slowly, the changes in factory production had a profound impact on skilled artisans and unskilled laborers alike, for they involved a fundamental restructuring of work habits and a new emphasis on workplace discipline.

The impact of these changes can be seen by examining the boot and shoe industry. As late as the 1840s, almost every shoe was custom-made by a single skilled artisan, who worked in a small, independent shop. These shoemakers were aristocrats in the world of la-one function: putting the shoe on the last (a form shaped like a person's foot), attaching the heel, trimming the sole, "finishing" the leather with stain and polish, and so forth. Thus instead of crafting a pair of shoes from start to finish, each team member specialized in only one part of the process.

Not only did the nature of the work change under the new factory system of shoe manufacture, but workers lost the freedom to drink on the job and to take time off for special occasions. A working-class culture that had reinforced group solidarity was now dismissed by owners and shop foremen as wasteful and inefficient.

In the 1880s, as shoe factories became larger and more mechanized, traditional skills largely vanished. Sophisticated sewing and buffing machines allowed shoe companies to replace skilled operatives with lower-paid, less skilled women and children. By 1890 women made up more than 35 percent of the work force in an industry once dominated by men.

In many other industries, skilled artisans found their responsibilities and relation to the production process changing. With the exception of some skilled construction crafts such as carpentry and bricklaying, artisans no longer participated in the production process *as a whole*. Like the laborer whose machine nailed heels on 4,800 shoes a day, even "skilled" workers in the new factories specializing in consumer goods found themselves performing numbingly repetitious and monotonous tasks.

### The Hardships of Industrial Labor

The expansion of the factory system not only altered the nature of skilled work but also spawned an unprecedented demand for unskilled labor. By the 1880s nearly one-third of the 750,000 workers employed in the railroad and steel industries, for example, were common laborers.

In the construction trades, the machine and tool industries, and garment making, the services of unskilled laborers were procured under the so-called contract system. To avoid the problems of hiring, managing, and firing their own workers, large companies negotiated an agreement with a subcontractor to take responsibility for employee relations. A foreman or boss employed by the subcontractor supervised gangs of unskilled day laborers. These common workers were seasonal help, hired in times of need and laid off in slack periods. The steel industry employed them to shovel ore in the yards and to move ingots inside the mills. The foremen drove

**Shoeworkers**
*Shoeworkers pose near their machines in Haverhill, Massachusetts, c. 1880. For them as well as for others, work became increasingly repetitive and routinized.*

bor. Taught in an apprentice system, they took pride in their work and controlled the quality of their products. In some cases they hired and paid their own helpers.

Around these shoemakers there evolved a distinctive working-class culture, subdivided along ethnic lines. Foreign-born English, German, and Irish shoe workers each set up ethnic trade organizations and joined affiliated benevolent associations (see Chapter 9). They took time off for religious observances, funerals, and holidays; drank sociably on the job; and helped one another weather accidents or sicknesses. Bound together by their potent religious and ethnic ties, they observed weddings and funerals according to old-country traditions and relaxed together at the local saloon after work. Living in tenements and boardinghouses within the same tight-knit ethnic neighborhood, they developed a strong ethnic and community pride.

As early as the 1850s, even before the widespread use of machinery, changes in the ready-made shoe trade had eroded the status of skilled labor. In 1851 Cincinnati's Filey and Chapin Company broke down the manufacturing process into a sequence of repetitive, easily mastered tasks. Skilled shoe artisans now worked in a "team" of four men, each responsible for

the gangs hard; in the Pittsburgh area, the workers called the foremen "pushers."

Notoriously transient, unskilled laborers drifted from city to city and from industry to industry. As the first hired during good times and the first let go in bad, they sometimes worked for one-third the wages of a typical skilled artisan. In the late 1870s, unskilled laborers earned $1.30 a day, whereas bricklayers and blacksmiths earned more than $3.00. Only unskilled southern mill workers, whose wages averaged a meager 84¢ a day in these years, earned less.

Unskilled and skilled workers alike not only put in up to twelve-hour shifts but also faced grave hazards to their health and safety. The alarming incidence of industrial accidents stemmed from a variety of circumstances, including dangerous factory conditions, workers' inexperience, and the rapid pace of the production process. Hamlin Garland graphically described the perilous environment of a steel-rail mill at Carnegie's Homestead Steel Works in Pittsburgh (see A Place in Time). One steelworker recalled that on his first day at the mill, "I looked up and a big train carrying a big vessel with fire was making towards me. I stood numb, afraid to move, until a man came to me and led me out of the mill." Under such conditions the accident rate in the steel mills was extremely high.

In the coal mines and cotton mills, child laborers typically entered the workforce at age eight or nine. These youngsters not only faced the same environmental hazards as adults but were especially prone to injury because of the pranks and play that they engaged in on the job. (When supervision was lax in the cotton mills, for example, child workers would grab the belts that powered the machines and see who could ride them farthest up toward the drive shaft in the ceiling before letting go and falling to the floor.) In the coal industry, children were commonly employed as slate pickers. Sitting at a chute beneath the breakers that crushed the coal, they removed pieces of slate and other impurities. The cloud of coal dust that swirled around them made them vulnerable to black lung disease—a disorder that could progress into emphysema and tuberculosis. Children and others who toiled in the cotton mills, constantly breathing in cotton dust, fell ill with brown lung, another crippling disease.

For adult workers, the railroad industry was one of the most perilous. In 1889, the first year that the Interstate Commerce Commission compiled reliable statistics, almost two thousand railwaymen were killed on the job and more than twenty thousand were injured.

Disabled workers and widows received only minimal financial aid from employers. Until the 1890s the courts considered employer negligence to be one of the normal risks borne by the employee. Railroad and factory owners regularly fought against the adoption of state safety and health standards, on the grounds that the economic costs would be excessive. For sickness and accident benefits, workers joined fraternal organizations and ethnic clubs, part of whose monthly dues benefited those in need. But in most cases, the amounts set aside were too low to be of much help. When a worker was killed or maimed in an accident, the family became dependent on relatives or kindly neighbors for assistance and support.

### Immigrant Labor

Outside the South, factory owners turned to unskilled immigrant laborers for the muscle needed in the booming factories, mills, railroads, and heavy-construction industries. In Philadelphia, where native-born Americans and recent German immigrants dominated the highly skilled metalworking trades, Irish newcomers remained mired in unskilled horse-carting and construction occupations until the 1890s, when the "new immigrants" from southern and eastern Europe replaced them (see Chapter 19). In the Northeast poverty-stricken French-Canadians filled the most menial positions in the textile mills. On the West Coast, Chinese immigrants performed the dirtiest and most physically demanding jobs in mining, canning, and railroad construction.

Writing home in the 1890s, eastern European immigrants described the hazardous and draining work in the steel mills. "Wherever the heat is most insupportable, the flames most scorching, the smoke and soot most choking, there we are certain to find compatriots bent and wasted in toil," reported one Hungarian. Yet those immigrants disposed to live frugally in a boardinghouse and to work an eighty-four-hour week could save fifteen dollars a month, far more than they could have earned in the old country.

Although most immigrants worked hard, few adjusted easily to the rat race of the factory world. The rural peasants from southern and eastern Europe who immigrated after 1890 found it especially difficult to abandon their irregular work habits for the unrelenting factory schedules. Unlike farm routines, which followed seasonal changes in daylight hours, factory operations were dictated by the invariable speed of the machines. A brochure that the International Harvester Corporation used to teach English to its Polish workers attempted to instill the "proper" values. Lesson 1 read:

> I hear the whistle. I must hurry.
> I hear the five minute whistle.
> It is time to go into the shop.
> I take my check from the gate board and hang
>     it on the department board.
> I change my clothes and get ready to work.
> The starting whistle blows.
> I eat my lunch.
> It is forbidden to eat until then.
> The whistle blows at five minutes of starting
>     time.
> I get ready to go to work.
> I work until the whistle blows to quit.
> I leave my place nice and clean.
> I put all my clothes in the locker.
> I must go home.

As this "lesson" reveals, factory work tied the immigrants to a rigid timetable very different from the pace of farm life.

When immigrant workers resisted the tempo of factory work, drank on the job, or took unexcused absences, employers used a variety of tactics to enforce discipline. Some sponsored temperance societies and Sunday schools to teach habits of punctuality and sobriety. Others cut wages and put workers on the piecework system, paying them only for the items produced. Employers sometimes also provided low-cost housing to gain leverage against work stoppages: if the workers went on strike, the boss could simply evict them.

Workers often fought attempts to tighten factory discipline by demanding a say in production quotas or asserting traditional rights, such as the custom in the cigar-making industry of allowing one employee to read to others as they worked. Seeking to re-create a village atmosphere within the workplace, immigrant factory help often persuaded employers to hire friends and family members.

In the face of immigrant labor's desires for a more sociable, humane working environment, the proliferation of machines in the factories frequently sparked employer-employee tensions. When the factory owner's interest in increasing output corresponded with the immigrant's desire to maximize income, the offer of long hours at the machines was accepted and even welcomed. But when the employer cut wages or

unreasonably accelerated the work schedule, unrest boiled to the surface.

## Women and Work in Industrializing America

Women's work experiences in the nineteenth century were shaped by marital status, social class, and race. Married women in all classes widely accepted an ideology of domesticity (see Chapter 20) and remained at home, raised children, and looked after the household. Although all married women supported their families by cooking, cleaning, and taking care of youngsters, the well-to-do could hire maids and cooks to ease their burdens. Working-class married women, in contrast, not only lacked such assistance but also often had the added responsibility of earning money at home to make ends meet.

For working-class married women, home work—working for wages at home by sewing, button-making, taking in boarders, or doing laundry—had predated industrialization. The growth of cities and the expansion of the economy enabled unscrupulous entrepreneurs to exploit this captive work force. Cigar manufacturers would buy or lease a tenement and require their twenty families to live and work there. In the clothing industry, similarly, manufacturers hired out finishing needlework tasks to lower-class married women and their children, who labored long hours in their crowded apartments.

In contrast to lower-class married women who had no choice but to accept home work, young, working-class single women often viewed outside work as an opportunity. In 1870 only 13 percent of all women worked outside the home. Sixty percent of these found jobs in domestic employment as cooks, maids, cleaning ladies, and laundresses. But most working women intensely disliked the long hours, dismally low pay, and social stigma attached to being a "servant." Therefore, with the exception of black working women, who were prevented by discrimination from changing occupations, when jobs in industry expanded in the last quarter of the century, growing numbers of single women abandoned domestic employment for better-paying, less-demeaning work in the textile, food-processing, and garment industries. Between 1870 and 1900, the number of women working outside the home nearly tripled, and by the turn of the century, women made up 17 percent of the country's labor force.

A variety of factors propelled this rise in the employment of single females. Changes in agriculture prompted many young farm women to seek employment in the industrial sector (see Chapter 19), and immigrant parents often sent their daughters to the factories to supplement meager family incomes. Plant managers, in turn, welcomed young immigrant women as a ready source of inexpensive unskilled labor. But factory owners assumed that many of these women would marry within a short time and thus treated them as temporary help and kept their wages low. Late in the century, young women in the clothing industry earned as little as five dollars for seventy hours of work.

Despite their paltry wages, long hours, and often unpleasant working conditions, many young women relished the income they gained through factory employment and joined the work force in increasing numbers. Although the financial support that these working women contributed to their families was significant few working women were paid enough to provide homes for themselves. Rather than fostering their independence, therefore, industrial work simply enmeshed them more deeply in a family economy that depended on their earnings.

When the typewriter and the telephone came into general use in the 1890s, office work became more specialized, and women with a high school education moved into clerical and secretarial jobs earlier filled primarily by men. They were attracted by the clean, safe working conditions and relatively good pay. First-rate typists could earn six to eight dollars a week, which compared favorably with factory wages. Even though women were excluded from managerial positions, office work carried higher prestige and was generally steadier than work in the factory or shop.

Despite the growing number of women workers, when the late-nineteenth-century popular press touted the possibilities of moving up the ladder of success in industrial America, it left out women completely. Women's work outside the home was seen as temporary. Their real achievement was defined in terms of marriage and the family. For women, success might be measured, for example, in the vicarious satisfaction they experienced when a husband received a promotion or a son earned a raise. Few people even considered the pos-

**Women in the Workplace**
*Women worked long hours at the National Cash Register Company in Dayton, Ohio, in the repetitive job of making parts for locks under the watchful eye of a male supervisor.*

sibility that a woman could attain national or even local prominence in the emerging corporate order.

## Hard Work and the Gospel of Success

Although women were generally excluded from the equation, influential opinion molders in these years preached that any man could achieve success in the new industrial era. In *Ragged Dick* (1867) and scores of later tales, Horatio Alger, a Unitarian minister turned dime novelist, recounted the adventures of poor but honest lads who rise through ambition, initiative, and self-discipline. In his stories shoe-shine boys stop runaway horses and are rewarded by rich benefactors who give them a start in business. The career of Andrew Carnegie was often offered as proof that the United States remained the land of opportunity and "rags to riches."

Not everyone embraced this belief. In an 1871 essay, Mark Twain chided the public for its naïveté and cynically suggested that business success was more likely to come to those who lied and cheated. In testimony given in 1883 before a Senate committee investigating labor conditions, a New Yorker named Thomas B. McGuire dolefully recounted how he had been forced out of the horse-cart business by larger, better-financed concerns. Declared McGuire: "I live in a tenement house, three stories up, where the water comes in through the roof, and I cannot better myself. My children will have to go to work before they are able to work. Why? Simply because this present system . . . is all for the privileged classes, nothing for the man who produces the wealth." Only with starting capital of ten thousand dollars—then a large sum—said McGuire, could the independent entrepreneur hope to compete with the large companies.

What are the facts? Certainly Carnegie's rise from abject poverty to colossal wealth was the rare exception, as recent studies of nearly two hundred of the largest corporations reveal. Ninety-five percent of the industrial leaders came from middle- and upper-class backgrounds. However, even if skilled immigrants and native-born working-class Americans had little chance to move into management in the largest corporations, they did have considerable opportunity to rise to the top in *small* companies. Although few of them reaped immense fortunes, many attained substantial incomes.

The position of immigrant workers in San Francisco in many ways reflected the possibilities and perils of moving up within the working class. In the 1860s the Irish-born Donahue brothers grew wealthy from the Union Iron Works they had founded where six hundred men built heavy equipment for the mining industry. In contrast to these Irish entrepreneurs, however, the nearly fifteen thousand Chinese workers who returned to the city after the Central Pacific's rail line was com-

pleted in 1869 were consigned by prejudice to work in cigar, textile, and other light industry factories. Even successful Chinese entrepreneurs faced discrimination. When a Chinese merchant, Mr. Yung, refused to sell out to the wealthy Charles Crocker, a dry goods merchant turned railroad entrepreneur who was building a mansion on Nob Hill, Crocker built a thirty-foot-high "spite fence" around Yung's house so that it would be completely sealed from view.

Thus, while some skilled workers became owners of their own companies, the opportunities for advancement for unskilled immigrant workers were considerably more limited. Some did move to semiskilled or skilled positions. Yet most immigrants, particularly the Irish, Italians, and Chinese, moved far more slowly than the sons of middle- and upper-class Americans who began with greater educational advantages and family financial backing. The upward mobility possible for such unskilled workers was generally mobility *within* the working class. Immigrants who got ahead in the late nineteenth century went from rags to respectability, not rags to riches.

One positive economic trend in these years was the rise in real wages, representing gains in actual buying power. Average real wages climbed 31 percent for unskilled workers and 74 percent for skilled workers between 1860 and 1900. Overall gains in purchasing power, however, were often offset by personal injuries and unemployment during slack times or economic slumps. The position of unskilled immigrant laborers was particularly shaky. Even during a prosperous year like 1890, one out of every five nonagricultural workers was unemployed at least one month. During the depressions of the 1870s and 1890s, wage cuts, extended layoffs, and irregular employment pushed those at the very base of the industrial workforce to the brink of starvation.

Thus the overall picture of late-nineteenth-century economic mobility is complex. At the top of the scale, the rich grew richer. In 1890 a mere 10 percent of American families owned 73 percent of the nation's wealth. At the bottom of the scale, the most recent immigrants, particularly the unskilled, struggled to make ends meet. During the 1890s only about 45 percent of American industrial laborers earned more than the five-hundred-dollar poverty line annually. Nevertheless, in between the very rich and the very poor, skilled immigrants and small shopkeepers were swelling the ranks of the middle class. So although the standard of living for millions of Americans rose, the gap between the poor and the well-off remained a yawning abyss.

**The Spite Fence, San Francisco**
*To punish a Chinese neighbor, wealthy railroad magnate Charles Crocker built a high fence around the neighbor's house to force him to sell out.*

# Labor Unions and Industrial Conflict

Toiling long hours for low wages, often under dangerous and degrading conditions, some late-nineteenth-century workers turned to labor unions for help. But the unions faced formidable obstacles to increasing their membership. With desperately poor immigrants pouring into the country, employers could always hire newcomers willing to work for lower wages and even to serve as strikebreakers.

Ethnic and racial divisions within the work force further hampered unionizing efforts. In mill towns like Troy, New York, for example, French-Canadian and Irish Catholic workers worshiped, socialized, and married largely within their own ethnic group. The same was true of Pennsylvania coal miners and steelworkers who had immigrated from various southern and eastern European countries.

Furthermore, relatively prosperous skilled craftsworkers felt little kinship with low-paid common laborers. And even the skilled artisans, who were divided into different trades, saw little reason for cooperative effort. Thus when craft-based unions did challenge management and go on strike, they represented only a tiny percentage of the work force.

Labor-organizing efforts reflected these realities. Two groups, the National Labor Union and the Knights of Labor, attempted to build a mass labor movement that would unite skilled and unskilled workers regardless of their specialty. After impressive initial growth, however, both efforts collapsed. The most successful labor movement of the period, the American Federation of Labor (AFL), represented an amalgamation of powerful independent craft unions. The AFL survived and grew, but it still represented only a small portion of the total labor force.

With unions so weak, labor unrest generally took the form of unplanned, wildcat walkouts when conditions became intolerable, and these actions, born of desperation, sometimes exploded into violence. This, in turn, whipped up middle-class fears of labor unrest, further impeding the development of a strong labor movement.

## *Organizing the Workers*

The Civil War marked a watershed in the development of labor organizations. Labor unions were nothing new. From the eighteenth century on, skilled workers had organized local trade unions to fight wage reductions and provide rudimentary benefits for their members in times of illness or accident. By the 1850s some tradesmen had even organized national associations along craft lines. But the effectiveness of these organizations was limited. The main challenge that labor leaders faced in the postwar period was how to boost the unions' clout. Some believed that this goal could be achieved by forming one big association that would transcend craft lines and pull in a mass membership.

One person inspired by this vision was Philadelphian William H. Sylvis, who in 1863 was elected president of the Iron Molders' International Union, an organization of iron-foundry workers. Strongly built and bearded, with a "face and eyes beaming with intelligence," Sylvis traveled the country exhorting iron molders to organize. Within a few years, Sylvis had built his union from "a mere pygmy" to a membership of eighty-five hundred.

In 1866, acting on his dream of a nationwide association to represent all workers, Sylvis called a convention in Baltimore that formed the National Labor Union (NLU). The new organization not only endorsed the eight-hour-day movement but also, reflecting the lingering aura of pre–Civil War utopianism, embraced a wide range of goals, including currency and banking reform, an end to convict labor, a federal department of labor, and restriction on immigration—especially Chinese immigration—since many regarded immigrants as responsible for driving wages down. The NLU under Sylvis's leadership also endorsed the cause of working women and elected a woman as one of its national officers. It urged black workers to organize as well, though in racially separate unions.

In the winter of 1866–1867, Sylvis's own union became locked in a harrowing strike with the nation's foundry owners. When the strike failed miserably, Sylvis turned to national political reform. He invited a number of reformers to the 1868 NLU convention, including woman-suffrage advocates Susan B. Anthony and Elizabeth Cady Stanton, who, according to a reporter, made "no mean impression on the bearded delegates." But the NLU suffered a shattering blow when Sylvis died suddenly in 1869. Despite a claim of 300,000 members, it faded quickly. After a brief incarnation in 1872 as the National Labor Reform party, it vanished from the scene.

But the dream of a national labor movement lived on in a new organization, the Noble and Holy Order of the Knights of Labor, founded in 1869 by nine Philadelphia tailors led by Uriah H. Stephens, head of the Garment Cutters of Philadelphia. A secret society modeled on the Masonic order (see Chapter 10), the Knights welcomed all wage earners or former wage earners; they excluded only bankers, doctors, lawyers, stockbrokers, professional gamblers, and liquor dealers. Calling for a great association of all workers, the Knights demanded equal pay for women, an end to child labor and convict labor, a graduated income tax, and the cooperative employer-employee ownership of factories, mines, and other businesses.

The Knights grew slowly at first. But membership rocketed in the 1880s after Terence V. Powderly replaced Stephens as the organization's head. A young Scranton machinist of Irish-Catholic immigrant origins, Powderly was an unlikely labor leader. He was short and slight, with a blond drooping mustache, elegant attire, and a fastidious, somewhat aloof manner. One journalist expressed surprise at finding such a fashionable man as the leader of "the horny-fisted sons of toil." But Powderly's oratorical eloquence, coupled with a series of successes in labor clashes, brought in thousands of new members.

During its growth years in the early 1880s, the Knights of Labor reflected both its idealistic origins and Powderly's collaborative vision. Powderly opposed strikes, which he considered "a relic of barbarism,"

and organized producer and consumer cooperatives. A teetotaler, he also urged temperance upon the membership. Powderly advocated the admission of blacks into local Knights of Labor assemblies, although he recognized the strength of racism and allowed local assemblies to be segregated in the South. Under his leadership the Knights welcomed women members; by 1886 women organizers such as the feisty Irish-born Mary Harris Jones, known as Mother Jones, had recruited thousands of workers, and women made up an estimated 10 percent of the union's membership.

Powderly also supported restrictions on immigration—and a total ban on Chinese immigration. This policy reflected the widespread fear among union members of immigrants working so cheaply that they would steal jobs from others. In the West such fears were directed particularly against the Chinese, and they were heightened when California railroad magnate Leland Stanford declared, "[O]pen the door and let everybody come who wants to come . . . until you get enough [immigrants] here to reduce the price of labor to such a point that its cheapness will stop their coming." In 1877 San Francisco workers demonstrating for an eight-hour workday destroyed twenty-five Chinese-run laundries and terrorized the local Chinese population. In 1880 both major party platforms included anti-Chinese immigration plans. Two years later, Congress passed the Chinese Exclusion Act, placing a ten-year moratorium on Chinese immigration. Nevertheless, for those Chinese who remained in the United States, sporadic labor violence continued.

Although inspired by Powderly's vision of a harmonious and cooperative future, most rank-and-file Knights of Labor strongly disagreed with Powderly's anti-strike position. In 1883–1884 local branches of the Knights led a series of spontaneous strikes that elicited only reluctant support from the national leadership. In 1885, however, when Jay Gould tried to eradicate the Knights of Labor from his Wabash railroad by firing active union members, Powderly and his executive board instructed all Knights employed by the Wabash line to walk off the job and those working for other lines to refuse to handle Wabash cars. This highly effective action crippled the Wabash's operations.

## The Eight-Hour-Day Movement

*Striking artisans from more than three hundred companies filled New York streets for weeks in 1872 in a campaign to reduce the workday from ten hours to eight hours. As is evident in this illustration, the eight-hour movement gained additional support from local saloons catering to German immigrants.*

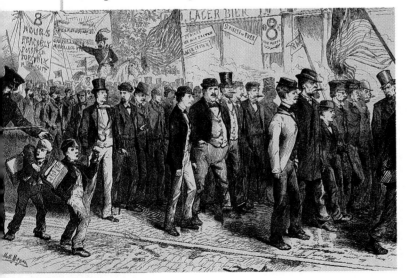

To the nation's amazement, the arrogant Jay Gould met with Powderly and cancelled his campaign against the Knights of Labor. "The Wabash victory is with the Knights," declared a St. Louis newspaper; "no such victory has ever before been secured in this or any other country."

With this apparent triumph, membership in the Knights of Labor soared. By 1886 more than 700,000 workers were organized in nearly six thousand locals. Turning to political action that fall, the Knights mounted campaigns in nearly two hundred towns and cities nationwide, electing several mayors and judges (Powderly himself had served as mayor of Scranton since 1878) and claimed a role in electing a dozen congressmen. In state legislatures they secured passage of laws banning convict labor, and at the national level they lobbied successfully for a law against the importation of foreign contract labor. Conservatives warned darkly that the Knights could cripple the economy and take over the country if they chose.

But in fact, the organization's strength soon waned. Workers became disillusioned when a series of unauthorized strikes failed in 1886. The national reaction to the Haymarket riot (see below) also contributed to the decline. By the late 1880s, the Knights of Labor was but a shadow of its former self. Nevertheless, the organization had given a major impetus to the labor movement and had awakened in thousands of workers a sense of group solidarity and potential strength. Powderly, who survived to 1924, always remained proud of his role "in forcing to the forefront the cause of misunderstood and downtrodden humanity."

As the Knights of Labor weakened, another national labor organization, pursuing more immediate and practical goals, was gaining strength. The skilled craft unions had long been uncomfortable with labor organizations like the Knights that welcomed skilled and unskilled alike. They were also concerned that the Knights' emphasis on broad reform goals would undercut their own commitment to better wages and to protecting the interests of their particular crafts. The break came in May 1886 when the craft unions left the Knights of Labor to form the American Federation of Labor (AFL).

From the first the AFL replaced the Knights' grand visions with practical tactics aimed at bread-and-butter issues. This philosophy was vigorously pursued by Samuel Gompers, the English immigrant cigar maker who became head of the AFL in 1886 and led it for nearly forty years, until his death in 1924. Gompers believed in "trade unionism, pure and simple." The stocky, mustachioed labor leader had lost faith in utopian social reforms and recognized that "the poor, the hungry, have not the strength to engage in a conflict even when life is at stake." To stand up to the corporations, Gompers asserted, labor would have to harness the bargaining power of the *skilled* workers, whom employers could not easily replace, and concentrate on the practical goals of raising wages and reducing hours.

A master tactician, Gompers believed that the trend toward large-scale industrial organization necessitated a comparable degree of organization by labor. He also recognized, however, that the skilled craft unions that had come together to form the AFL retained a strong commitment to controlling their own affairs. The challenge was to persuade the craftsworkers from the various trades to join forces without violating their sense of craft autonomy. Gompers's solution was to organize the AFL as a *federation* of trade unions, each retaining control of its own members but all linked by an exe-

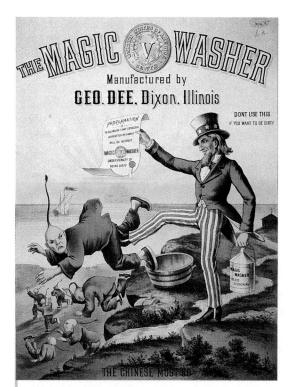

**Ethnic and Racial Hatred**
*Conservative business owners used racist advertising such as this trade card stigmatizing Chinese laundry workers to promote their own products and to associate their company with patriotism.*

cutive council to coordinate strategy during boycotts and strike actions. "We want to make the trade union movement under the AFL as distinct as the billows, yet one as the sea," he told a national convention.

Focusing the federation's efforts on short-term improvements in wages and hours, Gompers carefully sidestepped divisive political issues. The new organization's platform did, however, demand an eight-hour workday, employers' liability, and mine-safety laws. By 1904, under Gompers's conservative tutelage, the AFL had grown to more than 1.6 million strong.

Although the unions held up an ideal toward which many might strive, labor organizations as a whole in the late nineteenth century remained rather weak. Less than 5 percent of the work force joined union ranks. Split between skilled artisans and common laborers, separated along ethnic and religious lines, and divided over tactics, the unions battled with only occasional effectiveness against the growing power of corporate enterprise. Lacking financial resources, they typically watched from the sidelines during economic hard times as unorganized workers launched wildcat strikes that sometimes turned violent.

### Strikes and Labor Violence

Americans had lived with a high level of violence from the nation's beginnings, and the nineteenth century, with its international and civil wars, urban riots, and Indian-white conflict, was no exception. Terrible labor clashes toward the end of the century were part of this continuing pattern, but they nevertheless shocked and dismayed contemporaries. From 1881 to 1905, there erupted close to 37,000 strikes, in which nearly 7 million workers participated. Some of these strikes involved property damage and looting. To a shaken middle class, unaware of the hardships suffered by workers, the United States seemed on the verge of a class war.

In a period of chronic labor unrest, certain years stood out. One such year was 1877. The trouble actually began in 1873, when a Wall Street crash triggered a major depression. Six thousand businesses closed the following year, and many more cut wages and laid off workers in a desperate effort to survive. Striking Pennsylvania coal miners were fired and evicted from their homes. Tramps roamed the streets in New York and Chicago. The tension took a deadly turn in 1877 during a wildcat railroad strike. Ignited by a wage reduction on the Baltimore and Ohio Railroad in July, the strike exploded up and down the railroad lines, spreading

quickly to New York, Pittsburgh, St. Louis, Kansas City, Chicago, and San Francisco. Rioters in Pittsburgh torched Union Depot and the Pennsylvania Railroad roundhouse. By the time the newly installed president Rutherford B. Hayes had called out the troops and quelled the strike two weeks later, nearly one hundred people had died, and two-thirds of the nation's railroads stood idle.

The railroad strike stunned middle-class America. The religious press responded hysterically. "If the club of the policeman, knocking out the brains of the rioter, will answer, then well and good," declared one Congregational journal, "[but if not] then bullets and bayonets . . . constitute the one remedy. . . . Napoleon was right when he said that the way to deal with a mob was to exterminate it." The same middle-class Americans who worried about corporate abuse of power at the top echelons also grew terrified of mob violence from the bottom ranks of society.

Employers capitalized on the public hysteria to crack down on labor. Many required their workers to sign "yellow dog" contracts in which they promised not to strike or join a union. Some hired Pinkerton agents to serve as their own private police force and, when necessary, turned to the federal government and the U.S. Army to suppress labor unrest.

More strikes and violence followed in the 1880s. On May Day 1886, 340,000 workers walked off their jobs in support of the campaign for an eight-hour workday. Strikers in Cincinnati virtually shut down the city for nearly a month. Also in 1886, Chicago police shot and killed four strikers at the McCormick Harvester plant on May 3. At a protest rally the next evening in the city's Haymarket Square, someone threw a bomb from a nearby building, killing or fatally wounding seven po-

**Labor Rally Poster, 1886**
*Business interests tried to smear labor unions as violence-prone and dominated by foreign radicals. Published in both German and English, this labor poster lent credence to such attacks.*

licemen. The police in turn fired wildly into the crowd and killed four demonstrators.

Public reaction was immediate. Business leaders and middle-class citizens lashed out at labor activists and particularly at the sponsors of the Haymarket meeting, most of whom were associated with a German-language anarchist newspaper, the *Arbeiter Zeitung*. Eight were arrested and tried. Although no evidence connected them directly to the bomb throwing, all were convicted, and four were executed. One committed suicide in prison. In Haymarket's aftermath still more Americans became convinced that the nation was in the grip of a deadly foreign conspiracy, and animosity toward labor unions intensified.

Confrontations between capital and labor became particularly violent in the West. When the Mine Owners' Protective Association cut wages at the work sites along Idaho's Coeur d'Alene river in 1892, the miners, who were skilled in the use of dynamite, blew up a mill and captured the guards sent to defend it. Mine owners responded by mustering the Idaho National Guard to round up more than three hundred men and crush their union. Back east that same year, armed conflict broke out at the Carnegie Steel Company plant in Homestead, Pennsylvania, when managers cut wages, locked out the workers, and destroyed their labor union (see A Place in Time).

The most systematic use of troops to smash union power came in 1894, during a strike against the Pullman Palace Car Company. George Pullman, a manufacturer of elegant dining, parlor, and sleeping cars for the nation's railroads, in 1880 had constructed a factory and town, called Pullman, ten miles south of Chicago. The carefully planned community provided solid brick houses for the workers; beautiful parks and playgrounds; and even its own sewage-treatment plant. Alongside these benefits were drawbacks: Pullman closely policed workers' activities, outlawed saloons, and insisted that his properties turn a profit.

When the depression of 1893 hit, Pullman slashed workers' wages without reducing their rents. In reaction thousands of workers joined the newly formed American Railway Union and went on strike. They were led by a fiery young organizer, Eugene V. Debs, who vowed "to strip the mask of hypocrisy from the pretended philanthropist and show him to the world as an oppressor of labor." Union members working for the nation's largest railroads refused to switch Pullman cars, thus paralyzing rail traffic in and out of Chicago.

In response to the crisis, the General Managers' Association, an organization of top railroad executives,

set out to break the union. The General Managers imported strikebreakers from among jobless easterners and asked U.S. attorney general Richard Olney, who sat on the board of directors of three major railroad networks, for a federal injunction (court order) against the strikers for allegedly refusing to move railroad cars carrying U.S. mail.

In fact, union members had volunteered to switch mail cars onto any trains that did not carry Pullman cars, and it was the railroads' managers who were delaying the mail by refusing to send their trains without the full complement of cars. Nevertheless, Olney, supported by President Grover Cleveland and citing the Sherman Anti-Trust Act, secured an injunction against the leaders of the American Railway Union for restraint of commerce. When the union refused to obey the injunction and order its members back to work, Debs was arrested and federal troops poured in. During the ensuing riot, seven hundred freight cars were burned, thirteen people died, and fifty-three were wounded. By July 18 the strike had been crushed.

By playing upon a popular identification of strikers with anarchism and violence, crafty corporate leaders like Frick and Pullman persuaded state and federal officials to cripple organized labor's ability to bargain with business. When the Supreme Court (in the 1895 case *In re Debs*) upheld Debs's prison sentence and legalized the use of injunctions against labor unions, the judicial system gave business a potent new weapon with which to restrain labor organizers. Despite successive attempts by the National Labor Union, Knights of Labor, American Federation of Labor, and American Railway Union to build a strong working-class movement, aggressive employer associations and conservative state and local officials hamstrung their efforts. In sharp contrast to Great Britain and Germany, where state officials often mediated disputes between labor and capital, federal and state officials in the United States increasingly sided with manufacturers. American unions—ineffective in the political arena, blocked by state officials, and frustrated by court decisions—failed to expand their base of support. Post–Civil War labor turmoil had sapped the vitality of organized labor and given it a negative public image that it would not shed until the 1930s.

## Social Thinkers Probe for Alternatives

The widespread industrial disorder was particularly unsettling when juxtaposed with the growing evidence of working-class destitution. In 1879, after observing three

## Homestead: The Town and the Mill

On a rainy fall day in 1893, the writer Hamlin Garland crossed the Monongahela River on a ferry and debarked at a grimy industrial town near Pittsburgh. On assignment for *McClure's* magazine, Garland was investigating the "perilous trade" of steel making at Homestead, Pennsylvania, where the Carnegie Steel Company ran a major mill. One year before, state troops had suppressed a violent strike there. Garland had been sympathetic to the strikers, and he harbored grim expectations as he approached the plant.

From the banks of the polluted Monongahela, he could see the town and the mill sprawled over a hillside. Near the water's edge stood clusters of large sheds topped by tall smokestacks.

### Homestead Workers
*Shirts rolled up to expose their brawny arms, Homestead workers prided themselves on possessing the strength and toughness to work in the dangerous mills.*

Farther up the hill, Garland noted rows of dingy workers' houses, covered with soot and dust. All in all, the place seemed "as squalid and unlovely as could be imagined," he reported. "The streets of the town were horrible; the buildings were poor; the sidewalks were sunken and full of holes." Everywhere "groups of pale, lean men slouched in faded garments, grimy with the soot and grease of the mills."

Barely two decades earlier, the site of Homestead had been pastureland. In 1870 two large farms, the McClure and West homesteads, dominated the area, surrounded by smaller farms. The next year, a commercial venture, the Homestead Bank and Life Insurance Company, bought up the land and subdivided it into building lots. The company

planned to create a residential suburb from which commuters could easily reach Pitts-burgh—only seven miles away—on a new railroad line. But Homestead's suburban days were short-lived. In 1878, when the town's population reached six hundred, a glass factory was built. Three years later a steel mill was constructed on the riverbank, and in 1886 Carnegie's company purchased the mill. The Homestead facilities proved ideal for steel making. The Monongahela ensured an ample water supply. Running through a region of bituminous coal mines, the river provided a conduit for fuel as well. New railroads brought in iron ore from Michigan mines and later from Minnesota. Within five years Carnegie had doubled the mill's capital and expanded its work force. By 1892 the sheds of the Carnegie works ranged over sixty acres. The town had 11,000 residents, of whom 3,800 were mill employees.

Producing steel was inherently dangerous. Deaths from burns and other accidents were commonplace. Men worked twelve-hour shifts, and daily faced white-hot ingots, fast-moving overhead cranes, and exploding furnaces. To Garland, the mill was hell itself: "A roar of a hundred lions, a thunder as of cannons, flames that made the electric light look like a twinkling blue star, jarring clang of falling iron, burst of spluttering flakes of fire, scream of terrible saws, shifting of mighty trucks with hiss of steam!"

From within this industrial inferno, the Amalgamated Association of Iron and Steel Workers had won recognition in 1889. Andrew Carnegie had at first accepted the union, but he later had decided, despite public statements to the contrary, that it had to be destroyed. Following Carnegie's instructions, company president Henry Clay Frick informed the union of its dismissal in June

1892. One by one, the mills were shut down and the workers locked out. Mobilizing in self-defense, the workers on the night of July 6 identified two barges making their way up the river toward the mills. The boats carried more than three hundred armed men from the Pinkerton National Detective Agency. When the Pinkertons tried to disembark, a day-long battle ensued in which seven union members and three Pinkertons died. A week later, the governor of Pennsylvania sent eight thousand National Guardsmen to restore order.

By December the mills had resumed full operation, the union had been broken, and the town of Homestead had been transformed by the influx of nearly three thousand strikebreakers lured by the promise of jobs during a downturn in the national economy. Although the steel mills that Ham-

lin Garland visited seemed unchanged, Homestead as a community was devastated. Many former workmen were ruined. "The atmosphere was at times heavy with disappointment and hopelessness," commented another visitor. Not until World War I would steel workers again try to reform the oppressive work conditions in the steel industry.

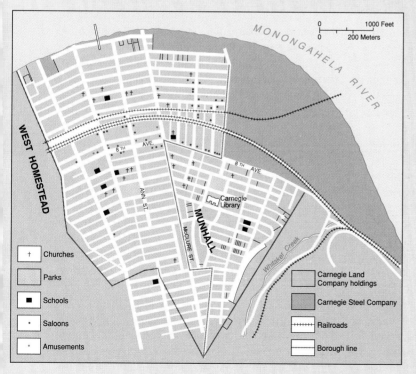

Churches †

Parks ▢

Schools ■

Saloons ·

Amusements ·

Carnegie Land Company holdings

Carnegie Steel Company

Railroads ++++++++

Borough line

### Homestead Life

*An oppressive atmosphere hung over Homestead. The heat, particularly unbearable in summer, provided work for numerous water boys in the mills. As for the quality of the air, one observer noted that "the idiosyncrasy of this town is smoke. It rolls sullenly in slow folds from the great chimneys of the iron-foundries, and settles down in black, slimy pools on the muddy streets."*

### Homestead

*The Carnegie Steel mills not only physically dominated the town but also occupied the most desirable land near the river. This location provided easy access to the barges that brought in supplies.* (Source: Pittsburgh Survey. Maps under direction of Shelby Harrison, 1908.)

men rummaging through garbage to find food, Walt Whitman wrote, "If the United States, like the countries of the Old World, are also to grow vast crops of poor, desperate, dissatisfied, nomadic, miserably-waged populations, such as we see looming upon us of late years . . . , then our republican experiment, notwithstanding all its surface-successes, is at heart an unhealthy failure."

Whitman's bleak speculations were part of a general public debate over the social meaning of the new industrial order. At stake was a larger issue: should government become the mechanism for helping the poor and regulating big business?

Defenders of capitalism preached the laissez-faire ("hands-off") argument, insisting that government should never attempt to control business. They buttressed their case by citing Scottish economist Adam Smith, who had argued in *The Wealth of Nations* (1776) that self-interest acted as an "invisible hand" in the marketplace, automatically regulating the supply of and demand for goods and services. In "The Gospel of Wealth," an influential essay published in 1889, Andrew Carnegie justified laissez-faire by applying to human society the evolutionary theories of British scientist Charles Darwin. "The law of competition," Carnegie argued, "may be sometimes hard for the individual, [but] it is best for the race, because it insures the survival of the fittest in every department." Ignoring the scramble among businesses in the late nineteenth century to *eliminate* competition, Carnegie praised an unregulated competitive environment as a source of positive long-term social benefits.

Tough-minded Yale professor William Graham Sumner shared Carnegie's disapproval of government interference. In his combative book *What Social Classes Owe to Each Other* (1883), Sumner asserted that inexorable natural laws controlled the social order: "A drunkard in the gutter is just where he ought to be. . . . The law of survival of the fittest was not made by man, and it cannot be abrogated by man. We can only, by interfering with it, produce the survival of the unfittest." The state, declared Sumner, owed its citizens nothing but law, order, and basic political rights.

This conservative, laissez-faire brand of Social Darwinism (as such ideas came to be called) did not go unchallenged. In *Dynamic Sociology* (1883), Lester Frank Ward, a geologist with the U.S. Geological Survey, argued that contrary to Sumner's claim, the supposed "laws" of nature *could* be circumvented by human will. Just as scientists had applied their knowledge to breeding superior livestock, government experts could use

the power of the state to regulate big business, protect society's weaker members, and prevent the heedless exploitation of natural resources.

Henry George, a self-taught San Francisco newspaper editor and economic theorist, proposed to solve the nation's uneven distribution of wealth through what he called the single tax. In *Progress and Poverty* (1879), he noted that speculators reaped huge profits from the rising price of land that they neither developed nor improved. By taxing this "unearned increment," the government could obtain the funds necessary to ameliorate the misery caused by industrialization. The result would bring the benefits of socialism—a state-controlled economic system that distributed resources according to need—without socialism's great disadvantage, the stifling of individual initiative. George's program was so popular that he lectured around the country and only narrowly missed being elected mayor of New York in 1886.

The vision of a harmonious industrialized society was vividly expressed in the utopian novel *Looking Backward* (1888) by Massachusetts newspaper editor Edward Bellamy. Cast as a fantastic glimpse into the future, Bellamy's novel tells of Julian West, who falls asleep in the year 1888 and awakens in the year 2000 to find a nation without poverty or strife. In this future world, West learns, a completely centralized, state-run economy and a new religion of solidarity have combined to create a society in which everyone works for the common welfare. Bellamy's vision of a conflict-free society where all share equally in industrialization's benefits so inspired middle-class Americans fearful of corporate power and working-class violence that nearly five hundred local Bellamyite organizations, called Nationalist clubs, sprang up to try to turn his dream into reality.

Ward, George, and Bellamy did not deny the benefits of the existing industrial order; they simply sought to humanize it. These utopian reformers envisioned a harmonious society whose members all worked together. Marxist socialists advanced a different view. Elaborated by German philosopher and radical agitator Karl Marx (1818–1883) in *Das Kapital* (1867) and other works, Marxism rested on the proposition (which Adam Smith had also accepted) that the labor required to produce a commodity was the only true measure of that commodity's value. Thus any profit made by the capitalist employer was "surplus value" appropriated from the exploited workers. As competition among capitalists increased, Marx predicted, wages would decline to starvation levels, and more and more capitalists would be driven out of business. At last society would be divided between a shrinking bourgeoisie (capitalists, merchants, and middle-class professionals) and an impoverished proletariat (the workers). At this point the proletariat would revolt and seize control of the state and of the means of production and distribution. Although Marx's thought was dominated by an insistence on class struggle as the essence of modern history, his eyes were also fixed on the shining vision of the communist millennium that the revolution would eventually usher in—a classless utopia in which the state would "wither away" and all exploitation would cease. To lead the working class in its coming showdown with capitalism, Marx and his collaborator Friedrich Engels helped found a series of socialist parties in Europe, whose strength grew steadily beginning in the 1870s.

Despite Marx's keen interest in the United States, Marxism proved to have little appeal in late-nineteenth-century America outside a tiny group of primarily German-born immigrants. The Marxist-oriented Socialist Labor party (1877) had attracted only about fifteen hundred members by 1890. More alarming to the public at large was the handful of anarchists, again mostly immigrants, who rejected Marxist discipline and preached the destruction of capitalism, the violent overthrow of the state, and the immediate introduction of a stateless utopia. In 1892 Alexander Berkman, a Russian immigrant anarchist, attempted to assassinate Henry Clay Frick, the manager of Andrew Carnegie's Homestead Steel Works. Entering Frick's office with a pistol, Berkman shot him in the neck and then tried to stab him. But a carpenter by chance working in Frick's office overpowered the assailant. Rather than igniting a workers' insurrection that would usher in a new social order, as he had hoped, Berkman's act simply earned him a long prison sentence and confirmed the middle-class stereotype of "labor agitators" as lawless and violent.

## CONCLUSION

By 1900 industrialization had propelled the United States into the forefront of the world's major powers, lowered the cost of goods through mass production, generated thousands of jobs, and made available a wide range of new consumer products. Few Americans would readily have given up their new material benefits.

Despite these advantages, all thinking people recognized that industrialization's cost was high. The rise of the giant corporations had been achieved through savage competition, exploited workers, shady business practices, polluted factory sites, and the collapse of an economic order built on craft skills and an apprenticeship system that had forged bonds between skilled and unskilled labor. Outbursts of labor violence, and the ominous phenomenon of urban slums and grinding poverty, showed starkly that all was not well in industrial America.

To improve their reputations, the great capitalists channeled at least a part of their fortunes into ostentatious public benefactions, including art museums, university endowments, and symphony orchestras. In contrast to Europe, where fortunes remained within the family, some U.S. millionaires developed a lively tradition of private philanthropy.

Nevertheless, Americans remained profoundly ambivalent about the new industrial order. Caught between their desire for the higher standard of living that industrialization made possible and their fears of capitalist power and social chaos, Americans of the 1880s and 1890s sought strategies that would preserve those benefits while alleviating the undesirable social byproducts. Efforts to regulate railroads at the state level, and such national measures as the Interstate Commerce Act and the Sherman Anti-Trust Act, as well as the fervor with which the ideas of a utopian theorist like Edward Bellamy were embraced, represented early manifestations of this impulse. In the Progressive Era of the early twentieth century, Americans would redouble their efforts to formulate political and social responses to the nation's economic transformation after the Civil War.

## FOR FURTHER READING

Edward L. Ayers, *The Promise of the New South: Life After Reconstruction* (1992). A comprehensive overview of economic and social change within the post–Civil War South.

Thomas Dublin, *Transforming Women's Work: New England Lives in the Industrial Revolution* (1994). An insightful examination of the changing nature of women's work and its impact on family finances.

Albro Martin, *Railroads Triumphant: The Growth, Rejection, and Rebirth of a Vital American Force* (1992). An excellent analysis of the railroads' impact on industrial and urban development in the late nineteenth century.

Walter Licht, *Industrializing America: The Nineteenth Century* (1995). A useful overview of the economic transformation of the American economy in the late nineteenth century.

Kim Voss, *The Making of American Exceptionalism: The Knights of Labor and Class Formation in the Nineteenth Century* (1993). A comparative analysis of American labor's attempts to mobilize workers in the face of business opposition.

# 19

# The Transformation
# of Urban America

**Washington Street, Indianapolis, at Dusk,** by Theodore Groll, c. 1892–1895

Incensed by the appalling crowding in New York City tenement housing in 1890, newspaper reporter Jacob Riis exploded in anger. He had toured congested inner-city apartments, poking into attics and cellars where families were jammed together so tightly that their members had to sleep in shifts. Riis published his findings in a dramatic exposé entitled *How the Other Half Lives* (1890).

With a sure eye for the distressing detail, he guided the reader into a typical Cherry Street tenement. "Be a little careful, please!" he warned. "The hall is dark and you might stumble over the children pitching pennies back there. . . . Here is a door. Listen! That short hacking cough, that tiny, helpless wail—what do they mean? They mean that the soiled bow of white you saw on the door downstairs will have another story to tell— Oh! a sadly familiar story—before the day is at an end. The child is dying of measles. With half a chance it might have lived; but it had none. That dark bedroom killed it."

To Riis, such tenements were significant not only as the homes of the immigrant poor and destitute but also as the incubators of disease and vice. With three of its wards averaging more than 285,000 people per square mile, New York City in 1890 epitomized for Riis the depths to which conditions in urban America had sunk.

Riis's grim view of tenement life, which reflected his secure middle-class position, contrasted sharply with many immigrants' remembrances of the tenement districts' vibrant street life, resonating with the melodies of organ grinders and the cries of peddlers and soda dispensers. Although their new homes in the tenements were crowded, immigrants often congregated elbow-to-elbow in the hallways; left apartment doors open to invite visitors; and joked, sang, and played music to re-create the village intimacy remembered from their homelands. "How the people did enjoy that music," reminisced Samuel Chotzinoff, an East Sider from New York. "Everyone would be at their windows listening. . . . Then the people would clap their hands; it was inspiring in a neighborhood like that." For Chotzinoff, the energy and creativity of urban life were forces to be admired and celebrated.

Their perspectives differed markedly, but Riis and Chotzinoff each recalled an era of bounding population growth that had transformed New York and other American cities in the late nineteenth century. Not only on the East Coast but south to New Orleans and west to San Francisco, cities had swelled at an astonishing pace. Between 1870 and 1900, New Orleans's population nearly doubled, Buffalo's tripled, and Chicago's increased more than fivefold. By the turn of the century, Philadelphia, New York, and Chicago had each passed the 1-million-person mark, and 40 percent of all Americans lived in cities. In 1900 New York's 3.4 million inhabitants alone almost exactly equaled the nation's entire urban population in 1850.

The spectacular urban growth, fueled by migration from the New England countryside and an influx of nearly 11 million foreign immigrants between 1870 and 1900, created a dynamic new environment for economic development. Mushrooming cities made possible an unparalleled concentration of resources and markets that in turn dramatically stimulated national economic expansion. Like the frontier, the city symbolized opportunity for all comers.

Yet the city's unprecedented scale and diversity threatened traditional expectations about community life and social stability. Rural America had been a place of face-to-face personal relations, where a homogeneous population shared the same likes and dislikes. In contrast, the city was a seething cauldron where a medley of immigrant groups contended with one another and with native-born Americans for jobs, power, and influence. Moreover, the same rapid growth that energized manufacturing and production strained

**Girl and Baby**
*Photographed by Jacob Riis on the grimy doorstep of their tenement house, this baby and his older sister were meant to show the impoverished life of immigrants.*

city services and generated terrible housing and sanitation problems.

Native-born American city dwellers found the noise, stench, and congestion of this transformed landscape disturbing. Like Jacob Riis, they worried about the newcomers' squalid tenements, fondness for drink, and strange social customs. Thus when native-born reformers set about cleaning up the city and "Americanizing" the foreigners, they sought not only to improve the physical environment but also to destroy the distinctive customs that made immigrant culture different from their own. Resenting the attack on their way of life, recent arrivals like Chotzinoff fought back and resisted change.

The late nineteenth century thus witnessed an intense struggle among these diverse urban constituencies to control the city politically and benefit from its economic and cultural potential. The stakes were high, for America was increasingly becoming an urban nation.

This chapter focuses on five major questions:

♦ What factors shaped the ways in which U.S. cities expanded in the late nineteenth century?

♦ What did immigrants contribute to urban life in America?

♦ Why did some immigrants prosper more than others?

♦ How and why did political bosses gain so much power in post–Civil War cities?

♦ How did civic leaders attempt to reform the urban poor? Why did their attempts yield mixed results?

# Urban Expansion

Between 1840 and 1900 two major changes took place in the American urban landscape: continuous innovations in transportation technology transformed the size and appearance of cities; these same urban areas now also became linked in extensive regional networks that were closely connected to the surrounding countryside. Fed by industrial expansion and waves of immigrants seeking jobs, urban America grew at a dizzying rate and spawned a vast array of new opportunities and perplexing problems.

### *The New Urban World*

The rapid growth of cities large and small after the Civil War created a national urban network—an interconnected web of regional metropolises, specialized manufacturing cities, and smaller subordinate communities of varying size and function. Linked by rail lines and waterways, major cities like Boston, New York, Philadelphia, Chicago, Cincinnati, and San Francisco became regional centers that provided manufacturing plants and financial services for the surrounding countryside. Chicago, for example, emerged in the 1850s in the upper Midwest as the region's center for the shipping and marketing of lumber, meat, and grain. A scant thirty years later, its factories employed the largest industrial work force—over 75,000 people—west of the Appalachians. Manufacturing nearly a quarter of a billion dollars worth of goods, the city's diverse industries also polluted the region's waterways and littered the landscape. Smaller cities, while equally destructive of the environment, often specialized in particular products or processes: for example, Holyoke, Massachusetts, in paper; Birmingham, Alabama, in steel; Minneapolis, Minnesota, in milling and lumber; Butte, Montana, in mining; Corning, New York, in glass; and Kansas City, Missouri, in processing and shipping beef.

Whatever the source of their growth, hundreds of cities expanded so briskly in the post–Civil War years that the nature of urban life was forever changed. In contrast to rural and small-town America, where the seasonality of agriculture dictated the rhythms of daily existence, cities pulsed with people rushing to beat deadlines. Moreover, whereas small-town residents knew their neighbors and shared their outlook, city dwellers lived in a world of strangers and confronted ethnic and class differences at every turn. Even the concept of time took on a new meaning in the city. Rural dwellers went to bed early, but urbanites walked about, played, and shopped late into the night. One social worker wrote, "Every night the brightly lighted main thoroughfares, with the gleaming store-windows, . . . provide a promenade for thousands who find in walk and talk along the pavement a cheap form of social entertainment."

## A Revolution in Transportation

Until the first quarter of the nineteenth century, most cities functioned as compact communities covering perhaps a three-square-mile area. Within these "walking" cities, so called because a person could easily walk from one end to the other, rich and poor lived in close proximity, with the wealthy near the commercial center and the poor scattered in basements around town. The development of new transportation systems, beginning in the 1830s with the stagecoach and continuing with the steam ferry and the horse-drawn streetcar, created a technological revolution that turned these older cities literally inside out. The rich and wellborn moved to the city's edge, while the poor migrated inward, settling in abandoned mansions that were subdivided and then subdivided again to accommodate their increasing numbers.

The first urban transportation networks, operating regularly scheduled city stagecoaches (omnibuses) over fixed routes, appeared in New York in the 1820s. Over the next two decades, smoother-riding horse-drawn streetcars, pulled by a single powerful horse along railway tracks in the streets, replaced them. By the 1880s, 415 horsecar companies carried 188 million passengers a year over more than six thousand miles of track. The horsecars provided easy transportation between city dwellers' places of work and their residences, which increasingly were separated.

The horsecars did have drawbacks. Extra animals were sometimes needed to pull the cars up hills, and hitching and unhitching them could take ten minutes. Observers recoiled as they watched panting horses, whipped by drivers, strain to pull the crowded cars. Many looked away in disgust as creatures that had stumbled and fallen were destroyed where they lay. In New York alone, an estimated fifteen thousand overworked beasts died each year in the 1880s.

Horse droppings were another problem. Health officials in Rochester, New York, estimated in 1900 that the excrement produced yearly by the city's fifteen thousand horses would fill a hole one acre in area and 175 feet deep and would breed 16 billion flies. Added to the mud and garbage that befouled city streets, the stinking heaps of dung moved officials to explore alternate transportation options.

Steam railroads were an obvious first choice. But they were designed for long hauls rather than short runs, and they functioned most efficiently when they pulled a large number of cars. To improve travel within the city, local officials explored more flexible alternatives that included cable cars and electric streetcars.

Chicago pioneered the most extensive cable-car system. Run by a circulating underground cable to which a conductor attached each vehicle, Chicago's cable cars by 1887 operated over more than eighty-six miles of track. More sanitary, better on hills, and quieter than horsecars and steam railways, cable cars marked a significant improvement in urban transportation. But high construction costs restricted cable operation to the most heavily traveled routes, and eventually cable cars proved profitable only in hilly cities such as San Francisco.

By the 1890s electric streetcars, called trolleys because of the four-wheeled spring mechanism that trolled along the overhead wires, had replaced horsecars and cable cars in most cities. First installed in Richmond, Virginia, and Montgomery, Alabama, electric streetcar systems shaped the urban environment in important ways. Unlike European transportation companies, which charged according to the distance traveled, American streetcar firms adopted a flat-fee policy, usually five cents per ride with free transfers. This uniform-fare system enabled families to move farther and farther from the city's center without increasing their transportation expenses, thereby encouraging urban sprawl. Recognizing that the expansion of streetcar lines would substantially raise land values, most street-

**Los Angeles Electric Railway Company, 1887**
*Electric trolley cars were quieter, cleaner, and less smelly than horse-pulled cars. Like most trolley lines in Los Angeles, this one was built to provide access to a new real estate development. Within three days, all building lots had been sold.*

**Dead Horse in Street**
*So many horses, like this one in New York at the turn of the century, died from overwork that they sometimes remained in the streets for several days before they could be removed.*

car companies ran their transportation operations at a loss, purchased land at the city's periphery, and earned towering profits from the sale of real estate. When the suburban lands became fully settled, however, many streetcar companies went broke.

Streetcar lines, which radiated outward from the heart of the city like spokes on a wheel, also helped revitalize the city center. With crosstown routes so limited, commuters who wished to visit a different part of the city had to pass through the downtown. The practical effect of this arrangement was to improve commercial opportunities in the central business district. In 1874 Philadelphia merchant John Wanamaker, recognizing the potential created by the growing streetcar network, turned an old downtown railroad freight depot into an elaborate department store. Wanamaker's success in Philadelphia was duplicated by Morris Rich in Atlanta, Adam Gimbel and Rowland H. Macy in New York, Marshall Field in Chicago, and Joseph L. Hudson in Detroit. The inexpensive convenience of traveling by trolley made shopping downtown a new form of recreation for millions of Americans.

**Urban Growth; 1880–1890**

| City | 1880 Population | 1890 Population | Percent Increase |
|------|------|------|------|
| Austin, Texas | 11,013 | 14,575 | 32.34 |
| Boston | 362,893 | 448,477 | 23.58 |
| Chicago | 503,185 | 1,099,850 | 118.57 |
| Cleveland | 160,146 | 261,353 | 63.19 |
| Dallas | 10,358 | 38,067 | 267.51 |
| Denver | 35,629 | 106,713 | 199.51 |
| New York | 1,206,299 | 1,515,301 | 25.61 |
| Lincoln, Nebraska | 13,003 | 55,154 | 324.16 |
| Los Angeles | 11,183 | 50,395 | 350.64 |
| Omaha | 30,518 | 140,452 | 360.23 |
| Philadelphia | 847,170 | 1,046,964 | 23.58 |
| Portland, Oregon | 17,577 | 46,385 | 163.92 |
| Salt Lake City | 20,768 | 44,843 | 115.92 |
| San Francisco | 233,959 | 298,997 | 27.70 |
| Topeka, Kansas | 15,452 | 31,007 | 100.67 |

*Source:* Abstract, The Eleventh Census, 1890 (Washington, D.C.: U.S. Government Printing Office, 1896).

## A Mobile Population

The expansion of streetcar systems, coupled with the completion of regional railroad networks, dramatically affected urban residential stability. Historians have long recognized that the immigrants and transplanted farm people who flooded into American cities in the late nineteenth century tended to move frequently. Only recently has it been discovered that the old elites in most of these cities were highly transient as well. Indeed, a fever to move seized much of the population in these years.

The reasons for this frenzied mobility were many. As city neighborhoods became crowded with people and congested with traffic, those who could headed for outlying residential areas, now conveniently accessible by streetcar. Others pulled up stakes in quest of cheaper or more fashionable homes available on the city's periphery.

A parallel movement *between* cities matched the frenetic residential shifts *within* cities. Both upper- and working-class urban families drifted from city to city in hopes of increasing their income or bettering their living conditions. Most cities, although growing in overall numbers because of the inpouring of newcomers, lost more than half their current inhabitants every decade. Historical demographers calculate that most U.S. cities in this period experienced an astonishing turnover of about three or four times their total population every ten years.

Contemporaries like Jacob Riis viewed the unprecedented migration of the middle and upper classes to the suburban fringe, away from downtown congestion, as a selfish attempt to escape responsibility for improving inner-city neighborhoods. An immigrant himself, Riis complained that the privileged classes were deserting the poor. In a sense, he was correct. Although many well-to-do city dwellers were concerned about the destitute, they placed the happiness, health, and safety of their own families first.

Thus mobility and change were the norm in nineteenth-century urban society. New transportation systems facilitated considerable residential movement.

Searching for new ways to better their lives, both rich and poor changed residences and jobs frequently. Just as the frontier West lured seekers of fresh beginnings and extravagant wealth, the city beckoned to the restless and ambitious with myriad exciting opportunities for advancement.

## Migrants and Immigrants

The growing concentration of industries in urban settings produced demands for thousands of new workers in these years. The promise of good wages and a broad range of jobs drew many rural and small-town dwellers to the cities. So great was the migration from rural areas, especially New England, that some farm communities vanished from the map.

Young farm women led the exodus cityward. With the growing mechanization of farming in the late nineteenth century, farm work was increasingly male work. At the same time, rising sales of factory-produced goods through mail-order catalogs serving country areas reduced rural needs for women's labor on subsis-

tence tasks. So young farm women flocked to the cities, where they competed for jobs with immigrant, black, and city-born white women.

From 1860 to 1890, the prospect of a better life also attracted nearly 10 million northern European immigrants to East Coast and midwestern cities, where they joined the more than 4 million who had settled there in the 1840s and 1850s. Germans made up the largest group, numbering close to 3 million. Behind them nearly 2 million English, Scottish, and Welsh immigrants and almost 1.5 million Irish came in search of new jobs and new opportunities. Moreover, by 1900 more than 800,000 French-Canadians had migrated south to work in the New England mills, and close to a million Scandinavian newcomers had put down roots in the rich farmlands of Wisconsin and Minnesota.

In the 1890s these "old immigrants" from northern and western Europe were joined by swelling numbers of "new immigrants"—Italians, Slavs, Greeks, and Jews from southern and eastern Europe, Armenians from the Middle East, and, in Hawaii, Japanese from Asia. In the next three decades, these new immigrants, often from peasant backgrounds, would boost America's foreign-born population by more than 18 million.

Whether old immigrants or new, the surge of foreigners owed much to improvements in steam-powered vessels. After the Civil War, the introduction of large, swift, oceangoing steamships had not only reduced the time required for the Atlantic voyage from three months to two or three weeks but it also spawned a competition for passengers that drove down the cost of ocean passage.

The overwhelming majority of immigrants settled in cities in the northeastern and north-central states, with the Irish predominating in New England and the Germans in the Midwest. The impact of their numbers was staggering. In 1890 New York City (including Brooklyn, still a

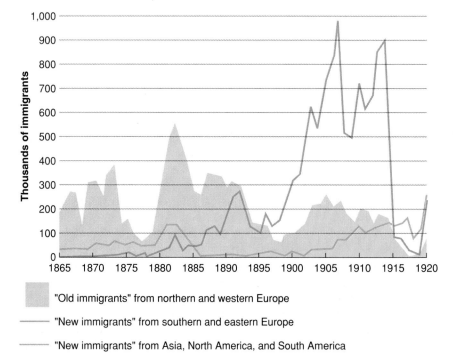

**The Changing Face of U.S. Immigration, 1865–1920**

*Between 1865 and 1895, the majority of newcomers to America hailed from northern and western Europe. But the early twentieth century witnessed a surge of immigration from southern and eastern Europe.*

"Old immigrants" from northern and western Europe

"New immigrants" from southern and eastern Europe

"New immigrants" from Asia, North America, and South America

**Jakob Mithelstadt
and Family, 1905**
*The Mithelstadts were Russian
Germans who arrived in New
York City on the S.S.* Pretoria. *The
poorest immigrants traveled in
steerage, below-deck cargo areas that lacked portholes and
originally housed the cables to
the ship's rudder.*

legally separate municipality) contained twice as many
Irish as Dublin, as many Germans as Hamburg, half as
many Italians as Naples, and 2½ times the Jewish population of Warsaw. That same year four out of five people living in greater New York had been born abroad or
were children of foreign parents.

Many of these recent immigrants had come voluntarily, in pursuit of economic betterment. Others were
forced out of their home countries by overpopulation,
crop failure, famine, violence, or industrial depression.
Emigration from England, for example, spurted during
downswings in the British economy in 1873 and 1883.
On the Continent, German peasants and artisans,
squeezed by overpopulation and threatened by church
reorganizations that they opposed, left in large numbers in the 1880s. In contrast to the European immigrants who left because of problems at home, more
than 100,000 Japanese laborers were lured to Hawaii in
the 1890s to work on the lucrative sugar plantations by
promises of considerable income.

Even among the Europeans, some ambitious individuals, including many single young men, immigrated
in the belief that their opportunities would be better in
the United States than in their homeland. Birger
Osland, an eighteen-year-old Norwegian, explained his
reasons for leaving to a friend: "My father is a schoolteacher and has, besides me, two younger sons, so that
it often strains his resources to keep us in school here.
. . . Besides . . . as I now probably have a foundation
upon which I can build my own further education, I

have come to feel that the most sensible thing I can do
is to emigrate to America." Although single women
were less likely than men to come on their own, Irish
women often did so and sent their earnings back
home. Most commonly, however, wives and children
waited in the old country until the family breadwinner
had secured a job and saved enough money to pay for
their passage to America.

Would-be immigrants first had to travel to a European port city—Hamburg was a major port of embarkation—where they booked passage on a steamship. The cramped, often stormy Atlantic journey
featured poor food, little privacy, and rudimentary sanitary facilities. Immigrants arrived tired, fearful, and in
some cases very sick.

Further complications awaited the travelers upon
reaching their destination, often New York City on the
East Coast or San Francisco on the West. Before customs officials allowed them to enter the country, they
inspected the newcomers for physical handicaps and
contagious diseases. After 1892, those with "loathsome" infections such as leprosy, trachoma (a contagious viral disease of the eye), or venereal disease
were refused admittance and deported. Immigrants
who passed the physical examination then had their
names recorded. If a customs inspector had difficulty
pronouncing a foreign name, he often Anglicized it.
One German Jew became flustered when asked for his
name and mumbled, "Schoyn vergessen [I forget]."
The inspector, who did not understand Yiddish, wrote

"Sean Ferguson" on the man's roster. In this manner, numerous immigrants ended up with "Americanized" names.

New York state established a special facility for admitting immigrants in 1855 at Castle Garden. Later, when the numbers swelled, the federal government took control and built a new station on Ellis Island in 1892. On the West Coast, Angel Island in San Francisco bay served a similar purpose after 1910. At the immigrant processing centers, America's newest residents exchanged foreign currency for U.S. dollars, purchased railroad tickets, and arranged lodgings. In other cities immigrants were hounded by tavernkeepers, peddlers, and porters who tried to exploit their ignorance of the English language and American ways. "When you land in America," wrote one Swedish resident to friends back home, "you will find many who will offer their services, but beware of them because there are so many rascals who make it their business to cheat the immigrants."

Those who arrived with sufficient cash, including many German artisans and Scandinavian farmers, commonly traveled west to Chicago, Milwaukee, and the rolling prairies beyond. But most of the Irish, and later the Italians, who hailed largely from poor peasant backgrounds, remained in eastern cities like Boston, New York, and Philadelphia. Those Irish and Italians who did go west typically made the trip in stages, moving from job to job on the railroad and canal systems.

### Adjusting to an Urban Society

For many immigrants the stress of adjusting to urban life in a new society was eased by the fact that they could settle among compatriots who had preceded them. If a map of New York City's streets and neighborhoods were colored in by nationality, Jacob Riis observed in 1890, it "would show more stripes than on the skin of a zebra, and more colors than any rainbow." The streets of Manhattan between the West Side Irish neighborhoods and the East Side German neighborhoods teemed with tenements housing Poles, Hungarians, Russians, Italians, and Chinese.

Late-nineteenth-century social commentators often assumed that each nationality group clumped together for reasons of national clannishness. But in fact, the process was far more subtle and complex. Most immigrants preferred to live near others not merely of their own nationality but from their own village or region in the old country. On New York's Lower East Side, for example, Italians did not form a single "Little Italy" but rather divided into many different subgroups: Neapolitans and Calabrians at Mulberry Bend, Genoese on Baxter Street, northern Italians west of Broadway, and Tyrolese Italians on Sixty-ninth Street near the Hudson River.

Within these ethnic neighborhoods, immigrants suffered incredibly crowded conditions. As early as 1853, the five-story Gotham Court tenement in New York City housed five hundred people. A decade later, when the owner added limited plumbing, the number of occupants jumped to eight hundred.

In 1879 New York reformers, concerned about the lack of light and fresh air in the tenements, passed a law that forced landlords to construct buildings with central ten-foot by four-foot air shafts. Dubbed "dumbbell tenements" because of their shape, the new buildings represented only a slight improvement over their predecessors. Although overcrowding was worst in Manhattan, cramped, low-grade housing also characterized immigrant districts in Boston, Philadelphia, San Francisco, and other cities. At the turn of the century, investigators in San Francisco's Chinatown found fami-

**Chinatown**

*As is evident in this photograph of San Francisco at the turn of the century, Chinese immigrant workers often retained their traditional ways of dress and lived in the most congested part of town.*

lies packed so densely into tenements that beds were attached to walls like shelves and used in shifts.

For all the adversity, many immigrant families enjoyed richly satisfying lives. Within the tight ethnic neighborhoods of major U.S. cities, immigrants could speak their native language, purchase traditional foods, attend old-world church services, and celebrate their festivals. Indeed, the immigrants' constant struggle to preserve old-world traditions transformed American urban life in the late nineteenth century by creating a diverse, pluralistic, civic culture in which a variety of different ethnic groups vied with native-born Americans for power and recognition.

In the competition to get ahead, some immigrant groups adjusted far more easily than others. Those with a background in the skilled trades and a familiarity with Anglo-American customs had relatively few problems. English-speaking immigrants from the British Isles, particularly those from mill, mining, and manufacturing districts, found comparable work and established a comfortable life. Ethnic groups that formed a substantial percentage of a city's population also had a major advantage. The Irish, for example, who by the 1880s made up nearly 16 percent of New York's population, 8 percent of Chicago's, and 17 percent of Boston's, facilitated Irish immigrants' entry into the American mainstream by dominating Democratic politics and controlling the hierarchy of the Catholic church in all three cities. Similarly the Germans in Milwaukee, composing about a third of the city's population in 1880, owned several major breweries, tanneries, and iron foundries and held leadership positions in local government and civic organizations.

Ironically, however, the larger immigrant groups' domination of urban institutions often made the adjustment to American society *more* difficult for members of smaller immigrant groups. Germans and other well-organized and skilled foreigners tended to exclude less-skilled newcomers from desirable jobs. English and German dominance of the building trades, for example, enabled those nationalities to limit the numbers of Italians hired. Not surprisingly, Italians accounted for only 18 percent of New York City's skilled brick masons in 1900 but made up 55 percent of the male barbers and 97 percent of the poorly paid bootblacks.

Another reason smaller immigrant groups had difficulty adjusting to American society was that many of their members had no intention of staying permanently. Young Chinese and Italian males often journeyed to American shores simply to earn enough

money to return home and buy land or set themselves up in business. Expecting only a brief stay, they made little effort to learn English or understand American customs. Of the Italians who immigrated to New York before 1914, nearly 50 percent went back to Italy. Although the rate of re-migration was greatest among Chinese and Italians, significant numbers of immigrants of other nationalities eventually returned to their homelands as well.

Various factors thus influenced the ability of immigrants of different national origins to adapt to urban society in America. Nevertheless, as the number of foreigners in U.S. cities ballooned toward the turn of the century, all immigrant groups, irrespective of size, faced increasing hostility from native-born Americans, who not only disliked the newcomers' social customs but also feared their growing influence.

## Slums and Ghettos

Every major city had its share of rundown, overcrowded slum neighborhoods. Generally clustered within walking distance of manufacturing districts, slums developed when landlords subdivided old buildings and packed in too many residents. The poorer the renters, the worse the slum. Slums became ghettos when laws, prejudice, and community pressure prevented the tenement inhabitants from renting elsewhere. During the 1890s Italians in New York, blacks in Philadelphia and Chicago, Mexican-Americans in Los Angeles, and Chinese in San Francisco increasingly became locked in segregated ghettos.

For a number of reasons, foreigners of Italian origin in particular were pushed into substandard housing. As we have seen, most unskilled young Italian male immigrants in these years had little alternative to accepting the lowest-paying jobs. To maximize their meager savings, they took the cheapest housing available—generally badly deteriorated tenements. Because many viewed their stay in America as temporary, they endured terrible filth and congestion.

To urban reformers like Danish-born Jacob Riis, who brought their own cultural biases to the effort to improve urban sanitation and housing, the Italians themselves appeared to be at the heart of the slum problem. In *How the Other Half Lives,* he singled out a district called the Bend, at the intersection of Mulberry and Baxter streets, as the worst of New York's slums, and he emphasized its Italian character. "Half of the people in 'the Bend' are christened Pasquale . . . ," he

**Garbage Box, First Ward, Chicago, c. 1900**
*Lacking space for recreation, immigrant children played atop garbage boxes in crowded alleys. Concerned for their health, Jane Addams wrote that "this slaughter of the innocents, this infliction of suffering on the newborn, is so gratuitous and so unfair, that it is only a question of time until an outraged sense of justice shall be aroused on behalf of these children."*

wrote patronizingly. "When the police do not know the name of an escaped murderer, they guess at Pasquale and send the name out on an alarm; in nine cases out of ten it fits." While acknowledging the destructive effects of substandard housing and inadequate health care, Riis nonetheless blamed the Italian residents themselves for the district's crime, filth, disease, and appallingly high infant death rate. Other middle-class observers of urban poverty used the terms *slum* and *foreign colony* interchangeably. This tendency to fault the slum dwellers for their own plight was characteristic of even well-intentioned reformers and helped shape—as well as distort—middle-class perceptions of the immigrant city.

Meanwhile, sobering evidence of the decay of urban America under the pressure of unremitting population growth mounted. Social workers in Chicago in the 1890s found conditions that matched those in New York City. Surveying a thirty-block section between Halsted Street and the Chicago River that was home to twenty-six different ethnic groups, they found that only about a quarter of the people had access to a bathroom with running water. The rest relied on repulsive outhouses, called privy vaults, located in yards or under porches. In an especially graphic report, the social workers de-

plored the district's "filthy and rotten tenements, the dingy courts and tumble-down sheds, the foul stables and dilapidated outhouses, the broken sewer-pipes, the piles of garbage fairly alive with diseased odors, and the numbers of children filling every nook, working and playing in every room, eating and sleeping in every window-sill, pouring in and out of every door, and seeming literally to pave every scrap of 'yard.' "

Health conditions in such districts almost defied description. Epidemics of typhoid fever, smallpox, and diphtheria periodically ravaged the slums, while slower killers like tuberculosis claimed many more victims (see A Place in Time). The immigrant city was particularly unsparing of its children. Juvenile diseases such as whooping cough, measles, and scarlet fever took a fearful toll, and infant mortality was very high. In one immigrant ward in Chicago in 1900, 20 percent of all infants died in their first year of life.

Furthermore, because tenements often bordered the industrial districts, residents had to put up with the noise, pollution, and foul odors of tanneries, foundries, factories, and packing houses. Because most factories used coal-fired steam engines as their energy source, and because coal was also the preferred heating fuel for most apartment houses and businesses, vast quantities of soot and coal dust drifted skyward daily. In tenements near factories and warehouses, the atmosphere was hazy gray with smoke, and the buildings themselves took on a dingy, grimy patina.

Although the immigrants' situation was grim, the position of blacks was worse. In contrast to most immigrants, who stayed in the shabbiest tenements only until they could afford better housing, blacks were trapped in segregated districts. Driven out of the skilled trades and excluded from most factory work, blacks took menial jobs whose low pay left them little income for housing. Racist city dwellers used high rents, real estate covenants, and neighborhood pressure to exclude them from areas inhabited by whites. Because the numbers of northern urban blacks in 1890 remained relatively small—for example, they composed only 1.2 percent of Cleveland's population and 1.3 percent of Chicago's—they could not overcome whites' concerted campaigns to shut them out.

By the turn of the century, growing competition between immigrants and black migrants moving up from the South led to further efforts to segregate blacks in the poorest sections of northern cities—in Chicago, a long, narrow "Black Belt" on the South Side; in Cleveland, the Central Avenue District. Blacks in such cities faced intimidation as well as segregation. A Washington,

D.C., black newspaper, the *Bee,* asserted in the 1880s that white police officers, particularly the Irishmen on the force, "delight in arresting every little colored boy they see on the street, who may be doing something not at all offensive, and allow the white boys to do what they please."

Rivalry over housing and jobs sometimes sparked racial violence. Most frequently the victim of an attack was a single individual, but sometimes interracial clashes escalated into a full-scale riot, as in New York City during the summer of 1900. The melee was touched off when Arthur J. Harris, a young black man, knifed and killed a plainclothes policeman in lower Manhattan who he believed was mishandling his wife. News of the murder spread quickly among whites, and the district seethed with anger. "Men and women poured by the hundreds from the neighboring tenements," reported a local newspaperman. "Negroes were set upon wherever they could be found and brutally beaten."

## Fashionable Avenues and Suburbs

As remains true today, the same cities that harbored slums, suffering, and violence also boasted neighborhoods of dazzling opulence. The wealthy built monumental residences on exclusive thoroughfares just out-side the downtown: Fifth Avenue in New York, Commonwealth Avenue in Boston, Euclid Avenue in Cleveland, and Summit Avenue in St. Paul.

In the 1870s and 1880s, wealthy city dwellers began moving to the suburbs to distance themselves further from the crowded tenement districts. Promoters of the suburban ideal, playing on the romantic rural nostalgia popular at the time, skillfully contrasted the rolling lawns and sheltered houses on the city's periphery with the teeming streets, noisy saloons, and mounds of garbage and excrement downtown. Soon many major cities could boast of their own stylish suburbs: Haverford, Ardmore, and Bryn Mawr outside Philadelphia; Brookline near Boston; and Shaker Heights near Cleveland.

Middle-class city dwellers followed the precedents set by the wealthy. Skilled artisans, shopkeepers, clerks, accountants, and sales personnel moved either to new developments at the city's edge or to outlying suburban communities (although those at the lower fringe of the middle class typically rented apartments in neighborhoods closer to the city center). In the 1890s Chicago developer Samuel Eberly Gross created entire low-cost subdivisions north and west of the city and advertised homes for as little as ten dollars a month. Lawyers, doctors, small businessmen, and other professionals moved farther out along the main thoroughfares served

**Toledo Street with Trees**
*This spacious, tree-lined street in Toledo, Ohio, typified the prosperous suburban developments at the turn of the century.*

**Philadelphia Streets**
*Although middle-class suburbanites could take the trolley into the city, they invariably ran through congested streets like this one in Philadelphia in 1897 filled with horse carriages, wagons, and immigrant workers.*

## Immigrant Milwaukee

On August 5, 1894, a mob of more than three thousand furious Polish citizens on Milwaukee's South Side fought a pitched battle with police and health department officials. A smallpox epidemic had broken out in the city, and the health department had ordered infected persons to be taken by ambulance to a city isolation hospital. A distraught mother who had recently lost another child to smallpox refused to let the city "kill" her sick two-year-old daughter by hospitalizing her. "I can give better care and nourishment here than they can give in the hospital," she yelled at the authorities. Confronted by a violent crowd armed with clubs, knives, and stones, the health department crew beat a hasty retreat. The local newspaper later reported that for more than a month after this incident, "mobs of Pomeranian and Polish women armed with baseball bats, potato mashers, clubs, bed slats, salt and pepper, and butcher knives, lay in wait all day for . . . the Isolation Hospital van."

The smallpox riots of 1894 reflected deep antagonisms between city officials and ethnic groups in Milwaukee. The confrontations pitted reform-minded political appointees and sanitary engineers seeking to establish citywide health ordinances against immigrants seeking to preserve their traditions. The conflicts exposed the reformers' mixed motives, for beneath their drive to improve city sanitation lay a desire to destroy the foreign customs of Milwaukee's immigrants.

Tensions first surfaced in Milwaukee during a period of rapid growth. Settled in 1836 at a natural harbor formed on Lake Michigan, the city witnessed a tenfold population gain from 1850 to 1890, swelling from 20,000 to more than 200,000 residents. Germans,

**East Water St. Looking South, Color Lithograph** (Detail), c. 1898
*By 1890 the thriving downtown center of Milwaukee, with its efficient trolley-car system and tall office buildings, was surrounded by immigrant neighborhoods on the near north and near south sides.*

who made up Milwaukee's largest immigrant group, predominated in the early years of settlement and concentrated heavily on the city's West Side. Then in the 1870s, large numbers of Poles and other eastern Europeans poured in, drawn by the unskilled jobs available in the rolling mills and blast furnaces of heavy industries such as the Milwaukee Iron Company and the E. P. Allis Company. Bartholomew Koperski, a Polish laborer, was typical of the many Poles who clustered in small, ill-ventilated houses in wards on the city's South Side. A railroad-car inspector, Koperski lived with his wife and six children in the upstairs of a twenty-two- by forty-foot cottage. He rented the basement to George Krzyzaniak, a twenty-nine-year-old Polish carpenter, his wife, and their two children. Although the city's health department inspectors reported that most immigrants' homes were in "good sanitary condition," less than half had indoor plumbing.

The Koperskis and their compatriots belonged to a close ethnic community whose ties were cemented by their common language and their powerful religious bonds. Milwaukee's Poles founded their own Catholic churches; published their own Polish-language newspaper, *Krytyka* (*The Critic*); and figured prominently in ward politics. During smallpox epidemics the Milwaukee health department tried to establish citywide health policies that quarantined infected houses, banned public funerals, and forced diseased persons into isolation hospitals, but the cohesive Polish wards fought back. Accustomed to nursing the sick at home, the Poles protested city efforts to cart invalids off to hospitals and then ban family members from visiting them. Furthermore, with a strong tradition of elaborate church funerals for their deceased loved ones, they refused to accept

the idea of burials without formal church rites.

At the height of the epidemic, a local alderman spoke out for his constituents. He raged that the Poles were being treated as "the scum of Milwaukee." "I don't blame the people down here for being worked up," he told a newspaper reporter. "The patients at the hospitals are not treated like human beings, and the way the dead are buried is brutal." He was particularly incensed by the position taken by Milwaukee's health commissioner, Walter Kempster, a native-born American who asserted, "I am here to enforce the laws, and I shall enforce them if I have to break heads to do it."

The debate over city quarantine policies between Kempster and Milwaukee's South Siders rekindled a conflict dating from nearly six months earlier, when Kempster was first appointed health commissioner. Hired because of his medical credentials, Kempster, a Republican, had ignored his party's suggested list of candidates to fill the twenty-six openings in his department. Incensed by Kempster's failure to reward any of their constituents with a job, Polish city council members had agitated for his removal. Now the

smallpox epidemic provided an additional avenue for those longing to unseat Kempster. In the crisis his adversaries denounced him as a symbol of arbitrary government authority and a subverter of immigrant culture and personal liberty.

As the deadly epidemic continued into the autumn months, the city council passed a new ordinance barring the health commissioner from hospitalizing victims without their consent. Still upset by his handling of the Polish South Siders, the council dismissed Kempster in February 1895. Milwaukee's battle over city health policies thus revealed a larger struggle between immigrant groups and public administrators: a tug-of-war for political control of the city.

Not until after 1900 did Milwaukee and other cities establish enforceable health regulations and vaccination policies that in time lowered the nationwide mortality rate from smallpox and other diseases. And only with massive educational campaigns in the Progressive Era were ethnic groups persuaded that local government had a legitimate need to interfere with their social customs in matters that concerned the welfare of all citizens.

## Milwaukee's Polish Community

*Polish residents of Milwaukee stand proudly before St. Josephat's Church, still under construction in this photograph from the early twentieth century.*

by the street railway, where they purchased homes with large lots.

In time, a pattern of informal residential segregation by income took shape in the cities and suburbs. Built up for families of a particular income level, certain neighborhoods and suburbs developed remarkably similar standards for lot size and house design. Commuters who rode the new street railways out from the city center could identify the changing neighborhoods along the way as readily as a geologist might distinguish different strata on a washed-out riverbank.

So by 1900 whirring trolley cars and hissing steam-powered trains had burst the boundaries of the compact midcentury city. Within this expanded city, sharp dissimilarities in building height and neighborhood quality set off business sectors from fashionable residential avenues and strikingly differentiated squalid manufacturing districts from parklike suburban subdivisions. Musing about urban America in 1902, James F. Muirhead, a popular Scottish guidebook author, wrote that New York and other U.S. cities reminded him of "a lady in a ball costume, with diamonds in her ears, and her toes out at her boots." To Muirhead, urban America had become a "land of contrasts" in which the spatial separations of various social groups and the radically unequal living conditions for rich and poor had heightened the sense of ethnic and class consciousness. Along with the physical change in American cities, in short, had come a new awareness of class and cultural disparities.

# The Urban Challenge

Although middle- and upper-class Americans were abandoning their downtown residences in the 1880s and 1890s, the business and professional activities of countless merchants, manufacturers, and others remained centered in the vibrant heart of the city. These old-stock citizens were deeply troubled by the strikes and riots that periodically swept through the cities. Urban critics blamed the disorder on the immigrant masses, who did not, they concluded, share their own cultural views on self-discipline and moral improvement.

Convinced that urgent steps must be taken to stem what seemed a rising tide of riot, robbery, and rotten government, these concerned citizens waged a continuous battle in the late nineteenth century to eradicate urban crime, reform "boss" politics, and assimilate the

immigrants into mainstream American society. Their efforts were motivated by a powerful blend of altruism and self-interest.

## *Policing the City*

Would-be reformers worried not only about the organized mass protests of disgruntled workers but about the crime that inevitably increased as city populations grew denser. In his novel *Ragged Dick* (1868), Unitarian minister Horatio Alger detailed the variety of scams and tricks that victimized rural visitors to the city. Shopkeepers swindled the unsuspecting by giving them incorrect change. Pickpockets and thieves stole handbags and purses. Worst of all, Irish street gangs, led by toughs like Alger's fictional Mickey Maguire, sometimes beat up and robbed the innocent.

Horatio Alger and other writers who associated crime with the growth of cities did not exaggerate. In Philadelphia, for example, both the population and the number of homicides nearly tripled in the second half of the century. As city dailies splashed reports of violence across their front pages, reformers worried publicly about urbanites' easy access to cheap handguns.

In their desire to maintain public order, city officials in the 1830s and 1840s had established police forces to supplement the traditional night watch that had patrolled the streets after dark to keep an eye out for fires. Unlike their European counterparts, these police forces were civilian enterprises, separate from the military and controlled by local officials. Following the example set by New York in 1853, other American cities had outfitted their municipal police forces with badges and uniforms and authorized officers to carry revolvers.

Initially, however, these new urban police forces had an odd, ill-defined assortment of responsibilities. In New York City they cleaned streets and inspected boilers. In Baltimore, Philadelphia, and New York, they ran lodging houses for the homeless and distributed supplies to the poor. In St. Louis they supervised the sanitation of vegetable markets.

The police sometimes battled immigrant gangs like Baltimore's Blood Tubs and New York City's Bowery Boys, but they made little headway in suppressing the rowdy street life, drinking, gambling, and prostitution that flourished within the immigrant working class. Middle-class civic leaders particularly feared the immigrants' neighborhood saloons, which offered a free lunch with a five-cent beer, provided meeting rooms, spread news of job openings, and sometimes, in back rooms, furnished gambling tables and offered prostitutes' services.

State legislatures, dominated in these years by rural, native-born citizens who deplored the immigrants' drinking and gambling, regularly passed laws banning these practices, curtailing Sunday business operations, and regulating saloons. Caught between moralistic state legislators and immigrant communities resentful of outside meddling, the police tried to steer a middle course, tacitly allowing the saloons to remain open on Sunday, for example, as long as their patrons behaved properly in public.

An investigation conducted in 1894 by New York State senator Clarence Lexow uncovered considerable evidence that the New York City police not only failed to suppress illegal activities but in effect often licensed them. In return for regular payoffs, Lexow reported, the police permitted gamblers, prostitutes, and saloonkeepers to operate more or less at will in poor neighborhoods, provided that they remained discreet. A portion of these payoffs, Lexow further revealed, ended up in the hands of local political bosses who hired and fired the police. Instead of fighting vice, a shocked Lexow concluded, the police were conniving in it.

In city after city in the late nineteenth century, reformers strove to professionalize law enforcement by transferring the hiring and firing of police officers from political bosses to independent, nonpartisan boards of commissioners. Not until the 1890s, however, did most urban police forces adopt a professional attitude toward their work. Pressured by reformers such as young Theodore Roosevelt, who headed New York City's Board of Police Commissioners from 1895 to 1897, civic leaders gradually removed the police department from the political patronage system and set up regular hiring procedures. Unable to enforce the strict morality desired by rural, native-born state legislators, many urban police departments by the turn of the century had shifted their attention from trying to control the "dangerous classes" to deterring criminal behavior.

## *Governing the City*

The competition for authority over the police revealed a deeper power struggle within urban politics. Amid the furiously haphazard growth of cities, political power had become fragmented and decentralized. The urgent demands placed on public utilities, rapid-transit systems, and fire and police departments forced cities to raise taxes, issue bonds, and create a host of new

**"Let Us Prey," 1871**
*Cartoonist Thomas Nast hated William Marcy Tweed's ostentatious style. Pictured here as the chief vulture standing over the body of New York City, Boss Tweed wears an enormous diamond, a symbol of his insatiable greed.*

municipal departments and positions. Since large sums of money could be made by dominating any segment of this process, state and local politicians fought desperately for control of the city and the right to run these lucrative urban services.

Complicating the contest for control of city politics was the fact that both city governments and state legislatures claimed to have jurisdiction over the urban environment. Ostensibly to curb abuse in urban government, state legislatures altered city charters, bestowed special contracts and monopolies on certain railroad and utility magnates, and tried to minimize taxes by reducing the expenses of city government and limiting city services.

This kind of outside interference in local affairs had by midcentury encouraged the rise of a new kind of professional politician, the "boss." The boss presided over the city's "machine"—an unofficial political organization designed to keep a particular party or faction in office. Whether or not officially serving as mayor, the boss, assisted by local ward or precinct "captains," wielded enormous influence in city government. Often a former saloonkeeper or labor leader, the boss knew his constituents well. Cincinnati's George B. Cox was a typical boss, though more honest than many. The son of British immigrants, Cox worked his way up from being a newsboy and lookout for gamblers to tending bar and eventually acquired his own saloon. Elected to the Cincinnati city council in 1879, Cox in time became head of the city's Republican machine, which swung elections to the GOP, controlled key public offices, and acted as a broker among competing corporate and political interests.

For better or worse, the political machine was America's unique contribution to the challenge of municipal government in an era of pell-mell urban growth. Typified by Tammany Hall, the Democratic organization that dominated New York City politics from the 1830s to the 1930s, machines emerged in Baltimore, Philadelphia, Atlanta, San Francisco, and a host of other cities in the Gilded Age. Organized in a pyramid, the machine consisted of precinct or election-district captains who worked on the block or neighborhood level and who in turn reported to ward bosses. The ward bosses, frequently saloonkeepers, turned out the vote at election time in return for patronage jobs, contracts, and political appointments from city hall. At the apex of this pyramid sat the city boss, who controlled party activities throughout the city.

By the turn of the century, many urban machines ruled supreme. Working through the local ward captains, the machine rode herd on the tangle of municipal bureaucracies, rewarding its friends and punishing its enemies through its control of taxes, licenses, and inspections. The machine gave tax breaks to favored contractors in return for large payoffs and slipped them insider information about upcoming street and sewer projects. At the neighborhood level, the ward boss sometimes acted as a welfare agent, helping the needy and protecting the troubled. It was important to the boss that he be viewed as being generous to his constituents. To spend three dollars to cover a fine for a juvenile offense meant a lot to the poor, but it was small change to a boss who raked in millions from public-utility contracts and land deals. If the machine helped alleviate some of the poor's suffering in the Gilded Age, however, it hopelessly entangled urban social services with corrupt politics and often prevented the political process from responding to the real problems of the city's neediest inhabitants.

Bosses like George Cox in Cincinnati, Ohio, and "Big Jim" Pendergast in Kansas City, Missouri—and even those in smaller cities such as Rochester, Omaha, and Memphis—transformed urban politics into a new form of entrepreneurship. They could be as ambitious and ruthless as any Gilded Age captain of industry. Like the Carnegies and the Rockefellers, the city bosses pioneered new forms of social organization and extemporized managerial innovations even as they consolidated their personal power, and in some cases they amassed vast fortunes. At times greedy and utterly unscrupulous, they nevertheless paid lip service to immigrant and working-class concerns in a society increasingly dominated by the middle and upper classes.

Under New York City's boss William Marcy Tweed, the Tammany Hall machine epitomized the slimy depths to which extortion and contract padding could sink. Although between 1869 and 1871, Tweed gave $50,000 to the poor and $2,250,000 to schools, orphanages, and hospitals, his machine also dispensed sixty thousand patronage positions and pumped up the city's debt by $70 million through graft and inflated contracts. The details of the Tweed ring's massive fraud and corruption were widely reported in newspapers and brilliantly satirized in *Harper's Weekly* by German immigrant cartoonist Thomas Nast, who in one cartoon portrayed Tweed and his cronies as vultures picking at the city's bones. Tweed bellowed in fury. "I don't care a straw for your newspaper articles—my constituents don't know how to read," he told *Harper's,* "but they can't help seeing them damned pictures." Convicted of fraud and extortion, Tweed was sentenced to jail in 1873, served two years, escaped to Spain, was reapprehended and reincarcerated, and died in jail in 1878.

Not all bosses were as crooked and covetous as Tweed. Boss Cox of Cincinnati, who steadfastly maintained he had never received an illegal payoff, gained the backing of local good-government reformers—"goo-goos" to their opponents—by supporting voter-registration laws and by placing the police and fire departments under independent bipartisan boards. He also supported the construction of a new city waterworks as well as the improvement of parks and recreational facilities. Although Cox's opponents never believed that his administration was as free from corruption as he claimed, they did not overthrow his political machine until 1897.

Despite the stereotype of city bosses as coarse and crude—British observer James Bryce described them as "vulgar figures with good coats"—not all bosses fit that mold. San Francisco boss Abraham Ruef had graduated from the University of California at eighteen years of age with highest honors and spoke seven languages. Ed Flynn, the boss of the Bronx, New York, was a brilliant lawyer. Whatever their backgrounds, however, bosses represented a new political organization that stressed grass-roots ties to the neighborhood and ward. Standing amid the real estate promoters, local businessmen, wealthy entrepreneurs, civic reformers, and other groups vying for power and pursuing their various agendas in the cockpit of urban politics, the boss made sure that the concerns of his constituents were heard. In this ceaseless struggle among competing groups with vastly different interests, the boss displayed a flexible, pragmatic, and opportunistic approach to meeting the day-to-day challenges of urban life.

Nevertheless, by the turn of the century, the bosses faced well-organized assaults on their power, led by an urban elite whose members sought to restore "good government." In this atmosphere the bosses increasingly forged alliances with civic organizations and reform leagues. The results, although never entirely satisfactory to any of the parties involved, paved the way for new sewer and transportation systems, expanded parklands, and improved public services—a record of considerable accomplishment, given the magnitude of the problems created by urban growth.

### *Battling Poverty*

In contrast to the political bosses' piecemeal attempts to help the urban poor, middle-class city leaders sought comprehensive solutions for relieving poverty. Jacob Riis and other reformers believed that the basic cause of urban distress was the immigrants' lack of self-discipline and self-control. Consequently, Riis and the other charity reformers focused on moral improvement and ignored the crippling impact of low wages and dangerous working conditions. Although many reformers genuinely sympathized with the suffering of the lower classes, the humanitarians ultimately turned their campaigns to help the destitute into missions to Americanize the immigrants and eliminate customs that they perceived as offensive and self-destructive.

Poverty-relief workers first targeted their efforts at the young, who were thought to be most malleable. Energized by the religious revivals of the 1830s and 1840s (see Chapter 10), early Protestant social reformers started charitable societies to help transient youths and street waifs. In 1843 Robert M. Hartley, a former employee of the New York Temperance Society, organized the New York Association for Improving the Condition of the Poor to urge poor families to change their ways. Expanding to Baltimore, Philadelphia, and Boston, Hartley's association also demanded pure-milk laws, public baths, and better housing.

Hartley's voluntaristic approach was supplemented at midcentury by the more coercive tactics of Charles Loring Brace, who in 1853 founded the New York Children's Aid Society. Brace admired "these little traders of the city . . . battling for a hard living in the snow and mud of the street" but worried that they might join the city's "dangerous classes." Brace not only established dormitories, reading rooms, and workshops where the boys could learn practical skills but he also sometimes swept children off the streets, shipped them to the country, and hired them out as farmhands.

Where Brace's Children's Aid Society gave vulnerable adolescents an alternative to living in the slums, the Young Men's Christian Association (YMCA), founded in England in 1841 and exported to America ten years later, provided decent housing and wholesome recreational facilities for country boys new to the city. More than any other institutions, the YMCA and later the YWCA (Young Women's Christian Association) worked to overcome the dislocation experienced by the thousands of rural Americans who migrated to the city in the post–Civil War years. In the Protestant tradition of moral improvement, both organizations subjected their members to considerable supervision and expelled them for drinking and other forbidden behavior.

The departure of young people—especially farmers' daughters—from older rural areas was truly startling. Between 1840 and 1900, almost half the townships in Vermont lost more than a quarter of their population, and young adults led the exodus. Like Carrie Meeber, the heroine in Theodore Dreiser's *Sister Carrie* (1900), youthful rural migrants drawn to the city's greater economic opportunities were awed by the glamour and glitter of urban life. Far from home, with few friends and no place to stay, they easily fell victim to the city's flashy con artists and fast talkers. The YMCA and the YWCA supplied such country innocents safe temporary lodgings and reassuring reminders of home.

By 1900 more than fifteen hundred YMCAs acted as a haven for nearly a quarter-million men. But YMCA (and YWCA) leaders reached only a small portion of the young adult population. Some whom they sought to

**YMCA, c. 1890**
*Designed to function as a wholesome alternative to the vices of city life, the Young Men's Christian Association helped newcomers adjust to an urban environment by providing reading room libraries and evening classes as well as gyms, swimming pools, handball courts, and other recreational facilities.*

help were put off by the organizations' close supervision and highly moralistic stance. Others, eager to assert their independence in their new urban environment, preferred not to ask for help. And although charity workers made some progress in their efforts to aid youth, the strategy was too narrowly focused to stem the rising tide of urban problems.

### New Approaches to Social Work

The inability of the Children's Aid Society, the YMCA, the YWCA, and other relief organizations to cope with the urban poor's explosive growth in the 1870s and 1880s convinced many middle-class Americans that urban poverty had reached epidemic proportions. The Reverend Josiah Strong, secretary of the American Home Missionary Society and minister of Cincinnati's Central Congregational Church, expressed this fear in his book *Our Country; Its Possible Future and Its Present Crisis* (1885). Asserting that the cities were "multiplying and focalizing the elements of anarchy and destruction," Strong attributed the urban menace to immigration and Catholicism. Critical of the immigrants' attachment to their saloons and beer halls, he pleaded for a cooperative effort among the Protestant churches to battle the dual plagues of intemperance and destitution.

Even before Strong mounted the battlements, social reformers had begun developing more coercive strategies for fighting poverty. One of the earliest and most effective agencies was the Salvation Army. A church es-

tablished along pseudomilitary lines in England in 1865 by Methodist minister "General" William Booth, the Salvation Army sent its uniformed volunteers to America in 1880 to provide food, shelter, and temporary employment for families. Known for its rousing music and attention-getting street meetings, the group ran soup kitchens and day nurseries and dispatched its "slum brigades" to carry the message of morality to the immigrant poor.

Funded by donations, the Salvation Army functioned both to aid and to control an urban lower-class population whose fondness for saloons, dance halls, and streetside entertainment threatened the middle-class conception of a stable society. The organization's strategy was simple. Attract the poor with marching bands and lively preaching; follow up with offers of food, assistance, and employment; and then teach them the solid middle-class virtues of temperance, hard work, and self-discipline.

A similar approach to poor relief was implemented by the New York Charity Organization Society (COS), founded in 1882 by Josephine Shaw Lowell. Of a prominent Boston family, the strong-willed Lowell had been widowed when her husband of a few months was killed during the Civil War, and she wore black for the rest of her life.

Adopting what they considered a scientific approach to make aid to the poor more efficient, the COS leaders divided New York City into districts, compiled files on all aid recipients, and sent "friendly visitors" into the tenements to counsel families on how to improve their lives. Convinced that moral deficiencies lay at the root of poverty, and that the "promiscuous charity" of overlapping welfare agencies undermined poor people's desire to work, the COS tried to foster self-sufficiency in its charges.

Although the COS and similar groups in Boston, Philadelphia, and other cities did serve as useful coordinators for relief efforts, critics justly accused them of being more interested in controlling the poor than in alleviating their suffering. More often than not, the friendly visitors wore cultural blinders and expected to effect change by imposing middle-class standards. In the 1890s Chicago journalist George Ade cruelly ridiculed the typical friendly visitor as "235 pounds of Sunshine." The earnest Salvation Army workers and COS volunteers no doubt accomplished some good, but unable to see slum problems from the vantage point of the poor, they failed, for the most part, in their underlying objective: to convert the poor to their own standards of morality and decorum.

### The Moral-Purity Campaign

The failure of Josephine Shaw Lowell and other like-minded social disciplinarians to eradicate urban poverty and crime prompted other reformers to push for even tougher measures against sin and immorality. In 1872 Anthony Comstock, a pious young dry-goods clerk, founded the New York Society for the Suppression of Vice. The organization demanded that municipal authorities close down gambling and lottery operations and censor obscene publications. Toward the end of his career in the early twentieth century, Comstock became a target of ridicule for his naive judgments about literature and art. (He dismissed George Bernard Shaw as "a foreign writer of filth" and raided the New York Art Students' League for displaying nude sculptures.) But in his heyday, Comstock's purity crusade gained widespread public support from middle- and upper-class civic leaders deeply frustrated by the lack of progress in flushing away urban vice.

Nothing symbolized the contested terrain between middle- and lower-class culture better than prostitution. Considered socially degenerate by some and a source of recreation by others, prostitution both exploited women and offered them large salaries and unbounded personal freedom. After the Civil War, the number of brothels—specialized houses where prostitutes plied their trade—expanded rapidly. Then in the

1880s, saloons, tenements, and cabarets, often controlled by political machines, displaced them. Even though immigrant women do not appear to have made up the majority of big-city prostitutes, reformers often labeled them as the major source of the problem.

In 1892 houses of prostitution, along with gambling dens and saloons, became targets for the reform efforts of New York Presbyterian minister Charles Parkhurst. Blaming the "slimy, oozy soil of Tammany Hall" and the New York City police—"the dirtiest, crookedest, and ugliest lot of men ever combined in semi-military array outside of Japan and Turkey"—for the city's rampant criminal evil, he organized the City Vigilance League in 1892 to clean up the city. Two years later, a nonpartisan Committee of Seventy elected a new mayor who pressured city officials to enforce the laws against prostitution, gambling, and Sunday liquor sales.

The purity campaign, however, lasted scarcely three years. Irish and German neighborhoods boisterously rallied in defense of their cherished saloons. Individuals who once championed Parkhurst's efforts scoffed at his self-righteous and bombastic rhetoric and deserted his movement; the city's reform coalition fell apart. Regaining power in 1897, Tammany Hall installed a new police chief who was once again content to regulate rather than root out vice. Even though Parkhurst politically controlled the mayor's office and had the backing of a reform coalition, his attempt to legislate morality had failed. New York City's population was too large, and its ethnic constituencies were too diverse, for middle- and upper-class reformers to curb all the illegal activities flourishing within the sprawling metropolis.

### The Social Gospel

Meanwhile, a handful of Protestant ministers in the 1870s and 1880s began to explore several radical alternatives for aiding impoverished city dwellers. Instead of focusing on their alleged moral flaws and character defects, these ministers argued that the rich and the well-born deserved part of the blame for urban poverty and thus had a responsibility to do something about it.

William S. Rainsford, the Irish-born minister at New York City's Saint George's Episcopal Church, pioneered the development of the so-called institutional church movement, whereby large downtown churches in once elite districts that had been overrun by immigrants would provide their new neighbors with social services as well as a place to worship. With the financial help of his wealthy church warden J. Pierpont Morgan, Rainsford organized a boys' club, built church recreational facilities for the destitute on the Lower East Side, and established an industrial training program.

Some conservatives tongue-lashed the churchman and his unorthodox approach. Charles A. Dana of the *New York Sun* branded Rainsford a "conspicuous representative of a school of unwise and mischievous social agitators." Unfazed, Rainsford redoubled his criticism of middle-class churchgoers for their lack of concern for the immigrant poor. Dismissing the moralists' assumption that alcohol abuse resulted entirely from a lack of will power, Rainsford argued that excessive drinking in immigrant wards was simply a by-product of life in the slums, where millions were trapped in often desperate circumstances. For Rainsford and those who shared his view, moral-purity campaigns to close saloons on Sunday were far less important than the prosecution of slum landlords and sweatshop owners who victimized the poor.

Although Rainsford and the members of his Institutional Church League could claim some successes in their own neighborhoods, their efforts in the end fell short, owing to the magnitude of slum conditions. But their sympathetic approach to urban destitution marked an important dimension of a crusade by a group of late-nineteenth-century ministers to awaken American Protestants to the realities of the immigrant city.

Supporting that drive were the leaders of the so-called Social Gospel movement, another effort within Protestantism to right contemporary social wrongs. The Social Gospel movement was launched in the 1870s by Washington Gladden, who for most of his career served as the minister of a large Congregational church in Columbus, Ohio. Dismayed by the way many middle-class churchgoers ignored the plight of urban slum dwellers, Gladden insisted that true Christianity commits men and women to fight social injustice head on, wherever it exists. Thus, in response to the wave of violent strikes in 1877, he urged church leaders to become mediators in the conflict between business and labor.

If Gladden set the tone for the Social Gospel, Walter Rauschenbusch, a minister at a German Baptist church in New York's notorious "Hell's Kitchen" neighborhood, articulated the movement's central philosophy. Educated in Germany, Rauschenbusch returned to the United States in the 1880s and was strongly influenced by Henry George's and Edward Bellamy's criticism of laissez-faire ideology. Enlarging the traditional Protestant focus on individual conversion, Rauschenbusch sought in such books as *Christianity and the Social Crisis* (1907) to apply Jesus' teachings to society itself. A truly Christian society, he said, would unite all churches, reorganize the industrial system, and work for international peace.

Although the Social Gospel's appeal for Christian unity led in 1908 to the formation of the Federal Council of Churches, the movement's biting attack on what its leaders blasted as the complacent Christian support of the status quo attracted only a handful of Protestants. But their earnest voices blended with a growing chorus of critics bemoaning the nation's urban woes.

## The Settlement-House Movement

By the 1880s many concerned citizens had become convinced that reform pressures applied from the top down by the Charity Organization Society and the purity crusaders, however well intentioned, were not only ineffective but wrongheaded. Simple passage of laws did not ensure obedience. Rejecting Parkhurst's contemptuous attitude toward the poor, and the Charity Organization Society's tendency to blame poverty on individual moral failure, a younger generation of charity workers led by Jane Addams developed a new weapon against destitution: the settlement house. Like the Social Gospelers, they began by recognizing that the physical hardships of slum life were often beyond the control of individuals. Stressing the environmental causes of poverty, settlement house advocates insisted that relief workers take up residence in poor neighborhoods where, in Addams's words, they could see firsthand "the struggle for existence, which is so much harsher among people near the edge of pauperism."

The youngest daughter of a successful Illinois businessman, Addams had graduated from Rockford College in 1882 and toured Europe a year later with her friend Ellen Gates Starr. Impressed by Toynbee Hall, a charity workers' residence situated deep in a London slum, the two women returned to Chicago in 1889, purchased and repaired the dilapidated Charles J. Hull mansion on South Halsted Street, and opened Hull House as an experiment in the settlement house approach.

Jane Addams's hostility toward the methods and philosophy of the Charity Organization Society and other coercive agencies came from disillusioning personal experience. During her first years at Hull House,

Addams had accepted Josephine Shaw Lowell's model for managing the poor. But in her autobiography, *Twenty Years at Hull House* (1910), Addams explained why she later rejected Lowell's self-assured methods. Once, attempting to get a jobless shipping clerk to help himself, she encouraged him to take a job as a canal digger. Following her advice, the clerk had contracted pneumonia and died a week later. "I learned," Addams wrote sadly, "that life cannot be administered by definite rules and regulations; that wisdom to deal with man's difficulties comes only through some knowledge of his life and habits as a whole; and that to treat an isolated episode is almost sure to invite blundering."

Drawing on the popular middle-class ideal of true womanhood as supportive and self-sacrificing, the indefatigable Addams turned Hull House into a social center for recent immigrants. Getting to know the Italian newcomers around her was a top priority. She invited them to plays; sponsored art projects; held classes in English, civics, cooking, and dressmaking; and encouraged them to preserve their traditional crafts. Disturbed by the depth of the neighborhood poverty that she witnessed, Addams set up a kindergarten, a laundry, an employment bureau, and a day nursery for working mothers. Hull House also sponsored recreational and athletic programs and dispensed legal aid and health care. In the hope of upgrading the shockingly filthy and overcrowded housing in its environs, Addams and her coworkers published systematic studies of city housing conditions and tirelessly pressured politicians to enforce sanitation regulations. For a time, demonstrating her principle of direct engagement with the lives of the poor, Addams even served as garbage inspector for her immigrant ward.

By 1895 at least fifty settlement houses had opened in cities around the nation. Settlement house leaders trained a generation of young college students, many of whom would later serve as state and local government officials. Florence Kelley, for example, who had worked at Hull House, in 1893 became the chief factory inspector in Illinois. For Kelley as for other young female settlement workers, settlement houses functioned as a supportive sisterhood of reform through which they developed skills in working with municipal governments. Many settlement house veterans would later draw on their experience in these years and play an influential role in the regulatory movements of the Progressive Era (see Chapter 22). Through their sympathetic attitudes toward the immigrants and their systematic publication of data about slum conditions, settlement house work-

**Greeting Neighbors at Hull House**
*Settlement house workers were eager to work with immigrant families in order to insure that the children received proper health care and nutrition. In addition to establishing its own nursery, Hull House in Chicago provided classes for parents and helped find them jobs.*

ers gave turn-of-the-century Americans new hope that the city's problems could be overcome.

But in their attempt to bridge the gap between rich and poor and to promote class cooperation and social harmony, settlement houses had mixed success. Although many immigrants deeply appreciated the settlement houses' resources and activities, they widely felt that the reformers were uninterested in increasing their political power. Limited by their own commitment to social order and class harmony, settlement house advisers tended to overlook immigrant organizations and their leaders. Although Hull House, one of the most successful of these efforts, attracted two thousand visitors per week in 1894, this was only a fraction of the more than seventy thousand people who dwelled in a six-block radius of the building. "They're like the rest," complained one immigrant, "a bunch of people planning for us and deciding what is good for us without consulting us or taking us into their confidence."

# Reshaping the Urban Environment

While reformers battled slum conditions and municipal corruption in the decades after the Civil War, landscape architects and city planners sought to reshape the urban masses by transforming their physical surroundings. In city after city, they redesigned the street system, installed new sewer and water mains, leveled hills, filled in swamps, created new parks, and paved broad boulevards and tree-lined parkways. These self-proclaimed saviors of American cities also established monumental public libraries, endowed huge art museums, and constructed theaters and symphony halls.

Although the motivation for rebuilding cities was simple—profit and business growth—sponsors of the new urban landscape also hoped that the cultural institutions and recreational facilities would make the city more appealing in ways that would tame and restrain the masses. Although they never entirely achieved either goal, they did significantly restructure America's cities in the second half of the nineteenth century.

**Boston Public Gardens, 1893**
by Edward Emerson Simmons

## *Rebuilding the City*

Frederick Law Olmsted was one of the earliest and most successful promoters of this vision. A self-taught scientific farmer, surveyor, and journalist, he had teamed up with English architect Calvert Vaux in 1858 to develop "Greensward," the original plan for Central Park in New York City. Olmsted and Vaux consciously designed the park as a spacious, tranquil country refuge within the city, a picturesque alternative to the monotonous straight-line grid of the urban streets. Buoyed by their success with Central Park, they went on to design major parks for Brooklyn, Chicago, Philadelphia, and Boston.

When Olmsted and other architects called for revitalizing the urban environment through the application of planning and design principles, they took as a model the development of Boston's fashionable Back Bay district.

Until 1857 this area was a 450-acre tidal flat covered with water. Beginning that year, the state undertook a massive engineering project to reclaim the land. Between 1857 and 1900, special gravel trains ran around the clock between the Back Bay and Needham, nine miles away, filling in the low areas and eventually raising the ground level by an average of twenty feet. The state deeded some of the lots thus created to the contractors as payment for the filling work, reserved others for educational and philanthropic organizations, and sold the rest as building lots. Each deed specified the height of the building that could be constructed on the lot, the distance that the building should be set back from the street, and the construction materials that could be used.

Under the careful regulations of the Back Bay commissioners, the district, with its array of cultural attractions, became a mecca for upper-class Bostonians. In addition to the public library, the Back Bay eventually contained two colleges, two museums, five schools, and twelve churches. In the eyes of many social reformers, Back Bay Boston thus represented the ideal urban environment that could be created through city planning.

Although many other cities determined to follow the precedent set by Boston, they often ran into great obstacles. For example, in contrast to Boston's achievement, the expansion of Chicago in the post–Civil War era was a

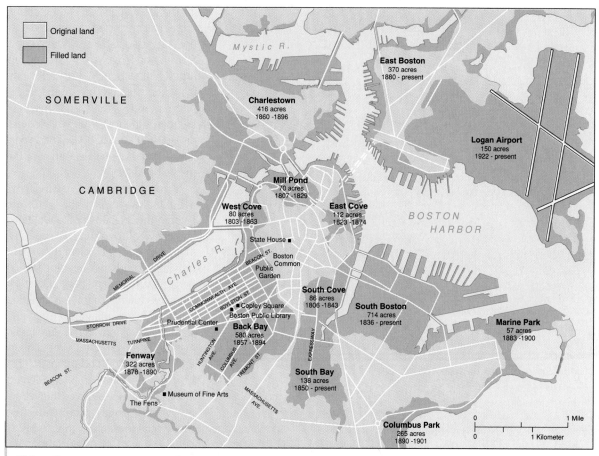

Legend:
- Original land
- Filled land

SOMERVILLE

*Mystic R.*

Charlestown
416 acres
1860 -1896

East Boston
370 acres
1880 - present

Logan Airport
150 acres
1922 - present

CAMBRIDGE

Mill Pond
70 acres
1807 -1829

West Cove
80 acres
1803 -1863

East Cove
112 acres
1823 -1874

*BOSTON HARBOR*

*Charles R.*

MEMORIAL DRIVE

State House

BEACON ST.
Boston Common

Public Garden

COMMONWEALTH AVE.

BOYLSTON ST.

Copley Square
Boston Public Library

South Cove
86 acres
1806 -1843

South Boston
714 acres
1836 - present

STORROW DRIVE

Prudential Center

Back Bay
580 acres
1857 -1894

Marine Park
57 acres
1883 -1900

MASSACHUSETTS TURNPIKE

HUNTINGTON AVE.

COLUMBUS AVE.

TREMONT ST.

EXPRESSWAY

Fenway
322 acres
1878 -1890

BEACON ST.

Museum of Fine Arts

The Fens

South Bay
138 acres
1850 - present

MASSACHUSETTS AVE.

Columbus Park
265 acres
1890 -1901

0    1 Mile
0    1 Kilometer

## Urban Improvement: Expanding the City of Boston

*Contractors used round-the-clock gravel trains to fill in Boston's smelly tidal flats. The city not only gained valuable new land but also cleverly transformed a storage basin for river flood waters into the Back Bay Fens, the first in a string of connected urban parks.*

planner's nightmare. Chicago was America's shock city, the extreme example of the many problems spawned by unregulated growth. Between 1850 and 1870, the city's population rose like a tidal wave, increasing from 30,000 to nearly 300,000. The influx not only strained city services but also inundated neighborhoods. So brisk was the rate of increase that architects, builders, and city officials could only react to crises as they arose. Nevertheless, the sheer magnitude of change forced Chicagoans to innovate in ways that were sometimes copied elsewhere.

For example, the expansion of the city in the 1840s left residents with swampy, unpaved streets that remained quagmires for most of the year. To remedy this soggy situation, the city council in 1855 decided to raise the level of the streets. Over the next twenty years, own-

ers jacked up their buildings to meet the new grade level. In 1857 one British traveler noted in amazement that "the Briggs House, a gigantic hotel, five stories high, solid masonry, weighing 22,000 tons, was raised four and a half feet, and new foundations built below. The people were in it all the time, coming and going, eating and sleeping—the whole business of the hotel proceeding without interruption."

Chicago faced a new crisis in October 1871 when a raging fire destroyed more than 61,000 buildings and leveled nearly four square miles in the central city. The entire commercial district was gutted, and nearly a hundred thousand people were left homeless. The urgent need for downtown reconstruction provided an unprecedented opportunity for Chicago architects, engineers, and civic leaders. In the next two decades,

**Chicago's Auditorium Building, 1889**
*Architects Louis Sullivan and Dankmar Adler pioneered new skyscraper forms by using structural steel for support, elevator systems for accessibility, and a complete electrical system for illumination.*

these groups cooperatively pioneered exciting new methods for tall-office-building construction. Their experimentation made possible a new American building type, the skyscraper.

The skyscraper depended on three technological innovations: fireproofing, the internal metal frame, and the elevator. Although all three were available before the fire, not until the 1880s did Chicago architects, in rebuilding the city's business district, combine them in a distinctive commercial style. By placing the metal frame on an expanded foundation and installing motorized steam and electric elevators, Chicago architects increased the city's building heights from four to twenty-two stories. Once the commanding size of Chicago skyscrapers had demonstrated the technical feasibility and commercial advantages of constructing tall, metal-supported buildings on small, expensive urban lots, other American cities began to raise their skylines as well.

The dramatic rebuilding of the urban environment in Boston and Chicago, together with the inspiring example of Chicago's World's Columbian Exposition in 1892–1893 (see Chapter 18), encouraged business leaders and reformers in many smaller cities to swing

into action. By the turn of the century, municipal art societies, park and outdoor art associations, and civic improvement leagues had sprung up around the country. City after city launched planning programs to replace muddy streets and unsightly billboards in the downtown business districts with broad boulevards, sparkling fountains, and gleaming marble public buildings.

Known collectively as the city-beautiful movement, this crusade favored the interests of the wellborn and the wealthy. Although advocates of the movement asserted that improving the urban landscape would benefit both rich and poor alike, they were less interested in upgrading the quality of immigrant housing and sanitary conditions in the slums than in making the city's public buildings impressive and monumental. Like the followers of the architect Richard Morris Hunt, they believed that attractive, monumental civic architecture and landscape design would inevitably produce better citizens and reduce the dangers of urban immorality and social disorder. In the early twentieth century, the city-beautiful impulse would evolve into a comprehensive city-planning movement (see Chapter 22) inspired by even more soaring visions of a transformed urban environment.

## Toward a Metropolitan America

While the city-beautiful advocates drafted their plans for the urban future, harried city hall bureaucrats, municipal administrators, and civic engineers wrestled with such practical matters as inadequate water supplies, antiquated sewer systems, and basic municipal services that seemed continually to lag behind the pace of urban growth.

Around midcentury, city dwellers began to recognize that the most dangerous aspect of urban life was the deplorable quality of the water and sewer systems. Most urbanites in the 1870s still relied on private wells, outhouses, and cesspools. Sewer systems, where they existed, were primitive and ineffective. One sanitary engineer described city sewer systems as "reservoirs of liquid filth, ever oozing through the defective joints, and polluting the very earth upon which the city stands."

Chicago poured its sewage directly into Lake Michigan, continually contaminating the source of its water supply and contributing directly to the frequent cholera, typhoid, and diphtheria epidemics that ravaged the city; Chicago's typhoid death rate alone reached 174 per 100,000 people in 1891. In New Jersey, Paterson and Passaic dumped their sewage directly into the Passaic River right above Newark's freshwater intakes.

Early attempts by city officials to construct interconnected sewer systems fell victim to local politics. In Washington, D.C., for example, the first contractors hired to build the system, who were chosen for their political contacts, proved grossly incompetent. They produced lateral sewers that could not run uphill into the main trunk lines. In New Orleans, a city subject to outbreaks of yellow fever and malaria, efforts to construct a citywide system in 1892 failed because of political ineptitude and contractor inexperience. Similarly, in St. Louis and Cincinnati, where politicians awarded contracts based on patronage, early, inadequate systems had to be replaced within a decade, at enormous expense.

Gradually and painfully, however, cities began to develop the centralized administrative structures that their size required, including the managerial tools to build and run effective sewer and water systems. To halt the further pollution of Lake Michigan, Chicago city officials in 1889 persuaded the state legislature to create a 185-square-mile sanitary district encompassing the city and its environs, supervised by elected officials with independent taxing authority. Between 1894 and 1899, the city built the enormous Ship and Sanitary Canal, which reversed the flow of the Chicago River to carry the city's processed sewage downstate. In Boston, too, engineers and civic officials in 1889 set up the centralized Metropolitan Sewage Commission, a permanent bureaucracy empowered to acquire land, oversee sewer construction, and formulate long-term expansion plans. By 1900 sewer and water systems established elsewhere had cut mortality rates from typhoid fever nationwide by 65 percent.

The movement to centralize control over water and sewer facilities was emblematic of a broader process of physical and political consolidation in urban America in the late nineteenth century. As cities exploded in size, they added unincorporated surrounding land (a process called annexation) and absorbed adjacent mu-

**House Moving**
*A central part in rebuilding American cities at the end of the century involved moving houses. As this photograph from San Francisco in 1908 attests, a huge house could be moved using horses, chains, and winches.*

nicipalities (consolidation). Through annexation and consolidation, city governments found that they could better coordinate transportation, water, and sewer networks and also increase tax revenues. In 1859 Philadelphia annexed five surrounding suburbs, quadrupling its population with the stroke of a pen. Chicago followed suit in 1889, adding 133 square miles in an area that is now the far South Side. The largest such consolidation occurred in 1898, when Brooklyn, Queens, Staten Island, and the Bronx joined Manhattan to form the New York City that we know today. In the process, New York added nearly 2 million people to its population and ballooned in size from forty-four to nearly three hundred square miles.

Practically every large American city broadened its boundaries in these years. The trend toward annexation was supported by merchants and business elites who saw it as another way to undercut the political power of the immigrant wards that in their view stood in the way of progress. The good-government reformers, waving the banner of civic efficiency, hailed annexation as a step toward making the police and fire departments and other municipal agencies more professional. Land speculators and real estate promoters welcomed annexation as a way of securing the municipal water and sewer systems that would sharply increase the worth of their holdings. Most middle-class suburbanites, eager for access to efficient city services, went along with the process. Not until the mid-twentieth century would outlying suburban communities, valuing local autonomy and wary of big-city tax rates and social problems, successfully fight off annexation.

## CONCLUSION

The movement toward a metropolitan America represented the culmination of a long struggle to control the changing urban world in the decades after the Civil War. The mind-boggling urban expansion of these years, drawing in millions of rural Americans and foreign immigrants alike, brought a concentration of economic power, an expansion of consumer markets, and a cornucopia of lucrative investment possibilities. For a nation in which seven out of ten people still lived on farms or in towns of fewer than 2,500 inhabitants, as was true of America in 1880, the big cities' sheer size and diversity sometimes seemed overwhelming, while the battles for power and wealth that raged in urban America proved both exciting and deeply disturbing. It is hardly surprising that observers of the time like Jacob Riis threw up their hands at conditions in the nation's metropolises.

While the social critics had their say, the urban population itself wrestled with the stresses and tensions of a social environment unfamiliar to many and undergoing tremendous flux. Middle- and upper-class urban residents were troubled not only by the new industrial city's massive physical problems—housing, schooling, transportation, sanitation, police and fire protection, and all the rest—but even more by the city's corrosive effect on traditional values and expectations. Migrants from America's farms and homogeneous small towns suddenly found themselves in an impersonal, ever-changing, fast-paced commercial world where antagonistic economic interests and ethnic and racial groups grappled for influence and power.

Predictably many of the native-born urban newcomers responded by attempting to re-create in the city the familiar features of rural life. They agitated for parks and playgrounds to bring nature into the metropolis, crusaded for temperance to dam the river of alcohol that washed over the immigrant wards, and campaigned for political reforms that would end boss rule and restore to them familiar forms of local government.

Immigrants, too, had to adjust to city life. Recently uprooted, in many cases, from centuries-old rhythms of peasant life or from the ghettos of eastern Europe, these newly arrived aliens had to adapt to the unremitting demands of industrial labor, to a babble of unfamiliar languages, to the mortal hazards and casual indignities of tenement life, and to the head-spinning diversity of the American urban scene. Faced with discrimination and hostility, older immigrants clung as long as they could to their traditional ways, their ethnic foods, their street and saloon culture, and their cherished religious institutions. Remarkably impervious to the assaults of middle-class political opponents, the pieties of would-be uplifters, or the efforts of moral reformers to legislate behavior, the immigrants rallied round a familiar figure, the boss. Of all the urban actors in these years the bosses demonstrated the most versatility in learning how to wield the levers of power in the strange new world of the Gilded Age city.

The city, then, was a place of constant contention among wildly different groups—poverty-stricken foreign immigrants, recent arrivals from the American hinterland, old urban elites, newly minted capitalist tycoons, an uneasy middle class, growing numbers of blacks—that eyed each other warily through layers of suspicion and mistrust. In view of these social realities, it is hardly surprising that the beautifiers and planners who sought through monumental architecture, classic statuary, and broad avenues to force the city into a single cultural mold only partially achieved their aims.

What finally emerged from the boisterous and bruising conflict was a gradual recognition that all city dwellers shared a basic interest in such mundane matters as clean water, adequate sewers, regular garbage collection, and reliable fire protection. Out of this realization blossomed a conception of what some called the service city—a city that could efficiently meet the collective needs of its diverse inhabitants while they pursued their personal or group interests. By 1900 cities across America had established administrative structures and developed trained bureaucracies with broad responsibility for sanitation, transportation, street lights, public health, parks, police, and so on. A metropolitan America had taken shape. In the process, urban growth profoundly altered American politics, culture, and thought.

Despite dark warnings of chaos and social upheaval, a remarkable degree of order and stability prevailed in urban America as the nineteenth century closed. After a generation of unchecked growth, political struggle, and social unrest, the nation's cities had evolved governmental forms sufficient to assure at least an adequate quality of life for all and to intervene when necessary to protect the welfare of the urban populace. This enlarged conception of government only slowly penetrated the arena of national politics, but the lessons so painfully learned in the late-nineteenth-century cities would significantly shape the progressive movement that lay ahead.

## FOR FURTHER READING

Paul Boyer, *Urban Masses and Moral Order in America, 1820–1920* (1978). A richly detailed analysis of reformers' attempts to control city life.

Ruth H. Crocker, *Social Work and Social Order: The Settlement Movement in Two Industrial Cities, 1889–1930* (1992). An important, balanced assessment of the settlement house movement.

William Cronon, *Nature's Metropolis: Chicago and the Great West* (1991). An innovative study of the link between urban growth and regional economic prosperity in the Midwest.

Kenneth T. Jackson, *Crabgrass Frontier: The Suburbanization of the United States* (1985). A stimulating comparative study of city expansion and suburban development in Europe and America.

Martin V. Melosi, ed., *Pollution and Reform in American Cities, 1870–1930* (1980). A pioneering examination of the environmental impact of U.S. industrial and urban growth.

Walter Nugent, *Crossings: The Great Transatlantic Migrations, 1870–1914* (1992). A thoughtful overview of the reasons for the major migrations to the Americas.

Carl Smith, *Urban Disorder and the Shape of Belief: The Great Chicago Fire, the Haymarket Bomb, and the Model Town of Pullman* (1995). An innovative study of the ways in which the nineteenth-century responses to urban disorders shaped contemporary perceptions about city life.

David Ward, *Poverty, Ethnicity, and the American City, 1840–1925* (1989). A penetrating analysis of the relationship among immigration, ethnicity, and the changing structure of industrial capitalism.

Judy Yung, *Unbound Feet: A Social History of Chinese Women in San Francisco* (1995). A search for a family history that offers insights into Chinese immigration practices and the ways in which women's experiences of immigration were different from men's.

# 20 Daily Life, Popular Culture, and the Arts, 1860–1900

**Slide, Kelly, Slide**
*by Frank O. Small*

On a sweltering day in August 1899, Scott Joplin, a young, black pianist and composer, signed an unusual contract with his music publisher in Sedalia, Missouri. Instead of receiving an outright payment for his new sheet music composition, "Maple Leaf Rag," Joplin would earn one cent for every copy sold. At a time when most composers were paid a small fixed fee per composition, the contract signaled a new era in the popular music industry. Over the next two decades, "Maple Leaf Rag" would sell more than half a million copies a year and make Joplin the king of ragtime, the popular, syncopated dance music that overnight had become a national sensation.

Scott Joplin's meteoric rise from unknown saloon piano player to renowned composer reflected not only the extraordinary expansion and commercialization of the entertainment industry at the turn of the century but also the class and racial tensions that pervaded popular culture. Although Joplin himself in the next decade and a half would publish more than seventy-five songs or piano rags, his success was tainted by white competitors who stereotyped his compositions as "Negro music" and "Coon songs." Joplin, who dreamed of gaining national recognition as an opera composer, remained frustrated by publishers' refusal to accept his work. Opera was considered serious music, a high art form controlled by the upper classes; blacks, even those with Joplin's talent, could not enter the field. Scott Joplin died in 1917, an admired leader in the entertainment industry whose genius for serious music would not be recognized for another half century. As Joplin's experience revealed, racial discrimination could reinforce the barriers of social class.

Scott Joplin's thwarted economic progress was not unusual. Countless others faced similar difficulties in moving up the economic ladder and adjusting to the social changes taking place at the turn of the century.

American society was slowly shifting from a producer economy that stressed work and thrift to a consumer economy in which new forms of entertainment, leisure time activities, and material possessions were becoming the hallmarks of personal identity. Not everyone would gain access to this expanding world of consumption.

Nevertheless, Joplin's success as a ragtime composer was mirrored in the upward mobility of numerous men and women whose improved earnings now enabled them to enjoy new levels of comfort and convenience in their everyday lives. In the closing decades of the nineteenth century, these people had profited from the ways in which industrialization had not only introduced an unprecedented range of innovative products but also opened up new jobs and destroyed older ones, in the process rearranging the occupational structure and altering the distribution of income within society. These changes, together with the expansion of white-collar occupations, created new expectations for family life and fostered a growing class awareness.

While the middle and upper classes prospered, immigrants, farmers, and the urban working classes—the overwhelming majority of the population—improved their families' economic position only slowly and slightly. In one sense, therefore, the onslaught of consumer products and leisure activities actually widened the gulf between the haves and the have-nots and intensified the sense of class consciousness among rich and poor.

While the very rich lived in a world apart, and the middle class embraced its particular behavior code and cultural pursuits, the working class to whom Joplin had first appealed created its own vigorous culture in the form of dance halls, saloons, vaudeville theaters, social clubs, and amusement parks in the bustling immigrant cities. Middle-class reformers who strove to remake this

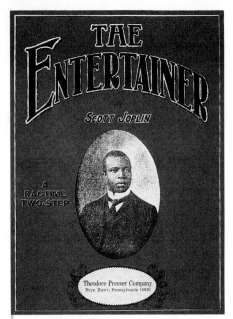

### Scott Joplin Music

*Despite Scott Joplin's desire to be recognized for his talent as an opera composer, publishers of his music preferred his popular ragtime compositions, such as his 1902 piano rag, "The Entertainer."*

working-class culture into their own image of propriety were soon frustrated. In the long run it was the culture of the masses that would prove more influential in the shaping of modern America.

This chapter will focus on five major questions:

♦ How did the changing standard of living among the middle and upper classes reinforce their awareness of class difference? How were racial stereotypes used to reinforce these distinctions?

♦ What was Victorian morality, and in what ways did it influence social conventions and patterns of everyday life?

♦ In what ways did changes in the occupational structure and in educational institutions affect the roles of women?

♦ How did the conflict between the working classes and those above them help reshape attitudes toward leisure and recreation at the turn of the century?

♦ Why did Americans of different social classes grow disenchanted with Victorian social and intellectual ideals?

## Everyday Life in Flux

In the second half of the nineteenth century, in virtually every industry, mechanization increased output, decreased prices, and encouraged the development of new consumer products that transformed the living standard for many Americans. In the clothing trades, for instance, the widespread use of sewing machines profoundly changed the apparel industry. Before the Civil War, handmade shirts required nearly thirty thousand stitches and took fourteen hours to complete. Most people wore hand-me-downs, and styles were simple. By the 1880s, however, complete shirts of standardized size could be machine-sewn in less than two hours.

As a result, personal wardrobes for the middle and elite classes expanded dramatically. Clothes closets became commonplace household features, supplementing the small bureaus or armoires that had previously sufficed to hold the family apparel. Dress became an ever-more-important badge of social class.

Innovations in food technology, among them breakfast cereals, changed eating habits. In 1878 physician John Harvey Kellogg of Battle Creek, Michigan, marketed Granola—a wheat, corn, and oat mixture that he advertised as healthier than the then standard breakfast of sausage, eggs, and potatoes. Competitors soon rushed into the field. Charles W. Post, for example, developed Grape Nuts Flakes and Postum, a breakfast drink made from bran, wheat, and molasses that he touted as an alternative to overstimulating, unhealthful coffee. By the turn of the century, health-conscious middle- and upper-class Americans had adopted the new cereals and hot drinks as their normal breakfast foods.

Not all inventions lived up to their promoters' claims. Lydia Pinkham's famous vegetable extract "for all those painful Complaints and Weaknesses so common to our best female population" contained nearly 23 percent alcohol. Other so-called health compounds featured significant amounts of opium. Countless patent medicines, including one that promised to "POSITIVELY CURE" backache in two hours and deafness in two days, were totally ineffective. But they were eagerly snatched up by a society that had come to believe that material and physical improvements were now within everyone's reach.

Although some products failed to work as claimed, the overall impact of late-nineteenth-century industrialization was to significantly improve the level of comfort and convenience for many middle- and upper-class American families. In 1870 most urban women had

CHRONOLOGY

**CHRONOLOGY**

**1865** Vassar College founded.

**1869** Cornell University founded.

First intercollegiate football game.

The Great Atlantic & Pacific Tea Company (A&P) organizes a chain of food stores.

**1871** Thomas Eakins, *The Champion Single Sculls.*

**1875** Smith College founded.

Frances Willard joins the Woman's Christian Temperance Union.

Henry Clay Work, "My Grandfather's Clock."

**1876** National League of baseball players organized.

**1879** F. W. Woolworth opens his "Five and Ten Cent Store" in Utica, New York.

**1884** Mark Twain, *Adventures of Huckleberry Finn.*

Bryn Mawr College founded.

**1886** Richard Warren Sears starts Sears, Roebuck.

**1891** Stanford University founded.

University of Chicago founded.

Columbia University adds Barnard College as a coordinate institution for women.

Basketball invented at Springfield College in Massachusetts.

**1892** Joseph Mayer Rice writes his exposé of public education in *Forum* magazine.

General Federation of Women's Clubs organized.

**1893** Stephen Crane, *Maggie: A Girl of the Streets.*

**1895** Coney Island amusement parks open in Brooklyn.

**1899** Scott Joplin, "Maple Leaf Rag."

Kate Chopin, *The Awakening.*

Thorstein Veblen, *The Theory of the Leisure Class.*

**1900** Theodore Dreiser, *Sister Carrie.*

shopped daily, baked their own bread, and canned their own fruits and vegetables. They spent hours preparing food, doing laundry by hand, firing up smoky stoves and furnaces, and carrying "slop jars" containing human excrement to malodorous waste-collection tanks. By 1900, in contrast, the spread of indoor plumbing, efficient stoves and furnaces, commercially prepared foods, and mechanical washing machines had greatly eased this domestic burden. Well-to-do urban families began to take for granted central heating, electric lights, telephone service, and a range of other household innovations unknown earlier.

### Bringing New Commodities to Rural and Small-Town America

While the new products made possible by swift industrialization gradually changed the lives of city dwellers, mail-order houses and chain stores reoriented the standards of rural and small-town consumers. The changes began with Aaron Montgomery Ward, a traveling salesman from Chicago. In 1872 Ward circulated among his rural customers a list of products for sale at a 40 percent discount. For farmers hesitant to deal with a distant, unknown merchant, he promised the unconditional right to return merchandise. Within a dozen years Ward's catalog offered nearly ten thousand items to rural customers.

**The Veribest, c. 1900**
*Meat packing companies promoted packaged meats as time-savers for busy homemakers and as a guarantee of high quality. As the product name and the medals on the young cook suggest, Armour hoped that customers would think that this canned meat had won prestigious awards at the recent world's fairs in Chicago or St. Louis.*

Ward soon ran into competition from Richard Warren Sears, a flamboyant young Minnesota railroad agent whose taste for marketing was first whetted when he sold a case of watches left at his station. Moving to Chicago in 1887, he established a mail-order company (now Sears, Roebuck) that could ship farmers a wide range of products, including agricultural implements, clothing, medicine, furniture, stoves, guns, tools, and baby carriages. Sears built customer loyalty by guaranteeing low prices and publishing testimonials from satisfied patrons. The firm carried many products at different prices to suit all pocketbooks. Pump organs, for example, ranged from "Our AA Grade Home Favorite" at $64.95 to "Our Happy Home Organ, Grade B," at $22.00.

To personalize their increasingly impersonal products, advertisers specifically targeted women as society's primary consumers. As one advertising company acknowledged, "She who 'rocks the cradle' and 'rules the world' is directly and indirectly head of the buying department of every home." By identifying women with the consumption of new products, therefore, advertisers helped create a consumer culture segregated by gender in which the world of shopping was increasingly divided into men's and women's products.

The down-home marketing of Sears, Ward's, and their emulators inspired such trust in rural and small-town readers that they sometimes sought advice on personal problems. One lonely farmer wrote to Montgomery Ward's proposing marriage to the "girl wearing hat number —— on p. 153 of your catalog."

The chain store offered another mechanism for bringing low-priced mass-produced goods to consumers outside large cities. F. W. Woolworth, a farm boy from upstate New York, in 1879 opened a "Five and Ten Cent Store" in Utica that sold goods like crochet needles, safety pins, soap, and thimbles from a "five-cent counter." Increasing his volume and multiplying his stores, Woolworth appealed to those Americans who either lacked the money to buy more expensive goods or simply wished to economize. Woolworth's, together with the Great Atlantic and Pacific Tea Company (A&P), which consolidated several separate food stores into one operation in 1869, pioneered the creation of nationwide "chains" that stressed low prices and consumer savings.

Under a barrage of advertising, consumers by the 1890s faced new choices daily about what they should buy. More conscious than ever before of the sparkling array of material options open to them, the American

people were slowly drawn into a milieu in which the goods and services purchased increasingly dictated one's position and status in society. At the same time that material possessions made possible new realms of comfort and convenience, they also reinforced a pervasive sense of widening class differences.

### A Shifting Class Structure

Patterns of consumption, culture, and everyday life reflect a society's class structure, and in late-nineteenth-century America, this structure underwent important modifications. From the colonial period on, social class had been loosely defined by occupation and income. Contemporaries readily identified the rich, the "middling ranks," and the poor in every community. But in the post–Civil War era, fundamental changes in the nature of work, together with shifts in residential location, massive immigration, and new patterns of consumption, redefined and sharpened the conception of social class. In addition to income and occupation, lifestyle and self-identification now became important determinants of social rank.

The working class felt the impact of these changes first and most keenly. At midcentury skilled artisans, who exercised considerable authority over their work and viewed themselves as independent entrepreneurs, had dominated the working class. Common laborers, who exchanged simple muscle power for a daily wage, identified with the artisans above them and hoped eventually to acquire skilled positions themselves. Although skilled artisans earned between five hundred and nine hundred dollars yearly, or from two to ten times the wages of common laborers, both segments of the working class shared a common outlook and sense of class identity. In Pittsburgh and other cities, craftsworkers and laborers lived on the same streets, attended the same churches, and patronized the same saloons. They believed in the value of hard physical labor, prided themselves on their physical strength, and helped one another in times of need.

Beginning in the 1870s, however, the bond between craftsworkers and unskilled laborers began to dissolve as new production methods restructured the work process. By the 1880s the widespread use of machinery had destroyed the jobs of many skilled artisans. The Bessemer steel-making process, for example, eliminated the need for the skilled puddlers who controlled production in the iron industry. With fewer skilled positions available, the only people willing to undertake the

**Telephone Operators, 1885**

*The anonymity of the new technology of the telephone sometimes led to flirtations between male callers and the young women who manually transferred calls. Mark Twain's narrator in* A Connecticut Yankee in King Arthur's Court *(1889) is so infatuated with telephone operators that he names his first child Hello Central.*

dangerous, low-paying steel-mill jobs were unskilled foreign immigrants who desperately needed work. Thus by the turn of the century, a rift had developed within the working class. Cut off from the common laborers who formed a substratum below them, skilled artisans identified more and more with the middle class.

As the working class fragmented, the expansion of the middle class, which would vastly accelerate in the early twentieth century, was already under way. After the Civil War, the demand for trained personnel increased in all economic sectors. Growing municipal bureaucracies, school systems, and police forces required specially trained employees. National corporations hired armies of clerks, accountants, and salespeople to manage their operations. Bustling department stores, insurance agencies, and food companies established accounting and sales divisions. These middle-class personnel worked in clean company headquarters and city offices physically separated from the sooty factories and noisy mills that employed manual laborers.

In contrast to members of the working class, who were paid by the hour or according to the level of production, middle-class clerical and professional workers received weekly or monthly salaries. The salaries of the middle class, moreover, were considerably higher than even those of skilled craftsworkers. In Detroit, where very few skilled artisans took home more than $500

yearly, city clerks, bookkeepers, and inspectors earned between $500 and $1,000, and other middle-class jobs often paid more than $1,000 a year.

Middle-class employees' higher earnings and steady work significantly changed their outlook and expectations. Freed from worries about making ends meet, many adopted long-term strategies for maximizing their purchasing power. They devoted more resources to educating their children, buying expensive items such as sewing machines and pianos on credit, and otherwise improving household comforts and conveniences. A shorter workweek, moreover, gave middle-class employees more time to spend with their families and greater opportunities for socializing and recreation.

The very wealthy, meanwhile, did not hesitate to flaunt their riches, thus honing public awareness of growing class divisions in industrial America. The Carnegies, Morgans, Rockefellers, and Fricks used their immense fortunes to build elaborate houses and country estates. Railroad financier Jay Gould, the owner of Lyndhurst—a Gothic castlelike home in Tarrytown, New York, with a 380-foot-long greenhouse filled with exotic plants—was typical of a generation for whom a palatial house offered the ultimate proof of victory on the capitalist battlefield.

As a result of workplace restructuring, the expansion of the middle class, and the rise in enormous fortunes, income distribution in America by the turn of the century had become severely skewed. Statistics are imprecise, but a knowledgeable observer estimated in 1896 that of the nation's 12.5 million families, approximately 5.5 million were working class and earned less than $500 annually; 5.5 million were middle class and had incomes from $500 to $5,000; and the remaining 1.5 million, or the 12 percent whose incomes were over $5,000, were rich. This privileged 12 percent, however, owned *86 percent* of the nation's wealth. In contrast, the middle class, whose families made up 44 percent of the population, possessed only 12.5 percent of the aggregate wealth, and the working class, who composed the bottom 44 percent of the nation's people, struggled to survive with a mere 1.5 percent of the wealth.

### The Changing Family

This lopsided distribution of resources had an important impact on family life. The level of family income not only determined access to household technology and consumer goods but also affected family size, life expectancy, infant mortality, and relationships between parents and children. Historians are cautious in their use of aggregate federal census statistics from the era, which blur differences among social classes as well as between rural and urban Americans and between ethnic groups and the native-born. Nevertheless, such data *can* give us a broad overview of the changes in family structure in the post–Civil War years.

Between 1860 and 1900, these statistics reveal, most Americans lived in nuclear families; that is, families made up of only parents and their children. Often boarders and servants resided with the nuclear family, but grandparents and other relatives typically did not. And families were becoming smaller, largely because mothers bore fewer children, continuing a trend begun in the early nineteenth century. For white women, the number of live births* fell from an average of 5.42 children in 1850 to 3.56 in 1900. But those children who were born had a better chance of surviving to adulthood, as indicated statistically by a rise in life expectancy from 38.4 years to 46.3 years for males and from 40.5 years to 48.3 years for females. Overall, the size of the average nuclear family stabilized at five or six members.

Like all averages, however, these figures obscure the significant differences created by social class, race,

---

* As measured by the fertility rate: the average number of children born to each female between the ages of fourteen and forty-five.

and ethnicity. For example, because of a very high rate of infant mortality among black males, their average life expectancy at birth in 1900, the first year for which we have statistics, was only 22.5 years, less than half that for whites. Similarly, the decline in family size was not uniformly distributed. Farmers and the urban working class, relying on the labor of their children to make ends meet, continued to have large families. Immigrant and farm families with six to eight children remained common. The urban middle and upper classes, by contrast, who did not need their children's earnings, chose to limit their family size. In Buffalo, New York, an industrial city with many immigrants, the difference in the average number of children in families of various occupational groups in 1900 was striking: 5.7 for laborers, 5.2 for skilled workers, and only 3.5 for business owners and company managers.

These statistics reveal how significantly middle- and upper-class families differed from their working-class counterparts. The correlation of high income with smaller family size indicates that the middle and upper classes were practicing birth control, either by periodically abstaining from sexual intercourse, by other forms of contraception, or by abortion. Whatever the method, smaller families meant more free time for women, more attention to the education and training of children, and greater opportunity for leisure and recreation.

### Working-Class Family Life

The dramatic impact of income level on the nature of family life becomes most evident when we look at black and immigrant working-class households. Because many such households hovered at or fell below the poverty level, they had to rely on the labor of the children and on a network of relatives who could pitch in during times of need. The poorer the family, the more dependent it became on the cooperative work of all its members simply to survive.

Black families in the post–Civil War South, freed from slavery with few possessions and little money, relied heavily on their extended families for help and support. Although most blacks lived in nuclear, two-parent families, they counted on the close proximity of cousins, aunts, uncles, and other relatives to assist them with child care, housing, and expenses. For blacks, the extended kinship network replaced the nuclear family as the dominant institution in their daily lives.

The case of Joseph Sutton, who lived at Miles River Neck in Talbot County, Maryland, typified postwar blacks' reliance on relatives. In 1889, when Sutton was four, his father died. His mother, unable to run the farm by herself, moved to Baltimore to find work, leaving Sutton with his grandmother, who became, in effect, his surrogate parent. Three years later, at age seven, he moved in with his uncle, a nearby tenant farmer. There, for several years, Sutton took care of a baby cousin who was named after his great-grandmother, a common practice that symbolically reinforced the cohesiveness of the extended family. Thanks to these strong family bonds, Sutton overcame the loss of his own parents and eventually was able to buy a farm and form a stable family of his own.

Although often better off than their black counterparts, poor white farm families in the South and Midwest also depended heavily on the effort of all family members to survive. While the men and older boys worked in the fields, the farm wife with her younger children ran the house and kept the kitchen garden. In addition to preparing meals, drawing water, tending the stove fire, cleaning the house, feeding chickens, taking care of the milk shed, and doing laundry, farm women sewed and mended clothes, knitted hats and gloves, wove tablecloths, churned butter, made soap, and trimmed the oil lamps that illuminated the home in this age before electricity.

The same was true for urban working-class families, for whom the contributions of women, young adults, and children often spelled the difference between survival and modest prosperity. The average urban family of five or six members in the 1890s needed an annual income of between six hundred and eight hundred dollars to live comfortably. Although prices for food, rent, and other necessities dropped between 1865 and 1890, and real wages increased by almost 50 percent, most working-class families still did not have a high enough income to live on the father's earnings alone. As in rural America, survival thus became a cooperative family effort.

To supplement their income, urban working-class families often rented rooms to boarders, and the women commonly took in laundry. If a husband became sick or lost his job, a wife might even take a job in a garment factory alongside her elder daughters, who usually worked in manufacturing plants until they married. Immigrant children commonly went to work at the age of ten or twelve and were expected to turn over their earnings to their parents. As children grew older and wanted to spend part of their earnings on themselves, however, tensions within working-class families sometimes erupted into outright rebellion.

Where parents were able to keep control, working-class families, by pooling the wages of all family members, were often able to set aside enough money to purchase a house, which functioned as both a residence and a kind of insurance. If the principal breadwinner fell sick or became unemployed, families could take in boarders or use the house as collateral on a loan.

The other common strategy used by working- and middle-class families to support elderly parents was the creation of what historians call a stem family arrangement. In the stem phase, as children grow up, get married, and move away from home to form their own nuclear families, one child remains in the parental household even after marrying. That child provides old-age care for the parents, often continuing in the same line of work or in some cases taking over the family farm or business, in return for assuming ownership of the house when the parents die. Particularly for working-class Americans, the stem family brought security to infirm and aged parents.

Successful working-class families took pleasure not only in their material gains but also in their accomplishments in the face of

**The Walters, Lubert County, Georgia, 1896**
*Southern black families such as the Walters clan depended on extended kin networks for assistance and emotional support.*

difficult odds. "We had to live pretty close," proudly commented a Massachusetts carpenter in 1890 who was raising six children, "but we did it, and now we have the house all paid for, so there is no longer any rent." The cooperative family ethic, which stressed mutual support and reliance on a network of relatives, thus enabled working-class Americans to survive and in some cases even get ahead in the rapidly changing economic environment of the late nineteenth century. But the cooperative pattern also accentuated the differences between poor families and their middle- and upper-class counterparts who managed comfortably on the salary of the main breadwinner alone.

# Middle-Class Society and Culture

Spared the struggle for survival that confronted most Americans after the Civil War, society's middle and upper ranks faced a different challenge: how to rationalize their access to the material benefits of the emerging consumer society. To justify the position of society's wealthier members, ministers, advice-book writers, and other commentators appealed to Victorian morality, a set of social ideas widely extolled by the privileged classes of England and America during the long reign (1837–1901) of Britain's Queen Victoria.

Proponents of Victorian morality argued that the financial success of the middle and upper classes was linked to their superior talent, intelligence, morality, and self-control. They also believed that women were the driving force for moral improvement: while men engaged in the world's work, women would provide the gentle, elevating influence that would lead society in its upward march.

While authoritative voices preached the certitudes of Victorian morality, thereby defending the status of America's upper classes, a network of institutions, from elegant department stores and hotels to elite colleges and universities, reinforced the privileged position of these groups in society.

## *Manners and Morals*

The Victorian world-view, which first emerged in the 1830s and 1840s, rested on a number of fundamental assumptions. One was that human nature was malleable: people could improve themselves. Hence, Victorian Americans were intensely moralistic and eager

to reform practices they considered evil or undesirable. A second assumption concerned the social value of work. Spokesmen for Victorian morality believed that a commitment to working hard not only developed personal self-discipline and self-control, it also helped advance the progress of the nation. Finally, Victorian Americans stressed the importance of good manners and the value of literature and the fine arts as marks of a truly civilized society. Although this genteel outlook set a standard that was often violated in practice, particularly by the middle classes and the rich, it remained an ideal that was widely preached as the norm for all society.

Before the Civil War, advocates for Victorian morality such as Brooklyn clergyman Henry Ward Beecher had energized the crusades against slavery and intemperance by appealing to the ethical standards of this new moral code. After the war, however, Beecher and other preachers became less interested in social reform and more preoccupied with the importance of polite manners and social protocol. Following their advice, middle- and upper-class families in the 1870s and 1880s increasingly defined their own social standing not only in terms of income but also of behavior. Good manners, especially a knowledge of dining and entertaining etiquette, became an important badge of status.

In her popular advice book *The American Woman's Home* (1869), Catharine Beecher (the sister of Henry Ward Beecher) reflected a typical Victorian self-consciousness about proper manners. The following list of dinner-table behaviors, she said, should be avoided by those of "good breeding":

> Reaching over another person's plate; standing up to reach distant articles, instead of asking to have them passed; . . . using the table-cloth instead of napkins; eating fast, and in a noisy manner; putting large pieces in the mouth; . . . [and] picking the teeth at the table. . . .

For Beecher and other molders of manners, meals became important rituals that differentiated the social classes. Not only were they occasions for displaying the elaborate china and silver that wealthy families exclusively possessed, but they also provided telltale clues to a family's level of refinement and sophistication.

The Victorian code—with its emphasis on morals, manners, and proper behavior—thus served to heighten the sense of class differences for the post–Civil War generation and to create visible distinctions among social groups. Prominent middle- and upper-class Vic-

**Middle-class Family Portrait**

*This portrait of the R.A. Acheson family in Watertown, Nebraska, pictures the family members with their favorite possessions—the daughter with her doll, and her mother with her pump organ.*

torians made bold claims about their sincere interest in helping others improve themselves. More often than not, however, their self-righteous, intensely moralistic outlook simply widened the gap that income disparities had already opened.

### The Cult of Domesticity

Victorian views on morality and culture, coupled with rising pressures on consumers to make decisions about a mountain of domestic products, had a subtle but important impact on middle-class expectations about women's role within the home. From the 1840s on, many architects, clergymen, and other promoters of the so-called cult of domesticity (see Chapter 9) had idealized the home as "the woman's sphere," a protected retreat where she could express her special maternal gifts, including a sensitivity toward children and an aptitude for religion. "The home is the wife's province," asserted one writer; "it is her natural field of labor . . . to govern and direct its interior management."

During the 1880s and 1890s, advocates of this cult of domesticity added a new obligation to the traditional woman's role as director of the household: to foster an artistic environment that would nurture her family's cultural improvement. For many Victorian Americans of the comfortable classes, houses became

statements of cultural aspiration. Excluded from the world of business and commerce, many middle- and upper-class women devoted considerable time and energy to decorating their home, seeking to make it, as one advice book suggested, "a place of repose, a refuge from the excitement and distractions of outside . . . , provided with every attainable means of rest and recreation."

Not all middle-class women pursued this domestic ideal. For some, housework and family responsibilities overwhelmed the concern for artistic accomplishment. For others, the artistic ideal itself was not to their taste. Sixteen-year-old Mary Putnam complained privately to a friend that she played the piano because of "an abstract general idea . . . of a father coming home regularly tired at night (from the plow, I believe the usual legend runs), and being solaced by the brilliant yet touching performance of a sweet only daughter upon the piano." She then confessed that she detested the piano. Increasingly, women in the 1880s and 1890s sought other outlets for their creative energies.

### Department Stores and Hotels

Although Victorian social thought justified the privileged status of the well-to-do, many thrifty people who had grown up in the early nineteenth century found it difficult to accept the new preoccupation with accumulation and display. To dull their pangs of guilt, merchandisers in the 1880s stressed the high quality and low cost of the objects they sold, encouraging Americans to loosen their purse strings and enjoy prosperity without inner reservations.

A key agent in modifying attitudes toward consumption was the department store. In the final quarter of the nineteenth century, innovative entrepreneurs led by Rowland H. Macy in New York, John Wanamaker in Philadelphia, and Marshall Field in Chicago built the giant department store into an urban institution and transformed the shopping experience for the millions of middle- and upper-class consumers who were their greatest patrons.

Merchants like Wanamaker and Macy helped overcome the middle and upper classes' reluctance to spend by advertising their products at "rock-bottom"

prices and fighting price wars to convince customers of the validity of their claims. To avoid keeping their stock too long, they held giant end-of-the-season clearance sales at drastically marked-down prices.

The major downtown establishments sought to make shopping an adventure. Not only did the rapid turnover of merchandise create a sense of constant novelty, but the mammoth stores themselves became imitation palaces, complete with stained-glass sky-lights, marble staircases, brilliant chandeliers, and plush carpets.

Department stores lavished care and attention on shoppers, especially women. Richly appointed lounges supplied with newspapers and stationery, elegant restaurants serving modestly priced lunches, salespeople who greeted shoppers at the door, and glittering holiday decorations enticed visitors to linger and buy on impulse. Brigades of female salesclerks answered questions and suggested to middle- and upper-class customers that they were of the ranks that deserved to be served. The large urban department store thus functioned as a kind of social club and home away from home for comfortably fixed women. For these women, shopping became an adventure, a form of entertainment, and a means of affirming one's place in society.

The stately metropolitan hotels that proliferated in the late nineteenth century provided further examples of high fashion and elite taste. After Boston's Tremont Hotel established a prototype for refined elegance and technological innovation in the 1830s by offering its guests indoor plumbing and speaking tubes (the predecessor of telephones), cities across America aspired to build top-notch hotels. By the 1880s innovative hotels were setting new standards for design excellence.

The Waldorf Astoria in New York, the Palmer House in Chicago, and San Francisco's Palace became public shrines, epitomizing efficient organization and ultra-smart taste. Built in 1892 in the German Renaissance style, the Waldorf Astoria was a self-contained community with offices, restaurants, ballrooms, courtyards, and five hundred guest rooms. Household reformers

**Cliff House, Point Lobos**
*Dramatic seaside hotels, like this one in San Francisco, set the standard for leisure and recreation. For ten cents, one could sit on the balcony in the summer, sip a cool drink, and watch the sea lions in the surf below.*

writing in the 1890s held up the highly organized restaurants and laundry systems of the big hotels as models for efficient cooperative-apartment complexes.

Whether one marveled at their efficiency or gazed in wonder at their splendid gilt mirrors and plush carpets, the grand hotels, like the giant department stores, set the pattern for luxury, convenience, and service. In his 1904 travel book *The American Scene,* writer Henry James described the first-class hotel as "a synonym for civilization." In a society that shunned aristocratic pretensions, hotels and department stores made luxury acceptable by clothing it in the guise of efficiency and simple good taste. They provided a setting where newly affluent members of society could indulge and pamper themselves, if only for an hour or a day.

### The Transformation of Higher Education

At a time when relatively few Americans possessed even a high school education, U.S. colleges and universities represented another institutional stronghold of the business and professional elite and of the moderately well-to-do middle class. In 1900, despite enrollment increases in the preceding decades, only 4 percent of the nation's eighteen- to twenty-one-year-olds were enrolled in institutions of higher learning.

Wealthy capitalists gained status and a measure of immortality by endowing colleges and universities. Leland Stanford and his wife Jane Lathrop Stanford launched Stanford University in 1885 with a bequest of $24 million in memory of a dead son; John D. Rockefeller donated $34 million to the University of Chicago in 1891. Industrialists and businessmen dominated the boards of trustees of many educational institutions and forced their conservative views on the faculty and administrators. Sardonic economist Thorstein Veblen called these business-oriented academic managers "Captains of Erudition."

Not only the classroom experience but also social contacts and athletic activities—especially football—prepared affluent young men for later responsibilities in business and the professions. Adapted by American college students in 1869 from English rugby, football was largely an elite sport. But the game, initially played without pads or helmets, was marred by violence in its early years. In 1905 eighteen students died of playing-field injuries. Many college presidents therefore dismissed football as a dangerous waste of time and money. When the University of Michigan in 1873 challenged Cornell to a game in Ann Arbor, Cornell's president Andrew D. White huffily telegraphed back, "I will not permit thirty men to travel four hundred miles merely to agitate a bag of wind."

But eager alumni and coaches strongly defended the new sport. Some—among them Henry Lee Higginson, the Civil War veteran and Boston banker who gave Harvard "Soldier's Field" stadium as a memorial to those who had died in battle—praised football as a character-building sport. Other defenders of the sport, including famed Yale coach Walter Camp, insisted that football could function as a surrogate frontier experience in an increasingly urbanized society. By 1900 football had become a popular fall ritual, and team captains were campus heroes. The sport served to stimulate alumni giving and built goodwill for these select institutions that otherwise remained far outside the experience of the average American.

Although postsecondary education remained confined to a small minority, more than 150 new colleges

**Army and Navy Football Players**

*The first Army-Navy football game was played in 1891. Walter Camp, the popular Yale coach, thought that the new sport provided excellent training for war. "The knowledge of when, where, and how to make an attack," he wrote, "is the critical thing which distinguishes great generalship, whether in war or football."*

and universities were founded between 1880 and 1900, and enrollments more than doubled. While wealthy capitalists endowed some institutions, others, such as the state universities of the Midwest, were financed largely through public funds. Many colleges, including some that would evolve into first-rate institutions, were founded and largely funded by various religious denominations.

These years also witnessed a fundamental debate in higher education over what should be taught and how it should be presented. Impetus for reform came from new discoveries in science and medicine. Most physicians in the 1850s had attended medical school for only two sixteen-week terms. They typically received their degree without ever having visited a hospital ward or examined a patient. Then came the Civil War, which graphically exposed the abysmal state of American medical education. Twice as many soldiers died from infections as from wounds. Doctors were so poorly trained and ignorant about sanitation that they often infected soldiers' injuries when they probed wounds with hands wiped on pus-stained aprons. "The ignorance and general incompetency of the average graduate of American medical schools, at the time when he receives the degree which turns him loose upon the community," wrote Harvard president Charles W. Eliot in 1870, "is something horrible to contemplate."

In the 1880s and the 1890s, the public's well-justified skepticism about doctors encouraged leading medical professors, many of whom had studied in France and Germany, to begin restructuring American medical education. Using the experimental method developed by German scientists, they insisted that medical students in graduate school programs be trained in biology, chemistry, and physics, including laboratory experience. By 1900 graduate medical education had been placed on a firm professional foundation. Similar reforms took place in graduate programs in architecture, engineering, and law.

These changes were part of a larger transformation in higher education after the Civil War that gave rise to a new institution, the research university. Unlike even the best of the mid-nineteenth-century colleges, whose narrow, unvarying curriculum focused on classical languages, theology, logic, and mathematics, the new research universities offered courses in a wide variety of subject areas, established various professional schools, and encouraged faculty members to pursue basic research. For Andrew D. White, the first president of Cornell University (1869), the objective was to create an environment "where any person can find instruction in any study." At Cornell, the University of Wisconsin at Madison, Johns Hopkins, Harvard, and other institutions, this new conception of higher education laid the groundwork for the central role that America's universities would play in the intellectual, cultural, and scientific life of the twentieth century. Despite these significant changes, with all their portents for the future, however, higher education still remained largely the privilege of a few as the nineteenth century ended. The era when college attendance would become the norm rather than the rare exception lay many years ahead.

## Working-Class Leisure in the Immigrant City

In colonial America the subject of leisure time had been linked by ministers to "idleness," the dangerous first step leading to sin and wickedness. Disapproval of leisure also characterized the overwhelmingly rural culture of the early nineteenth century, in which the unremitting routines of farm labor left little time for relaxation. Family picnics, horse races, county fairs, revival meetings, and holiday observances such as the Fourth of July and Christmas had provided occasional permissible diversion, but most Americans continued to view leisure activities skeptically, and the line between relaxation and laziness was never clearly drawn. Henry Clay Work's popular song "My Grandfather's Clock" (1876), which praised the ancient timepiece for "wasting no time" and working "ninety years, without slumbering," bore witness to the tenacity of this deep-seated reverence for work and suspicion of leisure.

After the Civil War, as immigration soared, urban populations shot up, and factories multiplied, striking new patterns of leisure and amusement emerged, most notably among the urban working class. Middle-class educators and moralists continued to ponder the distinction between "wholesome" and "unwholesome" recreation, but they were little heeded in the throbbing immigrant cities. After spending long hours in factories, mills, and behind department-store counters, or working as domestic servants in the homes of the wealthy, working-class Americans eagerly sought relaxation and diversion. They thronged the streets, patronized saloons and dance halls, cheered at boxing matches and baseball games, and organized boisterous group picnics and holiday celebrations. As amusement parks, vaudeville theaters, sporting clubs, and racetracks provided further outlets for workers' need for entertainment, leisure became a big business catering to a mass public.

For millions of working-class Americans, leisure time took on increasing importance as factory work became ever more routinized and impersonal. Although many recreational activities involved both men and women, others particularly attracted one gender or the other. Whereas saloons offered an intensely male environment where patrons could share good stories, discuss and bet on sporting events, and momentarily put aside pressures of job and family, young working women shared confidences with friends in informal social clubs, tried out new fashions in street promenading, and found excitement in neighborhood dance halls and amusement park excursions.

## Streets, Saloons, and Boxing Matches

No segment of the population had a greater need for amusement and recreation than the urban working class. Hours of tedious, highly disciplined, and physically exhausting labor left workers tired but thirsting for excitement and escape at the end of the day. A banner carried by the Worcester, Massachusetts, carpenters' union in an 1889 demonstration for the eight-hour workday summed up the importance of workers' leisure hours: "EIGHT HOURS FOR WORK, EIGHT HOURS FOR REST, AND EIGHT HOURS FOR WHAT WE WILL."

City streets provided recreation that anyone could afford. Relaxing after a day's work, shop girls and laborers clustered on busy corners, watching shouting pushcart peddlers and listening to organ grinders and buskers play familiar melodies. For a penny or a nickel, they could buy bagels, baked potatoes, soda, and a variety of other foods and drinks. Especially in the summer, when the heat and humidity within the tenements reached unbearable levels, the streets became a buzzing hive of neighborhood social life. One immigrant later fondly recalled his boyhood on the streets of New York's Lower East Side: "Something was always happening, and our attention was continually being shifted from one excitement to another."

The streets were open to all, but other leisure institutions drew mainly a male clientele. For example, in cities like Baltimore, Milwaukee, and Cincinnati with a strong German immigrant flavor, gymnastic clubs (called *Turnverein*) and singing societies (*Gesang-*

**McSorley's Bar,** by John Sloan, 1912
*Neighborhood saloons were places where friends could get together. In his novel* Sister Carrie, *Theodore Dreiser admiringly described "the long bar . . . [with its] blaze of lights, polished woodwork, colored and cut glassware and many fancy bottles."*

*verein*) provided both companionship and the opportunity to perpetuate old-world cultural traditions.

For workmen of all ethnic backgrounds, saloons offered companionship, conviviality, and five-cent beer, often with a free lunch thrown in. New York City had an estimated ten thousand saloons by 1900 and Denver nearly five hundred. As neighborhood gathering places, saloons reinforced group identity and became centers for immigrant politics. Saloonkeepers, who often doubled as local ward bosses, performed small services for their patrons, including finding jobs and writing letters for illiterate immigrants. Sports memorabilia and pictures of prominent prizefighters adorned saloon walls. With their rich mahogany bars, etched glass, shiny brass rails, and elegant mirrors, saloons provided a taste of high-tone luxury to their factory patrons. Although working-class women rarely joined their husbands at the saloon, they frequently sent a son or daughter to the corner pub for a "growler"—a large tin pail of beer.

The conventions of saloon culture thus stood in marked contrast to both the socially isolating routines of factory labor and the increasingly private and family-centered social life of the middle class. Nevertheless, it would be a mistake to view the old-time saloon through a haze of sentimental nostalgia. In the rougher saloons, prostitution and criminal activity flourished. Moreover, the problem of family violence related to drunkenness was a real one, and the widespread custom of "treating," or buying drinks for one's friends, although revealing an appealing spirit of comradeship, often meant that even less money from a workman's limited weekly pay was available to meet urgent family needs.

For working-class males, bare-knuckles prizefighting became one of the most popular amusements. Drawing its heroes from the poorer ranks of society, the ring became an arena where lower-class men could assert their individuality and physical prowess. In East Coast cities, blacks, Irish, and Germans formed their own "sporting clubs" and used athletics to bolster their self-confidence and reaffirm their racial or ethnic identity.

### The Rise of Professional Sports

Contrary to the prevailing myth, schoolboy Abner Doubleday did not invent baseball in Cooperstown, New York, in 1839. As an English game called rounders, the pastime had existed in one form or another since the seventeenth century. But if Americans did not create baseball, they unquestionably took this informal children's game and turned it into a major professional

sport. The first organized baseball team, the New York Knickerbockers, was formed in 1845. Then in the 1860s the rules were codified, and the sport assumed its modern form. Overhand pitches replaced those formerly thrown underhand. Fielders, who now wore gloves, had to catch the ball on the fly to make an out instead of fielding it on one bounce. Games were standardized at nine innings, and bases were spaced ninety feet apart, as they are today.

In that same decade, promoters organized professional clubs and began to charge admission and compete for players. The Cincinnati Red Stockings, the first team to put its players under contract for the whole season, gained fame in 1869 by touring the country and ending the season with fifty-seven wins and no losses. Team owners organized the National League in 1876, took control from the players by requiring them to sign a reserve contract that forbade them to play for a rival organization, and limited each city to one professional team. Soon the owners were filling baseball parks with crowds of from ten thousand to twelve thousand fans and earning enormous profits. By the 1890s baseball had become big business.

Although baseball attracted a national following at all social levels, the working class particularly took the sport to heart. The most profitable teams were those from major industrial cities with a large working-class population. Workers attended the games when they could and avidly followed their team's progress when they could not. Some saloons reported scores on black-

**FOR THE HEAVY-WEIGHT CHAMPIONSHIP OF THE WORLD.**

**World's Heavyweight Boxing Championship, 1892**
*In dethroning ring champion John L. Sullivan, "Gentleman Jim" Corbett demonstrated that speed and finesse were more than a match for brute strength.*

boards. In Cleveland just after the turn of the century, Mayor Tom Johnson erected a bulletin board downtown that recorded game results.

Newspapers thrived on baseball. Joseph Pulitzer introduced the first separate sports page when he bought the *New York World* in 1883, and much of the sporting news in the *World* and other papers was devoted to baseball. For the benefit of German immigrants, the New York *Staats Zeitung* published a glossary of German equivalents of baseball terms: for example, "umpire" was *Umparteiischer*. Baseball, declared novelist Mark Twain in a burst of hyperbole, had become "the very symbol . . . and visible expression of the drive and push and rush and struggle of the raging, tearing, booming nineteenth century."

Although no other organized sport attracted as large a following as baseball, horse racing and boxing contests were also widely covered in the popular press and drew big crowds of spectators and bettors. But whereas races like Louisville's Kentucky Derby became important social events for the rich, professional boxing aroused more passionate devotion among the working class. By far the most popular sports hero of the nineteenth century was heavyweight fighter John L. Sullivan, "the Boston Strong Boy." Of Irish immigrant stock, Sullivan began boxing in 1877 at the age of nineteen. His first professional fight came in 1880 when he knocked out John Donaldson, "the Champion of the West," in a Cincinnati beer hall. With his massive physique, handlebar mustache, and arrogant swagger, Sullivan was enormously popular among immigrants. Barnstorming across the country, he vanquished a succession of local strong men, invariably wearing his trademark green tights with an American flag wrapped around his middle. Cleverly, Sullivan also refused to fight blacks, in deference, he said, to the wishes of his fans. This policy conveniently allowed him to avoid facing the finest boxer of the 1880s, the Australian black Peter Jackson.

Sullivan loved drink and high living, and by the end of the eighties, he was sadly out of shape. But when the editor of the *Police Gazette*, a sensational tabloid, designed a new heavyweight championship belt—allegedly containing two hundred ounces of silver and encrusted with diamonds and pure gold—and awarded it to Sullivan's rival Jake Kilrain, the champion had to defend himself. The two met on a sweltering, hundred-degree day in New Orleans in July 1889, in the last bare-knuckles championship match. After seventy-five short but grueling rounds, Kilrain's managers threw in the towel. Newspapers around the nation banner-headlined the story. Contemptuously returning the championship belt to the *Police Gazette* after having had it appraised at $175, Sullivan went on the road in a melodrama written specifically for him. Playing the role of a blacksmith, he (in the words of a recent historian of bare-knuckles boxing) "pounded an anvil, beat a bully, and mutilated his lines." But his fans did not care: he was one of them, and they adored him. As one admirer wrote,

> His colors are the Stars and Stripes,
>   He also wears the green,
> And he's the grandest slugger that
>   The ring has ever seen.

## Vaudeville, Amusement Parks, and Dance Halls

In contrast to the male preserve of saloons and prize-fights, the world of vaudeville shows, amusement parks, and neighborhood dance pavilions not only welcomed all comers regardless of gender but in some cases proved particularly congenial to working-class women.

Vaudeville evolved out of the pre–Civil War minstrel shows, in which white comedians made up as blacks had performed songs and comic sketches (see Chapter 11). Vaudeville performances offered a succession of acts, all designed for mass appeal. The shows typically opened with a trained animal routine or a dance number, followed by a musical interlude featuring sentimental favorites such as "On the Banks of the Wabash Far Away" mixed in with new hits such as "Meet Me in St. Louis, Louis," a jaunty spoof of a young wife's frustration with her stick-in-the-mud husband.

Comic skits followed, ridiculing the trials of urban life, satirizing the ineptitude of the police and municipal officials, poking fun at the babel of accents in the immigrant city, and mining a rich vein of broad ethnic humor and stereotypes. After further musical numbers and acts by ventriloquists, pantomimes, and magicians, the program ended with a "flash" finale such as flying-trapeze artists swinging against a black background. By the 1880s vaudeville was drawing larger crowds than any other form of theater, and understandably so: not only did it provide an inexpensive evening of lighthearted entertainment, but also in the comic sketches, immigrant audiences could laugh at their own experience as they saw it translated into slapstick and caricature.

Where vaudeville offered psychological escape from the stresses of working-class life by exploiting its comic potential, amusement parks provided physical escape, at least for a day. The prototype of the sprawling urban amusement parks was New York's Coney Island, a section of Brooklyn's oceanfront that in the 1870s evolved into a resort for the masses. At Coney Island young couples who rode through the dark Tunnel of Love, sped down the dizzying roller coaster in Steeplechase Park, or watched belly dancers in the carnival atmosphere of the sideshows were encouraged to surrender to the spirit of exuberant play, forget the restrictions and demands of the industrial world, and lose themselves in fantasy.

By the end of the nineteenth century, New York City had well over 300,000 female wage earners, most of them young, unmarried women working as seamstresses, laundresses, typists, domestic servants, or department store clerks. For this army of low-paid young working women and their counterparts in other cities, the amusement parks with their exhilarating rides and crowded dance halls exerted a powerful lure. Here they could meet friends, spend time with young men beyond the watchful eyes of parents, show off their new dresses, and try out the latest dance steps. As a twenty-year-old German immigrant woman who worked as a servant in a wealthy household observed: "I have heard some of the high people with whom I have been living say that Coney Island is not tony. The trouble is that these high people don't know how to dance. I have to laugh when I see them at their balls and parties. If only I could get out on the floor and show them how—they would be astonished." For such women, the brightly decorated dance pavilion, the exciting music, and the spell of a warm summer night could seem a magical release from the drudgery of daily life.

## Ragtime

Since slavery days, black Americans had sustained a strong, creative musical culture, and thus it is not surprising that blacks made a major contribution to the popular music of the late nineteenth century, in the form of ragtime. Nothing could illustrate more sharply the differences between the culture of the middle class and that of the working class than the contrasting styles of popular music each favored. The middle class preferred hymns or songs that taught a lesson or conveyed a moral. Ragtime, by contrast, which originated in the 1880s with black musicians in the saloons and brothels of the South and Midwest, was played strictly for entertainment (see A Place in Time).

Ragtime developed out of the rich tradition of sacred and secular songs through which African Americans had long eased the burdens of their lives. Like spirituals, ragtime used syncopated rhythms and complex harmonies, but it blended these with marching-band musical structures to create a distinctive style. A favorite of "honky-tonk" piano players, ragtime was introduced to the broader public in the 1890s and became a national sensation.

The reasons for the sudden ragtime craze were complex. Inventive, playful, with catchy syncopations and an infectious rhythm in the bass clef, the music displayed a fresh originality that had an appeal all its own. But part of ragtime's popularity also came from its origin in brothels and its association with blacks, who

**Coney Island**

*Denounced by conservative reformers as "Sodom by the Sea," the Coney Island amusement park, as its guidebook implied, offered thrilling rides and a carnival atmosphere which stood in marked contrast to the decorous manners of starched, strait-laced, polite society.*

were widely stereotyped in the 1890s as sexual, sensual, and uninhibited by the rigid Victorian social conventions that restricted whites' behavior. The "wild" and complex rhythms of ragtime, therefore, were widely interpreted to be a freer and more "natural" expression of elemental feelings about love and affection.

The white working class's fascination with ragtime and vaudeville's blackface acts has been the subject of considerable recent scrutiny by historians. Some have interpreted it as a mechanism that enabled the white working class to mock upper-class ideals. By pretending to act like the popular stereotypes of blacks, white working-class youth could challenge traditional family structures, the virtue of sexual self-denial, and the adult role expectations about working hard. Popular culture thereby made fun of the ideals of thrift and propriety that had been promoted in marketplace and domestic ideology. But other historians have argued that blackface buffoonery, with its grotesque, demeaning caricatures of African Americans, reinforced prejudice against blacks and restricted blacks' escape from lower-class status. Paradoxically, therefore, the popularity of black music and blackface vaudeville acts reinforced a sense of white solidarity while at the same time strengthening the unbreachable wall separating whites from African Americans.

Ragtime's great popularity thus proved a mixed blessing for blacks. It testified to the achievements of brilliant composers like Joplin, helped break down the barriers faced by blacks in the music industry, and contributed to a spreading rebellion against the repressiveness of Victorian standards. But for some whites, ragtime simply confirmed their stereotype of blacks as primitive and sensual, a bias that underlay the racism of the period and helped justify segregation and discrimination.

In sum, from many perspectives the factories and immigrant slums of late-nineteenth-century America present a grim picture. The realities of overwork, poverty, disease, and inhumane living conditions hover darkly over the history of the period. Yet in the face of such realities, the laboring masses avidly pursued a colorful variety of leisure-time activities that affirmed their social solidarity and sustained their spirits. The vitality, gaiety, and sheer energy of this working-class culture remind us that however bleak their lives, the members of the urban working class remained strong and resilient in these years, conscious of their human worth and determined to celebrate it.

# Cultures in Conflict

In the late nineteenth century the United States was embroiled in class conflict and cultural unrest. Part of this turmoil raged within the middle class itself. Victorian morality and genteel cultural standards were never totally accepted even within the elite and middle classes, and as the century ended, ethical questionings and new cultural stirrings intensified. Women stood at the center of the era's cultural turbulence. Thwarted by a restrictive code of feminine propriety, middle-class women made their dissatisfactions heard. Developments as diverse as the rise of women's clubs, the growth of women's colleges, and an 1890s bicycle fad contributed to the emergence of what some began to call the new woman.

But although Victorian culture was challenged from within the middle class itself, a widening chasm divided the well-to-do from the immigrant cities' teaming hordes of laborers. Perhaps in no period of American history have class conflicts—cultural as well as economic—been more open and raw. As native-born middle-class leaders nervously eyed the rambunctious and sometimes disorderly culture of city streets, saloons, boxing clubs, dance halls, and amusement parks, they correctly perceived a massive if unconscious challenge to their own cultural and social standing. While some middle-class reformers promoted the public school as an institution for imposing middle-class values on the urban masses, others battled the hydra-headed manifestations of urban "vice" and "immorality." But ultimately it was the polite mores of the middle class, not urban working-class culture, that proved the more vulnerable. By 1900 the Victorian social and moral ethos was crumbling on every front.

## *The Genteel Tradition and Its Critics*

What was this genteel culture that aroused such opposition? In the 1870s and 1880s, a group of upper-class writers and magazine editors, led by Harvard art history professor Charles Eliot Norton and New York editors Richard Watson Gilder of *The Century* magazine and E. L. Godkin of *The Nation*, codified Victorian standards for literature and the fine arts. With the support of artistic allies in Boston and New York, they joined forces in a campaign designed to improve American taste in interior furnishings, textiles, ceramics, wallpaper, and books. By fashioning rigorous criteria for ex-

## New Orleans, Louisiana

From its French and Spanish beginnings in the eighteenth century, New Orleans remained a unique city in the 1890s. Its popular culture fused elements from the culinary and musical traditions of the varied groups in its population, especially its free blacks and Creoles of color. The latter were the offspring of Africans and "Cajuns"—descendants of the Acadians, the eighteenth-century exiles from French Canada who had settled along the swampy bayous of the Mississippi Delta south of the city.

During the early nineteenth century, New Orleans's large free-black and "colored" Creole population had enjoyed a degree of independence found nowhere else in the South among people of color. Free blacks had established their own churches and fraternal societies, formed their own militia, and borne arms. Both wealthy and poor free blacks had created a distinctive culture melding African and French customs. In the Vieux Carré, the old French part of the city, slaves and free blacks joined together on Sunday afternoons to play drums, banjos, and violins. Young people danced and sang, mingling African voodoo rhythms with Roman Catholic liturgical melodies.

During the Civil War and Reconstruction, however, the humiliating occupation of New Orleans by federal troops had left a legacy of southern white bitterness against the black population. Then in the 1880s and 1890s, as Italian immigrants swelled the city's population, racial tensions were rekindled. Despite the discord, festivals like Mardi Gras, with its riotous parades and boisterous balls, continued. The city won notoriety for its racetrack betting, gambling, and prostitution. Sightseers flocked to New Orleans to savor its spicy Creole food, drink in its smoky

bars, and visit its seedy bordellos and raunchy dance halls. Its sidewalks thronged with commercial travelers, longshoremen, country folk in the city for a day, and racetrack bettors. "One is apt to see here at some hour of the day anybody from a St. Louis capitalist to the man who came the night before with no change of linen, and seven dollars sewn in his waistcoat," wrote a visiting journalist. Appropriately, promoters chose New Orleans as the site of the September 1892 championship boxing match in which "Gentleman Jim" Corbett defeated John L. Sullivan.

Among the city's liveliest traditions was the marching band. A product of the eighteenth-century military, whose drummers and fifers helped identify regiments' locations amidst battlefield

chaos, the marching band by the mid-nineteenth century had become a fixture in cities and towns across America, and prominently so in New Orleans. Saturday nights, young and old alike ambled to the city-park bandstand to hear local groups belt out the stirring marches of John Philip Sousa and other composers.

New Orleans's black brass bands in particular pioneered new playing styles that captured national attention. Having snapped up the affordable used musical instruments piled high in pawn shops after the Civil War, blacks in New Orleans—unfettered by written scores and formal music lessons—developed innovative styles for bugles, trombones, and the newly invented piston-valve trumpets. Every black social organization,

### The Queen City Band of Sedalia, Missouri
*Marching bands helped popularize ragtime music. When he lived in Sedalia, Missouri, Scott Joplin often allowed the Queen City Band, pictured here in the 1890s, to give the first performance of his new compositions.*

club, fire station, and lodge boasted its own twelve-member brass marching band. The bands played at picnics, parades, dances, church socials, circuses, minstrel shows, athletic contests, and holiday gatherings. By the 1880s many brass bands gained fame for playing in the new "ratty," "raggy," unscored, syncopated style, with its echoes of the older call-and-response African-American singing style that featured one person shouting a phrase and in turn being answered by the group. Brass bands were also known for their custom of playing religious hymns "straight" on the way to the cemetery and then "jazzing them up" on the way home. Within the bands—which often also played in bars and brothels—individual soloists such as coronetist Charles "Buddy" Bolden became famous for improvisational blues solos. These soulful performances were the forerunners of a new musical style, "jazz," that emerged in the 1890s and became a national rage after the turn of the century.

Although the popularity of these musicians—later immortalized in Irving Berlin's song "Alexander's Ragtime Band"—increasingly attracted middle-class white audiences and seemed to imply a growing general acceptance of black musicians, racial prejudice in New Orleans continued to shape local practices. If a black band marched into a white neighborhood, the residents commonly pelted the musicians with rocks.

In 1897, seeking to isolate and regulate prostitution, city administrators created a special district, named Storyville after Sydney Story, the councilman who proposed the new quarter. Storyville's glittering saloons and ubiquitous houses of prostitution hired some of the best black ragtime piano players. Other black musicians, excluded from some white establishments, could find jobs only in the racially segregated bars and cabarets of the two-block "Tango Belt" surrounding Storyville. Musically talented Creoles of color—the proud descendants of free-black mulattos whose musical training had assured them positions in local orchestras and opera houses—could secure employment only in these districts, where they worked alongside criminals and prostitutes.

For all its uniqueness, New Orleans typified larger strands in the turn-of-the-century American fabric. (The city's cultural diversity also anticipated trends that in the twentieth century would make all the United States a truly multicultural society.) And the complex history of early jazz in New Orleans paralleled the ironic relationship of popular culture and racism in the larger society. White middle-class America, like the one of New Orleans, would soon embrace this African-American musical contribution. Captivated by New Orleans "Dixieland" jazz, they would idolize its best practitioners, including the great trumpeter Louis Armstrong, a veteran of the New Orleans brass marching bands. Yet these middle-class Americans, like their counterparts in New Orleans, would see no contradiction in celebrating jazz while harboring deep prejudices against the very people from whose culture this vital new music had emerged.

### Valve Trombone

*Members of New Orleans's Reliance Brass Band played this pre–World War I vintage trombone. The band's founder, "Papa" Jack Laine, was known as the father of white jazz.*

### Ragtime Sheet Music

*The nearly universal popularity of ragtime music was confirmed when sheet-music publishers on New York's 28th Street, an area nicknamed Tin Pan Alley, brought out Irving Berlin's "Alexander's Ragtime Band." Although Berlin was a Russian Jewish immigrant and the song had hardly a trace of ragtime in it, the connection with the New Orleans ragtime tradition made the tune an instant hit.*

cellence in writing and design, they hoped to create a coherent national artistic culture.

In the 1880s Norton, Godkin, and Gilder, joined by the editors of other highbrow periodicals such as the *Atlantic Monthly* and *North American Review,* set up new guidelines for serious literature. They lectured the middle class about the value of high culture and the insights to be gained from the fine arts. They also censored their own publications to remove all sexual allusions, vulgar slang, disrespectful treatments of Christianity, and unhappy endings.

Expanding their combined circulation to nearly 200,000 copies and opening their magazines to a variety of new authors, Godkin and the other editors of these "quality" periodicals created an important forum for serious writing. Novelists Henry James, who published virtually all of his work in the *Atlantic,* and William Dean Howells, who served as editor of the same magazine, helped to lead this elite literary establishment. James believed that "it is art that *makes* life, . . . [There is] no substitute whatever for [its] force and beauty. . . ." This so-called art for art's sake movement also made its influence felt through the work of architects, jewelers, and interior decorators.

Although these upper-class magazines initially provided an important forum for new writers, their editors' strident elitism and imperialistic desire to control the nation's literary standards soon aroused opposition. Samuel Langhorne Clemens, better known as Mark Twain, spoke for many young writers when he declared as early as 1869 that he was through with "literature and all that bosh." Attacking aristocratic literary conventions, Twain and other authors who shared his concerns explored new forms of fiction and worked to broaden literature's appeal to the general public.

These efforts by a younger generation of writers to chart new directions for American literature rested on fundamental changes taking place in the publishing industry. To compete with elite periodicals costing twenty-five to thirty-five cents, new magazines like *Ladies' Home Journal, Cosmopolitan,* and *McClure's* lowered their prices to a dime or fifteen cents and tripled or quadrupled their circulation. Supporting themselves through advertising, these magazines encouraged new trends in fiction while mass-marketing new products. Their energetic editors sought writers who could provide accurate depictions from the "whirlpool of real life" and create a new civic consciousness to heal the class divisions that splintered American society in the 1890s.

Some of these authors have been labeled regionalists because they captured the distinctive dialect and details of local life in their environs. In *The Country of the Pointed Firs* (1896), for example, Sarah Orne Jewett wrote of the New England village life that she knew from her own neighbors in South Berwick, Maine. Others, most notably William Dean Howells, have been called realists because of their focus on a truthful depiction of the commonplace and the everyday, especially in urban areas. Still others have been categorized as naturalists because their stories take on a fatalistic cast and stress the economic and psychological determinants of life. Stephen Crane's *Maggie: A Girl of the Streets* (1892), a bleak story of an innocent girl's exploitation and ultimate suicide in the harsh environment of an urban slum, is generally considered the first American naturalistic novel. Yet in practice, these categories are imprecise and often overlap. What many of these writers shared, irrespective of labels, was a skepticism toward literary conventions and an intense desire to understand and portray in words the society around them.

The careers of Mark Twain and Theodore Dreiser highlight the changes in the publishing industry and the evolution of new forms of writing. Both authors grew up in the Midwest, outside the East Coast literary establishment; Twain was born near Hannibal, Missouri, in 1835, and Dreiser in Terre Haute, Indiana, in 1871. As young men both worked as newspaper reporters and traveled widely in search of new financial opportunities. Both learned from direct and sometimes bitter personal experience about the greed, speculation, and fraud that figured centrally in Gilded Age life.

Of the two, Twain more incessantly sought a mass-market audience. With his drooping mustache, white hair, and white suits, Twain deliberately turned himself into a media personality, lecturing from coast to coast, founding his own publishing house, and selling his books through door-to-door salesmen. The name Mark Twain became his trademark, identifying him to readers as a literary celebrity much as the labels Coca-Cola and Ivory Soap won instant consumer recognition.* Although Dreiser possessed neither Twain's flamboyant personality nor his instinct for salesmanship, he, too, learned to crank out feature articles for mass magazines heavily dependent on advertising.

---

* *Mark Twain* was originally a boatman's term indicating the two-fathom depth at which steamboats could safely navigate on the Mississippi River, which flows past Clemens's native Hannibal.

**Sarah Orne Jewett and Mark Twain**
*Jewett and Twain not only broke from highbred literary standards but also created unique personal styles through their studied poses and distinctive attire.*

Drawing on their own experiences, Twain and Dreiser wrote about the human impact of the wrenching social changes taking place around them: the flow of people to the expanding cities and the relentless scramble for power, wealth, and fame. In the *Adventures of Huckleberry Finn* (1884), Twain presents a classic narrative of two runaways, the rebellious Huck and the slave Jim, drifting down the Mississippi in search of freedom. Their journey southward, which contrasts the idyllic life on the raft with the tawdry, fraudulent world of the small riverfront towns, is at the same time a journey of identity that brings with it a deeper understanding of contemporary American society.

Dreiser's *Sister Carrie* (1900) also tells of a journey. But in this case, the main character, Carrie Meeber, an innocent and attractive girl on her way from her Wisconsin farm home to Chicago, is first seduced by a traveling salesman and then moves in with Hurstwood, the married proprietor of a fancy saloon. Driven by her desire for expensive department store clothes and lavish entertainment, Carrie is an opportunist incapable of feeling guilt. She follows Hurstwood to New York, knowing that he has stolen the receipts from his saloon, abandons him when his money runs out, and pursues her own career in the theater.

Twain and Dreiser broke decisively with the genteel tradition's emphasis on manners and decorum. *Century* magazine readers complained that *Huckleberry Finn* was coarse and "destitute of a single redeeming

quality." The publisher of *Sister Carrie* was so repelled by Dreiser's novel that he printed only a thousand copies (to fulfill the legal terms of his contract) and then stored them in a warehouse, refusing to promote them.

Growing numbers of scholars and critics similarly challenged the self-serving certitudes of Victorian mores, including assumptions that moral worth and economic standing were closely linked and that the status quo of the 1870s and 1880s represented a social order decreed by God and nature alike. Whereas Henry George, Lester Ward, and Edward Bellamy elaborated their visions of a cooperative and harmonious society (see Chapter 18), economist Thorstein Veblen in *The Theory of the Leisure Class* (1899) offered a caustic critique of the lifestyles of the new capitalist elite. Raised in a Norwegian farm community in Minnesota, Veblen looked at the captains of industry and their families with a jaundiced eye, mercilessly documenting their "conspicuous consumption" and lamenting the widening economic gap between "those who worked without profit" and "those who profited without working."

Within the new discipline of sociology, Annie MacLean exposed the exploitation of department store clerks, Walter Wyckoff uncovered the hand-to-mouth existence of unskilled laborers, and W. E. B. Du Bois documented the suffering and hardships faced by blacks in Philadelphia. The publication of these social scientists' writings, coupled with the economic depression and seething labor agitation of the 1890s, made it increasingly difficult for turn-of-the-century middle-class Americans to accept the smug, self-satisfied belief in progress and gentility that had been a hallmark of the Victorian outlook.

## Modernism in Architecture and Painting

The challenge to the genteel tradition also found strong support among architects and painters. By the 1890s Chicago architects William Holabird, John Wellborn Root, and others had tired of copying European designs. Breaking with established architects such as Richard Morris Hunt, the designer of French chateaux for New York's Fifth Avenue, these Chicago architects followed the lead of Louis Sullivan, who argued that a building's form should follow its function. In their view, banks should look like the financial institutions they were, not like Greek temples. Rejecting the pretentiousness of prevailing elite mores and striving to evolve functional American design standards, the Chicago architects looked for inspiration to the future—to modernism—not to the past.

Frank Lloyd Wright's "prairie-school" houses, first built in the Chicago suburb of Oak Park in the 1890s, represented a typical modernist break with past styles. Wright scorned the bulky Victorian house with its large attic and basement. His designs, which featured broad, sheltering roofs and low silhouettes, used interconnecting rooms to create a sense of spaciousness.

The call of modernism, with its rejection of Victorian refinement, influenced late-nineteenth-century American painting as well. The watercolors of Winslow Homer, a magazine illustrator during the Civil War, revealed nature as brutally tough and unsentimental. In Homer's grim, elemental seascapes, lone men struggle against massive waves that constantly threaten to overwhelm them. Thomas Eakins's canvases of swimmers, boxers, and rowers (such as his well-known *Champion Single Sculls*, painted in 1871) similarly captured moments of vigorous physical exertion in everyday life. To make his paintings realistic, Eakins studied anatomy and dissected cadavers at a medical school. He also insisted on using nude models in his drawing classes at the Pennsylvania Academy of Fine Arts. When he removed the loincloth of a male model, proper Philadelphians demanded his dismissal, even though his students overwhelmingly supported him.

The revolt by architects and painters against Victorian standards was symptomatic of a larger shift in middle-class thought. This shift resulted from fundamental economic changes that had spawned a far more complex social environment than that of the past. As Protestant minister Josiah Strong perceptively observed in 1898, the transition from muscle to mechanical power had "separated, as by an impassable gulf, the simple, homespun, individualistic world of the . . . past, from the complex, closely associated life of the present." The increasingly evident gap between rural or small-town life—a world of quiet parlors and flickering kerosene lamps—and life in the big, glittering cities of iron and glass made nineteenth-century Americans acutely aware of differences in upbringing and wealth. Given the disparities between rich and poor, between rural and urban, and between native-born Americans and recent immigrants, it is no wonder that pious Victorian platitudes about proper manners and graceful arts seemed out of touch with the new social realities.

Distrusting the idealistic Victorian assumptions about social progress, middle-class journalists, novelists, artists, and politicians nevertheless remained divided over how to replace them. Not until the progressive period would social reformers draw on a new expertise in social research and an enlarged conception of the federal government's regulatory power to break sharply with their Victorian predecessors' social outlook.

## From Victorian Lady to New Woman

Although middle-class women figured importantly in the revolt against Victorian refinement, their role was complex and ambiguous. Dissatisfaction with the cult of domesticity did not necessarily lead to open rebellion. Many women, although chafing against the constraints of deference and the assumption that they should limit their activities to the home, remained committed to playing a nurturing and supportive role within the family. In fact, early advocates of a "widened sphere" for women often fused the traditional Victorian ideal of womanhood with a firm commitment to political action.

The career of temperance leader Frances Willard illustrates how the cult of domesticity, with its celebration of special female virtues, could evolve into a broader view of women's social and political responsibilities. Like many of her contemporaries, Willard believed that women by nature were compassionate and nurturing. She was also convinced that drinking encouraged thriftlessness and profoundly threatened family life. Resigning as dean of women and professor of English at Northwestern University in 1874, Willard devoted her energies full-time to the temperance cause. Five years later she was elected president of the newly formed Woman's Christian Temperance Union (WCTU).

Willard took the traditional cult of domesticity's belief that women had unique moral virtues and transformed it into a rationale for political action. The domestication of politics, she asserted, would protect the family and improve public morality. Choosing as the union's badge a bow of white ribbon, symbolizing the purity of the home, she launched a crusade in 1880 to win the franchise for women so that they could vote to outlaw liquor. Willard soon expanded the WCTU's activities to include welfare work, prison reform, labor arbitration, and public health. Under her leadership the WCTU, with a membership of nearly 150,000 by 1890, became the nation's first mass organization of women. Through it, women gained experience as lobbyists, organizers, and lecturers, in the process undercutting the assumption of "separate spheres."

An expanding network of women's clubs offered another means by which middle- and upper-class women could hone their skills in civic affairs, public speaking, and intellectual analysis. In the 1870s many well-to-do women met weekly to study topics of mutual interest. These club women soon became involved in social-welfare projects, public library expansion, and tenement reform. By 1892 the General Federation of Women's Clubs, an umbrella organization established that year, boasted 495 affiliates and a hundred thousand members.

Another major impetus to an expanded role for women came from a younger generation of college women. Following the precedent set by Oberlin College in 1836, coeducational private colleges and public universities in the Midwest enrolled increasing numbers of women in these years, whereas Columbia, Brown, and Harvard universities in the East admitted women to the affiliated but separate institutions of Barnard (1889), Pembroke (1891), and Radcliffe (1894), respectively. Nationally, the percentage of colleges admitting women jumped from 30 percent to 71 percent between 1880 and 1900. By the turn of the century, women made up more than one-third of the total college-student population.

Initially, female collegiate education reinforced the prevailing concepts of femininity. The earliest women's colleges—Mount Holyoke (1837), Vassar (1865), Wellesley and Smith (1875), and Bryn Mawr (1884)—

**Cigar-Box Label,** c. 1910
*Vassar College promoted the new image of womanhood by stressing the interconnections among education, athletics, and ethics.*

were founded to prepare women for marriage, motherhood, and Christian service. But participation in college organizations, athletics, and dramatics enabled female students to learn traditionally "masculine" strategies for gaining power. The generation of women educated at female institutions in the late nineteenth century developed the self-confidence to break with the Victorian ideal of passive womanhood and to compete on an equal basis with men by displaying strength, aggressiveness, and intelligence—popularly considered male attributes. By 1897 the U.S. commissioner of education noted, "[I]t has become an historical fact that women have made rapid strides, and captured a greater number of honors in proportion to their numbers than men."

Victorian constraints on women were further loosened at the end of the century when a bicycling vogue swept urban America. Fearful of waning vitality, middle- and upper-class Americans explored various ways to improve their vigor. Some used health products such as cod liver oil and sarsaparilla for "weak blood." Others played basketball, invented in 1891 by a physical education instructor at Springfield College in Massachusetts to keep students in shape during the winter months. But bicycling, which could be done individually or in groups, quickly became the most popular sport for those who wished to combine exercise with recreation.

Bicycles of various designs had been manufactured since the 1870s, but bicycling did not become a national craze until the invention in the 1880s of the so-

**Bicycling**
*In popular magazine pictures, such as this one, bicycling was often portrayed as a social activity where men and women could meet and date.*

called safety bicycle, with its smaller wheels, ball-bearing axles, and air-filled tires. By the 1890s over a million Americans owned bicycles.

Bicycling especially appealed to young women who had chafed under the restrictive Victorian attitudes toward female exercise, which held that proper young ladies must never sweat and that the female body must be fully covered at all times. Pedaling along in a shirtwaist or "split" skirt, a woman bicyclist made an implicit feminist statement suggesting that she had broken with genteel conventions and wanted to explore new activities beyond the traditional sphere.

Changing attitudes toward femininity and women's proper role also found expression in gradually shifting ideas about marriage. Charlotte Perkins Gilman, a suffrage advocate and speaker for women's rights, asserted that women would make an effective contribution to society only when they won economic independence from men through work outside the home (see Chapter 22). One very tangible indicator of women's changing relationship to men was the substantial rise in the divorce rate between 1880 and 1900. In 1880 one in every twenty-one marriages ended in divorce. By 1900 the rate had climbed to one in twelve. Women who brought suit for divorce increasingly cited their husbands' failure to act responsibly and to respect their autonomy. Accepting such arguments, courts frequently awarded the wife alimony, a monetary settlement payable by the ex-husband to support her and their children.

Women writers generally welcomed the new female commitment to independence and self-sufficiency. In the short stories of Mary Wilkins Freeman, for example, women's expanding role is implicitly compared to the frontier ideal of freedom. Freeman's characters fight for their beliefs without concern for society's reaction. Feminist Kate Chopin pushed the debate to the extreme by having Edna Pontellier, the married heroine of her 1899 novel *The Awakening,* violate social conventions by first falling in love with another man and then taking her own life when his ideas about women prove as narrow and traditional as those of her husband.

Despite the efforts of these and other champions of the new woman, attitudes changed slowly. The enlarged conception of women's role in society exerted its greatest influence on middle-class women who had enjoyed the privilege of higher education, possessed some leisure time, and could reasonably hope for success in journalism, education, social work, and nursing. For female immigrant factory workers and for shop girls who worked sixty hours a week to try to make ends meet, however, the ideal remained a more distant goal. So although many women were seeking more independence and control over their lives, most still viewed the home as their primary responsibility.

### Public Education as an Arena of Class Conflict

The agitation over women's role remained largely confined to the middle class, but a very different controversy, over the scope and function of public education, engaged Americans of all socioeconomic levels. This debate starkly highlighted the class and cultural divisions in late-nineteenth-century society. Viewing the public schools as an instrument for indoctrinating and controlling the lower ranks of society, middle-class educators and civic leaders from the 1870s on campaigned to expand public schooling and bring it under centralized control. Not surprisingly, the reformers' efforts aroused considerable opposition from ethnic and religious groups whose outlook and interests differed sharply from theirs.

Thanks to the crusade for universal public education started by Horace Mann and other antebellum educational reformers, most states by the Civil War had public school systems, and more than half the nation's children were receiving some formal education. But most attended school for only three or four years, and few went on to high school. Concerned that many Americans lacked sufficient knowledge to participate wisely in public affairs or function effectively in the labor force, middle-class educational activists in the 1870s worked to raise the overall educational level and to increase the number of years that children spent in school.

One such reformer was William Torrey Harris, a Victorian moralist who viewed the public schools as a "great instrumentality to lift all classes of people into . . . civilized life." First as superintendent of the St. Louis public schools in the 1870s, and later as the federal commissioner of education, Harris urged teachers to instill in their students a sense of order, decorum, self-discipline, and civic loyalty. Believing that modern industrial society depended on citizens' conforming to the timetables of the factory and the train, he envi-

sioned the schools as models of punctuality and precise scheduling: "The pupil must have his lessons ready at the appointed time, must rise at the tap of the bell, move to the line, return; in short, go through all the evolutions with equal precision."

To achieve these goals and to wrest control of the schools from neighborhood leaders and ward politicians, reform-minded educators like Harris elaborated a philosophy of public education stressing punctuality, centralized administration, compulsory-attendance laws, and a tenure system to insulate teachers from political favoritism and parental pressure. By 1900 thirty-one states required school attendance of all children from eight to fourteen years of age.

But the steamroller methods used by Harris and like-minded administrators to systematize public education quickly prompted protests. New York pediatrician Joseph Mayer Rice, who in 1892 toured thirty-six cities and interviewed twelve hundred teachers, scornfully criticized an educational establishment that stressed singsong memorization and prisonlike discipline.

Rice's biting attack on public education overlooked the real advances in reading and computation made in the previous two decades. Nationally, despite the influx of immigrants, the illiteracy rate for individuals ten years and older dropped from 17 percent in 1880 to 13 percent in 1890, largely because of the expansion of urban educational facilities. But Rice was on target in as-

**Interior Urban School**
*Photographers were careful to picture public elementary schools, such as this one on New York's Lower East Side in 1886, as models of immigrant children's decorum and good behavior.*

sailing many teachers' rigid emphasis on silence, docility, and unquestioning obedience to the rules. When a Chicago school inspector found a thirteen-year-old boy huddled in the basement of a stockyard building and ordered him back to school, the weeping boy blurted out, "[T]hey hits ye if yer don't learn, and they hits ye if ye whisper, and they hits ye if ye have string in yer pocket, and they hits ye if yer seat squeaks, and they hits ye if ye don't stan' up in time, and they hits ye if yer late, and they hits ye if ye ferget the page."

By the 1880s several different groups found themselves in opposition to centralized urban public school bureaucracies. Although many working-class families valued education, those who depended on their children's meager wages for survival resisted the attempt to force their sons and daughters to attend school past the elementary grades. Although some immigrant families made great sacrifices to enable their children to get an education, many withdrew their offspring from school as soon as they had learned the rudiments of reading and writing, and sent them to work.

Furthermore, Catholic immigrants objected to the overwhelmingly Protestant orientation of the public schools. Distressed by the use of the King James Bible and by the schools' failure to observe saints' days, Catholics set up separate parochial school systems. In response, Republican politicians, resentful of the Catholic immigrants' overwhelming preference for the Democratic party, tried unsuccessfully in 1875 to pass a constitutional amendment cutting off all public aid to church-related schools. Catholics in turn denounced federal aid to public schools as intended "to suppress Catholic education, gradually extinguish Catholicity in this country, and to form one homogeneous American people after the New England Evangelical type."

At the other end of the social scale, upper-class parents who did not wish to send their children to immigrant-thronged public schools enrolled their daughters in female seminaries such as Emma Willard's in Troy, New York, and their sons in private academies and boarding schools like St. Paul's in Concord, New Hampshire. Shielding their privileged students from the temptations of urban life and preparing them to go on to college, these institutions reinforced the elite belief that higher education should be the preserve of the well-to-do.

The proliferation of private and parochial schools, together with the controversies over compulsory education, school funding, and classroom decorum, reveal the extent to which public education had become entangled in ethnic and class differences. Unlike Germany and Japan, which standardized and centralized their national education systems in the late nineteenth century, the United States, reflecting its social heterogeneity, instead created a diverse system of locally run public and private institutions that allowed each segment of society to retain some influence over the schools attended by its own children. Amid the disputes, school enrollments dramatically expanded. In 1870 fewer than 72,000 students attended the nation's 1,026 high schools. By 1900 the number of high schools had jumped to more than 5,000, and the number of students to more than half a million.

## CONCLUSION

By the 1890s class conflict was evident not just in the struggles to control public education but in practically every area of daily life, from mealtime manners to popular entertainment and recreation. Caught up in the material benefits of a prospering industrial society, middle- and upper-class Americans battled against what they deemed "indecent" lower-class behavior in all its forms, from dancing to ragtime, gambling, and prizefighting to playing baseball on Sunday and visiting bawdy boardwalk sideshows. Even public parks became arenas of class conflict. Whereas the elite favored the large, impeccably groomed urban parks that would serve as models of orderliness and propriety, working people fought for neighborhood parks where they could picnic, play ball, drink beer, and escape the stifling heat of tenement apartments.

Although the well-to-do classes often appeared to have the upper hand in these clashes, significant dissension surfaced early within their own ranks. The aged poet Walt Whitman was not alone in his sentiments when he lamented, in his essay *Democratic Vistas* (1881), how "certain portions of the people" were trying to force their cultural standards and moral values on the great mass of the population, who were thereby made to feel "degraded, humiliated, [and] of no account." Other critics, among them Charlotte Perkins Gilman, faulted middle-class society broadly for its obsession with polite manners, empty social rituals, and restrictions on the occupations open to women.

By the end of the century, this contest for power between the elite classes on the one hand and the immigrants and workers on the other seemed headed toward a partial resolution in a series of compromises that neither side had anticipated or expected. As Victorian morality eroded, undermined by dissension from within and opposition from without, new standards emerged that blended elements of earlier positions. In the sports of boxing and baseball, for example, new rules regulated behavior in the ring and on the field. Despite the professionalization of sports, however, it was immigrant heroes who captured the popular imagination as the older elite vision of sport as a vehicle for instilling self-discipline and self-control was transformed into a new commitment to sports as spectacle and entertainment. Like it or not, sports had become big business and an important part of the new consumerism.

Similar patterns of compromise and change took place in other areas. Vaudeville houses, lambasted by the affluent for their risqué performances, evolved into the nation's first movie theaters. Ragtime music, with its syncopated rhythms, gave rise to jazz. In short, the raffish, disreputable, raucous, and frequently denounced working-class culture of the late-nineteenth-century immigrant city can be seen, in retrospect, as nothing less than the fertile seedbed of twentieth-century mass culture. And everywhere, popular culture became increasingly dominated by commercial interests that capitalized on the disposable income created by the nation's explosive industrial growth and encouraged the popular fondness for material goods, leisure, sports, and other entertainments.

## ─ FOR FURTHER READING ─

Henry F. Bedford, ed., *Their Lives and Numbers: The Condition of Working People in Massachusetts, 1870–1900* (1995). An excellent introduction to one of the most detailed studies of working-class life conducted in the nineteenth century.

Martin J. Burke, *The Conundrum of Class: Public Discourse on the Social Order in America* (1995). A pioneering study into the ways in which nineteenth-century Americans tried to understand class difference.

Elliot Gorn and Warren Goldstein, *A Brief History of American Sports* (1993). A skillful analysis of the impact of urbanization, industrialization, and commercialization on American sports.

William Leach, *Land of Desire: Merchants, Power, and the Rise of a New American Culture* (1993). A balanced examination of the innovative advertising and merchandising strategies that underlaid the shift to a consumer culture in the 1890s.

Sheila M. Rothman, *Woman's Proper Place: A History of Changing Ideals and Practices, 1870 to the Present* (1978). A perceptive study of shifting attitudes toward women's proper role in society.

Olivier Zunz, *Making America Corporate, 1879–1920* (1990). A pioneering exploration of corporate capitalism's impact on the creation of a consumer culture.

# Politics and Expansion in an Industrializing Age

Woolworth Building, New York City

July 2, 1881, was a muggy summer day in Washington, D.C., and President James A. Garfield was leaving town for a visit to western Massachusetts. At 9:30 A.M., as he strolled through the railroad station, shots rang out. Garfield fell, a bullet in his back. The shooter, Charles Guiteau, immediately surrendered.

At first, doctors thought the president would recover. But Garfield, a veteran who had seen the long-term effects of gunshot wounds, knew better. "I am a dead man," he told them. His doctors tried everything. Alexander Graham Bell, inventor of the telephone, brought in a metal-detecting device to search for the bullet. But as the doctors probed the wound with bare hands and unsterilized instruments, blood poisoning set in. On September 19, Garfield died.

The nation mourned. An Ohio farm boy, Will Boyer, was shocked to hear the news from another farmer as he walked along a country road. Garfield embodied the American dream of the self-made man. Born in a log cabin in Ohio (the last log-cabin president), he had worked his way through Williams College, preached in the Disciples of Christ Church, taught at Hiram College, practiced law, and won election to the Ohio senate. He fought in the Civil War, in 1863 went to Congress, and in 1880 was elected president—thereby sealing his death warrant.

As for Guiteau, the jury rejected his insanity plea, and in June 1882 he was hanged. For years, children sang a ditty:

> My name is Charles Guiteau
> My name I'll not deny,
> I shot President Garfield,
> And I know that I must die.

A decent, well-meaning man, Garfield also embodied a political generation that often seemed more preoccupied with the spoils of office than with the problems of ordinary people. In Congress Garfield was tainted by the 1873 Crédit Mobilier scandal and other corruption charges. His presidential nomination resulted from a split in the Republican party between two rival factions, the Stalwarts and the Half-Breeds, that vied with each other mainly over the power to distribute patronage jobs. At the 1880 convention, when the delegates could not choose between Ulysses S. Grant, the Stalwart candidate seeking a third term, and two Half-Breed senators, James G. Blaine of Maine and Ohio's John Sherman, Garfield emerged as a compromise choice.

But Garfield's selection of James G. Blaine as secretary of state outraged the Stalwarts, and his call for an investigation of a scandal involving post office fraud further upset Republican officeholders. This venomous political climate helped precipitate Garfield's murder. The obscure Guiteau, a Stalwart who had supported Garfield, expected to be rewarded with a high diplomatic post. When this failed to materialize, his delusionary mental state worsened. Viewing Garfield's death as "a political necessity," he firmly believed that the Stalwarts would hail him as a hero. (Indeed, he had selected as his gun a .44-caliber "British Bulldog" pistol because it would look good in a museum.)

Garfield's assassination built support for civil-service reform—one of the few reforms of a lackluster political era. In an age of burgeoning factories, rising immigration, explosive urban growth, and economic hardship among millions of Americans in crowded slums and on struggling western farms, the political system of the 1870s and 1880s—which Garfield epitomized and to which we now turn—often seemed paralyzed, obsessed with power jockeying at the top. Although powerful or well-organized groups such as corporate leaders or Union army veterans received a respectful hearing in Washington, many Americans did

J. G. BLAINE, THE SONOROUS SENATOR OF THE SANGUINARY SHIRT.

**Caricature of James G. Blaine**
*The quintessential Gilded Age Politician.*

not. But agrarian reform energies, rolling in from the Great Plains, arose to challenge the status quo. And in 1898, another Republican president, William McKinley (who would also die of an assassin's bullet), led the nation into a short but portentous war that propelled the United States into the role of an imperial power. These eventful two decades are the subject matter of Chapter 21.

This chapter focuses on five major questions:

♦ What major domestic issues did politicians address in the late nineteenth century? Why were these issues important to people?

♦ What social or economic groups had the greatest political clout in these years? Which groups had less political influence or were excluded altogether?

♦ Why did discontent spread across parts of rural America in these years, and what organizational forms did this discontent take?

♦ What were some of the social and political effects of the severe economic depression of 1893–1897?

♦ Why did expansionist pressures build in America in the late nineteenth century? In what specific ways was this expansionist impulse expressed?

# Party Politics in an Era of Social and Economic Upheaval

Geography, ethnicity, economic interests, and myriad state and local issues shaped American politics in the 1870s and 1880s. Two major issues preoccupied lawmakers nationally. The first involved the nature and size of the money supply. The second issue was civil-service reform, aimed at awarding government jobs on the basis of merit rather than political connections.

## *Patterns of Party Strength*

Although voters elected only one Democratic president, Grover Cleveland, between 1860 and 1912, presidential elections often proved extremely close. In 1876 and 1888 the defeated Democrat actually received more popular votes than the Republican victor. Control of the two houses of Congress was often divided between Republicans and Democrats.

Each party had its centers of regional strength. The Democrats ruled the South; southern sections of border states like Ohio; and northern cities with large immigrant populations. In the South the white elite that controlled the Democratic party dominated political life. White southerners, Democratic since President Andrew Jackson's day and embittered by the Civil War, viewed Republicans as villains who had devastated the South and set up carpetbag governments in the defeated Confederacy. In election after election, the "solid South" rolled up crushing Democratic majorities. Similarly, in Boston, New York, and other northern cities, powerful Democratic bosses ensured the national party ticket strong support at election time. Not all big-city political machines were Democratic, but many were.

The Republicans reigned in rural and small-town New England, Pennsylvania, and the upper Midwest. They also won votes in the northern cities from the native-born middle class and business and professional men, including the growing ranks of white-collar workers.

The Grand Army of the Republic (GAR), a social and political lobbying organization of northern Civil War veterans, represented another potent Republican bloc. The letters GAR, said one wit, stood for "Generally All Republican." To solidify this vote, the Republicans ran a series of former Union Army generals for president and voted generous veterans' benefits.

These regional divisions also reflected different economic interests. Politically powerful groups fre-

## CHRONOLOGY

**1867** Grange organized.

**1873** Panic of 1873.

Coinage Act demonetizes silver.

**1877** Rutherford B. Hayes becomes president after disputed election.

*Munn* v. *Illinois*.

**1878** Congress requires U.S. Treasury to purchase silver.

**1880** James Garfield elected president.

**1881** Assassination of Garfield; Chester A. Arthur becomes president.

**1883** Pendleton Civil Service Act.

**1884** Grover Cleveland elected president.

*Wabash* v. *Illinois*.

**1887** Cleveland urges tariff reform and vetoes veterans' pension bill.

Interstate Commerce Act.

**1888** Benjamin Harrison elected president.

**1889** United States, Great Britain, and Germany establish protectorate over Samoan Islands.

National Farmers' Alliance formed.

**1890** Sherman Silver Purchase Act.

Sherman Anti-Trust Act.

McKinley Tariff pushes tariffs to all-time high.

**1891** Crisis between United States and Chile over attack on U.S. sailors.

**1892** Cleveland elected to second term as president.

**1893** Panic of 1893; depression of 1893–1897 begins.

Drain of treasury's gold reserve.

Repeal of Sherman Silver Purchase Act.

Overthrow of Queen Liliuokalani of Hawaii.

Chicago World's Fair (Columbian Exposition).

**1894** "Coxey's Army" marches on Washington.

Pullman strike.

Wilson-Gorman Tariff.

**1895** Supreme Court declares federal income tax unconstitutional.

Bankers' loans end drain on gold reserve.

United States intervenes in Venezuela–British Guiana boundary dispute.

**1896** Free-silver forces capture Democratic party and nominate William Jennings Bryan.

William McKinley elected president.

**1897** Dingley Tariff.

**1898** Spanish-American War.

**1898–1902** United States suppresses guerrilla uprising in Philippines.

**1899** First United States Open Door notes on China.

United States helps put down Boxer uprising.

**1900** Currency Act officially places United States on gold standard.

Second Open Door notes on China.

McKinley reelected; Theodore Roosevelt elected vice president.

**1901** Platt Amendment retains U.S. role in Cuba.

Assassination of McKinley; Theodore Roosevelt becomes president.

**1902** Philippines Government Act.

**1903** Hay–Herrán Treaty rejected by Colombia.

"Revolution" in Panama organized by Philippe Bunau-Varilla.

Hay–Bunau-Varilla Treaty.

**1914** Completion of Panama Canal.

---

quently clashed over the tariff, currency, public-land policy, and government support for railroads and internal improvements.

These geographic patterns of party strength were not absolute. The Republicans made efforts to dent the "solid South" and to attract urban-immigrant voters. Democratic candidates often fared well in the Republican strongholds of New England and the Midwest. Family tradition, ethnic ties, religious affiliation, and local is-

sues often determined an individual's vote. Nor did economic status always determine party affiliation. Most businessmen were Republican, but not all. In 1888 a top Republican cautioned the party not to assume that the "great corporation interest" would automatically support the Republicans.

State and local party leaders managed campaigns. They chose the candidates, raised money, organized rallies, and—if their candidate won—distributed public

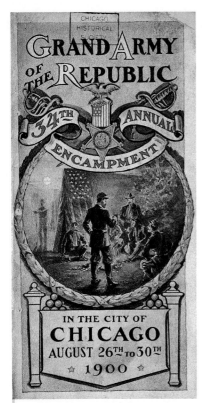

**Poster Announcing GAR Encampment, Chicago, 1900**
*In addition to their nostalgic annual reunions, Union army veterans, organized as the Grand Army of the Republic, were a potent force in Republican party politics, lobbying for pensions and other benefits.*

jobs to party workers. In Indiana ten thousand Republican workers canvassed the state in 1884, gathering data about party affiliation from every voter.

Chieftains like the former saloonkeepers "Big Jim" Pendergast of Kansas City, a Democrat, and George B. Cox of Cincinnati, a Republican, controlled urban politics (see Chapter 19). These bosses turned out the vote by taking care of constituents, giving ward leaders and party loyalists municipal jobs, and on occasion financing campaigns with "contributions" extracted from city employees or from companies doing business with the city.

With the two parties so evenly matched, "swing states" where elections could go either way—Connecticut, New York, New Jersey, Indiana, and Illinois—held the balance of power. By no coincidence, most presi-

dential and vice-presidential candidates came from these critical states.

Most women did not yet have the vote, and blacks were losing it in the post-Reconstruction South. But of eligible white males, more than 80 percent often voted, and in particularly hard-fought state and local elections, the ratio could rise to 95 percent. Voter participation a century later would equal scarcely half that level.

Because only men could vote in most states, political parties functioned in part as male social organizations. This is one reason woman suffrage aroused such resistance: it threatened a political subculture that offered men emotional as well as material rewards.

### The Stakes of Politics

The politicians and political issues of earlier eras sometimes seem dim and remote. The novelist Thomas Wolfe in 1935 described his schoolboy impressions of America's late-nineteenth-century presidents: "[T]heir gravely vacant and bewhiskered faces melted, swam together in the sea-depths of a past intangible, immeasurable, and unknowable." In fact, these politicians were vivid, flesh-and-blood individuals, intensely engaged with their own careers and with matters of public concern.

Similarly, late-nineteenth-century electoral campaigns centered on issues important to specific interest groups—among them the tariff, the currency supply, and veterans' benefits. The import duties charged on many commodities, from steel to sugar, directly impacted powerful economic interests and even entire regions. Government policies affecting the money supply or veterans' pensions similarly concerned millions of Americans.

To be sure, elections also involved emotional side issues. Orators resorted to patriotic rhetoric or flattered various immigrant groups. Southern office seekers made crude racist appeals, whereas Republican candidates in the North often "waved the bloody shirt," reminding voters that their party had led the nation during the Civil War and that the Confederacy's leaders had all been Democrats. As Rutherford B. Hayes advised a Republican campaigner in 1876: "Our strong ground is the dread of a solid south, rebel rule, etc., etc. . . . [T]hese topics…[lead] people away from 'hard times,' which is our deadliest foe."

And although the two parties addressed some issues of contemporary concern, the most glaring problems attracted little notice. Except for the Interstate

Commerce Act of 1887 and the largely symbolic Sherman Anti-Trust Act of 1890, Washington generally ignored the social consequences of industrialization. Indeed, the capital sometimes seemed caught in a time warp as the rest of society plunged into the modern era.

Why this neglect? First of all, the capitalist elite, with massive political clout, firmly resisted regulation. But the federal government's weakness had other causes as well. After Johnson's impeachment, Grant's passivity, and Hayes's disputed election, the presidency was a much diminished office.

In the legislative branch, party discipline hardly existed as senators guarded their political turf and displayed little concern for large national issues. The parties were organized to win elections, not to govern. One former senator, looking back on these years, recalled that each senator "shone in his sphere, within which he tolerated no intrusion from the President or from anybody else." As for the House of Representatives, political scientist (and future president) Woodrow Wilson described it in 1885 as a "mass of jarring elements."

Furthermore, most Americans did not *expect* the federal government to intervene in economic or social affairs. Many embraced the doctrine of laissez-faire—the belief that unregulated competition represented the best path to progress. By this view, the federal government should promote economic development but not regulate the industries that it subsidized.

Rather than looking to Washington, people tended to turn to local or state authorities, sometimes resulting in fierce political contests. On the Great Plains, angry farmers demanded that their state legislatures regulate railroad rates. In the cities, immigrant groups competed for political power while native-born reformers periodically attempted to oust the political machines.

Moreover, city and state governments vied with each other for control. Cities often could not change their system of government, alter their tax structure, or regulate municipal utilities without state approval. When Chicago wanted to issue permits to street popcorn vendors, the Illinois legislature had to pass a special act.

In most state legislatures the rural districts held disproportionate influence. In Connecticut, for example, villages of a few hundred people had the same voting strength in the legislature as Hartford and Bridgeport. This issue, too, sparked political battles.

Grass-roots political rivalries often pitted ethnic and social groups against one another. In New York

City immigrant Catholics and native-born Protestants fought over tax support to parochial schools. In 1889 Wisconsin's native-born Republican legislators passed a law requiring all children to attend English-language schools. This was aimed at eliminating the Catholic and Lutheran parochial schools where immigrant children studied mainly in German, Swedish, or Norwegian.

Electoral skirmishes between ethnic groups often centered on cultural differences, as native-born Protestants tried to force on the immigrants their own views on gambling, prostitution, temperance, and Sabbath observance. No issue aroused more conflict than prohibition. Irish whiskey drinkers, German beer drinkers, and Italian wine drinkers were equally outraged by anti-liquor legislation. State and local prohibition proposals always roused passionate voter interest.

Thus Gilded Age* politics formed an intricate mosaic of individuals, groups, and parties pursuing varied interests in city halls, statehouses, and Washington, D.C. But despite all the activity, the political system still often failed to address the social problems of an urbanizing, industrializing nation.

### The Hayes White House: Virtue Restored

In this era of locally based politics and a diminished presidency, the state leaders who ran party politics tended to favor appealing but pliable presidential candidates.

Rutherford B. Hayes fit the mold perfectly. A lawyer and Civil War general wounded in action, Hayes had won admiration as an honest governor of Ohio. His major presidential achievement was to restore respect for the office after the Grant scandals. With his flowing beard, the benevolent Hayes brought dignity and decorum to the White House. In part, this reflected the influence of his wife, Lucy, an intelligent, college-educated woman of great moral earnestness. The Hayeses and their five children often gathered after dinner for hymns and family prayers.

In contrast to the bibulous Grant, Hayes drank only moderately. He also recognized the political strength of the temperance movement. "Lemonade Lucy" Hayes supported the Woman's Christian Temperance Union. After one White House dinner, Hayes's secretary of

---

* Gilded Age: A term often applied to late-nineteenth-century America, from the title of an 1873 novel by Samuel Clemens and Charles Dudley Warner.

state grumbled, "It was a brilliant affair. The water flowed like champagne."

Hayes's diaries and voluminous correspondence make clear that he was intelligent, thoughtful, even reform-minded, and no mere stooge of the capitalist elite. After his presidency he devoted himself to such worthwhile causes as African-American education. But Hayes understood the political and economic realities of his day, and he adapted to them.

## Regulating the Money Supply

In the 1870s, politicians confronted a tough problem of economic policy: how to create a money supply adequate for a growing economy without producing inflation. Americans' almost superstitious reverence for gold and silver added to the difficulty of establishing a coherent monetary policy. The only trustworthy money, many believed, was gold or silver, or certificates exchangeable for these precious metals. Reflecting this notion, all the *federally* issued currency in circulation in 1860 consisted of gold or silver coins or U.S. Treasury notes redeemable for gold or silver. (Currency from some sixteen hundred state banks was also in circulation, worsening a chaotic monetary situation.)

To complicate matters, opposing groups clashed over the money question. Bankers and creditors, most business leaders, economists, and politicians believed that economic stability required a strictly limited currency supply. Debtors—especially southern and western farmers—favored expanding the money supply to make it easier for them to pay off their debts.

The monetary debate focused on a specific question: should the Civil War paper "greenbacks" that were still in circulation be retained and even expanded, or phased out, leaving only a currency backed by gold (see Chapter 16)? The hard times associated with the Panic of 1873 sharpened this dispute.

The Greenback party (founded 1877) advocated an expanded money supply and other measures to benefit workers and farmers. In the 1878 midterm elections, with the support of labor organizations angered by the government's hostility in the labor unrest of 1877, Greenback candidates won fourteen seats in Congress.

As prosperity returned, the Greenback party faded, but the money issue did not. The debate now focused on the coinage of silver. In 1873, with little silver being mined, Congress instructed the U.S. mint to stop making silver coins. Silver had been "demonetized." But new discoveries in Nevada soon increased the silver supply, and debtor groups now demanded that the government resume the coinage of silver.

Enthusiastically backed by the silver-mine owners, silver forces won a partial victory in 1878, when Congress required the treasury to buy up to $4 million worth of silver each month and mint it into silver dollars. But the treasury, dominated by monetary conservatives, sabotaged the law's intent by refusing to circulate the silver dollars that it minted.

Frustrated silver advocates tried a new approach in the Sherman Silver Purchase Act of 1890. This measure instructed the treasury to buy, at current market prices, 4.5 million ounces of silver monthly—almost precisely the output of the nation's silver mines. The act further required the government to issue treasury notes, redeemable in gold or silver, equivalent to the cost of these purchases. This law did slightly increase the money supply; but as silver prices fell in 1893 and after, the government paid far less for its monthly purchases and therefore issued fewer treasury notes. The controversy over silver dragged on.

## The Spoils System

For decades successful candidates in national, state, and local elections had rewarded supporters and contributors with jobs ranging from cabinet seats and ambassadorships to lowly municipal posts. To its defenders, this system, originally called rotation in office, seemed the most democratic means of filling government positions, and it provided upward mobility for lucky appointees.

But unqualified and incompetent applicants often got jobs simply because of their party loyalty. Once in office, these appointees had to contribute to the reelection campaigns of their political patrons. Because of such abuses, this mode of filling public jobs came to be called the spoils system after the old expression, "To the victor belong the spoils."

As we have seen, bitter patronage battles in the 1870s split the Republican party into two hostile factions that differed over little except who would have the right to distribute patronage jobs. The Stalwarts' leader was Senator Roscoe Conkling of New York. Senator James G. Blaine of Maine led the Half-Breeds.

For years, a small but influential group of elite, native-born reformers had campaigned for a professional civil service based on merit. Well bred, well educated, and well heeled, these reformers despised the immigrants for whom the public payroll could be a ticket out of poverty. They favored a civil service staffed by "gentlemen . . . who need nothing and want nothing from government except the satisfaction of using their talents." Whatever their class biases, these reformers had a point. A professional civil service was needed as government grew more complex.

Advocates of professionalization included Missouri senator Carl Schurz, editor E. L. Godkin, and social-welfare leader Josephine Shaw Lowell. They gave speeches, wrote editorials, and in 1881 founded the National Civil Service Reform League.

Cautiously embracing the civil-service cause, President Hayes in 1877 launched an investigation of the corruption-riddled New York City customs office and ordered the resignation of two high officials. Both men had ties to Conkling: one, Chester A. Arthur, was Conkling's top lieutenant in passing out jobs. When the two ignored Hayes's order, the president suspended them. Hayes's action won praise from civil-service reformers, but Conkling simply ridiculed "snivel service" and "Rutherfraud B. Hayes."

## Civil-Service Reform Succeeds

When Congressman James A. Garfield, with ties to the Half-Breeds, won the 1880 Republican presidential nomination, the delegates, to soften the blow to Conkling, chose as Garfield's running mate Chester A. Arthur, the Conkling loyalist Hayes had recently fired! Since Garfield enjoyed excellent health, the choice of the totally unqualified Arthur seemed safe.

The Democrats nominated a career army officer from Pennsylvania, Winfield Scott Hancock, and the Greenbackers gave the nod to Congressman James B. Weaver of Iowa. Garfield's managers stressed his Civil War record and his log-cabin birth. By a razor-thin margin of under 40,000 votes (of 9.2 million cast), Garfield edged out Hancock; Weaver trailed far behind.

When Garfield chose Blaine as secretary of state and named a Conkling opponent as the New York City

**The Sacred Elephant**
*Having yielded to reformers' pressure and enacted a civil-service law, the Republican party prepared for the 1884 electoral campaign. This cartoon by Thomas Nast represents an early use of the elephant as symbol of the Republican party.*

customs collector, Conkling in a political maneuver resigned from the Senate. He hoped that the New York legislature would reelect him and thereby strengthen his political power. But Conkling miscalculated. The legislature chose another senator and ended Conkling's career.

Garfield's assassination in 1881, which brought to the White House Vice President Arthur, the very symbol of patronage corruption, gave a powerful emotional thrust to the cause, as civil-service reformers portrayed the fallen president as a spoils-system martyr. In 1883 Congress enacted a civil-service law introduced by Senator George Pendleton of Ohio (Garfield's home state) and drafted by the Civil Service Reform League. The Pendleton Civil Service Act set up a commission to pre-

## The Election of 1880

| Candidates | Parties | Electoral Vote | Popular Vote | Percentage of Popular Vote |
|---|---|---|---|---|
| JAMES A. GARFIELD | Republican | 214 | 4,453,295 | 48.5 |
| Winfield S. Hancock | Democratic | 155 | 4,414,082 | 48.1 |
| James B. Weaver | Greenback-Labor | | 308,578 | 3.4 |

pare competitive examinations and establish standards of merit for a variety of federal jobs; it also forbade political candidates from soliciting contributions from government workers.

The Pendleton Act initially covered only about 12 percent of federal employees but was gradually expanded. The creation of a professional civil service helped bring the federal government in step with the modernizing trends transforming society.

As for Chester A. Arthur, the fact that he proved to be a mediocre president pleasantly surprised those who had expected him to be an utter disaster. Some feared that Roscoe Conkling would be "the power behind the throne," but in fact, Arthur supported civil-service reform and proved quite independent. Still, the easygoing Arthur was at best a caretaker president. Fed up with the feuding Republicans, the voters in 1882 gave the Democrats a strong majority in the House of Representatives. In 1884, for the first time since the 1850s, they would put a Democrat in the White House: Grover Cleveland.

## Politics of Privilege, Politics of Exclusion

Although no radical, Cleveland challenged powerful interests by calling for cuts in the tariff and in veterans' pensions. Aroused interest groups rallied to defeat him in the 1888 election, one of the most corrupt in American history. The Republican administration of 1889–1893 was dominated by corporate interests and the veterans' lobby. Elsewhere in the nation, debt-ridden, drought-stricken farmers mounted a spirited protest movement while in the Post-Reconstruction South the white majority took steps to deny the region's black citizens their most basic rights.

### 1884: Cleveland Victorious

At a tumultuous Chicago convention in 1884, the Republicans nominated their best-known leader, James G. Blaine. A gifted orator with a keen memory for names and faces, Blaine spoke for the younger, more dynamic wing of the Republican party eager to shed the taint of "Grantism," promote economic development, and take a greater interest in foreign policy.

But Blaine's name had been smirched in the tawdry politics of the Gilded Age. Historian Henry Adams surely had him in mind when he wrote that the political history of this era offered "little but damaged reputations." In Blaine's 1876 senatorial campaign, his opponents had published letters in which Blaine, as speaker of the house, offered political favors to a railroad company in exchange for stock. One of these communications ended with "Burn this letter," which Democrats gleefully chanted whenever Blaine ran for office thereafter. For civil-service reformers, Blaine epitomized the hated patronage system. To E. L. Godkin, he "wallowed in spoils like a rhinoceros in an African pool."

Sensing Blaine's vulnerability, the Democrats chose a sharply contrasting nominee, Grover Cleveland of New York. In a meteoric political rise from reform mayor of Buffalo to governor, Cleveland had fought the bosses and spoilsmen. Short, rotund, and resembling a bulldog, Cleveland was his own man.

The shrewdness of the Democrats' choice became apparent when Godkin, Carl Schurz, and other Republican reformers bolted to Cleveland. They were promptly nicknamed Mugwumps, an Algonquian term for a renegade chief.

But Cleveland had liabilities, including the fact that as a young man he had fathered an illegitimate child. Cleveland admitted the indiscretion, but the Republicans still jeered at rallies: "Ma, Ma, where's my pa?"

**The Election of 1884**

| Candidates | Parties | Electoral Vote | Popular Vote | Percentage of Popular Vote |
|---|---|---|---|---|
| GROVER CLEVELAND | Democratic | 219 | 4,879,507 | 48.5 |
| James G. Blaine | Republican | 182 | 4,850,293 | 48.2 |
| Benjamin F. Butler | Greenback-Labor | | 175,370 | 1.8 |
| John P. St. John | Prohibition | | 150,369 | 1.5 |

Cleveland also faced opposition by Tammany Hall, the New York City Democratic machine that he had fought as governor. If Tammany's immigrant voters stayed home on election day, Cleveland could lose his own state. But in October a New York City clergyman denounced the Democrats as the party of "Rum, Romanism, and Rebellion." Blaine failed to repudiate the remark immediately. The Cleveland campaign managers widely publicized this triple insult—to Catholics, to patriotic Democrats tired of the "bloody shirt," and to drinkers. This blunder and the Mugwumps' defection allowed Cleveland to carry New York State by twelve hundred votes, and with it the election.

### Tariffs and Pensions

In some respects, Cleveland fits the passive image of Gilded Age presidents. He had early embraced the belief that government must not meddle in the economy. In Andrew Jackson's day, laissez-faire had been a radical idea, endorsed by ambitious small entrepreneurs who wanted business conditions favorable to competition; by the 1880s it had become the rallying cry of a corporate elite opposed to any public regulation or oversight.

Sharing this outlook, Cleveland displayed a limited grasp of industrialization's impact. Vetoing a bill that would have provided seeds to drought-stricken farmers in Texas, he warned that people should not expect the government to solve their problems. Small wonder, then, that ordinary Americans often found national politics irrelevant. A trade-union leader, testifying in 1885 before a congressional committee investigating labor conditions, advised both parties to "take up some live issue instead of raking over the dead ashes of the past."

One public matter did arouse Cleveland's energies: the tariff, an issue involving a tangle of conflicting economic and political interests. Tariff duties were a major source of revenue in this era before a federal income tax, so the tariff was really a form of taxation. But which imported goods should be subject to duties, and how much? Opinions diverged radically.

The producers of such commodities as coal, hides, timber, and wool demanded tariff protection against foreign competition, and industries that had prospered behind tariff walls—iron and steel, textiles, machine tools—wanted protection to continue. Many workers in these industries agreed, convinced that high tariffs meant higher wages. Other manufacturers, however, while seeking protection for their finished products, wanted low tariffs on the raw materials they required. Massachusetts shoe manufacturers, for example, urged high duties on imported shoes but low duties on imported hides. Most farmers, by contrast, hated the protective tariff, charging that it inflated farm-equipment prices and, by impeding trade, made it hard to sell American farm products abroad.

**The Gendering of Labor in Corporate America**
*Machinist at Tabor Manufacturing Company in Philadelphia (below); artificial flower makers work at machines for pressing out petals (right).*

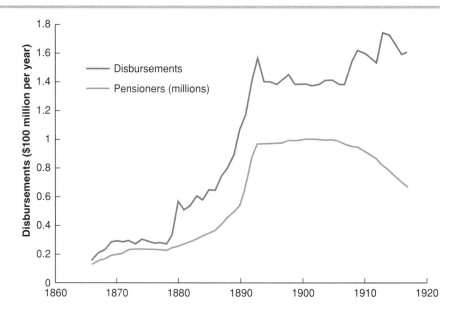

**Civil War Pensions and Pensioners, 1866–1917**

*The pension system for Union army veterans represented a major federal welfare program in the late nineteenth and early twentieth centuries.*

*Source:* William H. Glasson, *Federal Military Pensions in the United States* (New York: Oxford University Press, 1918), p. 273.

Above all, the tariff was a political football. In general, the business-oriented Republicans advocated high tariffs and the Democrats, with their agrarian base, favored lower rates. But in reality a legislator's vote on a tariff bill depended almost entirely on the economic interests of his state or district.

Cleveland's call for lower tariffs arose initially from the fact that in the 1880s the high tariff, generating millions of dollars in federal revenue, was feeding a growing budget surplus. This surplus tempted legislators to distribute it in the form of veterans' pensions or expensive public-works programs, commonly called pork-barrel projects, in their home districts. With his horror of paternalistic government, Cleveland viewed the budget surplus as a corrupting influence.

In his annual message to Congress in 1887, Cleveland argued that lower tariffs would not only cut the federal surplus but also reduce prices and slow the development of trusts. Although the Democratic campaign of 1888 gave little attention to the issue, Cleveland's talk of lowering the tariff struck many corporate leaders as highly threatening.

Cleveland stirred up another hornet's nest when he took on the Grand Army of the Republic. Veterans' disability pensions cost the government millions of dollars annually. No one opposed pensions for the deserving, but by the 1880s fraudulent claims had become a public scandal. The GAR urged veterans to file claims; and no matter how outrageous, these were routinely approved by Congress and the president. One veteran got a disability pension for poor eyesight that he blamed on wartime diarrhea.

Unlike his predecessors, Cleveland investigated these claims—and rejected many of them. In 1887 he vetoed a bill that would have pensioned all disabled veterans (even if their disability had nothing to do with military service) and their dependents. The pension list should be an honor roll, he declared, not a refuge for frauds.

### 1888: Big Business and the GAR Strike Back

By 1888 some influential interest groups had concluded that Cleveland must go. When Blaine decided not to challenge him, the Republicans turned to Benjamin Harrison of Indiana, the grandson of William Henry Harrison.

A corporation lawyer and former senator, Benjamin Harrison was so aloof that some ridiculed him as the human iceberg. His campaign managers learned to whisk him away after speeches before anyone could talk with him or experience his flabby handshake.

Harrison's managers also developed a new style of electioneering. Instead of sending the candidate around the country, they brought delegations to Indianapolis, where Harrison read them flowery speeches targeted to their interests. Solemnly Harrison told an audience

## The Election of 1888

| Candidates | Parties | Electoral Vote | Popular Vote | Percentage of Popular Vote |
|---|---|---|---|---|
| BENJAMIN HARRISON | Republican | 233 | 5,477,129 | 47.9 |
| Grover Cleveland | Democratic | 168 | 5,537,857 | 48.6 |
| Clinton B. Fisk | Prohibition | | 249,506 | 2.2 |
| Anson J. Streeter | Union Labor | | 146,935 | 1.3 |

of awed little girls, "Some of the best friends I have are under ten years of age."

The Republicans hammered at the tariff issue. Falsely portraying Cleveland as an advocate of "free trade"—the elimination of all tariffs—they warned of the bad effects of such a step. The high protective tariff, they argued, ensured prosperity, decent wages for industrial workers, and a healthy home market for farmers.

The Republicans amassed a $4 million campaign fund from worried business leaders. (Because the Pendleton Civil Service Act had outlawed campaign contributions by government workers, political parties depended more than ever on corporate donors.) This war chest purchased not only posters and buttons but also votes.

In one of the campaign's "dirty tricks," a Republican leader, pretending to be a British-born naturalized citizen named Charles Murchison, wrote to the British ambassador to ask how he should vote. The ambassador fell into the trap and advised a vote for Cleveland. Capitalizing on the anti-British feeling then prevalent, especially among Irish immigrants, the Republicans cynically publicized the "Murchison letter" as a shocking attempt by a foreign power to meddle in an American election.

Despite such chicanery, Cleveland got almost 100,000 more votes than Harrison. But Harrison carried the key states of Indiana and New York and won in the electoral college. The Republicans held the Senate and regained the House. When Harrison piously observed that Providence had aided the Republican cause, his campaign chairman snorted: "Providence hadn't a damn thing to do with it. . . . [A] number of men . . . approach[ed] the gates of the penitentiary to make him president."

Harrison swiftly rewarded his supporters. He appointed as commissioner of pensions a GAR official who on taking office declared "God help the surplus!" The pension rolls soon ballooned from 676,000 to nearly a million. This massive pension system (which was coupled with medical care in a network of veterans' hospitals) has been described as America's first large-scale public-welfare program.

In 1890 the triumphant Republicans also enacted the McKinley Tariff, which pushed rates to an all-time high.* Rarely has the federal government been so subservient to entrenched economic interests and so out of touch with the plight of the disadvantaged as during the 1880s.

But discontent was rising. The midterm election of 1890, when the Democrats gained sixty-six congressional seats to win control of the House of Representatives, awakened the nation to a tide of political activism engulfing the agrarian South and West. This activism, spawned by chronic problems in rural America, had a long history.

### The Granger Movement

As we saw in Chapter 17, Great Plains farming proved far riskier than many had anticipated. Terrible grasshopper infestations between 1873 and 1877 consumed nearly half the midwestern wheat corp. Although overall production surged after 1870, the abundant harvests undercut prices. Wheat tumbled from $2.95 a bushel in 1866 to $1.06 in 1880. Countless farmers who had borrowed heavily to finance their homesteads and expensive new machinery went bankrupt or barely survived. One struggling Minnesota farmer wrote the governor in 1874: "[W]e can see nothing but starvation in the future if relief does not come."

When relief did not come, the farmers responded by setting up cooperative ventures. Under the leadership of Oliver H. Kelley, a Department of Agriculture

---

* To pass the tariff, the Republican leadership did agree to a measure of interest to farmers and debtors: the Sherman Silver Purchase Act (see p. 603).

clerk, midwestern farmers in 1867 formed the Grange, or "Patrons of Husbandry," as it was officially called. Membership climbed to more than 1.5 million in the trying years of the early 1870s. Patterned after the Masonic Order, the Grange offered information, emotional support, and fellowship. For the inexperienced homesteader, it made available a library of the latest findings on planting and livestock raising. For the lonely farm family, the Grange organized biweekly social gatherings, including cooperative meals and lively songfests.

But the Grange's central concern was farmers' economic plight. An 1874 circular announced the organization's primary purpose: to help farmers "buy less and produce more, in order to make our farms more self-sustaining." Grangers embraced the Jacksonian belief that the products of the soil were the basis of all honorable wealth and that the producer classes—people who worked with their hands—formed the true backbone of society. Members sought to restore self-sufficiency to the family farm. Ignoring the contradiction in farmers' banding together to help individuals become more independent, they negotiated special discounts with farm-machinary dealers and set up "cash-only" cooperative stores and grain-storage elevators to cut out the "middlemen"—the bankers, grain brokers, and merchants who made money at their expense.

Grangers vehemently attacked the railroads, which routinely gave discounts to large shippers, bribed state legislators, and charged higher rates for short runs than for long hauls. These practices stung hard-pressed farmers. Although professing to be nonpolitical, Grangers in Illinois, Wisconsin, Minnesota, and Iowa lobbied state legislatures in 1874 to pass laws fixing maximum rates for freight shipments.

The railroads appealed to the Supreme Court to declare these "Granger laws" unconstitutional. But in *Munn* v. *Illinois* (1877), the Court not only rejected the railroads' appeal but also upheld an Illinois law setting a maximum rate for the storage of grain. The regulation of grain elevators, declared the Court's majority, was legitimate under the federal Constitution's grant of police powers to states. When the Court in *Wabash* v. *Illinois* (1886) modified this position by prohibiting states from regulating *interstate* railroad rates, Congress passed the Interstate Commerce Act (1887), reaffirming the federal government's power to investigate and oversee railroad activities and establishing a new agency, the Interstate Commerce Commission (ICC), to do just that. Although the commission failed to curb the railroads' monopolis-

tic practices, it did establish the principle of federal regulation of interstate transportation.

Despite promising beginnings, the Grange movement soon faltered. The railroads, having lost their battle on the national level, lobbied state legislatures and won repeal of most of the rate-regulation laws by 1878. Moreover, the Grange system of cash-only cooperative stores failed because few farmers had ample cash. Ultimately the Grange ideal of complete financial independence proved unrealistic. Under the conditions that prevailed on the Plains, it was impossible to farm without borrowing money.

How valid was the Grangers' analysis of the farmers' problems? The Grangers blamed greedy railroads and middlemen for their difficulties, but the situation was not that simple. The years 1873–1878 saw the entire economy in a depression; railroad operators and merchant middlemen, no less than farmers, had to scramble to survive. And although farm commodity prices did fall between 1865 and 1900, the wholsale prices of manufactured goods, including items needed on the farm, fell in the same period as well—often faster than farm prices. Even the railroads' stiff freight charges could be justified in part by the sparcity of western settlement and the seasonality of grain shipments.

Still, the farmers and the Grange leaders who voiced their grievances had reason to complain. Farmers who had no control over the prices of their crops were at the mercy of local merchants and farm-equipment dealers who exercised monopolistic control over the prices that *they* could charge. Similarly, railroads sometimes would transport wheat to only one mill. Some even refused to stop at small towns to pick up local wheat shipments. Policies like these struck the farmers as completely arbitrary and made them feel powerless. Hamlin Garland captured farmers' despair in his *Main-Travelled Roads* (1891) and *Son of the Middle Border* (1917), describing barely surviving families who "rose early and toiled without intermission, till the darkness fell on the plain, then tumbled into bed, every bone and muscle aching with fatigue."

When the prices of corn, wheat, and cotton briefly revived after 1878, many farmers deserted the Grange. Although the Grange lived on as a social and educational institution, it lost its economic clout because it was ultimately unable to improve its members' financial position. For all its weaknesses, the Grange movement did lay the groundwork for an even more powerful wave of agrarian protest.

## The Alliance Movement

While the Grange was centered in the Midwest and the Great Plains, the alliance movement first arose in the South and West, where farmers grappled with many of the same problems. In the cotton South, small planters found themselves trapped by the crop-lien system, mortgaging future harvests to cover current expenses. Mired in debt, many gave up their land and became tenants or sharecroppers. About a third of southern farmers were tenants by 1900. One historian has aptly called the South in these years "a giant pawnshop."

The alliance movement began in Texas in the late 1870s as poor farmers gathered to discuss their hardships. Soon an organization took shape, promoted by activists who organized hundreds of local alliances.

The alliance idea advanced eastward across the lower South, especially after Texan Charles W. Macune, a self-trained lawyer and a physician, assumed leadership in 1887. By 1889 Macune had merged several regional organizations into the National Farmers' Alliance and Industrial Union, or Southern Alliance. A parallel black organization, the National Colored Farmers' Alliance, had meanwhile emerged in Arkansas and spread to other southern states.

Like the Grange, the alliance initially advocated farmers' cooperatives to purchase equipment and supplies and to market their cotton. These cooperatives mostly failed, however, because farmers lacked the capital to finance them.

Still, by 1890 the Southern Alliance boasted 3 million members, with an additional 1.2 million claimed by the National Colored Farmers' Alliance. Alliance members generally comprised not only the poorest farmers but also those most dependent on a single crop and most geographically isolated. As they attended alliance rallies and picnics, read the alliance newspaper, and listened to alliance speakers, hard-hit farm families felt less cut off—and increasingly aware of their political potential. As an Arkansas member wrote in 1889, "Reform never begins with the leaders, it comes from the people."

Meanwhile, alliance fever hit the Great Plains as well. In the drought-plagued years 1880 and 1881, alliances sprang up in Kansas, Nebraska, Iowa, and Minnesota. But the protest spirit faded as renewed rainfall

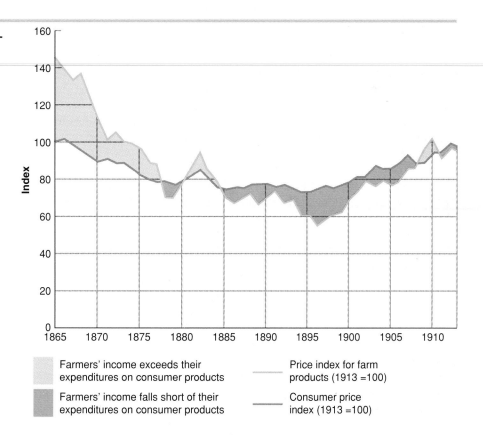

**Consumer Prices and Farm-Product Prices, 1865–1913**

*As cycles of drought and debt battered Great Plains wheat growers, a Kansas farmer wrote: "At the age of 52, after a long life of toil, economy, and self-denial, I find myself and family virtually paupers."*

Index

| | Farmers' income exceeds their expenditures on consumer products |
| | Farmers' income falls short of their expenditures on consumer products |

Price index for farm products (1913 =100)

Consumer price index (1913 =100)

**Farming on the Great Plains**
*John Painter, a Populist leader, poses with his family and others outside their farmhouse in Broken Bow, Nebraska.*

revived confidence and lured thousands of settlers to the northern plains. The boom triggered frenzied land speculation. Kansas farms that had sold for $6.25 an acre in the 1860s went for $270 an acre in 1887. Railroads promoting settlement along their routes fed the boom mentality.

In 1886–1887, however, came a painful awakening as drought returned. From 1887 to 1897, only two Great Plains wheat crops were worth harvesting. Searing winds shriveled the half-ripe grain as locusts and chinch bugs gnawed away the rest. To make matters worse, wheat prices fell as world production increased.

Many settlers returned East. "In God we trusted, in Kansas we busted," some scrawled on their wagons. Western Kansas lost 50 percent of its population between 1888 and 1892. But others hung on, and the Northwestern Alliance grew rapidly. By 1890 the Kansas Alliance claimed 130,000 members, followed closely by alliances in Nebraska, the Dakotas, and Minnesota. Like the Southern Alliance, the Northwestern Alliance first experimented with cooperatives and gradually turned to politics.

Southern Alliance leaders Tom Watson of Georgia and Leonidas Polk of North Carolina urged southern farmers, black and white, to act together. For a time, this message of racial cooperation in the interest of reform offered promise. In Kansas, meanwhile, Jerry Simpson, a rancher who lost his stock in the hard winter of 1886–1887, became a major alliance leader. Mary E. Lease, a Wichita lawyer, burst on the scene in 1890 as a fiery alliance orator.

Other women too, veterans of the Granger or prohibition cause, rallied to the new movement, founding the National Women's Alliance (NWA) in 1891. De-

clared the NWA: "Put 1,000 women lecturers in the field and revolution is here." By no coincidence, a strong feminist strain pervades Ignatius Donnelly's *The Golden Bottle* (1892), a novel portraying the agrarian reformers' social vision.

As the movement swelled, the opposition turned nasty. When Jerry Simpson mentioned the silk stockings of a conservative politician in his district and noted that *he* had no such finery, a hostile newspaper editor labeled him "Sockless Jerry" Simpson, the nickname he carried to his grave. When Mary Lease advised Kansas to "raise less corn and more hell," another editor sneered: "[Kansas] has started to raise hell, as Mrs. Lease advised, and [the state] seems to have an overproduction. But that doesn't matter. Kansas never did believe in diversified crops."

From all this activity, a political agenda took form. In 1889 the Southern and Northwestern Alliances loosely merged and adopted a political litmus test for candidates in the 1890 midterm elections. Their objectives included tariff reduction, a graduated income tax, public ownership of the railroads, federal funding for irrigation research, a ban on landownership by aliens, and "the free and unlimited coinage of silver."

The 1890 elections revealed the depth of agrarian disaffection. Southern Democrats who endorsed alliance goals won four governorships and control of eight state legislatures. On the Great Plains, alliance-endorsed candidates secured control of the Nebraska legislature and gained the balance of power in Minnesota and South Dakota. In Kansas the candidates of the alliance-sponsored People's party demolished all opposition. Three alliance-backed senators, together with some fifty congressmen (including Watson and

Simpson), went to Washington as angry winds from the hinterlands buffeted the political system.

But differences soon surfaced. Whereas Northwestern Alliance leaders favored a third party, the Southern Alliance, despite Watson's and Polk's advice, rejected such a move, fearing it would weaken the southern Democratic party, the bastion of white supremacy.

By 1892, however, some Southern Alliance leaders had reluctantly adopted the third-party idea, since many Democrats whom they had backed in 1890 had ignored the alliance agenda once in office. In February 1892 alliance leaders organized the People's Party of the United States, generally called the Populist party. At the party convention that August, cheering delegates nominated for president the former Civil War general and Greenback nominee James B. Weaver of Iowa, now white-maned. Courting the South, they chose as Weaver's running mate the Virginian James Field, who had lost a leg fighting for the Confederacy.

The Populist platform restated the alliance goals while adding a call for the direct popular election of senators and other electoral reforms. It also endorsed a plan devised by alliance leader Charles Macune by which farmers could store their nonperishable commodities in government warehouses, receive low-interest loans using the crops as collateral, and then sell the stored commodities when market prices rose. Ignatius Donnelly's ringing preamble pronounced the nation on "the verge of moral, political, and material ruin" and called for a return of the government "to the hands of 'the plain people' with which class it originated."

As the Populists geared up for the 1892 campaign, another group of citizens with far more profound grievances found themselves pushed even further to the margins of American public life.

### African Americans After Reconstruction

The end of Reconstruction in 1877 and the restoration of power to the southern white elites, the so-called redeemers (see Chapter 16), spelled bad news for southern blacks. The redeemer coalition of large landowners, merchants, and "New South" industrialists had little interest in the ex-slaves except as a docile labor force or as political pawns. However, southern white opinion demanded an end to the hated "Negro rule," and local Democratic party officials pursued this objective. Suppressing the black vote was a major goal. At first, black disfranchisement was achieved by intimida-

tion, terror, and vote fraud, as blacks were either kept from the polls or forced to vote Democratic. Then in 1890 Mississippi amended its state constitution in ways that effectively excluded most black voters, and other southern states soon followed suit.

Because the Fifteenth Amendment (1870) guaranteed all male citizens' right to vote, disfranchisement had to be accomplished indirectly by such means as literacy tests, poll taxes, and property requirements. The racist intent of these devices became obvious when procedures were introduced to ensure that they affected only *black* voters. One stratagem, the so-called grandfather clause, exempted from these electoral requirements anyone whose ancestor had voted in 1860.

Black disfranchisement proceeded erratically over the South, but by the early twentieth century, it was essentially complete. And disfranchisement was only part of the system of white supremacy laboriously erected in the South. In a parallel development that culminated in the early twentieth century, state after state passed laws imposing strict racial segregation in many realms of life (see Chapter 22).

Black caterers, barbers, bricklayers, carpenters, and other artisans lost their white clientele. Blacks who went to prison—sometimes for minor offenses—faced the convict-lease system, by which cotton planters, railroad builders, coal-mine operators, and other employers "leased" prison gangs and forced them to work under slave-labor conditions.

The convict-lease system not only enforced the racial hierarchy but also played an important economic role as industrialization and agricultural change came to the South. The system brought income to hard-pressed state governments and provided factories, railroads, mines, and large-scale farms with a predictable, controllable, and cheap labor supply. The system also intimidated free laborers; as one observer commented: "[O]n account of the convict employment, strikes are of rare occurrence." Recognizing this danger, free miners in Tennessee successfully agitated against the employment of convict labor in their state in the 1890s. Thousands died under the brutal convict-labor system. It survived into the early decades of the twentieth century, ultimately succumbing to humanitarian protest and to economic changes that made it unprofitable.

The ultimate enforcer of southern white supremacy was the lynch rope. Through the 1880s and 1890s, an average of about a hundred blacks were lynched annually in the United States, mainly in the South. The stated reasons, often the rape of a white woman, frequently

**Southern Prison Chain-Gang, 1898.**
*The southern chain-gang and convict-lease system gave rise to appalling abuses in the late nineteenth century, reducing thousands of African American men and youths to slavery-like conditions.*

arose from rumor and unsubstantiated accusations. (The charge of "attempted rape" could cover a wide range of behaviors unacceptable to whites.)

The lynch mob demonstrated whites' absolute power. In *Festival of Violence,* their 1995 computer-assisted study of 2,805 Southern lynchings, Stewart E. Tolnay and E. M. Beck found that more than 80 percent involved black victims. Lynchings most commonly occurred in the Cotton Belt, and they tended to peak at times of economic distress when cotton prices were falling and job competition between poor whites and poor blacks was most intense. By no coincidence, lynching peaked in 1892 as many poor blacks embraced the farmers' alliance movement and rallied to the Populist party banner. Fifteen black Populists were killed in Georgia alone, it has been estimated, during that year's acrimonious campaign.

The relationship between southern agrarian protest and white racism was complex. Some Populists, like Georgia's Tom Watson, sought to build an interracial movement. Watson denounced lynching and the convict-lease system. When a black Populist leader pursued by a lynch mob took refuge in his house during the 1892 campaign, Watson summoned two thousand armed white Populists to defend him. But most white Populists, abetted by rabble-rousers like "Pitchfork Ben" Tillman of South Carolina, clung to racism; Watson complained that most poor whites "would joyously hug the chains of . . . wretchedness rather than do any experimenting on [the race] question."

The white elite, eager to drive a wedge in the protest movement, inflamed lower-class white racism. Addressing an alliance audience in 1889, conservative Atlanta editor Henry W. Grady warned against division among white southerners; the region's only hope, he said, was "the clear and unmistakable domination of the white race." But even as they raised the bugaboo of "Negro rule," the white elite manipulated the urban black vote as a weapon against agrarian radicalism, driving Tom Watson to despair. On balance, the rise of southern agrarian protest deepened racial hatred and ultimately worsened blacks' situation.

While southern blacks suffered racist oppression, the federal government stood aside. A generation of northern politicians paid lip service to egalitarian principles but failed to apply them to blacks.

The Supreme Court similarly abandoned blacks. The Fourteenth Amendment (1868) had granted blacks citizenship and the equal protection of the laws, and the Civil Rights Act of 1875 outlawed racial discrimination on juries, in public places such as hotels and theaters, and on railroads, streetcars, and other such conveyances. But the Supreme Court soon ripped gaping holes in these protective laws.

In the *Civil Rights Cases* (1883), the Court declared the Civil Rights Act of 1875 unconstitutional. The Fourteenth Amendment protected citizens only from *governmental* infringement of their civil rights, the justices ruled, not from acts by private citizens such as railroad conductors. In *Plessy* v. *Ferguson* (1896), the justices upheld a Louisiana law requiring segregated railroad cars. Racial segregation was constitutional, the Court held, if equal facilities were made available to each race. (In a prophetic dissent, Associate Justice John Marshall Harlan observed, "Our Constitution is color blind." Segregation, he added, violated the constitutional principle of equality before the law.)

With the Supreme Court's blessing, the South segregated its public school system, ignoring the caveat that such separate facilities must be equal. White children studied in nicer buildings, used newer equipment, and were taught by higher-paid teachers. Not until 1954 did the Court abandon this "separate but equal" doctrine. Rounding out their dismal record, the justices in 1898 upheld the poll tax and literacy tests by which southern states had disfranchised blacks.

Few northerners protested the South's white-supremacist society. Until the North condemned lynching outright, declared the aged abolitionist Frederick Douglass in 1892, "it will remain equally involved with the South in this common crime." The restoration of sectional harmony, in short, came at a high price: acquiescence by the North in the utter debasement of the South's African-American citizenry. Further, the separatist principle endorsed in *Plessy* had a pervasive impact, affecting blacks nationwide, Mexicans in Texas, Asians in California, and other groups.

Blacks responded in various ways to their plight. The best-known black southerner of the period, Booker T. Washington, counseled patience, accommodation, and learning useful skills (see Chapter 22). Many blacks responded resourcefully to a racist society. Black churches provided emotional support, as did black fraternal lodges like the Knights of Pythias.

Some African Americans started businesses to serve their community. Two black-owned banks, in Richmond and Washington, D.C., were chartered in 1888. The North Carolina Mutual Insurance Company, organized in 1898 by John Merrick, a prosperous Durham barber, evolved into a major enterprise. Bishop Henry M. Turner of the African Methodist Episcopal church urged blacks to return to Africa and build a great Christian nation. Turner made several trips to Africa in pursuit of his proposal.

African-American protest never wholly died out. Frederick Douglass urged that blacks press for full equality. "Who would be free, themselves must strike the first blow," he proclaimed in 1883. Blacks should meet violence with violence, insisted militant New York black leader T. Thomas Fortune.

Other blacks answered southern racism by leaving the region. In 1879 several thousand moved to Kansas (see Chapter 16). Some ten thousand migrated to Chicago between 1870 and 1890. Blacks who moved north soon found, however, that although white supremacy was not official policy, public opinion sanctioned many forms of de facto discrimination. Northern black laborers, for example, encountered widespread prejudice. The Knights of Labor welcomed blacks and by the mid-1880s had an estimated sixty thousand black members. Its successor, the American Federation of Labor, officially forbade racial discrimination, but in practice many of its member unions excluded blacks.

The rise of the so-called solid South, firmly established on racist foundations, had important political implications. For one thing, it made a mockery of the two-party system in the South. For years, the only meaningful election south of the Potomac was the Democratic primary. Only in the 1960s, in the wake of sweeping social and economic changes, would a genuine two-party system emerge in the South. The large bloc of southern Democrats elected to Congress each year, accumulating seniority and power, exerted a great and often reactionary influence on public policy. Above all, they mobilized instantly to quash any threat to southern white supremacy. Finally, southern Democrats wielded enormous clout in the national party. No Democratic contender for national office unacceptable to them stood a chance.

But above all, the caste system that evolved in the post-Reconstruction South shaped the consciousness of those caught up in it, white and black alike. As white novelist Lillian Smith has written, describing her girlhood in turn-of-the-century Florida and Georgia, "From

**The Knights of Labor**
*Black delegate Frank J. Farrell introduces Terence V. Powderly, head of the Knights of Labor, at the organization's 1886 convention. The Knights were unusual in accepting both black and female workers.*

the day I was born, I began to learn my lessons. . . . I learned it is possible to be a Christian and a white southerner simultaneously; to be a gentlewoman and an arrogant callous creature at the same moment; to pray at night and ride a Jim Crow car the next morning; . . . to glow when the word *democracy* was used, and to practice slavery from morning to night."

# The 1890s: Politics in a Depression Decade

The 1890s was one of the most difficult and unsettled decades in American history. Grover Cleveland, elected to a second term in 1892, faced a business panic, an erosion of the government's fiscal stability, and a terrible depression. The early 1890s also brought labor violence as well as the emergence of the Populist party. The crises of the 1890s laid bare the paralysis of the federal government—dominated by a capitalist elite and wedded to the principle of laissez-faire—when confronted by the new social realities of factories, urban slums, immigrant workers, and desperate farmers.

## *1892: Populists Challenge the Status Quo*

The Populist party platform, adopted in July 1892, offered an angry catalog of agrarian demands. That same month, thirteen people died in a gun battle between strikers and strikebreakers at the Homestead steel plant near Pittsburgh, and President Harrison sent federal troops to Coeur d'Alene, Idaho, where a silver-mine strike had turned violent. Events seemed to justify the Populists' warnings of chaos ahead.

Faced with domestic turmoil and fearful that the powerful European socialist movement would spread to the United States, both major parties acted cautiously. The Republicans renominated Harrison and adopted a platform that ignored escalating unrest. The Democrats turned again to Grover Cleveland, who in

four years out of office had made clear his growing conservatism and his opposition to the Populists. Cleveland won by more than 360,000 votes—a decisive margin in this era of close elections. A public reaction against labor violence and the McKinley Tariff hurt Harrison, while Cleveland's support for the gold standard won conservative business support.

Populist strength proved spotty. James B. Weaver got just over a million votes—8.5 percent of the total—and the Populists elected five senators, ten congressmen, and three governors. The new party carried Kansas and registered some appeal in the West and in Georgia, Alabama, and Texas, where the alliance movement had taken deep root. But it made no dent in New England, the urban East, or the traditionally Republican farm regions of the Midwest. It even failed to show broad strength in the upper Great Plains. "Beaten! Whipped! Smashed!" moaned the Minnesota Populist Ignatius Donnelly in his diary.

Throughout most of the South, racism, ingrained Democratic loyalty, distaste for a ticket headed by a former Union general, and widespread intimidation and vote fraud kept the Populist vote under 25 percent. This failure killed the prospects for interracial agrarian reform in the region. After 1892 southern politicians seeking to appeal to poor whites—including a disillusioned Tom Watson—stayed within the Democratic fold and laced their populism with racism.

## *The Panic of 1893: Capitalism in Crisis*

Cleveland soon confronted a major crisis: an economic collapse in the railroad industry, which quickly spread. In the economic boom of the 1880s, railroads had led the way, triggering speculation among investors. Some railroads had fed the speculative mania by issuing more stock (and enticing investors with higher dividends) than their business prospects warranted.

Weakened by agricultural stagnation, railroad growth slowed in the early 1890s, affecting many re-

**The Election of 1892**

| Candidates | Parties | Electoral Vote | Popular Vote | Percentage of Popular Vote |
|---|---|---|---|---|
| GROVER CLEVELAND | Democratic | 277 | 5,555,426 | 46.1 |
| Benjamin Harrison | Republican | 145 | 5,182,690 | 43.0 |
| James B. Weaver | People's | 22 | 1,029,846 | 8.5 |
| John Bidwell | Prohibition | | 264,133 | 2.2 |

lated industries, including iron and steel. The first hint of trouble ahead came in February 1893 with the failure of the Philadelphia and Reading Railroad.

This bankruptcy came at a time of weakened confidence in the gold standard—the government's pledge to redeem paper money for gold on demand. This diminished confidence had several sources. First, when a leading London investment bank collapsed in 1890, hard-pressed British investors sold millions of dollars worth of stock in American railroads and other corporations and converted their dollars to gold, draining U.S. gold reserves. Second, Congress's lavish veterans' benefits and pork-barrel appropriations during the Harrison administration drained government resources just as tariff revenues were dropping because of the high McKinley Tariff. Third, the 1890 Sherman Silver Purchase Act further strained the gold reserve. This measure required the government to pay for its monthly silver purchases with treasury certificates redeemable for either silver or gold, and many certifcate holders chose to convert them to gold. Finally, the election of Grover Cleveland in 1892 further eroded confidence in the dollar. Although Cleveland endorsed the gold standard, his party harbored many advocates of inflationary policies.

Between January 1892 and March 1893, when Cleveland took office, the gold reserve had fallen sharply to around $100 million, the minimum considered necessary to support the dollar. This decline alarmed those who viewed the gold standard as the only sure evidence of the government's financial stability.

The collapse of a railroad early in 1893 thus triggered an economic crisis whose preconditions already existed. Fear fed on itself as panicky investors converted their stock holdings to gold. Stock prices plunged in May and June; the gold reserve sank to $59 million; by the end of the year, seventy-four railroads and more than fifteen thousand commercial institutions, including six hundred banks, had failed. After the Panic of 1893 came four years of hard times.

### The Depression of 1893–1897

By 1897 about a third of the nation's railroad mileage was in bankruptcy. Just as the railroad boom had spurred the industrial prosperity of the 1880s, so the railroad crisis of the early 1890s battered the entire

**Coxey's Army**

*Jacob Coxey's "army" of the unemployed reaches the outskirts of Washington, D.C., in 1894. Note the new electrical or telephone poles.*

economy as banks and other businesses failed. A full-scale depression gripped the nation.

The crisis took a heavy human toll. Industrial unemployed soared into the 20–25 percent range, leaving millions of factory workers with no money to feed their families and heat their homes. Recent immigrants faced disaster. Jobless men tramped the streets and rode freight trains from city to city seeking work. Immigrant wives and mothers struggled to care for their families with no money coming in.

The unusually harsh winters of 1893 and 1894 made matters worse. In New York City, where the crisis quickly swamped local relief agencies, a minister reported actual starvation. Amid the suffering, a rich New Yorker named Bradley Martin threw a lavish costume ball costing several hundred thousand dollars. Popular outrage over this flaunting of wealth in a prostrate city forced Martin and his family to move abroad.

Rural America, already hard-hit by declining agricultural prices, faced ruin. Farm prices dropped by more than 20 percent between 1890 and 1896. Corn plummeted from 50¢ to 21¢ a bushel; wheat, from 84¢ to 51¢. Cotton sold for 5¢ a pound in 1894.

Some desperate Americans turned to protest. The populist movement, already strong, gained momentum.

In Chicago, workers at the Pullman factory reacted to successive wage cuts by walking off the job in June 1894 (see Chapter 18). In Massillon, Ohio, self-taught monetary expert Jacob Coxey proposed as a solution to unemployment a $500 million public-works program funded with paper money not backed by gold but simply designated "legal tender" (just as it is today). A man of action as well as ideas, Coxey organized a march on Washington to lobby for his scheme. Thousands joined him en route, and several hundred actually reached Washington in late April 1894.

Police arrested Coxey and other leaders when they attempted to enter the Capitol grounds, and his "army" broke up. Although some considered Coxey eccentric, his proposal closely resembled programs that the government would adopt during the depression of the 1930s.

As unrest intensified, fear clutched middle-class Americans. A church magazine demanded that troops put "a pitiless stop" to outbreaks of unrest. To some observers, a bloody upheaval seemed imminent.

### Conservatives Hunker Down

In the face of suffering and turmoil, Cleveland retreated into a laissez-faire fortress. Boom-and-bust economic cycles were inevitable, he insisted, echoing the conventional wisdom of the day; the government could do nothing.

Failing to grasp the larger picture, Cleveland focused on a single peripheral issue: defending the gold standard. As the gold reserve dwindled, he blamed the Sherman Silver Purchase Act, and in August 1893 he called on Congress to repeal it. Silver advocates protested, but Congress followed Cleveland's wishes.

Nevertheless, the gold drain continued. In early 1895, with the gold reserve down to $41 million, Cleveland turned to Wall Street. Bankers J. P. Morgan and August Belmont agreed to lend the government $62 million in exchange for U.S. bonds at a special discount. With this loan, the government purchased gold to replenish its reserve. Meanwhile, Morgan and Belmont resold the bonds for a substantial profit. This complicated deal did help restore confidence in the government's economic stability. The gold drain stopped, and when the treasury offered $100 million in bonds early in 1896, they sold quickly.

Cleveland saved the gold standard, but at a high price. His dealings with Morgan and Belmont, and the bankers' handsome profits on the deal, confirmed radi-

cals' suspicions of an unholy alliance between Washington and Wall Street. Cleveland's readiness to use force against the Pullman strikers and against Jacob Coxey's peaceful marchers deepened such suspicions.

In the ongoing maneuverings of competing interest groups, corporate interests held the whip hand, as a battle over the tariff made clear. Although Cleveland favored tariff reform, the Congress of 1893–1895—despite its Democratic majorities—generally yielded to high-tariff lobbyists. The Wilson-Gorman Tariff of 1894 lowered duties somewhat but made so many concessions to protectionist interests that Cleveland disgustedly allowed it to become law without his signature.

Hinting at changes ahead, the Wilson-Gorman Tariff imposed a modest income tax of 2 percent on all income over $4,000 (about $40,000 in purchasing power today). But in *Pollock v. Farmers' Loan & Trust Co.* (1895), the Supreme Court narrowly held the law unconstitutional, ruling that the federal government could impose such a direct tax on personal property only if it were apportioned according to the population of each state. Whether one looked at the executive, the legislature, or the judiciary, Washington's subordination to a single interest group, the monied class, seemed absolute.

Cleveland's policies split the Democratic party. Farm leaders and silver Democrats condemned his opposition to the Sherman Silver Purchase Act. South Carolina's Ben Tillman, running for the Senate in 1894, proclaimed, "[T]his scoundrel Cleveland . . . is an old bag of beef and I am going to Washington with a pitchfork and prod him in his fat old ribs." This split in the Democratic ranks affected the elections of 1894 and 1896 and reshaped politics as the century ended.

The depression also helped reorient social thought. Middle-class charitable workers long convinced that individual character flaws caused poverty now realized—as socialists proclaimed and as the poor well knew—that even sober and hardworking people could succumb to economic forces beyond their control. As the social-work profession took form in the early twentieth century, its members spent less time preaching to the poor and more time investigating the social sources of poverty.

Laissez-faire ideology weakened in the 1890s as many depression-worn Americans adopted a broadened view of the government's role in dealing with the social consequences of industrialization. In the early twentieth century, this new view would activate powerful political energies. The depression, in short, not only brought suffering, it also taught lessons.

# The Watershed Election of 1896

Republican gains in the 1894 midterm election revealed the depths of revulsion against Cleveland and the Democrats, who were blamed for the hard times. As 1896 approached, the monetary question became the overriding symbolic issue. Conservatives clung to the gold standard; agrarian radicals rallied to the banner of "free silver." At the 1896 Democratic convention, the nomination went to a young champion of the silver cause, William Jennings Bryan. Despite Bryan's eloquence, Republican William McKinley emerged victorious. His triumph laid the groundwork for a political realignment that would influence American politics for a generation.

## *1894: Protest Grows Louder*

With the depression at its worst and President Grover Cleveland deeply unpopular, the midterm election of 1894 spelled Democratic disaster. The Republicans, gaining 5 seats in the Senate and 117 in the House, won both houses of Congress. They also secured control of several key states—including New York, Illinois, and Wisconsin—as immigrant workers, battered by the depression, abandoned their traditional Democratic allegiance.

Populist candidates garnered nearly 1.5 million votes in 1894—an increase of more than 40 percent over their 1892 total. Populism's most impressive gains occurred in the South. Although several western states that had voted Populist in 1892 returned to their traditional Republican allegiance in 1894, the overall results heartened Populist leaders.

## *The Silver Issue*

The serious economic divisions that split Americans in the mid-1890s focused especially on a symbolic issue: free silver.

Cleveland's rigid defense of the gold standard forced his opponents into an equally exaggerated obsession with silver, obscuring the genuine issues that divided rich and poor, creditor and debtor, and farmer and city dweller. Whereas conservatives tirelessly up-

held the gold standard, agrarian radicals extolled silver as a universal panacea. They were urged on and sometimes financed by western silver-mine owners who stood to profit if silver again became a monetary metal.

Each side had a point. Gold advocates recognized that a nation's paper money must be based on more than a government's ability to run printing presses and that uncontrolled inflation could be catastrophic. The silver advocates knew from experience how tight-money policies depressed prices and devastated farmers. Unfortunately, these underlying realities were rarely expressed clearly.

The silverites' most influential propaganda, William H. Harvey's widely distributed *Coin's Financial School* (1894), explained the monetary issue in simplified partisan terms, denounced "the conspiracy of Goldbugs," and insisted that the free coinage of silver would banish debt and end the depression.

## *Silver Advocates Capture the Democratic Party*

At the 1896 Democratic convention in Chicago, western and southern delegates adopted a platform—including a demand for the free and unlimited coinage of silver at the ratio to gold of sixteen to one—that in effect repudiated the Cleveland administration.

The front-running candidate was Congressman Richard Bland of Missouri, a silverite. But behind the scenes, the groundwork was being laid for the nomination of a dark horse, William Jennings Bryan, a thirty-six-year-old Nebraska lawyer and politician. During two terms in Congress (1891–1895), he championed western agrarian interests.

A famous orator, Bryan delivered his big convention speech in the debate over the platform. In an era before electronic amplification, his booming voice easily reached the upper gallery of the cavernous hall. Bryan praised western farmers and scorned advocates of the gold standard. By the time he reached his rousing conclusion—"You shall not press down upon the brow of labor this crown of thorns, you shall not crucify mankind upon a cross of gold"—the wildly cheering delegates had identified their candidate (see A Place in Time).

The silverites' capture of the Democratic party presented a dilemma to the Populists. They, too, advocated free silver, but only as one reform among many. To back Bryan would be to abandon the broad Populist program. Furthermore, fusion with the Democrats

## Chicago, Illinois

Barely sixty years old in the 1890s, Chicago was already a booming, bustling city of more than 1.5 million people, second in population only to New York. The Midwest's commercial, industrial, railroad, and agricultural hub, the city's stockyards teemed with livestock destined for slaughter and the packing houses. Along fashionable North Side streets like Lake Shore Drive stood the proud mansions of the city's great tycoons—men like Leander McCormick, who made farm equipment; Potter Palmer, who built hotels; Marshall Field, who owned a big department store; and Philip Armour, who slaughtered hogs. In

the sprawling South Side working-class wards, immigrants from scores of countries crowded in tenements but somehow preserved their distinctive ethnic identity. Along the notorious Levee, saloons and brothels flourished, including the elegant Everleigh Club, run by two sisters from Kentucky, Ada and Minna Everleigh. A maze of elevated trains brought Chicagoans to the crowded downtown area, the Loop, where in the 1880s the world's first skyscrapers, thrusting eight and ten stories in the air, had transformed the skyline. Presiding over it all were colorful, easygoing politicians with nicknames like Bathhouse John and Hinky Dink.

### A Busy Chicago Slaughterhouse

*From across the Midwest and Great Plains, the railroads funneled cattle, hogs, and other livestock into Chicago. Workers in blood-drenched slaughterhouses like this converted the animals into steaks, chops, and sausage for the dining tables of urban America.*

Visiting Chicago in the 1890s was a must for European tourists, who were invariably overwhelmed by its throbbing vitality and stark contradictions. A British journalist in 1897 called Chicago the "queen and guttersnipe of cities, cynosure and cesspool of the world," where public-spiritedness and flagrant civic corruption existed side by side.

Native-born writers, too, found the metropolis on Lake Michigan both alluring and repellent. The novelist Theodore Dreiser, who worked in Chicago as a journalist in the early 1890s, later tried to recapture his mixed impressions: "By its shimmering lake it lay, a king of shreds and patches, a . . . yokel with an epic in its mouth, a tramp, a hobo among cities, with the grip of Caesar in its mind, the dramatic force of Euripides in its soul. A very bard of a city this, singing of high deeds and high hopes, its heavy brogans buried deep in the mire of circumstance." A fictional Chicago reformer in Henry B. Fuller's *With the Procession* (1895) complains, "This town of ours labors under one peculiar disadvantage: it is the only great city in the world to which all its citizens have come for the one common, avowed object of making money."

In 1893 Chicago organized the magnificent Columbian Exposition, ostensibly to honor Christopher Columbus but mostly to celebrate itself. In a swampy area along Lake Michigan rose glistening exhibition halls, statuary, and a shimmering reflecting lagoon. A dizzying array of mechanical, artistic, and agricultural exhibits was on display from many states and nations. The Woman's Building, organized by Bertha Palmer, Potter Palmer's wife, housed exhibits from nearly fifty countries. Numerous conferences were held, including a "world's parliament of religions." On the Midway Plaisance—the fair's

popular amusement section—farm folk gaped at belly dancers from the Middle East and rode the world's first Ferris wheel. At night the exhibition buildings were outlined by strands of electric lights—the first that many Americans had seen. For hundreds of thousands of visitors, the Chicago world's fair provided memories for a lifetime. For urban planners, the "White City" that sprang up as if by magic that summer was a tantalizing foretaste of beautiful cities of the future. The man chiefly responsible for the fair's design, Chicago architect Daniel H. Burnham, more than lived up to his motto: "Make no little plans, they have no magic to stir men's blood." The fair ended literally with a bang. On the last day, as Mayor Carter H. Harrison was attending the closing ceremonies, he was shot and killed by a disappointed office seeker.

The world's fair delayed the arrival of the depression of 1893–1897 to Chicago, but when the crisis hit, it hit hard. More than two hundred thousand Chicagoans were out of work during the winter of 1893–1894. Many crowded into city hall each night to sleep on the floor; there, at least, they could be warm. In the city's dumps, men, women, and even small children picked over the garbage, searching for food. Tension gripped the city. When Governor John Peter Altgeld, charging a miscarriage of justice, in 1893 pardoned three men sentenced to hang after the Haymarket bombing of 1886, he was denounced by the city's elite, and his political career was over. In 1894, when workers at George Pullman's factory went out on strike, federal troops put down the disturbances.

Then in the hot July of 1896, the Democrats poured into town for their convention. The Nebraska delegation arrived in a special fourteen-car train festooned with banners for William

Jennings Bryan. Reflecting the desperate economic plight of the Great Plains, they took rooms at the Clifton House, a cheap, run-down hotel. The delegation of wealthy New York "Gold Democrats," led by millionaire financier and horse-racing enthusiast William C. Whitney, arrived in a special New York Central train and stayed at the city's finest hotel.

On the convention's second night, Bryan dined with his wife Mary and a friend at the Saratoga Restaurant. They watched as delegates surged along Dearborn Street, demonstrating for the Democratic front-runner, Missouri congressman Richard Bland. Said Bryan quietly, "These people don't know it, but they will be cheering for me just this way by this time tomorrow night. I will make the greatest speech of my life tomorrow." He was right. The next day, he gave his rousing "Cross of Gold" speech, and the nomination was his.

Even for Chicago, the overgrown boomtown of the West, it had been quite a week—and quite a decade.

**William Jennings Bryan**

### The 1893 Chicago World's Fair
*The fair's harmonious architecture and sylvan tranquillity, captured in this painting by Theodore Robinson, contrasted sharply with the grimy, throbbing city beyond.*

could destroy their influence as a third party. Yet the Populist leaders recognized that a separate Populist ticket would likely siphon votes from Bryan and ensure a Republican victory. Reluctantly, the Populists endorsed Bryan, while preserving a shred of independence (and confusing voters) by naming their own vice-presidential candidate, Tom Watson of Georgia. The Populists were learning the difficulty of organizing an independent political movement in a nation wedded to the two-party system.

The Republicans, meanwhile, had nominated former governor William McKinley, who as an Ohio congressman had given his name to the McKinley Tariff of 1890. The Republican platform embraced the high protective tariff and endorsed the gold standard.

### 1896: Conservatism Triumphant

Bryan tried to sustain the momentum of the Chicago convention. Crisscrossing the nation by train, he delivered his free-silver campaign speech to hundreds of audiences in twenty-nine states. One skeptical editor compared him to Nebraska's notoriously shallow Platte River: six inches deep and a mile wide at the mouth.

McKinley's campaign was shrewdly managed by Mark Hanna, a Cleveland industrialist. Dignified and aloof, McKinley could not match Bryan's popular touch; to one critic, he always seemed to be "determinedly looking for his pedestal." Accordingly, Hanna built the campaign not around the candidate but around posters, pamphlets, and newspaper editorials that warned of the dangers of free silver, caricatured Bryan as a rabid radical, and portrayed McKinley and the gold standard as twin pillars of prosperity. One poster pictured businessmen and factory workers carrying a giant gold coin on which stood a regal McKinley as the sun of "PROGRESS" rose behind him.

Drawing on a war chest possibly as large as $7 million, Hanna spent lavishly. J. P. Morgan and John D. Rockefeller together contributed half a million dollars, far more than Bryan's total campaign contributions. Like Benjamin Harrison in 1888, McKinley stayed home in Canton, Ohio, emerging from time to time to read speeches to visiting delegations. Carefully orchestrated by Hanna, McKinley's deceptively bucolic "front-porch" campaign involved elaborate organization. All told, some 750,000 people trekked to Canton that summer.

On election day, McKinley beat Bryan by over 600,000 votes. He swept the Northeast and the Midwest and even carried three farm states beyond the Mississippi—Iowa, Minnesota, and North Dakota—as well as

**William McKinley's "Front-Porch" Campaign, 1896**
*McKinley (front row, sixth from left) poses with an Italian-American brass band from Buffalo, New York, in front of his home in Canton, Ohio.*

## The Election of 1900

| Candidates | Parties | Electoral Vote | Popular Vote | Percentage of Popular Vote |
|---|---|---|---|---|
| WILLIAM MCKINLEY | Republican | 292 | 7,218,491 | 51.7 |
| William Jennings Bryan | Democratic; Populist | 155 | 6,356,734 | 45.5 |
| John C. Wooley | Prohibition | | 208,914 | 1.5 |

California and Oregon. Bryan's strength was limited to the South and the sparsely settled Great Plains and mountain states. The Republicans retained control of Congress.

Why did Bryan lose despite the depression and the protest spirit abroad in the land? Certainly Republican scare tactics played a role. But Bryan's candidacy carried its own liabilities. His core constituency, while passionately loyal, was limited. Seduced by free silver and Bryan's lung power, the Democrats had upheld a platform and a candidate with little appeal for factory workers, the urban middle class, or the settled family farmers of the midwestern corn belt. Urban voters, realizing that higher farm prices, a major free-silver goal, also meant higher food prices, went heavily for McKinley. Bryan's weakness in urban America reflected cultural differences as well. To urban Catholics and Jews, this moralistic, teetotaling Nebraskan thundering like a Protestant revival preacher seemed utterly alien.

Finally, despite their telling critique of laissez-faire capitalism, the Populists' effort to define a humane and democratic alternative relied heavily on visions of a premodern economic order of independent farmers and entrepreneurs. Although appealing, this vision bore little relationship to the new corporate order taking shape in America.

The McKinley administration quickly translated its conservative platform into law. The Dingley Tariff (1897) pushed rates to all-time high levels, and the Currency Act of 1900 officially committed the United States to the gold standard. With returning prosperity, rising farm prices after 1897, and the discovery of gold in Alaska and elsewhere, these measures aroused little protest. Bryan won renomination in 1900, but the fervor of 1896 was missing. The Republican campaign theme of prosperity easily won McKinley a second term.

The elections of 1894 and 1896 produced a Republican majority that, except for Woodrow Wilson's two presidential terms (1913–1921), would dominate national politics until the election of Franklin D. Roosevelt in 1932. Bryan's defeat and the Republicans' emergence as the party of prosperity and the sound dollar killed the Populist party and drove the Democrats back to their regional base in the South. But although populism collapsed, a new reform movement called progressivism was emerging. Many of the Populists' reform proposals would be enacted into law in the progressive years.

All this lay in the future, however. The most stirring events of the McKinley years occurred abroad. As prosperity returned at home, the United States flexed its muscles beyond the seas.

## The Election of 1896

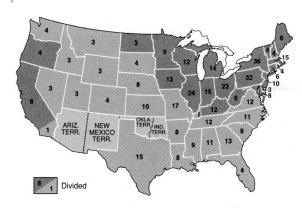

| | Electoral Vote | Popular Vote | Percentage of Popular Vote |
|---|---|---|---|
| **Republican** William McKinley | 271 | 7,102,246 | 51.1 |
| **Democratic** William J. Bryan | 176 | 6,492,559 | 47.7 |
| **Minor parties** | – | – | 315,398 | 1.2 |

# Expansionist Stirrings and War with Spain

The same corporate elite that dominated late-nineteenth-century domestic politics influenced U.S. foreign policy as well, contributing to surging expansionist pressures. Not only business leaders but also politicians, statesmen, and editorial writers insisted that national greatness required America to match Europe's imperial expansion. Fanned by sensationalistic newspaper coverage of a Cuban struggle for independence and elite calls for greater American international assertiveness, war between the United States and Spain broke out in 1898.

## Roots of Expansionist Sentiment

Since the first European settlers colonized North America's Atlantic coast, the newcomers had been an expansionist people. By the 1840s the push westward had acquired a name: Manifest Destiny. The expansionist impulse had faded as the Civil War and then industrialization absorbed American energies, but it revived strongly after 1880 as politicians and opinion molders proclaimed America's global destiny.

The example set by other nations fed this welling-up of expansionist sentiment. By the 1890s, Great Britain, France, Belgium, Italy, Germany, and Japan were busily collecting colonies from North Africa to the Pacific islands. National greatness, it appeared, demanded an empire.

In corporate circles, meanwhile, the opinion spread that continued prosperity required overseas markets. With industrial capacity expanding and the labor force growing, foreign markets offered a "safety valve" for potentially explosive pressures in the U.S. economy. Secretary of State James Blaine warned in 1890 that U.S. productivity was outrunning "the demands of the home market" and insisted that American business must look abroad.

Advocates of a stronger navy further fueled the expansionist mood. In *The Influence of Sea Power upon History* (1890), Alfred T. Mahan equated sea power with national greatness and urged a U.S. naval buildup. Since a strong navy required bases abroad, Mahan and other naval advocates supported the movement to acquire foreign territories, especially Pacific islands with good harbors.

Religious leaders proclaimed America's mission to spread Christianity. With U.S. missionaries spreading over the globe, this call exerted a powerful appeal. The expansionist argument sometimes took on a racist tinge. As Josiah Strong put it in his 1885 work *Our Country*, "God is training the Anglo-Saxon race for its mission"—a mission of Christianizing and civilizing the world's "weaker races."

A group of Republican expansionists led by Senator Henry Cabot Lodge of Massachusetts, diplomat John Hay, and Theodore Roosevelt of New York, preached imperial greatness and military might. "I should welcome almost any war," declared Roosevelt in 1897, "…this country needs one." A series of diplomatic skirmishes between 1885 and 1895 revealed the newly assertive American mood and paved the way for the war that Roosevelt desired.

In the mid-1880s, quarrels between the United States and Great Britain over fishing rights in the North Atlantic and in the Bering Sea off Alaska reawakened Americans' latent anti-British feelings as well as the old dream of acquiring Canada. A poem published in the *Detroit News* (adapted from an English music-hall song) supplied the nickname that critics would apply to the promoters of expansion—jingoists:

> We do not want to fight,
> But, by jingo, if we do,
> We'll scoop in all the fishing grounds
> And the whole dominion too!

The fishing-rights dispute was resolved in 1898, but by then attention had shifted to Latin America. In 1891, as civil war raged in Chile, U.S. officials seized a Chilean vessel that was attempting to buy guns in San Diego. Soon after, a mob in Valparaiso, Chile, killed two unarmed sailors on shore leave. President Harrison practically called for war. Only when Chile apologized and paid an indemnity was the incident closed.

Another Latin American conflict, in 1895, arose from a boundary dispute between Venezuela and British Guiana. The disagreement worsened after gold was discovered in the contested territory. When the British rejected a U.S. arbitration offer and condescendingly insisted that America's revered Monroe Doctrine had no standing in international law, a livid Grover Cleveland asked Congress to set up a commission to settle the disputed boundary even without Britain's approval. As patriotic fervor pulsed through the nation, the British in 1897 accepted the commission's findings.

## Pacific Expansion

Meanwhile, the U.S. Navy focused on the Samoan Islands in the South Pacific, where it sought access to the port of Pago Pago as a refueling station. Britain and Germany had ambitions in Samoa as well, and in March 1889 the United States and Germany narrowly avoided a naval clash when a hurricane wrecked both fleets. Secretary of State Blaine's wife wrote to one of their children, "Your father is now looking up Samoa on the map." Once he found it, negotiations began, and the United States, Great Britain, and Germany established a three-way "protectorate" over the islands.

Attention had by that time shifted to the Hawaiian Islands, which had both strategic and economic significance for the United States. New England trading vessels had visited Hawaii as early as the 1790s, and in the 1820s had come Yankee missionaries. By the 1860s American-owned sugar plantations worked by Chinese and Japanese laborers dotted the islands. Under an 1887 treaty (negotiated after the planters had forcibly imposed a new constitution on Hawaii's native ruler, Kalākaua), the United States built a naval base at Pearl Harbor, near Honolulu. American economic dominance and the influx of foreigners angered Hawaiians. In 1891 they welcomed to the Hawaiian throne Liliuokalani, a strong-willed woman hostile to Americans.

Meanwhile, in 1890, the framers of the McKinley Tariff, pressured by domestic sugar growers, eliminated the duty-free status enjoyed by Hawaiian sugar. Facing ruin as Hawaii's wholesale sugar prices plunged 40 percent, the planters in January 1893 deposed

### U.S. Territorial Expansion in the Late Nineteenth Century

*The major period of U.S. territorial expansion abroad came in a short burst of activity in the late 1890s, when newspapers and some politicians beat the drums for empire.*

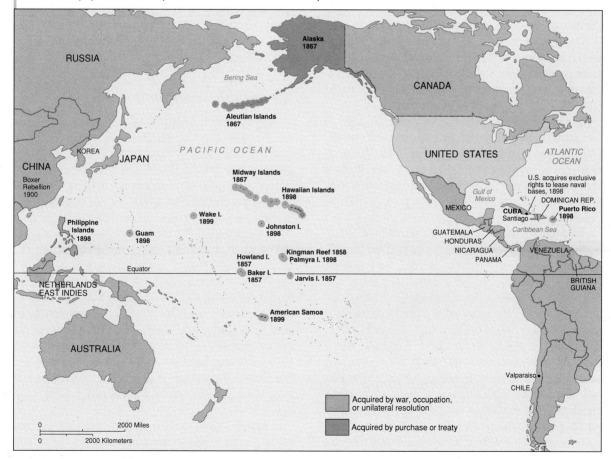

Queen Liliuokalani, proclaimed the independent Republic of Hawaii, and requested U.S. annexation. The U.S. State Department's representative in Hawaii cabled Washington: "The Hawaiian pear is now fully ripe, and this is the golden hour for the United States to pluck it." But the grab for Hawaii troubled Grover Cleveland, who sent a representative to investigate the situation. This representative's report questioned whether the Hawaiian people actually desired annexation.

Cleveland's scruples infuriated expansionists, however, and when William McKinley succeeded Cleveland in 1897, the acquisition of Hawaii moved rapidly forward. In 1898 Congress proclaimed Hawaii an American territory. Sixty-one years later, it joined the Union as the fiftieth state.

### Crisis over Cuba

By 1898 American attention had shifted to the Spanish colony of Cuba, ninety miles off Florida, where in 1895 an anti-Spanish rebellion had broken out. This revolt, organized by the Cuban writer José Martí and other Cuban exiles in New York City, won little support from U.S. business, which had $50 million invested in Cuba and annually imported $100 million worth of sugar and other products from the island. Nor did the rebels initially secure the backing of Washington, which urged Spain to grant Cuba a degree of autonomy.

But the rebels' cause aroused popular sympathy in the United States. This support increased with revelations that the Spanish commander in Cuba, Valeriano Weyler, was herding vast numbers of Cubans into concentration camps. Malnutrition and disease turned these camps into hellholes in which perhaps 200,000 Cubans died.

Fueling American anger was the sensationalized reporting of two competing New York City newspapers, William Randolph Hearst's *Journal* and Joseph Pulitzer's *World*. The Journal's color comic strip, "The Yellow Kid," provided a name for Hearst's debased editorial approach: yellow journalism. The Hungarian immigrant Pulitzer normally had higher standards, but in the cutthroat battle for readers, Pulitzer's *World* matched the *Journal's* sensationalism. Both editors exploited the Cuban crisis. Headlines turned rumor into fact, and feature stories detailed "Butcher" Weyler's atrocities. When a young Cuban woman was jailed for resisting a rape attempt by a Spanish officer, a Hearst reporter helped the woman escape and brought her triumphantly to New York.

In 1897 a new, more liberal Spanish government sought a peaceful resolution of the Cuban crisis. But Hearst and Pulitzer continued to inflame the public. On February 8, 1898, Hearst's *Journal* published a private letter by Spain's minister to the United States that described McKinley as "weak" and "a bidder for the admiration of the crowd." Irritation over this incident turned to outrage when on February 15 an explosion rocked the U.S. battleship *Maine* in Havana harbor and killed 266 crewmen. A painstaking review of the evidence in 1976 concluded that a shipboard ammunition explosion, set off by a fire in a coal bunker, had caused the blast. But at the time neither Washington nor the yellow press was in any mood to view the tragedy as accidental. Newspaper headlines screamed of a "Spanish mine," and war spirit flared high.

Despite further Spanish concessions, McKinley sent a war message to Congress on April 11, and legislators enacted a joint resolution recognizing Cuba's independence and authorizing force to expel the Spanish. An amendment introduced by Senator Henry M. Teller of Colorado renounced any U.S. interest in "sovereignty, jurisdiction, or control" in Cuba and pledged that America would leave the island alone once independence was assured.

### The Spanish-American War

The brief war with Spain involved only a few days of actual combat. The first action came on May 1, 1898, when a U.S. fleet commanded by George Dewey steamed into Manila Bay in the Philippines and destroyed or captured all ten Spanish ships anchored there, at the cost of 1 American and 381 Spanish lives. In mid-August U.S. troops occupied the capital, Manila.

In Cuba the fighting centered on the military stronghold of Santiago de Cuba on the southeastern coast. On May 19 a Spanish battle fleet of seven aging vessels under Pascual Cervera sailed into the Santiago de Cuba harbor, where five U.S. battleships and two cruisers blockaded them. On July 1, in the war's only significant land action, American troops seized two strongly defended Spanish garrisons on El Caney Hill and San Juan Hill overlooking Santiago de Cuba. Leading the volunteer "Rough Riders" unit in the capture of San Juan Hill was Theodore Roosevelt, who at last got his taste of war.

On July 3 Cervera attempted to pierce through the American blockade to the open sea. U.S. naval fire raked the archaic Spanish vessels and sank them. Spain

**African American Soldiers of the Tenth U.S. Cavalry in Cuba, July 1898**

*These men posed shortly after the capture of San Juan Hill. Black troops played an important role in the Spanish-American War, but they were also subject to harassment and discrimination.*

lost 474 men in this gallant but doomed show of the flag. Americans might have found a cautionary lesson in this sorry end to four hundred years of Spanish rule in the New World, but few had time for somber musings. The *Washington Post* observed, "A new consciousness seems to have come upon us—the consciousness of strength—and with it a new appetite, the yearning to show our strength. . . , [t]he taste of empire. . . ." John Hay was more succinct. It had been, he wrote Roosevelt, "a splendid little war."

Many who served in Cuba found the war far from splendid. Ill trained and poorly equipped, the troops went into summer combat in the tropics wearing heavy woolen uniforms. While 379 American soldiers died in combat, more than 5,000 succumbed to food poisoning, yellow fever, malaria, and other diseases during and after the war.

Several thousand black troops fought in Cuba. Some, such as the 24th Infantry and 10th Cavalry, were seasoned regular-army veterans transferred from bases in the West. Others were volunteers from various states. At assembly points in Georgia, and then at the embarkation port, Tampa, Florida, these troops encountered the racism of a Jim Crow society. Tampa restau-

rants and bars refused them service; Tampa whites disparaged them. On June 6, after weeks of racist treatment, some black troops exploded in riotous rage, storming into restaurants, bars, and other establishments that had barred them. White troops from Georgia restored order. Although white and black troops sailed to Cuba on the same transport ships (actually hastily converted freighters), the ships themselves were segregated, with black troops often confined to the lowest quarters in the stifling heat, denied permission to mingle on deck with the other units, and in other ways discriminated against.

Despite the racism, African Americans served with distinction once they reached Cuba. Black troops played key roles in the taking of both San Juan Hill and El Caney Hill; of the total U.S. troops involved in the latter action, some 15 percent were black.

The Spanish sought an armistice on July 17, and in the peace treaty signed that December in Paris, Spain recognized Cuba's independence and, after a U.S. payment of $20 million, ceded the Philippines, Puerto Rico, and the Pacific island of Guam to the United States. Americans now possessed an island empire stretching from the Caribbean to the Pacific.

## Deepening Imperialist Ventures: The Philippines, China, Panama

The end of the Spanish-American War proved only an interlude in this period of expansionism. A few anti-imperialists protested, but to little effect. In the Philippines, America fought a brutal four-year war against Filipinos struggling for independence. In China, Washington took diplomatic and military steps to ensure an "open door" for U.S. commerce. Closer to home, dubious maneuvering by President Theodore Roosevelt cleared the way for the construction of an American canal across the Isthmus of Panama.

### *The Platt Amendment*

From 1898 to 1902, the U.S. Army governed Cuba under the command of General Leonard Wood. Wood's administration improved public health, education, and sanitation but nevertheless violated the spirit of the 1898 Teller Amendment (see page 610).

The troops eventually withdrew, though under conditions that limited Cuban sovereignty. The 1901 Platt

Amendment, attached to an army appropriations bill offered by a Connecticut senator at the request of the War Department, authorized American withdrawal only after Cuba agreed not to make any treaty with a foreign power limiting its independence and not to borrow beyond its means. The United States also reserved the right to intervene in Cuba when it saw fit and to maintain a naval base there. With U.S. troops still occupying the island, the Cuban constitutional convention of 1901 accepted the Platt Amendment, which remained in force until 1934. Under its terms the United States established a naval base at Guantánamo Bay, near Santiago de Cuba, which it still maintains. U.S. investments in Cuba, some $50 million in 1898, soared to half a billion dollars by 1920.

### Guerrilla War in the Philippines

An urgent problem faced President McKinley as the Spanish-American War ended: what to do about the Philippines. This group of Pacific islands had a population of more than 5 million in 1898. At the war's outset, few Americans knew that the Philippines belonged to Spain or even where they were. Without a map, McKinley later confessed, "I could not have told where those darn islands were within two thousand miles."

**The Philippines Quagmire**

*Anticipating the Vietnam War, the U.S. suppression of the Philippines' independence struggle involved American troops in a long and nasty guerrilla campaign. One of the men in this 1900 photograph scrawled on the back: "27 hours on march, mud and rain, 24 hours without food."*

But the victory over Spain whetted the appetite for expansion. To the U.S. business community, the Philippines offered a stepping-stone to the China market. McKinley, reflecting the prevailing mood as always, reasoned that the Filipinos were unready for self-government and would be gobbled up if set adrift in a world of imperial rivalries. McKinley further persuaded himself that American rule would enormously benefit the Filipinos, whom he called "our little brown brothers." A devout Methodist, he explained that America's mission was "to educate the Filipinos, and to uplift and civilize and Christianize them, and by God's grace do the very best we could by them." (In fact, most Filipinos were already Christian—a legacy of centuries of Spanish rule.) Having prayerfully reached his decision, McKinley instructed the American peace negotiators in Paris to insist on U.S. acquisition of the Philippines.

But uplifting the Filipinos required a struggle. In 1896 young Emilio Aguinaldo had organized a Filipino independence movement to drive out Spain. In 1898, with arms supplied by George Dewey, Aguinaldo's forces had captured most of Luzon, the Philippines' main island. When the Spanish surrendered, Aguinaldo proclaimed Filipino independence and drafted a democratic constitution. Feeling betrayed when the peace treaty ceded his country to the United States, Aguinaldo ordered his rebel force to attack Manila, the American base of operations. Seventy thousand more U.S. troops were shipped to the Philippines, and by the end of 1899, this initial Filipino resistance had been crushed.

But these hostilities were only the opening phase of a long guerrilla conflict. Before it ended, over 125,000 American men had served in the Philippines, and 4,000 had been killed. As many as 20,000 Filipino independence fighters died. As in the later Vietnam War, casualties and suffering ravaged the civilian population as well. Aguinaldo was captured in March 1901, but large-scale guerrilla fighting went on through the summer of 1902.

In 1902 a special Senate committee heard testimony from veterans of the Philippines war about the execution of prisoners, the torture of suspects, and the burning of villages. The humanitarian mood of 1898, when Americans had rushed to save Cuba from the cruel Spaniards, seemed remote indeed.

By the Philippine Government Act (1902), Congress vested authority in a governor general to be appointed by the president. But the act also provided for an elected Filipino assembly and promised eventual self-government. Progress toward this goal inched forward, with intervals of semimilitary rule. In 1946, nearly half a century after Admiral Dewey's guns had boomed in Manila Bay, independence finally came to the Filipinos.

### Critics of Empire

Some Americans opposed imperialism. Although few in number, the critics, like the Mugwumps who had challenged the spoils system, were influential. Indeed, some of them, like Carl Schurz and E. L. Godkin, *were* former Mugwumps. Other anti-imperialists included William Jennings Bryan, settlement house founder Jane Addams, novelist Mark Twain, and Harvard philosopher William James. Steel king Andrew Carnegie gave thousands of dollars to the cause. In 1898 these critics of empire formed the Anti-Imperialist League.

For the United States to rule other peoples, the anti-imperialists believed, was to violate the principles of the Declaration of Independence and the Constitution. As one of them wrote, "Dewey took Manila with the loss of one man—and all our institutions." The military fever that accompanied expansionism also dismayed the anti-imperialists. Some labor leaders feared that imperial expansion would lead to competition from cheap foreign labor and products.

In February 1899 the anti-imperialists failed by one vote to prevent Senate ratification of the expansionist peace treaty with Spain. McKinley's overwhelming re-election victory in 1900 and the defeat of the expansionist critic William Jennings Bryan eroded the anti-imperialists' cause. Nevertheless, at a time of jingoistic rhetoric and militaristic posturing, they had upheld an older and finer vision of America.

### The "Open Door": Competing for the China Market

As the Philippines war dragged on, American policy makers turned their attention farther west—to China. Their objective was not territorial expansion but protection of U.S. commercial opportunities. Proclaimed

Indiana senator Albert J. Beveridge in 1898, "American factories are making more than the American people can use; American soil is producing more than they can consume....[T]he trade of the world must and shall be ours."

The China market beckoned. Textile producers dreamed of massive sales to China's millions; investors envisioned large-scale railroad construction. China was especially vulnerable to foreign intervention as the 250-year-old Manchu Dynasty grew weaker. In 1896 a consortium of New York capitalists formed a company to promote trade and railroad investment in China.

But other nations, too, were eyeing the China market. Some pressured the weak Manchu regime to designate certain ports and regions as spheres of influence where they would have exclusive trading and development rights. In 1896 Russia won both the right to build a railway across Manchuria and a twenty-five-year lease on a large section of the region. In 1897 Germany forcibly secured a ninety-nine-year lease on a Chinese port as well as mining and railroad rights in the adjacent province. The British won various concessions, too.

In September 1899 Secretary of State John Hay addressed notes to the major European powers with economic interests in China, asking them not to interfere with American trading rights in China. Specifically, Hay requested that they open the ports within their spheres of influence to all nations. The six nations gave non-committal answers, but Hay blithely announced that the principle of an "Open Door" to American business had been accepted.

These Open Door notes show how commercial considerations influenced American foreign policy. They reflected what has been called a quest for "informal empire," in contrast to the acquisition of overseas colonies. In this kind of economic expansionism, Washington played a supporting but subordinate role to private enterprise—a kind of "imperialism" that fit neatly with the ideology of laissez-faire.

As Hay pursued his Open Door efforts, a more immediate threat to all foreign interests emerged in China. For years, antiforeign feeling had simmered in China, fanned by an aged Manchu empress disgusted by the growth of Western influence. In 1899 a fanatical antiforeign secret society known as the Harmonious Righteous Fists (called "Boxers" by Western journalists) killed thousands of foreigners as well as Chinese Christians. In June 1900 the Boxers occupied Beijing (Peking), the Chinese capital, and laid siege to the district housing the foreign legations. The United States

**U.S. Troops in China, 1900**
*On a dirt road flanked by stone elephants, mounted American troops sent by President McKinley prepare to march on Beijing as part of an international force assembled to suppress the Boxer Rebellion. This intervention signaled a deepening U.S. involvement in Asia.*

contributed 2,500 soldiers to an international army that marched on Beijing, drove back the Boxers, and rescued the occupants of the besieged legations.

The defeat of the Boxer uprising further weakened China's government. Fearing the regime's collapse, which would allow the imperial powers to carve up China, John Hay in 1900 issued a second, more important series of Open Door notes. He reaffirmed the principle of open trade in China for all nations and announced America's determination to preserve China's territorial and administrative integrity. In the 1930s, when Japanese expansionism menaced China's survival, Hay's policy helped shape the American response.

### The Panama Canal: Hardball U.S. Diplomacy

Traders had long dreamed of a navigable canal across the ribbon of land joining North and South America that would eliminate the hazardous voyage around South America. In 1879 a French company had secured a twenty-five-year concession from Colombia to build a canal across the Isthmus of Panama, then part of Colombia. But mismanagement and yellow fever plagued the project, and ten years and $400 million later, it went bankrupt, with the canal half completed. Seeking to recoup some of its losses, the French company offered its assets, including the still-unexpired concession from Colombia, to the United States for $109 million.

In the expansionist climate of the 1890s, this offer aroused interest. Some favored an alternative route across Nicaragua, but in 1902, after the French had lowered their price to $40 million, Congress authorized President Theodore Roosevelt* to accept the French offer and the Panama route. The following year, Secretary of State Hay signed an agreement with the Colombian representative, Tomás Herrán, granting the United States a ninety-nine-year lease on the proposed path of the canal, in return for a down payment of $10 million and an annual fee of $250,000.

But the Colombian senate rejected the Hay-Herrán agreement, deciding instead to negotiate a new concession with the United States. This shrewd action outraged Roosevelt, who privately denounced the Colombians as "greedy little anthropoids."

Determined to have his canal, Roosevelt found a willing collaborator in Philippe Bunau-Varilla, an official of the bankrupt French company. Dismayed that his company might lose its $40 million, Bunau-Varilla, from a New York hotel room, organized a "revolution" in Panama. While his wife stitched a flag, he wrote a declaration of independence and a constitution for the new nation. When the "revolution" occurred as scheduled on November 3, 1903, a U.S. warship hovered offshore. Proclaiming Panama's independence, Bunau-Varilla appointed himself its first ambassador to the United States. Three days later, Washington recognized

---

\* Elected vice president in 1900, Roosevelt had become president upon McKinley's assassination in September 1901.

the newly hatched nation. Bunau-Varilla next signed a treaty with John Hay granting the United States a ten-mile-wide strip of land across Panama "in perpetuity" (that is, forever) on the same financial terms earlier rejected by Colombia. Theodore Roosevelt later summed up the episode: "I took the Canal Zone, and let Congress debate, and while the debate goes on, the canal does also."

The first challenge confronting the U.S. canal builders was the yellow fever that had haunted the French. A drainage project eradicated the fever-bearing mosquito—a remarkable public-health achievement. Construction began in 1906, and in August 1914 the first ship passed through the canal.

In 1921, implicitly acknowledging the dubious methods used to acquire the Canal Zone, the Senate voted a payment of $25 million to Colombia. But the political price paid by the United States for the Panama Canal was high. The ill feeling generated by Theodore Roosevelt's high-handed actions, combined with other instances of U.S. interventionism, long shadowed U.S.–Latin American relations.

## CONCLUSION

The opening of the Panama Canal concluded thirty years of expansionism that proclaimed America's debut on the world stage and underscored the global reach of U.S. capitalism. But amid foreign diversions, the fundamental question of late-nineteenth-century American politics remained: could a government designed for the needs of a small agrarian society serve a nation of factories and immigrant-crowded cities? Down to 1900, the answer was by no means clear. Although issues such as patronage, the tariff, veterans' benefits, and monetary policy generated much oratory and some action, the dominant ideology of laissez-faire severely limited government activism.

Rising agrarian discontent in the 1890s, sharpened by the depression of 1893–1897, underscored the urgency of certain social problems in these years. The Populist party, spawned by rural hardship, challenged the ideas of the laissez-faire ideologists and corporate leaders who largely determined public issues. Although populism as an organized political force disintegrated after Bryan's ill-fated free-silver campaign of 1896, the movement's insistence that government play an assertive role in solving social and economic problems helped form the political environment of the progressive movement, to which we now turn.

## FOR FURTHER READING

Edward L. Ayers, *The Promise of the New South: Life After Reconstruction* (1992). A richly textured work that explores the complexity of the topic and pays close attention to nonelite men and women.

Robert L. Beisner, *From the Old Diplomacy to the New, 1865–1900,* 2d ed. (1986). A valuable study tracing the roots of expansionism.

W. Fitzhugh Brundage, *Lynching in the New South: Georgia and Virginia, 1880–1930* (1993). A careful analysis of lynching in two southern states over a fifty-year period.

William F. Holmes, ed., *American Populism* (1994). A well-selected set of nineteen scholarly essays interpreting the agrarian reform movement and surveying its varied aspects.

Ari Hoogenboom, *Rutherford B. Hayes: Warrior and President* (1995). A detailed, sympathetic, and balanced assessment of an able and decent public figure constrained by the political realities of his time; a good introduction to the political and economic issues of post-Reconstruction America.

Morton Keller, *Affairs of State: Public Life in Late-Nineteenth-Century America* (1977). An excellent account of politics and government.

Robert C. McMath, *American Populism: A Social History, 1877–1898* (1993). A well-written study summing up recent scholarship on populism, especially its social and cultural dimensions.

John Offner, *An Unwanted War* (1992). A good recent history of the diplomacy leading up to the Spanish-American War.

Stewart E. Tolnay and E. M. Beck, *A Festival of Violence: An Analysis of Southern Lynchings, 1882–1930* (1995). A careful study of more than 2,800 lynchings, exploring the circumstances and linking patterns to social and economic conditions.

# 22

# The Progressive Era

**Six O'clock, Winter, 1912**
*by John Sloan*

It was late Saturday afternoon on March 25, 1911, but at the Triangle Shirtwaist factory in New York City, hundreds of young women and a few men were still at work. The clatter of sewing machines jammed into the eighth- and ninth-floor workrooms filled the air. Suddenly fire broke out. Feeding on bolts of cloth, the fire soon turned the upper floors into an inferno. Panicked workers rushed for the doors, only to find some of them locked. Other doors opened inward (a fire-law violation) and were jammed shut by the crush of bodies.

There were a few miraculous escapes. Young Pauline Grossman crawled to safety across a narrow alleyway when three male employees formed a human bridge. As others tried to cross, however, the weight became too great, and the three men fell to their deaths. Dozens of workers leaped from the windows to certain death on the sidewalk below.

Immigrant parents searched the scenes of death all night for their daughters; newspaper reporters could hear "a dozen pet names in Italian and Yiddish rising in shrill agony above the deeper moan of the throng." Sunday's headlines summed up the grim count: 141 dead.

The Triangle fire offered particularly horrifying evidence of what many citizens had recognized for years: all was not well in urban-industrial America. Industrialization, for all its benefits, had also taken a heavy human toll and changed American life. By the 1890s, the fabled "land of opportunity" seemed a myth as corporations grew ever larger. For the immigrants in unsafe factories and unhealthy slums, life was often a desperate cycle of poverty, exhausting labor, and early death. As a new middle class of white-collar workers and urban professionals consolidated its position, a revived women's movement demanded the vote.

From this volatile social stew surged a wave of reform that came to be called the progressive movement.

Originally historians portrayed this movement in political-cartoon fashion as an inspiring triumph of "the people" over sinister corporations and crooked bosses. More recently, historians have added complexity to this picture, noting the role of special-interest groups (sometimes including big business) in promoting specific reforms as well as the movement's darker side, its blind spots, and above all, its rich and sometimes contradictory diversity.

Fundamentally, the progressive reform movement was a response to the vast changes that since the Civil War had obliterated the familiar contours of an older, simpler America. Whatever their specific agenda, all progressives grappled with the new social world of corporations, factories, cities, and immigrants.

Of course, reform was nothing new, but progressivism differed from earlier reform movements. For example, the reformers of the 1830s and 1840s had typically viewed government as irrelevant or even hostile to their aims. Individuals and small, self-selected groups, they had insisted, must lead the way to a better social order. Progressive reformers, by contrast, viewed *government* as a major ally. And far from glorifying the individual or withdrawing from society, they saw organizations and social engagement as essential to reform.

Emerging in the 1890s, first at the city and state levels, myriad organizations, many composed exclusively of women, pursued varied reform objectives. Under the influence of journalists, novelists, religious leaders, social thinkers, and politicians, this diffuse progressive impulse took on national dimensions. At the federal level, a spirit of government activism energized Washington. By 1917, when reform gave way to war, America's political and social landscape looked very different. This chapter looks first at the social changes that spawned progressivism and then at the movement itself.

This chapter focuses on four major questions:

♦ Is "progressivism" simply a label used by historians to describe many divergent and even contradictory activities by different interest groups, or was there an authentic "progressive movement" united by common values, strategies, and concerns?

♦ What social realities associated with America's new urban-industrial order particularly disturbed progressives at the city and state level? What approaches did they take to address these problems?

♦ How did the reform impulse find expression at the national level in these years? Which politicians and issues are particularly identified with progressivism as a national movement?

♦ How did progressive reform affect ordinary Americans, including women, immigrants, poor city dwellers, and African Americans?

# The Changing American Society and Economy

Explosive urban growth and corporate consolidation transformed the United States in the early twentieth century. As native-born Americans poured cityward, they met a tide of immigrants. The American city, with its elite, its growing middle class, and its new immigrants, shaped the era's social character. Prosperity and new forms of business organization transformed American capitalism in these years, but as we saw in Chapter 18, not everyone benefited equally from economic growth. Industrial workers endured long hours, low

**Seamstress**
*141 died in the Triangle fire*

wages, dangerous working conditions, and pressures to increase productivity. Through labor unions and the ballot box, workers organized to improve their lot.

## *Immigrant Masses and a New Urban Middle Class*

Through all the events of the early twentieth century, urbanization remained a constant. By 1920, when the nation's urban population surpassed the 50 percent mark, sixty-eight U.S. cities boasted more than 100,000 inhabitants. New York City grew by 2.2 million from 1900 to 1920, Chicago by 1 million.

Like the heroine of Theodore Dreiser's novel *Sister Carrie* (1900), the new urbanites often came from farms and small towns. But the big source of urban growth continued to be immigration. More than 17 million newcomers arrived from 1900 to 1917 (many passing through New York City's immigration center, Ellis Island), and most of them became city dwellers.

As in the 1890s, the influx was mainly from southern and eastern Europe, but more than 200,000 Japanese and 40,000 Chinese also arrived between 1900 and 1920, as well as thousands of Mexicans who migrated northward to work on the railroad. As before, most immigrants came for economic reasons. But other factors influenced their decision as well. Whereas many Mexicans fled revolutionary upheavals at home, religious persecution drove many eastern European Jews to America. The Jews of the Russian Empire were confined to a region known as the Pale, where even in the best of times they suffered discrimination. Periodically, murderous anti-Semitic campaigns called pogroms swept over Russia, forcing Jews to flee for their lives. Hundreds of thousands of these eastern European Jewish immigrants settled on New York's Lower East Side.

The immigrants of the early twentieth century, like their predecessors, crowded into slum tenements, row houses, and rickety three-story structures called triple deckers. The ability of authorities to provide safe water, plumbing, garbage collection, and fire protection—not to mention decent schools and parks—chronically lagged behind the pace of urban growth. Municipal corruption often compounded the problem. Health conditions were appalling, with death rates sometimes reaching twice the national average.

For years, reform-minded ministers, settlement house leaders, and journalists had been reminding middle-class America of the conditions festering in the immigrant slums. As the message at last began to

## CHRONOLOGY

**1889** Jane Addams founds Hull House in Chicago.

**1895** Anti-Saloon League founded.

**1898** Charlotte Perkins Gilman, *Women and Economics.*

**1899** Thorstein Veblen, *The Theory of the Leisure Class.*

**1900** International Ladies' Garment Workers' Union (ILGWU) founded.

Socialist Party of America organized.

Theodore Dreiser, *Sister Carrie.*

Carrie Chapman Catt becomes president of the National American Woman Suffrage Association (NAWSA).

**1901** Assassination of McKinley; Theodore Roosevelt becomes president.

**1902** Roosevelt mediates coal strike.

National Reclamation Act.

Jane Addams, *Democracy and Social Ethics.*

**1903** W. E. B. Du Bois, *The Souls of Black Folk.*

**1904** Roosevelt elected president.

*Northern Securities* case.

Lincoln Steffens, *The Shame of the Cities.*

Ida Tarbell, *History of the Standard Oil Company.*

**1905** Industrial Workers of the World (IWW) organized.

Niagara Movement established by W. E. B. Du Bois and others.

Gifford Pinchot appointed head of U.S. Forest Service.

**1906** Hepburn Act.

Upton Sinclair, *The Jungle.*

Pure Food and Drug Act.

Meat Inspection Act.

*Lochner* v. *New York.*

Antiquities Act.

**1907** Walter Rauschenbusch, *Christianity and the Social Crisis.*

William James, *Pragmatism.*

**1908** *Muller* v. *Oregon.*

William Howard Taft elected president.

**1909** Payne-Aldrich Tariff.

Ballinger-Pinchot controversy.

National Association for the Advancement of Colored People (NAACP) founded.

Herbert Croly, *The Promise of American Life.*

**1910** Mann Act.

Mann-Elkins Act.

**1911** Triangle Shirtwaist Company fire.

Supreme Court orders dissolution of Standard Oil Company.

**1912** Republican party split; Progressive (Bull Moose) party founded.

Woodrow Wilson elected president.

Hague Opium Treaty.

**1913** Underwood-Simmons Tariff.

Federal Reserve Act.

Sixteenth Amendment added to the Constitution.

Seventeenth Amendment added to the Constitution.

Thirty thousand march for woman suffrage in New York.

**1914** Federal Trade Commission Act.

Clayton Antitrust Act.

Narcotics Act.

**1915** D. W. Griffith, *The Birth of a Nation.*

**1916** Federal Farm Loan Act.

Keating-Owen Act.

Adamson Act.

Workmen's Compensation Act.

Wilson reelected.

John Dewey, *Democracy and Education.*

Margaret Sanger opens nation's first birth-control clinic in Brooklyn, New York.

National Park Service created.

**1919** Eighteenth Amendment added to the Constitution.

**1920** Nineteenth Amendment added to the Constitution.

sink in, a growing awareness of the urban problem helped lay the groundwork for the progressive reform movement.

Along with immigration, a subtler change was transforming the cities as well: the vast expansion of a native-born middle class. From 1900 to 1920, the white-collar work force jumped from 5.1 million to 10.5 million—more than double the rate for the work force as a whole. As industry grew, the number of secretaries, civil engineers, and people in advertising increased at a phenomenal pace.

This new white-collar class included such diverse groups as corporate technicians and bureaucrats; the owners and managers of local businesses; and professionals such as lawyers, physicians, and teachers. Existing professional societies such as the American Bar

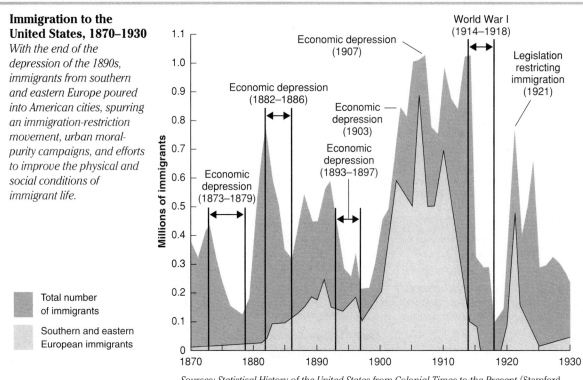

**Immigration to the United States, 1870–1930**

*With the end of the depression of the 1890s, immigrants from southern and eastern Europe poured into American cities, spurring an immigration-restriction movement, urban moral-purity campaigns, and efforts to improve the physical and social conditions of immigrant life.*

Total number of immigrants

Southern and eastern European immigrants

*Sources: Statistical History of the United States from Colonial Times to the Present* (Stamford, Conn.: Fairfield Publishers, 1965); and report presented by Senator William P. Dillingham, Senate document 742, 61st Congress, 3rd session, December 5, 1910: Abstracts of Reports to the Immigration Commission.

Association and the National Education Association grew rapidly. Scores of new professional groups arose, from the American Association of Advertising Agencies (1917) to the American Association of University Professors (1915). The age of organization had dawned, bringing with it new professional allegiances, a new emphasis on certification and licensing; and in general a more standardized, routinized society.

Ambitious, well educated, and valuing self-discipline and social stability, the members of this newly self-conscious middle class were aware of their numbers and eager to make their influence felt. They had a keen and uneasy sense of their rank: beneath the aristocratic old families and new corporate elite, above the immigrant masses in the slums. For many middle-class Americans, membership in a national professional society provided a sense of identity that might earlier have come from neighborhood, church, or political party affiliation.

For the women of this new urban middle class, the city offered both opportunities and frustrations. Immi-grant girls took jobs as servants or factory operatives; middle-class women became schoolteachers, secretaries, typists, clerks, and telephone operators. The number of women in such white-collar jobs surged from 949,000 in 1900 to 3.4 million in 1920. The number of women earning college degrees, although still small, more than tripled in this twenty-year period.

But for middle-class married women caring for the home and children and hedged in by an ideology of domesticity, city life could mean isolation and frustration. The divorce rate crept up, from one in twelve marriages in 1900 to one in nine by 1916. As we shall see, many middle-class women joined the new female white-collar workers and college graduates in leading a resurgent women's movement.

## African Americans in a Racist Age

Of the nation's 10 million blacks in 1900, more than two-thirds lived in the rural South as sharecroppers and tenant farmers. For them, devastating floods and infes-

**Japanese Immigrant Railroad Workers**
*America's phenomenal post–Civil War industrial growth would have been impossible without the millions of immigrants who labored long hours for low wages.*

**The Gendering of Labor in Corporate America**
*Male bookkeepers and female "type-writers" at the headquarters of the Metropolitan Life Insurance Company in New York City.*

tations of the cotton boll weevil, which spread to the United States from Mexico in the 1890s, worsened an already difficult situation and drove many southern blacks off the land. By 1910 over 20 percent of the southern black population was urban-dwelling. Black men in the cities took jobs in factories, mines, docks, and railroads or became carpenters, plasterers, or bricklayers. Many black women became domestic servants, seamstresses, or workers in laundries and tobacco factories. By 1910, 54 percent of America's black women held jobs.

Across the South, legally enforced racism peaked in the early twentieth century. Local "Jim Crow" laws segregated streetcars, schools, parks, and even cemeteries. The facilities provided for blacks, including the schools, were invariably far inferior. A number of Southern cities imposed residential segregation by law until the Supreme Court restricted it in 1917. Most labor unions excluded black workers. In some courts, black and white witnesses took the oath on separate Bibles! Disfranchised and trapped in a cycle of poverty, poor education, and discrimination, southern blacks faced formidable obstacles.

Fleeing poverty and racism, and drawn by job opportunities, 200,000 blacks migrated to the North between 1890 and 1910. Wartime conditions drew still more in 1917–1918 (see Chapter 23), and by 1920, 1.4 million African Americans lived in the North. They found conditions only slightly better. In northern cities, as in the South, open racism intensified after 1890, as depression and immigration heightened social tensions. (Ironically, the immigrants themselves, competing with blacks for jobs and housing, sometimes exhibited the most intense racial prejudice.) Segregation, though not imposed by law, was a fact of life, enforced by custom and sometimes by violence. Blacks lived in run-down "colored districts," attended dilapidated schools, and worked at the lowest-paying jobs. Their ballots—usually cast for the Republican party, the party of Lincoln—brought little political influence. Republican leaders tolerated only those black politicians who confined themselves to distributing low-level patronage jobs and otherwise kept silent. Even the newest of the mass media, the movies, reinforced racism. D. W. Griffith's *The Birth of a Nation* (1915) disparaged blacks and glorified the Ku Klux Klan.

**Confederate Troops in a Scene from D. W. Griffith's *The Birth of a Nation* (1915)**
*Griffith's technically innovative movie glorified the Confederacy and the Ku Klux Klan, feeding the up-surge of racism in early-twentieth-century America.*

African-American males who volunteered for military service entered a rigidly segregated world where they often faced hostility not only from white soldiers and officers, but from civilians who lived near the bases. The deadly violence that erupted in Brownsville, Texas, in 1906, discussed later in this chapter, was only the best known of many such racially charged encounters.

Smoldering racism elsewhere also occasionally exploded in violence. Antiblack rioters in Atlanta in 1906 murdered twenty-five blacks and burned many black homes. Lynching had peaked in the 1890s, but from 1900 to 1920, an average of about seventy-five still occurred yearly. In certain cases, trumped-up charges justified the murder of blacks whose assertive behavior or economic aspirations whites found intolerable. Some lynchings involved incredible sadism, with large crowds in attendance, and the victim's body mutilated. Authorities did little to stop the practice. At a 1916 lynching in Texas, the mayor warned the mob not to damage the hanging tree, since it was on city property.

For all their adversity, or in part because of it, blacks developed group cohesion and a vigorous culture. Black religious life, centered in the African Methodist Episcopal church, was a bulwark of support. African-American women in northern cities, drawing on strategies dating to the slavery era, relied on networks of relatives and neighbors to provide child care when both parents worked. A handful of black colleges and universities such as Fisk in Nashville and Howard in Washington, D.C., carried on against heavy odds. Dedicated teachers and administrators persevered to build a network of black colleges. John Hope (1868–1936), a Brown University graduate who taught classics at Atlanta's Morehouse College and in 1906 became its president, assembled a distinguished faculty, championed the cause of African-American higher education, and vigorously fought racial segregation. His sister Jane (Hope) Lyons was dean of women at Spelman College, another black educational institution in Atlanta.

The urban black community also included several black-owned insurance companies and banks and a small elite of entrepreneurs, teachers, ministers, and lawyers. A black prizefighter, Jack Johnson, won the heavyweight boxing championship in 1908. Although major league baseball excluded blacks, a thriving Negro League attracted a big following in black America.

Meanwhile, new African-American musical idioms emerged. Scott Joplin turned the music of black bars and "honky-tonks" into ragtime, which became highly popular. The blues, rooted in the chants of southern sharecroppers, gained recognition with the songs of W. C. Handy, including the classic "St. Louis Blues" (1914). Among urban blacks, jazz was gaining popularity (see A Place in Time, Chapter 20). Originating in New Orleans in the 1890s, jazz moved northward around the First World War, eventually to win recognition as America's greatest original musical achievement.

## Corporate Boardrooms, Factory Floors

The late-nineteenth-century corporate consolidation that produced such giants as Carnegie Steel and Standard Oil accelerated in the early twentieth century. For a time, more than 260 companies annually were swallowed up in mergers. This era also gave rise to holding companies—giant conglomerates that owned a number of corporations engaged in the same kind of business. The $1.4 billion United States Steel Company, which arose in 1901 when financiers led by J. P. Morgan bought Andrew Carnegie's steel business and combined it with others, controlled 80 percent of all U.S. steel production. Repeating the same pattern, Morgan in 1902 consolidated six competing companies into the International Harvester Company to gain control of the farm-implement business. William C. Durant in 1908 founded the General Motors Company, which, with backing from the Du Pont Corporation, bought up various independent automobile manufacturers, from the inexpensive Chevrolet to the luxury Cadillac.

Many workers benefited from the prevailing good times. Industrial workers' average annual real wages (defined, that is, in terms of actual purchasing power) rose from $532 in the late nineteenth century to $687 by 1915. In railroading and other unionized industries, wages climbed still higher. But even with the dollar worth far more than today such wages could barely support a family.

To survive, entire families went to work. Two-thirds of immigrant girls entered the labor force in the early 1900s, working as factory help or domestics or in small establishments like laundries and bakeries. Child-labor statistics, although sketchy, suggest that in 1910 the nonfarm labor force included at least 1.6 million children aged ten to fifteen working in factories, mills, tenement sweatshops, and street trades such as shoe shining and newspaper vending. The total may have been higher, since many "women workers" listed in the census were in fact young girls. One investigator found a girl of five working at night in a South Carolina textile mill.

For all laborers, the hours were long and the hazards great. Despite the 8-hour movement of the 1880s, the av-

**Child Worker**
*A young girl sells newspapers near an elevated train station in New York City, 1896.*

### Children in the Labor Force,[*] 1880–1930

|  | 1880 | 1890 | 1900 | 1910 | 1920 | 1930 |
|---|---|---|---|---|---|---|
| Total number of children aged 10–15 (in millions) | 6.6 | 8.3 | 9.6 | 10.8 | 12.5 | 14.3 |
| Total number of children employed (in millions) | 1.1 | 1.5 | 1.7 | 1.6 | 1.4 | 0.7 |
| Percentage of children employed | 16.8 | 18.1 | 18.2 | 15.0 | 11.3 | 4.7 |

* Nonagricultural workers.
*Source: The Statistical History of the United States from Colonial Times to the Present* (Stamford, Conn.: Fairfield Publishers, 1965).

**Frederick W. Taylor (1856–1915)**

*Taylor's efforts to rationalize—and speed up—industrial production through the principles of "Scientific Management" contributed to a vogue of "efficiency" in Progressive-era America.*

erage worker in 1900 still toiled 9½ hours a day. Some southern textile mills required workdays of 12 or 13 hours. Few employers accepted responsibility for work-related accidents and illnesses. Vacations and retirement benefits were practically unheard of.

For new industrial workers accustomed to rural labor, the discipline of the time clock and the machine forced major adjustments. Efficiency experts used time-and-motion studies to speed up production and to make human workers as predictable as machines. In *Principles of Scientific Management* (1911), Frederick W. Taylor explained how to increase output by standardizing job routines and rewarding the fastest workers. *Efficiency* became a popular catchword.

## Workers Organize; Socialism Advances

Confronting such conditions, workers continued to organize. The American Federation of Labor (AFL) grew from fewer than half a million members in 1897 to some 4 million by 1920. But this was still only about 20 percent of the nonfarm labor force. With thousands of immigrants hungry for jobs, union activities could be risky. The boss could always fire an "agitator" and hire a docile newcomer. Judicial hostility also plagued the labor movement. In one of many anti-union court decisions, the Supreme Court in the 1908 *Danbury Hatters* case found union boycotts in support of strikes a "conspiracy in restraint of trade" and thus a violation of the Sherman Anti-Trust Act.

The AFL's strength remained in the skilled trades and not in the factories and mills where most immigrants and women worked. A few unions did try to reach the laborers at the lower end of the scale. The International Ladies' Garment Workers' Union (ILGWU), organized in 1900 by immigrants working in New York City's needle trades, conducted a successful strike in 1909 and another after the 1911 Triangle fire.

For the women on the picket lines, these strikes were both exhilarating and frightening. Some were beaten by police; others fired. The 1909 strike began when young Clara Lemlich jumped up as the speech-making droned on at a protest rally and passionately called for a strike. Thousands of women garment workers stayed off the job the next day.

Another union that targeted the most exploited workers was the Industrial Workers of the World (IWW), nicknamed the Wobblies, founded in Chicago in 1905. The IWW's colorful leader was William D. "Big Bill" Haywood, a giant of a man and a compelling orator. Born in Salt Lake City, Haywood became a miner as a boy and in 1896 joined the militant, Denver-based Western Federation of Miners. In 1905 he was acquitted of complicity in the assassination of an antilabor former governor of Idaho, Frank Steunenberg.

Never large, the Wobblies' membership probably peaked at around thirty thousand, mostly western miners, lumbermen, fruit pickers, and itinerant laborers. But it captured the imagination of the cultural rebels of New York City's Greenwich Village, where Haywood often visited. Its greatest success came in 1912, when it won a bitter textile strike in Lawrence, Massachusetts. This victory owed much to two women: Elizabeth Gurley Flynn, a fiery Irish-American IWW orator, and Margaret Sanger, a leader of the birth-control movement, who publicized the cause by sending strikers' children to sympathizers in New York City for temporary care.

Despite much fire-breathing rhetoric, the IWW's reputation for violence was much exaggerated. Nevertheless, it faced harassment through arrests and prosecution by government officials, especially during World War I, and by 1920 its strength was broken.

Other workers, as well as some middle-class Americans, turned to socialism. All socialists advocated an end to capitalism and backed public ownership of factories, utilities, railroads, and communications systems, but they differed on how to achieve these goals. The revolutionary ideology of German social theorist Karl Marx won a few converts, but the vision of democratic socialism achieved at the ballot box proved more appealing. In 1900 democratic socialists formed the Socialist Party of America (SPA). They included Morris Hillquit, a Russian-Jewish immigrant and New York City labor organizer; Victor Berger, the leader of the German socialists of Milwaukee; and Eugene V. Debs, the Indi-

**Eugene V. Debs (1855–1926)**
*The much-beloved, much-reviled Socialist leader speaks in Canton, Ohio, in 1918, shortly before he was jailed for his opposition to U.S. intervention in World War I.*

ana labor leader. The SPA's most popular speaker, Debs was its presidential candidate five times between 1900 and 1920.

Socialism's high-water mark came around 1912, when SPA membership stood at 118,000. Debs won over 900,000 votes for president that year (about 6 percent of the total), and the Socialists elected a congressman (Berger) and hundreds of municipal officials. The Intercollegiate Socialist Society carried the message to college and university campuses. The party also boasted thirteen daily newspapers and some three hundred weeklies, many published in foreign languages for immigrant members.

The upsurge in Socialist votes represented only one sign of rising discontent. As the social consequences of industrialization became ever more palpable, the demand for government action first voiced by the Populists in the 1890s grew more insistent.

# The Progressive Movement Takes Shape

Intellectuals increasingly challenged the ideological foundations of a business-dominated social order, and writers and journalists publicized the human toll of industrialization. Soon reform thundered over the nation as activists sought to make government more democratic, eradicate dangerous conditions in cities and factories, and curb corporate power. Awed by the energy and diversity of these efforts, Americans grouped them under a single label: the progressive movement.

## Progressivism: An Overview

What was progressivism? First, at the most basic level, it was a political response to industrialization and its social by-products: immigration, urban growth, the growth of corporate power, and the widening of class divisions. Second, it was distinct from populism, the reform movement that preceded it. Whereas populism attracted aggrieved farmers, progressivism's strength lay in the cities. Progressivism enlisted far more journalists, academics, and social theorists than did populism. Finally, the progressives were *reformers,* not radicals. They wanted to remedy the social evils spawned by capitalism, not destroy the system itself.

But which aspects of the new industrial capitalist order most needed attention, and what remedies were required? These basic questions stirred deep disagreements. Indeed, progressivism was never a wholly cohesive, unified movement; instead, it constituted an array of reform activities that sometimes overlapped and sometimes diverged. Many reformers insisted that restoring democracy required stricter regulation of business, from local transit companies to the almighty trusts. Others, emphasizing the humanitarian theme, called for laws to protect workers and the urban poor. Still others concentrated on reforming the structure of government, especially at the municipal level. Finally, some reformers, viewing immigration, urban immorality, and social disorder as the central problems, fought for immigration restriction, the abolition of prostitution and saloons, and other social-control strategies. All this contributed to the mosaic of progressive reform.

And who were the progressives? Like the movement itself, they comprised a diverse lot. The native-born Protestant middle class, including the new white-collar professionals, was certainly central, but on issues affecting factory workers and slum dwellers, the urban-immigrant political machines—and workers themselves—provided critical support. Even corporate leaders helped shape business-regulation measures when pressure for such regulation became irresistible.

The initial reform impetus came not from the political parties but from private groups with names like the Playground Association of America and the American League for Civic Improvement. In this era of organiza-

tions, all the major progressive reforms drew strength from organized interest groups.

Closely related to this organizational impulse was the progressives' emphasis on a "scientific" approach to social problems. Scientific and technological expertise underlay the new industrial order, and progressives tended to believe that such expertise would also solve the social problems spawned by industrialism. Progressives marshaled social research, expert opinion, and statistical data to support their various causes.

Some historians, stressing progressivism's technological and managerial aspects, portray it as an organizational stage that all modernizing societies pass through. This is a useful perspective, provided one realizes that "progressivism" was not some automatic process unfolding independently of human will. Eloquent leaders, gifted journalists, earnest ministers, and energetic organizers all played a role. Human emotion—whether indignation over child labor, intense moralism, fear of the alien, visions of a happier future, or political ambition—drove the movement forward. Progressivism, in short, was not an impersonal historical force. The term is a useful general description of the activities and concerns of many thousands of individual Americans in the early twentieth century.

### Intellectuals Lay the Groundwork

A group of turn-of-the-century thinkers helped reorient American social thought and, in the process, lay the ideological foundation for progressivism. William Graham Sumner and other Gilded Age intellectuals had argued that Charles Darwin's theory of evolutionary progress through natural selection supported an ideology of unrestrained economic competition. The assault on this version of Social Darwinism, launched by Lester Ward, Edward Bellamy, and the Social Gospel leaders, intensified as the new century opened.

One innovator was the eccentric but brilliant Thorstein Veblen, a Norwegian-American from Minnesota who earned a Ph.D. from Yale in 1884. In *The Theory of the Leisure Class* (1899),

**A Poor Neighborhood in Philadelphia, c. 1915**
*Scenes like this in the immigrant wards of America's great cities stirred middle-class reformers to action at the turn of the century.*

Veblen brilliantly satirized the lifestyles of the Gilded Age business elite. Later he would argue that engineers, shaped by the discipline of the machine, were better fitted to lead society than the business class. Veblen epitomized the admiration for efficiency, science, and technical expertise so central to the progressive impulse.

Historians, too, contributed to the new currents of thought. In *An Economic Interpretation of the Constitution* (1913), for example, Charles A. Beard gave ammunition to progressive reformers seeking to curb big business by arguing that the Constitution makers of 1787 had served the interests of the moneyed class of their day. Mary Ritter Beard (Charles Beard's wife and collaborator), in such books as *Woman's Work in Municipalities* (1915), spotlighted groups that traditional histories ignored.

Harvard philosopher William James, meanwhile, in his influential 1907 essay *Pragmatism,* argued that truth emerges not from abstract theorizing but from experience. James's emphasis on the fluidity of knowledge and the importance of practical action contributed to the progressive mood of reformism and skepticism toward established orthodoxies.

James much admired Jane Addams, whose settlement house serving Chicago's immigrants exemplified his pragmatic philosophy. In *Democracy and Social Ethics* (1902), Addams criticized excessive individualism and called for a new social ideology rooted in awareness of modern society's complex interdependence.

No thinker better captured progressives' faith in the power of ideas to transform society than Herbert Croly. The son of Manhattan journalist David Croly and the feminist Jane Cunningham, Croly grew up in a cosmopolitan world where social issues were hotly debated. In *The Promise of American Life* (1909), Croly called for an activist government of the kind Alexander Hamilton had advocated, but one that would serve *all* citizens, not merely the capitalist class. To build public support for this enlarged view of government, Croly argued, socially engaged intellectuals must play a key role. In 1914 he founded the *New Republic* magazine to promote progressive ideas.

### New Ideas About Education and the Law

With public school enrollment leaping from about 7 million children in 1870 to more than 23 million in 1920, progressive intellectuals realized that here was a potent engine of social change. The philosopher John Dewey helped transform educational ideas. A just and harmonious society, he insisted, could be built through the intelligent application of the scientific method to social problems. Intelligence, he believed, should be viewed as above all an instrument of social action.

The public schools, Dewey maintained, could be incubators of reform if they embraced the new ethic of social interdependence. Banishing bolted-down chairs and desks from his model school at the University of Chicago, he encouraged children to interact with one another. The ideal school, he said in *Democracy and Education* (1916), would be an "embryonic community" where children shared a harmonious process of intellectual inquiry and social growth. A democratic socialist, Dewey saw educational reform as one step in a broad social and economic transformation.

Colleges and universities also caught the new spirit of civic idealism. Once havens of "useless and harmless recluses," proclaimed the University of Michigan's president in 1899, universities must dedicate themselves to the public good. Princeton's president Woodrow Wilson summed up the new mood in his 1902 inaugural address, "Princeton for the Nation's Service."

Fresh ideas suffused the legal profession as well. For decades, conservative judges, citing ancient precedents, had upheld corporate interests and struck down reform legislation. A few jurists, however, had argued for a more flexible view. In *The Common Law* (1881), law professor Oliver Wendell Holmes had insisted that law must evolve as society changes. In a phrase much quoted by progressives, he had declared, "The life of the law has not been logic; it has been experience." Appointed to the Supreme Court in 1902, Holmes issued a series of eloquent dissents from the opinions of the conservative Court majority.

### Novelists and Journalists Spread the Word

Novelists and journalists stirred reform energies by conveying to middle-class readers the details of corporate wrongdoing, municipal corruption, slum conditions, and factory life. Advances in printing and photo reproduction assured their message a mass audience and sharpened its emotional impact.

In the depression year 1894, Chicago journalist and reformer Henry Demarest Lloyd produced *Wealth Against Commonwealth,* a biting exposé of the Standard Oil Company. Several early-twentieth-century novelists offered compelling indictments of corporate

**Lincoln Steffens
(1866–1936)**

*Steffens, the quintessential muckraker, targeted urban political corruption in* The Shame of the Cities *(1904). Visiting revolutionary Russia in 1919, he declared: "I have seen the future, and it works."*

greed and urban social conditions. In *The Octopus* (1901), Frank Norris portrayed the struggle between California railroad owners and wheat growers. In *Susan Lenox: Her Fall and Rise* (1917), David Graham Phillips explored the links between slum life, political corruption, and prostitution. Theodore Dreiser's *The Financier* (1912) featured a hard-driving business tycoon utterly devoid of a social conscience.

Especially influential in forging the progressive spirit were articles exposing urban political corruption and corporate wrongdoing published in mass-circulation magazines such as *McClure's* and *Collier's*. President Theodore Roosevelt disparagingly nicknamed the authors "muckrakers," but the name stuck as a badge of honor. New York journalist Lincoln Steffens began the exposé vogue in October 1902 with a *McClure's* article on municipal dishonesty in St. Louis, and it soon spread widely.

The muckrakers' journalistic emphasis on facts rather than abstractions could be very powerful. Some reform-minded journalists actually lived for a time as waitresses, store clerks, factory laborers, slum residents, or homeless persons to chronicle more accurately the grim side of life in urban-industrial America. In a 1903 series on working women, for example, Maria Van Vorst discribed her experiences as a "worker" in a Massachusetts shoe factory where women's fingernails literally rotted off as they continually immersed their hands in caustic dyes.

The muckrakers touched a nerve. The circulation of *McClure's* and *Collier's* soared. Some magazine exposés later appeared in book form, including Lincoln Steffens's *The Shame of the Cities* (1904); Ida Tarbell's damning *History of the Standard Oil Company* (1904); and David Graham Phillips's *Treason of the Senate* (1906).

Artists and photographers played a role as well. Painters George Luks, John Sloan, and others, a group later dubbed the "Ashcan School," painted realistic canvases of New York's teeming immigrant life. Lewis Hine continued the tradition of Jacob Riis by photographing factory laborers, especially children with their stunted bodies and sad expressions.

### *Reforming the Political Process*

Progressivism's beginnings lie in the 1890s, as native-born urban elites and middle classes organized reform crusades against corrupt city governments. New York City experienced a succession of anti-Tammany reform spasms in which Protestant clergy helped to rally the forces of righteousness against the bosses. In Detroit the reform administration of Mayor Hazen Pingree (1890–1897) brought honesty to city hall, lowered transit fares, made the tax structure more fair, and provided public baths and other amenities for the city's poor. Pingree once slapped a health quarantine on a brothel where a local business leader was paying a visit, and refused to let the man leave until he promised to back Pingree's reforms.

In 1907 newspaper editor Fremont Older led a crusade against San Francisco's corrupt boss Abe Reuf. Attorney Hiram Johnson, who took over the prosecution of the case when the original prosecutor was gunned down in court, obtained a conviction of Reuf and his cronies. Sternly self-righteous, Johnson embodied the reform spirit—one observer called him "a volcano in perpetual eruption"—and he rode the fame of the Reuf case to the California governorship and the U.S. Senate.

In Toledo, Ohio, a colorful eccentric named Samuel M. "Golden Rule" Jones led the reform crusade. A self-made businessman converted to the Social Gospel, Jones introduced profit sharing in his factory, and as mayor he established playgrounds, free kindergartens, and lodging houses for homeless transients.

As the urban political-reform movement matured, it moved beyond good works or simply "throwing the rascals out." It now also involved analysis of the roots of urban misgovernment, including the uncontrolled private monopolies that provided such basic city services as water, gas, electricity, and public transportation. Municipal reformers passed laws regulating the rates these utilities could charge, taxing them more equitably, and curbing their political influence. The reform mayor of

Cleveland, Tom Johnson, went so far as to advocate public ownership of these companies.

Reflecting the Progressive Era vogue of expertise and efficiency, some municipal reformers advocated *structural* changes in city government. They wanted to substitute professional managers and administrators, chosen in citywide elections, for mayors and aldermen elected on a ward-by-ward basis. Natural disasters sometimes gave a boost to this particular reform. Dayton, Ohio, went to a city-manager system after a ruinous flood in 1913. Supposedly above politics, these experts were expected to run the city like an efficient business.

Who were these municipal reformers? This varied, depending on the issue. The native-born middle class, led by clergymen, newspaper editors, and other opinion molders, provided the initial impetus and core support. Business interests often pushed for citywide elections and the city-manager system—reforms that diminished the immigrant wards' political clout and increased that of the corporate elite. On matters of immediate practical concern to ordinary city dwellers, such as improved municipal services, the reform movement won support from the immigrants and even from political bosses who realized that explosive urban growth was swamping the old, informal system of responding to their constituents' needs.

The municipal-reform effort soon expanded to encompass electoral reform at the state level. By 1910, for example, all states had replaced the old system of voting, by which the voter brought to the polls a preprinted ballot bearing the name of a specific candidate, with the secret ballot, which made it hard to rig elections. Another electoral reform, the direct primary, which originated in Wisconsin in 1903, provided for the selection of candidates for public office by each political party's rank-and-file members rather than by the party bosses.

Some western states inaugurated electoral reforms known as initiative, referendum, and recall. By an initiative, voters can instruct the legislature to consider a specific bill. In a referendum, they can actually enact a law or (in a nonbinding referendum) express their views on a proposed measure. By a recall petition, voters can remove a public official from office by mustering enough signatures. This flurry of electoral reform crested in 1913 with the ratification of the Seventeenth Amendment to the Constitution, providing for the direct election of U.S. senators by the voters at large.

These electoral changes sought to democratize voting, but party leaders and interest groups soon learned to manipulate the new electoral machinery. Ironically, the new procedures appear to have weakened party loyalty and reduced voter interest. Voter-participation rates declined steeply in the early twentieth century, while political activity by organized interest groups increased.

### Protecting Workers, Beautifying the City

If municipal governance, utility regulation, and electoral reform represented the brain of progressivism, the impulse to improve conditions in factories, mills, and slums represented its heart. By 1907, some thirty states had outlawed child labor. A 1903 Oregon law limited women in industry to a ten-hour workday. Other reformers concentrated on industrial safety, welfare programs, and disability benefits for injured workers.

Such measures won support from political bosses in cities with large immigrant populations, such as New York, Cleveland, and Chicago. State senator Robert F. Wagner, a leader of Tammany Hall (New York City's Democratic machine), headed the investigating committee set up after the 1911 Triangle fire. Thanks to this committee's efforts, New York State enacted fifty-six worker-protection laws, including ones permitting pregnancy leaves, and requiring chairs with backs for garment workers. By 1914, spurred by the Triangle disaster, twenty-five states had passed laws making employers liable for job-related injuries or deaths.

Other urban reformers pursued such practical goals as better garbage collection and street cleaning, milk inspection, and public-health programs. In a reform measure that served as a model for many cities and states, the New York legislature in 1901 tightened the regulations governing tenement houses. Drawing on the earlier efforts of Frederick Law Olmsted and others (see Chapter 19), urban-beautification advocates campaigned for parks, boulevards, and street lights and for laws against billboards, smoky factories, and unsightly overhead electrical wires.

An influential voice for urban beautification was Daniel Burnham, chief architect of the 1893 Chicago world's fair. In 1902 Burnham spearheaded a drive to revive Charles L'Enfant's original plan for Washington, D.C. Burnham also developed innovative city plans for Cleveland and San Francisco. But his most impressive achievement was his master plan of 1909 for Chicago, a visionary blueprint for making the city both efficient and aesthetically harmonious. Burnham recommended transforming the lakefront with parks, a museum, and a recreational complex; speeding traffic flow by constructing diagonal avenues across the city's rigid street-grid system; and redesigning the city's congested major thoroughfare, Michigan Avenue.

In Burnham's dream city, Chicago's focal point would be a great new civic center containing a majestic city hall and a vast plaza. Although not all of Burnham's plan was adopted, Chicago in the 1910–1920 decade did spend more than $300 million on urban-development projects based on his ideas. Many urban beautifiers in the Progressive Era shared Burnham's conviction that parks, imposing squares, and monumental public buildings would surely create an orderly, civic-minded urban populace.

### Corporate Regulation

The conviction that big business must be regulated, inherited from the populists, suffused the progressive outlook. Few Americans wanted to destroy the giant corporations, but many became convinced that these enterprises that had benefited from the government's economic policies should also be subject to public supervision. Many states enacted legislation regulating railroads, mines and mills, and other businesses. Public-health officials, factory inspectors, and other regulators monitored corporate America as never before.

No state pursued regulation more avidly than Wisconsin under Governor Robert La Follette (1901–1906). As a Republican congressman in the 1880s, La Follette had feuded with the state party leadership, and in 1900 he won the governorship as an independent. Soon "Fighting Bob" began transforming state government just as various reform mayors were transforming municipal government. Challenging the business interests long dominant in Wisconsin politics, the La Follette administration adopted the direct primary system, set up a railroad regulatory commission, increased corporate taxes, and passed a law limiting campaign spending.

Reflecting progressivism's faith in scientific expertise, La Follette consulted regularly with reform-minded professors at the nearby University of Wisconsin, and set up a legislative reference library so lawmakers could inform themselves about issues rather than relying on political lobbyists. La Follette's reforms gained national attention as the "Wisconsin Idea."

## Progressivism and Social Control: The Movement's Coercive Dimension

The belief that the negative consequences of urban-industrial growth could be remedied through research, legislation, and enlightened social control underlay progressivism's confident spirit but also gave it a repressive, moralistic edge. Indeed, progressive social thought included a number of ingredients—an assurance of moral and intellectual superiority, high confidence in the social applications of science, a readiness to use state power to regulate behavior—that could all too readily turn coercive. While some progressives focused on such problems as child labor, industrial safety, and corporate regulation, others addressed issues of personal behavior. The social problems these reformers addressed were real, but their moralistic rhetoric and the remedies they proposed often betrayed an impulse to impose morality by law.

### Moral Control in the Cities

Fearful of urban social disorder, some reformers campaigned against gambling, amusement parks, dance halls, and the newest moral menace, the movies. The first commercial films were brief comic sequences like *The Sneeze,* but with *The Great Train Robbery* (1903), the movies began to tell stories. In 1914 came Theda Bara in *A Fool There Was,* with its provocative line "Kiss me, my fool!"

Quaint as they seem today, these early movies struck many middle-class Americans as dangerously immoral. Screened in poor neighborhoods in five-cent halls called nickelodeons, they allowed immigrant youth briefly to escape parental supervision. As a New York City garment worker who lived with her Italian immigrant parents later recalled, "The one place I was allowed to go by myself was the movies. My parents wouldn't let me go anywhere else."

This freedom from oversight was precisely what worried progressives. Warning of "nickel madness," they demanded film censorship. Several states and cities set up censorship boards.

Building on the moral-purity crusade of the 1890s, the reformers also targeted prostitution, a major social problem. Male procurers lured young women into the business and then took a share of their income. Women's paltry wages for factory work or domestic

**Instructing Movie Audiences
in Proper Behavior**
*Managers struggled to impose decorum as early
movie audiences, drawn mainly from the ranks of
urban immigrants, freely commented on the film or
otherwise made their opinions known.*

service attracted many to this more lucrative occupation. One prostitute wrote that she was unwilling "to get up at 6:30 . . . and work in a close stuffy room . . . until dark for $6 or $7 a week" when an afternoon with a man could bring in far more. Her math, if not her moral judgment, was accurate.

Addressing this issue in true progressive fashion, the reformers investigated what they called "the social evil." The American Social Hygiene Association (1914), financed by John D. Rockefeller, Jr., sponsored medical research on venereal disease, underwrote "vice investigations" in various cities, and drafted model municipal statutes against prostitution.

Soon this social issue took on symbolic overtones for middle-class reformers as a symptom of urban America's rampant immorality. A "white slave" hysteria gripped the country. Sensationalized books, articles, and films warned that innocent farm girls were being kidnapped and forced into a life of sin in the city. The Mann Act (1910) made it illegal to transport a woman across a state line "for immoral purposes." Amid much fanfare, the red-light districts of New Orleans, Chicago, and other cities were shut down or forced to operate more discreetly.

Hostility toward immigrants, fear of the city, and anxieties about changing sexual mores all fed into the antiprostitution crusade. In 1913 the African-American boxer Jack Johnson was convicted under the new law for transporting a white prostitute across state lines. Tipped off by neighbors and aggrieved spouses, authorities exploited the vague language of the Mann Act to pry into private sexual behavior. Scam artists deliberately entrapped men into Mann Act violations and then blackmailed them.

## Battling Alcohol and Drugs

Temperance had long been part of the American reform agenda, but in the Progressive Era the reformers' tactics and objectives shifted significantly. Earlier campaigns had focused on persuading individuals to give up drink. But with the founding of the Anti-Saloon League (ASL) in 1895, the emphasis shifted to the *legal* abolition of alcoholic beverages.

The ASL was a typical progressive organization. Full-time professionals ran the national office, and Protestant ministers staffed a network of state committees.

**Jack Johnson (1878–1946)**
*Winning the heavyweight title in 1908, the
flamboyant Johnson defeated a
succession of white challengers and became a lightning rod for the volatile
racial tensions of the era. James Earl Jones
starred in a 1970 movie about
Johnson,* The Great White Hope.

The ASL presses in Westerville, Ohio, produced propaganda documenting the role of alcohol and the saloon in health problems, family disorder, political corruption, and workplace inefficiency, and promoted prohibition as the answer.

Alcohol abuse was serious. Annual per capita consumption in 1906–1910 was 2.6 gallons. Alcoholism contributed to domestic abuse, various public health problems, and other social pathologies. But like the antiprostitution crusade, the prohibition campaign was also a symbolic battleground in the culture wars between native-born citizens and the new immigrants. The ASL, while it raised legitimate issues, also embodied Protestant America's impulse to control the immigrant city.

Supported by the Woman's Christian Temperance Union and influential church agencies, the ASL's crusade picked up steam. The Eighteenth Amendment, outlawing the manufacture, sale, or transport of alcoholic beverages, was adopted in 1919.

The Progressive Era also marks the point when Americans first addressed the issue of drug abuse—and for good reason. Opium, derived from poppies, was smoked by Chinese immigrants in "opium dens" dedicated to the purpose. Physicians and patent-medicine manufacturers freely used opium and its derivatives morphine and heroin. (The Bayer drug company marketed heroin commercially in 1898.) Cocaine, extracted from coca leaves, was widely used as well. Coca-Cola contained cocaine until about 1900.

The Progressive Era regulatory impulse quickly targeted these dangerous drugs. Federal efforts included not only the Pure Food and Drug Act but also the Hague Opium Treaty of 1912, a U.S. initiative. The Narcotics Act of 1914, a follow-up to the Hague Treaty, strictly regulated heroin, morphine, cocaine, and other addictive substances. In their battle against drugs, as in their environmental concerns, the progressives anticipated issues that would still confront the nation as the twentieth century closed.

### Immigration Restriction

If the immigrant city posed threats, some reformers concluded, the answer lay in excluding immigrants. Prominent Bostonians formed the Immigration Restriction League in 1894 to promote a literacy test as a means of cutting the influx of immigrants. The American Federation of Labor, fearing job competition, also endorsed restriction.

This reform won support from many progressives. Characteristically, they documented their case with a flourish of scientific expertise. In 1911 a congressional commission produced a massive statistical study allegedly proving the new immigrants' innate degeneracy. Sociologist Edward A. Ross, a prominent pro-

**Ellis Island, 1920**
*Early-twentieth-century immigrants faced rigorous tests that reflected not only public-health concerns but also a rising exclusionary sentiment that culminated in the restrictive Immigration Act of 1924.*

gressive, in 1914 described the typical recent immigrants as "low-browed, big-faced persons of obviously low mentality."

Led by Senator Henry Cabot Lodge of Massachusetts, Congress passed literacy-test bills in 1896, 1913, and 1915, only to see them vetoed by a succession of presidents. In 1917, however, such a bill became law over President Woodrow Wilson's veto. Would-be immigrants also faced rigorous physical examinations and tests in which legitimate public-health concerns became mixed up with anti-immigrant stereotypes of entire ethnic groups as mental or physical defectives. This, too, was part of progressivism's mixed legacy.

### Eugenics: Scientific Bigotry

The starkest example of the perversion of "science" in the Progressive Era was the eugenics movement. Eugenics is the control of reproduction to alter a plant or animal species. Some American eugenicists believed that society itself could be improved through genetic control. In 1904 the Carnegie Foundation funded a genetics research center on Long Island. The director, Charles B. Davenport, a well-known zoologist, was also a racist, anti-Semite, and advocate of immigration restriction. Inspired by Davenport and other eugenicists, certain states legalized the forced sterilization of criminals, sex offenders, and persons adjudged mentally deficient. In the 1927 case *Buck* v. *Bell*, the Supreme Court upheld the constitutionality of such laws.

A similar outlook pervaded Madison Grant's *The Passing of the Great Race* (1916). Grant, in many respects an embodiment of the best in progressivism, supported many civic causes. Yet in *The Passing* he used pseudoscientific data to justify a vicious diatribe against Jews, blacks, and southern and eastern Europeans. Jesus, he insisted, was not really a Jew but an unrecognized "Nordic." Anticipating ideas that Adolf Hitler would soon bring to fruition, Grant called for racial segregation, immigration restriction, and the forced sterilization of "unfit" groups, including "worthless race types."

### Racism and Progressivism

As Grant's work suggests, racism rose to a high pitch during the Progressive Era. Individual progressives like settlement house leader Lillian Wald and muckraker Ray Stannard Baker protested racial injustice. Settlement house worker Mary White Ovington helped found the National Association for the Advancement of Colored People (see below) and wrote *Half a Man* (1911), a study of the emotional scars of racial prejudice. But the progressive movement as a whole did little as blacks were lynched, disfranchised, and discriminated against. Many progressives viewed blacks, like immigrants, not as potential reform allies but as a source of social menace and danger to be studied and controlled.

In the South, progressive reformers often led the movement for black disfranchisement and segregation. Southern woman-suffrage leaders argued that granting women the vote would strengthen white supremacy. Numerous southern politicians—including Governor James K. Vardaman of Mississippi and Senator Ben Tillman of South Carolina—supported progressive reforms while simultaneously pursuing viciously antiblack policies.

Racism pervaded Washington during Woodrow Wilson's presidency (1913–1921). Born in Virginia and reared in Georgia, Wilson displayed a patronizing attitude toward blacks. He praised the racist movie *The Birth of a Nation* and acquiesced as southerners in his cabinet and in the Congress (some of them powerful committee chairmen) imposed rigid segregation on all levels of the government.

## Blacks and Women Organize

For blacks and women, especially those of the urban middle class, the early twentieth century was a time of intense activity and intellectual ferment. Both groups had ample reason for dissatisfaction, and both organized to address those grievances.

### Controversy Among African Americans

The nation's foremost black leader from the 1890s until his death in 1915 was Booker T. Washington. Born in slavery in Virginia in 1856, the son of a slave woman and her white master, Washington at the age of sixteen enrolled at a freedmen's school in Hampton, Virginia. In 1881 Washington organized in Alabama a state vocational school for blacks that eventually became Tuskegee University.

Although Washington secretly contributed to organizations fighting racial discrimination, his public message was one of accommodation to a racist society. In

**A New Black Leadership**

*Ida Wells-Barnett, crusader against lynching, and W. E. B. Du Bois, outspoken critic of Booker T. Washington and author of the classic* The Souls of Black Folk. *The challenge, wrote Du Bois, was to find a way "to be both a Negro and an American."*

chisement "a fatal blow . . . to the Negro's political rights and liberty." Another opponent was the formidable black journalist Ida Wells-Barnett. Driven from Memphis in 1892 when a mob destroyed her offices, she settled in Chicago and mounted a national anti-lynching campaign. Wells-Barnett sharply criticized Booker T. Washington's virtual silence on the subject.

Washington's most potent challenge came from W. E. B. Du Bois (1868–1963). America's first black Ph.D. (from Harvard in 1895), Du Bois taught from 1896 to 1910 at Atlanta University. A cultivated scholar of refined manners and a distinguished appearance, Du Bois set forth his differences with Washington in *The Souls of Black Folk* (1903). Rejecting Washington's call for patience and the exclusive cultivation of manual skills, Du Bois demanded for blacks the same intellectual opportunities open to whites. Furthermore, he declared, blacks must actively resist all forms of racism. Du Bois's assertiveness and militance set the direction of African-American activism in the new century.

### The Founding of the NAACP

In 1905, under Du Bois's leadership, blacks who favored vigorous resistance to racism and rejected Booker T. Washington's accommodationist position held a conference at Niagara Falls. For the next few years, participants in the "Niagara Movement" met annually.

Meanwhile, a group of white reformers had also grown dissatisfied with Washington's cautiousness. Their leader was newspaper publisher Oswald Garrison Villard, grandson of abolitionist William Lloyd Garrison. In 1909 Villard and his allies, with Du Bois and other blacks from the Niagara Movement, formed the National Association for the Advancement of Colored People (NAACP). Rejecting Washington's approach, the NAACP called for vigorous activism, including legal challenges, to achieve political equality for blacks and full integration into American life. Attracting the urban black middle class, the NAACP by 1914 had six thousand members in fifty branches.

### Revival of the Woman-Suffrage Movement

As late as 1910, women could vote in only four thinly populated western states: Wyoming, Utah, Colorado, and Idaho. In six state referenda after 1896, woman suffrage failed. But the progressive reform movement, in which women played a leading role, infused the cause

a famous address in Atlanta in 1895, he insisted that the first task of America's blacks must be to acquire useful vocational skills. Once blacks proved their economic value, he predicted, racism would fade; meanwhile, they must patiently accept their lot.

Washington lectured widely, and once dined at the White House with Theodore Roosevelt. His autobiography, *Up From Slavery* (1901), recounted his rise from poverty through honesty, hard work, and the help of kindly patrons—themes familiar to a generation reared on Horatio Alger.

Many blacks revered Washington, but northern blacks increasingly challenged his ideas. With racism rising and blacks' status worsening, Washington's accommodationist message and his optimistic predictions seemed unrealistic. William Monroe Trotter, the editor of a black newspaper, the *Boston Guardian,* in 1902 called Washington's acceptance of black disfran-

**A Revived Women's Movement**
*As the drive for woman suffrage gained momentum, activists put up posters in Washington State (above) and demonstrated in New York State in 1912 (right). New York State granted women the vote in 1917, and in 1920 the Nineteenth Amendment was ratified.*

with new vitality. Middle-class women found disfranchisement especially galling, particularly when recently arrived immigrant men could vote. A vigorous suffrage movement in Great Britain reverberated in America as well.

Like progressivism itself, the renewal of the women's movement started at the grassroots, as local suffragists developed innovative forms of publicity, including street meetings and parades. Suffrage campaigns in California (1911) and New York (1915), though unsuccessful, gave evidence of a fresh drive and militancy.

New leaders translated this energy into a revitalized national movement. When Susan B. Anthony retired in 1900 from the presidency of the National American Woman Suffrage Association (NAWSA), Carrie Chapman Catt of Iowa succeeded her. Under Catt's shrewd direction, NAWSA adopted the so-called Winning Plan: grassroots organization with tight central coordination.

As suffragists lobbied legislators, distributed literature, and organized parades and rallies, state after state fell into the suffrage column. A key victory came in 1917 when New York State voters approved a woman-suffrage referendum.

NAWSA's membership remained largely white, native-born, and middle class. Few black, immigrant, or working-class women joined, and some upper-class women *opposed* the reform. The leader of the "Antis," Josephine Dodge, a wealthy New York City widow, in 1911 formed the National Association Opposed to Woman Suffrage. Women already had behind-the-scenes influence, Dodge argued; to invade the male realm of politics would only tarnish their moral and spiritual role.

Not all suffragists accepted Catt's strategy. One who did not was Alice Paul, who as a student in Great Britain had observed the militant tactics of the British suffragists. Impatient with NAWSA's state-by-state approach, Paul in 1913 founded the Congressional Union, later renamed the Woman's party, to bring direct pressure on the federal government to enact a woman-suffrage amendment. Focusing their protests on "the party in power"—in this case, the Democrats—Paul and her followers in the war year 1917 picketed the White House round the clock. They posted large signs accusing President Wilson of hypocrisy in championing democracy abroad while opposing woman suffrage at home. Several of the demonstrators were

**Emma Goldman (1869–1940)**
*Anarchist, radical editor, birth-control advocate, and lecturer on avant-garde topics, Goldman, standing in an open car, addresses a predominantly male audience in 1915 in New York City's Union Square.*

arrested, jailed, and when they went on a hunger strike, force-fed.

Thanks in part to women's role in the war effort (see Chapter 23), the tide turned at last. The Nineteenth Amendment, granting women the vote, was ratified in 1920. That November, women across America went to the polls.

## Breaking Out of the "Woman's Sphere"

The suffrage movement did not exhaust women's organizational energies. Women's club members, settlement house leaders, and individual female activists joined in a wide range of reform efforts. These included the campaigns to bring playgrounds and day nurseries to the slums, to abolish child labor, to improve conditions for women workers, and to ban unsafe foods and quack remedies. As Jane Addams observed, the same nurturing impulse that led women to care for their own children also drew them into broader political activism in an industrial era when hazards often came from outside the home as well as inside.

Entrenched cultural assumptions about woman's "sphere" weakened as women became active on many fronts. Penologist Katherine Bement Davis served in these years as the innovative superintendent of a woman's reformatory in Bedford Hills, New York, and then as New York City's commissioner of correc-

**Woman Suffrage Before the Nineteenth Amendment**
*Beginning with Wyoming in 1869, woman suffrage made steady gains in western states before 1920. Further east, key victories came in New York (1917) and Michigan (1918). But much of the East remained an anti-woman-suffrage bastion throughout the period.*

tions. Anarchist Emma Goldman crisscrossed the country lecturing on politics, feminism, and modern drama while coediting a radical monthly, *Mother Earth*. And in 1914 Margaret Sanger began her crusade for birth control, a term that she coined. Sanger fled to Europe to escape arrest on obscenity charges directed against her journal *The Woman Rebel* but returned in 1916 to open the nation's first birth-control clinic, in Brooklyn, New York.

Representative of a vanguard group of women in higher education were Marion Talbot, first dean of women at the University of Chicago; Ellen Richards, who taught home economics at the Massachusetts Institute of Technology; and M. Carey Thomas, president of Bryn Mawr College.

The era's leading feminist intellectual, Charlotte Perkins Gilman, was divorced and living in California when she wrote *Women and Economics* (1898). This influential work probed the origins of female subordination; explored the cultural process of gender stereotyping; and linked the inferior status of women to their economic dependence upon men. Confining women to the domestic sphere, Gilman argued, though necessary at an earlier evolutionary stage, had become outdated and inefficient. She advocated economic independence for women through equality in the workplace; the consolidation of cooking, cleaning, and other domestic tasks; and state-run day-care centers.

Alice Hamilton and Florence Kelley typify women's central role in progressive reform. Hamilton, a Northwestern University bacteriologist, worked with Jane Addams at Hull House. In 1910, combining her scientific expertise with her reform impulses, she conducted a major study of lead poisoning in industry. Appointed an investigator for the U.S. Bureau of Labor in 1911, she became an expert on—and campaigner against—work-related health hazards.

Florence Kelley, the daughter of a Republican congressman from Pennsylvania, became a Hull House resident in 1891. Investigating conditions in factories and sweatshops, Kelley in 1893 helped secure passage of an Illinois law prohibiting child labor and limiting working hours for women. In 1899 she became general secretary of the National Consumers' League, which mobilized consumer pressure to lobby for improved factory conditions. Campaigning for a federal child-labor law, Kelley angrily asked, "Why are seals, bears, reindeer, fish, wild game in the national parks, buffalo, [and] migratory birds all found suitable for federal protection, but not children?"

# National Progressivism— Phase I: Roosevelt and Taft

By around 1905 these varied reform activities were coalescing into a national movement. Symbolically, in 1906 Wisconsin governor Robert La Follette went to Washington as a U.S. senator. Five years before, progressivism had found its first national leader, Theodore Roosevelt.

Bombastic, self-righteous, and jingoistic—but also brilliant, politically savvy, and endlessly interesting—Roosevelt, "TR," became president in 1901 and, for the next 7½ years, made the White House a volcano of activism. Skillfully orchestrating public opinion, the popular young president pursued his goals: labor mediation, consumer protection, conservation, business virtue, and engagement abroad. Roosevelt's activist approach to the presidency permanently enlarged the powers of the office. TR's hand-picked successor, William Howard Taft, lacked the master's political genius, however, and his administration floundered amid sniping among former allies.

## *Roosevelt's Path to the White House*

On September 6, 1901, in Buffalo, anarchist Leon Czolgosz shot William McKinley. It seemed at first that the president would survive, and Vice President Theodore Roosevelt proceeded with a planned hiking trip in New York's Adirondack Mountains. But on September 14, McKinley died. At age forty-two, Theodore Roosevelt was president of the United States.

Many politicians shuddered at the thought of the impetuous Roosevelt as president. Republican kingmaker Mark Hanna exclaimed, "My God, that damned cowboy in the White House!" Roosevelt did, indeed, display many traits associated with the West. The son of an aristocratic

**Teddy Roosevelt Cream Pitcher, c. 1910**
*TR captivated the national imagination like no president since Lincoln. With a gun in one hand and a book in the other, this bit of Americana suggested two of Roosevelt's many interests: hunting and scholarship.*

New York family of Dutch origins, Theodore was sickly as a child. But at the age of eleven, he began a body-building program that, combined with summers in Wyoming, transformed him into a model of physical fitness. When his young wife died in 1884, he stoically carried on. Two years on a Dakota ranch (1884–1886) further toughened him and deepened his enthusiasm for what he termed "the strenuous life."

Plunging into politics at a time when most members of his social class considered it unfit for gentlemen, he served as a state assemblyman, New York City's police commissioner, and a U.S. civil-service commissioner. In 1898, fresh from his Cuban exploits (see Chapter 21), he was elected New York's governor. Two years later, the state's Republican boss, eager to be rid of him, arranged for Roosevelt's nomination as vice president. (Complained Roosevelt, "I would . . . rather be anything, say a history professor, than Vice-President.")

Like everything else he did, Roosevelt found the presidency energizing. "I have been President emphatically . . . ," he once boasted; "I believe in a strong executive." He enjoyed public life and loved the limelight. "When Theodore attends a wedding he wants to be the bride," a relative observed, "and when he attends a funeral he wants to be the corpse." With his toothy grin, machine-gun speech, and amazing energy, Roosevelt dominated the political landscape. When he refused to shoot a bear cub on a hunting trip, a shrewd toy maker marketed a cuddly new product, the Teddy Bear.

### Labor Disputes and Corporate Regulation

The new president's political skills were quickly tested. In May 1902 the United Mine Workers Union (UMW) called a strike to gain not only higher wages and shorter hours but also recognition as a union. The mine own-

ers refused even to talk to the UMW leaders. After five months, with winter looming, TR acted. Summoning the two sides to the White House and threatening to take over the mines, he won their reluctant acceptance of an arbitration commission to settle the dispute. The commission granted the miners a 10 percent wage increase and reduced their working day from ten to nine hours.

TR's approach to labor disputes differed from that of his predecessors, who typically called out the troops to break strikes. Though not consistently prolabor, he defended workers' right to organize. When a prominent mine owner insisted that the miners' welfare be left to those "to whom God in his infinite wisdom has given control of the property interests of the country," Roosevelt derided such "arrogant stupidity."

With his elite background, TR neither feared nor much liked the tycoons of capitalism. The prospect of spending time with "big-money men," he once wrote a friend, "fills me with frank horror." Conservative at heart, he believed that big corporations were essential to national greatness. But he also embraced the progressive conviction that corporate behavior must be regulated. A strict moralist, he held corporations, like individuals, to a high standard.

At the same time, Roosevelt the political realist also understood that many Washington politicians did not share such views—among them Senator Nelson Aldrich of Rhode Island, a wily defender of business interests. Roosevelt's presidency thus involved continuing tension among his moralism, his conservatism, his progressive impulses, and his recognition of the power realities in capitalist America. The first test soon came.

When J. P. Morgan in 1901 formed the United States Steel Company, the nation's first billion-dollar corporation, public uneasiness over business consolidation deepened. As always, TR dashed to the head of the parade. His 1902 State of the Union message gave high

### The Election of 1904

| Candidates | Parties | Electoral Vote | Popular Vote | Percentage of Popular Vote |
|---|---|---|---|---|
| THEODORE ROOSEVELT | Republican | 336 | 7,628,461 | 57.4 |
| Alton B. Parker | Democratic | 140 | 5,084,223 | 37.6 |
| Eugene V. Debs | Socialist | | 402,283 | 3.0 |
| Silas C. Swallow | Prohibition | | 258,536 | 1.9 |

priority to breaking up business monopolies, or "trust-busting." Roosevelt's attorney general soon filed suit against the Northern Securities Company, a giant holding company recently formed to control railroading in the Northwest, for violation of the Sherman Anti-Trust Act. On a speaking tour that summer, Roosevelt called for a "square deal" for all Americans and denounced special treatment for powerful capitalists. "We don't wish to destroy corporations," he insisted, "but we do wish to make them subserve the public good." In 1904, on a 5 to 4 vote, the Supreme Court ordered the Northern Securities Company dissolved.

The Roosevelt administration filed forty-three other antitrust lawsuits. In two key cases not decided until 1911, the Supreme Court ordered the breakup of the Standard Oil Company and the reorganization of the American Tobacco Company to make it less monopolistic.

As the 1904 election neared, Roosevelt made peace with the Republicans' big-business wing, writing cordial letters to J. P. Morgan and other magnates. When the convention that unanimously nominated Roosevelt in Chicago adopted a probusiness platform, $2 million in corporate campaign contributions poured in. The Democratic convention, meanwhile, eager to purge the party of the taint of radicalism, embraced the gold standard and nominated a conservative New York judge, Alton B. Parker.

Trouncing the lackluster Parker, Roosevelt turned to one of his major goals: railroad regulation. He now regarded corporate regulation, rather than dramatic bursts of trust-busting, as a more promising long-term strategy, and this shift underlay his central role in the passage of the Hepburn Act (1906). The Elkins Act (1903) had stiffened the penalties against railroad rebates to favored shippers, and the Hepburn Act imposed further regulations. This measure empowered the Interstate Commerce Commission to set maximum railroad rates and to examine railroads' financial records. It also required standardized bookkeeping to make such inspection easier and curtailed the railroads' distribution of free passes.

The Hepburn Act displayed TR's knack for political bargaining, as he skillfully fenced with Senator Aldrich and other conservatives. In one basic compromise, he agreed to delay tariff reform in return for railroad regulations. Although the measure did not fully satisfy some reformers, it did significantly increase the government's regulatory powers.

## Consumer Protection and Racial Issues

No progressive reform aroused more popular support than the campaign against unsafe and falsely labeled food, drugs, and medicine. Upton Sinclair's *The Jungle* (1906) graphically described the foul conditions in some meatpacking plants. Wrote Sinclair in one vivid passage: "It was too dark in these [packing-house] storage places to see well, but a man could run his hand over these piles of meat and sweep off handfuls of dried dung of rats. These rats were nuisances, and the packers would put poisoned bread out for them, they would die, and then rats, bread, and meat would go into the hoppers together." (The socialist Sinclair also detailed the exploitation of immigrant workers but this message proved less potent. "I aimed at the nation's heart, but hit it in the stomach," he later lamented.)

Other muckrakers exposed useless or dangerous patent medicines, many of which contained cocaine, opium, or a heavy dose of alcohol. One tonic "recommended for treatment of the alcohol habit" itself contained 26.5 percent alcohol! The peddlers of these potions freely claimed that they could cure cancer, grow hair, and restore sexual potency.

Sensing the public mood, Roosevelt supported the Pure Food and Drug Act and the Meat Inspection Act, both passed in 1906. The former outlawed the sale of adulterated foods or drugs and required accurate ingredient labels; the latter imposed strict sanitary requirements for meatpackers and created a program of federal meat inspection. The more reputable food-processing, meatpacking, and medicinal companies, eager to regain public confidence, supported these regulatory measures.

On racial matters, Roosevelt compiled a marginally better record than that of many other politicians in this dismally racist age. On the positive side, he appointed a black as head of the Charleston customhouse despite white opposition, and he closed a Mississippi post office rather than yield to demands that he dismiss the black postmistress. In a gesture of symbolic import, he met with Booker T. Washington at the White House. The worst blot on his record came in 1906, when he dishonorably discharged an entire regiment of 167 black soldiers, including Congressional Medal of Honor winners, stationed in Brownsville, Texas, because some unidentified members of the regiment, goaded by racist taunts, had staged a raid on the town in

**Early-Twentieth-Century Girl Scouts Discover Nature**

*The scouting movement, originating in England, was one of many expressions of a rising back-to-nature movement in an era of rapid urban growth and industrialization.*

which a civilian was killed. The "Brownsville Incident" incensed black Americans. (In 1972, when most of the men involved were long dead, Congress removed the dishonorable discharges from their records.)

## *The Conservation Movement*

By 1900, decades of urban-industrial growth and western expansion had taken a heavy toll on the land. In the West, land-use disputes burst into the political arena as mining and timber interests, farmers, ranchers, sheep growers, and preservationists advanced competing claims.

Whereas business interests and boosters preached exploitation of the West's resources, groups such as the Sierra Club sought to preserve wilderness areas for their beauty and aesthetic appeal. Socially prominent easterners also embraced the wilderness cause. Thanks to their efforts, Congress in 1891 authorized the president to designate public lands as forest reserves. Under this act, presidents Harrison and Cleveland set aside some 35 million acres.

In the early twentieth century, a wilderness vogue swept America. Amid cities and factories, the unspoiled

wilderness offered the promise of tranquillity and solace. As Sierra Club president John Muir observed, "I never saw a discontented tree." Popular writers evoked the tang of the campfire and the lure of the primitive. Summer camps, which began in the 1890s, as well as the Boy Scouts (1910) and Girl Scouts (1912), gave city children a taste of wilderness living.

The wilderness vogue seeped into politics. Resource-management issues frequently pitted state and local authorities against the federal government. Local politicians, echoing their region's business groups, charged that the preservationists' wilderness campaign jeopardized western economic development.

Between the wilderness enthusiasts and the developers stood a cadre of government professionals who saw the public domain as a resource to be managed scientifically. This position found its ablest advocate in Gifford Pinchot. Appointed by President Roosevelt in 1905 to head the new U.S. Forest Service, Pinchot campaigned not for preservation but for conservation—the planned, regulated use of forest lands for public and commercial purposes.

Wilderness advocates viewed Pinchot's Forest Service warily. They welcomed his opposition to mindless exploitation but worried that Pinchot's multiuse approach would lead to commercial development in unspoiled wilderness areas. As one Sierra Club member wrote, "It is true that trees are for human use. But there are aesthetic uses as well as commercial uses—uses for the spiritual wealth of us all, as well as for the material wealth of some." Professional conservationists, in turn, dismissed the wilderness advocates as sentimental amateurs.

Theodore Roosevelt was by temperament a preservationist. In 1903 he spent a blissful few days camping in California's Yosemite National Park with John Muir. "When I hear of the destruction of a species," he wrote, "I feel just as if all the works of some great writer had perished." But Roosevelt the politician backed the conservationists' call for planned development. In this spirit he supported the National Reclamation Act of 1902 that earmarked the proceeds of public-land sales in the West for water management in the arid Southwest and set up the Reclamation Service to plan and construct dams and irrigation projects.

As historian William Cronon has noted, this measure (also known as the Newlands Act for its sponsor, an aptly named Nevada congressman) ranks with the Northwest Ordinance for its importance in promoting the development of a vast region of the continent.

**Teddy Roosevelt at Yosemite**

*TR loved the West, where he had found revitilization as a youth. As president he promoted wilderness preservation and better management of natural resources.*

Under director Frederick H. Newell, the Reclamation Service undertook projects that made possible settlement and productivity in the vast arid region between the Rockies and the Pacific Coast. The Roosevelt Dam in Arizona spurred the growth of Phoenix; the Arrowrock Dam on the Boise River converted thousands of barren acres in southern Idaho into fertile farmland. The law required those who profited from these reclamation projects to repay the government for the construction costs, creating a revolving fund for further projects. The Newlands Act and other federal measures of these years made possible the development of the West from a series of isolated "island settlements" into an interconnected and thriving region.

The competition for scarce water resources in the West sometimes led to bitter political battles. The Los Angeles basin, for example, with 40 percent of California's population in 1900, found itself with only 2 percent of the state's available surface water. In 1907 the city used highly dubious maneuvers to derail a Reclamation Service project intended for the farmers of California's Owens Valley, more than 230 miles to the north, and instead diverted the precious water to Los Angeles.

Meanwhile President Roosevelt also backed Pinchot's multiuse land-management program. Following Pinchot's advice, Roosevelt set aside 200 million acres of public land (85 million of them in Alaska) as national forests, mineral reserves, and potential water-power sites. But this, too, provoked opposition in the West, and in 1907 Congress rescinded the president's authority to create national forests in six timber-rich western states. Roosevelt signed the bill, but only after designating 16 million acres in the six states as national forests!

With Roosevelt's blessing, Pinchot organized a White House conservation conference for the nation's governors in 1908. Here experts discussed the utilitarian benefits of resource management. John Muir and other wilderness preservationists were not invited. But the struggle between wilderness purists and multiuse advocates went on (see A Place in Time).

Using magazine articles to rally public support, preservationists won key victories in these years. For example, campaigns by private citizens saved a large grove of California's giant redwoods and a lovely stretch of the Maine coastline from commercial depredation. Women reformers played a key role in many of these efforts.

The national-park system also grew stronger in these years. Beginning with Yellowstone in 1872, thirteen national parks had been created by 1916, but with

### The Election of 1908

| Candidates | Parties | Electoral Vote | Popular Vote | Percentage of Popular Vote |
| --- | --- | --- | --- | --- |
| WILLIAM H. TAFT | Republican | 321 | 7,675,320 | 51.6 |
| William Jennings Bryan | Democratic | 162 | 6,412,294 | 43.1 |
| Eugene V. Debs | Socialist | | 420,793 | 2.8 |
| Eugene W. Chafin | Prohibition | | 253,840 | 1.7 |

## Hetch Hetchy Valley, California

At the turn of the century, one of the loveliest spots in California's Sierras was Hetch Hetchy Valley. The Indian name referred to the Valley's grassy meadows. Here glaciers and the Tuolumne River had carved deep, sharp-edged gorges of spectacular beauty.

But when officials of San Francisco, 150 miles away, visited Hetch Hetchy, they saw not only beauty but a solution to their city's serious water problems. A dam at the valley's mouth would create a vast reservoir that could supply water for San Francisco and pay for itself as a hydroelectric power source.

**John Muir in Hetch Hetchy Valley, 1895,**
by Gilbert Dellinger, 1963
*This painting, based on a photograph, portrays the influential nature writer and Sierra Club president in the valley he loved and fought unsuccessfully to save.*

Because Hetch Hetchy lay within Yosemite National Park, created by Congress in 1890, the secretary of the interior at first rejected San Francisco's application to dam the Tuolumne. But the city applied again in 1908, two years after an earthquake and fire devastated San Francisco, and this time the secretary approved. The application needed congressional approval as well, however. Opponents of the plan geared up confidently for a campaign to defeat it.

The Sierra Club and its president, John Muir, a revered nature writer and wilderness advocate, led the opposition. Muir loved Yosemite, and the plan for a water-power project in the park dismayed him. Going public, Muir and his associates alerted wilderness groups across the nation and published magazine articles describing the beauty of the valley that would be forever hidden under the waters of the reservoir.

Muir compared the flooding of Hetch Hetchy to the willful destruction of a great cathedral. Amid rampant urban growth, he argued, Americans needed wilderness for their spiritual well-being. He wrote bitterly, "These temple destroyers, devotees of ravaging commercialism, seem to have a perfect contempt for Nature, and instead of lifting their eyes to the God of the Mountains, lift them to the Almighty Dollar."

But the project had attracted powerful backers, including Gifford Pinchot, head of the U.S. Forest Service. Pinchot advocated a multiuse approach to national forests and wilderness areas, and the Hetch Hetchy project fit his vision.

San Francisco authorities pushed hard for the plan. The reservoir, they argued, could support a variety of recreational activities. The San Francisco *Chronicle* called the dam's critics "hoggish and mushy esthetes." San Francisco's chief engineer ridiculed them as "short-haired women and long-haired men."

President Theodore Roosevelt at first endorsed the plan. However, he then vacillated as opposition grew. In the national parks, he said in 1908, "all wild things should be protected and the scenery kept wholly unmarred."

The battle culminated in 1913 with hearings before the Public Lands Committee of the U.S. House of Representatives. Both sides mounted a final effort. Opponents rallied public opinion through more magazine articles; backers lobbied members of Congress. Pinchot, testifying in support of the application, offered his own utilitarian definition of conservation: "The fundamental principle . . . is that of use, to take every part of the land and its resources and put it to that use . . . which . . . will serve the most people." A California congressman pointed out that the "old barren rocks" of Hetch Hetchy Valley had a market value of only about $300,000, whereas the proposed dam would be worth many times that amount. Another legislator posed the issue in dramatic terms: "We all love the sound of whispering winds amid the trees," he said, but "the wail of a hungry baby will make us forget it."

Late in 1913, despite a blizzard of opposition mail, both houses of Congress passed the Hetch Hetchy dam bill by large margins. Within a year John

Muir was dead of pneumonia—but really, some said, he had died of a broken heart.

The dam project proceeded slowly, at twice the estimated cost. The first water reached San Francisco in 1934. The vision of Hetch Hetchy reservoir as a vacation paradise remained unfulfilled. Writes environmental historian Stephen Fox: "As the water level rose and fell with the changing seasons the shoreline was marred by slimy mud and decaying vegetation. Nothing could grow at the edge of the artificial lake. Under moonlight, with tree trunks scattered around like so many bodies, it resembled a battlefield one day after the fight: a wasteland bearing stark testimony to man's befuddled ingenuity."

But though the dam's opponents lost this battle, historians point out that the struggle had a larger meaning: for the first time, over a five-year period, the American public debated the aesthetic implications of a major public-works project. In the nineteenth century, such a debate would have been unthinkable. Hetch Hetchy helped put wilderness preservation on the public agenda.

Hetch Hetchy retains its power to stir emotions. In 1987 Secretary of the Interior Donald Hodel made headlines by proposing that the reservoir be drained and the valley be restored to its natural state. This, Hodel said, would relieve overcrowding in Yosemite Valley, forty miles to the south. Environmentalists expressed interest; San Francisco officials reacted with the same outrage their predecessors had shown seventy-five years before toward opponents of their cherished project. Whether Hodel's ideas will ever be implemented remains to be seen. Meanwhile, Hetch Hetchy Valley lies submerged under three hundred feet of water, buried but not forgotten.

## Hetch Hetchy: From the Sublime to the Utilitarian

*California's lovely Hetch Hetchy Valley was a favorite subject of nineteenth-century artists, as this romantic painting by Albert Bierstadt, dating from the 1870s, reveals. When the Tuolumne River was dammed to create a reservoir for San Francisco, only the mountainous peaks above the waterline stood, silent reminders of the wild grandeur that had been sacrificed.*

no overall management despite growing numbers of park visitors. To oversee these preserves, Congress in 1916 created the National Park Service. Earlier, the Antiquities Act (1906) had protected archaeological sites, especially in the Southwest. A number of sites preserved under this law eventually became national parks.

Environmental health hazards roused progressives' concern as well. With factories polluting the air and discharging poisons into rivers, some urban reformers campaigned for restrictive legislation. Roosevelt was sympathetic, especially when personally affected. A power plant spewing black smoke near the White House roused him to threaten legal action.

Along with millions of acres of national forest, Roosevelt created fifty-three wildlife reserves, sixteen national monuments, and five new national parks. Just as important, Roosevelt kept environmental concerns in the public mind. Declaring conservation "the most vital internal question" facing America in his first State of the Union message, he gave priority to an issue that reverberates still.

### Taft in the White House

Roosevelt had pledged not to run in 1908, and to the sorrow of millions, he kept his promise. The Republican party's most conservative elements easily regained party control. They nominated Roosevelt's choice, Secretary of War William Howard Taft, for president but

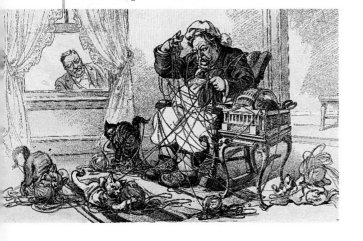

**"Goodness Gracious! I Must Have Been Dozing"**
*This 1910 cartoon in the humor magazine* Puck *lampoons President Taft's mounting political difficulties and suggests ex-president Theodore Roosevelt's unhappiness with his designated successor.*

chose a conservative vice-presidential nominee and, influenced by the National Association of Manufacturers, drafted an extremely conservative platform. (It called for "revision" of the tariff but failed to specify in which direction.)

On the Democratic side, the defeat of conservative Alton B. Parker in 1904 opened the door for a third White House run by William Jennings Bryan. Nominating the Nebraskan, the Democrats called for a lower tariff, denounced the trusts, and embraced the cause of labor.

With Roosevelt's endorsement, Taft coasted to victory. But the Democrats made gains—Bryan bested Parker's 1904 vote total by 1.3 million—and progressive Republican state candidates outran the national ticket. Overall, the outcome suggested a lull in the reform movement, not its end.

To the delight of conservatives, Roosevelt departed to hunt big game in Africa. Quipped Senator Aldrich, "Let every lion do its duty." But even with TR an ocean away, his presence remained vivid. "When I am addressed as 'Mr. President,'" Taft wrote him, "I turn to see whether you are not at my elbow."

Taft, from an old political family in Cincinnati, differed markedly from Roosevelt. Whereas TR kept in fighting trim, the sedentary Taft was obese. Roosevelt sparred in a boxing ring that he set up in the White House; Taft preferred golf. TR loved speech-making and battles with the forces of evil; Taft disliked controversy. His happiest days would come later, as chief justice of the United States.

Pledged to carry on TR's program, Taft supported the Mann-Elkins Act (1910), which strengthened the Interstate Commerce Commission's rate-setting powers and extended its regulatory authority to telephone and telegraph companies. On the antitrust front, the Taft administration actually prosecuted more cases than had Roosevelt. But Taft characteristically proceeded without much publicity; and to the public, TR remained the quintessential "trust-buster."

### A Divided Republican Party

During the Roosevelt administration, a small group of reform-minded Republicans including Senators La Follette and Albert Beveridge of Indiana and Congressman George Norris of Nebraska, nicknamed the Insurgents, challenged their party's congressional leadership. In 1909 the Insurgents turned against President Taft after a bruising battle over the tariff.

Taft at first backed the Insurgents' call for a lower tariff. But in 1909, when high-tariff advocates in the Senate, led by Nelson Aldrich, pushed through the Payne-Aldrich Act, raising the rates on hundreds of items, Taft not only signed the bill but praised it extravagantly. The battle between conservative Republicans and progressive Insurgents was on.

A major Insurgent target was Speaker of the House Joseph G. Cannon of Illinois. Wielding near-absolute power, the arch-conservative Cannon kept most reform bills from even reaching a vote. In March 1910, the Insurgents joined with the Democrats to remove Cannon from the pivotal Rules Committee. This was a direct slap at Taft, who supported Cannon.

Relations between Taft and Roosevelt eroded as TR's allies sent him stormy letters detailing Taft's lack of reform zeal. The so-called Ballinger-Pinchot affair brought matters to a head. Taft's interior secretary, Richard Ballinger, was a Seattle lawyer who disliked federal controls and believed in private development of natural resources. In one of several decisions galling to conservationists, Ballinger approved the sale, to a group of Seattle businessmen, of several million acres of public lands in Alaska containing coal deposits. This group in turn sold its holdings to a consortium of New York bankers that included J. P. Morgan. When Department of the Interior official Louis Glavis protested these actions, he was fired. In true muckraking style, Glavis published an article in *Collier's* blasting Ballinger's actions. When Gifford Pinchot of the Forestry Service likewise criticized Ballinger in congressional testimony early in 1910, he, too, got the ax. TR's supporters seethed.

Upon Roosevelt's return to America in June 1910, Pinchot met the boat. In the 1910 midterm election, Roosevelt campaigned for Insurgent candidates. In a speech that alarmed conservatives, he called for more regulation of business, censured judges who struck down progressive laws, and endorsed the radical idea of reversing judicial rulings by popular vote. Naming his reviving crusade, TR borrowed from Herbert Croly's *The Promise of American Life* and proposed a "New Nationalism" that would engage the federal government powerfully in reform.

The Democrats captured the House in 1910, and a coalition of Democrats and Insurgent Republicans controlled the Senate. As the reform tide rose, TR sounded more and more like a presidential candidate. Meanwhile, however, a new challenger for leadership of the progressive movement had emerged.

# National Progressivism— Phase II: Woodrow Wilson

In the 1912 election, Roosevelt and Woodrow Wilson, together with Socialist Eugene Debs, offered competing visions of reform. Wilson won, and in his first term he played a key leadership role as Congress enacted an array of reform measures.

## *The Four-Way Election of 1912*

In February 1912, now openly opposed to Taft, Roosevelt announced his candidacy for the Republican nomination. But Taft wanted a second term, and a Republican battle loomed. For a time, Senator Robert La Follette's candidacy attracted reform-minded Republicans, but when Roosevelt entered the race, it quickly collapsed. Further complicating the picture was the growing strength of the Socialist party

In a series of Republican state primaries and conventions, Roosevelt generally walloped Taft. But Taft controlled the party machinery, and at the Republican convention that met in Chicago, many of Roosevelt's

**The Election of 1912**

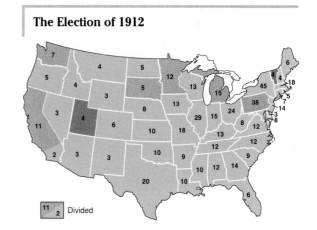

| | | Electoral Vote | Popular Vote | Percentage of Popular Vote |
|---|---|---|---|---|
| **Democratic** Woodrow Wilson | | 435 | 6,296,547 | 41.9 |
| **Progressive (Bull Moose)** Theodore Roosevelt | | 88 | 4,118,571 | 27.4 |
| **Republican** William H. Taft | | 8 | 3,486,720 | 23.2 |
| **Socialist** Eugene V. Debs | | – | 900,672 | 6.1 |

hard-won delegates were disqualified. Outraged, TR's backers stalked out of the convention and soon reassembled in Chicago to form a third party, the Progressive party. What had been a general term for a broad reform movement became the official name of a political organization.

"I feel fit as a bull moose," Roosevelt trumpeted, thereby giving his organization its nickname: the Bull Moose party. Riding an emotional high, the cheering delegates nominated their hero by acclamation, designated Hiram Johnson as his running mate, and adopted a platform that endorsed practically every reform cause of the day, including tariff reduction, woman suffrage, business regulation, the abolition of child labor, the eight-hour workday, workers' compensation, the direct primary, and the popular election of senators. The new party attracted a diverse array of followers, from a former J. P. Morgan partner to settlement house leader Jane Addams, united by their admiration for the charismatic Roosevelt.

Meanwhile, the new political spirit had also infused the Democratic party, spawning reform at the local and state level. In New Jersey, voters in 1910 elected a political novice, Woodrow Wilson, as governor. A "Wilson for President" boom soon arose, and when the Democrats assembled in Baltimore in June 1912, Wilson won the nomination, defeating the frontrunner, Speaker of the House Champ Clark of Missouri.

In the campaign, Taft more or less gave up, happy to have kept his party safe for conservatism. Whereas socialist Debs proposed an end to capitalism and a socialized economic order, Roosevelt and Wilson offered less radical prescriptions. TR continued to preach his New Nationalism: government regulation of big business in the public interest. Wilson, by contrast, speaking of the "New Freedom," evoked an earlier era of small entrepreneurs and free competition. "The history of liberty," he said, "is the history of the limitation of governmental power, not the increase of it."

Roosevelt garnered 630,000 more votes than Taft, but the divided Republicans proved no match for the united Democrats. Wilson won the presidency and the Democrats also took both houses of Congress. More than 900,000 voters opted for Debs and socialism.

The 1912 election linked the Democrats firmly with reform (except on the issue of race)—a link that Franklin D. Roosevelt would build upon in the 1930s. The breakaway Progressive party demonstrated the strength of the reform impulse among grassroots Republicans while leaving the party itself in the grip of its most conservative elements.

## Woodrow Wilson: The Scholar as President

The son and grandson of Presbyterian ministers, Wilson grew up in southern towns in a churchly atmosphere that shaped his oratorical style and his moral outlook. Although slow in school (probably because of the learning disorder dyslexia), Wilson graduated from Princeton and earned a Ph.D. in political science from Johns Hopkins University. He taught at Princeton and in 1902 became its president. Initially successful, he gradually lost support because of a rigid unwillingness to compromise. In 1910, having lost several battles at Princeton, he left the academic world to enter politics. Three years later he was president of the United States.

As national leader, Wilson exhibited the same strengths and weaknesses he had earlier displayed at Princeton. Impressive in bearing, with piercing gray eyes, he was an eloquent orator. But the idealism that inspired people could also alienate them. Wilson could be a master of political statesmanship. "He can walk on dead leaves and make no more noise than a tiger," declared one awed politician. But he could also retreat into a fortress of absolute certitude that tolerated no opposition. During his years as president, all these facets of his personality would come into play.

### Tariff and Banking Reform

Tariff reform—long a goal of southern and agrarian Democrats—headed Wilson's agenda. Breaking a precedent dating from Thomas Jefferson's day, Wilson on April 8, 1913, read his tariff message to Congress in person. A low-tariff bill quickly passed the House but bogged down in the Senate. Demonstrating his flair for leadership, Wilson denounced the tariff lobbyists flooding into Washington. His censure led to a Senate investigation of lobbyists and of senators who personally profited from high tariffs. In the aftermath of the publicity, the Senate slashed tariff rates even more than the House. The Underwood-Simmons Tariff reduced rates an average of 15 percent.[*]

In June 1913 Wilson again went before Congress, this time to call for banking and currency reform. Everyone agreed that the nation's banking system needed overhauling. Totally decentralized, American banks needed a strong central institution—a "lender of last resort" to help them weather fiscal crises such as the

---

[*] Underwood-Simmons also imposed an income tax, as authorized by the newly ratified Sixteenth Amendment.

Panic of 1907, in which many banks had failed. But beyond agreement on the need for reform, the consensus evaporated. The nation's bankers, whose Senate spokesman was Nelson Aldrich, favored a privately controlled central bank similar to Andrew Jackson's old enemy, the Bank of the United States. Progressive reformers wanted a publicly controlled central banking system. Others, including influential Virginia congressman Carter Glass, were leery of any central banking authority, public or private.

No banking expert, Wilson listened to all sides. He did, however, insist that the monetary system must ultimately be under public control. As the bargaining went on, Wilson played a critical behind-the-scenes role. The result was the Federal Reserve Act of December 1913.

A compromise among the various viewpoints, the Federal Reserve Act created a network of twelve regional Federal Reserve banks under mixed public and private control. Each regional bank was authorized to issue currency, called Federal Reserve notes, to the private banks in its district. These banks, in turn, could use this money to make loans to corporations and individual borrowers. (Each dollar bill today bears the name of the Federal Reserve Bank that issued it.) Overall control of the system was assigned to the heads of the twelve regional banks and a Washington-based Federal Reserve Board consisting of the secretary of the treasury, the comptroller of the currency, and seven other members appointed by the president for fourteen-year-terms. All national banks were required to join the new system and deposit a portion of their assets in their regional Federal Reserve Bank.

As established in 1913, the Federal Reserve's decision-making authority was highly diffused. But eventually "the Fed" would grow into a strong central monetary institution, adopting fiscal policies to guard against financial panics, promote economic growth, and dampen inflationary pressures. The Federal Reserve Act stands as President Wilson's greatest legislative achievement.

### Corporate Regulation

Wilson and Congress turned next to that perennial progressive cause, business regulation. Although candidate Wilson had shown little sympathy for the regulatory approach (with its implicit recognition that giant corporations were here to stay), as president he shepherded through Congress two key regulatory measures. These embodied somewhat different strategies. The first, the Federal Trade Commission Act (1914), re-flected an administrative approach. This law created a new "watchdog" agency, the Federal Trade Commission (FTC), with power to investigate suspected violations of federal regulatory statutes, to require regular reports from corporations, and to issue "cease and desist" orders (subject to court review) when it found unfair methods of business competition.*

The second of these laws, the Clayton Antitrust Act (1914), took the more traditional approach of listing specific illegal activities. The Sherman Act of 1890, although outlawing business practices "in restraint of trade," had been vague about details. The Clayton Act spelled out a series of illegal practices, such as selling at a loss to kill off the competition.

Because some of the "watchdogs" Wilson appointed to the FTC were conservatives with big-business links, this agency proved less effective than reformers had hoped. But with the added clout of the Clayton Act, the Wilson administration filed antitrust suits against nearly a hundred corporations.

### Labor Legislation and Farm Aid

Sympathetic to labor, and leading a party historically identified with working people, Wilson supported the American Federation of Labor, defended workers' right to organize, and endorsed a Clayton Act clause that exempted strikes, boycotts, and picketing from the antitrust laws' prohibition of actions "in restraint of trade." In 1916 (a campaign year) Wilson and the congressional Democrats pushed through three important worker-protection laws: the Keating-Owen Act, barring from interstate commerce products manufactured by child labor[†]; the Adamson Act, establishing an eight-hour workday for interstate railway workers; and the Workmen's Compensation Act, providing accident and injury protection to federal workers.

Wilson also supported the Federal Farm Loan Act and the Federal Warehouse Act (1916), which enabled farmers, using land or crops as security, to secure low-interest federal loans. The Federal Highway Act (1916), providing matching funds for state highway programs, benefited not only the new automobile industry but also farmers plagued by bad roads.

---

\* The Federal Trade Commission replaced an earlier agency, the Bureau of Corporations, set up in 1903.

† This measure was declared unconstitutional in 1918. Later a 1919 law that placed a special tax on all goods manufactured by child labor was also ruled unconstitutional. But these laws paved the way for the final abolition of child labor by the Fair Labor Standards Act of 1938.

**The Election of 1916**

| Candidates | Parties | Electoral Vote | Popular Vote | Percentage of Popular Vote |
|---|---|---|---|---|
| WOODROW WILSON | Democratic | 277 | 9,127,695 | 49.4 |
| Charles E. Hughes | Republican | 254 | 8,533,507 | 46.2 |
| A. L. Benson | Socialist | | 585,113 | 3.2 |
| J. Frank Hanly | Prohibition | | 220,506 | 1.2 |

## Progressivism and the Constitution

The probusiness tilt typical of the courts in the late nineteenth century shifted a bit in the Progressive Era. Evidence of the changing judicial climate came in *Muller* v. *Oregon* (1908), in which the Supreme Court upheld an Oregon ten-hour law for women laundry workers. Defending the constitutionality of the Oregon law was Boston attorney Louis Brandeis, who offered economic, medical, and sociological evidence of the harmful effects of long hours on women workers. Rejecting a legal claim long made by business, the High Court held that such worker-protection laws did not violate employers' rights under the due-process clause of the Fourteenth Amendment. *Muller* v. *Oregon* marked a breakthrough in making the legal system more responsive to new social realities.

In 1916 Woodrow Wilson nominated Brandeis to the Supreme Court. Disapproving of Brandeis's innovative approach to the law, the conservative American Bar Association protested, as did the *New York Times,* the president of Harvard, and Republican leaders in Congress. Anti-Semites opposed Brandeis because he was a Jew. But Wilson stood by his nominee, and after a fierce battle, the Senate approved.

The Progressive Era also produced four amendments to the Constitution, the first since 1870. The Sixteenth (ratified in 1913) granted Congress the authority to tax income, thus ending a long legal battle.* Quickly exercising its new authority, Congress in 1913 imposed

_____

* A Civil War income tax had been phased out by 1872. The Wilson-Gorman Tariff Act of 1894 had included a provision for an income tax (see Chapter 21), but a conservative U.S. Supreme Court, in *Pollack* v. *Farmers' Loan and Trust* (1895), had not only ruled this measure unconstitutional but blasted it as "communistic." The *Pollack* decision spurred the campaign for a constitutional amendment that succeeded in 1913.

a graduated federal income tax with a maximum rate of 7 percent on incomes in excess of $500,000.

The Seventeenth Amendment (1913) mandated the direct election of U.S. senators by the people, rather than senators' selection by state legislatures as required by Article I of the Constitution. This amendment brought to fruition a reform first advocated by the Populists as a way of making the Senate more responsive to the popular will.

The next two amendments culminated reform campaigns that we have already examined. The Eighteenth (1919) established nationwide prohibition, and the Nineteenth (1920) granted women the vote. This remarkable wave of amendments underscored how profoundly the progressive impulse had transformed the political landscape.

## 1916: Wilson Edges Out Hughes

Wilson easily won renomination in 1916. The Republicans turned to the bearded Charles Evans Hughes, a Supreme Court justice and former New York governor. The Progressive party again courted Theodore Roosevelt, but TR's reformist interests had given way to an obsession with drawing the United States into the European war. At his urging, the Progressives endorsed Hughes and effectively committed suicide. Because of the war, the issue of military preparedness figured importantly in the campaign (see Chapter 23).

With the Republicans now more or less reunited, the election was extremely close. Wilson won in the popular vote, but the electoral-college outcome remained in doubt for several weeks as the California tally seesawed back and forth. Ultimately, Wilson carried the state by fewer than four thousand votes, and with it, the election.

But war and its aftermath, not reform, would occupy Wilson's second term.

## CONCLUSION

Following the flurry of worker-protection legislation in 1916, the progressive movement lost momentum as the nation's attention turned from reform to war. A few reform measures enacted in the 1920s and a 1924 presidential campaign by Senator Robert La Follette under a revived Progressive party banner, would offer reminders of the progressive agenda. But the movement's zest and drive clearly waned with the coming of World War I.

Yet progressivism left a remarkable legacy, not only in specific laws but also in a changed view of government. To be sure, this altered perspective had ideological roots in the American past, including Jeffersonian optimism about human perfectibility, Jacksonian opposition to special privilege, conservative fears of "the masses," and the rising status of science and social research that had come with advances in higher education and in such academic disciplines as economics, sociology, and statistics.

But the progressives combined these diverse ingredients in creative new ways. By 1916 a consensus had taken hold that government should properly play a central social and economic role. The progressive movement expanded the meaning of democracy and challenged the cynical view that government was nothing but a tool of the rich. Theodore Roosevelt and Woodrow Wilson, together with governors like Robert La Follette and mayors like Tom Johnson, vastly enlarged the role of the executive in American government. But progressives did not seek "big government" for its own sake. Rather, they recognized that in an era of gargantuan industries, sprawling cities, and concentrated corporate power, government's role had to grow correspondingly to serve the public interest, achieve a decent common life, and protect the more vulnerable members of society.

Unquestionably, this ideal often faltered in practice. The reform laws and regulatory agencies inspired by moral indignation and a vision of social justice often fell short of their purpose, as emotional fervor gave way to bureaucratic routine. Indeed, reforms that the progressives envisioned as serving the larger society sometimes in practice mainly benefited special interests. Corporations that initially fought regulation proved remarkably adept at manipulating the new regulatory state to their own advantage. Unquestionably, too, progressivism had its illiberal and coercive dimensions; and on the issue of racial justice, its record was generally dismal.

After all this has been acknowledged, however, the Progressive Era stands as a time when American politics seriously confronted the social upheavals wrought by industrialization. It was also a time when Americans learned to think of their government neither as remote and irrelevant nor as a plaything of the powerful but rather as an arena of possibility where public issues and social problems could be thrashed out. Twenty years later, another great reform movement, the New Deal, would draw heavily on progressivism's legacy.

## FOR FURTHER READING

Alan Dawley, *Struggles for Justice: Social Responsibility and the Liberal State* (1991). A thoughtful study placing the progressive movement in a larger historical and ideological context.

Kenneth Finegold, *Experts and Politicians: Reform Challenges to Machine Politics in New York, Cleveland, and Chicago* (1995). A political scientist offers helpful analytic models of the differing political alignments that underlay reform efforts in various cities.

Noralee Frankel and Nancy S. Dye, eds., *Gender, Class, Race, and Reform in the Progressive Era* (1991). Selected essays exploring progressivism from various social perspectives.

Arthur S. Link and Richard L. McCormick, *Progressivism* (1983). Lucid, sensible unraveling of progressivism's diverse strands and comprehensive discussion of current interpretations.

Clyde A. Milner II, Carol A. O'Connor, and Martha A. Sandweiss, eds., *Oxford History of the American West* (1994). A compilation of valuable essays by Carl Abbott, William Cronon, and others on Progressive Era environmental measures affecting the West, and useful bibliographic essays.

Robert B. Westbrook, *John Dewey and American Democracy* (1991). The definitive intellectual biography of an influential philosopher and social thinker.

# 23

# World War I

**New York City, 1917**
*Bidding farewell to U.S. troops about to embark for France.*

It was 1917 and Jane Addams was troubled. On April 6, by overwhelming margins, Congress had supported President Woodrow Wilson's call for a declaration of war on Germany.

Addams belonged to the Daughters of the American Revolution (DAR); her father had served in the Illinois legislature with Abraham Lincoln. Yet she also believed in the cause of peace and deplored her nation's decision for war. As founder and director of Hull House, a Chicago settlement house, Addams had witnessed the tensions among different ethnic groups and had worked to overcome them. Indeed, in *Newer Ideals of Peace* (1907), she had insisted that the multi-ethnic "internationalism" of America's immigrant neighborhoods offered proof that national and ethnic hostilities could be disarmed. But Addams had also observed how war spirit can inflame a people. During the Spanish-American War, she had watched as little boys in the Hull House neighborhood had played at killing "Spaniards."

When war had erupted in Europe in 1914, Addams had worked to resolve the conflict and to keep America out of the fray. A founder of the Woman's Peace Party in January 1915, she had attended an International Congress of Women that April at the Hague that called upon the warring nations to submit their differences to arbitration. Addams had personally met with Woodrow Wilson to enlist his support for abitration, but with no success.

Now war had come to America, and Addams had to take a stand. Deepening her dilemma, many of her associates and friends were lining up behind Wilson. John Dewey, a frequent Hull House visitor, endorsed the war in a series of editorials in the *New Republic* magazine. Theodore Roosevelt, whose 1912 presidential campaign Addams had enthusiastically supported,

was now beating the drums for war. Government propaganda agencies were working overtime.

Despite the pressures, however, Addams concluded that she must remain faithful to her own conscience and oppose the war. The reaction was swift. Editorial writers who had earlier praised her settlement house work now either fell silent or denounced her. The DAR expelled her. For years after, the DAR, the American Legion, and other patriotic organizations would attack Addams for her "disloyalty" in 1917.

Addams did not sit out the war on the sidelines. Joining Herbert Hoover's Food Administration, she traveled across America, giving speeches urging increased food production to aid refugees and other innocent war victims.

Once the war ended, Addams resumed her work for peace. In 1919 she was elected first president of the Women's International League for Peace and Freedom. In 1922 she described her wartime anguish and isolation in a moving book, *Peace and Bread in Time of War.* In 1931 she won the Nobel Peace Prize. In the 1960s, some opponents of the Vietnam War would look for inspiration to Jane Addams's example in an earlier war.

Addams's experience underscores how deeply World War I affected American life. Whether they donned a uniform, worked on a farm or in a factory, or simply experienced U.S. life in wartime—whether they supported or opposed the conflict—every American was touched in some way by the war. And beyond its effect on individuals, the war's social, economic, and political ramifications lasted for years. Indeed, well before 1917, events abroad had increasingly impinged on Americans' consciousness. These larger global realities, and especially World War I, are the focus of this chapter.

This chapter focuses on five major questions:

♦ What general motivations or objectives underlay America's varied diplomatic involvements in Asia and Latin America in the early years of the twentieth century?

♦ Considering both immediate provocations and broader factors, why did the United States enter the European war in April 1917?

♦ How did America's participation in the war affect the home-front climate?

♦ In what specific ways did the role of the federal government in the U.S. economy, and in American life more generally, change in 1917–1918?

♦ How would you assess the role of President Woodrow Wilson in the creation of the League of Nations, and in the Senate's rejection of U.S. membership in the League?

**World War I Sheet Music**
*Tin Pan Alley helps whip up the war spirit.*

## Defining America's World Role

The Spanish-American War and the occupation of the Philippines signalled an era of intensified U.S. involvement abroad, especially in Asia and Latin America. These foreign engagements reflected a growing determination to assert American might, to protect and extend U.S. business investments abroad, and to impose American standards of good government worldwide. Progressivism's self-righteous, coercive side, evident in the domestic realm, emerged in America's dealings with other nations as well.

### *The Roosevelt Corollary in Latin America and the Balance of Power in Asia*

Although the Panama Canal remains Theodore Roosevelt's foreign-policy triumph, his response to other foreign crises underscores his belief that the United States must protect U.S. interests in Latin America, and preserve the balance of power in Asia. Roosevelt summed up his approach in a 1901 speech at the Minnesota state fair: "Speak softly and carry a big stick." (He followed the second part of this rule more consistently than the first.)

In 1904, when several European nations threatened to invade the Dominican Republic, a Caribbean island nation that had defaulted on its debts, Roosevelt re-

acted swiftly. If anyone were to intervene, he believed, it should be the United States. Although the United States had no territorial ambitions in Latin America, Roosevelt declared in December 1904, "chronic wrongdoing" by any Latin American nation would justify U.S. intervention.

This pronouncement soon came to be known as the Roosevelt Corollary to the Monroe Doctrine of 1823, which had warned European powers against meddling in Latin America. The Roosevelt Corollary announced that under certain circumstances, the United States had the right to precisely such meddling. Suiting actions to words, the United States operated the Dominican Republic's customs service for two years and took over the management of its foreign debt.

Meanwhile, the imperial rivalries that had swirled over China in the 1890s continued, briefly casting President Theodore Roosevelt in the unfamiliar role of peacemaker. In 1900, exploiting the turmoil caused by the Boxer uprising (see Chapter 21), Russian troops occupied the Chinese province of Manchuria, where Russia promoted its commercial interests by building railroads. This alarmed the Japanese, who had their own plans for Manchuria and nearby Korea. In February 1904, a Japanese surprise attack destroyed the Russian naval force at Port Arthur, Manchuria. In the Russo-Japanese War that followed, Japan completely dominated.

Roosevelt was happy to see Russian expansionism checked, but believed that a total Japanese victory would not only disrupt the balance of power in the Far

## CHRONOLOGY

| | | |
|---|---|---|
| **1905** | President Theodore Roosevelt mediates the end of the Russo-Japanese War. | |
| **1906** | At the request of Roosevelt, San Francisco ends segregation of Asian schoolchildren. | |
| **1907** | Roosevelt sends the "Great White Fleet" around the world. | |
| **1912** | U.S. Marines occupy Nicaragua. | |
| **1914** | U.S. troops occupy Vera Cruz, Mexico. | |
| | Archduke Franz Ferdinand of Austria assassinated. | |
| | World War I begins; President Woodrow Wilson proclaims American neutrality. | |
| | Wilson protests British interception of U.S. merchant ships. | |
| **1915** | U.S. Marines occupy Haiti and the Dominican Republic. | |
| | Woman's Peace party organized. | |
| | Wilson's "strict accountability" note protests German U-boat attacks. | |
| | British liner *Lusitania* sunk by German U-boat. | |
| | U.S. "preparedness" movement begins. | |
| | Germany restricts U-boat campaign. | |

**1915** *(continued)*
Wilson permits U.S. bank loans to Allies.

**1916** U.S. punitive expedition invades Mexico, seeking Pancho Villa.

After *Sussex* sinking, Germany pledges not to attack merchant ships without warning.

Wilson reelected.

**1917** U.S. troops withdraw from Mexico.

Germany resumes unrestricted U-boat warfare; United States breaks diplomatic relations.

United States enters the war.

Selective Service Act sets up national draft.

War Industries Board, Committee on Public Information, and Food Administration created.

Espionage Act passed.

NAACP march in New York City protests antiblack riot in East St. Louis and upsurge in lynchings.

Bolsheviks seize power in Russia; Russia leaves the war.

New York State passes woman-suffrage referendum.

U.S. government operates the nation's railroads.

**1918** Wilson outlines Fourteen Points for peace.

Sedition Amendment to Espionage Act passed.

National War Labor Board created.

American Expeditionary Force (AEF) helps stop Germans at Château-Thierry and Belleau Wood, closes St. Mihiel salient, and plays key role in the Meuse-Argonne campaign.

Midterm election (November 5).

Armistice signed (November 11).

**1919** Eighteenth Amendment added to the Constitution.

Peace treaty, including League of Nations covenant, signed at Versailles.

Racial violence in Chicago.

Wilson suffers paralyzing stroke.

Versailles treaty, with League covenant, rejected by Senate.

**1920** "Red raids" organized by Justice Department.

Nineteenth Amendment added to the Constitution.

Warren G. Harding elected president.

---

East but also threaten America's role in the Philippines. Accordingly, in June 1905 TR invited Japan and Russia to a peace conference at Portsmouth, New Hampshire. In September the two rivals signed a peace treaty. Russia recognized Japan's rule in Korea and made other territorial concessions. After this outcome, curbing Japanese expansionism—peacefully, if possible—became America's major objective in Asia. For his role in ending the Russo-Japanese War, Roosevelt received the Nobel Peace Prize.

Meanwhile, U.S.-Japanese relations soured when the San Francisco school board, in 1906, reflecting West Coast hostility to Asian immigrants, assigned all Asian children to segregated schools. Summoning the school board to Washington, Roosevelt persuaded them to reverse this discriminatory policy. In return, the administration in 1908 negotiated a "gentlemen's agreement" with Japan by which Tokyo pledged to stop the emigration of Japanese laborers to America. Racist attitudes continued to poison U.S.-Japanese relations, however. In 1913 the California legislature prohibited Japanese aliens from owning land.

While Californians warned of the "yellow peril," Japanese journalists, eyeing America's increasing military strength and involvements in Asia, spoke of a "white peril." In 1907 Roosevelt ordered sixteen gleaming white U.S. battleships on a "training operation" to Japan. Although officially treated as a courtesy call, the visit of this "Great White Fleet" pointedly underscored America's growing naval might.

**TR and the Great White Fleet, 1909**
*President Theodore Roosevelt greets the crew of the*
U.S.S. Constitution *as the fleet returns from a world
cruise designed to impress other nations with America's
emergence as a world power.*

### Dollar Diplomacy in China and Nicaragua

The foreign policy of the Taft administration (1909–
1913) focused on advancing American commercial
interests abroad—a policy some called dollar diplomacy. Since 1899, when Secretary of State John Hay
wrote the first of his "Open Door" notes (see Chapter
21), Washington had tried in vain to secure a share in
China's economic development. Pursuing this goal, the
Taft administration persuaded a group of U.S. bankers
to explore investments in China. But when their agent
in China proposed an American-financed railroad in
Manchuria, he got nowhere. Not only did the U.S.
bankers reject the idea, but the Russians and Japanese
at once signed a treaty carving up Manchuria for commercial purposes, freezing out the Americans.

Closer to home, in Nicaragua, dollar diplomacy
fared better. In 1911 a U.S.-supported revolution in
Nicaragua brought to power Adolfo Díaz, an officer of
an American-owned Nicaraguan mining property. In
response to Díaz's overtures, American bankers lent his
government $15 million in exchange for control of
Nicaragua's national bank, customs service, and
national railroad.

When a revolt against Díaz broke out in 1912, Taft
ordered in the marines to protect the bankers' investment. Except for one brief interval, marines occupied
Nicaragua until 1933, protecting the U.S. investment.

### Wilson and Latin America

Criticizing his Republican predecessors' expansionist
policies, Wilson pledged in 1913 that the United States
would "never again seek one additional foot of territory
by conquest." But he, too, soon intervened in Latin
America. In 1915, after upheavals in Haiti and the Dominican Republic (two nations sharing the same
Caribbean island, Santo Domingo), Wilson sent in the
marines. A Haitian constitution favorable to U.S. commercial interests was ratified in 1918 by a lopsided margin in a vote supervised by the marines. Under Major
General Smedley ("Old Gimlet Eye") Butler, marines
brutally suppressed Haitian resistance to U.S. rule. The
marines remained in the Dominican Republic until
1924, and in Haiti until 1934.

In 1913–1914, before the Haitian and Dominican
crises, Wilson's major foreign preoccupation was with
Mexico, a nation divided between a landowning elite
and a mass of poor peasants. In a turbulent era for Mexico, Wilson tried to promote good government, protect
U.S. investments, and safeguard U.S. citizens traveling
in Mexico or living along its border.

In 1911 rebels led by the democratic reformer Francisco Madero had ended the thirty-year rule of the autocratic president Porfirio Díaz. Forty thousand Americans had settled in Mexico under Díaz's regime, and
U.S. investors had poured some $2 billion into Mexican
oil wells and other ventures. Early in 1913, just as Wilson took office, Mexican troops loyal to General Victo-
riano Huerta, a full-blooded Indian, overthrew and
murdered Madero.

Reversing the long-standing American policy of recognizing all governments, Wilson refused to recognize
Huerta's regime, which he called "a government of
butchers." Authorizing arms sales to Huerta's rival,
General Venustiano Carranza, Wilson also ordered the
port of Vera Cruz blockaded to prevent a shipment of
German arms from reaching Huerta. Announced Wilson, "I am going to teach the South American republics
to elect good men."

In April 1914, tightening the screws on Huerta,
seven thousand U.S. troops occupied Vera Cruz and engaged Huerta's forces. Sixty-five Americans and some
five hundred Mexicans were killed or wounded. Bow-

**Woodrow Wilson, Schoolteacher**
*This 1914 political cartoon captures the patron-*
*izing self-righteousness of Wilson's approach*
*to Latin America that planted the seeds of*
*long-term resentments.*

ing to U.S. might, Huerta abdicated, Carranza took power, and the U.S. troops withdrew.

But the turmoil continued. In January 1916 a bandit chieftain in northern Mexico, Pancho Villa, murdered sixteen American mining engineers whom he had pulled from a train. Soon after, Villa's gang burned the town of Columbus, New Mexico, and killed nineteen inhabitants. Enraged, Americans demanded action. Wilson dispatched a large punitive expedition into Mexico under General John J. Pershing. When Pancho Villa not only eluded Pershing but brazenly staged another cross-border raid into Texas, Wilson ordered 150,000 National Guardsmen to the Mexican border. This massive military response to a comparatively minor problem would long embitter U.S.-Mexican relations.

Although soon overshadowed by World War I, these involvements in Asia and Latin America illuminate American foreign-policy goals in these years. These goals reflected a search for order on U.S. terms—an international system founded on an ideological blend of liberalism, democracy, and capitalistic enterprise. Washington planners envisioned a harmonious, stable global order of democratic societies that would welcome both American liberal political

values and the expansion of American capitalistic enterprise.

President Wilson summed up this view in a speech to business leaders: "[Y]ou are Americans and are meant to carry liberty and justice and the principles of humanity wherever you go. . . .[G]o out and sell goods that will make the world more comfortable and more happy, and convert them to the principles of America."

These involvements also portended future trends. The diplomatic maneuvering between the United States and Japan signaled a clash of interests, compounded by racism, that in 1941 would culminate in war. The revolutionary and nationalistic energies stirring in Latin America would transform the politics of this region half a century later. And of more immediate concern, Wilson's vision of an American-based world order, evident in these episodes, would soon find expression in his response to the crisis unfolding in Europe.

## War in Europe

When war burst upon Europe in 1914, most Americans wished only to remain aloof. For nearly three years, the United States stayed officially neutral. But opinion gradually shifted. Emotional ties to the British and French, economic considerations, the vision of a world remade in America's image, and German violations of Wilson's definition of neutral rights all combined by April 1917 to suck the United States into the maelstrom.

### The Coming of War

Europe remained at peace through much of the nineteenth century and beyond. Some believed that war was a thing of the past. Beneath the surface, however, ominous developments, including a complex web of military alliances, belied such hopes. Germany, Austria, and Italy signed a mutual-defense treaty in 1882. In turn, France signed military treaties with Russia and Great Britain.

Beyond the formal alliances stirred imperial ambitions and nationalistic passions. The Ottoman Empire, centered in Turkey, once dominant across southeastern Europe, receded in the 1870s, leaving in its wake such newly independent nations as Romania, Bulgaria, and Serbia.

Serbian patriots dreamed of uniting the large ethnic group known as Slavs, including those living in

CHAPTER 23 World War I

Bosnia-Herzegovina, Serbia's neighbor to the west. This dream, called Pan-Slavism, powerfully molded turn-of-the-century politics in southeastern Europe. Russia, home to millions of Slavs, supported the Pan-Slavic cause.

Meanwhile, however, the Austro-Hungarian Empire, with its capital in Vienna, also saw opportunities for expansion as the Ottoman Empire faded. In 1908 Austria-Hungary annexed Bosnia-Herzegovina, alarming Russia and infuriating Serbia.

Germany, ruled by Kaiser Wilhelm II, also displayed expansionist impulses. Many Germans believed that their recently created nation had lagged in the race for empire. Expansion, modernization, and military power became the order of the day in Berlin.

At a still deeper level, many Europeans felt a vague restlessness as the twentieth century began. Life seemed too soft. Like Theodore Roosevelt on the eve of the Spanish-American War, some longed for war as a way of strengthening character and adding excitement to a languid age.

Such was the context, then, in June 1914, when Archduke Franz Ferdinand of Austria made a state visit with his wife to Bosnia. As they rode in an open touring car through Sarajevo, the Bosnian capital, a young Pan-Slavic nationalist gunned them down. In response, Austria on July 28 declared war on Serbia. Russia, which had a secret treaty with Serbia, mobilized for war. Germany declared war on Russia and on Russia's ally France. Great Britain, linked by treaty to France, declared war on Germany. An assassin's bullet had plunged Europe into war.

### The American People's Initial Responses

Proclaiming American neutrality, President Wilson urged the nation to be neutral "in thought as well as in action." Most Americans, grateful that an ocean lay between them and the war, fervently agreed. A popular song summed up the mood: "I Didn't Raise My Boy to Be a Soldier."

Wilson's call to remain neutral in thought proved difficult, however. Strong economic ties bound the United States and Britain. Americans of British ancestry, including Wilson himself, felt an emotional bond with England. As early as August 1914, Wilson privately mused that victory for militaristic Germany would be a disaster. Many well-to-do Americans had traveled in England. Schoolbooks stressed the English origins of American institutions. The English language itself—the

language of Shakespeare, Dickens, and the King James Bible—deepened the bond. British propaganda subtly stressed the British-American link.

But not all Americans felt ties with the British. Many German-Americans sympathized with Germany's cause. Irish-Americans envisioned the prospect that a German victory might free Ireland from the British yoke. Some Scandinavian immigrants identified more with Germany than with England on a cultural level. But these cultural and ethnic cross-currents did not at first override the commitment to neutrality. For most Americans, as for the Wilson administration, staying out of the conflict became the chief goal.

### The Perils of Neutrality

Neutral in 1914, America went to war in 1917, with strong popular support. What caused this turnabout?

First of all, Wilson's vision of a world order in America's image conflicted with his neutrality. An international system based on liberalism, democracy, and capitalism would have been impossible, he believed, in a world dominated by imperial Germany. Furthermore, Wilson gradually became convinced that even an Allied* victory would not ensure a liberal peace without a U.S. role in the postwar settlement. And to shape the peace, America would have to fight the war.

This global vision influenced Wilson's handling of the immediate issue that dragged the United States into the conflict: neutral nations' rights on the high seas. When the war began, Britain started intercepting U.S. merchant ships bound for Germany, declaring their cargo contraband that could aid Germany's war effort. Recalling earlier conflicts with England over neutral rights during the War of 1812, Wilson protested vehemently.

Wilson's protests intensified late in 1914 and early in 1915, when Britain declared the North Sea a war zone, planted it with mines, and blockaded all German ports. By choking off Germany's imports, including food, Britain hoped to bring Germany to its knees. The United States protested in vain. Britain was determined to exploit its naval advantage, even if it meant alienating U.S. public opinion.

---

\* During World War I, Great Britain, Russia, France, and later Italy were called the Allies. Germany and Austria-Hungary were called the Central Powers. The United States entered the war in 1917 as an "Associate Power" of the Allies, thereby distinguishing its war conduct and aims from those of the other Allies.

But it was Germany, not England, that ultimately pushed the United States from neutrality to war. If Britannia ruled the waves, Germany controlled the ocean depths with its torpedo-equipped submarines, or U-boats. In February 1915 Berlin proclaimed the waters around Great Britain a war zone and warned off all ships. Germany would be held to "strict accountability," Wilson declared, for any loss of American ships or lives. Nevertheless, several Americans died as U-boats torpedoed British ships and a U.S. tanker.

On May 1, 1915, in a small notice published in U.S. newspapers, the German embassy cautioned Americans against travel on British or French vessels. Six days later, a U-boat sank the British liner *Lusitania* off the Irish coast, with the loss of 1,198 lives, including 128 Americans. As newspaper headlines screamed the news, U.S. public opinion turned sharply anti-German. (The *Lusitania*'s cargo holds, historians later discovered, had carried munitions destined for England.)

Wilson, demanding a series of specific pledges that Germany would cease unrestricted submarine warfare, insisted that America, without going to war, could persuade the belligerents to recognize the principle of neutral rights. The president said, "There is such a thing as a man being too proud to fight."

The *Lusitania* disaster exposed deep divisions in U.S. public opinion. Many Americans, now ready for war, ridiculed Wilson's "too proud to fight" speech. Theodore Roosevelt called for war and heaped scorn on the president's "abject cowardice." The National Security League, a lobby of bankers and industrialists, promoted armament and universal military training and organized "preparedness" parades in major cities. By late 1915, Wilson himself was calling for a military buildup.

Many others, however, not only German-Americans and pacifists but millions who had taken Wilson's neutrality speeches seriously, deplored the drift toward war. Some feminists and reformers warned that the war spirit eroded the humanitarian values central to progressive reform. Jane Addams lamented that the international movements to reduce infant mortality and improve care for the aged had been "scattered to the winds by the war."

As early as August 1914, fifteen hundred women had marched down New York's Fifth Avenue, protesting the war. Carrie Chapman Catt and other feminists joined Jane Addams in forming the Woman's Peace party. Late in 1915 automaker Henry Ford chartered a vessel to take a group of pacifists and other war oppo-

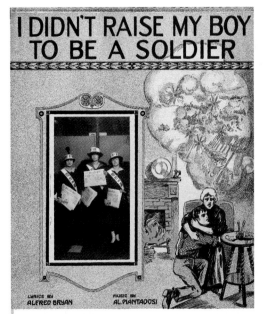

**Opposing War**

*This popular song of 1915 conveys the antiwar sentiment that swept America after the European war began in 1914.*

nents to Scandinavia to persuade the belligerents to accept neutral mediation and fulfill his dream of ending the war by Christmas.

Divisions surfaced even within the Wilson administration. Believing Wilson's *Lusitania* notes too hostile to Germany, Secretary of State William Jennings Bryan resigned in June 1915. His successor, the lawyer Robert Lansing, usually let Wilson act as his own secretary of state.

Some neutrality advocates concluded that incidents like the *Lusitania* crisis were inevitable if Americans continued to sail on belligerent ships. Early in 1916 Congress considered a measure to forbid such travel (the Gore-McLemore Resolutions), but President Wilson successfully opposed it, insisting that the principle of neutral rights must be upheld.

For a time, Wilson's approach seemed to work. Germany secretly ordered U-boat captains to spare passenger ships and agreed to pay compensation for the American lives lost in the *Lusitania* sinking. In August 1915, when a U-boat sank a British passenger vessel, the *Arabic*, killing two Americans, Germany pledged that such incidents would not recur. In March 1916, however, when a German sub sank a French passenger ship, the *Sussex,* in the English Channel, injuring several Americans and violating its pledge, Wilson threatened to break diplomatic relations—a step toward war. In response, Berlin pledged not to attack merchant vessels without warning, provided that Great Britain, too, observed "the rules of international law." Ignoring this qualification, Wilson announced Germany's acceptance of American demands; for the rest of 1916, the crisis over neutral rights eased.

The neutrality debate also involved questions of U.S. financial support to the warring nations. Early in the war, Secretary of State Bryan had rejected banker J. P. Morgan's request to extend a loan to France as "inconsistent with the true spirit of neutrality." But economic considerations, combined with outrage over the *Lusitania* sinking, undermined this policy. In August 1915 Treasury Secretary William G. McAdoo warned Wilson of dire economic consequences if a lack of funds forced cuts in Allied purchases of munitions and agricultural commodities in the United States. "To maintain our prosperity, we must finance it," McAdoo insisted. Only substantial loans to Great Britain, agreed Secretary of State Lansing, could prevent "a serious financial situation" in the United States, including "unrest and suffering among the laboring classes." Should America let the neutrality principle "stand in the way of our national interests?" asked Lansing rhetorically.

Swayed by such arguments, and personally sympathetic to the Allied cause, Wilson permitted the Morgan bank to lend $500 million to the British and French governments. By April 1917, U.S. banks had lent $2.3 billion to the Allies, in contrast to only $27 million to Germany.

### Stalemate in the Trenches

While Americans focused on neutral rights, the land war settled into a grim stalemate. Germany initially planned to defeat the French and British in six weeks, but an autumn 1914 German drive into France bogged down along the Marne River, stymied by dogged British and French resistance. The two sides then dug in, forming a line of trenches across France from the English Channel to the Swiss border. For more than three years, this line scarcely changed. Occasional offensives took a terrible human toll. A German offensive in February 1916 began with the capture of two forts near the town of Verdun and ended that June with the French recapture of the same two forts, now nothing but rubble, at a

horrendous cost in human life. For those caught up in it, trench warfare was a ghastly inferno of mud, lice, rats, artillery bursts, poison gas, and random death.

British propaganda portrayed the atrocities allegedly committed by "the Huns" (a derogatory term for the Germans), such as impaling babies on bayonets. After the war, much of this propaganda was exposed as false. Documents seized in 1915 revealing German espionage in U.S. war plants further discredited the German cause.

### The Election of 1916

The war dominated the 1916 presidential election, in which Woodrow Wilson edged out Charles Evans Hughes. The Democrats' campaign theme emerged when a convention speaker, praising Wilson's handling of a series of foreign crises, aroused wild applause as he ended each account with the refrain "We didn't go to war."

The Republican Hughes flip-flopped, criticizing Wilson for lack of aggressiveness and rebuking him for pursuing policies that risked war. Theodore Roosevelt, prodding Hughes toward greater militance (and thereby hurting Hughes's chances with antiwar voters), campaigned more for war than for the Republican ticket. The only difference between Wilson and the bearded Hughes, he jeered, was a shave. While Hughes did well among Irish-Americans and German-Americans, who considered Wilson too pro-British, Wilson's policies won him support from women voters in western states that had adopted woman suffrage. Above all, Wilson's victory, close as it was, revealed the strength of the popular desire for peace as late as November 1916.

### The United States Enters the War

Early in 1917 Germany's leaders took a fateful step: they resumed unrestricted submarine warfare. From 1914 on, a sharp debate had raged in Berlin between political leaders who favored limiting U-boat warfare to keep America neutral versus military planners who wanted to utilize Germany's U-boats to the maximum. As the war dragged on, the generals' position grew stronger. Even if the United States declared war, they argued, unrestricted U-boat warfare could bring victory before an American army reached the front. With billions in American loans already financing the Allied war effort, they contended, a formal U.S. declaration of war meant little. On January 31, 1917, Germany re-

**Go to War; "No Expense!"**
*Shortly after Congress declared war in April 1917, new recruits leave a New York City Armory beneath a banner urging more young men to sign up.*

sumed unlimited U-boat attacks—a decision almost certain to pull the United States into the war.

Events now rushed forward with grave inevitability. Wilson broke diplomatic relations on February 3. During February and March, U-boats sank five American ships. On February 24, British intelligence informed Washington of a telegram from the German foreign secretary, Alfred Zimmermann, to the German ambassador in Mexico. If Mexico would join in a war against the United States, the cable said, Germany would restore Mexico's "lost territories" of Texas, Arizona, and New Mexico.

On April 2, Wilson delivered his war message to Congress. After a short but bitter debate, the Senate voted 82 to 6 for war, and the House 373 to 50. Three key factors—German attacks on American shipping, U.S. economic investment in the Allied cause, and American cultural links to the Allies, especially England—had propelled the United States into the war.

# Mobilizing at Home, Fighting in France

Compared to European nations, the United States was scarred relatively lightly by World War I. The European states fought for more than four years; the United States, for nineteen months. Their armies suffered casualties of 70 percent or more; the American army's casualty rate was 8 percent. The fighting left parts of France and Belgium brutally scarred; the American homeland was untouched. Nevertheless, the war marked a profound turning point for America. It changed not only the lives of the men who fought in it, but also the American home front and the nation's government and economy.

## *Raising an Army*

April 1917 found America's military woefully unprepared. The regular army consisted of 120,000 men, few with combat experience, plus some 80,000 recently federalized National Guardsmen. An aging officer corps dozed away the years until retirement.* Ammunition reserves were paltry. The War Department was a snake pit of jealous bureaucrats, one of whom hoarded thousands of typewriters as the war approached.

While the brilliant army chief of staff Peyton C. Marsh handled the task of bringing order to the military, Wilson's secretary of war, Newton D. Baker, took on

---

* The last Civil War veteran in the army, Colonel John Clem (a drummer boy at the Battle of Shiloh), had retired only two years before.

the challenge of raising an army. The reform mayor of Cleveland, Baker was a poor administrator but a public-relations genius. The Selective Service Act of May 1917 required all young men between twenty-one and thirty (later expanded to eighteen and forty-five) to register with local civilian draft boards for military service. Mindful of the Civil War draft riots, Baker planned the first official draft-registration day, June 5, 1917, as a "festival and patriotic occasion."

Each registrant received a number, and draftees were chosen by lottery. By November 1918 more than 24 million men had registered, of whom nearly 3 million were drafted. Volunteers and National Guardsmen swelled the total to 4.3 million. Thanks to a precedent-breaking decision by Secretary of the Navy Josephus Daniels, eleven thousand women served in the navy in World War I, working as nurses, secretaries, and telephone operators.

The War Department originally planned for several months of training, but some draftees embarked for France after only a few weeks. Thousands of draftees sweated through the new "IQ" (intelligence quotient) tests. Entertainment and recreational facilities were provided by volunteer organizations monitored by the Commission on Training Camp Activities, a War Department agency that oversaw the recruits' moral welfare (see A Place in Time).

### Building an Army

*Uniformed young women dubbed "Marinettes" post marine recruitment posters in New York City.*

## Organizing the Economy for War

As historian Ellis Hawley shows in *The Great War and the Search for a Modern Order* (2d ed., 1992), the administrative innovations of the war years also accelerated longer-term processes of social reorganization. The rationalization of mass production; the government's regulatory role; the collaboration between government, business, and labor; and the rise of new professional and managerial elites—all these advances were furthered by the war. In tracing the roots of the modern American state, the years 1917–1918 are crucial.

Along with military mobilization, the war also introduced unprecedented government oversight of the economy. Populists and progressives had long urged more public control of corporations. Now wartime brought an elaborate supervisory apparatus.

In 1916 Congress had created an advisory body, the Council of National Defense, to oversee the government's preparedness program. In 1917 this council set up the War Industries Board (WIB) to coordinate military purchasing, assure production efficiency, and provide weapons, equipment, and supplies to the military. Wilson reorganized the WIB in March 1918 and put Bernard Baruch in charge. A South Carolinian of German-Jewish background, Baruch had made a fortune as a Wall Street stock speculator. Wilson, awed by his practical knowledge, called him Dr. Facts. Under Baruch, the WIB exercised enormous control over the industrial sector. It allocated raw materials, established production priorities, and induced competing companies to standardize and coordinate their production processes to save scarce commodities. The standardization of bicycle manufacturing, for example, saved two thousand tons of steel. Acting under the authority of the Lever Food and Fuel Control Act of August 1917, a law of far-reaching scope, Wilson set up two more powerful new agencies, the Fuel Administration and the Food Administration. The fuel administration controlled coal output, regulated fuel prices and consumption, and in March 1918 introduced daylight-saving time—an idea first proposed by Benjamin Franklin in the 1770s.

Herbert Hoover headed the Food Administration. Born in poverty in Iowa, Hoover

**Herbert Hoover, Humanitarian**
*During and after the war, the future president coordinated relief efforts to send food and clothing to war-torn Europe. In 1917–1918 he also headed the U.S. Food Administration.*

**Home-Front Mobilization**
*The U.S. Food Administration flooded the nation with posters urging wartime food conservation.*

had prospered as a mining engineer in Asia. He was organizing food relief in Belgium when Wilson brought him back to Washington. The Food Administration oversaw the production and allocation of wheat, meat, and sugar to assure adequate supplies for the army as well as for the desperately food-short Allies.

These regulatory agencies relied on voluntary cooperation—reinforced by official pressure—to achieve their objectives. For example, a barrage of Food Administration posters, magazine ads, and other propaganda urged Americans to conserve food. Housewives signed pledges to observe "meatless days" and "wheatless days." President Wilson pitched in by pasturing a flock of sheep on the White House lawn. Slogans such as "Serve Beans by All Means" promoted substitutes for scarce commodities.

Harriot Stanton Blatch, daughter of women's rights pioneer Elizabeth Cady Stanton, headed the Food Administration's Speakers' Bureau, which spread the conservation message. Blatch also organized the Woman's Land Army, which recruited female volunteers to replace male farm workers.

These agencies were only the tip of the regulatory iceberg. Nearly five thousand government boards, ultimately controlled by President Wilson, supervised home-front activities during the war. These included

the Railroad Administration, the Shipping Board, and the National War Labor Board, which resolved labor-management disputes that jeopardized production. When a railroad tie-up during the winter of 1917–1918 threatened the flow of supplies to Europe, the government took over the system. Within a few months, the Railroad Administration, headed by Treasury Secretary William McAdoo, transformed the thousands of miles of track owned by nearly three thousand competing companies into an efficient national transportation system.

American business, much criticized by progressive reformers, utilized the war emergency to improve its image. Corporate executives served as administrators of the wartime regulatory agencies. Factory owners distributed prowar propaganda to workers. Trade associations mobilized their productive strength behind the war.

The war sped up the ongoing process of corporate consolidation and economic integration. Prodded by Washington, businesses cooperated to make the production and distribution process more rational and efficient. In place of trust-busting, the government now encouraged industrial cooperation. The number of major corporate mergers in 1917–1918 jumped sharply. Commenting on the epidemic of "mergeritis," one magazine observed, "The war has accelerated . . . a tendency

1915

## A World War I Military Training Camp

lattsburgh, New York, nestled along Lake Champlain 160 miles north of Albany, has military associations dating to the War of 1812. In September 1814 a nearby naval engagement on the lake resulted in the surrender of four British ships and the withdrawal to Canada of an occupying British army. After the war, the government established a military barracks at Plattsburgh. Here, in 1915, General Leonard Wood, a leading proponent of "preparedness," began a summer military-training camp for wealthy New Yorkers who could pay their own expenses. His goal was to train officers for the coming war. (The camp was white-only; African-Americans were excluded.) A 1917 handbook for Wood's Plattsburgh program evoked the spirit of a boys' camp more than a military center: "The food is plain but . . . as a rule distinctly edible, especially when the open air life begins to develop unusual appetites. . . . The shower baths . . . and the 'latrines' [are] . . . open to the heavens . . . The lake offers splendid bathing and no suit is required . . ."

Woods's program of upper-class officers' training, dubbed "the Plattsburgh idea," was widely imitated. Financier Bernard Baruch funded three such camps. In May 1917 the War Department established similar officers' training camps throughout America. Except for one in Iowa, all were white-only.

When the United States went to war in April 1917, Plattsburgh became one of many military encampments where young men were trained, as either officers or foot soldiers, for combat in France. From Camp Upton on Long Island to Camp Lewis in Washington State, raw recruits encountered military discipline for the first time. One Plattsburgh trainee wrote home, "We drilled and fought dummies with bayonets until we couldn't see straight."

The War Department also sought to protect the morals of young men cut off from the watchful eye of family and community. The Commission on Training Camp Activities, directed by Raymond B. Fosdick, introduced educational and recreational programs. Trainees boxed; played volleyball and tennis; attended movies and amateur vaudeville shows; and participated in group sings featuring such ditties as

> Good-bye Ma, good-bye Pa,
> Good-bye mule with your old
>   he-haw.
> I may not know what the war's
>   about,
> But you bet, by gosh, I'll soon find
>   out.

The American Library Association and the Carnegie Foundation provided books and libraries. YMCA workers staffed base clubs, encouraged trainees to write home, and offered classes in literacy and academic subjects (including French slang) as well as Bible studies and religious services.

At Plattsburgh, local women opened a "Hostess House" to provide a touch of domesticity, and the idea soon

*General Leonard Wood at Plattsburg training camp, 1916.*

spread. In *Keeping Our Fighters Fit* (1918), Fosdick praised the Hostess Houses for "keeping the memories of home alive . . . by supplying . . . a substitute for home."

The Commission on Training Camp Activities also presented films, lectures, and posters on the dangers of alcohol and prostitution. Any soldier disabled by venereal disease, one poster warned, "is a Traitor!" Camp commanders confined trainees to the base until nearby towns closed all brothels and saloons, and authorities banned liquor sales near training camps. The camps' antiliquor, antiprostitution policy strengthened these national moral-reform campaigns. Indeed, proclaimed Fosdick, the training camps' objective was no less than "cleaning up the whole United States." Secretary of War Baker summed up the goal this way: "I want [our soldiers] to have . . . a set of social habits replacing those of their homes and communities . . . , so that when they get overseas and are removed from the reach of our comforting and restraining hand, they will have . . . a moral and intellectual armor for their protection."

Recruits also encountered intelligence testing. Led by Robert M. Yerkes, president of the American Psychological Association, psychologists were eager to show the practical utility of their fledgling new academic profession. They touted the value of intelligence ("IQ") tests for determining individuals' academic and vocational prospects. The tests could show which recruits had officer potential and which were incompetent, said Yerkes, and in this way psychology would "help to win the war." Persuaded, the War Department approved universal testing of all enlistees in December 1917.

Some military officers dismissed the psychological testers as "mental meddlers." Of one recruit who received a low IQ rating, the base commander commented, "[He is] a model of loyalty, reliability, cheerfulness, . . . and general helpfulness. . . . What do we care about his 'intelligence'?" Nevertheless, this wartime program helped accustom Americans to the idea of intelligence tests, psychological profiles, and the growing role of professionals in personnel management.

When the psychologists announced that a high percentage of the recruits had tested at the "Moron" level, editorial writers anxiously discussed the tide of imbecility supposedly sweeping the nation. The tests revealed not only many recruits' lack of formal education, but also the test writers' cultural biases. One question asked whether *mauve* was a drink, a color, a fabric, or a food. Another—at a time when automobiles were still a rarity in rural America—asked in which city a particular auto, the Overland, was built. The test results also confirmed racial and ethnic stereotypes: native-born recruits of northern European origins most often received "Superior" ratings; African-Americans and recent immigrants received the lowest standings.

In short, Plattsburgh and other World War I training camps not only prepared young men for combat in France. They also revealed much about American society in these years, including the social concerns of the day, and the changes looming on the horizon.

Plattsburgh's association with the military continued. During World War II, the training camp site became a U.S. Air Force base. In 1955, as the Cold War raged, a nuclear-bomber unit was stationed here. But the Cold War's end brought cutbacks, and in 1995, Plattsburgh Air Force Base closed its doors. But while the city's proud military history receded into memory, the IQ tests introduced at Plattsburgh and other bases in 1917–1918 did not. In fact, for better or worse, intelligence testing by the 1990s had become a ubiquitous feature of American life—another example of the First World War's long reach.

*A World War I recruit ponders an intelligence test.*

that was already irresistible. . . . Instead of punishing companies for acting in concert, the government is now in some cases forcing them to unite."

Overall, the war proved highly profitable for U.S. business. Although Congress imposed an excess-profits tax, the system had many loopholes, and wartime profits soared. For example, after-tax profits in the copper industry jumped from 12 percent in 1913 to 24 percent in 1917.

This colossal regulatory apparatus fell apart quickly after the war, but its influence lingered. The wartime mergers, coordination, and climate of business-government cooperation affected the evolution of American business. The old laissez-faire suspicion of government, already weakened, eroded further in 1917–1918. In the 1930s, when the nation faced a different crisis, the government activism of World War I would be remembered. Many New Deal agencies (see Chapter 25) closely resembled the wartime agencies of 1917–1918.

### With the AEF in France

About 2 million soldiers went to France in 1917–1918 as members of the American Expeditionary Force (AEF) under General John J. Pershing. Ironically, Pershing was of German origin; his family name had been Pfoersching. A West Point graduate and commander of the 1916 expedition against Pancho Villa, Pershing was an iron-willed officer with a ramrod bearing, steely eyes, and trim mustache. The death of his wife and three of their children in a fire in 1915 had further hardened him.

For most men of the AEF, the war at first seemed a great adventure. Plucked from towns and farms, they were en route to Europe! They made the voyage on crowded freighters or, for a lucky few, captured German passenger liners. Once in France, freight cars marked "HOMMES 40, CHEVAUX 8" (40 men, 8 horses) took them to the front. Then began the routine of marching, training—and waiting. The Young Men's Christian Association (YMCA), Red Cross, and Salvation Army, including many young American women volunteers, provided a touch of home.

France offered not only hospitality and culture, but other diversions as well, and the U.S. military mobilized lectures, posters, and films to warn recruits of the danger of venereal disease. One poster declared, "A German bullet is cleaner than a whore." When the French premier, Georges Clemenceau, offered to provide prostitutes for the American troops (as was the custom for French soldiers), Secretary of War Baker exclaimed, "For God's sake, don't show this to the President, or he'll stop the war."

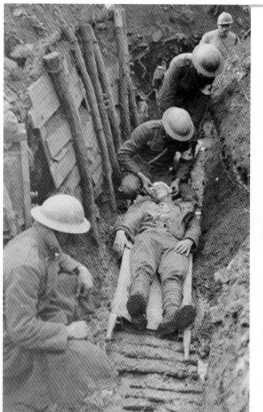

**The Faces of War**
*A wounded U.S. marine receives first aid in a trench near Toulon, France, in March 1918; fresh U.S. troops arrive in war-weary London in August 1917.*

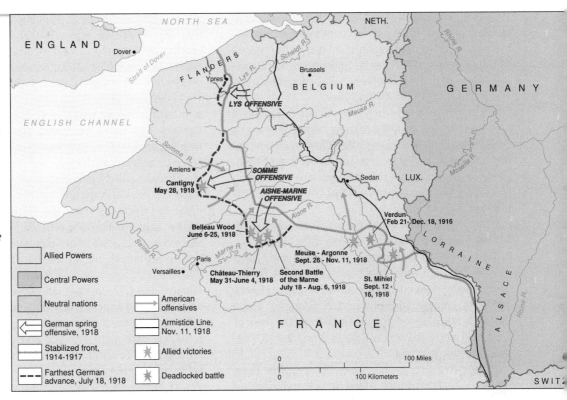

**The United States on the Western Front, 1918**

*American troops first saw action in the campaign to throw back Germany's spring 1918 offensive in the Somme and Aisne-Marne sectors. The next heavy American engagement came that autumn as part of the Allies' Meuse-Argonne offensive that ended the war.*

On the Western Front, aerial dogfights between German and Allied reconnaissance planes offered spectacular sideshows. Germany's legendary "Red Baron," Manfred von Richthofen, shot down eighty British and French planes before his luck ran out in April 1918. In 1916 a group of American volunteers joined the French air corps as the *Lafayette Escadrille.* Secretary of War Baker, convinced of the airplane's military importance, pushed a plane construction program. Few were actually built, however—a rare failure of the U.S. war-production program.

When the United States entered the conflict, Allied prospects looked bleak. Germany's resumption of unrestricted U-boat warfare took a horrendous toll on Allied shipping: 1.5 million tons in March and April 1917. A failed French offensive on the Marne that spring caused such losses that French troops mutinied. A British offensive along the French-Belgian border faltered near Passchendaele, Belgium, in November 1917, having gained four miles at a cost of more than 400,000 killed and wounded. That same month, the Italian army suffered a disastrous defeat at Caporetto near the Austrian border.*

---

* Initially neutral, Italy entered the war in 1915 on the side of the Allies.

Making matters worse for the Allies in 1917, Russia left the war. Russia for years had been seething with discontent. Peasants, industrial workers, intellectuals inspired by Western liberal values, and revolutionaries who embraced the communist ideology of Karl Marx all joined in a March 1917 revolutionary uprising that overthrew the repressive and incompetent government of Tsar Nicholas II. A provisional government under the liberal Alexander Kerensky took power. But Kerensky's government faltered as one faction of the revolutionary party, called Bolsheviks (the Russian word for *majority*), maneuvered to seize power. The Bolsheviks gained the initiative in April when its top leaders, including Vladimir Lenin, returned from exile in Switzerland.

On November 6, 1917 (October 24 by the Russian calendar), a Bolshevik coup led by Lenin and Leon Trotsky, another exile recently arrived from New York City, overthrew Kerensky and seized power. Capitalizing on the war weariness of the Russian people, the Bolsheviks signed an armistice with Germany, the Treaty of Brest-Litovsk, which freed many thousands of German troops on the Russian front for fighting in France.

In these desperate circumstances, the French and British generals urgently wished to absorb the Americans into already established units. But for both military and political reasons, Pershing and his superiors in

Washington insisted that the AEF be "distinct and separate." A believer in aggressive combat, Pershing abhorred the defensive mentality ingrained by three years of trench warfare. Further, he understood that America's voice at the peace table would be stronger if the AEF remained a distinct fighting force.

In March 1918, however, when Germany launched a major offensive along the Somme, aimed at France's ports on the English Channel, the Allies created a unified command under French general Ferdinand Foch. Some American troops were thrown into the fighting around Amiens and Armentières that stemmed the German advance.

The second phase of the Germans' spring 1918 offensive came in May along the Aisne River, where they broke through to the Marne and faced a nearly open route to Paris, fifty miles away. On June 4, as the French government prepared for evacuation, American forces arrived in strength. Parts of three U.S. divisions* and a marine brigade helped stop the Germans at the town of Château-Thierry and nearby Belleau Wood, a huge German machine-gun nest.

These two German offensives had punched deep holes (or *salients*) in the Allied line. A final German drive aimed at the cathedral city of Rheims between these two salients was stopped with the help of some 85,000 American troops. This was the war's turning point. At enormous cost, the Germans' last desperate effort to break the Allied line had been defeated.

### Turning the Tide

The final Allied offensive began on July 18, 1918. Of the 1 million American soldiers now in France, 270,000 fought in the drive to push the Germans back from the Marne. Rain pelted down as the Americans moved into position on the night of July 17. One wrote in his diary, "Trucks, artillery, infantry columns, cavalry, wagons, caissons, mud, MUD, utter confusion." Meanwhile, more than 100,000 AEF members joined in a parallel British offensive north of the Somme to expel the Germans from that area.

Pershing's first independent command came in September, when Foch authorized an AEF campaign to close a German salient around the town of St. Mihiel on the Meuse River, about 150 miles east of Paris. Eager to

---

* In World War I an AEF division at full strength consisted of 27,000 men and 1,000 officers, plus 12,000 support troops. Each division was split into four infantry regiments.

test his offensive strategy, Pershing assembled nearly 500,000 American and 100,000 French soldiers. Shelling of German positions began at 1:00 A.M. on September 11. Recorded an American in his diary, "[I]n one instant the entire front . . . was a sheet of flame, while the heavy artillery made the earth quake." Within four days the salient was closed, in part because some German units were already withdrawing when the attack began. Even so, St. Mihiel cost the United States seven thousand casualties.

The war's last battle began on September 26, as some 1.2 million Americans joined in the struggle to drive the Germans from the Meuse River and the dense Argonne Forest north of Verdun, a region scarred by four years of trench warfare. The stench of poison gas hung in the air, and bloated rats scurried in the mud, gorging on human remains. Americans now endured the filth, vermin, and dysentery familiar to veterans of the trenches. Frontline troops would never forget the terror of combat. As shells streaked overhead one dark night, recalled a veteran, "We simply lay and trembled from sheer nervous tension." Some welcomed injuries as a ticket out of the battle zone. Others collapsed emotionally and were hospitalized for "shell shock."

The AEF's assignment was to advance to the city of Sedan and cut the Sedan-Mezières Railroad, a major German supply route. In the way lay three long, heavily fortified German trenches, called *Stellung*. "We are not men anymore, just savage beasts," wrote a young American. Death came in many forms, and without ceremony. Bodies, packs, rifles, photos of loved ones, and letters from home sank indiscriminately into the all-consuming mud.

Adding to the horror, an influenza epidemic took many lives at the front as well as in training camps and cities back home. The strain reached even the iron-willed Pershing. One day as he rode in his staff car, he buried his head in his hands and moaned his dead wife's name: "Frankie, Frankie, my God, sometimes I don't know how I can go on."

Religious principles and ethical scruples faded as young men struggled to survive. "Love of thy neighbor is forgotten," recalled one, with "all the falsities of a sheltered civilization." The war's brutality would shape the literature of the 1920s as writers such as Ernest Hemingway stripped away the illusions obscuring the reality of mass slaughter.

But the AEF at last overran the dreadful *Stellung*, and the survivors slogged northward. In early November

**African Americans at the Front**
*Black troops of the 369th Infantry Regiment in the trenches near Maffrecourt, France, in 1918. Most African-American soldiers were assigned to non-combat duty, such as unloading supplies and equipment.*

the Sedan-Mezières railroad was cut. The AEF had fulfilled its assignment, at a cost of 26,277 dead.

### African-Americans in the AEF

More than 260,000 blacks volunteered or were drafted in World War I, and 50,000 went to France. Racism pervaded the military, as it did American society. The navy assigned blacks only to menial positions, and the marines excluded them altogether. When the war began, the army retired its senior black officer, Colonel Charles Young, on medical grounds.

One racist senator from Mississippi warned that the sight of "arrogant, strutting" black soldiers would trigger race riots. Blacks in training camps experienced crude racial abuse. Tension reached the breaking point in Houston in August 1917, when some black soldiers, endlessly goaded by local whites, seized weapons from the armory and killed seventeen whites. After a hasty trial with no appeal process, thirteen black soldiers were hanged and forty-one imprisoned for life. Not since the Brownsville Incident of 1906 (see Chapter 22) had black confidence in military justice been so shaken.

Once in France, blacks worked mainly as messboys (mealtime aides), laborers, or stevedores (ship-cargo handlers). Although reflecting a pattern of discrimination, these assignments in fact vitally aided the war effort. Working sometimes in twenty-four-hour shifts, black stevedores unloaded mountains of supplies with impressive efficiency.

One all-black division, the 92d, saw combat in the Meuse-Argonne. In addition, four black infantry regiments served with distinction under French command. One entire regiment received the French Croix de Guerre, and several hundred individual black soldiers were awarded French decorations for bravery.

The Germans showered the 92d division with leaflets describing racism in America and urging blacks to defect, but none did. Some whites of the AEF pressed the French to treat the blacks as inferiors. Most French people ignored this advice, however, and at least superficially treated blacks as equals. For blacks in the AEF, this eye-opening experience would remain with them after the war.

## Promoting the War and Suppressing Dissent

As neutralist sentiment faded, patriotic fervor gripped American society in 1917–1918. It reflected in part an elaborate government propaganda campaign to whip up war fever. As patriotism spread, it brought in its wake stifling intellectual conformity as well as intolerance for radical or dissenting ideas. Fueling this repressive spirit, government authorities and private vigilante groups hounded and arrested socialists, pacifists, and other dissidents and in the process trampled citizens' constitutional rights.

### Advertising the War

To President Wilson, the war at home was as important as the war in France. "It is not an army we must shape and train for war, it is a nation," he declared. Wilson understood that millions of Americans opposed the war. The opponents of the war represented many diverse viewpoints, but collectively they posed a formidable barrier to Wilson's dream of rallying the nation behind his crusade for a finer world order.

Seeking initially to overcome domestic opposition by persuasion, the administration drew upon the new professions of advertising and public relations to sell the war. Treasury Secretary McAdoo (who had married Woodrow Wilson's daughter Eleanor in 1914) orches-

**Financing the War; Mobilizing the Homefront**
*A patriotic war-bond poster; movie star Douglas Fairbanks at a New York City war-bond rally.*

trated a series of five government bond drives, called Liberty Loans, that financed about two-thirds of the $35.5 billion (including loans to the Allies) that World War I cost the United States.

McAdoo promoted the loan drives with ballyhoo. Posters exhorted citizens, "FIGHT OR BUY BONDS." Liberty Loan parades featured flags, banners, and marching bands. Movie stars like Mary Pickford and Charlie Chaplin worked for the cause. Schoolchildren purchased "thrift stamps" convertible into war bonds. Beneath the hucksterism ran a note of coercion. Only "a friend of Germany," McAdoo warned, would refuse to buy bonds.

The balance of the government's war costs came from taxes. Using its new power to tax incomes granted by the Sixteenth Amendment, Congress imposed stiff wartime taxes that rose as high as 70 percent at the top income levels. War-profits taxes, excise taxes on liquor and luxuries, and increased estate taxes also helped finance the war.

George Creel, a progressive reformer and journalist, headed Washington's most effective wartime propaganda agency, the Committee on Public Information (CPI). Established in April 1917, ostensibly to combat wartime rumors with facts, the Creel committee in re-

ality proclaimed the government's version of events and discredited all who questioned that version.

Twenty-one separate CPI divisions handled different aspects of the campaign. One division distributed posters drawn by leading illustrators. Another wrote propaganda releases that appeared in the press as "news" with no indication of their source. The *Saturday Evening Post* and other popular magazines published CPI ads that warned against spies, saboteurs, and anyone who "spreads pessimistic stories" or "cries for peace." Theaters screened CPI propaganda films bearing such titles as *The Kaiser: The Beast of Berlin.*

Particularly targeting immigrants, the CPI poured foreign-language pamphlets into immigrant neighborhoods and supplied prowar editorials to the foreign-language press. At a CPI media event held at Mount Vernon on July 4, 1918, an Irish-born tenor sang "The Battle Hymn of the Republic" while immigrants from thirty-three nations filed reverently past George Washington's tomb.

The CPI also targeted workers. Factory posters refuted the socialists' charge that this was a capitalists' war. Labor leader Samuel Gompers headed a prowar "American Alliance for Labor and Democracy" funded by the CPI.

A network of 75,000 CPI volunteers, called "four-minute men," gave short talks to movie-theater audiences and other gatherings. Creel later calculated that this small army of propagandists delivered 7.5 million speeches.

## Intellectuals, Cultural Leaders, and Reformers Present Arms

Teachers, writers, religious leaders, and magazine editors overwhelmingly supported the war. These custodians of culture saw the conflict as a struggle to defend threatened values. Historians wrote essays contrasting Germany's glorification of brute force with the Allies' loftier ideals. In *The Marne* (1918), expatriate American writer Edith Wharton expressed her love for her adopted nation, France. The war poems of Alan Seeger enjoyed great popularity in wartime America. A Harvard graduate who volunteered to fight for France and died in action in 1916, Seeger held a romantic vision of war and a "sense of being the instrument of Destiny." that many Americans longed to share. An artillery barrage was for him "the magnificent orchestra of war."

Many progressive reformers who had applauded Wilson's domestic program now cheered his war. The wartime climate of government activism and sacrifice, they believed, would encourage further reform activity. Herbert Croly, Walter Lippmann, and other progressive intellectuals associated with the *New Republic* magazine zealously supported the war. In gratitude, Wilson administration officials regularly briefed the *New Republic*'s editors on the government's policies.

John Dewey joined the prowar chorus. In a series of *New Republic* pieces in 1917–1918, Dewey condemned the war's opponents. Socially engaged intellectuals, he said, must accept reality and shape it toward positive social goals, not stand aside in self-righteous isolation. The war, he went on, presented exciting "social possibilities." Domestically, the wartime growth of government power could be channeled to reform purposes once peace returned. Internationally, America's entry into the war could transform an imperialistic struggle into a global democratic crusade.

## Wartime Intolerance

Responding to all this propaganda, some Americans became almost hysterical in their hatred of all things German, their hostility to aliens and dissenters, and their strident patriotism. Isolated acts by German saboteurs, including the blowing up of a New Jersey munitions dump, fanned the flames. German-Americans and others suspected of harboring pro-German sentiments were forced to kiss the flag or recite the Pledge of Allegiance. A woman in Canton, Ohio, was wrapped in a flag, marched to a bank, and ordered to buy a war bond. In Collinsville, Illinois, a mob lynched the German-born Robert Prager in April 1918. When a jury freed the mob leaders, a jury member shouted, "Nobody can say we aren't loyal now." The *Washington Post,* although deploring the lynching, saw it as evidence of "a healthful and wholesome awakening in the interior of the country."

An Iowa politician charged that "90 percent of all the men and women who teach the German language are traitors." German books vanished from libraries, towns with German names changed them, and on some restaurant menus, "liberty sandwich" and "lib-erty cabbage" replaced "hamburger" and "sauerkraut." A popular evangelist, Billy Sunday, proclaimed, "If you turn hell upside down you will find 'Made in Germany' stamped on the bottom."

Even the music world suffered. The Boston Symphony Orchestra dismissed its conductor, Karl Muck, for having accepted a decoration from the kaiser. Leopold Stokowski of the Philadelphia Orchestra dropped German opera, songs, and contemporary orchestral music from the repertoire. (He did retain Bach, Beethoven, Mozart, and Brahms, however.)

The zealots fell with special ferocity on war critics and radicals. A Cincinnati mob horsewhipped a pacifist minister. Theodore Roosevelt branded antiwar senator Robert La Follette "an unhung traitor." Columbia University fired two antiwar professors. In Bisbee, Arizona, vigilantes forced twelve hundred miners who belonged to the Industrial Workers of the World onto a freight train and shipped them into the New Mexico desert without food, water, or shelter.

## Opponents of the War

Despite the climate of intolerance, a few Americans opposed the war. Some were ethnic Germans with ties to the land of their forebears. Others were religious pacifists, including Quakers, Mennonites, and members of other historic peace churches. One of the votes against war in the House of Representatives was cast by the pacifist Jeannette Rankin of Montana, the first woman elected to Congress. "I want to stand by my country," she declared on the House floor, "but I cannot vote for war."

Of some 65,000 men who registered as conscientious objectors (COs), 21,000 were drafted. Assigned to noncombat duty on military bases, such as cleaning latrines, these COs sometimes experienced considerable abuse. When two Hutterite brothers who had refused to wear military uniforms died in prison, their bodies were dressed in uniforms before they were shipped home.

Woodrow Wilson heaped scorn on the pacifists. "What I am opposed to is not [their] feeling . . . , but their stupidity," he told a labor audience in November 1917; "my heart is with them, but my mind has contempt for them. I want peace, but I know how to get it, and they do not."

Socialist leaders such as Eugene Debs and Victor Berger opposed the war on political grounds. They regarded it as a capitalist contest for markets, with the

**Carrie Chapman Catt**
*The head of the National American Woman Suffrage Association supported the U.S. war effort in 1917–1918 while insisting that the suffrage campaign go forward as well.*

soldiers as cannon fodder. The U.S. declaration of war, they insisted, reflected mainly Wall Street's desire to protect its loans to England and France. Other socialists supported the war, however, dividing the party. The war split the women's movement as well. Some leaders like Jane Addams opposed it. Others endorsed it while keeping their own goals firmly in view. In *Mobilizing Woman-Power* (1918), Harriot Stanton Blatch offered a feminist variant of Woodrow Wilson's theme: women should support the war, she said, in order to have a role in shaping the peace. Anna Howard Shaw, a former president of the National American Woman Suffrage Association (NAWSA), chaired the Woman's Committee of the wartime Council of National Defense, using this largely symbolic post to bring a feminist perspective to wartime policy.

Carrie Chapman Catt, Shaw's successor as president of NAWSA, joined Jane Addams in founding the Woman's Peace party in 1915, but she supported U.S. entry into the war in 1917, sharing to some extent Wilson's vision of a more liberal postwar world order. Catt continued to direct her main energies to the suffrage cause, however, insisting that this was NAWSA's "number one war job." For this, some superpatriots accused her of disloyalty.

The war's most incisive critic was Randolph Bourne, a young journalist. Although Bourne admired John Dewey, he rejected Dewey's prowar position and dissected his arguments in penetrating essays published in 1917–1918. Like moths near a flame, Bourne said, intellectuals found power mesmerizing. He dismissed the belief that liberal reformers could direct the war to their own purposes. "If the war is too strong for you to prevent," he asked, "how is it going to be weak enough for you to control and mould to your liberal purposes?"

Eventually, Dewey, Lippmann, and other prowar intellectuals came to agree with Bourne. By 1919 Dewey conceded that the war, far from promoting liberalism, had encouraged reaction and intolerance. Randolph Bourne did not live to see his vindication, however. He died in 1918, at thirty-two, of influenza.

### Suppressing Dissent by Law

Wartime intolerance also surfaced in federal laws and official actions. The Espionage Act of June 1917 set stiff fines and prison sentences for a variety of loosely defined antiwar activities. The even more severe Sedition Amendment (May 1918) imposed heavy penalties on anyone convicted of using "disloyal, profane . . . or abusive language" about the government, the Constitution, the flag, or the military.

Wilson's attorney general, Thomas W. Gregory of Texas, employed these laws to stamp out dissent. Opponents of the war, proclaimed Gregory, should expect no mercy "from an outraged people and an avenging government." Under this sweeping legislation and similar state laws, the authorities arrested some fifteen hundred pacifists, socialists, IWW leaders, and other war critics. One socialist, Rose Pastor Stokes, found herself facing ten years in prison (the sentence was later commuted) for telling an audience, "I am for the people, and the government is for the profiteers." Kate Richards O'Hare, a midwestern socialist organizer, served more than a year in jail for allegedly telling a North Dakota audience, "The women of the United States are nothing more than brood sows, to raise children to get into the army and be made into fertilizer." Eugene Debs was sentenced to ten years in a federal penitentiary for a speech discussing the economic causes of war.

The Espionage Act also authorized the postmaster general to censor a wide variety of suspect material—a provision enforced by Postmaster General Albert S. Burleson, a reactionary superpatriot. Burleson suppressed a number of socialist periodicals. In January 1919 Congressman-elect Victor Berger received a twenty-year prison sentence (later set aside by the Supreme Court) and was denied his seat in the House of Representatives for publishing antiwar articles in his socialist newspaper, the *Milwaukee Leader.* According to socialist Norman Thomas, Burleson "didn't know socialism from rheumatism," but he pushed on with his repressive crusade. A patriotic group calling itself the

American Protective League, and local "Councils of Defense," operating with vague governmental authorization, further enforced ideological conformity. Alarm over the 1917 Bolshevik revolution in Russia further fueled these wartime attacks on domestic radicals.

A few citizens protested. Muckraking journalist Upton Sinclair wrote to President Wilson to deplore that a man of Albert Burleson's "childish ignorance" should wield such power; but Wilson did little to restrain the excesses. Nor did the U.S. Supreme Court. In three 1919 decisions, the Court upheld the Espionage Act convictions of antiwar activists. In one, *Schenck* v. *United States,* Justice Oliver Wendell Holmes, Jr., justified such repression when the exercise of the constitutional right of free speech posed a "clear and present danger" to the nation. In another decision, the Supreme Court upheld Eugene V. Debs's, conviction. Although the war was over, Woodrow Wilson refused to commute Debs's sentence.*

The wartime mood, originally one of idealism and high resolve, had degenerated into suspicion, narrow conformity, and persecution of all who failed to meet the zealots' notions of "100 percent Americanism." The effects of this ugly wartime climate would linger long after the armistice was signed.

# Economic and Social Trends in Wartime America

World War I affected millions of industrial workers, farmers, women, and blacks in important ways. The wartime mood also furthered some progressive reforms and gave a significant boost to the moral-reform movement.

## *Boom Times in Industry and Agriculture*

For all its horrendous toll, World War I brought prosperity to the U.S. economy. From 1914 to 1918, factory output grew by more than one-third. Even as several million men entered military service, the civilian work force grew by 1.3 million from 1916 to 1918, including many women and blacks. Unemployment dwindled as "Help Wanted" signs appeared most often in war-related industries such as shipbuilding, munitions,

---

* President Warren Harding released the aging Debs in December 1921, but his rights as a U.S. citizen were not restored.

steel, and textiles. Wages rose as well, but so did prices, which soared by 60 percent during the war. With manual labor in demand, however, the real wages of *unskilled* workers increased by nearly 20 percent from 1914 to 1918.

Samuel Gompers, the prowar head of the American Federation of Labor, urged workers not to strike during the war. (Some maverick AFL locals, as well as members of the more radical Industrial Workers of the World, ignored Gompers and went on strike anyway.) Despite the strike ban, union membership rose from 2.7 million in 1916 to more than 5 million by 1920. In part, this growth reflected the pro-union policies of the National War Labor Board, which guaranteed workers' right to organize and to bargain collectively with management.

The economic boom brought social disruption as well as prosperity. The stream of job seekers pouring into industrial centers strained housing, schools, and municipal services. The changes in social behavior took many forms. For example, the consumption of cigarettes, which soldiers and workers could conveniently carry in their uniform pockets, soared from 14 billion in 1914 to 48 billion in 1918. Automobile production quadrupled, from 460,000 in 1914 to 1.8 million in 1917. (The output of cars dipped briefly in 1918, as steel went for military production.)

Agriculture profited, too. With European farm production disrupted, U.S. agricultural prices more than doubled in 1913–1918, and farmers' real income rose significantly. Planters who sold cotton for 12¢ a pound in 1913 received 29¢ a pound by 1918. Corn prices surged upward at a similar rate.

This agricultural boom proved a mixed blessing. Many farmers borrowed heavily to expand production, and when farm prices fell after the war, they faced a credit squeeze. In the 1920s and 1930s, many hard-pressed farmers would look back to the war years as the last period of real prosperity.

## *Blacks Migrate Northward*

The war speeded up the exodus of southern blacks. An estimated half-million African-Americans moved north during the war, and most settled in cities. Each day, fresh arrivals from the South trudged through the railroad stations of Philadelphia, New York, Detroit, and Pittsburgh. Chicago's black population grew from 44,000 in 1910 to 110,000 in 1920; Cleveland's, from

8,000 to 34,000.

Economic opportunity beckoned. As the war disrupted immigration from Europe, American industry turned to the black population, still heavily southern and rural, to help take up the slack. Black newspapers like the *Chicago Defender* spread the word of job opportunities across the South. Some companies sent labor agents south to recruit black workers. Letters and word-of-mouth reports swelled the ranks of blacks heading north. One southern black, newly settled near Chicago, wrote home, "Nothing here but money, and it is not hard to get." A Pittsburgh newcomer presented a more balanced picture: "They give you big money for what you do, but they charge you big things for what you get."

To the southern black sharecropper confronting blatant racism, the prospect of a salary of three dollars a day or more, in a region where racism seemed less intense, appeared a heaven-sent opportunity. By 1920, 1.5 million African-Americans were working in northern factories or other urban-based jobs.

These newcomers brought with them their social institutions—above all, the church. Storefront "holiness" churches sprang up to meet the spiritual needs of deeply religious migrants from the South. The concentration of blacks in New York City laid the groundwork for the Harlem Renaissance, a cultural flowering of the 1920s. This migration also strengthened black activist organizations. Membership in the recently founded National Association for the Advancement of Colored People (NAACP) doubled in 1918–1919. The Jamaican black nationalist Marcus Garvey in 1916 moved his Universal Negro Improvement Association (UNIA) from Jamaica to New York City. By 1919, with branches in most northern cities, the UNIA stood poised for explosive growth.

Once the initial elation faded, African-Americans newly arrived in northern cities often found that they had exchanged one set of problems for another. White workers resented the labor competition, and white homeowners lashed out as jammed black neighborhoods spilled over into surrounding areas.

A bloody outbreak occurred on July 2, 1917, in East St. Louis, Illinois—home to thousands of recently arrived southern blacks. In a coordinated action, a white mob torched black homes and then shot the residents as they fled for their lives. At least thirty-nine blacks died, including a two-year-old who was shot and then thrown into a burning house.

A few weeks later, a silent march down New York's Fifth Avenue organized by the NAACP protested racist violence. One banner bore the slogan "Mr. President, Why Not Make AMERICA Safe for Democracy?" But growing racial tension, like other wartime social trends, did not end with the return of peace.

## Women and the War

From one perspective, World War I seems a uniquely male experience. Male politicians and statesmen led their nations into war. Male generals sent other men

**Migration of the Negro Series: No. 1, During the World War,** *by Jacob Lawrence, 1940–41*

into battle. Yet any event as vast as war touches all of society, not just half of it. The war affected women differently, but it affected them profoundly.

Women's movement leaders like Carrie Chapman Catt and Anna Howard Shaw hoped that the war would lead to equality and greater opportunity for women. And for a brief moment, the war did indeed seem to promise dramatic gains for women. Not only did thousands of women serve directly in the military and in volunteer agencies at home and in France, but in 1917–1918, about 1 million women worked in industry. More thousands held other jobs, from streetcar conductors to bricklayers. "Out of . . . repression into opportunity is the meaning of the war to thousands of women," wrote Florence Thorne of the American Federation of Labor in 1917.

Such hopes glowed brightly as the woman suffrage movement sped toward victory in 1917–1918 on a tide of wartime idealism. Through their wartime service, President Wilson wrote Catt, women had earned the right to vote. New York in 1917 passed a state woman-suffrage referendum that had been rejected two years before. In 1919, barraged by prosuffrage petitions from the states, the House and Senate by overwhelming margins passed a woman-suffrage amendment to the Constitution. The Nineteenth Amendment was ratified in 1920.

Beyond this achievement, however, hopes that the war would permanently better women's status proved unfounded. Relatively few women actually entered the work force for the first time in 1917–1918; most simply moved from poor-paying jobs to somewhat better-paying ones. And despite women's protests and War Labor Board rulings, even in these better-paying jobs most earned less than the men they replaced.

As the war ended, women lost their jobs to returning veterans. The New York labor federation advised, "The same patriotism which induced women to enter industry during the war should induce them to vacate their positions after the war." Male streetcar workers in Cleveland went on strike to force women conductors off the job.

Despite the spurt in employment during the war, the percentage of working women actually fell slightly from 1910 to 1920. As industrial researcher Mary Van Kleeck wrote in 1921, when the emergency ended, traditional male attitudes toward women "came to life once more." Randolph Bourne's bleak vision again proved prophetic. The darker side of the war spirit— prejudice, intolerance, and conformism—survived af-

ter the return of peace; the war's more positive side effects, such as greater gender equality in the workplace, proved more ephemeral.

## The War and Progressivism

What were the war's effects on the progressive reform movement? Historians paint a mixed picture. Overall, the war stifled reform energies and ushered in a decade of reaction. During the war itself, socialists and other critics of the capitalist system endured hostility and persecution. And while the war brought increased corporate regulation—a major progressive goal—the regulatory agencies were often dominated by the very business interests supposedly being supervised.

Yet some reform causes gained momentum during the war. The woman-suffrage campaign surged forward, and the years 1917–1918 also saw gains in the movement to better the condition of industrial workers. Spurred by social-justice progressives, the War Labor Board encouraged workers to join unions and pushed war plants to introduce the eight-hour workday, which by the war's end became the norm in U.S. industry. The wartime government also pressed factory owners to observe the federal ban on child labor, to provide worker-compensation benefits and to open their plants to safety and sanitation inspectors. William McAdoo's Railroad Administration, moreover, recognized railway workers' right to unionize. Another wartime agency, the United States Housing Corporation, built housing projects for workers, including some that encompassed schools, playgrounds, and recreational centers.

Responding to the argument that worker-protection laws would help to win the war by promoting social stability and industrial efficiency, several states during the war set wage-and-hour rules and enacted various protections and benefits for factory laborers. This flurry of social-justice reform activity quieted with the return of peace. But the laws remained on the books, creating precedents for future reform efforts.

The war also strengthened the coercive, moral-control component of the progressive movement, including the drive for prohibition. Exploiting the anti-German hysteria, prohibitionists pointed out that the nation's biggest breweries bore such German names as Pabst, Schlitz, and Anheuser-Busch. Beer, they hinted, was part of a German plot to undermine America's moral fiber and fighting qualities. And with Herbert Hoover preaching food conservation, they portrayed as unpatriotic and wasteful the use of grain to make whiskey and gin. Secretary of War Baker prohibited liquor sales near military camps and even forbade soldiers in uniform to buy a drink (see A Place in Time). Thus when the Eighteenth Amendment—banning the manufacture, shipment, or sale of alcoholic beverages—passed Congress in December 1917, it was widely seen as a war measure. Ratified in 1919, the prohibition amendment went into effect on January 1, 1920.

Extending the Progressive Era antiprostitution campaign, the War Department closed brothels near military bases; Congress appropriated $4 million to combat prostitution and venereal disease, especially among war workers; and sixty Young Women's Christian Association (YWCA) lecturers toured the nation for the Commission on Training Camp Activities, warning women to uphold standards of sexual morality. "Do Your Bit to Keep Him Fit," urged one wartime pamphlet addressed to women.

In San Antonio, Texas, a major military hub, an antiprostitution leader reflected the war mood when he declared, "We propose to fight vice . . . with the cold steel of the law, and to drive in the steel from the point to the hilt until the law's supremacy is acknowledged." Among the 110 red-light districts closed on military orders was New Orleans's famed Storyville. Jazz musicians who had been performing in Storyville's brothels and clubs moved up the Mississippi, carrying their music to Memphis, St. Louis, Kansas City, and Chicago. Thus the moral reformism of World War I helped to bring jazz northward.

This groundswell of moral-reform activity convinced some that traditional codes of behavior, weakening before the war, had now been restored. One antiprostitution crusader exulted: "Young men of today . . . are nearer perfection in conduct, morals, and ideals than any similar generation of young men in the history of the world. Their minds have been raised to ideals that would never have been attained save by the heroism of . . . the World War."

Taking the long view, the war severely retarded the social-justice, proworker side of progressivism, despite some wartime gains. As we saw in Chapter 22, Congress in 1916 had enacted a cluster of laws protecting workers. This legislation had rallied left-learning progressives, trade unionists, and some socialists behind Wilson. But the government's wartime repression of radicals and antiwar dissenters fractured this fragile coalition and laid the groundwork for a decade of reaction. The 1918 midterm election signalled the shift: the

Democrats lost both houses of Congress to a Republican party now dominated by conservatives. Not until the 1930s would the reform coalition foreshadowed in 1916 again emerge as a potent political force.

## Joyous Armistice, Bitter Aftermath

In November 1918 the war that had battered Europe for more than four years ended at last. Woodrow Wilson dominated the peace conference but failed in his most cherished objective: American membership in the League of Nations. At home, as racism and intolerance worsened, the electorate repudiated Wilsonianism and in 1920 sent Republican Warren G. Harding to the White House.

### Wilson's Fourteen Points

From the moment the United States went to war, President Wilson planned to put a "Made in America" stamp on the peace. U.S. involvement, he and his liberal supporters believed, could transform a sordid power conflict into a crusade for a more democratic world order. Many Americans looked to the president to translate that vision into reality.

As the nation mobilized in 1917, Wilson recruited a group of scholarly advisers called the Inquiry to translate his vision into specific war aims. The need for a clear statement of America's war objectives grew urgent after the Bolsheviks seized power in Russia late in 1917 and published many of the self-serving secret treaties signed by the European powers prior to 1914.

In a speech to Congress in January 1918, Wilson summed up U.S. war aims. These came to be called the "Fourteen Points." Eight of these goals dealt with territorial settlements in postwar Europe, pledging self-determination and autonomy for peoples formerly dominated by the Austro-Hungarian or the Ottoman empires. A ninth point insisted that colonial disputes be resolved in the interests of the colonized peoples as well as of the European colonial powers. The remaining five points offered Wilson's larger postwar vision: a world of unrestricted navigation, freer trade, reduced armaments, openly negotiated treaties rather than secret pacts, and "a general association of nations" to resolve conflicts peacefully. The Fourteen Points helped solidify American support for the war, especially among liberals. The high-minded objectives seemed proof that the nation had gone to war not for selfish reasons but out of noble motives. Could Wilson achieve his goals? That remained to be seen.

## Armistice

With the failure of Germany's spring 1918 offensive and Allied advances on several fronts, the German high command in early October proposed to Wilson an armistice based on the Fourteen Points. The British and French hesitated, but when Wilson threatened a separate peace, they agreed. Meanwhile, in Berlin, Kaiser Wilhelm II had abdicated and a German republic had been proclaimed.

As dawn broke over the Forest of Compiègne on November 11, 1918, Marshal Foch and his German counterparts, seated in Foch's private railway car, signed an armistice ending hostilities at 11:00 A.M. An American air ace, Captain Edward Rickenbacker, flew over the lines at precisely 11:00 A.M. and watched as the booming guns fell silent and as troops cautiously emerged and approached each other. Rockets burst over the front that night, not in anger now but in relief and celebration. Back home, cheering throngs filled the streets, many carrying hand-lettered signs. "LONG LIVE PEACE," blazed one in Chicago. "Everything for which America has fought has been accomplished," Wilson hopefully proclaimed.

Soon crowded troop transports were ferrying proud and relieved soldiers home. One returnee, artillery captain Harry Truman of Missouri, in a letter to his fiancée, Bess Wallace, described his feelings upon entering New York Harbor:

> Dear Bess,
>
> I've never seen anything that looks so good as the Liberty Lady in New York Harbor and the mayor's welcoming boat, which came down the river to meet us. You know the men have seen so much and have been in so many hard places that it takes something real to give them a thrill, but when the band on that boat played "Home Sweet Home" there were not many dry eyes. The hardest of hard-boiled cookies even had to blow his nose a time or two.

## The Versailles Peace Conference

**Woodrow Wilson: Peacemaker**
*On July 4, 1919, a confident President Wilson speaks to crew members and others aboard the* U.S.S. George Washington *en route home after the Versailles peace conference. Political realities would soon cruelly mock Wilson's optimistic vision of the postwar world order.*

The fighting was over; the task of forging a peace treaty remained. Eager to play a central role, Wilson made a crucial decision: he would lead the American delegation to the peace conference. This was probably a mistake. The strain of protracted bargaining soon took its toll on his frail nerves and slim reserve of energy.

Wilson compounded his mistake in naming the peace commission: the sole Republican was an elderly diplomat who lacked influence in the party. The appointment of one or two prominent Republicans might have spared Wilson future grief. A further ill omen came in the 1918 midterm elections. Despite Wilson's plea to the electorate to strengthen his hand at the peace conference by voting Democratic, the Republicans gained control of both houses of Congress.

Nevertheless, spirits soared on December 4, 1918, as the *George Washington,* a converted German liner, steamed out of New York bearing Woodrow Wilson to Europe—the first president to cross the Atlantic while in office. Ships' whistles blared as a jaunty Wilson waved his hat to the crowd on the docks. The giddy mood continued when Wilson reached France. In Paris shouts of "Voodrow Veelson" rang out as he rode in a parade up the Champs-Élysées, the city's ceremonial boulevard. When Wilson visited England, children at the dock in Dover spread flowers in his path. In Italy an exuberant local official compared his visit to the Second Coming of Jesus Christ.

The euphoria faded quickly, however, when the peace conference began at the palace of Versailles near Paris, led by the Allied heads of state: President Wilson; Italy's Vittorio Orlando; the aged and cynical Georges Clemenceau of France, determined to avenge Germany's defeat of France in 1871; and David Lloyd George of Great Britain, of whom Wilson said, "He is slippery as an eel, and I never know when to count on him."

These European statesmen represented vindictive nations that had suffered greatly in the war. Their goals bore little relationship to Wilson's liberal vision. As Clemenceau remarked, "God gave us the Ten Commandments and we broke them. Mr. Wilson has given us the Fourteen Points. We shall see."

Differences surfaced quickly. Orlando demanded a port for Italy on the eastern Adriatic. Japan insisted on keeping the trading rights that it had seized from Germany in the Chinese province of Shandong (Shantung). Clemenceau was obsessed with revenge. At one point, an appalled Wilson threatened to leave the conference.

Reflecting this poisonous climate, the peace treaty signed by a sullen German delegation on June 28, 1919, was harshly punitive. Germany was disarmed, stripped of its colonies, forced to admit sole blame for the war, and saddled with whopping reparation payments to the Allies.* France regained the provinces of Alsace and Lorraine lost to Germany in 1871 and took control for fifteen years of Germany's coal-rich Saar Basin. The treaty demilitarized a zone thirty miles east of the Rhine to the French border and transferred a slice of eastern Germany to Poland. All told, Germany lost one-tenth of its population and one-eighth of its territory. The treaty granted Japan's Shandong claims and gave Italy a slice of Austrian territory in which lived 200,000 German-speaking inhabitants.

Planting the seeds of future conflict—and underscoring that this had indeed been a *world* war—the treaty makers rejected the efforts of colonized peoples to free themselves of European rule. For example, Ho Chi Minh, a young Vietnamese nationalist who would later become head of his nation, visited Versailles in an unsuccessful effort to secure Vietnamese independence from the French.

Wilson's idealistic emphasis on self-determination and democracy, however, did influence some of the treaty's provisions. Germany's former colonies (as well as those of Turkey in the Middle East) went to the various Allies under a "mandate" or trusteeship system that in theory would eventually lead to independence. The treaty also recognized the independence of Poland; the Baltic states of Estonia, Latvia, and Lithuania (territories that Germany had seized in a harsh peace treaty with Bolshevik Russia in March 1918); and two new nations carved from the old Austro-Hungarian and Ottoman empires: Czechoslovakia and Yugoslavia.

On balance, however, the Versailles treaty proved a disaster. Not only did it arouse resentment in Germany, but its framers made little effort to come to terms with revolutionary Russia. Indeed, in August 1918 a fourteen-nation Allied army had landed at various Russian ports, ostensibly to protect Allied war matériel and secure the ports from German attack. But these troops were soon actively assisting Russian forces seeking to overthrow the new Bolshevik government.

Some seven thousand U.S. troops participated in this intervention, remaining until April 1920. Like nearly every political leader of his day, Woodrow Wilson strongly opposed Bolshevism. Having welcomed the liberal Russian revolution of March 1917, he viewed Lenin's October coup and Russia's withdrawal from the war as a betrayal of the Allied cause and of his hopes for a liberal Russian future.

The Versailles treaty reflected this hostility. Its territorial settlements in eastern Europe were designed to weaken Russia. Before leaving Versailles, Wilson and the other Allied leaders agreed to support a Russian military leader who was continuing to fight the Bolsheviks. David Fogelsong's *America's Secret War Against Bolshevism* (1995), based on intensive research, makes clear that the Wilson administration played a leading behind-the-scenes role in this entire effort to bring down the new communist regime. Not until 1933 did the United States recognize the Soviet Union.

## The Fight over the League of Nations

Dismayed by the treaty's vindictive features, Wilson focused on his one shining achievement at Versailles: the

---

* These reparations were set at $56 billion, including the pensions that the Allied governments would ultimately pay their veterans, but quickly negotiated downward. When Germany stopped reparations in 1932, only $9 billion had been paid.

*A 1918 cartoon portrays Senate opposition to U.S. membership in the League of Nations. At President Wilson's insistence, the covenant to establish the League had been incorporated in the Versailles treaty.*

creation of a new international organization, the League of Nations. The agreement or "covenant" to establish the League, written into the peace treaty itself, engaged Wilson's deepest emotions. The League embodied his vision of a liberal, harmonious, and rational world order.

But Wilson's dream would soon lie in ruins. A warning sign had come in February 1919, when thirty-nine Republican senators and senators-elect, including Henry Cabot Lodge, signed a letter rejecting the League in its present form. Wilson had retorted defiantly, "You cannot dissect the Covenant from the treaty without destroying the whole vital structure."

When Wilson in July 1919 sent the treaty to the Senate for ratification, Lodge bottled it up in the Foreign Relations Committee. Furious at Lodge's tactics, and convinced that he could rally popular opinion to his cause, Wilson left Washington on September 3 for a western speaking tour. Covering more than nine thousand miles by train, Wilson defended his beloved League in thirty-seven speeches in twenty-two days.

Crowds were large and friendly. People wept as Wilson described his visits to American war cemeteries in France, and cheered his vision of a world free of war.

But the grueling trip left Wilson exhausted. On September 25, in Colorado, he collapsed. "I just feel as if I am going to pieces," the president, bursting into tears, told his physician, Cary Grayson. The train sped back to Washington, where Wilson suffered a devastating stroke on October 2. For a time, he lay paralyzed and near death. Despite a partial recovery, Wilson spent the rest of his term mostly in bed or in a wheelchair, a reclusive invalid, his mind clouded, his fragile emotions betraying him into vindictive actions and outbursts. He broke with close advisers; refused to see the British ambassador; and dismissed Secretary of State Lansing, whom he accused of disloyalty. In January 1920 Dr. Grayson advised resignation on medical grounds, but Wilson refused.

Wilson's strong-willed second wife, Edith Galt, played a highly manipulative role during these difficult months, fiercely guarding her incapacitated husband.* She and Dr. Grayson hid his condition from the public, controlled his access to information, and decided who could see him. Cabinet members, congressional leaders, and even the vice president, Thomas R. Marshall, were barred from the White House. When one political leader seeking a meeting told Mrs. Wilson that "the welfare of the country" was involved, she snapped, "I am not thinking of the country now, I am thinking of my husband."[†]

Under these trying circumstances, the League drama unfolded. On September 10, 1919, the Foreign Relations Committee at last sent the treaty to the Senate, but with a series of amendments. The Senate split into three groups over the League issue: Democrats who supported the League covenant without changes; Republican "Irreconcilables," led by Hiram Johnson, Robert La Follette, and Idaho's William Borah, who opposed the League absolutely; and Republican "Reservationists" led by Lodge, who demanded changes in the League covenant as a condition of their support. The Reservationists' key objection focused on Article 10 of the covenant, which pledged each member nation to preserve the political independence and territorial integrity of all other members. This blank-check provi-

---

* Wilson's first wife, Ellen, had died in August 1914.

† The Twenty-fifth Amendment to the Constitution, ratified in 1967, set up procedures for the transfer of power to the vice president from a president unable to perform the duties of the office.

sion, the Reservationists believed, limited America's freedom of action in foreign affairs and Congress's constitutional right to declare war. That right must be spelled out explicitly in the League covenant, they insisted.

Had Wilson been willing to compromise, the Senate would probably have ratified the Versailles treaty, and the United States would have joined the League. But Wilson's illness aggravated his tendency toward rigidity. From his isolation in the White House, he instructed the Democratic senators to vote against the treaty with Lodge's reservations. Although international-law specialists believed that these reservations would not significantly weaken U.S. participation in the League, Wilson rejected them as "a knife thrust at the heart of the treaty."

Despite the positive responses to Wilson's western tour, the American people did not rally behind the League. The reactionary political mood that Wilson's own administration had helped create during the war did not encourage a grand gesture of political idealism once the war was over. As the editor of *The Nation* magazine observed, "If [Wilson] loses his great fight for humanity, it will be because he was deliberately silent when freedom of speech and the right of conscience were struck down in America."

On November 19, 1919, pro-League Democrats obeying Wilson's instructions and anti-League Irreconcilables joined forces to defeat the Versailles treaty with Lodge's reservations. A second vote the following March produced the same result. The United States would not join the League. A president elected amid much enthusiasm in 1912, applauded when he called for war in 1917, and adulated when he arrived in Europe in 1918, lay isolated and sick, his leadership repudiated. What might have been Woodrow Wilson's moment of triumph had turned to ashes in his grasp.

### Racism and Red Scare

The wartime spirit of "100 percent Americanism" left a bitter aftertaste. The years 1919–1920 saw new racial violence and fresh antiradical hysteria.

Mobs lynched seventy-six blacks in 1919, the worst toll in fifteen years. The victims included ten veterans, several still in uniform. Some lynchings involved incredible brutality. In Omaha a mob shot a black prisoner more than a thousand times, mutilated him, and hanged his body in a busy intersection.

The bloodiest violence occurred in 1919 in Chicago, where the influx of southern blacks had pushed racial tension to a high level. On a hot July afternoon, whites at a Lake Michigan beach threw stones at a black youth swimming offshore. When he sank and drowned, black neighborhoods erupted. A thirteen-day reign of terror followed as white and black marauders terrorized the streets with random attacks and arson. Black gangs stabbed an Italian peddler; white gangs pulled blacks from streetcars and shot or whipped them. The outbreak left fifteen whites and twenty-three blacks dead, over five hundred injured, and more than a thousand families, mostly black, homeless.

The wartime antiradical panic crested in the Red Scare of 1919–1920. Fears of "bolshevism" deepened when a rash of strikes broke out in 1919. When Seattle's labor unions organized a peaceful general strike early in 1919, the mayor, accusing the strikers of seeking to "duplicate the anarchy of Russia," called for federal troops. Anxiety crackled again in April, when packages mailed to various public officials proved to contain bombs. One such bomb blew off the hands of a senator's maid; another damaged the home of Attorney General A. Mitchell Palmer.

In September 350,000 steelworkers went on strike protesting low pay and long hours. Mill owners broke the strike in part by taking out newspaper ads describing the walkout as a bolshevik plot engineered by "Red agitators."

The antiradical paranoia soon took political form. In November 1919 the House of Representatives refused to seat the Milwaukee socialist Victor Berger. Berger's district promptly reelected him, but the House stood firm. The New York legislature expelled several socialist members. The Justice Department, setting up a countersubversion division under young J. Edgar Hoover, future head of the Federal Bureau of Investigation, arrested hundreds of suspected communists and radicals. In December 1919, 249 Russian-born aliens were deported. One deportee was the radical Emma Goldman, a leader of the birth-control movement. The government's antiradical crusade won enthusiastic support from the American Legion, a newly founded veterans' association, and the National Association of Manufacturers.

On January 2, 1920, in a dragnet coordinated by the Justice Department, federal marshals and local police in thirty-two cities raided the homes of suspected radicals and the headquarters of radical organizations.

**J. Edgar Hoover, Newly Appointed Director of the Federal Bureau of Investigation, 1924**
*Earlier, during the postwar "Red Scare" of 1919–1920, Hoover headed the Justice Department's General Intelligence Division that investigated radicals and alleged subversives.*

Attorney General Palmer, ambitious for higher office, coordinated these "Red raids." A Quaker who had compiled a strong reform record as Congressman, Palmer totally succumbed to the postwar anticommunist hysteria. Defending his actions, Palmer later described the menace he believed the nation faced in 1919:

> The blaze of revolution was sweeping over every American institution of law and order . . . eating its way into the homes of the American workman, its sharp tongues of revolutionary heat . . . licking at the altars of the churches, leaping into the belfry of the school bell, crawling into the sacred corners of American homes, . . . burning up the foundations of society.

The Red Scare subsided as Palmer's lurid predictions failed to materialize. When a bomb exploded in New York City's financial district in September 1920, killing thirty-eight people, most Americans saw the event as the work of an isolated fanatic, not evidence of approaching revolution.

### The Election of 1920

In this unsettled climate, the election of 1920 approached. Wilson, wholly out of touch with political reality, toyed with seeking a third term but was dissuaded. Treasury Secretary McAdoo and Attorney General Palmer, both harbored presidential hopes. But when the Democrats convened in San Francisco, the delegates sang "How Dry I Am" (prohibition had just taken effect), tepidly backed Wilson's League position, and nominated James M. Cox, the mildly progressive governor of Ohio. They chose as Cox's running mate the young assistant secretary of the navy, Franklin D. Roosevelt, who possessed a potent political name.

Without search warrants or arrest warrants, they arrested more than 4,000 persons (of whom some 550 were deported), and ransacked homes and offices, seizing papers and records.

These raids involved gross violations of civil rights and simple decency. Marshals arrested one woman in her bedroom. In Lynn, Massachusetts, police arrested thirty-nine men and women meeting to plan a cooperative bakery. In Boston, police paraded scores of arrested persons through the streets in handcuffs and chains and then confined them in crowded, unheated, and unsanitary cells.

### The Election of 1920

| Candidates | Parties | Electoral Vote | Popular Vote | Percentage of Popular Vote |
|---|---|---|---|---|
| WARREN G. HARDING | Republican | 404 | 16,143,407 | 60.4 |
| James M. Cox | Democratic | 127 | 9,130,328 | 34.2 |
| Eugene V. Debs | Socialist | | 919,799 | 3.4 |
| P. P. Christensen | Farmer-Labor | | 265,411 | 1.0 |

The confident Republicans, meeting in Chicago, had trouble agreeing on a candidate. Party leaders at last turned to Senator Warren G. Harding of Ohio, an amiable politician whose principal qualification was his availability. As one Republican leader observed: "There ain't any first raters this year. . . . We got a lot of second raters, and Harding is the best of the second raters." For vice president, they chose Governor Calvin Coolidge of Massachusetts, who won attention in 1919 with his denunciation of a Boston policemen's strike.

Wilson proclaimed the election a "solemn referendum" on the League, but the nation was psychologically drained, both by the war and by the emotional roller-coaster ride—from idealism to disillusionment—of the Wilson presidency. "The bitterness toward Wilson is everywhere . . .," wrote a Democratic campaign worker; "he hasn't a friend."

Harding promised a return to "normalcy"—no more crusades, no more cavalcades of reform. His campaign speeches were empty of content but vaguely reassuring. William McAdoo would later describe them as "an army of pompous phrases moving over the landscape in search of an idea."

Harding and Coolidge piled up a landslide victory: 16 million popular votes against 9 million for Cox and Roosevelt. Nearly a million voters, at least in part to protest the wartime repression of radicals, defiantly cast their ballots for the socialist Eugene V. Debs, then in an Atlanta penitentiary.

The election dashed all hope for American entry into the League of Nations. During the campaign Harding had spoken vaguely of some form of "international organization," but with victory assured, he bluntly announced that the League question was "dead." Senator Lodge exulted that the voters had ripped "Wilsonism" up by the roots. The sense of national destiny and high purpose that Woodrow Wilson had evoked so eloquently in April 1917 survived only as an ironic memory as Americans impatiently turned to a new president, a new decade, and a new era.

## CONCLUSION

The early twentieth century, an era of reform at home, also saw intensifying U.S. involvement abroad, reflecting the same economic and cultural forces that were shaping home-front policy. Focused initially on Latin America and Asia, after 1914 this new globalism in-

creasingly centered on the European war, which in 1917 became an America war as well.

By conservative estimate, the First World War cost 10 million dead and 20 million wounded. Included in this toll were 112,000 American dead—49,000 in battle and the rest from influenza and other diseases. For those not in uniform, the war often produced a flush of prosperity but also hardships, ranging from sugar shortages to the loss of loved ones.

The war's social, political, economic, and technological impact extended far beyond the battlefield. The conflict brought marked advances in the technology of slaughter, for example, from U-boat torpedoes and primitive aerial bombs to toxic gases and more efficient machine guns.

The war furthered the goals of some reformers, bringing to fruition the woman-suffrage and prohibition causes, for example. To promote economic mobilization, the federal government expanded its regulatory power over corporations and measures were enacted to assure war workers' well-being and efficiency. But in a larger sense, the war and its aftermath severely undermined the best side of progressivism: its openness to new ideas, its commitment to social justice, and its humanitarian concern for the underdog. As conformism and fear of radicalism set in, the prewar reform impulse withered. This climate of reaction intensified in 1919–1920, as an emotionally spent American people repudiated Wilsonian idealism.

The war also changed the lives of millions of ordinary workers, farmers, blacks, and women, and enhanced the standing of social workers, psychologists, engineers, public-relations specialists, advertisers, and other professionals who contributed expertise to the cause. Internationally, despite the wrangles that kept America out of the League of Nations, the conflict propelled the United States to the center of world politics and left the nation's businesses and financial institutions poised for global expansion.

Some of these changes endured; others proved fleeting. Cumulatively, however, their effect was profound. The nation that celebrated the armistice in November 1918 was very different from the one that Woodrow Wilson had solemnly taken into battle only nineteen months earlier.

## FOR FURTHER READING

Nancy K. Bristow, *Making Men Moral: Social Engineering During* the Great War (1996). Perceptive study of the Commission on Training Camp Activities.

Robert H. Ferrell, Woodrow Wilson and World War I, 1917–1921 (1985). A vigorously written critical synthesis; especially good on the peace negotiations.

Martin Gilbert, The First World War: A Complete History (1994). Weak on strategy, but vividly conveys the grim experience of ordinary soldiers.

Meiron and Susie Harries, The Last Days of Innocence: America at War, 1917–1918 (1997). Readable and well-researched overview history of both the military and the home-front aspects of the war.

David M. Kennedy, Over Here: The First World War and American Society (1980). Deeply researched interpretive study of the home front during the war.

Thomas J. Knock, To End All Wars: World War I and the Quest for a New World Order (1992). A compelling study of the origins of Wilson's internationalism and of the links between domestic reform and foreign policy.

Ronald Schaffer, America in the Great War: The Rise of the War Welfare State (1991). Explores the war's effect on corporate organization and business-government links, as well as wartime initiatives to benefit industrial workers.

# The 1920s

**Tongues (Holy Rollers),** by Archibald J. Motley, Jr., 1929

Sam Groipen of Medford, Massachusetts, was washing the windows of his grocery store, the Cooperative Cash Market, in June 1928 when a meat truck pulled up in front of the A&P supermarket next door. Sam knew the meaning of this seemingly ordinary event: his days as an independent grocer were numbered. A Russian-Jewish immigrant, Sam had opened his market in 1923, the year that he married. At first Sam and his wife did well. Sam served the customers; his wife kept the books. They knew their patrons by name and extended credit to those short on cash.

In 1925, however, the chain stores came. A&P moved in next door, then First National and Stop & Shop across the street. At first the chains did not hurt Sam's business. Small by today's standards, they carried only brand-name groceries, not meat or fish. But the Medford A&P added meat and fish in 1928. Sam watched as former customers—some of whom still owed him money—walked past his door on their way to a supermarket. "I felt like I was being strangled," he later recalled; "those bastard chains were destroying me."

In 1935 Sam Groipen sold out. Abandoning his dream of prospering as an independent businessman, he joined the giant Prudential Life Insurance Company. Eventually, Sam's bitterness toward the chains softened. "I have been mellowed by the system," he reflected.

Groipen's experience paralleled that of many independent entrepreneurs in the 1920s who found themselves competing with great corporations. Still in its early stages in the 1920s, this process of corporate consolidation would transform American society in the years ahead.

In the 1920s the nation's vast productive capacity burst forth with a tidal wave of automobiles, radios, electrical appliances, and other consumer goods. This stimulated the economy and transformed the lives of ordinary Americans. Ingrained patterns of diet, dress, travel, entertainment, and even thought shifted markedly as the economic order evolved.

These technological changes, following decades of immigration and urban growth, spawned social tensions. While Republican presidents espoused conservative political and cultural values, conflicts ripped at the social fabric. But this same ferment also stimulated creativity in literature and the arts. We turn in Chapter 24 to the decade of the 1920s, when so many features of modern American mass culture first became boldly evident.

This chapter focuses on four major questions:

♦ What economic developments underlay the prosperity of the 1920s, and how did those developments affect different social groups in America?

♦ What political values shaped American public life in this era of Republican ascendancy? How did Herbert Hoover's social and political thought differ from that of Harding and Coolidge?

♦ What is meant by "mass culture"? What developments helped create a mass culture in the 1920s, and how thoroughly did it penetrate American society?

♦ The 1920s was a time of both cultural creativity and social tensions. Can you identify any developments in American society in these years that contributed to *both* the creativity and the tensions?

# A New Economic Order

Fueled by new consumer products, advertising, and innovative forms of corporate organization, the economy surged in the 1920s. But not everyone benefited. Key industries declined, and farmers suffered chronic economic woes. Still, the overall picture seemed rosy, and most Americans celebrated a thriving business culture.

## *A Decade of Prosperity*

The war-induced boom lasted until 1920, when the rush of demobilization disrupted the economy. As the government canceled contracts and returning veterans sought jobs, a sharp recession struck. Recovery came in 1922, however, and for the next few years the economy hummed. Unemployment fell to as low as 3 percent, prices held steady, and the gross national product grew by 43 percent from 1922 to 1929.

New consumer goods, including home electrical products, contributed to the prosperity. Many factories were already electrified, but now the age of electricity dawned for urban households as well. By the mid-1920s, with more than 60 percent of the nation's homes wired for electricity, a parade of electrical appliances, from refrigerators, washing machines, and vacuum cleaners to fans, razors, and mixers, crowded the stores. The manufacture of such appliances, as well as of hydroelectric generating plants and equipment for the electrical industry itself, provided a massive economic stimulus.

The 1920s business boom rested, too, on the automobile. At first a plaything of the rich, the automobile was quickly democratized. As early as 1904, Ransom E. Olds had offered his sporty Oldsmobiles for $650. Henry Ford of Detroit, having built his first prototype in 1896, introduced the low-priced Model T in 1908; by 1916 seven hundred thousand had been sold.

In the 1920s the automobile came into its own. Registrations jumped from about 8 million in 1920 to more than 23 million in 1930, by which time some 60 percent of U.S. families owned automobiles. Ford led the market until mid-decade, when General Motors Corporation (GM) spurted ahead by touting a range of colors (the Model T came only in black) and greater comfort. GM's lowest-priced car, named for French au-

## Economic Expansion, 1920–1929

*After a brief postwar downturn, the American economy surged in the 1920s.*

**Index of Industrial Production (1913=100)**

*Source:* U.S. Department of Commerce, *Long-Term Economic Growth* (Washington, D.C.: U.S. Government Printing Office, October 1966), 169.

**Traffic Jam, 1920s-Style**
*Bumper-to-bumper traffic in Forest Park, St. Louis, in the Twenties*

## CHRONOLOGY

**1915** Modern Ku Klux Klan founded.

**1919** Volstead Act (Prohibition).

**1920–1921** Sharp postwar recession; agricultural prices plummet.

**1920** Warren G. Harding elected president.

Radio station KDKA, Pittsburgh, broadcasts election returns.

Eighteenth Amendment to the Constitution takes effect.

F. Scott Fitzgerald, *This Side of Paradise*.

Sinclair Lewis, *Main Street*.

**1921** Recovery from recession; economic boom begins; agriculture remains depressed.

Sheppard-Towner Act.

National Woman's party founded by Alice Paul.

*Shuffle Along*, all-black musical review.

**1921–1922** Washington Naval Arms Conference.

**1922** Supreme Court declares child-labor law unconstitutional.

Fordney-McCumber Tariff restores high rates.

Herbert Hoover, *American Individualism*.

Sinclair Lewis, *Babbitt*.

T. S. Eliot, *The Wasteland*.

**1923** Harding dies; Calvin Coolidge becomes president.

Supreme Court strikes down minimum-wage law for women.

Jean Toomer, *Cane*.

**1924** Teapot Dome scandals investigated.

National Origins Act.

Calvin Coolidge elected president.

McNary-Haugen farm bill introduced.

**1925** Scopes trial.

Ku Klux Klan scandal in Indiana.

Alain Locke, *The New Negro*.

Dorothy and DuBose Heyward, *Porgy*.

F. Scott Fitzgerald, *The Great Gatsby*.

**1926** Ernest Hemingway, *The Sun Also Rises*.

Langston Hughes, *The Weary Blues*.

**1927** *The Jazz Singer*, first sound movie.

Coolidge vetoes the McNary-Haugen bill.

Henry Ford introduces the Model A.

Execution of Sacco and Vanzetti.

Charles A. Lindbergh's transatlantic flight.

**1928** Kellogg-Briand Pact.

Herbert Hoover elected president.

**1929** Federal Farm Board created.

Sheppard-Towner program terminated.

*Hallelujah,* first all-black movie.

Ernest Hemingway, *A Farewell to Arms*.

Robert and Helen Lynd, *Middletown*.

**1930** Smoot-Hawley Tarrif.

**1933** Repeal of the Eighteenth Amendment

---

tomotive designer Louis Chevrolet, proved especially popular. Rising to the challenge, Ford in 1927 introduced the stylish Model A in a variety of colors. By the end of the decade, the automobile industry accounted for about 9 percent of all wages in manufacturing and had stimulated such related industries as rubber, gasoline and petroleum, advertising, and highway construction.

The business boom stimulated capitalist expansion. To supply their overseas markets, Ford, GM, General Electric, and other big corporations built production facilities abroad. Other U.S. firms acquired foreign processing facilities or sources of raw materials. Swift, Armour, and other meatpackers built plants in Argentina; Anaconda Copper acquired Chile's biggest copper mine; and the mammoth United Fruit Company established processing factories throughout Latin America. American capital also flowed to Europe, especially Germany, as investors loaned postwar European nations money to repay war debts and modernize their economies. Total U.S. private investment abroad—a scant $3.5 billion in 1914—exceeded $17 billion by 1930.

But the era of multinational corporations, global flow of capital, and thriving international trade still lay in the future in the 1920s. Economic nationalism prevailed as the industrialized nations, including the United States, erected high tariff barriers. As a percentage of the gross national product, U.S. exports actually fell from 1913 to 1929. But change was underway as U.S. industry flexed its muscles and organized for mass consumer production. Manufactured goods, less than half the value of total U.S. exports in 1913, rose to 61 percent by the end of the 1920s.

## New Modes of Producing, Managing, and Selling

Building on the industrial feats of the war years, the 1920s saw striking increases in productivity. New assembly-line techniques boosted the per capita output of industrial workers by some 40 percent during this decade. At the sprawling Ford plants near Detroit, workers stood in one place and performed repetitive tasks as an endless chain conveyed the partly assembled vehicles past them.

*Fordism* became a synonym worldwide for American industrial prowess and assembly-line production. In the Soviet Union, which purchased 25,000 Ford tractors in the 1920s, the people "ascribed a magical quality to the name of Ford," a 1927 visitor reported.

Corporate consolidation, spurred by the war, continued. By the late 1920s, over a thousand companies a year vanished through merger. Corporate giants dominated the major industries: Ford, GM, and Chrysler in automobiles; General Electric and Westinghouse in electricity; and so forth. In the public-utilities field, consolidation became epidemic. Samuel Insull of the Chicago Edison Company, for example, built a $3.5 billion empire of local power companies. By 1930 one hundred corporations controlled nearly half the na-

*Small neighborhood stores faced competition from supermarkets in the 1920s.*

tion's business. Without actually merging, companies that made the same product often cooperated through trade associations on such matters as pricing, product specifications, and division of markets.

As American capitalism streamlined its operations, more bureaucratic management structures arose. Like the federal government and many professional societies, corporations rationalized their operations in the twenties. They set up specialized divisions responsible for product development, market research, economic forecasting, employee relations, and so forth. The day-to-day oversight of this new corporate structure increasingly fell to professional managers.

The modernization of business affected wage policies as well. Rejecting the conventional wisdom that employers should pay the lowest wages possible, "enlightened" business leaders concluded that higher wages would generate higher productivity. Henry Ford led the way in 1914 by paying his workers five dollars a day, well above the average factory worker's wage. Other companies soon followed his lead.

New systems for distributing goods emerged as well. Automobiles reached consumers through vast dealer networks. By 1926 the number of Ford dealerships approached ten thousand. Chain stores accounted for about a quarter of all retail sales by 1930. The A&P grocery chain boasted 17,500 stores by 1928. Installment buying was another mass-marketing innovation. By 1929 credit purchases accounted for 75 percent of automobile sales, and other big-ticket items were increasingly bought on credit as well.

Above all, the 1920s business boom bobbed along on a frothy sea of advertising. In 1929 corporations spent some $1.8 billion promoting their wares via radio, billboards, newpapers, and magazines, and the advertising business employed some 600,000 people. The barons of advertising ranked among the corporate elite of the 1920s. Chicago ad man Albert Lasker owned the Chicago Cubs baseball team as well as his own golf course.

As they still do, the advertisers of the twenties used celebrity endorsements ("Nine out of ten screen stars care for their skin with Lux toilet soap"), promises of social success, and threats of social embarrassment. Beneath a picture of a sad young woman, for example, a Listerine mouthwash ad proclaimed,

> She was a beautiful girl and talented too. . . .Yet in the one pursuit that stands foremost in the mind of every girl and woman—marriage—she was a failure.

The young woman's problem was *halitosis,* or bad breath. The remedy, of course, was Listerine, and lots of it.

Beyond touting specific products, advertisers redefined popular aspiration by offering a seductive vision of a new era of abundance. Portraying a fantasy world of elegance, grace, and boundless pleasure, advertisers aroused desires that the new consumer-oriented capitalist system happily fulfilled. As one critic wrote in 1925,

> [W]hen all is said and done, advertising . . . creates a dream world: smiling faces, shining teeth, school girl complexions, cornless feet, perfect fitting [underwear], distinguished collars, wrinkleless pants, odorless breath, regularized bowels, . . . charging motors, punctureless tires, perfect busts, shimmering shanks, self-washing dishes—backs behind which the moon was meant to rise.

Business influence in the 1920s saturated the culture. As the *Independent* magazine put it in 1921: "America stands for one idea: Business. . . . Thru business, properly conceived, managed, and conducted, the human race is finally to be redeemed." Presidents Harding and Coolidge lauded business values and hobnobbed with businessmen. Magazines profiled corporate leaders. A 1923 opinion poll ranked Henry Ford as a leading presidential prospect. In *The Man Nobody Knows* (1925), ad man Bruce Barton described Jesus Christ as a managerial genius who "picked up twelve men from the bottom ranks of business and forged them into an organization that conquered the world." In *Middletown* (1929), a study of Muncie, Indiana, sociologists Robert and Helen Lynd observed, "More and more of the activities of life are coming to be strained through the bars of the dollar sign."

## Women in the New Economic Era

In the decade's advertising, glamorous women smiled behind the steering wheel, happily operated their new appliances, and smoked cigarettes in romantic settings. (One ad man promoted cigarettes for women as "torches of freedom.") In the advertisers' dream world, housework became an exciting challenge. As one ad put it: "Men are judged . . . according to their power to delegate work. Similarly the wise woman delegates to electricity all that electricity can do."

But what of women in the workplace? The rise of the assembly line, offering physically less demanding work, theoretically should have increased job opportunities for women; but in fact, male workers dominated the automobile plants and other assembly-line factories. Although the number of working women increased by more than 2 million in the 1920s, the *proportion* of such women hardly changed, hovering at about 24 percent.

Women workers often faced wage discrimination. In 1929, for example, a male trimmer in the meatpacking industry received fifty-two cents an hour, a female trimmer, thirty-seven cents. The weakening of the union movement in the 1920s (see below) particularly hit women workers. By 1929 the proportion of women workers belonging to unions fell to a miniscule 3 percent.

Corporate bureaucratization increased female job opportunities somewhat. By 1930 some 2 million women—one-fifth of the total female labor force—had become secretaries, typists, or filing clerks. Few women gained admission to capitalism's managerial ranks, however. Indeed, large corporations rearranged their office space to draw clear gender distinctions between male managers and female clerks. Nor did the professions open their doors to women. With medical schools imposing a 5 percent quota on female admissions, the number of women physicians actually declined from 1910 to 1930.

The proportion of female high school graduates going to college slowly increased, however, from 8 percent in 1920 to 12 percent in 1930. Nearly 50,000 women received college degrees in 1930, almost triple the 1920 figure. And despite the hurdles, college women increasingly combined marriage and career. Most took clerical jobs or entered traditional "women's professions" such as nursing, librarianship, social work and teaching. A handful, however, followed the lead of Progressive Era feminist trailblazers to become researchers and scholars in colleges and universities.

## Workers in a Business Age

Organized labor faced tough sledding in the twenties. Union membership fell from 5 million in 1920 to 3.4 million in 1929. Several factors underlay this decline. For one thing, overall wage rates climbed steadily in the 1920s. Aggregate wage statistics conceal many inequities and regional variations, but the prevailing pattern of fatter pay envelopes hobbled the union movement.

So did changes in the industrial process. The trade unions' strength lay in established industries like printing, railroading, coal mining, and the building trades. These older craft-based unions were ill suited to the new mass-production industries.

Management hostility further weakened organized labor. Henry Ford hired thugs to intimidate union organizers. In Marion, North Carolina, deputy sheriffs who shot and killed six striking textile workers were acquitted, but a union organizer went to jail. Violence also marked a 1929 strike in Gastonia, North Carolina, by the communist-led National Textile Workers Union. When armed thugs representing the mill-owners invaded union headquarters, the police chief was shot. In a later exchange, strike leader and singer Ella May Wiggins was killed.

The anti-union campaign took subtler forms as well. Manufacturers' associations renamed the non-union shop the "open shop" and dubbed it the "American Plan" of labor relations. Some firms set up employee associations and provided cafeterias and recreational facilities for workers. A few big corporations such as U.S. Steel sold their workers company stock at special prices. Some publicists praised "welfare capitalism" (the term for this new approach to labor relations) as evidence of corporate America's heightened ethical awareness. In reality, it mainly reflected the desire to prevent the formation of independent unions with real clout.

Black membership in labor unions by 1929 stood at only about 82,000—mostly longshoremen, miners, and railroad porters. The American Federation of Labor officially prohibited racial discrimination, but most AFL unions in fact barred African-Americans from membership. Corporations often hired blacks as strikebreakers, increasing organized labor's hostility toward them. Black strikebreakers, denounced as "scabs," took such work out of dire need. As a jobless black character says in Claude McKay's 1929 novel *Home to Harlem*, "I got to live, and I'll scab through hell to live."

Of the regional variations that skewed the wage picture, that between North and South loomed largest. In 1928 the average unskilled laborer in New England earned forty-seven cents an hour, in contrast to twenty-eight cents in the South. Textile corporations moved south in search of lower wage rates, devastating many New England mill towns.

Not only women but also blacks, Mexican-Americans, and recent immigrants clustered at the bottom of the wage scale. Black workers, many of them recent migrants from the rural South, faced special difficulties. "Last hired and first fired," they were generally confined to the most menial jobs.

### Ailing Agriculture

Agriculture's wartime prosperity gave way to hard times in the 1920s. Wheat, corn, and hay prices plummeted as the government's heavy purchases for the army dwindled, European agriculture revived, and the nation's high protective tariff depressed agricultural exports. From 1919 to 1921, farm income fell by some 60 percent. When farmers compensated by increasing productivity, large surpluses and still weaker prices resulted. Agricultural workers' real earnings fell sharply in the postwar recession of 1920–1921 and remained depressed for the rest of the decade. Farmers who had borrowed heavily to buy land and equipment during the war now felt the squeeze as payments came due.

Farm organizations, including the American Farm Bureau Federation (1920), turned to Washington for help. In 1924 farmers rallied behind a price-support

**Hollywood Glamor / Workplace Racism, 1927**
*Suave actor Adolphe Menjou boards a train attended by African-American porters, one of the occupations open to blacks in a racially stratified labor force. The original caption of this publicity shot probably staged by the hat industry reads: "[Menjou] is no follower of the hatless fad. Here he is embarking on a trip with the twenty-eight hats he considers essential to the well-dressed man's wardrobe."*

plan, the McNary-Haugen bill.* After two defeats, the McNary-Haugen bill passed in 1927 and 1928, but President Calvin Coolidge vetoed it both times. In the 1928 election, many angry farmers abandoned their traditional Republican ties and voted Democratic. This abortive effort to help financially strapped farmers underscored the conservative political climate of the 1920s.

# Republicans in Power

Politics in the 1920s reflected the decade's business orientation. The Republicans controlled Congress and supplied two presidents who mirrored the prevailing cultural mood. In this climate former progressives and feminists faced difficult times.

## *The Harding and Coolidge Years*

The Republican party continued in the 1920s to attract northern farmers, corporate leaders, small businesspeople, and some skilled workers. The Democrats' base remained the white South and the political machines of the immigrant cities.

With Republican progressives having bolted to Theodore Roosevelt in 1912, GOP conservatives controlled the 1920 convention and chose Senator Warren G. Harding of Marion, Ohio, as their presidential candidate. As a struggling newspaper editor, Harding had married the local banker's daughter, who prodded him to enter politics. He was elected to the Senate in 1915. A genial backslapper, the floridly handsome Harding enjoyed good liquor, good stories, a good poker game, and occasional encounters with his mistress, Nan Britton.

This amiable nonentity overwhelmed his Democratic opponent and fellow Ohioan James M. Cox (see Chapter 23). After the stresses of war and Wilson's lofty sermons, Harding's blandness and vacuous oratory had a soothing appeal.

Harding did make some notable cabinet appointments: Henry C. Wallace, the editor of an Iowa farm periodical, became secretary of agriculture; Charles

* Under this plan, the government would annually purchase the surplus of six basic farm commodities—cotton, corn, rice, hogs, tobacco, and wheat—at their average price in 1909–1914 (when farm prices were high). The government would then sell these surpluses on the world market at prevailing prices and make up the resulting losses through a tax on domestic sales of these commodities.

Evans Hughes, former New York governor and 1916 presidential candidate, secretary of state; and Andrew W. Mellon, a Pittsburgh financier, treasury secretary. Herbert Hoover, the wartime food czar, dominated the cabinet as secretary of commerce.

Harding also made some disastrous appointments: his political manager, Harry M. Daugherty, as attorney general; a Senate pal, Albert B. Fall of New Mexico, as secretary of the interior; a wartime draft dodger, Charles Forbes, as director of the Veterans' Bureau. It was these men who set the tone of the Harding years: an aura of back-room sleaze reminiscent of the Grant administration.

By 1922, as Washington rumor hinted at criminal activity in high places, Harding confessed to a friend, "I have no trouble with my enemies. . . . But . . . my goddamn friends . . . , keep me walking the floor nights." In July 1923, vacationing in the West, Harding suffered a heart attack; on August 2, in a San Francisco hotel, he died.

In 1924 a Senate investigation exposed the full scope of the scandals. Charles Forbes, convicted of stealing Veterans' Bureau funds, evaded prison by fleeing abroad. The bureau's general counsel committed suicide, as did an aide to Attorney General Daugherty accused of influence peddling. Daugherty himself narrowly escaped conviction in two criminal trials. Interior Secretary Fall went to jail for secretly leasing government oil reserves, one in Teapot Dome, Wyoming, to two oilmen while accepting "loans" from them totaling $400,000. Like "Watergate" in the 1970s, "Teapot Dome" became a shorthand label for a sordid tangle of presidential scandals.

Vice President Calvin Coolidge, on a family visit in Vermont, took the presidential oath by lantern light from his father, a local magistrate. Coolidge brought a different style to the White House. Raised in Vermont, the painfully shy Coolidge had attended Amherst College in Massachusetts, where he had struggled to eliminate all rural traces from his speech. Whereas Harding was convivial and talkative, Coolidge's naps and taciturnity became legendary. As he was leaving after a visit to California, a radio reporter asked for a parting message to the people of the state. "Good-bye," Coolidge responded.

The moral tone improved, but the government continued to reflect the prevailing probusiness climate. The Fordney-McCumber Tariff (1922) and the Smoot-Hawley Tariff (1930) pushed rates to all-time highs, benefiting domestic manufacturers. Prodded by Treasury Secretary Andrew Mellon, Congress in 1926 and

## The Election of 1924

| Candidates | Parties | Electoral Vote | Popular Vote | Percentage of Popular Vote |
|---|---|---|---|---|
| CALVIN COOLIDGE | Republican | 382 | 15,718,211 | 54.0 |
| John W. Davis | Democratic | 136 | 8,385,283 | 28.8 |
| Robert M. La Follette | Progressive | 13 | 4,831,289 | 16.6 |

again in 1928 lowered the income-tax and inheritance tax rates for the well-to-do. The Supreme Court under Chief Justice William Howard Taft, appointed by Harding in 1921, overturned several reform measures opposed by business interests, including a 1919 federal law imposing punitive taxes on the products of child labor. Coolidge rejected an aid request from Mississippi River flood victims with the prim reminder that the government had no duty to protect citizens "against the hazards of the elements."

Vetoing the McNary-Haugen farm bill, Coolidge warned of "the tyranny of bureaucratic regulation and control." The measure would benefit farmers at the expense of the general public, he went on, ignoring the fact that business had long benefited from high tariffs and other special-interest measures.

### Retreat from Internationalism

President Harding's most notable achievement was the Washington Naval Arms Conference. After the war ended in 1918, the United States, Great Britain, and Japan edged toward a dangerous (and costly) naval-arms race. In 1921 President Harding called for a conference to deal with the problem. When the gathering convened in Washington, Secretary of State Hughes startled the delegates by proposing a specific ratio of ships among the world's naval powers.

In February 1922 the three nations, together with Italy and France, pledged to reduce their battleship tonnage by specified amounts and to halt all battleship construction for ten years. The United States and Japan also agreed to respect each other's territorial holdings in the Pacific. Although this treaty ultimately failed to prevent war, it did represent an early arms-control effort.

Apart from this initiative, America followed a unilateralist foreign policy in the 1920s. As U.S. corporate interests spread worldwide, politically the nation turned inward, joining neither the League of Nations nor the League-sponsored Court of International Jus-

tice (the World Court). The United States did participate informally in some League activities, but in general, symbolic gestures replaced meaningful international engagement. In 1928 the United States and France, eventually joined by sixty other nations, signed the Kellogg-Briand Pact renouncing aggression and calling for the outlawry of war. Lacking any enforcement mechanism, this high-sounding document did nothing to prevent World War II.

Washington did actively pursue the $22 billion it claimed the Allies owed in war debts and Germany in reparation payments. A joint study commission considerably scaled back these claims in 1924, but high U.S. tariff barriers and economic problems in Europe, including runaway inflation in Germany, made repayment of even these reduced claims unrealistic.

### Progressive Stirrings, Democratic Divisions

The progressive spirit survived at least feebly in the legislative branch. Congress staved off Andrew Mellon's proposals for even deeper tax cuts for the rich. Senator George Norris of Nebraska prevented the Coolidge administration from selling a federal hydroelectric facility at Muscle Shoals, Alabama, to automaker Henry Ford for a pittance. And in 1927 Congress created the Federal Radio Commission, extending to this new industry the principle of government regulation of business.

In 1922, a midterm election year, labor and farm groups formed the Conference for Progressive Political Action (CPPA), which helped defeat conservative Republicans. In July 1924, CPPA delegates revived the Progressive party; adopted a prolabor, profarmer platform, and nominated Senator Robert La Follette for president. The Socialist party and the American Federation of Labor endorsed the nomination.

Split between urban and rural wings, the Democrats met in New York City for their 1924 convention. The delegates defeated by one vote a resolution condemning the Ku Klux Klan. In the contest for the presidential nomination, the party's rural, Protestant, southern wing backed Woodrow Wilson's treasury secretary, William G. McAdoo; the big-city delegates rallied behind Governor Alfred E. Smith of New York, a Roman Catholic of Irish immigrant origins.

As the balloting dragged on in the stifling convention hall, humorist Will Rogers joked: "New York invited you folks here as guests, not to live." After 102 ballots the exhausted delegates nominated John W. Davis, an obscure New York corporation lawyer.

Calvin Coolidge easily won the Republican nomination. The Republican platform praised the high Fordney-McCumber Tariff and urged tax and spending cuts. With the economy humming, Coolidge got nearly 16 million votes, about twice Davis's total. La Follette garnered 4.8 million votes, respectable for a third-party candidate but far short of victory. La Follette's Progressive party candidacy divided the Democratic vote, contributing to Coolidge's landslide victory.

### Women and Politics in the 1920s: A Dream Deferred

Suffragists' hope that votes for women would transform politics survived briefly after the war. The major parties in 1920 endorsed several platform planks drafted by the League of Women Voters. Polling places shifted from saloons to schools and churches. The Women's Joint Congressional Committee, formed by a coalition of women's groups in 1919, lobbied for child-labor laws, protection of women workers, and federal support for education. The Sheppard-Towner Act (1921), passed in response to such lobbying, funded rural prenatal and baby-care centers staffed by public-health nurses.

Overall, however, the Nineteenth Amendment had little political impact. Women who had worked for suffrage and other reforms now scattered across the political spectrum. Some voted Republican, some Democratic, others Socialist. Some supported La Follette in 1924. Many withdrew from politics altogether.

As the women's movement splintered, it lost focus. Drawing middle-class and professional women, the League of Women Voters abandoned activism for "nonpartisan" studies of civic issues. Carrie Chapman Catt and Jane Addams turned their energies to the peace movement.

Alice Paul's National Woman's party campaigned for an equal-rights amendment to the Constitution, but advocates of laws protecting women workers condemned her position. The amendment could hurt female factory workers, these critics charged, by jeopar-

dizing gender-based protective legislation. In any event, the proposed amendment went nowhere.

The conservative and materialistic climate of the 1920s underlay this disarray. Jane Addams and other women's rights leaders faced accusations of communist sympathies by right-wing groups. Many young women, bombarded by ads that defined liberation in terms of consumption, rejected the prewar feminists' earnest civic idealism. One young woman in 1927 ridiculed "the old school of fighting feminists" for their lack of "feminine charm" and their "constant clamor about equal rights."

In such a climate, the few reforms achieved by organized women's groups often proved short-lived. The Supreme Court struck down child-labor laws (1922) and women's protective laws (1923). A 1924 child-labor constitutional amendment passed Congress after heavy lobbying by women's organizations, but only a few states ratified it. And the Sheppard-Towner rural health-care program, denounced by the American Medical Association as an assault on physicians' monopoly of the health business, expired in 1929. The

**Alice Paul (1885–1977)**
*A student in England during the British suffrage campaign, Paul brought its militant tactics back to America. In the 1920s and after, she advocated an equal rights amendment to the Constitution.*

federal Children's Bureau, created in 1912, languished in the hostile, antireformist political environment of the 1920s.

# Mass Society, Mass Culture

The myriad new consumer products of the 1920s were harbingers of profound social and cultural change. Not only these products, but also the corporate order and technological processes that spawned them, would alter America forever.

### *Cities, Cars, Consumer Goods*

In the 1920 census, for the first time, the urban population outnumbered the rural. The United States had become a nation of cities.

African-Americans led the migration cityward. By 1930 more than 40 percent of the nation's 12 million blacks lived in cities, 2 million of them in Chicago, Detroit, New York, and other metropolitan centers of the North and West. The first black congressman since Reconstruction, Oscar De Priest, was elected in 1928 from Chicago's South Side.

Although small-town values remained strong, the nation in the 1920s became increasingly urbanized, not only numerically but also culturally. Even when the powerful shaping agencies of the culture—radio, the

**Christmas in Consumerland**
*Giving a modern twist to an ancient symbol, this advertising catalog of the 1920s offered an enticing array of new electric products for the home.*

movies, the advertising agencies, the mass magazines—nostalgically evoked rural values, they did so from big-city offices and studios.

For city women, this meant less housework. When the Lynds interviewed working-class women in Muncie in 1925, nearly 75 percent said that they spent less time on housework than had their mothers. Vacuum cleaners supplanted brooms and dustpans. Wood-burning stoves became a memory. Store-bought clothes replaced homemade apparel. Electric refrigerators supplanted the old oak iceboxes.

In some ways, however, the new technology reversed the trend toward the socialization of housework advocated by reformers like Charlotte Perkins Gilman. In the early twentieth century, for example, many urban wives had patronized commercial laundries. But with the arrival of the electric washing machine and iron, this task moved back into the home.

Food preparation and even diet also shifted in response to economic and technological change. The rise of the supermarket undermined the annual ritual of canning. Similarly, by the mid-1920s a majority of urban housewives used commercially baked bread rather than baking their own. With the advent of refrigeration, supermarkets, and motor transport, fresh fruits, vegetables, and salads became available year-round.

For social impact, nothing matched the automobile. Traffic jams, parking problems, and the soaring rate of deaths in auto accidents (more than 26,000 in 1924) attracted worried comment. A Muncie resident challenged the Lynds: "Why . . . do you need to study what's changing this country? I can tell you . . . in just four letters: A-U-T-O."

Thanks to the A-U-T-O, family vacations, rare a generation earlier, enjoyed a great vogue. City dwellers rediscovered the beauty of the land—along with thousands of other Ford owners. The automobile, by giving farm dwellers easier access to the city, diminished the isolation of rural life.

The automobile could also erode family cohesion. Young people welcomed the freedom from parental oversight that it offered. They could now on a whim drive to a dance or party in a distant city.

The automobile's effects on individuality were similarly mixed. While car owners, unlike train passengers, could travel when and where they wished, the automobile in many ways further standardized American life. One-room schoolhouses stood empty as buses carried children to consolidated schools. Neighborhood markets declined as people drove to more distant chain

### The Automobile Age: Passenger Cars Registered in the United States, 1900–1992

*From a plaything for the rich, the automobile emerged after 1920 as the basic mode of transportation for the masses, in the process transforming American life in countless ways.*

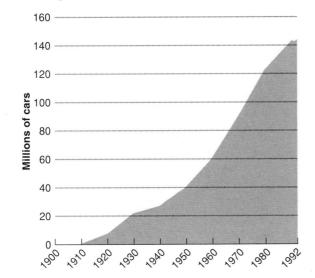

*Sources: Historical Statistics of the United States, Colonial Times to 1970* (Washington, D.C.: U.S. Government Printing Office, 1975), 716; *Statistical Abstract of the United States, 1994* (Washington, D.C.: U.S. Government Printing Office,

stores. Along with the automobile came the first suburban department stores, the first shopping center (in Kansas City), and the first fast-food chain (A & W Root Beer).

Even at $300 or $400, and despite a thriving used-car market, the automobile remained too expensive for many. Thus the "automobile suburbs" that sprang up beyond the streetcar lines attracted mainly the prosperous; the urban poor remained behind. This urban-suburban social division would widen in the decades ahead.

The automobile's farm cousin, the tractor, transformed agriculture. The number of tractors soared from 246,000 in 1920 to 920,000 in 1930. As farmers borrowed money to buy mechanized equipment, the rural debt crisis worsened.

### *Soaring Energy Consumption and a Threatened Environment*

The spread of electrical products and motorized vehicles had implications for the environment and natural resources. With electrical use more than tripling in the 1920s, U.S. generating plants in 1929 consumed vast quantities of coal, oil, and natural gas. In 1929, meeting the insatiable appetites of the nation's 20 million automobiles, U.S. refineries produced 435 million barrels of gasoline using more than a billion barrels of crude oil.

Domestic oil production rose by some 250 percent in the 1920s, setting off fevered activity in the oilfields of Texas, Oklahoma, and elsewhere. The Teapot Dome scandal arose directly from the decade's rising oil demand. As wildcatters made and lost fortunes, corporate giants like Standard, Texaco and Gulf solidified their dominance of the industry. Oil imports crept up as well. The natural gas found with petroleum seemed so abundant that much of it was simply burned off. In short, the profligate consumption of nonrenewable fossil fuels, though small by later standards, and not yet recognized as a problem, already characterized American society by the 1920s.

The wilderness that had inspired early-nineteenth-century Americans came under heavy siege a hundred years later. Power plants and automobile engines pumped pollutants into the atmosphere. The automobile opened once-pristine regions to easy human access. As ribbons of asphalt and cement snaked across the land, gas stations, billboards, restaurants, and tourist cabins followed.

A few protested. The Sierra Club and the Audubon Society worked to preserve wilderness and wildlife. In 1923 the Izaak Walton League, an organization devoted to recreational fishing, persuaded Congress to halt a private-development scheme to drain the Mississippi River wetlands from Lake Pepin in Minnesota to Rock Island, Illinois. Instead this beautiful stretch of the river was declared a wildlife preserve. Aldo Leopold of the U.S. Forest Service warned of the dangers of unchecked technology. For too long in the United States, wrote Leopold in 1925, "a stump was our symbol of progress."

Few listened. To most Americans of the 1920s, pollution and a contracting wilderness seemed small prices to pay for radio, the movies, electric appliances, and motorized transportation. The expansive, confident generation of the 1920s had little time for

**East River from the 30th Story of the Sheridan Hotel,** by Georgia O'Keeffe, 1928. *Better known for her later paintings inspired by the New Mexico desert, O'Keeffe in this painting of a New York City scene incidentally recorded the atmospheric pollution issuing from factory smokestacks, one of many warnings of environmental problems ahead.*

the environmental issues that would raise alarms two generations later.

### Routinized Work, Mass-Produced Pleasure

The new assembly-line techniques affected the way industrial employees viewed their work and themselves. The essence of the assembly line was repetitive labor; managers discouraged expressions of individuality and even talking or laughter that could divert workers from their task. Ford employees learned to speak without moving their lips and adopted an expressionless mask that some called "Fordization of the face."

As work became more routine, its psychic rewards diminished. Life on the assembly line did not foster pride in the specialized skill that came from years of farming or mastering a craft. Nor did the assembly line offer much prospect of advancement. In Muncie, factories employing over four thousand workers announced only ten openings for foremen in 1924 and 1925. The changing nature of work doubtless contributed—along with more disposable income—to the rising interest in leisure-time activities, as workers sought in their free hours the fulfillment missing in the workplace.

Standardized amusement helped fill leisure-time hours. The mass production of culture was hardly new in America, of course, but the process accelerated in the 1920s.

Mass-circulation magazines flourished. By 1922 ten American magazines boasted a circulation of more than 2.5 million. Some featured sex, crime, and "true confessions"; others fiction, cartoons, and stories. The venerable *Saturday Evening Post,* with its Norman Rockwell covers and its fiction featuring small-town life, specialized in prepackaged nostalgia.

In 1921 DeWitt and Lila Wallace started *Reader's Digest,* a magazine that condensed articles originally published elsewhere. The journalistic counterpart of the Model T or the A&P, the *Digest* offered conventional views in a standardized format and simple prose.

Even bookselling saw major changes. The cozy old-style bookstores declined as publishers marketed their wares through department stores or mail-order houses such as the Book-of-the-Month Club and the Literary Guild, both established in 1926. Often accused of debasing literary tastes, these ventures did help sustain a common national culture in an increasingly market-driven society.

Radio and the movies accelerated the standardization of culture. The radio era began on November 2, 1920, when station KDKA in Pittsburgh reported Warren Harding's election. In 1921 New York's WEAF began a regular news program, and that autumn a Newark station broadcast the World Series (the Giants beat the Yankees). In 1922 five hundred new stations began operations. By 1927 radio sales approached 7 million.

**Moviemaking at Warner Brothers Hollywood Studio**
*Pioneering in sound films in a movie-mad decade, Warner Brothers Pictures earned profits of more than $17 million in 1929.*

**Radio Mania**
*A 1920s furniture store capitalizes on the radio vogue with a display of the latest Atwater Kent models.*

In 1926 three big corporations—General Electric, Westinghouse, and the Radio Corporation of America—formed the first radio network, the National Broadcasting Company (NBC). The Columbia Broadcasting System (CBS) followed in 1927. Gauging audience preferences through market research, the networks soon ruled radio broadcasting. From Maine to California, Americans laughed at the same jokes, hummed the same tunes, and absorbed the same commercials.

WEAF broadcast the first sponsored program in 1922, and soon the commercialization of the new medium was complete. The first network comedy show, the enormously popular (and mildly racist) "Amos 'n' Andy" (1928), brought prosperity to its sponsor, Pepsodent toothpaste.

The movies attracted all social levels as they expanded from the immigrant slums into elegant uptown theaters with names like "Majestic," "Ritz," and "Palace." The silent-film era produced such stars as the comedian Charlie Chaplin, the romantic Rudolph Valentino, and "America's sweetheart" Mary Pickford. Director Cecil B. De Mille, the son of an Episcopal clergyman, pioneered lavish biblical spectacles such as *The Ten Commandments* (1923).

After Al Jolson's *The Jazz Singer* (1927) introduced sound to the movies, a new generation of screen idols arose, including the western hero Gary Cooper and the aloof Scandinavian beauty Greta Garbo. Walt Disney's Mickey Mouse made his debut in a 1928 animated cartoon, *Steamboat Willy.* By 1930 weekly movie attendance approached 80 million.

Like radio, movies became more standardized. By 1930 such Hollywood giants as Metro-Goldwyn-Mayer, Warner Brothers, and Columbia turned out the vast majority of American films. Predictable plots and typecast stars prevailed.

Moviegoers entered a celluloid world far removed from reality. One movie ad promised "all the adventure, all the romance, all the excitement you lack in your daily life." These mass-produced fantasies shaped behavior and values, especially of the young. In the words of writer John Dos Passos, Hollywood offered a "great bargain sale of five-and-ten-cent lusts and dreams." The film industry also stimulated consumption by presenting alluring images of the good life. Cecil B. DeMille's popular romantic comedies such as the lavish *Road to*

*Yesterday* (1925), in tandem with department stores, mass magazines, and the advertising industry, opened new vistas of consumer abundance.

Influential as it was, however, the new standardized mass culture penetrated society only unevenly, as various groups modified, adapted, and even rejected it. It made only scant inroads in large parts of rural America, and met strong resistance among evangelical Christians deeply suspicious of modernity. Mexican-American agricultural workers preserved traditional festivals and leisure activities despite their migratory life and the "Americanization" efforts of non-Hispanic priests and bosses. In big-city black neighborhoods, uninhibited rent parties featured dancing to local musicians or to blues and jazz records produced by companies oriented to this market. Along with the national radio shows, local stations also carried programs providing ethnic music, news, and community announcements for urban immigrant enclaves. Country music enlivened radio programming in the South. Despite the craze for professional sports, local athletic leagues flourished as well. Along with the great movie palaces, neighborhood theaters provided opportunities for conversation, announcements, live music, and sometimes jeering and catcalls for the film being shown.

The *Chicago Defender*, the voice of the city's black middle class, deplored the raucousness of movie theaters in poor black neighborhoods, where "during a death scene . . . you are likely to hear the orchestra jazzing away on 'Clap Hands, Here Comes Charlie.' " In short, despite the mass culture's growing power, the American cultural scene still remained vividly diverse in the 1920s.

## Fads, Celebrities, and Heroes

A succession of fads and media-promoted events—or pseudoevents—diverted millions of Americans in the 1920s. In 1921 Atlantic City launched a bathing-beauty competition grandly called the Miss America Pageant. In 1924 a crossword-puzzle craze swept the country.

A few larger-than-life celebrities dominated professional sports: Babe Ruth of the New York Yankees, who hit sixty home runs in 1927; Ty Cobb, the Detroit Tigers' manager, whose earlier record of 4,191 major-league hits stood for many years; prizefighters Jack Dempsey and Gene Tunney, whose heavyweight title fights in 1926 and 1927 drew thousands of fans and massive radio audiences. Ruth was a coarse, heavy-drinking womanizer; Cobb, an ill-tempered racist. Yet the alchemy of publicity transformed them into exciting gladiators with lovable nicknames like the Sultan of Swat (Ruth) or the Georgia Peach (Cobb).

This media-created celebrity culture illuminates the anxieties and aspirations of ordinary Americans in these years. For young women in a period of confusing social change, the beauty pageants offered one kind of ideal to which she could aspire. For the man whose sense of mastery had been shaken by unsettling developments from feminism to Fordism, cheering a sports hero like Dempsey or Ruth could momentarily restore a sense of pride and self-confidence.

The psychological meaning of this hero worship emerged with particular clarity in the response to Charles A. Lindbergh, the young pilot who flew solo across the Atlantic on May 20–21, 1927. A Minnesotan of Swedish ancestry, Lindbergh was a

**The Lindbergh Saga Begins**
*Charles A. Lindbergh in "The Spirit of St. Louis" takes off from Roosevelt Field, Long Island, May 20, 1927, as photographers record the start of the epic flight.*

stunt flyer and airmail pilot who decided to compete for a $25,000 prize offered by a New York hotel for the first nonstop New York–Paris flight. Lindbergh's daring flight in his monoplane, *The Spirit of St. Louis,* captured the popular imagination and attracted a blaze of media attention. In New York, thousands turned out for a ticker-tape parade. Radio, newspapers, magazines, and movie newsreels provided saturation coverage.

President Coolidge predictably praised Lindbergh's achievement as a triumph of corporate technology, but many editorialists saw it as evidence that the individual still counted in an era of standardization and mechanization. To conservatives, Lindbergh's solid virtues and self-effacing modesty proved that the old verities survived. Native-born midwesterners embraced the Minnesotan as one of their own and insisted that he, not urban immigrants, most truly represented America.

Overall, the new mass media had mixed social effects. Certainly they promoted cultural standardization and uniformity of thought and to a degree stifled local and regional diversity. But radio, the movies, and the mass magazines also helped forge a national culture and introduced fresh viewpoints and new ways of behaving. The mass media also hammered home a powerful message: an individual's horizons need not be limited by his or her immediate environment. The mass culture of the 1920s opened a larger world for ordinary Americans. If that world was often vacuous and tawdry, it could also be exciting, stimulating, and provocative.

# Cultural Ferment and Creativity

The American experience in the 1920s involved more than political scandals, assembly lines, and mass culture. This was also a decade of bubbling creativity. While some young people—and their parents— challenged traditional codes of behavior, writers, artists, musicians, and scientists compiled a record of remarkable achievement. African-Americans, meanwhile, asserted their pride and collective energy through a cultural flowering known as the Harlem Renaissance.

### *The Jazz Age and the Postwar Crisis of Values*

The war and its sour aftermath sharpened the cultural restlessness of the prewar years. As Randolph Bourne wrote in 1918 of the war's cultural implications, "One

has a sense of having come to a sudden, short stop at the end of an intellectual era." The postwar period confirmed Bourne's premonition. In *The Wasteland* (1922), poet T. S. Eliot evoked images of a shattered culture. Another poet, Ezra Pound, made the same point more brutally in 1920. America had gone to war, he wrote, to save "a botched civilization; . . . an old bitch gone in the teeth."

The postwar crisis of values took many forms. Some young people—especially affluent college students—boisterously assailed older conventions of decorous behavior. Taking advantage of the decade's prosperity and the freedom offered by the automobile, they threw parties, drank bootleg liquor, flocked to jazz clubs, and danced the Charleston. When asked about her favorite activity, a California college student replied, "I adore dancing; who doesn't?"

The young also discussed sex more freely than their elders and in some cases indulged more openly in sexual activity. Wrote novelist F. Scott Fitzgerald, "None of the Victorian mothers had any idea how casually their daughters were accustomed to be kissed." The ideas of Sigmund Freud, the Viennese founder of psychoanalysis, enjoyed a popular vogue in the 1920s—often in distorted form. In *Love and the Machine Age* (1930), Floyd Dell, a prewar Greenwich Village rebel, criticized male-dominated marriages, and called for a new "companionate marriage" based on sexual equality.

For all the talk about sex, the 1920s' "sexual revolution" is known largely from anecdotes and journalistic accounts. Premarital sexual intercourse may have increased, but it remained exceptional, and widely disapproved. What can be documented is a change in courtship patterns. "Courting" had once implied a serious intention of marriage. In the 1920s the more informal ritual of dating evolved. Casual dating allowed young people to test compatibility and gain social confidence without necessarily contemplating marriage. The twenties brought greater erotic freedom, but within clear bounds. Despite moralists' charges of collapsing standards, most 1920s youth drew a clear line between permissible and impermissible behavior. The double standard, which held women to a stricter code of conduct, remained in force. Whereas young men could boast of their sexual adventures, young women reputed to be "fast" faced ostracism.

Despite the double standard, the postwar changes in behavior did have a liberating effect on women. Female sexuality was acknowledged more openly. Skirt lengths crept up, makeup (once the badge of a prostitute) became more acceptable, and the elaborate armor of petticoats and corsets was drastically reduced. The awesome matronly bosom of the late nineteenth century mysteriously deflated in the twenties as a more boyish figure became the fashion ideal.

With the medical risks of tobacco as yet undiscovered, many young women took up cigarettes, especially college students and urban workers. For some, smoking became a women's rights issue. As a woman student at the University of Illinois put it, "[W]hy [should] men . . . be permitted to smoke while girls are expelled for doing it?"

Moral guardians protested. A Methodist bishop denounced the new dances that brought "the bodies of men and women in unusual relation to each other." When the women's college Bryn Mawr permitted students to smoke on campus in 1925, denunciations erupted.

According to F. Scott Fitzgerald, around 1922 adults began to imitate the rebelliousness of the young. Middle-aged Americans "discovered that young liquor will take the place of young blood," he wrote, "and with a whoop the orgy began." But cultural generalizations by novelists do not necessarily reflect historical reality. During the years of Fitzgerald's alleged national orgy, for example, the U.S. divorce rate remained constant and millions of Americans firmly rejected alcohol.

**Doing the Charleston: A St. Louis Dance Contest, 1925**
*Media events like this helped shape the image of the 1920s as frivolous and pleasure mad. Originating among African-Americans of Charleston, South Carolina, the Charleston was popularized by the all-black Broadway musical review of 1923,* Runnin' Wild.

The most enduring twenties stereotype is the *flapper*—the sophisticated, pleasure-mad young woman. The term apparently originated with a drawing by magazine illustrator John Held jr. depicting a fashionable young woman with her rubber boots open and flapping.

Although the flapper stereotype was largely a creation of journalists, fashion designers, and advertisers, it did play a significant cultural role. In the nineteenth century, the idealized woman on her moral pedestal had symbolized an elaborate complex of cultural ideals. The semimythic flapper, with her bobbed hair, defiant cigarette, lipstick, and short skirt, similarly epitomized youthful rebelliousness and signaled more changes ahead.

Indeed the entire Jazz Age was partially a media and novelistic creation. Fitzgerald's romanticized treatment of the affluent postwar young, *This Side of Paradise* (1920), spawned many imitators. A Princeton dropout, Fitzgerald was only twenty-four when his best-selling novel appeared. With his sculpted profile, blond hair, and striking green eyes, he not only wrote about the Jazz Age but lived it. Flush with royalties, he and his wife Zelda partied away the early twenties in New York, Paris, and the French Riviera. A moralist at heart, Fitzgerald both admired and deplored Jazz Age behavior. His *The Great Gatsby* (1925) captured not only the gilded existence of the superrich and the social climbers of the 1920s but also the selfishness and romantic illusions that ruled their lives.

The upheaval in manners and morals summed up in the "Jazz Age" label was genuine but limited to a narrow social stratum. Old values did not vanish overnight. Millions of Americans adhered to traditional ways and traditional standards. Most farmers, blacks, industrial workers, and recent immigrants found economic survival more pressing than boozy parties, the latest dance craze, or the newest fads and fashions.

But like the flapper, the Jazz Age stereotype did capture a part of the postwar scene, especially the brassy, urban mass culture and the hedonism so different from the idealism and social commitment of the Progressive Era and the war years. After the 1929 stock market crash (see Chapter 25), nostalgia-tinged memories of the Jazz Age would underscore the contrast between the supposedly carefree 1920s and the grim 1930s.

### Alienated Writers

Like Fitzgerald, many young writers found the cultural turbulence of the 1920s a creative stimulus. The decade's most talented writers were equally hostile to the moralistic pieties of the old order and the business pieties of the new.

The definitive literary skewering of postwar America came in the novels of Sinclair Lewis. In *Main Street* (1920), Lewis caustically depicted the provincial smugness and cultural barrenness of a fictional midwestern farm town, Gopher Prairie, based on his native Sauk Centre, Minnesota. In *Babbitt* (1922) he skewered a larger city, Zenith, in the character of George F. Babbitt, a real estate agent trapped in stifling middle-class conformity.

Lewis's novels found their journalistic counterpart in the work of H. L. Mencken, a Baltimore newspaperman who in 1924 launched *The American Mercury* magazine, the bible of the decade's alienated intellectuals. Mencken championed writers like Sinclair Lewis and Theodore Dreiser while ridiculing small-town Americans, Protestant fundamentalists, the middle class "Booboisie," and the politicians. His devastating essays on Wilson, Harding, Coolidge, and Bryan are classics of political satire. Asked why he remained in a nation so contemptible, Mencken replied, "Why do people visit zoos?"

Some young writers spent the 1920s abroad, often in France. One famous expatriate, Ernest Hemingway, had grown up in Oak Park, Illinois, became a reporter, and suffered serious wounds while serving as a Red Cross volunteer on the Italian front during the war. In 1921, at twenty-two, Hemingway settled in Paris and began to write. In *The Sun Also Rises* (1926), he portrayed a group of American and English young people, variously shattered by the war, as they drift around Spain.

For this generation of writers, World War I was a seminal experience. The best of the war novels, Hemingway's *A Farewell to Arms* (1929), loosely based on the author's own experiences in Italy, depicted the war's futility and the leaders' empty rhetoric. Avoiding the stilted prose and lofty abstractions of much prewar literature, Hemingway invented a terse, pared-down style. In a famous passage, the narrator says

> I was always embarrassed by the words sacred, glorious, and sacrifice and the expression in vain. We . . . had read them, on proclamations that were slapped up . . . over other proclamations, now for a long time, and I had seen nothing sacred, and the things that were glorious had no glory and the sacrifices were like the stockyards at Chicago if nothing was done with the meat except to bury it.

**Ernest Hemingway in 1918**
*Severely wounded on the Italian front, Hemingway would go on to write one of the great war novels,* A Farewell to Arms *(1929).*

But though writers gagged at Wilsonian rhetoric, village narrowness, and business cant, they remained American at heart. A confident desire to create a vital national culture inspired their literary efforts, as it had earlier inspired Hawthorne, Melville, and Whitman.

The social changes of these years energized African-American cultural life as well. Blacks' growing concentration in the urban North, especially in New York City, contributed to a cultural flowering of the 1920s known as the Harlem Renaissance. This surge of artistic creativity took many forms, from all-black Broadway musical reviews to poems and novels (see A Place in Time).

The Harlem Renaissance was important to different groups for different reasons. Black women writers and performers gained an important career boost. Young whites in rebellion against Victorian propriety romanticized black life, as expressed in the Harlem Renaissance, as freer and less inhibited. And cultural nationalists both black and white saw in the Renaissance a promising step toward an authentically *American* modernist culture, not one originating in London or Paris.

## Harlem in the Twenties

*B*raving chilly breezes, New Yorkers cheered warmly on February 17, 1919, as the all-black 15th Infantry Regiment, back from France, paraded up Fifth Avenue. Led by Lieutenant James Europe's band, thousands of black troops marched in formation. Banners blazed: "OUR HEROES—WELCOME HOME." When the parade reached Harlem, north of Central Park, discipline collapsed amid joyous reunions. A new day seemed at hand for black America, and Harlem stood at its center.

The part of Manhattan Island that the early Dutch settlers had called Nieuw Haarlem was in transition by 1920. An elite suburb in the late nineteenth century, Harlem evolved rapidly during the First World War as its black population swelled. Some 400,000 southern blacks in search of wartime work migrated northward from 1914 to 1918, and the influx continued in the 1920s. That decade, New York City's black community surged from 152,000 to 327,000. Most of the newcomers settled in Harlem, where handsome old brownstone apartments were subdivided to house them. But racism and lack of education took their toll. Black Harlem had a small middle class of entrepreneurs, ministers, and funeral directors, but most Harlemites held low-paying, unskilled jobs. Many found no work at all. Overcrowding and the population spurt gave rise to social problems and high rates of tuberculosis, infant mortality, and venereal disease.

But Harlem also became a vibrant center of black cultural activity in the twenties. On the musical-comedy stage, the 1921 hit *Shuffle Along* launched a series of popular all-black reviews. The 1923 show *Runnin' Wild* sparked the Charleston dance craze. The Cotton Club and other Harlem cabarets featured such jazz geniuses as Duke Ellington, Fletcher Henderson, and Jelly Roll Morton. Muralist Aaron Douglas, concert tenor Roland Hayes, and singer-actor Paul Robeson contributed to the cultural ferment.

Above all, the Harlem Renaissance was a literary movement. The poet Langston Hughes drew upon the oral traditions of transplanted southern blacks in *The Weary Blues* (1926). The Jamaican writer Claude McKay evoked Harlem's throbbing, sometimes sinister nightlife in *Home to Harlem* (1928). In his avant-garde work *Cane* (1923), Jean Toomer used poems, drama, and short stories to convey the thwarted efforts of a young northern mulatto to penetrate the mysterious, sensual world of the black South. In her novel *Quicksand* (1928), Nella Larsen, a native of the Danish West Indies, told of a mulatto woman's struggle with her own sexuality and with the divergent cultural worlds of Denmark, the West Indies, the American South, and Harlem.

In essays and conversations at late-night parties, talented young blacks explored the challenge of finding a distinct

### Jazz Pianist, Composer, and Band Leader Ferdinand (Jelly Roll) Morton
*Rooted in the rich musical traditions of African-Americans, jazz shaped the rhythm and beat of the Harlem Renaissance.*

cultural voice in white America. The gentle philosopher Alain Locke, a former Rhodes scholar who taught at Howard University in Washington, D.C., assembled essays, poems, and short stories in *The New Negro* (1925), a landmark work that hailed the Harlem Renaissance as black America's "spiritual coming of age." Wrote Locke: "Harlem, I grant you, isn't typical, but it is significant. It is prophetic."

White America quickly took notice. Book publishers courted black authors. Charlotte Mason, a wealthy Park Avenue matron, funded the aspiring writers Langston Hughes and Zora Neale Hurston. The novelist and photographer Carl Van Vechten introduced black artists and writers to editors, publishers, and producers. White writers discovered and sometimes distorted black life. Eugene O'Neill's play *The Emperor Jones,* produced in 1921, starred Charles Gilpin as a fear-crazed West Indian tyrant. King Vidor's 1929 movie *Hallelujah,* featuring an all-black cast, romanticized plantation life and warned of the city's dangers. The 1925 novel *Porgy,* by Dubose and Dorothy Heyward, offered a sympathetic but sentimentalized picture of Charleston's black community. Reworked as a drama, *Porgy* won the Pulitzer Prize in 1927; George Gershwin's musical adaptation, *Porgy and Bess,* appeared in 1935.

In a decade of prohibition and shifting sexual mores, Harlem seemed to offer sensuality, eroticism, and escape from taboos. Prostitutes, speakeasies, and cocaine were indeed readily available. The whites who packed the late-night jazz clubs and the pulsating dance reviews and who patronized black writers and artists widely praised black culture for its "spontaneous," "primitive," or "spiritual" qualities. Harlem, writes historian Nathan Huggins, offered the

hope of recovering "that essential self one somehow lost on the way to civility." Few whites bothered to examine the more prosaic realities of Harlem life. The Cotton Club, controlled by gangsters, featured black performers but barred most blacks from the audience. Observed black writer Rudolph Fisher in 1927: "White people [once] went to Negro cabarets to see how Negroes acted; now Negroes go to these same cabarets to see how white people act."

And with patronage came subtle attempts at control. When Langston Hughes in the 1930s began to write about urban poverty rather than Africa or black spirituality, Charlotte Mason angrily withdrew her support. Wrote Hughes later, "Concerning Negroes, she felt that they were America's great link with the primitive. . . . But unfortunately I did not feel the rhythms of the primitive surging through me . . . I was only an American Negro. I was not Africa. I was Chicago and Kansas City and Broadway and Harlem."

The Harlem Renaissance lacked a political framework or organic ties to the larger African-American experience. Indeed, Alain Locke in *The New Negro* urged talented blacks to shift from "the arid fields of controversy and debate to the productive fields of creative expression." The writers and artists of the Renaissance ignored the racism, discrimination, and economic troubles faced by most African-Americans in the 1920s. They reacted with hostility to Marcus Garvey and his efforts to mobilize the urban black masses.

With the stock market crash in 1929 and the onset of the Great Depression, the Harlem Renaissance ended. In the 1930s, a new generation of writers led by Richard Wright would launch a more politically engaged black cultural movement. Looking back in 1935, Alain Locke would write sadly: "The rosy enthusiasm and hopes of 1925 were cruelly deceptive mirages. [The Depression] revealed a Harlem that the social worker knew all along, but had not been able to dramatize. There is no cure or saving magic in poetry and art

for precarious marginal employment, high mortality rates, and civic neglect." Langston Hughes tersely assessed the movement in his 1940 autobiography: "The ordinary Negroes hadn't heard of the Negro Renaissance. And if they had, it hadn't raised their wages any."

But for all its naïveté, the Harlem Renaissance left an important legacy. The post–World War II literary flowering that began with Ralph Ellison's *Invisible Man* (1952) and continued with the works of James Baldwin, Toni Morrison, Alice Walker, and others owed a substantial debt to the Harlem Renaissance. Walker, in particular, would pay generous tribute to Zora Neale Hurston. For black writers in the West Indies and in French West Africa, "Harlem" would become a core motif, a symbol of both racial oppression and racial achievement. A fragile flower battered by the cold winds of the depression, the Harlem Renaissance nevertheless stands as a monument to African-American cultural creativity even under difficult circumstances.

**Poet and Novelist Langston Hughes,** by Winold Reiss

## Achievements in Architecture, Painting, and Music

The creative energies of the 1920s found many outlets. A burst of architectural activity, for example, transformed the urban skyline. By 1930 the United States boasted 377 buildings over 70 stories tall. The skyscraper, proclaimed one writer, "epitomizes American life and American civilization."

Cultural critic Lewis Mumford, by contrast, denounced America's gargantuan and impersonal cities, with their "audacious towers, [and] . . . endless miles of asphalted pavements." As an alternative, Mumford advocated decentralization and a revitalization of regional cultures.

Artists of the twenties turned to America itself for inspiration—either the real nation around them or an imagined one. Whereas muralist Thomas Hart Benton evoked a half-mythic America of cowboys, pioneers, and riverboat gamblers, Edward Hopper portrayed a nation of faded towns and lonely cities. Hopper's painting *Sunday* (1926), in which a man slumps on the curb

of an empty sidewalk in front of a row of abandoned stores, conveyed both the dreariness and the potential beauty of urban America.

Other 1920s painters offered more upbeat images. John Sloan's vibrant *Main Street Gloucester* (1921), conveys a very different mood from that of Sinclair Lewis's *Main Street*, published the year before. Charles Sheeler recorded on film a dramatic series of images of Ford's River Rouge plant near Detroit. Wisconsin native Georgia O'Keeffe came to New York City in 1918 when the photographer Alfred Stieglitz (whom she married in 1924) mounted a show of her work. O'Keeffe's 1920s paintings evoked both the congestion and the excitement of the city.

The ferment of the 1920s reached the musical world as well. Composer Aaron Copland later recalled the excitement of the early twenties: "The conviction grew inside me that the two things that seemed always to have been so separate in America—music and the life about me—must be made to touch."

While Copland drew upon folk traditions for inspiration, others evoked the new urban-industrial America. Composer Frederick Converse's 1927 tone poem about the automobile, "Flivver Ten Million," for example, featured such episodes as "Dawn in Detroit," "May Night by the Roadside," and "The Collision." Conductor Walter Damrosch brought classical music to millions of radio listeners with his "Music Appreciation Hour" on NBC.

Above all, American music in the 1920s meant jazz. The Original Dixieland Jazz Band—white musicians imitating the black jazz bands of New Orleans—debuted at Reisenweber's Cabaret in New York City in January 1917, and a jazz vogue soon began.

The white bands that promoted jazz in the twenties also drained it of

**The Great White Way,** by Howard Thain, 1925
*This painting radiates the vibrancy, bright lights, and raucous commercialism of New York City, the nation's premier metropolis in the booming 1920s.*

much of its energy. The popular white band leader Paul Whiteman offered watered-down "jazz" versions of standard tunes and light classical works. Of the white composers who wrote in a jazz idiom, George Gershwin, with his *Rhapsody in Blue* (1924) and *An American in Paris* (1928), was the most brilliantly original.

Meanwhile, black musicians preserved the spirit of authentic jazz. Guitar picker Hudie Ledbetter (nick-named Leadbelly) performed his blues and work songs before appreciative black audiences. Singers like Bessie Smith and Gertrude ("Ma") Rainey drew packed audiences on Chicago's South Side and recorded on black-oriented record labels. Trumpeter Louis ("Satchmo") Armstrong and band leader Fletcher Henderson did some of their most creative work in the 1920s, while the black pianist, composer, and band leader Duke Ellington performed to packed audiences at Harlem's Cotton Club. The spread of phonograph recordings, along with radio, helped both to popularize and to standardize this rambunctious new music, which so captured the spirit of the 1920s.

### Advances in Science and Medicine

In a different field of endeavor, the creativity of the 1920s found expression in important scientific and medical developments. The first long-range television transmission, from New York City to Washington, occurred in 1927. In nuclear physics Arthur H. Compton of the University of Chicago won the Nobel Prize in 1927 for his work on x-rays, and Ernest O. Lawrence of the University of California laid the theoretical groundwork that led to the construction of the first cyclotron.

In medical research, Harvey Cushing of Harvard Medical School made dramatic advances in neurosurgery, and at the University of Wisconsin, chemist Harry Steenbock discovered how to create vitamin D in milk using ultraviolet rays. Advances in the treatment of such killers as diphtheria, whooping cough, measles, and influenza helped produce a significant lengthening of life-expectancy rates.

Meanwhile, in 1919 a physicist at Clark University in Massachusetts, Robert Goddard, published a little-noticed scientific article entitled "A Method of Reaching Extreme Altitudes." Goddard studied rocketry throughout the 1920s and in 1926 launched a small liquid-fuel rocket. Ridiculed at the time, Goddard's predictions of lunar landings and space exploration proved prophetic.

**March 1926: Beginnings of the Space Age**
*Dr. Robert H. Goddard (1882–1945), physics professor at Clark University and a pioneer of rocketry, stands with one of his prototype models.*

In *Science and the Modern World* (1925), Harvard philosopher Alfred North Whitehead underscored science's growing role. Although "individually powerless," Whitehead concluded, scientists were "ultimately the rulers of the world." While some citizens welcomed this prospect, for others it was simply one more in an array of disorienting social changes that made the 1920s an unusually stressful and conflict-ridden decade.

## A Society in Conflict

Despite prosperity and superficial gaiety, society faced severe strains in the 1920s. While the economy had become increasingly standardized, the cultural homogeneity of an earlier day had collapsed under the combined assault of immigration, technology, urban growth, and Darwinian evolutionary theory. As a consequence, rural Americans uneasily surveyed the mushrooming cities; native-born Protestants apprehensively eyed the swelling ranks of Catholics and Jews; and traditionalists viewed the revolution in manners and morals with dismay. A series of highly charged episodes and movements highlighted the social tensions of these years.

## Immigration Restriction, Hispanic Newcomers

Fed by wartime superpatriotism, the old impulse to turn America into a nation of like-minded, culturally identical people revived in the 1920s. The National Origins Act of 1924 restricted annual immigration from any one foreign country to 2 percent of the total number of persons of that "national origin" in the United States in 1890. Since the great influx of southern and eastern Europeans had come after 1890, the intent of this provision was clear: to reduce the immigration of these people. As Calvin Coolidge observed upon signing the law, "America must be kept American." The law excluded Asians entirely, gratuitously insulting the Chinese and Japanese. In 1923 the U.S. Supreme Court upheld a California law limiting Japanese immigrants' right to own or lease farmland.

In 1929 Congress changed the base year for determining "national origins" to 1920, but even under this formula, the annual quota for Poland stood at a mere 6,500; for Italy, 5,800; and for Russia, 2,700. This quota system, which survived into the 1960s, represented a strong counterattack by rural, native-born America against the immigrant cities. Total immigration fell from 1.2 million in 1914 to 280,000 in 1929.

Because most restrictionists viewed Asia and southern and eastern Europe as the sources of "undesirables," these laws placed no restraints on immigration from the Western Hemisphere. In fact, immigration from French Canada and Latin America soared in the 1920s. Poverty and domestic political turmoil propelled thousands of Mexicans northward. By 1930 at least 2 million Mexican-born people lived in the United States, most of them in the Southwest. California's Mexican-American population mushroomed from 90,000 to nearly 360,000 in the 1920s.

Many of these were migratory farm workers who earned paltry wages in the region's large-scale agribusinesses. In California, Mexican migrant labor sustained the state's citrus industry. Grove owners belonging to cooperatives such as the Southern California Fruit Growers Exchange (Sunkist), hired itinerant workers on a seasonal basis, providing substandard housing in isolated settlements the workers called *colonias.* The growers bitterly opposed the migrants' attempts to form labor unions.

Though deeply religious, the Mexican-Americans found little support from the U.S. Catholic Church. Earlier, European Catholic immigrants had attended ethnic parishes and worshiped in their own languages, but by the 1920s the church's policy had changed. In "Anglo" parishes with non-Hispanic priests, the Spanish-speaking Mexican newcomers faced discrimination and pressure to abandon their language, traditions, and folk beliefs.

The Mexican-American community was split between alien migrant workers and earlier immigrants who had become U.S. citizens. The strongest Mexican-American organization in the 1920s, the Texas-based League of United Latin American Citizens, ignored the migrant laborers and their problems.

## The Sacco-Vanzetti Case

The nativist, antiradical sentiments that underlay the postwar Red Scare and the immigration-restriction movement emerged starkly in a Massachusetts murder case that quickly became a *cause célèbre.* On April 15, 1920, robbers shot and killed the paymaster and guard of a shoe factory in South Braintree, Massachusetts, and stole two cash boxes. The police charged two Italian immigrants, Nicola Sacco and Bartolomeo Vanzetti, with the murders. A jury found them guilty in 1921. After repeated delays and appeals, and a review of the case by a prestigious commission, they died in the electric chair on August 23, 1927.

These bare facts do not begin to convey the passions the case aroused. Sacco and Vanzetti were avowed anarchists, and from the start the prosecution harped on their radicalism. The judge, a conservative Republican, made plain his hostility to the defendants, whom he privately called "those anarchist bastards."

The Sacco-Vanzetti case mirrored divisions in the larger society. While nativists and conservatives, ignoring issues raised by the defense, insisted that these alien anarchists must die, prominent liberals, socialists, writers, and artists rallied around the convicted men. As Sacco and Vanzetti went to the chair, the writer John Dos Passos summed up his feelings in a bitter poem that ended:

> All right you have won you will kill the brave
> men our friends tonight
> . . . all right we are two nations.

Were Sacco and Vanzetti guilty? The case against them was circumstantial and far from airtight. However, later research on Boston's anarchist community and ballistics tests on Sacco's gun, pointed to their guilt. But the poisonous political climate that tainted the trial remains indisputable, as does the case's symbolic importance in exposing the splits in American society in the 1920s.

### The Ku Klux Klan

The nativism of the immigration-restriction movement erupted even more viciously in the revived Ku Klux Klan. The original Klan had faded by the 1870s, but in November 1915, a group of hooded men gathered at Stone Mountain, Georgia, and revived it. D. W. Griffith's glorification of the Klan in *The Birth of a Nation* provided further inspiration.

The movement attracted little notice until 1920, when two Atlanta entrepreneurs organized a national membership drive. Sensing the appeal of the Klan's ritual and its nativist, white-supremacist ideology, they devised a recruitment scheme involving a ten-dollar membership fee divided among the salesman (called the Kleagle), the local sales manager (King Kleagle), the district sales manager (Grand Goblin), and "Imperial Wizard" William J. Simmons—with a rake-off to themselves. The enterprising pair also sold Klan robes and masks ($6.50), the horse robe that every member had to buy ($8.00), and the genuine Chatta-hoochee River water used in initiation rites ($10.00 a bottle). This elaborate scam succeeded beyond their wildest dreams.

Estimates of the recruits to the Klan or its auxiliary, Women of the Klan, in the early twenties range as high as 5 million. From its southern base, the Klan spread through the Midwest and indeed across the country from Connecticut and Long Island to the West Coast, especially among the blue-collar and lower-white-collar ranks of cities and towns where native-born Protestants remained dominant. In 1922 a Texas dentist, Hiram Wesley Evans, who called himself "the most average man in America," became Imperial Wizard. Admitting the Klan's image as a haven of "hicks" and "rubes," Evans urged the college-bred to support the great cause.

Under the umbrella term "100 percent American-ism," the thrust of Klan bigotry varied from region to region: antiblack in the South; more often Catholics and Jews in the North and West. In the Southwest the Klan singled out violators of prohibition for vigilante action.

The Klan filled important needs for its members. Although corrupt at the top, it was not a movement of criminals or fanatics; observers commented on the members' ordinariness. The Klan's promise to restore the nation to an imagined purity—racial, ethnic, and moral—appealed to ill-educated, religious, and economically marginal Americans confronting a rapidly changing society. For small businessmen caught between organized labor and the new corporate order, the Klan's white-supremacist ideology offered a racist vocabulary for articulating economic anxieties. Those made uneasy by woman suffrage and by changing sexual mores among the young welcomed the Klan's pledge to fight for the "purity of white womanhood."

Klan membership gave a sense of importance and group cohesion to native-born citizens who felt disoriented and marginalized by the new social order of immigrants, big cities, and mass culture. The rituals and the burning crosses added drama and excitement to drab lives.

But if the individual Klan member seems more pathetic than sinister, the movement was not therefore insignificant. Klan members resorted to intimidation, threats, beatings, and even murder in their racist quest for a purified America.

**October 1922: The Ku Klux Klan on the March**
*Amid a crush of onlookers, and carrying a large American flag, KKK members parade through downtown Anderson, Indiana.*

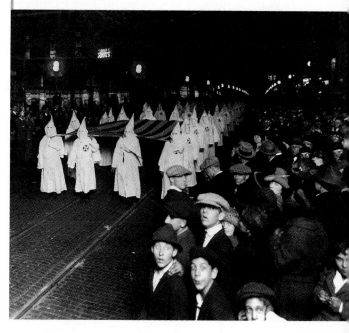

In several states, the Klan exerted substantial political power. In Oklahoma the Klan-controlled legislature impeached and removed an anti-Klan governor. In Oregon the Klan elected a governor and pushed through legislation requiring public school attendance of all children, a slap at the state's Catholic schools.

The Klan collapsed with shocking suddenness. In March 1925 Indiana's politically influential Grand Dragon, David Stephenson, raped his young secretary. When she swallowed poison the next day, Stephenson panicked and refused to call a physician. The woman died several weeks later, and Stephenson went to jail. From prison he revealed details of political corruption in Indiana. Its high moral pretensions in shreds, the Klan faded.

### The Garvey Movement

Among African-Americans the decade's social strains produced a different kind of mass movement. For most blacks, escape from southern rural poverty and racism led only to northern ghetto poverty and more racism.

**Marcus Garvey (1887–1945)**
*Jamaican-born Garvey, shown here in New York City in 1922, attracted many poor and working-class urban African-Americans with the parades and regalia of his Universal Negro Improvement Association and its message of black pride, self help, and African nationalism.*

Many poor urban blacks turned to the spellbinding Marcus Garvey and his Universal Negro Improvement Association (UNIA). In a society where white represented the ideal, Garvey glorified all things black. Urging black economic solidarity, he founded a chain of UNIA grocery stores and other businesses. He called on the world's blacks to return to "Motherland Africa" and establish there a powerful nation.

An estimated eighty thousand blacks joined the UNIA, and thousands more felt the lure of Garvey's oratory; the uplift of the UNIA parades, uniforms, and flags; and the seduction of Garvey's dream of a return to Africa. Garvey's movement unsettled not only white America but also the middle-class leaders of the NAACP and the black church. W. E. B. Du Bois was one of his sharpest critics.

In 1923 a federal court convicted Garvey of fraud in connection with one of his business ventures. In 1927, after two years' imprisonment, he was deported to Jamaica and the UNIA collapsed. But as the first mass movement in black America, it revealed both the discontent and the activist potential in the urban ghettos. "In a world where black is despised," commented a black newspaper upon Garvey's deportation, "he taught his followers that black is beautiful."

### Fundamentalism and the Scopes Trial

American Protestantism underwent severe trials in the half-century before 1920. The prestige of science had grown steadily, challenging religion's cultural standing. Scholars had probed the Bible's historical origins, and psychologists had explained religion in terms of human emotional needs. And all the while, Catholic and Jewish immigrants had poured in.

Liberal Protestantism had responded by accepting the findings of science and emphasizing the Social Gospel. But a reaction was building. This reaction came to be known as fundamentalism, after *The Fundamentals,* a series of tracts published in 1909–1914. Fundamentalists insisted on the inerrancy of every word in the Bible, a literalistic reading of the Genesis version of Creation, and Jesus' virgin birth and resurrection. Religious liberals and "modernists," they insisted, had abandoned these truths.

In the early 1920s, fundamentalists focused especially on the theory of evolution advanced in Charles Darwin's *Origin of Species* (1859), which seemed to them a blatant rejection of biblical truth. Legislators in twenty states in 1921–1922 introduced bills to prohibit the teaching of evolution in the public schools, and several southern states enacted such legislation. Texas governor Miriam ("Ma") Ferguson personally censored textbooks that discussed evolution. "I am a Christian mother," she declared, "and I am not going to let that kind of rot go into Texas textbooks." Fundamentalism's best-known champion, William Jennings Bryan, endorsed the anti-evolution cause.

When the Tennessee legislature in 1925 outlawed the teaching of evolution in the public schools, the American Civil Liberties Union (ACLU) offered to defend any teacher willing to challenge this law. A young high school biology teacher in Dayton, Tennessee, John T. Scopes, accepted the offer. Scopes summarized Darwin's theory to his class and was arrested. Famed criminal lawyer Clarence Darrow headed the defense team and Bryan assisted the prosecution. Journalists poured into Dayton, Chicago radio station WGN broadcast the proceedings live, and the Scopes "monkey trial" became a media sensation.

When cross-examined by Darrow, Bryan insisted on the literal accuracy of every story in the Bible and revealed his ignorance of vast realms of scientific knowledge. Although the jury found Scopes guilty, the Dayton trial marked an embarrassing setback for fundamentalism. When Bryan died of a heart attack a few days later, H. L. Mencken wrote a harshly satirical column that mercilessly derided Bryan and the "gaping primates" who idolized him.

Fundamentalism diminished as a force in mainstream Protestantism, but many local congregations and radio preachers still embraced the traditional faith. So, too, did the popular evangelist Billy Sunday, who used publicity techniques and a flamboyant pulpit style to denounce the loose living and modernism of the 1920s.

Zealous new denominations and independent "full gospel" churches promoted the cause. Charismatic evangelist Aimee Semple McPherson, who anticipated the TV evangelists of a later day, regularly filled her cavernous Angelus Temple in Los Angeles and reached thousands more by radio. Radiating drama and beauty, the white-gowned McPherson won a vast following through her cheerful sermons and theatrical talent. On one occasion she employed a gigantic electric scoreboard to illustrate the triumph of good over evil. Her followers, mainly transplanted midwestern farmers, embraced her fundamentalist theology while reveling in her

mass enterainment techniques. When she died in 1944, her International Church of the Foursquare Gospel had over six hundred branches in the United States and abroad. Embarrassed at Dayton, fundamentalism was far from dead as the 1920s ended.

## Prohibition

The societal fissures highlighted by the Klan movement and the Scopes trial extended as well to the battle to rid the United States of alcoholic beverages. Temperance reform had deep nineteenth-century roots, and, as we saw in Chapter 22, prohibition had won wide support among progressives as a legitimate response to the social problems associated with alcohol abuse. But the prohibition cause also had a symbolic dimension, as native-born Americans struggled to maintain cultural and political dominance over the immigrant cities.

When the Eighteenth Amendment took effect in January 1920, prohibitionists rejoiced. Billy Sunday proclaimed,

> The reign of tears is over. The slums will soon be only a memory. We will turn our prisons into factories and our jails into storehouses and corncribs. Men will walk upright now. Women will smile and children will laugh.

At first, Sunday's dream seemed attainable. Saloons closed; liquor advertising stopped; arrests for drunkenness dwindled. In 1921 alcohol consumption stood

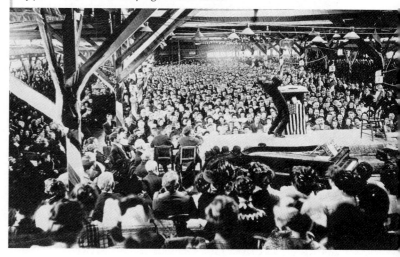

**Hoopla and Hallelujah: Billy Sunday in Action**
*The colorful ex-baseball player attracted vast audiences to his heavily promoted revival campaigns in the 1920s.*

at about one-third the prewar level. Yet prohibition was gradually discredited, and in 1933 it ended. What went wrong? Essentially, the prohibition debacle illustrates the virtual impossibility, in a democracy, of enforcing rules of behavior with which a great many citizens disagree.

From the beginning, the Volstead Act, the 1919 prohibition law, was underbudgeted and only sporadically enforced, especially in strongly antiprohibition states. New York, for example, repealed its prohibition-enforcement law as early as 1923. Would-be drinkers grew bolder as enforcement faltered. For rebellious young people, alcohol's illegality added to its appeal. "[P]rohibition has been an incentive for young folks to learn to drink," declared a University of Wisconsin student. "It is the natural reaction of youth to rules and regulations." Every city boasted speakeasies where customers could buy drinks, and rumrunners routinely smuggled in liquor from Canada and the West Indies. Shady entrepreneurs sold flavored industrial-grade alcohol to a gullible public. People concocted their own home brew, and the demand for sacramental wine increased amazingly. By 1929 alcohol consumption had risen to about 70 percent of the prewar level.

Organized crime helped circumvent the law. In Chicago, rival gangs fought bloody wars to control the liquor business. Chicago witnessed 550 gangland killings in the 1920s. By 1929 Chicago mob king Al Capone controlled a network of speakeasies generating annual profits of $60 million. Although not typical, Chicago's crime wave appeared to prove prohibi-

tion's failure. A reform designed to produce a more orderly, law-abiding America was having precisely the opposite effect.

Thus prohibition, too, became a battleground in the decade's cultural wars. The "drys"—usually native-born Protestants—praised it as a necessary social reform. The "wets"—liberals, alienated intellectuals, Jazz Age rebels, big-city immigrants—condemned it as moralistic meddling and made it a butt of humor. At Trinity College in Connecticut, the student newspaper suggested that as their class gift, the seniors erect a distillery on campus "with the proceeds going to the college."

Prohibition figured in the 1928 presidential campaign. Democratic candidate Al Smith openly endorsed repeal of the Eighteenth Amendment. By contrast, Republican Herbert Hoover praised prohibition as "a great social and economic experiment, noble in motive and far-reaching in purpose." Once elected, Hoover appointed a commission to study the matter. In a confusing 1931 report, the commission conceded the breakdown of prohibition but urged its retention. A New York journalist parodied the findings:

> Prohibition is an awful flop.
>   We like it.
> It can't stop what it's meant to stop.
>   We like it.
> It's left a trail of graft and slime,
> It's filled our land with vice and crime,
> It don't prohibit worth a dime,
>   Nevertheless we're for it.

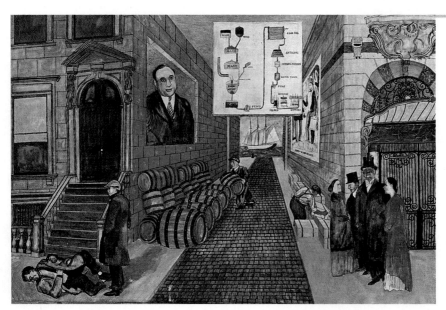

**Prohibition Alley Scene,** by Ben Shahn, c. 1934 *In this fanciful painting, incorporating a portrait of gangster Al Capone, Shahn linked the crime and violence of bootlegging with the respectable citizenry who patronized speakeasies that sold illicit liquor.*

By 1933, the year that brought repeal of the Eighteenth Amendment, prohibition seemed little more than a relic from another age.

# Hoover at the Helm

Herbert Hoover, elected president in 1928, seemed an excellent bet to sustain the nation's prosperity. No standpat conservative, Hoover brought to the White House a distinctive social and political philosophy that reflected his background in engineering.

## The Election of 1928

A Hollywood casting agent could not have chosen two individuals who better personified the social and cultural schisms of the 1920s than the presidential candidates of 1928.

Al Smith, the governor of New York, easily won the Democratic nomination. The urban-immigrant wing of the party had gained strength since the deadlocked convention of 1924. A Catholic and a "wet," Smith, with his brown derby hat perpetually askew, exuded the flavor of immigrant New York City. Originally a machine politician, and basically conservative in his social ideas, he represented progressivism's urban-immigrant component through his championing of social welfare measures. His political intimates included several reform-minded women, notably Frances Perkins, the head of the state industrial board, and Belle Moskowitz, a key adviser.

Secretary of Commerce Herbert Hoover won the Republican nomination with equal ease after Calvin Coolidge chose not to run. Some conservative party leaders, however, did not wholly trust the brilliant but aloof Hoover, who had never run for public office and indeed had spent much of his adult life abroad.

Born in Iowa and orphaned at an early age, Hoover had put himself through Stanford University and made a fortune as a mining engineer in China and Australia. His service as wartime food administrator won him a place in the Harding and Coolidge cabinets.

Hoover, disdaining handshaking and baby kissing, instead issued "tons of reports on dull subjects" (in Mencken's jaundiced view) and delivered radio speeches in a boring monotone. The dullness of Hoover's campaign obscured the originality of some of his ideas. Smith, by contrast, campaigned spiritedly throughout the country. This may actually have hurt his cause, however, because many Americans did not warm to his big-city wisecracking and accent.

Whether Smith's Catholicism helped or hurt his candidacy remains debatable, but he unquestionably faced a backlash of prejudice. Hoover urged religious tolerance, and Smith denied any conflict between his faith and the duties of the presidency, but some Protestants remained suspicious. Rumors circulated that the Vatican would relocate to the United States if Smith won. (A postelection joke had the defeated Smith sending the pope a one-word telegram: "Unpack.")

The decisive campaign issue was probably not religion but prosperity. Republican orators took credit for the booming economy and warned that a Smith victory would mean "soup kitchens instead of busy factories." In his nomination acceptance speech, Hoover foresaw "the final triumph over poverty." Seeking to defuse the prosperity issue, Smith chose as his campaign manager a General Motors vice president who released lists of well-known capitalists who backed Smith.

Nevertheless, Hoover won in a landslide, grabbing 58 percent of the vote and even making deep inroads in the Democratic "solid South." Smith won a meager 87 electoral votes, compared to 444 for Hoover. In a stark comment on the prevailing political climate, the Socialist party candidate, Norman Thomas, received only 267,000 votes—less than a third of Eugene V. Debs's 1920 total.

Beneath the Hoover landslide, however, lay evidence of an emerging political realignment. Smith did well in the rural Midwest, where hard-pressed farmers

### The Election of 1928

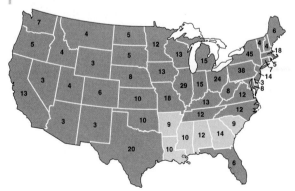

| | | Electoral Vote | Popular Vote | Percentage of Popular Vote |
|---|---|---|---|---|
| **Republican** Herbert C. Hoover | | 444 | 21,391,993 | 58.2 |
| **Democratic** Alfred E. Smith | | 87 | 15,016,169 | 40.9 |
| **Minor parties** | – | – | 330,725 | 0.9 |

## Presidential Voting by Selected Ethnic Groups in Chicago, 1924, 1928, and 1932

| | Percent Democratic | | |
| --- | --- | --- | --- |
| | 1924 | 1928 | 1932 |
| Blacks | 10 | 23 | 21 |
| Czechoslovaks | 40 | 73 | 83 |
| Germans | 14 | 58 | 69 |
| Italians | 31 | 63 | 64 |
| Jews | 19 | 60 | 77 |
| Lithuanians | 48 | 77 | 84 |
| Poles | 35 | 71 | 80 |
| Swedes | 15 | 34 | 51 |
| Yugoslavs | 20 | 54 | 67 |

*Source:* John M. Allswang, *A House for All Peoples: Ethnic Politics in Chicago, 1890–1936* (Lexington: University Press of Kentucky, 1971).

abandoned their normal Republican allegiance. In northern cities, Catholic and Jewish immigrants (and their offspring) voted Democratic in record numbers. In 1924 the nation's twelve largest cities had gone Republican; in 1928 Smith carried all twelve. Should prosperity end, these portents suggested, the Republican party would be in trouble.

### Herbert Hoover's Social Thought

As 1929 dawned, Americans looked hopefully to their new president, whom admirers dubbed the Great Engineer. Hoover entered the White House with a well-developed social creed expounded in his 1922 book *American Individualism.* Although a self-made man himself, Hoover was no cheerleader for laissez-faire competition. Nor, in contrast to Harding and Coolidge, did he uncritically praise big business. His Quakerism, humanitarian activities, and engineering experience combined with his Republican party loyalties to produce a unique social outlook.

Like Theodore Roosevelt (whom he had supported in 1912), Hoover disapproved of cutthroat capitalist competition. Rational economic development, he insisted, demanded corporate cooperation in marketing, wage policy, raw-material allocation, and product standardization. The economy, in short, should operate like an efficient machine.

Believing that business had broad social obligations, Hoover welcomed the growth of welfare capitalism. But above all, he believed in voluntarism. The cooperative, socially responsible economic order that he envisioned must arise from the voluntary action of capitalist leaders, not government coercion—down that path lay totalitarianism—or from labor-management power struggles.

Hoover had put his philosophy into practice as secretary of commerce. Seeking to accelerate the decade's trend toward corporate consolidation, he had convened more than 250 conferences where business leaders discussed such issues as unemployment, pricing policies, labor-management relations, and the virtues of trade associations. He urged higher wages to increase consumer purchasing power, and in 1923 he persuaded the steel industry on grounds of efficiency to adopt an eight-hour workday.

Hoover's ideology had its limitations. He showed more interest in cooperation among capitalists than among consumers or workers. His belief that capitalists would voluntarily embrace cooperation, social service, and enlightened labor policies overestimated the role of altruism in business decision making. And his firm opposition to government economic intervention brought him grief when such intervention became urgently necessary.

Hoover in his early months as president compiled an impressive record. He set up the President's Council on Recent Social Trends to gather data for policy makers' guidance. He created commissions to study public-policy issues. Responding to the farm problem, he secured passage of legislation that established a Federal Farm Board (1929) to promote cooperative commodity marketing. This, he hoped, would raise farm prices while preserving the voluntarist principle.

As the summer of 1929 turned to autumn, the Hoover administration seemed off to a promising start. But while Hoover applied his engineering skills to the business of government, a crisis was approaching that would overwhelm and ultimately destroy his presidency.

### CONCLUSION

Reacting against the exalted idealism of the war, America in the 1920s pursued a cautions, often unilateralist foreign policy, shying away from Wilson's vision of global leadership. The myth of U.S. "isolationism" in the twenties is belied, however, by aggressive corporate expansion, continued U.S. involvement in Latin America, and Washington's vigorous pursuit of U.S. interests in such matters as reparations payments.

On the domestic front, the era remains memorable for the picture it presents of an entire people grappling with massive technological and social change. Like world travelers groggy from jet lag, Americans of the twenties sought to adapt to the rise of a mass-culture, mass-production, urban world that had emerged, seemingly almost overnight. Radio, the automobile, the movies, electrical appliances—all so familiar today— were still exciting novelties in 1920s America.

In Republican-dominated Washington, the new corporate, consumerist culture was generally celebrated ("The business of America is business" [Calvin Coolidge]) or treated with solemn deference. The more interesting responses to these changes unfolded outside the political arena. Whereas the conservative political leadership of the decade typically fell back on inherited ideologies, the rest of society seethed in ferment. Ironically, the same stresses that produced bitter social conflicts also stimulated a rich cultural and literary flowering. The champions of prohibition and fundamentalism, the troubled folk who joined the Klan, the urban blacks who cheered Marcus Garvey, the artists and writers of the Harlem Renaissance, the early jazz musicians, and the novelists and poets who revitalized American literature were all, in their different ways, trying to make sense of an unfamiliar and often threatening new social order. Historians rightly deplore the political failures and reactionary social movements of the twenties, but that ought not obscure the decade's positive and lasting achievements.

## FOR FURTHER READING

Charles C. Alexander, *Here the Country Lies: Nationalism and the Arts in Twentieth Century America* (1980). A useful revisionist study whose chapters on the 1920s stress the decade's positive achievements.

Loren Bartiz, ed., *The Culture of the Twenties* (1970). A rich collection of primary documents with a helpful introductory essay.

Paul Carter, *The Twenties in America* (1968) and *Another Part of the Twenties* (1977). Two essays offering refreshingly personal interpretive judgments.

Lynn Dumenil, *The Modern Temper: America in the 1920s* (1995). Offers a wealth of fresh insights, especially on often neglected groups and movements.

Ellis W. Hawley, *The Great War and the Search for a Modern Order* (1979). An economic study that traces the emergence (and collapse in 1929) of the first mass-consumption society.

George Hutchinson, *The Harlem Renaissance in Black and White* (1995). Original new study linking the Harlem Renaissance to larger cultural and intellectual movements.

Nancy MacLean, *Behind the Mask of Chivalry: The Making of the Second Ku Klux Klan* (1994). Explores Klan members' anxieties about corporate growth, feminism, sexuality, and other issues of the 1920s.

Joan Shelley Rubin, *The Making of Middle-Brow Culture* (1992). An interpretive study of the Book-of-the-Month Club and other 1920s institutions by which high culture reached a larger public.

# Crash, Depression, and New Deal

**Drought Stricken Area,** by Alexander Hogue, 1934

Rugged Campobello Island, lying off Eastport, Maine, was sunlit that August afternoon in 1921. In the waters off the island bobbed a small sailboat. At the helm, with several of his children, was thirty-nine-year-old Franklin D. Roosevelt. Assistant secretary of the navy during World War I, Roosevelt had been the Democratic party's vice-presidential candidate in 1920. But all this was far from his mind now. He loved sailing, and he loved Campobello Island.

Suddenly the idyllic afternoon took an ominous turn as Roosevelt spotted a fire. Beaching the boat, he and the children frantically beat back the spreading flames.

The exertion left Roosevelt unusually fatigued. Next morning his left leg dragged as he tried to walk. Soon all sensation in both legs disappeared. He had suffered an attack of poliomyelitis (infantile paralysis), a viral infection that most often struck children but sometimes adults as well. Except for a cumbersome shuffle with crutches and heavy metal braces, he would never walk again.

This illness changed the lives of both Franklin Roosevelt and his wife Eleanor. For Franklin, it seemed the end of his career. But he endured endless therapy and gradually reentered politics. In 1928, laboriously mounting the podium at the Democratic National Convention, he nominated his friend Al Smith for president. That fall, he himself was elected governor of New York.

Somewhat superficial and even arrogant before 1921, this privileged only child became, through his ordeal, more understanding of the disadvantaged and far more determined. "If you had spent two years in bed trying to wiggle your big toe," he once said, "after that everything else would seem easy!"

Eleanor Roosevelt at first devoted herself to her husband's care and to the child-rearing responsibilities that now fell upon her. But she also encouraged his return to politics, firmly resisting her domineering mother-in-law's efforts to take her son back to the family home at Hyde Park, New York, and turn him into an invalid. Eleanor became her husband's eyes and ears. Already involved with social issues, she now joined the executive board of the New York Democratic party and edited the women's division newsletter. Painfully shy, she forced herself to make public speeches.

The Roosevelts would soon need the qualities of character they had acquired. Elected president in 1932, in the midst of the worst depression in American history, Franklin Roosevelt dominated U.S. politics until his death in 1945. The depression-fighting phase of Roosevelt's presidency, commonly called the New Deal, spawned an array of laws, agencies, and programs that historians ever since have tried to whip into coherent form. And, indeed, certain patterns do emerge. In the so-called First New Deal (1933–1935), the dual themes were relief and recovery through a united national effort. In 1935, responding to political challenges on the left and right, the New Deal took a more radical course. In the so-called Second New Deal (1935–1938), the administration placed less emphasis on unity and more on business regulation and on policies benefiting workers, small farmers, sharecroppers, migrant laborers, and others at the lower end of the scale.

The laws and agencies that made up the New Deal were shaped by many political cross-currents and countless individuals. But in the public mind, the New Deal meant Roosevelt. Loved by some almost as a member of the family and reviled by others as a demagogue or worse, Roosevelt is recognized today as a consummate politician whose administration set the national political agenda for a generation.

This chapter focuses on five major questions:

♦ What factors contributed to the 1929 stock market crash and the Depression that followed, and what were the immediate social and political effects of these events?

♦ What Depression-fighting strategy underlay the so-called First New Deal of 1933–1934, and what measures were adopted to implement this strategy?

♦ Why did the Roosevelt administration partially change course in 1935, and what strategies underlay the so-called Second New Deal of 1935–1938?

♦ Was the overwhelming support that African-Americans gave to the New Deal justified? Give reasons for your answer.

♦ Which New Deal programs proved unsuccessful, and why? Which had the greatest long-term impact on American society?

# Crash and Depression

The prosperity of the 1920s came to a jolting climax in October 1929 with the collapse of the stock market. The Wall Street crash proved only the overture to a de-

pression that reached every household in the land. President Hoover struggled with the crisis, but his ideological commitment to private initiative and his horror of governmental coercion limited his effectiveness. In November 1932 voters turned to the Democratic party and its new leader, Franklin Roosevelt.

## *Black Thursday*

Stock prices had risen steadily through much of the 1920s, but in 1928–1929, this upward movement became a frenzied spiral as speculators plunged into the market. Prices of automotive, radio, aviation, and other glamour stocks floated into the stratosphere.

In 1925 the market value of all stocks had stood at about $27 billion; in early October 1929, with an estimated 9 million Americans playing the market, it hit $87 billion. With stockbrokers lending speculators up to 75 percent of a stock's cost, credit or "margin" buying spread. The Federal Reserve Board's easy-credit policies and Treasury Secretary Andrew Mellon's continual pressure for income-tax cuts had increased the volume of money available for speculation.

A torrent of optimistic pronouncements drew more people into the market. "Everybody Ought to Be Rich," proclaimed General Motors executive John Raskob in

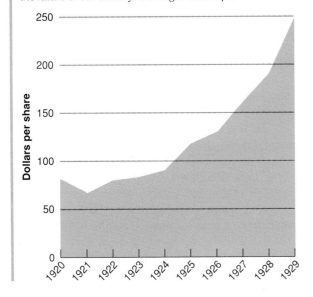

### Stock Market Prices in the 1920s

*After rising moderately in the early 1920s, stock market prices shot up later in the decade. Looking at such statistics, Herbert Hoover declared in 1929: "I have no fears for the future of our country. It is bright with hope."*

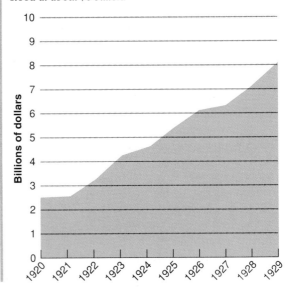

### Consumer Borrowing in the 1920s

*Americans plunged heavily into debt in the 1920s to play the stock market and to buy their new Fords, Chevrolets, and other consumer products. By 1929 their total debt stood at about $8 billion.*

**1929** Stock market crash; onset of depression.

**1930** President Hoover's Emergency Committee for Employment.

**1931** Farmers' Holiday Association.

**1932** Reconstruction Finance Corporation.

Glass–Steagall Act.

Veterans' bonus march.

Franklin D. Roosevelt elected president.

**1933** Repeal of Eighteenth Amendment (end of Prohibition).

Federal Deposit Insurance Corporation created.

Emergency Banking Act.

Civilian Conservation Corps (CCC).

Federal Emergency Relief Act (FERA).

Tennessee Valley Authority (TVA).

Agricultural Adjustment Administration (AAA).

National Recovery Administration (NRA).

Public Works Administration (PWA).

Civil Works Administration (CWA).

**1934** Securities and Exchange Commission (SEC).

National Planning Board.

Civil Works Emergency Relief Act.

Democrats gain in midterm elections.

Taylor Grazing Act.

**1935** Supreme Court declares NRA unconstitutional.

Emergency Relief Appropriation Act.

Works Progress Administration (WPA).

National Youth Administration.

Resettlement Administration.

Rural Electrification Administration (REA).

National Labor Relations Act (Wagner Act).

Social Security Act.

Banking Act.

Public Utilities Holding Company Act.

NAACP campaign for federal antilynching law.

Huey Long assassinated.

Revenue Act.

**1936** Supreme Court declares AAA unconstitutional.

Soil Conservation and Domestic Allotment Act.

Roosevelt wins landslide reelection victory.

**1937** Roosevelt's "court-packing" plan defeated.

Hugo Black appointed to the Supreme Court.

Farm Security Administration (FSA).

National Housing Act.

**1937–1938** The "Roosevelt recession."

**1938** Fair Labor Standards Act.

Agricultural Adjustment Act of 1938.

Republicans gain heavily in midterm elections.

Stanley Reed appointed to the Supreme Court.

**1939** Hatch Act.

Marian Anderson concert at Lincoln Memorial.

Felix Frankfurter and William O. Douglas appointed to the Supreme Court.

---

a *Ladies' Home Journal* article. President Calvin Coolidge in March 1929 declared stocks "cheap at current prices."

With corporations eager for their share of the speculators' money, new securities, observes one historian, "were manufactured almost like cakes of soap." "Investment trusts," akin to the mutual funds of a later day, though totally unregulated, offered novices the benefit of the supposedly superior wisdom of more seasoned investors.

The prosperity driving this speculative frenzy was precarious. Agriculture remained depressed, as did mining, textiles, and other industries. Automobile production slowed as the 1920s wore on. The construction industry declined sharply in 1928–1929—an omen few heeded.

In 1928 the Federal Reserve Board tried to dampen speculation by raising the interest rate on federal reserve notes, and early in 1929 "the Fed" warned member banks to tighten their lending policies. But with speculators willing to pay up to 20 percent interest for money to buy more stock, lending institutions poured additional millions into the money market—an act akin to dumping gasoline on a raging fire. The Fed tightened credit again in September. This time the action was effective, but with catastrophic consequences.

The collapse came on October 24, 1929—"Black Thursday." As prices fell, trading grew panicky. Some stocks found no buyers at all: they had literally become worthless. Anxious speculators huddled around the ticker-tape machines in brokers' offices. At midday a group of New York bankers temporarily allayed the panic by issuing a reassuring statement and ostentatiously buying some $30 million worth of stocks. But prices plunged again on Monday. The climax came on Tuesday, October 29, when a record 16 million stocks changed hands in frantic trading. In the ensuing weeks, feeble upswings in stock prices alternated with further plunges.

On Black Thursday Herbert Hoover, in the first of a long series of optimistic statements, pronounced the economy "sound and prosperous." But few listened. By mid-November the loss in the market value of stocks stood at $30 billion. Stock prices recovered somewhat in early 1930, suggesting that the worst might be over. But the economy had deeper problems.

### Onset of the Depression

Many economists shared Hoover's optimism. After a stock-market shakeout, analysts predicted, business would revive. Instead, the economy went into a long tailspin, producing a full-scale depression.

What were the underlying causes of this depression? Many economists focus on the structural factors that made 1920s' prosperity so unstable. For example, increased productivity did not generate equivalent wage increases but rather took the form of higher corporate profits. In 1929 the 40 percent of Americans at the lower end of the economic scale received only about 12 percent of the total national income. This reduced consumer purchasing power. At the same time, the decade's gains in productivity encouraged overproduction. By the summer of 1929, the automobile, housing, textile, tire, and other durable-goods industries were seriously overextended.

The decline in farm prices in the 1920s was another major structural weakness in the economy. Further, important sectors of industry—including railroads, steel, textiles, and mining— were lagging technologically in the 1930s and could not attract the kind of investment needed to stimulate recovery.

A second interpretation, the "monetarist" school identified with the economist Milton Friedman, focuses on the banking system's collapse in the early 1930s which they in turn blame on Federal Reserve System policies. The Fed, they charge, failed to assure an adequate money supply that would have enabled the economy to bounce back from the crash. The money supply did indeed shrink dramatically in the early 1930s, though the reasons remain under debate.

All analysts position the U.S. depression within a global economic crisis. European economies—already enfeebled by massive war debt payments and a

**The Stock Market Crash Hits Home**
*A bankrupt investor named Walter Thornton tries to sell his roadster for $100 cash the day after the 1929 stock-market crash.*

**The Faces of Despair**
*Farmers in a Spottsylvania, Virginia, courthouse watch impassively as their land is auctioned off for nonpayment of their mortgages.*

heavy trade imbalance with the United States—collapsed in 1931. This larger crisis depressed U.S. exports, but also fed the fear psychology that aggravated the instability.

Whatever the combination of causes, the depression's chilling impact on the U.S. economy is all too clear. From 1929 to 1932, the gross national product dropped from $104 billion to $59 billion and farm prices, already low, fell by nearly 60 percent. A third of the nation's railway mileage fell into bankruptcy in the early thirties. By early 1933 more than 5,500 banks had closed their doors, and unemployment stood at 25 percent, or nearly 13 million workers. Many who still had jobs faced cuts in pay and hours.

### The Depression's Human Toll

The grim message embedded in these figures found confirmation in the hopelessness etched in the expressions of the jobless waiting in breadlines, sleeping on park benches, or trudging the streets. Men hopped freight trains and rode from city to city, hoping to find work. Others sold pencils or apples to earn a few dollars. Americans reared on the ethic of hard work and self-support found chronic unemployment a shattering psychic blow.

Because most of the jobless had families, the unemployment figures must be multiplied several times over to reflect the magnitude of the distress. Similarly,

the epidemic of bank closings robbed millions of families of desperately needed savings. Blacks, Hispanics, southern sharecroppers, and other groups endured particular hardships (see Chapter 26).

Heartrending scenes unfolded as farm families lost their homes. In 1933 alone over 5 percent of the nation's farms underwent mortgage foreclosures or forced sales because of tax delinquency, with Iowa and the Dakotas especially hard hit. At some of these sales, angry neighbors dominated the auction, bought the foreclosed farm for a trivial sum, and returned it to the evicted family.

For depression-era children, poor diet and inadequate medical and dental care often led to long-term health problems. Malnutrition, rickets, pellagra, and other diet-related ills among children increased alarmingly. By early 1933, local school boards stung by dwindling tax revenues shortened the school year and even closed schools.

Newspapers conveyed the human meaning of the crisis by focusing on dramatic vignettes. The *New York Times* described "Hoover Valley"—a section of Central Park where jobless men had built makeshift shelters of boxes and packing crates. In winter, the homeless sometimes wrapped themselves in thick layers of newspapers they sardonically called Hoover blankets. The suicide rate climbed nearly 30 percent between 1928 and 1932. In Youngstown, Ohio, a fifty-seven-year-old jobless father of ten jumped to his death from a

## The Statistics of Hard Times

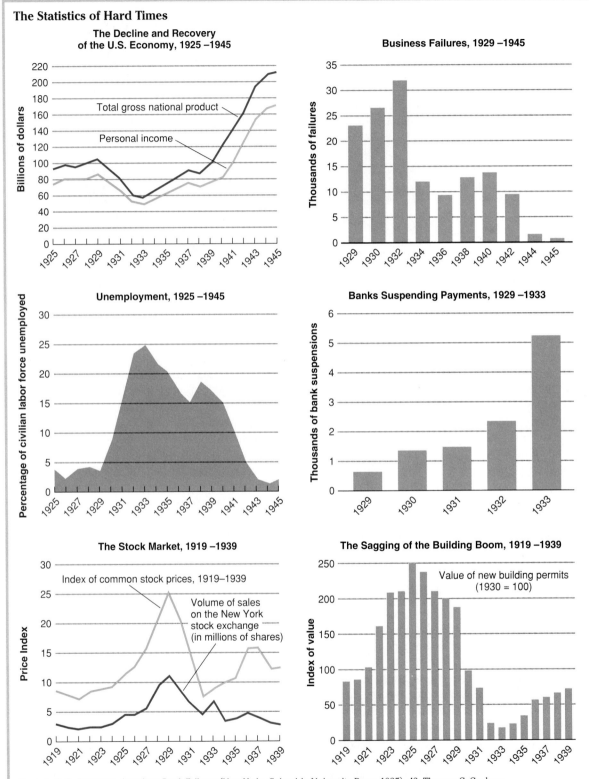

### The Decline and Recovery of the U.S. Economy, 1925–1945

### Business Failures, 1929–1945

### Unemployment, 1925–1945

### Banks Suspending Payments, 1929–1933

### The Stock Market, 1919–1939

### The Sagging of the Building Boom, 1919–1939

*Sources:* C. D. Bremmer, *American Bank Failures* (New York: Columbia University Press, 1935), 42; Thomas C. Cochran, *The Great Depression and World War II: 1929–1945* (Glenview, Illinois: Scott, Foresman, 1968); *Historical Statistics of the United States, Colonial Times to 1970* (Washington, D.C.: U.S. Government Printing Office, 1975).

bridge as his family faced eviction. Although extreme, such stories underscored the depression's social cost.

### Hoover's Response

Historically, Americans had viewed depressions as acts of nature: little could be done but to ride out the storm. Some of Hoover's advisers continued to espouse such views. Hoover himself disagreed. Drawing upon the legacy of progressive reform and his service as U.S. food administrator during World War I, he initially confronted to the economic crisis with bold determination. But his approach also reflected his strong belief in the character-building value of localism and private initiative.

Acting on these convictions, Hoover called business leaders to the White House and pledged them to maintain wages and employment. Viewing unemployment as a local issue, he urged municipal and state governments to create public-works projects. In October 1930 he set up an Emergency Committee for Employment to coordinate voluntary relief efforts. Seeking a nongovernmental response to the liquidity crisis, Hoover in 1931 persuaded the nation's largest banks to set up a private lending agency, the National Credit Corporation, from which hard-pressed smaller banks could borrow money for business loans.

Still the crisis worsened, and as early as November 1930, the voters rendered a harsh verdict on Hoover's policies. In that year's midterm election, the Republicans lost the House of Representatives and gave up eight Senate seats.

In fact, Hoover's antidepression strategy failed. Unemployment mounted, and in 1931, despite their pledges to the president, U.S. Steel, General Motors, and other big corporations announced major wage cuts. The crisis quickly swamped private charities and local welfare agencies. Philadelphia, with more than 300,000 jobless by 1932, first cut weekly relief payments to $4.23 per family and then in June suspended them entirely. One charitable leader later described Philadelphia's destitute as "reduced . . . to . . . the status of a stray cat prowling for food, for which a kind soul occasionally sets out a plate of table scraps or a saucer of milk."

By 1932, with an election looming and his voluntarist approach discredited, Hoover took a series of steps that added up to an unprecedented federal response to economic crisis. In January, at Hoover's recommendation, Congress set up and appropriated $2 billion for a new agency, the Reconstruction Finance Corporation (RFC), to make loans to major economic institutions such as banks and insurance companies. By July the RFC had pumped $1.2 billion into the economy. In February Hoover signed the Glass-Steagall Act, allocating $750 million for loans to private businesses. And in July, Hoover signed a bill authorizing the RFC to give $2 billion to state and local governments for job-creating public-works programs.

Ironically, Hoover reaped little political benefit from these measures. He supported the RFC and the $2 billion public-works bill very grudgingly, warning that such measures could open the door to "socialism and collectivism."

Hoover increasingly blamed great global forces for the depression and argued that only international measures would help. Some of his proposals, such as a one-year moratorium on war-debt and reparations payments by European nations, made sense but seemed irrelevant to the urgent plight of ordinary Americans. Dreading a budget deficit, Hoover in 1931 called for a tax increase and thereby further alienated hard-pressed voters.

As Hoover communicated with the public through impersonal press releases that urged self-help and local initiative and endlessly saw prosperity "just around the corner," relations with the news media soured. When he appointed a new press secretary heartily disliked by White House reporters, one journalist called it the first known instance of a rat boarding a sinking ship. An administration launched so auspiciously in 1929 by a president widely viewed as a great humanitarian and a managerial genius was ending in bitterness and failure.

### Mounting Discontent and Protest

An ominous mood spread over the nation. In 1931 midwestern farmers organized the Farmers' Holiday Association to force prices up by withholding grain and livestock from the market. As wholesale milk prices sank to two cents a quart, dairy farmers dumped thousands of gallons of milk in Iowa and Wisconsin. Farmers who opposed the boycott faced angry reprisals. Violence threatened some city streets when jobless people were evicted from homes and apartments, their meager possessions piled up on the sidewalk.

The most alarming protest came from World War I veterans. In 1924 Congress had voted a veterans' bonus in the form of twenty-year endowment policies against which the veterans might receive government loans. In June 1932 some ten thousand veterans, many jobless, descended on Washington to lobby for passage of a bill

## The Election of 1932

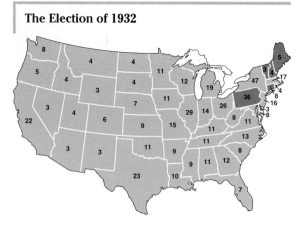

| | | Electoral Vote | Popular Vote | Percentage of Popular Vote |
|---|---|---|---|---|
| **Democratic** Franklin D. Roosevelt | | 472 | 22,809,638 | 57.4 |
| **Republican** Herbert C. Hoover | | 59 | 15,758,901 | 39.7 |
| **Minor parties** | – | – | 1,153,306 | 2.9 |

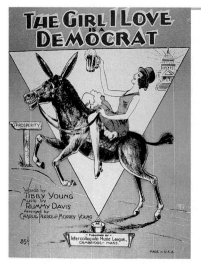

**Democratic Sheet Music, c. 1932**
*Though linking prosperity to prohibition repeal, this long-forgotten tune never attained the popularity of the song the Democrats made their own in 1932, "Happy Days Are Here Again."*

converting these endowments into immediate cash payments. When Congress rejected the bill, most of the "bonus marchers" went home, but about two thousand stayed on, building makeshift shelters in a section of the city called Anacostia Flats.

A nervous Herbert Hoover ordered the army to confine the veterans to Anacostia Flats. The officer given this duty, General Douglas MacArthur, decided to break up the settlement entirely. On July 28 a force of one thousand soldiers armed with tear gas, tanks, and machine guns drove the veterans from their encampment and burned it to the ground. For many Americans, the

image of using armed force on peaceful demonstrators—and veterans at that—symbolized the Hoover administration's utter bankruptcy.

### The Election of 1932

Although Herbert Hoover won renomination at the 1932 Republican convention, an atmosphere of intense gloom prevailed.

The Democrats, by contrast, scented victory as they gathered in Chicago. Their platform, crafted to erase the party divisions of the 1920s, appealed to urban voters with a call for repeal of prohibition, to farmers with support for agricultural aid programs, and to fiscal conservatives with a demand for a balanced budget and a federal spending cut.

Several Democratic hopefuls vied to challenge Hoover. These included Al Smith, the party's 1928 standard-bearer; Texas's John Nance ("Cactus Jack") Garner, Speaker of the House of Representatives; and Franklin D. Roosevelt, governor of New York. Although another deadlocked convention seemed a possibility, Roosevelt eventually emerged as the nominee.

Breaking precedent, FDR flew to Chicago to accept the nomination in person. Not realizing that he was naming an era, Roosevelt in his rousing acceptance speech pledged "a new deal for the American people."

Despite this ringing phrase, Roosevelt's campaign gave little sense of his agenda. He called for "bold persistent experimentation" and for attention to "the forgotten man at the bottom of the economic pyramid," yet he also attacked Hoover's "reckless" spending and insisted that "only as a last resort" should the federal government play a larger economic role.

But Roosevelt exuded confidence and high spirits. Above all, he was not Hoover! On November 8, FDR and his running mate John Nance Garner received nearly 23 million votes, as compared to fewer than 16 million for Hoover. Both houses of Congress went heavily Democratic. After twelve years of Republican rule, the Democrats were back in the saddle. But what did this mean in terms of fighting the depression? The nation waited to see.

## The New Deal Takes Shape

The Roosevelt years began amid excitement and feverish activity. Enjoying strong majorities in Congress, FDR proposed a staggering array of emergency measures, most of which passed by large margins. These measures reflected differing and sometimes contradictory approaches, but the contours of a depression-fighting strategy nevertheless emerged. This strategy involved three components: *industrial recovery* through business-government cooperation and pump-priming federal spending; *agricultural recovery* through subsidized crop reduction; and *short-term emergency relief*—funneled through state and local agencies when possible, but provided directly by the federal government if necessary. Hovering over this bustle loomed confident Franklin Roosevelt, cigarette holder jauntily tilted upward, a symbol of renewed hope.

## New Beginnings

Although short on specifics, FDR's inaugural address dedicated his administration to helping a people in crisis. "The only thing we have to fear," he intoned, "is fear itself." Americans responded with an outpouring of support, as half a million approving letters deluged the White House.

In some ways, Roosevelt seemed an unlikely figure to rally Americans in their moment of crisis. Like his distant cousin Theodore, FDR was of the social elite. His Dutch-immigrant ancestors had been merchants and landowners in New York for nearly three centuries, and he himself was the product of Harvard College and Columbia Law School. But during a term in the state senate (1911–1913) and as governor of New York, he had built close ties with the urban-immigrant wing of the state Democratic party. When the depression struck, he had introduced innovative measures in New York, including unemployment insurance and a public-works program.

Possessing a generalized desire to revive the economy while preserving capitalism and democracy, Roosevelt had no detailed agenda for achieving these goals. Little interested in theory, he encouraged competing proposals, compromised (or papered over) differences, and then backed the measures he sensed could be sold to Congress and the public.

Roosevelt brought to Washington a circle of advisers nicknamed the brain trust. This group included Columbia University professor Rexford G. Tugwell and lawyer Adolph A. Berle. Heirs of the progressive reform tradition, Tugwell and Berle rejected laissez-faire ideology and advocated federal economic planning and corporate regulation.

Roosevelt heeded his advisers, but they did not (as some critics charged) control him. In fact, the New Deal reflected many ideological and political

**Eleanor Roosevelt Visits a West Virginia Coal Mine, 1933**

*A* New Yorker *cartoon of 1933 portrayed one coal miner exclaiming to another: "Oh migosh, here comes Mrs. Roosevelt." But reality soon caught up with humor, as the First Lady immersed herself in the plight of the poor and the exploited.*

crosscurrents. FDR by temperament sought a broad range of opinions.

Eleanor Roosevelt played a key White House role. A niece of Theodore Roosevelt, she had a keen social conscience expressed in settlement house work and Florence Kelley's National Consumers' League. She helped shape FDR's ideas by exposing him to reformers, social workers, and advocates of minority rights. Recalled Rexford Tugwell: "No one who ever saw Eleanor Roosevelt sit down facing her husband, and holding his eyes firmly, say to him 'Franklin, I think you should . . . ,' or 'Franklin, surely you will not . . .' will ever forget the experience."

She traveled ceaselessly and served as an astute observer for her wheelchair-bound husband.* (With sly wit a Washington newspaper once headlined "MRS.

---

\* Ironically, this couple who had such emotional rapport with the American people had long been emotionally distant from each other. Each found intimacy outside marriage: Franklin through a long-term relationship with his wife's social secretary, Lucy Mercer, and Eleanor with Lorena Hickok, a former journalist and aide to the New Deal relief administrator Harry Hopkins.

ROOSEVELT SPENDS NIGHT AT WHITE HOUSE.") In 1935 she began a syndicated newspaper column, "My Day."

Roosevelt's top political adviser, Postmaster General James A. Farley, had managed FDR's two gubernatorial campaigns. He distributed patronage jobs, managed FDR's 1932 and 1936 campaigns, and smoothed White House relations with state and local Democratic leaders. Bored by policy issues, Jim Farley had a master's sense of politics.

Roosevelt's cabinet reflected the New Deal's diversity. Secretary of Labor Frances Perkins, the first woman cabinet member, had served as industrial commissioner of New York during FDR's years as governor. Interior Secretary Harold L. Ickes, prickly but able, had helped organize liberal Republicans for Roosevelt in 1932. Secretary of Agriculture Henry A. Wallace of Iowa held the same post his father had occupied in the 1920s. Treasury Secretary Henry Morgenthau, Jr., FDR's neighbor and political ally from New York days, though a fiscal conservative, tolerated the unbalanced budgets necessary to finance New Deal antidepression programs.

Below the cabinet rank, a host of newcomers poured into Washington in 1933—former progressive reformers, political scientists, economics professors, bright young lawyers. These newcomers energized the capital. They drafted bills, vied for the president's ear,

### Major Measures Enacted During the "Hundred Days" (March 9–June 16, 1933)

| March 9 | Emergency Banking Relief Act |
|---|---|
| 20 | Economy Act |
| 31 | Unemployment Relief Act (Civilian Conservation Corps) |
| May 12 | Agricultural Adjustment Act |
| 12 | Federal Emergency Relief Act |
| 18 | Tennessee Valley Authority |
| 27 | Federal Securities Act |
| June 13 | Home Owners' Refinancing Act |
| 16 | Farm Credit Act |
| 16 | Banking Act of 1933 (Federal Deposit Insurance Corporation) |
| 16 | National Industrial Recovery Act (National Recovery Administration; Public Works Administration) |

and debated conflicting strategies of reform and recovery. From this pressure-cooker environment emerged the laws, programs, and agencies that historians encompass within a single catchall label: the New Deal.

## The Hundred Days

Between March 9 and June 16, 1933, Congress enacted more than a dozen important measures, making the turbulent "Hundred Days" a period of remarkable legislative productivity. Rooted in the experience of the Progressive Era and World War I, and even in the Hoover presidency, these measures sharply increased federal involvement in the nation's economic life.

First addressing the banking crisis, FDR on March 5 ordered all banks to close for four days. At the end of this so-called bank holiday, he proposed an Emergency Banking Act, which sailed through Congress. This law permitted healthy banks to reopen with a Treasury Department license, set up procedures for managing failed banks, and enlarged the government's regulatory power over banking. In the first of a series of radio talks dubbed "fireside chats," the president assured Americans that they could again entrust their money to banks. A second banking act, passed in June, created the Federal Deposit Insurance Corporation (FDIC) to insure all bank deposits up to five thousand dollars and to separate deposit banking from investment banking.

In keeping with his budget-balancing campaign pledges, FDR on March 10 proposed, and Congress soon passed, an economy measure cutting federal workers' salaries, slashing veterans' pensions and benefits, and otherwise trimming spending.

Other early New Deal measures proved more innovative. On March 31, Congress created the Civilian Conservation Corps (CCC) to employ jobless youths in such projects as reforestation, park maintenance, and erosion control. By 1935 half a million young men were earning $35 a month in CCC camps. Even this small sum helped families with no income at all.

Two new federal agencies addressed the mortgage-foreclosure crisis. The Home Owners Loan Corporation (HOLC) helped people refinance their home mortgages. The Farm Credit Administration did the same for rural Americans facing the loss of their farms.

The principal relief measure of the early New Deal, the Federal Emergency Relief Act (May 1933), revealed the continued preferences for local relief. This measure appropriated $500 million to replenish the relief coffers of states and cities. To administer this program, FDR appointed Harry Hopkins, a former social worker who would emerge as a powerful New Deal figure. A gaunt chain smoker who enjoyed parties and the racetrack, Hopkins enlivened the Washington scene.

Another early New Deal measure incorporating ideas from the past was the Tennessee Valley Authority (TVA). During World War I, the government had built a hydroelectric plant on the Tennessee River in Alabama to power a nearby nitrate plant. In the 1920s Senator George W. Norris of Nebraska had unsuccessfully urged the reactivation of this facility to supply electric power to nearby farmers.

TVA expanded Norris's idea through a commitment to the economic and social development of the entire poverty-stricken Tennessee River valley. TVA built a hydroelectric network that supplied cheap power to the region while also developing a flood-control system, recreational facilities, and a soil-conservation program. Under director David E. Lilienthal, TVA proved one of the New Deal's most popular achievements.

Later, TVA would become controversial. In the 1950s President Dwight Eisenhower attacked it as "creeping socialism." Still later, environmentalists, advocates of energy conservation, and opponents of nuclear power (which TVA championed) offered various criticisms. In the 1930s, however, TVA and the planning vision it embodied won general praise.

The two most important measures of the Hundred Days, the Agricultural Adjustment Act and the National Recovery Act, sought to promote economic recovery. Both evolved from debates among advocates of differing ideas that had been around for some time.

To help farmers, some favored the approach of the McNary-Haugen bill of the 1920s by which the government would buy agricultural surpluses and sell them abroad. Others, however, advocated reduced production. They noted that farmers had responded to declining prices by *increasing* output, a process that pushed prices still lower.

The advocates of production cuts won out. As a first step to this goal, the government in the summer of 1933 paid southern cotton planters to plow under much of their crop and midwestern farmers to slaughter some 6 million piglets and pregnant sows—moves that proved to be public-relations nightmares.

Pursuing the same goal more systematically, the Agricultural Adjustment Act set up a program by which producers of the major agricultural commodities—including hogs, wheat, corn, cotton, and dairy products—received payments, called subsidies, in re-

**The Tennessee Valley Authority: Electrifying Rural America**
*Power-generating dynamos at the TVA's Pickwick Landing Dam in Tennessee, which began operations in 1938.*

turn for cutting production. A tax on grain mills and other food processors financed these subsidies. (Consumers, of course, ultimately paid this tax in the form of higher food prices.) A new federal agency, the Agricultural Adjustment Administration (AAA), supervised the program. The goal was *parity*: a restoration of farmers' purchasing power to what it had been in 1909–1914—a time of prosperity in rural America.

The National Industrial Recovery Act (NIRA) drew upon the trade associations that Herbert Hoover had promoted as secretary of commerce and that Washington had encouraged during the war. Now the enemy was the depression, but a comparable spirit of common purpose again united the nation—at least briefly.

Under this law, representatives of the major industries, granted immunity from antitrust prosecution, drafted codes of "fair competition" for their industries. These codes set production limits, prescribed wages and working conditions, and forbade price cutting and unfair competitive practices. The National Recovery Administration (NRA) oversaw the codes.

The NRA aimed to promote recovery by breaking the cycle of wage cuts, falling prices, and layoffs. But reformers like Frances Perkins and Senator Robert F. Wagner of New York saw further potential. Under pressure from Perkins, the NRA's textile-industry code banned child labor—long a goal of reformers. And through Wagner's efforts, Section 7a of the law prohibited employers from discriminating against union members and affirmed workers' right to organize and bargain collectively.*

The NRA's flamboyant head, Hugh Johnson, who had served with the War Industries Board in 1917–1918, organized parades in major cities to persuade consumers to buy only from companies that subscribed to an NRA code. The NRA symbol, the blue eagle, and its slogan, "We Do Our Part," adorned roadside billboards and magazine ads.

The National Industrial Recovery Act also appropriated some $3.3 billion for a public-works program to employ the jobless and stimulate the economy. The agency created to oversee this program, the Public Works Administration (PWA), was directed by Secretary of the Interior Harold Ickes.

The NRA echoed Hoover's theme of business-government cooperation, and indeed implementation of the NRA codes depended on voluntary business support. In his speeches of 1933–1935, FDR always included the corporations as key players in the "all-American team" fighting the depression.

Moreover, the probusiness Reconstruction Finance Corporation, dating from the Hoover era, remained active. Under its chairman Jesse H. Jones, a Houston banker, the RFC lent billions of dollars at favorable rates to banks, insurance companies, and even a large department-store chain. Jones also extended government loans for new business ventures, making the RFC a potent financial instrument serving corporate America.

A few early New Deal measures, however, anticipated a more adversarial approach to business. In fact, the 1929 crash had produced a strong antibusiness reaction that found expression in a Senate investigation of Wall Street conducted in 1932–1934. This probe revealed that not one of the twenty partners of the Morgan Bank had paid any income tax in 1931 or 1932. People jeered when the president of the New York Stock

Exchange told a Senate committee considering regulatory legislation: "You gentlemen are making a big mistake. The Exchange is a perfect institution."

Reflecting this public mood, Congress passed the Federal Securities Act. This law required corporations to inform the Federal Trade Commission fully on all stock offerings and made executives personally liable for any misrepresentation of securities issued by their companies. The following year Congress curbed the purchase of stock on credit (a practice that had contributed to the 1929 debacle) and created the Securities and Exchange Commission (SEC), to oversee the stock market.

Congress adjourned on June 16, 1933, and the Hundred Days ended. For many Americans this burst of legislative activity, with its array of "alphabet-soup" agencies whose initials few could keep straight, came to symbolize both the dynamism and the confusion of the Roosevelt years. How these new programs and agencies would work in practice remained to be seen.

### The NRA Bogs Down

A brief economic recovery in the summer of 1933 proved illusory. As the depression continued, problems and controversy plagued the New Deal.

The National Recovery Administration faced particular problems, related in part to the personality of the hard-driving, hard-drinking Hugh Johnson. But the NRA's difficulties went deeper. As the unity spirit faded, corporate America chafed under NRA regulation. Code violations increased. Small businesses complained that the codes favored large businesses. The agency itself, meanwhile, became bogged down in drafting trivial codes. The shoulder-pad industry had its own code; burlesque-house owners adopted an NRA code specifying how much flesh strippers could display. The trade associations that supervised the codes used them mainly to restrict competition and maintain prices, not to stimulate economic expansion.

Beset by problems, the NRA sank of its own weight. Johnson departed in 1934, and in May 1935 the Supreme Court unanimously declared the NRA unconstitutional. The Court cited two reasons: first, the act granted the president regulatory powers that constitutionally belonged to the legislative branch; second, the NRA was regulating commerce within states, violating the constitutional provision limiting federal regulation to *inter*state commerce. Few mourned the NRA. As a recovery measure, it had failed.

---

* Under the NIRA, the bargaining agent could be an employer-sponsored "company union." The 1935 Wagner Act, by contrast, forbade bargaining by employer-sponsored unions.

## Troubled Agriculture

The New Deal's early agricultural program did better, but it too proved controversial. Thanks to drought as well as the AAA, farm production declined and commodity prices rose, as planners had hoped. In 1933–1937, farm income increased by 50 percent.

But the AAA did little to help landless farm laborers or migrant workers; indeed, its crop-reduction subsidies actually hurt southern tenants and sharecroppers, as cotton growers banked the subsidy checks, removed the acreage from production, and evicted the sharecroppers. One Georgia sharecropper wrote Harry Hopkins: "I have Bin farming all my life But the man I live with Has Turned me loose . . . I can't get a Job so Some one said Rite you."

Some victims of this process resisted. In 1934 the interracial Southern Tenant Farmers' Union, led by the Socialist party, emerged in Arkansas. Declared one black sharecropper at the organizing meeting: "The same chain that holds my people holds your people too. . . . [We should] get together and stay together." The landowners struck back with a terror campaign, chasing down union organizers as their ancestors had once hunted runaway slaves.

Nature itself seemed to conspire against strapped farmers, as parching drought in the mid-1930s turned the Great Plains into a dust bowl (see A Place in Time). Hit by depression and drought alike, many poor farmers of the South and Great Plains left the land. Some migrated to the cities, expanding already huge relief rolls. Others packed their few belongings into old cars and headed west, facing new hardships as migrant agricultural workers in California and Arizona.

In 1933–1935 debate raged between New Dealers intent on raising agricultural income as a whole and others who urged special attention to the poorest farmers. At first FDR backed the former group. In the later New Deal, however, as we shall see the advocates of a more class-based farm policy would score significant legislative victories.

**Agriculture During the Great Depression**
*The depression hit rural America with brutal ferocity, as the statistics on commodity prices and farm mortgages show.*

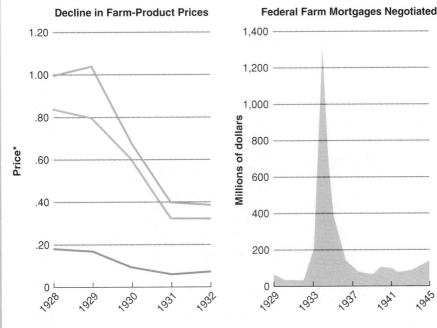

Decline in Farm-Product Prices

Federal Farm Mortgages Negotiated

——— Cotton
········· Corn
——— Wheat

* The graph shows the price per pound for cotton and the price per bushel for corn and wheat.
*Source: Historical Statistics of the United States, Colonial Times to 1970* (Washington, D.C., Government Printing Office, 1975), 511, 517.

## Cimarron County, Oklahoma

Although the depression were not enough, searing drought and howling dust storms compounded the misery of the 1930s across the Great Plains. Journalists dubbed the region the dust bowl, and the name stuck.

The rains failed in 1930, devastating wheat and livestock on the southern Plains. The dust came in 1934. A storm that began in early May whipped tons of dust across the nation. Massive amounts filtered down on Chicago alone. Before finally blowing out to sea, the storm darkened East Coast cities from Boston to Savannah.

Through 1939 each spring and summer brought a new scourge of dust. The worst year was 1937, with seventy-two major storms. The locus shifted from year to year, but hardest hit were western Kansas and Oklahoma, northwestern Texas, and eastern Colorado and New Mexico. Some storms—"black blizzards"—arose suddenly. One in Kansas roared in so quickly that the date, April 14, 1935, became known as Black Sunday. "Sand blows" started more insidiously but proved equally nerve-racking. By 1938 some 10 million acres had lost five inches or more of topsoil; another 13.5 million acres had suffered less severe but still serious erosion.

Survivors never forgot the experience. The skies blackened; trains derailed; blinded automobile drivers proceeded on foot, only to become hopelessly lost. A child died when he wandered away and suffocated in a dust drift. The dust sifted into houses and coated everything with a thick film. Night brought little relief: "A trip for water to rinse the grit from our lips," wrote a Kansas woman, "and then back to bed with washcloths over our noses. We try to lie still, because every turn stirs the dust on the blankets."

Some reacted with resignation; others, with gallows humor. Proclaimed one sign: "Great Bargains in Real Estate. Bring Your Own Container." Religious fundamentalists saw the dust storms as a portent of the Second Coming. Dorothea Lange and other New Deal photographers compiled a memorable visual record of the storms' aftermath; amateur photographers caught scenes of the dust clouds rolling in. Painter Alexandre Hogue created haunting images of dead cattle and abandoned tractors in mounds of dust. Woody Guthrie, the balladeer of the dust bowl, grew up in Okemah, Oklahoma, and Pampa, Texas, before migrating to California in 1937. Guthrie's song "The Great Dust Storm" began:

> It fell across our city like a
> curtain
> of black rolled down,
> We thought it was our judgment,
> we thought
> it was our doom.

In the heart of the Dust Bowl lay Cimarron County, Oklahoma, at the tip of the state's panhandle. After the displacement of the local Plains Indians to

**Fleeing a Dust Storm, Cimarron County, 1934**
*This famous photograph by Arthur Rothstein captured the desolation of the dust-choked Oklahoma land.*

reservations, the region had been settled by Mexican shepherds, Anglo cattle ranchers, and, in the 1890s, wheat growers. In the 1920s the Santa Fe Railroad chugged in, and some people prospered. Farm-implement dealers in the principal town, Boise City, did a thriving business. The 1931 wheat harvest approached 6 million bushels. But then spreading drought and swirling dust spelled catastrophe. As early as 1933, a Texas newspaper reported: "Not a blade of wheat in Cimarron County, Oklahoma; cattle dying. . . . Humans suffering from dust fever—milk cows going dry, turned into pasture to starve, hogs in such pitiable shape that buyers will not have them." Newspapers reported forced sales of farms.

With their livelihood destroyed, families packed their scant possessions into old jalopies, abandoned foreclosed farms and bank debts, and rumbled off in the night. The county's population fell by 40 percent in the 1930s, from over 4,000 to about 2,500.

The farmers who fled Cimarron County were part of a vast tide of migrants. From 1935 to 1937, a government study found, 34 percent of the farm families in forty dust bowl counties pulled up stakes, leaving ten thousand empty houses and 9 million abandoned acres. During the decade as a whole, nearly 3.5 million people left the Great Plains; Oklahoma's population sank more than 18 percent. Most moved only a short distance, into a city or a nearby state, but many pushed on to California or the Pacific Northwest. Though coming from various states, they all bore a derisive nickname: Okies.

The federal government tried to help. Congress voted $525 million in emergency drought relief in 1934. The Roosevelt administration sent fact-finding teams, launched public-works pro-

jects, and provided emergency farm loans. Dust Bowl wheat farmers gladly accepted federal payments under the Agricultural Adjustment Act for not cultivating their bone-dry land. The Taylor Grazing Act of 1934 addressed another environmental problem on the Plains: overgrazing by cattle herds. This law created the Grazing Service (later the Bureau of Land Management) to protect the remaining public lands in the West.

Although journalists sometimes portrayed the drought as unnatural and wholly unforeseen, agricultural specialists had long recognized that periodic drought and low rainfall make grain farming precarious beyond the 100th meridian, which bisects central Kansas. Drought had laid waste the region in the 1890s, and climatologists traced extended dry spells as far back as the thirteenth century. Nor were dust storms simply an inevitable corollary of drought. Environmental historian Donald Worster, in *Dust Bowl: The Southern Plains in the 1930s* (1979), documents the practices that caused the erosion that in turn produced the dust storms. Through the early twentieth century, settlers had used ever more

powerful tractors and combines (which harvest and thresh wheat in one operation across a sixteen-foot swath) to cultivate more and more acres. Going into debt to buy farm equipment, wheat-planting "sod-busters" had plowed up the grama-buffalo grass and other native short grasses, leaving 33 million acres exposed to parching winds.

Even without the drought, the transition to large-scale mechanized farming would have driven many small farmers off the land, prey to debt and tumbling wheat prices. Indeed, from 1910 to 1930, *before* the drought, notes James Gregory in *American Exodus* (1989), the number of agricultural workers on the southern Plains fell by some 340,000. And even in the 1930s, most who left the region did not come from the areas hardest hit by drought and dust. In short, the depression-era crisis on the southern Plains was a complex phenomenon with complex causes. But because of journalists, photographers, novelists, and folk singers, it was the "dust bowl" image that captured the popular imagination and shaped perceptions of the depression years on the Great Plains.

### Oklahoma Farm Family, 1939

*Battered by drought, dust, debt, and depression, rural Oklahomans endured especially hard times in the 1930s. Many gave up and moved on, sometimes in the dark of night to evade bank creditors.*

719b

## *Controversy over Relief Strategy*

As high unemployment continued, relief administrator Harry Hopkins convinced Roosevelt that only direct federal relief could prevent mass suffering and perhaps violent upheaval. Late in 1933 FDR named Hopkins to lead a temporary public works agency, the Civil Works Administration (CWA). Through the winter, the CWA expended nearly a billion dollars on short-term work projects for the jobless. When the CWA check arrived, one Iowa woman recalled, "The first thing I did was to . . . buy a dozen oranges. . . . I had forgotten what they were like."

When spring came, FDR abolished the CWA. No one would starve in warm weather, he believed. Although his conservative critics did not realize it, FDR shared their horror of creating a permanent underclass living on welfare payments. But persistent mass unemployment, coupled with the inability of local agencies to cope, made further federal relief programs inevitable.

Behind the scenes, Hopkins and Harold Ickes were struggling to control federal relief policy. The supercautious Ickes went over every PWA proposal with a fine-tooth comb. The PWA built many enduring projects, but the deliberate approach of "Honest Harold" and his staff left billions in relief funds stalled in the pipeline.

In contrast, Hopkins sought above all to put people to work and get money circulating. Even make-work projects like raking leaves and collecting litter had merit, in his view, if they achieved these goals. Given the urgency of the unemployment crisis, Hopkins's approach proved more influential in shaping federal relief policy.

## *The New Deal at High Noon: Popularity and Problems*

Despite the New Deal's brave beginnings, the depression continued as 1934 ended. Problems afflicted the NRA, conflict flared over farm policy, and the need for relief spending was expanding rather than tapering off.

But the New Deal remained popular, reflecting both its achievements and FDR's political skills. Assisted by speechwriters and publicists, Roosevelt commanded the political stage, marshalling support for his programs with buoyancy and self-assurance. Shrewdly pursuing his national unity theme, Roosevelt continued to exhort everyone to join in the battle for economic recovery. Just as Americans had united in 1917 against a foreign foe, he proclaimed, they must now come together to defeat the depression. Although Republican newspaper publishers remained hostile, FDR enjoyed excellent relations with the working press. He loved bantering with reporters, and they reciprocated by presenting a flattering picture of his administration.

In contrast to Hoover, Roosevelt loved public appearances and took naturally to radio. He treated radio listeners not as an anonymous mass but as three or four family members in a living room. To many, he seemed almost a family member himself. Frances Perkins later described his manner during his "fireside chats." "His head would nod and his hands would move in simple, natural, comfortable gestures. His face would smile and light up as though he were actually sitting on the front porch or in the parlor with them." Roosevelt's mastery of radio provided a model for his successors in the era of television.

**FDR's Christmas Message, 1943**
*Beginning in the depths of the Depression in 1933 and continuing through World War II, President Franklin Roosevelt's confident and folksy "fireside chats" reassured an anxious nation.*

The 1934 midterm election ratified the New Deal's popularity. Reversing the usual pattern, the Democrats *increased* their majorities in both the House and the Senate. As for FDR, Kansas journalist William Allen White observed, "He's been all but crowned by the people."

Some observers viewed the New Deal as essentially complete and anticipated a period of consolidation. But a different mood prevailed in the White House and in Congress. As the election returns rolled in, Harry Hopkins turned to a group of New Deal friends and declared, "Boys, this is our hour!" A new surge of activism, rivaling that of the Hundred Days, lay ahead.

# The New Deal Changes Course

As the mood of national unity faded, conservatives criticized the New Deal for going too far and radicals for not going far enough. Shelving the unity theme, Roosevelt veered leftward. With an eye on 1936, FDR in 1935 pushed through a bundle of reform measures so impressive that some call this phase the Second New Deal.

### *Challenges from Right and Left*

Although the early New Deal was hardly radical, some conservative business leaders soon concluded that it threatened capitalism's survival. In 1934 several top corporate figures, joined by Al Smith and other disgruntled Democrats, formed the American Liberty League, dedicated to the proposition that the Roosevelt program pointed the way to socialism. Early in 1935 the U.S. Chamber of Commerce blasted the New Deal. Anti-Roosevelt jokes circulated among the rich, many of whom denounced "that man in the White House" as a traitor to his class.

Opposition came, too, from demagogues who offered the poor a variety of social and economic panaceas. Detroit Catholic priest and radio spellbinder Charles E. Coughlin won an audience of millions. At first Coughlin backed the New Deal, but by 1935 he was condemning FDR as a "great betrayer and liar," making anti-Semitic allusions, and peddling his own panaceas, including nationalization of the banks. As a priest and a native of Canada, Coughlin himself could not run for office, but his radio followers, organized as the National Union of Social Justice and drawn mainly from the lower-middle class, were a potent force.

Meanwhile, California physician Francis E. Townsend proposed that the government pay two hundred dollars monthly to all retired citizens over sixty, requiring only that they spend the money within thirty days. Such a plan would not only help the elderly and stimulate the economy, Townsend insisted, but also open up jobs by encouraging early retirement. The scheme would have quickly bankrupted the nation, but many older citizens, especially in southern California rallied to Townsend's banner.

FDR's wiliest rival was the flamboyant Huey Long of Louisiana. A country lawyer who won the Louisiana governorship in 1928, Long dominated the state while building highways, schools, and public housing. He roared into Washington as a senator in 1932, preaching his "Share Our Wealth" program: a 100 percent tax on all annual incomes over $1 million and appropriation of all fortunes in excess of $5 million. With this money Long would give every family a comfortable income, a house, a car, old-age benefits, and free college education. Although he played the buffoon, Long was highly intelligent. One senator compared him to a horsefly: "He would light on one part of you, sting you, and then, when you slapped at him, fly away to land elsewhere and sting again."

"Every man a king," proclaimed Long, and millions responded. By 1935 he boasted 7.5 million supporters.

**Huey Long with Two Louisiana Political Cronies**
*Until Long's assassination in September 1935, many feared that his demagogic program of massive wealth redistribution might seriously threaten Franklin Roosevelt's 1936 reelection bid.*

His baiting of the rich appealed to many Americans resentful of the nation's wide disparities of wealth. As Long's 1935 book *My First Days in the White House* made clear, the presidency was his goal. An assassin's bullet cut Long down that September, but the even more demagogic Gerald L. K. Smith took over his Share Our Wealth organization.

Adding to Roosevelt's worries, economic recovery proved elusive. National income in 1934 rose about 25 percent above 1933 but still hovered far below the 1929 level. Millions had been jobless for three or four years. The rising frustration found expression in 1934 in nearly two thousand strikes, some of them communist-led, from New York taxi drivers to San Francisco dockworkers.

Rather than withdrawing, as Hoover had done, Roosevelt outflanked his opponents and regained the political high ground in 1935 with a series of legislative initiatives.

### The Second New Deal: Expanding Federal Relief

In his January 1935 State of the Union address, Roosevelt called for broad social reform. He soon fleshed out the rhetoric with a program involving six central elements: an enlarged public-works program, assistance to the rural poor, support for organized labor, social-welfare benefits for older Americans and other disad-vantaged groups, stricter business regulation, and heavier taxes on the well-to-do.

With unemployment still very high, Congress in April 1935 passed the Emergency Relief Appropriation Act with an initial grant of $5 billion. Roosevelt swiftly set up the Works Progress Administration (WPA), headed by Harry Hopkins. Like the temporary Civil Works Administration of 1933–1934, the WPA funneled assistance directly from the federal government to individuals.

Roosevelt insisted that the WPA provide *work,* not handouts, for the jobless. Over its eight-year life, the WPA employed more than 8 million Americans; pumped $11 billion into the economy; constructed or improved 650,000 miles of roads; built or repaired 124,000 bridges; and erected 125,000 schools, hospitals, post offices, and other public buildings.

The WPA also assisted writers, performers, and artists. In the South, WPA workers collected the reminiscences of ex-slaves. The Federal Writers' Project (FWP) employed out-of-work authors to produce state guides as well as the histories of ethnic and immigrant groups. Black novelist Richard Wright's first book, *Uncle Tom's Children* (1938), was written with FWP support.

The Federal Theatre Project (FTP) gave work to unemployed actors. One FTP project, the Living Newspaper, which dramatized contemporary social issues, was criticized as New Deal propaganda. But FTP drama companies touring small-town America gave many

**Construction of a Dam,** by William Gropper (1897–1977)
*The New Deal's Federal Arts Project commissioned murals for post offices and other public buildings. Gropper, whose work often exposed social injustice and class inequalities, painted this upbeat mural for the Department of the Interior building in Washington, D.C.*

their first taste of theater. Artists working for the Federal Arts Project designed posters, offered school courses, and decorated post offices and courthouses with murals.

Under the popular Federal Music Project (FMP), jobless musicians gave performances, often featuring American composers, in schools, hospitals, and parks, and at public ceremonies, especially in smaller communities. By 1938 more than 30 million Americans had attended an FMP concert.

Other New Deal agencies distributed relief funds as well. The National Youth Administration provided part-time work for more than 2 million high school and college youths. And Harold Ickes's Public Works Administration, after its slow start, now picked up steam. Expending more than $4 billion over its life span, PWA employed thousands of workers on some 34,000 construction projects, including dams, bridges, and public buildings. Among the PWA's undertakings were the Triborough Bridge and the Lincoln Tunnel in New York City and the awesome Grand Coulee Dam on the Columbia River.

With monumental relief spending came monumental federal budget deficits, cresting at $3.6 billion in 1934 and $4.4 billion in 1936. These deficits were covered by government borrowing. According to the British economist John Maynard Keynes, deficit spending in a depression was good policy. When faced with an economic downturn and chronic unemployment, said Keynes, governments should use deficit spending to fund public-works programs, thereby increasing purchasing power and stimulating recovery. The New Deal philosophy, however, was not Keynesian. Because all the dollars spent on public-works programs were withdrawn from the economy through taxation or government borrowing, the stimulus effect was nil. For FDR, deficit spending was a deplorable necessity, not a positive instrument of government policy.

### The Second New Deal: Turning Leftward

Roosevelt's 1935 legislative proposals reflected a sharp leftward shift. In 1933 Roosevelt had stressed national unity and attempted unprecedented centralized economic planning and control. By 1935 the political struggles inevitable in a democracy made up of diverse social classes and diverse interest groups were reviving. Reflecting the new political reality, Roosevelt abandoned the effort to devise programs with universal appeal. Stung by conservative criticism and gathering dis-

content, he now offered a program frankly geared to workers, the poor, and the disadvantaged.

Social-justice advocates like Secretary of Labor Frances Perkins, as well as Eleanor Roosevelt, helped shape this program. But so, too, did hard-headed politics. Looking ahead to 1936, Roosevelt's political advisers feared that the followers of Coughlin, Townsend, and Long could siphon off enough votes to deny Roosevelt a second term. This worry helped shape FDR's 1935 political agenda.

The New Deal's leftward turn was evident as its agricultural policy increasingly highlighted the plight of sharecroppers, migrants, and other poor farmers—a plight the New Deal's own policies had helped create, as we have seen. The Resettlement Administration (1935), directed by Rexford Tugwell, made loans to help small farmers buy their own farms and to enable sharecroppers and tenants tilling exhausted soil to re-

**Major Later New Deal Legislation**
(November 1933–1938)

| | |
|---|---|
| **1933 (Nov.)** | Civil Works Administration |
| **1934** | Civil Works Emergency Relief Act |
| | Home Owners' Loan Act |
| | Securities Exchange Act (Securities and Exchange Commission) |
| | Communications Act (Federal Communications Commission) |
| | Federal Farm Bankruptcy Act |
| | National Housing Act (Federal Housing Administration) |
| **1935** | Emergency Relief Appropriations Act (Works Progress Administration) |
| | National Labor Relations Act (Wagner Act) |
| | Revenue Act of 1935 |
| | Social Security Act |
| | Public Utilities Holding Company Act |
| | Banking Act of 1935 |
| | Resettlement Administration |
| | Rural Electrification Act |
| **1937** | National Housing Act of 1937 |
| | Bankhead-Jones Farm Tenancy Act |
| **1938** | Fair Labor Standards Act |
| | Agricultural Adjustment Act of 1938 |

## The Welfare State Begins

*One of the New Deal's most enduring legacies, the federal Social Security program, launched in 1935, would ease the lives of millions of older Americans. By the 1990s, with life expectancy rising and the baby-boom generation approaching retirement, Social Security faced serious funding problems.*

tutional, including Section 7a partially protecting union members' rights, FDR called for a labor law that would survive constitutional scrutiny.

The National Labor Relations Act of July 1935 guaranteed collective-bargaining rights, permitted closed shops,* and outlawed such management practices as blacklisting labor "agitators." The law created the National Labor Relations Board (NLRB) to supervise shop elections and deal with labor-law violations. The Wagner Act, as it was called, stimulated a wave of unionization (see Chapter 26).

The Social Security Act of 1935 especially stands out for its long-range significance. Drafted by a committee chaired by Frances Perkins, this measure had a complex parentage, including the ideas of Progressive Era reformers and the social-welfare programs of England and Germany. It established a mixed federal-state system of old-age pensions for workers; survivors' benefits for the victims of industrial accidents; unemployment insurance; and aid for dependent mothers and children and persons with disabilities.

Taxes paid in part by employers and in part by wages withheld from workers' paychecks funded the pension and survivors' benefit features of the program. This payroll-withholding provision withdrew money from circulation and contributed to a recession in 1937. But it made sense politically, because workers would fight any effort to repeal a pension plan to which they had contributed. As Roosevelt put it, "With those taxes in there, no damned politician can ever scrap my social security program."

The Social Security Act set benefit payments at a low level and contained no provision for farmers, domestic workers, or the self-employed. However, it established the principle of federal responsibility for social welfare and created the framework for a vastly expanded welfare system in the future.

The Second New Deal's radical thrust found expression, also, in two business regulatory measures of 1935. The Banking Act strengthened the Federal Reserve

settle in more productive areas. Although Tugwell's agency did not fulfill expectations and lasted only two years, it did keep the difficulties of poor farmers in the public eye.

The Rural Electrification Administration, also started in 1935, made low-interest loans to utility companies and farmers' cooperatives to extend electricity to the 90 percent of rural America that still lacked it. By 1941, 40 percent of U.S. farms enjoyed electric power.

The agricultural-recovery program suffered a setback in January 1936 when the Supreme Court declared the Agricultural Adjustment Act unconstitutional. The processing tax that funded the AAA's subsidies was an illegal use of the government's tax power, the Court ruled. To replace the AAA, Congress passed the Soil Conservation and Domestic Allotment Act, which paid farmers to plant grasses and legumes instead of soil-depleting crops such as wheat and cotton (which also happened to be the major surplus commodities).

Organized labor won a key victory in 1935 again thanks to New York senator Robert Wagner. During the New Deal's early, national-unity phase, FDR had opposed Wagner's campaign for a prolabor law, criticizing it as "special interest" legislation. Wagner patiently built congressional support for his bill, however. In May 1935, when the Supreme Court ruled the NIRA unconsti-

---

* In a closed shop, all employees must join the union as a condition of employment, so that the union bargaining agent can negotiate with management as the representative of the entire work force.

Board's control over the nation's financial system, and money supply. The Public Utilities Holding Company Act, targeting the sprawling public-utility empires that had proliferated in the 1920s, restricted gas and electric companies to one geographic region.

And finally, the Revenue Act of 1935 raised taxes on corporations, on the well-to-do, and on gifts and estates. Though this tax law had many loopholes and was not quite the "soak the rich" measure some believed, it did express the Second New Deal's somewhat more class-conscious spirit.

By September 1935, when Congress adjourned, the Second New Deal was complete. Laws had been enacted in the interests of the jobless, the elderly, the rural poor, and the blue-collar workers; regulating business more strictly; and somewhat increasing the taxes paid by the wealthy. Such measures as social security, the Wagner Act, and the Fair Labor Standards Act had defined the basic contours of the modern activist welfare state.

Without embracing the radical panaceas espoused by Coughlin, Townsend, or Long, FDR had directed his program to the inequities on which they had thrived. Despite the "antibusiness" label critics pinned on him, FDR insisted that the New Deal had *saved* capitalism by checking its excesses and addressing its undesirable social consequences.

In the 1920s, as through much of post–Civil War American history, the business class had dominated government, leaving other groups on the margins. Certainly the influence of business continued after 1933, as the Reconstruction Finance Corporation's generous corporate loans make clear. However, as the New Deal evolved, it increasingly acted as a broker for *all* organized interest groups—not just business but also agriculture, labor, and other sectors. And in the charged political climate of 1935, with an election looming, New Deal strategists reached beyond organized groups to address the fears and grievances of a far broader spectrum of the American people, from sharecroppers to mothers with dependent children.

In the process, the New Deal vastly increased the power and prestige of the presidency. Roosevelt so dominated the politics of the 1930s, and peppered Congress with so many messages and bills, that Americans began to expect their president to offer "programs," address large national issues, and shape the terms of public debate. This decisively altered the balance of power between the White House and Congress. In this sense, the New Deal's importance lies not only in the laws passed, but in the way it redefined the role of the executive and, more broadly still, the role of the modern nation-state.

## The Election of 1936: The New Deal at High Tide

With the Second New Deal in place and unemployment declining, FDR faced the 1936 campaign with confidence. "There's one issue . . . ," he told an aide; "it's myself, and people must be either for me or against me."

The Republicans' candidate, Governor Alfred Landon of Kansas, belonged to his party's long dormant progressive wing. A fiscal conservative who nevertheless believed that government must address social issues, Landon proved an earnest if inept campaigner. ("Wherever I have gone in this country, I have found Americans," he revealed in one speech.) Desperate Republican campaigners lambasted Roosevelt's alleged dictatorial ambitions and charged that the social security law would require all workers to wear metal dog tags.

FDR struck back with his usual zest. Only the forces of "selfishness and greed" opposed him, he declared at an election-eve rally in New York City, adding: "They are united in their hatred for me—and I welcome their hatred."

## The Election of 1936

| Candidates | Parties | Electoral Vote | Popular Vote | Percentage of Popular Vote |
|---|---|---|---|---|
| FRANKLIN D. ROOSEVELT | Democratic | 523 | 27,752,869 | 60.8 |
| Alfred M. Landon | Republican | 8 | 16,674,665 | 36.5 |
| William Lemke | Union | | 882,479 | 1.9 |

In the most crushing electoral victory since 1820, FDR carried every state but Maine and Vermont. Landon lost even his home state of Kansas. Pennsylvania went Democratic for the first time since 1856. The Democrats increased their already top-heavy majorities in Congress. Decades of Republican dominance in national politics lay in ruin.

The Roosevelt landslide buried his minor-party opponents as well. Socialist Norman Thomas received under 200,000 votes. The Communist party's presidential candidate garnered only about 80,000 votes. And Congressman William Lemke of North Dakota—the candidate of the coalition of Coughlinites, Townsendites, and Huey Long supporters that had appeared so formidable early in 1935—polled fewer than 900,000 votes.

In *Building a Democratic Political Order* (1996), political scientist David Plotke sees the years 1935–1936 as crucial to the emergence of a long-lasting new order in American politics. Having defined his "progressive liberalism" with such measures as the Wagner Act and the Social Security Act, Plotke argues, FDR in the 1936 election shrewdly marginalized his challengers on the Right and Left and rallied a potent coalition of interest groups behind the Democratic party.

### The New Democratic Coalition

As a minority party much of the time from 1860 to 1930, the Democrats had counted on three bases of support: the white South, parts of the West, and big-city Democratic organizations. FDR retained these centers of strength. The West, the South, and the cities all went for Roosevelt in 1936.

FDR rarely challenged state or local Democratic leaders who produced the votes, whether they supported the New Deal or not. In Virginia he even *withdrew* support from a pro–New Deal governor who clashed with the state's conservative but powerful Democratic senators, Harry Byrd and Carter Glass. When the Democratic boss of Jersey City, Frank Hague, faced mail tampering charges, FDR told Jim Farley: "Tell Frank to knock it off . . . , but keep this thing quiet because we need Hague's support if we want New Jersey."

FDR extended the party's traditional base in forging a new Democratic majority. Five partially overlapping voter groups made up this potent coalition: farmers, urban immigrants, unionized industrial workers, northern blacks, and women.

Midwestern farmers, long rock-ribbed Republicans, liked the New Deal's agricultural program and switched to Roosevelt. In Iowa, where Democrats had been lucky to garner 20 percent of the vote in the 1920s, FDR won decisively in 1936.

Building on Al Smith's urban breakthrough in 1928, FDR carried the nation's twelve largest cities in 1936. Not only did New Deal relief programs aid the urban masses, but Roosevelt wooed them persuasively at election time. When the presidential campaign entourage swept through cities like New York and Boston, cheering crowds lined the route. Solidifying his urban support, FDR appointed many representatives of the newer urban-immigrant groups, including Catholics and Jews, to New Deal positions.

Organized labor, led by figures like Sidney Hillman of the Clothing Workers and John L. Lewis of the Mine Workers, also joined the New Deal coalition. The unions pumped money into Roosevelt's campaigns (although far less than business gave to the Republicans), and union members voted overwhelmingly for Roosevelt. Despite his early foot dragging on the Wagner bill, FDR's reputation as a "friend of labor" proved unassailable.

FDR even won some business support in 1936, particularly from corporations that benefited from his programs, such as the electrical companies that provided equipment for the TVA and PWA hydroelectric projects, and exporters who profited from the later New Deal's free-trade policies.

Although most southern blacks remained disfranchised, the northern urban black population played a growing role in electoral politics. As late as 1932, two-thirds of northern black voters went for Hoover, leading one annoyed black editor to advise his readers: "[T]urn Lincoln's picture to the wall. That debt has been paid in full."

The New Deal era saw a historic shift. In 1934 Chicago's black voters elected a Democrat in place of their Republican congressman, Oscar DePriest. In 1936 northern blacks voted in record numbers, 76 percent of them for FDR. In Harlem, Roosevelt won a crushing 81 percent of the vote.

Solid reasons underlay this shift. Last hired and first fired, blacks experienced unemployment rates in the 1930s even higher than those for the work force as a whole. Thus jobless blacks benefited heavily from New Deal relief programs.

Many blacks perceived the New Deal as a force for racial justice, but the record is mixed at best. The racially discriminatory clauses written into some NRA codes led black activists to dismiss the agency as "Negroes Ruined Again." Some New Deal agencies tolerated racial bias. The TVA, for example, barred blacks from its "model town" in Tennessee.

Although lynchings increased in the 1930s, as some whites translated their economic woes into racial aggression, Roosevelt kept aloof from the NAACP's campaign to make lynching a federal crime. An antilynching bill passed the House of Representatives in 1935, but southern racist senators—all Democrats—killed it with a filibuster. To protect his legislative program, and avoid alienating southern white voters, FDR stood aside from the struggle. Concluded the NAACP bitterly, "[Blacks] ought to realize by now that . . . the Roosevelt administration [has] nothing for them."

In other ways, however, FDR and the New Deal did work modestly to advance the black cause. Assuring an audience at Howard University, a black institution in Washington, D.C., that there would be "no . . . forgotten races" in his administration, Roosevelt supported efforts to rid New Deal agencies of racism and he appointed more than a hundred blacks to policy-level and judicial positions. The highest-ranking New Dealer, Mary McLeod Bethune, served as director of minority affairs in the National Youth Administration. The daughter of ex-slaves, Bethune was a Florida educator and head of the National Council of Negro Women. A close friend of Eleanor Roosevelt's, Bethune led the so-called black cabinet that acted as a link between the administration and black organizations. In addition, the "Roosevelt Supreme Court" that took shape after 1936 issued important antidiscrimination rulings in cases involving voting rights, wage inequity, jury selection, and real estate bias.

Thanks in large part to Eleanor Roosevelt, the New Deal also supported racial justice in symbolic ways. In 1938, when a meeting in Birmingham, Alabama, of the interracial Southern Conference for Human Welfare was segregated in compliance with local statutes, Mrs. Roosevelt pointedly placed her chair halfway between the white and black delegates. In 1939, when the Daughters of the American Revolution barred a performance by black contralto Marian Anderson in Washington's Constitution Hall, Mrs. Roosevelt resigned from the organization and New Deal officials arranged a concert by Anderson at the Lincoln Memorial. Seventy-five thousand turned out.

White racists, including powerful Democrats, seethed at the New Deal's overtures to blacks. When a

black minister rose to deliver the invocation at the 1936 Democratic convention, Senator Ed Smith of South Carolina noisily stalked out. "This mongrel meeting ain't no place for a white man," he fumed.

In short, black support for FDR reflected more than purely economic calculations. Although not high on the New Deal's agenda, racial justice and civil rights did win support in Roosevelt's White House.

The Roosevelt administration courted women voters. The head of the Democratic party's women's division, Molly Dewson, a close friend of the Roosevelts, led this effort. In the 1936 campaign, Dewson mobilized fifteen thousand women who went door to door distributing millions of colorful flyers describing New Deal programs. "[W]e did not make the old-fashioned plea that our nominee was charming," she later recalled; " . . . we appealed to [women's] intelligence."

Believing that women had a special interest in issues relating to the home, Dewson stressed how social security, the National Youth Administration, and other New Deal programs strengthened the family. Unlike earlier feminists, Dewson did not push a specifically feminist agenda or women's rights legislation. New Deal efforts for economic recovery and social welfare, she argued, offered the best promise of advancement for both sexes.

Dewson did, however, use her influence to push the appointment of women to federal policy-level positions. FDR appointed not only the first woman cabinet member but also the first woman ambassador and unprecedented numbers of female federal judges. Through Dewson's efforts, the 1936 Democratic platform committee reflected a fifty-fifty gender balance.

**1934: Protesting Lynching**
*This young Howard University student demonstrates with a rope around her neck to protest the lack of federal action against the lynching of African Americans. The year 1933 saw twenty-eight lynchings in the United States.*

But symbolic gestures and the appointment of a few blacks and women had limited impact at best. Racism and sexism pervaded American society when FDR took office, and his administration, preoccupied with the economic crisis, did relatively little to change things. That would await a later reform generation.

## The New Deal, the Environment, and the West

Environmental issues loomed large in the 1930s, reflecting Roosevelt's own deep commitment to conservation. As early as 1910, serving in the New York Senate, he had sought to regulate tree cutting that threatened wildlife. As president, Roosevelt approached conservation passionately. Under his prodding, the Civilian Conservation Corps planted trees, thinned forests, and built hiking trails.

Soil conservation emerged as a New Deal priority. The Great Plains dust storms of 1933–1935 resulted not only from drought but from overgrazing and unwise farming practices. By the 1930s, 9 million acres of farmland had been lost to erosion, not only on the Great Plains, but in the South and elsewhere, with another 80 million acres in jeopardy.

The Soil Conservation Service of the Department of Agriculture set up demonstration projects across the nation. Farmers learned the value of contour plowing, terracing, crop rotation, and soil-strengthening grasses. The Taylor Grazing Act of 1934—enacted as dust clouds from the West darkened the skies over Washington, D.C.—restricted the grazing on public lands that had contributed to the problem. The TVA helped control the devastating floods that worsened soil erosion in the Tennessee Valley region.

New Deal planners also worked to further the national-park movement. Olympic National Park in Washington, Shenandoah National Park in Virginia, and Kings Canyon National Park in California all date from the 1930s.

Wildlife preservation also gained ground, under the Biological Survey of the Department of Agriculture. By 1940 the government had established some 160 new wildlife refuges. Roosevelt even closed a Utah artillery range that threatened a nesting site of the endangered trumpeter swan.

The wilderness movement, earlier championed by John Muir and Aldo Leopold, won powerful new adherents, including Robert Marshall of the U.S. Forest Service. In 1935 Marshall, Leopold, and others formed the Wilderness Society to lobby for the cause. Under pressure from wilderness advocates, Congress set aside a large portion of Kings Canyon National Park as wilderness area.

The wilderness and wildlife movements brought together an unusual coalition: New Deal planners, hunters, people who cherished the wilderness on aesthetic grounds, and firearms companies financially interested in preserving wildlife for hunters. The National Wildlife Federation (1936), for example, a leading voice for wildlife preservation, was largely funded by the gun industry.

From a contemporary perspective, the New Deal's environmental record presents gaps and blind spots. Matters of grave concern today, such as atmospheric pollution, dwindling fossil fuels, pesticide hazards, and the pressures of population on limited global resources, received little attention. Most New Dealers viewed ever-rising levels of mass consumption as desirable. The vast hydroelectric projects of the 1930s, while they made sense at a time when much of rural America still lacked electric power, fed an ideology of boundless energy consumption that today seems heedless and wasteful. Nor did the ecological effects of these projects attract much attention. The Grand Coulee Dam, for example, destroyed salmon spawning on much of the Columbia River's tributary system.

Still, when viewed in context rather than from a later perspective, the New Deal's environmental record remains impressive. The Roosevelt administration focused attention on conservation to a degree that had not been true for twenty years and would not again be true for a generation.

The New Deal, especially its conservation and environmental policies, profoundly affected the American West, from the Great Plains to the Pacific. Hard hit by the depression, the West was especially susceptible to the expansion of federal power in the 1930s because so much of its land was federally owned. Eighty-seven percent of Nevada was public land, and in ten other Western states, the federal government owned 35 percent or more of the land.

All the major New Deal agencies and programs had an impact in the West. The ribbons of highways that linked the rest of America to the West, such as the Lincoln Highway from Philadelphia to San Francisco, Yellowstone Trail from Chicago to Seattle, and Route 66 from St. Louis to Los Angeles, were improved and up-

**The Arts and Conservation Under the New Deal**
*This striking poster illustrates the work of two New Deal agencies. Designed by Albert Bender, an artist employed by the WPA's Federal Arts Project, it promoted the Civilian Conservation Corps (CCC), which put city youth to work in the great outdoors. Above, a CCC volunteer plants Ponderosa pines in 1938 in a Montana national forest.*

graded in the 1930s. The Agricultural Adjustment Administration, the Farm Security Administration, the Soil Conservation Service, and the Resettlement Administration, and such measures as the Taylor Grazing Act of 1934, set new conditions for western agriculture, from the grain and cattle country of the Great Plains to the citrus groves and truck farms of the West Coast with their dependence on migrant labor.

Some of the largest projects of Harold Ickes's Public Works Administration arose in the West. The PWA constructed thousands of public buildings in the West (246 in Washington State alone), from courthouses and post offices to tourist facilities such as beautiful Timberline Lodge on Oregon's Mount Hood. Above all, the PWA in the West built dams—not only Grand Coulee, but also Shasta on the Sacramento River, Bonneville on the Columbia, Glen Canyon on the Colorado. Boulder Dam, later Hoover Dam, on the Colorado, although authorized by Congress in 1928, was completed by the PWA. These great dams of the West—among the largest engineering projects in human history—provided hydroelectric power for vast regions while also contributing to flood control, irrigation, and soil conservation.

Abundant electric power—plus legalized gambling—propelled Las Vegas, Nevada, from a hamlet of 5,000 people in 1930 to a city of 750,000 in the 1990s. San Francisco's majestic Golden Gate Bridge (1933-1937), one of the largest in the world, stands as a monument to the public energies mobilized in the West by the New Deal.

Another New Deal initiative with special importance for the West was the National Planning Board of 1934, later renamed the National Resources Planning Board. As the name suggests, this agency facilitated state and regional planning for inventorying and conserving natural resources, including water, soil, timber, and minerals. Despite the West's celebrated "rugged individualism," the New Deal's emphasis on planning reshaped the public life of the region. Thanks to the New Deal, writes Carl Abbott of Portland State University, the West by 1940 "had new resources in place for an economic takeoff—new electric power, new expertise in large-scale construction, workers with new skills for an industrial economy, and a renewed commitment to the progressive agenda of efficient resource development."

# The New Deal Draws to a Close

No sooner had Roosevelt won his landslide victory in 1936 than he launched an ill-conceived attack on the Supreme Court that weakened him politically. In the wake of this divisive fight, an embattled FDR confronted a newly energized conservative opposition that helped bring the New Deal to an end. But its legacy remained; in the span of a few years, the nation's political agenda had been rewritten.

## *FDR and the Supreme Court*

Fresh from electoral triumph, Roosevelt went after the one branch of government that seemed immune to his New Deal vision: the Supreme Court. The Court in 1937 comprised nine elderly men; one had served as a justice since 1910, another since 1914. Four justices were archconservatives who abhorred the New Deal. Joined by others of more moderate views, these conservatives had invalidated the NRA, the AAA, and progressive state laws.

Roosevelt feared that key measures of the Second New Deal, including social security and the Wagner Act, would meet a similar fate. Indeed, some lawyers were so sure that the Social Security Act would be found unconstitutional that they advised their business clients to ignore it.

In February 1937 FDR proposed a sweeping court-reform bill that would have allowed the president to appoint an additional Supreme Court member for each justice over the age of seventy, up to a total of six. Roosevelt blandly insisted that this proposal reflected his concern for the heavy workload of aging justices, but his political motivation was obvious.

FDR evidently believed that his personal popularity would translate into support for his Court plan, but it did not. Congress and the public greeted it with skepticism that soon turned sharply hostile. The size of the Supreme Court (unspecified in the Constitution) had been modified several times in the early years of the Republic, but the membership of nine, dating to 1869, had taken on an almost sacrosanct quality. Conservatives blasted the "court-packing" scheme. Some feared a Rooseveltian power grab in the wake of the president's electoral triumph; others resented the disingenuous way that FDR had presented the plan. Even some New Dealers disapproved. When the Senate voted down the scheme in July, FDR quietly gave up the fight. For one of the rare times in his presidency, it seemed Roosevelt had suffered an embarrassing defeat.

**Life in a Small Southern Town**

*In a fleeting moment captured on film by Dorothea Lange, this 1936 shot of a Clarksdale, Mississippi, plantation owner speaks volumes about racial and class realities in the rural South.*

But was it a defeat? One conservative justice retired in May 1937; others announced retirement plans. In April and May, the Court upheld several key New Deal measures, including the Wagner Act, as well as a state minimum-wage law. This outcome may have been Roosevelt's objective all along. Not only FDR's direct challenge to the Supreme Court, but his landslide 1936 victory, sent powerful political signals that the justices heeded. From 1937 to 1939, to replace justices who retired or died, FDR appointed four new members to the Supreme Court—Hugo Black, Stanley F. Reed, Felix Frankfurter, and William O. Douglas—laying the groundwork for a liberal majority that would long outlive Roosevelt and his New Deal.

## The Roosevelt Recession

As the Supreme Court fight ended, FDR faced a more serious crisis: after improving in 1936 and early 1937, the economy again plunged ominously in August 1937. Industrial production slumped. Steel output sank from 80 percent to 19 percent of capacity. Bleak unemployment statistics again dominated the headlines: after dropping to around 7 million in early 1937, the jobless toll soared to 11 million in early 1938—more than 20 percent of the work force.

What caused this short but severe "Roosevelt recession"? Federal policies that reduced consumer income played a role. The new social-security program's payroll taxes withdrew some $2 billion from circulation. Furthermore, FDR, concerned about mounting deficits, had seized upon the signs of recovery to terminate the PWA and to cut back the WPA and other New Deal relief programs. Although these steps did reduce the federal deficit, they also contributed to the economic downturn of 1937–1938. So, too, did a drastic contraction of the money supply instigated by the Federal Reserve Board to forestall inflation.

Echoing Hoover, FDR assured his cabinet, "Everything will work out all right if we just sit tight and keep quiet." Meanwhile, however, some New Dealers had been persuaded by the Keynesian call for deficit spending as the key to recovery. Aware that FDR would have to be persuaded by political rather than economic arguments, they recruited Harry Hopkins to warn the president of a political backlash if breadlines and soup kitchens returned. Convinced, FDR in April 1938 authorized heavy new relief spending, and WPA work-relief checks soon rained down on the parched economy.

The PWA received a new lease on life. By late 1938, conditions were improving. Unemployment declined, and industrial output increased.

## The End of the New Deal

Preoccupied by the Supreme Court fight, the 1937–1938 recession, and a menacing world situation (see Chapter 26), FDR offered few reform initiatives in his second term. Congress, however, enacted several significant measures. The Farm Tenancy Act of 1937, for example, created a new agency, the Farm Security Administration (FSA), replacing Rexford Tugwell's Resettlement Administration. FSA made low-interest loans enabling tenant farmers and sharecroppers to buy family-size farms. Although the FSA did little to help the poorest tenants and sharecroppers (who were considered bad credit risks), it lent more than $1 billion through 1941, assisting thousands of tenant families to become farm owners.

The FSA also established a network of well-run camps offering clean, sanitary shelter and medical services to migrant farm workers, many of whom lived in wretched, unhealthful conditions. In its most innovative program, the FSA commissioned talented photographers to preserve on film the lives of tenants, migrants, and uprooted dust bowl families. In carrying out this assignment, FSA photographers created a haunting album of stark depression-era images.

Other measures set precedents for the future. The Housing Act of 1937, sponsored by Senator Wagner, appropriated $500 million for urban slum clearance and public-housing projects. The Fair Labor Standards Act of 1938 banned child labor and set a national minimum wage of forty cents an hour and a maximum workweek of forty hours. Passed after much political logrolling, this measure reflected not only humanitarianism but also some northern legislators' desire to undermine the competitive edge of the South, with its low wage scales. Although riddled with exceptions, this law set important regulatory precedents and improved conditions for some of the nation's hardest-working and lowest-paid workers.

The Agricultural Adjustment Act of 1938, adopted as surpluses and low prices continued to beset farmers, set up procedures for limiting production of basic commodities such as cotton, wheat, corn, and tobacco. It also created a mechanism by which the government, in years of big harvests and low prices, would make loans to farmers and store their surplus crops in government warehouses.* When prices, rose, farmers could repay their loans and market their commodities at a profit. This measure helped stabilize farm prices and set the basic framework of federal agricultural policy for decades to come.

The later 1930s also brought a surge in union membership (see Chapter 26). This labor activism, stimulated in part by Section 7a of the NIRA and by the Wagner Act, showed the New Deal's continuing role in transforming the social contours of American life.

Despite such achievements, the New Deal's pace after 1935 clearly slowed. This reflected in part the rise of an anti–New Deal congressional coalition of Republicans and conservative southern Democrats. Sensing FDR's vulnerability after the Supreme Court fight, this opposition became more outspoken. Virginia Democrat Carter Glass, for example, in attacking the New Dealers, proclaimed, "Thomas Jefferson would not speak to these people."

In 1937, at a moment when nerves were already rubbed raw by the Court fight, Congress rejected FDR's proposal to reorganize the executive branch by regrouping existing agencies, bureaus, and commissions into twelve superdepartments. The plan made administrative sense, but critics claimed that it would create a virtual White House dictatorship.

The conservative coalition also slashed relief appropriations, launched an investigation of the NLRB, cut corporate taxes in 1938, and in July 1939 killed the WPA's Federal Theatre Project. Suspecting FDR of using WPA staff for campaign purposes, the conservatives in 1939 passed the Hatch Act, forbidding federal workers from participating in electoral campaigns.

The Fair Labor Standards Act of 1938 became law only after intense White House lobbying and watering down by conservatives. As recovery proceeded, noted Harry Hopkins, Congress and the public seemed to become "bored with the poor, the unemployed, the insecure."

Although FDR campaigned actively in the midterm election of 1938, the Republicans gained heavily in the House and Senate and won a net of thirteen governorships. Roosevelt also tried to purge several prominent

anti–New Deal Democratic senators, but his major targets, including senators Walter George of Georgia, Ed Smith of South Carolina, and Millard Tydings of Maryland, all won renomination and went on to victory.

Focusing on foreign affairs in his January 1939 State of the Union message, FDR proposed no new domestic measures and spoke merely of the need to "preserve our reforms." The New Deal was over.

## CONCLUSION

The New Deal in its six-year life compiled a stunning record. To be sure, not all New Deal programs succeeded. Nor did the New Deal achieve full recovery. As late as 1939, some 9.5 million Americans, or more than 17 percent of the labor force, were out of work. Only in 1943, as war plants boomed, did the nation finally achieve full employment.

Nevertheless, the New Deal still stands as a watershed in American history. The basic ideological framework of the Democratic political order that took shape in the 1930s would prevail at least into the 1970s. The nation had seen many eras of reform, but the New Deal stood for reforms of a new kind. The progressives, for example, convinced of the righteousness of their cause, had set out to eradicate evil from American life, whether exploitative corporate power or gambling, drink, and prostitution. The New Dealers, by contrast, sought not to purify the nation but to use their expertise to solve the practical problems of business stagnation, unemployment, and the maldistribution of economic resources. Even their *style* differed from that of earlier reform eras. As historian William E. Leuchtenberg has written, "If the archetypical progressive was Jane Addams singing 'Onward Christian Soldiers,' the representative New Dealer was Harry Hopkins betting on the horses at Laurel Race Track."

Any evaluation of the New Deal must confront Franklin D. Roosevelt. Neither saint nor superman, he could be devious, as in the Supreme Court fight, and his administrative skills left much to be desired. But Roosevelt's strengths outweighed his liabilities. Unlike some of his opponents on the Left and Right, he adopted an open, experimental approach in grappling with the nation's problems. He once compared himself to a football quarterback, deciding which play to call next after seeing how the last one worked out. In the desperate conditions of the early depression years, the nation urgently needed such tolerance for innovation.

---

* These payments came directly from the federal treasury rather than from a processors' tax, a feature that had caused the Agricultural Adjustment Act of 1933 to be declared unconstitutional (see above).

Above all, Roosevelt's optimism reenergized a demoralized people. "We Americans of today . . . ," observed the president to an audience of young people in 1939, "are characters in the living book of democracy. But we are also its author. It falls upon us now to say whether the chapters that are to come will tell a story of retreat or a story of continued advance."

## — FOR FURTHER READING —

Anthony J. Badger, *The New Deal: The Depression Years, 1933–1940* (1989). Good recent overview of the period and its politics.

Blanche D. Coll, *Safety Net: Welfare and Social Security, 1929–1979* (1995). Balanced, well-written history, focusing on the politics of the Social Security Act and its aftermath.

Paul Conkin, *The New Deal,* 2d ed. (1975). A concise, balanced assessment.

Steve Fraser and Gary Gerstle, eds., *The Rise and Fall of the New Deal Order, 1930–1980* (1989). Incisive critical essays on the New Deal's long-term legacy.

William E. Leuchtenberg, *Franklin D. Roosevelt and the New Deal* (1983). A comprehensive, readable overview, rich in illuminating detail.

David Plotke, *Building a Democratic Political Order: Reshaping American Liberalism in the 1930s and 1940s* (1996). Insightful work examining the emergence of a new political order in the 1930s and tracing it through World War II and the early postwar era.

Albert U. Romasco, *The Politics of Recovery: Roosevelt's New Deal* (1983). A study particularly useful for the New Deal's policies toward business.

Harvard Sitkoff, *A New Deal for Blacks* (1978). An exploration of the Roosevelt administration's policies toward black Americans.

Susan Ware, *Beyond Suffrage: Women and the New Deal* (1981). A study of the network of women who held high office in the New Deal.

# 26 American Life in a Decade of Crisis at Home and Abroad

**Hoeing Tobacco,** by Robert Gwathmey
*The 1930s was a decade of cultural as well as political creativity.*

It was January 11, 1937, and in Flint, Michigan, the temperature was sixteen degrees. For ten days some one hundred strikers had occupied Fisher Body plant No. 2, which made bodies for General Motors cars. Nearby, other strikers were occupying the larger Fisher Body plant No. 1. To force a showdown, GM executives cut off the heat to plant No. 2 and locked the main gate, preventing supporters from carrying food to the strikers inside. Some 150 picketers and a crowd of onlookers milled about uneasily.

Around 8:00 P.M., after strikers broke the lock on the main gate, thirty Flint policemen in riot gear rolled up in squad cars; fifty more soon joined them. When the police fired tear-gas canisters into the plant, the occupiers doused them with fire hoses.

Masterminding the strategy was Victor Reuther, a brother of Walter Reuther, president of the local United Auto Workers (UAW) union. Victor issued directions to the strikers through a loudspeaker powered by his car battery. One participant later recalled his voice as "an inexhaustible, furious flood pouring courage into the men."

As the police advanced, the workers beat them back with a shower of empty bottles, nuts and bolts, and car-door hinges. When the picketers overturned a sheriff's car—with the sheriff inside—the police fired into their ranks, injuring fourteen.

At one point, Genora Johnson, the young wife of a striker, took the loudspeaker and urged women in the crowd to join the picketers. Many did so, running a gauntlet of police. As the ranks of the picketers grew, the police gunfire stopped. After a five-hour standoff, the police withdrew. Thanks in part to Victor Reuther's bullhorn and the quick thinking of Genora Johnson, the UAW's strike against GM went on to eventual victory.

To grasp the full meaning of the Great Depression, we must move from Wall Street, the halls of Congress, and New Deal agencies out into the world of auto plants, harvest fields, artists' studios, and ordinary people's homes. And we must look abroad as well, for in these years powerful nations came under the control of militaristic dictatorships that raised again the specter of war and added to the pervasive sense of crisis.

This chapter focuses on five major questions:

♦ What factors underlay the wave of unionization in the later 1930s, and what sectors of the American labor force were most affected?

♦ What was the impact of the depression and the New Deal on those Americans already on the economic margins, including many women, African-Americans, Hispanics, and Indians?

♦ What caused the upsurge of patriotism and cultural nationalism in the later 1930s, and what were some of its manifestations?

♦ What was the Good Neighbor policy, and how did it influence U.S. policies and actions in Latin America?

♦ How did the Roosevelt administration, and the American people as a whole, respond to the rise of fascism and militarism abroad in the 1930s?

## The American People in the Depression Decade

The depression that crashed over 1930s America left economic, social, and emotional havoc in its wake. A bird's-eye view of its human toll conveys some of the reality, but a full grasp of the depression's impact also demands attention to particular groups of Americans who experienced special hardships and, in some cases, unique opportunities.

For industrial workers, the New Deal created a more favorable climate for unionization. But workers still often had to fight for the right to organize. Some female and minority workers shared in the benefits of union membership, but for others, the depression worsened an already difficult situation. The 1930s witnessed a backlash against working women and feminist goals in general, and hard-pressed blacks and Hispanic-Americans faced even more desperate circumstances.

Native Americans, meanwhile, received well-meaning but in some ways misguided attention from New Dealers. And the depression touched the most basic social group of all, the family. While some families experienced conflict and disruption, others grew closer in the face of adversity.

## The Plight of a People

The depression brought enormous human suffering. Despite the New Deal, unemployment in the 1930s never fell below about 14 percent, and for much of the decade, it was considerably higher. As late as 1939, the total of jobless men and women stood at nearly 9 million. In rural America bankruptcies, foreclosures, and abandoned farms multiplied. A quarter of all farm families had to accept public or private assistance during the 1930s.

In some cities the jobless rate far exceeded the national average. In Toledo in 1932, for example, it stood at 80 percent. And many workers were forced to take jobs below their level of training: college alumni pumped gas; business-school graduates sold furniture. A retired navy captain became an usher in a movie theater.

Others eked out their income by peddling products to neighbors as poor as themselves. "I'll never forget watching my mother trying to sell Two-in-One Shoe Polish door to door," one child later remarked.

Poor diet and lack of funds for medical and dental visits laid the groundwork for long-term problems. "[D]entistry . . . was out of the question," novelist John Dos Passos recalled; "without dough you couldn't have a tooth filled." The savings of older Americans evaporated when hard times hit. By 1935 one million Americans over sixty-five were on relief.

Psychologists described "unemployment shock": jobless persons who walked the streets seeking work and then lay awake at night worrying. When shoe soles wore out, cardboard or folded newspapers had to

**Striking auto workers**
*In a new wave of labor militancy, some 1930s strikers occupied the plants where they worked.*

serve. Shoe tacks pierced worn rubber heels, cutting the skin. "You pass . . . shoe-shops where a tack might be bent down," one young man recalled, "but you can't pull off a shoe and ask to have *that* done—for nothing."

As for the young people of the 1930s, one observer compared them to a team of runners waiting for a starting gun that never sounded. High school enrollment increased sharply, as many youths, seeing no job prospects, simply stayed in school.

For the chronically disadvantaged, the depression represented simply one more hardship. But the jobless rolls also included millions who had achieved a measure of affluence before 1929. Some of these newly impoverished individuals went to great lengths to maintain appearances, even when they had barely enough to eat. Advertisements of the 1930s, promoting products ranging from mouthwashes and deodorants to encyclopedias and correspondence courses, exploited feelings of shame and played on people's fears of having their failings and pretenses exposed. Ads in women's magazines extolled low-cost meals and other budget-trimming strategies.

The depression deeply marked those who lived through it. Habits of scrimping and saving acquired in the 1930s often survived into more affluent times. As Caroline Bird has written in *The Invisible Scar,* a social history of the 1930s, the depression for many boiled down to "a dull misery in the bones."

## CHRONOLOGY

**1922** Benito Mussolini gains power in Italy.

**1930** *Little Caesar,* gangster movie starring Edward G. Robinson.

*Animal Crackers,* classic Marx Brothers comedy.

**1930–1936** John Dos Passos, *U.S.A.* trilogy.

**1931–1932** Japan invades Manchuria and creates puppet government.

**1932–1935** James T. Farrell, *Studs Lonigan* trilogy.

**1933** Nathanael West, *Miss Lonelyhearts.*

Jack Conroy, *The Disinherited.*

*She Done Him Wrong* and *I'm No Angel,* Mae West movie hits.

Roosevelt proclaims Latin American "Good Neighbor" policy.

Roosevelt's economic nationalism undermines London Economic Conference.

United States plays role in rise of Cuban strongman Fulgencio Batista.

Adolf Hitler becomes chancellor of Germany and assumes dictatorial powers.

**1934** Indian Reorganization Act.

Nathanael West, *A Cool Million.*

**1934–1936** Nye committee investigations.

Strikes by Mexican-American agricultural workers in the West.

**1935** Supreme Court reverses conviction of the "Scottsboro Boys."

Harlem ghetto riot.

Clifford Odets, *Waiting for Lefty.*

Walter Millis, *The Road to War: America, 1914–1917.*

Sinclair Lewis, *It Can't Happen Here.*

Nazi anti-Semitic laws in Germany.

**1935–1937** Neutrality Acts.

**1935–1938** Peace movement sweeps U.S. campuses.

**1935–1939** Era of the Popular Front.

**1936** William Faulkner, *Absalom, Absalom!*

*Mr. Deeds Goes to Town,* Frank Capra movie.

**1936–1937** Autoworkers' sit-down strike against General Motors (December 1936–February 1937).

**1936–1939** Spanish Civil War.

**1937** U.S. Steel, General Motors, and Chrysler sign union contracts.

Ten strikers shot dead in "Memorial Day Massacre" at Republic Steel Company in South Chicago.

Japan invades China.

Roosevelt delivers "Quarantine" speech.

**1938** Formation of Congress of Industrial Organizations (CIO).

Thornton Wilder, *Our Town.*

Carnegie Hall concert by Benny Goodman.

*War of the Worlds* broadcast on CBS radio.

Nazis occupy Austria.

Munich Pact gives Sudetenland to Hitler.

*Kristallnacht,* night of Nazi terror against German and Austrian Jews.

United States protests Japanese violation of Open Door principle in China.

**1939** John Steinbeck, *The Grapes of Wrath.*

New York World's Fair.

Nazis invade Czechoslovakia.

Nazi-Soviet Pact.

FDR submits $1.3 billion military budget.

*St. Louis,* carrying Jewish refugees from Naziism, refused landing permission in Florida.

**1940** Richard Wright, *Native Son.*

William Faulkner, *The Hamlet.*

Ernest Hemingway, *For Whom the Bell Tolls.*

*The Grapes of Wrath,* movie directed by John Ford.

**1941** James Agee and Walker Evans, *Let Us Now Praise Famous Men.*

## Industrial Workers Unionize

The economic crisis energized organized labor. Between 1900 and 1930, the number of unskilled or semi-skilled factory workers had soared from 3.7 million to 7.7 million. Yet most of these workers remained unorganized. For years managers of such major industries as steel, automobiles, and textiles had blocked attempts to unionize their workers. The prosperity and probusiness mood of the 1920s had further weakened the labor movement.

But in the 1930s hard times and a favorable government climate bred a new labor militancy. When the Wagner Act of 1935 guaranteed labor's right to engage in collective bargaining, tremors of activism shook the American Federation of Labor. In November 1935 John

L. Lewis of the United Mine Workers (UMW) and Sidney Hillman of the Amalgamated Clothing Workers, frustrated by the AFL's slowness in organizing factory workers, started the Committee for Industrial Organization (CIO) within the AFL. Young CIO activists preached unionization in Pittsburgh steel mills, Detroit auto plants, Akron rubber factories, and southern textile mills. Unlike the craft-based AFL unions, these CIO unions welcomed all workers in a particular industry, regardless of race, gender, or degree of skill.

In 1936 a CIO-sponsored organizing committee geared up for a major strike to win union recognition by the steel industry. The target was giant U.S. Steel, described by John L. Lewis as "the crouching lion in the pathway of labor." (In fact, Lewis had already secretly worked out a settlement with the head of U.S. Steel, who had decided to stop fighting unionization.) In March 1937 U.S. Steel recognized the steelworkers' union, granted a wage increase, and accepted a forty-hour workweek. Other big steel companies followed suit, and soon 400,000 steelworkers had signed union cards.

Meanwhile, organizers had mapped a campaign to unionize General Motors, an antiunion stronghold. Their leader was a redheaded young autoworker and labor activist, Walter Reuther. Born in 1907 in Wheeling West Virginia, Reuther was of German-immigrant stock. His socialist father idolized Eugene V. Debs. When the depression hit, Reuther and his brother Victor rediscovered their socialist roots, working for a time in the Soviet Union. In December 1936, employees at GM's two body plants in Flint stopped work and occupied the factories. Keeping their action peaceful, the strikers carefully protected the equipment and the cars on the assembly lines. This "sit-down strike" paralyzed GM's production.

Although women workers did not participate in the occupation of the plants (to avoid gossip that might discredit the strike), they picketed on the outside. In addition, strikers' wives, sisters, and daughters organized the Women's Auxiliary to support the strike. This auxiliary opened a kitchen to feed the striking workers, set up a speakers' bureau, and marched through downtown Flint.

The January 1937 showdown with the police at Fisher Body plant No. 2 led to the formation of the Women's Emergency Brigade, whose members remained on twenty-four-hour alert for picket duty. Complete with red berets and armbands, the Emergency Brigade members played a key role during the rest of the strike and discovered the exhilaration of working-class solidarity. As one woman wrote in the UAW newspaper, "I only wish I'd gotten mad long ago . . . , but I didn't have time for anything outside of my own small circle. I'm living for the first time with a definite goal."

Fighting unionization, GM called in the police to harass the sit-down strikers, sent spies to union meetings, and threatened to fire strikers. GM also asked the Roosevelt administration and the governor of Michigan to summon troops and expel the strikers by force. Although FDR disapproved of the sit-down tactic, he refused to call out troops.

On February 11, GM signed a contract recognizing the United Automobile Workers (UAW). Bearded workers who had vowed not to shave until victory was won streamed out of the plants. Chrysler soon fell into line, and by the end of 1937, the UAW boasted more than 400,000 members. Unionization of the electrical and rubber industries moved forward as well.

In 1938 the Committee for Industrial Organization broke with the AFL to become the Congress of Industrial Organizations, a 2-million-member association of industrial unions including the autoworkers, steelworkers, and electrical workers. In response to the CIO challenge, the AFL began to adapt to the changed nature of the labor force. Overall, union membership in the United States shot from under 3 million in 1933 to over 8 million in 1941.

Some big corporations fought on. Henry Ford, for example, hated unions, and his loyal lieutenant, a tough brawler named Harry Bennett, organized a squad of union-busting thugs to fight the UAW. In 1937 Bennett's men viciously beat Walter Reuther and other UAW officials outside Ford's River Rouge plant near Detroit. Not until 1941 did Ford yield to the union's pressure.

The Republic Steel Company, headed by a union hater named Tom Girdler, dug in as well. Even after U.S. Steel and other major steelmakers signed with the CIO, Republic and a group of smaller companies known collectively as "Little Steel" resisted. In May 1937 workers in twenty-seven Little Steel plants, including Republic's factory in South Chicago, walked off the job. Anticipating the strike, Girdler had assembled an arsenal of riot guns and tear gas. On May 30, Memorial Day, a mass of strikers approached a force of 264 police guarding the factory. When someone threw a large stick at the police, they responded with a hail of gunfire that left four strikers dead, six others dying, and scores wounded. An investigative committee headed by Senator Robert M. La Follette, Jr., found that the killings had been "clearly avoidable by the police." In 1941 Tom Girdler and the rest of Little Steel signed union agreements with the CIO.

Another holdout against unionization was the textile industry, with over 600,000 workers, mostly in the South and 40 percent female. The AFL's United Textile Workers had faltered badly in the 1920s owing to a series of failed strikes, a lack of AFL support, and a policy of admitting only skilled workers. In 1934 the CIO launched a textile workers' recruitment drive, but the mill owners viciously fought back. The 1930s ended with most textile workers still unorganized.

**The Growth of Labor Union Membership, 1933–1946**

Virtually untouched by the unionizing wave of the 1930s was a large pool of low-paid workers—domestics; agricultural laborers; department-store clerks; and restaurant and laundry workers, for example—who tended to be women, blacks, or recent immigrants. Despite the rapid growth of union membership in the 1930s, more than three-quarters of nonfarm workers remained unorganized as the decade ended. Nevertheless, the unionization of key sectors of America's industrial work force in the 1930s ranks as one of the decade's most memorable developments.

Why did powerful corporations finally cave in to unionization after resisting so long? Certainly workers' militance and the tactical skill of a new generation of labor leaders played a major role. But above all, labor's successes reflected a changed government climate. Where the government had once helped break strikes, Roosevelt and key state officials like the governor of Michigan refused to intervene on the side of management. (The South Chicago police, who acted as a kind of private army for Tom Girdler, were a rare exception to this pattern—at least in the North.) The Fair Labor Standards Act of 1938 and the oversight role of the National Labor Relations Board (see Chapter 25) made clear that Washington would no longer automatically back management in labor disputes. Once corporate managers realized this, most quickly accepted unionization.

Organized labor's apparent unity at the end of the 1930s concealed some complex tensions. A hard core of activists, many of whom believed in radical social change, had led the unionizing drive. But most rank-and-file industrial workers in the 1930s, while they welcomed unionization, had no desire to overthrow the capitalist system. Indeed, many initially held back from striking, fearful for their jobs. But once the CIO's militant minority showed that by organizing picket lines and sit-down strikes they could win union contracts and tangible gains for union members, workers by the thousands signed up. With the influx of rank-and-file workers, though, the influence of the radical leadership cadres diminished, and the unions became more conservative. Reuther himself reflected the shift and sought to rein in the more radical spirits in the CIO unions. "We must demonstrate that we are a disciplined, responsible organization," he intoned in 1939; "that we not only have power, but that we have *power under control*." After World War II, in a very different political climate, Reuther would take the lead in purging from the CIO some of the same leftists and communists who had led the organizational battles of the 1930s.

### Gender Aspects of the Depression

Senator Robert Wagner called the working woman in the depression "the first orphan in the storm." Indeed, for the 25 percent of American women employed in 1930, the depression brought difficult times. The female jobless rate stood at more than 20 percent through much of the decade. Women desperate to continue working often did so only by taking lower-paying jobs. A female factory worker who lost her job, for example, might take work as a waitress. Young women entering the job market for the first time often had to settle for temporary or part-time work.

Heavy competition from displaced male workers reduced the proportion of women even in such white-collar "women's professions" as librarianship, social work, and public school teaching. Women who did cling to their jobs confronted gender-based wage discrimination. In 1939, for example, the average woman teacher in the United States earned nearly 20 percent less than the average male with comparable experience.

Married women workers faced harsh criticism. Although most worked out of economic necessity, people still complained that they had no right to hold jobs with so many men out of work. Many cities refused to employ married women as teachers and even fired women teachers who got married.

Secretary of Labor Frances Perkins, though a woman, lined up with the labor leaders and others critical of married women who worked. A number of the NRA codes authorized lower pay for women workers. The minimum-wage clause of the Fair Labor Standards Act of 1938 helped some women workers, but did not cover many categories, including the more than 2 million women who worked for wages in private households.

The unionization drive of the later 1930s had a similarly mixed effect on women workers. Some benefited from the campaign to organize the mass-production industries. For example, more than six thousand female workers at a GM parts factory in Detroit helped plan and carry out the labor action that led to a union contract in 1937.

But the most heavily female sectors of the labor force—textile, clerical, service, and sales work—were precisely the ones most resistant to unionization. The campaign to unionize the textile industry failed, as did a drive to organize clerical workers. By the 1930s office work had been almost completely feminized, and most women office employees earned far less than male factory workers. A 1937 CIO campaign to unionize mostly female clerical workers riled not only male bosses but also many male union leaders, and it made little progress.

Despite the roadblocks, the proportion of women working for wages crept up in the 1930s. Furthermore, the percentage of wage-earning *married* women increased markedly, from 11.7 percent in 1930 to 15.6 percent a decade later. In short, neither depression nor criticism could reverse the long-term movement of women into the workplace; indeed, the crisis may have accelerated that movement, as married women took jobs to augment the family income. As one working wife explained: "One day in '32 [my husband] just went fishing . . . and he fished for the rest of the bad times. . . . So at twenty-eight, with two little girls, . . . I took a job as a salesclerk in the J. C. Penney, and worked through the Depression."

### Blacks, Hispanic Americans, and Native Americans Cope with Hard Times

The depression slowed the urbanization of African-Americans. Some 400,000 southern blacks moved to northern cities in the 1930s—far fewer than in the

1920s or the 1940s. In 1940 about 77 percent of the nation's 12 million blacks still lived in the South.

Rural or urban, blacks endured hardships. Tenant farmers and sharecroppers often faced eviction, in part because of the New Deal's farm policies. Among black industrial workers the jobless rate far outran the rate for whites, largely because of racism and discriminatory union policies. A 1936 Chicago study reported a general view "that Negroes should not be hired as long as there are white men without work." Although black workers benefited from the CIO's nondiscriminatory policy, workplace racism remained a fact of life.

Lynchings and miscarriages of justice continued as well, especially in the South. Twenty-four blacks died by lynching in 1933. In 1931 an all-white jury in Scottsboro, Alabama, sentenced eight black youths to death on highly suspect charges of rape. After heavy publicity and an aggressive defense, the Supreme Court in 1935 ordered a new trial for the "Scottsboro Boys" because of the exclusion of blacks from the jury and the denial of legal counsel to the defendants. Five of the group were again convicted, however, and served long prison terms.

Blacks did not accept racism and discrimination passively. The NAACP battled in courts and legislatures against lynching, segregation, and the denial of voting rights. An Urban League campaign against white-owned businesses in black neighborhoods that employed only whites spread from St. Louis to other cities. Under the banner "DON'T SHOP WHERE YOU CAN'T WORK," black protesters marched and boycotted businesses that refused to hire blacks. In March 1935 hostility against white-owned businesses in Harlem, fueled by more diffuse anger over racism and joblessness, ignited a riot that caused an estimated $200 million in damage and left three blacks dead.

The Communist party publicized racist conditions as part of a depression-era recruitment effort in the black community. The International Labor Defense Committee, a group linked to the Communist party, supplied lawyers for the "Scottsboro Boys'" defense. But despite a few notable recruits (including the young writer Richard Wright), blacks did not join the Communist party at any higher rate than other Americans.

To some extent, the depression diverted attention from racial issues. But the rising tempo of black activism gave warning that discrimination and inequality could not be ignored forever.

The more than 2 million Hispanic-Americans, too, faced trying times in the 1930s. Some were citizens long settled in the Southwest, but most were recent ar-

**Young Mexican Cotton Picker in the 1930s**
*Whether in agricultural labor or urban barrios, Mexican-Americans endured harsh conditions during the depression.*

**Fighting Racism in the Courts, 1935**
*NAACP lawyer Thurgood Marshall (left) meets with his client Donald Gaines (center), an Amherst College graduate denied admission to the University of Maryland Law School because of his race. Marshall would later become a justice of the U.S. Supreme Court.*

**A New Deal for American Indians, 1935**
*Delegates from Montana's Flathead tribe watch as Secretary of the Interior
Harold Ickes signs their tribal constitution, adopted under the Indian
Reorganization Act of 1934.*

rivals from Mexico, Puerto Rico, Cuba, and elsewhere, and most were manual laborers. Some worked in the steel or meatpacking industries; many, especially those from Mexico, were migratory agricultural laborers. As the depression deepened, the Mexican-born farm workers of the Southwest, welcomed for years as a source of cheap labor, faced rising hostility.

So, too, did Asian-American farmers and agricultural workers. California continued its efforts to prevent Japanese-Americans from owning land, and in 1934 Congress set the annual quota for immigrants from the new Commonwealth of the Philippines at fifty—lower than that for any other nation. Congress even offered free travel "home" for Filipinos who had emigrated to the United States.

The influx into California and Arizona of thousands of "Okies" fleeing the dust bowl worsened the job crisis for local farm workers. By 1937 more than half of Arizona's cotton workers were out-of-staters who had supplanted Mexican-American laborers.

With their traditional patterns of migratory work disrupted, Mexican-Americans poured into the Hispanic neighborhoods, called barrios, of many southwestern cities. Here, too, they met discrimination, sometimes in the form of such crude signs as "NO NIGGERS, MEXICANS, OR DOGS ALLOWED."

Lacking work, some half a million Mexicans returned to their native land in the 1930s. Many did so voluntarily; thousands of others were expelled by immigration officials and local authorities (see A Place in Time).

Mexican-American farm workers who remained endured appalling labor conditions and near-starvation wages. A wave of protests and strikes (some led by Communist party organizers) swept California in these years. In 1933 strawberry pickers in El Monte, pea pickers in Hayward, grape pickers in Lodi and Fresno, and cotton workers in the San Joaquin Valley struck for higher wages. A labor organization called the Confederación de Uniones de Campesinos y Obreros Mexicanos (Confederation of Unions of Mexican Workers and Farm Laborers) emerged from the El Monte strike. Under its impetus, more strikes erupted in 1935–1936, from the celery fields and citrus groves around Los Angeles to the lettuce fields of the Salinas Valley.

Organizations like the Associated Farmers of California and the California Fruit Growers Exchange (which marketed its citrus under the brand name Sunkist) fought the unions. Sometimes the owners' anti-union tactics turned violent. In October 1933 bullets ripped into a cotton pickers' union hall in Pixley, California, killing two men and wounding others.

The Mexican-American farm workers gained a few hard-fought successes. Striking cotton pickers, for example, increased the rate for a hundred pounds of cotton from 60¢ to 75¢. These strikes awakened at least some Americans to the plight of one of the nation's most exploited groups.

The 1930s also revived attention to the nation's 330,000 Native Americans, most of whom existed in a world of poverty, scant education, poor health care, and bleak prospects. The Dawes Act of 1887 (see Chapter 17) had dissolved the tribes as legal entities, allocated some tribal lands to individual Indians, and offered the rest for sale. By the 1930s, whites held about two-thirds of the land that Indians had possessed in 1887, including much of the most valuable acreage.

Aroused by reports documenting the failure of the Dawes Act, a growing number of reformers had become convinced that its approach should be reversed. Among them was John Collier, a reformer who had lived for a time among the Pueblo Indians of New Mexico. To preserve what he saw as the spiritual beauty and harmony of traditional Indian life, Collier in 1923 had founded the American Indian Defense Association.

Appointed commissioner of Indian affairs in 1933, Collier cadged funds from various New Deal agencies to construct schools, hospitals, and irrigation systems on reservations, and to preserve sites of cultural importance. By the end of 1933 twelve thousand Indian youths were working on CCC projects on Indian lands. Native American workers for whom these projects provided jobs would later recall the 1930s as a time of prosperity.

Pursuing his larger vision of a renewed tribal life, Collier in 1934 presented to Congress a bill halting the sale of tribal land, restoring the remaining unallocated lands to tribal control, creating new reservations, and expanding existing ones. The bill also provided for tribal councils with broad governing powers and required Indian schools to teach Native American history and traditional arts and handicrafts.

Collier's visionary bill sparked angry opposition in western states. Some Indian leaders criticized it as a plan to transform the reservations into living museums and to treat Native Americans as an exotic minority cut off from modern life. The Seneca of New York warned that no single law could cover the diverse situation of America's many different tribes. Indians who had succeeded as individual property owners or entrepreneurs rejected the bill's tribalist assumptions. The bill did, indeed, reflect the idealism of well-meaning outsiders rather than the views of the nation's diverse Native American population.

The compromise law that emerged, the Indian Reorganization Act of 1934, halted the sale of tribal lands and enabled tribes to regain title to unallocated lands. But Congress scaled back Collier's vision of tribal self-government and dropped his rhetorical calls for the renewal of traditional tribal culture.

The law required tribal approval, and of those that voted, 181 tribes, representing 130,000 Indians, approved, while 77, comprising 86,000 persons, disapproved. America's largest tribe, the 40,000-strong Navajo, voted no, largely because the law—seeking to prevent soil depletion—restricted grazing rights. The voting made clear that Indian policy would remain contentious. But the law did reflect greater acceptance of cultural diversity and an abandonment of the view that Indians must conform to the social and cultural norms of the white majority.

## Family Life and Population Trends

For parents, life in the 1930s often meant a struggle to make ends meet and hold the family together. They patched clothes, stretched food resources, and when necessary, turned to public assistance. A young wife described in a *Scribner's* magazine article the humiliation of welfare-office visits and the frustration of not being allowed to buy such "luxuries" as fresh fruit with her food coupons.

For the neediest families, among them blacks, Hispanics, and southern sharecroppers, the depression imposed added misery on poverty-blighted lives. In his novel *Native Son* (1940), Richard Wright vividly portrayed the desperate conditions of depression-era family life in Chicago's black slums.

But life at the bottom had forced blacks, as well as others among the very poor, to develop survival skills lacked by more affluent families. Emotional resilience and the patterns of mutual aid helped black families get through the depression despite appalling unemployment rates. In New York's Harlem, a charismatic black religious leader calling himself Father Divine institutionalized this cooperative spirit by organizing kitchens that distributed thousands of free meals daily.

The marriage rate tumbled in the early thirties, as young people confronted harsh economic realities. The birthrate also dropped sharply, as couples postponed a family or limited its size. Such planning became easier with the spread of birth-control devices such as condoms and diaphragms.

A declining birthrate plus immigration restrictions held population growth in the 1930s to a scant 7 percent, in contrast to an average of 20 percent per decade in 1900–1930. The crisis also temporarily stalled the growth of cities. In fact, many jobless young people returned to live with their parents on farms.

By contrast, another long-term demographic trend, the westward movement, continued unabated. Not only dust-bowl farmers but many thousands of hard-hit families sought brighter opportunities in the West, especially in California. The West Coast's share of the population rose dramatically in the 1930s, and Los Angeles jumped from tenth to fifth among U.S. cities.

The depression's psychological effects struck families as well as individuals. In households with a tradition of male authority, the husband's loss of a job and

**1930s**

## The Los Angeles Barrio

*I*n the early 1930s, the depths of the depression, a party went on in the heart of Los Angeles's Mexican barrio. The members of the Nava family planned to return to their native Mexico the next day, and their friends bade them good-bye. Without work or money, the Navas had accepted an offer made to all barrio residents by the welfare authorities: free transportation back to Mexico . . . one-way only.

But as it happened, the Navas never boarded the train for Mexico. That night their eight-year-old son Julián suffered a ruptured appendix and was rushed to the hospital. He survived, but in the aftermath of the crisis, the family decided to remain in Los Angeles.

The Navas were only one of many thousands of Los Angeles families of Mexican origin whose lives were disrupted by the depression. Mexicans had first migrated to the city in large numbers in the early twentieth century, to take jobs laying track for the Pacific Electric Railroad. The 1910 census reported 8,917 Mexicans in Los Angeles, but knowledgeable local observers put the figure at closer to 20,000.

Mexicans continued to pour into the city even after the railroad-construction boom ended. They took the lowest-paying urban jobs and found seasonal employment as agricultural workers. By 1930 the Mexican population of Los Angeles County stood at 167,000—the largest concentration of Mexicans in the world outside Mexico City. Most lived in "Sonora Town," the sprawling barrio of East Los Angeles.

When the depression hit, unemployment soared in the barrio, and the newcomers, once welcomed as a source of cheap labor, were now denounced as a drain on scarce relief funds. In January 1931 the Los Angeles County welfare director telegraphed Washington, asking that a team of immigration officials be sent to the city to supervise the deportation of Mexicans. The presence of federal representatives, he said, would "have a tendency to scare many thousands of alien deportables out of this district, which is the result intended."

Arriving as requested, immigration officers conducted dragnet raids in the barrio and made highly publicized arrests of Mexican aliens lacking proper documentation. In one raid in February 1931, police surrounded a downtown park popular with the Mexicans and held some four hundred adults and children captive for over an hour.

Meanwhile, Los Angeles welfare officials announced their plan of free one-way transportation to Mexico. The cost of sending a full trainload of returnees (called *repatriados*) to Mexico, they calculated, would be more than offset by annual savings in relief payments. Though the plan was "voluntary," those who refused to become *repatriados* found their relief payments cut off and, later in the 1930s, their applications for jobs in the WPA, PWA, or other New Deal work programs rejected. Under combined federal and local pressure, an estimated seventy thousand Mexicans left Los Angeles in 1931 alone.

Underlying this deportation drive was not only concern about welfare costs but prejudice. Some native-born Angelenos referred to the newcomers contemptuously as "greasers"; papers played up stories of barrio gang wars and crimes involving Mexicans. The Mexican community did not accept

**Los Angeles Barrio,** *c. 1930*
*This photograph was taken in Chavez Ravine, now the site of Dodger Stadium.*

**Designer's Sketch for a "Zoot Suit"**

this injustice passively, however. The city's Spanish-language newspaper, *La Opinión*, and the barrio's business association denounced the intimidating tactics of immigration and welfare officials.

As the worst of the depression passed and the deportations and "voluntary" departures diminished, the rhythm of life in the barrio resumed, presenting a fascinating picture of a community suspended between two cultures. Radios covered with colorful *serapes* broadcast both the latest popular songs and the native folk melodies of Mexico, called *rancheros*. Supermarket food supplemented such traditional fare as enchiladas, tamales, and burritos. Though influenced by the cosmopolitan life around them, the Mexicans of Los Angeles spoke Spanish in the barrio, lit votive candles to the Virgin Mary in their churches, and perpetuated traditional remedies and folk beliefs dating back centuries.

The younger generation, gathering on the barrio's sidewalks in the warm southern California evenings, developed a distinctive street culture involving endless conversation, dramatic hairdos, a swaggering air of bravado, and flamboyant styles of dress: short skirts, black stockings, and perilously high heels for the girls; widely draped, deeply pleated "zoot suits" for the boys.

Whereas some of the barrio's young people turned to the vibrant street life, others concentrated on making their way in the larger society. Among the latter was Julián Nava. After high school and World War II naval service, Nava went on to Pomona College and Harvard University. In the 1960s, by then a history professor at San Fernando State College, he was elected to the Los Angeles School Board. In 1971 he became the board's president, with responsibility for a school system enrolling 650,000 students and operating on an annual budget of $750 million.

Julián Nava had come a long way since that depression-era night when an appendicitis attack had changed the course of his life. And Los Angeles had come a long way as well. The once despised Mexican minority had become an integral part of the city's fabric, affecting in countless ways its culture, its music, its religion, its cuisine, and the very texture of its life.

**Mexican Men Outside Los Angeles Relief Office**

consequent erosion of self-esteem often had a devastating impact. "I would rather turn on the gas and put an end to the whole family than let my wife support me," one man told a social investigator. Desertions increased, and the divorce rate, after a dip in the early and mid-thirties, edged upward, hitting a then all-time high by 1940.

Children found vacation plans canceled, birthdays with few presents, and mealtimes tense with anxious discussions. Maria Tighe of Long Island, who was seven years old when the stock market crashed, could recall years later sneaking to 6:00 A.M. mass so her friends would not see her shoes provided by the welfare bureau. Elena Columbo, a child in Maynard, Massachusetts, in the thirties, remembered her dread at being sent to collect the food distributed by municipal authorities: "I used to cry. . . . Everyone would see you there. I was ashamed."

But depression-era Americans also rediscovered traditional skills. They painted their own houses and repaired their own cars. Baking and canning revived. Many would later recall this as a time when adversity had strengthened the spirit of mutual help. "The feeling among people was beautiful," a Wisconsin man recalled. "Supposing . . . a hunter[shot]. . . some ducks or some game, they'd have their friends over and share it."

But sharing and making do could not wholly erase the depression's harsh impact on family life. The experience of a Cleveland railroad worker's family, recalled by one of the daughters, vividly conveys that impact:

> My father lost his job and we moved into a double-garage. The landlord didn't charge us rent for seven years. We had a coal stove, and we had to each take turns . . . to warm our legs. It was awfully cold when you opened those garage doors. We would sleep with rugs and blankets over the top of us [and] dress under the sheets. . . . In the morning we'd . . . get some snow and put it on the stove and melt it and wash around our faces. . . . [We] put on two pairs of socks on each hand and two pairs of socks on our feet, and long underwear and . . . Goodwill shoes. Off we'd walk, three, four miles to school.

## The American Cultural Scene in the Thirties

The depression's cultural impact matched its social effects. Whereas radio and the movies presented escapist fare, writers, artists, and social thinkers offered a more probing view of American life and ideology. In the de-

moralized early thirties, this view tended to be highly critical. By the end of the thirties, however, a more positive tone reflected the renewal of hope stimulated by the New Deal as well as the rallying of American intellectuals against militaristic dictatorships abroad.

### Avenues of Escape: Radio and the Movies

The standardization of mass culture, underway in the 1920s, accelerated in the 1930s. Each evening, millions of Americans gathered around their Silvertone or Atwater Kent radio consoles to listen to network news commentators, musical programs, and—above all—comedy shows. Radio humor flourished in the 1930s, when the real world was grim. Comedians like Jack Benny and the husband-and-wife team George Burns and Gracie Allen attracted millions.

So, too, did the fifteen-minute afternoon domestic dramas known as soap operas (thus called because soap companies usually sponsored them). Despite the soap operas' monotonous, assembly-line quality, many listeners became deeply involved with these daily dollops of romance and melodrama. Some wrote earnest letters to the soap-opera characters advising them how to handle their problems.

The soap-opera audience consisted mostly of housewives. Identifying with the ordeals of the radio heroines, these women gained at least temporary escape from their own difficulties. As one female listener put it, "I can get through the day better when I hear they have sorrows, too."

The movies, too, proved extremely popular in depression America, when most people could still afford the quarter that it cost to see a show. The introduction of double features in 1931 and of drive-in theaters in 1933 further boosted attendance. In 1939, 65 percent of Americans went to the movies at least once a week. The motion picture, declared one Hollywood executive, had become "as necessary as any other daily commodity."

What did these millions see? A few movies dealt realistically with such social issues as labor unrest in the coal industry (*Black Fury*) and the sharecroppers' plight (*Cabin in the Cotton*). Two documentaries made by Pare Lorentz for the Farm Security Administration, *The River* and *The Plow That Broke the Plains,* evoked the human and environmental toll of a century of westward expansion.

Warner Brothers studio (which had close ties with the administration) made a series of movies in 1934–1936 celebrating the New Deal. And in *Mr. Deeds*

*Goes to Town* (1936) and *Mr. Smith Goes to Washington* (1939), director Frank Capra, the son of Italian immigrants, offered an unabashedly idealistic message: that "the people" would always triumph over entrenched interests.

The gangster movies of the early thirties, drawing inspiration from real-life criminals like John Dillinger and the legendary Bonnie Parker and Clyde Barrow, served up a different style of film realism. Photographed in black and white, motion pictures like *Little Caesar* (1930) and *The Public Enemy* (1931) offered harsh, gritty images of urban America: looming skyscrapers; squealing tires in menacing, rain-swept streets; lonely bus depots and all-night diners; the rat-tat-tat of machine guns as rival gangs battled it out. When civic groups protested the gangster movies' glorification of crime, Hollywood reversed the formula to make the police and "G-men" (FBI agents) the heroes, while retaining the same level of violence.

The stars of the gangster movies, such as Edward G. Robinson and James Cagney, represented 1930s-style variants of the earlier Horatio Alger heroes, fighting their way upward against the odds. Their portrayals resonated with depression-era moviegoers, for whom the odds often seemed equally discouraging and the social environment equally menacing.

But above all, the movies offered escape—the chance briefly to forget the depression. The Hollywood publicist who claimed that the movies "literally laughed the big bad wolf of the depression out of the public mind" exaggerated, but cinema's escapist function in the thirties is clear. Musicals such as *Gold Diggers of 1933* (with its theme song "We're in the Money") offered dancing, music, and cheerful plots involving the triumph of pluck over adversity. Walt Disney's *Snow White and the Seven Dwarfs* (1937) was a triumph of animation, and *The Wizard of Oz* (1939) became a beloved American classic.

The Marx Brothers provided the depression decade's zaniest movie moments. In comedies like *Animal Crackers* and *Duck Soup*, these vaudeville troupers of Jewish-immigrant origins created an anarchic world that satirized authority, fractured the English language, and defied logic. In *Animal Crackers*, for example, Groucho and Chico planned a search for a stolen painting:

GROUCHO: Suppose nobody in the house took the painting?
CHICO: Go to the house next door.
GROUCHO: Suppose there isn't any house next door?
CHICO: Then we gotta build one.

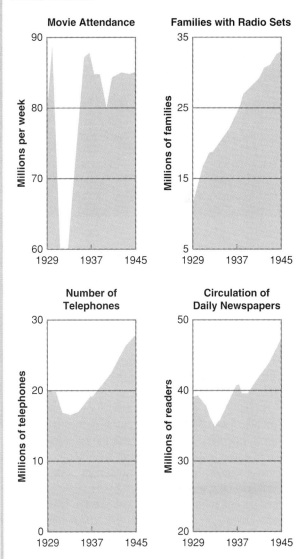

**Mass Communication and Entertainment, 1929–1945**
*The media provided both information and diversion amid hard times. Boasted one movie-industry leader in 1934: "No medium has contributed more greatly than film to . . . the national morale during a period featured by revolution . . . in other countries."*

*Sources:* American Telephone and Telegraph Company, Federal Communications Commission, *The Film Daily,* and the National Broadcasting Company.

At a time when the established order and the conventional wisdom seemed unreliable at best, the Marx Brothers' mockery matched the American mood.

Hollywood in the thirties dealt with blacks and women largely in stereotypes. Paul Robeson made a

**Hollywood Escapism in Depression America**

*A quartet of boys in Scott's Run, West Virginia (left), ponders whether an upcoming low-budget movie called "Hard-Rock Harrigan" will be worth the admission charge; child star Shirley Temple (above) with the brilliant tap dancer Bill Robinson in "Rebecca of Sunnybrook Farm" (1938).*

film recreating his stage role in *The Emperor Jones,* but black performers usually found themselves confined to such roles as the scatterbrained maid played by Butterfly McQueen in *Gone with the Wind* or the indulgent house servant (played by tap dancer Bill Robinson) patronized by child star Shirley Temple in *The Little Colonel* (1935). Under the denigrating screen name Stepin Fetchit, black actor Lincoln Perry played a slapstick role as the slow-moving, slow-talking butt of humor in many movies.

Fulfillment for women, Hollywood continued to preach, lay only in marriage and domesticity. A few films, however, chipped away at the stereotype. In the 1936 comedy *Wedding Present,* Joan Bennett played a strong-willed professional. Another star, Mae West, invented a new, more assertive stereotype. Brassy, openly sexual, and fiercely independent, West in *I'm No Angel, She Done Him Wrong,* and other 1930s hits mocked conventional morality, wittily toyed with her suitors, and made it clear that she would take orders from no one.

### The Literature of the Early Thirties

Matching the nation's mood, American fiction of the early depression exuded disillusionment and cynicism. Sinclair Lewis and H. L. Mencken had satirized the middle class in the 1920s, but their successors in the early thirties challenged the fundamental premises of American ideology far more radically.

In his *Studs Lonigan* trilogy (1932–1935), Chicago-born James T. Farrell offered a bleak picture of the hero's empty existence. The product of a chaotic working-class Irish-immigrant neighborhood much like that of Farrell's own boyhood, young Lonigan lacks any way of making sense of his fragmented urban world. He stumbles through life, trying to piece together a coherent world view from the bits of mass culture that drift his way.

In *U.S.A.* (1930–1936), another trilogy, John Dos Passos drew a dark panorama of twentieth-century America as a money-mad, exploitive society devoid of social or spiritual coherence. As one character says, "Everything you've wanted crumbles in your fingers as you grasp it."

Nathanael West, drawing on his experiences as a night clerk in a seedy Manhattan hotel, created in *Miss Lonelyhearts* (1933) a surreal story of a newspaper advice columnist so oppressed by the stream of human misery flowing across his desk that he retreats into apathy and ultimately insanity. In West's *A Cool Million* (1934), a parody of the Alger success novels, young Lemuel Pitkin comes to New York to seek his fortune only to be cheated, betrayed, beaten, imprisoned, and eventually murdered.

Some radical novelists of the early thirties even more explicitly attacked capitalism and its exploitation of workers. The Communist party encouraged such fiction through writers' clubs and contests to discover literary talent among the proletariat. Some interesting work emerged. Jack Conroy's *The Disinherited* (1933), a novel dealing with labor violence in the Missouri coal fields, gained force from the fact that Conroy's father and brother had died in a mine disaster.

Radical playwrights brought the class struggle to the stage. Clifford Odets's *Waiting for Lefty* (1935) offered noble workers and evil bosses and ended with the audience chanting "Strike! Strike! Strike!" Marc Blitzstein's radical musical *The Cradle Will Rock* (1937) was originally funded by the WPA's Federal Theatre Project. When nervous WPA officials ordered the performance postponed shortly before the opening-night curtain, the cast and audience defiantly walked to another theater, and the show went on.

### The Later Thirties: The Popular Front and Cultural Nationalism

Initially, the U.S. Communist party vehemently attacked Franklin Roosevelt and the New Deal. But in 1935 Soviet dictator Joseph Stalin promulgated a new policy. Fearful of attack by Nazi Germany, Stalin now called for a worldwide alliance, or "Popular Front," against Hitler and his Italian fascist* counterpart, Benito Mussolini. Responding to the new Soviet line, U.S. communist leaders praised Franklin Roosevelt, described communism as "twentieth century Americanism," and recruited noncommunist writers and intellectuals to the antifascist cause.

Few events aroused more passionate emotions in these years than the Spanish Civil War. In July 1936 Spanish fascist general Francisco Franco launched a revolt against Spain's legally elected government, a coalition of liberals, socialists, communists, and anarchists. Franco's cause won support from Spanish conservatives, monarchists, landowners, industrialists, and the Roman Catholic hierarchy. Hitler and Mussolini provided military aid.

In America, the cause of the anti-Franco Spanish Loyalists (those loyal to the elected government in Madrid) won support from writers, artists, and intellectuals who backed the Popular Front. Poet Archibald MacLeish, speaking at a writers' congress in New York City in 1937, embraced the Loyalist cause. No longer could writers stand aloof, he insisted. The time for political commitment had come.

---

* Fascism (derived from the *Fascisti,* a political organization founded in Italy in 1919): a form of government involving one-party dictatorship, state control of production, extreme nationalism, hostility to minority groups, and the forcible suppression of all opposition, including labor unions.

Writer Ernest Hemingway, who visited Spain in 1936–1937, firmly supported the Loyalists. His novel *For Whom the Bell Tolls* (1940) told of a young American who joins a Loyalist guerrilla band and eventually dies for the cause. *For Whom the Bell Tolls* contrasted with Hemingway's disillusioned novels of the 1920s. Reflecting on his new-found capacity for political engagement, Hemingway later wrote, "The Spanish Civil War offered something which you could believe in wholly and completely, and in which you felt an absolute brotherhood with the others who were engaged in it."

The Popular Front collapsed on August 24, 1939, when the Soviet Union and Nazi Germany signed a nonaggression pact and divided Poland between them. This cynical pact shocked idealistic Americans who had embraced the Popular Front. Overnight, enthusiasm for working with the communists under the banner of "antifascism" faded. Membership in the U.S. Communist party dwindled as well. But while it lasted, the Popular Front had influenced U.S. politics and culture and alerted Americans to the rise of fascism in Europe.

The emergence of fascism and the renewal of political engagement inspired by the Popular Front, coupled with the achievements of the Roosevelt administration, stimulated a broad shift in the cultural climate in the mid-1930s. The New Deal's programs for writers, artists, and musicians contributed to this cultural resurgence as well. The satirical tone of the 1920s and the cynicism of the early 1930s now gave way to a more hopeful view of America and the American people. In John Steinbeck's *The Grapes of Wrath* (1939), for example, an uprooted dust-bowl family, the Joads, experience many setbacks as they make their way from Oklahoma to California along Route 66. But they never give up, and they always help others. As Ma Joad puts it, "They ain't gonna wipe us out. Why, we're the people—we go on."

Another expression of the new cultural spirit began in 1936 when journalist James Agee and photographer Walker Evans spent several weeks living with Alabama sharecropper families while researching an article on rural poverty for the business magazine *Fortune*. But *Fortune* rejected the work that Agee produced, and not until 1941 was it published as *Let Us Now Praise Famous Men*. Enhanced by Walker Evans's haunting photographs, Agee's intensely personal masterpiece evoked the strength and decency of Americans living on society's margins.

The more positive mood found expression on the stage as well. Thornton Wilder's play *Our Town* (1938)

**Nineteen-Thirties America in Black-and-White**
*Walker Evans was one of a number of gifted photographers who created a lasting visual portfolio of American life during the Great Depression. Evans captured this moment at an auto repair shop in Atlanta, Georgia.*

mances as well as in recording sessions of his mainly white orchestra.

The Count Basie band started at Kansas City's Reno Club, where, as Basie later recalled, "We played from nine o'clock in the evening to five or six the next morning, including the floor shows, and the boys in the band got eighteen dollars a week and I got twenty one." In 1936 Basie moved on to New York, and for the next decade, swing ruled popular music.

The cultural nationalism of the later 1930s heightened interest in regional literature and art. Wallace Stegner wrote about Iowa in *Remembering Laughter* (1937), and Zora Neale Hurston's *Their Eyes Were Watching God* (1937) explored a black woman's search for fulfillment in rural Florida. In such works as *Absalom, Absalom!* (1936) and *The Hamlet* (1940), William Faulkner of Mississippi continued the saga of his mythic Yoknapatawpha County and its fictional population of McCaslins, Compsons, Sartorises, and the upstart Snopses.

Painters Thomas Hart Benton of Missouri (a descendant of the nineteenth-century senator of the same name), John Steuart Curry of Kansas, and Grant Wood of Iowa struck a strongly regional note. Wood's best ideas, he insisted, "came while milking a cow." But Curry, who taught art at the University of Wisconsin, warned that regionalism could not substitute for talent. "Your greatness will not be found in Europe or in New York, or in the Middle West, or in Wisconsin," he reminded his students, "but within yourself."

Americans in these years also discovered their folk-art heritage. Galleries mounted shows of Amish quilts, New Hampshire weather vanes, itinerant colonial portraiture, and lovingly crafted children's toys. A 1938 show at New York's Museum of Modern Art introduced Horace Pippin, a black Philadelphia laborer whose right arm had been shattered in World War I. In such paintings as *John Brown Going to His Hanging,* Pippin revealed a genuine, if untutored, talent. The same museum in 1939 featured seventy-nine-year-old Anna "Grandma" Moses of Hoosick Falls, New York. Paintings of scenes from her girlhood became highly popular.

The cultural nationalism as the thirties ended generated a fascination with the nation's past. Americans flocked to historical re-creations such as Henry Ford's Greenfield Village near Detroit and to Colonial

portrayed a turn-of-the-century New England town where life's everyday routines become, in memory, infinitely precious. William Saroyan's *The Time of Your Life* (1939) affectionately celebrated the foibles and virtues of a colorful collection of American "types" in a San Francisco waterfront bar.

Composers, too, reflected this swell of cultural nationalism. In such works as *Billy the Kid* (1938), Aaron Copland drew upon American legends and folk melodies. George Gershwin adapted Dubose and Dorothy Heyward's 1920s play about black life in Charleston for his 1935 opera *Porgy and Bess.*

And jazz, that quintessentially American music, surged in popularity in the later thirties, thanks to the big bands of Benny Goodman, Count Basie, Glenn Miller, and others who developed a more flowing jazz style known as swing. Goodman, son of a Chicago immigrant family, got his start on the clarinet at Jane Addams's Hull House. The swing era dates from August 1935, when the Goodman band played to a sellout audience at Los Angeles's Palomar Ballroom, featuring arrangements by the great Fletcher Henderson. Another high point came in 1938, when the Goodman band performed at New York's Carnegie Hall, citadel of classical music. Jazz had arrived. One of Goodman's contributions was to include black musicians like pianist Teddy Wilson and vibraphonist Lionel Hampton in live perfor-

**Bringing in the Maple Sugar,** by Anna "Grandma" Moses, c. 1939
*A mood of patriotism and nostalgia for simpler times contributed to the popularity of folk artists in the later 1930s.*

Williamsburg in Virginia, restored by the Rockefeller Foundation. In 1936–1939 Texans restored the Alamo in San Antonio, the "Cradle of Texas Liberty." Historical novels like Margaret Mitchell's romantic epic of the Old South, *Gone with the Wind* (1936) became best sellers. Poet Carl Sandburg won a Pulitzer Prize in 1939 for a eulogistic biography of Abraham Lincoln. And critic Van Wyck Brooks, who in the 1920s had dismissed the American literary tradition, struck a new note with *The Flowering of New England* (1936), praising the writers who had flourished in New England a century earlier.

As the 1930s ended, Americans viewed their nation with a newly appreciative eye. It had survived the economic crisis. The social fabric remained whole; revolution had not come. As other societies collapsed into dictatorships, American democracy endured.

### *The Age of Streamlining*

This restored confidence found expression in a style of industrial design called streamlining, which transformed the appearance of thousands of products. Streamlining originated in the 1920s with a group of industrial designers including Norman Bel Geddes, Walter Teague, and Raymond Loewy. Inspired by the romance of flight, they introduced smoothly flowing curves and parabolas into industrial designs.

Behind these aesthetic principles lay a social vision: that harmonious and functional consumer products would inspire a more harmonious and functional society. As cultural historian Jeffrey Meikle puts it, "The streamlined society would be as smooth and uncomplicated as an egg—a mechanical egg with no possibility of unruly life breaking out from within."

Streamlining appealed to American business in the 1930s. It made products more attractive to consumers—a vital consideration at a time of slow sales. When Sears, Roebuck hired Raymond Loewy to streamline its Coldspot refrigerators in the 1930s, sales surged. Streamlining also helped business rebuild its tarnished reputation. At first, business had tried to bolster its image with ad pronouncements in defense of the free-enterprise system. But by mid-decade corporations began to stress the wonderful benefits that business brought to society. The Du Pont Corporation's slogan "Better Things for Better Living Through Chemistry," summed up the new theme. Streamlined product designs reinforced corporate America's campaign to reinvent itself as the benevolent shaper of the future.

Products ranging from automobiles to cigarette lighters emerged in sleek new forms. The prosaic pencil sharpener metamorphosed into a gleaming, aerodynamic work of art poised for takeoff. Museums exhibited streamlined product designs. The modernistic service stations Geddes designed for Texaco, he boasted, would make lubrication "a stimulating experience" rather than merely a boring necessity.

Under the theme "The World of Tomorrow," the 1939 New York World's Fair represented the high point of both the streamlining vogue and corporate America's public-relations blitz. The fair's instantly famous logo was the Trylon and Perisphere: a seven-hundred-foot needle symbolizing the event's "lofty purpose" and a large globe that seemed to float on a circular pool of water. Inside the Perisphere, visitors found "Democracity," a revolving diorama portraying an orderly, harmonious city of the future.

The hit of the fair was Futurama, the General Motors exhibit designed by Norman Bel Geddes. Visitors entered a darkened circular auditorium where, amid piped-in music and a resonant recorded narration, a vision of America in the distant year 1960 unfolded—an America dominated by a highway network complete with multiple lanes, cloverleafs, and stacked interchanges. A brilliant public-relations investment, Futurama built support for the costly interstate highway system that the growing number of vehicles would soon make essential—a system that would become a reality in the 1950s.

Along with such wonders as television and automatic dishwashers, the 1939 World's Fair did, indeed, offer a first glimpse of "The World of Tomorrow"—a smoothly functioning technological utopia made possible by the nation's corporations. As a business magazine editorialized, "If there are any doubters left, a visit to the New York World's Fair should convince them that American business has been the vehicle which carried the discoveries of science and the benefits of machine production to the doorstep of American consumers." The fair epitomized corporate capitalism's version of America's cultural nationalism and reviving optimism as the thirties ended.

## Undercurrents of Apprehension

But muted fear belied the surface confidence. The economic crisis had eased, but dangers loomed beyond the seas. The anxiety triggered by the menacing world situation surfaced in unexpected ways. One such moment came on October 31, 1938, when CBS radio aired an adaptation of H. G. Wells's science-fiction story *War of the Worlds* directed by Orson Welles. In realistic detail, the broadcast reported the landing of a spaceship near Princeton, New Jersey, the emergence of aliens with lethal ray guns, and their advance toward New York City.

**Streamlining**
*Industrial designers of the 1930s whetted consumer demand and shaped the decade's aesthetics with their radically redesigned products. This experimental locomotive of 1934 was a gleaming triumph of streamlining.*

**New York World's Fair, 1939**
*Despite the fair's dreamy vision of a future made bright by technology, world events looked grim as the 1930s ended.*

The show sparked a national panic. For a few hours, horrified listeners from coast to coast firmly believed that the end was at hand. Opinion researchers later concluded that of some 6 million listeners, 20 percent had reacted in fear and even hysteria. Some jumped in their cars and sped off into the night. Others prayed. A few attempted suicide.

Beneath the panic about "Martians" lay a far more rational fear: of approaching war. For a decade, while Americans had coped with the depression, the international situation had steadily worsened. By October 1938 radio news bulletins were warning of impending war between Germany and England.

The panic triggered by Orson Welles's Halloween prank quickly changed to sheepish embarrassment, but the fear aroused by more realistic dangers only escalated. By the time the New York World's Fair offered its vision of "The World of Tomorrow," the actual world of 1939 had become very scary indeed.

# The United States in a Menacing World

Apart from efforts to improve relations with Latin America, the early Roosevelt administration remained largely aloof from the rest of the world. But while the United States grappled with the depression, Italy, Germany, and Japan grew increasingly aggressive and militaristic. Americans reacted with ambivalence. Vowing not to bumble into war once again as in 1917, millions in the United States supported neutrality and peace. Others, however, insisted that America must help embattled democracies abroad. All the while, the world edged closer to the precipice.

## *FDR's Nationalism and the Good Neighbor Policy*

Focusing on domestic recovery, FDR initially pursued a policy that put U.S. economic interests above all other considerations. Secretary of State Cordell Hull believed in free trade and international economic cooperation, but Roosevelt showed little interest.

Indeed, in the summer of 1933, while Hull was attending a London economic conference called by the leading trading nations to stabilize their currencies, Roosevelt dispatched a blunt message to England: the president had no interest in any plan that might undercut his New Deal recovery program. Without American cooperation, the conference broke up.

Roosevelt did, however, adopt an internationalist approach in Latin America, where bitterness over decades of "Yankee imperialism" ran high. In his 1933 inaugural address, FDR announced a "Good Neighbor" policy, rejecting the "Big Stick" tactics of his distant cousin Theodore, who had insisted on Washington's right to use force to correct "wrongdoing" in Latin America. At a conference in Uruguay in 1933, the United States endorsed a statement of principles that declared, "No state has the right to intervene in the internal or external affairs of another."

Under this policy Roosevelt withdrew the last U.S. troops from the Dominican Republic and Haiti. He also worked out a treaty with Panama reducing the U.S. role in Panamanian affairs and increasing Panama's commercial rights in the Canal Zone. At the same time, however, the United States remained closely identified with the repressive regimes of Raphael Trujillo in the Dominican Republic and Anastasio Somoza in Nicaragua.

The Good Neighbor policy faced major tests in Cuba and Mexico. In Cuba falling sugar exports related to high U.S. tariffs on imported sugar triggered an economic crisis. This in turn led to a revolutionary uprising in 1933 that brought to power the leftist Grau San Martín. The United States opposed the San Martín government, but rather than sending in the marines, the administration pursued a less direct but no less effective course of action. In 1934, with the connivance of the U.S. ambassador to Cuba and after a "visit" by U.S. warships, San Martín was overthrown by a conservative coalition dominated by strongman Fulgencio Batista. To shore up the Batista regime, Washington lowered the tariff on Cuban sugarcane. As Cuban exports to the United States rose, Batista consolidated his power. He would rule Cuba on and off until 1959, when he was overthrown by Fidel Castro.

In Mexico a reform government came to power in 1936 and promptly nationalized several oil companies owned by U.S. and British corporations. Washington once again refrained from military intervention. Conceding Mexico's right to nationalize the companies but insisting on fair compensation, the United States pressured Mexico economically by suspending U.S. purchases of Mexican silver. After lengthy negotiations, Mexico and the oil companies hammered out a mutually agreeable compensation figure.

Although Washington continued to intervene in Latin America in various ways, the Good Neighbor policy did diminish the more heavy-handed forms of interference, including military occupation. The better relations fostered by Roosevelt's policy would prove important in the future, when the United States sought to build hemispheric solidarity against the Axis powers in World War II, and later against the Soviet Union in the Cold War.

## The Rise of Fascism in Europe and Asia

Meanwhile, powerful political forces raged elsewhere in the world. As early as 1922, amid economic problems and social unrest, Benito Mussolini and his Fascist party came to power in Italy and within a few years suppressed all dissident voices and imposed one-party rule.

A greater menace unfolded in Germany with the rise of Adolf Hitler. An embittered war veteran given to demagogic harangues, Hitler exploited the German people's resentment of the harsh Versailles treaty and the inability of Germany's government to control runaway inflation in the 1920s. Briefly jailed in 1923 after a failed grab for power, Hitler took the opportunity to dictate his political manifesto, *Mein Kampf* (My Struggle), replete with fanatic nationalism and anti-Semitism.

Depression struck Germany in 1929 as it did the United States. As the economy deteriorated, Hitler's National Socialist (Nazi) party gained strength. On January 30, 1933, five weeks before Franklin Roosevelt took the oath as president of the United States, Hitler became the chancellor of Germany. The two men's lives would fatefully intertwine for the next twelve years until they died within two weeks of each other in April 1945—Roosevelt as leader of a victorious nation; Hitler, a suicide in his Berlin bunker.

Crushing potential rivals, Hitler quickly established a dictatorship. A racist who believed that Germany must be purified of all "inferior" taint, Hitler instituted a program to drive out German Jews, whom he further blamed for Germany's defeat in World War I.

Hitler in 1935 announced plans for a half-million-man army. A year later, Nazi troops reoccupied the German-speaking Rhineland, a region demilitarized under the Versailles treaty. Early in 1938, to the cheers of Austrian Nazis, Hitler proclaimed an *Anschluss* (union) between Austria and Germany, and German tanks rolled into Vienna. Mussolini, intent on building an African empire, invaded helpless Ethiopia in 1935. These moves caused protests but little action in London, Paris, Washington, and Geneva, the headquarters of the League of Nations.

Hitler next turned to the Sudetenland, a part of neighboring Czechoslovakia containing some 3 million ethnic Germans. The Sudetenland must be part of Germany, Hitler insisted, and he thundered his determination to take it. At a conference in Munich on September 29–30, 1938—a conference that excluded the Czechs—British prime minister Neville Chamberlain and his French counterpart yielded to Hitler's demands and agreed to turn over the Sudetenland to Germany. A weakened Czechoslovakia, stripped of a third of its population and territory, faced the formidable German army. Interpreting this appeasement of Hitler as a diplomatic victory, Chamberlain proclaimed "peace in our time."* Millions sighed in relief; war had been avoided.

Meanwhile, in Japan, militarists had gained control of the government and launched a fateful course of expansion. In 1931–1932 Japanese troops occupied the Chinese province of Manchuria and installed a puppet government. In July 1937 the Japanese unleashed a full-scale war against China itself.

In 1936 Germany, Italy, and Japan had signed treaties of alliance and mutual defense. The alignment that would soon join forces in war had been forged.

## The American Mood: No More War

The American people's response reflected a deep revulsion against war. Novelists of the 1920s had repudiated the exalted rhetoric of the World War I era, and by the mid-1930s millions of Americans had concluded that the decision for war in April 1917 had been a ghastly mistake.

Walter Millis's *The Road to War* (1935) and other books argued that the United States had been dragged into war by bankers and arms merchants desperate to protect their millions in loans and weapons sales to England and France. More sensational exposés of the international arms traffic bore such titles as *Merchants of Death* and *One Hell of a Business*. Other works probed the propaganda techniques by which American support for the war had been mobilized.

---

* This notorious capitulation would have a long rhetorical afterlife in Western diplomacy. Throughout the Cold War, U.S. officials often cautioned that any concessions to the communists risked "another Munich." In the 1960s Secretary of State Dean Rusk and others often invoked the Munich analogy in warning against U.S. withdrawal from Vietnam. Even the furled black umbrella Chamberlain carried at Munich became a shorthand icon for appeasement.

## European Aggression Before World War II

*Less than twenty years after the end of World War I, war again loomed in Europe as Hitler launched Germany on a course of military and territorial expansion.*

In a series of hearings between 1934 and 1936, a congressional committee headed by Senator Gerald Nye, a North Dakota Republican, investigated the involvement of U.S. banks and corporations in financing World War I and supplying arms to the Allies. Nye's committee also documented these groups' lobbying and public-relations activities in support of U.S. intervention.

These books and investigations hit home. In January 1937, pollsters found, 70 percent of Americans believed that the United States should have stayed out of World War I. What had seemed at the time an act of idealism now struck many as a surrender to corporate interests.

All this produced a widespread determination to keep the United States out of future wars. The United States, protected by two oceans, many Americans concluded, could safely remain aloof from the upheavals elsewhere in the world. A *New York Times* reviewer said that Millis's *Road to War* should be made "required reading before anything more [is] said or written about American participation in another European war."

As a peace movement spread across college and university campuses in 1935–1938, students organized antiwar rallies and marches. "SCHOLARSHIPS, NOT BATTLESHIPS," some posters read. In a "peace strike" in 1936, half a million students boycotted classes and attended antiwar events.

Novelists and playwrights expressed the national mood. The German antiwar novel *All Quiet on the Western Front* became a best seller in the United States, and two antiwar dramas of 1936—Irwin Shaw's *Bury the Dead* and Robert E. Sherwood's *Idiot's Delight*—strengthened the mid-decade peace movement. In Shaw's play six U.S. soldiers killed in battle refuse to stay buried despite desperate efforts to get them underground and out of sight.

A series of Neutrality Acts passed in 1935–1937 reflected the popular longing for peace. Trying to prevent a repeat of 1917, these measures outlawed arms sales or loans to nations at war and forbade Americans from

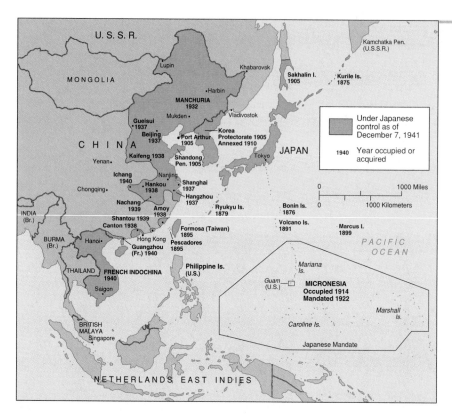

**Japanese Expansion Before World War II**

*Dominated by militarists, Japan pursued an expansionist policy in Asia in the 1930s, extending its sphere of economic and political influence. In July 1937, having already occupied the Chinese province of Manchuria, Japan attacked China proper.*

traveling on the ships of belligerent powers. In 1937, responding to the conflict in Spain, Congress extended the neutrality legislation to cover civil wars as well.

Critics of the Neutrality Acts (including President Roosevelt, who had signed them reluctantly) pointed out that they failed to distinguish between aggressors and victims. When Japan invaded China in 1937, FDR refused to invoke the Neutrality Act (on the technicality that neither side had formally declared war) so he could extend loans to the embattled Chinese.

The effort to legislate peace peaked early in 1938, when Indiana congressman Louis Ludlow proposed a constitutional amendment requiring a national referendum on any U.S. declaration of war except in cases of direct attack. Only by a narrow margin, and after an appeal from President Roosevelt, did Congress reject the Ludlow Amendment.

### Hesitant Response to the Fascist Challenge

Americans reacted only slowly to the fascist and militaristic regimes in Italy, Germany, and Japan. Indeed, many initially admired Mussolini. He had imposed discipline and in general energized Italy with a flurry of government activity.

Even Hitler found some American fans. As late as 1939, the German-American Bund, a pro-Nazi organization, filled New York's Madison Square Garden with twenty thousand sympathizers. A Hollywood writer and anti-Semite named William Dudley Pelley organized a U.S. fascist movement. Some Americans—including Joseph P. Kennedy, U.S. ambassador to Great Britain (and father of future president John F. Kennedy)—found Hitler at least tolerable because of his rabid anticommunism.

Even for Americans unsympathetic to fascism, Hitler and Mussolini seemed at first less figures of menace than of ridicule. Political cartoonists had a field day with Mussolini's jutting jaw and Hitler's mustache. The goose-stepping marches of fascist troops appeared more like comic-opera routines than omens of horror.

From the first, however, some Americans viewed fascism with grave alarm. The Popular Front was one expression of this antifascist impulse. As early as 1933 Harvard literature professor Howard Mumford Jones warned that Nazi book burnings and suppression of free speech menaced freedom everywhere. Newspaper columnist Dorothy Thompson, expelled from Nazi Germany in 1934, emerged as a powerful voice denouncing Hitlerism.

Whatever their feelings about fascism, most Americans opposed a U.S. military response. Since neither the League of Nations nor Europe itself seemed capable of resisting Hitler and Mussolini, why should the United States become involved?

President Roosevelt, fascinated by global politics and recognizing the role of power in world affairs, advocated strengthened defenses and as early as 1933 promoted naval expansion. At the same time, personalizing international affairs just as he did domestic issues, he communicated constantly with world leaders, including Hitler and Mussolini, seeking accommodation.

Bowing to antiwar sentiment, FDR never pushed ahead of public opinion. In 1935 he even assured a visiting Australian leader that America would never again under any circumstances enter a foreign war. In a 1937 speech, he suggested a "quarantine" of aggressor nations to stop "the epidemic of world lawlessness," but when the public reacted coolly, he backed off. For much of the decade, FDR urged negotiations as the best way to deal with Hitler. Thus, he sent a telegram of praise to Prime Minister Chamberlain after the 1938 Munich Pact and assured the State Department that he was "not a bit upset" over the agreement handing the Sudetenland over to Germany.

Various factors figured in America's hesitant response to the disturbing events in Europe. Since the 1790s, U.S. foreign policy had sought to avoid entanglement in Old World quarrels. This isolationist impulse was reinforced in the interwar years by the conviction that American intervention in World War I had been a mistake, and, after 1929, by the domestic economic crisis that overshadowed events abroad.

The only real confrontation with Hitlerism was in the arena of sports. At the 1936 Olympics in Berlin, African-American track star Jesse Owens had confounded Nazi racial theories by winning four gold medals and breaking or tying three world records. In 1938, in a sports event heavy with symbolism, black American boxer Joe Lewis knocked out German fighter Max Schmeling in the first round of their heavyweight championship fight in New York City. But while Americans might cheer these pinpricks at Hitler's pretensions, they shied away from any action that might threaten war.

Washington responded more uneasily to Japanese aggression against China, though initially with only verbal protests. Thanks to a long involvement in China by U.S. business interests and missionaries, Americans regarded that nation with special interest. Whereas religious groups looked upon China as a mission field ripe for harvest, government policy makers held to the old dream of China's boundless potential as an outlet for American goods. As U.S. corporations increasingly felt "the need of foreign markets," Secretary of State Hull wrote FDR in 1935, they would turn to Asia, one of "the great potential markets of the world." On such grounds the United States still adhered to its Open Door policy, guaranteeing all nations equal commercial access in China.

Japan's aggression in Manchuria and then against all China, threatened this Open Door principle. On a practical and immediate level, the closing of China to U.S. trade meant the loss of $100 million in annual cotton sales. Concern that Japanese goods, particularly textiles, might someday flood the world market sharpened Washington's uneasiness over Tokyo's aggressive policies. In the privacy of the cabinet, Roosevelt as early as 1934 speculated about the possibility of war with Japan.

Publicly, however, Washington (which was in no position militarily to do otherwise) reacted to Japan's moves in China with largely symbolic gestures. Both the Hoover and Roosevelt administrations refused to recognize Japan's puppet regime in Manchuria, and after the Japanese invasion of 1937, Washington extended modest loans to China and urged Americans to boycott Japanese silk. In 1938 the U.S. ambassador to Japan, Joseph Grew, protested Japan's violation of the

**Portents of Things to Come: Adolph Hitler, 1934**
*As troops and onlookers give the Nazi salute, a smiling Hitler arrives at a youth rally in Berlin.*

Open Door principle—a protest the Japanese quickly rejected. Apart from these cautious steps, the United States did little as Japan tightened its grip on China.

### 1938–1939: The Gathering Storm

The interlude of reduced tension that followed the Munich Pact proved brief. Chamberlain's "peace in our time" lasted precisely 5½ months. At 6:00 A.M. on March 15, 1939, Nazi troops crashed across the border into Czechoslovakia. By evening they had lofted the Nazi swastika flag in Prague. Within another five months came the Nazi-Soviet Pact, giving Hitler a green light to invade Poland.

In the United States, the worsening situation sharpened the debate over America's role. Some continued to urge the United States to keep free of the approaching conflict. Recalling how U.S. involvement in the 1914–1918 war had shattered the progressive reform movement and spawned a climate of reaction, the opponents of intervention warned that the same thing could happen again. The nation should concentrate on its own problems, they urged. As historian Carl Becker put it, "The place to save democracy is at home."

But opinion was shifting rapidly. As pacifist and neutralist sentiment weakened, the voices urging greater activism grew insistent. Warning of fascism's "cancerous spread," Lewis Mumford in 1938 issued "A Call to Arms" in the *New Republic* magazine. Archibald MacLeish, having earlier championed the cause of Spain, now urged decisive action against Hitlerism itself. MacLeish (appointed Librarian of Congress in 1939) coupled his calls for intervention with attacks on the writers and intellectuals of the 1920s who, he claimed, had undermined American patriotism and made it harder to rouse the nation against fascism.

After the fall of Czechoslovakia, a now aroused President Roosevelt called on Hitler and Mussolini to pledge not to invade thirty-one specific nations, which he listed. A jeering Hitler, reading FDR's message to the German Reichstag (legislative assembly) as his Nazi followers roared with laughter, proclaimed sarcastically: "Mr. President, I fully understand that the vastness of your nation and the immense wealth of your country allow you to feel responsible for . . . the whole world. . . . I, sir, am placed in a much more modest . . . sphere. . . ." In Rome Mussolini mocked Roosevelt's physical disability, joking that the president's paralysis must have reached his brain.

Roosevelt did more than send messages. In October 1938 he asked Congress for a $300 million military appropriation; in November he instructed the Army Air Corps to plan for an annual production of twenty thousand planes; in January 1939 he submitted to Congress a $1.3 billion defense budget. Hitler and Mussolini, he said, were "madmen" who "respect force and force alone."

### America and the Jewish Refugees

Once in power, the Nazis had quickly translated their hatred of Jews into official policy. In 1935 a series of measures denied German Jews citizenship and many legal rights. In 1938 the campaign grew more brutal, with the aim of forcing all Jews out of the country. The Nazis barred Jews from concerts or plays, expelled Jewish students from schools and universities, and required Jews to register all their property. Using as a pretext the assassination of a German official in Paris by a Jewish youth, Hitler levied a "fine" of $400 million on the entire Jewish population of Germany.

This remorseless campaign reached a crescendo of violence on November 9–10, 1938: *Kristallnacht*, or "the Night of Broken Glass." In a coordinated rampage carried out all over Germany and Austria, Nazi thugs vandalized Jewish homes, burned synagogues, and wrecked and looted thousands of Jewish-owned businesses. Not even Jewish hospitals, old people's homes, or children's boarding schools escaped the terror.

No longer could anyone mistake Hitler's malignant intent. Indeed, this repression foreshadowed the policy of extermination that would soon emerge as Hitler's "final solution" to the "Jewish problem." Jews, who had been leaving Germany in great numbers since 1933, now streamed out by the thousands, seeking whatever haven they could find. In 1933–1938 some sixty thousand came to the United States.

Distinguished scholars, musicians, writers, artists, and scientists were among the victims of fascism who found refuge in America. (Mostly Jewish, this group included some non-Jews who opposed Hitler, such as novelist Thomas Mann and theologian Paul Tillich.) The fleeing immigrants included pianist Rudolph Serkin, composer Béla Bartók, architect Walter Gropius, political theorist Hannah Arendt, future secretary of state Henry Kissinger, and scores more of equal distinction. It also comprised a brilliant cadre of physicists—Leo Szilard, James Franck, Edward Teller, Enrico Fermi—who would play a central role in building the atomic bomb. American scientific, cultural, and intellectual life of the twentieth century would have been much diminished had it not been for these talented refugees.

**Henry Kissinger (left) with His Brother Walter, Germany, c. 1934.**
*The future secretary of state was one of the lucky ones. His family escaped Nazi Germany in 1938.*

In general, however, the United States proved reluctant to grant sanctuary to the mass of Nazism's Jewish victims. The sixty thousand Jews admitted by the end of 1938 composed but a small ripple of the refugee tide, and Congress consistently rejected efforts to open the doors more widely by liberalizing the immigration law with its discriminatory quotas (see Chapter 24).

Nor did President Roosevelt prove much more receptive. To be sure, Roosevelt deplored Hitler's persecution of the Jews. After *Kristallnacht*, he told a news conference of his shock that "such things could occur in a twentieth-century civilization." And through FDR's efforts, a conference held at Evian, France, in 1938 set up an Inter-Governmental Committee on Refugees. But apart from this largely symbolic gesture, Roosevelt did little to translate his generalized sympathy for the Jews into concrete action.

Roosevelt's attitude mirrored that of the American populace as a whole. Although most Americans, according to the public-opinion polls, deplored the persecution of the Jews, only a minority favored admitting more refugees. When asked in 1938 if the immigration act should be amended to admit "a larger number of Jewish exiles from Germany," 75 percent responded no. When a bill was proposed in 1939 to admit twenty thousand German refugee children (most of whom would have been Jewish), 66 percent of Americans opposed even this humanitarian measure. Isolationist and anti-immigrant sentiments, perhaps intensified by latent anti-Semitism, severely limited America's response to the tragedy of European Jewry.

The implications of such attitudes became clear in June 1939 when the *St. Louis,* a vessel loaded with Jewish refugees, after being turned away from Cuba, asked permission to discharge its human cargo at Fort Lauderdale, Florida. Not only did immigration officials say no, but according to the *New York Times,* a Coast Guard cutter stood by "to prevent possible attempts by refugees to jump off and swim ashore." With the lights of America within view, the *St. Louis* turned eastward and sailed back across the Atlantic, carrying its stateless passengers to a fate that for many meant death at the hands of the Nazis.

## CONCLUSION

The depression and the New Deal affected America in profound and unpredictable ways. Individuals and families experienced severe strains. Some weakened; others gained strength from the ordeal. For workers, the later New Deal's prolabor stance stimulated a wave of unionizing activity, from steel mills and auto plants to southern textile mills and California agricultural fields. The depression brought a reaction against women workers, even as it prompted activist protest in black America. While writers and intellectuals of the early 1930s wrote capitalism's obituary, corporate America demonstrated its resilience. The mass media prospered by providing escapist fare, and businesses enticed consumers with streamlined design innovations and the probusiness themes woven through the New York World's Fair. As the 1930s wore on and powerful antidemocratic forces arose abroad, intellectuals, writers, painters, and photographers took a more positive view of America, rediscovering and affirming the richness of its regional cultures and folk traditions. By 1939 the world looked dark; it would soon look darker still.

## FOR FURTHER READING

Caroline Bird, *The Invisible Scar* (1966). Moving look at the depression's human and psychological toll.

Lizabeth Cohen, *Making a New Deal: Industrial Workers in Chicago, 1919–1939* (1990). A well-researched interpretive study of working-class culture and the union movement.

Robert Dallek, *Franklin D. Roosevelt and American Foreign Policy, 1932–1945* (1979). A fine study stressing FDR's responsiveness to domestic political currents.

Anthony Heilbut, *Exiled in Paradise: German Refugee Artists and Intellectuals in America from the 1930s to the Present* (1983). Good account of a refugee movement that profoundly influenced American culture.

Jeffrey Meikle, *Twentieth Century Limited: Industrial Design in America, 1925–1939* (1979). Fascinating study of the streamlining movement, with a good chapter on the New York World's Fair.

Arnold A. Offner, *American Appeasement: United States Foreign Policy and Germany, 1933–1938* (1969). A comprehensive and well-written study.

Susan Ware, *Holding Their Own: American Women in the 1930s* (1982). A good overview incorporating recent scholarly research.

Robert H. Zieger, *The CIO, 1935–1955* (1995). Major new study, especially valuable on the CIO's evolution and the tensions between the leadership and the rank-and-file.

# Waging Global War
## 1939–1945

**Let's Give Him Enough and On Time**
*By Norman Rockwell*

Americans who lived through World War II retained vivid images of the war's beginning and end. Even years later, most recalled their shock and indignation upon hearing the news on December 7, 1941, of the Japanese attack on the American naval base at Pearl Harbor, Hawaii, that brought the United States into the conflict. And they cherished their memories of the celebrations that greeted President Harry S Truman's announcement of the Japanese surrender on August 14, 1945.

Their forty-five months of global war finally over, Americans celebrated with exuberance. Virtually all Americans had considered the nation's participation in the war as just and necessary, and they now rejoiced in triumph. From New York to San Francisco, church bells pealed, car horns blew, confetti streamed out of office buildings, and millions poured into the streets waving flags and embracing strangers. "Any girl in downtown San Diego got kissed and thrown in Horton Plaza fountain," recalled Patricia Livermore. "I got thrown in ten times." After growing up in a small agricultural community in southern Indiana, Livermore had boarded a bus and headed, along with nearly 100,000 others in 1941, for a defense job in San Diego—reputed to be the "rip-roaringest coast boom town." She soon found work at Consolidated-Vultee, an aircraft manufacturer, where she worked six eight-hour days a week, shared a room with seven women in a company dormitory, and faced repeated insults from male workers who resented how efficiently she did "men's work." Still, Livermore felt herself to be an important contributor to the war effort, earned more money than she had dreamed possible, and developed a sense of self-respect and self-sufficiency that made her look back proudly on the war years.

For most Americans it was indeed "the good war." Despite the deaths of more than 300,000 Americans and the wounding of at least twice as many, U.S. losses paled beside the many millions of casualties suffered by Asian and European peoples. Moreover, the United States escaped the physical devastation that engulfed Europe and Asia. In fact, the war made the United States once again a land of opportunity and hope: it lifted the nation out of the depression, redistributed income, and transformed the nation into a genuinely middle-class society. It gave millions who had languished in the depression a second chance, and millions more a first chance. Women and most minorities especially savored the novel joys of independence and prosperity. At the same time, the war profoundly changed national institutions and behavior. It reshaped the economy as well as the role and power of government. It disrupted family relationships and traditional social values. And it ended American isolationism, pushing the United States to the forefront of world affairs. As the poet Archibald MacLeish noted in 1943, "This war is not a war only, but an end and a beginning—an end to things known and a beginning of things unknown. We have smelled the wind in the streets that changes weather. We know that whatever the world will be when the war ends, the world will be different."

This chapter focuses on five major questions:

♦ What measures were taken by FDR and the Congress to mobilize the nation for war?

♦ How did World War II affect the American economy?

♦ What were the major effects of World War II on American society, including minorities and women?

♦ What were the war goals of the Allied powers? How did these goals affect the strategies for waging war and the consequences for the postwar peace?

♦ Why did President Truman decide to drop the atomic bombs on Japan in 1945? What arguments have been raised to support and to condemn the decision?

# Into the Storm, 1939–1941

Twenty years after World War I ended, Germany and Japan unleashed aggression that drew the United States into a second global conflict. Initially relying on neutrality to keep America at peace, President Roosevelt resorted to economic intervention following the lightning German victories in western Europe in the spring of 1940. Then, as the fascist menace grew, FDR extended greater material assistance to the Allies, principally Great Britain. Although reluctant to ask a divided Congress to declare war against the Berlin-Rome-Tokyo Axis, FDR understood that his uncompromising conduct toward Germany and Japan could cause the United States to be "pushed," as he said, into a worldwide war. Japan's attack on the U.S. fleet at Pearl Harbor would provide the push.

## *Storm in Europe*

Adolf Hitler precipitated war by demanding that Poland return to Germany the city of Danzig (Gdansk), lost after World War I. When Poland refused, Nazi troops poured into Poland on September 1, 1939. Two days later, Britain and France, honoring commitments to Poland, declared war on Germany. Although FDR invoked the Neutrality Acts (see Chapter 26), he refused to ask Americans to be impartial. Even a neutral, he declared, "cannot be asked to close his mind or his conscience." Determined to avoid an Allied defeat, the president successfuly prodded Congress to revise the Neutrality Acts to allow the belligerents to purchase arms in the United States—if those nations paid cash and carried the arms away in their own ships. Roosevelt had tailored the "cash-and-carry" provision to fit a public mood that favored *both* aiding the Allies *and* staying out of the war.

A quiet lull followed the fall of Poland in September 1939 (a "phony war," some said). Suddenly, Hitler's army waged a *Blitzkrieg* (lightning war). First conquering Denmark and Norway in April 1940, Nazi *panzer* (armored) divisions then swept over Belgium, Holland, and Luxembourg in May, stormed into France, and sped toward the English Channel to capture retreating British and French forces. Narrowly escaping disaster, the British used almost every craft in England to evacuate most of its army and some French troops from the French coastal town of Dunkirk. German troops nevertheless quickly took Paris and forced France to surrender. Hitler dic-

**Balham High Road During the London Blitz**
*The massive German bombing of England prompted President Roosevelt to propose legislation that would permit him to lend or lease supplies to nations whose defense was vital to American security.*

## CHRONOLOGY

**1939** Germany invades Poland; World War II begins.

Soviet Union invades Poland.

**1940** Germany conquers the Netherlands, Belgium, France, Denmark, Norway, and Luxembourg.

Germany, Italy, and Japan sign the Tripartite Pact.

Selective Service Act.

Franklin Roosevelt elected to an unprecedented third term.

**1941** Lend-Lease Act.

Roosevelt establishes the Fair Employment Practices Commission (FEPC).

Germany invades the Soviet Union.

Japan attacks Pearl Harbor; the United States enters World War II.

War Powers Act.

**1942** Battles of Coral Sea and Midway halts Japanese offensive.

Internment of Japanese-Americans.

Revenue Act expands graduated income-tax system.

Allies invade North Africa (Operation Torch).

First successful atomic chain reaction.

CORE founded.

**1943** Soviet victory in Battle of Stalingrad.

Coal miners strike; Smith-Connally War Labor Disputes Act.

**1943** Detroit and Los Angeles race riots.

Allied invasion of Italy.

Big Three meet in Tehran.

**1944** Allied invasion of France (Operation Overlord).

GI Bill of Rights.

Roosevelt wins fourth term.

Battle of the Bulge.

**1945** Big Three meet in Yalta.

Battles of Iwo Jima and Okinawa.

Roosevelt dies; Harry S Truman becomes president.

Germany surrenders.

Truman, Churchill, and Stalin meet in Potsdam.

United States drops atomic bombs on Hiroshima and Nagasaki; Japan surrenders.

---

tated the armistice to the French in the same spot and very railway car in which Germany had surrendered in 1918.

Hitler now took aim at Great Britain. During the summer and fall of 1940, in the Battle of Britain, Hitler first sought to use the *Luftwaffe* (German air force) to soften England for a German invasion. Hitler then tried to terror-bomb Britain into submission. Round-the-clock aerial assaults wounded or killed thousands of civilians, destroyed Coventry, and reduced parts of London to rubble. Prime Minister Winston Churchill pleaded for more U.S. aid. Most Americans favored additional support for Britain. But a large and vocal isolationist minority opposed it as wasteful of materials needed for defense or as a ruse to draw Americans into a war not vital to U.S. interests.

### The Election of 1940

Not until the eve of the Democratic convention in July did Roosevelt reveal that, given the world crisis, he would consent to a "draft" from his party to run again. The Axis threat forced conservative Democrats to accept both FDR for a third term and the nomination of ultraliberal Henry Wallace as his running mate. It had an even greater impact on the Republicans, who passed over the anti-interventionist front-runners and nominated an all-out internationalist who championed greater aid to the British, Wendell Willkie of Indiana.

To overcome the no-third-term sentiment, Roosevelt played the role of a chief executive too busy with defense and diplomacy to engage in politics. He undercut GOP criticisms by appointing Republicans to his cabinet: Henry Stimson as secretary of war and Frank Knox as secretary of the navy. The president also signed two major bills that had bipartisan backing, dramatically increasing funds for rearmament and instituting the first peacetime draft in U.S. history. In September, with Willkie's public support, FDR engineered a "destroyers-for-bases" swap with England, sending fifty vintage ships to Britain in exchange for leases on

## The Election of 1940

| Candidates | Parties | Electoral Vote | Popular Vote | Percentage of Popular Vote |
|---|---|---|---|---|
| FRANKLIN D. ROOSEVELT | Democratic | 449 | 27,307,819 | 54.8 |
| Wendell L. Willkie | Republican | 82 | 22,321,018 | 44.8 |

British naval and air bases in the Western Hemisphere. Although FDR claimed the agreement was a way of keeping the country out of war, it infuriated isolationists.

The American isolationist camp in the 1930s had included members of both major parties and representatives from both the Right and Left (see Chapter 26). But in 1940 the arch-conservative America First Committee took the lead in mobilizing public opinion against Roosevelt and against the drift toward war. Largely financed by Henry Ford, the committee featured pacifist Charles Lindbergh as its most popular speaker. A majority of Americans, however, supported Roosevelt's effort to assist Great Britain while avoiding entry in the war. Reassured by the president's promise never to "send an American boy to fight in a European war," 55 percent of the voters chose to give Roosevelt an unprecedented third term.

### Neutrality

*Leading isolationist in the U.S. Senate took the view that, protected by the Atlantic Ocean, the nation could safely remain aloof from the conflict in Europe.*

### *From Isolation to Intervention*

Roosevelt now called upon the United States to be the "great arsenal of democracy." Because England did not have the money to purchase essential materials, he asked Congress to rescind the "cash" provision of the cash-and-carry legislation and to permit him to lend or lease supplies instead. While Roosevelt likened the plan to loaning a garden hose to a neighbor whose house was on fire, isolationist Senator Robert Taft compared it to "chewing gum": after a neighbor uses it, "you don't want it back." A large majority of Americans nonetheless favored lend-lease, and Congress approved the bill in March 1941. Shipments to England began at once, and after Hitler invaded the USSR in June, U.S. war supplies flowed to the Soviet Union. Despite American hostility toward communism, Roosevelt insisted that Nazi Germany was the chief danger to the United States. To defeat Hitler, FDR confided, "I would hold hands with the Devil."

Roosevelt next turned his sights on the German submarines that were destroying British ships more rapidly than they could be replaced. In April American ships began to assist the British in tracking German U-boats. Then the U.S. Navy started convoying British ships carrying lend-lease supplies, with orders to destroy enemy ships if necessary to protect the shipments. U.S. forces also occupied Greenland and Iceland to keep these strategic Danish islands out of Nazi hands.

In August Roosevelt met with Churchill aboard a warship off Newfoundland. They issued a document, the Atlantic Charter, that condemned international aggression, affirmed the right of national self-determination, and endorsed the principles of disarmament and collective security. The next month, after a German submarine fired at an American destroyer, Roosevelt authorized naval patrols to shoot on sight all Axis vessels operating in the western Atlantic. On October 31 a U-boat torpedoed and sank the *Reuben James,* killing 115 American sailors.

On a collision course with Germany, Roosevelt persuaded Congress in November to permit the arming of merchant ships and their entry into belligerent ports. Virtually nothing now remained of the neutrality legislation adopted by Congress in the 1930s to keep the United States out of war. Although not prepared for a major war, America was already fighting a limited one, and full-scale war seemed imminent.

## Toward Pearl Harbor

Hitler's triumphs in western Europe encouraged Japan to expand further into Asia. They also left the United States virtually alone to oppose Japan's expansion. Viewing Germany as the primary threat, the Roosevelt administration sought to apply just enough pressure to deter the Japanese without provoking Tokyo to war before the United States had built the "two-ocean navy" authorized by Congress in 1940. "It is terribly important for the control of the Atlantic for us to keep peace in the Pacific," Roosevelt told Harold Ickes in mid-1941. "I simply have not got enough navy to go around—and every episode in the Pacific means fewer ships in the Atlantic."

Both Japan and the United States hoped to avoid war, but neither would compromise. Japan's desire to create a Greater East Asia Co-Prosperity Sphere (an empire embracing much of China, Southeast Asia, and the western Pacific) matched America's insistence on the Open Door in China and status quo in the rest of Asia. The Japanese considered the U.S. demand that they give up their Asian conquests just a ploy to deny Japan's rise to world power. And the United States viewed Japan's talk of legitimate national aspirations a smoke screen to hide its aggression. Decades of "yellow peril" propaganda, moreover, had hardened American attitudes toward Japan. Widely depicted as bowlegged little people with buck teeth and thick spectacles, the Japanese appeared pushovers for the American navy. And with isolationists as virulently anti-Japanese as internationalists, no significant groups organized to prevent a war with Japan.

The two nations became locked in a deadly dance, matching step for step. Early in 1940, believing that economic coercion would force the Japanese out of China, the United States allowed its Treaty of Trade and Navigation (1911) with Japan to expire. In July Japan retaliated by initiating plans to implement its New Order in Asia. FDR then halted the sale of aviation gasoline and

scrap metal to Japan. Tokyo responded in September by occupying northern Indochina, a French colony, and signing the Tripartite Pact with Germany and Italy. Each Axis power pledged to help the others in the event of a U.S. attack. Washington answered by embargoing products vital to Japan.

Taking advantage of a defeated France, the Japanese overran the rest of Indochina in July 1941. FDR then froze all Japanese assets in the United States and clamped a total prohibition on trade with Japan. Tokyo had two choices: submit to the United States to gain a resumption of trade or conquer new lands to obtain vital resources. In October the expansionist General Hideki Tojo replaced the more conciliatory Prime Minister Fumimaro Konoye. Watching Japan's fuel meters drop toward empty, Tojo set the first week in December as a deadline for a preemptive attack if the United States did not yield.

By late November U.S. intelligence's deciphering of Japan's top diplomatic code alerted the Roosevelt administration that war was imminent. Negotiators made no concessions, however, during the eleventh-hour talks under way in Washington. "I have washed my hands of it," Secretary of State Hull told Secretary of War Stimson on November 27, "and it is now in the hands of you and Knox—the Army and the Navy." War warnings went out to all commanders in the Pacific that same day, advising that negotiations were deadlocked and that a Japanese attack was expected. But where? Most U.S. officials assumed that a Japanese offensive would continue southward, striking Malaya or the Philippines. But the Japanese gambled on a knockout punch; they hoped that a surprise raid on Pearl Harbor would destroy America's Pacific fleet and compel a Roosevelt preoccupied with Germany to seek accommodation with Japan.

On Sunday morning, December 7, 1941, Japanese dive-bombers and torpedo planes attacked Pearl Harbor on the Hawaiian island of Oahu. Pounding the harbor and nearby airfields, the Japanese sank or crippled nearly a score of warships, destroyed or damaged some 350 aircraft, killed more than 2,400 Americans, and wounded another 1,200. American forces suffered their most devastating loss in history. Some critics would later charge that Roosevelt knew the attack on Pearl Harbor was coming and deliberately left the fleet exposed in order to bring the United States into the war against Germany. That accusation of conspiracy is unsupported by documentary evidence. Roosevelt and

**Remember Pearl Harbor**
*At Minneapolis's Northern Pump Co., nightshift workers heralded the new year 1942 with a demonstration of national unity and determination. Rather than resorting to drafting workers or compelling them to work in certain areas, the government relied primarily on what FDR called "voluntary cooperation" to fill the labor shortages in war-related jobs.*

his advisers knew that war was close but did not expect an assault on Pearl Harbor. Neither did the U.S. military officials at Pearl Harbor, who took special precautions only against possible sabotage by the Japanese in Hawaii. American leaders, in part because of their own prejudices, underestimated the resourcefulness, skill, and daring of the Japanese. They simply did not believe that Japan would dare to attack an American stronghold nearly five thousand miles from home base. At the same time, Japanese leaders counted on a paralyzing blow to compel the Americans, unready for a two-ocean war, to compromise rather than fight against Japan. That miscalculation ensured Roosevelt an aroused and united nation to avenge an attack that he said "will live in infamy."

Even isolationists quickly rallied behind the war effort. On December 8, a unanimous Senate, and the House with only one dissenting vote—by Montana's Jeannette Rankin, who had also cast a nay vote against U.S. entry into WWI—declared war against Japan. Three days later Hitler declared war on the "half Judaized and the other half Negrified" American people, and Mussolini followed suit. The Congress quickly reciprocated, declaring that a state of war existed with both Germany and Italy. The United States faced a global war that it was not yet ready to fight.

## On the Defensive

In the aftermath of Pearl Harbor, U-boats wreaked havoc in the North Atlantic and prowled the Caribbean and the East Coast of the United States. Every twenty-four hours, five more Allied vessels went to the bottom. German submarines even bottled up the Chesapeake Bay for nearly six weeks. By the end of 1942, U-boat "wolf packs" had sunk more than a thousand Allied ships, offsetting the pace of American ship production. The United States was losing the Battle of the Atlantic.

Similarly, the war news from Europe and Africa was, as Roosevelt admitted, "all bad." Hitler had planted the swastika across an enormous swath of territory, from the outskirts of Moscow and Leningrad—a thousand miles deep into Russia—to the Pyrenees on the Spanish-French border, and from northern Norway to the Libyan desert. In the spring of 1942, the onrushing Germans inflicted more than 250,000 casualties on the Soviet army in the Crimea, and Hitler launched a powerful offensive to seize the Caucasian oil fields. In North Africa, the famed "Desert Fox," German General Erwin Rommel, and his *Afrika Korps* swept toward Cairo and the Suez Canal, the British oil lifeline. It seemed as if the Mediterranean would be an Axis sea and Hitler would be in India to greet Tojo marching across Asia even before the United States was ready to fight.

Japan followed its victory at Pearl Harbor by seizing Guam, Wake Island, and Hong Kong. In February 1942 the British suffered the loss of most of its Pacific fleet in the Battle of the Java Sea and saw Japan take Singapore on Malaya, the key to Southeast Asia. The following month the rubber-and-oil-rich Dutch East Indies fell, as did Burma in April. Then, having pushed the U.S. garrison on the Philippines first onto the Bataan peninsula and then onto the tiny island of Corregidor, Japan took more than eleven thousand American soldiers prisoner early in May. The land of the rising sun now controlled hundreds of islands in the Pacific and the entire eastern perimeter of the Asian mainland from Siberia to India.

## America Mobilizes for War

In December 1941 American armed forces numbered just 1.6 million and only 15 percent of industrial output went to war production. Pearl Harbor changed everything. Congress immediately passed a War Powers Act granting the president unprecedented authority to regulate American life. Volunteers and draftees swelled the armed forces: by war's end more than 15 million men and nearly 350,000 women had served. To direct this military engine, Roosevelt formed the Joint Chiefs of Staff, made up of representatives of the army, navy, and army air force. (Only a minor "corps" within the army as late as June 1941, the air force would grow more dramatically than any other branch of the service, achieve virtual autonomy, and play a vital role in combat strategy.) The changing nature of modern warfare also led to the creation of the Office of Strategic Services (OSS), forerunner of the Central Intelligence Agency. In 1942 those responsible for managing America's growing war machine moved into the world's largest building, the newly constructed Pentagon. And like the Pentagon, which was intended to house civilian agencies after the war, the far-reaching wartime domestic changes would also persist and significantly alter American attitudes, behavior, and institutions.

### *Organizing for Victory*

To organize the conversion of American industry to war production, Roosevelt created the War Production

Board (WPB). Its tasks included allocating scarce materials, limiting the production of civilian goods, and distributing contracts among manufacturers. Roosevelt also established a National War Labor Board (NWLB) with the authority to set wages and hours and to mediate disputes between management and labor; a War Manpower Commission (WMC) to supervise mobilization for the military and industry; and an Office of Price Administration (OPA) to ration scarce products and control inflation by setting prices on consumer items. Roosevelt in late 1942 persuaded James F. Byrnes to leave the Supreme Court to become his "assistant president" in charge of the domestic war effort, and in May 1943 he formally appointed Byrnes to head the new, all-powerful Office of War Mobilization (OWM).

"The Americans can't build planes," a Nazi commander had jeered, "only electric iceboxes and razor blades." But soon after February 1942, when the last civilian car came off an assembly line, the United States achieved a miracle of war production. A merry-go-round factory switched to fashioning gun mounts, a pinball-machine maker converted to armor-piercing shells, and overall, by late 1942, more than a third of the economy was committed to war production. More new industrial plants would be built in the first three years of the war than in the previous fifteen years of peace. Whole new industries would be created. To compensate for the loss of the nation's crude-rubber supply stemming from Japan's conquests in Southeast Asia, the government invested $700 million in some fifty new synthetic-rubber plants. By the end of the war, the United States, once the world's largest importer of crude rubber, had become the world's largest exporter of synthetic rubber.

The United States also became the world's greatest manufacturer of armaments, producing more war material than its Axis enemies combined. "To American production," Stalin would toast FDR and Churchill, "without which the war would have been lost." Indeed, the 300,000 military aircraft, 2.6 million machine guns, 6 million tons of bombs, and much more assembled by Americans would essentially win the war. In addition, the United States built more than 5,000 cargo ships and 86,000 warships. Henry J. Kaiser, who had supervised the construction of Boulder Dam, introduced prefabrication to cut the time needed to produce a Liberty-class merchant ship from six months in 1941 to less than two weeks in 1943. In 1945 Kaiser, dubbed "Sir Launchalot," and other shipbuilders completed a cargo ship a day.

Such breakneck production had its costs. The size and powers of the federal government swelled as defense spending zoomed from 9 percent of the GNP in 1940 to 46 percent in 1945, and the budget soared from $9 billion to $98 billion. Federal civilian employees mushroomed from 1.1 million to 3.8 million. The executive branch, directing the war effort, grew the most; and an alliance formed between the defense industry and the military. (A generation later, Americans would call these concentrations of power the imperial presidency and the military-industrial complex.) And because the government sought the greatest volume of war production in the shortest possible time, it encouraged corporate profits. "If you are going to try to go to war in a capitalist country," Secretary of War Stimson pointed out, "you have to let business make money out of the process or business won't work."

"Dr. New Deal," Roosevelt aptly put it in 1943, had given way to "Dr. Win the War." To encourage business to convert to war production and expand its capacity, the government guaranteed profits, provided generous tax write-offs and subsidies, and suspended antitrust prosecutions. Two-thirds of all war-production spending went to the hundred largest firms, greatly accelerating the trend toward economic concentration.

### A War Economy

The United States spent more than $320 billion ($250 million a day) to defeat the Axis—ten times more than the cost of World War I and nearly twice the amount that had been spent by the government since its founding. That spending ended the depression and stimulated an industrial boom that produced unprecedented prosperity for most Americans. It doubled U.S. industrial output and the GNP per capita, created 17 million new jobs, increased corporate after-tax profits 70 percent, and raised the real wages or purchasing power of industrial workers by 50 percent.

The federal government poured nearly $40 billion into the West, more than any other region, and four times as much as it had in the preceding decade, making the West an economic powerhouse. The West Coast became the center of the massive aircraft and shipbuilding industries. California alone secured more than 10 percent of all federal funds, and by 1945 nearly half of the personal income in that state was derived from the federal government.

A newly prospering South also contributed to the emergence of a dynamic Sunbelt. In an arc stretching from the coastal Southeast to the coastal Southwest, the billions spent by Uncle Sam on military bases and the needs of the armed forces meant hundreds of thousands of jobs in the textile, oil and natural gas, chemical, and aluminum industries, as well as in the shipyards of Norfolk, Virginia, Mobile, Alabama, and New Orleans, and the aircraft plants in Dallas–Fort Worth and Marietta, Georgia. The South's industrial capacity increased by 40 percent, and per capita income tripled. Boom times, moreover, led hundreds of thousands of sharecroppers and farm tenants to leave the land for better-paying industrial jobs. While the South's farm population decreased by 20 percent in the 1940s, its urban population grew 36 percent.

Full employment, longer workweeks, time-and-a-half pay for overtime, and the increased hiring of minorities, women, the elderly, and other underemployed groups brought a middle-class standard of living to millions of families. In California, the demand for workers in the shipyards and aircraft factories opened opportunities for thousands of Chinese-Americans who had previously been confined to menial jobs within their own ethnic communities. In San Diego, nearly four retirees in ten returned to work. Deafening factories hired the hearing-impaired, and aircraft plants employed dwarfs as inspectors because of their ability to crawl inside small spaces. The war years produced the only significant twentieth-century shift in the distribution of income toward greater equality. The earnings of the bottom fifth of all workers rose by 68 percent, and those of the middle class doubled. The richest 5 percent, conversely, saw their share of total disposable income drop from 23 to 17 percent.

In agriculture, large-scale commercial farmers particularly profited from the combination of a peak parity rate paid by the government, higher consumer prices, and increased productivity, thanks to improved fertilizers and more mechanization. At the same time, many sharecroppers, tenants, farm laborers, and small farmers left the land, reducing the agricultural population 17 percent. As the consolidation of many small farms into fewer large ones proceeded, commercial farming became dominated by corporations rather than individuals, and organized agriculture (later called agribusiness) took its seat in the council of power, alongside organized labor, big government, and big business.

Organized labor grew mightier as union membership leaped from 9 million in 1940 to 14.8 million in 1945 (35 percent of nonagricultural employment). This

**Producing for Victory**
*The 1942 dual launching of warships at Charleston, South Carolina, Navy Yard. By war's end the United States had built almost 100,000 new ships of one kind or another.*

C. T. 46—Dual Launching at Charleston, South Carolina Navy Yard

growth resulted from the huge increase in the workforce and the NWLB's "maintenance-of-membership" rule, which automatically enrolled new workers in unions and required workers to retain their union membership through the life of a contract. In return, unions agreed not to strike and to limit wage increases to 15 percent (the so-called Little Steel formula). Many unions, in lieu of higher pay, negotiated unprecedented fringe benefits for their members, including paid vacation time and health insurance and pension plans. Most of organized labor patriotically responded to the war, following the lead of CIO head Phillip Murray who exhorted his membership to "heed the call of the Commander in Chief and Work, Work, Work, PRODUCE, PRODUCE, PRODUCE."

Some unionists broke the no-strike pledge. Most were "wildcat strikes," not authorized by union officials, and of brief duration. All told, strikes amounted to less than one-tenth of 1 percent of total working time during the war and barely affected war production. In the most glaring exception, the iron-willed head of the United Mine Workers (UMW), John L. Lewis, led more than half a million coal-field workers out of the pits three times in 1943. Although the miners ultimately forced wage concessions from the government, their victory cost the union movement dearly. Public animosity toward labor rose, many states passed laws to limit union power, and over Roosevelt's

veto, Congress passed the Smith-Connally War Labor Disputes Act of 1943, which empowered the president to seize plants or mines if strikes interrupted war production.

Far more than strikes, inflation threatened the wartime economy, as increased spending power chased fewer available goods and services. Not until October 1942, however, did Congress enact the Anti-Inflation Act, giving the OPA authority to control wages, prices, and rents. Although never popular, the OPA did manage to curtail inflation: the 28 percent increase in the cost of living for 1940–1945 compared most favorably with the 62 percent rate of inflation for 1914–1918. As part of its effort to combat inflation, as well as to conserve scarce materials, the OPA also instituted a rationing program. Under the slogan "Use it up, wear it out, make it do or do without," the OPA rationed gasoline, coffee, sugar, butter, cheese, and meat. Americans endured "meatless Tuesdays" and cuffless trousers, ate sherbet instead of ice cream, and put up with imitation chocolate that tasted like soap and imitation soap that did not lather. Americans also planted 20 million victory gardens, served as air-raid wardens, and organized collection drives to recycle cooking grease and used paper and tires, while their children, known as "Uncle Sam's Scrappers" and "Tin-Can Colonels," scoured their neighborhoods for scrap metal and other valuable trash.

Buying war bonds also gave civilians a sense of involvement in the distant war and further limited inflation by decreasing consumer purchasing power. Responding to the Treasury Department's claim that war bonds "mean bullets in the bellies of Hitlers hordes!" schoolchildren bought war stamps to paste in an album until they had accumulated stamps worth $18.75, enough to buy a bond that was redeemable for $25 ten years later. Small investors bought about $40 billion in "E" bonds, mainly through payroll-deduction plans, while wealthier individuals and corporations purchased some $60 billion in bonds. This provided about half the money needed for the war, and Roosevelt sought to raise the rest by drastically increasing taxes. Although Congress refused the president much of what he sought, the Revenue Act of 1942 raised the tax rate from 60 percent to 94 percent for those in the highest income bracket and imposed income taxes on middle- and lower-income Americans for the first time, quadrupling the number who paid taxes. Beginning in 1943, the payroll-deduction system automatically withheld income taxes from wages and salaries. By 1945 the federal government took in nearly twenty times the tax revenue that it had in 1940.

### Science and the War

Recognizing the importance of wartime scientific and technological developments, Winston Churchill dubbed it "a wizard war." Even before the United States had entered the war, Roosevelt formed a committee to organize scientists for a weapons race against the Axis, and in 1941 he created the Office of Scientific Research and Development (OSRD) for the development of new ordnance and medicines. OSRD spent more than $1 billion to generate radar and sonar devices, rocket weapons, and proximity fuses. It advanced the development of jet aircraft and high-altitude bombsights, and its employment of scientists to devise methods for utilizing new weapons resulted in a brand-new field called operational analysis. OSRD also hastened the widespread use of DDT and other insecticides, contributed to improvements in blood-transfusion techniques, and helped produce copious supplies of "miracle drugs," notably penicillin, to combat infections, and synthetic drugs like Atabrine to substitute for scarce quinine. These advances, along with innovations like the Mobile Auxiliary Surgical Hospital (MASH), saved thousands of lives, halving the

World War I death rate of wounded soldiers who reached medical installations, and improved the health of the nation as well. Life expectancy rose by three years during the war, and infant mortality fell by more than a third. But in these endeavors, neither government nor industry evidenced much concern for the environment. While DDT helped control malaria and other insect-borne diseases, its toxicity and those of other insecticides was largely ignored. The production of synthetic rubber fouled the air with sulfur dioxide and carbon monoxide.

The project to develop an atomic bomb began in August 1939 when physicist Albert Einstein, a Jewish refugee from Hitler's Germany, warned Roosevelt that Nazi scientists were seeking to use atomic physics to construct a weapon of extraordinary destructiveness. The president promptly established an advisory committee on uranium and in late 1941 launched a massive Anglo-American secret program—the Soviets were excluded—to produce an atomic bomb. In 1942 the participating physicists, both Americans and Europeans, achieving a controlled atomic reaction, acquired the basic knowledge necessary to develop the bomb. In 1943–1944 the Manhattan Engineering District—the code name for the atomic project—stockpiled uranium and plutonium, and in 1945 the team assembled two bombs that could utilize those fissionable materials. By then the Manhattan Project had secretly employed more than 120,000 people and spent nearly $2 billion.

Just before dawn on July 16, 1945, a blinding fireball with "the brightness of several suns at midday" rose over the desert at Alamogordo, New Mexico. A huge, billowing mushroom cloud followed. With a force of twenty thousand tons of TNT, the blast shattered windows more than a hundred miles away. "A few people laughed, a few people cried," recalled J. Robert Oppenheimer, the Manhattan Project's scientific director. "Most people were silent. I remembered the line from the Hindu scripture, the Bhagavad-Gita: 'Now I am become Death, the destroyer of worlds.' " The atomic age had begun.

### Propaganda and Politics

People as well as science and machinery had to be mobilized for the global conflict. To sustain a spirit of unity and fan the fires of patriotism, the Roosevelt administration managed public opinion. The Office of Censorship, established in December 1941, examined letters going overseas and worked with publishers and broadcasters to suppress information that might hinder the war effort. A year passed before casualty and damage figures from Pearl Harbor were disclosed. Fearing that images of killed American servicemen would demoralize the public, photographs and newsreels showing American war dead were banned until 1943. Then, concerned that the public had become overconfident, the media was prompted to display pictures of American servicemen killed by the enemy. Lifting its ban on atrocity stories about Japan's treatment of American prisoners, government propaganda intensified hatred for Japan and prepared the public for the massive killing of Japanese civilians that was expected from the American air campaign against the home islands.

To shape public opinion and sell the faraway war to the American people, Roosevelt created the Office of War Information (OWI) in June 1942. The OWI employed more than four thousand artists, writers, and advertising specialists to explain the war and to counter enemy propaganda. The OWI depicted the war as a mortal struggle between good and evil and harped on the necessity of destroying, not merely defeating, the enemy.

Hollywood answered the OWI directive—"Will this help win the war?"—by highlighting the heroism and unity of the American forces, while inciting hatred of the enemy. Films about the war portrayed the Japanese, in particular, as treacherous and cruel, as the beast in the jungle, as "slant-eyed rats." Jukeboxes blared songs like "We're Gonna Have to Slap the Dirty Little Jap." Because the American home front was spared, U.S. propaganda stressed the enemy's "bestiality" in order to motivate support for the war effort. It also represented the war as a struggle to preserve the "American way of life," usually depicted in uplifting images of small-town, middle-class, white Americans enjoying a bountiful consumer society.

With the administration thus concentrated on winning the war on every front, Republican critics seized the initiative on domestic political matters. Full employment and higher wages undercut the Democrats' class appeal. And angered by wartime shortages and military losses abroad, many voters in 1942 shunned liberal candidates associated with FDR. In addition, many of the young, urban, working-class men and women of the Roosevelt coalition who had just gone into the armed services or migrated to a better job

**All Have a Role to Play**
*This poster by the famous artist Thomas Hart Benton emphasized the need for all Americans to do their part in winning the war—by buying war bonds and laboring in factories and fields, as well as by fighting in the armed forces and, not incidently, contributing their artistic talents.*

failed to meet residency requirements or to obtain absentee ballots. Consequently, the GOP gained nine seats in the Senate and forty-six in the House in 1942, and the conservative coalition of southern Democrats and Republicans now held the power to make or break all legislation. Resentful of the expansion of executive authority, and determined to preserve states' rights while curbing labor unions and welfare spending, the conservatives abolished the CCC and WPA and rebuffed all liberal proposals to extend the New Deal.

Despite the increasing influence of the conservative coalition in Congress, the war expanded government and executive power to an unprecedented degree. As never before, Washington managed the economy, shaped public opinion, determined research, and influenced people's daily lives.

But with more than $300 billion expended on the war effort, economic despondency gave way to buoyant prosperity. Unemployment ended. Millions entered the middle class. Big business prospered and grew bigger, more highly concentrated, and increasingly intertwined with the military. The "miracle of production" strengthened confidence in business leaders and in the government's fiscal role in maintaining a robust economy. The achievements of mobilization made the United States second to none in economic and military power and transformed Americans' expectations of what their federal government could be.

# War and American Society

Some 15 million Americans went to war. Most saw themselves as civilians in uniform and referred to themselves as GIs, after the "Government Issue" stamp on their gear, to emphasize the temporary nature of their military service. Like cartoonist Bill Mauldin's scruffy GI characters Willy and Joe, they griped about regimentation and were more interested in dry socks than in ideology. They knew little of the big strategies, and cared less. They fought because fighting was necessary and mostly sought small comforts and to stay alive. Reluctant warriors, they had few aims beyond returning to a familiar, secure United States.

But their war dragged on for almost four years, transforming them in the process. Millions who had never been far from home traveled to unfamiliar cities and remote lands, shedding their parochialism. Sharing tents and foxholes with Americans of different religions, ethnicities, and classes, their military stint acted as a "melting pot" experience that freed them of some prewar prejudices. Many of the thousands of gay men and lesbians who served in the armed forces (despite the military's efforts to exclude them) also found wartime liberating. Emancipated from traditional expectations and the close scrutiny of family and neighbors, and living in overwhelmingly all-male or all-female environments, allowed them to meet likeminded gay men and women and to express their sexual orientation. Some of those suspected of being gay were discharged as undesirables, sent to psychiatric hospitals, or imprisoned in so-called queer stockades. This led gays to think more about their right to equal treatment and opportunity, and in 1945 gay veterans established the Veteran's Benevolent Association, the first major gay organization in the United States. In countless ways, the war modified how GIs saw themselves, and others. It broadened personal horizons and sowed the seeds of a more tolerant and diverse national culture.

At the same time, physical misery, chronic exhaustion, and, especially, intense combat took a heavy toll, leaving lasting psychological as well as physical wounds. Both American and Japanese troops saw the other in racist images, as animals to be exterminated, and brutality became as much the rule as the exception. Both machine-gunned hostile flyers in parachutes; both tortured and killed prisoners; both mutilated enemy dead. In the fight against Germany, cruelties and atrocities also occurred, although on a lesser scale. A battalion of the 2nd Armored Division, calling itself "Roosevelt's Butchers," boasted that it shot all the SS soldiers it captured. Pilots laughed at the bodies they exploded out of trucks. Some became cynical about human life. Some languish in veterans' hospitals, still having nightmares about the war.

For most GIs, however, the wartime experience positively changed their sense of future possibilities. Many acquired skills in jobs that they had barely known existed. Under the Servicemen's Readjustment Act, or "GI Bill of Rights," enacted by Congress in June 1944, several million veterans who had been unable to afford a higher education before the war would enroll in college, the springboard for their entry into the growing middle class.

Returning GIs also found that America had changed as much as they had. "Home, the one really profound goal that obsesses every one of the Americans marching on foreign shores," wrote combat journalist Ernie Pyle, would never be the same again. Sweeping alterations in society challenged established values, redefined traditional relationships, and created new problems. Adjusting to this new world could be difficult, often painful, and for some impossible.

### *The New Mobility*

Nothing transformed the social topography more than the vast internal migration of an already mobile people. Along with the 15 million men who moved because of military service, as least as many Americans relocated to be near their husbands and fathers in the armed forces or to secure new economic opportunities, especially in the Pacific Coast states. Nearly a quarter of a million would find jobs in the shipyards of the Bay area and at least as many in the aircraft industry that arose in the orange groves of southern California. More than 100,000 worked in the Puget Sound shipyards and half as many in the nearby Boeing plants. Others flocked to the world's largest magnesium plant in Henderson, Nevada, to the huge Geneva Steel Works near Provo, Utah, and to the Rocky Mountain Arsenal and Remington Rand arms plant outside Denver. At least 6 million people left farms to work in urban areas, including several million southern blacks and whites. This mass uprooting of people from familiar settings made Americans both more cosmopolitan, and more lonely, alienated, and frustrated. Lifestyles became freewheeling as Americans moved far from their hometowns and their traditional values. Housing shortages left millions living in converted garages, trailer camps, even their own cars. Some workers in Seattle lived in chicken coops. And the swarms of migrants to Mobile, attracted by a new aluminum plant, two massive shipyards, an air base, and an army supply depot, transformed a sleepy fishing village into a symbol of urban disorder. There, and elsewhere, overcrowding along with wartime separations strained family and community life. High rates of divorce, mental illness, family violence, and juvenile delinquency reflected the disruptions caused in part by the lack of privacy, the sense of impermanence, the absence of familiar settings, and the competition for scarce facilities. Few boom communities had the resources to supply their suddenly swollen populations with needed transportation, recreation, and social services. Urban blight and conflicts between newcomers and old-timers accelerated.

### Education and Entertainment

The war-production boom that created both overcrowded communities and ghost towns played havoc with the nation's school systems. More than 350,000 teachers joined the armed services or took better-paying war work, leaving schools badly understaffed. Students, too, abandoned school in record numbers. High school enrollments sank as the full-time employment of teenagers rose from 900,000 in 1940 to 3 million in 1944.

The loss of students to war production and the armed services forced colleges to admit large numbers of women and to contract themselves out to the armed forces. Military training programs sent nearly a million servicemen to college to acquire skills in engineering, foreign languages, and the sciences. The military presence was all-pervasive. Harvard University awarded four military-training certificates for every academic degree it conferred, and the chancellor of one branch of the University of California announced that his school was "no longer an academic tent with military sideshows. It is a military tent with academic sideshows." Higher education became ever more dependent on the federal government, and most universities sought increased federal contracts and subsidies, despite their having to submit to greater government interference and regulation. The universities in the West themselves received some $100 billion from OSRD, more money than had been spent on scientific research by all the western universities since their founding.

The war profoundly affected American culture. The media, emphasizing mass production and targeting mass audiences as never before, emerged from the war more highly organized and with greater concentrations of power. Expenditures on books and theater entertainment doubled between 1941 and 1945. Between 60 million and 100 million Americans a week (in a population of 135 million) went to the movies, and the film industry reached its zenith in 1945–1946. Hollywood turned out a spate of war films that reinforced the image of Japanese as fiends, portrayed GIs as heroes, and intensified Americans' appetites for unconditional surrender. *Mission to Moscow* (1943) glorified Soviet heroism. But as the war dragged on, people tired of propaganda, and Hollywood reemphasized romance and nostalgia with such stars as Katherine Hepburn and Judy Garland.

Similarly, popular music early in the war featured patriotic themes. "Goodbye, Mama, I'm Off to Yokohama" became the first hit of 1942. As the war continued, themes of lost love and loneliness dominated lyrics. Numbers like "They're Either Too Young or Too Old" expressed the laments of women separated from the men they loved. So, too, did the dozens of "dream songs," in which love denied by the real world could be achieved only in a dream. By 1945 bitterness rather than melancholy pervaded the lyrics of best-selling records, and songs like "Saturday Night Is the Loneliest Night of the Week" revealed impatience for the war's end.

In bookstores, nonfiction ruled the roost. Few war novels were published, but Marion Hargrove's *See*

*Here, Private Hargrove,* a comic account of boot-camp experiences, and John Hersey's *A Bell for Adano,* the story of an Italian-American in the occupation of Sicily, became instant classics. Magazines, however, were the biggest sellers: every popular periodical increased its circulation. *Life, Look,* and *Time* satisfied Americans' hunger for battle reports and the prospects for peace. Wendell Willkie's *One World* (1943) became the fastest-selling title in publishing history to that time, with 1 million copies snapped up in two months. A euphoric vision of a world without military alliances and spheres of influence, this brief volume expressed hope that an international organization would extend peace and democracy through the postwar world. The Government Printing Office published Armed Services Editions, paperback reprints of classics and new re-

leases; and the nearly 350 million copies distributed free to soldiers speeded up the American acceptance of quality paperbacks, introduced in 1939 by the Pocket Book Company.

An avid interest in wartime news also spurred the major radio networks to increase their news programs from 4 percent to nearly 30 percent of broadcasting time, and enticed Americans to listen to the radio an average of $4^1/_2$ hours a day. Daytime radio serials, like those featuring Dick Tracy tracking down Axis spies, reached the height of their popularity, as did juvenile comic books, in which a platoon of new superheroes, including Captain America and Captain Marvel, saw action on the battlefield. Even Bugs Bunny donned a uniform to combat America's foes.

## Women and the Family

While military culture fostered a "pin-up" mentality toward women, emphasizing the differences between "femininity" and "masculinity," millions of American women donned pants, put their hair in bandannas, and went to work in defense plants. Reversing a decade of efforts to exclude women from the labor force, the federal government in 1942 urged women into war production. Songs like "We're the Janes Who Make the Planes" appealed to women to take up war work, and propaganda called upon them to "help save lives" and to "release able-bodied men for fighting." More than 6 million women entered the labor force during the war, increasing the number of employed women to 19 million. Less than a quarter of the labor force in 1940, women constituted well over a third of all workers in 1945.

The characteristics of female wage earners changed. Predominantly young and single before the war, 75 percent of the new women workers were married, 60 percent were over thirty-five, and more than 33 percent had children under the age of fourteen. They tended blast furnaces, operated cranes, greased locomotives, drove taxis, welded hulls, loaded shells, and worked in coke plants and rolling mills. On the Pacific Coast, more than one-third of all workers in aircraft and shipbuilding were women. "Rosie the Riveter," holding a pneumatic gun in arms bulging with muscle, became the symbol of the woman war worker: she was, in the words of a popular song, "making history working for victory."

Yet wartime also strengthened traditional convictions. Men fought. Women were neither drafted nor ex-

### Rosie the Riveter

*Memorialized in song and story, "Rosie the Riveter" symbolized the woman war workers who assumed jobs in heavy industry to take up the slack for the absent 15 million men in the armed services. Here a very real Rosie the Riveter is doing her job in April 1943 at the Baltimore manufacturing plant for Martin PMB Mariners. Although sometimes scorned by male workers, the dedication and efficiency of most female workers won them the praise of male plant supervisors.*

pected to volunteer. This allowed gender discrimination to flourish throughout the war. Women earned only about 65 percent of what men did for the same work. Government propaganda portrayed women's war work as only a temporary response to an emergency. "A woman is a substitute," claimed a War Department brochure, "like plastic instead of metal." Work was pictured as an extension of women's traditional roles as wives and mothers. A newspaperwoman wrote of the "deep satisfaction which a woman of today knows who has made a rubber boat which may save the life of her aviator husband, or helped fashion a bullet which may avenge her son!" Given the concern about jobs for veterans after the war, the public attitude toward women's employment changed little in World War II. In 1945 only 18 percent of the respondents in a poll approved of married women working.

Traditional notions of a woman's place, and the stigma attached to working mothers, also shaped government resistance to establishing child-care centers for women employed in defense. "A mother's primary duty is to her home and children," the Labor Department's Children's Bureau stated. "This duty is one she cannot lay aside, no matter what the emergency." New York Mayor Fiorello LaGuardia proclaimed that the worst mother was better than the best nursery. Funds for federal child-care centers covered fewer than 10 percent of defense workers' children, and the young suffered. Terms like *eight-hour orphans* and *latch-key children* described unsupervised children forced to fend for themselves. Fueling the fears of those who believed that the employment of women outside the home would cause the family to disintegrate, juvenile delinquency increased fivefold and the divorce rate zoomed from 16 per 100 marriages in 1940 to 27 per 100 in 1944.

Yet the impact of war on women and the family proved multifaceted and even contradictory. As the divorce rate soared, so did marriage rates and birthrates. Although some women remained content to roll bandages for the Red Cross, more than 300,000 women joined the armed forces and for the first time in American history were given regular military status and served in positions other than that of nurse. As WACs and WAVEs they replaced men in such noncombat jobs as mechanics and radio operators, and about a thousand women served as civilian pilots with the WASPs (Women's Airforce Service Pilots). When they left the service, moreover, they had the same rights and privileges as the male veterans.

Despite lingering notions of separate spheres, female workers gained unprecedented employment opportunities and public recognition. Although many eagerly gave up their jobs at the end of the war, just as many did not relish losing the income and self-esteem they had gained in contributing to the war effort. As Inez Sauer, who went to work for Boeing in Seattle, recalled,

> My mother warned me when I took the job that I would never be the same. She said, "You will never want to go back to being a housewife." She was right, it definitely did. At Boeing I found a freedom and an independence I had never known. After the war I could never go back to playing bridge again, being a clubwoman and listening to a lot of inanities when I knew there were things you could use your mind for. The war changed my life completely.

Overall, women gained a new sense of their potential. They proved their capabilities. The war widened their world and challenged sexist notions as nothing had before. It left its mark on a generation of women and, more vitally, on the sons and daughters they later raised.

## Racism and Pluralism

The war also opened doors of opportunity for many blacks. It heightened blacks' aspirations and widened cracks in the wall of white racist attitudes and policy.

Recognizing that the government needed the loyalty and labor of a united people, black leaders entered World War II determined to secure equal rights. In 1942 civil-rights spokesmen insisted that African-American support of the war hinged on America's commitment to racial justice. They called for a "Double V" campaign for victory over discrimination as well as over the Axis.

Membership in the NAACP multiplied nearly ten times, reaching half a million in 1945. The association pressed for anti–poll tax and antilynching legislation, decried discrimination in defense industries and in the armed services, and sought to end black disfranchisement. The campaign for voting rights gained momentum when the Supreme Court, in *Smith* v. *Allwright* (1944), ruled Texas's all-white primary unconstitutional. The decision eliminated a bar that had existed in eight southern states, although these states promptly resorted to other devices to minimize voting by blacks.

**Tuskegee Airmen**
*The pilots of the 99th Pursuit Squadron, the first African-American aerial fighting unit, trained at a field adjacent to Alabama's all-black Tuskegee Institute and became known as the "Tuskegee Airmen." They entered combat over North Africa in June 1943 and won much praise for their battles against the Luftwaffe. However, most blacks throughout the war were confined to noncombat service.*

A new civil-rights organization, the Congress of Racial Equality (CORE), founded in 1942, advanced the strategy of nonviolent resistance to challenge Jim Crow. Employing the same forms of direct action that Mohandas Gandhi used in his campaign for India's independence, CORE inspired interracial groups in other cities to begin experimenting with nonviolent direct action to end racial discrimination. Also during 1942, A. Philip Randolph, president of the Brotherhood of Sleeping Car Porters, labored to build his March-on-Washington Committee into an all-black mass protest movement that would engage in civil disobedience.

In 1941 Randolph had called for a "thundering march" of 100,000 blacks on Washington "to wake up and shock white America as it has never been shocked before." He warned Roosevelt that if the president did

not abolish discrimination in the armed services and the defense industry, African Americans would besiege Washington. FDR agreed to compromise.

In June 1941 Roosevelt issued Executive Order 8802, the first presidential directive on race since Reconstruction. It prohibited discriminatory employment practices by federal agencies and all unions and companies engaged in war-related work, and established the Fair Employment Practices Commission (FEPC) to enforce this policy. Although the FEPC lacked effective enforcement powers, booming war production and a labor supply depleted by the draft resulted in the employment of some 2 million African Americans in industry and 200,000 in the federal civil service. Between 1942 and 1945, the proportion of blacks in war-production work rose from 3 percent to 9 percent. Black membership in labor unions doubled to 1,250,000, and the number of skilled and semiskilled black workers tripled. Formerly mired in low-paying domestic and farm jobs, some 300,000 black women found work in factories and the civil service. "Hitler was the one that got us out of the white folks' kitchen," recalled one black women who went to work for Boeing in Seattle, a city whose black population rose from four thousand to forty thousand during the war. Overall, the average wage for African Americans increased from $457 to $1,976 a year, compared with a gain of $1,064 to $2,600 for whites.

About 1 million African Americans served in the armed forces. Wartime needs forced the military to end policies of excluding blacks from the marines and coast guard, restricting them to jobs as mess boys in the navy, and confining them to noncombatant units in the army. The all-black 761st Tank Battalion gained distinction fighting in Germany, and the 99th Pursuit Squadron won eighty Distinguished Flying Crosses for its combat against the *Luftwaffe* in Europe. In 1944 both the army and navy began experiments in integration in their training facilities, on ships, and on the battlefield. The great mass of blacks, however, served throughout the war in segregated service units commanded by white officers. Ironically, the Red Cross maintained separate black and white blood banks, even though a black physician, Dr. Charles Drew, had invented the process of storing blood plasma. The failure of military authorities to protect black servicemen off the post, and the use of white military police to keep blacks "in their place," sparked rioting on army bases. At least fifty black soldiers died in racial conflicts during the war. "I used to sing gospel songs until

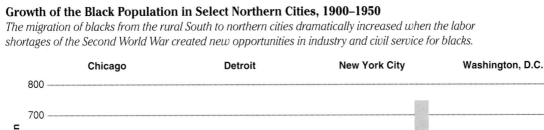

## Growth of the Black Population in Select Northern Cities, 1900–1950

*The migration of blacks from the rural South to northern cities dramatically increased when the labor shortages of the Second World War created new opportunities in industry and civil service for blacks.*

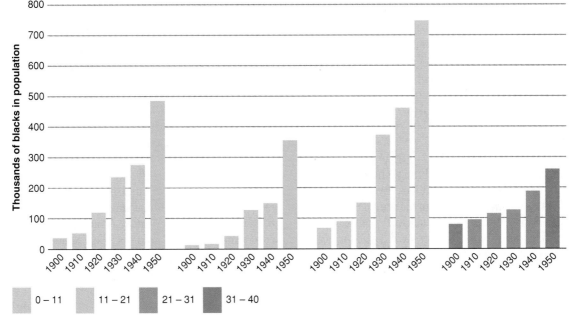

**Blacks as a Percentage of Total City Population**

I joined the Army," recalled blues-guitar great B. B. King, "then I sang the blues."

Violence within the military mirrored the growing racial tensions on the home front. As blacks protested against discrimination, many whites stiffened their resistance to raising blacks from their inferior economic and social positions. Numerous clashes occurred. The bloodiest race riot exploded in Detroit in June 1943. After thirty hours of racial beatings, shootings, burning, and looting, twenty-five African Americans and nine whites lay dead, more than seven hundred had been injured, and over $2 million of property had been destroyed. The fear of continued violence led to a greater emphasis on racial tolerance by liberal whites and to a reduction in the militancy of African-American leaders.

Yet the war brought significant changes that would eventually result in a successful drive for black civil rights. Over 700,000 blacks migrated from the South. This exodus turned a southern problem into a national concern. It created a new attitude of independence in blacks freed from the stifling constraints of caste. And greater educational and employment opportunities for the blacks who left the rural South engendered hopefulness. As the growing numbers of blacks in the industrial cities of the North began to vote, moreover, they held the balance of power in close elections. This prompted politicians in both major parties to extend greater recognition to blacks and to pay more attention to civil rights.

Blacks' optimism also flowed from the new prominence of the United States as a major power in a predominantly nonwhite world. Japanese propaganda appeals to the peoples of Asia and Latin America emphasized lynchings and race riots in the United States. For the first time, Americans had to confront the peril that white racism posed to their national security. In addition, the horrors of Nazi racism made Americans more sensitive to the harm caused by their own white-supremacist attitudes and practices. As a former governor of Alabama complained, Nazism has "wrecked the theories of the master race with which we were so contented so long."

Swedish economist Gunnar Myrdal, in his massive study of race problems, *An American Dilemma* (1944), concluded that "not since Reconstruction had there been more reason to anticipate fundamental changes in American race relations." Black veterans especially, with a new sense of self-esteem that came from participating in the victorious war effort, returned to civilian life with high expectations. Like the athlete Jackie Robinson, who as a young lieutenant had refused to take a seat at the rear of a segregated bus and had fought and won his subsequent court martial, blacks faced the postwar era resolved to gain all the rights enjoyed by whites.

## War and Diversity

Wartime winds of change also brought new opportunities and problems to other minorities. Twenty-five thousand Native Americans served in the armed forces during the war. Navajo "code talkers," for example, performed a valuable service for the U.S. military, confounding the Japanese by using the Navajo language to relay secret messages between U.S. command centers. "Were it not for the Navajos, the Marines would never have taken Iwo Jima," one Signal Corps officer declared. Another fifty thousand Indians left the reservation to work in defense industries, mainly on the West Coast. The Rosebud Reservation in South Dakota lost more than a quarter of its population to migration during the war. It was the first time most had lived in a non-Indian world, and the average income of Native American households tripled during the war. Such economic improvement encouraged many Indians to remain outside the reservation and to try and become assimilated into mainstream life. But formalized anti-Indian discrimination, particularly in smaller towns near reservations, such as Gallup, New Mexico, and Billings, Montana, forced a majority of Native Americans back to their reservations, which had suffered severely from budget cuts during the war. Prodded by those who coveted Indian lands, lawmakers demanded that Indians be taken off the backs of the taxpayers and "freed from the reservations" to make their own way like other Americans. To mobilize against the campaign to end all reservations and trust protections, Native Americans in 1944 organized the National Congress of American Indians.

To relieve labor shortages in agriculture, caused by conscription and the movement of rural workers to city factories, the government negotiated an agreement with Mexico in July 1942 to import *braceros,* or temporary workers. Classified as foreign laborers and not as immigrants, an estimated 200,000 *braceros,* half of them in California, received short-term contracts guaranteeing adequate wages, medical care, and decent living conditions. But farm owners frequently violated the terms of these contracts and also encouraged an influx of illegal migrants from Mexico desperate for employment. Unable to complain about their working conditions without risking arrest and deportation, hundreds of thousands of Mexicans became illegal aliens, exploited by agribusinesses. At the same time, tens of thousands of Chicanos left agricultural work for jobs in factories, shipbuilding yards, and steel mills. By 1943 about half a million Chicanos lived in Los Angeles County, 10 percent of the total population. In New Mexico nearly 20 percent of the Mexican American farm laborers escaped from rural poverty to urban jobs. Even as their occupational status and material conditions improved, most Mexican Americans remained in communities, called *colonias,* segregated from the larger society.

Much of the hostility toward Mexican Americans focused on young gang members who wore "zoot suits"—a fashion that originated in Harlem and emphasized long, broad-shouldered jackets and pleated trousers tightly pegged at the ankles. Known as *pachucos,* zoot-suited Mexican Americans aroused the ire of servicemen stationed in Los Angeles. After a series of minor clashes, bands of sailors from nearby bases and soldiers on leave in Los Angeles rampaged through the city in early June 1943, stripping *pachucos,* cutting their long hair, and beating them. Military authorities looked the other way. City police intervened only to arrest Mexican Americans. *Time* magazine described the violence as "the ugliest brand of mob action since the coolie race riots of the 1870s," yet Los Angeles officials praised the servicemen for having rioted, and the city council made the wearing of a zoot suit a misdemeanor. Nothing was done about the substandard housing, disease, and racism Hispanics had to endure, or the discrimination against them in the military. Still, 350,000 Mexican Americans served in the armed forces, volunteering in much higher numbers than that warranted by their percentage of the population and earning a disproportionate number of citations for distinguished service and seventeen Medals of Honor. And as did gay, black, and Native American veterans, returning Mexican-American GIs organized new groups, like the American GI Forum, to press for equal rights.

Despite the lip service paid to tolerance, American Jews also discovered that even a war against Nazism did not end traditional prejudices. Anti-Semitism persisted in restrictive covenants to prevent the sale of homes to Jews, in employment ads that stated that only Protestants or Catholics need apply, in rigid quota systems to limit the number of Jews in universities, and in "gentlemen's agreements" to exclude Jews from certain professions. Public-opinion polls throughout the war revealed that a significant minority of Americans blamed either Wall Street Jews or Jewish communists for the war and thought Hitler justified in his treatment of Jews.

When the Holocaust—the name later given to the Nazis' systematic effort to exterminate all European Jewry—became known in the United States early in 1942, most Americans viewed it as just a Jewish problem, of no concern to them. Most discounted the reports of Nazi genocide. Not until late November, with some 2.5 million Jews already dead, did the State Department admit knowledge of the massacres. Fourteen months then passed before Roosevelt established the War Refugee Board (WRB) to assist in the rescue and relocation of those condemned to the concentration camps. Even then, most Americans still did not believe that Hitler was systematically murdering European Jews; the anti-Semitic prejudices of State Department officials kept even the legal quota of Jewish immigrants from eastern Europe from entering the United States during the war; military officials scoffed at the notion that they could free and transport large numbers of Jews to safety; and Roosevelt and his advisers maintained that the liberation of the Jews depended solely on a speedy Allied victory. Thus, American planes flying over Auschwitz in southern Poland bombed factories, but left intact the gas chambers, crematoria, and railway lines leading to the death camp, in order, U.S. officials claimed, not to divert air power from more vital raids elsewhere and thereby prolong the war. "How could it be," historian David Wyman has asked, "that Government officials knew that a place existed where 2,000 helpless human beings could be killed in less than an hour, knew that this occurred over and over again, and yet did not feel driven to search for some way to wipe such a scourge from the earth?"

Although probably little could have been done to save most of Hitler's victims, the feeble U.S. response to Germany's "final solution" reflected American leaders' single-minded concentration on winning the war as quickly and with as little suffering to the United States as possible. U.S. inaction was also colored by Britain's wish to placate its Arab allies by keeping Jewish settlers out of Palestine, the congressional and public fears of an influx of destitute Jews into the United States, and the hesitancy of many American Jewish leaders to

**The Holocaust**
*Entering Germany in 1945, American and Russian soldiers discovered the horrors that the Nazis had perpetrated on European Jews and others. One anonymous American GI wrote of the ghastly concentration-camp scenes, "I've seen what wasn't ever meant for human eyes to see."*

press the matter and risk increasing anti-Semitism at home. Because of the State Department's obstruction of rescue efforts, the WRB saved the lives of only 200,000 Jews and 20,000 non-Jews. Six million other Jews, about 75 percent of the European Jewish population, were gassed, shot, and incinerated, as were several million gypsies, communists, homosexuals, Polish Catholics, and others deemed unfit to live in the Third Reich.

## *The Internment of Japanese Americans*

Only a tiny minority of Americans refused to support the war effort. While about 37,000 conscientious objectors to war, mostly Quakers and Mennonites, accepted noncombat service as medical corpsmen and as orderlies in public-health hospitals, some 5,500, primarily Jehovah's Witnesses, refused to serve in any way and were imprisoned. The worst abuse of civil liberties was the internment of about 37,000 first-generation Japanese immigrants (*Issei*) and nearly 75,000 native-born Japanese American citizens of the United States (*Nisei*) in relocation centers guarded by military police. The policy reflected forty years of anti-Japanese sentiment on the West Coast, rooted in racial prejudice and economic rivalry, as well as fear of Japanese sabotage after Pearl Harbor. Self-serving politicians and farmers who wanted Japanese American land had long decried the "yellow peril," and following the attack on Pearl Harbor, they whipped up the rage and fears of many white Californians. Numerous patriotic associations and newspapers clamored for action. The army general in charge of the Western Defense Command proclaimed, "A Jap is a Jap. It makes no difference whether he is an American citizen or not." In February 1942 Roosevelt gave in to the pressure and authorized the evacuation of all Japanese-Americans from the West Coast, despite the fact that not a single Japanese American had been apprehended for espionage or sedition and neither the FBI nor military intelligence had uncovered any evidence of disloyal behavior by Japanese Americans. Hawaii was the exception to this policy. Despite the large number of Hawaiians of Japanese ancestry, no internment policy was implemented there (see A Place in Time).

Forced to sell their lands and homes at whatever prices they could obtain, Japanese Americans were herded into barbed-wire-encircled detention camps in the most desolate areas of the West. Few Americans protested their incarceration. Stating that it would not question government claims of military necessity during time of war, the Supreme Court upheld the constitutionality of the evacuation in the *Korematsu* case (1944). By then the hysteria had subsided and the government had begun a program of gradual release, allowing some Nisei to attend college or take factory jobs (but not on the West Coast), and about eighteen thousand to serve in the military. The 442nd Regimental Combat Team, entirely Japanese-American, became the most decorated unit in the military. In 1982 a special government commission officially concluded in its report, *Personal Justice Denied,* that internment "was not justified by military necessity." It formally blamed the Roosevelt administration's action on "race prejudice, war hysteria, and a failure of political leadership" and apologized to Japanese Americans for "a grave injustice." In 1988 Congress voted to pay $20,000 compensation to each of the nearly 62,000 Japanese-American internees still alive.

**Mother in Jerome Camp,**
by Henry Sugimoto, 1943
*This painting expresses the loyalty and patriotism of the Japanese Americans detained in concentration camps, who, despite losing their liberty and most of their worldly goods, volunteered for combat duty and fought gallantly in the European theater.*

# The Battlefront, 1942–1944

The industrial and military might of the United States turned the tides of war. And diplomacy followed the fortunes of war. Allied unity gradually diminished as Germany and Japan weakened and as the United States, Britain, and the Soviet Union each sought wartime strategies and postwar arrangements best suited to its own national interest.

## *The Allied Drive in Europe*

After Pearl Harbor, British and American officials agreed to concentrate first on defeating Germany and then to smash Japan. But they differed on where to mount an attack. Stalin demanded a second front, an invasion of western Europe to relieve the pressure on the Soviet army, which faced 200 German divisions along a two-thousand-mile-front. Roosevelt concurred. But Churchill feared a premature landing on the continent would lead to a bloody stalemate like that of

## World War II in Europe and Africa

*The momentous German defeats at Stalingrad and in Tunisia early in 1943 marked the turning point in the war against the Axis. By 1945 the Allied conquest of Hitler's "thousand-year" Reich was imminent.*

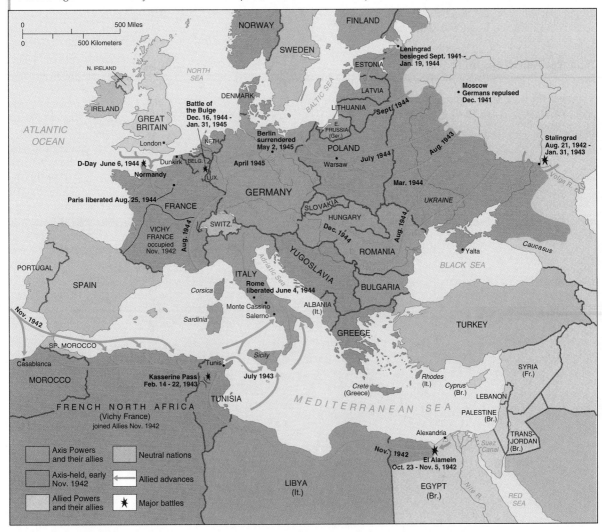

## Wartime Hawaii

*M*uch as the war came to the United States initially and most dramatically at Pearl Harbor, the outlines of an increasingly multicultural United States emerging from the Second World War could be seen first and most clearly in Hawaii. The nearly one million soldiers, sailors, and marines stopping in Hawaii on their way to the battlefront, as well as the more than one hundred thousand men and women who left the mainland to find war work on the islands, expected the Hollywood image of a simple Pacific paradise: blue sky, green sea, and white sand; palm trees and tropical sunsets; exotic women with flowers in their hair. They found instead a complex multiracial and multiethnic society. The experience would change them, as they in turn would change the islands.

Before December 7, 1941, few Americans knew where Pearl Harbor was or even that Hawaii was a part of their country, a colonial possession, a territory annexed by the U.S. government in 1898. Few realized that Honolulu, a tiny fishing village when Captain James Cook sailed by the difficult entrance to its harbor in 1778, had subsequently become the major maritime center of a kingdom, the seat of a territorial government, and a gritty port city that would serve as the major staging ground for the war to be waged in the Pacific. And few knew that this American outpost, as a result of successive waves of immigration beginning in the 1870s by Chinese, Portuguese, Japanese, and Filipinos, had a population in 1940 in which native Hawaiians and white Americans (called *haoles,* which in Hawaiian means "strangers") each constituted only 15 percent of the islands' inhabitants.

The approximately 160,000 Hawaiians of Japanese ancestry—including some 100,000 second-generation Japanese, or *Nisei,* who had been born in Hawaii and were therefore U.S. citizens—composed Hawaii's largest ethnic group, more than a third of the population. Japan's attack on Pearl Harbor immediately raised fears of sabotage or espionage by Hawaiians of Japanese descent. Rumors flew of arrow-shaped signs cut in the sugarcane fields to direct Japanese planes to military targets and of *Nisei* women waving kimonos to signal Japanese pilots. But in stark contrast to the

### Japanese-Americans Go to War

*The 442d Regimental Combat Team fought some of the bloodiest battles of the war.*

wholesale incarceration of the Japanese in the Pacific coast states, where the dangers of subversive activities were slight in comparison to Hawaii, official military and administrative policy in the islands was to maintain traditional interracial harmony throughout the war, and to treat all law-abiding inhabitants of Japanese ancestry justly and humanely. "This is America and we must do things the American way," announced Hawaii's military governor. "We must distinguish between loyalty and disloyalty among our people." There was no mass internment of the *Nisei* and *Issei* (those who emigrated from Japan) as there was on the mainland; and they committed no acts of sabotage.

For the *Issei,* loyalty to the United States had become an obligation, a matter of honor. To eliminate potential associations with the enemy, they destroyed old books, photographs of relatives, and brocaded *obi* (kimono sashes) and replaced portraits of the Japanese emperor with pictures of President Roosevelt. A burning desire to prove that they were true Americans prompted many of their Hawaiian-born children, often referred to as AJAS (Americans of Japanese ancestry), to become "superpatriots." AJAS contributed heavily to war-bond drives and sponsored their own "Bombs on Tokyo" campaign; they cleared areas for new military camps; and they converted the halls of Buddhist temples, Shinto shrines, and Japanese-language schools (all closed for the duration, and reopened after the war) into manufactories of bandages, knit socks, sweaters, and hospital gowns (the latter sewed for the Red Cross and Office of Civil Defense). Their newly expanded contact with other Hawaiians, including *haoles,* hastened their assimilation into the larger Hawaiian society. In addition, AJAS served in the military campaigns in the Pacific as interpreters—translating, interrogating, intercepting transmissions, and cracking enemy codes; and they fought in Europe with the all-*Nisei* 442d Regimental Combat Team, the most highly decorated organization in the U.S. Army. These contributions gave the Japanese in Hawaii, as it did other ethnic groups, a new sense of their worth and dignity. The war experience aroused expectations of equal opportunity and treatment, of full participation in island politics, of no longer accepting a subordinate status to *haoles.*

Additionally, the attitudes of many Hawaiians toward *haoles* changed as native islanders witnessed a large number of whites doing manual labor for the first time. Their view that whites would always hold superior positions in society—as bosses, plantation owners, business leaders, and politicians—was turned topsy-turvy by the flood of Caucasian mainland war workers, mostly from the fringes of respectability, and easily stereotyped as drunks and troublemakers. The hordes of white servicemen crowding into Honolulu's Hotel Street vice district for liquor, for tattoos, for posed pictures with hula girls in grass skirts, for three-dollar sex at the many brothels, and then for treatment at prophylaxis stations to ward off venereal diseases also tarnished traditional notions of white superiority. And the hundreds of white prostitutes (mostly from California) who brazenly operated in Honolulu further mocked the belief that those with white skin had a "natural" right to rule those of a darker hue.

Much as the influx of mainland whites changed the attitudes of the people of Hawaii, the Hawaiian experience, in turn, changed the outlooks of many of the servicemen and war workers stationed there. In Honolulu, they grew accustomed to women holding full-time jobs as a far higher percentage of women worked outside the home than was the case on the mainland. Given the scarcity of "available" white women, moreover, the men gradually became less uneasy about interracial dating, joking that "the longer you were on the island, the lighter [skinned] the girls became." And not a few GIS ultimately married women of Chinese, Filipino, or Hawaiian ancestry. Most of the whites who had come to Hawaii had never lived where whites did not constitute a majority and where *they* were the ones who were different. Most had never before encountered or conversed with those of African or Asian ancestry. Suddenly, they were in the midst of a mixture of ethnic and racial groups unmatched anywhere in the United States, in the midst of a society of people of diverse cultures working together for a common cause. So also were the nearly thirty thousand African-American servicemen and workers who arrived in the islands before the war's end. Having experienced nothing like the fluid and relaxed racial relations of Hawaii's multiethnic society, blacks discovered an alternative to the racist America they knew. Some chose never to go back to the mainland. Others returned home to the states to press for the rights and freedoms they had first tasted in Hawaii. In so many ways, wartime Hawaii, termed "the first strange place" by historians Beth Bailey and David Farber, would anticipate the "strangeness" of U.S. society today.

**Coming Home**
*Returning to Hawaii, a member of the "Fighting 442d" Regimental Combat Team is embraced by his grateful father.*

World War I, and he wanted the Americans to assist the British forces in North Africa trying to maintain England's control of the Suez Canal. Roosevelt gave in, to Stalin's dismay, and in November 1942 an Allied army commanded by U.S. General Dwight D. Eisenhower landed in Morocco and Algeria. They pressed eastward to entrap the German troops being pushed across Libya by British forces from Egypt. Eventually surrounded by the Allied armies, over a quarter of a million Germans surrendered in Tunisia in May 1943, despite Hitler's orders to fight to the death.

On the eastern front, a more lethal battle raged. Thousands died each day as huge Soviet and German armies slugged it out in the Battle of Stalingrad (August 1942–January 1943). There the Russian snow turned red with blood; in four months the Soviet Union and Germany each suffered more battle deaths than the United States did in the entire war. In early 1943 the Red Army emerged victorious: it saved Stalingrad, hung on at besieged Leningrad, and began an offensive across a thousand-mile-wide front.

### "Full Victory—Nothing Else!"

*Commander-in-Chief of the Allied Expeditionary Force General Dwight D. ("Ike") Eisenhower gives the order of the day to U.S. paratroopers in England on the eve of D-Day.*

Again Stalin pleaded for a second front, again Churchill objected, and again Roosevelt gave in and agreed to the British plan: an invasion of Sicily in the summer of 1943. In little more than a month the Allies seized Sicily, and then stormed ashore in Italy. Italian military officials deposed Mussolini and surrendered to the Allies on September 8. But as Allied forces moved up the Italian peninsula, German troops poured into Italy. Facing elite Nazi divisions in strong defensive positions, the Allies spent eight months inching their way 150 miles to Rome, and were still battling through the mud and snow of northern Italy when the war in Europe ended in 1945.

By the winter of 1943–1944, the Allies had turned the tide in the Atlantic, kept the Nazis in retreat along the eastern front, and begun round-the-clock bombardment of Germany. American science and industry, as much as the American navy, won the Battle of the Atlantic. Technical squads developed not only sophisticated radar and sonar systems but also better torpedoes and depth charges, and produced ever-increasing quantities of destroyers and aircraft. Britain's Royal Air Force by night and the U.S. Army Air Force by day rained thousands of tons of bombs on German cities. In raids on Hamburg in July 1943, Allied planes dropping incendiary bombs mixed with high explosives killed nearly 100,000 people and leveled the city, much as they had done earlier to Cologne and would do later to Dresden. Novelist Kurt Vonnegut, then an American prisoner of war in Dresden, described the day-after in his novel *Slaughterhouse Five* (1969): "The sky was black with smoke. The sun was an angry little pinhead. Dresden was like the moon now, nothing but minerals. The stones were hot. Everybody else in the neighborhood was dead."

Meanwhile, the Soviet offensive in 1943 reclaimed Russian cities and towns held by the Nazis. In July German and Soviet divisions fought the largest tank battle in history near the city of Kursk in the Ukraine. There the victorious Red Army gained the strategic offensive and drove the Germans out of Soviet territory by mid-1944. Advancing swiftly, they plunged into Poland in July and established a puppet government, took control of Romania

**Entry into Coutances,**
by Aaron Bohrad
*Breaking the lodgment in which the Germans had them contained in Normandy, General Omar Bradley's 1st Army and the U.S. 8th Air Force turned the German 7th Army's retreat into a rout by late July 1944.*

in late August and of Bulgaria two weeks later, and assisted communist guerrillas led by Josip Broz Tito in liberating Yugoslavia in October.

As the Soviets swept across eastern Europe, Allied forces in England prepared for Operation Overlord, the code name for the largest amphibious invasion in history. Early on the morning of June 6, 1944—D-Day— nearly 200,000 American, British, and Canadian troops, accompanied by 600 warships and more than 10,000 planes, stormed a sixty-mile stretch of the Normandy coast. Led by General Eisenhower, now Supreme Commander of the Allied Expeditionary Force in Western Europe, they established beachheads and gradually pushed inland. Within a month another million Allied troops and 170,000 vehicles came ashore, smashing through the German lines in late July. By summer's end they had secured most of Belgium and Luxembourg, and had driven the Germans almost entirely out of France.

Then, in the face of supply problems and stiffened German resistance, the Allied offensive ground to a halt. In mid-December, as the Allies regrouped for a full-scale assault on Germany, Hitler in a desperate gamble counterattacked with his last reserves against the American position in the forest of Ardennes in Belgium and Luxembourg. The Battle of the Bulge— named for the eighty-mile-long and fifty-mile-wide "bulge" that the German troops drove inside the American lines—raged for nearly a month. The bloodiest fight in its history, in which more than 70,000 Americans

died, were wounded, or were taken prisoner, ended with American forces on the banks of the Rhine, the German Army depleted, and the end of the European war in sight.

## *The War in the Pacific*

The day after the Philippines fell to Japan in mid-May 1942, the U.S. and Japanese fleets clashed in the Coral Sea off northeastern Australia. For the first time in history, a naval battle was fought entirely by planes from opposing aircraft carriers. Each side lost a carrier, but the Battle of the Coral Sea stopped the Japanese advance on Australia. The following month near Midway Island, in another huge battle waged entirely by carrier-based planes, the United States regained naval superiority in the central Pacific. Knowing the plans and location of the more powerful imperial armada, as a result of the U.S. Signal Corps deciphering of the Japanese secret naval code, American dive-bombers sank four aircraft carriers and destroyed several hundred planes. No longer an offensive threat, the Japanese now had to fight to try and hold what they had previously won.

In August 1942 the marines waded ashore at Guadalcanal in the Solomon Islands to begin the American counteroffensive. Facing fierce resistance—as well as an armada of tropical diseases—it would take U.S. forces six months to drive the Japanese off the island. By then, more than 25,000 Japanese troops had been

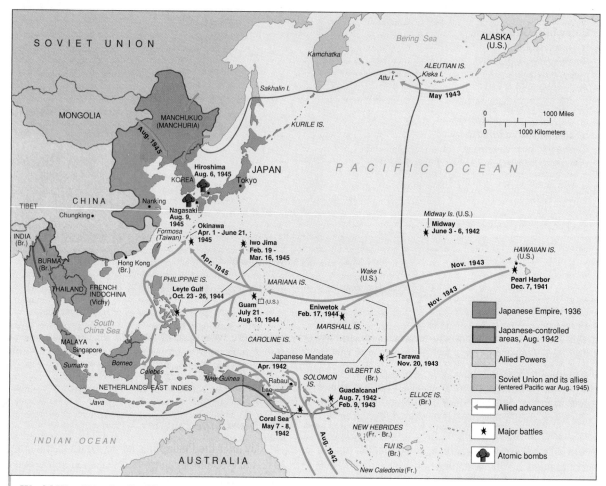

**World War II in the Pacific**

*American ships and planes stemmed the Japanese offensive at the Battles of the Coral Sea and Midway Island. Thereafter, the Japanese were on the defensive against American amphibious assaults and air strikes.*

killed, a gruesome preview of the island battles to come.

For the next two years American troops pursued a two-pronged advance toward Japan. Under General Douglas MacArthur, who had vowed "I shall return" to the Philippines, the army advanced north from Australia, "leapfrogging" from one strategic island to the next. A second force, led by Admiral Chester Nimitz, "island-hopped" across the central Pacific, seizing strategic bases on the Gilbert, Marshall, and Mariana Islands, and putting Tokyo within range of American B-29s, which could carry seven tons of bombs. By late 1944 U.S. planes were incinerating cities in Japan. Moreover, American victories at the battles of the Philippine Sea and Leyte Gulf in 1944 annihilated what

remained of imperial air and sea power, and gave American forces control of both the air and shipping lanes of the home islands. Confronted with certain defeat, factions within the Japanese military nevertheless vowed to keep fighting and stymied efforts by civilians in the government to negotiate a peace.

## The Grand Alliance

Two primary goals motivated Roosevelt's wartime strategy: the total defeat of the Axis at the least possible cost in American lives, and the establishment of a world order strong enough to preserve peace, open trade, and ensure national self-determination in the postwar era. Aware that only a common enemy fused the Grand

Alliance together, Roosevelt tried to promote harmony by concentrating on military victory and postponing divisive postwar matters.

But Churchill and Stalin had other goals. Britain wanted to create a balance of power in Europe and retain its imperial possessions. As Churchill said, he had "not become the King's First Minister to preside over the liquidation of the British Empire." The Soviet Union wanted a permanently weakened Germany and a sphere of influence in eastern Europe to protect itself against future attacks from the West. To hold together this fragile alliance, FDR relied on personal diplomacy to mediate conflicts.

The first president to travel by plane while in office, Roosevelt arrived in Casablanca, Morocco's main port, in January 1943 to confer with Churchill. They resolved to attack Italy before invading France and proclaimed that the war would continue until the Axis accepted "unconditional surrender." By so doing, they sought to reduce Soviet mistrust of the West, which had deepened because of the postponement of the second front. Ten months later, in Cairo, Roosevelt met with Churchill and Jiang Jieshi (Chiang Kai-shek), the anticommunist head of the Chinese government. To keep China in the war, FDR promised the return of Manchuria and Taiwan to China and a "free and independent Korea." From Cairo, FDR and Churchill continued on to Tehran, Iran's capital, to meet with Stalin. Here they set the invasion of France for June 1944, and agreed to divide Germany into zones of occupation and to impose reparations on the Reich. Most importantly to Roosevelt, Stalin pledged to enter the war against Japan after Hitler's defeat.

### The Election of 1944

As 1944 unfolded, Roosevelt turned his attention to politics. Increasing conservative strength led FDR to dump the liberal Henry A. Wallace from the ticket and accept Harry S Truman as his vice-presidential candidate. A moderate senator from Missouri, Truman was not unacceptable to any major faction in the party.

Dubbed "the new Missouri Compromise," this ticket restored a semblance of unity to the Democrats for the 1944 campaign.

The Republicans nominated moderate New York governor Thomas E. Dewey. Dewey had a difficult time criticizing the commander-in-chief without appearing unpatriotic, and increasing reports of victory in Europe and the Pacific neutralized GOP charges that Roosevelt had mismanaged the war. Despite his appearing haggard, the electorate sent FDR back to the White House for an unprecedented fourth term. But with just 53 percent of the popular vote, Roosevelt won by the narrowest margin since 1916, and the power of the conservative coalition in Congress was left intact. A weary, frail Roosevelt, already suffering from hypertension and heart disease, now directed his waning energies toward defeating the Axis and constructing an international peacekeeping system.

## Triumph and Tragedy, 1945

The spring and summer of 1945 brought stunning changes. In Europe the collapse of the Third Reich saw a new balance of power emerge. In Asia continued Japanese reluctance to surrender led to the use of the atomic bombs, the beginning of the nuclear age. And in the United States a new president, Harry Truman, presided over both the end of World War II and the start of the Cold War.

### The Yalta Conference

By the time Roosevelt, Churchill, and Stalin met in the Soviet city of Yalta in February 1945, the military situation favored the Soviet Union. The Red Army had overrun Poland, Romania, and Bulgaria; driven the Nazis out of Yugoslavia; penetrated Austria, Hungary, and Czechoslovakia; and was massed just fifty miles from Berlin. American forces, in contrast, were still recover-

**The Election of 1944**

| Candidates | Parties | Electoral Vote | Popular Vote | Percentage of Popular Vote |
|---|---|---|---|---|
| FRANKLIN D. ROOSEVELT | Democratic | 432 | 25,606,585 | 53.5 |
| Thomas E. Dewey | Republican | 99 | 22,014,745 | 46.0 |

**Yalta Conference, 1945**
*The palaces where Roosevelt, Churchill, Stalin, and their advisers gathered were still standing, but the rest of Yalta had been reduced to ruin during the German occupation.*

ing from the Battle of the Bulge and faced stiff resistance on the route to Japan. The Joint Chiefs of Staff, contemplating the awesome cost in American casualties of an invasion of Japan, insisted that Stalin's help was worth almost any price. And Stalin was in a position to make demands. The Soviet Union had suffered most in the war against Germany, it already dominated eastern Europe, and, knowing that the United States did not want to fight a prolonged war against Japan, Stalin had the luxury of deciding whether and when to enter the Pacific war.

The Yalta accords reflected these realities. Stalin again vowed to declare war on Japan "two or three months" after Germany's surrender, and in return Churchill and Roosevelt reneged on their arrangement with Jiang Jieshi (made in Cairo) and promised the Soviet Union concessions in Manchuria and the territories it had lost in the Russo-Japanese War (1904). Unable to reach agreement about the future of Germany, the Big Three delegated a final settlement of the reparations issue to a postwar commission, and left vague the matter of partitioning Germany and its eventual reunification. Similarly without specific provisions or timetables, the conference called for interim governments in eastern Europe "broadly representative of all democratic elements" and, ultimately, for freely elected permanent

governments. On the matter dearest to FDR's heart, the negotiators accepted a plan for a new international organization and agreed to convene a founding conference of the new United Nations in San Francisco in April 1945.

Stalin, however, proved adamant about the nature of the postwar Polish government. Twice in the twentieth century German troops had used Poland as a pathway for invading Russia. Stalin would not expose his land again, and after the Red Army had captured Warsaw in January 1945, he installed a procommunist regime—the Lublin Poles—and brutally subdued the anticommunist Poles. Refusing to recognize the Lublin government, Roosevelt and Churchill called for free, democratic elections. But at Yalta they sidestepped this crucial issue by accepting Stalin's vague pledge to include some prowesterners in the new Polish government and to allow elections "as soon as possible." Short of going to war against the Soviet Union while still battling Germany and Japan, FDR could only hope that Stalin would keep his word.

### Defeat and Death

As the Soviets prepared for their assault on Berlin, American troops in March 1945 crossed the Rhine and encircled the Ruhr Valley, Germany's industrial heartland. Churchill now proposed a rapid thrust to Berlin. But Eisenhower, with Roosevelt's backing, overruled Churchill. They saw no point in risking high casualties to rush to an area of Germany that had already been designated as the Soviet occupation zone. So Eisenhower advanced methodically along a broad front until the Americans met the Russians at the Elbe River at the end of April. By then the Red Army had taken Vienna and reached the suburbs of Berlin. On April 30, as Soviet troops approached his headquarters, Hitler committed suicide. Berlin fell to the Soviets on May 2, and on May 8 a new German government surrendered unconditionally.

Jubilant Americans celebrated Victory in Europe (V-E) Day, but the rejoicing subsided quickly as attention turned to the Pacific. During the last weeks of the war against Germany, moreover, Allied troops had liberated those still alive in the concentration and death camps, and Americans had been stunned by the newsreels of the gas chambers at Auschwitz, the human ovens at Dachau, the corpses stacked like cordwood at Belsen. They learned with horror of the systematic murder of 6 million Jews and 1 million others by the Nazis. And they mourned a death closer to home. On April 12 the exhausted president abruptly clutched his head, moaned of a "terrific headache," and fell unconscious. A cerebral hemorrhage ended his life. As the nation grieved, Roosevelt's unprepared successor assumed the burden of ending the war and dealing with the Soviet Union.

"I don't know whether you fellows ever had a load of hay or a bull fall on you," Harry S Truman told reporters on his first full day in office, "but last night the moon, the stars, and all the planets fell on me." An unpretentious politician, awed by his new responsibilities, Truman struggled to continue FDR's policies. But Roosevelt had made no effort to familiarize his vice president with the course of world affairs. Perhaps sensing his own inadequacies, Truman adopted a tough pose. In office less than two weeks, he lashed out at Soviet ambassador V. M. Molotov that the United States was tired of waiting for the Russians to carry out the Yalta agreement on free elections in Poland, and he threatened to cut off lend-lease aid if the Soviet Union did not cooperate. The Truman administration then reduced U.S. economic assistance to the Soviets and stalled on their request for a $1 billion reconstruction loan. Simultaneously, Stalin strengthened his grip on eastern Europe, ignoring the promises he had made at Yalta.

The United States would neither concede the Soviet sphere of influence in eastern Europe nor take steps to terminate it. Although Truman still sought Stalin's cooperation in establishing the United Nations and in defeating Japan, Soviet-American relations deteriorated. By June 1945, when the Allied countries succeeded in framing the United Nations Charter, hopes for a new international order had dimmed, and the United Nations emerged as a diplomatic battleground. Truman, Churchill, and Stalin met at Potsdam, Germany, from July 16 to August 2, to complete the postwar arrangements begun at Yalta. But the Allied leaders could barely agree even to demilitarize Germany and to punish Nazi war criminals. All the major divisive issues were postponed and left to the Council of Foreign Ministers to resolve later. Given the diplomatic impasse, only military power remained to determine the contours of the postwar world.

### The Atomic Bombs

Meanwhile, the war with Japan ground on. Early in 1945 an assault force of marines invaded Iwo Jima, 700 miles from Japan. There the marines battled thousands of Japanese soldiers hidden in tunnels and behind concrete bunkers and pillboxes. Securing the five-square-mile island would cost the marines 25,000 casualties. In June American troops waded ashore on Okinawa, 350 miles from Japan and a key staging area for the planned U.S. invasion of the Japanese home islands. Death and destruction engulfed Okinawa: after eighty-three days of fighting, some 80,000 civilians had suffered casualties and nearly the entire Japanese garrison of 110,000 men lay dead. Victory had cost the United States nearly 50,000 casualties, more than that at Normandy.

If the capture of these small islands had brought such bloodshed, officials wondered, what would the assault on the Japanese home islands be like? Although a naval blockade and daily bombing were exhausting Japan (on March 9–10 a fleet of B-29s dropped napalm- and magnesium-bombs on Tokyo, entirely burning to the ground sixteen square miles of the city and killing some 84,000), the Japanese Cabinet showed no readiness to surrender. In June the U.S. Joint Chiefs of Staff scheduled an invasion of Kyushu, the southernmost island of Japan, for November 1945, and, if necessary, of the main island of Honshu in 1946. Because Japan still had an army of more than 2 million, and at least twice as many civilians trained in the use of arms, the Joint Chiefs estimated that American casualties in the two campaigns might possibly exceed 1 million.

The successful detonation of an atomic blast at Alamogordo in mid-July, however, gave Truman an alternative to the planned invasions. While meeting with Stalin and Churchill in Potsdam, Truman, on July 25, ordered that an atomic bomb be used if Japan did not surrender before August 3. The next day he warned Japan to surrender unconditionally or face "prompt and utter destruction." Japan rejected the Potsdam Declaration on July 28. On August 6 a B-29 named the *Enola Gay* took off from the Marianas island of Tinian and dropped a uranium bomb on Hiroshima, plunging the city into what Japanese novelist Masuji Ibuse termed "a hell of unspeakable torments." The 300,000 degrees centigrade fireball incinerated houses and pulverized people. More than seventy thousand died in the searing flash of heat, and many of the seventy thousand injured later died from serious burns and radiation poisoning. On August 8 Stalin declared war on Japan and U.S. planes dropped leaflets on Japan warning that another bomb would soon be dropped if it did not immediately surrender. The next day, at high noon, a B-29, the *Bock's Car*, dropped a plutonium bomb, flattening Nagasaki, killing 35,000 and injuring more than 60,000. On August 14 Japan accepted the American terms of surrender, which implicitly permitted the emperor to

**Garden at Hiroshima,** by Standish Backus *A few years after the triumphant celebrations that came with the war's end, an American painter produced this powerful antiwar statement.*

retain his throne but subordinated him to the U.S. commander of the occupation forces. On the battleship *Missouri,* General MacArthur formally received the Japanese surrender on September 2, 1945. The war was over.

Many have questioned whether the war had to end with the United States resorting to atomic weapons. Some believe that racist American attitudes toward the Japanese motivated the decision to drop the bombs. As war correspondent Ernie Pyle wrote, "The Japanese are looked upon as something inhuman and squirmy—like some people feel about cockroaches or mice." Yet from the very beginnings of the Manhattan Project, those involved regarded Germany as the target; and considering the indiscriminate ferocity of the Allied bombings of Hamburg and Dresden that killed many tens of thousands of civilians, there is little reason to assume that the Allies would not have dropped atomic bombs on German cities had they been available. Others contend that demonstrating the bomb's terrible destructiveness on an uninhabited island would have moved Japan to surrender. We will never know for sure. American policy makers had rejected a demonstration bombing because the United States had an atomic arsenal of only two bombs, and they did not know whether the mechanism for detonating them in the air would work. Still others argue that Japan was

ready to surrender and that an invasion of the home islands was unnecessary. Again, we cannot know for sure. All that is certain is that as late as July 28, 1945, Japan refused a demand for surrender, and not until after the bombing of Hiroshima did the Japanese government discuss acceptance of the Potsdam Declaration.

The rapidly worsening relations between the United States and the USSR has led others to believe that Truman dropped the atomic bombs primarily to intimidate Stalin. By the late spring of 1945, the emerging conflict between the Americans and Soviets had led Truman to want an end to the Pacific war before Stalin could enter and then demand concessions. Truman also understood that using the awesome new bombs might give the United States leverage to oust the communists from eastern Europe. Referring to the Soviets, President Truman noted just before the atomic test at Alamogordo, "If it explodes, as I think it will, I'll certainly have a hammer on those boys." And Truman's new secretary of state, James Byrnes, thought that the bomb would "make Russia more manageable" and would "put us in a position to dictate our own terms at the end of the war."

The president and his advisers believed that the atomic bombs would strengthen their hand against the Soviets; but that was not the foremost reason the bombs were dropped. As throughout the war, American leaders in August 1945 relied on production and technology to win the war with the minimum loss of American life. Every new weapon was put to use; the concept of "total war" easily accommodated the bombing of masses of civilians; and the atomic bomb was one more item in an awesome arsenal that had already wreaked enormous destruction on the Axis. No responsible official counseled that the United States should accept the deaths of thousands of Americans while not using a weapon developed with 2 billion taxpayer dollars. Indeed, to the vast majority of Americans, the atomic bomb was, in Churchill's words, "a miracle of deliverance" that shortened the war and saved lives. "I was a 21-year-old second lieutenant leading a rifle platoon," wrote one veteran later:

> When the bombs dropped and news began to circulate that the invasion of Japan would not take place, that we would not be obliged to run up the beaches near Tokyo, assault-firing while being mortared and shelled, for all the fake manliness of our façades, we cried with relief and joy. We were going to live. We were going to grow up to adulthood after all.

that widened their public spheres and heightened their expectations. Fighting and winning the greatest war in history, moreover, was a vital coming-of-age experience for an entire generation that did much to give postwar American society a "can do" spirit.

The United States, Britain, and the Soviet Union each fought the war in a manner best suited to enlarge or preserve its sphere of influence in the world. To keep the Allies united and force the unconditional surrender of the Nazis and the Japanese, Roosevelt gave in to Churchill's pleas to delay a second front in Europe until 1944 and reluctantly accepted Soviet dominance in eastern Europe. Then to end the war in the Pacific as rapidly as possible, to minimize American losses, and perhaps to gain leverage over the Soviet Union, Truman ordered the dropping of atomic bombs on Japan. It ended the war, and the last remnants of American isolationism. Most dramatically, the United States had become the world's superpower; and the mass destruction of the war and the total defeat of the Axis had left in their wakes a new international conflict—the Cold War—that would see the United States play a role in global affairs that would have seemed inconceivable to most Americans just five years before.

## CONCLUSION

The atomic bombs ended the deadliest war in history. More than 14 million men under arms, including more than 300,000 Americans, had died. Another 25 million civilians had perished. Much of Asia and Europe was rubble. Although physically unscathed, the United States had changed profoundly. Mobilizing for war transformed the scope and authority of the federal government, vastly expanding presidential powers. It ended the unemployment of the depression and stimulated an unprecedented economic boom, enabling millions of Americans to become middle-class citizens; it tilted the national economic balance toward the South Atlantic, Gulf, and Pacific coasts; it accelerated trends toward bigness in business, agriculture, and labor; and it involved the military in the economy as never before. The war also catalyzed vital changes in racial and social relations—providing women and African Americans with broadened opportunities and new experiences

## FOR FURTHER READING

Michael C. C. Adams, *The Best War Ever* (1994). A wide-ranging interpretation of the experience of war on the homefront and abroad.

Beth Bailey and David Farber, *The First Strange Place: The Alchemy of Race and Sex in World War II Hawaii* (1992). A wide-ranging survey of the war's impact on Hawaiian society.

John Dower, *War Without Mercy* (1986). An insightful look at racism among the Americans and the Japanese.

Warren Kimball, *The Juggler: Franklin Roosevelt as Wartime Statesman* (1991). A study of the president's war aims and postwar vision.

Gerald D. Nash, *The American West Transformed: The Impact of the Second World War* (1985) and *World War II and the West: Reshaping the Economy* (1990). Two in-depth examinations of the changes in the West wrought by the war.

Holly Cowan Shulman, *The Voice of America* (1991). An in-depth account of America's wartime propaganda policies and programs.

David Wyman, *The Abandonment of the Jews* (1985). A critical assessment of the United States' role in the Holocaust.

# Cold War America
## 1945–1952

**McCarthyism and the Hollywood Witch Hunts**
*By Thomas Maitland Cleland*

On the day that Franklin Roosevelt died, the new president, Harry S Truman, hurried to console his predecessor's widow. "Is there anything *I* can do for you?" he inquired. "Is there anything *we* can do for you?" Eleanor Roosevelt responded, "for *you* are the one in trouble now." The self-educated, plainspoken Missourian who had met with FDR only twice during his eighty-two days as vice president suddenly faced a succession of crises at home and abroad. Truman had often quipped, "If you can't stand the heat, get out of the kitchen." And now the temperature in his White House shot up as domestic discord deepened, his relations with Congress and the Republicans worsened, and U.S.-Soviet relations crackled with nuclear tensions. Optimistic that there would not soon be another war, confident that the nation could solve any problems that arose, ordinary Americans rushed to grab a share of the good life. They married, had babies, made Dr. Benjamin Spock's child-care manual the hottest-selling title since the sales lists began in 1895, took instant pictures of their families on the first Polaroid cameras, bought cars with automatic transmissions, and moved to split-level houses in suburbs. But the peace of mind that they yearned for eluded them, for World War II had wrought decisive and disturbing changes in American society and around the globe. Disagreement over the postwar fate of Eastern Europe sparked a confrontation in which the Soviet Union and the United States each sought to reshape the postwar world to serve its own national interests. An uncompromising Truman squared off against an obsessive Stalin, each intensifying the insecurities of the other. A new form of international conflict—a Cold War, or state of mutual hostility short of direct armed confrontation—emerged, in which the two superpowers used all their resources to thwart the other's objectives.

The Cold War changed America. Abandoning its historic aloofness from events outside the Western Hemisphere, the United States plunged into a global struggle to contain the Soviet Union and stop communism. The nation that only a few years before had no military alliances, a small defense budget, and limited troops built a massive military establishment, signed mutual-defense pacts with some forty countries, directly intervened in the affairs of allies and enemies alike, erected military bases on every continent, and embarked on a seemingly limitless nuclear-arms race. To halt the expansion of communism, the United States dispatched its youth to fight in Korea, as their sons and younger brothers would later fight in Vietnam.

The Cold War's political and social effects proved equally decisive. Preoccupation with the Soviet threat discredited the Left. Conservatism, diminished during the New Deal, came roaring back, calling for the curtailment of Washington's role in domestic economic and social matters and the expansion of the federal government to lead the fight against communism at home and abroad. The anxieties provoked by fears of communist aggression and domestic subversion also spawned a second "Red Scare," reminiscent of 1919, with witch hunts undermining civil liberties. The reckless hurling of unfounded charges of disloyalty added McCarthyism to the American vocabulary. McCarthyism destroyed careers, silenced criticism, fueled intolerance, and discredited the Truman administration. Accordingly, the American people in 1952 turned to Dwight D. Eisenhower to deliver the calm stability for which they longed.

This chapter focuses on five major questions:

♦ How did the postwar policies of both the United States and the Soviet Union contribute to the beginnings of the Cold War?

♦ In what ways was the foreign policy of the Truman administration the right policy given the times and circumstances?

♦ What is the doctrine of containment, and how was it implemented from 1947 to 1950?

♦ What accounts for the demise of the New Deal spirit after World War II; and what effects did this have on the Truman presidency, especially his domestic program?

♦ What were the main domestic and international factors leading to the postwar Red Scare, and why did Americans react to it as they did?

## The Postwar Political Setting

In background and bearing, Harry Truman could not have been more unlike FDR. Born in 1884, the son of a Missouri horse and mule trader, Truman worked on his grandfather's farm until serving as an artillery captain in World War I. He then operated a men's clothing store in Kansas City and, as a member of "Boss" Tom Pendergast's Democratic party machine, dabbled in local politics. Elected to the Senate in 1934, the partisan Truman supported FDR without appearing to be a committed New Dealer. Thus, unopposed by any major group within the Democratic party, Truman won the vice-presidential nomination in 1944 as a safe alternative to the ultraliberal Henry A. Wallace and the strongly conservative James F. Byrnes.

**The Postwar Housing Shortage**
*Would-be homeowners and contractors waited in line for as long as three days for the building permits the FHA began issuing after V-J Day.*

After FDR's death, however, liberals voiced dismay at this "usurper" in the White House, as the feisty Truman made it clear that he would rule in his own way. He replaced New Dealers in the cabinet with moderates and gave key posts to political cronies, whom the press, recalling Harding's corrupt "Ohio Gang," dubbed the "Missouri Gang." Truman also displeased conservatives by urging Congress to adopt a twenty-one-point economic-reform program and by emphasizing his role as the champion of the common people against the special interests.

Deeply concerned for the public welfare, Truman displayed on his desk a motto of Mark Twain: "Always do right. This will gratify some people, and astonish the rest." He wanted government to help people, but without major changes to the status quo. "I don't want any experiments," he confided to an aide. "The American people have been through a lot of experiments and they want a rest." They would not get it, however, as Truman confronted assertive Republicans, a deeply divided Democratic party, and a Congress eager to reclaim the leadership that FDR had wrested from it.

### Demobilization and Reconversion

As soon as the war ended, GIs and civilians alike wanted those who had served in the military "home alive in '45." Troops demanding transport ships barraged Congress with threats of "no boats, no votes." On a single day in December 1945, sixty thousand postcards arrived at the White House with the message, "Bring the Boys Home by Christmas." Truman bowed to popular demand. American military strength dropped from 12 million men at war's end to just 1.5 million by 1948.

The psychological problems of readjustment faced by returning veterans were intensified by a soaring divorce rate, a drastic housing shortage, and, as war plants closed, the fear of mass unemployment and economic depression. Defense spending dropped from $76 billion in 1945 to under $20 billion in 1946, and more than a million defense jobs initially vanished. But late in 1946 an economic boom began. Reconversion—the transition from wartime production to the manufacturing of consumer goods—ushered in a quarter-century of ever-expanding prosperity.

This economic growth resulted, in part, from the Servicemen's Readjustment Act of 1944. Popularly called the GI Bill of Rights, it gave $14.5 billion to veterans to attend college, receive professional training, pur-

## CHRONOLOGY

**1945** Truman proposes twenty-one-point program of economic reforms.

**1946** Employment Act.

Winston Churchill delivers his "iron curtain" speech.

Coal miners' strike.

More than a million GIs enroll in college.

Inflation soars to more than 18 percent.

Republicans win control of Congress.

**1947** Truman Doctrine.

Truman orders Federal Employee Loyalty Program.

Taft-Hartley Act.

Marshall Plan proposed to aid Europe.

President's Committee on Civil Rights issues *To Secure These Rights*.

**1948** Communist coup in Czechoslovakia.

State of Israel founded.

Soviet Union begins blockade of Berlin; United States begins airlift.

Congress approves Marshall Plan.

Truman orders an end to segregation in the armed forces.

Communist leaders put on trial under the Smith Act.

Truman elected president.

**1949** North Atlantic Treaty Organization (NATO) established.

East and West Germany founded as separate nations.

Communist victory in China.

Soviet Union detonates an atomic bomb.

**1950** Truman authorizes building a hydrogen bomb.

Soviet spy ring at Los Alamos uncovered.

Alger Hiss convicted of perjury.

Joseph McCarthy launches anticommunist crusade.

Korean War begins.

Julius and Ethel Rosenberg arrested as atomic spies.

McCarran Internal Security Act.

Truman accepts NSC-68.

China enters the Korean War.

**1951** Douglas MacArthur dismissed from his Korean command.

Supreme Court upholds Smith Act.

Rosenbergs convicted of espionage.

**1952** First hydrogen bomb exploded.

Dwight D. Eisenhower elected president; Republicans win control of Congress.

chase homes, and start businesses. Designed to forestall a postwar depression and prevent a political extremism that feeds on the grievances of demobilized servicemen, as well as to honor and reward those who had served the country, the GI Bill helped transform the United States from a nation of renters to one of homeowners, and to more than triple the number of Americans graduating from college. By the time the program ended in 1956, 2.2 million veterans had gone to college, 3.5 million to technical school, and another 700,000 had received advanced agricultural instruction.

Another catalyst to economic expansion was a 1945 tax cut of $6 billion that enabled corporations to invest in new factories and equipment. Wartime savings and a pent-up demand for consumer goods boosted postwar growth and prosperity still more. The men and women who had endured the Great Depression and Second World War craved the "good life," and now they had $140 billion in bank accounts and wartime bonds with which to purchase it. As advertise-

ments promising "a Ford in your future" and an "all-electric kitchen of the future" furthered the rage to consume, sales of homes, cars, and appliances skyrocketed. Scores of new products—televisions, hi-fi sets, filter cigarettes, automatic transmissions, freezers, and air conditioners—soon defined the middle-class lifestyle. Wartime advances in science and technology, especially in electronics and plastics, also led to the development of whole new industries and radically boosted productivity in others.

The Bretton Woods Agreement (1944) of the wartime Allies played a key role in the successful reconversion of the American economy as well. In addition to valuing ("pegging") other currencies in relation to the dollar, Bretton Woods created the International Monetary Fund (IMF), the General Agreement on Tariffs and Trade (GATT), and the World Bank. Together, they solidified the United States' favorable position in international trade and finance. With many nations in ruin, American firms could import raw materials cheaply;

with little competition from other industrial countries, they could increase exports to record levels. Moreover, the wartime advances in science and technology that led to the development of new industries and a 35 percent jump in the productivity of American workers between 1945 and 1955 further bolstered the notion of the postwar years as the dawn of "the American century."

## *Truman's Troubles*

The hunger to enjoy the fruits of affluence left Americans with little appetite for more New Deal reforms. Truman's only major legislative accomplishment in the 79th Congress, the Employment Act of 1946, committed the federal government to ensuring economic growth and established the president's Council of Economic Advisers to help secure it. Congress, however, had gutted from the proposed bill both the goal of full employment and the enhanced executive powers to achieve that objective. Similarly, Congress passed an Indian Claims Commission Act, which minimized federal responsibilities toward Indians despite its stated purpose of correcting past violations of Indian rights. Congress also blocked Truman's requests for public housing, a higher minimum wage, social security expansion, a permanent Fair Employment Practices Commission, and anti–poll tax bill, federal aid to education, and government medical insurance.

Congressional hostility to wartime controls and inconsistent presidential leadership worsened the nation's chief economic problem: inflation. As consumer demand outran the supply of goods, intensifying the pressure on prices, the Office of Price Administration (OPA) continued to enforce price controls. But food producers, manufacturers, and retailers opposed controls strenuously; and while some consumers favored the OPA, others deplored it as a bothersome relic of the war. In June 1946 Congress both extended the OPA's life and deprived it of power. Truman vetoed the bill, effectively ending all price controls. The cost of food shot up immediately. Within a week the price of beef doubled. "PRICES SOAR, BUYERS SORE, STEERS JUMP OVER THE MOON," headlined the New York *Daily News*.

Congress then passed, and Truman signed, a second bill extending price controls in a very weakened form. Protesting any price controls, however, farmers and meat producers threatened to withhold food from the market. Acknowledging that "meatless voters are opposition voters," Truman lifted controls on food prices just before the 1946 midterm elections. The

**President Truman with Union Supporters**
*Following his veto of the Taft-Hartley bill and 1948 election victory, won, in large part, by the strong backing of organized labor, a smiling Truman dons a hard hat with copper miners in Butte, Montana.*

Democrats fared poorly anyway, and shortly after the elections Truman ended all price controls. By then the consumer price index had jumped nearly 25 percent since the end of the war.

The staggering increase in the cost of living, on top of the end of wartime bonuses and overtime, intensified organized labor's demand for higher wages. When employers resisted, 4.5 million workers went on strike in 1946. Soon after 750,000 steelworkers returned to their jobs following an eighty-day strike, 400,000 United Mine Workers shut down the coalfields for forty days. Eighteen days later, railway engineers and trainmen announced that they would totally shut down the nation's railroad system for the first time in history. Truman exploded. "If you think I'm going to sit here and let you tie up this whole country," he shouted at the heads of the two unions, "you're crazy as hell." In May he went before Congress to ask for authority to draft workers who struck vital industries. Before he could finish his speech, the brotherhoods gave in. Still, his threat alienated most labor leaders.

By autumn 1946, having antagonized virtually every major interest group, Truman appeared nearly unable to govern. Less than a third of those polled approved of his performance. "To err is Truman," some gibed. One commentator suggested that the Democrats nominate Hollywood humorist W. C. Fields for president: "If we're going to have a comedian in the White House, let's have a good one." Summing up the public discontent with inflation, strikes, and shortages, the Republicans asked, "Had enough?" In the 1946 elections they captured twenty-five governorships and, for the first time since 1928, won control of Congress.

# Anticommunism and Containment

By late 1946 the simmering antagonisms between Moscow and Washington had come to a boil. The U.S. and USSR abandoned their wartime alliance of convenience and struggled for advantage in the power vacuum left by the defeat of Germany and Japan, the exhaustion and bankruptcy of Western Europe, and the crumbling of colonial empires in Asia and Africa. Misperception and misunderstanding mounted as the two powers sought the upper hand, each feeding the other's fears and setting the stage for a dangerous conflict.

## *Confrontation and Polarization*

The destiny of Eastern Europe, especially Poland, stood at the heart of U.S.-USSR strife. Wanting to end the Soviet Union's vulnerability to invasions from the West, Stalin insisted on a buffer of nations friendly to Russia along its western flank, as well as a demilitarized and deindustrialized Germany. He considered a Soviet sphere of influence in Eastern Europe essential to Russian security, a just reward for bearing the brunt of the war against Germany, and no different than the American spheres of influence in Western Europe, Japan, and Latin America. Stalin also believed that Roosevelt and Churchill at Yalta had implicitly accepted a Soviet zone in Eastern Europe.

With the 10-million-strong Red Army occupying half of Europe at the war's end, Stalin installed pro-Soviet puppet governments in Bulgaria and Romania, while other communist regimes came to power in Albania and Yugoslavia. Ignoring the Yalta Declaration of Liberated Europe, Stalin also barred free elections in Poland and brutally suppressed the democratic parties there. Poland, he said, was "not only a question of honor for Russia, but one of life and death."

Stalin's insistence on dominance in Eastern Europe collided with Truman's unwillingness to concede Soviet supremacy beyond Russia's borders. What Stalin saw as critical to Russian security, Truman viewed as a violation of national self-determination, a betrayal of democracy, and a cover for communist aggression. His administration resolved to be tough in dealing with Moscow. It did so, in part, because Truman and his advisers believed that the appeasement of dictators only fed their appetites for expansion. It did so, as well, because those in Truman's inner circle considered that traditional balance-of-power politics and spheres of influence had precipitated both world wars, and that only a new world order maintained by the United Nations could guarantee peace.

In addition, Truman thought that accepting the "enforced sovietization" of Eastern Europe would betray American war aims and condemn nations rescued from Hitler's tyranny to yet another totalitarian dictatorship. He also worried that a Soviet stranglehold on Eastern Europe would hurt American businesses desiring access to raw materials there or wanting to sell their goods to East European countries. And Truman understood that the Democratic party would invite political disaster if he reneged on the Yalta agreements. The Democrats counted on winning most of the votes of the 6 million Polish-Americans and millions of other Americans of Eastern European origin, who remained keenly interested in the fates of their homelands. Not appearing "soft on communism" was a political necessity.

Combativeness fit the temperament of the feisty Truman. Eager to prove that he was in command, the president matched Stalin's refusal to hold free elections in Poland with his own insistence on Polish self-determination and democracy. Encouraged by America's monopoly of atomic bombs and its undisputed position as the world's economic superpower, the president hoped that the United States could control the terms of postwar settlements.

## *The Cold War Begins*

Truman's assertiveness inflamed Stalin's mistrust of the West and deepened the Soviets' obsession with their own security. Stalin stepped up his confiscation of materials and factories from occupied territories and forced his satellite nations to close their doors to American trade and influence. In a February 1946 speech that Washington considered a "declaration of World War III," Stalin asserted that there could be no lasting peace with capitalism and vowed to overcome the American lead in weaponry.

Two weeks later, a long telegram from George F. Kennan, an American diplomat in Moscow, arrived in

**A Cold War Confection**
*Celebrating the first public American atom-bomb tests, con-
ducted on the Bikini Atoll in 1946, navy admirals Blandy and
Lowery, assisted by Mrs. Blandy, slice an "atomic cake" in
the Pentagon.*

Fleet to the Black Sea in the spring of 1946 and threatened to send in American combat troops unless Stalin
withdrew Soviet soldiers from oil-rich Iran. In June he
submitted an atomic-energy control plan to the United
Nations that required the Soviet Union to stop all work
on nuclear weapons and to submit to U.N. inspections
before the United States would destroy its own atomic
arsenal. As expected, the Soviets rejected the American
proposal and offered an alternative plan equally unacceptable to the United States. With mutual hostility escalating, the Soviets and Americans rushed to develop
their own doomsday weapons. In 1946 Congress established the Atomic Energy Commission (AEC) to control
nuclear development and declared that the utilization
of fissionable materials should be for civilian purposes
"so far as practicable." From the outset, however, at
least 90 percent of the AEC's effort focused on weapons.

Thus, less than a year after American and Soviet soldiers had jubilantly met at the Elbe River to celebrate
Hitler's defeat, the Cold War had begun. It would be
waged by economic pressure, nuclear intimidation,
propaganda, and subversion rather than by direct
U.S.–Soviet military confrontation. It would affect
American life as decisively as any military engagement
that the nation had fought.

### European Crisis, American Commitment

On February 21, 1947, the British officially informed
the United States that they could no longer afford to
assist Greece and Turkey in their struggles against
communist-supplied guerilla insurgencies and Soviet
pressure for access to the Mediterranean. A stricken
Britain asked the United States to bear the costs of
thwarting communism in the eastern Mediterranean.
The harsh European winter, the most severe in memory, intensified the sense of urgency in Washington. The
economies of Western Europe had come to a standstill.
Famine and tuberculosis plagued the Continent. European colonies in Africa and Asia were in revolt. Cigarettes and candy bars circulated as currency in Germany, and the communist parties in France and Italy
appeared on the verge of toppling democratic coalition
governments. Truman resolved to meet the challenge.

The president first had to build support for a radical
departure from the American tradition of avoiding entangling alliances. In a tense White House on February
27, the new secretary of state, former army chief of staff
George C. Marshall, presented the case for aid to
Greece and Turkey. Congressional leaders balked, more
concerned about inflation at home than civil war in

Washington. Kennan described Soviet expansionism as
moving "inexorably along a prescribed path, like a toy
automobile wound up and headed in a given direction,
stopping only when it meets some unanswerable
force." Therefore, Kennan concluded, U.S. policy must
be the "long-term, patient but firm and vigilant containment of Russian expansive tendencies." The idea
that only strong, sustained U.S. resistance could "contain" Soviet expansionism suited the mood of Truman,
who a month earlier had insisted that the time had
come "to stop babying the Soviets" and "to get tough
with Russia." That the United States could block Soviet
aggression by applying firm diplomatic, economic, and
military counterpressure also suited the mood of Republican leaders who insisted on "no compromise"
with the USSR. "Containment" quickly became Washington gospel.

In early March 1946 Truman accompanied Winston
Churchill to Westminster College in Missouri, where
the former British prime minister delivered a speech
warning of a new threat to the democracies, this time
from Moscow. Stalin, he said, had drawn an iron curtain across the eastern half of Europe, and the threat of
further Soviet aggression required an alliance of the
English-speaking peoples and the maintenance of an
Anglo-American monopoly of atomic weapons.

Convinced that American firmness could check Soviet expansionism, Truman dispatched part of the Sixth

Greece. But Dean Acheson, the newly appointed under-secretary of state, seized the moment. He defined the issue not as one of assisting the Greek oligarchy and the Turkish military regime but rather as a universal struggle of freedom against tyranny. "Like apples in a barrel infected by the corruption of one rotten one," he warned, the fall of Greece or Turkey would open Asia, Western Europe, and the oil fields of the Middle East to the Red menace. "The Soviet Union [is] playing one of the greatest gambles in history," Acheson concluded. "We and we alone are in a position to break up that play." Shaken, the congressional leaders agreed to support the administration's request if the president could "scare hell out of the country."

Truman could and did. On March 12, 1947, addressing a joint session of Congress, he asked for $400 million in military assistance to Greece and Turkey. In a world endangered by the spreading tentacles of communism, Truman said, the United States must support free peoples everywhere "resisting attempted subjugation by armed minorities or by outside pressures." If we fail to act now, the president concluded, "we may endanger the peace of the world—and we shall surely endanger the welfare of our own nation." Called the Truman Doctrine—and meant to be as comprehensive as the Monroe Doctrine's "Keep Out" sign posted on the Western Hemisphere—the president's declaration committed Americans to an open-ended global struggle against communism. Endorsed by the Republican-controlled Congress, the Truman Doctrine laid the foundation for American Cold War policy for much of the next four decades.

In June the administration proposed massive U.S. assistance for European recovery. Advocated by the secretary of state, and thus called the Marshall Plan, it was to be another weapon in the arsenal against the spread of communism. With food in Western Europe scarce, the president wanted to end the economic devastation that could readily be exploited by communists. Ostensibly to help the hungry and homeless of all European nations, Truman calculated, correctly, that the USSR and its satellites would reject American aid because of the conditions and controls linked to it. The administration also accurately foresaw that Western European economic recovery would expand sales of American goods abroad and promote prosperity in the United States. Although denounced by the Left as a "Martial Plan" and by isolationist voices on the Right as a "Share-the-American-Wealth Plan," the Marshall Plan fulfilled its sponsors' hopes. By 1952 the economic and social chaos thought to spawn communism had

**American Food for a Hungry Europe**
*Grateful English mothers line up for orange juice sent by the United States to assist Europeans devastated by the Second World War.*

been overcome in the sixteen nations that shared the $17 billion in aid provided by the Marshall Plan. Western Europe had revived, and U.S. business, not coincidentally, boomed.

### Confrontation

Reacting to the Truman Doctrine and the Marshall Plan, the Soviet Union tightened its control in Eastern Europe. Communist takeovers added Hungary and Czechoslovakia to the Soviet sphere in 1947 and 1948. Stalin then turned his sights on Germany. The 1945 Potsdam Agreement had divided Germany into four separate zones (administered by France, Great Britain, the Soviet Union, and the United States) and created a joint four-power administration for Germany's capital, Berlin, lying 110 miles within the Soviet-occupied eastern zone. As the Cold War intensified, the Western powers moved toward uniting their zones into an anticommunist German state. Stalin responded, in June 1948, by blocking all rail and highway routes through the Soviet zone into Berlin, calculating that the Western powers, unable to provision the 2 million Berliners under their control, would either have to abandon plans to create a West German nation or to accept a communist Berlin.

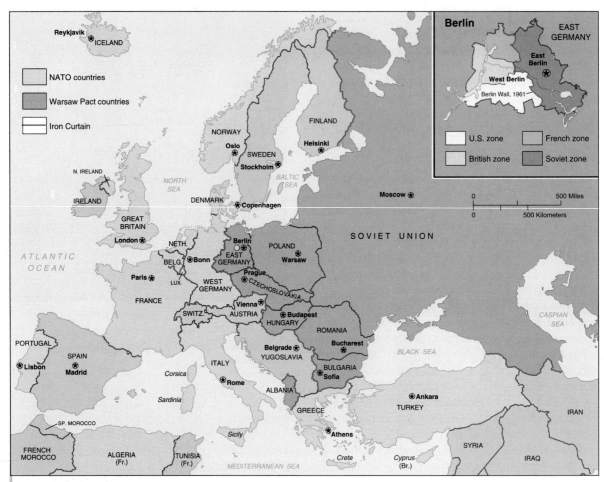

**The Postwar Division of Europe**

*The wartime dispute between the Soviet Union and the Western Allies over Poland's future hardened after World War II into a Cold War that split Europe into competing American and Russian spheres of influence. Across an "iron curtain," NATO countries faced the Warsaw Pact nations.*

Truman resolved neither to abandon Berlin to the Soviets nor to shoot his way into the city and possibly set off World War III. Instead he ordered a massive airlift to provide Berliners with the thousands of tons of food and fuel necessary for survival. American cargo planes landed at West Berlin's Templehof Airport every three minutes around the clock, bringing a mountain of supplies. To prevent the Soviets from shooting down the defenseless planes, Truman ordered a fleet of B-29s, the only planes capable of delivering atomic bombs, to bases in England in July 1948. Truman hinted that he would use "the bomb" if necessary. Tensions rose. The president confided in his diary that "we are very close to war." Meanwhile, for nearly a year,

"Operation Vittles" provided the blockaded city with a precarious lifeline.

In May 1949 the Soviets ended the blockade. Stalin's gambit had failed. The airlift highlighted America's determination and technological prowess, revealed Stalin's willingness to use innocent citizens as pawns, and dramatically heightened anti-Soviet feeling in the West. Truman spoke for the vast majority of Americans when he claimed that "there isn't any difference between the totalitarian Russian government and the Hitler government. . . . They are all alike . . . police state governments." U.S. public opinion polls revealed an almost unanimous belief that "Russia is an aggressive, expansion-minded nation" and an overwhelming de-

**The Berlin Airlift, 1948**
*German children watching an American plane in "Operation Vittles" bring food and supplies to their beleagured city. The airlift kept a city of 2 million people alive for nearly a year and made West Berlin a symbol of the West's resolve to contain the spread of Soviet communism.*

mand for "firmness and increased 'toughness' in relations with Russia."

Continuing fears of a Soviet attack on Western Europe strenthened support for a rearmed West German state and for an Atlantic collective security alliance. In May 1949 the United States, Britain, and France ended their occupation of Germany and approved the creation of the Federal Republic of Germany (West Germany). A month earlier, ten nations of Western Europe had adopted the North Atlantic Treaty, establishing a military alliance with the United States and Canada. Each nation pledged that an attack on one would be considered an attack on all, which would be met with armed force. For the first time in its history, the United States had entered into a peacetime military alliance. Senator Robert Taft of Ohio, speaking for a small band of Republican senators, warned that such an agreement would provoke the Soviets to respond in kind, stimulate a massive arms race, and open the floodgates of American military aid to Europe. But the Senate overwhelmingly approved the treaty, and in July the United States officially joined the North Atlantic Treaty Organization (NATO), marking the formal end of U.S. isolationism.

Two days after the Senate ratification, Truman asked Congress to authorize $1.3 billion for military assistance to NATO nations. To underscore his determination to contain communism, the president persuaded General Dwight D. Eisenhower to become the supreme commander of the new mutual defense force and authorized the stationing of four American army divisions in Europe as the nucleus of the NATO armed force. The Soviet Union responded by creating the German Democratic Republic (East Germany) in 1949, by exploding its own atomic bomb that same year, and by setting up a rival Eastern bloc military alliance, the Warsaw Pact, in 1955. The United States and Soviet Union had divided Europe into two armed camps.

## The Cold War Heats Up

Moscow-Washington hostility similarly carved Asia into contending military camps. The Soviets created a sphere of influence in Manchuria, the United States denied Moscow a role in postwar Japan, and the two superpowers partitioned a helpless Korea.

Under the rule of General Douglas MacArthur, Japan became a prosperous constitutional democracy firmly anchored in the American orbit by the end of the 1940s. As commander of the occupation forces, MacArthur sanctioned the construction of American military bases near the Soviet Union's Asian rim and encouraged U.S. businesses to invest in Japan. Under a U.N. mandate, moreover, the United States assumed control of Japan's prewar island empire and used the islands as air and naval bases and as atomic test sites. MacArthur could well boast that the Pacific had become "an Anglo-Saxon lake." To contain communism, the Truman administration also assisted in crushing a procommunist insurgency in the Philippines and aided the efforts of France to reestablish its colonial rule in Indochina (Vietnam, Laos, and Cambodia), despite American declarations for national self-determination and against imperialism.

## The Atomic West

ooking for an isolated site that could be easily guarded and that had some buildings for temporary use, General Leslie Groves and Robert Oppenheimer found it late in 1942 at the Los Alamos Ranch School atop a circular mesa in the Pajarito ("Little Bird") Plateau twenty miles northwest of Sante Fe, New Mexico. Only a poor jagged road led to the financially troubled school secluded by the ponderosa pine–covered Jemez Range to the west and, to the east, by the Sangre de Cristo ("Blood of Christ") Mountains—named by the first Spanish explorers of the area because of the blood-red glow behind the peaks at sunset. The army quickly took possession of the school and its surrounding 54,000 acres, supposedly for a "demolition range." It code-named Los Alamos "Project Y" and transformed what was more informally called the Hill into a "temporary" town of army-style barracks, old log cabins and adobe buildings, crude laboratories, and unpaved roads without street names. On that

windswept outpost patrolled by armed MPS and surrounded by high barbed-wire fence, some five thousand scientists and engineers—called "longhairs" and "plumbers" by the soldiers enforcing the regimen and regimentation dictated by rigid security requirements—developed the atomic bombs that left Hiroshima and Nagasaki in ashes.

With the war over, most of the scientists at Los Alamos considered their job done. Almost all hoped to replace military control over the site with democratic decision making and to convert weapons of war into tools of peace. Fed up with wood-burning kitchen stoves, irregular food supplies, and close military monitoring, they sought to return to pure science and teaching careers. Some, as Oppenheimer noted, had "learned sin" and felt guilty for what they had accomplished. By September 1945 State Highway 4, the rutted road connecting Los Alamos to Sante Fe, was clogged daily by a stream of departing trailers. By then, however, an atomic-arms race with the Soviet Union

had already begun, and Washington had decided to retain Los Alamos as a weapons-research center to improve and stockpile atomic bombs. To do otherwise, said Norris Bradbury, who succeeded Oppenheimer as director of the Los Alamos National Laboratory in October, would "weaken the nation's bargaining power" and ultimately prove suicidal.

There would be no return to a pre-atomic America. Science and national security had become inseparable. In Los Alamos, canteens gave way to restaurants, bathless cabins to comfortable homes, and dirt tracks to gracefully curved streets laid out according to the most up-to-date standards of urban design. Modern office and administrative complexes sprang up to serve the needs of a rapidly growing scientific community, and permanent concrete laboratories replaced wooden structures. But the wartime patterns of cooperation between the military, corporations, and university science remained, as did an atomic culture emphasizing rigid compartmentalization and classification of work, censorship, and secrecy. Not until the late 1950s did the gates come down that had kept Los Alamos a closed city. And the systems of behavior and belief that had guided the Manhattan Project spread, like the radioactive winds it spawned, to more and more of the postwar West.

In New Mexico, the Sandia National Laboratories operated by Western Electric joined Los Alamos in developing atomic bombs and soon had the largest payroll in the state; Las Cruces became a major testing site for new weaponry; and Albuquerque, billing itself "Atomic City," ranked in the top ten metropolitan areas in the amount of federal research and development contracts. Because of the cheap electricity generated by the Bonneville and Grand Coulee

*AEC Chairman Gordon Dean (3rd from right in front row) and other officials, scientists, and news photographers view a 1952 atomic bomb test.*

dams, the Hanford Engineer Works in Washington continued to produce plutonium for atomic bombs, and Seattle's Boeing Airplane Company to manufacture the planes that could deliver them. Touting the postwar slogan "Air power is peace power," Boeing employed more Washingtonians in the Evergreen State than logging and lumbering.

Immediately after the war, moreover, proponents of air power established the Rand Corporation (a contraction of the *r* and *d* of research & development) as a branch of the Douglas Aircraft Corporation in Los Angeles to retain the services of scientists and engineers returning to civilian life. It became an independent unit in 1948, mainly supported by the air force, and moved to Santa Monica, where it devised nuclear strategies. Californians also prospered from the defense expen-

*A mannequin used to gauge the effects of an atomic blast on the human body at the Atomic Energy Commission's test site at Yucca Flat, Nevada, in 1955.*

ditures going to Lockheed, as well as from the atomic research at the Lawrence Radiation Laboratory of the University of California, Berkeley, the rocketry work done at the California Institute of Technology's Jet Propulsion Laboratory in Pasadena, and the Lawrence Livermore National Laboratory established by Edward Teller in 1952 for new nuclear weaponry.

With the decision to build a hydrogen bomb and the start of the Korean War in 1950, the Four Corners area on the Colorado Plateau became, in the words of *National Geographic,* "the land of the weekend prospector." The once sleepy cattle town of Moab, Utah, suddenly proclaimed itself "The Uranium Capital of the World." Grants, New Mexico, grew from a ranching town of five hundred to the nation's largest uranium-milling center with a population of ten thousand. In Colorado, the Rocky Flats facility north of Denver built triggers for the new nuclear bombs, the Martin Marietta Corporation established a missile plant in the suburb of Littleton, and the command post coordinating the North American air defense was sunk deep beneath Cheyenne Mountain. Universities in the West soon garnered a lion's share of National Science Foundation grants. Utah led the nation in military expenditures per capita. And silos dotting Montana and Idaho housed the nuclear missiles targeted at Moscow and Beijing. The Cold War and atomic-arms race had vastly furthered the modernization, prosperity, and urbanization of the West. The region paid with serious environmental costs.

Although officials of the Atomic Energy Commission knew of the pathological and genetic dangers of nuclear particles as early as 1950, they kept their medical studies hidden from the public. The race for nuclear supe-

**Outside Las Vegas**
*A mushrooming atomic cloud dwarfs Army troops observing a bomb detonation during a 1951 series of AEC-Department of Defense tests.*

riority against the Soviets took precedence over the safety of Americans. While workers at Hanford sang of glowing in the dark in a ghoulish ditty they called "Plutonium Blues," radioactive liquids continued to be dumped into leaky tanks and trenches along the Columbia River. Nothing about health hazards was said to those working in the uranium processing plants of Uravan, Colorado, and Monticello, Utah, or to the residents of the nearby Navajo reservation. Nor were the dangers of radioactivity conveyed to those who lived downwind of the Nuclear Test Site, near Las Vegas, where more than a hundred atmospheric detonations of atomic devices in the 1950s sent pink-orange clouds of ash, dust, and gases over towns in Arizona, Nevada, and Utah, causing a sudden spurt of acute leukemia deaths and abnormally high cancer rates in the region. Soil in the Los Alamos area still remains contaminated with plutonium residue from the Second World War, and the only movement at the Trinity Site of the original atomic explosion comes from wind-whipped sands in the desert called Jornado del Muerto—"Journey of Death."

In China, however, U.S. efforts to block communism failed. The Truman administration initially tried to mediate the civil war between the Nationalist government of Jiang Jieshi (Chiang Kai-shek) and the communist forces of Mao Zedong (Mao Tse-tung). At the same time, it sent nearly $3 billion in aid to the Nationalists between 1945 and 1949. American dollars, however, could not force Jiang's corrupt government to reform itself and to win the support of the Chinese people, whom it had widely alienated. As Mao's well-disciplined and motivated troops marched south, Jiang's soldiers mutinied or surrendered without a fight. Unable to stem revolutionary sentiment or to hold the countryside—where the communists, in Mao's words, "swam like fishes in the peasant sea"—Jiang's regime collapsed. By the end of 1949 he had fled to exile on Taiwan (Formosa), an island east of mainland China.

Mao's establishment of the communist People's Republic of China shocked Americans. The most populous nation in the world, which Americans had hoped would be a counterforce to Asian communism and a market for American exports, had instead become "Red China." Most Americans rejected the Truman administration's explanation that it could have done nothing to alter the outcome of the civil war; like John Foster Dulles, the leading Republican authority on foreign affairs, many considered Mao's victory "the worst defeat the United States has suffered in its history." The communization of China especially embittered midwestern and western conservatives who believed that America's future lay in Asia, not Europe. Many on the Right blamed "pro-Communists in the State Department" for Jiang's failure.

As the China debate raged, the president announced in September 1949 that the Soviet Union had exploded an atomic bomb. Suddenly the world had changed, shattering illusions of American invincibility. While military leaders and politicians pressed Truman to develop a yet more powerful weapon, ordinary Americans sought safety in civil defense. Public schools held atomic-air-raid drills. "We took the drills seriously," recalled novelist Annie Dillard; "surely Pittsburgh, which had the nation's steel, coke, and aluminum, would be the enemy's first target." Many cities issued metal identification tags to all schoolchildren. Four million Americans volunteered to be Sky Watchers, looking for Soviet planes. More than a million purchased or constructed their own family bomb shelters. Those who could not afford one were advised by the Federal Civil Defense Administration to "jump in

any handy ditch or gutter . . . bury your face in your arms . . . never lose your head."

On January 31, 1950, Truman ended the dispute among his advisers and authorized the Atomic Energy Commission to develop a fusion-based hydrogen bomb (H-bomb) estimated to have the force of one million tons of TNT. In November 1952 the United States exploded its first thermonuclear bomb in the Marshall Islands. Far exceeding initial estimates, it delivered a force equal to 10.4 million tons of TNT, projected a radioactive cloud twenty-five miles into the stratosphere, and blasted a canyon a mile long and 175 feet deep in the ocean floor. Nine months later the Russians also detonated a hydrogen bomb. The balance of thermonuclear terror escalated.

Early in 1950, a reeling Truman had also called for a top-secret review of defense policy by the National Security Council. Its report, NSC-68, completed in April, emphasized the Soviet Union's military power and aggressive intentions. To counter the USSR's "design for world domination"—the mortal challenge posed by the Soviet Union "not only to this Republic but to civilization itself"—NSC-68 called for a vast U.S. military buildup. It advocated a large standing army and a 400 percent increase in military appropriations. Truman hesitated to swallow this expensive prescription. An aide to Secretary of State Acheson recalled, "We were sweating over it, and then, with regard to NSC-68, thank God Korea came along." By the end of 1950, Truman had ordered the implementation of NSC-68 and more than tripled the defense budget.

### The Korean War

After Japan's defeat in World War II, the United States and Soviet Union temporarily divided Korea at the thirty-eighth parallel for purposes of military occupation. This line then solidified into a political frontier between the American-supported Republic of Korea, usually called South Korea, and the Soviet-backed Democratic People's Republic of Korea in the north, each claiming the sole right to rule all of Korea.

On June 24, 1950, North Korean troops swept across the thirty-eighth parallel to attack South Korea. Truman immediately considered the invasion to be Soviet-directed aggression, rather than an internal Korean matter. He never doubted that Stalin was using Korea as a test of U.S. will and its containment policy.

"Korea is the Greece of the Far East," Truman maintained. "If we are tough enough now, if we stand up to them like we did in Greece . . . they won't take any next

**U.S. Marines Battling for Seoul, September 1950**

*From the start Truman believed that the Soviet Union had orchestrated the North Korean invasion of South Korea. He steadfastly maintained that "if the Russian totalitarian state was intending to follow in the path of the dictatorship of Hitler and Mussolini, they [had to] be met head on in Korea."*

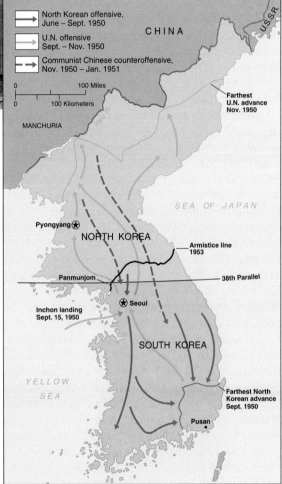

**The Korean War, 1950–1953**

*The experience of fighting an undeclared and limited war for the limited objective of containing communism confused the generation of Americans who had just fought an all-out war for the total defeat of the Axis. General MacArthur spoke for the many who were frustrated by the Korean conflict's mounting costs in blood and dollars: "There is no substitute for victory."*

steps." Mindful of the failure of appeasement at Munich, he believed that the communists were doing in Korea exactly what Hitler and Mussolini and the Japanese had done in the 1930s: "Nobody had stood up to them. And that is what led to the Second World War." With China on his mind as well, Truman needed to prove to Republican critics that the Democrats would stand up to "the Reds" and not allow another country to "fall" to the communists.

The president decided to intervene. Without consulting Congress, Truman quickly secured the United Nations' backing to repel the North Korean attack and restore the border of South Korea. (Because the Soviet Union was then boycotting the Security Council, to protest the U.N.'s failure to seat Mao Zedong's Chinese government in place of the exiled Jiang Jieshi regime in Taiwan, it could not utilize its veto.) On June 27 Truman appointed General Douglas MacArthur to command the U.N. effort and ordered American forces to South Korea's aid. The cold war had turned hot. Although the intervention was officially a U.N. "police action," most of the naval and air support and nearly half the troops fighting under the U.N. flag came from the United States; South Korea supplied some 43 percent of the forces, and fourteen other nations contributed fewer than 10 percent of the U.N. troops.

North Korea rapidly pushed the U.N. forces to the southeastern tip of the peninsula. Then in a brilliant amphibious maneuver on September 15, MacArthur's troops landed at Inchon, a port city near Seoul, and routed the North Koreans. Within two weeks MacArthur's forces had driven them back across the thirty-eighth parallel. Heartened, Truman then gave MacArthur the green light to cross the border and crush the North Korean army. The police action to chase the invaders out of South Korea now became a war to create a noncommunist, unified Korean nation.

As U.N. troops pushed north, nearing the Yalu River, the Chinese warned that they would not "stand idly by" and "let the Americans come to the border." Dismissing the threat of Chinese involvement, an overconfident MacArthur deployed his forces in a thin line below the river. On November 25 thirty-three Chinese divisions (about 300,000 men) counterattacked. Within two weeks they had driven the U.N. forces back below the thirty-eighth parallel; and by winter's end, the fighting had stabilized at roughly the original border between the two Koreas.

Truman then again reversed course and sought a negotiated peace based on the original objective of restoring the integrity of South Korea. MacArthur rocked the boat, however, seeking to be allowed to bomb and blockade China, to "unleash" Jiang Jieshi's troops against the communist regime, and to seek total victory even at the risk of an all-out war with China. Truman refused: "We are trying to prevent a world war—not to start one." Worried that U.S. involvement in Korea might tempt Stalin to aggression in Europe, Truman insisted that the conflict be a limited war for a limited objective—to hold the line in Korea. But MacArthur had no stomach for stalemate, "In war," he declared, "there is no substitute for victory."

When MacArthur refused to stop publicly criticizing administration policy, Truman relieved him of command on April 10, 1951, provoking a dramatic clash between civil and military authority. The president regarded "Mr. Prima Donna, Brass Hat, Five Star MacArthur" as a dangerously ambitious man who wanted to subvert civilian control of the military and plunge the United States into nuclear war. The Joint Chiefs of Staff endorsed Truman's decision, as did the secretary of state, General George Marshall, who said, "The s.o.b. should have been fired two years ago." But public opinion backed the general. The very idea of limited war, of containing rather than defeating the enemy, baffled many Americans; and the mounting toll of American casualties in pursuit of a stalemate angered them. It all seemed so senseless. Despite the warning by General Omar Bradley, the chairman of the Joint Chiefs of Staff, that MacArthur's proposals "would in-

volve us in the wrong war at the wrong place in the wrong time and with the wrong enemy," a growing number of Americans listened sympathetically to Republican charges that "this country today is in the hands of a secret coterie which is directed by agents of the Soviet Union."

In July 1951 truce talks began, but they dragged on for two years as both sides fought a restricted yet deadly war. By the time the wrangling over prisoner repatriation and the cease-fire line ended on July 26, 1953, this "limited" war had cost the United States 54,246 American lives, another 103,284 wounded or missing, and some $54 billion. The conflict also accelerated implementation of NSC-68 and the expansion of containment into a global policy. From 1950 to 1953, defense spending zoomed from $13 billion to $60 billion—from one-third to two-thirds of the entire federal budget. The United States acquired new bases around the world, committed itself to rearm West Germany, and joined a mutual-defense pact with Australia and New Zealand. Increased military aid flowed to Jiang Jieshi on Taiwan, and American dollars supported the French army fighting the communist Ho Chi Minh in Indochina (Vietnam, Laos, and Cambodia). By 1954 the United States would be paying three-quarters the cost of France's Indochinese war.

Truman's intervention in Korea preserved a precarious balance of power by preventing the South Korean regime from falling to its rival in the north. It underscored the administration's commitment to the anticommunist struggle, as well as the shift of that struggle's focus from Europe to Asia. Containment originally advanced to justify U.S. aid to Greece and Turkey served in the early 1950s as the ideological foundation for a major war in Korea and, ominously, for a deepening U.S. involvement in Vietnam. By committing U.S. troops to battle with neither a declaration of war nor congressional approval, Truman set precedents for future undeclared wars and added to the powers of an increasingly "imperial" presidency. Finally, the shock of China's "fall" and the frustrations of the Korean War heightened public unhappiness with Democratic rule and set off domestic shock waves that would have broad future consequences.

## The Truman Administration at Home

When World War II ended, Americans wanted to bring the boys home and enjoy the peace. Since 1929 they had known little but the sufferings and shortages of de-

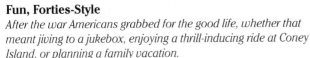

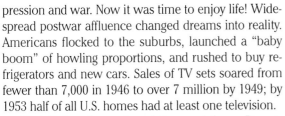

**Fun, Forties-Style**
*After the war Americans grabbed for the good life, whether that meant jiving to a jukebox, enjoying a thrill-inducing ride at Coney Island, or planning a family vacation.*

pression and war. Now it was time to enjoy life! Widespread postwar affluence changed dreams into reality. Americans flocked to the suburbs, launched a "baby boom" of howling proportions, and rushed to buy refrigerators and new cars. Sales of TV sets soared from fewer than 7,000 in 1946 to over 7 million by 1949; by 1953 half of all U.S. homes had at least one television.

Not all Americans shared the good times. Poverty remained a stark fact of life for millions. Minorities experienced the grim reality of racism. And the struggle of African Americans for equality would become the civil-rights movement that in a few years would sweep the South.

But family and making a living, not public issues, preoccupied most Americans, and the New Deal's reform energies subsided into complacency. Although Truman sought to extend liberalism, the mood of the times was against him. A growing conservative movement wanted to reduce, not expand, the power of government and that of organized labor. The fear of communism bred domestic repression, stifled dissent, and rewarded unquestioning conformity. Ultimately, it made it possible for the junior senator from Wisconsin to ride roughshod over principles of decency and fair play in the early 1950s.

### The Eightieth Congress

The Republicans of the Eightieth Congress interpreted the 1946 elections as a mandate to reverse the New Deal. As "Mr. Republican," Senator Robert A. Taft of Ohio declared, "We have got to break with the corrupting idea that we can legislate prosperity, legislate equality, legislate opportunity." Determined "to meat-axe government frills," the Republican-controlled Congress defeated bills to raise the minimum wage and to provide federal funds for education and housing.

Truman and the conservatives waged their major battle over the pro-union Wagner Act of 1935 (see

Chapter 25). The rash of postwar strikes had created a consensus for curbing union power. In 1947 more than twenty states passed laws to restrict union activities, and Congress passed the Taft-Hartley Act (the Labor-Management Relations Act), barring the closed shop, outlawing secondary boycotts, requiring union officials to sign loyalty oaths that they were not communists, and permitting the president to call an eighty-day cooling-off period to delay any strike that might endanger national safety or health. Although hardly the "slave labor bill" that the union leadership claimed, it did help to deradicalize organized labor, making it less of a social justice movement and more of a special interest group. It also weakened labor's new organizing drives, especially in the nonunion South and West, hastening the relocation of labor-intensive industries in the Northeast and Midwest, such as textiles, to the Sunbelt. Labor leaders demanded a presidential veto.

With an eye on the upcoming 1948 presidential election, Truman vetoed the bill. Congress easily overrode the veto. But Truman had taken a major step toward regaining labor's support. The president realized that his only hope for election lay in reforging FDR's majority coalition. To this end, he played the role of a staunch New Dealer to the hilt, offering favors to every group. He proposed that Congress repeal Taft-Hartley, raise the minimum wage and social security benefits, and enact federal aid to education, housing, and health insurance, as well as high price supports for farmers. Wooing Eastern European ethnic voters, Truman stressed his opposition to communism and endorsement of laws to admit more wartime refugees. Deeply sympathetic toward the hundreds of thousands of Jewish survivors of the Nazi concentration camps that flooded into Palestine and met bitter resistance from Arabs who had settled there, Truman also needed the votes of Jewish Americans. So, over vigorous protests from Western European leaders and his own foreign policy advisers, who feared losing the support of the rich oil-producing Arab states, the president extended diplomatic recognition to the new state of Israel immediately after it proclaimed independence on May 14, 1948.

**Wipe Out Discrimination,** *by Milton Ackoff, 1949*
*The publication of* To Secure These Rights *catapulted civil-rights issues to the forefront during the Truman years.*

### The Politics of Civil Rights

Truman also made the federal protection of civil rights part of his liberal agenda. Although, like FDR, he wanted the backing of southern white Democrats and therefore initially shied away from involvement in racial issues, the accelerating civil-rights movement, and the violence it provoked, called for a White House response.

After the war, many African Americans, especially veterans, demanded the right to vote. Voter-registration drives had raised the number of southern blacks registered to vote from 2 percent in 1940 to 12 percent in 1947, and fearful of further gains as well as of a bold new spirit among African Americans, some southern whites brutally asserted their dominance. In 1946 whites killed several black war veterans in rural Georgia who had voted that year, flogged to death an "uppity" black tenant farmer in Mississippi, blowtorched a young black in Louisiana for daring to enter a white woman's house, and blinded a black soldier for failing to sit in the rear of a bus in South Carolina. In Columbia, Tennessee, in 1946, whites rioted against blacks who insisted on their rights. The police then arrested seventy blacks and did nothing as a white mob broke into the jail to murder two black prisoners.

In September 1946 Truman met with a delegation of civil-rights leaders. Horrified by their accounts of racial terrorism, he promised action. The president believed that all Americans should enjoy the full rights of citizenship, regardless of race. He also understood the political importance of the growing black vote, particularly in northern cities. Truman realized, too, that white racism damaged U.S. relations with much of the world. The USSR highlighted the mistreatment of African Americans, both to undercut U.S. appeals to the non-white peoples of Africa, Asia, and Latin America, and to counter criticism of its own repression behind the Iron Curtain.

Truman acted in late 1946 by establishing the first President's Committee on Civil Right. The committee's 1947 report, *To Secure These Rights,* dramatized the inequities of life in Jim Crow America; it emphasized all the compelling moral, economic, and international reasons why the government should act; and it specifically called for federal legislation against lynching and the poll tax, for antidiscrimination measures in employment, housing, and public facilities, and for an end to segregation in the military. In February 1948 Truman called on Congress to enact many of the committee's proposals.

Southern segregationists reacted immediately—accusing Truman of "kissing the feet of minorities," of "stabbing the South in the back," and warning of a

Dixie boycott of the national Democratic ticket. Truman backtracked. Cowed by the prospect of major southern defections, he dropped his plans to submit civil-rights bills to Congress and endorsed a weak civil-rights plank for the Democratic platform.

At the Democratic convention in July 1948, liberals and urban politicians who needed the votes of African Americans rejected the president's feeble civil-rights plank and committed the party to enact Truman's initial proposals. In protest, thirty-five delegates from Alabama and Mississippi stalked out of the convention. They joined other southern segregationists to form the States' Rights Democratic party and nominated Governor Strom Thurmond of South Carolina for the presidency. The "Dixiecrats" hoped to win enough electoral votes to deny Truman reelection and thereby restore their dominance in the Democratic party and preserve the segregationist "southern way of life." Placing their electors on the ballot as the regular Democratic ticket in several states, they posed a significant roadblock to Truman's chances of victory.

## The Election of 1948

Truman's electoral hopes faded further when left-wing Democrats joined with communists to launch a new Progressive party and nominate Henry A. Wallace for president. Claiming that "we are whipping up another holy war against Russia," Wallace threatened Truman's chances in key northern states, where many urban Democrats saw FDR's third-term vice president as the true heir of New Deal liberalism.

To capitalize on Democratic divisions, Republicans bypassed conservative senator Robert A. Taft and nominated moderate governor Thomas E. Dewey of New York. Confident of victory, Dewey ran a complacent campaign designed to offend the fewest people. His bland appeals for unity made him seem aloof and smug.

Truman, in contrast, campaigned tirelessly, blasting the "no-good, do-nothing" Republican-controlled Eightieth Congress. To shouts of "Give 'em hell, Harry," the president crisscrossed the country hammering away at the GOP as the party of "privilege, pride, and plunder" just waiting "to do a hatchet job on the New Deal." Political pundits applauded Truman's spunk but predicted a sure Dewey victory.

A surprised nation awoke the day after the election to learn that the president had squeaked to the biggest upset in U.S. history. Ironically, the Progressives and

**The Election of 1948**

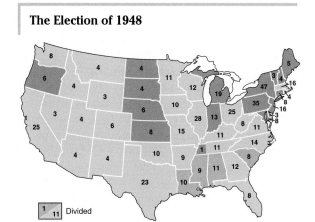

| | Electoral Vote | Popular Vote | Percentage of Popular Vote |
|---|---|---|---|
| **Democratic** Harry S Truman | 303 | 24,105,812 | 49.5 |
| **Republican** Thomas E. Dewey | 189 | 21,970,065 | 45.1 |
| **States' Rights** Strom Thurmond | 39 | 1,169,063 | 2.4 |
| **Minor parties** | – | 1,442,667 | 3.0 |

Dixiecrats had helped Truman. Their extremism had kept both moderate liberals and conservatives safely in the Democratic fold. The Berlin crisis, a coup in Czechoslovakia, and Wallace's failure to repudiate communist support forced most liberals away from the Progressives. And although the support for Thurmond portended that, on the issue of race, life-long southern Democrats would desert the national party, not enough yet considered the threat great enough to bolt. As the attorney general of Virginia explained, "The only sane and constructive course to follow is to remain in the house of our fathers—even though the roof leaks, and there be bats in the belfry, rats in the pantry, a cockroach in the kitchen and skunks in the parlor." Moreover, Dixiecrat defections had freed Truman to campaign as a champion of civil rights.

In July 1948 Truman had issued executive orders barring discrimination in federal employment and creating a committee to ensure "equality of treatment and opportunity for all persons in the armed services without regard to race, color, religion or national origin."

### A. Philip Randolph

*Leading a group of protesters at the 1948 Democratic national convention, Randolph vowed: "I am prepared to oppose a Jim Crow army till I rot in jail." Soon after, however, President Truman issued Executive Order 9981, asserting equality of treatment and opportunity for all members of the armed services, and a pleased Randolph called off his protest.*

Truman had also benefited from two Supreme Court decisions that African Americans applauded. In 1946 the Court had declared segregation in interstate bus transportation unconstitutional (*Morgan* v. *Virginia*); and in 1948 it outlawed restrictive housing covenants that forbade the sale or rental of property to minorities (*Shelley* v. *Kraemer*). Blacks also took heart from the growing number of cities and states that legislated against racial discrimination in employment and in public accommodations, and from the change in social attitudes symbolized by the Brooklyn Dodgers' decision to break major-league baseball's color barrier with Jackie Robinson, the grandson of a slave. They voted accordingly, giving Truman an even higher percentage of the black vote than FDR ever had.

Truman succeeded in 1948 primarily by recreating the New Deal coalition. He seized every opportunity to remind working-class Americans that the Republican "gluttons of privilege" planned to "turn the clock back" and strip them of the benefits they had gained under FDR. "In a sense," wrote one journalist, "Roosevelt won his greatest victory after his death."

### *The Fair Deal*

Despite his narrow victory margin, Truman tried to translate his election into a mandate for liberalism. In his 1949 State of the Union message, he proposed an ambitious social and economic program that he called the Fair Deal.

The Eighty-first Congress complied with Truman's requests to extend existing programs but rejected the president's new proposals. It raised the minimum wage; increased social security benefits and coverage; expanded appropriations for public power, conservation, and slum clearance; and authorized the construction of nearly a million low-income housing units. It also enacted the Displaced Persons Act, which allowed entry to 205,000 survivors of the Nazi forced-labor and death camps. But Congress rejected federal aid to education, national health insurance, civil-rights legislation, larger farm subsidies, and repeal of Taft-Hartley.

The failure to adopt much of the Fair Deal stemmed in part from Truman's own turn from domestic reform to a greater absorption in foreign and military affairs. In part it reflected the power of the conservative coalition in Congress, and Truman's dependence on those conservatives to support his containment policies. And increasing prosperity had sapped public enthusiasm for more reform. In 1949, according to the Hickock Manufacturing Company, the belt size of the average American man had expanded to thirty-four inches, up from a depression-years average of thirty-one inches. The postwar congresses mirrored the full-belly sense of well-being that many Americans felt and reflected the popular anxieties over communism that doomed hopes for liberal reform.

## The Politics of Anticommunism

As the Cold War worsened, some Americans concluded that the roots of the nation's foreign difficulties lay in domestic treason and subversion. How else could the communists have taken China and built an atomic bomb? Desperately afraid, millions of Americans enlisted in a crusade that sought scapegoats for the nation's problems and equated dissent with disloyalty.

Similar intolerance had prevailed in the Know-Nothing campaign of the 1850s and the Red Scare of 1919–1920. And since its establishment in 1938, the House Committee on Un-American Activities (later called the House Un-American Activities Committee, or HUAC) had served as a platform for right-wing denunciations of the New Deal as a communist plot. Only the extreme Right initially took such charges seriously. But after World War II, mounting numbers of Democrats as well as Republicans climbed aboard the anti-Red bandwagon.

This second Red Scare (see Chapter 23) influenced both governmental and personal actions. Millions of Americans were subjected to security investigations and loyalty oaths. Anticommunist extremism destroyed the Left and undermined labor militancy. The trampling of civil liberties spawned a "silent generation" of college students and widespread political apathy, and the purge of controversial government officials ensured foreign-policy rigidity and the postponement of liberal domestic reforms.

### *Loyalty and Security*

The Cold War brought legitimate concerns about American security. The Communist party had claimed 80,000 members during the Second World War, and many more Americans had sympathized with its goals. No one knew how many of them now occupied sensitive positions in the government or defense industry. In mid-1945 a

government raid on the offices of a procommunist magazine, *Amerasia,* revealed that classified documents had been given to the periodical by two State Department employees and a naval intelligence officer. Then a Russian defector to the West brought with him documents showing that a major spy network had given atomic secrets to the Soviets during the war. Some Republicans rushed to accuse the Democratic administration of being soft on communism.

The president responded, a week after his Truman Doctrine speech of March 1947, by issuing Executive Order 9835, which established the Federal Employee Loyalty Program to root out subversives in the government. It was the first such program established by a president, the first in peacetime, the first under which a person could be dismissed for political beliefs. Although the probe initially included safeguards, many of the investigating boards came to ignore individual rights in their drive for absolute security. Soon civil servants suspected of disloyalty were neither allowed to face their accusers nor allowed to require investigators to reveal sources.

Instead of focusing on potential subversives in high-risk areas, review boards extended the probe to the as-

**The Red Menace, 1949**
*Although Hollywood generally avoided overtly political films, it released a few dozen explicitly anticommunist films in the postwar era. Depicting American communists as vicious hypocrites, if not hardened criminals, Hollywood's Cold War movies, like its blacklist, were an effort to protect its imperiled public image after HUAC's widely publicized investigation of the movie industry.*

sociations and beliefs of every government worker. Mere criticism of American foreign policy could result in an accusation of disloyalty. Clouds of suspicion hovered over those who liked foreign films, or favored the unionization of federal workers or civil rights for blacks. "Of course the fact that a person believes in racial equality doesn't *prove* he's a communist," mused an Interior Department loyalty board chairman, "but it certainly makes you look twice, doesn't it?" Some lost jobs because they had friends who were radicals or had once belonged to organizations now declared disloyal. Of the 4.7 million jobholders and applicants who underwent loyalty checks by 1952, 560 were fired or denied a job on security grounds, and some ten thousand resigned or withdrew their applications. Although no evidence of espionage or subversion was uncovered, the loyalty probe, rather than calming public jitters, gave credibility to the growing Red Scare and spread fear among government employees. "Why lead with your chin?" became a dominant reflex. "If communists like apple pie and I do," claimed one federal worker, "I see no reason why I should stop eating it. But I would."

### The Anticommunist Crusade

The pall of conformity cast by Truman's loyalty inquest fed mounting anticommunist hysteria. It promoted fears of communist infiltrators and legitimized other efforts to expose subversives. Universities banned controversial speakers. Popular magazines featured articles like "Reds Are After Your Child." Even Marvel comics joined the fray: "Beware, commies, spies, traitors, and foreign agents! Captain America, with all loyal, free men behind him, is looking for you, ready to fight until the last one of you is exposed for the yellow scum you are."

By the end of Truman's term, thirty-nine states had created loyalty programs, most with virtually no procedural safeguards. In legislation reminiscent of the Sedition Act of 1918, Connecticut made it a crime to print any "scurrilous or abusive matter" about the government, the armed forces, military uniforms, and the flag. Michigan invalidated all bequests to organizations judged subversive. Imprisonment awaited anyone in Massachusetts who knowingly allowed a meeting place to be used by communists. Schoolteachers, college professors, and state and city employees throughout the nation had to sign loyalty oaths or lose their jobs. So did professional wrestlers in Indiana.

In 1947 the House Un-American Activities Committee began hearings to expose communist influence in American life. HUAC's investigations blurred distinctions between dissent and disloyalty, between radicalism and subversion. Those who refused to answer HUAC questions sometimes lost their livelihoods, and lives. In Washington, D.C., a man lost his license to sell secondhand furniture because he had invoked the Fifth Amendment when questioned about his past; a woman who did the same was so effectively boycotted that she had to sell her thriving drugstore and leave town. Rather than answer HUAC's questions, a Stanford University biochemist took poison and killed himself. In a suicide note he blasted the committee for wrecking careers and lives: "The scientific mind cannot flourish in an atmosphere of fear, timidity, and imposed conformity."

HUAC also left its mark on the entertainment industry. When a group of prominent film directors and screenwriters refused to cooperate in 1947, HUAC had them cited for contempt and sent to federal prison. The threat of further investigations prompted the movie colony, financially dependent on favorable press and public opinion, to exile its dissenters. Hollywood established a blacklist barring the employment of anyone with a slightly questionable past. Familiar faces disappeared from the movie screen; a similar blacklist in broadcasting silenced some of radio's most talented voices. One studio even canceled a film on Longfellow, explaining that Hiawatha had tried to stop wars between Indian tribes and that some might see the Indian's effort as communist propaganda for peace. Another withdrew plans to film the story of Robin Hood because he took from the rich and gave to the poor. HUAC also frightened the labor movement into expelling its communist unions and officers and avoiding progressive causes. Fearful of appearing "red," or even "pink," most unions now focused on just securing better pay and benefits for their members.

The presidential campaign of 1948 poured yet more fuel on the fires of national anxiety. Truman ran as America's chief anticommunist, lambasting Henry Wallace as a Stalinist dupe and accusing the Republicans of being "unwittingly the ally of the communists." In turn, the GOP dubbed the Democrats "the party of treason." Republican congressman Richard Nixon of California charged that Democrats bore responsibility for "the unimpeded growth of the communist conspiracy in the United States."

To blunt the force of such accusations, Truman's Justice Department prosecuted eleven top leaders of the American Communist party under the Smith Act of 1940, which outlawed any conspiracy advocating the overthrow of the government. In 1951, in *Dennis* v. *the United States*, the Supreme Court affirmed the conviction and jailing of the communists, despite the absence of any acts of violence or espionage by them. In upholding the constitutionality of the Smith Act, the Court declared that Congress had the power to curtail freedom of speech when national security required such restriction. This decision cleared the way for the prosecution of nearly one hundred other communist functionaries.

Ironically, the Communist party was fading into obscurity at the very time when politicians magnified the threat that it posed. By 1950 its membership had shrunk to fewer than thirty thousand. Yet Truman's attorney general warned that American Reds "are everywhere—in factories, offices, butcher stores, on street corners, in private businesses—and each carries in himself the germ of death for society."

### Hiss and the Rosenbergs

Nothing set off more alarms of a Red conspiracy in Washington than the case of Alger Hiss. In the midst of the 1948 presidential campaign, HUAC conducted a hearing in which Whittaker Chambers, a senior editor at *Time* magazine and former Soviet agent who had broken with the communists in 1938, identified Hiss as an underground party member in the 1930s. Chambers, the rumpled, repentant ex-communist, appeared a tortured soul crusading to save the West from the Red peril. The elegant Hiss, in contrast, seemed the very symbol of the liberal establishment. A graduate of Johns Hopkins University and Harvard Law School, Hiss had clerked for Supreme Court Justice Oliver Wendell Holmes before working for the New Deal and the wartime State Department (even serving as a presidential adviser at Yalta and helping to organize the founding conference of the United Nations).

Most liberals believed Hiss's denials of any communist affiliation or of even knowing Chambers. They saw him as a victim of conservatives bent on tarnishing New Deal liberalism. Coming to his defense, Truman denounced Chambers's allegation as a "red herring" to deflect attention from the failures of the Eightieth Congress.

But to many who harbored suspicions of the Rooseveltian liberal tradition, Chambers's persistence and Hiss's fumbling retreat intensified fears that the Democratic administration might be teeming with communists. Under rigorous questioning by Richard Nixon, the former New Dealer relented and admitted that he had

known Chambers and had even let Chambers have his car and live in his apartment. Still, Hiss denied ever having been a communist. Chambers then broadened his accusation, claiming that Hiss had committed espionage in the 1930s by giving him secret State Department documents to be transmitted to the Soviet Union. To prove his charge, Chambers produced microfilm copies of confidential government papers that had been reproduced on a typewriter once owned by Hiss.

Hiss protested his innocence, but a grand jury indicted him for perjury, or lying under oath. (The statute of limitations for espionage prevented a charge of treason.) A first trial ended in a hung jury, but a second resulted in a conviction in January 1950. Hiss was sentenced to five years in federal prison. Congressional conservatives were emboldened. Who knew how many other bright young New Dealers had betrayed the country?

**Ethel and Julius Rosenberg**
*Charged with plotting to transfer atomic secrets to the Soviet Union during World War II, the Rosenbergs were found guilty of conspiring to commit espionage and electrocuted on June 19, 1953. Although they and their defenders protested their innocence to the end, Soviet documents made public in the 1990s identified Julius Rosenberg as a secret communist agent.*

Just as the Hiss affair ended, another case alarmed Americans about their government's internal security. In February 1950, the British arrested Klaus Fuchs, a German-born scientist involved in the Manhattan Project, for passing atomic secrets to the Soviets during the Second World War. Fuchs's confession led to the arrest of his American accomplice, Harry Gold, who then implicated David Greenglass, a machinist who had worked at Los Alamos. Greenglass named his sister and brother-in-law, Ethel and Julius Rosenberg, as co-conspirators in the wartime atomic spy network. The children of Jewish immigrants, the Rosenbergs insisted that they were victims of anti-Semitism and were being persecuted for their leftist beliefs. But a jury in March 1951 found the Rosenbergs guilty of conspiring to commit espionage. The trial judge, declaring their crime "worse than murder" and the cause of communist aggression in Korea, sentenced them to die in the electric chair. Offered clemency if they named other spies, neither Rosenberg would confess. On June 19, 1953, they were executed—the first and last American civilians to lose their lives for espionage.

Although both Alger Hiss and the Rosenbergs had protested their innocence to their end, and their defenders continued to do so for decades after, Soviet secret documents released by the National Security Agency in the 1990s implicated Hiss and Julius Rosenberg, without confirming Ethel's guilt. At the time, however, few Americans could separate fact from fantasy. For some, only a conspiracy could explain U.S. weakness and Soviet might. Frustrated by their unexpected failure in 1948, Republicans eagerly exploited the fearful mood and abandoned restraint in accusing the "Commiecrats" of selling out America.

## McCarthyism

No individual would scourge Democrats as audaciously and inflict as many mortal wounds as Republican senator Joseph R. McCarthy of Wisconsin. Desperate for a winning issue on which to run for reelection in 1952, McCarthy noted the attention accorded his fellow Republicans for their attacks on the Democrats as "soft on communism." Following suit, in February 1950, McCarthy told a West Virginia audience that the United States now found itself in a "position of impotency" because of "the traitorous actions" of high officials in the Truman administration. "I have here in my hands a list of 205," McCarthy claimed as he waved a laundry ticket, "a list of names known to the Secretary of State

as being members of the Communist party and who nevertheless are still working and shaping policy." Although McCarthy offered no evidence to support his charges, his senatorial stature and brazen style gave him a national forum. McCarthy repeated his accusation in other speeches in the next few days, reducing his numbers to 81 and then 57 and toning down the rhetoric of his indictment from "card-carrying communists" to "subversives" to "bad risks." A Senate committee investigating the matter branded McCarthy's charges "a fraud and a hoax," but the junior senator from Wisconsin persisted.

Buoyed by the partisan usefulness of Senator McCarthy's onslaught, Republicans encouraged even more accusations. "Joe, you're a dirty s.o.b.," declared Ohio senator John Bricker, "but there are times when you've got to have an s.o.b. around, and this is one of them." Even the normally fair-minded Robert Taft

**McCarthyism**
*A term invented by cartoonist Herblock, McCarthyism to most liberals and Democrats meant the use of lies, slander, and innuendo to attack and discredit the Democratic party for "twenty years of treason."*

urged McCarthy "to keep talking, and if one case doesn't work, try another." He did just that, and *McCarthyism* became a synonym for public charges of disloyalty without sufficient regard for evidence.

As the Korean War dragged on, McCarthy's efforts to "root out the skunks" escalated. He ridiculed "the elegant and alien Acheson—Russian as to heart, British as to manner," as the "Red Dean of the State Department." He called Truman's dismissal of MacArthur "the greatest victory the communists have ever won." And he charged George Marshall with having "aided and abetted a communist conspiracy so immense as to dwarf any previous such venture in the history of man."

McCarthy's attacks appealed most to midwestern Republicans indignant about the welfare state and the Europe-first emphasis of Truman's foreign policy. For them, anticommunism was a weapon of revenge against liberals and internationalists, and a means to regain the controlling position that conservative forces had once held. McCarthy also won a devoted following among blue-collar workers who identified with the senator's charge that a person was either a true American who detested "communists and queers" or an "egg sucking phony liberal." Laborers praised his demand that the war against communism be fought with brass knuckles, not kid gloves. His flag-waving patriotic appeals held a special attraction for traditionally Democratic Catholic ethnics, who sought to gain acceptance as "100 percent Americans" through displays of anticommunist zeal. Countless Americans also shared McCarthy's hatred of privilege and gentility, of the "bright young men who are born with silver spoons in their mouths," of the "striped-pants boys in the State Department." And his conspiratorial explanation offered a simple answer to the perplexing questions of the Cold War.

McCarthy's political power rested on the Republican establishment's support and on Democrats' fears of antagonizing him. The backing of McCarthy by his GOP colleagues made Democratic condemnations of the senator's tactics seem mere partisan criticism. And

when he helped Republican candidates in the 1950 congressional elections to unseat Democrats who had denounced him, McCarthy appeared invincible. "Look out for McCarthy" became the Senate watchword. "Joe will go that extra mile to destroy you," warned the new majority leader, Lyndon B. Johnson of Texas. However much Democratic members of Congress detested him, few dared incur his wrath.

Over Truman's veto federal lawmakers in 1950 adopted the McCarran Internal Security Act. It required all communist groups to register with the attorney general, forbade the entry into the United States of anyone suspected of communism, and authorized the arrest and detention during a national emergency of "any person as to whom there is reason to believe might engage in acts of espionage or sabotage." As part of this effort, a Senate committee sought to root out homosexuals holding government jobs. The linking of disloyalty with homosexuality in turn legitimated the armed forces effort to dismiss "queers" and the raiding of gay bars by city police. The McCarran-Walter Immigration and Nationality Act of 1952, also enacted over Truman's veto, maintained the quota system that severely restricted immigration from southern and eastern Europe, and increased the attorney general's authority to exclude and deport aliens suspected of supporting communism.

## The Election of 1952

By 1952 public apprehension about the loyalty of government employees combined with frustration over the Korean stalemate to sink Democratic presidential hopes to their lowest level since the 1920s. Both business and labor also resented Truman's decision to freeze wages and prices during the Korean conflict. And revelations of bribery and influence peddling by some of Truman's old political associates gave the Republicans ammunition for charging the party in power with "plunder at home, and blunder abroad." In a late-1951 Gallup poll, Truman's standing dropped to an all-time low of 23 percent, and early in 1952, after he had

**The Election of 1952**

| Candidates | Parties | Electoral Vote | Popular Vote | Percentage of Popular Vote |
|---|---|---|---|---|
| DWIGHT D. EISENHOWER | Republican | 442 | 33,936,234 | 55.1 |
| Adlai E. Stevenson | Democratic | 89 | 27,314,992 | 44.4 |

lost the New Hampshire presidential primary to Senator Estes Kefauver of Tennessee, Truman announced that he would not seek reelection.

Dispirited Democrats drafted the governor of Illinois, Adlai Stevenson, to be their nominee. While his eloquence turned some "madly for Adlai," Stevenson's lofty speches failed to stir most voters. He could not disassociate himself from the unpopular Truman. Nor could he overcome the widespread sentiment that twenty years of Democratic rule was enough and that, as the Republicans proclaimed, "It's time for a change."

Compounding Democratic woes, the GOP nominated popular war hero Dwight D. Eisenhower. In 1948 Eisenhower had rejected Democratic pleas that he head their ticket, insisting that "lifelong professional soldiers should abstain from seeking higher political office." But in 1952 he answered the call of the moderate wing of the Republican party, opposed to the isolationist and conservative forces arrayed with Ohio senator Robert A. Taft. Eisenhower's supporters outmaneuvered Taft's and succeeded in getting "Ike" nominated on the first ballot. As a concession to the hard-line anticommunists in the party, Eisenhower accepted as his running mate Senator Richard M. Nixon of California, the former HUAC Red hunter who had exposed Alger Hiss and had won a seat in the Senate in 1950 by red-baiting his opponent, Helen Gahagan Douglas, as "pink right down to her underwear."

Eisenhower and Nixon proved unbeatable. With his captivating grin and unimpeachable record of public service, Eisenhower projected both personal warmth and the vigorous authority associated with military command. His smile, wrote one commentator, "was . . . a smile of infinite reassurance," promising benevolence and caring. Ike symbolized the stability for which Americans yearned. At the same time, Nixon kept public apprehensions at the boiling point. He accused the Democrats of treason, derided the Democratic candidate as "Adlai the appeaser . . . who got a Ph.D. from Dean Acheson's College of Cowardly Communist Containment," and charged that a Stevenson victory would bring "more Alger Hisses, more atomic spies."

The GOP ticket stumbled when newspapers revealed the existence of a "slush fund" created by California business leaders to keep Nixon in "financial comfort." However, Nixon saved his candidacy with a heart-tugging television defense. Eisenhower followed with a pledge to "go to Korea" to end the stalemated war.

It worked: 62.7 percent of those eligible to vote (compared to just 51.5 percent in 1948) turned out in 1952 and gave the Republican ticket 55 percent of its ballots. Ike did best in the suburbs and with women, and he even won nearly half the votes of southerners, cracking the once-solid South and carrying thirty-nine states. He also managed to pull enough Republicans into office on his coattails to give the GOP control of both houses of Congress by small margins.

Dan Collins was typical of the many Americans who voted for Eisenhower in 1952. Collins had suffered through the depression and fought in World War II. In 1946 he returned to Boston and civilian status, "hoping to relax, get rich, and enjoy a bit of the good life." He earned more money in construction than he had previously dreamed possible and gained reassurance from his family values, religion, and patriotism. But Soviet expansionism abroad, coupled with fears of communist infiltration at home, intruded on his peace of mind. By 1951 Collins had concluded that "McCarthy must be on target in attacking those liberals in Washington." The following year, believing the Truman administration "riddled with Reds and corruption," Collins, a staunch Democrat, decided that "it was time to give the other guys a chance."

## CONCLUSION

The 1952 election ended both two decades of uninterrupted Democratic control of the White House and the first phase of a postwar era that would be shaped and dominated by the Cold War. The power vacuum left by the defeat of the Axis, the devastation of Europe, and the demise of colonialism in Asia and Africa provided the field upon which an assertive United States, eager to protect and expand its influence and power in the world, sought to contain a Soviet Union obsessed with its own security and self-interests. To that end, the United States aided Greece and Turkey in 1947 and established the Marshall Plan to promote economic recovery in Western Europe, then massively airlifted supplies into Berlin for a year to frustrate Soviet efforts to blockade that city, approved the creation of the Federal Republic of Germany (West Germany), established the North Atlantic Treaty Organization (NATO) in 1949, and went to war in Korea the following year.

American fear of the spread of international communism abroad also spawned anxiety about communist subversion within the United States. Truman's own Cold War rhetoric and efforts to safeguard American security encouraged others to seek scapegoats for the failures of the United States to get its way everywhere in the world, and legitimated conservative accusations that equated dissent with disloyalty, quashed the Left, and scourged the Democrats. This postwar Red Scare, along with the economic prosperity furthered by reconversion and the pent-up demand for consumer goods, weakened the appeal of liberal reform. Truman and the Democrats would protect or expand most of the measures of the New Deal still in place, but fail to enact the bold initiatives of the Fair Deal in education, health insurance, and civil rights. Now a Republican would assume the presidency, and Americans looked with hope at Ike's infectious grin as an omen of better times ahead.

## FOR FURTHER READING

Richard M. Fried, *Nightmare in Red: The McCarthy Era in Perspective* (1990). A cogent account of McCarthyism's rise and fall.

Alonzo L. Hamby, *Man of the People: A Life of Harry S Truman* (1995). A thoroughly researched account of Truman's life and presidency.

Melvyn Leffler, *A Preponderance of Power: National Security, the Truman Administration, and the Cold War* (1992). The most comprehensive and incisive history of the Cold War's early stages.

James T. Patterson, *Grand Expectations: The United States, 1945–1974* (1996). A magisterial account of all the major political, diplomatic, economic, and cultural events of the period.

Athan Theoharis and John Stuart Cox, *The Boss: J. Edgar Hoover and the Great American Inquisition* (1988). A biographical analysis highlighting the FBI's role in the 1950s Red Scare.

Graham White and John Maze, *Henry A. Wallace: His Search for a New World Order* (1995). An insightful analysis of Wallace, the Progressive party, and the demise of the Left.

Vladislav Zubok and Constantine Pleshakov, *Inside the Kremlin's Cold War* (1996). Russian historians offer new insights on Stalin's foreign policies.

# America at Midcentury

**Happy New Year**
*by Ben Prins*

"It starts with these giant ants that crawl out of the ground from that place in New Mexico where they tested the atomic bomb—Alamogordo. They're desperate for sugar, and they rip apart anybody who gets in their way. It ends in the sewers of Los Angeles—and it's *really* scary!"

The year was 1954, and moviegoers shivered in terror at *Them!*, the giant-ant film that was part of a wave of mutant movies pouring out of Hollywood in the fifties. In *The Incredible Shrinking Man*, the unlucky hero is accidentally exposed to "atomic dust" and begins to shrink. In *The Attack of the Fifty-Foot Women,* the process is reversed. Nuclear radiation also spawned a giant octopus in *It Came from Beneath the Sea,* unleashed *The Attack of the Crab Monsters,* and was responsible for the *Invasion of the Body Snatchers* by pods from outer space.

The vogue for science fiction and monster movies revealed anxieties underlying the apparent complacency of the 1950s, particularly the fear of the atmospheric nuclear tests that pumped into the world's environment radioactive clouds containing strontium 90, a cancer-causing chemical that accumulates in the teeth and bone marrow, especially of children.

Added to this were public fears of communism, of juvenile delinquency, and of homosexuality (usually depicted as an "alien" lifestyle, and associated with blackmail by Soviet agents). As such fears dimmed, the late 1960s saw an outpouring of nostalgia for the "nifty fifties." In the distorting mirror of memory, the decade came to seem a peaceful time of prosperity and easy living, of cheap gasoline and big cars, of new suburban homes and family togetherness. The mass media portrayed the fifties as a sunny time when almost everybody liked Ike and loved Lucy. Hollywood films and TV programs re-created the lives of the "typical" fifties teenagers, who wore white bucks and poodle skirts, did the bunny hop, and idolized Elvis Presley.

Like most historical generalizations, this image of the fifties contains elements of truth. Many Americans did enjoy the fruits of the decade's consumer culture. Having endured the hard times of the depression and war years, they reveled in a prosperity presided over by a popular president. They trusted Dwight Eisenhower and welcomed the thaw in the Cold War that came after the Korean War. Some high schoolers did lead the carefree, fun-filled existence captured in later media images.

Behind the stereotypes lies a reality far more complex. For this decade also saw scientists end the scourge of polio, unravel the structure of DNA, the nucleic-acid molecule in cells that determines inherited characteristics, and send satellites into space. It was a time of hydrogen bombs and intercontinental ballistic missiles, as well as of Women Strike for Peace, an organization of mostly middle-class housewives concerned about radioactivity in the atmosphere and the possibility of nuclear war. It was an era, too, of intense political passions, kindled by Senator Joseph McCarthy, the Warren Court, and civil-rights leader Martin Luther King, Jr. The advent of an automated and computerized postindustrial society, television's growing power, and the baby boom transformed society, as did mass suburbanization and a remarkable internal migration. Midcentury America encompassed peace and a widening Cold War, prosperity and persistent poverty, civil-rights triumphs and rampant racism. Although the fifties were good years for many Americans, they were also a time when the seeds of future crises were sown.

This chapter focuses on five major questions:

♦ Why is Eisenhower said to have practiced the politics of moderation? What evidence from his domestic and foreign policies supports this view?

♦ What were the objectives, successes, and failures of the civil-rights movement in the 1950s?

◆ What explains the rise and fall of McCarthyism in the early 1950s?

◆ What were the principal changes in foreign policy initiated by Eisenhower? How successfully did these changes accomplish Eisenhower's goals?

◆ How did television and developments like Levittown affect American life? How accurate is the fifties' reputation as a period of conservatism and conformity?

# The Eisenhower Presidency

Rarely in U.S. history has a president better fit the national mood than did Dwight David Eisenhower. Exhausted by a quarter-century of upheaval—the depression, World War II, the Cold War—Americans craved peace and stability. And Eisenhower delivered. He ended "Truman's folly" in Korea, kept the nation prosperous and out of war, and inspired confidence. He gave a nation weary of partisanship a sense of unity, and he pleased most Americans with his moderate policies.

Immensely popular, Eisenhower epitomized the virtues and hopes of many Americans. The most distinguished general of the Second World War, he projected the image of a plain but good man. He expressed complicated issues in simple terms yet governed a complex urban, technological society. At once the hero who had vanquished Hitler and a grandfatherly figure with twinkling blue eyes, Ike comforted an anxious people.

### The General as Chief Executive

Born on October 14, 1890, in Denison, Texas, Dwight Eisenhower grew up in Abilene, Kansas, in a poor, strongly religious family. More athletic than studious, he graduated from the U.S. Military Academy at West Point in 1915. In directing the Allied invasion of North Africa in 1943 and of Western Europe in 1944, Eisenhower proved himself a brilliant war planner and organizer. He emerged from the war a national hero, especially lauded for his managerial ability and talent for conciliation.

Eisenhower's approach to the presidency reflected his wartime leadership style. He concentrated on "the big picture" while laboring to reconcile contending factions. His restrained view of presidential authority reflected his conviction that FDR had concentrated too much power in his own hands and that Truman had demeaned the dignity of the presidency by openly feuding with Congress. He rarely intervened publicly in the legislative process, shunned using his office as a "bully pulpit," and assured his cabinet that he would "stay out of its hair." Preferring an orderly chain of command, he delegated much power to subordinates. Athough scoffed at by Democrats as a bumbler who preferred golf to government, who "reigned but did not rule," Eisenhower's image of passivity actually masked an active and occasionally ruthless politician.

**Ike at the White House, 1958**
*Like a benign grandfather, Dwight D. Eisenhower appealed to Americans by his confident presence and air of command as much as by his moderation, balanced judgment, and apparent aloofness from partisanship.*

### *"Dynamic Conservatism"*

Determined to govern the nation on business principles, Eisenhower staffed his administration with corporate executives. "Eight millionaires and a plumber," jested one journalist. Eisenhower in his first year worked with Congress to reduce the size of government and its budget. He also promoted the private development of hydroelectric and nuclear power, and won congressional approval for the Submerged Lands Act, which turned over to California, Louisiana, and Texas the oil-rich tidelands that the Supreme Court had previously awarded to the federal government.

In the main, the Eisenhower administration followed a centrist course. More pragmatic than ideological, he wished to reduce taxes, contain inflation, and govern efficiently. Facing powerful pressure groups and, after 1954, Democratic majorities in both houses of Congress, he accommodated himself to large-scale labor organizations and social welfare policies. Summing up the president's views, his brother and adviser

## CHRONOLOGY

| | | |
|---|---|---|
| **1944** | Mark I calculator begins operation. | |
| **1946** | Dr. Benjamin Spock, *Baby and Child Care.* | |
| | ENIAC, the first electronic computer, begins operation. | |
| **1947** | Levittown, New York, development started. | |
| **1948** | Bell Labs develops the transistor. | |
| **1950** | Asociación Nacional México-Americana established. | |
| **1952** | Dwight D. Eisenhower elected president. | |
| | Ralph Ellison, *The Invisible Man.* | |
| **1953** | Korean War truce signed. | |
| | CIA-supported coup in Iran. | |
| | Earl Warren appointed U.S. chief justice. | |
| | House Concurrent Resolution 108. | |
| **1954** | Army-McCarthy hearings. | |
| | *Brown* v. *Board of Education of Topeka.* | |

| | | |
|---|---|---|
| **1954** | *(continued)* | |
| | Fall of Dienbienphu; Geneva Conference. | |
| | CIA intervention in Guatemala. | |
| | "Father Knows Best" begins on TV. | |
| **1955** | Salk polio vaccine developed. | |
| | AFL-CIO merger. | |
| | First postwar U.S.–Soviet summit meeting. | |
| | James Dean stars in *Rebel Without a Cause.* | |
| | Montgomery bus boycott begins. | |
| **1956** | Interstate Highway Act. | |
| | Suez crisis. | |
| | Soviet intervention in Poland and Hungary. | |
| | Allen Ginsberg, *Howl.* | |
| | Eisenhower reelected. | |
| **1957** | Eisenhower Doctrine announced. | |
| | Civil Rights Act (first since Reconstruction). | |
| | Jack Kerouac, *On the Road.* | |

| | | |
|---|---|---|
| **1957** | *(continued)* | |
| | Little Rock school-desegregation crisis. | |
| | Soviet Union launches *Sputnik.* | |
| | Peak of "baby boom" (4.3 million births). | |
| **1958** | U.S. troops sent to Lebanon. | |
| | National Defense Education Act. | |
| | United States and Soviet Union halt atomic tests. | |
| | National Aeronautics and Space Administration (NASA) founded. | |
| **1959** | Fidel Castro comes to power in Cuba. | |
| | Khrushchev and Eisenhower meet at Camp David. | |
| **1960** | National Liberation Front of South Vietnam (NLF) established. | |
| | U-2 incident. | |
| | Second Civil Rights Act. | |
| **1961** | Eisenhower notes military-industrial complex. | |
| **1962** | Rachel Carson, *Silent Spring.* | |

Milton Eisenhower declared, "We should keep what we have, catch our breath for a while, and improve administration; it does not mean moving backward."

Eager to avoid a depression, Eisenhower relied heavily on the Council of Economic Advisers (CEA), despite conservative calls for its abolition. Following the advice of CEA head Arthur Burns (the only government official other than the secretary of state who had a weekly appointment with Ike), the president advocated using "any and all weapons in the federal arsenal, including changes in monetary and credit policy, modifications of the tax structure, and a speedup in the construction of public works" to stimulate the economy and check business downturns. When recessions struck in 1953 and 1957, Eisenhower abandoned a balanced budget and increased spending to restore prosperity.

The president labeled his ideas "dynamic conservatism" and "modern Republicanism." Whatever the slogan, Eisenhower went along with Congress when it extended social security benefits to more than 10 million Americans; raised the minimum wage from seventy-five cents to a dollar an hour; added 4 million workers to those eligible for unemployment benefits; and increased federally financed public housing for low-income families. He also approved construction of the St. Lawrence Seaway, linking the Great Lakes and the Atlantic Ocean, and creation of the Department of Health, Education and Welfare. In 1956 Eisenhower backed the largest and most expensive public-works program in American history: the Interstate Highway Act, authorizing the building of a 41,000-mile system of expressways. The freeways accelerated suburban growth, heightened dependency on cars and trucks, hastened the decline of the nation's rail lines, contributed to the decay of its central cities and the pollution of its air, and drastically increased gasoline consumption.

Republicans renominated Ike by acclamation in 1956, and voters gave him a landslide victory over Democrat Adlai Stevenson. With the GOP crowing "Everything's booming but the guns," Eisenhower won by the greatest popular majority since FDR's in 1936 and carried all but seven states.

### The Downfall of Joseph McCarthy

Although he despised McCarthy—calling him a "pimple on the path to progress"—Eisenhower considered it beneath his dignity to "get into the gutter with that guy" and feared confronting the senator. Instead, he tried to steal McCarthy's thunder by tightening security requirements for government employees; when that failed, he allowed McCarthy to grab plenty of rope in hopes that the demagogue would hang himself. McCarthy did so in 1954, when he accused the army of harboring communist spies. The army then charged McCarthy with using his influence to gain preferential treatment for a member of his staff who had been drafted. The resulting nationally televised Senate investigation in 1954 brought McCarthy down.

A national audience witnessed McCarthy's boorish behavior firsthand. His dark scowl, raspy voice, endless interruptions ("point of order, Mr. Chairman, point of order"), and disregard for the rights of others repelled many viewers. He behaved like the bad guy in a TV western, observed novelist John Steinbeck: "He had a stubble of a beard, he leered, he sneered, he had a nasty laugh. He bullied and shouted. He looked evil." In June, McCarthy slurred the reputation of a young lawyer assisting Joseph Welch, the army counsel. Suddenly the mild-mannered Welch turned his wrath on McCarthy—"Until this moment, Senator, I think I really never gauged your cruelty or your recklessness. . . . Have you no sense of decency?" The gallery burst into applause.

With the spell of the inquisitor broken, the GOP no longer needing him to drive the "Commiecrats" from power, the Democrats eager to be rid of their scourge, and Eisenhower applying pressure behind the scenes, the Senate voted in December 1954 to censure McCarthy for contemptuous behavior. This powerful rebuke—only the third in the Senate's history—demolished McCarthy as a political force. McCarthyism, Ike gloated, had become "McCarthywasism."

In 1957 McCarthy died a broken man, suffering from the effects of alcoholism. But the fears he exploited lingered. Congress annually funded the House Un-American Activities Committee's search for suspected radicals, and state and local governments continued to require teachers to take loyalty oaths. McCarthyism also remained a rallying call of conservatives disenchanted with the postwar consensus. Young conservatives like William F. Buckley, Jr. (a recent Yale graduate who founded the *National Review* in 1955), and such organizations as the Christian Anti-Communist Crusade and the John Birch Society, persisted in claiming that domestic communism remained a major subversive threat. Stressing victory over communism, rather than its containment, the self-proclaimed "new conservatives" (or radical right, as their opponents called them) also criticized the "creeping socialism" of Truman and Eisenhower, advocated a return to traditional moral standards, and attacked the Supreme Court.

### The Warren Court

Liberalized by the presence of a new chief justice, Earl Warren (1953), and three other Eisenhower appointees, the Supreme Court incurred conservatives' wrath for defending the rights of persons accused of subversive beliefs. In *Jencks* v. *United States* (1957), the Court held that the accused had the right to inspect government files used by the prosecution. In *Yates* v. *United States* (also 1957), the justices overturned the convictions of Communist party officials under the Smith Act (see Chapter 28), emphasizing the distinc-

### The Election of 1956

| Candidates | Parties | Electoral Vote | Popular Vote | Percentage of Popular Vote |
|---|---|---|---|---|
| DWIGHT D. EISENHOWER | Republican | 457 | 35,590,472 | 57.6 |
| Adlai E. Stevenson | Democratic | 73 | 26,022,752 | 42.1 |

tion between unlawful concrete acts and the teaching of revolutionary ideology. *Yates* essentially ended further prosecutions of communists, and right-wing opponents of the decision demanded limitations on the Court's powers and plastered "Impeach Earl Warren" posters on highway billboards.

These condemnations paled beside those of segregationists following *Brown* v. *Board of Education of Topeka* (May 17, 1954). In a unanimous ruling reversing *Plessy* v. *Ferguson* (see Chapter 21), the Court held that separating schoolchildren "solely because of their race generates a feeling of inferiority as to their status in the community that may affect their hearts and minds in a way unlikely ever to be undone" and thus violated the equal-protection clause of the Fourteenth Amendment. "In the field of public education," the nine justices concluded, "the doctrine of 'separate but equal' has no place. Separate educational facilities are inherently unequal." A year later, the High Court ordered federal district judges to monitor compliance with *Brown*, requiring only that desegregation proceed "with all deliberate speed"—an oxymoron that vaguely implied the necessity for gradualism.

The border states complied, but when white southerners rejected the Court's ruling, Eisenhower refused to try to force their acceptance. "I don't believe you can change the hearts of men with laws or decisions," he observed. Although not a racist, he never publicly endorsed the *Brown* decision and privately called his appointment of Earl Warren "the biggest damn fool mistake I ever made."

Public opinion polls in 1954 indicated that some 80 percent of white southerners opposed the *Brown* decision, and encouraged by Ike's silence, white resistance stiffened. White Citizens Councils sprang up, and the Ku Klux Klan revived. Declaring *Brown* "null, void, and of no effect," southern legislatures claimed the right to "interpose" themselves against the federal government and adopted a strategy of "massive resistance" to thwart compliance with the law. They denied state aid to local school systems that desegregated and even closed down public schools ordered to desegregate. Most effectively, the states enacted pupil placement laws that permitted school boards to assign black and white children to different schools.

In 1956 more than a hundred members of Congress signed the Southern Manifesto, denouncing *Brown* as "a clear abuse of judicial power." White southern politicians competed to "outnigger" each other in opposition to desegregation. When a gubernatorial candidate in Alabama promised to go to jail to defend segregation, his opponent swore that he would die for it. Segregationists also resorted to violence and economic reprisals against blacks to maintain all-white schools. At the end of 1956, not a single black attended school with whites in the Deep South, and few did so in the Upper South.

## The Laws of the Land

Southern resistance reached a climax in September 1957 when Arkansas governor Orval E. Faubus mobilized the state's National Guard to bar nine African-American students from entering Little Rock's Central High School under a federal court order. After another court order forced Faubus to withdraw the guardsmen, a mob of whites blocked the black students' entry.

On national television, Eisenhower condemned this "disgraceful occurrence," ordering those obstructing federal law "to disperse forthwith." When the mob defied him, the president federalized the Arkansas National Guard and, for the first time since Reconstruction, dispatched federal troops to protect blacks' rights. To ensure the safety of the black students, soldiers patrolled Central High for the rest of the year. Rather than accept integration, however, Faubus shut down Little

**Little Rock, 1957**
*Elizabeth Eckford, age 15, one of the nine black students to desegregate Central High School, endures abuse on her way to school, September 4, 1957. Forty years later, the young white woman shouting insults asked for forgiveness.*

Rock's public high schools for two years. At the end of the decade, fewer than 1 percent of African-American students in the Deep South attended desegregated schools.

This resistance by white southerners, the flouting of the law of the land, strengthened the determination of African Americans to force the South to comply with desegregation. And Little Rock in particular foreshadowed television's vital role in the demise of Jim Crow. The contrast between the images of howling white racists and those of the clean-cut and resolute black students, projected so vividly on the TV screen, immensely aided the civil-rights cause. According to a 1957 public-opinion poll, fully 90 percent of whites outside the South approved the use of federal troops in Little Rock.

Most northern whites also favored legislation to enfranchise southern African Americans. Despite his personal reservations, Eisenhower proposed a voting-rights bill in the midst of the 1956 presidential campaign. The Civil Rights Act of 1957, the first civil-rights law since Reconstruction, established a permanent commission on civil rights with broad investigatory powers but did little to guarantee the ballot to blacks. The Civil Rights Act of 1960 only slightly strengthened the first measure's enforcement provisions. Neither act empowered federal officials to register African Americans to vote. Like the *Brown* decision, the laws revealed a changing attitude by the federal government and further encouraged blacks to fight for their due.

## The Cold War Continues

Internationally, the Eisenhower administration continued Truman's containment policy. Joseph Stalin's death in 1953 and Dwight Eisenhower's resolve to reduce the risk of nuclear war brought a thaw in the Cold War. But ideological deadlock still gripped the United States and the Cold War did not end. Nor did American determination to stop the spread of communism.

### Truce in Korea

Honoring his campaign pledge, Eisenhower went to Korea in December 1952, but he could not bring home a settlement. The fate of thousands of prisoners of war (POWs) who did not want to return to China or North Korea remained the sticking point in negotiations. Influenced by Eisenhower's hint that the United States

might use nuclear weapons to end the stalemate and by the uncertainty in the communist world after Stalin's death in March, North Korea agreed to an armistice in July 1953. A panel of representatives from neutral nations would oversee POW returns and Korea remained divided at the thirty-eighth parallel. Although Eisenhower claimed that communist aggression had been checked and the policy of containment vindicated, conservative critics condemned the truce as peace without honor.

### Ike and Dulles

Eager to ease Cold War tensions, Eisenhower first sought to quiet the Republican right-wing clamor for efforts to roll back the Red tide. To do so he chose as his secretary of state John Foster Dulles.

A rigid Presbyterian whose humorlessness led some to dub him "Dull, Duller, Dulles," the secretary of state talked of a holy war against "atheistic communism," "liberating" the captive peoples of Eastern Europe, and unleashing Jiang Jieshi against Communist China. Believing that the Soviet Union understood only force, Dulles insisted on the necessity of "brinksmanship," the art of never backing down in a crisis, even if it meant risking war.

Such saber-rattling pleased the Right, but Eisenhower preferred conciliation. Partly because he feared a nuclear war with the Soviet Union, which had tested its own H-bomb in 1953, Eisenhower refused to translate Dulles's rhetoric into action. The president understood the limits of American power. When East German workers rioted in 1953 and the Hungarians and Poles revolted in 1956, the United States did nothing to prevent the Soviets from crushing these insurrections.

### Waging Peace

As Hiroshima-size atomic bombs gave way to multi-megaton thermonuclear weapons in the American and Soviet arsenals, Eisenhower labored to reduce the probability of mutual annihilation. He proposed an "atoms for peace" plan, whereby both superpowers would contribute fissionable materials to a new U.N. agency for use in industrial projects. Meanwhile, mounting fears over radioactive fallout from atmospheric atomic tests, especially the 1954 U.S. test series in the Pacific that spread strontium 90 over a wide area, heightened world concern about the nuclear-arms race.

Dec 9, 1961    THE    Price 25 cents

**NEW YORKER**

**The Space-Age Toy Shop, 1950s**
*Through the eyes of two innocent children ogling a
fantastic assortment of toy doomsday weapons,
the cartoonist captured modern society's fascination with the space-age tools of global destruction.*

In 1955 Eisenhower and the Soviet leaders met in
Geneva for the first East-West summit conference since
the Second World War. Mutual talk of "peaceful coexistence" led reporters to hail the "spirit of Geneva." Although the two nations could not agree on a specific
plan for nuclear-arms control, Moscow suspended further atmospheric tests of nuclear weapons in March
1958 and the United States followed suit.

Still, the Cold War continued. Dulles negotiated
mutual-defense pacts with any nation that would join
the United States in opposing communism. Dulles's
"pactomania," as some called it, committed the United
States to the defense of forty-three nations. Primarily
the administration relied on the U.S. nuclear arsenal to
deter the Soviets. Tailored to suit fiscally conservative
Republicans, the "New Look" defense program
promised "more bang for the buck" by emphasizing
nuclear weapons and reducing conventional forces. It
resulted in spurring the Soviets to seek "more rubble
for the ruble" by enlarging their own nuclear stockpile.

Meanwhile, the focus of the Cold War shifted
from Europe to the Third World, the largely nonwhite
developing nations. There the two superpowers waged
war by proxy, using local guerrillas and military juntas
to battle in isolated deserts and steamy jungles. There
too, the Central Intelligence Agency (CIA) fought a
covert war against those thought to be imperiling
American interests.

### The Clandestine CIA

To command the CIA, Eisenhower chose Allen Dulles, a
veteran of wartime OSS cloak-and-dagger operations
and the brother of the secretary of state. Established in
1947 to coordinate foreign intelligence gathering, the
CIA became increasingly involved in secret operations
to undermine regimes friendly to communism. By
1957 half its personnel and 80 percent of its budget
were devoted to "covert action"—subverting governments, putting foreign leaders (like King Hussein of
Jordan) on its payroll, supporting foreign political parties (such as the Liberal Democratic Party of Japan),
and subsidizing foreign newspapers and labor unions
that hewed to a pro-American line. The CIA also used
American businessmen and journalists, as well as college students and professors, as "fronts" in its clandestine activities.

Led by a grandson of Teddy Roosevelt, the CIA's Operation Ajax in 1953 toppled the popularly elected Iranian government and returned the deposed shah to his
throne. The United States thus gained a loyal ally on
the Soviet border, and American oil companies prospered from Iranian oil concessions. But the seeds of
Iranian hatred of America had been sown—an enmity
that would haunt the United States a quarter-century
later.

In 1953, to ensure a pro-American government, the
CIA intervened in elections in the Philippines. In 1954 a
CIA-trained band of mercenaries overthrew the incum-
bent government in Guatemala that had seized lands
from the American-owned United Fruit Company. The
new pro-American regime then restored United Fruit's
properties and trampled all political opposition.

### Conflict in Vietnam

The most extensive CIA covert operations during the
1950s took place in Indochina. As a result of Mao Zedong's victory in China and the outbreak of war in Korea, the United States viewed Indochina as a strategic
arena in the Cold War. The Truman administration

had furnished the French (who were seeking to reconquer their former colony of Vietnam) with large-scale military assistance to fight the Vietminh, a broad-based Vietnamese nationalist coalition led by the communist Ho Chi Minh (see Chapter 28). By 1954 American aid accounted for three-quarters of French expenditures. Still, the French tottered near defeat. In early 1954 the Vietminh trapped twelve thousand French troops in the valley of Dienbienphu.

France appealed for U.S. intervention. But the president demurred, unwilling to commit U.S. troops to a jungle war against a popular liberation movement: "I cannot conceive of a greater tragedy for America." On May 7, 1954, the French surrendered at Dienbienphu, and in July an international conference in Geneva arranged a cease-fire and divided Vietnam at the seventeenth parallel pending elections in 1956 to choose the government of a unified nation.

Though opposed to committing the United States to another Asian land war, Eisenhower feared the consequences of a communist takeover in Vietnam and refused to sign the Geneva Peace Accords. He made his concern graphic in his "domino theory": If Vietnam fell, nearby Thailand, Burma, and Indonesia, and ultimately all of America's Asian allies, would follow.

Eisenhower ignored the Geneva settlement. The CIA mission in Vietnam helped install Ngo Dinh Diem, a fiercely anticommunist Catholic, first as premier of France's puppet state and then, in 1955, as president of an independent South Vietnam. CIA agents worked with Diem to train his armed forces and secret police, to eliminate political opposition, and to block the election to reunify Vietnam specified by the Geneva agreements. As Eisenhower later admitted, the United States did not want the election held because "possibly 80 percent of the population would have voted for the communist Ho Chi Minh as their leader." Washington pinned its hopes on Diem to maintain a noncommunist South Vietnam.

But the autocratic Diem never rallied public support. His Catholicism alienated the predominantly Buddhist population; and his refusal to institute land reform and to end corruption spurred opposition. In 1957 former Vietminh guerrillas began attacks against the Saigon regime, and in December 1960 they organized as the National Liberation Front of South Vietnam (NLF). Backed by North Vietnam, the insurgents attracted broad support. And as Diem's rule weakened, he relied more and more on the billions of dollars and the growing corps of U.S. advisers that the Eisenhower administration supplied. Although Diem spurned U.S.

requests to make the reforms that might undercut the NLF's appeal, the United States resolved to "sink or swim with Ngo Dinh Diem."

### *Antiwesternism in the Middle East*

As troubles simmered in Vietnam, Eisenhower faced his greatest crisis in the Middle East. Egyptian nationalist Gamal Abdel Nasser came to power in 1954 determined to modernize his nation. To woo him, the United States offered money to build a huge dam on the Nile at Aswan. Eisenhower, however, would not sell Nasser the arms he wanted. The communists would, and did. Dulles then canceled the offer of a loan, and Nasser responded by nationalizing the Suez Canal.

Britain, seeing the canal as the lifeline of its empire, decided to take it back by force. It was supported by France, fearful of Arab nationalism in its Algerian colony; and by Israel, alarmed by Arab hit-and-run raids along its borders and by Nasser's blockade of the Gulf of Aqaba, its only Red Sea outlet. On October 29, 1956, Israeli armored columns struck the Sinai Peninsula, and two days later British and French troops invaded Egypt, taking Port Said. The conflict enraged Eisenhower. America's closest allies had failed to consult him, and Moscow was threatening nuclear retaliation if France and Britain did not withdraw. "Goddamn it, we're going to apply sanctions, we're going to the United Nations, we're going to do everything that there is so we can stop this thing," Eisenhower fumed, forcing his allies to back down and, just nine days after the invasion began, to promise to withdraw their troops.

The Suez crisis had vital consequences. It intensified anti-Western sentiment in the Third World and enhanced Nasser's stature. It enabled the Soviet Union to recover much of the prestige it had lost as a consequence of its suppression of the revolt in Hungary. And it resulted in the United States replacing Britain and France as the protector of Western interests in the Middle East. Anxious to keep the oil of Iran, Iraq, Kuwait, and Saudi Arabia (about 60 percent of the world's known reserves) flowing to the West, the president in January 1957 announced the Eisenhower Doctrine, a proclamation that the United States was "prepared to use armed force" in the Middle East against "aggression from any country controlled by international communism." To prove he meant it, Eisenhower ordered fourteen thousand marines into Lebanon in July 1958 to quell a threatened revolt against the pro-Western regime.

## Frustrations Abroad

Such interventions stigmatized the United States as a foe of national liberation, social reform, and popular democracy among neutralists and nationalists in the Third World. Shouting "yanqui imperialism," angry crowds in Peru and Venezuela spat at Vice President Nixon and stoned his car in 1958. The following year, Fidel Castro overturned a dictatorial regime in Cuba. Denouncing the domination of Cuba by business interests in the United States, Castro confiscated American properties without compensation. Eisenhower retaliated by embargoing Cuban sugar and plotting to eliminate Castro. In 1960 anti-American riots rocked Japan, forcing Eisenhower to cancel his visit to the United States' strongest Asian ally.

A tougher blow struck Eisenhower on May 1, 1960, two weeks before a scheduled summit conference with Soviet premier Nikita Khrushchev, when the Soviets shot down a U.S. spy plane far inside their border. Khrushchev displayed to the world the captured CIA pilot and the photos he had taken of Soviet missile sites. Eisenhower took full responsibility for the U-2 missions but refused to apologize to the Soviet Union. The summit collapsed.

## The Eisenhower Legacy

Just before leaving office, Eisenhower offered Americans a farewell and warning. The demands of national security, he stated, had produced the "conjunction of an immense military establishment and a large arms industry that is new in the American experience." Swollen Cold War defense budgets had made the health of the economy dependent on military expenditures. Defense contracts had become the staff of life for scholars at research universities, for politicians from districts housing air and naval bases, and for executives at the United States' largest corporations. This combination of interests, Eisenhower believed, exerted enormous leverage and threatened the traditional subordination of the military in American life. "We must guard against the acquisition of unwarranted influence . . . by the military-industrial complex. The potential for the disastrous rise of misplaced power exists and will persist."

The president concluded that he had avoided war but could not affirm that lasting peace was in sight. Most scholars agreed. He ended the war in Korea, avoided direct military intervention in Vietnam, began relaxing tensions with the Soviet Union, and cooperated in achieving a lull in the atmospheric testing of doomsday weapons. Yet he had also presided over an accelerating nuclear-arms race and a widening Cold War and had allowed the CIA to intervene in local conflicts around the globe.

Eisenhower the moderate pleased neither Left nor Right in domestic affairs. Conservatives grumbled that Ike's memoir should have been titled *More of the Same* rather than *Mandate for Change.* Liberals faulted him

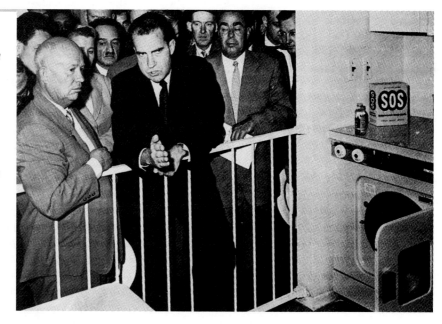

**The Great Debate, July 24, 1959**
*At the opening of the American National Exhibit in Moscow, Vice President Richard Nixon and Soviet Premier Nikita Khrushchev engaged in a "kitchen debate," arguing not about the strength of their rockets or bombs but about the relative merits of American and Soviet washing machines and television sets.*

for passivity in the face of McCarthyism and racism, joking that his White House was the tomb of the well-known soldier. Yet, rather than what ideologues thought Americans should want or what critics insisted the country needed, Eisenhower gave a majority of voters what they wanted. They yearned for reassurance, and Eisenhower supplied it. As lucky as he was skillful, Eisenhower led the nation during a great economic boom; and in an age of upheaval, he furnished what Americans most desired: a breathing spell in which to relish the comforts of life.

## The Affluent Society

In 1958 economist John Kenneth Galbraith published *The Affluent Society,* a study of postwar America whose title reflected the broad-based prosperity that made the 1950s seem the fulfillment of the American dream. By the end of the decade, about 60 percent of all American families owned homes; 75 percent, cars; and 87 percent, at least one TV. The gross national product in the 1950s increased 50 percent as a consequence of heavy government spending, a huge upsurge in productivity, and a steadily increasing demand for consumer goods and services.

Three brief recessions and a rising national debt, almost $290 billion by 1961, evoked concern but did little to halt economic growth or stifle optimism. The United States had achieved the world's highest living standard ever. By 1960 the average worker's income, adjusted for inflation, was 35 percent higher than in 1945. With just 6 percent of the world's population, the United States produced and consumed nearly half of everything made and sold on earth.

### The New Industrial Society

Federal spending constituted a major source of economic growth, nearly doubling in the 1950s to $180 billion, as did the outlays of state and local governments. Federal expenditures (accounting for 17 percent of the GNP in the mid-1950s, compared to just 1 percent in 1929) built roads and airports, financed home mortgages, supported farm prices, and provided stipends for education. But more than *half* the federal budget—about 10 percent of the GNP—went to defense spending. Continued superpower rivalry in atomic munitions, missile-delivery systems, and the space race kept the federal government the nation's main financier of both scientific and technological research and development (R&D).

For the West, especially, it was as if World War II never ended, as the new Air Force Academy in Colorado Springs signified. Politicians from both parties labored to keep defense spending flowing westward. Both liberal and conservative members of Congress from California sought contracts for Lockheed, as did those from Texas for General Dynamics, and those from Washington for Boeing. In the late 1950s California alone received half the space budget and a quarter of all major military contracts. By then, as well, Denver had the largest number of federal employees outside Washington, D.C.; Albuquerque R&D boasted more Ph.D. degrees per capita than any other U.S. city; and over a third of those employed in Los Angeles depended on defense industries. The Mormon dream of an agricultural utopia had become a Utah that led the nation in receiving expenditures per capita on space and defense

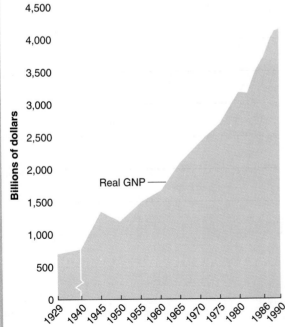

**Gross National Product, 1929–1990**

*Following World War II, the United States achieved the highest living standard in world history. Between 1950 and 1970, the real GNP, which factors out inflation and reveals the actual amount of goods and services produced, steadily increased. However, in 1972, 1974–1975, 1980, and 1982 the real GNP declined.*

Real GNP

*Source:* Economic Report of the President, 1991.
*Note:* Data shown in 1982 dollars.

research. Government spending had transformed the independent, individualistic West of cowboys, miners, and farmers into a new West of bureaucrats, manufacturers, and scientists dependent on federal funds.

Government-financed science transformed U.S. industry. Funded by the AEC and utilizing Navy scientists, the Duquesne Light Company in 1954 began construction in Shippingport, Pennsylvania, of the nation's first nuclear-power plant. Chemicals surged from the fiftieth-largest industry before the war to the nation's fourth-largest in the 1960s. As chemical fertilizers and pesticides contaminated groundwater supplies, and as the expansion of plastics for consumer products reduced landfill space, Americans—unaware of the hidden perils—marveled at the fruits and vegetables they could buy and delighted in their Dacron suits, Orlon shirts, Acrilan socks, and Teflon-coated pots and pans.

Electronics became the fifth-largest American industry, providing industrial equipment and consumer appliances. Electricity consumption tripled in the 1950s as industry automated and consumers, learning "to live better electrically," as commercials urged, purchased electric washers and dryers, freezers, blenders, television sets, and stereos, as well as electric blankets, electric garage-door openers, and electric pencil sharpeners. Essential to the expansion in both the chemical and the electronics industry was the availability of inexpensive petroleum. With domestic crude-oil production increasing close to 50 percent and petroleum imports rising from 74 million to 371 million barrels between 1945 and 1960, oil replaced coal as the nation's main energy source. Hardly anyone paid attention when a physicist in 1953 warned that "adding 6 billion tons of carbon dioxide to the atmosphere each year is warming up the Earth."

Plentiful, cheap gasoline fed the growth of the automobile and aircraft industries. The nation's third-largest industry in the 1950s, aerospace depended heavily on

**The New West**

*Symbolic of the defense spending and investment that helped the West's economy flourish, Seattle's Boeing plant in 1951 began production of the first of the B-52 Stratofortress heavy bombers. They would continue rolling off the Boeing assembly line until the end of the decade.*

defense spending and federally funded research. The manufacture of jet aircraft, ballistic missiles, and space equipment employed more people than did logging and timbering in Washington; and just the four metropolitan areas of Seattle, Dallas–Fort Worth, San Diego, and Los Angeles accounted for nearly all of the nation's aircraft production. The automobile industry, still the titan of the American economy, also utilized technological R&D. Where it had once partially replaced human labor with machinery, it now used automation to control the machines. Between 1945 and 1960, the industry halved the number of hours and workers required to produce a car. Other manufacturers followed suit, investing $10 billion a year throughout the fifties on labor-saving machinery.

## The Age of Computers

The computer was a major key to the technological revolution. In 1944 International Business Machines (IBM), cooperating with Harvard scientists, had produced the Mark I calculator, a slow, cumbersome device of five hundred miles of wiring and three thousand electromechanical relays to decipher secret Axis codes. Two years later, to improve artillery accuracy, the U.S.

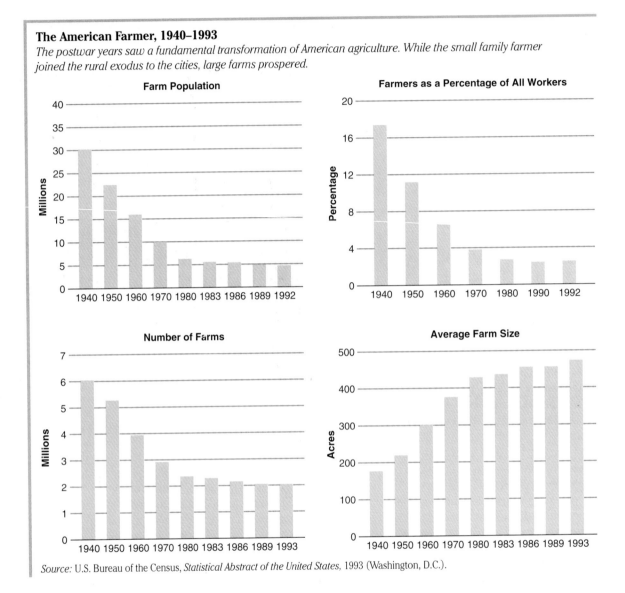

**The American Farmer, 1940–1993**

*The postwar years saw a fundamental transformation of American agriculture. While the small family farmer joined the rural exodus to the cities, large farms prospered.*

*Source:* U.S. Bureau of the Census, *Statistical Abstract of the United States,* 1993 (Washington, D.C.).

Army developed ENIAC, the first electronic computer. Still unwieldly, with tens of thousands of vacuum tubes and resistors, ENIAC reduced the time required to multiply two tenth-place numbers from Mark I's three seconds to less than three-thousandths of a second. Then came the development of operating instructions, or programs, that could be stored inside the computer memory; the substitution of printed circuits for wired ones; and in 1948, at Bell Labs, the invention of tiny, solid-state transistors that ended reliance on radio tubes.

The computer fundamentally changed the American economy and society. Sales of electronic comput-

ers to industry rose from twenty in 1954 to more than a thousand in 1957, and to more than two thousand in 1960. Major manufacturers used them to monitor production lines, track inventory, and ensure quality control. The government, which used three machines in computing the 1950 census returns, employed several hundred on the 1960 census. They became as indispensable to Pentagon strategists playing war games as to the Internal Revenue Service, as integral to meteorologists as to scientists "flying" rockets on the drawing board. By the mid-1960s more than thirty thousand mainframe computers would be used by banks, insurance firms, stock brokerages, hospitals, and universities. They enabled fewer workers to do more in less time than ever before, changing the nature of work as well as its landscape.

The first major step in the development of the high-technology complex known as Silicon Valley came with the opening of the Stanford Industrial Park in 1951. Seeking to develop its landholdings around Palo Alto, and to attract financial aid from business and government, Stanford University utilized its science and engineering faculties to design and produce products for the Fairchild Semiconductor and Hewlett-Packard companies. As this relationship became a model followed by other high-tech firms, apricot and cherry orchards throughout the Santa Clara Valley gave way to glass buildings in industrial parks for computer and aerospace firms, for microwave and pharmaceutical laboratories. Initially a far cry from the dirt and noise of eastern factories, these campus-like facilities would eventually choke the valley with traffic congestion, housing developments, and smog.

**Scientific Agriculture, 1955**

*A Pennsylvania farmer surveying the array of synthetic fertilizers, insecticides, and chemicals he annually uses on his 78-acre farm.*

## Concentration and Consolidation

Rapid technological advances accelerated the growth and power of big business. In 1950 twenty-two U.S. firms had assets of more than $1 billion; ten years later more than fifty did. By 1960 one-half of 1 percent of all companies earned more than half the total corporate income in the United States. The wealthiest, which could afford huge R&D outlays, became oligopolies, swallowing up weak competitors. Just as three television networks monopolized the nation's airwaves, so three automobile and three aluminum companies produced more than 90 percent of America's cars and aluminum, and a handful of firms controlled the lion's share of assets and sales in steel, petroleum, chemicals, and electrical machinery. Corporations also formed conglomerates by merging companies in unrelated industries, and acquired overseas facilities to become "multinational" enterprises. Despite talk of "people's capitalism," the oil-rich Rockefeller family alone owned more corporate stock than all the nation's wage earners combined.

Growth and consolidation brought further bureaucratization. "Executives" replaced "capitalists." Divorced from the ownership of the corporations they ran, professional managers oversaw R&D, production, advertising, sales, accounting, investment, and labor relations. Rewarded in their own careers for "fitting in" and for bowing to the dictates of the group rather than adhering to personal values, sociologist David Riesman contrasted their "other-directed" behavior with the "inner-directed" orientation of small businesspeople and professionals of earlier years, guided by the values they had learned in their youth.

Changes in American agriculture paralleled those in industry. Farming grew increasingly scientific and mechanized. Between 1949 and 1969, the percentage of cotton harvested by machine rose from 10 to 96 percent; and overall, between 1945 and 1960, technology cut the work hours necessary to grow crops by half, forcing many farm families to migrate to cities. In 1956 alone, one-eleventh of the farm population left the land.

**Rachel Carson**
*The mother of modern ecology, Carson exposed the dangers of pesticides to animal and human life in her 1962 bestseller* Silent Spring, *an enormously influential work that helped redefine the way humans look at their place in nature.*

Meanwhile, well-capitalized farm businesses, running "factories in the field," prospered by using more and more machines and chemicals.

Few Americans understood the extent to which the fertilizers, herbicides, and pesticides that brought huge gains in yields also poisoned the environment until the publication of Rachel Carson's *Silent Spring* in 1962. A former researcher for the Fish and Wildlife Service, Carson demonstrated the problems caused by the use of the insecticide DDT and its spread through the food chain. Her depiction of a "silent spring" caused by the death of songbirds from DDT toxicity led many states to ban the use of DDT, and the federal government to follow suit in 1972. Still, the incentives for cultivating more land, and more marginal land, provided by chemicals led to further ravages. As the Army Corps of Engineers and the Bureau of Reclamation raced to dam the waters of the West, they turned the Columbia and Missouri Rivers into rows of slack-water reservoirs, killing fish and wildlife, as well as immersing hundreds of square miles of Indian tribal lands.

## Blue-Collar Blues

Consolidation also transformed the labor movement. In 1955 the AFL and CIO merged, bringing 85 percent of union members into a single organization. Although its leadership promised aggressive unionism, the movement's old militancy was dead.

Organized labor had, in part, fallen victim to its own success. The benefits earned at the bargaining table bred complacency. Higher wages, shorter workweeks, paid vacations, health-care coverage, and automatic wage hikes tied to the cost of living led most workers to view themselves as middle class, not as an aggrieved proletariat. Labor turbulence quieted.

A decrease in the number of blue-collar workers further sapped organized labor. As automation reduced the number of laborers in coal mines, auto plants, and steel mills, membership in those once mighty industrial unions dropped by more than half. Most of the new jobs in the 1950s were in the service sector and in public employment, which banned collective bargaining by labor unions.

In 1956, for the first time in U.S. history, white-collar workers outnumbered blue-collar workers; by 1970 they would comprise 65 percent of the work force, leading some to conclude that the United States had become a "postindustrial" society. Although this belief minimized the fact that more service jobs involved manual labor than intellect, and that most clerical, food preparation, and sales work was as routinized as any factory job, few unions sought to woo the service worker. The percentage of the labor force in unions dropped from a high of 36 percent in 1953 to 31 percent in 1960.

## Prosperity and the Suburbs

As real income (adjusted for inflation) rose, Americans spent a lesser percentage of their income on necessities and more on the powered lawnmowers, air conditioners, and striped toothpaste that they longed for after the deprivations of the 1930s and the scarcities of the war years. They heaped their shopping carts with frozen, dehydrated, and fortified foods. And when they lacked cash, they borrowed. In 1950 Diner's Club issued the first credit card, and American Express followed in 1958. Installment buying, home mortgages, and auto loans raised Americans' total private indebtedness in the 1950s from $73 billion to $196 billion. To keep America buying, advertising expenditures tripled: busi-

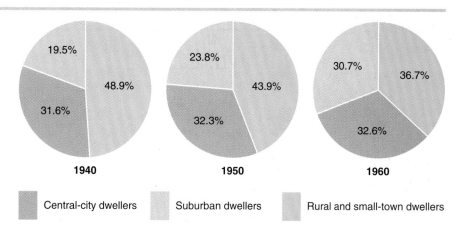

### Urban, Suburban, and Rural Americans, 1940–1960

*In the fifteen years following World War II, more than 40 million Americans migrated to the suburbs, where, as one father put it, "a kid could grow up with grass stains on his pants." Over the same period, fourteen of the fifteen largest U.S. cities lost population.*

*Source:* Adapted from U.S. Bureau of the Census, *Current Censuses,* 1930–1970 (Washington, D.C.: U.S. Government Printing Office).

1940 — 19.5%, 48.9%, 31.6%
1950 — 23.8%, 43.9%, 32.3%
1960 — 30.7%, 36.7%, 32.6%

Central-city dwellers   Suburban dwellers   Rural and small-town dwellers

ness spent more on advertising each year than the nation spent on public education.

Responding to the slogan "You auto buy now," Americans purchased 58 million new cars during the 1950s. Manufacturers enticed people to trade in and up by offering bigger and flashier models, more chrome and two-tone colors, extra-powerful engines, like Pontiac's 1955 "Sensational Strato-Streak V-8," that could propel riders more than twice as fast as any speed limit, and, inspired by the silhouette of the Lockheed P-38 fighter plane, tail-fins. Seat belts, however, remained an unadvertised extra-cost option. With these trends came increases in highway deaths, air pollution, oil consumption, and "autosclerosis"—clogged urban arteries.

Government policy as well as "auto mania" spurred white Americans' exodus to the suburbs. As federal spending on highways skyrocketed from $79 million in 1946 to $2.6 billion in 1960, once-remote areas came within "commuting distance" for urban workers. The income tax code stimulated home sales by allowing deductions for home-mortgage interest payments and for property taxes, and both the Federal Housing Administration (FHA) and Veterans Administration (VA) offered low-interest loans.

Eighty-five percent of the 13 million new homes built in the 1950s were in the suburbs. They drew the many Americans in search of single-family dwellings that promised greater privacy, roominess, and comfort. Others fled the crime and grime of the central cities, seeking to distance themselves from the millions of newly urbanized minorities. And many headed for suburbia in quest of communities oriented toward children and education (see A Place in Time).

While social critics lampooned the "split-level trap" of "ticky-tacky" houses in "disturbia," most suburbanites enjoyed their new lifestyles, tranquil surroundings, and like-minded neighbors. To a nation of immigrants, most from countries where only the elite owned prop-

### Made for Each Other

*The two-tone '55 Chevy Bel Air convertible and a California suburban drive-in. As Americans flocked to the new suburban communities the number of cars in the country increased by 133 percent between 1945 and 1960; and as Americans raced to buy the latest, flashiest model, almost as many cars were junked each year in the mid-1950s as were manufactured.*

## Levittown, U.S.A.

Alfred and William Levitt revolutionized home construction much as Henry Ford did automobile production and Henry Kaiser shipbuilding. Their pioneering use of mass-production techniques to construct a large, inexpensive housing development opened the gates for an exodus from the cities to the suburbs. Their success stimulated a host of imitators and a record 1.65 million housing starts in 1955.

Following the Second World War, Levitt & Sons purchased fifteen hundred acres of potato fields on Long Island's Hempstead Plain, some thirty miles from midtown Manhattan. In response to the housing shortage, the Levitts quickly built 2,000 homes and rented them for just sixty-five dollars a month to married veterans eager to escape from their in-laws' residences or cramped apartments where landlords frowned on children. Using the standardized construction techniques that they had first employed in erecting low-cost housing units for wartime navy workers in Norfolk, Virginia, the Levitts then rapidly built and rented 2,000 more homes. In 1948 they began to offer the houses for sale. The company recognized that working Americans' ever-greater demand for suburban housing—a demand fueled by the easy availability of low-cost mortgages from the FHA and the VA, extensive car ownership, and the expanding U.S. highway system—promised a bonanza of profits. By 1951 the Levitts had built and sold another 13,500 homes.

To erect their 720-square-foot Cape Cod or ranch-style houses as quickly and cheaply as possible, the Levitts established their own lumber mill, nail factory, and electrical-supply company. They employed mainly unskilled, nonunion laborers, each of whom was trained to perform just one task. Everything moved on a fixed timetable as Levitt & Sons made "a factory of the whole building site." First came the bulldozers and trenching machines to strip and ditch each 60- by 100-foot lot in twenty-seven minutes. Another crew poured the concrete foundation. The next day "convoys of trucks moved over the pavements, tossing out prefabricated sidings at 8:00 A.M., toilets at 9:30, sinks and tubs at 10:00, sheetrock at 10:45, flooring at 11:00." One man did nothing but move from house to house bolting Bendix washing machines to the floor.

The homes all looked alike, down to the blinds on the windows. Each had two bedrooms; a bath; a kitchen equipped with an electric refrigerator, a range, and a washing machine; an expansion attic; and a living room with a fireplace, picture window, and built-in television set. Deeds to the property required door chimes, not buzzers, prohibited picket fences, mandated regular lawn mowing, and even specified when the wash could be hung to dry in the backyard. All the town streets curved at the same angle, and a tree was planted every twenty-eight feet.

### Levittown, Long Island, in 1949

*The popularity of this typical Levittown house, providing comfortable living space for this family of five on a lot sixty feet by one hundred feet, made the Levitts the nation's largest home builder.*

Critics decried the tasteless, monotonous conformity of Levittown; but young marrieds, as they were called, avidly purchased the Levitts' houses. Levittown's comforts and conveniences sharply contrasted with living conditions in the Quonset huts, trailer parks, and stuffy apartments to which many postwar Americans had become accustomed. One veteran, Wilbur Schaetzl, considered the crowded, violence-ridden Brooklyn neighborhood from which he had moved "so awful I'd rather not talk about it. Getting into this house was like being emancipated." Laura Forman, who had one child and was expecting a second, found Levittown to be a "paradise for children—and mothers. Soon after we moved in, neighbors I hadn't even met yet came in to help. Because my husband was working, they packed my bags, drove me to the hospital, and took care of my other baby. And they wouldn't let me buy anything for the new baby either. That carriage isn't mine and neither is the crib." Such small-town friendliness also appealed to Izzy Stark, who had previously lived in an apartment house without ever knowing his neighbors. Stark's Levittown friends "were closer than kin. When the girls go to a garden club meeting, we boys get together and baby-sit and play poker. Or one night we'll all go bowling or to the movies. And now we're all taking some of these adult education courses down at the school one night a week. I'm taking 'How to Finish Your Attic' and Bob and Harry are learning photography." Despite the long commute to his office in Manhattan (he would travel half a million miles, or twenty times around the world, before he retired), Stark had achieved "his dream house."

To meet the galloping demand for its low-cost homes, in the early 1950s Levitt & Sons bought eight square miles of spinach farmland on the Delaware River in Bucks County, Pennsylvania, and constructed a second Levittown of sixteen thousand homes. Still another followed in Willingboro, New Jersey. Each endeavor mirrored the Levitts' concern for planned orderliness. In the Bucks County development, they situated schools, churches, baseball fields, shopping centers, parking lots, and offices for doctors and dentists at symmetrical points outside the residential clusters. In Willingboro they integrated the houses and the recreational and shopping facilities within the various neighborhoods. But that was all that the Levitts wished to integrate. Fearful that the admission of blacks would provoke "white flight" from the communities that they designed, Levitt & Sons excluded African Americans. Not until the mid-1960s, when blacks brought suit to be allowed to purchase a home in Levittown, New Jersey, did the Levitts sell their first home to a nonwhite. As late as 1990, Long Island's Levittown had an African-American population of just 0.03 percent.

The enormous success of the Levittown ventures reflected the shift in population in the 1950s. The United States in these years increasingly became a nation of white suburbs and nonwhite cities. As the suburbs attracted not only more and more private homeowners but also more and more commerce and industry, the cities fell victim to shrinking tax bases just as their need for social services zoomed. Levittown and such similar suburban communities as Oak Meadows outside Chicago and Parkmerced near San Francisco had changed the face of America.

### Suburban Leisure Time

*Working and/or relaxing in one's backyard became the primary weekend activity in the nation's burgeoning suburbs in the 1950s.*

erty, having a home of one's own was the essence of the American dream.

While the urban population rose 10 percent in the 1950s, 18 million Americans moved to the suburbs—doubling its numbers. A freeway system designed to lure shoppers into downtown Los Angeles instead became the highway out of the city. Bulldozers ripped out three thousand acres of orange groves a day in LA County to make way for new housing developments, and Orange County, bordering Los Angeles, doubled its population in the 1940s and then tripled that in the 1950s. For the first time in the twentieth century, more Americans were homeowners than renters. By 1960 the suburban population equaled that of the central cities, and by 1970 the suburbs contained two-thirds of the metropolitan-area population and the cities only one-third—exactly the reverse of 1950.

Americans moved not only from city to suburb but from North to South and from East to West. Many ex-servicemen who had first glimpsed the West in military camps returned to take up residence, as did others lured by job opportunities, the climate, and the pace of life. California's population alone went from 9 to 19 million between 1945 and 1964. The fifth-largest state in 1940, California would supplant New York in 1963 as the most populous. This shift of millions of people from the North and East to the South and West changed the United States in many fundamental ways. Drawn to the Sunbelt by low taxes, low energy costs, and anti-union right-to-work laws, industrialists transferred not only their plants and corporate headquarters but also their conservative politics. So too, senior citizens, attracted to places like Sun City, Arizona, "a complete community geared to older Americans," brought a more conservative outlook to the South and West. By 1980 the population of the Sunbelt, which stretched from the Old Confederacy across Texas to southern California, would exceed that of the North and East. The political power of the Republican party would rise accordingly.

## Consensus and Conservatism

Not everyone embraced the fifties' materialism or sank unquestioningly into a deep cushion of contentment. Intellectuals found a wide audience for their criticism of the shallow quality of life in "an America of mass housing, mass markets, massive corporations, massive government, mass media, and massive boredom."

These critics targeted "organization men" bent on getting ahead by going along, "status seekers" pursuing external rewards to compensate for inner insecurities, and "other-directed" Americans who took their cues from the opinions and behavior of peers. Some satirized the modern office, where "rows of blank-looking girls" sat "with blank, white folders in their blank hands, all blankly folding blank papers." Others took aim at "the packaged society," with its people "all items in a national supermarket—categorized, processed, labeled, priced, and readied for merchandising."

This social criticism oversimplified reality. It ignored ethnic, class, and social diversity. It overlooked the acquisitiveness and conformity of earlier generations—the peer-group pressures in small-town America. It failed to gauge the currents of dissent swirling beneath the surface. It caricatured rather than characterized American society.

Still, this criticism spotlighted the elevation of comfort over challenge, of safety over risk, and of private pleasures over public affairs. Americans, indeed, hungered for security, seeking refuge in "the good life." And perhaps more than ever before, a large majority agreed about fundamental democratic values, rejecting radicalism at home and opposing the spread of communism abroad.

## Togetherness and the Baby Boom

In 1954 *McCall's* magazine coined the term *togetherness* to celebrate the "ideal" couple: the man and woman who married young and centered their lives on home and children. Americans in the 1950s wed at an earlier age than their parents and had more babies sooner. The fertility rate (the number of births per thousand women), 80 in 1940, peaked at 123 in 1957, when an American baby was born every seven seconds.

At the same time, medical science banished many childhood diseases. Antibiotics virtually wiped out diphtheria and typhoid fever, while the Salk and Sabin vaccines ended the dread of poliomyelitis (polio). From the 58,000 American children afflicted in 1952, the number of new polio cases reported would drop to 5,700 in 1958. The decline in childhood mortality helped to raise American life expectancy from 65.9 years in 1945 to 70.9 years in 1970 and, coupled with the "baby boom," brought a 19 percent increase in the U.S. population during the 1950s—a larger jump than in any previous decade. Moreover, by 1960 children under fourteen made up one-third of the population.

The immense size of the baby-boom generation (the 76 million born between 1946 and 1964) guaranteed its historical importance. Its movement through each stage of life has been as contorting as the digestion of a pig by a boa constrictor. First came the bulge in baby carriages in the late 1940s, then in school construction, then in college enrollments, then in the 1970s—as they began to have families—in home construction and sales, and then in the 1980s and 1990s retirement investments that sent the stock market soaring. In the 1950s the baby boom also made child rearing a huge concern, reinforcing the idea that women's place was in the home. With Americans convinced of the psychological importance of early childhood experiences, motherhood became an increasingly vital calling.

No one did more to emphasize that children needed the love and care of full-time mothers than Dr. Benjamin Spock; only the Bible outsold his *Baby and Child Care* (1946) in the fifties. Spock urged mothers to create an atmosphere of warmth and intimacy for their children so that they could mature into well-adjusted adults. Crying babies were to be comforted so that they would not feel rejected. Breast feeding came back into vogue. Spock's advice led to less scolding and spanking and more "democratic" family discussions. In some homes it produced a "filiarchy" in which kids ruled the roost and their needs and wants predominated.

## Domesticity

For the most part, popular culture in the 1950s glorified marriage and parenthood, emphasizing women's role as a helpmate to her husband and a full-time mother to her children. As Debbie Reynolds declared in *The Tender Trap* (1955): "A woman isn't a woman until she's been married and had children." Television almost always pictured women as mothers at home. Women's magazines regularly featured articles with titles like "Cooking to Me Is Poetry." Hollywood depicted career women as neurotic. And millions of teenage girls swooned to Paul Anka singing "You're Having My Baby" and read *Seventeen* magazine's advice to them in 1957: "In dealing with a male, the art of saving face is essential. Traditionally he is the head of the family, the dominant partner, the man in the situation. Even on those occasions when you both know his decision is wrong, more often than not you will be wise to go along with his decision."

Education reinforced these notions. While girls learned typing and cooking, boys were channeled into

**Jonas Salk**
*Dr. Jonas Salk of the University of Pittsburgh developed a process of using dead polio virus particles to stimulate the immune system, ending the dreaded polio scourge of American children. "The reward for work well done," he said, "is the chance to do more." When he died at age 80, Salk was working on a vaccine for AIDS.*

carpentry and courses leading to professional careers. Guidance counselors cautioned young women not to "miss the boat" of marriage by pursuing higher education. "Men are not interested in college degrees but in the warmth and humanness of the girls they marry," stressed a textbook on the family. While a higher percentage of women than men graduated from high school in the 1950s, more men than women went on to college. And of those women who went, almost two-thirds failed to complete a degree. They dropped out, people joked, to get their M.R.S. degree and a Ph.T.— "Putting Hubbie Through."

Nevertheless, profound changes were under way. Despite the wave of layoffs of women workers after World War II, women quickly returned to the work force. By 1952, 2 million more women worked outside the home than had during the war; and by 1960 one-third of the labor force was female, and one out of three married women worked outside the home. Of all women workers that year, 60 percent were married while 40 percent had school-age children.

Forced back into the old cage of low-paying, dead-end, gender-segregated jobs, most women worked to add to the family income, not to challenge stereotypes. Yet, despite organized feminism ebbing to its lowest point of the century, many working women developed a heightened sense of expectations and empowerment. Transmitted to their daughters, it would lead to a feminist resurgence in the late 1960s.

### Religion and Education

"Today in the U.S.," *Time* claimed in 1954, "the Christian faith is back in the center of things." Leading religious popularizers—evangelist Billy Graham, Roman Catholic bishop Fulton J. Sheen, and Protestant minister Norman Vincent Peale—had syndicated newspaper columns, best-selling books, and radio and television programs. The Hollywood religious extravaganzas *Ben Hur* and *The Ten Commandments* were the most watched films; popular singers crooned such hits as "I Believe" and "The Man Upstairs"; and TV advertisements proclaimed that "the family that prays together stays together." Dial-a-Prayer offered telephone solutions for spiritual problems. Congress added "under God" to the Pledge of Allegiance and required "IN GOD WE TRUST" on all U.S. currency.

Millions embraced evangelical fundamentalism and became "born-again" Christians. In 1950 Billy Graham founded his Evangelistic Association with a single secretary in a one-room office. By 1958 Graham's weekly column appeared in 125 newspapers and his staff of more than two hundred answered ten thousand letters a week. Likewise, Oral Roberts, a Pentecostal Holiness preacher, perfected mass-mailing techniques and televised appeals to build a huge, nationwide fundamentalist organization. Both preached against the hedonism and secularism of modern life; and they appealed mainly to poorer, less educated Americans and to those alienated by the rapidity of cultural and social change.

"Everybody should have a religious faith," President Eisenhower declared, "and I don't care what it is." Most Americans agreed. Religious attendance swelled, and the percentage of people who said they belonged to a church or synagogue increased from 49 percent in 1940 to 55 percent in 1950 to a record-high 69 percent in 1959. For many, however, the intensity of religious faith declined, and mainstream churches, emphasizing Americanism and fellowship, downplayed sin and evil.

Similarly, education flourished in the 1950s yet seemed intellectually shallower than in prior decades. Swelled by the baby boom, primary school enrollment rose 10 million in the 1950s (compared to 1 million in the 1940s). California opened a new school every week throughout the decade and still faced a classroom shortage. The proportion of college-age Americans in higher education climbed from 15 percent in 1940 to more than 40 percent by the early 1960s. At every level, disciples of John Dewey promoted sociability and self-expression over science, math, and history. The "well-rounded" student became more prized than the highly skilled or knowledgeable pupil. Surveys of college students found them conservative, conformist, and careerist, a "silent generation" seeking security and comfort, much as their elders did.

### The Culture of the Fifties

American culture reflected the expansive spirit of a prosperous era as well as an undercurrent of discontent. With increasing leisure and fatter paychecks, Americans spent one-seventh of the 1950s GNP on fun and entertainment. Yellowstone National Park lured four times as many people through its gates each summer as lived in Wyoming; Glacier National Park attracted more visitors than lived in Montana. Spectator sports boomed, new symphony halls opened, and book sales doubled in the 1950s.

With the opening of a major exhibit of abstract expressionists by the Museum of Modern Art in 1951, New York replaced Paris as the capital of the art world. Like the immense canvases of Jackson Pollock and the cool jazz of trumpeter Miles Davis, introspection and improvisation characterized the major novels of the era. Their highly personal yearnings sharply contrasted with the political engagement and social realism of literature in the 1930s. Novels such as John Cheever's *The Wapshot Chronicles* (1957) and John Updike's *Rabbit Run* (1960) presented characters dissatisfied with jobs and home, longing for a more vital and authentic existence, yet incapable of decisive action. J. D. Salinger's popular *The Catcher in the Rye* (1951) offered an adolescent version of the alienated, ineffectual 1950s literary hero. Young Holden Caulfield, expelled from prep school, is repelled by the "phoniness" of the adult world and considers a break for freedom. But he returns home, suffers a nervous collapse, and retreats to an inner realm of imagined heroism.

Southern, African-American, and Jewish-American writers turned out the decades's most vital fiction. William Faulkner continued his dense saga of a family in Yoknapatawpha County, Mississippi, in *The Town* (1957) and *The Mansion* (1960), while Eudora Welty evoked southern small-town life in *The Ponder Heart* (1954). The black experience found memorable ex-

**Motorola Color TV**
*The television set, so grandly advertised and displayed, itself was a symbol of postwar affluence, and both advertising and programming, which featured largely middle-class, consumption-oriented suburban families, stimulated the consumer culture. Overall, TV powerfully reinforced the conservative, celebratory values of everyday American life in the 1950s.*

pression in James Baldwin's *Go Tell It on the Mountain* (1953) and Ralph Ellison's *Invisible Man* (1951). Bernard Malamud's *The Assistant* (1957) explored the Jewish immigrant world of New York's Lower East Side, and Philip Roth's *Goodby Columbus* (1959) dissected the very different world of upwardly mobile Jews.

The many westerns, musicals, and costume spectacles churned out by Hollywood further reflected the diminished interest in political issues. Movies about contemporary life for the most part portrayed Americans as one big, happy, white, middle-class family, exalting material success and romantic love. Minorities and the poor remained invisible, and the independent career-women in films of the 1940s were replaced by "dumb blondes" and cute helpmates. But as TV viewing soared, movie attendance dropped 50 percent and a fifth of the nation's theaters became bowling alleys and supermarkets. Hollywood tried to recoup by developing Cinerama and 3-D films. No technological wizardry however—including Smell-O-Vision and its rival Aroma-Rama—could stem television's exploding popularity. By 1960 TV showed more than five times as much film footage as Hollywood produced, and dozens of abandoned movie lots and theaters had been converted into TV locations and studios.

## The Message of the Medium

No cultural medium ever grew so huge so quickly, and so reinforced the public mood, as American television

in the 1950s. From several thousand in 1946, the number of households with TV sets soared to 5 million in 1950. Set ownership then rose at a rate of nearly 5 million a year. By 1955 three-fourths of all households owned at least one set, and by 1960 some 90 percent did.

Business capitalized on the phenomenon. Introduced in 1952, *TV Guide* soon outsold all other periodicals and by 1960 was published in fifty-three separate regional editions. The TV dinner, first marketed in 1954, altered the nation's eating habits. By the mid-fifties the three networks each had larger advertising revenues than any other communications medium in the world.

Geared to its initial small audience, early television showcased talent and creativity. High-quality shows, including opera, appeared in prime time, as did documentaries like Edward R. Murrow's "See It Now," sophisticated comedies like "Your Show of Shows," and original dramas on "Playhouse 90." But as the price of TV sets rapidly came down, allowing those less well-off and less educated to purchase them, the network's desire to appeal to a mass audience transformed television into a cautious celebration of conformity and consumerism. "The message of the media is the commercial," one critic noted, as corporations spent fortunes hawking their products. Expenditures for television advertising rose from $170 million in 1950 to $2 billion in 1960, and to get the largest possible audiences the networks appealed to the lowest common denominator of taste. (As radio comedian Fred Allen

## The Television Revolution, 1950–1994

*As televisions became commonplace in the 1950s, TV viewing altered the nature of American culture and politics.*

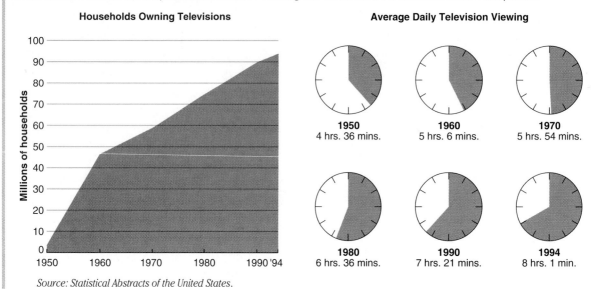

**Households Owning Televisions**

**Average Daily Television Viewing**

**1950** 4 hrs. 36 mins.  **1960** 5 hrs. 6 mins.  **1970** 5 hrs. 54 mins.

**1980** 6 hrs. 36 mins.  **1990** 7 hrs. 21 mins.  **1994** 8 hrs. 1 min.

*Source: Statistical Abstracts of the United States.*

observed, "They call television a medium because it's rare when it is well done.")

Decrying TV's mediocrity in 1961, the head of the Federal Communications Commission dared broadcasters to watch their own shows for a day: "I can assure you that you will observe a vast wasteland." A

### Father Knows Best

*Sitting on the couch, Jim and Margaret Anderson (played by Robert Young and Jane Wyatt) preside over their kids Betty, Kathy, and Bud. Typical of TV programming in the 1950s,* Father Knows Best *projected an image of American life that was white, middle-class, and suburban and that reinforced the concept of domesticity.*

steady parade of soaps, unsophisticated comedies, and violent westerns led others to call TV the "idiot box." The ethnic, working-class families shown on television in the 1940s, "The Goldbergs" and "Life of Riley," gave way to a succession of middle-class, suburban families like the Nelsons ("Ozzie and Harriet") and the Cleavers ("Leave It to Beaver"). They portrayed harmonious families, perfectly coiffed moms who loved to vacuum in high heels, frisky yet ultimately obedient kids, and all-knowing dads who never lost their tempers. And while Buffalo Bob asked all the children watching "The Howdy Doody Show" each Friday afternoon to worship "at the church or synagogue of your choice," most children's programs featured gunplay and mayhem.

Measuring television's impact is difficult. Depending on the many factors that differentiate individuals, people read the "texts" of TV (or of movies or music or books) their own way and so receive their own personal messages or signals from the mass media. Still, most observers agree that TV reflected existing values and institutions. It reinforced the rising consumerism of the era, spawning such mass fads as Barbie dolls and hula hoops, and strengthened gender and racial stereotypes. TV rarely showed African Americans and Latinos—except in prison scenes; it extolled male violence in fighting evil; and it portrayed women as either zany madcaps ("My Friend Irma") or self-effacing moms ("The Donna Reed Show").

Television also changed the political life of the nation. Millions watched Senator Estes Kefauver grill mobsters about their ties to city governments. At least 20 million observed the combative Senator Joseph McCarthy bully and slander witnesses during the hearings on disloyalty in the army. The 58 million who witnessed Richard Nixon's appeal for support in the "Checkers" speech helped save his place on the GOP ticket. And Eisenhower's pioneering use of brief "spot advertisements" following popular TV programs combined with Stevenson's avoidance of televised appearances clinched Ike's smashing presidential victories. In 1960 John F. Kennedy's "telegenic" image would play a significant role in his winning the presidency. Television vastly increased the cost of political campaigning while decreasing the content level of political discussion. It helped produce a more national culture, diminishing provincialism as well as regional and class differences, while its overwhelming portrayal of a contented citizenry reinforced complacency and obscured the reality of "the other America."

## The Other America

"I am an invisible man," declared the African-American narrator of Ralph Ellison's *Invisible Man*; "I am invisible, understand, simply because people refuse to see me." Indeed, few white, middle-class Americans perceived the extent of social injustice in the United States. "White flight" from cities to suburbs produced physical separation of the races and classes. New expressways walled off ghettos and rural poverty from middle-class motorists speeding by. Popular culture focused on affluent Americans enjoying the "good life." In the consensus of the Eisenhower era, deprivation had disappeared.

### *Poverty and Urban Blight*

In reality, poverty was rife and dire. Although the number of families living in poverty (then defined as a family of four with a yearly income of less than $3,000) had declined from 34 percent in 1947 to 22 percent in 1960, this still left 35 million Americans below the "poverty line"—victims of disease and squalor. Many were senior citizens. A Senate report in 1960 found that at least half of Americans sixty-five or older "cannot afford decent housing, proper nutrition, adequate medical care, or necessary recreation." Eight million of the aged existed on annual incomes below $1,000.

**The Other America**
*The quality of life for citizens like these poor white children substantiated Michael Harrington's claim that too much had been made of American affluence in the 1950s.*

At least a third of the poor lived in depressed rural areas, where the 2 million migrant farm workers experienced the most abject poverty. Observing a Texas migratory-labor camp in 1955, a journalist reported that 96 percent of the children had consumed no milk in the previous six months; eight out of ten adults had eaten no meat; and most slept "on the ground, in a cave, under a tree, or in a chicken house." In California's Imperial Valley, the infant death rate among migrant workers was more than seven times the statewide average.

The bulk of the poor huddled in decaying inner-city slums. Displaced southern blacks and Appalachian whites, Native Americans forced off reservations, and newly arrived Hispanics strained cities' already inadequate facilities. Nearly 200,000 Mexican-Americans herded into San Antonio's Westside barrio; a local newspaper described them as living like cattle in a stockyard, "with roofed-over corrals for homes and chutes for streets." A visitor to New York City's slums in 1950 found "25 human beings living in a dark and airless coal cellar ten feet below the street level. . . . No animal could live there long, yet here were 17 children, the youngest having been born here two weeks before." Trapped in a vicious cycle of want and a culture of poverty, children of the poor started school at a disadvantage, quickly fell behind, and lacking encouragement or expectation of success, dropped out. Living with neither hope nor the necessary skills to enter the mainstream of American life, they bequeathed a similar legacy to their children.

The pressing need for low-cost housing went unanswered. In 1955 less than 200,000 of the 810,000 public housing units called for in the Housing Act of 1949 had been built; a decade later a total of only some 320,000 had been constructed. "Slum clearance" generally meant "Negro clearance," and "urban renewal" meant "poor removal," as developers razed low-income neighborhoods to put up parking garages and more expensive housing. The Los Angeles barrio of Chavez Ravine was bulldozed to construct Dodger Stadium. At the same time, landlords, realtors, and bankers deliberately excluded nonwhites from decent housing. Half of the housing in New York's heavily black Harlem predated 1900. There, a dozen people might share a tiny apartment with broken windows, faulty plumbing, and gaping holes in the walls. Harlem's rates of illegitimate births, infant deaths, narcotics use, and crime towered above the averages for the city and the nation. "Where flies and maggots breed, where the plumbing is stopped up and not repaired, where rats bite helpless infants," black social psychologist Kenneth Clark observed, "the conditions of life are brutal and inhuman."

**Rosa Parks**

*In December 1956 Parks did what would have been unthinkable a year earlier: she took a seat in front of a white passenger on a Montgomery, Alabama, bus. Her refusal to stand for racism set in motion the Montgomery bus boycott, the emergence of Martin Luther King Jr. as a national leader, and the massive nonviolent civil disobedience phase of the civil rights movement.*

### Blacks' Struggle for Justice

The collision between the hopes raised by the 1954 *Brown* decision and the indignities of persistent discrimination and segregation sparked a new phase in the civil-rights movement. To sweep away the separate but rarely equal Jim Crow facilities in the South, African Americans tried new tactics, founded new organizations, and followed new leaders. They utilized nonviolent direct-action protest to engage large numbers of blacks in their own freedom struggle and to arouse white America's conscience.

In the 1950s racism still touched even the smallest details of daily life. In Montgomery, Alabama, black bus riders had to surrender their seats so that no white rider would stand. Although more than three-quarters of all passengers, blacks had to pay their fares at the front of the bus, leave and reenter through the back door, sit only in the rear, and then give up their seats to any standing white passengers. In December 1955 a strong-willed black woman named Rosa Parks refused to get up so that a white man could sit. She was arrested. In protest, Montgomery's black leaders organized a boy-

cott of the buses. "There comes a time when people get tired," declared Martin Luther King, Jr., an eloquent twenty-seven-year-old African-American minister who articulated the anger of Montgomery blacks, "tired of being segregated and humiliated; tired of being kicked about by the brutal feet of oppression." The time had come, King continued, to cease being patient "with anything less than freedom and justice." With this speech what would become a year-long bus boycott by fifty thousand black Montgomerians began. "My soul has been tired for a long time," an old woman told a minister who had stopped his car to offer her a ride; "now my feet are tired, and my soul is resting."

But the city leaders would not budge. This resistance forced the blacks to challenge the constitutionality of bus segregation. In November 1956 the U.S. Supreme Court affirmed a lower-court decision outlawing segregation on the buses.

The Montgomery bus boycott demonstrated African-American strength and determination. It shattered the myth that blacks favored segregation and that only outside agitators fought Jim Crow. It affirmed for blacks everywhere the possibility of social change. It gave the nation in Dr. King a persuasive African-American leader whose oratory simultaneously inspired black activism and touched white consciences.

King's philosophy of civil disobedience fused the spirit of Christianity with the strategy of nonviolent resistance. His emphasis on direct action gave every African American an opportunity to become involved; and his insistence on nonviolence diminished the likelihood of bloodshed. Preaching that they must lay their bodies on the line to provoke crises that would force whites to confront their racism, King urged his followers to love their enemies. By so doing, he believed, blacks would convert their oppressors and build a community of true brotherhood. In 1957 King and a group of black ministers formed the Southern Christian Leadership Conference (SCLC) to lead the fight against Jim Crow.

## Poverty and Prejudice

Native Americans and Hispanic-Americans, however, made less headway in ending the discrimination against them. High unemployment on the Caribbean island and cheap airfares to North America brought a steady stream of the newest minority group, Puerto Ricans (who as U.S. citizens could enter the mainland without restriction), to New York City. From seventy thousand in 1940 to a quarter of a million in 1950 and then nearly a million in 1960, El Barrio in New York City's East Harlem had a larger Puerto Rican population, and more bodegas, than San Juan in the late 1960s.

There they suffered from inadequate schools, minimal sanitation services, and harsh police harassment, and were denied middle-class jobs and political recognition. More than half lived in inadequate housing. Like countless earlier immigrants, they gained greater personal freedom in the United States while losing the security of a strong cultural tradition.

Family frictions flared in the transition from Puerto Rican to American ways. Parents felt upstaged by children who learned English and obtained jobs that were closed to them. The relationship between husbands and wives changed as women found readier access to jobs than did men. One recent migrant explained, "Whether I have a husband or not I work . . . and if my husband dare to complain, I throw him out. That is the difference; in Puerto Rico I should have to stand for anything a man asks me to do because he pays the rent. Here I belong to myself." However, although old values

weakened and Puerto Ricans tried to embrace American ways, they encountered prejudice because of their skin color and Spanish language.

Mexican-Americans suffered the same indignities. Most of them were also underpaid and overcharged, discriminated against, and segregated from mainstream American life. The presence of countless "undocumented aliens" compounded their woes.

After World War II, the advent of new irrigation systems added 7.5 million acres to the agricultural lands of the Southwest and stimulated demand for cheap Mexican labor. To stem the tide of illegal Mexican immigrants, Congress in 1951 enacted a "temporary worker" program that brought in seasonal laborers, called *braceros.* Many stayed on without authorization, joining a growing number of other illegal Latino migrants. Between 1953 and 1955 the Eisenhower administration's "Operation Wetback" deported more than 3 million allegedly undocumented entrants, in many cases without recourse to due process. Periodic roundups, however, did not substitute for a sound labor policy or an effective enforcement strategy, and millions of Mexicans continued to cross the poorly guarded two-thousand-mile border. The *bracero* program itself peaked in 1959, admitting 450,000 workers. Neither the Asociación Nacional México-Americana (founded in 1950) nor the League of United Latin American Citizens (LULAC) could stop their exploitation or the widespread violations of the rights of Mexican-American citizens.

The Mexican-American population in Los Angeles County doubled, to more than 600,000, and the *colonias* of Denver, El Paso, Phoenix, and San Antonio grew proportionately as large. The most rural of all major ethnic groups in 1940, the percentage of Mexican-Americans living in urban areas rose to 65 percent in 1950, and to 85 percent by 1970. As service in World War II gave Hispanics an increased sense of their own American identity and a claim on the rights supposedly available to all American citizens, so urbanization meant better educational and employment opportunities. Unions like the United Cannery, Agricultural, Packing and Allied Workers of America sought higher wages and better working conditions for their Mexican-American members, and such middle-class organizations as LULAC, the GI Forum, and the Unity League, emphasizing the American side of their identity, campaigned to desegregate schools and public facilities. In 1954 the Supreme Court banned the exclusion of Mexican-Americans from Texas jury lists, and the mobilization of Hispanic voters led to the election of the

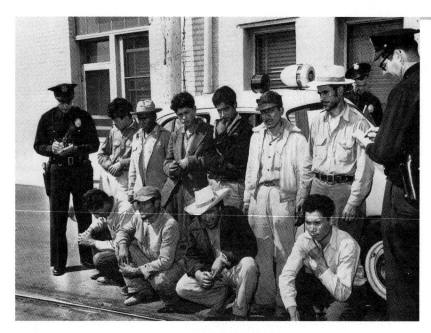

**A Periodic Roundup**
*Los Angeles police remove a group of undocumented Mexican immigrants from a freight train and prepare to send them back across the border.*

first Mexican-American mayor, in El Paso in 1958. Both the existence of millions of undocumented aliens and the continuation of the *bracero* program, however, stigmatized all people of Mexican descent and depressed their wages. The median income of Hispanics was less than two-thirds that of Anglos. At least a third lived in poverty.

Native Americans remained the poorest, most ignored, minority—their death rate three times the national average. Unemployment rates on reservations reached 70 percent for the Blackfeet of Montana and the Hopi of New Mexico, and a staggering 86 percent among the Choctaw of Mississippi. After World War II Congress veered away from John Collier's efforts to reassert Indian sovereignty and cultural autonomy and moved toward the goal of assimilation. This meant terminating treaty relationships with Indian tribes, thus ending the federal trusteeship of Indians. Some favored it as a move toward Indian self-sufficiency; others for an end to the communal culture of Indians; and still others because it meant access to Indian lands and mineral resources. Between 1954–1962 Congress passed a dozen termination bills, withdrawing financial support from 61 reservations.

First applied to Menominees of Wisconsin and the Klamaths of Oregon, who owned valuable timberlands, the policy proved disastrous. Further impoverishing the Indians whom it affected, the law transferred more than 500,000 acres of Native American lands to non-Indians. To speed the sale of Indian lands to developers,

the government established the Voluntary Relocation Program. Designed to lure Indians off the reservations and into urban areas, relocation offices provided Native Americans with moving costs, assistance in finding housing and jobs, and living expenses until they obtained work. "We're like wheat," said one Hopi woman who went to the city. "The wind blows, we bend over. . . . You can't stand up when there's wind."

By the end of the decade, about sixty thousand Indians had left the reservations for urban America. Some soon became assimilated into middle-class America. Most could not find work, and ended up on state welfare rolls living in rundown shantytowns. A third returned to the reservation. Not surprisingly, the National Congress of American Indians vigorously opposed termination, and most tribal politicians defended Indian sovereignty, treaty rights, federal trusteeship, and the special status of Indians.

## Seeds of Disquiet

Late in the fifties self-scrutiny and apprehension ruffled the placid surface of American life. Academics spotlighted shortcomings in the system and questioned the nation's goals and values. Periodic recessions, rising unemployment, and the growing national debt made Khrushchev's 1959 threat to bury the United States economically, and his boast that "your grandchildren will live under communism," ring in American ears. Third

World anticolonialism, especially in Cuba, diminished Americans' sense of national pride and power. Adding to the disquiet were the growing alienation of American youth and a technological breakthrough by the Soviet Union.

## Sputnik

On October 4, 1957, the Soviet Union launched the first artificial earth satellite, *Sputnik* ("Little Traveler"). Weighing 184 pounds and a mere twenty-two inches in diameter, it circled the earth at eighteen thousand miles per hour. *Sputnik* dashed the American myth of unquestioned technological superiority; and when *Sputnik II*, carrying a dog, went into a more distant orbit on November 3, critics charged that Eisenhower had allowed a "technological Pearl Harbor." Democrats warned of a "missile gap" between the United States and the Soviet Union.

The Eisenhower administration disparaged the Soviet achievement. But Eisenhower pushed behind the scenes to have the American Vanguard missile hastily readied to launch a satellite. On December 6, with millions watching on TV, the Vanguard rose six feet in the air before exploding. Newspapers mockingly rechristened the missile "Flopnik."

Eisenhower did not find it a laughing matter. He doubled the funds for missile development to $4.3 billion in 1958 and raised the level to $5.3 billion in 1959. He also established the Science Advisory Committee, whose recommendations led to the creation of the National Aeronautics and Space Administration (NASA) in July 1958. By the end of the decade, the United States had launched several space probes and successfully tested the Atlas intercontinental ballistic missile (ICBM).

Critics had long complained that Americans honored football stars more than outstanding students and had pointed out that the Soviet Union produced twice as many scientists and engineers as the United States. Suddenly, *Sputnik* provided the impetus for a crash program to improve American education. Political barriers to federal aid for education crumbled, and funds from Washington built new classrooms and laboratories, raised teacher salaries, and installed instructional television systems in schools. In 1958 Congress passed the National Defense Education Act, which provided loans to students and funds for teacher training and for the development of new instructional materials in the sciences, mathematics, and foreign languages.

Americans now banked on higher education to ensure national security. The number of college students,

**"Wonder Why We're Not Keeping Pace?"**
**A Response to Sputnik**
*To account for the USSR's lead in the space race, cartoonist Herblock focuses on American weaknesses rather than Soviet strengths.*

1.5 million in 1940 and 2.5 million in 1955, skyrocketed to 3.6 million in 1960. That year the U.S. government funneled $1.5 billion to universities, a hundredfold increase over 1940.

Linked directly to the Cold War, federal aid to education raised unsettling questions. By 1960 nearly a third of scientists and engineers on university faculties worked full-time on government research, primarily defense projects. Some would soon dub it the "military-industrial-*educational* complex."

## A Rebellion of Youth

As unsettling to some adults as *Sputnik*, American adolescents grew culturally restive as they searched for self-definition. Few adults considered the social implications of their affluence on the young, or the consequences of having a generation of teenagers who could stay in school instead of working. Few thought about the effects of growing up in an age when traditional values like thrift and self-denial had declining relevance, and of maturing at a time when young people had the leisure and money to shape their own subculture. And

**"Tutti Frutti, Aw rutti"**
*During a 1956 concert, the hip-bucking, tight-panted Elvis "the Pelvis" Presley elicits the usual passionate reactions from his female fans.*

despite talk of family togetherness, fathers were often too busy to give much attention to their children, and mothers sometimes spent more time chauffeuring their young than listening to them. Indeed, much of what adults knew about "teenagers" (a noun that first came into widespread use in 1956) they learned from the mass media, which focused on the sensational and the superficial.

Accounts of juvenile delinquency abounded. News stories painted high schools as war zones, city streets as jungles ruled by gangs, and teenagers as zipgun-armed hoodlums. In truth, the delinquency rate had remained stable. Nevertheless, male teenagers who sported black leather motorcycle jackets, bandied street slang, and slicked back their hair in the "ducktail" look aroused adult alarm.

Also dismaying to parents, young Americans embraced rock-and-roll. In 1951 Alan Freed, the host of a classical music program on Cleveland radio, had observed white teenagers dancing to and buying rhythm-and-blues records. Rhythm-and-blues had traditionally been recorded by and for blacks. In 1952 he started a

new radio program called "Moondog's Rock and Roll Party." Its popularity soared, and in 1954 Freed took his program to New York City, where he made rock-and-roll into a national craze.

Just as white musicians in the 1920s and 1930s had adapted black jazz for white audiences, so white performers in the 1950s transformed rhythm-and-blues into "Top Ten" rock-and-roll and made it part of the thriving culture of consumption. In 1954 Bill Haley and the Comets dropped the sexual allusions from Joe Turner's "Shake, Rattle, and Roll," added country-and-western guitar riffs, and had the first major white rock-and-roll hit. When Haley performed "Rock Around the Clock" in *The Blackboard Jungle,* a 1955 film about juvenile delinquency, many parents linked rock-and-roll with disobedience and crime. Red-hunters saw it as a communist plot to corrupt youth; segregationists claimed it a ploy "to mix the races"; and religious groups condemned it as the "devil's music."

Nothing confirmed this worry as much as Elvis Presley swaggering onto the music scene. Born in Tupelo, Mississippi, Elvis was a nineteen-year-old truck driver in 1954 when, on impulse, he paid four dollars to record two songs at a Memphis studio. Melding the pentecostal music of his boyhood with the hillbilly boogie that he heard on the "Grand Ole Opry" radio shows, and peppering in the frank sexuality of rhythm-and-blues, Presley transformed the bland popular music that youth found wanting.

Ironically, Presley himself craved respectability. Even as his lyrics invited rebelliousness, he was collecting society's material symbols of success and status, including a fleet of Cadillacs and a Memphis mansion that would become a shrine after his death.

Still, his smirking lips and bucking hips shocked middle-class white adults. And the more adults condemned rock-and-roll, the more teenagers loved it. Record sales tripled between 1954 and 1960, and Dick Clark's "American Bandstand" became the decade's biggest TV hit.

Much as teens cherished rock-and-roll for its frankness and exuberance, they elevated the characters played by Marlon Brando in *The Wild One* (1954) and by James Dean in *Rebel Without a Cause* (1955) to cult status for their overturning of respectable society's mores, and they delighted in *Mad* magazine's ridiculing of the phony and pretentious in middle-class America. Rejecting Detroit's standards, male teenagers customized their cars to make personal statements—which parents rarely understood.

## *Portents of Change*

Nonconformist writers known as the Beats expressed a more fundamental revolt against middle-class society. In Allen Ginsberg's *Howl* (1956) and Jack Kerouac's *On the Road* (1957), the Beats scorned competition and materialism and scoffed at the "square" America described by Kerouac as "rows of well-to-do houses with lawns and television sets in each living room with everybody looking at the same thing and thinking the same thing at the same time." The Beats romanticized society's outcasts—the mad ones, wrote Kerouac, "the ones who never yawn or say a commonplace thing, but burn, burn, burn like fabulous yellow roman candles exploding like spiders across the stars." And they glorified uninhibited sexuality, spontaneity, and spirituality in the search for "It," the ultimate authentic experience.

The college youth who were the Beats' greatest admirers rejected complacency and cautiousness. Protesting capital punishment and the continuing investigations of the House Un-American Activities Committee, they also decried the nuclear-arms race. In 1958 and 1959, thousands participated in Youth Marches for Integrated Schools in Washington. Together with the Beats and rock music, this vocal minority of the "silent generation" heralded a youth movement that would explode in the 1960s.

## CONCLUSION

The disquiet of the late fifties underlined the paradox of midcentury America. Mightier than any nation in history, the United States basked in prosperity. Simultaneously Americans felt uneasiness as the Cold War continued and booming times brought unsettling social changes.

Still, most Americans approved of Eisenhower's politics of moderation. They applauded his incremental expansion of bedrock New Deal programs like social security and the start of new projects like the interstate highway system. They liked his efforts to reduce taxes and lessen government interference with private enterprise. Moreover, Ike's ending of the U.S. war in Korea, opposition to American military intervention in Vietnam, halt to atmospheric testing of nuclear weapons, and relaxation of tensions with the Soviet Union brought a sense of relief. Ike's moderation appealed to a society seeking security and refuge in the good life—something increasing numbers of Americans sought in communities like Levittown, where traditional gender roles, togetherness, and domesticity were idealized and young American families went on a consumer buying spree to keep up with their neighbors' purchases of new automobiles and home appliances. They especially bought the newfangled televisions, whose programming reaffirmed existing American values and prejudices while reinforcing conformity, complacency, and consumerism.

Although there was no shortage of social critics attacking the materialism and monotony of life in the 1950s, most white, middle-class, adult Americans were content to enjoy their larger paychecks and increased leisure time. Ignoring the churnings beneath the guise of stability, they would leave for another decade the incendiary problems of poverty, urban decay, and racial injustice, and the explosive consequences of a younger generation hungering for self-definition and unwilling to accept their parents' cautious embrace of the status quo.

## FOR FURTHER READING

William H. Chafe, *The American Woman: Her Changing Social, Economic, and Political Roles, 1920–1970*, rev. ed. (1988). An incisive examination of discrimination against women and their efforts to overcome it.

Kenneth Jackson, *Crabgrass Frontier: The Suburbanization of the United States* (1985). An indispensable social history of suburban growth.

Jacqueline Jones, *The Dispossessed: America's Underclasses from the Civil War to the Present* (1992). A thorough analysis of the roots of modern poverty.

Karal Ann Marling, *As Seen on TV: The Visual Culture of Everyday Life in the 1950s* (1994). The influence of the medium is assessed.

Elaine Tyler May, *Homeward Bound: American Families in the Cold War Era* (1988). A social history of how the Cold War influenced gender roles, marriage, parenting, and family life.

John Modell, *Into One's Own: From Youth to Adulthood in the United States, 1920–1975* (1989). An important, insightful survey of the coming of age of American youth.

Chester Pach, Jr., and Elmo Richardson, *The Presidency of Dwight D. Eisenhower* (1991). A fair, balanced, and thoughtful overview.

Stephen J. Whitfield, *The Culture of the Cold War* (1991). A keensighted meditation on postwar cultural phenomena.

# 30

## The Turbulent
## Sixties

**Selma to Montgomery March, 1965**

In January 1960, four African-American freshmen at North Carolina Agricultural and Technical (A&T) College in Greensboro discussed their humiliation over not being allowed to eat alongside white diners at lunch counters in the South. Middle class in aspirations, the children of urban civil servants and industrial workers, they believed that the Supreme Court's *Brown* decision of 1954 should have ended the indignities of racial discrimination and segregation. But the promise of change had outrun reality. Massive resistance to racial equality still proved the rule throughout Dixie. In 1960 most southern blacks could neither vote nor attend integrated schools. They could not enjoy a cup of coffee alongside whites in a public restaurant. Impatient yet hopeful, the A&T students could not accept the inequality that their parents had endured. They had been inspired by the Montgomery bus boycott led by Martin Luther King, Jr., as well as by successful African independence movements in the late fifties in Ghana, the Belgian Congo, and other former European colonial possessions.

On the afternoon of February 1, the four young African Americans entered the local Woolworth's and sat down at the lunch counter. "We don't serve colored here," the waitress replied when the freshmen asked for coffee and doughnuts. The students remained seated. They would not be moved. They vowed to sit in until the store closed and to repeat their request the next day and beyond, until they were served. On February 2 more than twenty A&T students joined them in their protest. The following day, over sixty sat in. By the end of the week, the students overflowed Woolworth's and sat in at the lunch counter in the nearby S. H. Kress store. Six months later, after prolonged peaceful sit-ins, boycotts, and demonstrations, Greensboro's white civic leaders grudgingly allowed blacks to sit down at a restaurant and be served.

Meanwhile, the example of the Greensboro "coffee party" had inspired similar sit-ins throughout North Carolina and in neighboring states. By April 1960 sit-ins had disrupted seventy-eight southern communities, and by September 1961 some seventy thousand students had sat in to desegregate eating facilities as well as to "kneel in" in churches, "sleep in" in motel lobbies, "wade in" on restricted beaches, "read in" at public libraries, "play in" at city parks, and even "watch in" at segregated movie theaters.

The courage of the students transformed the struggle for racial equality. Their activism emboldened black adults to voice their dissatisfaction, and it brought young African Americans a new sense of self-respect and strength. "I myself desegregated a lunch counter, not somebody else, not some big man, some powerful man, but little me," claimed a student. "I walked the picket line and I sat in and the walls of segregation toppled." Each new victory convinced thousands more that "nothing can stop us now."

The winds of change stirred by the sit-ins had many counterparts that also punctured the apathy and self-satisfaction of the 1950s. That same year, socialist Michael Harrington investigated the plight of the poor in an America that barely acknowledged their existence. Ralph Nader, a recent graduate of Harvard Law School, sounded the alarm that many automobiles were "unsafe at any speed." Also in 1960, mother and author Betty Friedan began writing a pathbreaking critique of sexism, *The Feminine Mystique.*

These endeavors symbolized a spirit of new beginnings, of impatience and idealism. It would lead many to embrace John Kennedy's New Frontier and to rally behind Lyndon Johnson's Great Society. Both administrations' rhetorical emphasis on social justice generated fervent hopes and soaring expectations. But the assassination of cherished leaders, ongoing racial strife, and a frustrating war in Vietnam would terminate optimism, and a reaction by the majority who opposed radical change would curtail reform. The promise of a new decade would end in discord and disillusionment.

This chapter focuses on five major questions:

♦ How successful was the New Frontier in domestic affairs, especially the areas of civil rights and the economy? in foreign affairs?

♦ What were the similarities and differences between Kennedy's and Johnson's goals and accomplishments?

♦ In what ways did Lyndon Johnson's Great Society raise false hopes and encourage a violent reaction?

♦ What were the major successes and failures of the black movements for civil rights and socioeconomic progress from 1964 to 1968? What factors instigated the increase of black militancy in this period?

♦ How did the United States get involved in Vietnam and to what extent was President Johnson responsible for the tragedy of Vietnam?

### The Sit-Ins

*The sit-ins of 1960 initiated the student phase of the civil rights movement. Across the South, young black activists challenged segregation by staging nonviolent demonstrations to demand access to public facilities. Their courage and commitment reinvigorated the movement, leading to still greater grassroots activism.*

# The New Frontier, 1960–1963

Projecting an image of vigor and proposing new approaches to old problems, John F. Kennedy personified the energy and self-confidence of American youth in 1960. His wealthy father, Joseph P. Kennedy, had held appointive office under Franklin D. Roosevelt, until his outspoken isolationism ended his public career. Seething with unfulfilled ambitions, he raised his sons to attain the political power that had eluded him. He instilled in each a passion to excel and to rule. Despite a severe back injury, John Kennedy served in the navy in World War II, and the elder Kennedy persuaded a popular novelist to write articles lauding John's heroism in rescuing his crew after their PT boat had been sunk in the South Pacific.

Esteemed as a war hero, John Kennedy used his charm and his father's connections to win election in 1946 to the House of Representatives from a Boston district where he had never lived. Kennedy did little to distinguish himself in the Congress, but the voters of Massachusetts, captivated by his personality and pleased with his moderately liberal voting record, sent him to the Senate in 1952 and overwhelmingly reelected him six years later. By then Kennedy had a beautiful wife, Jacqueline, and a Pulitzer Prize for *Profiles in Courage*, a book written largely by a staff member.

Only Kennedy's religion, Roman Catholicism, threatened his political future. No Catholic had ever been elected president; and the 1928 defeat of Alfred E. Smith had convinced many politicians that none ever could be. Nevertheless, Kennedy won a first-ballot victory at the 1960 Democratic convention. Just forty-two years old, he sounded the theme of a "New Frontier"—for reform at home and victory abroad, for "more sacrifice instead of more security."

### *The Election of 1960*

"All at once you had something exciting," recalled Don Ferguson, a University of Nebraska student. "You had a guy who had little kids and who liked to play football on his front lawn. Kennedy was talking about pumping new life into the nation and steering it in new directions." But most voters, middle aged and middle class, wanted the stability and continuation of Eisenhower's "middle way" promised by the Republican candidate, Vice President Richard M. Nixon. Although scorned by liberals for his McCarthyism, Nixon was better known

## CHRONOLOGY

| | |
|---|---|
| **1960** | Sit-ins to protest segregation begin. |
| | John F. Kennedy elected president. |
| **1961** | Peace Corps and Alliance for Progress created. |
| | Bay of Pigs invasion. |
| | Freedom rides. |
| | Berlin Wall erected. |
| **1962** | Michael Harrington, *The Other America*. |
| | Cuban missile crisis. |
| **1963** | Civil-rights demonstrations in Birmingham. |
| | March on Washington. |
| | Test-Ban Treaty between the Soviet Union and the United States. |
| **1963** | *(Continued)* |
| | Kennedy assassinated; Lyndon B. Johnson becomes president. |
| | Betty Freidan, *The Feminine Mystique*. |
| **1964** | Freedom Summer in Mississippi. |
| | California becomes most populous state. |
| | Civil Rights Act. |
| | Gulf of Tonkin incident and resolution. |
| | Economic Opportunity Act initiates War on Poverty. |
| | Johnson elected president. |
| **1965** | Bombing of North Vietnam and Americanization of the war begin. |
| | Assassination of Malcolm X. |
| **1965** | *(Continued)* |
| | Civil-rights march from Selma to Montgomery. |
| | César Chávez's United Farm Workers strike in California. |
| | Teach-ins to question U.S. involvement in War in Vietnam begin. |
| | Voting Rights Act. |
| | Watts riot in Los Angeles. |
| **1966** | Stokely Carmichael calls for Black Power. |
| | Black Panthers formed. |
| | National Organization for Women (NOW) founded. |
| **1967** | Massive antiwar demonstrations. |
| | Race riots in Newark, Detroit, and other cities. |

and more experienced than Kennedy, a Protestant, and closely identified with the still popular Ike.

Nixon fumbled his opportunity by conceding that Kennedy and he shared the same policies and, primarily, by agreeing to meet his challenger in televised debates. More than 70 million tuned in to the first televised debate between presidential candidates—a broadcast that secured the dominance of television in American politics. The contrast between a haggard, pale Nixon, still recuperating from a knee infection that had hospitalized him for two weeks, and a dynamic, tanned Kennedy was striking. The telegenic Democrat radiated confidence; his opponent appeared insecure as he sweated visibly. Radio listeners judged the debate a draw. But the far more numerous television viewers declared Kennedy the victor. He shot up in the polls, and Nixon never regained the lead.

Kennedy also benefited from the humiliating U-2 incident and an economic recession, as well as from his selection of Senate majority leader Lyndon B. Johnson, a Protestant and moderate from Texas, as his running mate. Still, the election was the closest since 1888. Kennedy's tiny margin of victory reflected both a reluc-

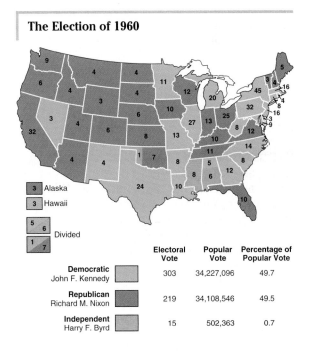

**The Election of 1960**

| | Electoral Vote | Popular Vote | Percentage of Popular Vote |
|---|---|---|---|
| **Democratic** John F. Kennedy | 303 | 34,227,096 | 49.7 |
| **Republican** Richard M. Nixon | 219 | 34,108,546 | 49.5 |
| **Independent** Harry F. Byrd | 15 | 502,363 | 0.7 |

**The Kennedys at Hyannisport, Cape Cod**

*In the Age of Television, when style and image often counted for more than substance, the glamorous Kennedys ruled the political roost. The youthful bravura, glitter, and romance associated with the president and his wife Jacqueline would in time generate the myth of Camelot—a legendary era when a dashing, attractive JFK and his beautiful wife presided over a brilliant, chivalric court.*

tance to change and lingering fears of a Catholic president. His religion cost him millions of votes in the heavily Protestant South. But his capture of 80 percent of the Catholic vote in the closely contested midwestern and northeastern states played a crucial role in his electoral college victory. Although Nixon carried more states than Kennedy, the Democrat's popularity with urban minorities gave Kennedy a slender triumph.

Kennedy set the tone of a new era at his inauguration, proclaiming that "the torch has been passed to a new generation of Americans." He recruited a host of young technocrats and academics—the "best and brightest" in author David Halberstam's wry phrase—who contrasted sharply with the staid businessmen of the Eisenhower administration. For attorney general the president selected his thirty-five-year-old brother Robert Kennedy. "I see nothing wrong with giving Robert some legal experience before he goes out to practice law," JFK joked.

"America's leading man," novelist Norman Mailer called him. Kennedy's dynamic style played well on TV. He exuded promise and purpose. The first president to allow his press conferences to be televised live, JFK

brought a special aura to the White House. Aided by his wife, the elegant Jacqueline, he adorned his presidency with the trappings of culture and excellence, inviting distinguished artists to perform at the White House and embellishing his speeches with quotations from Emerson. The media, awed by Kennedy's grace and taste, as well as by his wit and wealth, nurtured his image as both a vibrant, dashing hero and an adoring husband. The public knew nothing of his fragile health, frequent use of mood-altering drugs to alleviate pain, or extramarital affairs. He remained personally popular throughout his presidency.

### Kennedy's Domestic Record

Media images obscured Kennedy's lackluster domestic record. There was no New Frontier in domestic affairs. This was due, in part, to Kennedy's passive leadership. He was more a moderate than a liberal, did not care deeply about domestic matters, and would not personally court congressional leaders. Moreover, he lacked the votes on Capitol Hill to overcome the conservative coalition that had stymied liberalism since 1938. Citing Thomas Jefferson—"Great innovations should not be forced on slender majorities"—he rarely asked Congress to enact reform measures: "There is no sense in raising hell, and then not being successful." Accordingly, the Kennedy years saw little of significance in social legislation.

Instead, JFK made economic growth his domestic priority. To stimulate the economy, he combined increased defense and space expenditures with inducements to private enterprise to invest in capital growth. In 1961 he persuaded Congress to boost the defense budget by 20 percent, vastly increasing America's stockpile of nuclear missiles as well as strengthening the military's conventional forces and establishing the Special Forces ("Green Berets") to engage in guerrilla warfare. To stimulate the economy and enhance American power yet more, Kennedy also got Congress to finance a "race to the moon," an effort that would cost more than $25 billion to land astronauts Neil Armstrong and Buzz Aldrin on the lunar surface in 1969.

Accepting unbalanced budgets as a price of stimulating economic growth, Kennedy proposed lower business taxes through investment credits and generous depreciation allowances. Most business groups, however, remained cool to the Democratic president, and angrily resented his anti-inflationary efforts to force U.S. Steel to cancel an increase in its prices. Eager to woo the business community, Kennedy in 1963 rejected proposals for increased social spending and instead advocated lower personal and corporate taxes to encourage investment and consumption.

When the Kennedy presidency suddenly ended in November 1963, the proposed tax cut was still bottled up in Congress (an apt symbol of JFK's overall failure in domestic legislation). Military spending, however, and the continuation of technological innovation, heightened productivity, low-cost energy, and the expansion of world trade had already doubled the rate of economic growth, decreased unemployment, and held increases in inflation to 1.3 percent a year. The United States was in the midst of its longest uninterrupted economic boom ever. Still, some liberals grumbled about "the third Eisenhower administration," with its promotion of corporate profits and military spending at the expense of those most in need and the environment.

Environmentalism had its roots in both the older conservation movement, emphasizing the efficient use of resources, and the preservation movement, focusing on preserving "wilderness." Concern for the health of the ecosystem and the basic biological well-being of the planet grew during the fallout scare of the 1950s and intensified with the publication in 1962 of Rachel Carson's *Silent Spring* (see Chapter 29). Additionally, postwar prosperity made large numbers of Americans less concerned with increased production and more concerned with the quality of life. Responding to the furor set off by Carson's documentation of the hazards of DDT and environmental pollution, Kennedy appointed an advisory committee on pesticides, and Congress in 1963 passed a Clean Air Act, regulating automotive and industrial emissions. After decades of heedless pollution, hardly helped by the introduction of aluminum pop-top cans in 1963, Washington hesitatingly began to deal with environmental problems.

### Kennedy and Civil Rights

JFK neither anticipated nor welcomed the crusade for civil rights that engulfed the South in the 1960s. He straddled the issue for two years, fearing that the struggle for racial equality would divide the nation, split the Democratic party, immobilize Congress in lengthy filibusters, and jeopardize his reelection hopes.

Thus Kennedy treated racial problems as a thorny thicket to be tiptoed around rather than a moral issue requiring decisive leadership. He balanced his selection of an unprecedented number of African Americans for high office with the appointment of white racists to federal judgeships. He sought to speed desegregation by litigation yet remained aloof from attempts to enact civil rights legislation, and he stalled for two years before issuing the weakest possible executive order banning discrimination in federally financed housing.

But civil rights activists kept pressure on the president. In the spring of 1961, the Congress of Racial Equality (CORE), an interracial protest group founded in 1942, organized a "freedom ride" through the Deep South to dramatize the widespread violation of a 1960 Supreme Court decision outlawing segregation in interstate transportation. It aroused white wrath, leading to the savage beating of the freedom riders and the burning of their bus in Anniston, Alabama, and their being mauled by a white mob in Birmingham. Only after further assaults on the freedom riders in Montgomery did Kennedy dispatch federal marshals to end the violence. And not until after scores more freedom rides and the arrest of hundreds of young protesters did the president press the Interstate Commerce Commission to enforce the Supreme Court's ruling.

Kennedy again used federal force to quell white racist violence in the fall of 1962. When a federal court ordered the University of Mississippi to enroll James Meredith, a black air force veteran, angry whites rioted. Rallying behind Confederate flags, troublemakers attacked the federal marshals who had escorted Meredith to "Ole Miss." The clash left two dead, hundreds injured, and the campus shrouded in tear gas. Federal troops finally restored order—and upheld the right of a black American to attend the university of his home state.

### The African American Revolution

With mounting numbers of African Americans demonstrating to secure racial equality, Kennedy could no longer temporize. The climax came in Birmingham. Determined to provoke a confrontation that would expose the violent extremism of southern white racism and force Kennedy's hand, Martin Luther King, Jr., initiated a series of marches, sit-ins, and pray-ins on Good Friday, 1963. Birmingham police commissioner Eugene "Bull" Connor scoffed that King would soon "run out of niggers." But as thousands of schoolchildren joined King's crusade, Connor grew impatient and tried to crush the black movement with overwhelming force. He unleashed his men, armed with electric cattle prods, high-pressure water hoses, and snarling attack dogs, on the nonviolent demonstrators. The ferocity of Connor's attacks, chronicled on television news programs, filled the world with revulsion.

"The civil-rights movement should thank God for Bull Connor," JFK remarked. "He's helped it as much as Abraham Lincoln." Indeed, Connor's vicious tactics seared the nation's conscience. And the combination of growing white support for equal rights and African-American activism pushed Kennedy to arrange a settlement that ended the demonstrations in return for the desegregation of Birmingham's stores and the upgrading of black workers. By mid-1963 the rallying cry "Freedom Now!" reverberated through the land as the number and magnitude of protests soared. Concerned about America's image abroad and about the "fires of frustration and discord" raging at home, Kennedy believed that if the federal government did not lead the way toward "peaceful and constructive" changes in race relations, blacks would turn to far more militant leaders and methods. When Governor George Wallace refused to allow two black students to enter the University of Alabama in June 1963, Kennedy acted forthrightly. He forced Wallace—who had pledged "Segregation now! Segregation tomorrow! Segregation forever!"—to capitulate to a court desegregation order.

On June 11 the president went on television to define civil rights as "a moral issue" and to declare that "race has no place in American life or law." Describing the plight of blacks in the Jim Crow America of 1963, he asked, "Who among us would be content to have the color of his skin changed and stand in his place? Who among us would then be content with the counsels of patience and delay?" A week later Kennedy proposed a comprehensive civil-rights measure. Although House liberals moved to toughen Kennedy's proposal, most members of Congress did not heed the president's plea.

To compel Congress to act, nearly 250,000 Americans converged on the Capitol on August 28 (see A Place in Time). But neither Kennedy's nor King's eloquence could quell the rage of the bitterest opponents of civil rights. The night of the president's address, Medgar Evers, the head of the Mississippi branch of the NAACP, was murdered by a sniper in Jackson, Mississippi. In September the bombing of a black church in Birmingham killed four girls attending Sunday School. And still, southern obstructionism kept the civil-rights bill stymied in Congress, with little hope of passage.

## New Frontiers Abroad, 1960–1963

Proclaiming in his inaugural address that "we shall pay any price, bear any burden, oppose any foe to assure the survival and success of liberty," Kennedy launched

**Birmingham, 1963**
*The ferocious attempts by local authorities, led by Eugene "Bull" Connor, to repel nonviolent black protesters with fire hoses (capable of 100 pounds of water pressure per square inch), electrically charged cattle prods, and snarling, biting police dogs—shown nightly on TV—made white supremacy an object of revulsion throughout most of the country and forced the Kennedy administration to intervene to end the crisis.*

a major buildup of the nation's military arsenal. He gave foreign policy his top priority and surrounded himself with Cold Warriors who shared his belief that American security depended upon superior force and the willingness to use it. At the same time, he gained congressional backing for new programs of economic assistance to Third World countries to counter the appeal of communism, and he created the Peace Corps. By 1963 five thousand Peace Corps volunteers were serving two-year stints as teachers, sanitation engineers, crop specialists, and health workers in more than forty Third World nations.

## Cold War Activism

Kennedy's first foreign-policy crisis came in the spring of 1961. To eliminate a communist outpost on America's doorstep, Kennedy approved plans drawn up by the Eisenhower administration for fifteen hundred anti-Castro exiles, "La Brigada," to storm Cuba's Bay of Pigs. The scheme, conceived by the CIA and endorsed by the Joint Chiefs of Staff, assumed that the invasion would trigger a general uprising of the Cuban people to dethrone Fidel Castro. It was a fiasco. Deprived of air cover by Kennedy's desire to conceal U.S. involvement, the invaders were easily quashed by Castro's superior forces after they landed at the Bay of Pigs. The president expressed regret at the outcome but refused to apologize for violating Cuba's sovereignty. And for the remainder of his presidency he continued to harass the communist regime and to support efforts to assassinate Castro.

In July 1961, on the heels of the Bay of Pigs failure, Kennedy met in Vienna with Soviet premier Nikita Khrushchev to try to resolve the matters of a peace treaty with Germany and the presence of Western forces in Berlin (see Chapter 28). Comparing the American troops in that divided city to "a bone stuck in the throat," Khrushchev threatened war unless the West retreated. A shaken Kennedy returned to the United States and declared the defense of West Berlin "the great testing place of Western courage and will." He doubled draft calls, ordered more than 150,000 reservists to active duty, and asked Congress for an additional $3 billion defense appropriation. The threat of nuclear war escalated. Suddenly,

the Soviets sealed off their zone of the city in mid-August and began construction of the Berlin Wall to end the exodus of brains and talent to the West. Moscow then signed a separate peace treaty with East Germany. Berlin, Germany, Europe—all remained divided between East and West. Neither side could claim victory, but Kennedy believed his toughness had proved America's willingness to honor its commitments.

## To the Brink of Nuclear War

In mid-October 1962 American aerial photographs revealed that the Soviet Union had begun constructing missile bases in Cuba and had placed there intermediate-range nuclear missiles, capable of striking much of the United States. Smarting from the Bay of Pigs disaster, fearing unchecked Soviet interference in the Western Hemisphere, and believing that his own credibility was on the line, Kennedy responded vigorously. In a major televised address on October 22, he denounced "this clandestine, reckless, and provocative threat to world peace" and demanded that the missiles be removed. The United States, he asserted, would "quarantine" Cuba—impose a naval blockade—to prevent delivery of more missiles and would dismantle by force the missiles already in Cuba if the Soviets did not do so.

**JFK at the Berlin Wall**
*June 26, 1963, President John F. Kennedy and East German policemen stare at each other across the wall dividing East and West Berlin.*

## Washington, D.C.

In 1963 the racially separate and unequal nation's capital more closely resembled a divided southern city than a showplace of democracy. Beyond the gleaming marble façades of Washington's public buildings sprawled slums as appalling as any in the nation. The flight of the white middle class to suburban Maryland and Virginia had abandoned large residential sections of Washington to African Americans. Within the shadow of the Capitol, more than 40 percent of the city's families lived below the poverty level in a ghetto of wretched, rat-infested rooming houses. No other American city exceeded the District of Columbia in rates of infant mortality, venereal disease, and arrests for prostitution and drugs. And although, as the seat of the federal government, Washington could boast the highest per capita income of any American city, a large proportion of its citizens subsisted on welfare. Most African Americans fortunate enough to have jobs held low-paying government posts or served as the waiters, maids, and cooks for the whites in power. Many had no work at all.

It was to the Washington of stately white monuments that civil-rights groups planned to march in 1963 to dramatize grass-roots support for federal action against racial discrimination and segregation. To improve the chances of the civil-rights bill proposed by President Kennedy, they bypassed the drab streets of the black ghetto and rallied on the Mall, the very symbol of American nationhood and democracy.

As the sun rose over Washington on August 28, radio news bulletins predicted that the crowd would fall short of the 100,000 people expected. But throughout the morning a seemingly endless caravan of cars, buses, trains, and planes brought in an estimated quarter-million pilgrims from every part of the country and from abroad—powerful evidence of the new consensus in favor of a strong civil-rights act. More than 150,000 blacks mingled with some 75,000 whites on the grassy slopes surrounding the Washington Monument. In the spirit of a church outing, they shared picnic lunches, sang songs of the movement, and then surged toward the Lincoln Memorial, holding aloft banners proclaiming such messages as "WE SEEK THE FREEDOM IN 1963 PROMISED IN 1863" and "A CEN-

**A National Disgrace** *Abject poverty flourished just minutes from the Capitol Building as the civil-rights crusaders gathered on the Mall.*

TURY-OLD DEBT TO PAY." Massed along the banks of the reflecting pool, the crowd gloried in its immense size and patiently endured several hours of speechmaking by African Americans deploring discrimination and by whites confessing guilt over their belated commitment to racial justice.

Finally, in the late afternoon, after the wilting Washington heat and humidity had turned their clothes soggy, after many on the fringes of the crowd had withdrawn to the shade of old elms and oaks, the huge assemblage stilled as Martin Luther King, Jr., stood at the lectern in the shadow of the Great Emancipator. In a husky voice, King described the oppression of blacks, promised to continue the struggle until they gained all their civil rights, and in rising tones claimed that African Americans would never be satisfied as long as they remained victimized by ghettoization and powerlessness. "[W]e will not be satisfied," King thundered, "until justice rolls down like the waters and righteousness like a mighty stream." As his followers shouted their approval, King put aside his text and, in the familiar cadences of the southern preacher that he was, spoke of a broader vision.

"I have a dream," King chanted again and again as the crowd roared amens in response, "that someday, in the red hills of Georgia, the sons of former slaves and slave owners could sit together at the table of brotherhood . . . that even Mississippi could become an oasis of freedom and justice . . . that boys and girls of both races in Alabama could join hands and walk together as sisters and brothers" . . . that his four children could live in a nation where they would be judged on the basis of their character and not the color of their skin . . . that freedom could ring throughout America . . . that "all of

God's children, black men and white men, Jews and Gentiles, Protestants and Catholics, will be able to join hands and sing in the words of that old Negro spiritual 'Free at last! Free at last! Thank God almighty, we are free at last!'"

King's oratory on that muggy August afternoon in 1963 did not speed the slow progress of the civil-rights bill through Congress. It did not end racism or erase poverty and despair. It did not prevent the ghetto riots that lay ahead, or the white backlash that would ultimately smother the civil-rights movement and destroy King himself. But King had turned a political rally into a historic event. In one of the great speeches of history, he recalled America to the ideals of justice and equality, proclaiming that the color of one's skin ought never be a burden or a liability in American life. In five years King would be dead, murdered by a white racist. But his dream lives. It is the promise of America, a vital reminder of what the United States could be.

**March on Washington for Jobs and Freedom, 1963**
*Originally proposed by African-American trade unionist A. Philip Randolph, the March on Washington generated an outpouring of support far too powerful for President Kennedy to ignore.*

**Martin Luther King, Jr.**
*King warned of the "whirlwind of revolt" that would consume the nation if blacks' civil rights continued to be denied.*

847b

**Anti-Diem Buddhist Protests**
*After Diem's troops fired on Buddhists attempting to celebrate Buddha's 2,587th birthday, Buddhist monk Thich Quang Duc burned himself to death in downtown Saigon in June 1963. It was the first of several self-immolations in South Vietnam. Photographs and videotapes of these horrific protests, shown around the world, helped to convince the Kennedy administration that Diem's leadership of South Vietnam could no longer be supported.*

Kennedy's ultimatum, and Khrushchev's defiant response that the quarantine was "outright banditry," rocked the world. Never before had the two superpowers come so close to the brink of nuclear catastrophe. Apprehension mounted as the Soviet technicians worked feverishly to complete missile launch pads and as Soviet missile-carrying ships steamed toward the U.S. blockade. Americans stayed glued to their radios and television sets. As they waited, 180 U.S. naval ships in the Caribbean prepared to confront the Soviet freighters; B-52s armed with nuclear bombs took to the air; and nearly a quarter-million troops assembled in Florida to invade Cuba. A solemn secretary of state Dean Rusk reported, "We're eyeball to eyeball."

"I think the other fellow just blinked," a relieved Rusk announced on October 25. The Cuba-bound Soviet ships stopped dead in the water, and Kennedy received a message from Khrushchev that Moscow would remove the missiles in exchange for an American promise never to invade Cuba. As Kennedy prepared to accept the Soviet offer, a second, far more belligerent, message arrived from Khrushchev insisting that American missiles be withdrawn from Turkey as part of the deal. Hours later an American reconnaissance plane was shot down over Cuba. It was "the blackest hour of the crisis," recalled a Kennedy aide. Various presidential advisers urged an immediate invasion. But the president, heeding Robert Kennedy's advice, decided to ignore the second Soviet message and

accept the original offer. That night, October 27, the president's brother met secretly with the Soviet ambassador to inform him that this was the only way to avoid nuclear war. The next morning Khrushchev pledged to remove the missiles in return for Kennedy's noninvasion promise. Less publicly, Kennedy subsequently removed U.S. missiles from Turkey.

The full dimensions of the crisis became known only after the end of the Cold War. In January 1992 the Russian military disclosed that Soviet forces in Cuba had possessed thirty-six nuclear warheads for their twenty-four intermediate-range missiles, as well as nine tactical nuclear weapons intended to be used against invading U.S. troops. Soviet field commanders had independent authority to use these weapons. Worst of all, Kennedy had not known that the Soviets already had the capability to launch a nuclear strike from Cuba.

"We do not need to speculate," said a shaken McNamara in 1992, "about what would have happened had the U.S. attack been launched, as many in the U.S. government—military and civilian alike—were recommending to the President on October 27th and 28th. We can predict the results with certainty. . . . No one should believe that U.S. troops could have been attacked by tactical nuclear warheads without the U.S.'s responding with nuclear warheads. . . . And where would it have ended? In utter disaster."

Staring over the brink of nuclear war chastened both Kennedy and Khrushchev. They agreed to install a

Kremlin–White House "hot line" so that the two sides could communicate instantly in future crises. In June 1963 Kennedy publicly called for a relaxation of super-power tensions, and two months later the two nations agreed to a treaty outlawing atmospheric and undersea nuclear testing. These efforts ushered in a new phase of the Cold War, later called *détente,* in which the superpowers tilted toward negotiation rather than confrontation. But the Cuban missile crisis also had the unintended consequence of accelerating the race for evermore destructive weaponry. It confirmed American belief in the need for nuclear superiority to prevent war while convincing Russian leaders that they must overtake the American lead in nuclear missiles to avoid future humiliation. And so the nuclear arms race escalated.

### Kennedy and Indochina

In early 1961 a crisis flared in Laos, a tiny, landlocked nation created by the Geneva agreement in 1954 (see Chapter 29). There a civil war between American-supported forces and Pathet Lao rebels seemed headed for a communist triumph. Considering Laos strategically insignificant, Kennedy agreed in July 1962 to a face-saving compromise that restored a neutralist government but left communist forces dominant in the countryside. The accord both stiffened Kennedy's resolve not to allow further communist gains in Indochina and bolstered North Vietnam's impression of American spinelessness.

Determined not to give further ground in Southeast Asia, Kennedy ordered massive shipments of weaponry to South Vietnam and increased the number of American forces stationed there from less than 700 in early 1961 to more than 16,000 by the end of 1963. Like his predecessor, JFK thought that letting "aggression" go unchecked could lead to a wider war and believed that if communists forcibly took over one nation in a region, others would soon follow (the domino theory). Like Eisenhower, Kennedy assumed international communism to be a monolithic force, a single global enemy under the direct control of Moscow and Beijing. He viewed the conflicts fomented by the communist leadership as tests of America's, and his own, will. He would show the world that the United States was not the "paper tiger" that Mao Zedong (Mao Tse-tung) mocked.

To counter the success of the National Liberation Front, or Vietcong, in the countryside, the United States uprooted Vietnamese peasants and moved them into fortified villages, or "strategic hamlets." Kennedy also pressed the autocratic Diem to make the economic and political reforms that might win him popular support. Diem, instead, brutally crushed demonstrations by students and Buddhist monks. In mid-1963 Buddhist monks were setting themselves on fire to protest Diem's repression, and Diem's own generals were plotting a coup.

Frustrated American policy makers concluded that only a new government could prevent a Vietcong victory. They gave assurances of support to South Vietnamese army officers planning Diem's overthrow, and on November 1 the military leaders staged their coup, captured Diem and his brother, and shot them. The United States promptly recognized the new government (the first of nine South Vietnamese regimes in the next five years) but found it no better able than Diem's to defeat the Vietcong. JFK would either have to increase significantly the involvement of American combat forces or withdraw and seek a negotiated settlement.

What Kennedy would have done is unknown, and a matter of debate among historians. For less than a month after Diem's death, President Kennedy himself fell to an assassin's bullet. His admirers contend that by late 1963 a disillusioned Kennedy was favoring the withdrawal of American forces after the 1964 election. "It is their war," he said publicly. "We can help them, we can send them equipment, we can send our men out there as advisers, but in the final analysis it is their people and their government who have to win or lose the struggle."

Yet skeptics note that the president followed this comment with a ringing restatement of his belief in the domino theory and a promise that America would not withdraw from the conflict. Virtually all his closest advisers, moreover, held that an American victory in Vietnam was essential to check the advance of communism in Asia. They would also counsel Kennedy's successor accordingly.

### The Thousand-Day Presidency

On November 22, 1963, during a trip to Texas to improve his chances for victory in the 1964 presidential election, a smiling JFK and Jackie rode in an open car along Dallas streets lined with cheering crowds. As the motorcade slowed to turn, shots rang out. The president slumped. Bullets had shattered his skull and throat. While the driver sped the mortally wounded president to a nearby hospital—where the doctors pronounced Kennedy dead—Secret Service agents rushed Lyndon Johnson to Air Force One to be sworn in as president.

Sorrow and disbelief numbed the nation. During the next four days millions of Americans sat stunned in front of TV sets, staring at the steady stream of mourners filing by the slain president's coffin in the Capitol rotunda; at the countless replays of the murder of Kennedy's accused assassin, Lee Harvey Oswald, in the Dallas city jail by a nightclub owner; at the somber state funeral, with the president's small son saluting his father's casket; and at the grieving family lighting an eternal flame at Arlington National Cemetery. Few who watched would ever forget. Television's extraordinary power to convey high national drama with incredible poignancy intensified the sense of personal and national loss, and elevated the fallen leader to heroic stature.

### Funeral of a President

*The elaborate state funeral, planned by Jacqueline Kennedy and watched on television by much of the nation, was modeled on that of Lincoln's in 1865. Here the president's wife, whose attractiveness and social finish lent so much to the Kennedy's public image, is surrounded by her children and brothers-in-law.*

The assassination made a martyr of JFK, magnifying his accomplishments. More admired in death than in life, the public repeatedly ranked him with Washington, Lincoln, and Roosevelt as a "great" president. Emphasizing "might have beens," Kennedy loyalists have focused on his intelligence and grace, his ability to change and grow, his new directions on Soviet relations and racial equality. His detractors, however, stress the gap between rhetoric and substance, the discrepancy between his artfully contrived public image and his compulsive, even reckless, sexual behavior. Some deplore his aggressive conduct of the Cold War; others condemn his stirring, unrealistic, ever-grander expectations about social change at home.

In fact, there was no "New Frontier" in domestic matters. Only one-third of his legislative proposals became law. Constrained by the lack of a liberal majority, Kennedy frequently compromised with conservative, and segregationist, congressional leaders. Partly because his own personal behavior made him beholden to J. Edgar Hoover, JFK allowed the FBI unprecedented authority to infringe on civil liberties—even as the CIA was apparently conniving with the Mafia to assassinate Fidel Castro. (The tangled web of plots and policies that enmeshed John and Robert Kennedy, Hoover, organized crime, and the national security agencies remains to be sorted out by scholars.) And there was no "New Frontier" for environmental protection, for slowing corporate consolidation, or for women (JFK appointed fewer women to high-level federal posts than had his predecessors and was the first president since Hoover not to have a woman in the cabinet).

Internationally, Kennedy left a mixed record. He secured the world's first nuclear-test-ban treaty, yet also initiated a massive nuclear-arms buildup. He recognized the need for social reform in Latin America but failed to fund the Alliance for Progress adequately. He ended the conflict in Laos while expanding America's war in Vietnam. Despite gradually changing from an unabashed Cold Warrior to a leader who questioned the necessity of conflict with the Soviets and appeared ready to take risks for peace, JFK nevertheless insisted on maintaining U.S. global superiority and halting the spread of international communism.

Still, JFK had fired the energies and imaginations of millions of Americans. He gave reformers new hope, aroused the poor and the powerless, and challenged youth to fight for what ought to be. He stimulated social criticism and political activism. Like other heroes, Kennedy left the stage before his glory tarnished. He would leave to his successor both soaring expectations at home and a deteriorating entanglement in Vietnam. That legacy, as well as his assassination itself, would shatter illusions, leading an increasing number of Americans to no longer believe their government, to no longer have faith in the future.

## The Great Society

Distrusted by liberals as "a Machiavelli in a Stetson," regarded as a usurper by Kennedy loyalists, Lyndon Baines Johnson had achieved his highest ambition— but only through the assassination of a president in Johnson's home state, Texas. Though just nine years older than JFK, he seemed a relic of the past, a back-room wheeler-dealer, as crude as Kennedy was smooth, as insecure as his predecessor was self-confident.

Yet Johnson had substantial political assets. He had served in Washington almost continuously since 1932, as congressional aide, New Deal administrator, congressman, senator, majority leader, and vice president. No modern president came to office with more national political experience. He knew when to flatter, when to bargain, when to threaten. He excelled in wooing allies, neutralizing opponents, building coalitions, and achieving results. He loved the political maneuvering and legislative detail that Kennedy loathed, and his being a close associate of Capitol Hill power brokers significantly improved chances for the passage of the blocked JFK bills.

His first two years as president were extraordinarily successful. He deftly handled the transition of power, won a landslide victory in 1964, and guided through Congress the greatest array of social-reform legislation in American history.

But Johnson would not rest on his laurels. LBJ's swollen yet fragile ego could not abide the sniping of the Kennedy crowd, and he frequently complained that the media did not give him "a fair shake as president." Wondering aloud, "Why don't people like me?" Johnson pressed on—to do more, to do it bigger and better—to surpass his predecessors and vanquish all foes at home and abroad. Ironically, in seeking consensus and affection, Johnson would divide the nation and leave office repudiated.

## Toward the Great Society

Calling for quick passage of the tax-cut and civil rights bills as a memorial to JFK, Johnson used his skills to good effect. In February 1964 Congress passed a $10

billion tax-reduction bill, producing a surge in capital investment and personal consumption that further stimulated the economy and subsequently led to increased tax revenues and a lower budget deficit. In July, following a three-month filibuster, the lawmakers passed the Civil Rights Act of 1964—the most significant law in the history of American race relations. It banned discrimination and segregation in public accommodations; granted the federal government new powers to fight black disfranchisement and school segregation; and forbade discrimination in employment— creating the Equal Employment Opportunity Commission (EEOC) to enforce the ban on job discrimination by race, religion, national origin, or sex.

In his boldest domestic initiative, Johnson then declared "unconditional war on poverty in America." The public approval that greeted this sweeping effort owed much to Michael Harrington's *The Other America* (1962), which documented that one-fifth to one-fourth

### Lyndon Johnson at His Texas Ranch, 1964
*Recalling the utter chaos in the days after John Kennedy's murder, LBJ later told his biographer: "We were like a bunch of cattle caught in the swamp, simply circling 'round and 'round. . . . There is but one way to get cattle out of the swamps. And that is for the man on the horse to take the lead, to assume command, to provide direction. In the period of confusion after the assassination, I was that man."*

of the nation lived in poverty. Largely invisible in an affluent America, some 40 million people dwelled in substandard housing and subsisted on inadequate diets. Unaided or minimally assisted by a social-welfare bureaucracy, they lived with little hope in a culture of poverty, deprived of the education, medical care, and employment opportunities that most Americans took for granted. More than just being deprived of material things, Harrington asserted, to be poor "is to be an internal alien, to grow up in a culture that is radically different from the one that dominates the society."

LBJ proposed an array of training programs and support services to bring these "internal exiles" into the mainstream. He wanted to be the president who completed what his hero, FDR, had started; and he believed that a nation as rich and resourceful as the United States had the money and skills to improve the lot of all its citizens. Designed to promote greater opportunity, not to redistribute income or wealth, to offer a "hand up, not a handout," and enacted by Congress in August 1964, the Economic Opportunity Act established the Office of Economic Opportunity to fund and coordinate a Job Corps that would train young people in marketable skills; VISTA (Volunteers in Service to America), a domestic peace corps to work in poverty areas; Project Head Start, to provide compensatory education for preschoolers from disadvantaged families; the Community Action Program, to encourage the "maximum feasible participation" of the poor themselves in the decisions that affected them; and an assortment of public-works and training programs.

Summing up his goals in 1964, Johnson offered a cheering crowd in Ann Arbor, Michigan, his vision of the Great Society. First must come "an end to poverty and racial injustice," proclaimed LBJ, but that would be just the beginning. The Great Society would also be a place where all children could enrich their minds and enlarge their talents, where people could renew their contact with nature and sate their hunger for community, and where they would be "more concerned with the quality of their goals than the quantity of their goods."

## The 1964 Election

Johnson's plans for a Great Society horrified the "new conservatism" of the 1960s as expressed by William F. Buckley's *National Review,* by the college student movement Young Americans for Freedom (YAF), and by the extremist John Birch Society, which even accused Eisenhower and Chief Justice Warren of supporting a communist conspiracy. The most persuasive criticism of LBJ's program came from Arizona's Senator Barry Goldwater. A product of the twentieth-century West, Goldwater was an outsider fighting the power of Washington and the eastern establishment, a fervent anticommunist, and a proponent of individual freedom. His opposition to big government, deficit spending, racial liberalism, and most social-welfare programs found a receptive audience in the South, on Sunbelt golf courses, and in working-class neighborhoods.

Johnson's support for civil rights particularly frightened southern segregationists and the growing number of blue-collar workers in northern cities who dreaded the integration of their communities, schools, and workplaces. Many chose to support Alabama's governor George Wallace in the spring 1964 Democratic primaries. With little money and less organization, Wallace aroused passionate support, capturing 34 percent of the Democratic vote in Wisconsin, 30 percent in Indiana, and 43 percent in Maryland.

Buoyed by this "white backlash" against racial liberalism, conservatives took control of the GOP in 1964. At a raucous Republican convention in which the liberal Nelson Rockefeller was booed so loudly that his speech could not be heard, right-wing activists nominated Goldwater, and cheered his declaration "that extremism in defense of liberty is no vice . . . and that moderation in pursuit of justice is no virtue."

Determined to offer the nation "a choice not an echo," Goldwater lauded his opposition to the civil rights act and the censure of McCarthy. He denounced the War on Poverty in Appalachia, called in Tennessee for the sale of the TVA to private interests, opposed high price supports for farmers in the Midwest, and advo-

### The Election of 1964

| Candidates | Parties | Electoral Vote | Popular Vote | Percentage of Popular Vote |
|---|---|---|---|---|
| LYNDON B. JOHNSON | Democratic | 486 | 43,126,506 | 61.1 |
| Barry M. Goldwater | Republican | 52 | 27,176,799 | 38.5 |

cated scrapping social security in St. Petersburg, Florida, a major retirement community. Goldwater also accused the Democrats of a "no win" strategy in the Cold War, intimating that he might use nuclear weapons against Cuba and North Vietnam. His campaign appealed most to those angered by the Cold War stalemate, by the erosion of traditional moral values, and by the increasing militancy of African Americans. While his campaign slogan "In your heart you know he's right" summed up the zeal of his followers, it allowed his liberal opponents to quip "In your guts you know he's nuts."

Goldwater's crusade thus enabled Johnson and his running mate, the liberal Senator Hubert Humphrey of Minnesota, to run as the moderates. They depicted Goldwater as a trigger-happy extremist not to be trusted with the nuclear button. When Goldwater charged that the Democrats had dillydallied in Vietnam rather than pursuing a total victory, Johnson appeared the apostle of restraint. "We are not going to send American boys nine or ten thousand miles from home," the president assured the American people in October, "to do what Asian boys ought to be doing for themselves."

Unsurprisingly, LBJ won a landslide victory, with 43 million to Goldwater's 27 million. The GOP carried only Arizona and five Deep South states, and lost five hundred of the state legislative seats that it had held. Com-

## Major Great Society Programs

### 1964

**Tax Reduction Act** cuts by some $10 billion the taxes paid primarily by corporations and wealthy individuals.

**Civil Rights Act** bans discrimination in public accommodations, prohibits discrimination in any federally assisted program, outlaws discrimination in most employment, and enlarges federal powers to protect voting rights and to speed school desegregation.

**Economic Opportunity Act** authorizes $1 billion for a "war on poverty" and establishes the Office of Economic Opportunity to coordinate Head Start, Upward Bound, VISTA, the Job Corps, and similar programs.

### 1965

**Elementary and Secondary Education Act,** the first general federal-aid-to-education law in American history, provides more than $1 billion to public and parochial schools for textbooks, library materials, and special-education programs.

**Voting Rights Act** suspends literacy tests and empowers "federal examiners" to register qualified voters in the South.

**Medical Care Act** creates a federally funded program of hospital and medical insurance for the elderly (Medicare) and authorizes federal funds to the states to provide free health care for welfare recipients (Medicaid).

**Omnibus Housing Act** appropriates nearly $8 billion for low- and middle-income housing and for rent supplements for low-income families.

**Immigration Act** ends the discriminatory system of national-origins quotas established in 1924.

**Appalachian Regional Development Act** targets $1 billion for highway construction, health centers, and resource development in the depressed areas of Appalachia.

**Higher Education Act** appropriates $650 million for scholarships and low-interest loans to needy college students and for funds for college libraries and research facilities.

**National Endowments for the Arts and the Humanities** are created to promote artistic and cultural development.

### 1966

**Demonstration Cities and Metropolitan Development Act** provides extensive subsidies for housing, recreational facilities, welfare, and mass transit to selected "model cities" and covers up to 80 percent of the costs of slum clearance and rehabilitation.

**Motor Vehicle Safety Act** sets federal safety standards for the auto industry and a uniform grading system for tire manufacturers.

**Truth in Packaging Act** broadens federal controls over the labeling and packaging of foods, drugs, cosmetics, and household supplies.

mentators proclaimed the death of conservatism. But Goldwater's coalition of antifederal government westerners, economic and religious conservatives, and blue-collar workers and white southerners opposed to racial liberalism presaged the Right's future triumph. In fact, nearly 40 percent of the electorate had voted for the uncompromisingly conservative Goldwater. That would be more a beginning than an end. But in the short run, the Democrats secured huge majorities of 68 to 32 in the Senate and 295 to 140 in the House, which nullified the conservative coalition's power to block the president's proposals. For the first time in a quarter-century, the liberals had a working majority.

## Triumphant Liberalism

"Hurry, boys, hurry," an exhilarated LBJ urged his aides. "Get that legislation up to the hill and out. Eighteen months from now ol' Landslide Lyndon will be Lame-Duck Lyndon." Johnson flooded Congress with Great Society proposals—sixty-three of them in 1965 alone. And he got most of what he requested (see box on page 853).

The Eighty-ninth Congress—"the Congress of Fulfillment" to the president, and Johnson's "hip-pocket Congress" to his opponents—enlarged the War on Poverty and passed another milestone civil-rights act. It enacted a Medicare program that provided health insurance for the aged under social security, and a Medicaid program that allocated federal funds to the states to provide medical care for the indigent. The legislators also enacted the first-ever general aid to education, granting federal funds to every level from kindergarten to graduate school. Appalachia, one of the nation's poorest regions, received redevelopment aid. New laws provided federal funds to revitalize inner-city neighborhoods, to construct low-income housing, and to supplement the rents paid by impoverished tenants. Congress also created new departments of transportation and of housing and urban development (the latter headed by Robert Weaver, the first African-American cabinet member), established the National Endowments for the Arts and the Humanities, and promoted auto safety and consumer rights. Of enormous future significance, it adopted a new immigration law, abolishing the national-origins quotas of the 1920s. Los Angeles International Airport replaced Ellis Island as the symbolic port of entry to the United States, and one out of every four legal immigrants settled in California.

The Great Society also sought to reduce pollution and to protect and preserve nature. Congress established the Redwood National Park, strengthened the Clean Water and Clean Air acts, protected endangered species and wildlands, preserved scenic rivers and millions of acres of wilderness, defeated efforts to dam the Colorado River and flood the lower Grand Canyon, and lessened the number of junkyards and billboards.

Surveying the many measures enacted, the Speaker of the House claimed: "It is the Congress of accomplished hopes. It is the Congress of realized dreams." But for many Americans the Great Society remained more a dream than a reality. Although some programs improved the quality of life, as many failed or faded away—in part because they were flawed, ill conceived, and based on faulty assumptions; in part because the liberal consensus unraveled; in part because they were underfunded. The war against poverty was, in the words of Martin Luther King, Jr., "shot down on the battlefields of Vietnam."

In 1966 Johnson spent twenty times more to wage war in Vietnam than to fight poverty. By then, as well, a rising wave of black militancy and urban riots had alienated "middle America," and the bitter divisiveness caused by the war had shattered LBJ's consensus. The Democrats' loss of forty-seven House seats in 1966 sealed the Great Society's fate.

## The Warren Court in the Sixties

By the mid-sixties the liberal Supreme Court was also under siege. Its decisions from *Brown* v. *Board of Education* (1954) onward had incensed the Right. Kennedy's appointment of two liberals to the Court, and Johnson's selection of the even more liberal Abe Fortas and Thurgood Marshall, the Court's first black justice, further angered conservatives as the Warren court handed down decisions that changed the tenor of American life.

In a series of landmark cases (see box on page 855), the Court prohibited Bible reading and prayer in public schools, limited local power to censor books and films, and overturned state bans on contraceptives. In *Baker* v. *Carr* and related decisions, the Court held that apportionment in all legislative bodies be determined on the basis of "one man, one vote," ending rural overrepresentation and increasing the political power of cities and suburbs. The Court's upholding of the rights of the accused in criminal cases, just as crime rates soared, particularly unsettled many Americans.

Criticism of the Supreme Court reached a climax in 1966 when it ruled in *Miranda* v. *Arizona* that police must warn all suspects that anything they said could be

## Major Decisions of the Warren Court

**1954**

*Brown* v. *Board of Education of Topeka* rejects the separate-but-equal concept and outlaws segregation in public education.

**1957**

*Watkins* v. *U.S.* restricts Congress's investigatory power to matters directly pertinent to pending legislation.

*Yates* v. *U.S.* limits prosecutions under the Smith Act to the advocacy of concrete revolutionary action and disallows prosecutions for the preaching of revolutionary doctrine.

**1962**

*Baker* v. *Carr* holds that the federal courts possess jurisdiction over state apportionment systems to ensure that the votes of all citizens carry equal weight.

*Engel* v. *Vitale* prohibits prayer in the public schools.

**1963**

*Abington* v. *Schempp* bans Bible reading in the public schools.

*Gideon* v. *Wainwright* requires states to provide attorneys at public expense for indigent defendants in felony cases.

*Jacobellis* v. *Ohio* extends constitutional protection to all sexually explicit material that has any "literary or scientific or artistic value."

**1964**

*New York Times Co.* v. *Sullivan* expands the constitutional protection of the press against libel suits by public figures.

*Wesberry* v. *Sanders* and *Reynolds* v. *Sims* hold that the only standard of apportionment for state legislatures and congressional districts is "one man, one vote."

**1966**

*Miranda* v. *Arizona* requires police to advise a suspect of his or her constitutional right to remain silent and to have a counsel present during interrogation.

**1967**

*Loving* v. *Virginia* strikes down state antimiscegenation laws, which prohibit marriage between persons of different races.

**1968**

*Katzenbach* v. *Morgan* upholds federal legislation outlawing state requirements that a prospective voter must demonstrate literacy in English.

*Green* v. *County School Board of New Kent County* extends the *Brown* ruling to require the assignment of pupils on the basis of race, to end segregation.

used against them in court and that they could choose to remain silent. The Warren court had gone further than any previous Court in protecting the rights of the underprivileged and free expression. And in 1968 both Richard Nixon and George Wallace would win favor by promising to appoint judges who emphasized "law and order" over individual liberty.

## The Changing Struggle for Equality, 1964–1968

The drive for black equality crested and then receded in the two years following the 1963 March on Washington. The movement ended legal discrimination and black disfranchisement and gained improved opportunities for education and employment. But major problems remained: poverty, unemployment, crime, drug addiction, and family disorganization. Persistent white racism, moreover, discouraged many blacks; they doubted that they would ever be seen as equals in America, and some became increasingly hostile to whites. For them, the civil-rights movement had generated hopes it could not fulfill and had kindled a racial pride that rejected integration as a desirable goal. "The paths of Negro-white unity that had been converging," wrote Martin Luther King, Jr., "crossed at Selma and like a giant X began to diverge."

### The Voting Rights Act of 1965

In 1964 CORE and SNCC activists, believing that the ballot box held the key to power for African Americans in the South, mounted a major campaign to register black

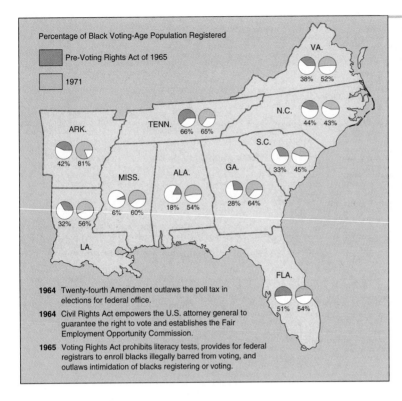

Percentage of Black Voting-Age Population Registered

■ Pre-Voting Rights Act of 1965

□ 1971

VA. 38% 52%

N.C. 44% 43%

TENN. 66% 65%

ARK. 42% 81%

S.C. 33% 45%

MISS. 6% 60%

ALA. 18% 54%

GA. 28% 64%

LA. 32% 56%

FLA. 51% 54%

**1964** Twenty-fourth Amendment outlaws the poll tax in elections for federal office.

**1964** Civil Rights Act empowers the U.S. attorney general to guarantee the right to vote and establishes the Fair Employment Opportunity Commission.

**1965** Voting Rights Act prohibits literacy tests, provides for federal registrars to enroll blacks illegally barred from voting, and outlaws intimidation of blacks registering or voting.

**Voter Registration of African Americans in the South, 1964–1971**

*As blacks overwhelmingly registered to vote as Democrats, some former segregationist politicians, among them George Wallace, started to court the black vote, and many southern whites began to cast their ballots for Republicans, inaugurating an era of real two-party competition in the South.*

voters. Focusing on the state most hostile to equal rights, they organized the Mississippi Freedom Summer Project of 1964. A thousand college-student volunteers assisted blacks in registering to vote and in organizing "Freedom Schools" that taught black history and emphasized African-American self-worth. Harassed by Mississippi law-enforcement officials and Ku Klux Klansmen, the volunteers endured the firebombing of black churches and civil-rights headquarters, as well as arrests.

Although they registered only 1,200 blacks to vote, the civil-rights workers enrolled nearly 60,000 disfranchised blacks in the Mississippi Freedom Democratic Party (MFDP) and took their case to the national Democratic convention in August 1964. They insisted that the convention seat MFDP delegates in place of the all-white delegation chosen by the Mississippi Democratic party. To head off a walkout by southern whites, LBJ forged a compromise that offered two at-large seats to the MFDP and barred from all future conventions any delegations from states that disfranchised blacks. It both angered southern segregationists and alienated the militants in the civil rights movement.

Determined to win a strong voting-rights law, Martin Luther King, Jr., and the SCLC organized mass

protests in Selma, Alabama, in March 1965. Blacks were half the population of Dallas County, where Selma was located, yet only 1 percent was registered to vote. Selma's county sheriff, Jim Clark, every bit as violence-prone as Birmingham's "Bull" Connor, attacked the protesters brutally. Showcased on TV, the attacks provoked national outrage and increased support for a voting-rights bill.

Signed by the president in August 1965, the Voting Rights Act expanded black suffrage in the South and transformed southern politics. The law authorized federal examiners to register voters and to suspend literacy tests in areas where fewer than half the minority residents of voting age were registered. Together with the Twenty-fourth Amendment, ratified in 1964, which outlawed the poll tax in federal elections, and a 1966 Supreme Court decision striking down the poll tax in *all* elections, the law boosted the number of registered black voters in the South from 1 million in 1964 to 3.1 million in 1968. For the first time since Reconstruction, southern blacks were a political force to be reckoned with.

The civil-rights movement had altered, not revolutionized, race relations. Black voting power led to the

**Black Power**

*Rejecting the faith long held by African Americans in the United States and in the professed intentions of white America to remedy injustices, advocates of black power insisted on controlling their own movement and institutions, shaping their own agenda and programs, and defining their own demands and destiny.*

defeat of white supremacists like Sheriff Jim Clark and caused other once ardent segregationists, like George Wallace, to seek black support. Equal access to public accommodations gave African Americans a greater sense of dignity. "Now if we do want to go to McDonald's we can go to McDonald's," mused a black woman in Atlanta. "It's just knowing! It's a good feeling." But with discrimination lingering in many spheres and black unemployment disproportionately high, the anger bubbling below the surface of the urban ghetto finally boiled over.

### The Long, Hot Summers

On August 11, 1965, five days after the voting-rights-bill signing, a confrontation between white police and young blacks in Watts, Los Angeles's largest black district, ignited the most destructive race riot in decades. For six days nearly fifty thousand blacks looted shops, firebombed white-owned businesses, and sniped at police officers, fire fighters, and National Guard troops. When the riot ended, 34 people were dead, 900 injured, 4,000 arrested, and $30 million of property devastated. In rapid succession blacks in Chicago and in Springfield, Massachusetts, took to the streets, looting, burning, and battling police.

In the summer of 1966, more than a score of ghetto outbreaks erupted in northern cities. Blacks rioted to force whites to pay heed to the squalor of the slums, to the savage behavior of police in the ghetto, and to urban poverty—issues that the civil-rights movement had ignored. Frustrated by the allure of America's wealth portrayed on TV and by what seemed the empty promise of civil-rights laws, African-American mobs stoned passing motorists, ransacked stores, torched white-owned buildings, and hurled bricks at the troops sent to quell the disorder. The following summer brought nearly 150 racial outbreaks and 40 riots—the most intense and destructive period of racial violence in U.S. history. Then in 1968, following the assassination of Martin Luther King, Jr. (see Chapter 31), black uprisings flared in the ghettos of a hundred cities. Overall, the 1964–1968 riot toll would include some 200 dead, 7,000 injured, 40,000 arrested, and $200 million of property destroyed.

A frightened, bewildered nation asked why such rioting was occurring just when blacks were beginning to achieve their goals. Militant blacks explained the riots as revolutionary violence to overthrow a racist, reactionary society. The Far Right saw them as evidence of a communist plot. Conservatives described the riots as senseless outbursts by a small number of troublemakers. The administration's National Advisory Commission on Civil Disorders (the Kerner Commission) indicted "white racism" for fostering an "explosive mixture" of poverty, slum housing, poor education, and police brutality in America's cities. Warning that "our nation is moving toward two societies, one black, one white—separate and unequal," the commission recommended increases in federal expenditures to assist urban blacks. Johnson, aware of the white backlash, ignored the advice, and most whites approved his inaction. Alarmed by demands for "Black Power," they preferred that their taxes go to strengthening local police forces instead of improving ghetto conditions.

### "Black Power"

The demand for Black Power sounded in 1966 expressed the disappointment of many African Americans at the slow pace of racial change and their bitterness toward a white society that blocked their aspirations. Less an ideology than a cry of fury and frustration, Black Power owed much to the teachings of Malcolm X. A former pimp and drug dealer, he had converted to the Nation of Islam, or Black Muslim, faith while in prison. Founded in Detroit in 1931 by Elijah Poole (who took the Islamic name Elijah Muhammad), the Nation of Islam was an expression of the separatist and nationalist impulses long present in the black community: racial solidarity and uplift, self-sufficiency and self-help. It insisted that blacks "wake up, clean up, and stand up" to achieve true independence. It rejected integration as a goal. The Black Muslims' most powerful orator, Malcolm X urged African Americans to be proud of their blackness and their African roots, to see themselves with their "own eyes not the white man's," and to separate themselves from the "white devil." He insisted that blacks seize their freedom "by any means necessary": "If ballots won't work, bullets will." In February 1965, after he broke with the Nation of Islam, Malcolm X was assassinated. But he was not silenced. His account of his life and beliefs, *The Autobiography of Malcolm X* (1965) became the main text for the rising Black Power movement.

Inspired by Malcolm X's example, militant blacks challenged the means and ends of the civil rights movement. CORE and SNCC in 1966 changed from interracial organizations committed to achieving integration nonviolently to all-black groups advocating racial separatism and Black Power. The most notorious champion of self-determination for African-American communities was the Black Panther party. To overthrow white oppressors it urged black men to become "panthers—smiling, cunning, scientific, striking by night and sparing no one." Its violent confrontations with the police left some of its supporters dead and many more in prison, and its extremism attracted little support from African Americans. Most blacks still lauded Martin Luther King, Jr., and supported the traditional civil rights groups.

Nevertheless, Black Power partisans exerted a significant influence on the movement. They helped to organize scores of community self-help groups and institutions that did not depend on whites, to establish black studies programs at colleges, to unite black voters to elect black candidates, and to encourage African Americans to see that "black is beautiful." "Say it loud—I'm black and I'm proud," sang James Brown, and as never before African Americans rejected skin bleaches and hair straighteners, and took pride in soul food and soul music. "I may have lost hope," young SCLC leader Jesse Jackson had students repeating with him, "but I am . . . somebody. . . . I am . . . black . . . beautiful . . . proud. . . . I must be respected." This theme would soon reverberate through other social movements.

### Ethnicity and Activism

Native Americans, now numbering nearly 800,000, also demonstrated to publicize their plight and to awaken self-respect and cultural pride. In 1961 representatives of sixty-seven tribes drew up a Declaration of Purposes, criticizing the termination policy. And in 1964 hundreds of Indians lobbied in Washington for the inclusion of Native Americans in the War on Poverty, claiming that Indians suffered the worst poverty, the highest disease and death rates, and the poorest education and housing of any group in the United States. President Johnson responded by establishing the National Council on Indian Opportunity in 1965, to channel antipoverty funds into Indian communities, and in 1968 he asked Congress for still more federal aid for Indians.

By 1968 activists were demanding "Red Power" and insisting on the name "Native American." They agitated for preferential hiring, Native American studies programs, and reimbursement for lands taken from them in violation of federal laws and treaties. The Puyallup in Washington held "fish-ins" in 1968 to assert old treaty rights to fish in the Columbia River and Puget Sound. The Wampanoag Indians in Massachusetts transformed Thanksgiving Day into a National Day of Mourning. The Navajo and Hopi began protesting strip-mining in the Southwest. And in San Francisco Bay those calling themselves "Indians of All Tribes" began a two-year sit-in at the former prison on Alcatraz Island to dramatize a history of broken promises over land claims. The most militant group, the American Indian Movement (AIM), founded in 1967 by Chippewas, Sioux, and Ojibwa from the Northern Plains, emphasized Indians' rights to control their own affairs. AIM, like the Black Panthers, set up armed patrols to protect Indians from police harassment.

Mexican-Americans also challenged whites' dominance. Using the tactics and ideas pioneered by the civil rights movement, César Chávez, a migrant farmworker since childhood, founded the National Farm Workers Association (later the United Farm Workers—UFW) to gain union recognition and improved working conditions for the mostly Mexican-American farm laborers in California. A charismatic leader who like Martin Luther King, Jr., used religion and nonviolent resistance to fight for social change, Chávez led his followers in the Delano vineyards to strike in 1965. Many similar efforts had been smashed in the past. But Chávez undertook a series of personal hunger strikes and organized consumer boycotts to dramatize the farm workers'

struggle—*La Causa*—as part of the common struggle of the entire Mexican-American community and as part of the larger national movement for civil rights and social justice. Just as the UFW flag featured a black Aztec eagle and the Virgin of Guadalupe, Chávez combined Mexican heritage, religion, and labor militancy to win union recognition, gain better wages for field hands, and stimulate ethnic consciousness and pride.

In the mid-1960s, as well, young Hispanic activists began using the formerly pejorative terms *Chicano* and *Chicana* as labels of collective identity and solidarity for all those of Mexican and Latin American descent. Rejecting assimilation, they demanded bilingual and bicultural education, fought for Chicano studies programs, and insisted on Chicana-only organizations. In New Mexico, they founded the Alianza to recapture territory usurped by whites. In Colorado the Crusade for Justice, and in Texas La Raza Unida, exemplified the new militancy, as did the United Mexican-American Students on campuses in the Southwest. Young Chicanos in California organized the Brown Berets, modeled on the Black Panthers, and in the name of "Chicano Power" demanded control over all those institutions most affecting them.

Like their counterparts, young activists who rejected the term "Oriental" increasingly called them-

### Native Americans on Alcatraz Island, 1969

*After taking over the island, the American Indian Movement demanded government funds to develop it into an Indian cultural center and university. In 1971 federal officials removed the demonstrators.*

### César Chávez

*To dramatize the plight of migrant workers, Chávez drew on the tactics of the civil-rights movement. In 1965 he led striking grape pickers with the slogan "God Is Beside You on the Picket Line."*

selves "Asian-Americans," to signify a new ethnic consciousness among peoples with their roots in the Far East. And they too campaigned for special educational programs and for the election of Asian-Americans to office. None of these movements for ethnic pride and power could sustain the fervent activism and media attention that they attracted in the late sixties. But by elevating the consciousness and nurturing the confidence of the younger generation, each contributed to the cultural pride of its respective group.

## A Second Feminist Wave

Following the victory of the woman-suffrage campaign in 1920, the feminist movement lost momentum and hit a low point in the 1950s. Then the rising tempo of activism in the 1960s stirred a new spirit of self-awareness and dissatisfaction among educated women. A revived feminist movement emerged, profoundly altering women's view of themselves and their role in American life.

Several events fanned the embers of discontent into a flame. John F. Kennedy, who personally exploited women in a series of fleeting sexual encounters both before and after his marriage, established the Presidential Commission on the Status of Women. Its 1963 report documented occupational inequities suffered by women that were similar to those endured by minority groups. Women received less pay than men for comparable or identical work and had far less chance of moving into professional or managerial careers. Women were 51 percent of the population, but only 7 percent of the doctors and less than 4 percent of the lawyers. The women who served on the presidential commission successfully urged that the Civil Rights Act of 1964 prohibit gender-based as well as racial discrimination in employment.

Dismayed by the Equal Employment Opportunity Commission's reluctance to enforce the ban on discrimination by gender, Bella Abzug, Aileen Hernandez, and others formed the National Organization for Women (NOW) in 1966. Defining itself as a civil-rights group for women, NOW lobbied for equal opportunity, filed lawsuits against gender discrimination, and mobi-

lized public opinion "to bring American women into full participation in the mainstream of American society *NOW*."

NOW's popularity owed much to the publication of Betty Friedan's *The Feminine Mystique* (1963). Calling it "the problem that has no name," Friedan deplored the narrow view that women should seek fulfillment solely as wives and mothers. Suburban domesticity, Friedan argued, left many women with feelings of emptiness, with no sense of accomplishment, and afraid to ask "the silent question—'Is this all?'" Friedan asserted that women must pursue careers and establish "goals that will permit them to find their own identity." *The Feminine Mystique* revealed to disillusioned women that they were not alone in their unhappiness. Friedan's demand for "something more than my husband, my children, and my home" rang true to many middle-class women who found the creativity of homemaking and the joys of motherhood exaggerated.

### The Feminine Mystique

*Analogous to the civil rights groups of the early 1960s, many feminist groups later in the decade mobilized to demand equality before the law and equal participation in the economic and political life of the nation. In challenging the institutions and attitudes that oppressed them, including the use of words like chicks, the women's movement raised questions about some of America's most cherished beliefs and behavior.*

'I don't know what you chicks are complaining about. We're just trying to protect your feminine mystique.'

Still another catalyst for feminism came from the involvement of younger women in the civil-rights and anti–Vietnam War movements. Women activists gained confidence in their own potential, an ideology to describe oppression and justify revolt, and experience in the strategy and tactics of organized protest. Their involvement also made them conscious of their own second-class status, as men in these movements had monopolized the positions of power, relegated women to menial jobs, and sexually exploited them.

In 1968 militant feminists adopted the technique of "consciousness raising" as a recruitment device and a means of transforming women's perceptions of themselves and society. Tens of thousands of women assembled in small groups to share experiences and air grievances. They soon realized that others felt dissatisfaction similar to their own. "When I saw that what I always felt were my own personal hangups was as true for every other woman in that room as it was for me! Well, that's when *my* consciousness was raised," a participant recalled. Women learned to regard their personal, individual problems as shared problems with social causes and political solutions—"the personal is political." These sessions opened eyes, and minds. "It wasn't just whining, it was trying to figure out *why*, why we felt things and what we could do to make our marriages more equal and our lives better." This new consciousness brought a sense of "sisterhood" and a commitment to end sexism.

Women's liberation groups sprang up across the nation, employing a variety of publicity-generating and confrontational tactics. In 1968 radical feminists crowned a sheep Miss America to dramatize that such contests degraded women, and set up "freedom trash cans" in which women could discard high-heeled shoes, bras, curlers, and other items that they considered demeaning. They established health collectives and day-care centers, founded abortion-counseling services, demanded equality in education and the workplace, and protested the negative portrayals of women in the media, in advertising, and in language. Terms such as *sexism* and *male chauvinist pig* entered the American vocabulary.

Despite a gulf between radicals and reformers, quarreling factions set aside their differences in August 1970 to join in the largest women's rights demonstration ever. Commemorating the fiftieth anniversary of woman suffrage, the Women's Strike for Equality brought out tens of thousands of women nationwide to parade for the right to equal employment and safe, legal abortions. By then the women's movement had already pressured many financial institutions to issue credit to single women and to married women in their own name; filed suit against hundreds of colleges and universities to secure salary raises for women faculty members victimized by discrimination; ended newspapers' practice of listing employment opportunities under separate "Male" and "Female" headings; and gained guidelines that required corporations receiving federal funds to adopt nondiscriminatory hiring practices and equal pay scales. By 1970, moreover, more than 40 percent of all women held full-time jobs outside the home.

In contrast to the 1950s, the changed consciousness of the feminist movement opened a larger world of choices and opportunities for American women. Domesticity remained an option, but it was no longer the *only* option. Women were taking control of their own lives and defining their own goals, in their own language. Accepting a Grammy award for "I Am Woman," singer Helen Reddy thanked God for all "She" had done.

## The Lost Crusade in Vietnam, 1964–1968

More than any other issue, America's deepening involvement in Vietnam shattered the consensus that LBJ desired. Developments in Vietnam ensnared his administration as Diem's successors proved equally unable to defeat the Vietcong.

Johnson had to choose between intervening decisively or withdrawing from Vietnam. While privately describing Vietnam as "a raggedy-ass fourth-rate country" undeserving of American blood and dollars, LBJ feared that an all-out American military effort might provoke Chinese or Soviet entry and lead to World War III. And he foresaw that full-scale engagement in "that bitch of a war" would destroy "the woman I really loved—the Great Society." Yet Johnson did not want the United States to appear weak. Only American strength and resolve, he believed, would prevent a wider war. He also worried that a pullout would leave him vulnerable to conservative attack. "I am not going to lose Vietnam," he insisted. "I am not going to be the president who saw Southeast Asia go the way China went."

Trapped between unacceptable alternatives, Johnson widened America's limited war, hoping that U.S. firepower would force Ho Chi Minh to the bargaining table. But the North Vietnamese and NLF calculated that they would gain more by outlasting the United States than by negotiating. So the war ground on, devastating Southeast Asia and dividing the United States as nothing had since the Civil War.

### *The Gulf of Tonkin Resolution*

In 1964 Johnson took steps to impress North Vietnam with America's commitment to defend South Vietnam and to block his opponent, Barry Goldwater, from capitalizing on Vietnam in the presidential campaign. In February he ordered the Pentagon to prepare for air strikes against North Vietnam. In May his advisers drafted a congressional resolution authorizing an escalation of American military action, and in June the president appointed General Maxwell Taylor, a proponent of

greater American involvement in the war, as ambassador to Saigon. Then, in early August, North Vietnamese patrol boats allegedly clashed with two American destroyers in the Gulf of Tonkin (see map). Evidence of the attack was unclear, yet Johnson announced that Americans had been victims of "open aggression on the high seas." Never saying that the U.S. ships had been aiding the South Vietnamese in secret raids against North Vietnam, Johnson condemned the attacks as unprovoked.

He ordered air strikes on North Vietnamese naval bases and asked Congress to pass the previously prepared resolution authorizing him to "take all necessary measures to repel any armed attack against the forces of the United States and to prevent further aggression." Assured by the president that this meant no "extension of the present conflict," the Senate passed the Gulf of

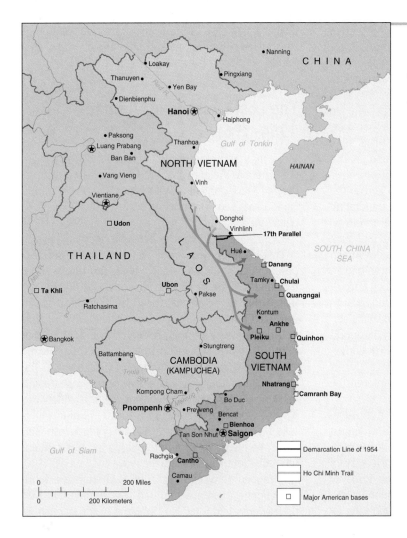

**The Vietnam War, to 1968**
*Wishing to guarantee an independent, noncommunist government in South Vietnam, Lyndon Johnson remarked in 1965: "We fight because we must fight if we are to live in a world where every country can shape its own destiny. To withdraw from one battlefield means only to prepare for the next."*

Tonkin Resolution 88 to 2, and the House 416 to 0. LBJ called the resolution "grandma's nightshirt—it covered everything." He considered it a mandate to commit U.S. forces as he saw fit. *But,* having once used force against North Vietnam made it more likely to do so again, and the resolution gave him a blank check to determine the level of force—making massive intervention more likely. And leaving himself open to the charge of misleading the people and the Congress, LBJ's credibility would ultimately become his Achilles heel. At this moment of triumph, his political downfall had begun.

### Americanization of the War

Early in 1965 Johnson cashed his blank check, ordering "Operation Rolling Thunder," the bombing of North Vietnam. Designed to inflict just enough damage to force Hanoi to negotiate, to boost the morale of the Saigon government, and to stop the flow of soldiers and supplies coming from North Vietnam, the bombing accomplished none of its purposes. So, LBJ escalated America's air war. Between 1965 and 1968, the U.S. would drop 800 tons of bombs a day on North Vietnam, three times the tonnage dropped by all the combatants in World War II.

Unable to turn the tide by bombing, Johnson committed U.S. combat troops to Vietnam. They pursued a "meat-grinder" or attrition strategy to force the communists to the peace table by inflicting losses on their forces at a rate that exceeded the enemy's ability to recruit additional troops. This required 185,000 Americans in Vietnam by the end of 1965; 385,000 a year later; and 485,000 (a greater military force than the U.S. had deployed in Korea) after another year. But the Vietcong still controlled most of the countryside, and Hanoi, determined to battle on until the United States lost the will to fight, matched each American troop increase with its own. No end was in sight.

### Opposition to the War

First on college campuses and then across the country, a growing number of Americans began to oppose the war. A week after the marines splashed ashore at Danang, South Vietnam, in March 1965, students and faculty at the University of Michigan conducted the first

**Infantry Patrol in a Clearing**, by Roger Blum
*An unconventional war without fronts or territorial objectives, the Vietnam War generally involved small units of American troops engaging NLF and NVA forces in rice paddies, jungles, and swamps.*

teach-in to raise questions about U.S. intervention. All-night discussions of the war followed at other universities; and some 25,000 people, mainly students, attended a rally in Washington that spring to protest U.S. meddling in what they considered a Vietnamese civil war. In 1966 large-scale campus protests against the war erupted. Students angrily demonstrated against the draft and against university research for the Pentagon. "Yesterday's ivory tower," observed the president of Hunter College, "has become today's foxhole."

Liberal intellectuals and clergy joined the chorus of opposition to the war. Some decried the massive aerial bombing of an underdeveloped nation; some feared the prospect of spiraling escalation; some doubted that the United States could win at any reasonable cost and feared the demise of the Great Society. In 1967 prominent critics of the war, ranging from Senator Robert Kennedy to George Kennan, from Dr. Benjamin Spock to Martin Luther King, Jr, spurred hundreds of thousands of Americans to participate in antiwar marches and demonstrations.

Critics also noted that the war's toll fell most heavily on the poor. Owing to college deferments, the use of influence, and a military-assignment system that shunted the better educated to desk jobs, lower-class

**LBJ's Vietnam Nightmare**
*The Vietnam War spelled Johnson's undoing. Young peace demonstrators made known their feelings about the president's role in the war during a massive antiwar protest at the Pentagon in October 1967 (above); a cartoonist caricatured Johnson as being haunted by the ghosts of Vietnam (right).*

youths were twice as likely to be drafted and, if drafted, twice as likely to be assigned to combat duty as those from the middle class. About 80 percent of the enlisted men who fought in Vietnam came from poor and working-class families.

TV coverage of the war further eroded support. Scenes of shocking cruelty, of fleeing refugees, of children maimed by U.S. bombs, and of dying Americans, replayed in living rooms night after night, laid bare the horror of the war and undercut the optimism of government officials. Americans shuddered as they watched napalm (a burning glue that adheres to skin and clothing) and defoliants lay waste to Vietnam's countryside and leave thousands of civilians dead or mutilated. They saw American troops, supposedly winning the hearts and minds of the Vietnamese, up-

root peasants, burn their villages, and desecrate their burial grounds.

Yet at the height of the antiwar movement most Americans either supported the war or remained undecided. Many expressed the sentiment "I want to get out, but I don't want to give up." They acknowledged that, in Secretary of Defense Robert McNamara's words, "the picture of the world's greatest superpower killing or seriously injuring a thousand noncombatants a week, while trying to pound a tiny backward country into submission on an issue whose merits are hotly disputed, is not a pretty one." But they did not see Americans as the aggressor in Vietnam, they believed the "domino theory," and they were not prepared to accept a communist victory over the United States.

Equally disturbing to the majority was how polarized the nation had grown. "Hawks" would accept little short of total victory, whereas "doves" insisted on an end to fighting regardless of the consequences. Civility, too, was a casualty. As Johnson lashed out at his critics as "nervous Nellies" and refused to de-escalate the conflict, the young paraded outside the White House taunting "Hey, hey, LBJ, how many kids did you kill today?" A virtual prisoner in the White House, unable to speak in public without being shouted down, Johnson and the Great Society, too, were casualties of the far-off war.

## CONCLUSION

The charming Kennedy style that captivated the media, and through them the public, combined an aura of "can do" vigor with intellectual curiosity and youthful glamour. It obscured the reality of an unexceptional domestic record. Not until Johnson became president did the more significant measures proposed by Kennedy become law. Then, in addition to a civil-rights act and a tax cut, LBJ pushed and prodded Congress to enact his Great Society legislation—promoting health, education, voting rights, urban renewal, immigration reform, federal support for the arts and humanities, protection of the environment, and a war against poverty—the most sweeping liberal measures since the New Deal. They made the United States a more caring and just nation. Thus, the landmark civil-rights acts, ending the legality of Jim Crow, racial discrimination, and black disfranchisement, provided for improving educational and employment opportunities for African Americans, nurtured the self-esteem of blacks, and inspired others to fight for equality and dignity. But they left largely untouched the maladies of the northern black ghetto. There, unfulfilled expectations and frustrated hopes would explode into urban rioting and increasing black militancy. That swelled the backlash of southern whites and blue-collar workers fed up with efforts to force racial integration and special governmental efforts to assist African Americans, undermining support for the Great Society.

Most of all, however, it was America's deepening involvement in Vietnam that destroyed both the programs LBJ most cared about and his presidency itself. He had inherited from his predecessor a seriously deteriorating limited war. The United States could leave and cede Vietnam to the communists, or it could launch an all-out military campaign that might trigger a nuclear or world war. Johnson chose to gradually increase the pressure on North Vietnam to negotiate a compromise, and within three years a half-million American troops were stationed in Vietnam and more bombs had exploded on that country than had been dropped in World War II. Yet the end was still not in sight, and despite LBJ's boast that the United States could afford both guns and butter, the skyrocketing billions spent on the war left the Great Society starved for funding, ensuring that victory in the war against poverty remained as elusive as victory over the Vietcong.

## FOR FURTHER READING

Irving Bernstein, *Promises Kept: John F. Kennedy's New Frontier* (1991), and Thomas Reeves, *A Question of Character: A Life of John F. Kennedy* (1991). Two conflicting interpretations of the man and his presidency.

David Burner, *Making Peace with the 1960s* (1996). A thought-provoking examination of the decade and liberalism's demise.

William Chafe, *The Unfinished Journey: America Since World War II*, rev. ed. (1999). An interpretive history of social change emphasizing issues of class, gender, and race.

Sara Evans, *Personal Politics* (1979). An analysis of the roots of modern feminism in the civil-rights movement and in the New Left.

Robert Gottlieb, *Forcing the Spring: The Transformation of the American Environmental Movement* (1996). A valuable study of the movement's changes.

Ernest R. May and Philip D. Zelikow, eds., *The Kennedy Tapes: Inside the White House During the Cuban Missile Crisis* (1997). A transcript, with explanatory text, that reveals the roles played by the president and his advisers in dealing with this tense matter.

Charles Payne, *I've Got the Light of Freedom: The Organizing Tradition and the Mississippi Freedom Struggle* (1995). An exhaustive study of the civil-rights struggles.

Harvard Sitkoff, *The Struggle for Black Equality, 1954–1992* (1993). A dramatic account of the terror-laced struggle against white racism.

# 31

## A Troubled Journey:
## From Port Huron to Watergate

Vietnam Ambushed Patrol, Dakto, 1969

A small group of students from the University of California, Berkeley, had participated in the Mississippi Freedom Summer Project of 1964. Back at school that autumn, the civil-rights activists set up tables to collect money and to solicit recruits near the campus gate, a place traditionally open to political activities. On September 14, prodded by local conservatives, the university banned these enterprises from the area. Organizing as the Berkeley Free Speech Movement, a coalition of student groups insisted on the right to campus political activity. As one member noted: "A student who has been chased by the KKK in Mississippi is not easily scared by academic bureaucrats." Matters came to a head on October 1, when the university ordered the arrest of Jack Weinberg, a student who had set up a table in defiance of the ban.

As the police dragged Weinberg to a patrol car, hundreds of students surrounded the vehicle and sat down, blocking its exit. The sit-in continued for thirty-two hours, until Berkeley's administrators dropped the charges against Weinberg. But late in November, again pressured by influential conservatives, the university leveled charges against several students who had led the earlier demonstration. A mass occupation of the university administration building and the arrest of more than five hundred students followed. The ensuing weeks saw the campus convulsed by demonstrations and a strike by nearly 70 percent of the student body. Angered by what they perceived as a stifling education institution eager to do the research and train the technicians desired by U.S. industry and the government, the students found their voice in junior philosophy major Mario Savio, who had confided to a friend: "I'm tired of reading about history. I want to make it."

Placing the Free Speech Movement in a broad context, Savio claimed that the university, serving the interests of corporate America, treated students like interchangeable robots. Urging them to fight against the education machine repressing them, Savio cried out, "There is a time when the operation of the machine becomes so odious, makes you so sick to heart, that . . . you've got to put your bodies upon the gears and upon the wheels, upon the levers, upon all the apparatus, and you've got to make it stop." Savio touched a nerve, and by the time Berkeley officials rescinded their restrictions on campus political advocacy early in 1965, the spirit of protest had spread to other campuses.

In 1965, 41 percent of all Americans were under the age of twenty. American youths deluged colleges and spawned a student movement and counterculture that gave the decade its distinctive aura. Their assault on traditional policies and values produced vital changes. It swept away the well-kept world of the fifties, when "nice" girls did not have sex or pursue careers and when African Americans did not have an effective voice or a guaranteed vote. It also led to a preoccupation with self and a conservative resurgence.

Both agent in and beneficiary of the era's turbulence and political realignment, Nixon won the presidency in 1968 and gained a stunning reelection victory in 1972. Winning high marks for his management of world affairs, Nixon ended U.S. involvement in Vietnam and inaugurated a period of détente with China and the Soviet Union. But flouting the very laws he had pledged to uphold, Nixon, to avoid impeachment, resigned in disgrace in 1974. His legacy was a public disrespect for politics seldom matched in U.S. history.

This chapter focuses on five major questions:

- Why and how did the 1960s become a decade of political protest and cultural insurgency? Why might 1968 be seen as a turning point in postwar American life?
- If President Nixon had chosen to end U.S. involvement in the Vietnam War in 1969, how might the course of domestic events have changed?

♦ What were the strategies by which the Republicans sought to build a new political majority? How did they contribute to Nixon's landslide reelection victory in 1972?

♦ How might the criminal and political abuses associated with Watergate have led to the impeachment of President Nixon, and what was the impact of Watergate on the American political system?

♦ Did the events of 1973–1974, culminating in the resignations of Nixon and Agnew, prove that the political system worked or that it failed? Explain.

# The Youth Movement

In the 1950s the number of American students pursuing higher education rose from 1 million to 4 million, and in the 1960s the number doubled again, to 8 million. By then more than half the U.S. population was under age thirty. Their sheer numbers gave them a collective identity and ensured that their actions would have impact.

Most baby boomers followed conventional paths in the 1960s. They sought a secure place in the system, not its overthrow. They preferred beer to drugs and football to political demonstrations. They joined fraternities and sororities and majored in subjects that would equip them for the job market. Whether or not they went to college—and fewer than half did—the vast majority had their eyes fixed on a good salary, a new car, a traditional family, and a pleasant home. Many disdained the long-haired protesters and displayed the same bumper stickers as their elders: "My Country—Right or Wrong" or "America—Love It or Leave It."

## *Toward a New Left*

However, an insurgent minority, mostly liberal arts majors and graduate students, got the lion's share of attention. They welcomed the idealism of the civil-rights movement and the rousing call of President Kennedy for service to the nation. They admired the mavericks and outsiders of the fifties: Martin Luther King, Jr.; iconoclastic comedian Mort Sahl; Beat poet Allen Ginsberg; and pop-culture rebels like Elvis Presley and James Dean.

Determined not to be a "silent generation," sixty students adopted the Port Huron Statement in June 1962. A broad critique of American society and a call for more genuine human relationships, it announced the formation of "a new left"—Students for a Democratic Society (SDS). Inspired by the activism of black youth in the sit-ins and freedom rides, SDS envisioned a nonviolent youth movement transforming the United States into a "participatory democracy" in which all citizens would make the decisions on which their lives and well-being depended. SDS assumed such a system would value love and creativity, and would cure the ills of materialism, militarism, and racism.

A generation of idealistic activists found their agenda in the Port Huron Statement. Most never joined SDS, instead associating themselves with what they

**Berkeley Free Speech Movement, 1965**
*The first wave of a storm of protest at many colleges and universities, the Berkeley Free Speech Movement of 1964–1965 began as a protest against the university administration's restrictions on political activity on campus and then broadened into struggles against racism and, especially, the war in Vietnam.*

## CHRONOLOGY

**1960**  Birth-control pill marketed.

**1963**  Bob Dylan releases "Blowin' in the Wind."

**1964**  Berkeley Free Speech Movement (FSM).

The Beatles arrive in the United States and "I Want to Hold Your Hand" tops the charts.

**1965**  Ken Kesey and Merry Pranksters stage first "acid test."

**1966**  Abolition of automatic student deferments from the draft.

**1967**  March on the Pentagon.

Israeli-Arab Six-Day War.

**1968**  Tet offensive.

President Lyndon Johnson announces that he will not seek reelection.

Martin Luther King, Jr., assassinated; race riots sweep nation.

Students take over buildings and strike at Columbia University.

Robert F. Kennedy assassinated.

Violence mars Democratic convention in Chicago.

Vietnam peace talks open in Paris.

Richard Nixon elected president.

**1969**  Apollo 11 lands first Americans on the moon.

Nixon begins withdrawal of U.S. troops.

Woodstock festival.

March Against Death in Washington, D.C.

Lieutenant William Calley charged with murder of civilians at My Lai.

**1970**  United States invades Cambodia.

Students killed at Kent State and Jackson State universities.

Nixon proposes Huston Plan.

Environmental Protection Agency established.

OSHA created.

Earth Day first celebrated.

The Beatles disband; Janis Joplin and Jimi Hendrix die of drug overdoses.

**1971**  United States invades Laos.

*Swann* v. *Charlotte-Mecklenburg Board of Education.*

*New York Times* publishes Pentagon Papers.

Nixon institutes wage-and-price freeze.

South Vietnam invades Laos with the help of U.S. air support.

**1972**  Nixon visits China and the Soviet Union.

SALT I agreement approved.

Break-in at the Democratic National Committee headquarters in Watergate complex.

Nixon reelected in landslide victory.

Christmas bombing of North Vietnam.

**1973**  Vietnam cease-fire agreement signed.

Trial of Watergate burglars.

Senate establishes Special Committee on Presidential Campaign Activities to investigate Watergate.

President Salvador Allende ousted and murdered in Chile.

Vice President Spiro Agnew resigns; Gerald Ford appointed vice president.

*Roe* v. *Wade.*

Yom Kippur War; OPEC begins embargo of oil to the West.

Saturday Night Massacre.

**1974**  Supreme Court orders Nixon to release Watergate tapes.

House Judiciary Committee votes to impeach Nixon.

Nixon resigns; Ford becomes president.

---

vaguely called "the Movement" or "the New Left." Unlike the Left of the 1930s, they rejected Marxist ideology and Stalinist party discipline; they emulated SNCC's rhetoric and style; and like the Berkeley Free Speech Movement students, they too would be radicalized by what they saw as the rigidity of campus administrators, the insensitivity of the nation's bureaucratic processes, and mainstream liberalism's inability to bring far-reaching change. Only a radical rejection of compromise and consensus, they concluded, could restructure society along humane and democratic lines. By 1965

Mario Savio's call for students to throw their bodies upon "the machine" until it ground to a halt was reverberating on campuses nationwide.

### From Protest to Resistance

The movement took many forms. Students held sit-ins to halt compulsory ROTC (Reserve Officer's Training Corps) programs. They protested dress codes and parietal rules. They marched to demand changes in the grading system and for fewer required courses. They threatened to close down universities unless they admitted more minority students and stopped research for the military-industrial complex. The escalation of the war in Vietnam, and the abolition of automatic student deferments from the draft in January 1966, made the Movement a mass movement. Popularizing the slogan "Make Love—Not War," SDS organized draft-card burnings, and harassed campus recruiters for the military and for the Dow Chemical Company—the chief producer of napalm and Agent Orange, chemicals used in Vietnam to burn villages and defoliate forests. In 1967 SDS leaders encouraged even more provocative acts of defiance. With the rallying cries "From Protest to Resistance" and "The Streets Belong to the People," they conducted civil disobedience at selective service centers and counseled students to flee the country rather than be drafted. At the Spring Mobilization to End the War in Vietnam, which attracted a half-million antiwar protesters to New York's Central Park, SDS members led the chants of "Hell, no, we won't go!" By 1968 SDS claimed 100,000 members on 300 campus chapters.

That spring saw at least 40,000 students on a hundred campuses demonstrate against war and racism. Most stayed peaceful. Some became violent. In April militant Columbia University students took over the administration building and held a dean captive to denounce the university's proposed expansion into Harlem to construct a gymnasium. The protest then expanded into a demonstration against the war and the university's military research. A thousand students barricaded themselves into campus buildings, declaring them "revolutionary communes." Outraged by the harshness of the police who retook the buildings by storm, the moderate majority of Columbia students joined a boycott of classes that shut down the university. The high point of the Movement came in mid-1969 with the New Mobilization, a series of huge antiwar demonstrations culminating with the March Against Death. Three hundred thousand protesters came to Washington, D.C., in November to march through the cold streets carrying candles and signs with the names of soldiers killed or villages destroyed in Vietnam.

### The Waning of Student Violence

A crescendo of violence in the spring of 1970 marked the effective end of the student movement as a political force. On April 30, 1970, Richard M. Nixon, LBJ's successor, jolted a war-weary nation by announcing that

**March Against Death, November 1969**
*Following the October 15 "moratorium," in which some 2 million Americans took to the streets to demand an end to the war, nearly 50,000 demonstrators paraded silently around the White House the next month to commemorate those Americans who had been killed in Vietnam.*

he had ordered U.S. troops to invade Cambodia, a neutral Indochinese nation that North Vietnamese forces used as a staging area. Nixon had previously announced that the United States would pursue peace by "Vietnamizing" the ground fighting (that is, using South Vietnamese troops instead of Americans) while stepping up the bombing to force the North Vietnamese to the negotiating table. Students, lulled by periodic announcements of troop withdrawals from Vietnam, suddenly felt betrayed. They exploded in hatred for Nixon and the war.

At Kent State University in Ohio, as elsewhere, student fears and frustrations unleashed new turmoil. Radicals broke windows and tried to firebomb the ROTC building. Nixon branded the protesters "bums," his vice president compared them to Nazi storm troopers, and in Ohio the governor ordered three thousand National Guardsmen to tense Kent and slapped martial law on the university. In full battle gear, the troops rolled onto the campus in armored personnel carriers.

The day after the guard's arrival six hundred Kent State students peacefully demonstrated against the

**"My God, They're Killing Us"**
*Following rioting downtown and the firebombing of the ROTC building, Ohio Governor James Rhodes called in the National Guard to stop the antiwar protests at Kent State University. On May 4, after retreating from rock-throwing students, nervous guardsmen turned and began to shoot. When the firing stopped, four students lay dead and 11 were left wounded.*

Cambodian invasion. Suddenly a campus policeman boomed through a bullhorn: "This assembly is unlawful! This is an order—disperse immediately!" Students shouted back: "Pigs off campus!" Some threw stones. "Prepare to move out," the guard commander ordered his men, "and disperse this mob." With bayonets fixed, the guardsmen moved toward the rally and laid down a blanket of tear gas. Hundreds of demonstrators and onlookers, choking and weeping, ran from the advancing troops. Guardsmen in Troop G, poorly trained in crowd control, sighted their rifles and fired a volley. When the shooting stopped, four students lay dead, two of them women merely passing by on their way to lunch.

Ten days later, Mississippi state patrolmen fired into a women's dormitory at Jackson State College, killing two black students. Nationwide, students reeled from shock and angrily protested. A wave of student strikes followed, closing down four hundred colleges, many of which had seen no previous unrest. Hundreds of thousands of once-moderate students now identified themselves as "radical or far Left."

The United States was badly divided, as if in a civil war. Although most students blamed Nixon for widening the war and applauded the demonstrators' goals, more Americans blamed the victims for the violence and criticized students for undermining U.S. foreign policy. This was especially true of the working class. Both a class resentment of privileged college students and a fear of social chaos animated its condemnation of protesters. In New York City hundreds of construction workers chanting "All the way with the USA" roughly broke up a demonstration to protest the murders at Kent State. And many Kent townspeople shared the view of a local merchant who asserted that the guard had "made only one mistake—they should have fired sooner and longer." A local ditty promised, "The score is four, and next time more."

The campus disorders following the invasion of Cambodia were the final spasm of a dwindling movement. When a bomb planted by three antiwar radicals destroyed a science building at the University of Wisconsin in the summer of 1970, killing a graduate student, most young people condemned the tactic. With the resumption of classes in the fall, the fad of "streaking"—racing across campus in the nude—more reminiscent of the twenties than the sixties, signaled the end of the student uprising. Frustrated by their failure to end the war, much less to revolutionize American society, antiwar activists turned to other causes—especially the women's and ecology movements—to mystic cults and rural communes, to careers and parenthood. A handful of radicals went underground, committing terrorist acts that resulted in a government crackdown on the remains of the antiwar movement. The New Left was finished, a victim of government repression, its own internal contradictions, and Nixon's winding down the war in Vietnam.

The aftereffects of campus activism lingered long after the end of the New Left. Festering resentment over the youth revolt would stoke the fires of conservatism among middle-class Americans; and a right-wing backlash, fueled in no small part by opposition to student radicalism, would unite religious fundamentalists, southern segregationists, and blue-collar workers.

This rejection of liberalism propelled conservatives like Ronald Reagan to prominence. In 1966 he won California's governorship by denouncing Berkeley demonstrators and the blacks who rioted in Watts. The actor-turned-politician then won a resounding reelection victory by condemning still more vigorously young militants and radicals. "If it takes a bloodbath, let's get it over with," he declared. "No more appeasement!" Sounding the same theme, conservatives gained office nationwide. And memories of student radicalism would continue to strengthen conservatism's appeal for the rest of the century.

The New Left had, however, help catalyze public opposition to the Vietnam War. It mobilized campuses into a force that the government could not ignore, and it made continued U.S. involvement in Vietnam difficult. The Movement also aided in liberalizing many facets of campus life and making university governance less authoritarian. Dress codes and curfews virtually disappeared; ROTC went from a requirement to an elective; minority recruitment increased; and students assisted in shaping their education.

Some New Left veterans continued their activism into the 1970s, joining the environmental, consumer rights, and antinuclear movements. Female students in the Movement of the sixties formed the backbone of a resurgent women's movement in the seventies. All this fell short of the New Left vision of remaking the social and political order. While masses of students could be mobilized in the short run against the Vietnam War, only a few made long-term commitments to radical politics. The generation that the New Left had hoped to organize as the vanguard of radical change preferred pot to politics, and rock to revolution.

## The Youth Culture

The alienation and hunger for change that drew some youths into radical politics led many more to cultural rebellion, to "getting their heads straight." They joined communes and tribes to cohabit in harmony and noncompetition; they rejected monogamy and reason as

**Avenue of the Americas, 1969,** by Raphael Soyer
*To distance themselves from the traditional norms of middle-class respectability, the disaffected young adopted new lifestyles and new forms of dress and recreation. Their sense of alienation and rebelliousness is captured in this painting of a late sixties urban street scene.*

"hangups"; and in urban areas such as Chicago's Old Town or Atlanta's Fourteenth Street—"places where you could take a trip without a ticket"—they experimented with drugs. Historian Theodore Roszak called them "a 'counter culture': meaning, a culture so radically disaffiliated from the mainstream assumptions of our society that it scarcely looks to many as a culture at all, but takes on the alarming appearance of a barbarian intrusion."

Surveys estimated that at least half the college students in the late sixties tried marijuana and that a minority used hallucinogenic or mind-altering drugs, particularly LSD. The high priest of LSD was Timothy Leary, a former Harvard psychologist fired in 1963 for encouraging students to experiment with drugs—to "tune in, turn on, drop out." On the West Coast, writer Ken Kesey and his followers, the Merry Pranksters, promoted hallucinogens by conducting "acid tests" (distributing free tablets of LSD in orange juice) and created the "psychedelic" craze of Day-Glo-painted bodies gyrating to electrified rock music under flashing strobe lights. Influenced by LSD's reality-bending effects, the counterculture sought a world without rules, one in which magic and mysticism replaced science and reason. Jim Morrison's rock group the Doors took inspiration and its name from Aldous Huxley's paean to hallucinogens, *The Doors of Perception,* and bands like the Grateful Dead, closely associated with Kesey, launched the San Francisco sound of "acid rock"—the perfect marriage of "sex, drugs, and rock-and-roll."

Distancing themselves from middle-class respectability, youths flaunted outrageous personal styles. They showed disdain for consumerism by wearing surplus military clothing, torn jeans, and tie-dyed T-shirts. Young men sported shaggy beards and long hair—a sign of freedom to do as they pleased to the young, but to parents a symbol of disrespect and contempt for social conventions.

Popular music both echoed and shaped the youth culture. Early in the sixties, folk music had been the vogue on college campuses. Songs protesting racism and injustice mirrored the idealistic, nonviolent commitment of the civil-rights movement. Bob Dylan sang hopefully of changes "blowin' in the wind" that would transform society. Then Beatlemania swept the country in 1964. It was time to heed one's hormones and have fun. Moving quickly beyond their early romantic songs like "I Want to Hold Your Hand," the English group soon gloried in the youth culture's drugs ("I'd love to turn you on"), sex ("why don't we do it in the road?"),

and radicalism ("you say you want a revolution?"). They would be joined by Rolling Stones mayhem, the Motown beat, and acid rockers.

In August 1969, 400,000 young people gathered for the Woodstock festival in New York's Catskill Mountains to celebrate their vision of freedom and harmony. For three days and nights they reveled in rock music and openly shared drugs, sexual partners, and contempt for the Establishment. The counterculture heralded the festival as the dawning of an era of love and peace, the Age of Aquarius.

In fact, the counterculture's luster had already dimmed. The pilgrimage of "flower children" to the Haight-Ashbury district of San Francisco (see A Place in Time) and to New York's East Village in 1967 brought in its wake a train of muggers, rapists, and dope peddlers. In December 1969 Charles Manson and his "family" of runaways ritually murdered a pregnant movie actress and four of her friends. Then a Rolling Stones concert at the Altamont Raceway near San Francisco deteriorated into a violent melee in which several concertgoers died. In 1970 the Beatles disbanded. On his own, Beatle John Lennon sang: "The dream is over. What can I say?"

## The Sexual Revolution

The counterculture's "do your own thing" and "if it feels good, do it" approach to sex corresponded with an overall atmosphere of greater permissiveness. These shifts in attitudes and behaviors constituted a sexual revolution that would flourish until the mid-1980s, when the AIDS epidemic and the "graying" of the "baby boomers" chilled the ardor of open sexuality.

Most commentators linked the increase in sexual permissiveness to waning fears of unwanted pregnancy. In 1960 oral contraceptives reached the market, and by 1970 12 million women were taking "the Pill." Even more women used the intrauterine device (or IUD, later banned as unsafe) or the diaphragm for birth control. And states gradually legalized abortion. In 1970 in New York state, one fetus was legally aborted for every two babies born. Then in 1973 the Supreme Court in *Roe* v. *Wade* struck down all remaining state laws infringing on a woman's right to abortion during the first trimester (three months) of pregnancy.

The Supreme Court also declared unconstitutional most laws restricting "sexually explicit" materials, and mass culture exploited the new permissiveness. *Playboy* featured ever-more-explicit erotica, and women's periodicals encouraged their readers to enjoy recre-

## Haight-Ashbury

ordering Golden Gate Park by the bay, the Haight-Ashbury district of San Francisco in 1965 became a haven for dropouts seeking an alternative to the competitive, materialistic values of the "straight" world. They were attracted to the two-square-mile area of rundown Victorian homes by the seemingly carefree lifestyle of the artists and "beatniks" who had moved there after being forced out of nearby North Beach. Fittingly, in a city once notorious for its opium dens, and whose original name, Yerba Buena, meant "good herb," Haight-Ashbury emerged as the capital of hippiedom, mainly because of the availability there of hallucinogenic drugs, which California did not outlaw until late 1966.

A distinctive counterculture developed in "Hashbury," as some called the district. The Psychedelic Shop on Haight Street supplied drug paraphernalia. Restaurants served organic or macrobiotic meals. The Free Medical Clinic dispensed aid for bad drug trips and venereal diseases. Disciples of the Radha Krishna Temple roamed the streets in flowing orange robes, preaching universal peace and chanting the Hare Krishna. Underground newspapers like *The Oracle* provided commentaries on drugs, radical politics, mysticism, and rock music.

Such local groups as the Grateful Dead and Country Joe and the Fish gave free concerts in the park and

**Janis Joplin with Big Brother and the Holding Company**
*Joplin once summed up her approach to her career and life for a reporter: "If I miss, I'll never have a second chance. . . . I gotta risk it. I never hold back, man. I'm always on the outer limits of probability." Along with Jim Morrison and Jimi Hendrix, other musical stars of the counterculture, Joplin died from a drug overdose.*

popularized psychedelic ballrooms like the Fillmore West. The Diggers—who took their name from the seventeenth-century English radicals who defined property owning as theft—distributed free food and clothing. And many residents lived communally, sharing work, meals, and sex.

Early in 1967, the first Human Be-In at Golden Gate Park made Haight-Ashbury a focus of media attention. Seeking to titillate their audiences, reporters and television crews dwelled on the twenty thousand "flower children" who rang bells, danced ecstatically, shared drugs, and handed sticks of smoking incense to the police.

Accounts of the festival played up Timothy Leary's preaching of the virtues of LSD, Beat poet Allen Ginsberg's chanting of Buddhist mantras, and the Jefferson Airplane's "acid rock" music. Soon everyone was talking about hippies. *Time* put them on its cover. About 75,000 runaways, drug addicts, and bewildered children crowded into the Haight for the 1967 "summer of love."

Close behind them came gawking tourists, "weekend hippies" looking for easy sex and exotic drugs, heroin addicts, and a legion of robbers and rapists. The Haight-Ashbury denizens' complete trust in strangers and faith in love and peace faded quickly as crime soared, drug users died, and narcotics agents cracked down on the abusers. "Love is the password in the Haight-Ashbury," observed one reporter, "but paranoia is the style. Nobody wants to go to jail."

"Hashbury" deteriorated into a slum overrun by dope dealers and criminals. Those who could, pursued their dream of living a life of love and sharing on communal farms in northern California, in Colorado, in southern Illinois. But whether in the hills of Vermont or the "big island" of Hawaii or the deserts of New Mexico, they often found, as did one disillusioned hippie, that "we were together at the level of peace and freedom and love. We fell apart over who would cook and wash the dishes and pay the bills."

**The Haight-Ashbury Scene**

*By 1967, as the popular song "Are You Going to San Francisco?" drifted over American airwaves, Haight-Ashbury was the scene of a mass immigration of youth. A Merry Prankster outside a bus adorned with psychedelic imagery (left) and orange-gowned Hare Krishnas (right).*

873b

ational sex. The commercial success of films given "R" or "X" ratings led Broadway producers to present plays featuring frontal nudity, mimed sex acts, and mock orgies. Even television taboos tumbled as network censors allowed off-color jokes and frank discussions of previously forbidden subjects. By 1970, when the Federal Commission on Obscenity and Pornography recommended the end of all restrictions on pornographic materials available to adults, most barriers to expressions of sexuality had already fallen.

Attitudinal changes brought behavioral changes, and vice versa. The divorce rate nearly doubled in the 1970s; many couples chose to live together without benefit of a marriage license; and by the mid-1970s three-quarters of all college students had engaged in sexual relations before their senior year. The use of contraceptives (and to some extent, even of abortion) spread to women of all religious backgrounds—including Roman Catholics, despite the Catholic Church's stand against "artificial" birth control. The national birthrate plunged steadily throughout the 1960s and 1970s.

Stimulated by the other protest movements in the sixties, gay liberation emerged publicly in late June 1969 after New York City police raided the Stonewall Inn, a gay bar in Greenwich Village, and the homosexual patrons fought back. A surge of "gay pride" and confrontations followed. The new Gay Liberation movement that emerged both built on the reform-minded Mattachine Society and the Daughters of Bilitis, as well as other earlier "homophile" efforts to lobby government officials to end discrimination and legal oppression, and went far beyond them in openly asserting its sexual orientation. Its supporters came primarily from the gay subcultures found in the largest cities. By 1973 some eight hundred openly gay groups were fighting for equal rights for homosexuals, for incorporating lesbianism into the women's movement, and for removing the stigma of immorality and depravity attached to being gay. That year, they succeeded in getting the American Psychiatric Association to rescind its official view of homosexuality as a mental disorder.

What some hailed as sexual liberation others bemoaned as moral decay. Offended by the sudden visibility of openly gay men and lesbians and by "topless" bars, X-rated theaters, and "adult" bookstores, many Americans applauded politicians who promised a war on smut. The public association of the counterculture and the sexual revolution with student demonstrations and ghetto riots swelled the tide of conservatism as the decade ended.

## 1968: The Politics of Strife

The social and cultural turmoil of the sixties unfolded against a backdrop of frustration with the war in Vietnam and an intensifying political crisis. The stormy year 1968 brought these developments together explosively. Converging in the presidential campaign, the swirling currents of strife precipitated the first major realignment in American politics since the New Deal.

### *The Tet Offensive in Vietnam*

In January 1968 liberal Democratic senator Eugene McCarthy of Minnesota, a Vietnam War critic, announced that he would challenge LBJ for the presidential nomination. Experts thought that McCarthy, a witty intellectual, had no chance of unseating Johnson, who had

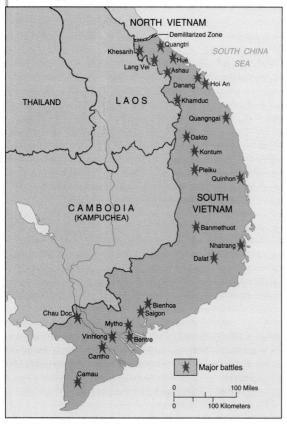

**The Tet Offensive, January–February 1968**
*Although the Tet offensive proved a major tactical defeat for the communists, it effectively undermined American public support for the war.*

won the presidency in 1964 by the largest margin of votes in American history. The last time such an insurgency had been attempted, in 1912, even the charismatic Teddy Roosevelt had failed. Yet McCarthy persisted, determined that at least one Democrat enter the primaries on an antiwar platform.

Suddenly America's hopes for victory in Vietnam sank, and with them LBJ's political fortunes. On January 31—the first day of Tet, the Vietnamese New Year—the National Liberation Front (NLF) and the North Vietnamese mounted a huge offensive, attacking more than a hundred South Vietnamese towns and even the U.S. embassy in Saigon. After a month of ferocious fighting, U.S. troops repelled the offensive, killing 37,000 enemy forces and inflicting a major military defeat on the communists.

The media, however, emphasized the staggering number of American casualties and the immense scope of the Tet offensive. The realization that no area of South Vietnam was secure from the enemy, and that a foe whom the president had repeatedly claimed was beaten could initiate such daring attacks, jolted Americans. Many stopped believing reports of battlefield success coming from the White House and doubted that the United States could win the war at an acceptable cost.

After Tet, McCarthy's criticism of the war won new sympathizers. *Time, Newsweek,* and the *Wall Street Journal* published editorials urging a negotiated settlement. NBC anchorman Frank McGee concluded that "the grand objective—the building of a free nation—is not nearer, but further, from realization." The nation's most respected newscaster, Walter Cronkite of CBS, observed that "it seems now more certain than ever that the bloody experience of Vietnam is to end in a stalemate." "If I've lost Walter," President Johnson sighed, "then it's over. I've lost Mr. Average Citizen." Johnson's approval rating dropped to 35 percent. The number of Americans who described themselves as prowar "hawks" slipped from 62 percent in January to 41 percent in March, while the proportion of antiwar "doves" climbed from 22 percent to 42 percent.

### A Shaken President

Beleaguered, Johnson pondered a change in American policy. When the Joint Chiefs of Staff requested an additional 206,000 men for Vietnam, the president turned to old friends and advisers. Former secretary of state Dean Acheson told the president that "the Joint Chiefs of Staff don't know what they're talking about." Clark

**A Despondent LBJ**
*The president felt trapped by the war in Vietnam, as if he were being "chased on all sides by a giant stampede coming at me from all directions. . . . The whole situation was unbearable to me. After 37 years of public service, I deserved something more than being left alone in the middle of a plain, chased by stampedes on every side."*

Clifford, the new secretary of defense, became "convinced that the military course we were pursuing was not only endless but hopeless."

Meanwhile, nearly five thousand college students had dropped their studies to stuff envelopes and ring doorbells for Eugene McCarthy in the New Hampshire primary contest. To be "clean for Gene," they cut their long hair and dressed conservatively so as not to alienate potential supporters. McCarthy astonished the experts by winning nearly half the popular vote as well as twenty of the twenty-four nominating-convention delegates in a state regarded as conservative.

After this upset, twice as many students converged on Wisconsin to canvass its more liberal Democratic voters. They expected a resounding McCarthy triumph in the nation's second primary. Hurriedly, on March 16, Senator Robert Kennedy entered the Democratic contest, also promising to end the war. Projecting the familiar Kennedy glamour and magnetism, Kennedy was the one candidate who Johnson feared could deny him renomination. Indeed, millions viewed Kennedy as the rightful heir to the White House. Having secured the passionate support of minorities, the poor, and working-class ethnic whites, Kennedy was described by one columnist as "our first politician for the pariahs, our great national outsider."

On March 31, exactly three years after the marines had first splashed ashore at Danang, Johnson informed a surprised television audience, "I'm taking the first step to de-escalate the conflict": a halt to the bombing in North Vietnam. Catching even his closest aides off guard, LBJ added that he wanted to devote all his efforts to the search for peace. "Accordingly," he concluded, "I shall not seek, and I will not accept, the nomination of my party for another term as your president." Johnson was embittered by the personal abuse he had suffered: "I tried to make it possible for every child of every color to grow up in a nice house, eat a solid breakfast, to attend a decent school and to get a good and lasting job," he grumbled. "But look at what I got instead. Riots in 175 cities. Looting. Burning. Shooting. . . . Young people by the thousands leaving the university, marching in the streets. . . ." Reluctant to polarize the nation and his party further, LBJ called it quits. "The only difference between the [John F.] Kennedy assassination and mine," he lamented, "is that I am alive and it has been more tortuous." Two days later, pounding the final nail into Johnson's political coffin, McCarthy trounced the president in the Wisconsin primary.

### Robert Kennedy

*Running an energy-charged campaign in 1968, the dynamic "Bobby" seemed to inspire either wild devotion or deep dislike. He became the Democrats' chief advocate for the disadvantaged and leading critic of the Vietnam War.*

## *Assassinations and Turmoil*

On April 4, three days after the Wisconsin primary, Martin Luther King, Jr., was killed in Memphis, Tennessee, where he had gone to support sanitation workers striking for union recognition and better working conditions. The assassin was James Earl Ray, a white escaped convict. As the news spread, black ghettoes in 125 cities burst into violence. Twenty blocks of Chicago's West Side went up in flames, and Mayor Richard Daley ordered police to shoot to kill arsonists. In Washington, D.C., under night skies illuminated by seven hundred fires, army units in combat gear set up machine-gun nests outside the Capitol and White House. The rioting, which left 46 dead, 3,000 injured, and nearly 27,000 in jail, stood in ironic contrast to King's hopeful message of reconciliation.

Meanwhile, the Democratic contest for the presidential nomination became a three-cornered scramble as LBJ's vice president, Hubert Humphrey, entered the race as the favorite of the party bosses, labor chieftains, and supporters of Johnson's Vietnam policy. McCarthy stood as the candidate of the "new politics"—a moral crusade against the war directed mainly to affluent, educated liberals. Kennedy matched McCarthy's moral outrage at the war. "Don't you understand," he lectured students, "that what we are doing to the Vietnamese is not very different than what Hitler did to the Jews"—and campaigned as the tribune of the less privileged, the sole candidate who appealed to white ethnics and the minority poor. But on June 5, 1968, as he celebrated victory in the California primary, the brother of the murdered president was himself assassinated, by a Palestinian refugee, Sirhan Sirhan, who loathed Kennedy's pro-Israeli views.

The dream of peace and justice turned to despair. "I won't vote," a youth said. "Every good man we get they kill." "We shall not overcome" concluded a Kennedy speech writer: "From this time forward things would get worse, not better. Our best political leaders were part of memory now, not hope."

Other Democrats turned to third-party candidate George Wallace or to the GOP's Richard Nixon. Appealing to those disgusted with inner-city riots and antiwar demonstrations, Nixon promised to end the war in Vietnam honorably, to restore "law and order," and to heed "the voice of the great majority of Americans, the forgotten Americans, the non-shouters, the non-demonstrators, those who do not break the law, people who pay their taxes and go to work, who send their children to school, who go to their churches, . . . who love this country." Tapping into the same wellspring of anger and alienation, Wallace pitched a fiery yet folksy message to blue-collar workers and southern whites fed up with black militants, hippies, and student protesters. He promised, if elected, to crack down on rioters and "long-hair, pot-smoking, draft-card-burning youth."

In August 1968 violence outside the Democratic National Convention in Chicago reinforced the appeal of both Wallace and Nixon. Thousands descended on the city to protest the Vietnam War. Radicals among them wanted to provoke a confrontation to discredit the Democrats, and anarchistic "Yippies" (Youth International party) sought to ridicule the political system by threatening to dump LSD in Chicago's water system and to release greased pigs in the city's crowded Loop area.

Remembering the rioting that Chicago had suffered in the wake of King's assassination, Mayor Richard Daley took a hard line against the demonstrators, giving his police a green light to attack "the hippies, the Yippies, and the flippies." The savagery of the Chicago police, however, fulfilled the radicals' wish for mass disorder. On August 28, as a huge national television audience looked on and as protesters chanted, "The whole world is watching," Daley's bluecoats clubbed demonstrators and bystanders alike. The brutality on the streets overshadowed Humphrey's nomination and tore the Democrats further apart, fixing Americans' image of them as the party of dissent and disorder.

## Conservative Resurgence

Nixon capitalized on the turmoil. His TV commercials flashed images of campus and ghetto uprisings. Portraying himself as the candidate of the great Silent Majority, "the working Americans who have become forgotten Americans," he criticized the Supreme Court for safeguarding the rights of criminals and revolutionaries, promised to appoint tough "law and order" judges, vowed to get people off welfare rolls and on payrolls, and asserted that "our schools are for education—not integration."

Capitalizing on the same revulsions and resentments, George Wallace raged across the political landscape. He stoked the fury of the working class toward welfare mothers, school integrationists, "bearded anarchists, smart-aleck editorial writers, and pointy-headed professors looking down their noses at us." Promising to keep peace in the streets if it took "thirty

**Mayor Daley** by Bernard Perlin, 1968
*In this artistic commentary on the Democratic convention in Chicago, Bernard Perlin depicts a dour Mayor Daley caught between the crowds of protesters and delegates in the foreground and the ghetto tenements in the background. Note the varied ages, races, and genders of the protesters on the left and how the two streams—of demonstrators and convention delegates—merge in front of Daley, suggesting that both are part of the same legitimate political process.*

thousand troops armed with three-foot bayonets," he vowed that "if any demonstrator ever lays [sic] down in front of my car, it'll be the last car he'll lie down in front of."

By September Wallace had climbed to 21 percent in voter-preference polls. Although he articulated deeply held resentments against costly welfare programs, ghetto rioting, and student uprisings, Wallace still seemed too extreme, like Goldwater four years earlier, especially after his running mate suggested dropping "nukes on Vietnam." Other potential supporters, believing Wallace had no real chance of winning, chose not to vote or switched to his opponents. Still, 14 percent of the electorate—primarily young, lower-middle-class, small-town workers—cast their votes for Wallace.

Nixon and Humphrey split the rest of the vote almost evenly. With just 43.4 percent of the popular vote and only 301 electoral votes, Nixon's victory was the narrowest triumph since Woodrow Wilson's. Still, with Humphrey receiving just 38 percent of the white vote (12 million votes less than Johnson in 1964), and not even close to half the labor vote, the long-dominant New Deal coalition was shattered. The 1968 election brought the inauguration of both a new president and a new political era.

The 57 percent of the electorate who voted for Nixon or Wallace would dominate American politics for the rest of the century. While the Democratic party fractured into a welter of contending interest groups, the Republicans attracted a new majority of Americans who lived in the suburbs or the Sunbelt. Capitalizing on the shift in political power from the older industrial cities and states of the Northeast and Midwest to the rapidly growing southern and western rims, the GOP won the allegiance of those most concerned with the traditional values of family, religion, and patriotism, upset by high taxes, and opposed to racial integration and special efforts to assist minorities. Throughout the South and West, the Democrats would carry only Texas and Washington in 1968, and not a single state four years later. The new conservative coalition, yearning for stability at home, looked hopefully to the Republi-

can president to end the Vietnam War and to restore social harmony.

## Nixon and World Politics

A Californian of Quaker origins, Richard Milhous Nixon had worked with the wartime Office of Price Administration before joining the navy. Elected to Congress in 1946, he soon won prominence as a member of HUAC investigating Alger Hiss. Nixon advanced to the Senate in a 1950 campaign highlighted by charges of disloyalty against his Democratic opponent. After two terms as Eisenhower's vice president, his loss to Kennedy in 1960 and his unsuccessful 1962 bid for the California governorship seemingly ended his political career. But Nixon persevered, campaigned vigorously for GOP candidates in 1966, and won his party's nomination and the presidency in 1968 by promising to restore domestic tranquillity.

Nixon, however, really wanted to make his mark in foreign affairs. Considering himself a master of *realpolitik*—a pragmatic, practical approach stressing national interest rather than theoretical or ethical goals—he sought both to check Soviet expansionism and to reduce superpower conflict, to limit the nuclear arms race and enhance America's economic well-being. He planned to get the United States out of Vietnam and begin a new era of détente—an easing of tensions—with the communist world. To manage his diplomacy, Nixon chose Henry Kissinger, a refugee from Hitler's Germany and a Harvard professor of international relations. Like the president, Kissinger also desired to centralize decision making in the White House, maintain the highest degree of secrecy, and engage in intrigue.

### *Vietnamization*

Nixon's grand design hinged on ending the Vietnam War. It was sapping American military strength, worsening inflation, and thwarting détente. Announcing the Nixon Doctrine in August 1969, the president redefined America's role in the Third World to be that of a helpful partner rather than a military protector: nations facing communist subversion could count on U.S. support, but they would have to defend themselves. Sales of American military supplies abroad jumped from $1.8 billion to $15.2 billion in the next six years.

The Nixon Doctrine reflected the president's understanding of the war weariness of both the electorate

**The Election of 1968**

| 3 | Alaska |
| 4 | Hawaii |
| 3 | Washington, D.C. |
| 1 / 12 | Divided |

|  | Electoral Vote | Popular Vote | Percentage of Popular Vote |
|---|---|---|---|
| **Republican** Richard M. Nixon | 301 | 31,770,237 | 43.4 |
| **Democratic** Hubert H. Humphrey | 191 | 31,270,533 | 42.7 |
| **American Independent** George C. Wallace | 46 | 9,906,141 | 13.5 |
| **Minor parties** | – | – | 239,908 | 0.4 |

and the U.S. troops in Vietnam. Johnson's decision to negotiate rather than escalate had left American troops with the sense that little mattered except survival. Morale plummeted. Discipline collapsed. Army desertions rocketed from 27,000 in 1967 to 76,000 in 1970, and absent-without-leave (AWOL) rates rose even higher. Racial conflict became commonplace. Drug use soared: the Pentagon estimated that two out of three soldiers in Vietnam were smoking marijuana and that one in three had tried heroin. The army reported hundreds of cases of "fragging"—the assassination of officers and noncommissioned officers by their own troops.

The toll of atrocities also mounted as the inconclusive war dragged on. Increasing instances of Americans' dismembering enemy bodies, torturing captives, and murdering civilians came to light. In March 1968, in the hamlet of My Lai, an army unit led by Lieutenant William Calley massacred several hundred South Vietnamese. The soldiers gang-raped girls, lined up women and old men in ditches and shot them, and then burned the village. Revelations of such incidents, and the increasing number of returning soldiers who joined the Vietnam Veterans Against the War, undercut the already diminished support for the war.

Despite pressure to end the war, Nixon would not sacrifice U.S. prestige. Seeking "peace with honor," he acted on three fronts. First was "Vietnamization," replacing American troops with South Vietnamese. Hardly a new idea, the French had tried *jaunissement* or "yellowing" in 1951, and it had not worked. By 1972 the more than half million U.S. forces in Vietnam when Nixon took office had been reduced to 30,000—and it still had not worked. Second, bypassing South Vietnamese leaders who feared that any accord with the communists would doom them, Nixon sent Kissinger to negotiate secretly with North Vietnam's foreign minister, Le Duc Tho. Third, to force concessions from the communists despite U.S. withdrawal, Nixon escalated the bombing of North Vietnam and secretly ordered air strikes on the communist supply routes in Cambodia and Laos. He told an aide,

> I want the North Vietnamese to believe I've reached the point where I might do *anything* to stop the war. We'll just slip the word to them that "for God's sake, you know Nixon is obsessed about communism. We can't restrain him when he's angry—and he has his hand on the nuclear button"—and Ho Chi Minh himself will be in Paris in two days begging for peace.

**"The Blind Leading the Blind," 1971**
*Cartoonist David Levine depicted four presidents as being blind with regard to American involvement in Vietnam: Eisenhower, who first made an equivocal U.S. commitment in the faraway Asian nation; Kennedy, who deepened that commitment; Johnson, under whose administration the war escalated into a major conflict; and finally Nixon, who expanded American bombing targets to neutral Cambodia.*

Reprinted with permission from *The New York Review of Books*, Copyright © 1971 NYREV, Inc.

## LBJ's War Becomes Nixon's War

But the secret air raids against Cambodia neither made Hanoi beg for peace nor disrupted communist supply bases. They did, however, undermine the stability of that tiny republic and precipitated a civil war between pro-American and communist factions. In early 1970 North Vietnam increased its infiltration of troops into Cambodia, both to aid the Khmer Rouge (Cambodian communists) and to escalate its war in South Vietnam. Nixon responded with a joint U.S.–South Vietnamese incursion into Cambodia at the end of April 1970. The invaders seized large caches of arms and bought time for Vietnamization. But the costs were high. The invasion ended Cambodia's neutrality, widened the war throughout Indochina, and provoked massive American protests against the war, culminating in the student deaths at Kent State and Jackson State universities.

In 1971 Nixon combined Vietnamization and secret diplomacy with renewed blows against the enemy. In February he invaded Laos with South Vietnamese troops to destroy the communist bases there and to restrict the flow of supplies and men southward from

North Vietnam. The South Vietnamese, however, were routed. Emboldened by its success, North Vietnam mounted a major campaign in the south in April 1972—the Easter Offensive. With less than 100,000 U.S. troops in Vietnam, Nixon retaliated by mining North Vietnam's harbors and unleashing B-52s on its major cities. "The bastards have never been bombed like they are going to be bombed this time," he vowed.

## America's Longest War Ends

The 1972 bombing helped to break the impasse in the Paris peace talks, stalemated since 1968. In late October, just days before the presidential election, Kissinger announced that "peace is at hand." The cease-fire agreement that he had negotiated with Le Duc Tho required the withdrawal of all U.S. troops; provided for the return of American prisoners of war; and allowed North Vietnamese troops to remain in South Vietnam.

Kissinger's negotiation ensured Nixon's reelection, but South Vietnam's President Thieu refused to sign a cease-fire permitting communist troops to remain in the South. An angry Le Duc Tho then pressed Kissinger for additional concessions. And Nixon again resorted to massive B-52 raids. The 1972 Christmas bombing of Hanoi and Haiphong, the heaviest and most destructive of the entire war, roused fierce opposition in Congress and the United Nations, but achieved its objective, dissolving the deadlock. Secretly, Nixon also reassured Thieu that the United States would "respond with full force should the settlement be violated by North Vietnam," ending Saigon's recalcitrance.

The Paris Accords, signed in late January 1973, essentially restated the terms of the October truce. The agreement ended hostilities between the United States and North Vietnam yet left unresolved the differences between North Vietnam and the Thieu regime, guaranteeing that Vietnam's future would yet be settled on the

---

## The Vietnam War: A Chronology

**1945** Ho Chi Minh announces Declaration of Independence from France.

**1950** French-controlled Vietnam receives U.S. financial aid and military advisers.

**1954** Dienbienphu falls to Ho's Vietminh.

Geneva Accords end Indochina War and temporarily divide Vietnam at the seventeenth parallel.

Ngo Dinh Diem becomes South Vietnam's premier.

**1955** Diem establishes the Republic of Vietnam.

U.S. advisers take over training of South Vietnamese army (ARVN).

**1960** National Liberation Front (Vietcong) formed.

**1961** President John Kennedy markedly increases military aid to South Vietnam.

**1962** Strategic-hamlet program put in operation.

**1963** Buddhist protests commence.

ARVN coup overthrows and assassinates Diem.

16,000 U.S. military personnel in Vietnam.

**1964** General William Westmoreland takes charge of U.S. Military Assistance Command in South Vietnam.

Gulf of Tonkin incident and subsequent U.S. congressional resolution.

**1964** (continued)

United States bombs North Vietnam.

23,300 U.S. military personnel in Vietnam.

**1965** First American combat troops arrive in South Vietnam, at Danang.

184,000 U.S. military personnel in Vietnam.

**1966** B-52s attack North Vietnam for first time.

Senate Foreign Relations Committee opens hearings on U.S. in Vietnam.

385,000 U.S. military personnel in Vietnam.

**1967** Major antiwar demonstrations in New York and San Francisco; protest march on the Pentagon.

485,600 U.S. military personnel in Vietnam.

**1968** North Vietnamese forces surround Khesanh.

Tet offensive.

My Lai massacre.

President Lyndon Johnson announces partial bombing halt and decision not to run for reelection.

Peace talks begin in Paris.

General Creighton Abrams replaces Westmoreland as commander of American troops in Vietnam.

536,000 U.S. military personnel in Vietnam.

battlefield. Even before the ink on the treaty had dried, both North and South Vietnam, seeking military advantage, began to violate its terms.

The war in Vietnam would continue despite 58,000 American deaths, 300,000 wounded, and an expenditure of at least $150 billion. Twenty percent of the Americans who served in Vietnam, nearly 500,000, moreover, received less-than-honorable discharges—a measure of the high desertion rate, the rampant drug use, the spread of antiwar sentiment even in the military, and the immaturity of the troops (the average U.S. soldier in Vietnam was just nineteen years old, seven years younger than the average American GI in World War II).

Virtually all who survived, wrote one marine, returned "as immigrants to a new world. For the culture we had known dissolved while we were in Vietnam, and the culture of combat we lived in so intensely . . . made us aliens when we returned." Reminders of a war that Americans wished to forget, most veterans were ignored when they returned home. Beyond media attention to the psychological difficulties that they faced in readjusting to civilian life, which principally fostered an image of veterans as disturbed and dangerous, the nation paid little heed to those who had served and sacrificed.

Most Americans wanted "to put Vietnam behind us" and just forget. The bitterness of many veterans, as of embattled hawks and doves, moderated with time. Few gave much thought to the 2 million casualties and the devastation in Vietnam, or to the suffering in Laos, or the price paid by Cambodia. After the war had spread there, the fanatical Khmer Rouge took power and killed 3 million Cambodians—40 percent of the population.

"We've adjusted too well," complained Tim O'Brien, a veteran and novelist of the war, in 1980. "Too many of us have lost touch with the horror of war. . . . It

---

**1969** United States begins bombing North Vietnamese bases in Cambodia.

Provisional Revolutionary Government (PRG) formed by Vietcong.

First U.S. troop withdrawal announced after American military personnel in Vietnam reach peak strength of 543,400 in April.

Ho Chi Minh dies.

Nationwide antiwar protests in October.

475,200 U.S. military personnel in Vietnam.

**1970** United States and South Vietnamese forces join in Cambodian incursion.

Student protests force some four hundred colleges and universities to close following Kent State killings.

Cooper-Church amendment limits U.S. role in Cambodia.

Senate repeals Gulf of Tonkin Resolution.

334,600 U.S. military personnel in Vietnam.

**1971** United States provides air support for South Vietnamese invasion of Laos.

Antiwar rally of 400,000 in Washington.

Daniel Ellsberg releases Pentagon Papers to the *New York Times*.

**1972** North Vietnam launches first ground offensive since 1968.

U.S. bombing and mining of North Vietnamese ports.

**1972** *(continued)*

Last U.S. ground troops leave South Vietnam.

Preliminary peace agreement reached; National Security Adviser Henry Kissinger announces that "peace is at hand."

South Vietnam rejects peace treaty.

United States bombs Hanoi and Haiphong.

24,200 U.S. military personnel in Vietnam.

**1973** Peace agreement signed in Paris by North and South Vietnam, the Vietcong, and the United States.

End of U.S. draft.

Congress passes War Powers Act.

First American POWs released in Hanoi.

U.S. bombing in Southeast Asia ends.

Fewer than 250 U.S. military personnel in Vietnam.

**1974** South Vietnam announces new outbreak of war.

**1975** North Vietnamese offensive captures Danang.

Senate rejects President Gerald Ford's request for emergency aid for South Vietnam.

South Vietnam surrenders following North Vietnam's capture of Saigon.

Khmer Rouge takes control in Cambodia.

Pro-Hanoi People's Democratic Republic established in Laos.

would seem that the memories of soldiers should serve, at least in a modest way, as a restraint on national bellicosity. But time and distance erode memory. We adjust, we lose the intensity. I fear that we are back where we started. I wish we were more troubled."

## *Détente*

Disengagement from Vietnam helped Nixon achieve a turnabout in Chinese-American relations and détente with the communist superpowers. These developments, the most significant shift in U.S. foreign policy since the start of the Cold War, created a new relationship among the United States, the Soviet Union, and China.

Presidents from Truman to Johnson had refused to recognize the People's Republic of China, allow its admission to the United Nations, or permit American allies to trade with the communist giant. But by 1969 a widening Sino-Soviet split made the prospect of improved relations attractive to both Mao Zedong and Nixon. China wanted to end its isolation, the United States wanted to play one communist power off against the other, and both wanted to thwart USSR expansionism in Asia.

In the fall of 1970, Nixon opened what Kissinger called "the three-dimensional game" by referring to China as the People's Republic rather than Red China. Eventually Kissinger began secret negotiations with Beijing, and in mid-1971 Nixon announced that he would go to the People's Republic "to seek the normalization of relations." In February 1972 Air Force One landed in China, the first visit ever by a sitting American president to the largest nation in the world. Although differences between the two powers delayed official diplomatic relations until 1979, Nixon's trip, the Chinese foreign minister said, bridged "the vastest ocean in the world, twenty-five years of no communication."

Equally significant, Nixon went to Moscow in May 1972 to sign agreements with the Soviets on trade, technological cooperation, and the limitation of nuclear weapons. The Strategic Arms Limitation Talks (SALT I), ratified by the Senate in October 1972, limited both the U.S. and USSR to two hundred antiballistic missiles (ABMs) and two ABM systems. SALT I reflected the belief that the fear of destruction offered the surest guarantee against nuclear war and that mutual fear could be maintained only if neither side built nationwide missile-defense systems. SALT I slowed, but did not end, the costly and dangerous nuclear-arms race. The first step toward strategic arms control since the start of the Cold War, it reduced Soviet-American tensions and, in an election year, enhanced Nixon's stature.

### Nixon in China

*One of the great triumphs of his administration was the rapprochment with the People's Republic of China. Planned in total secrecy, Nixon's trip to China in February 1972 stunned the world and gave the president the aura of a bold, imaginative statesman.*

## *Shuttle Diplomacy*

Not even rapprochment with China, détente with the Soviet Union, or the American withdrawal from Vietnam could ensure global stability. The Middle East, in particular, remained an arena of conflict. After the Six-day War of 1967, in which Israeli forces routed the forces of Egypt, Jordan, and Syria, and seized strategic territories from the three nations, the Arab states continued to refuse to negotiate with Israel or to recognize its right to exist. Palestinians, many of them refugees since the creation of Israel in 1948, and made far more numerous by the Israeli victory in 1967, turned increasingly to the militant Palestinian Liberation Organization (PLO), which demanded Israel's destruction.

War exploded again in October 1973 when Egypt and Syria launched surprise attacks against Israel on Yom Kippur, the most sacred Jewish holy day. Only massive shipments of military supplies from the United States enabled a reeling Israel to stop the assault and then counterattack. In retaliation, oil-producing Arab states embargoed shipments of oil to the United States and its allies. The five-month embargo dramatized U.S. dependence on foreign energy sources. It spawned acute fuel shortages, which spurred coal production in Montana and Wyoming, triggered an oil boom on Alaska's North Slope, and provided the impetus for constructing more nuclear-power plants. Most immediately, it sharply increased petroleum prices, intensifying inflation.

The energy crisis at home and the fear of rising Soviet influence in the Arab world spurred Kissinger to engage in "shuttle diplomacy." Flying from one Middle East capital to another for two years, he negotiated a cease-fire in the war, pressed Israel to give up the additional Arab territory it had taken, and persuaded the Arabs to end the oil embargo. Although Kissinger's diplomacy failed to deal with the Palestinian issue, leaving it to fester and erupt in continuing violence, it succeeded in excluding the Soviets from a major role in Middle Eastern affairs.

To counter Soviet influence, the Nixon administration also supplied arms and assistance to the shah of Iran, the white supremacist regime of South Africa, and President Ferdinand Marcos in the Philippines. Nixon-Kissinger realpolitik based American aid on a nation's opposition to the Soviet Union, not on the nature of its government. Thus the administration assisted antidemocratic regimes in Argentina, Brazil, Nigeria, and South Korea, as well as the Portuguese colonial authorities in Angola.

When Chileans elected a Marxist, Salvador Allende, president in 1970, Nixon secretly funneled $10 million to the CIA to fund opponents of the leftist government. The United States also cut off economic aid to Chile, blocked banks from granting loans, and successfully pressed the World Bank to lower Chile's credit rating. A military junta in September 1973 overthrew the Chilean government and killed Allende. Nixon quickly recognized the dictatorship, and economic aid and investment once again flowed to Chile.

The administration's active opposition to Allende reflected the extent to which American policy remained committed to containing communist influence. At the same time, Nixon understood the limits of U.S.

power and the changed realities of world affairs. Discarding the model of a bipolar conflict that had shaped American foreign policy since 1945, Nixon took advantage of the Chinese-Soviet rift to improve American relations with both nations. His administration also improved the U.S. position in the Middle East and ended American involvement in Vietnam. The politician who had built his reputation as a hard-line Cold Warrior had initiated a new era of détente.

# Domestic Problems and Divisions

Although Richard Nixon yearned to be remembered as an international statesman, domestic affairs kept intruding. He displayed creativity in seeking to reform the welfare system and in grappling with complex economic problems. But the underside of Nixon's complex personality appealed to the darker recesses of national character and intensified the fears and divisions among Americans.

### *Richard Nixon: Man and Politician*

Close observers of Nixon noted the multiple levels of his character, the calculated public persona of a politician beneath which hid a shadowy Nixon who rarely revealed himself. The public Nixon exhibited great intelligence and endurance, yet also displayed the rigid self-control of a man monitoring his own every move. Largely hidden was the insecure Nixon, suspicious and filled with anger. Seething with resentments and fears, he saw life as a series of crises to be met and surmounted. His conviction that enemies lurked everywhere, waiting to destroy him, verged on paranoia. Accordingly, he sought to annihilate, not merely defeat, his partisan enemies, particularly those of the "eastern liberal establishment" who had long opposed him.

Probing the source of his furies, some viewed him as the classic outsider: reared in pinched surroundings, physically awkward, unable to relate easily to others. Although propelled to the heights of national power, Nixon remained fearful that he would never be fully accepted. At the beginning of his administration, Nixon's strengths stood out. He spoke of national reconciliation, took bold initiatives in the international arena, and dealt with domestic problems responsibly. But the darker side ultimately prevailed and drove him from office in disgrace.

## The Nixon Presidency

Nixon began his presidency with a moderation reminiscent of Eisenhower, offering the respite from unrest desired by most Americans. Symbolic of this positive start, a united nation joined the president in celebrating the first successful manned mission to the moon. On July 21, 1969, the lunar module of Apollo 11 descended to the Sea of Tranquillity. As millions watched on television, astronaut Neil Armstrong walked on the moon's surface and proclaimed, "That's one small step for man, one giant leap for mankind." Americans took pride in the fact that the United States had come from behind to win the space race. They thrilled as Armstrong and Buzz Aldrin planted an American flag and a plaque reading, "Here men from planet earth first set foot on the moon, July 1969 A.D. We came in peace for all mankind."

The first newly elected president since 1849 whose party controlled neither house of Congress, Nixon initially approved an extension of liberal programs, including an increase in social security benefits, subsidized housing for low- and middle-income families, an expansion of the Job Corps, and the vote for eighteen-year-olds. More grudgingly, he also accepted Democratic

### "Earth Day," May 4, 1970

*Designed to alert people about the threats to the air, land, and water, the first Earth Day signaled the emergence of the modern environmental movement. It would put pressure on the federal government to take major steps in cleaning up the nation's environment and educate a generation of Americans to understand the ecology of the planet as a delicate, interconnected series of elements, in which damage to any single element damages many others.*

legislation targeting the negative effects of material growth. New laws limited pesticide use, further protected endangered species and marine mammals, controlled strip-mining practices, safeguarded coastal lands, regulated consumer-product safety and the transportation of hazardous materials, and established maximum levels for the emissions of pollutants into the air. The National Environmental Policy Act (1969) required federal agencies to prepare an environmental-impact analysis of all proposed projects and established the Environmental Protection Agency (EPA) to enforce environmental regulations. In 1970 Congress also created the Occupational Safety and Health Administration (OSHA) to enforce health and safety standards in the workplace.

Growing environmental awareness led 20 million Americans to gather in parks for the first Earth Day in April 1970. Their speeches and demonstrations spotlighted such problems as thermal pollution, dying lakes, oil spills, and dwindling resources, and introduced Americans to the idea of "living lightly on the earth." Organic gardening, vegetarianism, solar power, recycling, composting, and preventive health care came into vogue, as did zero population growth—the birthrate should not exceed the death rate.

Conservatives grumbled at a bigger, costlier, and more intrusive government—under Nixon, the number of pages in the Federal Register detailing federal regulations tripled. Race-conscious employment regulations for all federal contractors (including quotas to increase minority access to skilled jobs) displeased them even more. And they grew still angrier when Nixon unveiled his Family Assistance Plan, a bold effort to replace the unwieldy welfare system with a guaranteed minimum annual income, $1,600 for a family of four. Although the House passed the measure, liberals, who thought the money too minimal and opposed the requirement that welfare recipients had to register for employment or job training, joined with conservatives, who disliked both the cost and the principle of the program, to kill it in the Senate.

## A Troubled Economy

Nixon inherited the dire fiscal consequences of Johnson's effort to wage the Vietnam War and finance the Great Society—to have both "guns and butter"—by deficit financing. He faced a "whopping" budget deficit of $25 billion in 1969 and an inflation rate of 5 percent. As mounting energy prices threatened worse inflation, Nixon cut government spending and encouraged the

### Brother, Can You Spare a Gallon ?

*To retaliate against the United States for its support of Israel in the October 1973 Middle East war, Arab nations first imposed an embargo on oil shipments and then quadrupled the price of crude oil. The long lines of waiting cars at gas stations and the sharp rise in inflation crystallized the extent to which America's economic dominance in the world had been undermined.*

### The Energy Crisis: Crude-Oil Imports and Gasoline Prices

*Not until the 1980s, through the combination of a deep recession and fuel conservation, did U.S. petroleum imports finally begin dropping off (top). OPEC's ability to act as a supercartel in setting oil prices sent the cost of filling a car's gas tank skyrocketing in the 1970s (bottom).*

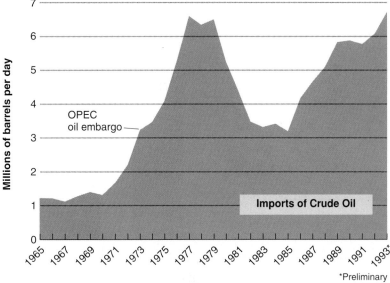

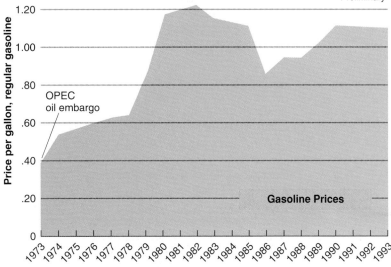

*Source:* Energy Information Administration, Annual Energy Review, 1993.

Federal Reserve Board to raise interest rates. The result was the first recession since Eisenhower and galloping inflation, a combination economists called "stagflation," and Democrats termed "Nixonomics."

Accelerating inflation wiped out some families' savings and lowered the standard of living of many more. It sparked a wave of strikes as workers sought wage hikes to keep up with the cost of living. It encouraged the wealthy to invest in art and real estate rather than technology and new factories. That meant more plant shutdowns, fewer industrial jobs, and millions of displaced workers seeing their savings depleted, their mortgages foreclosed, their health and pension benefits lost. The president had to act.

Nixon lurched from one policy to another in a futile effort to curb inflation while curing the recession. Early in 1971, declaring "I am now a Keynesian," he resorted to deficit spending and proposed an unbalanced federal

### Inflation, 1946–1993

*Inflation, which had been moderate during the two decades following the Second World War, began to soar with the escalation of the war in Vietnam in the mid-1960s. In 1979 and 1980 the nation experienced double-digit inflation in two consecutive years for the first time since World War I.*

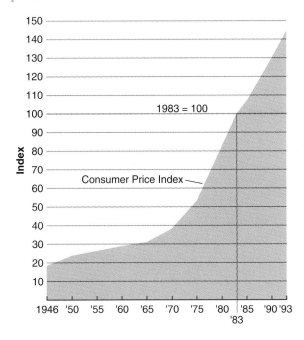

budget. That produced the largest budget deficit since World War II. Again in mid-1971 Nixon changed course, devaluing the dollar and imposing a ninety-day freeze on wages, prices, and rents as well as limits on future increases. These moves gave the economy a shot in the arm while reducing both inflation and the trade deficit. But in January 1973, now safely reelected, Nixon changed course yet again and replaced his wage-and-price ceilings with "voluntary restraints" and "guidelines." Inflation zoomed to 9 percent, then to 12 percent in 1974 as the OPEC boycott quadrupled the price of crude oil, and remained a major problem throughout the 1970s.

### Law and Order

Despite his public appeals for unity, Nixon hoped to divide the American people in ways that would make him unbeatable in the 1972 election. To outflank George Wallace and win the support of blue-collar workers, southern segregationists, and northern ethnics—those whom political theorist Kevin Phillips described as "in motion between a Democratic past and a Republican future"—Nixon opposed court-ordered busing and took a tough stand against criminals, drug users, and radicals.

The president used the full resources of the government against militants. The IRS audited their tax returns; the Small Business Administration denied them loans; the FBI illegally wiretapped them; and the National Security Agency intercepted their communications. While the Justice Department worked with local law officials to disrupt and immobilize the Black Panthers, the CIA illegally investigated and compiled dossiers on thousands of American citizens. The Nixon administration also prosecuted antiwar activists and black radicals in highly publicized trials.

To crush his political opponents, Nixon used unspent 1968 campaign funds to create a secret task force that spied on liberal journalists and congressional Democrats. He drew up an "enemies list" of prominent adversaries to be harassed by the government. "Anyone who opposes us, we'll destroy," warned a top White House official. "As a matter of fact, anyone who doesn't support us, we'll destroy."

Widening his offensive against the antiwar movement, Nixon in 1970 approved the Huston Plan to use the CIA and FBI illegally to wiretap and infiltrate radical organizations, and to break into the homes and offices of militants in order to gather or plant evidence. But FBI chief J. Edgar Hoover opposed the plan, which would be controlled by the White House, as a threat to the bureau's independence and power. Blocked, Nixon then created his own secret unit to monitor and discredit his opposition and to ensure executive secrecy. Nicknamed "the plumbers" because of their assignment to stop government leaks, the team was head by ex-FBI agent G. Gordon Liddy and former CIA operative E. Howard Hunt.

The plumbers first targeted Daniel Ellsberg, a former Defense Department analyst who had turned over to the press the Pentagon Papers, a secret documentary history of U.S. involvement in Vietnam. On June 13 the *New York Times* began publishing the documents, revealing a long history of White House lies to Congress, foreign leaders, and the American people. Although the papers contained nothing damaging about his administration, Nixon, fearing that they would undermine trust in government and establish a precedent for publishing classified material, sought to bar their publication. The

Supreme Court, however, ruled that their publication was protected by the First Amendment. Livid, Nixon directed the Justice Department to indict Ellsberg for theft and ordered the plumbers to break into the office of Ellsberg's psychiatrist to search for information that might discredit the man who had become a hero to the antiwar movement.

### The Southern Strategy

While attacking radicalism, Nixon courted whites upset by the drive for racial equality. The administration opposed extending the Voting Rights Act of 1965, sought to weaken enforcement of the Fair Housing Act of 1968, pleaded for a postponement in the desegregation of Mississippi's schools, and argued against busing as a means to desegregate public schools. In 1971, when the Supreme Court upheld busing as a constitutional and necessary tactic, Nixon condemned the ruling and asked Congress to enact a moratorium on busing.

The strategy to woo Wallace supporters also guided Nixon's nominations for the Supreme Court. To reverse the Warren court's liberalism, he sought strict constructionists; that is, judges who would not "meddle" in social issues or be "soft" on criminals. In 1969 he appointed Warren Burger to replace the retiring Earl Warren as chief justice. Although the Senate then twice rejected southern conservatives nominated by Nixon for the high court, the president had, by 1973, appointed three additional justices to the Supreme Court. Harry Blackmun of Minnesota, Lewis Powell of Virginia, and William Rehnquist of Arizona, along with Burger, steered the Court in a decidedly more moderate direction. While ruling liberally in cases involving abortion, desegregation, and the death penalty, the Burger court shifted to the right in rulings on civil liberties, community censorship, and police power.

As the 1970 congressional elections neared, Nixon encouraged his vice president, Spiro T. Agnew, to step up his attacks on the Democrats as the party of "hooligans, hippies, and radical liberals." Agnew did so. He assailed the opposition as "sniveling hand-wringers," intellectuals as "an effete corps of impudent snobs," and the news media as "nattering nabobs of negativism." Liberals deplored Agnew's alarming alliterative allegations, but much of the rest of the country found them on target. Although the party of the president had

**Driving Southward and Backwards**
*To outflank George Wallace and win the votes of both southern whites and urban blue-collar workers in the North, Nixon's "Southern Strategy" included delaying school desegregation plans and strong opposition to busing children to achieve racial balance in the schools.*

suffered significant losses in every off-year election since 1934, the GOP took comfort in losing just nine House seats and winning two Senate seats.

### The Election of 1972

Nixon's reelection appeared certain. He faced a deeply divided Democratic party. His diplomatic successes and winding down of the Vietnam War appealed to moderate voters. And his southern strategy and law-and-order posture attracted Democrats who had voted for George Wallace in 1968. His only possible worry, another third-party candidacy by Wallace, vanished on May 15, 1972. While campaigning, Wallace was shot. Paralyzed from the waist down, he withdrew from the race, leaving Nixon a monopoly on the white backlash.

Capitalizing on the support of antiwar activists, the Senate's most outspoken dove, George McGovern of South Dakota, blitzed the Democratic primaries. He gained additional support from new party rules requiring state delegations to include minority, female, and youthful delegates in approximate proportion to their numbers. Actress Shirley MacLaine approvingly described California's delegation as "looking like a couple of high schools, a grape boycott, a Black Panther rally, and four or five politicians who walked in the wrong door." A disapproving labor leader grumbled about "too much hair and not enough cigars at this convention." McGovern won the nomination on the first ballot.

**The Election of 1972**

| Candidates | Parties | Electoral Vote | Popular Vote | Percentage of Popular Vote |
|---|---|---|---|---|
| RICHARD M. NIXON | Republican | 520 | 47,169,911 | 60.7 |
| George S. McGovern | Democratic | 17 | 29,170,383 | 37.5 |

Perceptions of McGovern as inept and radical drove away all but those most committed to him. After pledging to stand behind his vice presidential running mate Thomas Eagleton "1,000 percent" when it became known that the Missouri senator had received electric-shock therapy for depression, McGovern dumped him and suffered the embarrassment of having several prominent Democrats publicly decline to run with him. McGovern's endorsement of income redistribution, the decriminalization of marijuana, immediate withdrawal from Vietnam, a $30 billion defense-budget cut, and pardons for those who had fled the United States to avoid the draft, exposed him to GOP ridicule as the candidate of the radical fringe.

Remembering his so-narrow loss to Kennedy in 1960 and all-too-slim victory in 1968, Nixon left no stone unturned. To do whatever was necessary to win, he appointed his attorney general, John Mitchell, to head the Committee to Re-Elect the President (CREEP). Millions of dollars in campaign contributions financed "dirty tricks" to create dissension in Democratic ranks and an espionage unit to spy on the opposition. Led by Liddy and Hunt of the White House plumbers, the Republican undercover team received Mitchell's approval to wiretap telephones at the Democratic National Committee headquarters in the Watergate apartment/office complex in Washington. Early in the morning of June 17, 1972, a security guard foiled the break-in to install the bugs. Arrested were James McCord, the security coordinator of CREEP, and several other Liddy and Hunt associates.

A White House cover-up began immediately. Nixon proclaimed "categorically" that "no one in the White House staff, no one in this administration, presently employed, was involved in this bizarre incident." Nixon ordered staff members to expunge Hunt's name from the White House telephone directory, to buy the silence of those arrested with $400,000 in hush money and hints of a presidential pardon, and to direct the CIA to halt the FBI's investigation of the Watergate break-

in on the pretext that the inquiry would damage national security.

With the McGovern campaign a shambles and Watergate contained, Nixon won overwhelmingly, amassing nearly 61 percent of the popular vote and 520 electoral votes. The southern strategy had worked to perfection. Strongly supported only by minorities and low-income voters, McGovern carried just Massachusetts and the District of Columbia. The election solidified the 1968 realignment.

However, the GOP gained only twelve seats in the House and lost two in the Senate. This demonstrated the growing difficulty of unseating incumbents, the rise in ticket-splitting, and the decline of both party loyalty and voter turnout. Only 55.7 percent of eligible voters went to the polls (down from 63.8 percent in 1960). Whether indifferent to politics or disenchanted with the choices offered, a growing number of citizens no longer bothered to participate in the electoral process.

## The Crisis of the Presidency

In his second inaugural address, Nixon pledged "to make these four years the best four years in America's history." Ironically, they would rank among its sorriest. His vice president would resign in disgrace, his closest aides would go to jail, and he would serve barely a year and a half of his second term before resigning to escape impeachment.

### The Watergate Cover-Up

The scheme to conceal the connection between the White House and the accused Watergate burglars had succeeded during the 1972 campaign. But after the election federal judge "Maximum John" Sirica, known for his tough treatment of criminals, refused to accept the defendants' claim that they had acted on their own. Threatening severe prison sentences, Sirica coerced

James McCord of CREEP into confessing that White House aides had known in advance of the break-in and that the defendants had committed perjury during the trial. Meanwhile, two *Washington Post* reporters, Carl Bernstein and Bob Woodward, following clues furnished by "Deep Throat,"* an unnamed informant in the Nixon administration, wrote a succession of front-page stories linking the break-in to illegal contributions and "dirty tricks" by CREEP.

In February 1973 the Senate established the Special Committee on Presidential Campaign Activities to investigate. As the trail of revelations led closer to the Oval Office, Nixon fired his special counsel, who refused to be a scapegoat, and announced the resignations of his two major assistants. Pledging to get to the bottom of the scandal, Nixon appointed Secretary of Defense Elliot Richardson, a Boston patrician of unassailable integrity, as his new attorney general, and instructed Richardson to appoint a special Watergate prosecutor with broad powers of investigation and subpoena. Richardson selected Archibald Cox, a Harvard law professor and a Democrat.

In May the special Senate committee began a televised investigation. Chaired by the wily Sam ("I'm just a plain country lawyer") Ervin of North Carolina, an expert on constitutional law, the hearings revealed the existence of a White House "enemies list," the president's use of government agencies to harass opponents, and administration favoritism in return for illegal campaign donations. Most damaging to Nixon, the hearings exposed the White House's active involvement in the Watergate cover-up. But the Senate still lacked concrete evidence of the president's criminality, the smoking gun that would prove Nixon's guilt. Because it was his word against that of his former counsel, who testified that Nixon directed the cover-up, the president expected to survive the crisis.

But another presidential aide dropped a bombshell by testifying that Nixon had installed a secret taping system that recorded all conversations in the Oval Office. Both the Ervin committee and Cox insisted on access to the tapes, but Nixon refused, claiming executive privilege. In October, when Cox sought a court order to obtain the tapes, Nixon ordered Richardson to fire him. Instead, Richardson resigned in protest, as did the deputy attorney general. The third-ranking official in the Department of Justice, Solicitor General Robert

---

* Deep Throat was also the title of a notorious pornographic film of the time.

Bork, dumped Cox. The furor stirred by this "Saturday Night Massacre" sent Nixon's public-approval rating rapidly downward. Even as Nixon named a new special prosecutor, Leon Jaworski, the House Judiciary Committee began impeachment proceedings.

## *A President Disgraced*

Adding to Nixon's woes that October, Vice President Agnew, charged with income-tax evasion and accepting bribes, pleaded no contest—"the full equivalent to a plea of guilty," according to the trial judge. Dishonored, Agnew left office with a three-year suspended sentence, a $10,000 fine, and a letter from Nixon expressing "a great sense of personal loss." Popular House minority leader Gerald R. Ford of Michigan replaced Agnew.

In March 1974 special prosecutor Jaworski and the House Judiciary Committee subpoenaed the president for the tape recordings of Oval Office meetings following the Watergate break-in. Nixon then released edited transcripts of the tapes, filled with gaps and the phrase "expletive deleted." Despite the excisions, the president

**White House Counsel John Dean**
*After being sworn in before the Senate Select Committee on Campaign Practices in May 1973, Dean testified that President Nixon himself had been involved in the cover-up of the Watergate burglary and other incriminating matters.*

YOUR SET DOES NOT NEED ADJUSTING. THESE THINGS HAVE REALLY BEEN HAPPENING IN THE UNITED STATES.

NEW DISCLOSURES Watergate And The White House

©1973 HERBLOCK

**Startling Watergate Revelations**
*Week after week, throughout 1973, came new head-lines of scandal, revealing the extent to which Presi-dent Nixon and the men around him had bribed defendants to keep their silence, committed perjury, engaged in wiretapping and "dirty tricks," evaded in-come taxes, tampered with evidence, and participated in a criminal conspiracy to obstruct justice.*

emerged as petty and vindictive. "We have seen the pri-vate man and we are appalled," declared the staunchly Republican *Chicago Tribune*.

Nixon's sanitized version of the tapes satisfied nei-ther Jaworski nor the House Judiciary Committee. Both pressed for unedited tapes. In late July the Supreme Court rebuffed the president's claim to executive privilege. Citing the president's obligation to provide evidence necessary for the due process of law, Chief Justice Burger ordered Nixon to release the unexpur-gated tapes.

In late July the House Judiciary Committee adopted three articles of impeachment, accusing President Nixon of obstruction of justice for impeding the Water-gate investigation, of abuse of power for his partisan

use of the FBI and IRS, and of contempt of Congress for refusing to obey a congressional subpoena to release the tapes. Checkmated, Nixon conceded in a televised address on August 5 that he had withheld relevant evi-dence. He then surrendered the subpoenaed tapes. They contained the smoking gun proving that the presi-dent had ordered the cover-up, obstructed justice, sub-verted one government agency to prevent another from investigating a crime, and lied about his role for more than two years. Impeachment and conviction were now certainties. On August 9, 1974, Richard Nixon be-came the first president to resign, and Gerald Ford took office as the nation's first chief executive to have been elected neither president nor vice president.

## CONCLUSION

Unlike the generations that preceded and succeeded them, the baby boomers who constituted the student movement and counterculture of the 1960s took mate-rial comfort and their own importance for granted. Most came from affluent, liberal, and indulgent house-holds. Longing for connectedness and meaning in their lives, as well as personal liberty, they sought a more hu-mane and democratic United States, a less racist and materialist society, an end to the war in Vietnam, and an America freer to enjoy "sex, drugs, and rock-and-roll." Accordingly, the United States, although hardly the Aquarian dream of those who were intoxicated by the bubble of limitless possibility, did become a more tolerant, diverse, and open society. And America's longest war, with its immense costs in lives and dollars and in polarizing the nation and diverting it from its greater needs, did finally end.

But not before the war claimed President Nixon as its final casualty. Nixon had won a landslide reelection victory in 1972, primarily because of his large-scale withdrawal of American troops from Vietnam, lessen-ing of hostilities with China and the Soviet Union, and a domestic program that courted whites upset by black militancy, radicalism, and the upsurge of criminality and breakdown of traditional values. By then, however, the secret schemes he had put in place initially to spy upon and destroy those who opposed his Vietnam poli-cies had started to unravel. The arrest of the Watergate burglars and the subsequent attempted cover-up of White House involvement eventually led to revelations of a host of "dirty tricks" and criminal acts that resulted in the indictment of nearly fifty Nixon administration officials, the jailing of a score of the president's associates, including his attorney general, and the House Judiciary Committee voting to impeach the president on charges of abuses of power in his harassment of opponents, obstruction of justice, and contempt of Congress. To avoid certain conviction, Nixon resigned. As his successor, Gerald Ford, took the oath of office, many Americans took pride in the smooth continuity of the political system and in its ability to curb excesses and abuses. Still others worried that so many Americans had for so long just shrugged off Watergate as politics as usual or that the Nixon scandals might never have come to light if not for coercion by a federal judge and the president's desire to tape and preserve his conversations. All that was sure was a deepening public distrust of politicians and disillusionment with government in general.

## FOR FURTHER READING

Terry H. Anderson, *The Movement and the Sixties: Protest in America from Greensboro to Wounded Knee* (1995). A comprehensive study of dissent in this era.

William Berman, *America's Right Turn: From Nixon to Bush* (1994). A valuable overview of the politics of conservatism.

William Chafe, *Never Stop Running: Allard Lowenstein and the Struggle to Save American Liberalism* (1993). The strife of the 1960s through the prism of a key liberal activist.

Charles Kaiser, *The Gay Metropolis: 1940–1996* (1997). A history, mostly concerned with New York City, that traces the gains homosexuals have made in equality and acceptance.

Stanley Kutler, ed., *Abuse of Power* (1997). Transcripts of Nixon's Oval Office recordings.

Herbert Parmet, *Richard Nixon and His America* (1990). A solid survey of the presidency and the era.

Robert Schulzinger, *Henry Kissinger: Doctor of Diplomacy* (1989). A balanced examination of Kissinger-Nixon foreign policies.

David Steigerwald, *The Sixties and the End of Modern America* (1995). A good brief overview.

# 32

# Turning Inward: Society and Politics from Ford to Bush

**"Denny's Arco"** by Stephen Hopkins, 1987

In October 1985 *Forbes* business magazine hailed "the richest man in America": Sam Walton of Bentonville, Arkansas. Walton was founder of the Wal-Mart Corporation, one of the discount chains that transformed mass marketing in the United States after 1960. Estimating his net worth at "$20 or $25 billion," he lived modestly in Bentonville, generally wore a Wal-Mart baseball cap, and still went to the local barbershop for his haircuts.

Born in Oklahoma in 1918, Walton grew up in Missouri. While his father, a mortgage agent, repossessed farms during the Great Depression, young Sam sold milk, rabbits, and magazine subscriptions door-to-door. After graduation from the University of Missouri, World War II army service, and marriage to Helen Robson, he became the manager of a Ben Franklin variety store in Newport, Arkansas, in 1945.

Sam and Helen (with a loan from Helen's father, a rancher and businessman) opened their own Walton's Five and Dime in Bentonville in 1950 and a second one in nearby Fayetteville two years later. From the first, he demonstrated the initiative that characterized his career: he scoured the region for bargain-priced merchandise that he then sold at a small markup. As the Fayetteville store manager recalled: "Sam used to come down . . . driving an old fifty-three Plymouth. He had that car so loaded up he barely had room to drive. And would you like to guess what he had in it? Ladies' panties. Three for $1.00 and four for $1.00 and nylon hose."

The first Wal-Mart store opened in 1962, and soon Wal-Marts were spreading across Arkansas, Oklahoma, Missouri, and beyond. "We just started repeating what worked, stamping out stores cookie-cutter style," Walton recalled. The time was right, as the boom years created rich opportunities for merchandisers. Walton innovated discount retailing, together with other chains including Woolco (spun off from the Woolworth five-and-dime empire) and K-Mart, started by the S. S. Kresge Company, another dime-store pioneer. With jobs tight and inflation eroding consumer buying power in the 1970s, Wal-Mart grew phenomenally, its rock-bottom prices a boon to low-income families. Thanks to successive stock splits, 100 shares of Wal-Mart stock purchased for $1,650 in 1970 were worth about $3 million by 1990.

Sam Walton also created a unique corporate culture that included promotional gimmicks such as "shopping cart bingo," employee rallies punctuated by cheers and company songs, and stunts including Walton's 1984 grass-skirted hula dance on Wall Street because he lost a bet about annual sales volume.

Sam Walton had his critics. He fought off unions by introducing a profit-sharing plan to supplement Wal-Mart's low wages. Many of Wal-Mart's senior officers resigned in 1974 amid a bitter management battle. Above all, criticism came from small-town merchants driven out of business by Wal-Mart's high-volume, price-slashing approach to marketing. Walton felt no sympathy for these failed competitors. "[Their] customers were the ones who shut [them] down. They voted with their feet. . . . Wal-Mart has actually [saved] quite a number of small towns . . . by offering low prices and saving literally billions of dollars for the people who live there, as well as by creating hundreds of thousands of jobs."

On March 17, 1992, President George Bush flew to Bentonville to give Walton the Medal of Freedom, the nation's highest civilian award. Said Bush: "Sam Walton embodies the entrepreneurial spirit and epitomizes the American dream." Two weeks later, Walton died of bone cancer.

**Sam Walton**
*Founder of the Wal-Mart chain and an entrepreneurial genius.*

By 1997 some 5,300 Wal-Mart Stores, Warehouse Outlets, and Sam's Wholesale Clubs could be found in most states, Canada, and Puerto Rico. Wal-Mart Corporation, employing 675,000, that year reported sales of nearly $100 billion.

The Wal-Mart phenomenon was part of a transformation in the U.S. economy in the 1970s and 1980s. The service sector grew rapidly as discount stores and fast-food outlets like McDonald's spread. High-tech industries prospered as well. But other sectors of the economy, notably the steel mills, auto plants, and factories of the old industrial heartland, grew weaker, battered by imports. Sam Walton may have lived "the American dream," as George Bush claimed, but for many, the dream was proving more elusive.

This chapter focuses on five major questions:

♦ What evidence suggests that the activist mood of the 1960s faded in the 1970s and early 1980s, and what evidence suggests that on some issues the spirit of protest remained very much alive?

♦ To what extent was President Carter himself to blame for the "malaise" he detected in America in 1979, and to what extent was Carter a victim of forces beyond his control?

♦ What were the key themes of the political ideology that Ronald Reagan brought to the presidency? What specific steps did his administration take to translate this ideology into practice?

♦ How did the Reagan administration express its intense opposition to communism, and how did U.S. relations with the world's chief communist nation, the Soviet Union, evolve over the course of the Reagan presidency?

♦ In what ways did the end of the Cold War make for a safer world? In what ways did it heighten global dangers and conflicts?

## After the Sixties: Changing Social and Cultural Contours

American social and cultural trends of the 1970s and 1980s reflected both the afterglow of 1960s activism and a reaction against that turbulent decade. Some causes, notably environmentalism and feminism, gained ground in the seventies. Women poured into the work force, enrolled in professional schools, and launched careers. But the divisiveness of 1968–1970 took its toll, and in its aftermath many young adults turned to personal goals and material acquisition.

While many Americans prospered, others remained mired in poverty. The African-American experience epitomizes the decade's divergent trends. While many blacks moved into the middle class, others found themselves cut off from the traditional avenues of upward mobility.

Radicals of the 1960s had celebrated sexual freedom and feminists had demanded reproductive choice, but the post-1970 years brought fierce debates over abortion, as well as more cautious sexual behavior as the AIDS epidemic spread. The pace of change led to a search for moral certitude and spiritual solace, producing a resurgence of religion.

### *America Turns Inward*

Social activism did not disappear in the aftermath of the 1960s, but while some issues attracted even more attention, others faded. Although the reform impetus in the sixties had initially come from the Left, after 1968 it was just as likely to surface on the Right.

The revived women's movement gained ground in the seventies. And the heightened environmental consciousness remained central as Americans worried about air and water pollution and endangered species. A campaign to save the whales from extinction at the hands of whaling fleets won many recruits. The hazards of nuclear power aroused particular attention in the later 1970s, culminating in 1979 when a near-catastrophic accident crippled the Three Mile Island nuclear-power plant near Harrisburg, Pennsylvania. A movie released at the same time, *China Syndrome,* raised further alarms about nuclear power. It starred Jane Fonda, an antiwar activist of the sixties, illustrating some political activists' shift of focus to new issues.

But millions of young people turned from public to private concerns. While the collapse of the liberal con-

## CHRONOLOGY

**1966**   Founding of National Organization for Women (NOW).

**1972**   Equal Rights Amendment passed by Congress.

**1973**   Major rise in OPEC prices; Arab oil boycott.

*Roe* v. *Wade*.

**1974**   Richard Nixon resigns presidency; Gerald Ford sworn in.

Whip Inflation Now (WIN) campaign.

Indian Self-Determination Act.

Ford-Brezhnev meeting.

**1975**   South Vietnamese government falls.

*Mayagüez* incident.

**1976**   Jimmy Carter elected president.

**1977**   Panama Canal treaties ratified.

Introduction of Apple II computer.

**1978–1980**   Double-digit inflation and soaring interest rates.

**1979**   Menachem Begin and Anwar el-Sadat sign peace treaty at White House.

Second round of OPEC price increases.

Accident at Three Mile Island nuclear plant.

Carter and Leonid Brezhnev sign SALT II agreement in Vienna.

Carter restores full diplomatic relations with the People's Republic of China.

**1980**   Carter withdraws SALT II agreement from Senate after Soviet invasion of Afghanistan.

Iran hostage crisis preoccupies nation.

Ronald Reagan elected president.

**1981**   Major cuts in taxes and domestic spending, coupled with large increases in military budget.

**1981–1983**   Severe recession (late 1981–early 1983).

**1982**   Equal Rights Amendment dies.

CIA organizes contra war against Nicaragua's Sandinista government.

800,000 rally in Central Park for nuclear-weapons freeze.

Stock-market boom begins.

**1983**   239 U.S. Marines die in Beirut terrorist attack.

U.S. invasion of Grenada.

U.S. deploys Pershing II and cruise missiles in Europe.

Reagan proposes Strategic Defense Initiative (Star Wars).

Soviets down Korean airliner, killing 269.

**1984**   Geraldine Ferraro chosen as vice presidential running mate on Democratic ticket.

Reagan defeats Walter Mondale in landslide.

**1984–1986**   Congress bars military aid to contras.

**1985**   Rash of airline hijackings and other terrorist acts.

**1986**   Congress passes South African sanctions.

U.S. air raid on Libya.

William Rehnquist becomes chief justice of the United States.

Antonin Scalia joins Supreme Court.

Immigration Reform and Control Act.

Federal deficit rises to $221 billion.

**1987**   Congressional hearings on Iran-contra scandal.

Stock market crash.

Trade deficit reaches $170 billion.

**1988**   Oliver North, John Poindexter, and other Iran-contra figures indicted.

Reagan signs INF Treaty in Moscow.

**1988**   *(continued)*

George Bush elected president.

Anthony Kennedy joins Supreme Court.

**1989**   Oliver North convicted of Iran-contra role.

Massive Alaskan oil spill by *Exxon Valdez*.

Supreme Court, in several 5–4 decisions, restricts civil-rights laws.

U.S. invasion of Panama; Manuel Noriega overthrown.

China's rulers crush prodemocracy movement.

Berlin Wall is opened.

**1990**   Federal Clean Air Act passed.

President Bush and Congress agree on five-year budget-deficit reduction package.

Iraq invades Kuwait.

Recession begins.

Germany reunified; Soviet troops start withdrawal from Eastern Europe.

David H. Souter joins Supreme Court.

**1991**   Gulf War (Operation Desert Storm).

United States and USSR sign treaty reducing strategic nuclear arms by 25 percent.

Upheavals in Soviet Union as economy nears collapse, Communist party is disbanded, and Soviet republics declare independence.

Clarence Thomas seated on Supreme Court.

**1992**   Recession recovery is slow, joblessness high.

Supreme Court approves Pennsylvania restriction on abortion but upholds *Roe* v. *Wade*.

Arkansas governor Bill Clinton elected president.

sensus in the wreckage of Vietnam and the fragmentation of the New Left left a vacuum of political leadership on the Left, the Watergate debacle temporarily slowed the conservative backlash. With politics in disarray, more personal preoccupations beckoned. And after 1980 Ronald Reagan's celebration of individual autonomy easily translated into a self-centered materialism. Apart from more military spending, Reagan offered little in the way of a common social agenda. In these circumstances, the "campus radical" of the 1960s gave way to a new social stereotype, the "yuppie" (young urban professional), preoccupied with physical fitness and consumption. Reversing the middle-class flight from the city, many yuppies purchased and restored run-down inner-city apartments or town houses. This process, known as gentrification, often had the effect of pushing out poorer and elderly residents.

Physical well-being became a middle-class obsession—sometimes to good effect. Yuppies jogged and exercised, ate "natural" foods free of pesticide residues and chemical additives, and stopped smoking as medical evidence linked cigarettes to lung cancer, heart disease, and other maladies. Transcendental Meditation and other "consciousness-raising" techniques won devoted followers. But self-improvement could easily turn

selfish. Historian Christopher Lasch summed up the era in the title of his 1978 book *The Culture of Narcissism;* writer Tom Wolfe called it simply the Me Generation.

Average daily TV viewing time crept up from about six hours in 1970 to nearly seven by 1990. Prime-time soap operas like "Dallas," chronicling the steamy affairs of a mythical Texas oil family, captivated millions. A variety of new cable television channels offered everything from business reports to rock music to first-run films. Faced with cable competition, the networks' share of the market declined.

The Disney Corporation, having opened its Southern California theme park, Disneyland, in 1955, launched the even bigger Disneyworld in Florida in 1982. Blockbuster movies like *Jaws* (1975), *Star Wars* (1977), and *E.T.* (1982) offered escapist fare for millions. Baseball's World Series, football's Super Bowl, and the National Basketball Association playoffs attracted vast television audiences. Superstar sports celebrities earned multimillion-dollar salaries and even more from product endorsements.

A revolution in consumer electronics shaped the era as well. By the early 1990s, 70 percent of U.S. households had VCRs (videocassette recorders), enabling users to tape TV shows for later viewing and to rent movies on cassette. As entertainment became more privatized, many families now stayed at home with the VCR, instead of going out to the movies. In the music field, the compact disc, in which laser beams "read" millions of dots molded into three miles of concentric circles on each disc, offered remarkably high-quality sound.

And this was the era of the personal computer. A product of World War II, the computer moved into the home when two young Californians, Steven Jobs and Stephen Wozniak, developed a small-scale model. In 1977 the Apple II computer hit the market. Sales reached $118 million by 1980, and computer businesses mushroomed in a region south of San Francisco nicknamed "Silicon Valley" (after the silicon computer chip). IBM, which launched its PC (personal computer) in 1981, quickly grabbed 40 percent of the market. By 1997, 44 percent of all U.S. households owned personal computers.

**The Lovable Droids C3PO and R2D2
in the 1977 Movie *Star Wars***
*A wave of escapist films with an undercurrent of concern about space-age warfare and automation helped set the tone of American popular culture in the 1970s.*

### The Women's Movement: Gains and Uncertainties

Of all the legacies of the 1960s, perhaps the most far-reaching was a revitalized women's movement. As the civil-rights and antiwar movements politicized thousands of middle-class young women, many began to examine their own status in society. The National Organization for Women (NOW) boasted nearly fifty thousand members by the mid-1970s. Feminist support groups and Gloria Steinem's *Ms.* magazine (founded in 1972) spread the message.

With the movement's growth came political clout. The National Women's Political Caucus (1971) promoted a feminist agenda. By 1972 many states had liberalized their abortion laws and outlawed gender discrimination in hiring. That same year, Congress passed an Equal Rights Amendment (ERA) to the Constitution ("Equality of rights under the law shall not be denied or abridged by the United States or any State on the basis of sex"). When twenty-eight states quickly ratified it, ultimate adoption seemed assured.

In 1973 came *Roe* v. *Wade,* a landmark case in which the Supreme Court, by a 7–2 vote, proclaimed women's constitutional right to abortion.* The majority decision, written by Justice Harry Blackmun, relied heavily on the right to privacy, which Blackmun grounded in the due-process clause of the Fourteenth Amendment.

The women's movement became more divided in the later 1970s and the 1980s, as moderates deplored the sometimes strident rhetoric of more radical feminists. Movement activists also remained mostly middle-class and white. Many homemakers and religious conservatives resented some feminists' tendency to downgrade family values while praising female autonomy and careerist goals. In *The Second Stage* (1981), Betty Friedan urged feminists to add family issues to their agenda.

As the movement gained visibility, its opposition hardened. In 1972 President Nixon vetoed a bill setting up a national network of day-care centers, criticizing its "communal approach to child-rearing." Amid the antifeminist backlash, the ERA amendment died in 1982, three states short of the three-fourths required for ratification.

No issue relating to women aroused more controversy than abortion. In the wake of *Roe* v. *Wade,* a "Right to Life" movement led by Roman Catholic and conservative Protestant groups pressed for a constitu-

---

* The decision gave women virtually unrestricted abortion rights in the first trimester of pregnancy, in consultation with a physician, while granting states increasing regulatory rights as the pregnancy progressed.

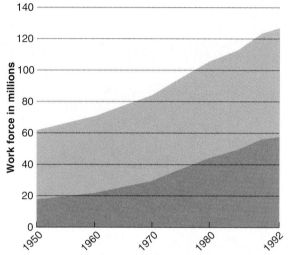

### Women in the Work Force, 1950–1992

*Since 1960 the proportion of American women who are gainfully employed has surged upward. As a result, young women coming of age in the 1990s had far different expectations about their lives than had their grandmothers or even their mothers.*

*Sources: Statistical Abstract of the United States, 1988* (Washington, D.C.: U.S. Government Printing Office, 1987), 373; *World Almanac and Book of Facts, 1989* (New York: Pharos Books, 1988), 152; *Statistical Abstract of the United States, 1993* (Washington, D.C., U.S. Government Printing Office, 1993), 400, 401.

tional amendment outlawing abortions. Abortion, opponents charged, undermined respect for human life; it was "the murder of the unborn." "Pro-life" advocates held rallies and picketed pregnancy-counseling centers. Phyllis Schlafly, a prominent conservative, emerged as a leading crusader against abortion, the Equal Rights Amendment, and other feminist causes. In 1976 Congress cut off Medicaid funding for most abortions, in effect putting this procedure out of reach of the poor.

Most feminists adopted a "pro-choice" stance, arguing that reproductive decisions should rest with the individual woman and her physician and not the government. Public-opinion polls reflected deep divisions, although a majority favored the "pro-choice" position. The number of abortions rose from about 750,000 in 1973 to more than 1.5 million in 1980 and then leveled off.

The proportion of women working outside the home leaped from 35 percent in 1960 to about 58 percent in 1992. Along with the women's movement, another reason for this trend was the soaring cost of living.

**Abortion Wars, 1989**
*"Pro Choice" and "Pro Life" demonstrators express their views in this battle of slogans at a Massachusetts clinic. A radical fringe of anti-abortion activists went beyond peaceful demonstrations to violence.*

Many families found they could not manage on a single income. Although many women workers remained at the low end of the pay scale, this, too, was changing. From 1977 to 1992, the proportion of management positions held by women rose from 24 percent to 42 percent (though *top* management still remained a male preserve). The ratio of female lawyers and physicians also edged upward, reaching about 18 percent by 1992, while the proportion of women in medical schools and law schools climbed steeply.

These changes affected fertility patterns. The birthrate dropped steadily after 1960, reaching a low in 1976. By 1980 the statistically average American family had 1.6 children. The number of unmarried couples living together—most of them childless—jumped from 523,000 in 1970 to 3.5 million by 1993.

Some conservatives worried that women's changing roles would weaken the family. Working women themselves acknowledged the stresses of their situation, torn between career and family pressures.

Feminists recognized, too, that a long road lay ahead in overcoming ingrained patterns of gender discrimination. Working women's average earnings still lagged well behind those of men. And although change was in the air, the workplace remained largely gender segregated. Such fields as nursing and secretarial work overwhelmingly employed women, whereas men dominated the higher-prestige professions like law and medicine, particularly at the upper ranks.

The eighties was not a favorable decade for confronting these inequities. The Reagan administration, suspicious of government activism on social issues, opposed many feminist goals. The Reagan budget cuts fell heavily on programs serving women and children. As single mothers swelled the welfare rolls, observers spoke of the "feminization of poverty."

### The American Birthrate, 1960–1991

*Families of four or five children or even more were once common in the United States. But from 1960 to the mid-1970s, the U.S. birthrate fell by nearly half.*

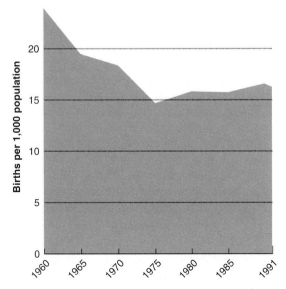

*Source: Statistical Abstract of the United States, 1994* (Washington, D.C.: U.S. Government Printing Office, 1994), 76.

As the 1980s ended, feminist leaders could take satisfaction in many gains achieved. But they also recognized that major challenges loomed and complex issues remained unresolved.

### The Two Worlds of Black America

The conservative trends of the 1970s and 1980s impacted African Americans as well. The Reagan administration, distrusting government, was cool toward calls for government action to remedy past racial injustices. Reagan's appointees to the U.S. Civil Rights Commission, the agency charged with enforcing civil-rights laws, shared the president's suspicion of federal activism. This governmental foot dragging came at a time when the African-American community faced many difficulties.

The story of black America in the 1970s and 1980s was really two very different stories. On one hand, millions of blacks experienced significant upward mobility. The civil-rights movement had opened many doors. In 1965 black students accounted for under 5 percent of college enrollments; by 1990 the figure had risen to 12 percent, as the proportion of black high-school graduates going on to college nearly matched that of whites. By 1990 some 46 percent of black workers held white-collar jobs. TV's *Cosby Show,* a popular comedy of the later 1980s in which Bill Cosby played an obstetrician married to a lawyer, portrayed this upwardly mobile black world. Many African Americans worked steadily in blue-collar jobs as well.

But outside this world lay the grim world of inner-city slums. In this world, comprising about a third of the black population, up to half the young people never finished high school and the jobless rate hovered as high as 60 percent.

Although racism was a factor, economic trends played a role as well. Structural changes in the economy since World War II had eliminated many unskilled jobs once held by the urban poor. The recessions of the 1970s and early 1980s battered the black underclass, and job cuts in steel, automaking, and other industries hit black skilled workers. Inflation and rising demands for a trained work force further battered the poor and uneducated, while welfare payments lagged behind rising living costs.

Cocaine and other drugs pervaded the urban ghettos in the 1970s and 1980s. Black children earned up to a hundred dollars a day as lookouts for drug dealers. By their early teens, some became dealers themselves.

This is not to suggest that only the poor or minorities abused drugs. They were found at all social levels in the 1970s, including the world of yuppies, sports celebrities, show-business figures, and young corporate executives. Despite a tough antidrug law (the Comprehensive Drug Abuse Act of 1970), the consumption of such substances was widely tolerated and was even glorified in some movies, songs, and rock concerts. But in the inner cities, drug use was particularly pervasive—and devastating.

With drugs came violence. In the 1980s a young black male was six times as likely to be murdered as a young white male. In Los Angeles two major gangs, the Bloods and the Crips, accounted for more than four hundred killings in 1987. Warned Jewelle Taylor Gibbs of the School of Social Welfare at Berkeley in 1988: "Young black males in America's inner cities are an endangered species. . . ., [the] rejects of our affluent society."

Single women—most of them young, poor, and uneducated—accounted for 66 percent of all black births in 1994. Scarcely beyond childhood themselves, many of these single mothers depended on welfare payments for survival. Caught in a cycle of dependence, these millions threatened to become a permanent undercaste in American society.

Buffeted by complex social and economic forces, the United States' predominantly nonwhite inner cities came to pose a major social challenge. Addressing these problems, governments extended "affirmative action" programs to groups previously discriminated against. Governments set aside a percentage of building contracts for minority contractors, for example, while some educational institutions reserved a certain number of openings for minority applicants. Such programs faced court challenges, however. In *Bakke* v. *U.S.* (1978), the Supreme Court overthrew the affirmative-action plan of a California medical school that reserved a specific number of spaces for minority applicants. In 1989 the High Court invalidated a Richmond, Virginia, requirement that 30 percent of building contracts be awarded to minority businesses.

### New Patterns of Immigration

America's growth from 204 million people in 1970 to 267 million in 1997 reflects a steady influx of immigrants, both legal and illegal. Whereas most immigrants once came from Europe, some 45 percent of the more recent arrivals have come from the Western Hemisphere and 30 percent from Asia.

Thanks to both immigration and a high birthrate, Hispanics compose the nation's fastest-growing ethnic group. The 1997 Hispanic population stood at some 29 million (up from 9 million in 1970), consisting mainly of Mexican-Americans concentrated in the Southwest; and Cubans, Puerto Ricans, Haitians, and other West Indians living mainly in New York, Florida, Illinois, and New Jersey.

As in the past, economic need drew these newcomers. In oil-rich Mexico, for example, an oil price collapse in the 1980s worsened the nation's chronic poverty, spurring many to seek jobs in the north. But these immigrants, like their predecessors, often did not escape hardship and poverty. In 1990 nearly 20 percent of Mexican-Americans and 30 percent of Puerto Ricans lived below the poverty line.

Preserving their language and traditions, Hispanic newcomers influenced U.S. culture. In Los Angeles, with nearly a million Mexican-Americans, Spanish business signs and movie marquees proliferated; large parts of Miami seemed wholly Hispanic (see A Place in Time).

Estimates of the number of illegal aliens in the United States ranged as high as 12 million by the early 1990s. Working long hours with few legal protections, these migrants, mostly Mexicans and Haitians (as well as Puerto Ricans, who are U.S. citizens), sweated in the garment trades, cleaned houses and cared for children, and labored in agricultural fields. Addressing this problem, the Immigration Reform and Control Act of 1986 outlawed the hiring of illegal aliens, strengthened border controls, and offered legal status to aliens who had lived in the United States since January 1, 1982.

Immigration from Asia climbed as newcomers from Korea, Vietnam, and the Philippines arrived in California and spread eastward. Prizing higher education, many Asian immigrants moved up rapidly. The

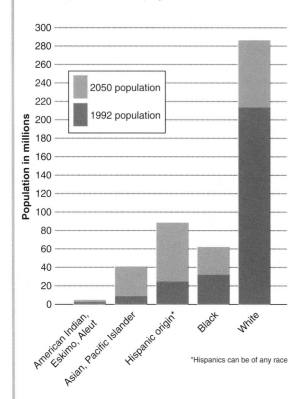

**Changing Demographics**

*The U.S. population by race and Hispanic origin in 1992 and 2050 (Census Bureau projections).*

Legend:
- 2050 population
- 1992 population

Y-axis: Population in millions (0 to 300)

X-axis categories: American Indian, Eskimo, Aleut; Asian, Pacific Islander; Hispanic origin*; Black; White

*Hispanics can be of any race

*Source: Statistical Abstract of the United States, 1994* (Washington, D.C.: U.S. Government Printing Office, 1994), 17, 18.

**New Americans, 1994**

*Beneath the political icons and popular-culture imagery of their adopted nation, children of Hmong (Laotian) immigrants study at Lincoln Elementary School, Wausau, Wisconsin.*

younger generation, torn between the new and the old, generally retained a strong group identity while taking advantage of the larger society's opportunities. All these ethnic trends made contemporary America a far more diverse and vibrant place than it had been a generation earlier.

## Brightening Prospects for Native Americans

In the 1950s the federal government had sought to terminate all Indian-aid programs and promote Indians' gradual absorption into the general population. Protesting this destructive policy, and influenced by the protest climate of the sixties, members of the militant American Indian Movement (AIM) occupied Alcatraz Island in San Francisco Bay in 1969, the Bureau of Indian Affairs in Washington in 1972, and a trading post at Wounded Knee, South Dakota (site of the 1890 Indian massacre by the U.S. Army), in 1973.

This militance spurred a shift in federal policy. Rejecting both the assimilationist and paternalistic approaches, President Nixon in 1970 called for greater autonomy for Native Americans in managing their own affairs. The Indian Self-Determination Act of 1974 granted tribes control of federal-aid programs on the reservations and oversight of their own schools.

In the 1990 census, more than 1.7 million persons identified themselves as American Indians, in contrast to fewer than 800,000 in 1970. This upsurge, far greater than could be accounted for by natural increase, doubtless reflected not only growing ethnic pride but also job opportunities available under federal affirmative-action guidelines, as well as economic advantages associated with tribal membership.

Federal legislation in 1961 had given tribes the right to buy or develop land for commercial or industrial projects, and a number of tribes undertook commercial ventures ranging from resorts to mining and logging operations, or permitted food-processing companies, electronics firms, and other businesses to build factories on tribal lands, providing much-needed jobs and income. Certain tribes took advantage of their exemption from state gambling laws to open casinos, although some Native American leaders saw in casinos a threat to Indian culture.

Indian tribes also reasserted long-ignored treaty rights. The Indian Claims Commission, a federal agency set up in 1946, worked overtime after 1970. In 1971 the native peoples of Alaska won 40 million acres of land and nearly $1 billion in settlement of long-standing claims. In 1980 the Sioux were awarded $107 million for South Dakota lands taken from them, and the Penobscot Indians in Maine won claims based on a federal law of 1790. In 1988 the tiny Puyallup tribe of Washington State received $162 million in settlement of their claim that the city of Tacoma occupied land granted them by treaty in the 1850s. The Puyallups announced plans to restore salmon runs on the Puyallup River and construct a deep-water port on Puget Sound.

High rates of unemployment, alcoholism, and disease persisted both on the reservations and among urbanized Indians. But the renewal of tribal life, new federal policies, and the courts' willingness to honor ancient treaties clearly represented an advance. In popular culture representations, movies such as *Little Big Man* (1970) and *Dances with Wolves* (1990), while prone to sentimentalizing Indian culture, were an improvement over the hostile stereotypes of earlier cowboy-and-Indian movies.

**Wounded Knee, South Dakota, 1973**

*In a gesture of symbolic protest, activists of the American Indian Movement (AIM) occupied Wounded Knee, scene of the 1890 massacre of 300 Sioux by the U.S. Army.*

## Miami, Florida

So tangled and complex has the U.S. social web become by the 1990s that some observers fear its unraveling. No American city poses the issue of multiculturalism more starkly than Miami, where ethnic diversity is not simply a *part* of the story; in many respects, it *is* the story.

Thrusting up along Biscayne Bay near Florida's southern tip, Miami's fifteen miles of sun-drenched beaches, breathtaking skyline of flamboyant skyscrapers, and pastel-tinted Art Deco buildings all proclaim the nation's southernmost major city. When Ponce de Leon reached the bay in 1513, Calusas Indians inhabited the area. Spain claimed the region until 1819, when the Adams-Onís Treaty ceded title to the United States. Florida entered the union in 1845, about the time the settlement on Biscayne Bay began to be called Miami. Sporadic Indian resistance—the so-called Seminole Wars—

persisted into the 1850s. (A small tribe of Native Americans, the Miccosukee, lives on a nearby reservation.)

A frenzied land boom in the 1920s collapsed in the wake of a killer hurricane, but Miami prospered after 1945 as GIS who had trained in the area returned to live and as northern "snowbirds" fled south each winter, many eventually to become permanent residents. Miami Beach proved especially popular with Jewish retirees from New York. One of these, the novelist I. B. Singer, recalled his first visit in 1948: "Miami Beach resembled a small Israel. . . . Yiddish resounded around us in accents as thick as those you would hear in Tel Aviv." By 1975 Miami's Jewish population had reached 300,000, most of them over age sixty.

But today's Miami exudes primarily a Hispanic flavor. Cubans fled their island country en masse after Fidel Castro seized power in 1959, and by 1973,

300,000 had settled in Miami. Thousands more, the so-called Mariel boat people who left with Castro's approval, arrived in 1980. By 1990, 49 percent of the 2 million inhabitants of Dade County (comprising Miami and its environs) were of Cuban birth or descent.

Cuban-Americans influence not only Miami's cultural ambience but its political and economic agenda. Cuban-born Xavier Saurez became mayor in 1985. Far from being a struggling minority, Cuban-Americans compose a confident, fully developed ethnic community. "Little Havana," the sprawling downtown district centered on *Calle Ocho* (Eighth Street), boasts not only churches, restaurants, and shops but also banks, medical centers, law offices, insurance companies, and construction firms, employing professionals of all kinds.

Other Hispanic groups also call Miami home. Jamaicans have long been present, and the 1980s brought emigrants from troubled Nicaragua, El Salvador, and especially Haiti. Although U.S. immigration officials intercept and repatriate Haitian refugees arriving by sea, this community continues to grow. "Little Haiti," a district of some 60,000 people anchored by Notre Dame d'Haiti Church, enhances Miami's ethnic ambience.

The African American community, making up some 18 percent of the population, is centered in Liberty City, Richmond Heights, and other enclaves. While Richmond Heights is middle class and well-to-do, the black population overall ranks among the city's poorest. In contrast to the situation in other multiethnic cities, Miami's African Americans and Hispanics have not collaborated in pursuit of common goals. While many native-born blacks feel alienated and exploited, Hispanic newcomers of whatever skin color

*The Café Cubano in Miami's "Little Havana."*

tend to view the United States more positively as a place of freedom and opportunity. Politically, the two communities diverge radically. While African Americans generally vote Democratic, the staunchly anticommunist Cubans are mostly conservative Republicans.

Ethnic diversity generates a distinctive Miami style. Jewish delis coexist with Hispanic restaurants. Snapper, *paella*, conch fritters, stone crabs, Haitian curried goat, potent Cuban coffee, black beans and rice, and an array of salsas tempt local palates. In prosperous times, ethnic lines blur in a shared pursuit of the good life. A recession in the 1970s drove the jobless rate to 13 percent, but the economy bounced back in the 1980s. For the affluent, a prevailing love of sports finds many outlets: sailing, windsurfing, sports car rallies, horseracing at Hialeah, the annual Orange Bowl extravaganza, and avid support for the Miami Dolphins professional football team, the Miami Heat basketball team, and the University of Miami Hurricanes.

With its ceaseless round of parades, fairs, and festivals, the city seems dedicated to the pleasure principle. Casual dress and gold jewelry for both sexes set the tone. One annual event draws thousands of chocolate lovers. The beaches encourage a narcissism that some call Miami's "body culture." Cosmetic surgery thrives. Fashion photography, capitalizing on the ever-present sunlight, is big business. Journalist Patrick May sums up the city this way: "Non-stop entertainment. Over a stage backdropped by fruit salad sunsets and palm tree props, the curtain for 100 years has risen faithfully each dawn. And there it stands, tongue firmly in cheek, hogging the spotlight. The show-off of American cities admiring itself in a full-length mirror."

But behind the façade lie problems. Indeed, Miami is a microcosm of troubling contemporary issues. Racial tensions simmer near the surface. Black neighborhoods erupted in violence in 1968 and again in 1980 when a Tampa jury acquitted a white police officer in a black man's death. As the Hispanic population has grown, non-Hispanic whites have moved out. Civic leaders bemoan "Anglo flight," and a commonly seen bumper sticker gibes: "Will the last American leaving Miami please bring the flag?"

With Spanish the native tongue of half the residents, language is contested terrain. In many neighborhoods, English is rarely spoken, heard on radio or TV, or seen on billboards, magazine stands, or store signs. Other languages thrive as well. In 1994 a reporter observed a Vietnamese, a Spanish-speaking Colombian, and a French-speaking Haitian vainly trying to communicate at an auto-repair shop. (They eventually diagnosed the problem: a faulty distributor.) In 1980 the Dade County commissioners proclaimed English the official language for government business. Florida voters imposed the same rule statewide in 1988. But many thousands of Miamians continue to conduct their daily lives without resort to English.

Miami's links with organized crime go far back. Rum-running and gambling proliferated in the 1920s, and underworld figures wielded great political and economic clout. Mobster Al Capone retired here in the 1930s. Today, a $12 billion annual wholesale drug traffic drives up the crime statistics. Fast boats smuggle in cocaine from "mother ships" hovering offshore; commercial aircraft arriving from South America unwittingly transmit drugs. Dade County's 1981 homicide toll of 621 earned it the dubious title "Murder Capital USA." A popular TV show of 1984–1989, "Miami Vice," glamorized the city's sleazy underside along with its tropical setting, laid-back fashions, and stage-set architecture. While drug wars and domestic disputes account for most of the bloodshed, the killing of several tourists during robbery attempts tarnished the city's appeal in the early 1990s. "Miami wears its crime like cheap perfume," observes a guidebook half boastfully; "it's hard to ignore."

On another front, decades of development have taken a heavy toll on fragile wetlands and unspoiled wilderness areas. The nearby Everglades, once spread over 4 million acres, has dwindled to one-tenth its former size. Of the exotic wildlife that formerly inhabited this fragile ecosystem, only a fraction survives.

Crime, ethnic tensions, environmental degradation, cultural diversity, hedonistic pleasure seeking—for better or worse, Miami has it all. In this vibrant, garish, future-oriented city, many of the most urgent social issues facing contemporary America emerge in particularly stark fashion.

*A mother and her daughters in Miami's Little Haiti District.*

### Sexuality in the Era of AIDS

As we saw in Chapter 31 many gay men and lesbians "came out of the closet" in the 1970s and openly avowed their sexual preference. They rallied, paraded, and organized to fight job discrimination and harassment. Religious conservatives, however, deplored this trend as evidence of society's moral disintegration. "God . . . destroyed the cities of Sodom and Gomorrah because of this terrible sin," thundered evangelist Jerry Falwell.

The freer attitude toward sex changed in the 1980s, however, with the proliferation of sexually transmitted diseases, including AIDS (acquired immune deficiency syndrome), first diagnosed in the United States in 1981. By 1998 more than 380,000 Americans had died of AIDS, and an estimated 1–1.2 million more either had the disease or carried HIV, the causative virus. Public-health officials warned that a vaccine lay far in the future. AIDS spread mainly among sexually active homosexuals and bisexuals, intravenous drug users sharing needles, and those having sexual intercourse with members of these high-risk groups.* Nevertheless, medical authorities warned of the need for caution and urged the wider use of condoms. This message was driven home when basketball superstar Earvin ("Magic") Johnson of the Los Angeles Lakers and Olympic gold-medal-winning diver Greg Louganis announced that they had the HIV virus.

AIDS provided some Americans with an excuse to express their hatred of homosexuals, but the disease also stimulated a massive medical-research effort. Hospices in many communities provided care and support to sufferers and a large AIDS quilt bearing the names of victims toured the nation.

Fearful of AIDS and other sexually transmitted diseases, Americans grew more cautious in their sexual behavior. The exuberant slogan of the 1960s, "Make Love, Not War," gave way to a more somber one: "Safer Sex."

### The Evangelical Renaissance

Religion flourished in post-1970 American. Religion has always loomed large in American history, but after 1970 it played an especially sensitive cultural and political role.

This revival of religious interest took many forms. Some joined the Reverend Sun Myung Moon's Unification church (whose adherents some called "moonies") and the International Society for Krishna Consciousness, whose saffron-robed followers added an exotic note on city streets and college campuses. Another manifestation of religious resurgence was the rapid growth of evangelical Protestant denominations such as the 2-million-member Assemblies of God church and the 14-million-strong Southern Baptist Convention, which believed in the Bible's verbatim truth, in a "born-again" religious conversion, and in personal piety and strict morality.

Evangelical Christians had pursued social reform before the Civil War, and many modern-day evangelicals also turned to political activity, but of a conservative variety. As one observed in 1985: "I always thought that churches should stay out of politics. Now it seems almost a sin *not* to get involved." Jerry Falwell's pro-Reagan Moral Majority registered an estimated 2 million new voters in 1980 and 1984. While targeting domestic issues such as abortion, pornography, and

**Combating the AIDS Scourge**
*A public-service poster in San Francisco seeks to spread information about AIDS prevention.*

GANNETT SHELTER POSTERS

**WHAT'S STOPPING YOU?**
because what you don't know CAN hurt you.
AIDS TESTING IS AVAILABLE FOR EVERYONE CALL 621-4858

AIDS

---

* Babies born to women with AIDS were also at risk. Early in the epidemic, some persons contracted AIDS through blood transfusions.

public school prayer, evangelicals also embraced a militantly anticommunist world view.

Falwell's organization disbanded after 1984, but the Reverend Pat Robertson's Christian Coalition took its place. Mobilizing conservative Christians to elect candidates to local school boards and the like, the coalition's long-range aim was expanded political influence at the national level.

A network of Christian bookstores, radio stations, and television evangelists fueled evangelicalism's rejuvenation. Along with Falwell's "Old Time Gospel Hour," popular broadcasts included Pat Robertson's "700 Club," Jim and Tammy Bakker's "PTL" (Praise the Lord) program, Oral Roberts's telecasts from Oklahoma, and Jimmy Swaggart's from Louisiana. Many of these shows aired on Robertson's CBN (Christian Broadcasting Network). With their constant pleas for money, the televangelists repelled many Americans, but millions embraced their spiritual message.

The "electronic church" suffered after 1987 as sexual and financial scandals swirled around some of its luminaries, but the growing influence of evangelical religion continued. In *The Culture of Disbelief* (1993), Stephen J. Carter, a professor at Yale Law School, called on politicians, the media, and the legal profession to cease "trivializing" religion and to recognize its importance for millions of Americans. In a world of change, evangelicals found certitude in their faith. In the process, they profoundly influenced late-twentieth-century American life.

# Years of Malaise: Post-Watergate Politics and Diplomacy

Richard Nixon's failed presidency had a dispiriting effect on the nation's political culture, as Gerald Ford and then Jimmy Carter grappled—mostly ineffectually—with a tangle of domestic and foreign problems. As oil prices soared, the U.S. economy fell prey to inflation, unemployment, and recession. A foreboding sense of limits—both on economic growth and on the ability of government to solve problems—gripped many Americans. Globally, the period 1974–1980 brought mostly humiliations, from the sorry end of the Vietnam intervention to Iran's seizure of U.S. hostages. The stark simplicities of the Cold War blurred as complex problems arose in Asia, the Mideast, Latin America, and Africa—a region coming to be called the Third World.

The confident days of the 1950s and early 1960s, when Americans, enjoying an expansive economy, had felt assured of their role as leaders of the "Free World" and equal to whatever challenges arose, now seemed remote indeed. A nation long convinced that it was immune to the historical forces that hedged in other societies seemed adrift, buffeted by forces beyond its control. By 1980 the accumulation of frustration had generated a strong political revolt.

## *The Caretaker Presidency of Gerald Ford*

Gerald R. Ford took the presidential oath on August 9, 1974. A Michigan congressman who had served as minority leader before becoming vice president, Ford conveyed a likeable decency, if little evidence of brilliance. After the trauma of Watergate, America viewed Nixon's successor with relief and cautious hope.

Ford's period of grace ended a month into his term, however, when he pardoned Richard Nixon for "any and all crimes" committed while in office—thus shielding the ex-president from prosecution for his Watergate role. Ford said he wanted to help heal the body politic, but many Americans reacted with outrage.

On domestic issues Ford proved more conservative than Nixon, vetoing a variety of environmental, social-welfare, and public-interest measures, among them a 1974 "freedom of information" bill granting citizens greater access to government records. The Democratic Congress, however, overrode most of these vetoes.

Economic problems occupied Ford's attention. Beginning in 1973, oil prices shot up as a result of the Arab oil embargo (see Chapter 31) and price hikes by the Organization of Petroleum Exporting Countries (OPEC), a thirteen-nation consortium formed in 1960. The impact on the United States, which imported more than one-third of its oil, was severe. The soaring cost of gasoline, heating oil, and other petroleum-based products worsened already serious inflation. Consumer prices rose by 23 percent in 1974–1975. In October 1974 Ford unveiled a program of voluntary restraint dubbed "Whip Inflation Now" (WIN), but prices continued to zoom. When the Federal Reserve Board tried to cool the economy by raising the discount rate, a severe recession resulted. Unemployment approached 11 percent by 1975. Tax receipts dropped as business stagnated, and the federal deficit increased. Ford proposed a tax cut and other measures to stimulate consumer spending, but economic headaches continued.

**No Gas!**

*As the 1973 oil crisis hit home, panicky motorists, like these in Boston, rushed to gas stations to fill up, making the situation worse.*

The oil crisis hit the U.S. auto industry hard, as Americans stopped buying Detroit's gas-guzzlers. GM, Ford, and Chrysler laid off more than 225,000 workers in 1974. Smaller, fuel-efficient foreign imports increased their market share from 17 to 33 percent in the 1970s.

On the diplomatic front, Ford retained Henry Kissinger as secretary of state and supported the effort to improve relations with China and the Soviet Union (see Chapter 31). Meeting at Vladivostok, Siberia, in 1974, Ford and Soviet leader Leonid Brezhnev worked on a new arms-control treaty, SALT II, limiting each side to twenty-four hundred nuclear missiles.

The national morale suffered another blow in April 1975 when the South Vietnamese government fell, ending in failure two decades of U.S. effort in Vietnam. The TV networks chronicled desperate helicopter evacuations from the roof of the U.S. embassy in Saigon (soon renamed Ho Chi Minh City) as North Vietnamese troops closed in. A few weeks later, when Cambodia seized a U.S. merchant ship, the *Mayagüez,* a frustrated Ford ordered a military rescue. This hasty show of force freed the thirty-nine *Mayagüez* crew members but cost the lives of forty-one U.S. servicemen.

As the nation entered the election year 1976—also the bicentennial of the Declaration of Independence—Americans found little cause for cheer and ample reason to repudiate the party in power.

## The Outsider as Insider: President Jimmy Carter

Gerald Ford won the Republican nomination in 1976 despite a challenge from the former governor of California, Ronald Reagan. Among a large field of Democratic hopefuls was Jimmy Carter, a wealthy Georgia peanut grower who had served as governor of his home state but remained unknown nationally. But Carter swept the primaries by stressing themes that appealed to post-Watergate America. He emphasized his status as an outsider to Washington, pledged never to lie to the American people, and avowed his religious faith as a "born-again" Christian. Winning the nomination, Carter chose as his running mate Senator Walter Mondale, a liberal Democrat from Minnesota.

Carter's early lead in the polls eroded as voters sensed a lack of clarity in his program, but he hung on to win by a narrow margin. (Less than 54 percent of those eligible had bothered to vote—a gauge of post-Watergate apathy.) The vote broke sharply along class lines: the well-to-do went for Ford; the poor, overwhelmingly for Carter. The Georgian swept the South and received 90 percent of the black vote.

Carter rejected the trappings of what some in Nixon's day had labeled the imperial presidency. On inauguration day, with his wife and daughter, he walked from the Capitol to the White House. In an echo of Franklin D. Roosevelt's radio chats, he delivered some of his television speeches wearing a casual sweater and seated in an easy chair by a fireplace. Responding to major social movements, he appointed a number of women and members of minority groups to federal judgeships.

Populist symbolism and gestures of inclusiveness aside, Carter never managed to articulate a clear political philosophy. Liberals and conservatives both claimed him; no one knew where he stood. Intensely private, he relied on young staff members from Georgia and avoided socializing with politicians. "Carter couldn't get the Pledge of Allegiance through Congress," groused one legislator. An intelligent, disciplined man who had worked as a nuclear-submarine engineer after graduating from the U.S. Naval Academy, Carter focused on specific problems but lacked a larger political vision.

Carter fought the recession with a tax cut and public-works programs. Thanks in part to these efforts, the unemployment rate dropped to around 5 percent by late 1978. But he showed little sympathy for any social-welfare measures involving federal spending.

## The Election of 1976

| Candidates | Parties | Electoral Vote | Popular Vote | Percentage of Popular Vote |
|---|---|---|---|---|
| JIMMY CARTER | Democratic | 297 | 40,827,394 | 49.9 |
| Gerald R. Ford | Republican | 240 | 39,145,977 | 47.9 |

Carter proposed administrative reforms in the civil service and the executive branch of government, but his poor relations with Congress often frustrated even these efforts. His calls for a national health-insurance program, overhaul of the welfare system, and reform of the income tax laws fell flat.

Carter did better on foreign policy, but here, too, the negatives outweighed the positives. As a candidate he had urged increased attention to human rights and his secretary of state, Cyrus Vance, worked to combat abuses in Chile, Argentina, Ethiopia, South Africa, and elsewhere. Human-rights problems in countries considered vital to U.S. security, such as South Korea and the Philippines, were downplayed. Carter also tried to adapt to a world no longer dominated by the superpowers. He sought better relations, for example, with the new nations of Africa.

In Panama and China, Carter pursued initiatives launched by his predecessors. Since 1964, when anti-American riots had rocked Panama, successive administrations had been negotiating a more equitable treaty relationship. The Carter administration completed negotiations on treaties transferring the Panama Canal and the Canal Zone to the Panamanians by 1999. Although these agreements protected U.S. security interests, conservatives attacked them as proof of America's post-Vietnam loss of nerve. But in a rare congressional success, Carter won Senate ratification of the treaties in 1977 by a vote of 68–32, 1 more than the two-thirds required.

After China's long-time leader Mao Zedong (Mao Tse-tung) died in 1976, his successor, Deng Xiaoping, expressed interest in closer links with the United States. Carter restored full diplomatic relations with the People's Republic of China on January 1, 1979, thus opening the door to scientific, cultural, and commercial exchanges.

Toward the Soviet Union Carter showed both conciliation and toughness, with toughness winning out. In a 1979 meeting in Vienna, Carter and Leonid Brezhnev signed the SALT II agreement, which Carter sent to the Senate for ratification. Advocates of a strong

**Jimmy and Rosalynn Keep in Shape**
*As a fitness vogue swept the nation in the 1970s, President Carter and his wife took to the jogging track, reenforcing the folksy image Carter sought to project.*

military criticized it, however, charging that it favored the Soviets.

SALT II dissolved entirely in January 1980 when the Soviet Union invaded Afghanistan. The reasons were complex, but many Americans viewed it as proof of Moscow's expansionist designs on the Middle East. As U.S.-Soviet relations soured, Carter withdrew the SALT II agreement from the Senate and adopted a series of anti-Soviet measures, including a boycott of the 1980 Summer Olympics in Moscow. Carter's hard-line Soviet policy reflected the influence of national security adviser Zbigniew Brzezinski, a Polish-born political scientist who advocated a tough stance toward Moscow.

Under Brzezinski's influence, the administration's human-rights pronouncements mainly targeted the Soviet Union.

### *The Middle East: Peace Accords and Hostages*

Carter's proudest achievement and his bitterest setback came in the Middle East. Despite Kissinger's efforts, a state of war still prevailed between Israel and Egypt. When Egyptian leader Anwar el-Sadat unexpectedly flew to Israel in November 1977 to negotiate with Israeli prime minister Menachem Begin, Carter saw an opening. In September 1978, Carter hosted Sadat and Begin at Camp David, the presidential retreat in Maryland, where they agreed on the "framework" of a peace treaty. On March 26, 1979, the two leaders signed a formal peace treaty at the White House. The Camp David Accords set a timetable for a transition to greater autonomy for the West Bank and Gaza Strip Palestinians.

But events soon dashed Carter's hopes for a comprehensive Middle Eastern settlement. Prime Minister Begin insisted that despite the Camp David Accords Israel could continue to build Jewish settlements in the occupied territories. The other Arab states

rejected the accords, and in 1981 Islamic fundamentalists assassinated Sadat. Tension in the region remained high and peace as elusive as ever. Limited though it was, however, Camp David was the high point of Carter's presidency.

A fresh Middle Eastern crisis erupted in 1979. For years, Iran had been ruled by the shah Mohammed Reza Pahlavi, who had been restored to power with CIA help in 1953 as head of a repressive but pro-U.S. regime. Resistance was led by Iran's Shiite Muslim spiritual head, Ayatollah Ruhollah Khomeini, from his exile in Paris. In January 1979, as Shiite unrest peaked, the shah fled Iran. Khomeini, returning in triumph, imposed strict Islamic rule and preached hatred of the United States.

In early November Carter admitted the shah to the United States for cancer treatment. Shortly after, Khomeini supporters stormed the U.S. embassy in Tehran and seized more than fifty American hostages. Thus began a 444-day ordeal that nearly paralyzed the Carter administration. TV images from Tehran of blindfolded hostages, anti-American mobs, and U.S. flags being used as garbage bags rubbed American nerves raw. A rescue attempt in April 1980 failed as a U.S. helicopter and transport plane collided in the Iranian desert, killing eight GIs. Secretary of State Vance, who had opposed the rescue effort, resigned. Not until inauguration day, January 20, 1981, after Carter had left office, did the Iranian authorities release the hostages.

### *A Sea of Troubles as Carter's Term Ends*

Inflation worsened as Carter's term wore on. Prices rose by more than 13 percent in both 1979 and 1980. The decade's second oil crisis hit in 1979. As OPEC boosted oil prices to more than $30 a barrel, Americans accustomed to paying 30¢ for a gallon of gasoline saw prices edging toward $1 a gallon. As lines formed at gas stations, tempers flared. In 1979 alone, U.S. consumers paid $16.4 billion in added costs related to the oil-price increases. Carter's Council on Wage and Price Stability exhorted workers and manufacturers to hold the line, but repeated oil-price hikes perpetuated the inflationary spiral.

As the Federal Reserve Board pushed the discount rate higher, bank interest rates reached 20 percent by 1980. With mortgages and business loans prohibitively expensive, economic activity stalled, producing "stagflation"—a combination of business stagnation and price inflation.

**Iran Hostage Crisis, 1979**
*As the Iranians staged scenes like this at the U.S. embassy in Baghdad for the TV cameras, American frustration soared and President Carter's political fortunes plunged.*

Pondering the oil crisis, Carter drew a larger lesson: the nation's profligate waste of fossil-fuel resources must give way to a new ethic of conservation. Carter recognized that two key factors underlying U.S. economic growth—cheap, unlimited energy and the lack of foreign competition—could no longer be counted on. The era of endless expansion was over, Carter concluded, and the nation must adopt a philosophy of restraint.

Congress in 1975 had set fuel-efficiency standards for cars and imposed a national speed limit of fifty-five miles per hour, but Carter sought to do more. In 1977 he created the Department of Energy and proposed various taxes on oil and gasoline consumption, tax credits for conservation measures, and research on alternative-energy resources. Congress passed a considerably watered-down energy bill in 1978.

As with Herbert Hoover earlier, Americans turned against the remote figure in the White House. When Carter's approval rating hit 26 percent in the summer of 1979 (lower than Nixon's at the depths of Watergate), the president retreated to Camp David for a period of reflection and then delivered a television address that seemed to shift the blame to the American people for their collective "crisis of confidence." A cabinet reshuffle followed, but the whole exercise deepened suspicions that Carter himself was a big part of the problem.

By mid-1980, as the Iranian hostage crisis deepened, Carter's approval rating had sunk to an appalling 23 percent. The Democrats glumly renominated him, but defeat in November loomed.

Carter's sudden emergence in 1976 illustrated how, in the TV era, a relative unknown could bypass party power brokers and gain a national following almost overnight. At a moment when Americans longed to see integrity and competence restored to the presidency, he seemed at first a godsend. Keenly analytical, he identified many emerging issues: energy policy; tax, welfare, and health-care reform; the need to redefine America's world role. But he lacked the political skills that might have inspired the nation to confront those problems productively. By the end of his term, a victim both of his own flaws and of forces beyond his control, Carter was discredited. A postpresidential career devoted to humanitarian service and the resolution of international conflicts helped to restore Carter's reputation, but when he left office in January 1981, few expressed regrets.

## The Reagan Revolution

In 1980 voters turned to a candidate who promised to break with the recent past: Ronald Reagan. Reagan's unabashed patriotism appealed to a nation still traumatized by Vietnam. His promise to reverse the Democrats' "tax and spend" policies and his attacks on the social-welfare ideology of the New Deal, the Fair Deal, and the Great Society resonated with millions of middle-class and blue-collar Americans.

As president, Reagan revived national pride. His economic policies at first caused a recession but eventually brought down inflation and triggered a consumer buying spree and a surge of speculative investment. But these same policies laid the groundwork for economic difficulties after his departure.

Reagan in his first term revived the belligerent rhetoric of the early Cold War, intensified the arms competition with the Soviets, and supplied weapons and money to anticommunist forces in Latin America. But Reagan also found himself enmeshed in foreign problems that did not readily fit into his Cold War world view.

### *Background of the Revolution*

What underlay Reagan's appeal? First, voters were frightened by the prospect of chronic stagflation, and

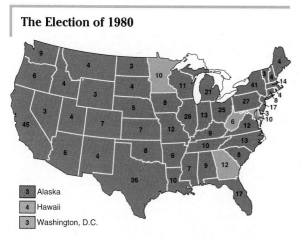

**The Election of 1980**

| | | Electoral Vote | Popular Vote | Percentage of Popular Vote |
|---|---|---|---|---|
| **Republican** Ronald Reagan | | 489 | 43,899,248 | 50.8 |
| **Democratic** Jimmy Carter | | 49 | 35,481,435 | 41.0 |
| **Independent** John B. Anderson | – | – | 5,719,437 | 6.6 |
| **Minor parties** | – | – | 1,395,558 | 1.6 |

3 Alaska
4 Hawaii
3 Washington, D.C.

Reagan promoted a seemingly painless panacea: a dramatic tax cut that would stimulate the economy and thereby boost tax revenues so that the budget could be balanced, reducing inflationary pressures. His fellow Republican George Bush, a rival for the nomination, ridiculed this plan as "voodoo economics," but it impressed many voters. Moreover, Reagan's tributes to self-help and private enterprise exerted great appeal as an alternative to the New Deal–Great Society ideology of government activism. Decades of Cold War rhetoric had left Americans determined to stay ahead of the Soviets militarily and to play a forceful world role. Reagan's uncomplicated patriotism, his calls for military strength, and his paeans to America's continued greatness soothed a battered national psyche.

Reagan also embraced the ideology of the so-called New Right: a cultural conservatism stressing social and moral issues. The social turmoil and sexual revolution of the 1960s; the women's movement; rising rates of abortion and divorce; the more open expression of homosexuality; the pervasiveness of sex and violence in the mass media; and "secular humanism" in school textbooks—all upset millions of Americans, who longed for a restoration of morality and "traditional values." Jerry Falwell's Moral Majority and other groups eagerly translated such concerns into political action.

Demographics also played a role in Reagan's success. Whereas New York City, Chicago, Detroit, and other Northeast and upper Midwest cities lost population during the 1970s, Texas, California, Florida, and other Sunbelt states, historically conservative politically and suspicious of Washington, rapidly gained. In 1978 Californians passed Proposition 13, a referendum calling for sharp cuts in state taxes. Elsewhere in the West, ranchers and developers demanded a return of federal lands to state control.

Ronald Reagan, a skillful actor and seasoned public speaker, combined these themes and concerns into a potent message. Belying his sixty-nine years, he conveyed a youthful jauntiness. At a time of national malaise, he seemed to offer confident, assured leadership. Time would reveal gaps between substance and image in Reagan's appeal, but in 1980 a majority of voters found it irresistible.

### The Man Behind the Movement

Reagan grew up in Dixon, Illinois, the son of an alcoholic father and a pious mother active in the Disciples of Christ church. After graduating from Eureka College, he worked as a sports announcer in Des Moines and in 1937 set out for Hollywood. His fifty-four films proved forgettable, but he was active in union politics as president of the Screen Actors' Guild. In 1954 he became a corporate spokesman for the General Electric Company. A New Dealer in the 1930s, Reagan had moved to the right in the 1950s. In a 1964 TV speech for presidential candidate Barry Goldwater, he eloquently praised American individualism and the free-enterprise system.

Elected governor of California in 1966 with the help of a group of California millionaires, Reagan continued to popularize conservative ideas while proving himself capable of compromise. He nearly won the Republican presidential nomination in 1976, and in 1980 he easily disposed of his principal opponent, George Bush, whom he then chose as his running mate.

Like his one-time political hero Franklin Roosevelt, Reagan promised the American people a new deal. But

**Hail to the (Virtual) Chief**
*A master of television, President Reagan was at his best in carefully staged appearances, such as this one at the 1984 Republican National Convention.*

unlike FDR's New Deal, Reagan's offered smaller government, reduced taxes and spending, and untrammelled free enterprise.

Hammering at the question "Are you better off now than you were four years ago?" Reagan garnered almost 51 percent of the popular vote to Carter's 41 percent.* Republicans gained eleven Senate seats, and with them, for the first time since 1955, a majority. These Senate victories revealed the power of conservative political-action groups (PACs), which used computerized mass mailings focusing on emotional issues like abortion and gun control. (PACs were not confined to conservatives; organizations of all ideological stripes used them.)

Reaping the benefits of Richard Nixon's southern strategy, Reagan carried every southern state except Carter's own Georgia as well as every state west of the Mississippi except Minnesota and Hawaii. Over half the nation's blue-collar workers voted Republican. Of FDR's New Deal political alliance, only black voters remained firmly Democratic.

## *Reaganomics*

The new president's economic program, called Reaganomics by the media, boiled down to the belief that U.S. capitalism, if freed from heavy taxes and government regulation, would achieve wonders of productivity. Reagan's first budget message proposed a 30 percent reduction in federal income taxes over three years. Trimming this proposal slightly, Congress voted a 25 percent income tax cut: 5 percent in 1981 and 10 percent in 1982 and 1983.

To make up for the lost revenues, Reagan proposed massive cuts in such programs as school lunches, student loans, job training, and urban mass transit. Congress went along to some extent, slashing more than $40 billion from domestic spending (less than Reagan had requested). Conservative, mostly southern Democrats, nicknamed boll weevils, joined Republicans in voting these cuts. Journalists harked back to FDR's "Hundred Days" of 1933 to find a time when government had shifted gears so dramatically. Economists warned that the tax cut, even with reduced spending, would produce huge federal deficits, but Reagan insisted that lower tax rates would stimulate business growth and thereby push up total tax revenues.

---

\* An independent candidate, liberal Republican congressman John Anderson, collected most of the balance.

Reaganomics also meant drastic cutbacks in federal regulation of business. Deregulation had begun under Carter, but Reagan extended it into new areas such as banking, the savings-and-loan industry, transportation, and communications. The head of the Federal Communications Commission hacked away at federal rules governing the broadcast industry. The secretary of transportation cut back on the regulations Congress had passed in the 1970s to reduce air pollution and improve vehicle efficiency and safety. Secretary of the Interior James Watt opened federal wilderness areas, forest lands, and coastal waters to developers. But although the Reagan administration's attack on "big government" affected certain federal functions, particularly in the regulatory realm, it had little overall effect. The century-long growth of the federal budget and of the federal bureaucracy continued in the 1980s.

While implementing Reaganomics, the administration also faced the immediate problem of inflation. The Federal Reserve Board led the charge, pushing the discount rate ever higher. This harsh medicine, coupled with a drop in oil prices, did its job. Inflation fell to around 4 percent in 1983 and held steady thereafter.

## *Recession and Boom Times*

The high interest rates necessary to curb inflation again spawned a recession. By late 1982, unemployment stood at 10 percent. As funding for social programs dried up, the plight of the poor worsened. Blacks and Hispanics of the inner cities suffered severely.

The Reagan recession also contributed to falling exports. (As foreign investors bought dollars to earn high American interest rates, the dollar rose in value vis-à-vis foreign currencies, making U.S. goods more expensive abroad.) The decline in exports—coupled with big increases in imports of TVs, stereos, and automobiles from Japan and other countries—propelled the U.S. trade deficit (the gap between exports and imports) from $31 billion in 1981 to $111 billion in 1984.

The industrial heartland reeled under the triple blow of slumping exports, foreign competition, and technological obsolescence. The aging steel mills, auto companies, and other industries of the Midwest and Great Lakes region laid off hordes of workers; some plants closed. In 1979–1983, 11.5 million American workers lost jobs as a result of plant closings or slack work. Farmers suffered as well. Wheat exports fell 38 percent from 1980 to 1985, and corn exports by

49 percent. In foreclosure sales evocative of the 1930s, many family farms were lost.

Soaring federal deficits added to the economic muddle. Reagan's tax cuts reduced federal revenues without immediately producing the predicted business boom, while increased military appropriations far exceeded domestic spending cuts. With the economy sputtering, budget deficits mounting, and critics denouncing him as callous toward the poor, Reagan in 1982–1983 accepted a reduced rate of military spending, a slowing of funding cuts in social programs, emergency job programs, and various tax increases disguised as "revenue-enhancement measures."

Despite a stock-market upturn, the economy remained worrisome throughout 1982. In the elections that fall, the Democrats gained twenty-six House seats. Like too many recent presidents, Reagan appeared headed for failure. But 1983 brought an economic rebound. Encouraged by tax cuts, a drop in interest rates, and, above all, by evidence that inflation had been tamed at last, consumers went on a buying binge. Unemployment dropped, the gross national product rose nearly 10 percent, and Reagan's reputation revived.

With better times came a wave of stock-market speculation reminiscent of the 1920s. The bull market began on August 12, 1982, when the Dow Jones average stood at 777, and it lasted for five years. Entrepreneurs like Donald Trump, a Manhattan real estate tycoon, and Ivan Boesky, an apparent genius at stock transactions, became celebrities. E. F. Hutton and other brokerage firms advertised heavily to lure new investors. Corporate mergers proliferated. Chevron bought Gulf for $13 billion in 1984; GE acquired RCA (and its NBC subsidiary) for $6.3 billion in 1986. And the stock market roared on. Banks and savings-and-loan companies, newly deregulated and flush with the deposits of eager investors, lent billions to developers planning shopping malls, luxury apartments, retirement villages, and office buildings.

But the Wall Street feeding frenzy had its down side. In 1985 E. F. Hutton officials pled guilty to manipulating funds in ways that defrauded hundreds of banks. Ivan Boesky went to prison after his 1986 conviction for insider trading (profiting through advance knowledge of planned corporate actions). Then on October 19, 1987, came a stock market crash. The Dow plunged 508 points as one-fifth of the paper value of the nation's stocks evaporated. Thanks to prompt government action to ease credit the market soon recovered, but the 1987 collapse did remind giddy investors that stocks can go down as well as up.

Even during the great bull market, economic problems remained. The trade gap widened; the deficit passed $200 billion in 1986; and many farmers, inner-city poor, and displaced industrial workers did not share in the boom times. But by mid-1988—just in time for Reagan's reelection campaign—the overall economic picture looked brighter than it had in years.

## Reagan Confronts the "Evil Empire"

The anti-Soviet rhetoric of the late 1970s intensified during Reagan's first term. Addressing a convention of Protestant evangelicals, the president blasted the Soviet Union as "the focus of evil in the modern world." Anti-Soviet fury exploded in September 1983, when the Russians shot down a Korean passenger plane that had strayed into their airspace, killing all 269 aboard.*

The administration's anti-Soviet obsession influenced its policy toward El Salvador and Nicaragua, two poor nations caught up in revolutionary turmoil. The Reagan White House backed the Salvadoran military junta in its suppression of a leftist insurgency backed by Cuba and Nicaragua. A moderate won the 1984 presidential election with U.S. support, but the killing of suspected leftists went on.

In Nicaragua the Carter administration initially extended aid to the Sandinista revolutionaries who overthrew dictator Anastasio Somoza in 1979. But Reagan reversed this policy, claiming that the leftist Sandinistas were turning Nicaragua into a procommunist state like Castro's Cuba. The CIA in 1982 organized and financed a ten-thousand-man anti-Sandinista guerrilla army, called the contras, based in neighboring Honduras and Costa Rica. The contras, many with links to the deposed Somoza regime, conducted raids, planted mines, and carried out sabotage inside Nicaragua.

Fearing another Vietnam, Americans grew alarmed as details of this U.S.-run "covert" war leaked out. Congress voted a yearlong halt in U.S. military aid to the contras in December 1982 and imposed a two-year ban in October 1984. But Reagan's enthusiasm for the contras held steady. Secret contra aid, funded from right-wing sources and foreign governments, and organized within the White House, continued despite congressional prohibitions. A 1988 truce between the Sandinistas and the contras, arranged by Central American leaders, won grudging backing by Reagan, still hoping for a contra victory.

---

* Moscow claimed that the plane had been spying but later abandoned this excuse.

Reagan's militarization of American foreign policy fell heavily on the tiny West Indian island of Grenada, where a 1983 coup had brought a radical leftist government to power. On October 25, 1983, two thousand U.S. Marines invaded Grenada and installed a government friendly to the United States. Democrats voiced sharp criticism, but most Grenadians, as well as other West Indian governments, expressed their approval.

### Tragedy and Frustration in the Middle East

Hoping to stem the spread of radical Islamic fundamentalism, the United States tilted toward Saddam Hussein's Iraq in its long war with Iran, although Washington also courted perceived "moderates" in Iran. Meanwhile, the administration viewed the conflicts among Israel, the faction-ridden PLO, and Syria through the prism of Soviet-Western rivalries.

In August 1981 Israel and the PLO concluded a cease-fire, but the PLO continued building up its forces and carved out a sanctuary in southern Lebanon. In June 1982, when the Abu Nidal group—extremists within the PLO who advocated all-out struggle with Israel—critically wounded Israel's ambassador to Great Britain, Israeli troops invaded Lebanon, defeated the PLO militarily, and forced its leaders to evacuate Lebanon. The invasion also intensified the civil war among Lebanese Christian and Muslim factions. A Christian militia took the opportunity to massacre Palestinians in a refugee camp near Beirut.

After the Beirut massacre, two thousand American marines entered Lebanon as part of a multinational peacekeeping force. But the Muslim militias saw the Americans as favoring Israel and the Christian side. In October 1983, a Shiite Muslim crashed an explosive-laden truck into a poorly guarded barracks, killing 239 marines. Reagan had not made clear how the deployment served U.S. interests, and the disaster further discredited his Lebanese policy. By early 1984 he withdrew the marines.

Disappointment also dogged Reagan's attempt to promote a wider Middle Eastern settlement. In September 1982, the president tried to use the Lebanese crisis to jump-start Arab-Israeli peace talks along the lines envisioned by the Camp David Accords, and he stressed the urgency of the Palestinian question. The administration tried to bring Arafat and Jordan's King Hussein together for a "Jordanian solution" to the West Bank question. But this effort was scuttled by Syrian opposition to being excluded from the process, by the PLO's reluctance to come under a Jordanian "umbrella," and by Israel's security fears.

### Military Buildup and Antinuclear Protest

Convinced that the United States had grown dangerously weak since Vietnam, Reagan launched a massive military expansion. The Pentagon's budget swelled from $171 billion in 1981 to more than $300 billion by 1985. With the subsequent collapse of the Soviet Union, Reagan's supporters would claim that Moscow's efforts to match Reagan's military buildup was the final blow to an already weak Soviet economy.

**The Nuclear-Freeze Campaign, 1982**

*A movement to halt the nuclear arms race arose in the early Reagan years. These New York City marchers on June 12, 1982, were part of a rally that drew 800,000 demonstrators to Central Park.*

Others, however, traced the Soviet collapse primarily to structural weaknesses within the USSR itself.

The Reagan military buildup included nuclear weapons. Secretary of State Alexander Haig spoke of the possible utility of "nuclear warning shots" in a conventional war, and other administration officials mused about the "winnability" of nuclear war. Despite popular protests in parts of Europe, the administration in 1983 deployed 572 cruise and Pershing II missiles in Western Europe, fulfilling a NATO decision, counterbalancing Soviet missiles in Eastern Europe.

The Federal Emergency Management Agency promulgated a nuclear-war defense plan whereby city residents would flee to small towns. A Defense Department official argued that backyard shelters would provide protection in a nuclear conflagration. "With enough shovels," he asserted, "everybody's going to make it."

Such talk, coupled with the military buildup, the faltering arms-control process, and Reagan's anti-Soviet rhetoric, sparked a grass-roots reaction as many Americans perceived a growing threat of nuclear war. This response took the form of a campaign for a superpower freeze on the manufacture and deployment of nuclear weapons. Early in 1982 several New England town meetings adopted freeze resolutions; that summer, antinuclear protesters packed New York's Central Park; freeze resolutions passed that November in nine states, including California and Wisconsin.

Responding to the pressure, the administration in June 1982 proposed the removal of all medium-range nuclear missiles from Europe and resumed talks with the Soviets on strategic-arms reductions. To neutralize the freeze movement, Reagan in March 1983 proposed the Strategic Defense Initiative (SDI), a system of space-based lasers and other high-tech defenses against nuclear missiles. Quickly nicknamed Star Wars, SDI drew upon Americans' deep faith in technology. The Pentagon launched an SDI research program, but critics warned of the project's prohibitive cost, technical implausibility, and the likelihood that it would further escalate the nuclear-arms race.

### Reagan Reelected

As the 1984 election neared, liberal Democrats and many independents criticized the Reagan presidency for runaway military spending, Cold War belligerence, massive budget deficits, cuts in social programs, and assaults on the government's regulation of corpora-

tions. To critics, jingoism abroad and selfishness at home summed up the meaning of Reaganism.

But many Americans applauded Reagan's attacks on big government and his get-tough policy toward the Soviets. Rhetoric aside, the administration had some solid achievements to its credit, notably an end to rampant inflation and a booming economy. Reagan's personal popularity, moreover, remained high. Some dubbed him the Teflon president—nothing seemed to stick to him. Feminists welcomed his 1981 nomination of Sandra Day O'Connor as the first woman justice on the U.S. Supreme Court. And Americans admired Reagan's jaunty response when a ricocheting bullet fired by a mentally disturbed young man struck him in the chest as he left a Washington hotel on March 30, 1981. Rushed to the hospital, Reagan walked in under his own steam, quipping to the physicians, 'Please tell me you're all Republicans."* By 1984 many citizens believed that Reagan had delivered on his promise to revitalize the free-enterprise system, rebuild U.S. military might, and make the nation again "stand tall" in the world.

The 1984 Republican convention, staged for television, accented themes of patriotism, prosperity, and the personality of Ronald Reagan. The Democratic hopefuls included Gary Hart, a former Colorado senator, and Jesse Jackson, a Chicago black leader who proposed a "rainbow coalition" of African Americans, Hispanics, displaced workers, and other outsiders in Reagan's America.

But former vice president Walter Mondale won the nomination, securing endorsements from labor unions, party bigwigs, and various interest groups. His vice-presidential choice, New York congresswoman Geraldine Ferraro, thus became the first woman to run on a major-party presidential ticket.

Amid general prosperity, Reagan and Bush won 59 percent of the popular vote and carried every state but Mondale's Minnesota and the District of Columbia. Many traditionally Democratic voters, especially blue-collar workers, again defected to Reagan. Despite Ferraro's presence on the Democratic ticket, a higher percentage of women voted Republican in 1984 than in 1980.

Reagan's ideological appeal and his mastery of television, combined with a booming economy, had car-

---

* The attack disabled Reagan's press secretary, James Brady, who with his wife Sarah later became a leader in the campaign for toughened gun-control laws.

ried the day. Though the Democrats retained control of Congress and remained strong at the state and local level, the Republicans' post-1968 dominance of presidential politics—interrupted only by Jimmy Carter's single term—continued.

# Problems and Opportunities in Reagan's Second Term

In his first term, Ronald Reagan set the political agenda: tax cuts, deregulation, expanded military spending. In his second term, events began to overtake the Reagan White House. The budget deficit and trade gap continued to grow, and the so-called Iran-contra scandal erupted in 1986. But all this was eclipsed by a dramatic easing of Cold War tensions capped by Reagan's historic trip to Moscow in 1988. Despite problems and scandals, Reagan left office in 1989 with high approval ratings.

## Tax Reform, Budget Deficits, and Trade Gaps

Reagan's second term brought significant legislative achievements, including the Immigration Reform and Control Act of 1986 and a tax-reform law that made the system fairer by eliminating many deductions and establishing uniform rates for people at comparable income levels. The law also removed some 6 million low-income Americans from the income-tax rolls. Reagan also reshaped the Supreme Court and the federal judiciary in his own conservative image.

But sky-high federal deficits—the legacy of Reaganomics—grew worse. The deficit gushed to over $200 billion in 1985 and 1986 and hovered at about $150 billion in 1987 and 1988. This, coupled with a trade gap that surged to more than $152 billion in 1986 and 1987, were Reagan's principal economic legacies to his successor.

## Middle East Encore: Talks and Terrorism

The Middle East continued to spell trouble. In December 1987 a Palestinian uprising against Israeli occupation began in Gaza and the West Bank. In response, Secretary of State George Shultz tried to bring Jordan and the Palestinians into negotiations with Israel over a Palestinian autonomy plan. But the Israeli government rejected the "land for peace" formula and refused to negotiate with the Palestinians until the uprising ended; and the Palestinians rejected Shultz's proposals as not going far enough toward creating a Palestinian state. Despite U.S. opposition, Israel continued to build Jewish settlements in the disputed West Bank region.

A deadly by-product of the Middle East conflict came in the later 1980s in the form of kidnappings, airplane hijackings, airport attacks, and other terrorist acts linked to Palestinians and their backers, including Muammar el-Qaddafi, Libya's ruler. In April 1986, after a Libyan-directed bombing of a Berlin nightclub popular with American GIs, U.S. bombers hit five Libyan military sites. In the worst of the terrorist incidents, a Pan Am jet flying from London to New York in December 1988 crashed in Scotland, killing all 259 aboard, including many Americans. Experts quickly identified a concealed bomb as the cause. In 1991, the U.S. and Great Britain formally blamed Libya for the Pan Am bombing. But Qaddafi denied the charges and refused until 1999 to extradite the accused officials for trial.

## The Iran-Contra Scandal

The Mideast also spawned the worst scandal to hit the Reagan presidency. Late in 1986 a Beirut newspaper reported that in 1985 the United States had shipped, via Israel, 508 antitank missiles to the anti-American government of Iran. Admitting the sale, Reagan said that the aim had been to encourage "moderate elements" in Tehran and to gain the release of American hostages held in Lebanon by pro-Iranian groups. In February 1987 a presidentially appointed investigative

**The Election of 1984**

| Candidates | Parties | Electoral Vote | Popular Vote | Percentage of Popular Vote |
|---|---|---|---|---|
| RONALD REAGAN | Republican | 525 | 54,451,521 | 58.8 |
| Walter Mondale | Democratic | 13 | 37,565,334 | 40.5 |

panel placed heavy blame on Reagan's chief of staff, Donald Regan, who resigned.

But more details soon spilled out, including the explosive revelation that Lieutenant Colonel Oliver North, a National Security Council aide, had diverted the profits from the Iran arms sales to the Nicaraguan contras (opponents of Nicaragua's Marxist government) at a time when Congress had forbidden such aid. In November 1986, just before FBI investigators arrived, North and his secretary, as they later admitted, altered and deleted sensitive computer files and destroyed incriminating documents. North also implicated CIA director William Casey in illegalities, but Casey's death in May 1987 thwarted this line of investigation.

In the summer of 1987, a joint House-Senate committee investigated the charges. The nation watched in fascination as "Ollie" North, resplendent in his marine uniform, portrayed himself as a true patriot, and as former national security adviser John Poindexter testified that he had deliberately concealed the fund-diversion scheme from Reagan.

The committee found no proof of Reagan's personal knowledge of illegalities, but roundly criticized the lax management style and disregard for the law that had fed the scandal. Meanwhile, early in 1988, a court-appointed special prosecutor, Lawrence Walsh, indicted Poindexter, North, and others. In 1989 a federal jury convicted North of obstructing a congressional inquiry and destroying and falsifying official documents. A federal judge reversed this conviction in 1991 on the technicality that some testimony used against North had been given under a promise of immunity. Although less damaging than Watergate, the Iran-contra scandal dogged the Reagan administration's final years as a serious abuse of executive power.

### More Scandals and Embarrassments

Other revelations plagued Reagan's second term, including allegations of bribery and conspiracy in military-procurement contracts. Ironically, Reagan's closest associates caused some of his worst problems. His old friend Attorney General Edwin Meese became a target of investigation for allegedly using his influence to promote ventures in which he had a financial interest. Meese resigned in July 1988. In *For the Record* (1988), former chief of staff Donald Regan, still smarting over his forced resignation, portrayed Reagan as little more than an automaton: "Every moment of every public appearance was scheduled, every word was scripted, every place where Reagan was expected to

stand was chalked with toe marks." In 1989 came revelations that former interior secretary James Watt and other prominent Republicans had been paid hundreds of thousands of dollars for using their influence on behalf of housing developers seeking federal subsidies.

Reagan's popularity seemed unaffected by all this dirty linen. Drawing on his conservative convictions and his training as an actor, Reagan possessed an uncanny ability to articulate the beliefs and aspirations of millions of Americans. Moreover, Reagan benefited from an unanticipated turn of events abroad that would end his presidency on a note of triumph.

### Reagan's Mission to Moscow

A dramatic warming of Soviet-American relations began early in Reagan's second term. Meeting at Geneva in 1985 and Reykjavík, Iceland, in 1986, Reagan and Soviet leader Mikhail Gorbachev revived the lifeless arms-control negotiations. Beset by economic problems at

**President Reagan Visits Red Square**
*As the Cold War crumbled, President Reagan flew to Moscow in 1988 to sign a nuclear-arms reduction treaty with Soviet premier Mikhail Gorbachev.*

**Milestones in Nuclear-Arms Control**

| Year | Event | Provisions |
|------|-------|------------|
| 1963 | Limited Test Ban Treaty | Prohibits atmospheric, underwater, and outer-space nuclear testing. |
| 1967 | Outer Space Treaty | Prohibits weapons of mass destruction and arms testing in space. |
| 1968 | Non-Proliferation Treaty | Promotes peaceful international uses of nuclear energy; aims to stop the global proliferation of nuclear weaponry. |
| 1972 | Strategic Arms Limitation Treaty (SALT I) | Limits for five years U.S. and Soviet deployment of strategic weapons systems. |
| | Anti-Ballistic Missile (ABM) Treaty | Restricts U.S. and Soviet testing and deployment of defensive systems. |
| 1974 | Threshold Test Ban Treaty | Establishes limits on size of underground tests. |
| 1979 | Strategic Arms Limitation Treaty (SALT II) (Unratified) | Limits strategic launch vehicles and delivery craft and restricts the development of new missiles. (The treaty was never ratified, but the United States and the Soviet Union observed its terms.) |
| 1982 | Strategic Arms Reduction (START) Talks | Seeks 50 percent reduction in U.S. and Soviet strategic nuclear weapons. |
| 1988 | Intermediate-Range Nuclear Forces (INF) Treaty | Commits the United States and the Soviet Union to withdraw their intermediate-range nuclear missiles from Eastern and Western Europe and to destroy them. |
| 1991 | START Treaty | Provides for a 25 percent cut in U.S. and Soviet strategic nuclear weapons. |

home, Gorbachev pursued an easing of superpower tensions to gain a breathing space for domestic reform.

In 1987 the two sides agreed on a treaty providing for the removal of 2,500 U.S. and Soviet missiles from Europe. This treaty for the first time eliminated an entire class of *existing* nuclear weapons rather than merely limiting the number of *future* weapons as SALT I had done. This agreement, in turn, led to Reagan's historic visit to Moscow in May 1988, where the two leaders established a cordial personal relationship.

After Nixon's political disgrace, Ford's caretaker presidency, and Carter's problem-ridden tenure, Ronald Reagan served two full terms, helped restore national pride and had the good fortune to hold office as the Cold War thawed and the Soviet menace faded. Domestically, he chalked up a mixed record. Inflation was tamed, and after 1983 the economy turned upward. But the federal deficit soared, and the administration largely ignored serious social issues and structural weaknesses in the economy. Despite Reagan's popularity, his image faded quickly. From the perspective of the later 1990s, the Reagan years seemed more an interlude of nostal-

gia and drift than of positive achievement—a time when individual gain look precedence over the public sphere. But détente, derailed in the late 1970s, was not only back on track but barreling ahead.

## The Election of 1988

As the 1988 election approached, Vice President George Bush easily bested Kansas senator Robert Dole to win the Republican presidential nomination. A large group of contenders for the Democratic nomination eventually narrowed to two: Jesse Jackson and Massachusetts governor Michael Dukakis. Jackson, preaching concern for the poor and urging a full-scale war on drugs, ran well in the primaries. But Dukakis victories in major primary states like New York and California proved decisive. As his running mate, Dukakis chose Texas senator Lloyd Bentsen.

Accepting the Republican nomination, Bush called for a "kinder, gentler America" and pledged: "Read my lips: no new taxes." As his running mate, Bush selected Senator Dan Quayle of Indiana, the son of a wealthy

### The Election of 1988

| | Electoral Vote | Popular Vote | Percentage of Popular Vote |
|---|---|---|---|
| **Republican** George H. Bush | 426 | 47,946,422 | 54.0 |
| **Democratic** Michael S. Dukakis | 112 | 41,016,429 | 46.0 |

Alaska 3
Hawaii 4
Washington, D.C. 3

newspaper publisher. In the campaign he stressed Reagan's achievements while distancing himself from the Iran-contra scandal. Emphasizing peace and prosperity, he pointed to better Soviet relations, low inflation, and the 14 million new jobs created during the eighties—an achievement unmatched by any other industrial nation.

A TV commercial aired by Bush supporters, playing on racist stereotypes, featured a black man who committed rape and murder after his release under a Massachusetts prisoner-furlough program. Bush assailed Dukakis's veto of a bill requiring Massachusetts schoolchildren to recite the Pledge of Allegiance, even though the Supreme Court had declared such laws unconstitutional. In response, Dukakis emphasized his accomplishments as governor. "This election is not about ideology, it's about competence," he insisted. He hammered at the failures of the "Swiss-cheese" Reagan economy and urged "Reagan Democrats" to return to the party. But Dukakis seemed edgy and defensive, and his dismissal of ideology made it difficult for him to define his vision of America. Even Dukakis supporters wearied of his stock phrases and his repeated boasts of his managerial skills.

Both candidates avoided serious issues in favor of TV-oriented "photo opportunities" and "sound bites." Bush visited flag factories and military plants. Dukakis proved his toughness on defense by posing in a tank. Editorial writers grumbled about the "junk-food" campaign, but fleeting visual images, catchy phrases, and

twenty-second spots on the evening news had seemingly become the essence of presidential politics.

On November 8, Bush carried forty states and garnered 54 percent of the vote. Dukakis prevailed in only ten states plus the District of Columbia. The Democrats, however, retained control of both houses of Congress and most state legislatures.

## The Bush Years: Resolve Abroad, Drift at Home

George Bush was a patrician in politics. The son of a Connecticut senator, he had attended Yale and fought in World War II before entering the Texas oil business. He had served in Congress, lost a Senate race, and directed the CIA before being tapped as Ronald Reagan's running mate in 1980.

As president, Bush compiled an uneven record. Internationally, his administration responded positively to upheavals in the Soviet Union, reacted decisively when Iraq invaded Kuwait, took positive steps in Latin America, and worked to ease Israeli-Palestinian tensions. But on domestic issues, Bush substituted platitudes for policy. In retrospect, the Bush interlude seems primarily a postscript to the Reagan era.

### The Cold War Ends

The collapse of Soviet power proceeded with breathtaking rapidity. When Gorbachev refused to send troops to prop up unpopular Marxist regimes in Eastern Europe, they gave way to new democratic, noncommunist governments. In November 1989, the Berlin Wall, a grim Cold War symbol, was opened and Germany reunited for the first time since 1945. The Baltic republics—Estonia, Latvia, and Lithuania—forcibly annexed by the Soviet Union on the eve of World War II, declared independence. Calls for autonomy resounded within the other Soviet republics as well.

The Cold War was over. In August 1991 President Bush and Mikhail Gorbachev signed a treaty in Moscow reducing their strategic nuclear arsenals by 25 percent. The nuclear-arms race seemed over as well. Secretary of Defense Dick Cheney proposed a 25 percent reduction in U.S. military forces over five years. With the Soviet-sponsored Warsaw Pact ended, NATO announced plans for a 50 percent troop reduction.

As the Soviet Communist party's centralized control collapsed, the nation's economy sank into crisis. Soviet reformers called for a market economy on the Western capitalist model, but the opposition still posed a threat. On August 21, 1991, hard-line Communist party leaders in Moscow tried to overthrow Gorbachev. But hundreds of thousands of Muscovites, rallied by Boris Yeltsin, president of the Russian Republic, protectively surrounded the Russian parliament and the coup failed. Gorbachev briefly returned to power, but Yeltsin increasingly assumed the dominant role.

Exuberant crowds toppled statues of Lenin and other communist leaders across the Sovet Union. Leningrad reverted to its tsarist name, St. Petersburg. As the various Soviet republics rushed to independence, Mikhail Gorbachev was overwhelmed by forces he himself had unleashed. The coup attempt stripped the last shred of legitimacy from the Soviet Communist party. And later that year most of the Soviet republics proclaimed the end of the USSR. Bowing to the inevitable, Gorbachev resigned.

Dealing with these complexities was Secretary of State James Baker, a long-time Bush ally who had served as chief of staff and treasury secretary under Reagan. Bush and Baker proceeded cautiously as the Soviet empire disintegrated. America's influence was limited, in any event, as long-suppressed forces of nationalism and ethnicity burst forth in Eastern Europe and in the former Soviet Union itself.

One issue of vital concern was the future of the Soviet arsenal of 27,000 nuclear weapons, based not only in Russia but in newly independent Ukraine, Belarus, and Kazakhstan. Baker worked to ensure the security and orderly dismantling of these weapons and to prevent the flow of nuclear-weapons technology and know-how to other nations. As strategic talks with Yeltsin and other leaders went forward, Bush announced further major reductions in the U.S. nuclear arsenal.

In some respects, the Cold War's end made it easier to settle regional conflicts. For decades the superpowers had given aid to their client states and rebel forces throughout the Third World. As the Cold War faded, the prospect for resolving local disputes brightened.

Evidence for this change appeared in Latin America. In Nicaragua, Bush abandoned Reagan's failed policy of financing the contra's war against the leftist Sandinista government. Instead, Bush and Congress worked out a program aimed at reintegrating the contras into Nicaraguan life and politics. In the 1990 elections in Nicaragua, the victory went to a multiparty anti-Sandinista coalition.

**End of the Berlin Wall, November 1989**
*As East German border guards watch passively, a West Berliner pounds away at the hated symbol of a divided city.*

Monumental problems linked to poverty, ignorance, and economic exploitation still plagued Latin America, however, and open guerrilla war continued in Peru. The flow of cocaine and heroin to U.S. cities from South America and Central America posed a serious problem. Indeed, in December 1989 concern over the drug traffic led to a U.S. invasion of Panama to capture the nation's strongman ruler, General Manuel Noriega. Formerly on the CIA payroll, Noriega had accepted bribes to permit drugs to pass uninterruptedly through Panama on their way north. Convicted of drug trafficking, Noriega was given a life prison term.

America's relations with the Philippines, a former colony and long-time U.S. ally, shifted as well. Resistance to the corrupt government of President Ferdinand Marcos intensified after the 1983 assassination of opposition leader Benigno Aquino. After a fraud-ridden election in 1986, Aquino's widow, Corazon, proclaimed

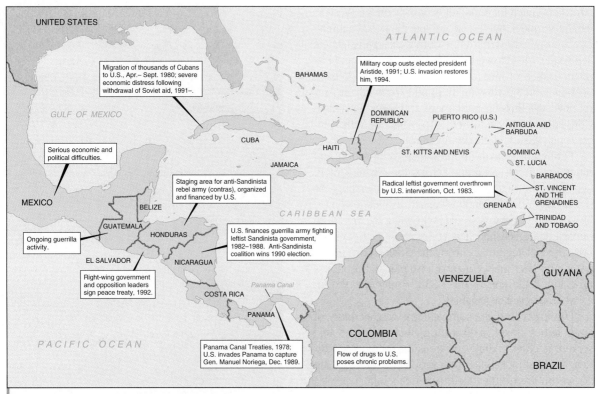

### The United States in Latin America and the Caribbean

*Plagued by poverty, population pressures, repressive regimes, and drug trafficking, Latin America saw turmoil and conflict—but also some hopeful developments—in the 1980s and 1990s.*

herself president and Marcos went into exile in Hawaii. In 1991, over Aquino's opposition, the Philippines legislature ended the agreement by which the United States had maintained two naval bases in the islands. With the Cold War over, the Bush administration accepted this decision and closed the bases.

South Africa had emerged as a focus of debate in Reagan's second term; Anglican bishop Desmond Tutu, a leader of South Africa's blacks, had rallied American support against South Africa's policy of racial segregation, called apartheid. In 1986, over a Reagan veto, Congress had imposed economic sanctions against South Africa, including a ban on U.S. business investments in South Africa. These sanctions, with similar actions by other nations, brought change to South Africa. In 1990 the government released black leader Nelson Mandela after a long imprisonment and opened negotiations with Mandela's African National Congress. When South Africa scrapped much of the nation's apartheid policy in 1991, President Bush lifted the economic sanctions.

China proved an exception to the world trend toward greater freedom. The United States' improved relations with China suffered a grievous setback in 1989, when the Chinese army crushed a prodemocracy demonstration by masses of unarmed students in Beijing's Tiananmen Square, killing an estimated four hundred to eight hundred young men and women. A wave of repression, arrests, and public executions followed. The Bush administration protested, curtailed diplomatic contacts, and urged international financial institutions to postpone loans to China. But Bush refrained from breaking diplomatic relations or canceling trade agreements with China, leaving these and other foreign-policy headaches to his successor.

As Cold War worries diminished, trade issues loomed large. The towering U.S. trade deficit with Japan stirred special concern. Although this gap dropped from its 1987 high of $55 billion, it hovered at $43 billion in 1991. Early in 1992, facing a recession and rising unemployment in an election year, President Bush turned a planned Asian trip into a trade mission.

He took along a team of U.S. business leaders, including the heads of the "big three" American auto companies, who tried, with little success, to persuade the Japanese to buy more U.S. products. When Bush collapsed and vomited from a sudden attack of flu at a state dinner in Tokyo, some found the mishap unhappily symbolic. As the Bush administration tried to chart a course in a world no longer dominated by superpower rivalry, one regional provocation elicited a clearcut, forceful response.

## Operation Desert Storm

On August 2, 1990, Iraq invaded the oil-rich sheikdom of Kuwait, with which it had a long-running dispute over the vast Rumaila oilfield. Iraq's dictator, Saddam Hussein, had dismissed Kuwait's independent-nation status as a creation of Western imperialists and asserted Iraq's historic claims to the region.

Under Saddam, Iraq for years had threatened not only Israel but the Arab nations as well. The Iraqi military buildup, including both chemical- and nuclear-weapons programs, had worried many governments in the 1980s. During the Iran-Iraq war from 1980 to 1988, however, the United States had tilted in Iraq's favor and even assisted in Iraq's military buildup, because Iran was rabidly anti-American. But Iranian hostility to the United States eased after the death of Ayatollah Khomeini in 1989, removing this incentive to placate Iraq. When Iraq invaded Kuwait, Washington reacted quickly.

Avoiding Lyndon Johnson's mistakes in the Vietnam era, Bush built a consensus for action in the Congress, at the U.N., and among the American people.

**Kuwait, 1991**
*Burning oilfields, set ablaze by retreating Iraqis, provide an eerie backdrop to motorized U.S. troops participating in Operation Desert Storm, the high point of the Bush presidency.*

**February 25 – 28, 1991**

**Operation Desert Storm: The Ground War**
*Preceding the ground operations that ended the war was a massive air assault. Iraq's Scud missile attacks on Israel and Saudi Arabia provided TV drama but had little effect on the war's outcome.*

He also articulated a clear military objective—Iraq's withdrawal from Kuwait—and deployed more than 400,000 troops in Saudi Arabia to achieve that goal. The U.N. imposed economic sanctions against Iraq and insisted that Saddam withdraw from Kuwait by January 15, 1991.

On January 12, after somber debate, the Senate by a 52 to 47 vote and the House (250–183) endorsed military action against Iraq. Most Democrats voted against war, favoring continued economic sanctions instead.

The air war began on January 16. For six weeks, U.S. B-52 and F-16 bombers, flying up to 3,000 sorties daily, pounded Iraqi troops, supply depots, and command targets in Iraq's capital, Baghdad. The air forces of other nations participated as well. In retaliation, Saddam ordered Soviet-made Scud missiles fired against Tel Aviv and other Israeli cities, as well as against the Saudi capital, Riyadh. Americans watched transfixed as CNN carried live coverage of U.S. Patriot missiles streaking off to intercept incoming Scuds. Indeed, as seen on TV, the war often seemed a glorified video game. The reality of an estimated 100,000 Iraqi deaths, military and civilian, hardly impinged on the national consciousness.

On February 23, 200,000 U.S. troops under General H. Norman Schwarzkopf moved across the desert toward Kuwait. Although rain turned the roadless sands to soup, the army ground on. Within three days Iraqi soldiers were in full flight or surrendering en masse. U.S. forces destroyed 3,700 Iraqi tanks while losing only three. With Iraqi resistance crushed, President Bush declared a cease-fire and members of Kuwait's ruling al-Sabah family returned from Cairo and other safe havens where they had sat out the war. Total American casualties numbered 148 dead—including 35 killed inadvertently by U.S. firepower—and 467 wounded.

Despite some campus protests, the war enjoyed broad public support. As the victory celebrations receded, however, the war's political aftermath came into focus. Saddam still held power. His army brutally suppressed uprisings against his rule by Shiite Muslims in the south and a large Kurdish ethnic minority in the north. With little alternative, Saddam agreed to grant U.N. inspection teams full access to his weapons-production facilities. Within a few years, however, Saddam would renege on this agreement. What seemed a stunning military success in 1991 appeared in a more ambiguous light a few years later, as Saddam Hussein's Iraq continued to preoccupy the United States and its U.N. allies.

## Domestic Discontents

The tax cuts, Pentagon spending, and deregulatory fervor of the "Reagan revolution" had roused entrepreneurial energies, fueled a stock-market surge, and set off an economic boom that gave the 1980s a glow of prosperity. In the early 1990s, however, the longer-term effects of Reaganism began to be felt. As the economy soured, the go-go eighties seemed remote. Bush's term brought rising economic discontent, especially among the middle class.

First came the collapse of the savings-and-loan (S&L) industry, which had long provided home loans to borrowers and a secure return to depositors. As interest rates rose in the late seventies, the S&Ls had been forced to pay high interest to attract deposits, even though most of their assets were in long-term, fixed-rate mortgages. In the early eighties, money freed up by the Reagan tax cuts flowed into S&Ls, with their high rates of return. In the fever to deregulate, the rules governing S&Ls were eased. Caught up in the high-flying mood of the eighties, S&Ls nationwide made risky loans on speculative real estate ventures. As the economy cooled, many of these investments went bad. In 1988–1990, nearly six hundred S&Ls failed, especially in the Southwest, wiping out many depositors.

Because the government insures savings-and-loan deposits, the Bush administration in 1989 set up a program to repay depositors and sell millions of dollars worth of foreclosed office towers and apartment buildings in a depressed real estate market. Estimates of the cost of the bailout topped $400 billion. " 'Savings and loan,' " wrote a journalist, "had become synonymous with 'bottomless pit.' "

The deficit, another problem linked to the Reagan tax cuts and military spending, continued to mount. In 1990, after testy negotiations, Congress and Bush agreed on a five-year deficit-reduction plan involving spending cuts and tax increases. Bush would pay a high political price for this retreat from his 1988 campaign pledge, "Read my lips: no new taxes."

Despite this agreement, the red ink flowed on. The deficit reached $290 billion in 1992. The total federal debt surpassed $3 trillion. The Gulf War, the S&L bailout, and soaring welfare and Medicare/Medicaid payments combined to undercut the budget-balancing effort.

To make matters worse, recession struck in 1990. Retail sales slumped; housing starts declined. The U.S. auto industry, battered by Japanese imports, fared disastrously. In December 1991 GM unveiled plans to cut its work force by more than seventy thousand. Hard times hung on into 1992, with a jobless rate of more than 7 percent. As the slowdown cut tax revenues, states slashed social-welfare funding. Michigan reduced AFDC payments by 17 percent, and other states planned similar cuts. The number of Americans below the poverty line rose by 2.1 million in 1990, to about 34 million. As the economy stumbled, the plight of the poor roused resentment rather than sympathy. Political strategists diagnosed a middle-class phenomenon they called "compassion fatigue." Declared Ohio's governor, "Most Ohioans have had enough welfare, enough poverty, enough drugs, enough crime."

In this bleaker economic climate, many Americans looked back on Reagan's policies with skepticism. If 1984 was "morning in America," wrote a columnist, quoting a Reagan campaign slogan, this was the "morning after." For most middle-class Americans, the situation was more anxiety-producing than desperate. Still, a gloomy economic picture clouded much of Bush's term.

Hard times worsened conditions in the inner cities. In April 1992 an outbreak of civil disorder, arson, and looting erupted in a poor black district of Los Angeles and spread to other parts of the city. The immediate cause was black rage and incredulity (shared by many others) over a jury's acquittal of four white Los Angeles police officers whose beating of a black motorist had been filmed on videotape. For several days the explosion of anger and pent-up frustration raged, leaving some forty persons dead and millions in property damage, and reminding the nation yet again of the desperate conditions in its inner cities.

Reflecting the priorities of the middle-class white majority, the Bush administration did little to address these issues. In 1990, when Congress passed a bill broadening federal protection against job discrimination, Bush vetoed it, claiming that it encouraged racial quotas in hiring.* When Bush came to Atlanta in 1992 on the birthday of Martin Luther King, Jr., King's daughter, a minister, asked bitterly, "How dare we celebrate in the midst of a recession, when nobody is sure whether their jobs are secure?"

The recession also stung public school budgets. Bush proclaimed himself the "education president" but addressed the issue only fitfully. Bush called for national testing of schoolchildren, supported a voucher system by which parents could enroll their children in private schools at public expense, and urged corporate

* In 1991, announcing that his concerns had been met, Bush signed a similar bill.

**South Central Los Angeles, 1992**
*Violenced erupted in this predominantly African-American, but ethnically mixed, part of the city after a white jury acquitted white policemen who had been videotaped beating an African-American motorist. Here a Korean-American merchant suggests the inadvisability of looting his shop.*

America to fund experimental schools. But such proposals hardly matched the magnitude of the problem.

The environmental issue was spotlighted in March 1989 when a giant oil tanker, the *Exxon Valdez,* ran aground in Alaska's Prince William Sound and spilled more than 10 million gallons of crude oil. The accident fouled coastal and marine habitats, killed thousands of sea otters and shore birds, and jeopardized Alaska's herring and salmon industries. That summer the Environmental Protection Agency (EPA) reported that air pollution in more than one hundred cities exceeded federal standards. In 1991 the EPA reported that pollutants were depleting the ozone shield over the United States—the layer that protects human life from cancer-causing solar radiation—at twice the rate scientists had predicted.

Squeezed between rising public concern and corporate calls for a go-slow policy, the Bush administration compiled a mixed record on the environment. Bush deplored the *Exxon Valdez* spill but defended oil exploration and drilling. In a bipartisan effort, the White House and the Democratic Congress passed a toughened Federal Clean Air Act in 1990. (California and other states enacted even stricter laws, tightening

**Cleaning Up After the *Exxon Valdez* Disaster**
*Volunteers collect and bag sea otters killed in the* Exxon Valdez *oil spill of March 1989, a catastrophe that focused attention on industrialization's mounting ecological toll.*

automobile-emission standards, for example.) In addition, the government began the costly task of disposing of radioactive wastes and cleaning up nuclear facilities that in some cases had been contaminating the soil and ground water for years.

But the Bush administration more often dismissed environmental concerns. Vice President Quayle ridiculed environmentalists; the administration scuttled treaties on global warming and mining in Antarctica, backed oil exploration in Alaskan wilderness preserves, and proposed to open vast tracts of protected wetlands to development. Bush's defensive, self-serving 1992 speech to a United Nations–sponsored international environmental conference in Rio de Janeiro further alienated environmentalists.

### The Supreme Court Moves Right

Like all presidents, Reagan and Bush sought to perpetuate their political ideology through their Supreme Court appointments. In addition to the Sandra Day O'Connor nomination, Reagan in 1986 named William Rehnquist chief justice to replace Warren Burger and chose another conservative, Antonin Scalia, to fill the Burger vacancy. When a third vacancy opened in 1987, Reagan nominated Robert Bork, a judge and legal scholar whose rigidity and doctrinaire opposition to judicial activism led the Senate to reject him. Reagan's next nominee withdrew after admitting that he had smoked marijuana. Reagan's third choice, Anthony Kennedy, a conservative California jurist, won quick confirmation.

President Bush made two Court nominations: David Souter in 1990 and Clarence Thomas in 1991. Souter, a New Hampshire judge, won easy confirmation. The Thomas nomination, however, proved very controversial. Bush nominated him to replace the retiring Thurgood Marshall, a black who had fought segregation as an NAACP lawyer. Thomas, also an African American, was notable mainly for espousing conservative causes and opposing affirmative-action programs. Having risen from poverty to attend Yale Law School and to head the Equal Employment Opportunity Commission (EEOC), Thomas viewed individual effort, not government programs, as the avenue of black progress. Noting Thomas's thin record as a federal appeals judge, critics charged Bush with playing the politics of race.

The nomination became more controversial when a former Thomas associate at EEOC, Anita Hill, charged him with sexual harassment. As the Senate Judiciary Committee explored Hill's accusations, the face-off dominated the nation's TV screens and heightened awareness of the harassment issue. In the end Thomas won confirmation, 52–48.

With these Reagan-Bush appointments, the social-activist thrust of the Court that had been inaugurated in Franklin Roosevelt's day and sustained in the 1950s and 1960s under Earl Warren and other justices was blunted. As we have seen, the Court took a generally skeptical view of affirmative-action programs. In a series of 5–4 rulings in 1989, the Court upheld a Missouri law limiting women's right to an abortion and imposed restrictions on civil-rights laws aimed at protecting the employment rights of women and minorities and remedying past inequities. In the 1990–1991 term, the Court narrowed the rights of arrested persons and upheld federal regulations barring physicians in federally funded clinics from discussing abortion with their clients. (A poll found that 71 percent of Americans opposed this intrusion in the doctor-patient relationship.) In a 5–4 decision in 1992, the Supreme Court upheld a Pennsylvania law placing various restrictions on abortion. The majority, however, led by a centrist group comprising Souter, O'Connor, and Kennedy, did affirm *Roe* v. *Wade,* the 1973 decision upholding women's constitutional right to an abortion.

### The Politics of Frustration

In the afterglow of Operation Desert Storm, George Bush's approval ratings hit 88 percent—only to fall below 50 percent as the recession eroded the nation's confidence. Bush proclaimed economic recovery his "No. 1 priority." But late in 1991 the *New York Times* damningly commented: "George Bush remains mystifyingly incomplete: shrewd and energetic in foreign policy . . . , clumsy and irresolute at home. . . . The domestic Bush flops like a fish, leaving the impression that he doesn't know what he thinks or doesn't much care, apart from the political gains to be extracted from an issue." In January 1992 Bush unveiled a package of recession-fighting proposals, including tax breaks for home buyers, lower taxes on capital gains, and tax incentives for business investment. Democrats dismissed this initiative as politically motivated and inadequate to the problem.

With Bush seemingly invulnerable after Operation Desert Storm, top Democrats stayed out of the 1992 presidential race. But Governor Bill Clinton of Arkansas took the plunge and, despite doubts about his character and stories of marital infidelity, defeated other hopefuls in the primaries. As his running mate, Clinton chose Senator Al Gore of Tennessee. At the party's convention in July, Clinton pledged an activist government addressing the environment, health care, and the economy. On abortion, he was strongly pro-choice. As Clinton oriented the party toward the middle class and muted its concern with the poor, traditional liberals and black leaders expressed uneasiness.

President Bush easily quashed a primary challenge by conservative columnist Pat Buchanan, but the Republican right dominated the party convention. Buchanan and evangelist Pat Robertson gave divisive speeches urging a GOP crusade in defense of "family values" and against abortion, sexual permissiveness, radical feminism, and gay rights. Delegates who belonged to Robertson's Christian Coalition cheered, but moderate Republicans deplored this rightward turn.

**"Read My Lips: No New Taxes"**
*As president, George Bush broke his 1988 campaign pledge not to raise taxes, contributing to his loss to Bill Clinton four years later.*

One gauge of voter disaffection was the presidential race of political outsider H. Ross Perot. At the peak of "Perotmania," nearly 40 percent of the voters supported the Texan, who had grown rich as founder and head of a data-processing firm. The nation's economic problems were simple, Perot insisted on TV talk shows; only party politics stood in the way of solving them. As president he would conduct electronic "town meetings" by which voters would judge his proposals. Where this left Congress remained unclear. Perot's autocratic ways and thin-skinned response to criticism turned off many supporters, and in July 1992 he left the race. But he reentered in time to take part in the televised presidential debates.

Bush attacked Clinton's character and charged that he had evaded the draft during the Vietnam War and later obscured the truth. Sensing voter anger over his failure to confront economic distress, Bush promised to put James A. Baker in charge of domestic affairs in a second term. Clinton, meanwhile, focused on the stagnant economy and the problems of the middle class. He pledged to work for a national health-care system, welfare reform, and a federal industrial policy to promote economic recovery and new technologies.

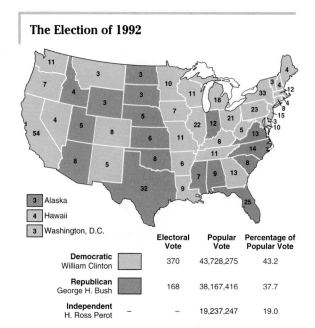

## The Election of 1992

|  | Electoral Vote | Popular Vote | Percentage of Popular Vote |
|---|---|---|---|
| **Democratic** William Clinton | 370 | 43,728,275 | 43.2 |
| **Republican** George H. Bush | 168 | 38,167,416 | 37.7 |
| **Independent** H. Ross Perot | – | – | 19,237,247 | 19.0 |

3 Alaska
4 Hawaii
3 Washington, D.C.

The voters spoke on November 3, when 43 percent chose Clinton. Bush trailed with 38 percent, and Perot amassed 19 percent—the largest share for a third party since Teddy Roosevelt's Bull Moose party got 27 percent in 1912.

Carrying such key swing states as California, Ohio, and New Jersey, Clinton lured back many blue-collar and suburban "Reagan Democrats" and made strides toward reclaiming the South for the Democrats. Younger voters, who had tilted Republican in 1984 and 1988, went for Clinton in 1992.

Most incumbents in Congress won reelection. In Pennsylvania, Republican senator Arlen Specter, a Judiciary Committee member who had roused women's anger by his harsh questioning of Anita Hill, narrowly beat back a challenge by a feminist political novice. But Congress was becoming less of a white male club and more representative of U.S. society as a whole. Thirty-eight African Americans and seventeen Hispanics won election. Colorado elected Native American Ben Nighthorse Campbell to the Senate, and a California congressional district sent the first Korean-American to Washington.

California became the first state to elect two women senators, Barbara Boxer and Diane Feinstein. Illinois sent the first African-American woman to the Senate, Carol Moseley Braun. Overall, the new Congress included fifty-three women: six in the Senate and forty-seven in the House. This outcome gave credence to those who had proclaimed 1992 the "Year of the Woman."

The 1992 election marked a shift of voter attention to domestic issues as the Cold War faded. With Democrats in control of both the legislative and executive branches of government, the end of the much-deplored Washington "gridlock" seemed possible. Formidable challenges confronted the new Congress and the new White House team. In the hopeful beginnings of his term, President Bill Clinton eagerly engaged those challenges.

## CONCLUSION

American culture in the 1970s and 1980s revealed sharply contradictory tendencies. On one hand, in reaction against the 1960s, a distinctly conservative mood prevailed. Recoiling from the activism and social conflicts of the later sixties, millions of middle-class Americans and even ex-radicals turned to personal pursuits and careerist goals. But at the same time, reformist energies rooted in the 1960s found expression in a revived women's movement, a gay-rights campaign, and a variety of environmentalist and consumer causes. But given the prevailing conservative climate, this activism stirred opposition as well as support.

On the economic front, these years brought equally divergent tendencies. In the 1970s a series of economic problems related to rising oil prices brought simultaneous economic stagnation and inflation that soured the national mood and shadowed the presidencies of Gerald Ford and Jimmy Carter. The economy in the 1980s was similarly mixed, with recessions at the beginning and at the end of the Reagan-Bush era bracketing a boom that suffused parts of Reagan's America with a glow of prosperity. As the economic cycle fluctuated, however, one unhappy constant remained: millions of Americans—mostly in the inner cities and mostly darker skinned minorities—seemed permanently frozen out of a high-tech economy that increasingly demanded education and specialized skills.

On the international front, the quartet of presidents from Ford to Bush grappled with a rapidly changing world in which solutions seemed maddeningly elusive. The Mideast, in particular, riven by ancient conflicts, brought moments of achievement interspersed with frustration and tragedy. As the Cold War rumbled on, seemingly forever, U.S.-Soviet relations worsened in the late 1970s and early 1980s. But the situation reversed with breathtaking speed as precipitous events in the Soviet Union produced nothing less than the end of the Cold War—certainly the most momentous event of the time period covered in this chapter. Beginning during Reagan's second term, this amazing development unfolded fully during George Bush's watch. Bush effectively forged an international coalition and rallied home-front support in shaping a military response to the first post-Cold War world crisis, Iraq's invasion of Kuwait. But more complex issues clearly lay ahead in a world no longer dominated by a conflict between two nuclear-armed superpowers. Unfortunately for Bush, his Gulf War burst of popularity quickly faded, as Americans became frustrated by his ineffectiveness on domestic issues, and by a worsening economic climate. This unpopularity translated into defeat at the polls in 1992, as a new historical era—or at least a new presidential administration—loomed on the horizon.

## FOR FURTHER READING

Robert Bellah et al., *Habits of the Heart* (1985). Reflections on the discontents of the American middle class in the early 1980s, drawn from extensive interviews.

Michael R. Beschloss and Strobe Talbott, *At the Highest Levels: The Inside Story of the End of the Cold War* (1994). A historian and a journalist-turned-diplomat collaborate on an early but informed account of the Cold War's demise.

Paul Boyer, ed., *Reagan as President* (1990). Contemporary speeches, articles, and editorials commenting on Reagan and his program, with an introduction by the editor.

Peter Carroll, *It Seemed Like Nothing Happened* (1983). A perceptive overview history of the 1970s.

Thomas Byrne Edsall with Mary D. Edsall, *Chain Reaction: The Impact of Race, Rights, and Taxes on American Politics* (1992). Insightful analysis of the social and economic sources of the rise of a conservative voting majority.

Haynes Johnson, *Sleepwalking Through History: America in the Reagan Years* (1991). A thoughtful account of American politics and culture in the 1980s by a seasoned *Washington Post* reporter.

J. Anthony Lucas, *Common Ground: A Turbulent Decade in the Lives of Three American Families* (1986). A skilled journalist offers an insightful, nuanced account of urban life in the 1980s as experienced by three Boston-area families.

Carl H. Nightingale, *On the Edge: A History of Poor Black Children and Their American Dreams* (1993). Moving presentation of the effect of inner-city poverty on its most vulnerable victims.

Garry Wills, *Reagan's America: Innocents at Home* (1987). A stimulating, wide-ranging work by a distinguished political writer.

# 33 Bright Prospects and Nagging Uncertainties for a New Century

**Massachusetts High School Students and a Teacher Admire Their Computer Web Page**

INTERNET

Wendy Scribner was thrilled when she received her Ph.D. in English from New York University in 1989. An older student, she had spent ten years writing her doctoral dissertation while teaching part-time to support her family, including a disabled spouse and two young sons. But now, she hoped, the doctoral degree would bring the career she dreamed of: a tenured position in a college or university, sharing her love of literature with students.

But Wendy Scribner's career didn't proceed quite as she had hoped. She found herself competing for scarce jobs with hundreds of other equally qualified new Ph.D.s. By 1998, at age fifty-six, instead of her dream career, she was working long hours as a part-time teacher at New York City Technical College in Brooklyn and Pace University in Manhattan. On a typical day she left home early to catch a train to Brooklyn, returned to Manhattan in the afternoon (crossing the Brooklyn Bridge on foot) to teach at Pace until 9:15 P.M. After a stop for groceries she arrived home exhausted, with time only for a hurried conversation with her family and a quick snack. For a while she also taught summer school and evening remedial classes to earn money for such extras as an air conditioner, but this proved too exhausting. As a part-time "adjunct" faculty member, Ms. Scribner had no real connection to the schools where she taught. She lacked even an office, desk, and telephone of her own. She was a resourceful and dedicated teacher, but her difficult life took its toll.

Thousands of part-time adjunct faculty taught in American universities and colleges in the 1990s. One study found that the percentage of part-time faculty in U.S. higher education soared from 22 percent in 1970 to more than 40 percent in 1993. Having pursued the training they believed would assure them a secure career, they found themselves pawns in a shifting academic job market, shuttling between institutions or holding a succession of temporary positions. A combination of enrollment pressures and budget cuts (coupled with an overproduction of Ph.D.s) provided the ingredients of the situation. Resenting their status as "cheap labor" and "second-class" faculty, these eager would-be educators earned scarcely enough to live on, worked long hours in substandard conditions, and often lacked medical coverage or retirement benefits.

The precarious employment situation in higher education mirrored the conditions in large sectors of the American labor market as the twentieth century ended. Overall, the economic picture seemed rosy. The stock market soared to unheard-of levels in the 1990s, inflation was tamed, and unemployment fell to low levels. But in an era of downsizing, cost-cutting, and efficiency pressures in both the private and the public sectors, many Americans experienced anxiety as they competed in a changing job market. Despite the boom times, the old confidence that the future would be brigher than the past—a confidence that had faded amid the energy crisis and stagflation of the 1970s—remained elusive.

Deepening career anxieties despite the robust economy was only one of many realities—political, diplomatic, economic, social, and cultural—that made the twentieth century's final years intensely interesting. Although reasons for optimism abounded, nagging doubts persisted. Here are some issues to keep in mind as you explore contemporary American history in this final chapter.

This chapter focuses on five major questions:

♦ What were the key themes of Bill Clinton's 1992 presidential campaign and the early years of his presidency?

♦ How did Clinton's priorities and approaches—and the constraints on his power—evolve over the course of his two terms, and why?

♦ With the collapse of the Soviet Union and the end of the Cold War, how successfully did the United States adapt to its new role as the world's only remaining superpower?

♦ What were the major economic trends in 1990s' America and the world? How universally shared was the booming U.S. prosperity of the mid- and later 1990s?

♦ What social and cultural trends of the 1990s seem most likely to shape the course of American history as the twenty-first century dawns?

# The Clinton Era I: Debating Domestic Policy

George Bush was a World War II veteran, shaped by Pearl Harbor, FDR, and Bing Crosby. William Jefferson Clinton—or Bill Clinton, as he preferred—was a baby boomer, formed by Vietnam, JFK, and the Beatles.

Born in Arkansas in 1946, he admired Elvis Presley, played the saxophone, and thought of becoming a pop musician. But graduation from Georgetown University and Yale Law School, and a stint at Oxford University as a Rhodes scholar, roused an interest in politics. After marrying his law-school classmate Hillary Rodham, he was elected governor of Arkansas in 1979, at age thirty-two.

**U.S. Health Spending, 1960–1993**

*Source:* Department of Health and Human Services, in *The Economist*, March 19, 1994.

Clinton began his presidency with high energy. But his administration soon encountered rough waters, and the 1994 midterm election produced a Republican landslide.

## Shaping a Domestic Agenda

Both Clinton and Vice President Albert Gore belonged to the New Democratic Coalition, a group of moderates who sought to shed the party's reputation for high taxes and heavy spending on social programs. Trying to win back middle-class and blue-collar voters, Clinton's campaign stressed Middle America's concerns: the recession, health care, and runaway welfare costs. But Clinton also embraced causes that had inspired activists of his generation, including abortion rights, environmental concerns, and feminism.

Clinton named women to head the Departments of Justice, Energy, and Health and Human Services; the Council of Economic Advisors; the Environmental Protection Agency; the United Nations delegation; and (in 1994) the Bureau of the Budget. To fill a Supreme Court vacancy in 1993, he nominated Judge Ruth Bader Ginsberg of New York, a champion of women's rights. (To fill a second vacancy in 1994, Clinton nominated moderate liberal Stephen G. Breyer, a federal appeals-court judge in Boston.) Clinton appointed his wife to head the Task Force on National Health-Care Reform.

Clinton's early weeks in office proved rocky. His effort to fulfill a campaign pledge to end the exclusion of homosexuals from military service provoked much controversy. A study commission eventually crafted a compromise summed up in the phrase "Don't ask, don't tell."

As the nation confronted a recession and high budget deficits, Clinton promised to focus "like a laser beam" on the economy. His economic program, offered in February 1993, proposed spending cuts (especially in military appropriations) and tax increases to ease the budget deficit. Clinton also proposed new spending to stimulate job creation and economic growth. In August Congress passed an economic plan that incorporated Clinton's spending cuts and tax increases but not his economic-stimulus package. Enactment of even a modified budget plan spared Clinton a major early embarrassment.

Clinton also endorsed the North American Free Trade Agreement (NAFTA). Negotiated by the Bush administration, this pact admitted Mexico to the free-trade zone earlier created by the United States and Canada. While critics warned that low-wage jobs

## CHRONOLOGY

**1984–1986** Congress bars military aid to contras.

**1985** Rash of airline hijackings and other terrorist acts.

**1986** Congress passes South African sanctions.

U.S. air raid on Libya.

William Rehnquist becomes chief justice of the United States.

Antonin Scalia joins Supreme Court.

**1987** Congressional hearings on Iran-contra scandal.

Stock market crash.

Trade deficit reaches $170 billion.

**1988** Oliver North, John Poindexter, and other Iran-contra figures indicted.

Reagan signs INF Treaty in Moscow.

George Bush elected president.

Anthony Kennedy joins Supreme Court.

**1989** Oliver North convicted of Iran-contra role.

Massive Alaskan oil spill by *Exxon Valdez*.

Supreme Court, in several 5–4 decisions, restricts civil-rights laws.

U.S. invasion of Panama; Manuel Noriega overthrown.

China's rulers crush prodemocracy movement.

Berlin Wall is opened.

**1990** Federal Clean Air Act passed.

President Bush and Congress agree on five-year budget-deficit reduction package.

Iraq invades Kuwait.

Recession begins.

Germany reunified; Soviet troops start withdrawal from Eastern Europe.

David H. Souter joins Supreme Court.

**1991** Gulf War (Operation Desert Storm).

United States and USSR sign treaty reducing strategic nuclear arms by 25 percent.

Upheavals in Soviet Union as economy nears collapse, Communist party is disbanded, and Soviet republics declare independence.

Clarence Thomas seated on Supreme Court.

**1992** Recession recovery is slow, joblessness high.

Supreme Court approves Pennsylvania restriction on abortion but upholds *Roe* v. *Wade*.

U.S. intervention in Somalia to provide humanitarian aid.

Arkansas governor Bill Clinton elected president.

**1993** Congress enacts modified version of Clinton economic plan.

Congress approves NAFTA treaty.

Recession ends.

Congress debates health-care reform (1993–1994).

Ruth Bader Ginsberg joins Supreme Court.

World Trade Center bombed.

**1994** Christian Coalition gains control of Republican party in several states.

Somalia intervention ends.

United States seeks ouster of military junta in Haiti.

Nelson Mandela elected president of South Africa.

Israeli-PLO accord on limited Palestinian self-rule in Gaza and Jericho.

G-7 nations meet in Naples.

Stephen G. Breyer joins Supreme Court.

Republican victory in 1994 elections.

---

would flee to Mexico, NAFTA backers, including most economists, predicted a net gain in jobs as Mexican markets opened to U.S. products. The House in November 1993 passed NAFTA by a comfortable margin, thus handing Clinton another welcome victory.

An improving economy eased pressures on the administration to devise an economic-stimulus program. A rebound that began in 1992 picked up steam in 1993

and 1994. Thanks to the addition of 3.5 million jobs in 1994, the unemployment rate fell to 5.4 percent, the lowest in more than four years.

Inflation remained under control as well, owing in part to interest-rate increases imposed by the Federal Reserve Board to cool the surging economy. A weakening of the OPEC oil cartel also helped check inflation. In constant dollars, crude oil cost about the same in 1993

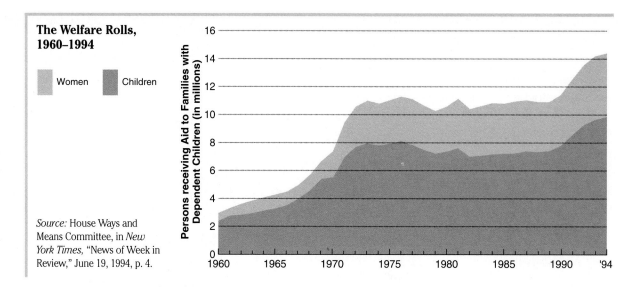

**The Welfare Rolls, 1960–1994**

Women · Children

Persons receiving Aid to Families with Dependent Children (in millions)

*Source:* House Ways and Means Committee, in *New York Times,* "News of Week in Review," June 19, 1994, p. 4.

as in 1973, before the cycle of price spurts. And the 1994 federal deficit dropped to $220 billion, with a further decline in prospect.

Meanwhile, Hillary Rodham Clinton's health-care task force, working mainly in secret, devised a sweeping reform plan. Providing universal coverage, including the estimated 39 million people lacking medical insurance, the plan mandated that employers pay 80 percent of workers' health-insurance costs and, to cover start-up expenses, proposed stiff new taxes on tobacco. The proposal also addressed the problem of spiraling costs. From 1980 to 1992, Medicare and Medicaid payments ballooned from 8 percent to 14 percent of the federal budget. Health-insurance premiums soared as well. Without controls, analysts calculated, U.S. health spending would soon consume nearly 20 percent of the Gross Domestic Product. The plan's cost-containment provisions included regional health-care purchasing cooperatives, caps on health-insurance premiums and on Medicare and Medicaid payments, and a national health board to monitor costs.

Lobbyists for the insurance industry, tobacco companies, the medical profession, retired persons, business organizations, and hospital associations all mobilized against the plan. President Clinton offered to compromise but insisted that universal coverage was not negotiable.

By the fall of 1994, after months of lobbying and partisan wrangling, health-care reform was stalled, at a heavy cost to the Clinton presidency. Public sentiment for piecemeal change had been misinterpreted by the administration as support for a total overhaul of the health-care system. Appearing secretive and patronizing, Hillary Clinton's task force had ignored political realities. But the problems that had given rise to the effort persisted, and health care remained on the political agenda.

As the economy improved, crime and welfare reform topped voter concerns. In response, Clinton in 1994 proposed an anti-crime bill to fund drug treatment, more prisons and police officers, boot camps for first-time offenders, and a ban on assault weapons. After much partisan maneuvering, Congress enacted a crime bill similar to Clinton's initial proposal.

In addition, Clinton in 1994 introduced a welfare-reform bill, fulfilling a campaign pledge to "end welfare as we know it." This measure reflected concerns that the biggest welfare system, Aid to Families with Dependent Children (AFDC), was creating a permanent dependent class. With 14.3 million women and children on AFDC's rolls—a 31 percent jump since 1989—the program cost $63 billion annually in direct payments, food stamps, and Medicaid benefits. Under Clinton's bill, all AFDC recipients would have to go to work after two years, in a public-service job if necessary. The bill included job training and child-care provisions, as well as measures to force absent fathers ("deadbeat dads") to support their offspring. It also permitted states to deny extra payments to mothers who bore more children while on welfare. Although Congress took no action on Clinton's bill, welfare reform, too, remained high on the public agenda.

By mid-1994 Clinton's approval ratings had dropped to 42 percent. Many found him too ready to compromise and too inclined to flit from issue to issue. Exploiting the "character issue," critics publicized Clinton's involvement while governor in a shady real estate speculation, the Whitewater Development Company. Hillary Rodham Clinton's profit of $100,000 in a $1,000 commodities investment raised more questions, as did the 1993 suicide of the Clintons' close friend, assistant White House counsel Vincent Foster. Charges of sexual harassment, first aired during the campaign, resurfaced in 1994 when Paula Jones, an Arkansas state employee, alleged in a lawsuit that as governor, Clinton had solicited sexual favors.

As Clinton proved vulnerable, the political climate turned nasty. Radio commentator Rush Limbaugh won celebrity with his jeering attacks on liberals. Televangelist Jerry Falwell offered a videotape suggesting that Clinton had arranged the murder of political enemies. The Christian Coalition, founded by TV preacher Pat Robertson, mobilized voters at the local level. By 1994, with some nine hundred chapters nationwide, the Christian Coalition had gained control of several state Republican parties. Although a minority of the electorate, the religious Right, with its passion and organizational energy, represented a potent and unpredictable force in American politics of the 1990s.

### 1994: A Sharp Right Turn

Bill Clinton had won in 1992 as a "new Democrat" offering fresh ideas, but by 1994 many voters saw him as simply an old Democrat of the big-government, "tax-and-spend" variety. His early call for an end to the ban on homosexuals in the military convinced some that special-interest groups controlled the White House agenda. To his critics, Clinton's failed health-care plan epitomized the dead end of a New Deal/Great Society style of top-down reform. The "character issues" swirling around Clinton worsened his political fortunes, as did the view of him as hopelessly indecisive. Commented the Rev. Jesse Jackson: "When the president comes to a fork in the road, he chooses the fork."

At the same time, a movement to downsize government, reform the welfare system, slash taxes and spending, and shift power to the states gained momentum among the middle class. A bubbling brew of cultural and social issues added to the disaffection. These included such emotional topics as abortion, pornography, school prayer, "radical feminism," and an alleged collapse of "family values." Adding to the brew was a

**The Republican Revolution, 1994**
*Led by House Minority Whip Newt Gingrich, Republican congressional candidates gather at the Capitol in September 1994 to sign the "Contract with America," a prelude to dramatic GOP gains in the midterm elections that November.*

reaction against affirmative-action programs designed to aid minorities and women.

A network of conservative organizations orchestrated the rightward swing. As the Christian Coalition mobilized evangelicals, the National Rifle Association (NRA) contributed to candidates who opposed restrictions on firearms. Conservative think tanks such as the Heritage Foundation funded studies critiquing liberal policies. Right-wing radio commentators continued to denounce the "liberal elite."

Normally, prosperity helps the party in power, but not in 1994, in part because the recovery did little for ordinary Americans. The actual buying power of the average worker's paycheck fell from 1986 to 1990, and remained flat thereafter. Automation, foreign competition, and the weakness of organized labor all combined to keep wages down. In October 1994 an ominous 58 percent of Americans told pollsters they did not feel better off despite the economic upturn.

In the summer of 1994, Republican Congressman Newt Gingrich of Georgia shrewdly translated the disgruntled mood into Republican votes. In a photogenic ceremony on the Capitol steps, some 300 Republican candidates signed Gingrich's "Contract with America," pledging tax cuts, congressional term limits, tougher crime laws, a balanced-budget amendment, and other popular reforms.

In a Republican landslide that November, voters gave the GOP control of both houses of Congress for the first time since 1954; increased the number of Republican governors to thirty-one; and cut down such Democratic giants as New York governor Mario Cuomo and Texas governor Ann Richards.

Evangelical Christians flocked to the polls, mostly to vote for GOP candidates. Republican strategists hailed the election as the death knell of an activist, big-government tradition dating to the New Deal, and a further step in a conservative resurgence launched by Barry Goldwater in 1964. Republican governors like Wisconsin's Tommy Thompson, a champion of welfare reform, insisted that the states, not Washington, D.C., were now the best source of policy ideas. In the Senate, Republican Robert Dole of Kansas became majority leader; the reactionary Jesse Helms of North Carolina ascended to the chairmanship of the Foreign Relations Committee; and ninety-two-year-old Strom Thurmond of South Carolina, presidential candidate of the States Rights (Dixiecrat) party in 1948, headed the Arms Services Committee.

In the House of Representatives, a jubilant horde of 230 Republicans, 73 of them newly elected, proclaimed Newt Gingrich Speaker by acclamation, made Rush Limbaugh an "honorary member," and set about translating the "Contract with America" into law. One early bill forbade unfunded mandates, by which Washington had imposed regulations on the states without providing money to cover the costs. The House also passed a constitutional amendment requiring a balanced federal budget. The Senate, however, narrowly rejected the admendment. On the cultural front, House Republicans targeted such "liberal elite" institutions as the Public Broadcasting Corporation and the National Endowments for the Arts and the Humanities. Other "Contract with America" issues, including increased military spending, repeal of the 1993 ban on assault weapons (the NRA's top priority), and a constitutional amendment permitting prayer in the schools, awaited their turn.

GOP leaders also promised an array of tax credits and benefits for the middle class and the wealthy that, if enacted, would have gutted the Tax Reform Act of 1986, designed to eliminate tax breaks and loopholes.

The promise of tax cuts coupled with increased defense spending threatened worse budget deficits, but Republican leaders insisted that large savings could be achieved in other parts of the budget. Where these savings would come from was unclear, since the biggest budget items apart from defense were interest payments on the national debt and two programs sacred to the middle class, social security and Medicare.

The torrent of bills, hearings, and press releases of early 1995 recalled the heady days of Lyndon Johnson's Great Society and even the first Hundred Days of FDR's New Deal. Now, however, the activist energy came from conservatives, not from liberals.

At first, President Clinton appeared stunned by the altered political landscape. He went hunting the day the new Congress convened, and was photographed carrying a dead duck. A rambling State of the Union address echoed the Republican agenda, including tax cuts, welfare reforms, and a smaller federal government.

For a time, House Speaker Newt Gingrich displayed an intellectual cockiness that struck many as arrogance. Gingrich stumbled in January 1995 when he first accepted, and then turned down, a $4.5 million book-royalty advance from a publishing house owned by Rupert Murdoch, a publishing tycoon with vital interests in federal legislation. Journalists also focused on Gingrich's network of political action groups, dubbed "Newt, Inc.," funded by corporate contributors and conservative foundations, with its $16 million war chest. Lampooning liberals as "left-wing elitists" trapped in the past and unable to think creatively about the future, the Georgia firebrand challenged the entire structure of social programs and federal-state relations that had evolved since the New Deal, and articulated the political values of an earlier era of laissez-faire, sink-or-swim individualism.

In a troubling demonstration of voter apathy, only 38 percent of eligible voters went to the polls in 1994, so the great shift rightward was actually achieved by about one-fifth of the total electorate. Still, a significant ideological change did appear to be under way, challenging a social-welfare legacy stretching back to the progressive era. In their railings against "Washington," the conservative ideologists of the 1990s echoed the Antifederalists of the 1780s, terrified of the centralized power the new Constitution would create.

## Welfare Reform

In the aftermath of the Republican sweep in 1994, welfare reform took on fresh urgency. Critics of the existing welfare system offered two principal arguments. The first was cost. The largest welfare programs, Medicaid and Aid to Families with Dependent Children (AFDC), together with food stamps, cost about $125 billion in 1994. Though dwarfed by the benefits that flowed to the middle class through social security, Medicare, farm subsidies, and various tax deductions, this was still a substantial drain on the budget. The second argument for welfare reform was ideological: the belief that the system undermined the work ethic and trapped the poor in a cycle of dependence.

The debate raised serious policy issues and ethical questions. Would cutting welfare penalize children for their parents' actions? In depressed urban areas, would the government provide public employment to individuals dropped from the welfare rolls if no private-sector jobs were available?

Welfare reform transcended party divisions. Clinton had pledged in 1992 to "end welfare as we know it" and in 1994 had introduced a welfare-reform bill. A broad consensus held that the present system had failed and that welfare should be a short-term bridge to gainful employment, not a lifelong entitlement. Many observers also saw a link between a system that automatically paid higher benefits for each child, and the soaring rate of out-of-wedlock births, which by the mid-1990s constituted about one-third of all births. The debate, therefore, was not over *whether* changes were needed, but *what* changes. While Clinton favored federally funded child-care, job-training, and work programs to ease the transition from welfare to employment, conservative Republicans believed that the market and state and local agencies could best handle these problems. Clinton vetoed two welfare bills that lacked the safeguards he thought essential.

At last in August 1996, Clinton signed a landmark welfare reform bill. Reversing sixty years of federal welfare policy, the law ended the largest federal program, AFDC. Instead, states were told to develop their own welfare programs with federal block grants while abiding by tough federal rules limiting most welfare recipients to two years of continuous coverage, with a lifetime total of five years. The law also granted states authority to withdraw Medicaid coverage once welfare benefits had been terminated.

Supporters argued that ending welfare as a lifetime entitlement would encourage initiative and personal responsibility. Critics warned of the effects on poor children and on ill-educated welfare mothers in inner cities lacking jobs and social services. The law had been passed during an economic boom; what would happen when the good times ended?

Clinton's approval of a Republican welfare bill disappointed liberals, including Senator Edward Kennedy, and such mainstays of the Democratic coalition as

**Welfare to Work**
*A former welfare recipient in Georgia receives training for a new job.*

women's groups, minority organizations, and advocacy groups for children and the poor. But in the election summer of 1996, still smarting from the repudiation of 1994, Clinton had adjusted to the shifting political winds and moved to the right.

In the short run, the law achieved its goal. By December 1998, the welfare rolls had dropped by 38 percent to a thirty-year low of 7.6 million people, down from 14.1 million in January 1993.

### Campaign '96 and After: Tobacco Regulation and Campaign-Finance Reform

After the rout of 1994, Clinton's prospects looked bleak. But Clinton had acquired the nickname "the Comeback Kid" after losing and then regaining the Arkansas governorship, and he now again hit the comeback trail. While Clinton's missteps of 1993 proved costly, he gained generally good marks for signing the budget-balancing and welfare-reform bills. Simultaneously, the Republicans suffered black eyes in 1995 when Newt Gingrich, battling Clinton over the budget, twice allowed a partial government shutdown.

Clinton got another lucky break as well: a weak Republican opponent in 1996. When General Colin Powell, the popular former chairman of the Joint Chiefs of Staff, declined to run, Senator Bob Dole of Kansas easily bested a weak field of GOP contenders. Dole was a party stalwart who had battled back from near-fatal World War II injuries, and many felt that, at age seventy-three, he deserved the nomination. But Dole campaigned lethargically, delivering wooden speeches devoid of ideas. Some Republicans grumbled that Dole's talented wife Elizabeth, a former cabinet member and now head of the American Red Cross, would have made a stronger candidate.

Clinton won with just under 50 percent of the vote, to Dole's 41 percent. (Ross Perot garnered 8 percent.) The Republicans retained control of Congress, though Gingrich and most other GOP legislators were considerably less combative than after their 1994 triumph. At times they seemed more preoccupied with intraparty intrigues than with proposing new initiatives.

Launching his second term, Clinton initially pursued a cautious course, distancing himself from his party's New Deal–Great Society past. In 1997 he signed a Republican bill providing some tax cuts while establishing a timetable for a balanced budget by 2002. (In fact, as the economic boom continued, Clinton beat that deadline by three years.) Many Clinton proposals involved no legislation or federal spending. To improve

### The Political Doles

*Bob Dole and his wife Elizabeth launch Dole's 1996 presidential bid on primary day in Manchester, New Hampshire. By 1999, Bob Dole was appearing in TV commercials for Viagra, a new pill for male sexual dysfunction, while Elizabeth Dole was launching her own presidential bid.*

student discipline, he advocated school uniforms. To promote early-childhood development, he urged parents to read to their children. He set up a citizens' commission to lead a national dialogue on race.

Clinton tepidly defended affirmative-action programs, but public opinion (especially among non-Hispanic whites) was flowing the other way. The Supreme Court in 1995 restricted the awarding of federal contracts on the basis of race, and in 1996 California voters barred racial or ethnic preferences in state agencies, including the state's university system.

Clinton did act forcefully on one issue: the perils of tobacco. In 1997, to forestall state lawsuits to recover the medical costs of treating smoking-related diseases, the tobacco industry, after negotiations with the attorneys general of forty states, agreed to pay some $368 billion to settle pending liability suits and to reimburse the states for tobacco-related medical costs. The agreement also strictly limited tobacco advertising, especially to young people. If teenage smoking did not decline by 60 percent by 2007, the industry would face heavy fines. In return, the tobacco companies gained protection from future class-action lawsuits.

Since the agreement required government approval, the debate now shifted to Washington. Legislators close to the tobacco companies such as Jesse Helms defended the industry, but President Clinton and others called for tougher penalties, higher taxes on cigarettes, rejection of the blanket immunity provision, and stronger measures to stop teenage smoking. The demands intensified as more evidence surfaced of the industry's manipulation of nicotine levels and deliberate targeting of children. The administration supported a tough bill aimed at cutting cigarette smoking, especially among teenagers, through stricter regulation and higher cigarette taxes. But the tobacco industry struck back with a $40 million lobbying campaign and heavy contributions to key legislators, killing the bill for the moment. Commented Arizona's maverick Republican legislator (and Vietnam war hero) Senator John McCain, a champion of the bill: "Some Republicans might be vulnerable to the charge that their party is in the pocket of the tobacco companies."

Late in 1998, the tobacco industry reached a new settlement, scaled back to some $200 billion, with forty-six states. The industry's woes persisted, however. President Clinton continued to push for tougher federal regulation of tobacco and for legal action to recover Medicare costs arising from smoking-related illnesses. The industry also faced a wave of private suits. In 1999,

**"I Solemnly Swear…"**
*Tobacco-industry executives prepare to testify before the House Commerce Committee in January 1998. Political and legal issues related to smoking loomed large in the 1990s, as cigarettes' deadly effects became more widely understood.*

a California jury awarded a lung-cancer victim a whopping $51 million in her suit against Philip Morris Company. Even if reduced on appeal, as seemed likely, the award sent a chill through the industry.

Big Tobacco's successful purchase of politicians' votes highlighted another hot issue in Clinton's second term: campaign-finance reform. The cost of television advertising had long been driving up campaign expenses, and the 1996 campaign was particularly outrageous. A 1997 Senate inquiry examined abuses in the 1996 campaign, including illegal contributions by Asian businesses. One Democratic fundraiser, John Huang, with links to Indonesian and possibly Chinese corporate interests, raised $3.4 million, of which nearly half was eventually returned as illegal. After one event at a Los Angeles Buddhist temple arranged by Huang and attended by Vice President Gore, Buddhist priests and nuns sworn to poverty had contributed over $100,000 dollars to the Democratic cause.

Neither party leapt to curb these abuses. Clinton paid lip service to reform while endlessly appearing at fundraising events. Early in 1998, the Senate shelved a modest campaign-finance bill introduced by John McCain and Russ Feingold (D-Wisconsin). Like the tobacco addicts Clinton deplored, American politicians had become addicted to the contributions that poured in from lobbying groups of all kinds. As scandal and legal charges swirled around the White House (see next section), the momentum for campaign-finance reform

faltered, though the issues remained very much alive.

In his January 1998 State of the Union address, Clinton set goals for his final three years and, in effect, opened the 1998 midterm campaign. For the first time in thirty years, Clinton boasted, his 1999 budget would include a modest surplus. As the politics of plenty replaced the politics of scarcity, some Republican leaders called for big tax cuts. Clinton, however, offered a politically shrewd alternative. First, he proposed to use a projected tobacco settlement to provide tax credits for college-tuition costs, give school boards grants to hire more teachers, increase the government's medical-research budget, and fund other social programs. But most of the surplus, Clinton argued, should go to reduce the national debt and, especially, strengthen the social security system, which, economists calculated, faced eventual bankrupcy as the nation's 76 million baby boomers retired. Clinton's call to "Save social security first" not only made fiscal sense but made Republican tax-cut proposals appear fiscally irresponsible.

With this address, Clinton sought to define his second term. After the health-care setback, Clinton had abandoned large-scale programs in favor of small, incremental proposals that appealed to progressives without alienating moderates. While offering some initiatives to help the poor (such as enrolling the nation's 3 million uninsured low-income children in Medicaid),

Clinton also introduced proposals that targeted the middle class (such as college-tuition tax credits and extending Medicare to early retirees) and fiscal conservatives (reducing the national debt, shoring up social security). Some liberals jeered at Clinton's program as "Progressivism Lite," but it was politically astute. Under normal conditions, the speech would have been a major step in Clinton's political comeback and a strong claim for his place in history.

## Impeachment and Beyond

But conditions were not normal. Even as Clinton spoke, scandal enveloped the White House. Charges of serial adultery had long clung to Clinton and indeed had briefly surfaced in the 1992 campaign. Now, in January 1998, as Paula Jones's sexual-harassment suit moved forward (after a May 1997 Supreme Court ruling permitting civil suits against sitting presidents), a new crisis erupted. Seeking to establish a pattern of sexual harassment, Jones's lawyers subpoenaed President Clinton to testify. At his testimony, on January 17, they quizzed him about reports of a sexual relationship with a White House intern, Monica Lewinsky. The president denied the story, as did Lewinsky in an affidavit in the Jones case. As the rumors became public (at first via an Internet website devoted to political gossip), Clinton insisted to his advisors, family, cabinet members, and the American people in a television address that the stories were utterly false. Ever-loyal Hillary Clinton spoke darkly of "a vast right-wing conspiracy."

But unbeknownst to Clinton, a bombshell awaited. In hours of telephone conversations secretly and illegally taped in 1997 by Monica Lewinsky's "friend" Linda Tripp, Lewinsky had graphically described an intermittent sexual relationship with Clinton starting in 1995, when she was twenty-one years old, and continuing through early 1997, including trysts in the Oval Office. On January 12, 1998, Tripp had passed the tapes to Kenneth Starr, an independent counsel appointed in 1994 by Attorney General Janet Reno to investigate the Whitewater matter. At Starr's request, FBI agents fitted Tripp with a concealed recording device and secured further Lewinsky evidence. (Persisent charges would later surface that Starr's office had informed Jones's lawyers about the Tripp tapes before Clinton's testimony, as part of a sting operation.)

Although a judge dismissed the Jones suit, Starr—having secured Justice Department permission to expand his inquiry—now focused on whether Clinton had committed perjury in his Jones testimony and had

tried to persuade Lewinsky to lie as well. In August, after threats of a long jail term and a promise of immunity, Lewinsky acknowledged the affair in testimony before Starr's grand jury. She even provided, under court order, a dress allegedly containing physical evidence of her sexual contact with Clinton. (DNA tests confirmed the accuracy of her claim.) Soon after, in his own testimony before Starr's grand jury, videotaped at the White House, Clinton conceded that he had engaged in "conduct that was wrong" with Lewinsky but insisted that his denial of a "sexual relationship" in his testimony in the Jones case had been technically accurate, under his rather narrow definition of the term. In a brief television address, Clinton confessed to "a relationship with Ms. Lewinsky that was not appropriate," acknowledged having "misled" the American people, but again called his testimony "legally accurate" and attacked Starr as politically motivated.

The scandal set off a media frenzy and provided endless grist for TV's late-night comedians, for Internet humor, and for conservative radio talk-show hosts. Adding more fuel, another White House volunteer told Starr's grand jury—and the nation via CBS's popular *Sixty Minutes* program—about unwanted sexual advances by Clinton. When Starr released Clinton's grand-jury testimony, the president's tortuous definitions of what constituted a "sexual" relationship—and even, at one point, his discussion of the meaning of the word "is"—became the target of more derisive humor.

What was going on? Other presidents had pursued extramarital affairs with impunity, but by the 1990s the cultural and legal context differed radically. The women's movement and sexual-harassment laws had made such behavior increasingly objectionable. In a media-saturated age, politicians lived in the constant glare of public scrutiny. Indeed, politicians themselves had eroded the distinction between public and private by parading intimate personal details for political advantage. Unsurprisingly, then, the Clinton scandal unfolded on television and in tabloid headlines. Finally, the independent-counsel law, a legacy of Watergate, meant that Clinton faced not only public disgrace but legal and constitutional consequences from Starr's seemingly endless investigations.

In September, Starr presented a 4,800-word report to the House Judiciary Committee narrating the Clinton-Lewinsky affair in explicit and lurid detail and finding "substantial and credible" grounds for impeachment. The president, Starr charged, had committed perjury in both the Jones civil suit and his grand-jury testimony; had influenced others to commit perjury by various means, including instructing his friend Vernon Jordan to help Lewinsky find a job; and had obstructed justice by using his secretary to retrieve gifts he had given Lewinsky, coaching his secretary on his innocent version of events, and taking other actions.

After acrimonious hearings, the intensely partisan Judiciary Committee, chaired by Congressman Henry Hyde of Illinois, on a straight party-line vote, forwarded four articles of impeachment to the full House of Representatives. In an equally partisan vote, the House in late December approved and forwarded to the Senate two articles of impeachment charging Clinton with perjury in his grand-jury testimony and with obstruction of justice through a pattern of activities intended to conceal the truth. For the first time since Andrew Johnson's day, a president of the United States had been impeached.

But polling data sent the Republicans an ominous message: most Americans did not support impeachment. The clearest signal came in the November 1998 midterm elections, as the House impeachment process unfolded. Contrary to predictions of massive Democratic losses, the Democrats not only held their own in the Senate and in state races but actually gained five seats in the House. In the aftermath of this stinging setback, Speaker Newt Gingrich, the Republicans' darling in 1994, abruptly resigned both the speakership and his House seat. His apparent successor as speaker, Robert Livingston of Louisiana, similarly resigned and left Congress a few weeks later as a magazine prepared a report on his adulterous relationships.

Since conviction and removal of a president requires a two-thirds Senate vote, and since the Republicans held only a 55-45 Senate majority, the impeachment effort seemed foredoomed to eventual failure. Nevertheless, the new Senate early in 1999 conducted a full-scale trial. As Chief Justice William Rehnquist presided, resplendent in a black robe with gold bars on the sleeves, the 100 senators sat silently as thirteen Republican members of the House Judiciary Committee, acting as the impeachment managers, presented their case and as White House lawyers sought to rebut what one called a "witches' brew of speculation." Three witnesses—Monica Lewinsky, Vernon Jordan, and White House advisor Sidney Blumenthal—were deposed, and portions of their videotaped testimony shown to the Senate.

Throughout, opinion-poll ratings of Clinton's performance as president remained remarkably high, soaring to nearly 70 percent as the impeachment process proceeded. Most citizens, it appeared, were sharply

**Ken Starr Meets the Press, January 1998**
*Independent Counsel Starr's dogged investigations into legal issues arising from President Clinton's affair with a White House intern set off a media frenzy, which in turn set off a round of hand-wringing about the state of American journalism.*

distinguishing between the president's private behavior and his public role. Meanwhile, the approval ratings of Kenneth Starr and the Republican-controlled Congress—not to mention the faithless Linda Tripp—sank to abysmal levels. A solid majority of Americans clearly wanted the impeachment to end and Clinton to remain in office. While the public clearly found Clinton's behavior shameful and irresponsible, most people remained unconvinced that it had imperiled the republic or met the "high crimes and misdemeanors" standard set by the Constitution as the only grounds for impeachment and removal.

Again earning his nickname "the comeback kid," Clinton in January 1999, in the midst of the trial, delivered a confident State of the Union address that was generally rated a stunning success. Rise above "the clash of controversy," the president exhorted the bemused legislators, and in "a spirit of civility and bipartisanship" address the people's business.

With the economy booming and Clinton dominating the vast middle ground of American politics on most issues, a majority of citizens appeared willing to tolerate his personal flaws. Further, as the process unfolded, the feeling grew that whatever Clinton's mis-

**The Comeback Kid Comes Back**
*Political cartoonists enjoyed a field day with the impeachment of Bill Clinton, which, in the short run at least, did more damage to the Republicans than it did to Clinton, whose approval ratings remained high.*

deeds, he was also the target of a campaign by conservative Republican zealots grimly determined to drive him from office. Offering a British perspective, the *Economist* of London observed in early January 1999: "[A]s the machinery of impeachment was gleefully cranked up, it soon felt wrong. The sense of shame and sadness that now engulfs many thoughtful Americans comes not so much from sympathy with this particular president—whose lying defiance deserves none—as from worry at the precedents that have been set for political vendettas against elected presidents in the future."

On February 12, 1999, after three days of closed-door deliberation, the Senate rejected the impeachment charges and ended the trial. Both charges fell short of the required two-thirds vote; indeed, neither won even a simple majority. With several Republicans joining the Democrats in voting to dismiss, the obstruction-of-justice charge failed by a 50-50 vote, and the perjury charge by an even wider margin of 45 ayes, 55 nays. Some senators who voted to dismiss said they found the House case circumstantial and unconvincing; others were convinced by the evidence but found that Clinton's offenses, while deplorable and even illegal, did not rise to the constitutional level of impeachment. In a brief statement, President Clinton again expressed contrition and urged the nation to move on. While the House managers warned darkly of a double

standard of justice, most Americans simply felt relief that the long ordeal was over.

Despite this outcome, Clinton clearly had suffered grievous damage—mostly self-inflicted. Despite all his strengths, his character flaws, whose consequences he had long managed to avoid in a charmed political life, had overtaken him at last, eroding his leadership and tarnishing his historical standing. But the Republican party, ironically, had been damaged even more by its apparent surrender to its most extreme and moralistic elements. Democrats, mired in gloom when the scandal first erupted, now looked to the 2000 election with growing confidence.

With the impeachment process over, the Clinton administration and the Republican Congress returned to an array of pressing issues. As the booming economy continued to generate huge budget surpluses, each party assumed predictable positions. While Republicans called for big across-the-board tax cuts, the administration favored more modest and targeted cuts while stressing the need to strengthen Medicare and social security and beef up the military after a decade of post–Cold War budget cuts. Clinton also reiterated in sweeping, broad-brush fashion such familiar and popular themes as the need for better schools, health-care reform, more effective anticrime programs, child-care and other initiatives to strengthen welfare-to-work efforts, plans to encourage personal savings, renewed warfare with Big Tobacco, and greater safeguards for women and parents against discriminatory practices in the workplace.

With the impeachment dragon slain, a tarnished but still formidable Bill Clinton looked to the waning years of his roller-coaster presidency. Amid domestic distractions, global problems continued to challenge the nation.

## The Clinton Era II: The Quest for a Coherent Foreign Policy

In contrast to George Bush, Bill Clinton preferred domestic issues to foreign policy. Yet the United States remained the world's only superpower after the demise of the Soviet Union, and its post–Cold War global role inevitably invited scrutiny.

In Eastern Europe, the Soviet collapse unleashed bitter ethnic conflicts. As Yugoslavia broke up in 1991, Serbian forces in Bosnia launched a campaign of "ethnic cleansing" to drive out Muslims and Croats. Advised by his first-term Secretary of State Warren Christopher, Clinton supported a U.N.-peacekeeping effort and contributed U.S. airpower to NATO bombing raids on Serb positions. But when the Serbs took U.N. peacekeepers hostage following NATO air strikes in 1995, NATO suspended the attacks. Encouraged, the Serbs overran a Muslim enclave and menaced other U.N.-designated "safe areas."

Later in 1995 the State Department flew the leaders of Bosnia's warring factions to Dayton, Ohio, for intensive talks. The resulting Dayton Accords imposed a cease-fire and established a framework for governing the region. President Clinton committed 20,000 U.S. troops to a NATO force to oversee the accords. Conditions remained unstable, but the cease-fire generally held. By 1998 some 8,000 GIs remained in Bosnia.

In the former Soviet Union, Russia endured inflation, shortages, and economic chaos as centralized control yielded to a market-oriented system. The Clinton administration supported President Boris Yeltsin and pledged economic aid to Russia and the Ukraine but otherwise watched from the sidelines. Despite worsening conditions in Russia and strained diplomatic relations following Moscow's brutal attack on the breakaway republic of Chechnya early in 1995, the administration continued to view Yeltsin as Russia's best hope. Relations with Washington remained testy as Russia adopted a more vocal and independent foreign-policy course, though with little hint of a return to Cold War hostilities.

In another indication of how radically the Soviet collapse had reconfigured Europe's balance of power, NATO in 1997 admitted three new members from the former Soviet bloc: Hungary, Poland, and the Czech Republic. Russia protested, but to little effect.

The domestic political constraints on post–Cold War U.S. power became clear in Africa and the Caribbean. In the East African nation of Somalia, a U.S. intervention undertaken by President Bush in 1992 as a humanitarian response to famine ended bleakly in 1994 as U.S. forces became embroiled in conflict between warring Somali factions. In the central African nation of Rwanda, hatreds between the Hutu majority and the Tutsi minority flared into genocidal violence in 1994. Hutu militia massacred as many as a half-

**Sarajevo, May 1995**
*Grieving relatives bury a five-year-old boy killed in the shelling of Sarajevo by Bosnian Serbs. As the Serbs pursued their campaign of "ethnic cleansing" against Bosnia's Muslim population, scenes like this became tragically frequent.*

million Tutsi. When Tutsi rebels struck back, terrified Hutus fled into neighboring Zaire, creating a massive refugee crisis. Traumatized by the Somali fiasco, the Clinton administration did little.

On a brighter note, South Africa's move to multiracial democracy, hastened by the economic sanctions imposed by the United States and other nations, culminated in 1994 as Nelson Mandela, long imprisoned by the apartheid government, won the presidency in South Africa's first free elections.

In Haiti a 1991 military junta overthrew President Jean-Bertrand Aristide and terrorized his supporters. Thousands of Haitians fleeing poverty and repression set out for Florida in small, leaky craft. African-American leaders kept attention focused on the crisis, as did the 300,000 U.S.-born Haitians. To dislodge the junta, Clinton in July 1994 assembled an invasion flotilla off Haiti's coast. In September, however, ex-president Jimmy Carter persuaded the junta leaders to accept voluntary exile. Backed by a U.S. occupation force, Aristide resumed the presidency, giving Clinton a modest diplomatic success.

In the Middle East, negotiations between the Israelis and the Palestine Liberation Organization produced in 1994 an agreement on limited Palestinian self-rule. PLO leader Yasir Arafat and Israeli prime minister

## The Mideast Crises, 1980–Present

*Despite the long history of Mideast violence and animosity, the end of the Cold War and negotiations among the hostile parties gave promise by the mid-1990s of at least a partial easing of tensions in the region.*

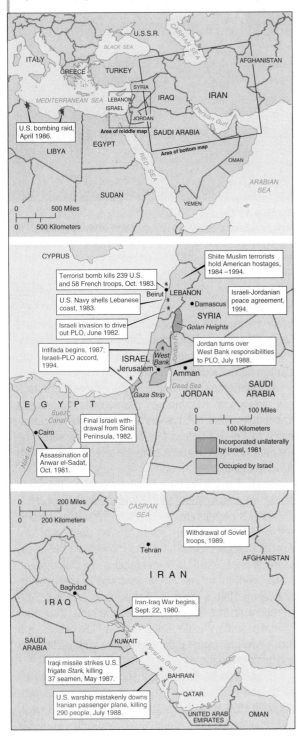

Yitzhak Rabin signed the agreement in Washington. Terrorism continued, however, including the 1993 bombing of the World Trade Center in New York City that killed six people and injured more than a thousand. Shiite terrorists linked to a radical Egyptian sheik were quickly arrested; in 1997 the group's leader was convicted and imprisoned for life. An Israeli fanatic murdered twenty-nine Muslim worshipers in Hebron in 1994. In 1995 a young Israeli assassinated Prime Minister Rabin. Israel's next election brought to power Benjamin Netanyahu of the hard-line Likud party. A series of suicide bombings by Palestinian extremists in Jerusalem, Tel Aviv, and other centers in 1996–1997 killed some eighty Israelis and injured hundreds. Accusing Yasir Arafat of condoning terrorism, Netanyahu stalled on the agreed-upon withdrawal of Israeli forces from West Bank areas and tolerated the construction of Jewish housing in disputed districts. The dilemma fell into the lap of Madeleine K. Albright, appointed secretary of state early in 1997 (thereby becoming the highest-ranking woman in U.S. government history). Albright pressured the Israelis and the Palestinians to settle their differences, but as of 1998 little progress was evident. The death in 1999 of Jordan's King Hussein, long a moderating force in the region, further darkened hopes for peace.

### Another Step on the Rocky Path to Mideast Peace

*President Clinton presides as Israeli Prime Minister Yitzhak Rabin and PLO Chairman Yasir Arafat shake hands after signing a peace accord at the White House, September 13, 1993.*

North Korea, under communist strongman Kim Il Sung, posed another diplomatic challenge for Clinton. In violation of the 1970 Nuclear Nonproliferation Treaty, North Korea began reprocessing spent fuel rods from nuclear-power plants into weapons-grade plutonium. In 1994, with pledges of $9 billion in international assistance in the balance and facing U.N. economic sanctions (and following a visit by Jimmy Carter), Kim pledged to stop making plutonium. But in the shadowy arena of post–Cold War diplomacy, such agreements often seemed written in sand. In 1998 U.S. intelligence detected evidence that North Korea was reneging on its pledge, leading to a fresh round of diplomatic action.

On the foreign-relations front, the 1994 Republican landslide signaled a turn inward. Newt Gingrich's Contract with America largely ignored foreign policy, and key Republican legislators pushed isolationist views. Jesse Helms, the new chair of the Senate Foreign Relations Committee, denounced the United Nations, criticized international environmental treaties, and saw little good in U.N. peacekeeping efforts or America's $14 billion foreign-aid program. Congressional Republicans refused to pay America's $1 billion in overdue U.N. dues and in 1996 pressured the administration to oppose a second term for U.N. secretary general Boutras Boutras Ghali. Facing Pentagon objections, the Clinton administration even refused to sign a multinational treaty banning land mines. This upsurge of isolationism dismayed those who saw an intimate link between America's prospects and the fate of the world, including societies mired in poverty.

A renewed crisis in Iraq highlighted the complexities of post–Cold War diplomacy. After the Persian Gulf War, the United Nations had imposed trade sanctions on Iraq and set up an inspection system to prevent Saddam Hussein from building chemical, biological, or nuclear weapons. Late in 1997 Saddam refused the U.N. inspection team access to certain sites. Dispatching ships, bombers, cruise missiles, and thirty thousand troops to the Persian Gulf, President Clinton sought to rally U.N. and U.S. support for a military strike, as George Bush had done in 1991. But France, Russia, and various Arab states resisted. At home the administration faced hard questions about how bombing would further the goal of unrestricted inspections. Some called for Saddam's removal, but whether even that risky course would serve U.S. interests seemed dubious. Washington drew back from military action after the new U.N. secretary general, Kofi Annan of Ghana, secured Saddam's agreement to open inspection, but in mid-1998 Iraq again barred the weapons-inspection program, and the crisis atmosphere continued. By 1999 the U.N. arms-inspection system had collapsed, and U.S. bombers and Iraqi antiaircraft were engaging in sporadic exchanges in the Iraqi "no-fly zone" established after the Persian Gulf War. The Iraqi situation underscored the difficulty of bringing U.S. military might to bear in complex local situations, and the challenge of mobilizing nations with diverse interests for collective action, and the pitfalls involved in rallying post–Cold War U.S. public opinion behind a military option whose purpose and outcome seemed murky.

Along with the continuing Iraqi crisis, other events of 1998 erased any doubt that despite the Cold War's end, urgent global security challenges remained. In May the stakes in the long-simmering dispute between India and Pakistan over Kashmir escalated sharply when India tested a nuclear bomb. Pakistan, despite urgent pleas from the United States and other powers, quickly followed suit. Fears of nuclear proliferation rose sharply, recalling the anxious days of the superpower nuclear-arms race.

Then, in August, deadly terrorist bombs simultaneously exploded at the U.S. embassies in Kenya and Tanzania, killing 12 Americans and some 250 Africans, and wounding hundreds more. Two weeks later, after intense consultations with his military and national security advisers, and despite the distractions of the Lewinsky scandal, President Clinton ordered cruise missile strikes on a suspected chemical-weapons factory in Khartoum, Sudan, and a terrorist training camp in Afghanistan. These sites, the administration charged, were part of a terrorist network linked to the embassy bombings and financed by Osama bin Laden, a wealthy Saudi exile and fanatical hater of America. Warning of probable retaliatory attacks, the administration advised Americans to prepare for a protracted period of combatting shadowy terrorist groups. "[W]e are involved here in a long-term struggle . . . ," declared Secretary of State Albright; "This is, unfortunately, the war of the future."

While the precarious Bosnian ceasefire held, Washington and NATO enjoyed less success in capturing Serbian war criminals and in combatting Serbia's aggressive boss, Slobodan Milosevic. Indeed, in 1998 Milosevic launched a bloody repression of Serbia's southern province Kosovo, inhabited mostly by Muslin ethnic Albanians. Ever since the 1389 Battle of Kosovo against Ottoman Turks, the Serbs had regarded this region as "sacred land," and Milosevic cynically stirred up these ancient feelings. In March 1999, as the situation worsened, NATO under U.S. leadership launched a major bombing assault on Serbian military and government facilities in Kosovo and in Serbia proper, including the capital, Belgrade. Russia protested the attack on its traditional ally Serbia, but the raids continued into the spring. In response, Milosevic stepped up the forced expulsion of ethnic Albanians from Kosovo. Amid horrendous scenes of suffering and killing, Serbian forces drove hundreds of thousands of Kosovars across the borders into Macedonia, Albania, and Montenegro, poverty-stricken regions overwhelmed by the human tide. Along with the challenge of curbing Milosevic's aggression, NATO and the United States now also faced a refugee crisis on a scale unseen in Europe since World War II. President Clinton, desperate to avoid U.S. casualties and haunted by memories of Vietnam, insisted that the United States would not commit ground forces to the conflict. American public opinion wavered, appalled by the human suffering but deeply wary of U.S. military involvement.

The continuing Balkans crisis underscored—were more evidence needed—that the end of the Cold War did not mean an end to conflict and danger for America and its allies. It also illustrated the difficulty of applying

**Kosovo, 1999**
*As the 1990s ended, NATO and the United States launched a bombing campaign again Serbia, in an effort to halt President Slobodan Milosevic's "ethnic cleansing" campaign against Kosovo's ethnic Albanians. Here, an elderly ethnic Albanian peers from the trunk of a car filled with refugees fleeing Kosovo.*

U.S. power in complex regional conflicts and of coordinating international peacekeeping efforts in the absence of a Soviet threat capable of unifying the West and rallying public opinion behind forceful action.

In 1999 the administration called for increased military appropriations and for modification of the 1972 Anti-Ballistic Missile Treaty to cope with regional conflicts and with threats of rogue states or terrorist groups that might possess not only conventional explosives but possibly nuclear, chemical, or biological weapons. The widely anticipated post–Cold War era of peace and security seemed an ever-receding mirage.

### Diplomacy in the Era of a Global Economy

Foreign policy in the 1990s increasingly involved economic issues. As the NAFTA agreement made plain, the expansion of foreign trade ranked high on Clinton's foreign-policy agenda. The U.S. trade deficit, after several years of decline, shot up to $133 billion in 1993, including a $59 billion trade gap with Japan. Emulating George Bush, Clinton seized every opportunity to pressure the Japanese to buy more U.S. goods.

Again like Bush, Clinton chose to preserve trading ties with China despite Beijing's human-rights abuses. In 1994, while deploring the repression of dissidents, Clinton extended China's "most favored nation" trading status with the United States. In 1997, despite protests from human-rights activists, the administration approved a state visit to America by Chinese president Jiang Zemin. In 1998 President Clinton, accompanied by a vast entourage of more than a thousand officials and journalists, paid a return state visit to China. Congress grew increasingly skeptical of the administration's policy of "constructive engagement" with China as the Chinese government continued its human-rights abuses, military threats to Taiwan, and restrictive trade practices. But the effort to build better relations continued, reflecting hard economic realities: China had become the fourth most important U.S. trading partner. At the 1994 annual meeting of the Group of Seven (G-7), the world's leading economic powers, Clinton declared: "Trade as much as troops will increasingly define the ties that bind nations in the twenty-first century." On a six-nation tour of Africa in 1998, Clinton called for "trade not aid" and urged more U.S. investment and business activity in that continent.

Certainly trade increasingly defined U.S. relations with Europe. In 1993 the nations of the European Community (EC) created a stronger organization, the European Union (EU). With fifteen member states pledged to achieving a common currency and coordinated economic policies, the EU loomed as a formidable trading bloc.

In 1994 the Senate ratified a new trading agreement negotiated by the World Trade Organization (formerly known as GATT, the General Agreement on Tariffs and Trade, established in 1947). The agreement provided for a gradual lowering of trade barriers worldwide and set up mechanisms for resolving trade disputes.

The link between trade and diplomacy was illustrated early in 1995 when the Mexican peso collapsed, jeopardizing not only foreign investors but the flow of foreign trade. President Clinton, concluding that the crisis affected America's vital interests, offered $40 billion in loan guarantees to stabilize the situation. At about the same time, Clinton threatened heavy punitive tariffs on imports from China to pressure Beijing to halt the black-market pirating of U.S. movies, CDs, and computer software. In the administration's view the economic issues clearly outweighed the resulting strained relations.

The importance of foreign economic developments to American interests again became evident in 1997–1998 when the economies of several Asian nations, including South Korea, Malaysia, and Indonesia, collapsed as a result of corruption, excessive debt, and mismanagement. As currencies lost value, prices soared, jobs disappeared, and citizens panicked. Treating the crisis as a threat to U.S. economic and strategic interests, State Department officials warned of political chaos and regional instability. Federal Reserve Board chairman Alan Greenspan cautioned that Asia's economic turmoil could threaten U.S. prosperity if falling U.S. exports to Asia worsened the trade deficit* and if the affected nations defaulted on Western loans. Political and social chaos especially threatened Indonesia, the world's fourth-most-populous nation, ruled by the autocratic sixty-seven-year-old President Suharto. Working through the International Monetary Fund, the Clinton administration sought to bail out Indonesia's faltering economy and to reduce corruption in Suharto's regime.

The impact of distant economic developments on America's strategic interests and domestic economic health was further illustrated in 1998 by events in Russia and Japan. Russia's continued efforts to convert to a free-market economy resulted in a deepening economic crisis and devaluation of the ruble in the summer of 1998, causing political turmoil and threat-

**The Clintons in Africa, March 1998**
*As scandal swirled around the White House, the president and his wife made a whirlwind tour of Africa. Here, wearing colorful kinta cloth, they appeared at a rally with Ghana president Jerry Rawlings.*

ening to topple President Boris Yeltsin. Having just helped put together a $22.6 billion package of loans and credits, Washington could only watch anxiously as its former Cold War adversary threatened to sink into chaos. The once-sizzling Japanese economy, which began to turn downward in 1992, weakened further in 1998 as Asia's economic crisis spread. Japan's banks tottered, the Tokyo stock market fell, and the yen lost value, unsettling the U.S. stock market and further jeopardizing U.S. exports and investments in Asia. Recognizing the threat to U.S. prosperity, the Clinton administration urged the Japanese government to undertake needed economic reforms.

By 1999 the economies of Brazil and other South American nations teetered toward collapse as well. Although the short-term U.S. economic prognosis remained bright, questions proliferated as to how long the American boom could go on amid economic crises elsewhere.

### A New World Order?

As the bipolar world that had emerged after World War II collapsed, so too did the Cold War that for forty years had shaped the United States' foreign policy, economy, and culture. Victory in that epic struggle brought a

---

* This, in fact, quickly happened. In January 1998 the U.S. trade deficit rose to its highest level in a decade.

sense of long effort rewarded and an occasion to reaffirm such basic principles as democracy, individual rights, and freedom of expression that had outlasted the dogmas of totalitarianism.

But the Cold War's end also brought a realization that the world had suddenly become a more complicated place. The post–Cold War era saw "a good deal of talk about a new world order," observed political scientist Richard Barnet in 1992, "but, for all the talk, the nightly news is a kaleidoscope of disorder." Totalitarian regimes had collapsed, and the threat of nuclear holocaust had subsided, but trouble spots around the world still clamored for attention. Like firefighters battling many small blazes rather than one raging conflagration, policymakers accustomed to Cold War strategizing coped with a tangle of seemingly unrelated issues.

Africa, Bosnia, Iraq, the Mideast, Indonesia, Japan, Russia, Northern Ireland, Kosovo—all claimed Washington's attention. Clinton's domestic troubles and legal difficulties further weakened his role as foreign-policy leader. Amidst the confusion, the public's attention wandered. In a 1997 poll, only 20 percent of Americans said they followed foreign news, down from 80 percent in the 1980s, with the sharpest drop among young people. From 1989 to 1995, foreign-news coverage on network television fell by more than 50 percent. Post–Cold War America, commented one cultural observer in 1998, "has no mission other than to keep itself entertained." Congress did little better. In a hasty 1998 Senate debate on the important issue of NATO expansion, senators complained about the diversion from domestic issues.

Taking a broader view, four large-scale developments helped define America's post–Cold War global role:

- First, *the growing centrality of economic and trade issues.* As commercial considerations; multinational corporations; and global systems of communications, finance, and marketing increasingly defined international relations, the task of defining America's foreign-policy interests and purposes in this new trade-driven era posed a major challenge.

- Second, in contrast to this economic globalization, *a turning inward toward various forms of fundamentalism.* Muslim fundamentalists, reacting against Western secularism, searched for Islamic purity. In India, a fundamentalist Hindu government gained power in 1998, replacing the secularist Congress party that had ruled since 1948. In America, too, a fundamentalist outlook suspicious not only of

the outside world, but of the U.S. government itself, was widespread. This struggle between fundamentalism and inward-turning isolationism, on the one hand, and the dynamic of a globalized economy and communications system, on the other, posed a dilemma for diplomats in all world capitals, including Washington.

- Third, *a new gulf dividing the world:* not East/West, this time, but North-South. While the prosperous nations built their trading systems, the chasm has grown between the industrialized societies of the Northern Hemisphere, with their high living standards and stable birthrates, and a Southern Hemisphere scourged by poverty, disease, illiteracy, crushing population growth, and a dangerous gap between the masses and the ruling elites. The destabilizing potential of this vast disparity was only too obvious.

- Finally, *the uncertain role of international organizations in the post–Cold War era.*

Some Americans, including Washington politicians, adopted a go-it-alone foreign policy, favoring unilateral, Washington-imposed approaches rather than patient multinational diplomacy. Congress's refusal to pay America's U.N. dues, and even demands for withdrawal from the U.N., expressed this attitude in a particularly stark fashion.

Others, however, hoped that in the post–Cold War era, the United Nations, long a pawn of the superpowers' conflict, could at last function in the way envisioned by its more idealistic supporters in 1945. And indeed, in 1994 more than seventy thousand U.N. representatives from seventy nations performed peacekeeping duties in fourteen world trouble spots from El Salvador to Somalia. U.N. agencies also addressed environmental and public-health issues that transcended national boundaries. In 1998, as we saw, U.N. Secretary General Kofi Annan helped avert, at least for a time, a U.S. military attack on Iraq. How the world organization would evolve, amid contradictory global trends toward economic consolidation and ideological separatism, remained to be seen.

Opinion polls indicated that most Americans supported international approaches to world problems and generally supported the United Nations. The data also suggested that despite flagging attention to foreign affairs, Americans could become deeply engaged when they understood an issue in human terms, or when they grasped how events abroad affected U.S. interests. Clearly, Americans needed time to adjust to a new historical age in which international issues could not be reduced to simplistic Cold War slogans. A stable, humane, and open international order will not arise automatically. It will require clear thinking, committed effort, and active engagement by citizens as well as policy makers.

## An Overview of America in 2000

A concluding overview as the United States stands on the cusp of a new millennium offered many reasons for confidence. For all its flaws, American democracy survived. Taken overall, the economy exuded a glow of health. A society that was "multicultural" from the beginning was growing increasingly diverse. Religious faith remained strong for many, and technological advances offered multiple benefits, from medical breakthroughs to instant global communications.

But not everyone shared in the prosperity. New patterns of immigration brought social problems as well as benefits. For some, ethnic and cultural diversity and differing moral values stirred conflict and anxiety. And the technological wonders that inspired awe also provoked uneasy debate (see A Place in Time). Many Americans appeared alienated from their society and cynical about their government as the 1990s ended. Nevertheless, as the twenty-first century dawned, the nation's prospects seemed in many respects more hopeful than they had for years.

### *Two-and-a-Half Cheers for the Economy*

The economic boom of the 1990s proved remarkably long-lived. By 1999 America had enjoyed one of the longest sustained periods of growth in the postwar era. The stock market, starting at around 2700 in 1990, rose to well over 10,000 by spring 1999. Inflation remained stable, and in early 1999 the jobless rate stood at 4.3 percent—a twenty-five-year low.

The boom had vast social and political ramifications. It fueled the welfare-reform campaign and raised the prospect of budget surpluses after years of deficits. Business mergers proliferated as corporations maneuvered to improve their profitability. For many Americans, a rising stock market brought unprecedented levels of personal wealth. By 1997, 28 percent of American householders' assets were in stocks—a fifty-year high. The time just a few years earlier when America's economy had looked anemic in contrast to Japan and other Asian nations seemed remote by the late 1990s.

**Boom Times**
*As the economy soared and energy worries faded, vans and sport-utility vehicles exempt from fuel-efficiency regulations crowded the highways. Here, at the Texas state fair, potential buyers admire a new "concept vehicle" from General Motors.*

**New York Stock Exchange, August 1998**
*Despite economic crises elsewhere, U.S. stock prices soared as the 1990s wore on, fueled especially by computer and information-technology stocks.*

Still, economists cautioned that with such a large share of Americans saving in the stock market, the inevitable downturn could jeopardize the financial well-being of millions. And Americans continued to import more than they exported. The U.S. trade deficit in 1994 hit $108 billion. By 1998, as the declining value of Asian

## Cybermind

"Cybermind" is not a physical place. It has no streets, no zipcode, no latitude and longitude coordinates. But from another perspective, Cybermind is every bit as "real" as the thirty-two other Places in Time described in earlier chapters. For Cybermind is a site on the Internet, the global computer-based communications system that burst on the cultural scene in the 1990s. Each day, Cybermind subscribers log on to their computers, gain access to the Internet with a few keystrokes, and seek out Cybermind's electronic site to scroll through the latest comments or contributions of other Cybermind participants. Some do so silently—it's called "lurking"—while others add their thoughts and reflections on the topic under discussion, or introduce a new topic for consideration. Scattered around the world, most Cybermind participants have never met. Some use pseudonyms, masking their "real" identity. They may be of any race or ethnic group; male or female; gay or straight; old or young; a graduate student or a building custodian. All that is known of them by other Cybermind members is what they choose to reveal in their Internet communications—the words that appear on the display screen. Occasionally, some members arrange a "fleshmeet"—a get-together with other members in real time at a real place—but such encounters are exceptional, and often fraught with anxiety.

But if Cybermind enjoys only a virtual reality, it is a reality nonetheless, and it plays an important role in its members' lives. This became sadly evident in July 1994 when a message flashed to Cybermind members reporting the death of Michael Current, one of the two administrators of Cybermind, and an active participant in all its discussions. One member, Katie Argyle, later described her initial reaction: "In over five years of online activity this was the first time someone whom I had never met in the flesh, but who was very familiar to me in textual form, had died and would post no more. I thought it wasn't real. I thought it was a hoax, and so did many others." But as the realization sank in that the message was no hoax, and not just an example of the wordplay beloved of Internet users, expressions of shock and loss raced from computer to computer. Argyle went on: "The [Cybermind] list grieved as one, strengthening the bonds between its members. . . . [T]he emotional force of the postings, the emotional impact on Cybermind members, and the willingness to grieve in public, [are] very striking." Another Cybermind member put it more simply in his communication: "Can anyone still doubt that we are a community?" But just as Cybermind is a new kind of "place," so do its citizens constitute a new kind of "community"—a community whose members may live thousands of miles apart and who, even if they lived in the same town, would not recognize each other if they passed on the street.

Cybermind—this Place in Time but not in space—is one of many thousands of sites on the Internet, a communications system that began to transform American and indeed global culture as the twentieth century ended. A by-product of U.S. military research in the Cold War era, the Internet originally served only a few hundred Pentagon strategists, government-funded re-

*A young couple prepare's its income taxes using a laptop computer.*

searchers, and computer specialists. But by the 1990s, anyone with a computer and the proper software could roam the Internet at will. By the end of the decade, the Internet was attracting millions of users worldwide. Some, like the members of Cybermind, joined discussion groups that shared specific interests, from space travel to mushrooms to the Titanic disaster to Bible prophecy. Others used their home or laptop computers to shop, play video games, check on library holdings, follow breaking news stories, read book reviews, make travel plans, scout the weather in distant cities, explore recent medical and scientific research, seek out long-lost friends, or launch a quest for a new relationship. In the darker corners of the Internet lurked pornographers, pedophiles, and sexual predators, stirring alarm among parents, politicians, and religious groups. Universities, museums, and institutions of all kinds set up "home pages" describing themselves to interested browsers. So did many individuals, offering family news and even photographs and recorded messages to anyone who cared to "hit" their site. Others used the Internet simply as a convenient form of communication, dashing off an e-mail (electronic mail) question to a friend across the country or around the world, and receiving an answer within minutes.

As usual with a pervasive new technology, the Internet was both welcomed and deplored. Archivists and historians feared that with so much of communication taking ephemeral electronic form, fewer and fewer written records would be preserved. (This simply intensified a problem as old as the telephone.) Social psychologists cautioned that a generation reared on the Internet and videogames could lose

track of the distinction between the "real world" and the virtual world of the computer screen. Others worried that the sense of self would blur as people took on a new "identity," or multiple identities, in the anonymous electronic world of the Internet.

But for better or worse, the Internet seemed here to stay. Indeed, as social forecasters looked to the future, they predicted that the pace of change in communications technology, driven by ever tinier and more powerful computer chips, would accelerate in the twenty-first century. The "global village" once foreseen by the communications specialist Marshall McLuhan seemed on the verge of becoming a reality—at least for people in the developed world affluent enough to afford the necessary equipment. On the cusp of a new century, the potential for more and more virtual Places in Time such as Cybermind seemed almost infinite.

*In a Manhattan neighborhood nicknamed Silicon Alley, a cafe invites patrons to "sip'n surf" the Internet.*

*A young college student studies on his laptop and listens to a CD while awaiting a train on his way to classes.*

currencies made their exports more affordable, the trade deficit remained high.

In the global economy of the 1990s, foreign investors flocked into the lucrative American market. By 1990 foreign investment in the United States totaled $630 billion. The Australian tycoon Rupert Murdoch (who eventually became a U.S. citizen) acquired large chunks of the American entertainment and communications industry. In 1998 a German publishing giant acquired the venerable U.S. publishing firm Random House for $1.4 billion. Of course, the investment flowed the other way as well. As American fast-food chains, soft drinks, movies, pop music, and TV programs spread globally, other nations fretted about being swamped by U.S. mass culture. The international flow of capital, ignoring national boundaries, had become a fact of life.

At home, the benefits of prosperity were unevenly distributed. From 1979 to 1996, the portion of income that flowed to the wealthiest 20 percent of the population increased by 13 percent, while the share going to the poorest 20 percent dropped by 22 percent. Commented Harvard economist Richard Freeman: "The U.S. has the most unequal distribution of income among advanced countries—and the degree of inequality has increased more here than in any comparable country." This widening gap stirred uneasiness as the century ended. The 1997 blockbuster movie *Titanic*, which portrayed the stark social-class divisions aboard a doomed oceanliner in 1912, reminded moviegoers of the continuing reality of class differences.

As corporations maintained their competitive edge through "downsizing" and cost cutting, personal economic worries and job uneasiness gnawed at many Americans despite the good times. Adjusted for inflation, real wages remained flat through much of the 1990s. And the long-term growth of the service sector continued. The service sector included many high-income positions, but also many low-paying, low-skilled jobs in sales, fast-food outlets, custodial work, telemarketing, and similar jobs. More than a fifth of the U.S. labor force in 1994 was either temporary or part-time, enjoying few benefits or advancement prospects.

Manufacturing, by contrast, employed only 17 percent of nonagricultural workers in the mid-1990s. Although domestic steel production increased in the 1980s and 1990s, the number of steelworkers fell from 460,000 in 1979 to 160,000 in 1998, in part as a result of automation and cost-cutting efficiencies by upstart minimills using nonunion labor. As industrial employment declined, so did union membership. In 1945 some 35 percent of U.S. workers belonged to unions; by 1997, the figure was 14.1 percent. With these declining numbers, unions' political clout weakened. President Clinton successfully campaigned for the NAFTA treaty despite protests from organized labor.

**The Economic Boom of the 1990s**

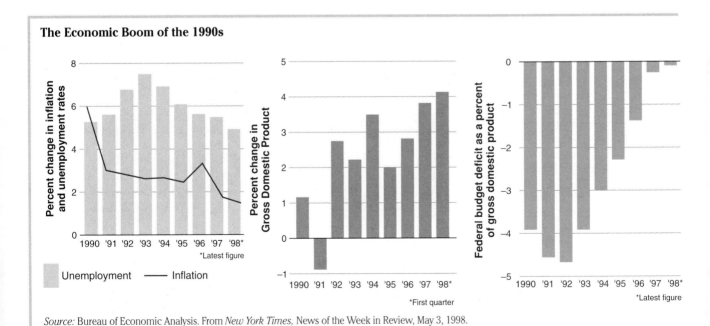

*Source:* Bureau of Economic Analysis. From *New York Times*, News of the Week in Review, May 3, 1998.

**The Two Worlds of Black America**
*A homeless family (below) in a makeshift shelter under an interstate highway in Miami, Florida; an African American judge (left) confers with a defendant in a Texas courtroom.*

Job-market success increasingly required advanced training and special skills. For many young people, displaced industrial workers, and erstwhile welfare recipients thrown into the labor force, this posed problems. In 1997 about 16 percent of job-seeking youths aged sixteen to nineteen were unemployed, three times the national average. The employment picture of the later 1990s also concealed some disturbing racial and ethnic variables. In 1997 the jobless rate for Hispanics stood at almost 8 percent, and for blacks over 10 percent. As we saw in the chapter introduction, even advanced academic training did not guarantee success in the uncertain job market of the 1990s. In short, despite the economic boom, many Americans felt a nagging sense of narrowing possibilities.

### Problems and Promise in a Multicultural America

These income and employment disparities underscored larger divisions in American society. Within the African-American community, deep social and economic fissures remained. The average annual earnings of college-educated blacks hovered at around $30,000 by the mid-1990s, and the income of black married couples approached that of non-Hispanic white married couples. The number of black-owned businesses, including such giants as TLC Beatrice International, a

foods company, reached some 600,000. Reversing a long trend, some 370,000 blacks moved from North to South in 1990–1995, strengthening the thriving black middle-class and professional communities in Atlanta and other cities.

But the chronic social problems of inner-city blacks and other minorities persisted as well. Some 800,000 African Americans were in prison in 1998, most of them young males convicted of drug-related crimes. The suicide rate among teenage blacks rose steadily from 1980 to 1995. Movies such as *Boyz 'N the Hood* (1991), set in Los Angeles, portrayed the grim inner-city reality. Drug-related carnage, peaking in the early 1990s, took a fearful toll. In April 1994 James Darby, a black third-grader in New Orleans, as part of a school assignment, wrote to President Clinton expressing his fear of urban violence. A week later, walking home from a Mother's Day picnic, James was shot dead. High rates of out-of-wedlock pregnancies among teenage black girls continued into the mid-nineties as well, reducing the young mothers' opportunities for education and employment and narrowing their children's prospects. A 1994 Census Bureau report found 57 percent of African-American children living with a single parent, usually the mother.

But black-led revitalization efforts, coupled with the admittedly uneven prosperity of the 1990s, offered hopes of change. In October 1995 thousands of black males came to Washington, D.C., for a "Million Man March" to affirm their obligations as husbands and fathers. With the improving economy, the African-American poverty rate, the inner-city murder rate, and the birthrate among unmarried black teenage girls all fell significantly in the later 1990s. Early evidence supported the contention of welfare reformers that eliminating automatic benefit increases for each new baby would further reduce teen pregnancy in the inner cities.

In the continuing battle against urban violence, several big cities filed suit against the major gun manufacturers for negligent marketing practices in cases involving injury and death caused by unregistered firearms. With annual sales of $1.4 billion, the manufacturers deliberately overproduced guns, the suits alleged, knowing that many of them would enter the black market. In one such suit in 1999, a Brooklyn, New York, jury awarded a victim nearly $4 million.

Among Native Americans, the reassertion of tribal pride and activism continued in the 1990s. Citing Article VI of the U.S. Constitution, which describes all treaties approved by Congress as "the supreme law of the land," and assisted by groups like the Indian Law Resource Center of Helena, Montana, tribes pursued their campaign to enforce the 331 Indian treaties ratified between 1778 and 1871. But this movement roused antagonisms, as non-Indians, including some prominent Western politicians, complained that the treaty-rights movement was going too far.

The growth of Indian-run businesses stirred further controversy. In Utah, the tiny Skull Valley Band of Goshute Indians, proclaiming themselves an independent nation, offered to lease the valley for nuclear-waste disposal, alarming environmentalists. The Omaha Indians of Nebraska opened a cigarette factory, dismaying public-health advocates.

The proliferation of Indian gambling casinos, approved by Congress in 1988, stirred intense debate. By the late 1990s Indian casinos such as the giant Foxwoods Casino run by the Mashantucket Pequots in Connecticut were earning $6 billion annually. The competition for lucrative casino licenses was so intense that Indian tribes became major political contributors, pouring $7 million into the 1996 campaign. While the casinos brought needed capital into Indian communities, many citizens deplored the spread of gambling, states battled to extract more tax revenues from the casinos, and many Indians lamented the erosion of traditional values.

Despite new sources of income, such chronic problems as alcoholism, joblessness, and poor education persisted in Indian communities. But the tribes fought back, supporting tribal colleges and community centers, and using casino earnings to fund alcohol-treatment centers that drew upon such Native American traditions as the sweat lodge and respect for the wisdom of elders.

New patterns of immigration continued to change the face of America as the twentieth century ended. By 1996 America's foreign-born population included 6.7 million newcomers from Mexico, 772,000 from Cuba, and 701,000 from El Salvador, along with 1.2 million from the Philippines, 801,000 from China, 757,000 from India, and 740,000 from Vietnam. The newcomers continued to cluster in big cities, from Miami and New York on the East Coast to Los Angeles, San Francisco, Houston, and Seattle in the West.

The Hispanic population, fueled by immigration and high natural increase, grew with special rapidity. By the mid-1990s, when Hispanics represented about 10 percent of the population, Hispanic women accounted for 18 percent of all births. With both white and African-American birthrates declining, demographers predicted that Hispanics would surpass blacks as the nation's largest minority by 2005, and comprise 25 percent of the population by 2050.

**Mexican Americans in Los Angeles**

*The nation's Hispanic population soared as the twentieth century ended. Here, a couple dances to the music of a pick-up band in an informal community gathering spot called "the Hill."*

The highly diverse Hispanic population resisted easy generalizations. Many were well educated, prosperous, upwardly mobile, and members of stable families. Many others, however, remained trapped in an inner-city reality of gangs, addiction, failing schools, and teen pregnancy. Despite the importance of religion and family in traditional Hispanic culture, in 1994 a third of all Hispanic children lived with a single parent—typically the mother.

Some of the new immigrants were college educated, and around 12 percent held graduate degrees. These newcomers usually moved into skilled jobs. But most were young and ill educated and gravitated toward the lowest-paid ranks of the labor force as gardeners, maids, nannies, unskilled laborers, and migrant agricultural workers. About 6 percent ended up on welfare, twice the rate for native-born Americans. For the children of the immigrant poor, exposed to TV and magazine images of the good life, the frustrations of thwarted expectations could be intense.

But all immigrant and minority groups mobilized their social and organizational potential to address problems, lobby politically, and campaign for community betterment. The largest Hispanic advocacy group, *La Raza*, worked to promote Hispanic interests. By the early 1990s, in California alone, more than four thousand Hispanics held public office. Asian-Americans, on campuses and in city neighborhoods, organized as well, sometimes acting collectively and sometimes in specific national groups.

By 2050, population experts calculate, no single racial or ethnic group will be a majority in America. Non-Hispanic whites, in other words, will simply become another "minority" in America's ethnic fabric. In a parallel development, growing numbers of Americans of mixed racial and ethnic origins, like the golfer Tiger Woods, resisted being pigeonholed in any single category. Amid these shifting demographic realities, what did it mean to be an "American" in a truly multiethnic, multicultural society? What would bind together such a diverse population?

The separatist pressures seemed strong. At the UCLA law school, for example, blacks, Latinos, and Asians each had their own student association and their own law review. Similar divisions arose across American society. In the 1992 Los Angeles riots (see Chapter 32), Korean-American merchants became a target of black rage. When President Clinton in 1997 appointed a commission to lead a national discussion on race, it was criticized for focusing on black-white issues,

**Tiger Woods, Golf Champion**
*Woods, of mixed Asian and African American ancestry, exults after winning the 1997 Masters tournament in Augusta, Georgia.*

rather than on the more complex ethnic realities of late twentieth-century America.

Language became a major battleground. While some Anglo politicians campaigned to make English America's "official language," advocates for various immigrant groups called for public school instruction in children's native tongue, or at least bilingual classes. However, a 1998 study of immigrant children found that while most spoke their native tongue at home, 88 percent preferred to learn and speak English.

The continuing phenomenon of "white flight" intensified the separatist tendency. As immigrants arrived in the cities, native-born whites tended to move out. Between 1990 and 1995, both Los Angeles and New York lost more than 1 million native-born inhabitants, approximately equal to the new arrivals from Asia and Latin America. Cities such as Las Vegas, Phoenix, Portland, Denver, and Austin attracted whites departing from larger metropolitan centers with growing immigrant populations.

Some social observers feared the fragmentation of the nation into enclaves determined by ethnicity, national origin, or skin color, each competing to advance its own interests. While countertrends toward a more cosmopolitan culture could be seen, particularly among the well-educated professional classes, much other evidence did indeed show the continuing strength of racial and ethnic identities. This was hardly surprising at a time when inequities of income and opportunity still remained linked to race and ethnicity. It was also unsurprising, perhaps, that Americans who felt alienated and adrift in the anonymity of modern mass society should seek security and reassurance in a seemingly unambigious group identity.

In his 1908 play *The Melting Pot,* the English Jewish immigrant Israel Zangwill foresaw the assimilation of immigrants into a common "American" type. By the century's end, the "melting pot" metaphor had faded, in part because its proponents had so often tacitly assumed that "Americanized" immigrants would abandon their ethnic roots, cultural traditions, and ways of behaving. But if there was to be no "melting pot," what would hold this diverse and multicultural society together? Certainly Americans shared a common identity as consumers of products and of the mass culture's diversions. Was this enough? This remained an unresolved question for the dawning new century.

### Protecting an Imperiled Environment

In 1984 gases from a U.S.-owned chemical plant in Bhopal, India, killed seventeen hundred villagers. This tragedy, coupled with the Three Mile Island crisis and the *Exxon Valdez* disaster, grimly underscored modern technology's human and environmental risks. The 1990s brought growing awareness of environmental dangers, but also intensified efforts to meet the challenge.

With the Cold War over, Americans faced the estimated $150 billion cost of cleaning up the nation's nuclear-weapons facilities, including tons of weapons-grade uranium and plutonium. The Hanford Nuclear Reservation near Richland, Washington, was a vast dump of radioactive waste. The permanent disposal of this material, as well as of radioactive fuel rods from aging nuclear-power plants, roused intense political controversy and grass-roots protests. In 1997 scientists reported more water seepage than expected into the man-made cave intended for nuclear-waste storage at one proposed site, Nevada's Yucca Mountain.

Acid rain and threatened global warming posed further environmental hazards. Acid rain, bearing sulphur dioxide and other pollutants from U.S. factories and auto exhaust, threatened Appalachian forests and marine life in Canadian lakes. As carbon dioxide from fossil-fuel emissions generated a layer of heat-retaining gases in the lower atmosphere, and as fluorocarbons from spray cans, refrigerator equipment, and other sources depleted the protective upper-atmosphere ozone layer, scientists warned of increased solar radiation and a global warming trend—the "greenhouse effect"—with catastrophic potential, including greater skin cancer risks.

Concern about hazards associated with pesticides and various food additives increased in the 1990s. Hamburgers tainted with a deadly strain of *E. coli* bacteria, purchased at fast-food outlets in the Northwest, killed four children in 1993. In 1997 the government ordered the recall of 25 million pounds of hamburger from one processing plant.

While environmental problems remained, gains were recorded as well. The Environmental Protection Agency reported dramatically improved air quality in most American cities from 1987 to 1995, and sharp reductions in emissions of lead, carbon monoxide, and other pollutants. In 1996–1997, President Clinton secured passage of a bill strengthening pesticide regulation and announced new air-quality standards to reduce soot and ground-level ozone. In 1997 the EPA allocated special federal funds to clean up more than one thousand hazardous-waste sites.Despite waning enthusiasm for governmental activism in the 1980s and 1990s, support for environmental protection remained strong, as Republican legislators learned in 1995–1996 when they attacked the EPA. U.N.-sponsored environmental conferences at Rio de Janeiro in 1992 and Kyoto in 1997 highlighted environmental protection as a common global concern. The Kyoto conference focused on a treaty to reduce the emissions contributing to global warming. When negotiations stalled, Vice President Gore flew to Japan to push the process forward. A treaty did emerge, though U.S. adherence to the standards awaited Senate ratification.

### A Truce in the Culture Wars?

On the cultural front, the Christian Coalition's effort to take over the Republican party was only part of a larger campaign to reverse what conservatives saw as America's moral decay. In earlier times, the cultural wars had raged along sectarian lines, with native-born Protestants battling Catholic and Jewish immigrants. Now the lines were redrawn, focusing on an array of emotion-laden issues touching deeply held values. During the Cold War, the source of evil had been clear: the global communist conspiracy, centered in Moscow. Now, many Americans translated the same apocalyptic worldview to the home front, and searched for the enemy within.

As the abortion controversy continued, some "pro-life" advocates turned from peaceful protest to violence. In 1995 an anti-abortion activist fatally shot a physician and his bodyguard outside a Florida abortion clinic and an unstable young man murdered two people and wounded five others at a clinic near Boston. In 1997 bombers struck abortion clinics in Tulsa and Atlanta.

In the worst outburst of domestic terrorism, on April 19, 1995, a bomb demolished an Oklahoma City federal building, killing 168 people. The bomber struck precisely two years after a government raid on the Waco, Texas, compound of the Branch Davidians, an apocalyptic religious sect charged with firearms violations. The 1993 Waco raid ended tragically when fire enveloped the compound as federal tanks moved in, leaving some eighty Branch Davidians dead. In the Oklahoma City blast, the authorities soon arrested Timothy McVeigh, a Gulf War veteran outraged over the Waco incident. McVeigh and his coconspirator, Terry Nichols, had vague links to one of many secretive right-wing militia groups that sprang up in the 1990s. These organizations were often racist, anti-Semitic, obsessed with conspiracy theories, and deeply suspicious of the government. In 1997 McVeigh was convicted of murder and sentenced to death. Nichols, convicted of involuntary manslaughter, escaped the death penalty.

Adding to the national jitters over violence-prone loners and shadowy antigovernment groups was a series of bombs mailed between 1978 and 1995 to individuals whose business or professional activities could be interpreted as anti-environmental. The bombs killed three people and injured twenty-eight others. In 1996 authorities arrested Theodore Kaczynski, a Harvard-trained mathematician and obsessive opponent of modern technology, in his remote Montana cabin. Kaczynski was convicted but escaped the death penalty by reason of mental incapacity.

Although overall crime rates declined as the crack-cocaine epidemic peaked, the late 1900s brought a rash of school shootings, culminating in April 1999 when two high-school students in Littleton, Colorado,

shot and killed a teacher and twelve of their fellow students before turning their guns on themselves. These episodes produced anxious discussions of America's obsession with firearms, of a breakdown of parental authority, and of the influence of violence in the mass media on impressionable children and adolescents. In the aftermath of the Littleton horror, President Clinton intensified his campaign for tougher gun-control laws.

The culture wars were fought mainly with words and gestures, though, not bullets and bombs. In 1995 a Smithsonian Institution exhibit marking the fiftieth anniversary of the atomic bombing of Japan was canceled when veterans' organizations and some politicians attacked it for allegedly overemphasizing the bombs' destructiveness and for being overly critical of Truman's decision.

The culture wars unfolded on many fronts, from televangelists' programs and radio talk shows, to school-board protests and boycotts of TV shows deemed morally offensive. The National Endowment for the Arts became a target for supposedly funding "indecent" art. Republican legislators cut funding for the Public Broadcasting System as too liberal and "elitist." Conservative cultural warriors also called for a constitutional amendment permitting prayer in the classroom and a renewal of religion, morality, and "family values."

Conservatives attacked history textbooks for promoting "multiculturalism," for being insufficiently patriotic, and for pandering to the forces of "political correctness." In literary studies, conflict raged between conservative traditionalists and "deconstructionists" who probed the way writers of the past had reenforced an imperialist and patriarchal social order. The rapidly growing evangelical and charismatic churches continued to denounce the wickedness of society and the government's role in the decline of morality. In October 1997 some 700,000 men belonging to a conservative Protestant religious movement called Promise Keepers rallied in Washington, D.C., for a day of prayer, hymn singing, and pledges to reclaim the moral and spiritual leadership of their households.

As the year 2000 approached, the popularizers of Bible prophecy intensified their warnings that history's final crisis was near. Pat Robertson's *The New World Order* (1991) saw much of American history as a vast conspiracy that would soon culminate in the rule of the Antichrist. The swirling charges of infidelity and lying levied against President Clinton simply underscored for conservatives the moral rot they saw eating away at America.

As the 1990s ended, however, the cultural wars seemed to be diminishing. The Christian Coalition lost momentum when its politically savvy director, Ralph Reed, resigned in 1997. By 1998, leaders of the Christian Coalition and other groups were expressing open frustration with Republican politicians who courted conservative Christian votes but failed to fight for the conservatives' cultural agenda when they gained power.

In academia, too, the cultural wars lost steam. Wrote sociologist Todd Gitlin in 1998: "The pendulum has swung away from adding trendy new courses and toward reinstating a humanities core that emphasizes classics. At the same time, . . . many conservatives have lost heart for a free-for-all. Administrators are inclined to organize truces." In *One Nation After All* (1998), sociologist Alan Wolfe reported on his extensive interviews with middle-class Americans across the nation. Wolfe found his interviewees suspicious of extremist positions and broadly accepting of diversity. The old virtues of tolerance and live-and-let-live, Wolfe suggested, were thriving in middle America. To be sure, Wolfe's conclusions reflected the outlook of a comfortable class that had prospered in the 1990s, and they excluded the perspectives of the poor and most immigrant newcomers, as well as of highly ideological activist organizations whose influence did not depend entirely on numbers.

But Wolfe's study did illuminate the outlook of the vast American middle class, and the generosity of spirit that runs through the interviews offered reassurance amid warnings of social fragmentation and irreconcilable cultural divisions. As one of Wolfe's interviewees reflected: "I wish more people would recognize [that] we can't just stand back and whine about the ways things are and . . . about how terrible the changes will be. We've got to move forward and trust that we can . . . get to a solution eventually." In its tempered, matter-of-fact optimism and its avoidance of extremist language, such a perspective captured a deep-seated American pragmatic approach to social problems and struck an encouraging note as a new century dawned.

## CONCLUSION

America changed with dizzying rapidity as the twentieth century ended. Politically, the repudiation of New Deal–style liberalism led to a major welfare-reform initiative and other policy changes. A strong economy erased the budget deficit and gave the decade a glow of prosperity, but millions in the inner cities remained economically marginal or mired in poverty. New immigration patterns, meanwhile, made the nation ever more multiethnic and multicultural—stirring anxiety in some quarters. At the same time, the personal computer continued to transform American life, with the promise of greater changes ahead. The rise of multinational conglomerates made mass-market consumption a global phenomenon, from fast foods and sneakers to movies, TV, pop music, videogames, and theme parks. These developments, coupled with such emotion-laden issues as abortion and homosexuality, fueled the bitter controversies—the "culture wars"—that punctuated the decade.

Internationally, U.S. policy makers faced a new global situation characterized by regional trouble spots and crises that required analysis on their own terms, not simply as pawns in a global superpower struggle. The 1990s also saw a close intertwining of trade and diplomacy that suggested a long-term shift in the nature of foreign relations.

Through most of the decade, political leadership was divided between a Republican Congress that started out ambitiously after its 1994 triumph but soon bogged down and a Democratic presidential administration eager to shed the "liberal" label. The price of this centrism often seemed a loss of vision and an opportunism driven by polls rather than principle. In Bill Clinton, the nation had a highly intelligent president with a mastery of policy issues and an easy empathy ("I feel your pain"), but with character flaws that continually threatened to overshadow his strengths. For all his defects, Clinton nevertheless caught the mood of the 1990s and, at times at least, articulated a political vision—tempered by experience and skeptical of grand initiatives—but nevertheless still committed to the perennial American dream of a more just and humane social order.

## FOR FURTHER READING

Many titles listed in Chapter 32's bibliography are relevant for Chapter 33 as well. Discussions of trends in contemporary America may also be found in such journals as *The American Prospect, The Atlantic Monthly, Business Week, Christianity Today, Commentary, The Economist* (London), *Fortune, Harper's Magazine, Monthly Labor Review* (U.S. Department of Labor), *The New Republic, National Review, The Nation, Nation's Business, New York Times Magazine, The Progressive, Scientific American,* and *U.S. News and World Report.*

Mary Jo Bane and David T. Ellwood, *Welfare Realities: From Rhetoric to Reform* (1994). Ellwood, assistant secretary of health and human services in the Clinton administration, and his coauthor explore the complexities of welfare reform.

Robert Bellah et al., *The Good Society* (1991). Thoughtful reflections on the sources of community in the American historical experience.

David Callahan, *Unwinnable Wars: American Power and Ethnic Conflict* (1997). Sober, carefully argued analysis of the implications of ethnic conflicts for U.S. interests and foreign policy.

David Maraniss, *First in His Class: A Biography of Bill Clinton* (1995). Explores the sources of Clinton's political drive and his almost desperate need to be liked.

Gary B. Nash, Charlotte Crabtree, and Ross E. Dunn, *History on Trial: Culture Wars and the Teaching of the Past* (1997). Readable account of one battleground in the culture wars, by three survivors.

Richard J. Payne, *Getting Beyond Race: The Changing American Culture* (1998). An argument for moving beyond the emphasis on division and difference.

Mark Robert Rank, *Living on the Edge: The Realities of Welfare in America* (1994). A compelling look at the human face of some of society's most marginal members.

Rickie Solinger, ed., *Abortion Wars: A Half Century of Struggle* (1998). Scholars offer historical perspectives on a contentious issue.

Kenneth Starr, *The Starr Report: The Official Report of the Independent Counsel's Investigation of the President* (1998). The document that triggered the impeachment of President Clinton.

*Statistical Abstract of the United States, 1999. The National Data Book* (1999). A treasure trove of information on economic and social trends, from the budget to college enrollments.

Peter Trubowitz, *Defining the National Interest: Conflict and Change in American Foreign Policy* (1998). Examines the domestic economic and political considerations that shape the U.S. government's approach to foreign affairs.

Alan Wolfe, *One Nation After All: What Middle Class Americans Really Think . . .* (1998). A sociologist reports on his extensive firsthand interviews, and finds reason for optimism about middle-class attitudes on a variety of issues.

# *Appendix*

# DECLARATION OF INDEPENDENCE

**IN CONGRESS, JULY 4, 1776**

THE UNANIMOUS DECLARATION OF THE THIRTEEN UNITED STATES OF AMERICA

When, in the course of human events, it becomes necessary for one people to dissolve the political bands which have connected them with another, and to assume, among the powers of the earth, the separate and equal station to which the laws of nature and of nature's God entitle them, a decent respect to the opinions of mankind requires that they should declare the causes which impel them to the separation.

We hold these truths to be self-evident: That all men are created equal; that they are endowed by their Creator with certain unalienable rights; that among these are life, liberty, and the pursuit of happiness; that, to secure these rights, governments are instituted among men, deriving their just powers from the consent of the governed; that whenever any form of government becomes destructive of these ends, it is the right of the people to alter or to abolish it, and to institute new government, laying its foundation on such principles, and organizing its powers in such form, as to them shall seem most likely to effect their safety and happiness. Prudence, indeed, will dictate that governments long established should not be changed for light and transient causes; and accordingly all experience hath shown that mankind are more disposed to suffer, while evils are sufferable, than to right themselves by abolishing the forms to which they are accustomed. But when a long train of abuses and usurpations, pursuing invariably the same object, evinces a design to reduce them under absolute despotism, it is their right, it is their duty, to throw off such government, and to provide new guards for their future security. Such has been the patient sufferance of these colonies; and such is now the necessity which constrains them to alter their former systems of government. The history of the present King of Great Britain is a history of repeated injuries and usurpations, all having in direct object the establishment of an absolute tyranny over these states. To prove this, let facts be submitted to a candid world.

He has refused his assent to laws, the most wholesome and necessary for the public good.

He has forbidden his governors to pass laws of immediate and pressing importance, unless suspended in their operation till his assent should be obtained; and, when so suspended, he has utterly neglected to attend to them.

He has refused to pass other laws for the accommodation of large districts of people, unless those people would relinquish the right of representation in the legislature, a right inestimable to them, and formidable to tyrants only.

He has called together legislative bodies at places unusual, uncomfortable, and distant from the depository of their public records, for the sole purpose of fatiguing them into compliance with his measures.

He has dissolved representative houses repeatedly, for opposing, with manly firmness, his invasions on the rights of the people.

He has refused for a long time, after such dissolutions, to cause others to be elected; whereby the legislative powers, incapable of annihilation, have returned to the people at large for their exercise; the state remaining, in the mean time, exposed to all the dangers of invasions from without and convulsions within.

He has endeavored to prevent the population of these states; for that purpose obstructing the laws of naturalization of foreigners; refusing to pass others to encourage their migration hither, and raising the conditions of new appropriation of lands.

He has obstructed the administration of justice, by refusing his assent to laws for establishing judiciary powers.

He has made judges dependent on his will alone, for the tenure of their offices, and the amount and payment of their salaries.

He has erected a multitude of new offices, and sent hither swarms of officers to harass our people and eat out their substance.

He has kept among us, in times of peace, standing armies, without the consent of our legislatures.

He has affected to render the military independent of, and superior to, the civil power.

He has combined with others to subject us to a jurisdiction foreign to our constitution, and unacknowledged by our laws, giving his assent to their acts of pretended legislation:

For quartering large bodies of armed troops among us;

For protecting them, by a mock trial, from punishment for any murders which they should commit on the inhabitants of these states;

For cutting off our trade with all parts of the world;

For imposing taxes on us without our consent;

For depriving us, in many cases, of the benefits of trial by jury;

For transporting us beyond seas, to be tried for pretended offenses;

For abolishing the free system of English laws in a neighboring province, establishing therein an arbitrary government, and enlarging its boundaries, so as to render it at once an example and fit instrument for introducing the same absolute rule into these colonies;

For taking away our charters, abolishing our most valuable laws, and altering fundamentally the forms of our governments;

For suspending our own legislatures, and declaring themselves invested with power to legislate for us in all cases whatsoever.

He has abdicated government here, by declaring us out of his protection and waging war against us.

He has plundered our seas, ravaged our coasts, burned our towns, and destroyed the lives of our people.

He is at this time transporting large armies of foreign mercenaries to complete the works of death, desolation, and tyranny already begun with circumstances of cruelty and perfidy scarcely paralleled in the most barbarous ages, and totally unworthy of the head of a civilized nation.

He has constrained our fellow-citizens, taken captive on the high seas, to bear arms against their country, to become the executioners of their friends and brethren, or to fall themselves by their hands.

He has excited domestic insurrection among us, and has endeavored to bring on the inhabitants of our frontiers the merciless Indian savages, whose known rule of warfare is an undistinguished destruction of all ages, sexes, and conditions.

In every stage of these oppressions we have petitioned for redress in the most humble terms; our repeated petitions have been answered only by repeated injury. A prince, whose character is thus marked by every act which may define a tyrant, is unfit to be the ruler of a free people.

Nor have we been wanting in our attentions to our British brethren. We have warned them, from time to time, of attempts by their legislature to extend an unwarrantable jurisdiction over us. We have reminded them of the circumstances of our emigration and settlement here. We have appealed to their native justice and magnanimity; and we have conjured them by the ties of our common kindred, to disavow these usurpations, which would inevitably interrupt our connections and correspondence. They, too, have been deaf to the voice of justice and of consanguinity. We must, therefore, acquiesce in the necessity which denounces our separation, and hold them, as we hold the rest of mankind, enemies in war, in peace friends.

We, therefore, the representatives of the United States of America, in General Congress assembled, appealing to the Supreme Judge of the world for the rectitude of our intentions, do, in the name and by the authority of the good people of these colonies, solemnly publish and declare, that these United Colonies are, and of right ought to be, FREE AND INDEPENDENT STATES; that they are absolved from all allegiance to the British crown, and that all political connection between them and the state of Great Britain is, and ought to be, totally dissolved; and that, as free and independent states, they have full power to levy war, conclude peace, contract alliances, establish commerce, and do all other acts and things which independent states may of right do. And for the support of this declaration, with a firm reliance on the protection of Divine Providence, we mutually pledge to each other our lives, our fortunes, and our sacred honor.

JOHN HANCOCK [*President*]
[*and fifty-five others*]

# THE ARTICLES OF CONFEDERATION AND PERPETUAL UNION

BETWEEN THE STATES OF NEW HAMPSHIRE, MASSACHUSETTS BAY, RHODE ISLAND AND PROVIDENCE PLANTATIONS, CONNECTICUT, NEW YORK, NEW JERSEY, PENNSYLVANIA, DELAWARE, MARYLAND, VIRGINIA, NORTH CAROLINA, SOUTH CAROLINA, GEORGIA.*

## Article 1.

The stile of this confederacy shall be "The United States of America."

## Article 2.

Each State retains its sovereignty, freedom and independence, and every power, jurisdiction, and right, which is not by this confederation expressly delegated to the United States, in Congress assembled.

## Article 3.

The said states hereby severally enter into a firm league of friendship with each other for their common defence, the security of their liberties and their mutual and general welfare; binding themselves to assist each other against all force offered to, or attacks made upon them, or any of them, on account of religion, sovereignty, trade, or any other pretence whatever.

## Article 4.

The better to secure and perpetuate mutual friendship and intercourse among the people of the different states in this union, the free inhabitants of each of these states, paupers, vagabonds, and fugitives from justice excepted, shall be entitled to all privileges and immunities of free citizens in the several states; and the people of each State shall have free ingress and regress to and from any other State, and shall enjoy therein all the privileges of trade and commerce, subject to the same duties, impositions, and restrictions, as the inhabitants thereof respectively; provided, that such restrictions shall not extend so far as to prevent the removal of property, imported into any State, to any other State of which the owner is an inhabitant; provided also, that no imposition, duties, or restriction, shall be laid by any State on the property of the United States, or either of them.

If any person guilty of, or charged with treason, felony, or other high misdemeanor in any State, shall flee from justice and be found in any of the United States, he shall, upon demand of the governor or executive power of the State from which he fled, be delivered up and removed to the State having jurisdiction of his offence.

Full faith and credit shall be given in each of these states to the records, acts, and judicial proceedings of the courts and magistrates of every other State.

## Article 5.

For the more convenient management of the general interests of the United States, delegates shall be annually appointed, in such manner as the legislature of each State shall direct, to meet in Congress, on the 1st Monday in November in every year, with a power reserved to each State to recall its delegates, or any of them, at any time within the year, and to send others in their stead for the remainder of the year.

No State shall be represented in Congress by less than two, nor by more than seven members; and no person shall be capable of being a delegate for more than three years in any term of six years; nor shall any person, being a delegate, be capable of holding any office under the United States, for which he, or any other for his benefit, receives any salary, fees, or emolument of any kind.

Each State shall maintain its own delegates in a meeting of the states, and while they act as members of the committee of the states.

*This copy of the final draft of the Articles of Confederation is taken from the *Journals*, 9:907–925, November 15, 1777.

In determining questions in the United States, in Congress assembled, each State shall have one vote.

Freedom of speech and debate in Congress shall not be impeached or questioned in any court or place out of Congress: and the members of Congress shall be protected in their persons from arrests and imprisonments, during the time of their going to and from, and attendance on Congress, *except for treason,* felony, or breach of the peace.

## Article 6.

No State, without the consent of the United States, in Congress assembled, shall send any embassy to, or receive any embassy from, or enter into any conference, agreement, alliance, or treaty with any king, prince, or state; nor shall any person, holding any office of profit or trust under the United States, or any of them, accept of any present, emolument, office or title, of any kind whatever, from any king, prince, or foreign state; nor shall the United States, in Congress assembled, or any of them, grant any title of nobility.

No two or more states shall enter into any treaty, confederation, or alliance, whatever, between them, without the consent of the United States, in Congress assembled, specifying accurately the purposes for which the same is to be entered into, and how long it shall continue.

No State shall lay any imposts or duties which may interfere with any stipulations in treaties entered into by the United States, in Congress assembled, with any king, prince, or state, in pursuance of any treaties already proposed by Congress to the courts of France and Spain.

No vessels of war shall be kept up in time of peace by any State, except such number only as shall be deemed necessary by the United States, in Congress assembled, for the defence of such State or its trade; nor shall any body of forces be kept up by any State, in time of peace, except such number only as, in the judgment of the United States, in Congress assembled, shall be deemed requisite to garrison the forts necessary for the defence of such State; but every State shall always keep up a well regulated and disciplined militia, sufficiently armed and accoutred, and shall provide, and constantly have ready for use, in public stores, a due number of field pieces and tents, and a proper quantity of arms, ammunition and camp equipage.

No State shall engage in any war without the consent of the United States, in Congress assembled, unless such State be actually invaded by enemies, or shall have received certain advice of a resolution being formed by some nation of Indians to invade such State, and the danger is so imminent as not to admit of a delay till the United States, in Congress assembled, can be consulted; nor shall any State grant commissions to any ships or vessels of war, nor letters of marque or reprisal, except it be after a declaration of war by the United States, in Congress assembled, and then only against the kingdom or state, and the subjects thereof, against which war has been so declared, and under such regulations as shall be established by the United States, in Congress assembled, unless such States be infested by pirates, in which case vessels of war may be fitted out for that occasion, and kept so long as the danger shall continue, or until the United States, in Congress assembled, shall determine otherwise.

## Article 7.

When land forces are raised by any State for the common defence, all officers of or under the rank of colonel, shall be appointed by the legislature of each State respectively, by whom such forces shall be raised, or in such manner as such State shall direct; and all vacancies shall be filled up by the State which first made the appointment.

## Article 8.

All charges of war and all other expences, that shall be incurred for the common defence or general welfare, and allowed by the United States, in Congress assembled, shall be defrayed out of a common treasury, which shall be supplied by the several states, in proportion to the value of all land within each State, granted to or surveyed for any person, as such land and the buildings and improvements thereon shall be estimated according to such mode as the United States, in Congress assembled, shall, from time to time, direct and appoint.

The taxes for paying that proportion shall be laid and levied by the authority and direction of the legislatures of the several states, within the time agreed upon by the United States, in Congress assembled.

## Article 9.

The United States, in Congress assembled, shall have the sole and exclusive right and power of determining on peace and war, except in the cases mentioned in the

6th article; of sending and receiving ambassadors; entering into treaties and alliances, provided that no treaty of commerce shall be made, whereby the legislative power of the respective states shall be restrained from imposing such imposts and duties on foreigners as their own people are subjected to, or from prohibiting the exportation or importation of any species of goods or commodities whatsoever; of establishing rules for deciding, in all cases, what captures on land or water shall be legal, and in what manner prizes, taken by land or naval forces in the service of the United States, shall be divided or appropriated; of granting letters of marque and reprisal in times of peace; appointing courts for the trial of piracies and felonies committed on the high seas, and establishing courts for receiving and determining, finally, appeals in all cases of captures; provided, that no member of Congress shall be appointed a judge of any of the said courts.

The United States, in Congress assembled, shall also be the last resort on appeal in all disputes and differences now subsisting, or that hereafter may arise between two or more states concerning boundary, jurisdiction or any other cause whatever; which authority shall always be exercised in the manner following: whenever the legislative or executive authority, or lawful agent of any State, in controversy with another, shall present a petition to Congress, stating the matter in question, and praying for a hearing, notice thereof shall be given, by order of Congress, to the legislative or executive authority of the other State in controversy, and a day assigned for the appearance of the parties by their lawful agents, who shall then be directed to appoint, by joint consent, commissioners or judges to constitute a court for hearing and determining the matter in question; but, if they cannot agree, Congress shall name three persons out of each of the United States, and from the list of such persons each party shall alternately strike out one, in the petitioners beginning, until the number shall be reduced to thirteen; and from that number not less than seven, nor more than nine names, as Congress shall direct, shall, in the presence of Congress, be drawn out by lot; and the persons whose names shall be drawn, or any five of them, shall be commissioners or judges to hear and finally determine the controversy, so always as a major part of the judges who shall hear the cause shall agree in the determination; and if either party shall neglect to attend at the day appointed, without shewing reasons which Congress shall judge sufficient, or, being present, shall refuse to strike, the Congress shall proceed to nominate three persons out of each State, and the secretary of Congress shall strike in behalf of such party absent or refusing; and the judgment and sentence of the court to be appointed, in the manner before prescribed, shall be final and conclusive; and if any of the parties shall refuse to submit to the authority of such court, or to appear or defend their claim or cause, the court shall nevertheless proceed to pronounce sentence or judgment, which shall, in like manner, be final and decisive, the judgment or sentence and other proceedings being, in either case, transmitted to Congress, and lodged among the acts of Congress for the security of the parties concerned: provided, that every commissioner, before he sits in judgment, shall take an oath, to be administered by one of the judges of the supreme or superior court of the State where the cause shall be tried, "well and truly to hear and determine the matter in question, according to the best of his judgment, without favour, affection, or hope of reward": provided, also, that no State shall be deprived of territory for the benefit of the United States.

All controversies concerning the private right of soil, claimed under different grants of two or more states, whose jurisdictions, as they may respect such lands and the states which passed such grants, are adjusted, the said grants, or either of them, being at the same time claimed to have originated antecedent to such settlement of jurisdiction, shall, on the petition of either party to the Congress of the United States, be finally determined, as near as may be, in the same manner as is before prescribed for deciding disputes respecting territorial jurisdiction between different states.

The United States, in Congress assembled, shall also have the sole and exclusive right and power of regulating the alloy and value of coin struck by their own authority, or by that of the respective states; fixing the standard of weights and measures throughout the United States; regulating the trade and managing all affairs with the Indians not members of any of the states; provided that the legislative right of any State within its own limits be not infringed or violated; establishing and regulating post offices from one State to another throughout all the United States, and exacting such postage on the papers passing through the same as may be requisite to defray the expences of the said office; appointing all officers of the land forces in the service of the United States, excepting regimental officers; appointing all the officers of the naval forces, and commissioning all officers whatever in the service of the United States; making rules for the government and regulation of the said land and naval forces, and directing their operations.

The United States, in Congress assembled, shall have authority to appoint a committee to sit in the recess of Congress, to be denominated "a Committee of the States," and to consist of one delegate from each State, and to appoint such other committees and civil officers as may be necessary for managing the general affairs of the United States, under their direction; to appoint one of their number to preside; provided that no person be allowed to serve in the office of president more than one year in any term of three years; to ascertain the necessary sums of money to be raised for the service of the United States, and to appropriate and apply the same for defraying the public expences; to borrow money or emit bills on the credit of the United States, transmitting, every half year, to the respective states, an account of the sums of money so borrowed or emitted; to build and equip a navy; to agree upon the number of land forces, and to make requisitions from each State for its quota, in proportion to the number of white inhabitants in such State; which requisitions shall be binding; and, thereupon, the legislature of each State shall appoint the regimental officers, raise the men, and cloathe, arm, and equip them in a soldier-like manner, at the expence of the United States; and the officers and men so cloathed, armed, and equipped, shall march to the place appointed and within the time agreed on by the United States, in Congress assembled; but if the United States, in Congress assembled, shall, on consideration of circumstances, judge proper that any State should not raise men, or should raise a smaller number than its quota, and that any other State should raise a greater number of men than the quota thereof, such extra number shall be raised, officered, cloathed, armed, and equipped in the same manner as the quota of such State, unless the legislature of such State shall judge that such extra number cannot be safely spared out of the same, in which case they shall raise, officer, cloathe, arm, and equip as many of such extra number as they judge can be safely spared. And the officers and men so cloathed, armed, and equipped, shall march to the place appointed and within the time agreed on by the United States, in Congress assembled.

The United States, in Congress assembled, shall never engage in a war, nor grant letters of marque and reprisal in time of peace, nor enter into any treaties or alliances, nor coin money, nor regulate the value thereof, nor ascertain the sums and expences necessary for the defence and welfare of the United States, or any of them: nor emit bills, nor borrow money on the credit of the United States, nor appropriate money, nor agree upon the number of vessels of war to be built or purchased, or the number of land or sea forces to be raised, nor appoint a commander in chief of the army or navy, unless nine states assent to the same; nor shall a question on any other point, except for adjourning from day to day, be determined, unless by the votes of a majority of the United States, in Congress assembled.

The Congress of the United States shall have power to adjourn to any time within the year, and to any place within the United States, so that no period of adjournment be for a longer duration than the space of six months, and shall publish the journal of their proceedings monthly, except such parts thereof, relating to treaties, alliances or military operations, as, in their judgment, require secrecy; and the yeas and nays of the delegates of each State on any question shall be entered on the journal, when it is desired by any delegate; and the delegates of a State, or any of them, at his, or their request, shall be furnished with a transcript of the said journal, except such parts as are above excepted, to lay before the legislatures of the several states.

### Article 10.

The committee of the states, or any nine of them, shall be authorized to execute, in the recess of Congress, such of the powers of Congress as the United States, in Congress assembled, by the consent of nine states, shall, from time to time, think expedient to vest them with; provided, that no power be delegated to the said committee for the exercise of which, by the articles of confederation, the voice of nine states, in the Congress of the United States assembled, is requisite.

### Article 11.

Canada acceding to this confederation, and joining in the measures of the United States, shall be admitted into and entitled to all the advantages of this union; but no other colony shall be admitted into the same, unless such admission be agreed to by nine states.

### Article 12.

All bills of credit emitted, monies borrowed and debts contracted by, or under the authority of Congress before the assembling of the United States, in pursuance of the present confederation, shall be deemed and considered as a charge against the United States, for payment and satisfaction whereof the said United States and the public faith are hereby solemnly pledged.

### Article 13.

Every State shall abide by the determinations of the United States, in Congress assembled, on all questions which, by this confederation, are submitted to them. And the articles of this confederation shall be inviolably observed by every State, and the union shall be perpetual; nor shall any alteration at any time hereafter be made in any of them, unless such alteration be agreed to in a Congress of the United States, and be afterwards confirmed by the legislatures of every State.

These articles shall be proposed to the legislatures of all the United States, to be considered, and if approved of by them, they are advised to authorize their delegates to ratify the same in the Congress of the United States; which being done, the same shall become conclusive.

# Constitution of the United States of America

**PREAMBLE**

We the people of the United States, in order to form a more perfect union, establish justice, insure domestic tranquillity, provide for the common defense, promote the general welfare, and secure the blessings of liberty to ourselves and our posterity, do ordain and establish this CONSTITUTION for the United States of America.

## Article I

**Section 1.**  All legislative powers herein granted shall be vested in a Congress of the United States, which shall consist of a Senate and a House of Representatives.

**Section 2.**  The House of Representatives shall be composed of members chosen every second year by the people of the several States, and the electors in each State shall have the qualifications requisite for electors of the most numerous branch of the State Legislature.

No person shall be a Representative who shall not have attained to the age of twenty-five years, and been seven years a citizen of the United States, and who shall not, when elected, be an inhabitant of that State in which he shall be chosen.

Representatives and direct taxes shall be apportioned among the several States which may be included within this Union, according to their respective numbers, *which shall be determined by adding to the whole number of free persons, including those bound to service for a term of years and excluding Indians not taxed, three-fifths of all other persons.* The actual enumeration shall be made within three years after the first meeting of the Congress of the United States, and within every subsequent term of ten years, in such manner as they shall by law direct. The number of Representatives shall not exceed one for every thirty thousand, but each State shall have at least one Representative; *and until such enumeration shall be made, the State of New Hampshire shall be entitled to choose three, Massachusetts eight, Rhode Island and Providence Plantations one, Connecticut five, New York six, New Jersey four, Pennsylvania eight, Delaware one, Maryland six, Virginia ten, North Carolina five, South Carolina five, and Georgia three.*

When vacancies happen in the representation from any State, the Executive authority thereof shall issue writs of election to fill such vacancies.

The House of Representatives shall choose their Speaker and other officers; and shall have the sole power of impeachment.

**Section 3.**  The Senate of the United States shall be composed of two Senators from each State, *chosen by the legislature thereof,* for six years; and each Senator shall have one vote.

*Immediately after they shall be assembled in consequence of the first election, they shall be divided as equally as may be into three classes. The seats of the Senators of the first class shall be vacated at the expiration of the second year, of the second class at the expiration of the fourth year, and of the third class at the expiration of the sixth year,* so that one-third may be chosen every second year; *and if vacancies happen by resignation or otherwise, during the recess of the legislature of any State, the Executive thereof may make temporary appointments until the next meeting of the legislature, which shall then fill such vacancies.*

No person shall be a Senator who shall not have attained to the age of thirty years, and been nine years

---

Note: Passages that are no longer in effect are printed in italic type.

a citizen of the United States, and who shall not, when elected, be an inhabitant of that State for which he shall be chosen.

The Vice President of the United States shall be President of the Senate, but shall have no vote, unless they be equally divided.

The Senate shall choose their other officers, and also a President *pro tempore,* in the absence of the Vice President, or when he shall exercise the office of the President of the United States.

The Senate shall have the sole power to try all impeachments. When sitting for that purpose, they shall be on oath or affirmation. When the President of the United States is tried, the Chief Justice shall preside: and no person shall be convicted without the concurrence of two-thirds of the members present.

Judgment in cases of impeachment shall not extend further than to removal from the office, and disqualification to hold and enjoy any office of honor, trust or profit under the United States; but the party convicted shall nevertheless be liable and subject to indictment, trial, judgment and punishment, according to law.

**Section 4.**   The times, places and manner of holding elections for Senators and Representatives shall be prescribed in each State by the legislature thereof; but the Congress may at any time by law make or alter such regulations, except as to the places of choosing Senators.

The Congress shall assemble at least once in every year, and such meeting *shall be on the first Monday in December, unless they shall by law appoint a different day.*

**Section 5.**   Each house shall be the judge of the elections, returns and qualifications of its own members, and a majority of each shall constitute a quorum to do business; but a smaller number may adjourn from day to day, and may be authorized to compel the attendance of absent members, in such manner, and under such penalties, as each house may provide.

Each house may determine the rules of its proceedings, punish its members for disorderly behavior, and with the concurrence of two-thirds, expel a member.

Each house shall keep a journal of its proceedings, and from time to time publish the same, excepting such parts as may in their judgment require secrecy; and the yeas and nays of the members of either house on any question shall, at the desire of one-fifth of those present, be entered on the journal.

Neither house, during the session of Congress, shall, without the consent of the other, adjourn for more than three days, nor to any other place than that in which the two houses shall be sitting.

**Section 6.**   The Senators and Representatives shall receive a compensation for their services, to be ascertained by law and paid out of the treasury of the United States. They shall in all cases except treason, felony and breach of the peace, be privileged from arrest during their attendance at the session of their respective houses, and in going to and returning from the same; and for any speech or debate in either house, they shall not be questioned in any other place.

No Senator or Representative shall, during the time for which he was elected, be appointed to any civil office under the authority of the United States, which shall have been created, or the emoluments whereof shall have been increased, during such time; and no person holding any office under the United States shall be a member of either house during his continuance in office.

**Section 7.**   All bills for raising revenue shall originate in the House of Representatives; but the Senate may propose or concur with amendments as on other bills.

Every bill which shall have passed the House of Representatives and the Senate, shall, before it become a law, be presented to the President of the United States; if he approve he shall sign it, but if not he shall return it with objections to that house in which it originated, who shall enter the objections at large on their journal, and proceed to reconsider it. If after such reconsideration two-thirds of that house shall agree to pass the bill, it shall be sent, together with the objections, to the other house, by which it shall likewise be reconsidered, and, if approved by two-thirds of that house, it shall become a law. But in all such cases the votes of both houses shall be determined by yeas and nays, and the names of the persons voting for and against the bill shall be entered on the journal of each house respectively. If any bill shall not be returned by the President within ten days (Sundays excepted) after it shall have been presented to him, the same shall be a law, in like manner as if he had signed it, unless the Congress by their adjournment prevent its return, in which case it shall not be a law.

Every order, resolution, or vote to which the concurrence of the Senate and House of Representatives may be necessary (except on a question of adjournment) shall be presented to the President of the United

States; and before the same shall take effect, shall be approved by him, or being disapproved by him, shall be repassed by two-thirds of the Senate and House of Representatives, according to the rules and limitations prescribed in the case of a bill.

**Section 8.**   The Congress shall have power

To lay and collect taxes, duties, imposts, and excises, to pay the debts and provide for the common defense and general welfare of the United States; but all duties, imposts and excises shall be uniform throughout the United States;

To borrow money on the credit of the United States;

To regulate commerce with foreign nations, and among the several States, and with the Indian tribes;

To establish an uniform rule of naturalization, and uniform laws on the subject of bankruptcies throughout the United States;

To coin money, regulate the value thereof, and of foreign coin, and fix the standard of weights and measures;

To provide for the punishment of counterfeiting the securities and current coin of the United States;

To establish post offices and post roads;

To promote the progress of science and useful arts by securing for limited times to authors and inventors the exclusive right to their respective writings and discoveries;

To constitute tribunals inferior to the Supreme Court;

To define and punish piracies and felonies committed on the high seas and offenses against the law of nations;

To declare war, grant letters of marque and reprisal, and make rules concerning captures on land and water;

To raise and support armies, but no appropriation of money to that use shall be for a longer term than two years;

To provide and maintain a navy;

To make rules for the government and regulation of the land and naval forces;

To provide for calling forth the militia to execute the laws of the Union, suppress insurrections, and repel invasions;

To provide for organizing, arming, and disciplining the militia, and for governing such part of them as may be employed in the service of the United States, reserv-

ing to the States respectively the appointment of the officers, and the authority of training the militia according to the discipline prescribed by Congress;

To exercise exclusive legislation in all cases whatsoever, over such district (not exceeding ten miles square) as may, by cession of particular States, and the acceptance of Congress, become the seat of government of the United States, and to exercise like authority over all places purchased by the consent of the legislature of the State, in which the same shall be, for erection of forts, magazines, arsenals, dock-yards, and other needful buildings;—and

To make all laws which shall be necessary and proper for carrying into execution the foregoing powers, and all other powers vested by this Constitution in the government of the United States, or in any department or officer thereof.

**Section 9.**   *The migration or importation of such persons as any of the States now existing shall think proper to admit shall not be prohibited by the Congress prior to the year 1808; but a tax or duty may be imposed on such importation, not exceeding $10 for each person.*

The privilege of the writ of habeas corpus shall not be suspended, unless when in cases of rebellion or invasion the public safety may require it.

No bill of attainder or ex post facto law shall be passed.

No capitation, or other direct, tax shall be laid, unless in proportion to the census or enumeration herein before directed to be taken.

No tax or duty shall be laid on articles exported from any State.

No preference shall be given by any regulation of commerce or revenue to the ports of one State over those of another; nor shall vessels bound to, or from, one State, be obliged to enter, clear, or pay duties in another.

No money shall be drawn from the treasury, but in consequence of appropriations made by law; and a regular statement and account of the receipts and expenditures of all public money shall be published from time to time.

No title of nobility shall be granted by the United States: and no person holding any office of profit or trust under them, shall, without the consent of the Congress, accept of any present, emolument, office, or title, of any kind whatever, from any king, prince, or foreign state.

**Section 10.** No State shall enter into any treaty, alliance, or confederation; grant letters of marque and reprisal; coin money; emit bills of credit; make anything but gold and silver coin a tender in payment of debts; pass any bill of attainder, ex post facto law, or law impairing the obligation of contracts, or grant any title of nobility.

No State shall, without the consent of Congress, lay any imposts or duties on imports or exports, except what may be absolutely necessary for executing its inspection laws: and the net produce of all duties and imposts, laid by any State on imports or exports, shall be for the use of the treasury of the United States; and all such laws shall be subject to the revision and control of the Congress.

No State shall, without the consent of Congress, lay any duty of tonnage, keep troops or ships of war in time of peace, enter into any agreement or compact with another State, or with a foreign power, or engage in war, unless actually invaded, or in such imminent danger as will not admit of delay.

## Article II

**Section 1.** The executive power shall be vested in a President of the United States of America. He shall hold his office during the term of four years, and, together with the Vice President, chosen for the same term, be elected as follows:

Each state shall appoint, in such manner as the legislature thereof may direct, a number of electors, equal to the whole number of Senators and Representatives to which the State may be entitled in the Congress; but no Senator or Representative, or person holding an office of trust or profit under the United States, shall be appointed an elector.

*The electors shall meet in their respective States, and vote by ballot for two persons, of whom one at least shall not be an inhabitant of the same State with themselves. And they shall make a list of all the persons voted for, and of the number of votes for each; which list they shall sign and certify, and transmit sealed to the seat of government of the United States, directed to the President of the Senate. The President of the Senate shall, in the presence of the Senate and the House of Representatives, open all the certificates, and the votes shall then be counted. The person having the greatest number of votes shall be the President,*

*if such number be a majority of the whole number of electors appointed; and if there be more than one who have such majority, and have an equal number of votes, then the House of Representatives shall immediately choose by ballot one of them for President; and if no person have a majority, then from the five highest on the list said house shall in like manner choose the President. But in choosing the President the votes shall be taken by States, the representation from each State having one vote; a quorum for this purpose shall consist of a member or members from two-thirds of the States, and a majority of all the States shall be necessary to a choice. In every case, after the choice of the President, the person having the greatest number of votes of the electors shall be the Vice President. But if there should remain two or more who have equal votes, the Senate shall choose from them by ballot the Vice President.*

The Congress may determine the time of choosing the electors and the day on which they shall give their votes; which day shall be the same throughout the United States.

No person except a natural-born citizen, *or a citizen of the United States at the time of the adoption of this Constitution,* shall be eligible to the office of President; neither shall any person be eligible to that office who shall not have attained to the age of thirty-five years, and been fourteen years a resident within the United States.

In case of the removal of the President from office or of his death, resignation, or inability to discharge the powers and duties of the said office, the same shall devolve on the Vice President, and the Congress may by law provide for the case of removal, death, resignation, or inability, both of the President and Vice President, declaring what officer shall then act as President, and such officer shall act accordingly, until the disability be removed, or a President shall be elected.

The President shall, at stated times, receive for his services a compensation, which shall neither be increased nor diminished during the period for which he shall have been elected, and he shall not receive within that period any other emolument from the United States, or any of them.

Before he enter on the execution of his office, he shall take the following oath or affirmation:—"I do solemnly swear (or affirm) that I will faithfully execute the office of the President of the United States, and will to the best of my ability preserve, protect and defend the Constitution of the United States."

**Section 2.** The President shall be commander in chief of the army and navy of the United States, and of the militia of the several States, when called into the actual service of the United States; he may require the opinion, in writing, of the principal officer in each of the executive departments, upon any subject relating to the duties of their respective offices, and he shall have power to grant reprieves and pardons for offenses against the United States, except in cases of impeachment.

He shall have power, by and with the advice and consent of the Senate, to make treaties, provided two-thirds of the Senators present concur; and he shall nominate, and by and with the advice and consent of the Senate, shall appoint ambassadors, other public ministers and consuls, judges of the Supreme Court, and all other officers of the United States, whose appointments are not herein otherwise provided for, and which shall be established by law: but Congress may by law vest the appointment of such inferior officers, as they think proper, in the President alone, in the courts of law, or in the heads of departments.

The President shall have power to fill up all vacancies that may happen during the recess of the Senate, by granting commissions which shall expire at the end of their next session.

**Section 3.** He shall from time to time give to the Congress information of the state of the Union, and recommend to their consideration such measures as he shall judge necessary and expedient; he may, on extraordinary occasions, convene both houses, or either of them, and in case of disagreement between them, with respect to the time of adjournment, he may adjourn them to such time as he shall think proper; he shall receive ambassadors and other public ministers; he shall take care that the laws be faithfully executed, and shall commission all the officers of the United States.

**Section 4.** The President, Vice President and all civil officers of the United States shall be removed from office on impeachment for, and on conviction of, treason, bribery, or other high crimes and misdemeanors.

## Article III

**Section 1.** The judicial power of the United States shall be vested in one Supreme Court, and in such inferior courts as the Congress may from time to time ordain and establish. The judges, both of the Supreme and inferior courts, shall hold their offices during good behavior, and shall, at stated times, receive for their services a compensation which shall not be diminished during their continuance in office.

**Section 2.** The judicial power shall extend to all cases, in law and equity, arising under this Constitution, the laws of the United States, and treaties made, or which shall be made, under their authority;—to all cases affecting ambassadors, other public ministers and consuls;—to all cases of admiralty and maritime jurisdiction;—to controversies to which the United States shall be a party;—to controversies between two or more States;—*between a State and citizens of another State;*—between citizens of different States;—between citizens of the same State claiming lands under grants of different States, and between a State, or the citizens thereof, and foreign states, citizens or subjects.

In all cases affecting ambassadors, other public ministers and consuls, and those in which a State shall be party, the Supreme Court shall have original jurisdiction. In all the other cases before mentioned, the Supreme Court shall have appellate jurisdiction, both as to law and fact, with such exceptions, and under such regulations, as the Congress shall make.

The trial of all crimes, except in cases of impeachment, shall be by jury; and such trial shall be held in the State where said crimes shall have been committed; but when not committed within any State, the trial shall be at such place or places as the Congress may by law have directed.

**Section 3.** Treason against the United States shall consist only in levying war against them, or in adhering to their enemies, giving them aid and comfort. No person shall be convicted of treason unless on the testimony of two witnesses to the same overt act, or on confession in open court.

The Congress shall have power to declare the punishment of treason, but no attainder of treason shall work corruption of blood, or forfeiture except during the life of the person attainted.

## Article IV

**Section 1.** Full faith and credit shall be given in each State to the public acts, records, and judicial proceedings of every other State. And the Congress may by general laws prescribe the manner in which such acts, records, and proceedings shall be proved, and the effect thereof.

**Section 2.** The citizens of each State shall be entitled to all privileges and immunities of citizens in the several States.

A person charged in any State with treason, felony, or other crime, who shall flee from justice, and be found in another State, shall on demand of the executive authority of the State from which he fled, be delivered up, to be removed to the State having jurisdiction of the crime.

*No person held to service or labor in one State, under the laws thereof, escaping into another, shall, in consequence of any law or regulation therein, be discharged from such service or labor, but shall be delivered up on claim of the party to whom such service or labor may be due.*

**Section 3.** New States may be admitted by the Congress into this Union; but no new State shall be formed or erected within the jurisdiction of any other State; nor any State be formed by the junction of two or more States, or parts of States, without the consent of the legislatures of the States concerned as well as of the Congress.

The Congress shall have power to dispose of and make all needful rules and regulations respecting the territory or other property belonging to the United States; and nothing in this Constitution shall be so construed as to prejudice any claims of the United States, or of any particular State.

**Section 4.** The United States shall guarantee to every State in this Union a republican form of government, and shall protect each of them against invasion; and on application of the legislature, or of the executive (when the legislature cannot be convened), against domestic violence.

## Article V

The Congress, whenever two-thirds of both houses shall deem it necessary, shall propose amendments to this Constitution, or, on the application of the legislatures of two-thirds of the several States, shall call a convention for proposing amendments, which, in either case, shall be valid to all intents and purposes, as part of this Constitution, when ratified by the legislatures of three-fourths of the several States, or by conventions in three-fourths thereof, as the one or the other mode of ratification may be proposed by the Congress; provided *that no amendments which may be made prior to the year one thousand eight hundred and eight shall in any manner affect the first and fourth clauses in the ninth section of the first article;* and that no State, without its consent, shall be deprived of its equal suffrage in the Senate.

## Article VI

All debts contracted and engagements entered into, before the adoption of this Constitution, shall be as valid against the United States under this Constitution, as under the Confederation.

This Constitution, and the laws of the United States which shall be made in pursuance thereof; and all treaties made, or which shall be made, under the authority of the United States, shall be the supreme law of the land; and the judges in every State shall be bound thereby, anything in the Constitution or laws of any State to the contrary notwithstanding.

The Senators and Representatives before mentioned, and the members of the several State legislatures, and all executive and judicial officers, both of the United States and of the several States, shall be bound by oath or affirmation to support this Constitution; but no religious test shall ever be required as a qualification to any office or public trust under the United States.

## Article VII

The ratification of the conventions of nine States shall be sufficient for the establishment of this Constitution between the States so ratifying the same.

Done in Convention by the unanimous consent of the States present, the seventeenth day of September in the year of our Lord one thousand seven hundred and eighty-seven and of the Independence of the United States of America the twelfth. In witness whereof we have hereunto subscribed our names.

[Signed by]
G° WASHINGTON
*Presidt and Deputy from Virginia*
[*and thirty-eight others*]

## AMENDMENTS TO THE CONSTITUTION

### Article I*

Congress shall make no law respecting an establishment of religion, or prohibiting the free exercise thereof; or abridging the freedom of speech, or of the press; or the right of the people peaceably to assemble, and to petition the government for a redress of grievances.

### Article II

A well-regulated militia being necessary to the security of a free State, the right of the people to keep and bear arms shall not be infringed.

### Article III

No soldier shall, in time of peace, be quartered in any house without the consent of the owner, nor in time of war, but in a manner to be prescribed by law.

### Article IV

The right of the people to be secure in their persons, houses, papers, and effects, against unreasonable searches and seizures, shall not be violated, and no warrants shall issue but upon probable cause, supported by oath or affirmation, and particularly describing the place to be searched, and the persons or things to be seized.

### Article V

No person shall be held to answer for a capital, or otherwise infamous crime, unless on a presentment or indictment of a grand jury, except in cases arising in the land or naval forces, or in the militia, when in actual service in time of war or public danger; nor shall any person be subject for the same offense to be twice put in jeopardy of life or limb; nor shall be compelled in any criminal case to be a witness against himself, nor be deprived of life, liberty, or property, without due process of law; nor shall private property be taken for public use without just compensation.

### Article VI

In all criminal prosecutions, the accused shall enjoy the right to a speedy and public trial, by an impartial jury of the State and district wherein the crime shall have been committed, which district shall have been previously ascertained by law, and to be informed of the nature and cause of the accusation; to be confronted with the witnesses against him; to have compulsory process for obtaining witnesses in his favor, and to have the assistance of counsel for his defense.

### Article VII

In suits at common law, where the value in controversy shall exceed twenty dollars, the right of trial by jury shall be preserved, and no fact tried by a jury shall be otherwise reexamined in any court of the United States, than according to the rules of the common law.

### Article VIII

Excessive bail shall not be required, nor excessive fines imposed, nor cruel and unusual punishments inflicted.

### Article IX

The enumeration in the Constitution, of certain rights, shall not be construed to deny or disparage others retained by the people.

### Article X

The powers not delegated to the United States by the Constitution, nor prohibited by it to the States, are reserved to the States respectively, or to the people.

### Article XI
[*Adopted 1798*]

The judicial power of the United States shall not be construed to extend to any suit in law or equity, commenced or prosecuted against one of the United States by citizens of another State, or by citizens or subjects of any foreign state.

### Article XII
[*Adopted 1804*]

The electors shall meet in their respective States, and vote by ballot for President and Vice President, one of whom, at least, shall not be an inhabitant of the same State with themselves; they shall name in their ballots the person voted for as President, and in distinct ballots the person voted for as Vice President, and they shall make distinct lists of all persons voted for as President, and of all per-

*The first ten Amendments (Bill of Rights) were adopted in 1791.

sons voted for as Vice President, and of the number of votes for each, which lists they shall sign and certify, and transmit sealed to the seat of government of the United States, directed to the President of the Senate;—the President of the Senate shall, in the presence of the Senate and House of Representatives, open all the certificates and the votes shall then be counted;—the person having the greatest number of votes for President shall be the President, if such number be a majority of the whole number of electors appointed; and if no person have such majority, then from the persons having the highest numbers not exceeding three on the list of those voted for as President, the House of Representatives shall choose immediately, by ballot, the President. But in choosing the President, the votes shall be taken by States, the representation from each State having one vote; a quorum for this purpose shall consist of a member or members from two-thirds of the States, and a majority of all the States shall be necessary to a choice. And if the House of Representatives shall not choose a President whenever the right of choice shall devolve upon them, before *the fourth day of March* next following, then the Vice President shall act as President, as in the case of the death or other constitutional disability of the President.

The person having the greatest number of votes as Vice President shall be the Vice President, if such a number be a majority of the whole number of electors appointed; and if no person have a majority, then from the two highest numbers on the list the Senate shall choose the Vice President; a quorum for the purpose shall consist of two-thirds of the whole number of Senators, and a majority of the whole number shall be necessary to a choice. But no person constitutionally ineligible to the office of President shall be eligible to that of Vice President of the United States.

## Article XIII
*[Adopted 1865]*

**Section 1.** Neither slavery nor involuntary servitude, except as a punishment for crime whereof the party shall have been duly convicted, shall exist within the United States, or any place subject to their jurisdiction.

**Section 2.** Congress shall have power to enforce this article by appropriate legislation.

## Article XIV
*[Adopted 1868]*

**Section 1.** All persons born or naturalized in the United States, and subject to the jurisdiction thereof, are citizens of the United States and of the State wherein they reside. No State shall make or enforce any law which shall abridge the privileges or immunities of citizens of the United States; nor shall any State deprive any person of life, liberty, or property, without due process of law; nor deny to any person within its jurisdiction the equal protection of the laws.

**Section 2.** Representatives shall be apportioned among the several States according to their respective numbers, counting the whole number of persons in each State, excluding Indians not taxed. But when the right to vote at any election for the choice of Electors for President and Vice President of the United States, Representatives in Congress, the executive and judicial officers of a State, or the members of the legislature thereof, is denied to any of the male inhabitants of such State, being twenty-one years of age and citizens of the United States, or in any way abridged, except for participation in rebellion, or other crime, the basis of representation therein shall be reduced in the proportion which the number of such male citizens shall bear to the whole number of male citizens twenty-one years of age in such State.

**Section 3.** No person shall be a Senator or Representative in Congress or Elector of President and Vice President, or hold any office, civil or military, under the United States, or under any State, who, having previously taken an oath, as a member of Congress, or as an officer of the United States, or as a member of any State legislature, or as an executive or judicial officer of any State, to support the Constitution of the United States, shall have engaged in insurrection or rebellion against the same, or given aid and comfort to the enemies thereof. Congress may, by a vote of two-thirds of each house, remove such disability.

**Section 4.** The validity of the public debt of the United States, authorized by law, including debts incurred for payment of pensions and bounties for services in suppressing insurrection or rebellion, shall not be questioned. But neither the United States nor any State shall assume or pay any debt or obligation incurred in aid of insurrection or rebellion against the United States, or any claim for the loss or emancipation of any slave; but all such debts, obligations, and claims shall be held illegal and void.

**Section 5.** The Congress shall have the power to enforce, by appropriate legislation, the provisions of this article.

## Article XV
[*Adopted 1870*]

**Section 1.** The right of citizens of the United States to vote shall not be denied or abridged by the United States or by any State on account of race, color, or previous condition of servitude.

**Section 2.** The Congress shall have power to enforce this article by appropriate legislation.

## Article XVI
[*Adopted 1913*]

The Congress shall have power to lay and collect taxes on incomes, from whatever source derived, without apportionment among the several States, and without regard to any census or enumeration.

## Article XVII
[*Adopted 1913*]

**Section 1.** The Senate of the United States shall be composed of two Senators from each State, elected by the people thereof, for six years; and each Senator shall have one vote. The electors in each State shall have the qualifications requisite for electors of [voters for] the most numerous branch of the State legislatures.

**Section 2.** When vacancies happen in the representation of any State in the Senate, the executive authority of such State shall issue writs of election to fill such vacancies: Provided, that the Legislature of any State may empower the executive thereof to make temporary appointments until the people fill the vacancies by election as the Legislature may direct.

**Section 3.** This amendment shall not be so construed as to affect the election or term of any Senator chosen before it becomes valid as part of the Constitution.

## Article XVIII
[*Adopted 1919; repealed 1933*]

**Section 1.** *After one year from the ratification of this article the manufacture, sale, or transportation of intoxicating liquors within, the importation thereof into, or the exportation thereof from the United States and all territory subject to the jurisdiction thereof, for beverage purposes, is hereby prohibited.*

**Section 2.** *The Congress and the several States shall have concurrent power to enforce this article by appropriate legislation.*

**Section 3.** *This article shall be inoperative unless it shall have been ratified as an amendment to the Constitution by the legislatures of the several States, as provided by the Constitution, within seven years from the date of the submission thereof to the States by the Congress.*

## Article XIX
[*Adopted 1920*]

**Section 1.** The right of citizens of the United States to vote shall not be denied or abridged by the United States or by any State on account of sex.

**Section 2.** The Congress shall have the power to enforce this article by appropriate legislation.

## Article XX
[*Adopted 1933*]

**Section 1.** The terms of the President and Vice President shall end at noon on the 20th day of January, and the terms of Senators and Representatives at noon on the 3d day of January, of the years in which such terms would have ended if this article had not been ratified; and the terms of their successors shall then begin.

**Section 2.** The Congress shall assemble at least once in every year, and such meeting shall begin at noon on the 3d of January, unless they shall by law appoint a different day.

**Section 3.** If, at the time fixed for the beginning of the term of the President, the President-elect shall have died, the Vice President-elect shall become President. If a President shall not have been chosen before the time fixed for the beginning of his term, or if the President-elect shall have failed to qualify, then the Vice President-elect shall act as President until a President shall have qualified; and the Congress may by law provide for the case wherein neither a President-elect nor a Vice President-elect shall have qualified, declaring who shall then act as President, or the manner in which one who is to act shall be selected, and such persons shall act accordingly until a President or Vice President shall have qualified.

**Section 4.** The Congress may by law provide for the case of the death of any of the persons from whom the House of Representatives may choose a President whenever the right of choice shall have devolved upon them, and for the case of the death of any of the persons from whom the Senate may choose a Vice President whenever the right of choice shall have devolved upon them.

**Section 5.** Sections 1 and 2 shall take effect on the 15th day of October following the ratification of this article.

**Section 6.** This article shall be inoperative unless it shall have been ratified as an amendment to the Constitution by the Legislatures of three-fourths of the several States within seven years from the date of its submission.

## Article XXI
[*Adopted 1933*]

**Section 1.** The eighteenth article of amendment to the Constitution of the United States is hereby repealed.

**Section 2.** The transportation or importation into any State, Territory, or Possession of the United States for delivery or use therein of intoxicating liquors, in violation of the laws thereof, is hereby prohibited.

**Section 3.** This article shall be inoperative unless it shall have been ratified as an amendment to the Constitution by conventions in the several States, as provided in the Constitution, within seven years from the date of submission thereof to the States by the Congress.

## Article XXII
[*Adopted 1951*]

**Section 1.** No person shall be elected to the office of President more than twice, and no person who has held the office of President, or acted as President, for more than two years of a term to which some other person was elected President shall be elected to the office of President more than once. But this article shall not apply to any person holding the office of President when this article was proposed by the Congress, and shall not prevent any person who may be holding the office of President, or acting as President, during the

term within which this article becomes operative from holding the office of President or acting as President during the remainder of such term.

**Section 2.** This article shall be inoperative unless it shall have been ratified as an amendment to the Constitution by the legislatures of three-fourths of the several States within seven years from the date of its submission to the States by the Congress.

## Article XXIII
[*Adopted 1961*]

**Section 1.** The District constituting the seat of Government of the United States shall appoint in such manner as the Congress may direct:

A number of electors of President and Vice President equal to the whole number of Senators and Representatives in Congress to which the District would be entitled if it were a State, but in no event more than the least populous State; they shall be in addition to those appointed by the States, but they shall be considered for the purposes of the election of President and Vice President, to be electors appointed by a State; and they shall meet in the District and perform such duties as provided by the twelfth article of amendment.

**Section 2.** The Congress shall have the power to enforce this article by appropriate legislation.

## Article XXIV
[*Adopted 1964*]

**Section 1.** The right of citizens of the United States to vote in any primary or other election for President or Vice President, for electors for President or Vice President, or for Senator or Representative in Congress, shall not be denied or abridged by the United States or any State by reason of failure to pay any poll tax or other tax.

**Section 2.** The Congress shall have the power to enforce this article by appropriate legislation.

## Article XXV
[*Adopted 1967*]

**Section 1.** In case of the removal of the President from office or of his death or resignation, the Vice President shall become President.

**Section 2.** Whenever there is a vacancy in the office of the Vice President, the President shall nominate a Vice President who shall take office upon confirmation by a majority vote of both Houses of Congress.

**Section 3.** Whenever the President transmits to the President pro tempore of the Senate and the Speaker of the House of Representatives his written declaration that he is unable to discharge the powers and duties of his office, and until he transmits to them a written declaration to the contrary, such powers and duties shall be discharged by the Vice President as Acting President.

**Section 4.** Whenever the Vice President and a majority of either the principal officers of the executive departments or of such other body as Congress may by law provide, transmit to the President pro tempore of the Senate and the Speaker of the House of Representatives their written declaration that the President is unable to discharge the powers and duties of his office, the Vice President shall immediately assume the powers and duties of the office as Acting President.

Thereafter, when the President transmits to the President pro tempore of the Senate and the Speaker of the House of Representatives his written declaration that no inability exists, he shall resume the powers and duties of his office unless the Vice President and a majority of either the principal officers of the executive department[s] or of such other body as Congress may by law provide, transmit within four days to the President pro tempore of the Senate and the Speaker of the House of Representatives their written declaration that the President is unable to discharge the powers and duties of his office. Thereupon Congress shall decide the issue, assembling within forty-eight hours for that purpose if not in session. If the Congress, within twenty-one days after receipt of the latter written declaration,

or, if Congress is not in session, within twenty-one days after Congress is required to assemble, determines by two-thirds vote of both Houses that the President is unable to discharge the powers and duties of his office, the Vice President shall continue to discharge the same as Acting President; otherwise, the President shall resume the powers and duties of his office.

## Article XXVI
*[Adopted 1971]*

**Section 1.** The right of citizens of the United States, who are eighteen years of age or older, to vote shall not be denied or abridged by the United States or by any State on account of age.

**Section 2.** The Congress shall have power to enforce this article by appropriate legislation.

## Article XXVII*
*[Adopted 1992]*

No law, varying the compensation for services of the Senators and Representatives, shall take effect, until an election of Representatives shall have intervened.

---

*Originally proposed in 1789 by James Madison, this amendment failed to win ratification along with the other parts of what became the Bill of Rights. However, the proposed amendment contained no deadline for ratification, and over the years other state legislatures voted to add it to the Constitution; many such ratifications occurred during the 1980s and early 1990s as public frustration with Congress's performance mounted. In May 1992 the Archivist of the United States certified that, with the Michigan legislature's ratification, the article had been approved by three-fourths of the states and thus automatically became part of the Constitution. But congressional leaders and constitutional specialists questioned whether an amendment that took 202 years to win ratification was valid, and the issue had not been resolved by the time this book went to press.

## Growth of U.S. Population and Area

| Census | Population | Percentage of Increase over Preceding Census | Land Area Square Miles | Population per Square Mile |
|---|---|---|---|---|
| 1790 | 3,929,214 | | 867,980 | 4.5 |
| 1800 | 5,308,483 | 35.1 | 867,980 | 6.1 |
| 1810 | 7,239,881 | 36.4 | 1,685,865 | 4.3 |
| 1820 | 9,638,453 | 33.1 | 1,753,588 | 5.5 |
| 1830 | 12,866,020 | 33.5 | 1,753,588 | 7.3 |
| 1840 | 17,069,453 | 32.7 | 1,753,588 | 9.7 |
| 1850 | 23,191,876 | 35.9 | 2,944,337 | 7.9 |
| 1860 | 31,443,321 | 35.6 | 2,973,965 | 10.6 |
| 1870 | 39,818,449 | 26.6 | 2,973,965 | 13.4 |
| 1880 | 50,155,783 | 26.0 | 2,973,965 | 16.9 |
| 1890 | 62,947,714 | 25.5 | 2,973,965 | 21.2 |
| 1900 | 75,994,575 | 20.7 | 2,974,159 | 25.6 |
| 1910 | 91,972,266 | 21.0 | 2,973,890 | 30.9 |
| 1920 | 105,710,620 | 14.9 | 2,973,776 | 35.5 |
| 1930 | 122,775,046 | 16.1 | 2,977,128 | 41.2 |
| 1940 | 131,669,275 | 7.2 | 2,977,128 | 44.2 |
| 1950 | 150,697,361 | 14.5 | 2,974,726* | 50.7 |
| 1960† | 178,464,236 | 18.4 | 2,974,726 | 59.9 |
| 1970 | 204,765,770 | 14.7 | 2,974,726 | 68.8 |
| 1980 | 226,504,825 | 10.6 | 2,974,726 | 76.1 |
| 1990 | 248,709,873 | 9.8 | 2,974,726 | 83.6 |

*As remeasured in 1940.
†Not including Alaska (pop. 226,167) and Hawaii (632,772).

## Admission of States into the Union

| State | Date of Admission | State | Date of Admission |
|---|---|---|---|
| 1. Delaware | December 7, 1787 | 26. Michigan | January 26, 1837 |
| 2. Pennsylvania | December 12, 1787 | 27. Florida | March 3, 1845 |
| 3. New Jersey | December 18, 1787 | 28. Texas | December 29, 1845 |
| 4. Georgia | January 2, 1788 | 29. Iowa | December 28, 1846 |
| 5. Connecticut | January 9, 1788 | 30. Wisconsin | May 29, 1848 |
| 6. Massachusetts | February 6, 1788 | 31. California | September 9, 1850 |
| 7. Maryland | April 28, 1788 | 32. Minnesota | May 11, 1858 |
| 8. South Carolina | May 23, 1788 | 33. Oregon | February 14, 1859 |
| 9. New Hampshire | June 21, 1788 | 34. Kansas | January 29, 1861 |
| 10. Virginia | June 25, 1788 | 35. West Virginia | June 20, 1863 |
| 11. New York | July 26, 1788 | 36. Nevada | October 31, 1864 |
| 12. North Carolina | November 21, 1789 | 37. Nebraska | March 1, 1867 |
| 13. Rhode Island | May 29, 1790 | 38. Colorado | August 1, 1876 |
| 14. Vermont | March 4, 1791 | 39. North Dakota | November 2, 1889 |
| 15. Kentucky | June 1, 1792 | 40. South Dakota | November 2, 1889 |
| 16. Tennessee | June 1, 1796 | 41. Montana | November 8, 1889 |
| 17. Ohio | March 1, 1803 | 42. Washington | November 11, 1889 |
| 18. Louisiana | April 30, 1812 | 43. Idaho | July 3, 1890 |
| 19. Indiana | December 11, 1816 | 44. Wyoming | July 10, 1890 |
| 20. Mississippi | December 10, 1817 | 45. Utah | January 4, 1896 |
| 21. Illinois | December 3, 1818 | 46. Oklahoma | November 16, 1907 |
| 22. Alabama | December 14, 1819 | 47. New Mexico | January 6, 1912 |
| 23. Maine | March 15, 1820 | 48. Arizona | February 14, 1912 |
| 24. Missouri | August 10, 1821 | 49. Alaska | January 3, 1959 |
| 25. Arkansas | June 15, 1836 | 50. Hawaii | August 21, 1959 |

## Presidential Elections, 1789–1996

| Year | States in the Union | Candidates | Parties | Electoral Vote | Popular Vote | Percentage of Popular Vote |
|---|---|---|---|---|---|---|
| 1789 | 11 | GEORGE WASHINGTON | No party designations | 69 | | |
| | | John Adams | | 34 | | |
| | | Minor candidates | | 35 | | |
| 1792 | 15 | GEORGE WASHINGTON | No party designations | 132 | | |
| | | John Adams | | 77 | | |
| | | George Clinton | | 50 | | |
| | | Minor candidates | | 5 | | |
| 1796 | 16 | JOHN ADAMS | Federalist | 71 | | |
| | | Thomas Jefferson | Democratic-Republican | 68 | | |
| | | Thomas Pinckney | Federalist | 59 | | |
| | | Aaron Burr | Democratic-Republican | 30 | | |
| | | Minor candidates | | 48 | | |
| 1800 | 16 | THOMAS JEFFERSON | Democratic-Republican | 73 | | |
| | | Aaron Burr | Democratic-Republican | 73 | | |
| | | John Adams | Federalist | 65 | | |
| | | Charles C. Pinckney | Federalist | 64 | | |
| | | John Jay | Federalist | 1 | | |
| 1804 | 17 | THOMAS JEFFERSON | Democratic-Republican | 162 | | |
| | | Charles C. Pinckney | Federalist | 14 | | |
| 1808 | 17 | JAMES MADISON | Democratic-Republican | 122 | | |
| | | Charles C. Pinckney | Federalist | 47 | | |
| | | George Clinton | Democratic-Republican | 6 | | |
| 1812 | 18 | JAMES MADISON | Democratic-Republican | 128 | | |
| | | DeWitt Clinton | Federalist | 89 | | |
| 1816 | 19 | JAMES MONROE | Democratic-Republican | 183 | | |
| | | Rufus King | Federalist | 34 | | |
| 1820 | 24 | JAMES MONROE | Democratic-Republican | 231 | | |
| | | John Quincy Adams | Independent Republican | 1 | | |
| 1824 | 24 | JOHN QUINCY ADAMS | Democratic-Republican | 84 | 108,740 | 30.5 |
| | | Andrew Jackson | Democratic-Republican | 99 | 153,544 | 43.1 |
| | | William H. Crawford | Democratic-Republican | 41 | 46,618 | 13.1 |
| | | Henry Clay | Democratic-Republican | 37 | 47,136 | 13.2 |
| 1828 | 24 | ANDREW JACKSON | Democratic | 178 | 642,553 | 56.0 |
| | | John Quincy Adams | National Republican | 83 | 500,897 | 44.0 |
| 1832 | 24 | ANDREW JACKSON | Democratic | 219 | 687,502 | 55.0 |
| | | Henry Clay | National Republican | 49 | 530,189 | 42.4 |
| | | William Wirt | Anti-Masonic | 7 } | 33,108 | 2.6 |
| | | John Floyd | National Republican | 11 } | | |

Because candidates receiving less than 1 percent of the popular vote are omitted, the percentage of popular vote may not total 100 percent. Before the Twelfth Amendment was passed in 1804, the electoral college voted for two presidential candidates; the runner-up became vice president.

## Presidential Elections, 1789–1996 *(cont.)*

| Year | States in the Union | Candidates | Parties | Electoral Vote | Popular Vote | Percentage of Popular Vote |
|------|---------------------|------------|---------|----------------|--------------|----------------------------|
| 1836 | 26 | MARTIN VAN BUREN | Democratic | 170 | 765,483 | 50.9 |
|      |    | William H. Harrison | Whig | 73 | | |
|      |    | Hugh L. White | Whig | 26 | 739,795 | 49.1 |
|      |    | Daniel Webster | Whig | 14 | | |
|      |    | W. P. Mangum | Whig | 11 | | |
| 1840 | 26 | WILLIAM H. HARRISON | Whig | 234 | 1,274,624 | 53.1 |
|      |    | Martin Van Buren | Democratic | 60 | 1,127,781 | 46.9 |
| 1844 | 26 | JAMES K. POLK | Democratic | 170 | 1,338,464 | 49.6 |
|      |    | Henry Clay | Whig | 105 | 1,300,097 | 48.1 |
|      |    | James G. Birney | Liberty | | 62,300 | 2.3 |
| 1848 | 30 | ZACHARY TAYLOR | Whig | 163 | 1,360,967 | 47.4 |
|      |    | Lewis Cass | Democratic | 127 | 1,222,342 | 42.5 |
|      |    | Martin Van Buren | Free Soil | | 291,263 | 10.1 |
| 1852 | 31 | FRANKLIN PIERCE | Democratic | 254 | 1,601,117 | 50.9 |
|      |    | Winfield Scott | Whig | 42 | 1,385,453 | 44.1 |
|      |    | John P. Hale | Free Soil | | 155,825 | 5.0 |
| 1856 | 31 | JAMES BUCHANAN | Democratic | 174 | 1,832,955 | 45.3 |
|      |    | John C. Frémont | Republican | 114 | 1,339,932 | 33.1 |
|      |    | Millard Fillmore | American | 8 | 871,731 | 21.6 |
| 1860 | 33 | ABRAHAM LINCOLN | Republican | 180 | 1,865,593 | 39.8 |
|      |    | Stephen A. Douglas | Democratic | 12 | 1,382,713 | 29.5 |
|      |    | John C. Breckinridge | Democratic | 72 | 848,356 | 18.1 |
|      |    | John Bell | Constitutional Union | 39 | 592,906 | 12.6 |
| 1864 | 36 | ABRAHAM LINCOLN | Republican | 212 | 2,206,938 | 55.0 |
|      |    | George B. McClellan | Democratic | 21 | 1,803,787 | 45.0 |
| 1868 | 37 | ULYSSES S. GRANT | Republican | 214 | 3,013,421 | 52.7 |
|      |    | Horatio Seymour | Democratic | 80 | 2,706,829 | 47.3 |
| 1872 | 37 | ULYSSES S. GRANT | Republican | 286 | 3,596,745 | 55.6 |
|      |    | Horace Greeley | Democratic | * | 2,843,446 | 43.9 |
| 1876 | 38 | RUTHERFORD B. HAYES | Republican | 185 | 4,034,311 | 48.0 |
|      |    | Samuel J. Tilden | Democratic | 184 | 4,288,546 | 51.0 |
|      |    | Peter Cooper | Greenback | | 75,973 | 1.0 |
| 1880 | 38 | JAMES A. GARFIELD | Republican | 214 | 4,453,295 | 48.5 |
|      |    | Winfield S. Hancock | Democratic | 155 | 4,414,082 | 48.1 |
|      |    | James B. Weaver | Greenback-Labor | | 308,578 | 3.4 |
| 1884 | 38 | GROVER CLEVELAND | Democratic | 219 | 4,879,507 | 48.5 |
|      |    | James G. Blaine | Republican | 182 | 4,850,293 | 48.2 |
|      |    | Benjamin F. Butler | Greenback-Labor | | 175,370 | 1.8 |
|      |    | John P. St. John | Prohibition | | 150,369 | 1.5 |
| 1888 | 38 | BENJAMIN HARRISON | Republican | 233 | 5,477,129 | 47.9 |
|      |    | Grover Cleveland | Democratic | 168 | 5,537,857 | 48.6 |
|      |    | Clinton B. Fisk | Prohibition | | 249,506 | 2.2 |
|      |    | Anson J. Streeter | Union Labor | | 146,935 | 1.3 |

*When Greeley died shortly after the election, his supporters divided their votes among the minor candidates.

Because candidates receiving less than 1 percent of the popular vote are omitted, the percentage of popular vote may not total 100 percent.

## Presidential Elections, 1789–1996 *(cont.)*

| Year | States in the Union | Candidates | Parties | Electoral Vote | Popular Vote | Percentage of Popular Vote |
|------|------|------|------|------|------|------|
| 1892 | 44 | GROVER CLEVELAND | Democratic | 277 | 5,555,426 | 46.1 |
|      |    | Benjamin Harrison | Republican | 145 | 5,182,690 | 43.0 |
|      |    | James B. Weaver | People's | 22 | 1,029,846 | 8.5 |
|      |    | John Bidwell | Prohibition | | 264,133 | 2.2 |
| 1896 | 45 | WILLIAM McKINLEY | Republican | 271 | 7,102,246 | 51.1 |
|      |    | William J. Bryan | Democratic | 176 | 6,492,559 | 47.7 |
| 1900 | 45 | WILLIAM McKINLEY | Republican | 292 | 7,218,491 | 51.7 |
|      |    | William J. Bryan | Democratic; Populist | 155 | 6,356,734 | 45.5 |
|      |    | John C. Wooley | Prohibition | | 208,914 | 1.5 |
| 1904 | 45 | THEODORE ROOSEVELT | Republican | 336 | 7,628,461 | 57.4 |
|      |    | Alton B. Parker | Democratic | 140 | 5,084,223 | 37.6 |
|      |    | Eugene V. Debs | Socialist | | 402,283 | 3.0 |
|      |    | Silas C. Swallow | Prohibition | | 258,536 | 1.9 |
| 1908 | 46 | WILLIAM H. TAFT | Republican | 321 | 7,675,320 | 51.6 |
|      |    | William J. Bryan | Democratic | 162 | 6,412,294 | 43.1 |
|      |    | Eugene V. Debs | Socialist | | 420,793 | 2.8 |
|      |    | Eugene W. Chafin | Prohibition | | 253,840 | 1.7 |
| 1912 | 48 | WOODROW WILSON | Democratic | 435 | 6,296,547 | 41.9 |
|      |    | Theodore Roosevelt | Progressive | 88 | 4,118,571 | 27.4 |
|      |    | William H. Taft | Republican | 8 | 3,486,720 | 23.2 |
|      |    | Eugene V. Debs | Socialist | | 900,672 | 6.0 |
|      |    | Eugene W. Chafin | Prohibition | | 206,275 | 1.4 |
| 1916 | 48 | WOODROW WILSON | Democratic | 277 | 9,127,695 | 49.4 |
|      |    | Charles E. Hughes | Republican | 254 | 8,533,507 | 46.2 |
|      |    | A. L. Benson | Socialist | | 585,113 | 3.2 |
|      |    | J. Frank Hanly | Prohibition | | 220,506 | 1.2 |
| 1920 | 48 | WARREN G. HARDING | Republican | 404 | 16,143,407 | 60.4 |
|      |    | James N. Cox | Democratic | 127 | 9,130,328 | 34.2 |
|      |    | Eugene V. Debs | Socialist | | 919,799 | 3.4 |
|      |    | P. P. Christensen | Farmer-Labor | | 265,411 | 1.0 |
| 1924 | 48 | CALVIN COOLIDGE | Republican | 382 | 15,718,211 | 54.0 |
|      |    | John W. Davis | Democratic | 136 | 8,385,283 | 28.8 |
|      |    | Robert M. La Follette | Progressive | 13 | 4,831,289 | 16.6 |
| 1928 | 48 | HERBERT C. HOOVER | Republican | 444 | 21,391,993 | 58.2 |
|      |    | Alfred E. Smith | Democratic | 87 | 15,016,169 | 40.9 |
| 1932 | 48 | FRANKLIN D. ROOSEVELT | Democratic | 472 | 22,809,638 | 57.4 |
|      |    | Herbert C. Hoover | Republican | 59 | 15,758,901 | 39.7 |
|      |    | Norman Thomas | Socialist | | 881,951 | 2.2 |
| 1936 | 48 | FRANKLIN D. ROOSEVELT | Democratic | 523 | 27,752,869 | 60.8 |
|      |    | Alfred M. Landon | Republican | 8 | 16,674,665 | 36.5 |
|      |    | William Lemke | Union | | 882,479 | 1.9 |

Because candidates receiving less than 1 percent of the popular vote are omitted, the percentage of popular vote may not total 100 percent.

**Presidential Elections, 1789–1996** *(cont.)*

| Year | States in the Union | Candidates | Parties | Electoral Vote | Popular Vote | Percentage of Popular Vote |
|------|------|------|------|------|------|------|
| 1940 | 48 | FRANKLIN D. ROOSEVELT | Democratic | 449 | 27,307,819 | 54.8 |
|      |    | Wendell L. Willkie | Republican | 82 | 22,321,018 | 44.8 |
| 1944 | 48 | FRANKLIN D. ROOSEVELT | Democratic | 432 | 25,606,585 | 53.5 |
|      |    | Thomas E. Dewey | Republican | 99 | 22,014,745 | 46.0 |
| 1948 | 48 | HARRY S TRUMAN | Democratic | 303 | 24,105,812 | 49.5 |
|      |    | Thomas E. Dewey | Republican | 189 | 21,970,065 | 45.1 |
|      |    | Strom Thurmond | States' Rights | 39 | 1,169,063 | 2.4 |
|      |    | Henry A. Wallace | Progressive |  | 1,157,172 | 2.4 |
| 1952 | 48 | DWIGHT D. EISENHOWER | Republican | 442 | 33,936,234 | 55.1 |
|      |    | Adlai E. Stevenson | Democratic | 89 | 27,314,992 | 44.4 |
| 1956 | 48 | DWIGHT D. EISENHOWER | Republican | 457 | 35,590,472 | 57.6 |
|      |    | Adlai E. Stevenson | Democratic | 73 | 26,022,752 | 42.1 |
| 1960 | 50 | JOHN F. KENNEDY | Democratic | 303 | 34,227,096 | 49.7 |
|      |    | Richard M. Nixon | Republican | 219 | 34,108,546 | 49.5 |
|      |    | Harry F. Byrd | Independent | 15 | 502,363 | .7 |
| 1964 | 50 | LYNDON B. JOHNSON | Democratic | 486 | 43,126,506 | 61.1 |
|      |    | Barry M. Goldwater | Republican | 52 | 27,176,799 | 38.5 |
| 1968 | 50 | RICHARD M. NIXON | Republican | 301 | 31,770,237 | 43.4 |
|      |    | Hubert H. Humphrey | Democratic | 191 | 31,270,533 | 42.7 |
|      |    | George C. Wallace | American Independent | 46 | 9,906,141 | 13.5 |
| 1972 | 50 | RICHARD M. NIXON | Republican | 520 | 47,169,911 | 60.7 |
|      |    | George S. McGovern | Democratic | 17 | 29,170,383 | 37.5 |
| 1976 | 50 | JIMMY CARTER | Democratic | 297 | 40,827,394 | 49.9 |
|      |    | Gerald R. Ford | Republican | 240 | 39,145,977 | 47.9 |
| 1980 | 50 | RONALD W. REAGAN | Republican | 489 | 43,899,248 | 50.8 |
|      |    | Jimmy Carter | Democratic | 49 | 35,481,435 | 41.0 |
|      |    | John B. Anderson | Independent |  | 5,719,437 | 6.6 |
|      |    | Ed Clark | Libertarian |  | 920,859 | 1.0 |
| 1984 | 50 | RONALD W. REAGAN | Republican | 525 | 54,451,521 | 58.8 |
|      |    | Walter F. Mondale | Democratic | 13 | 37,565,334 | 40.5 |
| 1988 | 50 | GEORGE H. W. BUSH | Republican | 426 | 47,946,422 | 54.0 |
|      |    | Michael S. Dukakis | Democratic | 112 | 41,016,429 | 46.0 |
| 1992 | 50 | WILLIAM J. CLINTON | Democratic | 370 | 43,728,275 | 43.2 |
|      |    | George H. W. Bush | Republican | 168 | 38,167,416 | 37.7 |
|      |    | H. Ross Perot | Independent |  | 19,237,247 | 19.0 |
| 1996 | 50 | WILLIAM J. CLINTON | Democratic |  |  |  |
|      |    | Robert Dole | Republican |  |  |  |
|      |    | H. Ross Perot | Independent |  |  |  |

Because candidates receiving less than 1 percent of the popular vote are omitted, the percentage of popular vote may not total 100 percent.

## Vice President and Cabinet Members, 1789–1998

### The Washington Administration (1789–1797)

| | | |
|---|---|---|
| Vice President | John Adams | 1789–1797 |
| Secretary of State | Thomas Jefferson | 1789–1793 |
| | Edmund Randolph | 1794–1795 |
| | Timothy Pickering | 1795–1797 |
| Secretary of Treasury | Alexander Hamilton | 1789–1795 |
| | Oliver Wolcott | 1795–1797 |
| Secretary of War | Henry Knox | 1789–1794 |
| | Timothy Pickering | 1795–1796 |
| | James McHenry | 1796–1797 |
| Attorney General | Edmund Randolph | 1789–1793 |
| | William Bradford | 1794–1795 |
| | Charles Lee | 1795–1797 |
| Postmaster General | Samuel Osgood | 1789–1791 |
| | Timothy Pickering | 1791–1794 |
| | Joseph Habersham | 1795–1797 |

### The John Adams Administration (1797–1801)

| | | |
|---|---|---|
| Vice President | Thomas Jefferson | 1797–1801 |
| Secretary of State | Timothy Pickering | 1797–1800 |
| | John Marshall | 1800–1801 |
| Secretary of Treasury | Oliver Wolcott | 1797–1800 |
| | Samuel Dexter | 1800–1801 |
| Secretary of War | James McHenry | 1797–1800 |
| | Samuel Dexter | 1800–1801 |
| Attorney General | Charles Lee | 1797–1801 |
| Postmaster General | Joseph Habersham | 1797–1801 |
| Secretary of Navy | Benjamin Stoddert | 1798–1801 |

### The Jefferson Administration (1801–1809)

| | | |
|---|---|---|
| Vice President | Aaron Burr | 1801–1805 |
| | George Clinton | 1805–1809 |
| Secretary of State | James Madison | 1801–1809 |
| Secretary of Treasury | Samuel Dexter | 1801 |
| | Albert Gallatin | 1801–1809 |
| Secretary of War | Henry Dearborn | 1801–1809 |
| Attorney General | Levi Lincoln | 1801–1805 |
| | Robert Smith | 1805 |
| | John Breckinridge | 1805–1806 |
| | Caesar Rodney | 1807–1809 |
| Postmaster General | Joseph Habersham | 1801 |
| | Gideon Granger | 1801–1809 |
| Secretary of Navy | Robert Smith | 1801–1809 |

### The Madison Administration (1809–1817)

| | | |
|---|---|---|
| Vice President | George Clinton | 1809–1812 |
| | Elbridge Gerry | 1813–1814 |
| Secretary of State | Robert Smith | 1809–1811 |
| | James Monroe | 1811–1817 |
| Secretary of Treasury | Albert Gallatin | 1809–1813 |
| | George Campbell | 1814 |
| | Alexander Dallas | 1814–1816 |
| | William Crawford | 1816–1817 |
| Secretary of War | William Eustis | 1809–1812 |
| | John Armstrong | 1813–1814 |
| | James Monroe | 1814–1815 |
| | William Crawford | 1815–1817 |
| Attorney General | Caesar Rodney | 1809–1811 |
| | William Pinkney | 1811–1814 |
| | Richard Rush | 1814–1817 |
| Postmaster General | Gideon Granger | 1809–1814 |
| | Return Meigs | 1814–1817 |
| Secretary of Navy | Paul Hamilton | 1809–1813 |
| | William Jones | 1813–1814 |
| | Benjamin Crowninshield | 1814–1817 |

### The Monroe Administration (1817–1825)

| | | |
|---|---|---|
| Vice President | Daniel Tompkins | 1817–1825 |
| Secretary of State | John Quincy Adams | 1817–1825 |
| Secretary of Treasury | William Crawford | 1817–1825 |
| Secretary of War | George Graham | 1817 |
| | John C. Calhoun | 1817–1825 |
| Attorney General | Richard Rush | 1817 |
| | William Wirt | 1817–1825 |
| Postmaster General | Return Meigs | 1817–1823 |
| | John McLean | 1823–1825 |
| Secretary of Navy | Benjamin Crowninshield | 1817–1818 |
| | Smith Thompson | 1818–1823 |
| | Samuel Southard | 1823–1825 |

### The John Quincy Adams Administration (1825–1829)

| | | |
|---|---|---|
| Vice President | John C. Calhoun | 1825–1829 |
| Secretary of State | Henry Clay | 1825–1829 |
| Secretary of Treasury | Richard Rush | 1825–1829 |
| Secretary of War | James Barbour | 1825–1828 |
| | Peter Porter | 1828–1829 |
| Attorney General | William Wirt | 1825–1829 |
| Postmaster General | John McLean | 1825–1829 |
| Secretary of Navy | Samuel Southard | 1825–1829 |

### The Jackson Administration (1829–1837)

| | | |
|---|---|---|
| Vice President | John C. Calhoun | 1829–1833 |
| | Martin Van Buren | 1833–1837 |
| Secretary of State | Martin Van Buren | 1829–1831 |
| | Edward Livingston | 1831–1833 |
| | Louis McLane | 1833–1834 |
| | John Forsyth | 1834–1837 |
| Secretary of Treasury | Samuel Ingham | 1829–1831 |
| | Louis McLane | 1831–1833 |
| | William Duane | 1833 |
| | Roger B. Taney | 1833–1834 |
| | Levi Woodbury | 1834–1837 |
| Secretary of War | John H. Eaton | 1829–1831 |
| | Lewis Cass | 1831–1837 |
| | Benjamin Butler | 1837 |
| Attorney General | John M. Berrien | 1829–1831 |
| | Roger B. Taney | 1831–1833 |
| | Benjamin Butler | 1833–1837 |
| Postmaster General | William Barry | 1829–1835 |
| | Amos Kendall | 1835–1837 |
| Secretary of Navy | John Branch | 1829–1831 |
| | Levi Woodbury | 1831–1834 |
| | Mahlon Dickerson | 1834–1837 |

### The Van Buren Administration (1837–1841)

| | | |
|---|---|---|
| Vice President | Richard M. Johnson | 1837–1841 |
| Secretary of State | John Forsyth | 1837–1841 |
| Secretary of Treasury | Levi Woodbury | 1837–1841 |
| Secretary of War | Joel Poinsett | 1837–1841 |
| Attorney General | Benjamin Butler | 1837–1838 |
| | Felix Grundy | 1838–1840 |
| | Henry D. Gilpin | 1840–1841 |
| Postmaster General | Amos Kendall | 1837–1840 |
| | John M. Niles | 1840–1841 |
| Secretary of Navy | Mahlon Dickerson | 1837–1838 |
| | James Paulding | 1838–1841 |

### The William Harrison Administration (1841)

| | | |
|---|---|---|
| Vice President | John Tyler | 1841 |
| Secretary of State | Daniel Webster | 1841 |
| Secretary of Treasury | Thomas Ewing | 1841 |
| Secretary of War | John Bell | 1841 |
| Attorney General | John J. Crittenden | 1841 |
| Postmaster General | Francis Granger | 1841 |
| Secretary of Navy | George Badger | 1841 |

### The Tyler Administration (1841–1845)

| | | |
|---|---|---|
| Vice President | None | |
| Secretary of State | Daniel Webster | 1841–1843 |
| | Hugh S. Legaré | 1843 |
| | Abel P. Upshur | 1843–1844 |
| | John C. Calhoun | 1844–1845 |
| Secretary of Treasury | Thomas Ewing | 1841 |
| | Walter Forward | 1841–1843 |
| | John C. Spencer | 1843–1844 |
| | George Bibb | 1844–1845 |
| Secretary of War | John Bell | 1841 |
| | John C. Spencer | 1841–1843 |
| | James M. Porter | 1843–1844 |
| | William Wilkins | 1844–1845 |
| Attorney General | John J. Crittenden | 1841 |
| | Hugh S. Legaré | 1841–1843 |
| | John Nelson | 1843–1845 |
| Postmaster General | Francis Granger | 1841 |
| | Charles Wickliffe | 1841 |
| Secretary of Navy | George Badger | 1841 |
| | Abel P. Upshur | 1841 |
| | David Henshaw | 1843–1844 |
| | Thomas Gilmer | 1844 |
| | John Y. Mason | 1844–1845 |

### The Polk Administration (1845–1849)

| | | |
|---|---|---|
| Vice President | George M. Dallas | 1845–1849 |
| Secretary of State | James Buchanan | 1845–1849 |
| Secretary of Treasury | Robert J. Walker | 1845–1849 |
| Secretary of War | William L. Marcy | 1845–1849 |
| Attorney General | John Y. Mason | 1845–1846 |
| | Nathan Clifford | 1846–1848 |
| | Isaac Toucey | 1848–1849 |
| Postmaster General | Cave Johnson | 1845–1849 |
| Secretary of Navy | George Bancroft | 1845–1846 |
| | John Y. Mason | 1846–1849 |

### The Taylor Administration (1849–1850)

| | | |
|---|---|---|
| Vice President | Millard Fillmore | 1849–1850 |
| Secretary of State | John M. Clayton | 1849–1850 |
| Secretary of Treasury | William Meredith | 1849–1850 |
| Secretary of War | George Crawford | 1849–1850 |
| Attorney General | Reverdy Johnson | 1849–1850 |
| Postmaster General | Jacob Collamer | 1849–1850 |
| Secretary of Navy | William Preston | 1849–1850 |
| Secretary of Interior | Thomas Ewing | 1849–1850 |

## The Fillmore Administration (1850–1853)

| | | |
|---|---|---|
| Vice President | None | |
| Secretary of State | Daniel Webster | 1850–1852 |
| | Edward Everett | 1852–1853 |
| Secretary of Treasury | Thomas Corwin | 1850–1853 |
| Secretary of War | Charles Conrad | 1850–1853 |
| Attorney General | John J. Crittenden | 1850–1853 |
| Postmaster General | Nathan Hall | 1850–1852 |
| | Sam D. Hubbard | 1852–1853 |
| Secretary of Navy | William A. Graham | 1850–1852 |
| | John P. Kennedy | 1852–1853 |
| Secretary of Interior | Thomas McKennan | 1850 |
| | Alexander Stuart | 1850–1853 |

## The Pierce Administration (1853–1857)

| | | |
|---|---|---|
| Vice President | William R. King | 1853 |
| Secretary of State | William L. Marcy | 1853–1857 |
| Secretary of Treasury | James Guthrie | 1853–1857 |
| Secretary of War | Jefferson Davis | 1853–1857 |
| Attorney General | Caleb Cushing | 1853–1857 |
| Postmaster General | James Campbell | 1853–1857 |
| Secretary of Navy | James C. Dobbin | 1853–1857 |
| Secretary of Interior | Robert McClelland | 1853–1857 |

## The Buchanan Administration (1857–1861)

| | | |
|---|---|---|
| Vice President | John C. Breckinridge | 1857–1861 |
| Secretary of State | Lewis Cass | 1857–1860 |
| | Jeremiah S. Black | 1860–1861 |
| Secretary of Treasury | Howell Cobb | 1857–1860 |
| | Philip Thomas | 1860–1861 |
| | John A. Dix | 1861 |
| Secretary of War | John B. Floyd | 1857–1861 |
| | Joseph Holt | 1861 |
| Attorney General | Jeremiah S. Black | 1857–1860 |
| | Edwin M. Stanton | 1860–1861 |
| Postmaster General | Aaron V. Brown | 1857–1859 |
| | Joseph Holt | 1859–1861 |
| | Horatio King | 1861 |
| Secretary of Navy | Isaac Toucey | 1857–1861 |
| Secretary of Interior | Jacob Thompson | 1857–1861 |

### The Lincoln Administration (1861–1865)

| | | |
|---|---|---|
| Vice President | Hannibal Hamlin | 1861–1865 |
| | Andrew Johnson | 1865 |
| Secretary of State | William H. Seward | 1861–1865 |
| Secretary of Treasury | Samuel P. Chase | 1861–1864 |
| | William P. Fessenden | 1864–1865 |
| | Hugh McCulloch | 1865 |
| Secretary of War | Simon Cameron | 1861–1862 |
| | Edwin M. Stanton | 1862–1865 |
| Attorney General | Edward Bates | 1861–1864 |
| | James Speed | 1864–1865 |
| Postmaster General | Horatio King | 1861 |
| | Montgomery Blair | 1861–1864 |
| | William Dennison | 1864–1865 |
| Secretary of Navy | Gideon Welles | 1861–1865 |
| Secretary of Interior | Caleb B. Smith | 1861–1863 |
| | John P. Usher | 1863–1865 |

### The Andrew Johnson Administration (1865–1869)

| | | |
|---|---|---|
| Vice President | None | |
| Secretary of State | William H. Seward | 1865–1869 |
| Secretary of Treasury | Hugh McCulloch | 1865–1869 |
| Secretary of War | Edwin M. Stanton | 1865–1867 |
| | Ulysses S. Grant | 1867–1868 |
| | Lorenzo Thomas | 1868 |
| | John M. Schofield | 1868–1869 |
| Attorney General | James Speed | 1865–1866 |
| | Henry Stanbery | 1866–1868 |
| | William M. Evarts | 1868–1869 |
| Postmaster General | William Dennison | 1865–1866 |
| | Alexander Randall | 1866–1869 |
| Secretary of Navy | Gideon Welles | 1865–1869 |
| Secretary of Interior | John P. Usher | 1865 |
| | James Harlan | 1865–1866 |
| | Orville H. Browning | 1866–1869 |

### The Grant Administration (1869–1877)

| | | |
|---|---|---|
| Vice President | Schuyler Colfax | 1869–1873 |
| | Henry Wilson | 1873–1875 |
| Secretary of State | Elihu B. Washburne | 1869 |
| | Hamilton Fish | 1869–1877 |
| Secretary of Treasury | George S. Boutwell | 1869–1873 |
| | William Richardson | 1873–1874 |
| | Benjamin Bristow | 1874–1876 |
| | Lot M. Morrill | 1876–1877 |

### The Grant Administration  (1869–1877)   (cont.)

| | | |
|---|---|---|
| Secretary of War | John A. Rawlins | 1869 |
| | William T. Sherman | 1869 |
| | William W. Belknap | 1869–1876 |
| | Alphonso Taft | 1876 |
| | James D. Cameron | 1876–1877 |
| Attorney General | Ebenezer Hoar | 1869–1870 |
| | Amos T. Ackerman | 1870–1871 |
| | G. H. Williams | 1871–1875 |
| | Edwards Pierrepont | 1875–1876 |
| | Alphonso Taft | 1876–1877 |
| Postmaster General | John A. J. Creswell | 1869–1874 |
| | James W. Marshall | 1874 |
| | Marshall Jewell | 1874–1876 |
| | James N. Tyner | 1876–1877 |
| Secretary of Navy | Adolph E. Borie | 1869 |
| | George M. Robeson | 1869–1877 |
| Secretary of Interior | Jacob D. Cox | 1869–1870 |
| | Columbus Delano | 1870–1875 |
| | Zachariah Chandler | 1875–1877 |

### The Hayes Administration (1877–1881)

| | | |
|---|---|---|
| Vice President | William A. Wheeler | 1877–1881 |
| Secretary of State | William M. Evarts | 1877–1881 |
| Secretary of Treasury | John Sherman | 1877–1881 |
| Secretary of War | George W. McCrary | 1877–1879 |
| | Alex Ramsey | 1879–1881 |
| Attorney General | Charles Devens | 1877–1881 |
| Postmaster General | David M. Key | 1877–1880 |
| | Horace Maynard | 1880–1881 |
| Secretary of Navy | Richard W. Thompson | 1877–1880 |
| | Nathan Goff, Jr. | 1881 |
| Secretary of Interior | Carl Schurz | 1877–1881 |

### The Garfield Administration (1881)

| | | |
|---|---|---|
| Vice President | Chester A. Arthur | 1881 |
| Secretary of State | James G. Blaine | 1881 |
| Secretary of Treasury | William Windom | 1881 |
| Secretary of War | Robert T. Lincoln | 1881 |
| Attorney General | Wayne MacVeagh | 1881 |
| Postmaster General | Thomas L. James | 1881 |
| Secretary of Navy | William H. Hunt | 1881 |
| Secretary of Interior | Samuel J. Kirkwood | 1881 |

### The Arthur Administration (1881–1885)

| | | |
|---|---|---|
| Vice President | None | |
| Secretary of State | F. T. Frelinghuysen | 1881–1885 |
| Secretary of Treasury | Charles J. Folger | 1881–1884 |
| | Walter Q. Gresham | 1884 |
| | Hugh McCulloch | 1884–1885 |
| Secretary of War | Robert T. Lincoln | 1881–1885 |
| Attorney General | Benjamin H. Brewster | 1881–1885 |
| Postmaster General | Timothy O. Howe | 1881–1883 |
| | Walter Q. Gresham | 1883–1884 |
| | Frank Hatton | 1884–1885 |
| Secretary of Navy | William H. Hunt | 1881–1882 |
| | William E. Chandler | 1882–1885 |
| Secretary of Interior | Samuel J. Kirkwood | 1881–1882 |
| | Henry M. Teller | 1882–1885 |

### The Cleveland Administration (1885–1889)

| | | |
|---|---|---|
| Vice President | Thomas A. Hendricks | 1885–1889 |
| Secretary of State | Thomas F. Bayard | 1885–1889 |
| Secretary of Treasury | Daniel Manning | 1885–1887 |
| | Charles S. Fairchild | 1887–1889 |
| Secretary of War | William C. Endicott | 1885–1889 |
| Attorney General | Augustus H. Garland | 1885–1889 |
| Postmaster General | William F. Vilas | 1885–1888 |
| | Don M. Dickinson | 1888–1889 |
| Secretary of Navy | William C. Whitney | 1885–1889 |
| Secretary of Interior | Lucius Q. C. Lamar | 1885–1888 |
| | William F. Vilas | 1888–1889 |
| Secretary of Agriculture | Norman J. Colman | 1889 |

### The Benjamin Harrison Administration (1889–1893)

| | | |
|---|---|---|
| Vice President | Levi P. Morton | 1889–1893 |
| Secretary of State | James G. Blaine | 1889–1892 |
| | John W. Foster | 1892–1893 |
| Secretary of Treasury | William Windom | 1889–1891 |
| | Charles Foster | 1891–1893 |
| Secretary of War | Redfield Proctor | 1889–1891 |
| | Stephen B. Elkins | 1891–1893 |
| Attorney General | William H. H. Miller | 1889–1891 |
| Postmaster General | John Wanamaker | 1889–1893 |
| Secretary of Navy | Benjamin F. Tracy | 1889–1893 |
| Secretary of Interior | John W. Noble | 1889–1893 |
| Secretary of Agriculture | Jeremiah M. Rusk | 1889–1893 |

## The Cleveland Administration (1893–1897)

| | | |
|---|---|---|
| Vice President | Adlai E. Stevenson | 1893–1897 |
| Secretary of State | Walter Q. Gresham | 1893–1895 |
| | Richard Olney | 1895–1897 |
| Secretary of Treasury | John G. Carlisle | 1893–1897 |
| Secretary of War | Daniel S. Lamont | 1893–1897 |
| Attorney General | Richard Olney | 1893–1895 |
| | James Harmon | 1895–1897 |
| Postmaster General | Wilson S. Bissell | 1893–1895 |
| | William L. Wilson | 1895–1897 |
| Secretary of Navy | Hilary A. Herbert | 1893–1897 |
| Secretary of Interior | Hoke Smith | 1893–1896 |
| | David R. Francis | 1896–1897 |
| Secretary of Agriculture | Julius S. Morton | 1893–1897 |

## The McKinley Administration (1897–1901)

| | | |
|---|---|---|
| Vice President | Garret A. Hobart | 1897–1899 |
| | Theodore Roosevelt | 1901 |
| Secretary of State | John Sherman | 1897–1898 |
| | William R. Day | 1898 |
| | John Hay | 1898–1901 |
| Secretary of Treasury | Lyman J. Gage | 1897–1901 |
| Secretary of War | Russell A. Alger | 1897–1899 |
| | Elihu Root | 1899–1901 |
| Attorney General | Joseph McKenna | 1897–1898 |
| | John W. Griggs | 1898–1901 |
| | Philander C. Knox | 1901 |
| Postmaster General | James A. Gary | 1897–1898 |
| | Charles E. Smith | 1898–1901 |
| Secretary of Navy | John D. Long | 1897–1901 |
| Secretary of Interior | Cornelius N. Bliss | 1897–1899 |
| | Ethan A. Hitchcock | 1899–1901 |
| Secretary of Agriculture | James Wilson | 1897–1901 |

## The Theodore Roosevelt Administration (1901–1909)

| | | |
|---|---|---|
| Vice President | Charles Fairbanks | 1905–1909 |
| Secretary of State | John Hay | 1901–1905 |
| | Elihu Root | 1905–1909 |
| | Robert Bacon | 1909 |
| Secretary of Treasury | Lyman J. Gage | 1901–1902 |
| | Leslie M. Shaw | 1902–1907 |
| | George B. Cortelyou | 1907–1909 |

### The Theodore Roosevelt Administration (1901–1909)   (cont.)

| | | |
|---|---|---|
| Secretary of War | Elihu Root | 1901–1904 |
| | William H. Taft | 1904–1908 |
| | Luke E. Wright | 1908–1909 |
| Attorney General | Philander C. Knox | 1901–1904 |
| | William H. Moody | 1904–1906 |
| | Charles J. Bonaparte | 1906–1909 |
| Postmaster General | Charles E. Smith | 1901–1902 |
| | Henry C. Payne | 1902–1904 |
| | Robert J. Wynne | 1904–1905 |
| | George B. Cortelyou | 1905–1907 |
| | George von L. Meyer | 1907–1909 |
| Secretary of Navy | John D. Long | 1901–1902 |
| | William H. Moody | 1902–1904 |
| | Paul Morton | 1904–1905 |
| | Charles J. Bonaparte | 1905–1906 |
| | Victor H. Metcalf | 1906–1908 |
| | Truman H. Newberry | 1908–1909 |
| Secretary of Interior | Ethan A. Hitchcock | 1901–1907 |
| | James R. Garfield | 1907–1909 |
| Secretary of Agriculture | James Wilson | 1901–1909 |
| Secretary of Labor and Commerce | George B. Cortelyou | 1903–1904 |
| | Victor H. Metcalf | 1904–1906 |
| | Oscar S. Straus | 1906–1909 |
| | Charles Nagel | 1909 |

### The Taft Administration (1909–1913)

| | | |
|---|---|---|
| Vice President | James S. Sherman | 1909–1912 |
| Secretary of State | Philander C. Knox | 1909–1913 |
| Secretary of Treasury | Franklin MacVeagh | 1909–1913 |
| Secretary of War | Jacob M. Dickinson | 1909–1911 |
| | Henry L. Stimson | 1911–1913 |
| Attorney General | George W. Wickersham | 1909–1913 |
| Postmaster General | Frank H. Hitchcock | 1909–1913 |
| Secretary of Navy | George von L. Meyer | 1909–1913 |
| Secretary of Interior | Richard A. Ballinger | 1909–1911 |
| | Walter L. Fisher | 1911–1913 |
| Secretary of Agriculture | James Wilson | 1909–1913 |
| Secretary of Labor and Commerce | Charles Nagel | 1909–1913 |

## The Wilson Administration (1913–1921)

| | | |
|---|---|---|
| Vice President | Thomas R. Marshall | 1913–1921 |
| Secretary of State | William J. Bryan | 1913–1915 |
| | Robert Lansing | 1915–1920 |
| | Bainbridge Colby | 1920–1921 |
| Secretary of Treasury | William G. McAdoo | 1913–1918 |
| | Carter Glass | 1918–1920 |
| | David F. Houston | 1920–1921 |
| Secretary of War | Lindley M. Garrison | 1913–1916 |
| | Newton D. Baker | 1916–1921 |
| Attorney General | James C. McReynolds | 1913–1914 |
| | Thomas W. Gregory | 1914–1919 |
| | A. Mitchell Palmer | 1919–1921 |
| Postmaster General | Albert S. Burleson | 1913–1921 |
| Secretary of Navy | Josephus Daniels | 1913–1921 |
| Secretary of Interior | Franklin K. Lane | 1913–1920 |
| | John B. Payne | 1920–1921 |
| Secretary of Agriculture | David F. Houston | 1913–1920 |
| | Edwin T. Meredith | 1920–1921 |
| Secretary of Commerce | William C. Redfield | 1913–1919 |
| | Joshua W. Alexander | 1919–1921 |
| Secretary of Labor | William B. Wilson | 1913–1921 |

## The Harding Administration (1921–1923)

| | | |
|---|---|---|
| Vice President | Calvin Coolidge | 1921–1923 |
| Secretary of State | Charles E. Hughes | 1921–1923 |
| Secretary of Treasury | Andrew Mellon | 1921–1923 |
| Secretary of War | John W. Weeks | 1921–1923 |
| Attorney General | Harry M. Daugherty | 1921–1923 |
| Postmaster General | Will H. Hays | 1921–1922 |
| | Hubert Work | 1922–1923 |
| | Harry S. New | 1923 |
| Secretary of Navy | Edwin Denby | 1921–1923 |
| Secretary of Interior | Albert B. Fall | 1921–1923 |
| | Hubert Work | 1923 |
| Secretary of Agriculture | Henry C. Wallace | 1921–1923 |
| Secretary of Commerce | Herbert C. Hoover | 1921–1923 |
| Secretary of Labor | James J. Davis | 1921–1923 |

### The Coolidge Administration (1923–1929)

| | | |
|---|---|---|
| Vice President | Charles G. Dawes | 1925–1929 |
| Secretary of State | Charles E. Hughes | 1923–1925 |
| | Frank B. Kellogg | 1925–1929 |
| Secretary of Treasury | Andrew Mellon | 1923–1929 |
| Secretary of War | John W. Weeks | 1923–1925 |
| | Dwight F. Davis | 1925–1929 |
| Attorney General | Henry M. Daugherty | 1923–1924 |
| | Harlan F. Stone | 1924–1925 |
| | John G. Sargent | 1925–1929 |
| Postmaster General | Harry S. New | 1923–1929 |
| Secretary of Navy | Edwin Denby | 1923–1924 |
| | Curtis D. Wilbur | 1924–1929 |
| Secretary of Interior | Hubert Work | 1923–1928 |
| | Roy O. West | 1928–1929 |
| Secretary of Agriculture | Henry C. Wallace | 1923–1924 |
| | Howard M. Gore | 1924–1925 |
| | William M. Jardine | 1925–1929 |
| Secretary of Commerce | Herbert C. Hoover | 1923–1928 |
| | William F. Whiting | 1928–1929 |
| Secretary of Labor | James J. Davis | 1923–1929 |

### The Hoover Administration (1929–1933)

| | | |
|---|---|---|
| Vice President | Charles Curtis | 1929–1933 |
| Secretary of State | Henry L. Stimson | 1929–1933 |
| Secretary of Treasury | Andrew Mellon | 1929–1932 |
| | Ogden L. Mills | 1932–1933 |
| Secretary of War | James W. Good | 1929 |
| | Patrick J. Hurley | 1929–1933 |
| Attorney General | William D. Mitchell | 1929–1933 |
| Postmaster General | Walter F. Brown | 1929–1933 |
| Secretary of Navy | Charles F. Adams | 1929–1933 |
| Secretary of Interior | Ray L. Wilbur | 1929–1933 |
| Secretary of Agriculture | Arthur M. Hyde | 1929–1933 |
| Secretary of Commerce | Robert P. Lamont | 1929–1932 |
| | Roy D. Chapin | 1932–1933 |
| Secretary of Labor | James J. Davis | 1929–1930 |
| | William N. Doak | 1930–1933 |

## The Franklin D. Roosevelt Administration (1933–1945)

| | | |
|---|---|---|
| Vice President | John Nance Garner | 1933–1941 |
| | Henry A. Wallace | 1941–1945 |
| | Harry S Truman | 1945 |
| Secretary of State | Cordell Hull | 1933–1944 |
| | Edward R. Stettinius, Jr. | 1944–1945 |
| Secretary of Treasury | William H. Woodin | 1933–1934 |
| | Henry Morgenthau, Jr. | 1934–1945 |
| Secretary of War | George H. Dern | 1933–1936 |
| | Henry A. Woodring | 1936–1940 |
| | Henry L. Stimson | 1940–1945 |
| Attorney General | Homer S. Cummings | 1933–1939 |
| | Frank Murphy | 1939–1940 |
| | Robert H. Jackson | 1940–1941 |
| | Francis Biddle | 1941–1945 |
| Postmaster General | James A. Farley | 1933–1940 |
| | Frank C. Walker | 1940–1945 |
| Secretary of Navy | Claude A. Swanson | 1933–1940 |
| | Charles Edison | 1940 |
| | Frank Knox | 1940–1944 |
| | James V. Forrestal | 1944–1945 |
| Secretary of Interior | Harold L. Ickes | 1933–1945 |
| Secretary of Agriculture | Henry A. Wallace | 1933–1940 |
| | Claude R. Wickard | 1940–1945 |
| Secretary of Commerce | Daniel C. Roper | 1933–1939 |
| | Harry L. Hopkins | 1939–1940 |
| | Jesse Jones | 1940–1945 |
| | Henry A. Wallace | 1945 |
| Secretary of Labor | Frances Perkins | 1933–1945 |

## The Truman Administration (1945–1953)

| | | |
|---|---|---|
| Vice President | Alben W. Barkley | 1949–1953 |
| Secretary of State | Edward R. Stettinius, Jr. | 1945 |
| | James F. Byrnes | 1945–1947 |
| | George C. Marshall | 1947–1949 |
| | Dean G. Acheson | 1949–1953 |
| Secretary of Treasury | Fred M. Vinson | 1945–1946 |
| | John W. Snyder | 1946–1953 |
| Secretary of War | Robert P. Patterson | 1945–1947 |
| | Kenneth C. Royall | 1947 |
| Attorney General | Tom C. Clark | 1945–1949 |
| | J. Howard McGrath | 1949–1952 |
| | James P. McGranery | 1952–1953 |

*The Truman Administration (1945–1953)   (cont.)*

| | | |
|---|---|---|
| Postmaster General | Frank C. Walker | 1945 |
| | Robert E. Hannegan | 1945–1947 |
| | Jesse M. Donaldson | 1947–1953 |
| Secretary of Navy | James V. Forrestal | 1945–1947 |
| Secretary of Interior | Harold L. Ickes | 1945–1946 |
| | Julius A. Krug | 1946–1949 |
| | Oscar L. Chapman | 1949–1953 |
| Secretary of Agriculture | Clinton P. Anderson | 1945–1948 |
| | Charles F. Brannan | 1948–1953 |
| Secretary of Commerce | Henry A. Wallace | 1945–1946 |
| | W. Averell Harriman | 1946–1948 |
| | Charles W. Sawyer | 1948–1953 |
| Secretary of Labor | Lewis B. Schwellenbach | 1945–1948 |
| | Maurice J. Tobin | 1948–1953 |
| Secretary of Defense | James V. Forrestal | 1947–1949 |
| | Louis A. Johnson | 1949–1950 |
| | George C. Marshall | 1950–1951 |
| | Robert A. Lovett | 1951–1953 |

*The Eisenhower Administration (1953–1961)*

| | | |
|---|---|---|
| Vice President | Richard M. Nixon | 1953–1961 |
| Secretary of State | John Foster Dulles | 1953–1959 |
| | Christian A. Herter | 1959–1961 |
| Secretary of Treasury | George M. Humphrey | 1953–1957 |
| | Robert B. Anderson | 1957–1961 |
| Attorney General | Herbert Brownell, Jr. | 1953–1958 |
| | William P. Rogers | 1958–1961 |
| Postmaster General | Arthur E. Summerfield | 1953–1961 |
| Secretary of Interior | Douglas McKay | 1953–1956 |
| | Fred A. Seaton | 1956–1961 |
| Secretary of Agriculture | Ezra T. Benson | 1953–1961 |
| Secretary of Commerce | Sinclair Weeks | 1953–1958 |
| | Lewis L. Strauss | 1958–1959 |
| | Frederick H. Mueller | 1959–1961 |
| Secretary of Labor | Martin P. Durkin | 1953 |
| | James P. Mitchell | 1953–1961 |
| Secretary of Defense | Charles E. Wilson | 1953–1957 |
| | Neil H. McElroy | 1957–1959 |
| | Thomas S. Gates, Jr. | 1959–1961 |
| Secretary of Health, Education, and Welfare | Oveta Culp Hobby | 1953–1955 |
| | Marion B. Folsom | 1955–1958 |
| | Arthur S. Flemming | 1958–1961 |

## The Kennedy Administration (1961–1963)

| | | |
|---|---|---|
| Vice President | Lyndon B. Johnson | 1961–1963 |
| Secretary of State | Dean Rusk | 1961–1963 |
| Secretary of Treasury | C. Douglas Dillon | 1961–1963 |
| Attorney General | Robert F. Kennedy | 1961–1963 |
| Postmaster General | J. Edward Day | 1961–1963 |
| | John A. Gronouski | 1963 |
| Secretary of Interior | Stewart L. Udall | 1961–1963 |
| Secretary of Agriculture | Orville L. Freeman | 1961–1963 |
| Secretary of Commerce | Luther H. Hodges | 1961–1963 |
| Secretary of Labor | Arthur J. Goldberg | 1961–1962 |
| | W. Willard Wirtz | 1962–1963 |
| Secretary of Defense | Robert S. McNamara | 1961–1963 |
| Secretary of Health, Education, and Welfare | Abraham A. Ribicoff | 1961–1962 |
| | Anthony J. Celebrezze | 1962–1963 |

## The Lyndon Johnson Administration (1963–1969)

| | | |
|---|---|---|
| Vice President | Hubert H. Humphrey | 1965–1969 |
| Secretary of State | Dean Rusk | 1963–1969 |
| Secretary of Treasury | C. Douglas Dillon | 1963–1965 |
| | Henry H. Fowler | 1965–1969 |
| Attorney General | Robert F. Kennedy | 1963–1964 |
| | Nicholas Katzenbach | 1965–1966 |
| | Ramsey Clark | 1967–1969 |
| Postmaster General | John A. Gronouski | 1963–1965 |
| | Lawrence F. O'Brien | 1965–1968 |
| | Marvin Watson | 1968–1969 |
| Secretary of Interior | Stewart L. Udall | 1963–1969 |
| Secretary of Agriculture | Orville L. Freeman | 1963–1969 |
| Secretary of Commerce | Luther H. Hodges | 1963–1964 |
| | John T. Connor | 1964–1967 |
| | Alexander B. Trowbridge | 1967–1968 |
| | Cyrus R. Smith | 1968–1969 |
| Secretary of Labor | W. Willard Wirtz | 1963–1969 |
| Secretary of Defense | Robert F. McNamara | 1963–1968 |
| | Clark Clifford | 1968–1969 |
| Secretary of Health, Education, and Welfare | Anthony J. Celebrezze | 1963–1965 |
| | John W. Gardner | 1965–1968 |
| | Wilbur J. Cohen | 1968–1969 |
| Secretary of Housing and Urban Development | Robert C. Weaver | 1966–1969 |
| | Robert C. Wood | 1969 |
| Secretary of Transportation | Alan S. Boyd | 1967–1969 |

---

### The Nixon Administration (1969–1974)

| | | |
|---|---|---|
| Vice President | Spiro T. Agnew | 1969–1973 |
| | Gerald R. Ford | 1973–1974 |
| Secretary of State | William P. Rogers | 1969–1973 |
| | Henry A. Kissinger | 1973–1974 |
| Secretary of Treasury | David M. Kennedy | 1969–1970 |
| | John B. Connally | 1971–1972 |
| | George P. Shultz | 1972–1974 |
| | William E. Simon | 1974 |
| Attorney General | John N. Mitchell | 1969–1972 |
| | Richard G. Kleindienst | 1972–1973 |
| | Elliot L. Richardson | 1973 |
| | William B. Saxbe | 1973–1974 |
| Postmaster General | Winton M. Blount | 1969–1971 |
| Secretary of Interior | Walter J. Hickel | 1969–1970 |
| | Rogers Morton | 1971–1974 |
| Secretary of Agriculture | Clifford M. Hardin | 1969–1971 |
| | Earl L. Butz | 1971–1974 |
| Secretary of Commerce | Maurice H. Stans | 1969–1972 |
| | Peter G. Peterson | 1972–1973 |
| | Frederick B. Dent | 1973–1974 |
| Secretary of Labor | George P. Shultz | 1969–1970 |
| | James D. Hodgson | 1970–1973 |
| | Peter J. Brennan | 1973–1974 |
| Secretary of Defense | Melvin R. Laird | 1969–1973 |
| | Elliot L. Richardson | 1973 |
| | James R. Schlesinger | 1973–1974 |
| Secretary of Health, Education, and Welfare | Robert H. Finch | 1969–1970 |
| | Elliot L. Richardson | 1970–1973 |
| | Caspar W. Weinberger | 1973–1974 |
| Secretary of Housing and Urban Development | George Romney | 1969–1973 |
| | James T. Lynn | 1973–1974 |
| Secretary of Transportation | John A. Volpe | 1969–1973 |
| | Claude S. Brinegar | 1973–1974 |

---

### The Ford Administration (1974–1977)

| | | |
|---|---|---|
| Vice President | Nelson A. Rockefeller | 1974–1977 |
| Secretary of State | Henry A. Kissinger | 1974–1977 |
| Secretary of Treasury | William E. Simon | 1974–1977 |
| Attorney General | William Saxbe | 1974–1975 |
| | Edward Levi | 1975–1977 |
| Secretary of Interior | Rogers Morton | 1974–1975 |
| | Stanley K. Hathaway | 1975 |
| | Thomas Kleppe | 1975–1977 |

### The Ford Administration (1974–1977)   (cont.)

| | | |
|---|---|---|
| Secretary of Agriculture | Earl L. Butz | 1974–1976 |
| | John A. Knebel | 1976–1977 |
| Secretary of Commerce | Frederick B. Dent | 1974–1975 |
| | Rogers Morton | 1975–1976 |
| | Elliott L. Richardson | 1976–1977 |
| Secretary of Labor | Peter J. Brennan | 1974–1975 |
| | John T. Dunlop | 1975–1976 |
| | W. J. Usery | 1976–1977 |
| Secretary of Defense | James R. Schlesinger | 1974–1975 |
| | Donald Rumsfeld | 1975–1977 |
| Secretary of Health, Education, and Welfare | Caspar Weinberger | 1974–1975 |
| | Forrest D. Mathews | 1975–1977 |
| Secretary of Housing and Urban Development | James T. Lynn | 1974–1975 |
| | Carla A. Hills | 1975–1977 |
| Secretary of Transportation | Claude Brinegar | 1974–1975 |
| | William T. Coleman | 1975–1977 |

### The Carter Administration (1977–1981)

| | | |
|---|---|---|
| Vice President | Walter F. Mondale | 1977–1981 |
| Secretary of State | Cyrus R. Vance | 1977–1980 |
| | Edmund Muskie | 1980–1981 |
| Secretary of Treasury | W. Michael Blumenthal | 1977–1979 |
| | G. William Miller | 1979–1981 |
| Attorney General | Griffin Bell | 1977–1979 |
| | Benjamin R. Civiletti | 1979–1981 |
| Secretary of Interior | Cecil D. Andrus | 1977–1981 |
| Secretary of Agriculture | Robert Bergland | 1977–1981 |
| Secretary of Commerce | Juanita M. Kreps | 1977–1979 |
| | Philip M. Klutznick | 1979–1981 |
| Secretary of Labor | Ray F. Marshall | 1977–1981 |
| Secretary of Defense | Harold Brown | 1977–1981 |
| Secretary of Health, Education, and Welfare | Joseph A. Califano | 1977–1979 |
| | Patricia R. Harris | 1979 |
| Secretary of Health and Human Services | Patricia R. Harris | 1979–1981 |
| Secretary of Education | Shirley M. Hufstedler | 1979–1981 |
| Secretary of Housing and Urban Development | Patricia R. Harris | 1977–1979 |
| | Moon Landrieu | 1979–1981 |
| Secretary of Transportation | Brock Adams | 1977–1979 |
| | Neil E. Goldschmidt | 1979–1981 |
| Secretary of Energy | James R. Schlesinger | 1977–1979 |
| | Charles W. Duncan | 1979–1981 |

## The Reagan Administration (1981–1989)

| | | |
|---|---|---|
| Vice President | George Bush | 1981–1989 |
| Secretary of State | Alexander M. Haig | 1981–1982 |
| | George P. Shultz | 1982–1989 |
| Secretary of Treasury | Donald Regan | 1981–1985 |
| | James A. Baker III | 1985–1988 |
| | Nicholas Brady | 1988–1989 |
| Attorney General | William F. Smith | 1981–1985 |
| | Edwin A. Meese III | 1985–1988 |
| | Richard Thornburgh | 1988–1989 |
| Secretary of Interior | James Watt | 1981–1983 |
| | William P. Clark, Jr. | 1983–1985 |
| | Donald P. Hodel | 1985–1989 |
| Secretary of Agriculture | John Block | 1981–1986 |
| | Richard E. Lyng | 1986–1989 |
| Secretary of Commerce | Malcolm Baldridge | 1981–1987 |
| | C. William Verity, Jr. | 1987–1989 |
| Secretary of Labor | Raymond Donovan | 1981–1985 |
| | William E. Brock | 1985–1988 |
| | Ann Dore McLaughlin | 1988–1989 |
| Secretary of Defense | Caspar Weinberger | 1981–1988 |
| | Frank Carlucci | 1988–1989 |
| Secretary of Health and Human Services | Richard Schweiker | 1981–1983 |
| | Margaret Heckler | 1983–1985 |
| | Otis R. Bowen | 1985–1989 |
| Secretary of Education | Terrel H. Bell | 1981–1985 |
| | William J. Bennett | 1985–1988 |
| | Lauro F. Cavazos | 1988–1989 |
| Secretary of Housing and Urban Development | Samuel Pierce | 1981–1989 |
| Secretary of Transportation | Drew Lewis | 1981–1983 |
| | Elizabeth Dole | 1983–1987 |
| | James L. Burnley IV | 1987–1989 |
| Secretary of Energy | James Edwards | 1981–1982 |
| | Donald P. Hodel | 1982–1985 |
| | John S. Herrington | 1985–1989 |

## The Bush Administration (1989–1993)

| | | |
|---|---|---|
| Vice President | J. Danforth Quayle III | 1989–1993 |
| Secretary of State | James Baker III | 1989–1993 |
| Secretary of Treasury | Nicholas Brady | 1989–1993 |
| Attorney General | Richard Thornburgh | 1989–1991 |
| | William Barr | 1991–1993 |
| Secretary of Interior | Manuel Lujan | 1989–1993 |
| Secretary of Agriculture | Clayton Yeutter | 1989–1991 |
| | Edward Madigan | 1991–1993 |

## The Bush Administration (1989–1993)   (cont.)

| | | |
|---|---|---|
| Secretary of Commerce | Robert Mosbacher | 1989–1992 |
| | Barbara Franklin | 1992–1993 |
| Secretary of Labor | Elizabeth Dole | 1989–1990 |
| | Lynn Martin | 1991–1993 |
| Secretary of Defense | Richard Cheney | 1989–1993 |
| Secretary of Health and Human Services | Louis Sullivan | 1989–1993 |
| Secretary of Education | Lauro Cavazos | 1989–1990 |
| | Lamar Alexander | 1990–1993 |
| Secretary of Housing and Urban Development | Jack Kemp | 1989–1993 |
| Secretary of Transportation | Samuel Skinner | 1989–1991 |
| | Andrew Card | 1992–1993 |
| Secretary of Energy | James Watkins | 1989–1993 |
| Secretary of Veterans' Affairs | Edward Derwinski | 1989–1993 |

## The Clinton Administration (1993–      )

| | | |
|---|---|---|
| Vice President | Albert W. Gore, Jr. | 1993– |
| Secretary of State | Warren Christopher | 1993–1997 |
| | Madeline Albright | 1997– |
| Secretary of Treasury | Lloyd Bentsen | 1993–1994 |
| | Robert Rubin | 1995– |
| Attorney General | Janet Reno | 1993– |
| Secretary of Interior | Bruce Babbitt | 1993– |
| Secretary of Agriculture | Michael Espy | 1993–1994 |
| | Dan Glickman | 1994– |
| Secretary of Commerce | Ronald Brown | 1993–1996 |
| | Mickey Kantor | 1996–1997 |
| | William Daley | 1997– |
| Secretary of Labor | Robert Reich | 1993–1997 |
| | Alexis Herman | 1997– |
| Secretary of Defense | Les Aspin | 1993–1994 |
| | William Perry | 1994–1997 |
| | William Cohen | 1997 |
| Secretary of Health and Human Services | Donna Shalala | 1993– |
| Secretary of Education | Richard Reilly | 1993– |
| Secretary of Housing and Urban Development | Henry Cisneros | 1993–1997 |
| | Andrew Cuomo | 1997– |
| Secretary of Transportation | Federico Peña | 1993–1997 |
| | Rodney Slater | 1997– |
| Secretary of Energy | Hazel O'Leary | 1993–1997 |
| | Federico Peña | 1997–1998 |
| | Bill Richardson | 1998– |
| Secretary of Veterans' Affairs | Jesse Brown | 1993–1998 |
| | Togo West | 1998– |

## Supreme Court Justices

| Name | Term of Service | Appointed By |
| --- | --- | --- |
| JOHN JAY | 1789–1795 | Washington |
| James Wilson | 1789–1798 | Washington |
| John Rutledge | 1790–1791 | Washington |
| William Cushing | 1790–1810 | Washington |
| John Blair | 1790–1796 | Washington |
| James Iredell | 1790–1799 | Washington |
| Thomas Johnson | 1792–1793 | Washington |
| William Paterson | 1793–1806 | Washington |
| JOHN RUTLEDGE* | 1795 | Washington |
| Samuel Chase | 1796–1811 | Washington |
| OLIVER ELLSWORTH | 1796–1800 | Washington |
| Bushrod Washington | 1799–1829 | J. Adams |
| Alfred Moore | 1800–1804 | J. Adams |
| JOHN MARSHALL | 1801–1835 | J. Adams |
| William Johnson | 1804–1834 | Jefferson |
| Brockholst Livingston | 1807–1823 | Jefferson |
| Thomas Todd | 1807–1826 | Jefferson |
| Gabriel Duvall | 1811–1835 | Madison |
| Joseph Story | 1812–1845 | Madison |
| Smith Thompson | 1823–1843 | Monroe |
| Robert Trimble | 1826–1828 | J. Q. Adams |
| John McLean | 1830–1861 | Jackson |
| Henry Baldwin | 1830–1844 | Jackson |
| James M. Wayne | 1835–1867 | Jackson |
| ROGER B. TANEY | 1836–1864 | Jackson |
| Philip P. Barbour | 1836–1841 | Jackson |
| John Cartron | 1837–1865 | Van Buren |
| John McKinley | 1838–1852 | Van Buren |
| Peter V. Daniel | 1842–1860 | Van Buren |
| Samuel Nelson | 1845–1872 | Tyler |
| Levi Woodbury | 1845–1851 | Polk |
| Robert C. Grier | 1846–1870 | Polk |
| Benjamin R. Curtis | 1851–1857 | Fillmore |
| John A. Campbell | 1853–1861 | Pierce |
| Nathan Clifford | 1858–1881 | Buchanan |
| Noah H. Swayne | 1862–1881 | Lincoln |
| Samuel F. Miller | 1862–1890 | Lincoln |
| David Davis | 1862–1877 | Lincoln |

*Note:* The names of Chief Justices are printed in capital letters.
*Although Rutledge acted as Chief Justice, the Senate refused to confirm his appointment.

## Supreme Court Justices  *(cont.)*

| Name | Term of Service | Appointed By |
| --- | --- | --- |
| Stephen J. Field | 1863–1897 | Lincoln |
| SALMON P. CHASE | 1864–1873 | Lincoln |
| William Strong | 1870–1880 | Grant |
| Joseph P. Bradley | 1870–1892 | Grant |
| Ward Hunt | 1873–1882 | Grant |
| MORRISON R. WAITE | 1874–1888 | Grant |
| John M. Harlan | 1877–1911 | Hayes |
| William B. Woods | 1881–1887 | Hayes |
| Stanley Matthews | 1881–1889 | Garfield |
| Horace Gray | 1882–1902 | Arthur |
| Samuel Blatchford | 1882–1893 | Arthur |
| Lucious Q. C. Lamar | 1888–1893 | Cleveland |
| MELVILLE W. FULLER | 1888–1910 | Cleveland |
| David J. Brewer | 1890–1910 | B. Harrison |
| Henry B. Brown | 1891–1906 | B. Harrison |
| George Shiras, Jr. | 1892–1903 | B. Harrison |
| Howell E. Jackson | 1893–1895 | B. Harrison |
| Edward D. White | 1894–1910 | Cleveland |
| Rufus W. Peckham | 1896–1909 | Cleveland |
| Joseph McKenna | 1898–1925 | McKinley |
| Oliver W. Holmes | 1902–1932 | T. Roosevelt |
| William R. Day | 1903–1922 | T. Roosevelt |
| William H. Moody | 1906–1910 | T. Roosevelt |
| Horace H. Lurton | 1910–1914 | Taft |
| Charles E. Hughes | 1910–1916 | Taft |
| EDWARD D. WHITE | 1910–1921 | Taft |
| Willis Van Devanter | 1911–1937 | Taft |
| Joseph R. Lamar | 1911–1916 | Taft |
| Mahlon Pitney | 1912–1922 | Taft |
| James C. McReynolds | 1914–1941 | Wilson |
| Louis D. Brandeis | 1916–1939 | Wilson |
| John H. Clarke | 1916–1922 | Wilson |
| WILLIAM H. TAFT | 1921–1930 | Harding |
| George Sutherland | 1922–1938 | Harding |
| Pierce Butler | 1923–1939 | Harding |
| Edward T. Sanford | 1923–1930 | Harding |
| Harlan F. Stone | 1925–1941 | Coolidge |
| CHARLES E. HUGHES | 1930–1941 | Hoover |
| Owen J. Roberts | 1930–1945 | Hoover |
| Benjamin N. Cardozo | 1932–1938 | Hoover |

## Supreme Court Justices  *(cont.)*

| Name | Term of Service | Appointed By |
| --- | --- | --- |
| Hugo L. Black | 1937–1971 | F. Roosevelt |
| Stanley F. Reed | 1938–1957 | F. Roosevelt |
| Felix Frankfurter | 1939–1962 | F. Roosevelt |
| William O. Douglas | 1939–1975 | F. Roosevelt |
| Frank Murphy | 1940–1949 | F. Roosevelt |
| HARLAN F. STONE | 1941–1946 | F. Roosevelt |
| James F. Byrnes | 1941–1942 | F. Roosevelt |
| Robert H. Jackson | 1941–1954 | F. Roosevelt |
| Wiley B. Rutledge | 1943–1949 | F. Roosevelt |
| Harold H. Burton | 1945–1958 | Truman |
| FREDERICK M. VINSON | 1946–1953 | Truman |
| Tom C. Clark | 1949–1967 | Truman |
| Sherman Minton | 1949–1956 | Truman |
| EARL WARREN | 1953–1969 | Eisenhower |
| John Marshall Harlan | 1955–1971 | Eisenhower |
| William J. Brennan, Jr. | 1956–1990 | Eisenhower |
| Charles E. Whittaker | 1957–1962 | Eisenhower |
| Potter Stewart | 1958–1981 | Eisenhower |
| Byron R. White | 1962–1993 | Kennedy |
| Arthur J. Goldberg | 1962–1965 | Kennedy |
| Abe Fortas | 1965–1970 | L. Johnson |
| Thurgood Marshall | 1967–1991 | L. Johnson |
| WARREN E. BURGER | 1969–1986 | Nixon |
| Harry A. Blackmun | 1970–1994 | Nixon |
| Lewis F. Powell, Jr. | 1971–1987 | Nixon |
| William H. Rehnquist | 1971–1986 | Nixon |
| John Paul Stevens | 1975– | Ford |
| Sandra Day O'Connor | 1981– | Reagan |
| WILLIAM H. REHNQUIST | 1986– | Reagan |
| Antonin Scalia | 1986– | Reagan |
| Anthony Kennedy | 1988– | Reagan |
| David Souter | 1990– | Bush |
| Clarence Thomas | 1991– | Bush |
| Ruth Bader Ginsburg | 1993– | Clinton |
| Stephen Breyer | 1994– | Clinton |

# Additional Bibliography

## Chapter 1

### History and Anthropology

Harold E. Driver, *Indians of North America,* 2d ed. (1969); Charles Hudson, *The Southeastern Indians* (1976); Alice B. Kehoe, *North American Indians: A Comprehensive Account,* 2d ed. (1992); Eleanor Burke Leacock and Nancy Oestreich Lurie, eds., *North American Indians in Historical Perspective* (1971).

### Archaeology

Linda S. Cordell, *Prehistory of the Southwest* (1984); Stuart J. Fiedel, *Prehistory of the Americas,* 2d ed. (1992); Melvin Fowler, *The Cahokia Atlas: A Historical Atlas of Cahokia Archaeology* (1989); Patricia Galloway, ed., *The Southeastern Ceremonial Complex: Artifacts and Analysis* (1989); Jesse B. Jennings, ed., *Ancient North Americans* (1983); Frances Joan Mathien and Randall H. McGuire, eds., *Ripples in the Chichimec Sea: New Considerations of Southwestern-Mesoamerican Interactions* (1986); Karl Schleiser, ed., *Plains Indians, A.D. 500–1500* (1994); Lynda Norene Shaffer, *Native Americans Before 1492: The Moundbuilding Centers of the Eastern Woodlands* (1992); Bruce D. Smith, ed., *The Mississippian Emergence* (1990) and *Rivers of Change: Essays on Early Agriculture in Eastern North America* (1992); Stephen E. Williams, *Towns and Temples along the Mississippi* (1990).

### Spirituality and World Views

Donald Bahr et al., *The Short, Swift Time of Gods on Earth: The Hohokam Chronicles* (1994); Robert L. Hall, *An Archaeology of the Soul: North American Indian Belief and Ritual* (1997); Åke Hultkrantz, *The Religions of the American Indians* (1979); Lee Irwin, *The Dream Seekers: Native American Visionary Traditions of the Great Plains* (1994); Paul Radin, *The Trickster: A Study in American Indian Mythology* (1972); Elisabeth Tooker, ed., *Native North American Spirituality of the Eastern Woodlands* (1979); Christopher Vecsey, *Imagine Ourselves Richly: Mythic Narratives of North American Indians* (1988); Ray A. Williamson, *Living the Sky: The Cosmos of the American Indian* (1987); Paul Zolbrod, *Diné bahané: The Navajo Creation Story* (1984).

### Demography

Ann F. Ramenofsky, *Vectors of Death: The Archaeology of European Contact* (1987); Russell Thornton, *American Indian Holocaust and Survival: A Population History Since 1492* (1987); John W. Verano and Douglas H. Ubelaker, eds., *Disease and Demography in the Americas* (1992).

## Chapter 2

### Africa and Slavery

J. F. A. Ajayi and Michael Crowder, eds., *History of West Africa,* vol. I (1972); Robin Blackburn, *The Making of New World Slavery: From the Baroque to the Modern, 1492–1800* (1997); Philip Curtin, *The Atlantic Slave Trade: A Census* (1969) and *Economic Change in Precolonial Africa: Senegambia in the Era of the Slave Trade* (1975); Winthrop D. Jordan, *White Over Black: American Attitudes Toward the Negro, 1550–1812* (1968); R. A. Kea, *Settlements, Trade, and Politics on the Seventeenth-century Gold Coast* (1982); Robin Law, *The Slave Coast of West Africa, 1550–1750: The Impact of the Atlantic Slave Trade on an African Society* (1991); Paul E. Lovejoy, *Transformations in Slavery: A History of Slavery in Africa* (1983); Patrick Manning, *Slavery and African Life: Occidental, Oriental, and African Slave Trades* (1990); Walter Rodney, *A History of the Upper Guinea Coast, 1545–1800* (1970).

### Europe

Fernand Braudel, *The Mediterranean and the Mediterranean World in the Age of Philip II,* 2d ed. (1966; English trans., 1972) and *Civilization and Capitalism, 15th–18th Centuries* (3 vols., 1979; English trans., 1981); Robin Briggs, *Witches and Neighbours: The Social and Cultural Context of European Witchcraft* (1996); Peter Burke, *Popular Culture in Early Modern Europe* (1978); Natalie Z. Davis, *Society and Culture in Early Modern France* (1975) and *Women on the Margins: Three Seventeenth-Century Lives* (1995); Ralph Davis, *Rise of the Atlantic Economies* (1973); Anthony Fletcher, *Gender, Sex, and Subordination in England, 1500–1800* (1995); J. R. Hale, *War and Society in Renaissance Europe, 1450–1620* (1985); George Huppert, *After the Black Death: A Social History of Early Modern Europe* (1986); Lisa Jardine, *Worldly Goods: A New History of the Renaissance* (1996); Sherrin Marshall, ed., *Women in Reformation and Counter-Reformation Europe: Public and Private Worlds* (1989); Stephen Ozment, *The Age of Reform, 1250–1550* (1980); Simon Schama, *An Embarrassment of Riches: Dutch Culture in the Golden Age* (1987); Keith Wrightson, *English Society, 1580–1680* (1982).

### European Expansion and Colonization

Kenneth R. Andrews, *Trade, Plunder, and Settlement: Maritime Enterprise and the Genesis of the British Empire, 1480–1630* (1984); Nicholas P. Canny, *The Elizabethan Conquest of Ireland: A Pattern Established, 1565–1576* (1976); W. J. Eccles, *France in America,* rev. ed. (1990); J. H. Elliott, *The Old World and the New, 1492–1650* (1970); Stephen J. Greenblatt, *Marvelous Possessions: The Wonder of the New World* (1991); Karen Ordahl Kupperman, *Roanoke: The Abandoned Colony* (1984); James Lockhart and Stuart B. Schwartz, *Early Latin America: A History of Colonial Spanish America and Brazil* (1983); Anthony Pagden, *European Encounters with the New World: From Renaissance to Romanticism* (1993); J. H. Parry, *The Establishment of the European Hegemony: Trade and Expansion in the Age of Renaissance* (1966); William D. Phillips, Jr., and Carla Rahn Phillips, *The Worlds of Christopher Columbus* (1992); Oliver Rink, *Holland on the Hudson: An Economic and Social History of Dutch New York* (1986); Gordon Sayre, *Les Sauvages Américains: Representations of Native Americans in French and English Colonial Literature* (1997); Patricia Seed, *Ceremonies of Possession in Europe's Conquest of the New World, 1492–1640* (1995); David J. Weber, *The Spanish Frontier in North America* (1992).

**B-1**

### Native Americans

James Axtell, *After Columbus: Essays in the Ethnohistory of Colonial North America* (1988); Charles Hudson and Carmen C. Tesser, eds., *The Forgotten Centuries: Indians and Europeans in the American South, 1521–1704* (1994); Francis Jennings, *The Invasion of America: Indians, Colonialism, and the Cant of Conquest* (1975); Calvin Martin, *Keepers of the Game: Indian-Animal Relationships and the Fur Trade* (1978); Daniel K. Richter, *The Ordeal of the Longhouse: The Peoples of the Iroquois League in the Era of European Colonization* (1992); Neal Salisbury, *Manitou and Providence: Indians, Europeans, and the Making of New England, 1500–1643* (1982); David Hurst Thomas, *Columbian Consequences* (3 vols., 1989–1991); Russell Thornton, *American Indian Holocaust and Survival: A Population History Since 1492* (1987); Bruce G. Trigger, *Natives and Newcomers: Canada's "Heroic Age" Reconsidered* (1985).

## *Chapter 3*

### New England

Virginia DeJohn Anderson, *New England's Generation: The Great Migration and the Formation of Society and Culture in the Seventeenth Century* (1991); Cornelia Hughes Dayton, *Women Before the Bar: Gender, Law, and Society in Connecticut, 1639–1789* (1995); Andrew Delbanco, *The Puritan Ordeal* (1989); John Demos, *A Little Commonwealth: Family Life in Plymouth Colony* (1970) and *Entertaining Satan: Witchcraft and the Culture of Early New England* (1982); Stephen Foster, *The Long Argument: English Puritanism and the Shaping of New England Culture, 1570–1700* (1991); Richard Godbeer, *The Devil's Dominion: Magic and Religion in Early New England* (1992); Philip F. Gura, *A Glimpse of Sion's Glory: Puritan Radicalism in New England, 1620–1660* (1984); David D. Hall, *Worlds of Wonder, Days of Judgment: Popular Religious Belief in Early New England* (1990); Stephen Innes, *Creating the Commonwealth: The Economic Culture of Puritan New England* (1995); Carol F. Karlsen, *The Devil in the Shape of a Woman: Witchcraft in Colonial New England* (1987); David Thomas Konig, *Law and Society in Puritan Massachusetts, 1629–1692* (1979); Janice Knight, *Orthodoxies in Massachusetts: Rereading American Puritanism* (1994); John F. Martin, *Profits in the Wilderness: Entrepreneurship and the Founding of New England Towns in the Seventeenth Century* (1991); Carla Gardina Pestana, *Quakers and Baptists in Colonial Massachusetts* (1991); Robert Blair St. George, *Conversing by Signs: Poetics of Implication in Colonial New England Culture* (1998); Laurel Thatcher Ulrich, *Good Wives: Image and Reality in the Lives of Women in Northern New England, 1650–1763* (1982); Daniel Vickers, *Farmers and Fishermen: Two Centuries of Work in Essex County, Massachusetts, 1630–1850* (1994).

### The Southern Colonies and the West Indies

Hilary M. Beckles, *White Servitude and Black Slavery in Barbados, 1627–1715* (1989); Timothy H. Breen and Stephen Innes, *"Myne Own Ground": Race and Freedom on Virginia's Eastern Shore, 1640–1676* (1980); Kathleen M. Brown, *Good Wives, Nasty Wenches, and Anxious Patriarchs: Gender, Race, and Power in Colonial Virginia* (1996); Lois Green Carr et al., *Colonial Chesapeake Society* (1988); James Deetz, *Flowerdew Hundred:*

*The Archaeology of a Virginia Plantation, 1619–1864*; Richard S. Dunn, *Sugar and Slaves: The Rise of the Planter Class in the English West Indies, 1624–1713* (1972); James Horn, *Adapting to a New World: English Society in the Seventeenth-Century Chesapeake* (1994); Daniel C. Littlefield, *Rice and Slavery: Ethnicity and the Slave Trade in Colonial South Carolina* (1981); Darret B. Rutman and Anita S. Rutman, *A Place in Time: Middlesex County, Virginia, 1650–1750* (1984); Peter H. Wood, *Black Majority: Negroes in Colonial South Carolina from 1670 Through the Stono Rebellion* (1974).

### The Middle Colonies

Thomas J. Archdeacon, *New York City, 1664–1710: Conquest and Change* (1976); Thomas Burke, *Mohawk Frontier: The Dutch Community of Schenectady, New York, 1661–1710* (1991); Richard S. Dunn and Mary Maples Dunn, eds., *The World of William Penn* (1986); Joyce D. Goodfriend, *Before the Melting Pot: Society and Culture in Colonial New York City, 1664–1730* (1991); Barry Levy, *Quakers and the American Family: British Settlement in the Delaware Valley* (1988); Donna Merwick, *Possessing Albany, 1630–1710: The Dutch and English Experiences* (1990); Gary B. Nash, *Quakers and Politics: Pennsylvania, 1681–1726* (1968); Robert C. Ritchie, *The Duke's Province: A Study of New York Politics and Society, 1664–1691* (1977); Oliver A. Rink, *Holland on the Hudson: An Economic and Social History of Dutch New York* (1986).

### French and Spanish Colonies

Amy Turner Bushnell, *Situado and Sabana: Spain's Support System for the Presidio and Mission Provinces of Florida* (1994); Donald E. Chipman, *Spanish Texas, 1519–1821* (1992); Leslie Choquette, *Frenchmen into Peasants: Modernity and Tradition in the Peopling of French Canada* (1997); W. J. Eccles, *Canada Under Louis XIV, 1663–1701* (1964); Ramón A. Gutiérrez, *When Jesus Came, the Corn Mothers Went Away: Marriage, Sexuality, and Power in New Mexico, 1500–1846* (1991); Richard Colebrook Harris, *The Seigneurial System in Early Canada* (1966); Andrew L. Knaut, *The Pueblo Revolt of 1680: Conquest and Resistance in Seventeenth-Century New Mexico* (1995).

### Indian-European Relations

James Axtell, *The Invasion Within: The Contest of Cultures in Colonial North America* (1985); Frederic W. Gleach, *Powhatan's World and Colonial Virginia: A Conflict of Cultures* (1997); Robert S. Grumet (ed.), *Northeastern Indian Lives, 1632–1816* (1996); Francis Jennings, *The Invasion of America: Indians, Colonialism, and the Cant of Conquest* (1975); Elizabeth A. H. John, *Storms Brewed in Other Men's Worlds: The Confrontation of Indians, Spanish, and French in the Southwest, 1540–1795* (1975); Andrew L. Knaut, *The Pueblo Revolt of 1680: Conquest and Resistance in Seventeenth-Century New Mexico* (1995); James H. Merrell, *The Indians' New World: Catawbas and Their Neighbors from European Contact Through the Era of Removal* (1989); Daniel K. Richter, *The Ordeal of the Longhouse: The Peoples of the Iroquois League in the Era of European Colonization* (1992); Neal Salisbury, *Manitou and Providence: Indians, Europeans, and the Making of New England, 1500–1643* (1982); Ian K. Steele, *Warpaths: Invasions of North America* (1994); Richard White, *The Middle Ground: Indians, Empires, and Republics in the Great Lakes Region, 1650–1815* (1991).

## Chapter 4

### Rebellion and Imperial Warfare

John Demos, *The Unredeemed Captive: A Family Story from Early America* (1994); Richard R. Johnson, *Adjustment to Empire: The New England Colonies, 1675–1715* (1981); David S. Lovejoy, *The Glorious Revolution in America, 1660–1692* (1972).

### Anglo-American Society and Economy

Kathleen M. Brown, *Good Wives, Nasty Wenches, and Anxious Patriarchs: Gender, Race, and Power in Colonial Virginia* (1996); Richard L. Bushman, *The Refinement of America: People, Houses, Cities* (1992); Cary Carson et al., eds., *Of Consuming Interests: The Style of Life in the Eighteenth Century* (1994); Stephen Innes, ed., *Work and Labor in Early America* (1988); Allan Kulikoff, *Tobacco and Slaves: The Development of Southern Cultures in the Chesapeake, 1680–1800* (1986); Barry Levy, *Quakers and the American Family: British Settlement in the Delaware Valley* (1988); Judith A. McGaw, ed., *Early American Technology: Making and Doing Things from the Colonial Era to 1850* (1994); A. G. Roeber, *Palatines, Liberty, and Property: German Lutherans in Colonial British America* (1993); Sharon V. Salinger, *"To Serve Well and Faithfully": Labor and Indentured Servants in Pennsylvania, 1682–1800* (1987); Marylynn Salmon, *Women and the Law of Property in Early America* (1986); Timothy Silver, *A New Face on the Countryside: Indians, Colonists, and Slaves in South Atlantic Forests, 1500–1800* (1990); Laurel Thatcher Ulrich, *Good Wives: Image and Reality in the Lives of Women in Northern New England, 1650–1763* (1982).

### Blacks and Slavery

Jeffrey Bolster, *Black Jacks: African American Seamen in the Age of Sail* (1997); Sylvia R. Frey and Betty Wood, *Come Shouting to Zion: African Protestantism in the American South and British Caribbean to 1830* (1998); Michael A. Gomez, *Exchanging Our Country Marks: The Transformation of African Identities in the Colonial and Antebellum South* (1998); Gwendolyn Midlo Hall, *Africans in Colonial Louisiana: The Development of Afro-Creole Culture in the Eighteenth Century* (1992); Edgar J. McManus, *Black Bondage in the North* (1973); Edmund S. Morgan, *American Slavery, American Freedom: The Ordeal of Colonial Virginia* (1975); Philip D. Morgan, *Slave Counterpoint: Black Culture in the Eighteenth-Century Chesapeake and Lowcountry* (1998); William D. Piersen, *Black Yankees: The Development of an Afro-American Subculture in Eighteenth-Century New England* (1988); Mechal Sobel, *The World They Made Together: Black and White Values in Eighteenth-Century Virginia* (1987); Peter H. Wood, *Black Majority: Negroes in Colonial South Carolina from 1670 Through the Stono Rebellion* (1974).

### Indian-European Relations

James Axtell, *The Invasion Within: The Contest of Cultures in Colonial North America* (1985); Colin G. Calloway, ed., *After King Philip's War: Presence and Persistence in Indian New England* (1997) and *New Worlds for All: Indians, Europeans, and the Remaking of Early America* (1997); Gregory Evans Dowd, *A Spirited Resistance: The North American Indian Struggle for Unity, 1745–1815* (1992); Tom Hatley, *The Dividing Paths: Cherokees and South Carolinians Through the Era of Revolution* (1993); Preston Holder, *The Hoe and the Horse on the Plains: A Study of Cultural Development Among North American Indians* (1970); Elizabeth A. H. John, *Storms Brewed in Other Men's Worlds: The Confrontations of Indians, Spanish, and French in the Southwest, 1540–1795* (1975); Daniel K. Richter, *The Ordeal of the Longhouse: The Peoples of the Iroquois League in the Era of European Colonization* (1992); Daniel H. Usner, Jr., *Indians, Settlers, and Slaves in a Frontier Exchange Economy: The Lower Mississippi Valley Before 1783* (1992); Richard White, *The Middle Ground: Indians, Empires and Republics in the Great Lakes Region, 1650–1815* (1991).

### French and Spanish Colonies

J. M. Bumsted, *The Peoples of Canada: A Pre-Confederation History* (1992); Donald E. Chipman, *Spanish Texas, 1519–1821* (1992); Leslie Choquette, *Frenchmen into Peasants: Modernity and Tradition in the Peopling of French Canada* (1997); W. J. Eccles, *The French in North America* (1998); Allan Greer, *Peasant, Lord, and Merchant: Rural Society in Three Quebec Parishes, 1740–1840* (1985); Naomi Griffiths, *The Contexts of Acadian History, 1686–1784* (1992); Ramón A. Gutiérrez, *When Jesus Came, the Corn Mothers Went Away: Marriage, Sexuality, and Power in New Mexico, 1500–1846* (1991); Richard Colebrook Harris, *The Seigneurial System in Early Canada* (1966); Jesús de la Teja, *San Antonio de Béxar: A Community on New Spain's Northern Frontier* (1995); David J. Weber, *The Spanish Frontier in North America* (1992).

### The Enlightenment, Religion, and Politics

Bernard Bailyn, *The Origins of American Politics* (1968); Patricia Bonomi, *Under the Cope of Heaven: Religion, Society, and Politics in Colonial America* (1986); Richard D. Brown, *Knowledge Is Power: The Diffusion of Information in Early America, 1700–1865* (1991); Jon Butler, *Awash in a Sea of Faith: Christianizing the American People* (1990); Frank Lambert, *"Pedlar in Divinity": George Whitefield and the Transatlantic Revivals* (1994); Harry S. Stout, *The New England Soul: Preaching and Religious Culture in Colonial New England* (1988); Michael Warner, *The Letters of the Republic: Publication and the Public Sphere in Eighteenth-Century America* (1990); Marilyn J. Westerkamp, *Triumph of the Laity: Scots-Irish Piety and the Great Awakening, 1625–1760* (1988); Esmond Wright, *Franklin of Philadelphia* (1986).

## Chapter 5

### The Military Background

Fred Anderson, *A People's Army: Massachusetts Soldiers and Society in the Seven Years' War* (1984); Sylvia R. Frey, *The British Soldier in America: A Social History of Military Life in the Colonial Period* (1981); John Shy, *Toward Lexington: The Role of the British Army in the Coming of the American Revolution* (1965); Ian K. Steele, *Betrayals: Fort William Henry and the "Massacre"* (1990).

### Native Americans and the Frontier

Gregory Evans Dowd, *A Spirited Resistance: The North American Indian Struggle for Unity, 1745–1815* (1992); Tom Hatley, *The Dividing Paths: Cherokees and South Carolinians Through the Era of Revolution* (1993); Eric Hinderaker, *Elusive Empires:*

*Constructing Colonialism in the Ohio Valley, 1673–1800* (1997); Dorothy V. Jones, *License for Empire: Colonialism by Treaty in Early America* (1982); Francis Jennings, *Empire of Fortune: Crowns, Colonies and Tribes in the Seven Years' War in America* (1988); Michael N. McConnell, *A Country Between: The Upper Ohio Valley and Its Peoples, 1724–1774* (1992).

### Constitutional Issues

Richard L. Bushman, *King and People in Provincial Massachusetts* (1985); Jack P. Greene, *Peripheries and Center: Constitutional Development in the Extended Politics of the British Empire and the United States, 1607–1788* (1987); Jerrilyn G. Marston, *King and Congress* (1987); Edmund S. Morgan, *Inventing the People: The Rise of Popular Sovereignty in England and America* (1988); J. G. A. Pocock, *Three British Revolutions: 1641, 1688, 1776* (1980); J. R. Pole, *Political Representation in England and the Origins of the American Republic* (1966); John Philip Reid, *Constitutional History of the American Revolution,* 4 vols. (1986–1993).

### Religious and Intellectual Dimensions

Ruth H. Bloch, *Visionary Republic: Millennial Themes in American Thought, 1756–1800* (1985); Jay Fleigelman, *Prodigals and Pilgrims: The American Revolution Against Patriarchal Authority, 1750–1800* (1982) and *Declaring Independence: Jefferson, Natural Language, and the Culture of Performance* (1993); Jack P. Greene and William G. McLoughlin, *Preachers and Politicians: Two Essays on the Origin of the American Revolution* (1977); Nathan O. Hatch, *The Sacred Cause of Liberty: Republican Thought and the Millennium in Revolutionary New England* (1977); Rhys Isaac, *The Transformation of Virginia, 1740–1790* (1982); Susan Juster, *Disorderly Women: Sexual Politics and Evangelicalism in Revolutionary New England* (1994); Linda K. Kerber, *Women of the Republic: Intellect and Ideology in Revolutionary America* (1980); Garry Wills, *Inventing America: Jefferson's Declaration of Independence* (1978).

### Politics and Resistance

David Ammerman, *In the Common Cause: American Response to the Coercive Acts of 1774* (1974); John L. Brooke, *The Heart of the Commonwealth: Society and Political Culture in Worcester County, Massachusetts, 1713–1861* (1989); Richard D. Brown, *Revolutionary Politics in Massachusetts: The Boston Committees of Correspondence and the Towns, 1772–1774* (1970); David W. Conroy, *In Public Houses: Drink and the Revolution of Authority in Colonial Massachusetts* (1995); Marc Egnal, *A Mighty Empire: The Origins of the American Revolution* (1988); David Hackett Fischer, *Paul Revere's Ride* (1994); Eric Foner, *Tom Paine and Revolutionary America* (1976); Sylvia Frey, *Water from the Rock: Black Resistance in a Revolutionary Age* (1991); Jesse Lemisch, *Jack Tar vs. John Bull: The Role of New York's Seamen in Precipitating the Revolution* (1997); Robert Middlekauff, *The Glorious Cause: The American Revolution, 1763–1789* (1982); Edmund S. Morgan and Helen M. Morgan, *The Stamp Act Crisis: Prologue to Revolution,* rev. ed. (1963); Gary B. Nash, *The Urban Crucible: The Northern Seaports and the Origins of The American Revolution,* abridged ed. (1986); John Sainsbury, *Disaffected Patriots: London Supporters of Revolutionary America, 1769–1782* (1987); Peter Shaw, *American Patriots and the Rituals of Revolution* (1981); George F. E. Rudé,

*Wilkes and Liberty: A Social Study of 1763 to 1774* (1962); Neil R. Stout, *The Perfect Crisis: The Beginnings of the Revolutionary War* (1976); Peter D. G. Thomas, *The Townshend Duties Crisis: The Second Phase of the American Revolution, 1767–1773* (1987); Robert W. Tucker and David C. Hendrickson, *The Fall of the First British Empire: Origins of the War of American Independence* (1982); Ann Fairfax Withington, *Toward a More Perfect Union: Virtue and the Formation of American Republics* (1991); Gordon S. Wood, *The Radicalism of the American Revolution* (1991); Rosemarie Zagarri, *A Woman's Dilemma: Mercy Otis Warren and the American Revolution* (1995).

## Chapter 6

### The Military Struggle

Richard Buel, Jr., *Dear Liberty: Connecticut's Mobilization for the Revolutionary War* (1980); Robert M. Calhoon, *The Loyalists in Revolutionary America, 1760–1781* (1973); E. Wayne Carp, *To Starve the Army at Pleasure: Continental Army Administration and American Political Culture, 1775–1783* (1984); John Mack Faragher, *Daniel Boone: The Life and Legend of an American Pioneer* (1992); James T. Flexner, *Washington: The Indispensable Man* (1974); Barbara Graymont, *The Iroquois in the American Revolution* (1972); Don Higginbotham, *The War of American Independence: Military Attitudes, Policies, and Practice, 1763–1789* (1983); Ronald Hoffman and Thad W. Tate, eds., *An Uncivil War: The Southern Backcountry During the American Revolution* (1985); Isabel Thompson Kelsay, *Joseph Brant, 1743–1807: Man of Two Worlds* (1984); Mark V. Kwansey, *Washington's Partisan War, 1775–1783* (1997); Holly A. Mayer, *Belonging to the Army: Camp Followers and Community during the American Revolution* (1996); Elizabeth A. Perkins, *Border Life: Experience and Memory in the Revolutionary Ohio Valley* (1998); Steven Rosswurm, *Arms, Country, and Class: The Philadelphia Militia and the "Lower Sort" in the Era of the American Revolution* (1987); John Shy, *A People Numerous and Armed: Reflections on the Military Struggle for American Independence* (1976);

### Society and Economy

Ira Berlin and Ronald Hoffman, eds., *Slavery and Freedom in the Age of the American Revolution* (1983); Joy Day Buel and Richard Buel, Jr., *The Way of Duty: A Woman and Her Family in Revolutionary America* (1984); Ronald Hoffman et al., eds., *The Economy of Early America: The Revolutionary Period, 1763–1790* (1988); Rhys Isaac, *The Transformation of Virginia, 1740–1790* (1982); Michael Kammen, *A Season of Youth: The American Revolution and the Historical Imagination* (1978); Susan Juster, *Disorderly Women: Sexual Politics and Evangelicalism in Revolutionary New England* (1994); Duncan J. MacLeod, *Slavery, Race, and the American Revolution* (1974); Mary Beth Norton, *Liberty's Daughters: The Revolutionary Experience of American Women, 1750–1800* (1980); Gary B. Nash, *Race and Revolution* (1990); Gary B. Nash and Jean R. Soderlund, *Freedom by Degrees: Emancipation in Pennsylvania and Its Aftermath* (1991); Anthony F. C. Wallace, *The Death and Rebirth of the Seneca* (1969); Gordon S. Wood, *The Radicalism of the American Revolution* (1992);.

## Politics and Constitutionalism

Lance Banning, *The Sacred Fire of Liberty: James Madison and the Founding of the Federal Republic* (1995); Richard Beeman et al., eds., *Beyond Confederation: Origins of the Constitution and American National Identity* (1987); Michael Bellesisles, *Revolutionary Outlaws: Ethan Allen and the Struggle for Independence* (1993); Herman Belz et al., eds., *To Form a More Perfect Union: The Critical Ideas of the Constitution* (1992); John L. Brooke, *The Heart of the Commonwealth: Society and Political Culture in Worcester County, Massachusetts, 1713–1861* (1989); Robert A. Gross, ed., *In Debt to Shays: The Bicentennial of an Agrarian Rebellion* (1993); Van Beck Hall, *Politics Without Parties: Massachusetts, 1780–1791* (1972); Owen S. Ireland, *Religion, Ethnicity, and Politics: Ratifying the Constitution in Pennsylvania* (1995); Donald S. Lutz, *Origins of American Constitutionalism* (1988); Cathy D. Matson and Peter S. Onuf, *Union of Interests: Political and Economic Thought in Revolutionary America* (1990); Jackson T. Main, *The Antifederalists: Critics of the Constitution, 1781–1788* (1961); Forrest McDonald, *Novus Ordo Seclorum: The Intellectual Origins of the Constitution* (1985); Robert Middlekauff, *Benjamin Franklin and His Enemies* (1996); Jack N. Rakove, *The Beginnings of National Politics: An Interpretive History of the Continental Congress* (1979); Norman K. Risjord, *Chesapeake Politics, 1781–1800* (1978); Sheila L. Skemp, *William Franklin: Son of a Patriot, Servant of a King* (1990); David P. Szatmary, *Shays' Rebellion: The Making of an Agrarian Insurrection* (1980); Gordon S. Wood, *The Creation of the American Republic, 1776–1787* (1969); Rosemarie Zagarri, *A Woman's Dilemma: Mercy Otis Warren and the American Revolution* (1995).

# *Chapter 7*

## Early National Society

Robin Blackburn, *The Overthrow of Colonial Slavery, 1776–1848* (1988); Jeanne Boydston, *Home and Work: Housework, Wages, and the Ideology of Labor in the Early Republic* (1990); Ira Berlin, *Slaves Without Masters: The Free Negro in the Antebellum South* (1974); James Essig, *Bonds of Wickedness: American Evangelicals Against Slavery, 1770–1808* (1982); Paul A. Gilje, ed., *Wages of Independence: Capitalism in the Early American Republic* (1997); Alfred N. Hunt, *Haiti's Influence on Antebellum America* (1989); Joan M. Jensen, *Loosening the Bonds: Mid-Atlantic Farm Women, 1750–1850* (1986); Jan Lewis, *The Pursuit of Happiness: Family and Values in Jefferson's Virginia* (1983); Gary B. Nash, *Forging Freedom: The Formation of Philadelphia's Black Community, 1720–1840* (1990); Howard B. Rock, *Artisans of the New Republic: The Tradesmen of New York City in the Age of Jefferson* (1979); Billy G. Smith, *The "Lower Sort": Philadelphia's Laboring People, 1750–1800* (1990); Merril D. Smith, *Breaking the Bonds: Marital Discord in Pennsylvania, 1730–1830* (1991); Charles G. Steffen, *The Mechanics of Baltimore: Workers and Politics in the Age of Revolution, 1763–1812* (1984); Alan Taylor, *Liberty Men and Great Proprietors: The Revolutionary Settlement on the Maine Frontier, 1760–1820* (1990); Shane White, *Somewhat More Independent: The End of Slavery in New York City, 1770–1810* (1991); T. Stephen Whitman, *The Price of Freedom: Slavery and Manumission in Baltimore and Early National Maryland* (1997); Betty Wood, *Women's Work, Men's Work: The Informal Slave Economies of Lowcountry Georgia* (1995).

## Diplomatic, Military, and Western Affairs

Stephen Aron, *How the West Was Lost: Kentucky from Daniel Boone to Henry Clay* (1996); Colin G. Calloway, *Crown and Calumet: British-Indian Relations, 1783–1815* (1987); Andrew R. L. Cayton and Frederika J. Teute, eds., *Contact Points: American Frontiers from the Mohawk Valley to the Mississippi, 1750–1830* (1998); Gregory Evans Dowd, *A Spirited Resistance: The North American Indian Struggle for Unity, 1745–1815* (1992); John Mack Faragher, *Daniel Boone: The Life and Legend of an American Pioneer* (1992); Reginald Horsman, *The Frontier in the Formative Years, 1783–1815* (1970); Richard H. Kohn, *Eagle and Sword: The Federalists and the Creation of the Military Establishment in America, 1783–1802* (1975); Daniel G. Lang, *Foreign Policy in the Early Republic: The Law of Nations and the Balance of Power* (1985); Peter Onuf and Nicholas Onuf, *Federal Union, Modern World: The Law of Nations in an Age of Revolutions, 1776–1814* (1993); Thomas P. Slaughter, *The Whiskey Rebellion: Frontier Epilogue to the American Revolution* (1986); Richard White, *The Middle Ground: Indians, Empires, and Republics in the Great Lakes Region, 1650–1815* (1991); J. Leitch Wright, *Britain and the American Frontier, 1783–1815* (1975).

## Political and Economic Affairs

Lance Banning, *The Jeffersonian Persuasion: Evolution of a Party Ideology* (1978); Richard Beeman, *The Old Dominion and the New Nation, 1788–1801* (1972); Richard Buel, Jr., *Securing the Revolution: Ideology in American Politics, 1789–1815* (1972); John E. Crowley, *The Privileges of Independence: Neomercantilism and the American Revolution* (1993); Jacob E. Cooke, *Alexander Hamilton* (1982); Marcus Cunliffe, *George Washington: Man and Monument* (1958); Michael Durey, *Transatlantic Radicals and the Early American Republic* (1997); Joseph J. Ellis, *American Sphinx: The Character of Thomas Jefferson* (1996) and *Passionate Sage: The Character and Legacy of John Adams* (1993); Paul Finkleman, *Slavery and the Founders: Race and Liberty in the Age of Jefferson* (1996); John F. Hoadley, *Origins of American Political Parties, 1789–1803* (1986); Ralph Ketcham, *Presidents Above Party: The First American Presidency, 1789–1829* (1984); Joyce Lee Malcolm, *To Keep and Bear Arms: The Origins of an Anglo-American Right* (1994); Drew R. McCoy, *The Elusive Republic: Political Economy in Jeffersonian America* (1980); Conor Cruise O'Brien, *The Long Affair: Thomas Jefferson and the French Revolution, 1785–1800* (1996); Peter S. Onuf, ed., *Jeffersonian Legacies* (1993); Thomas L. Pangle, *The Spirit of Modern Republicanism: The Moral Vision of the American Founders and the Followers of Locke* (1988); Bernard Schwartz, *The Great Rights of Mankind* (1977); James Roger Sharp, *American Politics in the Early Republic: The New Nation in Crisis* (1993); Herbert E. Sloan, *Thomas Jefferson and the Problem of Debt* (1995); James M. Smith, *Freedom's Fetters: The Alien and Sedition Laws and American Civil Liberties*, rev. ed. (1966); David Waldstreicher, *In the Midst of Perpetual Fetes: The Making of American Nationalism, 1776–1820* (1997); Alfred F. Young, *The Democratic Republicans of New York: The Origins, 1763–1797* (1967).

## Chapter 8

### Political Ideologies

Joyce Appleby, *Capitalism and a New Social Order: The Republican Vision of the 1790s* (1984); Lance Banning, *The Jeffersonian Persuasion: Evolution of a Party Ideology* (1978); Drew McCoy, *The Elusive Republic: Political Economy in Jeffersonian America* (1980); Steven Watts, *The Republic Reborn* (1987).

### Political Parties

James Banner, *To the Hartford Convention: The Federalists and the Origins of Party Politics in the Early Republic, 1789–1815* (1967); Noble E. Cunningham, *The Jeffersonian Republicans and Power: Party Operations, 1801–1809* (1963); David Hackett Fischer, *The Revolution of American Conservatism: The Federalist Party in the Era of Jeffersonian Democracy* (1965); Ronald P. Formisano, *The Transformation of Political Culture: Massachusetts Parties, 1790s–1840s* (1983); Linda K. Kerber, *Federalists in Dissent: Imagery and Ideology in Jeffersonian America* (1970); Shaw Livermore, *The Twilight of Federalism: The Disintegration of the Federalist Party, 1815–1830* (1962); Alan Taylor, *Liberty Men and Great Proprietors: The Revolutionary Settlement on the Maine Frontier* (1990); James S. Young, *The Washington Community: 1800–1828* (1966).

### Political Leaders

Thomas P. Abernethy, *The Burr Conspiracy* (1954); Maurice G. Baxter, *Henry Clay and the American System* (1995); Andrew Burstein, *The Inner Jefferson* (1995); Robert Dawidoff, *The Education of John Randolph* (1979); Milton Lomask, *Aaron Burr*, 2 vols. (1979, 1982); Samuel Eliot Morison, *Harrison Gray Otis, 1765–1848: The Urbane Federalist* (1962); Robert Shalhope, *John Taylor of Caroline: Pastoral Republican* (1978); Herbert Sloan, *Principle and Interest: Thomas Jefferson and the Problem of Debt* (1995).

### Law and the Judiciary

Leonard Baker, *John Marshall: A Life in Law* (1974); Albert J. Beveridge, *John Marshall*, 4 vols. (1916–1919); Richard E. Ellis, *The Jeffersonian Crisis: Courts and Politics in the Young Republic* (1971); Charles G. Haines, *The Role of the Supreme Court in American Government and Politics, 1789–1835* (1944); Peter C. Hoffer and N. E. H. Hull, *Impeachment in America, 1635–1805* (1984); Morton J. Horwitz, *The Transformation of American Law, 1780–1860* (1977).

### The War of 1812 and Its Prologue

Pierre Berton, *The Invasion of Canada* (1980); Roger H. Brown, *The Republic in Peril* (1964); A. L. Burtt, *The United States, Great Britain, and British North America* (1940); Harry L. Coles, *The War of 1812* (1965); Donald R. Hickey, *The War of 1812: A Forgotten Conflict* (1989); Reginald Horsman, *The Causes of the War of 1812* (1962); Bradford Perkins, *Prologue to War: England and the United States, 1805–1812* (1961); Julius W. Pratt, *Expansionists of 1812* (1925); Burton Spivak, *Jefferson's English Crisis: Commerce, Embargo, and the Republican Revolution* (1979).

### Nationalism and Sectionalism

Harry Ammon, Jr., *James Monroe: The Quest for National Identity* (1971); George Dangerfield, *The Awakening of American Nationalism, 1815–1828* (1965) and *The Era of Good Feelings* (1952); Don E. Fehrenbacher, *The South and Three Sectional Crises* (1980); Glover Moore, *The Missouri Compromise, 1819–1821* (1953); Donald L. Robinson, *Slavery in the Structure of American Politics, 1765–1820* (1971).

### John Quincy Adams and the Monroe Doctrine

Samuel F. Bemis, *John Quincy Adams and the Foundations of American Foreign Policy* (1949); Walter LaFeber, ed., *John Quincy Adams and the American Continental Empire* (1965); Ernest R. May, *The Making of the Monroe Doctrine* (1975); Dexter Perkins, *Hands Off: A History of the Monroe Doctrine* (1951) and *The Monroe Doctrine, 1823–1826* (1927); Frank Owsley, Jr., and Gene Smith, *Filibusters and Expansionists* (1997); Greg Russell, *John Quincy Adams and the Public Virtues of Diplomacy* (1995).

## Chapter 9

### Agriculture and the Westward Movement

Stephen Aron, *How the West Was Lost: The Transformation of Kentucky from Daniel Boone to Henry Clay* (1996); Charles Danhof, *Change in Agriculture: The Northern United States, 1820–1870* (1969); Robert Feller, *The Public Lands in Jacksonian Politics* (1984); Paul W. Gates, *The Farmer's Age: Agriculture, 1815–1860* (1960); William H. Goetzmann, *Explorations and Empire: The Explorer and the Scientist in the Winning of the American West* (1966); Hildegard B. Johnson, *Order Upon the Land* (1976); Malcolm Rohrbough, *The Land Office Business: The Settlement and Administration of American Public Lands, 1789–1837* (1968); Michael Williams, *Americans and Their Forests* (1989).

### Indians

Robert F. Berkhofer, Jr., *The White Man's Indian: Images of the American Indian from Columbus to the Present* (1979); John R. Finger, *The Eastern Band of Cherokees, 1819–1900* (1984); Michael D. Green, *The Politics of Indian Removal: Creek Government and Society in Crisis* (1982); Joseph Herring, *The Enduring Indians of Kansas* (1990); William G. McLoughlin, *Cherokee Renascence in the New Republic* (1987); Roy H. Pearce, *The Savages of America* (1965); Richard Slotkin, *Regeneration Through Violence: The Mythology of the American Frontier, 1600–1860* (1973); Wilcomb E. Washburn, *The Indian in America* (1975); J. Leitch Wright, Jr., *Creeks and Seminoles* (1986).

### The Transportation Revolution

Albert Fishlow, *American Railroads and the Transformation of the Ante-Bellum Economy* (1965); Robert W. Fogel, *Railroads and American Economic Growth: Essays in Econometric History* (1964); Carter Goodrich, *Government Promotion of American Canals and Railroads, 1800–1890* (1960); Erik F. Haites, James Mak, and Gary M. Walton, *Western River Transportation: The Era of Early Internal Development, 1800–1860* (1975); R. E. Shaw, *Erie Water West* (1966); Carol Sheriff, *The Artificial River* (1996); George R. Taylor, *The Transportation Revolution, 1815–1860* (1951).

### Communities

Jeffrey S. Adler, *Yankee Merchants and the Making of the Urban West* (1991); Stuart Blumin, *The Urban Threshold: Growth and*

*Change in a Nineteenth-Century American Community* (1976); Steven Bullock, *Revolutionary Brotherhood: Freemasonry and the Transformation of the American Social Order, 1730–1840* (1996); Don H. Doyle, *The Social Order of a Frontier Community: Jacksonville, Illinois, 1825–1870* (1978); Clyde Griffen and Sally Griffen, *Natives and Newcomers: The Ordering of Opportunity in Mid-Nineteenth-Century Poughkeepsie* (1978); David Hamer, *New Towns in the New World* (1990); Paul Johnson, *A Shopkeeper's Millennium: Society and Revivals in Rochester, New York, 1815–1837* (1978); Steven J. Ross, *Workers on the Edge: Work, Leisure, and Politics in Industrializing Cincinnati, 1788–1890* (1985); Richard C. Wade, *The Urban Frontier* (1964); Anthony F. C. Wallace, *Rockdale: The Growth of an American Village in the Early Industrial Revolution* (1977); Peter Way, *Common Labour: Workers and the Digging of North American Canals, 1780–1860* (1994).

### Immigrants

Rowland Berthoff, *British Immigrants in Industrial America* (1953); Kathleen N. Conzen, *Immigrant Milwaukee, 1836–1860* (1976); Jay P. Dolan, *The Immigrant Church: New York's Irish and German Catholics, 1815–1860* (1975); Oscar Handlin, *Boston's Immigrants: A Study in Acculturation,* rev. ed. (1959); Marcus L. Hansen, *The Atlantic Migration, 1607–1860* (1940); Philip Taylor, *The Distant Magnet: European Emigration to the United States of America* (1971); Carl Wittke, *The Irish in America* (1956).

### Technology

Siegfried Giedion, *Mechanization Takes Command* (1948); H. J. Habakkuk, *American and British Technology in the Nineteenth Century* (1962); Otto Mayr and Robert C. Post, eds., *Yankee Enterprise: The Rise of the American System of Manufactures* (1981); Merritt R. Smith, *Harpers Ferry Armory and the New Technology* (1977).

### Manufacturing and Economic Growth

W. Elliot Brownlee, *Dynamics of Ascent* (1974); Stuart Bruchey, *The Roots of American Economic Growth, 1607–1861* (1965); Christopher Clark, *The Roots of Rural Capitalism: Western Massachusetts, 1780–1860* (1990); Thomas C. Cochran, *Frontiers of Change: Early Industrialism in America* (1981); Alan Dawley, *Class and Community: The Industrial Revolution in Lynn* (1976); Thomas Dublin, *Women at Work: The Transformation of Work and Community in Lowell, Massachusetts, 1826–1860* (1979) and *Transforming Women's Work* (1994); Bruce Laurie, *Working People of Philadelphia, 1800–1850* (1980); Judith A. McGaw, *Most Wonderful Machine: Mechanization and Social Change in Berkshire Paper Making, 1815–1885* (1987); Douglass North, *The Economic Growth of the United States, 1790–1860* (1961); Ronald Schultz, *The Republic of Labor: Philadelphia Artisans and the Politics of Class, 1720–1830* (1993); Peter Temin, *The Jacksonian Economy* (1969); Philip Scranton, *Proprietary Capitalism* (1983); Barbara Tucker, *Samuel Slater and the Origins of the American Textile Industry, 1790–1860* (1984).

### Rich and Poor

Elizabeth Blackmar, *Manhattan for Rent, 1785–1850* (1989); Martin Burke, *The Conundrum of Class* (1995); Leonard P. Curry, *The Free Black in Urban America, 1800–1850* (1981); Paul A. Gilje, *The Road to Mobocracy: Popular Disorder in New York City, 1763–1834* (1987); Peter Knights, *The Plain People of Boston, 1830–1860* (1971); Edward Pessen, *Riches, Class, and Power Before the Civil War* (1973); Stephan Thernstrom, *Poverty and Progress* (1964).

### Professions

Daniel H. Calhoun, *Professional Lives in America: Structure and Aspiration, 1750–1850* (1965); Donald M. Scott, *From Office to Profession: The New England Ministry, 1750–1850* (1978); Richard Shryock, *Medical Licensing in America, 1650–1965* (1967); William B. Skelton, *An American Profession of Arms: The Army Officer Corps, 1784–1861* (1993).

### Women and the Family

Jeanne Boydston, *Home and Work* (1990); Nancy F. Cott, *The Bonds of Womanhood: 'Woman's Sphere' in New England, 1780–1835* (1977); Suzanne Lebsock, *The Free Women of Petersburg: Status and Culture in a Southern Town, 1784–1860* (1984); James C. Mohr, *Abortion in America: The Origins and Evolution of National Policy, 1800–1900* (1978); Glenda Riley, *Women and Indians on the Frontier, 1825–1915* (1984); Ellen K. Rothman, *Hands and Hearts: A History of Courtship in America* (1987); Mary Ryan, *Cradle of the Middle Class: The Family in Oneida County, New York, 1790–1865* (1981); Kathryn K. Sklar, *Catharine Beecher: A Study in American Domesticity* (1973); Christine Stansell, *City of Women: Sex and Class in New York, 1789–1860* (1986); Gwendolyn Wright, *Building the Dream: A Social History of Housing in America* (1981).

## *Chapter 10*

### Political Leaders

Donald B. Cole, *Martin Van Buren and the American Political System* (1984); Richard B. Latner, *The Presidency of Andrew Jackson: White House Politics, 1829–1837* (1979); John Niven, *Martin Van Buren and the Romantic Age* (1983); Merrill D. Peterson, *The Great Triumvirate: Webster, Clay and Calhoun* (1987); Leonard L. Richards, *The Life and Times of Congressman John Quincy Adams* (1986); Major L. Wilson, *The Presidency of Martin Van Buren* (1984).

### Political Parties

Jean H. Baker, *Affairs of Party: The Political Culture of Northern Democrats in the Mid-Nineteenth Century* (1983); Ronald P. Formisano, *The Birth of Mass Political Parties, 1827–1861* (1971) and *The Transformation of American Political Culture: Massachusetts Parties, 1790s–1840s* (1983); Paul Goodman, *Towards a Christian Republic: Antimasonry and the Great Tradition in New England, 1826–1836* (1988); Daniel W. Howe, *The Political Culture of the American Whigs* (1980); Robert V. Remini, *The Election of Andrew Jackson* (1963) and *Andrew Jackson and the Course of American Empire* (1977); Harry L. Watson, *Jacksonian Politics and Community Conflict: The Emergence of the Second American Party System in Cumberland County, North Carolina* (1981); Sean Wilentz, *Chants Democratic: New York City and the Rise of the American Working Class, 1788–1850* (1983).

### Banking and the Economy

Bray Hammond, *Banks and Politics in America from the Revolution to the Civil War* (1957); John M. McFaul, *The Politics of Jack-*

*sonian Finance* (1972); William G. Shade, *Banks or No Banks: The Money Question in Western Politics* (1972); James Roger Sharp, *The Jacksonians Versus the Banks: Politics in the United States After the Panic of 1837* (1970); Peter Temin, *The Jacksonian Economy* (1965).

### Religious Revivals

Sydney E. Ahlstrom, *A Religious History of the American People*, 2 vols. (1975); Leonard J. Arrington, *The Mormon Experience* (1979) and *Brigham Young: American Moses* (1985); John Boles, *The Great Revival, 1787–1805* (1972); Paul Conkin, *The Uneasy Center* (1995); Whitney Cross, *The Burned-Over District* (1950); Nathan O. Hatch, *The Democratization of American Christianity* (1989); Donald G. Mathews, *Religion in the Old South* (1977); Stephen J. Stein, *The Shaker Experience in America* (1992).

### Relationships Between Religion and Reform

Gilbert Barnes, *The Anti-Slavery Impulse* (1933); Richard Cardwardine, *Evangelicals and Politics in Antebellum America* (1993); Clifford S. Griffin, *Their Brothers' Keepers: Moral Stewardship in the United States* (1960); Mary Ryan, *Cradle of the Middle Class: The Family in Oneida County, New York, 1790–1865* (1981); Timothy L. Smith, *Revivalism and Social Reform* (1957).

### Temperance

Jed Dannenbaum, *Drink and Disorder: Temperance Reform in Cincinnati from the Washingtonian Revival to the WCTU* (1984); Ian Tyrrell, *Sobering Up: From Temperance to Prohibition in Antebellum America* (1979).

### Educational Reform

Carl F. Kaestle, *Pillars of the Republic: Common Schools and American Society, 1780–1860* (1983); Carl F. Kaestle and Maris A. Vinovskis, *Education and Social Change in Nineteenth-Century Massachusetts* (1980); Michael B. Katz, *The Irony of Early School Reform* (1968); Stanley K. Schultz, *The Culture Factory: Boston Public Schools 1789–1860* (1973).

### Abolitionists

Robert H. Abzug, *Passionate Liberator: Theodore Weld Dwight and the Dilemma of Reform* (1890); William Cheek and Aimee Lee Cheek, *John Mercer Langston and the Fight for Black Freedom, 1829–1865* (1989); David B. Davis, *The Problem of Slavery in the Age of Revolution, 1770–1823* (1975); Hugh Davis, *Joshua Leavitt: Evangelical Abolitionist* (1990); Lawrence J. Freidman, *Gregarious Saints: Self and Community in American Abolitionism, 1830–1870* (1982); Louis Gerteis, *Morality and Utility in American Antislavery Reform* (1987); Blanche Glassman Hersh, *The Slavery of Sex: Feminist Abolitionists in America* (1978); William Lee Miller, *Arguing Against Slavery* (1996); William McFeely, *Frederick Douglass* (1991); Jane A. Pease and William H. Pease, *They Who Would Be Free: Blacks' Search for Freedom, 1830–1861* (1974); Lewis Perry, *Radical Abolitionism: Anarchy and the Government of God in Antislavery Thought* (1973); Benjamin Quarles, *Black Abolitionists* (1969); Leonard L. Richards, *"Gentlemen of Property and Standing": Anti-Abolition Mobs in Jacksonian America* (1970); Ronald G. Walters, *The Antislavery Appeal: American Abolitionists After 1830* (1976); Bertram Wyatt-Brown, *Lewis Tappan and the Evangelical War Against Slavery* (1969).

### Women's Rights

Lois Banner, *Elizabeth Cady Stanton* (1980); Barbara J. Berg, *The Remembered Gate—The Woman and the City, 1800–1860* (1978); Carl N. Degler, *At Odds: Women and the Family in America from the Revolution to the Present* (1980); Ellen C. DuBois, *Feminism and Suffrage: The Emergence of an Independent Women's Movement in America, 1848–1869* (1978); Lori D. Ginzberg, *Women and the Work of Benevolence* (1990); Elisabeth Griffith, *In Her Own Right: The Life of Elizabeth Cady Stanton* (1984); Gerda Lerner, *The Grimké Sisters from South Carolina: Rebels Against Slavery* (1967); Jean Fagan Yellin, *Women and Sisters: The Antislavery Feminists in American Culture* (1989).

### Institutional Reformers

Gerald W. Grob, *Mental Institutions in America: Social Policy to 1875* (1973); W. David Lewis, *From Newgate to Dannemora: The Rise of the Penitentiary* (1965); Robert Mennel, *Thorns and Thistles* (1973); David Rothman, *The Discovery of the Asylum* (1971).

### Utopian Communities

Michael Barkun, *Crucible of the Millennium* (1986); Arthur E. Bestor, *Backwoods Utopias: The Sectarian and Owenite Phases of Communitarian Utopianism in America, 1663–1829* (1950); Michael Fellman, *The Unbounded Frame: Freedom and Community in Nineteenth-Century American Utopianism* (1973); Lawrence Foster, *Women, Family, and Utopia* (1991); Carl J. Guarneri, *Utopian Alternative: Fourierism in Nineteenth-Century America* (1991); Carol Kolmerten, *Women in Utopia* (1990).

## Chapter 11

### Technology, Progress, and the Standard of Living

Ruth Schwartz Cowan, *More Work for Mother: The Ironies of Household Technology from the Open Hearth to the Microwave* (1983); Durand Echeverria, *Mirage in the West: A History of the French Image of American Society to 1815* (1957); H. J. Habakkuk, *American and British Technology in the Nineteenth Century* (1962); Dolores Hayden, *The Grand Domestic Revolution: A History of Feminist Designs for American Homes, Neighborhoods, and Cities* (1981); David A. Hounshell, *From the American System to Mass Production, 1800–1932* (1984); John F. Kasson, *Civilizing the Machine: Technology and Republican Values in America, 1776–1900* (1976); Jack Larkin, *Reshaping Everyday Life, 1790–1849* (1988); Susan Strasser, *Never Done: A History of American Housework* (1983).

### Railroads

Eugene Alvarez, *Travel on Southern Antebellum Railroads, 1828–1860* (1974); Alfred D. Chandler, *The Visible Hand: The Managerial Revolution in American Business* (1977); Stewart H. Holbrook, *The Story of American Railroads* (1947); Edward C. Kirkland, *Men, Cities and Transportation: A Study in New England History, 1820–1900* (1948); Robert J. Parks, *Democracy's Railroads: Public Enterprise in Michigan* (1972); John F. Stover, *American Railroads* (1961).

### Disease and Health

John D. Davies, *Phrenology: Fad and Science* (1955); John S. Haller, Jr., *American Medicine in Transition, 1840–1910* (1981);

Stephen Nissenbaum, *Sex, Diet, and Debility in Jacksonian America: Sylvester Graham and Health Reform* (1980); Martin S. Pernick, *A Calculus of Suffering: Pain, Professionalism, and Anesthesia in Nineteenth-Century America* (1985); Charles Rosenberg, *The Cholera Years: The United States in 1832, 1849, and 1866* (1962); Paul Starr, *The Social Transformation of American Medicine* (1982).

### Popular Culture

Richard D. Brown, *Knowledge Is Power: The Diffusion of Information in Early America, 1700–1865* (1989); Daniel A. Cohen, *Pillars of Salt, Monuments of Grace: New England Crime Literature and the Origins of American Popular Culture, 1674–1860* (1993); Ann Fabian, *Card Sharps, Dream Books, and Bucket Shops: Gambling in 19th-Century America* (1990); David Grimsted, *Melodrama Unveiled: American Theater and Culture, 1800–1850* (1968); Karen Halttunen, *Confidence Men and Painted Women: A Study in Middle-Class Culture in America, 1830–1870* (1982); Neil Harris, *Humbug: The Art of P. T. Barnum* (1973); Dan Schiller, *Objectivity and the News: The Public and the Rise of Commercial Journalism* (1981); Michael Schudson, *Discovering the News: A Social History of American Newspapers* (1978); Donald Scott, "The Popular Lecture," *Journal of American History* 66 (March 1980): 791–809; Robert C. Toll, *Blacking Up: The Minstrel Show in Nineteenth-Century America* (1974); Ronald J. Zboray, *A Fictive People: Antebellum Economic Development and the American Reading Public* (1993).

### Literature

Nina Baym, *Woman's Fiction: A Guide to Novels By and About Women in America, 1820–1870* (1978); Nina Baym, *Novels, Readers, and Reviewers: Responses to Fiction in Antebellum America* (1984); Vincent Buranelli, *Edgar Allan Poe* (1977); Charles Capper, *Margaret Fuller* (1992); William Charvat, *The Profession of Authorship in America, 1800–1870* (edited by Matthew J. Bruccoli, 1968); Cathy Davidson, *Revolution and the Word* (1986); Steven Fink, *Prophet in the Marketplace: Thoreau's Development as a Professional Writer* (1992); David Levin, *History as Romantic Art: Bancroft, Prescott, Motley, and Parkman* (1963); Lucy Maddox, *Removals: Nineteenth-Century American Literature and the Politics of Indian Affairs* (1991); James Mellow, *Nathaniel Hawthorne in His Time* (1980); David S. Reynolds, *Walt Whitman's America* (1995); Benjamin T. Spencer, *The Quest for Nationality: An American Literary Campaign* (1957); Tony Tanner, *The Reign of Wonder: Naiveté and Reality in American Literature* (1965); Larzer Ziff, *Literary Democracy: The Declaration of Cultural Independence in America* (1981).

### Visual Arts

Elizabeth Barlow, *Frederick Law Olmsted's New York* (1972); Thomas Bender, *Toward an Urban Vision: Ideas and Institutions in Nineteenth-Century America* (1975); Albert Fein, *Frederick Law Olmsted and the Environmental Tradition* (1972); Neil Harris, *The Artist in American Society: The Formative Years, 1790–1860* (1966); Lee Clark Mitchell, *Witness to a Vanishing America* (1981); Raymond J. O'Brien, *Landscape and Scenery of the Lower Hudson Valley* (1981); Nancy Rash, *The Painting and Politics of George Caleb Bingham* (1991); Laura Wood Roper, *FLO: A Biography of Frederick Law Olmsted* (1973); Bryan J. Wolf, *Romantic Re-Vision: Culture and Consciousness in Nineteenth-Century American Painting and Literature* (1982).

## Chapter 12

### The Economic and Social Structure of the White South

William L. Barney, *The Road to Secession* (1972); Fred Bateman and Thomas Weiss, *A Deplorable Scarcity: The Failure of Industrialism in the Slave Economy* (1981); Orville V. Burton and Robert McMath, eds., *Class, Conflict, and Consensus* (1982); Mary B. Chesnut, *A Diary from Dixie* (edited by Ben Ames Williams, 1949); Blanche Henry Clark, *The Tennessee Yeoman, 1840–1860* (1942); Catherine G. Clinton, *The Plantation Mistress: Women's World in the Old South* (1982); Barbara J. Fields, *Slavery and Freedom on the Middle Ground: Maryland During the Nineteenth Century* (1985); Elizabeth Fox-Genovese, *Within the Plantation Household: Black and White Women of the Old South* (1988); Eugene Genovese, *The Political Economy of Slavery* (1965); Steven Hahn, *The Roots of Southern Populism: Yeomen Farmers and the Transformation of the Georgia Upcountry, 1850–1890* (1983); Suzanne Lebsock, *The Free Women of Petersburg: Status Culture in a Southern Town, 1784–1860* (1984); Stephanie McCurry, *Masters of Small Worlds* (1995); Forrest McDonald and Grady McWhiney, "The Antebellum Southern Herdsman: A Reinterpretation," *Journal of Southern History* 41 (May 1975): 147–166; Frank L. Owsley, *Plain Folk of the Old South* (1949); Anne F. Scott, *The Southern Lady: From Pedestal to Politics, 1830–1930* (1970); Herbert Weaver, *Mississippi Farmers, 1850–1860* (1945); Ralph A. Wooster, *Politicians, Planters, and Plain Folk* (1975); Gavin Wright, *The Political Economy of the Cotton South* (1978).

### The Values of the White South

David F. Allmendinger, Jr., *Ruffin: Family and Reform in the Old South* (1990); Edward L. Ayers, *Vengeance and Justice: Crime and Punishment in the Nineteenth-Century American South* (1984); David T. Bailey, *Shadow on the Church: Southwestern Evangelical Religion and the Issue of Slavery, 1783–1860* (1985); Dickson D. Bruce, *Violence and Culture in the Antebellum South* (1979); William J. Cooper, *The South and the Politics of Slavery, 1829–1856* (1978); James D. Essig, *The Bonds of Wickedness: American Evangelicals Against Slavery, 1770–1808* (1982); Drew G. Faust, *A Sacred Circle: The Dilemma of the Intellectual in the Old South, 1840–1860* (1977) and *James Henry Hammond and the Old South: A Design for Mastery* (1982); John Hope Franklin, *The Militant South* (1966); George M. Fredrickson, *The Black Image in the White Mind: The Debate on Afro-American Character and Destiny, 1817–1914* (1971) and *White Supremacy: A Comparative Study in American and South African History* (1981); Alison G. Freehling, *Drift Toward Dissolution: The Virginia Slavery Debate of 1831–1832* (1982); Elliott J. Gorn, "'Gouge and Bite, Pull Hair and Scratch': The Social Significance of Fighting in the Southern Backcountry," *American Historical Review* 90 (February 1985): 18–43; Michael Hindus, *Prison and Plantation: Crime, Justice, and Authority in Massachusetts and South Carolina, 1767–1878* (1980); John McCardell, *The Idea of a Southern Nation: Southern Nationalists and Southern Nationalism* (1979); Donald G. Mathews, *Religion in the Old South* (1977); Mitchell Snay, *Gospel of Disunion: Religion and Separatism in the Antebellum South* (1993); Ronald Takaki, *A Pro-Slavery Crusade:*

*The Agitation to Reopen the African Slave Trade* (1980); J. Mills Thornton, *Politics and Power in a Slave Society: Alabama, 1800–1860* (1978); Larry E. Tise, *Proslavery: A History of the Defense of Slavery in America, 1701–1840* (1987); Bertram Wyatt-Brown, *Southern Honor: Ethics and Behavior in the Old South* (1982).

### Black Experience and Culture in the Old South

Ira Berlin, *Slaves Without Masters: The Free Negro in the Antebellum South* (1974); John Blassingame, *The Slave Community* (1972); Leonard P. Curry, *The Free Black in Urban America, 1800–1850: The Shadow of the Dream* (1981); Carl N. Degler, *Neither Black Nor White: Slavery and Race Relations in Brazil and the United States* (1971); Dena J. Epstein, *Sinful Tunes and Spirituals: Black Folk Music to the Civil War* (1977); Claudia D. Goldin, *Urban Slavery in the American South, 1820–1860* (1976); Herbert G. Gutman, *The Black Familiy in Slavery and Freedom, 1759–1925* (1976); Jacqueline Jones, *Labor of Love, Labor of Sorrow: Black Women, Work, and the Family from Slavery to the Present* (1985); Lawrence W. Levine, *Black Culture and Black Consciousness: Afro-American Folk Thought from Slavery to Freedom* (1977); Ann P. Malone, *Sweet Chariot: Slave Family and Household Structure in Nineteenth-Century Louisiana* (1992); Thomas D. Morris, *Southern Slavery and the Law* (1996); Stephen B. Oates, *The Fires of Jubilee* (1975); Leslie H. Owens, *This Species of Property: Slave Life and Slave Culture in the Old South* (1976); Albert J. Raboteau, *Slave Religion* (1978); George P. Rawick, *From Sundown to Sunup: The Making of a Black Community* (1972); Jon Michael Spencer, *Black Hymnody* (1992); Robert S. Starobin, *Industrial Slavery in the Old South* (1970); Brenda R. Stevenson, *Life in Black and White: Family and Community in the Slave South* (1996); Michael Tadman, *Speculators and Slaves: Traders and Slaves in the Old South* (1989).

## *Chapter 13*

### Immigration, Nativism, and Labor Protest

Tyler Anbinder, *Nativism and Slavery: The Northern Know Nothings and the Politics of the 1850s* (1992); Lee Benson, *The Concept of Jacksonian Democracy: New York as a Test Case* (1961); Ray A. Billington, *The Protestant Crusade, 1800–1860: A Study of the Origins of Nativism* (1938); R. A. Burchell, *The San Francisco Irish, 1848–1880* (1980); Kathleen Conzen, *Immigrant Milwaukee, 1836–1860* (1976); Hasia R. Diner, *Erin's Daughter in America* (1983); Oscar Handlin, *Boston's Immigrants*, rev. ed. (1969); Bruce Laurie, *Working People of Philadelphia, 1800–1850* (1980); Bruce Levine, *The Spirit of 1848: German Immigrants, Labor Conflict, and the Coming of the Civil War* (1992); Lawrence J. McCaffrey, *The Irish Diaspora in America* (1984); Kerby A. Miller, *Emigrants and Exiles: Ireland and the Irish Exodus to North America* (1985); Norman Ware, *The Industrial Worker, 1840–1860* (1964); Sean Wilentz, *Chants Democratic: New York City and the Rise of the American Working Class, 1788–1850* (1984); Carl Wittke, *The Irish in America* (1956).

### The Far West

John W. Caughey, *The California Gold Rush* (1975); Malcolm Clark, Jr., *Eden Seekers: The Settlement of Oregon, 1818–1862* (1981); Douglas H. Daniels, *Pioneer Urbanities: A Social and Cultural History of Black San Francisco* (1980); Arnoldo De Leon,

*They Called Them Greasers: Anglo Attitudes Toward Mexicans in Texas, 1821–1900* (1983); John Mack Faragher, *Women and Men on the Overland Trail* (1979); William H. Goetzmann, *Exploration and Empire: The Explorer and the Scientist in the Winning of the American West* (1966); Neal Harlow, *California Conquered: War and Peace on the Pacific, 1846–1850* (1982); Theodore J. Karaminski, *Fur Trade and Exploration: Opening of the Far Northwest, 1821–1852* (1983); Frederick Merk, *History of the Westward Movement* (1978); Leonard Pitt, *The Decline of the Californios: A Social History of the Spanish-Speaking Californians, 1846–1890* (1966); John I. Unruh, Jr., *The Plains Across: Overland Emigrants and the Trans-Mississippi West, 1840–1860* (1979); David J. Weber, *The Mexican Frontier, 1821–1846: The American Southwest Under Mexico* (1982) and *The Spanish Frontier in North America* (1992).

### The Politics and Diplomacy of Expansion

K. Jack Bauer, *The Mexican War, 1846–1848* (1974); Paul H. Bergeron, *The Presidency of James K. Polk* (1987); William C. Binkley, *The Texas Revolution* (1952); Gene M. Brack, *Mexico Views Manifest Destiny* (1976); Seymour Connor and Odie Faulk, *North America Divided: The Mexican War, 1846–1848* (1971); William J. Cooper, *Liberty and Slavery: Southern Politics to 1860* (1983); Bernard DeVoto, *The Year of Decision, 1846* (1943); Norman A. Graebner, *Empire on the Pacific: A Study in American Continental Expansion* (1955); Thomas R. Hietala, *Manifest Design: Anxious Aggrandizement in Late Jacksonian America* (1985); Reginald Horsman, *Race and Manifest Destiny: The Origins of American Racial Anglo-Saxonism* (1981); Robert W. Johannsen, *To the Halls of the Montezumas: The Mexican War in the American Imagination* (1985); Ernest McPherson Lander, Jr., *Reluctant Imperialist: Calhoun, the South Carolinian, and the Mexican War* (1980); Frederick Merk, *Slavery and the Annexation of Texas* (1972); David M. Pletcher, *The Diplomacy of Annexation: Texas, Oregon, and the Mexican War* (1973); Joseph G. Raybeck, *Free Soil: The Election of 1848* (1970); John H. Schroeder, *Mr. Polk's War: American Opposition and Dissent, 1846–1848* (1971); Charles G. Sellers, *James K. Polk: Jacksonian, 1795–1843* (1957); Joel H. Silbey, *The Shrine of Party: Congressional Voting Behaviour, 1841–1852* (1967); Otis A. Singletary, *The Mexican War* (1960).

## *Chapter 14*

### The Compromise of 1850 and Its Aftermath

Thomas F. Gossett, *Uncle Tom's Cabin and American Culture* (1985); Holman Hamilton, *Prologue to Conflict: The Crisis and Compromise of 1850* (1964); Peter Knupfer, *The Union as It Is: Constitutional Unionism and Sectional Compromise, 1787–1861* (1991); Thomas D. Morris, *Free Men All: The Personal Liberty Laws of the North, 1780–1861* (1974); Chaplain W. Morrison, *Democratic Politics and Sectionalism: The Wilmot Proviso Controversy* (1967); Mark Stegmaier, *Texas, New Mexico, and the Compromise of 1850* (1996); Albert J. Von Frank, *The Trials of Anthony Burns* (1998).

### Political Realignment, 1852–1856

Tyler Anbinder, *Nativism and Slavery: The Northern Know Nothings and the Politics of the 1850s* (1992); Eugene Berwanger, *The Frontier Against Slavery: Western Anti-Negro Prejudice in the*

*Slavery Extension Controversy* (1967); Michael F. Holt, *Political Parties and American Political Development from the Age of Jackson to the Age of Lincoln* (1992); James A. Rawley, *Race and Politics: "Bleeding Kansas" and the Coming of the Civil War* (1969); Geoffrey W. Wolff, *The Kansas-Nebraska Bill* (1977).

### The South and the Sectional Crisis

Charles H. Brown, *Agents of Manifest Destiny: The Lives and Times of the Filibusterers* (1978); John Hope Franklin, *The Militant South, 1800–1861* (1970) and *A Southern Odyssey: Travelers in the Antebellum North* (1976); Michael P. Johnson and James L. Roark, eds., *No Chariot Let Down: Charleston's Free People of Color on the Eve of the Civil War* (1984); John McCardell, *The Idea of a Southern Nation: Southern Nationalists and Southern Nationalism, 1830–1861* (1979); Robert E. May, *The Southern Dream of a Caribbean Empire, 1854–1861* (1973); Rollin G. Osterweiss, *Romanticism and Nationalism in the Old South* (1949); Ronald L. Takaki, *A Proslavery Crusade: The Agitation to Reopen the African Slave Trade* (1971); J. Mills Thornton, *Politics and Power in a Slave Society* (1978).

### The Disruption of the Union

William L. Barney, *The Road to Secession* (1972); Steven A. Channing, *Crisis of Fear: Secession in South Carolina* (1970); David Donald, *Charles Sumner and the Coming of the Civil War* (1960); Don E. Fehrenbacher, *The Dred Scott Case* (1978) and *Prelude to Greatness: Lincoln in the 1850s* (1962); Paul W. Finkelman, ed., *His Soul Goes Marching On: Responses to John Brown and the Harpers Ferry Raid* (1995); George B. Forgie, *Patricide in the House Divided: A Psychological Interpretation of Lincoln and His Age* (1979); Henry V. Jaffa, *Crisis of the House Divided: An Interpretation of the Lincoln-Douglas Debates* (1959); Robert W. Johannsen, *Stephen A. Douglas* (1973); Michael Johnson, *Secession and Conservatism in the Lower South: The Social and Ideological Bases of Secession in Georgia, 1860–1861* (1983); Albert J. Kirwan, *John J. Crittenden: The Struggle for the Union* (1962); Milton Klein, *President James Buchanan: A Biography* (1962); Michael Morison, *Slavery and the American West* (1997); Paul C. Nagel, *One Nation Indivisible: The Union in American Thought* (1964); Allan Nevins, *The Emergence of Lincoln* (2 vols., 1950); Roy F. Nichols, *The Disruption of American Democracy* (1948); Stephen B. Oates, *To Purge This Land with Blood: A Biography of John Brown* (1970); David Potter, *Lincoln and His Party in the Secession Crisis* (1942); Kenneth Stampp, *And the War Came: The North and the Secession Crisis, 1860–1861* (1970).

## *Chapter 15*

### General

Daniel Aaron, *The Unwritten War* (1973); William L. Barney, *Flawed Victory* (1975); Catherine Clinton and Nina Silber, eds., *Divided Houses: Gender and the Civil War* (1992); David P. Crook, *Diplomacy During the Civil War* (1975); David Donald, ed., *Why the North Won the Civil War* (1960); Eric Foner, *Politics and Ideology in the Age of the Civil War* (1980); Paul G. Gates, *Agriculture and the Civil War* (1965); Harold Hyman, *A More Perfect Union* (1975); James M. McPherson, *Ordeal by Fire* (1982); Mary Elizabeth Massey, *Bonnet Brigades: American Women and the Civil War* (1966); Allan Nevins, *The War for the Union*, 4 vols.

(1959–1971); Lewis P. Simpson, *Mind and the American Civil War* (1989); Maris A. Vinovskis, *Toward a Social History of the American Civil War: Exploratory Essays* (1990); Edmund Wilson, *Patriotic Gore* (1961).

### Lincoln

LaWanda Cox, *Lincoln and Black Freedom* (1981); David Donald, *Lincoln Reconsidered: Essays on the Civil War Era*, 2d ed. (1956); James M. McPherson, *Abraham Lincoln and the Second American Revolution* (1990); Mark E. Neely, Jr., *The Last Best Hope on Earth: Abraham Lincoln and the Promise of America* (1993); Stephen B. Oates, *With Malice Toward None: The Life of Abraham Lincoln* (1979); Phillip Shaw Paludan, *The Presidency of Abraham Lincoln* (1994); James R. Randall, *Lincoln the President*, 4 vols. (1944–1955); Benjamin Thomas, *Abraham Lincoln* (1952); T. Harry Williams, *Lincoln and the Radicals* (1941) and *Lincoln and His Generals* (1952); Garry Wills, *Lincoln at Gettysburg: The Words That Remade America* (1992); Douglas L. Wilson, *Honor's Voice: The Transformation of Abraham Lincoln* (1998).

### The Military Experience

Michael Barton, *Good Men: The Character of Civil War Soldiers* (1981); Richard G. Beringer et al., *Why the South Lost the Civil War* (1986); Bruce Catton, *Mr. Lincoln's Army* (1951), *Glory Road* (1952), and *A Stillness at Appomattox* (1953); Shelby Foote, *The Civil War: A Narrative*, 3 vols. (1958–1974); Joseph T. Glatthaar, *The March to the Sea and Beyond* (1985) and *Partners in Command: The Relationships Between Leaders in the Civil War* (1994); Paddy Griffith, *Battle Tactics of the Civil War* (1989); Edward Hagerman, *The American Civil War and the Origins of Modern Warfare* (1988); Herman Hattaway, *Shades of Blue and Gray* (1997); Herman Hattaway and Archer Jones, *How the North Won: A Military History of the Civil War* (1984); Alvin M. Josephy, Jr., *The Civil War in the American West* (1991); Maury Klein, *Days of Defiance: Sumter, Secession, and the Coming of the Civil War* (1997); Gerald F. Linderman, *Embattled Courage: The Experience of Combat in the American Civil War* (1987); James M. McPherson, *What They Fought for, 1861–1865* (1994) and *For Causes and Comrades: Why Men Fought in the Civil War* (1997); Carol Reardon, *Pickett's Charge in History and Memory* (1997).

### The Black Experience

Ira Berlin et al., eds., *Freedom, A Documentary History of Emancipation, 1861–1867* (1982–1993); Dudley Cornish, *The Sable Arm: Negro Troops in the Union Army* (1956); John Hope Franklin, *The Emancipation Proclamation* (1963); Louis S. Gerteis, *From Contraband to Freeman: Federal Policy Toward Southern Blacks, 1861–1865* (1973); Joseph T. Glatthaar, *Forged in Battle: The Civil War Alliance of Black Soldiers and White Officers* (1990); James M. McPherson, ed., *The Negro's Civil War* (1965); Benjamin Quarles, *The Negro in the Civil War* (1953); Willie Lee Rose, *Rehearsal for Reconstruction: The Port Royal Experiment* (1964).

### The Southern Experience

Thomas B. Alexander and Richard E. Beringer, *The Anatomy of the Confederate Congress* (1972); Paul D. Escott, *After Secession: Jefferson Davis and the Failure of Southern Nationalism* (1978); Eli N. Evans, *Judah P. Benjamin* (1987); Drew Gilpin

Faust, *The Creation of Confederate Nationalism* (1988) and *Southern Stories: Slaveholders in Peace and War* (1992); Douglas Southall Freeman, *R. E. Lee: A Biography*, 4 vols. (1934–1935); Gary W. Gallagher, *The Confederate War* (1997); Mark Grimsley, *The Hard Hand of War: Union Military Policy Toward Southern Civilians, 1861–1865* (1995); Clarence Mohr, *On the Threshold of Freedom: Masters and Slaves in Civil War Georgia* (1986); Robert M. Myers, ed., *The Children of Pride: A True Story of Georgia and the Civil War* (1972); Alan T. Nolan, *Lee Considered: General Robert E. Lee and Civil War History* (1991); George C. Rable, *Civil Wars: Women and the Crisis of Southern Nationalism* (1989); James L. Roark, *Masters Without Slaves: Southern Planters in the Civil War and Reconstruction* (1978); Emory M. Thomas, *The Confederate Nation, 1861–1865* (1979); Bell I. Wiley, *The Plain People of the Confederacy* (1943) and *Road to Appomattox* (1956).

**The Northern Experience**

Adrian Cook, *Armies of the Streets: The New York City Draft Riots of 1863* (1974); George M. Fredrickson, *The Inner Civil War: Northern Intellectuals and the Crisis of the Union* (1965); David Gilchrist and W. David Lewis, eds., *Economic Change in the Civil War Era* (1965); Frank L. Klement, *The Copperheads of the Middle West* (1960) and *Dark Lanterns: Secret Political Societies, Conspiracies, and Treason Trials in the Civil War* (1984); William S. McFeely, *Grant: A Biography* (1981); James H. Moorhead, *American Apocalypse: Yankee Protestants and the Civil War* (1978); Stephen B. Oates, *A Woman of Valor: Clara Barton and the Civil War* (1994); Phillip Shaw Paludan, *"A People's Contest": The Union and the Civil War, 1861–1865* (1988); Joel Silbey, *A Respectable Minority: The Democratic Party in the Civil War Era, 1860–1868* (1977); George W. Smith and Charles Judah, eds., *Life in the North During the Civil War* (1968); Hans L. Trefousse, *The Radical Republicans* (1968).

**Personal Narratives**

Eliza Frances Andrews, *Wartime Journal of a Georgia Girl* (1908); David Donald, ed., *Inside Lincoln's Cabinet: The Civil War Diaries of Salmon P. Chase* (1959); Ulysses S. Grant, *Memoirs and Selected Letters* (1990); Rupert S. Hallard, ed., *The Letters and Diaries of Laura M. Towne* (1970); T. W. Higginson, *Army Life in a Black Regiment* (1867); Mary Ashton Livermore, *My Story of the War* (1881); W. T. Sherman, *Memoirs* (1990); C. Vann Woodward, ed., *Mary Chesnut's Civil War* (1982).

## *Chapter 16*

**Reconstruction Politics**

Richard H. Abbott, *The Republican Party and the South, 1855–1877* (1986); Herman Belz, *Emancipation and Equal Rights: Politics and Constitutionalism in the Civil War Era* (1978); Michael Les Benedict, *A Compromise of Principle: Congressional Republicans and Reconstruction, 1863–1869* (1974) and *The Impeachment and Trial of Andrew Johnson* (1973); W. R. Brock, *An American Crisis: Congress and Reconstruction, 1865–1867* (1963); Fawn Brodie, *Thaddeus Stevens: Scourge of the South* (1959); Richard O. Curry, ed., *Radicalism, Racism, and Party Realignment: The Border States During Reconstruction* (1969); David Donald, *Charles Sumner and the Rights of Man* (1970) and *The Politics of Reconstruction, 1863–1867* (1965);

Ellen Carol DuBois, *Feminism and Suffrage: The Emergence of an Independent Women's Movement in America, 1848–1869* (1978); William Gillette, *The Right to Vote: Politics and Passage of the Fifteenth Amendment* (1969); William C. Harris, *With Charity for All: Lincoln and the Reconstruction of the Union* (1997); Harold Hyman, *A More Perfect Union: The Impact of the Civil War and Reconstruction on the Constitution* (1973); Stanley I. Kutler, *Judicial Power and Reconstruction* (1968); Eric McKitrick, *Andrew Johnson and Reconstruction* (1960); James C. Mohr, *Radical Republicans in the North: State Politics During Reconstruction* (1976); William E. Nelson, *The Fourteenth Amendment* (1988); Hans Trefousse, *Andrew Johnson: A Biography* (1989) and *Thaddeus Stevens: Nineteenth-Century Egalitarian* (1997).

**The South**

Dan C. Carter, *When the War Was Over: Self-Reconstruction in the South, 1865–1867* (1985); William Cohen, *At Freedom's Edge: Black Mobility and the Southern White Quest for Racial Control, 1861–1915* (1991); Richard Nelson Current, *Those Terrible Carpetbaggers* (1988); Don H. Doyle, *New Men, New Cities, New South: Atlanta, Nashville, Charleston, Mobile, 1860–1910* (1990); Stephen Hahn, *The Roots of Southern Populism* (1983); William C. Harris, *The Day of the Carpetbagger: Republican Reconstruction in Mississippi* (1979); Otto Olsen, ed., *Reconstruction and Redemption in the South* (1980); Michael Perman, *Reunion Without Compromise: The South and Reconstruction, 1865–1868* (1973) and *The Road to Redemption: Southern Politics, 1869–1879* (1984); Howard N. Rabinowitz, *Race Relations in the Urban South, 1865–1890* (1978); George C. Rable, *But There Was No Peace: The Role of Violence in the Politics of Reconstruction* (1984); Mark W. Summers, *Railroads, Reconstruction, and the Gospel of Prosperity* (1984); Allen W. Trelease, *White Terror: The Ku Klux Klan Conspiracy and Southern Reconstruction* (1971); Ted Tunnell, *Crucible of Reconstruction: War, Radicalism, and Race in Louisiana, 1862–1877* (1984); Jonathan M. Wiener, *Social Origins of the New South: Alabama, 1860–1885* (1978); Gavin Wright, *Old South, New South: Revolutions in the Southern Economy Since the Civil War* (1986).

**Emancipation and the Freedmen**

Ira Berlin et al., eds., *Freedom, A Documentary History of Emancipation, 1861–1867* (1982–1993); Carol Rothrock Bleser, *The Promised Land: The History of the South Carolina Land Commission, 1869–1890* (1969); W. E. B. Du Bois, *Black Reconstruction in America, 1860–1880* (1935); Barbara Jeanne Fields, *Slavery and Freedom on the Middle Ground: Maryland During the Nineteenth Century* (1985); Eric Foner, *Nothing but Freedom: Emancipation and Its Legacies* (1983) and *Politics and Ideology in the Age of the Civil War* (1980), Chapters 6–7; Herbert G. Gutman, *The Black Family in Slavery and Freedom, 1750–1925* (1976); Robert Higgs, *Competition and Coercion: Blacks in the American Economy, 1865–1914* (1977); Thomas Holt, *Black over White: Negro Political Leadership in South Carolina During Reconstruction* (1977); Gerald Jaynes, *Branches Without Roots: Genesis of the Black Working Class in the American South, 1862–1882* (1986); Jacqueline Jones, *Soldiers of Light and Love: Northern Teachers and Georgia Blacks, 1865–1873* (1980) and *Labor of Love, Labor of Sorrow: Black Women, Work, and the Family from Slavery to the Present* (1985), Chapter 2; Peter Kolchin, *First Freedom: The Responses of Alabama's Blacks to*

*Emancipation and Reconstruction* (1972); Lawrence W. Levine, *Black Culture and Black Consciousness: Afro-American Folk Thought from Slavery to Freedom* (1977); William S. McFeely, *Yankee Stepfather: General O. O. Howard and the Freedmen* (1966); Nell Irvin Painter, *Exodusters* (1977); James Roark, *Masters Without Slaves: Southern Planters in the Civil War and Reconstruction* (1978); William Preston Vaughan, *Schools for All: The Blacks and Public Education in the South, 1865–1877* (1974); Joel Williamson, *The Crucible of Race: Black-White Relations in the American South Since Emancipation* (1984).

### National Trends

Paul H. Buck, *The Road to Reunion, 1865–1900* (1937); Adrian Cook, *The Alabama Claims* (1975); Ari M. Hoogenboom, *Outlawing the Spoils: A History of the Civil Service Reform Movement* (1961); William S. McFeely, *Grant: A Biography* (1981); David Montgomery, *Beyond Equality: Labor and the Radical Republicans, 1862–1872* (1967); Walter T. K. Nugent, *The Money Question During Reconstruction* (1967) and *Money and American Society, 1865–1880* (1968); Keith I. Polakoff, *The Politics of Inertia: The Election of 1876 and the End of Reconstruction* (1973); John C. Sproat, *"The Best Men": Liberal Reformers in the Gilded Age* (1968); Mark W. Summers, *The Era of Good Stealings* (1993); Irwin Unger, *The Greenback Era: A Social and Political History of American Finance* (1964); Allen Weinstein, *Prelude to Populism: Origins of the Silver Issue, 1867–1878* (1970); C. Vann Woodward, *Reunion and Reaction: The Compromise of 1877 and the End of Reconstruction* (rev. ed., 1956).

## *Chapter 17*

### The Western Mystique

William Cronon, George Miles, and Jay Gitlin, eds., *Under the Open Sky: Rethinking America's Western Past* (1992); William H. Goetzmann, *Exploration and Empire* (1966); Anne F. Hyde, *The American Vision: Far Western Landscape and National Culture, 1820–1920* (1990); Howard R. Lamar, *The Far Southwest, 1846–1912* (1966); Roderick Nash, *Wilderness and the American Mind* (1973); Kevin Starr, *Americans and the California Dream, 1850–1915* (1973);

### Native Americans

David W. Adams, *Education for Extinction: American Indians and the Boarding School Experience, 1875–1928* (1995); Gary C. Anderson, *Sitting Bull and the Paradox of Lakota Nationhood* (1996); Robert F. Berkhofer, Jr., *The White Man's Indian* (1978); Michael C. Coleman, *American Indian Children at School, 1850–1930* (1993); Michael Green, *The Creeks* (1990); Frederick E. Hoxie, *A Final Promise: The Campaign to Assimilate the Indians, 1880–1920* (1984) and *Parading Through History: The Making of the Crow Nation in America, 1805–1935* (1995); David R. Lewis, *Neither Wolf Nor Dog: American Indians, Environment, and Agrarian Change* (1994); Janet A. McDonnell, *The Dispossession of the American Indian, 1887–1934* (1991); Theda Perdue, *The Cherokee* (1989); Francis Paul Prucha, *The Great Father: The United States Government and the American Indians* (2 vols., 1984); Glenda Riley, *Women and Indians on the Frontier, 1825–1915* (1984); Willard H. Rollings, *The Comanche* (1989); Robert M. Utley, *The Last Days of the Sioux Nation* (1963), *Frontier Regulars: The United States Army and the Indian, 1866–1891*

(1973), *The Indian Frontier of the American West, 1846–1890* (1984) and *The Lance and the Shield: The Life and Times of Sitting Bull* (1993); Richard White, *The Roots of Dependency: Subsistence, Environment, and Social Change Among the Choctaws, Pawnees, and Navajos* (1983).

### The Process of Settlement

Richard Griswold del Castillo, *La Familia: Chicano Families in the Urban Southeast, 1848 to the Present* (1984); Arnoldo De Leon, *They Called Them Greasers: Anglo Attitudes Toward Mexicans in Texas, 1821–1900* (1983); Sarah Deutsch, *No Separate Refuge: Culture, Class, and Gender on the Anglo-Hispanic Frontier in the Early Southwest, 1880–1940* (1987); Katherine Harris, *Long Vistas: Women and Families on Colorado Homesteads* (1993); Paul W. Gates, *Jeffersonian Dream: Studies in the History of American Land Policy and Development* (1996); Jon Gjerde, *The Minds of the West: Ethnocultural Evolution in the Rural Middle West, 1830–1917* (1997); Robert V. Hine, *Community on the American Frontier* (1980); Richard Hogan, *Class and Community in Frontier Colorado* (1990); Julie R. Jeffrey, *Frontier Women* (1979); Maury Klein, *Union Pacific: Birth of a Railroad, 1862–1893* (1987); Bradford Luckingham, *Minorities in Phoenix: A Profile of Mexican American, Chinese American, and African American Communities, 1860–1992* (1994); Dean L. May, *Three Frontiers: Family, Land, and Society in the American West, 1850–1900* (1994); D. Aidan McQuillan, *Prevailing over Time: Ethnic Adjustment on the Kansas Prairies, 1875–1925* (1990); Timothy R. Mahoney, *River Towns in the Great West* (1990); David Montejano, *Anglos and Mexicans in the Making of Texas, 1836–1986* (1987); Peggy Pascoe, *Relations of Rescue: The Search for Female Moral Authority in the American West, 1874–1939* (1990); Jane M. Pederson, *Between Memory and Reality: Family and Community in Rural Wisconsin, 1870–1970* (1992); Kenneth L. Stewart and Arnoldo De Leon, *Not Room Enough: Mexicans, Anglos, and Socioeconomic Change in Texas, 1850–1900* (1993); Robert J. Rosenbaum, *Mexicano Resistance in the Southwest* (1981).

### The Bonanza West

Susan Armitage and Elizabeth Jameson, eds., *The Woman's West* (1987); Anne M. Butler, *Daughters of Joy, Sisters of Misery* (1985); William Cronon, *Nature's Metropolis: Chicago and the Great West* (1991); Hiram M. Drache, *The Day of the Bonanza* (1964); Monroe L. Billington, *New Mexico's Buffalo Soldiers, 1866–1900* (1991); Marion S. Goldman, *Gold Diggers & Silver Miners: Prostitution and Social Life on the Comstock* (1981); Christopher M. Klyza, *Who Controls Public Lands? Mining, Forestry, and Grazing Policies, 1870–1990* (1996); Wilson P. Rodman, *Mining Frontiers of the Far West* (1963); William R. Savage, *The Cowboy Hero* (1986); Richard W. Slatta, *Cowboys of the Americas* (1990); Duane A. Smith, *Mining America: The Industry and the Environment* (1987); Donald E. Worcester, *The Chisholm Trail* (1980).

### The Frontier Legend

John M. Faragher, ed., *Rereading Frederick Jackson Turner: "The Significance of the Frontier in American History" and Other Essays* (1994); Roderick Nash, *The Rights of Nature: A History of Environmental Ethics* (1989); Albert Runte, *Yosemite: The Embattled Wilderness* (1990); Henry Nash Smith, *Virgin Land: The American West as Symbol and Myth* (1950); Frederick Turner,

*Rediscovering America: John Muir in His Time and Ours* (1985); G. Edward White, *The Eastern Establishment and the Western Experience* (1968); Thurman Wilkins, *John Muir: Apostle of Nature* (1995); Rupert Wilkinson, *American Tough: The Tough-Guy Tradition and American Character* (1984); Donald Worster, *Nature's Economy: A History of Ecological Ideas* (1977) and *Rivers of Empire* (1985).

## Chapter 18

### The Character of Industrial Change

Stephen Brier, ed., *Who Built America? Working People and the Nation's Economy, Politics, Culture, and Society* (1992); Charles W. Calhoun, ed., *The Gilded Age: Essays in Modern America* (1995); Alfred D. Chandler, Jr., *The Visible Hand: The Managerial Revolution in American Business* (1977); Victoria C. Hattam, *Labor Visions and State Power: The Origins of Business Unionism in the United States* (1993); Ari and Olive Hoogenboom, *A History of the ICC: From Panacea to Palliative* (1976); Thomas P. Hughes, *Networks of Power: Electrification in Western Society, 1880–1930* (1983); Maury Klein, *The Flowering of the Third America: The Making of an Organizational Society, 1850–1920* (1993); Naomi R. Lamoreaux, *The Great Merger Movement in American Business, 1895–1904* (1985); Harold Livesay, *Andrew Carnegie and the Rise of Big Business* (1975); Martin V. Melosi, *Coping with Abundance: Energy and Environment in Industrial America* (1985); Andre Millard, *Edison and the Business of Innovation* (1990); Olivier Zunz, *Making America Corporate, 1870–1920* (1990).

### The New South

James C. Cobb, *Industrialization and Southern Society, 1877–1984* (1984) and *The Most Southern Place on Earth: The Mississippi Delta and the Roots of Regional Identity* (1992); Paul M. Gaston, *The New South Creed: A Study in Southern Mythmaking* (1970); Dewey W. Grantham, *The South in Modern America: A Region at Odds* (1995); Steven Hahn and Jonathan Prude, eds., *The Countryside in the Age of Capitalist Transformation: Essays in the Social History of Rural America* (1985); Jacquelyn D. Hall et al., *Like a Family: The Making of a Southern Cotton Mill World* (1987); Michael Shirley, *From Congregation Town to Industrial City: Culture and Social Change in a Southern Community* (1994); Roger L. Ransom and Richard Sutch, *One Kind of Freedom: The Economic Consequences of Emancipation* (1977); Peter Wallenstein, *From Slave South to New South: Public Policy in Nineteenth-Century Georgia* (1987); Jonathan M. Wiener, *Social Origins of the New South: Alabama, 1860–1885* (1978); C. Vann Woodward, *Origins of the New South, 1877–1913* (1951); Gavin Wright, *Old South, New South: Revolutions in the Southern Economy Since the Civil War* (1986).

### Industrial Work and the Work Force

Ava Baron, *Work Engendered: Toward a New History of American Labor* (1991); John Bodnar, *Immigration and Industrialization: Ethnicity in an American Mill Town* (1977); David Brody, *In Labor's Cause: Main Themes on the History of the American Worker* (1993); Ileen A. DeVault, *Sons and Daughters of Labor: Class and Clerical Work in Turn-of-the-Century Pittsburgh* (1990); Melvyn Dubovsky, *The State and Labor in Modern Amer-*

*ica* (1994); William F. Hartford, *Working People of Holyoke: Class and Ethnicity in a Massachusetts Mill Town, 1850–1960* (1990); Alice Kessler-Harris, *Out to Work: A History of Wage-Earning Women in the United States* (1982); S. J. Kleinberg, *The Shadow of the Mills: Working-Class Families in Pittsburgh, 1870–1907* (1989); Angel Kwolek-Folland, *Engendering Business: Men and Women in the Corporate Office, 1870–1930* (1994); Bruce Levine, ed., *Who Built America?* (1991); J. Carroll Moody and Alice Kessler-Harris, eds., *Perspectives on American Labor History: The Problems of Synthesis* (1989); David Montgomery, *The Fall of the House of Labor: The Workplace, the State, and American Labor Activism, 1865–1925* (1987); Peter Rachleff, *Black Labor in Richmond, 1865–1890* (1984); Stephen J. Ross, *Workers on the Edge: Work, Leisure, and Politics in Industrializing Cincinnati, 1788–1890* (1985); Peter R. Shergold, *Working Class Life* (1982); Stephan Thernstrom, *The Other Bostonians: Poverty and Progress in the American Metropolis, 1880–1970* (1973).

### Industrial Conflict

Paul Avrich, *The Haymarket Tragedy* (1984); Robert C. Bannister, *Social Darwinism: Science and Myth in Anglo-American Social Thought* (1979); Stanley Bruder, *Pullman* (1967); Mari Jo Buhle, *Women and American Socialism, 1870–1920* (1983); David P. Demarest, Jr., ed., *'The River Ran Red': Homestead 1892* (1992); Margaret M. Marsh, *Anarchist Women, 1870–1920* (1981); David Montgomery, *Workers' Control in America: Studies in the History of Work, Technology, and Labor Struggles* (1979); Alun Munslow, *Discourse and Culture: The Creation of America, 1870–1920* (1992); Richard J. Oestreicher, *Solidarity and Fragmentation: Working People and Class Consciousness in Detroit* (1986); William Serrin, *Homestead: The Glory and the Tragedy of an American Steel Town* (1992); Shelton Stromquist, *A Generation of Boomers: The Pattern of Railroad Labor Conflict in Nineteenth-Century America* (1993); John L. Thomas, *Alternative America: Henry George, Edward Bellamy, Henry Demarest Lloyd, and the Adversary Tradition* (1983); Daniel J. Walkowitz, *Worker City, Company Town: Iron and Cotton Workers Protest in Troy and Cohoes, New York, 1855–1884* (1978).

## Chapter 19

### Urban Growth and Expansion

Thomas J. Archdeacon, *Becoming American: An Ethnic History* (1983); Ronald H. Bayor and Timothy J. Meagher, eds., *The New York Irish* (1996); Selma Berrol, *East Side/East End: Eastern European Jews in London and New York, 1870–1920* (1994); John E. Bodnar, *The Transplanted: A History of Immigrants in Urban America* (1985); Brian J. Cudahy, *Cash, Tokens, and Transfers: A History of Urban Mass Transit in North America* (1990); Roger Daniels, *Coming to America: A History of Immigration and Ethnicity in American Life* (1990); Lawrence H. Fuchs, *The American Kaleidoscope: Race, Ethnicity, and the Civic Culture* (1990); Susan A. Glenn, *Daughters of the Shtetl: Life and Labor in the Immigrant Generation* (1990); William Issel and Robert W. Cherny, *San Francisco, 1865–1932: Politics, Power, and Urban Development* (1986); Kathie Friedman-Kasaba, *Memories of Migration: Gender, Ethnicity and Work in the Lives of Jewish and Italian Women in New York, 1870–1924* (1996); Judith W. Leavitt, *The*

*Healthiest City: Milwaukee and the Politics of Health Reform* (1982); Stephen J. Leonard and Thomas J. Noel, *Denver: Mining Camp to Metropolis* (1990); Mario Maffi, *Gateway to the Promised Land: Ethnic Cultures in New York's Lower East Side* (1995); Peter McCaffery, *When Bosses Ruled Philadelphia: The Emergence of the Republican Machine, 1867–1933* (1993); James S. Pula, *Polish Americans: An Ethnic Community* (1995).

### The Problems of the City

Jane Addams, *Twenty Years at Hull House* (1910); Allen F. Davis, *Spearheads for Reform: The Social Settlements and the Progressive Movement, 1890–1914* (1967); Robert M. Fogelson, *Big-City Police* (1977); Timothy J. Gilfoyle, *City of Eros: New York City, Prostitution, and the Commercialization of Sex, 1790–1920* (1992); Lori Ginzberg, *Women and the Work of Benevolence: Morality, Politics, and Class in the Nineteenth-Century United States* (1990); Eric Homberger, *Scenes From the Life of a City: Corruption and Conscience in Old New York* (1994); Alan M. Kraut, *Silent Travelers: Germs, Genes, and the "Immigrant Menace"* (1994); Kenneth L. Kusmer, *A Ghetto Takes Shape: Black Cleveland, 1870–1930* (1976); Roger Lane, *Policing the City: Boston, 1822–1885* (1967) and *William Dorsey's Philadelphia and Ours: On the Past and Future of the Black City in America* (1991); Elisabeth Lasch-Quinn, *Black Neighbors: Race and the Limits of Reform in the American Settlement House Movement, 1890–1945* (1993); Terrence J. McDonald, *The Parameters of Urban Fiscal Policy: Socioeconomic Change and Political Culture in San Francisco, 1860–1906* (1986) and with William Riordan, eds., *Plunkett of Tammany Hall* (1994); Henry F. May, *Protestant Churches and Industrial America* (1963); Gwendolyn Mink, *Old Labor and New Immigrants in American Political Development: Union, Party, and State, 1875–1920* (1986); Eric H. Monkkonen, *Police in Urban America, 1860–1920* (1981) and *America Becomes Urban: The Development of U.S. Cities and Towns, 1780–1980* (1988); Marian J. Morton, *And Sin No More: Social Policy and Unwed Mothers in Cleveland, 1855–1990* (1993); Lucy E. Salyer, *Laws Harsh as Tigers: Chinese Immigrants and the Shaping of Modern Immigration Law* (1995); Karen Sawislak, *Smoldering City: Chicagoans and the Great Fire, 1871–1874* (1995); Christine M. Rosen, *The Limits of Power: Great Fires and the Process of City Growth in America* (1986); Shelia Rothman, *Living in the Shadow of Death: Tuberculosis and the Social Experience of Illness in American History* (1994); Henry L. Taylor, Jr., ed., *Race and the City: Work, Community, and Protest in Cincinnati, 1820–1970* (1993).

### Transforming the City's Physical Environment

Elizabeth C. Cromley, *Alone Together: A History of New York's Early Apartments* (1990); John Duffy, *The Sanitarians: A History of American Public Health* (1990); Albert Fein, *Frederick Law Olmsted and the American Environmental Tradition* (1972); James Gilbert, *Perfect Cities: Chicago's Utopias of 1893* (1991); David C. Hammack, *Power and Society: Greater New York at the Turn of the Century* (1982); William H. Jordy, *American Buildings and Their Architects* (vol. 3 of *Progressive and Academic Ideals at the Turn of the Century*) (1972); Lawrence W. Kennedy, *Planning a City on a Hill: Boston Since 1630* (1992); David G. Lowe, *Stanford White's New York* (1992); John Ottensmann, *The Changing Spatial Structure of American Cities* (1975); Roy Rosenzweig and Elizabeth Blackmar, *The Park and the People: A History of Central Park* (1992); David Schuyler, *The New Urban Landscape: The Redefinition of City Form in Nineteenth-Century America* (1986).

## Chapter 20

### Daily Life

Stuart Blumin, *The Emergence of the Middle Class: Social Experience in the American City, 1760–1900* (1989); Clifford E. Clark, Jr., *The American Family Home, 1800–1960* (1986); Francis G. Couvares, *The Remaking of Pittsburgh: Class and Culture in an Industrializing City, 1877–1919* (1984); Helen Damon-Moore, *Magazines for the Millions: Gender and Commerce in the "Ladies Home Journal" and the "Saturday Evening Post," 1880–1910* (1994); William F. Hartford, *Working People of Holyoke: Class and Ethnicity in a Massachusetts Mill Town, 1850–1960* (1990); Jacqueline Jones, *Labor of Love, Labor of Sorrow: Black Women, Work, and the Family from Slavery to the Present* (1985) and *The Dispossessed: America's Underclasses from the Civil War to the Present* (1992); S. J. Kleinberg, *The Shadow of the Mills: Working-Class Families in Pittsburgh, 1870–1907* (1989); Jessica Foy and Thomas J. Schlereth, eds., *American Home Life, 1876–1915* (1992); Matthew Schneirov, *The Dream of a New Social Order: Popular Magazines in America, 1893–1914* (1994); Michael Shirley, *From Congregation Town to Industrial City: Culture and Social Change in a Southern Community* (1994); Olivier Zunz, *The Changing Face of Inequality: Urbanization, Industrial Development, and Immigrants in Detroit, 1880–1920* (1982).

### The Culture of the Middle Class

Lawrence A. Cremin, *American Education: The Metropolitan Experience, 1876–1980* (1988); Judy Hilkey, *Character Is Capital: Success Manuals and Manhood in Gilded Age America* (1997); Helen L. Horowitz, *Alma Mater: Design and Experience in Women's Colleges from Their Nineteenth-Century Beginnings to the 1930s* (1984); John F. Kasson, *Rudeness and Civility: Manners in Nineteenth-Century Urban America* (1990); Angel Kwolek-Foland, *Engendering Business: Men and Women in the Corporate Office, 1870–1930* (1994); Steven Mintz and Susan Kellogg, *Domestic Revolutions: A Social History of American Family Life* (1988); Michael Oriard, *Reading Football* (1993); Thomas Schlereth, ed., *Victorian America: Transformations in Everyday Life* (1991); Barbara M. Solomon, *In the Company of Educated Women: A History of Women and Higher Education in America* (1985); Louise L. Stevenson, *The Victorian Homefront: American Thought and Culture, 1860–1880* (1991); Susan Strasser, *Satisfaction Guaranteed: The Making of the American Mass Market* (1989); David Tyack and Elisabeth Hansot, *Learning Together: A History of Coeducation in American Schools* (1990); Laurence R. Veysey, *The Emergence of the American University* (1965).

### Working-Class Leisure and Recreation

Robert C. Allen, *Horrible Prettiness: Burlesque and American Culture* (1991); John C. Burnham, *Bad Habits: Drinking, Smoking, Taking Drugs, Gambling, Sexual Misbehavior, and Swearing in American History* (1993); Thomas Dublin, *Transforming Women's Work: New England Lives in the Industrial Revolution*

(1994); Perry Duis, *The Saloon: Public Drinking in Chicago and Boston, 1880–1920* (1983); Elliot J. Gorn, *The Manly Art: Bare-Knuckle Prize Fighting in America* (1986); Karen Halttunen, *Confidence Men and Painted Women: A Study of Middle-Class Culture in America, 1830–1870* (1982); Neil Harris, *Cultural Excursions: Marketing Appetites and Cultural Tastes in Modern America* (1990); John F. Kasson, *Amusing the Millions: Coney Island at the Turn of the Century* (1978); Peter Levine, *A. G. Spalding and the Rise of Baseball: The Promise of American Sport* (1985); Mary E. Odem, *Delinquent Daughters: Protecting and Policing Adolescent Female Sexuality in the United States, 1885–1920* (1995); Steven A. Riess, *City Games: The Evolution of American Urban Society and the Rise of Sports* (1995) and *Sport in Industrial America, 1850–1920* (1995); Roy Rosenzweig, *Eight Hours for What We Will: Workers and Leisure in an Industrial City, 1870–1920* (1983); Robert W. Snyder, *The Voice of the City: Vaudeville and Popular Culture in New York* (1989); James C. Whorton, *Crusaders for Fitness: The History of Health Reformers* (1984).

### The Clash of Cultures

Edward A. Berlin, *King of Ragtime: Scott Joplin and His Era* (1993); Burton J. Bledstein, *The Culture of Professionalism: The Middle Class and the Development of Higher Education in America* (1976); Ruth Borodin, *Francis Willard: A Biography* (1986); Robert Crunden, *American Salons: Encounters with European Modernism, 1885–1917* (1993); Emory Elliott, ed., *Columbia Literary History of the United States* (1988); Lori Ginsberg, *Women and the Work of Benevolence: Morality, Politics, and Class in the Nineteenth-Century United States* (1990); T. J. Jackson Lears, *No Place of Grace: Antimodernism and the Transformation of American Culture, 1880–1920* (1981); Lawrence W. Levine, *Highbrow/Lowbrow: The Emergence of Cultural Hierarchy in America* (1988); R. Laurence Moore, *Selling God: American Religion in the Marketplace of Culture* (1994); David Nasaw, *Schooled to Order: A Social History of Public Schooling in the United States* (1979); Martin Paulsson, *The Social Anxieties of Progressive Reform: Atlantic City, 1854–1920* (1994); Burton W. Peretti, *The Creation of Jazz: Music, Race, and Culture in Urban America* (1992); David B. Tyack, *The One Best System: A History of American Urban Education* (1974); Morton White, *Social Thought in America: The Revolt Against Formalism* (1947).

## *Chapter 21*

### Gilded Age Politics and Voting Patterns: General

Peter H. Argersinger, "The Value of the Vote: Political Representation in the Gilded Age," *Journal of American History* 76 (June 1989): 59–90; Paula Baker. "The Domestication of Politics: Women and American Political Society, 1780–1920," *American Historical Review* 89 (June 1984): 620–647, and *The Moral Framework of Public Life: Gender, Politics and the State in Rural New York, 1870–1930* (1991); Richard F. Hamm, *Shaping the Eighteenth Admendment: Temperance Reform, Legal Culture, and the Polity, 1880–1920* (1995); Richard J. Jensen, *The Winning of the Midwest: Social and Political Conflict, 1888–1896* (1971); David J. Rothman, *Politics and Power: The United States Senate, 1869–1901* (1966).

### Monetary Issues and Civil-Service Reform

Milton Friedman and A. J. Schwartz, *A Monetary History of the United States* (1963); Ari A. Hoogenboom, *Outlawing the Spoils: The Civil Service Movement* (1961); Gerald W. McFarland, *Mugwumps, Morals, and Politics, 1884–1920* (1975); John Sproat, *"The Best Men": Liberal Reformers in the Gilded Age* (1968); Allen Weinstein, *Prelude to Populism: Origins of the Silver Issue* (1970).

### Pensions, the Tariff, Agrarian Protest, Populism

Peter H. Argersinger, *The Limits of Agrarian Radicalism: Western Populism and American Politics* (1995); Gene Clanton, *Populism: The Humane Preference in America, 1890–1900* (1991); Stephen Cresswell, *Multiparty Politics in Mississippi, 1877–1902* (1995); Lawrence Goodwyn, *The Populist Moment: A Short History of the Agrarian Revolt in America* (1978); Steven Hahn, *The Roots of Southern Populism: Yeoman Farmers and the Transformation of the Georgia Upcountry, 1850–1890* (1983); Donald B. Marti, *Women of the Grange: Mutuality and Sisterhood in Rural America, 1866–1920* (1991); Megan J. McClintock, "Civil War Pensions and the Reconstruction of Union Families," *Journal of American History* 83 (September 1996): 456–480; Joanne Reitano, *The Tariff Question in the Gilded Age: The Great Debate of 1888* (1994); Theda Skocpol, *Protecting Soldiers and Mothers: The Political Origins of Social Policy in the United States* (1992); Tom E. Terrill, *The Tariff, Politics, and American Foreign Policy, 1874–1901* (1973).

### Black History in the Late Nineteenth Century

Kenneth M. Hamilton, *Black Towns and Profit: Promotion and Development in the Trans-Appalachian West, 1877–1915* (1991); Louis R. Harlan, *Booker T. Washington: The Making of a Black Leader, 1865–1901* (1972); J. Morgan Kousser, *The Shaping of Southern Politics: Suffrage Restriction and the Establishment of the One-Party South* (1974); Alex Lichtenstein, *Twice the Work of Free Labor: The Political Economy of Convict Labor in the South* (1996); Neil R. McMillan, *Dark Journey: Black Mississippians in the Age of Jim Crow* (1989); Matthew J. Mancini, *One Dies, Get Another: Convict Leasing in the American South, 1866–1928* (1996); Howard N. Rabinowitz, *Race Relations in the Urban South* (1978); C. Vann Woodward, *The Origins of the New South, 1877–1913* (1971).

### The Election of 1896, McKinley, and Bryan

Peter H. Argersinger, " 'A Place on the Ballot': Fusion Politics and Antifusion Laws," *American Historical Review* 85 (April 1980): 287–306; Paolo E. Coletta, *William Jennings Bryan* (3 vols., 1964–1969); Robert F. Durden, *The Climax of Populism: The Election of 1896* (1965); Lewis L. Gould, *The Presidency of William McKinley* (1980).

### Roots of American Expansion; Anti-Imperialism

Robert L. Beisner, *Twelve Against Empire: The Anti-Imperialists, 1898–1900* (1968); Walter LeFeber, *New Empire: American Expansionism, 1860–1898* (1963); Ernest R. May, *American Imperialism* (1968); Thomas J. Osborne, *"Empire Can Wait": American Opposition to Hawaiian Annexation, 1893–1898* (1981); Emily S. Rosenberg, *Spreading the American Dream: American Economic and Cultural Expansion, 1890–1945* (1982); Mark Russell Shulman, *Navalism and the Emergence of American Sea Power, 1882–1893* (1995); E. Berkeley Tompkins, *Anti-Imperialism in the United States: The Great Debate, 1890–1920* (1970).

### The Spanish-American War and the Philippines

H. W. Brands, *Bound to Empire: The United States and the Philippines* (1992); H. Paul Jeffers, *Colonel Roosevelt: Theodore Roosevelt Goes to War, 1897–1898* (1996); Walter LaFeber, *Inevitable Revolutions: The United States in Central America* (1983); Gerald F. Linderman, *The Mirror of War: American Society and the Spanish-American War* (1974); Glenn A. May, *Social Engineering in the Philippines: The Aims, Execution, and Impact of American Colonial Policy, 1900–1913* (1980); Stuart Creighton Miller, *"Benevolent Assimilation": The American Conquest of the Philippines, 1899–1903* (1982); Ian Mugridge, *The View from Xanadu: William Randolph Hearst and United States Foreign Policy* (1995); John Edward Weems, *The Fate of the Maine* (1992); Richard E. Welch, *Response to Imperialism: The United States and the Philippine-American War* (1979); Edward Van Zile Scott, *The Unwept: Black American Soldiers and the Spanish-American War* (1996).

### U.S.-Chinese Relations; The Panama Canal

Michael L. Coniff, *Panama and the United States: The Forced Alliance* (1992); Michael Hunt, *The Making of a Special Relationship: The United States and China to 1914* (1983); Walter LaFeber, *The Panama Canal* (1979); Thomas J. McCormick, *China Market: America's Quest for Informal Empire, 1893–1901* (1967); David McCullough, *The Path Between the Seas: The Creation of the Panama Canal, 1870–1914* (1977); Marilyn B. Young. *The Rhetoric of Empire: American China Policy, 1895–1901* (1968).

## Chapter 22

### Society and the Economy

David Brody, "The American Worker in the Progressive Age: A Comprehensive Analysis" in David Brody, *Workers in Industrial America: Essays on the Twentieth-Century Struggle*, 2d ed. (1985); Ardis Cameron, *Radicals of the Worst Sort: Laboring Women in Lawrence, Massachusetts, 1860–1912* (1993); Susan A. Glenn, *Daughters of the Shtetl: Life and Labor in the Immigrant Generation* (1990); Alice Kessler-Harris, *Out to Work: A History of Wage-Earning Women in the United States* (1982); Elaine Tyler May, *Great Expectations: Marriage and Divorce in Post-Victorian America* (1980).

### The Progressive Impulse

John D. Buenker, *Urban Liberalism and Progressive Reform* (1973); Nancy F. Cott, *A Woman Making History: Mary Ritter Beard Through Her Letters* (1991); Lawrence A. Cremin, *The Transformation of the Schools: Progressivism in American Education, 1876–1957* (1971); Robert Crunden, *Ministers of Reform: The Progressives' Achievement in American Civilization* (1982); Allen F. Davis, *Spearheads for Reform: The Social Settlements and the Progressive Movement, 1890–1914*, 2d ed., (1984); Eldon J. Eisenach, *The Lost Promise of Progressivism* (1994); Dewey W. Grantham, *Southern Progressivism: The Reconcilia-*

tion of Progress and Tradition* (1983); William A. Link, *The Paradox of Southern Progressivism* (1992); Richard L. McCormick, "The Discovery That Business Corrupts Politics: A Reappraisal of the Origins of Progressivism," *American Historical Review* 86 (1981): 247–274; Mark Pittenger, "A World of Experience: Constructing the 'Underclass' in Progressive America," *American Quarterly*, March 1997; Alan Ryan, *John Dewey and the High Tide of American Liberalism* (1995); Judith Ann Trolander, *Professionalism and Social Change: From the Settlement House Movement to Neighborhood Centers* (1987); Robert Wiebe, *Businessmen and Reform: A Study of the Progressive Movement* (1962) and *The Search for Order, 1877–1920* (1967); Clarence E. Wunderlin, Jr., *Visions of a New Industrial Order: Social Science and Labor Theory in America's Progressive Era* (1992).

### Reforming Municipal Government

Ruth H. Crocker, *Social Work and Social Order: The Settlement Movement in Two Industrial Cities, 1889–1930* (1992); Samuel P. Hays, "The Politics of Reform in Municipal Government in the Progressive Era," *Pacific Northwest Quarterly* 55 (1964): 157–169; Melvin G. Holli, *Reform in Detroit: Hazen S. Pingree and Urban Politics* (1969); Martin Paulson, *The Social Anxieties of Progressive Reform: Atlantic City, 1854–1920* (1994); Bradley R. Rice, *Progressive Cities: The Commission Government Movement in America, 1901–1920* (1977); Martin J. Schiesl, *The Politics of Efficiency: Municipal Administration and Reform in America, 1880–1920* (1977).

### Moral Reform, Labor Relations, and Social Control

Paul Boyer, *Urban Masses and Moral Order in America, 1820–1920* (1978); Mark T. Connelly, *The Response to Prostitution in the Progressive Era* (1980); Mark H. Haller, *Eugenics: Hereditarian Attitudes in American Thought* (1963); Richard F. Hamm, *Shaping the Eighteenth Amendment: Temperance Reform, Legal Culture, and the Polity, 1880–1920* (1995); Barbara Meil Hobson, *Uneasy Virtue: The Politics of Prostitution and the American Reform Tradition* (1987); Alan M. Kraut, *Silent Travelers: Germs, Genes, and the "Immigrant Menace"* (1994); David Langum, *Crossing Over the Line: Legislating Morality and the Mann Act* (1994); Joseph A. McCartin, *Labor's Great War: The Struggle for Industrial Democracy and the Origins of Modern American Labor Relations, 1912–1921* (1997); John F. McClymer, *War and Welfare: Social Engineering in America, 1890–1925* (1980); W. J. Rorabaugh, *The Alcoholic Republic* (1979); Ruth Rosen, *The Lost Sisterhood: Prostitution in America: 1900–1918* (1982); Peter Temin, *Taking Your Medicine: Drug Regulation in the United States* (1980); William O. Walker III, *Opium and Foreign Policy: The Anglo-American Search for Order in Asia, 1912–1954* (1991).

### Women in the Progressive Movement

Ellen Chesler, *Woman of Valor: Margaret Sanger and the Birth Control Movement in America* (1992); Ellen Fitzpatrick, *Endless Crusade: Women Social Scientists and Progressive Reform* (1990); Lynn D. Gordon, *Gender and Higher Education in the Progressive Era* (1990); Thomas J. Jablonsky, *The Home, Heaven, and Mother Party: Female Anti-Suffragists in the United States, 1868–1920* (1994); Ann J. Lane, *To Herland and Beyond: The Life and Work of Charlotte Perkins Gilman* (1990); Marian J.

Morton, *Emma Goldman and the American Left* (1992); Robyn Muncy, *Creating a Female Dominion in American Reform, 1890–1935* (1991).

### African-American Life and Thought

Garna L. Christian, *Black Soldiers in Jim Crow Texas, 1899–1917* (1995); Louis R. Harlan, *Booker T. Washington: Wizard of Tuskegee, 1901–1915* (1983); Charles F. Kellogg, *NAACP: The History of the National Association for the Advancement of Colored People, 1909–1920* (1967); Elliott M. Rudwick, *W. E. B. Du Bois* (1969); Joe W. Trotter, Jr., ed., *The Great Migration in Historical Perspective: New Dimensions of Race, Class, and Gender* (1991).

### Progressivism in National Politics

Kendrick A. Clements, *The Presidency of Woodrow Wilson* (1992); Paolo E. Coletta, *The Presidency of William Howard Taft* (1973); Lewis L. Gould, *The Presidency of Theodore Roosevelt* (1991); Nick Salvatore, *Eugene V. Debs* (1982); David Steigerwald, *Wilsonian Idealism in America* (1994); Melvin I. Urofsky, *Louis D. Brandeis and the Progressive Tradition* (1981); Bernard A. Weisberger, *The LaFollettes of Wisconsin: Love and Politics in Progressive America* (1994).

### Progressives and the Environment

Stephen R. Fox, *The American Conservation Movement: John Muir and His Legacy* (1981); Clayton R. Koppes, "Shifting Themes in American Conservation," in Donald Worster, ed., *The Ends of the Earth* (1988); Carolyn Merchant, "Women of the Progressive Conservation Movement, 1900–1916," *Environmental Review* 8 (Spring 1984): 57–85; Roderick Nash, *Wilderness and the American Mind* (1967); Elmo R. Richardson, "The Struggle for the Valley: California's Hetch Hetchy Controversy, 1905–1913," *California Historical Society Quarterly* 38 (1959): 249–258; Thurman Wilkins, *John Muir: Apostle of Nature* (1995).

## *Chapter 23*

### The United States in Asia and Latin America

Lloyd C. Gardner, *Safe for Democracy: The Anglo-American Response to Revolution, 1913–1923* (1984); Linda B. Hall, *Oil, Banks, and Politics: The United States and Post-Revolutionary Mexico, 1917–1923* (1995); Friedrich Katz, *The Secret War in Mexico: Europe, the United States, and the Mexican Revolution* (1981); Lester E. Langley, *The Banana Wars: An Inner History of American Empire, 1900–1934* (1983); James Reed, *The Missionary Mind and America's East Asian Policy, 1911–1915* (1983); Thomas Schoonover, *The United States in Central America, 1860–1911* (1991).

### The Road to War, Wartime Diplomacy, and the Russian Revolution

Lloyd E. Ambrosius, *Woodrow Wilson and the American Diplomatic Tradition* (1987); John M. Blum, *Woodrow Wilson and the Politics of Morality* (1956); David S. Fogelsong, *America's Secret War Against Bolshevism: U.S. Intervention and the Russian Civil War, 1917–1920* (1995); John L. Gaddis, *Russia, the Soviet Union, and the United States* (1978); Lloyd C. Gardner, *Safe for Democracy: The Anglo-American Response to Revolution, 1913–1923* (1984); Georg Schild, *Between Ideology and Realpolitik: Woodrow Wilson and the Russian Revolution, 1917–1921* (1995).

### The Battlefield Experience

John Whiteclay Chambers II, *To Raise an Army: The Draft in Modern America* (1987); Edward M. Coffman, *The War to End All Wars: The American Military Experience in World War I* (1968); Paul Fussell, *The Great War and Modern Memory* (1975); Lee Kennett, *The First Air War, 1914–1918* (1991); Bernard Nalty, *Strength for the Fight: A History of Black Americans in the Military* (1986); Frank E. Vandiver, *Black Jack: The Life and Times of John J. Pershing* (1977).

### The Government Mobilizes for War

Daniel R. Beaver, *Newton D. Baker and the American War Effort, 1917–1919* (1966); Kathleen Burk, *Britain, America and the Sinews of War* (1985); Robert D. Cuff, *The War Industries Board* (1973); Ellis W. Hawley, *The Great War and the Search for a Modern Order: A History of the American People and Their Institutions, 1917–1933*, 2d ed. (1992); Daniel J. Kevles, "Testing the Army's Intelligence: Psychologists and the Military in World War I," *Journal of American History*, December 1968; Franz Samelson, "Putting Psychology on the Map: Ideology and Intelligence Testing," in Allan R. Buss, ed., *Psychology in Social Context* (1979): 103–168; Jordan A. Schwarz, *The Speculator: Bernard M. Baruch in Washington, 1917–1965* (1981).

### American Society and Culture in World War I

Allen F. Davis, "Welfare, Reform and World War I," *American Quarterly* 19 (1967): 516–533; Maurine W. Greenwald, *Women, War and Work* (1980); Jeffrey Haydu, *Making American Industry Safe for Democracy: Comparative Perspectives on the State and Employee Representation in the Era of World War I* (1997); Florette Henri, *Black Migration: Movement Northward, 1900–1920* (1975); Joseph A. McCartin, *Labor's Great War: The Struggle for Industrial Democracy and the Origins of Modern American Labor Relations, 1912–1921* (1997); John F. McClymer, *War and Welfare: Social Engineering in America, 1890–1925* (1980); Barbara J. Steinson, *American Women's Activism in World War I* (1982); Jacqueline van Voris, *Carrie Chapman Catt: A Public Life* (1987).

### Patriotism, Dissent, and Repression

Ray H. Abrams, *Preachers Present Arms: The Role of the American Churches and Clergy in World Wars I and II* (1969); George T. Blakey, *Historians on the Homefront: American Propagandists for the Great War* (1970); Bruce Clayton, *Forgotten Prophet: The Life of Randolph Bourne* (1984); Alfred E. Cornebise, *War as Advertised: The Four Minute Men and America's Crusade, 1917–1918* (1984); Christopher Gibbs, *The Great Silent Majority: Missouri's Resistance to World War I* (1988); Carol S. Gruber, *Mars and Minerva: World War I and the Uses of Higher Learning in America* (1975); Michael T. Isenberg, *War on Film* (1981); Michael Pearlman, *To Make Democracy Safe for America: Patricians and Preparedness in the Progressive Era* (1984); Harold C. Peterson and Gilbert Fite, *Opponents of War, 1917–1918* (1968);

William Preston, Jr., *Aliens and Dissenters: Federal Suppression of Radicals, 1903–1933* (1966); Maurice Rickards, *Posters of the First World War* (1968); Stephen Vaughn, *Holding Fast the Inner Lines: Democracy, Nationalism, and the Committee on Public Information* (1980); Larry Wayne Ward, *The Motion Picture Goes to War: The U.S. Government Film Effort During World War I* (1985).

### Aftermath: Red Scare, Failed Peace, and Disillusionment

David Brody, *Labor in Crisis: The Steel Strike of 1919* (1965); Stanley A. Coben, *A. Mitchell Palmer: Politician* (1963); Stanley Cooperman, *World War I and the American Novel* (1970); Arno Mayer, *Politics and Diplomacy of Peacemaking* (1967); Robert K. Murray, *Red Scare: A Study in National Hysteria, 1919–1920* (1955); Stewart I. Rochester, *American Liberal Disillusionment in the Wake of World War I* (1977); Klaus Schwabe, *Woodrow Wilson, Revolutionary Germany, and Peacemaking, 1918–1919* (1985); Ralph Stone, *The Irreconcilables: The Fight Against the League of Nations* (1970); William M. Tuttle, Jr., *Race Riot: Chicago in the Red Summer of 1919* (1970); Arthur J. Walworth, *Wilson and His Peacemakers* (1986); William C. Widenor, *Henry Cabot Lodge and the Search for an American Foreign Policy* (1980).

## *Chapter 24*

### Economic Trends, Labor Unions, Workers' Lives

Guy Alchon, *The Invisible Hand of Planning: Capitalism, Social Science, and the State in the 1920s* (1985); Irving Bernstein, *The Lean Years: A History of the American Worker, 1920–1933* (1966); Lizbeth Cohen, *Making a New Deal: Industrial Workers in Chicago, 1919–1939* (1990); Lisa M. Fine, *The Souls of the Skyscraper: Female Clerical Workers in Chicago, 1870–1930* (1990); Gilbert C. Fite, *American Farmers: The New Minority* (1981); Chris Friday, *Organizing Asian American Labor: The Pacific Coast Salmon Industry, 1870–1942* (1994); H. M. Gitelman, "Welfare Capitalism Reconsidered," *Labor History,* Winter 1992; Jacqueline Dowd Hall, *Like a Family: The Making of a Southern Cotton Mill World* (1987); Angel Kwolek-Folland, *Engendering Business: Men and Women in the Corporate Office, 1870–1930* (1994); Roland Marchand, *Advertising the American Dream: Making Way for Modernity, 1920–1940* (1985); John A. Salmond, *Gastonia 1929: The Story of the Loray Mill Strike* (1995); Susan Strasser, *Satisfaction Guaranteed: The Making of the American Mass Market* (1989); Mira Wilkins, *The Maturing of Multinational Enterprise: American Business Abroad from 1914 to 1970* (1974).

### Politics and International Relations

Hendrik Booraem V, *The Provincial: Calvin Coolidge and His World, 1885–1895* (1994); Thomas Buckley, *The United States and the Washington Conference, 1921–1922* (1970); Douglas B. Craig, *After Wilson: The Struggle for the Democratic Party, 1920–1934* (1992); L. Ethan Ellis, *Republican Foreign Policy, 1921–1933* (1968); Kriste Lindenmeyer, *"A Right to Childhood": The U.S. Children's Bureau and Child Welfare, 1912–1946* (1997); Charles L. Mee, *The Ohio Gang: The World of Warren G. Harding* (1981); Robert K. Murray, *The Politics of Normalcy: Governmental Theory and Practice in the Harding–Coolidge Era* (1973); Joan Hoff-Wilson, *American Business and Foreign Policy* (1971).

### Mass Culture

James J. Flink, *The Car Culture* (1975); Sumiko Higashi, *Cecil B. DeMille and American Culture: The Silent Era* (1994); Gwenyth L. Jackaway, *Media at War: Radio's Challenge to the Newspapers, 1924–1939* (1995); Lary May, *Screening Out the Past: The Birth of Mass Culture and the Motion Picture Industry* (1980); Janice Radway, *A Feeling for Books: The Book of the Month Club, Literary Taste, and Middle Class Desire* (1997); Susan Smulyan, *Selling Radio: The Commercialization of American Broadcasting, 1920–1934* (1994).

### Youth, Dissident Writers, and Intellectuals

Beth A. Bailey, *From Front Porch to Back Seat: Courtship in Twentieth-Century America* (1988); George Chauncey, *Gay New York: Gender, Urban Culture, and the Making of the Gay Male World, 1890–1940* (1994); Douglas Clayton, *Floyd Dell: The Life and Times of an American Rebel* (1994); Stanley Coben, *Rebellion Against Victorianism: The Impetus for Cultural Change in 1920s America* (1991); Paula Fass, *The Damned and the Beautiful: American Youth in the 1920s* (1977); Nathan G. Hale, Jr., *The Rise and Crisis of Psychoanalysis in the United States . . . 1917–1985* [*Freud in America,* Vol. 2] (1995); Fred Hobson, *Mencken: A Life* (1994); Frederick J. Hoffman, *The Twenties: American Writing in the Postwar Decade,* rev. ed. (1962); David O. Levine, *The American College and the Culture of Aspiration, 1915–1940* (1986).

### Women in the 1920s

Kathleen M. Blee, *Women and the Klan: Racism and Gender in the 1920s* (1991); Dorothy M. Brown, *Setting a Course: American Women in the 1920s* (1987); Nancy Cott, *The Grounding of Modern Feminism* (1987); Stanley Lemons, *The Woman Citizen: Social Feminism in the 1920s* (1973); Leslie Woodcock Tentler, *Wage-Earning Women: Industrial Work and Family in the United States, 1900–1930* (1979); Daniel J. Walkowitz, "The Making of a Feminine Professional Identity: Social Workers in the 1920s," *American Historical Review* 95 (October 1990): 1051–1075.

### African Americans, Jazz, the Harlem Renaissance

Robert E. Hemenway, *Zora Neale Hurston: A Literary Biography* (1977); Thomas J. Hennessey, *From Jazz to Swing: African-American Jazz Musicians and Their Music, 1890–1935* (1994); David L. Lewis, *When Harlem Was in Vogue* (1981); William H. Kenney, *Chicago Jazz: A Cultural History* (1993); Kathy H. Ogren, *The Jazz Revolution: Twenties America and the Meaning of Jazz* (1989); Gilbert Osofsky, *Harlem: The Making of a Ghetto* (1968); Burton W. Peretti, *The Creation of Jazz: Race and Culture in Urban America* (1992); Arnold Rampersad, *The Life of Langston Hughes* (2 vols., 1986–1988); Judith Stein, *The World of Marcus Garvey: Race and Class in Modern Society* (1985); Tyrone Tillery, *Claude McKay* (1992); Cheryl A. Wall, *Women of the Harlem Renaissance* (1995); Irma Watkins-Owens, *Blood Relations: Caribbean Immigrants and the Harlem Community, 1900–1930* (1996).

### Hispanic Life and Culture

Jay P. Dolan et al., eds., *Mexican Americans and the Catholic Church, 1900–1965* (1994), *Puerto Rican and Cuban Catholics in the U.S., 1900–1965* (1994), and *Hispanic Catholic Culture in the U.S., Issues and Concerns* (1994); Gilbert G. González, *Labor and Community: Mexican Citrus Worker Villages in a Southern California County, 1900–1950* (1994); Camille Guerin-Gonzales, *Mexican Workers and American Dreams: Immigration, Repatriation, and California Farm Labor, 1900–1939* (1994); David G. Gutiérrez, *Walls and Mirrors: Mexican Americans, Mexican Immigrants, and the Politics of Ethnicity* (1995); Martha Menchaca, *The Mexican Outsider: A Community History of Marginalization and Discrimination in California* (1995).

### Religious Trends

Edith L. Blumhofer, *Aimee Semple McPherson* (1993); Lyle W. Dorsett, *Billy Sunday and the Redemption of Urban America* (1991); David Mark Epstein, *Sister Aimee: The Life of Aimee Semple McPherson* (1993); Henry L. Feingold, *A Time for Searching: Entering the Mainstream, 1920–1945* [*The Jewish People in America*, Vol. 3] (1992); George M. Marsden, *Fundamentalism and American Culture* (1980); Martin E. Marty, *The Noise of Conflict, 1919–1941* [*Modern American Religion*, Vol. 2] (1991); William Vance Trollinger, *God's Empire: William Bell Riley and Midwestern Fundamentalism* (1990).

### Cultural Tensions and Symbolic Events

Paul Avrich, *Sacco and Vanzetti: The Anarchist Background* (1991); Norman H. Clark, *Deliver Us from Evil: An Interpretation of American Prohibition* (1976); Kenneth T. Jackson, *The Ku Klux Klan in the City, 1915–1930* (1967); Edward J. Larson, *Trial and Error: The American Controversy over Creation and Evolution* (1989); Shawn Lay, ed., *The Invisible Empire in the West: Toward a New Historical Appraisal of the Ku Klux Klan in the 1920s* (1992); Leonard J. Moore, *Citizen Klansmen: The Ku Klux Klan in Indiana, 1921–1928* (1991); Francis Russell, *Tragedy in Dedham: The Story of the Sacco-Vanzetti Case* (1971); David E. Ruth, *Inventing the Public Enemy: The Gangster in American Culture, 1918–1934* (1996).

### Herbert Hoover and the 1928 Election

David Bruner, *Herbert Hoover: The Public Life* (1979); E. Paula Elder, *Governor Alfred E. Smith: The Politician as Reformer* (1983); Ellis W. Hawley, ed., *Herbert Hoover as Secretary of Commerce* (1981); Joan Hoff-Wilson, *Herbert Hoover: Forgotten Progressive* (1975); Allan J. Lichtman, *Prejudice and the Old Politics: The Presidential Election of 1928* (1979).

## *Chapter 25*

### Onset of the Great Depression

Roger Daniels, *The Bonus March* (1971); John Kenneth Galbraith, *The Great Crash, 1929* (1961); John A. Garraty, *The Great Depression* (1986); Albert U. Romasco, *The Poverty of Abundance: Hoover, the Nation, the Depression* (1965); John Shover, *Cornbelt Rebellion: The Farmers' Holiday Association* (1965); Peter Temin, *Did Monetary Forces Cause the Great Depression?* (1976) and *Lessons from the Great Depression* (1989); Studs Terkel, *Hard Times* (1970).

### The New Deal Era: Biographical Studies

Jeanne Nienaber Clarke, *Roosevelt's Warrior: Harold L. Ickes and the New Deal* (1996); Blanche Wiesen Cook, *Eleanor Roosevelt*, vol. 1 (1992); Searle F. Charles, *Minister of Relief: Harry Hopkins and the Depression* (1963); Doris Kearns Goodwin, *No Ordinary Time: Franklin and Eleanor Roosevelt* (1994); William Ivy Hair, *The Kingfish and His Realm: The Life and Times of Huey P. Long* (1991); J. Joseph Huthmacher, *Robert F. Wagner and the Rise of Urban Liberalism* (1968); Steven M. Neuse, *David E. Lilienthal: The Journey of an American Liberal* (1996); Sean J. Savage, *Roosevelt: The Party Leader, 1932–1945* (1991); Jordan Schwarz, *The New Dealers: Power Politics in the Age of Roosevelt* (1993); Geoffrey C. Ward, *Before the Trumpet: The Young Franklin D. Roosevelt* (1985) and *A First-Class Temperament: The Emergence of Franklin Roosevelt* (1989).

### The New Deal: General Studies and Assessments

Matthew J. Dickinson, *Bitter Harvest: FDR, Presidential Power, and the Growth of the Presidential Branch* (1997); Lyle Dorsett, *Franklin D. Roosevelt and the City Bosses* (1977); Gerald H. Gamm, *The Making of New Deal Democrats: Voting Behavior and Realignment in Boston, 1920–1940* (1989); Colin Gordon, *New Deals: Business, Labor, and Politics in America, 1920–1935* (1994); Mark Leff, *The Limits of Symbolic Reform: The New Deal and Taxation, 1933–1939* (1984); William E. Leuchtenberg, *The FDR Years: On Roosevelt and His Legacy* (1995); Theodore Rosenof, *Economics in the Long Run: New Deal Theorists and Their Legacies* (1997).

### The Early New Deal

Richard P. Adelstein, " 'The Nation as an Economic Unit': Keynes, Roosevelt, and the Managerial Idea," *Journal of American History* 78 (June 1991): 160–187; Bernard Bellush, *The Failure of NRA* (1975); Walter L. Creese, *TVA's Public Planning: The Vision, the Reality* (1990); Otis L. Graham, Jr., *Toward a Planned Society: From Roosevelt to Nixon* (1976); Nancy L. Grant, *TVA and Black Americans: Planning for the Status Quo* (1990); James N. Gregory, *American Exodus: The Dust Bowl Migration and Okie Culture in California* (1989); Peter H. Irons, *The New Deal Lawyers* (1982); Richard H. Maidment, *The Judicial Response to the New Deal* (1991); Van L. Perkins, *Crisis in Agriculture: The AAA and the New Deal* (1969); Donald Worster, *Dust Bowl* (1979).

### The Later New Deal

Carl Abbott, "The Federal Presence," in Clyde A. Milner II et al., eds., *The Oxford History of the American West* (1994); Kenneth J. Bindas, *All of This Music Belongs to the Nation: The WPA's Federal Music Project and American Society* (1995); Alan Brinkley, *Voices of Protest: Huey Long, Father Coughlin, and the Great Depression* (1982); David E. Conrad, *The Forgotten Farmers: The Story of the Sharecroppers and the New Deal* (1965); Stephen Fox, *The American Conservation Movement*, ch. 6, "Franklin D. Roosevelt and New Deal Conservation" (1985); Richard Lowitt, *The New Deal and the West* (1984); William F. MacDonald, *Federal Relief Administration and the Arts* (1969); Karal Ann Marling, *Wall-to-Wall America: A Cultural History of Post-Office Murals in the Great Depression* (1982); Charles McKinley and Robert W. Frase, *Launching Social Security* (1970); Paul C. Pitzer, *Grand Coulee: Harnessing a Dream* (1994); Nancy J. Weiss, *Farewell to the Party of Lincoln: Black Politics in the Age of FDR* (1983).

## Conservative Opposition; The End of the New Deal

Alan Brinkley, *The End of Reform: New Deal Liberalism in Recession and War* (1995); Dewey W. Grantham, *The Democratic South* (1963); James T. Patterson, *Congressional Conservatives and the New Deal* (1967); Milton Plesur, "The Republican Congressional Comeback of 1938," *Review of Politics* 24 (1962): 525–562; Charles M. Price and Joseph Boskin, "The Roosevelt Purge . . .," *Journal of Politics* 28 (1966): 660–670; Clyde P. Weed, *The Nemesis of Reform: The Republican Party During the New Deal* (1994).

## *Chapter 26*

### American Labor and Society in the 1930s

George Chauncey, *Gay New York: Gender, Urban Culture, and the Making of the Gay Male World, 1890–1940* (1994); John A. Clausen, *American Lives: Looking Back at the Children of the Great Depression* (1993); Melvyn Dubofsy and Warren Van Tine, *John L. Lewis: A Biography* (1977); Sidney Fine, *Sitdown: The General Motors Strike of 1936–1937* (1969); Mario T. Garcia, *Mexican Americans: Leadership, Ideology and Identity, 1930–1960* (1989); Gary Gerstle, *Working-Class Americanism: The Politics of Labor in a Textile City, 1914–1960* (1989); Cheryl Lynn Greenberg, *"Or Does It Explode?": Black Harlem in the Great Depression* (1991); David G. Gutierrez, *Walls and Mirrors: Mexican Americans, Mexican Immigrants, and the Politics of Ethnicity* (1995); Nelson Lichtenstein, *The Most Dangerous Man in Detroit: Walter Reuther and the Fate of American Labor* (1995); Robert S. McElvaine, ed., *Down and Out in the Great Depression* (1983); Ruth M. Milkman, "Women's Work and the Economic Crisis: Some Lessons from the Great Depression," in Nancy Cott and Elizabeth Pleck, eds., *A Heritage of Her Own* (1979), pp. 507–541; Richard A. Reiman, *The New Deal and American Youth* (1992); Pamela Riney-Kehrberg, *Rooted in Dust: Surviving Drought and Depression in Southwestern Kansas* (1994); Lois Scharf, *To Work and to Wed: Female Employment, Feminism, and the Great Depression* (1980); Catherine McNichol Stock, *Main Street in Crisis: The Great Depression and the Old Middle Class on the Northern Plains* (1992); Susan Ware, *Still Missing: Amelia Earhart and the Search for Modern Feminism* (1993); Jill Watts, *God, Harlem U.S.A.: The Father Divine Story* (1992); Devra Weber, *Dark Sweat, White Gold: California Farm Workers, Cotton, and the New Deal* (1994); Marsha L. Weisiger, *Land of Plenty: Oklahomans in the Cotton Fields of Arizona, 1933–1942* (1995); Beth S. Wenger, *New York Jews and the Great Depression* (1996).

### Cultural Trends in the Depression Decade

Matthew Baigell, *The American Scene: Painting in the 1930s* (1974); Andrew Bergman, *We're in the Money: Depression America and Its Films* (1971); Terry A. Cooney, *Balancing Acts: American Thought and Culture in the 1930s* (1995); Michael Denning, *The Culture Front: The Laboring of American Culture in the Twentieth Century* (1996); Malcolm Goldstein, *The Political State: American Drama and Theatre of the Great Depression* (1974); Nancy Helber and Julia Williams, *The Regionalists* (1967); Henry Jenkins, *Who Made Pistachio Nuts? Early Sound Comedies and the Vaudeville Aesthetic* (1992); Harvey Klehr, *The Heyday of American Communism: The Depression Decade* (1984); Giuliana Muscio, *Hollywood's New Deal* (1997); Marlene Park and Gerald Markowitz, *Democratic Vistas: Post Offices and Public Art in the New Deal* (1984); Richard H. Pells, *Radical Visions and American Dreams: Culture and Social Thought in the Depression Years* (1973); William Stott, *Documentary Expression and Thirties America* (1973); Martin Williams, *Jazz in Its Own Time* (1989); Douglas Wixson, *Worker-Writer in America: Jack Conroy and the Tradition of Midwestern Literary Radicalism, 1898–1990* (1994).

### U.S. Foreign Policy and the Fascist Challenge

Patricia Clavin, *The Failure of Economic Diplomacy: Britain, Germany, France, and the United States, 1931–1936* (1996); Robert Cohen, *When the Old Left Was Young: America's First Mass Student Movement, 1929–1941* (1993); Wayne S. Cole, *Roosevelt and the Isolationists, 1932–1945* (1983); Robert A. Divine, *The Reluctant Belligerent* (1979); Lloyd C. Gardner, *Economic Aspects of New Deal Diplomacy* (1964); Thomas N. Guinsburg, *The Pursuit of Isolation in the United States Senate from Versailles to Pearl Harbor* (1982); Fredrick B. Pike, *FDR's Good Neighbor Policy* (1995); John E. Wiltz, *In Search of Peace: The Senate Munitions Inquiry, 1934–1936* (1963); David S. Wyman, *Paper Walls: America and the Refugee Crisis, 1938–1941* (1985).

## *Chapter 27*

### Military Operations

Ed Cray, *General of the Army: George C. Marshall, Soldier and Statesman* (1990); Michael Doubler, *Closing with the Enemy: How GIs Fought the War in Europe* (1994); John Ellis, *Brute Force: Allied Strategy and Tactics in the Second World War* (1990); Akira Iriye, *Power and Culture: The Japanese-American War, 1941–1945* (1981); Lee Kennett, *G.I.: The American Soldier in World War II* (1987); Michael Sherry, *The Rise of American Air Power* (1987); Ronald H. Spector, *Eagle Against the Sun: The American War with Japan* (1984); Mark A. Stoler, *The Politics of the Second Front: American Military Planning and Diplomacy in Coalition Warfare, 1941–1945* (1977).

### Mobilization

Alan Clive, *State of War: Michigan in World War II* (1979); George Q. Flynn, *The Draft, 1940–1973* (1993); Mark S. Foster, *Henry J. Kaiser: Builder in the Modern American West* (1989); Paul A. C. Koistinen, *The Military-Industrial Complex: A Historical Perspective* (1980); Nelson Lichtenstein, *Labor's War at Home: The CIO in World War II* (1983); Judy Barrett Litoff and David C. Smith, eds., *We're In This War, Too: World War II Letters from American Women in Uniform* (1994); David R. Segal, *Recruiting for Uncle Sam: Citizenship and Military Manpower Policy* (1989); Bradley F. Smith, *The Shadow Warriors: The OSS and the Origins of the CIA* (1983); Peter Soderbergh, *Women Marines: The World War II Era* (1992); B. H. Sparrow, *From the Outside In: World War II and the American State* (1996); Allan M. Winkler, *The Politics of Propaganda: The Office of War Information, 1942–1945* (1978).

### American Society

Karen Anderson, *Wartime Women: Sex Roles, Family Relations, and the Status of Women During World War II* (1981); Alison R. Bernstein, *American Indians and World War II* (1991); Allan

Berube, *Coming Out Under Fire: The History of Gay Men and Women in World War II* (1990); Dominic Capeci and Martha Wilkerson, *Layered Violence: The Detroit Rioters of 1943* (1991); Roger Daniels, *Prisoners Without Trial* (1993); John D'Emilio, *Sexual Politics, Sexual Communities: The Making of a Homosexual Minority in the United States* (1983); Lewis Ehrenberg and Susan Hirsch, eds., *The War in American Culture* (1996); Lillian Faderman, *Odd Girls and Twilight Lovers, A History of Lesbian Life in Twentieth-Century America* (1994); Mario T. Garcia, *Mexican-Americans: Leadership, Ideology, and Identity, 1930–1960* (1989); Maureen Honey, *Creating Rosie the Riveter: Class, Gender, and Propaganda During World War II* (1984); Peter Irons, *Justice at War: The Inside Story of the Japanese-American Internment* (1983); Walter Jackson, *Gunnar Myrdal and America's Conscience* (1990); Amy Kesselman, *Fleeting Opportunities: Women Shipyard Workers in Portland and Vancouver During World War II and Reconversion* (1990); Deborah E. Lipstadt, *Beyond Belief: The American Press and the Coming of the Holocaust* (1993); Ruth Milkman, *Gender at Work: The Dynamics of Job Discrimination by Sex During World War II* (1987); Merl Reed, *Seedtime for the Modern Civil Rights Movement* (1991); George H. Roeder, Jr., *The Censored War: American Visual Experience During World War II* (1993); Viki Ruiz, *Cannery Women, Cannery Lives: Mexican Women, Unionization, and the California Food Processing Industry* (1987); Page Smith, *Democracy on Trial: The Japanese American Evacuation and Relocation in World War II* (1995); William Tuttle, Jr., *"Daddy's Gone to War": The Second World War in the Lives of America's Children* (1993).

### Diplomacy

Russell D. Buhite, *Decision at Yalta* (1986); Wayne S. Cole, *Roosevelt and the Isolationists, 1932–1945* (1983); Waldo Heinrichs, Jr., *Threshold of War* (1988); James H. Madison, ed., *Wendell Wilkie: Hoosier Internationalist* (1992); Verne Newton, ed., *FDR and the Holocaust* (1996); Keith Sainsbury, *Churchill and Roosevelt at War* (1994); Jonathan Utley, *Going to War with Japan* (1985); Donald Watt, *How War Came* (1989).

### The Atomic Bomb

Gar Alperovitz, *Atomic Diplomacy: Hiroshima and Potsdam*, rev. ed. (1995); Herbert Feis, *The Atomic Bomb and the End of World War II* (1966); Gregg Herken, *The Winning Weapon: The Atomic Bomb in the Cold War, 1945–1950* (1980); Michael Hogan, ed., *Hiroshima in History and Memory* (1995); Leon Sigal, *Fighting to a Finish* (1995); John Ray Skates, *The Invasion of Japan, Alternative to the Bomb* (1994).

## *Chapter 28*

### General Works

William Graebner, *The Age of Doubt: American Thought and Culture in the 1940s* (1991); David Halberstam, *The Fifties* (1993); William Pemberton, *Harry S. Truman: Fair Dealer and Cold Warrior* (1989); Gary W. Reichard, *Politics as Usual: The Age of Truman and Eisenhower* (1988).

### The Cold War

H. W. Brands, *The Devil We Knew: Americans and the Cold War* (1993); Gregory Fossedal, *Our Finest Hour: Will Clayton, The Marshall Plan and the Triumph of Democracy* (1993); Michael Hogan, *The Marshall Plan* (1987); Timothy P. Ireland, *Creating the Entangling Alliance: The Origins of NATO* (1981); Robert H. Johnson, *Improbable Dangers: U.S. Perceptions of Threat in the Cold War and After* (1994); Bruce R. Kuniholm, *The Origins of the Cold War in the Near East* (1980); Ralph Levering, *The Cold War* (1994); T. J. McCormick, *America's Half Century: United States Foreign Policy in the Cold War* (1992); Robert L. Messer, *The End of an Alliance* (1982); Wilson Miscamble, *George F. Kennan and the Making of American Foreign Policy* (1992); David Painter, *Oil and the American Century* (1986); H. Schaffer, *Chester Bowles: New Dealer in the Cold War* (1993).

### The Cold War in Asia

Roy Appleman, *Disaster in Korea* (1992); Clay Blair, *The Forgotten War* (1988); Thomas Christensen, *Useful Adversaries* (1996); June Grasso, *Harry Truman's Two-China Policy* (1987); John Halliday and Bruce Cumings, *Korea: The Unknown War* (1989); Gary Hess, *The U.S. Emergence as a Southeast Asian Power* (1986); Andrew Rotter, *The Path to Vietnam* (1987); Howard Schonberger, *Aftermath of War: Americans and the Remaking of Japan* (1989); William Stueck, *The Korean War: An International History* (1995); Shu Guang Zhang, *Deterrence and Strategic Culture: Chinese-American Confrontations* (1993).

### The Cold War at Home

Paul Boyer, *By the Bomb's Early Light* (1985); Nadine Cohodas, *Strom Thurmond and the Politics of Southern Change* (1993); Marjorie Garber and Rebecca Walkowitz, eds., *Secret Agents: The Rosenberg Case, McCarthyism, and Fifties America* (1995); Steven Gillon, *Politics and Vision: The ADA and American Liberalism* (1987); Harvey Klehr and Ronald Radosh, *The Amerasia Spy Case* (1996); Joel Kovel, *Red Hunting in the Promised Land* (1994); Gary May, *Un-American Activities: The Trials of William Remington* (1994); David M. Oshinski, *A Conspiracy So Immense: The World of Joe McCarthy* (1983); Ronald Radosh and Joyce Milton, *The Rosenberg File* (1983); Raye C. Ringholz, *Uranium Frenzy: Boom and Bust on the Colorado Plateau* (1989); Hal Rothman, *On Rims and Ridges: The Los Alamos Area since 1880* (1992); Ellen Schrecker, *No Ivory Tower: McCarthyism and the Universities* (1986); Allen Weinstein, *Perjury: The Hiss-Chambers Case* (1978); Stephen Whitfield, *The Culture of the Cold War* (rev. ed., 1996).

## *Chapter 29*

### The Eisenhower Administration

Gunter Bischof and Stephen E. Ambrose, eds., *Eisenhower: A Centenary Assessment* (1995); Fred Greenstein, *The Hidden-Hand Presidency* (1982); Elizabeth Huckaby, *Crisis at Central High: Little Rock, 1957–1958* (1980); Richard Melanson and David Mayers, eds., *Reevaluating Eisenhower* (1986); Nicol Rae, *The Decline and Fall of the Liberal Republicans* (1989); David W. Reinhard, *The Republican Right Since 1945* (1983).

### Foreign Affairs and Policies

David Anderson, *Trapped by Success: The Eisenhower Administration and Vietnam* (1991); Howard Ball, *Justice Downwind: America's Nuclear Testing Program in the 1950s* (1986); Henry Brands, Jr., *Cold Warriors* (1988); John Gaddis, *We Now Know:*

*Rethinking Cold War History* (1997); Walter L. Hixson, *Parting the Curtain: Propaganda, Culture, and the Cold War, 1945–1961* (1997); Richard Immerman, *The CIA in Guatemala* (1982); Burton Kaufman, *The Arab Middle East and the United States* (1996); Gabriel Kolko, *Confronting the Third World* (1988); Andrew Rotter, *The Path to Vietnam* (1987).

### The Economy and the Affluent Society

David P. Calleo, *The Imperious Economy* (1982); Daniel Clark, *Like Night and Day: Unionization in a Southern Mill Town* (1997); Gilbert C. Fite, *American Farmers* (1981); Mark I. Gelfand, *A Nation of Cities* (1975); James R. Green, *The World of the Worker* (1980); Dolores Hayden, *Redesigning the American Dream* (1984); Donald Katz, *Home Fires: An Intimate Portrait of One Middle-Class Family in Postwar America* (1992); Linda Lear, *Rachel Carson: Witness for Nature* (1997); J. R. Oakley, *God's Country: America in the Fifties* (1986); Gwendolyn Wright, *Building the Dream: A Social History of Housing in America* (1981).

### Culture and Conservatism

James Baughman, *The Republic of Mass Culture: Journalism, Filmmaking, and Broadcasting Since 1941* (1992); Joel Foreman, ed., *The Other Fifties: Interrogating Midcentury American Icons* (1997); Landon Y. Jones, *Great Expectations: America and the Baby Boom Generation* (1980); George Lipsitz, *Class and Culture in Cold War America* (1981); William O'Neill, *American High* (1986); Richard Pells, *The Liberal Mind in a Conservative Age: American Intellectuals in the 1940s and 1950s* (1984); Lynn Spigel, *Make Room for TV* (1992); Ella Taylor, *Prime-Time Families: Television Culture in Postwar America* (1989); Alan M. Wald, *The New York Intellectuals* (1987).

### Feminism and Women's History

S. Paige Baty, *American Monroe: The Making of a Body Politic* (1995); Wini Breines, *Young, White, and Miserable: Growing Up Female in the Fifties* (1992); Stephanie Coontz, *The Way We Never Were* (1992); Ruth Schwartz Cowan, *More Work for Mother* (1983); Myra Dinnerstein, *Women Between Two Worlds* (1992); Eugenia Kaledin, *Mothers and More: American Women in the 1950s* (1984); Joanne Meyerowitz, ed., *Not June Cleaver: Women and Gender in Postwar America* (1994); Leila Rupp and Verta Taylor, *Survival in the Doldrums* (1987); Rickie Solinger, *Wake Up Little Susie: Single Pregnancy and Race Before Roe v. Wade* (1992).

### The Other America

Rodolfo Acuna, *Occupied America: A History of Chicanos* (1981); Larry W. Burt, *Tribalism in Crisis: Federal Indian Policy, 1953–1961* (1982); Thomas Cripps, *Making Movies Black: The Hollywood Message Movie from World War II to the Civil Rights Era* (1993); Donald Fixico, *Termination and Relocation: Federal Indian Policy, 1945–1970* (1986); Juan Ramon Garcia, *Operation Wetback: The Mass Deportation of Mexican Undocumented Workers in 1954* (1980); Mario Garcia, *Mexican Americans: Leadership, Ideology, and Identity, 1930–1960* (1989); Peter Guralnick, *Last Train to Memphis: The Rise of Elvis Presley* (1994); Elena Padilla, *Up from Puerto Rico* (1958); Linda Reed, *Simple Decency & Common Sense* (1992); Harvard Sitkoff, *The Struggle for Black Equality, 1954–1992* (1993); Thomas J. Sugrue, *The Origins of the Urban Crisis* (1996); Stuart Svonkin, *Jews Against Prejudice* (1997); Steven Watson, *The Birth of the Beat Generation* (1995).

## Chapter 30

### John F. Kennedy and the New Frontier

Thomas Brown, *JFK: History of an Image* (1988); James Giglio, *The Presidency of John F. Kennedy* (1991); Seymour Hersh, *The Dark Side of Camelot* (1997); Jim F. Heath, *Decade of Disillusionment: The Kennedy-Johnson Years* (1975); Bruce Miroff, *Pragmatic Illusions: The Presidential Politics of JFK* (1976); Herbert Parmet, *Jack* (1980) and *JFK* (1983); Garry Wills, *The Kennedy Imprisonment* (1983).

### Foreign Affairs in the Sixties

James Arnold, *The First Domino* (1991); Michael Beschloss, *The Crisis Years* (1991); Bernard Firestone, *The Quest for Nuclear Stability* (1982); Aleksandr Fursenko and Timothy Naftali, *'One Hell of a Gamble': Khrushchev, Castro, and Kennedy, 1958–1964* (1998); John Girling, *America and the Third World* (1980); Walter LaFeber, *Inevitable Revolutions: The United States in Central America* (1985); Richard Mahoney, *JFK: Ordeal in Africa* (1983); Ernest R. May and Philip D. Zelikow, eds., *The Kennedy Tapes: Inside the White House During the Cuban Missile Crisis* (1997); Philip Nash, *The Other Missiles of October: Eisenhower, Kennedy, and the Jupiters, 1957–1963* (1998); Deborah Shapley, *Promises and Power: The Life and Times of Robert McNamara* (1993); Peter Wyden, *Bay of Pigs* (1980).

### Lyndon B. Johnson and the Great Society

E. Berkowitz and Kim McQuaid, *Creating the Welfare State* (1992); Irving Bernstein, *Guns or Butter: The Presidency of Lyndon Johnson* (1996); Michael R. Beschloss, *Taking Charge: The Johnson White House Tapes, 1963–1964* (1997); Richard Cloward and Frances Fox Piven, *Poor People's Movements* (1978); Paul Conkin, *Big Daddy from the Pedernales* (1986); Mark Gelfand, *A Nation of Cities* (1975); Michael Katz, *The Undeserving Poor: From the War on Poverty to the War on Welfare* (1989); Doris Kearns, *Lyndon Johnson and the American Dream* (1977); Charles Morris, *A Time of Passion* (1984); Charles Murray, *Losing Ground: American Social Policy, 1950–1980* (1984); John Schwartz, *America's Hidden Success: Twenty Years of Public Policy* (1983); D. Zarefsky, *President Johnson's War on Poverty: Rhetoric and History* (1986).

### The Pursuit of Equality

Taylor Branch, *Parting the Waters: America in the King Years* (1988); Elaine Brown, *A Taste of Power: A Black Woman's Story* (1992); Eric Burner, *And Gently He Shall Lead Them: Robert Parris Moses and Civil Rights in Mississippi* (1994); Clayborne Carson, *In Struggle: SNCC and the Black Awakening of the 1960s* (1981); David Chappell, *Inside Agitators: White Southerners in the Civil Rights Movement* (1994); E. C. Clark, *The Schoolhouse Door: Segregation's Last Stand at the University of Alabama* (1993); W. M. Dulaney and Kathleen Underwood, eds., *Essays on the American Civil Rights Movement* (1993); Alice Echols, *Daring to Be Bad: Radical Feminism in America* (1989); Mario García, *Mexican-Americans: Leadership, Ideology, and Identity* (1989); Hugh Davis Graham, *The Civil Rights Era* (1989); James Gwynne, ed., *Malcolm X—Justice Seeker* (1993); Cynthia Harrison, *On Account of Sex: The Politics of Women's Issues, 1945–1968* (1988); K. Mills, *This Little Light of Mine: The Life of Fannie Lou Hamer* (1993); Carlos Munoz, Jr., *Youth, Identity, Power: Chicano Movement* (1989); Joane Nagel, *American Indian Ethnic Renewal*

(1996); James Ralph, Jr., *Northern Protest: Martin Luther King, Jr., Chicago, and the Civil Rights Movement* (1993); Mark Stern, *Calculating Visions: Kennedy, Johnson and Civil Rights* (1992); Joe Wood, ed., *Malcolm X: In Our Own Image* (1992).

### The Vietnam War at Home and at the Front

David Anderson, *Trapped by Success* (1991); C. Appey, *Working Class War* (1992); Eric Bergerud, *The Dynamics of Defeat* (1991); Larry Berman, *Lyndon Johnson's War* (1989); Robert Buzzanco, *Masters of War: Military Dissent and Politics in the Vietnam Era* (1996); Phillip Davidson, *Vietnam at War* (1991); Frances FitzGerald, *Fire in the Lake* (1972); George Herring, *LBJ and Vietnam* (1995); Gary Hess, *Vietnam and the United States* (1990); Lloyd Gardner, *Pay Any Price: Lyndon Johnson and the Wars for Vietnam* (1995); David Levy, *The Debate over Vietnam* (1990); Neil Sheehan, *A Bright Shining Lie* (1988); Fred Turner, *Echoes of Combat: The Vietnam War in American Memory* (1996); Tom Wells, *The War Within: America's Battle over Vietnam* (1994); Marilyn Young, *The Vietnam Wars* (1991).

## *Chapter 31*

### The New Left and Student Movements

Alexander Bloom and Winifred Breines, eds., *Takin' It to the Streets: A Sixties Reader* (1995); Wini Breines, *Community and Organization in the New Left* (1989); Paul Buhle, ed., *History and the New Left: Madison, Wisconsin, 1950–1970* (1989); Peter Clecak, *Radical Paradoxes* (1973); Peter Collier and David Horowitz, *Destructive Generation: Second Thoughts About the Sixties* (1989); C. DeBenedetti and C. Chatfield, *An American Ordeal: The Antiwar Movement of the Vietnam Era* (1990); David Farber, *Chicago '68* (1988) and *The Age of Great Dreams: America in the 1960s* (1994); Lewis Gann and Peter Duignan, *The New Left and the Cultural Revolution of the 1960s: A Reevaluation* (1995); Todd Gitlin, *The Sixties: Years of Hope, Days of Rage* (1987); David L. Goines, *The Free Speech Movement: Coming of Age in the 1960s* (1993); Kenneth Heineman, *Campus Wars* (1992); Maurice Isserman, *If I Had a Hammer: The Death of the Old Left—and the Birth of the New Left* (1989); Charles Kaiser, *1968 in America* (1988); Joseph Kelner and James Munves, *The Kent State Coverup* (1980); Peter Levy, *The New Left and Labor in the 1960s* (1994); C. Manes, *Green Rage: Radical Environmentalism* (1990); James Miller, *Democracy Is in the Streets* (1987); Charles Reich, *The Greening of America* (1970); Theodore Roszak, *The Making of a Counterculture* (1969); M. Small and W. Hoover, eds., *Give Peace a Chance: Exploring the Vietnam Antiwar Movement* (1992); Alan Wald, *Writing from the Left: New Essays on Radical Culture and Politics* (1994); Jon Wiener, *Come Together* (1991).

### The Politics of 1968

Paul Berman, *A Tale of Two Utopias: The Political Journey of the Generation of 1968* (1996); Mary C. Brennan, *Turning Right in the Sixties: The Conservative Capture of the GOP* (1995); Dan Carter, *The Politics of Rage* (1995); Marshall Frady, *Wallace* (1970); Louis Gould, *1968: The Election That Changed America* (1993); Richard Lemons, *The Troubled Americans* (1970); Joe McGinniss, *The Selling of the President, 1968* (1969); Kevin Phillips, *The Emerging Republican Majority* (1969); Richard Scammon and Ben Wattenberg, *The Real Majority* (1970); Herbert Schandler, *The Unmaking of a President* (1977); Jeff Shesol, *Mutual Contempt: Lyndon Johnson, Robert Kennedy, and the Feud That Defined a Decade* (1997); Irwin Unger and Debi Unger, *Turning Point: 1968* (1988); Jules Witcover, *The Year the Dream Died: Revisiting 1968 in America* (1997).

### Nixon-Kissinger Foreign Policies

Lloyd Gardner, *A Covenant with Power* (1984) and *The Great Nixon Turnaround* (1973); Stephen Green, *Living by the Sword: America and Israel in the Middle East, 1968–1987* (1988); Arnold Isaacs, *Without Honor: Defeat in Vietnam and Cambodia* (1983); Henry Kissinger, *White House Years* (1979) and *Years of Upheaval* (1982); Walter LaFeber, *Inevitable Revolutions* (1993); Robert Litwack, *Détente and the Nixon Doctrine* (1984); Timothy Lomperis, *The War Nobody Lost—and Won* (1984); Robert McMahon, *The Cold War on the Periphery* (1994); Stephen Rabe, *The Road to OPEC* (1982); Franz Schurmann, *The Foreign Policies of Richard Nixon* (1987); William Shawcross, *Side-Show: Kissinger, Nixon, and the Destruction of Cambodia* (1979); Melvin Small, *Johnson, Nixon, and the Doves* (1988); William Slater, *Chile and the United States* (1990).

### The Nixon Administration

Jonathan Aitken, *Nixon: A Life* (1994); Stephen Ambrose, *The Triumph of a Politician* (1989); Fawn Brodie, *Richard Nixon: The Shaping of His Character* (1981); Vincent Burke, *Nixon's Good Deed: Welfare Reform* (1974); David Calleo, *The Imperious Economy* (1982); Jody Carleson, *George Wallace and the Politics of Powerlessness* (1981); Ronald Formisano, *Boston Against Busing: Race, Class, and Ethnicity in the 1960s and 1970s* (1991); J. Greene, *The Limits of Power: The Nixon and Ford Administrations* (1992); Roger Morris, *Richard Milhous Nixon* (1990); James Reichley, *Conservatives in an Age of Change: The Nixon and Ford Administrations* (1981); Kirkpatrick Sale, *Power Shift* (1976); Michael Tanzer, *The Energy Crisis* (1974).

### Watergate

John Dean, *Blind Ambition* (1976); James Doyle, *Not Above the Law* (1977); John Ehrlichman, *Witness to Power* (1982); Jim Houghan, *Secret Agenda: Watergate, Deep Throat and the CIA* (1984); J. Anthony Lukas, *Nightmare: The Underside of the Nixon Years* (1976); Kim McQuaid, *The Anxious Years: America in the Vietnam-Watergate Era* (1989); Richard Nixon, *RN: The Memoirs of Richard Nixon* (1978); John Sirica, *To Set the Record Straight* (1979); Maurice Stans, *The Terrors of Justice* (1984); Athan Theoharis, *Spying on Americans* (1978).

## *Chapter 32*

### The Ford and Carter Years

Patrick Anderson, *Electing Jimmy Carter: The Campaign of 1994* (1994); William C. Berman, *America's Right Turn: From Nixon to Bush* (1994); James Bill, *The Eagle and the Lion: . . . American-Iranian Relations* (1987); Douglas Brinkley, *The Unfinished Presidency: Jimmy Carter's Journey Beyond the White House* (1998); Raymond L. Garthoff, *Détente and Confrontation: American-Soviet Relations from Nixon to Reagan* (1987); John Robert Greene, *The Presidency of Gerald R. Ford* (1995); Steven B. Hunt, *The Energy Crisis* (1978); Burton I. Kaufman, *The Presidency of James Earl Carter, Jr.* (1993); George D. Moffett III, *The Limits of*

*Victory: . . . The Panama Canal Treaties* (1983); Peter R. Odell, *Oil and World Power,* 5th ed. (1979); William B. Quandt, *Camp David* (1987); A. James Riechley, *Conservatives in an Age of Change* (1980); David Schoenbaum, *The United States and the State of Israel* (1993); Lars Shoultz, *Human Rights and U.S. Policy Toward Latin America* (1981); Gaddis Smith, *Morality, Reason, and Power* (1986) [Carter's foreign policy]; Strobe Talbott, *Endgame* (1979) [SALT II].

### The Reagan Presidency

William J. Broad, *Teller's War: The Top-Secret Story Behind the Star Wars Deception* (1992); Thomas Carothers, *In the Name of Democracy: U.S. Policy Toward Latin America in the Reagan Years* (1991); Paul S. Dempsey, *The Social and Economic Consequences of Deregulation* (1988); Jane Feuer, *Seeing Through the Eighties: Television and Reaganism* (1995); Benjamin Friedman, *Day of Reckoning: The Consequences of American Economic Policy Under Reagan and After* (1988); Jack W. Germond and Jules Witcover, *Blue Smoke and Mirrors: How Reagan Won and Why Carter Lost the Election of 1980* (1981); David E. Kyvig, ed., *Reagan and the World* (1990); Jonathan Lash, *A Season of Spoils: The Story of the Reagan Administration's Attack on the Environment* (1984); John D. Martz, *United States Policy in Latin America* (1995); Morris H. Morley, *Washington, Somoza, and the Sandinistas* (1994); Frances Fox Piven and Richard A. Cloward, *The New Class War: Reagan's Attack on the Welfare State and Its Consequences* (1982); Michael Schaller, *Reckoning with Reagan: America and Its President in the 1980s* (1992); C. Brant Short, *Ronald Reagan and the Public Lands: America's Conservation Debate, 1979–1984* (1989); Charles D. Smith, *Palestine and the Arab-Israeli Conflict,* 2d ed. (1992); Sidney Weintraub and Marvin Goodstein, eds., *Reaganomics in the Stagflation Economy* (1983).

### The Bush Presidency; End of the Cold War; Persian Gulf War

Rick Arkinson, *Crusade: The Untold Story of the Persian Gulf War* (1993); Michael L. Coniff, *Panama and the United States: The Forced Alliance* (1992); Michael Duffy, *Marching in Place: The Status Quo Presidency of George Bush* (1992); Alan Friedman, *Spider's Web: The Secret History of How the White House Illegally Armed Iraq* (1993); John Lewis Gaddis, *The United States and the End of the Cold War* (1992); Raymond L. Garthoff, *The Great Transition: American-Soviet Relations and the End of the Cold War* (1994); Jack W. Germond and Jules Witcover, *Whose Broad Stripes and Bright Stars* (1989) [the 1988 campaign]; Ken Gross, *Ross Perot: The Man Behind the Myth* (1992); Roger Hilsman, *George Bush vs. Saddam Hussein* (1992); Michael J. Hogan, ed., *The End of the Cold War: Its Meaning and Implications* (1992); Martin Lowy, *High Rollers: Inside the Savings and Loan Debacle* (1991); John R. MacArthur, *Second Front: Censorship and Propaganda in the Gulf War* (1992); David Mervin, *George Bush and the Guardianship Presidency* (1996); Richard Rose, *The Post-Modern President: George Bush Meets the World* (1991); *U.S. News & World Report, Triumph Without Victory* (1992) [the Persian Gulf War].

### Social and Cultural Trends in the 1970s and 1980s

Carl Abbott, *The New Urban America: Growth and Politics in the Sunbelt Cities* (1981); Frank D. Bean et al., *Mexican and Central American Population and U.S. Immigration Policy* (1989);

Michael A. Bernstein and David A. Adler, eds., *Understanding American Economic Decline* (1994); Bongyoun Choy, *Koreans in America* (1979); John Crewden, *The Tarnished Door: The New Immigrants and the Transformation of America* (1983); Douglas Glasgow, *The Black Underclass* (1980); Andrew Hacker, *Two Nations: Black and White, Separate, Hostile, Unequal* (1992); Sylvia Ann Hewlett, *When the Bow Breaks: The Cost of Neglecting Our Children* (1991); Dennis Heyck, ed., *Barrios and Borderlands: Cultures of Latinos and Latinas in the U.S.* (1993); Lloyd D. Johnson et al., *Trends in Drug Use . . . 1975–1989* (National Institute on Drug Abuse, 1991); Christopher Lasch, *The Culture of Narcissism* (1978); Nicholas Mills, ed., *Culture in an Age of Money* (1991); Michael Moritz, *The Little Kingdom: The Private Story of Apple Computer* (1984); Edwin Shur, *The Awareness Trap: Self-Absorption Instead of Social Change* (1976); James B. Stewart, *Den of Thieves* (1991) [Wall Street trading scandals of the 1980s]; Vance Trimble, *Sam Walton: The Inside Story of America's Richest Man* (1990); Reed Ueda, *Postwar Immigrant America* (1994); Sam Walton, *Made in America* (1992); William Julius Wilson, *The Truly Disadvantaged: The Inner City, the Underclass, and Public Policy* (1987).

### Women's Issues; Gay and Lesbian History; Sexuality

Barbara Hinkson Craig and David M. O'Brien, *Abortion and American Politics* (1993); Sara Evans, *Personal Politics: The Roots of Women's Liberation in the Civil Rights Movement and the New Left* (1979); Jo Freeman, *The Politics of Women's Liberation* (1979); David J. Garrow, *Liberty and Sexuality: The Right to Privacy and the Making of* Roe v. Wade (1994); Roger Rosenblatt, *Life Itself* (1992) [the abortion debate]; Leigh W. Rutledge, *The Gay Decades: From Stonewall to the Present* (1992); Barry D. Schoub, *AIDS and HIV in Perspective* (1994); Suzanne Staggenborg, *The Pro-Choice Movement* (1991); Mark Thompson, ed., *Long Road to Freedom: . . . The Gay and Lesbian Movement* (1994); Winifred D. Wandersee, *On the Move: American Women in the 1970s* (1988).

### Religion in Modern America

Paul Boyer, *When Time Shall Be No More: Prophecy Belief in Modern American Culture* (1992); Donald W. Dayton and Robert K. Johnston, eds., *The Variety of American Evangelicalism* (1991); Ethics and Public Policy Center, *No Longer Exiles: The Religious New Right in American Politics* (1993); Michael Lienesch, *Redeeming America: Piety and Politics in the New Christian Right* (1993); Mark Noll, *One Nation Under God? Christian Faith and Political Action in America* (1988); Garry Wills, *Under God: Religion and American Politics* (1990); Robert Wuthnow, *The Restructuring of American Religion: Society and Faith Since World War II* (1988).

## *Chapter 33*

### Domestic Politics in the Clinton Years

Vincent Bugliosi, *No Island of Sanity: Paula Jones v. Bill Clinton* (1998); E. J. Dionne, *They Only Look Dead: Why Progressives Will Dominate the Next Political Era* (1996); Elizabeth Drew, *Whatever It Takes: The Real Struggle for Political Power in America* (1997); Stanley B. Greenberg and Theda Skocpol, eds., *The New Majority: Toward a Popular Progressive Politics* (1997); Jacob S. Hacker, *The Road to Nowhere: The Genesis of President*

*Clinton's Plan for Health Security* (1997); Roderick P. Hart, *Seducing America: How Television Charms the Modern Voter* (1994); Webb Hubbell, *Friends in High Places: Our Journey from Little Rock to Washington, D.C.* (1997); Kathleen Hall Jamieson, *Packaging the Presidency: . . . Presidential Campaign Advertising* (3d ed., 1996); Todd E. Jones, ed., *Affirmative Action: Social Justice or Reverse Discrimination?* (1997); Linda Killian, *The Freshmen: What Happened to the Republican Revolution* (1998); Charles Noble, *Welfare as We Knew It: A Political History of the American Welfare State* (1997); Tom Rosenstiel, *Strange Bedfellows: How Television and the Presidential Candidates Changed American Politics, 1992* (1993); James B. Stewart, *Blood Sport: The President and His Adversaries* (1996); Bob Woodward, *The Agenda: Inside the Clinton White House* (1994) and *The Choice: How Clinton Won* (1996).

**Post–Cold-War Foreign Policy**

Benjamin R. Barber, *Jihad vs. McWorld* (1996); Wayne Bert, *The Reluctant Superpower: United States Policy in Bosnia, 1991–1995* (1997); Mark I. Clifford, *Troubled Tiger: Businessmen, Bureaucrats, and Generals in South Korea* (1994); *Foreign Affairs* 76 (September/October 1997), special issue on "The World Ahead"; John Lewis Gaddis, *Now We Know: Rethinking Cold War History* (1997); Samuel P. Huntington, *The Clash of Civilizations and the Remaking of World Order* (1996); Jim Rohwer, *Asia Rising* (1995); Robert W. Tucker and David C. Hendrickson, *The Imperial Temptation: The New World Order and America's Purposes* (1992); Stansfield Turner, *Caging the Nuclear Genie* (1997); Daniel Yergin and Thane Gustafson, *Russia 2010* (1993).

**Economic and Social Trends in the 1990s**

Thomas D. Boston and Catherine L. Ross, eds., *The Inner City: Urban Poverty and Economic Development in the Next Century* (1997); Fergus M. Bordewich, *Killing the White Man's Indian: Reinventing Native-Americans at the End of the Twentieth Century* (1996); Ellis Cose, *The Rage of a Privileged Class: Why Are Middle-Class Blacks Angry* (1993); Geoffrey Fox, *Hispanic Nation: Culture, Politics, and the Constructing of Identity* (1996); Denis Lynn Daly Heyck, ed., *Barrios and Borderlands: Cultures of Latinos and Latinas in the United States* (1993); Bill Ong Hing, *Making and Remaking Asian America Through Immigration Policy, 1950–1990* (1993); Susan D. Holloway et al., *Through My Own Eyes: Single Mothers and the Cultures of Poverty* (1997); Jong-deuk Jung, *A Study of Korean Immigration in America* (1991); Jonathan Kozol, *Amazing Grace: The Lives of Children and the Conscience of a Nation* (1995); Ruth Milkman, *Farewell to the Factory: Auto Workers in the Late Twentieth Century* (1998); Joel Millman, *The Other Americans: How Immigrants Renew Our Country, Our Economy, and Our Values* (1997); Joan K. Peters, *When Mothers Work: Loving Our Children Without Sacrificing Ourselves* (1997); Joseph Tilden Rhea, *Race Pride and the American Identity* (1998); Peter Skerry, *Mexican Americans: The Ambivalent Minority* (1993); Robert C. Smith, *Racism in the Post–Civil Rights Era: Now You See It, Now You Don't* (1995); William Wei, *The Asian American Movement* (1993); Tom Wicker, *Tragic Failure: Racial Integration in America* (1996); William Julius Wilson, *When Work Disappears: The World of the New Urban Poor* (1996).

**Technology, Science, Medicine, Environmentalism, Computers**

Paul Boyer, *Fallout: A Historian Reflects on America's Half-Century Encounter with Nuclear Weapons* (1998); Francis Cairncross, *The Death of Distance: How the Communications Revolution Will Change Our Lives* (1997); Arthur L. Caplan, *Am I My Brother's Keeper? The Ethical Frontiers of Biomedicine* (1997); Al Gore, *Earth in the Balance: Ecology and the Human Spirit* (1992); Richard Kluger, *Ashes to Ashes* (1996) [tobacco and public health]; Gina Kolata, *Clone: The Road to Dolly, and the Path Ahead* (1997); Carrick Mollenkamp et al., *The People v. Big Tobacco* (1998); Philip Shabecoff, *A Fierce Green Fire: The American Environmental Movement* (1994); Daniel E. Sichel, *The Computer Revolution: An Economic Perspective* (1997); Mark Sloutka, *War of the Worlds: Cyberspace and the High-Tech Assault on Reality* (1995); Paul Starr, *The Logic of Health Care Reform* (1992); Don Tapscott, *Growing Up Digital: The Rise of the Net Generation* (1998); Sherry Turkle, *Life on the Screen: Identity in the Age of the Internet* (1995); James Wallace, *Overdrive: Bill Gates and the Race to Control Cyberspace* (1997).

**The Struggle for the American Soul: The Culture Wars of the 1990s**

T. Alexander Aleinikoff, "A Multicultural Nationalism?" *The American Prospect* 36 (January–February 1998): 80–86; William J. Bennett, *The Devaluing of America: How to Win the Fight for Our Culture and Our Children* (1992); Joel A. Carpenter, *Revive Us Again: The Reawakening of American Fundamentalism* (1997); Stephen L. Carter, *The Culture of Disbelief: How American Law and Politics Trivialize Religious Devotion* (1993); Cynthia Gorney, *Articles of Faith: A Frontline History of the Abortion Wars* (1998); James L. Guth et al., *The Bully Pulpit: The Politics of Protestant Clergy* (1997); Robert Hughes, *Culture of Complaint: The Fraying of America* (1993); Martin Harwit, *An Exhibit Denied* (1996) [the Smithsonian controversy]; David Hollinger, *Post-Ethnic America: Beyond Multiculturalism* (1995); Robert Kuttner, *Everything for Sale: The Virtues and Limits of Markets* (1996); George Lakoff, *Moral Politics: What Conservatives Know that Liberals Don't* (1997); Philip Lamy, *Millennium Rage: Survivalists, White Supremacists, and the Doomsday Prophecy* (1996); Christopher Lasch, *The Revolt of the Elites and the Betrayal of Democracy* (1995); Michael Lienesch, *Redeeming America: Piety and Politics in the New Christian Right* (1993); Edward T. Linenthal and Tom Engelhardt, eds., *History Wars: The Enola Gay and Other Battles for the American Past* (1996); Edward N. Luttwack, *The Endangered American Dream* (1993); William Martin, *With God on Our Side: The Rise of the Religious Right in America* (1996); Walter Benn Michaels, *Our America: Nativism, Modernism, and Pluralism* (1995); Richard Moe and Carter Wilkie, *Changing Places: Rebuilding Community in the Age of Sprawl* (1997); Joseph S. Nye et al., eds., *Why People Don't Trust Government* (1997); Ralph Reed, *Active Faith: How Christians Are Changing the Soul of American Politics* (1996); Robert J. Samuelson, *The Good Life and Its Discontents: The American Dream in an Age of Entitlement, 1945–1995* (1995); Michael J. Sandel, *Democracy's Discontent: America in Search of a Public Philosophy* (1996); James D. Tabor and Eugene V. Gallagher, *Why Waco? Cults and the Battle for Religious Freedom in America* (1995); Justin Watson, *The Christian Coalition: Dreams of Restoration, Demands for Recognition* (1997).

# *Photograph Credits*

**Prologue**   *p. xxxii*, Courtesy of the Gerald Peters Gallery, Santa Fe, NM; *p. xxxvi*, Eric Meola/The Image Bank; *p. xxxviii (top)*, Charles Kennard/Stock Boston; *(bottom)*, Steve Proehl/The Image Bank; *p. xxxix (top)*, Craig Aurness/West Light; *(bottom)*, Richard Elliott Sisk/Panoramic Images; *p. xl*, Joe Jacobson/Panoramic Images; *p. xlii (bottom)*, Jim Brandenburg/Minden Pictures; *(top)*, Eric Meola/The Image Bank; *p. xliii (top)*, Don Landwehrle/The Image Bank; *(bottom)*, Edward Bower/The Image Bank; *p. xliv (top)*, John Aldridge/The Picture Cube; *(center)*, Steve Dunwell/The Image Bank; *(bottom)*, Bo Zaunders/The Stock Market; *p. xlv*, Peter Cole/New England Stock Photo.

**Chapter 1**   *p. xlviii*, Werner Forman Archive/Museum of the American Indian/Art Resource, NY; *p. 2*, Courtesy of the Peabody Essex Museum, Salem, MA, photograph by Mark Sexton; *p. 3*, Courtesy of the National Museum of the American Indian, Smithsonian Institution; *p. 6 (top)*, Museum of Mankind/The British Museum; *(bottom)*, Santa Barbara Museum of Natural History; *p. 7*, Werner Forman Archive Maxwell Museum of Anthropology/Art Resource, NY; *p. 8*, William M. Ferguson; *p. 10 (top)*, Georg Gerster/Comstock Inc.; *(bottom)*, James A. Ford and Clarence H. Webb. "Poverty Point, a late archaic site in Louisiana." NY, American Museum of Natural History, 1956 (Anthropological Papers, Vol. 46, Part 1); *p. 11a*, Cahokia Mounds State Historic Site, painting of Cahokia by William R. Iseminger; *p. 11b (both)*, Cahokia Mounds Historic Site; *p. 12*, By permission of the Houghton Library, Harvard University.

**Chapter 2**   *p. 18*, Courtesy of the John Carter Brown Library at Brown University; *p. 20, (detail)* The Metropolitan Museum of Art, Gift of J.P. Morgan, 1900 (00.18.2); *p. 23*, Courtesy of Entwistle Gallery, London/Werner Forman Archives/Art Resource, NY; *p. 25,(detail)* Harvey D. Parker Collection. Courtesy of the Museum of Fine Arts, Boston; *p. 27*, The Granger Collection; *p. 31*, American Museum of Natural History, Else Sackler/Lee Boltin; *p. 32*, Museum of Mankind, © The British Museum; *p. 34*, cliché (negative) © Bibliothèque Nationale de Paris, France; *p. 35*, "Manuscrito Pictorio Mexicano de Mediados del Siglo XVI," by Lienzo de Tlaxcala, Tozzer Library, Harvard University; *p. 38*, Arizona State Museum, University of Arizona, photograph by Helga Teiwes; *p. 40*, I. N. Phelps Stokes Collection, Miriam and Ira D. Wallach Division of Art, Prints & Photographs, The New York Public Library; Astor, Lenox and Tilden Foundations; *p. 41*, By kind permission of the Marquess of Tavistock and the Trustees of the Bedford Estate; *p. 41b (top), (detail)* Carte Géographique de la Nouvelle France by Samuel de Champlain; *(bottom left)*, Bibliothèque Nationale/Giraudon/Art Resource, NY; *(bottom right)*, By permission of Houghton Library, Harvard University, photograph by Barry Donahue; *p. 43*, © The British Museum; *p. 44*, Courtesy of Plimoth Plantation, Inc., Plymouth, Massachusetts.

**Chapter 3**   *p. 46*, Museum of Art, Rhode Island School of Design; Gift of Mr. Robert Winthrop, photograph by Del Bogart; *p. 48*, American Antiquarian Society; *p. 51 (left)*, Drawing from John Underhill's News from America, 1638; *(right)*, Courtesy of the Pilgrim Society, Plymouth, Massachusetts; *p. 55*, Peabody Essex Museum, Salem, MA, photograph by Jeffrey Dykes; *p. 60, (detail)* "From the records of the Court of Oyer & Terminer 1692, property of the Supreme Judicial Court, Division of Archives and Records Preservation." On deposit at Peabody Essex Museum, Salem, Massachusetts; *p. 63 (all)*, Courtesy of Flowerdew Hundred Foundation; *p. 68*, The New York Public Library, Arent's Tobacco Collection, Print Collection, Mirian and Ira D. Wallach Division of Art, Prints & Photographs; Aster, Lenox and

Tilden Foundations; *p. 70*, Library Company of Philadelphia; *p. 71*, Burgerbibliothek Bern; *p. 74*, Collection of the New York Historical Society; *p. 76 (left)*, Library of Congress; *(right)*, The Historical Society of Pennsylvania; *p. 77a*, Courtesy of the Museum of New Mexico Neg. #11409; *p. 77b*, Photograph by John K. Hillers, Courtesy of Museum of New Mexico. Neg. #16096; *p. 78*, The Public Archives of Canada.

**Chapter 4**   *p. 80*, Courtesy of Winterthur Museum; *p. 82*, The Granger Collection; *p. 84*, Courtesy of Winterthur Museum; *p. 87, (detail)* The Library Company of Philadelphia; *p. 90*, Peabody Essex Museum, Salem, Massachusetts; *p. 93*, Wethersfield Historical Society; *p. 95*, Chicago Historical Society; *p. 96*, © The British Museum; *p. 98*, Newport Historical Society #NHS53.3; *p. 99*, Courtesy of Maryland State Archives, Special Collections MSA SC 1497-277; *p. 101*, Peabody Museum, Harvard University, photograph by Hillel Burger; *p. 102*, Mackinac State Historic Park; *p. 103*, Courtesy of Winterthur Museum; *p. 104*, The Royal Library, Copenhagen; *p. 105*, Bob Daemmrich/Stock Boston; *p. 105a*, From the exhibition "Fort Mose: Colonial America's Black Fortress of Freedom" produced by the Florida Museum of Natural History; *p. 105b (both)*, From the exhibition "Fort Mose: Colonial America's Black Fortress of Freedom" produced by the Florida Museum of Natural History; *p. 107*, Maryland Historical Society, Baltimore, Maryland; *p. 109 (both)*, John Neubauer; *p. 110*, Print Department, Public Library of the City of Boston.

**Chapter 5**   *p. 112*, Library of Congress; *p. 114*, Courtesy of the Print Collection, Lewis Walpole Library, Yale University; *p. 116*, Library of Congress; *p. 118*, Courtesy of Winterthur Museum; *p. 119*, © 1995 Indianapolis Museum of Art, The James E. Roberts Fund; *p. 120*, Courtesy of Winterthur Museum; *p. 123*, Manuscripts & Archives Division, New York Public Library; *p. 125*, Library of Congress; *p. 127*, American Antiquarian Society; *p. 130*, Deposited by the City of Boston, courtesy of the Museum of Fine Arts, Boston; *p. 131*, Colonial Williamsburg Foundation; *p. 132*, Historical Society of Pennsylvania; *p. 135*, Museum of Fine Arts, Boston, bequest of Winslow Warren; *p. 139*, American Antiquarian Society; *p. 141*, Kirby Collection of Historical Paintings, Lafayette College, Easton, Pennslyvania; *p. 141a*, American Antiquarian Society; *p. 141b (top)*, John Carter Brown Library at Brown University; *(bottom)*, Courtesy of the Concord Museum, Concord, Massachusetts.

**Chapter 6**   *p. 144*, West Point Museum Collections, United States Military Academy; *p. 146*, Print Collection, Miriam & Ira D. Wallach Division of Art, Prints and Photographs, The New York Public Library; Astor, Lenox and Tilden Foundations; *p. 149, (detail)* Collection of the New York Historical Society; *p. 151 (top), (detail)* Courtesy of the Museum of Fine Arts, Boston, Deposited by City of Boston; *(bottom)*, Graphic Arts Collections, Visual Materials Division, Department of Rare Books and Special Collections, Princeton University Libraries; *p. 153*, Chicago Historical Society; *p. 157*, Geography & Map Division, Library of Congress; *p. 158*, Anne S. K. Brown Military Collection, Brown University Library; *p. 159a*, Washington University Gallery of Art, St. Louis, Gift of Nathaniel Phillips, 1890; *p. 159b*, The Filson Club Historical Society, Louisville, Kentucky; *p. 161, (detail)* Boston Athenaeum; *p. 162*, The Frick Art Reference Library; *p. 171*, National Gallery of Canada, Ottawa; *p. 173*, Henry Grosinsky, Life Magazine © Time Warner Inc.; *p. 174, (detail)* Colonial Williamsburg Foundation.

**Chapter 7**   *p. 180*, Chrylser Museum of Art, Norfolk, Virginia, Gift of Edgar and William Bernice Chrysler Garbisch; *p. 182, (detail)*

Chicago Historical Society; *p. 185,* Collection of the New York Historical Society; *p. 186,* Collection of the New York Historical Society; *p. 188,* Courtesy of Donaldson, Lufkin & Jenrette Collection of Americana; *p. 193,* Smithsonian Institution Photo #BAE 1169-L-3; *p. 195, (detail)* Chicago Historical Society; *p. 197,* The Brooklyn Museum, #39.536.1, Gift of the Crescent Hamilton Athletic Club; *p. 199,* Private Collection; *p. 200,* National Museum of American Art, Washington, DC/Art Resource, NY; *p. 202,* Library of Congress; *p. 205,* Monticello/Thomas Jefferson Memorial Foundation, Inc.; *p. 205a,* Rare Book Department, The Free Library of Philadelphia; *p. 205b (top), (detail)* Delaware Art Museum, Wilmington, Gift of Absalom Jones School, Wilmington; *(bottom),* Chicago Historical Society; *p. 208,* Maryland Historical Society, Baltimore, Maryland.

**Chapter 8** *p. 210, (detail)* The Minneapolis Institute of Arts, William Hood Dunwoody Fund; *p. 212,* Library of Congress; *p. 213a (left),* Courtesy of Robert M. Hinklin Jr., Inc., Spartanburg, South Carolina; *p. 213a (right),* Monticello/Thomas Jefferson Memorial Foundation; *(left),* Larry Lee/Corbis/West Light; *p. 213b (right),* Monticello/Thomas Jefferson Memorial Foundation; *p. 214,* Franklin D. Roosevelt Library; *p. 215,* Boston Athenaeum; *p. 218 (top left and right),* Courtesy of the Independence National Historical Park; *(bottom),* Peabody Museum, Harvard University, photograph by Hillel Burger; *p. 222,* G.W. Blunt White Library Manuscript Collection/Mystic Seaport Museum, Inc.; *p. 224,* The Granger Collection; *p. 226,* The New Haven Colony Historical Society, Gift of Mrs. Philip Galpin; *p. 228,* © The White House Historical Association; *p. 229,* National Archives of Canada; *p. 231,* Corbis-Bettmann.

**Chapter 9** *p. 236, (detail),* Gift of the Fred Sanders Company in memory of its founder, Fred Sanders, © The Detroit Institute of Arts; *p. 238,* Hudson Bay Company Archives/Provincial Archives of Manitoba; *p. 240 (left),* The Walters Art Gallery, Baltimore; *(top right),* Buffalo Bill Historical Center, Cody, Wyoming; As a Memorial to Jeanette J. Leonard, on behalf of her husband Dr. Kenneth O. Leonard; *(bottom right),* Missouri Historical Society, St. Louis; *p. 241,* Library of Congress; *p. 242,* William L. Clements Library, University of Michigan, Ann Arbor; *p. 243a,* Woolaroc Museum, Bartlesville, Oklahoma; *p. 243b,* From the Collection of Gilcrease Museum, Tulsa; *p. 247,* Museum d'Histoire Naturelle, No. 62003-2; *p. 248,* The New York Historical Society; *p. 252,* University of Massachusetts, Lowell; *p. 254,* Cincinnati Public Library; *p. 256,* Library of Congress; *p. 260,* Giampietro Gallery, 50 East 78th, New York, NY 10021.

**Chapter 10** *p. 264,* The Saint Louis Art Museum; *p. 266,* Special Collections, Skillman Library, Lafayette College, Easton, PA; *p. 269,* The New Haven Colony Historical Society, Gift of Dr. Charles Purvis, 1898; *p. 272 (bottom),* George Eastman House; *(top),* The National Portrait Gallery, Washington, DC/Art Resource, NY; *p. 275,* Collection of the New York Historical Society; *p. 279,* Library of Congress; *p. 281,* Collection of the New York Historical Society; *p. 283,* Courtesy of Museum of Fine Arts, Brigham Young University. All rights reserved; *p. 285,* National Academy of Design, New York City; *p. 288,* Boston Athenaeum; *p. 290 (right),* Chicago Historical Society; *(left),* National Women's Party; *p. 291 (left),* Free Library of Philadelphia; *(right),* Courtesy of the Eastern State Penitentiary Historic Site; *p. 291a,* Courtesy of the Oneida Community Mansion House; *p. 291b (both),* Courtesy of the Oneida Community Mansion House.

**Chapter 11** *p. 294, (detail)* From the collections of Henry Ford Museum & Greenfield Village; *p. 296 (left),* Library of Congress; *(right),* Iconograhics Collection/State Historical Society of Wisconsin; *p. 298,* Library of Congress; *p. 300,* The Granger Collection; *p. 303,* Courtesy of George Eastman House; *p. 304,* Library of Congress; *p. 305,* Museum of the City of New York, Anonymous gift; *p. 306,* Historic Cherry Hill CH.1963.2193, Courtesy of Albany Institute of History & Art; *p. 309,* Corbis-Bettmann; *p. 309a,* National Portrait Gallery, London; *p. 309b (top),* From "Domestic Manners of the Americans,"

by Fanny Trollope, Harvard College Library; *(bottom),* The Cincinnati Historical Society; *p. 310,* Culver Pictures; *p. 312,* The Louisa May Alcott Memorial Association; *p. 314,* Brown University Library, reproduction photograph by John M. Miller; *p. 317 (top left),* Rare Books and Manuscripts Division, New York Public Library; Astor, Lenox and Tilden Foundation; *p. 317 (bottom and top right),* National Museum of American Art, Washington, DC/Art Resource, NY; *p. 318,* Courtesy of The New York Historical Society.

**Chapter 12** *p. 320,* Virginia Historical Society; *p. 327,* Tulane University Art Collection, New Orleans; *p. 328,* The Gibbes Museum of Art/Carolina Art Association; *p. 329,* Hunter Museum of American Art, Chattanooga, TN, Gift of Mr. & Mrs. Thomas B. Whiteside; *p. 331,* Collection of Dr. Richard Saloom; *p. 333 (both),* Chicago Historical Society; *p. 335a (both),* South Carolina Library; *p. 335b (left),* South Carolina State Museum; *(right),* Museum of Early Southern Decorative Arts; *p. 337,* Collection of the New York Historical Society; *p. 339,* National Archives of Canada/C-115001; *p. 341,* From the Permanent Collection of the University Art Museum, University of Southwestern Louisiana, Lafayette; *p. 343,* Historic Mobile Preservation Society Archives; *p. 345,* Courtesy Museum of the Confederacy, Richmond, VA. Photograph by Katherine Wetzel; *p. 347 (left),* Schomberg Center for Research in Black Culture, New York Public Library; *(right),* Howard University Gallery of Art, Washington, DC.

**Chapter 13** *p. 350,* National Museum of American Art, Washington, DC/Art Resource, NY; *p. 355,* The Metropolitan Museum of Art, The Edward W. C. Arnold Collection of New York Prints, Maps and Pictures, Bequest of W. C. Arnold, 1954. #54.90.166; *p. 356, (detail)* Museum of the City of New York, Gift of Mrs. Robert M. Littlejohn; *p. 360,* Santa Barbara Mission Archive-Library; *p. 362,* Daughters of the Republic of Texas Library, Gift of the Yanaguana Society; *p. 364,* The Granger Collection; *p. 370,* National Portrait Gallery, Smithsonian Institution/Art Resource, NY; *p. 373 (left),* Courtesy of the Decorative & Industrial Arts Department of the Chicago Historical Society, Uniform #1920.38; *(right),* Chicago Historical Society; *p. 375,* Library of Congress; *p. 375a,* Courtesy of George Eastman House; *p. 375b,* Courtesy of University Archives, Bancroft Library; *p. 376,* "California Forty-niner." Artist unknown, Daguerreotype with applied coloring, quarter-plate c. 1850, Amon Carter Museum, Fort Worth, TX, #P1983.20.

**Chapter 14** *p. 378, (detail)* The Metropolitan Museum of Art, Gift of Mr. & Mrs. Carl Stoeckel, 1897; *p. 382,* National Portrait Gallery, Smithsonian Institution/Art Resource, NY; *p. 385,* National Portrait Gallery, Smithsonian Institution/Art Resource, NY; *p. 395,* Chicago Historical Society; *p. 396 (left),* National Portrait Gallery, Washington, DC/Art Resource, NY; *(right),* Library of Congress; *p. 398 (left),* Courtesy of the Decorative and Industrial Arts Department of the Chicago Historical Society; *(right),* Chicago Historical Society; *p. 401,* National Portrait Gallery, Washington, DC/Art Resource, NY; *p. 401a,* Courtesy of The Charleston Museum, Charleston, South Carolina; *p. 401b (top),* Courtesy of the Decorative and Industrial Arts Department of the Chicago Historical Society; *(bottom),* Library of Congress; *p. 402,* Library of Congress.

**Chapter 15** *p. 404,* Courtesy Drake House Museum, Plainfield, NJ; *p. 405,* (Civil War drum), Index of American Design © 1999 Board of Trustees, National Gallery of Art, Washington DC; *p. 408,* Cook Collection, Valentine Museum, Richmond, Virginia; *p. 411,* Corbis-Bettmann; *p. 414,* Geography & Map Division, Library of Congress; *p. 416 (top),* Library of Congress; *(bottom),* Antietam National Battlefield, Sharpsburg, Maryland, photograph by Larry Sherer; *p. 419,* Corbis-Bettmann; *p. 420,* The Museum of American Political Life, University of Hartford, photograph by Sally Anderson Bruce; *p. 422,* Gift of Edgar William and Bernice Chrysler Garbisch, © Board of Trustees, National Gallery of Art, Washington; *p. 423,* Chicago Historical Society; *p. 423b (both),* The Western Reserve Historical Society; *p. 424,* Library of Congress; *p. 426,* Corbis; *p. 429,* Library of Congress; *p. 432*, Museum of the City of New York, Gift of Mrs. J. West Roosevelt, #38.120.3; *p. 433*, Library of Congress; *p. 437 (top right)*, National Portrait Gallery, Washington, DC/Art Resource, NY; *(bottom)*, Corbis-Bettmann; *p. 438*, Collection of the New York Historical Society.

**Chapter 16**   *p. 440*, William Gladstone Collection; *p. 442*, Library of Congress; *p. 445*, National Portrait Gallery, Washington, DC/Art Resource, NY; *p. 446, Harpers Weekly*, 1866; *p. 447*, Corbis-Bettmann; *p. 452*, Schlesinger Library, Radcliffe College; *p. 453*, The Granger Collection; *p. 454*, The Museum of the Confederacy, Richmond, Virginia, photograph by Katherine Wetzel; *p. 456 (left)*, Decorative and Industrial Arts, Chicago Historical Society; *(right)*, Tennessee State Museum Collection, photograph by June Dorman; *p. 457a*, Library of Congress; *p. 457b (both)*, Courtesy of the Atlanta History Center, Atlanta, Georgia; *p. 458*, William Gladstone Collection; *p. 460*, From the Collection of the South Carolina Historical Society; *p. 463 (left)*, Brown Brothers; *(right), Harpers Weekly*, 1871; *p. 467, Harpers Weekly*, October 24, 1874; *p. 468 (both)*, Kansas State Historical Society.

**Chapter 17**   *p. 472*, National Anthropological Archives, Smithsonian Institution; *p. 474*, Gilcrease Museum, Tulsa, Oklahoma; *p. 476*, Courtesy of the Burton Historical Collection, Detroit Public Library; *p. 479 (both)*, Corbis-Bettmann; *p. 481a*, Cumberland Historical Society, Carlisle, Pennsylvania; *p. 481b (both)* Cumberland Historical Society, Carlisle, Pennsylvania; *p. 482 (top)*, The Huntington Library, San Marino, California; *(bottom)*, National Museum of Natural History, Smithsonian Institution; *p. 485 (right)*, Nebraska State Historical Society; *(left)*, Milwaukee Public Museum; *p. 486*, Courtesy of the Sioux City Public Museum, Sioux City, Iowa; *p. 487*, Minnesota Historical Society; *p. 490*, Fine Arts Museum/Museum of New Mexico; *p. 492 (left)* National Cowboy Hall of Fame and Western Heritage Center, Oklahoma City, Oklahoma; *(right)*, California Historical Society, FN-22101; *p. 494*, Denver Public Library, Western History Department; *p. 497*, Courtesy of Edward E. Ayer Collection, The Newberry Library, Chicago; *p. 499*, Lent by the Department of the Interior Museum, National Museum of American Art, Washington, DC/Art Resource, NY.

**Chapter 18**   *p. 502*, Pennsylvania Historical & Museum Committee, Bureau of Historic Sites and Museums, Anthracite Museum Complex; *p. 504*, Courtesy of the Hagley Museum and Library; *p. 506*, Corbis-Bettmann; *p. 509*, Corbis-Bettmann; *p. 512*, Corbis-Bettmann; *p. 513 (left)*, Electricity & Modern Physics Collection, Smithsonian Institution; *(right)*, Library of Congress; *p. 514 (top)*, Archives Center of the National Museum of American History, Smithsonian Institution, Negative #89-363; *(bottom)*, Culver Pictures, Inc.; *p. 515*, Courtesy of the Boston Public Library, Print Department; *p. 517, Harper's Weekly*, March 26, 1877; *p. 518*, Library of Congress; *p. 520*, Courtesy of the Trustees of the Haverhill Public Library, Special Collections Department; *p. 523*, Library of Congress; *p. 524*, California Historical Society, Luke Fay Collection, FN-00507; *p. 526*, Museum of American Political Life, University of Hartford, photograph by Steven Laschever; *p. 527*, Library of Congress; *p. 528*, Chicago Historical Society; *p. 529a*, Carnegie Library of Homestead, reproduction by Randolph Harris; *p. 529b (both)*, Library of Congress.

**Chapter 19**   *p. 532*, Gift of a Couple Old Hoosiers, © 1997 Indianapolis Museum of Art; *p. 534*, Corbis-Bettmann/UPI Newsphotos; *p. 536 (right)*, Detroit Publishing Company/Library of Congress; *(left)*, Security Pacific Collection, Los Angeles Public Library; *p. 539*, Courtesy of the Ellis Island Immigration Museum; *p. 540*, California Historical Society; *p. 542*, Chicago Historical Society; *p. 543 (left)*, Library of Congress; *(right)*, National Archives; *p. 543a* Courtesy of Milwaukee County Historical Society; *p. 543b*, State Historical Society of Wisconsin; *p. 545, Harper's Weekly*, 1871; *p. 548*, The Granger Collection; *p. 551*, University of Illinois at Chicago, The University Library, Jane Addams Memorial Collection; *p. 552*, Edward Emerson Simmons (1852–1931), Boston Public Gardens, 1893, oil on canvas, 18x26 in. (45.7x66 cm), Daniel J. Terra Collection, 34.1984, © 1966 Courtesy of Terra Museum of American Art, Chicago; *p. 554*, Corbis/Angelo Hornak; *p. 555*, Milwaukee Public Museum.

**Chapter 20**   *p. 558*, Courtesy of the Boston Public Library, Print Department; *p. 560*, The Granger Collection; *p. 561*, Corbis-Bettmann; *p. 563*, By permission of AT&T Archives; *p. 565*, Courtesy of University Archives, Bancroft Library; *p. 567*, Solomon D. Butcher Collection, Nebraska State Historical Society; *p. 568 (top)*, The Granger Collection; *(bottom)*, Colorado Historical Society #WHJ-32888; *p. 569 (both)*, West Point Museum Collections, U.S. Military Academy, photograph by Paul Warchol; *p. 571*, © The Detroit Institute of Arts, Founders Society Purchase; *p. 572*, From the Collections of Henry Ford Museum and Greenfield Village; *p. 574*, Brooklyn Historical Society; *p. 575a*, Courtesy of Fisk University, Special Collection; *p. 575b (both)*, Courtesy New Orleans Jazz Club Collection, Louisiana State Museum, photograph © Jan White Brantley; *p. 577 (left)*, The Granger Collection; *(right)*, North Wind Picture Archives; *p. 579*, The Gifted Line, John Grossman, Inc.; *p. 580*, Corbis-Bettmann; *p. 581*, Corbis-Bettmann.

**Chapter 21**   *p. 584*, Brown Brothers; *p. 586*, Library of Congress; *p. 588*, Chicago Historical Society; *p. 591*, Harvard College Library; *p. 593 (left)*, Frederick Winslow Taylor Collection, Stevens Institute of Technology; *(right)*, Lewis W. Hine Collection, US History, Local History & Genealogy Division, The New York Public Library; *p. 598*, Solomon D. Butcher Collection, Nebraska State Historical Society; *p. 600*, Corbis; *p. 601*, The Granger Collection; *p. 603*, Library of Congress; *p. 605a*, Chicago Historical Society; *p. 605b (top)*, Library of Congress; *(bottom)*, Courtesy of the Manoogian Collection; *p. 606*, Political History Division, National Museum of American History, Smithsonian Institution; *p. 611*, National Archives; *p. 612*, National Archives; *p. 614*, U.S. Signal Corps Photo/National Archives.

**Chapter 22**   *p. 616*, The Phillips Collection, Washington, DC, acquired 1922; *p. 618*, The Granger Collection; *p. 621 (left)*, Denver Public Library, Western History Department; *(right)*, Courtesy of MetLife Archives; *p. 622*, Corbis-Bettmann; *p. 623*, Alice Austen, Staten Island Historical Society; *p. 624*, Corbis-Bettmann; *p. 625*, Corbis-Bettmann; *p. 626*, City Archives of Philadelphia; *p. 628*, Corbis-Bettmann; *p. 631 (both)*, Corbis-Bettmann; *p. 632*, Corbis-Bettmann; *p. 634 (top)*, University of Chicago Library, Department of Special Collections; *(bottom)*, Archives of the University of Massachusetts at Amherst; *p. 635 (right)*, Corbis-Bettmann; *(left)*, Special Collections Division, University of Washington Libraries, Negative #UW1527; *p. 636*, Corbis-Bettmann; *p. 637*, Museum of American Political Life, University of Hartford, photograph by Sally Anderson-Bruce; *p. 640*, Brown Brothers; *p. 641*, Library of Congress; *p. 641a*, University of the Pacific; *p. 641b (top)*, Wadsworth Atheneum, Hartford, CT, Bequest of Mrs. Theodore Lyman in memory of her husband; *(bottom)*, Corbis-Bettmann/UPI Newsphotos; *p. 642*, Theodore Roosevelt Collection, Harvard College Library.

**Chapter 23**   *p. 648*, Corbis-Bettmann/UPI Newsphotos; *p. 650*, Collection of Picture Research Consultants; *p. 652*, Naval Historical Center; *p. 653*, The Granger Collection #4E1063.77; *p. 655*, Culver Pictures; *p. 655 (inset photograph)*, Corbis; *p. 657*, Corbis-Bettmann; *p. 658*, National Archives; *p. 659 (left)*, Corbis-Bettmann/UPI Newsphotos; *(right)*, Poster Collection, Hoover Institution Archives, Stanford University; *p. 659a*, Culver Pictures; *p. 659b*, Corbis-Bettmann; *p. 660 (left)*, National Archives; *(right)*, Hulton Getty/Gamma-Liaison; *p. 663*, U.S. Army Military History Institute; *p. 664*, Brown Brothers; *p. 666*, Library of Congress; *p. 668*, The Phillips Collection, Washington, DC, acquired 1942; *p. 671*, National Archives; *p. 673*, Courtesy of *OAH Magazine of History*, Spring, 1994; *p. 675*, Library of Congress.

**Chapter 24** *p. 678*, Chicago Historical Society, Collection of Archie Motley and Valerie Gerrard Browne; *p. 680*, Brown Brothers; *p. 682*, Corbis-Bettmann/UPI Newsphotos; *p. 684*, Culver Pictures; *p. 687*, Library of Congress; *p. 688*, Courtesy of The Strong Museum, Rochester, NY © 1999; *p. 690*, New Britain Museum of American Art, Connecticut, Stephen Lawrence Fund, photograph by E. Irving Blomstrann; *p. 691 (right)*, Atlanta History Center; *(left)*, Warner Brothers Archive; *p. 692*, Brown Brothers; *p. 694*, Missouri Historical Society; *p. 695*, Corbis; *p. 695a*, Archive Photos; *p. 695b*, National Portrait Gallery, Washington, DC/Art Resource, NY; *p. 696*, The New York Historical Society; *p. 697*, Corbis-Bettmann; *p. 699*, W. A. Swift Collection, Archives and Special Collections, Ball State University Libraries; *p. 700*, Corbis-Bettmann; *p. 701*, Brown Brothers; *p. 702*, Museum of the City of New York.

**Chapter 25** *p. 706*, Dallas Museum of Art, Dallas Art Association Purchase 1945.6 © 1999, Estate of Alexandre Hogue, courtesy Cline Gallery of Fine Art, New Mexico; *p. 710*, Corbis-Bettmann; *p. 711*, Corbis-Bettmann/UPI Newsphotos; *p. 714*, The Granger Collection; *p. 715*, Corbis-Bettmann/UPI Newsphotos; *p. 717*, Courtesy of TVA Office of Natural Resources; *p. 719a*, Library of Congress; *p. 719b*, Corbis-Bettmann/UPI Newsphotos; *p. 720*, Courtesy of the Franklin D. Roosevelt Library; *p. 721*, National Archives; *p. 722*, National Museum of American Art, Washington, DC/Art Resource, NY; *p. 724*, Library of Congress; *p. 727*, Corbis-Bettmann; *p. 729 (left)*, US Forest Service; *(right)*, Library of Congress; *p. 730*, Library of Congress.

**Chapter 26** *p. 734*, Georgia Museum of Art, University of Georgia/Eva Underhill Holbrook Memorial Collection of American Art, Gift of Alfred H. Holdbrook; *p. 736*, Detroit Free Press Photo; *p. 738*, Corbis-Bettmann; *p. 741 (both)*, Library of Congress; *p. 742*, Corbis-Bettmann; *p. 743a*, Dick Whittington; *p. 743b (bottom)*, Library of Congress; *p. 743b (top)*, D.C. Heath Photo Archives; *p. 746 (left)*, Resettlement Administration/Library of Congress; *(right)*, Corbis-Bettmann; *p. 748*, Corbis-Bettmann; *p. 749*, © 1989, Grandma Moses Properties Co., NY; *p. 750 (top)*, Penn Central Collection, Hagley Museum and Library, Wilmington, Delaware; *(bottom)*, Archive Photos; *p. 755*, AKG London; *p. 757*, Corbis-Bettmann/UPI Newsphotos.

**Chapter 27** *p. 758*, U.S. Army Center of Military History; *p. 760*, William Vandivert/Life Magazine © Time, Inc.; *p. 762*, National Archives; *p. 764*, Myron H. Davis, Life Magazine © Time, Inc.; *p. 767*, Curt Teich Postcard Archives; *p. 769*, Library of Congress; *p. 772*, National Archives; *p. 774*, USAF; *p. 777*, U.S. Army; *p. 778*, Madeleine Sugimoto and Naomi Tagawa Collection, Japanese-American National Museum; *p. 779a*, Hawaii State Archives; *p. 779b*, Photograph by Robert B. Ebert for the Honolulu Star-Bulletin/Hawaii State Archives; *p. 780*, Imperial War Museum; *p. 781*, U.S. Army Center of Military History, Exhibits Branch; *p. 784*, U.S. Army /Franklin D. Roosevelt Library; *p. 786*, Navy Art Collection.

**Chapter 28** *p. 788*, Courtesy of Edenhurst Gallery, Los Angeles, Daniel Nicoderr, Thomas Gianetto, and Donald Merrill; *p. 790*, H. Armstrong Roberts; *p. 792*, Corbis-Bettmann; *p. 794*, Stock Montage; *p. 795*, National Archives; *p. 797*, Corbis-Bettmann; *p. 797a*, J. R. Eyerman/Life Magazine © Time, Inc.; *p. 797b (bottom)*, Loomis Dean/Life Magazine © Time, Inc.; *(top)*, National Archives; *p. 799*, Corbis-Bettmann; *p. 801 (top right)*, AP/Wide World Photos, Inc.; *(bottom right)*, Henry Ford Museum and Greenfield Village; *(left)*, Library of Congress; *p. 802*, Milton Ackoff, Wipe Out Discrimination, 1949, Offset lithography, printed in color 43-7/8 in. x 32-3/4 in. The Museum of Modern Art, New York, Gift of the Congress of Industrial Organization, © The Museum of Modern Art, New York; *p. 804*, Corbis-Bettmann; *p. 805*, The Michael Barson Collection/Past Perfect; *p. 807*, The Michael Barson Collection/Past Perfect; *p. 808*, "I Have Here in My Hand . . ." from *Herblock: A Cartoonist's Life* (Macmillian Publishing Company, 1993).

**Chapter 29** *p. 812*, © The Curtis Publishing Company; *p. 814*, Eisenhower Library; *p. 817*, Wide World Photos, Inc.; *p. 819*, Cover drawing by Kovarsky © 1989, 1961, The New Yorker Magazine, Inc.; *p. 821*, Wide World Photos, Inc.; *p. 823*, Courtesy of Boeing Defense & Space Group; *p. 825*, Corbis-Bettmann; *p. 826*, Alfred Eisenstaedt/Life Magazine © Time, Inc.; *p. 827*, © 1992 Cindy Lewis; *p. 827a*, Bernard Hoffmann/Life Magazine © 1950 Time, Inc.; *p. 827b*, © Curtis Publishing Company; *p. 829*, © Yousuf Karsh/Woodfin Camp & Associates; *p. 831*, Courtesy of Motorola Museum © 1999 Motorola, Inc.; *p. 832*, Culver Pictures, Inc; *p. 833*, Elliot Erwitt/Magnum Photos, Inc.; *p. 834*, Corbis-Bettmann; *p. 836*, Corbis-Bettmann; *p. 837*, "Wonder Why We're Not Keeping Pace" from *Herblock's Special for Today* (Simon & Schuster, 1958); *p. 838*, Corbis-Bettmann.

**Chapter 30** *p. 840*, Dan Budnick/Woodfin Camp & Associates; *p. 842*, Wide World Photos, Inc.; *p. 844*, © The Mark Shaw Collection/Photo Researchers; *p. 846*, Charles Moore/Black Star; *p. 847*, Corbis-Bettmann; *p. 847a*, Corbis-Bettmann; *p. 847b (top)*, Fred Ward/Black Star; *(bottom)*, Bob Adelman/Magnum Photos, Inc.; *p. 848*, Wide World Photos, Inc.; *p. 850*, David S. Boyer/National Geographic Society Image Collection; *p. 851*, Wide World Photos, Inc.; *p. 857*, Corbis-Bettmann; *p. 859 (left)*, Wide World Photos, Inc.; *(right)*, Bob Fitch/Black Star; *p. 860*, Bill Sanders/The Milwaukee Journal; *p. 863*, U.S. Army Center of Military History; *p. 864 (top left)*, Corbis-Bettmann; *(bottom right)*, Cartoon by Paul Szep © The Boston Globe.

**Chapter 31** *p. 866*, Larry Burrows/Life Magazine © Time, Inc.; *p. 868*, University of California at Berkeley, Bancroft Library; *p. 870*, Corbis-Bettmann; *p. 871*, John Filo; *p. 872*, Private Collection; *p. 873a (top left)*, Gene Anthony/Black Star; *(bottom right)*, Elliot Landy/Magnum; *p. 873b (right)*, M.L. Carlebach/Black Star; *(left)*, Gene Anthony/Black Star; *p. 875*, Jack Knightlinger/LBJ Library; *p. 876*, Cornel Cappa/Magnum Photos, Inc.; *p. 877*, Collection of Philip J. & Suzanne Schiller; *p. 879*, Reprinted with permission from The New York Review of Books, © 1971 NYRB, Inc.; *p. 882*, Wally McNamee/Woodfin Camp & Associates; *p. 884*, Ken Regan/Camera 5; *p. 885*, Gordon Douglas/FPG; *p. 887*, Cartoon News International; *p. 889*, Gjon Mili/Life Magazine © Time, Inc.; *p. 890*, © 1973 Herblock.

**Chapter 32** *p. 892*, Courtesy of Modernism Gallery, San Francisco; *p. 894*, Rob Nelson/Black Star; *p. 896*, Movie Stills Archive; *p. 898*, Rob Crandall/Stock, Boston; *p. 900*, Leonard Freed/Magnum Photos, Inc.; *p. 901*, Corbis/Bettmann/UPI Newsphotos; *p. 901a*, Susan Greenwood/Gamma Liaison; *p. 901b*, Alex Webb/Magnum Photos; *p. 902*, Herb Snitzer/Stock Boston; *p. 904*, Arthur Grace/Stock Boston; *p. 905*, Corbis; *p. 906*, Sipa Press; *p. 908*, J. L. Atlan/Sygma; *p. 911*, Corbis/Bettmann; *p. 914*, AP/Wide World Photos; *p. 917*, Corbis/Bettmann/Reuters; *p. 919*, Bruno Barbey/Magnum Photos, Inc.; *p. 921*, Rus Ruelas/L.A. Daily News/Sygma; *p. 922*, Corbis-Bettmann; *p. 923*, Courtesy of the George Bush Presidential Library.

**Chapter 33** *p. 926*, Seth Resnick/Stock Boston; *p. 931*, AP/Wide World Photos; *p. 933*, Brooks Kraft/Sygma; *p. 934*, AP/Wide World Photos; *p. 935*, Agence France Presse/Corbis/Bettmann; *p. 937*, Richard Ellis/Sygma; *p. 938*, Tribune Media Services, Inc. All rights reserved. Reprinted with permission; *p. 939*, Christopher Morris/Black Star; *p. 940*, AP/Wide World Photos; *p. 942*, Corbis/AFP; *p. 943*, AP/Wide World Photos; *p. 945 (top)*, Bob Daemmrich/Stock Boston; *(bottom)*, AP/Wide World Photos; *p. 945a*, Bob Daemmrich/Stock Boston; *p. 945b (top)*, Mark Mellett/Stock Boston; *(bottom)*, Dorothy Littell Greco/Stock Boston; *p. 947 (right)*, Christopher Brown, Stock Boston; *(left)*, Bob Daemmrich; *p. 948*, Lee CeLano/Gamma/Liaison; *p. 949*, David Tulis/Atlanta Journal Constitution/Sygma.

CANADA

Vancouver I.

Seattle
Olympia ★
Spokane
WASHINGTON
Portland
Salem ★
Eugene
OREGON

Great Falls
Helena
MONTANA

*Missouri R.*

NORTH DAKOTA
★ Bismarck
Fargo

IDAHO
Boise

*Snake R.*

WYOMING

Cheyenne ★

SOUTH DAKOTA
★ Pierre

BLACK HILLS

Sioux Falls

Reno
Carson City
Sacramento ★
San Francisco
San Jose
Fresno

*GREAT BASIN*

Salt Lake City

Boulder
Denver ★

COLORADO

GREAT PLAINS

NEBRASKA

*Platte R.*

Omaha
Lincoln ★

NEVADA

UTAH

KANSAS

Topeka

*SIERRA NEVADA*

Las Vegas

*Arkansas R.*

Wichita

CALIFORNIA

Los Angeles

ARIZONA

Santa Fe
Albuquerque

Amarillo

Oklahoma City ★

Tulsa

OKLAHOMA

San Diego

Phoenix ★

NEW MEXICO

Lubbock

*Red R.*

Dallas

PACIFIC OCEAN

Tucson

El Paso

Ft. Worth

TEXAS

GULF OF CALIFORNIA

Austin ★

San Antonio

ROCKY MOUNTAINS

MEXICO

HAWAII

Niihau    Kauai
         Oahu
Honolulu ★  Molokai
    Lanai    Maui
      Kaho'olawe
         *Hawaii*

PACIFIC OCEAN

0    100    200 Miles
0  100   200 Kilometers

RUSSIA

*Bering Strait*

ARCTIC OCEAN

BROOKS RANGE

*Yukon R.*

ALASKA

ALASKA RANGE

Anchorage

CANADA

Juneau ★

BERING SEA

GULF OF ALASKA

*A l e u t i a n   I s l a n d s*

0    200    400 Miles
0  200   400 Kilometers